W9-BIS-443

Principles Volume

BUSINESS LAW

Principles for Today's Commercial Environment

BUSINESS LAW

Principles for Today's Commercial Environment

4e

DAVID P. TWOMEY
Professor of Law
Carroll School of Management
Boston College
Member of the Massachusetts and Florida Bars

MARIANNE MOODY JENNINGS
Professor Emeritus of Legal and Ethical Studies
W. P. Carey School of Business
Arizona State University
Member of the Arizona Bar

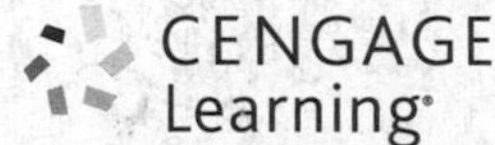

Australia • Brazil • Japan • Korea • Mexico • Singapore • Spain • United Kingdom • United States

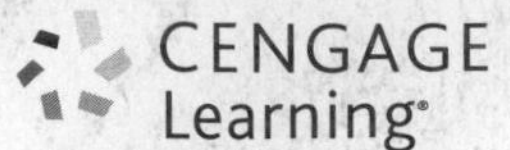

Business Law: Principles for Today's Commercial Environment, 4e
David P. Twomey, Marianne Moody Jennings

Senior Vice President, Global Product Management Higher Education: Jack W. Calhoun

Vice President and General Manager, Social Science & Qualitative Business: Erin Joyner

Product Director: Rob Dewey

Sr. Product Manager: Vicky True

Content Developer: Ted Knight

Product Assistant: Tristann Jones

Senior Brand Manager: Kristen Hurd

Associate Market Development Manager: Roy Rosa

Content Project Manager: Darrell E. Frye

Sr. Media Developer: Kristen Meere

Manufacturing Planner: Kevin Kluck

Production Service: MPS Limited

Sr. Art Director: Michelle Kunkler

Cover and Internal Designer: Beckmeyer Design

Cover Image: © FloridaStock/Shutterstock; © Stéphane Bidouze/iStockphoto; © Sean Nel/iStockphoto; © Charles Plant/Shutterstock

Rights Acquisitions Specialist: Amber Hosea

Marketing Coordinator: Christopher P. Walz

Library of Congress Control Number: 2012956483

ISBN 13: 978-1-133-58824-5

ISBN 10: 1-133-58824-7

Cengage Learning
200 First Stamford Place, 4th Floor
Stamford, CT 06902
USA

Printed in Canada
1 2 3 4 5 6 7 15 14 13

contents

preface

Regardless of the day of the week, newspapers and magazines constantly carry stories about law and business together. Raj Rajaratnam of the now-defunct Galleon Hedge Fund was convicted of insider trading even as his former employees entered guilty pleas and a Goldman Sachs director was convicted of passing inside information along to Raj. The U.S. Supreme Court issued a landmark constitutional decision when it held that the Commerce Clause did not permit Congress to require citizens to purchase health insurance, but yet upheld the law that imposed that requirement. Mortgage foreclosures hit record levels as questions about who owned the promissory notes arose as courts tried to determine who could actually start the foreclosure proceedings. MF Global collapsed into bankruptcy because employees violated one of Wall Street's critical regulations that prohibits the use of client funds for hedging. The problem of cyberbullying resulted in cases, new laws, and company policies on employee use of social media. Those who did business with Bernie Madoff, and their auditors, faced questions regarding their liability to those who lost money in the failed Madoff firm.

Here in the United States and around the world fascinating legal questions arose and all of those questions affected businesses. What damages is Qantas airlines entitled to when it must ground its entire Airbus 380 fleet because the manufacturer has found a defect that affects safety? Did Goldman Sachs intentionally misrepresent the risk on mortgage-based obligations? If so, are they criminally liable? And who is responsible for crimes committed by companies? As major corporations have continued to experience significant criminal, legal, and ethical difficulties since the last edition in 2009, we can see how important it is for business managers to understand the law and the foundations of ethics. When a manager has a void in knowledge on law and ethics, running a company can be tricky business. Employers are learning the complexities of access to employee e-mails and text messages, and lenders are learning the importance of complete and accurate paperwork when they create a mortgage.

When an entrepreneur is struggling with the decision of whether to incorporate or create an LLC, or the shareholders of Disney are grappling with issues about their rights when their CEO makes a bad decision, the law is there. No business or manager can hope to succeed without an understanding of the laws and legal environment of business. Students in business must be prepared with both knowledge of the law and the skill of applying it in the business setting. We learn principles and application through interaction with examples and by working our way through dilemmas, issues, and problems. This fourth edition of *Business Law* continues its emphasis on the student's learning process while still providing a detailed and rigorous case approach.

Features of the Text

The features of this text make the business and law connection easily understood and offer students clarity for grasping the often challenging complexities of law. The features are summarized in the following sections, which offer an overview of this edition.

Learning Outcomes

Students will better see and understand the relationship between legal concepts and their application in real-life situations by using the new chapter Learning Outcomes. These are also featured at the end of each chapter—along with the Summary and new Key Terms list—in the all-encompassing "Make the Connection" section. The Learning Outcomes also encourage students to utilize the existing text pedagogy by serving as a direct reference point for selected *For Example* call-outs, case summaries, and feature boxes.

Sports and Entertainment Law

Using pop culture, this feature teaches students about law and ethics in a way that is sure to engage them. How does a court handle the fact that Leona Helmsley left a large portion of her estate to her dog? The bankruptcies of celebrities and sports figures provide some insight into what poor money management can do to substantial assets. And what about football fans' rights to transfer their season tickets to others? Can the team prohibit the transfer of those tickets as a license restriction? What are their rights? What are the rights of the teams and stadium owners? Students have the chance to explore the law through these examples of sports figures' and entertainers' brushes with the law.

Clarity

The writing style has been evolving and, once again, we have changed those passages that fell victim to the passive voice. The writing is clear and lively. The examples are student-friendly, and the discussions of law are grounded in the book's strong connection to business. The principles of law are taught in the language and examples of business. Students can relate to the examples, which provide memorable illustrations of complex but critical legal concepts. Several chapters, including the chapter that covers antitrust, have been substantially reorganized and rewritten.

CPA Helps

As always, the text provides coverage for all the legal topics covered on the CPA exam. Several topics have been eliminated from the content for the CPA exam as of October 2009. However, the exam lags behind the content change, so the eliminated topics may continue to appear on the exam for six to 18 months. Below is the new business law/regulatory content for the CPA exam. The topics of property, bailments, insurance, and estates will be eliminated going forward with more emphasis on federal regulation, including in the areas of antitrust and employment law.

Business Law (17%–21%)

A. Agency

1. Formation and termination
2. Authority of agents and principals
3. Duties and liabilities of agents and principals

B. Contracts

1. Formation
2. Performance
3. Third-party assignments
4. Discharge, breach, and remedies

C. Uniform Commercial Code

1. Sales contracts
2. Negotiable instruments
3. Secured transactions
4. Documents of title and title transfer

D. Debtor-Creditor Relationships

1. Rights, duties, and liabilities of debtors, creditors, and guarantors
2. Bankruptcy and insolvency

E. Government Regulation of Business

1. Federal securities regulation
2. Other federal laws and regulations (antitrust, copyright, patents, money laundering, labor, employment, and ERISA)

F. Business Structure (Selection of a Business Entity)

1. Advantages, disadvantages, implications, and constraints
2. Formation, operation, and termination
3. Financial structure, capitalization, profit and loss allocation, and distributions
4. Rights, duties, legal obligations, and authority of owners and management

Business organizations, now a substantial portion of the exam, remain a focus of eight chapters with up-to-date coverage of Sarbanes-Oxley and Dodd-Frank and their impact on business forms and disclosures. This edition continues to feature sample CPA exam questions at the end of those chapters that include legal areas covered on the exam. Answers for the odd-numbered CPA exam questions in each of the appropriate chapters are given in the Instructor's Manual along with explanations for the answers. This edition of the book also continues to use a CPA highlight icon to alert students to those areas that are particularly critical in preparing for the law portion of the CPA exam.

Innovative Chapters

Restructured and updated for this edition, the Cyberlaw chapter (Chapter 11) provides students with a look at how the Internet and new technology have resulted in new interpretations of existing laws as well as new laws that govern the unique commerce issues involving these tools. Bloggers and Tweeters beware, for the law has caught up with you. The chapter provides a nice introductory tool for instructors who want to show how much the law affects this new generation of Internet-savvy students.

Cases

Specially selected cases appear in abundance and are still at the core of this text. Most chapters include three to five cases, many of them with 2012 decision dates. Landmark decisions also appear. To highlight the charm and induce the student's recall of the principles of the cases, a one-line title appears above each case. These can be a humorous introduction, a play on words, or a simple memorable description of the parties or facts of the case. The one-line introduction is intriguing for students and makes the strong cases even more memorable.

e-Commerce and Cyberlaw

This feature covers e-mail privacy, Internet taxes, identity theft, contract formation on the Internet, e-commerce employment rules, electronic signatures, and more. Chapter 26 includes a new cyberlaw feature on returns and revocation of acceptance for online sellers and buyers.

Chapter 8, the criminal law chapter, includes great detail on the new and evolving computer crimes. Chapter 34 covers fraudulent title issues on Craigslist and the rights of the parties.

Thinking Things Through

This feature is designed to help students apply the law they have learned from the chapter and cases to a hypothetical or another case that varies slightly from the examples in the reading. With these problems built into this feature the reading, students have the chance to really think through what they have just read and studied with regard to the law presented in that chapter. This feature can be used to promote classroom discussion or as an assignment for analysis. For example, in Chapter 25, students can walk through an example on a customer biting into an undeveloped peanut in a Goo Goo candy bar and whether there is liability on the part of the manufacturer. Do people expect to bite into undeveloped peanuts in a candy bar? What is the test for product liability when a natural item in food results in harm?

Major Regulatory Reforms: Dodd-Frank, the Consumer Financial Protection Bureau

Businesses continue to be dramatically affected not only by laws at the federal level, but also by complex and intricate new federal regulatory schemes. Dodd-Frank affects everything from corporate governance to consumer rights in financing. This dramatic piece of legislation and the new Consumer Financial Protection Bureau with its expansive authority, enjoy coverage throughout this edition.

Ethical Focus

In addition to Chapter 3, which is devoted exclusively to the current issues in business ethics, each chapter continues to provide students with an ethical dilemma related to that particular area of law. The Ethics & the Law feature presents problems in each area of law. Students will be able to analyze ethical issues and problems that are very real and very challenging for anyone in business—for example, the issues involved in the state of Ohio's release of Joe the Plumber's divorce and child custody records after he asked then-presidential candidate Barack Obama a question about his views, Claremont-McKenna's inflation of SAT scores to ensure its outstanding ranking among the best colleges, and Wi-Fi Piggybacking.

Critical Thinking

The American Assembly of Collegiate Schools of Business (AACSB) mandate on critical thinking is addressed by this text. The Thinking Things Through feature asks students to analyze a problem that requires application of the law and examination of slight changes in factual patterns from examples in the text and the cases. For example, in the negotiable instruments chapters, students can look at a sample instrument in one problem and apply the requirements for negotiability to determine whether the instrument is indeed negotiable. In the Ethics & the Law feature, students must connect ethical thought with law and public policy and walk through the logic of application and results. End-of-chapter problems are, for the most part, real cases that summarize fact patterns and ask the students to find the applicable laws in the chapter and determine applicability and results. The fact patterns in the chapter problems are detailed and realistic and offer students the chance to test their mastery of the chapter concepts.

For Additional Help in Teaching and Learning

For more detailed information about any of the following ancillaries, contact your local South-Western sales representative or visit **www.CengageBrain.com**.

INSTRUCTOR'S RESOURCE CD (IRCD) (ISBN: 1285186613). The IRCD contains the Instructor's Manual in Microsoft® Word files as well as the ExamView® testing software files, Microsoft® Word test bank files, and PowerPoint® lecture slides.

INSTRUCTOR'S MANUAL. The Instructor's Manual is prepared by Marianne Jennings, one of the textbook authors. It provides instructor insights, chapter outlines, and teaching strategies for each chapter. Discussion points are provided for Thinking Things Through, Ethics & the Law vignettes and for each case referenced in the new Learning Outcomes. Also included are answers to CPA questions. Download the Instructor Manual at **www.CengageBrain.com** or access it from the IRCD.

EXAMVIEW® TESTING SOFTWARE—COMPUTERIZED TESTING SOFTWARE. This testing software contains all of the questions in the printed test bank. This program is an easy-to-use test creation software compatible with Microsoft® Windows. Instructors can add or edit questions, instructions, and answers; and they can select questions by previewing them on the screen, selecting them randomly, or selecting them by number. Instructors can also create and administer quizzes online, whether over the Internet, a local area network (LAN), or a wide-area network (WAN). The ExamView® testing software is only available on the IRCD.

TEST BANK. The Test Bank includes thousands of true/false, multiple-choice, and case questions. The test bank is only available on the IRCD or textbook companion Web site (**www.CengageBrain.com**).

MICROSOFT® POWERPOINT® LECTURE REVIEW SLIDES. PowerPoint® slides are available for use by instructors for enhancing their lectures. Download these slides at **www.CengageBrain.com** or access them on the IRCD.

COURSEMATE. **CourseMate** with Engagement Tracker: CourseMate brings course concepts to life with interactive learning tools and an eBook. CourseMate now includes the KnowNOW! Blog, the most current solution for the most convenient online news and classroom application. KnowNOW! brings news into your course with discipline-specific online pages and applications. **www.cengage.com/coursemate**

Instant Access Code ISBN: 9781285194240

BUSINESS LAW DIGITAL VIDEO LIBRARY. This dynamic video library features more than ninety video clips that spark class discussion and clarify core legal principles. The library is organized into five series: Legal Conflicts in Business (includes specific modern business and e-commerce scenarios); Ask the Instructor (presents straightforward explanations of concepts for student review); Drama of the Law (features classic business scenarios that spark classroom participation); and Real World Legal (explores conflicts that arise in a variety of business environments). Access for students is free when bundled with a new textbook, or it can be purchased at **www.cengagebrain.com**.

Instant Access Code ISBN: 9781285458496

CENGAGE LEARNING CUSTOM SOLUTIONS. **Cengage Learning Custom Solutions** can provide your students exactly what they need to succeed—remove extra coverage you normally skip, replace chapters with coverage that better matches your approach, supplement your text with additional cases or readings from our legal, business ethics, or our new "pop culture" case collections, and include your own material to create a complete and efficient course resource. With a customized product your students are paying for "exactly what they need" and receive a greater value for their dollar. Learn more about all our services at **www.cengage.com/custom**.

acknowledgements

The development and revision of a textbook represents teamwork in its highest form. We thank the innumerable instructors, students, attorneys, and managers who have added to the quality of this textbook through its many editions. In particular, we thank the following reviewers who provided their honest and valuable commentary to this text:

Robert A. Arnold
Thomas More College

Weldon M. Blake, JD
Bethune-Cookman University

Bob Blinderman
WTAMU and Amarillo College

Norman Bradshaw
Alvin Community College

Thomas L. Brooks, Jr.
Purdue University

Myra Bruegger
Southeastern Community College

Barry Bunn
Valencia Community College

Jarrod Y. Burch, JD
Saint Leo University and American Intercontinental University

Deborah Carter
Coahoma Community College

Shoshana Dennis
San Diego City College

Andrea Foster
John Tyler Community College

Leslie L. Francis
CUNY-York College

Kimberly Goudy
Central Ohio Technical College

Patrick J. Griffin, CPA, LL.M, JD
Lewis University

Francis A. Hatstat, MBA, JD
Bellevue College

David Lewis Jordan
Emmanuel College

Virginia Edgerton Law, JD
Saint Leo University

Paolo Longo, Jr.
Valencia Community College

Linda McCarley
Bevill State Community College

Derek Mosley
Meridian Community College

Michael Murphy
Langston University – Tulsa

Jeffrey D. Penley, JD
Catawba Valley Community College

Simone I. Rosenberg
Valencia Community College – East Campus

Joseph A. Spadaro
Naugatuck Valley Community College

Darrell H. Thompson
Mountain View College

Cathy Trecek
Iowa Western Community College

Thomas K. Ware
Johnson State College

Lisa Wilhite
Bevill State Community College

We also thank the instructors who have reviewed previous editions of this text:

Dean Alexander
Miami-Dade Community College

Robert A. Arnold
Thomas More College

John T. Ballantine
University of Colorado

Todd Barnet
Pace University

Marie F. Benjamin
Valencia Community College

Kenneth V. Bevan
Valencia Community College

Robert Boeke
Delta College

Greg Cermigiano
Widener University

David A. Clough
Naugatuck Valley Community College

Anne Cohen
University of Massachusetts

Thomas S. Collins
Loras College

Lawrence J. Danks
Camden County College

Darrell Dies
Illinois State University

De Vee E. Dykstra
University of South Dakota

Adam Epstein
University of Tennessee

Phillip Evans
Kutztown University of Pennsylvania

Deborah Lynn Bundy Ferry
Marquette University

Darrel Ford
University of Central Oklahoma

Edward J. Gac
University of Colorado

Teresa R. Gillespie
Northwest University

David Grigg
Pfeiffer University

Ronald Groeber
Ball State University

Heidi Helgren
Delta College

Florence Elliot Howard
Stephen F. Austin University

Richard Hurley
Francis Marion University

Lawrence A. Joel
Bergen Community College

Michael A. Katz
Delaware State University

Thomas E. Knothe
Viterbo University

Ruth Kraft
Audrey Cohen College

Claire La Roche
Longwood College

Susan D. Looney
Mohave Community College

Roy J. Millender, Jr.
Westmont College

Steven Murray
Community College of Rhode Island

Ann Olazábal
University of Miami

Neal Orkin
Drexel University

Ronald Picker
St. Mary's of the Woods College

Francis Polk
Ocean County College

Robert Prentice
University of Texas at Austin

Linda Reppert
Marymount University

Richard J. Riley
Samford University

Gary Sambol
Rutgers University School of Business

Samuel L. Schrager
University of Connecticut

Lester Smith
Eastern New Mexico University

Michael Sugameli
Oakland University

Cathy L. Taylor
Park University and Webster University

Mike Teel
Samford University

Bob Vicars
Bluefield State University

James Welch
Kentucky Wesleyan College

We extend our thanks to our families for their support and patience as we work our long hours to ensure that each edition is better than the last.

about the authors

Professor David Twomey has been a member of the Business Law Department in the Carroll School of Management at Boston College since 1968. As department chair for over a decade, and four-term chairman of the school's Education Policy Committee, he served as a spokesperson for a strong legal and ethical component in both the undergraduate and graduate curriculum. The author of some 34 editions of textbooks on labor, employment, and business law topics, the 15th edition of his *Labor & Employment Law* book was published in 2012. His articles have appeared in journals such as *Best's Review, The American Business Law Journal, The Labor Law Journal, The Massachusetts Law Quarterly, The Florida Bar Journal*, and *The Business Law Review*.

He has served as arbitrator in over two thousand labor-management disputes throughout the country. His service includes appointments by Presidents Ronald Reagan, George H. W. Bush, William J. Clinton, and George W. Bush to eight Presidential Emergency Boards, whose recommendations served as a basis for the resolution of major disputes in the rail and airline industries.

After service in the U.S. Marine Corps, he graduated from Boston College, earned his M.B.A. at the University of Massachusetts, Amherst, and a J.D. degree at Boston College Law School. He is a member of the Massachusetts and Florida Bars and a member of the National Academy of Arbitrators.

Professor Marianne M. Jennings, Emeritus Professor of Legal and Ethical Studies, taught at the W. P. Carey School of Business, Arizona State University, from 1977 through 2011. She has six textbooks and four monographs in circulation with the 7th edition of her business ethics case book published in January 2011 and the 22nd and 7th editions of two other textbooks to be published in 2013. She was director of the Lincoln Center for Applied Ethics from 1995 to 1999. She has worked with government agencies, professional organizations, colleges and universities, and Fortune 500 companies on ethics training and culture. She is a contributing editor of *Corporate Finance Review* and *Real Estate Law Journal.* Two of her books have been named *Library Journal*'s book of the year and her books have been translated into three languages. Her book, *The Seven Signs of Ethical Collapse*, was published by St. Martin's Press and has been used as a primer by numerous organizations for creating and sustaining an ethical culture. In 2011, she was named one of the Top 100 Thought Leaders by Trust Across America and in 2012, she was named one of the 100 most influential people in business ethics by *Ethisphere* magazine.

PART 1

The Legal and Social Environment of Business

© Manuel Gutjahr/iStockphoto.com

The Nature and Sources of Law

learningoutcomes

After studying this chapter, you should be able to

LO.1 Discuss the nature of law

LO.2 List the sources of law

LO.3 Describe the classifications of law

Why have law? If you have ever been stuck in a traffic jam or jostled in a crowd leaving a stadium, you have observed the need for order to keep those involved moving in an efficient and safe manner. The issues with bloggers' use of others' materials and continuing downloading of music and films without compensation to copyright holders illustrate the need for rules and order in this era of new technology. When our interactions are not orderly, whether at our concerts or through our e-mail, all of us and our rights are affected. The order or pattern of rules that society uses to govern the conduct of individuals and their relationships is called **law**. Law keeps society running smoothly and efficiently.

A. Nature of Law and Legal Rights

Law consists of the body of principles that govern conduct and that can be enforced in courts or by administrative agencies. The law could also be described as a collection or bundle of rights.

1. Legal Rights

A **right** is a legal capacity to require another person to perform or refrain from performing an act. Our rights flow from the U.S. Constitution, state constitutions, federal and state statutes, and ordinances at the local levels, including cities, counties, and boroughs. Within these sources of rights are also duties. A **duty** is an obligation of law imposed on a person to perform or refrain from performing a certain act.

Duties and rights coexist. No right exists in one person without a corresponding duty resting on some other person or persons. For example, if the terms of a lease provide that the premises will remain in a condition of good repair so that the tenant can live there comfortably, the landlord has a corresponding duty to provide a dwelling that has hot and cold running water.

2. Individual Rights

The U.S. Constitution gives individuals certain rights. Those rights include the right to freedom of speech, the right to due process or the right to have a hearing before any freedom is taken away, and the right to vote. There are also duties that accompany individual rights, such as the duty to speak in a way that does not cause harm to others. For example, individuals are free to express their opinions about the government or its officials, but they would not be permitted to yell "Fire!" in a crowded theater and cause unnecessary harm to others. The rights given in the U.S. Constitution are rights that cannot be taken away or violated by any statutes, ordinances, or court decisions. These rights provide a framework for the structure of government and other laws.

3. The Right of Privacy

One very important individual legal right is the right of privacy, which has two components. The first is the right to be secure against unreasonable searches and seizures by the government. The Fourth Amendment of the U.S. Constitution guarantees this portion of the **right of privacy**.[1] A police officer, for example, may not search your home unless the officer has a reasonable suspicion (which is generally established through a warrant) that your home contains evidence of a crime, such as illegal drugs. If your home or business is searched unlawfully, any items obtained during that unlawful search could be excluded as evidence in a criminal trial because of the Fourth Amendment's exclusionary rule.

For Example, in the murder trial of O.J. Simpson, Judge Lance Ito excluded some of the evidence the police had obtained from inside Mr. Simpson's Ford Bronco, which was parked on the street outside his home. Judge Ito ruled that the officers should have first obtained a warrant for the locked vehicle, which was not going to be taken anywhere because Mr. Simpson was out of town at that time. The *Arizona v. Gant* case deals with an issue of a warrantless search of a vehicle.

[1] Police officers who record the arrest of a DUI suspect have not violated the suspect's privacy. *State v. Morris*, 214 P.3d 883 (Ut. App. 2009)

Arizona v. Gant, 556 U.S. 332 (2009)

Searches of Cars When Drivers Are Cuffed

Rodney Gant was arrested for driving with a suspended license and handcuffed in the back seat of the squad car of the arresting officers. After handcuffing Mr. Gant, the arresting officers searched his car and found cocaine in the pocket of a jacket lying on the back seat of Gant's vehicle. Mr. Gant was charged with possession of cocaine (as well as driving with a suspended license).

Mr. Gant's lawyer challenged the search of his client's vehicle on the grounds that there were not exigent circumstances. That is, locked in and handcuffed as he was, there was no emergency or reason to believe that Mr. Gant would spring into action and hide, destroy, or swallow the cocaine. As a result, his lawyer argued that the officers needed a warrant. Without the warrant, his lawyer argued, the cocaine could not be used as evidence in the case.

The cocaine evidence was admitted, and Mr. Gant was convicted and appealed. The Court of Appeals of Arizona reversed. The United States Supreme Court granted Arizona's petition for *certiorari*, and subsequently vacated and remanded. The Court of Appeals of Arizona remanded for an evidentiary hearing on the legality of the warrantless search. On remand, the trial court found no violation. Defendant appealed again. The Court of Appeals of Arizona reversed the decision and the Supreme Court of Arizona affirmed that reversal. Arizona appealed.

JUDICIAL OPINION

STEVENS, Justice [A] search incident to arrest may only include "the arrestee's person and the area 'within his immediate control'—construing that phrase to mean the area from within which he might gain possession of a weapon or destructible evidence." That limitation, which continues to define the boundaries of the exception, ensures that the scope of a search incident to arrest is commensurate with its purposes of protecting arresting officers and safeguarding any evidence of the offense of arrest that an arrestee might conceal or destroy.

Gant clearly was not within reaching distance of his car at the time of the search. An evidentiary basis for the search was also lacking in this case. Because police could not reasonably have believed either that Gant could have accessed his car at the time of the search or that evidence of the offense for which he was arrested might have been found therein, the search in this case was unreasonable.

A rule that gives police the power to conduct such a search whenever an individual is caught committing a traffic offense, when there is no basis for believing evidence of the offense might be found in the vehicle, creates a serious and recurring threat to the privacy of countless individuals. Indeed, the character of that threat implicates the central concern underlying the Fourth Amendment—the concern about giving police officers unbridled discretion to rummage at will among a person's private effects.

Police may search a vehicle incident to a recent occupant's arrest only if the arrestee is within reaching distance of the passenger compartment at the time of the search or it is reasonable to believe the vehicle contains evidence of the offense of arrest. When these justifications are absent, a search of an arrestee's vehicle will be unreasonable unless police obtain a warrant or show that another exception to the warrant requirement applies. The Arizona Supreme Court correctly held that this case involved an unreasonable search. Accordingly, the judgment is affirmed.

QUESTIONS

1. Would the decision have been different if Mr. Gant were standing along the side of the road, uncuffed?
2. Would the decision have been different if Mr. Gant had been arrested for suspicion of driving under the influence of cocaine?

A second aspect of the right of privacy protects individuals against intrusions by others. Your private life is not subject to public scrutiny when you are a private citizen. This right is provided in many state constitutions and exists through interpretation at the federal level through the landmark case of *Roe v. Wade*,[2] in which the U.S. Supreme Court established a right of privacy that gives women the right to choose whether to have an abortion.

These two components of the right to privacy have many interpretations. These interpretations are often found in statutes that afford privacy rights with respect to certain types of conduct. **For Example,** a federal statute provides a right of privacy to bank customers that prevents their banks from giving out information about their accounts except to law enforcement agencies conducting investigations. Some laws protect the rights of students. **For Example,** the Family

[2] 410 U.S. 113 (1973).

Ethics & the Law

Twitter, Facebook, Google, and Your Job Application

A study by the social monitoring service, Reppler, found the following about employers:

- 91 percent of the employers polled use social networking sites (Twitter, Facebook, and LinkedIn) to screen prospective employees. Some employers even ask for applicants' passwords as a condition of employment.
- 69 percent say they have rejected a job applicant because of something they saw on one of these social platforms.
- 47 percent of employers do their checks of these social networking sites immediately after receiving their job applications.
- 76 percent of employers check Facebook.
- 53 percent check Twitter.
- 48 percent check LinkedIn.
- 68 percent of employers say that they have hired someone because they liked what they saw on these social networking sites.

One employer commented that these searches are so simple that it would be irresponsible to not do them. Experts tell college students to remember that what may seem to be fun can later come back to haunt you when you begin your professional career. Their advice is to watch what you post and what you write. Discuss privacy rights and whether there is any legal issue when information is posted voluntarily on the Internet. Is there an ethical issue with these types of searches?

Source: Shea Bennett, "91% of Employers Use Twitter, Facebook, and LinkedIn to Screen Job Applicants," **www.alltwitter.com**, October 24, 2011.

Educational Rights and Privacy Act of 1974 (FERPA, also known as the *Buckley Amendment*) prevents colleges and universities from disclosing students' grades to third parties without the students' permission. From your credit information to your Social Security number, you have great privacy protections.

4. Privacy and Technology

Technology creates new situations that may require the application of new rules of law. Technology has changed the way we interact with each other, and new rules of law have developed to protect our rights. Today, business is conducted by computers, wire transfers of funds, e-mail, electronic data interchange (EDI) order placements, and the Internet. We still expect that our communication is private. However, technology also affords others the ability to eavesdrop on conversations and intercept electronic messages. The law has stepped in to reestablish that the right of privacy still exists even in these technologically nonprivate circumstances. Some laws now make it a crime and a breach of privacy to engage in such interceptions of communications.[3] (See Chapter 11)

E-Commerce & Cyberlaw

A University's Access to Your Computer

Scott Kennedy, a computer system administrator for Qualcomm Corporation in San Diego, California, discovered that somebody had obtained unauthorized access (or "hacked into," in popular parlance) the company's computer network. Kennedy contacted the Federal Bureau of Investigation (FBI). Working together, Kennedy and the FBI were able to trace the intrusion to a computer on the University of Wisconsin at Madison network. They contacted Jeffrey Savoy, the University of Wisconsin computer network investigator, who found evidence that someone using a computer on the university network was in fact hacking into the Qualcomm system and that the user had gained unauthorized access to the university's system as well. Savoy traced the source of intrusion to a computer located in university housing, the room of Jerome Heckenkamp, a computer science graduate student at the university. Savoy knew that Heckenkamp had been terminated from his job at the university computer help desk two years earlier for similar unauthorized activity.

While Heckenkamp was online and logged into the university's system, Savoy, along with detectives, went to Heckenkamp's room. The

[3] *Luangkhot v. State*, 722 S.E.2d 193 (Ga. App. 2012).

E-Commerce & Cyberlaw—*Contd.*

door was ajar, and nobody was in the room. Savoy entered the room and disconnected the network cord that attached the computer to the network. In order to be sure that the computer he had disconnected from the network was the computer that had gained unauthorized access to the university server, Savoy wanted to run some commands on the computer. Detectives located Heckenkamp, explained the situation, and asked for Heckenkamp's password, which Heckenkamp voluntarily provided. Savoy then ran tests on the computer and copied the hard drive without a warrant. When Heckenkamp was charged with several federal computer crimes, he challenged the university's access to his account and Savoy's steps that night, including the copy of the hard drive, as a breach of his privacy. Was Heckenkamp correct? Was his privacy breached?

[*U.S. v. Heckenkamp*, 482 F.3d 1142 (9th Cir. 2007)]

B. Sources of Law

Several layers of law are enacted at different levels of government to provide the framework for business and personal rights and duties. At the base of this framework of laws is constitutional law.

5. Constitutional Law

Constitutional law is the branch of law that is based on the constitution for a particular level of government. A **constitution** is a body of principles that establishes the structure of a government and the relationship of that government to the people who are governed. A constitution is generally a combination of the written document and the practices and customs that develop with the passage of time and the emergence of new problems. In each state, two constitutions are in force: the state constitution and the federal Constitution.

6. Statutory Law

Statutory law includes legislative acts. Both Congress and the state legislatures enact statutory law. Examples of congressional legislative enactments include the Securities Act of 1933 (Chapter 46), the Sherman Antitrust Act (Chapter 5), the bankruptcy laws (Chapter 35), and consumer credit protection provisions (Chapter 33). At the state level, statutes govern the creation of corporations, probate of wills, and the transfer of title to property. In addition to the state legislatures and the U.S. Congress, all cities, counties, and other governmental subdivisions have some power to adopt ordinances within their sphere of operation. Examples of the types of laws found at this level of government include traffic laws, zoning laws, and pet and bicycle licensing laws.

7. Administrative Law

Administrative regulations are rules promulgated by state and federal administrative agencies, such as the Securities and Exchange Commission and the National Labor Relations Board. For example, most of your rights related to your wages, hours worked, and overtime pay have been promulgated by the Department of Labor. These regulations generally have the force of statutes.

8. Private Law

Even individuals and businesses create their own laws, or **private law**. Private law consists of the rules and regulations parties agree to as part of their contractual relationships. **For Example,** landlords develop rules for tenants on everything from parking to laundry room use. Employers develop rules for employees on everything from proper computer use to posting pictures and information on bulletin boards located within the company walls. Homeowner associations have rules on everything from your landscaping to the color of your house paint.

9. Case Law, Statutory Interpretation, and Precedent

Law also includes principles that are expressed for the first time in court decisions. This form of law is called **case law**. Case law plays three very important roles. The first is one of clarifying the meaning of statutes, or providing statutory interpretation. **For Example,** a man who was sentenced to house arrest left his house but still wanted to count the time as part of his sentence.[4] A court decision held that you must actually be in the house to have the time count. The second role that courts play is in creating precedent. When a court decides a new question or problem, its decision becomes a **precedent**, which stands as the law in future cases that involve that particular problem.

Using precedent and following decisions is also known as the doctrine of **stare decisis**. However, the rule of *stare decisis* is not cast in stone. Judges have some flexibility. When a court finds an earlier decision to be incorrect, it overrules that decision. **For Example,** in 1954, the U.S. Supreme Court departed from the general rule of *stare decisis* in *Brown v. Board of Education.*[5] In that case, the Court decided that its 1896 decision *Plessy v. Ferguson,*[6] that held separate facilities for blacks were equal to facilities for whites, was incorrect.

The third role courts play is in developing a body of law that is not statutory but addresses long standing issues. Court decisions do not always deal with new problems or make new rules. In many cases, courts apply rules as they have been for many years, even centuries. These time-honored rules of the community are called the **common law**. **For Example,** most of law that we still follow today in determining real property rights developed in England, beginning in 1066. Statutes sometimes repeal or redeclare the common law rules. Many statutes depend on the common law for definitions of the terms in the statutes.

10. Other Forms of Law: Treaties and Executive Orders

Law also includes treaties made by the United States and proclamations and executive orders of the president of the United States or of other public officials.

11. Uniform State Laws

To facilitate the national nature of business and transactions, the National Conference of Commissioners on Uniform State Laws (NCCUSL), composed of representatives from every state, has drafted statutes on various subjects for adoption by the states. The best example of such laws is the Uniform Commercial Code (UCC).[7] (See Chapters 23–31, Chapter 34.) The UCC regulates the sale and lease of goods; commercial paper, such as checks; fund transfers; secured transactions in personal property; banking; and letters of credit. Having the same principles of law on contracts for the sale of goods and other commercial transactions in most of the 50 states makes doing business easier and less expensive. Other examples of uniform laws across the states include the Model Business Corporations Act (Chapter 44), the Uniform Partnership Act (Chapter 42), and the Uniform Residential Landlord Tenant Act (Chapter 51). The Uniform Computer Information Transactions Act (UCITA) as well as the Uniform Electronic Transactions Act (UETA) are two uniform laws that have taken contract law from the traditional paper era to the paperless computer age.

C. Classifications of Law

12. Substantive Law vs. Procedural Law

Substantive law creates, defines, and regulates rights and liabilities. The law that determines when a contract is formed is substantive law. **Procedural law** specifies the steps that must be followed in enforcing those rights and liabilities. For example, once that contract is formed, you have rights to enforce that contract, and the steps you take through the court system to recover your damages for a breach of contract are procedural laws. The laws that prohibit computer theft are substantive laws. The prosecution of someone for computer theft follows procedural law.

[4] *Com. v. Stafford,* 29 A.3d 800 (Pa. Super. 2011).

[5] 349 U.S. 294 (1954).

[6] 163 U.S. 537 (1895).

[7] The UCC has been adopted in every state, except that Louisiana has not adopted Article 2, Sales. Guam, the Virgin Islands, and the District of Columbia have also adopted the UCC. The NCCUSL has adopted amendments to Article 8, Investment Securities (1977 and 1994), and Article 9, Secured Transactions (1999, and as amended 2001). There have been new articles of the UCC: Article 2A, Leases, and Article 4A, Funds Transfers. The United Nations Convention on Contracts for the International Sale of Goods (CISG) has been adopted as the means for achieving uniformity in sale-of-goods contracts on an international level. Provisions of CISG were strongly influenced by Article 2 of the UCC.

Sports & Entertainment Law

MLB and Steroids

On March 17, 2005, former and current major league baseball (MLB) players, Commissioner Bud Selig, and the parents of young baseball players who had taken their own lives after taking steroids testified before the U.S. House of Representatives Government Reform Committee. The House held the hearings to determine whether government regulation of baseball is necessary.

Committee Chair Tom Davis made an opening statement with the following excerpts:

> *Fourteen years ago, anabolic steroids were added to the Controlled Substance Act as a Schedule III drug, making it illegal to possess or sell them without a valid prescription. Today, however, evidence strongly suggests that steroid use among teenagers—especially aspiring athletes—is a large and growing problem.*
>
> *Today we take the committee's first steps toward understanding how we got here, and how we begin turning those numbers around. Down the road, we need to look at whether and how Congress should exercise its legislative powers to further restrict the use and distribution of these substances.*
>
> *Our specific purpose today is to consider MLB's recently negotiated drug policy; how the testing policy will be implemented; how it will effectively address the use of prohibited drugs by players; and, most importantly, the larger societal and public health ramifications of steroid use.*

Mark McGwire, now a retired MLB player and a record holder, stated during the hearings:

> *Asking me, or any other player, to answer questions about who took steroids in front of television cameras will not solve this problem. If a player answers 'no,' he simply will not be believed. If he answers 'yes,' he risks public scorn and endless government investigations. My lawyers have advised me that I cannot answer these questions without jeopardizing my friends, my family, or myself. I intend to follow their advice.**

Give a list of all the laws, rights, and duties you can find in this information.

***http://reform.house.gov/GovReform/Hearings/EventSingle.aspx?EventID=637**. Click on *Mark McGwire.*

13. Criminal Law vs. Civil Law

Criminal laws define wrongs against society. **Civil laws** define the rights of one person against another. Criminal law violations carry fines and imprisonment as penalties. Civil laws carry damage remedies for the wronged individual. **For Example,** if you run a red light, you have committed a crime and you will be punished with a fine and points on your license. If you run a red light and strike a pedestrian, you will also have committed a civil wrong of injury to another through your carelessness. Civil laws provide that in addition to taking care of your wrong to society, you must take care of your wrong to the pedestrian and pay damages for the cost of her injuries (see Chapter 8 for more information about recovery of damages for accidents such as this).

14. Law vs. Equity

Equity is a body of law that provides justice when the law does not offer an adequate remedy or the application of the law would be terribly unfair. Equity courts developed in England as a means of getting to the heart of a dispute and seeing that justice was done. **For Example,** Christian Louboutin shoes have a distinctive red bottom that is their trademark. Yves Saint Laurent began producing its shoes with a red bottom. Common and statutory law provide for Louboutin to collect damages—the amount the company lost in sales through the copycat efforts of Yves Saint Laurent. However, if the Yves Saint Laurent shoes continue in production, Louboutin is never adequately compensated. Equity provides for an injunction, a court order to stop Yves Saint Laurent from making the red-soled shoes.[8] At one time, the United States had separate law courts and equity courts, but, today, these courts have been combined so that one court applies principles of both law and equity. A party may ask for both legal and equitable remedies in a single court.[9] **For Example,** suppose a homeowner contracts to sell

[8] *Christian Louboutin S.A. v. Yves Saint Laurent America, Inc.*, 778 F. Supp. 2d 445 (S.D.N.Y. 2011).

[9] For example, Jennifer Lopez and Marc Anthony filed suit against the manufacturer of a British company that produces baby carriages for using their images on its Web site and in ads without permission; they asked for $5 million in damages as well as an injunction to stop use of their photos and likenesses in the company's ads. *Lopez v. Silver Cross*, 2009 WL 481386 (CD Cal). The case was settled prior to the dissolution of the Lopez and Anthony marriage. The terms of the settlement are not known, but Silver Cross no longer uses the images of Lopez and Anthony in its ads.

his home to a buyer. If the homeowner then refuses to go through with the contract, the buyer has the legal remedy of recovering damages. The rules of equity go further and could require the owner to convey title to the house, an equitable remedy known as *specific performance.* Equitable remedies may also be available in certain contract breaches (see Chapters 2, 12, and 20).

LawFlix

And Justice for All (1979) (R)

An excellent film that gives an overview of the judicial system in Maryland. Rights, precedent, and the role of lawyers are all topics for satire and analysis in the movie.

MAKE THE CONNECTION

SUMMARY

Law provides rights and imposes duties. One such right is the right of privacy, which affords protection against unreasonable searches of our property and intrusion into or disclosure of our private affairs.

Law consists of the pattern of rules established by society to govern conduct and relationships. These rules can be expressed as constitutional provisions, statutes, administrative regulations, and case decisions. Law can be classified as substantive or procedural, and it can be described in terms of civil or criminal law. Law provides remedies in equity in addition to damages.

The sources of law include constitutions, federal and state statutes, administrative regulations, ordinances, and uniform laws generally codified by the states in their statutes. The courts are also a source of law through their adherence to case precedent under the doctrine of *stare decisis* and through their development of time-honored principles called the common law.

LEARNING OUTCOMES

After studying this chapter, you should be able to clearly explain:

A. Nature of Law and Legal Rights

LO.1 Discuss the nature of law and legal rights
See *Arizona v. Gant*, p. 5.
See Ethics & the Law on p. 6 for a discussion of employers checking Twitter, Facebook, and LinkedIn for information about potential employees.

See E-Commerce & Cyberlaw, p. 6.

B. Sources of Law

LO.2 List the sources of law
See the *For Example* discussion of landlords developing rules for tenants on everything from parking to laundry room use on p. 7.
See the list and explanation of uniform laws on p. 8.
See the Sports & Entertainment Law discussion of steroids in baseball on p. 9.

C. Classifications of Law

LO.3 Describe the classifications of law
See the discussion of law, equity, procedural, substantive, criminal, and civil on pp. 8–9.
See the Christian Louboutin example on its red-bottomed shoe being copied and footnote 9 with the discussion of the Jennifer Lopez/Marc Anthony suit on p. 9.

Explain uniform state laws.

KEY TERMS

administrative regulations
case law
civil law
common law
constitution
criminal law
duty
equity
law
precedent
private law
procedural law
right of privacy
right
stare decisis
statutory law
substantive law

QUESTIONS AND CASE PROBLEMS

1. On January 9, 2007, two Springfield, Missouri, Police Department officers made a traffic stop of a vehicle driven by Claude X. The purpose of the stop was to arrest X's passenger, Melissa Owen, who had a pending warrant for check-kiting. Once the officers made visual contact with Owen, the officers stopped X's car and instructed Owen to get out of the car. Ms. Owen did not bring her belongings with her when she got out of the car. One of the officers called dispatch to verify Owen's warrant and requested backup from a K–9 officer. Another officer arrived at the scene with his service dog, Marko. X was told to get out of the car so that it could be searched. X did get out of the car but then also locked it and refused to allow the officers to search. X was handcuffed for obstruction and the officers took away his keys to the car.

   At that time, Marko searched (sniffed) the exterior of X's car. Marko alerted to the car's rear bumper. The officers began to search the trunk of the vehicle and found containers with drugs in them along with a weighing scale. X's lawyer moved to have the evidence excluded because the drugs were found without a warrant. Should the judge exclude the evidence or is it admissible? Be sure to refer to the *Arizona v. Gant* case on p. 6 in developing your answer and explaining why. [*U.S. v. Claude X,* 648 F.3d 599 (8th Cir.)]

2. The Family Educational Rights and Privacy Act (FERPA) protects students' rights to keep their academic records private. What duties are imposed and upon whom because of this protection of rights? Discuss the relationship between rights and duties.

3. List the sources of law.

4. What is the difference between common law and statutory law?

5. Classify the following laws as substantive or procedural:

   a. A law that requires public schools to hold a hearing before a student is expelled.

   b. A law that establishes a maximum interest rate for credit transactions of 24 percent.

   c. A law that provides employee leave for the birth or adoption of a child for up to 12 weeks.

   d. A law that requires the county assessor to send four notices of taxes due and owing before a lien can be filed (attached) to the property.

6. What do uniform laws accomplish? Why do states adopt them? Give an example of a uniform law.

7. Cindy Nathan is a student at West University. While she was at her 9:00 A.M. anthropology class, campus security entered her dorm room and searched all areas, including her closet and drawers. When Cindy returned to her room and discovered what had happened, she complained to the dorm's senior resident. The senior resident said that this was the university's property and that Cindy had no right of privacy. Do you agree with the senior resident's statement? Is there a right of privacy in a dorm room?

8. Professor Lucas Phelps sent the following e-mail to Professor Marlin Jones: "I recently read the opinion piece you wrote for the *Sacramento Bee* on affirmative action. Your opinion is incorrect, your reasoning and analysis are poor, and I am

embarrassed that you are a member of the faculty here at Cal State Yolinda." Professor Jones forwarded the note from Professor Phelps to the provost of the university and asked that Professor Phelps be disciplined for using the university e-mail system for harassment purposes. Professor Phelps objected when the provost contacted him: "He had no right to forward that e-mail to you. That was private correspondence. And you have no right of access to my e-mail. I have privacy rights." Do you agree with Professor Phelps? Was there a breach of privacy?

9. Under what circumstances would a court disregard precedent?

10. What is the difference between a statute and an administrative regulation?

11. The Eminem ad for Chrysler that ran during the Super Bowl in February 2011 was rated as one of the best ads for the game. In May 2011, Audi ran an ad at a German auto show that had the "feel" of the Eminem Chrysler "Lose Yourself" ad. Subsequently, the German auto show ad made its way onto the Internet.

    The German ad caught the attention of Eminem and 8 Mile, Eminem's publishing company. They notified Audi that the ad constituted an unauthorized use of their intellectual property. Explain what rights Eminem and 8 Mile have and how the courts can help.

12. Give examples of areas covered by federal laws. Give examples of areas covered by city ordinances. What are the limitations on these two sources of laws? What could the laws at these two levels not do?

13. What is the principle of *stare decisis?*

14. Explain how Twitter, Facebook, and LinkedIn have resulted in the development of new laws and precedent.

15. During the 2001 baseball season, San Francisco Giants player Barry Bonds hit 73 home runs, a new record that broke the one set by Mark McGwire in 2000 (72 home runs). When Mr. Bonds hit his record-breaking home run, the ball went into the so-called cheap seats. Alex Popov was sitting in those seats and had brought along his baseball glove for purposes of catching any hits that might come into the stands.

    Everyone sitting in the area agreed that Mr. Popov's glove touched Bonds's home-run ball. Videotape also shows Mr. Popov's glove on the ball. However, the ball dropped and, following a melee among the cheap-seat fans, Patrick Hayashi ended up with Bonds's home-run ball.

    Mr. Popov filed suit for the ball, claiming it as his property. Such baseballs can be very valuable. The baseball from Mr. McGwire's record-breaking home run in 2000 sold for $3 million. List those areas of law that will apply as the case is tried and the owner of the baseball is determined.

CHAPTER 2

The Court System and Dispute Resolution

learningoutcomes

After studying this chapter, you should be able to

LO.1 Explain the federal and state court systems

LO.2 Describe court procedures

LO.3 List the forms of alternative dispute resolution and distinguish among them

Despite carefully negotiated and well-written contracts and high safety standards in the workplace or in product design and production, businesses can end up in a lawsuit. **For Example,** you could hire the brightest and most expensive lawyer in town to prepare a contract with another party and believe the final agreement is "bulletproof." However, even a bulletproof contract does not guarantee performance by the other party, and you may have to file a suit to collect your damages.

Business disputes can be resolved in court or through alternative dispute resolution. This chapter covers the structure of the court system and the litigation process as well as the forms of alternative dispute resolution.

A. The Court System

A **court** is a tribunal established by government to hear evidence, decide cases brought before it, and provide remedies when a wrong has been committed. As discussed in Chapter 1, sometimes courts prevent wrongs by issuing the equitable remedy of an injunction. **For Example,** in March 2012, a federal court issued an injunction against Cardinal Health because it was shipping too much oxycodone to pharmacies in Florida, and the FDA had discovered that the prescriptions were fraudulent. The FDA needed to stop the flow of the drug while it pulled the prescriptions.[1]

1. The Types of Courts

Each type of court has the authority to decide certain types or classes of cases. The authority of courts to hear cases is called **jurisdiction**. One form of jurisdiction, **subject matter jurisdiction**, covers the type of cases the court has the authority to hear. Courts that have the authority to hear the original proceedings in a case (the trial court) are called courts of **original jurisdiction**. **For Example,** in a court of original jurisdiction witnesses testify, documents are admitted into evidence, and the jury, in the case of a jury trial, hears all the evidence and then makes a decision.

Other types of subject matter jurisdiction give courts the authority over particular legal topic areas. A court with **general jurisdiction** has broad authority to hear general civil and criminal cases. When a general jurisdiction trial court hears criminal cases, it serves as the trial court for those charged with crimes. General trial courts also have the authority to hear civil disputes, such as breach of contract cases and personal injury lawsuits.

A court with **limited or special jurisdiction** has the authority to hear only particular kinds of cases. **For Example,** many states have courts that can hear only disputes in which the damages are $10,000 or less. Other examples of limited or special jurisdiction courts are juvenile courts, probate courts, and domestic relations courts. States vary in the names they give these courts, but these courts of special or limited jurisdiction have very narrow authority for the types of cases they hear. In the federal court system, limited or special jurisdiction courts include bankruptcy courts and the U.S. Tax Court.

A court with **appellate jurisdiction** reviews the work of a lower court. **For Example,** a trial court may issue a judgment that a defendant in a breach of contract suit should pay $500,000 in damages. That defendant could appeal the decision to an appellate court and seek review of the decision itself or even the amount of the damages.[2] An **appeal** is a review of the trial and decision of the lower court. An appellate court does not hear witnesses or take testimony. An appellate court, usually a panel of three judges, simply reviews the transcript and evidence from the lower court and determines whether there has been **reversible error.** A reversible error is a mistake in applying the law or a mistake in admitting evidence that affected the outcome of the case. An appellate court can **affirm** or **reverse** a lower court decision or **remand** that decision for another trial or additional hearings. The *Yates v. State* case deals with an appeal and reversal of a lower court decision.

[1] *Holiday CVS, L.L.C. v. Holder*, 839 F. Supp. 2d 145 (D.D.C. 2012).

[2] A case that is sent back for a redetermination of damages is remanded for what is known as *remittur*. For example, an appeal of Oracle's $1.3 billion verdict against SAP was sent back for another determination of damages, with the judge indicating $272 million was in the right range. *Oracle USA, Inc. v. SAP AG*, 2012 WL 29095 (N.D. Cal.).

Yates v. State, 171 S.W.3d 215 (Tex. App. 2005)

Law and Order on TV and in the Court

Andrea Pia Yates (Appellant) (Andrea) and Russell Yates were married on April 17, 1993. Their first child, Noah, was born in February 1994; their second child, John, was born in December 1995; and their third child, Paul, was born in September 1997. During this time, the Yates family moved from place to place living in a recreational vehicle. In 1998, they moved from the recreational vehicle to a converted bus and continued to live in a trailer park.

In February 1999, a fourth child, Luke, was born. On June 18, 1999, Andrea suffered severe depression and tried to commit suicide by taking an overdose of an antidepressant that had been prescribed for her father. She was admitted to the psychiatric unit of Methodist Hospital. After her release, she began seeing a psychiatrist as an outpatient. On July 20, 1999, Mr. Yates found Andrea in the bathroom, holding a knife to her neck. She was admitted to Spring Shadows Glen Hospital where a physician classified her among the five sickest patients she had ever seen. When she was discharged, her treating physician warned Mr. Yates that having another baby could result in a severe psychotic episode. Following her release in August 1999, the Yates family moved from the converted bus to a house and in November 2000, Andrea had her fifth child, Mary. Several months later her father died and Andrea experienced another depression and resulting hospitalization. Upon her discharge, her treating physician recommended that someone stay with her at all times and that she not be left alone with her children.

During April 2001, Mr. Yates' mother came to the house each day and described Andrea as almost catatonic, unresponsive, trembling, and scratching her head until she created bald spots. She did not eat.

On June 20, 2001, at 9:48 A.M., Mrs. Yates called 9-1-1 and told the operator that she needed a police officer to come to her home. She also called Mr. Yates at his work and told him that he needed to come home, because the kids were hurt. He asked, "Which ones?" She responded, "All of them."

Within minutes of the 9-1-1 call, several police officers arrived at the Yates' home. They discovered four dead children, soaking wet and covered with a sheet, lying on appellant's bed. The fifth child, Noah, was still in the bathtub, floating face down.

Mrs. Yates was charged with capital murder and entered a plea of "not guilty by reason of insanity."

At trial, ten psychiatrists and two psychologists testified regarding Andrea's mental illness. The tenth psychiatrist, Dr. Park Dietz, who interviewed Mrs. Yates and was the State's sole mental-health expert in the case, testified that Yates, although psychotic on June 20, knew that what she did was wrong.

On cross-examination, Mrs. Yates's counsel asked Dr. Dietz about his consulting work with the television show *Law & Order*, which Mrs. Yates was known to watch. The testimony was as follows:

Q. Now, you are, are you not, a consultant on the television program known as *Law & Order?*

A. Two of them.

Q. Okay. Did either one of those deal with postpartum depression or women's mental health?

A. As a matter of fact, there was a show of a woman with postpartum depression who drowned her children in the bathtub and was found insane and it was aired shortly before the crime occurred.

The second mention of *Law & Order* came during Dr. Lucy Puryear's testimony. Dr. Puryear testified as follows:

Q. You know she watched *Law & Order* a lot; right?

A. I didn't know. No.

Q. Did you know that in the weeks before June 20th, there was a *Law & Order* episode where a woman killed her children by drowning them in a bathtub, was defended on the basis of whether she was sane or insane under the law, and the diagnosis was postpartum depression and in the program the person was found insane, not guilty by reason of insanity? Did you know that?

A. No.

If I had known she watched that show, I would have ask[ed] her about it, yes.

In his final argument appellant's attorney referred to Dr. Dietz's testimony by stating, "Or maybe even we heard some evidence that she saw some show on TV and knew she could drown her children and get away with it."

The prosecutor, in his final argument, made the following reference to Dietz's testimony about the *Law & Order* episode:

> *She gets very depressed and goes into Devereux. And at times she says these thoughts came to her during that month. These thoughts came to her, and she watches Law & Order regularly, she sees this program. There is a way out. She tells that to Dr. Dietz. A way out.*

The jury returned a guilty verdict. Mrs. Yates's counsel discovered that Dr. Dietz had given false testimony. The producer of *Law & Order* spoke to counsel by telephone and

Continued

said he could not recall such an episode. An attorney representing the producer, after talking to Dr. Dietz and researching the shows, verified to counsel that there was no show with a plot as outlined by Dr. Dietz. Dr. Dietz acknowledged that he had made an error in his testimony. Mrs. Yates appealed the guilty verdict on the grounds that the testimony about the show constituted reversible error.

JUDICIAL OPINION

NUCHIA, Justice... The State recognizes that the State's knowing use of perjured testimony that is likely to materially affect the judgment violates the Due Process Clause of the Fourteenth Amendment of the United States Constitution. The State argues that it did not know that the testimony was false, did not use the false information, and the information was not material. We agree that this case does not involve the State's knowing use of perjured testimony. At the hearing on appellant's motion for mistrial, appellant did not complain that there had been prosecutorial misconduct. Rather, appellant stated, "[M]ake no mistake, the issue is not whether or not the State was aware and we have no reason to believe the State was aware that such a program did not exist. The issue is that the defense of insanity was rebutted by the testimony of Dr. Dietz relative to an act of premeditation, that is a planned and/or a deceptive act on Mrs. Yates' part, that is something that would give her an idea, a way out of these particular allegations. And that was relayed to this jury and we believe that the jury relied upon the presentation of Dr. Dietz as well as the cross-examination by [the State's attorney] of Dr. Puryear relative to this particular issue."

It is uncontested that the testimony of Dr. Dietz regarding his consultation on a *Law & Order* television show having a plot remarkably similar to the acts committed by appellant was untrue and that there was no *Law & Order* television show with such a plot. However, the State asserts that it is "very questionable whether it can be said that the trial prosecutors used Dr. Dietz' testimony on cross-examination, especially in light of the fact that it played absolutely no role in the development of Dr. Dietz' conclusion that the appellant knew that her conduct was wrong...."

The record reflects that the State used Dr. Dietz's testimony twice. First, the State used the testimony to cross-examine Dr. Puryear, who had seen appellant for several months while appellant was in the county jail, asking Dr. Puryear whether she knew that appellant watched *Law & Order* and whether she knew that there was an episode with a plot line mirroring appellant's acts. In so doing, the State repeated those facts that were common to appellant's acts and the referenced episode, thus emphasizing those facts already stated by Dr. Dietz. Second, the State connected the dots in its final argument by juxtaposing appellant's depression, her dark thoughts, watching *Law & Order* and seeing "a way out." Thus, the State used Dr. Dietz's false testimony to suggest to the jury that appellant patterned her actions after that *Law & Order* episode. We emphasize that the State's use of Dr. Dietz's false testimony was not prosecutorial misconduct. Rather, it served to give weight to that testimony.

The State argues that Dr. Dietz's testimony regarding the *Law & Order* episode was not material. The State asserts that "there is no reasonable likelihood" that the testimony "could have affected the judgment of the jury," but does not make any argument to support such a conclusory statement. We conclude that the testimony, combined with the State's cross-examination of Dr. Puryear and closing argument, was material. The materiality of the testimony is further evidenced by the fact that appellant's attorney felt compelled to address it in his own closing argument.

The State also asserts that Dr. Dietz did not suggest that appellant used the plot of the show to plan killing her children. Although it is true that Dr. Dietz did not make such a suggestion, the State did in its closing argument.

Five mental health experts testified that appellant did not know right from wrong or that she thought what she did was right. Dr. Dietz was the only mental health expert who testified that appellant knew right from wrong. Therefore, his testimony was critical to establish the State's case. Although the record does not show that Dr. Dietz intentionally lied in his testimony, his false testimony undoubtedly gave greater weight to his opinion.

We conclude that there is a reasonable likelihood that Dr. Dietz's false testimony could have affected the judgment of the jury. We further conclude that Dr. Dietz's false testimony affected the substantial rights of appellant. We reverse the trial court's judgment and remand the cause for further proceedings.[3]

QUESTIONS

1. What was Mrs. Yates' family and mental health history?
2. What was the significance of the *Law & Order* show testimony?
3. Why does the appellate court find that the false testimony about the *Law & Order* segment was reversible error?

[3] Mrs. Yates was found to be criminally insane in her 2006 retrial and is now institutionalized.

2. The Federal Court System

The federal court system consists of three levels of courts. Figure 2-1 illustrates federal court structure.

(A) Federal District Courts. The **federal district courts** are the general trial courts of the federal system. They are courts of original jurisdiction that hear both civil and criminal matters. Criminal cases in federal district courts are those in which the defendant is charged with a violation of federal law (the U.S. Code). In addition to the criminal cases, the types of civil cases that can be brought in federal district courts include (1) civil suits in which the United States is a party, (2) cases between citizens of different states that involve damages of $75,000 or more, and (3) cases that arise under the U.S. Constitution or federal laws and treaties.

Federal district courts are organized within each of the states. There are 94 federal districts (each state has at least one federal district and there are 89 federal districts in the United States with the remaining courts found in Puerto Rico, Guam, etc.). Judges and courtrooms are assigned according to the caseload in that geographic area of the state.[4] Some states, such as New York and California, have several federal districts because of the population base and the resulting caseload. Figure 2-2 shows the geographic structure of the federal court system, including the appellate circuits.

The federal system has additional trial courts with limited jurisdiction, differing from the general jurisdiction of the federal district courts. These courts include, for example, the federal bankruptcy courts, Indian tribal courts, Tax Court, Court of Federal

FIGURE 2-1 *The Federal Court System*

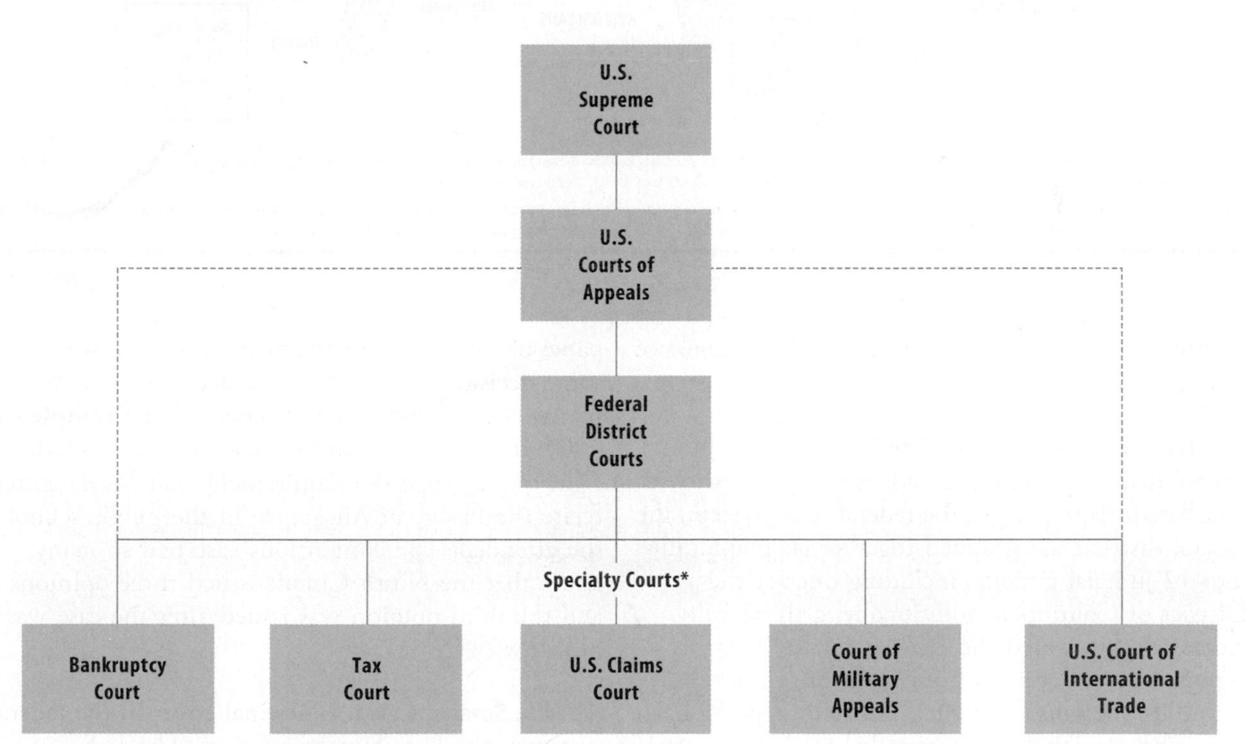

*Appeals often go directly to U.S. Courts of Appeals.

[4] For complete information about the courts and the number of judgeships, go to 28 U.S.C. §§81-144 and 28 U.S.C. §133.

FIGURE 2-2 *The Thirteen Federal Judicial Circuits*

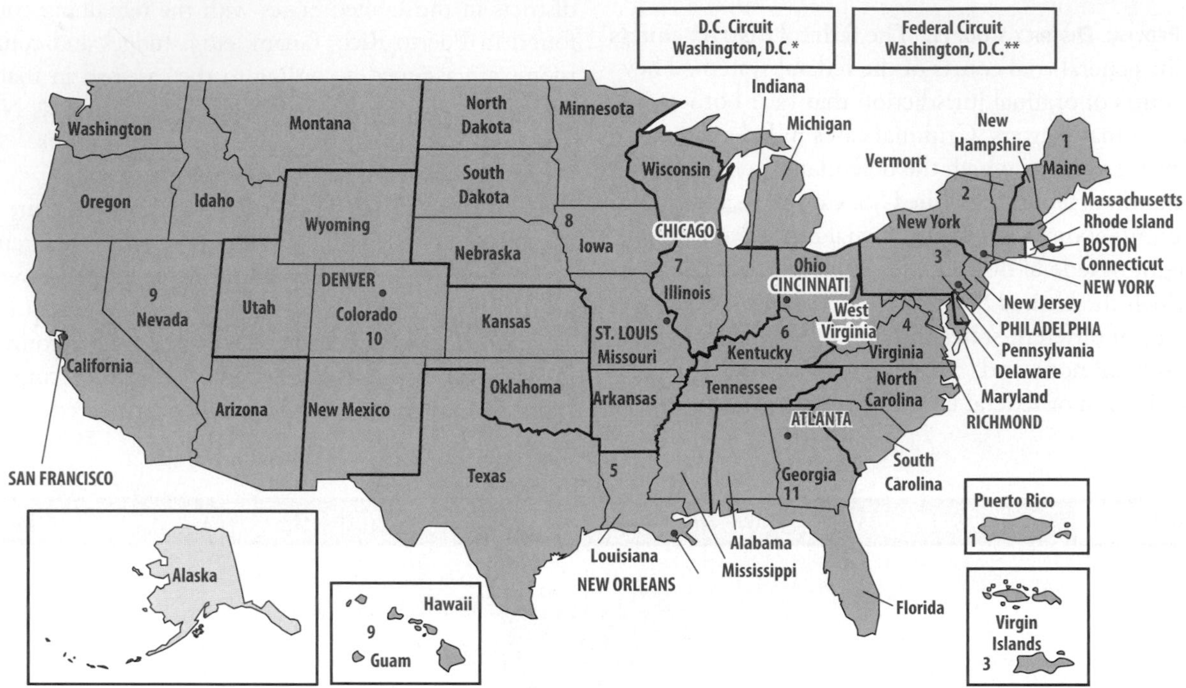

*A sizable portion of the caseload of the D.C. Circuit comes from the federal administrative agencies and offices located in Washington, D.C., such as the Securities and Exchange Commission, the National Labor Relations Board, the Federal Trade Commission, the Secretary of the Treasury, and the Labor Department, as well as appeals from the U.S. District Court of the District of Columbia.

**Rather than being defined by geography like the regional courts of appeals, the Federal Circuit is defined by subject matter, having jurisdiction over such matters as patent infringement cases, appeals from the Court of Federal Claims and the Court of International Trade, and appeals from administrative rulings regarding subject matter such as unfair import practices and tariff schedule disputes.

Claims, Court of Veterans Appeals, and the Court of International Trade.

(B) U.S. COURTS OF APPEALS. The final decision in a federal district court can be appealed to a court with appellate jurisdiction. In the federal court system, the federal districts are grouped together geographically into 12 judicial circuits, including one for the District of Columbia. Additionally, a thirteenth federal circuit, called the *Federal Circuit,* hears certain types of appeals from all of the circuits, including specialty cases such as patent appeals. Each circuit has an appellate court called the U.S. Court of Appeals, and the judges for these courts review the decisions of the federal district courts. Generally, a panel of three judges reviews the cases. However, some decisions, called ***en banc*** decisions, are made by the circuit's full panel of judges. **For Example,** in 2003, the Ninth Circuit heard an appeal on a father's right to challenge the requirement that his daughter recite the Pledge of Allegiance in the public school she attended. The contentious case had so many issues that the Ninth Circuit issued three opinions and the third opinion was issued after the case was heard *en banc.*[5]

(C) U.S. SUPREME COURT. The final court in the federal system is the U.S. Supreme Court. The U.S. Supreme Court has appellate jurisdiction over cases that are appealed from the federal courts of appeals

[5] *Newdow v. U.S. Congress,* 292 F.3d 597 (9th Cir. 2002) (*Newdow I*); *Newdow v. U.S. Congress,* 313 F.3d 500, 502 (9th Cir. 2002) (*Newdow II*); and *Newdow v. U.S. Congress,* 328 F.3d 466, 468 (9th Cir. 2003) (*Newdow III*). The U.S. Supreme Court eventually heard the case. *Elkgrove Unified School District v. Newdow,* 542 U.S. 1 (2004). Another *en banc* hearing occurred at the Ninth Circuit over the issues in the California gubernatorial recall election. The three-judge panel held that the voting methods in California violated the rights of voters and therefore placed a stay on the election. However, the Ninth Circuit then heard the case *en banc* and reversed the decision of the original three-judge panel. The recall election then proceeded.

as well as from state supreme courts when a constitutional issue is involved in the case or a state court has reversed a federal court ruling. The U.S. Supreme Court does not hear all cases from the federal courts of appeals but has a process called granting a **writ of *certiorari***, which is a preliminary review of those cases appealed to decide whether a case will be heard or allowed to stand as ruled on by the lower courts.[6]

The U.S. Supreme Court is the only court expressly created in the U.S. Constitution. All other courts in the federal system were created by Congress pursuant to its Constitutional power. The Constitution also makes the U.S. Supreme Court a court of original jurisdiction. The U.S. Supreme Court serves as the trial court for cases involving ambassadors, public ministers, or consuls and for cases in which two states are involved in a lawsuit. **For Example,** the U.S. Supreme Court has served for a number of years as the trial court for a Colorado River water rights case in which California, Nevada, and Arizona are parties.

3. State Court Systems

(A) General Trial Courts. Most states have trial courts of general jurisdiction that may be called superior courts, circuit courts, district courts, or county courts. These courts of general and original jurisdiction usually hear both criminal and civil cases. Cases that do not meet the jurisdictional requirements for the federal district courts would be tried in these courts. Figure 2-3 illustrates a sample state court system.

(B) Specialty Courts. Most states also have courts with limited jurisdiction, sometimes referred to as *specialty courts.* **For Example,** most states have juvenile courts, or courts with limited jurisdiction over criminal matters that involve defendants who are under the age of 18. Other specialty courts or lesser courts in state systems are probate and family law courts.

(C) City, Municipal, and Justice Courts. Cities and counties may also have lesser courts with limited jurisdiction, which may be referred to as *municipal courts* or *justice courts.* These courts generally handle civil matters in which the claim made in the suit is an amount below a certain level, such as $5,000 or $10,000. These courts may also handle misdemeanor types of offenses, such as traffic violations or violations of noise ordinances, and the trials for them.

(D) Small Claims Courts. Most states also have **small claims courts** at the county or city level. These are courts of limited jurisdiction where parties with small amounts in dispute may come to have a third party, such as a justice of the peace or city judge, review their disputes and determine how they should be resolved. A true small claims court is one in which the parties are not permitted to be represented by counsel. Rather, the parties present their cases to the judge in an informal manner without the strict procedural rules that apply in courts of general jurisdiction. Small claims courts provide a faster and inexpensive means for resolving a dispute that does not involve a large amount of claimed damages.

(E) State Appellate Courts. Most states also have intermediate-level courts similar to the federal courts of appeals. They are courts with appellate jurisdiction that review the decisions of lower courts in that state. Decisions of the general trial courts in a state would be appealed to these courts.

(F) State Supreme Courts. The highest court in most states is generally known as the *state supreme court,* but a few states, such as New York, may call their highest court the *court of appeals;* Maine and Massachusetts, for example, call their highest court the *supreme judicial court.* State supreme courts primarily have appellate jurisdiction, but some states' courts do have original jurisdiction, such as in Arizona, where counties in litigation have their trial at the supreme court level. Most state supreme courts also have a screening process for cases. They are required to hear some cases, such as criminal cases in which the defendant has received the death penalty. A decision of a state supreme court is final except in those circumstances in which a federal law or treaty or the U.S. Constitution is involved. Cases with these federal subject matter issues can then be appealed to the U.S. Supreme Court.

[6] For example, the Supreme Court refused to grant *certiorari* in a Fifth Circuit case on law school admissions at the University of Texas. However, it granted *certiorari* in a later case involving law school admissions at the University of Michigan. *Gratz v. Bollinger,* 539 U.S. 244 (2003). The U.S. Supreme Court granted certiorari. *Fisher v. University of Texas,* 132 S.Ct. 1536 (2012).

FIGURE 2-3 *Sample State Court System*

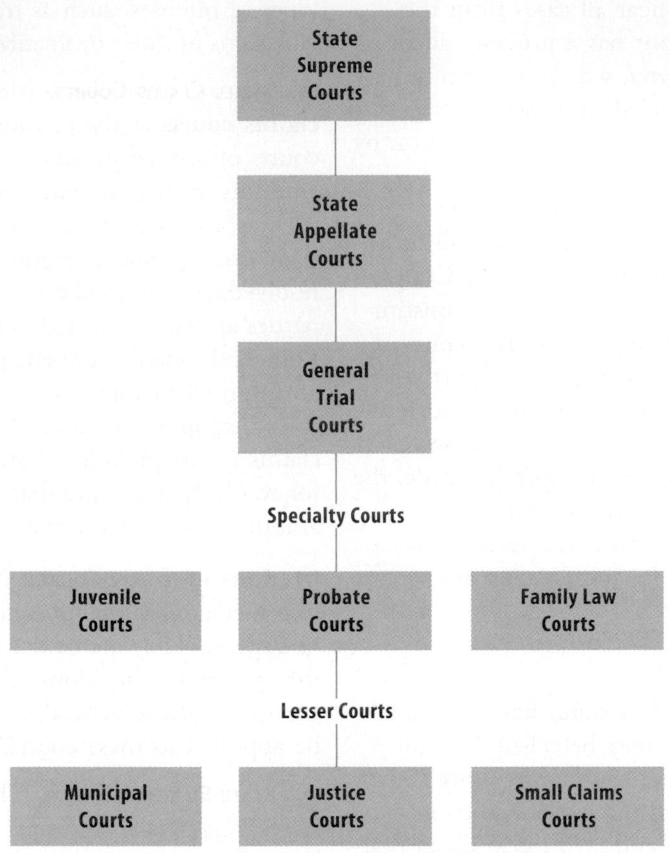

B. Court Procedure

Once a party decides to use the court system for resolution of a dispute, that party enters a world with specific rules, procedures, and terms that must be used to have a case proceed.

4. Participants in the Court System

The **plaintiff** is the party that initiates the proceedings in a court of original jurisdiction. In a criminal case in which charges are brought, the party initiating the proceedings would be called the **prosecutor**. The party against whom the civil or criminal proceedings are brought is the **defendant**. A **judge** is the primary officer of the court and is either an elected or an appointed official who presides over the matters brought before the court. Attorneys or lawyers are representatives for the plaintiff and the defendant for purposes of presenting their cases. Lawyers and clients have a privilege of confidentiality known as the **attorney-client privilege**. Lawyers cannot disclose what their clients tell them unless the client is committing, or plans to commit, a crime.

A **jury** is a body of citizens sworn by a court to reach a verdict on the basis of the case presented to them. Jurors are chosen for service based on lists compiled from voter registration and driver's license records.

5. Which Law Applies—Conflicts of Law

When a lawsuit is brought, there is not just the question of where a case will be tried but also of what law will be applied in determining the rights of the parties. The principle that determines when a court applies the law of its own state—the law of the forum—or some foreign law is called *conflict of laws.* Because there are 50 state court systems and a federal court system, as well as a high degree of interstate activity, conflicts of law questions arise frequently.

Some general rules apply. For example, the law of the state in which the court is located governs the case on procedural issues and rules of evidence. In contract litigation, the court applies the law of the state in which the contract was made for determining issues of formation. Performance disputes and damages for nonperformance are generally governed by the law of the state where the contract is to be performed. International contracts follow similar rules. **For Example,** a California court will apply Swiss law to a contract made in Switzerland that is to be performed in that country.

However, it is becoming more common for the parties to specify their choice of law in their contract. In the absence of a law-selecting provision in the contract, there is a growing acceptance of the rule that a contract should be governed by the law of the state that has the most significant contacts with the transaction.

For Example, assume the buyer's place of business and the seller's plant are located in Nebraska, and the buyer is purchasing goods from the seller to resell to Nebraska customers. Many courts will hold that this is a contract governed by the law of Nebraska. In determining which state has the most significant contacts, the court considers the place of contracting, negotiating, and performing; the location of the subject matter of the contract; and the domicile (residence), states of incorporation, and principal place of business of the parties.

6. Initial Steps in a Lawsuit

The following steps in a lawsuit generally apply in cases brought in courts of original jurisdiction. Not every step applies in every case, but understanding litigation steps and terms is important for businesspeople.

(A) Commencement of a Lawsuit. A lawsuit begins with the filing of a **complaint**. The complaint generally contains a description of the wrongful conduct and a request for damages, such as a monetary amount. **For Example,** a plaintiff in a contract suit would describe the contract, when it was entered into, and when the defendant stopped performance on the contract. A copy of the contract would be attached to the complaint.

(B) Service of Process. Once the plaintiff has filed the complaint with the proper court, the plaintiff has the responsibility of notifying the defendant that the lawsuit has been filed. The defendant must be served with **process**. Process, often called a *writ, notice,* or *summons,* is delivered to the defendant and includes a copy of the complaint and notification that the defendant must appear and respond to the allegations in the complaint.

(C) The Defendant's Response and the Pleadings. After the defendant is served with process in the case, the defendant is required to respond to or **answer** the complaint within the time provided under the court's rules. In answering the plaintiff's complaint, the defendant has several options. For example, the defendant could make a **motion to dismiss**, which is a request to the court to dismiss the lawsuit on the grounds that, even if everything the plaintiff said in the complaint were true, there is still no right of recovery. A motion to dismiss is also called a **demurrer**.

A defendant could also respond and deny the allegations. **For Example,** in a contract lawsuit, the defendant-seller could say he did not breach the contract but stopped shipment of the goods because the plaintiff-buyer did not pay for the goods in advance as the contract required. A defendant could also **counterclaim** in the answer, which is asking the court for damages as a result of the underlying dispute. **For Example,** the defendant-seller in the contract lawsuit might ask for damages for the plaintiff-buyer's failure to pay as the contract required.

All documents filed in this initial phase of the case are referred to as the **pleadings**. The pleadings are a statement of the case and the basis for recovery if all the facts alleged can be proved.

(D) Discovery. The Federal Rules of Civil Procedure and similar rules in all states permit one party to obtain from the adverse party information about all witnesses, documents, and any other items relevant to the case. **Discovery** requires each side to name its potential witnesses and to provide each side the chance to question those witnesses in advance of the trial. Each party also has the opportunity to examine, inspect, and photograph books, records, buildings, and machines. Even examining the physical or mental condition of a party is part of discovery when it has relevance in the case. The scope of discovery is extremely broad because the rules permit any questions that are likely to lead to admissible evidence.

Deposition.

A **deposition** is the testimony of a witness taken under oath outside the courtroom; it is transcribed by a court reporter. Each party is permitted to question the witness. If a party or a witness gives testimony at the trial that is inconsistent with her deposition testimony, the prior inconsistent testimony can be used to **impeach** the witness's credibility at trial.

Depositions can be taken either for discovery purposes or to preserve the testimony of a witness who will not be available during the trial. Some states now permit depositions to be videotaped. A videotape is a more effective way of presenting deposition testimony than reading that testimony at trial from a reporter's transcript because jurors can see the witness and the witness's demeanor and hear the words as they were spoken, complete with inflection.[7]

Other Forms of Discovery.

Other forms of discovery include medical exams, particularly in cases in which the plaintiff is claiming damages for physical injuries. Written **interrogatories** (questions) and written **requests for production of documents** are discovery requests that can be very time consuming to the answering party and often lead to pretrial legal disputes between the parties and their attorneys as a result of the legal expenses involved.

(E) Motion for Summary Judgment. If a case has no material facts in dispute, either party can file a **motion for summary judgment**. Using affidavits or deposition testimony obtained in discovery, the court can find that there are no factual issues and decide the case as a matter of law. **For Example,** suppose that the parties can agree that they entered into a life insurance contract but dispute whether the policy applies when there is a suicide. The facts are not in dispute; the law on payment of insurance proceeds in the event of a suicide is the issue. Such a case is one that is appropriate for summary judgment.

(F) Designation of Expert Witnesses. In some cases, such as those involving product safety, the parties may want to designate an expert witness. An **expert witness** is a witness who has some special expertise, such as an economist who gives expert opinion on the value of future lost income or a scientist who testifies about the safety of a prescription drug. There are rules for naming expert witnesses as well as for admitting into evidence any studies or documents of the expert.[8] The purpose of these rules is to avoid the problem of what has been called *junk science,* or the admission of experts' testimony and research that has not been properly conducted or reviewed by peers.

7. The Trial

(A) Selecting a Jury. Jurors drawn for service are questioned by the judge and lawyers to determine whether they are biased or have any preformed judgments about the parties in the case. Jury selection is called ***voir dire* examination**. **For Example,** in the trial of Martha Stewart, the multimedia home and garden diva, it took a great deal of time for the lawyers to question the potential jurors about their prior knowledge concerning the case, which had received nationwide attention and much media coverage. Lawyers have the opportunity to remove jurors who know parties in the case or who indicate they have already formed opinions about guilt or innocence. The attorneys question the potential jurors to determine if a juror should be *challenged for cause* (e.g., when the prospective juror states he is employed by the plaintiff's company). Challenges for cause are unlimited, but each side can also exercise six to eight peremptory challenges.[9] A peremptory challenge is a challenge that is used to strike (remove) a juror for any reason except on racial grounds.[10]

[7] At the civil trial of O.J. Simpson for the wrongful death of Nicole Brown Simpson and Ronald Goldman, Daniel Petrocelli used a videotape of Mr. Simpson's deposition very effectively in impeaching Mr. Simpson's testimony at trial. Daniel Petrocelli, *Triumph of Justice: The Final Judgment on the Simpson Saga* (1998).

[8] *Daubert v. Merrell Dow Pharmaceuticals, Inc.,* 509 U.S. 579 (1993).

[9] The number of peremptory challenges varies from state to state and may also vary within a particular state depending on the type of case. For example, in Arizona, peremptory challenges are unlimited in capital cases.

[10] *Felkner v. Jackson,* 131 S.Ct. 1305 (2011).

Thinking Things Through

Why Do We Require Sworn Testimony?

There is a difference between what people say in conversation (and even what company executives say in speeches and reports) and what they are willing to say under oath. Speaking under oath often means that different information and recollections emerge. The oath is symbolic and carries the penalty of criminal prosecution for perjury if the testimony given is false.

The *Wall Street Journal* has reported that the testimony of executives in the Microsoft antitrust trial and their statements regarding their business relationships outside the courtroom are quite different. For example, the following quotations indicate some discrepancies. Eric Benhamou, the chief executive officer (CEO) of Palm, Inc., said:

> *We believe that the handheld opportunity remains wide open .... Unlike the PC industry, there is no monopoly of silicon, there is no monopoly of software.*

However, at the Microsoft trial, another officer of Palm, Michael Mace, offered the following testimony:

> *We believe that there is a very substantial risk that Microsoft could manipulate its products and its standards in order to exclude Palm from the marketplace in the future.*

Likewise, Microsoft has taken different positions inside and outside the courtroom. For example, an attorney for Microsoft stated that Microsoft had "zero deployments of its interactive TV middleware products connected to cable systems in the United States." However, Microsoft's marketing materials provide as follows:

> *Microsoft's multiple deployments around the world—now including Charter—show Microsoft TV is ready to deploy now and set the standard for what TV can be.**

Explain why the executives had differing statements. For more information on the Microsoft antitrust cases, go to **www.usdoj.gov** or **www.microsoft.com**.

*Rebecca Buckman and Nicholas Kulish, "Microsoft Trial Prompts an Outbreak of Doublespeak," Wall Street Journal, April 15, 2002, B1, B3.

(B) Opening Statements. After the jury is chosen, the attorneys for each of the parties make their **opening statements** to the jury. An opening statement, as one lawyer has explained, makes a puzzle frame for the case so jurors can follow the witnesses and place the pieces of the case—the various forms of evidence—within the frame.

(C) The Presentation of Evidence. Following the opening statements, the plaintiff presents his case with witnesses and other evidence. A judge rules on the **admissibility** of evidence. Evidence can consist of documents, testimony, expert testimony, medical information from exams, and even physical evidence.

In the case of testimony, the attorney for the plaintiff conducts **direct examination** of his witnesses during his case, and the defense attorney conducts **cross-examination** of the plaintiff's witnesses. The plaintiff's attorney can then ask questions again of his witnesses in what is called **redirect examination**. Finally, the defense attorney may question the plaintiff's witnesses again in **recross-examination**. The defendant presents her case after the plaintiff's case concludes. During the defendant's case, the lawyer for the defendant conducts direct examination of the defendant's witnesses, and the plaintiff's lawyer can then cross-examine the defendant's witnesses.

(D) Motion For a Directed Verdict. A motion for a **directed verdict** asks the court to grant a verdict because even if all the evidence that has been presented by each side were true, there is either no basis for recovery or no defense to recovery. **For Example,** suppose that a plaintiff company presented evidence that an employee who quit working for the company posted on his Facebook page, "I just wasn't happy there." The company might not feel good about the former employee's post, but there is no false statement and no breach of privacy. The evidence is true, but there is no legal right of recovery. The defendant employee would be entitled to a directed verdict. A directed verdict means that the party has not presented enough evidence to show that there is some right of recovery under the law.

(E) Closing Arguments or Summation. After the witnesses for both parties have been examined and all the evidence has been presented, each attorney makes a

Ethics & the Law

Injustice, Misconduct, and Senator Stevens

The late Senator Ted Stevens (from Alaska) was tried in the fall of 2008 on charges that he lied on his financial disclosure forms by not disclosing the work a contractor performed on his Alaska home. He was convicted just days before the 2008 federal elections and he lost his Senate seat. However, the verdict and all of the charges were dismissed in 2009 on a motion by the U.S. attorney general, Eric Holder, when the Department of Justice discovered that prosecutors withheld exculpatory evidence, evidence that would have helped Senator Stevens. Sadly, Senator Stevens was killed in a plane crash in 2010. A 525-page report released in 2012 concluded that several prosecutors withheld evidence that Mr. Stevens had asked several times to be billed for the work on his home so that he could pay and make the necessary financial disclosures about its value. Also, one of the witness's background was shaky, something that would have caused his credibility to come into question at the trial. The jury never heard this evidence and neither Senator Stevens nor his lawyers were given the documents and interviews that would have helped his case. No criminal charges will be brought against the prosecutors who withheld the evidence. However, does that mean that their conduct was ethical? What is the obligation of lawyers when they discover evidence that favors the other side in a case?

[*In re Special Proceedings*, 842 F. Supp. 2d 232 (D.D.C. 2012)]

closing argument. These statements are also called **summations**; they summarize the case and urge the jury to reach a particular verdict.

(F) Motion for Mistrial. During the course of a trial, when necessary to avoid great injustice, the trial court may declare a **mistrial**. A mistrial requires a do-over, a new jury. A mistrial can be declared for jury or attorney misconduct. **For Example,** if a juror were caught fraternizing with one of the lawyers in the case, objectivity would be compromised and the court would most likely declare a mistrial. See also eCommerce & Cyber Law on p. 27 for more information on juror misconduct and case dismissals.

(G) Jury Instructions and Verdict. After the summation by the attorneys, the court gives the jurors **instructions** on the appropriate law to apply to the facts presented. The jury then deliberates and renders its verdict. After the jury verdict, the court enters a judgment. If the jury is deadlocked and unable to reach a verdict, known as a hung jury or a mistrial, the case is reset for a new trial at some future date.

(H) Motion for New Trial; Motion for Judgment *n.o.v.* A court may grant a **judgment *non obstante veredicto*** or a **judgment *n.o.v.*** (notwithstanding the verdict) if the verdict is clearly wrong as a matter of law. The court can set aside the verdict and enter a judgment in favor of the other party. Perhaps one of the most famous judgments n.o.v. occurred in Boston in 1997 when a judge reversed the murder conviction of nanny Louise Woodward, who was charged with the murder of one of her young charges.

8. Posttrial Procedures

(A) Recovery of Costs/Attorney Fees. Generally, the prevailing party is awarded costs. Costs include filing fees, service-of-process fees, witness fees, deposition transcript costs, and jury fees. Costs do not include compensation spent by a party for preparing the case or being present at trial, including the time lost from work because of the case and the fee paid to the attorney, although lost wages from an injury are generally part of damages.

Attorney fees may be recovered by a party who prevails if a statute permits the recovery of attorney fees or if the complaint involves a claim for breach of contract and the contract contains a clause providing for recovery of attorney fees.

(B) Execution of Judgment. After a judgment has been entered or all appeals or appeal rights have ended, the losing party must pay that judgment. The winning party can also take steps to execute, or carry out, the judgment. The **execution** is accomplished by the seizure and sale of the losing party's assets by the sheriff according to a writ of execution or a writ of possession.

FIGURE 2-4 ***Dispute Resolution Procedures***

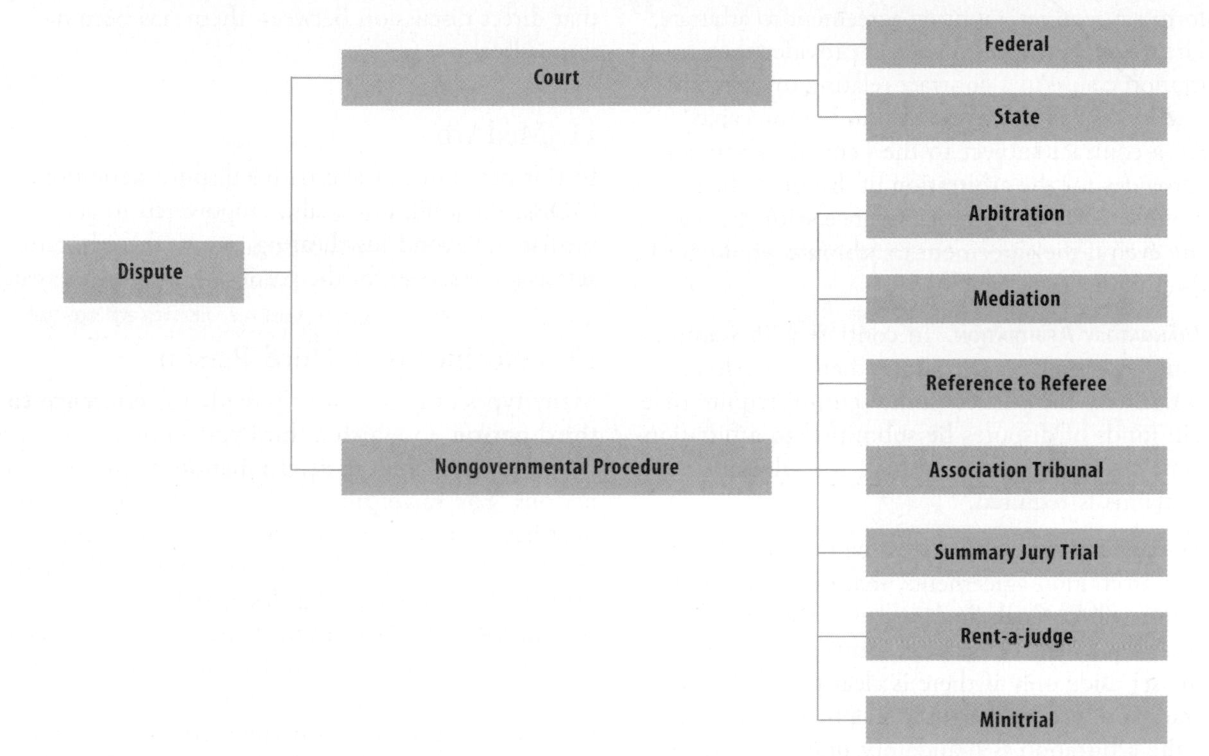

Garnishment is a common method of satisfying a judgment. When the judgment debtor is an employee, the appropriate judicial authority in the state garnishes (by written notice to the employer) a portion of the employee's wages on a regular basis until the judgment is paid.

C. Alternative Dispute Resolution (ADR)

Parties can use means other than litigation to resolve disagreements or disputes. Litigation takes significant time and money, so many businesses use alternative methods for resolving disputes. Those methods include arbitration, mediation, and several other formats. Figure 2-4 provides an overall view of alternative dispute resolution procedures.

9. Arbitration

In **arbitration**, arbitrators (disinterested persons selected by the parties to the dispute) hear evidence and determine a resolution. Arbitration enables the parties to present the facts before trained experts familiar with the industry practices that may affect the nature and outcome of the dispute. Arbitration first reached extensive use in the field of commercial contracts and is encouraged as a means of avoiding expensive litigation and easing the workload of courts.[11]

A number of states have adopted the Uniform Arbitration Act.[12] Under this act and similar statutes, the parties to a contract may agree in advance that all

[11] *Warfield v. Beth Israel Deaconess Medical Center, Inc.*, 910 N.E.2d 317 (Mass. 2009). Arbitration has existed in the United States since 1920 when New York passed an arbitration statute. For a look at the history of arbitration, see Charles L. Knapp, "Taking Contracts Private: The Quiet Revolution in Contract Law," 71 *Fordham L. Rev.* 761 (2002).

[12] On August 3, 2000, the National Conference of Commissioners on Uniform State Laws unanimously passed major revisions to the Uniform Arbitration Act (UAA). These revisions were the first major changes in 45 years to the UAA, which is the basis of arbitration law in 49 states, although not all states have adopted it in its entirety. Thirty-five states and the District of Columbia have adopted the 1955 version. Only 13 states have adopted the UAA 2000 revisions. Uniform Laws Annotated, Section 1 (2012); see also Donald L. Carpo & John B. LaRocco, "A Comparison of Litigation, Arbitration, and Mediation," 63 *Dispute Resolution J.* 48 (2008).

disputes arising under it will be submitted to arbitration. In some instances, the contract will name the arbitrators for the duration of the contract. The uniform act requires a written agreement to arbitrate.[13]

The Federal Arbitration Act[14] provides that an arbitration clause in a contract relating to an interstate transaction is valid, irrevocable, and enforceable. When a contract subject to the Federal Arbitration Act provides for the arbitration of disputes, the parties are bound to arbitrate in accordance with the federal statute even if the agreement to arbitrate would not be binding under state law.

(A) Mandatory Arbitration. In contrast with statutes that merely regulate arbitration when it is selected voluntarily by the parties, some statutes require that certain kinds of disputes be submitted to arbitration. In some states, by rule or statute, the arbitration of small claims is required.

(B) Finality of Arbitration. Most parties provide, within their arbitration agreements, that the decision of the arbitrator will be final. Such a clause is binding on the parties, even when the decision seems to be wrong, and can be set aside only if there is clear proof of fraud, arbitrary conduct, or a significant procedural error.[15]

If the arbitration is mandatory under statute or rule, the losing party generally may appeal such arbitration to a court.[16] The appeal proceeds just as though there had never been any prior arbitration. This new court proceeding is called a **trial *de novo*** and is necessary to preserve the constitutional right to a jury trial. As a practical matter, however, relatively few appeals are taken from arbitration decisions.

10. Mediation

In **mediation**, a neutral person acts as a messenger between opposing sides of a dispute, carrying to each side the latest settlement offer made by the other. The mediator has no authority to make a decision, although in some cases the mediator may make suggestions that might ultimately be accepted by the disputing parties.

The use of mediation has the advantage of keeping discussions going when the disputing parties have developed such fixed attitudes or personal animosity that direct discussion between them has become impossible.

11. MedArb

In this new form of alternative dispute resolution (ADR), the arbitrator is also empowered to act as a mediator. Beyond just hearing a case, the arbitrator acts as a messenger for the parties on unresolved issues.

12. Reference to a Third Person

Many types of transactions provide for **reference to a third person**, in which a third person or a committee makes an out-of-court determination of the rights of persons. **For Example,** employees and an employer may have agreed as a term of the employment contract that claims of employees under retirement plans will be decided by a designated board or committee. In a sales contract, the seller and buyer can select a third person to determine the price to be paid for goods. Construction contracts often include a provision for disputes to be referred to the architect in charge of the construction with the architect's decision being final.

These referrals often eliminate the disputes or pursuit of remedies. **For Example,** fire insurance policies commonly provide that if the parties cannot agree on the amount of the loss, each will appoint an appraiser, the two appraisers will appoint a third appraiser, and the three will determine the amount of the loss the insurer is required to pay.

13. Association Tribunals

Many disputes never reach the courts because both parties to a dispute belong to a group or an association, and the **association tribunal** created by the group or association disposes of the matter. Trade associations commonly require their members to employ out-of-court methods of dispute settlement.

[13] *Fawzy v. Fawzy*, 973 A.2d 347 (N.J. 2009).

[14] 9 U.S.C §§114 *et seq.*

[15] *Apache Bohai Corp. LDC v. Texaco China BV*, 480 F.3d 397 (5th Cir. 2007).

[16] *U.S. v. Park Place Associates*, 563 F.3d 907 (9th Cir. 2009).

E-Commerce & Cyberlaw

The Googling Juror

Referred to as the "Google Mistrial," a federal judge in Florida declared a mistrial after a juror told that judge that he had been doing research on the Internet on the drug trial in which he was serving. When the judge declared the mistrial, eight other jurors confessed that they had been doing the same thing.

Judges have long warned jurors about using outside sources, including the Internet, but BlackBerries and iPhones have proven to be mighty tempting for jurors. Some jurors are using Facebook to announce when verdicts are coming. One juror even looked up evidence that had been excluded by the judge in the case. When asked why he violated the judge's order, the juror said simply, "Well, I was curious." Another juror contacted the defendant through Facebook, and another mistrial resulted.

A judge in Arkansas is reviewing a request for a reversal of a $12.6 million jury verdict against a company from one of the company's lawyers based on the court's discovery that one of the jurors was using Twitter to send out postings about how the trial was proceeding. An excerpt from the posting follows:

> *"Oh, and nobody buy Stoam. It's bad mojo and they'll probably cease to Exist now that their wallet is $12m lighter ... So, Jonathan, what did you do today? Oh nothing really, I just gave away TWELVE MILLION DOLLARS of somebody else's money."**

What is the problem with jurors using these electronic tools during their cases?

*John Schwartz, "As Jurors Turn to Google and Twitter, Mistrials Are Popping Up," *New York Times*, March 18, 2009, p. A1.

For Example, the National Association of Home Builders requires its member builders to employ arbitration. The National Automobile Dealers Association provides for panels to determine warranty claims of customers. The decision of such panels is final as to the builder or dealer, but the consumer can still bring a regular lawsuit after losing before the panel. Members of an association must use the association tribunal, which means they cannot bypass the association tribunal and go directly to a law court.[17]

14. Summary Jury Trial

A **summary jury trial** is a dry-run or mock trial in which the lawyers present their claims before a jury of six persons. The object is to get the reaction of a sample jury. No evidence is presented before this jury, and it bases its opinion solely on what the lawyers state. The determination of the jury has no binding effect, but it has value in that it gives the lawyers some idea of what a jury might think if there were an actual trial. This type of ADR has special value when the heart of a case is whether something is reasonable under all circumstances. When the lawyers and their clients see how the sample jury reacts, they may moderate their positions and reach a settlement.

15. Rent-A-Judge

Under the **rent-a-judge plan**, the parties hire a judge to hear the case. In many states, the parties voluntarily choose the judge as a "referee," and the judge acts under a statute authorizing the appointment of referees. Under such a statute, the referee hears all evidence just as though there were a regular trial, and the rented judge's determination is binding on the parties unless reversed on appeal if such an appeal (like a court trial) is permitted under the parties' agreement.

16. Minitrial

When only part of a case is disputed, the parties may stay within the framework of a lawsuit but agree that only the disputed issues will be taken to trial and submitted to a jury. **For Example,** if there is no real dispute over who is liable but the parties disagree as to the damages, the issue of damages alone may be submitted to the jury. This shortened trial is often called a **minitrial**. A minitrial may use a retired judge to make a decision on just the disputed issues. The parties may also specify whether this decision will be binding on the parties. As a practical matter, the evaluation of a case by a neutral person often brings the opposing parties together to reach a settlement.

[17] The securities industry follows this process as well.

17. Judicial Triage

The court systems, experiencing heavy caseloads, now practice **judicial triage**. Judges examine cases from a timeliness perspective. For example, in asbestos cases, judges are now evaluating plaintiffs on the basis of "how sick they are" and expediting trials for those plaintiffs who are the most ill from the alleged effects of asbestos that are the subject of their suits. The trials of those who do not have medical documentation of current illness are postponed and placed on the inactive docket until the court can get to them or until the plaintiffs become sick. Using triage, one judge has been able to bring to trial 40 percent of all asbestos cases between 1992 and 2003. Since then, multiple settlements have slowed the rate of litigation.[18]

18. Contract Provisions

The parties' contract may pave the way for the settlement of future disputes by including clauses that require the parties to use one of the means of ADR. Other provisions in contracts that serve to keep the parties calm with the hope of resolving differences without a lawsuit include waiting periods before a suit can be filed and obligations to continue performing even as they try to resolve differences and issues.

LawFlix

Class Action (1991) (R)

Here is a good movie to illustrate discovery and the ethics of withholding paperwork.

Twelve Angry Men (1957) (G)

A movie that shows the jury process, rights of parties in court, jury instructions, and group think, all wrapped up in terrific dialogue.

[18] Susan Warren, "Swamped Courts Practice Plaintiff Triage," *Wall Street Journal*, January 27, 2003, B1, B3.

MAKE THE CONNECTION

SUMMARY

Courts have been created to hear and resolve legal disputes. A court's specific power is defined by its jurisdiction. Courts of original jurisdiction are trial courts, and courts that review the decisions of trial courts are appellate courts. Trial courts may have general jurisdiction to hear a wide range of civil and criminal matters, or they may be courts of limited jurisdiction—such as a probate court or the Tax Court—with the subject matter of their cases restricted to certain areas.

The courts in the United States are organized into two different systems: the state and federal court systems. There are three levels of courts, for the most part, in each system, with trial courts, appellate courts, and a supreme court in each. The federal courts are federal district courts, federal courts of appeals, and the U.S. Supreme Court.

In the states, there may be specialized courts, such as municipal, justice, and small claims courts, for trial courts. Within the courts of original jurisdiction, there are rules for procedures in all matters brought before them. A civil case begins with the filing of a complaint by a plaintiff, which is then answered by a defendant. The parties may be represented by their attorneys. Discovery is the pretrial process used by the parties to find out the evidence in the case. The parties can use depositions, interrogatories, and document requests to uncover relevant information.

The case is managed by a judge and may be tried to a jury selected through the process of *voir dire*, with the parties permitted to challenge jurors on the basis of cause or through the use of their peremptory challenges. The trial begins following discovery and involves opening statements and the presentation of evidence, including the direct examination and cross-examination of witnesses. Once a judgment is entered, the party who has won can collect the judgment through garnishment and a writ of execution.

Alternatives to litigation for dispute resolution are available, including arbitration, mediation, MedArb, reference to a third party, association tribunals, summary jury trials, rent-a-judge plans, minitrials, and judicial triage. Court dockets are relieved and cases consolidated using judicial triage, a process in which courts hear the cases involving the most serious medical issues and health conditions first. Triage is a blending of the judicial and alternative dispute resolution mechanisms.

LEARNING OUTCOMES

After studying this chapter, you should be able to clearly explain:

A. The Court System

LO.1 Explain the federal and state court systems

See Figure 2-1 on p. 17 and accompanying text.

See Figure 2-3 on p. 20 and accompanying text.

B. Court Procedure

LO.2 Describe court procedures

See the discussion of steps in litigation that begins on p. 21.

See the *For Example* discussion of the Martha Stewart *voir dire* example on p. 22.

C. Alternative Dispute Resolution (ADR)

LO.3 List the forms of alternative dispute resolution and distinguish among them

See the discussion of arbitration that begins on p. 25.

See the discussion of other forms of ADR, mediation, minitrials, rent-a-judge, MedArb, judicial triage, and referral to a third party that begins on p. 26.

See the discussion of employee and employer referrals of disputes to a designated board or committee on p. 26.

KEY TERMS

admissibility
affirm
answer
appeal
appellate jurisdiction
arbitration
association tribunal
attorney-client privilege
complaint
counterclaim
court
cross-examination
defendant
demurrer
deposition
direct examination
directed verdict
discovery
en banc
execution
expert witness
federal district courts
garnishment
general jurisdiction
impeach
instructions
interrogatories
judge
judgment n.o.v. or judgment *non obstante verdict*
judicial triage
jurisdiction
jury
limited (special) jurisdiction
mediation
minitrial
mistrial
motion for summary judgment
motion to dismiss
opening statements
original jurisdiction
plaintiff
pleadings
process
prosecutor
recross-examination
redirect examination
reference to a third person
remand
rent-a-judge plan
requests for production of documents
reverse
reversible error
small claims courts
subject matter jurisdiction
summary jury trial
summations
trial *de novo*
voir dire examination
writ of *certiorari*

QUESTIONS AND CASE PROBLEMS

1. List the steps in a lawsuit. Begin with the filing of the complaint, and explain the points at which there can be a final determination of the parties' rights in the case.
2. Explain why a business person would want to use alternative dispute resolution methods. Discuss the advantages. What disadvantages do you see?
3. Ralph Dewey has been charged with a violation of the Electronic Espionage Act, a federal statute that prohibits the transfer, by computer or disk or other electronic means, of a company's proprietary data and information. Ralph is curious. What type of court has jurisdiction? Can you determine which court?
4. Jerry Lewinsky was called for jury duty. When *voir dire* began, Jerry realized that the case involved his supervisor at work. Can Jerry remain as a juror on the case? Why or why not?
5. Carolyn, Elwood, and Isabella are involved in a real estate development. The development is a failure, and Carolyn, Elwood, and Isabella want to have their rights determined. They could bring a lawsuit, but they are afraid the case is so complicated that a judge and jury not familiar with the problems of real estate development would not reach a proper result. What can they do?
6. Larketta Randolph purchased a mobile home from Better Cents Home Builders, Inc., and financed her purchase through Green Tree Financial Corporation. Ms. Randolph signed a standard form contract that required her to buy Vendor's Single Interest insurance, which protects the seller against the costs of repossession in the event of default. The agreement also provided that all disputes arising from the contract would be resolved by binding arbitration. Larketta found that there was an additional $15 in finance charges that were not disclosed in the contract. She and other Green Tree customers filed a class-action suit to recover the fees. Green Tree moved to dismiss the suit because Larketta had not submitted the issue to arbitration. Larketta protests, "But I want the right to go to court!" Does she have that right? What are the rights of parties under a contract with an arbitration clause? [*Green Tree Financial Corp. v. Randolph*, 531 U.S. 79]
7. John Watson invested $5,000,000 in SmartRead, Inc., a company that was developing an electronic reading device. Within a few months, the $5,000,000 was spent but SmartRead never developed the reading device. John filed suit against directors of SmartRead for their failure to supervise SmartRead's CEO in his operation of the company. The directors used an expert on corporate governance to testify that the directors had done all that they could to oversee the company. The expert did not disclose that he had served as a director of a company and had been found to be negligent in his role there and had been required to pay $370,000 to shareholders. The directors won the case. Is there anything Watson can do?
8. Indicate whether the following courts are courts of original, general, limited, or appellate jurisdiction:
   a. Small claims court
   b. Federal bankruptcy court
   c. Federal district court
   d. U.S. Supreme Court
   e. Municipal court
   f. Probate court
   g. Federal court of appeals
9. The Nursing Home Pension Fund filed suit against Oracle Corporation alleging that Larry Ellison, the company's CEO, misled investors in 2001 about the true financial condition of the company. During the time of the alleged misrepresentation, Mr. Ellison was working with a biographer on his life story and there are videotapes of Mr. Ellison's interviews with his biographer as well as e-mails between the two that discuss Oracle. Could the Nursing Home Pension Fund have access to the tapes and e-mails? Explain how. [*Nursing Home Pension Fund, Local 144 v. Oracle Corp.*, 380 F.3d 1226 (9th Cir.)]
10. Mostek Corp., a Texas corporation, made a contract to sell computer-related products to

North American Foreign Trading Corp., a New York corporation. North American used its own purchase order form, on which appeared the statement that any dispute arising out of an order would be submitted to arbitration, as provided in the terms set forth on the back of the order. Acting on the purchase order, Mostek delivered almost all of the goods but failed to deliver the final installment. North American then demanded that the matter be arbitrated. Mostek refused to do so. Was arbitration required? [*Application of Mostek Corp.*, 502 N.Y.S.2d 181 (App. Div.)]

11. Ceasar Wright was a longshoreman in Charleston, South Carolina, and a member of the International Longshoremen's Association (AFL-CIO). Wright used the union hiring hall. The collective bargaining agreement (CBA) of Wright's union provides for arbitration of all grievances. Another clause of the CBA states: "It is the intention and purpose of all parties hereto that no provision or part of this Agreement shall be violative of any Federal or State Law."

    On February 18, 1992, while Wright was working for Stevens Shipping and Terminal Company (Stevens), he injured his right heel and back. He sought permanent compensation from Stevens and settled his claims for $250,000 and another $10,000 in attorney fees. Wright was also awarded Social Security disability benefits.

    In January 1995, Wright, whose doctor had approved his return to work, returned to the hiring hall and asked to be referred for work. Wright did work between January 2 and January 11, 1995, but when the companies realized Wright had been certified as permanently disabled, they deemed him not qualified for longshoreman work under the CBA and refused to allow him to work for them.

    Wright did not file a grievance under the union agreement but instead hired a lawyer and proceeded with a claim under the Americans with Disabilities Act. The district court dismissed the case because Wright had failed to pursue the grievance procedure provided by the CBA. Must Wright pursue the dispute procedure first, or can he go right to court on the basis of his federal rights under the Americans with Disabilities Act? [*Wright v. Universal Maritime Service Corp.*, 525 U.S. 70]

12. Winona Ryder was arrested for shoplifting from Saks Fifth Avenue in California. One of the members of the jury panel for her trial was Peter Guber, a Hollywood executive in charge of the production of three films in which Ms. Ryder starred, including *Bram Stoker's Dracula, The Age of Innocence,* and *Little Women.* If you were the prosecuting attorney in the case, how could you discover such information about this potential juror, and what are your options for excluding him from selection? [Rick Lyman, "For the Ryder Trial, a Hollywood Script," *New York Times*, November 3, 2002, SL-1]

13. Two doctors had a dispute over who was doing how much work at their clinic. Their dispute was submitted to arbitration and the arbitrator held in favor of the less experienced doctor. The senior doctor wants the arbitration set aside. Is it possible for the arbitrator's decision to be set aside?

14. Martha Simms is the plaintiff in a contract suit she has brought against Floral Supply, Inc., for its failure to deliver the green sponge Martha needed in building the floral designs she sells to exclusive home decorators. Martha had to obtain the sponge from another supplier and was late on seven deliveries. One of Martha's customers has been called by Martha's lawyer as a witness and is now on the witness stand, testifying about Martha's late performance and the penalty she charged. The lawyer for Floral Supply knows that Martha's customer frequently waives penalties for good suppliers. How can Floral Supply's lawyer get that information before the jury?

15. What would happen if lawyers for one side withheld evidence in a case? How could the party affected have the problem corrected?

Business Ethics, Social Forces, and the Law

learningoutcomes

After studying this chapter, you should be able to

LO.1 Define business ethics

LO.2 Discuss why ethics are important in business

LO.3 Describe how to recognize and resolve ethical dilemmas

Each day businesspeople work together on contracts and projects. Their completion of the work is partially the result of the laws that protect contract rights. Much of what businesspeople do, however, is simply a matter of their word. Executives arrive at a 9:00 A.M. meeting because they promised they would be there. An employee meets a deadline for an ad display board because she said she would. Business transactions are completed through a combination of the values of the parties and the laws that reflect those values and the importance of one's word in business.

This chapter takes you behind the rules of law to examine the objectives in establishing rules for business conduct. Ethical principles, social norms, and business needs contribute to the standards that govern businesses and their operations.

A. What Is Business Ethics?

Ethics is a branch of philosophy dealing with values that relate to the nature of human conduct and values associated with that conduct. Balancing the goal of profits with the values of individuals and society is the focus of **business ethics**. Some economists make the point that insider trading is an efficient way to run that market. To an economist, inside information allows those with the best information to make the most money. This view ignores some issues: What about those who trade stock who do not have access to that information? What will happen to the stock market if investors perceive there is not a level playing field? In the U.S. Supreme Court decision *United States v. O'Hagan*[1] on insider trading, Justice Ruth Ginsburg noted, "Investors likely wouldn't invest in a market where trading based on misappropriated nonpublic information is unchecked." The field of business ethics deals with the balance between society's values and the need for businesses to remain profitable.

1. The Law as the Standard for Business Ethics

Philosophers debate the origin of moral and ethical standards as well as which of those standards should be applied. One view of ethics is simply following what codified or **positive law** requires. The test of whether an act is legal is a common moral standard used frequently in business. Codified law, or law created by governmental authority, is used as the standard for ethical behavior. Absent illegality, all behavior is ethical under this simple standard. The phrase "AS IS," on a contract (see Chapter 25 for further discussion), means by law that there are no warranties for the goods being sold. **For Example,** if a buyer purchases a used car and the phrase "AS IS" is in the contract, the seller has no legal obligation, in most states, if the transmission falls apart the day after the buyer's purchase. Following a positive law standard, the seller who refuses to repair the transmission has acted ethically. However, ethical standards are different. We know there was no legal obligation to fix the transmission, but was it fair that the car fell apart the day after it was purchased?

2. The Notion of Universal Standards for Business Ethics

Another view of ethics holds that standards exist universally and cannot be changed or modified by law. In many cases, universal standards stem from religious beliefs. In some countries today, the standards for business are still determined by religious tenets. **Natural law** imposes higher standards of behavior than those required by positive law and they must be followed even if those higher standards run contrary to codified law. **For Example,** in the early nineteenth century when slavery was legally permissible in the United States, a positive law standard supported slavery. However, slavery violates the natural law principle of individual freedom and would be unethical. **Civil disobedience** is the remedy natural law proponents use to change positive law.

Former Supreme Court Justice Sandra Day O'Connor, who was second in her class at Stanford Law School (the late Chief Justice William Rehnquist

[1] 521 U.S. 657 (1997).

was first), was offered a job as a receptionist for a law firm while her male classmates were hired as attorneys. At that time, no law prohibited discrimination against women, so law firms' hiring practices, using only a positive law standard, were ethical. However, if the natural law standard of equality is applied, the refusal to hire Sandra O'Connor as a lawyer, a position for which she was qualified, was a violation of the natural law principle of equality and unethical.

3. Ethical Theories and Standards

There are many different views about the correct theory or standard we should apply when we face ethical dilemmas. Some of those theories and standards are covered here.

(A) THE CATEGORICAL IMPERATIVE AND IMMANUEL KANT. Philosopher Immanuel Kant does not allow any resolution of an ethical dilemma in which human beings are used as a means by which others obtain benefits. **Kant's categorical imperative** theory, reduced to simplest terms, is that you cannot use others in a way that gives you a one-sided benefit. Everyone must operate under the same usage rules. In Kant's words, "One ought only to act such that the principle of one's act could become a universal law of human action in a world in which one would hope to live." **For Example,** if you hit a car in a parking lot and damaged it but you could be guaranteed that no one saw you do it, would you leave a note on the other car with contact information? If you answered, "No, because that's happened to me 12 times before and no one left me a note," then you are unhappy with universal behaviors but are unwilling to commit to universal standards of honesty and disclosure to remedy those behaviors.

International business presents some interesting Kantian dilemmas. For example, there are some U.S. companies that use suppliers in developing nations. Those suppliers have employees in sweatshop atmospheres who work for pennies per hour. The pennies-per-hour wage seems unjust. However, suppose the company was operating under one of its universal principles: Always pay a fair wage to those who work for it. A "fair wage" in that country might be pennies, and the company owner could argue, "I would work for that wage if I lived in that country." The company owner could also argue, "But, if I lived in the United States, I would not work for that wage, would require a much higher wage, and would want benefits, and we do provide that to all of our U.S. workers."

The company has developed its own ethical standard that is universally applicable, and those who own the company could live with it if it was applied to them, but context is everything under the categorical imperative. The basic question is: Are you comfortable living in a world operating under the standards you have established, or would you deem them unfair or unjust?

There is one more part to Kant's theory: You not only have to be fair but also have to want to do it for all the right reasons. Kant wants you to adopt and accept these ethical standards because you do not want to use other people as a means to your enrichment at their expense.

(B) THE CONTRACTARIANS AND JUSTICE. John Locke and John Rawls developed what is sometimes called the **theory of justice** and sometimes referred to as the **social contract**. Rawls and Locke believe that Kant was wrong in assuming that we could all have a meeting of the minds on what were the good rules for society. Locke and Rawls preferred just putting the rules into place with a social contract. Under this theory we imagine what it would be like if we had no rules or laws at all. If we started with a blank slate, or *tabula rasa* as these philosophers would say, rational people would agree—perhaps in their own self-interest, or perhaps to be fair—that certain universal rules must apply. Rational people, thinking through the results and consequences if there were not rules, would develop rules that would result in fairness. **For Example,** we would probably develop rules such as "Don't take my property without my permission" and "I would like the same rights in court that rich people have even if I am not so rich." Locke and Rawls want us to step back from the emotion of the moment and make universal principles that will survive the test of time.

(C) RIGHTS THEORY. The **rights theory** is also known as an **entitlement theory** and is one of the more modern theories of ethics. Robert Nozick is the key modern-day philosopher on this theory, which has two big elements: (1) everyone has a set of rights, and (2) it is up to the governments to protect those rights. **For Example,** there are rights issues related to sweatshops, abortion, slavery, property ownership and use, justice (as in court processes), animal rights, privacy, and euthanasia. Nozick dealt with all the controversial and emotional issues of ethics including everything from human dignity in suffering to third-trimester abortions.

(D) ETHICAL EGOISM THEORY: AYN RAND AND ATLAS. Ethical egoism holds that we all act in our own self-interest and that all of us should limit our judgment to our own ethical egos and not interfere with the exercise of ethical egoism by others. This view holds that everything is determined by self-interest. We act as we do and decide to behave as we do because we have determined that it is in our own self-interest.

Ayn Rand, who wrote books about business and business leaders' decisions in ethical dilemmas, such as *The Fountainhead* and *Atlas Shrugged*, was an ethical egoist. These two famous books made Ms. Rand's point about ethical dilemmas: the world would be better if we did not feel so guilty about the choices we make in ethical dilemmas and just acknowledged that it is all self-interest.

(E) THE UTILITARIAN THEORY: BENTHAM AND MILL. Utilitarians resolve ethical dilemmas by doing the most good for the most people. For example, suppose that the FBI has just arrested a terrorist who is clearly a leader in a movement that plans to plant bombs in the nation's trains, subways, and airports. This individual has critical information about upcoming planned attacks but refuses to speak. A utilitarian would want the greatest good for the greatest number and would feel that harsh interrogation methods would be justified to save thousands of lives. Rights theorists would disagree with using torture to obtain the information because human rights must be protected.

(F) MORAL RELATIVISTS. Moral relativists resolve ethical dilemmas according to time and place. For example, suppose that you live in a neighborhood in which drug dealers are operating a crystal meth lab or crack house, something that is causing violence in your neighborhood. A relativist would feel justified in committing arson to get rid of the drug house. Another classic example would be a parent stealing a

Thinking Things Through

Corrupt Climates: Good or Bad for Business?

As you examine the following list of countries, those in the column labeled "Least Corrupt" (countries in which government officials are least likely to accept bribes) and those in the column marked "Most Corrupt" (countries in which government officials are most likely to accept bribes), can you comment on the business climates in them? What can you conclude about following the cultural practices of paying bribes? Who is harmed when a company pays bribes?

Least Corrupt (Least Likely to Accept Bribes)

- Denmark
- Finland
- New Zealand
- Sweden
- Singapore
- Switzerland
- Australia
- Norway
- Canada
- Netherlands
- Iceland
- Luxembourg
- Germany
- Hong Kong
- Barbados
- Belgium
- Japan
- United Kingdom
- United States
- Chile
- Uruguay
- Bahamas
- France
- Santa Lucia
- Austria
- Ireland
- Qatar/United Arab Emirates (tied)

Most Corrupt (Most Likely to Accept Bribes)

- Somalia
- Korea (North)
- Myanmar
- Afghanistan
- Uzbekistan
- Turkmenistan
- Sudan
- Iraq
- Haiti
- Venezuela
- Equatorial Guinea
- Burundi
- Libya
- Democratic Republic of Congo
- Chad
- Yemen
- Kyrgyzstan
- Guinea
- Cambodia
- Zimbabwe
- Paraguay
- Papua New Guinea
- Nepal
- Laos
- Kenya

*From 2012 Transparency International annual survey, **http://www.transparency.org**.

loaf of bread to feed a starving child. Moral relativists resolve ethical dilemmas by weighing competing factors at the moment and then taking the lesser of the evils as the solution. **For Example,** Google and other Internet service providers have agreed to do business in China despite the restrictions the Chinese government places on the use of the Internet and the content of search engines. Such restrictions in the United States would be an unconstitutional violation of our First Amendment. In China, however, government control of information is legal. Google and others testified before Congress that some entry, however restricted, was better for the Chinese people than no access at all. Their decision weighed the conflicting values and concluded that they would use the standard of honoring the law of China despite the censorship.

(G) Plato and Aristotle: Virtue Ethics. Aristotle and Plato taught that solving ethical dilemmas requires training, that individuals solve ethical dilemmas when they develop and nurture a set of virtues. Aristotle encouraged his students to solve ethical dilemmas using virtues such as honesty, justice, and fairness.

4. The Business Stakeholder Standard of Behavior

Businesses have different constituencies, referred to as **stakeholders**, often with conflicting goals for the business. Shareholders, for example, may share economists' view that earnings, and hence dividends, should be maximized. Members of the community where a business is located are also stakeholders in the business and have an interest in preserving jobs. The employees of the business itself are stakeholders and certainly wish to retain their jobs. Balancing the interests of these stakeholders is a standard used in resolving ethical dilemmas in business.

As Figure 3-1 indicates, stakeholder analysis requires a view of an issue from different perspectives in a transparent way. **Stakeholder analysis** measures the impact of a decision on various groups and then asks whether public disclosure of that decision is defensible. The questions provide insight in a variety of situations and ethical dilemmas. **For Example,** if a lender gives a loan to a debtor without checking income, the lapse seems harmless. But, suppose someone purchases that loan believing the debtor met the standards and the lender verified income. The debtor defaults on the loan. The purchaser has to write down or write off the loan. If enough loans that were not documented go into default, you create the kind of ripples in the real estate and stock markets that occurred in late 2008. Stakeholder analysis helps you to see that the decisions we make in business are not made in isolation or limited in their impact. Figure 3-1 summarizes ethical analysis.

In other ethical dilemmas, a business faces the question of taking voluntary action or simply complying with the law. Some experts maintain that the shareholders' interest is paramount in resolving these conflicts among stakeholders. Others maintain that a business must assume some responsibility for social issues and their resolution. Economist Milton

FIGURE 3-1 *Guidelines for Analyzing a Contemplated Action*

1. **Define the problem from the decision maker's point of view.**
2. **Identify who could be injured by the contemplated action.**
3. **Define the problem from the opposing point of view.**
4. **Would you (as the decision maker) be willing to tell your family, your supervisor, your CEO, and the board of directors about the planned action?**
5. **Would you be willing to go before a community meeting, a congressional hearing, or a public forum to describe the action?**
6. **With full consideration of the facts and alternatives, reach a decision about whether the contemplated action should be taken.**

Ethics & the Law

Hopping Plankers

Plankers are subway riders who hop the turn styles, that is they do not pay. Plankers have a pool that they all contribute to with the funds being used to pay their fines if they are arrested for riding for free. Plankers feel public transportation should be free. Discuss which ethical theories and standards the plankers are following. List the stakeholders in the plankers' actions.

Friedman expresses his views on resolving the conflicts among stakeholders as follows:

> *A corporate executive's responsibility is to make as much money for the shareholders as possible, as long as he operates within the rules of the game. When an executive decides to take action for reasons of social responsibility, he is taking money from someone else—from the stockholders, in the form of lower dividends; from the employees, in the form of lower wages; or from the consumer, in the form of higher prices. The responsibility of the corporate executive is to fulfill the terms of his contract. If he can't do that in good conscience, then he should quit his job and find another way to do good. He has the right to promote what he regards as desirable moral objectives only with his own money.*[2]

Many businesses feel an obligation to solve social problems because those problems affect their stakeholders. **For Example,** programs such as flextime, job sharing, and telecommuting for work are not legal requirements but voluntary options businesses offer their employees to accommodate family needs. These options are a response to larger societal issues surrounding children and their care but may also serve as a way to retain a quality workforce that is more productive without the worry of poor child care arrangements.

Some businesses are also involved in their communities through employees' volunteer work and companies' charitable donations. For example, a painting company in Phoenix donates paint, and its employees work on weekends painting Habitat for Humanity homes and helping churches get their facilities painted. Apple was able to capture future customers through its donations of computers to schools. Many companies also provide support for employees to participate in volunteer programs in their communities.

B. Why Is Business Ethics Important?

Ethics and values represent an important part of business success. Business ethics is important for more than the simple justification that "it's the right thing to do." This section covers the significance of ethics in business success.

5. The Importance of Trust

Capitalism succeeds because of trust. Investors provide capital for a business because they believe the business will provide a return on their investment. Customers are willing to purchase products and services from businesses because they believe the businesses will honor their commitments to deliver quality and then stand behind their product or service. Businesses are willing to purchase equipment and hire employees on the assumption that investors will continue to honor their commitment to furnish the necessary funds and will not withdraw their promises or funds. Business investment, growth, and sales are a circle of trust. Although courts provide remedies for breaches of agreements, no economy could grow if it were based solely on positive law and court-mandated performance. It is the reliance on promises, not the reliance on litigation, that produces good business relationships.

[2] "Interview: Milton Friedman," *Playboy*, February 1973. ©1973 *Playboy*.

6. Business Ethics and Financial Performance

Studies centering on a business's commitment to values and its financial performance suggest that those with the strongest value systems survive and do so successfully. According to the book *Building and Growing a Business Through Good Times and Bad* by Louis Grossman and Marianne Jennings,[3] an in-depth look at companies that paid 100 years of consistent dividends produced a common thread: the companies' commitment to values. All firms studied had focused on high standards for product quality, employee welfare, and customer service.

Poor value choices do have an effect on financial performance. A study of the impact of just breaches of federal law by companies showed that for five years after their regulatory or legal misstep, these companies were still struggling to recover the financial performances they had achieved prior to their legal difficulties.[4]

Over the past few years, there have been devastating stories of companies' fates after ethical lapses. For example, after the congressional hearings revealed that Goldman Sachs took positions in the market that were the opposite of recommendations to its clients, its revenue dropped 18 percent and its share price dropped 32 percent.[5] Columbia Health Care's share price dropped 58 percent and it experienced a 93 percent drop in earnings after it was charged with overbilling for Medicare reimbursements. Its share price dropped from $40 to $18. The nation's largest hospital chain had to spin off 100 hospitals and has paid record fines to settle the charges.[6] When the subprime lender New Century Financial announced that it was finally writing down all the subprime loans it had made that had gone into default but that it had been concealing, it was forced to declare bankruptcy because it was insolvent. On January 1, 2007, New Century had $1.75 billion in market capitalization, but by the middle of March, that figure was $55 million and its stock was delisted by the New York Stock Exchange.

Insurance broker Marsh & McLennan paid $850 million to former clients to settle price-fixing charges brought by then–New York Attorney General Eliot Spitzer. The 134-year-old company saw a drop in both its earnings (64 percent) and its share price (40 percent).[7] The financial crunch resulted in 3,000 employees losing their jobs. AIG, the insurance giant, paid $1.64 billion, to settle charges that it smoothed its earnings over time and was forced to reduce its reported earnings by $1.3 billion.[8] Its $73 share price dropped to $50 before the financial reporting allegations were settled. But AIG continued to underestimate its needed reserves and losses for the subprime mortgage market it had insured. By the fall of 2008, AIG had to be rescued by the federal government with a funds bailout. In 2011,

Ethics & the Law

AIG Bailout and Bonuses

In March 2009, after it received government assistance, AIG announced the payment of $100 million in bonuses to various executives and managers in the company. There was a great hue and cry from regulators, legislators, and the public. However, AIG maintained it was contractually obligated to pay the bonuses. For a time, AIG had to cover its name on its New York office building because of public protests. The executives who received the bonuses received death threats. Evaluate the ethical issues related to the bonus payments. Evaluate the ethical issues in the public response to those bonuses. Be sure to discuss AIG's argument on the legal requirements for the bonuses.

3 Greenwood Press (2002).

4 Melinda S. Baucus and David A. Baucus, "Paying the Piper: An Empirical Examination of Longer-Term Financial Consequences of Illegal Corporate Behavior," 40 *Academic Management Journal* 129 (1997).

5 Susanne Craig, "Goldman's Safer Position Eats Deeply Into Its Profits," *New York Times*, July 20, 2011, p. B4.

6 Lucette Lagnado, "Columbia/HCA Warns of Profit Decline," *Wall Street Journal*, September 10, 1987, A3.

7 Ian McDonald, "After Spitzer Probe, Marsh CEO Tries Corporate Triage," *Wall Street Journal*, August 29, 2005 A1, A5.

8 Ian McDonald and Liam Pleven, "AIG Reaches Accord with Regulators, Stock Rises but May Still Be a Bargain," *Wall Street Journal*, February 10, 2006, C1, C4.

MF Global had to declare bankruptcy after its risky bets on Greek bonds resulted in $1.6 billion in losses. Over 1,000 employees lost their jobs and the firm is being liquidated.[9]

7. The Importance of a Good Reputation

Richard Teerlink, the CEO of Harley-Davidson, once said, "A reputation, good or bad, is tough to shake.[10] A breach of ethics is costly to a firm not only in the financial sense of drops in earnings and possible fines. A breach of ethics also often carries with it a lasting memory that affects the business and its sales for years to come. **For Example,** the Peanut Corporation of America had to declare bankruptcy in 2009 after government officials discovered that its plant was the source of salmonella poisonings among those customers who had eaten peanut products that used Peanut Corporation's base in their production. Records showed that Peanut Corporation continued to produce the product even after salmonella warnings and questions arose. The company's name and image became so damaged that it could not continue to make sales. When an ethical breach occurs, businesses lose that component of trust important to customers' decisions to buy and invest.

8. Business Ethics and Business Regulation: Public Policy, Law, and Ethics

When business behavior results in complaints from employees, investors, or customers, laws or regulations are often used to change the behavior. **For Example,** the bankruptcy of Lehman Brothers, the near-collapse of Bear Stearns, and the losses at Merrill Lynch and AIG in 2008–2009 all resulted from the subprime mortgage financial derivative investment market, a market that had previously been a relatively regulation-free environment. The companies had billions of dollars of exposure because of their sales and purchases of financial instruments that were tied to the subprime mortgage market that ultimately resulted in high rates of foreclosure and nearly worthless loans. Congress, the Securities and Exchange Commission (SEC), and the Federal Reserve all stepped in to regulate virtually all aspects of mortgage transactions, including the lenders and others who were involved in packaging the loans into financial products.

Confusion among consumers about car leasing and its true costs and the fees applicable at the end of the lease terms caused the Federal Reserve (now the Consumer Financial Protection Bureau) to expand its regulation of credit to car leases. Figure 3-2 depicts the relationships among ethics, the social forces of customers and investors, and the laws that are passed to remedy the problems raised as part of the social forces movement.

Businesses that act voluntarily on the basis of value choices often avoid the costs and the sometimes arbitrariness of legislation and regulation. Voluntary change by businesses is less costly and is considered less intrusive.

Businesses that respond to social forces and the movements of the cycle of societal interaction often gain a competitive advantage. Businesses that act irresponsibly and disregard society's views and desire for change speed the transition from value choice to enforceable law. Businesses should watch the cycle of social forces and follow trends there to understand the values attached to certain activities and responses. These values motivate change either in the form of voluntary business activity or legislation. All values that precipitate change have one of several basic underlying goals. These underlying goals are discussed in the following sections.

(A) Protection of the State. A number of laws exist today because of an underlying goal or value of protection of the state. The U.S Patriot Act and airport security regulations are examples of government programs and regulations created with the protection and security of the state as the goal.

(B) Protection of the Person. A second social force is protection of the person. Criminal laws are devoted to protection of individuals and their properties. In addition, civil suits permit private remedies for wrongful acts toward people and their property. Over time, the protection of personal rights has expanded to include the rights of privacy and the protection of

[9] Mike Spector, Aaron Lucchetti, and Liam Pleven, "Corzine Firm's Final Struggles," *Wall Street Journal*, November 5–6, 2011, p. A1.

[10] David K. Wright, *The Harley-Davidson Motor Co.: An Official Ninety-Year History* (1993).

FIGURE 3-2 *The Endless Cycle of Societal Interaction*

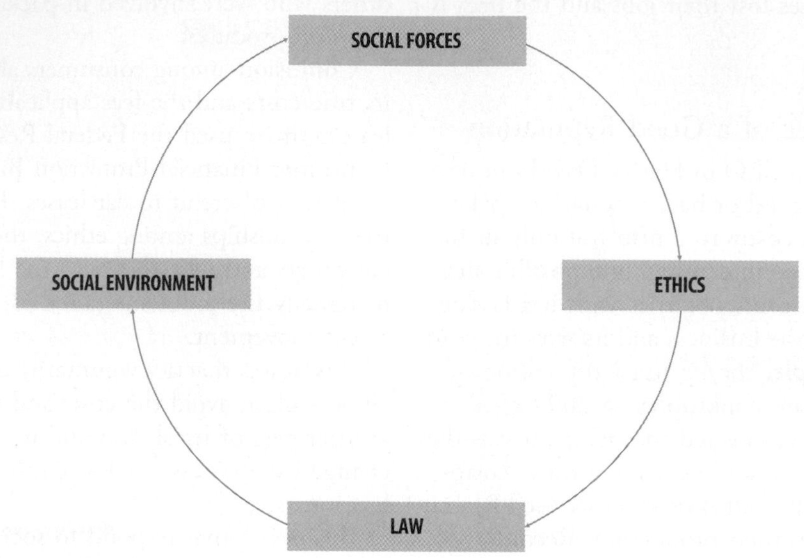

individuals from defamation. Laws continue to evolve to protect the reputations, privacy, and mental and physical well-being of individuals.

(c) Protection of Public Health, Safety, and Morals. Food-labeling regulations are an example of laws grounded in the value of protecting the safety and health of individuals. Food and restaurant inspections, mandatory inoculation, speed limits on roadways, mandatory smoke detectors and sprinkler systems in hotels, and prohibitions on the sale of alcohol to minors are all examples of laws based on the value of safety for the public. Zoning laws that prohibit the operation of adult bookstores and movie theaters near schools and churches are examples of laws based on moral values.

(d) Protection of Property: Its Use and Title. Someone who steals another's automobile is a thief and is punished by law with fines and/or imprisonment. A zoning law that prohibits the operation of a steel mill in a residential area also provides protection for property. A civil suit brought to recover royalties lost because of another's infringement of one's copyrighted materials is based on federal laws that afford protection for property rights in nontangible or intellectual property (see Chapter 10). Laws afford protection of title for all forms of property. The deed recorded in the land record is the legal mechanism for protecting the owner's title. The copyright on a software program or a song protects the creator's rights in that intellectual property. The title documents issued by a department of motor vehicles afford protection of title for the owner of a vehicle.

Those who have title to property are generally free to use the property in any manner they see fit. However, even ownership has restrictions imposed by law. A business may operate a factory on its real property, but if the factory creates a great deal of pollution, adjoining landowners may successfully establish it as a nuisance (see Chapter 49) that interferes with their use and enjoyment of their land. Environmental laws also emerged as regulation of land use in response to concerns about legal, but harmful, emissions by companies.

(e) Protection of Personal Rights. The desire for freedom from economic domination resulted in the free enterprise philosophy that exists in the United States today. Individual freedoms and personal rights continue as a focus of value discussions followed by legislation if those individual rights are violated.

Ethics & the Law

Ethics, Trust, and Markets

The cover of *Fortune* magazine from May 14, 2001, featured a picture of Wall Street financial analyst Mary Meeker and the words, "Can we ever trust again?"* The inside story focused on the relationship of underwriters, analysts, and brokerage houses with the high-tech companies whose stocks they were touting and selling, knowing there were questionable accounting practices and a lack of earnings at these companies. When the dot-com market bubble burst, the losses to shareholders were catastrophic. Those in the financial markets had too much at stake to be honest with investors. They did not break the law, however.

In 2002, when companies, such as Enron, WorldCom, and Tyco had to take write-downs because of years of overstating earnings, the market once again looked at analysts, wondering how they had failed to catch the accounting issues. The cover of *Fortune* read, "In Search of the Last Honest Analyst."**

During 2007, *Fortune* ran a cover with the pictures of the CEOs of the major Wall Street investment firms (such as Merrill Lynch, Bear Stearns, and Lehman Brothers) who had managed to lose trillions of investors' pension and 401(k) plans to risky investments in subprime mortgages that were marketed as low-risk investments. The cover's headline asked, "What Were They Smoking?"*** In 2011, following the collapse of Jon Corzine's MF Global hedge fund, a headline read, "Trustee Says More Cash Is Missing at MF Global." The estimated loss to investors at the firm was $1.6 billion.****

What do these headlines convey about the importance of trust and its role in markets?

*"Can We Ever Trust Again?" *Fortune*, May 14, 2001 (cover).
**"In Search of the Last Honest Analyst," *Fortune*, June 10, 2002 (cover).
***"What Were They Smoking?" *Fortune, November 26, 2007 (cover).*
****Michael J. de la Merced and Ben Protess, "Trustee Says More Cash Is Missing at MF Global," *New York Times, November 22, 2011, p. B1.*

(F) Enforcement of Individual Intent. When we voluntarily enter into a contract, we have a responsibility to fulfill the promises made in that agreement. Principles of honesty and the honoring of commitments are the ethical values at the heart of the parties' conduct in carrying out contracts. If, however, the parties do not keep their promises, the law does enforce transactions through sets of rules governing requirements for them. **For Example,** the law will carry out the intentions of the parties to a business transaction through judicial enforcement of contract rights and damages.

(G) Protection from Exploitation, Fraud, and Oppression. Many laws have evolved because businesses took advantage of others. Minors, or persons under legal age (see Chapter 14), are given special protections under contract laws that permit them to disaffirm their contracts so they are not disadvantaged by excessive commitments without the benefit of the wisdom of age and with the oppressive presence of an adult party.

The federal laws on disclosure in the sales of securities and shareholder relations (see Chapters 45 and 46) were developed following the 1929 stock market crash when many investors lost all they had because of the lack of candor and information by the businesses in which they were investing.

(H) Furtherance of Trade. Some laws are the result of social forces seeking to simplify business and trade. Credit laws, regulations, and protections have made additional capital available for businesses and provided consumers with alternatives to cash purchases. The laws on checks, drafts, and notes have created instruments used to facilitate trade.

(I) Protection of Creditors and Rehabilitation of Debtors. Mortgages, security interests, and surety relationships (see Chapters 32, 34, and 49) are mechanisms created by law to provide creditors the legal mechanisms for collecting their obligations.

When collection techniques became excessive and exploitative, new laws on debtors' rights were enacted. Debtors' prisons were abolished. Congress mandated disclosure requirements for credit contracts. The Fair Debt Collections Practices Act (see Chapter 33) limited collection techniques. The remedy of bankruptcy was afforded debtors under federal law to provide them an opportunity to begin a new economic life when their existing debts reached an excessive level and could no longer be paid in a timely fashion (see Chapter 35).

(J) Stability and Flexibility. Because of the desire for stability, courts will ordinarily follow former decisions unless there is a strong reason to depart from them. (See Chapter 1 for more discussion of precedent.) Similarly, when no former case bears on the point involved, a court will try to reach a decision that is a logical extension of some former decision or that follows a former decision by analogy rather than strike out on a new path to reach a decision unrelated to the past.

C. How to Recognize and Resolve Ethical Dilemmas

Business managers often find themselves in circumstances in which they are unclear about right and wrong and are confused about how to resolve the dilemmas they face. A recent survey showed that 98 percent of all Fortune 500 companies have codes of ethics designed to help their employees recognize and resolve ethical dilemmas. Nearly 99 percent of those firms provide their employees some form of training in ethics.[11] Almost 80 percent of companies now have an ethics officer. These codes of ethics provide employees information about categories of behavior that constitute ethical breaches. Regardless of the industry, the type of business, or the size of the company, certain universal categories can help managers recognize ethical dilemmas. Figure 3-3 provides a list of those categories.

FIGURE 3-3 *Categories of Ethical Behavior*

1. **Integrity and truthfulness**
2. **Promise keeping**
3. **Loyalty—avoiding conflicts of interest**
4. **Fairness**
5. **Doing no harm**
6. **Maintaining confidentiality**

9. Categories of Ethical Behavior

(A) Integrity and Truthfulness. A famous anonymous quote on truth is, "Circumstances beyond your control will cause the truth to come out, no matter what." As discussed earlier, trust is a key component of business relationships and of the free enterprise system. Trust begins with the belief that honesty is at the heart of relationships. Many contract remedies in law are based on the failure of the parties to be truthful with each other. **For Example,** if you purchase a home that has been certified as termite free but you discover termites in the home shortly after you move in, someone has not been truthful. If you also discover that two termite inspections were conducted and that the first one, which revealed there were termites, was concealed from you, your trust in both the sellers and their exterminators is diminished.

Integrity is the adherence to one's values and principles despite the costs and consequences. **For Example,** an executive contracted with a variety of companies to sell his hard-to-find computer components. When he was approached by one of his largest customers to break a contract with a small customer, the executive refused. The customer assured the executive it would be his last order with the company if he did not get more components. Despite facing the threat of losing a multimillion-dollar customer, the executive fulfilled his promises to the small purchasers. The executive kept his word on all of his contracts and demonstrated integrity.

(B) Promise Keeping. If we examined the types of things we do in a day, we will find that most of them are based on promises. We promise to deliver goods either with or without a contract. We promise to pay the dentist for our dental work. We promise to provide someone with a ride. Keeping those promises, regardless of whether there is a legal obligation to do so, is a key component of being an ethical person and practicing ethical business. Keeping promises is also evidence of integrity, for example.

(C) Loyalty—Avoiding Conflicts of Interest. An employee who works for a company owes allegiance to that company. Conduct that compromises that loyalty

[11] Jason Lunday, "The Need for More Effective Standards of Conduct," *Corporate Compliance Insights*, June 8, 2010, **http://www.corporatecomplianceinsights.com/the-need-for-more-effective-standards-of-conduct/**

Ethics & the Law

Lying to Get into a Top School

The University of California at Berkeley has implemented a new step in its admission process. The Haas School of Business has begun running background checks on students who have applied to determine whether the information in their applications is correct. The Wharton School implemented a similar procedure and charges applicants a $35 fee for these background checks.

Of the 100 students admitted to Berkeley's Haas School in the fall of 2003, 5 students were found to have offered false information on their admissions applications. The most common type of false information was the job titles they held, and the second most common type was their number of years of work experience. Haas admissions officers indicated that had the students not lied, they otherwise met the GMAT score and GPA standards for admission to Haas.

What risk do the students take in lying on their applications? What are the long-term consequences?

Source: "Cheaters Don't Make the Grade at Berkeley Business School," **www.azcentral.com**, March 14, 2003, AP wire reports.

is a **conflict of interest. For Example,** suppose that your sister operates her own catering business. Your company is seeking a caterer for its monthly management meetings. You are responsible for these meetings and could hire your sister to furnish the lunches for the meetings. Your sister would have a substantial contract, and your problems with meal logistics would be solved. Nearly all companies have a provision in their codes of ethics covering this situation. An employee cannot hire a relative, friend, or even her own company without special permission because it is a conflict of interest. Your loyalty to your sister conflicts with the loyalty to your employer, which requires you to make the best decision at the best price.

A conflict of interest arises when a purchasing agent accepts gifts from suppliers, vendors, or manufacturers' representatives. The purchasing agent has introduced into the buy-sell relationship an element of *quid pro quo,* or the supplier's expectation that the gift will bring about a return from the agent in the form of a contract. Some companies have zero tolerance for conflicts and establish a complete prohibition on employees accepting any gifts from suppliers and manufacturers. **For Example,** Wal-Mart buyers are not permitted to accept even a cup of coffee from potential merchandise suppliers, and Amgen's buyers can go out to dinner with a supplier only if Amgen pays.

Sports & Entertainment Law

Identity Theft and MLB

The Washington Nationals signed Esmailyn "Smiley" Gonzalez (aka Carlos Gonzalez), whom they believed to be a 19-year-old phenomenon, for $1.4 million. Mr. Gonzalez turned out to be a 23-year-old who had presented the Nationals with fake identification when he first signed for the minor leagues, with the ID placing his age at 16. After the Nationals signed, they realized that they did not have a wonder player and that his years left for playing were far less than they had figured. "You know, to say I'm disappointed doesn't begin to describe how I feel. I'm angry. I am very angry. We've been defrauded, and make no mistake—this wasn't a college kid with a fake ID that came in and did this. This was a deliberate, premeditated fraud with a lot more to this story, and we are going to get to the bottom of it. There were many, many people involved in this premeditated fraud."* Some fans and Mr. Gonzalez and his agent did not see any problem because they never misrepresented his skill. They say he was signed because of his skill, not his age. Should the Nationals have been told his real age? Is it fraud or is it an ethical issue? Both? What will the impact be on the sports agent?

*Chico Harlan, "I'm Angry, We've Been Defrauded," *Washington Post, September 21, 2010.* **http://voices.washingtonpost.com/nationalsjournal/2010/09/a_new_development_in_the_smile.html**

(D) Doing No Harm. Imagine selling a product that your company's internal research shows presents significant health dangers to its users. Selling the product without disclosure of the information is unfair. There is the additional ethical breach of physical harm to your customers and users. Ford designed and sold its Pinto with a fundamental flaw in the placement of the car's gas tank. Rear-end collisions in which a Pinto was involved resulted, even at very low speeds, in fires that engulfed the car so quickly that occupants could not always escape from it. An internal memo from engineers at Ford revealed that employees had considered doing an analysis of the risk of the tanks versus the cost of redesign but never did. The late Peter Drucker's advice on ethics for businesses is ***primum non nocere***, or "above all, do no harm." Such a rule might have helped Ford.

(E) Maintaining Confidentiality. Often the success of a business depends on the information or technology that it holds. If the competitive edge that comes from the business's peculiar niche or knowledge is lost through disclosure, so are its profits. Employees not only owe a duty of loyalty to their employers, but they also owe an obligation of confidentiality. Employees should not use, either personally or through a competitor, information they have obtained through their employer's work or research. Providing customer lists or leads is a breach of employees' obligation of confidentiality.

In addition, managers have responsibilities regarding their employees' privacy. Performance evaluations of individual employees are private and should never be disclosed or revealed, even in one-on-one conversations outside the lines of authority and the workplace.

10. Resolving Ethical Dilemmas

Recognizing an ethical dilemma is perhaps the easiest part of business ethics. Resolution of that dilemma is more difficult. The earlier section on stakeholders offers one model for resolution of ethical dilemmas (see Figure 3-1). Other models have been developed to provide managers analytical methods for resolving dilemmas in a timely fashion.

(A) Blanchard and Peale Three-Part Test. Dr. Kenneth Blanchard, author of the books on the *One-Minute Manager*, and the late Dr. Norman Vincent Peale developed a model for evaluating ethical breaches that is widely used among Fortune 500 companies.[12] To evaluate situations, ask the following three

E-Commerce & Cyberlaw

Piggybacking on Wireless Networks

A new issue that has evolved because of technology could require legal steps to stop it. People are "piggybacking" or tapping onto their neighbors' wireless Internet connection. The original subscriber pays a monthly fee for the service, but without security, people located in the area are able to tap into the wireless network, which bogs down the speed of the service. Once limited to geeks and hackers, the practice is now common among the ordinary folk who just want free Internet service.

One college student said, "I don't think it's stealing. I always find [P]eople out there … aren't protecting their connection, so I just feel free to go ahead and use it."* According to a recent survey, only about 30 percent of the 4,500 wireless networks onto which the surveyors logged were encrypted, and another survey shows that 32 percent of us do engage in Wi-Fi piggybacking.

An apartment dweller said she leaves her connection wide open because "I'm sticking it to the man. I open up my network, leave it wide open for anyone to jump on." One of the users of another's wireless network said, "I feel sort of bad about it, but I do it anyway. It just seems harmless." She said that if she gets caught, I'll just play the dumb card."

Some neighbors offer to pay those with wireless service in exchange for their occasional use rather than paying a wireless company for full-blown service. However, the original subscribers do not really want to run their own Internet service.

Do you think we need new legislation to cover this activity? What do you think of the users' statements? Is their conduct legal? Is it ethical?

*Michael Marriott, "Hey Neighbor, Stop Piggybacking on My Wireless," *New York Times*, March 5, 2006, A1, A23.

[12] Kenneth Blanchard and Norman Vincent Peale, *The Power of Ethical Management* (1986).

Ethics & the Law

Pumping Up the SAT Scores for a Good Ranking

Since 2005, Claremont McKenna, ranked #9 on *U.S. News & World Report's* best liberal arts colleges in the country, has been lopping on a few points here and there to its entering students' average SAT score before reporting those numbers to *U.S. News & World Report* and rating organizations such as the Princeton Review. For example, in 2010, its combined median score was reported as 1410, rather than its actual 1400. And its 75th percentile was reported at 1510, when it was, in reality, 1480.

Oops! Turns out the academic world is darn near as competitive as Wall Street when it comes to rankings and ratings. In fact, so competitive are those of the ivory tower that they used the same strategies: cook the books and hope no one notices.

Claremont McKenna's vice president and dean of admissions has been removed from his job title on the college Website. President Pamela B. Gann explained the problem and concluded, "As an institution of higher education with a deep and consistent commitment to the integrity of our academic activities, and particularly, our reporting of institutional data, we take this situation very seriously."

Indeed. Now, if we could just get the rankings and ratings organizations to respond with appropriate outrage. From Robert Franek of the Princeton Review, we have these thoughts, "That is a pretty mild difference in a point score. That said, 10 points, 20 points to a student that isn't getting that score on the SAT could be an important distinction." Yes, but even without the numbers difference, it is an important distinction. Claremont McKenna was not honest, and students who rely on reviews when such an obvious flaw is on the table deserve whatever fate awaits them at an institution that would pull a statistical stunt (however it may have impacted the rankings/ratings). Oh, and Mr. Franek finished with a flourish, "I feel like so many schools have a very clear obligation to college-bound students to report this information honestly." Actually, it would be all schools, not just "so many," and the reporting of correct data is not just a "clear obligation," it is an ethical responsibility.

Daniel E. Slotnik and Richard Pérez-Peña, "College Says It Exaggerrated SAT Figures for Rating," *New York Times*, Jan. 31, 2012, p. A12.

questions: Is it legal? Is it balanced? How does it make me feel?

In answering the questions on legality, a manager should look to positive law both within and outside the company. If the proposed conduct would violate antitrust laws, the manager's analysis can stop there. If the proposed conduct would violate company policy, the manager's analysis can stop. In the field of business ethics, there is little room for civil disobedience. Compliance with the law is a critical component of a successful ethics policy in any company.

The second question on balance forces the manager to examine the ethical value of fairness. A good follow-up question is, "How would I want to be treated in this circumstance?" Perhaps the decision to downsize must be made, but couldn't the company offer the employees a severance package and outplacement assistance to ease the transition?

The final question of the Blanchard and Peale model is conscience based. Although some managers may employ any tactics to maximize profits, this final question forces a manager to examine the physical impact of a decision: Does it cause sleeplessness or appetite changes? Personalizing business choices often helps managers to see the potential harm that comes from poor ethical choices.

(b) The Front-Page-of-the-Newspaper Test. This simple but effective model for ethical evaluation helps a manager visualize the public disclosure of proposed conduct. When he temporarily took over as the leader of Salomon Brothers after its bond-trading controversy, Warren Buffett described the newspaper test as follows:

> *Contemplating any business act, an employee should ask himself whether he would be willing to see it immediately described by an informed and critical reporter on the front page of his local paper, there to be read by his spouse, children, and friends. At Salomon, we simply want no part of any activities that pass legal tests but that we, as citizens, would find offensive.*[13]

[13] Janet Lowe, *Warren Buffett Speaks: Wit and Wisdom from the World's Greatest Investor* (New York: Wiley, 1997).

(c) Laura Nash Model. In her work, business ethicist Laura Nash has developed a series of questions to help businesspeople reach the right decision in ethical dilemmas. These are her questions: Have you defined the problem accurately? How would you define the problem if you stood on the other side of the fence? How did this situation occur in the first place? What is your intention in making this decision? How does the intention compare with the probable results? Whom could your decision or action injure? Can you discuss your decision with the affected parties? Are you confident that your position will be as valid over a long period of time as it seems now? Could you discuss your decision with your supervisor, coworkers, officers, board, friends, and family?

The Nash model requires an examination of the dilemma from all perspectives. Defining the problem and how the problem arose provides the business assistance in avoiding the dilemma again. **For Example,** suppose that a supervisor is asked to provide a reference for a friend who works for her. The supervisor is hesitant because the friend has not been a very good employee. The ethical dilemma the manager believes she faces is whether to lie or tell the truth about the employee. The real ethical dilemma is why the supervisor never provided evaluation or feedback indicating the friend's poor performance. Avoiding the problem in the future is possible through candid evaluations. Resolving the problem requires that the supervisor talk to her friend now about the issue of performance and the problem with serving as a reference.

One final aspect of the Nash model that businesspeople find helpful is a question that asks for a perspective on an issue from family and friends. The problem of groupthink in business situations is very real. As businesspeople sit together in a room and discuss an ethical dilemma, they can persuade each other to think the same way. The power of consensus can overwhelm each person's concerns and values. There is a certain fear in bringing up a different point of view in a business meeting. Proper perspective is often lost as the discussion centers around numbers. Therefore, bringing in the views of an outsider is often helpful. **For Example,** when McNeil, the manufacturer of Tylenol, faced the cyanide poisonings from contaminated capsules sold in the Chicago area, it had to make a decision about the existing Tylenol inventory. It was clear to both insiders and outsiders that the poison had not been put in the capsules at McNeil but after delivery to the stores. Despite the huge numbers involved in the recall and the destruction of inventory, the McNeil managers made the decision easily because they viewed the risk to their own families, that is, from the outside. From this standpoint, the issue became a question of human life, not of numbers.[14]

LawFlix

Breaking Away (1979) (PG)

In this story about "cutters" (a nickname for natives of Bloomington, Indiana), a recent high school graduate trains to be a first-class bike rider. He idolizes the Italian world racing team and enters an Indiana race to have the opportunity to compete with them. He does well in the race and manages to catch up and keep pace with the Italian team. As he rides alongside his idols, one of the members of the Italian team places a tire pump in his spoke. His bike crashes, he loses the race and is injured. He becomes disillusioned. Is this experience like business? Do unethical tactics get you ahead? Do nice guys finish last? Are there sanctions for unethical conduct?

Jaws (1975) (PG-13)

The movie that shot Steven Spielberg to directorial legend brings us the classic business dilemma of what to do when you have a high-risk/low-probability event that you know about but about which the public has no knowledge. Do you stop? But what about the economic losses?

[14] "Brief History of Johnson & Johnson" (company pamphlet, 1992).

LawFlix—*Contd.*

Hoosiers (1986) (PG)

Often called the "greatest sports movie ever made," this story of a coach with a history and a small-town team presents several life-defining ethical moments. In one, with advancement to the finals on the table, Coach Norman Dale grapples with whether he should allow one of his injured players to continue when he has no depth on his bench. What do you do when your values are in conflict?

The Family Man (2000) (PG-13)

Nicolas Cage plays a Wall Street billionaire who is suddenly given a suburban life in New Jersey with all of its family life and financial constraints. He is forced to examine who he really is and what is important.

MAKE THE CONNECTION

SUMMARY

Business ethics is the application of values and standards to business conduct and decisions. These values originate in various sources from positive (codified) law to natural law to ethical theories and standards and on to stakeholder values. Business ethics is important because trust is a critical component of good business relationships and free enterprise. A business with values will enjoy the additional competitive advantage of a good reputation and, over the long term, better earnings. When businesses make decisions that violate basic ethical standards, they set into motion social forces and cause the area of abuse to be regulated, resulting in additional costs and restrictions for business. Voluntary value choices by businesses position them for a competitive advantage.

The categories of ethical values in business are truthfulness and integrity, promise keeping, loyalty and avoiding conflicts of interest, fairness, doing no harm, and maintaining confidentiality.

Resolution of ethical dilemmas is possible through the use of various models that require a businessperson to examine the impact of a decision before it is made. These models include stakeholder analysis, the Blanchard and Peale test, the front-page-of-the-newspaper test, and the Laura Nash model.

LEARNING OUTCOMES

After studying this chapter, you should be able to clearly explain:

A. What Is Business Ethics?

LO.1 Define business ethics

See the discussion of the definition, balancing the goal of profits with the values of individuals and society on p. 33.

B. Why Is Business Ethics Important?

LO.2 Discuss why ethics are important in business

See "The Importance of Trust" on p. 37.
See "Business Ethics and Financial Performance" on p. 38.
See "The Importance of a Good Reputation" on p. 39.
See Ethics & the Law on market trust on p. 41.

C. How to Recognize and Resolve Ethical Dilemmas

LO.3 Describe how to recognize and resolve ethical dilemmas

See "Integrity and Truthfulness" on p. 42.

See "Promise Keeping" on p. 42.
See "Loyalty—Avoiding Conflicts of Interest" on p. 42.
See "Doing No Harm" on p. 44.
See "Maintaining Confidentiality" on p. 44.
See "Resolving Ethical Dilemmas" on p. 44.
See "Blanchard and Peale Three-Part Test" on p. 44.
See "The Front-Page-of-the-Newspaper Test" on p. 45.
See Ethics & the Law on pumping up SAT scores on p. 45.
See "Laura Nash Model" on p. 46.

KEY TERMS

business ethics
civil disobedience
conflict of interest
entitlement theory
ethical egoism
ethics
integrity
kant's categorical imperative
moral relativists
natural law
positive law
primum non nocere
rights theory
social contract
stakeholder analysis
stakeholders
theory of justice
utilitarians

QUESTIONS AND CASE PROBLEMS

1. Marty Mankamyer, the president of the United States Olympic Committee (USOC), resigned in early February 2003 following reports in *The Denver Post* that indicated she had demanded a commission from a fellow real estate broker in the Colorado Springs area, the home of the USOC, who had sold property to Lloyd Ward, the CEO of the USOC. Mr. Ward had purchased a 1.3-acre lot in Colorado Springs for $475,000 and had paid the listing broker, Brigette Ruskin, a commission.

   Ms. Mankamyer allegedly demanded a portion of the commission from Ms. Ruskin, and Ms. Ruskin sent her a check. Ms. Mankamyer had shown Mr. Ward and his wife properties in the area when they were being considered for the job and when he was considering taking the job. However, Mrs. Ward indicated that Ms. Mankamyer did not identify herself as a real estate agent and that she assumed that Ms. Mankamyer was showing the properties as a "goodwill gesture."[15] What conflicts of interest do you see here?

2. Ann Elkin, who works for Brill Co., has been sent out to conduct two customer evaluations, which have gone much more quickly than Ann anticipated. Her supervisor does not expect Ann back until after lunch. It is now 10:30 A.M., and Ann would like to run some personal errands and then go to lunch before returning to work at 1:00 P.M. Should Ann take the time? Would you? Why or why not? Be sure to consider the categories of ethical values and apply one or two models before reaching your conclusion.

3. Fred Sanguine is a New York City produce broker. Ned Santini is a 19-year-old college student who works for Sanguine from 4:00 A.M. until 7:00 A.M. each weekday before he attends classes at Pace University. Fred has instructed Ned on the proper packing of produce as follows: "Look, put the bad and small cherries at the bottom. Do the same with the strawberries and blueberries. Put the best fruit on top and hide the bad stuff at the bottom. This way I get top dollar on all that I sell." Ned is uncomfortable about the instructions, but, as he explains to his roommate,

[15] Richard Sandomir, "U.S. Olympic Chief Resigns in a Furor Over Ethics Issues," *New York Times*, February 5, 2003, A1, C17; Bill Briggs, *Realtor Waving Red Flag*, **www.denverpost.com**, February 4, 2003.

"It's not me doing it. I'm just following orders. Besides, I need the job."

Should Ned just follow instructions? Is the manner in which the fruit is packed unethical? Would you do it? Why or why not? Is anyone really harmed by the practice?

4. Alan Gellen is the facilities manager for the city of Milwaukee and makes all final decisions on purchasing items such as chairs, lights, and other supplies and materials. Alan also makes the final decisions for the award of contracts to food vendors at event sites. Grand Beef Franks has submitted a bid to be one of the city's vendors. Alan went to school with Grand Beef's owner, Steve Grand, who phones Alan and explains that Grand Beef owns a condominium in Maui that Alan could use. Steve's offer to Alan is: "All it would cost you for a vacation is your airfare. The condo is fully stocked with food. Just let me know."

   Should Alan take the offer? Would you? Be sure to determine which category of ethical values this situation involves and to apply several models as you resolve the question of whether Alan should accept the invitation.

5. A Dillard's customer brought in a pair of moderately expensive dress shoes, expressing a desire to return them because they just weren't quite right. As the manager processed the order, she checked inside the box to be sure that the shoes in the box were the shoes that matched the box – past experience dictated that follow-up on returns. The shoes were the correct ones for the box, but there was another issue. The shoes had masking tape on the bottom – masking tape that was dirty. When the manager returned to the customer she said, "You forgot to remove the masking tape from your shoes." The customer responded, "I only wore them once. That's all I needed them for."

   From Neiman Marcus to Saks to Dillard's, managers have to stay one step ahead of customers, or lessees, who buy, or lease for free, dresses and now shoes for one use with premeditated intent to return the merchandise. Stores now place tags strategically so that the dresses cannot be worn without cutting them off and there are no returns if the tags are cut off on formal wear.

   Ace Hardware and Home Depot have customers who "buy" a special tool, try to use it once, and then return it. The hardware/home improvement stores are left with opened packaging and used goods by buy-it-temporarily customers.

   List some consequences for this behavior by customers.

6. Adam Smith wrote the following in *The Theory of Moral Sentiments:*

   > *In the practice of the other virtues, our conduct should rather be directed by a certain idea of propriety, by a certain taste for a particular tenor of conduct, than by any regard to a precise maxim or rule; and we should consider the end and foundation of the rule, more than the rule itself.*[16]

   Do you think Adam Smith adhered to positive law as his ethical standard? Was he a moral relativist? Does his quote match stakeholder analysis? What would his ethical posture be on violating the law?

7. A new phenomenon for admissions to MBA programs is hiring consultants to help applicants hone their applications. About 20 percent of those who apply to the top MBA programs have hired consultants at a cost of $150 to $200 per hour to help them say and do the right things to be admitted. The total cost for most who use a consultant is $5,000. The consultants help with personal essays and applications. One admissions officer points out that one function of the consultant is to draw out and emphasize skills that the applicant may not see as important. For example, playing the piano is looked upon favorably because it shows discipline and focus.

   However, admissions committees are becoming adept at spotting the applications via consultant because, as the faculty describe it, these essays and applications have a certain "sameness" to them. The Fuqua School at North Carolina

[16] Adam Smith, *The Theory of Moral Sentiments* (Arlington House, 1969; originally published in 1769).

suggests that students simply call the admissions office and get comparable advice for free. Is it ethical to use an admissions consultant? When would you cross a line in using the consultant on the essay?

8. "I was very upset that there's that many dishonest people," said Andrea Reuland, the owner of Trigs Shell Station in Minocqua, Wisconsin.

   She lost $3 per gallon on 586 gallons of gas sold during a 45-minute period when local residents phoned others to come and get gas because an employee had made a mistake and entered the price at 32.9 cents vs. $3.299 per gallon.

   Eighty-seven percent of the people who responded to a survey about the incident said they would have done the same thing as the Minocqua residents.

   Describe who is affected by what buyers did by not paying the correct price for the gas. Describe a simple test for resolving an ethical dilemma such as this where you can get something for free or very little.

9. The state of Arizona mandates emissions testing for cars before drivers can obtain updated registrations. The state hires a contractor to conduct the emissions tests in the various emissions-testing facilities around the state. In October 1999, the Arizona attorney general announced the arrest of 13 workers at one of the emissions-testing facilities for allegedly taking payoffs of between $50 and $200 from car owners to pass their cars on the emissions tests when those cars fell below emissions standards and would not have been registered. Nearly half of the staff at the emissions facility were arrested.

   Why is it a crime for someone working in a government-sponsored facility to accept a payment for a desired outcome? Do the payoffs to the workers really harm anyone?

10. The president and athletic director at the University of California at Los Angeles (UCLA) fired the school's basketball coach because an expense form he had submitted for reimbursement had the names of two students he said had joined him for a recruiting dinner. The students had not been to the dinner. The coach was stunned because he had been at UCLA for eight years and had established a winning program. He said, "And to throw it all away on a meal?" Do you agree with the coach's assessment? Was it too harsh to fire him for one inaccurate expense form? Did the coach commit an ethical breach?

11. When some runners in the New York City Marathon hit the Queensboro Bridge, temptation sets in and, rather than finishing the last 10 miles through Harlem and the Bronx, they hop a ride on the subway and head toward the finish line at Central Park. A total of 46 runners used the subway solution to finish the race in the 2008 NYC Marathon. When one runner was questioned about his unusual time, he admitted to using the subway and said, "So I skipped a few boroughs. I didn't do anything illegal." How would you respond to his point that he did not break the law? Why should we worry about some runners?

12. David A. Vise, a Pulitzer Prize winner and a reporter for the *Washington Post,* wrote the book *The Bureau and the Mole.* When the book hit the market, Mr. Vise purchased 20,000 copies via Barnes & Noble.com, taking advantage of both free shipping offered by the publisher and a discounted initial price. Mr. Vise's book had already hit the *New York Times'* bestseller list in the week before the purchases. He used the books he purchased to conduct online sales of autographed copies of the books, and then returned 17,500 books and asked for his money back. However, that return of 17,500 books represented more books than a publisher generally runs for a book. Mr. Vise said that he did not intend to manipulate the market or profit from the transactions. He said his only intent was to "increase awareness of *The Bureau and the Mole.*"

    Mr. Vise's editor offered to pay Barnes & Noble for any expenses it incurred. Was it ethical to do what Mr. Vise did? Was he within his rights to return the books? What are his remedies? Does Barnes & Noble have any rights?

13. Former Enron Chief Financial Officer Andrew Fastow, in his testimony against his former bosses

at their criminal trial for fraud, said, "I thought I was being a hero for Enron. At the time, I thought I was helping myself and helping Enron to make its numbers." Mr. Fastow also added, however, "I lost my moral compass."

Are you able to classify Mr. Fastow into a particular ethical standard or principle?

14. Piper High School in Piper, Kansas, a town located about 20 miles west of Kansas City, experienced national attention because of questions about students and their term papers for a botany class. Christine Pelton, a high school science teacher, had warned students in her sophomore class not to use papers posted on the Internet for their projects. When their projects were turned in, Ms. Pelton noticed that the writing in some of the papers was well above the students' usual quality and ability. She found that 28 of her 118 students had taken substantial portions of their papers from the Internet. She gave these students a zero grade on their term paper projects with the result that many of the students were going to fail the course for that semester. The students' parents protested, and the school board ordered Ms. Pelton to raise the grades.

She resigned in protest. She received a substantial number of job offers from around the country following her resignation. Nearly half of the high school faculty as well as its principal announced their plans to resign at the end of the year. Several of the parents pointed to the fact that there was no explanation in the Piper High School handbook on plagiarism. They also said that the students were unclear about what could be used, when they had to reword, and when quotations marks were necessary.

The annual Rutgers University survey on academic cheating has revealed that 15 percent of college papers turned in for grades are completely copied from the Internet.

Do you think such copying is unethical? Why do we worry about such conduct? Isn't this conduct just a function of the Internet? Isn't it accepted behavior?

15. Pharmaceutical companies, faced with the uphill battle of getting doctors to take a look at their new products, have created complex systems and programs for enticing doctors to come, sit, and absorb information about the new products.

Following is a list of the various type of benefits and gifts that drug companies have given doctors over the past few years to entice them to consider prescribing their new offerings:

- An event called "Why Cook?" in which doctors were given the chance to review drug studies and product information at a restaurant as their meals were being prepared—they could leave as soon as their meals were ready, and they were treated to appetizers and drinks as they waited
- Events at Christmas tree lots where doctors can come and review materials and pick up a free Christmas tree
- Flowers sent to doctors' offices on Valentine's Day with materials attached
- Manicures as they study materials on new drugs
- Pedicures as they study materials on new drugs
- Free car washes during which they study materials
- Free books with materials enclosed
- Free CDs with materials attached
- Bottles of wine with materials attached
- Events at Barnes & Noble where doctors can browse and pick out a book for themselves for free as long as they also take some materials on a new drug

Some doctors say that they can enjoy dinner on a drug company as often as five times per week. The American Medical Association (AMA) frowns on the "dine-and-dash" format because its rules provide that dinners are acceptable only as long as the doctors sit and learn something from a featured speaker. The AMA also limits gifts to those of a "minimal value" that should be related to their patients, such as note pads and pens with the new drug's name imprinted on them. The chairman of the AMA Committee on Ethics says the following about gifts, "There are doctors who say, 'I always do what's best for my patients, and these gifts and dinners and trips do not influence me.' They are wrong."[17]

In which category of ethical issues do these gifts fall? Do you think doctors act ethically in accepting gifts, meals, and favors? The Food and Drug Administration recently issued rules about such favors and perks. Why?

[17] Chris Adams, "Doctors on the Run Can 'Dine 'n' Dash' in Style in New Orleans," *Wall Street Journal*, May 14, 2001, A1, A6.

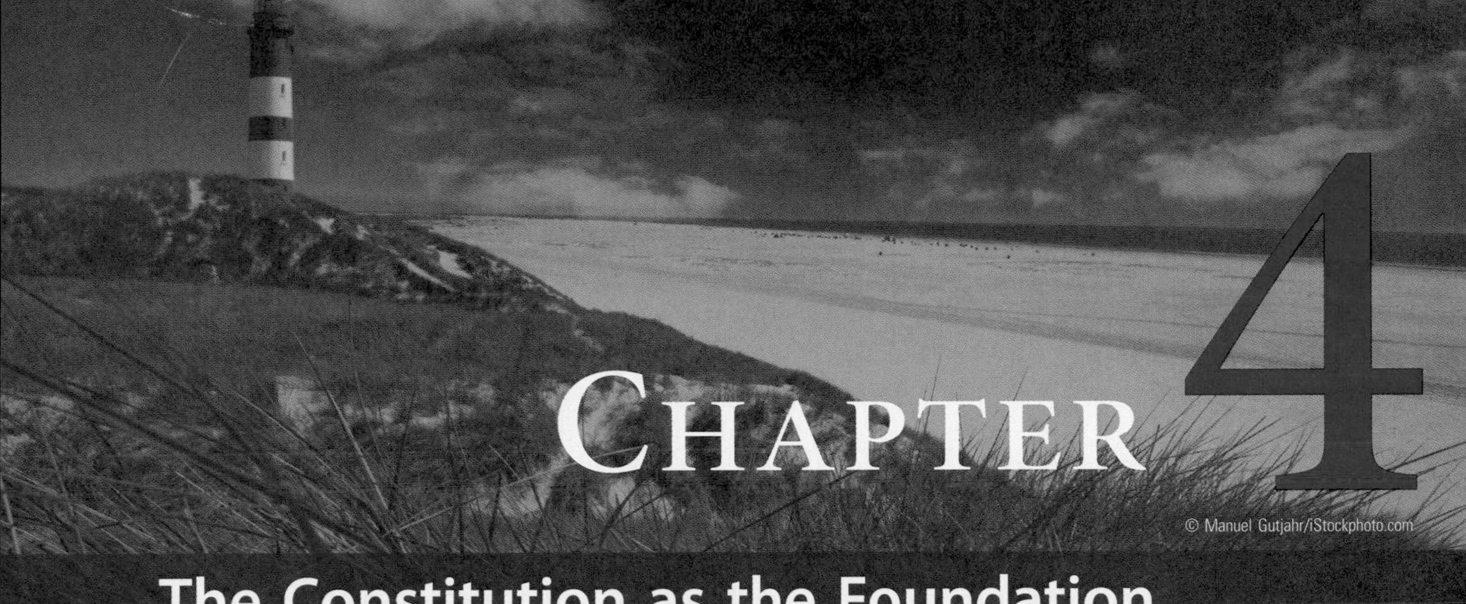

© Manuel Gutjahr/iStockphoto.com

The Constitution as the Foundation of the Legal Environment

learningoutcomes

After studying this chapter, you should be able to

LO.1 Describe the U.S. Constitution and the Federal System

LO.2 Explain the relationship between the U.S. Constitution and the States

LO.3 Discuss interpreting and amending the Constitution

LO.4 List and describe the significant federal powers

LO.5 Discuss constitutional limitations on governmental power

This chapter introduces you to the powers of government and to the protections that you have for your rights. The Constitution of the United States establishes the structure and powers of government but also the limitations on those powers. This Constitution forms the foundation of our legal environment.

A. The U.S. Constitution and the Federal System

By establishing a central government to coexist with the governments of the individual states, the U.S. Constitution created a federal system. In a **federal system,** a central government has power to address national concerns, while the individual states retain the power to handle local concerns.

1. What a Constitution Is

A **constitution** is the written document that establishes the structure of the government and its relationship to the people. The U.S. Constitution was adopted in 1789 by the 13 colonies that had won their independence from King George.[1]

2. The Branches of Government

The U.S. Constitution establishes a **tripartite** (three-part) government: a **legislative branch** (Congress) to make the laws, an **executive branch** (the president) to execute or enforce the laws, and a **judicial branch** (courts) to interpret the laws.[2] The national legislature or Congress is a **bicameral** (two-house) body consisting of the Senate and the House of Representatives. Members of the Senate are popularly elected for a term of six years. Members of the House of Representatives are popularly elected for a term of two years. The president is elected by an electoral college whose membership is popularly elected. The president serves for a term of four years and is eligible for reelection for a second term. Judges of the United States are appointed by the president with the approval of the Senate and serve for life, subject to removal only by impeachment because of misconduct. (See Chapter 2 for a discussion of the federal court system.)

B. The U.S. Constitution and the States

The Constitution created certain powers within the national government that would have been exercised by the individual states, which are given their powers by the people of the state. Figure 4-1 illustrates the delegation of powers. Likewise, the states, as the power-granting authorities, reserved certain powers for themselves.

3. Delegated and Shared Powers

(A) Delegated Powers. The powers given by the states to the national government are described as *delegated powers.* Some of these **delegated powers** are given exclusively to the national government. **For Example,** the national government alone may declare war or establish a currency.

(B) Shared Powers. The powers delegated to the national government that may still be exercised by the states are **shared powers**. **For Example,** the grant of power to the national government to impose taxes did not destroy the state power to tax. In other cases, a state may provide regulation along with, but subject to the supremacy of, federal law. **For Example,** regulation of the use of navigable waterways within a state is an example of joint state and federal regulation.

4. Other Powers

(A) State Police Power. The states possess the power to adopt laws to protect the general welfare, health, safety, and morals of the people. This authority is called the **police power. For Example,** states may require that businesses be licensed with state agencies to protect persons dealing with the business. State exercise of the police power may not unreasonably interfere with federal powers.

(B) Prohibited Powers. The Constitution also prohibits both states and the federal government from doing certain things. **For Example,** neither states nor the

[1] To examine the U.S. Constitution, go to **www.constitution.org** and click on "Founding Documents," or refer to Appendix 2.

[2] *Free Enterprise Fund v. Public Company Accounting Oversight Board,* 130 S. Ct. 3138 (2010).

FIGURE 4-1 *Governments of the United States*

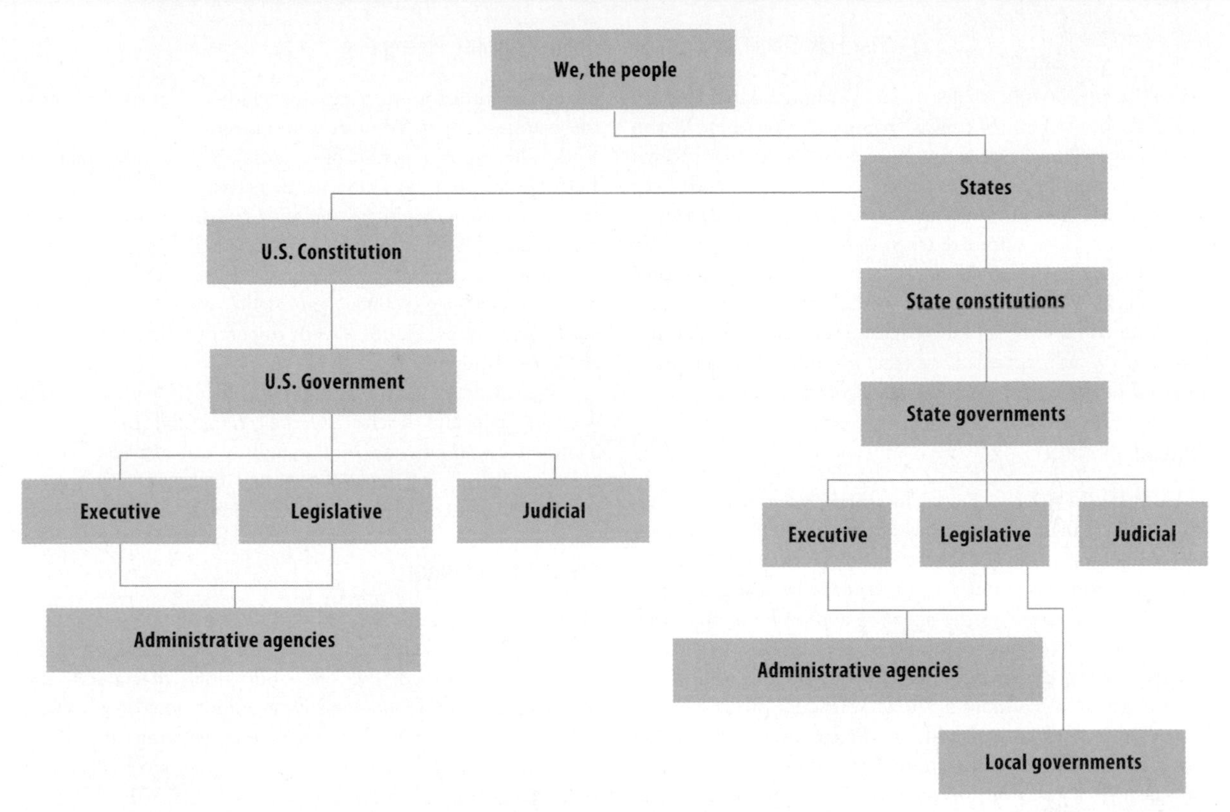

national government may adopt ***ex post facto* laws,** which make criminal an act that has already been committed but was not criminal when it was committed. Laws that increase the penalty for an act already committed above the penalty in force when the act was committed are also *ex post facto* laws.

5. Federal Supremacy

States cannot enact conflicting state regulation if the congressional intent to regulate exclusively can be inferred from the details of congressional regulation. **Preemption** means that the federal regulatory scheme is controlling.

(A) Express Federal Regulation. The Constitution and statutes passed by Congress are the supreme law of the land. They cancel out any conflicting state law.[3] When a direct conflict exists between federal and state statutes, federal law prevails.

In some cases, however, no obvious conflict occurs because the federal statute covers only part of the subject matter. In such cases, the question becomes whether a state law can regulate the areas not regulated by Congress or whether the partial regulation made by Congress preempts, or takes over, the field so as to preclude state legislation. The *Wyeth v. Levine* case deals with an issue of federal preemption.

(B) Silence of Congress. In some situations, the silence of Congress in failing to cover a particular subject area indicates that Congress does not want any law on the matter. However, when national uniformity is essential, the silence of Congress generally means that

[3] U.S. Const., Art VI, cl 2. *Cuomo v. Clearinghouse Ass'n, LLC*, 557 U.S. 519 (2009).

Wyeth v. Levine, 555 U.S. 555 (2009)*

The Folk Singer Who Staged a Protest against Preemption

Diana Levine, a folk singer from Vermont, suffered from migraine headaches. She was being administered Wyeth Laboratory's Phenergan through a drip IV. Either because the IV needle entered Levine's artery or the drug escaped from the vein into her surrounding tissue, Ms. Levine developed gangrene. Doctors amputated her right hand and eventually her forearm. Levine could no longer work as a professional musician. Levine filed suit against both the clinic that administered the drug and Wyeth. She was awarded $7.4 million and Wyeth appealed on the grounds that the FDA approval of the drug preempted state tort suits by patients.

JUDICIAL OPINION

STEVENS, Justice ... Generally speaking, a manufacturer may only change a drug label after the FDA approves a supplemental application. There is, however, an FDA regulation that permits a manufacturer to make certain changes to its label before receiving the agency's approval. Among other things, this "changes being effected" (CBE) regulation provides that if a manufacturer is changing a label to "add or strengthen a contraindication, warning, precaution, or adverse reaction" or to "add or strengthen an instruction about dosage and administration that is intended to increase the safe use of the drug product," it may make the labeling change upon filing its supplemental application with the FDA; it need not wait for FDA approval. Wyeth argues that the CBE regulation is not implicated in this case because a 2008 amendment provides that a manufacturer may only change its label "to reflect newly acquired information." Resting on this language (which Wyeth argues simply reaffirmed the interpretation of the regulation in effect when this case was tried), Wyeth contends that it could have changed Phenergan's label only in response to new information that the FDA had not considered. And it maintains that Levine has not pointed to any such information concerning the risks of IV-push administration.

We need not decide whether the 2008 CBE regulation is consistent with the FDCA and the previous version of the regulation, as Wyeth and the United States urge, because Wyeth could have revised Phenergan's label even in accordance with the amended regulation. As the FDA explained in its notice of the final rule, "'newly acquired information'" is not limited to new data, but also encompasses "new analyses of previously submitted data."

Wyeth argues that if it had unilaterally added such a warning, it would have violated federal law governing unauthorized distribution and misbranding. But strengthening the warning about IV-push administration would not have made Phenergan a new drug.... And the very idea that the FDA would bring an enforcement action against a manufacturer for strengthening a warning pursuant to the CBE regulation is difficult to accept.

Absent clear evidence that the FDA would not have approved a change to Phenergan's label, we will not conclude that it was impossible for Wyeth to comply with both federal and state requirements.

We conclude that it is not impossible for Wyeth to comply with its state and federal law obligations and that Levine's common-law claims do not stand as an obstacle to the accomplishment of Congress' purposes in the FDCA. Accordingly, the judgment of the Vermont Supreme Court is affirmed.

DISSENTING OPINION

Justice ALITO, with whom THE CHIEF JUSTICE and Justice SCALIA join, dissenting. This case illustrates that tragic facts make bad law. The Court holds that a state tort jury, rather than the Food and Drug Administration (FDA), is ultimately responsible for regulating warning labels for prescription drugs. That result cannot be reconciled with *Geier v American Honda Motor Co.*, 529 US 861, 120 S Ct 1913, 146 L Ed 2d 914 (2000), or general principles of conflict preemption. I respectfully dissent. The Court frames the question presented as a "narro[w]" one—namely, whether Wyeth has a duty to provide "an adequate warning about using the IV-push method" to administer Phenergan. But that ignores the antecedent question of who—the FDA or a jury in Vermont—has the authority and responsibility for determining the "adequacy" of Phenergan's warnings. Moreover, it is unclear how a "stronger" warning could have helped respondent, after all, the physician's assistant who treated her disregarded at least six separate warnings that are already on Phenergan's labeling, so respondent would be hard pressed to prove that a seventh would have made a difference.

As noted above, when the FDA approved Phenergan's label, it was textbook medical knowledge that the "antecubital fossa" creates a high risk of inadvertent intra-arterial injection, given the close proximity of veins and arteries. According to the physician's assistant who injured respondent, however, "[i]t never crossed my mind" that an antecubital injection of Phenergan could hit an artery. Oblivious to the risks emphasized in Phenergan's warnings, the physician's assistant pushed a double dose of the drug into an antecubital artery over the course of "[p]robably about three to four minutes," notwithstanding respondent's complaints of a "'burn[ing]'" sensation that she subsequently described as "'one of the most

*For an earlier decision that concluded differently on preemption, see *Riegel v Medtronic*, 552 U.S. 312 (2008).

Continued

extreme pains that I've ever felt,'" And when asked why she ignored Phenergan's label and failed to stop pushing the drug after respondent complained of burning pains, the physician's assistant explained that it would have been "just crazy" to "worr[y] about an [intra-arterial] injection" under the circumstances.

The FDA, however, did not think that the risks associated with IV push—especially in the antecubital space—were "just crazy." That is why Phenergan's label so clearly warns against them.

To be sure, state tort suits can peacefully coexist with the FDA's labeling regime, and they have done so for decades. But this case is far from peaceful coexistence.

The FDA told Wyeth that Phenergan's label renders its use "safe." But the State of Vermont, through its tort law, said: "Not so."

The state-law rule at issue here is squarely preempted. Therefore, I would reverse the judgment of the Supreme Court of Vermont.

QUESTIONS

1. What argument does Wyeth make to establish preemption protection against the suit?
2. What does the majority of the court say about the right of Wyeth to change its label and how does that right affect the preemption argument?
3. What is the concern of the dissenting judges about allowing the suit?

the subject has been preempted for practical reasons by Congress and that no state law on the subject may be adopted.

(c) Effect of Federal Deregulation. The fact that the federal government removes the regulations from a regulated industry does not automatically give the states the power to regulate that industry. If under the silence-of-Congress doctrine the states cannot regulate, they are still barred from regulating after deregulation. **For Example,** deregulation of banks in the 1980s did not mean that the states could step in and regulate those banks.[4]

C. Interpreting and Amending the Constitution

The Constitution as it is interpreted today has changed greatly from the Constitution as originally written. The change has been brought about by interpretation, amendment, and practice.

6. Conflicting Theories

Shortly after the Constitution was adopted, conflict arose over whether it was to be interpreted strictly, so as to give the federal government the least power possible, or broadly, so as to give the federal government the greatest power that the words would permit. These two views may be called the *bedrock view* and the *living-document view*, respectively.

In the **bedrock view,** or strict constructionist or originalist view, the purpose of a constitution is to state certain fundamental principles for all time. In the **living-document view,** a constitution is merely a statement of goals and objectives and is intended to grow and change with time.

Whether the Constitution is to be liberally interpreted under the living-document view or narrowly interpreted under the bedrock view has a direct effect on the Constitution. For the last century, the Supreme Court has followed the living-document view. This view has resulted in strengthening the power of the federal government, permitting the rise of administrative agencies, and expanding the protection of human rights.

One view is not selected to the exclusion of the other. As contradictory as these two views sound, the Constitution remains durable. We do not want a set of New Year's resolutions that will soon be forgotten. At the same time, we know that the world changes, and therefore, we do not want a constitution that will hold us tied in a straitjacket of the past.

[4] For a discussion of preemption of state regulation of airline advertising when federal regulation of air travel is so pervasive see *New York v. Trans World Airlines*, 556 N.Y.S. 2d 803 (1990) and *Pan American World Airways, Inc. v. Abrams*, 764 F. Supp. 864, 868 (S.D.N.Y. 1991). See also footnote 3 and the *Cuomo* case from 2009.

FIGURE 4-2 *Amending the U.S. Constitution*

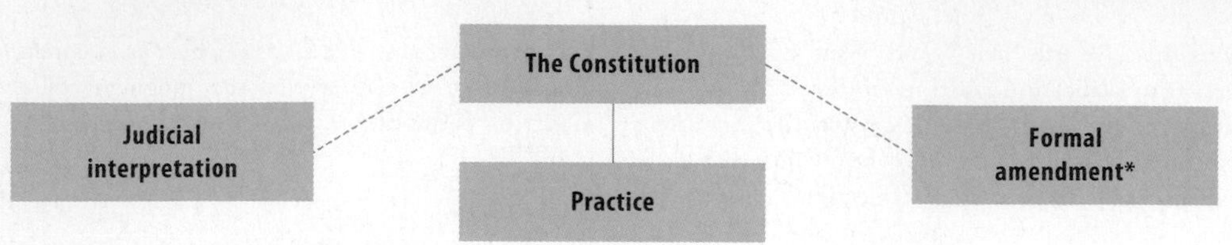

*Article V of the U.S. Constitution specifies the procedure for adopting amendments.

In terms of social forces that make the law, we are torn between our desire for stability and our desire for flexibility. We want a constitution that is stable. At the same time, we want one that is flexible.

7. Amending the Constitution

The Constitution has been amended in three ways: (1) expressly, (2) by interpretation, and (3) by practice. Figure 4-2 illustrates these three methods of amendment.

(A) CONSTITUTIONAL METHOD OF AMENDING. Article V of the Constitution gives the procedure to be followed for amending the Constitution. Relatively few changes have been made to the Constitution by this formal process, although thousands of proposals have been made. Since the time of its adoption, there have been only 27 amendments to the Constitution.[5]

(B) AMENDMENT BY JUDICIAL INTERPRETATION. The U.S. Supreme Court has made the greatest changes to the written Constitution by interpreting it. Generally, interpretation is used to apply the Constitution to a new situation that could not have been foreseen when the written Constitution was adopted.

(C) AMENDMENT BY PRACTICE. In practice, the letter of the Constitution is not always followed. Departure from the written Constitution began as early as 1793 when George Washington refused to make treaties as required by the Constitution, by and with the consent of the Senate. Washington began the practice of the president's negotiating a treaty with a foreign country and then submitting it to the Senate for approval. This practice has been followed since that time. Similarly, the electoral college was originally intended to exercise independent judgment in selecting the president, but it now automatically elects the official candidate of the party that elected the majority of the members of the electoral college.

8. The Living Constitution

The living Constitution has the following characteristics.

(A) STRONG GOVERNMENT. One of the characteristics of the new Constitution is strong government. Business enterprises are highly regulated and the economy is controlled through monetary policy.

(B) STRONG PRESIDENT. Instead of being merely an officer who carries out the laws, the president has become the political leader of a party, exerting strong influence on the lawmaking process.

(C) ECLIPSE OF THE STATES. Under constitutional interpretations, all levels of government have powers that they never possessed before, but the center of gravity has shifted from the states to the nation. When the Constitution was adopted in 1789, the federal government was to have only the very limited powers specified in Article I, Section 8, of the Constitution. Whatever regulation of business was permissible was to be imposed by the states. Today, the great bulk of the regulation of business is adopted by the federal government through Congress or its administrative agencies. As the U.S. economy moved from the local community stage to the nationwide and then

[5] Gregory Watson, a University of Texas at Austin student who was doing research for a paper for a class on the U.S. Constitution, ran across a 1789 proposed amendment to the Constitution that had never been ratified by the states. Watson wrote a paper and got a "C," but through a successful letter-writing campaign was able to get the 27th Amendment passed. The amendment reads, "No law, varying the compensation for the services of the Senators and Representatives, shall take effect, until an election of Representatives shall have intervened."

international stages, individual states could no longer provide effective regulation of business. Regulation migrated to the central government.

(D) Administrative Agencies. These units of government were virtually unheard of in 1789, and the Constitution made no mention of them. The vast powers of the new Constitution are exercised to a very large degree by administrative agencies. They are in effect a fourth branch of the government, not provided for in the written Constitution. More importantly, the administrative agencies are the ones that come in contact with the majority of businesspersons and citizens.

Agencies have had a significant amount of power delegated to them. The members and heads of the agencies, boards, or commissions are not elected by the voters (see Chapter 6). They are appointed by the president and, at certain levels of appointment in the agency, must be approved by Congress.

D. Federal Powers

The federal government possesses powers necessary to administer matters of national concern.

9. The Power to Regulate Commerce

The desire to protect commerce from restrictions and barriers set up by the individual states was a prime factor leading to the adoption of the Constitution of 1789. To protect commerce, Congress was given Article I, Section 8, Clause 3—now known as the **commerce clause**—the power "to regulate commerce with foreign nations, and among the several states, and with the Indian tribes."[6]

Until 1937, the Supreme Court held that this provision gave Congress the power to control or regulate only that commerce crossing a state line, such as an interstate railway train or an interstate telegraph message.

(A) The Commerce Power Becomes a General Welfare Power. In 1937, the Supreme Court began expanding the concept of interstate commerce. By 1946, the power to regulate interstate commerce had become very broad. By that year, the power had expanded to the point that it gave authority to Congress to adopt regulatory laws that were "as broad as the economic needs of the nation."[7] By virtue of this broad interpretation, Congress can regulate manufacturing, agriculture, mining, stock exchanges, insurance, loan sharking, monopolies, and conspiracies in restraint of trade. The far reach of the interstate commerce power is seen in the Freedom of Access to Clinic Entrances Act,[8] which prohibits obstruction of entrances to clinics, as well as in the commerce clause challenges to the Affordable Health Care Act, also known as Obama Care.[9]

The case that was the beginning point in the transition of the commerce clause was *NLRB v. Jones & Laughlin Steel*, 301 U.S. 1 (1937). The "affectation" doctrine expanded the authority of the federal government under the commerce clause. At that time, the Court concluded, "If it is interstate commerce that feels the pinch, it does not matter how local the squeeze."

(B) The Commerce Clause Today. Today, judicial review of the commerce clause typically finds some connection between the legislation and congressional authority. However, in the past five years, the U.S. Supreme Court has found some areas Congress may not regulate and has placed some limitations on the commerce clause. These constraints on the commerce clause focus on the nature of the underlying activity being regulated. So long as the federal regulation relates to economic/ commercial activity, it is constitutional. If, however, the underlying activity is not economic and has only an economic impact, the Supreme Court has imposed restrictions on congressional authority under the commerce clause.

For Example, in *U.S. v. Morrison*, 529 U.S. 598 (2000), the Supreme Court held that the Violence Against Women Act was unconstitutional because the underlying activity being regulated was violence, an activity that was not economic. Regulation of economic activity is required in order to survive constitutional scrutiny under the Commerce Clause.

The *National Federation of Independent Business v. Sebelius* case deals with a critical Commerce Clause issue and the constitutionality of Obama Care, the Affordable Health Care Act.

[6] For more details on the actual language in the U.S. Constitution, go to **www.constitution.org** and click on "Founding Documents," or refer to Appendix 2.

[7] *American Power & Light Co. v. Securities and Exchange Commission*, 329 U.S. 90 (1946).

[8] 18 USC §248.

[9] *United States v. Wilson*, 73 F.3d 675 (7th Cir. 1995), *cert. denied*, 519 U.S. 806 (1996), Florida ex rel. *National Federation of Independent Business v. Sebelius*, 132 S.Ct. 2566 (2012).

National Federation of Independent Business v. Sebelius, 132 S.Ct. 2566 (2012)

If I Don't Buy Something, Is That Economic Activity Congress Can Regulate?

Congress passed the Patient Protection and Affordable Care Act (also known as Obama Care) in order to increase the number of Americans covered by health insurance and decrease the cost of health care. One key provision in the law was the individual mandate, which requires most Americans to maintain "minimum essential" health insurance coverage. Attorneys general from several states, along with businesses, challenged this requirement (and other provisions of the law) as being unconstitutional under the Commerce Clause. From a series of federal court decisions below, some finding the law constitutional and others not, the affected parties appealed and the Supreme Court granted *certiorari.* Their cases were consolidated for the court's review.

JUDICIAL OPINION

ROBERTS, Chief Justice ... The Constitution grants Congress the power to "*regulate* Commerce." Art. I, § 8, cl. 3 The power to *regulate* commerce presupposes the existence of commercial activity to be regulated. If the power to "regulate" something included the power to create it, many of the provisions in the Constitution would be superfluous. For example, the Constitution gives Congress the power to "coin Money," in addition to the power to "regulate the Value thereof." And it gives Congress the power to "raise and support Armies" and to "provide and maintain a Navy," in addition to the power to "make Rules for the Government and Regulation of the land and naval Forces." If the power to regulate the armed forces or the value of money included the power to bring the subject of the regulation into existence, the specific grant of such powers would have been unnecessary. The language of the Constitution reflects the natural understanding that the power to regulate assumes there is already something to be regulated.

Our precedent also reflects this understanding. As expansive as our cases construing the scope of the commerce power have been, they all have one thing in common: They uniformly describe the power as reaching "activity." It is nearly impossible to avoid the word when quoting them.

The individual mandate, however, does not regulate existing commercial activity. It instead compels individuals to *become* active in commerce by purchasing a product, on the ground that their failure to do so affects interstate commerce. Construing the Commerce Clause to permit Congress to regulate individuals precisely *because* they are doing nothing would open a new and potentially vast domain to congressional authority. Every day individuals do not do an infinite number of things. In some cases they decide not to do something; in others they simply fail to do it. Allowing Congress to justify federal regulation by pointing to the effect of inaction on commerce would bring countless decisions an individual could *potentially* make within the scope of federal regulation, and—under the Government's theory—empower Congress to make those decisions for him.

Indeed, the Government's logic would justify a mandatory purchase to solve almost any problem. To consider a different example in the health care market, many Americans do not eat a balanced diet. That group makes up a larger percentage of the total population than those without health insurance. The failure of that group to have a healthy diet increases health care costs, to a greater extent than the failure of the uninsured to purchase insurance. Those increased costs are borne in part by other Americans who must pay more, just as the uninsured shift costs to the insured. Congress addressed the insurance problem by ordering everyone to buy insurance. Under the Government's theory, Congress could address the diet problem by ordering everyone to buy vegetables.

People, for reasons of their own, often fail to do things that would be good for them or good for society. Those failures—joined with the similar failures of others—can readily have a substantial effect on interstate commerce. Under the Government's logic, that authorizes Congress to use its commerce power to compel citizens to act as the Government would have them act.

That is not the country the Framers of our Constitution envisioned. James Madison explained that the Commerce Clause was "an addition which few oppose and from which no apprehensions are entertained." The Federalist No. 45, at 293. While Congress's authority under the Commerce Clause has of course expanded with the growth of the national economy, our cases have "always recognized that the power to regulate commerce, though broad indeed, has limits." The Government's theory would erode those limits, permitting Congress to reach beyond the natural extent of its authority, "everywhere extending the sphere of its activity and drawing all power into its impetuous vortex." The Federalist No. 48, at 309 (J. Madison). Congress already enjoys vast power to regulate much of what we do. Accepting the Government's theory would give Congress the same license to regulate what we do not do, fundamentally changing the relation between the citizen and the Federal Government.

The complicated decision resulted in the lower court decisions being both affirmed and reversed, but the individual mandate was declared unconstitutional under the Commerce Clause.

QUESTIONS

1. What was missing that the Court indicated was needed in order to find that the mandate was constitutional?
2. What was the purpose of the court's discussion of a healthy diet?
3. What sources does the court rely on for constitutional interpretation?

(c) **The Commerce Power as a Limitation on States.** The federal power to regulate commerce not only gives Congress the power to act but also prevents states from acting in any way that interferes with federal regulation or burdens interstate commerce. **For Example,** if the federal government establishes safety device regulations for interstate carriers, a state cannot require different devices. The *Rowe v. New Hampshire Motor Transport Association* case deals with an issue of a state law that affects interstate carriers and its constitutionality.

Rowe v. New Hampshire Motor Transport Association, 552 U.S 364 (2008)

Minors in Maine and a Major Commerce Clause Decision

Maine passed a law that prohibited anyone other than a Maine-licensed tobacco retailer from accepting an order for delivery of tobacco. The law required the retailer to arrange for delivery with a special receipt showing that someone over the age of 18 had received and signed for the tobacco products delivered. Out-of-state shippers and tobacco sellers challenged the law as one that favored Maine tobacco retailers. The state of Maine argued that its law was passed to prevent the public health hazard of minors becoming addicted to tobacco. The federal district court granted summary judgment for the shippers, and the court of appeals affirmed. The state of Maine appealed.

JUDICIAL OPINION

BREYER, Justice ... The provision requires the carrier to check each shipment for certain markings and to compare it against the Maine attorney general's list of proscribed shippers. And it thereby directly regulates a significant aspect of the motor carrier's package pickup and delivery service. In this way it creates the kind of state-mandated regulation that the federal Act pre-empts.

Maine replies that the regulation will impose no significant additional costs upon carriers. But even were that so (and the carriers deny it), Maine's reply is off the mark. As with the recipient-verification provision, the "deemed to know" provision would freeze in place and immunize from competition a service-related system that carriers do not (or in the future might not) wish to provide. To allow Maine to insist that the carriers provide a special checking system would allow other States to do the same. And to interpret the federal law to permit these, and similar, state requirements could easily lead to a patchwork of state service-determining laws, rules, and regulations. That state regulatory patchwork is inconsistent with Congress' major legislative effort to leave such decisions, where federally unregulated, to the competitive marketplace.

And to allow Maine directly to regulate carrier services would permit other States to do the same. Given the number of States through which carriers travel, the number of products, the variety of potential adverse public health effects, the many different kinds of regulatory rules potentially available, and the difficulty of finding a legal criterion for separating permissible from impermissible public-health-oriented regulations.

In this case, the state law is not general, it does not affect truckers solely in their capacity as members of the general public, the impact is significant, and the connection with trucking is not tenuous, remote, or peripheral. The state statutes aim directly at the carriage of goods, a commercial field where carriage by commercial motor vehicles plays a major role. The state statutes require motor carrier operators to perform certain services, thereby limiting their ability to provide incompatible alternative services; and they do so simply because the State seeks to enlist the motor carrier operators as allies in its enforcement efforts.

Maine adds that it possesses legal authority to prevent *any* tobacco shipments from entering into or moving within the State, and that the broader authority must encompass the narrower authority to regulate the *manner* of tobacco shipments. But even assuming purely for argument's sake that Maine possesses the broader authority, its conclusion does not follow. To accept that conclusion would permit Maine to regulate carrier routes, carrier rates, and carrier services, all on the ground that such regulation would not restrict carriage of the goods as seriously as would a total ban on shipments. And it consequently would severely undermine the effectiveness of Congress' pre-emptive provision. Indeed, it would create the very exception that we have just rejected, extending that exception to all other products a State might ban. We have explained why we do not believe Congress intended that result. *Supra,* at 996–998.

Finally, Maine says that to set aside its regulations will seriously harm its efforts to prevent cigarettes from falling into the hands of minors. The Solicitor General denies that this is so. He suggests that Maine, like other States, can prohibit all persons from providing tobacco products to minors; that it can ban all non-face-to-face sales of tobacco; that it might pass other laws of general applicability; and that it can, if necessary, seek appropriate federal regulation.

For these reasons, the judgment of the Court of Appeals is affirmed.

QUESTIONS

1. What is the effect of the Maine law, if allowed to stand, on interstate carriers?
2. If this law is constitutional, what will happen to interstate carriers and their activities within particular states?

States may not use their tax power for the purpose of discriminating against interstate commerce. **For Example,** a state cannot impose a higher tax on goods imported from another state than it imposes on the same kind of goods produced in its own territory.

State regulations designed to advance local interests may conflict with the commerce clause. Such regulations are invalid. For example, suppose a state has a health concern about having milk properly processed. One way to address the concern is to require all milk to be processed in-state. Such a regulation clearly favors that state's businesses and imposes a great burden on out-of-state milk producers. Such a regulation would be an unconstitutional exercise of state power because the state could simply require all milk sellers to be licensed. Licensing would allow the state to check the milk-processing procedures of all firms and accomplish the safety goal without imposing such a burden on out-of-state firms. *The Granholm v. Heald* case deals with the problem and constitutionality of state laws benefiting intrastate businesses in order to give them a competitive edge within the state.[10]

Granholm v. Heald, 544 U.S. 460 (2005)

Whining About Wine

Like many other states, Michigan and New York regulate the sale and importation of alcoholic beverages, including wine, through a three-tier distribution system. Separate licenses are required for producers, wholesalers, and retailers. Both the regulations and statutory frameworks in New York and Michigan prohibit out-of-state wine producers from selling their wines directly to consumers there. In-state wineries can sell directly to consumers. The impact of the prohibition on the out-of-state wine producers is that they are required to pay wholesaler fees and cannot compete with in-state wine producers on direct-to-consumer sales. The direct-to-consumer sales avenue has been a means for small wineries to compete. Also, technological improvements, in particular the ability of wineries to sell wine over the Internet, have helped make direct shipments an attractive sales channel.

Several wine producers filed suit in their federal districts challenging these laws that prohibit direct shipment. The district court granted summary judgment for the state of Michigan. The Sixth Circuit Court of Appeals reversed on the grounds that the out-of-state restrictions violated the commerce clause. The state of Michigan appealed. In the New York case, the district court found the out-of-state restrictions violative of the Commerce Clause and Second Circuit Court of Appeals reversed and upheld the New York statute as constitutional. The out-of-state wine producers appealed, and the Supreme Court agreed to hear the cases to resolve the conflict in the circuits.

JUDICIAL OPINION

KENNEDY, Justice ... We consolidated these cases and granted certiorari on the following question: "'Does a State's regulatory scheme that permits in-state wineries directly to ship alcohol to consumers but restricts the ability of out-of-state wineries to do so violate the ... Commerce Clause...?'"

Time and again this Court has held that, in all but the narrowest circumstances, state laws violate the Commerce Clause if they mandate "differential treatment of in-state and out-of-state economic interests that benefits the former and burdens the latter." This rule is essential to the foundations of the Union. The mere fact of nonresidence should not foreclose a producer in one State from access to markets in other States. States may not enact laws that burden out-of-state producers or shippers simply to give a competitive advantage to in-state businesses. This mandate "reflect[s] a central concern of the Framers that was an immediate reason for calling the Constitutional Convention: the conviction that in order to succeed, the new Union would have to avoid the tendencies toward economic Balkanization that had plagued relations among the Colonies and later among the States under the Articles of Confederation."

The rule prohibiting state discrimination against interstate commerce follows also from the principle that States should not be compelled to negotiate with each other regarding favored or disfavored status for their own citizens. States do not need, and may not attempt, to negotiate with other States regarding their mutual economic interests. Rivalries among the States are thus kept to a minimum, and a proliferation of trade zones is prevented.

Laws of the type at issue in the instant cases contradict these principles. They deprive citizens of their right to have access to the markets of other States on equal terms. State laws that protect

[10] *Minnesota v. Clover Leaf Creamery*, 449 U.S. 456 (1981).

Continued

local wineries have led to the enactment of statutes under which some States condition the right of out-of-state wineries to make direct wine sales to in-state consumers on a reciprocal right in the shipping State. The current patchwork of laws—with some States banning direct shipments altogether, others doing so only for out-of-state wines, and still others requiring reciprocity—is essentially the product of an ongoing, low-level trade war. Allowing States to discriminate against out-of-state wine "invite[s] a multiplication of preferential trade areas destructive of the very purpose of the commerce clause."

The discriminatory character of the Michigan system is obvious. Michigan allows in-state wineries to ship directly to consumers, subject only to a licensing requirement. Out-of-state wineries, whether licensed or not, face a complete ban on direct shipment. The differential treatment requires all out-of-state wine, but not all in-state wine, to pass through an in-state wholesaler and retailer before reaching consumers. These two extra layers of overhead increase the cost of out-of-state wines to Michigan consumers. The cost differential, and in some cases the inability to secure a wholesaler for small shipments, can effectively bar small wineries from the Michigan market.

The New York regulatory scheme differs from Michigan's in that it does not ban direct shipments altogether. Out-of-state wineries are instead required to establish a distribution operation in New York in order to gain the privilege of direct shipment.

The New York scheme grants in-state wineries access to the State's consumers on preferential terms. The suggestion of a limited exception for direct shipment from out-of-state wineries does nothing to eliminate the discriminatory nature of New York's regulations. In-state producers, with the applicable licenses, can ship directly to consumers from their wineries. Out-of-state wineries must open a branch office and warehouse in New York, additional steps that drive up the cost of their wine. For most wineries, the expense of establishing a bricks-and-mortar distribution operation in 1 State, let alone all 50, is prohibitive. It comes as no surprise that not a single out-of-state winery has availed itself of New York's direct-shipping privilege. We have "viewed with particular suspicion state statutes requiring business operations to be performed in the home State that could more efficiently be performed elsewhere." *Pike v. Bruce Church, Inc.* 397 U.S. 137, 145, 90 S.Ct. 844, 25 L.Ed.2d 174 (1970). New York's in-state presence requirement runs contrary to our admonition that States cannot require an out-of-state firm "to become a resident in order to compete on equal terms."

We have no difficulty concluding that New York, like Michigan, discriminates against interstate commerce through its direct-shipping laws.

Affirmed as to judgment of the Sixth Circuit Court of Appeals; reversed and remanded as to judgment of the Second Circuit Court of Appeals.

NOTE: There was a strong dissent in the case that indicated that because of the 21st Amendment the federal government (and the court) could not be involved in state liquor regulation and that the Commerce Clause could not be applied to these state laws on liquor sales.

QUESTIONS

1. What do the Michigan and New York statutes require?
2. Why did the U.S. Supreme Court grant *certiorari* in the cases? Why do you think the court heard and decided the two cases together?
3. What is the economic impact of the statutes on wineries, both in- and out-of-state? On wholesalers? On consumers?

10. The Financial Powers

The financial powers of the federal government include the powers to tax and to borrow, spend, and coin money.

(A) The Taxing Power. The federal Constitution provides that "Congress shall have power to lay and collect taxes, duties, imposts and excises, to pay the debts and provide for the common defence and general welfare of the United States."[11] Subject to the express and implied limitations arising from the Constitution, the states may impose such taxes as they desire and as their own individual constitutions and statutes permit. In addition to express constitutional limitations, both national and local taxes are subject to the unwritten limitation that they be imposed for a public purpose. Taxes must also be apportioned. A business cannot be taxed for all of its revenues in all 50 states. There must be apportionment of taxes, and there must be sufficient connection with the state.[12] The *Quill Corporation v. North Dakota* case deals with the issue of the sufficiency of the connection between the company and the taxing state.

[11] U.S. Const., Art 1, §8, cl 1. To read more of the U.S. Constitution, refer to Appendix 2, or go to **www.constitution.org** and click on "Founding Documents."

[12] *Polar Tankers, Inc. v. City of Valdez, Alaska*, 557 U.S. 1 (2009).

Quill Corporation v. North Dakota, 504 U.S. 298 (1992)

Is North Dakota a Taxing State?

Quill is a Delaware corporation with offices and warehouses in Illinois, California, and Georgia. None of its employees works or lives in North Dakota, and it owns no property in North Dakota.

Quill sells office equipment and supplies; it solicits business through catalogs and flyers, advertisements in national periodicals, and telephone calls. Its annual national sales exceed $200 million, of which almost $1 million are made to about 3,000 customers in North Dakota. The sixth largest vendor of office supplies in the state, it delivers all of its merchandise to its North Dakota customers by mail or common carriers from out-of-state locations.

As a corollary to its sales tax, North Dakota imposes a use tax upon property purchased for storage, use, or consumption within the state. North Dakota requires every "retailer maintaining a place of business in" the state to collect the tax from the consumer and remit it to the state. In 1987, North Dakota amended its statutory definition of the term "retailer" to include "every person who engages in regular or systematic solicitation of a consumer market in th[e] state." State regulations in turn define "regular or systematic solicitation" to mean three or more advertisements within a 12-month period. Thus, since 1987, mail-order companies that engage in such solicitation have been subject to the tax even if they maintain no property or personnel in North Dakota.

Quill has taken the position that North Dakota does not have the power to compel it to collect a use tax from its North Dakota customers. Consequently, the state, through its tax commissioner, filed an action to require Quill to pay taxes (as well as interest and penalties) on all such sales made after July 1, 1987. The trial court ruled in Quill's favor on a motion for summary judgment. The North Dakota Supreme Court reversed, and Quill appealed.

JUDICIAL OPINION

STEVENS, Justice ... This case, like *National Bellas Hess, Inc. v Department of Revenue of Ill.*, 386 U.S. 753, 87 S.Ct. 1389, 18 L.Ed.2d 505 (1967), involves a State's attempt to require an out-of-state mail-order house that has neither outlets nor sales representatives in the State to collect and pay a use tax on goods purchased for use within the State. In *Bellas Hess* we held that a similar Illinois statute violated the Due Process Clause of the Fourteenth Amendment and created an unconstitutional burden on interstate commerce. In particular, we ruled that a "seller whose only connection with customers in the State is by common carrier or the United States mail" lacked the requisite minimum contacts with the State.

In this case the Supreme Court of North Dakota declined to follow *Bellas Hess* because "the tremendous social, economic, commercial, and legal innovations" of the past quarter-century have rendered its holding "obsole[te]."

The Due Process Clause "requires some definite link, some minimum connection, between a state and the person, property or transaction it seeks to tax," and that the "income attributed to the State for tax purposes must be rationally related to 'values connected with the taxing State.'" Prior to *Bellas Hess,* we had held that that requirement was satisfied in a variety of circumstances involving use taxes. For example, the presence of sales personnel in the State, or the maintenance of local retail stores in the State, justified the exercise of that power because the seller's local activities were "plainly accorded the protection and services of the taxing State." We expressly declined to obliterate the "sharp distinction ... between mail order sellers with retail outlets, solicitors, or property within a State, and those who do no more than communicate with customers in the State by mail or common carrier as a part of a general interstate business."

Our due process jurisprudence has evolved substantially in the 25 years since *Bellas Hess,* particularly in the area of judicial jurisdiction. Building on the seminal case of *International Shoe Co. v Washington,* 326 U.S. 310, 66 S.Ct. 154, 90 L.Ed. 95 (1945), we have framed the relevant inquiry as whether a defendant had minimum contacts with the jurisdiction "such that the maintenance of the suit does not offend 'traditional notions of fair play and substantial justice.'"

Applying these principles, we have held that if a foreign corporation purposefully avails itself of the benefits of an economic market in the forum State, it may subject itself to the State's *in personam* jurisdiction even if it has no physical presence in the State.

Comparable reasoning justifies the imposition of the collection duty on a mail-order house that is engaged in continuous and widespread solicitation of business within a State. In "modern commercial life" it matters little that such solicitation is accomplished by a deluge of catalogs rather than a phalanx of drummers: the requirements of due process are met irrespective of a corporation's lack of physical presence in the taxing State. Thus, to the extent that our decisions have indicated that the Due Process Clause requires physical presence in a State for the imposition of duty to collect a use tax, we overrule those holdings as superseded by developments in the law of due process.

In this case, there is no question that Quill has purposefully directed its activities at North Dakota residents. We therefore agree with the North Dakota Supreme Court's conclusion that the Due Process Clause does not bar enforcement of that State's use tax against Quill.

Continued

Our interpretation of the "negative" or "dormant" Commerce Clause has evolved substantially over the years, particularly as that Clause concerns limitations on state taxation powers. Contrary to the suggestion of the North Dakota Supreme Court, this does not mean that Bellas Hess [is] "obsolete."

[w]e will sustain a tax against a Commerce Clause challenge so long as the "tax [1] is applied to an activity with a substantial nexus with the taxing State, [2] is fairly apportioned, [3] does not discriminate against interstate commerce, and [4] is fairly related to the services provided by the State." A vendor whose only contacts with the taxing State are by mail or common carrier lacks the "substantial nexus" required by the Commerce Clause.

The nexus requirements of the Due Process and Commerce Clauses are not identical. The two standards are animated by different constitutional concerns and policies.

Due process centrally concerns the fundamental fairness of governmental activity. Thus, at the most general level, the due process nexus analysis requires that we ask whether an individual's connections with a State are substantial enough to legitimate the State's exercise of power over him. We have, therefore, often identified "notice" or "fair warning" as the analytic touchstone of due process nexus analysis. In contrast, the Commerce Clause and its nexus requirement are informed not so much by concerns about fairness for the individual defendant as by structural concerns about the effects of state regulation on the national economy. That Clause prohibits discrimination against interstate commerce, and bars state regulations that unduly burden interstate.

The first and fourth prongs, which require a substantial nexus and a relationship between the tax and state-provided services, limit the reach of state taxing authority so as to ensure that state taxation does not unduly burden interstate commerce. Accordingly, contrary to the State's suggestion, a corporation may have the "minimum contacts" with a taxing State as required by the Due Process Clause, and yet lack the "substantial nexus" with that State as required by the Commerce Clause.

[a]lthough our Commerce Clause jurisprudence now favors more flexible balancing analyses, we have never intimated a desire to reject all established "bright-line" tests.

The bright-line rule of *Bellas Hess* furthers the ends of the dormant Commerce Clause. Undue burdens on interstate commerce may be avoided not only by a case-by-case evaluation of the actual burdens imposed by particular regulations or taxes, but also, in some situations, by the demarcation of a discrete realm of commercial activity that is free from interstate taxation. *Bellas Hess* followed the latter approach and created a safe harbor for vendors "whose only connection with customers in the [taxing] State is by common carrier or the United States mail." Under *Bellas Hess,* such vendors are free from state-imposed duties to collect sales and use taxes.

Like other bright-line tests, the *Bellas Hess* rule appears artificial at its edges: Whether or not a State may compel a vendor to collect a sales or use tax may turn on the presence in the taxing State of a small sales force, plant, or office. This artificiality, however, is more than offset by the benefits of a clear rule. Such a rule firmly establishes the boundaries of legitimate state authority to impose a duty to collect sales and use taxes and reduces litigation concerning those taxes.

Moreover, a bright-line rule in the area of sales and use taxes also encourages settled expectations and, in doing so, fosters investment by businesses and individuals. Indeed, it is not unlikely that the mail-order industry's dramatic growth over the last quarter century is due in part to the bright-line exemption from state taxation created in *Bellas Hess.*

Accordingly, Congress is now free to decide whether, when, and to what extent the States may burden interstate mail-order concerns with a duty to collect use taxes.

Reversed and remanded

QUESTIONS

1. Did Quill Corporation own any property in North Dakota? Were any Quill offices or personnel located in North Dakota?
2. What is the Commerce Clause issue in the case? Where does the "bright-line rule" fit into the decision?
3. What is the standard now for states collecting taxes from out-of-state companies? What is the requirement for a presence in a state for collecting taxes?

(B) THE SPENDING POWER. The federal government may use tax money and borrowed money "to pay the debts and provide for the common defence and general welfare of the United States."[13]

(C) THE BANKING POWER. The Constitution is liberally interpreted to allow the federal government to create banks and to regulate banks created under state laws. **For Example,** the Federal

[13] U.S. Const., Art 1, §8, cl 1. See **www.constitution.org**, or Appendix 2.

Reserve System is responsible for this regulatory oversight of banks.

E. Constitutional Limitations on Government

The constitutional limitations discussed in the following sections afford protections of rights for both persons and businesses.

11. Due Process

The power of government is limited by both the Fifth and Fourteenth Amendments to the Constitution. Those amendments respectively prohibit the national government and state governments from depriving any person "of life, liberty, or property without due process of law."[14]

(a) When Due Process Rights Arise. As a result of liberal interpretation of the Constitution, the **due process clause** now provides a guarantee of protection against the loss of property or rights without the chance to be heard. These amendments also guarantee that all citizens are given the same protections. **For Example,** the Supreme Court has extended the due process clause to protect the record or standing of a student.[15] A student cannot lose credit in a course or be suspended or expelled without some form of a hearing.

Because there are so many areas in which due process rights exist and require a chance to be heard, speeding up due process has resulted in the creation of **quasi-judicial proceedings**. In these types of proceedings, the parties need not go through the complex, lengthy, and formal procedures of a trial (described in Chapter 2). Rather, these proceedings have a hearing officer or administrative law judge (see Chapter 6) who conducts an informal hearing in which the rules of evidence and procedure are relaxed.

For Example, a student taking a grade grievance beyond a faculty member's decision will generally have his case heard by a panel of faculty and students as established by college or university rules. An employer appealing its unemployment tax rate will have the appeal heard by an administrative law judge.

(b) What Constitutes Due Process? Due process does not require a trial on every issue of rights. Shortcut procedures, such as grade grievance panels, have resulted as a compromise for providing the right to be heard along with a legitimate desire to be expeditious in resolving these issues.

12. Equal Protection of the Law

The Constitution prohibits the states and the national government from denying any person the equal protection of the law.[16] This guarantee prohibits a government from treating one person differently from another when there is no reasonable ground for classifying them differently.

(a) Reasonable Classification. Whether a classification is reasonable depends on whether the nature of the classification bears a reasonable relation to the wrong to be remedied or to the object to be attained by the law. The judicial trend is to permit the classification to stand as long as there is a rational basis for the distinction made.[17] Whether a rational basis exists is determined by answering whether the lawmaking body has been arbitrary or capricious.

The equal protection clause is the basis of many of the U.S. Supreme Court's most complicated decisions. **For Example,** during the 2000 presidential election, the U.S. Supreme Court faced an issue of equal protection with regard to the challenge then–vice president and presidential candidate Al Gore made to the undervotes in Florida's ballots. However, then–presidential candidate George W. Bush argued that counting the undervotes in some counties and not in others and applying different standards for counting or not counting the infamous dimpled chads, hanging chads, and other undervotes was unconstitutional because it deprived other Florida voters of equal protection because each vote is intended to count equally. Recounts in only some counties while using varying standards resulted in some counties being given greater weight in Florida's presidential election. The

[14] For more information on the language of the Fifth and Fourteenth Amendments, see the U.S. Constitution in Appendix 2, or go to **www.constitution.org**.

[15] That is, a student cannot be expelled without a chance to have his or her side of the story reviewed.

[16] U.S. Constitution, Fourteenth Amendment as to the states; modern interpretation of due process clause of the Fifth Amendment as to national government. Congress adopted the Civil Rights Act to implement the concept of equal protection.

[17] *Ileto v. Glock, Inc.*, 565 F.3d 1126 (9th Cir. 2006).

E-Commerce & Cyberlaw

Internet and Interstate

Collection of sales tax from Internet stores has been a stickler of an issue for businesses, state revenue officials, and the U.S. Supreme Court. All three were grappling with how to collect, what to collect, and whether anybody had any authority to collect. Internet sales represent a large, untapped source of revenue. A study from the Center for Business and Economic Research at the University of Tennessee estimates the lost tax revenue from untaxed Internet sales as $30 billion in 2011.

The merchants involved fell into several different legal groups in terms of their theories on whether tax was owed and whether they should just pay it, with or without the states having the authority to tax:

1. Those stores with physical presences in states (Wal-Mart and J.C. Penney) that just collected sales tax as if they were collecting it in a store in that state where the Internet purchaser was located
2. Those stores without a physical presence (Amazon) that did collect taxes, particularly in those states known for taking a hard-line approach
3. Those stores without a physical presence that do not collect taxes and maintain that it is unconstitutional to do so
4. Those stores with or without a physical presence that have collected taxes but held them until everyone could figure out the legal status of the companies.

What are the constitutional issues in this taxation question?

Note: Amazon.com filed suit in 2011 in nine states challenging their laws on collection of taxes from Amazon when it has no physical presence in those states. In July, 2012, some of the suits were settled. Amazon collects taxes now in Kentucky, New York, North Dakota, Texas, and Washington, and it will collect taxes in eight more states. A federal law is pending.

Source: Stu Woo, "Amazon Battles States Over Sales Tax," Wall Street Journal, August 3, 2011, p. A1.

U.S. Supreme Court agreed in a 7–2 decision that the recounts were unconstitutional on equal protection grounds.[18] However, the justices split 5–4 on the correct remedy for the unconstitutional recounts.

(b) Improper Classification. Laws that make distinctions in the regulation of business, the right to work, and the right to use or enjoy property on the basis of race, national origin, or religion are invalid. Also invalid are laws that impose restrictions on some, but not all, persons without any justification for the distinction.[19] **For Example,** a state statute taxing out-of-state insurance companies at a higher rate than in-state insurance companies violates the equal protection clause.[20]

13. Privileges and Immunities

The U.S. Constitution declares that "the citizens of each state shall be entitled to all privileges and immunities of citizens in the several states."[21] The so-called **privileges and immunities clause** means that a person going into another state is entitled to make contracts, own property, and engage in business to the same extent as the citizens of that state. **For Example,** a state cannot bar someone who comes from another state from engaging in local business or from obtaining a hunting or fishing license merely because the person is not a resident of that state.

14. Protection of the Person

The Constitution has no general provision declaring that the government shall not impair rights of persons. The Constitution does not mention the phrase "unalienable right" that was part of the Declaration of Independence.[22] However, the Bill of Rights, the first 10 amendments to the Constitution, does provide protections for freedom of speech, jury trials, and freedom of religion and association.[23]

[18] *Bush v. Gore*, 531 U.S. 98 (2000).

[19] *Associated Industries of Missouri v. Lohman*, 511 U.S. 641 (1994).

[20] *Metropolitan Life Ins. Co. v. Ward*, 470 U.S. 869 (1985).

[21] U.S. Const., Art IV, §2, cl 1. See **www.constitution.org** and click on "Founding Documents" to access more language of the Constitution, or see Appendix 2.

[22] The term *unalienable right* is employed in reference to natural right, fundamental right, or basic right. Apart from the question of scope of coverage, the adjective *unalienable* emphasizes the fact that the people still possess the right rather than having surrendered or subordinated it to the will of society. The word *alien* is the term of the old common law for transferring title or ownership. Today, we would say *transfer* and, instead of saying unalienable rights, would say *nontransferable* rights. Unalienable rights of the people were therefore rights that the people not only possessed but also could not give up even if they wanted to. Thus, these rights are still owned by everyone. It is important to note that the Declaration of Independence actually uses the word "unalienable" when describing the rights eventually placed in the Constitution as Amendments I–X, the Bill of Rights, not "inalienable."

[23] *North Coast Women's Care Medical Group, Inc. v. San Diego County Superior Court*, 189 P.3d 959 (Ca. 2008).

Thinking Things Through

Sweating It Out on Free Speech

In 1996, Nike was inundated with allegations about its labor practices in shoe factories around the world. Nike responded to the negative reports and allegations with a series of releases, advertisements, and op-ed pieces in newspapers around the country. *New York Times* columnist Bob Herbert wrote two columns that were sharply critical of Nike's conditions in plants throughout Asia. The columns compared then-CEO Philip Knight's compensation with the $2.20 per day wages of Nike workers in Indonesia.

After the columns appeared, CEO Knight wrote a letter to the editor in response to them. In that letter, he wrote, "Nike has paid, on average, double the minimum wage as defined in countries where its products are produced under contract. History shows that the best way out of poverty for such countries is through exports of light manufactured goods that provide the base for more skilled production."*

Marc Kasky filed suit against Nike in California, alleging that the op-ed pieces and letters in response to negative op-ed pieces about Nike violated the False Advertising Act of California. The act permits state agencies to take action to fine corporate violators of the act as well as to obtain remedies such as injunctions to halt the ads.

Nike challenged the suit on the grounds that such an interpretation and application of the advertising regulation violated its rights of free speech. The lower court agreed with Kasky and held that the advertising statute applied to Nike's defense of its labor practices, even on the op-ed pages of newspapers. The California Supreme Court, 45 P.3d 243 (Cal. 2002), ruled that Nike could be subject to regulatory sanctions for false advertising. Nike appealed to the U.S. Supreme Court. Should Nike's editorial be protected by the First Amendment? Discuss where this type of speech fits.

The opinion handed down in this case is only one sentence: "The writ of *certiorari* is dismissed as improvidently granted." 539 U.S. 645 (2003). Nike settled the case. Is this letter protected speech? Does the California statute, as applied to Nike's op-ed letters, violate the First Amendment?

*Roger Parloff, "Can We Talk?" *Fortune*, September 2, 2002, 02–110.

The Bill of Rights provides for the due process protections discussed earlier as well as those that prohibit unlawful searches and seizures. The Second Amendment provides for the right to keep and bear arms, an issue that has resulted in some conflicting decisions that the U.S. Supreme Court has begun to address.[24]

During the last six decades, the Supreme Court has been interpreting the rights in these amendments and has been finding constitutional protection for a wide array of rights of the person that are not expressly protected by the Constitution. **For Example,** judicial interpretations have concluded that the Constitution provides for the right of privacy, the right to marry the person one chooses,[25] protection from unreasonable zoning, protection of parental control, protection from discrimination because of poverty, and protection from gender discrimination.[26]

15. The Bill of Rights and Businesses as Persons

The Bill of Rights provides protections for individuals and also for corporations. **For Example,** the Fourth Amendment (see Chapter 8) provides protections against unreasonable searches. Individuals enjoy that protection in their homes, and corporations enjoy that protection with their files, offices, and business records. Businesses also enjoy freedom of speech protections under the First Amendment. The First Amendment provides that "Congress shall make no law … abridging the freedom of speech …"[27]

The U.S. Supreme Court has clarified the free speech rights of business through classification of the types of business speech. One form of business or commercial speech is advertising. This form of speech in which businesses tout their products is subject to regulation and restriction on form, content, and placement, and such regulation has been deemed constitutional.

[24] *District of Columbia v. Heller*, 554 U.S. 570 (2008).

[25] *Akron v. Akron Center for Reproductive Health, Inc.*, 462 U.S. 416 (1983); but see *Colorado v. Hill*, *cert.* granted, 527 US 1068 (2000). See also *Snyder v. Phelps*, 131 S.Ct. 1207 (2011). For more on commercial speech, see *Greater New Orleans Broadcasting Association, Inc., v. U.S.* 527 U.S. 173 (1999) and *U.S. v. Philip Morris USA Inc.*, 566 F.3d 1095 (D.C. Cir. 2009).

[26] In some cases, the courts have given the due process and equal protection clauses a liberal interpretation in order to find a protection of the person. *Davis v. Passman*, 442 U.S. 228 (1979) (due process); *Grutter v. Bollinger*, 530 U.S. 306 (2003) (equal protection).

[27] To read the full language of the First Amendment, go to Appendix 2, or to **www.constitution.org** and click on "Founding Documents."

(See Chapters 25 and 33 for more information on the regulation of advertising.) However, there are other forms of commercial speech. Businesses do have the right to participate in political processes such as creating political action committees and supporting or opposing ballot initiatives. Businesses often take positions and launch campaigns on ballot initiatives that will affect the taxes they will be required to pay. The courts are often balancing the power of corporate political speech, regulation of ads, and the right of corporations as citizens to speak.

The *Citizens United v. Federal Election Commission* case is a controversial decision that deals with the speech rights of corporations in influencing elections through ads, films, and commentary.

Citizens United v. Federal Election Commission, 558 U.S. 310 (2010)

The Case That Launched a Dust-Up between the President and a Justice*

In January 2008, Citizens United, a nonprofit corporation, released the film, *Hillary: The Movie (Hillary)*, a 90-minute documentary about then-senator, Hillary Clinton, who was a candidate for the Democratic Party's 2008 presidential nomination. Most of the commentators in the film were quite critical of Senator Clinton. *Hillary* was released in theaters and on DVD, but Citizens United wanted to increase distribution by making it available through video-on-demand.

Citizens United produced two 10-second ads and one 30-second ad for *Hillary*. Each ad included a short, pejorative statement about Senator Clinton, followed by the name of the movie and the movie's Website address. Citizens United wanted to run the ads on broadcast and cable television. The Federal Election Commission (FEC) wanted to stop Citizens United from running the ads and Citizens United brought suit, seeking a preliminary injunction against the FEC. The District Court denied Citizens United a preliminary injunction and granted the FEC summary judgment. Citizens United requested and was granted *certiorari.*

JUDICIAL OPINION

KENNEDY, Justice Courts, too, are bound by the First Amendment. We must decline to draw, and then redraw, constitutional lines based on the particular media or technology used to disseminate political speech from a particular speaker.

It is well known that the public begins to concentrate on elections only in the weeks immediately before they are held. There are short timeframes in which speech can have influence. The decision to speak is made in the heat of political campaigns, when speakers react to messages conveyed by others. A speaker's ability to engage in political speech that could have a chance of persuading voters is stifled if the speaker must first commence a protracted lawsuit. Today, Citizens United finally learns, two years after the fact, whether it could have spoken during the 2008 Presidential primary—long after the opportunity to persuade primary voters has passed.

[A] speaker who wants to avoid threats of criminal liability and the heavy costs of defending against FEC enforcement must ask a governmental agency for prior permission to speak. These onerous restrictions [give] the FEC power analogous to licensing laws implemented in 6th- and 17th-century England, laws and governmental practices of the sort that the First Amendment was drawn to prohibit. The law before us is an outright ban, backed by criminal sanctions.

[The BCRA] is a ban on corporate speech notwithstanding the fact that a PAC created by a corporation can still speak. Even if a PAC could somehow allow a corporation to speak—and it does not—the option to form PACs does not alleviate the First Amendment problems. PACs are burdensome alternatives; they are expensive to administer and subject to extensive regulations.

PACs have to comply with these regulations just to speak. This might explain why fewer than 2,000 of the millions of corporations in this country have PACs. Given the onerous restrictions, a corporation may not be able to establish a PAC in time to make its views known regarding candidates and issues in a current campaign. The BCRA prohibition on corporate independent expenditures is thus a ban on speech.

By taking the right to speak from some and giving it to others, the Government deprives the disadvantaged person or class of the right to use speech. The Government may not deprive the public of the right and privilege to determine for itself what speech and speakers are worthy of consideration.

Citizens United [also] challenges BCRA's disclaimer and disclosure provisions. Under BCRA, televised electioneering communications funded by anyone other than a candidate must include a disclaimer that " '________ is responsible for the content of this advertising.'

Disclaimer and disclosure requirements may burden the ability to speak, but they "impose no ceiling on campaign-related activities," and "do not prevent anyone from speaking," The Court has explained that disclosure is a less restrictive alternative to more comprehensive regulations of speech.

This transparency enables the electorate to make informed decisions and give proper weight to different speakers and

Continued

messages. [W]e affirm their application to *Hillary*. We find no constitutional impediment to the application of BCRA's disclaimer and disclosure requirements to a movie broadcast via video-on-demand.

The judgment of the District Court is reversed on restrictions on corporate independent expenditures. The judgment is affirmed with respect to BCRA's disclaimer and disclosure requirements.

QUESTIONS

1. Why does the court uphold the provisions of the BCRA that require disclosure of funding for ads?
2. What are the issues raised about controls on the funding of political ads?
3. What are the concerns of the court in making political speech criminal?

LawFlix

The Candidate (1972) (PG)

The movie depicts an idealist running for office who finds himself caught in the political process of fundraising, image-building, and winning. A number of scenes with speeches, fundraising, and principles in conflict provide excellent discussion issues with respect to government structure, the First Amendment, and campaign contributions.

MAKE THE CONNECTION

SUMMARY

The U.S. Constitution created the structure of our national government and gave it certain powers. It also placed limitations on those powers. It created a federal system with a tripartite division of government and a bicameral national legislature.

The national government possesses some governmental powers exclusively, while both the states and the federal government share other powers. In areas of conflict, federal law is supreme.

The U.S. Constitution is not a detailed document. It takes its meaning from the way it is interpreted. In recent years, liberal interpretation has expanded the powers of the federal government. Among the powers of the federal government that directly affect business are the power to regulate commerce; the power to tax and to borrow, spend, and coin money; and the power to own and operate businesses.

Among the limitations on government that are most important to business are the requirements of due process and the requirement of equal protection of the law. In addition, government is limited by the rights given to individuals such as freedom of speech, freedom of religion, and equal protection. The equal protection concept of the U.S. Constitution prohibits both the federal government and the state governments from treating one person differently from another unless there is a legitimate reason for doing so and unless the basis of classification is reasonable.

LEARNING OUTCOMES

After studying this chapter, you should be able to clearly explain:

A. The U.S. Constitution and the Federal System

LO.1 Describe the U.S. Constitution and the Federal System

See the discussion of the **tripartite** (three-part) government on p. 54.

B. The U.S. Constitution and the States

LO.2 Explain the relationship between the U.S. Constitution and the States

See the discussion of the federal system on p. 55.

See Figure 4-1 for an illustration of the delegation of powers.

C. Interpreting and Amending the Constitution

LO.3 Discuss interpreting and amending the Constitution

See the discussion of the bedrock and constructionist views on p. 57.

D. Federal Powers

LO.4 List and describe the significant federal powers

See the discussion of the commerce power on p. 59.

See the discussion of the taxing power beginning on p. 63.

See the discussion of the banking power on p. 65.

E. Constitutional Limitations on Government

LO.5 Discuss constitutional limitations on governmental power

See the discussion of the Bill of Rights on p. 68.

See the discussion of the Fourth Amendment on p. 68.

See the discussion of due process starting on p. 66.

See the *For Example* discussion of a student taking a grade grievance beyond a faculty member's decision on p. 66.

KEY TERMS

bedrock view
bicameral
commerce clause
constitution
delegated powers
due process clause
executive branch
ex post facto laws
federal system
judicial branch
legislative branch
living-document view
police power
preemption
privileges and immunities clause
quasi-judicial proceedings
shared powers
tripartite

QUESTIONS AND CASE PROBLEMS

1. Federal law requires most interstate truckers to obtain a permit that reflects compliance with certain federal requirements. The 1965 version of the law authorized states to require proof that a truck operator had such a permit. By 1991, 39 states had demanded such proof, requiring a $10 per truck registration fee and giving each trucker a stamp to affix to a multistate "bingo card" carried in the vehicle. Finding this scheme inefficient and burdensome, Congress created the current Single State Registration System (SSRS), which allows a trucking company to fill out one set of forms in one state, thereby registering in every participating state through which its trucks travel.

   A subsection of Michigan's Motor Carrier Act imposes on truck companies operating in interstate commerce an annual fee of $100 for each self-propelled motor vehicle operated by or on behalf of the motor carrier. The American Truckers Association (ATA) and others challenged the $100 fee as preempted by the extensive federal regulation of interstate trucking and trucking companies. The ATA and others appealed to the U.S. Supreme Court. What should the U.S. Supreme Court do? Be sure to discuss what portion of the Constitution applies to this issue. [*American Trucking Associations, Inc. v. Michigan Public Service Com'n,* 545 U.S. 429]

2. J.C. Penney, a retail merchandiser, has its principal place of business in Plano, Texas. It operates retail stores in all 50 states, including 10 stores in Massachusetts, and a direct mail catalog business. The catalogs illustrated merchandise available for purchase by mail order. The planning, artwork, design, and layout for these catalogs were completed and paid for outside of Massachusetts, primarily in Texas, and Penney contracted with independent printing companies located outside Massachusetts to produce the catalogs. The three major catalogs were generally printed in Indiana, while the specialty catalogs were printed in South Carolina and Wisconsin. Penney supplied the printers with paper, shipping wrappers, and address labels for the catalogs; the printers supplied the ink, binding materials, and labor. None of these materials was purchased in Massachusetts. Printed catalogs, with address labels and postage affixed, were transported by a common carrier from the printer to a U.S. Postal Service office located outside Massachusetts, where they were sent to Massachusetts addressees via third- or fourth-class mail. Any undeliverable catalogs were returned to Penney's distribution center in Connecticut.

   Purchases of catalog merchandise were made by telephoning or returning an order form to Penney at a location outside Massachusetts, and the merchandise was shipped to customers from a Connecticut distribution center. The Massachusetts Department of Revenue audited Penney in 1995 and assessed a use tax, penalty, and interest on the catalogs that had been shipped into Massachusetts. The position of the department was that there was a tax due of $314,674.62 on the catalogs that were used by Penney's Massachusetts customers. Penney said such a tax was unconstitutional in that it had no control or contact with the catalogs in the state. Can the state impose the tax? Why or why not? [*Commissioner of Revenue v. J.C. Penney Co., Inc.,* 730 N.E.2d 266 (Mass)]

3. Alfonso Lopez, Jr., a 12th-grade student at Edison High School in San Antonio, Texas, went to school carrying a concealed .38-caliber handgun and five bullets. School officials, acting on an anonymous tip, confronted Lopez. Lopez admitted that he had the gun. He was arrested and charged with violation of federal law, the Gun-Free School Zones Act of 1990. Lopez moved to dismiss his indictment on the grounds that the provision of the Gun-Free School Zones Act with which he was charged was unconstitutional in that it was beyond the power of Congress to legislate controls over public schools. The district court found the statute to be a constitutional exercise of congressional authority.

   Lopez was found guilty and sentenced to two years in prison. He appealed and challenged his conviction on the basis of the commerce clause. The Court of Appeals agreed with Lopez, found the Gun-Free School Zones Act an unconstitutional exercise of congressional authority, and reversed the conviction. The U.S. Attorney appealed. Who should win at the U.S. Supreme Court and why? [*United States v. Lopez,* 514 U.S. 549]

4. The University of Wisconsin requires all of its students to pay, as part of their tuition, a student activity fee. Those fees are used to support campus clubs and activities. Some students who objected to the philosophies and activities of some of the student clubs filed suit to have the fees halted. What constitutional basis do you think they could use for the suit? [*Board of Regents of Wisconsin System v. Southworth,* 529 U.S. 217]

5. The Crafts' home was supplied with gas by the city gas company. Because of some misunderstanding, the gas company believed that the Crafts were delinquent in paying their gas bill. The gas company had an informal complaint procedure for discussing such matters, but the Crafts had never been informed that such a procedure was available. The gas company

notified the Crafts that they were delinquent and that the company was shutting off the gas. The Crafts brought an action to enjoin the gas company from doing so on the theory that a termination without any hearing was a denial of due process. The lower courts held that the interest of the Crafts in receiving gas was not a property interest protected by the due process clause and that the procedures the gas company followed satisfied the requirements of due process. The Crafts appealed. Were they correct in contending that they had been denied due process of law? Why or why not? [*Memphis Light, Gas and Water Division v. Craft,* 436 U.S. 1]

6. In 2002, the Williamson family, riding in their 1993 Mazda minivan, was struck head-on by another vehicle. Thanh Williamson was sitting in a rear aisle seat, wearing a lap belt; she died in the accident. Delbert and Alexa Williamson were wearing lap-and-shoulder belts; they survived. Thanh's estate brought suit in a California state court to recover from Mazda for her wrongful death. The basis of the suit was that Mazda should have installed lap-and-shoulder belts on all seats, including the rear aisle seats, and that Thanh died because Mazda equipped her seat with only a lap belt instead. Federal safety requirements do not require lap-and-shoulder belts except for seats located next to doors and windows. Middle seats (aisle) can have a lap belt only. Mazda asked for a dismissal on the grounds that allowing Thanh's estate to recover would contradict federal law and that federal law preempts state tort laws on product liability. The trial court dismissed the suit as preempted by federal law, and the Court of Appeal affirmed. The U.S. Supreme Court granted *certiorari*. What should the court decide and why? [*Williamson v. Mazda Motor of America, Inc.* 131 S.Ct. 1131]

7. Montana imposed a severance tax on every ton of coal mined within the state. The tax varied depending on the value of the coal and the cost of production. It could be as high as 30 percent of the price at which the coal was sold. Montana mine operators and some out-of-state customers claimed that this tax was unconstitutional as an improper burden on interstate commerce. Decide. [*Commonwealth Edison Co. v. Montana,* 453 U.S. 609]

8. Ollie's Barbecue is a family-owned restaurant in Birmingham, Alabama, specializing in barbecued meats and homemade pies, with a seating capacity of 220 customers. It is located on a state highway 11 blocks from an interstate highway and a somewhat greater distance from railroad and bus stations. The restaurant caters to a family and white-collar trade, with a take-out service for "Negroes." (Note: This term is used by the Court in its opinion in the case.) In the 12 months preceding the passage of the Civil Rights Act, the restaurant purchased locally approximately $150,000 worth of food, $69,683 or 46 percent of which was meat that it bought from a local supplier who had procured it from outside the state. Ollie's has refused to serve Negroes in its dining accommodations since opening in 1927, and since July 2, 1964, it has been operating in violation of the Civil Rights Act. A lower court concluded that if it were required to serve Negroes, it would lose a substantial amount of business. The lower court found that the Civil Rights Act did not apply because Ollie's was not involved in "interstate commerce." Will the commerce clause permit application of the Civil Rights Act to Ollie's? [*Katzenbach v. McClung,* 379 U.S. 294]

9. Ellis was employed by the city of Lakewood. By the terms of his contract, he could be discharged only for cause. After working for six years, he was told that he was going to be discharged because of his inability to generate safety and self-insurance programs, because of his failure to win the confidence of employees, and because of his poor attendance. He was not informed of the facts in support of these conclusions and was given the option to resign. He claimed that he was entitled to a hearing. Is he entitled to one? Why or why not? [*Ellis v. City of Lakewood,* 789 P.2d 449 (Colo. App.)]

10. The Federal Food Stamp Act provided for the distribution of food stamps to needy households. In 1971, section 3(e) of the statute was amended to define households as limited to groups whose members were all related to each other. This was

done because of congressional dislike for the lifestyles of unrelated hippies who were living together in hippie communes. Moreno and others applied for food stamps but were refused them because the relationship requirement was not satisfied. An action was brought to have the relationship requirement declared unconstitutional. Is it constitutional? Discuss why or why not. [*USDA v. Moreno,* 413 U.S. 528]

11. New Hampshire adopted a tax law that in effect taxed the income of nonresidents working in New Hampshire only. Austin, a nonresident who worked in New Hampshire, claimed that the tax law was invalid. Was he correct? Explain. [*Austin v. New Hampshire,* 420 U.S. 656]

12. Gladys Mensing and other patients took the generic version of metoclopramide over a long period a time, which resulted in serious neurological damage. Ms. Mensing and others filed suit against the generic manufacturers under the Louisiana Products Liability Act. They alleged that despite mounting evidence of the connection between long-term use of metoclopramide and neurological damage, the manufacturers did not change their labels to provide warnings. The generic drug manufacturers argued that federal statutes and FDA regulations require generic manufacturers to use the same safety standards and labeling as their brand-name counterparts. They argued that it was impossible to simultaneously comply with both federal law and any state tort-law duty that required them to use a different label. What section of the U.S. Constitution will be used to resolve this issue? How will the court decide whether the manufacturers can be held liable? [*PLIVA, Inc. v. Mensing,* 131 S.Ct. 2567]

13. California passed a law that prohibited the sale or rental of "violent video games." The act defined violent video games as games "in which the range of options available to a player includes killing, maiming, dismembering, or sexually assaulting an image of a human being, if those acts are depicted" in a manner that "[a] reasonable person, considering the game as a whole, would find appeals to a deviant or morbid interest of minors." The association of video game manufacturers and developers brought suit, challenging the California statute as an unconstitutional violation of their First Amendment right and a violation of their due process rights because it is so vague. What should the U.S. Supreme Court hold on the constitutionality of the statute and why? [*Brown v. Entertainment Merchants Ass'n,* 131 S.Ct. 2729]

CHAPTER 5

© Manuel Gutjahr/iStockphoto.com

Government Regulation of Competition and Prices

learningoutcomes

After studying this chapter, you should be able to

LO.1 Explain the powers the government has to be sure free markets are working efficiently

LO.2 List the federal statutes that regulate horizontal markets and competition and give examples of each

LO.3 Describe the federal statutes that regulate the supply chain and vertical markets

LO.4 Discuss the remedies available to protect business competition

The government can regulate not just businesses but also business competition and prices. Antitrust laws were passed to help ensure that businesses compete fairly.

A. Power to Regulate Business

The federal government may regulate any area of business to advance the nation's economic needs.[1] Under the police power, states may regulate all aspects of business so long as they do not impose an unreasonable burden on interstate commerce or any activity of the federal government. (See Chapter 4 for a discussion of the protections and limits of the commerce clause.)

1. Regulation, Free Enterprise, and Deregulation

Milton Friedman, the Nobel economist, has written that government regulation of business interferes with the free enterprise system. Under a true free enterprise system, market forces would provide the necessary protections through the forces of demand and supply. Sometimes, however, the demand response, or market reaction, to problems or services is not rapid enough to prevent harm, and government regulation steps in to stop abuses. The antitrust laws step in when competitors create barriers to market entry or collude on prices or production in order to control prices.

2. Regulation of Unfair Competition

Each of the states and the federal government have statutes and regulations that prohibit unfair methods of competition. Unfair competition is controlled by both statutes and administrative agencies and regulations. The statutes that curb unfair competition are the Sherman Act, the Clayton Act, the Robinson-Patman Act, and the Federal Trade Commission Act.[2] Each of these statutes covers different types of anticompetitive behavior by competitors and each is discussed in the sections below.

B. Regulation of Horizontal Markets and Competitors

Antitrust laws regulate the relationships between and among competitors, known as horizontal restraints. The goal of these laws is to be sure that firms that are gaining customers are doing so because they offer better products and better customer service and not because they are manipulating the markets or their prices.

CPA 3. Regulation of Prices

Governments, both national and state, may regulate prices. Prices in various forms are regulated, including not only what a buyer pays for goods but also through credit terms and other charges. The Sherman Act is the federal law that regulates anticompetitive behavior among horizontal competitors.

(a) Prohibition on Price Fixing. Agreements among competitors, as well as "every contract, combination … or conspiracy" to fix prices, violate Section 1 of the Sherman Act.[3] Known as *horizontal price-fixing,* any agreements to charge an agreed-upon price or to set maximum or minimum prices between or among competitors are *per se*—in, through, or by themselves—a violation of the Sherman Act. Price-fixing can involve competitors agreeing to not sell below a certain price, agreeing on commission rates, agreeing on credit terms, or exchanging cost information. Price is treated as a sensitive element of competition, and discussion among competitors has also been deemed to be an attempt to monopolize. An agreement among real estate brokers to never charge below a 6 percent commission is price-fixing.[4] **For Example,** in 2001, Christie's and Sotheby's auction houses settled an antitrust lawsuit for charging the same commissions for many years.[5]

[1] *SKF, USA, Inc. v. Customs and Border Protection,* 556 F.3d 1337 (9th Cir. 2009).

[2] 15 U.S.C. §41 *et seq.* To review the Federal Trade Commission Act, go to **www.ftc.gov**.

[3] To view the full language of Section 1 of the Sherman Act, see 15 U.S.C. §1.

[4] *McClain v. Real Estate Board of New Orleans, Inc.,* 441 U.S. 942 (1980).

[5] Carol Vogel and Ralph Blumenthall, "Ex-Chairman of Sotheby's Gets a Year and a Day for Price-Fixing," *New York Times,* April 12, 2002, A26.

4. Prevention of Monopolies and Combinations

Monopolies and combinations that restrain trade are prohibited under the federal antitrust laws.

CPA **(A) The Sherman Act.** The **Sherman Antitrust Act** includes two very short sections that control monopolistic behavior. They provide:

> *[§1] Every contract, combination in the form of trust or otherwise, or conspiracy, in restraint of trade or commerce among the several states, or with foreign nations, is declared to be illegal.*
>
> *[§2] Every person who shall monopolize or attempt to monopolize, or combine or conspire with any other person or persons to monopolize any part of the trade or commerce among the several states, or with foreign nations, shall be deemed guilty of a felony.*[6]

The Sherman Act applies not only to buying and selling activities but also to manufacturing and production activities. Section 1 of the Sherman Act applies to agreements, conduct, or conspiracies to restrain trade, which can consist of price-fixing, tying, and monopolization. Section 2 prohibits monopolizing or attempting to monopolize by companies or individuals.

(B) Monopolization. To determine whether a firm has engaged in monopolization or attempts to monopolize, the courts determine whether the firm has **market power**, which is the ability to control price and exclude competitors. Market power is defined by looking at both the geographic and product markets. **For Example,** a cereal manufacturer may have 65 percent of the nationwide market for its Crispy Clowns cereal (the product market), but it may have only 10 percent of the Albany, New York, market because of a local competitor, Crunchy Characters. Crispy Clowns may have market power nationally, but in Albany, it would not reach monopoly levels.

Ethics & the Law

Marsh & McLennan

Marsh & McLennan (MMC) is best known as the world's largest insurance broker with 43,000 employees in its global operations.* MMC had a different way of achieving growth.

MMC should have been obtaining competing bids on employee insurance plans for the companies it represented. However, MMC developed a "pay-to-play" format for obtaining bids that allowed the insurers and MMC to profit. To be sure (1) that the policies were renewed and (2) that the renewal bonus was a given, MMC had all of its insurers agree to roll over on renewals. For example, if Insurer A was up for renewal, Insurers B and C would submit fake and higher bids that MMC would then take to the corporate client and, of course, recommend renewal at the lower rate.

One of the companies to complain about MMC's practices was Munich RE. One of its e-mails to an MMC executive (whose name was blacked out) wrote, "I am not some Goody Two Shoes who believes that truth is absolute, but I have a pretty strict ethical code about being truthful and honest. '[T]hrowing the quote' by artificially high numbers to lose is repugnant... because it is dishonest. [I]... comes awfully close to collusion and price-fixing."

Without admitting or denying guilt, MMC settled antitrust charges by agreeing to drop the commission system and pay $850 million to its clients as a means of compensating for what might have been overcharges. MMC also agreed to hire a new CEO. The value of MMC's shares dropped almost 50 percent within 10 days following the mid-October filing of suit by then New York Attorney General Spitzer against the company.**

MMC hired a new CEO who fired several senior executives despite the fact that there was no evidence that they had broken the law. When asked why he would fire them, Michael G. Cherkasky, a former district attorney in New York, said, "Freedom from criminal culpability is not our standard for executive leadership."***

*Monica Langley and Ianthe Jeanne Dugan, "How a Top Marsh Employee Turned the Tables on Insurers," *Wall Street Journal*, October 23, 204, A1, A9. Some put the number of employees at 60,000. *See also* Gretchen Morgenson, "Who Loses the Most at Marsh? Its Workers," *New York Times*, October 24, 2004, 3–1 (Sunday Business 1) and 9.

**"The Chatter," *New York Times*, November 14, 2004, BU2.

***Ian McDonald, "After Spitzer Probe, Marsh CEO Tries Corporate Triage," *Wall Street Journal*, August 29, 2005, A1.

[6] 15 U.S.C. §1. Free competition has been advanced by the Omnibus Trade and Competitiveness Act of 1988, 19 U.S.C. §2901 *et seq.*

Having a large percentage of a market is not necessarily a monopoly.[7] The Sherman Act requires that the monopoly position be gained because of a superior product or consumer preference, not because the company has engaged in purposeful conduct to exclude competitors by other means, such as preventing a competitor from purchasing a factory. **For Example,** perhaps one of the best known monopolization cases involved Microsoft. In the case, the Justice Department alleged that because Microsoft had 90 percent of the market for operating systems, it had and used monopoly power to control and market and did so by refusing to sell its operating system to companies that installed Netscape in lieu of or in addition to the Microsoft Explorer browser.[8] Today, Microsoft has filed antitrust complaints against Google along with Yelp and Expedia, alleging that Google drives those who use its search engine to its own specialized sites that compete with them.

5. Boycotts and Refusals to Deal

Under the Sherman Act, competitors are not permitted to agree not to deal with certain buyers. Boycotts among competitors are *per se* violations of the Sherman Act, which means that there are no defenses to these kinds of controls by competitors on markets. Sometimes boycotts have the best of intentions, but they are still illegal. For example, defense lawyers who went on strike in order to get a higher hourly rate for public defenders so that the indigent defendants would have quality representation still engaged in an illegal boycott.[9]

6. Mergers among Competitors

The Sherman Antitrust Act does not prohibit bigness. However, Section 7 of the Clayton Act provides that "no corporation … shall acquire the whole or any part of the assets of another corporation … where in any line of commerce in any section of the country, the effect of such acquisition may be substantially to lessen competition, or to tend to create a monopoly." If the Clayton Act is violated through ownership or control of competing enterprises, a court may order the violating defendant to dispose of such interests by issuing a decree called a **divestiture order**.[10] Courts examine market share and relevant markets to determine whether a merger would create a monopoly.

When large-size enterprises plan to merge, they must give written notice to the FTC and to the head of the Antitrust Division of the Department of Justice. This advance notice gives the department the opportunity to block the merger and thus avoid the loss that would occur if the enterprises merged and were then required to separate.[11] **For Example,** AT&T was required to notify the Justice Department when it proposed acquisition of T-Mobile because AT&T's market share was 37 percent and T-Mobile's was 16 percent. A merger (which was not approved) would have resulted in a company with a 51 percent share of the market.[12]

E-Commerce & Cyberlaw

E-mail's Revelations

In the U.S. Justice Department's case against Microsoft, a lawyer commented, "The Government does not need to put Mr. Gates on the stand because we have his e-mail and memoranda." There were 30 million pages of e-mail used as evidence in the Microsoft trial.

E-mail provides what is known as a *contemporaneous record of events* and has the added bonus that, for whatever psychological reason, those communicating with e-mail tend to be more frank and informal than they would be in a memo. E-mail can also contradict a witness's testimony and serve to undermine credibility. For example, when asked whether he recalled discussions with a subordinate about whether Microsoft should offer to invest in Netscape, Mr. Gates responded in his deposition, "I didn't see that as something that made

[7] *Bell Atlantic v. Twombly*, 550 U.S. 544 (2007).

[8] *United States v. Microsoft*, 253 F.2d 34 (D.C. Cir. 2001).

[9] *FTC v. Superior Court Trial Lawyers Ass'n*, 493 U.S. 411 (1990).

[10] *California v. American Stores Co.*, 492 U.S. 1301 (1989).

[11] Antitrust Improvement Act of 1976, 15 U.S.C. §1311 *et seq.*

[12] Thomas Catan and Spencer A. Ante, "U.S. Sues to Stop AT&T Deal," *Wall Street Journal*, September 9, 2011, p. A1.

E-Commerce & Cyberlaw—*Contd.*

sense." But Mr. Gates's e-mail included an urging to his subordinates to consider a Netscape alliance: "We could even pay them money as part of the deal, buying a piece of them or something."

E-mail is discoverable, admissible as evidence, and definitely not private. Employees should follow the admonition of one executive whose e-mail was used to fuel a million-dollar settlement by his company with a former employee: "If you wouldn't want anyone to read it, don't send it in e-mail."

The impact of e-mail in the Microsoft antitrust case on companies and their e-mail policies was widespread. For example, Amazon.com launched a companywide program called "Sweep and Keep," under which employees were instructed to purge e-mail messages no longer needed for conducting business. Amazon.com offered employees who immediately purged their e-mail free lattes in the company cafeteria. The company had a two-part program. The first portion included instructions on document retention and deletion. The second part of the program was on document creation and included the following warning for employees: "Quite simply put, there are some communications that should not be expressed in written form. Sorry, no lattes this time."

Source: Adapted from Marianne M. Jennings, *Business: Its Legal, Ethical and Global Environment*, 8th ed. (Cincinnati, OH: West Legal Studies in Business, 2009), ch. 16.

C. Regulation of the Supply Chain and Vertical Trade Restraints

7. Price Discrimination

The **Clayton Act** and **Robinson-Patman Act** prohibit price discrimination.[13] **Price discrimination** occurs when a seller charges different prices to different buyers for "commodities of like grade and quality," with the result being reduced competition or a tendency to create a monopoly.[14]

Price discrimination prohibits charging different prices to buyers as related to marginal costs. That is, volume discounts are permissible because the marginal costs are different on the larger volume of goods. However, the Robinson-Patman Act makes it illegal to charge different prices to buyers when the marginal costs of the seller for those goods are the same. Any added incentives or bonuses are also considered part of the price.

For Example, offering one buyer free advertising while not offering it to another as an incentive to buy would be a violation of the Robinson-Patman Act.

The Clayton Act makes both the giving and the receiving of any illegal price discrimination a crime.

CPA State statutes frequently prohibit favoring one competitor by giving a secret discount when the effect is to harm the competition.[15] A state may prohibit either selling below cost to harm competitors or selling to one customer at a secret price that is lower than the price charged other customers when there is no economic justification for the lower price.[16] Some state statutes specifically permit sellers to set prices so that they can match competitive prices, but not to undercut a competitor's prices.[17]

Price discrimination is expressly permitted when it can be justified on the basis of (1) a difference in grade, quality, or quantity; (2) the cost of transportation involved in performing the contract; (3) a good-faith effort to meet competition; (4) differences in methods or quantities, that is marginal cost differences; (5) deterioration of goods; or (6) a close-out sale of a particular line of goods. The *Utah Pie Co. v. Continental Baking Co.* is a case that involves price discrimination issues in the midst of a battle for a state market for frozen pies.[18]

[13] 15 U.S.C. §§1, 2, 3, 7, 8.

[14] 15 U.S.C. §13a. To read the full Clayton Act, go to **www.usdoj.gov** or **www.justice.gov** and plug in "Clayton Act" in a site search.

[15] *Eddins v. Redstone*, 35 Cal. Rptr. 2d 863 (2006).

[16] In *Weyerhaeuser v. Ross-Simons*, 549 U.S. 212 (2007), the U.S. Supreme Court ruled that predatory bidding is also a price discrimination issue. In a monopsony, a buyer tries to control a market by overbidding all its competitors and thereby cornering the market for supplies it needs to produce goods. However, if the bidder is actually just in need of the goods and bids higher for them, there is no anticompetitive conduct.

[17] *Home Oil Company, Inc. v. Sam's East, Inc.*, 252 F. Supp. 2d 1302 (M.D. Ala. 2003).

[18] 15 U.S.C. §§13, 21.

Utah Pie Co. v. Continental Baking Co., 386 U.S. 685 (1967)

Getting a Piece of the Pie Market

Utah Pie Company (petitioner) is a Utah corporation that for 30 years has been baking pies in its plant in Salt Lake City and selling them in Utah and surrounding states. It entered the frozen pie business in 1957 and was immediately successful with its new line of frozen dessert pies—apple, cherry, boysenberry, peach, pumpkin, and mince.

Continental Baking Company, Pet Milk, and Carnation (respondents), based in California, sell pies in Utah primarily on a delivered-price basis.

The major competitive weapon in the Utah pie market was price. Between 1958 and 1961, there was a deteriorating price structure for pies in the Utah market. Utah Pie was selling pies for $4.15 per dozen at the beginning of the period; at the time it filed suit for price discrimination, it was selling the same pies for $2.75 per dozen. Continental's price went from $5.00 per dozen in 1958 to $2.85 at the time suit was filed. Pet's prices went from $4.92 per dozen to $3.46, and Carnation's from $4.82 per dozen to $3.30.

Utah Pie filed suit, charging price discrimination by respondents based on allegations outlined in the opinion that follows. The district court found for Utah Pie. The court of appeals reversed, and Utah Pie appealed.

JUDICIAL OPINION

WHITE, J.… We deal first with petitioner's case against the Pet Milk Company…. Pet's initial emphasis was on quality, but in the face of competition from regional and local companies and in an expanding market where price proved to be a crucial factor, Pet was forced to take steps to reduce the price of its pies to the ultimate consumer. These developments had consequences in the Salt Lake City market which are the substance of petitioner's case against Pet.

First, Pet successfully concluded an arrangement with Safeway, which is one of the three largest customers for frozen pies in the Salt Lake market, whereby it would sell frozen pies to Safeway under the latter's own "Bel-air" label at a price significantly lower than it was selling its comparable "Pet-Ritz" brand in the same Salt Lake market and elsewhere….

Second, it introduced a 20-ounce economy pie under the "Swiss Miss" label and began selling the new pie in the Salt Lake market in August 1960 at prices ranging from $3.25 to $3.30 for the remainder of the period. This pie was at times sold at a lower price in the Salt Lake City market than it was sold in other markets.

Third, Pet became more competitive with respect to the prices for its "Pet-Ritz" proprietary label…. According to the Court of Appeals, in seven of the 44 months Pet's prices in Salt Lake were lower than prices charged in the California markets. This was true although selling in Salt Lake involved a 30- to 35-cent freight cost.

The burden of proving cost justification was on Pet and, in our view, reasonable men could have found that Pet's lower priced "Bel-air" sales to Safeway were not cost justified in their entirety.

The Court of Appeals almost entirely ignored other evidence which provides material support of the jury's conclusion that Pet's behavior satisfied the statutory test regarding competitive injury. This evidence bore on the issue of Pet's predatory intent to injure Utah Pie. As an initial matter, the jury could have concluded that Pet's discriminatory pricing was aimed at Utah Pie; Pet's own management, as early as 1959, identified Utah Pie as an "unfavorable factor," one which "d[u]g holes in our operation" and posed a constant "check" on Pet's performance in the Salt Lake City market. Moreover, Pet candidly admitted that during the period when it was establishing its relationship with Safeway, it sent into Utah Pie's plant an industrial spy to seek information that would be of use to Pet in convincing Safeway that Utah Pie was not worthy of its customers…. Finally, Pet does not deny that the evidence showed it suffered substantial losses on its frozen pie sales during the greater part of time involved in this suit, and there was evidence from which the jury could have concluded that the losses Pet sustained in Salt Lake City were greater than those incurred elsewhere. It would not have been an irrational step if the jury concluded that there was a relationship between the price and the losses.

It seems clear to us that the jury heard adequate evidence from which it could have concluded that Pet had engaged in predatory tactics in waging competitive warfare in the Salt Lake City market. Coupled with the incidence of price discrimination attributable to Pet, the evidence as a whole established, rather than negated, the reasonable possibility that Pet's behavior produced a lessening of competition proscribed by the Act.

Petitioner's case against Continental is not complicated. Continental was a substantial factor in the market in 1957. But its sales of frozen 22-ounce dessert pies, sold under the "Morton" brand, amounted to only 1.3 percent of the market in 1958, 2.9 percent in 1959, and 1.8 percent in 1960. Its problems were primarily that of cost and in turn that of price, the controlling factor in the market. In late 1960 it worked out a co-packing arrangement in California by which fruit would be processed directly from the trees into the finished pies without large intermediate packing, storing, and shipping expenses. Having improved its position, it attempted to increase its share of the Salt Lake City market by utilizing a

Continued

local broker and offering short-term price concessions in varying amounts. Its efforts for seven months were not spectacularly successful. Then in June 1961, it took the steps which are the heart of petitioner's complaint against it. Effective for the last two weeks of June it offered its 22-ounce frozen apple pies in the Utah area at $2.85 per dozen. It was then selling the same pies at substantially higher prices in other markets. The Salt Lake City price was less than its direct cost plus an allocation for overhead.... Utah's response was immediate. It reduced its price on all of its apple pies to $2.75 per dozen.... Continental's total sales of frozen pies increased from 3,350 dozen in 1960 to 18,800 dozen in 1961. Its market share increased from 1.8 percent in 1960 to 8.3 percent in 1961. The Court of Appeals concluded that Continental's conduct had had only minimal effect, that it had not injured or weakened Utah Pies as a competitor, that it had not substantially lessened competition and that there was no reasonable possibility that it would do so in the future.

Even if the impact on Utah Pie as a competitor was negligible, there remain the consequences to others in the market who had to compete not only with Continental's 22-ounce pie at $2.85 but with Utah's even lower price of $2.75 per dozen for both its proprietary and controlled labels.... The evidence was that there were nine other sellers in 1960 who sold 23,473 dozen pies, 12.7 percent of the total market. In 1961 there were eight other sellers who sold less than the year before—18,565 dozen or 8.2 percent of the total—although the total market had expanded from 184,569 dozen to 226,908 dozen. We think there was sufficient evidence from which the jury could find a violation of §2(a) by Continental.

Section 2(a) does not forbid price competition which will probably injure or lessen competition by eliminating competitors, discouraging entry into the market or enhancing the market shares of the dominant sellers. But Congress has established some ground rules for the game. Sellers may not sell like goods to different purchasers at different prices if the result may be to injure competition to either the sellers' or the buyers' market unless such discriminations are justified as permitted by the Act. In this case there was some evidence of predatory intent with respect to each of these respondents. There was also other evidence upon which the jury could rationally find the requisite injury to competition. The frozen pie market in Salt Lake City was highly competitive. At times Utah Pie was a leader in moving the general level of prices down, and at other times each of the respondents also bore responsibility for the downward pressure on the price structure. We believe that the Act reaches price discrimination that erodes competition as much as it does price discrimination that is intended to have immediate destructive impact. In this case, the evidence shows a drastically declining price structure which the jury could rationally attribute to continued or sporadic price discrimination.

[Reversed]

QUESTIONS

1. Describe the competitors in the Utah Pie frozen pie market.
2. Is it significant that the national competitors were selling their pies at different prices in Utah?
3. Does it matter that the size of the pie market (i.e., number of pies sold) increased during the period examined?

8. Exclusive Dealings and Territories

Sometimes manufacturers have sole outlets. Sole outlets are not *per se* violations. For restrictions on territories and outlets to be legal, there must be enough interbrand competition to justify no intrabrand competition. **For Example,** Coca-Cola can have exclusive distributorships in cities because Pepsi will always be there providing consumers with competitive choices in soft drinks.

9. Resale Price Maintenance

Resale price maintenance is an attempt by manufacturers to control the prices that retailers can charge for their goods. A "suggested retail price" is just that, a suggestion, and is not a violation of the antitrust laws. However, some manufacturers have policies of terminating retailers when they charge too little or charge too much. For example, Apple's iPads are the same price wherever you buy them. Minimum prices are justified in a competitive sense because without them, some retailers would cut the price but not offer the customer service the manufacturer wants for its brand. Retailers who charge more can be stopped by manufacturers who do not want to gouge consumers on prices. The *Khan* and *Leegin* cases illustrate these two principles of legal resale price maintenance.

Leegin Creative Leather Products, Inc. v. PSKS, Inc., 551 U.S. 877 (2007)

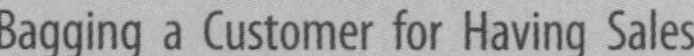

Bagging a Customer for Having Sales

Leegin Creative Leather Products, Inc. (Leegin) (petitioner), designs, manufactures, and distributes leather goods and accessories under the brand name "Brighton." The Brighton brand has now expanded into a full line of women's fashion accessories and is sold across the United States in over 5,000 retail stores. PSKS, Inc., (PSKS) (respondent) runs Kay's Kloset, a Brighton retailer in Lewisville, Texas, that carries about 75 different product lines, but was known as the place in that area to go for Brighton. Kay's ran Brighton ads and had Brighton days in its store.

Leegin's president, Jerry Kohl, who also has an interest in about 70 stores that sell Brighton products, believes that small retailers treat customers better, provide customers more services, and make their shopping experience more satisfactory than do larger, often impersonal retailers. In 1997, Kohl released a new strategic refocus for Brighton and instituted the "Brighton Retail Pricing and Promotion Policy," which banished retailers that discounted Brighton goods below suggested prices. In December 2002, Leegin discovered that Kay's Kloset had been marking down Brighton's entire line by 20 percent. Leegin stopped selling to the store.

PSKS sued Leegin for violation of the antitrust laws. Leegin asked to introduce expert testimony describing the procompetitive effects of its pricing policy. The jury awarded PSKS $1.2 million in damages and the judge trebled the damages and reimbursed PSKS for its attorney's fees and costs—for a judgment against Leegin of $3,975,000.80. The Court of Appeals affirmed. Leegin appealed. The U.S. Supreme Court granted *certiorari.*

JUDICIAL OPINION

KENNEDY, Justice

The question presented by the instant case is whether the Court should overrule the *per se* rule and allow resale price maintenance agreements to be judged by the rule of reason, the usual standard applied to determine if there is a violation of §1. The Court has abandoned the rule of *per se* illegality for other vertical restraints a manufacturer imposes on its distributors. Respected economic analysts, furthermore, conclude that vertical price restraints can have precompetitive effects.

The rule of reason is the accepted standard for testing whether a practice restrains trade in violation of §1. The rule of reason does not govern all restraints. Some types "are deemed unlawful *per se.*" The *per se* rule, treating categories of restraints as necessarily illegal, eliminates the need to study the reasonableness of an individual restraint in light of the real market forces at work, and, it must be acknowledged, the *per se* rule can give clear guidance for certain conduct. Restraints that are *per se* unlawful include horizontal agreements among competitors to fix prices, or to divide markets.

… [T]he *per se* rule is appropriate only after courts have had considerable experience with the type of restraint at issue, and only if courts can predict with confidence that it would be invalidated in all or almost all instances under the rule of reason. Though each side of the debate can find sources to support its position, it suffices to say here that economics literature is replete with procompetitive justifications for a manufacturer's use of resale price maintenance.

The justifications for vertical price restraints are similar to those for other vertical restraints. Minimum resale price maintenance can stimulate interbrand competition—the competition among manufacturers selling different brands of the same type of product—by reducing intrabrand competition—the competition among retailers selling the same brand. The promotion of interbrand competition is important because "the primary purpose of the antitrust laws is to protect [this type of] competition." A single manufacturer's use of vertical price restraints tends to eliminate intrabrand price competition; this in turn encourages retailers to invest in tangible or intangible services or promotional efforts that aid the manufacturer's position as against rival manufacturers. Resale price maintenance also has the potential to give consumers more options so that they can choose among low-price, low-service brands; high-price, high-service brands; and brands that fall in between.

Resale price maintenance can also increase interbrand competition by encouraging retailer services that would not be provided even absent free riding. It may be difficult and inefficient for a manufacturer to make and enforce a contract with a retailer specifying the different services the retailer must perform. Offering the retailer a guaranteed margin and threatening termination if it does not live up to expectations may be the most efficient way to expand the manufacturer's market share by inducing the retailer's performance and allowing it to use its own initiative and experience in providing valuable services. While vertical agreements setting minimum resale prices can have procompetitive justifications, they may have anticompetitive effects in other circumstances. Vertical price restraints also "might be used to organize cartels at the retailer level." A group of retailers might collude to fix prices to consumers and then compel a manufacturer to aid the unlawful arrangement with resale price maintenance. In that instance the manufacturer does not establish the practice to stimulate services or to promote its brand but to give inefficient retailers higher profits.

Resale price maintenance, furthermore, can be abused by a powerful manufacturer or retailer. A manufacturer might consider it has little choice but to accommodate the retailer's

Continued

demands for vertical price restraints if the manufacturer believes it needs access to the retailer's distribution network.

Vertical agreements establishing minimum resale prices can have either procompetitive or anticompetitive effects, depending upon the circumstances in which they are formed. Resale price maintenance, it is true, does have economic dangers. If the rule of reason were to apply to vertical price restraints, courts would have to be diligent in eliminating their anticompetitive uses from the market.

[Reversed].

QUESTIONS

1. What reasons did Leegin give for wanting the minimum price established for its retailers?
2. What points does the Court make about not having minimum prices in terms of reducing competition?
3. What risks are there in allowing minimum price requirements?

State Oil v. Khan, 522 U.S. 3 (1997)

Fill It Up: The Price Is Right and Fixed

Barkat U. Khan and his corporation (respondents) entered into an agreement with State Oil (petitioner) to lease and operate a gas station and convenience store owned by State Oil. The agreement provided that Khan would obtain the gasoline supply for the station from State Oil at a price equal to a suggested retail price set by State Oil, less a margin of 3.25 cents per gallon. Khan could charge any price he wanted, but if he charged more than State Oil's suggested retail price, the excess went to State Oil. Khan could sell the gasoline for less than State Oil's suggested retail price, but the difference would come out of his allowed margin.

After a year, Khan fell behind on his lease payments and State Oil gave notice of and began proceedings for eviction. The court had Khan removed and appointed a receiver for operation of the station. The receiver operated the gas station without the price constraints and received an overall profit margin above the 3.25 cents imposed on Khan.

Khan filed suit, alleging that the State Oil agreement was a violation of Section 1 of the Sherman Act because State Oil was controlling price. The district court held that there was no *per se* violation and that Khan had failed to demonstrate antitrust injury. The Court of Appeals reversed and State Oil appealed.

JUDICIAL OPINION

O'CONNOR, J.… Under §1 of the Sherman Act, 26 Stat. 209, as amended, 15 U.S.C. §1, "[e]very contract, combination…, or conspiracy, in restraint of trade" is illegal. In *Albrecht v. Herald Co.,* 390 U.S. 145, 88 S. Ct. 869, 19 L.Ed.2d 998 (1968), this Court held that vertical maximum price fixing is a per se violation of that statute. In this case, we are asked to reconsider that decision in light of subsequent decisions of this Court. We conclude that *Albrecht* should be overruled.

Although the Sherman Act, by its terms, prohibits every agreement "in restraint of trade," this Court has long recognized that Congress intended to outlaw only unreasonable restraints. As a consequence, most antitrust claims are analyzed "under a rule of reason," according to which the finder of fact must decide whether the questioned practice imposes an unreasonable restraint on competition, taking into account a variety of factors, including specific information about the relevant business, its condition before and after the restraint was imposed, and the restraint's history, nature, and effect.

Some types of restraints, however, have such predictable and pernicious anticompetitive effect, and such limited potential for procompetitive benefit, that they are deemed unlawful per se.

Thus, we have expressed reluctance to adopt per se rules with regard to "restraints imposed in the context of business relationships where the economic impact of certain practices is not immediately obvious."

Albrecht, decided the following Term, involved a newspaper publisher who had granted exclusive territories to independent carriers subject to their adherence to a maximum price on resale of the newspapers to the public. The Court concluded that it was per se unlawful for the publisher to fix the maximum resale price of its newspapers. The Court acknowledged that "[m]aximum and minimum price fixing may have different consequences in many situations," but nonetheless condemned maximum price fixing for

Continued

"substituting the perhaps erroneous judgment of a seller for the forces of the competitive market."

Our analysis is also guided by our general view that the primary purpose of the antitrust laws is to protect interbrand competition. "Low prices," we have explained, benefit consumers regardless of how those prices are set, and so long as they are above predatory levels, they do not threaten competition." Our interpretation of the Sherman Act also incorporates the notion that condemnation of practices resulting in lower prices to consumers is "especially costly" because "cutting prices in order to increase business often is the very essence of competition."

So informed, we find it difficult to maintain that vertically-imposed maximum prices could harm consumers or competition to the extent necessary to justify their per se invalidation. As Chief Judge Posner wrote for the Court of Appeals in this case:

"As for maximum resale price fixing, unless the supplier is a monopsonist he cannot squeeze his dealers' margins below a competitive level; the attempt to do so would just drive the dealers into the arms of a competing supplier. A supplier might, however, fix a maximum resale price in order to prevent his dealers from exploiting a monopoly position.... [S]uppose that State Oil, perhaps to encourage... dealer services... has spaced its dealers sufficiently far apart to limit competition among them (or even given each of them an exclusive territory); and suppose further that Union 76 is a sufficiently distinctive and popular brand to give the dealers in it at least a modicum of monopoly power. Then State Oil might want to place a ceiling on the dealers' resale prices in order to prevent them from exploiting that monopoly power fully. It would do this not out of disinterested malice, but in its commercial self-interest. The higher the price at which gasoline is resold, the smaller the volume sold, and so the lower the profit to the supplier if the higher profit per gallon at the higher price is being snared by the dealer."

Further, although vertical maximum price fixing might limit the viability of inefficient dealers, that consequence is not necessarily harmful to competition and consumers.

After reconsidering *Albrecht*'s rationale and the substantial criticism the decision has received, however, we conclude that there is insufficient economic justification for per se invalidation of vertical maximum price fixing. That is so not only because it is difficult to accept the assumptions underlying *Albrecht,* but also because *Albrecht* has little or no relevance to ongoing enforcement of the Sherman Act.

We approach the reconsideration of decisions of this Court with the utmost caution. *Stare decisis* reflects "a policy judgment that 'in most matters it is more important that the applicable rule of law be settled than that it be settled right."

But "[*s*]*tare decisis* is not an inexorable command." In the area of antitrust law, there is a competing interest, well-represented in this Court's decisions, in recognizing and adapting to changed circumstances and the lessons of accumulated experience. Thus, the general presumption that legislative changes should be left to Congress has less force with respect to the Sherman Act in light of the accepted view that Congress "expected the courts to give shape to the statute's broad mandate by drawing on common-law tradition."

In overruling *Albrecht,* we of course do not hold that all vertical maximum price fixing is per se lawful. Instead, vertical maximum price fixing, like the majority of commercial arrangements subject to the antitrust laws, should be evaluated under the rule of reason. In our view, rule-of-reason analysis will effectively identify those situations in which vertical maximum price fixing amounts to anticompetitive conduct.

There remains the question whether respondents are entitled to recover damages based on State Oil's conduct. Although the Court of Appeals noted that "the district judge was right to conclude that if the rule of reason is applicable, Khan loses," its consideration of this case was necessarily premised on *Albrecht*'s per se rule. Under the circumstances, the matter should be reviewed by the Court of Appeals in the first instance. We therefore vacate the judgment of the Court of Appeals and remand the case for further proceedings consistent with this opinion.

[Remanded.]

QUESTIONS

1. What were the price requirements for Khan's lease?
2. What happened when someone else took over Khan's station?
3. What does the court discuss about long-standing precedent and *stare decisis?*

10. Tying

It is a violation of the Sherman Act to force "tying" sales on buyers. **Tying** occurs when the seller makes a buyer who wants to purchase one product buy an additional product that he or she does not want.

The essential characteristic of a tying arrangement that violates Section 1 of the Sherman Act is the use of control over the tying product within the relevant market to compel the buyer to purchase the tied article that either is not wanted or could be purchased

Sports & Entertainment Law

Celebrity Issues and Antitrust

Public Interest Corporation (PIC) owned and operated television station WTMV-TV in Lakeland, Florida. MCA Television Ltd. (MCA) owns and licenses syndicated television programs. In 1990, the two companies entered into a licensing contract for several first-run television shows. With respect to all but one of these shows, MCA exchanged the licenses on a "barter" basis for advertising time on WTMV. However, MCA conditioned this exchange on PIC's agreeing to license the remaining show, *Harry and the Hendersons,* for cash as well as for barter. *Harry and the Hendersons* was what some in the industry would call a "dog," a show that was not very good that attempted to capitalize on a hit movie. PIC agreed to this arrangement, although it did not want *Harry and the Hendersons.* The shows that PIC did want were *List of a Lifetime, List of a Lifetime II, Magnum P.I.,* and 17 other miscellaneous features.

The relationship between the parties was strained over nonpayment, poor ratings performance of *Harry,* and other issues. When litigation resulted, PIC alleged that it had been subjected to an illegal tying arrangement. PIC requested damages for MCA's violation of the Sherman Act. What violation do you think occurred?

Source: Adapted from *MCA Television Ltd. v. Public Interest Corp.,* 171 F.3d 1265 (11th Cir. 1998).

elsewhere on better terms. **For Example,** in the Microsoft antitrust case, Microsoft was accused of requiring the purchase and use of its browser as a condition for purchasing its software. The Sherman Act also prohibits professional persons, such as doctors, from using a peer review proceeding to pressure another professional who competes with them in private practice and refuses to become a member of a clinic formed by them.

11. Mergers along the Supply Chain

Vertical mergers occur between firms that have buyer and seller relationships. The Clayton Act also applies to vertical mergers. The test is whether the vertical merger will foreclose or lessen competition. **For Example,** the Justice Department took a very close look at whether the merger between Live Nation and Ticketmaster would be anticompetitive because the largest U.S. event promoter was proposing a merger with the largest primary and secondary ticket seller in the world. The merger was eventually approved because there were still thriving smaller ticket sellers.

In addition to controlling business combinations, the federal government protects others. By statute or decision, associations of exporters, marine insurance associations, farmers' cooperatives, and labor unions are exempt from the Sherman Act with respect to agreements between their members. Certain pooling and revenue-dividing agreements between carriers are exempt from the antitrust law when approved by the appropriate federal agency. The Newspaper Preservation Act of 1970 grants an antitrust exemption to operating agreements entered into by newspapers to prevent financial collapse. The Soft Drink Interbrand Competition Act[19] grants the soft drink industry an exemption when it is shown that, in fact, substantial competition exists in spite of the agreements.

The general approach of the U.S. Supreme Court has been that these types of agreements should not be automatically, or *per se,* condemned as a restraint of interstate commerce merely because they create the power or potential to monopolize interstate commerce. It is only when the restraint imposed is unreasonable that the practice is unlawful. The Court applies the rule of reason in certain cases because the practice may not always harm competition.

D. Remedies for Anticompetitive Behavior

12. Criminal Penalties

A violation of either section of the Sherman Act is punishable by fine or imprisonment or both at the discretion of the court. The maximum fine for a

[19] 15 U.S.C. §3501 *et seq.*

corporation is $100 million. A natural person can be fined a maximum of $1,000,000 or imprisoned for a maximum term of ten years or both.

13. Civil Remedies

In addition to these criminal penalties, the law provides for an injunction to stop the unlawful practices.

Any individual or company harmed may bring a separate action for **treble damages** (three times the damages actually sustained). In addition to individual suits, there is the possibility that a state could bring a class-action suit if the antitrust violation has resulted in large numbers of buyers paying higher prices. **For Example,** Pilgrim's Pride agreed to pay $26 million in damages to dozens of poultry growers because of its closure of chicken-processing plants in order to bring down the price of chicken.

The attorney general of a state may bring a class-action suit to recover damages on behalf of those who have paid the higher prices. This action is called a *parens patriae* action on the theory that the state is suing as the parent of its people.

LawFlix

Antitrust (2001) (R)

This movie is based on the story of Bill Gates and Microsoft.

MAKE THE CONNECTION

SUMMARY

Regulation by government has occurred primarily to protect one group from the improper conduct of another group. The police power is the basis for government regulation. Regulation is passed when the free enterprise system fails to control abuses, as when companies engage in unfair methods of competition.

There are horizontal and vertical forms of anticompetitive behavior. The Sherman Act focuses on horizontal anticompetitive behavior such as price-fixing, boycotts, refusals to deal, and monopolization achieved through means other than fair competition.

The Sherman Antitrust Act prohibits price-fixing among competitors, monopolies that do not result from superior skill or products, boycotts, and mergers that lessen competition. The Clayton Act prohibits mergers or the acquisition of the assets of another corporation when this conduct would tend to lessen competition or create a monopoly. The Justice Department requires premerger notification for proposed mergers. Violation of the federal antitrust statutes subjects the wrongdoer to criminal prosecution and possible civil liability that can include treble damages.

Vertical trade restraints include price discrimination, some exclusive dealings arrangements, resale price maintenance, and some mergers among companies positioned vertically in the supply chain.

Prices have been regulated both by prohibiting setting the exact price or a maximum price and discrimination in pricing. Price discrimination between buyers is prohibited when the effect of such discrimination could tend to create a monopoly or lessen competition. Price discrimination occurs when the prices charged different buyers are different despite the same marginal costs. Another vertical antitrust issue is resale price maintenance. Resale price maintenance is control by the manufacturer of the price of its goods as they flow through the supply chain. Resale price maintenance is not illegal *per se* if the control is for purposes of providing customer service.

LEARNING OUTCOMES

After studying this chapter, you should be able to clearly explain:

A. Power to Regulate Business

LO.1 Explain the powers the government has to be sure free markets are working efficiently

See the *For Example* about Crispy Clowns Cereal on p. 77.

B. Regulation of Horizontal Markets and Competitors

LO.2 List the federal statutes that regulate horizontal markets and competition and give examples of each

See the Christie's and Sotheby's example on p. 76.

See the Marsh & McLennan Ethics & the Law on p. 77.

See the Microsoft monopolization discussion on p. 78.

C. Regulation of the Supply Chain and Vertical Trade Restraints

LO.3 Describe the federal statutes that regulate the supply chain and vertical markets

See the *Utah Pie* case on predatory pricing, pp. 80–81.

See the *Khan* oil case on price controls, pp. 83–84.

See the *Leegin* case on resale price maintenance, pp. 82–83.

See the Sports & Entertainment Law feature on tying, p. 85.

D. Remedies for Anticompetitive Behavior

LO.4 Discuss the remedies available to protect business competition

See a list of the penalties and remedies on p. 85.

KEY TERMS

Clayton Act
divestiture order
market power
price discrimination
Robinson-Patman Act
Sherman Antitrust Act
treble damages
tying

QUESTIONS AND CASE PROBLEMS

1. American Crystal Sugar Co. was one of several refiners of beet sugar in northern California, and it distributed its product in interstate commerce. American Crystal and the other refiners had a monopoly on the seed supply and were the only practical market for the beets. In 1939, all of the refiners began using identical form contracts that computed the price paid to the sugar beet growers using a "factor" common to all the refiners. As a result, all refiners paid the same price for beets of the same quality. Though there was no hard evidence of an illegal agreement, the growers brought suit under the Sherman Act against the refiners, alleging that they conspired to fix a single uniform price among themselves to hold down the cost of the beets. The growers sued for the treble damages available under the Sherman Act. Can they recover? [*Mandeville Island Farms v. American Crystal Sugar Co.,* 334 U.S. 219]

2. Penny Stafford, the owner of Belvi Coffee and Tea Exchange, located in Bellevue, Washington, brought an antitrust suit against Starbucks. She alleged that through its exclusive leases, Starbucks bans other coffee shops from competing. Starbucks has a 73 percent market share, has $8.4 billion in annual sales in the United States, and owns 7,551 of the 21,400 coffeehouses located in the United States. However, if Dunkin' Donuts, Krispy Kreme, and Tim Hortons are included in the gourmet coffee market, Starbucks holds only 43 percent of the coffee market. Starbucks purchased Seattle's Best Coffee (SBC) in 2003 and Torrefazione Italia the same year. Starbucks then

closed one-half of all SBC stores and all of the Torrefazione outlets. Starbucks runs 59 stores within a two-mile radius of downtown Seattle. Stafford said that Starbucks has exclusive leases with landlords so that the landlords cannot lease space in the same building to another coffee shop. Does such an exclusive lease violate any antitrust laws, or are such clauses permitted under the law?

3. David Ungar holds a Dunkin' Donuts franchise. The terms of his franchise agreement require him to use only those ingredients furnished by Dunkin' Donuts. He is also required to buy its napkins, cups, and so on, with the Dunkin' Donuts trademark on them. Is this an illegal tying arrangement? What if Dunkin' Donuts maintains that it needs these requirements to maintain its quality levels on a nationwide basis? [*Ungar v. Dunkin' Donuts of America, Inc.,* 429 U.S. 823]

4. During the 1980s, the NCAA, a voluntary unincorporated association of approximately 1,100 educational institutions, became concerned over the steadily rising costs of maintaining competitive athletic programs. As a way of containing those costs, the association imposed salary caps on college and university athletic coaches. The caps on salaries as well as limits on number and types of coaches were imposed pursuant to NCAA procedures and members' votes. A group of coaches filed suit, challenging the caps on salaries and hiring as being anti-competitive. The NCAA responded that it had a goal of containing athletic program costs as well as ensuring that entry-level coaching positions were available. Are the salary caps legal under the federal antitrust laws? [*Law v. National Collegiate Athletic Ass'n,* 134 F.3d 1010 (10th Cir.)]

5. Hines Cosmetic Co. sold beauty preparations nationally to beauty shops at a standard or fixed-price schedule. Some of the shops were also supplied with a free demonstrator and free advertising materials. The shops that were not supplied with them claimed that giving the free services and materials constituted unlawful price discrimination. Hines replied that there was no price discrimination because it charged everyone the same. What it was giving free was merely a promotional campaign that was not intended to discriminate against those who were not given anything free. Was Hines guilty of unlawful price discrimination? Explain.

6. Moore ran a bakery in Santa Rosa, New Mexico. His business was wholly intrastate. Meads Fine Bread Co., his competitor, engaged in an interstate business. Meads cut the price of bread in half in Santa Rosa but made no price cut in any other place in New Mexico or in any other state. This price-cutting drove Moore out of business. Moore then sued Meads for damages for violating the Clayton and Robinson-Patman Acts. Meads claimed that the price-cutting was purely intrastate and, therefore, did not constitute a violation of federal statutes. Was Meads correct? Why or why not? [*Moore v. Meads Fine Bread Co.,* 348 U.S. 115]

7. A&P Grocery Stores decided to sell its own brand of canned milk (referred to as private label milk). A&P asked its longtime supplier, Borden, to submit an offer to produce the private label milk. Bowman Dairy also submitted a bid, which was lower than Borden's. A&P's Chicago buyer then contacted Borden and said, "I have a bid in my pocket. You people are so far out of line it is not even funny. You are not even in the ballpark." The Borden representative asked for more details but was told only that a $50,000 improvement in Borden's bid "would not be a drop in the bucket." A&P was one of Borden's largest customers in the Chicago area. Furthermore, Borden had just invested more than $5 million in a new dairy facility in Illinois. The loss of the A&P account would result in underutilization of the plant. Borden lowered its bid by more than $400,000. The Federal Trade Commission charged Borden with price discrimination, but Borden maintained it was simply meeting the competition. Did Borden violate the Robinson-Patman Act? Does it matter that the milk was a private label milk, not its normal trade name Borden milk? [*Great Atlantic & Pacific Tea Co., Inc. v. FTC,* 440 U.S. 69]

8. Department 56 is a company that manufactures and sells collectible Christmas village houses and other replica items to allow collectors to create the

whimsical "Snow Village" town or "Dickens Christmas." Department 56 has only authorized dealers. Sam's Club, a division of Wal-Mart Stores, Inc., began selling Department 56 pieces from the Heritage Village Collection. Susan Engel, president and CEO of Department 56, refused to sell Department 56 products to Wal-Mart. Does her refusal violate any antitrust laws?

9. Dr. Edwin G. Hyde, a board-certified anesthesiologist, applied for permission to practice at East Jefferson Hospital in Louisiana. An approval was recommended for his hiring, but the hospital's board denied him employment on grounds that the hospital had a contract with Roux & Associates for Roux to provide all anesthesiological services required by the hospital's patients. Dr. Hyde filed suit for violation of antitrust laws. Had the hospital done anything illegal? [*Jefferson Parish Hosp. Dist. No. 2 v. Hyde,* 466 U.S. 2]

10. BRG of Georgia, Inc. (BRG), and Harcourt Brace Jovanovich Legal and Professional Publications (HJB) are the nation's two largest providers of bar review materials and lectures. HJB began offering a Georgia bar review course on a limited basis in 1976 and was in direct, and often intense, competition with BRG from 1977 to 1979 when the companies were the two main providers of bar review courses in Georgia. In early 1980, they entered into an agreement that gave BRG an exclusive license to market HJB's materials in Georgia and to use its trade name "Bar/Bri." The parties agreed that HJB would not compete with BRG in Georgia and that BRG would not compete with HJB outside of Georgia. Under the agreement, HJB received $100 per student enrolled by BRG and 40 percent of all revenues over $350. Immediately after the 1980 agreement, the price of BRG's course was increased from $150 to more than $400. Is their conduct illegal under federal antitrust laws? [*Palmer v. BRG of Georgia, Inc.,* 498 U.S. 46]

11. Favorite Foods Corp. sold its food to stores and distributors. It established a quantity discount scale that was publicly published and made available to all buyers. The top of the scale gave the highest discount to buyers purchasing more than 100 freight cars of food in a calendar year. Only two buyers, both national food chains, purchased in such quantities, and therefore, they alone received the greatest discount. Favorite Foods was prosecuted for price discrimination in violation of the Clayton Act. Was it guilty?

12. Run America, Inc., manufactures running shoes. Its shoe is consistently rated poorly by *Run Run Run* magazine in its annual shoe review. The number one shoe in *Run Run Run*'s review is the Cheetah, a shoe that Run America has learned is manufactured by the parent company of the magazine. Is this conduct a violation of the antitrust laws? Do you think it is ethical to run the shoe review without disclosing ownership?

13. The Quickie brand wheelchair is the most popular customized wheelchair on the market. Its market share is 90 percent. Other manufacturers produce special-use wheelchairs that fold, that are made of mesh and lighter frames, and that are easily transportable. These manufacturers do not compete with Quickie on customized chairs. One manufacturer of the alternative wheelchairs has stated, "Look, it's an expensive market to be in, that Quickie market. We prefer the alternative chairs without the headaches of customizations." Another has said, "It is such a drain on cash flow in that market because insurers take so long to pay. We produce chairs that buyers purchase with their own money, not through insurers. Our sales are just like any other product." Quickie entered the market nearly 40 years ago and is known for its quality and attention to detail. Buying a Quickie custom chair, however, takes time, and the revenue stream from sales is slow but steady because of the time required to produce custom wheelchairs. Has Quickie violated the federal antitrust laws with its 90 percent market share? Discuss.

14. Gardner-Denver is the largest manufacturer of ratchet wrenches and their replacement parts in the United States. Gardner-Denver had two different lists of prices for its wrenches and parts. Its blue list had parts that, if purchased in quantities of five or more, were available for substantially less than its white list prices. Did Gardner-Denver engage in price discrimination with its two price lists? [*D. E. Rogers Assoc., Inc. v. Gardner-Denver Co.,* 718 F.2d 1431 (6th Cir.)]

15. The Aspen ski area consisted of four mountain areas. Aspen Highlands, which owned three of those areas, and Aspen Skiing, which owned the fourth, had cooperated for years in issuing a joint, multiple-day, all-area ski ticket. After repeatedly and unsuccessfully demanding an increased share of the proceeds, Aspen Highlands canceled the joint ticket. Aspen Skiing, concerned that skiers would bypass its mountain without some joint offering, tried a variety of increasingly desperate measures to re-create the joint ticket, even to the point of in effect offering to buy Aspen Highland's tickets at retail price. Aspen Highlands refused even that. Aspen Skiing brought suit under the Sherman Act, alleging that the refusal to cooperate was a move by Aspen Highlands to eliminate all competition in the area by freezing it out of business. Is there an antitrust claim here in the refusal to cooperate? What statute and violation do you think Aspen Skiing alleged? What dangers do you see in finding the failure to cooperate to be an antitrust violation? [*Aspen Skiing Co. v. Aspen Highlands Skiing Corp.*, 472 U.S. 585]

CHAPTER 6

© Manuel Gutjahr/iStockphoto.com

Administrative Agencies

learningoutcomes

After studying this chapter, you should be able to

LO.1 Describe the nature and purpose of administrative agencies

LO.2 Discuss the legislative or rulemaking power of administrative agencies

LO.3 Explain the executive or enforcement function of administrative agencies

LO.4 Discuss the judicial power of administrative agencies including the rule on exhaustion of administrative remedies

Late in the nineteenth century, a new type of governmental structure began to develop to meet the highly specialized needs of government regulation of business: the administrative agency. The administrative agency is now typically the instrument through which government makes and carries out its regulations.

A. Nature of the Administrative Agency

An **administrative agency** is a government body charged with administering and implementing legislation. An agency may be a department, independent establishment, commission, administration, authority, board, or bureau. Agencies exist on the federal and state levels. One example of a federal agency is the Federal Trade Commission (FTC), whose structure is shown in Figure 6-1.

1. Purpose of Administrative Agencies

Federal administrative agencies are created to carry out general policies specified by Congress. Federal agencies include the Securities Exchange Commission (SEC), the Consumer Product Safety Commission (CPSC), and the Food and Drug Administration (FDA). The law governing these agencies is known as **administrative law**.

States also have administrative agencies that may have jurisdiction over areas of law affecting business, such as workers' compensation claims, real estate licensing, and unemployment compensation.

2. Uniqueness of Administrative Agencies

Administrative agencies differ from the legislative branch in that those who head up and operate are ordinarily appointed (in the case of federal agencies, by the president of the United States with the consent of the Senate).

In the tripartite structure of legislative, executive, and judicial branches, the judicial branch reviews actions of the executive and legislative branches to ensure that they have not exceeded their constitutional powers. However, governmental agencies combine legislative, executive, and judicial powers (see Figure 6-2). These agencies make the rules, conduct inspections to see that the rules have been or are being obeyed, and determine whether there have been violations of their rules. Because agencies have such broad powers, they are subject to strict procedural rules as well as disclosure requirements (discussed in the following section).

FIGURE 6-1 Structure of the Federal Trade Commission

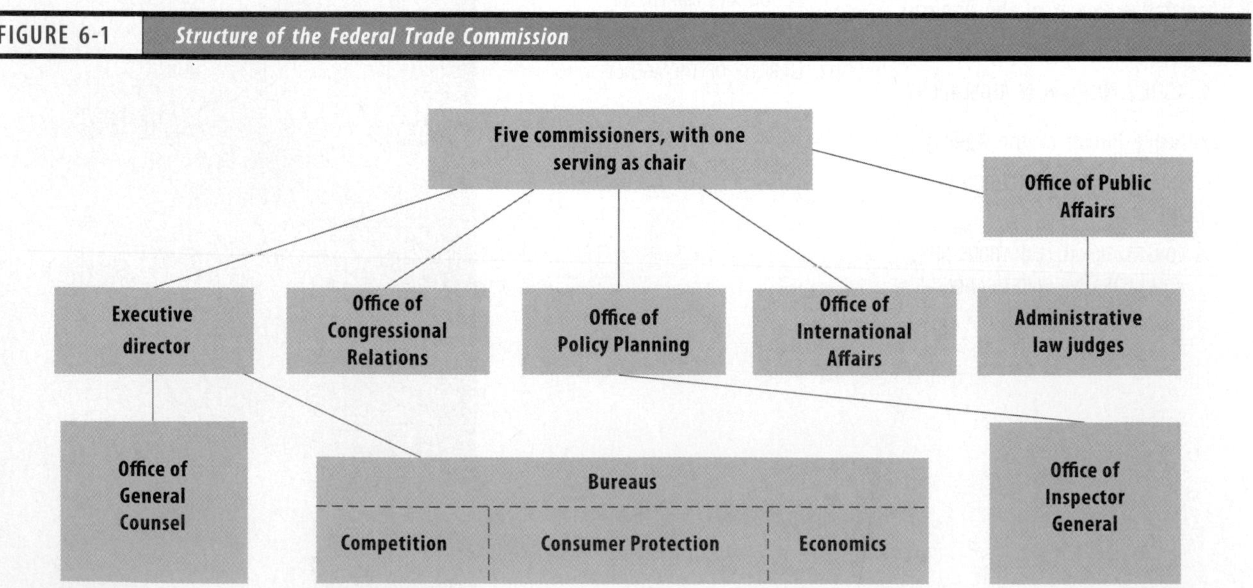

FIGURE 6-2 *The Administrative Chain of Command*

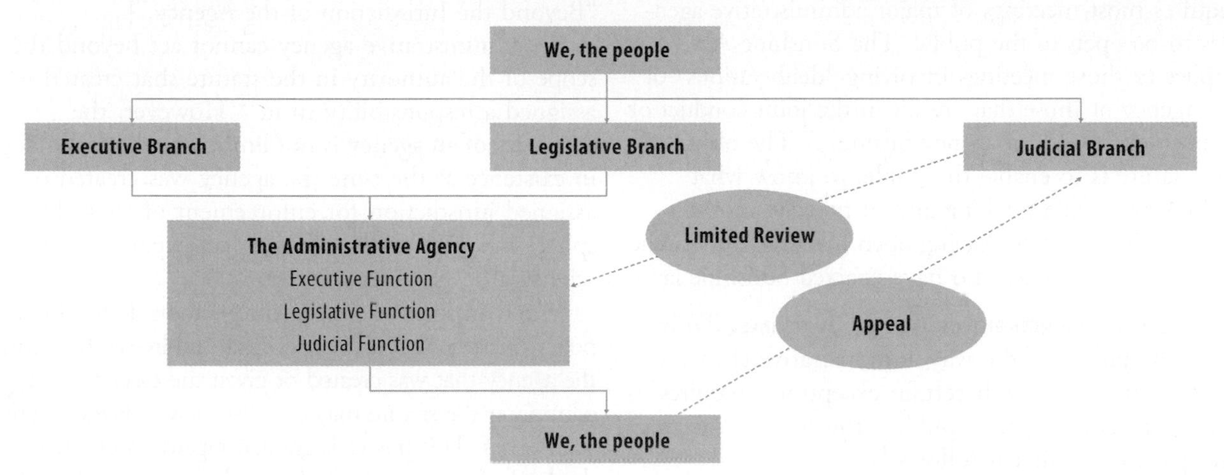

3. Open Operation of Administrative Agencies

The public has ready access to the activity of administrative agencies. That access comes in three ways: (1) open records, (2) open meetings, and (3) public announcement of agency guidelines. The actions and activities of most federal agencies that are not otherwise regulated are controlled by the **Administrative Procedure Act** (APA).[1] Many states have adopted statutes with provisions similar to those of the APA.

(A) Open Records. The **Freedom of Information Act**[2] (FOIA) provides that information contained in records of federal administrative agencies is available to citizens on proper request. The primary purpose of this statute is "to ensure that government activities be opened to the sharp eye of public scrutiny."[3] To ensure that members of the public understand how to obtain records, the FOIA provides that "[e]ach agency shall…publish in the *Federal Register* for the guidance of the public…the methods whereby the public may obtain information, make submittals or requests, or obtain decisions."[4] There are exceptions to this right of public scrutiny. They prevent individuals and companies from obtaining information that is not necessary to their legitimate interests and might harm the person or company whose information is being sought.[5] State statutes typically exempt from disclosure any information that would constitute an invasion of the privacy of others. However, freedom of information acts are broadly construed, and unless an exemption is clearly given, the information in question is subject to public inspection.[6] Moreover, the person claiming that there is an exemption that prohibits disclosure has the burden of proving that the exemption applies to the particular request made. Exemptions include commercial or financial information not ordinarily made public by the person or company that supplies the information to the agency as part of the agency's enforcement role.[7]

The FOIA's primary purpose is to subject agency action to public scrutiny. Its provisions are liberally interpreted, and agencies must make good-faith efforts to comply with its terms.

[1] Administrative Procedures Act 5 U.S.C. §550 *et seq.*

[2] 5 U.S.C. §552 *et seq.* The Electronic Freedom of Information Act Amendments of 1996 extend the public availability of information to electronically stored data.

[3] *Brady-Lunny v. Massey,* 185 F. Supp. 2d 928 (C.D. Ill. 2007). See also *Better Government Association v. Blagojevich,* 899 N.E.2d 382 (Ill. App. 2008).

[4] 5 U.S.C. §552(a)(1)(a).

[5] Additional protection is provided by the Privacy Act of 1974, 5 U.S.C. §552a(b); *Doe v. U.S. Dept. of Treasury,* 706 F. Supp. 2d 1 (D.D.C. 2009).

[6] Corporations have limited privacy rights. *FCC v. AT&T Inc.* 131 S.Ct. 1177 (2011).

[7] *Sun-Sentinel Company v. U.S. Dept. of Homeland Security,* 431 F. Supp. 2d 1258 (S.D Fla. 2006). For a state law example, see *Oklahoma Public Employees Ass'n v. State ex rel. Oklahoma Office of Personnel Management,* 267 P.3d 838 (Okla. 2011).

(B) Open Meetings. Under the Sunshine Act of 1976,[8] called the **open meeting law**, the federal government requires most meetings of major administrative agencies to be open to the public. The Sunshine Act[9] applies to those meetings involving "deliberations" of the agency or those that "result in the joint conduct or disposition of official agency business." The object of this statute is to enable the public to know what actions agencies are taking and to prevent administrative misconduct by having open meetings and public scrutiny. Many states also have enacted Sunshine laws.

(C) Public Announcement of Agency Guidelines. To inform the public of the way administrative agencies operate, the APA, with certain exceptions, requires that each federal agency publish the rules, principles, and procedures that it follows.[10]

B. Legislative Power of the Agency

An administrative agency has the power to make laws and does so by promulgating regulations with public input.

4. Agency's Regulations as Law

An agency may adopt regulations within the scope of its authority. The power of an agency to carry out a congressional program "necessarily requires the formulation of policy and the making of rules to fill any gap left by Congress."[11] If the regulation is not authorized by the law creating the agency, anyone affected by it can challenge the regulation on the basis that the agency has exceeded its authority. [See Section 11(c), "Beyond the Jurisdiction of the Agency."]

An administrative agency cannot act beyond the scope of the authority in the statute that created it or assigned a responsibility to it.[12] However, the authority of an agency is not limited to the technology in existence at the time the agency was created or assigned jurisdiction for enforcement of laws. The sphere in which an agency may act expands with new scientific developments.[13]

When an agency's proposed regulation deals with a policy question that is not specifically addressed by statute, the agency that was created or given the discretion to administer the statute may establish new policies covering such issues. This power is granted regardless of whether the lawmaker intentionally left such matters to the agency's discretion or merely did not foresee the problem. In either case, the matter is one to be determined within the agency's discretion, and courts defer to agencies' policy decisions.[14] **For Example,** the FCC has authority to deal with cell phones and cell phone providers even though when the agency was created, there were only the traditional types of land-line telephones.

Courts regard the administrative agency as holding all powers necessary to effectively perform the duties entrusted to it. When the agency establishes a rational basis for its rule, courts accept the rule and do not substitute their own judgment.[15] The *Massachusetts v. EPA* case deals with the issue of the scope of an agency's authority.

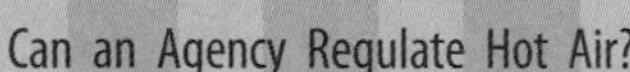

Can an Agency Regulate Hot Air?

On October 20, 1999, a group of 19 private organizations (petitioners) filed a rulemaking petition asking EPA to regulate "greenhouse gas emissions from new motor vehicles under § 202 of the Clean Air Act." These organizations argued that greenhouse gas emissions have significantly accelerated climate change, and that "carbon dioxide remains the most important contributor to [man-made] forcing of climate change."

---

[8] The Government in the Sunshine Act can be found at 5 U.S.C. §552b.

[9] 5 U.S.C. §552b(a)(2).

[10] APA codified at 5 U.S.C. §552. See Section 5(c) of this chapter for a description of the *Federal Register,* the publication in which these agency rules, principles, and procedures are printed.

[11] *National Elec. Mfrs. Ass'n v. U.S. Dept. of Energy,* 654 F.3d 496 (4th Cir. 2011).

[12] *Zuni Public School Dist. No. 89 v. Department of Educ.,* 550 U.S. 81 (2007).

[13] *United States v. Midwest Video Corp.,* 406 U.S. 649 (1972) (sustaining a commission regulation that provided that "no CATV system having 3,500 or more subscribers shall carry the signal of any television broadcast station unless the system also operates to a significant extent as a local outlet by cablecasting and has available facilities for local production and presentation of programs other than automated services").

[14] *Chevron, U.S.A., Inc. v. National Resources Defense Council, Inc.,* 467 U.S. 837 (1984).

[15] *Covad Communications Co. v. FCC,* 450 F.3d 528 (D.C. Cir. 2006).

Continued

Fifteen months after the petition was filed, the EPA requested public comment on "all the issues raised in [the] petition," adding a "particular" request for comments on "any scientific, technical, legal, economic or other aspect of these issues that may be relevant to EPA's consideration of this petition, including whether there was global warming due to carbon emissions." The EPA received more than 50,000 comments over the next five months.

On September 8, 2003, EPA entered an order denying the rulemaking petition because (1) the Clean Air Act does not authorize EPA to issue mandatory regulations to address global climate change; and (2) even if the agency had the authority to set greenhouse gas emission standards, it would be unwise to do so at this time. Massachusetts, other states, and private organizations filed suit challenging the EPA denial as arbitrary and capricious, violative of the APA, and *ultra vires* because of statutory mandates for EPA action.

The court of appeals dismissed the appeal from the agency denial and the Supreme Court granted *certiorari.*

JUDICIAL OPINION

STEVENS, Justice...In essence, EPA concluded that climate change was so important that unless Congress spoke with exacting specificity, it could not have meant the agency to address it.

While it may be true that regulating motor-vehicle emissions will not by itself *reverse* global warming, it by no means follows that we lack jurisdiction to decide whether EPA has a duty to take steps to *slow* or *reduce* it.

The Clean Air Act's sweeping definition of "air pollutant" includes "*any* air pollution agent or combination of such agents, including *any* physical, chemical ... substance or matter which is emitted into or otherwise enters the ambient air ... ." The statute is unambiguous. If EPA makes a finding of endangerment, the Clean Air Act requires the agency to regulate emissions of the deleterious pollutant from new motor vehicles.

EPA finally argues that it cannot regulate carbon dioxide emissions from motor vehicles because doing so would require it to tighten mileage standards, a job (according to EPA) that Congress has assigned to DOT. But that DOT sets mileage standards in no way licenses EPA to shirk its environmental responsibilities.

EPA has been charged with protecting the public's "health" and "welfare," a statutory obligation wholly independent of DOT's mandate to promote energy efficiency. The two obligations may overlap, but there is no reason to think the two agencies cannot both administer their obligations and yet avoid inconsistency.

Because greenhouse gases fit well within the Clean Air Act's capacious definition of "air pollutant," we hold that EPA has the statutory authority to regulate the emission of such gases from new motorvehicles.

In short, EPA has offered no reasoned explanation for its refusal to decide whether greenhouse gases cause or contribute to climate change. Its action was therefore "arbitrary, capricious, ... or otherwise not in accordance with law." We need not and do not reach the question whether on remand EPA must make an endangerment finding, or whether policy concerns can inform EPA's actions in the event that it makes such a finding. We hold only that EPA must ground its reasons for action or inaction in the statute.

The judgment of the Court of Appeals is reversed, and the case is remanded.

DISSENTING OPINION

Chief Justice ROBERTS, with whom Justice SCALIA, Justice THOMAS, and Justice ALITO join, dissenting. Global warming may be a "crisis," even "the most pressing environmental problem of our time." Indeed, it may ultimately affect nearly everyone on the planet in some potentially adverse way, and it may be that governments have done too little to address it. It is not a problem, however, that has escaped the attention of policymakers in the Executive and Legislative Branches of our Government, who continue to consider regulatory, legislative, and treaty-based means of addressing global climate change.

This Court's standing jurisprudence simply recognizes that redress of grievances of the sort at issue here "is the function of Congress and the Chief Executive," not the federal courts. I would vacate the judgment below and remand for dismissal of the petitions for review. Justice SCALIA, with whom THE CHIEF JUSTICE, Justice THOMAS, and Justice ALITO join, dissenting. I simply cannot conceive of what else the Court would like EPA to say.

The Court's alarm over global warming may or may not be justified, but it ought not distort the outcome of this litigation. This is a straightforward administrative law case, in which Congress has passed a malleable statute giving broad discretion, not to us but to an executive agency. No matter how important the underlying policy issues at stake, this Court has no business substituting its own desired outcome for the reasoned judgment of the responsible agency.

QUESTIONS

1. What authority is given to the EPA by statute? Why does the EPA not want to exercise authority over greenhouse gases?
2. Why does the majority conclude that "greenhouse gases" are included within that authority?
3. List the arguments the dissent makes against requiring the EPA to take action on greenhouse gases. What do you learn about the role of the issue of global warming in the dissent's analysis of the case vs. the analysis of the majority?

5. Agency Adoption of Regulations

(A) Congressional Enabling Act. Before an agency can begin rulemaking proceedings, it must be given jurisdiction by congressional enactment in the form of a statute. **For Example,** Congress has enacted broad statutes governing discrimination in employment practices and has given authority to the Equal Employment Opportunity Commission (EEOC) to establish definitions, rules, and guidelines for compliance with those laws. Sometimes an existing agency is assigned the responsibility for new legislation implementation and enforcement. **For Example,** the Department of Labor has been assigned the responsibility to handle the whistle-blower protection provisions of Sarbanes-Oxley that provide protection against retaliation and/or termination to those who report financial chicanery at their companies. The Department of Labor has been in existence for almost a century, but it was assigned a new responsibility and given new jurisdiction by Congress.

(B) Agency Research of the Problem. After jurisdiction is established, the agency has the responsibility to research the issues and various avenues of regulation for implementing the statutory framework. As the agency does so, it determines the cost and benefit of the problems, issues, and solutions. The study may be done by the agency itself, or it may be completed by someone hired by the agency. **For Example,** before red lights were required equipment in the rear windows of all cars, the Department of Transportation developed a study using taxicabs with the red lights in the rear windows and found that the accident rate for rear-end collisions with taxicabs was reduced dramatically. The study provided justification for the need for regulation as well as the type of regulation itself.

(C) Proposed Regulations. Following a study, the agency proposes regulations, which must be published. To provide publicity for all regulations, the **Federal Register Act**[16] provides that proposed administrative regulation be published in the ***Federal Register***. This is a government publication published five days a week that lists all administrative regulations, all presidential proclamations and executive orders, and other documents and classes of documents that the president or Congress directs to be published.

The Federal Register Act provides that printing an administrative regulation in the *Federal Register* is public notice of the contents of the regulation to persons subject to it or affected by it, but in addition, the Regulatory Flexibility Act,[17] passed during the Reagan administration, requires that all proposed rules be published in the trade journals of those trades that will be affected by the proposed rules. **For Example,** any changes in federal regulations on real property closings and escrows have to be published in real estate broker trade magazines. In addition to the public notice of the proposed rule, the agency must also include a "regulatory flexibility analysis" that "shall describe the impact of the proposed rule on small entities."[18] The goal of this portion of the APA was to be certain that small businesses were aware of proposed regulatory rules and their cost impact.

E-Commerce & Cyberlaw

Peer-to-Peer Sharing and the FCC's Authority

Several subscribers to Comcast's Internet services discovered that the company was interfering with their use of peer-to-peer networking applications. The subscribers asked the FCC to regulate the Internet management practices of Comcast. However, the court held that there was no statutory authority that permitted the FCC to regulate the internal practices of communication providers. **[*Comcast Corp. v. F.C.C.,* 600 F.3d 642 (C.A.D.C. 2010)]**

[16] 44 U.S.C. §1505 *et seq.*
[17] 5 U.S.C. §601 *et seq.*
[18] 5 U.S.C. §603(a).

Motor Vehicles Manufacturers Ass'n v. State Farm Mutual Ins. Co., 463 U.S. 29 (1983)

Seats Belts and Air Bags and Rules, Oh My!

The U.S. Department of Transportation (DOT), charged with enforcing the National Traffic and Motor Vehicle Safety Act of 1966 and reducing auto accidents, passed Standard 208 in 1967, which required that all cars be equipped with seat belts. When another study showed the DOT that people did not use the belts, the department began a study of passive restraint systems which showed that these devices—automatic seat belts and air bags—could prevent approximately 12,000 deaths a year and over 100,000 serious injuries.

In 1972, after many hearings and comments, the DOT passed a regulation requiring some type of passive restraint system on all vehicles manufactured after 1975. Because of changes in directors of the DOT and the unfavorable economic climate in the auto industry, the requirements for passive restraints were postponed. In 1981, the department proposed a rescission of the passive restraint rule. After receiving written comments and holding public hearings, the agency concluded there was no longer a basis for reliably predicting that passive restraints increased safety levels or decreased accidents. Furthermore, the agency found it would cost $1 billion to implement the rule, and it was unwilling to impose such substantial costs on auto manufacturers.

State Farm filed suit on the rescission of the rule on the basis that it was arbitrary and capricious. The Court of Appeals held that the rescission was, in fact, arbitrary and capricious. The auto manufacturers appealed.

JUDICIAL OPINION

WHITE, J.... The ultimate question before us is whether NHTSA's (National Highway Traffic Safety Administration) rescission of the passive restraint requirement of Standard 208 was arbitrary and capricious. We conclude, as did the Court of Appeals, that it was.

The first and most obvious reason for finding the rescission arbitrary and capricious is that NHTSA apparently gave no consideration whatsoever to modifying the standard to require that airbag technology be utilized. Standard 208 sought to achieve automatic crash protection by requiring automobile manufacturers to install either of two passive restraint devices: airbags or automatic seatbelts. There was no suggestion in the long rulemaking process that led to Standard 208 that if only one of these options were feasible, no passive restraint standard should be promulgated. Indeed, the agency's original proposed standard contemplated the installation of inflatable restraints in all cars. Automatic belts were added as a means of complying with the standard because they were believed to be as effective as airbags in achieving the goal of occupant crash protection.

The agency has now determined that the detachable automatic belts will not attain anticipated safety benefits because so many individuals will detach the mechanism. Even if this conclusion were acceptable in its entirety, standing alone it would not justify any more than an amendment of Standard 208 to disallow compliance by means of the only technology which will not provide effective passenger protection. It does not cast doubt on the need for a passive restraint standard or upon the efficacy of airbag technology. In its most recent rulemaking, the agency again acknowledged the life-saving potential of the airbag. Given the effectiveness ascribed to airbag technology by the agency, the mandate of the Safety Act to achieve traffic safety would suggest that the logical response to the faults of detachable seatbelts would be to require the installation of airbags. At the very least this alternative way of achieving objectives of the Act should have been addressed and adequate reasons given for its abandonment. But the agency not only did not require compliance through airbags, it did not even consider the possibility in its 1981 rulemaking. Not one sentence of its rulemaking statement discusses the airbags-only option. We have frequently reiterated that an agency must cogently explain why it had exercised its discretion in a given manner.

For nearly a decade, the automobile industry waged the regulatory equivalent of war against the airbag and lost—the inflatable restraint was proven sufficiently effective. Now the automobile industry has decided to employ a seatbelt system which will not meet the safety objectives of Standard 208. This hardly constitutes cause to revoke the standard itself. Indeed the Motor Vehicle Safety Act was necessary because the industry was not sufficiently responsive to safety concerns. The Act intended that safety standards not depend on current technology and would be "technology-forcing" in the sense of inducing the development of superior safety design.

It is not infrequent that the available data does not settle a regulatory issue and the agency must then exercise its judgment in moving from the facts and probabilities on the record to a policy conclusion. Recognizing that policy making in a complex society must account for uncertainty, however, does not imply that it is sufficient for an agency to merely recite the terms "substantial uncertainty" as a justification for its actions. The agency must explain the evidence which is available, and must offer a "rational connection between the facts found and the choice made."

In this case, the agency's explanation for rescission of the passive restraint requirement is not sufficient to enable us to conclude that the rescission was the product of reasoned decision making. We start with the accepted ground that if used, seatbelts unquestionably would save many thousands of lives and would prevent tens of thousands of crippling injuries.

Continued

Unlike recent regulations we have reviewed, the safety benefits of wearing seatbelts are not in doubt and it is not challenged that were those benefits to accrue, the monetary costs of implementing the standard would be easily justified.

Since 20 to 50 percent of motorists currently wear seatbelts on some occasions, there would seem to be grounds to believe that seatbelt use by occasional users will be substantially increased by the detachable passive belts. Whether this is the case is a matter for the agency to decide, but it must bring its expertise to bear on the question.

An agency's view of what is in the public interest may change, either with or without a change in circumstances. But an agency changing its course must supply a reasoned analysis. We do not accept all of the reasoning of the Court of Appeals but we do conclude that the agency has failed to supply the requisite "reasoned analysis" in this case. Accordingly, we remand the matter to the NHTSA for further consideration consistent with this opinion.

[Affirmed]

QUESTIONS

1. Why does the DOT want to withdraw the regulation?
2. What does the DOT need to withdraw the regulation?
3. Will the regulation go into effect?

(D) PUBLIC COMMENT PERIOD. Following the publication of the proposed rules, the public has the opportunity to provide input on the proposed rules. Called the *public comment period,* this time must last at least 30 days (with certain emergency exceptions) and can consist simply of letters written by those affected that are filed with the agency or of hearings conducted by the agency in Washington, D.C., or at specified locations around the country. An emergency exemption for the 30-day comment period was made when airport security measures and processes were changed following the September 11, 2001, attacks on the World Trade Center and the Pentagon that used domestic, commercial airliners.

(E) OPTIONS AFTER PUBLIC COMMENT. After receiving the public input on the proposed rule, an agency can decide to pass, or promulgate, the rule. The agency can also decide to withdraw the rule. **For Example,** the EEOC had proposed rules on handling religious discrimination in the workplace. The proposed rules, which would have required employers to police those wearing a cross or other religious symbol, met with so much public and employer protest that they were withdrawn. Finally, the agency can decide to modify the rule based on comments and then promulgate or, if the modifications are extensive or material, modify and put the proposed rule back out for public comment again. A diagram of the rule-making process can be found in Figure 6-3.

C. EXECUTIVE POWER OF THE AGENCY

The modern administrative agency has the power to execute the law and to bring proceedings against violators.

6. Enforcement or Execution of the Law

An agency has the power to investigate, to require persons to appear as witnesses, to require witnesses to produce relevant papers and records, and to bring proceedings against those who violate the law. In this connection, the phrase *the law* embraces regulations adopted by an agency as well as statutes and court decisions.

An agency may investigate to determine whether any violation of the law or of its rules generally has occurred. An agency may also investigate to determine whether additional rules need to be adopted, to ascertain the facts with respect to a particular suspected or alleged violation, and to see whether the defendant in a proceeding before it is complying with its final order. An agency may issue subpoenas to obtain information reasonably required by its investigation.[19]

7. Constitutional Limitations on Administrative Investigation

Although administrative agencies have broad enforcement authority, they remain subject to the constitutional protections afforded individuals and businesses.

[19] *EEOC v. Sidley, Austen, Brown and Wood,* 35 F.3d 696 (7th Cir. 2002).

FIGURE 6-3 *Steps in Agency Rulemaking*

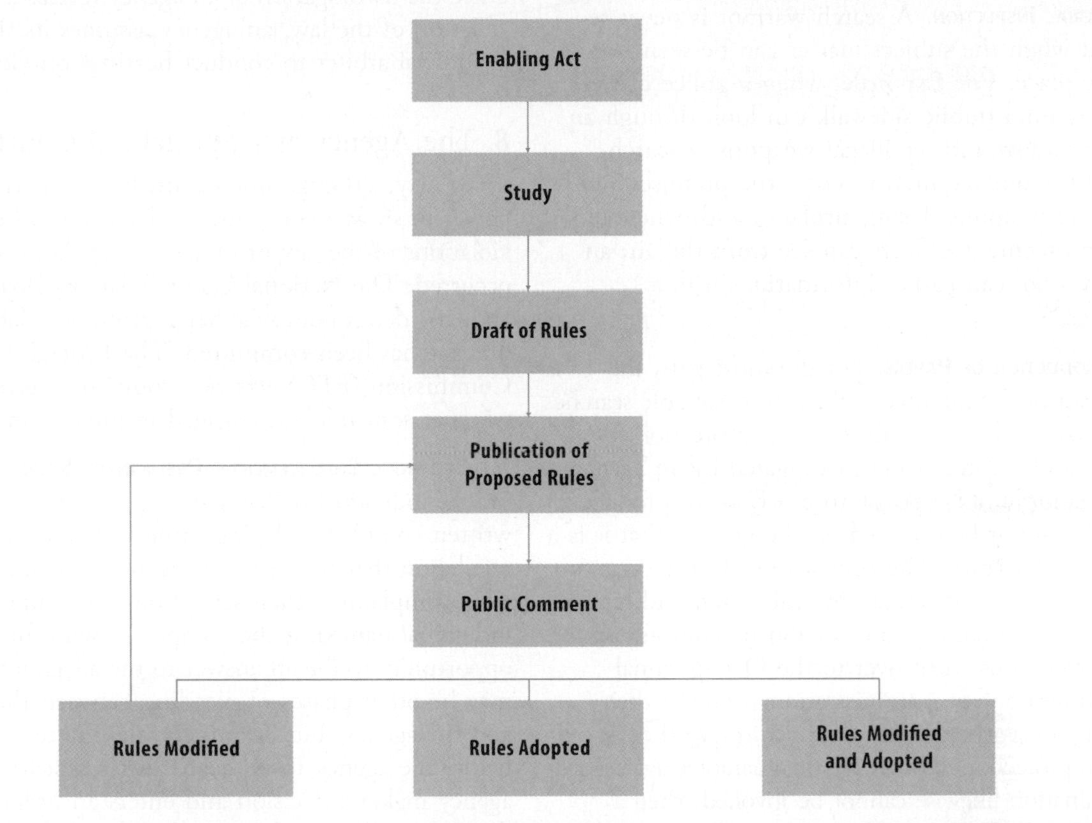

(A) INSPECTION OF PREMISES. Agency officials have the right to conduct inspections, pursuant to the warrant protections afforded by the Fourth Amendment (see Chapter 8). However, when violation of the law is dangerous to health and safety, a workplace inspection without advance notice or a search warrant

Ethics & the Law

Joe the Plumber's Privacy

In 1997, the Internal Revenue Service (IRS) disciplined employees who, out of curiosity, were looking up tax returns of famous people to see who made how much income. The IRS fired 23 employees, disciplined 349, and provided counseling for 472. During the 2008 election, the director of the Ohio Department of Job and Family Services ordered employees to look up the child support payment record of Samuel Joseph Wurzelbacher (Joe the Plumber), a man who had raised a controversial issue to then-candidate Barack Obama. Helen Jones-Kelley, the director, was a donor to the Obama campaign. Employees in the office complained about the search, and the director said, "Our practice is when someone is thrust quickly into the public spotlight, we often take a look." The Ohio Inspector General investigated the use of state computers for the search.

Is this practice so bad? What is wrong with just looking at data accessible at work? Why are we concerned about selective research about private citizens? Does it matter that the information was not released to the public?

is permitted when such a requirement could defeat the purpose of the inspection.

(B) Aerial Inspection. A search warrant is never required when the subject matter can be seen from a public place. **For Example,** when a police officer walking on a public sidewalk can look through an open window and see illegal weapons, a search warrant is not required to enter the premises and seize the weapons. Using airplanes and helicopters, law enforcement officers can see from the air; an agency, too, can gather information in this manner.[20]

(C) Production of Papers. For the most part, the constitutional guarantee against unreasonable searches and seizures does not afford much protection for papers and records being investigated by an agency. **For Example,** a subpoena to testify or to produce records cannot be opposed on the ground that it is a search and seizure. The constitutional protection is limited to cases of actual physical search and seizure rather than obtaining information by compulsion. Employers must turn over to the Occupational Health and Safety Administration (OSHA) their records on workplace injuries and lost workdays.

The protection afforded by the guarantee against self-incrimination likewise cannot be invoked when a corporate employee or officer in control of corporate records is compelled to produce those records even though he or she would be incriminated by them.[21] The privilege against self-incrimination cannot be invoked if records required to be kept by law are involved.

(D) Compliance Verification. To ensure that a particular person or business is obeying the law, including an agency's regulations and orders, the administrative agency may require proof of compliance. At times, the question of compliance may be directly determined by an agency investigation, involving an examination either of a building or plant or of witnesses and documents. An agency may require the regulated person or enterprise to file reports in a specified form.[22]

D. Judicial Power of the Agency

Once the investigation of an agency reveals a potential violation of the law, an agency assumes its third role of judicial arbiter to conduct hearings on violations.

8. The Agency as a Specialized Court

An agency, although not a court by law, may be given power to sit as a court and to determine whether any violations of the law or of agency regulations have occurred. The National Labor Relations Board (NLRB) determines whether a prohibited labor practice has been committed. The Federal Trade Commission (FTC) acts as a court to determine whether someone has engaged in unfair competition.

(A) Beginning Enforcement—Preliminary Steps. Either a private individual or company or an agency may file a written complaint alleging some violation of law or regulation that is within the agency's jurisdiction. This complaint is then served on the company or individual named in the complaint, who then has the opportunity to file an answer to the allegations. There may be other phases of pleading between the parties and the agency, but eventually, the matter comes before the agency to be heard. After a hearing, the agency makes a decision and enters an order either dismissing the complaint or directing remedies or resolutions.

(B) The Administrative Hearing. To satisfy the requirements of due process, an agency handling a complaint must generally give notice and hold a hearing at which all persons affected may be present. A significant difference between an agency hearing and a court hearing is that there is no right of trial by jury before an agency. **For Example,** a workers' compensation board may decide a claim without any jury. Similarly, a case in which an employer protests the unemployment tax rate assigned to her company by a state agency has no right to a jury trial. The lack of a jury does not deny due process (see Chapter 4). An administrative law judge (ALJ) hears the complaint

[20] *Dow Chemical Co. v. United States,* 476 U.S. 1819 (1986).

[21] *Braswell v. United States,* 487 U.S. 99 (1988); See also *Armstrong v. Guccione,* 470 F.3d 89 (2nd Cir. 2006).

[22] *United States v. Morton Salt Co.,* 338 U.S. 632 (1950).

and has the authority to swear witnesses, take testimony, make evidentiary rulings, and make a decision to recommend to the agency heads for action.

An agency hearing is ordinarily not subject to the rules of evidence. Another difference between an administrative hearing and a judicial determination is that an agency may be authorized to make an initial determination without holding a hearing. If its conclusion is challenged, the agency then holds a hearing. This procedural difference has important practical consequences because the result is that fewer persons go to the trouble of seeking such a hearing, which reduces the number of hearings and the amount of litigation in which an agency becomes involved. The government saves money and time with this abbreviated process.

Civil servants of administrative agencies have greater protections when it comes to due process. The Supreme Court has held that because a civil service employee may be removed only for cause, it is a denial of due process for a statute to authorize an agency to remove the employee without a hearing.[23] Just giving the employee the right to appeal such action is not sufficient. There must be some form of hearing prior to removing the employee to determine that there were not errors in the administrative action.

(c) Streamlined Procedure: Consent Decrees. **Informal settlements** or **consent decrees** are practical devices to cut across the procedures already outlined. In many instances, an alleged wrongdoer informally notified that a complaint has been made is willing to change. An agency's informing an alleged wrongdoer of the charge before filing any formal complaint is sound public relations, as well as expeditious policy. A matter that has already gone into the formal hearing stage may also be terminated by agreement, and a stipulation or consent decree may be filed setting forth the terms of the agreement. The Administrative Dispute Resolution Act of 1990 encourages the streamlining of the regulatory process and authorizes federal agencies to use alternative means of dispute resolution.[24]

(d) Form of Administrative Decision. When an administrative agency makes a decision, it usually files an opinion that sets forth findings of facts and reasons for that decision. In some instances, a statute expressly requires this type of opinion, but agencies usually file opinions so that the parties and the court (in the event of an appeal) will understand the agency's action and reasoning.[25]

9. Punishment and Enforcement Powers of Agencies

(a) Penalty. Within the last few decades, agencies have increasingly been given the power to impose a penalty and to issue orders that are binding on a regulated party unless an appeal is taken to a court, which reverses the administrative decision. **For Example,** the Occupational Safety and Health Act of 1970 provides for the assessment of civil penalties against employers who fail to end dangerous working conditions when ordered to do so by the administrative agency created by that statute.[26]

(b) Cease-and-Desist Order. Environmental protection statutes adopted by states commonly give a state agency the power to assess a penalty for violating environmental protection regulations. As an illustration of the issuance of binding orders, the FTC can issue a **cease-and-desist order** to stop a practice that it decides is improper. This order to stop is binding unless reversed on an appeal. **For Example,** the FTC can order a company to stop making claims in ads that have been determined by that agency to be deceptive.

10. Exhaustion of Administrative Remedies

All parties interacting with an agency must follow the procedure specified by the law. No appeal to a court is possible until the agency has acted on the party's matter before it. As a matter of policy, parties are required to exhaust administrative remedies before they may go into court or take an appeal.

As long as an agency is acting within the scope of its authority or jurisdiction, a party cannot appeal before the agency has made a final decision. The fact that the

[23] *Cleveland Board of Education v. Loudermill,* 470 U.S. 532 (1985); *Darr v. Town of Telluride, Colo.,* 495 F.3d 1243 (10th Cir. 2007).

[24] 5 U.S.C. §571 *et seq.*

[25] *Jordan v. Civil Service Bd., Charlotte,* 570 S.E.2d 912 (N.C. App. 2002).

[26] 29 U.S.C. §651 *et seq.*

complaining party does not want the agency to decide the matter or is afraid that the agency will reach a wrong decision is not grounds for bypassing the agency by going to court before the agency has acted.

Exceptions to the **exhaustion-of-administrative remedies** requirement are: (1) available remedies that provide no genuine opportunity for adequate relief; (2) irreparable injury that could occur if immediate judicial relief is not provided; (3) an appeal to the administrative agency that would be useless; or (4) a substantial constitutional question that the plaintiff has raised.

11. Appeal from Administrative Action and Finality of Administrative Determination

The statute creating the modern administrative agency generally provides that an appeal may be taken from the administrative decision to a particular court. The statute may provide the basis for an appeal. However, judicial precedent holds that courts may review administrative agency decisions on the bases covered in the following sections.

(A) Procedural Issues. If the procedure that an agency is to follow is specified by law, a decision of the agency that was made without following that procedure will be set aside and the matter sent back to the agency to proceed according to the required law.[27] An agency's actions, whether enforcement or rule promulgation, can be set aside if the agency has not followed the procedures required for rule making or, in the case of enforcement, the due process rights of the charged business or individual.

(B) Substantive Law or Fact Issues. When the question that an agency decides is a question of law, the court on appeal will reverse the agency if the court disagrees with the legal interpretation.[28] Courts tend to accept the agency's interpretation so long as it was reasonable even though it was not the only interpretation that could have been made.

A court will not reverse an agency's decision merely because the court would have made a different decision based on the same facts.[29] Because most disputes before an agency are based on questions of fact, the net result is that the agency's decision will be final in most cases.

Courts must give administrative agencies the freedom to do the work delegated to them and should not intervene unless the agency action is clearly unreasonable or arbitrary (see below). The agency action is presumed proper, and a person seeking reversal of the agency action has the burden to prove a basis for reversal.[30]

(C) Beyond the Jurisdiction of the Agency. When the question is whether an administrative action is in harmony with the policy of the statute creating the agency, an appellate court will sustain the administrative action if substantial evidence supports it.

(D) Arbitrary and Capricious. When an agency changes its prior decisions and customary actions, it must give its reasons. In the absence of such an explanation, a reviewing court cannot tell whether the agency changed its interpretation of the law for a valid reason or has made a mistake. The absence of an explanation means the agency action is arbitrary and requires reversal.[31]

A decision involving agency discretion will not be reversed in the absence of an error of law or a clear abuse of, or the arbitrary or capricious exercise of, discretion. The courts reason that because agency members were appointed on the basis of expert ability, it would be absurd for the court, which is unqualified technically to make a decision in the matter, to step in and determine whether the agency made the proper choice. Courts will not do so unless the agency has clearly acted wrongly, arbitrarily, or capriciously. As a practical matter, an agency's action is rarely found to be arbitrary or capricious. As long as an agency has followed proper procedure, the fact that the court disagrees with the agency's conclusion does not make that conclusion arbitrary or capricious.

In areas in which economic or technical matters are involved, it is generally sufficient that the agency had a reasonable basis for its decision. A court will not attempt to second-guess the agency about complex criteria with which an administrative agency is intimately familiar. However, if an agency's

[27] *Tingler v. State Board of Cosmetology*, 814 S.W.2d 683 (Mo. App. 1991).

[28] *Wallace v. Iowa State Bd. of Educ.*, 770 N.W.2d 344 (Iowa 2009).

[29] *Dorchester Associates LLC v. District of Columbia Bd. of Zoning Adjustment*, 976 A.2d 200 (D.C. 2009).

[30] See note 29.

[31] *Lorillard Tobacco Co. v. Roth*, 786 N.E.2d 7 (N.Y. App. 2003).

Hornbeck Offshore Services, L.L.C. et al., v. Salazar, 696 F. Supp. 2d 627 (E.D. La. 2010)

Drilling Down to Arbitrary and Capricious Rules

Hornbeck and others (plaintiffs) provide services to support offshore oil and gas drilling, exploration, and production activities in the Gulf of Mexico. Kenneth Salazar is the Secretary of the Department of Interior (DOI), a federal agency that includes the Minerals Management.

Following the BP Deepwater Horizon drilling platform explosion on April 20, 2010, and the resulting devastation and unprecedented disaster, the president asked DOI to conduct a study to determine what steps were needed to be taken to prevent another problem with oil rigs in the Gulf.

DOI did a 30-day study, consulting respected experts from state and federal governments, academic institutions, and industry and advocacy organizations. On May 27, 2010, DOI issued a Report that recommended a six-month moratorium on permits for new wells and an immediate halt to drilling operations on the 33 permitted wells in the Gulf of Mexico. The DOI Report also stated that "the recommendations contained in this report have been peer-reviewed by seven experts identified by the National Academy of Engineering." The experts pointedly observed that this statement was misleading and called it a "misrepresentation." Although the experts agreed with the safety recommendations contained in the body of the main report, five of the National Academy of Engineering experts and three of the other experts publicly stated that they "do not agree with the six month blanket moratorium" on floating drilling. They envisioned a more limited kind of moratorium, but a blanket moratorium was added after their final review and was never agreed to by them. The plaintiffs moved for a preliminary injunction against the DOI moratorium.

JUDICIAL OPINION

FELDMAN, District Judge.…The Administrative Procedure Act authorizes judicial review of final agency action. The APA cautions that an agency action may only be set aside if it is "arbitrary, capricious, an abuse of discretion, or not otherwise in accordance with law." The reviewing court must decide whether the agency acted within the scope of its authority, "whether the decision was based on a consideration of the relevant factors and whether there has been a clear error of judgment."

Normally, an agency rule would be arbitrary and capricious if the agency has relied on factors which Congress has not intended it to consider, entirely failed to consider an important aspect of the problem, offered an explanation for its decision that runs counter to the evidence before the agency, or is so implausible that it could not be ascribed to a difference in view or the product of agency expertise.

After reviewing the Secretary's Report and the Moratorium Memorandum, the Court is unable to divine or fathom a relationship between the findings and the immense scope of the moratorium. The Report describes the offshore oil industry in the Gulf and offers many compelling recommendations to improve safety. But it offers no time line for implementation. The Report patently lacks any analysis of the asserted fear of threat of irreparable injury or safety hazards posed by the 33 permitted rigs also reached by the moratorium. It is incident-specific and driven: Deepwater Horizon and BP only. None others. While the Report notes the increase in deepwater drilling over the past ten years and the increased safety risk associated with deepwater drilling, the parameters of "deepwater" remain confused. And drilling elsewhere simply seems driven by political or social agendas on all sides. The Report seems to define "deepwater" as drilling beyond a depth of 1,000 feet by referencing the increased difficulty of drilling beyond this depth; similarly, the shallowest depth referenced in the maps and facts included in the Report is "less than 1,000 feet." But while there is no mention of the 500 feet depth anywhere in the Report itself, "deepwater" [is now anything] more than 500 feet.

The Court recognizes that the compliance of the thirty-three affected rigs with current government regulations may be irrelevant if the regulations are insufficient or if MMS (Minerals Management Services), the government's own agent, itself is suspected of being corrupt or incompetent. Nonetheless, the Secretary's determination that a six-month moratorium on issuance of new permits and on drilling by the 33 rigs is necessary does not seem to be fact-specific and refuses to take into measure the safety records of those others in the Gulf. There is no evidence presented indicating that the Secretary balanced the concern for environmental safety with the policy of making leases available for development. There is no suggestion that the Secretary considered any alternatives: for example, an individualized suspension of activities on target rigs until they reached compliance with the new federal regulations said to be recommended for immediate implementation. The Deepwater Horizon oil spill is an unprecedented, sad, ugly, and inhuman disaster. What seems clear is that the federal government has been pressed by what happened on the Deepwater Horizon into an otherwise sweeping confirmation that all Gulf deepwater drilling activities put us all in a universal threat of irreparable harm. While the implementation of regulations and a new culture of safety are supportable by the Report and the documents presented, the blanket moratorium, with no parameters, seems to assume that because one rig failed and although no one yet fully knows why, all companies and rigs drilling

Continued

new wells over 500 feet also universally present an imminent danger.

[t]he Court has found the plaintiffs would likely succeed in showing that the agency's decision was arbitrary and capricious. An invalid agency decision to suspend drilling of wells in depths of over 500 feet simply cannot justify the immeasurable effect on the plaintiffs, the local economy, the Gulf region, and the critical present-day aspect of the availability of domestic energy in this country.

The plaintiffs' motion for preliminary injunction is granted.

QUESTIONS

1. Why is the problem with the experts' objections important in determining whether DOI's moratorium was arbitrary and capricious?
2. What is the significance of the difference between the factual information in the report and the terms of the moratorium?
3. What does the court see as alternatives to the moratorium?

recommendation parts ways with the underlying factual findings or the conclusions of its experts, then the court is likely to find that the actions of the agency were arbitrary and capricious. The judicial attitude is that for protection from laws and regulations that are unwise, improvident, or out of harmony with a particular school of thought, the people must resort to the ballot box, not to the court.

(E) CONSTITUTIONAL RIGHTS. Challenges to administrative agency rules and actions can also be based in constitutional rights.[32] For example, agency restrictions on language or religious freedom have been successfully challenged in court. EEOC regulations on employees wearing religious jewelry (such as necklaces with crosses) were withdrawn after the agency realized through congressional actions that the regulations could not survive a constitutional challenge. The *F.C.C. v. Fox Television Stations, Inc.* case deals with the issue of the constitutionality of an FCC action against broadcast networks.

F.C.C. v. Fox Television Stations, Inc., 132 S.Ct. 2307 (2012)

The Obscenity Case That Has Been Around As Long As Cher

In a case that has been around almost as long as Cher, the U. S. Supreme Court, once again, issued a decision related to three FCC charges against Fox and ABC Television. First, in the 2002 Billboard Music Awards, broadcast by Fox Television, the singer Cher exclaimed during an unscripted acceptance speech: "I've also had my critics for the last 40 years saying that I was on my way out every year. Right. So f * * * 'em." At the 2003 Billboard Music Awards, Nicole Richie made the following unscripted remark while presenting an award: "Have you ever tried to get cow s* * * out of a Prada purse? It's not so f * * *ing simple." The third incident involved an episode of *NYPD Blue*, a regular television show broadcast by respondent ABC Television Network. The episode, broadcast on February 25, 2003, showed the nude buttocks of an adult female character for approximately seven seconds and for a moment the side of her breast. During the scene, in which the character was preparing to take a shower, a child portraying her boyfriend's son entered the bathroom. A moment of awkwardness followed. The FCC received indecency complaints about all three broadcasts.

After these incidents, but before the FCC issued Notices of Apparent Liability to Fox and ABC, it issued a decision sanctioning NBC for a comment made by the singer Bono during the 2003 Golden Globe Awards. Upon winning the award for Best Original Song, Bono exclaimed: "'This is really, really, f* * *ing brilliant. Really, really great.'" The FCC found that the use of the F-word was "one of the most vulgar, graphic and explicit descriptions of sexual activity in the English language," and found that "any use of that word or a variation, in any context, inherently" indecent. The FCC then found that both Fox and ABC had violated commission standards for decency.

The networks appealed the findings of indecency and their fines ($1.4 million each). The U.S. Supreme Court (*FCC v. Fox Television Stations, Inc.* (Fox 1), 556 U.S. 502

[32] *CBS Corp. v. F.C.C.*, 663 F.3d 122 (3rd Cir 2011).

Continued

(2009) held that the FCC's findings were not arbitrary nor capricious and remanded the case for findings related to the network's First Amendment challenges to the fines. On remand, the Court of Appeals found that the FCC indecency policy failed to give broadcasters sufficient notice of what would be considered indecent. The Court of Appeals found that the commission was inconsistent as to which words it deemed patently offensive. The FCC standard was held to be void for vagueness. The FCC appealed.

JUDICIAL OPINION

KENNEDY, Justice…In 2001, the Commission issued a policy statement intended "to provide guidance to the broadcast industry regarding [its] caselaw interpreting 18 U.S.C. §1464 and [its] enforcement policies with respect to broadcast indecency." In that document the Commission restated that for material to be indecent it must depict sexual or excretory organs or activities and be patently offensive as measured by contemporary community standards for the broadcast medium.

A fundamental principle in our legal system is that laws which regulate persons or entities must give fair notice of conduct that is forbidden or required. It requires the invalidation of laws that are impermissibly vague. A conviction or punishment fails to comply with due process if the statute or regulation under which it is obtained "fails to provide a person of ordinary intelligence fair notice of what is prohibited, or is so standardless that it authorizes or encourages seriously discriminatory enforcement."

Regulated parties should know what is required of them so they may act accordingly. Precision and guidance are necessary so that those enforcing the law do not act in an arbitrary or discriminatory way. When speech is involved, rigorous adherence to those requirements is necessary to ensure that ambiguity does not chill protected speech.

The broadcasters claim they did not have, and do not have, sufficient notice of what is proscribed. Under the 2001 Guidelines in force when the broadcasts occurred, a key consideration was " 'whether the material dwell[ed] on or repeat[ed] at length' " the offending description or depiction. In the challenged orders now under review the Commission applied [a] new principle and determined that fleeting expletives and a brief moment of indecency were actionably indecent. The Commission policy in place at the time of the broadcasts gave no notice to Fox or ABC that a fleeting expletive or a brief shot of nudity could be actionably indecent; yet Fox and ABC were found to be in violation. The Commission's lack of notice to Fox and ABC that its interpretation had changed so the fleeting moments of indecency contained in their broadcasts were a violation.

As for the two fleeting expletives, the Government concedes that "Fox did not have reasonable notice at the time of the broadcasts that the Commission would consider non-repeated expletives indecent." The Government argues, nonetheless, that Fox "cannot establish unconstitutional vagueness on that basis ... because the Commission did not impose a sanction where Fox lacked such notice." This "policy of forbearance," as the Government calls it, does not suffice to make the issue moot.

Commission sanctions on broadcasters for indecent material are widely publicized. The challenged orders could have an adverse impact on Fox's reputation that audiences and advertisers alike are entitled to take into account.

With respect to ABC, the Government with good reason does not argue no sanction was imposed. The fine against ABC and its network affiliates for the seven seconds of nudity was nearly $1.24 million. The Government argues instead that ABC had notice that the scene in *NYPD Blue* would be considered indecent in light of a 1960 decision where the Commission declared that the "televising of nudes might well raise a serious question of programming contrary to 18 U.S.C. §1464." An isolated and ambiguous statement from a 1960 Commission decision does not suffice for the fair notice required when the Government intends to impose over a $1 million fine for allegedly impermissible speech. The Commission, furthermore, had released decisions before sanctioning ABC that declined to find isolated and brief moments of nudity actionably indecent. The Government can point to nothing that would have given ABC affirmative notice that its broadcast would be considered actionably indecent.

The Commission failed to give Fox or ABC fair notice prior to the broadcasts in question that fleeting expletives and momentary nudity could be found actionably indecent. Therefore, the Commission's standards as applied to these broadcasts were vague, and the Commission's orders must be set aside.

This opinion leaves the Commission free to modify its current indecency policy in light of its determination of the public interest and applicable legal requirements. And it leaves the courts free to review the current policy or any modified policy in light of its content and application.

The judgments of the United States Court of Appeals for the Second Circuit are vacated, and the cases are remanded for further proceedings consistent with the principles set forth in this opinion.

QUESTIONS

1. What must the FCC now do to make the standards constitutional?
2. Why were the cases taken up on appeal so many times?

(f) Arbitrary Enforcement Actions. Because of limited funding and staff, an agency must exercise discretion in deciding which cases it should handle. Ordinarily, a court will not reverse an agency's decision to do nothing about a particular complaint.[33] That is, the courts will not override an agency's decision to do nothing. Exceptions include acting arbitrarily in those enforcement actions as when an agency refuses to act in circumstances in which action is warranted and necessary.

12. Liability of the Agency

The decision of an agency may cause substantial loss to a business by increasing its operating costs or by making a decision that later is shown to be harmful to the economy. An agency is not liable for such loss when it has acted in good faith in the exercise of discretionary powers. An administrator who wrongly denies a person the benefit of a government program is not personally liable to that person.

LawFlix

Clear and Present Danger (1994) PG-13

The struggles of Jack Ryan involve more than Colombian drug lords; he must battle the political appointees and their overstepping of their agency's authority. The relationship between agencies and Congress is also depicted in the film.

[33] *Heckler v. Chaney*, 470 U.S. 821 (1985).

MAKE THE CONNECTION

SUMMARY

The administrative agency is unique because it combines the three functions that are kept separate under our traditional governmental system: legislative, executive, and judicial. By virtue of legislative power, an agency adopts regulations that have the force of law, although agency members are not elected by those subject to the regulations. By virtue of the executive power, an agency carries out and enforces the regulations, makes investigations, and requires the production of documents. By virtue of the judicial power, an agency acts as a court to determine whether a violation of any regulation has occurred. To some extent, an agency is restricted by constitutional limitations in inspecting premises and requiring the production of papers. These limitations, however, have a very narrow application in agency actions. When an agency acts as a judge, a jury trial is not required, nor must ordinary courtroom procedures be followed. Typically, an agency gives notice to the person claimed to be acting improperly, and a hearing is then held before the agency. When the agency has determined that there has been a violation, it may order that the violation stop. Under some statutes, the agency may go further and impose a penalty on the violator.

No appeal from an administrative agency's action can be made until every step available before the agency has been taken; that is, the administrative remedy must first be exhausted. An agency's actions can be reversed by a court if the agency exceeded its authority, the decision is not based in law or fact, the decision is arbitrary and capricious, the decision violates the laws or the rights of those affected by the agency's rule or actions, or, finally, the agency violated procedural steps.

Protection from secret government is provided by Sunshine laws that afford the right to know what most administrative agency records contain; by the requirement that most agency meetings be open to the public; by the invitation to the public to take part in rulemaking; and by publicity given, through publication in the *Federal Register* and trade publications, to the guidelines followed by the agency and the regulations it has adopted.

LEARNING OUTCOMES

After studying this chapter, you should be able to clearly explain:

A. Nature of the Administrative Agency

LO.1 Describe the nature and purpose of administrative agencies

See Section A(2) for a discussion of the unique nature of agencies, p. 92.

B. Legislative Power of the Agency

LO.2 Discuss the legislative or rulemaking power of administrative agencies

See the *EPA* case on pp. 94–95.

C. Executive Power of the Agency

LO.3 Explain the executive or enforcement function of administrative agencies

See the *FCC* case on pp. 104–105.

D. Judicial Power of the Agency

LO.4 Discuss the judicial power of administrative agencies including the rule on exhaustion of administrative remedies

See the *Salazar* case on pp. 103–104.

KEY TERMS

administrative agency
administrative law
Administrative Procedure Act
cease-and-desist order
consent decrees
exhaustion-of-administrative remedies
Federal Register
Federal Register Act
Freedom of Information Act
informal settlements
open meeting law

QUESTIONS AND CASE PROBLEMS

1. Following the events of September 11, 2001, in which four airplanes crashed as a result of the presence of terrorists on those flights, the FAA concluded that it needed to implement new procedures for airports and flights. The new procedures for security and flights took effect when the airports reopened five days later. Why did the FAA not need to go through the promulgation and public comment processes and time periods to have the new rules take effect?

2. The FDA was challenged by tobacco companies for its new rules that required the tobacco companies to put one of the FDA's 12 picture labels on its packaging. The tobacco companies argued that their First Amendment rights were violated by the rules, forcing them to speak in a certain way using government-mandated materials. The new labels were promulgated by both the FDA and the Department of Health and Human Services (HHS) pursuant to authority granted by Congress in 2009 under the Family Smoking Prevention and Tobacco Control Act.

   Under the law, the following nine textual statements were to be included on cigarette labels:

   WARNING: Cigarettes are addictive.

   WARNING: Tobacco smoke can harm your children.

   WARNING: Cigarettes cause fatal lung disease.

   WARNING: Cigarettes cause cancer.

   WARNING: Cigarettes cause strokes and heart disease.

   WARNING: Smoking during pregnancy can harm your baby.

   WARNING: Smoking can kill you.

   WARNING: Tobacco smoke causes fatal lung diseases in nonsmokers.

   WARNING: Quitting smoking now greatly reduces serious risks to your health.

The act required that these warnings and graphic labels take up 50 percent of the cigarette package label and 20 percent of all cigarette ads.

After publishing the proposed rule and receiving more than 1,700 comments, the FDA published its final rule in June 2011. Explain how the tobacco companies could challenge the rules. Discuss whether the rules will be set aside. [In the case of *R.J. Reynolds Tobacco Company et al. v. FDA et al.,* 696 F.3d 1205 (D.C. Cir.)]

3. The Tacoma-Pierce County Health Department conducted an investigation into the quality of care provided by ambulance service providers in its jurisdiction. On the basis of that investigation, the department issued a set of temporary rules and regulations that established minimum requirements for equipment, drugs, and service availability for ambulance service providers in Pierce County. The *Tacoma News* wanted to publish an article on the matter and sought discovery of everything that had led to the adoption of the regulations, including all details of the investigation made by the health department. The health department objected to disclosing the names of the persons who had volunteered information on which the department had based its action and the names of the ambulance companies. Were the names subject to a Freedom of Information Act (FOIA) request? [*Tacoma News, Inc. v. Tacoma-Pierce County Health Dept.,* 778 P.2d 1066 (Wash. App.)]

4. Congress adopted a law to provide insurance to protect wheat farmers. The agency in charge of the program adopted regulations to govern applications for this insurance. These regulations were published in the *Federal Register.* Merrill applied for insurance, but his application did not comply with the regulations. He claimed that he was not bound by the regulations because he never knew they had been adopted. Is he bound by the regulations? [*Federal Crop Ins. Corp. v. Merrill,* 332 U.S. 380]

5. Santa Monica adopted a rent control ordinance authorizing the Rent Control Board to set the amount of rents that could be charged. At a hearing before it, the board determined that McHugh was charging his tenants a rent higher than the maximum allowed. McHugh claimed that the action of the board was improper because there was no jury trial. Is McHugh correct? Why or why not? [*McHugh v. Santa Monica Rent Control Board,* 777 P.2d 911 (Cal.)]

6. New York City's charter authorized the New York City Board of Health to adopt a health code that it declared to have the force and effect of law. The board adopted a code that provided for the fluoridation of the public water supply. A suit was brought to enjoin the carrying out of this program on the grounds that it was unconstitutional and that money could not be spent to carry out such a program in the absence of a statute authorizing the expenditure. It was also claimed that the fluoridation program was unconstitutional because there were other means of reducing tooth decay; fluoridation was discriminatory by benefiting only children; it unlawfully imposed medication on children without their consent; and fluoridation was or may be dangerous to health. Was the code's provision valid? [*Paduano v. City of New York,* 257 N.Y.S.2d 531]

7. What is the *Federal Register?* What role does it play in rulemaking? What is the difference between the *Federal Register* and the Code of Federal Regulations?

8. The Consumer Product Safety Commission is reconsidering a rule it first proposed in 1997 that would require child-resistant caps on household products, including cosmetics. When the rule was first proposed in 1997, it was resisted by the cosmetics industry and abandoned. However, in May 2001, a 16-month-old baby died after drinking baby oil from a bottle with a pull-tab cap.

   The proposed rule would cover products such as baby oil and suntan lotion and any products containing hydrocarbons such as cleansers and spot removers. The danger, according to the commission, is simply the inhalation by children, not necessarily the actual ingestion of the products. Five children have died from inhaling such fumes since 1993, and 6,400 children under the age of five were brought into emergency rooms and/or hospitalized for treatment after breathing in hydrocarbons. There is no medical treatment for the inhalation of hydrocarbons.

Several companies in the suntan oil/lotion industry have supported the new regulations. The head of a consumer group has said, "We know these products cause death and injury. That is all we need to know."[34]

What process must the CPSC follow to promulgate the rules? What do you think of the consumer group head's statement? Will that statement alone justify the rulemaking?

9. The *Federal Register* contained the following provision from the Environmental Protection Agency on January 14, 2002:

We, the U.S. Fish and Wildlife Service (Service), announce the re-opening of the comment period on the proposed listing of Lomatium cookii *(Cook's lomatium) and* Limnanthes floccosa ssp. grandiflora *(large-flowered wooly meadowfoam) as endangered species under the Endangered Species Act of 1973, as amended (Act). We are re-opening the comment period to provide the public an opportunity to review additional information on the status, abundance, and distribution of these plants, and to request additional information and comments from the public regarding the proposed rule. Comments previously submitted need not be resubmitted as they will be incorporated into the public record as part of this extended comment period; all comments will be fully considered in the final rule.*

DATES: We will accept public comments until March 15, 2002.

What was the EPA doing and why? What could those who had concerns do at that point?

10. Macon County Landfill Corp. applied for permission to expand the boundaries of its landfill. Tate and others opposed the application. After a number of hearings, the appropriate agency granted the requested permission to expand. Tate appealed and claimed that the agency had made a wrong decision on the basis of the evidence presented. Will the court determine whether the correct decision was made? [*Tate v. Illinois Pollution Control Board,* 544 N.E.2d 1176 (Ill. App.)]

11. The planning commissioner and a real estate developer planned to meet to discuss rezoning certain land that would permit the real estate developer to construct certain buildings not allowed under the then-existing zoning law. A homeowners association claimed it had the right to be present at the meeting. This claim was objected to on the theory that the state's Open Meetings Act applied only to meetings of specified government units and did not extend to a meeting between one of them and an outsider. Was this objection valid?

12. The Michigan Freedom of Information Act declares that it is the state's policy to give all persons full information about the actions of the government and that "the people shall be informed so that they may participate in the democratic process." The union of clerical workers at Michigan State University requested the trustees of the university to give them the names and addresses of persons making monetary donations to the university. Michigan State objected because the disclosure of addresses was a violation of the right of privacy. Decide. [*Clerical-Technical Union of Michigan State University v. Board of Trustees of Michigan State University,* 475 N.W.2d 373 (Mich.)]

13. The Department of Health and Human Services has proposed new guidelines for the interpretation of federal statutes on gifts, incentives, and other benefits bestowed on physicians by pharmaceutical companies. The areas on which the interpretation focused follow:
    - Paying doctors to act as consultants or market researchers for prescription drugs
    - Paying pharmacies fees to switch patients to new drugs
    - Providing grants, scholarships, and anything more than nominal gifts to physicians for time, information sessions, and so on, on new drugs[35]

    The Office of Inspector General is handling the new rules interpretation and has established a public comment period of 60 days. Explain the

[34] Julian E. Barnes, "Safety Caps Are Considered for Cosmetics," *New York Times*, October 10, 2001, C1, C8.

[35] See 67 *Federal Register* 62057, October 3, 2002. Go to **www.oig.hhs.gov**. See also Robert Pear, "U.S. Warning to Drug Makers Over Payments," *New York Times*, October 1, 2002, A1, A23; Julie Appleby, "Feds Warn Drugmakers: Gifts to Doctors May Be Illegal," *USA Today*, October 2, 2002, 1A.

purpose of the public comment period. What ethical issues do the regulations attempt to address?

14. San Diego Air Sports (SDAS) Center operates a sports parachuting business in Otay Mesa, California. SDAS offers training to beginning parachutists and facilitates recreational jumping for experienced parachutists. It indicates that the majority of SDAS jumps occur at altitudes in excess of 5,800 feet. The jump zone used by SDAS overlaps the San Diego Traffic Control Area (TCA). Although the aircraft carrying the parachutists normally operate outside the TCA, the parachutists themselves are dropped through it. Thus, the air traffic controllers must approve each jump.

    In July 1987, an air traffic controller in San Diego filed an Unsatisfactory Condition Report with the Federal Aviation Administration (FAA), complaining of the strain that parachuting was putting on the controllers and raising safety concerns. The report led to a staff study of parachute jumping within the San Diego TCA. This was followed by a letter in March 1988 from the FAA to SDAS, informing SDAS that "[e]ffective immediately parachute jumping within or into the San Diego TCA in the Otay Reservoir Jump Zone will not be authorized." The FAA stated that the letter was final and appealable. SDAS challenged the letter in federal court on grounds that it constituted rulemaking without compliance with required Administrative Procedure Act (APA) procedures. Who is correct in this dispute and why? [*San Diego Air Sports Center, Inc. v. FAA,* 887 F.2d 966 (9th Cir.)]

15. The Endangered Species Act (ESA) charges the National Marine Fisheries Service (a federal agency) with the duty to "ensure" that any proposed action by the Council does not "jeopardize" any threatened or endangered species. The Steller sea lion is on the list of endangered species. The agency developed a North Pacific marine fishery plan that permitted significant harvest of fish by commercial fisheries in the area. Greenpeace, an environmental group, challenged the agency on the grounds that the plan was not based on a sufficient number of biological studies on the impact of the allowed fishing on the Steller sea lion. Greenpeace's biologic opinion concluded that the fishery plan would reduce the level of food for the sea lions by about 40 percent to 60 percent, if the juvenile fish were not counted in that figure. Greenpeace's expert maintained that counting juvenile fish was misleading because they were not capable of reproducing and the government agency's figure was, as a result, much lower at 22 percent. What would Greenpeace need to show to be successful in challenging the agency's fishery plan? [*Greenpeace, American Oceans Campaign v. National Marine Fisheries Service,* 237 F. Supp. 2d 1181 (W.D. Wash.)]

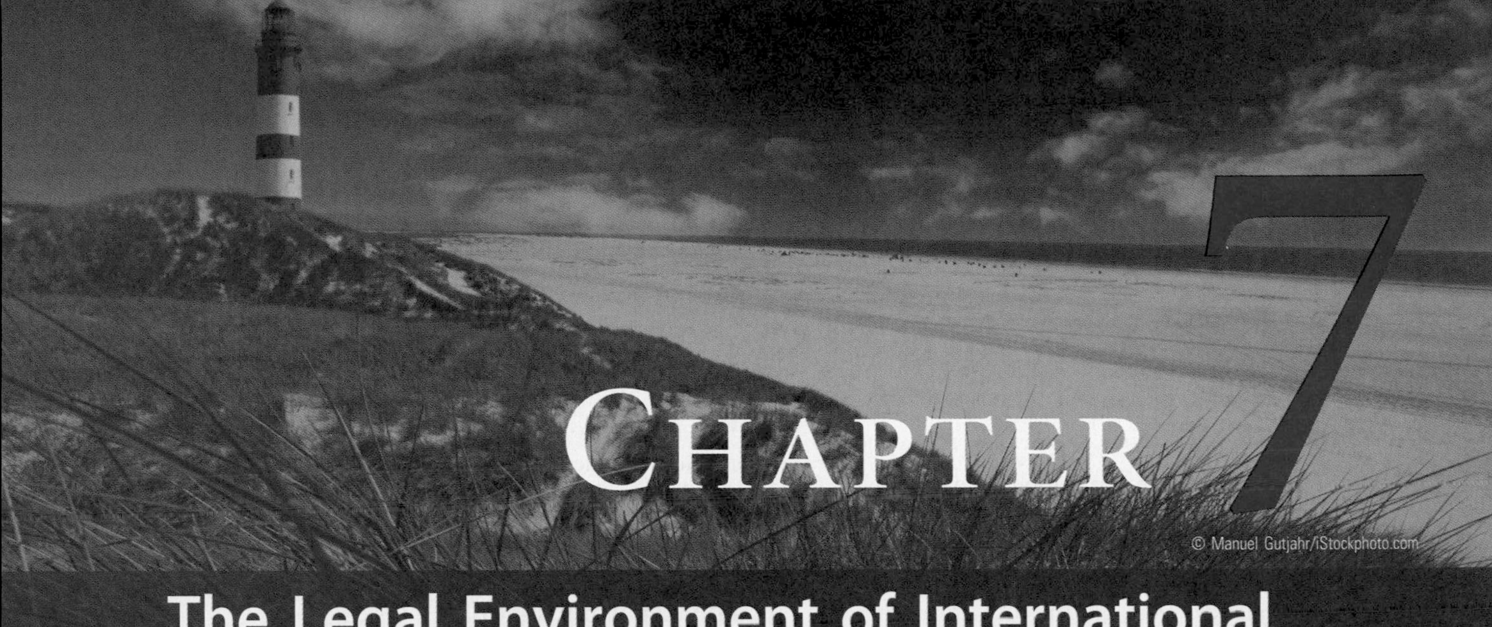

The Legal Environment of International Trade

learningoutcomes

After studying this chapter, you should be able to

LO.1 Explain which country's law will govern an international contract should a dispute arise

LO.2 Identify seven major international organizations, conferences, and treaties that affect the multinational markets for goods, services, and investments

LO.3 List the forms of business organizations for doing business abroad

LO.4 Explain the import protections afforded owners of U.S. intellectual property rights

LO.5 Explain the tariff barriers and nontariff barriers to the free movements of goods across borders

LO.6 Explain U.S. law regarding payment to foreign government officials as a means of obtaining business contracts with other governments, and compare U.S. law to laws and treaties applicable to most First World nations

The success or failure of the U.S. firms doing business in foreign countries may well depend on accurate information about the laws and customs of the host countries. In their domestic operations, U.S. business firms compete against imports from other nations. Such imported goods include Canadian lumber, Mexican machinery, Japanese automobiles, German steel, French wine, Chinese textiles, and Chilean copper. To compete effectively, U.S. firms should learn about the business practices of foreign firms. They should be alert to unfair trade practices that will put U.S. firms at a disadvantage. Such practices may include the violation of U.S. antitrust and antidumping laws or violation of international trade agreements. Individuals from all over the world participate in the U.S. securities markets. Special problems exist in the regulation and enforcement of U.S. securities laws involving financial institutions of countries with secrecy laws.

While this chapter focuses on the above aspects of the legal environment of international trade, the American people, nonprofit agencies, American businesses aware of their corporate social responsibilities, and government officials all are very much concerned about the working conditions of the people throughout the world who make the products sold in the United States. **For Example,** in 2012, Apple Inc. joined the Fair Labor Association (FLA), a Washington, D.C.–based nonprofit workers' rights group, and invited the FLA to investigate the performance of its largest suppliers, including Foxconn, China's largest private employer. The FLA report on Foxconn identified some 50 legal violations or policy gaps, including health and safety issues, excessive overtime, and low pay and overtime pay issues, which prompted Foxconn and Apple to agree to new reforms.[1] Nike, Inc., a U.S. apparel company with international operations, is also a participating member of the FLA, agreeing to uphold the FLA Workplace Code of Conduct and Compliance benchmarks.

A. General Principles

Nations enter into treaties and conferences to further international trade. The business world has developed certain forms of organizations for conducting that trade.

1. The Legal Background

Because of the complexity and ever-changing character of the legal environment of international trade, this section will focus on certain underlying elements.

(A) What Law Applies. When there is a sale of goods within the United States, one law typically applies to the transaction. Some variation may be introduced when the transaction is between parties in different states, but for the most part, the law governing the transaction is the U.S. law of contracts and the Uniform Commercial Code (UCC). In contrast, when an international contract is made, it is necessary to determine whether it is the law of the seller's country or the law of the importer's country that will govern. The parties to an international contract often resolve that question themselves as part of their contract, setting forth which country's law will govern should a dispute arise. Such a provision is called a **choice-of-law clause**. **For Example,** U.S. investors Irmgard and Mitchell Lipcon provided capital to underwriters at Lloyd's of London and signed choice-of-law clauses in their investment agreements binding them to proceed in England under English law should disputes arise. When the Lipcons realized that their investments were exposed to massive liabilities for asbestos and pollution insurance claims, they sued in U.S. district court in Florida for alleged U.S. securities acts violations. However, their complaints were dismissed based on the choice-of-law clauses in their contracts. The U.S. court of appeals stated that the Lipcons must "honor their bargains" and attempt to

[1] Apple Inc.'s reports on supplier responsibility and its supplier list may be accessed at **http://apple.com/suppliersresponsibility/**.

vindicate their claims in English courts under English law.[2]

The major trading countries of the world have entered into a number of treaties. When their citizens deal with each other and their respective rights are not controlled in their contract, their rights and liabilities are determined by looking at the treaty. These treaties are discussed in Section 7 of this chapter, including the United Nations Convention on Contracts for the International Sale of Goods (CISG), which deals with certain aspects of the formation and performance of international commercial contracts for the sale of goods.

(B) The Arbitration Alternative. Traditional litigation may be considered too time consuming, expensive, and divisive to the relationships of the parties to an international venture. The parties, therefore, may agree to arbitrate any contractual disputes that may arise according to dispute resolution procedures set forth in the contract.

Pitfalls exist for U.S. companies arbitrating disputes in foreign lands. **For Example,** were a U.S. company to agree to arbitrate a contractual dispute with a Chinese organization in China, it would find that the arbitrator must be Chinese. Also, under Chinese law, only Chinese lawyers can present an arbitration case, even if one party is a U.S. company. Because of situations like this, it is common for parties to international ventures to agree to arbitrate their disputes in neutral countries.

An arbitration agreement gives the parties more control over the decision-making process. The parties can require that the arbitrator have the technical, language, and legal qualifications to best understand their dispute. While procedures exist for the prearbitration exchange of documents, full "discovery" is ordinarily not allowed. The decision of the arbitrator is final and binding on the parties with very limited judicial review possible.

(C) Conflicting Ideologies. Law, for all people and at all times, is the result of the desire of the lawmaker to achieve certain goals. These are the social forces that make the law. In the eyes of the lawmaker, the attainment of these goals is proper and therefore ethical. This does not mean that we all can agree on what the international law should be because different people have different ideas as to what is right. This affects our views as to ownership, trade, and dealings with foreign merchants. **For Example,** a very large part of the world does not share the U.S. dislike of cartels. Other countries do not have our antitrust laws; therefore, their merchants can form a trust to create greater bargaining power in dealing with U.S. and other foreign merchants.

(D) Financing International Trade. There is no international currency. This creates problems as to what currency to use and how to make payment in international transactions. Centuries ago, buyers used precious metals, jewels, or furs in payment. Today, the parties to an international transaction agree in their sales contract on the currency to be used to pay for the goods. They commonly require that the buyer furnish the seller a **letter of credit**, which is a commercial device used to guarantee payment to a seller in an international transaction. By this, an issuer, typically a bank, agrees to pay the drafts drawn against the buyer for the purchase price. In trading with merchants in some countries, the foreign country itself will promise that the seller will be paid.

2. International Trade Organizations, Conferences, and Treaties

A large number of organizations exist that affect the multinational markets for goods, services, and investments. A survey of major international organizations, conferences, and treaties follows.

(A) GATT and WTO. The *General Agreement on Tariffs and Trade* 1994 (GATT 1994) is a multilateral treaty subscribed to by 127 member governments, including the United States.[3] It consists of the original 1947 GATT, numerous multilateral agreements negotiated since 1947, the Uruguay Round Agreements, and the agreement establishing the *World Trade Organization* (WTO). On January 1, 1995, the WTO took over responsibility for administrating and policing the objectives of the former GATT administrative structure. Since 1947 and the end of the World War II era, the goal of the GATT has been to liberalize world

[2] *Lipcon v. Underwriters at Lloyd's, London,* 148 F.2d 1285, 1299 (11th Cir. 1998).

[3] In December 2011, after 18 years of negotiating membership, Russia became a WTO member and joined the GATT. To secure admission, Russia undertook a series of commitments designed to provide meaningful market access to member countries and a solid legal and administrative framework to guarantee the implementation of contractual commitments.

trade and make it secure for furthering economic growth and human development. The current round of WTO negotiations began in Doha, Qatar, in 2001. As the talks continued in Cancun in 2003 and Hong Kong in 2005 the developed countries and developing countries divided on key issues such as agricultural subsidies. After 10 years, Doha Round negotiations have stalled and, although negotiations continue, the future of the Doha Round remains uncertain.

The GATT is based on the fundamental principles of (1) trade without discrimination and (2) protection through tariffs. The principle of trade without discrimination is embodied in its **most-favored-nation clause**. In treaties between countries, a most-favored-nation clause is one whereby any privilege subsequently granted to a third country in relation to a given treaty subject is extended to the other party to the treaty. In the application and administration of import and export duties and charges under the GATT most-favored-nation clause, all member countries grant each other equal treatment. Thus, no country gives special trading advantages to another. All member countries are equal and share the benefits of any moves toward lower trade barriers. Exceptions to this basic rule are allowed in certain special circumstances involving regional trading arrangements, such as the European Union (EU) and the North American Free Trade Agreement (NAFTA). Special preferences are also granted to developing countries. The second basic principle is protection for domestic industry, which should be extended essentially through a tariff, not through other commercial measures. The aim of this rule is to make the extent of protection clear and to make competition possible.

The WTO provides a **Dispute Settlement Body (DSB)** to enable member countries to resolve trade disputes rather than engage in unilateral trade sanctions or a trade war. The DSB appoints panels to hear disputes concerning allegations of GATT agreement violations, and it adopts (or rejects) the panels' decisions. If a GATT agreement violation is found and not removed by the offending country, trade sanctions authorized by a panel may be imposed on that country in an amount equal to the economic injury caused by the violation.

(B) CISG. The *United Nations Convention on Contracts for the International Sale of Goods* (CISG or convention) sets forth uniform rules to govern international sales contracts. National law, however, is sometimes required to fill gaps in areas not covered by the CISG. The CISG became effective on January 1, 1988, between the United States and the 60 other nations that had approved it.[4] The provisions of the CISG have been strongly influenced by Article 2 of the UCC.

However, as set forth in Chapter 23 on sales, several distinct differences exist between the convention and the UCC. Excluded from the coverage of the convention under Article 2 are the sale of goods for personal, family, or household uses and the sale of watercraft, aircraft, natural gas, or electricity; letters of credit; and auctions and securities.[5] The CISG is often viewed by foreign entities as a neutral body of law, the utilization of which can be a positive factor in successfully concluding negotiations of a contract. The parties to an international commercial contract may opt out of the convention. However, absent an express "opt-out provision," the CISG is controlling and preempts all state actions.

(C) UNCTAD. The *United Nations Conference on Trade and Development* (UNCTAD) represents the interests of the less developed countries. Its prime objective is the achievement of an international redistribution of income through trade. Through UNCTAD pressure, the developed countries agreed to a system of preferences, with quota limits, for manufactured imports from the developing countries.

(D) EU. The *European Economic Community* (EEC) was established in 1958 by the Treaty of Rome to remove trade and economic barriers between member countries and to unify their economic policies. It changed its name and became the *European Union* (EU) after the Treaty of Maastricht was ratified on November 1, 1993. The Treaty of Rome containing the governing principles of this regional trading group was signed by the original six nations of Belgium, France, West Germany, Italy, Luxembourg, and the Netherlands. Membership expanded by the entry of Denmark, Ireland, and Great Britain in 1973; Greece in 1981; Spain and Portugal in 1986; and Austria,

4 52 Fed. Reg. 6262.

5 C.I.S.G. art. 2(a)–(f).

Sweden, and Finland in 1995. Ten countries joined the EU in 2004: Cyprus, the Czech Republic, Estonia, Hungary, Latvia, Lithuania, Malta, Poland, Slovakia, and Slovenia. Bulgaria, Romania, Croatia, and Turkey expect to join in the coming years.

Four main institutions make up the formal structure of the EU. The first, the European Council, consists of the heads of state of the member countries. The council sets broad policy guidelines for the EU. The second, the European Commission, implements decisions of the council and initiates actions against individuals, companies, or member states that violate EU law. The third, the European Parliament, has an advisory legislative role with limited veto powers. The fourth, the European Court of Justice (ECJ) and the lower Court of First Instance make up the judicial arm of the EU. The courts of member states may refer cases involving questions on the EU treaty to these courts.

The Single European Act eliminated internal barriers to the free movement of goods, persons, services, and capital between EU countries. The Treaty on European Union, signed in Maastricht, Netherlands (the Maastricht Treaty), amended the Treaty of Rome with a focus on monetary and political union. It set goals for the EU of (1) single monetary and fiscal policies, (2) common foreign and security policies, and (3) cooperation in justice and home affairs.

(E) NAFTA. The *North American Free Trade Agreement* (NAFTA) is an agreement between Mexico, Canada, and the United States, effective January 1, 1994, that included Mexico in the arrangements previously initiated under the United States–Canada Free Trade Agreement of 1989. NAFTA eliminates all tariffs among the three countries over a 15-year period. Side agreements exist to prevent the exploitation of Mexico's lower environmental and labor standards.

Products are qualified for NAFTA tariff preferences only if they originate in one or more of the three member countries.

Documentation is required in a NAFTA *Certificate of Origin,* except for certain "low-value" items for which the statement of North American origin is recorded on an invoice. NAFTA ensures nondiscriminatory and open markets for a wide range of services and lowers barriers to U.S. investments in both Canada and Mexico. Although NAFTA does not create a common labor market, as does the European Union, the agreement provides temporary access for businesspersons across borders. The *DaimlerChrysler* case is an example of the interrelationship of the manufacturing and assembly process between the U.S. and Mexico and the tariff preferences when the finished goods are shipped back to the U.S. for sale.

DaimlerChrysler Corp. v U.S., 361 F.3d 1378 (Fed. Cir. 2004)

A Reason to Assemble Cars in Mexico

DaimlerChrysler assembles trucks in Mexico utilizing sheet metal components manufactured in the United States. The sheet metal is subject to painting in Mexico, consisting of primer coats followed by a color-treated coat and a clear coat, referred to as the top coats. After the assembly is completed, the trucks are shipped to and sold in the United States. The U.S. Customs Service believes the top coats are subject to duty payments. DaimlerChrysler asserts that the entire painting process is duty free. Subheading 9802.00.80 of the Harmonized Tariffs Schedule of the U.S. (HTSUS) provides duty-free treatment for:

> *Articles…assembled abroad in whole or in part of fabricated components, the product of the United States, which (a) were exported in condition ready for assembly without further fabrication, (b) have not lost their physical identity in such articles by change in form, shape or otherwise, and (c) have not been advanced in value or improved in condition abroad except by being assembled and except by operations incidental to the assembly process such as cleaning, lubricating and* painting. *[emphasis added by the court]*

From a judgment by the Court of International Trade in favor of the United States, DaimlerChrysler appealed.

JUDICIAL OPINION

PROST, C. J.…[T]he United States Supreme Court addressed the application and interpretation of HTSUS 9802.00.80 in *Haggar I*.…In answering that question in the affirmative, the Court specifically considered HTSUS 9802.00.80 and noted that it established two different categories of operations incidental to assembly—one specific and unambiguous and the other

Continued

general and ambiguous. "The statute under which respondent claims an exemption gives direction not only by stating a general policy (to grant the partial exemption where only assembly and incidental operations were abroad) but also by determining some specifics of the policy (finding that painting, for example, is incidental to assembly)." *Haggar I*, 526 U.S. at 393...

On appeal, DaimlerChrysler primarily argues that the Supreme Court's analysis in *Haggar I* provides that painting, without limitation, is an operation incidental to assembly. By using the term "painting" generally to describe a category of incidental operations, DaimlerChrysler argues, Congress unambiguously intended to include all painting, regardless of purpose. Because Customs' regulation regarding painting therefore conflicts with the clear statutory language, DaimlerChrysler continues, the Court of International Trade erred as a matter of law in applying this regulation so as to deny DaimlerChrysler a partial duty exemption....

The government counters that the statute cannot be read to cover all painting, only painting incidental to assembly. It argues that DaimlerChrysler reads too much into the Supreme Court's statements regarding painting in *Haggar I*, which are simply dicta....

We agree with DaimlerChrysler that the Supreme Court in *Haggar I* determined generally that painting is incidental to the assembly process. In order to qualify for the duty exemption, subheading 9802.00.80 requires that articles not be "advanced in value or improved in condition abroad except by being assembled and except by operations incidental to the assembly process such as cleaning, lubricating and *painting*." HTSUS 9802.00.80 (emphasis added). For purposes of interpreting subheading 9802.00.80, the Court in *Haggar I* found that it established both an unambiguous category and an ambiguous category of operations incidental to assembly. As noted, subheading 9802.00.80 "determin[es] some specifics of the policy (finding that *painting*, for example, *is incidental to assembly*)." *Haggar I*, 526 U.S. at 393, 119 S.Ct. 1392 (emphases added). Moreover, the Court concluded that subheading 9802.00.80 is "ambiguous in that the agency must use its discretion to determine how best to implement the policy *in those cases not covered by the statute's specific terms*." *Id.* (emphasis added)....

...Because subheading 9802.00.80 unambiguously covers painting operations broadly, DaimlerChrysler's entire painting process, including the application of the tops coats, qualifies for the partial duty exemption....

[Reversed]

QUESTIONS

1. What is the question at issue in this case?
2. How did the Court of Appeals decide the case?
3. Discuss the advantages and disadvantages regarding the U.S. economy and employment issues regarding USTSUS 9802.00.80.

(F) Regional Trading Groups of Developing Countries. In recent years, numerous trading arrangements between groups of developing countries have been established.

(G) IMF—World Bank. The *International Monetary Fund* (IMF) was created after World War II by a group of nations meeting in Bretton Woods, New Hampshire. The Articles of Agreement of the IMF state that its purpose is "to facilitate the expansion and balanced growth of international trade" and to "shorten the duration and lessen the disequilibrium in the international balance of payments of members." The IMF helps to achieve such purposes by administering a complex lending system. A country can borrow money from other IMF members or from the IMF by means of **special drawing rights (SDRs)** sufficient to permit that country to maintain the stability of its currency's relationship to other world currencies. The Bretton Woods conference also set up the *International Bank for Reconstruction and Development* (World Bank) to facilitate the lending of money by capital surplus countries—such as the United States—to countries needing economic help and wanting foreign investments after World War II.

(H) EX-IM Bank. The Export Import Bank (EX-IM Bank) is a United States federal agency that helps U.S. companies sell manufactured goods to foreign firms by providing loan guarantees and some forms of insurance. The bank was reauthorized in 2012, and its financing cap increased from \$100 billion to \$140 billion. Big exporters like Boeing, General Electric, and Caterpillar were supportive of the reauthorization, asserting that it supports U.S. jobs. Opponents including Delta Airlines opposed the reauthorization, contending that the bank effectively subsidizes foreigners that compete with the U.S. companies.

The bank has been self-sustaining, more than covering its operating costs and loan-default experience.

(I) OPEC. The *Organization of Petroleum Exporting Countries* (OPEC) is a producer cartel or combination. One of its main goals was to raise the taxes and royalties earned from crude oil production. Another major goal was to take control over production and exploration from the major oil companies. Its early success in attaining these goals led other nations that export raw materials to form similar cartels.
For Example, copper and bauxite-producing nations have formed cartels.

3. Forms of Business Organizations

The decision to participate in international business transactions and the extent of that participation depend on the financial position of the individual firm, production and marketing factors, and tax and legal considerations. There are a number of forms of business organizations for doing business abroad.

(A) Export Sales. A direct sale to customers in a foreign country is an **export sale**. A U.S. firm engaged in export selling is not present in the foreign country in such an arrangement. The export is subject to a tariff by the foreign country, but the exporting firm is not subject to local taxation by the importing country.

(B) Agency Requirements. A U.S. manufacturer may decide to make a limited entry into international business by appointing an agent to represent it in a foreign market. An **agent** is a person or firm with authority to make contracts on behalf of another—the **principal**. The agent will receive commission income for sales made on behalf of the U.S. principal. The appointment of a foreign agent commonly constitutes "doing business" in that country and subjects the U.S. firm to local taxation.

(C) Foreign Distributorships. A **distributor** takes title to goods and bears the financial and commercial risks for the subsequent sale. To avoid making a major financial investment, a U.S. firm may decide to appoint a foreign distributor. A U.S. firm may also appoint a foreign distributor to avoid managing a foreign operation with its complicated local business, legal, and labor conditions. Care is required in designing an exclusive distributorship for an EU country lest it would violate EU antitrust laws.

(D) Licensing. U.S. firms may select licensing as a means of doing business in other countries. **Licensing** involves the transfer of technology rights in a product so that it may be produced by a different business organization in a foreign country in exchange for royalties and other payments as agreed. The technology being licensed may fall within the internationally recognized categories of patents, trademarks, and "know-how" (trade secrets and unpatented manufacturing processes outside the public domain). These intellectual property rights, which are legally protectable, may be licensed separately or incorporated into a single, comprehensive licensing contract. **Franchising**, which involves granting permission to use a trademark, trade name, or copyright under specified conditions, is a form of licensing that is now very common in international business.

(E) Wholly Owned Subsidiaries. A firm seeking to maintain control over its own operations, including the protection of its own technological expertise, may choose to do business abroad through a wholly owned subsidiary. In Europe the most common choice of foreign business organization, similar to the U.S. corporate form of business organization, is called the *société anonyme* (S.A.). In German-speaking countries, this form is called *Aktiengesellschaft* (A.G.). Small and medium-sized companies in Europe now utilize a newly created form of business organization called the limited liability company (*Gesellschaft mit beschränkter Haftung,* or "GmbH" in Germany; *Società a responsabilità limitata,* or "S.r.l." in Spain). It is less complicated to form but is restrictive for accessing public capital markets.

A corporation doing business in more than one country poses many taxation problems for the governments in those countries where the firm does business. The United States has established tax treaties with many countries granting corporations relief from double taxation. Credit is normally given by the United States to U.S. corporations for taxes paid to foreign governments.

There is a potential for tax evasion by U.S. corporations from their selling goods to their overseas subsidiaries. Corporations could sell goods at less than the fair market value to avoid a U.S. tax on the full profit for such sales. By allowing the foreign subsidiaries located in countries with lower tax rates to make higher profits, a company as a whole would minimize its taxes. Section 482 of the Internal Revenue Code (IRC), however, allows the Internal Revenue Service (IRS) to reallocate the income between the parent and its foreign subsidiary. Intellectual property such as patent rights, internationally held and generating revenues outside the United States, provide a basis for U.S. multinational companies to legally minimize tax liability by shifting income internationally. **For Example,** global companies like Apple, Microsoft, Google, and Facebook may utilize tax avoidance techniques like the "Double Irish with a Dutch Sandwich," relying on transferring profits on international patent royalties to places like Ireland, with routing through the Netherlands, back to an Irish subsidiary, then to a Caribbean tax haven.[6]

(F) Joint Ventures. A U.S. manufacturer and a foreign entity may form a **joint venture**, whereby the two firms agree to perform different functions for a common result. The responsibilities and liabilities of such operations are governed by contract. **For Example,** General Motors Co. (GM) and its Chinese partner, Shanghai Automotive Industry Corp. (SAIC), formed an auto-making joint venture in 1995, selling 22,000 cars in 1999 and expanding to 2.6 million cars sold in 2011, with a profit of $1.5 billion for GM.[7]

B. Governmental Regulation

Nations regulate trade to protect the economic interests of their citizens or to protect themselves in international relations and transactions.

4. Export Regulations

For reasons of national security, foreign policy, or short supply of domestic products, the United States controls the export of goods and technology. The Export Administration Act[8] imposes export controls on goods and technical data from the U.S. Since April 2002, the Bureau of Industry and Security (BIS) of the Department of Commerce has issued Export Administration Regulations to enforce export controls.

Export Administration Regulations effective in 1996 simplify the process and enhance export trade by U.S. citizens.[9] These regulations eliminate the former system of general and validated licenses under which every export required a license. Under the 1996 *Simplification Regulations,* no license is required unless the regulations affirmatively require a license. However, when no license is required, the exporter must fill out a Shipper's Export Declaration and attach it to the bill of lading for shipment with the goods being exported.

(A) Determining If a License Is Needed. To determine whether a product requires a BIS export license, the exporter should review the Commerce Control List (CCL) to see whether the product to be exported is listed. Listed products have Export Control Classification Numbers (ECCNs) that conform to those used by the EU. If a product is on the list, the ECCN code will provide the reason for control, such as national security, missile technology, nuclear nonproliferation, chemical and/or biological weapons, antiterrorism, crime control, short supply, or UN sanctions.[10] The exporter should then consult the Commerce Country Chart to determine whether a license is needed to send the product to its proposed destination. **For Example,** western red cedar is on the Commerce Control List because of the "short supply" of this product. As a result, it is controlled to all destinations, and no reference to the Commerce Country Chart is necessary.

(B) Sanctions. Export licenses are required for the export of certain high-technology and military products. A company intending to ship "maraging 350 steel" to a user in Pakistan would find by checking the CCL and the ECCN code for the product that such steel is used in making high-technology products and has nuclear applications. Thus, an export license would be required. Because Pakistan is a nonsignatory nation of the Nuclear Non-Proliferation Treaty, the Department of Commerce would be expected to deny a license application for the use of this steel in a nuclear plant. However, a license to export this steel for the manufacture of high-speed turbines or compressors might be approved. The prospective purchaser must complete a "Statement of Ultimate Consignee and

[6] **http://www.nytimes.com/interactive/2012/04/28/business/Double-Irish-With-A-Dutch-Sandwich.html. http://www.npr.org/blogs/money/2010/10/21/130727655/google-s-tax-tricks-double-irish-and-dutch-sandwich.** See also James Barrett and Steven Hadjilogiou, "The Tax Benefits and Obstacles to U.S. Businesses in Transferring Foreign Intellectual Property to Foreign Affiliates," 89 *Fla. B. J.* No. 5, pp. 40–45 (May 2012).

[7] Sharon Terlep, "GM Seeks Sway in China," *Wall Street Journal*, April 19, 2012, at B3.

[8] The Export Administration Act of 1979 expired in August 1994 and was extended by Executive Orders signed by Presidents Clinton and G. W. Bush. The EAA is now extended annually by presidential notice.

[9] Simplification of Export Regulations, 61 Fed.Reg. 12,714 (1996).

[10] *Id.*

Purchaser" form with the application for an export license. The prospective purchaser must identify the "end use" for the steel and indicate where the purchaser is located and the location in Pakistan where a U.S. embassy official can make an on-site inspection of the product's use. Falsification of the information in the license application process is a criminal offense. Thus, if the exporter of maraging 350 steel asserted that it was to be used in manufacturing high-speed turbines when in fact the exporter knew it was being purchased for use in a nuclear facility, the exporter would be guilty of a criminal offense.[11]

Civil charges may also be brought against U.S. manufacturers who fail to obtain an export license for foreign sales of civilian items that contain any components that have military applications under the Arms Control Export Act. For example. between 2000 and 2003, Boeing Co. shipped overseas 94 commercial jets that carried a gyrochip used as a backup system in determining a plane's orientation in the air. This 2-ounce chip that costs less than $2,000 also has military applications and can be used to stabilize and steer guided missiles. Boeing is asserted to have made false statements on shipping documents to get around the export restrictions. Boeing argued that the State Department is without legal authority to regulate its civilian rather than military items. However, Boeing agreed to pay a $15 million fine for the violations.[12]

(c) Expert Assistance. The Department of Commerce's Exporter Assistance Staff provides assistance to exporters needing help in determining whether an export license is needed.[13] Licensed foreign-**freight forwarders** are in the business of handling the exporting of goods to foreign destinations. They are experts on U.S. Department of Commerce export license requirements. Licensed foreign-freight forwarders can attend to all of the essential arrangements required to transport a shipment of goods from the exporter's warehouse to the overseas buyer's specified port and inland destination. They are well versed in all aspects of ocean, air, and inland transportation as well as banking, marine insurance, and other services relating to exporting.

5. Protection of Intellectual Property Rights

U.S. laws protect **intellectual property rights**, which consist of trademarks, copyrights, patents, and trade secrets. (See Figure 10-1, p. 205, for a summary of intellectual property law.)

(a) Counterfeit Goods. The importation of counterfeit compact discs, tapes, computer software, and movies into the United States violates U.S. copyright laws. Importing goods, such as athletic shoes, jeans, or watches bearing counterfeits of U.S. companies' registered trademarks violates the Lanham Act. Possible remedies include injunctive relief, seizure and destruction of counterfeit goods that are found in the United States, damages, and attorney fees. U.S. firms injured by counterfeit trademarks may recover triple damages from the counterfeiters.[14]

(b) Patent and Trade Secrets. Importing machines or devices that infringe on U.S. patents not only violates U.S. patent laws but also the Tariff Act of 1930. **For Example,** the United States International Trade Commission (ITC) determined that the importation and sale of personal data and mobile communication devices by High Tech Computer Corp. of Taiwan (HTC) and its U.S. subsidiary HTC, America infringed on two patents of Apple Inc. of Cupertino, California, in violation of Section 337 of the Tariff Act of 1930. It ordered the exclusion of the articles from the United States, but allowed HTC to import refurbished handsets to be provided to consumers as replacement under warranty or insurance contracts until December 13, 2013.[15]

The International Trade Commission has authority under the Tariff Act of 1930 over "unfair methods of competition and unfair acts in the importation of articles into the United States." Accordingly, the ITC is allowed to investigate conduct occurring in a foreign country in the course of a trade secrets misappropriation case, in order to protect domestic industries from injuries arising out of unfair competition in the U.S. domestic marketplace, as developed in the *TianRui* case.

[11] See *United States v. Pervez,* 871 F.2d 310 (3d Cir. 1989), on the criminal application of the Export Administration Regulations to an individual who stated a false end use for "maraging 350 steel" (used in the nuclear industry) on his export application to ship this steel to Pakistan.

[12] Associated Press, "Boeing to Pay $15 Million Fine for Export of Military Technology," *The Boston Globe*, April 10, 2006, at E3.

[13] U.S. Export Assistance Centers located in major metropolitan areas throughout the United States provide small or medium-sized firms export assistance.

[14] 15 U.S.C. §1117(b); *Nintendo of America v. NTDEC*, 822 F. Supp. 1462 (D. Ariz. 1993).

[15] *In re Certain Personal Data and Communication Devices and Related Software*, U.S. International Trade Commission Investigation, No. 337-TA-710 (Dec. 19, 2011), **www.edis.usitc.gov**.

TianRui Group Co., Ltd. v. International Trade Commission, 661 F.3d 132 (Fed. Cir. 2011)

I hear the train a comin'
It's rollin' 'round the bend....*
And it ain't rollin' on cheatin' TianRui wheels!

*Johnny Cash: Folsom Prison Blues

Amsted Industries Inc. is a domestic manufacturer of cast steel railway wheels. It owns two secret processes for manufacturing such wheels, the "ABC process" and the "Griffin process." Amsted previously practiced the ABC process at its foundry in Calera, Alabama, but it no longer uses that process in the United States. Instead, Amsted uses the Griffin process at three of its domestic foundries. However, Amsted has licensed the "ABC process" to several firms with foundries in China. TianRui Group Company Limited manufactures cast steel railway wheels in China. TianRui hired nine employees away from one of Amsted's Chinese licensees, Datong ABC Castings Company, Limited. Datong had previously notified those employees through a written employee code of conduct that information pertaining to the ABC process was proprietary and confidential. Each employee had been advised that he had a duty not to disclose confidential information. In the proceedings brought by Amsted before the International Trade Commission (ITC), Amsted alleged that the former Datong employees disclosed information and documents to TianRui that revealed the details of the ABC process and thereby misappropriated Amsted's trade secrets. TianRui partnered with Standard Car Truck Company, Inc., to form the joint venture Barber TianRui Railway Supply, LLC, and has marketed TianRui wheels to United States customers. Other than Amsted, they are the only companies selling or attempting to sell cast steel railway wheels in the United States. The ITC determined that the importation of the articles violated the Tariff Act and issued a limited exclusion order. TianRui appealed to the United States Court of Appeals for the Federal Circuit.

JUDICIAL OPINION

BRYSON, C.J.... The Administrative law judge's findings establish that TianRui obtained access to Amsted's confidential information through former Datong employees, who were subject to duties of confidentiality imposed by the Datong code of employee conduct, and that TianRui exploited that information in producing the subject goods. TianRui does not take issue with those findings, which are sufficient to establish the elements of trade secret misappropriation under either Illinois law or the generally understood law of trade secrets, as reflected in the Restatement, the Uniform Trade Secrets Act, and previous Commission decisions under section 337....

In this case, TianRui argues that section 337 is inapplicable because Amsted's confidential information was disclosed in China. The legal issue for us to decide is thus whether section 337...applies to imported goods produced through the exploitation of trade secrets in which the act of misappropriation occurs abroad....

...[I]n this case the Commission has not applied section 337 to sanction purely extraterritorial conduct; the foreign "unfair" activity at issue in this case is relevant only to the extent that it results in the importation of goods into this country causing domestic injury. In light of the statute's focus on the act of importation and the resulting domestic injry, the Commission's order does not purport to regulate purely foreign conduct....

...Congress intended a...broad and flexible meaning when it used the...language to prohibit "unfair methods of competition" in importation. That provision was added to the law in the Tariff Act of 1922, Pub.L. No. 67–318, § 316(a), 42 Stat. 858, 943, pursuant to a recommendation of the Tariff Commission (the former name of the International Trade Commission) in a 1919 report. *See* U.S. Tariff Comm'n, *Dumping and Unfair Foreign Competition in the United States and Canada's Anti-dumping Law* (1919) ("1919 Report"). In its report, the Commission identified several deficiencies in U.S. trade laws, including the absence of any remedy for unfair competition other than dumping, *id.* at 11, and the lack of any adequate "governmental machinery" for investigating allegations of dumping, "one element of which must be found abroad," *id.* at 18. In a subsequent annual report, issued while the bill that was to become the 1922 Tariff Act was pending before Congress, the Commission renewed the recommendations from the 1919 report relating to unfair competition. *See* U.S. Tariff Comm'n, *Fifth Annual Report* 96 (1921).

In section 316 of the Tariff Act of 1922, Congress responded to the Commission's recommendation by declaring "unfair methods of competition and unfair acts in the importation of articles into the United States" to be unlawful. That Act authorized the Tariff Commission to investigate allegations of such conduct in accordance with rules that the Commission would promulgate, and it gave the President the authority to impose additional duties or to exclude articles that the Commission found to be in violation of that provision....

Thus, the question in this case is whether the disclosure of protected information in breach of that duty is beyond the reach of section 337 simply because the breach itself took place outside the United States. To answer that question in the

Continued

affirmative would invite evasion of section 337 and significantly undermine the effectiveness of the congressionally designed remedy....

...[T]he statutory prohibition on "unfair methods of competition and unfair acts in the importation of articles...into the United States" naturally contemplates that the unfair methods of competition and unfair acts leading to the prohibited importation will include conduct that takes place abroad. Because the statute applies to goods that are presented for importation, it would be a strained reading of the statute to bar the Commission from considering acts of trade secret misappropriation that occur abroad. In cases in which misappropriated trade secrets are used in the manufacture of the imported goods, the misappropriation will frequently occur overseas, where the imported goods are made. To bar the Commission from considering such acts because they occur outside the United States would thus be inconsistent with the congressional purpose of protecting domestic commerce from unfair methods of competition in importation such as trade secret misappropriation.

TianRui's second ground for appeal focuses on the requirement of section 337 that the acts of unfair competition threaten "to destroy or substantially injure an industry in the United States." 19 U.S.C. § 1337(a)(1)(A)(i). TianRui contends that in trade secret cases, the domestic industry must practice the misappropriated trade secret in order for the Commission to be authorized to grant relief. Because Amsted has no domestic operations practicing the misappropriated ABC process, TianRui argues that its imported wheels cannot be held to injure or threaten injury to any domestic industry within the meaning of section 337....

In sum, we conclude that the Commission did not err in defining the domestic industry in this case. The parties submitted evidence indicating that the imported TianRui wheels could directly compete with wheels domestically produced by the trade secret owner. That type of competition, the Commission concluded, is sufficiently related to the investigation to constitute an injury to an "industry" within the meaning of section 337(a)(1)(A). We hold that the Commission's conclusion in that regard is based on a proper construction of the statute and that its factual analysis of the effect of TianRui's imports on the domestic industry is supported by substantial evidence.

[Affirmed]

[MOORE, Circuit Judge, dissenting. The majority in this case expands the reach of both 19 U.S.C. § 1337 (§ 337) and trade secret law to punish TianRui Group Company Limited (TianRui) for its completely extraterritorial activities. As a court, however, we must act within the confines set out by the text of the law. Here, there is no basis for the extraterritorial application of our laws to punish TianRui's bad acts in China. As a result, I respectfully dissent....]

QUESTIONS

1. State the issue before the appeals court.
2. Does the commission's order in this case purport to regulate purely foreign conduct contravening the proper application of Section 337 of the Tariff Act?
3. Section 337 requires that the acts of unfair competition threaten "to destroy or substantially injure an industry in the United States." Since it is fact that there is no domestic manufacturer currently practicing the protected process, must the appeals court set aside the ITC's order?

(c) Gray Market Goods. A U.S. trademark holder may license a foreign business to use its trademark overseas. Exploiting geographic price differentials, a third party may import these foreign-made goods into the United States to compete against the U.S. manufacturer's goods. The foreign made goods are called **gray market goods**. The Copyright Act and the Lanham Act have been utilized with varying degrees of success by U.S. trademark and U.S. copyright owners in their effort to exclude gray market goods from the United States.

(1) The Copyright Act.

The Copyright Act of 1976 addresses the importation of copyrighted works and may apply to gray market goods. One provision of the act gives the copyright holder the exclusive right to distribute copies of the copyrighted work.[16] Another section, known as the *first sale doctrine*, states that a copyright owner may only influence the price at which their work is sold once; after that the subsequent owners may sell the copyrighted work for as much as they see fit.[17] One type of gray market issue occurs when

[16] 17 U.S.C. §106(3).

[17] 17 U.S.C. §109(2).

U.S. manufacturers sell their U.S.-made products overseas at deep discounts, and other firms reimport the products back to the United States for resale. The Supreme Court held that a copyrighted label on the product would not protect a U.S. manufacturer's claim of unauthorized importation because the copyright owner's rights cease upon the original sale to the overseas buyer.[18]

The first sale doctrine also applies to copyrighted works that are lawfully made and first sold abroad. Under a recent decision of the U.S. Supreme Court, importation of these goods for resale into the United States is not a violation of the Copyright Act. **For Example,** University of Southern California graduate student Supap Kirtsaeng, a citizen of Thailand, had friends in Thailand buy copies of foreign manufactured J. Wiley & Sons English language textbooks at Thai bookshops at low prices and imported and resold them in the U.S. at a profit. Copies of Wiley's foreign version English language textbooks state that they are not to be taken into the United States without permission. Before the U.S. Supreme Court, Wiley contended that the phrase "lawfully made under this title" in the section of the Copyright Act creating the first sale doctrine means "legally made in the United States" thus precluding Kirtsaeng's "first sale doctrine" defense. The Court majority disagreed, determining that the phrase was not geographic in nature but is referring to works that are "lawfully made" from those that are counterfeit.[19]

(2) The Lanham Trademark Act.

A gray market situation also arises when foreign products made by affiliates of U.S. companies have trademarks identical to U.S. trademarks but the foreign products are physically different from U.S. products. The Lanham Act applies.[20] **For Example,** Lever Brothers (Lever U.S.) manufactures a soap under the trademark Shield and a dishwashing liquid under the trademark Sunlight for sale in the United States. A British affiliate, Lever U.K., also makes products using the marks Shield and Sunlight. Because of different needs and tastes of U.S. and U.K. consumers, the products have physical differences. Third parties imported these U.K. products through unauthorized channels into the United States. Because of the confusion and dissatisfaction to American consumers the Customs Service was directed by the court of appeals to exclude the two products from sale in the United States, ruling that Section 42 of the Lanham Act bars importation of physically different foreign goods bearing a trademark identical to a valid U.S. trademark.[21]

(D) Other Protections. Intellectual property rights are also protected by international treaties, such as the Berne Convention, which protects copyrights; the Patent Cooperation Treaty; and the Madrid System of International Registration of Marks (the Madrid Protocol), a treaty providing for the international registration of marks applicable to more than 60 signatory countries, including the United States.[22]

6. Antitrust

Antitrust laws exist in the United States to protect the U.S. consumer by ensuring the benefits of competitive products from foreign competitors as well as domestic competitors. Competitors' agreements designed to raise the price of imports or to exclude imports from our domestic markets in exchange for not competing in other countries are restraints of trade in violation of our antitrust laws.[23]

The antitrust laws also exist to protect U.S. export and investment opportunities against privately imposed restrictions, whereby a group of competitors seeks to exclude another competitor from a particular foreign market. Antitrust laws exist in other countries where U.S. firms compete. These laws are usually directed not at breaking up cartels to further competition but at regulating them in the national interest.

(A) Jurisdiction. In U.S. courts, the U.S. antitrust laws have a broad extraterritorial reach. Our antitrust laws must be reconciled with the rights of other interested countries as embodied in international law.

[18] *Quality King v. L'Anza Research*, 523 U.S. 1435 (1998).

[19] *Kirtsaeng v. John Wiley & Sons Inc.*, 133 S. Ct. 1351 (2013). Academic textbooks publishers, and other copyright owners selling books, DVDs and CDs who once protected their American markets against cheaper gray market goods through the use of the Copyright Act, may now seek protections through their international distribution and licensing contracts.

[20] 15 U.S.C. §1124.

[21] *Lever Brothers Co. v. U.S.*, 981 F.2d 1330 (D.C. Cir. 1993).

[22] The Agreement on Trade-Related Aspects of Intellectual Property (TRIPS) is a WTO agreement that requires WTO members to adhere to certain treaties and guidelines in respecting copyright, trademark, and patent rights. Enforcement of such rights, however, varies, depending on national law.

[23] *United States v. Nippon Paper Industries Co. Ltd.*, 64 F. Supp. 2d 173 (1999).

(1) The Effects Doctrine.

Judge Learned Hand's decision in *United States v. Alcoa* established the **effects doctrine.**[24] Under this doctrine, U.S. courts assume jurisdiction and apply the antitrust laws to conduct outside of the United States where the activity of the business firms outside the United States has a direct and substantial effect on U.S. commerce. This basic rule has been modified to require that the effect on U.S. commerce also be foreseeable.

(2) The Jurisdictional Rule of Reason.

The jurisdictional rule of reason applies when conduct taking place outside the United States affects U.S. commerce but a foreign state also has a significant interest in regulating the conduct in question. The **jurisdictional rule of reason** balances the vital interests, including laws and policies, of the United States with those of the foreign country involved. This rule of reason is based on **comity**, a principle of international law, that means that the laws of all nations deserve the respect legitimately demanded by equal participants in international affairs.

(B) Defenses. Three defenses are commonly raised to the extraterritorial application of U.S. antitrust laws. These defenses are also commonly raised to attack jurisdiction in other legal actions involving international law.

(1) Act-of-State Doctrine.

By the **act-of-state doctrine**, every sovereign state is bound to respect the independence of every other sovereign state, and the courts of one country will not sit in judgment of another government's acts done within its own territory.[25] The act-of-state doctrine is based on the judiciary's concern over its possible interference with the conduct of foreign relations. Such matters are considered to be political, not judicial, questions.

(2) The Sovereign Compliance Doctrine.

The **sovereign compliance doctrine** allows a defendant to raise as an affirmative defense to an antitrust action the fact that the defendant's actions were compelled by a foreign state. To establish this defense, compulsion by the foreign government is required. The Japanese government uses informal and formal contacts within an industry to establish a consensus on a desired course of action. Such governmental action is not a defense for a U.S. firm, however, because the activity in question is not compulsory.

(3) The Sovereign Immunity Doctrine.

The **sovereign immunity doctrine** states that a foreign sovereign generally cannot be sued unless an exception to the Foreign Sovereign Immunities Act of 1976 applies.[26] The most important exception covers the commercial conduct of a foreign state.[27]

For Example, receivers for various insurance companies brought suit against the Vatican City State, contending that the Vatican's conduct fell within the commercial activity exception to the FSIA. Martin Frankel had engaged in a massive insurance fraud scheme, using front organizations to acquire and loot several insurance agencies. Masquerading as "David Rose," a philanthropist, he met Monsignor Emilio Cologiovani and convinced him to create a Vatican-affiliated entity, the St. Francis of Assisi Foundation (SFAF), which was used as part of Frankel's scam. The Court of Appeals held, however, that Cologiovani, acting with only apparent authority of the state, could not trigger the commercial activity doctrine.[28]

(C) Legislation. In response to business uncertainty as to when the antitrust laws apply to international transactions, Congress passed the Foreign Trade Antitrust Improvements Act of 1982. This act, in essence, codified the effects doctrine. The act requires a direct, substantial, and reasonably foreseeable effect on U.S. domestic commerce or exports by U.S. residents before business conduct abroad may come within the purview of U.S. antitrust laws.[29]

(D) Foreign Antitrust Laws. Attitudes in different countries vary toward cartels and business combinations. Because of this, antitrust laws vary in content and application. **For Example,** Japan has stressed

[24] 148 F.2d 416 (2d Cir. 1945).

[25] *Underhill v. Hernandez,* 108 U.S. 250, 252 (1897).

[26] See *Verlinden B.V. v. Central Bank of Nigeria,* 461 U.S. 574 (1983).

[27] See *Dole Food Co. v. Patrickson,* 538 U.S. 468 (2003), for a limited discussion of when a foreign state can assert a defense of sovereign immunity under the Foreign Sovereign Immunities Act of 1976 (FSIA). The FSIA allows certain foreign-state commercial entities not entitled to sovereign immunity to have the merits of a case heard in federal court. The U.S. Supreme Court held in the *Dole Food* case that a foreign state must itself own a majority of the shares of a corporation if the corporation is to be deemed an instrumentality of the state under the FSIA, and the instrumentality status is determined at the time of the filing of the complaint.

[28] *Dale v. Cologiovani,* 443 F.3d 425 (5th Cir. 2006).

[29] P.L. 97-290, 96 Stat. 1233, 15 U.S.C. §6(a).

consumer protection against such practices as price-fixing and false advertising. However, with regard to mergers, stock ownership, and agreements among companies to control production, Japanese law is much less restrictive than U.S. law.

Europe is a major market for U.S. products, services, and investments. U.S. firms doing business in Europe are subject to the competition laws of the EU.[30] The Treaty of Rome uses the term *competition* rather than *antitrust.* Articles 85 and 86 of the Treaty of Rome set forth the basic regulation on business behavior in the EU.[31] Article 85(1) expressly prohibits agreements and concerted practices that

1. even indirectly fix prices of purchases or sales or fix any other trading conditions;
2. limit or control production, markets, technical development, or investment;
3. share markets or sources of supply;
4. apply unequal terms to parties furnishing equivalent considerations, thereby placing one at a competitive disadvantage; or
5. make a contract's formation depend on the acceptance of certain additional obligations that, according to commercial usage, have no connection with the subject of such contracts.

Article 85(3) allows for an individual exemption if the agreement meets certain conditions, such as improving the production or distribution of goods, promoting technical or economic progress, and reserving to consumers a fair share of the resulting economic benefits.

Article 86 provides that it is unlawful for one or more enterprises having a dominant market position within at least a substantial part of the EU to take improper advantage of such a position if trade between the member states may be affected. **For Example,** the European Commission fined computer chip maker Intel $1.45 billion for abusing its dominance in the computer chip market by offering rebates which were conditioned on buying less of a rival's products, or not buying them at all. Intel disagrees with the decision and has appealed the Commission's ruling.[32]

7. Securities and Tax Fraud Regulation in an International Environment

Illegal conduct in the U.S. securities markets, whether this conduct is initiated in the United States or abroad, threatens the vital economic interests of the United States. Investigation and litigation concerning possible violations of the U.S. securities laws often have an extraterritorial effect. Conflicts with the laws of foreign countries may occur.

(A) Jurisdiction. U.S. district courts have jurisdiction over violations of the antifraud provisions of the Securities Exchange Act of 1934 when losses occur from sales to Americans living in the United States.[33] U.S. district courts also have jurisdiction when losses occur to Americans living abroad if the acts occurred in the United States. The antifraud provisions do not apply, however, to losses from sales of securities to foreigners outside the United States unless acts within the United States caused the losses.

(B) Impact of Foreign Secrecy Laws in SEC Enforcement. **Secrecy laws** are confidentiality laws applied to home-country banks. These laws prohibit the disclosure of business records or the identity of bank customers. **Blocking laws** prohibit the disclosure, copying, inspection, or removal of documents located in the enacting country in compliance with orders from foreign authorities. These laws impede, and sometimes foreclose, the SEC's ability to police its securities markets properly.

The *Banca Della Suizzera* case demonstrates how the SEC, in certain circumstances, can obtain discovery from foreign financial institutions in spite of secrecy laws.

The SEC is not limited to litigation when a securities law enforcement investigation runs into secrecy or blocking laws. For example, the SEC may rely on the 1977 Treaty of Mutual Assistance in Criminal Matters between the United States and Switzerland.[34] Although this treaty has served to deter the use of Swiss secrecy laws to conceal fraud in the United States, its benefits for securities enforcement have been limited. It applies only where there is a dual criminality—that is, the conduct

[30] The European Commission is the executive branch of the EU government and performs most of the EU's regulatory work. The Competition Commission oversees antitrust and mergers for the European Commission. New merger regulations took effect on May 1, 2004. The regulations require the Competition Commission to review proposed mergers and prohibit those mergers when the effects may "significantly impede effective competition" (called the *SIEC test*). The U.S. test prohibits mergers when the effect "may substantially lessen competition…." 15 U.S.C. §18 (2005). The wording of the EU and U.S. tests is relatively similar.

[31] See *Osakeyhtio v. EEC Commission*, 1988 Common Mkt. Rep. (CCH) ¶ 14,491 for discussion of the extraterritorial reach of the European Commission.

[32] Intel's appeal was heard before the Luxemburg-based General Court in July of 2012, *Intel v. Commission*, Case T-286109, and it is now awaiting the court's ruling.

[33] *Kauthar Sdn. Bhd. v. Sternberg*, 149 F.3d 659 (7th Cir. 1998).

[34] 27 U.S.T. 2021.

SEC v. Banca Della Suzzera Italiana, 92 F.R.D. 111 (S.D.N.Y. 1981)

The Long Reach of the SEC

Banca Della Suizzera Italiana (BSI), a Swiss bank with an office in the United States, purchased certain call options and common stock of St. Joe Minerals Corporation (St. Joe), a New York corporation, immediately prior to the announcement on March 11, 1981, of a cash tender offer by Joseph Seagram & Sons Inc. for all St. Joe common stock at $45 per share. On March 11, 1981, when BSI acted, the stock moved sharply higher in price. BSI instructed its broker to close out the purchases of the options and sell most of the shares of stock, resulting in an overnight profit of $2 million. The SEC noticed the undue activity in the options market and initiated suit against BSI. The SEC, through the Departments of State and Justice, and the Swiss government sought without success to learn the identity of BSI's customers involved in the transactions. The SEC believed that the customers had used inside information in violation of the Securities Exchange Act of 1934. The SEC brought a motion to compel disclosure. BSI objected on the ground that it might be subject to criminal liability under Swiss penal and banking laws if it disclosed the requested information.

JUDICIAL OPINION

POLLACK, D. J.…BSI claims that it may be subject to criminal liability under Swiss penal and banking law if it discloses the requested information. However, this Court finds the factors in § 40 of the Restatement of Foreign Relations* to tip decisively in favor of the SEC. Moreover, it holds BSI to be "in the position of one who deliberately courted legal impediments…and who thus cannot now be heard to assert its good faith after this expectation was realized." BSI acted in bad faith. It made deliberate use of Swiss nondisclosure law to evade in a commercial transaction for profit to it, the strictures of American securities law against insider trading.…

The first of the § 40 factors is the vital national interest of each of the States. The strength of the United States' interest in enforcing its securities laws to ensure the integrity of its financial markets cannot seriously be doubted. That interest is being continually thwarted by the use of foreign bank accounts. Congress, in enacting legislation on bank recordkeeping, expressed its concern over the problem over a decade ago.…

The Swiss government, on the other hand, though made expressly aware of the litigation, has expressed no opposition. In response to BSI's lawyers' inquiries, the incumbent Swiss Federal Attorney General…said only that a foreign court could not change the rule that disclosure required the consent of the one who imparted the secret and that BSI might thus be subject to prosecution. The Swiss government did not "confiscate" the Bank records to prevent violations of its law. …NEITHER THE UNITED STATES NOR THE SWISS GOVERNMENT has suggested that discovery be halted.…

The Court of Appeals in *United States v. National City Bank*, 396 F.2d 897 (2d Cir 1968), found the fact that the governments concerned had not intervened of great importance. It observed that "when foreign governments, including Germany, have considered their vital national interests threatened, they have not hesitated to make known their objections…to the issuing court." It is true that BSI may be subject to fines and its officers to imprisonment under Swiss law. However, this Court notes that there is some flexibility in the application of that law. Not only may the particular bank involved obtain waivers from its customers to avoid prosecution, but Article 34 of the Swiss Penal Code contains a "State of Necessity" exception that relieves a person of criminal liability for acts committed to protect one's own good, including one's fortune, from an immediate danger if one is not responsible for the danger and one cannot be expected to give up one's good.

Of course, given BSI's active part in the insider trading transactions alleged here, the Swiss government might well conclude—as this Court has—that BSI is responsible for the conflict it is in and that therefore the "State of Necessity" exception should not apply. However, that is certainly no cause for this Court to withhold its sanctions since the dilemma would be a result of BSI's bad faith. A party's good or bad faith is an important factor to consider, and this court finds that BSI, which deposited the proceeds of these transactions in an American bank account in its name and which certainly profited in some measure from the challenged activity, undertook such transactions fully expecting to use foreign law to shield it from the reach of our laws. Such "deliberate courting" of foreign legal impediments will not be countenanced.…

It would be a travesty of justice to permit a foreign company to invade American markets, violate American laws if

§ 40 reads as follows:

§ 40. Limitations on Exercise of Enforcement Jurisdiction. Where two states have jurisdiction to prescribe and enforce rules of law and the rules they may prescribe require inconsistent conduct upon the part of a person, each state is required by international law to consider, in good faith, moderating the exercise of its enforcement jurisdiction, in the light of such factors as

a. vital national interests of each of the states,
b. the extent and the nature of the hardship that inconsistent enforcement actions would impose upon the person,
c. the extent to which the required conduct is to take place in the territory of the other state,
d. the nationality of the person, and
e. the extent to which enforcement by action of either state can reasonably be expected to achieve compliance with the rule prescribed by that state.

Continued

they were indeed violated, withdraw profits and resist accountability for itself and its principals for the illegality by claiming their anonymity under foreign law....

...BSI is directed to complete its answers to all of the demands in the SEC's First Interrogatories, pertaining to St. Joe.

[So ordered]

[*Authors' Note:* Faced with the judge's opinion and the possibility of substantial fines, BSI obtained a waiver of the secrecy laws from its customer and produced the requested information.]

QUESTIONS

1. What are the dominant factors considered by a court when deciding whether to issue a subpoena or discovery order to a foreign bank in a secrecy jurisdiction?
2. Did the court find that the Swiss interest in bank secrecy outweighed the U.S. interest?
3. Did BSI act in good faith?
4. Did the court give significant weight to BSI's potential liability under Swiss law?

involved constitutes a criminal offense under the laws of both the United States and Switzerland.

(c) Offshore Tax Evasion. Switzerland and other countries with histories of banking secrecy have yielded to United States and EU pressures to help cut down on tax evaders. The United States and Switzerland have agreed in an amended tax treaty to increase the amount of tax information they share. Swiss banks have been reluctant to provide client information, asserting that it would violate Swiss Privacy laws. **For Example,** Swiss Bank UBS AG admitted that its bankers and managers referred U.S. clients to lawyers and accountants who set up secret offshore entities to conceal assets from the IRS, and it agreed to pay $780 million to settle the federal investigation in the U.S. and the Swiss government's investigations. Subsequently the Swiss Financial Markets Supervising Authority ordered UBS to reveal account details to the U.S. authorities for some 250 customers, asserting that "banking secrecy remains intact," while it "doesn't protect tax fraudsters."[35]

8. Barriers to Trade

The most common barrier to the free movement of goods across borders is a tariff. A wide range of nontariff barriers also restricts the free movement of goods, services, and investments. Government export controls used as elements of foreign policy have proven to be a major barrier to trade with certain countries.

(a) Tariff Barriers. A **tariff** is an import or export duty or tax placed on goods as they move into or out of a country. It is the most common method used by countries to restrict foreign imports. The tariff raises the total cost, and thus the price, of an imported product in the domestic market. Thus, the price of a domestically produced product not subject to the tariff is more advantageous.

The U.S. Customs and Border Protection Service (Customs) imposes tariffs on imported goods at the port of entry. The merchandise is classified under a tariff schedule, which lists each type of merchandise and the corresponding duty rate (or percentage). Customs also determines the "computed value" of the imported goods under very precise statutory formulas.[36] The total amount of the duty is calculated by applying the duty percentage to the computed value figure.[37] Customs also has authority to investigate fraudulent schemes to avoid or underpay customs' duties.[38]

In the *Sabritas* case, an importer challenged Customs' classification of imported taco shells and potato chips.

[35] See "The Swiss Bank UBS Is Set to Open Its Secret Files," *New York Times*, **www.globalpost.com/dispatch/europe/110109/irs-offshore-bank-accounts-tax-cheats-switzerland-ubs.**

[36] See Tariff Act of 1930, as amended, 19 U.S.C. §1401 a(e).

[37] It is common for importers to utilize customs brokers who research the tariff schedules to see whether a product fits unambiguously under one of the Customs Service's classifications. A broker will also research the classifications given to similar products. It may find that a fax switch may be classified as "other telephonic switching apparatus" at a tariff rate of 8.5 percent or "other telegraphic switching apparatus" with a tariff of 4.7 percent. Obviously, the importer desires to pay the lower rate, and the broker with the assistance of counsel will make a recommendation to the Customs Service for the lower rate, and Customs will make a ruling. The decisions of the Customs Service are published in the *Customs Bulletin*, the official weekly publication of the Customs Service. See *Command Communications v. Fritz Cos.*, 36 P.3d 182 (Colo.App. 2001). See also *Estee Lauder, Inc. v. United States*, 815 F. Supp. 2d 1287 (Ct. Int'l Trade 2012), where the importer successfully challenged Custom's classification of a cosmetic product and the court declined to adopt Custom's position because of the flawed analysis and application of the "rule" therefrom, which has been inconsistent and arbitrary.

[38] *U.S. v. Inn Foods, Inc.*, 560 F.3d 1338 (Fed. Cir. 2009).

Sabritas v. United States, 998 F. Supp. 1123 (Ct. Int'l Trade 1998)

Customs Crunch!

Frito-Lay, Inc., owns a Mexican affiliate, Sabritas, S.A. de C.V., and it imports taco shells and *Munchos* potato chips from Mexico to the United States. Customs classified these products as "other bakers' wares" under Section 1905.90.90 of the Tariff Schedule subject to a 10 percent duty rate. Frito-Lay contends before the Court of International Trade that the import of taco shells is properly classified as "bread," which carries duty-free status. It also contends that *Munchos* are properly classified as potato chips and entitled to duty-free treatment.

JUDICIAL OPINION

TSOUCALAS, S. J.…The issue of whether an imported article has been classified under an appropriate tariff provision entails a two-step process: (1) ascertaining the proper meaning of specific terms in the tariff provision; and (2) determining whether the article comes within the description of such terms as properly construed. *Sports Graphics, Inc. v. United States*, 24 F.3d 1390, 1391 (Fed.Cir.1994.…

[To] determine the common meaning of a tariff term, the Court may utilize standard dictionaries and scientific authorities, as well as its own understanding of the term. The Court may also consider the testimony of credible witnesses as an aid in its understanding, although such testimony is not dispositive.

TACO SHELLS

Frito-Lay contends its taco shells are not properly classified as other bakers' wares because they are more specifically provided for as bread or, alternatively, as "biscuits and similar baked products" under…1905.90.10. Customs disagrees with plaintiff, alleging, mostly through testimonial evidence, that the frying of taco shells necessarily removes them from classification as either bread or biscuits and similar baked products.…

An *eo nomine* provision, such as 1905.90.10, includes all forms of the named article, in this case bread. As bread is not specifically defined in the [tariff provision] or in the relevant legislative history, it is necessary for the Court to determine, as a matter of law, the common and commercial meaning of the term bread to decide whether Frito-Lay's taco shells can be classified as such.

Customs maintains that Frito-Lay bases its contention on an intermediate article, the tortilla, and argues that frying baked tortillas substantially transforms them into a different article of commerce such that they are removed from the realm of bread. Indeed, Customs' expert, food scientist Dr. Nicholas Pintauro, defined bread in the following narrow manner:

> *Bread is a product that is formulated with a cereal grain that's in a flour form, with other ingredients such as shortening, salt, baking powder or a leavening agent and it is prepared as a dough and that dough has to be treated, which we call kneading so that you could develop the protein that's in the cereal portion of that dough so that the protein is in the form that would encapsulate the gas that's generated by the leavening agent so that you get a rise out of the dough and then at the proper time, in the form of a loaf, that dough is baked.*

Tr. 164-65. Dr. Pintauro's definition necessarily precludes any unleavened or fried products from falling within the common and commercial meaning of bread. Nothing could be further from the truth.…

First, **Sharon T. Herbst,** *Barron's Cooking Guide: Food Lover's Companion* 49 (1990) (emphasis added), recognizes that a bread may be fried, as it defines bread as a "staple… made from flour, water (or other liquid) and usually a LEAVENER [that] can be baked…fried or steamed." The Court also deems it exceptionally significant that two recognized bread treatises devote entire chapters to fried breads. *See* **Judith Jones,** *The Book of Bread* (1982) & **Dolores Casela,** *A World of Breads* (1966).

To contend that the common and commercial meaning of bread is limited to baked leavened (or even unleavened) products ignores the reality that flat, fried, usually ethnic breads exist in the United States market and are generally accepted as forms of bread. As Dr. Pintauro noted on cross-examination, "ethnic bread is bread. Period." Tr. 236; *see also* Tr. 132 (testimony that tortillas, of which hard taco shells are a type, are consumed throughout the United States, but primarily in the south and southwest); *Atwood-Stone Co. v. United States* 5 Ct. Cust.App. 472, 474 (CCPA 1914) ("The term 'bread'…is broad enough to cover all articles of food made from the flour or meal of grain, whether it will 'raise' or not"). The taco shells at issue, in particular, are not only found in obscure Mexican restaurants, but also on grocery store shelves and in the world's largest Mexican food chain, Taco Bell, which operates outlets across the United States. Tr. 45–46; 132–33.

Contrary to Customs' argument, therefore, the Court finds that the hard, flat, corn-based taco shells at issue are not "bread of de minimis commercial significance" or an "ancient

Continued

or obscure product" but, rather, articles that are commonly and commercially known as bread in the United States....

MUNCHOS

Frito-Lay contends its *Munchos* should be classified under... A2005.20.20 because they are fabricated, as opposed to natural, potato chips, and so, are a type of potato chips....

In opposition, Customs contends *Munchos* are not prepared or preserved potatoes, and so, cannot be classified under...A2005, Customs further points to several physical characteristics that differentiate *Munchos* from natural potato chips, including bulk density, color, texture and flavor. Finally, Customs claims that the process of producing *Munchos*, as well as the ingredient composition and merchandising of *Munchos*, differ greatly from those of potato chips....

Potato chips are consistently defined in food and non-food related sources as snack articles produced from thin slices of whole potatoes that are fried. For instance, *Webster's Third New International Dictionary* at 1774, defines a potato chip as "a thin slice of raw white potato fried crisp in deep fat."...

Munchos are composed of several ingredients, including dehydrated potato flakes, corn meal and potato starch, while potato chips are produced entirely from sliced raw whole potatoes....

The physical characteristics of *Munchos* in their final form also set them apart from conventional, natural potato chips....

Upon consideration of the proffered testimonial and documentary evidence and based on the Court's *in camera* inspection of the subject potato crisps, the Court agrees with [Customs] that Munchos are not a form of potato chips and are, therefore, removed from the scope of the...provision for potato chips.

CONCLUSION

Consequently, the Court concludes that Customs properly classified plaintiff's import *Munchos* potato crisps under 1905.90.90. The court also concludes that plaintiff's import taco shells are properly classified as bread under 1905.90.10 and orders Customs to reliquidate these items accordingly.

QUESTIONS

1. Summarize the matter before the court.
2. What decisional process does the court follow in determining whether an imported article is properly classified under the appropriate tariff provision by the Customs Service?
3. Compare Frito-Lay's *Munchos* to its Lay's Potato Chips and Pringles potato chips. Review the ingredients of each product and the merchandising of each product. Should all of these products be subject to the same tax treatment by the Customs Service?

(B) NONTARIFF BARRIERS. Nontariff barriers consist of a wide range of restrictions that inhibit the free movement of goods between countries. An import quota, such as a limitation on the number of automobiles that can be imported into one country from another, is such a barrier. More subtle nontariff barriers exist in all countries. **For Example,** Japan's complex customs procedures resulted in the restriction of the sale of U.S. made aluminum baseball bats in Japan. The customs procedures required the individual uncrating and "destruction testing" of bats at the ports of entry. Government subsidies are also nontariff barriers to trade.

One U.S. law—the Turtle Law—prohibits the importation of shrimp from countries that allow the harvesting of shrimp with commercial fishing technology that could adversely affect endangered sea turtles. **For Example,** two U.S. importers sought an exemption, representing that their Brazilian supply of shrimp was caught in the wild by vessels using turtle excluder devices (TEDs). Because Brazil had failed to comply with the U.S. Turtle Law by requiring TEDs on its commercial shrimp fleet, even though it had seven years to do so, the exemption was not granted.[39]

(C) EXPORT CONTROLS AS INSTRUMENTS OF FOREIGN POLICY. U.S. export controls have been used as instruments of foreign policy in recent years. **For Example,** the United States has sought to deny goods and technology of strategic or military importance to unfriendly nations. The United States has also denied goods such as grain, technology, and machine parts, to certain countries to protest or to punish activities considered violative of human rights or world peace.

[39] *Earth Island Institute v. Christopher*, 948 F. Supp. 1062 (Ct. Int'l Trade 1996). See *Turtle Island Restoration Network v. Evans*, 284 F.3d 1282 (Fed. Cir. 2002), on the continuing litigation on this topic and the clash between statutory enforcement and political and diplomatic considerations.

9. Relief Mechanisms for Economic Injury Caused by Foreign Trade

Certain U.S. industries may suffer severe economic injury because of foreign competition. U.S. law provides protection against unfair competition from foreigners' goods and provides economic relief for U.S. industries, communities, firms, and workers adversely affected by import competition. U.S. law also provides certain indirect relief for U.S. exporters and producers who encounter unfair foreign import restrictions.

(A) Antidumping Laws and Export Subsidies. Selling goods in another country at less than their fair value is called **dumping**. The dumping of foreign goods in the United States is prohibited under the Tariff Act of 1930, as amended including the antidumping laws contained in the Uraguay Round Agreement Act of 1994.[40] Proceedings in antidumping cases are conducted by two federal agencies, which separately examine two distinct components. The International Trade Administration (ITA) of the Department of Commerce (commonly referred to in cases as simply "Commerce") investigates whether specified foreign goods are being sold in the United States at less than fair value (LTFV). The International Trade Commission (ITC) conducts proceedings to determine if there is an injury to a domestic industry as a result of such sales. Findings of both LTFV sales and injury must be present before remedial action is taken. Remedial action might include the addition of duties to reflect the difference between the fair value of the goods and the price being charged in the U.S. Commerce and ITC decisions may be appealed to the Court of International Trade. Decisions of this court are reviewable by the U.S. Court of Appeals for the Federal Circuit and then the U.S. Supreme Court.

A settlement may be reached through a suspension agreement, whereby prices are revised to eliminate any LTFV sales and other corrective measures are taken.

American producers have to take the initiative and shoulder the expense of assisting government's enforcement of antidumping laws, and when antidumping laws are violated, producers are entitled to a reward as injured parties.[41]

The 1979 act also applies to subsidy practices by foreign countries. If subsidized goods are sold in the United States at less than their fair value, the goods may be subject to a countervailing duty.

Canada and Mexico may appeal countervailing duty assessments by the United States to an arbitration panel established under NAFTA. The NAFTA panel, however, can determine only whether the U.S. determinations were made in accordance with U.S. law. An appeal can also be made by member states to the WTO Dispute Settlement Body, which can determine whether the United States breached its obligations under the WTO.

(B) Relief from Import Injuries. Title II of the Trade Act of 1974[42] provides relief for U.S. industries, communities, firms, and workers when any one or more of them are substantially adversely affected by import competition. The Department of Commerce, the secretary of labor, and the president have roles in determining eligibility. The relief provided may be temporary import relief through the imposition of a duty or quota on the foreign goods. Workers, if eligible, may obtain readjustment allowances, job training, job search allowances, or unemployment compensation.

For Example, trade adjustment assistance, including unemployment compensation and training and relocation allowances, was provided for former employees of Johnson Controls Battery Group plants in Garland, Texas; Bennington, Vermont; and Owosso, Michigan, because surveys of the customers of those plants by the Department of Labor indicated that increased imports of aftermarket batteries, the products produced at these closed plants, caused the shutdowns. Former workers of the closed Louisville battery plant were not provided assistance because this plant produced new car batteries, and the work was shifted to another Johnson Controls plant in the United States.[43]

(C) Retaliation and Relief against Foreign Unfair Trade Restrictions. U.S. exporters of agricultural or manufactured goods or of services may encounter unreasonable, unjustifiable, or discriminatory foreign import restrictions. At the same time, producers from

40 19 U.S.C. §1675b (2000). See *Allegheny Ludlum Corp. v. United States,* 287 F.3d 1365 (Fed. Cir. 2002).

41 The Continued Dumping and Subsidy Offset Act of 2000 (the Byrd Amendment), 19 U.S.C. 1679c(a) (2000).

42 P.L. 93-618, 88 Stat. 1978, 19 U.S.C. §§2251, 2298.

43 20 F. Supp. 2d 1288 (Ct. Int'l Trade 1998). See also *Former Employees of Merrill Corp. v. U.S.,* 387 F. Supp. 2d 1336 (Ct. Int'l Trade 2005).

the foreign country involved may be benefiting from trade agreement concessions that allow producers from that country access to U.S. markets. Prior trade acts and the Omnibus Trade and Competitiveness Act of 1988 contain broad authority to retaliate against "unreasonable," "unjustifiable," or "discriminatory" acts by a foreign country.[44] The authority to retaliate is commonly referred to as "Section 301 authority." The fear or actuality of the economic sting of Section 301 retaliation often leads offending foreign countries to open their markets to imports. Thus, indirect relief is provided to domestic producers and exporters adversely affected by foreign unfair trade practices.

Enforcement of the act is entrusted to the U.S. trade representative (USTR), who is appointed by the president. Under the 1988 act, mandatory retaliatory action is required if the USTR determines that (1) rights of the United States under a trade agreement are being denied or (2) actions or policies of a foreign country are unjustifiable and a burden or restrict U.S. commerce. The overall thrust of the trade provisions of the 1988 act is to open markets and liberalize trade.

10. Expropriation

A major concern of U.S. businesses that do business abroad is the risk of expropriation of assets by a host government. Firms involved in the extraction of natural resources, banking, communications, or defense-related industries are particularly susceptible to nationalization. Multinational corporations commonly have a staff of full-time political scientists and former Foreign Service officers studying the countries relevant to their operations to monitor and calculate risks of expropriation. Takeovers of U.S.-owned businesses by foreign countries may be motivated by a short-term domestic political advantage or the desire to demonstrate political clout in world politics. Takeovers may also be motivated by long-term considerations associated with planned development of the country's economy.

Treaty commitments, or provisions in other international agreements between the United States and the host country, may serve to narrow expropriation uncertainties. Treaties commonly contain provisions whereby property will not be expropriated except for public benefit and with the prompt payment of just compensation.

One practical way to mitigate the risk of investment loss as a result of foreign expropriation is to purchase insurance through private companies, such as Lloyd's of London. Commercial insurance is also available against such risks as host governments' arbitrary recall of letters of credit and commercial losses resulting from embargoes.

The Overseas Private Investment Corporation (OPIC) is a U.S. agency under the policy control of the secretary of state. OPIC supports private investments in less developed, friendly countries. OPIC also offers asset protection insurance against risk of loss to plant and equipment as well as loss of deposits in overseas bank accounts to companies that qualify on the basis of the involvement of a "substantial U.S. interest."

11. The Foreign Corrupt Practices Act

The Foreign Corrupt Practices Act of 1977, as amended, prohibits U.S. based companies and foreign companies listed on U.S. stock exchanges from paying anything of value to foreign officials to obtain or retain business with a foreign government. The law is jointly enforced by the Department of Justice and the Securities and Exchange Commission. It requires strict accounting standards and internal control procedures to prevent the hiding of improper payments to foreign officials. The act prohibits any offers, payments, or gifts to foreign officials—or third parties who might have influence with foreign officials—to influence a decision on behalf of the firm making the payment. It provides for sanctions against the company and fines and imprisonment for the employees or agents involved. Moreover, the individuals involved may be responsible for damages as a result of civil actions brought by competitors under federal and state antiracketeering acts.[45]

The act does not apply to payments made to low-level officials for expediting the performance of routine government services.

[44] P.L. 100-418, 102 Stat. 1346, 15 U.S.C. §4727.

[45] P.L. 95-213, 94 Stat. 1494, 15 U.S.C. §78a nt.

Ethics & the Law

Combating Bribery of Foreign Public Officials in International Business Transactions

Prior to 1999, German law prohibited bribery of domestic public officials (and did not prohibit bribery of foreign officials). Siemens AG, headquartered in Germany and Europe's largest engineering conglomerate, conducts business throughout the world. Employees were allowed to withdraw up to €1 million for bribes from three "cash desks" set up at Siemens's offices to facilitate the obtaining of government contracts throughout the world. And, until 1999, Siemens claimed tax deductions for these bribes, many of which were listed as "useful expenditures."

The Organization for Economic Cooperation and Development (OECD) works on global issues, endeavoring to help member countries sustain economic growth and employment. OECD adopted its Anti-Bribery Convention on November 21, 1997; its regulations came into effect in 1999. In 1999, member countries, including Germany, adopted laws combating bribery of foreign public officials in international business transactions. However, between 2001 and 2004 some $67 million was withdrawn from the Siemens "cash desks." The bribery had continued! Mark Pieth, chairman of the working group on bribery at the OECD, said: "People felt confident that they were doing nothing wrong."* With some 470,000 employee jobs at Siemens depending on the ability to obtain engineering and high-tech contracts throughout the world, were Siemens contracting agents justified in continuing to make "useful expenditures" to save jobs and their company from ruin? How could these expenditures be a bad thing?

On December 11, 2008, Siemens AG pleaded guilty to criminal violations of the United States Foreign Corrupt Practices Act and received a total criminal fine of $450 million. It also reached a settlement with the U.S. Securities and Exchange Commission for violation of the FCPA's antibribery, books and records, and internal control provisions and agreed to pay $350 million in disgorgement of profits. Moreover, it agreed to fines and disgorgement of profits of $569 million to settle an investigation by the Munich Public Prosecutor's Office. Siemens's bribery was a bad thing because bribery and corruption were criminal acts.** Moreover, it allowed the corporation to have an inherently unfair competitive advantage over other contract bidders. The convention helps ensure that public works projects are awarded on the basis of sound economic judgment rather than on the basis of who offers the biggest bribe. The notoriety of the Siemens prosecutions should send a strong and clear message to all trading partners that parties to the convention must not engage in bribery to obtain business deals.*** Siemens's board member Peter Solmssen believes it is a myth that firms have to pay bribes to do business in developing countries, and believes that Siemens can increase sales without paying bribes.

*"The Siemens Scandal: Bavarian Baksheesh," *The Economist*, **www.economist.com/business/displaystory.cfm?story_id=12814642**.

See also *"SEC Charges Seven Former Siemens Executives with Bribing Leaders in Argentina, News Release,"* SEC 2011-263. On December 13, 2011, the Securities and Exchange Commission charged seven former Siemens executives with violating the Foreign Corrupt Practices Act for their involvement in the company's decade-long bribery scheme to retain a $1 billion government contract to produce national identity cards for Argentine citizens. The scheme lasted from 1996 to early 2007. The SEC's Enforcement Director said: "Corruption erodes public trust and the transparency of our commercial markets, and undermines corporate governance." **www.sec.gov./news/press/2011/2011-263.htm.

***The current members of the Anti-Bribery Convention are Argentina, Australia, Austria, Belgium, Brazil, Bulgaria, Canada, Chile, Czech Republic, Denmark, Estonia, Finland, France, Germany, Greece, Hungary, Iceland, Ireland, Israel, Italy, Japan, Korea, Luxemburg, Mexico, Netherlands, New Zealand, Norway, Poland, Portugal, Slovak Republic, Slovenia, South Africa, Spain, Sweden, Switzerland, Turkey, United Kingdom, and the United States.

LawFlix

The In-Laws (1979) (PG)

Review the segment in the film in which money is paid by a dictator for the sale of U.S. currency plates. The dictator's plan is to create worldwide inflation. List the various laws and conventions Peter Falk and Alan Arkin violate through their sale of the plates.

MAKE THE CONNECTION

SUMMARY

The World Trade Organization, a multilateral treaty subscribed to by the United States and most of the industrialized countries of the world, is based on the principle of trade without discrimination. The United Nations Convention on Contracts for the International Sale of Goods provides uniform rules for international sales contracts between parties in contracting nations. The European Union is a regional trading group that includes most of western Europe. The North American Free Trade Agreement involves Mexico, Canada, and the United States and eliminates all tariffs between the three countries over a 15-year period.

U.S. firms may choose to do business abroad by making export sales or contracting with a foreign distributor to take title to their goods and sell them abroad. U.S. firms may also license their technology or trademarks for foreign use. An agency arrangement or the organization of a foreign subsidiary may be required to participate effectively in foreign markets. This results in subjecting the U.S. firm to taxation in the host country. However, tax treaties commonly eliminate double taxation.

The Export Administration Act is the principal statute imposing export controls on goods and technical data.

In choosing the form for doing business abroad, U.S. firms must be careful not to violate the antitrust laws of host countries. Anticompetitive foreign transactions may have an adverse impact on competition in U.S. domestic markets. U.S. antitrust laws have a broad extraterritorial reach. U.S. courts apply a "jurisdictional rule of reason," weighing the interests of the United States against the interests of the foreign country involved in making a decision on whether to hear a case. Illegal conduct may occur in U.S. securities markets. U.S. enforcement efforts sometimes run into foreign countries' secrecy and blocking laws that hinder effective enforcement.

Antidumping laws offer relief for domestic firms threatened by unfair foreign competition. In addition, economic programs exist to assist industries, communities, and workers injured by import competition.

The Foreign Corrupt Practices Act restricts U.S. firms doing business abroad from paying public officials "commissions" for getting business contracts from the foreign governments.

LEARNING OUTCOMES

After studying this chapter, you should be able to clearly explain:

A. General Principles

LO.1 Explain which country's law will govern an international contract should a dispute arise

See the choice of law example where the U.S. Court required the Lipcons to "honor their bargains" and vindicate their claims in an English Court on p. 112.

LO.2 Identify seven major international organizations, conferences, and treaties that affect the multinational markets for goods, services, and investments

See the discussion of the GATT-WTO, CISG, UNCTAD, EU, NAFTA, IMF-World Bank, and OPEC beginning on p. 113.

LO.3 List the forms of business organizations for doing business abroad

See the discussion of export sales, appointing of an agent, foreign distributorships, licensing, subsidiaries, and joint ventures beginning on p. 117.

B. Governmental Regulation

LO.4 Explain the import protections afforded owners of U.S. intellectual property rights

See the discussion on the legal remedies provided owners of U.S. copyrights and trademarks against counterfeit goods, p. 119.

See the example excluding certain foreign-made mobile phones because the devices infringed on two Apple Inc. patents, p. 119.
See the *TianRui* case whereby the ITC excluded cast steel railway wheels made in a foreign country with misappropriated trade secrets of a U.S. manufacturer, pp. 120–121.
See the application of the U.S. Copyright Act's *first sale doctrine's* to gray market goods, p. 121.
See the *Lever Brothers* example barring importation of physically difficult foreign goods bearing trademarks identical to valid U.S. trademarks, p. 122.

LO.5 Explain the tariff barriers and nontariff barriers to the free movements of goods across borders

See the *Sabritas* case on the applicability of tariff barriers on pp. 127–128.
See the U.S. embargo on all Brazilian shrimp example because of Brazil's failure to require turtle excluder devices on its shrimp boats p. 128.

LO.6 Explain U.S. law regarding payment to foreign government officials as a means of obtaining business contracts with other governments, and compare U.S. law to laws and treaties applicable to most First World nations

See the Ethics & the Law discussion of the tax deductions for "useful expenditures" (bribes) claimed by Siemens AG, p. 131.

KEY TERMS

act-of-state doctrine
agent
blocking laws
choice-of-law clause
comity
Dispute Settlement Body (DSB)
distributor
dumping
effects doctrine
export sale
franchising
freight forwarders
gray market goods
intellectual property rights
joint venture
jurisdictional rule of reason
letter of credit
licensing
most-favored-nation clause
principal
secrecy laws
sovereign compliance doctrine
sovereign immunity doctrine
special drawing rights (SDRs)
tariff

QUESTIONS AND CASE PROBLEMS

1. How does the selling of subsidized foreign goods in the United States adversely affect free trade?
2. Able Time Inc. imported a shipment of watches into the United States. The watches bore the mark "TOMMY," which is a registered trademark owned by Tommy Hilfiger. U.S. Customs seized the watches pursuant to the Tariff Act, which authorizes seizure of any "merchandise bearing a counterfeit mark." Tommy Hilfiger did not make or sell watches at the time of the seizure. Able argues that because Tommy Hilfiger did not make watches at the time of the seizure, the watches it imported were not counterfeit, and the civil penalty imposed by Customs was unlawful. The government argues that the mark was counterfeit and the Tariff Act does not require the owner of the registered mark to make the same type of goods as those bearing the offending mark. Decide. [*U.S. v. Able Time, Inc.*, 545 F.3d 824 (9th Cir.)].
3. PepsiCo has registered its PEPSI trademarks in the U.S. Patent and Trademark Office. PEPSI products are bottled and distributed in the United States by PepsiCo and by authorized bottlers pursuant to Exclusive Bottling Appointment agreements, which authorize local bottlers to bottle and distribute PEPSI products in their respective territories. Similarly, PepsiCo has appointed local bottlers to bottle and distribute PEPSI products in Mexico within particular territories. Pacific Produce, Ltd., has been engaged in the sale and distribution within the

United States and Nevada of PEPSI products that were manufactured and bottled in Mexico and intended for sale in Mexico ("Mexican product"). The Mexican product sold by Pacific Products in the United States has certain material differences from domestic PEPSI products sold by PepsiCo: (1) it contains inferior paper labels that improperly report nutritional information; (2) it does not comply with the labeling standards followed by PepsiCo in the United States; (3) it is sold in channels of trade different from PepsiCo's authorized distribution channels without "drink by" notice dates on the Mexican product and monitoring on the Mexican product for proper shipment and storage conditions; and (4) it conflicts with the bottle return policies of PepsiCo. The Mexican product with its "Marca Reg" and Spanish language bottle caps is well received by consumers in Pacific Produce distribution channels. Classify the goods being sold by Pacific Produce. State the applicable law governing a dispute between PepsiCo and Pacific Produce. How would you decide this case? [*PepsiCo, Inc. v. Pacific Produce, Ltd.*,70 F. Supp. 2d 1057 (C.D. Cal.)]

4. Ronald Sadler, a California resident, owned a helicopter distribution company in West Germany, Delta Avia. This company distributed U.S. made Hughes civilian helicopters in western Europe. Sadler's German firm purchased 85 helicopters from Hughes Aircraft Co. After export licenses were obtained in reliance on the purchaser's written assurance that the goods would not be disposed of contrary to the export license, the helicopters were exported to Germany for resale in western Europe. Thereafter, Delta Avia exported them to North Korea, which was a country subject to a trade embargo by the United States. The helicopters were converted to military use. Sadler was charged with violating the Export Administration Regulations. In Sadler's defense, it was contended that the U.S. regulations have no effect on what occurs in the resale of civilian helicopters in another sovereign country. Decide.

5. Mirage Investments Corp. (MIC) planned a tender offer for the shares of Gulf States International Corp. (GSIC). Archer, an officer of MIC, placed purchase orders for GSIC stock through the New York office of the Bahamian Bank (BB) prior to the announcement of the tender offer, making a $300,000 profit when the tender offer was made public. The Bahamas is a secrecy jurisdiction. The bank informed the SEC that under its law, it could not disclose the name of the person for whom it purchased the stock. What, if anything, may the SEC do to discover whether the federal securities laws have been violated?

6. United Overseas, Ltd. (UOL), is a U.K. firm that purchases and sells manufacturers' closeouts in Europe and the Middle East. UOL's representative, Jay Knox, used stationery listing a UOL office in New York to solicit business from Revlon, Inc., in New York. On April 1, 1992, UOL faxed a purchase order from its headquarters in England to Revlon's New York offices for the purchase of $4 million worth of shampoo. The purchase order on its face listed six conditions, none of which referred to a forum selection clause. When Revlon was not paid for the shampoo it shipped, it sued UOL in New York for breach of contract. UOL moved to dismiss the complaint because of a forum selection clause, which it stated was on the reverse side of the purchase order and provided that "the parties hereby agree to submit to the jurisdiction of the English Courts disputes arising out of the contract." The evidence did not show that the reverse side of the purchase order had been faxed with the April 1992 order. Should the court dismiss the complaint based on the "forum selection clause"? Read Chapter 32 on letters of credit and advise Revlon how to avoid similar litigation in the future. [*Revlon, Inc. v. United Overseas, Ltd.*, 1994 WL 9657 (S.D.N.Y)]

7. Reebok manufactures and sells fashionable athletic shoes in the United States and abroad. It owns the federally registered Reebok trademark and has registered this trademark in Mexico as well. Nathan Betech is a Mexican citizen residing in San Diego, California, with business offices there. Reebok believed that Betech was in the business of selling counterfeit Reebok shoes in Mexican border towns, such as Tijuana, Mexico. It sought an injunction in a federal district court in California ordering Betech to cease his counterfeiting activity and to refrain from destroying

certain documents. It also asked the court to freeze Betech's assets pending the outcome of a Lanham Act lawsuit. Betech contended that a U.S. district court has no jurisdiction or authority to enter the injunction for the activities allegedly occurring in Mexico. Decide. [*Reebok Int'l, Ltd. v. Marnatech Enterprises, Inc.,* 970 F.2d 552 (9th Cir.)]

8. Assume that before the formation of the European Union, the lowest-cost source of supply for a certain product consumed in France was the United States. Explain the basis by which, after the EU was formed, higher-cost German producers could have replaced the U.S. producers as the source of supply.

9. A complaint was filed with the U.S. Commerce Department's ITA by U.S. telephone manufacturers AT&T, Comidial Corp., and Eagle Telephones, Inc., alleging that 12 Asian manufacturers of small business telephones, including the Japanese firms Hitachi, NEC, and Toshiba and the Taiwanese firm Sun Moon Star Corp., were dumping their small business phones in the U.S. market at prices that were from 6 percent to 283 percent less than those in their home markets. The U.S. manufacturers showed that the domestic industry's market share had dropped from 54 percent in 1985 to 33 percent in 1989. They asserted that it was doubtful if the domestic industry could survive the dumping. Later, in a hearing before the ITC, the Japanese and Taiwanese respondents contended that their domestic industry was basically sound and that the U.S. firms simply had to become more efficient to meet worldwide competition. They contended that the United States was using the procedures before the ITA and ITC as a nontariff barrier to imports. How should the ITC decide the case? [*American Telephone and Telegraph Co. v. Hitachi,* 6 I.T.C. 1511]

10. Campbell Soup Co. imports tomato paste from a wholly owned Mexican subsidiary, Sinalopasta, S.A. de C.V. It deducted $416,324 from the computed value of goods shipped to the United States, which was the cost of transportation of the finished tomato paste from Sinalopasta's loading dock in Mexico to the U.S. border. The deduction thus lowered the computed value of the goods and the amount of duty to be paid the U.S. government by Campbell Soup Co. United States Customs questioned this treatment of freight costs. Tariff Act §140a(e)(1)(B) requires that profits and general expenses be included in calculating the computed value of goods, which in part quantify the value of the merchandise in the country of production. Is Campbell's position correct? [*Campbell Soup Co., Inc. v. United States,* 107 F.3d 1556 (Fed. Cir.)]

11. Roland Staemphfli was employed as the chief financial officer of Honeywell Bull, S.A. (HB), a Swiss computer company operating exclusively in Switzerland. Staemphfli purportedly arranged financing for HB in Switzerland through the issuance of promissory notes. He had the assistance of Fidenas, a Bahamian company dealing in commercial paper. Unknown to Fidenas, the HB notes were fraudulent. The notes were prepared and forged by Staemphfli, who lost all of the proceeds in a speculative investment and was convicted of criminal fraud. HB denied responsibility for the fraudulently issued notes when they came due. Fidenas's business deteriorated because of its involvement with the HB notes. It sued HB and others in the United States for violations of U.S. securities laws. HB defended, arguing that the U.S. court did not have jurisdiction over the transactions in question. Decide. [*Fidenas v. Honeywell Bull, S.A.,*606 F.2d 5 (2d Cir.)]

12. Marc Rich & Co., A.G., a Swiss commodities trading corporation, refused to comply with a grand jury subpoena requesting certain business records maintained in Switzerland and relating to crude oil transactions and possible violations of U.S. income tax laws. Marc Rich contended that a U.S. court has no authority to require a foreign corporation to deliver to a U.S. court documents located abroad. The court disagreed and imposed fines, froze assets, and threatened to close a Marc Rich wholly owned subsidiary that did business in the state of New York. The fines amounted to $50,000 for each day the company failed to comply with the court's order. Marc Rich appealed. Decide. [*Marc Rich v. United States,* 707 U.S. 633 (2d Cir.)]

13. U.S. Steel Corp. formed Orinoco Mining Co., a wholly owned corporation, to mine large deposits of iron ore that U.S. Steel had discovered in Venezuela. Orinoco, which was incorporated in Delaware, was subject to Venezuela's maximum tax of 50 percent on net income. Orinoco was also subject to U.S. income tax, but the U.S. foreign tax credit offset this amount. U.S. Steel purchased the ore from Orinoco in Venezuela. U.S. Steel formed Navios, Inc., a wholly owned subsidiary, to transport the ore. Navios, a Liberian corporation, was subject to a 2.5 percent Venezuelan excise tax and was exempt from U.S. income tax. Although U.S. Steel was Navios's primary customer, it charged other customers the same price it charged U.S. Steel. U.S. Steel's investment in Navios was $50,000. In seven years, Navios accumulated nearly $80 million in cash but had not paid any dividends to U.S. Steel. The IRS used IRC §482 to allocate $52 million of Navios's income to U.S. Steel. U.S. Steel challenged this action, contending Navios's charges to U.S. Steel were at arm's length and the same it charged other customers. Decide. [*United States Steel Corp. v. Commissioner,* 617 F.2d 942 (2d Cir.)]

14. National Computers, Inc., a U.S. firm, entered into a joint venture with a Chinese computer manufacturing organization, TEC. A dispute arose over payments due the U.S. firm under the joint venture agreement with TEC. The agreement called for disputes to be arbitrated in China, with the arbitrator being chosen from a panel of arbitrators maintained by the Beijing arbitration institution, Cietac. What advantages and disadvantages exist for the U.S. firm under this arbitration arrangement? Advise the U.S. firm on negotiating future arbitration agreements with Chinese businesses.

15. Sensor, a Netherlands business organization wholly owned by Geosource, Inc., of Houston, Texas, made a contract with C.E.P. to deliver 2,400 strings of geophones to Rotterdam by September 20, 1982. The ultimate destination was identified as the USSR. Thereafter, in June 1982, the president of the United States prohibited shipment to the USSR of equipment manufactured in foreign countries under license from U.S. firms. The president had a foreign policy objective of retaliating for the imposition of martial law in Poland, and he was acting under regulations issued under the Export Administration Act of 1979. Sensor, in July and August of 1982, notified C.E.P. that as a subsidiary of a U.S. corporation, it had to respect the president's embargo. C.E.P. filed suit in a district court of the Netherlands asking that Sensor be ordered to deliver the geophones. Decide. [*Compagnie Européenne des Pétroles v. Sensor Nederland,* 22 I.L.M. 66]

Crimes

learningoutcomes

After studying this chapter, you should be able to

LO.1 Discuss the nature and classification of crimes

LO.2 Describe the basis of criminal liability

LO.3 Identify who is responsible for criminal acts

LO.4 Explain the penalties for crimes and the sentencing for corporate crimes

LO.5 List examples of white-collar crimes and their elements

LO.6 Describe the common law crimes

LO.7 Discuss crimes related to computers

LO.8 Describe the rights of businesses charged with crimes and the constitutional protections afforded them

Society sets certain standards of conduct and punishes a breach of those standards as a crime. This chapter introduces the means by which government protects people and businesses from prohibited conduct.

A. General Principles

Detailed criminal codes and statutes define crimes and specify their punishment. Crimes vary from state to state but still show the imprint of a common law background through similar elements and structure.

1. Nature and Classification of Crimes

A **crime** is conduct that is prohibited and punished by a government. Crimes are classified as *common law* or *statutory* according to their origin. Offenses punishable by less than one year in prison are called **misdemeanors**. More serious crimes are called **felonies**, including serious business crimes such as bribery and embezzlement, which are punishable by confinement in prison for more than one year. Misdemeanors include weighing goods with uninspected scales or operating without a sales tax license. An act may be a felony in one state and a misdemeanor in another.[1]

2. Basis of Criminal Liability

A crime generally consists of two elements: (1) a mental state (scienter or intent) and (2) an act or omission. Harm may occur as a result of a crime, but harm is not an essential element of a crime.

(A) Mental State. Mental state, or intent, does not require an awareness or knowledge of guilt. In most crimes, the voluntary commission of the act is sufficient for proving mental state. Ignorance that a law is being broken does not mean there is not mental state. **For Example,** dumping waste without a permit is still a criminal act even when the party releasing the waste did not know about the permit requirement.

(B) Act or Omission. Specific statutes define the conduct that, when coupled with sufficient mental state, constitutes a crime. **For Example,** writing a check knowing you do not have the funds available is a crime. Likewise, the failure to file your annual income tax returns is also a crime. The *U.S. v. Erickson* case involves an issue of the criminal act of document falsification.

U.S. v. Erickson, 561 F.3d 1150 (10th Cir. 2009)

Making Stuff Up for the Grand Jury

Kathryn Erickson was the general manager of the Uintah Special Services District (USSD), a company that worked to obtain federal-mineral-lease revenues for road projects. She, along with her secretary, Cheryl McCurdy, administered the (USSD) from a small office in Vernal, Utah. Ms. Erickson's authority was limited and she was not permitted to enter into or modify contracts without board approval.

Mitchell Construction was a major contractor for USSD. In 1998, USSD awarded Mitchell Construction two contracts that were to be completed within the 1998 construction year.

During 1999 and 2000 Mitchell Construction continued to perform work on the projects covered by its 1998 contracts with USSD, despite their expiration. It submitted invoices to USSD and was paid for this work.

In June 1999 a federal grand jury began to investigate contracting irregularities at USSD and the Uintah County Road Department and issued a *subpoena duces tecum* to USSD requesting copies of "project contracts, invoices" between USSD and contractors.

While the office was preparing the response for the grand jury subpoena, Ms. McCurdy saw Ms. Erickson prepare a handwritten change order for a Mitchell contract and saw Ms. Erickson and Gilman N. Mitchell both sign it. The change order, which was backdated to January 13, 1999, extended the contract through December 31, 2000.

Ms. McCurdy later discovered that two other change orders had been created and backdated. She spent a day copying documents for the grand jury and recording, on a handwritten list, all of the documents that she had copied. However, she left Ms. Erickson in the office while she was working on the list in order to go home for dinner. Ms. Erickson called her and told her not to come back

[1] Some states further define crimes by seriousness with different degrees of a crime, such as first-degree murder, second-degree murder, and so on. Misdemeanors may be differentiated by giving special names to minor misdemeanors.

Continued

because all the copying was done. Later, Ms. McCurdy found on Ms. Erickson's desk a photocopy of the grand jury document list and saw that two entries not in her handwriting had been added. These entries were for change orders for contracts between Mitchell Construction and USSD. Ms. McCurdy reported the change to the government.

Ms. Erickson and Mr. Mitchell were each indicted by a grand jury on three counts of obstruction of justice by knowingly falsifying a document with the knowledge and intent that the grand jury would rely on it.

The jury returned a verdict of guilty against both Ms. Erickson and Mr. Mitchell on all three counts. The two appealed.

JUDICIAL OPINION

HARTZ, Circuit Judge…The Defendants were convicted of violating 18 U.S.C. § 1503, which prohibits "corruptly… influenc[ing], obstruct[ing], or imped[ing], or endeavor[ing] to influence, obstruct, or impede, the due administration of justice." We have identified three "core" elements of this offense: "(1) There must be a pending judicial proceeding; (2) the defendant must have knowledge or notice of the pending proceeding; and (3) the defendant must have acted corruptly with the specific intent to obstruct or impede the proceeding in its due administration of justice." In construing the elements of the offense, the Supreme Court has endorsed a nexus test, requiring that

> *[t]he action taken by the accused must be with an intent to influence judicial or grand jury proceedings; it is not enough that there be an intent to influence some ancillary proceeding, such as an investigation independent of the court's or grand jury's authority…. [T]he act must have a relationship in time, causation, or logic with the judicial proceedings. [I]f the defendant lacks knowledge that his actions are likely to affect the judicial proceeding, he lacks the requisite intent to obstruct.*

"The nexus limitation is best understood as an articulation of the proof of wrongful intent that will satisfy the *mens rea* requirement of 'corruptly' obstructing or endeavoring to obstruct." *United States v. Quattrone*, 441 F.3d 153, 170 (2d Cir.2006).

Ms. Erickson and Mr. Mitchell concede that the first two elements of the offense are not at issue: A grand-jury proceeding was pending at the time of the charged conduct and both Defendants knew of it. Moreover, although Defendants' briefs occasionally speak in general terms of the absence of evidence of intent, their specific arguments focus on the issue of nexus. The essence of their various arguments is that the government failed to show how their conduct affected the grand-jury investigation.

We are not persuaded.

Here, the Defendants created false documents to deliver to the grand jury in response to its subpoena. The evidence was sufficient to satisfy the nexus requirement.

Both Defendants insist that the government failed to present evidence that the grand jury was misled or otherwise affected by their submission of falsified change orders. But the required nexus is only that the charged conduct "have the natural and probable effect of interfering with the due administration of justice." Success is not necessary; "an 'endeavor' suffices."

Ms. Erickson also asserts that the backdated change orders did no more than memorialize the reality of what had happened during 1999 and 2000; that reality, she says, was that Mitchell Construction continued to do work for USSD and to submit invoices that its board duly paid. But a reasonable jury could reject this innocent explanation for the change orders. USSD board member Merlin Sinfield testified that the board trusted Ms. Erickson and did not scrutinize the paperwork she presented to it, which typically included multiple invoices for each check. Sinfield also testified that the board had not known of the change orders and that he now recognized that it was improper for USSD to pay Mitchell Construction after the paving contracts had run. In any event, the fraudulent documents compromised the grand jury's ability to make its own determination whether the work in 1999 and 2000 was authorized. A grand jury is obstructed whenever it is presented with manufactured evidence, even if the manufacturer thinks that the evidence supports "reality." Ms. Erickson's challenge to the sufficiency of the evidence on this ground fails.

In brief, we hold that knowingly submitting fraudulent documents in response to a grand-jury subpoena constitutes obstruction of justice, when, as here, a grand-jury proceeding is underway and the defendant knows of it. The evidence was therefore sufficient to convict Defendants of violating § 1503.

QUESTIONS

1. List the three requirements for proving an obstruction of justice case.
2. How does the court respond to the defendants' arguments that no one was hurt by what was done?
3. What would be an effective business policy for responding to subpoenas?

3. Responsibility for Criminal Acts

In some cases, persons who did not necessarily commit the criminal act itself are still held criminally responsible for acts committed by others.

(A) Corporate Liability. Corporations are held responsible for the acts of their employees. A corporation may also be held liable for crimes based on the failure of its employees to act. In the past decade, some of the nation's largest corporations have paid fines for crimes based on employees' failure to take action or for the actions they did take. **For Example,** Siemens, an international company, paid the largest fine in the history of the Foreign Corrupt Practices Act for paying bribes in order to win contracts in countries around the world, a total of $1.6 billion in fines, including $350 million in the United States.

(B) Officers and Agents of Corporations. One of the main differences between nonbusiness and business crimes is that more people in a company can be convicted for the same business crime. For nonbusiness crimes, only those who are actually involved in the act itself can be convicted of the crime. For business crimes, however, managers of firms whose employees commit criminal acts can be held liable if the managers authorized the conduct of the employees or knew about their conduct and did nothing or failed to act reasonably in their supervisory positions to prevent the employees from engaging in criminal conduct. **For Example,** the former security chief for Massey Mines was sentenced to three years in prison after being found guilty of notifying employees in advance of the arrival of federal mine inspectors at the company's mines.[2] The *U.S. v. Park* case deals with an issue of corporate officer liability.

United States v. Park, 421 U.S. 658 (1975)

Rats In the Warehouse and a CEO with a Fine

Acme Markets, Inc., was a national food retail chain headquartered in Philadelphia, Pennsylvania. At the time of the government action, John R. Park [respondent] was president of Acme, which employed 36,000 people and operated 16 warehouses.

In 1970, the Food and Drug Administration (FDA) forwarded a letter to Mr. Park describing, in detail, problems with rodent infestation in Acme's Philadelphia warehouse facility. In December 1971, the FDA found the same types of conditions in Acme's Baltimore warehouse facility. In January 1972, the FDA's chief of compliance for its Baltimore office wrote to Mr. Park about the inspection. The letter included the following language:

> *We note with much concern that the old and new warehouse areas used for food storage were actively and extensively inhabited by live rodents. Of even more concern was the observation that such reprehensible conditions obviously existed for a prolonged period of time without any detection, or were completely ignored.*
>
> *We trust this letter will serve to direct your attention to the seriousness of the problem and formally advise you of the urgent need to initiate whatever measures are necessary to prevent recurrence and ensure compliance with the law.*

After Mr. Park received the letter, he met with the vice president for legal affairs for Acme and was assured that he was "investigating the situation immediately and would be taking corrective action."

When the FDA inspected the Baltimore warehouse in March 1972, there was some improvement in the facility, but there was still rodent infestation. Acme and Park were both charged with violations of the Federal Food, Drug, and Cosmetic Act. Acme pleaded guilty. Mr. Park was convicted and fined $500; he appealed based on error in the judge's instruction, given as follows:

> *The individual is or could be liable under the statute, even if he did not consciously do wrong. However, the fact that the Defendant is president and is a chief executive officer of the Acme Markets does not require a finding of guilt. Though he need not have personally participated in the situation, he must have had a responsible relationship to the issue. The issue is, in this case, whether the Defendant, John R. Park, by virtue of his position in the company, had a position of authority and responsibility in the situation out of which these charges arose.*

The court of appeals reversed Mr. Park's conviction, and the government appealed.

[2] Ken Maher, "Ex-Massey Official Gets Three Years," *Wall Street Journal*, March 1, 2012, p. A3.

Continued

JUDICIAL OPINION

BURGER, C. J..... Central to the Court's conclusion [in *United States v Dotterweich*], 320 U.S. 277 (1943), that individuals other than proprietors are subject to the criminal provisions of the Act was the reality that "the only way in which a corporation can act is through the individuals who act on its behalf."

At the same time, however, the Court was aware of the concern...that literal enforcement "might operate too harshly by sweeping within its condemnation any person however remotely entangled in the proscribed shipment." A limiting principle, in the form of "settled doctrines of criminal law" defining those who "are responsible for the commission of a misdemeanor," was available. In this context, the Court concluded, those doctrines dictated that the offense was committed "by all who have...a responsible share in the furtherance of the transaction which the statute outlaws."

The Act does not, as we observed in *Dotterweich*, make criminal liability turn on "awareness of some wrongdoing" or "conscious fraud." The duty imposed by Congress on responsible corporate agents is, we emphasize, one that requires the highest standard of foresight and vigilance, but the Act, in its criminal aspect, does not require that which is objectively impossible. The theory upon which responsible corporate agents are held criminally accountable for "causing" violations of the Act permits a claim that a defendant was "powerless" to prevent or correct the violation to "be raised defensively at a trial on the merits." *U.S. v. Wiesenfield Warehouse Co.*, 376 U.S. 86 (1964). If such a claim is made, the defendant has the burden of coming forward with evidence, but this does not alter the Government's ultimate burden of proving beyond a reasonable doubt the defendant's guilt, including his power, in light of the duty imposed by the Act, to prevent or correct the prohibited condition.

Turning to the jury charge in this case, it is of course arguable that isolated parts can be read as intimating that a finding of guilt could be predicated solely on respondent's corporate position.... Viewed as a whole, the charge did not permit the jury to find guilt solely on the basis of respondent's position in the corporation; rather, it fairly advised the jury that to find guilt it must find respondent "had a responsible relation to the situation," and "by virtue of his position...had authority and responsibility" to deal with the situation. The situation referred to could only be "foods...held in unsanitary conditions in a warehouse with the result that it consisted, in part, of filth or...may have been contaminated with filth."

Park testified in his defense that he had employed a system in which he relied upon his subordinates, and that he was ultimately responsible for this system. He testified further that he had found these subordinates to be "dependable" and had "great confidence" in them.

[The rebuttal] evidence was not offered to show that respondent had a propensity to commit criminal acts, that the crime charged had been committed; its purpose was to demonstrate that respondent was on notice that he could not rely on his system of delegation to subordinates to prevent or correct unsanitary conditions at Acme's warehouses, and that he must have been aware of the deficiencies of this system before the Baltimore violations were discovered. The evidence was therefore relevant since it served to rebut Park's defense that he had justifiably relied upon subordinates to handle sanitation matters.

"[Reversed]"

QUESTIONS

1. How long had Mr. Park known about the rats in the warehouse?
2. Does it matter that a subordinate did not respond?
3. Do officers need to be certain their subordinates are reliable in order to avoid criminal liability?

(c) Federal Laws Targeting Officer and Director Criminal Responsibility. Following the Michael Milken and Ivan Boesky junk bond era on Wall Street in 1988, the Insider Trading and Securities Fraud Act of 1988 increased the criminal penalties for officers and directors who violated the law tenfold. In addition, the "white-collar kingpin" law imposed mandatory minimum sentences for corporate officers. Sarbanes-Oxley, which followed the 2000-era dot-com failures increased penalties for officers and directors from 5 years to 20 years, along with an increase in fines by 20 times. Under The Dodd-Frank Wall Street Reform and Consumer Protection Act, the types of white-collar executives covered under criminal laws increased to include brokers, insurers, and any financial services firms.

So-called "honest services" fraud has been refined by Dodd-Frank and court decisions.[3] Executives can no longer be convicted on the basis that something went wrong at their company. Proof of fraud requires something more than an officer just being an officer at the company—there must be active engagement in operations that led to the officer's committing fraud.

[3] *Skilling v. U.S.* 130 S.Ct. 2896 (2010).

(D) Penalty for Crime: Forfeiture. When a defendant is convicted of a crime, the court may also declare that the defendant's rights in any property used or gained from a crime (an instrument of that crime) be confiscated. Some types of instruments of the crime are automatically forfeited, such as the tools of a crime. **For Example,** the U.S. government confiscated from confessed $50-billion-Ponzi schemer, Bernie Madoff, everything from his yacht to his bank accounts to his seat on NASDAQ. Confiscation is, in effect, an increased penalty for the defendant's crime.

(E) Penalties for Business and White-Collar Crimes. Most common law criminal penalties were created with "natural" persons in mind, as opposed to "artificial" or corporate persons. A $100,000 fine may be significant to an individual but to a corporation with $3 billion in assets and hundreds of millions in income, such a fine could be viewed as a minimal cost of doing business.

As a result of these fine amount realities, corporate penalties and processes have been reformed. Congress, prosecutors, and the courts are in a continual process of developing penalties for corporations and white-collar crimes so that the result is both a deterrent effect as well as changes in cultures of corporations to prevent additional violations.

(E)(1) Computing New Penalties for Corporations. Criminal penalties have been increased to allow judges to fine corporations according to how much a bad decision would cost. For example, if a company develops a faulty product, net earnings could decline 10 to 20 percent. Criminal penalties can be assessed as a percentage of net income.

Rather than using fixed-amount fines for corporations, statutes and courts apply percentage of revenue penalties. **For Example,** a bad decision on a product line would cost a company 10 percent to 20 percent of its earnings. A criminal penalty could be imposed in the same percentage fashion with the idea that the company simply made a bad legal decision that should be reflected in earnings.

(E)(2) Corporate Integrity Agreements. Using a corporate integrity agreement (CIA), judges are able to, in effect, place corporations on probation. Under CIAs, companies are assigned monitors who are on-site and follow up to be sure the company is not committing any further violations. **For Example,** because of environmental law violations, ConEd was assigned a monitor from the National Resources Defense Council to observe the company's activities. CIAs do not require an admission of guilt, but generally require the payment of a fine and an agreement to "stay clean" for three to five years.

(E)(3) Federal Sentencing Guidelines. Another change in penalties for business and white-collar crimes has been the requirement for mandatory prison sentences for officers and directors who are convicted of crimes committed as they led their corporations. The human element of the corporation is then punished for the crimes that the business committed. The U.S. Sentencing Commission, established by Congress in 1984, has developed both federal sentencing guidelines and a carrot-and-stick approach to fighting business crime. If the managers of a company are involved and working to prevent criminal misconduct in the company and a crime occurs, the guidelines permit sentence reductions for the managers' efforts. If the managers do not adequately supervise conduct and do not encourage compliance with the law, the guidelines require judges to impose harsher sentences and fines. The guidelines, referred to as the **Federal Sentencing Guidelines** (or the *U.S. Sentencing Guidelines*), apply to federal crimes such as securities fraud, antitrust violations, racketeering, theft (embezzlement), Medicare fraud, and other business crimes. The sentencing guidelines permit a judge to place a guilty company on probation, with the length of the probation controlled by whether the company had prevention programs in place.

(E)(4) Mandatory Sentences for Officers of Corporations Who Mastermind Crimes. Following the collapse of companies such as Enron, WorldCom, and Adelphia, the U.S. Sentencing Commission (USSC) piloted the passage of the 2001 Economic Crime Package: Consolidation, Clarification, and Certainty. Amended guidelines, post-Enron, address the increased corporate and white-collar criminal penalties enacted under Sarbanes-Oxley (SOX) (see (E)(5) for more discussion of SOX), and consider the seriousness of the offense, the company's history of violations, its cooperation in the investigation, the effectiveness of its compliance program (often called an *ethics program*), and the role of senior management in the wrongdoing. Corporate managers found to have masterminded any criminal activity must be sentenced to prison time.[4] Figure 8-1 is a summary of

[4] *U.S. v. Booker*, 543 U.S. 220 (2005).

FIGURE 8-1 ***Roster of White-Collar Criminal Charges***

COMPANY/PERSON	ISSUE	STATUS
Andrew Fastow, former CFO of Enron (2004)	Multimillion-dollar earnings from serving as principal in SPEs of Enron created to keep debts off the company books; significant sales of shares during the time frame preceding company collapse	Resigned as CFO; appeared before Congress and took the Fifth Amendment; entered guilty plea to securities and wire fraud; sentence of 6 years; reduced to 5 years and 3 months; completed at the end of 2012
Galleon Group (hedge fund 2011). A Goldman Sachs director who fed information to Galleon Group was also convicted of insider trading.	Insider trading charges (securities fraud)	Twenty-three executives, including CEO, convicted or entered guilty pleas; Galleon's $3.7 billion fund liquidated; CEO sentenced to 11 years
Bernie Ebbers (2005) Former CEO, WorldCom	Fraud	Convicted; sentenced to 25 years
Computer Associates (2004)	Criminal investigation for securities fraud and obstruction following $2.2 billion restatement in sales	Company paid $225 million fine; former CEO entered guilty plea to felony charges; sentenced to 11 years; company changed name to CA, Inc.
Countrywide Mortgage (2009)	Insider trading; securities fraud	Former CEO Angelo Mozilo charged with insider trading, CFO and COO charged with failure to disclose firm's relaxed lending standards; settled cases for fines
Enron (2001)	Earnings overstated through mark-to-market accounting; off-the-book/special-purpose entities (SPEs) carried significant amounts of Enron debt not reflected in the financial statements; significant offshore SPEs (881 of 3,000 SPEs were offshore, primarily in Cayman Islands)	Company in bankruptcy; impetus for SOX; CFO Andrew Fastow and others entered guilty pleas; Jeffrey Skilling, former CEO, found guilty
HealthSouth (2003)	$2.7 billion accounting fraud; overstatement of revenues	Sixteen former executives indicted; 5 plead guilty; see Richard Scrushy
KPMG (2006)	Tax shelter fraud	Settled by paying a penalty of $456 million fine in lieu of indictment; 16 former partners and employees indicted; most charges dismissed
L. Dennis Kozlowski, former CEO of Tyco (2003)	Accused of improper use of company funds	Indicted in New York for failure to pay sales tax on transactions in fine art; hung jury on charges of looting Tyco; convicted on retrial with 15–25-year sentence; denied parole in 2012
Bernard Madoff (2009)	Ran a $50-billion Ponzi scheme through Madoff Securities	Entered guilty plea to all charges and refused to cooperate with investigators; 150-year sentence (at age of 71 in 2009, it is the equivalent of a life sentence)
Martha Stewart, CEO of Martha Stewart Living, Omnimedia, Inc., and close friend of Dr. Waksal (2003)	Sold 5,000 shares of ImClone one day before public announcement of negative FDA action on Erbitux	Indicted and convicted, along with her broker at Merrill Lynch, of making false statements and conspiracy; served sentence and probation
Richard Scrushy (2003)	Indicted for fraud and bribery for HealthSouth accounting fraud	Acquitted of all charges related to HealthSouth; convicted of bribing former governor of Alabama
Stanford Securities (2012)	$9 billion Ponzi scheme	CEO convicted of mail, wire, and securities fraud; Laura Pendergest-Holt, the former chief investment officer, entered a guilty plea to obstruction of an SEC investigation

the current penalties for federal crimes. Under a U.S. Supreme Court decision in 2005, *U.S. v. Booker,* judges may only use the guidelines as just that, guidelines; the sentencing ranges are no longer mandatory for judges.[5] Going outside those ranges, however, is carefully reviewed by appellate courts.[6] Federal judges can consider only evidence presented at trial in making their sentencing determinations. They can consider evidence of prior convictions, but only if that evidence was presented at trial or if the defendant has a chance to present evidence about those convictions at the sentencing.[7]

(E)(5) SARBANES-OXLEY REFORMS TO CRIMINAL PENALTIES. Part of SOX, passed by Congress following the collapses of Enron and WorldCom corporations, was the **White-Collar Crime Penalty Enhancement Act of 2002.**[8] This act increases penalties substantially. **For Example,** the penalties for mail and wire fraud are increased from a maximum of 5 years to a maximum of 20 years. Penalties for violation of pension laws increased from 1 year to 10 years and the fines increased from $5,000 to $100,000.[9] In addition, many federal statutes now require executives to reimburse their companies for any money earned as a result of illegal activity. **For Example,** the former CEO of UnitedHealth Group Inc. was required to pay back $448 billion in profits he had made from stock options that were granted illegally.[10]

(E)(6) CREATIVE PENALTIES FOR WHITE-COLLAR CRIME. Federal judges are developing new types of sentences in order to use those convicted to convince business people to avoid criminal conduct. **For Example,** in 2009, a federal judge required an executive who entered a guilty plea to spend his two years of probation writing

Thinking Things Through

Can a Pharmacy's License Be Revoked for Too Many Cash Sales of Oxycodone?

The Drug Enforcement Administration (DEA) has moved to revoke the controlled medication licenses of two pharmacies because the pharmacies were filling prescriptions for oxycodone (the painkiller) in excess of their monthly allowances for controlled substances. In addition, the DEA alleges that the pharmacies' corporate entities failed to conduct on-site inspections and failed to notice that 42 to 58 percent of all the sales of the substances were cash sales, something that is considered a red flag in the sale and distribution of controlled substances. In addition, the number of prescriptions filled continued to escalate.

The two pharmacies won an injunction against the revocation in federal district court. However, the DEA is hoping to persuade the judge to lift the injunction once it is able to show that the corporations should have known there was a problem. The rate of cash sales at these pharmacies was eight times the national rate for filling prescriptions with cash. Pharmacists at the drug stores, in interviews with the DEA agents, indicated that the customers paying cash for the oxycodone were "shady," and that they suspected that some of the prescriptions were not legitimate. One of the companies adjusted (increased) the levels of shipment of oxycodone to the pharmacies five times. In one on-site visit by a DEA agent, the following information emerged: one of every three cars that came to the drive-thru window had a prescription for oxycodone; many patients living at the same address had the same prescriptions for oxycodone from the same doctor.

Both companies, CVS and Cardinal Health, have indicated in court filings that they have changed their practices and provided training to pharmacy personnel so that they can spot these types of illegal prescriptions and report suspicious activity. Both pharmacy companies have terminated customers, meaning that they will no longer fill prescriptions for those customers.

The DEA seeks to hold the corporations responsible because of the lack of on-site presence and the failure to follow the numbers for sales and distribution at the pharmacies. Can the corporation be held liable when it was not actually participating in the distribution of the oxycodone?

Source: Timothy W. Martin and Devlin Barrett, "Red Flags Ignored, DEA Says," *Wall Street Journal,* February 21, 2012. p. B1.

[5] *U.S. v. Skilling,* 554 F.3d 529 (5th Cir. 2009).
[6] *Gall v. U.S.,* 552 U.S. 38 (2007).
[7] Miriam H. Baer, "Choosing Punishment," 92 *Boston Univ. Law Rev.* 577 (2010).
[8] 18 U.S.C. §1314 *et seq.*
[9] 18 U.S.C. §§1341 and 1343; 29 U.S.C. §1131.
[10] S. Almashat et al., "Rapidly Increasing Criminal and Civil Monetary Penalties Against the Pharmaceutical Industry: 1991 to 2010," *Public Citizen's Health Research Group,* December 16, 2010, available at **www.citizen.org/documents/rapidlyincreasingcriminalandcivilpenalti**

a book about what he did and offer guidance to business executives so that they can avoid his missteps. He was required to publish and distribute the book.[11] In 2010, a federal agency agreed to defer penalties if an officer agreed to travel around the country and speak to companies and executives about the mistakes he had made in order to help them understand the need for vigilance in stopping missteps that lead to crimes.

4. Indemnification of Crime Victims

Penalties are paid to the government. Typically, the victim of a crime does not benefit from the criminal prosecution and conviction of the wrongdoer, although courts can order that restitution be paid to victims.

The Victims of Crime Act of 1984 creates a federal Crime Victims Fund.[12] Using the fines paid into the federal courts as well as other monies, the federal government makes grants to the states to assist them in financing programs to provide assistance for victims of crime.[13] The Victim and Witness Protection Act of 1982 authorizes the sentencing judge in a federal district court to order, in certain cases, that the defendant make restitution (restoration) to the victim or pay the victim the amount of medical expenses or loss of income caused by the crime.[14]

Victims may also be entitled to bring civil actions for recovery of the damages they experience because a crime is committed. **For Example,** a company or individual violating federal antitrust laws is liable to the victim for three times the damages actually sustained.

B. White-Collar Crimes

White-collar crime is generally considered business crime, the type committed generally in the course of doing business and usually involving some form of deceit used to get gains.

5. Conspiracies

The crime of conspiracy is committed before the actual crime; it is the planning of the crime. A **conspiracy** is an agreement between two or more persons to commit an unlawful act or to use unlawful means to achieve an otherwise lawful result. Some conspiracy statutes do require that those charged must have done something to carry out the agreement before the crime of conspiracy is committed.

6. Crimes Related to Production, Competition, and Marketing

(A) Improper Use of Interstate Commerce. The shipment of improper goods or the transmission of improper information in interstate commerce is a federal crime. **For Example,** knowingly shipping food with salmonella would be a violation of the federal law that prohibits shipping adulterated foods, drugs, or cosmetics in interstate commerce.

The Communications Act of 1934, as amended, makes it a crime to manufacture or sell devices knowing their primary use is to unscramble satellite telecasts without having paid for the right to do so.[15]

(B) Securities Crimes. To protect the investing public, both state and federal laws have regulated the issuance and public sale of stocks and bonds. These statutes and the crimes associated with sales of securities are covered in Chapter 46.

7. Money Laundering

The federal government has adopted a Money Laundering Control Act (MLCA).[16] The act prohibits the knowing and willful participation in a financial transaction when the transaction is designed to conceal or disguise the source of the funds. The so-called *USA Patriot Act* that was passed on October 26, 2001, less than two months after the destruction of the World Trade Center and the damage to the Pentagon on September 11, 2001, includes a substantial number of changes and amendments to the

[11] Natasha Singer, "Judge Orders Former Bristol-Myers Executive to Write Book," *New York Times*, June 9, 2009, p. B3.

[12] 18 U.S.C. §3771. The act was amended in 2004 to include a type of bill of rights for crime victims, including assistance through the newly created Office for Victims of Crime.

[13] 18 U.S.C. §1401 *et seq.*

[14] 18 U.S.C. §3579, as amended by 18 U.S.C. §18.18; see *Hughey v. United States,* 495 U.S. 411 (1990). Some states likewise provide for payment into a special fund. Ex parte *Lewis*, 556 So.2d 370 (Ala. 1989). In 2002, Congress passed another victims' compensation statute, with this one providing relief and assistance to the victims of terrorist attacks in the United States. 42 U.S.C. §10603b.

[15] 47 U.S.C. §705(d)(1), (e)(4), 47 U.S.C. §605 (d)(1), (e)(4); *United States v. Harrell,* 983 F.2d 36 (5th Cir. 1993); but see *DIRECTV, Inc. v. Robson,* 420 F.3d 740 (6th Cir. 2000).

[16] 18 U.S.C. §§1956–1957 (2000). *U.S. v. Prince,* 214 F.3d 740 (6th Cir. 2000).

MLCA and the Bank Secrecy Act (BSA).[17] Both statutes have been used as means to control bribery, tax evasion, and money laundering. Their changes and amendments were designed to curb the funding of terrorist activities in the United States.

The Patriot Act expands the coverage of the law from banks and financial institutions to anyone involved in financial transactions, which includes securities brokers; travel agents; those who close real estate transactions; insurance companies; loan or finance companies; casinos; currency exchanges; check-cashing firms; auto, plane, and boat dealers; and branches and agencies of foreign banks located in the United States. The amendments make even small businesses subject to the requirements of disclosure under MLCA and BSA, such as reporting cash transactions in excess of $10,000.

In addition, the types of accounts covered have been expanded. The accounts covered are not only securities accounts but also money market accounts. Furthermore, banks are now more actively involved in supervising accounts and following through on government information furnished to the bank on suspicious transactions and activities as well as individuals. Banks are required to implement new policies to prevent the types of transactions tagged by the government and conduct internal investigations for suspicious transactions. Because of the required close-watch provisions of these laws, banks and others covered under the federal statutes have developed anti-money-laundering programs. These programs must include a "Know Your Customer" training segment that teaches employees how to spot suspicious customers and transactions.

8. Racketeering

Congress passed the **Racketeer Influenced and Corrupt Organizations (RICO) Act**[18] in 1970 as part of the Organized Crime Control Act. The law was designed primarily to prevent individuals involved in organized crime from investing money obtained through racketeering in legitimate businesses. However, the broad language of the act, coupled with a provision that allows individuals and businesses to sue for treble damages, has resulted in an increasing number of lawsuits against ordinary business persons not associated with organized crime.

(A) Criminal and Civil Applications. RICO authorizes criminal and civil actions against persons who use any income derived from racketeering activity to invest in, control, or conduct an enterprise through a pattern of *racketeering activity.*[19] In criminal and civil actions under RICO, a pattern of racketeering activity must be established by proving that at least two acts of racketeering activity—so-called *predicate acts*—have been committed within 10 years.[20] Conviction under RICO's criminal provisions may result in a $25,000 fine and up to 20 years' imprisonment as well as forfeiture of the property involved. A successful civil plaintiff may recover three times the actual damages suffered and attorney fees.[21]

(B) Expanding Usage. Civil RICO actions have been successful against business entities, such as accounting firms, labor unions, insurance companies, commercial banks, and stock brokerage firms. However, under the Private Securities Litigation Reform Act of 1995, securities fraud was eliminated as a **predicate act**, or a qualifying underlying offense, for private RICO actions, absent a prior criminal conviction.[22]

9. Bribery

Bribery is the act of giving money, property, or any benefit to a particular person to influence that person's judgment in favor of the giver.[23] At common law, the crime was limited to doing such acts to influence a public official.

The giving and the receiving of a bribe constitute separate crimes. In addition, the act of trying to

[17] 31 U.S.C. §531(h).

[18] 18 U.S.C. §§1961–1968.

[19] §1961. Definitions:
(1) "Racketeering activity" means any act or threat involving murder, kidnapping, gambling, arson, robbery, bribery, extortion, dealing in obscene matter, dealing in a controlled substance or listed chemical, or sports bribery; counterfeiting; theft from interstate shipment; embezzlement from pension and welfare funds; extortionate credit transactions; fraud; wire fraud; mail fraud; procurement of citizenship or nationalization unlawfully; reproduction of naturalization or citizenship papers; obstruction of justice; tampering with a witness, victim, or an informant; retaliating against a witness, victim, or an informant; false statement in application and use of passport; forgery or false use of passport; fraud and misuse of visas, permits, and other documents; racketeering; unlawful welfare fund payments; laundering of monetary instruments; use of interstate commerce facilities in the commission of murder-for-hire; sexual exploitation of children; interstate transportation of stolen motor vehicles; interstate transportation of stolen property; trafficking in counterfeit labels of phonorecords, computer programs or computer program documentation, or packaging and copies of motion pictures or other audiovisual works; criminal infringement of a copyright; trafficking in contraband cigarettes; and white slave traffic.

[20] Brian Slocum, "RICO and the Legislative Supremacy Approach to Federal Criminal Lawmaking," 31 *Loyola Univ. Chicago Law Journal* 639 (2000).

[21] *Criminal RICO: 18 U.S.C. 1961–1968: A Manual for Federal Prosecutors.* Washington, D.C.: U.S. Dept. of Justice, Criminal Division, Organized Crime and Racketeering Section, [2009].

[22] 15 U.S.C. §78(a), (n)–(t).

[23] *In re Mangone*, 923 N.Y.S.2d 679 (2011).

obtain a bribe may be a crime of solicitation of bribery in some states, while in other states bribery is broadly defined to include solicitation of bribes.

10. Commercial Bribery

Commercial bribery is a form of bribery in which an agent for another is paid or given something of value in order to make a decision on behalf of his or her principal that benefits the party paying the agent. **For Example,** a napkin supplier who pays a restaurant agent $500 in exchange for that agent's decision to award the restaurant's napkin contract to that supplier has engaged in commercial bribery.[24]

11. Extortion and Blackmail

Extortion and *blackmail* are crimes in which money is exchanged for either specific actions or restraint in taking action.

(A) Extortion. When a public officer makes an illegal demand, the officer has committed the crime of **extortion**. **For Example,** if a health inspector threatens to close down a restaurant on a false sanitation law charge unless the restaurant pays the inspector a sum of money, the inspector has committed extortion. (If the restaurant voluntarily offers the inspector the money to prevent the restaurant from being shut down because of actual violations of the sanitation laws, the crime committed would be bribery.)

(B) Blackmail. In jurisdictions where extortion is limited to the conduct of public officials, a nonofficial commits **blackmail** by making demands that would be extortion if made by a public official. Ordinarily, blackmail is the act of threatening someone with publicity about a matter that would damage the victim's personal or business reputation.

12. Corrupt Influence

Legislative bodies have increasingly outlawed certain practices that exert a corrupting influence on business transactions.

(A) Improper Political Influence. At the federal and state levels, it is a crime for one who holds public office to hold a financial interest in or to receive money from an enterprise that seeks to do business with the government. Such conduct is a conflict of interest between the official's duty to citizens and his or her personal financial interests. **For Example,** the former governor of Illinois, Rod Blagojevich, was convicted of seeking funds, fundraisers, and positions in exchange for political favors. To keep officials' conduct transparent, lobbyists must register in Washington, D.C.,[25] and adhere to statutory limits on gifts and contributions to political campaigns. Public officials must file annual disclosure forms about their financial positions as well as provide a disclosure of all gifts and their value.

(B) Foreign Corrupt Practices Act. The **Foreign Corrupt Practices Act (FCPA)** is a federal criminal statute that applies to businesses whose principal offices are in the United States; it is an antibribery and anticorruption statute covering these companies' international operations.[26] The FCPA prohibits making, authorizing, or promising payments or gifts of money or anything of value with the intent to corrupt. This prohibition applies to payments or gifts designed to influence official acts of foreign officials, parties, party officials, candidates for office, nongovernmental organizations (NGOs), or any person who transmits the gift or money to these types of persons.[27]

The FCPA does not prohibit **grease** or **facilitation payments**. These are payments made only to get officials to perform their normal duties or to perform them in a timely manner. Facilitation payments are those made to (1) secure a permit or a license, (2) obtain paper processing, (3) secure police protection, (4) provide phone, water, or power services, or (5) obtain any other similar action.

13. Counterfeiting

Counterfeiting is making, with fraudulent intent, a document or coin that appears to be genuine but is not because the person making it did not have the

[24] Connecticut's commercial bribery statute is a good example. It provides: *A person is guilty of commercial bribery when he confers, or agrees to confer, any benefit upon any employee, agent or fiduciary without the consent of the latter's employer or principal, with intent to influence his conduct in relation to his employer's or principal's affairs.* CGSA §53a-160 (2012). Other examples of commercial bribery statues can be found at Minn. Stat Ann §609.86 (Minnesota 2012); NH Rev Stat §638:8 (New Hampshire 2010); Alaska Stat §11.45.670 (Alaska 2012); and Ala. Code §13A-11-120 (Alabama 2012). Mississippi prohibits commercial bribery as well as sports bribery, which is paying the agent of a sports team in order to influence the outcome of a sporting event. Miss. Code Ann §97-9-10 (2010).

[25] Foreign Agents Registration Act, 22 U.S.C. §611 *et seq.*, as amended.

[26] 15 U.S.C. §78dd-1 *et seq.*

[27] A state-owned electric utility is considered an instrumentality of government. *United States v. Aguilar*, 783 F. Supp. 2d 1108 (C.D. Cal. 2011).

Ethics & the Law

Am I My Company's Keeper?

Think about the following statements by the former CEOs of companies that had accounting fraud.

CEO	QUOTE
Ken Lay, Enron	"Enron was an enormous corporation. How could I have known everything going on everywhere in the company?"
Richard Scrushy, HealthSouth	"You have to rely; you have to trust people. You have to believe. You have to delegate . . . I signed off on the information based on what was provided to me. And what I was told."
Bernie Ebbers, WorldCom	"Bernie Ebbers did not know about the accounting decisions of Scott Sullivan to reassign billions of dollars."
John Rigas, Adelphia	"John Rigas had a right to trust and rely on professionals and his own staff to get the financials right."

Are the CEOs responsible for knowing what goes on at their companies? Are they able to find out what is happening? Are they criminally responsible? Are they ethically responsible?

Source: Mike France, "The New Accountability," *BusinessWeek,* July 25, 2004. p. 30 at p. 32.

authority to make it. It is a federal crime to make, to possess with intent to transfer, or to transfer counterfeit coins, bank notes, or obligations or other securities of the United States. Various states also have statutes prohibiting the making and passing of counterfeit coins and bank notes. These statutes often provide, as does the federal statute, a punishment for the mutilation of bank notes or the lightening (of the weight) or mutilation of coins.

14. Forgery

Forgery consists of the fraudulent making or material altering of an instrument, such as a check, that attempts to create or changes a legal liability of another person.[28] Ordinarily, **forgery** consists of signing another's name with intent to defraud, but it may also consist of making an entire instrument or altering an existing one. It may result from signing a fictitious name or the offender's own name with the intent to defraud.

The issuing or delivery of a forged instrument to another person constitutes the crime of **uttering** a forged instrument. Sending a forged check through the channels of commerce or of bank collection constitutes an uttering of a forged instrument. The act of depositing a forged check into the forger's bank account by depositing it in an automatic teller machine constitutes uttering within the meaning of a forgery statute.[29]

15. Perjury

Perjury consists of knowingly giving false testimony in a judicial proceeding after having been sworn to tell the truth. Knowingly making false answers on any form filed with a government typically constitutes perjury or is subjected to the same punishment as perjury. In some jurisdictions, the false answers given in a situation other than in court or the litigation process is called the crime of *false swearing.* The penalties for perjury were increased substantially under SOX.

16. False Claims and Pretenses

Many statutes make it a crime to submit false claims or to obtain goods by false pretenses.

(A) False Claims. The federal false statement statute makes it a crime to knowingly and willfully make a false material statement about any matter within the jurisdiction of any department or agency of the United States. **For Example,** it is a crime for a

[28] Misrepresenting the nature of a document in order to obtain their signature on it is forgery. *State v. Martinez,* 74 Cal. Rptr. 3d 409 (2008).
[29] *Warren v. State,* 711 S.E.2d 108 (Ga. App. 2011).

contractor to make a false claim against the United States for payment for work that was never performed. It is also a crime to make false statements about income and assets on a student's application for federal financial aid.

(B) Obtaining Goods by False Pretenses. Almost all states have statutes that forbid obtaining money or goods under false pretenses.[30] An intent to defraud is an essential element of obtaining property by false pretenses.[31]

Examples of false pretense include delivering a check knowing that there is insufficient money in the bank account to cover the check.[32] False representations as to future profits in a business are also forms of false pretenses. Identity theft can be prosecuted under false pretenses statutes.[33]

Failing to perform on a contract is not a false pretense crime unless the contract had been entered into with the intent of not performing it.[34]

(C) Unauthorized Use of Automated Teller Machine. Obtaining money from an automated teller machine (ATM) by the unauthorized use of the depositor's ATM card is a federal crime.

(D) False Information Submitted to Banks. Knowingly making false statements in a loan application to a federally insured bank is a federal crime.[35] It is also a crime for a landowner to put a false value on land transferred to a bank as security for a loan.[36] **For Example,** many of the initial criminal charges in the subprime mortgage market collapse have involved mortgage brokers and appraisers who misrepresented property value or applicants' income in their mortgage applications for federally insured loans.

17. Bad Checks

Under a bad check statute, it is a crime to use or pass a check with the intent to defraud with the knowledge that there are insufficient funds in the bank to pay the check when it is presented for payment. Knowledge that the bad check will not be paid when presented to the bank is an essential element of the crime. The bad check statutes typically provide that if the check is not made good within a specified number of days after payment by the bank is refused, it is presumed that the defendant acted with the intent to defraud.[37] For more information on checks, see Chapters 28 and 31.

18. Credit Card Crimes

It is a crime to steal a credit card and, in some states, to possess the credit card of another person without that person's consent. Using a credit card without the permission of the card owner is the crime of obtaining goods or services by false pretenses or with the intent to defraud. Likewise, a person who continues to use a credit card with the knowledge that it has been canceled is guilty of the crime of obtaining goods by false pretenses. Federal law also makes it a crime to use counterfeit credit cards for purposes of obtaining goods, services, or cash. The statute now covers the use of credit card numbers on the Internet in order to obtain goods and services.[38]

19. Embezzlement

Embezzlement is the fraudulent conversion of another's property or money by a person to whom it has been entrusted.[39] Employees who take or sell their employer's property or funds for personal use have committed the crime of embezzlement. An agent employee commits embezzlement when he receives and keeps payments from third persons—payments the agent should have turned over to the principal. **For Example,** when an insured gives money to an insurance agent to pay the insurance company but the insurance agent uses the money to pay premiums on the policies of other persons, the agent is guilty of embezzlement. Generally, the intent to return or actual return of the property or money embezzled is no defense.

[30] *Mass. v. Cheromcka,* 850 N.E.2d 1088 (Mass. App. 2006).
[31] *State v. Moore,* 903 A.2d 669 (Conn. App. 2006).
[32] *U.S. v. Tudeme,* 457 F.3d 577 (Fed. App. 2006).
[33] *State v. Parker,* 2009 WL 1065988 (Ariz. App. 2009).
[34] *Higginbotham v. State,* 356 S.W.3d 584 (Tex. App. 2011).
[35] 18 U.S.C. §1014. See *United States v. Autorino,* 381 F.3d 48 (2nd Cir. 2004).
[36] *U.S. v. Rizk,* 660F.3d 1125 (9th Cir. 2011).
[37] *McMillan v. First Nat. Bank of Berwick,* 978 A.2d 370 (Pa. Super. 2009).
[38] 18 U.S.C. §1029. Fines for credit card fraud were increased in 2002 to levels between $50,000 and $100,000 per offense.
[39] *State v. Henry,* 73 So.3d 958 (La. App. 2011); *Stern v. Epps,* 464 Fed.Appx. 388 (5th Cir. 2012).

20. Obstruction of Justice: Sarbanes-Oxley (SOX)

Another SOX provision clarifies what constitutes obstruction of justice and increases the penalties for such an act. The new section makes it a felony for anyone, including company employees, auditors, attorneys, and consultants,

> *to alter, destroy, mutilate, conceal, cover up, falsify or make a false entry with the "intent to impede, obstruct, or influence the investigation or proper administration of any matter within the jurisdiction of any department or agency of the United States."* [40]

The statute goes on to address audit records specifically and requires auditors to retain their work papers related to a client's audit for at least five years. Any destruction of documents prior to that time constitutes a felony and carries a penalty of up to 20 years. The statute was passed in response to the conduct of Arthur Andersen, the audit firm for the collapsed Enron Corporation. Many of the firm's audit papers on Enron were destroyed, but the firm and partner-in-charge escaped criminal liability because the government could not establish that the senior managers in Andersen were aware of the shredding.[41]

21. Corporate Fraud: SOX

SOX also created a new form of mail and wire fraud. Ordinarily, mail or wire fraud consists of the use of the mail or telephones for purposes of defrauding someone of money and/or property. However, the

Sports & Entertainment Law

The NBA Referee, Gambling, and Some Tossed Games

Tim Donaghy, a referee for the NBA, entered a guilty plea to two federal felony charges in connection with his bets and tips on NBA games. The charges were conspiracy to engage in wire fraud and transmitting betting information via interstate commerce. Mr.Donaghy picked teams to win in games he was scheduled to referee. Mr. Donaghy committed the equivalent of insider trading on Wall Street by providing outsiders with information about games, players, and referees. He got $5,000 from his tippees for correct picks.

Mr. Donaghy began betting on games in 2003, but in December 2006 began passing along inside information to others who were also charged in the conspiracy. The communication was in code via cell phone. Mr.Donaghy explained at his sentencing that he had a gambling addiction problem and took medication under the treatment of a psychiatrist.

The NBA Commissioner, David Stern, referred to Mr. Donaghy as a "rogue referee," but said that the gambling charges were a wake-up call for the NBA and that it must not be "complacent."*

Mr. Donaghy's missteps were discovered as the federal government was conducting an investigation into the Gambino crime family, based in Brooklyn.

Commissioner Stern said that the NBA would be looking at the checks and balances that the NFL has built into its system including Las Vegas travel prohibitions on referees. The NFL also has significant background checks and ongoing monitoring of its referees.

Mr. Donaghy ran a basketball clinic for developmentally disabled boys in Springfield, PA (Mr. Donaghy's hometown) for almost a decade. He was a graduate of Villanova and had worked his way up to being one of the NBA's top referees, coming through the ranks of refereeing in both high school and the Continental Basketball Association. Mr. Donaghy had a wife and four children. His salary with the NBA during 2006 was $260,000. Mr. Donaghy was sentenced to 15 months in prison. After serving 11 months of his prison term, Mr. Donaghy was released to a halfway house, but was sent back to prison to finish out his term because of violations of the terms of his partial release. He wrote a book about his actions, *Personal Foul: A First-Person Account of the Scandal That Rocked the NBA*.

Why do you think Mr. Donaghy was engaged in gambling? Doesn't his civic activity paint a different picture of his character? Mr. Donaghy said in an interview about his book that what he did was no different from Wall Streeters who engaged in insider trading except, "I didn't affect the economy." How would you analyze his comparison?

*Roscoe Nance, "Scandal Is a 'Wakeup Call,' Stern Says," *USA Today*, August 16, 2007 p. 1C.

[40] 18 U.S.C. §1519. *U.S. v. Hunt*, 526 F.3d 739 (11th Cir. 2008).

[41] *Arthur Andersen LLP v. U.S.*, 544 U.S. 696 (2005). The obstruction conviction of the firm was reversed because of insufficient proof of the firm's actual knowledge of document destruction.

SOX form of mail or wire fraud is based on new requirements imposed on corporate officers to certify their financial statements when they are issued. If a corporate officer fails to comply with all requirements for financial statement certification or certifies financial statements that contain false material information, the officer and company have committed corporate fraud with penalties that range from fines of $1,000,000 and/or 10 years to $5,000,000 and/or 20 years for willful violation of the certification requirements.

22. The Common Law Crimes

In contrast to white-collar crimes, *common law crimes* are crimes that involve the use of force or the threat of force or cause injury to persons or damage to property. The following sections discuss crimes of force and crimes against property that affect businesses.

(A) Larceny. *Larceny* is the wrongful or fraudulent taking of the personal property of another by any person with fraudulent intent. Shoplifting is a common form of larceny. In many states, shoplifting is made a separate crime. In some states, all forms of larceny and robbery are consolidated into a statutory crime of theft. At common law, there was no crime known as theft.

(B) Robbery. *Robbery* is the taking of personal property from the presence of the victim by use of force or fear. Most states have aggravated forms of robbery, such as robbery with a deadly weapon. Snatching a necklace from the neck of the victim involves sufficient force to constitute robbery. When the unlawful taking is not by force or fear, as when the victim does not know that the property is being taken, the offense is larceny, but it cannot be robbery.

Some statutes may be aimed at a particular kind of robbery. **For Example,** carjacking is a federal crime under the Anti-Car Theft Act of 1992.[42]

(C) Burglary. At common law, *burglary* was the breaking and entering during the night into the dwelling house of another with the intent to commit a felony. Inserting the automatic teller card of another, without their knowledge or permission, into an automatic teller machine set in the wall of the bank may constitute an entry into the bank for the purpose of committing burglary.[43] Some states word their burglary statutes, however, so that there is no burglary in this automatic teller case. This act would be covered by other criminal statutes.

Modern statutes have eliminated many of the elements of the common law definition so that under some statutes it is now immaterial when or whether there was an entry to commit a felony. The elements of breaking and entering are frequently omitted. Under some statutes, the offense is aggravated and the penalty is increased, depending on the place where the offense was committed, such as a bank building, freight car, or warehouse. Related statutory offenses, such as the crime of possessing burglars' tools, have been created.

(D) Arson. At common law, *arson* was the willful and malicious burning of another's dwelling. The law was originally designed to protect human life, although arson has been committed just with the burning of the building even if no one is actually hurt. In most states, arson is a felony, so if someone is killed in the resulting fire, the offense is considered a felony-murder. Under the felony-murder rule, homicide, however unintended, occurring in the commission of a felony is automatically classified as murder. Virtually every state has created a special offense of burning to defraud an insurer.

(E) Riots and Civil Disorders. Damage to property in the course of a riot or civil disorder is ordinarily covered by other types of crimes such as the crime of larceny or arson. In addition, the act of assembling as a riotous mob and engaging in civil disorders is generally some form of crime in itself under either common law concepts of disturbing the peace or modern antiriot statutes, even without destruction or theft of property. However, statutes on civil disorders must be carefully drawn to avoid infringing on constitutionally protected free speech.

C. Criminal Law and the Computer

In some situations, ordinary crimes cover computer crimes situations. In other situations, new criminal law statutes are required.

[42] 18 §2119. See *U.S. v. Bell,* 608 F. Supp. 2d 1257 (Kan. 2009).

[43] *People v. Cardwell,* 137 Cal. Rptr.3d 525 (2012).

23. What Is a Computer Crime?

Generally, the term **computer crime** is used to refer to a crime that can be committed only by a person having some knowledge of the operation of a computer. Just as stealing an automobile requires knowledge of how to operate and drive a car, so the typical computer crime requires the knowledge of how the computer works.

Because the more serious and costly wrongs relating to computers do not fit into the ordinary definitions of crime, there are now computer-specific criminal statutes: Computer crimes can be committed against the computer, using the computer, or through the computer.

24. The Computer as Victim

A traditional crime may be committed by stealing or intentionally damaging a computer.

(A) Theft of Hardware. When a computer itself is stolen, the ordinary law relating to theft crimes should apply. Theft of a computer is subject to the same law as the theft of a truck or a desk.

(B) Theft of Software. When a thief takes software, whether in the form of a program written on paper or a program on a disk or memory stick, something has been taken, but it is not tangible property as larceny requires. Virtually every state makes stealing software a crime. Chapter 11 provides more information on crimes, software, and the Internet.

(C) Intentional Damage. The computer may be the "victim" of a crime when it is intentionally destroyed or harmed. In the most elementary form of damage, the computer could be harmed if it was smashed with an ax or destroyed in an explosion or a fire. In such cases, the purpose of the intentional damage is to cause the computer's owner the financial loss of the computer and the destruction of the information that is stored in it.

Intentional damage can result from more subtle means. Gaining access to the computer and then erasing or altering the data is also the crime of intentional damage. Likewise, interfering with the air conditioning so computers are damaged or malfunction would also be covered under intentional damage statutes. Planting a bug or virus in the software, causing the program to malfunction or to give incorrect output, is a form of intentional damage. Angry employees, former employees, and competitors have all been convicted of intentional damage.

25. Unauthorized Use of Computers

The unlawful use of a computer belonging to someone else is also a crime in some states. There are specific statutes at the state and federal levels that make it unlawful to use government computers without permission. One of the issues that is critical in criminal prosecution is whether the use was, in fact, "unauthorized." With Wi-Fi networks, the ease of access and openess has proven to be a challenge in prosecution for unauthorized use.[44]

26. Computer Raiding

Taking information from a computer without the consent of the owner is a crime. Whether theft is accomplished by instructing the computer to make a printout of stored information or by tapping into its data bank by electronic means is not important. In some states, taking information is known as the crime of "computer trespass."[45]

Both Congress and state legislatures have adopted statutes that make it a crime to gain unauthorized access to a computer or use information so gained to cause harm to the computer or its rightful user.[46] Again, the presence of Wi-Fi when there are unsecured users has complicated prosecutions for taking information.

27. Diverted Delivery by Computer

In many industries, a computer controls the delivery of goods. The person in charge of that computer or someone unlawfully gaining access to it may cause the computer to direct delivery to an improper place. That is, instead of shipping goods to the customers to whom they should go, the wrongdoer diverts the goods to a different place, where the wrongdoer or a confederate receives them.

[44] U.S.C. §1030(e)(6); for an article summarizing the issues, see Orin S. Kerr, "Cybercrime's Scope: Interpreting 'Access' and 'Authorization' in Computer Misuse Statutes", 78 *N.Y.U. L. Rev.* 1596, 1632-37 (2003).

[45] *Washington v. Riley,* 846 P.2d 1365 (Wash. 1993).

[46] The Counterfeit Access Device and Computer Fraud Act of 1984, 18 U.S.C. §1030 *et seq.;* Computer Fraud and Abuse Act of 1986, 18 U.S.C. §1001; Electronic Communications Privacy Act of 1986, 18 U.S.C. §2510; Computer Fraud Act of 1987, 15 U.S.C. §§272, 278, 40 U.S.C. §759; National Information Infrastructure Protection Act, 18 U.S.C. §1030 (protecting confidentiality and integrity on the Internet).

E-Commerce & Cyberlaw

They Were Bullies: Mean Girls in Cyberspace

It has been called the MySpace suicide case. On May 14, 2008, a federal grand jury indicted Lori Drew, 49, of Missouri, the so-called cyber bully. Ms. Drew had created a MySpace site for Josh Evans, a fictitious teen boy she used as a means of getting information from Megan Meier, a 13-year-old girl with whom Ms. Drew's daughter had had a falling-out. Josh pretended to be interested in Megan, but then said that she was "fat" and that the world would be a better place without her. Megan hanged herself within an hour of receiving the final comments from "Josh."

Ms. Drew was charged with one count of conspiracy and two counts of accessing computers without authorization and was convicted of three lesser charges. However, the judge dismissed the charges because of issues related to the meaning of the term "unauthorized use" and whether the federal statutes could be applied to what Ms. Drew did.

When the indictment was made public, Salvador Hernandez, assistant director of the FBI in Los Angeles, said, "Whether we characterize this tragic case as 'cyber-bullying,' cyberabuse, or illegal computer access, it should serve as a reminder that our children use the Internet for social interaction and that technology has altered the way they conduct their daily activities. As adults, we must be sensitive to the potential dangers posed by the use of the Internet by our children."*

Some states have now passed specific statutes to make cyber-bullying a crime.

Why would the judge not find a criminal violation? Is it a crime to bully over the Internet?

**U.S. v. Lori Drew*, 259 F.R.D. 449 (C.D. Cal. 2009).

Instructing the computer to give false directions can cause this fraudulent diversion of goods. Because the computer allows changes in delivery of goods through a mere keystroke, the depth of diversion cases is great. **For Example,** in one case, several hundred loaded freight cars disappeared. In another case, a loaded oil tanker was diverted to unload into a fleet of tank trucks operated by an accomplice of the computer operator.

28. Economic Espionage by Computer

The **Economic Espionage Act (EEA)** is a federal law[47] passed in response to several cases in which high-level executives took downloaded proprietary information from their computers to their new employers. The EEA makes it a felony to steal, appropriate, or take a trade secret as well as to copy, duplicate, sketch, draw, photograph, download, upload, alter, destroy, replicate, transmit, deliver, send, mail, or communicate a trade secret. The penalties for EEA violations are up to $500,000 and 15 years in prison for individuals and $10 million for organizations. When employees take new positions with another company, their former employers are permitted to check the departing employees' computer e-mails and hard drives to determine whether the employees have engaged in computer espionage.

29. Electronic Fund Transfer Crimes

The Electronic Fund Transfers Act (EFTA)[48] makes it a crime to use any counterfeit, stolen, or fraudulently obtained card, code, or other device to obtain money or goods in excess of a specified amount through an electronic fund transfer system. The EFTA also makes it a crime to ship in interstate commerce devices or goods so obtained or to knowingly receive goods that have been obtained by means of the fraudulent use of the transfer system.

30. Circumventing Copyright Protection Devices Via Computer

The Digital Millennium Copyright Act (DMCA)[49] makes it a federal offense to circumvent or create programs to circumvent encryption devices that copyright holders place on copyrighted material to

[47] 18 U.S.C. §1831.
[48] 15 U.S.C. §1693(n).
[49] 17 U.S.C. §512 (2010).

Ethics & the Law

Ethics and the Tobacco Class-Action Lawyer

Class-action lawyer Dickie Scruggs was portrayed in the 1999 movie "The Insider," which starred Russell Crowe as Jeffrey Wigand, the tobacco industry whistle-blower who obtained a $206 billion settlement from the tobacco companies (Mr. Scruggs's fee for the case was $1 billion). Almost a decade after the movie that made him a hero came out, Scruggs entered a guilty plea to bribery and was sentenced to five years in prison for his role in an attempt to bribe a federal judge.

Mr. Scruggs was representing insurance claimants against insurers for their damages from Hurricane Katrina. The judge presiding over the case contacted the FBI about a bribery attempt. One of the four lawyers working with Scruggs was approached by the FBI and agreed to wear a wire to catch Scruggs. The content of the tapes revealed both *actus reus* and *scienter*. Zachary Scruggs, Dickie's son, also entered a guilty plea. All of the remaining lawyers involved in the bribery scheme entered guilty pleas as well.

Those in the legal profession said they did not understand Scruggs's actions because he had the skill to win any case. "He didn't need to cheat," was the comment of a representative from the American Trial Lawyers Association. Scruggs's words at his sentencing were poignant: "I could not be more ashamed to be where I am today, mixed up in a judicial bribery scheme.... I realized I was getting mixed up in it. And I will go to my grave wondering why. I have disappointed everyone in my life–my wife, my family, my son, particularly.... I deeply regret my conduct. It is a scar and a stain on my soul that will be there forever."

Source: Abha Bhattarai, "Class-Action Lawyer Given 5 Years in a Bribery Case," *New York Times,* June 28, 2008, B3.

prevent unauthorized copying. **For Example,** circumventing the encryption devices on software or CDs or DVDs is a violation of the DMCA.

For Example, Dmitry Sklyarov, a Russian computer programmer, was the first person to be charged with a violation of the DMCA. Mr. Sklyarov was arrested in early 2002 at a computer show after giving a speech in Las Vegas at the Defcon convention on his product that he had developed to permit the circumvention of security devices on copyrighted materials. His program unlocks password-protected e-books and PDF files. He gave his speech and was returned to Russia in exchange for his agreement to testify in a case that will determine the constitutionality of DMCA.

The No Electronic Theft Act makes it a federal criminal offense to willfully infringe copyrighted material worth more than $1,000 using the Internet or other electronic devices even if the infringer does not profit from others' use of the material. **For Example,** sending along copyrighted articles on the Internet to friends, without permission from the site, would be a violation even though there is no profit.

31. Spamming

More states are addressing the use of computers to send unsolicited e-mails. For 2011, there were 7 trillion pieces of spam sent over the Internet. Criminal regulation began with very narrowly tailored statutes such as one in Washington that made it a crime to send an e-mail with a misleading title line. The specific criminal statutes on spamming are evolving, and Virginia became the first state to pass a criminal antispamming law. The statute prohibits sending "unsolicited bulk electronic mail" or spam and makes the offense a felony based on the level of activity.[50] Thirty-six states and the federal government now have some form of spamming regulation.[51] The penalties range from fines to imprisonment.

D. Criminal Procedure Rights for Businesses

The U.S. Constitution guarantees the protection of individual and corporate rights within the criminal justice system.

[50] *Gordon v. Virtumundo, Inc.,* 575 F.3d 1040 (9th Cir. 2009).

[51] Controlling the Assault of Non–Solicited Pornography and Marketing (CAN–SPAM), 15 U.S.C. §7701.

32. Fourth Amendment Rights for Businesses

(A) **Search and Seizure: Warrants.** The **Fourth Amendment** of the U.S. Constitution provides that "the right of the people to be secure in their persons, houses, papers, and effects, against unreasonable searches and seizures, shall not be violated." This amendment protects individual privacy by preventing unreasonable searches and seizures. Before a government agency can seize the property of individuals or businesses, it must obtain a valid **search warrant** issued by a judge or magistrate, based on probable cause, unless an exception to this warrant requirement applies. In other words, there must be good reason to search the location named. The Fourth Amendment applies equally to individuals and corporations. If an improper search is conducted, evidence obtained during the course of that search may be inadmissible in the criminal proceedings for the resulting criminal charges.[52]

(B) **Exceptions to the Warrant Requirement.** Exceptions to the warrant requirement are emergencies, such as a burning building, and the "plain-view" exception, which allows law enforcement officials to take any property that anyone can see, for no privacy rights are violated when items and property are left in the open for members of the public to see. **For Example,** you have an expectation of privacy in the garbage in your garbage can when it is in your house. However, once you move that garbage can onto the public sidewalk for pickup, you no longer have the expectation of privacy because you have left your garbage out in plain view of the public. The *Dow Chemical Co. v. U.S.* case deals with an issue of the plain view exception.

Dow Chemical Co. v. U.S., 476 U.S. 227 (1986)

Low-Flying Aircraft Bearing Federal Agents with Cameras

Dow Chemical (petitioner) operates a 2,000-acre chemical plant at Midland, Michigan. The facility, with numerous buildings, conduits, and pipes, is visible from the air. Dow has maintained ground security at the facility and has investigated flyovers by other, unauthorized aircraft. However, none of the buildings or manufacturing equipment is concealed.

In 1978, the Environmental Protection Agency (EPA) conducted an inspection of Dow. The EPA requested a second inspection, but Dow denied the request. The EPA then employed a commercial aerial photographer to take photos of the plant from 12,000, 3,000, and 1,200 feet. The EPA had no warrant, but the plane was always within navigable air space when the photos were taken.

When Dow became aware of the EPA photographer, it brought suit in federal district court and challenged the action as a violation of its Fourth Amendment rights. The district court found that the EPA had violated Dow's rights and issued an injunction prohibiting further use of the aircraft. The Court of Appeals reversed and Dow appealed.

JUDICIAL OPINION

BURGER, Chief Justice.... The photographs at issue in this case are essentially like those used in map-making. Any person with an airplane and an aerial camera could readily duplicate them. In common with much else, the technology of photography has changed in this century. These developments have enhanced industrial processes, and indeed all areas of life; they have also enhanced enforcement techniques. Whether they may be employed by competitors to penetrate trade secrets is not a question presented in this case. Governments do not generally seek to appropriate trade secrets of the private sector, and the right to be free of appropriation of trade secrets is protected by law.

That such photography might be barred by state law with regard to competitors, however, is irrelevant to the questions presented here. State tort law governing unfair competition does not define the limits of the Fourth Amendment. The Government is seeking these photographs in order to regulate, not compete with, Dow.

Dow claims first the EPA has no authority to use aerial photography to implement its statutory authority of "site inspection" under the Clean Air Act.

Congress has vested in EPA certain investigatory and enforcement authority, without spelling out precisely how this authority was to be exercised in all the myriad circumstances that might arise in monitoring matters relating to clean air and water standards.

[52] See, *Arizona v. Gant*, 556 U.S. 332 (2009) in which the U.S. Supreme Court held that evidence obtained searching the vehicle of a suspect who is handcuffed and locked in a police car cannot be used. A search warrant is needed when the suspect has no access to the evidence to destroy it.

Continued

Regulatory or enforcement authority generally carries with it all the modes of inquiry and investigation traditionally employed or useful to execute the authority granted. Environmental standards cannot be enforced only in libraries and laboratories, helpful as those institutions may be.

The EPA, as a regulatory and enforcement agency, needs no explicit statutory provisions to employ methods of observation commonly available to the public at large; we hold that the use of aerial photography is within the EPA's statutory authority.

DISSENTING OPINION

POWELL, MARSHALL, BRENNAN, and BLACKMUN, Justices...The Fourth Amendment protects private citizens from arbitrary surveillance by their Government. Today, in the context of administrative aerial photography of commercial premises, the Court retreats from that standard. It holds that the photography was not a Fourth Amendment "search" because it was not accompanied by a physical trespass and because the equipment used was not the most highly sophisticated form of technology available to the Government. Under this holding the existence of an asserted privacy interest apparently will be decided solely by reference to the manner of surveillance used to intrude on that interest. Such an inquiry will not protect Fourth Amendment rights, but rather will permit their gradual decay as technology advances.

EPA's aerial photography penetrated into a private commercial enclave, an area in which society has recognized that privacy interests may legitimately be claimed. The photographs captured highly confidential information that Dow had taken reasonable and objective steps to preserve as private.

QUESTIONS

1. Of what significance is the fact that Dow's plant could be seen from the air?
2. Did the EPA need a warrant for taking its aerial photographs?
3. What objections does the dissent raise to the decision?

Another exception allows officers to enter when they are needed to give aid because of an ongoing criminal act. **For Example,** officers who are able to see a fight through the windows of a house and resulting injuries can enter to render help.

Another exception would be that the person who lives in the property to be searched has given permission for the search. The *Georgia v. Randolph* case deals with a Fourth Amendment consent issue.

Georgia v. Randolph, 547 U.S. 103 (2006)

A Man's Home Is His Castle, but Can His Wife Still Turn on Him?

Scott Randolph and his wife, Janet, separated in late May 2001, when she left their Americus, Georgia, home and went to stay with her parents in Canada, taking their son and some belongings. In July, she returned to the Americus house with the child. No one is sure whether she had returned to reconcile or whether she had come to gather her remaining possessions.

On July 6, 2001, Janet called the police and told them that there were "items of drug evidence" in the house. Sergeant Murray asked Scott Randolph for permission to search the house, which he refused.

The sergeant turned to Janet for consent to search, which she readily gave. She led the officer upstairs to a bedroom that she identified as Scott's, where the sergeant noticed a section of a drinking straw with a powdery residue he suspected was cocaine. He then left the house to get an evidence bag from his car and to call the district attorney's office, which instructed him to stop the search and apply for a warrant. When Sergeant Murray returned to the house, Janet Randolph withdrew her consent. The police took the straw and the Randolphs to the police station. After getting a search warrant, the police returned to the house and seized further evidence of drug use, which served as the basis of Scott's indictment for possession of cocaine.

Scott Randolph moved to suppress the evidence, as products of a warrantless search. The trial court denied the motion, ruling that Janet had common authority to consent to the search.

The Court of Appeals of Georgia reversed, and the Georgia Supreme Court sustained the reversal. The state of Georgia appealed, and the U.S. Supreme Court granted *certiorari*.

Continued

JUDICIAL OPINION

SOUTER, Justice...To the Fourth Amendment rule ordinarily prohibiting the warrantless entry of a person's house as unreasonable per se, one "jealously and carefully drawn" exception recognizes the validity of searches with the voluntary consent of an individual possessing authority. None of our co-occupant consent-to-search cases, however, has presented the further fact of a second occupant physically present and refusing permission to search, and later moving to suppress evidence so obtained.

[S]hared tenancy is understood to include an "assumption of risk," on which police officers are entitled to rely, and although some group living together might make an exceptional arrangement that no one could admit a guest without the agreement of all, the chance of such an eccentric scheme is too remote to expect visitors to investigate a particular household's rules before accepting an invitation to come in.

The want of any recognized superior authority among disagreeing tenants is also reflected in the law's response when the disagreements cannot be resolved. The law does not ask who has the better side of the conflict; it simply provides a right to any co-tenant, even the most unreasonable, to obtain a decree partitioning the property and terminating the relationship. In sum, there is no common understanding that one co-tenant generally has a right or authority to prevail over the express wishes of another, whether the issue is the color of the curtains or invitations to outsiders.

Since we hold to the "centuries-old principle of respect for the privacy of the home," "it is beyond dispute that the home is entitled to special protection as the center of the private lives of our people." We have, after all, lived our whole national history with an understanding of "the ancient adage that a man's home is his castle [to the point that t]he poorest man may in his cottage bid defiance to all the forces of the Crown."

Disputed permission is thus no match for this central value of the Fourth Amendment, and the State's other countervailing claims do not add up to outweigh it. Yes, we recognize the consenting tenant's interest as a citizen in bringing criminal activity to light. And we understand a co-tenant's legitimate self-interest in siding with the police to deflect suspicion raised by sharing quarters with a criminal.

Nor should this established policy of Fourth Amendment law be undermined by the principal dissent's claim that it shields spousal abusers and other violent co-tenants who will refuse to allow the police to enter a dwelling when their victims ask the police for help. It is not that the dissent exaggerates violence in the home; we recognize that domestic abuse is a serious problem in the United States. But this case has no bearing on the capacity of the police to protect domestic victims. The dissent's argument rests on the failure to distinguish two different issues: when the police may enter without committing a trespass, and when the police may enter to search for evidence. No question has been raised, or reasonably could be, about the authority of the police to enter a dwelling to protect a resident from domestic violence; so long as they have good reason to believe such a threat exists, it would be silly to suggest that the police would commit a tort by entering, say, to give a complaining tenant the opportunity to collect belongings and get out safely, or to determine whether violence (or threat of violence) has just occurred or is about to (or soon will) occur, however much a spouse or other co-tenant objected. Thus, the question whether the police might lawfully enter over objection in order to provide any protection that might be reasonable is easily answered yes.

This case invites a straightforward application of the rule that a physically present inhabitant's express refusal of consent to a police search is dispositive as to him, regardless of the consent of a fellow occupant. Scott Randolph's refusal is clear, and nothing in the record justifies the search on grounds independent of Janet Randolph's consent. The State does not argue that she gave any indication to the police of a need for protection inside the house that might have justified entry into the portion of the premises where the police found the powdery straw (which, if lawfully seized, could have been used when attempting to establish probable cause for the warrant issued later).

The judgment of the Supreme Court of Georgia is therefore affirmed.

DISSENTING OPINION

Chief Justice ROBERTS, with whom Justice SCALIA joins, dissenting.

The Court creates constitutional law by surmising what is typical when a social guest encounters an entirely atypical situation. The rule the majority fashions does not implement the high office of the Fourth Amendment to protect privacy, but instead provides protection on a random and happenstance basis, protecting, for example, a co-occupant who happens to be at the front door when the other occupant consents to a search, but not one napping or watching television in the next room. And the cost of affording such random protection is great, as demonstrated by the recurring cases in which abused spouses seek to authorize police entry into a home they share with a nonconsenting abuser.

The correct approach to the question presented is clearly mapped out in our precedents: The Fourth Amendment protects privacy. If an individual shares information, papers, or places with another, he assumes the risk that the other person will in turn share access to that information or those papers or places with the government. And just as an individual who has shared illegal plans or incriminating documents with another cannot interpose an objection when that other person turns

Continued

the information over to the government, just because the individual happens to be present at the time, so too someone who shares a place with another cannot interpose an objection when that person decides to grant access to the police, simply because the objecting individual happens to be present.

A warrantless search is reasonable if police obtain the voluntary consent of a person authorized to give it. Co-occupants have "assumed the risk that one of their number might permit [a] common area to be searched." Just as Mrs. Randolph could walk upstairs, come down, and turn her husband's cocaine straw over to the police, she can consent to police entry and search of what is, after all, her home, too.

The majority's assumption about voluntary accommodation simply leads to the common stalemate of two gentlemen insisting that the other enter a room first.

If two friends share a locker and one keeps contraband inside, he might trust that his friend will not let others look inside. But by sharing private space, privacy has "already been frustrated" with respect to the lockermate. If two roommates share a computer and one keeps pirated software on a shared drive, he might assume that his roommate will not inform the government. But that person has given up his privacy with respect to his roommate by saving the software on their shared computer.

The same analysis applies to the question whether our privacy can be compromised by those with whom we share common living space. If a person keeps contraband in common areas of his home, he runs the risk that his co-occupants will deliver the contraband to the police.

In this sense, the risk assumed by a joint occupant is comparable to the risk assumed by one who reveals private information to another. If a person has incriminating information, he can keep it private in the face of a request from police to share it, because he has that right under the Fifth Amendment. If a person occupies a house with incriminating information in it, he can keep that information private in the face of a request from police to search the house, because he has that right under the Fourth Amendment. But if he shares the information—or the house—with another, that other can grant access to the police in each instance.

QUESTIONS

1. What factors in the case caused such strong opinions by the majority and dissenting judges?
2. What role did the issue of property law play in the decision and opinions?
3. Why did the issue of domestic violence come up in the opinion?

(C) Business Records and Searches. In many business crimes, the records that prove a crime was committed are not in the hands of the person who committed that crime. Accountants, attorneys, and other third parties may have the business records in their possession. In addition to the Fourth Amendment issues involved in seizing these records (a warrant is still required), there may be protections for the business defendants. The next section covers those protections.

(D) Protections for Privileged Records and Documents. All states recognize an attorney-client privilege, which means that an individual's conversations with her lawyer and the notes of those conversations are not subject to seizure unless the privilege is waived. In many of the prosecutions of companies, the Justice Department has asked companies to waive the attorney/client privilege so that it can have access to information that is then used to find other companies that may have participated in criminal activity. Some states recognize an accountant-client privilege and other privileges, such as those between priest and parishioner or doctor and patient. A privileged relationship is one in which the records and notes resulting from the contact between individuals cannot be seized even with a warrant (with some exceptions).

33. Fifth Amendment Self-Incrimination Rights for Businesses

(A) Self-Incrimination. The words "I take the Fifth" are used to invoke the constitutional protections against self-incrimination provided under the **Fifth Amendment** that prevents compelling a person to be a witness against himself. **For Example,** Mark McGwire, the former St. Louis baseball player, invoked the Fifth Amendment in his testimony during Congressional hearings on steroid use. Edith O'Brien, a lawyer for the collapsed investment fund, MF Global, refused to answer questions before Congress, claiming her right against self-incrimination. The Fifth Amendment protection applies only to individuals; corporations are not given Fifth Amendment protection. A corporation cannot prevent the disclosure of its books and records on the grounds of self-incrimination. The officers and employees of a corporation can assert the Fifth Amendment, but the records of the corporation belong to the corporation, not to them.

(b) *Miranda* Rights. The famous ***Miranda* warnings** come from a case interpreting the extent of Fifth Amendment rights. In *Miranda v. Arizona,*[53] the U.S. Supreme Court ruled that certain warnings must be given to persons who face custodial interrogation for the purposes of possible criminal proceedings. The warnings consist of an explanation to individuals that they have the right to remain silent; that if they do speak, anything they say can be used against them; that they have the right to have an attorney present; and that if they cannot afford an attorney, one will be provided for them. Failure to give the *Miranda* warnings means that any statements, including a confession, obtained while the individual was being interrogated cannot be used as evidence against that individual. The prosecution will have to rely on evidence other than the statements made in violation of *Miranda,* if such evidence exists. The *Dickerson v. U.S.* case deals with an interpretation of *Miranda* rights.

Dickerson v. U.S., 530 U.S. 428 (2000)

I Confess, but without *Miranda* You Can't Use It against Me

Charles Thomas Dickerson (petitioner) confessed to robbing a bank to field officers of the Federal Bureau of Investigation (FBI). At the time he confessed, he was not a suspect, was free to leave, and was not in custody. He was not, however, given his Miranda warnings before the FBI agents interrogated him about the robbery. Dickerson's lawyer moved to have his confession excluded from his trial because it was obtained in violation of Miranda. The federal district court suppressed the confession. The Court of Appeals reversed, noting that while the warnings had not been given, the confession was clearly voluntary. Mr. Dickerson appealed.

JUDICIAL OPINION

REHNQUIST, Chief Justice...In *Miranda v. Arizona,* 384 U.S. 436, 86 S.Ct. 1602, 16 L.Ed.2d 694 (1966), we held that certain warnings must be given before a suspect's statement made during custodial interrogation could be admitted in evidence. In the wake of that decision, Congress enacted 18
U.S.C. § 3501, which laid down a rule that the admissibility of such statements should turn only on whether or not they were voluntarily made. Section § 3501 provides:

"(a) In any criminal prosecution brought by the United States or by the District of Columbia, a confession ... shall be admissible in evidence if it is voluntarily given. Before such confession is received in evidence, the trial judge shall, out of the presence of the jury, determine any issue as to voluntariness."

The District Court granted [a] motion to suppress, and the Fourth Circuit reversed the District Court's suppression order. It agreed with the District Court's conclusion that petitioner had not received *Miranda* warnings before making his statement. But it went on to hold that § 3501, which in effect makes the admissibility of statements such as Dickerson's turn solely on whether they were made voluntarily, was satisfied in this case. It then concluded that our decision in *Miranda* was not a constitutional holding, and that, therefore, Congress could by statute have the final say on the question of admissibility.

The *Miranda* opinion itself begins by stating that the Court granted *certiorari* "to explore some facets of the problems ... of applying the privilege against self-incrimination to in-custody interrogation, *and to give concrete constitutional guidelines for law enforcement agencies and courts to follow.*" (emphasis added). In fact, the majority opinion is replete with statements indicating that the majority thought it was announcing a constitutional rule. Indeed, the Court's ultimate conclusion was that the unwarned confessions obtained in the four cases before the Court in *Miranda* "were obtained from the defendant under circumstances that did not meet constitutional standards for protection of the privilege."

After discussing the "compelling pressures" inherent in custodial police interrogation, the *Miranda* Court concluded that, "[i]n order to combat these pressures and to permit a full opportunity to exercise the privilege against self-incrimination, the accused must be adequately and effectively apprised of his rights and the exercise of those rights must be fully honored."

Given § 3501's express designation of voluntariness as the touchstone of admissibility, its omission of any warning requirement, and the instruction for trial courts to consider a nonexclusive list of factors relevant to the circumstances of a confession, we agree with the Court of Appeals that Congress intended by its enactment to overrule *Miranda.*

[53] 384 U.S. 436 (1966).

Continued

We disagree with the Court of Appeals' conclusion. *Miranda* announced a constitutional rule that Congress may not supersede legislatively. Following the rule of *stare decisis,* we decline to overrule *Miranda* ourselves. The judgment of the Court of Appeals is therefore reversed.

DISSENTING OPINION

SCALIA and THOMAS, Justices...[T]o justify today's result, the Court must adopt a significant *new,* if not entirely comprehensible, principle of constitutional law. As the Court chooses to describe that principle, statutes of Congress can be disregarded, not only when what they prescribe violates the Constitution, but when what they prescribe contradicts a decision of this Court that "announced a constitutional rule." As I shall discuss in some detail, the only thing that can possibly mean in the context of this case is that this Court has the power, not merely to apply the Constitution but to expand it, imposing what it regards as useful "prophylactic" restrictions upon Congress and the States. That is an immense and frightening antidemocratic power, and it does not exist.

QUESTIONS

1. What is the purpose of the *Miranda* decision?
2. What is the purpose of §3501 and why does the court refuse to apply it in this case?
3. What is the dissent's view on what has been done by this decision?

34. Due Process Rights for Businesses

Also included in the Fifth Amendment is the language of due process. **Due process** is the right to be heard, question witnesses, and present evidence before any criminal conviction can occur. Due process in criminal cases consists of an initial appearance at which the charges and the defendant's rights are outlined; a preliminary hearing or grand jury proceeding in which the evidence is determined to be sufficient to warrant a trial; an arraignment for entering a plea and setting a trial date when the defendant pleads innocent; a period of discovery for obtaining evidence; and a trial at which witnesses for the prosecution can be cross-examined and evidence presented to refute the charges. In addition to these procedural steps, the **Sixth Amendment** guarantees that the entire process will be completed in a timely fashion because this amendment guarantees a speedy trial.

LawFlix

Double Jeopardy (2000) R

Ashley Judd plays a woman on the run for false charges of killing her husband. But her husband faked his death and then she finds and kills him — can she be tried again?

Columbo (Seasons 1–6)

Detective Columbo is the bumbling, brilliant sleuth who crosses a few Fourth and Fifth Amendment lines here and there.

MAKE THE CONNECTION

SUMMARY

When a person does not live up to the standards set by law, this punishable conduct, called *crime,* may be common law or statutory in origin. Crimes are classified as *felonies,* which generally carry greater sentences and more long-term consequences, and *misdemeanors.*

Employers and corporations may be criminally responsible for their acts and the acts of their employees. The federal sentencing guidelines provide parameters for sentences for federal crimes and allow judges to consider whether the fact that a business promotes compliance with the law is a reason to reduce a sentence.

White-collar crimes include those relating to financial fraud. Sarbanes-Oxley reforms increased the penalties for financial fraud and added fraudulent financial statement certification as a crime. Other white-collar crimes include bribery, extortion, blackmail, and corrupt influence in politics and in business. Also included as white-collar crimes are counterfeiting, forgery, perjury, making false claims against the government, obtaining goods or money by false pretenses, using bad checks, false financial reporting, and embezzlement. The common law crimes include those that involve injury to person and/or property, such as arson and murder.

Statutes have expanded the area of criminal law to meet situations in which computers are involved. Both federal and state statutes make the unauthorized taking of information from a computer a crime. The diversion of deliveries of goods and the transfer of funds, the theft of software, and the raiding of computers are made crimes to some extent by federal laws. Newer federal statutes that apply to computers are the Economic Espionage Act, which prohibits downloading or copying information via computer to give to a competitor, and the Digital Millennium Copyright Act that prohibits circumventing or designing programs to circumvent encryption devices.

Criminal procedure is dictated by the Fourth, Fifth, and Sixth Amendments. The Fourth Amendment protects against unreasonable searches, the Fifth Amendment protects against self-incrimination and provides due process, and the Sixth Amendment guarantees a speedy trial.

LEARNING OUTCOMES

After studying this chapter, you should be able to clearly explain:

A. General Principles

LO.1 Discuss the nature and classification of crimes

See the discussion of crimes and misdemeanors on p. 138.

LO.2 Describe the basis of criminal liability

See the *For Example*, discussion of dumping waste and intent on p. 138.

See *U.S. v. Erickson* on pp. 138–139.

LO.3 Identify who is responsible for criminal acts

See *U.S. v. Park* on pp. 140–141.

See Thinking Things Through on p. 144.

See Ethics & the Law on p. 148, Am I My Company's Keeper?

LO.4 Explain the penalties for crimes and the sentencing for corporate crimes

See the discussion of the sentencing guidelines and the various cases related to them on p. 142.

B. White-Collar Crimes

LO.5 List examples of white-collar crimes and their elements

See the discussion that begins on p. 145.

See the Sports & Entertainment Law discussion of the NBA referee on p. 150.

LO.6 Describe the common law crimes

See the discussion that begins on p. 151.

C. Criminal Law and the Computer

LO.7 Discuss crimes related to computers

See the discussion that begins on p. 151.

See the E-Commerce & Cyberlaw discussion of cyber-bullying on p. 153.

D. Criminal Procedure Rights for Businesses

LO.8 Describe the rights of businesses charged with crimes and the constitutional protections afforded them

See the *Dow* case on pp. 155–156.

See the *Dickerson* case on pp. 159–160.

KEY TERMS

blackmail
computer crime
conspiracy
crime
due process
Economic Espionage Act (EEA)
embezzlement
extortion
facilitation payments
Federal Sentencing Guidelines
felonies
Fifth Amendment
Foreign Corrupt Practices Act (FCPA)
forgery
Fourth Amendment
grease payments
Miranda warnings
misdemeanors
predicate act
Racketeer Influenced and Corrupt Organizations (RICO) Act
search warrant
Sixth Amendment
uttering
white-collar crime
White-Collar Crime Penalty Enhancement Act of 2002

QUESTIONS AND CASE PROBLEMS

1. Bernard Flinn operated a business known as Harvey Investment Co., Inc./High Risk Loans. Flinn worked as a loan broker, matching those who came to him with lenders willing to loan them money given their credit history and the amount involved. From 1982 through 1985, Flinn found loans for five people. Indiana requires that persons engaged in the business of brokering loans obtain a license from the state. Flinn was prosecuted for brokering loans without having a license. He raised the defense that he did not know that a license was required and that, accordingly, he lacked the criminal intent to broker loans without having a license. Does Flinn have a good defense? [*Flinn v. Indiana,* 563 N.E.2d 536 (Ind.)]

2. H. J., Inc., and other customers of Northwestern Bell Corp. alleged that Northwestern Bell had furnished cash and tickets for air travel, plays, and sporting events and had offered employment to members of the Minnesota Public Utilities Commission in exchange for favorable treatment in rate cases before the commission. A Minnesota statute makes it a felony to bribe public officials. H. J. and other customers brought suit against Northwestern for violating the criminal bribery statute. Can the customers bring a criminal action? [*H. J., Inc. v. Northwestern Bell Corp.,* 420 N.W.2d 673 (Minn. App.)]

3. Baker and others entered a Wal-Mart store shortly after 3:00 A.M. by cutting through the metal door with an acetylene torch. They had moved some of the merchandise in the store to the rear door, but the police arrived before the merchandise could be taken from the store. Baker was prosecuted for larceny. He raised the defense that he was not guilty of larceny because no merchandise had ever left the store. Is there enough intent and action for a crime? [*Tennessee v. Baker,* 751 S.W.2d 154 (Tenn. App.)]

4. Gail drove her automobile after having had dinner and several drinks. She fell asleep at the wheel and ran over and killed a pedestrian. Prosecuted for manslaughter, she raised the defense that she did not intend to hurt anyone and because of the drinks did not know what she was doing. Was this a valid defense?

5. Dr. Doyle E. Campbell, an ophthalmologist, established his practice in southern Ohio in 1971. Many of Dr. Campbell's patients are elderly people who qualify for federal Medicare benefits and state Medicaid benefits. Under the existing financing system, a doctor who treats a Medicare patient is required to submit a "Medicare Health Insurance Claim Form" (HCFA Form 1500). The doctor is required to certify that "the services shown on this form were medically indicated and necessary for the health of the patient and were personally rendered by me or were rendered incident to my professional service by my employees." Claims Dr. Campbell submitted for his elderly patients ranged from \$900 to \$950, of

which $530 to $680 were covered by the Medicare program. The government alleged that Dr. Campbell billed Medicare for several treatments that were either not performed or not necessary. Dr. Campbell was charged with fraud for the paperwork he submitted. Has he committed a crime? [*United States v. Campbell,* 845 F.2d 1374 (6th Cir.)]

6. In the late 1980s, Life Energy Resources, Ltd. (LER), a New York corporation, was a multilevel marketing network. LER's marketing plan provided that members of the general public could purchase its products only through an official LER distributor or by becoming LER distributors themselves. Each potential distributor had to be sponsored by an existing distributor and was required to sign a distributorship agreement with LER stating that he or she would not make medical claims or use unofficial literature or marketing aids to promote LER products.

   Ballistrea and his partner Michael Ricotta were at the top of the LER distribution network. Two products sold by LER were the REM SuperPro Frequency Generator (REM) and the Lifemax Miracle Cream (Miracle Cream). The REM, which sold for $1,350 to distributors, was a small box powered by electricity that ran currents through the feet and body of the user.

   Ballistrea and Ricotta distributed literature and audiotapes to many potential downstream distributors and customers—some of whom were undercover government agents—touting the REM and the Miracle Cream. Other literature claimed that the Miracle Cream could alleviate the discomforts of premenstrual syndrome and reverse the effects of osteoporosis. The Food and Drug Administration charged Ballistrea and Ricotta with violating federal law for making medical claims concerning LER products. Their defense is that they never sold any of the products. They simply earned commissions as part of the marketing scheme and could not be held criminally liable on the charges. Are they correct? [*United States v. Ballistrea,* 101 F.3d 827 (2d Cir.)]

7. Carriage Homes, Inc., was a general contractor that built multifamily residential and land-development projects in Minnesota. John Arkell was Carriage Homes' chief executive officer, president, and sole shareholder. Carriage Homes built Southwinds, a condominium development of 38 residential units in Austin, Minnesota. The foundation elevations of some of the Southwinds units were lower than permitted under the State Building Code, causing storm water to pool in the units' driveways and garages. The city of Austin's development director sent Arkell a series of seven letters in 1999 and 2001 concerning the elevation problems, and Arkell gave the letters to the project managers, who failed to resolve the problems.

   Minnesota makes a violation of the State Building Code a misdemeanor. On May 30, 2001, the state charged Carriage Homes and Arkell with three misdemeanor counts each, alleging a violation of the Uniform Building Code (UBC).

   Carriage Homes pleaded guilty and was sentenced to a $1,000 fine. But Arkell pleaded not guilty, asserting that he could not be held criminally responsible for the violation. After a bench trial, the district court found Arkell guilty. He was sentenced to pay a fine, pay restitution to the condominium owners, and serve 90 days in jail, with 80 days stayed pending his compliance with sentencing conditions. Mr. Arkell appealed on the grounds that the employees and subcontractors had simply not followed his orders and he was not responsible for their failures. Is he correct? [*State v. Arkell,* 657 N.W.2d 883 (Minn. App. 2003)]

8. James Durham runs an art gallery. He has several paintings from unknown artists that he has listed for sale. The paintings always sell at his weekly auction for $20,000 to $50,000 above what James believes them to be worth. James learns that the bidders at the auctions are employed by an olive distributor located near the shipping yards of the city. What concerns should Durham have about the art, the bidders, and the large purchase prices?

9. Jennings operated a courier service to collect and deliver money. The contract with his customers allowed him a day or so to deliver the money that had been collected. Instead of holding collections until delivered, Jennings made short-term

investments with the money. He always made deliveries to the customers on time, but because he kept the profit from the investments for himself, Jennings was prosecuted for embezzlement. Was he guilty? [*New York v. Jennings,* 504 N.E.2d 1079 (N.Y.)]

10. In April 2006, a DC-9 aircraft landed in the port city of Ciudad del Carmen, located 500 miles east of Mexico City. When the plane's crew began directing security personnel away from the plane, the suspicious activity piqued the curiosity of local law enforcement officials. They decided to search the plane and found 128 suitcases packed with over 56 tons of cocaine. The cocaine was to have been delivered to Toluca, near Mexico City. In investigating the plane and individual involved, law enforcement agents discovered that the plane had been purchased with money that had been laundered through two U.S. banks, Wachovia Corp. and Bank of America Corp. Neither bank was actually aware that the money was being used to purchase a plane that would then be used for drug trafficking. Are the banks still criminally liable for breaking the rules? Explain why or why not. What if the banks were aware of large sums of money being run through particular customers' accounts? Would that knowledge make a difference?

11. Grabert ran Beck's, an amusement center in Louisiana. He held a license for video gambling machines. Louisiana makes it illegal to allow a minor to play a video gambling machine. A mother came into Grabert's center carrying her 23-month-old baby in her arms. She sat at the video poker machine with her child on her lap and proceeded to play. State troopers witnessed the baby pushing the buttons on the machine at least three times. The Department of Public Safety and Corrections revoked Grabert's video gaming license because a minor had been allowed to play the machines, and Grabert sought judicial review. The trial court reversed, and the department appealed. Has Grabert committed the crime of allowing a minor to engage in gaming? Is this the crime of allowing a minor to gamble? [*Grabert v. Department of Public Safety & Corrections,* 680 So.2d 764 (La. App.) cert. denied; *Grabert v. State through Dept. of Public Safety and Corrections,* 685 So.2d 126 (La.)]

12. The Banco Central administered a humanitarian plan for the government of Ecuador. Fernando Banderas and his wife presented false claims that the bank paid. After the fraud was discovered, the bank sued Banderas and his wife for damages for fraud and treble damages under the Florida version of RICO. Banderas and his wife asserted that they were not liable for RICO damages because there was no proof that they were related to organized crime and because the wrong they had committed was merely ordinary fraud. They had not used any racketeering methods. Is involvement with organized crime a requirement for liability under RICO? [*Banderas v. Banco Central del Ecuador,* 461 So.2d 265 (Fla. App.)]

13. Kravitz owned 100 percent of the stock of American Health Programs, Inc. (AHP). To obtain the Philadelphia Fraternal Order of Police as a customer for AHP, Kravitz paid money bribes to persons who he thought were officers of that organization but who in fact were federal undercover agents. He was prosecuted for violating RICO. He was convicted, and the court ordered the forfeiture of all of Kravitz's shares of AHP stock. Can a forfeiture be ordered? [*United States v. Kravitz,* 738 F.2d 102 (3d Cir.)]

14. Howell made long-distance telephone calls through the telephone company's computer-controlled switching system to solicit funding for a nonexistent business enterprise. What crimes did Howell commit? [*New Mexico v. Howell,* 895 F.2d 232 (N.M. App.)]

CHAPTER 9

© Manuel Gutjahr/iStockphoto.com

Torts

learningoutcomes

After studying this chapter, you should be able to

LO.1 Explain the difference between torts and crimes

LO.2 Identify the possible tort theories applicable to transmission of disease cases

LO.3 Distinguish between an assault and a battery

LO.4 Explain the three different torts of invasion of privacy

LO.5 Explain the torts of defamation and defenses

LO.6 Explain the elements of negligence and defenses

LO.7 Explain the tort of strict liability and why very few defenses are avaliable

The law of torts permits individuals and companies to recover from other individuals and companies for wrongs committed against them. Tort law provides rights and remedies for conduct that meets the elements required to establish that a wrong has occurred.

A. General Principles

Civil, or noncriminal, wrongs that are not breaches of contract are governed by tort law. This chapter covers the types of civil wrongs that constitute torts and the remedies available for those wrongs.

1. What Is a Tort?

Tort comes from the Latin term *tortus,* which means "crooked, dubious, twisted." Torts are actions that are not straight but are crooked, or civil, wrongs. A tort is an interference with someone's person or property. **For Example,** entering someone's house without his or her permission is an interference and constitutes the tort of trespass. Causing someone's character to be questioned is a wrong against the person and is the tort of defamation. The law provides protection against these harms in the form of remedies awarded after the wrongs are committed. These remedies are civil remedies for the acts of interference by others.

2. Tort and Crime Distinguished

A *crime* is a wrong that arises from a violation of a public duty, whereas a *tort* is a wrong that arises from a violation of a private duty. A crime is a wrong of such a serious nature that the appropriate level of government steps in to prosecute and punish the wrongdoer to deter others from engaging in the same type of conduct. However, whenever the act that is committed as a crime causes harm to an identifiable person, that person may recover from the wrongdoer for monetary damages to compensate for the harm. For the person who experiences the direct harm, the act is called a *tort*; for the government, the same act is called a *crime.*

When the same act is both a crime and a tort, the government may prosecute the wrongdoer for a violation of criminal law, and the individual who experiences the direct harm may recover damages. **For Example,** O. J. Simpson was charged by the state of California with the murder of his ex-wife, Nicole Brown Simpson, and her friend Ron Goldman. A criminal trial was held in which O. J. Simpson was acquitted. Simpson was subsequently sued civilly by the families of Nicole Simpson and Ron Goldman for the tort of wrongful death. The jury in the civil case found Simpson civilly liable and the court ordered him to pay nearly $20 million in damages plus interest. Only $382,000 of this judgment has actually been paid to the families.

3. Types of Torts

There are three types of torts: intentional torts, negligence, and strict liability. **Intentional torts** are those that occur when wrongdoers engage in intentional conduct. **For Example,** striking another person in a fight is an intentional act and would be the tort of battery and possibly also the crime of battery. Your arm striking another person's nose in a fast-moving crowd of people at a rock concert is not a tort or crime because your arm was pushed unintentionally by the force of the crowd. If you stretched out your arms in that crowd or began to swing your arms about and struck another person, you would be behaving carelessly in a crowd of people; and, although you may not have committed an intentional tort, it is possible that your careless conduct constitutes the tort of **negligence**. Careless actions, or actions taken without thinking through their consequences, constitute negligence. The harm to the other person's nose may not have been intended, but there is liability for these accidental harms under negligence. **For Example,** if you run a red light, hit another car, and injure its driver, you did not intend the result. However, your careless behavior of disregarding a traffic signal resulted in the injury, and you would have liability for your negligence to that driver.

In transmission of disease cases, depending on the facts, both intentional torts and negligence theories may apply. A person who knows or should know that he or she has herpes and fails to disclose that fact, or misrepresents that he or she is disease-free, may be liable to a sexual partner. The torts theories may include negligence, battery, intentional infliction of emotional distress, and fraud. In most cases, the three words "I have herpes" is fair notice of the danger of infection.[1] However, saying it is okay to have sex because the individual was not having an outbreak of the disease is actionable. **For Example,** Thomas R. disclosed to his girlfriend that he had herpes but nevertheless told her that it was "okay" to have sex with him because he was not then experiencing an outbreak of the disease. The jury's finding of negligence and fraudulent concealment in the transmission of the disease was upheld by the appeals court, and the plaintiff was awarded compensatory damages as well as $2.75 million in punitive damages.[2]

Strict liability is another type of tort that imposes liability without regard to whether there was any intent to harm or any negligence occurred. Strict liability is imposed without regard to fault. Strict or absolute liability is imposed because the activity involved is so dangerous that there must be full accountability. Nonetheless, the activity is necessary and cannot be prohibited. The compromise is to allow the activity but ensure that its dangers and resulting damages are fully covered through the imposition of full liability for all injuries that result. **For Example,** contractors often need to use dynamite to take a roadway through a mountainside or demolish a building that has become a hazard. When the dynamite is used, noise, debris, and possibly dangerous pieces of earth and building will descend on others' land and possibly on people. In most states, contractors are held strictly liable for the resulting damage from the use of dynamite. The activity is necessary and not illegal, but those who use dynamite must be prepared to compensate those who are injured as a result.

Other areas in which there is strict liability for activity include the storage of flammable materials and crop dusting. The federal government and the states have pure food laws that impose absolute liability on manufacturers who fail to meet the statutory standards for their products. Another area of strict liability is *product liability,* which is covered in Chapter 25.

B. Intentional Torts

4. Assault

An *assault* is intentional conduct that threatens a person with a well-founded fear of imminent harm coupled with the present ability to carry out the threat of harm. **For Example,** the angry assertion "I'm going to kick your butt" along with aggressive movement in the direction of the victim with the intent to carry out the threat is an assault, even though a third person intervenes to stop the intended action. Mere words, however, although insulting, are ordinarily insufficient to constitute an assault.

5. Battery

A *battery* is the intentional, wrongful touching of another person without that person's consent. Thus, a threat to use force is an assault, and the actual use of force is the battery. The single action of striking an individual can be both a crime and a tort. A lawsuit for the tort of battery provides a plaintiff with the opportunity to recover damages resulting from the battery. The plaintiff must prove damages, however.

6. False Imprisonment

False imprisonment is the intentional detention of a person without that person's consent.[3] The detention need not be for any specified period of time, for any detention against one's will is false imprisonment. False imprisonment is often called the *shopkeeper's tort* because so much liability has been imposed on store owners for their unreasonable detention of customers suspected of shoplifting. Requiring a customer to sit in the manager's office or not allowing a customer to leave the store can constitute the tort of false imprisonment. Shop owners do, however, need the opportunity to investigate possible thefts in their stores. As a result, all states have some form of privilege or protection for store owners called a *shopkeeper's privilege.*

The **shopkeeper's privilege** permits the store owner to detain a suspected shoplifter based on reasonable suspicion for a reasonable time without resulting liability for false imprisonment to the

[1] *R.A.P. v. B.J.P.*, 428 N.W.2d 103, 108 (Minn. App. 1988).

[2] *Behr v. Redmond*, 123 Cal. Rptr. 3d 97 (Cal. App. 2011).

[3] *Forgie-Buccioni v. Hannaford Bros. Inc.*, 413 F.3d 175 (1st Cir. 2005).

accused customer.[4] The privilege applies even if the store owner was wrong about the customer being a shoplifter, so long as the store owner acted based on reasonable suspicions and treated the accused shoplifter in a reasonable manner.

7. Intentional Infliction of Emotional Distress

The **intentional infliction of emotional distress** (IIED) is a tort involving conduct that goes beyond all bounds of decency and produces mental anguish in the harmed individual. This tort requires proof of outrageous conduct and resulting emotional distress in the victim. **For Example,** Erica Schoen, a 16-year employee of Freightliner, returned to work on light duty after surgery for a work-related shoulder injury. She was assigned to work out of the nurse's station under two employees who intentionally worked her beyond her restrictions, assigned her to humiliating work, repeatedly called her worthless, and used her as a personal servant—ordering her to get snacks, sodas, and lunches for them and not reimbursing her. After five months of this treatment, Erica brought the matter to the human resources manager, who told her, in part, "Nobody wants you. You're worthless. We build trucks down here…." Erica became hysterical and thereafter required psychiatric care. The jury awarded $250,000 for IIED, and it was upheld on appeal because the repetitive misconduct and its duration, ratified by the human resource manager, was intolerable.[5]

8. Invasion of Privacy

The right of privacy is the right to be free of unreasonable intrusion into one's private affairs. The tort of **invasion of privacy** actually consists of three different torts: (1) intrusion into the plaintiff's private affairs (for example, planting a microphone in an office or home); (2) public disclosure of private facts (for example, disclosing private financial information, such as a business posting returned checks from customers near its cash register in a public display); and (3) appropriation of another's name, likeness, or image for commercial advantage. This form of invasion of privacy is generally referred to as the *right of publicity.* The elements of this tort are (1) appropriation of the plaintiff's name or likeness for the value associated with it, and not in an incidental manner or for a newsworthy purpose, (2) identification of the plaintiff in the publication, and (3) an advantage or benefit to the defendant. The right to publicity is designed to protect the commercial interest of celebrities in their identities. **For Example,** popular and critically acclaimed rock and roll musician Don Henley, the founder and member of the band The Eagles, successfully sued a department store chain that ran an international newspaper advertisement for its Henley shirt, which stated in large letters as the focus of the ad "This is Don's henley." The ad (1) used the value associated with the famous name Don Henley to get consumers to read it, (2) the plaintiff was identifiable in the ad, and (3) the ad was created with the belief that use of the words "Don's henley" would help sell the product.[6]

Some states refer to the right of publicity as a cause of action for *commercial misappropriation of a name or likeness,* and provide two vehicles a plaintiff can use to protect the economic value of one's name, a common law action or a statutory remedy. The *Schlein* case involved a breach of contract action and an action for commercial misappropriation of his name.

Orthopedic Systems, Inc. v. Schlein, 135 Cal. Rptr. 3d 200 (Cal. App. 2011)

The Name Game: We Are Discontinuing Your Royalty on the "Schlein Ultra," Dr. Schlein

Orthopedic Systems, Inc. (OSI), and Dr. Schlein entered into a contract, whereby OSI would manufacture and sell an unpatented product originally designed by Dr. Schlein called the "Schlein Shoulder Positioner," which is to be used in arthroscopic shoulder surgery. The contract called for a 5% royalty of the list price less discounts. Over the years OSI's marketing brochures thanked "Allen P. Schlein M.D. for his assistance in the development of the product." OSI paid royalty checks from January 1991 to January

[4] *Limited Stores, Inc. v. Wilson-Robinson,* 876 S.W.2d 248 (Ark. 1994); see also *Wal-Mart Stores, Inc. v. Binns,* 15 S.W.3d 320 (Ark. 2000).
[5] *Schoen v. Freightliner LLC,* 199 P.3d 332 (Or. App. 2008).
[6] *Henley v. Dillard Department Stores,* 46 F. Supp. 2d 587 (N.D. Tex. 1999).

Continued

2005, when OSI paid its last royalty payment. In January 2005, OSI sent a letter to Dr. Schlein stating that in light of the fact that there is no patent protection on the product, it would be discontinuing the royalty. From January 2005 until July 29, 2005, OSI continued to market and sell the product using Dr. Schlein's name. OSI sued Dr. Schlein for declaratory relief and reformation of the royalty contract. Dr. Schlein cross-complained for breach of contract and commercial misappropriation of his name. The jury awarded Dr. Schlein $616,043 for failure to pay royalties under the contract. OSI earned $1,220,000 in profits attributed to the use of Dr. Schlein's name during the period from January 1, 2005 to July 31, 2005, after which OSI stopped using Schlein's name. The trial court declined to award the profits to Schlein, and both parties appealed.

JUDICIAL OPINION

REARDON, J.... [T]he issue is whether Dr. Schlein was entitled to the $1,220,000 in profits earned by OSI's use of his name....

California law has long recognized "the right to profit from the commercial value of one's identity as an aspect of the right of publicity." ... "What may have originated as a concern for the right to be left alone has become a tool to control the commercial use and, thus, protect the economic value of one's name." ... There are two vehicles a plaintiff can use to protect this right: a common law cause of action for commercial misappropriation and a section 3344 claim. To prove the common law cause of action, the plaintiff must establish: "(1) the defendant's use of the plaintiff's identity; (2) the appropriation of plaintiff's name or likeness to defendant's advantage, commercially or otherwise; (3) lack of consent; and (4) resulting injury." To prove the statutory remedy, a plaintiff must present evidence of "all the elements of the common law cause of action" and must also prove "a knowing use by the defendant as well as a direct connection between the alleged use and the commercial purpose."

Section 3344 governs the statutory remedy. Section 3344, subdivision (a) (section 3344(a)) provides in relevant part that "in any action brought under this section, the person who violated the section shall be liable to the injured party or parties in an amount equal to the greater of seven hundred fifty dollars ($750) or the actual damages suffered by him or her as a result of the unauthorized use, and any profits from the unauthorized use that are attributable to the use and are not taken into account in computing the actual damages."...

The human problem to be solved by section 3344(a) is the provision of a remedy to a person whose name, among other things, is misappropriated. That statute provides for damages (statutory or actual), as well as profits. We recognize there is some ambiguity regarding whether the minimum measure of damages is $750 plus profits or just $750.

In *Miller v. Collectors Universe, Inc.* (2008) 72 Cal.Rptr.3d 194 (*Miller*), the court traced the history of section 3344 in order to determine, inter alia, what the minimum statutory damages (i.e., the $750 award) set forth in subdivision (a) were meant to remedy. According to *Miller,* "[t]he statute's legislative history reveals section 3344(a) was intended to fill 'a gap which exist[ed] in the common law tort of invasion of privacy' as applied to noncelebrity plaintiffs whose names lacked 'commercial value on the open market.' [Citation.] Unlike an entertainment or sports star, noncelebrity plaintiffs often could not prove damages under the common law; therefore, section 3344(a) as originally enacted in 1971 'established a concrete remedy for the little man with a minimum ... payment,' 'a simple, civil remedy for the injured individual.' [Citation.]" Thus, the *Miller* court confirmed that section 3344 was enacted to provide a "practical remedy for a noncelebrity plaintiff whose damages are difficult to prove... ." (*Miller, supra,* at p. 72 Cal.Rptr.3d 194.)

We can conceive no rational basis for the Legislature to limit the $750 as an alternative to all other damages, including profits. If someone profits from the unauthorized use of another's name, it makes little sense to preclude the injured party from recouping those profits because he or she is entitled to statutory damages as opposed to actual damages....

An interpretation of section 3344(a) that limits the minimum measure of damages to $750 as an alternative to all other damages, including profits, would be contrary to the spirit of the statute and the long-recognized right to control the commercial use, and thus protect the economic value of one's name... .

We hold that under section 3344(a), an injured party may recover either the amount of damages specified in the statute or actual damages, whichever is greater, as well as profits from the unauthorized use... .

Accordingly, we modify the judgment so that it accurately reflects the jury's special verdict, namely its finding that Dr. Schlein was entitled to $1,220,000 as a result of OSI's unauthorized use of his name, and affirm the judgment as so modified.

[Modified and affirmed]

QUESTIONS

1. State the issue before the appeals court.
2. What must a plaintiff prove to establish a claim of commercial misappropriation of a name or likeness (right of publicity)?
3. May an injured party recover profits from the commercial misappropriations of his or her name, in addition to either the amount of damages specified in the statute, which is $750, or actual damages?

9. Defamation

Defamation is an untrue statement by one party about another to a third party. **Slander** is oral or spoken defamation, and **libel** is written (and in some cases broadcast) defamation. The elements for defamation are (1) a statement about a person's reputation, honesty, or integrity that is untrue; (2) publication (accomplished when a third party hears or reads the defamatory statement); (3) a statement directed at a particular person; and (4) damages that result from the statement.[7]

For Example, a false statement by the owner of a business that the former manager was fired for stealing when he was not would be defamation, and the former manager's damages could be his inability to find another position because of the statement's impact on his reputation.

In cases in which the victim is a public figure, such as a Hollywood celebrity or a professional sports player, another element is required, the element of malice, which means that what was said or written was done with the knowledge that the information was false or with reckless disregard for whether it was true or false.

The defenses to defamation include the truth. If the statement is true, even if it is harmful to the victim, it is not the tort of defamation.[8]

Some statements are privileged, and this privilege provides a full or partial defense to the tort of defamation. **For Example,** members of Congress enjoy an **absolute privilege** when they are speaking on the floor of the Senate or the House because public policy requires a free dialogue on the issues pending in a legislative body. The same absolute privilege applies to witnesses in court proceedings to encourage witnesses with information to come forward and testify. Where a witness granted immunity from prosecution testifies before a governmental agency, the witness is entitled to immunity from defamation lawsuits. **For Example,** Roger Clemens sued his former trainer, Brian McNamee, for defamation, contending that McNamee falsely stated to a congressional committee that Clemens had used steroids during his professional baseball career. This defamation claim was dismissed because McNamee's statements were entitled to absolute immunity on the reasoning that the proper administration of justice requires full disclosure from witnesses without fear of retaliatory lawsuits.[9]

The media enjoy a **qualified privilege** for stories that turn out to be false. Their qualified privilege is a defense to defamation so long as the information was released without malice and a retraction or correction is made when the matter is brought to their attention.

A *qualified privilege* to make a defamatory statement in the workplace exists when the statement is made to protect the interests of the private employer on a work-related matter, especially when reporting actual or suspected wrongdoing. **For Example,** Neda Lewis was fired from her job at Carson Oil Company for allegedly stealing toilet paper. The employee in charge of supplies noticed toilet paper was regularly missing from the ladies room, and one evening from a third-floor window overlooking the parking lot, she observed that the plaintiff's bag contained two rolls of toilet paper. She reported the matter to the executive secretary, who reported it to both the president and the CEO of the firm, who decided to fire her. Two other employees were also informed. The employer was able to successfully raise the defense of a qualified privilege to Ms. Lewis' defamation action for "false accusations of theft" since all of the employees involved were participants in the investigation and termination of the employee.[10]

A new statutory privilege has been evolving with respect to letters of recommendation and references given by employers for employees who are applying for jobs at other companies. Most companies, because of concerns about liability for defamation, will only confirm that a former employee did work at their firm and will provide the time period during which the person was employed. However, many employees who had histories that should have been revealed for safety reasons have been hired because no negative

[7] Regarding damages, where one publishes a slander that imputes to another a communicable disease, or would adversely affect that person's fitness for the proper conduct of a lawful business, trade, or profession, the words are actionable in themselves, and the law implies compensatory damages. Once compensatory damages are established the jury will assess punitive damages to punish the party who committed the wrong and to deter others from committing similar wrongs in the future. See *Tanner v. Ebbole*, 2011 WL 4425540 (Ala. App. 2011) where the jury returned "nominal" compensatory damages of $1 and punitive damages of $100,000 against Paul Averette, the owner of a competing tattoo business, for slanderous statements to several patrons that his competitor Chassity Ebbole had hepatitis, syphilis, gonorrhea, and AIDS and that she used "nasty needles."

[8] See *Stark v. Zeta Phi Beta Sorority Inc.*, 587 F. Supp. 2d 170 (D. D.C. 2008).

[9] *Clemens v. McNamee*, 608 F. Supp. 2d 811 (S.D. Tex. 2009). On June 18, 2012, Clemens was acquitted of all six counts of lying to Congress.

[10] *Lewis v. Carson Oil Co.*, 127 P.3d 1207 (Or. App. 2006).

information was released. Numerous states now have statutes that provide employers a qualified privilege with respect to references and recommendations. So long as the employer acts in good faith in providing information, there is no liability for defamation to the former employee as a result of the information provided.

10. Product Disparagement

Although the comparison of products and services is healthy for competition, false statements about another's products constitute a form of slander called **slander of title** or libel called **trade libel**; collectively, these are known as **product disparagement**, which occurs when someone makes false statements about another business, its products, or its abilities.[11] The elements of product disparagement are (1) a false statement about a particular business product or about its service in terms of honesty, reputation, ability, or integrity; (2) communication of the statement to a third party; and (3) damages.

11. Wrongful Interference with Contracts

The tort of **contract interference** or (tortious interference with contracts) occurs when parties are not allowed the freedom to contract without interference from third parties. While the elements required to establish the tort of contract interference are complex, a basic definition is that the law affords a remedy when a third party intentionally causes another to break a contract already in existence.[12] **For Example,** Nikke Finke, a newspaper reporter who had a contract with the *New York Post* to write stories about the entertainment industry for the *Post's* business section, wrote two articles about a lawsuit involving a literary agent and the Walt Disney Company over merchandising rights to the Winnie-the-Pooh characters. Finke reported that the trial court sanctioned Disney for engaging in "misuse of the discovery process" and acting in "bad faith" and ordered Disney to pay fees and costs of $90,000. Disney's president, Robert Iger, sent a letter to the *Post's* editor-in-chief, Col Allan, calling Finke's reporting an "absolute distortion" of the record and "absolutely false." Approximately two weeks after the Pooh articles were published, the *Post* fired Finke; her editor told her she was being fired for the Pooh articles. She sued Disney on numerous tort theories, including interference with her contract with the *Post*. Disney sought to have the complaint dismissed, which motion was denied by the court. The Court of Appeals concluded that Finke demonstrated a reasonable probability of proving that Iger's allegations that she made false statements in her article were themselves false; and it concluded that a jury could find Disney liable for intentional interference with contractual relations based on circumstantial evidence and negligent interference with contractual relations because it was reasonably foreseeable to Disney that the nature of its accusations against Finke would result in her termination from employment.[13]

12. Trespass

A **trespass** is an unauthorized action with respect to land or personal property. A *trespass to land* is any unpermitted entry below, on, across, or above the land of another. **For Example,** Joyce Ameral's home abutts the mid-way point of the 240-yard, par-4 ninth hole of the public Middlebrook Country Club. Balls sliced and hooked by golfers have damaged her windows and screens, dented her car, and made her deck too dangerous for daytime use. Her landscapers are forced to wear hard hats when cutting her lawn. In her lawsuit against the country club owner, the court ruled that the projection of golf balls onto Ameral's property constituted a continuing trespass and it enjoined the trespass.[14]

A *trespass to personal property* is the invasion of personal property without the permission of the owner. **For Example,** the use of someone's car without that person's permission is a trespass to personal property.

C. Negligence

The widest range of tort liability today arises in the field of negligence. Accidents happen! Property is damaged, and/or injuries result. The fact that an

[11] *Sannerud v. Brantz*, 879 P.2d 341 (Wyo. 1994). See *Suzuki Motor Corp. v. Consumers Union*, 230 F.3d 1110 (9th Cir. 2003), *cert denied* 540 U.S. 983 (2003), for an example of the complexity of a product disparagement action.

[12] See *Ventas, Inc. v. HCP, Inc.*, 647 F.3d 291 (6th Cir. 2011); *ASDI, Inc. v. Beard Research, Inc.*, 11 A.3d 749 (Del. 2010).

[13] *Finke v. The Walt Disney Co.*, 2 Cal. Rptr. 3d 436 (Cal. App. 2003).

[14] *Ameral v. Pray*, 831 N.E.2d 915 (Mass. App. 2005).

individual suffers an injury does not necessarily mean that the individual will be able to recover damages for the injury. **For Example,** Rhonda Nichols was shopping in the outdoor garden center at a Lowe's Home Center when a "wild bird" flew into the back of her head, causing injuries. Her negligence lawsuit against Lowe's was dismissed because the owner did not have a duty to protect her from a wild bird attack because it was not reasonably foreseeable.[15] Jane Costa was passively watching a Boston Red Sox baseball game at Fenway Park when a foul ball struck her in the face, causing severe and permanent injuries. Her negligence lawsuit against the Boston Red Sox was unsuccessful because it was held that the owners had no duty to warn Ms. Costa of the obvious danger of foul balls being hit into the stands.[16] Although cases involving injury to spectators at baseball games in other jurisdictions have turned on other tort doctrines, injured fans, like Ms. Costa, are left to bear the costs of their injuries. Only when an injured person can demonstrate the following four elements of negligence is a right to recover established: (1) a duty, (2) breach of duty, (3) causation, and (4) damages.[17] Several defenses may be raised in a negligence lawsuit.

13. Elements of Negligence

(A) Duty to Exercise Reasonable Care. The first element of negligence is a *duty*. There is a general duty of care imposed to act as a reasonably prudent person would in similar circumstances. **For Example,** Gustavo Guzman worked for a sub-contractor as a chicken catcher at various poultry farms where a Tyson Foods employee, Brian Jones, operated a forklift and worked with the catchers setting up cages to collect birds for processing at a Tyson plant. Contrary to Tyson's instructions "never to allow catchers to move behind the forklift or otherwise out of sight," Brian moved his forklift and struck Guzman, who suffered a serious spinal injury. A general contractor, Tyson Foods, owes a duty to exercise reasonable care to a subcontractor's employee, Gustavo Guzman.[18]

Professionals have a duty to perform their jobs at the level of a reasonable professional. For a professional such as an accountant, doctor, lawyer, dentist, or architect to avoid liability for **malpractice**, the professional must perform his or her skill in the same manner as, and at the level of, other professionals in the same field.

Those who own real property have a duty of care to keep their property in a condition that does not create hazards for guests. Businesses have a duty to inspect and repair their property so that their customers are not injured by hazards, such as spills on the floor or uneven walking areas. When customer safety is a concern, businesses have a duty to provide adequate security, such as security patrols in mall parking lots.

(B) Breach of Duty. The second element of negligence is the breach of duty imposed by statute or by the application of the reasonable person standard. The defendant's conduct is evaluated against what a reasonable person would have done under the circumstances. That is, when there is sufficient proof to raise a jury question, the jury decides whether the defendant breached the duty to the injured person from a reasonable person's perspective.[19] **For Example,** the jury in Guzman's lawsuit against Tyson Foods (the *Tyson* case), after weighing all of the facts and circumstances, determined that Tyson's employee's operation of the forklift constituted a breach of Tyson's duty of care to Guzman.

(C) Causation. A third element of negligence is *causation,* the element that connects the duty and the breach of duty to the injuries to the plaintiff. **For Example,** in Guzman's lawsuit, the forklift operator's careless conduct was the cause in fact of this worker's injuries. A "but for" test for causation is used. *But for* Tyson employee Brian Jones' negligent conduct in moving the forklift under the

15 *Nichols v. Lowe's Home Center, Inc.*, 407 F. Supp. 2d 979 (S.D. Ill. 2006).

16 *Costa v. Boston Red Sox Baseball Club*, 809 N.E.2d 1090 (Mass. App. 2004).

17 *Alfred v. Capital Area Soccer League, Inc.*, 669 S.E.2d 277 (N.C. App. 2008).

18 *Tyson Foods Inc. v. Guzman*, 116 S.W.3d 233 (Tex. App. 2003). But see *Pippin v. Hill-Rom Co., Inc.*, 615 F.3d 886 (8th Cir. 2010), where a shipper's failure to load cargo onto an independent truck driver's trailer, as required by the transportation contract, did not give rise to a cause of action for negligence, where the driver was injured loading the truck by himself. The shipper owed no duty to the driver, who chose to load the truck by himself.

19 A breach of duty may be established by the very nature of the harm to the plaintiff. The doctrine of *res ipsa loquitur* ("the event speaks for itself") provides a rebuttable presumption that the defendant was negligent when a defendant owes a duty to the plaintiff, the nature of the harm caused the plaintiff is such that it ordinarily does not happen in the absence of negligence, and the instrument causing the injury was in the defendant's exclusive control. An example of the doctrine is a lawsuit against a surgeon after a surgical device is discovered in a former patient months after the surgery by another physician seeking the cause of the patient's continuing pain subsequent to the operation.

circumstances surrounding the accident, Guzman would not have been injured.

Once the cause in fact is established, the plaintiff must establish *proximate cause*. That is, it must establish that the harm suffered by the injured person was a foreseeable consequence of the defendant's negligent actions. Foreseeability requires only the general danger to be foreseeable. In the *Tyson* case, the court determined that while there was some evidence that a jury could possibly infer that Tyson could not foresee an accident similar to the one involving Guzman, the evidence was legally sufficient to support the jury's finding that Tyson's negligence was foreseeable and the cause in fact of Guzman's injuries.

The landmark *Palsgraf v. Long Island Rail Road Co.* case established a limitation on liability for unforeseeable or unusual consequences following a negligent act.

Palsgraf v. Long Island Ry. Co., 162 N.E. 99 (N.Y. 1928)

The Scales Tipped on Causation

Helen Palsgraf (plaintiff) had purchased a ticket to travel to Rockaway Beach on the Long Island Railway (defendant). While she was standing on a platform at the defendant's station waiting for the train, another train stopped at the station. Two men ran to catch the train, which began moving as they were running. One of the men made it onto the train without difficulty but the other man who was carrying a package, was unsteady as he tried to jump aboard. Employees of the defendant helped pull the man in and push him onto the train car, but in the process the package was dropped. The package contained fireworks, and when it was dropped, it exploded. The vibrations from the explosion caused some scales (located at the end of the platform on which Palsgraf was standing) to fall. As they fell, they hit Palsgraf, who was injured. Palsgraf filed suit against the railroad for negligence.

JUDICIAL OPINION

CARDOZO, C. J.…The conduct of the defendant's guard, if a wrong in its relation to the holder of the package, was not a wrong in its relation to the plaintiff, standing far away. Nothing in the situation gave notice that the falling package had in it the potency of peril to persons thus removed. Negligence is not actionable unless it involves the invasion of a legally protected interest, the violation of a right. "Proof of negligence in the air, so to speak, will not do." The plaintiff, as she stood upon the platform of the station, might claim to be protected against intentional invasion of her bodily security. Such invasion is not charged. She might claim to be protected against unintentional invasion by conduct involving in the thought of reasonable men an unreasonable hazard that such invasion would ensue. These, from the point of view of the law, were the bounds of her immunity, with perhaps some rare exceptions, survivals for the most part of ancient forms of liability, where conduct is held to be at the peril of the actor. If no hazard was apparent to the eye of ordinary vigilance, an act innocent and harmless, at least to outward seeming, with reference to her, did not take to itself the quality of a tort because it happened to be a wrong, though apparently not one involving the risk of bodily insecurity, with reference to some one else.

A different conclusion will involve us, and swiftly too, in a maze of contradictions. A guard stumbles over a package which has been left upon a platform. It seems to be a bundle of newspapers. It turns out to be a can of dynamite. To the eye of ordinary vigilance, the bundle is abandoned waste, which may be kicked or trod on with impunity. Is a passenger at the other end of the platform protected by the law against the unsuspected hazard concealed beneath the waste? If not, is the result to be any different, so far as the distant passenger is concerned, when the guard stumbles over a valise which a truckman or a porter has left upon the walk? The passenger far away, if the victim of a wrong at all, has a cause of action, not derivative, but original and primary. His claim to be protected against invasion of his bodily security is neither greater nor less because the act resulting in the invasion is a wrong to another far removed. In this case, the rights that are said to have been violated, the interests said to have been invaded, are not even of the same order. The man was not injured in his person or even put in danger. The purpose of the act, as well as its effect, was to make his person safe. If there was a wrong to him at all, which may very well be doubted, it was a wrong to a property interest only, the safety of his package. Out of this wrong to property, which threatened injury to nothing else, there has passed, we are told, to the plaintiff by derivation or succession a right of action for the invasion of an interest of another order, the right to bodily security. The diversity of interests emphasizes the futility of the effort to build the plaintiff's right upon the basis of a wrong to some one else. The gain is one of emphasis, for a like result would follow if the interests were the same. Even then, the orbit of the danger as disclosed to the eye of reasonable vigilance would be the orbit of the duty. One who jostles one's neighbor in a crowd does not invade the rights of others standing at the outer fringe when the unintended contact casts a bomb upon the ground. The wrongdoer as to them is the man who carries the bomb, not the one who explodes it without

Continued

suspicion of the danger. Life will have to be made over, and human nature transformed, before prevision so extravagant can be accepted as the norm of conduct, the customary standard to which behavior must conform.

The risk reasonably to be perceived defines the duty to be obeyed, and risk imports relation; it is risk to another or to others within the range of apprehension. Here, by concession, there was nothing in the situation to suggest to the most cautious mind that the parcel wrapped in newspaper would spread wreckage through the station. If the guard had thrown it down knowingly and willfully, he would not have threatened the plaintiff's safety, so far as appearances could warn him. His conduct would not have involved, even then, an unreasonable probability of invasion of her bodily security. Liability can be no greater where the act is inadvertent.

DISSENTING OPINION

ANDREWS, J.…The proposition is this: Every one owes to the world at large the duty of refraining from those acts that may unreasonably threaten the safety of others. Such an act occurs. Not only is he wronged to whom harm might reasonably be expected to result, but he also who is in fact injured, even if he be outside what would generally be thought the danger zone.

As we have said, we cannot trace the effect of an act to the end, if end there is. Again, however, we may trace it part of the way. An overturned lantern may burn all Chicago. We may follow the fire from the shed to the last building. We rightly say the fire started by the lantern caused its destruction. A cause, but not the proximate cause. What we do mean by the word "proximate" is that, because of convenience, of public policy of a rough sense of justice, the law arbitrarily declines to trace a series of events beyond a certain point. This is not logic. It is practical politics.

The act upon which defendant's liability rests is knocking an apparently harmless package onto the platform. The act was negligent. For its proximate consequences the defendant is liable. If its contents were broken, to the owner; if it fell upon and crushed a passenger's foot, then to him; if it exploded and injured one in the immediate vicinity, to him. Mrs. Palsgraf was standing some distance away. How far cannot be told from the record—apparently 25 to 30 feet, perhaps less. Except for the explosion, she would not have been injured.… The only intervening cause was that, instead of blowing her to the ground, the concussion smashed the weighing machine which in turn fell upon her. There was no remoteness in time, little in space. And surely, given such an explosion as here, it needed no great foresight to predict that the natural result would be to injure one on the platform at no greater distance from its scene than was the plaintiff. Just how no one might be able to predict. Whether by flying fragments, by broken glass, by wreckage of machines or structures no one could say. But injury in some form was most probable.

Under these circumstances I cannot say as a matter of law that the plaintiff's injuries were not the proximate result of the negligence.

QUESTIONS

1. Do you think helping someone onto a moving train is a breach of duty? Do reasonable people do this?
2. Was Mrs. Palsgraf's injury foreseeable?
3. What is the court choosing to limit?

(D) DAMAGES. The plaintiff in a personal injury negligence lawsuit must establish the actual losses caused by the defendant's breach of duty of care and is entitled to be made whole for all losses. The successful plaintiff is entitled to compensation for (1) past and future pain and suffering (mental anguish), (2) past and future physical impairment, (3) past and future medical care, and (4) past and future loss of earning capacity. Life and work life expectancy are critical factors to consider in assessing damage involving permanent disabilities with loss of earning capacity. Expert witnesses are utilized at trial to present evidence based on worklife tables and present value tables to deal with these economic issues. The jury considers all of the evidence in the context of the elements necessary to prove negligence and all defenses raised, and it renders a verdict. **For Example,** in the *Tyson* case, the defendant presented evidence and argued that Gustavo Guzman was himself negligent regarding the accident. The jury found that both parties were negligent and attributed 80 percent of the fault to Tyson and 20 percent to Guzman (this is called *comparative negligence* and is discussed in the following section). The jury awarded Guzman $931,870.51 in damages ($425,000.00 for past physical pain and mental anguish, $150,000.00 for future physical pain and mental anguish, $10,000.00 for past physical impairment, $10,000.00 for future physical impairment, $51,870.51 for past medical care, $5,000.00 for future medical care, $70,000.00 for past lost earning capacity, and

$210,000.00 for future lost earning capacity). After deducting 20 percent of the total jury award for Guzman's own negligence, the trial court's final judgment awarded Guzman $745,496.41.

In some situations, the independent actions of two defendants occur to cause harm. **For Example,** Penny Shipler was rendered a quadriplegic as a result of a Chevrolet S-10 Blazer rollover accident. She sued the driver Kenneth Long for negligence and General Motors for negligent design of the Blazer's roof. She was awarded $18.5 million in damages. Because two causes provided a single indivisible injury, the two defendants were held jointly and severally liable.[20] Under *joint and several liability,* each defendant may be held liable to pay the entire judgment. However, should one defendant pay the entire judgment, that party may sue the other for "contribution" for its proportionate share.

In some cases in which the breach of duty was shocking, plaintiffs may be awarded *punitive damages.* However, punitive (also called *exemplary*) damages are ordinarily applied when the defendant's tortious conduct is attended by circumstances of fraud, malice, or willful or wanton conduct.[21]

14. Defenses to Negligence

(A) Contributory Negligence. A plaintiff who is also negligent gives the defendant the opportunity to raise the defense of **contributory negligence**, which the defendant establishes by utilizing the elements of negligence previously discussed, including the plaintiff's duty to exercise reasonable care for his or her own safety, the breach of that duty, causation, and harm. Under common law, the defense of contributory negligence, if established, is a complete bar to recovery of damages from the defendant.

The *Hardesty case* involves the application of the contributory negligence defense.

Hardesty v. American Seating Co., 194 F. Supp. 2d 447 (D. Md. 2002)

Keep Your Eye on the Ball in Sports: Keep Your Eye on the 300-Pound Boxes in Trucking

Lawrence Hardesty is an over-the-road tractor-trailer truck driver who picked up a load of stadium seating equipment for the NFL stadium under construction in Baltimore. The equipment was packaged in large corrugated cardboard boxes weighing several hundred pounds. The shipper, American Seating Co., loaded the trailer while Hardesty remained in the cab of his truck doing "paperwork" and napping. Considerable open space existed between the boxes and the rear door of the trailer. The evidence showed that Hardesty failed to properly examine the load bars used to secure the boxes from movement during transit. When Hardesty arrived at the Baltimore destination, he opened the rear trailer door and boxes at the end of the trailer fell out and injured him. Hardesty brought a personal injury negligence action against the shipper. American Seating Co. responded that Hardesty was contributorily negligent, thus barring his negligence claim.

JUDICIAL OPINION

DAVIS, D. J.…Under Maryland tort law, a negligence claim requires a showing of the following four elements: "(1) a duty owed to the plaintiff by the defendant; (2) a breach of that duty by the defendant; (3) a legally cognizable causal relationship between the breach of duty and the harm suffered; and (4) damages suffered by the plaintiff." Although the question "whether there is adequate proof of the required elements needed to succeed in a negligence action is [generally] a question of fact to be determined by the fact finder,…*the existence of a legal duty is a question of law to be decided by the court.*" Contributory negligence, "that degree of reasonable and ordinary care that a plaintiff fails to undertake in the face of an appreciable risk which cooperates with the defendant's negligence in bringing about the plaintiff's harm," is a complete bar to recovery.…

As a matter of law, Plaintiff's claim is barred by his own contributory negligence.…

QUESTIONS

1. How does the court define contributory negligence?
2. Is contributory negligence a complete bar to Hardesty's recovery of damages for his injuries in this case?
3. If Maryland applied a "comparative negligence" defense, as set forth in the following section of the text, rather than contributory negligence, would a more fair or just result have been reached in this case?

[20] *Shipler v. General Motors Corp.*, 710 N.W.2d 807 (Neb. 2006).

[21] See *Eden Electrical, Ltd. v. Amana Co.*, 370 F.3d 824 (8th Cir. 2004); and *University of Colorado v. American Cyanamid Co.*, 342 F.3d 1298 (Fed. Cir. 2003).

The contributory negligence defense has given way to the defense of comparative negligence in most states.

(B) Comparative Negligence. Because contributory negligence produced harsh results with no recovery of damages for an injured plaintiff, most states have adopted a fairer approach to handling situations in which both the plaintiff and the defendant are negligent; it is called *comparative negligence*. Comparative negligence is a defense that permits a negligent plaintiff to recover some damages but only in proportion to the defendant's degree of fault.[22] **For Example,** in the *Tyson* case, both the defendant and the plaintiff were found to be negligent. The jury attributed 80 percent of the fault for the plaintiff's injury to Tyson and 20 percent of the fault to the plaintiff, Guzman. While Guzman's total damages were $931,870, they were reduced by 20 percent, and the final judgment awarded Guzman was $745,496.

Some comparative negligence states refuse to allow the plaintiff to recover damages if the plaintiff's fault was more than 50 percent of the cause of the harm.[23]

(C) Assumption of the Risk. The assumption of the risk defense has two categories. *Express assumption of the risk* involves a written exculpatory agreement under which a plaintiff acknowledges the risks involved in certain activities and releases the defendant from prospective liability for personal injuries sustained as a result of the defendant's negligent conduct. Examples include ski lift tickets, white water rafting contracts, permission for high school cheerleading activities, and parking lot claim checks. In most jurisdictions these agreements are enforceable as written. However, in some jurisdictions they may be considered unenforceable because they violate public policy. **For Example,** Gregory Hanks sued the Powder Ridge Ski Resort for negligence regarding serious injuries he sustained while snowtubing at the defendant's facility. He had signed a release which explicitly provided that the snowtuber: *["fully] assume[s] all risks associated with [s]nowtubing*, even if due to the NEGLIGENCE" of the defendants [emphasis in original]. The Supreme Court of Connecticut found that the release was unenforceable because it violated the public policy by shifting the risk of negligence to the weaker bargainer.[24]

Implied primary assumption of the risk arises when a plaintiff has impliedly consented, often in advance of any negligence by the defendant, to relieve a defendant of a duty to the plaintiff regarding specific known and appreciated risks. It is a subjective standard, one specific to the plaintiff and his or her situation. **For Example,** baseball mom Delinda Taylor took her two boys to a Seattle Mariners baseball game and was injured during the pregame warm-up when a ball thrown by José Mesa got past Freddie Garcia, striking Taylor in the face and causing serious injuries. The defendant baseball team successfully raised the affirmative defense of implied primary assumption of the risk by showing that Mrs. Taylor had full subjective understanding of the specific risk of getting hit by a thrown baseball, and she voluntarily chose to encounter that risk.[25] Riding in a motorcycle procession on a Los Angeles freeway qualifies as an application of the implied primary assumption of the risk doctrine regarding involvement in a traffic collision.[26]

A number of states have either abolished the defense of assumption of the risk, reclassifying the defense as comparative negligence so as not to completely bar a plaintiff's recovery of damages, or have eliminated the use of the assumption of the risk terminology and handle cases under the duty, breach of duty, causation, and harm elements of negligence previously discussed.[27]

(D) Immunity. Governments are generally immune from tort liability.[28] This rule has been eroded by decisions and in some instances by statutes, such as the Federal Tort Claims Act. Subject to certain exceptions, this act permits the recovery of damages from the United States for property damage, personal injury, or death action claims arising from the negligent act or omission of any

[22] *City of Chicago v. M/V Morgan*, 375 F.3d 563 (7th Cir. 2004).
[23] *Davenport v. Cotton Hope Plantation*, 482 S.E.2d 569 (S.C. App. 1997).
[24] *Hanks v. Powder Ridge*, 885 A.2d 734 (Conn. 2005).
[25] *Taylor v. Baseball Club of Seattle*, 130 P.3d 835 (Wash. App. 2006).
[26] *Amezcua v. Los Angeles Harley-Davidson*, 132 Cal. Rptr. 3d 567 (Cal. App. 2011).
[27] See, for example, *Costa v. The Boston Red Sox Baseball Club*, 809 N.E.2d 1090 (Mass. App. 2004), where the court cites state precedent that "… the abolishment of assumption of the risk as an affirmative defense did not alter the plaintiff's burden … to prove the defendant owed [the plaintiff] a duty of care … and thus left intact the open and obvious damages rule, which operates to negate the existence of a duty to care."
[28] *Kirby v. Macon County*, 892 S.W.2d 403 (Tenn. 1994).

Sports & Entertainment Law

Liability for Injuries under the Sports Exception Doctrine

Charles "Booby" Clark played football for the Cincinnati Bengals as a running back on offense. Dale Hackbart played defensive free safety for the Denver Broncos. As a consequence of an interception by the Broncos, Hackbart became an offensive player, threw a block, and was watching the play with one knee on the ground when Clark "acting out of anger and frustration, but without a specific intent to injure," stepped forward and struck a blow to the back of Hackbart's head and neck, causing a serious neck fracture. Is relief precluded for injuries occurring during a professional football game? The answer is no. While proof of mere negligence is insufficient to establish liability during such an athletic contest, liability must instead be premised on heightened proof of reckless or intentional conduct on the part of the defendant. In the *Hackbart* case, the court determined that if the evidence established that the injury was the result of acts of Clark that were in reckless disregard of Hackbart's safety, Hackbart is entitled to damages.* Why didn't Hackbart pursue recovery under negligence law, contending that Clark had a general duty of care to act as a reasonably prudent person would in similar circumstances? Because football and other contact sports contain within the rules of the games inherent *unreasonable* risks of harm, a negligence theory is not applicable. What contact sports do you believe qualify under this "sports exception" doctrine for which proof of negligence is insufficient to establish liability for injuries sustained during the athletic contest? Is softball a contact sport for players? What about coaching or officiating decisions made in the middle of a fast-moving game?**

PGA golfer Walter Mallin sued PGA golfer John Paesani for injuries that Mallin sustained while competing in a PGA golf tournament when Paesani drove a golf ball that struck Mallin in the head on his right temple. Paesani contends that the "sports exception" doctrine applies and the negligence case must be dismissed. How would you decide this case?***

Hackbart v. Cincinnati Bengals, Inc., 601 F.2d 516 (10th Cir. 1979).

**See *Guillo v. DeKamp Junction, Inc.*, 959 N.E.2d 215 (Ill. App. 2011).

****Mallin v. Paesani*, 892 A.2d 1043 (Conn. Super, 2005).

employee of the United States under such circumstances that the United States, if a private person, would be liable to the claimant in accordance with the law of the place where the act or omission occurred. A rapidly growing number of states have abolished governmental immunity, although many still recognize it.

Until the early 1900s, charities were immune from tort liability, and children and parents and spouses could not sue each other. These immunities are fast disappearing. **For Example,** if a father's negligent driving of his car causes injuries to his minor child passenger, the child may recover from the father for his injuries.[29]

D. Strict Liability

The final form of tort liability is known as *strict liability*. When the standards of strict liability apply, very few defenses are available. Strict liability was developed to provide guaranteed protection for those who are injured by conduct the law deems both serious and inexcusable.

15. What Is Strict Liability?

Strict liability is an absolute standard of liability imposed by the law in circumstances the courts or legislatures have determined require a high degree of protection. When strict liability is imposed, the result is that the company or person who has caused injury or damages by the conduct will be required to compensate for those damages in an absolute sense. Few, if any, defenses apply in a situation in which the law imposes a strict liability standard. **For Example,** as noted earlier in the chapter, engaging in ultrahazardous activities, such as using dynamite to excavate a site for new construction, results in strict liability for the contractor performing the demolition. Any damages resulting from the explosion are the responsibility of that contractor, so the contractor is strictly liable.

[29] *Cates v. Cates*, 588 N.E.2d 330 (Ill. App. 1992); see also *Doe v. McKay*, 700 N.E.2d 1018 (Ill. 1998).

Thinking Things Through

Torts and Public Policy

Over a decade ago, a jury awarded 81-year-old Stella Liebeck nearly $3 million because she was burned after she spilled a cup of McDonald's coffee on her lap. Based on these limited facts, a national discussion ensued about a need for tort reform, and to this day "Stella Awards" are given on Web sites for apparently frivolous or excessive lawsuits. Consider the following additional facts and the actual damages awarded Stella Liebeck. Decide whether her recovery was just.

- McDonald's coffee was brewed at 195 to 205 degrees.
- McDonald's quality assurance manager "was aware of the risk [of burns] ... and had no plans to turn down the heat."
- Mrs. Liebeck spent seven days in the hospital with third degree burns and had skin grafts. Gruesome photos of burns of the inner thighs, groin, and buttocks were entered as evidence.
- The compensatory damages were $200,000, which were reduced to $160,000 because Mrs. Liebeck was determined to be 20 percent at fault.
- The jury awarded $2.7 million in punitive damages. The trial court judge reduced this amount to $480,000.
- The total recovery at the trial court for Mrs. Liebeck was $640,000. Both parties appealed, and a settlement was reached at what is believed to be close to the $640,000 figure.

Tort remedies have evolved because of public policy incentives for the protection of individuals from physical, mental, and economic damage. Tort remedies provide economic motivation for individuals and businesses to avoid conduct that could harm others.

The amount of the compensation and the circumstances in which compensation for torts should be paid are issues that courts, juries, and legislatures review. Many legislatures have examined and continue to review the standards for tort liability and damages.

The U.S. Supreme Court devoted several decisions in recent years to dealing with excessive punitive damages in civil litigation, and it has set "guideposts" to be used by courts in assessing punitive damages.* In *State Farm Mutual Automobile Insurance Co. v. Campbell*, compensatory damages for the plaintiffs at the trial court level were $1 million, and punitive damages, based in part on evidence that State Farm's nationwide policy was to underpay claims regardless of merit to enhance profits, were assessed at $145 million. The Supreme Court concluded that the facts of *Campbell* would likely justify a punitive damages award only at or near the amount of compensatory damages. Thus, even those who act very badly as State Farm Insurance did have a constitutionally protected right under the Due Process Clause of the Fourteenth Amendment to have civil law damages assessed in accordance with the Supreme Court's guideposts.

**BMW of North America v. Gore*, 517 U.S. 559 (1996); *Cooper Industries v. Leatherman Tool Group, Inc.*, 532 U.S. 424 (2001); *State Farm Insurance v. Campbell*, 538 U.S. 408 (2003); *Exxon Shipping Co. v. Baker*, 128 S. Ct. 2605, 2621 (2008).

16. Imposing Strict Liability

Strict liability arises in a number of different circumstances, but the most common are in those situations in which a statutory duty is imposed and in product liability. **For Example,** at both the state and federal levels, there are requirements for the use, transportation, and sale of radioactive materials, as well as the disposal of biomedical materials and tools. Any violation of these rules and regulations would result in strict liability for the company or person in violation.

Product liability, while more fully covered in Chapter 25, is another example of strict liability. A product that is defective through its design, manufacture, or instructions and that injures someone results in strict liability for the manufacturer.

LawFlix

Class Action (1991) (R)

This movie depicts the magnitude of damages and recovery when multiple injuries occur. The film provides insights on tort reform and the ethics of lawyers. You can learn about the magnitude of discovery and evidence.

Notting Hill (1999) (PG-13)

A story of famous star gets guy, dumps guy, gets guy back, dumps guy again, and then guy dumps famous star, and on and on. But, the guy owns a bookstore that sells travel books and he has a shoplifter. Hugh Grant, as the guy, illustrates perfection in exercising the shopkeeper's privilege.

MAKE THE CONNECTION

SUMMARY

A *tort* is a civil wrong that affords recovery for damages that result. The three forms of torts are intentional torts, negligence, and strict liability. A tort differs from a crime in the nature of its remedy. Fines and imprisonment result from criminal violations, whereas money damages are paid to those who are damaged by conduct that constitutes a tort. An action may be both a crime and a tort, but the tort remedy is civil in nature.

Selected intentional torts are false imprisonment, defamation, product disparagement, contract interference or tortious interference, and trespass. False imprisonment is the detention of another without his or her permission. False imprisonment is often called the *shopkeeper's tort* because store owners detain suspected shoplifters. Many states provide a privilege to store owners if they detain shoplifting suspects based on reasonable cause and in a reasonable manner. Defamation is slander (oral) or libel (written) and consists of false statements about another that damage the person's reputation or integrity. Truth is an absolute defense to defamation, and there are some privileges that protect against defamation, such as those for witnesses at trial and for members of Congress during debates on the floor. There is a developing privilege for employers when they give references for former employees. Invasion of privacy is intrusion into private affairs; public disclosure of private facts; or appropriation of someone's name, image, or likeness for commercial purposes.

To establish the tort of negligence, one must show that there has been a breach of duty in the form of a violation of a statute or professional competency standards or of behavior that does not rise to the level of that of a reasonable person. That breach of duty must have caused the foreseeable injuries to the plaintiff, and the plaintiff must be able to quantify the damages that resulted. Possible defenses to negligence include contributory negligence, comparative negligence, and assumption of risk.

Strict liability is absolute liability with few defenses.

LEARNING OUTCOMES

After studying this chapter, you should be able to clearly explain:

A. General Principles

LO.1 Explain the difference between torts and crimes

See the discussion on wrongs that are a violation of a private duty as torts, and wrongs that are a violation of a public duty as crimes, p. 166.

See the O. J. Simpson example of his acquittal of the crime of murder and his civil liability for the torts of wrongful death on p. 166.

LO.2 Identify the possible tort theories applicable to transmission of disease cases

See the transmission of herpes example on p. 167.

B. Intentional Torts

LO.3 Distinguish between an assault and a battery

See the "kick your butt" threat example of an assault on p. 167.

LO.4 Explain the three different torts of invasion of privacy

See the discussion of the intrusion into a person's private affairs, public disclosure of private facts, and right to publicity torts beginning on p. 168.

See the *Schlein* case involving commercial misappropriation of one's name on p. 169.

LO.5 Explain the torts of defamation and defenses

See the discussion of slander, libel, and trade libel beginning on p. 170.

See the discussion of the requirement of the enhanced element of malice for cases in which the victim is a public figure, p. 170.

C. Negligence

LO.6 Explain the elements of negligence and defenses

See the discussion of the elements of negligence: duty, breach of duty, and causation and damages beginning on p. 172.

See the discussion of the defenses of contributory negligence, comparative negligence, assumption of risk, and immunity beginning on p. 175.

D. Strict Liability

LO.7 Explain the tort of strict liability and why very few defenses are avaliable

See the dynamite excavation example, holding the contractor liable for any damages with no defenses because of the hazardous activity, p. 177.

KEY TERMS

absolute privilege
contract interference
contributory negligence
defamation
false imprisonment
intentional infliction of emotional distress
intentional torts
invasion of privacy
libel
malpractice
negligence
product disparagement
qualified privilege
shopkeeper's privilege
slander
slander of title
strict liability
tort
trade libel
trespass

QUESTIONS AND CASE PROBLEMS

1. Christensen Shipyards built a 155-foot yacht for Tiger Woods at its Vancouver, Washington, facilities. It used Tiger's name and photographs relating to the building of the yacht in promotional materials for the shipyard without seeking his permission. Was this a right of publicity tort because Tiger could assert that his name and photos were used to attract attention to the shipyard to obtain commercial advantage? Did the shipyard have a First Amendment right to present the truthful facts regarding their building of the yacht and the owner's identity as promotional materials? Does the fact that the yacht was named *Privacy* have an impact on this case? Would it make a difference as to the outcome of this case if the contract for building the yacht had a clause prohibiting the use of Tiger's name or photo without his permission?

2. ESPN held its Action Sports and Music Awards ceremony in April, at which celebrities in the fields of extreme sports and popular music such as rap and heavy metal converged. Well-known musicians Ben Harper and James Hetfield were there, as were popular rappers Busta Rhymes and LL Cool J. Famed motorcycle stuntman Evel Knievel, who is commonly thought of as the "father of extreme sports," and his wife Krystal were photographed. The photograph depicted Evel, who was wearing a motorcycle jacket and rose tinted sunglasses, with his right arm around Krystal and his left arm around another young woman. ESPN published the photograph on its "extreme sports" Web site with a caption that read "Evel Knievel proves that you're never too old to be a pimp." The Knievels brought suit against ESPN, contending that the photograph and caption were defamatory because they accused Evel of soliciting prostitution and implied that Krystal was a prostitute. ESPN contends that the caption was a figurative and slang usage

and was not defamatory as a matter of law. Decide. [*Knievel v. ESPN,* 393 F3.d 1068 (9th Cir.)]

3. While snowboarding down a slope at Mammoth Mountain Ski Area (Mammoth), 17-year-old David Graham was engaged in a snowball fight with his 14-year-old brother. As he was "preparing to throw a snowball" at his brother, David slammed into Liam Madigan, who was working as a ski school instructor for Mammoth, and injured him. Madigan sued Graham for damages for reckless and dangerous behavior. The defense contended that the claim was barred under the doctrine of assumption of the risk, applicable in the state, arising from the risk inherent in the sport that allows for vigorous participation and frees a participant from a legal duty to act with due care. Decide. [*Mammoth Mountain Ski Area v. Graham,* 38 Cal. Rptr. 3d 422 (Cal. App.)]

4. Following a visit to her hometown of Coalinga, Cynthia wrote "An Ode to Coalinga" (Ode) and posted it in her online journal on MySpace.com. Her last name did not appear online. Her page included her picture. The Ode opens with "The older I get, the more I realize how much I despise Coalinga" and then proceeds to make a number of extremely negative comments about Coalinga and its inhabitants. Six days later, Cynthia removed the Ode from her journal. At the time, Cynthia was a student at UC Berkeley, and her parents and sister were living in Coalinga. The Coalinga High School principal, Roger Campbell, submitted the Ode to the local newspaper, the *Coalinga Record*, and it was published in the Letters to the Editor section, using Cynthia's full name. The community reacted violently to the Ode, forcing the family to close its business and move. Cynthia and her family sued Campbell and the newpaper on the right-of-privacy theory of public disclosure of private facts. What are the essential elements of this theory? Was Cynthia and her family's right of privacy violated? [*Moreno v. Hanford Sentinel, Inc.,* 91 Cal. Rptr. 3d 858 (Cal. App.)]

5. JoKatherine Page and her 14-year-old son Jason were robbed at their bank's ATM at 9:30 P.M. one evening by a group of four thugs. The thieves took $300, struck Mrs. Page in the face with a gun, and ran. Mrs. Page and her son filed suit against the bank for its failure to provide adequate security. Should the bank be held liable? [*Page v. American National Bank & Trust Co.,* 850 S.W.2d 133 (Tenn.)]

6. A Barberton Glass Co. truck was transporting large sheets of glass down the highway. Elliot Schultz was driving his automobile some distance behind the truck. Because of the negligent way that the sheets of glass were fastened in the truck, a large sheet fell off the truck, shattered on hitting the highway, and then bounced up and broke the windshield of Shultz's car. He was not injured but suffered great emotional shock. He sued Barberton to recover damages for this shock. Barberton denied liability on the ground that Schultz had not sustained any physical injury at the time or as the result of the shock. Should he be able to recover? [*Schultz v. Barberton Glass Co.,* 447 N.E.2d 109 (Ohio)]

7. Mallinckrodt produces nuclear and radioactive medical pharmaceuticals and supplies. Maryland Heights Leasing, an adjoining business owner, claimed that low-level radiation emissions from Mallinckrodt damaged its property and caused a loss in earnings. What remedy should Maryland Heights have? What torts are involved here? [*Maryland Heights Leasing, Inc. v. Mallinckrodt, Inc.,* 706 S.W.2d 218 (Mo. App.)]

8. An owner abandoned his van in an alley in Chicago. In spite of repeated complaints to the police, the van was allowed to remain in the alley. After several months, it was stripped of most of the parts that could be removed. Jamin Ortiz, age 11, was walking down the alley when the van's gas tank exploded. The flames from the explosion set fire to Jamin's clothing, and he was severely burned. Jamin and his family brought suit brought against the city of Chicago to recover damages for his injuries. Could the city be held responsible for injuries caused by property owned by someone else? Why or why not? [*Ortiz v. Chicago,* 398 N.E.2d 1007 (Ill. App.)]

9. Carrigan, a district manager of Simples Time Recorder Co., was investigating complaints of mismanagement of the company's Jackson office.

He called at the home of Hooks, the secretary of that office, who expressed the opinion that part of the trouble was caused by the theft of parts and equipment by McCall, another employee. McCall was later discharged and sued Hooks for slander. Was she liable? [*Hooks v. McCall,* 272 So.2d 925 (Miss.)]

10. Defendant no. 1 parked his truck in the street near the bottom of a ditch on a dark, foggy night. Iron pipes carried in the truck projected nine feet beyond the truck in back. Neither the truck nor the pipes carried any warning light or flag, in violation of both a city ordinance and a state statute. Defendant no. 2 was a taxicab owner whose taxicab was negligently driven at an excessive speed. Defendant no. 2 ran into the pipes, thereby killing the passenger in the taxicab. The plaintiff brought an action for the passenger's death against both defendants. Defendant no. 1 claimed he was not liable because it was Defendant no. 2's negligence that had caused the harm. Was this defense valid? [*Bumbardner v. Allison,* 78 S.E.2d 752 (N.C.)]

11. Carl Kindrich's father, a member of the Long Beach Yacht Club before he died, expressed a wish to be "buried at sea." The Yacht Club permitted the Kindrich family the use of one of its boats, without charge, for the ceremony, and Mr. Fuller—a good friend of Carl's father—piloted the boat. Portable stairs on the dock assisted the attendees in boarding. Upon returning, Fuller asked for help to tie up the boat. The steps were not there, and Carl broke his leg while disembarking to help tie up the boat. Carl sued the Yacht Club for negligence in failing to have someone on the dock to ensure that the portable steps were available. The Yacht Club contended that it was not liable because Carl made the conscious decision to jump from the moving vessel to the dock, a primary assumption of risk in the sport of boating. The plaintiff contended that he was not involved in the sport of boating, and at most his actions constituted minimal comparative negligence, the type which a jury could weigh in conjunction with the defendant's negligence in assessing damages. Decide. [*Kindrich v. Long Beach Yacht Club,* 84 Cal. Rptr. 3d 824 (Cal. App.)]

12. Hegyes was driving her car when it was negligently struck by a Unjian Enterprises truck. She was injured, and an implant was placed in her body to counteract the injuries. She sued Unjian, and the case was settled. Two years later Hegyes became pregnant. The growing fetus pressed against the implant, making it necessary for her doctor to deliver the child 51 days prematurely by Cesarean section. Because of its premature birth, the child had a breathing handicap. Suit was brought against Unjian Enterprises for the harm sustained by the child. Was the defendant liable? [*Hegyes v. Unjian Enterprises, Inc.,* 286 Cal. Rptr. 85 (Cal. App.)]

13. Kendra Knight took part in a friendly game of touch football. She had played before and was familiar with football. Michael Jewett was on her team. In the course of play, Michael bumped into Kendra and knocked her to the ground. He stepped on her hand, causing injury to a little finger that later required its amputation. She sued Michael for damages. He defended on the ground that she had assumed the risk. Kendra claimed that assumption of risk could not be raised as a defense because the state legislature had adopted the standard of comparative negligence. What happens if contributory negligence applies? What happens if the defense of comparative negligence applies?

14. A passenger on a cruise ship was injured by a rope thrown while the ship was docking. The passenger was sitting on a lounge chair on the third deck when she was struck by the weighted end of a rope thrown by an employee of Port Everglades, where the boat was docking. These ropes, or heaving lines, were being thrown from the dock to the second deck, and the passenger was injured by a line that was thrown too high.

    The trial court granted the cruise line's motion for directed verdict on the ground there was no evidence that the cruise line knew or should have known of the danger. The cruise line contended that it had no notice that this "freak accident" could occur. What is the duty of a cruise ship line to its passengers? Is there liability here? Does it matter that an employee of the port city, not the cruise lines, caused the injury? Should the passenger be able to recover? Why or why not? [*Kalendareva v. Discovery Cruise Line Partnership,* 798 So.2d 804 (Fla. App.)]

15. Blaylock was a voluntary psychiatric outpatient treated by Dr. Burglass, who became aware that Blaylock was violence prone. Blaylock told Dr. Burglass that he intended to do serious harm to Wayne B[illegible] killed Wayn[illegible] Dr. Burglas[illegible] death of th[illegible] warning o[illegible] threat and[illegible] Should D[illegible] *Burglass,* [illegible]

Intellectual Property Rights and the Internet

learningoutcomes

After studying this chapter, you should be able to

LO.1 Explain the spectrum of distinctiveness used to classify trademarks and explain why distinctiveness is important

LO.2 Explain how personal names can acquire trademark protection

LO.3 List the remedies available for improper use of trademarks

LO.4 Explain what is and is not copyrightable; explain the fair use defense

LO.5 Explain the "new and not obvious" requirement necessary to obtain a patent

LO.6 List and explain the defensive measures employers take to preserve confidential business information

LO.7 Explain the extent of protection provided owners of software

Intellectual property comes in many forms: the writing by an author or the software developed by an employee, the new product or process developed by an inventor, the company name Hewlett-Packard, and the secret formula used to make Coca-Cola. Federal law provides rights to owners of these works, products, company names, and secret formulas that are called *copyrights, patents, trademarks*, and *trade secrets*. State laws provide protection for trade secrets. These basic legal principles are also applicable in an Internet and e-commerce context. This chapter discusses the federal and state laws governing intellectual property rights and their Internet context.

A. Trademarks and Service Marks

The Lanham Act, a federal law, grants a producer the exclusive right to register a trademark and prevent competitors from using that mark. This law helps assure a producer that it, not an imitating competitor, will reap the financial, reputation-related rewards of a desirable product. And trademarks reduce consumers' search costs, allowing them to make decisions that more closely coincide with their preferences.

1. Introduction

A mark is any word, name, symbol, device, or combination of these used to identify a product or service.[1] If the mark identifies a product, such as an automobile or soap, it is called a **trademark**. If it identifies a service, such as an airline or dry cleaner, it is called a **service mark**.

The owner of a mark may obtain protection from others using it by registering the mark in accordance with federal law at the United States Patent and Trademark Office (USPTO) in Washington, D.C.[2] To be registered, a mark must distinguish the goods or services of the applicant from those of others. Under the federal Lanham Act, a register, called the Principal Register, is maintained for recording such marks. Inclusion on the Principal Register grants the registrant the exclusive right to use the mark. Challenges may be made to the registrant's right within five years of registration, but after five years, the right of the registrant is incontestable.

A mark may be "reserved" before starting a business by filing an application for registration on the basis of the applicant's good-faith intent to use the mark. Once the mark is used in trade, then the USPTO will actually issue the registration with a priority date retroactive to the date the application was filed. The applicant has a maximum period of 36 months to get the business started and demonstrate that the mark is in "use in commerce."

2. International Registration

Under the Madrid System of International Registration of Marks (the Madrid Protocol), the United States became a party to a treaty providing for the international registration of marks in November 2003. Now U.S. companies that sell products and provide services in foreign countries may register their marks and obtain protection for them in more than 60 signatory countries by filing a single application in English for each mark with the U.S. Patent and Trademark Office.[3] Before the mark can be the subject of an international application, it must have already been registered or applied for with the U.S. Patent and Trademark Office (USPTO). A change in ownership of a mark can be accomplished by a single filing. Renewal is required every 10 years by paying a single renewal fee.

3. Registrable Marks

Trademark law categorizes marks along a spectrum of **distinctiveness**, based on their capacity to serve a source-identifying function. A mark is classified as (1) coined or fanciful (most distinctive), (2) arbitrary, (3) suggestive, (4) descriptive, and (5) generic (least distinctive). **For Example,** the mark EXXON is fanciful because it was designed by its owner to designate petroleum and related products. The name CENGAGE is a coined creation of the owner of this trademark and has no other meaning in English, but

[1] 15 U.S.C. §1127.

[2] *Lanham Act,* 15 U.S.C. §§1050–1127.

[3] Signatory countries include most U.S. trading partners with the exception of Canada and Mexico.

it serves to distinguish the products of its owner from all others. The mark APPLE for computers, an arbitrary mark, consists of a word in common usage that is arbitrarily applied in such a way that it is not descriptive or suggestive. The mark COPPERTONE for suntan lotion is a suggestive mark—requiring some imagination to reach a conclusion about the nature of the product. Coined or fanciful, arbitrary, and suggestive marks may be registered on the Principal Register under the Lanham Act without producing any actual evidence of the source-identifying attribution or the public perception of these marks.

Descriptive marks are those that convey an immediate idea of the ingredients, qualities, or characteristics of the goods or service, such as SPORTS ILLUSTRATED for a sports magazine. Because descriptive marks are not inherently capable of serving as source identifiers, such marks may only be registered on the Principal Register after the owner has provided sufficient evidence to establish that the public associates the term or phrase not only with a specific feature or quality, but also with a single commercial source. When a descriptive phrase becomes associated with a single commercial source, the phrase is said to possess "**acquired distinctiveness**" or "**secondary meaning**," and therefore functions as a trademark. **For Example,** when the public perceives the phrase SPORTS ILLUSTRATED as a particular sports magazine in addition to its primary meaning as a description of a specific feature or element, the phrase has "acquired distinctiveness" or "secondary meaning" and may receive trademark protection. In the *Harley-Davidson* case, the motorcycle manufacturer sought to appropriate the word *hog* as its trademark, and a local motorcycle shop sought to parody Harley's logo to promote its own products and services.

Harley-Davidson, Inc. v. Grottanelli, 164 F.3d 987 (2d Cir. 1999)

No Hogging Generic Terms

Harley-Davidson obtained a judgment against Ronald Grottanelli in the U.S. District for the Western District of New York for infringement of its bar-and-shield trademark, and the court enjoined his future use of that mark. The judgment also enjoined Grottanelli from using the word "hog" in reference to some of his products and services. Both parties appealed.

JUDICIAL OPINION

NEWMAN, J.…

1. The word "Hog" Applied to Motorcycles

Public use of the word "hog." In the late 1960s and early 1970s, the word "hog" was used by motorcycle enthusiasts to refer to motorcycles generally and to large motorcycles in particular. The word was used that way in the press at least as early as 1965, and frequently thereafter, prior to the 1980s when Harley first attempted to make trademark use of the term. Several dictionaries include a definition of "hog" as a motorcycle, especially a large one. The October 1975 issue of *Street Chopper* contained an article entitled "Honda Hog," indicating that the word "hog" was generic as to motorcycles and needed a tradename adjective.

Beginning around the early 1970s and into the early 1980s, motorcyclists increasingly came to use the word "hog" when referring to Harley-Davidson motorcycles. However, for several years, as Harley-Davidson's Manager of Trademark Enforcement acknowledged, the company attempted to disassociate itself from the word "hog." The Magistrate judge drew the reasonable inference that the company wished to distance itself from the connection between "hog" as applied to motorcycles and unsavory elements of the population, such as Hell's Angels, who were among those applying the term to Harley-Davidson motorcycles.

Harley-Davidson's use of the word "hog." In 1981, Harley-Davidson's new owners recognized that the term "hog" had financial value and began using the term in connection with its merchandise, accessories, advertising, and promotions. In 1983, it formed the Harley Owners' Group, pointedly using the acronym "H.O.G." In 1987, it registered the acronym in conjunction with various logos. It subsequently registered the mark "HOG" for motorcycles. That registration lists Harley-Davidson's first use as occurring in 1990.

Grottanelli's use of the word "hog." Grottanelli opened a motorcycle repair shop under the name "The Hog Farm" in 1969. Since that time his shop has been located at various sites in western New York. At some point after 1981, Grottanelli also began using the word "hog" in connection with events and merchandise. He has sponsored an event alternatively known as "Hog Holidays" and "Hog Farm Holidays," and sold products such as "Hog Wash" engine degreaser and a "Hog Trivia" board game.

Continued

2. The Bar-and-Shield Logo

Harley-Davidson's use of the logo. Since approximately 1909, Harley-Davidson has used variations of its bar-and-shield logo—a shield traversed across the middle by a horizontal bar. The words "Motor" and "Cycles" (or sometimes "Company") appear at the chief and base of the shield, respectively, and the name "Harley-Davidson" appears on the horizontal bar. Variations of the bar-and-shield logo were registered with the United States Patent and Trademark Office in 1982 and thereafter.

Grottanelli's use of the logo. By 1979, Grottanelli had begun using variants of Harley-Davidson's bar-and-shield logo. His 1979 advertisements include a hand-drawn copy of the bar-and-shield logo, with the name "Harley-Davidson" displayed on the horizontal bar. Since 1982, in response to letters of protest from Harley-Davidson, Grottanelli has replaced the words "Harley-Davidson" on the horizontal bar of his logo with the words "American-Made." He has also placed a banner at the bottom of his logo with the words "UNAUTHORIZED DEALER." In 1986, Grottanelli began using his current logo, which adds an eagle's wings behind the shield. This addition was apparently patterned after Harley-Davidson's bicentennial logo design mark, which included an eagle above the shield. Grottanelli's 1986 version of his logo also features a drawing of a pig wearing sunglasses. Grottanelli acknowledged at trial that his bar-and-shield logo is his version of Harley-Davidson's logo and that his version is "supposed to be similar, but confusing…[t]o a Harley-Davidson bar and shield."…

DISCUSSION

I. USE OF THE WORD "HOG"

…No manufacturer can take out of the language a word, even a slang term, that has generic meaning as to a category of products and appropriate it for its own trademark use.…

…In this case, one dictionary cites a generic use of "hog" to mean a large motorcycle as early as 1967, long before Harley's first trademark use of the word, and the recent dictionary editions continuing to define the word to mean a large motorcycle indicate that the word has not lost its generic meaning. We have observed that newspaper and magazine use of a word in a generic sense is "a strong indication of the general public's perception" that the word is generic. In this case, media use of "hog" to mean a large motorcycle began as early as 1935 and continued thereafter.

However, rather than recognize that the word "hog," originally generic as applied to motorcyles, cannot subsequently be appropriated for trademark use, the Magistrate Judge upheld Harley-Davidson's anti-dilution claim on the ground that its "HOG" mark has become a strong trademark. This was error. Even the presumption of validity arising from federal registration, *see Reese Publishing Co. v Hampton International Communications, Inc.,* 620 F.2d 7, 11 [205 USPQ 585] (2d Cir. 1980), cannot protect a mark that is shown on strong evidence to be generic as to the relevant category of products prior to the proprietor's trademark use and registration.…

…Harley-Davidson suggests…that it is entitled to trademark use of "HOG" as applied to motorcycles because a substantial segment of the relevant consumers began to use the term specifically to refer to Harley-Davidson motorcycles before the company made trademark use of the term. Some decisions have invoked this principle to accord a company priority as to its subsequent trademark use of a term. *See National Cable Television Ass'n, Inc. v American Cinema Editors, Inc.,* 937 F.2d 1572 [19 USPQ2d 1424] (Fed. Cir. 1991) (mark "ACE")*; Volkswagenwerk AG v Hoffman,* 489 F. Supp. 678 [209 USPQ 398] (D.S.C. 1980) (mark "BUG"). Whether or not we would agree with these decisions, they present a significantly different situation. Neither "ACE" nor "BUG" was a generic term in the language as applied, respectively, to a category of film editors or a category of automobiles prior to the public's use of the terms to refer to the American Cinema Editors and Volkswagen cars. By contrast, "hog" was a generic term in the language as applied to large motorcycles before the public (or at least some segments of it) began using the word to refer to Harley-Davidson motorcycles. The public has no more right than a manufacturer to withdraw from the language a generic term, already applicable to the relevant category of products, and accord it trademark significance, at least as long as the term retains some generic meaning.

For all of these reasons, Harley-Davidson may not prohibit Grottanelli from using "hog" to identify his motorcycle products and services. Like any other manufacturer with a product identified by a word that is generic, Harley-Davidson will have to rely on all or a portion of its tradename (or other protectable marks) to identify its brand of motorcycles, *e.g.,* "Harley Hogs."

II. BAR-AND-SHIELD LOGO

Parody defense. Grottanelli admits that his use of his bar-and-shield logo "purposefully suggests an association with Harley," but argues that his use is a protectable parody. We have accorded considerable leeway to parodists whose expressive works aim their parodic commentary at a trademark or a trademarked product, *see, e.g.,Cliffs Notes, Inc. v Bantam Doubleday Dell Publishing Group, Inc.,* 886 F.2d 490, 493–95 (2d Cir. 1989), *cf. Rogers, v Grimaldi,* 875 F.2d 994, 998 (2d Cir. 1989), but have not hesitated to prevent a manufacturer from using an alleged parody of a competitor's mark to sell a competing product, *see Deere & Co. v MTD Products, Inc.,* 41 F.3d 39 (2d Cir. 1994) (applying New York's anti-dilution statute). Grottanelli uses his

Continued

bar-and-shield logo on the signage of his business, in his newsletter, and on T-shirts. The signage on his business is, in effect, trademark use for a competing service, since, Harley-Davidson offers motorcycle repair services through its authorized dealers, and Grottanelli's placement of his bar-and-shield logo on his newsletter and T-shirts promotes his repair and parts business. In this context, parodic use is sharply limited. *See Deere,* 41 F.3d at 45 (citing *Wendy's International, Inc. v Big Bite, Inc.,* 576 F. Supp. 816 (S.D. Ohio 1983)).

In light of our ruling, we need not consider, with respect to Grottanelli's use of the term "hog," his defense of laches or both parties' challenge to the geographic scope of the injunction.

...Grottanelli's mark makes no comment on Harley's mark; it simply uses it somewhat humorously to promote his own products and services, which is not a permitted trademark parody use....

Disclaimer defense. Grottanelli gains no protection by coyly adding to his version of the bar-and-shield logo the wording "UNAUTHORIZED DEALER." We have alluded to commentary questioning the capacity of brief negating words like "not" or "no" in disclaimers adequately to avoid confusion.

...Whatever the worth of such disclaimers in other contexts, the use of the prefix "UN" before "AUTHORIZED DEALER" provides Grottanelli with no defense when used on signage designed to attract speeding motorcyclists. *See* Restatement (Third) of Unfair Competition § 21 cmt. c (noting that "[a]lthough in theory *prominent* disclaimer of association with the prior user can reduce or eliminate confusion, the courts have ordinarily found the use of disclaimers insufficient to avoid liability for infringement") [emphasis added]....

For all of these reasons, Grottanelli was properly enjoined from using his current bar-and-shield logo and any mark that so resembles Harley-Davidson's trademarked logo as to be likely to cause confusion.

CONCLUSION: The judgment of the District Court is affirmed to the extent it enjoined Grottanelli's use of his bar-and-shield logo and reversed to the extent that it enjoined his use of the word "hog."...

[Judgment affirmed]

QUESTIONS

1. If a term is classified as generic, may a manufacturer enforce trademark usage of that term if it shows that a substantial segment of the relevant consumer population believes the term refers to the products of that manufacturer?
2. Did the court accept Grottanelli's parody defense?
3. Did Grottanelli's disclaimer that he was an unauthorized dealer enable him to avoid liability for infringement of Harley's bar-and-shield logo?

Generic terms that describe a "genus" or class of goods such as soap, car, cola, or rosé wine are never registrable because they do not have a capacity to serve as a source identifier.

Ordinarily geographic terms are not registrable on the Principal Register. **For Example,** BOSTON BEER was denied trademark protection because it was a geographic term.[4] However, if a geographic term has acquired a secondary meaning, it would be registrable. **For Example,** the geographic term *Philadelphia* has acquired secondary meaning when applied to cream cheese products.

A personal name can acquire trademark protection if the name has acquired secondary meaning. **For Example,** the name "Paul Frank" is a personal name and as a trademark had acquired significant recognition and fame in the sale of t-shirts, clothing, and accessories designed by Paul Frank Sunich. Mr. Sunich had a falling out with Paul Frank Industries Inc. (PFI), and started his own t-shirt business using his own personal name, Paul Frank Sunich. The court rejected Mr. Sunich's contention that he had a right to use his full name as a trademark, because it was likely to cause consumer confusion with the established famous mark, and the court preliminarily enjoined him from using his "Paul Frank Sunich" mark with the sale of clothing or accessories. It did, however, permit him to use his full name, Paul Frank Sunich, in signatures, business meetings, and other such contexts where the name did not resemble a trademark or trade name, and did not appear on goods similar to those sold by PFI. Where Mr. Sunich's full name was used, there also had to be some clear explanation that Mr. Sunich was no longer affiliated with PFI. For example, his use of the Web site domain name **www.paulfranksunich.com** was not

[4] *Boston Beer Co. v. Slesar Bros. Brewing Co.,* 9 F.3d 812 (1st Cir. 1994).

enjoined so long as it maintained a message explaining that Mr. Sunich no longer worked for or with PFI.[5]

With a limited number of colors available for use by competitors, along with possible shade confusion, courts had held for some 90 years that color alone could not function as a trademark. The U.S. Supreme Court has overturned this rule, and now if a color serves as a symbol that distinguishes a firm's goods and identifies their source without serving any other significant function, it may, sometimes at least, meet the basic legal requirements for use as a trademark.[6] **For Example,** Owens-Corning Fiberglass Corp. has been allowed to register the color pink as a trademark for its fiberglass insulation products.

4. Remedies for Improper Use of Marks

A person who has the right to use a mark may obtain an injunction prohibiting a competitor from imitating or duplicating the mark. The basic question in such litigation is whether the general public is likely to be confused by the mark of the defendant and to believe wrongly that it identifies the plaintiff's mark.[7] If there is this danger of confusion, the court will enjoin the defendant from using the particular mark.

In some cases, the fact that the products of the plaintiff and the defendant did not compete in the same market was held to entitle the defendant to use a mark that would have been prohibited as confusingly similar if the defendant manufactured the same product as the plaintiff. **For Example,** it has been held that Cadillac, as applied to boats, is not confusingly similar to Cadillac as applied to automobiles; therefore, its use cannot be enjoined.[8]

In addition to broad injunctive relief, the prevailing party may recover lost profits and other actual damages. In cases of willful violations, the court has full discretion to award the plaintiff up to treble damages. In "exceptional cases" the court has discretion to award attorney's fees.

5. Abandonment of Exclusive Right to Mark

An owner who has an exclusive right to use a mark may lose that right. If other persons are permitted to use that mark, it loses its exclusive character and is said to pass into the English language and become generic. Examples of formerly enforceable marks that have made this transition into the general language are *aspirin, thermos, cellophane,* and *shredded wheat.* Nonuse for three consecutive years is prima facie evidence of abandonment.[9]

6. Trade Dress Protection

Firms invest significant resources to develop and promote the appearance of their products and the packages in which these products are sold so that they are clearly recognizable by consumers.

Trade dress involves a product's total image and, in the case of consumer goods, includes the overall packaging look in which each product is sold.

When a competitor adopts a confusingly similar trade dress, it dilutes the first user's investment and goodwill and deceives consumers, hindering their ability to distinguish between competing brands. The law of trade dress protection was initially settled by the U.S. Supreme Court in 1992,[10] and courts have subsequently become more receptive to claims of trade dress infringement under Section 43(a) of the Lanham Act. To prevail, a plaintiff must prove that its trade dress is distinctive and nonfunctional and the defendant's trade dress is confusingly similar to the plaintiff's.[11] **For Example,** Jose Cuervo International was found to have infringed upon Maker's Mark Distillery's red dripping-wax-seal trade dress element used on its bourbon bottles when it used a similar element on its tequila bottles. The court held that the wax seal was not functional because there was more than one way to seal a bottle. The strength of the mark and the likelihood of the confusion were additional factors supporting the court's decision.[12]

[5] *Paul Frank Industries Inc. v. Paul Sunich*, 502 F. Supp. 2d 1094 (C.D. Cal. 2007).

[6] *Qualitex Co. v. Jacobson Products Co., Inc.*, 514 U.S. 159 (1995).

[7] *Resource Lenders, Inc. v. Source Solutions, Inc.*, 404 F. Supp. 2d 1232 (E.D. Cal. 2005).

[8] *General Motors Corp. v. Cadillac Marine and Boat Co.*, 226 F. Supp. 716 (W.D. Mich. 1964). See also *Amstar Corp. v. Domino's Pizza Inc.*, 615 F.2d 252 (5th Cir. 1980), where the mark Domino as applied to pizza was not held to be confusingly similar to Domino as applied to sugar.

[9] *Doeblers' Pennsylvania Hybrids, Inc. v. Doebler*, 442 F.3d 812 (3rd Cir. 2006).

[10] *Two Pesos, Inc. v. Taco Cabana, Inc.*, 505 U.S. 763 (1992).

[11] *Clicks Billiards v. Sixshooters, Inc.*, 251 F.3d 1252 (9th Cir. 2001); and *Woodsland Furniture, LLC v. Larsen*, 124 P.3d, 1016 (Idaho 2005).

[12] *Maker's Mark Distillery, Inc. v. Jose Cuervo International*, 679 F.3d 410 (6th Cir. 2012).

7. Limited Lanham Act Protection of Product Design

Trade dress originally included only the packaging and "dressing" of a product, but in recent years, federal courts of appeals' decisions have expanded trade dress to encompass the design of a product itself. Some manufacturers have been successful in asserting Section 43(a) Lanham Act protection against "knockoffs"—that is, copies of their furniture designs, sweater designs, and handbag designs. In this context Samara Brothers, Inc., discovered that Wal-Mart Stores, Inc., had contacted a supplier to manufacture children's outfits based on photographs of Samara garments, and Wal-Mart was selling these so-called knockoffs. Samara sued Wal-Mart, claiming infringement of unregistered trade dress under Section 43(a) of the Lanham Act. The matter progressed to the U.S. Supreme Court, which considered whether a product's design can be distinctive and, therefore, protectable under Section 43(a) of the Lanham Act. The Court set aside the trial court's decision in favor of Samara Brothers and concluded that a product's design is not inherently distinctive and can only meet the "distinctiveness" element required in a Section 43(a) case by a showing of secondary meaning. That is, the manufacturer must show that the design has come to be known by the public as identifying the product in question and its origin. The matter was remanded for further proceeding consistent with the Court's decision.[13]

It is clear from the Supreme Court's *Wal-Mart Stores, Inc. v. Samara Bros, Inc.* decision that ordinarily only famous designers whose works are widely recognized by the public by their design alone, such as certain Tommy Hilfiger and Ralph Lauren garments, Dooney & Bourke handbags, and Movado watches, will be able to successfully pursue Section 43(a) trade dress protection for their designs against knockoff versions of their work sold under Wal-Mart or other private labels. Of course if a manufacturer's design is copied along with the manufacturer's labels or logo, the makers and sellers of these counterfeit goods are always in clear violation of the Lanham Act.[14] As discussed later, design patents also have limited applicability and protect new and nonobvious ornamental features of a product.

8. Prevention of Dilution of Famous Marks

The Federal Trademark Dilution Act of 1995 (FTDA)[15] provides a cause of action against the "commercial use" of another's famous mark or trade name when it results in a "dilution of the distinctive quality of the mark." The act protects against discordant uses, such as Du Pont shoes, Buick aspirin, and Kodak pianos. Unlike an ordinary trademark infringement action, a dilution action applies in the absence of competition and likelihood of confusion. The act was amended in 2005 to provide that a plaintiff need not prove actual injury to the economic value of the famous mark to prevail in the lawsuit. In addition, the revised act permits truthful comparative advertising and a "fair use" defense for parodying a famous mark.[16]

9. Internet Domain Names and Trademark Rights

An *Internet domain name* is a unique address by which an Internet resource can be identified and found by a Web browser accessing the Internet. Examples of commercial Internet domain names are "Amazon .com," "Priceline.com," and the publisher of this book, "Cengage.com." These domain names match the names of their respective businesses, and these domain names are also trademarks.

Any unused domain name can be registered on a first-come, first-served basis for a rather modest fee, so long as the name differs from a previously registered name by at least one character. **For Example,** Facebook, Inc., was allowed to bring a trademark dilution claim against Teachbook.com LLC, alleging that the TEACHBOOK mark "impairs the distinctiveness of the FACEBOOK mark."[17]

In 2012 the Internet Corporation for Assigned Names and Numbers (ICANN) initiated a process for selecting entities to manage new Web address

13 *Wal-Mart Stores, Inc. v. Samara Bros, Inc.*, 529 U.S. 205 (2000).

14 See *Gucci America Inc. v. Tyrell-Miller*, 678 F. Supp. 2d 117 (S.D.N.Y. 2008), where the court assessed Ms. Miller damages of $200,000 for each of the 15 trademark violations incurred for selling counterfeit Gucci handbags on her Web site.

15 15 U.S.C. §125(c)(1).

16 Trademark Dilution Revision Act (2005).

17 *Facebook, Inc. v. Teachbook.com LLC*, 819 F. Supp. 2d 764 (N.D. Ill. 2011).

endings, including, .app, .home, .music, and .fun. Trademark owners were allowed to file objections against applications if the name sought was confusingly similar to the objector's own trademark.

(A) Cybersquatters. Cybersquatters are individuals who register and set up domain names on the Internet that are identical, or confusingly similar, to existing trademarks that belong to others or are the personal names of famous persons. The cybersquatter hopes to sell or "ransom" the domain name to the trademark owner or the famous individual.

Because the extent of the legal remedies available to famous companies or famous individuals who have been victims of cybersquatters has not always been certain, Congress passed the Federal Anticybersquatting Consumer Protection Act (ACPA)[18] in 1999 to prohibit the practice of cybersquatting and cyberpiracy and to provide clear and certain remedies. However, to be successful in a ACPA lawsuit, the plaintiff must prove that the name is famous and that the domain name was registered in bad faith.[19] Remedies include (1) injunctive relief preventing the use of the name, (2) forfeiture of the domain name, and (3) attorney fees and costs. In addition, trademark owners may obtain damages and the profits that cybersquatters made from the use of the name.

A safe harbor exists under the ACPA for defendants who both "believed and had reasonable grounds to believe that the use of the domain name was fair use or otherwise lawful."[20] A defendant who acts even partially in bad faith in registering a domain name is not entitled to the shelter of the safe harbor provision. **For Example,** Howard Goldberg, the president of Artco, is an operator of Web sites that sell women's lingerie and other merchandise. He registered a domain name **www.victoriassecrets.net** to divert consumers to his Web sites to try to sell them his goods. The court rejected his ACPA safe harbor defense that he intended in good faith to have customers compare his company's products with those of Victoria's Secret. The fact that Victoria's Secret is a distinctive or famous mark deserving of the highest degree of trademark protection, coupled with the fact that the

E-Commerce & Cyberlaw

Metatags describe the contents of a Web site using keywords. Some search engines search metatags to identify Web sites related to a search. In *Playboy Enterprises, Inc. (PEI) v. WELLES,** PEI sued "Playmate of the year 1981" Terri Welles for using that and other phrases involving PEI's trademarks on her Internet Web site metatags. Some search engines that use their own summaries of Web sites, or that search the entire text of sites, would be likely to identify Welles's site as relevant to a search for "Playboy" or "Playmate," thus allowing Welles to trade on PEI's marks, PEI asserted. Remembering that the purpose of a trademark is not to provide a windfall monopoly to the mark owner but to prevent confusion over the source of products or services, the court applied a three-factor test for normative use to this case: (1) the product or service must be one not readily identifiable without the use of the mark, (2) only so much of the mark may be used as reasonably necessary to identify the product or service, and (3) the user must not suggest sponsorship or endorsement by the trademark holder.

Welles had no practical way of describing herself without using the trademark terms. The court stated, "We can hardly expect someone searching for Welles's site...to describe Welles without referring to Playboy—as the nude model selected by Mr. Hefner's organization."

The court stated that there is no descriptive substitute for the trademarks used in Welles's metatags, and to preclude their use would inhibit the free flow of information on the Internet, which is not a goal of trademark law. Moreover, the metatag use was reasonable use to identify her products and services and did not suggest sponsorship, thus satisfying the second and third elements of the court's test.

**Playboy Enterprises, Inc. v. Welles*, 279 F.3d 796 (9th Cir. 2002). See *ESS Entertainment 2000, Inc. v. Rockstar Videos Inc.*, 547 F.3d 1095 (9th Cir. 2008).

[18] Pub. L. 106, 113 Stat. 1536, 15 U.S.C. §1051.

[19] A plaintiff must meet the burden of proof, however, that its mark is "famous," in order to come within the protection of the ACPA, with the courts requiring the marks be highly distinctive and thus well known throughout the country. Among the marks courts have ruled not to be distinctive are "Blue Man Group," the performing group; "Clue," the board game; and "Trek," for bicycles. In contrast, marks that have been ruled famous include "Nike," "Pepsi," and "Victoria's Secret." See *Philbrick v. eNom Inc.*, 593 F. Supp. 2d 352, 367 (D. N.H. 2009). But see *DSPT International, Inc. v. Nahum*, 624 F.3d 1213 (9th Cir. 2010), where a former employee's actions of removing access to the Internet Web site at a domain name containing the employer's trademark, and withholding the domain name from the employer to obtain leverage in a dispute with the employer, constituted "cyberpiracy" under the language of Anti-Cybersquatting Protection Act.

[20] U.S.C. §1125(d)(1)(B)(ii).

defendant added a mere *s* to that mark and gave false contact information when he requested the domain name, indicates that he and his company acted in bad faith and intended to profit from the famous mark.[21]

(B) Dispute Avoidance. To avoid the expense of trademark litigation, it is prudent to determine whether the Internet domain name selected for your new business is an existing registered trademark or an existing domain name owned by another. Commercial firms provide comprehensive trademark searches for less than $500. Determining whether a domain name is owned by another may be done online at **www.internic.net/whois.html**.

The Internet Corporation for Assigned Names and Numbers (ICANN) provides fast-track arbitration procedures to protect trademark owners from conflicting online domain names under the auspices of the World Intellectual Property Organization (WIPO). **For Example,** Victoria's Secret stores arbitrated the "victoriassecrets.net" domain name held by Howard Goldberg's company, and the arbitration panel transferred the ownership of the name to Victoria's Secret stores. Victoria's Secret stores subsequently brought an action against Goldberg and Artco for damages and injunctive relief under trademark law and the ACPA.

B. Copyrights

A **copyright** is the exclusive right given by federal statute to the creator of a literary or an artistic work to use, reproduce, and display the work. Under the international treaty called the *Berne Convention*, copyright of the works of all U.S. authors is protected automatically in all Berne Convention nations that have agreed under the treaty to treat nationals of other member countries like their own nationals.

A copyright prevents not the copying of an idea but only the copying of the way the idea is expressed.[22] That is, the copyright is violated when there is a duplication of the words, pictures, or other form of expression of the creator but not when there is just use of the idea those words, pictures, or other formats express.

The Copyright Act does not apply extraterritorially. However, if the infringement is completed in the United States and the copied work is then disseminated overseas, there is liability under the act for the resulting extraterritorial damages. **For Example,** the Los Angeles News Service (LANS), an independent news organization, produced two copyrighted videotapes of the beating of Reginald Denny during the Los Angeles riots of April 1992, and LANS licensed them to NBC for use on the *Today Show* in New York. Visnews taped the works and transmitted them by satellite to Reuters in London, which provided copies to its overseas subscribers. The infringement by Visnews occurred in New York, and Visnews was liable for the extraterritorial damages that resulted from the overseas dissemination of the work.[23]

It is a violation of U.S. copyright law for satellite carriers to capture signals of network stations in the United States and transmit them abroad. **For Example,** PrimeTime's satellite retransmission of copyrighted NFL football games to satellite dish owners in Canada was held to be a violation of U.S. copyright law, notwithstanding testimony of PrimeTime's CEO that a law firm in Washington, D.C., told him that U.S. law did not pertain to the distribution of products in Canada. The NFL was awarded $2,557,500 in statutory damages.[24]

10. Duration of Copyright

Article 1, Section 8, of the U.S. Constitution empowered Congress to

> *promote the Progress of Science and useful Arts, by securing for limited times to Authors and Inventors the exclusive Right to their respective Writings and Discoveries.*

The first U.S. copyright statute was enacted soon after in 1790 and provided protection for any "book, map or chart" for 14 years, with a privilege to renew for an additional 14 years. In 1831, the initial 14-year term was extended to 28 years, with a privilege for an additional 14 years. Under the 1909 Copyright Act, the protection period was for 28 years, with a right of renewal for an additional 28 years.

[21] *Victoria's Secret Stores v. Artco*, 194 F. Supp. 2d 204 (S.D. Ohio 2002).
[22] *Attia v. New York Hospital*, 201 F.3d 50 (2d Cir. 2000).
[23] *Los Angeles News Service v. Reuters*, 149 F.3d 987 (9th Cir. 1998).
[24] *National Football League v. PrimeTime 24 Joint Venture*, 131 F. Supp. 2d 458 (S.D.N.Y. 2001).

The Copyright Act of 1976 set the duration of a copyright at the life of the creator of the work plus 50 years. Under the Sonny Bono Copyright Term Extension Act of 1998, the duration has been extended to the life of the creator plus 70 years.[25] If a work is a "work made for hire"—that is, a business pays an individual to create the work—the business employing the creator registers the copyright. Under the 1998 Extension Act, such a copyright has been extended by 20 years and now runs for 120 years from creation or 95 years from publication of the work, whichever period is shorter. After a copyright has expired, the work is in the public domain and may be used by anyone without cost.[26]

11. Copyright Notice

Prior to March 1, 1989, the author of an original work secured a copyright by placing a copyright notice on the work, consisting of the word *copyright* or the symbol ©, the year of first publication, and the name or pseudonym of the author. The author was also required to register the copyright with the Copyright Office. Under the Berne Convention Implementation Act of 1988,[27] a law that adjusts U.S. copyright law to conform to the Berne Convention, it is no longer mandatory that works published after March 1, 1989, contain a notice of copyright. However, placing a notice of copyright on published works is strongly recommended. This notice prevents an infringer from claiming innocent infringement of the work, which would reduce the amount of damages owed. To bring a copyright infringement suit for a work of U.S. origin, the owner must have submitted two copies of the work to the Copyright Office in Washington, D.C., for registration.

12. What Is Copyrightable?

Copyrights protect literary, musical, dramatic, and artistic work. Protected are books and periodicals; musical and dramatic compositions; choreographic works; maps; works of art, such as paintings, sculptures, and photographs; motion pictures and other audiovisual works; sound recordings; architectural works; and computer programs.

The work must be original, independently created by the author, and possess at least some minimal degree of creativity.[28] **For Example,** William Darden, a Web page designer, challenged the Copyright Office's denial of a copyright registration for a series of existing maps with some changes in the nature of shading, coloring, or font. A court found that the Copyright Office acted within its discretion when it denied Darden's registration with the finding by the examiner from the Visual Arts Section that the maps were "representations of the preexisting census maps in which the creative spark is utterly lacking or so trivial as to be virtually nonexistent."[29]

13. Copyright Ownership and the Internet

Businesses today commonly use offsite programming services to create copyrightable software, with the delivery of code over the Internet. As set forth previously, when a business pays an employee to create a copyrightable work, it is a "work for hire" and the business employing the creator owns and may register the copyright. On the other hand, if a freelancer is employed offsite to create software for a fixed fee without a contract setting forth the ownership of the work, the freelancer owns the work product and the company utilizing the freelancer has a license to use the work product but does not have ownership of it. To avoid disputes about ownership of custom software, a written contract that addresses these ownership and license questions is necessary.

14. Rights of Copyright Holders

A copyright holder has the exclusive right to (1) reproduce the work; (2) prepare derivative works, such as a script from the original work; (3) distribute copies of recordings of the work; (4) publicly perform the work, in the case of plays and motion pictures; and (5) publicly display the work, in the case of paintings, sculptures, and photographs. **For Example,** David LaChapelle is a photographer and director with a worldwide reputation

[25] P.L. 105-298, 112 Stat. 2827, 17 U.S.C. §302(b).

[26] Without the Sonny Bono Extension Act of 1998, the copyright on Mickey Mouse, created by Walt Disney Co. in 1928, was set to expire in 2003 and enter the public domain. Pluto, Goofy, and Donald Duck would have followed soon after.

[27] P.L. 100-568, 102 Stat. 2854, 17 U.S.C. §101 et seq.

[28] *Feist Publications Inc. v. Rural Telephone Services Co.*, 499 U.S. 340 (1991).

[29] *Darden v. Peters*, 402 F. Supp. 2d 638 (E.D. N.C. 2005).

for his unique body of work in fashion and editorial photography, defined by its saturating, vibrant colors and theatrical, often surreal composition. He charges up to $1 million to direct/produce a music video. "Def Jam" released a music video for Rihanna's song "S&M." Prospective directors of the music video had been asked by Rihanna or persons acting on her behalf to make a "LaChapelle-esque music video." LaChapelle contends that the defendants used protected expressions from eight of his photographs in the video and that an ordinary observer might find Rihanna's "Presence" to be substantially similar to LaChapelle's protectable expression in "Noisy Fame." Accordingly, the district court denied the defendant's motion to dismiss the copyright infringement case.[30]

The copyright owner may assign or license some of the rights listed and will receive royalty payments as part of the agreement. The copyright law also ensures royalty payments. **For Example,** Jessie Riviera is a songwriter whose songs are sung at public performances and are recorded by performers on records, tapes, and CDs. Jessie is entitled to royalties from the public performance of her works. Such royalties are collected by two performing rights societies, the American Society of Composers, Authors, and Publishers (ASCAP) and Broadcast Music, Inc. (BMI), which act on behalf of the copyright holders. Jessie is also entitled to so-called mechanical royalties that refer to the royalty stream derived from "mechanically" reproduced records, tapes, and CDs.[31] The principal payers of mechanical royalties are record companies, and the rates are set by the Copyright Royalty Tribunal.

In addition to rights under the copyright law and international treaties, federal and state laws prohibit record and tape piracy.

15. Limitation on Exclusive Character of Copyright

A limitation on the exclusive rights of copyright owners exists under the principle of *fair use*, which allows limited use of copyrighted material in connection with criticism, news reporting, teaching, and research. Four important factors to consider when judging whether the use made in a particular case is fair use include the following:

1. The purpose and character of the use, including whether such use is of a commercial nature or is for nonprofit educational purposes[32]
2. The nature of the copyrighted work
3. The amount and substantiality of the portion used in relation to the copyrighted work as a whole
4. The effect of the use on the potential market for or value of the copyrighted work[33]

In *American Geophysical Union v. Texas, Inc.*, the court applied the four statutory standards to determine whether the defendant's photocopying of scientific journal articles was fair use.

American Geophysical Union v. Texaco, Inc., 60 F.3d 913 (2d Cir. 1995)

Fair Use or Not Fair Use—That Is the Question

The American Geophysical Union and 82 other publishers of scientific and technical journals brought a class-action lawsuit against Texaco claiming that Texaco's unauthorized photocopying of articles from their journals constituted a copyright infringement. Texaco's defense was that the copying was fair use under Section 107 of the Copyright Act of 1976. To avoid extensive discovery, the parties agreed to focus on one randomly selected Texaco scientist, Dr. Donald Chickering, who had photocopies of eight articles from the *Journal of Catalysis* in his files. The trial court judge held that the copying of the eight articles did not constitute fair use, and Texaco appealed.

30 *LaChapelle v. Fenty*, 812 F. Supp. 2d 434 (S.D.N.Y. 2011).

31 The ASCAP was formed in 1914 by eminent American composers including Victor Herbert and John Philip Sousa. BMI was formed in 1939. Public performance royalties collected by these societies exceed $1.5 billion per year and are distributed according to elaborate formulas.

32 In *Princeton University Press v. Michigan Document Services, Inc.*, 99 F.3d 1381 (6th Cir. 1996), a commercial copyshop reproduced "coursepacks" and sold them to students attending the University of Michigan. The court refused to consider the "use" as one for nonprofit educational purposes because the use challenged was that of the copyshop, a for-profit corporation that had decided to duplicate copyrighted material for sale to maximize its profits and give itself a competitive edge over other copyshops by declining to pay the royalties requested by the holders of the copyrights.

33 See fair use analysis in *Perfect 10 v. Amazon.com, Inc.*, 487 F.3d 701, 719–725 (9th Cir. 2007).

Continued

JUDICIAL OPINION

NEWMAN, C. J.... Burdens of Proof and Standard of Review

Fair use serves as an affirmative defense to a claim of copyright infringement, and thus the party claiming that its secondary use of the original copyrighted work constitutes a fair use typically carries the burden of proof as to all issues in the dispute. Moreover, since fair use is a "mixed question of law and fact," *Harper & Row,* 471 U.S. at 560, 105 S.Ct. at 2230, we review the District Court's conclusions on this issue *de novo,* though we accept its subsidiary findings of fact unless clearly erroneous, see *Twin Peaks,* 996 F.2d at 1374....

FIRST FACTOR: PURPOSE AND CHARACTER OF USE

The first factor listed in section 107 is "the purpose and character of the use, including whether such use is of a commercial nature or is for nonprofit educational purposes." Especially pertinent to an assessment of the first fair use factor are the precise circumstances under which copies of the eight *Catalysis* articles were made. After noticing six of these articles when the original copy of the journal issue containing each of them was circulated to him, Chickering had them photocopied, at least initially, for the same basic purpose that one would normally seek to obtain the original—to have it available on his shelf for ready reference if and when he needed to look at it. The library circulated one copy and invited all the researchers to make their own photocopies. It is a reasonable inference that the library staff wanted each journal issue moved around the building quickly and returned to the library so that it would be available for others to look at. Making copies enabled all researchers who might one day be interested in examining the contents of an article in the issue to have the article readily available in their own offices. In Chickering's own words, the copies of the articles were made for "my personal convenience," since it is "far more convenient to have access in my office to a photocopy of an article than to have to go to the library each time I wanted to refer to it." Affidavit of Donald Chickering at 11 (submitted as direct trial testimony) [hereinafter *Chickering testimony*]. Significantly, Chickering did not even have occasion to use five of the photocopied articles at all, further revealing that the photocopies of the eight *Catalysis* articles were primarily made just for "future retrieval and reference." *Id....*

The photocopying of these eight *Catalysis* articles may be characterized as "archival"—*i.e.,* done for the primary purpose of providing numerous Texaco scientists (for whom Chickering served as an example) each with his or her own personal copy of each article without Texaco's having to purchase another original journal....

On balance, we agree with the District Court that the first factor favors the publishers; primarily because the dominant purpose of the use is a systematic institutional policy of multiplying the available number of copies of pertinent copyrighted articles by circulating the journals among employed scientists for them to make copies, thereby serving the same purpose for which additional subscriptions are normally sold, or, as will be discussed, for which photocopying licenses may be obtained.

SECOND FACTOR: NATURE OF COPYRIGHTED WORK

The second statutory fair use factor is "the nature of the copyrighted work." In assessing this factor, the District Court noted that the articles in *Catalysis* "are created for publication with the purpose and intention of benefiting from the protection of the copyright law," and that copyright protection "is vitally necessary to the dissemination of scientific articles of the sort that are at issue." 802 F.Supp. at 16. Nevertheless, the Court ultimately concluded that this factor favored Texaco because the photocopied articles were essentially factual in nature and the "scope of fair use is greater with respect to factual than nonfactual works."...

Ultimately...the manifestly factual character of the eight articles precludes us from considering the articles as "within the core of the copyright's protective purposes," *Campbell,* 114 S.Ct. at 1175; see also *Harper & Row,* 471 U.S. at 563, 105 S. Ct. at 2232 ("The law generally recognizes a greater need to disseminate factual works than works of fiction or fantasy."). Thus, in agreement with the District Court, we conclude that the second factor favors Texaco.

THIRD FACTOR: AMOUNT AND SUBSTANTIABILITY OF PORTION USED

The third statutory fair use factor is "the amount and substantiality of the portion used in relation to the copyrighted work as a whole." The District Court concluded that this factor clearly favors the publishers because Texaco copied the eight articles from *Catalysis* in their entirety....

Despite Texaco's claims that we consider its amount of copying "minuscule" in relation to the entirety of *Catalysis,* we conclude, as did the District Court, that Texaco has copied entire works. Though this conclusion does not preclude a finding of fair use, it militates against such a finding, see *Sony,* 464 U.S. at 449–50, 104 S.Ct. at 792–93, and weights the third factor in favor of the publishers....

FOURTH FACTOR: EFFECT UPON POTENTIAL MARKET OR VALUE

The fourth statutory fair use factor is "the effect of the use upon the potential market for or value of the copyrighted

Continued

work." Assessing this factor, the District Court detailed the range of procedures Texaco could use to obtain authorized copies of the articles that it photocopied and found that "whatever combination of procedure Texaco used, the publishers' revenues would grow significantly." The Court concluded that the publishers "powerfully demonstrated entitlement to prevail as to the fourth factor," since they had shown "a substantial harm to the value of their copyrights" as the consequence of Texaco's copying. See *id.* at 18–21.

Prior to *Campbell,* the Supreme Court had characterized the fourth factor as "the single most important element of fair use," *Harper & Row,* 471 U.S. at 566, 105 S.Ct. at 2233. However, *Campbell's* discussion of the fourth factor conspicuously omits this phrasing. Apparently abandoning the idea that any factor enjoys primacy, *Campbell* instructs that '[a]ll [four factors] are to be explored, and the results weighed together, in light of the purposes of copyright.' 114 S.Ct. at 1171....

Primarily because of lost licensing revenue, and to a minor extent because of lost subscription revenue, we agree with the District Court that "the publishers have demonstrated a substantial harm to the value of their copyrights through [Texco's] copying," 802 F.Supp. at 21, and thus conclude that the fourth statutory factor favors the publishers.

AGGREGATE ASSESSMENT

We conclude that three of the four statutory factors, including the important first and the fourth factors, favor the publishers. ...We therefore agree with the District Court's conclusion that Texaco's photocopying of eight particular articles from the *Journal of Catalysis* was not fair use.

Though we recognize the force of many observations made in Judge Jacob's dissenting opinion, we are not dissuaded by his dire predictions that our ruling in this case "has ended fair-use photocopying with respect to a large population of journals," 60 F.3d at 938–39, or, to the extent that the transactional licensing scheme is used, "would seem to require that an intellectual property lawyer be posted at each copy machine," *id.* at 937–38. Our ruling does not consider photocopying for personal use by an individual. Our ruling is confined to the institutional, systematic, archival multiplication of copies revealed by the record—the precise copying that the parties stipulated should be the basis for the District Court's decision now on appeal and for which licenses are in fact available. And the claim that lawyers need to be stationed at copy machines is belied by the ease with which music royalties have been collected and distributed for performances at thousands of cabarets, without the attendance of intellectual property lawyers in any capacity other than as customers....

[Affirmed]

QUESTIONS

1. Assess Texaco's position that the purpose and character of its use of the eight articles were for the legitimate reason of use in Dr. Chickering's research and they were not photocopied for resale.
2. Is the "market-effect" factor the single most important element of fair use?
3. Do you believe that the result of this decision will lead to the dire consequences of the posting of intellectual property lawyers at every copy machine, trying to enforce licensing schemes?

First Amendment privileges of freedom of speech and the press are preserved through the doctrine of *fair use,* which allows for use of portions of another's copyrighted work for matters such as comment and criticism. Parodies and caricatures are the most penetrating forms of criticism and are protected under the fair use doctrine. Moreover, while injunctive relief is appropriate in the vast majority of copyright infringement cases because the infringements are simply piracy, in the case of parodies and caricatures where there are reasonable contentions of fair use, preliminary injunctions to prevent publication are inappropriate. The copyright owner can be adequately protected by an award of damages should infringement be found. **For Example,** Suntrust Bank, the trustee of a trust that holds the copyright to Margaret Mitchell's *Gone with the Wind,* one of the all-time best-selling books in the world, obtained a preliminary injunction preventing Houghton Mifflin Co. from publishing Alice Randall's *The Wind Done Gone.* The Randall book is an irreverent parody that turns old ideas upside down. The Court of Appeals set aside the injunction of the federal district court because Houghton Mifflin had a viable fair use defense.[34]

[34] *Suntrust Bank v. Houghton Mifflin Co.,* 268 F.3d 1257 (11th Cir. 2001). See also *Brownmark Films, LLC. v. Comedy Partners,* 800 F. Supp. 2d 991 (E.D. Wis. 2011), where the federal district court dismissed a copyright infringement lawsuit against the South Park defendants on the basis of fair use defense, in an episode lampooning viral video crazes.

16. Secondary Liability for Infringement

An entity that distributes a device with the object of promoting its use to infringe copyrights as shown by clear expression or other active steps taken to foster the resulting acts of infringement is liable for these acts of infringement by third parties, regardless of the device's lawful uses. **For Example,** Grokster, Ltd., and StreamCast Networks, Inc., distributed free software products that allow all computer users to share electronic files through peer-to-peer networks, so called because users' computers communicate directly with each other, not through central servers. When these firms distributed their free software, each clearly voiced the objective that the recipients use the software to download copyrighted works. These firms derived profits from selling advertising space and streaming ads to the software users. Liability for infringement was established under the secondary liability doctrines of contributory or vicarious infringement.[35]

While copyright holders have historically chosen to litigate against the provider of new technologies rather than the users of the technology, the law is clear that copyright holders may sue individual infringers. **For Example,** Sony and other recording companies successfully sued Goucher College student Joel Tenenbaum for willfully downloading and distributing 30 copyrighted works, and the court assessed statutory damages at $675,000.[36]

17. Digital Millennium Copyright Act

The Digital Millennium Copyright Act of 1998 (DMCA)[37] was enacted to curb the pirating of software and other copyrighted works, such as books, films, videos, and recordings, by creating civil and criminal penalties for anyone who circumvents encryption software. The law also prohibits the manufacture, import, sale, or distribution of circumvention devices.

Title II of the DMCA provides a "safe harbor" for Internet Service Providers (ISP) from liability for direct, vicarious, and contributory infringement of copyrights provided the ISP (1) does not have actual knowledge of the infringing activity or expeditiously removed access to the problematic material upon obtaining knowledge of infringing activity, (2) does not receive financial benefit directly attributable to the infringing activity, and (3) responded expeditiously upon notification of the claimed infringement.

Ethics & the Law

The Death of Journalism?

Washington Post columnist Ian Shapira wrote a column entitled "How Gawker Ripped off My Newspaper Story."* He had written a profile on Washington-based "business coach" Anne Loehr, an expert on how people in their 20s and late teens behave in the workplace. He conducted an extensive phone interview with Loehr, attended one of her "Get Wise with Gen Ys" sessions and spent an additional day writing the story. Shapira is provided a living wage, health care, and retirement benefits by *The Post*. Gawker's eight-paragraph posting condensed Loehr's biography with a link to Shapira's story, and utilized Loehr's own words on various points of interest, followed by a "cut and paste" of Shapira's "stuff." It ended with the hyperlinked words "*Washington Post*."

The newspaper industry is in financial peril. Is there a line that can be drawn between the "fair use" doctrine allowing appropriate quoting and linking, and "parasitic" free-rider Web sites? Shapira asserts that current law allows "the Gawker's of the world to appropriate others' work, repurpose it, and sell ads against it with no payment to or legal recourse for the company that [paid the originator of the story]." Should the copyright law be amended to require those who sell ads against heavily excerpted articles to pay a fee to the originator? Is this payment the ethical thing to do?

***http://www.washingtonpost.com/wp-dyn/content/article/2009/07/31/AR2009073102476.html**

[35] *Metro-Goldwyn-Mayer Studios, Inc. v. Grokster, Ltd.*, 545 U.S. 913 (2005).
[36] *Sony v. Tenenbaum*, 660 F.3d 487 (1st Cir. 2011).
[37] 17 U.S.C. §1201.

C. Patents

Under Article 1, Section 8, of the U.S. Constitution, the founding fathers of our country empowered Congress to promote the progress of science by securing for limited times to inventors the exclusive rights to their discoveries. Federal patent laws established under Article 1, Section 8, protect inventors just as authors are protected under copyright law authorized by the same section of the U.S. Constitution.

Thomas Jefferson was the first administrator of the United States' patent system and was the author of the Patent Act of 1793. During his time of administrating the system Jefferson saw clearly the difficulty of deciding what should be patentable. Years after drafting the 1793 Act, he explained that in that Act "the whole was turned over to the judiciary, to be matured into a system, under which everyone might know when his actions were safe and lawful."[38] In practice Congress has left wide latitude for judicial construction of patent law, entrusting the courts to keep pace with advancing industrial and technological developments.

18. Types, Duration, and Notice

There are three types of patents, the rights to which may be obtained by proper filing with the United States Patent and Trademark Office (USPTO) in Washington, D.C. The types and duration of patents are as follows.

(a) Utility Patents. Inventions classified as *utility* or *functional patents* grant inventors of any new and useful process, machine, manufacture, or composition of matter or any new and useful improvement of such devices the right to obtain a patent.[39] Prior to 1995, utility patents had a life of 17 years from the date of grant. Under the Uruguay Round Trade Agreement Act, effective June 8, 1995, the duration of U.S. utility patents was changed from 17 years from the date of grant to 20 years from the date of filing to be consistent with the patent law of World Trade Organization (WTO) member states.

(b) Design Patents. A second kind of patent exists under U.S. patent law that protects new and nonobvious ornamental features that appear in connection with an article of manufacture.[40] These patents are called *design patents* and have a duration of 14 years. In order to establish design patent infringement, the patent holder has the difficult task of proving, by a preponderance of the evidence, that an ordinary observer (and not the eye of an expert) taking into account the prior art would believe the accused design to be the same as the patented design.[41] **For Example,** the Court of Appeals for the Federal Circuit (CAFC) held that defendant Swisa's Nail Buffer, which features buffer surfaces on all four of its sides, was not "the same as" and thus did not infringe on Egyptian Goddess, Inc.'s patented nail buffer design, which features buffer surfaces on three of its four sides.[42]

(c) Plant Patents. A third type of patent, called a *plant patent,* protects the inventors of asexually reproduced new varieties of plants. The duration is 20 years from the date of filing, the same duration applied to utility patents.

(d) Notice. The owner of a patent is required to mark the patented item or device using the word *patent* and must list the patent number on the device to recover damages from an infringer of the patent.

(e) The America Invents Act. Federal patent law was amended in 2011 by the America Invents Act (AIA).[43] Section 3 of the Act defines the effective filing date of a claimed invention as the actual filing date of the patent or application for a patent, replacing the current "first to invent" system with a "first to file system." The purpose of this change is to provide the inventor with greater certainty regarding the scope of protection and to promote international uniformity by harmonizing the U.S. patent system with systems used in Europe and other countries with which the United States conducts trade. The AIA provides the option of an expedited patent examination process, with the goal of processing applications within 12 months, as opposed to the ordinary processing period of three to

[38] See *Graham v. John Deere Co. of Kansas City,* 383 U.S.1, 10 (1966).
[39] 35 U.S.C. §101.
[40] 35 U.S.C. §173.
[41] *Gorham v. White,* 81 U.S. 511 (1871).
[42] *Egyptian Goddess, Inc. v. SWISA, Inc.,* 545 F.3d 665 (Fed. Cir. 2008).
[43] Pub. L. 112-29, H.R. 1249 enacted September 16, 2011, and effective as of March 16, 2013. Amended 35 U.S.C. §102.

four years. The USPTO fee for this service is an extra $4,800, with a 50 percent reduction for "small entity" inventors. Under the Act, the USPTO will also speed up the application process, at no additional cost, for inventions that reduce greenhouse emissions or provide energy conservation.

Challenges to patent grants can be made for up to nine months after the patent is granted. The post-grant review is made by a patent examiner.

19. Patentability

Section 101 of the 1952 Patent Act recognizes four categories of subject matter for patent eligibility: (1) processes, (2) machines, (3) manufactures, and (4) compositions of matter. However, even if a claim may be deemed to fit one of these categories, it may not be patent eligible. Phenomena of nature, though just discovered; mental processes; and abstract intellectual concepts are not patentable because they are the basic tools of scientific and technological work.[44] **For Example,** Prometheus Laboratories Inc. patented steps for testing the proper dosage level of drug treatments for individuals with gastrointestinal diseases. The Mayo Clinic developed its own test to determine toxicity-risk levels similar to that of Prometheus, and Prometheus sued Mayo for patent infringement. The Supreme Court held that the Prometheus patents were not patent eligible because they were merely instructions to apply the laws of nature.[45]

Once it is established that an invention is patent eligible, a patent may be obtained if the invention is something that is *new and not obvious* to a person of ordinary skill and knowledge in the art or technology to which the invention is related. Whether an invention is new and not obvious in its field may lead to highly technical proceedings before a patent examiner, the USPTO's Board of Patent Appeals, and the U.S. Court of Appeals for the Federal Circuit (CAFC). **For Example,** Thomas Devel's application for a patent on complementary DNA (cDNA) molecules encoding proteins that stimulated cell division was rejected by a patent examiner as "obvious" and the rejection was affirmed by the USPTO's Board of Patent Appeals. However, after a full hearing before the CAFC, which focused on the state of research in the field as applied to the patent application, Devel's patent claims were determined to be "not invalid because of obviousness."[46]

Once approved by the Patent and Trademark Office, a patent is presumed valid.[47] However, a defendant in a patent infringement lawsuit may assert a patent's invalidity as a defense to an infringement claim by showing the invention as a whole would have been obvious to a person of ordinary skill in the art when the invention was patented. This showing is called **prior art**. **For Example,** Ron Rogers invented and patented a tree-trimming device that is essentially a chain saw releasably mounted on the end of a telescoping pole. Rogers sued Desa International, Inc. (DIA) for patent infringement after DIA introduced the Remington Pole Saw, a chain saw releasably mounted on the end of a telescoping pole. DIA provided evidence of prior art, citing four preexisting patents dealing with "trimming tools on extension poles" that correlated with Rogers's patent. The court nullified Rogers's patent because it concluded the DIA had met its heavy burden of proof that releasably mounting a lightweight chain saw on the end of a telescoping pole assembly to trim trees would be obvious to a person of ordinary skill in the art.[48]

Patent law has expanded to include human-made microorganisms as patent-eligible subject matter, since such compositions are not nature's handiwork, but the inventor's own work.

20. Patentable Business Methods

A 1998 Court of Appeals for the Federal Circuit (CAFC) decision recognized "business methods" as a patent-eligible "process" under Section 101 of the

[44] *Gottschalk v. Benson*, 409 U.S. 63, 67 (1972).

[45] *Mayo Collaborative Services v. Prometheus Laboratories, Inc.*, 132 S.Ct. 1289, 1301 (2012). The Court explained in part its rationale: [E]ven though rewarding with patents those who discover new laws of nature and the like might well encourage their discovery, those laws and principles, considered generally, are "the basic tools of scientific and technological work." ... And so there is a danger that the grant of patents that tie up their use will inhibit future innovation premised upon them, a danger that becomes acute when a patented process amounts to no more than an instruction to "apply the natural law," or otherwise forecloses more future invention than the underlying discovery could reasonably justify.

[46] *In re Devel*, 51 F.3d 1552 (Fed. Cir. 1995).

[47] See *Microsoft Corp. v. i4i Limited Partnership*, 131 S.Ct. 2238 (2011), where the Supreme Court determined that defenses to patent infringement claims must be proven by clear and convincing evidence.

[48] See *KRS International Co. v. Teleflex, Inc.*, 500 U.S. 398 (2007) for the Supreme Court's recent "obviousness" patent decision, where the Court held that mounting an available sensor on a fixed pivot point of the prior art pedal was a design step well within the grasp of a person of ordinary skill in the relevant art and that the benefit of doing so would be obvious.

Patent Act.[49] A burgeoning number of business-method patents followed, with the U.S. Supreme Court referencing in its *eBay v. MercExchange* decision the "potential vagueness and suspect validity of some of these patents." A pure business-method patent consists basically of a series of steps related to performing a business process. **For Example,** Patent No. 6,846,131 sets forth a method of doing business with steps for Producing Revenue from Gypsum-Based Refuse Sites. So-called junk patents have also been issued as business-method patents. **For Example,** Patent No. 4,022,227, Method of Concealing Baldness, contains a series of steps for combing one's hair that amount to what is best known as a *comb-over*. Business methods are often in the form of software programs and encompass e-commerce applications.

Recent decisions of the U.S. Court of Appeals for the Federal Circuit, which specializes in patent issues, contained a much more restrictive approach to evaluating the patentability of business methods under Section 101 of the Patent Act.[50] The Supreme Court, however, declined to impose limitations on the Patent Act that are inconsistent with the Act's text, as set forth in the *Bilski v. Kappos* decision.

Bilski v. Kappos, 130 S. Ct. 3218 (2010)

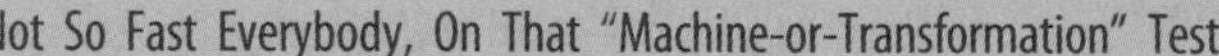

Not So Fast Everybody, On That "Machine-or-Transformation" Test

Bernard Bilski challenged the denial of his patent application for a method of hedging risk in the field of commodities trading in the energy market based on patent-eligible subject matter. The key claims are claims 1 and 4. Claim 1 describes a series of steps instructing how to hedge risk. Claim 4 puts the concept articulated in claim 1 into a simple mathematical formula. On appeal to the Federal Circuit Court of Appeals (*en banc*), it applied a "machine-or-transformation" test:

> *A claimed process is surely patent-eligible under § 101 if: (1) it is tied to a particular machine or apparatus, or (2) it transforms a particular article into a different state or thing.*

The court determined that Bilski's "business method" of hedging risk in the field of commodities trading was not patent eligible because it was neither "tied to a machine or apparatus," nor did it transform anything. The Supreme Court granted review of the decision.

JUDICIAL OPINION

KENNEDY, J.... Under the Court of Appeals' formulation, an invention is a "process" only if: "(1) it is tied to a particular machine or apparatus, or (2) it transforms a particular article into a different state or thing." This Court has more than once cautioned that courts should not read into the patent laws limitations and conditions which the legislature has not expressed....

This Court's precedents establish that the machine-or-transformation test is a useful and important clue, an investigative tool, for determining whether some claimed inventions are processes under § 101. The machine-or-transformation test is not the sole test for deciding whether an invention is a patent-eligible "process."...

The machine-or-transformation test may well provide a sufficient basis for evaluating processes similar to those in the Industrial Age—for example, inventions grounded in a physical or other tangible form. But there are reasons to doubt whether the test should be the sole criterion for determining the patentability of inventions in the Information Age. As numerous *amicus* briefs argue, the machine-or-transformation test would create uncertainty as to the patentability of software, advanced diagnostic medicine techniques, and inventions based on linear programming, data compression, and the manipulation of digital signals....

Section 101 similarly precludes the broad contention that the term "process" categorically excludes business methods....

The argument that business methods are categorically outside of § 101's scope is further undermined by the fact that federal law explicitly contemplates the existence of at least some business method patents. Under 35 U.S.C. § 273(b)(1), if a patent-holder claims infringement based on "a method in [a] patent," the alleged infringer can assert a defense of prior use. For purposes of this defense alone, "method" is defined as "a method of doing or conducting business." In other words, by allowing this defense the statute itself acknowledges that there may be business method patents....

A conclusion that business methods are not patentable in any circumstances would render § 273 meaningless....

[49] *State Street Bank v. Signature Financial Group*, 149 F.3d 1368 (Fed. Cir. 1998).

[50] See *In re Bilski*, 545 F.3d 943 (Fed. Cir. 2008) (en banc).

Continued

Interpreting § 101 to exclude all business methods simply because business method patents were rarely issued until modern times revives many of the previously discussed difficulties. At the same time, some business method patents raise special problems in terms of vagueness and suspect validity. See *eBay Inc. v. MercExchange, L.L. C.,* 547 U.S. 388, 397 (2006) (KENNEDY, J., concurring). The Information Age empowers people with new capacities to perform statistical analyses and mathematical calculations with a speed and sophistication that enable the design of protocols for more efficient performance of a vast number of business tasks. If a high enough bar is not set when considering patent applications of this sort, patent examiners and courts could be flooded with claims that would put a chill on creative endeavor and dynamic change....

... [E]ven if a particular business method fits into the statutory definition of a "process," that does not mean that the application claiming that method should be granted. In order to receive patent protection, any claimed invention must be novel, § 102, nonobvious, § 103, and fully and particularly described, § 112. These limitations serve a critical role in adjusting the tension, ever present in patent law, between stimulating innovation by protecting inventors and impeding progress by granting patents when not justified by the statutory design....

In light of ... precedents, it is clear that petitioners' application is not a patentable "process." Claims 1 and 4 in petitioners' application explain the basic concept of hedging, or protecting against risk: "Hedging is a fundamental economic practice long prevalent in our system of commerce and taught in any introductory finance class."... The concept of hedging, described in claim 1 and reduced to a mathematical formula in claim 4, is an unpatentable abstract idea.... Allowing petitioners to patent risk hedging would pre-empt use of this approach in all fields, and would effectively grant a monopoly over an abstract idea....

Today, the Court once again declines to impose limitations on the Patent Act that are inconsistent with the Act's text. The patent application here can be rejected under our precedents on the unpatentability of abstract ideas....

[Affirmed]

QUESTIONS

1. Did the Supreme Court reject the Court of Appeals' "machine-or-transformation test"?
2. What reasons are there to doubt whether the machine-or-transformation test should be the sole current criterion for determining the patentability of inventions?
3. Are business methods patentable?
4. How did the Court decide this case?

Believing that many business-method patents are obvious to persons of ordinary skill in their respective fields and have a chilling effect on consumer and public interests, a number of organizations have filed multiple reexamination requests with the USPTO to invalidate these patents.[51]

21. Infringement

The patent owner has the exclusive right to make, use, or sell the invention. The owner may bring suit for patent infringement for unauthorized use of a patent and obtain appropriate monetary damages and injunctive relief.[52] The Patent Act provides for the enhancement of damages upon proof of willful infringement and the award of reasonable attorney's fees in "exceptional cases."[53]

Under the act, the owner has "the right to exclude others from making, using, offering for sale or selling the invention."[54] In *eBay, Inc. v. MercExchange, LLC,* the U.S. Supreme Court dealt with the question of whether the patent holder had the right to obtain the permanent injunctive relief of stopping a business entity from "using" the patented technology in addition to obtaining damages for the patent violation. The threat of a court order may be used to seek high and often unreasonable licensing fees. Major technology companies contended that trial courts should consider multiple factors in deciding whether to issue a permanent injunction.

[51] See Electronic Frontier Foundation, Patent Busting Project at **www.eff.org/patent-busting** (April 2009).

[52] See also *Global-Tech Appliances, Inc. v. SEB S.A.*, 131 S.Ct. 2060 (2011), where induced infringement of a patent is also actionable. Global-Tech Appliances, Inc., located in Hong Kong, developed a cool-touch deep fryer for Sunbeam Products by copying the "T-Fal" fryer in violation of SEB's U.S. patent. The Supreme Court agreed that the evidence was sufficient for a jury to find that Global-Tech willfully blinded itself to the infringing nature of the sales it encouraged Sunbeam to make.

[53] See *In re Seagate Technology, LLC,* 497 F.3d 1360 (Fed. Cir. 2007), where the CAFC set a higher "willfulness" standard, requiring at least a showing of objective recklessness on the part of the infringer.

[54] 35 U.S.C. §154(a)(1).

EBay, Inc. v. MercExchange, LLC, 547 U.S., 388 (2006)

"Squeeze Play" Averted

eBay and its subsidiary half.com operate popular Internet Web sites that allow private sellers to list goods they wish to sell at either an auction or a fixed price (its "Buy it Now" feature). MercExchange, LLC, sought to license its business-method patent to eBay, but no agreement was reached. In Merc Exchange's subsequent patent infringement suit, a jury found that its patent was valid, that eBay had infringed the patent, and $29.5 million in damages were appropriate. However, the District Court denied MercExchange's motion for permanent injunctions against patent infringement absent exceptional circumstances. MercExchange appealed. The Federal Circuit Court of Appeals reversed, and the U.S. Supreme Court granted *certiorari*.

JUDICIAL OPINION

THOMAS, A.J.…According to well-established principles of equity, a plaintiff seeking a permanent injunction must satisfy a four-factor test before a court may grant such relief. A plaintiff must demonstrate: (1) that it has suffered an irreparable injury; (2) that remedies available at law, such as monetary damages, are inadequate to compensate for that injury; (3) that, considering the balance of hardships between the plaintiff and defendant, a remedy in equity is warranted; and (4) that the public interest would not be disserved by a permanent injunction.…The decision to grant or deny permanent injunctive relief is an act of equitable discretion by the district court, reviewable on appeal for abuse of discretion.

These familiar principles apply with equal force to disputes arising under the Patent Act.…To be sure, the Patent Act also declares that "patents shall have the attributes of personal property," § 261, including "the right to exclude others from making, using, offering for sale, or selling the invention," § 154(a)(1). According to the Court of Appeals, this statutory right to exclude alone justifies its general rule in favor of permanent injunctive relief. But the creation of a right is distinct from the provision of remedies for violations of that right. Indeed, the Patent Act itself indicates that patents shall have the attributes of personal property "[s]ubject to the provisions of this title," 35 U.S.C. § 261, including, presumably, the provision that injunctive relief "may" issue only "in accordance with the principles of equity," § 283.…

Because we conclude that neither court below correctly applied the traditional four-factor framework that governs the award of injunctive relief, we vacate the judgment of the Court of Appeals, so that the District Court may apply that framework in the first instance. In doing so, we take no position on whether permanent injunctive relief should or should not issue in this particular case, or indeed in any number of other disputes arising under the Patent Act.…

[Reversed and Remanded]

Chief Justice ROBERTS, with whom Justice SCALIA and Justice GINSBURG join, concurring. I agree with the Court's holding that "the decision whether to grant or deny injunctive relief rests within the equitable discretion of the district courts, and that such discretion must be exercised consistent with traditional principles of equity, in patent disputes no less than in other cases governed by such standards," *ante*, at 1841, and I join the opinion of the Court. That opinion rightly rests on the proposition that "a major departure from the long tradition of equity practice should not be lightly implied."…

Justice KENNEDY, with whom Justice STEVENS, Justice SOUTER, and Justice BREYER join, concurring.… To the extent earlier cases establish a pattern of granting an injunction against patent infringers almost as a matter of course, this pattern simply illustrates the result of the four-factor test in the contexts then prevalent. The lesson of the historical practice, therefore, is most helpful and instructive when the circumstances of a case bear substantial parallels to litigation the courts have confronted before.

In cases now arising trial courts should bear in mind that in many instances the nature of the patent being enforced and the economic function of the patent holder present considerations quite unlike earlier cases. An industry has developed in which firms use patents not as a basis for producing and selling goods but, instead, primarily for obtaining licensing fees. See FTC, To Promote Innovation: The Proper Balance of Competition and Patent Law and Policy, ch. 3, pp. 38–39 (Oct. 2003). For these firms, an injunction, and the potentially serious sanctions arising from its violation, can be employed as a bargaining tool to charge exorbitant fees to companies that seek to buy licenses to practice the patent. When the patented invention is but a small component of the product the companies seek to produce and the threat of an injunction is employed simply for undue leverage in negotiations, legal damages may well be sufficient to compensate for the infringement and an injunction may not serve the public interest. In addition injunctive relief may have different consequences for the burgeoning number of patents over business methods, which were not of much economic and legal significance in earlier times. The potential vagueness and suspect validity of some of these patents may affect the calculus under the four-factor test.…

QUESTIONS

1. What classification of patent is involved in this decision?
2. Did eBay win on the issue before the Supreme Court? Explain.
3. Summarize the position set forth in Justice Kennedy's concurring opinion.

Under the Supreme Court's "doctrine of equivalents," infringers may not avoid liability for patent infringement by substituting insubstantial differences for some of the elements of the patented product or process. The test for infringement requires an essential inquiry: Does the accused product or process contain elements identical or equivalent to each claimed element of the patented invention?[55]

D. Secret Business Information

A business may have developed information that is not generally known but that cannot be protected under federal law, or a business may want to avoid the disclosure required to obtain a patent or copyright protection of computer software. As long as such information is kept secret, it will be protected under state law relating to trade secrets.[56]

22. Trade Secrets

A **trade secret** may consist of any formula, device, or compilation of information that is used in one's business and is of such a nature that it provides an advantage over competitors who do not have the information. It may be a formula for a chemical compound, a process of manufacturing, treating, or preserving materials. **For Example,** shortly before he departed employment with Siemens, salesman J. J. David e-mailed the wiring schematics for the company's reverse osmosis water desalination units (R.O. units) to his future co-founder of Revo Water Systems, LLC, and also requested and was allowed to observe and assist in the construction of a unit. Two years later a Siemens technician discovered that a Revo unit was a copy of the Siemens R.O. units. Siemens successfully sued David and Revo for breach of the confidentiality agreement David had signed with Siemens. The measure of damages for misappropriation of a trade secret is the profit derived from the misappropriation of the trade secret, which in this case amounted to $908,160 over a 40-month period.[57]

To a limited extent, courts will protect certain confidential customer lists. However, courts will not protect customer lists if customer identities are readily ascertainable from industry or public sources or if products or services are sold to a wide group of purchasers based on their individual needs.[58]

23. Loss of Protection

When secret business information is made public, it loses the protection it had while secret. This loss of protection occurs when the information is made known without any restrictions. In contrast, there is no loss of protection when secret information is shared or communicated for a special purpose and the person receiving the information knows that it is not to be made known to others.

When a product or process is unprotected by a patent or a copyright and is sold in significant numbers to the public, whose members are free to resell to whomever they choose, competitors are free to reverse engineer (start with the known product and work backward to discover the process) or copy the article. **For Example,** Crosby Yacht Co., a boatbuilder on Cape Cod, developed a hull design that is not patented. Maine Boatbuilders, Inc. (MBI), purchased one of Crosby's boats and copied the hull by creating a mold from the boat it purchased. MBI is free to build and sell boats utilizing the copied hull.

24. Defensive Measures

Employers seek to avoid the expense of trade secret litigation by limiting disclosure of trade secrets to employees with a "need to know." Employers also have employees sign nondisclosure agreements, and they conduct exit interviews when employees with confidential information leave, reminding the employees of the employer's intent to enforce the nondisclosure agreement. In addition, employers have adopted industrial security plans to protect their unique knowledge from "outsiders," who may engage in theft, trespass, wiretapping, or other forms of commercial espionage.

[55] *Warner-Jenkinson v. Hilton Davis Chemical Co.*, 520 U.S. 17 (1997). But see *Festo Corp. v. Shoketsu*, 493 F.3d 1368 (Fed. Cir. 2007).

[56] The Uniform Trade Secrets Act was officially amended in 1985. It is now in force in Alabama, Alaska, Arizona, Arkansas, California, Colorado, Connecticut, Delaware, Florida, Georgia, Hawaii, Idaho, Illinois, Indiana, Iowa, Kansas, Kentucky, Louisiana, Maine, Minnesota, Mississippi, Montana, Nebraska, Nevada, New Hampshire, New Mexico, North Dakota, Ohio, Oklahoma, Oregon, Rhode Island, South Carolina, South Dakota, Utah, Vermont, Virginia, Washington, West Virginia, and Wisconsin. Trade secrets are protected in all states either under the uniform act or common law and under both criminal and civil statutes.

[57] *Siemens Water Technologies Corp. v. Revo Water Systems*, 74 So.3d 824 (La. App. 2011).

[58] *Xpert Automation Systems Corp. v. Vibromatic Co.*, 569 N.E.2d 351 (Ind. App. 1990).

25. Criminal Sanctions

Under the federal Industrial Espionage Act of 1996,[59] knowingly stealing, soliciting, or obtaining trade secrets by copying, downloading, or uploading via electronic means or otherwise with the intention that it will benefit a foreign government or agent is a crime. This act also applies to the stealing or purchasing of trade secrets by U.S. companies or individuals who intend to convert trade secrets to the economic benefit of anyone other than the owner. The definition of trade secret is closely modeled on the Uniform Trade Secrets Act and includes all forms and types of financial, business, scientific, technical, economic, and engineering information. The law requires the owner to have taken "reasonable and proper" measures to keep the information secret. Offenders are subject to fines of up to $500,000 or twice the value of the proprietary information involved, whichever is greater, and imprisonment for up to 15 years.

Corporations may be fined up to $10,000,000 or twice the value of the secret involved, whichever is greater. In addition, the offender's property is subject to forfeiture to the U.S. government, and import-export sanctions may be imposed.

E. Protection of Computer Software and Mask Works

Computer programs, chip designs, and mask works are protected from infringement with varying degrees of success by federal statutes, restrictive licensing, and trade secrecy.

CPA 26. Copyright Protection of Computer Programs

Under the Computer Software Copyright Act of 1980,[60] a written program is given the same protection as any other copyrighted material regardless of whether the program is written in source code (ordinary language) or object code (machine language). **For Example,** Franklin Computer Corp. copied certain operating-system computer programs that had been copyrighted by Apple Computer, Inc. When Apple sued Franklin for copyright infringement, Franklin argued that the object code on which its programs had relied was an uncopyrightable "method of operation." The Third Circuit held that computer programs, whether in source code or in object code embedded on ROM chips, are protected under the act.[61]

In determining whether there is a copyright violation under the Computer Software Copyright Act, courts will examine the two programs in question to compare their structure, flow, sequence, and organization. Moreover, the courts in their infringement analysis look to see whether the most *significant* steps of the program are similar rather than whether most of the program's steps are similar. To illustrate a copyright violation, substantial similarity in the structure of two computer programs for dental laboratory record-keeping was found—even though the programs were dissimilar in a number of respects—because five particularly important subroutines within both programs performed almost identically.[62]

The protection afforded software by the copyright law is not entirely satisfactory to software developers because of the distinction made by the copyright law of protecting expressions but not ideas. Also, Section 102(b) of the 1980 Computer Software Copyright Act does not provide protection for "methods of operation." A court has allowed a competitor to copy the identical menu tree of a copyrighted spreadsheet program because it was a noncopyrightable method of operation.[63]

As set forth previously, the Digital Millennium Copyright Act of 1998 was enacted to curb the pirating of a wide range of works, including software.

CPA 27. Patent Protection of Programs

Patents have been granted for computer programs; for example, a method of using a computer to translate from one language to another has been held patentable.

[59] P.L. 104–294, 18 U.S.C. §1831 et seq. (1996).
[60] Act of December 12, 1980, P.L. 96–517, 94 Stat. 3015, 17 U.S.C. §§101, 117.
[61] *Apple Computer Inc. v. Franklin Computer Corp.*, 714 F.2d 1240 (3d Cir. 1983).
[62] *Whelen Associates v. Jaslow Dental Laboratory*, 797 F.2d 1222 (3d Cir. 1986).
[63] *Lotus Development Corp. v. Borland International Inc.*, 49 F.3d 807 (1st Cir. 1995), aff'd, 516 U.S. 233 (1996).

FIGURE 10-1 ***Summary Comparison of Intellectual Property Rights***

TYPE OF INTELLECTUAL PROPERTY	TRADEMARKS	COPYRIGHTS	PATENTS	TRADE SECRETS
PROTECTION	WORDS, NAMES, SYMBOLS, OR DEVICES USED TO IDENTIFY A PRODUCT OR SERVICE	ORIGINAL CREATIVE WORKS OF AUTHORSHIP, SUCH AS WRITINGS, MOVIES, RECORDS, AND COMPUTER SOFTWARE	UTILITY, DESIGN, AND PLANT PATENTS	ADVANTAGEOUS FORMULAS, DEVICES, OR COMPILATION OF INFORMATION
APPLICABLE STANDARD	IDENTIFIES AND DISTINGUISHES A PRODUCT OR SERVICE	ORIGINAL CREATIVE WORKS IN WRITING OR IN ANOTHER FORMAT	NEW AND NONOBVIOUS, ADVANCED IN THE ART	NOT READILY ASCERTAINABLE, NOT DISCLOSED TO THE PUBLIC
WHERE TO APPLY	PATENT AND TRADEMARK OFFICE	REGISTER OF COPYRIGHTS	PATENT AND TRADEMARK OFFICE	NO PUBLIC REGISTRATION NECESSARY
DURATION	INDEFINITE SO LONG AS IT CONTINUES TO BE USED	LIFE OF AUTHOR PLUS 70 YEARS, OR 95 YEARS FROM PUBLICATION FOR "WORKS FOR HIRE"	UTILITY AND PLANT PATENTS, 20 YEARS FROM DATE OF APPLICATION; DESIGN PATENTS, 14 YEARS	INDEFINITE SO LONG AS SECRET IS NOT DISCLOSED TO PUBLIC

The disadvantage of patenting a program is that the program is placed in the public records and may thus be examined by anyone. This practice poses a potential danger that the program will be copied. To detect patent violators and bring legal action is difficult and costly.[64]

28. Trade Secrets

While primary protection for computer software is found in the Computer Software Copyright Act, industry also uses trade secret law to protect computer programs. When software containing trade secrets is unlawfully appropriated by a former employee, the employee is guilty of trade secret theft.[65]

[64] The USPTO has adopted guidelines for the examination of computer-related inventions, 61 C.F.R. §§7478–7502.

[65] The National Conference of Commissioners on Uniform State Laws (NCCUSL) has promulgated a new uniform law, the Uniform Computer Information Transactions Act (UCITA), to govern contracts involving the sale, licensing, maintenance, and support of computer software and books in digital form. This uniform act had been identified as Article 2B and was part of the comprehensive revisions to Article 2 of the Uniform Commercial Code. The act is supported by software publishers and opposed by software developers and buyers. The act can be obtained from the NCCUSL at **www.uniformlaws.org.** Information for and against the UCITA can be found at **www.ucitaonline.com.** The act has been adopted by Maryland and Virginia.

29. Restrictive Licensing

To retain greater control over proprietary software, it is common for the creator of the software to license its use to others rather than selling it to them. Such licensing agreements typically include restrictions on the use of the software by the licensee and give the licensor greater protection than that provided by copyright law. These restrictions commonly prohibit the licensee from providing, in any manner whatsoever, the software to third persons or subjecting the software to reverse engineering.[66]

30. Semiconductor Chip Protection

The Semiconductor Chip Protection Act (SCPA) of 1984[67] created a new form of industrial intellectual property by protecting mask works and the semiconductor chip products in which they are embodied against chip piracy. A **mask work** refers to the specific form of expression embodied in chip design, including the stencils used in manufacturing semiconductor chip products. A **semiconductor chip product** is a product placed on a piece of semiconductor material in accordance with a predetermined pattern that is intended to perform electronic circuitry functions. These chips operate microwave ovens, televisions, computers, robots, X-ray machines, and countless other devices. This definition of semiconductor chip products includes such products as analog chips, logic function chips like microprocessors, and memory chips like RAMS and ROMs.

(A) Duration and Qualifications for Protection. The SCPA provides the owner of a mask work fixed in semiconductor chip products the exclusive right for 10 years to reproduce and distribute the products in the United States and to import them into the United States. The protection of the act applies only to those works that, when considered as a whole, are not commonplace, staple, or familiar in the semiconductor industry.

(B) Limitation on Exclusive Rights. Under the SCPA's reverse engineering exemption, competitors may not only study mask works but may also use the results of that study to design their own semiconductor chip products embodying their own original masks even if the masks are substantially similar (but not substantially identical) so long as their products are the result of substantial study and analysis, not merely the result of plagiarism.

Innocent infringers are not liable for infringements occurring before notice of protection is given them and are liable for reasonable royalties on each unit distributed after notice has been given them. However, continued purchase of infringing semiconductors after notice has been given can result in penalties of up to $250,000.

(C) Remedies. The SCPA provides that an infringer will be liable for actual damages and will forfeit its profits to the owner. As an alternative, the owner may elect to receive statutory damages of up to $250,000 as determined by a court. The court may also order destruction or other disposition of the products and equipment used to make the products. **For Example,** Altera Corporation manufactures programmable logic devices. It was successful in the lawsuit against its competitor Clear Logic, Inc., which works from a different business model. Altera was successful in its lawsuit against Clear Logic under the SCPA, asserting that Clear Logic had copied the layout design of its registered mask works. It also was successful in its claim that Clear Logic induced breach of software licenses with Altera customers. Damages were assessed at $36 million.[68]

LawFlix

The Jerk (1979) (R)

Steve Martin invents a special handle for eyeglasses that is mass marketed by a businessman who gives him a percentage of the royalties from sales. Should Martin be paid?

[66] See *Fonar Corp. v. Domenick*, 105 F.3d 99 (2d Cir. 1997).
[67] P.L. 98-620, 98 Stat. 3347, 17 U.S.C. §901.
[68] *Altera Corp. v. Clear Logic Inc.*, 424 F.3d 1079 (9th Cir. 2005).

MAKE THE CONNECTION

SUMMARY

Property rights in trademarks, copyrights, and patents are acquired as provided primarily in federal statutes. A trademark or service mark is any word, symbol, design, or combination of these used to identify a product (in the case of a trademark) or a service (in the case of a service mark). Terms will fall into one of four categories: (1) generic, (2) descriptive, (3) suggestive, or (4) arbitrary or fanciful. Generic terms are never registrable. However, if a descriptive term has acquired a secondary meaning, it is registrable. Suggestive and arbitrary or fanciful marks are registrable as well. If there is likelihood of confusion, a court will enjoin the second user from using a particular mark.

A copyright is the exclusive right given by federal statute to the creator of a literary or an artistic work to use, reproduce, or display the work for the life of the creator and 70 years after the creator's death.

A patent gives the inventor an exclusive right for 20 years from the date of application to make, use, and sell an invention that is new and useful but not obvious to those in the business to which the invention is related. Trade secrets that give an owner an advantage over competitors are protected under state law for an unlimited period so long as they are not made public.

Protection of computer programs and the design of computer chips and mask works is commonly obtained, subject to certain limitations, by complying with federal statutes, by using the law of trade secrets, and by requiring restrictive licensing agreements. Many software developers pursue all of these means to protect their proprietary interests in their programs.

LEARNING OUTCOMES

After studying this chapter, you should be able to clearly explain:

A. Trademarks and Service Marks

LO.1 Explain the spectrum of distinctiveness used to classify trademarks and explain why distinctiveness is important

See the Cengage example, a coined most distinctive mark, p. 185.

See the Sports Illustrated example, a descriptive mark with acquired distinctiveness, p. 186.

See the *Harley Davidson* case where H.O.G. was found to be generic and not distinctive at all, pp. 186–188.

LO.2 Explain how personal names can acquire trademark protection

See the Paul Frank example on p. 188.

LO.3 List the remedies available for improper use of trademarks

See the applicable remedies of injunctive relief, lost profits, and attorney's fees, p. 189.

B. Copyrights

LO.4 Explain what is and is not copyrightable; explain the fair use defense

See the discussion on what is copyrightable on p. 193.

See the Darden example of a denial of a copyright because of lack of creativity, p. 193.

See the *Wind Done Gone* example of fair use parody p. 196.

C. Patents

LO.5 Explain the "new and not obvious" requirement necessary to obtain a patent

See the cDNA "not obvious" example on p. 199.

See the mounted chainsaw "obvious" example on p. 199.

See the *Bilski* decision where a patent application was found to be an unpatentable abstract idea not entitled to a grant of monopoly, pp. 200–201.

D. Secret Business Information

LO.6 List and explain the defensive measures employers take to preserve confidential business information

See the discussion on signing and enforcing nondisclosure agreements on p. 203.

E. Protection of Computer Software and Mask Works

LO.7 Explain the extent of protection provided owners of software

See the Apple Computer example on p. 204.

KEY TERMS

acquired distinctiveness
copyright
cybersquatters
distinctiveness
mask work
prior art
secondary meaning
semiconductor chip product
service mark
trade dress
trade secret
trademark

QUESTIONS AND CASE PROBLEMS

1. China is a signatory country to the Madrid Protocol on the international registration of trademarks. Starbucks opened its first café in China in 1999 and has added outlets in numerous locations including Shanghai and at the Great Wall and the imperial palace in Beijing. Xingbake Café Corp. Ltd. has imitated the designs of Starbuck's cafés in its business coffee café locations in Shanghai. *Xing* (pronounced "Shing") means star, and *bake*, or "bak kuh" is pronounced like "bucks." Does the Seattle, Washington, Starbucks Corporation have standing to bring suit in China against Xingbake Café Corp. Ltd? If so, on what theory? Decide.

2. Cable News Network with its principal place of business in Atlanta, Georgia, is the owner of the trademark CNN in connection with providing news and information services to people worldwide through cable and satellite television networks, Web sites, and news services. Its services are also available worldwide on the Internet at the domain name CNN.com. Maya Online Broadband Network (Maya HK) is a Chinese company. It registered the domain name CNNEWS.com with Network Solutions, Inc. The CNNews.com Web site was designed to provide news and information to Chinese-speaking individuals worldwide, making significant use of the terms *CNNews* and *CNNews.com* as brand names and logos that the Atlanta company contends resembles its logos. Maya HK has admitted that CNNews in fact stands for China Network News abbreviated as CNN. The Atlanta company had notified Maya HK of its legal right to the CNN mark before the Chinese company registered the CNNews.com domain name. Does the federal Anticybersquatting Consumer Protection Act apply to this case? If so, does a "safe harbor" exist under the ACPA for Maya HK in that most people who access its Web site in China have never heard of CNN? Decide. [*Cable News Network v. CNN News.com,* 177 F. Supp. 2d 506 (E.D. Va.)]

3. Sara Bostwick hired Christian Oth, Inc., to be her wedding photographer. The parties' written contract granted ownership of the copyright in all images created to Oth. Oth posted the wedding photos on its Web site. Bostwick e-mailed Oth to remove the photos from the Web site. Oth failed to do so and Bostwick sued, claiming that she had the sole and exclusive right to control her own wedding photos. Is she correct? [*Bostwick v. Christian Oth, Inc.* 936 N.Y.S.2d 176 (A.D.)]

4. Jim and Eric work for Media Technical Services (MTS) at Cramer University in Casper, Wyoming. For "expenses" of $5, Jim and Eric used MTS facilities after hours to burn discs of Pearl Jam's CD *Vitology* for 25 friends or friends of friends from school. When Mrs. Mullen, who is

in charge of MTS, discovered this and confronted them, Jim, a classics major, defended their actions, telling her, "It's *de minimis*...I mean, who cares?" Explain to Jim and Eric the legal and ethical ramifications of their actions.

5. Sullivan sold t-shirts with the name *Boston Marathon* and the year of the race imprinted on them. The Boston Athletic Association (BAA) sponsors and administers the Boston Marathon and has used the name *Boston Marathon* since 1917. The BAA registered the name *Boston Marathon* on the Principal Register. In 1986, the BAA entered into an exclusive license with Image, Inc., to use its service mark on shirts and other apparel. Thereafter, when Sullivan continued to sell shirts imprinted with the name *Boston Marathon*, the BAA sought an injunction. Sullivan's defense was that the general public was not being misled into thinking that his shirts were officially sponsored by the BAA. Without this confusion of source, he contended, no injunction should be issued. Decide. [*Boston Athletic Ass'n v. Sullivan,* 867 F.2d 22 (1st Cir.)]

6. The University of Georgia Athletic Association (UGAA) brought suit against beer wholesaler Bill Laite for marketing Battlin' Bulldog Beer. The UGAA claimed that the cans infringed its symbol for its athletic teams. The symbol, which depicted an English Bulldog wearing a sweater with a G and the word BULLDOGS on it, had been registered as a service mark. Soon after the beer appeared on the market, the university received telephone calls from friends of the university who were concerned that Battlin' Bulldog Beer was not the sort of product that should in any way be related to the University of Georgia. The university's suit was based on the theory of false designation of origin in violation of the Lanham Act. Laite contended that there was no likelihood of confusion because his bulldog was different from the university's and his cans bore the disclaimer "Not associated with the University of Georgia." Decide. [*University of Georgia Athletic Ass'n v. Laite,* 756 F.2d 1535 (11th Cir.)]

7. Twentieth Century Fox (Fox) owned and distributed the successful motion picture *The Commitments*. The film tells the story of a group of young Irish men and women who form a soul music band. In the film, the leader of the band, Jimmy, tries to teach the band members what it takes to be successful soul music performers. Toward that end, Jimmy shows the band members a videotape of James Brown's energetic performance of the song "Please, Please, Please." This performance came from Brown's appearance in 1965 on a television program called the *TAMI Show*. Portions of the 1965 performance are shown in *The Commitments* in seven separate "cuts" for a total of 27 seconds. Sometimes the cuts are in the background of a scene, and sometimes they occupy the entire screen. Brown's name is not mentioned at all during these relatively brief cuts. His name is mentioned only once later in the film, when Jimmy urges the band members to abandon their current musical interests and tune in to the great soul performers, including James Brown: "Listen, from now on I don't want you listening to Guns & Roses and The Soup Dragons. I want you on a strict diet of soul. James Brown for the growls, Otis Redding for the moans, Smokey Robinson for the whines, and Aretha for the whole lot put together." Would it be fair use under U.S. copyright law for Fox to use just 27 seconds of James Brown cuts in the film without formally obtaining permission to use the cuts? Advise Fox as to what, if anything, would be necessary to protect it from a lawsuit. [See *Brown v. Twentieth Century Fox Film Corp.*, 799 F. Supp. 166 (D. D.C.)]

8. The Greenwich Bank & Trust Co. (GB&T) opened in 1998 and by 2008 had expanded to a total of four branches in the Greenwich, Connecticut, community of 62,000 residents. A competitor using the name Bank of Greenwich (BOG) opened in December 2006. GB&T's parent entity sued BOG for trademark violation under the Lanham Act. BOG argued that GB&T's service mark is generic and is simply not entitled to Lanham Act protection because it combines the generic term "bank" and the geographic term "Greenwich." GB&T asserted that it had been the only bank in Greenwich using the word *Greenwich* in its name and had done so exclusively for nine years. It asserted that a geographic term is entitled to protection if it acquires secondary meaning.

GB&T introduced evidence regarding its advertising expenditures, sales success, and length of exclusivity of use along with evidence of actual consumer confusion. Decide. [*Connecticut Community Bank v. The Bank of Greenwich,* 578 F. Supp. 2d 405 (D. Conn.)]

9. The U.S. Polo Association (USPA) is a not-for-profit corporation that is the governing body of the sport of polo in the United States. It has been in existence since 1890 and derives the majority of its revenue from royalties obtained from licensing its trademarks. It owns more than 900 trademarks worldwide, including marks bearing the words "U.S. Polo Assn." with the depiction of two polo players for licensees on products sold in the apparel category. In 2009 it produced 10,000 units of a men's fragrance using packaging featuring its logo as used on apparel. Since 1978 PRL (Polo Ralph Lauren) and its licensee of PRL trademarks, L'Oreal, have used the mark known as the "Polo Player" logo on men's fragrances with its logo containing one player. The fragrance has been sold for 32 years and it was voted into the industry's Hall of Fame. PRL sued USPA. What must PRL establish to prevail in an action for trademark infringement? How would you decide this case? [*United States Polo Assn. v. PRL USA Holdings, Inc.,* 800 F. Supp. 2d 515 (S.D.N.Y.)]

10. Diehr devised a computerized process for curing rubber that was based on a well-known mathematical formula related to the cure time, and he devised numerous other steps in his synthetic rubber-curing process. The patent examiner determined that because abstract ideas, the laws of nature, and mathematical formulas are not patentable subject matter, the process in this case (based on a known mathematical formula) was also not patentable. Diehr contended that all of the steps in his rubber-curing process were new and not obvious to the art of rubber curing. He contended also that he did not seek an exclusive patent on the mathematical formula, except for its use in the rubber-curing process. Decide. [*Diamond v. Diehr,* 450 U.S. 175]

11. Aries Information Systems, Inc., develops and markets computer software specifically designed to meet the financial accounting and reporting requirements of such public bodies as school districts and county governments. One of Aries's principal products is the POBAS III accounting program. Pacific Management Systems Corporation was organized by Scott Dahmer, John Laugan, and Roman Rowan for marketing a financial accounting and budgeting system known as FAMIS. Dahmer, Laugan, and Rowan were Aries employees before, during, and shortly after they organized Pacific. As employees, they each gained access to Aries's software materials (including the POBAS III system) and had information about Aries's existing and prospective clients. Proprietary notices appeared on every client contract, source code list, and magnetic tape. Dahmer, Laugan, and Rowan signed an Employee Confidential Information Agreement after beginning employment with Aries. While still employees of Aries, they submitted a bid on behalf of Pacific to Rock County and were awarded the contract. Pacific's FAMIS software system is substantially identical to Aries's proprietary POBAS III system. Aries sued Pacific to recover damages for misappropriation of its trade secrets. Pacific's defense was that no "secrets" were misappropriated because many employees knew the information in question. Decide. [*Aries Information Systems, Inc. v. Pacific Management Systems Corp.,* 366 N.W.2d 366 (Minn. App.)]

12. The plaintiff, Herbert Rosenthal Jewelry Corporation, and the defendant, Kalpakian, manufactured jewelry. The plaintiff obtained a copyright registration of a jeweled pin in the shape of a bee. Kalpakian made a similar pin. Rosenthal sued Kalpakian for infringement of copyright registration. Kalpakian raised the defense that he was only copying the idea, not the way the idea was expressed. Was he liable for infringement of the plaintiff's copyright? [*Herbert Rosenthal Jewelry Corp. v. Kalpakian,* 446 F.2d 738 (9th Cir.)]

13. Mineral Deposits, Ltd. (MD, Ltd.), an Australian company, manufactures the Reichert Spiral, a device used for recovering gold particles from sand and gravel. The spiral was patented in Australia, and MD, Ltd., had applied for a patent in the United States. Theodore Zigan contacted MD, Ltd., stating he was interested in purchasing up to 200 devices for use in his gravel pit. MD,

Ltd., agreed to lend Zigan a spiral for testing its efficiency. Zigan made molds of the spiral's components and proceeded to manufacture 170 copies of the device. When MD, Ltd., found out that copies were being made, it demanded the return of the spiral. MD, Ltd., also sought lost profits for the 170 spirals manufactured by Zigan. Recovery was sought on a theory of misappropriation of trade secrets. Zigan offered to pay for the spiral lent him by MD, Ltd. He argued that trade secret protection was lost by the public sale of the spiral. What ethical values are involved? Was Zigan's conduct a violation of trade secret law? [*Mineral Deposits, Ltd. v. Zigan,* 773 P.2d 609 (Colo. App.)]

14. Village Voice Media, owners of the famous *Village Voice* newspaper in New York City, sent a letter to *The Cape Cod Voice*, a year-old publication located in Orleans, Massachusetts, objecting to the use of the word *Voice* in the title of its publication. It warned that the Cape Cod publication could cause "confusion as to the source affiliation with the famous Village Voice marks." The publisher of *The Cape Cod Voice* responded that "small places have a right to their own voices." The use of the word *Voice* was thus in dispute between these parties. Would you classify it as generic, descriptive, suggestive, arbitrary, or fanciful? How would you resolve this controversy? [*Cape Cod Times* Business Section, Amy Zipkin, *The New York Times*, October 16, 2004, G-1]

CPA QUESTIONS

1. Multicomp Company wishes to protect software it has developed. It is concerned about others copying this software and taking away some of its profits. Which of the following is true concerning the current state of the law?
   a. Computer software is generally copyrightable.
   b. To receive protection, the software must have a conspicuous copyright notice.
   c. Software in human readable source code is copyrightable but machine language object code is not.
   d. Software can be copyrighted for a period not to exceed 20 years.

2. Which of the following is not correct concerning computer software purchased by Gultch Company from Softtouch Company? Softtouch originally created this software.
   a. Gultch can make backup copies in case of machine failure.
   b. Softtouch can typically copyright its software for at least 75 years.
   c. If the software consists of compiled computer databases, it cannot be copyrighted.
   d. Computer programs are generally copyrightable.

3. Using his computer, Professor Bell makes 15 copies (to distribute to his accounting class) of a database in some software he has purchased for his personal research. The creator of this software is claiming copyright. Which of the following is correct?
   a. This is an infringement of copyright, since he bought the software for personal use.
   b. This is not an infringement of copyright, since databases cannot be copyrighted.
   c. This is not an infringement of copyright because the copies were made using a computer.
   d. This is not an infringement of copyright because of the fair use doctrine.

4. Intellectual property rights included in software may be protected under which of the following?
   a. Patent law
   b. Copyright law
   c. Both of the above
   d. None of the above

Cyberlaw

learningoutcomes

After studying this chapter, you should be able to

LO.1 Define cyberlaw

LO.2 Discuss the employment issues in cyberspace

LO.3 Explain user issues in cyberspace

LO.4 Discuss appropriation and other forms of unfair competition in cyberspace

LO.5 List and explain the contract issues in cyberspace

A. Types of Legal Issues in Cyberspace

1. What Is Cyberlaw?

Even though the law that is applied to resolve the problems of the new technologies and the new economy that have developed and grown on the Internet is often referred to as **cyberlaw**, you need not fear that you will be required to learn a whole new body of law. There have been and will continue to be changes in the law to accommodate new ways of doing business, but there has also been and will continue to be reliance on the fundamental principles that underlie our laws and the rights they protect. This chapter simply examines the issues and concerns in cyberspace and covers their resolution through a brief overview of new and existing laws. This chapter provides a framework for the challenges of legal issues in **cyberspace**.

2. What Are the Issues in Cyberlaw?

The legal issues of cyberspace can be broken down into four main areas: employment issues, user issues, appropriation and competition issues, and contract issues. Within each of these four areas of existing law are a number of new legal issues that have arisen because of the nature of cyberspace and the conduct of business there. That various cyberlaw issues can be grouped into traditional areas of law demonstrates the not-so-new nature of cyberlaw.

B. Employment Issues in Cyberspace

The lines between our jobs and personal lives are increasingly blurred. Just three years ago, the focus in the case law was on employee use of company e-mail systems to send personal messages. Today, personal blogs, social media profiles (such as Facebook), Tweets, and other online activities by employees result in increasing challenges for employers as they try to protect company information and balance employee rights and privacy.[1] Blogging has often resulted in employees disclosing private and/or negative information about their companies. Tweeting is instant and ongoing communication that could reveal, prematurely, information that the company does not want public. E-mails, Internet surfing, and blogging require a delicate balancing of rights and interests.[2]

3. Employers Are Accountable for Employee Electronic Content

Employers are held responsible for the content of employee e-mails and employers must have access and control rights over employee information that is released publicly through various electronic means. For example, e-mails that contain off-color jokes or suggestive comments create an atmosphere of harassment. (See Chapter 40 for more information on sexual harassment.)[3] Employers are also responsible when employees use e-mail or the Internet at work to violate intellectual property rights. Employers are also held accountable when employees use e-mails and blogs to defame fellow employees or competitors, vendors, or even customers.

Employee e-mail is spontaneous, candid, and discoverable. As a result, the content of employees' e-mail is often fertile territory for prosecutors who can find evidence of intent in employee e-mails and blogs. For example, in 2008, investigators uncovered e-mails of employees at Standard & Poor's, the investment rating agency, that indicated that while the employee/analysts were rating debt instruments as AAA, they were also having their doubts about them. One employee wrote, "These deals could have been structured by cows and we would still rate them."[4] Another e-mail read, "Rating agencies continue to create [an] even bigger monster—the CDO market. Let's hope we are all wealthy and retired by the time this house of cards falters."[5] These candid e-mails were a foundation for settlements paid by the analysts' firms and resulted in general reforms of the analyst industry.

E-mails provide a contemporaneous record of events that often defy our recollections. **For Example,** in 2011

[1] In 2009, Facebook had over one billion users and accounted for 72 percent of online social networking including MySpace, Twitter, and LinkedIn. Nicholas Carlson, "Chart of the Day: How Many Users Does Twitter Really Have?" *Business Insider*, March 31, 2011. **www.businessinsder.com/**.

[2] A survey found that 72 percent of businesses use social media for marketing purposes. Robert Ball, "Social Media Marketing: What's the Payoff for Your Business," *Huffington Post*, February 24, 2011. **www.huffingtonpost.com**.

[3] See *Garrity v. John Hancock Mut. Life Ins. Co.*, 2002 WL 974676 (D. Mass. 2002) (memorandum opinion), in which an employer's termination of an employee for sending an e-mail entitled, "The Top Ten Reasons Cookie Dough Is Better Than Men" was upheld on grounds that such content created an atmosphere of harassment. An employer was held liable for its failure to take action against an employee who used a company computer to post nude photographs of his daughter. *Doe v. XYC Corp.*, 887 A.2d 1156 (N.J. Super. Ct. 2005).

[4] Summary Report of Issues Identified in the Commission's Examination of Select Credit Rating Agencies, July 8, 2008.

[5] Ibid.

the indictment of former Penn State assistant football coach, Jerry Sandusky, for child sexual abuse, resulted in questions about whether university officials had failed to report past incidents of Mr. Sandusky's inappropriate involvement with children. The late and then–head football coach, Joe Paterno, denied any knowledge of a 1998 incident in the football program showers with a young boy. However, subsequent investigation uncovered e-mails that contradicted Coach Paterno's recollection. On May 13, 1998, Tim Curley, the university's athletic director, sent an e-mail to Gary Schultz, a university vice president of finance and operations, with the caption, "Jerry," and this message, "Anything new in this department? Coach is anxious to now where it stands."[6] Mr. Curley also requested updates on May 18 and May 30, 1998. As a result, Mr. Curley and Mr. Schultz were charged with perjury regarding their testimony of not knowing about previous incidents and Coach Paterno and Penn State were disciplined by the NCAA. The e-mail era means our own words often determine our consequences.

4. Employer Monitoring: What's Legal

Because they are held accountable for what employees do in cyberspace, employers use various methods for monitoring employees including using key-stroking software that allows the employer to see those messages employees typed but did not send, using blocking software that limits sites employees can visit, monitoring and searching e-mails, checking blogs for content, and examining items posted on Facebook, Twitter, and YouTube. The *U.S. v. King* case deals with an issue of employer access to employee computers when the computer is a personal laptop.

U.S. v. King, 509 F.3d 1338 (11th Cir. 2007)

Shared Drive + Shared Access = No Privacy

In February 2003, while serving as a civilian contractor, Michael D. King resided in a dormitory at the Prince Sultan Air Base in Saudi Arabia. During his stay in the dormitory, King kept his personal laptop computer in his room and connected it to the base network. All users of the base network signed agreements indicating that they understood their communications over and use of the base network were subject to monitoring. King believed that he had secured his computer so that others could not access the contents of its hard drive.

On February 23, 2003, an enlisted airman was searching the base network for music files when he came across King's computer on the network. The airman was able to access King's hard drive because it was a "shared" drive. In addition to finding music files on King's computer, the airman also discovered a pornographic movie and text files "of a pornographic nature." The airman reported his discovery to a military investigator who in turn referred the matter to a computer specialist. This specialist located King's computer and hard drive on the base network and verified the presence of pornographic videos and explicit text files on the computer. She also discovered a folder on the hard drive labeled "pedophilia." The computer specialist did not employ any "special means" to access King's computer because "everybody on the entire network" could obtain the same access.

The computer specialist then filed a report with the investigator detailing what she had found, and the investigator obtained a search warrant for King's room. During a search of his room, military officials seized King's computer and also found CDs containing child pornography. They then referred the matter to the FBI for investigation and King left Saudi Arabia and returned to Montgomery, Alabama.

Two years later, the government obtained an indictment charging King with possession of child pornography. After his arrest, the government searched his residence pursuant to a search warrant and found additional CDs and hard drives containing over 30,000 images of child pornography.

King entered a guilty plea and was sentenced to 108 months in prison. King then appealed his conviction on the grounds that there had been an illegal search and seizure of his computer and files.

PER CURIMA

King contends that the district court denied his motions to suppress based on the erroneous finding that he did not have a reasonable expectation of privacy in his computer files that were remotely accessed over a military computer network, because the search of those files by the computer specialist exceeded the scope of her authority to monitor usage of the

[6] Freeh Sporkin Sullivan, LLP, Report of the Special Investigative Counsel Regarding the Actions of the Pennsylvania State University Related to the Child Sexual Abuse Committed by Gerald A. Sandusky (2012), at p. 4.

Continued

base network. King asserts that he sought to protect his computer files through security settings, he never knowingly exposed them to the public, and he was unaware that the files were shared on the network. King further challenges the district court's alternative finding that the military officials conducted a proper workplace search, arguing that this was a criminal investigation into King's personal computer located in his private dorm room. Finally, King asserts that the subsequent search warrant was invalid, as it was based on information that was obtained improperly through the remote search of his computer files.

The Fourth Amendment's prohibition against unreasonable searches and seizures "protects an individual in those places where [he] can demonstrate a reasonable expectation of privacy against government intrusion," and "only individuals who actually enjoy the reasonable expectation of privacy have standing to challenge the validity of a government search." Accordingly, the threshold issue in this case is whether King had a legitimate expectation of privacy in the contents of his personal laptop computer when it was connected to the base network from his dorm room.

We have held that tenants of a multiunit apartment building do not have a reasonable expectation of privacy in the common areas of the building, where the lock on the front door is "undependable" and "inoperable." We have also held that even though a company has a subjective expectation of privacy in documents that are shredded and disposed of in a garbage bag that is placed within a private dumpster, the company's "subjective expectation of privacy is not one that society is prepared to accept as objectively reasonable" when the company fails to "take sufficient steps to restrict the public's access to its discarded garbage."

King has not shown a legitimate expectation of privacy in his computer files. His experience with computer security and the affirmative steps he took to install security settings demonstrate a subjective expectation of privacy in the files, so the question becomes "whether society is prepared to accept [King's] subjective expectation of privacy as objectively reasonable."

It is undisputed that King's files were "shared" over the entire base network, and that everyone on the network had access to all of his files and could observe them in exactly the same manner as the computer specialist did. As the district court observed, rather than analyzing the military official's actions as a search of King's personal computer in his private dorm room, it is more accurate to say that the authorities conducted a search of the military network, and King's computer files were a part of that network. King's files were exposed to thousands of individuals with network access, and the military authorities encountered the files without employing any special means or intruding into any area which King could reasonably expect would remain private. The contents of his computer's hard drive were akin to items stored in the unsecured common areas of a multiunit apartment building or put in a dumpster accessible to the public.

Because his expectation of privacy was unreasonable King suffered no violation of his Fourth Amendment rights when his computer files were searched through the computer's connection to the base network. It follows that his additional claim that the later search warrant was invalid because it incorporated information obtained from the search of his computer files also lacks merit.

[Affirmed]

QUESTIONS

1. Why does the court draw the comparisons with non-cyber searches?
2. What lessons should contractors learn from this case?

There were some efforts in the early days of cyberspace to apply existing law to ensure e-mail privacy. The Electronic Communications Privacy Act of 1986 (ECPA) prohibits the unauthorized access of "live" communications, as when someone uses a listening device to intercept a telephone conversation. However, e-mail and social media are stored information, and the question of this act's application for resolving the privacy issue is doubtful.[7] ECPA also has an exception for consensual interception. The Stored Communication Act (SCA) prohibits the unauthorized interception of electronic communications, generally meaning stored communication, not ongoing communication such as text messaging, tweeting, and instant messaging. However, the courts have held consistently that employees give consent to such monitoring, and there are no statutory violations when employers do live listening, interception, or recovery of sent communication that is stored and available electronically.[8] When employers have informal policies or policies that allow employees to reimburse their employers for private use of text services, the courts have held that monitoring and disclosure of those messages is a violation of the law.

[7] "Every circuit court to have considered the matter has held that an 'intercept' under the ECPA must occur contemporaneously with transmission." See *Fraser v. Nationwide Mut. Ins. Co.*, 352 F.3d 107, 113 (3d Cir. 2003).

[8] For detailed information on this issue, see Patricia Sanchez Abril, Avner Levin, and Alissa Del Riego "Blurred Boundaries: Social Media Privacy and the Twenty-First-Century Employee," 49 *American Business Law Journal* 63 (2012).

Ethics & the Law

When Social Media Get Back at Employers

A teacher posts negative information about her high school students on her Facebook page.

A flight attendant posts provocative pictures of herself in her airline's uniform on her Facebook page.

Medical students post information about their patients on their Facebook pages.

Domino's employees post a video on YouTube that shows them putting mucus on Domino's food as they prepare it.

Discuss the ethical obligations of employees to their employers when they are posting information on their Facebook pages.

5. Employer Screening of Applicants

If the employer will be doing prehiring monitoring, such as looking at MySpace.com and Facebook—and/or "Googling" the applicant's name—the applicant must be told of this monitoring at the time of the application. The information that we post on publicly available sites is not considered private, so employers, as long as they are maintaining consistent standards for all applicants, can examine what you have posted on the Internet.

Employers are also using Google and other Internet sources to track employee work excuses. One company's human resources official was on the phone with the company employment lawyer seeking to determine what action could be taken against an employee who was absent frequently but who claimed he was absent to care for his ill grandmother. While they were talking, the lawyer "Googled" the employee's name and found that he was being arraigned in federal court.

Schools, employment counselors, and lawyers are offering the following warnings about the dangers of social media and e-mail postings:[9]

1. Nothing is private on the Internet. People can see everything.
2. Be careful what you blog.
3. Protect your identity when in chat rooms.
4. Assume that everything you write and post will be seen.
5. You can clean up your name on Google using several services, but having no hits at all can lead to suspicions.
6. Think before you write, blog, post, or do anything on the Internet. The *City of Ontario v. Quon* case deals with an issue of employer monitoring of private texts on employer cell phones.

City of Ontario v. Quon, 130 S.Ct. 2619 (2010)

Text Me, If You Dare

Jeff Quon, a sergeant and member of the city of Ontario's SWAT team, "texted" Sergeant Steve Trujillo, dispatcher April Florio, and his wife Jerilyn Quon (Respondents) using Arch Wireless text-messaging services that were provided for him through the city of Ontario's contract with Arch.

Ontario Police Department (The city) (OPD) (Petitioners) had no official policy directly addressing the use of text messaging. However, the city did have a general "Computer Usage, Internet, and E-mail Policy" applicable to all employees. The policy provided that all software, programs, networks, Internet, e-mail, and other systems were to be used only for city of Ontario–related business. The policy also indicated that usages were monitored and recorded.

Quon attended a meeting during which SWAT team members and others were told that text messages would fall under the city's policy as public information and be therefore eligible for auditing.

[9] From Michelle Conlin, "You Are What You Post," *Business Week*, March 27, 2006, pp. 52–53. For a discussion of research on blogging, see Rainie, "The State of Blogging," Pew Internet and American Life Project, November 2005; available at **http://pewinternet.org/Reports/2005/The-State-of-Blogging.aspx**, and **www.technorati.com**.

Continued

Under the city's contract each pager was allotted 25,000 characters, after which the city had to pay overage charges. Quon's supervisor, Duke, told him that he was over by more than 15,000 characters and that he should reimburse the city for the overage charges so that he (the supervisor) would not have to audit the transmission and see how many messages were non–work related. Quon refused to pay and was told to cut down on his transmissions.

When Quon and another officer again exceeded the 25,000-character limit, his supervisor, Duke, stated that he was "tired of being a bill collector with guys going over the allotted amount of characters on their text pagers." Ontario's chief of police then requested an audit of the text messages.

Because city officials were not able to access the text messages themselves, they requested and obtained the messages from Arch Wireless. The audit of the messages revealed abuse of on-the-clock time through sheer numbers of personal texts and their sexually explicit content.

The officers were disciplined and challenged the discipline as a violation of their Fourth Amendment rights. The trial court found that there was a Fourth Amendment violation. The Ninth Circuit held that the search was unreasonable and the city appealed.

JUDICIAL OPINION

KENNEDY, Justice...Respondents contend that because Duke told Quon that an audit would be unnecessary if Quon paid for the overage, Quon reasonably could expect that the contents of his messages would remain private.

Cell phone and text message communications are so pervasive that some persons may consider them to be essential. That might strengthen the case for an expectation of privacy.

Even if Quon had a reasonable expectation of privacy in his text messages, petitioners did not necessarily violate the Fourth Amendment by obtaining and reviewing the transcripts. Although as a general matter, warrantless searches "are *per se* unreasonable under the Fourth Amendment," there are "a few specifically established and well-delineated exceptions" to that general rule. The Court has held that the "'special needs'" of the workplace justify one such exception.

The search here was reasonable under that approach. The search was justified at its inception because there were "reasonable grounds for suspecting that the search [was] necessary for a non investigatory work-related purpose." As a jury found, Chief Scharf ordered the search in order to determine whether the character limit on the City's contract with Arch Wireless was sufficient to meet the City's needs.

[R]eviewing the transcripts was reasonable because it was an efficient and expedient way to determine whether Quon's overages were the result of work-related messaging or personal use. The review was also not "'excessively intrusive.'" Although Quon had gone over his monthly allotment a number of times, OPD requested transcripts for only the months of August and September 2002. While it may have been reasonable as well for OPD to review transcripts of all the months in which Quon exceeded his allowance, it was certainly reasonable for OPD to review messages for just two months in order to obtain a large enough sample to decide whether the character limits were efficacious. And it is worth noting that during his internal affairs investigation, McMahon redacted all messages Quon sent while off duty, a measure which reduced the intrusiveness of any further review of the transcripts.

Even if he could assume some level of privacy would inhere in his messages, it would not have been reasonable for Quon to conclude that his messages were in all circumstances immune from scrutiny. Quon was told that his messages were subject to auditing. Under the circumstances, a reasonable employee would be aware that sound management principles might require the audit of messages to determine whether the pager was being appropriately used. Given that the City issued the pagers to Quon and other SWAT Team members in order to help them more quickly respond to crises—Quon could have anticipated that it might be necessary for the City to audit pager messages to assess the SWAT Team's performance in particular emergency situations.

That the search did reveal intimate details of Quon's life does not make it unreasonable, for under the circumstances a reasonable employer would not expect that such a review would intrude on such matters.

The Court of Appeals erred in finding the search unreasonable. It pointed to a "host of simple ways to verify the efficacy of the 25,000 character limit ... without intruding on [respondents'] Fourth Amendment rights."

This Court has "repeatedly refused to declare that only the 'least intrusive' search practicable can be reasonable under the Fourth Amendment." That rationale "could raise insuperable barriers to the exercise of virtually all search-and-seizure powers," because "judges engaged in *post hoc* evaluations of government conduct can almost always imagine some alternative means by which the objectives of the government might have been accomplished."

Finally, the Court must consider whether the search violated the Fourth Amendment rights of Jerilyn Quon, Florio, and Trujillo, the respondents who sent text messages

Continued

to Jeff Quon. Respondents argue that because "the search was unreasonable as to Sergeant Quon, it was also unreasonable as to his correspondents." They make no corollary argument that the search, if reasonable as to Quon, could nonetheless be unreasonable as to Quon's correspondents. In light of this litigating position and the Court's conclusion that the search was reasonable as to Jeff Quon, it necessarily follows that these other respondents cannot prevail.

The judgment of the Court of Appeals for the Ninth Circuit is reversed.

QUESTIONS

1. What general advice could you give a business about its access to employees' text messages based on the decision in this case?
2. Why are alternative methods for searching the decision not relevant?
3. How does the court deal with the issue of expectation of privacy on the parts of the officers' family and friends?

6. Employers' Right of Access to Employee E-Mails and Internet Use

Because employers are accountable for the content of employee e-mail, it is not a breach of privacy for employers to monitor employee e-mail and Internet usage. Monitoring the content of employee e-mails is important for keeping companies out of legal difficulties. However, employees may believe they have an expectation of privacy in their e-mails, even when those e-mails are sent from work. That belief may spring from the tort standards that protect private lives, communications, and information. The tort of **invasion of privacy**, or intrusion into private affairs, has application to cyberspace communication. Internet disclosure, without permission, of private information is a breach of privacy. Employers generally require employees to sign a document in which they acknowledge that by working at the company and using the company's e-mail and server that they have waived their right to privacy. Former Sun Microsoft Systems CEO, Scott McNealy, summed up employee rights to privacy when it comes to Internet use: "You have zero privacy. Get over it."[10]

Employers can monitor electronic communications from employees that are marked as private; e-mails that are sent from home and from private computers that use the company server; e-mails that do not involve company business; text messages sent using company phones; and tweets sent over company iPhones, BlackBerries, and other phone communication systems. Employees should be careful when using their work laptops for private communications. Courts have reached different conclusions, for example, on whether employees waive their attorney-client privilege when using their work computers or employer-issued cell phones to communicate with their employers.[11] The *Holmes v. Petrovich Development Company, LLC* case deals with an issue of an employee's e-mails communicating about a legal issue.

Holmes v. Petrovich Development Company, LLC, 119 Cal. Rptr. 3d 878 (Cal. App. 2011)

The E-Mail Detailed Pregnancy

Gina Holmes began working for Paul Petrovich as his executive assistant in early June 2004. The employee handbook, which Holmes read and signed, contained the following warnings, "[e]mployees who use the Company's Technology Resources to create or maintain personal information or messages have no right of privacy with respect to that information or message," and, "E-mail is not private communication, because others may be able to read or access the

[10] A. Michael Froomkin, "The Death of Privacy," 52 *Stanford Law Review*, 1461, 1462 (2000). Presented at the *Cyberspace and Privacy: A New Legal Paradigm? Symposium*, Stanford, CA, 2000.

[11] *Scott v. Beth Israel Med. Ctr.*, 847 N.Y.S.2d 436 (2007).

Continued

message. E-mail may best be regarded as a postcard rather than as a sealed letter… ." The handbook also states that company may "inspect all files or messages … at any time for any reason at its discretion."

Ms. Holmes told Petrovich in July 2004 that she was pregnant and that her due date was December 7, 2004. During her pregnancy, Ms. Holmes was put off when coworkers asked her questions about maternity leave and made "belly-monitoring" comments. She asked " [t]hat little group of hens" to stop, and they complied. Ms. Holmes discussed her belly getting big and baby names with Mr. Petrovich and felt the discussions were inappropriate but never said anything about being offended.

On Friday morning, August 6, 2004, Mr. Petrovich and Ms. Holmes discussed her maternity leave, which he assumed would start December 7. A few hours later Ms. Holmes e-mailed back that she estimated starting her maternity leave around November 15. Mr. Petrovich responded, "I need some honesty. How pregnant were you when you interviewed with me and what happened to six weeks? You have rights for sure and I am not going to do anything to violate any laws, but I feel taken advantage of and deceived for sure."

Ms. Holmes responded by explaining that she disclosed her pregnancy as soon as the tests from her amniocentesis came back that everything was "normal" with the baby. An amnio cannot be performed until the fourth month of pregnancy. Ms. Holmes added, "I am 39 years old, and therefore, there was a chance that there could be something 'wrong' or 'abnormal' with the baby. If there had been, I had decided not to carry the baby to term. That is a very personal choice, and not something that I wanted to have to share with people at work; so in order to avoid that, I waited until I knew that everything was o.k. before telling anyone I was pregnant. I've also had 2 miscarriages at 3 months into my pregnancy, and could not bear having to share that with co-workers again, as I have in the past. I feel that I have the right to make these decisions, and there is no deceipt [sic] or dishonesty involved with this. [T]here is no requirement in a job interview or application to divulge if you are pregnant or not; in fact, I believe it's considered unethical to even inquire as to such."

Mr. Petrovich forwarded the e-mail exchange to other employees who would need to be aware of the staffing and payroll issues.

On Monday morning, August 9, 2004, Holmes sent an e-mail to Petrovich indicating that she was very flexible and that she wanted to "work out the bumps along the way." Mr. Petrovich replied that he was pleased with her work and commitment to the job and concluded, "I want you to stay. It will work."

On August 10, 2004, Ms. Holmes used the company computer to e-mail an attorney, Joanna Mendoza. Ms. Holmes asked for a referral to an attorney specializing in labor law, specifically relating to pregnancy discrimination. Ms. Holmes forwarded a few of Mr. Petrovich's e-mails.

At 4:42 P.M. on the same day, Ms. Mendoza e-mailed Ms. Holmes that she should delete their attorney-client communications from her work computer because her employer might claim a right to access it.

On August 11, 2004, after her lunch with Ms. Mendoza, Ms. Holmes e-mailed Mr. Petrovich saying that she had cleared her things from her desk and would not be returning to work.

In September of 2005, Ms. Holmes filed a lawsuit against Mr. Petrovich and his company for sexual harassment, retaliation, wrongful termination in violation of public policy, violation of the right to privacy, and intentional infliction of emotional distress. She alleged that she was constructively terminated.

The trial court granted the motion for summary judgment. Ms. Holmes appealed.

JUDICIAL OPINION

SCOTLAND, JUDGE… Holmes points to the e-mails she exchanged with Petrovich on August 6 and 9, 2004, in which he implied she had deceived him about her pregnancy, stated he was offended that she had changed the period of time she would be absent for maternity leave, and asserted that her pregnancy was an extreme hardship on his business. She also complains that Petrovich unnecessarily forwarded to others her e-mail containing personal information. Holmes asserts that Petrovich did this to humiliate her. Petrovich said he sent the e-mails to in-house counsel and employees involved in human relations because he thought that Holmes was about to quit.

When viewed in context, the e-mails show nothing more than that Petrovich made some critical comments due to the stress of being a small business owner who must accommodate a pregnant woman's right to maternity leave. He recognized Holmes's legal rights, stated he would honor them, said he was not asking for her resignation, noted he had been pleased with her work, and simply expressed his feelings as a "human in a tough business where people are constantly trying to take advantage of me." He assured Holmes that "it will work." Rather than giving him a chance to honor his promise, Holmes quit.

Continued

"Constructive discharge occurs only when the employer coerces the employee's resignation, either by creating working conditions that are intolerable under an objective standard, or by failing to remedy objectively intolerable working conditions that actually are known to the employer."

Holmes argues that she was subjected to negative comments and accusations about her pregnancy, followed by Petrovich's retaliatory conduct when she told him she planned to exercise her leave rights; he retaliated by forwarding her sensitive personal information to others in the office, who had no reason to know about her prior miscarriages, amniocentesis, and potential termination of her pregnancy.

Here, Petrovich did not reduce Holmes's salary, benefits or work hours, and did not terminate her. He assured Holmes that she still had a job and that they would work things out. Holmes chose to quit because Petrovich expressed his concerns about the changes in her pregnancy leave dates and the need to replace her while she was on leave, and because he forwarded an e-mail that she wished to keep private. But she failed to demonstrate there was a triable issue of fact concerning whether he did these things to retaliate against her; she simply concluded that this was his motivation by taking out of context certain comments that he made.

A reasonable person would have talked to Petrovich, expressed dismay at his actions, given him an opportunity to explain or apologize, and waited to see if conditions changed after the air had cleared. Instead, Holmes chose to quit despite Petrovich's assurances that he wanted her to stay and that things would work out.

Holmes's remaining claims of error all arise from an alleged violation of her attorney-client privilege.

When Holmes e-mailed her attorney, she did not use her home computer to which some unknown persons involved in the delivery, facilitation, or storage may have access. Had she done so, that would have been a privileged communication unless Holmes allowed others to have access to her e-mails and disclosed their content. Instead, she used defendants' computer, after being expressly advised this was a means that was not private and was accessible by Petrovich, the very person about whom Holmes contacted her lawyer and whom Holmes sued. This is akin to consulting her attorney in one of defendants' conference rooms, in a loud voice, with the door open, yet unreasonably expecting that the conversation overheard by Petrovich would be privileged.

Holmes used her employer's company e-mail account after being warned that it was to be used only for company business, that e-mails were not private, and that the company would randomly and periodically monitor its technology resources to ensure compliance with the policy.

Holmes emphasizes that she believed her personal e-mail would be private because she utilized a private password to use the company computer and she deleted the e-mails after they were sent. However, her belief was unreasonable because she was warned that the company would monitor e-mail to ensure employees were complying with office policy not to use company computers for personal matters, and she was told that she had no expectation of privacy in any messages she sent via the company computer. Likewise, simply because she "held onto a copy of the fax," she had no expectation of privacy in documents she sent to her attorney using the company's facsimile machine, a technology resource that, she was told, would be monitored for compliance with company policy not to use it for personal matters.

It is inaccurate to say only one person had the ability to monitor e-mail sent and received on company computers. The company's controller, who had an administrative password giving her access to all e-mail sent by employees with private passwords, testified that the company's "IT person" as well as company owner Cheryl Petrovich also had such access to e-mail sent and received by company computers.

[Affirmed]

NOTE: The court did allow the case on intentional infliction of emotional distress and breach of privacy to continue with respect to the forwarded e-mail Mr. Petrovich sent to the group of employees.

QUESTIONS

1. Why did the court conclude that there was not an atmosphere of harassment?
2. Why does having a password not mean that your e-mail is private?
3. What can you learn about employer policies on e-mail from this case? What are some best practices employers should follow?

E-Commerce & Cyberlaw

Top Ten Tips for Employer Regulation of Social Media and E-Mail Content

1. Create policies for e-mail and social media use by employees.
2. Train employees on the policies and post the policies.
3. Be sure all employees have a copy of the policies.
4. Have employees sign off on the policies every year.
5. Help employees understand what can happen as a result of misuse of e-mail and social networking outlets.
6. Enforce your policies.
7. Explain that you cooperate with law enforcement agencies on e-mail and social media content.
8. Update policies as avenues for social media change and expand.
9. Have an electronic retention policy and train employees on retention of e-mails and other postings.
10. Tell employees that you monitor all sites and uses of company computers, phones, and social media accounts.

C. User Issues in Cyberspace

A second series of issues in cyberlaw is the use of information that Web sites have gleaned from their users.

7. Use of User Information

Each time you are online, there is the possibility that someone is gathering information about you—what you buy, what you are interested in, and even those to whom you are linked. **For Example,** if you use an airline's Web site to book your travel arrangements, that Web site has a profile of your travel habits. The airline knows how frequently you travel and where you travel. That type of targeted customer information is something other Web sites and retailers are willing to pay dearly for because they know their product is being considered by those most likely to purchase it. If you use Amazon.com to buy books, that Web site has relevant information about the types of books you read, your interests, and even some indications about your income level based on your spending habits.

Even though this issue of privacy may seem new and peculiar to cyberspace, it is, in fact, a rather old issue that has long been a concern of credit card companies. These companies' use and sale of information about their customers are restricted. Customers must be given the right to refuse such use of their names and other information for sale as part of lists for target marketing. Some state attorneys general are utilizing these credit card privacy rights to enforce privacy rights against Web site owners who sell information about their users. The Federal Trade Commission (FTC) has begun to take positions on all Internet issues that are identical to its stances on other types of commerce issues. **For Example,** if catalog companies are required to provide notice to customers about delays in shipment of goods to customers, Internet companies must comply with the same notification rules.

8. Identifying Users: Screen Names, Privacy, and Freedom of Speech

Another privacy issue that has arisen is whether plaintiffs in suits for defamation can successfully subpoena Internet Service Providers (ISPs) to obtain the identity of individuals who post statements in chat rooms and across the Internet, make defamatory remarks over the Internet, facilitate the downloading of music through their sites, and even allow the sharing of exam information that is proprietary. Music companies' actions against individuals who download music but do not pay for their songs requires the discovery of the identity of those who are doing the downloading. Can the music companies require the ISPs to disclose the names of their customers for purposes of preventing copyright infringement? There are now clear standards for determining disclosure of identity that tend to favor disclosure.[12] However, the courts have been very careful to distinguish releasing identity information when there is no illegal activity and what is posted

[12] *Columbia Pictures, Inc. v. Bunnell*, 245 F.R.D. 443 (C.D. Cal. 2007). However, the duty to preserve such information for discovery is still up in the air. *Healthcare Advocates, Inc. v. Harding, Earley, Follner & Frailey*, 497 F. Supp. 2d 627 (E.D. Pa. 2007).

on the Internet or Tweets is simply an expression of opinion. The key to releasing identity of posters is whether the posters were engaged in illegal or harmful activity. There is a difference between posting a nasty opinion and posting false information. Posting false information requires ISPs to disclose identity. Nasty opinions enjoy some First Amendment protection. Access to ISP identity information for illegal or actionable behavior on the Internet is now relatively routine.[13] The *Varrenti v. Gannett Co.* case deals with an issue of disclosure of the identity of bloggers sued for defamation.

Varrenti v. Gannett Co., Inc., 929 N.Y.S.2d 671 (2011)

Dissed on a Blog by Taxcut *et al.*

The local police chief and officers (Daniel P. Varrenti, Brian Winant, Adam Mesiti, and Stephen Mesiti) (plaintiffs) filed suit against Gannett Co (specifically its newspaper, the *Democrat & Chronicle*, a newspaper for Brockport, New York) and four John/Jane Does (defendants) who posted allegedly defamatory comments about the officers. The four posters are known online as "Taxcut," "brockportonian," "BkptStar," and "TaxpayerBWare."

The alleged defamatory statements were posted between January 17, 2011, and January 20, 2011, in response to two articles that were posted on the *Democrat & Chronicle's* Web site, one of which was "Brockport, Sweden and Clarkson Feud Over Fire, Ambulance Services." The following comments were posted by the four on January 17, 2011, and January 18, 2011:

> *Tom MudGun is Tom MudGun by any other name, and he smells as foul as the venom he dispenses. Now. According to Mr. Varrenti, we had almost 16,000 calls for service in Brockport. We have about 8,000 residents. That's 2 calls per resident. Have you made your call today? Chief V counts as a call for service every time an officer touches a doorknob, every call received for any reason, and I believe every time an officer waves at you. My! Crime has sure soared in Broke-port since Mr. V was hired. Mr. V has a 10 year, million dollar contract with Broke-port. He has found the pot of gold at the end of the rainbow. Just call him "The Million Dollar Dan."*
>
> *Regarding the competence of Broke-port's 100K a year cops, consider the following, Broke-port cops don't stop for pedestrians.*
>
> *Officer Masseti broke into a home thru a basement window (without a warrant) and arrested the residents. The case was thrown out of court, and no discipline given to officer. Why?*
>
> *Officers beat up a deaf kid because he could not hear their commands. Could that be a liability?*
>
> *"The Million Dollar Dan" could reign in over time, but he has a sweet heart deal with the cops. They both look the other way and ignore their mutual misdeeds.*
>
> *We don't need cops who harass and intimidate taxpayers who complain about the high cost, and we don't want them to manipulate elections so they can control the village board.*

In response to the second article, "Municipalities Discuss Forming Fire District," "BkptStar," wrote the following comment on January 20, 2011:

> *Dear Loone,*
>
> *If BPD is the best in the county, we are all in real trouble. They are sure not the cheapest. Why Varrenti didn't discipline the officers that beat up a deaf kid because he could not hear their commands? Why is Varrenti allowing his cops to rake in all the overtime they want?*

In addition, "brockportonian" and "TaxpayerBWare," wrote the following series of comments on January 20, 2011, in response to the second article, "Municipalities Discuss Forming Fire District:"

> *Mesiti is the least of the ones there to worry about. Someone should check into the cover ups, yes plural, of trouble the current union president got into. And, I wonder how much money was donated to the campaigns of the three blind mice by Broke-port police officers. THAT would be interesting to find out. It would definitely show allegiance.*
>
> *Replying to brockportonian: Regarding cover ups and the current union president, Brian Winant, are you referring to marijuana? Evidently the investigation will turn up more than the hours that they actually work. We keep hearing about all the overtime worked. I understand that their time sheets will be available to the public soon. If there are more cover ups regarding the corruption that has been allowed by the chif, million dollar dan, laughing all the way to the bank, I can't wait.*
>
> *"brockportonian":*
>
> *No, I am not talking about marijuana; that would be the least of their worries. Maybe the MCSO deputies who had to deal with the problem child would cooperate if forced through an investigation. What a shame, Brockport's good cop gone bad; hiding behind the badge. I feel sorry for the reputation he is giving all the other officers. I am sure they aren't like him. He sure puts on a good show.*

[13] See, e.g., *Laface Records, LLC v. Atlantic Recording Corp.*, 2007 WL 4286189, (W.D. Mich. 2007).

Continued

The court was asked to order Gannett to provide any identifying information regarding the four anonymous John/Jane Doe defendants so that the suit for defamation could proceed.

JUDICIAL OPINION

BARRY, Judge... It is well settled that the First Amendment protects anonymous speech. However, defamatory speech, whether anonymous or from identifiable sources, is not protected by the First Amendment.

The common factor that this Court must decide is whether plaintiffs have stated a prima facie cause of action for defamation.

The elements of a cause of action for defamation are "a false statement, published without privilege or authorization to a third party, constituting fault as judged by, at a minimum, a negligence standard, and, it must either cause special harm or constitute defamation per se." As public officials, the plaintiffs here must also prove that the asserted defamatory statements were made "'with actual malice'—that is, with knowledge that it was false or with reckless disregard of whether it was false or not."

However, "[e]xpressions of opinion, as opposed to assertions of fact, are deemed privileged and, no matter how offensive, cannot be the subject of an action for defamation." Whether a particular statement constitutes an opinion or an objective fact is a question of law for the Court to decide. To distinguish between opinion and fact, Courts should consider various factors, including "(1) whether the specific language in issue has a precise meaning which is readily understood; (2) whether the statements are capable of being proven true or false; and (3) whether either the full context of the communication in which the statement appears or the broader social context and surrounding circumstances are such as to signal readers or listeners that what is being read or heard is likely to be opinion, not fact."

"In distinguishing between actionable factual assertions and non-actionable opinions, courts must consider the content of the communication as a whole, as well as its tone and apparent purpose." Instead of "sifting through a communication for the purpose of isolating and identifying assertions of fact, the court should look to the over-all context in which the assertions were made and determine on that basis whether the reasonable reader would have believed that the challenged statements were conveying facts about the libel plaintiff.' "

Here, the Court concludes that based on the over-all context in which the alleged defamatory statements were made, a reasonable reader would conclude that the statements were the opinions of the anonymous John/Jane Doe defendants. The anonymous comments expressed opinions that the Village of Brockport Police Department was not properly serving the citizens of Brockport. The tone of the comments was sarcastic, hyperbolic, and based on rumors that the anonymous posters heard around the Village of Brockport and about the Department. Moreover, the apparent purpose of the comments made by the John/Jane Doe defendants was to call for an investigation into the Department's practices.

Here, the forum itself is inviting readers to comment on the articles posted on the Democrat & Chronicle's website, and the readers are expected to give their opinions in the comments section of the online article. As the Appellate Division, First Department, observed, the culture of Internet communications, as distinct from print media such as newspapers and magazines, has been characterized as encouraging a "freewheeling, anything-goes writing style."

Given this contextual background, the Court finds that the comments posted by the four John/Jane Doe defendants on the Democrat & Chronicle's website constitute expressions of protected opinion, and because opinions cannot form the basis of a defamation claim, defendant Gannett is not required to unmask the identities of the four anonymous internet commentators. Therefore, plaintiffs' applications by Order to Show Cause for an order compelling defendant Gannett to provide the names, addresses, and identities and/or any relevant pedigree information for the four John/Jane Doe defendants "Taxcut," "brockportonian," "BkptStar," and "TaxpayerBWare" are hereby denied.

QUESTIONS

1. Why is the context important in determining whether there is defamation?
2. Is Internet communication different from other forms of communication?
3. Why does the court not release the identity of the posters?

9. The Cloud and Privacy

Cloud computing is another technological development that has resulted in complex legal issues. With cloud computing (such as Google Docs), the information companies have could be intermingled with other users. In addition, the information is completely within the hands of a third party. One of the benefits of cloud computing is that companies have instantaneous access to computer processing services for a fee, something that does not require substantial capital expense and allows for rapid growth. However, legal rights, in terms of access to information, privacy rights, and information retrieval remain unresolved.[14]

[14] Shannon M. Curreri, Note, *Developments in the Law: Defining "Document" in the Digital Landscape of Electronic Discovery*, 38 *Loy. L.A. L. Rev.* 1541 (2005).

10. Cookies and Privacy

Technology has permitted companies to plant "cookies" on the computers of those who are using certain Internet sites. With those "cookies" in place, the Web site owner has a way to track the computer owner's activity. At least one court has held that a Web site operator's placing cookies on a user's computer is a violation of an unauthorized access statute that would provide the computer owner a right of action for that breach of the statute and privacy.[15]

11. Statutory Protections for Privacy in Cyberspace

Several federal laws and some state laws provide privacy protections, although somewhat limited, for Internet users. The Privacy Act of 1974 controls the use of information gathered about consumers, but it applies only to government-collected data such as information gathered by the Social Security Administration or the Internal Revenue Service. Furthermore, there are exceptions for the agencies for "routine use."[16] Some segments of the Computer Fraud and Abuse Act (CFAA) and the ECPA provide privacy protection for certain types of communications, such as financial information and its use and transfer.[17] These privacy laws are not general protections but address specific issues. For example, the Children's Online Privacy Protection Act (COPPA) targets online informational privacy but applies only to Web sites that collect information from children.[18]

Numerous state laws on privacy exist; the problem comes in enforcing those laws against Web site sponsors who have no presence in the state. (See the discussion of jurisdiction in Chapter 2.)

D. Appropriation and Other Forms of Unfair Competition in Cyberspace

The competition on the Internet is intense. Competitors have many opportunities for expanding their customer bases. However, they still must expand their businesses within the legal standards that apply to competition, regardless of where that competition occurs.

12. Appropriation Online

The tort of **appropriation** involves taking an image, likeness, or name for purposes of commercial advantage. A business cannot use someone's name or likeness for advertising or endorsement without permission. The use of that name or image in cyberspace does not change the nature of the protection that this form of the privacy tort provides. **For Example,** the use of Tiger Woods's name or picture on the Web site of a yacht company, without his permission, is appropriation, even if Mr. Woods actually owns one of the company's yachts. A screen saver program that uses a likeness of Richard, the million-dollar winner on the CBS television program *Survivor,* without his permission violated his privacy rights. The use of his likeness for the Conniver screen saver program with the *Survivor* logo was appropriation.

13. Unfair Methods of Competition in Cyberspace

Concealed identity bloggers can wreak havoc on competitors. **For Example,** John Mackey, the CEO of Whole Foods, using the name Rahodeb (his wife's name, Deborah, jumbled), posted over 1,000 messages in chat rooms that were dedicated to stock trading. During the period that Mr. Mackey was posting messages, Whole Foods stock quadrupled in value. The messages were flattering to Whole Foods and negative about Wild Oats, a competitor. On February 24, 2005, Mackey posted the following comment about Wild Oats CEO Perry Odak: "Perhaps the OATS Board will wake up and dump Odak and bring in a visionary and highly competent CEO [like Mackey]." Referred to as "sock-puppeting," this common practice also raises ethical issues.

[15] In re *Intuit Privacy Litigation,* 138 F. Supp. 2d 1272 (C.D. Cal. 2001); see also *In re Toys R Us, Inc., Privacy Litig.,* 2001 WL 34517252 (N.D. Cal.), in which the court reached a different conclusion. However, tapping into sites to gain competitive or proprietary information is a breach of privacy. *Creative Computing v. Getloaded.com LLC,* 386 F.3d 930 (9th Cir. 2004). See also *Rich v. City of Jacksonville,* 2010 WL 4403095 (M.D.Fla.).

[16] 5 U.S.C. §552a (2011).

[17] 18 U.S.C. §1030 and 18 U.S.C. §§2510–2520, 2701 (2011). *LVRC Holdings LLC v. Brekka,* 581 F.3d 1127 (9th Cir. 2009).

[18] 15 U.S.C. §§6501–6506.

Ethics & the Law

The Blogger Who Kissed and Told on Capitol Hill

Jessica Cutler, a staff member for Senator Mike DeWine, began a blog that detailed her sexual encounters with various government officials in Washington, D.C. Ms. Cutler did not identify anyone by name in her blog, but the level of detail in her posts had most of Washington figuring out who was who in the Cutler blog. Ms. Cutler was fired for "misusing an office computer." What ethical issues exist in Ms. Cutler's public revelations? Was it legal for the senator to terminate her employment? What advice could you offer employers that would come from this experience? What about defamation if her partners are not identified by name?

Source: April Witt, "Blog Interrupted," *Washington Post*, Apr. 15, 2004, W12.

E. Contract Issues in Cyberspace

14. Formation of Contracts in Cyberspace

Formation of a **contract** in cyberspace is simply the result of the desire for speed and better communication in business. If you wanted to form a contract with a New York seller 20 years ago and you were in Los Angeles, you drafted a proposal and mailed it to the seller. The back-and-forth negotiations took time through the mail. Then overnight delivery service arrived to speed up your cross-country negotiations. Next came faxes and their instantaneous exchanges of terms and negotiations. The amount of paperwork involved in transactions was still unchanged. Paperless contracts were born with the availability of electronic digital interchange (EDI). EDI is simply the electronic exchange of business forms. Contracts are formed using purchase orders and invoices submitted via computer.[19]

With the Internet, e-mail, and the ability to attach documents, cyberspace has provided business yet another method for forming contracts. And while the method is different, the rules for formation have not changed. The same laws that apply when contracts are formed in a business office govern the formation of contracts in cyberspace: there must be offer and acceptance.

Some issues that arise in contract formation in the new economy are, for example, whether a contract is formed when someone downloads a program from the Internet. The person may have paid for the program by credit card and simply downloaded it on the computer. Acceptance occurs when the click occurs—a contract is formed.[20] (See Chapters 12–17 for more information on contracts in cyberspace.)

The Electronic Signatures in Global and National Commerce Act (called **E-sign**) is a federal law that recognizes digital signatures as authentic for purposes of contract formation. Even though E-sign recognizes the validity of electronic signatures, state laws regulate the authenticity and security of signatures. The Uniform Electronic Transactions Act (UETA) and the Uniform Computer Information Transaction Act (UCITA) are two model laws drafted to allow states to adopt a uniform position. UETA is a uniform law that 46 states plus the District of Columbia have adopted.[21] Two states have adopted UCITA.[22]

15. Misrepresentation and Fraud in Cyberspace

The types of **misrepresentation** and fraud on the Internet range from promises of delivery not fulfilled to promises of performance not met. The majority of the fraud complaints received by the FBI relate to Internet auctions. These issues are not new legal issues; only the form of misrepresentation or fraud has changed. **For Example,** seven retailers signed a consent decree with the FTC, which required them to pay fines totaling $1.5 million to settle a complaint against them for late delivery of Christmas merchandise ordered over the Web. The consent decree that was the retailers signed based on the FTC mail-and-telephone rule requiring retailers to let customers know when they do not have a product or that there

[19] L. J. Kutten, Bernard D. Reams, and Allen E. Strehler, *Electronic Contracting Law* (Clark Boardman, 1991).

[20] *A.V. v. iParadigms, Ltd. Liability Co.*, 544 F. Supp. 2d 473 (E.D. Va. 2008).

[21] Forty-six jurisdictions have adopted UETA. The states that have not adopted it are Georgia, Illinois, New York, and Washington.

[22] Maryland Commercial Law §§22-101 to 22-816, and Virginia Code §§59.1-501.1 to 59.1-509.2. Both laws can be found online: **www.uetaonline.com** and **www.ucitaonline.com**.

Thinking Things Through

Twitter, Social Responsibility, the First Amendment, and Making Money

It's a tight rope task. The task is dealing with what account holders post on Twitter even as Twitter tries to make money as well as deal with governments in other countries that are not as tolerant of criticism and dissent as our First Amendment allows. For example, during the London Olympics, a Twitter account holder and British journalist, Guy Adams, was tweeting criticisms of NBC's coverage of the games. However, NBC is a Twitter partner. Mr. Adams' account was suspended after a Twitter employee working in the partnerships area of the company told NBC to file a complaint.

Hell hath no fury like those who wish to preserve their unalienable right to tweet. Their outrage caused Twitter's general counsel to apologize, restore the account, and explain that Mr. Adams' account was suspended because he had included an NBC executive's email address in his tweet, something that violates Twitter user policies.

Twitter's general counsel, Alexander Macgillivray, works diligently to balance Twitter's basic policy of not scrutinizing tweets along with the need to work with other countries' governments, and continue to make money through its partnerships, such as the one with NBC.

The basics of its international policy are that it does not remove any tweets unless someone asks and only if the tweet violates a country's laws. In addition, Twitter has some universal rules such as suspending the accounts of those who pretend to tweet as someone else. In one case, several accounts were suspended because the tweeters pretended to be the prime minister of India.

In the United States, Twitter does not experience government censorship, which leaves the tweeters to post what they wish, within user guidelines. However, the concern is that with its corporate partnerships, Twitter is beholden to those partners who may, as NBC did, request review of posts or even suspension of accounts for posting negative thoughts about those partners.

The other legal issues Twitter faces relate to, for example, defamation (libel) in the written posts. Posts often contain defamatory information, but Twitter enjoys a sort of quasi privilege that allows it to escape liability if it removes the post upon request.

What if Twitter allows its partners to have tweets removed? What happens when Twitter removes tweets because of government demands? Can Twitter balance the interests of its stakeholders?

will be a delay in the shipment. The existing notification rule was simply applied to Internet transactions.

In marketing **search engines**, some companies have misrepresented the capabilities of their products or have failed to disclose the methods they use to give preference to certain links and their order of listing when the search engine is used. The remedy for such misrepresentations and fraud on the Internet is the same as the remedy in situations with paper contracts. Misrepresentation and fraud are defenses to formation and entitle the party who was misled or defrauded to rescind the agreement and/or collect money damages.

In addition to contract remedies available for misrepresenting the nature of the search engine product and capabilities, a small group of search engine companies has proposed a code of ethics for search engine firms. Headed by Mike Adams, founder and owner of WebSeed.com, the rules are called "Search Engine Promotion Code of Ethics." Adams says that his industry needs reform and gave the following example of Dotsubmit.com, a former company that claimed it would submit its clients' Web sites to 10,000 search engines. Other problems include the lack of limitations on the number of pages from any domain, which means there is so much space used that consumers have difficulty finding what they are looking for.

Key provisions of the search engine code of ethics cover claims about search engine performance as well as the honoring of submission guidelines that impose requirements on Web sites seeking to be listed.

16. Tax Issues on Contracts in Cyberspace

The U.S. Constitution requires that there be some "nexus" between the taxing authority and the business paying the tax (see Chapter 4 for more information on constitutional issues in taxation), and many questions arise about the constitutionality of taxing Internet sales because of the lack of "bricks and mortar" in these businesses. Some Internet retailers are located in one state and have no contact, physically, with any other states. Their only contact is through the computers of their customers, who may be located in all 50 states. Is it constitutional for

Colorado to tax a New Jersey company operating out of a small office in Trenton? Courts will simply apply the standards of fairness and allocation that they have relied on in other eras as businesses grew in reach even though their physical locations did not change.

The Internet Tax Freedom Act (ITFA)[23] has been renewed. The ITFA provides that states and local governments cannot tax Internet access. Contrary to popular belief, ITFA does not suspend sales taxes on transactions over the Internet. To tax Internet sales, the seller must have some physical presence in the state or a pattern of distribution and doing business there. **For Example,** Nordstrom might not have stores located in a particular state, but it would be required to collect sales taxes from sales to residents of that state if it had warehouse facilities in that state. Refer to Chapter 3 for a full discussion of the Internet and sales tax. Online retailers have been negotiating tax rates and procedures with states. However, several states have passed laws that require those who purchase merchandise over the Internet declare the amount of goods they purchased and then pay sales tax on those goods on their state income tax returns.

LawFlix

The Net (1995) (PG-13)

In a movie that was ahead of its time, a computer programmer becomes a victim of identity theft when she holds too much information about the software companies for which she has done consulting work.

The Social Network (2010) (PG-13)

The film presents a fascinating picture of the start of Facebook and the resulting contract and intellectual property disputes that arose after the company became successful.

[23] 47 U.S.C. §151, originally enacted in 1998, and as amended 2010.

MAKE THE CONNECTION

SUMMARY

The term *cyberlaw* seems to indicate a new body of law that exists or is being created to manage all of the legal issues of the cybereconomy, cyberspace, and cybertechnology. Even though some new criminal statutes have been enacted to address specific types of computer crimes, the law, with its great flexibility, has been able to easily adapt to address many of the legal issues that affect the new economy in cyberspace.

There are four areas of issues in cyberlaw. The first area covers the rights of employers and employees in the workplace cyberspace. Employers are responsible for the content of their Web pages as well as for what employees send out via e-mail, Twitter, and Facebook. Employers have the right to monitor all communications from employees from their work computers. Employers can also use the social media devices for screening potential employees as long as they use the screening for all employees.

Cyberspace also presents legal issues for users such as when and if their anonymous identity online can be revealed by those who provide Internet services. If users are engaged in illegal or tortious activity online, then their identity can be revealed for litigation purposes. If, however, their right to free expression of opinion has been exercised, they can be protected. There are also statutory protections for privacy and required disclosures from retailers who are using information gleaned from users' online activity.

The third area deals with appropriation and competition in cyberspace. The use of trademarks and tradenames that are deceptive can be stopped through injunction for appropriation. In addition, anonymous postings of defamatory information about a competitor can also be halted by an injunction.

The final area that affects users relates to the formation of contracts and issues related to online fraud as well as who pays taxes on goods purchased from online retailers.

LEARNING OUTCOMES

After studying this chapter, you should be able to clearly explain:

A. Types of Legal Issues in Cyberspace

LO.1 Define cyberlaw

Explain how we develop cyberlaw. See p. 213 for an introduction and explanation

B. Employment Issues in Cyberspace

LO.2 Discuss the employment issues in cyberspace

Review the list of best practices for employers on monitoring employee electronic communication on p. 221.

Study the *Quon* case on employer access to texts on pp. 216–218.

C. User Issues in Cyberspace

LO.3 Explain user issues in cyberspace

Discuss the issue of defamation on the Web.

See the Ethics the Law discussion of the blogger who kissed and told, p. 225.

See Twitter Thinking Things Through on p. 226.

Refer to the discussion of cookies, p. 224.

Discuss the *U.S. v. King* military cloud case on pp. 214–215.

D. Appropriation and Other Forms of Unfair Competition in Cyberspace

LO.4 Discuss appropriation and other forms of unfair competition in cyberspace

See the Tiger Woods example on p. 224.

Refer to the Whole Foods CEO's conduct on p. 224.

E. Contract Issues in Cyberspace

LO.5 List and explain the contract issues in cyberspace

Explain the obligations of service providers to reveal identity and content.

See the *Gannett* case on pp. 222–223.

KEY TERMS

appropriation
contract
cyberlaw
cyberspace
E-sign
invasion of privacy
misrepresentation
search engines

QUESTIONS AND CASE PROBLEMS

1. Discuss whether employees would have the right of privacy in the following e-mail situations:
   a. E-mail sent in a company in which there is no warning given about the lack of privacy in e-mails. [*Smyth v. Pillsbury,* 914 F. Supp. 97 (E.D. Pa.)]
   b. An e-mail sent to coworkers from home using the employee's AOL account.
   c. An e-mail sent from a laptop while the employee is traveling for the company.
   d. An e-mail sent to a coworker over a company Internet system in a company in which the employer has promised privacy in e-mail. [*Commonwealth v. Proetto,* 771 A.2d 823 (Pa. Super.Ct.)]
   e. Employer monitoring of the e-mails of any employee when those e-mails were stored in a file folder marked "Personal." [*McLaren v. Microsoft Corp.,* 1999 WL 339015 (Tex. App.)]
   f. Employees using company e-mail for union organization purposes. [*Pratt & Whitney,* National Labor Relations Board General Counsel Advisory Memorandum Cases 12-CA-18446, 12-CA-18722, 12-CS-18863]
2. The *New York Times* discovered that 24 of the employees in its payroll processing center were sending "inappropriate and offensive e-mail in violation of corporate policy." Do the employees have any right to privacy with regard to the jokes they send over their e-mail accounts at

work? Applying what you have learned about the nature of cyberlaw, determine whether, under existing sexual harassment laws, a company could be held liable for harassment via e-mails.

3. Colleges and universities continue to work to help students understand that what they post on the Web is not private information and can often have unintended consequences. The following examples resulted in student disciplinary proceedings:
   - Several students at Ohio State University boasted on Facebook (a networking/socializing site) that they had stormed the field after Ohio State beat Penn State and had taken part in what erupted into a riot. Law enforcement officials were able to trace the students through the university system, and 50 Ohio State students were referred to the office of judicial affairs.
   - Students at the University of Mississippi stated on an open site that they wanted to have sex with a professor.
   - A student at Fisher College threatened to take steps to silence a campus police officer.

   Another problem with the open sites is that the students are posting personal information with which stalkers and others can access them. These nefarious individuals can then easily obtain students' cell phone numbers, addresses, whereabouts, and other information.

   The most popular college site, Facebook, indicates that students spend an average of 17 minutes per day on the site. A great deal of information can be conveyed during that time period. Students do so without thinking through the possibility that outsiders with bad intentions could be seeking and using information about them that is posted there.

   What legal and ethical issues do you see in the types of comments that students make on these sites and in the sites themselves? Why and how can the colleges and universities obtain information from these sites without a warrant?

4. On July 24, 2002, the Recording Industry Association of America (RIAA) served its first subpoena to obtain the identity of a Verizon subscriber alleged to have made more than 600 copyrighted songs available for downloading over the Internet through peer-to-peer file transfer software provided by KaZaA. Verizon claimed that because RIAA's subpoena related to material transmitted over Verizon's network—rather than stored on it—it fell outside the scope of the subpoena power. Should the subpoena be quashed as Verizon requests, or should it be honored? [In re *Verizon Internet Services, Inc.*, 257 F. Supp. 2d 244 (D.D.C.)]

5. Glenayre Electronics announced to its employees that it could inspect the laptops it furnished for its employees to use. An employee challenged the inspection of his laptop as a violation of his privacy. Could the company search the laptops? [*Muick v. Glenayre Electronics,* 280 F.3d 741 (7th Cir.)]

6. A state university provided a written notice to employees that their computers could be monitored and added a splash screen with the same notice that appears on the computers each time employees start their computers. Has the university done enough to allow monitoring without invading employee privacy? Would it make any difference if the employees had a password for their e-mail access and computer access? What about state public records law? Would employee e-mails be subject to public disclosure because the e-mails would be considered public record? [*U.S. v. Angevine,* 281 F.3d 1130 (10th Cir.)]

7. A hospital filed suit against an individual who began a blog that included disparaging information about the hospital, its physicians, and the results for patients who were treated there. The hospital wants the court to require the cable company to identify the blogger. What will the hospital have to show in order to get the blogger's identity revealed? [In re *Does 1–10*, 242 S.W.3d 805 (Tex. App.)]

8. Sony and others own the copyrights and exclusive licenses to their various sound recordings. Without permission, 40 unidentified individuals (called Does) used "Fast Track," an online media distribution system—or "peer to peer" ("P2P")

file-copying network—to download hundreds or thousands of copyrighted sound recordings. Sony was able to identify Cablevision as the Internet service provider (ISP) to which the Does subscribed. Sony did so by using a publicly available database to trace the Internet Protocol (IP) address for each Doe. As a condition of providing its Internet service, Cablevision requires its subscribers to agree to its "Terms of Service" under which "[t]ransmission or distribution of any material in violation of any applicable law or regulation is prohibited. This includes, without limitation, material protected by copyright, trademark, trade secret or other intellectual property right used without proper authorization." On January 26, 2004, the court issued an order granting Sony the right to serve a subpoena upon Cablevision to obtain the identity of each Doe by requesting the name, address, telephone number, e-mail address, and Media Access Control address for each defendant. On February 23, 2004, Cablevision complied with the subpoena and provided relevant information about the Jane and John Does. Discuss whether the release of identity was proper. [*Sony Music Entertainment Inc. v. Does*, 326 F. Supp. 2d 56 (S.D.N.Y.)]

9. Immunomedics, Inc., has discovered sensitive information about its technology posted on various Web sites and chat rooms. The information is so proprietary that it could have come only from company employees, all of whom have signed agreements not to disclose such information. Those who posted the information used screen names, and Immunomedics has asked the court to issue a subpoena to the ISP so that it can determine the identity of those posting the information and recover for breach of contract and trade secret infringement. Should the court issue the subpoena? [*Immunomedics, Inc. v. Does 1–10,* 775 A.2d 773 (N.J. Super.)]

10. Jane Doe filed a complaint against Richard Lee Russell and America Online (AOL) to recover for alleged emotional injuries suffered by her son, John Doe. Doe claimed that in 1994, Russell lured John Doe, who was then 11 years old, and two other minor males to engage in sexual activity with each other and with Russell. She asserted that Russell photographed and videotaped these acts and used AOL's chat rooms to market the photographs and videotapes and to sell a videotape. In her six-count complaint, Doe claimed that AOL violated criminal statutes and that AOL was negligent *per se* in distributing an advertisement offering "a visual depiction of sexual conduct involving [John Doe]" and by allowing Russell to sell or arrange to sell child pornography, thus aiding in the sale and distribution of child pornography, including obscene images of John Doe. Does Mrs. Doe have a cause of action? What laws discussed in this chapter apply? [*Doe v. America Online, Inc.,* 783 So.2d 1010 (Fla.)]

11. Customers of a chat room are using the chat room, Maphia, for access to each other and to transfer Sega games to each other. They are able to avoid paying the $19 to $60 the games cost for purchase in the stores. The users say they are simply transferring files and that there is no crime. The chat room says it cannot stop customers from interacting. Do you think there are any civil or criminal law violations in their conduct? [*Sega Enterprises, Ltd. v. Maphia,* 857 F. Supp. 679 (N.D.Cal.)]

PART 2

Contracts

© Manuel Gutjahr/iStockphoto.com

Nature and Classes of Contracts: Contracting on the Internet

learning outcomes

After studying this chapter, you should be able to

- **LO.1** Explain the meaning and importance of privity of a contract
- **LO.2** Describe the way in which a contract arises
- **LO.3** Distinguish between bilateral and unilateral contracts
- **LO.4** Explain the reasoning behind quasi-contract recovery
- **LO.5** Explain how Internet contracts involve the same types of issues as offline contracts.

Practically every business transaction affecting people involves a contract.

A. Nature of Contracts

This introductory chapter will familiarize you with the terminology needed to work with contract law. In addition, the chapter introduces quasi contracts, which are not true contracts but obligations imposed by law.

1. Definition of a Contract

A **contract** is a legally binding agreement.[1] By one definition, "a contract is a promise or a set of promises for the breach of which the law gives a remedy, or the performance of which the law in some way recognizes as a duty."[2] Contracts arise out of agreements, so a contract may be defined as an agreement creating an obligation.

The substance of the definition of a contract is that by mutual agreement or assent, the parties create enforceable duties or obligations. That is, each party is legally bound to do or to refrain from doing certain acts.

2. Elements of a Contract

The elements of a contract are (1) an agreement (2) between competent parties (3) based on the genuine assent of the parties that is (4) supported by consideration, (5) made for a lawful objective, and (6) in the form required by law, if any. These elements will be considered in the chapters that follow.

3. Subject Matter of Contracts

The subject matter of a contract may relate to the performance of personal services, such as contracts of employment to work developing computer software or to play professional football. A contract may provide for the transfer of ownership of property, such as a house (real property) or an automobile (personal property), from one person to another.

4. Parties to a Contract

The person who makes a promise is the **promisor**, and the person to whom the promise is made is the **promisee**. If the promise is binding, it imposes on the promisor a duty or obligation, and the promisor may be called the **obligor**. The promisee who can claim the benefit of the obligation is called the **obligee**. The parties to a contract are said to stand in **privity** with each other, and the relationship between them is termed **privity of contract**. **For Example,** when the state of North Carolina and the architectural firm of O'Brien/Atkins Associates executed a contract for the construction of a new building at the University of North Carolina, Chapel Hill, these parties were in privity of contract. However, a building contractor, RPR & Associates, who worked on the project did not have standing to sue on the contract between the architect and the state because the contractor was not in privity of contract.[3]

In written contracts, parties may be referred to by name. More often, however, they are given special names that better identify each party. For example, consider a contract by which one person agrees that another may occupy a house upon the payment of money. The parties to this contract are called *landlord* and *tenant*, or *lessor* and *lessee*, and the contract between them is known as a *lease*. Parties to other types of contracts also have distinctive names, such as *vendor* and *vendee* for the parties to a sales contract, *shipper* and *carrier* for the parties to a transportation contract, and *insurer* and *insured* for the parties to an insurance policy.

A party to a contract may be an individual, a partnership, a limited liability company, a corporation, or a government.[4] One or more persons may be on each side of a contract. Some contracts are three-sided, as in a credit card transaction, which involves the company issuing the card, the holder of the card, and the business furnishing goods and services on the basis of the credit card.

If a contract is written, the persons who are the parties and who are bound by it can ordinarily be

[1] The Uniform Commercial Code defines *contract* as "the total legal obligation which results from the parties' agreement as affected by [the UCC] and any other applicable rules of law." U.C.C. §1–201(11).

[2] Restatement (Second) of Contracts §1.

[3] *RPR & Associates v. O'Brien/Atkins Associates, P.A.*, 24 F. Supp. 2d 515 (M.D. N.C. 1998). See also *Roof Techs Int. Inc. v. State*, 57 P.3d 538, (Kan. App. 2002), where a layer of litigation was avoided regarding lawsuits involving the renovation of the Farrell Library at Kansas State University. The state was the only party in privity of contract with the architectural firm and would thus have to bring claims against the architectural firm on behalf of all of the contractors. Two subcontractors, the general contractor, and the owner of the library, the state of Kansas, used a settlement and liquidation agreement assigning all of the state's claims against the architect to the general contractor.

[4] See *Purina Mills, LLC v. Less*, 295 F. Supp. 2d 1017 (N.D. Iowa 2003) in which the pig-seller plaintiff, which converted from a corporation to a limited liability company (LLC) while the contract was in effect, was a proper party in interest and could maintain a contract action against defendant buyers.

determined by reading what the document says and seeing how it is signed. A contract binds only the parties to the contract. It cannot impose a duty on a person who is not a party to it. Ordinarily, only a party to a contract has any rights against another party to the contract.[5] In some cases, third persons have rights on a contract as third-party beneficiaries or assignees. A person cannot be bound, however, by the terms of a contract to which that person is not a party. **For Example,** in approximately 1995 Jeff and Mark Bass signed Marshall B. Mathers III, better known as rapper Eminem, to an exclusive record deal with FBT Productions LLC (FBT), their production company. In 2000 Aftermath Records entered into a direct contractual relationship with Eminem, transferring Eminem's recording services from FBT directly to Aftermath. Under the contract FBT became a "passive income participant," retaining a right to royalty income from Eminem's recordings. A dispute occurred regarding percentages of royalties due. Aftermath entered into an agreement with Eminem in 2009, setting the royalties for Eminem's *Recovery* and *Relapse* albums, asserting that all royalties, including royalties owed FBT were dictated by this 2009 agreement. FBT was not a party to the 2009 agreement and as such cannot be bound by it. A contract cannot bind a nonparty. Therefore, Aftermath was required to pay FBT royalties for the two albums at a higher rate in accordance with an earlier agreement.[6]

CPA 5. How a Contract Arises

A contract is based on an agreement. An agreement arises when one person, the **offeror**, makes an offer and the person to whom the offer is made, the **offeree**, accepts. There must be both an offer and an acceptance. If either is lacking, there is no contract.

6. Intent to Make a Binding Agreement

Because a contract is based on the consent of the parties and is a legally binding agreement, it follows that the parties must have an intent to enter into an agreement that is binding. Sometimes the parties are in agreement, but their agreement does not produce a contract. Sometimes there is merely a preliminary agreement, but the parties never actually make a contract, or there is merely an agreement as to future plans or intentions without any contractual obligation to carry out those plans or intentions.

7. Freedom of Contract

In the absence of some ground for declaring a contract void or voidable, parties may make such contracts as they choose. The law does not require parties to be fair, or kind, or reasonable, or to share gains or losses equitably.

B. Classes of Contracts

Contracts may be classified according to their form, the way in which they were created, their binding character, and the extent to which they have been performed.

CPA 8. Formal and Informal Contracts

Contracts can be classified as formal or informal.

(A) Formal Contracts. **Formal contracts** are enforced because the formality with which they are executed is considered sufficient to signify that the parties intend to be bound by their terms. Formal contracts include (1) **contracts under seal** where a person's signature or a corporation's name is followed by a scroll, the word *seal*, or the letters *L.S.*;[7] (2) contracts of record, which are obligations that have been entered before a court of record, sometimes called a **recognizance**; and (3) negotiable instruments.

CPA **(B) Informal Contracts.** All contracts other than formal contracts are called **informal** (or simple) **contracts** without regard to whether they are oral or written. These contracts are enforceable, not because of the form of the transaction but because they represent agreement of the parties.

9. Express and Implied Contracts

Simple contracts may be classified as *express contracts* or *implied contracts* according to the way they are created.

[5] *Hooper v. Yakima County*, 904 P.2d 1193 (Wash. App. 1995).

[6] *F.B.T. Productions, LLC v. Aftermath Records*, 2011 WL 5174766 (C.D. Cal. Oct. 31, 2011).

[7] Some authorities explain *L.S.* as an abbreviation for *locus sigilium* (place for the seal).

FIGURE 12-1 *Contractual Liability*

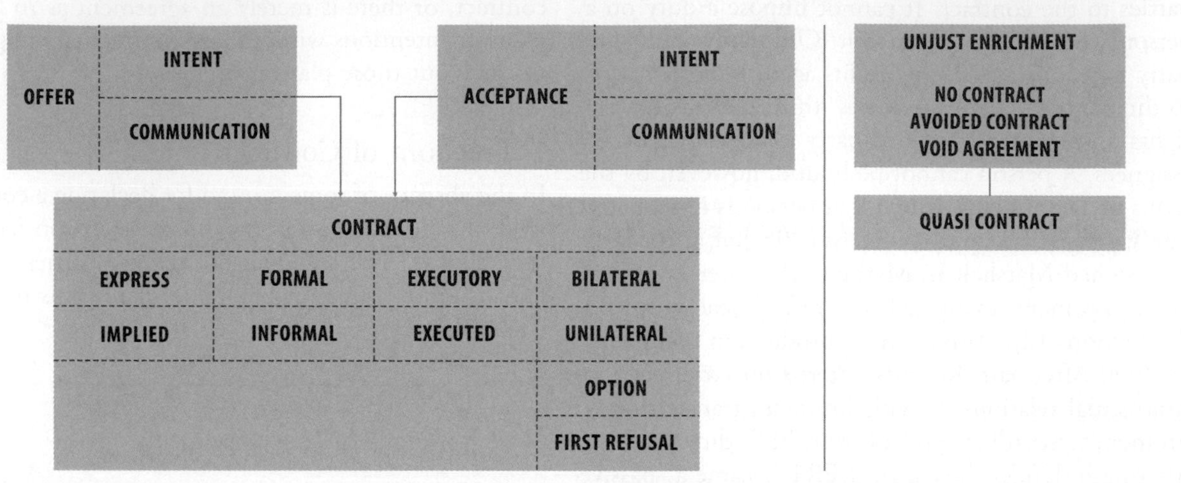

(A) Express Contracts. An **express contract** is one in which the terms of the agreement of the parties are manifested by their words, whether spoken or written.

(B) Implied Contracts. An **implied contract** (or, as sometimes stated, a *contract implied in fact*) is one in which the agreement is shown not by words, written or spoken, but by the acts and conduct of the parties.[8] Such a contract arises when (1) a person renders services under circumstances indicating that payment for them is expected and (2) the other person, knowing such circumstances, accepts the benefit of those services. **For Example,** when a building owner requests a professional roofer to make emergency repairs to the roof of a building, an obligation arises to pay the reasonable value of such services, although no agreement has been made about compensation.

An implied contract cannot arise when there is an existing express contract on the same subject.[9] However, the existence of a written contract does not bar recovery on an implied contract for extra work that was not covered by the contract.

CPA 10. Valid and Voidable Contracts and Void Agreements

Contracts may be classified in terms of enforceability or validity.

(A) Valid Contracts. A **valid contract** is an agreement that is binding and enforceable.

(B) Voidable Contracts. A **voidable contract** is an agreement that is otherwise binding and enforceable, but because of the circumstances surrounding its execution or the lack of capacity of one of the parties, it may be rejected at the option of one of the parties. **For Example,** a person who has been forced to sign an agreement that that person would not have voluntarily signed may, in some instances, avoid the contract.

(C) Void Agreements. A **void agreement** is without legal effect. An agreement that contemplates the performance of an act prohibited by law is usually incapable of enforcement; hence it is void. Likewise, it cannot be made binding by later approval or ratification.

[8] *Lindquist Ford, Inc. v. Middleton Motors, Inc.*, 557 F.3d 469, 481 (7th Cir. 2009). See also *Dynegy Marketing and Trade v. Multiut Corp.*, 648 F.3d 506 (7th Cir. 2011).
[9] *Pepsi-Cola Bottling Co. of Pittsburgh, Inc., v. PepsiCo, Inc.*, 431 F.3d 1241 (10th Cir. 2000).

11. Executed and Executory Contracts

Contracts may be classified as *executed contracts* and *executory contracts* according to the extent to which they have been performed.

(A) Executed Contracts. An **executed contract** is one that has been completely performed. In other words, an executed contract is one under which nothing remains to be done by either party.[10] A contract may be executed immediately, as in the case of a cash sale, or it may be executed or performed in the future.

(B) Executory Contracts. In an **executory contract**, something remains to be done by one or both parties.[11] **For Example,** on July 10, Mark agreed to sell to Chris his Pearl drum set for $600, the terms being $200 upon delivery on July 14, with $200 to be paid on July 21, and the final $200 being due July 28. Prior to the July 14 delivery of the drums to Chris, the contract was entirely executory. After the delivery by Mark, the contract was executed as to Mark and executory as to Chris until the final payment was received on July 28.

12. Bilateral and Unilateral Contracts

In making an offer, the offeror is in effect extending a promise to do something, such as pay a sum of money, if the offeree will do what the offeror requests. Contracts are classified as *bilateral* or *unilateral.* Some bilateral contracts look ahead to the making of a later contract. Depending on their terms, these are called *option contracts* or *first-refusal contracts.*

CPA **(A) Bilateral Contract.** If the offeror extends a promise and asks for a promise in return and if the offeree accepts the offer by making the promise, the contract is called a **bilateral contract**. One promise is given in exchange for another, and each party is bound by the obligation. **For Example,** when the house painter offers to paint the owner's house for $3,700 and the owner promises to pay $3,700 for the job, there is an exchange of promises, and the agreement gives rise to a bilateral contract.

(B) Unilateral Contract. In contrast with a bilateral contract, the offeror may promise to do something or to pay a certain amount of money only when the offeree does an act.[12] Examples of where **unilateral contracts** commonly appear are when a reward is offered, a contest is announced, or changes are made and disseminated in an employee manual. The offeree does not accept the offer by express agreement, but rather by performance. The *Aon Risk Services* case involved an assertion of the existence of a unilateral contract.

Aon Risk Services Inc. v. Meadors, 267 S.W.3d 603 (Ark. App. 2007)

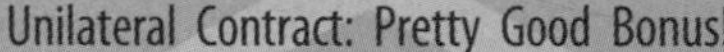

Unilateral Contract: Pretty Good Bonus!

Aon Risk Services, Inc. (ARS Arkansas), and Combined Insurance Companies are subsidiaries of Aon Corporation. The parent corporation issued an "Interdependency Memo" dated February 2000, which encouraged ARS brokerage offices to place insurance business with Aon-affiliated companies. It also set up a bonus pool for revenues generated under the plan, with Combined agreeing to pay "30% of annualized premium on all life products over 15-year term plus 15% 1st year for all other products." John Meadors saw the memo in February 2000, and believed it would entitle him to this compensation over and above his employment contract. Meadors put Combined in touch with Dillard's Department Stores and on March 24, 2000, Dillard's and Combined executed a five-year agreement whereby Dillard's employees could purchase life, disability, and other insurance policies through workplace enrollment. When Meadors did not receive bonus-pool money generated by the transaction, he sued his employer for breach of a unilateral contract. The employer's defense was that the memo was not sufficiently definite to constitute an offer.

JUDICIAL OPINION

VAUGHT, J. ... Meadors's theory at trial was that the Interdependency Memo formed a unilateral contract. There are several instances where unilateral contracts commonly appear, such as where a reward is offered, *e.g., Ark. Bankers' Ass'n v. Ligon* 174 *Ark.* 234, 295 S.W. 4 (1927), where a

[10] *Marsh v. Rheinecker*, 641 N.E.2d 1256 (Ill. App. 1994).

[11] *DiGennaro v. Rubbermaid, Inc.*, 214 F. Supp. 2d 1354 (S.D. Fla. 2002).

[12] See *Young v. Virginia Birth-Related Neurological Injury Compensation Program*, 620 S.E.2d 131 (Va. App. 2005).

Continued

contest is announced, *e.g.*, *Mears v. Nationwide Mut. Ins. Co.* 91 F.3d 1118 (8th Cir. 1996), or where changes are made and disseminated in an employee manual. *See Crain Indus., Inc. v. Case* 305 *Ark.* 566, 810 S.W.2d 910 (1991). In those situations, the offeree does not accept the offer by express agreement but by his performance. For example, in the case of a reward, the offeree accepts by performing the particular task, such as the capture of a fugitive, for which the reward is offered. Even though he has not directly communicated his acceptance, a contract is formed as the result of his performance. *See Ligon, supra* (recognizing that a unilateral contract is composed of an offer that invites acceptance in the form of actual performance), 17A AM. JUR. 2D *Contracts* § 5 (2d ed. 1991) (stating that, if performance occurs, then the offer has been accepted, and a contract is formed). The performance also constitutes consideration for the contract. 17A AM. JUR 2D *Contracts* § 5.

Definiteness of offer

ARS Arkansas argues first that the interdependency Memo was not sufficiently definite to constitute an offer for a unilateral contract. An offer is the manifestation of willingness to enter into a bargain, so made as to justify another person in understanding that his assent to the bargain is invited and will conclude it. An offer cannot be accepted so as to form a contract unless the terms are reasonably certain. *Restatement (Second) of Contracts* § 33 (1981). To bind the employer, an offer must be definite in form and must be communicated to the offeree. *See Hardie v. Cotter & Co.* 849 F.2d 1097 (18th Cir. 1988); *Dumas v. Kessler & Maguire Funeral Home, Inc.* 380 N. W.2d 544 (Minn. Ct. App. 1986). Whether a proposal is meant to be an offer for a unilateral contract is determined by the outward manifestations of the parties, and not by their subjective intentions. The principle issue is whether the employer's statements are intended as an offer and accepted as such or are merely statements of policy and practice. *id....*

ARS ... relies heavily on *Martens v. Minnesota Minning & Manufacturing Co.* 616 N.W. 2d 732 (Minn. 2000), but it is distinguishable. There, the Minnesota court held that a brochure touting equal compensation for technical and administrative employees was too indefinite to constitute an offer. The court noted that there was no suggestion that an individual would be entitled to specific pay, benefit level, or condition of employment, nor were there any criteria to determine when the rights to any benefits had been breached. Further, the prerogative to make decisions as to individual employee promotions, salaries, and so forth was clearly reserved to management based on an evaluation of the individual. By contrast, the interdependency Memo in this case does not merely set out general goals and philosophies of compensation. It sets out specific percentages of premiums that will go into the bonus pool as part of an "enhanced compensation structure." And, while no employee is entitled to a "formulaic" bonus and Managing Directors may decide how to allocate the bonus pool among their employees, their discretion is not unfettered. For example, managers cannot withhold payment of the pool amount; the Memo provides that the entire pool must be distributed annually. Thus, the mere inclusion of possible judgment calls by management as to the manner of distribution among its employees does not, under these circumstances, render the Memo too indefinite to operate as an offer for a unilateral contract....

CONCLUSION

We affirm the jury's verdict for breach of a unilateral contract against ARS Arkansas and reinstate Meador's damages of $2,406,522.60 pertaining to the Dillard's transaction....

QUESTIONS

1. Must an offeree accept an offer by express agreement in order for a legally enforceable contract to be formed?
2. Was the "Interdependency Memo" too indefinite to constitute an offer?

(c) Option and First-Refusal Contracts. The parties may make a contract that gives a right to one of them to enter into a second contract at a later date. If one party has an absolute right to enter into the later contract, the initial contract is called an **option contract**. Thus, a bilateral contract may be made today giving one of the parties the right to buy the other party's house for a specified amount. This is an option contract because the party with the privilege has the freedom of choice, or option, to buy or not buy. If the option is exercised, the other party to the contract must follow the terms of the option and enter into the second contract. If the option is never exercised, no second contract ever arises, and the offer protected by the option contract merely expires.

In contrast with an option contract, a contract may merely give a **right of first refusal**. This imposes only the duty to make the first offer to the party having the right of first refusal.

13. Quasi Contracts

In some cases, a court will impose an obligation even though there is no contract.[13] Such an obligation is called a **quasi contract**, which is an obligation imposed by law.

(A) Prevention of Unjust Enrichment. A quasi contract is not a true contract reflecting all of the elements of a contract set forth previously in this chapter. The court is not seeking to enforce the intentions of the parties contained in an agreement. Rather, when a person or enterprise receives a benefit from another, even in the absence of a promise to pay for the benefit, a court may impose an obligation to pay for the reasonable value of that benefit, to avoid *unjust enrichment*. The spirit behind the law of unjust enrichment is to apply the law "outside the box" and fill in the cracks where common civil law and statutes fail to achieve justice.[14]

A successful claim for unjust enrichment usually requires (1) a benefit conferred on the defendant,

FIGURE 12-2 *Contract*

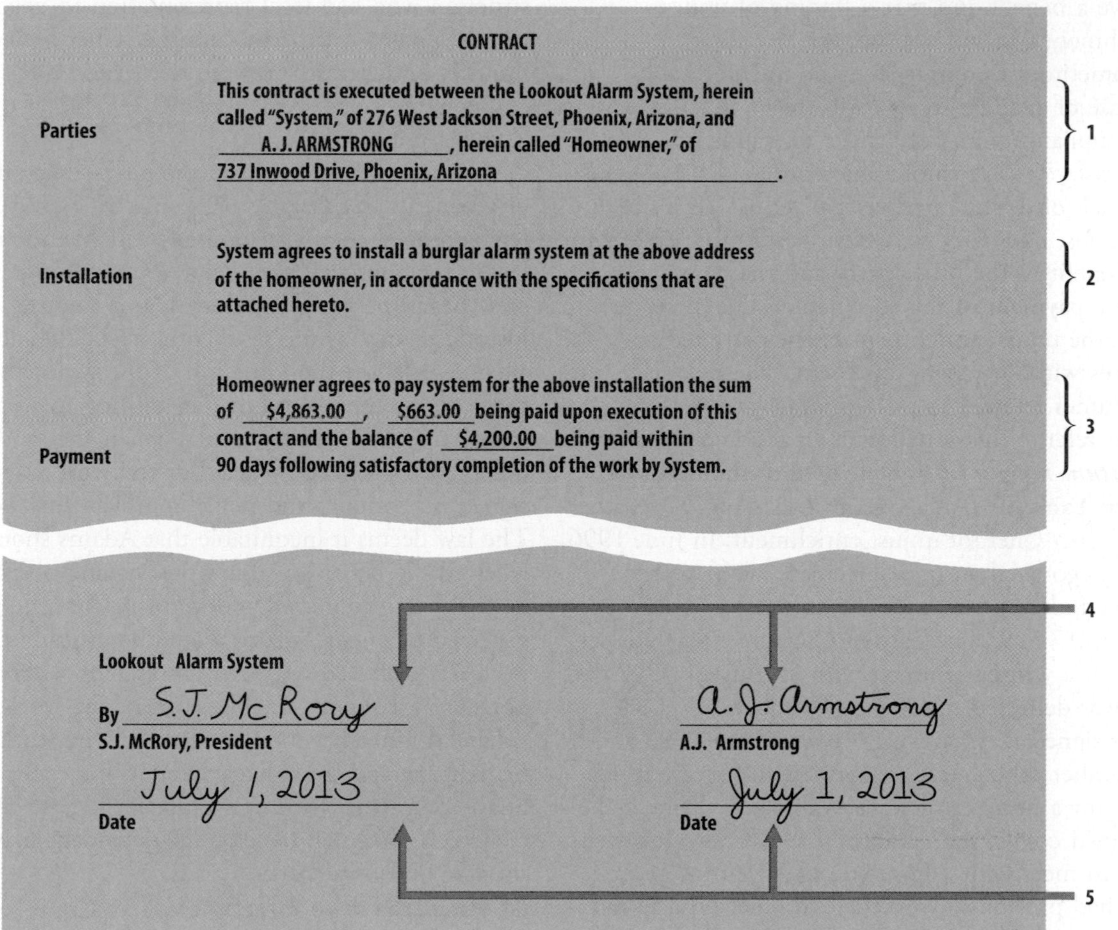

CONTRACT

Parties — This contract is executed between the Lookout Alarm System, herein called "System," of 276 West Jackson Street, Phoenix, Arizona, and A. J. ARMSTRONG, herein called "Homeowner," of 737 Inwood Drive, Phoenix, Arizona. (1)

Installation — System agrees to install a burglar alarm system at the above address of the homeowner, in accordance with the specifications that are attached hereto. (2)

Payment — Homeowner agrees to pay system for the above installation the sum of $4,863.00, $663.00 being paid upon execution of this contract and the balance of $4,200.00 being paid within 90 days following satisfactory completion of the work by System. (3)

Lookout Alarm System

By S.J. McRory
S.J. McRory, President

July 1, 2013
Date

A.J. Armstrong
A.J. Armstrong

July 1, 2013
Date

Note that this contract includes the following important information: (1) the name and address of each party, (2) the promise or consideration of the seller, (3) the promise or consideration of the buyer, (4) the signature of the two parties, and (5) the date.

[13] *Thayer v. Dial Industrial Sales, Inc.*, 85 F. Supp. 2d 263 (S.D.N.Y. 2000).
[14] *Hernandez v. Lopez*, 103 Cal. Rptr.3d 376, 381 (Cal. App. 2009).

(2) the defendant's knowledge of the benefit, and (3) a finding that it would be unjust for the defendant to retain the benefit without payment. The burden of proof is on the plaintiff to prove all of the elements of the claim. **For Example,** Hiram College sued Nicholas Courtad for $6,000 plus interest for tuition and other expenses. Because no evidence of a written contract was produced, the court considered it an unjust enrichment claim by the college. Courtad had attended classes for a few weeks and had not paid his tuition due to a problem with his financial aid package. Because he did not receive any credit hours toward a degree, which is the ultimate benefit of attending college, the court found that he did not receive a benefit and that a finding of unjust enrichment was not appropriate.[15]

Sometimes a contract may be unenforceable because of a failure to set forth the contract in writing in compliance with the statute of frauds. In other circumstances, no enforceable contract exists because of a lack of definite and certain terms. Yet in both situations, one party may have performed services for the benefit of the other party and the court will require payment of the reasonable value of services to avoid the unjust enrichment of the party receiving the services without paying for them. These damages are sometimes referred to as *restitution damages*. Some courts refer to this situation as an action or recovery in ***quantum meruit*** (as much as he or she deserved).

For Example, Arya Group, Inc. (Arya), sued the entertainer Cher for unjust enrichment. In June 1996, Cher negotiated an oral agreement with Arya to design and construct a house on her Malibu property for $4,217,529. The parties' oral agreement was set forth in a written contract with an August 1997 date and was delivered to Cher in October 1997. She never signed it. However, between June 1996 and November 1997, Arya performed and received payment for a number of services discharged under the unsigned contract. In August 1997, Cher requested Arya to meet with a home designer named Bussell who had previously worked with Cher on a Florida project, and Arya showed Bussell the plans and designs for the Malibu property and introduced her to his subcontractors. In November 1997, Cher terminated her agreement with Arya without paying the balance then due, as asserted by Arya, of $415,169.41. Arya claims that Cher and Bussell misappropriated the plans and designs Arya had prepared. Cher and the other defendants demurred to Arya's unjust enrichment complaint, pointing out that construction contracts must be evidenced in a writing signed by both parties under state law in order to be enforceable in a court of law. The appeals court determined that Arya's noncompliance with the state law requiring a signed written contract did not absolutely foreclose Arya from seeking damages for unjust enrichment if he could prove the assertions in the complaint that Cher was a sophisticated homeowner with previous involvement in residential construction who had legal representation in negotiating the agreement with Arya, and that Cher would be unjustly enriched if she were not required to compensate Arya for the reasonable value of the work already performed.[16]

A situation may arise over the mistaken conferrence of a benefit. **For Example,** Nantucket Island has a few approved colors for houses in its historic district. Using the approved gray color, Martin Kane and his crew began painting Sheldon Adams's house in the historic district as the result of a mistaken address. Adams observed the initiation of the work from his office across the street but did nothing to stop the painters. At the end of the day when the work was done, Adams refused to pay for the work, saying, "I signed no contract and never approved this work." The law deems it inequitable that Adams should have received the benefit of this work, having observed the benefit being conferred and knowing that the painters expected payment. Adams would be unjustly enriched if he were allowed to retain the benefit without payment for the reasonable value of the work. If Adams did not have knowledge that the work was being done and thus that payment was expected, quasi-contractual liability would not be imposed.

The mistake that benefits the defendant may be the mistake of a third party.

(B) Preclusion by an Express Contract. Courts award relief based on quasi-contractual principles, implying by law a contract where one did not exist in fact. Thus, where an express contract exists, it precludes an unjust enrichment claim.

[15] *Hiram College v. Courtad*, 834 N.E.2d 432 (Ohio App. 2005).

[16] *Arya Group, Inc. v. Cher*, 91 Cal. Rptr. 2d 815 (Cal. App. 2000). See also *Fischer v. Flax*, 816 A.2d 1 (2003).

Thinking Things Through

Twelve Years of Litigation

Brown University accepted the bid of Marshall Contractors, Inc. (Marshall), to build the Pizzitola Sports Facility on its Providence, Rhode Island, campus. The parties intended to execute a formal written contract. Brown decided to pay $7,157,051 for the project, but Marshall sought additional payment for items it deemed extras and not contemplated in its bid. Because the parties were unable to agree on the scope of the project as compared to the price Brown was willing to pay, they never executed the formal written contract. Nevertheless, in the context of this disagreement over terms and price, construction began in May 1987. When the parties could not resolve their disagreements as the project neared completion in January 1989, Marshall sued Brown University, seeking to recover the costs for what it deemed "changes." Brown asserted that an implied-in-fact contract existed for all work at the $7,157,051 figure because the contractor went ahead with the project knowing the money Brown would pay. The litigation ended up in the Supreme Court of Rhode Island, and in 1997, the court concluded that no express or implied-in-fact contract had ever been reached by the parties concerning the scope of the project and what costs were to be included in the price stipulated by Brown. The case was remanded to the trial court for a new trial. After a trial on the theories of *quantum meruit* and unjust enrichment, a jury awarded Marshall $1.2 million dollars, which was some $3.1 million less than Marshall sought. Brown University appealed, and on November 21, 2001, the Supreme Court of Rhode Island affirmed the jury verdict for the contractor, determining that the proper measure of damages on unjust enrichment and *quantum meruit* theories was "the reasonable value of the work done."*

In May 1987 when the parties could not reach agreement enabling the execution of a formal written contract, thinking things through at that point in time should have exposed the potential for significant economic uncertainties to both parties in actually starting the building process under such circumstances. In the spring of 1987 when all parties were unable to reach agreement, mediation or expedited arbitration by construction experts may well have resolved the controversy and yielded an amicable written contract with little or no delay to the project. Instead, the unsettled cost issues during the building process could have had an adverse impact on the "job chemistry" between the contractor and the owner, which may have adversely affected the progress and quality of the job. The 12 years of litigation that, with its economic and human resource costs, yielded just $1.2 million for the contractor was a no-win result for both sides. A primary rule for all managers in projects of this scope is to make sure the written contracts are executed before performance begins! Relying on "implied-in-fact" or quasi-contract legal theories is simply a poor management practice.

*ADP Marshall, Inc. v. Brown University, 784 A2d 309 (R.I. 2001).

(c) Extent of Recovery. When recovery is allowed in quasi contract, the plaintiff recovers the reasonable value of the benefit conferred on the defendant,[17] or the fair and reasonable[18] value of the work performed, depending on the jurisdiction and the circumstances of the case itself. The customary method of calculating damages in construction contract cases is actual job costs plus an allowance for overhead and profits minus amount paid.[19]

C. Contracting on the Internet

Doing business online for consumers is very similar to doing business through a catalog purchase or by phone. Before placing an order, a buyer is commonly concerned about the reputation of the seller. The basic purchasing principle of *caveat emptor* still applies: buyer beware! The Internet provides valuable tools to allow a buyer to research the reputation of the seller and its products. Online evaluations of companies and their products can be found at Web sites, such as Consumer Reports (**www.consumerreports.org**), Consumers Digest (**www.consumersdigest.com**), or the Better Business Bureau (**www.bbb.org**). E-consumers may have access to categorized histories of comments by other e-consumers, such as Planet Feedback ratings at **www.planetfeedback.com**.

The intellectual property principles set forth in Chapter 10—as well as the contractual principles,

[17] *Ramsey v. Ellis*, 484 N.W.2d 331 (Wis. 1992).
[18] *ADP Marshall, Inc. v. Brown University*, 784 A.2d 309 (R.I. 2001).
[19] *Miranco Contracting, Inc. v. Perel*, 871 N.Y.S.2d 310 (A.D. 2008).

the law of sales, and privacy laws you are about to study—all apply to e-commerce transactions. When you are purchasing an item online, you must carefully read all of the terms and conditions set forth on the seller's Web site when assessing whether to make a contemplated purchase. The proposed terms may require that any disputes be litigated in a distant state or be resolved through arbitration with restricted remedies, or there may be an unsatisfactory return policy, warranty limitations, or limitation of liability. Generally, the Web site terms become the contract of the parties and are legally enforceable.

The laws you have studied that prevent deceptive advertising by brick-and-mortar businesses also apply to Internet sites.[20] If an in-state site is engaging in false advertising, you may be able to exercise consumer protection rights through your state's attorney general's office, or you may find some therapeutic relief by reporting the misconduct to the Internet Scambusters site (**www.scambusters.com**).

From a seller's perspective, it is exceedingly helpful to have as much information as possible on your potential customers' buying habits. Federal law prohibits the collection of personal information from children without parental consent, and some states restrict the unauthorized collection of personal information. European Union countries have strict laws protecting the privacy of consumers. Sellers intending to collect personal information should obtain the consent of their customers, make certain that children are excluded, and make sure that the information is stored in a secure environment.

Advanced encryption technology has made the use of credit card payments through the Internet very safe. No computer system connected to the Internet is totally secure however. In the worst-case scenario, credit card issuers will not charge a user for more than the first $50 of unauthorized activity.

Internet contracts involve the same types of issues that are addressed in contracts offline but with certain technology-related nuances. The parties to the e-contracts must still negotiate their obligations in clear and unambiguous language, including such terms as quantity, quality, and price as well as warranties, indemnification responsibilities, limitations on liability, and termination procedures. The federal Electronic Signatures in Global and National Commerce Act (E-Sign) and the Uniform Electronic Transactions Act (UETA) mandate parity between paper and electronic contracts. The basic legal rules that govern contracts offline are the very same rules that govern online contracts, and basic civil procedure rules apply. **For Example,** California buyer Paul Boschetto bought a 1964 Ford Galaxy that had been advertised on eBay to be "in awesome condition" from a Milton, Wisconsin, resident, J. Hansing, for $34,106. On delivery Boschetto discovered that the car had rust, extensive dents, and would not start. His lawsuit against Hansing in U.S. District Court in California was dismissed for lack of personal jurisdiction.[21] (The formation of a contract with a nonresident defendant was not, standing alone, sufficient to create personal jurisdiction in California.)

Boxes identifying special Internet e-commerce topics are strategically placed throughout these chapters.

LawFlix

Paper Moon (1973) (PG)

In this movie for which Tatum O'Neal was given an Oscar, the ongoing issue between Annie and her alleged father is her recoupment of the money she says he promised. Discuss the contract issues (voidable [minor], formation, unilateral vs. bilateral, express, informal, etc.).

[20] See *MADCAP I, LLC v. McNamee*, 712 N.W.2d 16 (Wis. App. 2005) in which the court found genuine issues of material fact as to whether a business Web site falsely represented the size and nature of its business to induce the public to purchase products and services described on its Web site in violation of the state's fraudulent representations statute.

[21] *Boschetto v. Hansing*, 539 F.3d 1011 (9th Cir. 2008).

MAKE THE CONNECTION

SUMMARY

A contract is a binding agreement between two or more parties. A contract arises when an offer is accepted with contractual intent (the intent to make a binding agreement).

Contracts may be classified in a number of ways according to form, the way in which they were created, validity, and obligations. With respect to form, a contract may be either informal or formal, such as those under seal or those appearing on the records of courts. Contracts may be classified by the way they were created as those that are expressed by words— written or oral—and those that are implied or deduced from conduct. The question of validity requires distinguishing between contracts that are valid, those that are voidable, and those that are not contracts at all but are merely void agreements. Contracts can be distinguished on the basis of the obligations created as executed contracts, in which everything has been performed, and executory contracts, in which something remains to be done. The bilateral contract is formed by exchanging a promise for a promise, so each party has the obligation of thereafter rendering the promised performance. In the unilateral contract, which is the doing of an act in exchange for a promise, no further performance is required of the offeree who performed the act.

In certain situations, the law regards it as unjust for a person to receive a benefit and not pay for it. In such a case, the law of quasi contracts allows the performing person to recover the reasonable value of the benefit conferred on the benefited person even though no contract between them requires any payment. Unjust enrichment, which a quasi contract is designed to prevent, sometimes arises when there was never any contract between the persons involved or when there was a contract, but for some reason it was avoided or held to be merely a void agreement.

LEARNING OUTCOMES

After studying this chapter, you should be able to clearly explain:

A. Nature of Contracts

LO.1 Explain the meaning and importance of privity of a contract

See the example of the subcontractor, RPR & Associates, who worked on a project but could not sue the owner for payment, p. 234.

See the example involving rapper Eminem, FBT, and Aftermath Records, where FBT was not a party to the contract and thus not bound by it, p. 235.

LO.2 Describe the way in which a contract arises

See the discussion on offer and acceptance on p. 235.

B. Classes of Contracts

LO.3 Distinguish between bilateral and unilateral contracts

See the example of the Nantucket painters on p. 240.

See the *Aon Risk Services* case where an insurance agent won his case based on a unilateral contract theory, pp. 237–238.

LO.4 Explain the reasoning behind quasi-contract recovery

See the example whereby Cher had to pay a home designer for certain work even though there was no contract, p. 240.

C. Contracting on the Internet

LO.5 Explain how Internet contracts involve the same types of issues as offline contracts

See the eBay example on p. 242.

KEY TERMS

bilateral contract
contract
contract under seal
executed contract
executory contract
express contract
formal contract
implied contract
informal contract
obligee
obligor
offeree
offeror
option contract
privity
privity of contract
promisee
promisor
quantum meruit
quasi contract
recognizance
right of first refusal
unilateral contracts
valid contract
void agreement
voidable contract

QUESTIONS AND CASE PROBLEMS

1. What is a contract?
2. Fourteen applicants for a city of Providence, Rhode Island, police academy training class each received from the city a letter stating that it was a "conditional offer of employment" subject to successful completion of medical and psychological exams. The 14 applicants passed the medical and psychological exams. However, these applicants were replaced by others after the city changed the selection criteria. Can you identify an offer and acceptance in this case? Can you make out a bilateral or unilateral contract? [*Ardito et al. v. City of Providence, 213* F. Supp. 2d 358 (D.R.I.)]
3. Compare an implied contract with a quasi contract.
4. The Jordan Keys law firm represented the Greater Southeast Community Hospital of Washington, D.C., in a medical malpractice suit against the hospital. The hospital was self-insured for the first $1,000,000 of liability and the St. Paul Insurance Co. provided excess coverage up to $4,000,000. The law firm was owed $67,000 for its work on the malpractice suit when the hospital went into bankruptcy. The bankruptcy court ordered the law firm to release its files on the case to St. Paul to defend under the excess coverage insurance, and the Jordan Keys firm sued St. Paul for its legal fees of $67,000 expended prior to the bankruptcy under an "implied-in-fact contract" because the insurance company would have the benefit of all of its work. Decide. [*Jordan Keys v. St. Paul Fire,* 870 A.2d 58 (D.C.)]
5. Beck was the general manager of Chilkoot Lumber Co. Haines sold fuel to the company. To persuade Haines to sell on credit, Beck signed a paper by which he promised to pay any debt the lumber company owed Haines. He signed this paper with his name followed by "general manager." Haines later sued Beck on this promise, and Beck raised the defense that the addition of "general manager" showed that Beck, who was signing on behalf of Chilkoot, was not personally liable and did not intend to be bound by the paper. Was Beck liable on the paper? [*Beck v. Haines Terminal and Highway Co.,* 843 P.2d 1229 (Alaska)]
6. *A* made a contract to construct a house for *B*. Subsequently, *B* sued *A* for breach of contract. *A* raised the defense that the contract was not binding because it was not sealed. Is this a valid defense? [*Cooper v. G. E. Construction Co.,* 158 S.E.2d 305 (Ga. App.)]
7. Edward Johnson III, the CEO and principal owner of the world's largest mutual fund company, Fidelity Investments, Inc., was a longtime tennis buddy of Richard Larson. In 1995, Johnson asked Larson, who had construction experience, to supervise the construction of a house on Long Pond, Mount Desert Island, Maine. Although they had no written contract, Larson agreed to take on the project for

$6,700 per month plus lodging. At the end of the project in 1997, Johnson made a $175,000 cash payment to Larson, and he made arrangements for Larson to live rent-free on another Johnson property in the area called Pray's Meadow in exchange for looking after Johnson's extensive property interests in Maine. In the late summer of 1999, Johnson initiated a new project on the Long Pond property. Johnson had discussions with Larson about doing this project, but Larson asked to be paid his former rate, and Johnson balked because he had already hired a project manager. According to Johnson, at a later date he again asked Larson to take on the "shop project" as a favor and in consideration of continued rent-free use of the Pray's Meadow home. Johnson stated that Larson agreed to do the job "pro bono" in exchange for the use of the house, and Johnson acknowledged that he told Larson he would "take care" of Larson at the end of the project, which could mean as much or as little as Johnson determined. Larson stated that Johnson told him that he would "take care of" Larson if he would do the project and told him to "trust the Great Oracle" (meaning Johnson, the highly successful businessperson). Larson sought payment in March 2000 and asked Johnson for "something on account" in April. Johnson offered Larson a loan. In August during a tennis match, Larson again asked Johnson to pay him. Johnson became incensed, and through an employee, he ended Larson's participation in the project and asked him to vacate Pray's Meadow. Larson complied and filed suit for payment for work performed at the rate of $6,700 per month. Did Larson have an express contract with Johnson? What legal theory or theories could Larson utilize in his lawsuit? How would you decide this case if you believed Larson's version of the facts? How would you decide the case if you believed Johnson's version of the facts? [*Larson v. Johnson,* 196 F. Supp. 2d 38 (D. Me. 2002)]

8. While Clara Novak was sick, her daughter Janie helped her in many ways. Clara died, and Janie then claimed that she was entitled to be paid for the services she had rendered her mother. This claim was opposed by three brothers and sisters who also rendered services to the mother. They claimed that Janie was barred because of the presumption that services rendered between family members are gratuitous. Janie claimed that this presumption was not applicable because she had not lived with her mother but had her own house. Was Janie correct? [*In re Estate of Novak,* 398 N.W.2d 653 (Minn. App.)]

9. Dozier and his wife, daughter, and grandson lived in the house Dozier owned. At the request of the daughter and grandson, Paschall made some improvements to the house. Dozier did not authorize these, but he knew that the improvements were being made and did not object to them. Paschall sued Dozier for the reasonable value of the improvements, but Dozier argued that he had not made any contract for such improvements. Was he obligated to pay for such improvements?

10. When Harriet went away for the summer, Landry, a house painter, painted her house. He had a contract to paint a neighbor's house but painted Harriet's house by mistake. When Harriet returned from vacation, Landry billed her for $3,100, which was a fair price for the work. She refused to pay. Landry claimed that she had a quasi-contractual liability for that amount. Was he correct?

11. Margrethe and Charles Pyeatte, a married couple, agreed that she would work so that he could go to law school and that when he finished, she would go back to school for her master's degree. After Charles was admitted to the bar and before Margrethe went back to school, the two were divorced. She sued Charles, claiming that she was entitled to quasi-contractual recovery of the money that she had paid for Charles's support and law school tuition. He denied liability. Was she entitled to recover for the money she spent for Charles's maintenance and law school tuition? [*Pyeatte v. Pyeatte,* 661 P.2d 196 (Ariz. App.)]

12. Carriage Way was a real estate development of approximately 80 houses and 132 apartments. The property owners were members of the Carriage Way Property Owners Association. Each year, the association would take care of certain open neighboring areas, including a nearby lake, that were used by the property owners. The board of

directors of the association would make an assessment or charge against the property owners to cover the cost of this work. The property owners paid these assessments for a number of years and then refused to pay any more. In spite of this refusal, the association continued to take care of the areas in question. The association then sued the property owners and claimed that they were liable for the benefit that had been conferred on them. Were the owners liable? [*Board of Directors of Carriage Way Property Owners Ass'n v. Western National Bank,* 487 N.E.2d 974 (Ill. App.)]

13. When improvements or buildings are added to real estate, the real estate tax assessment is usually increased to reflect the increased value of the property. Frank Partipilo and Elmer Hallman owned neighboring tracts of land. Hallman made improvement to his land, constructing a new building and driveway on the tract. The tax assessor made a mistake about the location of the boundary line between Partipilo's and Hallman's land and thought the improvements were made on Partipilo's property. Instead of increasing the taxes on Hallman's land, the assessor wrongly increased the taxes on Partipilo's land. Partipilo paid the increased taxes for three years. When he learned why his taxes had been increased, he sued Hallman for the amount of the increase that Partipilo had been paying. Hallman raised the defense that he had not done anything wrong and that the mistake had been the fault of the tax assessor. Decide. [*Partipilo v. Hallman,* 510 N.E.2d 8 (Ill.App.)]

14. When a college student complained about a particular course, the vice president of the college asked the teacher to prepare a detailed report about the course. The teacher did and then demanded additional compensation for the time spent in preparing the report. He claimed that the college was liable to provide compensation on an implied contract. Was he correct? [*Zadrozny v. City Colleges of Chicago,* 581 N.E.2d 44 (Ill. App.)]

15. Smith made a contract to sell automatic rifles to a foreign country. Because the sale of such weapons to that country was illegal under an act of Congress, the U.S. government prosecuted Smith for making the contract. He raised the defense that because the contract was illegal, it was void and there is no binding obligation when a contract is void; therefore, no contract for which he could be prosecuted existed. Was he correct?

CPA QUESTIONS

1. Kay, an art collector, promised Hammer, an art student, that if Hammer could obtain certain rare artifacts within two weeks, Kay would pay for Hammer's postgraduate education. At considerable effort and expense, Hammer obtained the specified artifacts within the two-week period. When Hammer requested payment, Kay refused. Kay claimed that there was no consideration for the promise. Hammer would prevail against Kay based on:

   a. Unilateral contract.
   b. Unjust enrichment.
   c. Public policy.
   d. Quasi contract.

CHAPTER 13

© Manuel Gutjahr/iStockphoto.com

Formation of Contracts: Offer and Acceptance

learningoutcomes

After studying this chapter, you should be able to

LO.1 Decide whether an offer contains definite and certain terms

LO.2 Explain the exceptions the law makes to the requirement of definiteness

LO.3 Explain all the ways an offer can be terminated

LO.4 Explain what constitutes the acceptance of an offer

LO.5 Explain the implications of failing to read a clickwrap agreement

A *contract* consists of enforceable obligations that have been voluntarily assumed. Thus, one of the essential elements of a contract is an agreement. This chapter explains how the basic agreement arises, when there is a contract, and how there can be merely unsuccessful negotiations without a resulting contract.

A. Requirements of an Offer

An **offer** expresses the willingness of the offeror to enter into a contractual agreement regarding a particular subject. It is a promise that is conditional upon an act, a forbearance (a refraining from doing something one has a legal right to do), or a return promise.

CPA 1. Contractual Intention

To make an offer, the offeror must appear to intend to create a binding obligation. Whether this intent exists is determined by objective standards.[1] This intent may be shown by conduct. **For Example,** when one party signs a written contract and sends it to the other party, such action is an offer to enter into a contract on the terms of the writing.

There is no contract when a social invitation is made or when an offer is made in obvious jest or excitement. A reasonable person would not regard such an offer as indicating a willingness to enter into a binding agreement. The test for a valid, binding offer is whether it induces a reasonable belief in the offeree that he or she can, by accepting it, bind the offeror, as developed in the *Wigod* case.

Wigod v. Wells Fargo Bank, 673 F.3d 547 (7th Cir. 2012)

A Valid Offer!

The U.S. Department of the Treasury implemented the federal Home Affordable Mortgage Program (HAMP) to help homeowners avoid foreclosure amidst the sharp decline in the nation's housing market in 2008. In 2009, Wells Fargo Bank issued Lori Wigod a four-month "trial" loan modification under a Trial Period Plan (TPP). After the trial period, if the borrower complied with all of the terms of the TPP agreement, including making all required payments and providing all required documentation, and if the borrower's representations remained true and correct, the servicer, Wells Fargo, had to offer a permanent mortgage modification. Wigod alleged that she complied with these requirements and that Wells Fargo refused to grant a permanent modification. Wells Fargo contended that the TPP contained no valid offer. The trial court dismissed Wigod's claim. Wigod appealed.

JUDICIAL OPINION

HAMILTON, J.…

Valid Offer

… [T]he "test for an offer is whether it induces a reasonable belief in the recipient that he can, by accepting, bind the sender." *Boomer v. AT & T Corp.*, 309 F.3d 404, 415 (7th Cir. 2002); see also Restatement (Second) of Contracts § 24 (1981) ("An offer is the manifestation of willingness to enter into a bargain, so made as to justify another person in understanding that his assent to that bargain is invited and will conclude it.")....

Under contract law principles, when "some further act of the purported offeror is necessary, the purported offeree has no power to create contractual relations, and there is as yet no operative offer." 1 Joseph M. Perillo, *Corbin on Contracts* § 1.11, at 31 (rev. ed. 1993).... Thus, "a person can prevent his submission from being treated as an offer by [using] suitable language conditioning the formation of a contract on some further step, such as approval by corporate headquarters." *Architectural Metal Systems, Inc. v. Consolidated Systems, Inc.*, 58 F.3d 1227, 1230 (7th Cir. 1995) (Illinois law). Wells Fargo contends that the TPP did just that by making a permanent modification expressly contingent on the bank taking some later action.

That is not a reasonable reading of the TPP. Certainly, when the promisor conditions a promise on *his own* future action or approval, there is no binding offer. But when the promise is conditioned on the performance of some act *by the promisee* or a third party, there can be a valid offer. See 1 Richard A. Lord, *Williston on Contracts* § 4:27 (4th ed. 2011) … ("a promisor's sole discretion gives rise to no obligation.... However, the mere fact that an offer or agreement is subject to events not within the promisor's control … will not render the

[1] *Glass Service Co. v. State Farm Mutual Automobile Ins. Co.*, 530 N.W.2d 867 (Minn. App. 1995).

Continued

agreement illusory."); compare *McCarty*, 411 N.E.2d at 942 ("An offer is an act on the part of one person giving another person the legal power of creating the obligation called a contract."), with *Village of South Elgin v. Waste Management of Illinois, Inc.*, 810 N.E.2d 658, 672 (2004) ("A manifestation of willingness to enter into a bargain is not an offer if the person to whom it is addressed knows or has reason to know that the person making it does not intend to conclude a bargain until he has made a further manifestation of assent.").

Here the TPP spelled out two conditions precedent to Wells Fargo's obligation to offer a permanent modification: Wigod had to comply with the requirements of the trial plan, and her financial information had to remain true and accurate. But these were conditions to be satisfied by the promisee (Wigod) rather than conditions requiring further manifestation of assent by the promisor (Wells Fargo). These conditions were therefore consistent with treating the TPP as an offer for permanent modification....

In more abstract terms, then, when Wells Fargo executed the TPP, its terms included a unilateral offer to modify Wigod's loan conditioned on her compliance with the stated terms of the bargain. "The test for an offer is whether it induces a reasonable belief in the [offeree] that he can, by accepting, bind the [offeror]." *Architectural Metal Systems*, 58 F.3d at 1229, citing *McCarty*, 411 N.E.2d at 943; see also 1 *Williston on Contracts* § 4.10 (offer existed if the purported offeree "reasonably [could] have supposed that by acting in accordance with it a contract could be concluded"). Here a reasonable person in Wigod's position would read the TPP as a definite offer to provide a permanent modification that she could accept so long as she satisfied the conditions....

Once Wells Fargo signed the TPP Agreement and returned it to Wigod, an objectively reasonable person would construe it as an offer to provide a permanent modification agreement if she fulfilled its conditions.

[The Court of Appeals determined that Wigod had stated a breach of contract claim.]

Reversed and remanded.

QUESTIONS

1. Is there a valid, binding offer when the promisor conditions the promise on his own future action or approval?
2. Is there a valid offer when the promisor conditions the offer on an action or approval by the promisee or a third party?
3. What is the test to determine if an offer is binding?

(A) Invitation to Negotiate. The first statement made by one of two persons is not necessarily an offer. In many instances, there may be a preliminary discussion or an invitation by one party to the other to negotiate or to make an offer. Thus, an inquiry by a school as to whether a teacher wished to continue the following year was merely a survey or invitation to negotiate and was not an offer that could be accepted. Therefore, the teacher's affirmative response did not create a contract.

Ordinarily, a seller sending out circulars or catalogs listing prices is not regarded as making an offer to sell at those prices. The seller is merely indicating a willingness to consider an offer made by a buyer on those terms. The reason for this rule is, in part, the practical consideration that because a seller does not have an unlimited supply of any commodity, the seller cannot possibly intend to make a contract with everyone who sees the circular. The same principle is applied to merchandise that is displayed with price tags in stores or store windows and to most advertisements. An advertisement in a newspaper is ordinarily considered an invitation to negotiate and is not an offer that can be accepted by a reader of the paper.[2] However, some court decisions have construed advertisements as offers that called for an act on the part of the customer thereby forming a unilateral contract, such as the advertisement of a reward for the return of lost property.

Quotations of prices, even when sent on request, are likewise not offers unless the parties have had previous dealings or unless a trade custom exists that would give the recipient of the quotation reason to believe that an offer was being made. Whether a price quotation is to be treated as an offer or merely an invitation to negotiate is a question of the intent of the party giving the quotation.[3]

[2] *Zanakis-Pico v. Cutter, Dodge, Inc.*, 47 P.2d 1222 (Haw. 2002).

[3] Statutes prohibiting false or misleading advertising may require adherence to advertised prices.

(B) Agreement to Make a Contract at a Future Date. No contract arises when the parties merely agree that at a future date they will consider making a contract or will make a contract on terms to be agreed on at that time. In such a case, neither party is under any obligation until the future contract is made. Unless an agreement is reached on all material terms and conditions and nothing is left to future negotiations, a contract to enter a contract in the future is of no effect. **For Example,** Hewitt Associates provided employee benefits administrative services to Rollins, Inc. under a contract negotiated in 2001 to run through 2006. Prior to its expiration, the parties negotiated—seeking to agree to a multiyear extension of the 2001 agreement. They agreed to all of the material terms of the contract, except that Rollins balked at a $1.8 million penalty clause. Rollins's employees told Hewitt that the extension "was going to be signed." However, Rollins did not sign and the 2001 agreement expired. Hewitt's contention that the agreement was enforceable at the moment Rollins told Hewitt it was going to sign the new agreement was rejected by the court, stating that an agreement to reach an agreement is a contradiction in terms and imposes no obligation on the parties.[4]

2. Definiteness

An offer, and the resulting contract, must be definite and certain.[5] If an offer is indefinite or vague or if an essential provision is lacking,[6] no contract arises from an attempt to accept it. The reason is that courts cannot tell what the parties are to do. Thus, an offer to conduct a business for as long as it is profitable is too vague to be a valid offer. The acceptance of such an offer does not result in a contract that can be enforced. Statements by a bank that it was "with" the debtors and would "support" them in their proposed business venture were too vague to be regarded as a promise by the bank to make necessary loans to the debtors. In the *McCarthy* case, the court was faced with the question of whether a legally enforceable contract had been made where the parties expressed their intent to execute a subsequent purchase and sale agreement.

McCarthy v. Tobin, 706 N.E.2d 629 (Mass. 1999)

Offer to Purchase Is Controlling Legal Document

John McCarthy Jr. brought an action for specific performance against Ann Tobin claiming that the parties created a binding contract when they signed an offer to purchase (OTP) form on August 9, 1995. Robert DiMinico and his wife intervened because they thereafter agreed to purchase the property in question from Ms. Tobin. The trial court granted summary judgment for Tobin and the DiMinicos, which was vacated by the Appeals Court. The Supreme Judicial Court granted further appellate review.

JUDICIAL OPINION

ABRAMS, J.

1. *Firm offer*. The primary issue is whether the OTP executed by McCarthy and Tobin was a binding contract. Tobin and the DiMinicos argue that it was not because of the provision requiring the execution of a purchase and sale agreement. McCarthy urges that he and Tobin intended to be bound by the OTP and that execution of the purchase and sale agreement was merely a formality.

McCarthy argues that the OTP adequately described the property to be sold and the price to be paid. The remaining terms covered by the purchase and sale agreement were subsidiary matters which did not preclude the formation of a binding contract. We agree.

The controlling fact is the intention of the parties.... Tobin argues that language contemplating the execution of a final written agreement gives rise to a strong inference that she and McCarthy have not agreed to all material aspects of a transaction and thus that they do not intend to be bound....

Although the provisions of the purchase and sale agreement can be the subject of negotiation, "norms exist for their customary resolution."...

The interveners argue that McCarthy departed from the customary resolution of any open issues, and therefore manifested his intent not to be bound, by requesting several additions to the purchase and sale agreement. We agree with the Appeals Court, however, that McCarthy's revisions were "ministerial and nonessential terms of the bargain."...

The inference that the OTP was binding is bolstered by the notice printed on the form. McCarthy and Tobin were alerted to the fact that the OTP "create[d] binding obligations." The question is what those obligations were. The DiMinicos argue that the OTP

[4] *Hewitt Associates, LLC v. Rollins, Inc.*, 669 S.E.2d 551 (Ga. App. 2008).

[5] *Norton v. Correctional Medicare, Inc.*, 2010 WL 4103016 (N.D.N.Y. Oct. 18, 2010).

[6] *Peace v. Doming Holdings Inc.*, 554 S.E.2d 314 (Ga. App. 2001).

Continued

merely obligated the parties to negotiate the purchase and sale agreement in good faith. We disagree. The OTP employs familiar contractual language. It states that McCarthy "hereby offer[s] to buy" the property, and Tobin's signature indicates that "[t]his Offer is hereby accepted." The OTP also details the amount to be paid and when, describes the property bought, and specifies for how long the offer was open. This was a firm offer, the acceptance of which bound Tobin to sell and McCarthy to buy the subject property. We conclude that the OTP reflects the parties' intention to be bound.

[The court found that Tobin had waived the August 16 deadline by words and conduct attributable to her, including her lawyer's failure to object to the passage of the deadline and his continued dealing with McCarthy's lawyer to craft an agreement.]...

The judgment is vacated. The case is remanded to the Superior Court for the entry of a judgment in favor of McCarthy's claim for specific performance.

[Judgment for McCarthy]

QUESTIONS

1. State Tobin's position before the court.
2. Were there definite and certain terms agreed to by the parties regarding the purchase to Tobin's property?
3. Evaluate Ms. Tobin's strategy, after signing the OTP, of hiring an attorney to handle the purchase and sale agreement and closing.

The fact that minor, ministerial, and nonessential terms are left for future determination does not make an agreement too vague to be a contract.[7]

The law does not favor the destruction of contracts because that would go against the social force of carrying out the intent of the parties.[8] Consequently, when it is claimed that a contract is too indefinite to be enforced, a court will do its best to find the intent of the parties and thereby reach the conclusion that the contract is not too indefinite. **For Example,** boxing promoter Don King had both a Promotional Agreement and a Bout Agreement with boxer Miguel Angel Gonzalez. The Bout Agreement for a boxing match with Julio Cesar Chavez gave King the option to promote the next four of

Thinking Things Through

The Rules of Negotiations

Business agreements are often reached after much discussion, study, and posturing by both sides. Many statements may be made by both sides about the price or value placed on the subject of the transaction. Withholding information or presenting selective, self-serving information may be perceived by a party to the negotiations as protective self-interest. Does the law of contracts apply a duty of good faith and fair dealing in the negotiation of contracts? Does the Uniform Commercial Code provide for a general duty of good faith in the negotiation of contracts? Are lawyers under an ethical obligation to inform opposing counsel of relevant facts? The answer to all of these questions is no.

The Restatement (Second) of Contracts applies the duty of good faith and fair dealing to the performance and enforcement of contracts, not their negotiation*; so also does the UCC.** The American Bar Association's Model Rules of Professional Conduct, Rule 4.1 Comment 1 requires a lawyer to be "truthful" when dealing with others on a client's behalf, but it also states that generally a lawyer has "no affirmative duty to inform an opposing party of relevant facts."*** Comment 2 to Rule 4.1 contains an example of a "nonmaterial" statement of a lawyer as "estimates of price or value placed on the subject of a transaction."

The legal rules of negotiations state that—in the absence of fraud, special relationships, or statutory or contractual duties—negotiators are not obligated to divulge pertinent information to the other party to the negotiations. The parties to negotiations themselves must demand and analyze pertinent information and ultimately assess the fairness of the proposed transaction. Should a party conclude that

*Restatement (Second) of Contracts §105, comment (c).
**Uniform Commercial Code §1-203.
***American Bar Association Model Rule of Professional Conduct 4.1(a) Comment 1.

[7] *Hsu v. Vet-A-Mix, Inc.,* 479 N.W.2d 336 (Iowa App. 1991). But see *Ocean Atlantic Development Corp. v. Aurora Christian Schools, Inc.,* 322 F.3d 983 (7th Cir. 2003), where letter offers to purchase (OTP) real estate were signed by both parties, but the offers conditioned the purchase and sale of each property upon the subsequent execution of a purchase and sale agreement. The court held that the parties thus left themselves room to walk away from the deal under Illinois law, and the OTPs were not enforced.

[8] *Mears v. Nationwide Mut., Inc. Co.,* 91 F.3d 1118 (8th Cir. 1996).

Thinking Things Through—*Contd.*

the elements of a final proposal or offer are excessive or dishonest, that party's legal option is to walk away from the deal. Generally, the party has no basis to bring a lawsuit for lack of good faith and fair dealing in negotiations.

However, THINKING THINGS THROUGH, the ethical standards for negotiations set forth in Chapter 3 indicate that establishing a reputation for trustworthiness, candor, and reliability often leads to commercial success for a company's continuing negotiations with its customers, suppliers, distributors, lenders, unions, and employees.****

****For a contrary example, consider the following story. The Atlanta Braves baseball team's general manager Frank Wren negotiated with free agent baseball player Rafael Furcal's agent Paul Kinzer. When all terms had been negotiated, Kinzer asked for a written terms-of-agreement sheet signed by the Braves, which to Wren meant an agreement had been reached. Kinzer took the sheet to the L.A. Dodgers, who then reached an agreement to sign the shortstop. Braves President John Schuerholz said, "The Atlanta Braves will no longer do business with that company—ever. I told Arn Tellem that we can't trust them to be honest and forthright." "Braves GM Blasts Furcal's Agents," Associated Press, *The Boston Globe*, December 20, 2008, C-7.

Gonzalez's matches. The contract made clear that if Gonzalez won the Chavez match, he would receive at least $75,000 for the next fight unless the parties agreed otherwise, and if he lost, he would receive at least $25,000 for the subsequent fight unless otherwise agreed. The agreement did not explicitly state the purse for the subsequent match in the event of a draw. The Chavez match ended in a draw, and Gonzalez contended that this omission rendered the contract so indefinite that it was unenforceable. The court disagreed, stating that striking down a contract as indefinite and in essence meaningless is at best a last resort. The court held that although the contract was poorly drafted, the Promotional Agreement contained explicit price terms for which a minimum purse for fights following a draw may be inferred.[9] A court may not, however, rewrite the agreement of the parties in order to make it definite.

(A) Definite by Incorporation. An offer and the resulting contract that by themselves may appear "too indefinite" may be made definite by reference to another writing. **For Example,** a lease agreement that was too vague by itself was made definite because the parties agreed that the lease should follow the standard form with which both were familiar. An agreement may also be made definite by reference to the prior dealings of the parties and to trade practices.

FIGURE 13-1 *Offer and Acceptance*

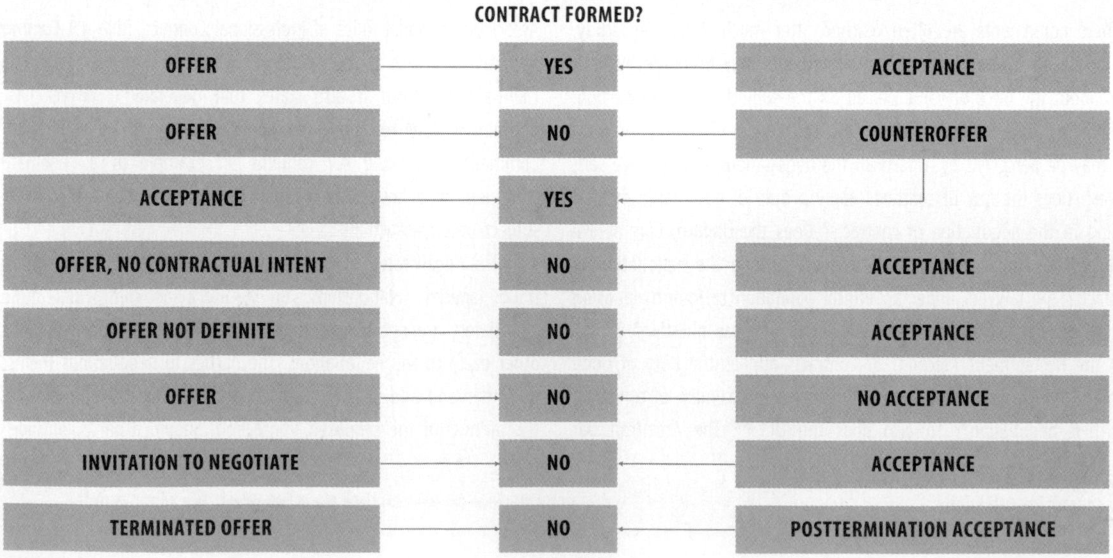

	CONTRACT FORMED?	
OFFER	YES	ACCEPTANCE
OFFER	NO	COUNTEROFFER
ACCEPTANCE	YES	(counteroffer)
OFFER, NO CONTRACTUAL INTENT	NO	ACCEPTANCE
OFFER NOT DEFINITE	NO	ACCEPTANCE
OFFER	NO	NO ACCEPTANCE
INVITATION TO NEGOTIATE	NO	ACCEPTANCE
TERMINATED OFFER	NO	POSTTERMINATION ACCEPTANCE

[9] *Gonzalez v. Don King Productions, Inc.*, 17 F. Supp. 2d 313 (S.D.N.Y. 1998); see also *Echols v. Pelullo*, 377 F.3d 272 (3rd Cir. 2004).

(B) IMPLIED TERMS. Although an offer must be definite and certain, not all of its terms need to be expressed. Some omitted terms may be implied by law. **For Example,** an offer "to pay $400" for a certain Movado timepiece does not state the terms of payment. A court, however, would not condemn this provision as too vague but would hold that it required that cash be paid and that the payment be made on delivery of the watch. Likewise, terms may be implied from conduct. As an illustration, when borrowed money was given to the borrower by a check on which the word *loan* was written, the act of the borrower in endorsing the check constituted an agreement to repay the amount of the check.

(C) "BEST EFFORTS" CLAUSES. While decades ago it was generally accepted that a duty defined only in terms of "best efforts" was too indefinite to be enforced, such a view is no longer widely held. **For Example,** Thomas Hinc, an inventor, executed a contract with Lime-O-Sol Company (LOS) for LOS to produce and distribute Hinc's secret ingredient Stain Remover. Under the contract, Hinc was to receive $10 per gallon sold. The contract contained a clause obligating both parties to use their "best efforts" to market the product "in a manner that seems appropriate." Ultimately, LOS never produced, marketed, or sold Stain Remover for the duration of the contract. The court rejected the defense that the "best efforts" provision was vague and unenforceable stating "[b]est efforts, as commonly understood, means, at the very least *some* effort. It certainly does not mean *zero* effort—the construction LOS urges here to escape any obligation under its contract."[10]

(D) DIVISIBLE CONTRACTS. When the agreement consists of two or more parts and calls for corresponding performances of each part by the parties, the agreement is a **divisible contract**. Thus, in a promise to buy several separate articles at different prices at the same time, the agreement may be regarded as separate or divisible promises for the articles.

(E) EXCEPTIONS TO DEFINITENESS. The law has come to recognize certain situations in which the practical necessity of doing business makes it desirable to have a contract, yet the situation is such that it is either impossible or undesirable to adopt definite terms in advance. In these cases, the indefinite term is often tied to the concept of good-faith performance or to some independent factor that will be definitely ascertainable at some time in the future. The indefinite term might be tied to market price, cost to complete, production, or sales requirements. Thus, the law recognizes binding contracts in the case of a **requirements contract**—that is, a contract to buy all requirements of the buyer from the seller.[11] **For Example,** an agreement between Honeywell International Inc. and Air Products and Chemicals Inc. whereby Air Products would purchase its total requirements of wet process chemicals from Honeywell was held to be an enforceable requirements contract.[12] The law also recognizes as binding an **output contract**—that is, the contract of a producer to sell the entire production or output to a given buyer. These are binding contracts even though they do not state the exact quantity of goods that are to be bought or sold. The *Delphi Corporation* case contains an interpretation of a requirements contract allowing the buyers to control the timing and quantity of deliveries.

In re Delphi Corp., 394 B.R. 342 (S.D.N.Y. 2008)

GM—In The Driver's Seat On Quantity and Timing!

Automodular entered into a series of purchase orders that obligated Delphi to purchase and Automodular to provide all of Delphi's requirements deliverable to the original equipment manufacturer (OEM), General Motors. Automodular receives directions from the OEM's final assembly plants, regardless of whether Automodular is under contract to the OEM or Delphi. The purchase orders ("Contracts") incorporated Delphi's terms that the Buyer, GM, could require Automodular to implement

[10] *Hinc v. Lime-O-Sol Company,* 382 F.3d 716 (7th Cir. 2004).

[11] *Simcala v. American Coal Trade, Inc.,* 821 So.2d 197 (Ala. 2001).

[12] *Honeywell International Inc. v. Air Products and Chemicals, Inc.,* 872 A.2d 944 (Sup. Ct. Del. 2005).

Continued

changes to the specifications or design of the goods or to the scope of any services covered by the Contracts. GM informed Automodular that it needed fewer components and directed Automodular to, among other requirements, reduce shifts, change the assembly line speed, and change the length of workers' shifts (the "Delphi changes"). As a result, Automodular requested a price increase per unit assembled from Delphi because Automodular believed that such an increase was warranted pursuant to the Contract's change-in-scope provision. Delphi, however, refused to negotiate any price increase and the matter was litigated.

JUDICIAL OPINION

MARRERO, D. J. ... In the instant matter, it was the clear intent of the parties to enter into requirement contracts. In a requirement contract, the parties do not fix a quantity term, but instead, the quantity will be the buyer's needs of the specific commodity over the contract's life. Specifically, this intent is demonstrated by language in the Contracts requiring Automodular to supply 100 percent of Delphi's particular subassembly needs, typically at a fixed price. Because the Contracts are requirement contracts, Delphi cannot generally be held liable under the Contracts for mere reductions in volume unless Delphi acted with bad faith. Automodular has not alleged that Delphi acted with bad faith in reducing its requirements, and the record clearly demonstrates that Delphi's reduced requirements were a result of GM's lowered demand, not bad faith on the part of Delphi.

Automodular counters that, although the Contracts may have been requirements contracts, it is entitled to an increase in price because the Delphi Changes altered the scope of services and were not merely reductions in requirements. Section 3 of the Terms states that:

> *Buyer may at any time request [Automodular] to implement changes to the specifications or design of the goods or to the scope of any services or work covered by this Contract, including work related to inspection, testing or quality control.... Buyer will equitably determine any adjustment in price or delivery schedules resulting from such changes....*

Automodular argues that by requiring the Delphi Changes, Delphi effectively altered the scope of the services or work covered by the Terms and that, pursuant to 3 of the Terms, Automodular is entitled to a price adjustment....

Section 2.5 states in relevant part that "[d]eliveries will be made in the quantities, on the dates, and at the times specified by Buyer in this Contract or any subsequent releases or instructions Buyer issues under this Contract," and that "[i]f the requirements of Buyer's customers or market, economic or other conditions require changes in delivery schedules, Buyer may change the rate of scheduled shipments or direct temporary suspension of scheduled shipments without entitling [Automodular] to a price adjustment or other compensation." (*Id.* § 2.5.) This provision demonstrates the intent of the parties to allow the buyer to effectively control the timing and quantity of deliveries without entitling Automodular to an adjustment in price.

...The express language in the Terms clearly demonstrates that the parties entered into requirement contracts, which did not allow for adjustments to price terms based on reductions in requirements.... Automodular is not entitled to a price adjustment pursuant to the Terms....

[Affirmed]

QUESTIONS

1. Ordinarily, in requirement contracts, where the parties do not fix a quantity figure, is the Buyer held liable for breach of contract for reductions in volumes over previous years?
2. When GM directed Automodular to reduce shifts, change assembly line speed, and change the length of workers' shifts, in fairness, was not Automodular allowed, even entitled, to a price adjustment to reflect actual increases in its costs of production?

CPA 3. Communication of Offer to Offeree

An offer must be communicated to the offeree. Otherwise, the offeree cannot accept even though knowledge of the offer has been indirectly acquired. Internal management communications of an enterprise that are not intended for outsiders or employees do not constitute offers and cannot be accepted by them. Sometimes, particularly in the case of unilateral contracts, the offeree performs the act called for by the offeror without knowing of the offer's existence. Such performance does not constitute an acceptance. Thus, without knowing that a reward is offered for information leading to the arrest of a particular criminal, a person may provide information that leads to the arrest of the criminal. In most states, if that person subsequently learns of the reward, the reward cannot be recovered.[13]

[13] With respect to the offeror, it should not make any difference, as a practical matter, whether the services were rendered with or without knowledge of the existence of the offer. Only a small number of states have adopted this view, however.

Not only must the offer be communicated but also it must be communicated by the offeror or at the offeror's direction.

CPA B. TERMINATION OF OFFER

An offeree cannot accept a terminated offer. Offers may be terminated by revocation, counteroffer, rejection, lapse of time, death or disability of a party, or subsequent illegality.

CPA 4. Revocation of Offer by Offeror

Ordinarily, an offeror can revoke the offer before it is accepted. If this is done, the offeree cannot create a contract by accepting the revoked offer. **For Example,** Bank of America (BOA) contended that it had reached a valid settlement agreement on December 17, 2010, with Jonathan Davidoff concerning his lawsuit against BOA seeking damages for slander of credit and breach of contract. At 3:08 P.M. on December 17, 2010, Davidoff revoked his offer to settle the matter. A few minutes later BOA counsel sent by e-mail the settlement agreements signed by the defendants and asked if Mr. Davidoff would "rescind his rejection." Davidoff clearly revoked the settlement offer prior to BOA's delivery of acceptance of the offer and no contract was formed.[14]

An ordinary offer may be revoked at any time before it is accepted even though the offeror has expressly promised that the offer will be good for a stated period and that period has not yet expired.

The fact that the offeror expressly promised to keep the offer open has no effect when no consideration was given for that promise.

(A) WHAT CONSTITUTES A REVOCATION? No particular form or words are required to constitute a revocation. Any words indicating the offeror's termination of the offer are sufficient. A notice sent to the offeree that the property that is the subject of the offer has been sold to a third person is a revocation of the offer. A customer's order for goods, which is an offer to purchase at certain prices, is revoked by a notice to the seller of the cancellation of the order, provided that such notice is communicated before the order is accepted.

(B) COMMUNICATION OF REVOCATION. A revocation of an offer is ordinarily effective only when it is made known to the offeree.[15] Until it is communicated to the offeree, directly or indirectly, the offeree has reason to believe that there is still an offer that may be accepted, and the offeree may rely on this belief. A letter revoking an offer made to a particular offeree is not effective until the offeree receives it. It is not a revocation when the offeror writes it or even when it is mailed or dispatched. A written revocation is effective, however, when it is delivered to the offeree's agent or to the offeree's residence or place of business under such circumstances that the offeree may be reasonably expected to be aware of its receipt.

It is ordinarily held that there is a sufficient communication of the revocation when the offeree learns indirectly of the offeror's revocation. This is particularly true in a land sale when the seller-offeror, after making an offer to sell the land to the offeree, sells the land to a third person and the offeree indirectly learns of such sale. The offeree necessarily realizes that the seller cannot perform the original offer and therefore must be considered to have revoked it.

If the offeree accepts an offer before it is effectively revoked, a valid contract is created.

(C) OPTION CONTRACTS. An *option contract* is a binding promise to keep an offer open for a stated period of time or until a specified date. An option contract requires that the promisor receive consideration—that is, something, such as a sum of money—as the price for the promise to keep the offer open. In other words, the option is a contract to refrain from revoking an offer.

(D) FIRM OFFERS. As another exception to the rule that an offer can be revoked at any time before acceptance, statutes in some states provide that an offeror cannot revoke an offer prior to its expiration when the offeror makes a firm offer. A **firm offer** is an offer that states that it is to be irrevocable, or irrevocable for a stated period of time. Under the Uniform Commercial Code, this doctrine of firm offer applies to a merchant's signed, written offer to buy or sell goods but with a maximum of three months on its period of irrevocability.[16]

[14] *Davidoff v. Bank of America*, 2011 WL 999564 (S.D. Fla. Oct. 18, 2010).
[15] *MD Drilling and Blasting, Inc. v. MLS Construction, LLC*, 889 A.2d 850 (Conn. App. 2006).
[16] U.C.C. §2-205.

5. Counteroffer by Offeree

The offeree rejects the offer when she ignores the original offer and replies with a different offer.[17] If the offeree purports to accept an offer but in so doing makes any change to the terms of the offer, such action is a **counteroffer** that rejects the original offer. An "acceptance" that changes the terms of the offer or adds new terms is a rejection of the original offer and constitutes a counteroffer.[18]

Ordinarily, if *A* makes an offer, such as to sell a used automobile to *B* for $3,000, and *B* in reply makes an offer to buy at $2,500, the original offer is terminated. *B* is in effect indicating refusal of the original offer and in its place is making a different offer. Such an offer by the offeree is known as a *counteroffer*. No contract arises unless the original offeror accepts the counteroffer.

Counteroffers are not limited to offers that directly contradict the original offers. Any departure from or addition to the original offer is a counteroffer even though the original offer was silent on the point added by the counteroffer.

6. Rejection of Offer by Offeree

If the offeree rejects the offer and communicates this rejection to the offeror, the offer is terminated. Communication of a rejection terminates an offer even though the period for which the offeror agreed to keep the offer open has not yet expired. It may be that the offeror is willing to renew the offer, but unless this is done, there is no longer any offer for the offeree to accept.

7. Lapse of Time

When the offer states that it is open until a particular date, the offer terminates on that date if it has not yet been accepted. This is particularly so when the offeror declares that the offer shall be void after the expiration of the specified time. Such limitations are strictly construed. **For Example,** Landry's Restaurant Minnesota Inc. extended a written, signed offer to Starlite L.P. to lease Starlite's real estate for a period of 20 years. The written offer stated that if a fully executed acceptance of the lease is not returned to Landry's Minnesota Inc. within six days of the written offer dated April 30, 1998, "the offer to lease … shall be deemed withdrawn and this lease shall be deemed null and void." Starlite signed and returned the lease agreement on May 11, 1998, five days after the May 6 deadline. Landry's Minnesota occupied the property and built a restaurant on it but vacated the property after nine years. Starlite sued the restaurant's parent corporation, Landry's Restaurants Inc., as guarantor of the lease, seeking payment for past due and ongoing rent. Starlite's lawsuit was not successful as no valid lease agreement existed because no contract could be properly formed when acceptance occurred after the written offer had expired.[19]

If the offer contains a time limitation for acceptance, an attempted acceptance after the expiration of that time has no effect and does not give rise to a contract.[20] When a specified time limitation is imposed on an option, the option cannot be exercised after the expiration of that time, regardless of whether the option was exercised within what would have been held a reasonable time if no time period had been specified.

If the offer does not specify a time, it will terminate after the lapse of a reasonable time. What constitutes a reasonable time depends on the circumstances of each case—that is, on the nature of the subject matter, the nature of the market in which it is sold, the time of year, and other factors of supply and demand. If a commodity is perishable or fluctuates greatly in value, the reasonable time will be much shorter than if the subject matter is of a stable value. An offer to sell a harvested crop of tomatoes would expire within a very short time. When a seller purports to accept an offer after it has lapsed by the expiration of time, the seller's acceptance is merely a counteroffer and does not create a contract unless the buyer accepts that counteroffer.

8. Death or Disability of Either Party

If either the offeror or offeree dies or becomes mentally incompetent before the offer is accepted, the offer is automatically terminated. **For Example,** Chet Wilson offers to sell his ranch to Interport, Inc., for $2.5 million. Five days later, Chet is killed in an aviation accident. Interport, Inc., subsequently writes

[17] *Bourque v. FDIC*, 42 F.3d 704 (1st Cir. 1994).
[18] *McLaughlin v. Heikkila*, 697 N.W.2d 231 (Minn. App. 2005).
[19] *Starlite Limited Partnership v. Landry's Restaurants, Inc.*, 780 N.W.2d 396 (Minn. App. 2010).
[20] *Century 21 Pinetree Properties, Inc. v. Cason*, 469 S.E.2d 458 (Ga. App. 1996).

to Chet Wilson Jr., an adult, that his father's offer is accepted. No contract is formed because the offer made by Chet died with him.

CPA 9. Subsequent Illegality

If the performance of the contract becomes illegal after the offer is made, the offer is terminated. **For Example,** if an offer is made to sell six semiautomatic handguns to a commercial firing range for $550 per weapon but a new law prohibiting such sales is enacted before the offer is accepted, the offer is terminated.

CPA C. ACCEPTANCE OF OFFER

An **acceptance** is the assent of the offeree to the terms of the offer. Objective standards determine whether there has been an agreement of the parties.

10. What Constitutes an Acceptance?

No particular form of words or mode of expression is required, but there must be a clear expression that the offeree agrees to be bound by the terms of the offer. If the offeree reserves the right to reject the offer, such action is not an acceptance.[21]

11. Privilege of Offeree

Ordinarily, the offeree may refuse to accept an offer. If there is no acceptance, by definition there is no contract. The fact that there had been a series of contracts between the parties and that one party's offer had always been accepted before by the other does not create any legal obligation to continue to accept subsequent offers.

CPA 12. Effect of Acceptance

The acceptance of an offer creates a binding agreement or contract,[22] assuming that all of the other elements of a contract are present. Neither party can subsequently withdraw from or cancel the contract without the consent of the other party. **For Example,** James Gang refused to honor an oral stock purchase agreement he made with Moshen Sadeghi under terms he assented to and that were announced on the record to a court as a mutual settlement of a dispute. Gang was not allowed subsequently to withdraw from the agreement, because it was an enforceable contract.[23]

CPA 13. Nature of Acceptance

An *acceptance* is the offeree's manifestation of intent to enter into a binding agreement on the terms stated in the offer. Whether there is an acceptance depends on whether the offeree has manifested an intent to accept. It is the objective or outward appearance that is controlling rather than the subjective or unexpressed intent of the offeree.[24]

In the absence of a contrary requirement in the offer, an acceptance may be indicated by an informal "okay," by a mere affirmative nod of the head, or in the case of an offer of a unilateral contract, by performance of the act called for.

The acceptance must be absolute and unconditional. It must accept just what is offered.[25] If the offeree changes any terms of the offer or adds any new term, there is no acceptance because the offeree does not agree to what was offered.

When the offeree does not accept the offer exactly as made, the addition of any qualification converts the "acceptance" into a counteroffer, and no contract arises unless the original offeror accepts such a counteroffer.

CPA 14. Who May Accept?

Only the person to whom an offer is directed may accept it. If anyone else attempts to accept it, no agreement or contract with that person arises.

If the offer is directed to a particular class rather than a specified individual, anyone within that class may accept it. If the offer is made to the public at large, any member of the public at large having knowledge of the existence of the offer may accept it.

When a person to whom an offer was not made attempts to accept it, the attempted acceptance has the effect of an offer. If the original offeror is willing to accept this offer, a binding contract arises. If the original offeror does not accept the new offer, there is no contract.

[21] *Pantano v. McGowan*, 530 N.W.2d 912 (Neb. 1995).
[22] *Ochoa v. Ford*, 641 N.E.2d 1042 (Ind. App. 1994).
[23] *Sadeghi v. Gang*, 270 S.W.3d 773 (Tex. App. 2008).
[24] *Cowan v. Mervin Mewes, Inc.*, 546 N.W.2d 104 (S.D. 1996).
[25] *Jones v. Frickey*, 618 S.E.2d 29 (Ga. App. 2005).

CPA 15. Manner and Time of Acceptance

The offeror may specify the manner and time for accepting the offer. When the offeror specifies that there must be a written acceptance, no contract arises when the offeree makes an oral acceptance. If the offeror calls for acceptance by a specified time and date, a late acceptance has no legal effect, and a contract is not formed. Where no time is specified in the offer, the offeree has a reasonable period of time to accept the offer. After the time specified in the offer or a reasonable period of time expires (when no time is specified in the offer), the offeree's power to make a contract by accepting the offer "lapses."

When the offeror calls for the performance of an act or of certain conduct, the performance thereof is an acceptance of the offer and creates a unilateral contract.

When the offeror has specified a particular manner and time of acceptance, generally, the offeree cannot accept in any other way. The basic rule applied by the courts is that the offeror is the master of the offer![26]

CPA **(A) Silence as Acceptance.** In most cases, the offeree's silence and failure to act cannot be regarded as an acceptance. Ordinarily, the offeror is not permitted to frame an offer in such a way as to make the silence and inaction of the offeree operate as an acceptance. Nor can a party to an existing contract effect a modification of that agreement without the other party's actual acceptance or approval. **For Example,** H. H. Taylor made a contract with Andy Stricker, a civil engineer, to design a small hotel. The parties agreed on an hourly rate with "total price not to exceed $7,200," and required that additional charges be presented to Taylor prior to proceeding with any changes. Andy was required to dedicate more hours to the project than anticipated but could not present the additional charges to Taylor because Taylor would not return his phone calls. He billed Taylor $9,035 for his services. Taylor's failure to act in not returning phone calls is not a substitute for the assent needed to modify a contract. Stricker is thus only entitled to $7,200.[27]

(B) Unordered Goods and Tickets. Sometimes a seller writes to a person with whom the seller has not had any prior dealings, stating that unless notified to the contrary, the seller will send specified merchandise and the recipient is obligated to pay for it at stated prices. There is no acceptance if the recipient of the letter ignores the offer and does nothing. The silence of the person receiving the letter is not an acceptance, and the sender, as a reasonable person, should recognize that none was intended.

This rule applies to all kinds of goods, books, magazines, and tickets sent through the mail when they have not been ordered. The fact that the items are not returned does not mean that they have been accepted; that is, the offeree is required neither to pay for nor to return the items. If desired, the recipient of the unordered goods may write "Return to Sender" on the unopened package and put the package back into the mail without any additional postage. The Postal Reorganization Act provides that the person who receives unordered mailed merchandise from a commercial sender has the right "to retain, use, discard, or dispose of it in any manner the recipient sees fit without any obligation whatsoever to the sender."[28] It provides further that any unordered merchandise that is mailed must have attached to it a clear and conspicuous statement of the recipient's right to treat the goods in this manner.

CPA 16. Communication of Acceptance

Acceptance by the offeree is the last step in the formation of a bilateral contract. Intuitively, the offeror's receipt of the acceptance should be the point in time when the contract is formed and its terms apply. When the parties are involved in face-to-face negotiations, a contract is formed upon the offeror's receipt of the acceptance. When the offeror hears the offeree's words of acceptance, the parties may shake hands, signifying their understanding that the contract has been formed.

CPA **(A) Mailbox Rule.** When the parties are negotiating at a distance from each other, special rules have developed as to when the acceptance takes effect based on the commercial expediency of creating a contract at the earliest period of time and the

[26] See *1-800 Contacts, Inc. v. Weigner*, 127 P.3d 1241 (Utah App. 2005).
[27] *Stricker v. Taylor*, 975 P.2d 930 (Or. App. 1999).
[28] Federal Postal Reorganization Act §3009.

E-Commerce & Cyberlaw

Contract Formation on the Internet

It is not possible for an online service provider or seller to individually bargain with each person who visits its Web site. The Web site owner, therefore, as offeror, places its proposed terms on its Web site and requires visitors to assent to these terms in order to access the site, download software, or purchase a product or service.

In a written contract, the parties sign a paper document indicating their intention to be bound by the terms of the contract. Online, however, an agreement may be accomplished by the visitor-offeree simply typing the words "I Accept" in an onscreen box and then clicking a "send" or similar button that indicates acceptance. Or the individual clicks an "I Agree" or "I Accept" icon or check box. Access to the site is commonly denied those who do not agree to the terms. Such agreements have come to be known as *clickwrap* agreements and in the case of software license agreements, *SLAs*. The agreements contain fee schedules and other financial terms and may contain terms such as a notice of the proprietary nature of the material contained on the site and of any limitations on the use of the site and the downloading of software. Moreover, the clickwrap agreements may contain limitations on liability, including losses associated with the use of downloaded software or products or services purchased from the site.

To determine whether a clickwrap agreement is enforceable, courts apply traditional principles of contract law and focus on whether the plaintiffs had reasonable notice of and manifested assent to the clickwrap agreement. Failure to read an enforceable clickwrap agreement, as with any binding contract, will not excuse compliance with its terms.

In *Specht v. Netscape Communications Corp.*,* the Internet users were urged to click on a button to download free software, but the offer did not make clear to the user that clicking the download button would signify assent to restrictive contractual terms and conditions. The court, in its 2002 decision, declined to enforce this clickwrap agreement. Internet sellers and service providers generally learned from the *Specht* decision, and most clickwrap agreements now provide sufficient notice and means for clear assent. For example, in *Feldman v. Google, Inc.*,** decided in 2007, the user was unsuccessful in challenging the terms of Google's "AdWords" Program clickwrap agreement. In order to activate an AdWords account, the user had to visit a Web page that displayed the agreement in a scrollable text box. The text of the agreement was immediately visible to the user, as was a prominent admonition in boldface to read the terms and conditions carefully, and with instructions to indicate assent if the user agreed to the terms.

Unlike the impermissible agreement in *Specht*, the user here had to take affirmative action and click the "Yes, I agree to the above terms and conditions" button in order to proceed to the next step. Clicking "Continue" without clicking the "Yes" button would have returned the user to the same Web page. If the user did not agree to all of the terms, he could not have activated his account, placed ads, or incurred charges.

*306 F.3d 17 (2d Cir. 2002).

***Feldman v. Google, Inc.*, 513 F. Supp. 2d 229 (E.D. Pa. 2007). See also *A.V. v. Iparadigms, LLC*, 554 F. Supp. 2d 473 (E.D. Va. 2008).

protection of the offeree. Under the so-called *mailbox rule,* a properly addressed, postage-paid mailed acceptance takes effect when the acceptance is placed into the control of the U.S. Postal Service[29] or, by judicial extension, is placed in the control of a private third-party carrier such as Federal Express or United Parcel Service.[30] That is, the acceptance is effective upon dispatch even before it is received by the offeror.

The offeror may avoid the application of this rule by stating in the offer that acceptance shall take effect upon receipt by the offeror.

CPA **(b) Determining the Applicable Means of Communication.** The modern rule on the selection of the appropriate medium of communication of acceptance is that unless otherwise unambiguously indicated in the offer, it shall be construed as inviting acceptance in any manner and by any medium reasonable under the circumstances.[31] A medium of communication is normally reasonable if it is one used by the offeror or if it is customary in similar transactions at the time and place the offer is received. Thus, if the offeror uses the mail to extend an offer, the offeree may accept by using the mail. Indeed, acceptance by mail is ordinarily reasonable when the parties are negotiating at a distance even if the offer is not made by mail.

CPA **(c) Telephone and Electronic Communication of Acceptance.** Although telephonic communication is very similar to face-to-face communication, most U.S.

[29] See *Adams v. Lindsell*, 106 Eng. Rep. 250 (K.B. 1818). Common law jurisdictions have unanimously adopted the mailbox rule, as has the Restatement (Second) of Contracts §63, and the U.C.C [see U.C.C §1-201(26),(38)].

[30] But see *Baca v. Trejo*, 902 N.E.2d 1108 (Ill App. 2009) whereby an Illinois Court determined that a statute deeming a document to be filed with a state court on the date shown by the U.S. Postal Service cancellation mark—the mailbox rule—does not apply to documents consigned to a private carrier, UPS. The court reasoned that courts should not have the task of deciding which carriers are acceptable.

[31] Restatement (Second) of Contracts §30; U.C.C. §2-206(1) (a).

courts, nevertheless, have applied the mailbox rule, holding that telephoned acceptances are effective where and when dispatched.

The courts have yet to address the applicability of the mailbox rule to e-mail. However, when the offeree's server is under the control of an independent entity, such as an online service provider, and the offeree cannot withdraw the message, it is anticipated that the courts will apply the mailbox rule, and acceptance will take effect on proper dispatch. In the case of companies that operate their own servers, the acceptance will take effect when the message is passed onto the Internet.

Facsimile transmissions are substantially instantaneous and could be treated as face-to-face communications. However, it is anticipated that U.S. courts, when called upon to deal with this issue, will apply the mailbox acceptance-upon-dispatch rule as they do with telephoned acceptances.

(D) Effects of the Mailbox Rule. If an offer requires that acceptance be communicated by a specific date and the acceptance is properly dispatched by the offeree on the final date, the acceptance is timely and the contract is formed, even though the offeror actually receives the acceptance well after the specified date has passed. **For Example,** by letter dated February 18, 1999, Morton's of Chicago mailed a certified letter to the Crab House accepting the Crab House's offer to terminate its restaurant lease. The Crab House, Inc., sought to revoke its offer to terminate the lease in a certified letter dated February 18, 1999, and by facsimile transmission to Morton's dated February 19, 1999. On February 22, 1999, the Crab House received Morton's acceptance letter; and on the same date Morton's received Crab House's letter revoking the offer to terminate the lease. Acceptance of an offer is effective upon dispatch to the Postal Service, and the contract springs into existence at the time of the mailing. Offers, revocations, and rejections are generally effective only upon the offeree's receipt. Morton's dispatch of its acceptance letter on February 18 formed an agreement to terminate the lease, and the fax dispatched on February 19 was too late to revoke the offer to terminate the lease.[32]

17. Auction Sales

At an auction sale, the statements made by the auctioneer to draw forth bids are merely invitations to negotiate. Each bid is an offer, which is not accepted until the auctioneer indicates that a particular offer or bid is accepted. Usually, this is done by the fall of the auctioneer's hammer, indicating that the highest bid made has been accepted.[33] Because a bid is merely an offer, the bidder may withdraw the bid at any time before it is accepted by the auctioneer.

Ordinarily, the auctioneer who is not satisfied with the amounts of the bids that are being made may withdraw any article or all of the property from the sale. Once a bid is accepted, however, the auctioneer cannot cancel the sale. In addition, if it had been announced that the sale was to be made "without reserve," the property must be sold to the person making the highest bid regardless of how low that bid may be.

In an auction "with reserve," the auctioneer takes bids as agent for the seller with the understanding that no contract is formed until the seller accepts the transaction.[34]

LawFlix

Funny Farm (1988) (PG)

Near the end of this Chevy Chase movie, two couples face a formation issue as one couple attempts to purchase a home. An offer, presented around a friendly kitchen table setting, is declined by the sellers. Do the buyers' threats to sue the sellers have any legal basis? While the buyers had made a special trip to see the land and felt that since they were offering more than the asking price that they had a contract, the sellers were free to reject the offer. Listing a house for a price is not an offer; it is an invitation for an offer.

[32] *Morton's of Chicago v. Crab House Inc.*, 746 N.Y.S.2d 317 (2002). *Kass v. Grais*, 2007 WL 2815498 (N.Y. Sup. Sept. 4, 2007).

[33] *Dry Creek Cattle Co. v. Harriet Bros. Limited Partnership*, 908 P.2d 399 (Wyo 1995).

[34] *Marten v. Staab*, 543 N.W.2d 436 (Neb. 1996). Statutes regulate auctions and auctioneers in all states. For example, state of Maine law prohibits an auctioneer from conducting an auction without first having a written contract with the consignor of any property to be sold, including (1) whether the auction is with reserve or without reserve, (2) the commission rate, and (3) a description of all items to be sold. See *Street v. Board of Licensing of Auctioneers*, 889 A.2d 319 ([Me.] 2006).

MAKE THE CONNECTION

SUMMARY

Because a contract arises when an offer is accepted, it is necessary to find that there was an offer and that it was accepted. If either element is missing, there is no contract.

An offer does not exist unless the offeror has contractual intent. This intent is lacking if the statement of the person is merely an invitation to negotiate, a statement of intention, or an agreement to agree at a later date. Newspaper ads, price quotations, and catalog prices are ordinarily merely invitations to negotiate and cannot be accepted.

An offer must be definite. If an offer is indefinite, its acceptance will not create a contract because it will be held that the resulting agreement is too vague to enforce. In some cases, an offer that is by itself too indefinite is made definite because some writing or standard is incorporated by reference and made part of the offer. In some cases the offer is made definite by implying terms that were not stated. In other cases, the indefinite part of the offer is ignored when that part can be divided or separated from the balance of the offer.

Assuming that there is in fact an offer that is made with contractual intent and that it is sufficiently definite, it still does not have the legal effect of an offer unless it is communicated to the offeree by or at the direction of the offeror.

In some cases, there was an offer but it was terminated before it was accepted. By definition, an attempted acceptance made after the offer has been terminated has no effect. The offeror may revoke the ordinary offer at any time. All that is required is the showing of the intent to revoke and the communication of that intent to the offeree. The offeror's power to revoke is barred by the existence of an option contract under common law or a firm offer under the Uniform Commercial Code. An offer is also terminated by the express rejection of the offer or by the making of a counteroffer, by the lapse of the time stated in the offer or of a reasonable time when none is stated, by the death or disability of either party, or by a change of law that makes illegal a contract based on the particular offer.

When the offer is accepted, a contract arises. Only the offeree can accept an offer, and the acceptance must be of the offer exactly as made without any qualification or change. Ordinarily, the offeree may accept or reject as the offeree chooses.

The acceptance is any manifestation of intent to agree to the terms of the offer. Ordinarily, silence or failure to act does not constitute acceptance. The recipient of unordered goods and tickets may dispose of the goods or use the goods without such action constituting an acceptance. An acceptance does not exist until the words or conduct demonstrating assent to the offer is communicated to the offeror. Acceptance by mail takes effect at the time and place when and where the letter is mailed or the fax is transmitted.

In an auction sale, the auctioneer asking for bids makes an invitation to negotiate. A person making a bid is making an offer, and the acceptance of the highest bid by the auctioneer is an acceptance of that offer and gives rise to a contract. When the auction sale is without reserve, the auctioneer must accept the highest bid. If the auction is not expressly without reserve, the auctioneer may refuse to accept any of the bids.

LEARNING OUTCOMES

After studying this chapter, you should be able to clearly explain:

A. Requirements of an Offer

LO.1 Decide whether an offer contains definite and certain terms

See the legal impact of a party's statement that the contract "was going to be signed" in the *Hewitt* example on p. 250.

See the *Wigod* case that discusses the test for a valid, binding offer, pp. 248–249.

B. Termination of an Offer

LO.2 Explain the exceptions the law makes to the requirement of definiteness

See the *Delphi* case on requirements contracts, pp. 253–254.

LO.3 Explain all the ways an offer can be terminated

See the discussion of revocation, counteroffer, rejection, lapse of time, death or disability of a party, or subsequent illegality, starting on p. 255.

See the *Davidoff* example of a revocation communicated to the offeree prior to acceptance, p. 255.

See the *Landry's Restaurants* example that illustrates the effect of an "acceptance" signed just a few days after the written offer had expired, p. 256.

C. Acceptance of an Offer

LO.4 Explain what constitutes the acceptance of an offer

See the *Sadeghi* example where acceptance of an offer created a binding contract, p. 257.

LO.5 Explain the implications of failing to read a clickwrap agreement

See the *Feldman* case as an example of an enforceable clickwrap agreement containing notice and manifested assent, p. 259.

KEY TERMS

acceptance
counteroffer
divisible contract
firm offer
offer
output contract
requirements contract

QUESTIONS AND CASE PROBLEMS

1. Bernie and Phil's Great American Surplus store placed an ad in the *Sunday Times* stating, "Next Saturday at 8:00 A.M. sharp, 3 brand new mink coats worth $5,000 each will be sold for $500 each! First come, First served." Marsha Lufklin was first in line when the store opened and went directly to the coat department, but the coats identified in the ad were not available for sale. She identified herself to the manager and pointed out that she was first in line in conformity with the store's advertised offer and that she was ready to pay the $500 price set forth in the store's offer. The manager responded that a newspaper ad is just an invitation to negotiate and that the store decided to withdraw "the mink coat promotion." Review the text on unilateral contracts in Section 12(B) of Chapter 12. Decide.

2. Brown made an offer to purchase Overman's house on a standard printed form. Underneath Brown's signature was the statement: "ACCEPTANCE ON REVERSE SIDE." Overman did not sign the offer on the back but sent Brown a letter accepting the offer. Later, Brown refused to perform the contract, and Overman sued him for breach of contract. Brown claimed there was no contract because the offer had not been accepted in the manner specified by the offer. Decide. [*Overman v. Brown,* 372 N.W.2d 102 (Neb.)]

3. Katherine mailed Paul an offer with definite and certain terms and that was legal in all respects stating that it was good for 10 days. Two days later she sent Paul a letter by certified mail (time stamped by the Postal Service at 1:14 P.M.) stating that the original offer was revoked. That evening Paul e-mailed acceptance of the offer to Katherine. She immediately phoned him to tell him that she had revoked the offer that afternoon, and he would surely receive it in tomorrow's mail. Was the offer revoked by Katherine?

4. Nelson wanted to sell his home. Baker sent him a written offer to purchase the home. Nelson made some changes to Baker's offer and wrote him that he, Nelson, was accepting the offer as amended. Baker notified Nelson that he was dropping out

of the transaction. Nelson sued Baker for breach of contract. Decide. What social forces and ethical values are involved? [*Nelson v. Baker,* 776 S.W.2d 52 (Mo. App.)]

5. Lessack Auctioneers advertised an auction sale that was open to the public and was to be conducted with reserve. Gordon attended the auction and bid $100 for a work of art that was worth much more. No higher bid, however, was made. Lessack refused to sell the item for $100 and withdrew the item from the sale. Gordon claimed that because he was the highest bidder, Lessack was required to sell the item to him. Was he correct?

6. Willis Music Co. advertised a television set at $22.50 in the Sunday newspaper. Ehrlich ordered a set, but the company refused to deliver it on the grounds that the price in the newspaper ad was a mistake. Ehrlich sued the company. Was it liable? Why or why not? [*Ehrlich v. Willis Music Co.,* 113 N.E.2d 252 (Ohio App.)]

7. When a movement was organized to build Charles City College, Hauser and others signed pledges to contribute to the college. At the time of signing, Hauser inquired what would happen if he should die or be unable to pay. The representative of the college stated that the pledge would then not be binding and that it was merely a statement of intent. The college failed financially, and Pappas was appointed receiver to collect and liquidate the assets of the college corporation. He sued Hauser for the amount due on his pledge. Hauser raised the defense that the pledge was not a binding contract. Decide. What ethical values are involved? [*Pappas v. Hauser,* 197 N.W.2d 607 (Iowa)]

8. *A* signed a contract agreeing to sell land he owned but reserved the right to take the hay from the land until the following October. He gave the contract form to *B*, a broker. *C*, a prospective buyer, agreed to buy the land and signed the contract but crossed out the provision regarding the hay crop. Was there a binding contract between *A* and *C*?

9. A. H. Zehmer discussed selling a farm to Lucy. After a 40-minute discussion of the first draft of a contract, Zehmer and his wife, Ida, signed a second draft stating: "We hereby agree to sell to W. O. Lucy the Ferguson farm complete for $50,000 title satisfactory to buyer." Lucy agreed to purchase the farm on these terms. Thereafter, the Zehmers refused to transfer title to Lucy and claimed they had made the contract for sale as a joke. Lucy brought an action to compel performance of the contract. The Zehmers claimed there was no contract. Were they correct? [*Lucy v. Zehmer,* 84 S.E.2d 516 (Va. App.)]

10. Wheeler operated an automobile service station, which he leased from W. C. Cornitius, Inc. The lease ran for three years. Although the lease did not contain any provision for renewal, it was in fact renewed six times for successive three-year terms. The landlord refused to renew the lease for a seventh time. Wheeler brought suit to compel the landlord to accept his offer to renew the lease. Decide. [*William C. Cornitius, Inc. v. Wheeler,* 556 P.2d 666 (Or.)]

11. Buster Cogdill, a real estate developer, made an offer to the Bank of Benton to have the bank provide construction financing for the development of an outlet mall, with funds to be provided at prime rate plus two percentage points. The bank's president Julio Plunkett thanked Buster for the proposal and said, "I will start the paperwork." Did Cogdill have a contract with the Bank of Benton? [*Bank of Benton v. Cogdill,* 454 N.E.2d 1120 (Ill. App.)]

12. Ackerley Media Group, Inc., claimed to have a three-season advertising Team Sponsorship Agreement (TSA) with Sharp Electronics Corporation to promote Sharp products at all Seattle Supersonics NBA basketball home games. Sharp contended that a valid agreement did not exist for the third season (2000–2001) because a material price term was missing, thus resulting in an unenforceable "agreement to agree." The terms of the TSA for the 2000–2001 third season called for a base payment of $144,200 and an annual increase "not to exceed 6% [and] to be mutually agreed upon by the parties." No "mutually agreed" increase was negotiated by the parties. Ackerley seeks payment for the base price of $144,200 only. Sharp contends that since no

price was agreed upon for the season, the entire TSA is unenforceable, and it is not obligated to pay for the 2000–2001 season. Is Sharp correct? [*Ackerley Media Group, Inc. v. Sharp Electronics Corp.*, 170 F. Supp. 2d 445 (S.D.N.Y.)]

13. L. B. Foster invited Tie and Track Systems Inc. to submit price quotes on items to be used in a railroad expansion project. Tie and Track responded by e-mail on August 11, 2006, with prices for nine items of steel ties. The e-mail concluded, "The above prices are delivered/Terms of Payment—to be agreed/Delivery—to be agreed/We hope you are successful with your bid. If you require any additional information please call." Just three of the nine items listed in Tie and Track's price quote were "accepted" by the project. L. B. Foster demanded that Tie and Track provide the items at the price listed in the quote. Tie and Track refused. L. B. Foster sued for breach of contract. Did the August 11 e-mail constitute an offer, acceptance of which could bind the supplier to a contract? If so, was there a valid acceptance? [*L. B. Foster v. Tie and Track Systems, Inc.*, 2009 WL 900993 (N.D. Ill.)

14. On August 15, 2003, Wilbert Heikkila signed an agreement with Kangas Realty to sell eight parcels of Heikkila's property. On September 8, 2003, David McLaughlin met with a Kangas agent who drafted McLaughlin's offer to purchase three of the parcels. McLaughlin signed the offer and gave the agent checks for each parcel. On September 9 and 10, 2003, the agent for Heikkila prepared three printed purchase agreements, one for each parcel. On September 14, 2003, David's wife, Joanne McLaughlin, met with the agent and signed the agreements. On September 16, 2003, Heikkila met with his real estate agent. Writing on the printed agreements, Heikkila changed the price of one parcel from $145,000 to $150,000, the price of another parcel from $32,000 to $45,000, and the price of the third parcel from $175,000 to $179,000. Neither of the McLaughlins signed an acceptance of Heikkila's changes to the printed agreements before Heikkila withdrew his offer to sell. The McLaughlins learned that Heikkila had withdrawn his offer on January 1, 2004, when the real estate agent returned the checks to them. Totally shocked at Heikkila's conduct, the McLaughlins brought action to compel specific performance of the purchase agreement signed by Joanne McLaughlin on their behalf. Decide. [*McLaughlin v. Heikkila*, 697 N.W.2d 231 (Minn. App.)]

CPA QUESTIONS

1. Able Sofa, Inc., sent Noll a letter offering to sell Noll a custom-made sofa for $5,000. Noll immediately sent a telegram to Able purporting to accept the offer. However, the telegraph company erroneously delivered the telegram to Abel Soda, Inc. Three days later, Able mailed a letter of revocation to Noll, which was received by Noll. Able refused to sell Noll the sofa. Noll sued Able for breach of contract. Able:
   a. Would have been liable under the deposited acceptance rule only if Noll had accepted by mail.
   b. Will avoid liability since it revoked its offer prior to receiving Noll's acceptance.
   c. Will be liable for breach of contract.
   d. Will avoid liability due to the telegraph company's error (Law, #2, 9911).

2. On September 27, Summers sent Fox a letter offering to sell Fox a vacation home for $150,000. On October 2, Fox replied by mail agreeing to buy the home for $145,000. Summers did not reply to Fox. Do Fox and Summers have a binding contract?
   a. No, because Fox failed to sign and return Summers's letter.
   b. No, because Fox's letter was a counteroffer.
   c. Yes, because Summers's offer was validly accepted.
   d. Yes, because Summers's silence is an implied acceptance of Fox's letter (Law, #2, 0462).

3. On June 15, Peters orally offered to sell a used lawn mower to Mason for $125. Peters specified that

Mason had until June 20 to accept the offer. On June 16, Peters received an offer to purchase the lawn mower for $150 from Bronson, Mason's neighbor. Peters accepted Bronson's offer. On June 17, Mason saw Bronson using the lawn mower and was told the mower had been sold to Bronson. Mason immediately wrote to Peters to accept the June 15 offer. Which of the following statements is correct?

a. Mason's acceptance would be effective when received by Peters.

b. Mason's acceptance would be effective when mailed.

c. Peters's offer had been revoked and Mason's acceptance was ineffective.

d. Peters was obligated to keep the June 15 offer open until June 20 (Law, #13, 3095).

Capacity and Genuine Assent

learningoutcomes

After studying this chapter, you should be able to

LO.1 Define contractual capacity

LO.2 Explain the extent and effect of avoidance of a contract by a minor

LO.3 Distinguish unilateral mistakes and mutual mistakes

LO.4 Explain the difference between intentional misrepresentation, negligent misrepresentation, and puffery

LO.5 Explain the difference between undue influence and duress

A *contract* is a binding agreement. This agreement must be made between parties who have the capacity to do so. They must also truly agree so that all parties have really consented to the contract. This chapter explores the elements of contractual capacity of the parties and the genuineness of their assent.

A. Contractual Capacity

Some persons lack contractual capacity, a lack that embraces both those who have a status incapacity, such as minors, and those who have a factual incapacity, such as persons who are insane.

1. Contractual Capacity Defined

Contractual capacity is the ability to understand that a contract is being made and to understand its general meaning. However, the fact that a person does not understand the full legal meaning of a contract does not mean that contractual capacity is lacking. Everyone is presumed to have capacity unless it is proven that capacity is lacking or there is status incapacity.[1] **For Example,** Jacqueline, aged 22, entered into a contract with Sunrise Storage Co. but later claimed it was not binding because she did not understand several clauses in the printed contract. The contract was binding. No evidence supported her claim that she lacked capacity to contract or to understand its subject. Contractual capacity can exist even though a party does not understand every provision of the contract.

(A) Status Incapacity. Over the centuries, the law has declared that some classes of persons lack contractual capacity. The purpose is to protect these classes by giving them the power to get out of unwise contracts. Of these classes, the most important today is the class identified as minors.

Until recent times, some other classes were held to lack contractual capacity in order to discriminate against them. Examples are married women and aliens. Still other classes, such as persons convicted of and sentenced for a felony, were held to lack contractual capacity in order to punish them. Today, these discriminatory and punitive incapacities have largely disappeared. Married women have the same contractual capacity as unmarried persons.

By virtue of international treaties, the discrimination against aliens has been removed.

(B) Factual Incapacity. A *factual incapacity* contrasts with incapacity imposed because of the class or group to which a person belongs. A factual incapacity may exist when, because of a mental condition caused by medication, drugs, alcohol, illness, or age, a person does not understand that a contract is being made or understand its general nature. However, mere mental weakness does not incapacitate a person from contracting. It is sufficient if the individual has enough mental capacity to understand, to a reasonable extent, the nature and effect of what he is doing.[2]

2. Minors

Minors may make contracts.[3] To protect them, however, the law has always treated minors as a class lacking contractual capacity.

(A) Who Is a Minor? At common law, any person, male or female, under 21 years of age was a minor. At common law, minority ended the day before the twenty-first birthday. The "day before the birthday" rule is still followed, but the age of majority has been reduced from 21 years to 18 years.

CPA **(B) Minor's Power to Avoid Contracts.** With exceptions that will be noted later, a contract made by a minor is voidable at the election of the minor. **For Example,** Adorian Deck, a minor, created a Twitter feed titled "@OMGFacts." The feed collected and republished interesting and trivial facts from other sources on the Internet. It was subscribed to by over 300,000 Twitter users, including some celebrities. Spatz, Inc. entered into a joint venture with Deck as described in a written contract signed by both parties, under which Spatz would expand the Twitter feed into a suite of Internet products, including a Web site and a YouTube.com video channel. In an "OMG-moment" prior to his 18th birthday, Deck notified

[1] *In re Adoption of Smith*, 578 So 2d 988 (La. App. 1991).

[2] *Fisher v. Schefers*, 656 N.W.2d 591 (Minn. App. 2003).

[3] *Buffington v. State Automobile Mut. Ins. Co.*, 384 S.E.2d 873 (Ga. App. 1989).

Spatz, Inc. that he wished to disaffirm the parties' agreement. This disaffirmation by a minor rescinded the entire contract, rendering it a nullity.[4] The minor may affirm or ratify the contract on attaining majority by performing the contract, by expressly approving the contract, or by allowing a reasonable time to lapse without avoiding the contract.

CPA ***(1) What Constitutes Avoidance?***

A minor may avoid or *disaffirm* a contract by any expression of an intention to repudiate the contract. Any act inconsistent with the continuing validity of the contract is also an avoidance.

CPA ***(2) Time for Avoidance.***

A minor can disaffirm a contract only during minority and for a reasonable time after attaining majority. After the lapse of a reasonable time, the contract is deemed ratified and cannot be avoided by the minor.

CPA ***(3) Minor's Misrepresentation of Age.***

Generally, the fact that the minor has misrepresented his or her age does not affect the minor's power to disaffirm the contract. Some states hold that such fraud of a minor bars contract avoidance. Some states permit the minor to disaffirm the contract in such a case but require the minor to pay for any damage to the property received under the contract.

In any case, the other party to the contract may disaffirm it because of the minor's fraud.

CPA **(c) Restitution by Minor after Avoidance.** When a minor disaffirms a contract, the question arises as to what the minor must return to the other contracting party.

(1) Original Consideration Intact.

When a minor still has what was received from the other party, the minor, on avoiding the contract, must return it to the other party or offer to do so. That is, the minor must put things back to the original position or, as it is called, restore the **status quo ante**.

(2) Original Consideration Damaged or Destroyed.

What happens if the minor cannot return what has been received because it has been spent, used, damaged, or destroyed? The minor's right to disaffirm the contract is not affected. The minor can still disaffirm the contract and is required to return only what remains. The fact that nothing remains or that what remains is damaged does not bar the right to disaffirm the contract. In states that follow the common law rule, minors can thus refuse to pay for what has been received under a contract or can get back what had been paid or given even though they do not have anything to return or return property in a damaged condition. There is, however, a trend to limit this rule.

(d) Recovery of Property by Minor on Avoidance. When a minor disaffirms a contract, the other contracting party must return the money received. Any property received from the minor must also be returned. If the property has been sold to a third person who did not know of the original seller's minority, the minor cannot get the property back. In such cases, however, the minor is entitled to recover the property's monetary value or the money received by the other contracting party.

CPA **(e) Contracts for Necessaries.** A minor can disaffirm a contract for necessaries but must pay the reasonable value for furnished necessaries.

(1) What Constitutes Necessaries?

Originally, **necessaries** were limited to those things absolutely necessary for the sustenance and shelter of the minor. Thus limited, the term would extend only to food, clothing, and lodging. In the course of time, the rule was relaxed to extend generally to things relating to the health, education, and comfort of the minor. Thus, the rental of a house used by a married minor is a necessary.

(2) Liability of Parent or Guardian.

When a third person supplies the parents or guardian of a minor with goods or services that the minor needs, the minor is not liable for these necessaries because the third person's contract is with the parent or guardian, not with the minor.

When necessary medical care is provided a minor, a parent is liable at common law for the medical expenses provided the minor child. However, at common law, the child can be held contractually liable for her necessary medical expenses when the parent is unable or unwilling to pay. In the *Schmidt* case, the court dealt with the public policy considerations behind this rule.

[4] *Deck v. Spatz, Inc.*, 2011 WL 775067 (E.D. Cal. Sept. 27, 2011).

Schmidt v. Prince George's Hospital, 784 A. 2d 1112 (Md. 2001)

The Concussion and Legal Repercussion

On March 7, 1997, 16-year-old Michelle Schmidt was involved in a two-vehicle auto collision. She was transported to the Shock Trauma Unit at Prince George's Hospital, where she was initially admitted as "Jane Doe," without an emergency contact person or telephone number, because she was unconscious at the time of arrival. Although the hospital later was able to identify her name and address, it was only able to determine that her father was "Mr. Schmidt," and it obtained a telephone number for him. Due to the severity of her injuries sustained in the collision, the hospital provided necessary emergency medical care for a brain concussion and an open scalp wound. As of her discharge on March 8, 1997, she had incurred hospital expenses in the amount of $1,756.24. Ms. Schmidt was insured with personal injury protection (PIP) benefits through her father's insurance company, Erie Insurance Group. Erie issued a check in the amount of $1,756.24 to "Lewis A. Schmidt for Minor, Michelle Schmidt" in reference to "Prince George's Hospital Center, Service Date 03-07-1997 to 03-08-1997." The check was negotiated, but the funds were not used to pay the hospital; rather, the funds apparently were used to purchase a replacement automobile for Ms. Schmidt. After Ms. Schmidt attained her eighteenth birthday and failed to pay the hospital, it brought suit against her. From a judgement for the hospital, she appealed to the seven justice Court of Appeals.

JUDICIALOPINION

HARRELL, J....

A.

In the absence of a statute to the contrary, the prevailing modern rule is that a minor's contracts are voidable; nevertheless, it also is well established that a minor may be liable for the value of necessaries furnished to him or her. This doctrine, eponymously referred to as the doctrine of necessaries, is well recognized in Maryland law. In *Monumental Building Association v Herman*, 33 Md. 128, (1870), our venerable predecessor explained somewhat the breadth and application of this doctrine.

By the common law, persons, under the age of twenty-one years* are not bound by their contracts, *except for necessaries,* nor can they do any act, to the injury of their property, which they may not avoid, when arrived at full age.

...Infants have this indulgence from their supposed want of judgment in their transactions with others, and the law takes this care of them to prevent them from being imposed upon, or overreached by persons of more years and experience.

They are allowed to contract for their benefit with power in most cases, to recede from their contract when it may prove prejudicial to them, *but in their contract for necessaries, such as board, apparel, medical aid, teaching and instruction, and other necessaries, they are absolutely bound, and may be sued and charged in execution;* but it must appear that the things were absolutely necessary, and suitable to their circumstances, and whoever trusts them does so at his peril, or as it is said, deals with them at arms' length.

Their power, thus to contract for necessaries, is for their benefit, because the procurement of these things is essential to their existence, and if they were not permitted so to bind themselves they might suffer. *Monumental,* 33 Md. at 131–32 (emphasis added)....

The rationales underlying [named precedent cases] recognize that public policy and justice demand that an injured minor have the right to recover incurred medical expenses from a third-party tortfeasor, where the child's parents are unable or unwilling to pay for those expenses, *because the medical provider may sue to recover them,* either during the child's minority or within the statute of limitations after the child has reached the age of majority. By parity of reasoning, it would seem that such a child, upon attaining adulthood, may be liable in contract to pay for medical necessaries provided to him or her while a minor, if the parents were unable or unwilling to pay for such necessaries. Before we may reach such a holding, however, it seems prudent to examine how, if at all, our sister states regard the unwillingness prong of this aspect of the doctrine of necessaries.

B.

There appears to be no case elsewhere that supplies a user-friendly, all-purpose definition or scope of the term "unwilling to pay" in connection with the doctrine of necessaries. The vast majority of these cases share two common traits; they are bereft of detailed or substantive analysis of the "unwillingness" standard, and the varying outcomes are largely fact-driven....

Some states appear to hold that, in order to find a parent "unwilling," thus making a child liable for his or her necessaries, a court should require hard and fast proof of default by the parents. Those states note that in order to meet the requirement of "unwilling," it must be shown that a parent was billed and/or sued and still refused to pay. We shall not subscribe to that requirement as an essential prerequisite to a finding of unwillingness.

There are a significant number of states that interpret their version of the doctrine of necessaries as placing liability on a child *only* when his or her parents are financially unable to pay....

...Overweighing the arguable unfairness to the minor in the balancing, at least in the present case, is the consideration of not placing hospitals and other emergency health care providers in a situation where apparently financially-able

*Effective 1 July 1973, the age of majority in Maryland was reduced from 21 to 18 years of age. Maryland Code (1957, 1998 Repl. Vol.), Art. I § 24.

Continued

individuals may avoid paying for necessary medical treatment through a contrivance similar to that demonstrated on the record of this case.

...The doctrine of necessaries states that a minor may be held liable for the necessaries, including medical necessaries, which he or she is afforded when his or her parents are either unable or unwilling to pay. Consistent with this principle, Respondent, on the present facts, could have: (a) sued Petitioner, while she was still a minor, and her father; or, (b), as was done in the present case, sued Petitioner upon her reaching the age of majority.

...The father's refusal to apply the insurance proceeds to the debt owed Respondent—the existence of which he was well aware of as it was the facial premise for which he and Petitioner supplied to Erie in the first place—is a clear indication of his unwillingness to pay for Petitioner's medical expenses at a time fairly contemporaneous with the provision of the medical services, i.e., within 60 days. We agree with the Circuit Court, which found that, as an adult, Petitioner is liable for the medical treatment expenses which she incurred while a minor. We find no error in the Circuit Court's conclusions that Petitioner could be held liable for those medical expenditures provided for her benefit under the doctrine of necessaries, which trumps her defense that she was under the disability of minority when she entered into the implied promise to pay Respondent for the needed medical treatment. Lastly, we agree that the record supports that Petitioner's father was unwilling to pay for his then minor daughter's medical necessaries, which, in turn, left Petitioner primarily liable for the debt to Respondent.**

[Judgment affirmed]

**On this record, Petitioner may have been able to implead her father in this litigation, whose parental duties during Petitioner's minority included paying for her necessaries, such as the medical expenses in issue. If Petitioner's father was able, but merely unwilling, to pay for her medical necessaries, it would not violate public policy for Petitioner, as an adult, to sue her parent for failure to provide for her necessaries...

DISSENTING OPINION

RAKER, J., dissenting, joined by BELL, C. J., and ELDRIDGE, J.:

The majority finds petitioner liable to respondent because her father was *unwilling* to pay for petitioner's medical expenses, not because her father was *unable* to pay....The majority believes that the father's failure to use insurance proceeds to pay the hospital for his daughter's medical bills is a "clear indication" of his unwillingness to pay for petitioner's medical expenses. There is little case law in this State, or any other state, to help us decide when a parent is unwilling to pay for his or her child's necessary medical costs. What little law there is, however, suggests that where a child is supported by his or her parents, the parents' failure or default on single necessary expense does not usually render the child liable for that expense.

QUESTIONS

1. What is the historical policy basis for the modern rule that minors' contracts are voidable; and what is the basis for the exception that minors may be liable for necessaries?
2. In layperson's terms, explain the public policy utilized to support the court's decision to hold Ms. Schmidt liable for the unpaid emergency care provided to her while she was a minor.
3. What is the dissent's view of the case?

CPA **(F) RATIFICATION OF FORMER MINOR'S VOIDABLE CONTRACT.** A former minor cannot disaffirm a contract that has been ratified after reaching majority.[5]

CPA ***(1) What Constitutes Ratification?***
Ratification consists of any words or conduct of the former minor manifesting an intent to be bound by the terms of a contract made while a minor.

CPA ***(2) Form of Ratification.***
Generally, no special form is required for ratification of a minor's voidable contract, although in some states a written ratification or declaration of intention is required.

CPA ***(3) Time for Ratification.***
A person can disaffirm a contract any time during minority and for a reasonable time after that but, of

[5] *Fletcher v. Marshall*, 632 N.E.2d 1105 (Ill. App. 1994).

necessity, can ratify a contract only after attaining majority. The minor must have attained majority, or the ratification would itself be regarded as voidable.

(G) CONTRACTS THAT MINORS CANNOT AVOID. Statutes in many states deprive a minor of the right to avoid an educational loan;[6] a contract for medical care; a contract made while running a business; a contract approved by a court; a contract made in performance of a legal duty; and a contract relating to bank accounts, insurance policies, or corporate stock.

(H) LIABILITY OF THIRD PERSON FOR A MINOR'S CONTRACT. The question arises as to whether parents are bound by the contract of their minor child. The question of whether a person cosigning a minor's contract is bound if the contract is avoided also arises.

(1) Liability of Parent.

Ordinarily, a parent is not liable on a contract made by a minor child. The parent may be liable, however, if the child is acting as the agent of the parent in making the contract. Also, the parent is liable to a seller for the reasonable value of necessaries supplied by the seller to the child if the parent had deserted the child.

(2) Liability of Cosigner.

When the minor makes a contract, another person, such as a parent or a friend, may sign along with the minor to make the contract more acceptable to the third person.

With respect to the other contracting party, the cosigner is bound independently of the minor. Consequently, if the minor disaffirms the contract, the cosigner remains bound by it. When the debt to the creditor is actually paid, the obligation of the cosigner is discharged.

If the minor disaffirms a sales contract but does not return the goods, the cosigner remains liable for the purchase price.

3. Mentally Incompetent Persons

A person with a mental disorder may be so disabled as to lack capacity to make a contract. An individual seeking to avoid the consequences of a contract due to incompetency must demonstrate that at the time the agreement was executed he or she was suffering from a mental illness or defect, which rendered the party incapable of comprehending the nature of the transaction, or that by reason of mental illness the party was unable to control his or her conduct.[7] **For Example,** a guardian established that Ms. Brunson suffered from a mental illness at the time the challenged mortgage documents were executed, and the contract was set aside by the court.[8] However, where a guardian's evidence was insufficient to demonstrate that at the time two mortgage transactions occurred, one in 1999 for $212,000 and a second in 2003 for $7,628.08, that Mr. and Mrs. Haedrich were incompetent or that Washington Mutual Bank knew or was put on notice of their purported incapacity, the court refused to vacate the judgments of foreclosure.[9]

(A) EFFECT OF INCOMPETENCY. An incompetent person may ordinarily avoid a contract in the same manner as a minor. Upon the removal of the disability (that is, upon becoming competent), the formerly incompetent person can either ratify or disaffirm the contract.

A mentally incompetent person or his estate is liable for the reasonable value of all necessaries furnished that individual.

A current trend in the law is to treat an incompetent person's contract as binding when its terms and the surrounding circumstances are reasonable and the person is unable to restore the other contracting party to the status quo ante.

(B) APPOINTMENT OF GUARDIAN. If a court appoints a guardian for the incompetent person, a contract made by that person before the appointment may be ratified or, in some cases, disaffirmed by the guardian. If the incompetent person makes a contract after a guardian has been appointed, the contract is void and not merely voidable.

4. Intoxicated Persons

The capacity of a party to contract and the validity of the contract are not affected by the party's being

[6] A Model Student Capacity to Borrow Act makes educational loans binding on minors in Arizona, Mississippi, New Mexico, North Dakota, Oklahoma, and Washington. This act was reclassified from a uniform act to a model act by the Commissioners on Uniform State Law, indicating that uniformity was viewed as unimportant and that the matter was primarily local in character.

[7] *Horrell v. Horrell*, 900 N.Y.S. 2d 666 (2d Dept. 2010).

[8] *In re* Doar, 900 N.Y.S. 2d 593 (Sup. Ct. Queens Co., Dec. 18, 2009).

[9] *JP Morgan Chase Bank v. Haedrich*, 918 N.Y.S. 2d 398 (Sup. Ct. Nassau County, Oct. 15, 2010).

impaired by alcohol at the time of making the contract so long as the party knew that a contract was being made.

If the degree of intoxication is such that a person does not know that a contract is being made, the contract is voidable by that person. On becoming sober, the individual may avoid or rescind the contract. However, an unreasonable delay in taking steps to set aside a known contract entered into while intoxicated may bar the intoxicated person from asserting this right.[10]

Excessive intoxication is a viable defense to contracts arising between casinos and their patrons. Thus, when a casino comes to court to enforce a marker debt against a patron, it seeks to enforce a contractual debt, and the patron is entitled to raise the common law defense that his capacity to contract was impaired by voluntary intoxication.[11]

The courts treat impairment caused by the use of drugs the same as impairment caused by the excessive use of alcohol.

CPA B. Mistake

The validity of a contract may be affected by the fact that one or both of the parties made a mistake. In some cases, the mistake may be caused by the misconduct of one of the parties.

5. Unilateral Mistake

A *unilateral mistake*—that is, a mistake by only one of the parties—as to a fact does not affect the contract when the mistake is unknown to the other contracting party.[12] When a contract is made on the basis of a

FIGURE 14-1 *Avoidance of Contract*

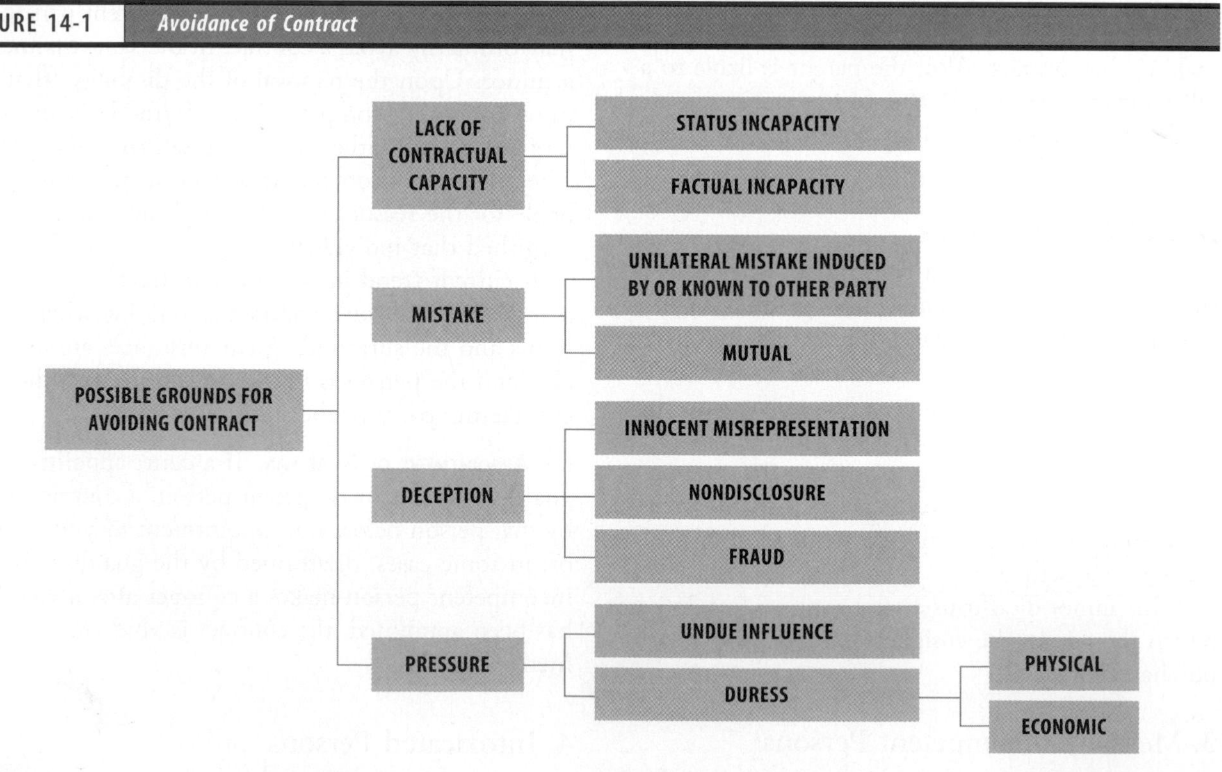

[10] *Diedrich v. Diedrich*, 424 N.W.2d 580 (Minn. App. 1988).
[11] See *Adamar of New Jersey v. Luber*, 2011 WL1325978 (D. N.J. Mar. 30, 2011).
[12] *Truck South Inc. v. Patel*, 528 S.E.2d 424 (S.C. 2000).

quoted price, the validity of the contract is not affected by the fact that the party furnishing the quotation made a mathematical mistake in computing the price if there was no reason for the other party to recognize that there had been a mistake.[13] The party making the mistake may avoid the contract if the other contracting party knew or should have known of the mistake.

6. Mutual Mistake

When both parties enter into a contract under a mutually mistaken understanding concerning a basic assumption of fact or law on which the contract is made, the contract is voidable by the adversely affected party if the mistake has a material effect on the agreed exchange.[14]

A contract based on *a mutual mistake in judgment* is not voidable by the adversely affected party. **For Example,** if both parties believe that a colt is not fast enough to develop into a competitive race horse and effect a sale accordingly, when the animal later develops into the winner of the Preakness as a three-year-old, the seller cannot rescind the contract based on mutual mistake because the mutual mistake was a mistake in judgment. In contrast, when two parties to a contract believe a cow to be barren at the time they contract for its sale, but before delivery of the animal to the buyer, it is discovered that the assumption was mistaken, such is a mutual mistake of fact making the contract void.[15]

7. Mistake in the Transcription or Printing of the Contract: Reformation

In some instances, the parties make an oral agreement, and in the process of committing it to writing or printing it from a manuscript, a phrase, term, or segment is inadvertently left out of the final, signed document. The aggrieved party may petition the court to **reform** the contract to reflect the actual agreement of the parties. However, the burden of proof is heightened to clear and convincing evidence that such a mistake was made. **For Example,** Jewell Coke Co. used an illustration to explain a complex pricing formula in its negotiations with the ArcelMittal steel mill in Cleveland, Ohio, for a long-term contract for the supply of blast furnace coke. The multiplier in the illustration was the actual intent of the parties, according to ArcelMittal, but during the drafting process the multiplier was accidently inverted, resulting in an overpayment of $100,000,000 when discovered, and which potentially could result in an overpayment of over $1 billion over the life of the contract. If proven, the court will reform the contract to reflect the intentions of the parties at the time the contract was made.[16]

C. Deception

One of the parties may have been misled by a fraudulent statement. In such situations, there is no true or genuine assent to the contract, and it is voidable at the innocent party's option.

8. Intentional Misrepresentation

Fraud is a generic term embracing all multifarious means that human ingenuity can devise and that are resorted to by one individual to get advantage over another. It is classified in the law as a *tort.* However, where a party is induced into making a contract by a material misrepresentation of fact, this form of fraudulent activity adversely affects the genuineness of the assent of the innocent party, and this type of fraud is the focus of our discussion in the chapters on contracts.

9. Fraud

Fraud is the making of a material misrepresentation (or false statement) of fact with (1) knowledge of its falsity or reckless indifference to its truth, (2) the intent that the listener rely on it, (3) the result that the listener does so rely, and (4) the consequence that the listener is harmed.[17]

To prove fraud, there must be a material misrepresentation of fact. Such a misrepresentation is one that is likely to induce a reasonable person to assent to a contract. **For Example,** Traci Hanson-Suminski purchased a used Honda Civic from Arlington Acura

[13] *Procan Construction Co. v. Oceanside Development Corp.*, 539 N.Y.S.2d 437 (App. Div. 2d 1989).

[14] See *Browning v. Howerton*, 966 P.2d 367 (Wash. App. 1998).

[15] See *Sherwood v. Walker*, 66 Mich. 568 (1887).

[16] *ArcelMittal Cleveland, Inc. v. Jewell Coke Co.*, 750 F. Supp. 2d 839 (N.D. Ohio 2010).

[17] *Maack v. Resource Design & Construction, Inc.*, 875 P.2d 570 (Utah 1994); *Bortz v. Noon*, 729 A.2d 555 (Pa. 1999).

for $10,899. On a test drive with salesperson Mike Dobin, Traci noticed a vibration in the steering wheel and asked if the car had been in an accident. Dobin said, "No, it's fine." The dealer put new tires on the car and Traci bought it. Traci testified that she would not have purchased the car if she had known it had been in an accident. Eight months later when she sought to trade the car for another car, she was shown a Carfax Vehicle History Report which indicated the car had been in an accident. The dealer testified that all its sales associates are trained to respond to questions about vehicle history with "I don't know." It asserted that Dobin's statement was mere puffery. The court found that Dobin's statement was a material misrepresentation of the car's history, inducing the plaintiff to purchase the car. It rejected outright the dealer's assertion of puffery, which it defined as meaningless superlatives that no reasonable person would take seriously.[18]

(A) Statement of Opinion or Value. Ordinarily, matters of opinion of value or opinions about future events are not regarded as fraudulent. Thus, statements that a building was "very good," it "required only normal maintenance," and the "deal was excellent" were merely matters of opinion. Therefore, a court considered the sophistication and expertise of the parties and the commercial setting of the transaction and enforced the contract "as is." The theory is that the person hearing the statement recognizes or should recognize that it is merely the speaker's personal opinion, not a statement of fact. A statement that is mere sales talk cannot be the basis of fraud liability. **For Example,** CEO Bernard Ellis sent a memo to shareholders of his Internet-related services business some four days before the expiration of a lockup period during which these shareholders had agreed not to sell their stock. In the memo, he urged shareholders not to sell their stock on the release date because in the event of a massive sell-off "our stock could plummet." He also stated, "I think our share price will start to stabilize and then rise as our company's strong performance continues." Based on Ellis's "strong performance" statement, a major corporate shareholder did not sell. The price of the stock fell from $40 a share to 29 cents a share over the subsequent nine-month period. The shareholder sued Ellis for fraud, seeking $27 million in damages. The court held that the first half of the sentence in question was framed as a mere opinion as to future events and thus was nonactionable; and as to the characterization of the company's performance as "strong," such a self-congratulatory comment constituted mere puffery on which no reasonable investor would rely.[19]

A statement of opinion may be fraudulent when the speaker knows of past or present facts that make the opinion false. **For Example,** Biff Williams, the sales manager of Abrasives International (AI), sold an exclusive dealership selling AI products to Fred Farkas for $100,000 down and a 3 percent royalty on all gross proceeds. Williams told Farkas, "You have the potential to earn $300,000 to $400,000 a year in this territory." He later added, "We have four dealerships making that kind of money today." Farkas was thus persuaded by the business potential of the territory and executed the purchase contract. He later found out AI had a total of just four distributorships at that time, and the actual earnings of the highest producer was $43,000. Assertions of opinions about the future profit potential alone may not amount to fraud, but the assertion of present fact—that four dealerships were presently earning $300,000 to $400,000 a year—was a material misstatement of fact that made the forecast sales potential for Farkas's territory a material misstatement of fact as well. Because there were reliance and damages, Farkas can rescind the contract based on fraud and recover all damages resulting from it.[20]

(B) Reliance on Statement. A fraudulent statement made by one party has no importance unless the other party relies on the statement's truth. **For Example,** after making thorough tests of Nagel Company's pump, Allstate Services Company ordered 100 pumps. It later sued Nagel on the ground that advertising statements made about the pumps were false. Allstate Services cannot impose fraud liability on Nagel for the advertisements, even if they were false, because it had not relied on them in making the purchase but had acted on the basis of its own tests.

[18] *Hanson-Suminski v. Rohrman Midwest Motors Inc.*, 858 N.E.2d 194 (Ill. App. 2008).
[19] *Next Century Communications v. Ellis*, 318 F.3d 1023 (11th Cir. 2003).
[20] The Federal Trade Commission and state agencies have franchise disclosure rules that will penalize the franchisor in this case. See Chapter 41.

If the alleged victim of the fraud knew that the statements were false because the truth was commonly known, the victim cannot rely on the false statements. When the statements of a seller are so "indefinite and extravagant" that reasonable persons would not rely on them, the statements cannot be the basis of a claim of fraud.[21] Trusting the honesty of salespersons or their disarming statements, an individual may knowingly agree in writing that no representations have been made to him or her, while at the same time believing and relying upon representation, which in fact have been made and in fact are false, but for which the individual would not have made the agreement. However, purchasers cannot assert justifiable reliance on statements made by sellers that directly contradict clear and specific terms of their written contracts.

Trusting the honesty of salespersons or their disarming statements, an individual may knowingly agree in writing that no representations have been made to him or her, while at the same time believing and relying upon representation which in fact have been made and in fact are false, and but for which the individual would not have made the agreement. However, as seen in the *Novare Group, Inc. v. Sarif* case, purchasers cannot assert justifiable reliance on statements made by sellers that directly contradict clear and specific terms of their written contracts.

Novare Group, Inc. v. Sarif, 718 S.E.2d 304 (Ga. 2011)

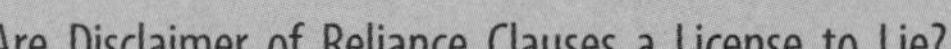

Are Disclaimer of Reliance Clauses a License to Lie?

David Sarif and seven other purchasers (Purchasers) each bought a unit at the 26-story Twelve Atlantic Station (Twelve) condominiums in 2005 and 2006. They sued the developers and the brokers for fraud in the inducement and negligent misrepresentation. They alleged that at the time of their purchases, the developers were advertising "spectacular city views" of Atlanta while they had already undertaken to develop the 46-story Atlantic Station tower directly across the street, and that their brokers were advising the Purchasers that any future development to the south of Twelve would be low- to mid-rise office buildings. Purchasers allege that they paid substantial premiums for their views of the city from the south side of the building, which is now blocked by the 46-story building. Each Purchaser signed an agreement containing a provision stating that "[t]he views from and natural light available to the Unit may change over time due to, among other circumstances, additional development and the removal or addition of landscaping"; a disclaimer at the top of the first page as required by the Georgia Condominium Act stating that "ORAL REPRESENTATIONS CANNOT BE RELIED UPON AS CORRECTLY STATING THE REPRESENTATIONS OF SELLER"; an express disclaimer in which Purchasers affirmed that they did not rely upon any representations or statements of the brokers; and a comprehensive merger clause. The Court of Appeals reversed the trial court's judgment for the defendants, and the Georgia Supreme Court granted *certiorari*.

JUDICIAL OPINION

HUNSTEIN, C.J.... It is well-settled law in Georgia that a party who has "the capacity and opportunity to read a written contract cannot afterwards set up fraud in the procurement of his signature to the instrument" based on oral representations that differ from the terms of the contract. *Craft v. Drake*, 260 S.E. 2d 475 (1979). Statements that directly contradict the terms of the agreement or offer future promises simply cannot form the basis of a fraud claim for the purpose of cancelling or rescinding a contract. *Id.* In fact, the only type of fraud that can relieve a party of his obligation to read a written contract and be bound by its terms is a fraud that prevents the party from reading the contract.

In *Craft*, the plaintiff alleged that a bank officer fraudulently induced him to execute certain notes by misrepresenting that plaintiff's home would not be used as collateral for the note. However, the express terms of the note specifically stated that the holder would have a security interest in any property held by the plaintiff at the time of

[21] *Eckert v. Flair Agency, Inc.*, 909 P.2d 1201 (Okla App. 1995) (seller's statement that house would never be flooded again). But see *Italian Cowboy Partners, Ltd. v. Prudential Insurance*, 341 S.W. 3d 323 (Tex. 2011) where a split decision of the Texas Supreme Court determined that the following contract language was not a disclaimer of reliance to negate the "justifiable reliance" element of a fraud claim.

> *Tenant acknowledges that neither Landlord nor Landlord's agents, employees or contractors have made any representations or promises with respect to the Site, the Shopping Center or this lease except as expressly set forth herein.*

The court determined that the property manager's representations to the future tenant that the building was problem free; no problems had been experienced by the prior tenant; and the building was a perfect restaurant site were false statements of fact known to be false when made. Testimony indicated that the manager herself had personally experienced a sewer gas odor in the prior tenant's restaurant she described as "almost unbearable" and "ungodly."

Continued

execution or subsequently acquired. The Court held that because the oral misrepresentation was directly contradicted by the language of the agreement and because the statements were promissory in nature as to future acts, the plaintiff was bound by the terms of the note he signed. See *Craft*, 260 S. E.2d 475.

The crux of Purchasers' argument here is that they are not bound by the terms of their agreements because Brokers promised "spectacular city views" from the south side of Twelve at the same time that Developers were moving forward with plans to erect a 46-story condominium across the street that would ultimately block Purchasers' views. Nevertheless, Purchasers all signed agreements that expressly state that the views may change over time, oral representations of the sellers could not be relied upon, Purchasers did not in fact rely upon any oral representations or statements of Brokers, and the entire agreement between the parties was set forth in the terms of the written contract.... There is no allegation in this case that Developers or Brokers tried to prevent the Purchasers from reading the terms of the agreements. Rather, the alleged misrepresentation upon which Purchasers premise their fraud claim is simply a promise regarding future events specifically a promise that their views would not be blocked. However, this Court made clear in *Craft* that future promises are not sufficient to sustain fraud-based claims. Purchasers are not entitled to back out of a written agreement whose terms expressly contradict the oral representations on which Purchasers claim to have relied. Accordingly, the Court of Appeals erred in holding that Purchasers were not bound by the agreements they signed ....

Justifiable reliance is an essential element of Purchasers' fraud [and] negligent misrepresentation ... claims. See ... *Real Estate Intl., Inc. v. Buggay*, 469 S.E.2d 242 (1996) (justifiable reliance is essential element of negligent misrepresentation claim). Since Purchasers are estopped from relying on a representation outside of the agreement, they cannot sustain any of the causes of action that require justifiable reliance. Therefore, the fraud [and] negligent misrepresentation ... claims fail, even construing the pleadings most favorably to Purchasers.

[Reversed.]

QUESTIONS

1. May a seller avoid liability for fraud and negligent misrepresentation involving its material misrepresentations of fact that induce a buyer to assent to a contract by having a disclaimer-of-reliance clause in a contract?
2. Knowing that the purchase and sales agreements contained contractual devices designed to negate the element of fraudulent reliance, and thus preclude fraudulent inducement lawsuits, were the developers and brokers accordingly given a license to lie?

(c) Proof of Harm. For an individual to recover damages for fraud, proof of harm to that individual is required. The injured party may recover the actual losses suffered as a result of the fraud as well as punitive damages when the fraud is gross or oppressive. The injured party has the right to have the court order the rescission or cancellation of the contract that has been induced by fraud.[22]

10. Negligent Misrepresentation

While fraud requires the critical element of a known or recklessly made falsity, a claim of negligent misrepresentation contains similar elements except it is predicated on a negligently made false statement. That is, the speaker failed to exercise due care regarding material information communicated to the listener but did not intend to deceive. When the negligent misrepresentation of a material fact that the listener relies on results in harm to the listener, the contract is voidable at the option of the injured party. If fraud is proven, as opposed to misrepresentation, recovery of punitive damages in addition to actual damages can occur. Because it may be difficult to prove the intentional falsity required for fraud, it is common for a lawsuit to allege both a claim of fraud and a claim of negligent misrepresentation.

For Example, Marshall Armstrong worked for Fred Collins, owner of Collins Entertainment, Inc., a conglomerate that owns and operates video games. Collins Entertainment's core product video poker was hurt by a court ruling that prohibited cash payouts, which adversely affected its business and resulted in a debt of $13 to $20 million to SouthTrust bank. Chief operating officer Armstrong, on his own time, came up with the idea of modifying bingo machines as a

[22] *Paden v. Murray*, 523 S.E.2d 75 (Ga. App. 2000).

new venture. To exploit this idea, Collins agreed to form a corporation called Skillpins Inc., that was unencumbered by the SouthTrust debt and to give Armstrong a 10 percent ownership interest. After a period, with some 300 Skillpins machines producing income, Armstrong discovered the revenues from the new venture on the debt-laden Collins Entertainment profit and loss statement, not that of Skillpins, Inc. Armstrong's suit for both fraud and intentional misrepresentation was successful. In addition to actual damages, he received $1.8 million in punitive damages for fraud.[23]

11. Nondisclosure

Under certain circumstances, nondisclosure serves to make a contract voidable, especially when the nondisclosure consists of active concealment.

(A) General Rule of Nonliability. Ordinarily, a party to a contract has no duty to volunteer information to the other party. **For Example,** if Fox does not ask Tehan any questions, Tehan is not under any duty to make a full statement of material facts. Consequently, the nondisclosure of information that is not asked for does not impose fraud liability or impair the validity of a contract.

(B) Exceptions. The following exceptions to the general rule of nonliability for nondisclosure exist.

(1) Unknown Defect or Condition.

A duty may exist in some states for a seller who knows of a serious defect or condition to disclose that information to the other party where the defect or condition is unknown to the other person and is of such a nature that it is unlikely that the other person would discover it. However, a defendant who had no knowledge of the defect cannot be held liable for failure to disclose it.[24]

(2) Confidential Relationship.

If parties stand in a **confidential relationship**, failure to disclose information may be regarded as fraudulent. **For Example,** in an attorney-client relationship,[25] the attorney has a duty to reveal anything that is material to the client's interest when dealing with the client. The attorney's silence has the same legal consequence as a knowingly made false statement that there was no material fact to be told the client.

(3) Active Concealment.

Nondisclosure may be more than the passive failure to volunteer information. It may consist of a positive act of hiding information from the other party by physical concealment, or it may consist of knowingly or recklessly furnishing the wrong information. Such conduct constitutes fraud. **For Example,** when Nigel wanted to sell his house, he covered the wooden cellar beams with plywood to hide extensive termite damage. He sold the house to Kuehne, who sued Nigel for damages on later discovering the termite damage. Nigel claimed he had no duty to volunteer information about the termites, but by covering the damage with plywood, he committed active fraud as if he had made a false statement that there were no termites.

D. Pressure

What appears to be an agreement may not in fact be voluntary because one of the parties entered into it as the result of undue influence or physical or economic duress.

CPA 12. Undue Influence

An aged parent may entrust all business affairs to a trusted child; a disabled person may rely on a nurse; a client may follow implicitly whatever an attorney recommends. The relationship may be such that for practical purposes, one person is helpless in the hands of the other. When such a confidential relationship exists, it is apparent that the parent, the disabled person, or the client is not exercising free will in making a contract suggested by the child, nurse, or attorney but is merely following the will of the other person. Because of the great possibility of unfair advantage, the law presumes that the dominating person exerts **undue influence** on the other person whenever the dominating person obtains any benefit from a contract made with the dominated person.

[23] *Armstrong v. Collins*, 621 S.E.2d 368 (S.C. App. 2005).
[24] *Nesbitt v. Dunn*, 672 So 2d 226 (La. App. 1996).
[25] *In re Boss Trust*, 487 N.W.2d 256 (Minn. App. 1992).

The contract is then voidable. It may be set aside by the dominated person unless the dominating person can prove that, at the time the contract was made, no unfair advantage had been taken.

The class of confidential relationships is not well defined. It ordinarily includes the relationships of parent and child, guardian and ward, physician and patient, and attorney and client, and any other relationship of trust and confidence in which one party exercises a control or influence over another.

Whether undue influence exists is a difficult question for courts (ordinarily juries) to determine. The law does not regard every influence as undue.

An essential element of undue influence is that the person making the contract does not exercise free will. In the absence of a recognized type of confidential relationship, such as that between parent and child, courts are likely to take the attitude that the person who claims to have been dominated was merely persuaded and there was therefore no undue influence.

CPA 13. Duress

A party may enter into a contract to avoid a threatened danger. The danger threatened may be a physical harm to person or property, called **physical duress**, or it may be a threat of financial loss, called **economic duress**.

(A) Physical Duress. A person makes a contract under **duress** when there is such violence or threat of violence that the person is deprived of free will and makes the contract to avoid harm. The threatened harm may be directed either at a near relative of the contracting party or against the contracting party. If a contract is made under duress, the resulting agreement is voidable at the victim's election.

Agreements made to bring an end to mass disorder or violence are ordinarily not binding contracts because they were obtained by duress.

One may not void a contract on grounds of duress merely because it was entered into with great reluctance and proves to be very disadvantageous to that individual.[26]

(B) Economic Duress. Economic duress is a condition in which one is induced by a wrongful act or threat of another to make a contract under circumstances that deprive one of the exercise of his own free will.[27] **For Example,** Richard Case, an importer of parts used to manufacture high-quality mountain bicycles, had a contractual duty to supply Katahdin Manufacturing Company's needs for specifically manufactured stainless steel brakes for the 2013 season. Katahdin's president, Bill Read, was in constant contact with Case about the delay in delivery of the parts and the adverse consequences it was having on Katahdin's relationship with its retailers. Near the absolute deadline for meeting orders for the 2013 season, Case called Read and said, "I've got the parts in, but I'm not sure I'll be able to send them to you because I'm working on next year's contracts, and you haven't signed yours yet." Case's 2014 contract increased the cost of parts by 38 percent. Read signed the contract to obtain the delivery but later found a new supplier and gave notice to Case of this action. The defense of economic duress would apply in a breach of contract suit brought by Case on the 2014 contract because Case implicitly threatened to commit the wrongful act of not delivering parts due under the prior contract, and Katahdin Company had no means available to obtain parts elsewhere to prevent the economic loss that would occur if it did not receive those parts.

LawFlix

Jerry Maguire (1996) (R)

Consider the marriage proposal, its validity, and Dorothy's later statement, "I did this. I made this happen. And the thing is, I can do something about it." What was Maguire's state of mind at the time of the proposal? Consider its possible hypothetical nature and the issues of whether it was a joke and the possible presence of undue influence (the young boy).

Matilda (1996)(PG)

A brilliant little girl with a strong moral compass who tries to instruct her family on many things erudite and her father specifically on what constitutes misrepresentation in selling used cars.

26 *Miller v. Calhoun/Johnson Co.*, 497 S.E.2d 397 (Ga. App. 1998).

27 *Hurd v. Wildman, Harrold, Allen, and Dixon*, 707 N.E.2d 609 (Ill. App. 1999).

MAKE THE CONNECTION

SUMMARY

An agreement that otherwise appears to be a contract may not be binding because one of the parties lacks contractual capacity. In such a case, the contract is ordinarily voidable at the election of the party who lacks contractual capacity. In some cases, the contract is void. Ordinarily, contractual incapacity is the inability, for mental or physical reasons, to understand that a contract is being made and to understand its general terms and nature. This is typically the case when it is claimed that incapacity exists because of insanity, intoxication, or drug use. The incapacity of minors arises because society discriminates in favor of that class to protect them from unwise contracts.

The age of majority is 18. Minors can disaffirm most contracts. If a minor received anything from the other party, the minor, on avoiding the contract, must return what had been received from the other party if the minor still has it.

When a minor disaffirms a contract for a necessary, the minor must pay the reasonable value of any benefit received.

Minors only are liable for their contracts. Parents of a minor are not liable on the minor's contracts merely because they are the parents. Frequently, an adult enters into the contract as a coparty of the minor and is then liable without regard to whether the minor has avoided the contract.

The contract of an insane person is voidable to much the same extent as the contract of a minor. An important distinction is that if a guardian has been appointed for the insane person, a contract made by the insane person is void, not merely voidable.

An intoxicated person lacks contractual capacity if the intoxication is such that the person does not understand that a contract is being made.

The consent of a party to an agreement is not genuine or voluntary in certain cases of mistake, deception, or pressure. When this occurs, what appears to be a contract can be avoided by the victim of such circumstances or conduct.

As to mistake, it is necessary to distinguish between unilateral mistakes that are unknown to the other contracting party and those that are known. Mistakes that are unknown to the other party usually do not affect the binding character of the agreement. A unilateral mistake of which the other contracting party has knowledge or has reason to know makes the contract avoidable by the victim of the mistake.

The deception situation may be one of negligent misrepresentation or fraud. The law ordinarily does not attach any significance to nondisclosure. Contrary to this rule, there is a duty to volunteer information when a confidential relationship exists between the possessor of the knowledge and the other contracting party.

When concealment goes beyond mere silence and consists of actively taking steps to hide the truth, the conduct may be classified as fraud. A statement of opinion or value cannot ordinarily be the basis for fraud liability.

The voluntary character of a contract may be lacking because the agreement had been obtained by pressure. This may range from undue influence through the array of threats of extreme economic loss (called *economic duress*) to the threat of physical force that would cause serious personal injury or damage to property (called *physical duress*). When the voluntary character of an agreement has been destroyed by deception, or pressure, the victim may avoid or rescind the contract or may obtain money damages from the wrongdoer.

LEARNING OUTCOMES

After studying this chapter, you should be able to clearly explain:

A. Contractual Capacity

LO.1 Define contractual capacity

See the example where Jacqueline, age 22, did not understand parts of a storage contract, p. 267.

LO.2 Explain the extent and effect of avoidance of a contract by a minor

See the *Adorian Deck* example where the creator of a Twitter feed, a minor, disaffirmed his joint venture contract, p. 267.

See the *Prince George's Hospital* case where a minor had to pay for medical necessaries, p. 269.

B. Mistake

LO.3 Distinguish unilateral mistakes and mutual mistakes

See the *Jewell Coke Co.* example of a remedy for a billion dollar mistake, p. 273.

See the example of the mutual mistake of fact regarding the fertility of a cow on p. 273.

C. Deception

LO.4 Explain the difference between intentional misrepresentation, negligent misrepresentation, and puffery

See the example of the purchase of the used Honda where the misrepresentation was found to be fraud not puffery on p. 273.

See the *Novare Group, Inc.* decision on the enforceability of disclaimer-of-liability clauses, pp. 275–276.

D. Pressure

LO.5 Explain the difference between undue influence and duress

See the Katahdin bicycle example on economic duress, p. 278.

KEY TERMS

confidential relationship
contractual capacity
duress
economic duress
fraud
necessaries
physical duress
reformation
status quo ante
undue influence

QUESTIONS AND CASE PROBLEMS

1. Lester purchased a used automobile from MacKintosh Motors. He asked the seller if the car had ever been in a wreck. The MacKintosh salesperson had never seen the car before that morning and knew nothing of its history but quickly answered Lester's question by stating: "No. It has never been in a wreck." In fact, the auto had been seriously damaged in a wreck and, although repaired, was worth much less than the value it would have had if there had been no wreck. When Lester learned the truth, he sued MacKintosh Motors and the salesperson for damages for fraud. They raised the defense that the salesperson did not know the statement was false and had not intended to deceive Lester. Did the conduct of the salesperson constitute fraud?

2. Helen, age 17, wanted to buy a Harley-Davidson "Sportster" motorcycle. She did not have the funds to pay cash but persuaded the dealer to sell the cycle to her on credit. The dealer did so partly because Helen said that she was 22 and showed

the dealer an identification card that falsely stated her age as 22. Helen drove the motorcycle away. A few days later, she damaged it and then returned it to the dealer and stated that she disaffirmed the contract because she was a minor. The dealer said that she could not because (1) she had misrepresented her age and (2) the motorcycle was damaged. Can she avoid the contract?

3. Paden signed an agreement dated May 28 to purchase the Murrays' home. The Murrays accepted Paden's offer the following day, and the sale closed on June 27. Paden and his family moved into the home on July 14, 1997. Paden had the home inspected prior to closing. The report listed four minor repairs needed by the home, the cost of which was less than $500. Although these repairs had not been completed at the time of closing, Paden decided to go through with the purchase. After moving into the home, Paden discovered a number of allegedly new defects, including a wooden foundation, electrical problems, and bat infestation. The sales agreement allowed extensive rights to inspect the property. The agreement provided:

   > *Buyer…shall have the right to enter the property at Buyer's expense and at reasonable times…to thoroughly inspect, examine, test, and survey the Property.… Buyer shall have the right to request that Seller repair defects in the Property by providing Seller within 12 days from Binding Agreement Date with a copy of inspection report(s) and a written amendment to this agreement setting forth the defects in the report which Buyer requests to be repaired and/or replaced.… If Buyer does not timely present the written amendment and inspection report, Buyer shall be deemed to have accepted the Property "as is."*

   Paden sued the Murrays for fraudulent concealment and breach of the sales agreement. If Mr. Murray told Paden on May 26 that the house had a concrete foundation, would this be fraud? Decide. [*Paden v. Murray*, 523 S.E.2d 75 (Ga. App.)]

4. High-Tech Collieries borrowed money from Holland. High-Tech later refused to be bound by the loan contract, claiming the contract was not binding because it had been obtained by duress. The evidence showed that the offer to make the loan was made on a take-it-or-leave-it basis. Was the defense of duress valid? [*Holland v. High-Tech Collieries, Inc.*, 911 F. Supp. 1021 (N.D. W.Va.)]

5. Thomas Bell, a minor, went to work in the Pittsburgh beauty parlor of Sam Pankas and agreed that when he left the employment, he would not work in or run a beauty parlor business within a 10-mile radius of downtown Pittsburgh for a period of two years. Contrary to this provision, Bell and another employee of Pankas's opened a beauty shop three blocks from Pankas's shop and advertised themselves as Pankas's former employees. Pankas sued Bell to stop the breach of the noncompetition, or restrictive, covenant. Bell claimed that he was not bound because he was a minor when he had agreed to the covenant. Was he bound by the covenant? [*Pankas v. Bell*, 198 A.2d 312 (Pa.)]

6. Aldrich and Co. sold goods to Donovan on credit. The amount owed grew steadily, and finally Aldrich refused to sell any more to Donovan unless Donovan signed a promissory note for the amount due. Donovan did not want to but signed the note because he had no money and needed more goods. When Aldrich brought an action to enforce the note, Donovan claimed that the note was not binding because it had been obtained by economic duress. Was he correct? [*Aldrich & Co. v. Donovan*, 778 P.2d 397 (Mont.)]

7. James Fitl purchased a 1952 Mickey Mantle Topps baseball card from baseball card dealer Mark Strek for $17,750 and placed it in a safe deposit box. Two years later, he had the card appraised, and he was told that the card had been refinished and trimmed, which rendered it valueless. Fitl sued Strek and testified that he had relied on Strek's position as a sports card dealer and on his representations that the baseball card was authentic. Strek contends that Fitl waited too long to give him notice of the defects that would have enabled Strek to contact the person who sold him the card and obtain relief. Strek asserts that

he therefore is not liable. Advise Fitl concerning possible legal theories that apply to his case. How would you decide the case? [See *Fitl v. Strek*, 690 N.W.2d 605 (Neb.)]

8. Willingham proposed to obtain an investment property for the Tschiras at a "fair market price," lease it back from them, and pay the Tschiras a guaranteed return through a management contract. Using a shell corporation, The Wellingham Group bought a commercial property in Nashville for $774,000 on December 14, and the very same day sold the building to the Tschiras for $1,985,000. The title insurance policy purchased for the Tschiras property by Willingham was for just $774,000. Willingham believes that the deal was legitimate in that they "guaranteed" a return on the investment. The Tschiras disagree. In a lawsuit against Willingham, what theory will the Tschiras rely on? Decide. [*Tschiras v. Willingham*, 133 F.3d 1077 (6th Cir.)]

9. Blubaugh was a district manager of Schlumberger Well Services. Turner was an executive employee of Schlumberger. Blubaugh was told that he would be fired unless he chose to resign. He was also told that if he would resign and release the company and its employees from all claims for wrongful discharge, he would receive about $5,000 in addition to his regular severance pay of approximately $25,000 and would be given job-relocation counseling. He resigned, signed the release, and received about $40,000 and job counseling. Some time thereafter, he brought an action claiming that he had been wrongfully discharged. He claimed that the release did not protect the defendants because the release had been obtained by economic duress. Were the defendants protected by the release? [*Blubaugh v. Turner*, 842 P.2d 1072 (Wyo.)]

10. Sippy was thinking of buying Christich's house. He noticed watermarks on the ceiling, but the agent showing the house stated that the roof had been repaired and was in good condition. Sippy was not told that the roof still leaked and that the repairs had not been able to stop the leaking. Sippy bought the house. Some time later, heavy rains caused water to leak into the house, and Sippy claimed that Christich was liable for damages. What theory would he rely on? Decide. [*Sippy v. Christich*, 609 P.2d 204 (Kan. App.)]

11. Pileggi owed Young money. Young threatened to bring suit against Pileggi for the amount due. Pileggi feared the embarrassment of being sued and the possibility that he might be thrown into bankruptcy. To avoid being sued, Pileggi executed a promissory note to pay Young the amount due. He later asserted that the note was not binding because he had executed it under duress. Is this defense valid? [*Young v. Pileggi*, 455 A.2d 1228 (Pa. Super.)]

12. Office Supply Outlet, Inc., a single-store office equipment and supply retailer, ordered 100 model RVX-414 computers from Compuserve, Inc. A new staff member made a clerical error on the order form and ordered a quantity that was far in excess of what Office Supply could sell in a year. Office Supply realized the mistake when the delivery trucks arrived at its warehouse. Its manager called Compuserve and explained that it had intended to order just 10 computers. Compuserve declined to accept the return of the extra machines. Is the contract enforceable? What additional facts would allow the store to avoid the contract for the additional machines?

13. The Printers International Union reached agreement for a new three-year contract with a large regional printing company. As was their practice, the union negotiators then met with Sullivan Brothers Printers, Inc., a small specialty shop employing 10 union printers, and Sullivan Brothers and the union agreed to follow the contractual pattern set by the union and the large printing company. That is, Sullivan Brothers agreed to give its workers all of the benefits negotiated for the employees of the large printing company. When the contract was typed, a new benefit of 75 percent employer-paid coverage for a dental plan was inadvertently omitted from the final contract the parties signed. The mistake was not discovered until six months after the contract took effect. Sullivan Brothers Printers, Inc. is reluctant to assume the additional expense. It contends that the printed

copy, which does not cover dental benefits, must control. The union believes that clear and convincing evidence shows an inadvertent typing error. Decide.

14. The city of Salinas entered into a contract with Souza & McCue Construction Co. to construct a sewer. City officials knew unusual subsoil conditions (including extensive quicksand) existed that would make performance of the contract unusually difficult. This information was not disclosed when city officials advertised for bids. The advertisement for bids directed bidders to examine carefully the site of the work and declared that the submission of a bid would constitute evidence that the bidder had made an examination. Souza & McCue was awarded the contract, but because of the subsoil conditions, it could not complete on time and was sued by Salinas for breach of contract. Souza & McCue counterclaimed on the basis that the city had not revealed its information on the subsoil conditions and was thus liable for the loss. Was the city liable? [*City of Salinas v. Souza & McCue Construction Co.*, 424 P.2d 921 (Cal. App. 3d)]

15. Vern Westby inherited a "ticket" from Anna Sjoblom, a survivor of the sinking of the *Titanic*, which had been pinned to the inside of her coat. He also inherited an album of postcards, some of which related to the *Titanic*. The ticket was a one-of-a-kind item in good condition. Westby needed cash and went to the biggest antique dealer in Tacoma, operated by Alan Gorsuch and his family, doing business as Sanford and Sons, and asked about the value of these items. Westby testified that after Alan Gorsuch examined the ticket, he said, "It's not worth nothing." Westby then inquired about the value of the postcard album, and Gorsuch advised him to come back later. On Westby's return, Gorsuch told Westby, "It ain't worth nothing." Gorsuch added that he "couldn't fetch $500 for the ticket." Since he needed money, Westby asked if Gorsuch would give him $1,000 for both the ticket and the album, and Gorsuch did so.

    Six months later, Gorsuch sold the ticket at a nationally advertised auction for $110,000 and sold most of the postcards for $1,200. Westby sued Gorsuch for fraud. Testimony showed that Gorsuch was a major buyer in antiques and collectibles in the Puget Sound area and that he would have had an understanding of the value of the ticket. Gorsuch contends that all elements of fraud are not present since there was no evidence that Gorsuch intended that Westby rely on the alleged representations, nor did Westby rely on such. Rather, Gorsuch asserts, it was an arm's-length transaction and Westby had access to the same information as Gorsuch. Decide. [*Westby v. Gorsuch*, 50 P.3d 284 (Wash. App.)]

CPA QUESTIONS

1. A building subcontractor submitted a bid for construction of a portion of a high-rise office building. The bid contained material computational errors. The general contractor accepted the bid with knowledge of the errors. Which of the following statements best represents the subcontractor's liability?
    a. Not liable, because the contractor knew of the errors.
    b. Not liable, because the errors were a result of gross negligence.
    c. Liable, because the errors were unilateral.
    d. Liable, because the errors were material (5/95, Law, #17, 5351).

2. Egan, a minor, contracted with Baker to purchase Baker's used computer for $400. The computer was purchased for Egan's personal use. The agreement provided that Egan would pay $200 down on delivery and $200 thirty days later. Egan took delivery and paid the $200 down payment. Twenty days later, the computer was damaged seriously as a result of Egan's negligence.

Five days after the damage occurred and one day after Egan reached the age of majority, Egan attempted to disaffirm the contract with Baker. Egan will:

a. Be able to disaffirm despite the fact that Egan was *not* a minor at the time of disaffirmance.

b. Be able to disaffirm only if Egan does so in writing.

c. Not be able to disaffirm because Egan had failed to pay the balance of the purchase price.

d. Not be able to disaffirm because the computer was damaged as a result of Egan's negligence (11/93, Law, #21, 4318).

Chapter 15

© Manuel Gutjahr/iStockphoto.com

Consideration

learningoutcomes

After studying this chapter, you should be able to

LO.1 Explain what constitutes consideration

LO.2 Distinguish between a "preexisting legal obligation" and "past consideration"

LO.3 Explain why promises based on moral obligations lack consideration

LO.4 List the exceptions to the requirement of consideration

LO.5 Explain the "fundamental idea" underlying promissory estoppel

Will the law enforce every promise? Generally, a promise will not be enforced unless something is given or received for the promise.

A. General Principles

As a general rule, one of the elements needed to make an agreement binding is consideration.

1. Consideration Defined and Explained

Consideration is what each party to a contract gives up to the other in making their agreement.

(a) Bargained-for Exchange. *Consideration* is the bargained-for exchange between the parties to a contract. In order for consideration to exist, something of value must be given or promised in return for the performance or promise of performance of the other.[1] The value given or promised can be money, services, property, or the forbearance of a legal right.

For Example, Beth offers to pay Kerry $100 for her used skis, and Kerry accepts. Beth has promised something of value, $100, as consideration for Kerry's promise to sell the skis, and Kerry has promised Beth something of value, the skis, as consideration for the $100. If Kerry offered to *give* Beth the used skis and Beth accepted, these parties would have an agreement but not an enforceable contract because Beth did not provide any consideration in exchange for Kerry's promise of the skis. There was no *bargained-for exchange* because Kerry was not promised anything of value from Beth.

(b) Benefit-Detriment Approach. Some jurisdictions analyze consideration from the point of view of a *benefit-detriment approach,* defining *consideration* as a benefit received by the promisor or a detriment incurred by the promisee.

As an example of a unilateral contract analyzed from a benefit-detriment approach to consideration, Mr. Scully, a longtime summer resident of Falmouth, states to George Corfu, a college senior, "I will pay you $3,000 if you paint my summer home." George in fact paints the house. The work of painting the house by George, the promisee, was a legal detriment to him. Also, the painting of the house was a legal benefit to Scully, the promisor. There was consideration in this case, and the agreement is enforceable.

2. Gifts

Promises to make a gift are unenforceable promises under the law of contracts because of lack of consideration, as illustrated previously in the scenario of Kerry promising to give her used skis to Beth without charge. There was no bargained-for exchange because Kerry was not promised anything of value from Beth. A completed gift, however, cannot be rescinded for lack of consideration.[2]

Charitable subscriptions by which individuals make pledges to finance the construction of a college building, a church, or another structure for charitable purposes are binding to the extent that the donor (promisor) should have reasonably realized that the charity was relying on the promise in undertaking the building program. Some states require proof that the charity has relied on the subscription.[3]

An agreement to give property for the consideration of love and affection does not transfer the property to the donee nor secure for the donee a right to sue to compel the completion of the contract. Love and affection alone have not been recognized as consideration for a contract.

Consideration is what distinguishes a contract from a gift. Merely moving into a home with another while engaged in a romantic relationship is not consideration for the formation of a contract giving a half-interest in the property as discussed in the *Williams v. Ormsby* case.

[1] *Brooksbank v. Anderson,* 586 N.W.2d 789 (Minn. App. 1998).
[2] *Homes v. O'Bryant,* 741 So.2d 366 (Miss. App. 1999).
[3] *King v. Trustees of Boston University,* 647 N.E.2d 1176 (Ma. 1995).

Williams v. Ormsby, 966 N.E.2d 255 (Ohio, 2012)

What's Love Got To Do With It...

Amber Williams and Frederick Ormsby lived together in a nonmarital relationship in a house deeded to Ormsby in 2004. The couple separated and attended couples counseling. Amber refused to move back into the house unless Frederick granted her a one-half interest in the property. On June 2, 2005, they signed a document purportedly making themselves equal partners in the home. Amber ended the relationship in September 2007, and she sought specific performance of the June 2, 2005, contract giving her a half-interest in the property. Frederick defended that "love and affection is insufficient consideration for a contract." The trial court determined that the agreement was not supported by consideration but was reversed by the court of appeals. The state supreme court voted to hear the case.

JUDICIAL OPINION

LANZINGER, J. …

DISTINCTION BETWEEN CONTRACT AND GIFT

The trial court concluded that the June 2005 agreement was nothing more than a written gratuitous promise because there was no consideration for that agreement. In fact, the requirement for consideration is what distinguishes a contract from a gift. The essential elements of an inter vivos gift are (1) an intention on the part of the donor to transfer the title and right of possession to the donee, (2) delivery by the donor to the donee, (3) relinquishment of ownership, dominion, and control over the gift by the donor, and (4) acceptance by the donee. Therefore, a gift is a voluntary transfer by the donor to the donee without any consideration or compensation.

Even if we were to construe the June 2005 agreement as a promise to make a gift of one-half interest in the property, we must still examine whether there is consideration, because even a written promise to make a gift is not binding on the promisor if the promise lacks consideration.…

THE JUNE 2005 AGREEMENT

With respect to the … document, signed in June 2005, the trial court found that the writing was not a valid contract, because there was no consideration to support it. The June document … stated that "for valuable consideration," the parties agree that although titled solely in Frederick's name, the house was owned jointly by Frederick and Amber and that they were equal partners. In addition, Amber's name would be placed on the deed at a time she specified, and she could file a lien against the house for her share of the property until it was retitled. This writing required Frederick to pay all expenses on the property, including taxes and insurance. If the house was sold, Amber and Frederick would divide the proceeds from the sale after expenses were paid. Finally, if their relationship ended and they chose not to sell the house, Frederick could elect to keep the house and pay Amber for her share of the property or to leave the house to Amber after being paid for his share.…

Love and Affection Are Not Consideration for a Contract

… [W]e conclude that our decision in *Flanders v. Blandy,* 12 N.E. 321 (1887), is instructive on whether moving into the home with another while engaging in a romantic relationship is consideration for the formation of a contract. In *Flanders,* a father had intended to give his daughter certain bonds worth $2,000 in addition to interest. But the daughter did not receive the bonds as a gift, because they were never delivered to her. Her father then delivered to her a written promise to pay her $2,000 with interest in lieu of the bonds. Upon her father's death, the daughter sought to enforce the written promise, but we held that her father's promise to give her the value of the bonds was not enforceable as a contract, because that promise lacked consideration.

We stated that a gift required a transfer to take effect "for the reason that, there being no consideration therefor, no action will lie to enforce it." *Id.* And we continued to explain why the father's written promise would not be enforced: "[a]n agreement to give *for the consideration of love and affection,* whether the gift is to be of goods and chattels or of a chose in action, *neither transfers the property* to the donee, *nor secures him a right by suit to compel a completion of the contract.*" (Emphasis added.) Thus, for more than a century, love and affection alone have not been recognized as consideration for a contract.…

… The evidence demonstrates that the only consideration offered by Amber for the June 2005 agreement was her resumption of a romantic relationship with Frederick. There is no detriment to Amber in the June 2005 document, only benefit. Essentially, this agreement amounts to a gratuitous promise by Frederick to give Amber an interest in property based solely on the consideration of her love and affection. Therefore, the June 2005 document is not an enforceable contract, because it fails for want of consideration. …

We hold that merely moving into a home with another while engaging in a romantic relationship is not consideration for the formation of a contract. To hold otherwise would open the door to palimony claims and invite a number of evidentiary problems.

[Judgment reversed.]

QUESTIONS

1. In the June 2005 agreement, what consideration did Amber offer in exchange for Frederick's granting her a half-interest in the property?
2. Is love and affection alone consideration for a contract?

3. Adequacy of Consideration

Ordinarily, courts do not consider the adequacy of the consideration given for a promise. The fact that the consideration supplied by one party is slight when compared with the burden undertaken by the other party is immaterial. It is a matter for the parties to decide when they make their contract whether each is getting a fair return. In the absence of fraud or other misconduct, courts usually will not interfere to make sure that each side is getting a fair return.

Because the adequacy of consideration is ignored, it is immaterial that consideration is so slight that the transaction is in part a "gift." However, the Internal Revenue Service may view a given transaction as part consideration, part gift, and assess a gift tax as appropriate.

The fact that the consideration turns out to be disappointing does not affect the binding character of the contract. Thus, the fact that a business purchased by a group of investors proves unprofitable does not constitute a failure of consideration that releases the buyers from their obligation to the seller.

4. Forbearance as Consideration

In most cases, consideration consists of the performance of an act such as providing a service, or the making of a promise to provide a service or goods, or paying money.[4] Consideration may also consist of **forbearance**, which is refraining from doing an act that an individual has a legal right to do, or it may consist of a promise of forbearance. In other words, the promisor may desire to buy the inaction or a promise of inaction of the other party.

The giving up of any legal right can be consideration for the promise of the other party to a contract. Thus, the relinquishment of a right to sue for damages will support a promise for the payment of money given in return for the promise to relinquish the right, if such is the agreement of the parties.

The promise of a creditor to forbear collecting a debt is consideration for the promise of the debtor to modify the terms of the transaction.

5. Illusory Promises

In a bilateral contract, each party makes a promise to the other. For a bilateral contract to be enforceable, there must be *mutuality of obligation*. That is, both parties must have created obligations to the other in their respective promises. If one party's promise contains either no obligation or only an apparent obligation to the other, this promise is an **illusory promise**. The party making such a promise is not bound because he or she has made no real promise. The effect is that the other party, who has made a real promise, is also not bound because he or she has received no consideration. It is said that the contract fails for lack of mutuality.

For Example, Mountain Coal Company promises to sell Midwest Power Company all the coal it may order for $48 per ton for the year 2013, and Midwest Power agrees to pay $48 for any coal it orders from Mountain Coal. Mountain Coal in its promise to Midwest Power has obligated itself to supply all coal ordered at a stated price. However, Midwest Power's promise did not obligate it to buy any coal whatsoever from Mountain Coal (note that it was not a requirements contract). Because Midwest has no obligation to Mountain Coal under its promise, there is no mutuality of obligation, and Midwest cannot enforce Mountain Coal's promise when the market price of coal goes to $55 a ton in the winter of 2013 as the result of severe weather conditions.

Consider as well the example of the Jacksonville Fire soccer team's contract with Brazilian soccer star Edmundo. Edmundo signed a contract to play for the Jacksonville franchise of the new International Soccer League for five years at $25 million. The extensive document signed by Edmundo set forth the details of the team's financial commitment and the details of Edmundo's obligations to the team and its fans. On page 4 of the document, the team inserted a clause reserving the right "to terminate the contract and team obligations at any time in its sole discretion." During the season, Edmundo received a $40 million five-year offer to play for Manchester United of the English Premier League, which he accepted. Because Jacksonville had a free way out of its obligation by the unrestricted cancellation provision in the contract, it thus made its promises to Edmundo illusory. Edmundo was not bound by the Jacksonville contract as a result of a lack of mutuality and was free to sign with Manchester United.

[4] *Prenger v. Baumhoer,* 914 S.W.2d 413 (Mo. App. 1996).

(A) Cancellation Provisions. Although a promise must impose a binding obligation, it may authorize a party to cancel the agreement under certain circumstances on giving notice by a certain date. Such a provision does not make this party's promise illusory, for the party does not have a free way out and is limited to living up to the terms of the **cancellation provision**. **For Example,** actress Zsa Zsa Gabor made a contract with Hollywood Fantasy Corporation to appear at a fantasy vacation in San Antonio, Texas, on May 2–4, for a $10,000 appearance fee plus itemized (extravagant) expenses. The last paragraph of the agreement stated: "It is agreed that if a significant acting opportunity in a film comes up, Ms. Gabor will have the right to cancel her appearance in San Antonio by advising Hollywood Fantasy in writing by April 15, 1991." Ms. Gabor sent a telegram on April 15, 1991, canceling her appearance. During the May 2 through 4 period, Ms. Gabor's only acting activity was a 14-second cameo role during the opening credits of *Naked Gun 2½*. In a lawsuit for breach of contract that followed, the jury saw this portion of the movie and concluded that Ms. Gabor had not canceled her obligation on the basis of a "significant acting opportunity," and she was held liable for breach of contract.[5]

(B) Conditional Promises. A *conditional promise* is a promise that depends on the occurrence of a specified condition in order for the promise to be binding. **For Example,** Mary Sparks, in contemplation of her signing a lease to take over a restaurant at Marina Bay, wanted to make certain that she had a highly qualified chef to run the restaurant's food service. She made a contract with John "Grumpy" White to serve as executive chef for a one-year period at a salary of $150,000. The contract set forth White's responsibilities and was conditioned on the successful negotiation of the restaurant lease with Marina Bay Management. Both parties signed it. Although the happening of the condition was within Mary's control because she could avoid the contract with Grumpy White by not acquiring the restaurant lease, she limited her future options by the contract with White. Her promise to White was not illusory because after signing the contract with him, if she acquired the restaurant lease, she was bound to hire White as her executive chef. Before signing the contract with White, she was free to sign any chef for the position. The contract was enforceable.

CPA B. Special Situations

The following sections analyze certain common situations in which a lawsuit turns on whether the promisor received consideration for the promise sued on.

6. Preexisting Legal Obligation

Ordinarily, doing or promising to do what one is already under a legal obligation to do is not consideration.[6] Similarly, a promise to refrain from doing what one has no legal right to do is not consideration. This preexisting duty or legal obligation can be based on statute, on general principles of law, on responsibilities of an office held, or on a preexisting contract.

For Example, Officer Mary Rodgers is an undercover police officer in the city of Pasadena, California, assigned to weekend workdays. Officer Rodgers promised Elwood Farnsworth that she would diligently patrol the area of the Farnsworth estate on weekends to keep down the noise and drinking of rowdy young persons who gathered in this area, and Mr. Farnsworth promised to provide a $500 per month gratuity for this extra service. Farnsworth's promise is unenforceable because Officer Rodgers has a preexisting official duty as a police officer to protect citizens and enforce the antinoise and public drinking ordinances.

CPA **(A) Completion of Contract.** Suppose that a contractor refuses to complete a building unless the owner promises a payment or bonus in addition to the sum specified in the original contract, and the owner promises to make that payment. The question then arises as to whether the owner's promise is binding. Most courts hold that the second promise of the owner is without consideration.

If the promise of the contractor is to do something that is not part of the first contract, then the promise of the other party is binding. **For Example,** if a bonus of $5,000 is promised in return for the promise of a contractor to complete the building at a date earlier

[5] *Hollywood Fantasy Corp. v. Gabor,* 151 F.2d 203 (5th Cir. 1998).
[6] *Willamette Management Associates, Inc. v. Palczynski,* 38 A.3d 1212 (Conn. App. 2012).

than that specified in the original agreement, the promise to pay the bonus is binding.

CPA (1) Good-Faith Adjustment.

A current trend is to enforce a second promise to pay a contractor a higher amount for the performance of the original contract when there are extraordinary circumstances caused by unforeseeable difficulties and when the additional amount promised the contractor is reasonable under the circumstances. The classic *Angel v. Murray* decision involves a good-faith adjustment.

Angel v. Murray, 322 A.2d 630 (R.I. 1974)

"You Had a Preexisting Legal Obligation," Said the Public Guardian, Mr. Angel.

John Murray was director of finance of the city of Newport. A contract was made with Alfred Maher to remove trash. Later, Maher requested that the city council increase his compensation. Maher's costs were greater than had been anticipated because 400 new dwelling units had been put into operation. The city council voted to pay Maher an additional $10,000 a year. After two such annual payments had been made, Angel and other citizens of the city sued Murray and Maher for a return of the $20,000. They said that Maher was already obligated by his contract to perform the work for the contract sum, and there was, accordingly, no consideration for the payment of the increased compensation. From a decision in favor of the plaintiffs, the city and Maher appealed.

JUDICIAL OPINION

ROBERTS, C. J.... It is generally held that a modification of a contract is itself a contract, which is unenforceable unless supported by consideration....

The preexisting duty rule is followed by most jurisdictions....

The primary purpose of the preexisting duty rule is to prevent what has been referred to as the "hold-up game." ... A classic example of the "hold-up game" is found in *Alaska Packers' Ass'n v Domenico,* 117 F 99 (9th Cir 1902). There 21 seamen entered into a written contract with Domenico to sail from San Francisco to Pyramid Harbor, Alaska. They were to work as sailors and fishermen out of Pyramid Harbor during the fishing season of 1900. The contract specified that each man would be paid $50 plus two cents for each red salmon he caught. Subsequent to their arrival at Pyramid Harbor, the men stopped work and demanded an additional $50. They threatened to return to San Francisco if Domenico did not agree to their demand. Since it was impossible for Domenico to find other men, he agreed to pay the men an additional $50. After they returned to San Francisco, Domenico refused to pay the men an additional $50. The court found that the subsequent agreement to pay the men an additional $50 was not supported by consideration because the men had a preexisting duty to work on the ship under the original contract, and thus the subsequent agreement was unenforceable.

Another example of the "hold-up game" is found in the area of construction contracts. Frequently, a contractor will refuse to complete work under an unprofitable contract unless he is awarded additional compensation. The courts have generally held that a subsequent agreement to award additional compensation is unenforceable if the contractor is only performing work which would have been required of him under the original contract....

These examples clearly illustrate that the courts will not enforce an agreement that has been procured by coercion or duress and will hold the parties to their original contract regardless of whether it is profitable or unprofitable. However, the courts have been reluctant to apply the preexisting duty rule when a party to a contract encounters unanticipated difficulties and the other party, not influenced by coercion or duress, voluntarily agrees to pay additional compensation for work already required to be performed under the contract. For example, the courts have found that the original contract was rescinded,... abandoned,... or waived.

Although the preexisting duty rule has served a useful purpose insofar as it deters parties from using coercion and duress to obtain additional compensation, it has been widely criticized as a general rule of law.... The modern trend appears to recognize the necessity that courts should enforce agreements modifying contracts when unexpected or unanticipated difficulties arise during the course of the performance of a contract, even though there is no consideration for the modification, as long as the parties agree voluntarily.

Under the Uniform Commercial Code, §2-209(1), ..."an agreement modifying a contract [for the sale of goods] needs no consideration to be binding."... Although at first blush this section appears to validate modifications obtained by coercion and duress, the comments to this section indicate that a modification under this section must meet the test of good faith imposed by the Code, and a modification obtained by extortion without a legitimate commercial reason is unenforceable.

The modern trend away from a rigid application of the preexisting duty rule is reflected by § 89D(a) of the American Law Institute's Restatement Second of the Law of Contracts, which provides: "A promise modifying a duty under a contract not fully performed on either side is binding (a) if the modification is fair and equitable in view of circumstances not anticipated by the parties when the contract was made...."

Continued

We believe that § 89D(a) is the proper rule of law and find it applicable to the facts of this case. It not only prohibits modifications obtained by coercion, duress, or extortion but also fulfills society's expectation that agreements entered into voluntarily will be enforced by the courts....

Section 89D(a), of course, does not compel a modification of an unprofitable or unfair contract; it only enforces a modification if the parties voluntarily agree and if (1) the promise modifying the original contract was made before the contract was fully performed on either side, (2) the underlying circumstances which prompted the modification were unanticipated by the parties, and (3) the modification is fair and equitable.

The evidence, which is uncontradicted, reveals that in June of 1968 Maher requested the city council to pay him an additional $10,000 for the year beginning on July 1, 1968, and ending on June 30, 1969. This request was made at a public meeting of the city council, where Maher explained in detail his reasons for making the request. Thereafter, the city council voted to authorize the Mayor to sign an amendment to the 1964 contract which provided that Maher would receive an additional $10,000 per year for the duration of the contract. Under such circumstances we have no doubt that the city voluntarily agreed to modify the 1964 contract.

Having determined the voluntariness of this agreement, we turn our attention to the three criteria delineated above. First, the modification was made in June of 1968 at a time when the five-year contract which was made in 1964 had not been fully performed by either party. Second, although the 1964 contract provided that Maher collect all refuse generated within the city, it appears this contract was premised on Maher's past experience that the number of refuse-generating units would increase at a rate of 20 to 25 per year. Furthermore, the evidence is uncontradicted that the 1967–1968 increase of 400 units "went beyond any previous expectation." Clearly, the circumstances which prompted the city council to modify the 1964 contract were unanticipated. Third, although the evidence does not indicate what proportion of the total this increase comprised, the evidence does indicate that it was a "substantial" increase. In light of this, we cannot say that the council's agreement to pay Maher the $10,000 increase was not fair and equitable in the circumstances.

[Judgment reversed and action remanded]

QUESTIONS

1. What was the basis for the plaintiff's suit?
2. How would the *Angel* case have been decided under the common law rule as to consideration?
3. Can an adversely affected contractor compell a modification of an unprofitable contract under the *Angel v Murray* decision?

(2) Contract for Sale of Goods.

When the contract is for the sale of goods, any modification made in good faith by the parties to the contract is binding without regard to the existence of consideration for the modification.

CPA (B) COMPROMISE AND RELEASE OF CLAIMS. The rule that doing or promising to do what one is already legally bound to do is not consideration applies to a part payment made in satisfaction of an admitted or *liquidated debt*. Thus, a promise to pay part of an amount that is admittedly owed is not consideration for a promise to discharge the balance. It will not prevent the creditor from demanding the remainder later. **For Example,** John owes Mark $100,000, which was due on March 1, 2010. On March 15, John offers to pay back $80,000 if Mark will agree to accept this amount as the discharge of the full amount owed. Mark agrees to this proposal, and it is set forth in writing signed by the parties. However, Mark later sues for the $20,000 balance. Mark will be successful in the lawsuit because John's payment of the $80,000 is not consideration for Mark's promise to discharge the full amount owed because John was doing only what he had a preexisting legal duty to do.

If the debtor pays the part payment before the debt is due, there is consideration because, on the day when the payment was made, the creditor was not entitled to demand any payment. Likewise, if the creditor accepts some article (even of slight value) in addition to the part payment, consideration exists.

A debtor and creditor may have a bona fide dispute over the amount owed or whether any amount is owed. Such is called an *unliquidated debt*. In this case, payment by the debtor of less than the amount claimed by the creditor is consideration for the latter's agreement to release or settle the claim. It is generally regarded as sufficient if the claimant believes in the merit of the claim.[7]

(c) Part-Payment Checks. When there is a good-faith dispute about the amount of a debt and the debtor tenders a check that states on its face "paid in full" and references the transaction in dispute, but the amount of the check is less than the full amount the creditor asserts is owed, the cashing of the check by the creditor discharges the entire debt.

(d) Composition of Creditors. In a **composition of creditors**, the various creditors of one debtor mutually agree to accept a fractional part of their claims in full satisfaction of the claims. Such agreements are binding and are supported by consideration. When creditors agree to extend the due date of their debts, the promise of each creditor to forbear is likewise consideration for the promise of other creditors to forbear.

7. Past Consideration

A promise based on a party's past performance lacks consideration.[8] It is said that **past consideration** is no consideration. **For Example,** Fred O'Neal came up with the idea for the formation of the new community bank of Villa Rica and was active in its formation. Just prior to the execution of the documents creating the bank, the organizers discussed that once the bank was formed, it would hire O'Neal, giving him a three-year contract at $65,000 the first year, $67,000 the second year, and $70,000 the third. In a lawsuit against the bank for breach of contract, O'Neal testified that the consideration he gave in exchange for the three-year contract was his past effort to organize the bank. The court stated that past consideration generally will not support a subsequent promise and that the purported consideration was not rendered to the bank, which had not yet been established when his promotion and organization work took place.[9] The presence of a bargained-for exchange is not present when a promise is made in exchange for a past benefit.[10]

8. Moral Obligation

In most states, promises made to another based on "moral obligation" lack consideration and are not enforceable.[11] They are considered gratuitous promises and unenforceable. **For Example,** while on a fishing trip, Tom Snyder, a person of moderate means, met an elderly couple living in near-destitute conditions in a rural area of Texas. He returned to the area often, and he regularly purchased groceries for the couple and paid for their medical needs. Some two years later, the couple's son, David, discovered what Tom had been doing and promised to reimburse Snyder for what he had furnished his parents. This promise, based on a moral obligation, is unenforceable. A "past consideration" analysis also renders David's promise as unenforceable.

Ethics & the Law

Alan Fulkins, who owns a construction company that specializes in single-family residences, is constructing a small subdivision with 23 homes. Tretorn Plumbing, owned by Jason Tretorn, was awarded the contract for the plumbing work on the homes at a price of $4,300 per home.

Plumbing contractors complete their residential projects in three phases. Phase one consists of digging the lines for the plumbing and installing the pipes that are placed in the foundation of the house. Phase two consists of installing the pipes within the walls of the home, and phase three is installing of the surface plumbing, such as sinks and tubs. However, industry practice dictates that the plumbing contractor receive one-half of the contract amount after completion of phase one.

Tretorn completed the digs of phase one for Fulkins and received payment of $2,150. Tretorn then went to Fulkins and demanded an additional $600 per house to complete the work. Fulkins said, "But you already have a contract for $4,300!" Tretorn responded, "I know, but the costs are killing me. I need the additional $600."

[7] *F. H. Prince & Co. v. Towers Financial Corp.*, 656 N.E.2d 142 (Ill. App. 1995).

[8] *Smith v. Locklear*, 906 So.2d 1273 (Fla. App. 2005).

[9] *O'Neal v. Home Town Bank of Villa Rica*, 514 S.E.2d 669 (Ga. App. 1999).

[10] But see *United Resource Recovery Corp v. Ranko Venture Management Inc.*, 854 F. Supp. 2d 645 (S.D.N.Y. 2008) where a past work agreement was unenforceable because it was based on past consideration—however, the individual could recover under a signed consulting agreement for which no compensation had been paid. See also *Travis v. Paepke*, 3 So.3d 131 (Miss. App. 2009).

[11] *Production Credit Ass'n of Manaan v. Rub*, 475 N.W.2d 532 (N.D. 1991). As to the Louisiana rule of moral consideration, see *Thomas v. Bryant*, 596 So.2d 1065 (La. App. 1992).

Ethics & the Law—*Contd.*

Fulkins explained the hardship of the demand, "Look, I've already paid you half. If I hire someone else, I'll have to pay them two-thirds for the work not done. It'll cost me $5,000 per house."

Tretorn responded, "Exactly. I'm a bargain because the additional $600 I want only puts you at $4,900. If you don't pay it, I'll just lien the houses and then you'll be stuck without a way to close the sales. I've got the contract all drawn up. Just sign it and everything goes smoothly."

Should Fulkins sign the agreement? Does Tretorn have the right to the additional $600? Was it ethical for Tretorn to demand the $600? Is there any legal advice you can offer Fulkins?

FIGURE 15-1 *Consideration and Promises*

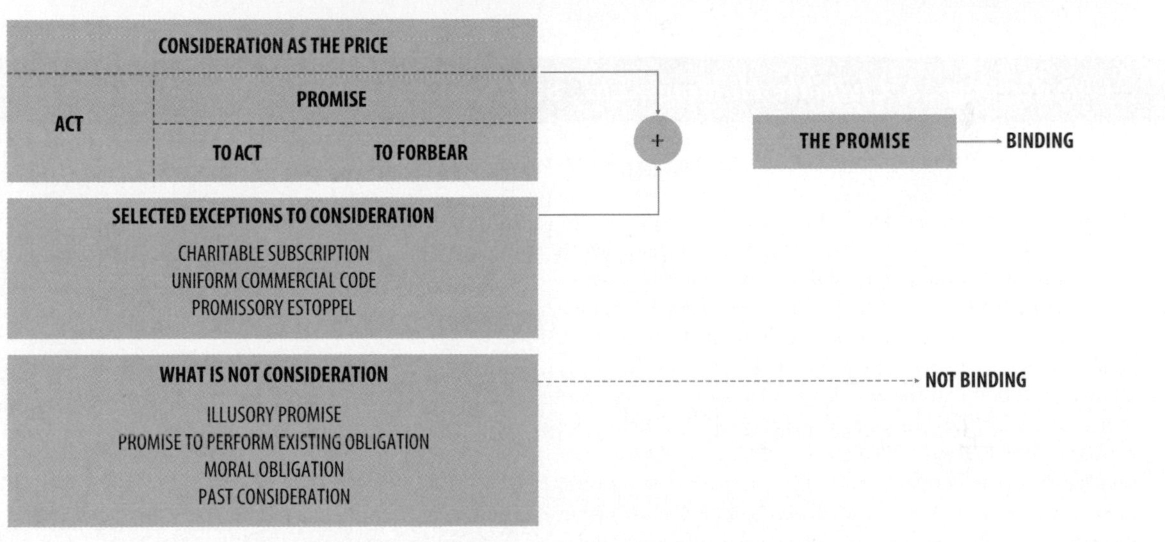

C. Exceptions to the Laws of Consideration

The ever-changing character of law clearly appears in the area of consideration as part of the developing law of contracts.

9. Exceptions to Consideration

By statute or decision, traditional consideration is not required in these situations:

(A) Charitable Subscriptions. Where individuals made pledges to finance the construction of buildings for charitable purposes, consideration is lacking according to technical standards applied in ordinary contract cases. For public policy reasons, the reliance of the charity on the pledge in undertaking the project is deemed a substitute for consideration.

(B) Uniform Commercial Code. In some situations, the Uniform Commercial Code abolishes the requirement of consideration. **For Example,** under the Code, consideration is not required for (1) a merchant's written, firm offer for goods stated to be irrevocable, (2) a written discharge of a claim for an alleged breach of a commercial contract, or (3) an agreement to modify a contract for the sale of goods.[12]

[12] U.C.C. §2-209(1).

(c) Promissory Estoppel. Under the doctrine of **promissory estoppel**, a promisor may be prevented from asserting that his or her promise is unenforceable because the promisee gave no consideration for the promise. This doctrine, sometimes called the *doctrine of detrimental reliance,* is applicable when (1) the promisor makes a promise that lacks consideration, (2) the promisor intends or should reasonably expect that the promisee will rely on the promise, (3) the promisee in fact relies on the promise in some definite and substantial manner, and (4) enforcement of the promise is the only way to avoid injustice.[13]

Damages recoverable in a case of promissory estoppel are not the profits that the promisee expected, but only the amount necessary to restore the promisee to the position he or she would have been in had the promisee not relied on the promise.[14]

Legal difficulties often arise because parties take certain things for granted. Frequently, they will be sure that they have agreed to everything and that they have a valid contract. Sometimes, however, they do not. The courts are then faced with the problem of leaving them with their broken dreams or coming to their rescue when promissory estoppel can be established. The *Chrysler* case is an example of the application of the doctrine of promissory estoppel.

Chrysler Corp. v. Chaplake Holdings, Ltd., 822 A.2d 1024 (Del. 2003)

Brits Rescued by Promissory Estoppel

Portman Lamborghini, Ltd. (Portman), was owned by Chaplake Holdings, Ltd., a United Kingdom company, which was owned by David Jolliffe and David Lakeman as equal shareholders. Between 1984 and 1987, Portman sold approximately 30 new Lamborghinis each year through its exclusive concession contract with the car maker. It was then the largest Lamborghini dealer in the world, since Lamborghini's production was just 250 cars per year. These cars sold at a retail price between $200,000 and $300,000. In 1987, Chrysler Corporation bought Lamborghini, and its chairman, Lee Iacocca, presented a plan to escalate production to 5,000 units within five years. The plan included the introduction of a new model, the P140, with a retail price of $70,000. Between 1987 and 1991, all of the Chrysler/Lamborghini top executives with whom Jolliffe and Lakeman and their top advisors came in contact provided the same message to them—Chrysler was committed to the Expansion Plan, and in order for Portman to retain its exclusive U.K. market, it must expand its operational capacity from 35 cars in 1987 to 400 cars by 1992. Accordingly, Portman acquired additional financing, staff, and facilities and built a new distribution center. An economic downturn in the United States and major development and production problems at Lamborghini led Chrysler to reduce its expansion investment by two-thirds. Factory production delays eroded Portman's profitability and success, and it entered into receivership in April 1992. Suit was brought on behalf of the Portman and Chaplake entities on a promissory estoppel theory against Chrysler, a Delaware corporation. The Jury awarded 569,321 to Portman for costs incurred in implementing the Expansion plan and awarded 462,686 to Chaplake for its investment in the plan. Chrysler appealed.

JUDICIAL OPINION

WALSH, J.... Under the doctrine of promissory estoppel a plaintiff must demonstrate by clear and convincing evidence that:

(i) a promise was made;

(ii) it was the reasonable expectation of the promisor to induce action or forbearance on the part of the promisee;

(iii) the promisee reasonably relied on the promise and took action to his detriment; and

(iv) such promise is binding because injustice can be avoided only by enforcement of the promise.

There were a series of promises made by Chrysler and its various representatives to Portman, Chaplake and their representatives. First, the comments of then-chairman Iacocca upon the acquisition of Lamborghini made clear Chrysler's plans to expand production over a period of five to six years. More importantly, between 1987 and 1991 [Chrysler/Lamborghini executives] Novaro, Richards, Molaschi and Levy made similar statements promising that the Lamborghini line would expand ten-fold, and that Portman would retain its exclusivity deal *only* if it expanded its operational capacity. By making these promises, Chrysler should have expected that Portman and Chaplake would be induced to expand its operations in accordance with the promised expansion of the Lamborghini line of automobiles.

Portman and Chaplake reasonably relied upon the promises made by Chrysler, and took action to their detriment. Over a period of several years, Portman and Chaplake were regularly updated regarding the progress of

[13] *Neuhoff v. Marvin Lumber and Cedar Co.,* 370 F.3d 197 (1st Cir. 2004).

[14] *Medistar Corp. v. Schmidt,* 267 S.W.3d 150 (Tex. App. 2008).

Continued

the Expansion Plan. Portman would not have implemented the Portman Plan in the absence of these promises. The reasonableness of Portman and Chaplake's reliance is bolstered by the fact that the promises emanated from many of the most senior officers involved with the Expansion Plan.

Lakeman and Jolliffe were sophisticated businessmen in their own right, and in crafting the Portman Plan they employed the services of highly sophisticated advisors. Nevertheless, the record establishes that *all* of the Chrysler/Lamborghini executives with whom Lakeman, Jolliffe, and their advisors came in contact provided the same message: Chrysler is committed to the Expansion Plan, and in order for Portman to retain its exclusivity in the U.K. market, it must expand its operational capacity accordingly. Therefore, it was not unreasonable for Lakeman and Jolliffe to rely upon the promises made by these executives.

Chrysler also argues that the existing written contracts between the parties governed the relationship, and therefore promissory estoppel is inapplicable. Here, Portman and Chaplake relied on promises from Chrysler executives. Those promises induced them to increase operational capacity and investment to a degree that would have been unnecessary *but for* the Expansion Plan and the role they were promised therein. The contracts governing other aspects of the business relationship are of no consequence to this analysis because the promises made regarding Portman's role in the Expansion Plan were in addition to the existing relationship. Finally, Chrysler correctly points out that the trial court failed to address the fourth element—or the so-called "avoidance of injustice" element—of the *Lord* test....

The prevention of injustice is the "fundamental idea" underlying the doctrine of promissory estoppel. *See Chrysler v Quimby,* 144 A.2d 123, 133 (Del.1958). Accordingly, the trial judge implicitly found that this element was satisfied, and the court did not err by failing to submit this element of the *Lord* test to the jury.

[Judgment affirmed]...

CASE QUESTIONS

1. State the four elements of a promissory estoppel claim.
2. What is the significance of the fourth element of promissory estoppel, "avoidance of injustice"?
3. How did the court deal with Chrysler's assertion that existing written contracts between the parties preclude the application of promissory estoppel?

LawFlix

Baby Boom (1987) (PG)

Review the scene near the end of the movie when Diane Keaton is presented with an offer for the purchase of her company, Country Baby. List the elements of consideration that Food Giant is paying for the company. Explain what Ms. Keaton's consideration is in exchange.

MAKE THE CONNECTION

SUMMARY

A promise is not binding if there is no consideration for the promise. Consideration is what the promisor requires as the price for his promise. That price may be doing an act, refraining from the doing of an act, or merely promising to do or to refrain. In a bilateral contract, it is necessary to find that the promise of each party is supported by consideration. If either promise is not so supported, it is not binding, and the agreement of the parties is not a contract. Consequently, the agreement cannot be enforced. When a promise is the consideration, it must be a binding promise. The binding character of a promise is not affected by the circumstance that there is a condition precedent to the performance promised. A promise to do what one is already obligated to do is not consideration, although some exceptions are made. Such exceptions include the rendering of a partial performance or a modified performance accepted as a good-faith adjustment to a changed situation, a compromise and release of claims, a part-payment check, and a compromise of creditors. Because consideration is the price that is given to obtain the promise, past benefits conferred on the promisor cannot be consideration.

A promise to refrain from doing an act can be consideration. A promise to refrain from suing or asserting a particular claim can be consideration. When consideration is forbearance to assert a claim, it is immaterial whether the claim is valid as long as the claim has been asserted in the good-faith belief that it was valid.

When the promisor obtains the consideration specified for the promise, the law is not ordinarily concerned with the value or adequacy of that consideration.

Under the doctrine of promissory estoppel a court may enforce a promise lacking consideration where it is the only way to avoid injustice.

LEARNING OUTCOMES

After studying this chapter, you should be able to clearly explain:

A. General Principles—Consideration

LO.1 Explain what constitutes consideration

See the *Williams v. Ormsby* case, which determined that love and affection is not recognized as consideration, p. 287.

See the "bargained for exchange" example involving Beth and Kerry, p. 286.

See the "benefit-detriment" approach to consideration example, p. 286.

See the discussion on forbearance as consideration on p. 288.

B. Special Situations

LO.2 Distinguish between a "preexisting legal obligation" and "past consideration"

See the preexisting duty example involving Officer Rodgers on p. 289.

See the *Angel v. Murray* case involving a good-faith adjustment exception to the preexisting duty rule, pp. 290–291.

See the example involving Fred O'Neal where he found out the past consideration is no consideration rule, p. 292.

LO.3 Explain why promises based on moral obligations lack consideration

See the example of the gratuitous deeds of Tom Snyder on p. 292.

C. Exceptions to The Laws of Consideration

LO.4 List the exceptions to the requirement of consideration

See the discussion on charitable subscriptions, the UCC, and promissory estoppel on p. 293.

LO.5 Explain the "fundamental idea" underlying promissory estoppel

See the *Chaplake Holdings* case where the court enforced Chrysler's promise in order to correct an injustice, pp. 294–295.

KEY TERMS

cancellation provision
composition of creditors
consideration
forbearance
illusory promise
past consideration
promissory estoppel

QUESTIONS AND CASE PROBLEMS

1. Sarah's house caught on fire. Through the prompt assistance of her neighbor Odessa, the fire was quickly extinguished. In gratitude, Sarah promised to pay Odessa $1,000. Can Odessa enforce this promise?

2. William E. Story agreed to pay his nephew, William E. Story II, a large sum of money (roughly equivalent to $50,000 in 2007 dollars) "if he would refrain from drinking liquor, using tobacco, swearing, and playing cards or billiards for money until he should come to be 21 years of age." William II had been using tobacco and occasionally drank liquor but refrained from using these stimulants over several years until he was 21 and also lived up to the other requirements of his uncle's offer. Just after William II's 21st birthday, Story acknowledged that William II had fulfilled his part of the bargain and advised that the money would be invested for him with interest. Story died, and his executor, Sidway, refused to pay William II because he believed the contract between Story and William II was without consideration. Sidway asserted that Story received no benefit from William II's performance and William II suffered no detriment (in fact, by his refraining from the use of liquor and tobacco, William II was not harmed but benefited, Sidway asserted). Is there any theory of consideration that William II can rely on? How would you decide this case? [*Hamer v. Sidway,* 124 N.Y. 538]

3. Dale Dyer, who was employed by National By-Products, Inc., was seriously injured at work as the result of a job-related accident. He agreed to give up his right to sue the employer for damages in consideration of the employer's giving him a lifetime job. The employer later claimed that this agreement was not binding because Dyer's promise not to sue could not be consideration for the promise to employ on the ground that Dyer in fact had no right to sue. Dyer's only remedy was to make a claim under workers' compensation. Was the agreement binding? [*Dyer v. National By-Products, Inc.,* 380 N.W.2d 732 (Iowa)]

4. Charles Sanarwari retained Stan Gissel to prepare his income tax return for the year 2006. The parties agreed on a fee of $400. Charles had done a rough estimate based on last year's return and believed he would owe the IRS approximately $2,000. When Stan's work was completed, it turned out that Charles would receive a $2,321 tax refund. Stan explained how certain legitimate advantages were used to reduce Charles's tax obligation. Charles paid for Stan's services and was so pleased with the work that he promised to pay Stan an additional $400 for the excellent job on the tax return when he received his tax refund. Thereafter, Stan and Charles had a falling out over a golf tournament where Charles was late for his tee time and Stan started without him, causing Charles to lose an opportunity to win the club championship. Stan was not paid the $400 promised for doing an excellent job on the tax return, and he sued Charles as a matter of principle. Decide.

5. Medistar is a real estate development company specializing in the development of medical facilities. Dr. Schmidt, the team physician for the San Antonio Spurs basketball team, sought to develop "The Texas Center for Athletes" medical center next to the Spurs facility and urged Medistar to obtain the real estate and develop the project on his group's behalf. Medistar spent more than $1 million and thousands of man-hours on the project from 2000 to July 12, 2004, when Dr. Schmidt's new group of investors purchased the property next to the Spur's facility for the project; subsequently, Medistar was informed that it would have no role in the project. Medistar asserts that it relied on Dr. Schmidt's assurances that it would be the developer of the project—and after four years and the $1 million in time and expenses it spent, it is unconscionable to be excluded from the project. Dr. Schmidt and associates contend that Medistar has presented no contractual agreement tying it to any legal obligation to Medistar. Is there a viable legal theory available to Medistar? If so what is the remedy? [*Medistar v. Schmidt,* 267 S.W.3d 150 (Tex. App.)]

6. Fedun rented a building to Gomer, who did business under the name of Mike's Cafe. Later,

Gomer was about to sell the business to Brown and requested Fedun to release him from his liability under the lease. Fedun agreed to do so. Brown sold the business shortly thereafter. The balance of the rent due by Gomer under the original lease agreement was not paid, and Fedun sued Gomer on the rent claim. Could he collect after having released Gomer? [*Fedun v. Mike's Cafe,* 204 A.2d 776 (Pa. Super.)]

7. Alexander Proudfoot Co. was in the business of devising efficiency systems for industry. It told Sanitary Linen Service Co. that it could provide an improved system for Sanitary Linen that would save Sanitary Linen money. It made a contract with Sanitary Linen to provide a money-saving system. The system was put into operation, and Proudfoot was paid the amount due under the contract. The system failed to work and did not save money. Sanitary Linen sued to get the money back. Was it entitled to do so? [*Sanitary Linen Service Co. v. Alexander Proudfoot Co.,* 435 F.2d 292 (5th Cir.)]

8. Sears, Roebuck and Co. promised to give Forrer permanent employment. Forrer sold his farm at a loss to take the job. Shortly after beginning work, he was discharged by Sears, which claimed that the contract could be terminated at will. Forrer claimed that promissory estoppel prevented Sears from terminating the contract. Was he correct? [*Forrer v. Sears, Roebuck & Co.,* 153 N.W.2d 587 (Wis.)]

9. Kemp leased a gas filling station from Baehr. Kemp, who was heavily indebted to Penn-O-Tex Oil Corp., transferred to it his right to receive payments on all claims. When Baehr complained that the rent was not paid, he was assured by the corporation that the rent would be paid to him. Baehr did not sue Kemp for the overdue rent but later sued the corporation. The defense was raised that there was no consideration for the promise of the corporation. Decide. [*Baehr v. Penn-O-Tex Corp.,* 104 N.W.2d 661 (Minn.)]

10. Bogart owed several debts to Security Bank & Trust Co. and applied to the bank for a loan to pay the debts. The bank's employee stated that he would take the application for the loan to the loan committee and "within two or three days, we ought to have something here, ready for you to go with." The loan was not made. The bank sued Bogart for his debts. He filed a counterclaim on the theory that the bank had broken its contract to make a loan to him and that promissory estoppel prevented the bank from going back on what the employee had said. Was this counterclaim valid?

11. Kelsoe worked for International Wood Products, Inc., for a number of years. One day Hernandez, a director and major stockholder of the company, promised Kelsoe that the corporation would give her 5 percent of the company's stock. This promise was never kept, and Kelsoe sued International for breach of contract. Had the company broken its contract? [*Kelsoe v. International Wood Products, Inc.,* 588 So.2d 877 (Ala.)]

12. Kathy left her classic 1978 Volkswagen convertible at Freddie's Service Station, requesting a "tune-up." When she returned that evening, Freddie's bill was $374. Kathy stated that Firestone and Sears advertise tune-ups for $70, and she asked Freddie, "How can you justify this bill?" Freddie responded, "Carburator work." Kathy refused to pay the bill and left. That evening, when the station closed, she took her other set of keys and removed her car, after placing a check in the station's mail slot. The check was made out to Freddie's Service Station for $200 and stated on its face: "This check is in full payment of my account with you regarding the tune-up today on my 1978 Volkswagen convertible." Freddie cashed the check in order to meet his business expenses and then sued Kathy for the difference owed. What result?

13. On the death of their mother, the children of Jane Smith gave their interests in their mother's estate to their father in consideration of his payment of $1 to each of them and his promise to leave them the property on his death. The father died without leaving them the property. The children sued their father's second wife to obtain the property in accordance with the agreement. The second wife claimed that the agreement was not a binding contract because the amount of $1 and future gifts given for the children's interests were so trivial and uncertain. Decide.

14. Radio Station KSCS broadcast a popular music program. It announced that it would pay $25,000 to any listener who detected that it did not play three consecutive songs. Steve Jennings listened to and heard a program in which two songs were followed by a commercial program. He claimed the $25,000. The station refused to pay on the ground that there was no consideration for its promise to pay that amount. Was the station liable? [*Jennings v. Radio Station KSCS,* 708 S.W.2d 60 (Tex. App.)]

15. Hoffman wanted to acquire a franchise for a Red Owl grocery store. (Red Owl was a corporation that maintained a system of chain stores.) An agent of Red Owl informed Hoffman and his wife that if they would sell their bakery in Wautoma, acquire a certain tract of land in Chilton (another Wisconsin city), and put up $6,000, they would be given a franchise. In reliance on the agent's promise, Hoffman sold his business and acquired the land in Chilton, but he was never granted a franchise. He and his wife sued Red Owl. Red Owl raised the defense that there had been only an assurance that Hoffman would receive a franchise, but because there was no promise supported by consideration, there was no binding contract to give him a franchise. Decide. [*Hoffman v. Red Owl Stores, Inc.,* 133 N.W.2d 267 (Wis.)]

Legality and Public Policy

learningoutcomes

After studying this chapter, you should be able to

LO.1 Explain the general contract principles on "illegality"

LO.2 Explain the implied obligation on all parties of good faith and fair dealing

LO.3 Understand that it is only in unusual situations that a contract provision will be unenforceable because it is unconscionable

LO.4 Explain the rationale for requiring licenses to carry on as a business, trade, or profession

LO.5 Distinguish between noncompete clauses after the sale of a business and noncompete clauses in employment contracts

A court will not enforce a contract if it is illegal, contrary to public policy, or unconscionable.

A. General Principles

An agreement is illegal either when its formation or performance is a crime or a tort or when it is contrary to public policy or unconscionable.

1. Effect of Illegality

Ordinarily, an illegal agreement is void. When an agreement is illegal, the parties are usually not entitled to the aid of the courts. Examples of illegal contracts where the courts have left the parties where they found them include a liquor store owner not being allowed to bring suit for money owed for goods (liquor) sold and delivered on credit in violation of statute and an unlicensed home improvement contractor not being allowed to enforce his contract for progress payments due him. If the illegal agreement has not been performed, neither party can sue the other to obtain performance or damages. If the agreement has been performed, neither party can sue the other to obtain damages or to set the agreement aside.[1]

Even if a contract appears to be legal on its face, it may be unenforceable if it was entered into for an illegal purpose. **For Example,** if zoning regulations in the special-purpose district of Washington, D.C., require that only a professional can lease space in a given building, and the rental agent suggests that two nonprofessionals take out the lease in their attorney's name, but all parties realize that the premises will be used only by the nonprofessionals, then the lease in question is illegal and unenforceable.[2]

2. Exceptions to Effect of Illegality

To avoid hardship, exceptions are made to the rules stated in Section 1.

(a) Protection of One Party. When the law that the agreement violates is intended to protect one of the parties, that party may seek relief. **For Example,** when, in order to protect the public, the law forbids the issuance of securities by certain classes of corporations, a person who has purchased them may recover the money paid.

(b) Unequal Guilt. When the parties are not ***in pari delicto***—equally guilty—the least guilty party is granted relief when public interest is advanced by doing so. **For Example,** when a statute is adopted to protect one of the parties to a transaction, such as a usury law adopted to protect borrowers, the person to be protected will not be deemed to be *in pari delicto* with the wrongdoer when entering into a transaction that the statute prohibits.

3. Partial Illegality

An agreement may involve the performance of several promises, some of which are illegal and some legal. The legal parts of the agreement may be enforced provided that they can be separated from the parts that are illegal.

When the illegal provision of a contract may be ignored without defeating the contract's basic purpose, a court will merely ignore the illegal provision and enforce the balance of the contract. Consequently, when a provision for the payment of an attorney's fee in a car rental agreement was illegal because a local statute prohibited it, the court would merely ignore the fee provision and enforce the balance of the contract.[3]

If a contract is susceptible to two interpretations, one legal and the other illegal, the court will assume that the legal meaning was intended unless the contrary is clearly indicated.

4. Crimes and Civil Wrongs

An agreement is illegal, and therefore void, when it calls for the commission of any act that constitutes a crime. To illustrate, one cannot enforce an agreement by which the other party is to commit an assault, steal property, burn a house, or kill a person. A contract to obtain equipment for committing a crime is illegal and cannot be enforced. Thus, a contract to manufacture and sell illegal slot machines is void.

An agreement that calls for the commission of a civil wrong is also illegal and void. Examples are agreements to slander a third person; defraud another; infringe another's patent, trademark, or copyright; or fix prices.

[1] *Sabia v. Mattituck Inlet Marina, Inc.,* 805 N.Y.S.2d 346 (A.D. 2005).

[2] *McMahon v. A, H, & B,* 728 A.2d 656 (D.C. 1999).

[3] *Harbour v. Arelco, Inc.,* 678 N.E.2d 381 (Ind. 1997).

5. Good Faith and Fairness

Every contract has an implied obligation that neither party shall do anything that will have the effect of destroying or injuring the right of the other party to receive the fruits of the contract. This means that in every contract there exists an implied covenant of **good faith** and fair dealing. **For Example,** Katy Lesser entered into a 10-year lease of retail space to operate a natural food store in South Burlington, Vermont. Her business prospered and in April of 1999 she signed a lease for additional space. For five years, the landlord continually rebuffed her efforts to meet and discuss plans to renovate the 1999 space to expand the grocery store, motivated solely by a desire to pressure the tenant to pay a portion of his legal fees in an unrelated zoning case. The court found that the landlord breached the obligation of good faith and fair dealing, causing the 1999 space to be essentially unusable from 1999 to 2004. The court awarded the tenant the rent she paid for this period less a storage fee adjustment.[4]

6. Unconscionable Clauses

Ordinarily, a court will not consider whether a contract is fair or unfair, is wise or foolish, or operates unequally between the parties. **For Example,** the Kramper Family Farm agreed to sell 17.59 acres of land to Dakota Industrial Development, Inc. (DID), for $35,000 per acre if the buyer constructed a paved road along the property by December 31. The contract also provided that if the road was not completed by the date set forth in the contract, the price per acre would be $45,000. When the road was not completed by the December 31 date, Family Farm sued DID for the additional $10,000 per acre. DID defended that to apply the contract according to its plain language would create an unconscionable result and was an unenforceable penalty provision contrary to public policy. The court refused to allow DID to escape its contractual obligations on the pretext of unconscionability and public policy arguments. The parties are at liberty to contract as they see fit, the court concluded, and generally, a court will not inquire into the adequacy of consideration inasmuch as the value of property is a matter of personal judgment by the parties to the contract. In this case, the price consisted of either $45,000 per acre, or $35,000 per acre with the road by a certain date.[5]

However, in certain unusual situations, the law may hold a contract provision unenforceable because it is too harsh or oppressive to one of the parties. This principle may be applied to invalidate a clause providing for the payment by one party of an excessive penalty on the breaking of a contract or a provision inserted by the dominant party that it shall not be liable for the consequences of intentional torts, fraud, or gross negligence. This principle is extended in connection with the sale of goods to provide that "if the court … finds the contract or any clause of the contract to have been unconscionable at the time it was made, the court may refuse to enforce the contract, or it may enforce the remainder of the contract without the unconscionable clause, or it may so limit the application of any unconscionable clause as to avoid any unconscionable result."[6]

(A) What Constitutes Unconscionability? A provision in a contract that gives what the court believes is too much of an advantage over a buyer may be held void as unconscionable.

(B) Determination of Unconscionability. Some jurisdictions analyze unconscionability as having two separate elements: procedural and substantive. Both elements must be present for a court to refuse to enforce a contract provision. Other jurisdictions analyze unconscionability by considering the doctrine of adhesion and whether the clause in question is unduly oppressive.

Procedural unconscionability has to do with matters of freedom of assent resulting from inequality of bargaining power and the absence of real negotiations and meaningful choice or a surprise resulting from hiding a disputed term in an unduly long document or fine print. Companywide standardized form contracts imposed on a take-it-or-leave-it basis by a party with superior bargaining strength are called **contracts of adhesion**, and they may sometimes be deemed procedurally unconscionable.

Substantive unconscionability focuses on the actual terms of the contract itself. Such unconscionability is indicated when the contract terms are so one-sided as

[4] *Century Partners, LP v. Lesser Goldsmith Enterprises*, 958 A.2d 627 (Vt. 2008).
[5] *Kramper Family Farm v. Dakota Industrial Development, Inc.*, 603 N.W.2d 463 (Neb. App. 1999).
[6] U.C.C. §2-302(1).

to shock the conscience or are so extreme as to appear unconscionable according to the mores and business practices of the time and place.

The U.S. Supreme Court has made clear that arbitration is an acceptable forum for the resolution of employment disputes between employees and their employers, including employment-related claims based on federal and state statutes.[7] The controlling arbitration agreement language is commonly devised and implemented by the employer. Under the Federal Arbitration Act (FAA), the employer can obtain a court order to stay court proceedings and compel arbitration according to the terms of the controlling arbitration agreement. The Supreme Court also made clear that in agreeing to arbitration of a statutory claim, a party does not forgo substantive rights afforded by the statute. In a growing number of court decisions, in effect employers are finding that courts will not enforce arbitration agreements in which the employer has devised an arbitration agreement that functions as a thumb on the employer's side of the scale.[8]

When a court finds that a contract or any clause of a contract was unconscionable at the time it was made, it may enforce the remainder of the contract without the unconscionable clause or refuse to enforce the entire agreement if the agreement is permeated by unconscionability. **For Example,** Sandra Menefee sued Geographic Expeditions, Inc. (GeoEx), for the wrongful death of her son while on a GeoEx expedition up Mount Kilimanjaro. GeoEx moved to compel arbitration under the parties' limitation of liability contract. The arbitration provision was found by the court to be procedurally and substantively unconscionable. GeoEx contended that the court should have severed the objectionable provisions and enforced the remainder of the arbitration clause. The court refused to do so because GeoEx designed its arbitration clause to impose arbitration not simply as an alternative to litigation, but as an inferior forum that would give it an advantage. In addition to limiting the plaintiffs' recovery, the agreement required them to indemnify GeoEx for its legal costs and fees if they pursued any claims covered by the release agreement, compounded by the requirement that plaintiffs pay half of any mediation fees and mediate and arbitrate in San Francisco, GeoEx's choice of venue, far from the plaintiffs' home in Colorado.[9]

B. Agreements Affecting Public Welfare

Agreements that may harm the public welfare are condemned as contrary to public policy and are not binding. Agreements that interfere with public service or the duties of public officials, obstruct legal process, or discriminate against classifications of individuals may be considered detrimental to public welfare and, as such, are not enforceable.

7. Agreements Contrary to Public Policy

A given agreement may not violate any statute but may still be so offensive to society that the courts feel that enforcing the contract would be contrary to public policy.

Public policy cannot be defined precisely but is loosely described as protection from that which tends to be injurious to the public or contrary to the public good or which violates any established interest of society. Contracts that may be unenforceable as contrary to public policy frequently relate to the protection of the public welfare, health, or safety; to the protection of the person; and to the protection of recognized social institutions. **For Example,** a woman entered into a services contract with a male in exchange for financial support. The record disclosed, however, that the association between the parties was one founded upon the exchange of money for sex. The court determined that the agreement for financial support in exchange for illicit sexual relations was violative of public policy and thus was unenforceable.[10] Courts are cautious in invalidating a contract on the ground that it is contrary to public policy because courts recognize that, on the one hand, they are applying a very vague standard and, on the other hand, they are restricting the freedom of the contracting parties to contract freely as they choose.[11]

[7] *Gilmer v. Interstate/Johnson Lane Corp.*, 500 U.S. 20 (1991); *Circuit City Stores, Inc. v. Adams*, 532 U.S. 105 (2001).
[8] See *Vassi/Kouska v. Woodfield Nissan Inc.*, 830 N.E.2d 619 (Ill. App. 2005).
[9] *Lhotka v. Geographic Expeditions, Inc.*, 104 Cal. Rptr. 3d 844 (Cal. App. 2010).
[10] *Anonymous v. Anonymous*, 740 N.Y.S.2d 341 (App. Div. 2002).
[11] *Beacon Hill Civic Ass'n v. Ristorante Toscano, Inc.*, 662 N.E.2d 1015 (Mass. 1996).

8. Gambling, Wagers, and Lotteries

Gambling contracts are illegal. Largely as a result of the adoption of antigambling statutes, wagers or bets are generally illegal. Private **lotteries** involving the three elements of prize, chance, and consideration (or similar affairs of chance) are also generally held illegal. In many states, public lotteries (lotteries run by a state government) have been legalized by statute. Raffles are usually regarded as lotteries. In some states, bingo games, lotteries, and raffles are legalized by statute when the funds raised are used for a charitable purpose.

Sales promotion schemes calling for the distribution of property according to chance among the purchasers of goods are held illegal as lotteries without regard to whether the scheme is called a *guessing contest,* a *raffle,* or a *gift.*

Giveaway plans and games are lawful so long as it is not necessary to buy anything or give anything of value to participate. If participation is free, the element of consideration is lacking, and there is no lottery.

An activity is not gambling when the result is solely or predominantly a matter of skill. In contrast, it is gambling when the result is solely a matter of luck. Rarely is any activity 100 percent skill or 100 percent luck.

C. Regulation of Business

Local, state, and national laws regulate a wide variety of business activities and practices.

9. Effect of Violation

Whether an agreement made in connection with business conducted in violation of the law is binding or void depends on how strongly opposed the public policy is to the prohibited act. Some courts take the view that the agreement is not void unless the statute expressly specifies this. In some instances, a statute expressly preserves the validity of the contract. **For Example,** if someone fails to register a fictitious name under which a business is conducted, the violator, after registering the name as required by statute, is permitted to sue on a contract made while illegally conducting business.

10. Statutory Regulation of Contracts

To establish uniformity or to protect one of the parties to a contract, statutes frequently provide that contracts of a given class must follow a statutory model or must contain specified provisions. **For Example,** statutes commonly specify that particular clauses must be included in insurance policies to protect the persons insured and their beneficiaries. Other statutes require that contracts executed in connection with credit buying and loans contain particular provisions designed to protect the debtor.

Consumer protection legislation gives the consumer the right to rescind the contract in certain situations. Laws relating to truth in lending, installment sales, and home improvement contracts commonly require that an installment-sale contract specify the cash price, the down payment, the trade-in value (if any), the cash balance, the insurance costs, and the interest and finance charges.

CPA 11. Licensed Callings or Dealings

Statutes frequently require that a person obtain a license, certificate, or diploma before practicing certain professions, such as law and medicine.[12] A license may also be required before carrying on a particular business or trade, such as that of a real estate broker, stockbroker, hotel keeper, or pawnbroker.

If a license is required to protect the public from unqualified persons, a contract made by an unlicensed person is unenforceable. **For Example,** a corporation that does not hold a required real estate broker's license cannot sue to recover fees for services as a broker. An unlicensed insurance broker who cannot recover a fee because of the absence of a license cannot evade the statutory requirement by having a friend who is a licensed broker bill for the services and collect the payment for him.

In some states an unlicensed contractor can neither enforce a home improvement contract against an owner, nor seek recovery in *quantum meruit.* **For Example,** a contractor who performed work on Adam Gottbetter's apartment in New York City and was not paid for its work was barred from pursuing its claim against the owner.[13]

[12] *Hakimi v. Cantwell,* 855 N.Y.S.2d 273 (App. Div. 2008).

[13] *Orchid Construction Corp. v. Gottbetter,* 932 N.Y.S.2d 100 (A.D. 2011).

CPA 12. Contracts in Restraint of Trade

An agreement that unreasonably restrains trade is illegal and void on the ground that it is contrary to public policy. Such agreements take many forms, such as a combination to create a monopoly or to obtain a corner on the market or an association of merchants to increase prices. In addition to the illegality of the agreement based on general principles of law, statutes frequently declare monopolies illegal and subject the parties to various civil and criminal penalties.[14]

CPA 13. Agreements Not to Compete

In the absence of a valid restrictive covenant, the seller of a business may compete with the buyer, or an ex-employee may solicit customers of the former employer.

A noncompetition covenant may be held invalid because of vagueness concerning the duration and geographic area of the restriction.[15] Moreover, if the agreement not to compete is not properly executed in accordance with state law, it will not be enforced. **For Example,** Holly Martinez worked for Avis Rent-A-Car at the New Bern, North Carolina, airport. When hired, she printed her name on the top of the form containing an agreement not to compete but did not sign it. On December 17, she resigned her position to return to school, saying that she planned to get a part-time job. The next day, she began working for Hertz Rent-A-Car at the counter adjacent to the Avis counter. Avis was unsuccessful in obtaining a restraining order to prevent Holly from working for its competitor because the agreement was not signed as required by state law.[16]

CPA (A) Sale of Business. When a going business is sold, it is commonly stated in the contract that the seller shall not go into the same or a similar business again within a certain geographic area or for a certain period of time, or both. In early times, such agreements were held void because they deprived the public of the service of the person who agreed not to compete, impaired the latter's means of earning a livelihood, reduced competition, and exposed the public to monopoly. To modern courts, the question is whether, under the circumstances, the restriction imposed on one party is reasonably necessary to protect the other party. If the restriction is reasonable, it is valid and enforceable. **For Example,** when Scott Gaddy, the majority stockholder of GWC Insurance Brokers, sold his business to Alliant for $4.1 million he agreed to refrain from competing in the insurance business in California for five years. Under California law, contracts not to compete are void, except for noncompetition covenants in connection with the sale of a business. The reason for the exception is to prevent the seller from depriving the buyer of the full value of the acquisition, including the sold company's goodwill. The court enforced the covenant against Gaddy.[17]

(B) Employment Contract. Restrictions to prevent competition by a former employee are held valid when reasonable and necessary to protect the interest of the former employer. **For Example,** a noncompete clause executed by Dr. Samuel Keeley that prohibited his "establishing a competing cardiovascular surgery practice within a 75-mile radius of Albany, Georgia, for a period of two years following the date of termination" was upheld in court and did not include more territory than necessary to protect the professional corporation's business interests.[18]

Public policy requires that noncompetition covenants be strictly construed in favor of freedom of action of the employee.[19] A restrictive covenant is not binding when it places a restriction on the employee that is broader than reasonably necessary to protect the employer. **For Example,** Illinois manufacturer Arcor's noncompete clause, which had a restricted area of "the United States and Canada" precluding competition by a former employee for a one-year period, was found to be unenforceable as an industrywide ban that constituted a "blanket prohibition on competition."[20] In determining the validity of a restrictive covenant binding an employee, the court balances the aim of protecting the legitimate interests of the employer with the right of the employee to follow gainful employment and provide services required by the public and other employers.

---

[14] Sherman Antitrust Act, 15 U.S.C. §§1–7; Clayton Act, 15 U.S.C. §§12–27; Federal Trade Commission Act, 15 U.S.C. §§41–58.

[15] *Vukovich v. Coleman*, 789 N.E.2d 520 (Ind. App. 2003).

[16] *New Hanover Rent-A-Car, Inc. v. Martinez*, 525 S.E.2d 487 (N.C. App. 2000).

[17] 72 Cal. Rptr. 3d 259 (Cal. App. 2008).

[18] *Keeley v. CSA*, P.C., 510 S.E.2d 880 (Ga. App. 1999).

[19] Noncompetition covenants are not valid in California. However, confidentiality agreements protecting trade secrets are enforceable in that state.

[20] *Arcor, Inc. v. Haas*, 842 N.E.2d 265 (Ill. App. 2005).

Thinking Things Through

Noncompete Clauses, Cause for Concern?

Some nine states do not enforce noncompete clauses in employment contracts, according to the research of Matt Marx who has dedicated his doctoral studies at Harvard to this topic. The states are (from west to east): California, Washington, Nevada, Montana, North Dakota, Minnesota, Oklahoma, West Virginia, and Connecticut. (New York and Oregon have significantly limited their applicability.) Marx had naively signed a two-year noncompete agreement out of MIT at SpeechWorks, a voice recognition start-up, and when he wanted to leave and continue in the voice recognition field, his options were to sit out the two-year noncompete period or go to work at a California firm, which he did. He is now researching whether enforcing noncompetes in a state can spur inventors, engineers, and entrepreneurs to move elsewhere to pursue development of their ideas.*

Does a state's innovation suffer when noncompete clauses handcuff employees to an employer, or force employees to take an unpaid leave for the noncompete period before continuing in their field with a new or start-up employer? THINKING THINGS THROUGH, prospective employees should carefully consider the impact noncompetes would have on their lives, and if they must sign one, carefully negotiate its duration and scope.**

*See Scott Kirsner, "Why 'Noncompete' Means 'Don't Thrive,'" *Boston Globe*, December 30, 2007, E-1; Scott Kirsner, "Start-ups Stifled by Noncompetes," *Boston Globe*, June 21, 2009, G-1.

**For a comprehensive study of the strength of noncompetition enforcement rankings by state, see Norman D. Bishara, "Fifty Ways to Leave Your Employer: Relative Enforcement of Covenants Not to Compete, Trends and Implications for Employee Mobility Policy," 13 *U. Pa. J. Bus. L.* 751 (2011).

(c) Effect of Invalidity. When a restriction of competition agreed to by the parties is invalid because its scope as to time or geographic area is too great, how does this affect the contract? Some courts trim the restrictive covenant down to a scope they deem reasonable and require the parties to abide by that revision.[21] This rule is nicknamed the "blue-pencil rule." **For Example,** Julie Murray signed a noncompete agreement, which was validly assigned to the purchaser of the Accounting Center of Lucas County, Inc. When the new owner changed from an hourly wage to commission pay for her tax preparation work, she objected and was terminated. The court found the 24-month

Ethics & the Law

William Stern and his wife were unable to have children because the wife suffered from multiple sclerosis and pregnancy posed a substantial health risk. Stern's family had been killed in the Holocaust, and he had a strong desire to continue his bloodline.

The Sterns entered into a surrogacy contract with Mary Beth Whitehead through the Infertility Center of New York (ICNY). William Stern and the Whiteheads (husband and wife) signed a contract for Mary Beth to be artificially inseminated and carry Stern's child to term, for which Stern was to pay Mary Beth $10,000 and ICNY $7,500.

Mary Beth was successfully artificially inseminated in 1985, and Baby M was born on March 27, 1986. To avoid publicity, the parents of Baby M were listed as "Mr. and Mrs. Whitehead," and the baby was called Sara Elizabeth Whitehead. On March 30, 1986, Mary Beth turned Baby M over to the Sterns at their home. They renamed the little girl Melissa.

Mary Beth became emotionally distraught and was unable to eat or sleep. The Sterns were so frightened by her behavior that they allowed her to take Baby M for one week to help her adjust. The Whiteheads took the baby and traveled throughout the East, staying in 20 different hotels and motels. Florida authorities found Baby M with Mary Beth's parents and returned her to the Sterns.

Mary Beth said the contract was one to buy a baby and was against public policy and therefore void. She also argued that the contract violated state laws on adoption and the severance of parental rights. The Sterns brought an action to have the contract declared valid and custody awarded to them.

Should the contract be valid or void? What types of behavior would be encouraged if the contract were declared valid? Is it ethical to "rent a womb"? Is it ethical to sell a child? See *In re Baby M*, *537 A.2d 15 (N.J. 1988)*.

[21] *Unisource Worldwide, Inc. v. Valenti*, 196 F. Supp. 2d 269 (E.D.N.Y. 2002).

noncompete restriction exceeded what was reasonable to protect the employer's legitimate business interests, and modified the time period to one year.[22] In the *Arcor* case, the court refused to "blue pencil" the covenant because to render the clause reasonable, the court would in effect be writing a new agreement, which is inappropriate.[23]

Other courts refuse to apply the blue-pencil rule and hold that the restrictive covenant is void or that the entire contract is void.[24] There is also authority that a court should refuse to apply the blue-pencil rule when the restrictive covenant is manifestly unfair and would virtually keep the employee from earning a living.

Courts have reexamined their precedents and overruled or gradually refined their rulings regarding non-competition provisions broadly barring former employees for working in any capacity for any other business in an industry, as seen in the *Home Paramount Pest Control* case.

Home Paramount Pest Control Companies, Inc. v. Shaffer, 718 S.E.2d 762 (Va. 2011)

Overlybroad and Unenforceable

Justin Shaffer while an employee of the Home Paramount Pest Control Companies Inc. (Home Paramount) signed an employment agreement (the Provision) providing that:

> *The Employee will not engage directly or indirectly or concern himself/herself in any manner whatsoever in the carrying on or conducting the business of exterminating, pest control, termite control and/or fumigation services as an owner, agent, servant, representative, or employee, and/or as a member of a partnership and/or as an officer, director or stockholder of any corporation, or in any manner whatsoever, in any city, cities, county or counties in the state(s) in which the Employee works and/or in which the Employee was assigned during the two (2) years next preceding the termination of the Employment Agreement and for a period of two (2) years from and after the date upon which he/she shall cease for any reason whatsoever to be an employee of [Home Paramount].*

Shaffer resigned from Home Paramount in 2009 and became an employee of Connor's Termite and Pest Control Inc. Home Paramount sued Shaffer and Connor's, claiming that Shaffer's employment by Connor's violated the provision. The defendants contended the provision was overlybroad and unenforceable. From a judgment for Shaffer, Home Paramount appealed.

JUDICIAL OPINION

MIMS, J.…The enforceability of a provision that restricts competition is a question of law that we review de novo.… It is enforceable if it "is narrowly drawn to protect the employer's legitimate business interest, is not unduly burdensome on the employee's ability to earn a living, and is not against public policy." The employer bears the burden of proving each of these factors. When evaluating whether the employer has met that burden, we consider the "function, geographic scope, and duration" elements of the restriction. These elements are "considered together" rather than "as three separate and distinct issues."

Home Paramount asserts that the circuit court erred by focusing on the language of the Provision prohibiting Shaffer from "engag[ing] indirectly or concern[ing] himself… in any manner whatsoever" in pest control "as an owner, agent, servant, representative, or employee, and/or as a member of a partnership and/or as an officer, director or stockholder of any corporation, or in any manner whatsoever." …

We have consistently assessed the function element of provisions that restrict competition by determining whether the prohibited activity is of the same type as that actually engaged in by the former employer. For example, in *Blue Ridge Anesthesia & Critical Care, Inc. v. Gidick,* 239 Va. 369, 389 S. E.2d 467 (1990), the employer was a medical equipment vendor. We upheld a provision that prohibited employees from "open[ing] or be[ing] employed by or act[ing] on behalf

[22] *Murray v. Accounting Center of Lucas County, Inc.*, 898 N.E.2d 89 (Ohio App. 2008).

[23] *Arcor, Inc. v. Haas*, 842 N.E.2d 265 (Ill. App. 2005).

[24] *SWAT 24 v. Bond*, 759 So.2d 1047 (La. App. 2000). Under California law, any "contract by which anyone is restrained from engaging in a lawful profession, trade or business is to that extent void." Cal B&P Code §16600. A noncompete provision is permitted, however, when "necessary to protect the employer's trade secrets." See *Lotona v. Aetna U.S. Healthcare Inc.*, 82 F. Supp. 2d 1089 (C.D. Cal. 1999), where Aetna was liable for wrongful termination when it fired a California employee for refusing to sign a noncompete agreement.

Continued

of any competitor of [the][e]mployer which renders the same or similar services." However, that provision included explicit language allowing employees to "work[ ] in the medical industry in some role which would not compete with the business" of the employer. We noted that "the former employees are not forbidden from working in *any* capacity for a medical equipment company, or from selling *any* type of medical equipment. They are only prohibited 'from working in the medical industry in some role which would ... compete with the business'" of the employer. (emphasis in original)....

In this case, the Provision is akin to those we found unenforceable.... On its face, it prohibits Shaffer from working for Connor's or any other business in the pest control industry in any capacity. It bars him from engaging even indirectly, or concerning himself in any manner whatsoever, in the pest control business, even as a passive stockholder of a publicly traded international conglomerate with a pest control subsidiary. The circuit court therefore did not err in requiring Home Paramount to prove it had a legitimate business interest in such a sweeping prohibition....

Because Home Paramount did not confine the function element of the Provision to those activities it actually engaged in, it bore the burden of proving a legitimate business interest in prohibiting Shaffer from engaging in all reasonably conceivable activities while employed by a competitor.

Although we weigh the function element of a provision that restricts competition together with its geographic scope and duration elements, the clear overbreadth of the function here cannot be saved by narrow tailoring of geographic scope and duration. Accordingly, we will affirm the circuit court's judgment that the Provision was overbroad and therefore unenforceable....

Home Paramount also argues that "[i]t has been settled law for more than 20 years that similar language of Home Paramount's non-compete agreement is not overly broad and is enforceable." Home Paramount thereby suggests that the doctrine of stare decisis compels us to uphold the Provision in this case. We disagree.

Stare decisis "is not an inexorable command." *McDonald v. City of Chicago,* 130 S.Ct. 3020, 3063(2010). It "was never meant to prevent a careful evolution of the law....

We acknowledge that the language of the provision we upheld in *Paramount Termite* is identical to the Provision. However, we have incrementally clarified the law since that case was decided in 1989. In the intervening twenty-two years, we have gradually refined its application.... Therefore, to the extent that *Paramount Termite* conflicts with any portion of our holding today, *Paramount Termite* is overruled.

Finally, Home Paramount argues the circuit court erred in failing to consider its evidence that Shaffer actually breached the Provision by soliciting its customers. However, the threshold question is whether the Provision is enforceable. Since the circuit court determined that the Provision cannot be enforced, the issue of its actual breach was not reached.

[Judgment affirmed.]

QUESTIONS

1. State the rule of law allowing the enforcement of noncompetition provisions in this jurisdiction.
2. Was Home Paramount able to prove that it had a legitimate business interest in prohibiting Shaffer from engaging in all reasonably conceivable activities while employed by its competitor Connor's Pest Control?
3. Does the fact that Shaffer actually solicited Home Paramount customers demonstrate that the noncompetition provision should be enforced?

14. Usurious Agreements

Usury is committed when money is loaned at a higher rate of interest than the law allows. Most states prohibit by statute charging more than a stated amount of interest. These statutes provide a maximum annual contract rate of interest that can be exacted under the law of a given state. In many states, the usury law does not apply to loans made to corporations.

When a lender incurs expenses in making a loan, such as the cost of appraising property or making a credit investigation of the borrower, the lender will require the borrower to pay the amount of such expenses. Any fee charged by a lender that goes beyond the reasonable expense of making the loan constitutes "interest" for the purposes of determining whether the transaction is usurious.[25]

[25] *Lentimo v. Cullen Center Bank and Trust Co.*, 919 S.W.2d 743 (Tex. App. 1996).

Thinking Things Through

Legality and Public Policy

Karl Llewellyn, the principal drafter of the law that governs nearly all sales of goods in the United States—the Uniform Commercial Code (UCC)—once wrote, "Covert tools are never reliable tools." He was referring to unfairness in a contract or between the contracting parties.

The original intent of declaring certain types of contracts void because of issues of imbalance was based in equity. Courts stepped in to help parties who found themselves bound under agreements that were not fair and open in both their written terms and the communications between the parties. One contracts scholar wrote that the original intent could be described as courts stepping in to help "presumptive sillies like sailors and heirs..." and others who, if not crazy, are "pretty peculiar."

However, as the sophistication of contracts and commercial transactions increased, the importance of accuracy, honesty, and fairness increased. Unconscionability is a contracts defense that permits courts to intervene where contracts, if enforced, would "affront the sense of decency." UNCONSCIONABILITY is a term of ethics or moral philosophy used by courts to prevent exploitation and fraud.

Penalites for violating usury laws vary from state to state, with a number of states restricting the lender to the recovery of the loan but no interest whatsoever; other states allow recovery of the loan principal and interest up to the maximum contract rate. Some states also impose a penalty on the lender such as the payment of double the interest paid on a usurious loan.

LawFlix

Midnight Run (1988) (R)

Is the contract Robert DeNiro has for bringing in Charles Grodin, an embezzler, legal? Discuss the issues of consideration and ethics as the bail bondsman puts another bounty hunter on the case and DeNiro flees from law enforcement agents in order to collect his fee. And finally, discuss the legality of DeNiro's acceptance of money from Grodin and his release of Grodin at the end of the movie.

MAKE THE CONNECTION

SUMMARY

When an agreement is illegal, it is ordinarily void and no contract arises from it. Courts will not allow one party to an illegal agreement to bring suit against the other party. There are some exceptions to this, such as when the parties are not equally guilty or when the law's purpose in making the agreement illegal is to protect the person who is bringing suit. When possible, an agreement will be interpreted as being lawful. Even when a particular provision is held unlawful, the balance of the agreement may be saved so that the net result is a contract minus the clause that was held illegal.

The term *illegality* embraces situations in unconscionable contract clauses in which the courts hold that contract provisions are unenforceable because they are too harsh or oppressive to one of the parties to a transaction. If the clause is part of a standard form contract drafted by the party having superior bargaining power and is presented on a take-it-or-leave-it basis (a contract of adhesion) and the substantive terms of the clause itself are unduly oppressive, the clause will be found to be unconscionable and not enforced.

Whether a contract is contrary to public policy may be difficult to determine because public policy is not precisely defined. That which is harmful to the public welfare or general good is contrary to public policy. Contracts condemned as contrary to public policy include those designed to deprive the weaker party of a benefit that the lawmaker desired to provide, agreements injuring public service, and wagers and private lotteries. Statutes commonly make the wager illegal as a form of gambling. The private lottery is any plan under which, for a consideration, a person has a chance to win a prize.

Illegality may consist of the violation of a statute or administrative regulation adopted to regulate business. An agreement not to compete may be illegal as a restraint of trade except when reasonable in its terms and when it is incidental to the sale of a business or to a contract of employment.

The charging by a lender of a higher rate of interest than allowed by law is usury. Courts must examine transactions carefully to see whether a usurious loan is disguised as a legitimate transaction.

LEARNING OUTCOMES

After studying this chapter, you should be able to clearly explain:

A. General Principles

LO.1 Explain the general contract principles on "illegality"

See the unenforceable illegal lease to non-professionals example on p. 301.

See the example where a contract to manufacture and sell illegal slot machines is void, p. 301.

LO.2 Explain the implied obligation on all parties of good faith and fair dealing

See the example of the Vermont landlord who deprived a tenant of her rights under a lease, p. 302.

B. Agreements Affecting Public Welfare

LO.3 Understand that it is only in unusual situations that a contract provision will be unenforceable because it is unconscionable

See the *Kramper Family Farm* example where the court refused to consider whether the contract was fair or unfair, wise or foolish, p. 302.

But see the *Geographic Expeditions* case that illustrates an unconscionable arbitration clause, p. 303.

C. Regulation of Business

LO.4 Explain the rationale for requiring licenses to carry on as a business, trade, or profession

See the discussion requiring licenses to protect the public from unqualified persons, p. 304.

LO.5 Distinguish between noncompete clauses in the sale of a business and noncompete clauses in employment contracts

See the example where the California court enforced a five-year noncompete clause against the seller of a business, p. 305.

See the example involving Julie Murray's noncompete clause and why it was modified from 24 months to one year, pp. 306–307.

See the *Home Paramount Pest Control* case that illustrates a trend barring enforcement of overlybroad noncompetition clauses, pp. 307–308.

KEY TERMS

contracts of adhesion
good faith
in pari delicto
lotteries
public policy
usury

QUESTIONS AND CASE PROBLEMS

1. When are the parties to an illegal agreement *in pari delicto*?

2. John Iwen sued U.S. West Direct because of a negligently constructed yellow pages advertisement. U.S. West Direct moved to stay litigation and compel arbitration under the yellow pages order form, which required advertisers to resolve all controversies through arbitration, but allowed U.S. West (the publisher) to pursue judicial remedies to collect amounts due it. Under the arbitration provision, Iwen's sole remedy was a pro rata reduction or refund of the cost of the advertisement. The order form language was drafted by U.S. West Direct on a take-it-or-leave-it basis and stated in part:

   Any controversy or claim arising out of or relating to this Agreement, or breach thereof, other than an action by Publisher for the collection of amounts due under this Agreement, shall be settled by final, binding arbitration in accordance with the Commercial Arbitration rules of the American Arbitration Association.

   If forced to arbitration, Iwen would be unable to recover damages for the negligently constructed yellow pages ad, nor could he recover damages for infliction of emotional distress and punitive damages related to his many efforts to adjust the matter with the company, which were ignored or rejected. Must Iwen have his case resolved through arbitration rather than a court of law? [*Iwen v. U.S. West Direct,* 977 P.2d 989 (Mont.)]

3. Sutcliffe Banton, dba Nemard Construction, furnished labor and materials (valued at $162,895) for improving Vicky Deafeamkpor's New York City residential property. She paid only $41,718, leaving $121,987 unpaid. Banton sued her and the jury awarded $90,000 in damages. Deafeamkpor moved for an order setting aside the jury's verdict because Banton was not properly licensed by New York City. Under NYC Code an unlicensed contractor may neither enforce a home improvement contract against an owner or recover in *quantum meruit*. The jury heard all the evidence regarding the materials and labor expended on Deafeamkpor's residence and concluded that the plaintiff performed satisfactory work valued at $90,000 for which he was not paid. Should the court allow the owner to take advantage of Banton and his employees and suppliers? What public policy would support such an outcome? Decide. [*Nemard Construction Corp. v. Deafeamkpor,* 863 N.Y.S.2d 846]

4. Eugene McCarthy left his position as director of sales for Nike's Brand Jordan division in June 2003 to become vice president of U.S. footwear sales and merchandising at Reebok, one of Nike's competitors. Nike sought a preliminary injunction to prevent McCarthy from working for Reebok for a year, invoking a noncompete agreement McCarthy had signed in Oregon in 1997 when Nike had promoted him to his earlier position as a regional footwear sales manager. The agreement stated in pertinent part:

   During EMPLOYEE'S employment by NIKE… and for one (1) year thereafter, ("the Restriction Period"), EMPLOYEE will not directly or indirectly… be employed by, consult for, or be connected in any manner with, any business engaged anywhere in the world in the athletic footwear, athletic apparel or sports equipment and accessories business, or any other business which directly competes with NIKE or any of its subsidiaries or affiliated corporations.

   McCarty contends that such a contract is a restraint of trade and should not be enforced. Nike contends that the agreement is fair and should be enforced. Decide. [*Nike, Inc. v. McCarthy,* 379 F.3d 576 (9th Cir.)]

5. Ewing was employed by Presto-X-Co., a pest exterminator. His contract of employment specified that he would not solicit or attempt to solicit customers of Presto-X for two years after the termination of his employment. After working several years, his employment was terminated. Ewing then sent a letter to customers of Presto-X stating that he no longer worked for Presto-X and that he was still certified by the state. Ewing set forth his home address and phone number, which the customers did not previously have. The letter ended with the statement, "I thank you for your

business throughout the past years." Presto-X brought an action to enjoin Ewing from sending such letters. He raised the defense that he was prohibited only from soliciting and there was nothing in the letters that constituted a seeking of customers. Decide. What ethical values are involved? [*Presto-X-Co. v. Ewing,* 442 N.W.2d 85 (Iowa)]

6. The Minnesota adoption statute requires that any agency placing a child for adoption make a thorough investigation and not give a child to an applicant unless the placement is in the best interests of the child. Tibbetts applied to Crossroads, Inc., a private adoption agency, for a child to adopt. He later sued the agency for breach of contract, claiming that the agency was obligated by contract to supply a child for adoption. The agency claimed that it was required only to use its best efforts to locate a child and was not required to supply a child to Tibbetts unless it found him to be a suitable parent. Decide. [*Tibbetts v. Crossroads, Inc.,* 411 N.W.2d 535 (Minn. App.)]

7. Siddle purchased a quantity of fireworks from Red Devil Fireworks Co. The sale was illegal, however, because Siddle did not have a license to make the purchase, which the seller knew because it had been so informed by the attorney general of the state. Siddle did not pay for the fireworks, and Red Devil sued him. He defended on the ground that the contract could not be enforced because it was illegal. Was the defense valid? [*Red Devil Fireworks Co. v. Siddle,* 648 P.2d 468 (Wash. App.)]

8. Onderdonk entered a retirement home operated by Presbyterian Homes. The contract between Onderdonk and the home required Onderdonk to make a specified monthly payment that could be increased by the home as the cost of operations increased. The contract and the payment plan were thoroughly explained to Onderdonk. As the cost of operations rose, the home continually raised the monthly payments to cover these costs. Onderdonk objected to the increases on the ground that the increases were far more than had been anticipated and that the contract was therefore unconscionable. Was his objection valid?

9. Smith was employed as a salesman for Borden, Inc., which sold food products in 63 counties in Arkansas, 2 counties in Missouri, 2 counties in Oklahoma, and 1 county in Texas. Smith's employment contract prohibited him from competing with Borden after leaving its employ. Smith left Borden and went to work for a competitor, Lady Baltimore Foods. Working for this second employer, Smith sold in 3 counties of Arkansas. He had sold in 2 of these counties while he worked for Borden. Borden brought an injunction action against Smith and Lady Baltimore to enforce the noncompete covenant in Smith's former contract. Was Borden entitled to the injunction? [*Borden, Inc. v. Smith,* 478 S.W.2d 744 (Ark.)]

10. All new employees of Circuit City Stores were required to sign a Dispute Resolution Agreement (DRA) mandating that employees submit all employment-related disputes to arbitration. Under the DRA Circuit City was not obligated to arbitrate its claims against employees and may bring lawsuits against employees. Remedies are limited under the DRA, including one year back pay limit and a two-year front pay limit, with cap on punitive damages of an amount up to the greater of the amount of back pay and front pay awarded or $5,000. In a civil lawsuit under state law a plaintiff is entitled to all forms of relief. The DRA requires that employees split the cost of the arbitrator's fees with the employer. An individual is not required to pay for the services of a judge. Adams filed a sexual harassment case against his employer in state court. Circuit City filed a petition in federal court to compel arbitration. Decide. [*Circuit City Stores, Inc. v. Adams,* 274 F.3d 889 (9th Cir.)]

11. Vodra was employed as a salesperson and contracting agent for American Security Services. As part of his contract of employment, Vodra signed an agreement that for three years after leaving this employment, he would not solicit any customer of American. Vodra had no experience in the security field when he went to work for American. To the extent that he became known to American's customers, it was because of being American's representative rather than because of his own reputation in the security field. After some years, Vodra left American and organized a competing company that solicited American's

customers. American sued him to enforce the restrictive covenant. Vodra claimed that the restrictive covenant was illegal and not binding. Was he correct? [*American Security Services, Inc. v. Vodra,* 385 N.W.2d 73 (Neb.)]

12. Potomac Leasing Co. leased an automatic telephone system to Vitality Centers. Claudene Cato signed the lease as guarantor of payments. When the rental was not paid, Potomac Leasing brought suit against Vitality and Cato. They raised the defense that the rented equipment was to be used for an illegal purpose—namely, the random sales solicitation by means of an automatic telephone in violation of state statute; that this purpose was known to Potomac Leasing; and that Potomac Leasing could therefore not enforce the lease. Was this defense valid? [*Potomac Leasing Co. v. Vitality Centers, Inc.,* 718 S.W.2d 928 (Ark.)]

13. The English publisher of a book called *Cambridge* gave a New York publisher permission to sell that book any place in the world except in England. The New York publisher made several bulk sales of the book to buyers who sold the book throughout the world, including England. The English publisher sued the New York publisher and its customers for breach of the restriction prohibiting sales in England. Decide.

14. A state law required builders of homes to be licensed and declared that an unlicensed contractor could not recover compensation under a contract made for the construction of a residence. Although Annex Construction, Inc., did not have a license, it built a home for French. When he failed to pay what was owed, Annex sued him. He raised the defense that the unlicensed contractor could not recover for the contract price. Annex claimed that the lack of a license was not a bar because the president of the corporation was a licensed builder and the only shareholder of the corporation, and the construction had been properly performed. Was Annex entitled to recover?

15. Yarde Metals, Inc., owned six season tickets to New England Patriots football games. Gillette Stadium, where the games are played, had insufficient men's restrooms in use for football games at that time, which was the subject of numerous newspaper columns. On October 13, 2002, a guest of Yarde Metals, Mikel LaCroix, along with others, used available women's restrooms to answer the call of nature. As LaCroix left the restroom, however, he was arrested and charged with disorderly conduct. The Patriots organization terminated all six of Yarde's season ticket privileges, incorrectly giving as a reason that LaCroix was ejected "for throwing bottles in the seating section." Yarde sued, contending that "by terminating the plaintiff's season tickets for 2002 and for the future arbitrarily, without cause and based on false information," the Patriots had violated the implicit covenant of good faith and fair dealing of the season tickets contract. The back of each Patriots ticket states:

    This ticket and all season tickets are revocable licenses. The Patriots reserve the right to revoke such licenses, in their sole discretion, at any time and for any reason.

    How would you decide this case? [*Yarde Metals, Inc. v. New England Patriots Ltd.,* 834 N.E.2d 1233 (Mass. App.)]

CPA QUESTIONS

1. West, an Indiana real estate broker, misrepresented to Zimmer that West was licensed in Kansas under the Kansas statute that regulates real estate brokers and requires all brokers to be licensed. Zimmer signed a contract agreeing to pay West a 5 percent commission for selling Zimmer's home in Kansas. West did not sign the contract. West sold Zimmer's home. If West sued Zimmer for nonpayment of commission, Zimmer would be:
    a. Liable to West only for the value of services rendered.
    b. Liable to West for the full commission.
    c. Not liable to West for any amount because West did not sign the contract.

d. Not liable to West for any amount because West violated the Kansas licensing requirements (5/92, Law, #25).

2. Blue purchased a travel agency business from Drye. The purchase price included payment for Drye's goodwill. The agreement contained a covenant prohibiting Drye from competing with Blue in the travel agency business. Which of the following statements regarding the covenant is *not* correct?

   a. The restraint must be *no* more extensive than is reasonably necessary to protect the goodwill purchased by Blue.
   b. The geographic area to which it applies must be reasonable.
   c. The time period for which it is to be effective must be reasonable.
   d. The value to be assigned to it is the excess of the price paid over the seller's cost of all tangible assets (11/87, Law, #2).

CHAPTER 17

© Manuel Gutjahr/iStockphoto.com

Writing, Electronic Forms, and Interpretation of Contracts

learningoutcomes

After studying this chapter, you should be able to

LO.1 Explain when a contract must be evidenced by a writing

LO.2 Explain the effect of noncompliance with the statute of frauds

LO.3 Explain the parol evidence rule and the exceptions to this rule

LO.4 Understand the basic rule of contract construction that a contract is enforced according to its terms

LO.5 State the rules for interpreting ambiguous terms in a contract

When must a contract be written? What is the effect of a written contract? These questions lead to the statute of frauds and the parol evidence rule.

A. Statute of Frauds

A *contract* is a legally binding agreement. Must the agreement be evidenced by a writing?

1. Validity of Oral Contracts

In the absence of a statute requiring a writing, a contract may be oral or written. Managers and professionals should be more fully aware that their oral communications, including telephone conversations and dinner or breakfast discussions, may be deemed legally enforceable contracts. **For Example,** suppose that Mark Wahlberg, after reviewing a script tentatively entitled *The Bulger Boys*, meets with Steven Spielberg to discuss Mark's playing mobster James "Whitey" Bulger in the film. Steven states, "You *are* 'Whitey,' Marky! The nuns at Gate of Heaven Grammar School in South Boston—or maybe it was St. Augustine's—they don't send for the Boston Police when they are troubled about drug use in the schools; they send for you to talk to the kids. Nobody messes with you, and the kids know it. This is true stuff, I think, and this fugitive's brother Bill comes out of the Southie projects to be president of U Mass." Mark likes the script. Steven and Mark block out two months of time for shooting the film this fall. They agree on Mark's usual fee and a "piece of the action" based on a set percentage of the net income from the film. Thereafter, Mark's agent does not like the deal. He believes there are better scripts for Mark. Incredibly brutal things are coming out about "Whitey" and his ties to drug dealers that tarnish the script. And with Hollywood accounting, a percentage of the "net" take is usually of little value. However, all of the essential terms of a contract have been agreed on, and such an oral agreement would be legally enforceable. As set forth in the following text, no writing is required for a services contract that can be performed within one year after the date of the agreement.

Certain contracts, on the other hand, must be evidenced by a writing to be legally enforceable. These contracts are covered by the **statute of frauds.**[1]

Because many oral contracts are legally enforceable, it is a good business practice in the preliminary stages of discussions to stipulate that no binding agreement is intended to be formed until a written contract is prepared and signed by the parties.

2. Contracts That Must be Evidenced by a Writing

The statute of frauds requires that certain kinds of contracts be evidenced by a writing or they cannot be enforced. This means that either the contract itself must be in writing and signed by both parties or there must be a sufficient written memorandum of the oral contract signed by the person being sued for breach of contract. A *part performance* doctrine or exception to the statute of frauds may exist when the plaintiff's part performance is "unequivocally referable" to the oral agreement.[2]

(a) Agreement that Cannot Be Performed within One Year After the Contract Is Made. A writing is required when the contract, by its terms or subject matter, cannot be performed within one year after the date of the agreement. An oral agreement to supply a line of credit for two years cannot be enforced because of the statute of frauds.

The *Bithoney* case is an application of the rule that contracts that cannot be performed within one year must be in writing. Did the court determine that an oral contract for severance pay was barred by the Statute of Frauds?

[1] The name is derived from the original Statute of Frauds and perjuries, which was adopted in 1677 and became the pattern for similar legislation in America. The 17th section of that statute governed the sale of goods, and its modern counterpart is §2-201 of the U.C.C. The 4th section of the English statute provided the pattern for U.S. legislation with respect to contracts other than for the sale of goods described in this section of the chapter. The English statute was repealed in 1954 except as to land sale and guarantee contracts. The U.S. statutes remain in force, but the liberalization by U.C.C. §2-201 of the pre-Code requirements with respect to contracts for the sale of goods lessens the applicability of the writing requirement. Additional movement away from the writing requirement is seen in the 1994 Revision of Article 8, Securities, which abolishes the statute of frauds provision of the original U.C.C. §8-319 and goes beyond by declaring that the one-year performance provision of the statute of frauds is not applicable to contracts for securities. U.C.C. §8-113 [1994 Revision].

[2] *Carey & Associates v. Ernst*, 802 N.Y.S.2d 160 (A.D. 2005).

Bithoney v. Fulton Dekalb Hospital, 721 S.E.2d 577 (Ga. App. 2011)

Not A Good Move, Doctor

Despite not having an executed employment agreement, Dr. William Bithoney sold his home in New York and moved to Atlanta in early October in anticipation of his October 15 start work date as an executive at Grady Memorial Hospital. But the night before his anticipated start, he was informed that Grady's governing body, the Fulton-DeKalb Hospital Authority, did not approve his hiring and would not permit him to commence work. He sued the Authority for breach of an oral contract for severance, claiming that he and Grady's CEO, Otis Story, had agreed that he would receive "a severance payment of 15 months salary if Grady terminated his employment without cause"! Subsequently, Bithoney received a draft employment contract from Grady, which included a provision that, in the event Bithoney was terminated without cause, he would receive "full severance payment," which would be "payable for 15 months from the effective date of said termination."

JUDICIAL OPINION

DILLARD, J....

Analysis

Under Georgia law, the Statute of Frauds requires, inter alia, that "[a]ny agreement that is not to be performed within one year of the making thereof" be in writing and signed by the party to be charged. To fall within the ambit of this statutory provision, a contract must be incapable of being performed within a year; "the possibility of performance of the contract within one year is sufficient to remove it from the Statute of Frauds." Thus, in the event that Bithoney's oral severance agreement contained a provision that it be paid over the span of 15 months' time, its enforcement is barred by the Statute of Frauds. If the payment terms were otherwise unspecified, the oral agreement would not fall within the statute.

In the case sub judice, the trial court based its finding that the 15-month payment schedule was a term of the severance agreement on Bithoney's deposition testimony. And as a result of the trial court's determination that Bithoney's deposition responses constituted a "clear and unambiguous" admission of the 15-month payment term, the trial court rejected Bithoney's averments that he and Story did not discuss how the severance was to be paid....

Although Bithoney is not a lawyer and may have been less sensitive to the significance attached to certain words, the Authority's counsel clearly and unambiguously asked if the draft employment agreement—which provided that the severance "shall be payable for 15 months from the effective date of said termination"—"contain[ed] a written description of the severance terms" that he and Story had agreed upon, and Bithoney answered in the affirmative. This representation mirrored the allegation made by Bithoney in his complaint and repeated in his interrogatory response that the draft employment agreement "contain[ed]," among other things, "the severance terms" agreed upon....

Thus, because we cannot say that there is no evidence to support the trial court's ruling, we are constrained to conclude that it did not *clearly err* in applying the rule of *Prophecy* to hold that enforcement of the oral severance agreement was barred by the Statute of Frauds....

[Judgment affirmed]

QUESTIONS

1. Assess the quality of Dr. Bithoney's decision to sell his house in New York and move to Atlanta without a properly executed employment agreement.
2. Why was the severance agreement subject to the statute of frauds?
3. How should the oral agreement have been structured to avoid application of the statute of frauds?

The year runs from the time the oral contract is made rather than from the date when performance is to begin. In computing the year, the day on which the contract was made is excluded.

No *part performance* exception exists to validate an oral agreement not performable within one year. **For Example,** Babyback's Foods negotiated a multiyear oral agreement to comarket its barbecue meat products with the Coca-Cola Co. nationwide and arranged to have several coolers installed at area grocery stores in Louisville under the agreement. Babyback's faxed to Coca-Cola a contract that summarized the oral agreement but Coca-Cola never signed it. Because Coca-Cola did not sign and no part performance exception exists for an oral agreement not performable within one year, Babyback's lawsuit was unsuccessful.[3]

When no time for performance is specified by the oral contract and complete performance could "conceivably occur" within one year, the statute of frauds is not applicable to the oral contract.[4]

[3] *Coca-Cola Co. v. Babyback's International Inc.*, 841 N.E.2d 557 (Ind. 2006).

[4] *El Paso Healthcare System v. Piping Rock Corp.*, 939 S.W.2d 695 (Tex. App. 1997).

FIGURE 17-1 *Hurdles in the Path of a Contract*

WRITING REQUIRED	
STATUTE OF FRAUDS	EXCEPTIONS
MORE THAN ONE YEAR TO PERFORM SALE OF LAND ANSWER FOR ANOTHER'S DEBT OR DEFAULT PERSONAL REPRESENTATIVE TO PAY DEBT OF DECEDENT FROM PERSONAL FUNDS PROMISE IN CONSIDERATION OF MARRIAGE SALE OF GOODS FOR $500 OR MORE MISCELLANEOUS	PART PERFORMANCE PROMISOR BENEFIT DETRIMENTAL RELIANCE
PAROL EVIDENCE RULE	EXCEPTIONS
EVERY COMPLETE, FINAL WRITTEN CONTRACT	INCOMPLETE CONTRACT AMBIGUOUS TERMS FRAUD, ACCIDENT, OR MISTAKE TO PROVE EXISTENCE OR NONBINDING CHARACTER OF CONTRACT MODIFICATION OF CONTRACT ILLEGALITY

When a contract may be terminated at will by either party, the statute of frauds is not applicable because the contract may be terminated within a year. **For Example,** David Ehrlich was hired as manager of Gravediggaz pursuant to an oral management agreement that was terminable at will by either Ehrlich or the group. He was entitled to receive 15 percent of the gross earnings of the group and each of its members, including rap artist Robert Diggs, professionally known as RZA, for all engagements entered into while he was manager under this oral agreement. Such an at-will contract is not barred by the statute of frauds.[5]

(1) Oral Extension of a Contract.

A contract in writing, but not required to be so by the statute of frauds because it is terminable at will, may be varied by a new oral contract, even if the original written contract provided that it should not be varied except by writing. However, the burden of proof on the party asserting the oral modification is a heavy one. The modification must be shown by "clear, unequivocal and convincing evidence, direct or implied." **For Example,** John Boyle is the sole shareholder of numerous entertainment-related companies called the Cellar Door Companies, valued at some $106,000,000. Through these companies, he controls much of the large concert business at outdoor amphitheaters in Virginia and North Carolina. Bill Reid worked for Boyle beginning in 1983 as president of one of Boyle's companies. Boyle conducted financial affairs with an "air of informality." Reid proposed to

[5] See *Ehrlich v. Diggs*, 169 F. Supp. 2d 124 (E.D.N.Y. 2001). See also *Sterling v. Sterling*, 800 N.Y.S.2d 463 (A.D. 2005), in which the statute of frauds was no bar to an oral partnership agreement, deemed to be at will, that continued for an indefinite period of time.

Boyle the need for an amphitheater in Virginia Beach, and Boyle promised him a "33 percent interest" "if he pulled it off." As a result of Reid's efforts, the 20,000-seat Virginia Beach Amphitheater opened in 1996. The Supreme Court of Virginia determined that clear and convincing evidence did support the oral modification of Reid's written contract, including the following excerpt from the Court's opinion:

> *Thomas J. Lyons, Jr., Boyle's friend for over 35 years, testified on behalf of Reid. Lyons and his wife attended a concert in July 1996 at the newly constructed Virginia Beach Amphitheater as guests of Boyle and his wife. Lyons complimented Boyle for the excellent work and effort that Reid had undertaken in making the amphitheater a reality. According to Lyons, Boyle stated: "Well that's why he's my partner… that's why he owns 35 percent in this—in the Amphitheater or this project." After Lyons finished his testimony, the chancellor remarked on the record that Boyle stood up from his seat and "hugged" Lyons, even though Lyons had just provided testimony detrimental to Boyle.*

Reid was thus entitled to a judgment equivalent to the value of his interest in the project, \$3,566,343.[6]

(B) Agreement to Sell or a Sale of an Interest in Land. All contracts to sell land, buildings, or interests in land, such as mortgages, must be evidenced by a writing.[7] Leases are also interests in land and must be in writing, except in some states where leases for one year or less do not have to be in writing.[8]
For Example, if Mrs. O'Toole orally agrees to sell her house to the Gillespies for \$250,000 and, thereafter, her children convince her that she could obtain \$280,000 for the property if she is patient, Mrs. O'Toole can raise the defense of the statute of frauds should she be sued for breach of the oral agreement. Under the *part performance doctrine,* an exception exists by which an oral contract for the sale of land will be enforced by a court of equity in a suit for specific performance if the buyer has taken possession of the land under an oral contract and has made substantial improvements, the value of which cannot easily be ascertained, or has taken possession and paid part of the purchase price.

(C) Promise to Answer for the Debt or Default of Another. If an individual *I* promises a creditor *C* to pay the debt of *D* if *D* does not do so, *I* is promising to answer for the debt of another. Such a promise is sometimes called a **suretyship** contract, and it must be in writing to be enforceable. *I*, the promisor, is obligated to pay only if *D* does not pay. *I*'s promise is a *collateral* or *secondary* promise, and such promises must be in writing under the statute of frauds.[9]

(1) Main Purpose of Exception.

When the main purpose of the promisor's promise to pay the debt of another is to benefit the promisor, the statute of frauds is not applicable, and the oral promise to pay the debt is binding.

For Example, an individual *I* hires a contractor *C* to repair *I*'s building, and the supplier *S* is unwilling to extend credit to *C*. In an oral promise by *I* to pay *S* what is owed for the supplies in question if *C* does not pay, *I* is promising to pay for the debt of another, *C*. However, the *main purpose* of *I*'s promise was not to aid *C* but to get his own house repaired. This promise is not within the statute of frauds.[10]

(D) Promise by the Executor or Administrator of a Decedent's Estate to Pay a Claim Against the Estate from Personal Funds. The **personal representative (executor** or **administrator)** has the duty of handling the affairs of a deceased person, paying the debts from the proceeds of the estate and distributing any balance remaining. The executor or administrator is not personally liable for the claims against the estate of the **decedent**. If the personal representative promises to pay the decedent's debts with his or her own money, the promise cannot be enforced unless it is evidenced by a writing.

[6] *Reid v. Boyle*, 527 S.E.2d 137 (Va. 2000).
[7] *Magnum Real Estate Services, Inc. v. Associates, LLC*, 874 N.Y.S.2d 435 (A.D. 2009).
[8] See, however, *BBQ Blues Texas, Ltd. v. Affiliated Business*, 183 S.W.3d 543 (Tex. App. 2006), in which Eddie Calagero of Affiliated Business and the owners of BBQ Blues Texas, Ltd., entered an oral commission agreement to pay a 10 percent commission if he found a buyer for the restaurant, and he did so. The oral agreement was held to be outside the statute of frauds because the activity of finding a willing buyer did not involve the transfer of real estate. The second contract between the buyer and seller of the restaurant, which involved the transfer of a lease agreement, was a separate and distinct agreement over which Calagero had no control.
[9] See *Martin Printing, Inc. v. Sone*, 873 A.2d 232 (Conn. App. 2005), in which James Kuhe, in writing, personally guaranteed Martin Printing, Inc., to pay for printing expenses of *Pub Links Golfer Magazine*, if his corporation, Abbey Inc., failed to do so. When Abbey, Inc., failed to pay, the court enforced Kuhe's promise to pay.
[10] See *Christian v. Smith*, 759 N.W.2d 447 (Neb. 2008).

If the personal representative makes a contract on behalf of the estate in the course of administering the estate, a writing is not required. The representative is then contracting on behalf of the estate. Thus, if the personal representative employs an attorney to settle the estate or makes a burial contract with an undertaker, no writing is required.

(E) Promises Made in Consideration of Marriage. Promises to pay a sum of money or give property to another in consideration of marriage must be in writing under the statute of frauds.

For Example, if Mr. John Bradley orally promises to provide Karl Radford $20,000 on Karl's marriage to Mr. Bradley's daughter Michelle—and Karl and Michelle marry—the agreement is not enforceable under the statute of frauds because it was not in writing.

Prenuptial or *antenuptial* agreements are entered into by the parties before their marriage. After full disclosure of each party's assets and liabilities, and in some states, income,[11] the parties set forth the rights of each partner regarding the property and, among other things, set forth rights and obligations should the marriage end in a separation or divorce. Such a contract must be in writing.

For Example, when Susan DeMatteo married her husband M. J. DeMatteo in 1990, she had a 1977 Nova and $5,000 in the bank. M. Joseph DeMatteo was worth as much as $112 million at that time, and he insisted that she sign a prenuptial agreement before their marriage. After full disclosure of each party's assets, the prenuptial agreement was signed and videotaped some five days before their marriage ceremony. The agreement gave Susan $35,000 a year plus cost-of-living increases, as well as a car and a house, should the marriage dissolve. After the couple divorced, Susan argued before the state's highest court that the agreement was not "fair or reasonable" because it gave her less than 1 percent of her former husband's wealth. The court upheld the agreement, however, pointing out that Susan was fully informed about her fiancé's net worth and was represented by counsel.[12] When there is full disclosure and representation, prenuptial agreements, like other contracts, cannot be set aside unless they are unconscionable, which in a domestic relations setting means leaving a former spouse unable to support herself or himself.

(F) Sale of Goods. As will be developed in Chapter 23, Nature and Form of Sales, contracts for the sale of goods priced at $500 or more must ordinarily be in writing under UCC §2-201.[13]

(G) Promissory Estoppel. The statute of frauds may be circumvented when the party seeking to get around the statute of frauds is able to prove an enhanced promissory estoppel. While one element of a routine promissory estoppel case requires that the promisee rely on the promise in some definite and substantial manner, an enhanced level of reasonable reliance is necessary in order to have enhanced promissory estoppel, along with proof of an unconscionable injury or unjust enrichment. **For Example,** an Indiana bakery, Classic Cheesecake Inc., was able to interest several hotels and casinos in Las Vegas in buying its products. On July 27, 2004, its principals sought a loan from a local branch office of J. P. Morgan Chase Bank in order to establish a distribution center in Las Vegas. On September 17, local bank officer Dowling told Classic that the loan was a "go." When credit quality issues surfaced, Dowling continued to make assurances that the loan would be approved. On October 12, however, she told Classic that the loan had been turned down. Classic claimed that the bank's breach of its oral promise to make the loan and Classic's detrimental reliance on the promise caused it to lose more than $1 million. The Indiana statute of frauds requires agreements to lend money to be in writing. Classic contended that the oral agreement in this case must be enforced on the basis of promissory estoppel and the company's unconscionable injury. Judge Posner of the Seventh Circuit upheld the dismissal of the claim, writing (in part):

> *. . . For the plaintiff to treat the bank loan as a certainty because they were told by the bank officer whom they were dealing with that it would be approved was unreasonable, especially if, as the plaintiffs' damages claim presupposes, the need for the loan was urgent. Rational businessmen know that there is many a slip 'twixt cup and lips,' that a loan is not approved until it is approved, that if a*

[11] See FLA. STAT. §732–702 (2).

[12] *DeMatteo v. DeMatteo*, 762 N.E.2d 797 (Mass. 2002). See also *Waton v. Waton*, 887 So.2d 419 (Fla. App. 2004).

[13] As will be presented in Chapter 23, under Revised Article 2, §2-201, the $500 amount is increased to $5,000. This revision has not yet been adopted by any states.

bank's employee tells you your loan application will be approved that is not the same as telling you it has been approved, and that if one does not have a loan commitment in writing yet the need for the loan is urgent one had better be negotiating with other potential lenders at the same time....[14]

CPA 3. Note or Memorandum

The statute of frauds requires a writing to evidence those contracts that come within its scope. This writing may be a note or memorandum as distinguished from a contract.[15] The statutory requirement is, of course, satisfied if there is a complete written contract signed by both parties.

(A) SIGNING. The note or memorandum must be signed by the party sought to be bound by the contract. **For Example,** in the previous scenario involving Mark Wahlberg and Steven Spielberg, suppose the parties agreed to do the film according to the same terms but agreed to begin shooting the film a year from next April, and Mark wrote the essential terms on a napkin, dated it, and had Steven sign it "to make sure I got it right." Mark then placed the napkin in his wallet for his records. Because the contract could not be performed within one year after the date of the agreement, a writing would be required. If Steven thereafter decided not to pursue the film, Mark could enforce the contract against him because the napkin-note had been signed by the party to be bound or "sought to be charged," Steven. However, if Mark later decided not to appear in the film, the agreement to do the film could not be enforced against Mark because no writing existed signed by Mark, the party sought to be charged.

Some states require that the authorization of an agent to execute a contract coming within the statute of frauds must also be in writing. In the case of an auction, it is usual practice for the auctioneer to be the agent of both parties for the purpose of signing the memorandum.

E-Commerce & Cyberlaw

Electronic Signatures in the Internet Age

A SIGNATURE authenticates a writing by identifying the signers through their distinctive marks. The act of signing a document calls to the attention of the signing parties the legal significance of their act and expresses authorization and assent to the body of the signed writing. An ELECTRONIC SIGNATURE, including technology having digital or wireless capabilities, means any electronic sound, symbol, or process attached to, or logically associated with, a contract or other electronic record and executed with the intent to sign the record. An ELECTRONIC RECORD means any contract or other record created or stored in an electronic medium and retrievable in a perceivable form.

Conducting business electronically over the Internet has many advantages for consumers, businesses, and governments by allowing the instant purchase of goods, information, and services, and the reduction of sales, administrative, and overhead expenses. To facilitate the expansion of electronic commerce and place electronic signatures and electronic contracts on an equal footing with written signatures and paper contracts, Congress enacted a federal electronic signatures law.

Under the Electronic Signatures in Global and National Commerce Act (E-Sign),* electronically signed contracts cannot be denied legal effect because the signatures are in electronic form, nor can they be denied legal effect because they are delivered electronically. Contracts or documents requiring a notarized signature can be satisfied by the electronic signatures of the notaries coupled with the enclosure of all other required information as part of the record.

One of the goals of E-Sign was to spur states to enact the Uniform Electronic Transactions Act (UETA). Under E-Sign, a state may "modify, limit or supersede" the provisions of the federal act by enacting UETA "as approved and recommended for enactment in all the states" by the National Conference of Commissioners on Uniform State Laws or enacting a law that is consistent with E-Sign.** Thus, for those states that enacted the official version of UETA or one consistent with E-Sign, the federal law is superseded by the state law. UETA is similar to

*Pub. L. 106-229, 114 Stat. 464, 15 U.S.C. §7001.

**§102(a) and 102(a)(2). Forty-eight states and the District of Columbia have enacted the UETA in some form.

[14] *Classic Cheesecake Co. Inc. v. J. P. Morgan Chase Bank*, 546 F.3d 839 (7th Cir. 2008).

[15] *McLinden v. Coco*, 765 N.E.2d 606 (Ind. App. 2002).

E-Commerce - Cyberlaw—*Contd.*

E-Sign. It specifies that e-signatures and e-records can be used in contract formation, in audits, and as evidence. Selective differences between E-Sign and UETA are identified below. For example, inventor Stewart Lamle sued toy maker Mattel, Inc., for breach of contract. The U.S. Court of Appeals for the Federal Circuit remanded the case for trial after resolving the motions before it. The facts reveal that after a June 11, 1997, meeting of the parties, Mattel employee Mike Bucher sent an e-mail dated June 26 to Lamle, which set forth the terms agreed to in principle at the meeting with the closing "Best regards, Mike Bucher" appearing at the end of the e-mail. The court resolved the issue of whether an e-mail is a writing "subscribed by the party to be charged or the party's agent" in Lamle's favor. The court stated that under the UETA, the e-signature satisfies the state's (California's) Statute of Frauds. Because the e-mail was sent in 1997 prior to the effective date on the UETA, January 1, 2000, an evaluation of state common law was necessary. The court stated that it could see no meaningful difference between a typewritten signature on a telegram, which is sufficient to be a signature under state law, and the typed signature on the June 26 e-mail. It concluded that the e-mail satisfies the Statute of Frauds, assuming that there was a binding oral agreement on June 11.***

(a) General Rule of Parity. E-Sign provides for parity of electronic and paper signatures, contracts, and records. Electronic signatures and contracts satisfy the statute of frauds to the same extent they would if embodied as paper contracts with handwritten signatures. Internet contracts are neither more nor less valid, legal, and binding than are offline paper contracts. The rules are the same! The UETA is comparable to E-Sign in that it treats e-signatures and e-records as if they were handwritten.****

(b) Identity Verification. Neither E-Sign nor UETA is a digital signature law in that neither requires security procedures or a certification authority for the verification of electronic signatures. The parties themselves determine how they will verify each other's identity. Some options are a credit card, a password or PIN, public-key cryptographic exchange of digital signatures, or biometric signatures.

(c) Exceptions. The E-Sign Act exempts documents and records on trust and estate law so that it does not cover wills, codicils, and testamentary trusts or commercial law matters such as checks, negotiable instruments, and letters of credit. The act also does not cover court documents and cancellation of health and life insurance. Generally, the UETA also does not apply to these documents and records set forth previously.

****Lamle v. Mattel, Inc.*, 394 F.3d 1355 (Fed. Cir. 2005); see also *Payoutone v. Coral Mortgage Bankers*, 602 F. Supp. 2d 1219 (D. Colo. 2009).

****UETA §7(a) and 7(b).

(d) Consumer Protection and Notice and Consent Requirements. Consumer protection laws remain intact under E-Sign. Protections exist for consumers to consent to receiving electronic contracts, records, and documents; and businesses must tell consumers of their right to receive hardcopy documents.

Consumers must consent to receiving documents electronically or confirm consent electronically. For example, a consumer and a business may have negotiated terms of a contract by telephone and agreed to execute their agreement by e-mail. The consumer is then sent an e-mail that contains a consent disclosure, which contains a hypertext markup language (HTML) link the consumer can use to test her ability to view the contract in HTML. The consumer then returns the e-mail message to the business, thereby confirming electronically her consent to use this electronic means.

The UETA, like E-Sign, defers to existing substantive law regarding consumer protection.

(e) Time and Place of Sending and Receipt. E-Sign does not contain a provision addressing basic contract requirements such as sending and delivery, leaving such matters to existing contract law. However, the UETA provides that an electronic record is sent when it (1) is properly directed to an information processing system designated or used by the recipient to receive such records and from which the recipient may recover that record; (2) is in a form that the recipient's system is able to process; and (3) enters an information processing system that is in the control of the recipient but outside the control of the sender. An electronic record is received when (1) it enters an information processing system designated or used by the recipient to receive such records and from which the recipient is able to obtain the record and (2) it is in a form that the recipient's system can process.*

(f) Errors. Unlike E-Sign, which leaves matters relating to errors to be resolved by existing state contract law, UETA creates a system for dealing with errors. For example, when Marv Hale clicks on "buy" to make an online purchase of 12 bottles of Napa Valley Supreme Chardonnay at $12.90 per bottle, the computer will produce the equivalent of an invoice that includes the product's name, description, quantity, and price to enable Marv to avoid possible error when forming the electronic contract. This procedure gives the buyer an opportunity to identify and immediately correct an error. When such a procedure is not in effect and an error is later discovered, prompt notice to the other party can cure the error under Section 10 of the UETA.**

*UETA §15.

**UETA §10(2)(A)-(C).

The signature may be an ordinary one or any symbol that is adopted by the party as a signature. It may consist of initials, figures, or a mark. In the absence of a local statute that provides otherwise, a signature may be made by pencil, pen, typewriter, print, or stamp. As will be discussed, electronic signatures have parity with on-paper signatures.

(B) CONTENT. The note or memorandum must contain all of the essential terms of the contract so the court can determine just what was agreed. If any essential term is missing, the writing is not sufficient. A writing evidencing a sale of land that does not describe the land or identify the buyer does not satisfy the statute of frauds. The subject matter must be identified either within the writing itself or in other writings to which it refers. A deposit check given by the buyer to the seller does not take an oral land sales contract out of the statute of frauds. This is so because the check does not set forth the terms of the sale.

The note or memorandum may consist of one writing or of separate papers, such as letters, or a combination of such papers. Separate writings cannot be considered together unless they are linked. Linkage may be express reference in each writing to the other or by the fact that each writing clearly deals with the same subject matter.

4. Effect of Noncompliance

The majority of states hold that a contract that does not comply with the statute of frauds is not enforceable.[16] If an action is brought to enforce the contract, the defendant can raise the defense that the alleged contract is not enforceable because it is not evidenced by a writing, as required by the statute of frauds.

(A) RECOVERY OF VALUE CONFERRED. In most instances, a person who is prevented from enforcing a contract because of the statute of frauds is nevertheless entitled to recover from the other party the value of any services or property furnished or money given under the oral contract. Recovery is not based on the terms of the contract but on a quasi-contractual obligation. The other party is to restore to the plaintiff what was received in order to prevent unjust enrichment at the plaintiff's expense. **For Example,** when an oral contract for services cannot be enforced because of the statute of frauds, the person performing the work may recover the reasonable value of the services rendered.

(B) WHO MAY RAISE THE DEFENSE OF NONCOMPLIANCE? Only a party to the oral contract may raise a defense that it is not binding because there is no writing that satisfies the statute of frauds. Third persons, such as an insurance company or the Internal Revenue Service, cannot claim that a contract is void because the statute of frauds was not satisfied.

B. PAROL EVIDENCE RULE

When the contract is evidenced by a writing, may the contract terms be changed by the testimony of witnesses?

5. Exclusion of Parol Evidence

The general rule is that parol or extrinsic evidence will not be allowed into evidence to add to, modify, or contradict the terms of a written contract that is fully integrated or complete on its face.[17] Evidence of an alleged earlier oral or written agreement within the scope of the fully integrated written contract or evidence of an alleged contemporaneous oral agreement within the scope of the fully integrated written contract is inadmissible as *parol evidence.*

Parol evidence is admissible, however, to show fraud, duress, or mistake and under certain other circumstances to be discussed in the following paragraphs.

The **parol evidence rule** is based on the theory that either there never was an oral agreement or, if there was, the parties abandoned it when they reached the stage in negotiations of executing their written contract. The social objective of the parol evidence rule is to give stability to contracts and to prevent the assertion of terms that did not exist or did not survive the bargaining of the parties so as to reach inclusion in the final written contract.

For Example, *L* (landlord), the owner of a new development containing a five-store mall, discusses leasing one of the stores to *T* (tenant), who is viewing

[16] The U.C.C. creates several statutes of frauds of limited applicability, in which it uses the phrase "not enforceable": §1-206 (sale of intangible personal property); §2-201 (sale of goods); and §8-319 (sale of securities).
[17] *Mayday v. Grathwohl*, 805 N.W.2d 285 (Minn. App. 2011).

the property with his sister *S,* a highly credible poverty worker on leave from her duties in Central America. *L,* in the presence of *S,* agrees to give *T* the exclusive right to sell coffee and soft drinks in the five-store mall. Soon *L* and *T* execute a detailed written lease for the store, which makes no provision for *T's* exclusive right to sell soft drinks and coffee in the mall. Subsequently, when two of the mall's new tenants begin to sell soft drinks and coffee, *T* brings suit against *L* for the breach of the oral promise granting him exclusive rights to sell soft drinks and coffee. *T* calls *S* as his first witness to prove the existence of the oral promise. *L,* through his attorney, will object to the admission of any evidence of a prior oral agreement that would add to or amend the fully integrated written lease, which set forth all restrictions on the landlord and tenant as to uses of the premises. After study of the matter, the court, based on the parol evidence rule, will not hear testimony from either *S* or *T* about the oral promise *L* made to *T.* In order to preserve his exclusive right to sell the drinks in question, *T* should have made certain that this promise was made part of the lease. His lawsuit will not be successful.

6. When the Parol Evidence Rule Does Not Apply

The parol evidence rule will not apply in certain cases. The most common of these are discussed in the following paragraphs.

(A) Ambiguity. If a written contract is **ambiguous** or may have two or more different meanings, parol evidence may generally be admitted to clarify the meaning.[18]

Parol evidence may also be admitted to show that a word used in a contract has a special trade meaning or a meaning in the particular locality that differs from the common meaning of that word.

(B) Fraud, Duress, or Mistake. A contract apparently complete on its face may have omitted a provision that should have been included. Parol evidence may be admitted to show that a provision was omitted as the result of fraud, duress, or mistake and to further show what that provision stated. Parol evidence is admissible to show that a provision of the written contract was a mutual mistake even though the written provision is unambiguous. When one party claims to have been fraudulently induced by the other to enter into a contract, the parol evidence rule does not bar proof that there was a fraud. **For Example,** the parol evidence rule does not bar proof that the seller of land intentionally misrepresented that the land was zoned to permit use as an industrial park. Such evidence does not contradict the terms of the contract but shows that the agreement is unenforceable.[19]

(C) Modification of Contract. The parol evidence rule prohibits only the contradiction of a complete written contract. It does not prohibit proof that the contract was thereafter modified or terminated. The *Bourg* case deals with an asserted oral modification of a written agreement.

Bourg v. Bristol Boat Co., 705 A.2d 969 (RI. 1998)

All Sail and No Anchor

On April 2, 1990, Christian Bourg hired Bristol Boat Co., Inc., and Bristol Marine Co. (defendants) to construct and deliver a yacht on July 1, 1990. However, the defendants did not live up to their promises and the contract was breached. On October 22, 1990, the defendants executed a written settlement agreement whereby Bourg agreed to pay an additional sum of $135,000 for the delivery of the yacht and to provide the defendants a loan of $80,000 to complete the construction of the vessel. Referencing the settlement agreement, the defendants at the same time executed a promissory note obliging them to repay the $80,000 loan plus interest in annual installments due on November 1 of each year, with the final payment due on November 1, 1994. The court stated in presenting the facts: "However, like the yacht itself, the settlement agreement soon proved to be just another hole in the water into which the plaintiff threw his money." Bourg sued the defendants after they failed to make certain payments on the note, and the court granted a motion

[18] *Berg v. Hudesman,* 801 P.2d 222 (Wash. 1990). This view is also followed by U.C.C. §2-202(a), which permits terms in a contract for the sale of goods to be "explained or supplemented by a course of dealing or usage of trade… or by course of performance." Such evidence is admissible not because there is an ambiguity but "in order that the true understanding of the parties as to the agreement may be reached." Official Code Comment to §2-202.

[19] *Edwards v. Centrex Real Estate Corp.,* 61 Cal. Rptr. 518 (Cal. App. 1997).

Continued

for summary judgment in favor of Bourg for $59,081. The defendants appealed.

The defendants asserted that the trial court was in error because "at the time of the execution of the promissory note and settlement agreement upon which Plaintiff relies, it was understood and agreed that a substantial part of the note would be paid for by services rendered by the defendants...."

JUDICIAL OPINION

FLANDERS, J.... [T]he statement in defendants' affidavit that the alleged oral modification was agreed to "[*at*] *the time of* the execution of the promissory note and settlement agreement" (emphasis added) eviscierates defendants' contention on appeal that it was in fact a subsequent oral modification. Rather, because the affidavit recites that the alleged oral side agreement was entered into *at the time of* the settlement agreement and promissory note, it would have constituted a contemporaneous modification that would merge into the integrated promissory note and settlement agreement and thus be barred from admission into evidence under the parol evidence rule. In short, this alleged contemporaneous oral modification was legally "immaterial in ascertaining the terms of the transaction" between plaintiff and defendants. *Fram Corp.*, 121 R.I. at 587–88, 401 A.2d at 1272.

Finally, although parties to an integrated written contract—that is, "one where the parties adopt a writing or writings as a final and complete expression of [their] agreement," *id.* at 587, 401 A.2d at 1272—can modify their understanding by a subsequent oral pact, to be legally effective there must be evidence of mutual assent to the essential terms of the modification and adequate consideration. Here the defendants adduced no competent evidence of either mutual assent to particular terms or of a specific consideration that would be sufficiently definite to constitute an enforceable subsequent oral modification to the parties' earlier written agreements. Thus legally this alleged oral alteration was all sail and no anchor.

[Judgment affirmed]

QUESTIONS

1. Did the parties have a fully integrated written contract concerning the loan of $80,000 and the promissory note?
2. Can a contemporaneous oral agreement that "it was understood and agreed that a substantial part of the note would be paid for by services rendered by the defendants" be given weight as evidence to contradict the 1990 written settlement agreement and note that called for annual cash payments to repay the $80,000 loan?
3. Must a subsequent oral modification to a written agreement meet the essential elements for contract formation, including an agreement, and consideration?

C. Rules of Construction and Interpretation

In interpreting contracts, courts are aided by certain rules.

7. Intention of the Parties

When persons enter into an agreement, it is to be presumed that they intend for their agreement to have some effect. A court will strive to determine the intent of the parties and to give effect to it. A contract, therefore, is to be enforced according to its terms.[20] A court cannot remake or rewrite the contract of the parties under the pretense of interpreting.[21]

No particular form of words is required, and any words manifesting the intent of the parties are sufficient. In the absence of proof that a word has a peculiar meaning or that it was employed by the parties with a particular meaning, a common word is given its ordinary meaning.

(A) Meaning of Words. Ordinary words are to be interpreted according to their ordinary meaning.[22] **For Example,** when a contract requires the gasoline dealer to pay the supplier for "gallons" supplied, the term *gallons* is unambiguous and does not require that an adjustment of the gallonage be made for the temperature.[23] When a contract calls for a businessperson to pay a builder for the builder's "costs," the

[20] See *Greenwald v. Kersh*, 621 S.E.2d 463 (Ga. App. 2005).
[21] *Abbot v. Schnader, Harrison, Segal & Lewis, LLP*, 805 A.2d 547 (Pa. Super. 2002).
[22] *Thorton v. D.F.W. Christian Television, Inc.*, 925 S.W.2d 17 (Tex. App. 1995).
[23] *Hopkins v. BP Oil, Inc.*, 81 F.3d 1070 (11th Cir. 1996).

term *costs* is unambiguous, meaning actual costs, not a lesser amount based on the builder's bid.[24]

If there is a common meaning to a term, that meaning will be followed even though the dictionary may contain additional meanings. If technical or trade terms are used in a contract, they are to be interpreted according to the area of technical knowledge or trade from which the terms are taken.

(B) Incorporation by Reference. The contract may not cover all of the agreed terms. The missing terms may be found in another document. Frequently, the parties executing the contract for storage will simply state that a storage contract is entered into and that the contract applies to the goods listed in the schedule attached to and made part of the contract. Likewise, a contract for the construction of a building may involve plans and specifications on file in a named city office. The contract will simply state that the building is to be constructed according to those plans and specifications that are "incorporated herein and made part of this contract." When there is such an **incorporation by reference**, the contract consists of both the original document and the detailed statement that is incorporated in it.

When a contract refers to another document, however, the contract must sufficiently describe the document or so much of it as is to be interpreted as part of the contract.

8. Whole Contract

The provisions of a contract must be construed as a whole in such a way that every part is given effect.

Every word of a contract is to be given effect if reasonably possible. The contract is to be construed as a whole, and if the plain language of the contract thus viewed solves the dispute, the court is to make no further analysis.[25]

In the *DHL Express* decision, the contract was read as a whole to determine the intention of the parties regarding the application of termination fees.

C.A. Acquisition Newco, LLC v. DHL Express (USA), Inc., 795 F. Supp. 2d 140 (D. Mass. 2011)

When You Permanently Reduced the Shipping Spots to Zero, You "Terminated" the Contract, Silly

C.A. Acquisition Newco LLC is a successor in interest to Cyphermint, Inc. (or "CI"), a New York corporation specializing in software development for self-service kiosks. DHL Express (USA), Inc., is an Ohio corporation with a principal place of business in Florida. It is a division of DHL International GmBH, a Deutsche Post Company and express carrier of documents and freight. Until 2008, DHL provided express pick-up and delivery, including same-day air delivery of letters and packages throughout the United States.

DHL entered into an agreement with Cyphermint, hoping to expand its customer base by offering domestic shipping services in retail locations, such as Walgreens and OfficeMax, via kiosks, or "Shipping Spots." Customers were able to use the kiosks' touch screen to pay for shipping costs and print shipping labels. The contract provided for an initial three-year term (August 1, 2006, through July 31, 2009) that automatically renewed for two more years unless either party gave notice of its election not to renew 90 days before the end of the initial contract. Under the contract, Cyphermint agreed to provide interactive software enabling customers to use DHL's services from the shipping spots. Section 10.5 of the contract governs termination fees:

> *There shall be no termination fees for any termination by either party, irrespective of the reason for such termination, except for a "Material Breach" or as provided pursuant to the "Statement of Work" (SOW).*

The SOW contains the following provision concerning termination fees:

> *Should DHL terminate this agreement for any reason other than a material breach by Cyphermint before its termination date DHL agrees to compensate CI in the amount of $50,000 per month for each month remaining in the initial term.*

In November 2008, DHL decided to end all domestic delivery service within the United States. CI requested early termination fees under Section 10.5 of the contract of $413,333.33. DHL refused to pay, contending that Section

[24] *Batzer Construction, Inc. v. Boyer*, 125 P.3d 773 (Or. App. 2006).
[25] *Covensky v. Hannah Marine Corp.*, 903 N.E.2d 422 (Ill. App. 2009).

Continued

2.8 of the contract gave DHL the discretion to control the number and placement of the shipping spots, and when it ended U.S. domestic operations, it exercised its discretion to reduce shipping spots to zero.

JUDICIAL OPINION

PONSOR, J.... Plaintiff argues that Defendant breached the Contract by ceasing all shipments under the Contract prior to its expiration and failing to pay the resultant termination fees pursuant to Section 10.5. Under Section 10.5, termination fees only arise in case of "a 'Material Breach' or as provided pursuant to the 'Statement of Work.'" The SOW states, "[s]hould DHL terminate this agreement for any reason other than a material breach by Cyphermint before its termination date DHL agrees to compensate Cyphermint in the amount of $50,000 per month for each month remaining in the initial term." Given Defendant's concession that it did not terminate the agreement as a result of a material breach by Cyphermint, Plaintiff reasons that Defendant was obligated to pay Plaintiff $50,000 per month for the remainder of the initial term.

Defendant responds that it never "terminated" the agreement and that, rather, it merely reduced the number of shipping spots pursuant to express language in the Contract. Defendant points to Section 2.8 of the MSA:

> Limitations on Scope of Obligations. *Nothing in this Agreement guarantees the number or placement of DHL Shipping Spot(s). DHL hereby acknowledges that the number of DHL Shipping Spots, [and] the placement, movement, and/or access of such units is solely within the discretion of DHL....*

Accordingly, Defendant argues that "[w]hen DHL made the global decision to cease its entire United States operations, it exercised its contractual discretion to limit its business with Newco to zero."

Plaintiff has the stronger argument. Contrary to Defendant's interpretation, finding that Defendant terminated the agreement by ending its support for the shipping spot project does not render meaningless Section 2.8. Section 2.8 vests Defendant with the discretion to control the number and placement of the shipping spots, but it does not, as Defendant suggests, permit Defendant to stop performing altogether for any reason or no reason, with no consequences. Such a construction is strained on its face and, when placed in context, is obviously contrary to the Contract's intent. It is also contrary to good sense. The proposition that reducing the shipping posts to zero is not the same as "termination" is Looking-Glass logic, recalling Humpty Dumpty's remark that "When *I* use a word ... it means just what I choose it to mean—neither more nor less." Lewis Carroll [Charles L. Dodgson], *Through the Looking-Glass* 72 (1872).

As noted, Section 10 of the Contract—the termination provision itself—incorporates by reference clear language in the SOW declaring that Defendant may *not* terminate the agreement except in the case of a material breach by Plaintiff. Thus, viewing the document as a whole—*i.e.,* from the perspective the court is obliged to take—disposes of Defendant's over-labored interpretation. In reviewing a document, a court must consider the document as a whole, rather than attempting to isolate certain portions of it.

Notably, even if the court were to accept Defendant's argument that Section 2.8 gave Defendant blanket authority to reduce or even eliminate the shipping spot project altogether, the outcome would remain the same. The relevant provision in the SOW provides for termination fees without regard to whether the termination was authorized. The only restriction placed on the recovery of such fees is that they will not be available in the case of a material breach by Cyphermint ("Should DHL terminate this agreement *for any reason other than a material breach* by Cyphermint....") (emphasis added)....

Regardless of the label Defendant uses, the undeniable effect of its actions was to bring the parties' performance to an immediate and permanent halt. A termination by any other name would end the contract just the same.

In sum, Defendant's termination of the Contract manifestly triggered Plaintiff's termination rights, including termination fees of $50,000 per month for the remaining term. The failure to pay such fees constitutes a breach of contract as a matter of law. Accordingly, Plaintiff's motion will be allowed, and Defendant's motion will be denied....

[Judgment for the plaintiff]

QUESTIONS

1. State DHL's position regarding its contractual obligations to CI's successor upon ceasing its U.S. domestic operations.
2. State the Cyphermint view of what was owed to it under the contract with DHL upon its ceasing U.S. domestic operations.
3. What rule of contract interpretation did the court apply in this case? State the court's decision.

9. Contradictory and Ambiguous Terms

One term in a contract may conflict with another term, or one term may have two different meanings. It is then necessary for the court to determine whether there is a contract and, if so, what the contract really means.

If the language within the four corners of the contract is unambiguous, the parties' intentions are determined from the plain meaning of the words, used in the contract, as a matter of law, by the judge. A contract term or provision is *ambiguous* if it is capable of more than one reasonable interpretation, because of the uncertain meaning of terms or missing terms. A finding of ambiguity is justified only if the language of the contract reasonably supports the competing interpretations.[26] It is the role of the judge—a question of law—to initially determine whether a contract is ambiguous. If the contract is ambiguous, it is the role of the jury—a question of fact—to determine which party's position is correct with the aid of extrinsic evidence.

(A) Nature of Writing. When a contract is partly a printed form or partly type-written and partly handwritten and the written part conflicts with the printed or typewritten part, the written part prevails. When there is a conflict between a printed part and a typewritten part, the latter prevails. Consequently, when a clause typewritten on a printed form conflicts with what is stated by the print, the conflicting print is ignored and the typewritten clause controls. This rule is based on the belief that the parties had given greater thought to what they typed or wrote for the particular contract as contrasted with printed words already in a form designed to cover many transactions. Thus, a typewritten provision to pay 90 cents per unit overrode a preprinted provision setting the price as 45 cents per unit.

When there is a conflict between an amount or quantity expressed both in words and figures, as on a check, the amount or quantity expressed in words prevails. Words control because there is less danger that a word will be wrong than a number.

(B) Ambiguity. A contract is ambiguous when the intent of the parties is uncertain and the contract is capable of more than one reasonable interpretation.[27] The background from which the contract and the dispute arose may help in determining the intention of the parties. **For Example,** when suit was brought in Minnesota on a Canadian insurance policy, the question arose whether the dollar limit of the policy referred to Canadian or U.S. dollars. The court concluded that Canadian dollars were intended. Both the insurer and the insured were Canadian corporations; the original policy, endorsements to the policy, and policy renewals were written in Canada; over the years, premiums had been paid in Canadian dollars; and a prior claim on the policy had been settled by the payment of an amount computed on the basis of Canadian dollars.

(C) Strict Construction Against Drafting Party. An ambiguous contract is interpreted strictly against the party who drafted it.[28] **For Example,** an insurance policy containing ambiguous language regarding coverage or exclusions is interpreted against the insurer and in favor of the insured when two interpretations are reasonably possible. This rule is a secondary rule that may be invoked only after all of the ordinary interpretive guides have been exhausted. The rule basically assigns the risk of an unresolvable ambiguity to the party creating it.[29]

10. Implied Terms

In some cases, a court will imply a term to cover a situation for which the parties failed to provide or, when needed, to give the contract a construction or meaning that is reasonable.

The court often implies details of the performance of a contract not expressly stated in the contract. In a contract to perform work, there is an implied promise to use such skill as is necessary to properly perform the work. When a contract does not specify the time for performance, a reasonable time is implied.

In every contract, there is an implied obligation that neither party shall do anything that will have the effect of destroying or injuring the right of the other party to receive the fruits of the contract. This means that in every contract there exists an implied covenant of **good faith** and fair dealing. When a contract may reasonably be interpreted in different ways, a court

[26] *QEP Energy Co. v. Sullivan*, 444 Fed. Appx. 284 (10th Cir. 2011).

[27] *Kaufman & Stewart v. Weinbrenner Shoe Co.*, 589 N.W.2d 499 (Minn. App. 1999).

[28] *Idaho Migrant Council, Inc. v. Warila*, 89 P.2d 39 (Wyo. 1995).

[29] *Premier Title Co. v. Donahue*, 765 N.E.2d 513 (Ill. App. 2002).

should make the interpretation that is in harmony with good faith and fair dealing. **For Example,** when a contract is made subject to the condition that one of the parties obtain financing, that party must make reasonable, good-faith efforts to obtain financing. The party is not permitted to do nothing and then claim that the contract is not binding because the condition has not been satisfied. Likewise, when a contract requires a party to obtain government approval, the party must use all reasonable means to obtain it.[30]

The Uniform Commercial Code imposes an obligation of good faith in the performance or enforcement of every contract.[31]

11. Conduct and Custom

The conduct of the parties and the customs and usages of a particular trade may give meaning to the words of the parties and thus aid in the interpretation of their contract.

(A) Conduct of the Parties. The conduct of the parties in carrying out the terms of a contract is the best guide to determine the parties' intent. When performance has been repeatedly tendered and accepted without protest, neither party will be permitted to claim that the contract was too indefinite to be binding. **For Example,** a travel agent made a contract with a hotel to arrange for trips to the hotel. After some 80 trips had already been arranged and paid for by the hotel at the contract price without any dispute about whether the contract obligation was satisfied, any claim by the travel agent that it could charge additional fees must be rejected.

(B) Custom and Usage of Trade. The customs and **usages of trade** or commercial activity to which the contract relates may be used to interpret the terms of a contract.[32] **For Example,** when a contract for the construction of a building calls for a "turn-key construction," industry usage is admissible to show what this means: a construction in which all the owner needs to do is to turn the key in the lock to open the building for use and in which all construction risks are assumed by the contractor.[33]

Custom and usage, however, cannot override express provisions of a contract that are inconsistent with custom and usage.

12. Avoidance of Hardship

As a general rule, a party is bound by a contract even though it proves to be a bad bargain. If possible, a court will interpret a contract to avoid hardship. Courts will, if possible, interpret a vague contact in a way to avoid any forfeiture of a party's interest.

When hardship arises because the contract makes no provision for the situation that has occurred, the court will sometimes imply a term to avoid the hardship.

LawFlix

The Santa Clause (1996) (PG)

When Scott Calvin (Tim Allen) tries on a Santa suit, he discovers that he has assumed all of Santa's responsibility. Calvin tries to challenge his acceptance of the terms of the agreement. Analyze the problems with offer, acceptance, and terms in very fine print (a magnifying glass is required). Do the terms of the suit contract apply when Calvin did not know them at the time he put on the suit?

[30] *Kroboth v. Brent*, 625 N.Y.S.2d 748 (A.D. 1995).

[31] U.C.C. §§1-201(19), 1-203.

[32] *Affiliated FM Ins. Co. v. Constitution Reinsurance Corp.*, 626 N.E.2d 878 (Mass. 1994).

[33] *Blue v. R.L. Glossen Contracting, Inc.*, 327 S.E.2d 582 (Ga. App. 1985).

MAKE THE CONNECTION

SUMMARY

An oral agreement may be a contract unless it is the intention of the parties that they should not be bound by the agreement without a writing executed by them. Certain contracts must be evidenced by a writing, however, or else they cannot be enforced. The statutes that declare this exception are called *statutes of frauds.*

Statutes of frauds commonly require that a contract be evidenced by writing in the case of (1) an agreement that cannot be performed within one year after the contract is made, (2) an agreement to sell any interest in land, (3) a promise to answer for the debt or default of another, (4) a promise by the executor or administrator of a decedent's estate to pay a claim against the estate from personal funds, (5) a promise made in consideration of marriage, and (6) a contract for the sale of goods for a purchase price of $500 or more.

To evidence a contract to satisfy a statute of frauds, there must be a writing of all essential terms. The writing must be signed by the defendant against whom suit is brought for enforcement of the contract.

If the applicable statute of frauds is not satisfied, the oral contract cannot be enforced. To avoid unjust enrichment, a plaintiff barred from enforcing an oral contract may in most cases recover from the other contracting party the reasonable value of the benefits conferred by the plaintiff on the defendant.

When there is a written contract, the question arises whether that writing is the exclusive statement of the parties' agreement. If the writing is the complete and final statement of the contract, parol evidence as to matters agreed to before or at the time the writing was signed is not admissible to contradict the writing. This is called the *parol evidence rule*. In any case, the parol evidence rule does not bar parol evidence when (1) the writing is ambiguous, (2) the writing is not a true statement of the agreement of the parties because of fraud, duress, or mistake, or (3) the existence, modification, or illegality of a contract is in controversy.

Because a contract is based on the agreement of the parties, courts must determine the intent of the parties manifested in the contract. The intent that is to be enforced is the intent as it reasonably appears to a third person. This objective intent is followed.

In interpreting a contract, ordinary words are to be given their ordinary meanings. If trade or technical terms have been used, they are interpreted according to their technical meanings. The court must consider the whole contract and not read a particular part out of context. When different writings are executed as part of the same transaction, or one writing refers to or incorporates another, all of the writings are to be read together as the contract of the parties.

When provisions of a contract are contradictory, the court will try to reconcile or eliminate the conflict. If this cannot be done, the conclusion may be that there is no contract because the conflict makes the agreement indefinite as to a material matter. In some cases, conflict is solved by considering the form of conflicting terms. Handwriting prevails over typing and a printed form, and typing prevails over a printed form. Ambiguity will be eliminated in some cases by the admission of parol evidence or by interpreting the provision strictly against the party preparing the contract, particularly when that party has significantly greater bargaining power.

LEARNING OUTCOMES

After studying this chapter, you should be able to clearly explain:

A. Statute of Frauds

LO.1 Explain when a contract must be evidenced by a writing

See the discussion and examples beginning on p. 316.

LO.2 Explain the effect of noncompliance with the statute of frauds

See the *Bithoney* case where a doctor's oral contract for severance was barred by the statute of frauds, p. 317.

See the example in which an oral contract cannot be enforced because it is not in writing, but the plaintiff may recover the reasonable value of the services rendered, p. 323.

B. Parol Evidence Rule

LO.3 Explain the parol evidence rule and the exceptions to this rule

See the example in which the tenant is not allowed to call a witness to testify about a prior oral agreement that would add to and alter the written lease, pp. 323–324.

See the exceptions based on ambiguity, fraud, duress, and mistake discussed on p. 324.

C. Rules of Construction and Interpretation

LO.4 Understand the basic rule of contract construction that a contract is enforced according to its terms

See the example of the interpretation of the word "costs" on pp. 325–326.

See the *DHL Express* case that illustrates the judicial common sense of interpreting the contract as a whole rather than a strained construction contrary to the contract's intent, pp. 326–327.

LO.5 State the rules for interpreting ambiguous terms in a contract

See the discussion on the nature of the writing beginning on p. 328.

KEY TERMS

administrator
ambiguous
decedent
executor
good faith
incorporation by reference
parol evidence rule
personal representative
statute of frauds
suretyship
usages of trade

QUESTIONS AND CASE PROBLEMS

1. Kelly made a written contract to sell certain land to Brown and gave Brown a deed to the land. Thereafter, Kelly sued Brown to get back a 20-foot strip of the land. Kelly claimed that before making the written contract, it was agreed that Kelly would sell all of his land to Brown to make it easier for Brown to get a building permit, but after that was done, the 20-foot strip would be reconveyed to Kelly. Was Kelly entitled to the 20-foot strip? What ethical values are involved? [*Brown v. Kelly,* 545 So.2d 518 (Fla. App.)]

2. Martin made an oral contract with Cresheim Garage to work as its manager for two years. Cresheim wrote Martin a letter stating that the oral contract had been made and setting forth all of its terms. Cresheim later refused to recognize the contract. Martin sued Cresheim for breach of the contract and offered Cresheim's letter in evidence as proof of the contract. Cresheim claimed that the oral contract was not binding because the contract was not in writing and the letter referring to the contract was not a contract but only a letter. Was the contract binding?

3. Lawrence loaned money to Moore, who died without repaying the loan. Lawrence claimed that when he mentioned the matter to Moore's widow, she promised to pay the debt. She did not pay it, and Lawrence sued her on her promise. Does she have any defense? [*Moore v. Lawrence,* 480 S.W.2d 941 (Ark.)]

4. Jackson signed an agreement to sell 79 acres of land to Devenyns. Jackson owned 80 acres and was apparently intending to keep for himself the acre on which his home was located. The written agreement also stated that "Devenyns shall have the option to buy on property _____," but nothing was stated in the blank space. Devenyns sued to enforce the agreement. Was it binding? [*In re Jackson's Estate,* 892 P.2d 786 (Wyo.)]

5. Boeing Airplane Co. contracted with Pittsburgh–Des Moines Steel Co. for the latter to construct a supersonic wind tunnel. R.H. Freitag Manufacturing Co. sold materials to York-Gillespie Co., which subcontracted to do part of the work. To persuade Freitag to keep supplying materials on credit, Boeing and the principal contractor both assured Freitag that he would be paid. When Freitag was not paid by the subcontractor, he sued Boeing and the contractor. They defended on the ground that the assurances given Freitag were not written. Decide. What ethical values are

involved? [*R.H. Freitag Mfg. Co. v. Boeing Airplane Co.,* 347 P.2d 1074 (Wash.)]

6. Louise Pulsifer owned a farm that she wanted to sell and ran an ad in the local newspaper. After Russell Gillespie agreed to purchase the farm, Pulsifer wrote him a letter stating that she would not sell it. He sued her to enforce the contract, and she raised the defense of the statute of frauds. The letter she had signed did not contain any of the terms of the sale. Gillespie, however, claimed that the newspaper ad could be combined with her letter to satisfy the statute of frauds. Was he correct? [*Gillespie v. Pulsifer,* 655 S.W.2d 123 (Mo.)]

7. In February or March, Corning Glass Works orally agreed to retain Hanan as management consultant from May 1 of that year to April 30 of the next year for a present value fee of $200,000. Was this agreement binding? Is this decision ethical? [*Hanan v. Corning Glass Works,* 314 N.Y. S.2d 804 (A.D.)]

8. Catherine (wife) and Peter (husband) Mallen had lived together unmarried for some four years when Catherine got pregnant and a marriage was arranged. Peter asked Catherine to sign a prenuptial agreement. Although his financial statement attached to the agreement did not state his income at $560,000 per year, it showed he was wealthy, and she had lived with him for four years and knew from their standard of living that he had significant income. Catherine contends that failure to disclose Peter's income was a nondisclosure of a material fact when the agreement was drawn up and that accordingly the agreement is not valid. Peter contends that he fully disclosed his net worth and that Catherine was well aware of his significant income. Further, he contends that disparities in the parties' financial status and business experience did not make the agreement unconscionable. Decide. [*Mallen v. Mallen,* 622 S.E.2d 812 (Ga. Sup. Ct.)]

9. Panasonic Industrial Co. (PIC) created a contract making Manchester Equipment Co., Inc. (MECI), a nonexclusive wholesale distributor of its products. The contract stated that PIC reserved the unrestricted right to solicit and make direct sales of the products to anyone, anywhere. The contract also stated that it contained the entire agreement of the parties and that any prior agreement or statement was superseded by the contract. PIC subsequently began to make direct sales to two of MECI's established customers. MECI claimed that this was a breach of the distribution contract and sued PIC for damages. Decide. What ethical values are involved? [*Manchester Equipment Co. Inc. v. Panasonic Industrial Co.,* 529 N.Y.S.2d 532 (App. Div.)]

10. A contract made for the sale of a farm stated that the buyer's deposit would be returned "if for any reason the farm cannot be sold." The seller later stated that she had changed her mind and would not sell, and she offered to return the deposit. The buyer refused to take the deposit back and brought suit to enforce the contract. The seller contended that the "any reason" provision extended to anything, including the seller's changing her mind. Was the buyer entitled to recover? [*Phillips v. Rogers,* 200 S.E.2d 676 (W. Va.)]

11. Integrated, Inc., entered into a contract with the state of California to construct a building. It then subcontracted the electrical work to Alec Fergusson Electrical Contractors. The subcontract was a printed form with blanks filled in by typewriting. The printed payment clause required Integrated to pay Fergusson on the 15th day of the month following the submission of invoices by Fergusson. The typewritten part of the contract required Integrated to pay Fergusson "immediately following payment" (by the state) to the general contractor. When was payment required? [*Integrated, Inc. v. Alec Fergusson Electrical Contractors,* 58 Cal. Rptr. 503 (Cal. App.)]

12. Norwest Bank had been lending money to Tresch to run a dairy farm. The balance due the bank after several years was $147,000. The loan agreement stated that Tresch would not buy any new equipment in excess of $500 without the express consent of the bank. Some time later,

Tresch applied to the bank for a loan of $3,100 to purchase some equipment. The bank refused to make the loan because it did not believe the new equipment would correct the condition for which it would be bought and would not result in significant additional income. Tresch then sued the bank, claiming that its refusal to make the loan was a breach of the implied covenant of good faith and fair dealing. Decide. [*Tresch v. Norwest Bank of Lewistown,* 778 P.2d 874 (Mont.)]

13. Physicians Mutual Insurance Co. issued a policy covering Brown's life. The policy declared that it did not cover any deaths resulting from "mental disorder, alcoholism, or drug addiction." Brown was killed when she fell while intoxicated. The insurance company refused to pay because of the quoted provision. Her executor, Savage, sued the insurance company. Did the insurance company have a defense? [*Physicians Mutual Ins. Co. v. Savage,* 296 N.E.2d 165 (Ind. App.)]

14. The Dickinson Elks Club conducted an annual Labor Day golf tournament. Charbonneau Buick-Pontiac offered to give a new car as a prize to anyone making "a hole in one on hole no. 8." The golf course of the club was only nine holes. To play 18 holes, the players would go around the course twice, although they would play from different tees or locations for the second nine holes. On the second time around, what was originally the eighth hole became the seventeenth hole. Grove was a contestant in the tournament. He scored 3 on the no. 8 hole, but on approaching it for the second time as the seventeenth hole, he made a hole in one. He claimed the prize car from Charbonneau. The latter claimed that Grove had not won the prize because he did not make the hole in one on the eighth hole. Decide. [*Grove v. Charbonneau Buick-Pontiac, Inc.,* 240 N.W.2d 8533 (N.D.)]

15. Tambe Electric Inc. entered into a written agreement with Home Depot to provide copper wire to Tambe at a price set forth in the writing, and allowing the contractor the option of paying for the wire over a period of time. Home Depot did not fulfill this written agreement and Tambe sued for $68,598, the additional cost it had to subsequently pay to obtain copper wire for its work. Home Depot defended that it had made an oral condition precedent requiring payment in full by Tambe at the time it accepted the price quoted in the written agreement. Decide. [*Tambe Electric v. Home Depot*, 856 N.Y.S.2d 373]

CPA QUESTIONS

1. Which of the following statements is true with regard to the statute of frauds?
   a. All contracts involving consideration of more than $500 must be in writing.
   b. The written contract must be signed by all parties.
   c. The statute of frauds applies to contracts that can be fully performed within one year from the date they are made.
   d. The contract terms may be stated in more than one document.

2. With regard to an agreement for the sale of real estate, the statute of frauds:
   a. Requires that the entire agreement be in a single writing.
   b. Requires that the purchase price be fair and adequate in relation to the value of the real estate.
   c. Does *not* require that the agreement be signed by all parties.
   d. Does *not* apply if the value of the real estate is less than $500.

3. In negotiations with Andrews for the lease of Kemp's warehouse, Kemp orally agreed to pay one-half of the cost of the utilities. The written lease, later prepared by Kemp's attorney, provided that Andrews pay all of the utilities. Andrews failed to carefully read the lease and signed it. When Kemp demanded that Andrews pay all of the utilities, Andrews refused, claiming that the

lease did not accurately reflect the oral agreement. Andrews also learned that Kemp intentionally misrepresented the condition of the structure of the warehouse during the negotiations between the parties. Andrews sued to rescind the lease and intends to introduce evidence of the parties' oral agreement about sharing the utilities and the fraudulent statements made by Kemp. Will the parol evidence rule prevent the admission of evidence concerning each of the following?

	Oral agreement regarding who pays the utilities	*Fraudulent statements by Kemp*
a.	Yes	Yes
b.	No	Yes
c.	Yes	No
d.	No	No

CHAPTER 18

© Manuel Gutjahr/iStockphoto.com

Third Persons and Contracts

learningoutcomes

After studying this chapter, you should be able to

LO.1 Explain the two types of intended third-party beneficiaries

LO.2 Explain why an incidental beneficiary does not have the right to sue as a third-party beneficiary

LO.3 Define an assignment

LO.4 Explain the general rule that a person entitled to receive money under a contract may generally assign that right to another person

LO.5 List the nonassignable rights to performance

A. Third-Party Beneficiary Contracts

Generally, only the parties to a contract may sue on it. However, in some cases a third person who is not a party to the contract may sue on the contract.

CPA 1. Definition

When a contract is intended to benefit a third person, such a person is an **intended beneficiary** and may bring suit on and enforce the contract. In some states, the right of the intended **third-party beneficiary** to sue on the contract is declared by statute. **For Example,** Ibberson Co., the general contractor hired by AgGrow Oils, LLC to design and build an oilseed processing plant, contracted with subcontractor Anderson International Corp. to supply critical seed processing equipment for the project. Anderson's formal proposal to Ibberson identified the AgGrow Oils Project, and the proposal included drawings of the planned AgGrow plant. Under state law, this contract made between the contractor and subcontractor for the express benefit of the third-party AgGrow Oils could be enforced by the intended third-party beneficiary AgGrow Oils. The project was a failure. AgGrow was successful in the lawsuit against Anderson under the Anderson-Ibberson contract, having the standing to sue as an intended third-party beneficiary of that contract.[1]

(A) Creditor Beneficiary. The intended beneficiary is sometimes classified as a *creditor beneficiary* when the promisee's primary intent is to discharge a duty owed to the third party.[2] **For Example,** when Max Giordano sold his business, Sameway Laundry, to Harry Phinn, he had three years of payments totaling $14,500 owing to Davco, Inc., on a commercial Davco shirt drying and pressing machine purchased in 2006. Max (the promisee) made a contract with Harry to sell the business for a stipulated sum. A provision in this contract selling the business called for Harry (the promisor) to make the Davco machine payments when due over the next three years. Should Harry fail to make payments, Davco, Inc., as an intended creditor beneficiary under the contract between Max and Harry, would have standing to sue Harry for breach of the payment provision in the contract.

CPA **(B) Donee Beneficiary.** The second type of intended beneficiary is a *donee beneficiary* to whom the promisee's primary intent in contracting is to give a benefit. A life insurance contract is such an intended third-party beneficiary contract. The promisee-insured pays premiums to the insurer under the contract of insurance so that, upon the death of the insured, the promisor-insurer would pay the sum designated in the contract to the beneficiary. The beneficiary's rights vest upon the insured's death, and the beneficiary can sue the insurance company upon the insured's death even though the insurance company never made any agreement directly with the beneficiary.

(C) Necessity of Intent. A third person does not have the status of an intended third-party beneficiary unless it is clear at the time the contract was formed that the parties intended to impose a direct obligation with respect to the third person.[3] In determining whether there is intent to benefit a third party, the surrounding circumstances as well as the contract may be examined.[4] There is a strong presumption that the parties to a contract intend to benefit only themselves.[5]

(D) Description. It is not necessary that the intended third-party beneficiary be identified by name. The beneficiary may be identified by class, with the result that any member of that class is a third-party beneficiary. **For Example,** a contract between the promoter of an automobile stock car race and the owner of the racetrack contains a promise by the owner to pay specified sums of money to each driver racing a car in certain races. A person driving in one of the designated races is a third-party beneficiary and can sue the owner on the contract for the promised compensation.

[1] *AgGrow Oils, LLC v. National Union Fire Ins.*, 420 F.3d 751 (8th Cir. 2005).

[2] The Restatement (Second) of Contracts §302 substitutes "intended beneficiary" for the terms "creditor" and "donee" beneficiary. However, some courts continue to use the classifications of creditor and donee third-party beneficiaries. Regardless of the terminology, the law continues to be the same. See *Continental Casualty v. Zurich American Insurance*, 2009 WL 455285 (D.C. Or. 2009).

[3] *American United Logistics, Inc. v. Catellus*, 319 F.3d 921 (7th Cir. 2003).

[4] See *Becker v. Crispell-Snyder, Inc.*, 763 N.W.2d 192 (Wis. App. 2009) for an example of complex circumstances surrounding a third-party beneficiary contract. The town of Somers, Wisconsin, entered into a contract with engineering firm Crispell-Synder (C-S) because it needed an engineering firm to oversee a new subdivision to be developed by the Beckers. Under this contract C-S would submit bills to the town for overseeing the development, and the town would pay C-S through a line of credit from the Beckers. The court held that the Beckers were third-party beneficiaries entitled to sue C-S for overcharging change orders.

[5] *Barney v. Unity Paving, Inc.*, 639 N.E.2d 592 (Ill. App. 1994).

2. Modification or Termination of Intended Third-Party Beneficiary Contract

Can the parties to the contract modify or terminate it so as to destroy the right of the intended third-party beneficiary? If the contract contains an express provision allowing a change of beneficiary or cancellation of the contract without the consent of the intended third-party beneficiary, the parties to the contract may destroy the rights of the intended beneficiary by acting in accordance with that contract provision.[6]

For Example, Roy obtained a life insurance policy from Phoenix Insurance Company that provided the beneficiary could be changed by the insured. Roy named his son, Harry, as the beneficiary. Later, Roy had a falling out with Harry and removed him as beneficiary. Roy could do this because the right to change the beneficiary was expressly reserved by the contract that created the status of the intended third-party beneficiary.

In addition, the rights of an intended third-party beneficiary are destroyed if the contract is discharged or ended by operation of law, for example, through bankruptcy proceedings.

3. Limitations on Intended Third-Party Beneficiary

Although the intended third-party beneficiary rule gives the third person the right to enforce the contract, it obviously gives no more rights than the contract provides. That is, the intended third-party beneficiary must take the contract as it is. If there is a time limitation or any other restriction in the contract, the intended beneficiary cannot ignore it but is bound by it.

If the contract is not binding for any reason, that defense may be raised against the intended third-party beneficiary suing on the contract.[7]

CPA 4. Incidental Beneficiaries

Not everyone who benefits from the performance of a contract between other persons is entitled to sue as a third-party beneficiary. If the benefit was intended, the third person is an intended beneficiary with the rights described in the preceding sections. If the benefit was not intended, the third person is an *incidental beneficiary*. **For Example,** real estate developer Ocean Atlantic Corp. purchased a series of bonds from American Southern Insurance Co. for the purpose of guaranteeing the performance of public improvement in a subdivision it was developing in Yorkville, Illinois. The bonds representing the surety contract between Ocean Atlantic and American Southern were issued in favor of the City of Yorkville. Ocean Atlantic hired subcontractor Aurora Blacktop, Inc., to perform several improvements, but the project stalled and Aurora was never paid for its work. Aurora lacked standing as a third-party beneficiary to enforce the subdivision bonds against American Southern because the contractual obligations ran only to the city. Aurora was deemed an incidental beneficiary rather than a third-party beneficiary.[8]

Whether or not a third party is an *intended* or *incidental* beneficiary, therefore, comes down to determining whether or not a reasonable person would believe that the promisee intended to confer on the beneficiary an enforceable benefit under the contract in question. The intent must be clear and definite or expressed in the contract itself or in the circumstances surrounding the contract's execution.

B. Assignments

The parties to a contract have both rights and duties. Can rights be transferred or sold to another person or entity? Can duties be transferred to another person?

5. Definitions

Contracts create **rights** and **duties** between the parties to the contract. An **assignment** is a transfer of contractual rights to a third party. The party owing a duty or debt under the contract is the **obligor** or **debtor**, and the party to whom the obligation is owed is the **obligee**. The party making the assignment is the **assignor**. The third party to whom the assignment is made is the **assignee**. **For Example,** Randy Marshall

[6] A common form of reservation is the life insurance policy provision by which the insured reserves the right to change the beneficiary. Section 142 of the Restatement (Second) of Contracts provides that the promisor and the promise may modify their contract and affect the right of the third-party beneficiary thereby unless the agreement expressly prohibits this or the third-party beneficiary has changed position in reliance on the promise or has manifested assent to it.

[7] *XL Disposal Corp. v. John Sexton Contractors Co.*, 659 N.E.2d 1312 (Ill. App. 1995).

[8] *City of Yorkville v. American Southern Insurance Co.*, 654 F.3d 713 (7th Cir. 2011).

FIGURE 18-1 Surfboard Transaction Diagram

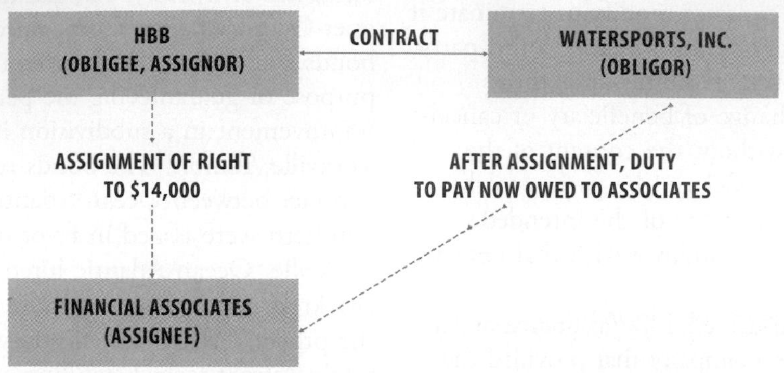

and Marilee Menendez own Huntington Beach Board (HBB) Company, LLC, a five-employee start-up company making top-of-the line surfboards. Marilee was able to sell 100 Duke Kahanamoku–inspired "longboards" to Watersports, Inc., a large retail sporting goods chain, for $140 per board. However, the best payment terms she could obtain were payment in full in 90 days. A contract containing these terms was executed, and the goods were delivered. To meet internal cash flow needs, HBB assigned its right to receive the $14,000 payment from the buyer to West Coast Financial Associates (Associates) and received $12,800 cash from Associates on execution of the assignment documents. Notice was given at that time to Watersports, Inc., of the assignment. The right to receive the payment due in 90 days under the sales contract has thus been transferred by the seller HBB (assignor) to the third party, Associates (the assignee), to whom the buyer, Watersports, Inc. (obligor), now owes the duty of payment. Under the law of assignments, Associates, the assignee, now has direct rights against the obligor, Watersports, Inc. (See Figure 18-1.)

6. Form of Assignment

Generally, an assignment may be in any form. Statutes, however, may require that certain kinds of assignments be in writing or be executed in a particular form. Any words, whether written or spoken, that show an intention to transfer or assign will be given the effect of an assignment.[9]

7. Notice of Assignment

An assignment, if otherwise valid, takes effect the moment it is made. The assignee should give immediate notice of the assignment to the obligor, setting forth the obligor's duty to the assignee, in order to prevent improper payment.[10]

If the obligor is notified in any manner that there has been an assignment and that any money due must be paid to the assignee, the obligor's obligation can be discharged only by making payment to the assignee.

If the obligor is not notified that there has been an assignment and that the money due must be paid to the assignee, any payment made by the obligor to the assignor reduces or cancels that portion of the debt. The only remedy for the assignee is to sue the assignor to recover the payments that were made by the obligor.

The Uniform Consumer Credit Code (UCCC) protects consumer-debtors making payments to an assignor without knowledge of the assignment[11] and imposes a penalty for using a contract term that would destroy this protection of consumers.[12]

[9] *JBM Investments, LLC v. Callahan Industries, Inc.*, 667 S.E.2d 429 (Ga. App. 2008).

[10] In some cases, an assignee will give notice of the assignment to the obligor in order to obtain priority over other persons who claim the same right or in order to limit the defenses that the obligor may raise against the assignee. U.C.C. §9-318.

[11] U.C.C.C. §2.412.

[12] U.C.C.C. §5.202.

8. Assignment of Right to Money

Assignments of contracts are generally made to raise money. **For Example,** an automobile dealer assigns a customer's credit contract to a finance company and receives cash for it. Sometimes assignments are made when an enterprise closes and transfers its business to a new owner.

A person entitled to receive money, such as payment for goods sold to a buyer or for work done under a contract, may generally assign that right to another person.[13] A **claim** or **cause of action** against another person may be assigned. Isaac Hayes, an Academy Award®–winning composer, producer, and the original voice of Chef in the television series South Park, assigned his copyright interests in several musical works in exchange for royalties from Stax Records.[14] A contractor entitled to receive payment from a building's owner can assign that right to a bank as security for a loan or can assign it to anyone else.

For Example, Celeste owed Roscoe Painters $5,000 for painting her house. Roscoe assigned this claim to the Main Street Bank. Celeste later refused to pay the bank because she had never consented to the assignment. The fact that Celeste had not consented is irrelevant. Roscoe was the owner of the claim and could transfer it to the bank. Celeste, therefore, is obligated to pay the assignee, Main Street Bank.

(A) Future Rights. By the modern rule, future and expected rights to money may be assigned. Thus, prior to the start of a building, a building contractor may assign its rights to money not yet due under an existing contract's payment on completion-phase schedule.

(B) Purpose of Assignment. The assignment of the right to money may be a complete transfer of the right that gives the assignee the right to collect and keep the money. In contrast, the assignment may be held for security. In this case, the assignee may hold the money only as a security for some specified obligation.

(C) Prohibition of Assignment of Rights. A clear and specific contractual prohibition against the assignment of rights is enforceable at common law. However, the UCC favors the assignment of contracts, and express contractual prohibitions on assignments are ineffective against (1) the assignment of rights to payment for goods or services, including accounts receivable,[15] and (2) the assignment of the rights to damages for breach of sales contracts.[16]

9. Nonassignable Rights

If the transfer of a right would materially affect or alter a duty or the rights of the obligor, an assignment is not permitted.[17]

(A) Assignment Increasing Burden of Performance. When the assignment of a right would increase the burden of the obligor in performing, an assignment is ordinarily not permitted. To illustrate, if the assignor has the right to buy a certain quantity of a stated article and to take such property from the seller's warehouse, this right can be assigned. However, if the sales contract stipulates that the seller should deliver to the buyer's premises and the assignee's premises are a substantial distance from the assignor's place of business, the assignment would not be given effect. In this case, the seller would be required to give a different performance by providing greater transportation if the assignment were permitted.

(B) Personal Services. Contracts for personal services are generally not assignable. **For Example,** were golf instructor David Ledbetter to sign a one-year contract to provide instruction for professional golfer Davis Love III, David Ledbetter could not assign his first assistant to provide the instruction, nor could Davis Love assign a protégé to receive instruction from Ledbetter. Professional athletes and their agents commonly deal with assignment or trading rights of the athletes in their contracts with professional sports franchises.

There is a split among jurisdictions regarding whether employee noncompetition covenants are assignable to the new owner of a business absent employee consent. That is, some courts permit a successor employer to enforce an employee's noncompetition agreement as an assignee of the original employer. However, a majority of states that have considered this issue have concluded that restrictive

[13] *Pravin Banker Associates v. Banco Popular del Peru*, 109 F.3d 850 (2d Cir. 1997).

[14] *Hayes v. Carlin America, Inc.*, 168 F. Supp. 2d 154 (S.D.N.Y 2001).

[15] U.C.C. §9-318(4). This section of the U.C.C. is applicable to most common commercial assignments.

[16] U.C.C. §2-210(2).

[17] *Aslakson v. Home Savings Ass'n*, 416 N.W.2d 786 (Minn. App. 1987) (increase of credit risk).

FIGURE 18-2 Limitations on Transfer of Rights and Duties

ASSIGNMENT OF RIGHT TO MONEY	ASSIGNMENT OF RIGHT TO PERFORMANCE	DELEGATION OF DUTIES
GENERALLY NO LIMITATION	INCREASE OF BURDEN PERSONAL SERVICES CREDIT TRANSACTION	PERSONAL OR NONSTANDARDIZED PERFORMANCE

covenants are personal in nature and not assignable. **For Example,** in September 2000, Philip Burkhardt signed a noncompetition agreement with his employer, NES Trench Shoring. On June 30, 2002, United Rentals Purchased NES with all contracts being assigned to United Rentals. Burkhardt stayed on with the new owner for five weeks and thereafter went to work for Traffic Control Services, a direct competitor of United. United was unsuccessful in its action to enforce the noncompetition covenant Burkhardt had signed with NES. Burkhardt's covenant with NES did not contain a clause allowing the covenant to be assigned to a new owner, and the court refused to enforce it, absent an express clause permitting assignment.[18]

(c) Credit Transaction. When a transaction is based on extending credit, the person to whom credit is extended cannot assign any rights under the contract to another. **For Example,** Jack Aldrich contracted to sell his summer camp on Lake Sunapee to Pat Norton for $200,000, with $100,000 in cash due at the closing and the balance due on an installment basis secured by a mortgage on the property to be executed by Norton. Several days later, Norton found a more desirable property, and her sister Meg was very pleased to take over the Sunapee contract. Pat assigned her rights to Meg. Jack Aldrich, having received a better offer after contracting with Pat, refused to consent to the assignment. In this situation, the assignment to Meg is prohibited because the assignee, Meg, is a different credit risk even though the property to serve as security remained unchanged.

CPA 10. Rights of Assignee

Unless restricted by the terms of the assignment or applicable law, the assignee acquires all the rights of the assignor.[19]

An assignee stands exactly in the position of the assignor. The assignee's rights are no more or less than those of the assignor. If the assigned right to payment is subject to a condition precedent, that same condition exists for the assignee. **For Example,** when a contractor is not entitled to receive the balance of money due under the contract until all bills of suppliers of materials have been paid, the assignee to whom the contractor assigns the balance due under the contract is subject to the same condition. As set forth previously, in some states the assignee of a business purchasing all of the assets and rights of the business has the right to enforce a confidentiality and noncompetition agreement against a former employee of the assignor, just as though it were the assignor.[20]

11. Continuing Liability of Assignor

The making of an assignment does not relieve the assignor of any obligation of the contract. In the absence of a contrary agreement, an assignor continues to be bound by the obligations of the original contract. **For Example,** boatbuilder Derecktor NY's assignment of obligations to a Connecticut boatbuilder did not release it from all liabilities under its boatbuilding contract with New York Water Taxi (NYWT); and NYWT was allowed to proceed against

[18] *Traffic Control Sources, Inc. v. United Rentals Northwest, Inc.*,87 P.3d 1054 (Nev. 2004).
[19] *Puget Sound National Bank v. Washington Department of Revenue*, 868 P.2d 127 (Wash. 1994).
[20] *Artromick International, Inc. v. Koch*, 759 N.E.2d 385 (Ohio App. 2001).

Derecktor NY for breach of contract–design and breach of contract–workmanship.[21]

When a lease is assigned, the assignee becomes the principal obligor for rent payments, and the leasee becomes a surety toward the lessor for the assignee's performance. **For Example,** Tri-State Chiropractic (TSC) held a five-year lease on premises at 6010 East Main Street in Columbus, Ohio. Without the leasor's consent, TSC assigned that lease to Dr. T. Wilson and Buckeye Chiropractic, LLC, prior to the expiration of the lease. TSC continues to be liable for rent as surety during the term of the lease, even if the leasor (owner) had consented to the assignment or accepted payment from the assignee.[22] In order to avoid liability as a surety, TSC would have to obtain a discharge of the lease by **novation**, in which all three parties agree that the original contract (the lease) would be discharged and a new lease between Dr. Wilson and the owner would take effect. A novation allows for the discharge of a contractual obligation by the substitution of a new contract involving a new party.[23]

12. Liability of Assignee

It is necessary to distinguish between the question of whether the obligor can assert a particular defense against the assignee and the question of whether any person can sue the assignee. Ordinarily, the assignee is not subject to suit by virtue of the fact that the assignment has been made.

(A) Consumer Protection Liability of Assignee. The assignee of the right to money may have no direct relationship to the original debtor except with respect to receiving payments. Consumer protection laws in most states, however, may subject the assignee to some liability for the assignor's misconduct. In the *Jackson v. Dewitt* case, the court was faced with deciding whether a finance company had an obligation to return money already paid to it by a homeowner under a retail installment security agreement between the homeowner and a contractor, which agreement had been assigned to the finance company by the contractor.

Jackson v. Dewitt, 592 N.W.2d 262 (Wis. App. 1999)

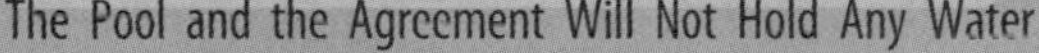

The Pool and the Agreement Will Not Hold Any Water

Homeowner Michael Jackson entered into a contract for the construction of an in-ground lap pool with James DeWitt. The contract provided for a 12 ft. by 60 ft. pool at an estimated cost of $21,000. At the time the contract was signed, Jackson paid DeWitt $11,400 in cash and financed $7,500 through a Retail Installment Security Agreement (RISA). Associates Financial Services Co. (Associates) provided DeWitt with all the forms necessary to document the financing of the home improvements. Consumer requests for financing were subject to Associates' approval, which was given for Jackson's lap pool. When the RISA was completed, DeWitt assigned it to Associates. Jackson made two monthly payments of $202.90 and a final payment of $7,094.20 while the lap pool was still under construction. When the pool was filled, it failed to hold water, and Jackson had the pool and deck removed. Jackson sued DeWitt for breach of contract. He asserted that all valid claims and defenses he had against DeWitt were also valid against the assignee, Associates. Jackson sought the return of the $7,500 he had financed from Associates. The trial court held that because Jackson had paid the entire balance of the loan before Associates knew of Jackson's claim he could not obtain relief from Associates under the consumer protection law § ATCP 110.06. Jackson appealed this decision.

JUDICIAL OPINION

ANDERSON, J.... WISCONSIN ADM.CODE § ATCP 110.06, governs home improvement contracts and provides:

1. *Every assignee of a home improvement contract takes subject to all claims and defenses of the buyer or successors in interest.*
2. *No seller shall enter into any home improvement contract wherein the buyer waives the right to assert against the seller or any assignee any claim or defense the buyer may have against the seller under the contract....*

To subject all assignees or holders of "home improvement" contracts, including Associates, to the claims and defenses of

[21] *New York Trans Harbor, LLC v. Derecktor Shipyards*, 841 N.Y.S.2d 821 (2007).

[22] *Schottenstein Trustees v. Carano*, 2000 WL 1455425 (Ohio. App. 2000).

[23] *Willamette Management Association, Inc. v. Palczynski*, 38 A.3d 1212 (Conn. App. 2012).

Continued

the consumer, fulfills the intent of WIS. ADM. CODE ch. ATCP 110. As one commentator has noted, ch. ATCP 110 "deals with a virtual laundry list of unfair or deceptive home improvement practices that have resulted in substantial financial losses to home owners over the years." Jeffries 57 MARQ. L. REV. at 578. The Wisconsin Supreme Court has also noted, "[T]he home improvement trade is subject to comprehensive and stringent rules designed to protect the consumer." To protect the homeowner when the contractor or seller has failed to fulfill the obligations imposed by ch. ATCP 110, the homeowner must be able to seek restitutionary relief wherever it is available. [It] provide[s] relief from the assignee or holder on a "home improvement contract" by making the assignee or holder subject to the claims and defenses of the buyer....

We conclude, from the statute and regulation, that a homeowner may proceed under § 100.20(5), STATS., when he or she has suffered pecuniary loss as a result of violations of WIS. ADM. CODE ch. ATCP 110. If the "home improvement contract" was financed with an "interlocking consumer loan," full payment before discovering the violations of the regulation does not eliminate the consumer's cause of action against the assignee or holder of the "home improvement contract."

Excel Management, like this case, involved contracts for the sale of swimming pools to consumers. *See Excel Management,* 111 Wis.2d at 483, 331 N.W.2d at 314. In *Excel Management,* like this case, the complaint alleged that the contracts were obtained in violation of WIS. ADM. CODE ch. ATCP 110. In *Excel Management,* like this case, the retailer used loan papers provided by the lender and assigned the completed contract to the lender. In *Excel Management,* like this case, the assigned contract contained a notice required by 16 C.F.R § 433.2, "Any holder of this consumer credit contract is subject to all claims and defenses which the debtor could assert against the seller of goods or services obtained pursuant hereto or with the proceeds hereof."

Considering these facts, the supreme court in *Excel Management,* readily concluded that although the contract was not a negotiable instrument, "[a]s an assignee of the contracts from Viking, First Savings takes each contract 'subject to all claims and defenses of the buyer of his successor in interest.'"... The supreme court commented that the warning language required by 16 C.F.R. § 433.2 clearly made the assignee of the contract aware that it took assignment of the contract subject to "any claims or defenses the buyer may assert." In *Excel Management,* the supreme court concluded that the consumers could bring actions against the assignees of their contracts for pecuniary losses stemming from the retailers' violations of the unfair trade statutes. *See id.* at 487, 331 N.W.2d at 316.

The factual similarity between this case and *Excel Management* requires us to reach a similar conclusion. Associates is an assignee of a "home improvement contract" that is governed by WIS. ADM. CODE § ATCP 110.06. The regulation provides, "Every assignee of a home improvement contract takes subject to all claims and defenses of the buyer or successors in interest." Section ATCP 110.06(1). Therefore, as the assignee of the RISA, Associates is subject to any claims Jackson may assert, without regard to the negotiability of the contract....

[Reversed]

QUESTIONS

1. Identify the parties to the retail installment sales agreement (RISA), identify their obligations, explain how Associates became involved, and identify Associates' legal status.
2. Assess the validity of this statement: "The contractor botched the pool installation job. The finance company merely facilitated the transaction for the benefit of both parties and is innocent of wrongdoing. The homeowner therefore should obtain relief solely from the contractor."
3. What did Jackson claim he was due from Associates?

(B) DEFENSES AND SETOFFS. The assignee's rights are no greater than those of the assignor.[24] If the obligor could successfully defend against a suit brought by the assignor, the obligor will also prevail against the assignee.

The fact that the assignee has given value for the assignment does not give the assignee any immunity from defenses that the other party, the obligor, could have asserted against the assignor. The rights acquired by the assignee remain subject to any limitations imposed by the contract.

13. Warranties of Assignor

When the assignment is made for a consideration, the assignor is regarded as providing an **implied warranty** that the right assigned is valid. The assignor also warrants that the assignor is the owner of the claim or right

[24] *Shoreline Communications, Inc. v. Norwich Taxi, LLC,* 797 A.2d 1165 (Conn. App. 2002).

FIGURE 18-3 Can a Third Person Sue on a Contract?

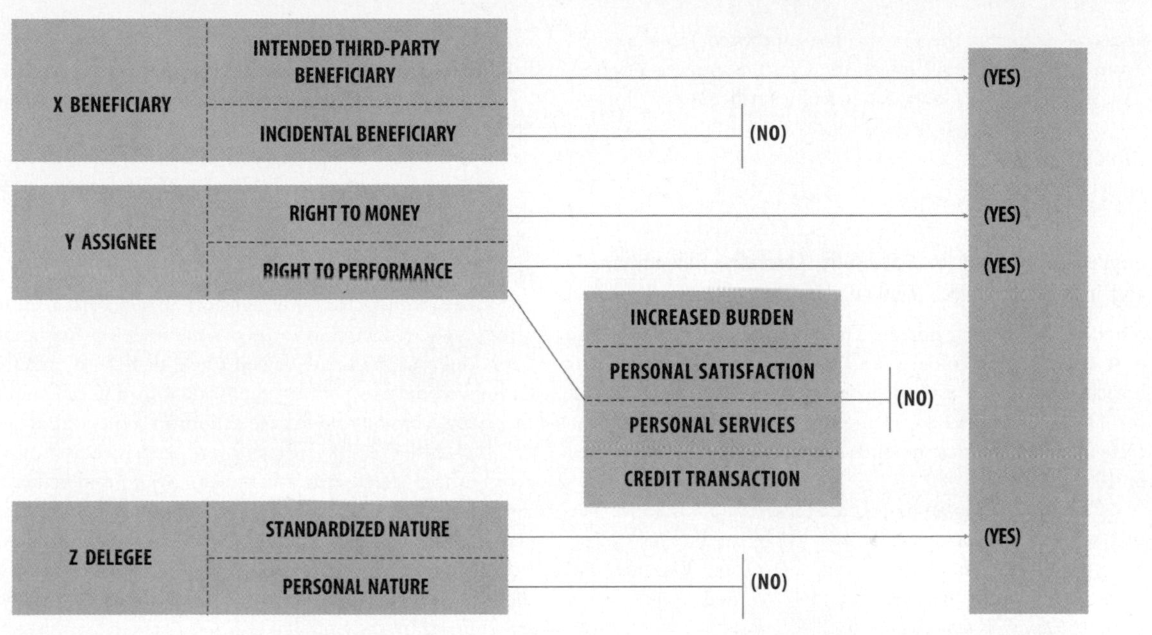

assigned and that the assignor will not interfere with the assignee's enforcement of the obligation.

14. Delegation of Duties

A **delegation of duties** is a transfer of duties by a contracting party to another person who is to perform them. Under certain circumstances, a contracting party may obtain someone else to do the work. When the performance is standardized and nonpersonal, so that it is not material who performs, the law will permit the **delegation** of the performance of the contract. In such cases, however, the contracting party remains liable in the case of default of the person doing the work just as though no delegation had been made.[25]

The *Winters* case is an example of a contracting party who had delegated a roof repair contract being held liable for damages caused by poor workmanship just as though no delegation had been made.

Federal Insurance Co. v. Winters, 345 S.W.3d 287 (Tenn. 2011)

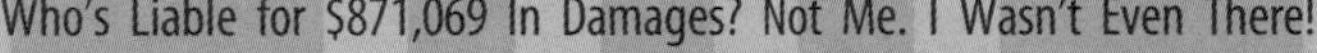

Who's Liable for $871,069 In Damages? Not Me. I Wasn't Even There!

The Emersons contracted with Martin Winters, the owner of Winters Roofing Company, to install a new roof on their home. When the new roof leaked, Winters agreed to fix the problems. Without the knowledge of the Emersons, Winters hired a subcontractor, Bruce Jacobs, to perform the repair work. Jacobs's use of a propane torch in repairing the roof resulted in a fire that caused $871,069 in damages to the house and personal property. Federal Insurance Co. sued Winters to recover sums it paid the Emersons for damages resulting from the fire. Winters defended that Federal had sued the wrong party because Winters did not participate in the repair work but had subcontracted the work out to Jacobs

[25] *Orange Bowl Corp. v. Warren*, 386 S.E.2d 293 (S.C. App. 1989).

Continued

and was neither at the job site nor supervised Jacobs's work. From a judgment for Winters, the Court of Appeals reversed. The state Supreme Court conducted a further review.

JUDICIAL OPINION

WADE, J....

Implied Duty to Perform Skillfully, Carefully, Diligently, and in a Workmanlike Manner

Since neither Federal nor the Defendant dispute the existence of a contract, the initial question is whether the Defendant breached its terms, express or implied. Federal contends that the Defendant breached its implied responsibility, while the Defendant argues that no such implied responsibility existed on his part.....

Cases from numerous jurisdictions support the principle that service contracts are accompanied by an implied obligation to perform the service skillfully, carefully, diligently, and in a workmanlike manner. *See, e.g., Reliable Elec. Co. v. Clinton Campbell Contractor, Inc., 459 P.2d 98, 101 (1969)* (explaining that someone who undertakes a service must perform the service in a "good workmanlike manner and in a manner befitting a skilled contractor")....

Non-delegable Duty to Perform Skillfully, Carefully, Diligently, and in a Workmanlike Manner

The question is whether the duty of the Defendant to replace the roof skillfully, carefully, diligently, and in a workmanlike manner could be delegated to a subcontractor. That is, may a contractor who has such a duty escape liability by subcontracting with a third party who breaches these implied responsibilities? This Court has not previously considered whether utilizing an independent contractor in performing a contract for services can absolve the contracting party from liability under the contract.

The Restatement (Second) of Contracts specifically addresses this issue, explaining that "neither delegation of performance nor a contract to assume the duty [under a contract] ... discharges any duty or liability of the delegating obligor." Restatement (Second) of Contracts § 318(3) (1981)....

The Supreme Court of Washington reached a similar result in *White Pass Co. v. St. John,* 427 P.2d 398 (1967). In that case, a contractor, after agreeing to renovate a ski lodge, hired a subcontractor, who used a flammable material on the floors and caused a fire. The court held that the contractor had an implied duty to perform the work with due care and ruled that he was responsible for the actions of a subcontractor who had breached this duty. Relying on persuasive authority, the court further stated that a contractor who "undertakes to do some particular thing ... cannot, by employing an independent contractor, avoid responsibility for an injury resulting from the nonperformance of any duty or duties which, under the express terms of the agreement, or by implication of law, are assumed by the undertaker."

[Court of Appeals decision affirmed; remanded for trial]

QUESTIONS

1. When Winters entered a contract with the Emersons to install a new roof, did he have an implied obligation to perform the service skillfully, carefully, diligently, and in a workmanlike manner?
2. May a contractor escape his responsibilities under his contract with a homeowner by subcontracting with a third party who breaches the implied responsibilities to perform the work in a skillful, careful, diligent, and workmanlike manner?

A contract may prohibit a party owing a duty of performance under a contract from delegating that duty to another.[26] **For Example,** Tom Joyce of Patriot Plumbing Co. contracts to install a new heating system for Mrs. Lawton. A notation on the sales contract that Tom Joyce will do the installation prohibits Patriot Plumbing from delegating the installation to another equally skilled plumber or to another company if a backlog of work occurs at Patriot Plumbing.

If the performance of a party to a contract involves personal skill, talents, judgment, or trust, the delegation of duties is barred unless consented to by the person entitled to the performance. Examples include performance by professionals such as physicians, dentists, lawyers, consultants, celebrities, artists, and craftpersons with unusual skills.

(A) Intention to Delegate Duties. An assignment of rights does not in itself delegate the performance of duties to the assignee. In the absence of clear language in the assignment stating that duties are or are not

[26] See *Physical Distribution Services, Inc. v. R. R. Donnelley*, 561 F.3d 792 (8th Cir. 2009).

delegated, all circumstances must be examined to determine whether there is a delegation. When the total picture is viewed, it may become clear what was intended. The fact that an assignment is made for security of the assignee is a strong indication there was no intent to delegate to the assignee the performance of any duty resting on the assignor.[27]

(B) Delegation of Duties under the UCC. With respect to contracts for the sale of goods, "an assignment of 'the contract' or of 'all my rights under the contract' or an assignment in similar general terms is an assignment of rights and, unless the language or the circumstances (as in an assignment for security) indicate the contrary, it is a delegation of performance of the duties of the assignor, and its acceptance by the assignee constitutes a promise … to perform those duties. This promise is enforceable by either the assignor or the other party to the original contract."[28]

LawFlix

It Could Happen to You (1996) (PG)

Discuss the legal, ethical, and contract issues involved in the first portion of the film in which a police officer (Nicholas Cage) promises to split a lottery ticket with a coffee shop waitress (Bridget Fonda) as her tip because he does not have enough money. The lottery ticket (purchased by Cage and his wife, Rosie Perez) is a winner, and Cage wrestles with his obligation to tell Fonda. You could discuss whether there was an assignment or whether Fonda was added as a third-party beneficiary after the fact.

[27] *City National Bank of Fort Smith v. First National Bank and Trust Co. of Rogers*, 732 S.W.2d 489 (Ark. App. 1987).
[28] U.C.C. §2-210(4).

MAKE THE CONNECTION

SUMMARY

Ordinarily, only the parties to contracts have rights and duties with respect to such contracts. Exceptions are made in the case of third-party beneficiary contracts and assignments.

When a contract shows a clear intent to benefit a third person or class of persons, those persons are called *intended third-party beneficiaries*, and they may sue for breach of the contract. A third-party beneficiary is subject to any limitation or restriction found in the contract. A third-party beneficiary loses all rights when the original contract is terminated by operation of law or if the contract reserves the right to change the beneficiary and such a change is made.

In contrast, an incidental beneficiary benefits from the performance of a contract, but the conferring of this benefit was not intended by the contracting parties. An incidental beneficiary cannot sue on the contract.

An assignment is a transfer of a right; the assignor transfers a right to the assignee. In the absence of a local statute, there are no formal requirements for an assignment. Any words manifesting the intent to transfer are sufficient to constitute an assignment. No consideration is required. Any right to money may be assigned, whether the assignor is entitled to the money at the time of the assignment or will be entitled or expects to be entitled at some time in the future.

A right to a performance may be assigned except when (1) it would increase the burden of performance, (2) the contract involves the performance of personal services, or (3) the transaction is based on extending credit.

When a valid assignment is made, the assignee has the same rights—and only the same rights—as the assignor. The assignee is also subject to the same defenses and setoffs as the assignor had been.

The performance of duties under a contract may be delegated to another person except when a personal element of skill or judgment of the original contracting party is involved. The intent to delegate duties may be expressly stated. The intent may also be found in an "assignment" of "the contract" unless the circumstances make it clear that only the right to money was intended to be transferred. The fact that there has been a delegation of duties does not release the assignor from responsibility for performance. The assignor is liable for breach of the contract if the assignee does not properly perform the delegated duties. In the absence of an effective delegation or the formation of a third-party beneficiary contract, an assignee of rights is not liable to the obligee of the contract for its performance by the assignor.

Notice is not required to effect an assignment. When notice of the assignment is given to the obligor together with a demand that future payments be made to the assignee, the obligor cannot discharge liability by payment to the assignor.

When an assignment is made for a consideration, the assignor makes implied warranties that the right assigned is valid and that the assignor owns that right and will not interfere with its enforcement by the assignee.

LEARNING OUTCOMES

After studying this chapter, you should be able to clearly explain:

A. Third-Party Beneficiary Contracts

LO.1 Explain the two types of intended third-party beneficiaries

See the Sameway Laundry example that illustrates how the "intended creditor beneficiary" can sue the buyer, p. 336.

See the text discussion explaining that a life insurance contract is an "intended" donee third-party beneficiary contract, p. 337.

LO.2 Explain why an incidental beneficiary does not have the right to sue as a third-party beneficiary

See the *City of Yorkville* example, in which a subcontractor was an incidental beneficiary with no standing to sue on performance bonds because the obligation ran only to the city, p. 337.

B. Assignments

LO.3 Define an assignment

See the text discussion explaining that an assignment is the transfer of contractual rights to a third party, p. 337.

See the *Huntington Beach Board* example that discusses the assignee's direct rights against the obligor, pp. 337–338.

LO.4 Explain the general rule that a person entitled to receive money under a contract may generally assign that right to another person

See the example of an automobile dealer assigning a customer's credit contract to a finance company in order to raise cash to buy more inventory, p. 339.

LO.5 List the nonassignable rights to performance

See the text discussion regarding increase of burden, personal services, and credit transactions beginning on p. 339.

KEY TERMS

assignee
assignment
assignor
cause of action
claim
debtor
delegation
delegation of duties
duties

implied warranty
intended beneficiary
novation
obligee
obligor
rights
third-party beneficiary

QUESTIONS AND CASE PROBLEMS

1. Give an example of a third-party beneficiary contract.

2. A court order required John Baldassari to make specified payments for the support of his wife and child. His wife needed more money and applied for Pennsylvania welfare payments. In accordance with the law, she assigned to Pennsylvania her right to the support payments from her husband. Pennsylvania then increased her payments. Pennsylvania obtained a court order directing John, in accordance with the terms of the assignment from his wife, to make the support-order payments directly to the Pennsylvania Department of Public Welfare. John refused to pay on the ground that he had not been notified of the assignment or the hearing directing him to make payment to the assignee. Was he correct? [*Pennsylvania v. Baldassari,* 421 A.2d 306 (Pa. Super.)]

3. Lee contracts to paint Sally's two-story house for $2,500. Sally realizes that she will not have sufficient money, so she transfers her rights under this agreement to her neighbor Karen, who has a three-story house. Karen notifies Lee that Sally's contract has been assigned to her and demands that Lee paint Karen's house for $2,500. Is Lee required to do so?

4. Assume that Lee agrees to the assignment of the house-painting contract to Karen as stated in question 3. Thereafter, Lee fails to perform the contract to paint Karen's house. Karen sues Sally for damages. Is Sally liable?

5. Jessie borrows $1,000 from Thomas and agrees to repay the money in 30 days. Thomas assigns the right to the $1,000 to Douglas Finance Co. Douglas sues Jessie. Jessie argues that she had agreed to pay the money only to Thomas and that when she and Thomas had entered into the transaction, there was no intention to benefit Douglas Finance Co. Are these objections valid?

6. Washington purchased an automobile from Smithville Motors. The contract called for payment of the purchase price in installments and contained the defense preservation notice required by the Federal Trade Commission regulation. Smithville assigned the contract to Rustic Finance Co. The car was always in need of repairs, and by the time it was half paid for, it would no longer run. Washington canceled the contract. Meanwhile, Smithville had gone out of business. Washington sued Rustic for the amount she had paid Smithville. Rustic refused to pay on the grounds that it had not been at fault. Decide.

7. Helen obtained an insurance policy insuring her life and naming her niece Julie as beneficiary. Helen died, and about a year later the policy was found in her house. When Julie claimed the insurance money, the insurer refused to pay on the ground that the policy required that notice of death be given to it promptly following the death. Julie claimed that she was not bound by the time limitation because she had never agreed to it, as she was not a party to the insurance contract. Is Julie entitled to recover?

8. Lone Star Life Insurance Co. agreed to make a long-term loan to Five Forty Three Land, Inc., whenever that corporation requested one. Five Forty Three wanted this loan to pay off its short-term debts. The loan was never made, as it was never requested by Five Forty Three, which owed the Exchange Bank & Trust Co. on a short-term debt. Exchange Bank then sued Lone Star for breach of its promise on the theory that the Exchange Bank was a third-party beneficiary of the contract to make the loan. Was the Exchange Bank correct? [*Exchange Bank & Trust Co. v. Lone Star Life Ins. Co.,* 546 S.W.2d 948 (Tex. App.)]

9. The New Rochelle Humane Society made a contract with the city of New Rochelle to capture and impound all dogs running at large. Spiegler, a minor, was bitten by some dogs while in her schoolyard. She sued the school district of New Rochelle and the Humane Society. With respect to the Humane Society, she claimed that she was a third-party beneficiary of the contract that the Humane Society had made with the city. She claimed that she could therefore sue the Humane Society for its failure to capture the dogs that had bitten her. Was she entitled to recover? [*Spiegler v. School District of the City of New Rochelle,* 242 N.Y.S.2d 430]

10. Zoya operated a store in premises rented from Peerless. The lease required Zoya to maintain liability insurance to protect Zoya and Peerless. Caswell entered the store, fell through a trap door, and was injured. She then sued Zoya and Peerless on the theory that she was a third-party beneficiary of the lease requirement to maintain liability insurance. Was she correct? [*Caswell v. Zoya Int'l,* 654 N.E.2d 552 (Ill. App.)]

11. Henry was owed $10,000 by Jones Corp. In consideration of the many odd jobs performed for him over the years by his nephew, Henry assigned the $10,000 claim to his nephew Charles. Henry died, and his widow claimed that the assignment was ineffective so that the claim was part of Henry's estate. She based her assertion on the ground that the past performance rendered by the nephew was not consideration. Was the assignment effective?

12. Industrial Construction Co. wanted to raise money to construct a canning factory in Wisconsin. Various persons promised to subscribe the needed amount, which they agreed to pay when the construction was completed. The construction company assigned its rights and delegated its duties under the agreement to Johnson, who then built the cannery. Vickers, one of the subscribers, refused to pay the amount that he had subscribed on the ground that the contract could not be assigned. Was he correct?

13. The Ohio Department of Public Welfare made a contract with an accountant to audit the accounts of health care providers who were receiving funds under the Medicaid program. Windsor House, which operated six nursing homes, claimed that it was a third-party beneficiary of that contract and could sue for its breach. Was it correct? [*Thornton v. Windsor House, Inc.,* 566 N.E.2d 1220 (Ohio)]

CPA QUESTIONS

1. On August 1, Neptune Fisheries contracted in writing with West Markets to deliver to West 3,000 pounds of lobster at $4.00 a pound. Delivery of the lobsters was due October 1, with payment due November 1. On August 4, Neptune entered into a contract with Deep Sea Lobster Farms that provided as follows: "Neptune Fisheries assigns all the rights under the contract with West Markets dated August 1 to Deep Sea Lobster Farms." The best interpretation of the August 4 contract would be that it was:
   a. Only an assignment of rights by Neptune.
   b. Only a delegation of duties by Neptune.
   c. An assignment of rights and a delegation of duties by Neptune.
   d. An unenforceable third-party beneficiary contract.

2. Graham contracted with the city of Harris to train and employ high school dropouts residing in Harris. Graham breached the contract. Long, a resident of Harris and a high school dropout, sued Graham for damages. Under the circumstances, Long will:
   a. Win, because Long is a third-party beneficiary entitled to enforce the contract.
   b. Win, because the intent of the contract was to confer a benefit on all high school dropouts residing in Harris.
   c. Lose, because Long is merely an incidental beneficiary of the contract.
   d. Lose, because Harris did not assign its contract rights to Long.

3. Union Bank lent $200,000 to Wagner. Union required Wagner to obtain a life insurance policy

naming Union as beneficiary. While the loan was outstanding, Wagner stopped paying the premiums on the policy. Union paid the premiums, adding the amounts paid to Wagner's loan. Wagner died, and the insurance company refused to pay the policy proceeds to Union. Union may:

a. Recover the policy proceeds because it is a creditor beneficiary.
b. Not recover the policy proceeds because it is a donee beneficiary.
c. Not recover the policy proceeds because it is not in privity of contract with the insurance company.
d. Not recover the policy proceeds because it is only an incidental beneficiary.

Discharge of Contracts

learningoutcomes

After studying this chapter, you should be able to

LO.1 List the three types of conditions that affect a party's duty to perform

LO.2 Explain the on-time performance rule

LO.3 Explain the adequacy of performance rules

LO.4 Explain four ways a contract can be discharged by agreement of the parties

LO.5 State the effect on a contract of the death or disability of one of the contracting parties

LO.6 Explain when impossibility or impracticability may discharge a contract

In the preceding chapters, you studied how a contract is formed, what a contract means, and who has rights under a contract. In this chapter, attention is turned to how a contract is ended or discharged. In other words, what puts an end to the rights and duties created by a contract?

A. Conditions Relating to Performance

As developed in the body of this chapter, the ordinary method of discharging obligations under a contract is by performance. Certain promises may be less than absolute and instead come into effect only upon the occurrence of a specified event, or an existing obligation may be extinguished when an event happens. These are conditional promises.

1. Classifications of Conditions

When the occurrence or nonoccurrence of an event, as expressed in a contract, affects the duty of a party to the contract to perform, the event is called a **condition**. Terms such as *if, provided that, when, after, as soon as, subject to,* and *on the condition that* indicate the creation of a condition.[1] Conditions are classified as *conditions precedent, conditions subsequent,* and *concurrent conditions.*

(a) Condition Precedent. A **condition precedent** is a condition that must occur before a party to a contract has an obligation to perform under the contract. **For Example,** a condition precedent to a contractor's (MasTec's) obligation to pay a subcontractor (Mid-America) under a "pay-if-paid" by the owner (Path-Net) clause in their subcontract agreement is the receipt of payment by MasTec from PathNet. The condition precedent—payment by the owner—did not occur due to bankruptcy, and therefore MasTec did not have an obligation to pay MidAmerica.[2]

(b) Condition Subsequent. The parties to a contract may agree that a party is obligated to perform a certain act or pay a certain sum of money, but the contract contains a provision that relieves the obligation on the occurrence of a certain event. That is, on the happening of a **condition subsequent**, such an event extinguishes the duty to thereafter perform. **For Example,** Chad Newly served as the weekend anchor on *Channel 5 News* for several years. The station manager, Tom O'Brien, on reviewing tapes in connection with Newly's contract renewal, believed that Newly's speech on occasion was slightly slurred, and he suspected that it was from alcohol use. In the parties' contract discussions, O'Brien expressed his concerns about an alcohol problem and offered help. Newly denied there was a problem. O'Brien agreed to a new two-year contract with Newly at $167,000 for the first year and $175,000 for the second year with other benefits subject to "the condition" that the station reserved the right to make four unannounced drug-alcohol tests during the contract term; and should Newly test positive for drugs or alcohol under measurements set forth in the contract, then all of Channel 5's obligations to Newly under the contract would cease. When Newly subsequently

Sports & Entertainment Law

Endorsement Contracts

Sports marketing involves the use of famous athletes to promote the sale of products and services in our economy. Should an athlete's image be tarnished by allegations of immoral or illegal conduct, a company could be subject to financial losses and corporate embarrassment. Endorsement contracts may extend for multiyear periods, and should a "morals" issue arise, a company would be well served to have had a

[1] *Harmon Cable Communications v. Scope Cable Television, Inc.,* 468 N.W.2d 350 (Neb. 1990).

[2] *MidAmerica Construction Management, Inc. v. MasTec North America, Inc.,* 436 F.3d 1257 (10th Cir. 2006). But see *International Engineering Services, Inc. v. Scherer Construction Co.,* 74 So.3d 53 (Fla. App. 2011), where a "pay-when-paid" provision was found to be ambiguous, resulting in the general contractor being liable for the payment to the subcontractor.

Sports & Entertainment Law—*Contd.*

broad morals clause in its contract that would allow the company at its sole discretion to summarily terminate the endorsement contract. Representatives of athletes, on the other hand, seek narrow contractual language that allows for termination of endorsement contracts only upon the indictment for a crime, and they seek the right to have an arbitrator, as opposed to the employer, make the determination as to whether the morals clause was violated. NBA player Latrell Spreewell's endorsement contract with Converse Athletic Shoe Co. was terminated by the company following his altercation with his coach P. J. Carlisimo; John Daly's endorsement contract with Callaway Golf was terminated by the company when he violated his good conduct clause that restricted gambling and drinking activities; and six-time Pro Bowl football player Chad Johnson (aka "Ochocinco") lost his endorsement deal with Zico Coconut Water after he was arrested in a domestic battery case involving his wife. And, Nike, RadioShack, and other sponsors ended their relationships with cyclist Lance Armstrong after a report detailing doping charges was issued by the U.S. Anti-Doping Agency.

Can the courts be utilized to resolve controversies over whether a "morals clause" has been violated? If so, is the occurrence of a morals clause violation a condition precedent or a condition subsequent?

failed a urinalysis test three months into the new contract, the happening of this event extinguished the station's obligation to employ and pay him under the contract. Conditions subsequent are strictly construed, and where ambiguous, are construed against forfeiture.[3]

(c) Concurrent Condition. In most bilateral contracts, the performances of the parties are *concurrent conditions*. That is, their mutual duties of performance under the contract are to take place simultaneously. **For Example,** concerning a contract for the sale and delivery of certain goods, the buyer must tender to the seller a certified check at the time of delivery as set forth in the contract, and the seller must tender the goods to the buyer at the same time.

B. Discharge by Performance

When it is claimed that a contract is discharged by performance, questions arise as to the nature, time, and sufficiency of the performance.

2. Normal Discharge of Contracts

A contract is usually discharged by the performance of the terms of the agreement. In most cases, the parties perform their promises and the contract ceases to exist or is thereby discharged. A contract is also discharged by the expiration of the time period specified in the contract.[4]

3. Nature of Performance

Performance may be the doing of an act or the making of payment.

(a) Tender. An offer to perform is known as a **tender**. If performance of the contract requires the doing of an act, the refusal of a tender discharges the party offering to perform and is a basis for that party to bring a lawsuit.

A valid tender of payment consists of an unconditional offer of the exact amount due on the date when due. A tender of payment is not just an expression of willingness to pay; it must be an actual offer to perform by making payment of the amount owed.

(b) Payment. When the contract requires payment, performance consists of the payment of money.

(1) Application of Payments.

If a debtor owes more than one debt to the creditor and pays money, a question may arise as to which debt has been paid. If the debtor specifies the debt to which the payment is to be applied and the creditor accepts the money, the creditor is bound to apply the money as specified.[5] Thus, if the debtor specifies that a payment is to be made for a current purchase, the creditor may not apply the payment to an older balance.

(2) Payment by Check.

Payment by commercial paper, such as a check, is ordinarily a conditional payment. A check merely

[3] *Cardone Trust v. Cardone,* 8 A.3d 1 (N.H. 2010).
[4] *Washington National Ins. Co. v. Sherwood Associates,* 795 P.2d 665 (Utah App. 1990).
[5] *Oakes Logging, Inc. v. Green Crow, Inc.,* 832 P.2d 894 (Wash. App. 1992).

suspends the debt until the check is presented for payment. If payment is then made, the debt is discharged; if not paid, the suspension terminates, and suit may be brought on either the debt or the check. Frequently, payment must be made by a specified date. It is generally held that the payment is made on time if it is mailed on or before the final date for payment.

4. Time of Performance

When the date or period of time for performance is specified in the contract, performance should be made on that date or within that time period.

(A) No Time Specified. When the time for performance is not specified in the contract, an obligation to perform within a reasonable time is implied.[6] The fact that no time is specified neither impairs the contract on the ground that it is indefinite nor allows an endless time in which to perform. What constitutes a reasonable time is determined by the nature of the subject matter of the contract and the facts and circumstances surrounding the making of the contract.

(B) When Time Is Essential. If performance of the contract on or within the exact time specified is vital, it is said that "time is of the essence." Time is of the essence when the contract relates to property that is perishable or that is fluctuating rapidly in value. When a contract fixes by unambiguous language a time for performance and where there is no evidence showing that the parties did not intend that time should be of the essence, failure to perform within the specified time is a breach of contract entitling the innocent party to damages. **For Example,** Dixon and Gandhi agreed that Gandhi would close on the purchase of a motel as follows: "Closing Date. The closing shall be held … on the date which is within twenty (20) days after the closing of Nomura Financing." Gandhi did not close within the time period specified, and Dixon was allowed to retain $100,000 in prepaid closing costs and fees as liquidated damages for Gandhi's breach of contract.[7]

(C) When Time Is Not Essential. Unless a contract so provides, time is ordinarily not of the essence, and performance within a reasonable time is sufficient. In the case of the sale of property, time is not regarded as of the essence when there has not been any appreciable change in the market value or condition of the property and when the person who delayed does not appear to have done so for the purpose of speculating on a change in market price.

(D) Waiver of Essence of Time Limitation. A provision that time is of the essence may be waived. It is waived when the specified time has expired but the party who could complain requests the delaying party to take steps necessary to perform the contract.

5. Adequacy of Performance

When a party renders exactly the performance called for by the contract, no question arises as to whether the contract has been performed. In other cases, there may not have been a perfect performance, or a question arises as to whether the performance satisfies the standard set by the contract.

CPA **(A) Substantial Performance.** Perfect performance of a contract is not always possible when dealing with construction projects. A party who in good faith has provided **substantial performance** of the contract may sue to recover the payment specified in the contract.[8] However, because the performance was not perfect, the performing party is subject to a counterclaim for the damages caused the other party. When a building contractor has substantially performed the contract to construct a building, the contractor is responsible for the cost of repairing or correcting the defects as an offset from the contract price.[9]

The measure of damages under these circumstances is known as "cost of completion" damages.[10] If, however, the cost of completion would be unreasonably disproportionate to the importance of the defect, the measure of damages is the diminution in value of the building due to the defective performance.

Whether there is substantial performance is a question of degree to be determined by all of the facts,

[6] *First National Bank v. Clark,* 447 S.E.2d 558 (W. Va. 1994).
[7] *Woodhull Corp. v. Saibaba Corp.,* 507 S.E.2d 493 (Ga. App. 1998).
[8] *Gala v. Harris,* 77 So.3d 1065 (La. App. 2012).
[9] Substantial performance is not a defense to a breach of contract claim, however. See *Bentley Systems Inc. v. Intergraph Corp.,* 922 So.2d 61 (Ala. 2005).
[10] *Hammer Construction Corp. v. Phillips,* 994 So.2d 1135 (Fla. App. 2008).

FIGURE 19-1 *Causes of Contract Discharge*

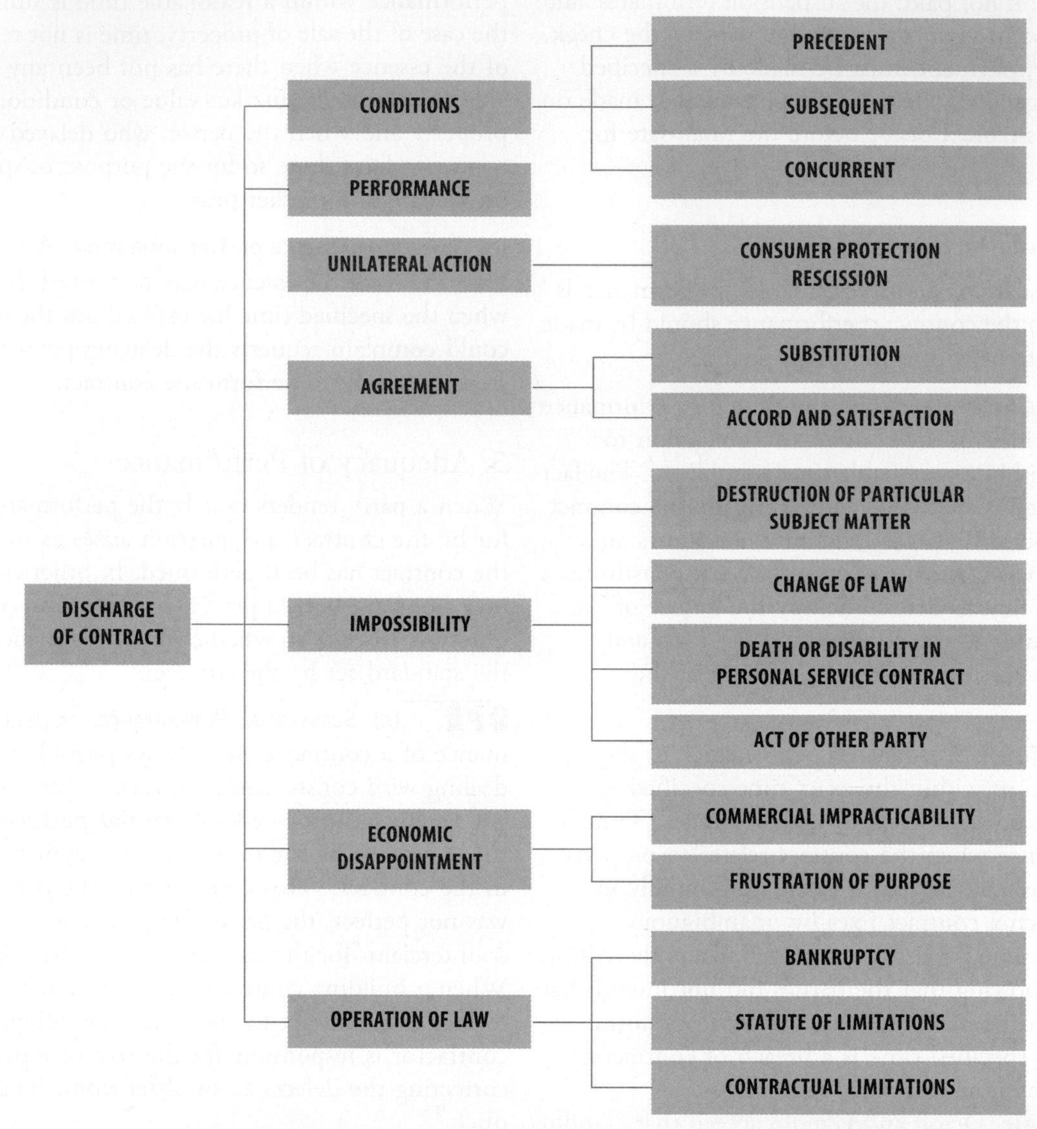

including the particular type of structure involved, its intended purpose, and the nature and relative expense of repairs.

For Example, a certain building contractor (BC) and a certain owner (O) made a contract to construct a home overlooking Vineyard Sound on Martha's Vineyard according to plans and specifications that clearly called for the use of General Plumbing Blue Star piping. The contract price was $1,100,000. Upon inspecting the work before making the final $400,000 payment and accepting the building, O discovered that BC had used Republic piping throughout the house. O explained to BC that his family had made its money by investing in General Plumbing, and he, therefore, would not make the final payment until the breach of contract was remedied. BC explained that Republic pipes were of the same industrial grade and quality as the Blue Star pipes. Moreover, BC estimated that it would cost nearly $300,000 to replace all of the pipes because of the destruction of walls and fixtures necessary to accomplish such a task. BC may sue O for $400,000 for breach of contract, claiming he had substantially performed the contract, and O may counterclaim for $300,000, seeking an offset for the cost of remedying the breach. The court will find in favor of the contractor and will not allow the $300,000 offset but will allow a "nominal" offset of perhaps $100 to $1,000 for the amount by which the Republic pipes diminished the value of the building. To have required the pipes to be replaced would amount to economic waste.[11]

When a contractor does not substantially perform its obligations under a contract, not only will the contractor not prevail in a breach of contract claim against a homeowner for extra work beyond the contract price but the contractor is liable for the reasonable cost of making the contractor's work conform to the contract. **For Example,** Superior Wall and Paver, LLC sued homeowners Pamela and Mark Gacek for $14,350 it claimed was still owed Superior as extra work, for concrete pavers it installed in the driveway of their residence. The Gaceks had previously paid the $45,000 contract price. The Gackes counterclaimed for $60,500 for the reasonable cost of making the contractor's work conform to the contract. The evidence established that Superior did not install a proper base of 3" to 4" of crushed limestone before installing the pavers as required by the contract, which caused the pavers to move, creating gaps between the pavers and causing water to flow into the garage. To correct the problem the pavers needed to be removed and the area excavated and replaced with a crushed limestone base before again installing the pavers. Superior claimed it had substantially performed the contract as a fully usable driveway, and the proper remedy, if any, was the diminution of the market value of the Gaceks' property due to any defective performance. Superior asserted the cost of redoing the entire job would be economic waste. The court determined that Superior had not substantially performed the contract and awarded the homeowners the cost of making Superior's work conform to the contract by having the job redone, rejecting Superior's assertion of economic waste.[12]

In most jurisdictions, the willfulness of the departure from the specifications of the contract does not by itself preclude some recovery for the contractor on the "cost of completion" basis but rather is a factor in consideration of whether there was substantial performance by the contractor.[13]

(B) Fault of Complaining Party. A party cannot complain that a performance was defective when the performance follows the terms of the contract required by the complaining party. Thus, a homeowner who supplied the specifications for poured cement walls could not hold a contractor liable for damages when the walls that were poured in exact compliance with those specifications proved defective.

(C) Performance to the Satisfaction of the Contracting Party or a Third Party. Sometimes an agreement requires performance to the satisfaction, taste, or judgment of the other party to the contract. When the contract specifically stipulates that the performance must satisfy the contracting party, the courts will ordinarily enforce the plain meaning of the language of the parties and the work must satisfy the contracting party—subject, of course, to the requirement that dissatisfaction be made in good faith. **For Example,** the Perrones' written contract to purchase the Hills' residence contained a clause making performance subject to inspection to the Perrones' satisfaction. During the house inspection, the inspector found a piece of wood in a crawl space that appeared to have been damaged by termites and had possibly been treated some 18 years before with chlordane. At the end of the inspection Mr. Perrone indicated that he would perform on the contract. Thereafter, he went on the Internet and found that chlordane is a highly toxic pesticide now banned from use as a termite treatment. As a result, the Perrones rescinded the contract under the buyer satisfaction

[11] See *Jacob & Youngs, Inc. v. Kent,* 230 N.Y. 239 (1921).

[12] *Superior Wall and Paver, LLC. v. Gacek,* 73 So.3d (Ala. App. 2011).

[13] But see *USX Corp. v. M. DeMatteo Construction Co.,* 315 F.3d 43 (1st Cir. 2002), for application of a common law rule that prohibits a construction contractor guilty of a willful breach of contract from maintaining any suit on the contract against the other party.

clause. The Hills sued, believing that speculation about a pesticide treatment 18 years ago was absurd. They contended that the Perrones had breached the contract without a valid reason. The court decided for the Perrones, since they exercised the "satisfaction clause" in good faith.[14] Good-faith personal satisfaction is generally required when the subject matter of the contract is personal, such as interior design work, tailoring, or the painting of a portrait.

With respect to things mechanical or routine performances, courts require that the performance be such as would satisfy a reasonable person under the circumstances.

When work is to be done subject to the approval of an architect, engineer, or another expert, most courts apply the reasonable person test of satisfaction.

C. Discharge by Action of Parties

Contracts may be discharged by the joint action of both contracting parties or, in some cases, by the action of one party alone.

6. Discharge by Unilateral Action

Ordinarily, a contract cannot be discharged by the action of either party alone. In some cases, however, the contract gives one of either party the right to cancel the contract by unilateral action, such as by notice to the other party. Insurance policies covering loss commonly provide that the insurer may cancel the policy upon giving a specified number of days' notice.

(A) Consumer Protection Rescission. A basic principle of contract law is that once made, a contract between competent persons is a binding obligation. Consumer protection legislation introduces into the law a contrary concept—that of giving the consumer a chance to think things over and to rescind the contract. Thus, the federal Consumer Credit Protection Act (CCPA) gives the debtor the right to rescind a credit transaction within three business days when the transaction would impose a lien on the debtor's home. **For Example,** a homeowner who mortgages his or her home to obtain a loan may cancel the transaction for any reason by notifying the lender before midnight of the third full business day after the loan is made.[15]

A Federal Trade Commission regulation gives the buyer three business days in which to cancel a home-solicited sale of goods or services costing more than $25.[16]

7. Discharge by Agreement

A contract may be discharged by the operation of one of its provisions or by a subsequent agreement. Thus, there may be a discharge by (1) the terms of the original contract, such as a provision that the contract should end on a specified date; (2) a mutual cancellation, in which the parties agree to end their contract; (3) a mutual **rescission**, in which the parties agree to annul the contract and return both parties to their original positions before the contract had been made; (4) the **substitution** of a new contract between the same parties; (5) a novation or substitution of a new contract involving a new party;[17] (6) an **accord and satisfaction**; (7) a release; or (8) a **waiver**.

(A) Substitution. The parties may decide that their contract is not the one they want. They may then replace it with another contract. If they do, the original contract is discharged by substitution.[18]

(B) Accord and Satisfaction. When the parties have differing views as to the performance required by the terms of a contract, they may agree to a different performance. Such an agreement is called an *accord.* When the accord is performed or executed, there is an accord and satisfaction, which discharges the original obligation. To constitute an accord and satisfaction, there must be a bona fide dispute, a proposal to settle the dispute, and performance of the agreement. As seen in the *MKL Pre-Press* case, to constitute an accord and satisfaction, there must be a bona fide dispute, a proposal to settle the dispute, and performance of the agreement.

[14] *Hill v. Perrones,* 42 P.3d 210 (Kan. App. 2002).
[15] If the owner is not informed of this right to cancel, the three-day period does not begin until that information is given. Consumer Credit Protection Act §125, 15 U.S.C. §1635(a), (e), (f).
[16] C.F.R. §429.1.
[17] *Eagle Industries, Inc. v. Thompson,* 900 P.2d 475 (Or. 1995). In a few jurisdictions, the term *novation* is used to embrace the substitution of any new contract, whether between the original parties or not.
[18] *Shawnee Hospital Authority v. Dow Construction, Inc.,* 812 P.2d 1351 (Okla. 1990).

MKL Pre-Press Electronics v. La Crosse Litho Supply, LLC, 840 N.E.2d 687 (Ill. App. 2005)

A Full Court Press to No Avail

In September 2002 La Crosse Litho Supply, LLC (La Crosse) entered a distribution agreement with MKL Pre-Press Electronics (MKL) for the distribution of MKL printing systems. La Crosse purchased a 7000 System unit from MKL for its end user Printing Plus with MKL technicians providing service and training for the unit. The 7000 System at Printing Plus failed on three occasions and ultimately repairs were unsuccessful. On September 30, 2003, La Crosse cancelled the distribution agreement. On October 2, 2003, La Crosse sent a letter to MKL's Sales V.P. Bill Landwer setting forth an itemized accounting of what it owed MKL Pre-Press with deductions for the purchase price of the failed 7000 System and other offsets. MKL sent a subsequent bill for repairs and services, to which La Crosse objected and stated it would not pay them. MKL's attorney sent a demand letter for $26,453.31. La Crosse's president, Randall Peters, responded by letter dated December 30, 2003, explaining that with an offset for training and warranty work it performed, "we are sending you the final payment in the amount of $1,696.47." He added, "[w]ith this correspondence, we consider all open issues between La Crosse Litho Supply and MKL Pre Press closed." Enclosed with the letter was a check for $1,696.47 payable to MKL Pre-Press. In the remittance portion of the check, under the heading "Ref," was typed "FINAL PAYM." The check was endorsed and deposited on either January 26 or 27, 2004. MKL sued La Crosse for $24,756.84. La Crosse defended that the tender and subsequent deposit of the check for $1,696.47 constituted an accord and satisfaction. Jill Fleming, MKL's office manager, stated that it was her duty to process checks and that she did not read Peters' letter. From a judgment for La Crosse, MKL appealed.

JUDICIAL OPINION

GREIMAN, J.... An accord and satisfaction is a contractual method of discharging debts or claims between the parties to such an agreement. In order for such an arrangement to exist, there must be: (1) a *bonafide* dispute as to the claims pending between the parties; (2) an unliquidated sum owed; (3) consideration; (4) a shared mutual intent to compromise the claims; and (5) execution of the agreement. The accord is the actual agreement between the parties, while the satisfaction is its execution or performance....

Where there is an honest dispute as to the amount owed and due between the parties and the debtor tenders an amount with the explicit understanding that it is full payment of all demands, the creditor's acceptance and negotiation of that amount constitutes an accord and satisfaction. *Koules v Euro–American Arbitrage, Inc.,* 689 N.E.2d 411 (1998). However, the partial payment of a fixed and certain demand due and not in dispute does not constitute satisfaction of the entire debt even where the creditor agrees to receive partial payment for the whole debt and gives a receipt for the whole demand. *Koules,* 689 N.E.2d 411.

As demonstrated by the October 2003 correspondence between Peters and Landwer concerning amounts still due and owing to plaintiff, plaintiff's subsequent invoices and Peters' objection there-to, and plaintiff's November 2003 demand letter, it is plainly apparent that a *bonafide* dispute existed as to the claims pending between the parties and an unliquidated sum was owed by defendant to plaintiff. The tender of the check by defendant and its deposit by plaintiff constituted consideration and execution. The only element remaining is a shared mutual intent by the parties to compromise the claims between them. Intent can be inferred from conduct; the act of knowingly accepting and depositing a check upon which conditional language has been added indicates the existence of an accord and satisfaction. Where creditor takes and keeps a debtor's reduced payment with actual or constructive knowledge of the condition, the creditor has accepted the debtor's offer, and the original debt is settled for the reduced amount....

Plaintiff additionally argues that the deposit of defendent's check by Fleming should not be imputed to it as an organization because Fleming had no responsibility to enter the organization into any sort of agreement like an accord and satisfaction and because the check contained no restrictive language indicating that it had been tendered in consideration of all claims pending between the parties. We disagree.

An organization's practice of authorizing its employee to endorse checks and deposit them into an account on its behalf cannot serve as a means of isolating the organization or its principals from the legal consequences that flow from the employee's actions in the scope of his or her duties. An employee whose authority includes depositing a check upon which restrictive language appeared will be presumed to have acted on behalf of the organization, and his or her acts will be imputed to the organization as a matter of law.

In this case, Fleming's affidavit clearly stated that it was within the scope of her duties to process and deposit checks on the plaintiff's behalf. She stated herself that she endorsed and deposited the check, the voucher portion of which clearly stated "FINAL PAYM." We cannot fathom what "FINAL PAYM" might mean, other than "final payment," meaning that defendant did not intend to send plaintiff any more money. Accordingly, we can only conclude that Fleming's conduct can and should be imputed to plaintiff and its principals, thereby constituting an accord and satisfaction....

[Affirmed]

Continued

QUESTIONS

1. What are the elements of an "accord and satisfaction"?
2. Was there a shared mutual intent to compromise the claims between the parties?
3. Is it fair to expect an office manager to know that by processing a check for $1,696.47 marked "final payment" that her company could lose the right to pursue its position that it was owed an additional $24,756.84?

D. Discharge by External Causes

Circumstances beyond the control of the contracting parties may discharge the contract.

8. Discharge by Impossibility

To establish impossibility a party must show (1) the unexpected occurrence of an intervening act; (2) that the risk of the unexpected occurrence was not allocated by agreement or custom; and (3) that the occurrence made performance impossible. The doctrine of impossibility relieves nonperformance only in extreme circumstances.[19] The party asserting the defense of impossibility bears the burden of proving "a real impossibility and not a mere inconvenience or unexpected difficulty."[20] Moreover, courts will generally only excuse nonperformance where performance is objectively impossible—that is, incapable performance by anyone. Financial inability to perform a contract that a party voluntarily entered into will rarely, if ever, excuse nonperformance. **For Example,** Ms. Robinson was employed by East Capital Community Development Group under a written employment contract for one year, but was terminated early for lack of funding. The contract did not reference that her continued employment was contingent on continued grant funding. The contract was objectively capable of performance. The defense of impossibility was rejected by the court.[21]

(A) Destruction of Particular Subject Matter. When parties contract expressly for, or with reference to, a particular subject matter, the contract is discharged if the subject matter is destroyed through no fault of either party. When a contract calls for the sale of a wheat crop growing on a specific parcel of land, the contract is discharged if that crop is destroyed by blight.

On the other hand, if there is merely a contract to sell a given quantity of a specified grade of wheat, the seller is not discharged when the seller's crop is destroyed by blight. The seller had made an unqualified undertaking to deliver wheat of a specified grade. No restrictions or qualifications were imposed as to the source. If the seller does not deliver the goods called for by the contract, the contract is broken, and the seller is liable for damages.

(B) Change of Law. A contract is discharged when its performance is made illegal by a subsequent change in the law. Thus, a contract to construct a nonfireproof building at a particular place is discharged by the adoption of a zoning law prohibiting such a building within that area. Mere inconvenience or temporary delay caused by the new law, however, does not excuse performance.

(C) Death or Disability. When the contract obligates a party to render or receive personal services requiring peculiar skill, the death, incapacity, or illness of the party that was either to render or receive the personal services excuses both sides from a duty to perform. It is sometimes said that "the death of either party is the death of the contract."

The rule does not apply, however, when the acts called for by the contract are of such a character that (1) the acts may be as well performed by others, such as the promisor's personal representatives, or (2) the contract's terms contemplate continuance of the obligations after the death of one of the parties. **For Example,** Lynn Jones was under contract to investor Ed Jenkins to operate certain Subway

[19] *Island Development Corp. v. District of Columbia,* 933 A.2d 340, 350 (D.C. 2007).
[20] *Bergmann v. Parker,* 216 A.2d 581 (D.C. 1966).
[21] *East Capital View Community Development Corp. v. Robinson,* 941 A.2d 1036 (D.C. 2008).

sandwich shops and to acquire new franchises with funding provided by Jenkins. After Jenkins's death, Jones claimed he was no longer bound under the contract and was free to pursue franchise opportunities on his own. The contract between Jones and Jenkins expressed that it was binding on the parties' "heirs and assigns" and that the contract embodied property rights that passed to Jenkins's widow. The agreement's provisions thus established that the agreement survived the death of Jenkins, and Jones was therefore obligated to remit profits from the franchise he acquired for himself after Jenkins's death.[22]

(D) ACT OF OTHER PARTY. Every contract contains "an implied covenant of good faith and fair dealing." As a result of this covenant, a promisee is under an obligation to do nothing that would interfere with the promisor's performance. When the promisee prevents performance or otherwise makes performance impossible, the promisor is discharged from the contract. Thus, a subcontractor is discharged from any obligation when it is unable to do the work because the principal contractor refuses to deliver the material, equipment, or money required by the subcontract. When the default of the other party consists of failing to supply goods or services, the duty may rest on the party claiming a discharge of the contract to show that substitute goods or services could not be obtained elsewhere.

9. Developing Doctrines

Commercial impracticability and frustration of purpose may excuse performance.

(A) COMMERCIAL IMPRACTICABILITY. The doctrine of *commercial impracticability* was developed to deal with the harsh rule that a party must perform its contracts unless it is absolutely impossible. However, not every type of impracticability is an excuse for nonperformance. **For Example,** I. Patel was bound by his franchise agreement with Days Inn, Inc., to maintain his 60-room inn on old Route 66 in Lincoln, Illinois, to at least minimum quality assurance standards. His inn failed five consecutive quality inspections over two years, with the inspector noting damaged guest rooms, burns in the bedding, and severely stained carpets. Patel's defense when his franchise was canceled after the fifth failed inspection was that bridge repairs on the road leading from I-55 to his inn had adversely affected his business and made it commercially impractical to live up to the franchise agreement. The court rejected his defense, determining that while the bridge work might have affected patronage, it had no effect on his duty to comply with the quality assurance standards of his franchise agreement.[23] Commercial impracticability is available only when the performance is made impractical by the subsequent occurrence of an event whose nonoccurrence was a basic assumption on which the contract was made.[24]

The defense of commercial impractability will not relieve sophisticated business entities from their contractual obligations due to an economic downturn, even one as drastic and severe as the recent recession. **For Example,** real estate developer Beemer Associates was not excused under this doctrine of commercial impracticability from performance of its construction loan payment obligation of $5,250,000 plus interest and fees where unanticipated changes in the financial and real estate markets made it unable to secure tenants at the expected rate.[25] Economic downturns and other market shifts do not constitute unanticipated circumstances in a market economy.[26]

(B) FRUSTRATION OF PURPOSE DOCTRINE. Because of a change in circumstances, the purpose of the contract may have no value to the party entitled to receive performance. In such a case, performance may be excused if both parties were aware of the purpose and the event that frustrated the purpose was unforeseeable.[27]

For Example, National Southern Bank rents a home near Willowbend Country Club on the southeastern shore of North Carolina for $75,000 a week

[22] *Jenkins Subway, Inc. v. Jones,* 990 S.W.2d 713 (Tenn. App. 1998).
[23] *Days Inn of America, Inc. v. Patel,* 88 F. Supp. 2d 928 (C.D. Ill. 2000).
[24] See Restatement (Second) of Contracts §261; U.C.C. §2-615.
[25] *LSREF2 Baron, LLC v. Beemer,* 2011 WL 6838163 (M.D. Fla. Dec. 29, 2011).
[26] *Flathead-Michigan I, LLC v. Peninsula Dev., LLC,* 2011 WL 940048 (E.D. Mich. March 16, 2011).
[27] The defense of frustration of purpose, or commercial frustration, is very difficult to invoke because the courts are extremely reluctant to allow parties to avoid obligations to which they have agreed. See *Wal-Mart Stores, Inc. v. AIG Life Insurance Co.,* 872 A.2d 611 (Del. Ch. 2005), denying application of the commercial frustration doctrine when the supervening event, the invalidation of hundreds of millions in tax deductions by the IRS, was reasonably foreseeable and could have been provided for in the contract.

to entertain business guests at the Ryder Cup matches scheduled for the week in question. Storm damage from Hurricane David the week before the event caused the closing of the course and the transfer of the tournament to another venue in a different state. The bank's duty to pay for the house may be excused by the doctrine of *frustration of purpose,* because the transfer of the tournament fully destroyed the value of the home rental, both parties were aware of the purpose of the rental, and the cancellation of the golf tournament was unforeseeable.

(c) Comparison to Common Law Rule. The traditional common law rule refuses to recognize commercial impracticability or frustration of purpose. By the common law rule, the losses and disappointments against which commercial impracticability and frustration of purpose give protection are merely the risks that one takes in entering into a contract. Moreover, the situations could have been guarded against by including an appropriate condition subsequent in the contract. A condition subsequent declares that the contract will be void if a specified event occurs.[28] The contract also could have provided for a readjustment of compensation if there was a basic change of circumstances. The common law approach also rejects these developing concepts because they weaken the stability of a contract.

An indication of a wider recognition of the concept that "extreme" changes of circumstances can discharge a contract is found in the Uniform Commercial Code. The UCC provides for the discharge of a contract for the sale of goods when a condition that the parties assumed existed, or would continue, ceases to exist.[29]

(d) Force Majeure. To avoid litigation over impossibility and impractability issues, modern contracting parties often contract around the doctrine of impossibility, specifying the failures that will excuse performance in their contracts. The clauses in which they do this are called *force majeure*—uncontrollable event—clauses. And they are enforced by courts as written.

And as seen in the *Union Pacific Railroad* case, they are enforced by courts as written.

Wisconsin Electric Power Co. v. Union Pacific Railroad Co., 557 Fd.3d 504 (7th Cir. 2009)

WEPCO Was Not Railroaded, It Was *Force Majeured*!

WEPCO, an electric utility, sued the Union Pacific Railroad Co. alleging that the railroad breached the *force majeure* provision of the parties' long-term coal-hauling contract, which ran from 1999 to 2005. The provision at issue provides that if the railroad is prevented by "an event of Force Majeure" from reloading its empty cars (after it has delivered coal to WEPCO) with iron ore destined for Geneva, Utah, it can charge the higher rate that the contract makes applicable to shipments that do not involve backhauling. The rate for coal shipped from one of the Colorado coal mines to WEPCO was specified as $13.20 per ton if there was a backhaul shipment but $15.63 if there was not. The iron ore that the railroad's freight trains would have picked up in Minnesota was intended for a steel mill in Utah. The steel company was bankrupt when the parties signed the contract. In November 2001 the steel mill shut down, and closed for good in February 2004. Two months later the railroad wrote WEPCO to declare "an event of Force Majeure" and that henceforth it would be charging WEPCO the higher rate applicable to shipments without a backhaul. WEPCO sued the railroad for breach of the force majeure provision in the contract.

JUDICIAL OPINION

POSNER, C. J.... The doctrine of impossibility in the common law of contracts excuses performance when it would be unreasonably costly (and sometimes downright impossible) for a party to carry out its contractual obligations. If the doctrine is successfully invoked, the contract is rescinded without liability....

...Parties can, however, contract around the doctrine, because it is just a gap filler, 2 E. Allan Farnsworth, *Farnsworth on Contracts* § 9.6, p. 643 (3d ed.2004)—a guess at what the parties would have provided in their contract had they thought about the contingency that has arisen and has prevented performance or made it much more costly.

..."In the case of a binding promise that it shall rain tomorrow, the immediate legal effect of what the promisor

[28] *Wermer v. ABI,* 10 S.W.3d 575 (Mo. App. 2000).
[29] U.C.C. §2-615.

Continued

does is, that he takes the risk of the event, within certain defined limits, as between himself and the promisee. He does no more when he promises to deliver a bale of cotton." O.W. Holmes, Jr., *The Common Law* 299–300 (1881). To defeat the application of the doctrine of impossibility the contract must state that the promisor must pay damages even if he commits a breach that could not have been prevented at a reasonable cost.

Modern contracting parties often do contract around the doctrine, though not by making the promisor liable for any and every failure to perform—rather by specifying the failures that will excuse performance. The clauses in which they do this are called force majeure ("superior force") clauses. The name suggests a purpose similar to that of the impossibility doctrine. But it is essential to an understanding of this case that a force majeure clause must always be interpreted in accordance with its language and context, like any other provision in a written contract, rather than with reference to its name....

The provision at issue in this case does not specify circumstances that would make performance impossible or infeasible in any sense, and does not excuse the performing party (the railroad) from performing the contract. The prevision is part of Article XI of the contract, and some of the other provisions in the article do specify contingencies that would excuse performance, including certain "acts of God." But the provision at issue merely provides that if the railroad is prevented by "an event of Force Majeure" from reloading its empty cars (after it has delivered coal to WEPCO) with iron ore destined for Geneva, Utah, it can charge the higher rate that the contract makes applicable to shipments that do not involve backhauling.

... A couple of months after the final closing the railroad wrote WEPCO to declare "an event of Force Majeure" and that henceforth it would be charging WEPCO the higher rate applicable to shipments without a backhaul. It did not attempt to make the rate change retroactive. Had it invoked the force majeure clause when the steel mill first shut down, WEPCO would have incurred an extra $7 million in shipping charges between then and the belated declaration of force majeure.

Despite this windfall, WEPCO argues that the railroad broke the contract by invoking the force majeure clause when it did. The fact that the railroad didn't invoke the clause earlier shows that the shutting down of the steel mill did not prevent the railroad from charging the low, backhaul rate. Well of course not; it is never "impossible" to offer a discount. But what the contract says is that the railroad may charge the higher rate if it is prevented from reloading its cars, rather than if it is prevented from charging a lower rate....

[Summary judgement for the railroad affirmed]

QUESTIONS

1. What is the purpose of a *force majeure* clause?
2. Did the court enforce the *force majeure* clause as written?

10. Temporary Impossibility

Ordinarily, a temporary impossibility suspends the duty to perform. If the obligation to perform is suspended, it is revived on the termination of the impossibility. If, however, performance at that later date would impose a substantially greater burden on the party obligated to perform, some courts discharge the obligor from the contract.

After the September 11, 2001, terrorist attack on the World Trade Center, New York City courts followed wartime precedents that had developed the law of temporary impossibility. Such impossibility, when of brief duration, excuses performance until it subsequently becomes possible to perform rather than excusing performance altogether. Thus, an individual who was unable to communicate her cancellation of travel 60 days prior to her scheduled travel as required by her contract, which needed to occur on or before September 14, 2001, could expect relief from a cancellation penalty provision in the contract based on credible testimony of attempted phone calls to the travel agent on and after September 12, 2001, even though the calls did not get through due to communication problems in New York City.[30]

(A) WEATHER. Acts of God, such as tornadoes, lightning, and floods, usually do not terminate a contract even though they make performance difficult. Thus, weather conditions constitute a risk that is assumed by a contracting party in the absence of a contrary agreement. Consequently, extra expense sustained by a contractor because of weather conditions is a risk that the contractor assumes in the absence of an express provision for additional compensation in such a case. **For Example,** Danielo Contractors made a

[30] See *Bugh v. Protravel International, Inc.,* 746 N.Y.S.2d 290 (Civ. Ct. N.Y.C. 2002).

contract to construct a shopping mall for the Rubicon Center, with construction to begin November 1. Because of abnormal cold and blizzard conditions, Danielo was not able to begin work until April 1 and was five months late in completing the construction of the project. Rubicon sued Danielo for breach of contract by failing to perform on schedule. Danielo is liable. Because the contract included no provision covering delay caused by weather, Danielo bore the risk of the delay and resulting loss.

Modern contracts commonly contain a "weather clause" and reflect the parties' agreement on this matter. When the parties take the time to discuss weather issues, purchasing insurance coverage is a common resolution.

11. Discharge by Operation of Law

A contract is discharged by **operation of law** by (1) an alteration or a material change made by a party, (2) the destruction of the written contract with intent to discharge it, (3) bankruptcy, (4) the operation of a statute of limitations, or (5) a contractual limitation.

(A) BANKRUPTCY. As set forth in the chapter on bankruptcy, even though all creditors have not been paid in full, a discharge in **bankruptcy** eliminates ordinary contract claims against the debtor.

CPA **(B) STATUTE OF LIMITATIONS.** A **statute of limitations** provides that after a certain number of years have passed, a contract claim is barred. The time limitation provided by state statutes of limitations varies widely. The time period for bringing actions for breach of an oral contract is two to three years. The period may differ with the type of contract—ranging from a relatively short time for open accounts (ordinary customers' charge accounts) to four years for sales of goods.[31] A somewhat longer period exists for bringing actions for breach of written contracts (usually four to ten years). **For Example,** Prate Installations, Inc., sued homeowners Richard and Rebecca Thomas for failure to pay for a new roof installed by Prate. Prate had sent numerous invoices to the Thomases over a four-year period seeking payment to no avail. The Thomases moved to dismiss the case under a four-year limitation period. However, the court concluded that the state's ten-year limitations period on written contracts applied.[32] The maximum period for judgments of record is usually 10 to 20 years.

A breach of contract claim against a builder begins to run when a home's construction is substantially complete. **For Example,** a breach of contract claim against home builder Stewart Brockett was time barred under a state's six-year statute of limitations for breach of contract actions inasmuch as the home in question was substantially completed in September 2001 and the breach of contract action commenced on June 17, 2008.[33]

(C) CONTRACTUAL LIMITATIONS. Some contracts, particularly insurance contracts, contain a time limitation within which suit must be brought. This is in effect a private statute of limitations created by the agreement of the parties.

A contract may also require that notice of any claim be given within a specified time. A party who fails to give notice within the time specified by the contract is barred from suing on the contract.

A contract provision requiring that suit be brought within one year does not violate public policy, although the statute of limitations would allow two years in the absence of such a contract limitation.[34]

LawFlix

Uncle Buck (1989) (PG-13)

John Candy plays ne'er-do-well Uncle Buck who promises to go to work at his girlfriend's tire store and marry her. When his brother calls in the middle of the night seeking help with his children, Buck tells his girlfriend (Chenise) that he can no longer honor his promise because he must go to the suburbs to care for his brother's children while his brother and sister-in-law travel to Indiana to be with his sister-in-law's very ill father.

Discuss Buck's excuse. Is it impossibility? Does the change in circumstances excuse Buck?

31 U.C.C. §2-725(1).
32 *Prate Installations, Inc. v. Thomas*, 842 N.E.2d 1205 (Ill. App. 2006).
33 *New York Central Mutual Fire Insurance Co. v. Gilder Oil Co.*, 936 N.Y.S. 2d 815 (Sup.Ct. A.D. 2011).
34 *Keiting v. Skauge*, 543 N.W.2d 565 (Wis. App. 1995).

MAKE THE CONNECTION

SUMMARY

A party's duty to perform under a contract can be affected by a condition precedent, which must occur before a party has an obligation to perform; a condition subsequent, that is, a condition or event that relieves the duty to thereafter perform; and concurrent conditions, which require mutual and often simultaneous performance.

Most contracts are discharged by performance. An offer to perform is called a *tender of performance*. If a tender of performance is wrongfully refused, the duty of the tenderer to perform is terminated. When the performance called for by the contract is the payment of money, it must be legal tender that is offered. In actual practice, it is common to pay and to accept payment by checks or other commercial paper.

When the debtor owes the creditor on several accounts and makes a payment, the debtor may specify which account is to be credited with the payment. If the debtor fails to specify, the creditor may choose which account to credit.

When a contract does not state when it is to be performed, it must be performed within a reasonable time. If time for performance is stated in the contract, the contract must be performed at the time specified if such time is essential (is of the essence). Ordinarily, a contract must be performed exactly in the manner specified by the contract. A less-than-perfect performance is allowed if it is a substantial performance and if damages are allowed the other party.

A contract cannot be discharged by unilateral action unless authorized by the contract itself or by statute, as in the case of consumer protection rescission.

Because a contract arises from an agreement, it may also be terminated by an agreement. A contract may also be discharged by the substitution of a new contract for the original contract; by a novation, or making a new contract with a new party; by accord and satisfaction; by release; or by waiver.

A contract is discharged when it is impossible to perform. Impossibility may result from the destruction of the subject matter of the contract, the adoption of a new law that prohibits performance, the death or disability of a party whose personal action was required for performance of the contract, or the act of the other party to the contract. Some courts will also hold that a contract is discharged when its performance is commercially impracticable or there is frustration of purpose. Temporary impossibility, such as a labor strike or bad weather, has no effect on a contract. It is common, though, to include protective clauses that excuse delay caused by temporary impossibility.

A contract may be discharged by operation of law. This occurs when (1) the liability arising from the contract is discharged by bankruptcy, (2) suit on the contract is barred by the applicable statute of limitations, or (3) a time limitation stated in the contract is exceeded.

LEARNING OUTCOMES

After studying this chapter, you should be able to clearly explain:

A. Conditions Relating to Performance

LO.1 List the three types of conditions that affect a party's duty to perform

See the "pay-if-paid" condition-precedent example on p. 351.

See the TV anchor's "failed urinalysis test" condition-subsequent example on pp. 351–352.

B. Discharge by Performance

LO.2 Explain the on-time performance rule

See the "mailed payment" example on p. 353.

See the "time is of the essence" example on p. 353.

LO.3 Explain the adequacy of performance rules

See the application of the substantial performance rule to the nonconforming new home piping example, pp. 354–355.

See the effect of failure to substantially perform a contract in the *Superior Wall and Paver* case, p. 355.

C. Discharge by Action of Parties

LO.4 Explain four ways a contract can be discharged by agreement of the parties

See the text discussion on rescission, cancellation, substitution, and novation on p. 356.

D. Discharge by External Causes

LO.5 State the effect on a contract of the death or disability of one of the contracting parties

See the Subway Sandwich Shops example on pp. 358–359.

LO.6 Explain when impossibility or impracticability may discharge a contract

See the Ryder Cup frustration-of-purpose example on pp. 359–360.

KEY TERMS

accord and satisfaction
bankruptcy
condition
condition precedent
condition subsequent
operation of law
rescission
statute of limitations
substantial performance
substitution
tender
waiver

QUESTIONS AND CASE PROBLEMS

1. CIT entered into a sale/leaseback contract with Condere Tire Corporation for 11 tire presses at Condere's tire plant in Natchez, Mississippi. Condere ceased making payments on these presses owned by CIT, and Condere filed for Chapter 11 bankruptcy. CIT thereafter contracted to sell the presses to Specialty Tires Inc., for $250,000. When the contract was made, CIT, Condere, and Specialty Tire believed that CIT was the owner of the presses and was entitled to immediate possession. When CIT attempted to gain access to the presses to have them shipped, Condere changed its position and refused to allow the equipment to be removed from the plant. When the presses were not delivered, Specialty sued CIT for damages for nondelivery of the presses, and CIT asserted the defense of impracticability. Decide. [*Specialty Tires, Inc. v. CIT,* 82 F. Supp. 2d 434 (W.D. Pa.)]

2. Lymon Mitchell operated a Badcock Home Furnishings dealership, under which as dealer he was paid a commission on sales and Badcock retained title to merchandise on display. Mitchell sold his dealership to another and to facilitate the sale, Badcock prepared a summary of commissions owed with certain itemized offsets it claimed that Mitchell owed Badcock. Mitchell disagreed with the calculations, but he accepted them and signed the transfer documents closing the sale on the basis of the terms set forth in the summary and was paid accordingly. After pondering the offsets taken by Badcock and verifying the correctness of his position, he brought suit for the additional funds owed. What defense would you expect Badcock to raise? How would you decide the case? Explain fully. [*Mitchell v. Badcock Corp.,* 496 S.E.2d 502 (Ga. App.)]

3. American Bank loaned Koplik $50,000 to buy equipment for a restaurant about to be opened by Casual Citchen Corp. The loan was not repaid, and Fast Foods, Inc., bought out the interest of Casual Citchen. As part of the transaction, Fast

Foods agreed to pay the debt owed to American Bank, and the parties agreed to a new schedule of payments to be made by Fast Foods. Fast Foods did not make the payments, and American Bank sued Koplik. He contended that his obligation to repay $50,000 had been discharged by the execution of the agreement providing for the payment of the debt by Fast Foods. Was this defense valid? [*American Bank & Trust Co. v. Koplik,* 451 N.Y.S.2d 426 (A. D.)]

4. Metalcrafters made a contract to design a new earth-moving vehicle for Lamar Highway Construction Co. Metalcrafters was depending on the genius of Samet, the head of its research department, to design a new product. Shortly after the contract was made between Metalcrafters and Lamar, Samet was killed in an automobile accident. Metalcrafters was not able to design the product without Samet. Lamar sued Metalcrafters for damages for breach of the contract. Metalcrafters claimed that the contract was discharged by Samet's death. Is it correct?

5. The Tinchers signed a contract to sell land to Creasy. The contract specified that the sales transaction was to be completed in 90 days. At the end of the 90 days, Creasy requested an extension of time. The Tinchers refused to grant an extension and stated that the contract was terminated. Creasy claimed that the 90-day clause was not binding because the contract did not state that time was of the essence. Was the contract terminated? [*Creasy v. Tincher,* 173 S.E.2d 332 (W. Va.)]

6. Christopher Bloom received a medical school scholarship created by the U.S. Department of Health and Human Services to increase the number of doctors serving rural areas. In return for this assistance, Bloom agreed to practice four years in a region identified as being underserved by medical professionals. After some problem with his postgraduation assignment, Bloom requested a repayment schedule from the agency. Although no terms were offered, Bloom tendered to the agency two checks totaling $15,500 and marked "Final Payment." Neither check was cashed, and the government sued Bloom for $480,000, the value of the assistance provided. Bloom claimed that by tendering the checks to the agency, his liability had been discharged by an accord and satisfaction. Decide. [*United States v. Bloom,* 112 F.3d 200 (7th Cir.)]

7. Dickson contracted to build a house for Moran. When it was approximately 25 percent to 40 percent completed, Moran would not let Dickson work any more because he was not following the building plans and specifications and there were many defects. Moran hired another contractor to correct the defects and finish the building. Dickson sued Moran for breach of contract, claiming that he had substantially performed the contract up to the point where he had been discharged. Was Dickson correct? [*Dickson v. Moran,* 344 So.2d 102 (La. App.)]

8. A lessor leased a trailer park to a tenant. At the time, sewage was disposed of by a septic tank system that was not connected with the public sewage system. The tenant knew this, and the lease declared that the tenant had examined the premises and that the landlord made no representation or guarantee as to the condition of the premises. Some time thereafter, the septic tank system stopped working properly, and the county health department notified the tenant that he was required to connect the septic tank system with the public sewage system or else the department would close the trailer park. The tenant did not want to pay the additional cost involved in connecting with the public system. The tenant claimed that he was released from the lease and was entitled to a refund of the deposit that he had made. Was he correct? [*Glen R. Sewell Street Metal v. Loverde,* 451 P.2d 721 (Cal. App.)]

9. Oneal was a teacher employed by the Colton Consolidated School District. Because of a diabetic condition, his eyesight deteriorated so much that he offered to resign if he would be given pay for a specified number of "sick leave" days. The school district refused to do this and discharged Oneal for nonperformance of his contract. He appealed to remove the discharge from his record. Decide. What ethical values are involved? [*Oneal v. Colton Consolidated School District,* 557 P.2d 11 (Wash. App.)]

10. Northwest Construction, Inc., made a contract with the state of Washington for highway construction. Part of the work was turned over under a subcontract to Yakima Asphalt Paving Co. The contract required that any claim be asserted within 180 days. Yakima brought an action for damages after the expiration of 180 days. The defense was that the claim was too late. Yakima replied that the action was brought within the time allowed by the statute of limitations and that the contractual limitation of 180 days was therefore not binding. Was Yakima correct?

11. The Metropolitan Park District of Tacoma gave Griffith a concession to run the district's parks. The agreement gave the right to occupy the parks and use any improvements found therein. The district later wished to set this agreement aside because it was not making sufficient money from the transaction. While it was seeking to set the agreement aside, a boathouse and a gift shop in one of the parks were destroyed by fire. The district then claimed that the concession contract with Griffith was discharged by impossibility of performance. Was it correct? [*Metropolitan Park District of Tacoma v. Griffith,* 723 P.2d 1093 (Wash.)]

12. Suburban Power Piping Corp., under contract to construct a building for LTV Steel Corp., made a subcontract with Power & Pollution Services, Inc., to do some of the work. The subcontract provided that the subcontractor would be paid when the owner (LTV) paid the contractor. LTV went into bankruptcy before making the full payment to the contractor, who then refused to pay the subcontractor on the ground that the "pay-when-paid" provision of the subcontract made payment by the owner a condition precedent to the obligation of the contractor to pay the subcontractor. Was the contractor correct? [*Power & Pollution Services, Inc. v. Suburban Power Piping Corp.,* 598 N.E.2d 69 (Ohio App.)]

13. Ellen borrowed money from Farmers' Bank. As evidence of the loan, she signed a promissory note by which she promised to pay to the bank in installments the amount of the loan together with interest and administrative costs. She was unable to make the payments on the scheduled dates. She and the bank then executed a new agreement that gave her a longer period of time for making the payments. However, after two months, she was unable to pay on this new schedule. The bank then brought suit against her under the terms of the original agreement. She raised the defense that the original agreement had been discharged by the execution of the second agreement and could not be sued on. Decide.

14. Beeson Company made a contract to construct a shopping center for Sartori. Before the work was fully completed, Sartori stopped making the payments to Beeson that the contract required. The contract provided for liquidated damages of $1,000 per day if Beeson failed to substantially complete the project within 300 days of the beginning of construction. The contract also provided for a bonus of $1,000 for each day Beeson completed the project ahead of schedule. Beeson stopped working and sued Sartori for the balance due under the contract, just as though it had been fully performed. Sartori defended on the ground that Beeson had not substantially completed the work. Beeson proved that Sartori had been able to rent most of the stores in the center. Was there substantial performance of the contract? If so, what would be the measure of damages? [*J.M. Beeson Co. v. Sartori,* 553 So.2d 180 (Fla. App.)]

15. New Beginnings provides rehabilitation services for alcohol and drug abuse to both adults and adolescents. New Beginnings entered into negotiation with Adbar for the lease of a building in the city of St. Louis, and subsequently entered into a three-year lease. The total rent due for the three-year term was $273,000. After the lease was executed, the city denied an occupancy permit because Alderman Bosley and residents testified at a hearing in vigorous opposition to the presence of New Beginnings in the neighborhood. A court ordered the permit issued. Alderman Bosley thereafter contacted the chair of the state's appointment committee and asked her to pull the agency's funding. He received no commitment from her on this matter. After a meeting with the state director of Alcohol and Drug Abuse where it

was asserted that the director said the funding would be pulled if New Beginnings moved into the Adbar location, New Beginnings's board decided not to occupy the building. Adbar brought suit for breach of the lease, and New Beginnings asserted it was excused from performance because of commercial impracticability and frustration of purpose. Do you believe the doctrine of commercial impracticability should be limited in its application so as to preserve the certainty of contracts? What rule of law applies to this case? Decide. [*Adbar v. New Beginnings,* 103 S.W.2d 799 (Mo. App.)]

CPA QUESTIONS

1. Parc hired Glaze to remodel and furnish an office suite. Glaze submitted plans that Parc approved. After completing all the necessary construction and painting, Glaze purchased minor accessories that Parc rejected because they did not conform to the plans. Parc refused to allow Glaze to complete the project and refused to pay Glaze any part of the contract price. Glaze sued for the value of the work performed. Which of the following statements is correct?
   a. Glaze will lose because Glaze breached the contract by not completing performance.
   b. Glaze will win because Glaze substantially performed and Parc prevented complete performance.
   c. Glaze will lose because Glaze materially breached the contract by buying the accessories.
   d. Glaze will win because Parc committed anticipatory breach.
2. Ordinarily, in an action for breach of a construction contract, the statute of limitations time period would be computed from the date the contract is:
   a. Negotiated.
   b. Breached.
   c. Begun.
   d. Signed.
3. Which of the following will release all original parties to a contract but will maintain a contractual relationship?

	Novation	*Substituted contract*
a.	Yes	Yes
b.	Yes	No
c.	No	Yes
d.	No	No

Breach of Contract and Remedies

learningoutcomes

After studying this chapter, you should be able to

LO.1 Explain what constitutes a breach of contract and an anticipatory breach of contract

LO.2 Describe the effect of a waiver of a breach

LO.3 Explain the range of remedies available for breach of contract

LO.4 Explain when liquidated damages clauses are valid and invalid

LO.5 State when liability-limiting clauses and releases are valid

What can be done when a contract is broken?

A. What Constitutes a Breach of Contract?

The question of remedies does not become important until it is first determined that a contract has been violated or breached.

1. Definition of Breach

A **breach** is the failure to act or perform in the manner called for by the contract. When the contract calls for performance, such as painting an owner's home, the failure to paint or to paint properly is a *breach of contract.* If the contract calls for a creditor's forbearance, the creditor's action in bringing a lawsuit is a breach of the contract.

2. Anticipatory Breach

When the contract calls for performance, a party may make it clear before the time for performance arrives that the contract will not be performed. This is referred to as an **anticipatory breach**.

(A) Anticipatory Repudiation. When a party expressly declares that performance will not be made when required, this declaration is called an **anticipatory repudiation** of the contract. To constitute such a repudiation, there must be a clear, absolute, unequivocal refusal to perform the contract according to its terms. **For Example,** Procter & Gamble (P&G) sought payment on four letters of credit issued by a Serbian bank, Investbanka. P&G presented two letters by June 8, prior to their expiration dates, with the necessary documentation for payment to Beogradska Bank New York, Investbanka's New York agent. A June 11 letter from Beogradska Bank broadly and unequivocally stated that the bank would not pay the letters of credit. Two additional letters of credit totaling $20,000 issued by Investbanka that expired by June 30 were not thereafter submitted to the New York agent bank by P&G. However, a court found that the bank had anticipatorily breached its obligations under those letters of credit by its broad renouncements in the June 11 letter, and judgments were rendered in favor of P&G.[1]

The *Tips* case deals with the issue of anticipatory repudiation and damages.

Tips v. Hartland Developers, Inc., 961 S.W.2d 618 (Tex. App. 1998)

Splitting Tips—Contract Price Less Cost of Completion

In 1985, Hartland Developers, Inc., agreed to build an airplane hangar for Robert Tips of San Antonio for $300,000, payable in three installments of $100,000, with the final payment due upon the completion of the building and the issuance of a certificate of completion by the engineer representing Tips. The evidence shows that Tips's representative Mr. Lavelle instructed Hartland to cease work on the building because Tips could no longer afford to make payments. Hartland ceased work as instructed before the completion of the building, having been paid $200,000 at that time. He sued Tips for breach of contract. On May 6, 1996, the trial court allowed Hartland the amount owing on the contract, $100,000, less the cost of completing the building according to the contract, $65,000, plus attorneys' fees and prejudgment and postjudgment interest. Tips appealed.

JUDICIALOPINION

HARDBERGER, C. J.…

Substantial Performance

Tips claims that the evidence is legally or factually insufficient to support the trial court's finding that Hartland had substantially performed under the agreement.…

We agree with Tips that Hartland had not substantially performed under the contract. However, we find this point

[1] *Procter & Gamble v. Investbanka,* 2000 WL 520630 (S.D.N.Y. 2000).

Continued

irrelevant to the resolution of this case. Substantial performance is a doctrine that allows *breaching* parties who have substantially completed their obligations to recover on a contract. WHITE & SUMMERS, CONTRACTS § 11–18(b) (3rd ed 1987). Hartland was not a breaching party. A contractor can recover on a contract when the failure to substantially perform is the fault of the other party. A party injured by the anticipatory breach of another may elect to sue for damages under the contract,...(if owner repudiates construction contract, contractor may sue in damages or for restitution); *Taylor Pub. Co. v Systems Marketing Inc.* 686 S.W.2d 213, 217 (when party obligated to make fixed payment absolutely repudiates the agreement, the obligee is entitled to recover [in an] action for damages and receive the present value of the payments payable under the agreement).

The trial judge based his damage assessment on anticipatory repudiation of contract. The evidence that Tips's representative, Lavelle, instructed Hartland to cease work on the project because Tips no longer could afford to make payments was sufficient to support this finding. *See Tennessee Gas Pipeline Co. v Lenape Resources Corp.,* 870 S.W.2d 286, 302 (Tex App.—San Antonio 1993) (anticipatory repudiation occurs when a party repudiates a contract before time for performance), *aff'd in part, rev'd in part,* 925 S.W.2d 565 (Tex. 1996)

OFFSET DAMAGES

Tips claims that the trial judge erred in not off-setting Hartland's award for its failure to provide electrical connections to the hangar. Tips also claims he should be compensated $11,000 for a temporary access ramp he was forced to construct in anticipation of a permanent ramp being installed. ...[W]e find that the $65,000 offset for the construction of a permanent ramp is sufficient compensation for that deficiency. However, we agree with Tips that the damages award must be offset by the cost of providing electrical outlets to the hangar.

Tips is entitled to an offset for electrical connections under a breach of contract theory. Damages for breach of contract are the contract price, less, the cost of completion. *Sage Street Assoc. v Northdale Const. Co.* 937 S.W.2d 425, 426 (Tex. 1996). The trial judge did not address in his findings of fact and conclusions of law whether the electrical connections were contemplated by the contract, but there was testimony at trial that they were, and electrical wiring is listed among Hartland's duties in the contract. A witness for Hartland admitted under cross examination that the work was part of the agreement and that it had not been completed. Tips testified that he had spent $23,000 to install connections. Hartland's damages should be further offset by this amount.

[Judgment affirmed as modified]

QUESTION

1. What facts did Hartland rely on to assert the anticipatory repudiation of the contract?
2. What is the measure of damages for a breach of a construction contract? Calculate what is owed Hartland excluding attorneys' fees and interest.
3. Why is prejudgment and postjudgment interest appropriate in a breach of contract lawsuit?

A refusal to perform a contract that is made before performance is required unless the other party to the contract does an act or makes a concession that is not required by the contract, is an anticipatory repudiation of the contract.[2]

A party making an anticipatory repudiation may retract or take back the repudiation if the other party has not changed position in reliance on the repudiation. However, if the other party has changed position, the party making the anticipatory repudiation cannot retract it. **For Example,** if a buyer makes another purchase when the seller declares that the seller will not perform the contract, the buyer has acted in reliance on the seller's repudiation. The seller will therefore not be allowed to retract the repudiation.

(B) ANTICIPATORY REPUDIATION BY CONDUCT. The anticipatory repudiation may be expressed by conduct that makes it impossible for the repudiating party to perform subsequently. **For Example,** while the Town of Mammoth Lakes, California, was claiming a willingness to move forward with a hotel/condominium project under its contract with the developer, in actuality, the evidence established that town officials refused to move forward and actively sought to

[2] *Chamberlain v. Puckett Construction,* 921 P.2d 1237 (Mont. 1996).

undermine the developer's rights under the development contract. The court affirmed a judgment of $30 million in damages and attorneys' fees.[3]

B. Waiver of Breach

The breach of a contract may have no importance because the other party to the contract waives the breach.

3. Cure of Breach by Waiver

The fact that one party has broken a contract does not necessarily mean that there will be a lawsuit or a forfeiture of the contract. For practical business reasons, one party may be willing to ignore or waive the breach. When it is established that there has been a **waiver** of a breach, the party waiving the breach cannot take any action on the theory that the contract was broken. The waiver, in effect, erases the past breach. The contract continues as though the breach had not existed.

The waiver may be express or it may be implied from the continued recognition of the existence of the contract by the aggrieved party.[4] When the conduct of a party shows an intent to give up a right, it waives that right.[5]

4. Existence and Scope of Waiver

It is a question of fact whether there has been a waiver.

(A) Existence of Waiver. A party may express or declare that the breach of a contract is waived. A waiver of a breach is more often the result of an express forgiving of a breach. Thus, a party allowing the other party to continue performance without objecting that the performance is not satisfactory waives the right to raise that objection when sued for payment by the performing party.

For Example, a contract promising to sell back a parcel of commercial property to Jackson required Jackson to make a $500 payment to Massey's attorney on the first of the month for five months, December through April. It was clearly understood that the payments would be "on time without fail." Jackson made the December payment on time. New Year's Day, a holiday, fell on a Friday, and Jackson made the second payment on January 4. He made $500 payments on February 1, March 1, and March 31, respectively, and the payments were accepted and a receipt issued on each occasion. However, Massey refused to convey title back to Jackson because "the January 4 payment was untimely and the parties' agreement had been breached." The court held that the doctrine of waiver applied due to Massey's acceptance of the late payment and the three subsequent payments without objection, and the court declared that Jackson was entitled to possession of the land.[6]

(B) Scope of Waiver. The waiver of a breach of contract extends only to the matter waived. It does not show any intent to ignore other provisions of the contract.

(C) Antimodification Clause. Modern contracts commonly specify that the terms of a contract shall not be deemed modified by waiver as to any breaches. This means that the original contract remains as agreed to. Either party may therefore return to, and insist on, compliance with the original contract.

In the example involving Jackson and Massey's contract, the trial court reviewed the contract to see whether the court was restricted by the contract from applying the waiver. It concluded: "In this case, the parties' contract did not contain any terms that could prevent the application of the doctrine of waiver to the acceptance of late payments."[7]

5. Reservation of Rights

It may be that a party is willing to accept a defective performance but does not wish to surrender any claim for damages for the breach. **For Example,** Midwest Utilities, Inc., accepted 20 carloads of Powder River Basin coal (sometimes called *Western coal*) from its

[3] *Mammoth Lakes Land Acquisition, LLC v. Town of Mammoth Lakes,* 120 Cal. Rptr. 3d 797 (Cal. Ct. of App. 3d Dist. 2010).
[4] *Huger v. Morrison,* 809 So.2d 1140 (La. App. 2002).
[5] *Stronghaven Inc. v. Ingram,* 555 S.E.2d 49 (Ga. App. 2001).
[6] *Massey v. Jackson,* 726 So.2d 656 (Ala. App. 1998).
[7] *Id.* at 659.

supplier, Maney Enterprises, because its power plants were in short supply of coal. Midwest's requirements contract with Maney called for Appalachian coal, a low-sulfur, highly efficient fuel, which is sold at a premium price per ton. Midwest, in accepting the tendered performance with a **reservation of rights**, gave notice to Maney that it reserved all rights to pursue damages for the tender of a nonconforming shipment.

C. Remedies for Breach of Contract

One or more **remedies** may be available to the innocent party in the case of a breach of contract. There is also the possibility that arbitration or a streamlined out-of-court alternative dispute resolution procedure is available or required for determining the rights of the parties.

6. Remedies Upon Anticipatory Repudiation

When an anticipatory repudiation of a contract occurs, the aggrieved person has several options. He may (1) do nothing beyond stating that performance at the proper time will be required, (2) regard the contract as having been definitively broken and bring a lawsuit against the repudiating party without waiting to see whether there will be proper performance when the performance date arrives, or (3) regard the repudiation as an offer to cancel the contract. This offer can be accepted or rejected. If accepted, there is a discharge of the original contract by the subsequent cancellation agreement of the parties.

FIGURE 20-1 *What Follows the Breach*

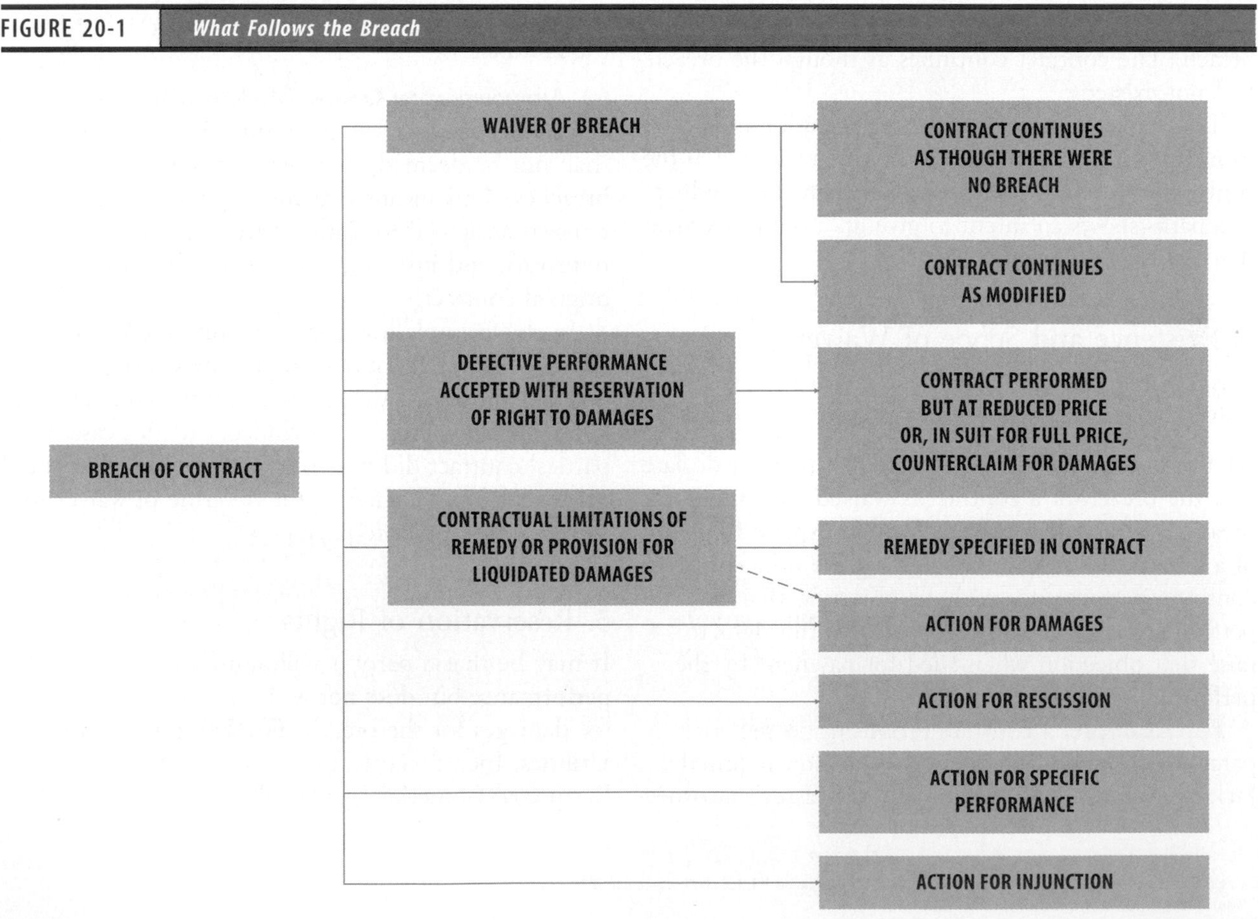

7. Remedies in General and the Measure of Damages

Courts provide a *quasi-contractual* or *restitution* remedy in which a contract is unenforceable because it lacked definite and certain terms or was not in compliance with the statute of frauds, yet one of the parties performed services for the other. The measure of damages in these and other quasi-contract cases is the reasonable value of the services performed, not an amount derived from the defective contract.

In cases when a person retains money or when a contemplated contract is not properly formed and no work is performed, the party retaining the benefit is obligated to make restitution to the person conferring the benefit. **For Example,** Kramer Associates, Inc. (KAI), a Washington D.C., consulting firm, accepted $75,000 from a Ghana-based corporation, Ikam, Ltd., to secure financing for a Ghana development project. No contract was ever executed, and KAI did virtually nothing to secure financing for the project. Restitution of the $75,000 was required.[8]

When there is a breach of contract, the regular remedy is an award of *monetary damages*. In unusual circumstances, when monetary damages are inadequate, the injured party may obtain **specific performance**, whereby the court will order that the contract terms be carried out.

The measure of monetary damages when there has been a breach of contract is the sum of money that will place the injured party in the same position that would have been attained if the contract had been performed.[9] That is, the injured party will be given the *benefit of the bargain* by the court.

8. Monetary Damages

Monetary damages are commonly classified as compensatory damages, nominal damages, and punitive damages. **Compensatory damages** compensate the injured party for the damages incurred as a result of the breach of contract. Compensatory damages have two branches, *direct damages* and *consequential* (or *special*) *damages*.

Injured parties that do not sustain an actual loss because of a breach of contract are entitled to a judgment of a small sum of money such as $1; these damages are called **nominal damages**.

Damages in excess of actual loss, imposed for the purpose of punishing or making an example of the defendant, are known as **punitive damages** or *exemplary damages*. In contract actions, punitive damages are not ordinarily awarded.[10]

(A) Direct and Consequential Damages. Direct damages (sometimes called *general damages*) are those that naturally flow from the given type of breach of contract involved and include *incidental damages*, which are extra expenditures made by the injured party to rectify the breach or mitigate damages. **Consequential damages** (sometimes called *special damages*) are those that do not necessarily flow from the type of breach of contract involved but happen to do so in a particular case as a result of the injured party's particular circumstances.[11]

Consequential damages may be recovered only if it was reasonably foreseeable to the defendant that the kind of loss in question could be sustained by the nonbreaching party if the contract were broken.

For Example, in early August, Spencer Adams ordered a four-wheel-drive GMC truck with a rear-end hydraulic lift for use on his Aroostook County, Maine, potato farm. The contract price was $58,500. He told Brad Jones, the owner of the dealership, that he had to have the truck by Labor Day so he could use it to bring in his crop from the fields before the first frost, and Brad nodded that he understood. The truck did not arrive by Labor Day as promised in the written contract. After a two-week period of gradually escalating recriminations with the dealership, Adams obtained the same model GMC truck at a dealership 40 minutes away in Houlton but at the cost of $60,500. He was also able to rent a similar truck from the Houlton dealer for $250 for the day while the new truck was being prepared. Farmhands had used other means of harvesting, but because of the lack of the truck, their work was set back by five

[8] *Kramer Associates, Inc. v. IKAM, Ltd.*, 888 A.2d 247 (D.C. 2005).

[9] *Leingang v. City of Mandan*, 468 N.W.2d 397 (N.D. 1991).

[10] A party who is not awarded actual damages but wins nominal damages can be considered a "prevailing party" for the purposes of a contractual attorney fee-shifting provision. *Brock v. King*, 629 S.E.2d 829 (Ga. App. 2006).

[11] See *Powell Electrical Systems, Inc. v. Hewlett Packard Co.*, 356 S.W.3d 113 (Tex. App. 2011).

days. As a result of the delays, 30 percent of the crop was still in the fields when the first frost came, causing damages expertly estimated at $320,000. The *direct damages* for the breach of contract in this case would be the difference between the contract price for the truck of $58,500 and the market price of $60,500, or $2,000. These direct damages naturally flow from the breach of contract for the purchase of a truck. Also, the *incidental damages* of $250 for the truck rental are recoverable direct damages. The $320,000 loss of the potato crop was a consequence of not having the truck, and this sum is arguably recoverable by Spencer Adams as *consequential or special damages*. Adams notified Brad Jones of the reason he needed to have the truck by Labor Day, and it should have been reasonably foreseeable to Jones that loss of a portion of the crop could occur if the truck contract was breached. However, because of Spencer Adams's obligation to mitigate damages (as discussed below), it is unlikely that Adams will recover the full consequential damages. Truck rental availability or the lack of availability within the rural area, alternative tractor usage, and the actual harvesting methods used by Adams all relate to the mitigation issue to be resolved by the jury.

(B) Mitigation of Damages. The injured party is under the duty to mitigate damages if reasonably possible.[12] In other words, damages must not be permitted to increase if an increase can be prevented by reasonable efforts. This means that the injured party must generally stop any performance under the contract to avoid running up a larger bill. The duty to mitigate damages may require an injured party to buy or rent elsewhere the goods that the wrongdoer was obligated to deliver under the contract. In the case of breach of an employment contract by the employer, the employee is required to seek other similar employment. The wages earned from other employment must be deducted from the damages claimed. The discharged employee, however, is not required to take employment of less-than-comparable work.

(1) Effect of Failure to Mitigate Damages. The effect of the requirement of mitigating damages is to limit recovery by the nonbreaching party to the damages that would have been sustained had this party mitigated the damages where it was possible to do so. **For Example,** self-described "sports nut" Gary Baker signed up for a three-year club-seat "package" that entitled him and a companion to tickets for 41 Boston Bruins hockey games and 41 Boston Celtics basketball games at the New Boston Garden Corporation's Fleet Center for approximately $18,000 per year. After one year, Baker stopped paying for the tickets, thinking that he would simply lose his $5,000 security deposit. Baker, a CPA, tried to work out a compromise settlement to no avail. New Boston sued Baker for breach of contract, seeking the balance due on the tickets of $34,866. At trial, Baker argued to the jury that although he had breached his contract, New Boston had an obligation to mitigate damages, for example, by treating his empty seats and those of others in the same situation as "rush seats" shortly before game time and selling them at a discount. New Boston argued that just as a used luxury car cannot be returned for a refund, a season ticket cannot be canceled without consequences. The jury accepted Baker's position on mitigation and reduced the amount owed New Boston by $21,176 to $13,690.[13]

9. Rescission

When one party commits a material breach of the contract, the other party may rescind the contract; if the party in default objects, the aggrieved party may bring an action for rescission. A breach is *material* when it is so substantial that it defeats the object of the parties in making the contract.[14]

An injured party who rescinds a contract after having performed services may recover the reasonable value of the performance rendered under restitutionary or quasi-contractual damages. Money paid by the injured party may also be recovered. **For Example,** the Sharabianlous signed a purchase agreement to buy a building owned by Berenstein Associates for $2 million. Thereafter the parties learned of

[12] *West Pinal Family Health Center, Inc. v. McBride*, 785 P.2d 66 (Ariz. 1989).
[13] Sacha Pfeiffer, "Disenchanted Fan Scores Win in Ticket Fight," *Boston Globe*, August 28, 1999, at B4.
[14] *Greentree Properties, Inc. v. Kissee*, 92 S.W.3d 289 (Mo. App. 2003).

environmental contamination on the property. Faced with uncertainty about the scope of the problem and the cost of the cleanup, the deal fell through and litigation ensued. The trial court rescinded the agreement based on mutual mistake of fact because neither party knew the full extent of the environmental hazard at the property. Damages available to parties upon mistake are more limited than those available in cases in which rescission is based on fault. The Sharabianlous were awarded $61,423.82 in expenses and an order returning their $115,000 deposit.[15]

The purpose of rescission is to restore the injured party to the position occupied before the contract was made. However, the party seeking restitutionary damages must also return what this party has received from the party in default.

For Example, Pedro Morena purchased real estate from Jason Alexander after Alexander had assured him that the property did not have a flooding problem. In fact, the property regularly flooded after ordinary rainstorms. Morena was entitled to the return of the purchase price and payment for the reasonable value of the improvements he made to the property. Alexander was entitled to a setoff for the reasonable rental value of the property during the time Morena was in possession of this property.

10. Action for Specific Performance

Under special circumstances, an injured party may obtain the equitable remedy of specific performance, which compels the other party to carry out the terms of a contract. Specific performance is ordinarily granted only if the subject matter of the contract is "unique," thereby making an award of money damages an inadequate remedy. Contracts for the purchase of land will be specifically enforced.[16]

Specific performance of a contract to sell personal property can be obtained only if the article is of unusual age, beauty, unique history, or other distinction. **For Example,** Maurice owned a rare Revolutionary War musket that he agreed to sell to Herb. Maurice then changed his mind because of the uniqueness of the musket. Herb can sue and win, requesting the remedy of specific performance of the contract because of the unique nature of the goods.

When the damages sustained by the plaintiff can be measured in monetary terms, specific performance will be refused. Consequently, a contract to sell a television station will not be specifically enforced when the buyer had made a contract to resell the station to a third person; the damages caused by the breach of the first contract would be the loss sustained by being unable to make the resale, and such damages would be adequate compensation to the original buyer.[17]

Ordinarily, contracts for the performance of personal services are not specifically ordered. This is because of the difficulty of supervision by the court and the restriction of the U.S. Constitution's Thirteenth Amendment prohibiting involuntary servitude except as criminal punishment.

11. Action for an Injunction

When a breach of contract consists of doing an act prohibited by the contract, a possible remedy is an **injunction** against doing the act. **For Example,** when the obligation in an employee's contract is to refrain from competing after resigning from the company and the obligation is broken by competing, a court may order or enjoin the former employee to stop competing. Similarly, when a vocalist breaks a contract to record exclusively for a particular label, she may be enjoined from recording for any other company. This may have the indirect effect of compelling the vocalist to record for the plaintiff.

12. Reformation of Contract by a Court

At times, a written contract does not correctly state the agreement already made by the parties. When this occurs, either party may seek to have the court reform or correct the writing to state the agreement actually made.

A party seeking reformation of a contract must clearly prove both the grounds for reformation and what the agreement actually was. This burden is particularly great when the contract to be reformed is written. This is so because the general rule is that parties are presumed to have read their written contracts and to have intended to be bound by them when they signed the contracts.

[15] *Sharabianlou v. Karp,* 105 Cal. Rptr. 3d 300 (Cal. App. 2010).
[16] *English v. Muller,* 514 S.E.2d 195 (Ga. 1999).
[17] *Miller v. LeSea Broadcasting, Inc.,* 87 F.3d 224 (7th Cir. 1996).

When a unilateral mistake is made and it is of such consequence that enforcing the contract according to its terms would be unreasonable, a court may reform the contract to correct the mistake.

D. Contract Provisions Affecting Remedies and Damages

The contract of the parties may contain provisions that affect the remedies available or the recovery of damages.

13. Limitation of Remedies

The contract of the parties may limit the remedies of the aggrieved parties. **For Example,** the contract may give one party the right to repair or replace a defective item sold or to refund the contract price. The contract may require both parties to submit any dispute to arbitration or another streamlined out-of-court dispute resolution procedure.

14. Liquidated Damages

The parties may stipulate in their contract that a certain amount should be paid in case of a breach. This amount is known as liquidated damages and may be variously measured by the parties. When delay is possible, **liquidated damages** may be a fixed sum, such as $1,000 for each day of delay. When there is a total default, damages may be a percentage of the contract price or the amount of the down payment.

(A) Validity. To be valid, a **liquidated damages clause** must satisfy two requirements: (1) The situation must be one in which it is difficult or impossible to determine the actual damages, and (2) the amount specified must not be excessive when compared with the probable damages that would be sustained.[18] The validity of a liquidated damages clause is determined on the basis of the facts existing when the clause was agreed to.

(B) Effect. When a liquidated damages clause is held valid, the injured party cannot collect more than the amount specified by the clause. The defaulting party is bound to pay such damages once the fact is established that there has been a default. The injured party is not required to make any proof as to damages sustained, and the defendant is not permitted to show that the damages were not as great as the liquidated sum.

(C) Invalid Clauses. If the liquidated damages clause calls for the payment of a sum that is clearly unreasonably large and unrelated to the possible actual damages that might be sustained, the clause will be held to be void as a penalty. **For Example,** a settlement agreement between 27 plaintiffs seeking recovery for injuries resulting from faulty breast implants and the implants' manufacturer, Dow Corning Corp., called for seven $200,000 payments to each plaintiff. The agreement also called for a $100 per day payment to each plaintiff for any time when the payments were late as "liquidated damages." The court held that the $100 per day figure was not a reasonable estimate of anticipated damages. Rather, it was an unenforceable "penalty" provision.[19]

When a liquidated damages clause is held invalid, the effect is merely to erase the clause from the contract, and the injured party may proceed to recover damages for breach of the contract. Instead of recovering the liquidated damages amount, the injured party will recover whatever actual damages he can prove. **For Example,** Richard Goldblatt and his wife Valerie breached a five-year restrictive covenant in a settlement agreement with the medical devices corporation that Goldblatt had cofounded, C.P. Motion, Inc. A liquidated damages provision in the settlement agreement that obligated Goldblatt and his wife to pay $250,000 per breach of the restrictive covenant was unenforceable as a penalty clause. The appeals court set aside a $4,969,339 judgment against the Goldblatts, determining that the parties could have agreed to arrive at actual damages by calculating a percentage of lost profits of specific lost clients or reclaiming any profits gained by the breaching parties. Because the liquidated damages clause was a penalty provision, C.P. Motion, Inc., may only recover the actual damages filed and proven at trial.[20]

[18] *Southeast Alaska Construction Co. v. Alaska*, 791 P.2d 339 (Alaska 1990).

[19] *Bear Stearns v. Dow Corning Corp.*, 419 F.3d 543 (6th Cir. 2005). See *RKR Motors Inc. v. Associated Uniform Rentals*, 995 So.2d 588 (Fla. App. 2008).

[20] *Goldblatt v. C. P. Motion, Inc.*, 77 So.3d 798 (Fla. App. 2011).

15. Attorneys' Fees

Attorneys' fees are a very significant factor in contract litigation. In Medistar Corporation's suit against Dr. David Schmidt, the jury awarded it $418,069 in damages under its promissory estoppel claim and in addition thereto the trial court judge allowed Medistar to recover $408,412 for its attorneys' fees. A state statute allows recovery of attorneys' fees for the prevailing party in a breach of partnership claim. On appeal the recovery of $408,412 in attorneys' fees was reversed since the jury awarded zero damages on Medistars' breach of partnership claim. The net result after payment of attorneys' fees—and not counting attorneys' fees for the appeal—was $9,657 for Medistar, after four years of "successful" litigation.[21]

The so-called "American rule" states that each party is responsible for its own attorneys' fees in the absence of an express contractual or statutory provision to the contrary.[22] Even in the event of a valid contractual provision for attorneys' fees, a trial court has the discretion to exercise its equitable control to allow only such sum as is reasonable, or the court may properly disallow attorneys' fees altogether on the basis that such recovery would be inequitable. **For Example,** although Evergreen Tree Care Services was awarded some monetary damages in its breach of contract suit against JHL, Inc., it was unsuccessful in its claim for attorneys' fees under a provision for attorneys' fees in the contract because the trial court exercised its equitable discretion, finding that both parties to the litigation came to court with "unclean hands," and that Evergreen failed to sufficiently itemize and exclude fees to discovery abuses.[23]

16. Limitation of Liability Clauses

A contract may contain a provision stating that one of the parties shall not be liable for damages in case of breach. Such a provision is called an **exculpatory clause**, or when a monetary limit to damages for breach of contract is set forth in the contract, it may be referred to as a **limitation-of-liability clause**.

(A) Content and Construction. If an exculpatory clause or a limitation-of-liability clause limits liability for damages caused only by negligent conduct, liability is neither excluded nor limited if the conduct alleged is found to be grossly negligent, willful, or wanton. **For Example,** Security Guards Inc. (SGI) provided services to Dana Corporation, a truck frame manufacturer under a contract that contained a limitation-of-liability clause capping losses at $50,000 per occurrence for damages "caused solely by the negligence" of SGI or its employees. When a critical alarm was activated by a fire in the paint shop at 5:39 p.m., the SGI guard on duty did not follow appropriate procedures, which delayed notification to the fire department for 15 minutes. Royal Indemnity Co., Dana's insurer, paid Dana $16,535,882 for the fire loss and sued SGI for $7 million, contending that the SGI guard's actions were grossly negligent and caused the plant to suffer increased damages. The court held that if SGI were to be found grossly negligent, the liability would not be limited to $50,000, and a jury could find damages far exceeding that amount.[24]

(B) Validity. As a general rule, experienced businesspersons are free to allocate liability in their contracts as they see fit. They have freedom to contract—even to make bad bargains or relinquish fundamental rights. However, courts in most states will not enforce a contract provision that *completely exonerates* a party from gross negligence or intentional acts.

(C) Releases. Release forms signed by participants in athletic and sporting events declaring that the sponsor, proprietor, or operator of the event shall not be liable for injuries sustained by participants because of its negligence are generally binding.[25] The *Cheley Colorado Camps* decision is such a case.

[21] *Medistar Corp. v. Schmidt*, 267 S.W.3d 150 (Tex. App. 2008).

[22] *Centimark v. Village Manor Associates, Ltd.*, 967 A.2d 550 (Conn. App. 2009).

[23] *Stafford v. JHL, Inc.*, 194 P.3d 315 (Wyo. 2008). See also *FNBC v. Jennessey Group, LLC*, 759 N.W.2d 808 (Iowa App. 2008).

[24] *Royal Indemnity Co. v. Security Guards, Inc.*, 255 F. Supp. 2d 497 (E.D. Pa. 2003).

[25] But see *Woodman v. Kera, LLC*, 760 N.W.2d 641 (Mich. App. 2008) where the Court of Appeals of Michigan held that a preinjury waiver signed by a parent on behalf of a five-year-old child was invalid.

Hamill v. Cheley Colorado Camps, Inc., 262 P.3d 945 (Colo. App. 2011)

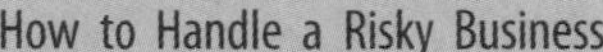

How to Handle a Risky Business

Chelsea Hamill attended Camp Cheley for three years. Before attending camp each summer her parents signed a liability/risk release form. In July 2004, when Hamill was 15 years old, she fell off a Cheley horse and broke her arm. Chelsea brought a negligence and gross negligence lawsuit against the summer camp. Hamill's mother testified at her deposition that she voluntarily signed the release after having "skimmed" it. The release language stated in part:

> *I, on behalf of myself and my child, hereby release and waive* any claim of liability against Cheley…*with respect to any injury…occurring to my child while he/she participates in any and all camp programs and activities.*
>
> *I give my permission for my child to participate in all camp activities, including those described above. I acknowledge and assume the risks involved in these activities, and for any damages, illness,* injury or death …*resulting from such risks for myself and my child.*
>
> *(Emphasis Added.)*

Hamill's mother's interpretation of the release is that prospective negligent claims were not waived. The camp disagreed. The trial court granted summary judgment in favor of the camp, and Hamill appealed.

JUDICIAL OPINION

LAKE, J. …

Parental Consent to Exculpatory Agreements Affecting Minors

Hamill argues that the exculpatory clauses in the agreement do not bar her negligence claims. She reasons … that her mother did not make an informed decision under … [state law] to release her prospective negligence claims. This statute states that "[s]o long as [a parent's] decision [to waive the child's claims] is voluntary and *informed,* the decision should be given the same dignity as decisions regarding schooling, medical treatment, and religious education."

We disagree with Hamill's position.

Degree of Risk

… [T]he undisputed facts in the record show that Hamill's mother knew the activities Cheley offered. Hamill had attended Cheley and ridden the camp horses for two years before the accident. The agreement clearly indicated that horseback riding was an activity available to campers. The agreement described many of the risks associated with horseback riding at camp, and notified Hamill's mother that it was impossible to list all risks.

…

The agreement included language that informed Hamill's mother that the equipment used by Cheley could fail and that the wranglers might "misjudge" situations. Both of these possibilities envision forms of negligence. As discussed above, the agreement itself directly contradicts Hamill's mother's objectively unreasonable interpretation of the contract that prospective negligence claims were not waived.

…

Hamill's mother testified at her deposition that she voluntarily signed the release after having "skimmed" it. She had signed the same agreement in 2002 and 2003 and agreed that, by signing the waiver, she understood that she was accepting certain risks of injury to her child. *See Rasmussen v. Freehling,* 159 Colo. 414, 417, 412 P.2d 217, 219 (1966) (if a person signs a contract without reading it, she is barred from claiming she is not bound by what it says); *Day,* 810 F. Supp. at 294 (a party signing a contract without reading it cannot deny knowledge of its contents, and is bound by what it says)….

That Hamill's mother may not have contemplated the precise mechanics of her daughter's fall does not invalidate the release and does not create a genuine issue of material fact. She knew her daughter would be riding horses and she was advised that there were risks, known and unknown, associated with the activity. Indeed, Hamill's mother acknowledged in her deposition testimony that when horseback riding, there is "a risk of a child being thrown or falling off a horse." Hamill's argument that her mother did not give informed consent, despite her signature on the agreement and the language in the agreement indicating the contrary, is not persuasive and does not create a genuine issue of material fact. As a matter of law, the agreement sufficiently informed Hamill's mother about the risks involved in horseback riding.

Extent of Injury

The broad release language in the agreement waiving "any claims of liability," for "any injury," even "death," evidences that Hamill's mother was informed that she was waiving Hamill's prospective claims, including negligence, and had sufficient information to assess the extent of possible injuries

Continued

to Hamill. At her deposition, Hamill's mother testified as follows:

Attorney: And, you know, you knew that someone such as Christopher Reeve had been tragically injured falling off a horse?

Ms. Hamill: Yes.

Attorney: Did you personally know Mr. Reeve?

Ms. Hamill: Yes.

Attorney: And so you were aware that there were significant risks associated with horseback riding?

Ms. Hamill: Yes.

Attorney: And you were aware that your daughter was going to be doing a significant amount of horseback riding?

Ms. Hamill: Yes.

The agreement did not need to include an exhaustive list of particularized injury scenarios to be effective.

Our review of the entire record leads us to conclude that there are no genuine issues of material fact. Hamill's mother had more than sufficient information to allow her to assess the extent of injury possible in horseback riding, and to make an "informed" decision before signing the release. *See Black's Law Dictionary* 346 (definition of informed consent).

We conclude that the agreement adequately disclosed the extent of potential injuries. Moreover, because the agreement was fairly entered into and the language clearly and unambiguously presents no genuine issue of material fact as to whether Hamill's mother was informed of the agreement's intent to release "all claims," including prospective negligence claims, the district court did not err in granting summary judgment for Cheley.

...

[The court concluded that the agreement was not contrary to public policy; nor was there any evidence of gross negligence on the part of the camp.]

[Judgment affirmed]

QUESTIONS

1. Does state law allow parents to make informed decisions to waive their children's prospective negligence claims in exculpatory agreements?
2. Was Hamill's mother sufficiently informed about the risks involved in horseback riding, including the extent of possible injury, so as to have made an informed decision when she signed the release? Should the camp have included a list of particularized injury scenarios to be effective?

LawFlix

The Goodbye Girl (1977) (PG)

Richard Dreyfuss plays Elliott Garfield, a struggling Shakespearean actor who lands in New York with a sublease on an apartment still occupied by divorcee Marsha Mason and her daughter. The two work out living arrangements, split rent and food, and deal with the issue of whether Mason has any rights. Review all aspects of contracts as the characters discuss subleases, rent payment, living arrangements, and food costs.

MAKE THE CONNECTION

SUMMARY

When a party fails to perform a contract or performs improperly, the other contracting party may sue for damages caused by the breach. What may be recovered by the aggrieved person is stated in terms of being direct or consequential damages. Direct damages are those that ordinarily will result from the breach. Direct damages may be recovered on proof of causation and amount. Consequential damages can be recovered only if, in addition to proving causation and amount, it is shown that they were reasonably within the contemplation of the contracting parties as a probable result of a breach of the contract. The right to recover consequential damages is lost if the aggrieved party could reasonably have taken steps to avoid such damages. In other words, the aggrieved person has a duty to mitigate or reduce damages by reasonable means.

In any case, the damages recoverable for breach of contract may be limited to a specific amount by a liquidated damages clause.

In a limited number of situations, an aggrieved party may bring an action for specific performance to compel the other contracting party to perform the acts called for by the contract. Specific performance by the seller is always obtainable for the breach of a contract to sell land or real estate on the theory that such property has a unique value. With respect to other contracts, specific performance will not be ordered unless it is shown that there was some unique element present so that the aggrieved person would suffer a damage that could not be compensated for by the payment of money damages.

The aggrieved person also has the option of rescinding the contract if (1) the breach has been made concerning a material term and (2) the aggrieved party returns everything to the way it was before the contract was made.

Although there has been a breach of the contract, the effect of this breach is nullified if the aggrieved person by word or conduct waives the right to object to the breach. Conversely, an aggrieved party may accept a defective performance without thereby waiving a claim for breach if the party makes a reservation of rights. A reservation of rights can be made by stating that the defective performance is accepted "without prejudice," "under protest," or "with reservation of rights."

LEARNING OUTCOMES

After studying this chapter, you should be able to clearly explain:

A. What Constitutes a Breach of Contract?

LO.1 Explain what constitutes a breach of contract and an anticipatory breach of contract

See the illustration of a painting contractor's failure to properly paint a house, p. 369.

See the *Mammoth Lakes* example involving anticipatory repudiation by conduct, p. 370.

B. Waiver of Breach

LO.2 Describe the effect of a waiver of a breach

See the application of the waiver doctrine as applied in the *Massey* example on p. 371.

C. Remedies for Breach of Contract

LO.3 Explain the range of remedies available for breach of contract

See Figure 20-1, "What Follows the Breach," on p. 372.

See the *Spencer Adams* example involving a range of monetary damages on pp. 373–374.

See the *Pedro Morena* example involving rescission of a contract on pp. 374–375.

See the rare Revolutionary War musket example of specific performance, p. 375.

D. Contract Provisions Affecting Remedies and Damages

LO.4 Explain when liquidated damages clauses are valid and invalid

See the Dow Corning faulty breast implants settlement agreement example in which liquidated damages of a $100 per day late payment were found to be unenforceable penalty provision, p. 376.

LO.5 State when liability-limiting clauses and releases are valid

See the *Cheley Camps* case that illustrates how the camp successfully raised a signed parental exculpatory release as a defense in a horseback riding injury case, pp. 378–379.

KEY TERMS

anticipatory breach
anticipatory repudiation
breach
compensatory damages
consequential damages
direct damages
exculpatory clause
injunction
limitation-of-liability clause
liquidated damages
liquidated damages clause
nominal damages
punitive damages
remedies
reservation of rights
specific performance
waiver

QUESTIONS AND CASE PROBLEMS

1. The Forsyth School District contracted with Textor Construction, Inc., to build certain additions and alter school facilities, including the grading of a future softball field. Under the contract, the work was to be completed by August 1. Various delays occurred at the outset of the project attributable to the school district, and the architect's representative on the job, Mr. Hamilton, told Textor's vice president, William Textor, not to be concerned about a clause in the contract of $250 per day liquidated damages for failure to complete the job by August 1. Textor sued the school district for breach of contract regarding payment for the grading of the softball field, and the District counterclaimed for liquidated damages for 84 days at $250 per day for failure to complete the project by the August 1 date. What legal basis exists for Textor to defend against the counter-claim for failure to complete the job on time? Was it ethical for the school district to bring this counterclaim based on the facts before you? [*Textor Construction, Inc. v. Forsyth R-III School District,* 60 S.W.3d 692 (Mo. App.)]

2. Anthony makes a contract to sell a rare painting to Laura for $100,000. The written contract specifies that if Anthony should fail to perform the contract, he will pay Laura $5,000 as liquidated damages. Anthony fails to deliver the painting and is sued by Laura for $5,000. Can she recover this amount?

3. Rogers made a contract with Salisbury Brick Corp. that allowed it to remove earth and sand from land he owned. The contract ran for four years with provision to renew it for additional four-year terms up to a total of 96 years. The contract provided for compensation to Rogers based on the amount of earth and sand removed. By an unintentional mistake, Salisbury underpaid Rogers the amount of $863 for the months of November and December 1986. Salisbury offered this amount to Rogers, but he refused to accept it and claimed that he had been underpaid in other months. Rogers claimed that he was entitled to rescind the contract. Was he correct? [*Rogers v. Salisbury Brick Corp.,* 882 S.E.2d 915 (S.C.)]

4. A contractor departed from the specifications at a number of points in a contract to build a house. The cost to put the house in the condition called for by the contract was approximately $14,000. The contractor was sued for $50,000 for breach of contract and emotional distress caused by the breach. Decide.

5. Protein Blenders, Inc., made a contract with Gingerich to buy from him the shares of stock of a small corporation. When the buyer refused to take and pay for the stock, Gingerich sued for specific performance of the contract on the ground that the value of the stock was unknown and could not be readily ascertained because it was not sold on the general market. Was he entitled to specific performance? [*Gingerich v. Protein Blenders, Inc.,* 95 N.W.2d 522 (Iowa)]

6. The buyer of real estate made a down payment. The contract stated that the buyer would be liable for damages in an amount equal to the down payment if the buyer broke the contract. The buyer refused to go through with the contract and demanded his down payment back. The seller refused to return it and claimed that he was

entitled to additional damages from the buyer because the damages that he had suffered were more than the amount of the down payment. Decide. [*Waters v. Key Colony East, Inc.,* 345 So.2d 367 (Fla. App.)]

7. Kuznicki made a contract for the installation of a fire detection system by Security Safety Corp. for \$498. The contract was made one night and canceled at 9:00 the next morning. Security then claimed one-third of the purchase price from Kuznicki by virtue of a provision in the contract that "in the event of cancellation of this agreement… the owner agrees to pay $33^{1/3}$ percent of the contract price, as liquidated damages." Was Security Safety entitled to recover the amount claimed? [*Security Safety Corp. v. Kuznicki,* 213 N.E.2d 866 (Mass.)]

8. FNBC is a business brokerage firm that assits in the purchase and sale of businesses. Jennings and Hennessey were independent contractors working for FNBC. They left FNBC, and FNBC sued them for breach of their contracts with FNBC. The trial court issued a permanent injuction prohibiting the former contractors from using proprietary information and the court awarded attorneys' fees under a clause in the contract that would obligate Jennings and Hennessey to indemnify FNBC against claims "brought by persons not a party to the provision." Jennings and Hennessey appealed the decision on attorneys' fees. Decide. [*FNBC v. Jennessey Group, LLC,* 759 N.W.2d 808 (Iowa App.)]

9. Melodee Lane Lingerie Co. was a tenant in a building that was protected against fire by a sprinkler and alarm system maintained by the American District Telegraph Co. (ADT). Because of the latter's fault, the controls on the system were defective and allowed the discharge of water into the building, which damaged Melodee's property. When Melodee sued ADT, its defense was that its service contract limited its liability to 10 percent of the annual service charge made to the customer. Was this limitation valid? [*Melodee Lane Lingerie Co. v. American District Telegraph Co.,* 218 N.E.2d 661 (N.Y.)]

10. JRC Trading Corp (JRC) bought computer software and hardware from Progressive Data Systems (PDS) for \$167,935, which it paid in full, to track movement of its trucks with inventory and to process transactions. The purchase agreement also called for a \$7,500 per year licensing fee for an 18-year period, and it stated that in the event of default PDS could "accelerate and declare all obligations of Customer as a liquidated sum." A dispute arose between the parties, and when the case was litigated the only actual contract charges owed PDS were the license fees of \$7,500 for two years. The application of the liquidated damages clause would yield an additional \$120,000 cash for PDS for the future fees for 16 years without any reduction for expenses or the present cash value for the not-yet-earned fees. JRC contends that actual damages were clearly ascertainable and that the liquidated damages clause was a penalty provision that should not be enforced. Progressive argued that the court must interpret the contract as written, stating that the court has no power to rewrite the contract. Decide. [*Jefferson Randolf Corp. v. PDS,* 553 S.E.2d 304 (Ga. App.)]

11. Ken Sulejmanagic, aged 19, signed up for a course in scuba diving taught by Madison at the YMCA. Before the instruction began, Ken was required to sign a form releasing Madison and the YMCA from liability for any harm that might occur. At the end of the course, Madison, Ken, and another student went into deep water. After Ken made the final dive required by the course program, Madison left him alone in the water while he took the other student for a dive. When Madison returned, Ken could not be found, and it was later determined that he had drowned. Ken's parents sued Madison and the YMCA for negligence in the performance of the teaching contract. The defendants raised the defense that the release Ken signed shielded them from liability. The plaintiffs claimed that the release was invalid. Who was correct? [*Madison v. Superior Court,* 250 Cal. Rptr. 299 (Cal. App.)]

12. Wassenaar worked for Panos under a three-year contract stating that if the contract were terminated wrongfully by Panos before the end of the three years, he would pay as damages the salary for the remaining time that the contract had to run. After three months, Panos terminated the

contract, and Wassenaar sued him for pay for the balance of the contract term. Panos claimed that this amount could not be recovered because the contract provision for the payment was a void penalty. Was this provision valid? [*Wassenaar v. Panos,* 331 N.W.2d 357 (Wis.)]

13. Soden, a contractor, made a contract to build a house for Clevert. The sales contract stated that "if either party defaults in the performance of this contract," that party would be liable to the other for attorneys' fees incurred in suing the defaulter. Soden was 61 days late in completing the contract, and some of the work was defective. In a suit by the buyer against the contractor, the contractor claimed that he was not liable for the buyer's attorneys' fees because he had made only a defective performance and because "default" in the phrase quoted meant "nonperformance of the contract." Was the contractor liable for the attorneys' fees? [*Clevert v. Soden,* 400 S.E.2d 181 (Va.)]

14. Protection Alarm Co. made a contract to provide burglar alarm security for Fretwell's home. The contract stated that the maximum liability of the alarm company was the actual loss sustained or $50, whichever was the lesser, and that this provision was agreed to "as liquidated damages and not as a penalty." When Fretwell's home was burglarized, he sued for the loss of approximately $12,000, claiming that the alarm company had been negligent. The alarm company asserted that its maximum liability was $50. Fretwell claimed that this was invalid because it bore no relationship to the loss that could have been foreseen when the contract was made or that in fact "had been sustained." Decide.

15. Shepherd-Will made a contract to sell Emma Cousar:

    5 acres of land adjoining property owned by the purchaser and this being formerly land of Shepherd-Will, Inc., located on north side of Highway 223. This 5 acres to be surveyed at earliest time possible at which time plat will be attached and serve as further description on property.

    Shepherd-Will owned only one 100-acre tract of land that adjoined Emma's property. This tract had a common boundary with her property of 1,140 feet. Shepherd-Will failed to perform this contract. Emma sued for specific performance of the contract. Decide. [*Cousar v. Shepherd-Will, Inc.,* 387 S.E.2d 723 (S.C. App.)]

CPA QUESTIONS

1. Master Mfg., Inc., contracted with Accur Computer Repair Corp. to maintain Master's computer system. Master's manufacturing process depends on its computer system operating properly at all times. A liquidated damages clause in the contract provided that Accur pay $1,000 to Master for each day that Accur was late responding to a service request. On January 12, Accur was notified that Master's computer system had failed. Accur did not respond to Master's service request until January 15. If Master sues Accur under the liquidated damages provision of the contract, Master will:
    a. Win, unless the liquidated damage provision is determined to be a penalty.
    b. Win, because under all circumstances liquidated damages provisions are enforceable.
    c. Lose, because Accur's breach was *not* material.
    d. Lose, because liquidated damage provisions violate public policy (5/93, Law, #25).

2. Jones, CPA, entered into a signed contract with Foster Corp. to perform accounting and review services. If Jones repudiates the contract prior to the date performance is due to begin, which of the following is *not* correct?
    a. Foster could successfully maintain an action for breach of contract after the date performance was due to begin.
    b. Foster can obtain a judgment ordering Jones to perform.
    c. Foster could successfully maintain an action for breach of contract prior to the date performance is due to begin.

d. Foster can obtain a judgment for the monetary damages it incurred as a result of the repudiation (5/89, Law, #35).

3. Which of the following concepts affect(s) the amount of monetary damages recoverable by the nonbreaching party when a contract is breached?

	Forseeability of damages	*Mitigation of damages*
a.	Yes	Yes
b.	Yes	No
c.	No	Yes
d.	No	No

PART 3

Sales and Leases of Goods

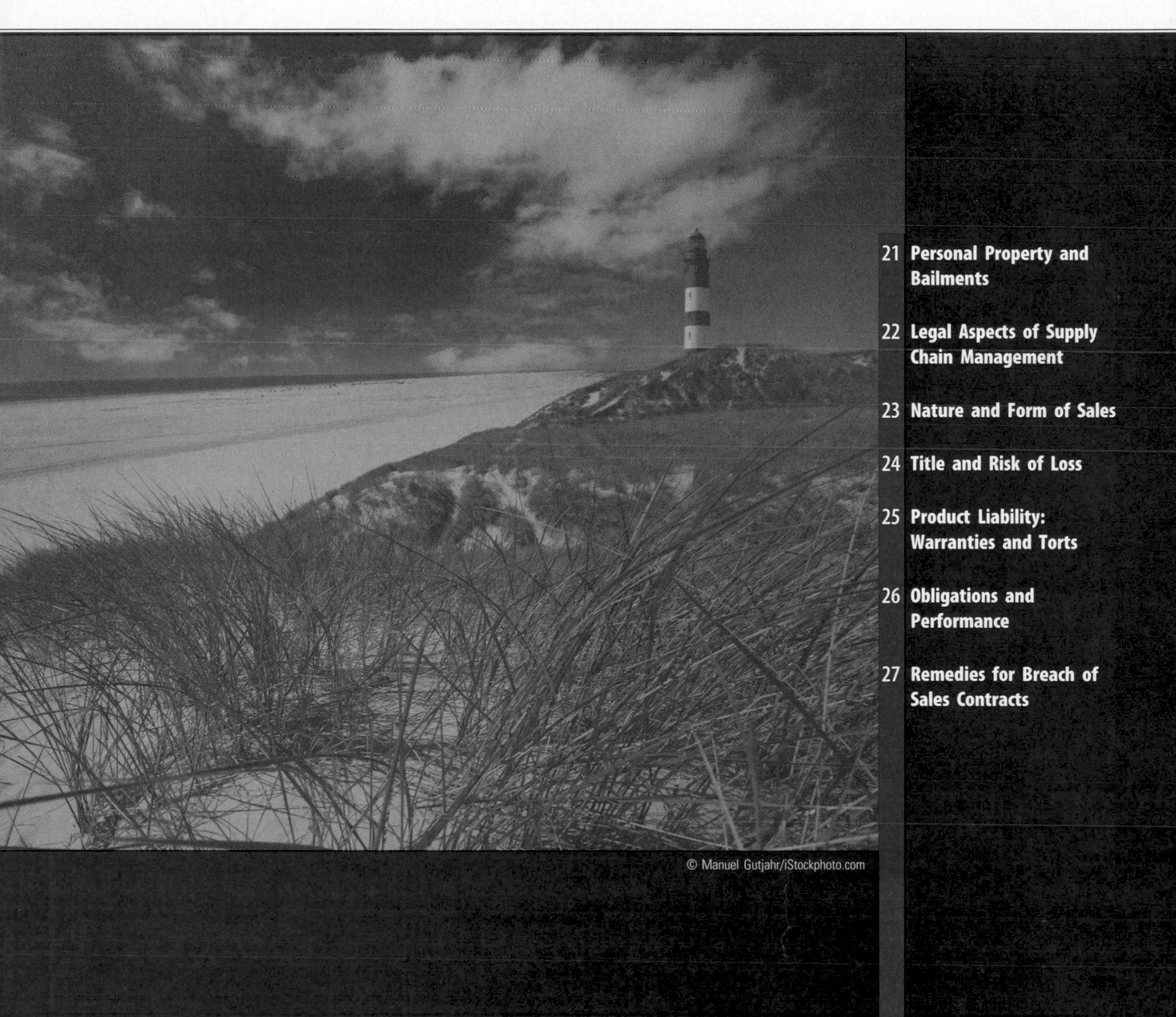

© Manuel Gutjahr/iStockphoto.com

Personal Property and Bailments

learningoutcomes

After studying this chapter, you should be able to

LO.1 Explain how title to personal property is acquired

LO.2 List and explain the various types of gifts

LO.3 Explain the legal theory whereby an owner can recover his or her property from the wrongful exclusionary retention of another

LO.4 Identify the elements necessary to create a bailment

LO.5 Explain the standard of care a bailee is required to exercise over bailed property

What is personal property? Who owns it? How is it acquired? Think of personal property as all things of value other than real estate. Many instances arise in which the owner of personal property entrusts it to another—a person checks a coat at a restaurant or leaves a watch with a jeweler for repairs; or a company rents a car to a tourist for a weekend. The delivery of personal property to another under such circumstances is a bailment.

A. Personal Property

1. Personal Property in Context

In common usage, the term *property* refers to a piece of land or a thing or an object. As a legal concept, however, property also refers to the rights that an individual may possess in the piece of land or that thing or that object.[1] Property includes the rights of any person to possess, use, enjoy, and dispose of a thing or object of value. A right in a thing is property, without regard to whether this right is absolute or conditional, perfect or imperfect, legal or equitable.

Real property means land and things embedded in the land, such as oil tanks. It also includes things attached to the earth, such as buildings or trees, and rights in any of these things. **Personal property** is property that is movable or intangible, or rights in such things. As described in Chapter 10, rights in intellectual property, such as writings, computer programs, inventions, and trademarks, are valuable business properties that are protected by federal statutes.

Personal property then consists of (1) whole or fractional rights in things that are tangible and movable, such as furniture and books; (2) claims and debts, which are called **choses in action**; and (3) intangible property rights, such as trademarks, copyrights, and patents.

2. Title to Personal Property

Title to personal property may be acquired in different ways. For example, property is commonly purchased. The purchase and sale of goods is governed by the law of sales. In this chapter, the following methods of acquiring personal property are discussed: gift, finding lost property, occupation, and escheat.

No title is acquired by theft. The thief acquires possession only, and if the thief makes a sale or gift of the property to another, the latter acquires only possession of the property. The true owner may reclaim the property from the thief or a thief's transferee. **For Example,** through a response to a classified ad, Ray purchased a Mongoose bicycle for his son from Kevin for $250, a favorable but fair price for this used bicycle. To protect himself, he obtained from Kevin a handwritten bill of sale that was notarized by a notary public. In fact, Kevin had stolen

FIGURE 21-1 *Inter Vivos Gift*

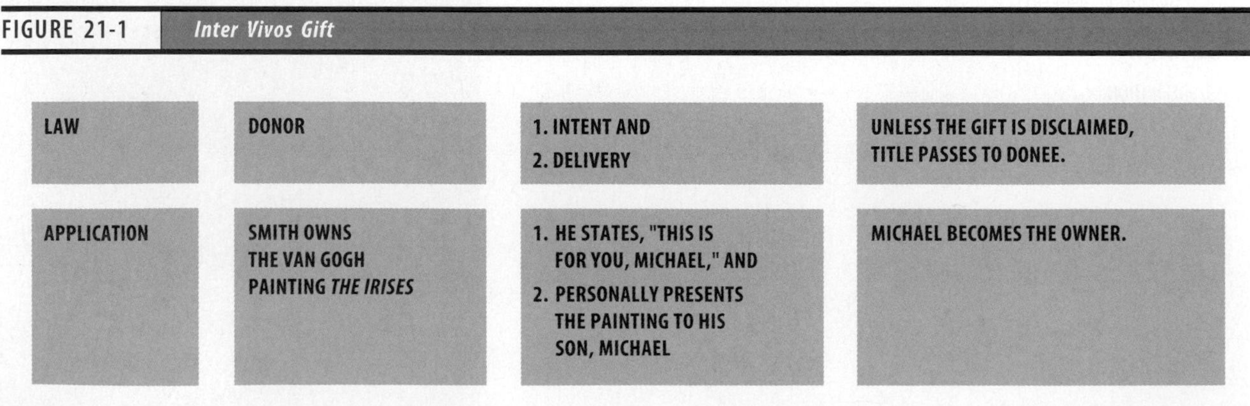

LAW	DONOR	1. INTENT AND 2. DELIVERY	UNLESS THE GIFT IS DISCLAIMED, TITLE PASSES TO DONEE.
APPLICATION	SMITH OWNS THE VAN GOGH PAINTING *THE IRISES*	1. HE STATES, "THIS IS FOR YOU, MICHAEL," AND 2. PERSONALLY PRESENTS THE PAINTING TO HIS SON, MICHAEL	MICHAEL BECOMES THE OWNER.

[1] *Presley Memorial Foundation v. Crowell*, 733 S.W.2d 89 (Tenn. App. 1987).

the bicycle. Its true owner, Juan, can reclaim the bike from Ray, even though Ray has a notarized bill of sale. Ray does not have legal title to the bicycle.

CPA 3. Gifts

Title to personal property may be transferred by the voluntary act of the owner without receiving anything in exchange—that is, by **gift**. The person making the gift, the **donor**, may do so because of things that the recipient of the gift, the **donee**, has done in the past or is expected to do in the future. However, such things are not deemed consideration and thus do not alter the "free" character of the gift. Five types of gifts are discussed below.

(A) Inter Vivos Gifts. The ordinary gift that is made between two living persons is an **inter vivos gift**. For practical purposes, such a gift takes effect when the donor (1) expresses an intent to transfer title and (2) makes delivery, subject to the right of the donee to disclaim the gift within a reasonable time after learning that it has been made.[2] Because there is no consideration for a gift, there is no enforceable contract, and an intended donee cannot sue for breach of contract if the donor fails to complete the gift.[3]

(1) Intent.

The intent to make a gift requires an intent to transfer title at that time. **For Example,** former ballet star Rudolf Nureyev made a valid gift when he extended deeds of gift granting ownership of his New York City apartment and its $5 million artwork collection to a nonprofit dance foundation even though he retained the right to visit the apartment and pay for its maintenance. He gave up the right to live in the apartment and executed all documents necessary to divest his domain over it.[4] In contrast, an intent to confer a benefit at a future date is not a sufficient intent to create any right in the intended donee.

A delivery of property without the intent to make a gift does not transfer title. **For Example,** Mrs. Simpson's $80,000 check to her daughter and son-in-law, Shari and Karl Goodman, to help them buy a house was not a gift if the transaction was structured as a loan, notwithstanding Shari and Karl's assertion that it was structured as a loan simply to avoid gift taxes. The legal documents setting up the loan transaction indicated that no gift was intended.[5]

CPA *(2) Delivery.*

Ordinarily, the delivery required to make a gift will be an actual handing over to the donee of the thing that is given.

The delivery of a gift may also be made by a **symbolic** or **constructive delivery**, such as by the delivery of means of control of property. Such means of control might be keys to a lock or keys to a garden tractor or papers that are essential to or closely associated with the ownership of the property, such as documents of title or a ship's papers. The *Fontane* case deals with the question of constructive delivery.

Fontane v. Colt Manufacturing Co., 814 A.2d 433 (Conn. App. 2003)

But You Gave It to Me in Front of All Those People?

On March 6, 1999, Colt Manufacturing Co., a handgun manufacturer, sponsored a farewell dinner for one of its officers, Marc Fontane. At the dinner, two Colt officials presented Fontane with a single-action, .45 caliber Colt revolver. After the presentation, an agent of Colt's took possession of the revolver for the purpose of improving it by installing ivory grips and adding engraving. Fontane inquired over a period of months as to when he would receive the revolver and was ultimately told "the gun has been sold and there will be no replacement." Fontane sued Colt for the conversion of the gift with the promised improvements. For a judgment for Fontane for the value of the gun in an improved state, Colt appealed.

[2] *Bishop v. Bishop*, 961 S.W.2d 770 (Ark. 1998).

[3] *Dellagrotta v. Dellagrotta*, 873 A.2d 101 (R.I. 2005).

[4] *Rudolf Nureyev Dance Foundation v. Noureeva-Francois*, 7 F. Supp. 2d 402 (S.D.N.Y. 1998).

[5] *Simpson v. Goodman*, 727 So.2d 555 (La. App. 1998). See also *Wright v. Mallet*, 894 A.2d 1016 (Conn. App. 2006) in which the evidence showed that a transfer of an interest in land was not intended to be a gift.

Continued

JUDICIAL OPINION

PER CURIAM…Where actual delivery has not occurred, the resolution of the issue of whether a donor has made a constructive delivery depends on the circumstances of each case. "For a constructive delivery, the donor must do that which, under the circumstances, will in reason be equivalent to an actual delivery. It must be as nearly perfect and complete as the nature of the property and the circumstances will permit." *Hebrew University Assn. v Nye supra* 148 Conn. at 232–33, 169 A.2d 641.,

In the present case, there is no dispute that the defendant effectuated its donative intent of giving the plaintiff a gift of, at the very least, an unimproved revolver when it actually presented the same, along with a presentation case, to the plaintiff at the dinner. The evidence also supports the court's finding that the defendant intended, in accordance with its customary practice, to give the plaintiff the revolver with improvements to be made thereto. In the present case, the court found that the circumstances did not permit the defendant to deliver to the plaintiff at the retirement dinner a fully improved revolver; the defendant had not made the improvements to the revolver by that time. The evidence further supports the court's finding that the defendant did what was practicable under the circumstances: It publicly presented the defendant with the unimproved revolver and then immediately took possession of the revolver for the purpose of making the improvements that it intended to be part of the gift.

We agree with the court that the constructive, or symbolic, form of delivery employed by the defendant was sufficient to consummate the gift of an improved revolver.

We have concluded that the court properly found that the defendant's gift consisted of an improved revolver. Accordingly, that gift is what the defendant, almost immediately after having presented the gift to the plaintiff, converted. We therefore conclude that the court properly found that the value of the converted gift was $8155.

[Affirmed]

QUESTIONS

1. What test did the court use to determine whether a donor has made a constructive delivery of the revolver?
2. Did the court determine that a constructive delivery took place?

Failure to meet the "delivery" requirement will result in an ineffective gift. **For Example,** Walter Brownlee signed a bill of sale and attached a list of valuable construction equipment to it and left it with his attorney with instructions that it be passed to his son Randy after Walter's death. By leaving the bill of sale with his attorney, Walter retained control over the property, and therefore it was never effectively delivered to Randy, resulting in an ineffective gift.[6] A completed gift is made, however, when a decedent mails a certified check to the donee prior to his death, even though the check is received after the decedent died.[7] **For Example,** Harry obtained a certified check from Colonial Bank in the amount of $80,000 on September 1, 2009, payable to Allan Foster. Harry mailed the check on September 2, 2009, and it arrived at Allan's home on September 3, 2009, several hours after Harry's death. Because the check was certified, the funds had already been subtracted from Harry's account, and Harry had relinquished all control and right over the certified check before his death, the check was a completed gift.

CPA (3) *Donor's Death.*

If the donor dies before doing what is needed to make an effective gift, the gift fails.[8] An agent or the executor or administrator of the estate cannot thereafter perform the missing step on behalf of the decedent.

For Example, Mary Manning, who was in poor health, wanted to give her college-age granddaughter, Phyllis, her antique 1966 Ford Mustang convertible. She sent her daughter, Nel, to obtain the car's title from a file in the basement but was too tired to sign it on Nel's return. Mary passed away the next day without signing the document. Nel, the executrix under Mary's will, cannot complete the delivery of the gift by signing the title because it is beyond the authority of an executrix. Even though donative

[6] *In re Estate of Walter Brownlee, Sr.*, 654 N.W.2d (S.D. 2002).
[7] *Foster v. Foster*, 2012 WL 29164 (Ala. App. Jan. 6, 2012).
[8] *Laverman v. Destocki*, 622 N.E.2d 1122 (Ohio App. 1994).

intent existed, no evidence of transfer of ownership and delivery to Phyllis occurred prior to Mary's death. Therefore, no valid gift was made.

(B) Gifts Causa Mortis. A **gift causa mortis** is made when the donor, contemplating imminent and impending death, delivers personal property to the donee with the intent that the donee shall own it if the donor dies. This is a conditional gift, and the donor is entitled to take the property back if (1) the donor does not die, (2) the donor revokes the gift before dying, or (3) the donee dies before the donor.

(C) Gifts and Transfers to Minors. Uniform acts provide for transferring property to a custodian to hold for the benefit of a minor.[9] When a custodian holds property for the benefit of a minor under one of the uniform acts, the custodian has discretionary power to use the property "for the support, maintenance, education, and benefit" of the minor, but the custodian may not use the custodial property for the custodian's own personal benefit. The gift is final and irrevocable for tax and all other purposes on complying with the procedures of the acts.

Under the uniform acts, custodianships terminate and the property is distributed when the minor reaches age 21.

(D) Conditional Gifts. A gift may be made subject to a condition, such as "This car is yours when you graduate" or "This car is yours unless you drop out of school." In the first example, the gift is subject to a condition precedent—graduation. A condition precedent must be satisfied before any gift or transfer takes place. In the second example, the gift is subject to a condition subsequent—dropping out of school.

Absent a finding of an intent to create a trust, a donative transaction will be analyzed as a gift subject to conditions. **For Example,** the gift by the Tennessee United Daughters of the Confederacy (UDC) to a building fund for Peabody College expressly reserved the right to recall the gift if the college failed to comply with the conditions of placing an inscription on the 1935 building naming it Confederate Memorial Hall. Peabody College for Teachers was merged into Vanderbilt University in 1979. In 2002, Vanderbilt decided to rename Confederate Memorial Hall. The Tennessee UDC's suit for the return of its gift was successful; the court decided it was not at liberty to relieve a party from its contractual obligations.[10]

Most courts regard an engagement ring as a conditional gift subject to the condition subsequent of a failure to marry. The inherent symbolism of the gift itself is deemed to foreclose the need to establish an express condition that there be a marriage.

Some jurisdictions require return of engagement rings only if the donor has not unjustifiably broken off the engagement. Most states now reject considerations of "fault" in the breaking of an engagement and always require the return of the ring to the donor when an engagement is broken. This "modern trend" is based on the theory that, in most cases, "fault" is impossible to determine, as discussed in the *Meyers* case.

Meyer v. Mitnick, 625 N.W.2d 136 (Mich. App. 2001)

Your Honor, Marriages Are Not Made in Heaven, You Say?

Dr. Barry Meyer and Robyn Mitnick became engaged on August 9, 1996, at which time Barry gave Robyn a custom-designed engagement ring that he purchased for $19,500. On November 8, 1996, Barry asked Robyn to sign a prenuptial agreement and Robyn refused. The engagement was broken during that meeting, with both Barry and Robyn contending the other party caused the breakup. Robyn did not return the ring, and Barry sued for its return. Robyn filed a countercomplaint, alleging that the ring was an unconditional gift and that because Barry broke the engagement, she was entitled to keep the ring.

[9] The Uniform Gifts to Minors Act (UGMA) is in effect in South Carolina and Vermont. The Uniform Transfers to Minors Act, which expands the type of property that can be made the subject of a gift, was originally proposed in 1983. It has been adopted, often with minor variations, in all states and the District of Columbia except South Carolina and Vermont.

[10] *Tennessee UDC v. Vanderbilt University*, 174 S.W.3d 98 (Tenn. Ct. App. 2005).

Continued

JUDICIAL OPINION

FITZGERALD, R. J.…Where a gift of personal property is made with the intent to take effect irrevocably, and is fully executed by unconditional delivery, it is a valid gift inter vivos.… Such a gift is absolute and, once made, cannot be revoked.…A gift, however, may be conditioned on the performance of some act by the donee, and if the condition is not fulfilled the donor may recover the gift.…We find the conditional gift theory particularly appropriate when the contested property is an engagement ring. The inherent symbolism of this gift forecloses the need to establish an express condition that marriage will ensue. Rather, the condition may be implied in fact or imposed by law in order to prevent unjust enrichment.…

Like the courts in other states…we find that engagement rings should be considered, by their very nature, conditional gifts given in contemplation of marriage. Once we recognize an engagement ring is a conditional gift, the question still remains: who gets the gift when the condition is not fulfilled? The general principles of law concerning a donor's right to the return of an engagement ring or its value when the marriage does not occur are contained in a collection of cases from multiple jurisdictions. …Generally, courts have taken two divergent paths. The older one rules that when an engagement has been unjustifiably broken by the donor, the donor shall not recover the ring. However, if the engagement is broken by mutual agreement, or unjustifiably by the donee, the ring should be returned to the donor. The critical inquiry in this fault-based line of cases is who was at "fault" for the termination of the relationship. The other rule, the so-called, "modern trend," holds that because an engagement ring is an inherently conditional gift, once the engagement has been broken the ring should be returned to the donor. Thus, the question of who broke the engagement and why, or who was "at fault," is irrelevant. This is the no-fault line of cases.

We find the reasoning of the no-fault cases persuasive. Because the engagement ring is a conditional gift, when the condition is not fulfilled the ring or its value should be returned to the donor no matter who broke the engagement or caused it to be broken. As stated by the court in *Aronow v Silver* 223 N.J. Super. 344 (1987), in concluding that fault is irrelevant in an engagement setting:

> *What fact justifies the breaking of an engagement? The absence of a sense of humor? Differing musical tastes? Differing political views? The painfully-learned fact is that marriages are made on earth, not in heaven. They must be approached with intelligent care and should not happen without a decent assurance of success. When either party lacks that assurance, for whatever reason, the engagement should be broken. No justification is needed. Either party may act. Fault, impossible to fix, does not count.*

In sum, we hold that an engagement ring given in contemplation of marriage is an impliedly conditional gift that is a completed gift only upon marriage. If the engagement is called off, for whatever reason, the gift is not capable of becoming a completed gift and must be returned to the donor.

[Judgment affirmed]

QUESTIONS

1. State the "older rule" regarding a donor's right to the return of an engagement ring.
2. What is the "modern trend" regarding return of engagement rings or their value to the donor after the breaking of an engagement?
3. Is fault a factor under the *Aronow v Silver* precedent case referred to by the court?

(E) Anatomical Gifts. Persons may make gifts of parts of their bodies, as in the case of kidney transplants. Persons may also make postdeath gifts. The Uniform Anatomical Gift Act[11] permits persons 18 years or older to make gifts of their bodies or any parts thereof. The gift takes effect on the death of the donor. The gift may be made to a school, a hospital, an organ bank, or a named patient. Such a gift may also be made, subject to certain restrictions, by the spouse, adult child, parent, adult brother or sister, or guardian of a deceased person. If a hospital misleads family members into consenting to tissue or organ donations that exceed their express wishes, such misconduct is sufficiently outrageous to support a claim for intentional infliction of emotional distress.[12]

CPA 4. Finding of Lost Property

Personal property is lost when the owner does not know where it is located but intends to retain title to or ownership of it. The person finding lost property

[11] This act has been adopted in every state.

[12] See *Perry v. Saint Francis Hospital*, 886 F. Supp. 1551 (D. Kan. 1995).

does not acquire title but only possession. Ordinarily, the finder of lost property is required to surrender the property to the true owner when the latter establishes ownership. Meanwhile, the finder is entitled to retain possession as against everyone else.

Without a contract with the owner or a statute so providing, the finder of lost property usually is not entitled to a reward or to compensation for finding or caring for the property.

(A) Finding in Public Place. If the lost property is found in a public place, such as a hotel, under such circumstances that to a reasonable person it would appear the property had been intentionally placed there by the owner and the owner would be likely to recall where the property had been left and to return for it, the finder is not entitled to possession of the property. The finder must give it to the proprietor or manager of the public place to keep it for the owner. This exception does not apply if it appears that the property was not intentionally placed where it was found. In that case, it is not likely that the owner will recall having left it there.

(B) Statutory Change. Some states have adopted statutes permitting the finder to sell the property or keep it if the owner does not appear within a stated period of time. In this case, the finder is required to give notice—for example, by newspaper publication—to attempt to reach the owner.

5. Occupation of Personal Property

In some cases, title to personal property may be acquired by occupation—that is, by taking and retaining possession of the property.

(A) Wild Animals. Wild animals, living in a state of nature, are not owned by any individual. In the absence of restrictions imposed by game laws, the person who acquires dominion or control over a wild animal becomes its owner. What constitutes sufficient dominion or control varies with the nature of the animal and the surrounding circumstances. If the animal is killed, tied, imprisoned, or otherwise prevented from going at its will, the hunter exercises sufficient dominion or control over the animal and becomes its owner. If the wild animal, subsequent to its capture, should escape and return to its natural state, it resumes the status of a wild animal.

As a qualification to the ordinary rule, the following exception developed. If an animal is killed or captured on the land of another while the hunter is on the land without permission of the landowner, the animal, when killed or captured, belongs not to the hunter but to the landowner.

(B) Abandoned Personal Property. Personal property is deemed abandoned when the owner relinquishes possession with the intention to disclaim title to it. Yesterday's newspaper thrown out in the trash is abandoned personal property. Title to abandoned property may be acquired by the first person who obtains possession and control of it. A person becomes the owner at the moment of taking possession of the abandoned personal property. If, however, the owner of property flees in the face of an approaching peril, property left behind is not abandoned. An abandonment occurs only when the owner voluntarily leaves the property.

(C) Conversion. The tort of conversion has its origins in the ancient common law writ of trover, created "as a remedy against the finder of lost goods who refused to return them."[13] Because of that origin, the tort of conversion was limited to property that could be lost and found (i.e., tangible personalty as opposed to real property).

As the nature of personal property evolved to the point that tangible documents represented highly valuable rights, such as promissory notes, stock certificates, insurance policies, and bank books, common law courts expanded the tort of conversion to include such documents within its definitional scope despite their intangible aspects, which, invariably, are primary components of the document's value. The concept of conversion today, which is the wrongful exclusionary retention of an owner's physical property, applies to an electronic record as much as it does to a paper record such as valuable stock certificates and bank books. **For Example,** a computerized client/investor list created by a real estate agent is "property" protected by the law of conversion.[14]

[13] Restatement, Second of Torts §242, comment d.

[14] *Shmueli v. Corcoran Group*, 802 N.Y.S.2d 871 (2005).

6. Escheat

Who owns unclaimed property? In the case of personal property, the practical answer is that the property will probably "disappear" after a period of time, or if in the possession of a carrier, hotel, or warehouse, it may be sold for unpaid storage charges. A growing problem arises with respect to unclaimed corporate dividends, bank deposits, insurance payments, and refunds. Most states have a statute providing for the transfer of such unclaimed property to the state government. This transfer to the government is often called by its feudal name of **escheat**. **For Example,** when James Canel's 280 shares of stock in Patrick Industries were turned over to the state treasurer's office by Harris Bank because his account at the bank had been inactive for more than five years, the property was presumed to be abandoned. Once Canel claimed the property, however, he was entitled to the return of the stock and the past dividends. The state was not entitled to retain the dividends under the court's reading of the state's Unclaimed Property Act.[15] Funds held by stores for layaway items for customers who fail to complete the layaway purchases are subject to escheat to the state. To provide for unclaimed property, many states have adopted the Uniform Unclaimed Property Act (UUPA),[16] formerly called the Uniform Disposition of Unclaimed Property Act, as referenced in the *Presley* case.

Presley v. City of Memphis, 769 S.W.2d 221 (Tenn. App. 1988)

The King Is Dead! Who Gets the Unrefunded Ticket Proceeds?

Elvis Presley contracted with Mid-South Coliseum Board (City of Memphis) for the rental of the Coliseum and for personnel to sell tickets for concerts on August 27 and 28, 1977; $325,000 worth of tickets were sold. On August 16, 1977, Elvis Presley died. Refunds were given to those who returned their tickets to the Coliseum Board. Ten years after his death, however, $152,279 worth of ticket proceeds remained unclaimed in the custody of the Board. This fund had earned $223,760 in interest. Priscilla Presley and the coexecutors of the estate of Elvis Presley brought an action claiming the unrefunded ticket proceeds for the canceled concerts. The state of Tennessee claimed that it was entitled to the proceeds under the Uniform Disposition of Unclaimed Property Act. From a judgment for the coexecutors, the state appealed.

JUDICIAL OPINION

HIGHERS, J.…Although the ticket may have some value as memorabilia apart from its intended function, such value was not the essence of the contract, had no bearing on the original proceeds, and has none now.

When Presley died, performance of the concert became impossible, and the contract was void.…The ticketholder was vested with a right to a refund of contract proceeds from the Coliseum as Presley's agent.…

Tennessee's version of the UDUPA is codified at T.C.A. § 66-29-101 et seq.…§ 66-29-113 requires that the holder of the [abandoned] property report that property to the state treasurer. After notice is given…the property is to be delivered to the treasurer.…

The owner may recover at any time no matter how remote.…

The state has asserted that the definition in T.C.A. § 66-29-111 is applicable to the case at bar. That statute provides in pertinent part as follows:

> *66-29-111. Miscellaneous property held for another person.—All property, not otherwise covered by this chapter, including any income or increment thereon and deducting any lawful charges, that is held or owing in this state in the ordinary course of the holder's business and has remained unclaimed by the owner for more than seven (7) years after it became payable or distributable is presumed abandoned.*

We agree with the state's assertion. The refunds in question have remained unclaimed in the more than seven years they have been held by the Coliseum in the ordinary course of its business. The ticketholder's right to a refund vested when the contract was voided. That right arose and the seven-year statutory period began when Elvis Presley died on August 16, 1977. Therefore, a presumption of abandonment as to

[15] *Canel v. Topinka*, 818 N.E.2d 311 (Ill. 2004).

[16] The 1981 or 1995 version of the Act has been adopted in Alaska, Arizona, Arkansas, Colorado, Florida, Hawaii, Idaho, Illinois, Indiana, Kansas, Louisiana, Maine, Michigan, Montana, Nevada, New Hampshire, New Jersey, New Mexico, North Carolina, North Dakota, Oklahoma, Oregon, Rhode Island, South Carolina, South Dakota, U.S. Virgin Islands, Utah, Virginia, Washington, West Virginia, Wisconsin, and Wyoming.

Continued

unclaimed refunds matured on August 16, 1984. The present action…does not qualify as a claim under the statute because the plaintiffs have no legal right to the funds. Any right they might have had was lost when the contract was voided.

The presumption of abandonment under the UDUPA is statutory and therefore independent of common law principles of abandonment….Intentional and voluntary relinquishment is not required under the statute. Statutory abandonment occurs when the conditions set out in the UDUPA exist….Only statutorily abandonment property is disposed of under the UDUPA….

We are well aware that this fund would not exist were it not for Elvis Presley's unique skills and talents while living and the legendary status he continues to hold in the years after his death….These considerations might in the absence of the Tennessee statute merit granting the windfall to Presley's estate. But Presley's death voided the contract represented by each ticket sold…and Presley's estate [has] no legal claim to the ticket proceeds. Granting the proceeds to either of them or to the Coliseum constitutes the type of windfall the drafters of UDUPA sought to address….We believe the drafters of the UDUPA and our legislature intended such windfalls to benefit the public rather than individuals in precisely the manner we hold here….

In summary, pursuant to the Tennessee UDUPA, we hold that the Coliseum must deliver all of the unclaimed ticket refunds and all of the accumulated interest thereon to the treasurer. Further, the treasurer shall publish the existence of the unclaimed funds and hold those amounts until such time as they are claimed by the rightful owners, the ticketholders.

[Judgment reversed and action remanded]

QUESTIONS

1. On what basis did the estate of Elvis Presley claim the unrefunded ticket proceeds and interest?
2. Present the state's legal position before the court.
3. Did the court think the intent of the drafters of the UDUPA would support the "windfall" in this case benefiting the estate of the individual whose legendary status generated the unclaimed funds? Explain.

CPA 7. Multiple Ownership of Personal Property

When all rights in a particular object of property are held by one person, that property is held in **severalty**. However, two or more persons may hold concurrent rights and interests in the same property. In that case, the property is said to be held in **cotenancy**. The various forms of cotenancy include (1) tenancy in common, (2) joint tenancy, (3) tenancy by entirety, and (4) community property.

(A) TENANCY IN COMMON. A **tenancy in common** is a form of ownership by two or more persons. The interest of a tenant in common may be transferred or inherited, in which case the taker becomes a tenant in common with the others. **For Example,** Brandt and Vincent restored an 18-foot 1940 mahogany-hulled Chris Craft runabout and own it as tenants in common. If Brandt sold his interest in the boat to Andrea, then Vincent and Andrea would be co-owners as tenants in common. If Brandt died before Vincent, a one-half interest in the boat would become the property of Brandt's heirs.

CPA **(B) JOINT TENANCY.** A **joint tenancy** is another form of ownership by two or more persons, but a joint tenancy has a *right of survivorship*.[17] On the death of a joint tenant, the remaining tenants take the share of the deceased tenant. The last surviving joint tenant takes the property as a holder in severalty. **For Example,** in Brandt and Vincent's Chris Craft case, if the boat were owned as joint tenants with a right of survivorship, Vincent would own the boat outright upon Brandt's death, and Brandt's heirs would obtain no interest in it.

A joint tenant's interest may be transferred to a third person, but this destroys the joint tenancy. If the interest of one of two joint tenants is transferred to a third person, the remaining joint tenant becomes a tenant in common with the third person. **For Example,** if Brandt sold his interest to Andrea, Vincent and Andrea would be co-owners as tenants in common.

Statutes in many states have modified the common law by adding a formal requirement to the creation of a joint tenancy with survivorship. At common law, such an estate would be created by a transfer of

[17] *Estate of Munier v. Jacquemin*, 899 S.W.2d 114 (Mo. App. 1995).

property to "*A* and *B* as joint tenants."[18] Under these statutes, however, it is necessary to add the words "with right of survivorship" or other similar words if a right of survivorship is desired.

If no words of survivorship are used, the transfer of property to two or more persons will be construed as creating a tenancy in common. Under such a statute, a certificate of deposit issued only in the name of "*A* or *B*" does not create a joint tenancy because it does not contain words of survivorship.

(c) Tenancy by Entirety. At common law, a **tenancy by entirety** or **tenancy by the entireties** was created when property was transferred to both husband and wife. It differs from joint tenancy in that it exists only when the transfer is to husband and wife. Also, the right of survivorship cannot be extinguished, and one spouse's interest cannot be transferred to a third person. However, in some jurisdictions, a spouse's right to share the possession and the profits may be transferred. This form of property holding is popular in common law jurisdictions because creditors of only one of the spouses cannot reach the property while both are living. Only a creditor of both the husband and the wife under the same obligation can obtain execution against the property.

For Example, a husband and wife, Rui and Carla Canseco, purchased a 2012 Lexus LS 460 for cash. It was titled in the names of "Rui J. *and* Carla T. Canseco." Later that year, State National Bank obtained a money judgment against Rui for $200,000, and the bank claimed entitlement to half the value of the Cansecos' car, which it asserted was Rui's share as a joint tenant. A tenancy by entirety had been created, however, so the bank could not levy against the auto. If the car had been titled "Rui *or* Carla T. Canseco," in most states the use of the word "or" would indicate that the vehicle was held in joint tenancy even if the co-owners are husband and wife. As such, Rui's half interest could be reached by the bank.

The tenancy by entirety is, in effect, a substitute for a will because the surviving spouse acquires the complete property interest on the death of the other. There are usually other reasons, however, why each spouse should make a will.

In many states, the granting of an absolute divorce converts a tenancy by the entireties into a tenancy in common.

8. Community Property

In some states, property acquired during the period of marriage is the **community property** of the husband and wife. Some statutes provide for the right of survivorship; others provide that half of the property of the deceased husband or wife shall go to the heirs of that spouse or permit such half to be disposed of by will. It is commonly provided that property acquired by either spouse during the marriage is **prima facie** community property, even though title is taken in the spouse's individual name, unless it can be shown that it was obtained with property possessed by the spouse prior to the marriage.

B. Bailments

9. Definition

A **bailment** is the relationship that arises when one person delivers possession of personal property to another under an agreement, express or implied, by which the latter is under a duty to return the property or to deliver it or dispose of it as agreed. The person who turns over the possession of the property is the **bailor**. The person who accepts is the **bailee**.

For Example, Arthur Grace, a world renowned photo-journalist, had an agreement with Sygma-Paris and Sygma-New York whereby Grace turned over his photographs to Sygma, and Sygma agreed to act as Grace's agent to license the images and administer the fee-setting process and delivery and return of the images. The *bailor*, Grace, terminated its agreement with the *bailee*, Sygma, in 2001, and the *bailee* was unable to return all of the photographs to Grace as obligated under the agreement. Sygma's system of keeping track of images was "completely inadequate"; hence, it was liable for $472,000 in damages to the *bailor* for the failure to return some 40,000 images.[19]

[18] Some states have modified the common law by creating a condition that whenever two or more persons are listed as owners of a bank account or certificate of deposit, a presumption of joint tenancy with right of survivorship arises unless expressly negated by the signature card or another instrument or by extrinsic proof. Thus, when Herbert H. Herring had his bank change the designated owners of a certificate of deposit to read, "Herbert H. Herring or [his grandson] Robert J. Herring," and no words indicating survivorship upon the death of either were on the certificate, nevertheless under a 1992 Florida statute creating a presumption of survivorship, which presumption was not rebutted, grandson Robert was declared the owner of the certificate. *In re Estate of H. H. Herring*, 670 So.2d 145 (Fla. App. 1996).

[19] *Grace v. Corbis Sygma*, 403 F. Supp. 2d 337 (S.D.N.Y. 2005).

10. Elements of Bailment

A bailment is created when the following elements are present.

(A) Agreement. The bailment is based on an *agreement.* This agreement may be express or implied. Generally, it contains all of the elements of a contract. The bailment transaction in fact consists of (1) a contract to bail and (2) the actual bailing of the property. Ordinarily, there is no requirement that the contract of bailment be in writing. The subject of a bailment may be any personal property of which possession may be given.[20] Real property cannot be bailed.

(B) Delivery and Acceptance. The bailment arises when, pursuant to the agreement of the parties, the property is delivered to the bailee and accepted by the bailee as subject to the bailment agreement.

In the absence of a prior agreement to the contrary, a valid delivery and acceptance generally require that the bailee be aware that goods have been placed within the bailee's exclusive possession or control. **For Example,** photography equipment belonging to Bill Bergey, the photographer of Roosevelt University's student newspaper, was stolen from the newspaper's campus office. Bergey believes that the university breached its duty as bailee because records showed that no campus police officer checked the building on the night of the theft. Bergey's case against the university on this bailment theory will fail, however, because the university did not know the equipment was left in the office. Without this knowledge, there was neither a bailment agreement nor acceptance of delivery by the university as a bailee.

11. Nature of the Parties' Interests

The bailor and bailee have different legal interests in the bailed property.

(A) Bailor's Interest. The bailor is usually the owner, but ownership by the bailor is not required. It is sufficient that the bailor have physical possession. **For Example,** Crella Magee delivered a blue fox jacket for summer storage to Walbro, Inc. When it was not returned, she sued Walbro for the replacement cost of the jacket, $3,400. Walbro's defense that Magee was not entitled to recover the replacement cost of the lost jacket because she did not prove ownership was rejected as irrelevant by the court, and the case was decided in favor of Magee.[21]

(B) Bailee's Interest. The bailee has possession of the property only. **For Example,** the Lackawanna Chapter for the Railway & Locomotive Historical

FIGURE 21-2 *Bailment of Personal Property*

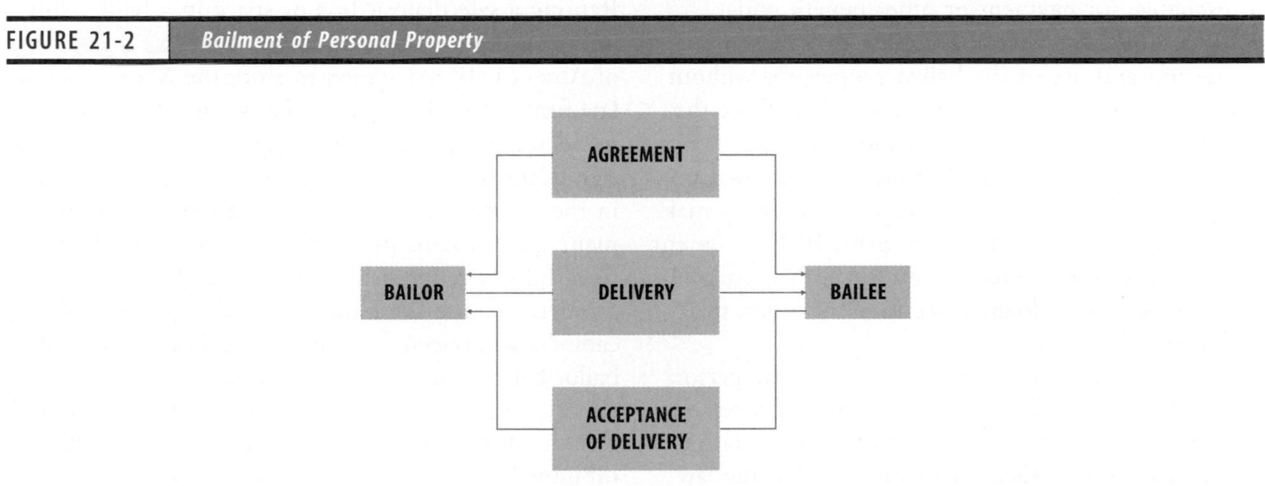

[20] *Stone v. CDI Corp.*, 9 S.W.3d 699 (Mo. App. 1999).

[21] *Magee v. Walbro, Inc.*, 525 N.E.2d 975 (Ill. App. 1988).

Society, Inc. and its predecessor held title to Engine No. 952, a now-rare camelback locomotive built in 1905 and retired in 1938. It was placed in the care of the St. Louis Transportation Museum in 1953 for "permanent exhibition." The Lackawanna Chapter sought the return of Engine No. 952 after more than 50 years, and the successor St. Louis Museum raised numerous defenses. Possession and control do not entitle the St. Louis Museum to continued possession that overcomes a lender's good title. The museum, as a bailee in a gratuitous bailment, has the duty to return the bailment property to the owner.[22]

Title to the property does not pass to the bailee, and the bailee cannot sell the property to a third person. If the bailee attempts to sell the property, such sale transfers only possession, and the owner may recover the property from the buyer.

12. Classification of Ordinary Bailments

Ordinary bailments are generally classified as being for (1) the sole benefit of the bailor, (2) the sole benefit of the bailee, or (3) the mutual benefit of both.

Bailments may or may not provide for compensation to the bailee. On the basis of compensation, bailments may be classified as (1) **bailments for mutual benefit** in which one party takes the personal property of another into her care or custody in exchange for payment or other benefit and (2) **gratuitous bailments** in which the transfer of possession and use of the bailed property is without compensation. Bailments for the sole benefit of the bailor or for the sole benefit of the bailee are sometimes described as gratuitous. The fact that no charge is made by the bailor does not necessarily make the transaction a gratuitous bailment. If the bailment is made to further a business interest of the bailor, as when something is loaned free to a customer, the bailment is not gratuitous.

A **constructive bailment** arises when one person has lawfully acquired possession of another's personal property other than by virtue of a bailment contract and holds it under such circumstances that the law imposes on the recipient of the property the obligation to keep it safely and redeliver it to the owner. **For Example,** the City of Chicago is the constructive bailee of an automobile impounded by Chicago police at the time of a driver's arrest for drunk driving. It has a duty to keep the automobile safely and turn it over to the owner upon payment of towing and storage fees. When this duty is delegated to a private contractor to tow and store, a constructive bailment for the mutual benefit of the contractor and the owner exists.

13. Renting of Space Distinguished

When a person rents space in a locker or building under an agreement that gives the renter the exclusive right to use that space, the placing of goods by the renter in that space does not create a bailment, for it does not constitute a delivery of goods into the possession of the owner of the space. **For Example,** Winston Hutton entered into a rental agreement for a storage space at Public Storage Management's self-storage facility in New York City, and his stored property was stolen from the space. Hutton had procured his own lock for the storage space, and the rental agreement provided that management would not have a key. Hutton's lawsuit was unsuccessful because the defendant did not take possession of the property. The legal relationship was not a bailment.[23] Renting a safe deposit box or space in a bank vault does create a bailment, however. **For Example,** Bank of America (BOA) agreed to store the Martin Lucas law firm's file cabinets in its bank vault for a monthly fee. A water pipe burst, flooding the vault and causing significant damage to original legal documents stored in the cabinets. BOA's contention that the arrangement did not constitute a bailment because the law firm did not relinquish exclusive control over the cabinets because the bank could not open the file cabinets was rejected by the court. The relation of bailor-bailee is not disturbed by the fact that a safe deposit company does not know and is not expected to know the contents of a safe deposit box or file cabinet.[24]

[22] *Lackawanna Chapter v. St. Louis County*, 497 F.3d 832 (8th Cir. 2007).
[23] *Hutton v. Public Storage Management, Inc.*, 676 N.Y.S.2d 887 (N.Y. City Civ. Ct. 1998).
[24] *Martin, Lucas, Chioffi, LLP v. Bank of America*, 714 F. Supp. 2d 303 (D. Conn. 2010).

14. Duties and Rights of the Bailee

The bailee has certain duties concerning performance, care, and return of the bailed property. The bailee must perform his part of a contract and is liable for ordinary contract damages for failure to perform the contract.

The bailee is under a duty to care for the bailed property, and the duty of care owed differs according to classification, based in terms of "benefit." A bailment may be for the sole benefit of the bailor. **For Example,** when Fred allows Mary, a college classmate from out of state, to store her books and furniture in his basement over the summer, Fred, the bailee, is liable only for gross negligence relating to damage to these stored belongings. A bailment may be for the sole benefit of the bailee, as when Mary allows Fred to borrow her Les Paul Gibson guitar. Fred, the bailee, is liable even for slight negligence in the case of any damage to the guitar. Most bailments, however, are mutual benefit bailments. **For Example,** when Harry rents for a fee a trailer from U-Haul, Inc., to transport his son's belongings to college, Harry, the bailee, is responsible for using reasonable or ordinary care under the circumstances while possessing and using the trailer. U-Haul, the bailor, has a duty to warn Harry of any known defects or defects that could be discovered on reasonable inspection.

A bailee has a right to receive payment for charges due for storage or repairs. A **bailee's lien** gives the bailee the right to keep possession of the bailed property until charges are paid. A bailee who is authorized by statute to sell the bailed property to enforce a charge or claim against the bailor must give such notice as is required by the statute. A bailee who sells without giving the required notice is liable for conversion of the property.

15. Breach of Duty of Care: Burden of Proof

Although a bailment is contractual in nature, an action for breach of duty of care by a bailee "sounds in tort." That is, the true nature of the liability is not contractual at all but based on tort principles.

When the bailor sues the bailee for damages to the bailed property, the bailor has the burden of proving that the bailee was at fault and that such fault was the proximate cause of the loss.[25] A prima facie right of the bailor to recover is established, however, by proof that the bailor delivered the property to the bailee in good condition and subsequently could not be returned by the bailee or was returned in a damaged condition. When this is done, the bailee has the burden of proving that the loss or damage was not caused by the bailee's failure to exercise the care required by law, which in the case of a mutual benefit bailment is that of an ordinary or due care, under all of the circumstances.

The *Hadfield* case involved a lawsuit where the bailee believed it was not responsible for damages to a bailed automobile, asserting that the bailment was for the sole benefit of the bailor, making it a gratuitous bailment in which the bailee can be held responsible only for gross negligence.

Hadfield v. Gilchrist, 538 S.E.2d 268 (S.C. App. 2000)

Towed into Court

Mark Hadfield, a medical student in Charleston, South Carolina, went to retrieve his 1988 Lincoln Continental from a parking space on private property near the medical school where his wife had parked the car earlier that day without permission. The property owner called Gilchrist Towing Co. and had the auto removed. When Hadfield discovered that the car had been towed, he telephoned Gilchrist Towing and was told that he would have to wait until the next morning to retrieve the car after paying towing and storage fees. The next morning after paying the charges, he went to the storage lot and found that his car had been extensively vandalized along with a number of other vehicles. The owner of the company, S.A. Gilchrist, refused to pay the estimated cost of repairs, $4,021.43. Hadfield brought suit contending that a constructive bailment for the mutual benefit of Hadfield and Gilchrist had been created, and that Gilchrist breached his duty of care to Hadfield. Gilchrist contended that he towed the vehicle pursuant to Charleston Municipal Ordinances, which are for the sole benefit of the vehicle owners, intended to preserve their property. As such the relationship created was a gratuitous

[25] *Fedrick v. Nichols*, 2008 WL 4117208 (Tex. App. 2008).

Continued

bailment, which limited his duty of care. Gilchrist contended he was not liable for the damages caused by unknown vandals.

JUDICIAL OPINION

ANDERSON, J.... Although contractual in nature, and involving the conveyance of personal property, an action for breach of the duty of care owed by a bailee sounds in tort. See Kurt Philip Autor, Note, Bailment Liability: Toward a Standard of Reasonable Care, 61 S. Car. L. Rev. 2117, 2124 (Sept. 1998)....

The burden of proof in this case rests first upon the bailor, Hadfield, to prove *prima facie* case. He must show: 1) the goods were delivered to the bailee in good condition; and 2) they were lost or returned in a damaged condition. See *Fortner v Carnes* 258 S.C. 455, 189 S. E. 2d 24 (1972) (burden is upon bailee to prove due or ordinary care on his part, to jury's satisfaction, if he is to relieve himself of liability for goods not returned in accordance with bailment contract; whether bailee has exercised due care with regard to stored goods has to be determined with reference to all circumstances of particular case); *Shoreland Freezers, Inc. v Textile Ice & Fuel Co.* 241 S.C. 537, 129 S.E.2d 424 (1963). When the bailor, Hadfield, has so proven, the burden is then shifted to the bailee, Gilchrist, to show that he has used ordinary care in the good's storage and safekeeping.... Hadfield testified before the magistrate regarding the "nice" condition of the vehicle prior to being towed, and the damage to his vehicle, and the other vehicles on the lot. In addition, he introduced photographs depicting the damage. Thus, Hadfield made out his *prima facie* case. The burden then shifted to Gilchrist to show that he used ordinary care in protecting the vehicle while in his care.

Gilchrist impounded the cars in a storage lot surrounded by a chain link fence. There was an individual on the clock at all times. The person on duty spent time in the office and only visited the storage lot to check on it. The vandal cut a hole in the fence and broke into six to eight cars on the night in question. The fact the guard was not on duty at the impound lot and, considering the only other security for the vehicles was the chain link fence, the magistrate and Circuit Court judge could have concluded Gilchrist failed to exercise ordinary care. As explicated above, the decision of whether or not Gilchrist used ordinary care is a question of fact. Based on our standard of review, we must affirm the decision of the Circuit Court on the facts if it is supported by any evidence, and this Court finds no error of law. We find the facts support the finding that Gilchrist breached his duty as a bailee to Hadfield....

DAMAGES

Gilchrist asserts the magistrate and the Circuit Court judge erred in the finding of damages. Yet, Gilchrist's own counsel stated: "And all they have proved is damages. There's no question that the plaintiffs were damaged."... Hadfield proffered the testimony of Rodney Smitz, an assistant manager at Rick Hendrick Collision Center, to explain the damages and the cost to repair the vehicle. Gilchrist's counsel did not cross-examine Smitz regarding the estimates. We find no merit in Gilchrist's argument that there was no evidence for the Circuit Court to calculate damages.

CONCLUSION

We rule that where a city ordinance is utilized as the legal justification for taking possession of a vehicle on private property the person or entity lawfully acquiring possession of the property under the ordinance becomes a constructive bailee as a matter of law. We find a constructive bailment, for the mutual benefit of Hadfield and Gilchrist, was created. Further, we hold an action for breach of the duty of care owed by a bailee, although contractual in nature, sounds in tort. We conclude the burden of proof in a constructive bailment case rests first upon a bailor to prove a prima facie case and, once so proven, the burden shifts to the bailee to show the use of ordinary care in the storage and safekeeping of the property.

[Judgment affirmed]

QUESTIONS

1. What type of bailment was created when Gilchrist took possession of Hadfield's car? Why is a determination about the type of bailment important?
2. Explain the burden of proof applicable in this case.
3. Explain the statement, "Although contractual in nature, and involving the conveyance of personal property, an action for breach of a duty of care owed by a bailee sounds in tort."

16. Liability for Defects in Bailed Property

In the case of a mutual benefit bailment, the bailor must not only inform the bailee of known defects but also make a reasonable investigation to discover defects. The bailor is liable for harm resulting from any such defects. If the bailment is for the sole benefit of the bailee, the bailor must inform the bailee of known defects.

In bailments for hire where the bailor is in the business of renting vehicles, machines, or equipment for use by bailees, such as Hertz or Avis car rental companies, Article 2A of the Uniform Commercial

Code provides an implied warranty of merchantability and fitness for a particular purpose for the protection of bailee customers.[26]

17. Contract Modification of Liability

An ordinary bailee may limit liability (except for willful misconduct) by agreement or contract. If the bailee seeks to limit liability for its own negligence, the wording of the contract must clearly express this intention so that the other party will know what is being contracted away.[27] In some states, statutes prohibit certain kinds of paid bailees, such as automobile parking garages, from limiting their liability for negligence. Statutes in some states declare that a party cannot bar liability for negligent violations of common law standards of care where a public interest is involved. **For Example,** Bruce Gardner left his Porsche 911 automobile to be repaired at Downtown Porsche Auto, signing a repair order standardized adhesion contract that stated Downtown was "not responsible for loss of cars…in case of…theft." The car was stolen while in the garage for repairs due to Downtown's negligence. The California appeals court determined that because automobile repair contracts "affect the public interest," Downtown's exculpatory clause was invalid as to public policy.[28]

When a bailee attempts to limit liability by printing a limitation on a claim check, the limitation must be called to the attention of the bailor in some reasonable fashion, such as a sign at point of purchase, before it may become part of the bailment contract. **For Example,** a claim check for a coat that purports to limit liability is ineffective without a reasonably placed sign notifying customers of the limitation.

LawFlix

The Goonies (1985)(PG)

This story is about children finding a lost treasure they wish to claim as theirs and use to stop the condemnation of their parents' properties by developers. The issue of who owns the treasure is a fascinating one for discussion.

[26] U.C.C. §§2A-212, 2A-213.
[27] *Hertz v. Klein Mfg., Inc.*, 636 So.2d 189 (Fla. App. 1994).
[28] *Gardner v. Downtown Porsche Auto*, 225 Cal. Rptr. 757 (1986).

MAKE THE CONNECTION

SUMMARY

Personal property consists of whole or fractional ownership rights in things that are tangible and movable, as well as rights in things that are intangible.

Personal property may be acquired by purchase. Personal property may also be acquired by gift when the donor has present intent to make a gift and delivers possession to the donee or makes a constructive delivery. Personal property may be acquired by occupation and under some statutes may be acquired by finding. The state may acquire property by escheat.

All rights in a particular object of property can be held by one individual, in which case it is said to be held *in severalty*. Ownership rights may be held concurrently by two or more individuals, in which case it is said to be held in cotenancy. The major forms of cotenancy are (1) tenancy in common, (2) joint tenancy, (3) tenancy by entirety, and (4) community property.

A bailment is the relationship that exists when tangible personal property is delivered by the bailor into the possession of the bailee under an agreement, express or implied, that the identical property will be returned or delivered in accordance with the agreement. No title is transferred by a bailment. The bailee has the right of possession. When a person comes into the possession of the personal property of another without the owner's consent, the law classifies the relationship as a constructive bailment.

Bailments may be classified in terms of benefit—that is, for the (1) sole benefit of the bailor, (2) sole benefit of the bailee, or (3) benefit of both parties (mutual benefit bailment). Some courts state the standard of care required of a bailee in terms of the class of bailment. Thus, if the bailment is for the sole benefit of the bailor, the bailee is required to exercise only slight care and is liable for gross negligence only. When the bailment is for the sole benefit of the bailee, the bailee is liable for the slightest negligence. When the bailment is for the mutual benefit of the parties, as in a commercial bailment, the bailee is liable for ordinary negligence. An ordinary bailee may limit liability except for willful misconduct or where prohibited by law.

A bailee must perform the bailee's part of the contract. The bailee has a lien on the bailed property until they have paid for storage or repair charges.

In a mutual benefit bailment, the bailor is under a duty to furnish goods reasonably fit for the purposes contemplated by the parties. The bailor may be held liable for damages or injury caused by the defective condition of the bailed property.

LEARNING OUTCOMES

After studying this chapter, you should be able to clearly explain:

A. Personal Property

LO.1 Explain how title to personal property is acquired

See the discussion of the acquisition of property by gift, the finding of lost property, occupation, and escheat, p. 389.

See the example of Steam Engine No. 952 where the museum had possession and control of the locomotive for over 50 years but could not overcome the lender's good title, pp. 397–398.

LO.2 List and explain the various types of gifts

See the discussion of inter vivos gifts, gifts causa mortis, gifts and transfers to minors, conditional gifts, and anatomical gifts, starting on p. 389.

LO.3 Explain the legal theory whereby an owner can recover his or her property from the wrongful exclusionary retention of another

See the example of the real estate agent who recovered her computerized client investment list from a former employer under the legal theory called "conversion," p. 393.

B. Bailments

LO.4 Identify the elements necessary to create a bailment

See the Roosevelt University example in which there could be no bailment created because there was no agreement or acceptance of delivery, p. 397.

LO.5 Explain the standard of care a bailee is required to exercise over bailed property

See the examples of duties owed according to classifications based in terms of benefits, p. 399.

KEY TERMS

bailee
bailee's lien
bailment
bailments for mutual benefit
bailor
choses in action
community property
constructive bailment
constructive delivery
cotenancy
donee
donor
escheat
gift
gift causa mortis
gratuitous bailments
inter vivos gift
joint tenancy
personal property
prima facie
real property
severalty
symbolic delivery
tenancy by entirety
tenancy by the entireties
tenancy in common

QUESTIONS AND CASE PROBLEMS

1. Can a creditor of both the husband and wife under the same obligation obtain an execution against a Winnebago mobile home owned by the husband and wife in tenancy by entirety?

2. Joe obtained a box of antique Lenox china dishes that had been left at the Mashpee town dump. He supplemented the sizable but incomplete set of dishes with other Lenox pieces found at antique dealers. At dinner parties, he proudly told of the origin of his china. When Marlene discovered that Joe had taken her dishes from the dump, she hired an attorney to obtain their return. What result?

3. Joyce Clifford gave a check for $5,000 to her nephew Carl to help with living expenses for his last year of college. The face of the check stated, "As a loan." Years later, Carl wrote to his aunt asking what he should do about the loan. She responded on her Christmas card simply, "On money—keep it—no return." After Joyce's death, her administrator sued Carl after discovering the "As a loan" canceled check. Decide.

4. Ruth and Stella were sisters. They owned a house as joint tenants with right of survivorship. Ruth sold her half interest to Roy. Thereafter, Stella died, and Roy claimed the entire property by survivorship. Was he entitled to it?

5. Mona found a wallet on the floor of an elevator in the office building where she worked. She posted several notices in the building about finding the wallet, but no one appeared to claim it. She waited for six months and then spent the money in the wallet in the belief that she owned it. Jason, the person who lost the wallet, subsequently brought suit to recover the money. Mona's defense was that the money was hers because Jason did not claim it within a reasonable time after she posted the notices. Is she correct? (Assume that the common law applies.)

6. In 1971, Harry Gordon turned over $40,000 to his son, Murray Gordon. Murray opened two $20,000 custodial bank accounts under the Uniform Gifts to Minors Act for his minor children, Eden and Alexander. Murray was listed as the custodian of both accounts. On January 9, 1976, both accounts were closed, and a single bank check representing the principal of the accounts was drawn to the order of Harry Gordon. In April 1976, Murray and his wife, Joan, entered into a separation agreement and were later divorced. Thereafter, Joan, on behalf of her children, Eden and Alexander, brought suit against Murray to recover the funds withdrawn in January 1976, contending that the deposits in both accounts were irrevocable gifts. Murray contended that the money was his father's and that it was never intended as a gift but was merely a means of avoiding taxes. Decide. [*Gordon v. Gordon,* 419 N.Y.S.2d 684 (App. Div.)]

7. New York's banking law provides that a presumption arises that a joint tenancy has been created when a bank account is opened in the names of two persons "payable to either or the survivor." While he was still single, Richard Coddington opened a savings account with his mother, Amelia. The signature card they signed stated that the account was owned by them as joint tenants with the right of survivorship. No statement as to survivorship was made on the passbook. Richard later married Margaret. On Richard's death, Margaret claimed a share of the account on the ground that it was not held in joint tenancy because the passbook did not contain words of survivorship and because the statutory presumption of a joint tenancy was overcome by the fact that Richard had withdrawn substantial sums from the account during his life. Decide. [*Coddington v. Coddington,* 391 N.Y.S.2d 760 (Sup. Ct. App. Div.)]

8. Martin Acampora purchased a shotgun at a garage sale years ago, never used the weapon, and did not know of any defects in it. His 31-year-old son Marty borrowed the shotgun to go duck hunting. As Marty attempted to engage the safety mechanism, the shotgun fired. The force of the shotgun's firing caused it to fall to the ground and to discharge another shot, which struck Marty in the hand. Classify the bailment in this case. What duty of care was owed by the bailor in this case? Is Martin liable to his son for the injury?

9. Baena Brothers agreed to reupholster and reduce the size of the arms of Welge's sofa and chair. The work was not done according to the contract, and the furniture when finished had no value to Welge and was not accepted by him. Baena sued him for the contract price. Welge counterclaimed for the value of the furniture. Decide. [*Baena Brothers v. Welge,* 207 A.2d 749 (Conn. Cir. Ct.)]

10. Schroeder parked his car in a parking lot operated by Allright, Inc. On the parking stub given him was printed in large, heavy type that the lot closed at 6:00 P.M. Under this information, printed in smaller, lighter type, was a provision limiting the liability of Allright for theft or loss. A large sign at the lot stated that after 6:00 P.M. patrons could obtain their car keys at another location. Schroeder's car was stolen from the lot sometime after the 6:00 P.M. closing, and he sued Allright for damages. Allright defended on the basis of the limitation-of-liability provision contained in the parking stub and the notice given Schroeder that the lot closed at 6:00 P.M. Decide. [*Allright, Inc. v. Schroeder,* 551 S.W.2d 745 (Tex. Civ. App.)]

11. John Hayes and Lynn Magosian, auditors for a public accounting firm, went to lunch at the Bay View Restaurant in San Francisco. John left his raincoat with a coatroom attendant, but Lynn took her new raincoat with her to the dining room, where she hung it on a coat hook near her booth. When leaving the restaurant, Lynn discovered that someone had taken her raincoat. When John sought to claim his raincoat at the coatroom, it could not be found. The attendant advised that it might have been taken while he was on his break. John and Lynn sued the restaurant, claiming that the restaurant was a bailee of the raincoats and had a duty to return them. Are both John and Lynn correct?

12. Rhodes parked his car in the self-service park-and-lock lot of Pioneer Parking Lot, Inc. The ticket that he received from the ticket meter stated the following: "NOTICE. THIS CONTRACT LIMITS OUR LIABILITY. READ IT. WE RENT SPACE ONLY. NO BAILMENT IS CREATED." Rhodes parked the car himself and kept the keys. There was no attendant at the lot. The car was stolen from the lot. Rhodes sued the parking lot on the theory that it had breached its duty as a bailee. Was there a bailment? [*Rhodes v. Pioneer Parking Lot, Inc.,* 501 S.W.2d 569 (Tenn.)]

13. Newman underwent physical therapy at Physical Therapy Associates of Rome, Inc. (PTAR), in Rome, Georgia, for injuries sustained in an auto accident. At a therapy session on February 6, it was necessary for Newman to take off two necklaces. She placed one of the necklaces on a peg on the wall in the therapy room, and the therapist placed the other necklace on another peg. After the session, Newman forgot to retrieve her jewelry from the wall pegs. When she called the next day for the forgotten jewelry, it could not be found. She sued PTAR for the value of the jewelry on a bailment theory. PTAR raised the defense that there was no bailment because Newman retained the right to remove the jewelry from the wall pegs. Decide. [*Newman v. Physical Therapy Associates of Rome, Inc.,* 375 S.E.2d 253 (Ga. App.)]

14. Charles and Nicolette went to Italy in November 2008, where Charles proposed marriage and presented Nicolette with a diamond ring. She accepted the proposal and the ring. On the same day, Nicolette asked Charles where he had purchased the ring. She became disappointed when he told her where he bought it, and she gave him back the ring, suggesting a different style she would like. He returned the ring to the jeweler and received a refund of $5,000. He then purchased a new ring for $12,000. Charles testified that near the end of November he "reproposed" and presented the second ring to Nicolette. The relationship soon soured and in late February 2009 Charles asked for the return of the ring. Contrary to Charles' testimony that he gave the second ring as an engagement ring in late November, Nicolette testified that he gave the second ring to her a few days before Christmas as a holiday gift. Was it an engagement ring or a holiday gift? What legal significance is there to how the gift is classified? Decide. [*Miller v. Chiaia,* 2011 WL 1367050 (Conn. Superior)]

15. Charter Apparel, Inc., supplied fabric to Marco Apparel, Inc., in December to manufacture

finished articles of clothing at its Walnut Grove, Mississippi, facilities. The fabric arrived just before the Christmas holiday shutdown and was stacked on cutting tables in the old building, which was known to have a roof that leaked. The evidence showed that no precautions were taken to cover the fabric and no guard was posted at the plant during the shutdown. Severe weather and freezing rain occurred during the shutdown, and it was discovered that the rain had leaked through the roof and destroyed more than $400,000 worth of the fabric. Marco denied that it was negligent and argued that it exercised ordinary care. It offered no evidence to rebut Charter's prima facie case or to rebut Charter's evidence of negligence. It asserted, however, that as a bailee it was not an insurer of goods against severe weather conditions. Decide. [*California Union Ins. v. City of Walnut Grove,* 857 F. Supp. 515 (S.D. Miss.)]

Legal Aspects of Supply Chain Management

learningoutcomes

After studying this chapter, you should be able to

LO.1 Identify and explain all of the features of a negotiable warehouse receipt

LO.2 List and explain the differences between the three types of motor carriers of goods

LO.3 Explain a common carrier's liability for loss or damage to goods

LO.4 Identify and explain the role of each of the persons or business entities involved in the sale of goods on consignment

LO.5 Describe a hotelkeeper's liability for loss of a guest's property

All bailments are not created equal. Because of the circumstances under which possession of the bailed property is transferred, the law imposes special duties in some cases on warehouses, common carriers, factors, and hotelkeepers. Documents of title facilitate the transportation, storage, and financing of goods in commerce.

A. Warehouses

The storage of goods in a warehouse is a special bailment.

1. Definitions

A **warehouse** is an entity engaged in the business of storing the goods of others for compensation. **Public warehouses** hold themselves out to serve the public generally, without discrimination.

A building is not essential to warehousing. Thus, an enterprise that stores boats outdoors on land is engaged in warehousing, for it is engaged in the business of storing goods for hire.

2. Rights and Duties of Warehouses

The rights and duties of a warehouse are for the most part the same as those of a bailee under a mutual benefit bailment.[1] A warehouse is not an insurer of goods. A warehouse is liable for loss or damage to goods stored in its warehouse when the warehouse is negligent.[2]

(a) Statutory Regulation. The rights and duties of warehouses are regulated by the UCC, Article 7. Article 7 was revised in 2003 and 32 states have adopted the revised version.[3] The purpose of revision was to provide a framework for the future development of electronic documents of title and to update the article for modern times in light of state, federal, and international developments, including the need for medium and gender neutrality. For example, the term utilized to designate a person engaged in storing goods for hire under Article 7 is *warehouseman*.[4] The revised act uses the term *warehouse*.[5] In addition, most states have passed warehouse acts defining the rights and duties of warehouses and imposing regulations. Regulations govern charges and liens, bonds for the protection of patrons, maintenance of storage facilities in a suitable and safe condition, inspections, and general methods of transacting business.

(b) Lien of Warehouse. The public warehouse has a lien against the goods for reasonable storage charges.[6] It is a **specific lien** in that it attaches only to the property on which the charges arose and cannot be asserted against any other property of the same owner in the possession of the warehouse. However, the warehouse may make a lien carry over to other goods by noting on the receipt for one lot of goods that a lien is also claimed for charges on the other goods. The warehouse's lien for storage charges may be enforced by sale after due notice has been given to all persons who claim any interest in the stored property.

3. Warehouse Receipts

A **warehouse receipt** is a written acknowledgment or record of an acknowledgment by a warehouse (bailee) that certain property has been received for storage from a named person called a **depositor** (bailor). The warehouse receipt is a memorandum of the contract between the **issuer**, the warehouse that prepares the receipt, and the depositor. No particular form is required, but usually the receipt (record) will provide:

> *(1) the location of the warehouse where the goods are stored, (2) the date of issuance of the receipt, (3) the consecutive number of the receipt, (4) information on the negotiability of the receipt, (5) the rate of storage and handling charges, (6) a description of the goods or the packages containing them, and*

[1] U.C.C. §7-204.

[2] General contract principles also apply. For example, in *Williamson v. Strictland & Smith Inc., 673 S.E.2d 858 (Ga. App. 2009)*, a warehouser successfully sued an onion farmer for breach of contract when the warehouser was unable to fill a large order because the majority of the farmer's onions stored at the warehouse were rotten.

[3] Revised Article 7 (2003) has been adopted by Alabama, Arizona, Arkansas, California, Colorado, Connecticut, Delaware, Hawaii, Idaho, Illinois, Indiana, Iowa, Kansas, Maryland, Minnesota, Mississippi, Montana, Nebraska, Nevada, New Hampshire, New Jersey, New Mexico, North Carolina, North Dakota, Oklahoma, Pennsylvania, Rhode Island, Tennessee, Texas, Utah, Virginia, and West Virginia. For more modern statutory drafting, the revised edition converts subparagraph designations from numbers to letters. For example, U.C.C. §7-307(1) is designated as Rev. U.C.C. §7-307(a).

[4] U.C.C. §7-102(1)(h).

[5] Rev. U.C.C. §7-102(a)(13).

[6] U.C.C. §7-209(1). The warehouse's lien provision of the UCC is constitutional as a continuation of the common law lien.

(7) a statement of any liabilities incurred for which the warehouse claims a lien or security interest.[7]

A warehouse receipt (as well as a bill of lading, discussed at a later point in this chapter) is considered a **document of title**—that is, a document that in the regular course of business or financing is treated as evidence that a person is entitled to receive, hold, and dispose of the document and the goods it covers.[8] Under revised Article 7 of the UCC, the term *record* is used in the definition of document of title, reflecting the present commercial reality of the use of electronic records as documents of title, in addition to traditional "written" documents of title inscribed on a tangible medium.[9] The person holding a warehouse receipt or the person specified in the receipt is entitled to the goods represented by the receipt. A warehouse receipt as a document of title can be bought or sold and can be used as security for a loan.

4. Rights of Holders of Warehouse Receipts

The rights of the holders of warehouse receipts differ depending on whether the receipts are nonnegotiable or negotiable.

CPA **(A) Nonnegotiable Warehouse Receipts.** A warehouse receipt in which it is stated that the goods received will be delivered to a specified person is a **nonnegotiable warehouse receipt**. A transferee of a nonnegotiable receipt acquires only the title and rights that the transferor had actual authority to transfer. Therefore, the transferee's rights may be defeated by a good-faith purchaser of the goods from the transferor of the receipt.

(B) Negotiable Warehouse Receipts. A warehouse receipt stating that the goods will be delivered "to the bearer" or "to the order of" any named person is a **negotiable warehouse receipt**.

(1) Negotiation.

If the receipt provides for the delivery of the goods "to the bearer," the receipt may be negotiated by transfer of the document. If the receipt provides for delivery of the goods "to the order of" a named individual, the document must be indorsed[10] and delivered by that person in order for the document to be negotiated.

(2) Due Negotiation.

If a receipt is duly negotiated, the person to whom it is negotiated may acquire rights superior to those of the transferor. A warehouse receipt is "duly negotiated" when the holder purchases the document in good faith without notice of any defense to it, for value, in an ordinary transaction in which nothing appears improper or irregular.[11] The holder of a duly negotiated document acquires title to the document and title to the goods.[12] The holder also acquires the direct obligation of the issuer to hold or deliver the goods according to the terms of the warehouse receipt. The rights of a holder of a duly negotiated document cannot be defeated by the surrender of the goods by the warehouse to the depositor.[13]

It is the duty of the warehouse to deliver the goods only to the holder of the negotiable receipt and to cancel this receipt on surrendering the goods.[14]

[7] U.C.C. §7-202(2)(a)–(i).

[8] U.C.C. §1-201(15).

[9] Rev. U.C.C. §1-201(b)(16). An "electronic" document of title is evidenced by a record consisting of information stored in an electronic medium. A "tangible" document of title is evidenced by a record consisting of information that is inscribed on a tangible medium.

[10] The spelling *endorse* is commonly used in business. The spelling *indorse* is used in the U.C.C.

[11] U.C.C. §7-501(4).

[12] U.C.C. §7-502(1).

[13] For electronic documents of title, Revised Article 7, Section 7-106, includes a list of how a party becomes a holder, and the result is that Article 7 creates a new concept of "control." That is, a holder who has control of a document of title (as evidenced by a record that may be electronic) has all the rights of a holder. The Revised Article states:

a. A person has control of an electronic document of title if a system employed for evidencing the transfer of interests in the electronic document reliably establishes that person as the person to which the electronic document was issued or transferred,

b. A system satisfies subsection (a) and a person is deemed to have control of an electronic document of title, if the electronic document is created, stored, and assigned in such a manner that:
   1. a single authoritative copy of the document exists which is unique, identifiable, and, except as otherwise provided in paragraphs (4), (5), and (6), unalterable.
   2. the authoritative copy identifies the person asserting control as:
      A. the person to which the document was issued; or
      B. if the authoritative copy indicates that the document has been transferred, the person to which the document was most recently transferred;
   3. the authoritative copy is communicated to and maintained by the person asserting control or its designated custodian;
   4. copies or amendments that add or change an identified assignee of the authoritative copy can be made only with the consent of the person asserting control;
   5. each copy of the authoritative copy and any copy of a copy is readily identifiable as a copy that is not the authoritative copy; and
   6. any amendment of the authoritative copy is readily identifiable as authorized or unauthorized.

[14] U.C.C. §7–403(3).

The rights of a purchaser of a warehouse receipt by due negotiation are not cut off by the fact that (1) an original owner was deprived of the receipt in "bearer" form by misrepresentation, fraud, mistake, loss, theft, or conversion or (2) a bona fide purchaser bought the goods from the warehouse.

A purchaser of a warehouse receipt who takes by due negotiation does not cut off all prior rights. If the person who deposited the goods with the warehouse did not own the goods or did not have power to transfer title to them, the purchaser of the receipt is subject to the title of the true owner. Accordingly, when goods are stolen and delivered to a warehouse and a warehouse receipt is issued for them, the owner of the goods prevails over the due-negotiation purchaser of the warehouse receipt.

Study Figure 22-1, and note all of the features of a negotiable warehouse receipt in the context of the following. **For Example,** Latham and Loud (L&L) sporting goods manufacturers' representatives in Cleveland, Ohio, hijacked a truckload of ice skates from Bartlett Shoe and Skate Company of Bangor, Maine. L&L warehoused the skates at the Northern Transfer Company warehouse, and received a negotiable warehouse receipt. Jack Preston, a large sporting goods retailer who had had previous business dealings with L&L and believed it to be operated by honest individuals, made a bona fide purchase of the receipt. Bartlett, the true owner, discovered that the skates were at Northern's warehouse and informed Northern of the hijacking. Northern delivered the skates to Bartlett; Latham and Loud have fled the country. Preston believed he was entitled to delivery of the skates because he acquired the negotiable receipt by due negotiation and informed Northern of his status before delivery of the skates to Bartlett. He contemplated legal action against Northern. Preston, however, is not entitled to the skates. Ordinarily, a purchaser of a warehouse receipt obtained by due negotiation takes title to the document and title to the goods. However, an exception exists in the case of theft. Thus, because of the theft by L&L, Preston's rights have been cut off by the true owner in this case. When conflicting claims exist, the warehouse can protect itself by instituting proceedings under UCC §7-603 to ascertain the validity of the conflicting claims.

CPA **(c) Warranties.** The transferor of a negotiable or nonnegotiable warehouse receipt makes certain implied warranties for the protection of the transferee. These warranties are that (1) the receipt is genuine, (2) its transfer is rightful and effective, and (3) the transferor has no knowledge of any facts that impair the validity or worth of the receipt.[15]

5. Field Warehousing

Ordinarily, stored goods are placed in a warehouse belonging to the warehouse company. In other instances, the owner of goods, such as a manufacturer, keeps the goods in the owner's own storage area or building. The warehouse may then take exclusive control over the area in which the goods are stored and issue a receipt for the goods just as though they were in the warehouse. Such a transaction has the same legal effect with respect to other persons and purchasers of the warehouse receipts as though the property were in fact in the warehouse. This practice is called **field warehousing** because the goods are not taken to the warehouse but remain "in the field."

The purpose of field warehousing is to create warehouse receipts that the owner of the goods may pledge as security for loans. The owner could, of course, have done this by actually placing the goods in a warehouse, but this would have involved the expense of transportation and storage.

CPA 6. Limitation of Liability of Warehouses

A warehouse may limit liability by a provision in the warehouse receipt specifying the maximum amount for which the warehouse can be held liable. This privilege is subject to two qualifications. First, the customer must be given the choice of storing the goods without such limitation if the customer pays a higher storage rate, and, second, the limitation must be stated for each item or for each unit of weight.[16] **For Example,** Chisholm Ltd., a Canadian Corporation, delivered ham products for storage to the Fulton Market Cold Storage Co.'s Chicago warehouse.

[15] U.C.C. §7-507. These warranties are in addition to any that may arise between the parties by virtue of the fact that the transferor is selling the goods represented by the receipt to the transferee. See Chapter 25 for a discussion of seller's warranties.

[16] U.C.C. §7-204(2); *Lobel v. Samson Moving & Storage, Inc.*, 737 N.Y.S.2d 24 (A.D. 2002).

FIGURE 22-1 ***Negotiable Warehouse Receipt***

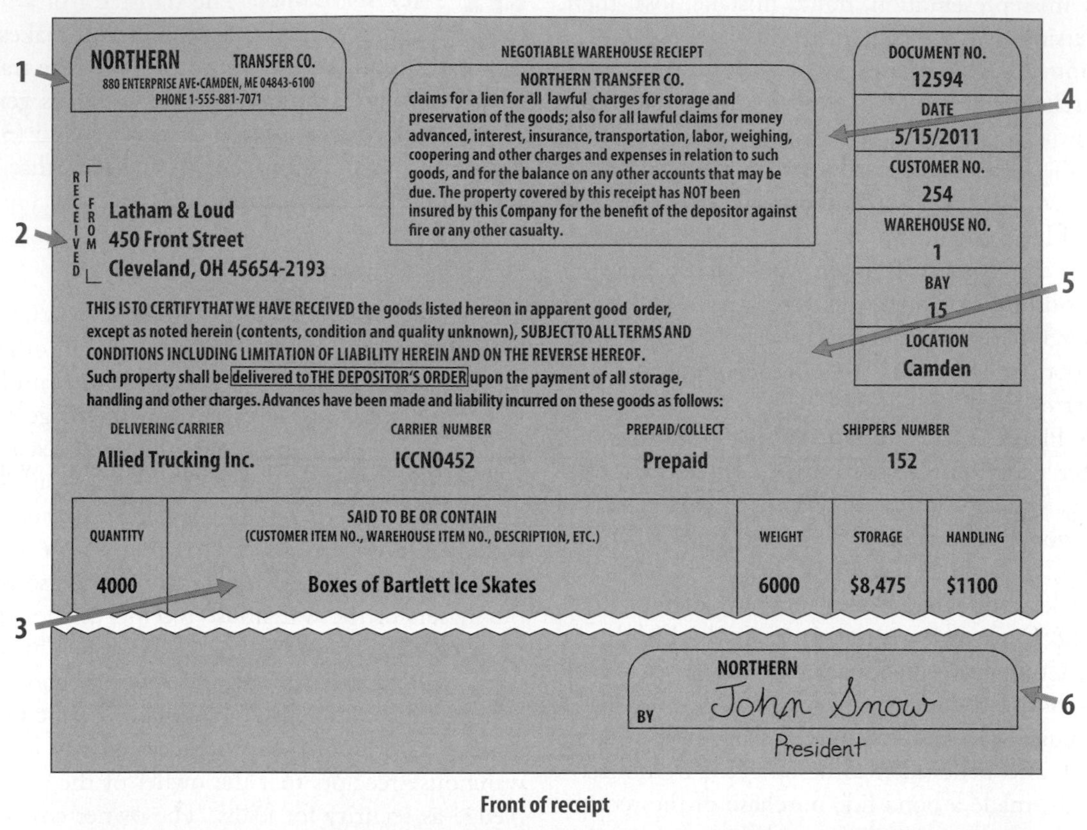

NORTHERN TRANSFER CO.
880 ENTERPRISE AVE•CAMDEN, ME 04843-6100
PHONE 1-555-881-7071

NEGOTIABLE WAREHOUSE RECIEPT

NORTHERN TRANSFER CO.
claims for a lien for all lawful charges for storage and preservation of the goods; also for all lawful claims for money advanced, interest, insurance, transportation, labor, weighing, coopering and other charges and expenses in relation to such goods, and for the balance on any other accounts that may be due. The property covered by this receipt has NOT been insured by this Company for the benefit of the depositor against fire or any other casualty.

DOCUMENT NO. 12594
DATE 5/15/2011
CUSTOMER NO. 254
WAREHOUSE NO. 1
BAY 15
LOCATION Camden

RECEIVED FROM
Latham & Loud
450 Front Street
Cleveland, OH 45654-2193

THIS IS TO CERTIFY THAT WE HAVE RECEIVED the goods listed hereon in apparent good order, except as noted herein (contents, condition and quality unknown), SUBJECT TO ALL TERMS AND CONDITIONS INCLUDING LIMITATION OF LIABILITY HEREIN AND ON THE REVERSE HEREOF. Such property shall be delivered to THE DEPOSITOR'S ORDER upon the payment of all storage, handling and other charges. Advances have been made and liability incurred on these goods as follows:

DELIVERING CARRIER	CARRIER NUMBER	PREPAID/COLLECT	SHIPPERS NUMBER
Allied Trucking Inc.	ICCNO452	Prepaid	152

QUANTITY	SAID TO BE OR CONTAIN (CUSTOMER ITEM NO., WAREHOUSE ITEM NO., DESCRIPTION, ETC.)	WEIGHT	STORAGE	HANDLING
4000	Boxes of Bartlett Ice Skates	6000	$8,475	$1100

NORTHERN
BY John Snow
President

Front of receipt

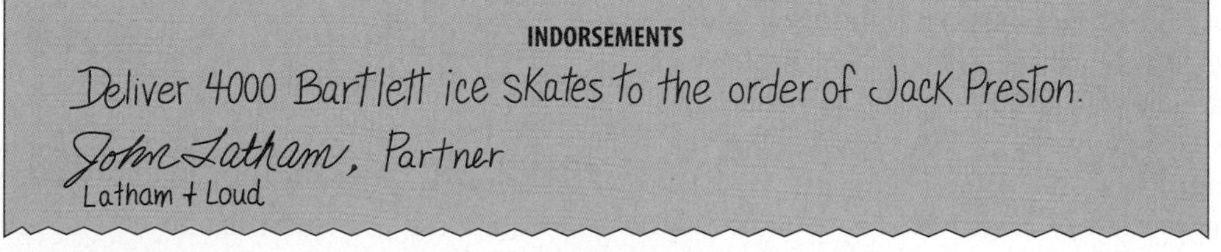

INDORSEMENTS

Deliver 4000 Bartlett ice skates to the order of Jack Preston.
John Latham, Partner
Latham + Loud

Reverse side

(1) Warehouse, (2) depositor, (3) goods, (4) warehouse's lien, (5) negotiable delivery terms, (6) warehouse's authorized agent. A negotiable warehouse receipt contains a promise to deliver the goods to the bearer or to the order of the depositor, unlike a nonnegotiable warehouse receipt, which promises only to deliver them to the depositor.

Fulton issued a warehouse receipt to Chisholm, stating in part:

> *Section 10(e): "in the event of loss, damage or destruction to stored goods for which the warehouseman is legally liable, storer declares and agrees that the warehouseman's liability for damages shall be limited to 50¢ per pound."* (id.)

The ham products were damaged due to freezer burn and Fulton sought to "work with" Chisholm to resolve the claim. When Chisholm would not budge off its demand for full compensation for the damage, Fulton reverted to the "fifty cents per pound" limitation of liability clause of the warehouse receipt. The limitation of liability clause based on the unit of weight of "50¢ per pound" was enforced by the court.[17]

General contract law determines whether a limitation clause is a part of the contract between the warehouse and the customer. **For Example,** warehouse Eastern Warehousing, Inc., and customer Delavau, Inc., executed a comprehensive contract for storage of a nutritional supplement after extensive negotiations between Eastern's chief operating officer and Delavau's president. The goods were damaged due to a leaking warehouse roof. Eastern was unsuccessful in its argument that the contract was formed when the goods were subsequently delivered to the warehouse and a preprinted warehouse receipt containing a limitation-of-liability provision was given to the customer's driver. The court ruled that the terms of the receipt were not part of the contract of the parties, and awarded Delavau $1,358,601 in damages.[18]

B. Common Carriers

The purpose of a bailment may be transportation. In this case, the bailee may be a common carrier.

7. Definitions

A **carrier** of goods is an individual or organization undertaking the transportation of goods regardless of the method of transportation or the distance covered. The **consignor** or shipper is the person who delivers goods to the carrier for shipment. The **consignee** is the person to whom the goods are shipped and to whom the carrier should deliver the goods.

A carrier may be classified as a common carrier, a contract carrier, or a private carrier. A **common carrier** holds itself out as willing to furnish transportation for compensation without discrimination to all members of the public who apply, assuming that the goods to be carried are proper and facilities of the carrier are available. A **contract carrier** transports goods under individual contracts, and a **private carrier** is owned and operated by the shipper. **For Example,** a truck fleet owned and operated by an industrial firm is a private carrier. Common carrier law or special bailment law applies to common carriers, ordinary bailment law to contract carriers, and the law of employment to private carriers.

The Federal Motor Carrier Safety Administration is the successor agency to the Interstate Commerce Commission and was created under the Interstate Commerce Commission Termination Act (ICCTA).[19] Under the ICCTA, Congress merged the separate classifications of common and contract carrier into one classification termed "motor carrier." However, as is seen in the *Fortunoff* case, the fundamental distinction between the types of carriage remains explicit in the act.

M. Fortunoff of Westbury Corp. v. Peerless Ins., 432 F.3d 127 (2nd Cir. 2005)

The Distinction Continues

M. Fortunoff of Westbury operates a chain of department stores in New York and New Jersey. In March of 1997 it entered into a contract with Frederickson Motor Express, whereby the carrier agreed "as contract carrier and independent contractor…to transfer shipments…as authorized in Carrier's contract carrier permit…issued by the ICC." The contract further provided: "Although carrier is authorized to operate…as a common carrier, each and every shipment tendered to carrier by shipper…shall be deemed to be a tender to carrier as a motor contract carrier…." Fortunoff's goods were damaged in transit, prompting it to make a claim against Frederickson. When the carrier went out of business, Fortunoff asserted the same claim against the carrier's insurer, Peerless Insurance Co., for $13,249.42 under the BMC-32

[17] *Chisholm, Ltd. v. Fulton Cold Storage Company LCC*, 2011 WL 6182347 (N.D. Ill. Dec. 13, 2011).
[18] *Delavau v. Eastern American Trading & Warehousing, Inc.*, 810 A.2d 672 (Pa. Super. 2002).
[19] 49 U.S.C. §13906 (a)(3) (2000) (amended 2005).

Continued

indorsement (the mandatory attachment to all common carrier insurance policies), which was part of Frederickson's insurance policy. From a judgment for Fortunoff, on the ground that the ICCTA mandated the extension of BMC-32 indorsements to all motor carriers, Peerless appealed.

JUDICIAL OPINION

CARDAMONE, C. J.…[The] question is whether 49 U.S.C. § 13906(a)(3) (2000) (amended 2005), enacted as part of the Interstate Commerce Commission Termination Act of 1995 (ICCTA or Termination Act), to replace the Motor Carrier Act's insurance provisions, allowed the Federal Motor Carrier Safety Administration (agency or FMCSA)—the successor agency to the Interstate Commerce Commission (ICC) in this area of regulation—to continue to distinguish between types of motor carriage when requiring cargo liability insurance.…

Although Congress' aim was to eliminate the separate registration requirements for common and contract carriers, we do not believe that fact is dispositive in this case. Rather, what is most important is the method by which Congress saw fit to implement the Termination Act. With respect to insurance, Congress left it to the Secretary of Transportation's discretion to require cargo liability insurance. As we have stated, § 13906(a)(3) replaced former § 10927(a)(3) and gave the Secretary discretion over whether "a registered motor carrier," including carriers once classified as common or contract, must insure cargo.…

…Congress' creation of one type of motor carrier did not also create only one type of carriage. Indeed, common carriage services, that is, those services offered to the general public at fixed rates without negotiated bilateral contracts, continue to be different from contract carriage services, which are those services performed on an ongoing basis for a shipper pursuant to a contract individualy negotiated at arm's length. This fundamental distinction remains explicit in the terms of the Termination Act. *See* 49 U.S.C § 14101 (2000) (requiring motor carriers to perform common carrier services and permitting them to perform contract carrier services.)

…[R]equiring cargo liability insurance for common carriage but not contract carriage is not an arbitrary distinction. Instead, it makes economic sense because of the different types of services performed, and the customers served, by common carriage. Although the licensing distinction between common and contract carriers was abolished by the ICCTA, such occurred in large part because most carriers had a common carrier certificate and a contract carrier permit and provided both types of services anyway. But the functional distinction between the two types of carriage survives, and is still highly relevant to deciding which motor carriers must have cargo liability insurance.…

In sum, we hold that the FMCSA's discretionary decision to require motor carriers to supply default cargo liability insurance only when performing common carriage services is consistent with the terms of the ICCTA, and the agency's decision is entitled to respect. As a consequence of this ruling we must reverse the district court's judgment in favor of plaintiff Fortunoff.…

[Reversed and remanded]

CASE QUESTIONS

1. State the issue in this case.
2. Can one trucking company engage in both common and contract carriage? What distinguishes a common motor carrier from a contract motor carrier?
3. Did the ICCTA abolish the distinction between the two types of carrier?

8. Bills of Lading

When the carrier accepts goods for shipment or forwarding, the carrier ordinarily issues to the shipper a **bill of lading** in the case of land or water transportation or an **airbill** for air transportation. This instrument is a document of title and provides rights similar to those provided by a warehouse receipt. A bill of lading is both a receipt for the goods and a memorandum of a contract stating the terms of carriage. Title to the goods may be transferred by a transfer of the bill of lading made with that intention.

Bills of lading for intrastate shipments are governed by the Uniform Commercial Code. For interstate shipments, bills of lading are regulated by the Federal Bills of Lading Act (FBLA).[20]

CPA **(A) Contents of Bill of Lading.** The form of the bill of lading is regulated in varying degrees by administrative agencies. Prior to the revisions to Article 7, negotiable bills of lading were printed on yellow paper, and nonnegotiable or straight bills of lading were printed on white paper. This color-coding may continue as commercial practice for those

[20] 49 U.S.C. §81 *et seq.*

documents reduced to written form, but new commercial practices will evolve regarding the use of "records."[21]

As against the good faith transferee of the bill of lading, a carrier is bound by the recitals in the bill as to the contents, quantity, or weight of goods.[22] This means that the carrier must produce the goods that are described or pay damages for failing to do so. This rule is not applied if facts appear on the face of the bill that should keep the transferee from relying on the recital.

(b) Negotiation. A bill of lading is a **negotiable bill of lading** when by its terms the goods are to be delivered "to the bearer" or "to the order of" a named person.[23] Any other bill of lading, such as one that consigns the goods to a named person, is a **nonnegotiable** or **straight bill of lading**. Like transferees of warehouse receipts who take by due negotiation, holders of bills of lading who take by due negotiation ordinarily also acquire title to the bills and title to the goods represented by them.

Rights of a transferee are defeated by the true owner, however, when a thief delivers the goods to the carrier and then negotiates the bill of lading. The thief had no title to the goods at any time.

(c) Warranties. By transferring for value a bill of lading, whether negotiable or nonnegotiable, the transferor makes certain implied warranties to the transferee. The transferor impliedly warrants that (1) the bill of lading is genuine, (2) its transfer is rightful and is effective to transfer the goods represented by it, and (3) the transferor has no knowledge of facts that would impair the validity or worth of the bill of lading.[24]

9. Rights of Common Carrier

A common carrier of goods has the right to make reasonable and necessary rules for the conduct of its business. It has the right to charge such rates for its services to yield it a fair return on the property devoted to the business of transportation.

As security for unpaid transportation and service charges, a common carrier has a lien on goods that it transports. The carrier's lien also secures demurrage, the costs of preservation of the goods, and the costs of sale to enforce the lien.[25]

10. Duties of Common Carrier

A common carrier is required (1) to receive and carry proper and lawful goods of all persons who offer them for shipment as long as the carrier has space, (2) to furnish facilities that are adequate for the transportation of freight in the usual course of business and to furnish proper storage facilities for goods awaiting shipment or awaiting delivery after shipment, (3) to follow the directions given by the shipper, (4) to load and unload goods delivered to it for shipment, but the shipper or consignee may assume this duty by contract or custom, and (5) to deliver the goods in accordance with the shipment contract.

Goods must be delivered at the usual place of delivery at the specified destination. When goods are shipped under a negotiable bill of lading, the carrier must not deliver the goods without obtaining possession of the bill, properly indorsed. When goods are shipped under a straight bill of lading, the carrier may deliver the goods to the consignee or the consignee's agent without receiving the bill of lading unless notified by the shipper to deliver the goods to someone else. If the carrier delivers the goods to the wrong person, the carrier is liable for breach of contract and for the tort of conversion.

CPA 11. Liabilities of Common Carrier

When goods are delivered to a common carrier for immediate shipment and while they are in transit, the carrier is absolutely liable for any loss or damage to the goods unless it can prove that the loss or damage was due solely to one or more of the following excepted causes: (1) an act of God, meaning a natural phenomenon that is not reasonably foreseeable, (2) an act of a public enemy, such as the military forces of an opposing government, as distinguished from ordinary robbers, (3) an act of a public authority, such as a health officer removing goods from the carrier, (4) an act of the shipper, such as fraudulent labeling or defective packing, or (5) the inherent nature of the goods, such as those naturally tending to spoil or deteriorate.

[21] The U.C.C. contains no provision regulating the form of the bill of lading and the use of records, including electronic tracking, now covered under Revised Article 7. This means that new commercial practices will evolve.

[22] U.C.C. §7-301(1).

[23] U.C.C. §7-104(1)(a).

[24] U.C.C. §7-507; F.B.L.A., 49 U.S.C. §§114, 116. When the transfer of the bill of lading is part of a transaction by which the transferor sells the goods represented thereby to the transferee, there will also arise the warranties that are found in other sales of goods.

[25] U.C.C. §7-307(1); F.B.L.A., 49 U.S.C. §105.

(A) Carrier's Liability for Delay. A carrier is liable for losses caused by its failure to deliver goods within a reasonable time. **For Example,** J.B. Hunt Transport, Inc., "lost" a shipment of boxed Christmas cards specially packaged for Target Stores, Inc., by the shipper, Paper Magic, Inc. The goods were shipped on October 16, 1998, and the invoice valued them at $130,080.48. Hunt located the shipment on February 5, 1999, and Target refused the goods because it was well after Christmas and the goods were worthless to Target. The cards were worthless to Paper Magic because they were packaged with Target's private label. The court found that awarding the shipper the invoice value was a permissible award under the Carmack Amendment to the Interstate Commerce Act.[26]

The carrier, however, is not liable for every delay. The shipper assumes the risk of ordinary delays incidental to transporting goods.

(B) Limitation of Liability of Carrier. In the absence of a constitutional or statutory prohibition, a common carrier generally has the right to limit its liability by contract.

Common carriers operating interstate may limit their liability for the negligent loss of consigned items to a stated dollar amount, such as $100 per package. Shippers, however, must be given a reasonable opportunity to select excess liability coverage for the higher value of their shipment, with payment of higher freight charges.[27]

The Carmack Amendment to the Interstate Commerce Act governs the liability of carriers for loss or damage in the interstate shipment of goods.[28] Shippers displeased with liability limitations permitted carriers under the Carmack Amendment may not sue a carrier under any state statute if the statute in any way enlarges the responsibility of a carrier for loss or damage to the goods.[29] The Carmack Amendment provides the exclusive remedy for loss or damage, and its purpose is to provide uniformity in the disposition of claims brought under a bill of lading or waybill. An insurer, as a subrogee of the owner or shipper, has standing to sue the carrier under a bill of lading.[30] The *Tronosjet* case involved a claim under the Carmack Amendment and a carrier's limitation of liability.

Tronosjet Maintenance, Inc. v. Con-way Freight, Inc., 2011 WL 3322800 (S.D. Tex. Aug. 2, 2011)

Damage to Cargo $165,000: Carrier Only Has to Pay $819.71: Can That Be Right?

On March 11, 2009, a Straight Bill of Lading (BOL) was issued by Con-way Freight, Inc., for a shipment of cargo from Canada to the United States. The BOL identified the shipper as the Tronosjet Maintenance, Inc., and the consignee as Montex Drilling, Fort Worth, Texas. The "SPECIAL AGREEMENT" box for declaring value and agreeing to pay for excess liability was blank. The BOL identified the cargo as three crates of landing gear. On March 13, 2009, the cargo was picked up in St. John, New Brunswick, Canada. On March 17, 2009, the cargo was transloaded to another trailer, carried from Canada across the border to the United States. On March 19, 2009, the cargo was transloaded to another trailer and physical damage to the crates was noted. On March 23, 2009, the damaged cargo was delivered to Montex Drilling in Fort Worth, Texas. Tronosjet seeks to recover $165,000 as full damages under the Carmack Amendment. Con-way claims that it owes just $819.71 because the claim is subject to the limitation of liability set forth in the BOL and Tariff CNWY 199.

JUDICIAL OPINION

LAKE, D. J.…Historically, a carrier could limit its liability under the Carmack Amendment by (1) maintaining a tariff filed with the Interstate Commerce Commission (I.C.C.), (2) obtaining the shipper's written agreement as to its choice of liability, (3) giving the shipper a reasonable

[26] *The Paper Magic Group, Inc. v. J.B. Hunt Transport, Inc.*, 318 F.3d 458 (3d Cir. 2003). See also *National Hispanic Circus, Inc. v. Rex Trucking*, 414 F.3d 546 (5th Cir. 2005).

[27] In *Sassy Doll Creations Inc. v. Watkins Motor Lines Inc.*, 331 F.3d 834 (11th Cir. 2003), the carrier was held liable for the full value of a lost shipment of perfume, $28,273.60, rather than $10,000.00, the carrier's established limitation of its liability. The bill of lading prepared by the carrier contained a declared value box, which the shipper filled in. However, the document did not contain any space for requesting excess liability coverage and thus did not give the shipper a reasonable opportunity to select a higher level of coverage as required by the Carmack Amendment to the Interstate Commerce Act.

[28] 49 U.S.C. §11707.

[29] *Dugan v. FedEx Corp.*, 2002 WL 31305208 (C.D. Cal. Sept. 26, 2002).

[30] *Onebeacon Insurance Co. v. Haas Industries, Inc.*, 634 F.3d 1092 (9th Cir. 2011).

Continued

opportunity to choose between two or more levels of liability, and (4) issuing a receipt or BOL prior to moving the shipment.

...

In 1995 Congress added a requirement that carriers "provide to the shipper, on request of the shipper, a written or electronic copy of the rate, classification, rules, and practices upon which any rate applicable to a shipment, or agreed to between the shipper and the carrier, is based." *Id.* (quoting I.C.C. Termination Act of 1995, Pub. L. No. 104–88.... Instead of maintaining a tariff in compliance with the I.C.C., a motor carrier must now, at the shipper's request, provide the shipper with "a written or electronic copy of the rate, classification, rules, and practices upon which any rate applicable to a shipment, or agreed to between the shipper and the carrier, is based." 49 U.S.C. § 14706(c)(1) (B).

[T]he BOL under which the cargo shipped states that "the shipment is received subject to Tariff CNWY–199, Carrier's pricing schedules, terms, conditions, and rules maintained at Carrier's general offices in effect on the date of issue of this Bill of Lading." Because Tronosjet does not dispute that Con-way not only maintained a tariff that incorporated both the limitation of liability at issue and a separate excess valuation charge for full liability, but also published that tariff on its website, and incorporated the tariff by reference into the BOL at issue, the court concludes that Con-way has presented undisputed evidence showing that...Con-way had established rates for different levels of liability and would have made these rates available to Tronosjet upon request.

Con-way Obtained Tronosjet's Written Agreement and Gave Tronosjet Reasonable Opportunity to Choose Between Two or More Levels of Liability

Con-way argues that Tronosjet could have elected to declare a value for its shipment and pay excess liability charges pursuant to the Special Agreement provision contained on the BOL, but that Tronosjet deliberately chose not to do so. Con-way explains that

> *[u]nder the plain terms of the Con-way BOL, Con-way's liability is limited to "CAN$2.00 per pound (CAN$4.41 per kilogram) per individual lost or damaged piece within the shipment, subject to a maximum total liability per shipment of CAN$20,000.00," or if the articles are "other than new articles," Con-way's liability is limited to ($0.10) ten cents (CAN$) per pound.*

Asserting that "[t]he Special Agreement provision on the through bill of lading gave [Tronosjet] a reasonable opportunity to select the level of liability," Con-way argues that by leaving blank the declared value spaces in the Special Agreement box of the BOL, Tronosjet made a deliberate choice not to take advantage of this opportunity but, instead, agreed to the limitation of liability contained in the Con-way tariff.

...

[T]he shipper must have had both reasonable notice of the liability limitation and the opportunity to obtain information necessary to make a deliberate and well-informed choice, and the carrier must have obtained the shipper's written agreement.... . Both the BOL and the applicable Con-way tariff clearly state that absent a declared value, Con-way's liability is limited. The court concludes that these statements on both the BOL issued for the shipment at issue and the applicable Con-way tariff provide sufficient notice of the limitation of liability and sufficient opportunity to shippers to reject that limitation by declaring the value of the shipment and agreeing to pay excess liability charges.... Accordingly, the court concludes that the BOL and tariff that Con-way has presented provide undisputed evidence that Con-way [gave]...Tronosjet a reasonable opportunity to choose between two or more levels of liability, and obtaining Tronosjet's written agreement to Con way's limitation of liability....

[Judgment for Con-way]

QUESTIONS

1. Did Tronosjet declare the value of the cargo of three crates of landing gear in the "SPECIAL AGREEMENT" box of the BOL?
2. Did the trucking firm have an obligation under the ICC Termination Act of 1995 to affirmatively notify Tronosjet that, absent a declared value, Con-way's liability was limited?
3. Is it "right" that the motor carrier caused $165,000 in damages to the cargo and that a court of law determined that the shipper's claim is limited to $819.71?

(c) Notice of Claim. The bill of lading and applicable government regulations may require that a carrier be given notice of any claim for damages or loss of goods within a specified time, generally within nine months.

(d) COD Shipment. A common carrier transporting goods under a COD (cash on delivery) shipment may not make delivery of the goods without first receiving payment. If it does, it is liable to the shipper for any resulting loss. Thus, if a FedEx or UPS driver were to accept a bad check from a consignee on a COD shipment, the carrier would be liable to the shipper for the amount owed.

There are two forms of COD payments in addition to cash—certified and cashier's checks.

(E) Rejected Shipments. When a common carrier tenders delivery of consigned goods to a consignee that refuses to accept the delivery, the carrier is no longer a common carrier but becomes a warehouse. When the carrier-turned-warehouse receives new shipping instructions from the owner, its status again changes to that of a common carrier.

(F) Complexities in Intercontinental and Domestic Shipping. In intercontinental ocean-to-inland shipping, carriers may or may not know whether they are dealing with an intermediary, such as a freight forwarding company rather than a cargo owner, or what legal obligations the cargo owner and intermediary have agreed upon. Moreover, the number of times goods change hands in the course of this intermodal transportation of goods adds to the complexities regarding liability limitations and other bills-of-lading issues such as forum selection clauses. **For Example,** James Kirby, Ltd, an Australian manufacturer, hired International Cargo Control (ICC) to arrange for the delivery of machinery from Australia to Huntsville, Alabama. The bill of lading that ICC issued to Kirby designated Savannah, Georgia, as the discharge port and Huntsville, Alabama, as the ultimate destination, and set ICC's liability limitation lower than the cargo's true value, using the default liability rule in the Carriage of Goods by Sea Act (COGSA) of $500 per package for the sea leg and a higher amount for the land leg. The bill also contained what is known as the "Himalaya Clause," which extends liability limitations to downstream carriers and contractors. When ICC hired a German shipping company, Hamburg Süd, to transport the containers, Hamburg Süd issued its own bill of lading to ICC. That bill of lading also adopted COGSA's default rule, extended it to any land damages, and extended it in a Himalaya Clause to "all agents… (including inland) carriers…." Hamburg Süd hired Norfolk Southern Railway (NS) to transport the machinery some 366 miles from Savannah to Huntsville. The train derailed, causing some $1.5 million in damages. Kirby sued NS for the full value of its loss, and NS, claiming the protections of the ICC and Hamburg Süd bills of lading, asserted that it owed just $500 per container. The U.S. Supreme Court held that "when it comes to liability limitations for negligence resulting in damage, an intermediary [ICC and Hamburg Süd] can negotiate reliable and enforceable agreements with the carrier it engages,"[31] thus upholding NS's limited liability of $500 per container. U.S. courts have also recognized the rule that a freight forwarder has a limited agency to bind a cargo owner to a forum selection clause by accepting a carrier's bill of lading.[32] The COGSA governs the terms of bills of lading by ocean carriers engaged in foreign trade. It does not limit the parties' ability to adopt forum-selection clauses.

C. Factors and Consignments

A **factor** is a special type of bailee who sells consigned goods as though the factor were the owner of those goods.

12. Definitions

Entrusting a person with the possession of property for the purpose of sale is commonly called **selling on consignment**.[33] The owner who consigns the goods for sale is the *consignor*. The person or agent to whom they are consigned is the factor or *consignee*; this individual may also be known as a **commission merchant**. A consignee's compensation is known as a **commission** or **factorage**. **For Example,** *consignor* Rolly Tasker Sails Co., Ltd. (RTS) would ship sails from Thailand to the *consignee*, Bacon & Associates of Annapolis, Maryland, with a bill of lading and an "invoice price" for each sail. Mrs. Bacon would then set her "retail fair market value price." Once a set of sails was sold,

[31] *Norfolk Southern Ry. Co. v. Kirby*, 543 U.S. 1433 (2004).
[32] *Maersk Sealand v. Ocean Express Miami (Quality Print)*, 550 F. Supp. 2d 484 (S.D.N.Y. 2008).
[33] *Amoco Oil Co. v. DZ Enterprises, Inc.*, 607 F. Supp. 595 (S.D.N.Y. 1985).

Mrs. Bacon would deposit a check to the consignor's account at Alex Brown Co. at the invoice price. Her *commission* was the difference between the retail price and the invoice price. This arrangement began in 1971, but began to unravel 27 years later. RTS was successful in its breach of *consignment agreement* lawsuit against Bacon for $345,327 in damages and $78,660 in interest.[34]

13. Effect of Factor Transaction

In a sale on consignment, the property remains the property of the owner-consignor, and the consignee acts as the agent of the owner to pass the owner's title to the buyer. A consignment sale is treated as a sale or return under Article 2 of the Uniform Commercial Code (UCC), and the factor-consignee has full authority to sell the goods for the consignor and can pass title to those goods. Thus, creditors of the consignee can obtain possession of the goods and have a superior right to them over the consignor. If, however, the owner-consignor complies with the security interest and perfection provisions of Article 9 of the UCC (Chapter 34), there is public notice of the consignment, and the goods will be subject to the claims of the owner's creditors, but not to those of the factor-consignee.[35]

If the consignor is not the owner, as when a thief delivers stolen goods to the factor, a sale by the factor passes no title and is an unlawful **conversion**.

D. Hotelkeepers

A hotelkeeper has a bailee's liability with respect to property specifically entrusted to the hotelkeeper's care. In addition, the hotelkeeper has special duties with respect to a guest's property brought into the hotel. The rules governing the special relationship between a hotelkeeper and a guest arose because of the special needs of travelers.

14. Definitions

The definitions of *hotelkeeper* and *guest* exclude lodging of a more permanent character, such as that provided by boardinghouse keepers to boarders.

(A) HOTELKEEPER. A **hotelkeeper** is an operator of a hotel, motel, or tourist home or anyone who is regularly engaged in the business of offering living accommodations to transient persons. In the early law, the hotelkeeper was called an *innkeeper* or a *tavernkeeper*.

(B) GUEST. A **guest** is a transient. The guest need not be a traveler or come from a distance. A person living within a short distance of a hotel who engages a room at the hotel and remains there overnight is a guest.

In contrast, a person who enters a hotel at the invitation of a guest or attends a dance or a banquet given at the hotel is not a guest. Similarly, the guest of a registered occupant of a motel room who shares the room with the occupant without the knowledge or consent of the management is not a guest of the motel because there is no relationship between that person and the motel.

15. Duration of Guest Relationship

The relationship of guest and hotelkeeper does not begin until a person is received as a guest by the hotelkeeper. The guest–hotelkeeper relationship does not automatically end when the hotel bill is paid.[36]

The relationship terminates when the guest leaves or ceases to be a transient, as when the guest arranges for a more or less permanent residence at the hotel. The transition from the status of guest to the status of boarder or lodger must be clearly indicated. It is not established by the mere fact that one remains at the hotel for a long period, even though it runs into months.

Circumstances arise when a hotel assumes an obligation to deliver packages to a guest from a person

[34] *Bacon & Associates, Inc. v. Rolly Tasker Sails Co. Ltd. (Thailand)*, 841 A.2d 53 (Md. App. 2004).

[35] Revised Article 2 (1999) modifies the rules on consignments slightly in that all transactions are treated as sales or return or sales on approval unless steps are taken to identify a transaction as a consignment and to comply with state laws on consignment. The new U.C.C. §2-326(a), (b), and (c) provides as follows:

> The provisions of this subsection are applicable even though an agreement purports to reserve title to the person making delivery until payment or resale or uses such words as "on consignment" or "on memorandum." However, this subsection is not applicable if the person making delivery
>
> a. complies with an applicable law providing for a consignor's interest or the like to be evidenced by a sign, or
>
> b. establishes that the person conducting the business is generally known by his creditors to be substantially engaged in selling the goods of others, or
>
> c. complies with the filing provisions of the Article on Second Transactions (Article 9).

[36] *Garrett v. Impac Hotels, LLC*, 87 S.W.3d 870 (Mo. App. 2002).

who is not a guest of the hotel. The hotelkeeper has a bailee's liability for the care of such packages. **For Example,** Richard St. Angelo, vice president of sales for jewelry manufacturer Don-Linn Inc., left two boxes of jewelry prototypes at the front desk of the Westin Hotel with instructions to deliver the boxes to the hotel's guest from Dillard's Inc., a national department store. This delivery took place. Thereafter, a Dillard's representative notified St. Angelo that Dillard's review of the products was complete and he could pick up the boxes at the hotel but specified no location. St. Angelo and the Westin staff later searched for the boxes, but they were never found. The manufacturer's lawsuit against the Westin asserting a breach of bailment was not successful. St. Angelo was not a guest at the Westin, thus the obligation assumed for the care of the packages initially left at the Westin was not as a hotelkeeper but a bailee. When the Westin surrendered the packages to Dillard's group, it completed its bailment agreement. No bailment or any other legal obligation between Don-Linn and the Westin was shown to exist with regard to the return of the jewelry prototypes.[37]

16. Hotelkeeper's Liability for Guest's Property

With respect to property expressly entrusted to the hotelkeeper's care, the hotelkeeper has a bailee's liability. At common law, the hotelkeeper was absolutely liable for damage to, or loss of, a guest's property unless the hotelkeeper could show that the damage or loss was caused solely by an act of God, a public enemy, an act of a public authority, the inherent nature of the property, or the fault of the guest.[38]

In most states, statutes limit or provide a method of limiting the common law liability of a hotelkeeper. The statutes may limit the extent of liability, reduce the liability of a hotelkeeper to that of an ordinary bailee, or permit the hotelkeeper to limit liability by contract or by posting a notice of the limitation. Some statutes relieve the hotelkeeper from liability when the guest has not complied with directions for depositing valuables with the hotelkeeper.[39] A hotelkeeper must substantially comply with such statutes in order to obtain their protection. The *Ippolito* case involved the application of a statute allowing hotels to limit common law liability for the loss of guests' property.

Ippolito v. Hospitality Management Associates, 575 S.E. 2d 562 (S.C. App. 2003)

Holiday Inn: We Complied With the Innkeeper's Statute! Ippolitos: No, You Didn't

While traveling from Florida to Connecticut, Mr. and Mrs. Ippolito stopped in Walterboro, South Carolina, and paid for a room at a Holiday Inn. At the hotel, Mr. Ippolito signed a registration card on which was written, " The management is not responsible for any valuables not secured in safety deposit boxes provided at the front office." In addition to the language on the registration card, notice that the hotel had safety deposit boxes available for guests' valuables was also printed on the pouch that enclosed the key-card to the Ippolitos' room. After bringing their luggage to the room, the Ippolitos walked to a nearby restaurant, and they returned approximately 40 minutes later. Upon their return, they noticed that pieces of their luggage, which contained jewelry valued at over $500,000 and approximately $8,000 in cash, were missing. The Ippolitos sued the innkeeper, alleging their property loss resulted from "...the negligence, gross negligence, reckless, willful, wanton and careless action..." of the innkeeper, including "...failing to post proper notices as required under South Carolina law."

The state's innkeeper statute requires the innkeeper to post notice in a "conspicuous manner" in the room occupied by the guest, and the guest must deposit money and jewels in the office safe. The Ippolitos testified that they did not see any notice of safety deposit boxes posted in their room. Police officer Sadler testified that, although he made no mention of it in his police report, he saw a notice posted on the back of the hotel room door indicating that the innkeeper had safety deposit boxes available. The jury awarded the Ippolitos $350,000 in actual damages. However, the jury found that

[37] *Don-Linn Jewelry Co. v. The Westin Hotel Co.*, 877 A.2d 621 (R.I. 2005).
[38] *Cook v. Columbia Sussex Corp.*, 807 S.W.2d 567 (Tenn. App. 1991).
[39] *Chappone v. First Florence Corp.*, 504 S.E.2d 761 (Ga. App. 1998). But see *World Diamond Inc. v. Hyatt Corp.*, 699 N.E.2d 980 (Ohio App. 1997), where the court held that when special arrangements have been made between the innkeeper and the guest, the innkeeper is liable for the loss of any property so received when the loss is caused by the innkeeper's negligence.

Continued

the Ippolitos were 40 percent comparatively negligent, and reduced the award to $210,000. The hotel appealed.

JUDICIAL OPINION

HEARN, C. J.... At trial, Mrs. Ippolito testified that, prior to the disappearance of their belongings, she looked around the hotel room for notice of the availability of hotel safety deposit boxes for her valuables, but saw no such notice. Mr. Ippolito also testified he did not see any notice of the availability of safety deposit boxes posted in the room; however, he admitted that if such notice was posted, he may have overlooked it. Despite not seeing a notice in the room, Mr. Ippolito testified he was aware that Innkeeper provided safety deposit boxes, but he chose not to request a box from the Innkeeper because "[he] felt that the less anybody knew what [he] had[,] the better."

Innkeeper provided testimony from several of its former and current employees regarding its security procedures and its dedication to adhering to those procedures, particularly for providing guests with notice of the availability of safety deposit boxes. Officer Arthur McTeer Sadler, who investigated the incident, also testified on Innkeeper's behalf, claiming that although he made no mention of it in his incident report, he saw a notice posted on the back of the hotel room door indicating Innkeeper had safety deposit boxes available.

...

LAW/ANALYSIS

Initially, we note this is a matter of first impression in South Carolina. Although our Innkeeper's Statute has been in place for over a century, until now, no appellate court in our state has interpreted the statute's meaning. S.C.Code Ann. § 45-1-40 (1976).

The first portion of the South Carolina Innkeeper's Statute states that Innkeepers who post a conspicuous notice in guests' rooms requiring guests to lock their doors, leave their keys at the office, and deposit money and jewels in the Innkeeper's safety deposit box are not liable for the loss of any baggage, money, or jewels left in the room. *Id.* Specifically, the statute states:

Whenever an innkeeper shall post and keep posted in a ***conspicuous manner*** *in the room occupied by any guest a notice requiring such guest to bolt the door of his room, or leaving his room to lock the door and leave the keys at the office, and also to deposit such money and jewels as are not ordinarily carried upon the person in the office safe, and the guest shall neglect to comply with the requirements of such notice, the innkeeper shall not be liable for the loss of any baggage of such guest which may be lost or stolen from his room or for the loss of any money or jewels not deposited in the safe.*

Id. *(emphasis added)*

...

Accordingly, if an innkeeper fails to post notice...the innkeeper's liability is not limited.

Innkeeper first argues the trial court erred in denying its... motion because it complied with the statute's notice requirements, thereby limiting its liability for property missing from the Ippolitos' hotel room. We disagree.

...

Here, the Ippolitos testified that neither of them saw any conspicuously posted notice in their room indicating that the hotel had safety deposit boxes available in which they could store their valuables. Although testimony from Officer Sadler, as well as several of Innkeeper's current and former employees, contradicts this evidence, the existence of conflicting evidence precludes us from finding as a matter of law that Innkeeper complied with the statute.

...

For the foregoing reasons, the trial court's decision is *[Affirmed]*

QUESTIONS

1. Did the innkeeper post a notice in the guests' room, in a conspicuous manner, of the availability of safety deposit boxes for valuables?
2. What is the effect of an innkeeper's failure to post a "conspicuous notice" in a guest's room?

17. Hotelkeeper's Lien

The hotelkeeper has a lien on the baggage of guests for the agreed charges or, if no express agreement was made, for the reasonable value of the accommodations furnished. Statutes permit the hotelkeeper to enforce this lien by selling the goods of the guests at a public sale. The lien of the hotelkeeper is terminated by (1) the guest's payment of the hotel charges, (2) any conversion of the guest's goods by the hotelkeeper, or (3) final return of the goods to the guest.

18. Boarders or Lodgers

The hotelkeeper owes only the duty of an ordinary bailee of personal property under a mutual benefit bailment to those persons who are permanent boarders or lodgers rather than transient guests.

A hotelkeeper has no lien on property of boarders or lodgers, as distinguished from guests, in the absence of an express agreement creating such a lien. A number of states, however, have adopted legislation giving a lien to keepers of boardinghouses or lodging houses.

LawFlix

Nine to Five (1980) (PG)

At the heart of the twists and turns in this boss/secretary caper are the warehouse receipts an executive is using to embezzle from his company. Analyze what the executive was doing with the documents.

MAKE THE CONNECTION

SUMMARY

A warehouse stores the goods of others for compensation and has the rights and duties of a bailee in an ordinary mutual benefit bailment. A warehouse issues a warehouse receipt to the depositor of the goods. This receipt is a document of title that ordinarily entitles the person in possession of the receipt to receive the goods. The warehouse receipt can be bought, sold, or used as security to obtain a loan. A nonnegotiable warehouse receipt states that the goods received will be delivered to a specified person. A negotiable warehouse receipt states that the goods will be delivered "to the bearer" or "to the order of " a named person. If a negotiable warehouse receipt is duly negotiated, the transferee may acquire rights superior to those of the transferor. A warehouse may limit its liability for loss or damage to goods resulting from its own negligence to an agreed valuation of the property stated in the warehouse receipt, provided the depositor is given the right to store the goods without the limitation at a higher storage rate.

A common carrier of goods is in the business of transporting goods received from the general public. It issues to the shipper a bill of lading or an airbill. Both of these are documents of title and provide rights similar to those provided by a warehouse receipt. A common carrier is absolutely liable for any loss or damage to the goods unless the carrier can show that the loss was caused solely by an act of God, an act of a public enemy, an act of a public authority, an act of the shipper, or the inherent nature of the goods. The carrier may limit its liability in the same manner as a warehouse.

A factor is a special type of bailee who has possession of the owner's property for the purpose of sale. The factor, or consignee, receives a commission on the sale.

A hotelkeeper is in the business of providing living accommodations to transient persons called guests. Subject to exceptions, at common law, hotelkeepers were absolutely liable for loss or damage to their guests' property. Most states, however, provide a method of limiting this liability. A hotelkeeper has a lien on the property of the guest for the agreed charges.

LEARNING OUTCOMES

After studying this chapter, you should be able to clearly explain:

A. Warehousers

LO.1 Identify and explain all of the features of a negotiable warehouse receipt

See the example of the bona fide purchase of a warehouse receipt of 4,000 pairs of ice skates on p. 409.

See Figure 22-1 in p. 410.

B. Common Carriers

LO.2 List and explain the differences between the three types of motor carriers of goods

See the *Fortunoff* case and distinctions made between "common" and "contract" carriers, pp. 411–412.

LO.3 Explain a common carrier's liability for loss or damage to goods

See the *Tronosjet* case applying the Carmack Amendment rule on carrier liability, pp. 414–415.

C. Factors and Consignments

LO.4 Identify and explain the role of each of the persons or business entities involved in the sale of goods on consignment

See the Rolly Tasker Sails example involving breach of a consignment agreement on pp. 416–417.

D. Hotelkeepers

LO.5 Describe a hotelkeeper's liability for loss of a guest's property

See the *Ippolito* case for a discussion of the common law rule on liability for loss of a guest's property and application of a statutory exemption, pp. 418–419.

KEY TERMS

airbill
bill of lading
carrier
commission merchant
commission
common carrier
consignee
consignor
contract carrier
conversion
depositor
document of title
factor
factorage
field warehousing
guest
hotelkeeper
issuer
negotiable bill of lading
negotiable warehouse receipt
nonnegotiable bill of lading
nonnegotiable warehouse receipt
private carrier
public warehouses
selling on consignment
specific lien
straight bill of lading
warehouse
warehouse receipt

QUESTIONS AND CASE PROBLEMS

1. What social forces are involved in the rule of law governing the liability of a common carrier for loss of freight?

2. American Cyanamid shipped 7,000 vials of DPT—a vaccine for immunization of infants and children against diphtheria, pertussis, and tetanus—from its Pearl River, New York, facility to the U.S. Defense Department depot in Mechanicsburg, Pennsylvania, by New Penn Motor Express, a common carrier. Cyanamid's bill of lading included a "release value," which stated the value of the property was declared as not exceeding $1.65 per pound. Cyanamid's shipment weighed 1,260 pounds. The bill of lading accepted by New Penn on picking up the DPT vaccine on February 6 also clearly stated that the shipment contained drugs and clearly warned to "protect from freezing." The bill further recited "rush…must be delivered by February 8, 1989." New Penn permitted the vaccine to sit in an unheated uninsulated trailer while it gathered enough other merchandise to justify sending a truck to Mechanicsburg. The DPT vaccine was delivered on February 10 in worthless condition, having been destroyed by the cold. New Penn admitted it owed $2,079 in damages pursuant to the bill of lading ($1.65 × 1,260 lb.). Cyanamid claimed that the actual loss was much greater, $53,936.75. It stated that because New Penn

breached its contract with Cyanamid, it could not invoke the benefits of that same contract, namely, the release value clause.

Was it ethical for New Penn to hold the vaccine while waiting for enough merchandise to justify the trip? How would you decide the case? [*American Cyanamid Co. v. New Penn Motor Express, Inc.*, 979 F.2d 301 (3d Cir.)]

3. Compare the liens of carriers, warehouses, and hotels in terms of being specific.
4. Compare the limitations of the liability of a warehouse and of a hotelkeeper.
5. Compare warehouse receipts and bills of lading as to negotiability.
6. Doyle Harms applied to his state's Public Utilities Commission for a Class B permit authorizing performance as a common carrier. Doyle testified that it was not his intention to haul in a different direction than he was already going, stating in part:

   > *No way, that's not what I'm asking for. I've got enough business of my own, it's just the times when you get done with a sale at the end of the day and you've got a half load and somebody else has a half load, then you'd be able to help each other out. It's kind of the name of the game in my mind.*

   He also testified that the application was so he could haul cattle for his own customers. State law defines a common carrier as "a motor carrier which holds itself out to the general public as engaged in the business of transporting persons or property in intrastate commerce which it is accustomed to and is capable of transporting from place to place in this state, for hire." Its property is "devoted to the public service." Should Doyle Harms be issued a common carrier permit? [*In re Harms,* 491 N.W.2d 760 (S.D.)]
7. Motorola manufactured cell phones for Nextel of Mexico at its facility in Plantation, Florida. Nextel used Westwind International to arrange transportation of the cell phones. Westwind utilized Transpro Logistics to administer the transportation process and Transpro entered a Broker Transportation Agreement (BTA) with Werner Enterprises, a common carrier, to transport the phones from Florida to Texas on a regular basis. The BTA incorporated Werner's tariff giving shippers the option of selecting Carmack Liability full-value coverage or the carrier's limitation of liability of a maximum of $200,000 per truckload shipment. In its contract with Nextel, Westwind notified Nextel that third-party carriers might limit their liability for loss, and stated that it would request excess valuation coverage only upon specific written instructions from Nextel. Nextel simply relied on Westwind to handle shipping issues. On October 8, 2004, a shipment of 7,958 cell phones valued at $1,251,673 was stolen from one of Werner's trucks. Werner contended it owed a maximum liability of $200,000 under its tariff. Nextel's insurer, Ace Seguros SA, sued Werner for the full value of the shipment, contending that contracts downstream by Westwind and Transpro cannot be imputed back to Nextel—and that the cargo owner Nextel had not been given the opportunity to choose between two or more levels of liability as required by the Carmack Amendment. Can intermediaries like Westwind and/or Transpro negotiate an enforceable agreement with a carrier it engages? Was Nextel given a reasonable opportunity to choose between two or more levels of liability? Decide. [*Werner Enterprises, Inc. v. Ace Seguros SA,* 554 F.3d 1319 (11th Cir.)]
8. Richard Schewe and others placed personal property in a building occupied by Winnebago County Fair Association, Inc. Prior to placing their property in the building, they signed a "Storage Rental Agreement" prepared by the County Fair Association, which stated: "No liability exists for damage or loss to the stored equipment from the perils of fire...." The property was destroyed by fire. Suit was brought against the County Fair Association to recover damages for the losses on the theory of negligence of a warehouse. The County Fair Association claimed that the language in the storage agreement relieved it of all liability. [*Allstate Ins. Co. v. Winnebago County Fair Ass'n, Inc.*, 475 N.E.2d 230 (Ill. App.)]
9. Buffett sent a violin to Strotokowsky by International Parcel Service (IPS), a common carrier.

Buffett declared the value of the parcel at $500 on the pick-up receipt given him by the IPS driver. The receipt also stated: "Unless a greater value is declared in writing on this receipt, the shipper hereby declares and agrees that the released value of each package covered by this receipt is $100.00, which is a reasonable value under the circumstance surrounding the transportation." When Strotokowsky did not receive the parcel, Buffett sued IPS for the full retail value of the violin—$2,000. IPS's defense was that it was liable for just $100. Decide.

10. Glen Smith contracted with Dave Watson, a common carrier, to transport 720 hives of live bees along with associated equipment from Idabel, Oklahoma, to Mandan, North Dakota. At 9:00 A.M. on May 24, 1984, while en route, Watson's truck skidded off the road and tipped over, severely damaging the cargo. Watson notified Smith about what had happened, and Smith immediately set out for the scene of the accident. He arrived at 6:00 P.M. with two bee experts and a Bobcat loader. They were hindered by the turned-over truck on top of the cargo, and they determined that they could not safely salvage the cargo that evening. The next day, an insurance adjuster determined that the cargo was a total loss. The adjuster directed a bee expert, Dr. Moffat, to conduct the cleanup; Moffat was allowed to keep the salvageable cargo, valued at $12,326, as compensation. Smith sued Watson for damages. Watson denied liability and further contended that Smith failed to mitigate damages. Decide. [*Smith v. Watson,* 406 N.W.2d 685 (N.D.)]

11. Garrett and his wife checked into the St. Louis Airport North Holiday Inn on March 29, taking advantage of the hotel's "Park and Fly" package, which provided one night of lodging to individuals, provided a shuttle service to Lambert International Airport, and allowed individuals to keep a vehicle on the hotel's parking lot for up to two weeks. When the Garretts returned from their vacation on April 17, they discovered that their vehicle was stolen. They sued the hotel, contending that a special relationship of an innkeeper and guest was created by the "Park and Fly" marketing package, and that the hotel's knowledge of criminal activity on its parking lot created a duty to warn the Garretts, which it failed to do. What status did the Garretts have with the hotel regarding the protection of their vehicle after boarding the plane on their vacation trip? Was there a bailment of the vehicle under the "Park and Fly" marketing package? [*Garrett v. IMPAC Hotels Inc.,* 87 S.W.3d 870 (Mo. App.)]

12. On March 30, Emery Air Freight Corp. picked up a shipment of furs from Hopper Furs, Inc. Hopper's chief of security filled in certain items in the airbill. In the box entitled ZIP Code, he mistakenly placed the figure "61,045," which was the value of the furs. The ZIP Code box was immediately above the Declared Value box. The airbill contained a clause limiting liability to $10 per pound of cargo lost or damaged unless the shipper makes a declaration of value in excess of the amount and pays a higher fee. A higher fee was not charged in this case, and Gerald Doane signed the airbill for the carrier and took possession of the furs. The furs were lost in transit by Emery, and Hopper sued for the value of the furs, $61,045. Emery's offer to pay $2,150, the $10-per-pound rate set forth in the airbill, was rejected. Hopper claimed that the amount of $61,045, which was mistakenly placed in the ZIP Code box, was in fact part of the contract set forth in the airbill and that Emery, on reviewing the contract, must have realized a mistake was made. Decide. [*Hopper Furs, Inc. v. Emery Air Freight Corp.,* 749 F.2d 1261 (8th Cir.)]

13. When de Lema, a Brazilian resident, arrived in New York City, his luggage consisted of three suitcases, an attaché case, and a cylindrical bag. The attaché case and the cylindrical bag contained jewels valued at $300,000. De Lema went from JFK Airport to the Waldorf Astoria Hotel, where he gave the three suitcases to hotel staff in the garage, and then he went to the lobby to register. The assistant manager, Baez, summoned room clerk Tamburino to assist him. De Lema stated, "The room clerk asked me if I had a reservation. I said, 'Yes. The name is José Berga de Lema.' And I said, 'I want a safety deposit box.' He said, 'Please fill out your registration.'" While de Lema was filling out the registration form, paying $300 in cash as an advance, and

Tamburino was filling out a receipt for that amount, de Lema had placed the attaché case and the cylindrical bag on the floor. A woman jostled de Lema, apparently creating a diversion, and when he next looked down, he discovered that the attaché case was gone. De Lema brought suit against the hotel for the value of the jewels stolen in the hotel's lobby. The hotel maintained a safe for valuables and posted notices in the lobby, garage, and rooms as required by the New York law that modifies a hotelkeeper's common law liability. The notices stated in part that the hotel was not liable for the loss of valuables that a guest had neglected to deliver to the hotel for safekeeping. The hotel's defense was that de Lema had neglected to inform it of the presence of the jewels and to deliver the jewels to the hotel. Is the hotel liable for the value of the stolen jewels? [*De Lema v. Waldorf Astoria Hotel, Inc.*, 588 F. Supp. 19 (S.D.N.Y.)]

14. Frosty Land Foods shipped a load of beef from its plant in Montgomery, Alabama, to Scott Meat Co. in Los Angeles via Refrigerated Transport Co. (RTC), a common carrier. Early Wednesday morning, December 7, at 12:55 A.M., two of RTC's drivers left the Frosty Land plant with the load of beef. The bill of lading called for delivery at Scott Meat on Friday, December 9, at 6:00 A.M. The RTC drivers arrived in Los Angeles at approximately 3:30 P.M. on Friday, December 9. Scott notified the drivers that it could not process the meat at that time. The drivers checked into a motel for the weekend, and the load was delivered to Scott on Monday, December 12. After inspecting 65 of the 308 carcasses, Scott determined that the meat was in off condition and refused the shipment. On Tuesday, December 13, Frosty Land sold the meat, after extensive trimming, at a loss of $13,529. Frosty Land brought suit against RTC for its loss. Decide. [*Frosty Land Foods v. Refrigerated Transport Co.*, 613 F.2d 1344 (5th Cir.)]

15. Tate hired Action-Mayflower Moving & Storage to ship his belongings. Action prepared a detailed inventory of Tate's belongings, loaded them on its truck, and received the belongings at its warehouse, where they would be stored until Tate asked that they be moved. Months later, a dispute arose, and Tate asked Action to release his property to a different mover. Tate had prepaid more than enough to cover all charges to this point. Action refused to release the goods and held them in storage. After allowing storage charges to build up for 15 months, Action sold Tate's property under the warehouser's public sale law. Tate sued Action for damages. Decide. [*Tate v. Action-Mayflower Moving & Storage, Inc.*, 383 S.E.2d 229 (N.C. App.)]

CPA QUESTIONS

1. A common carrier bailee generally would avoid liability for loss of goods entrusted to its care if the goods are:
   a. Stolen by an unknown person.
   b. Negligently destroyed by an employee.
   c. Destroyed by the derailment of the train carrying them due to railroad employee negligence.
   d. Improperly packed by the party shipping them.
2. Under a nonnegotiable bill of lading, a carrier who accepts goods for shipment must deliver the goods to:
   a. Any holder of the bill of lading.
   b. Any party subsequently named by the seller.
   c. The seller who was issued the bill of lading.
   d. The consignee of the bill of lading.
3. Under the UCC, a warehouse receipt:
   a. Is negotiable if, by its terms, the goods are to be delivered to bearer or to the order of a named person.
   b. Will not be negotiable if it contains a contractual limitation on the warehouse's liability.
   c. May qualify as both a negotiable warehouse receipt and negotiable commercial paper if the instrument is payable either in cash or by the delivery of goods.

d. May be issued only by a bonded and licensed warehouser.

4. Under the Documents of Title Article of the UCC, which of the following acts may limit a common carrier's liability for damages to the goods in transit?

a. Vandalism

b. Power outage

c. Willful acts of third person

d. Providing for a contractual dollar liability limitation

Nature and Form of Sales

learningoutcomes

After studying this chapter, you should be able to

LO.1 Define a sale of goods and explain when UCC Article 2 applies to contracts

LO.2 Distinguish between an actual sale of goods and other types of transactions in goods

LO.3 Describe how contracts are formed under Article 2, and list the differences in formation standards between the UCC and common law

LO.4 Explain when a contract for the sale of goods must be in writing

LO.5 List and explain the exceptions to the requirement that certain contracts be in writing

LO.6 Discuss the purpose of the United Nations Convention on Contracts for the International Sale of Goods

Chapters 12 through 20 examined the common law of contracts. That source of contract law applies to contracts whose subject matter is land or services. However, there is another source of contract law, **Article 2** of the Uniform Commercial Code (UCC).

Article 2 was revised substantially by the National Conference of Commissioners on Uniform State Laws (NCCUSL) and the American Law Institute (ALI) in August 2003. Because no state has adopted Revised Article 2, its future remains a question. Revised Article 2 is covered only briefly in this chapter and Chapters 24–27.

UCC Article 2 governs the sale of everything from boats to televisions to compact discs and applies to contracts for the sale of goods. Article 2 exists as a result of the work of businesspeople, commercial transactions lawyers, and legal experts who together have developed a body of contract law suitable for the fast pace of business. Article 2 continues to be refined and modified to ensure seamless laws for transactions in goods across the country.[1]

A. Nature of Sales

A *sale of goods* is defined under Article 2 as transfer of title to tangible personal property for a price.[2] This price may be a payment of money, an exchange of other property, or the performance of services.

The parties to a sale are the person who owns the goods, the seller or vendor, and the person to whom the title is transferred, the buyer or vendee.

CPA 1. Subject Matter of Sales

Goods, as defined under the UCC, consist of all forms of tangible personal property, including specially manufactured goods—everything from a fan to a painting to a yacht.[3] Article 2 does not cover (1) investment securities, such as stocks and bonds, the sale of which is regulated by Article 8 of the UCC; (2) insurance policies, commercial paper, such as checks, and promissory notes because they are regulated under Articles 3 and 4 of the UCC; and (3) real estate, such as houses, factories, farms, and land itself.[4]

(A) Nature of Goods. Article 2 applies not only to contracts for the sale of familiar items of personal property, such as automobiles or chairs, but also to the transfer of commodities, such as oil, gasoline, milk, and grain.[5]

(B) Existing and Future Goods. Goods that are already manufactured or crops already grown and owned by the seller at the time of the transaction are called **existing goods**. All other goods are called **future goods**, which include both goods that physically exist but are not owned by the seller and goods that have not yet been produced, as when a buyer contracts to purchase custom-made office furniture.

2. Sale Distinguished from Other Transactions

Other types of transactions in goods are not covered by Article 2 because they are not transfers of title to the goods.

(A) Bailment. A **bailment** is not a sale because only possession is transferred to a **bailee**. Title to the property is not transferred. (For more information on bailments, their nature, and the rights of the parties, see Chapter 21.) A lease of goods, such as an automobile, is governed by Article 2A of the UCC, which is covered later in Section D of this chapter.

(B) Gift. A **gift** is a gratuitous (free) transfer of the title to property. The Article 2 definition of a sale

[1] The UCC Article 2 (prior to the 2003 revisions) has been adopted in 49 states plus the Virgin Islands and the District of Columbia. Louisiana adopted only Article 1; 1990 Revision of Article 3; 1990 Amendments to Article 4; Article 4A (Funds Transfers); 1995 Revision of Articles 5 and 7; 1994 Revision of Article 8; and 2000 Revision of Article 9. The newest revisions of Article 2 were reconciled in July, 2003. The changes in Revised Article 2 are noted briefly throughout this chapter and Chapters 24–27.

[2] UCC §2-105(1). *General Mills Operations, LLC v. Five Star Custom Foods, Ltd.*, 798 F. Supp. 2d 1148 (D. Minn. 2011); *M K Intern., Inc. v. Central Oil & Supply Corp.*, 87 So.3d 165 (La.App. 2012).

[3] *State v. Cardwell*, 718 A.2d 594 (Conn. 1998) (concert tickets are goods); *In re Grede Foundries, Inc.*, 435 B.R. 593 (W.D. Wisc. 2010) (electricity is a good); *Leal v. Holtvogh*, 702 N.E.2d 1246 (Ohio App. 1998) (transfer of part interest in a horse is a good); *Bergeron v. Aero Sales*, 134 P.3d 964 (Or. App. 2006) (jet fuel is a good); *Rite Aid Corp. v. Levy-Gray*, 894 A.2d 563 (Md. 2006) (prescription drug is a good); *Willis Mining v. Noggle*, 509 S.E.2d 731 (Ga. App. 1998) (granite blocks are goods); *Sterling Power Partners, L.P. v. Niagra Mohawk Power Corp.*, 657 N.Y.S.2d 407 (1997) (electricity is a good); *Gladhart v. Oregon Vineyard Supply Co.*, 994 P.2d 134 (Or. App. 1999) (grape plants bought from nursery are goods); *Dantzler v. S.P. Parks, Inc.*, 40 UCC Rep.Serv.2d 955 E.D. Pa. 1988) (purchase of ticket to amusement ride is not transaction in goods); *Rossetti v. Busch Entm't Corp.*, 87 F. Supp. 2d (E.D. Pa. 2000) (computer software programs are goods); and *Saxton v. Pets Warehouse, Inc.*, 691 N.Y.S.2d 872 (1999) (dog is a good).

[4] However, Article 2 does apply to the sale of rare coins. *Bowers and Merena Auctions, LLC, v. James Lull*, 386 B.R. 261, 65 UCC Rep. Ser. 2d 194 (Haw. 2008).

[5] UCC §2-105(1)–(2). *Venmar Ventilation, Inc. v. Von Weise USA, Inc.*, 68 UCC Serv. 2d 373 (D. Minn. 2009); *Marcus Dairy, Inc. v. Rollin Dairy Corp.*, 67 UCC Rep. Serv. 2d 777 (D. Conn. 2008).

requires that the transfer of title be made for a price. Gifts are not covered under Article 2.[6]

(c) Contract for Services. A contract for services, such as a contract for painting a home, is not a sale of goods and is not covered under Article 2 of the UCC. Contracts for services are governed by common law principles.

(d) Contract for Goods and Services. If a contract calls for both rendering services and supplying materials to be used in performing the services, the contract is classified according to its dominant element. **For Example,** a homeowner may purchase a security system. The homeowner is paying for the equipment that is used in the system as well as for the seller's expertise and installation of that system. Is the homeowner's contract governed by Article 2, or is it a contract for services and covered under the common law of contracts?

If the service element dominates, the contract is a service contract and is governed by common law rather than Article 2. If the goods make up the dominant element of the contract, then the parties' rights are determined under Article 2.[7] In the home security system contract example, the question requires comparing the costs of the system's parts versus the costs of its installation. In some contracts, the equipment costs are minimal, and installation is key for the customer. In more sophisticated security systems, the installation is a small portion of the overall contract price, and the contract would be governed by the UCC.[8] The *Paramount Contracting Co. v. DPS Industries, Inc.* case deals with an interesting analysis of goods vs. services.

Paramount Contracting Co. v. DPS Industries, Inc., 709 S.E.2d 288 (Ga.App. 2011)

Dirt Is Cheap, But It Is Still a Good

Paramount, a civil engineering firm and general contractor, submitted a bid to perform the construction of runway improvements at the Atlanta Hartsfield–Jackson International Airport. Paramount included DPS's quote for supplying the fill dirt for the project in its bid. DPS's written quote described its work as "furnish[ing] and haul[ing]/deliver[ing] borrow dirt from DPS's location to the job site," and specifically excluded the provision of "traffic control, dust control, security and escort services" from the scope of work. The quote provides that the dirt would be delivered for a price of "$140/Truck Load."

After Paramount was awarded the airport project, it contacted DPS about the amount of dirt and numbers of trucks that it would need for the airport project. DPS believed that the parties had a contract, and it sent a letter to Paramount confirming that it was "holding approximately 45,000 [cubic yards] of borrow dirt ready to be hauled in to your project once we receive [the] 10–day notice from you." Paramount did not respond.

Over the next two months, DPS sent other letters to Paramount about their agreement, but Paramount did not respond. After a meeting of executives from the two companies met, Paramount sent the following:

> *[Y]ou insisted that we give commitment to you for buying the dirt before you will give us price [for other work]. This really was a surprise to us.... Also please note that we have never committed to buy all the fill materials from you. In the last meeting you were informed that we intend to purchase some materials from you and it may be through other subcontractors. Our decisions will be conveyed to you as soon as possible.*

Ultimately, Paramount bought the dirt it needed from another vendor. DPS sued Paramount for breach of contract. The jury found for DPS. Paramount appealed.

JUDICIAL OPINION

BLACKWELL, Judge.

The question of formation depends on [whether the contract is] governed by Article 2 of the Commercial Code or the common law. []it is easier, generally speaking, to form a binding contract under Article 2 than under the common law. Article 2 applies only to contracts for the sale of goods, and it does not apply to contracts for the mere provision of services or labor. When a transaction involves both the sale of a good and the provision of services or labor, whether the transaction is governed by Article 2 depends upon

[6] The adoption of a dog from an animal shelter is not the sale of goods. *Slodov v. Animal Protective League*, 628 N.E.2d 117 (Oh. App. 1993).

[7] Trees and shrubs as part of a landscaping contract are sales of goods. *Kaitz v. Landscape Creations, Inc.*, 2000 Mass.App.Div. 140, 2000 WL 694274 (Mass.App.Div.), 42 UCC Rep.Serv.2d 691.

[8] *TK Power, Inc. v. Textron, Inc.*, 433 F. Supp. 2d 1058 (N.D. Cal. 2006), see also *Lesiak v. Central Valley Ag Co-op., Inc.*, 808 N.W.2d 67 (Neb. 2012) (a contract for the sale and application of herbicide was primarily a contract for the sale of the herbicide and was governed by the UCC).

Continued

the "predominant purpose" of the transaction. When the predominant element of a contract is the sale of goods, the contract is viewed as a sales contract and [Article 2] applies, even though a substantial amount of service is to be rendered in installing the goods.

DPS said that the parties contemplated only that DPS would sell and deliver dirt, and DPS urged that Article 2 applies because the sale of goods—the dirt that DPS offered to furnish to Paramount—was the predominant purpose of the contemplated transaction. Paramount, on the other hand, said that the parties also contemplated that DPS would perform other tasks, such as placing and compacting dirt at the construction site.

It was for the jury to weigh the conflicting evidence, resolve this disputed issue of fact, and determine exactly what the contemplated transaction involved. So long as the evidence would permit a rational jury to resolve this issue in a way that would lead to a conclusion that the sale of goods was the predominant purpose of the contemplated transaction.

The evidence is consistent with a finding that the sale of dirt was the predominant purpose of the contemplated transaction. The DPS quote contains representations and warranties about the quality of the dirt. The pricing was based on the quantity of dirt furnished, not the miles driven or time spent to deliver the dirt. DPS did not provide separate pricing for the sale of the dirt and its delivery. Paramount itself characterized the transaction repeatedly as one for the sale and furnishing of dirt, not the hauling of dirt.

Paramount relies on testimony that the costs of furnishing and hauling dirt would amount to approximately $70 or $80 per load, and that these costs would include both the expenses of operating a backhoe to load trucks and the expenses of operating the trucks. Paramount says that these cost factors all relate to hauling dirt and establish, therefore, that most of the transaction costs were related to hauling, not furnishing, the dirt.

Under Article 2, dirt is a "good" only if it is severed from the land by the seller, so the separation of dirt from the land is a necessary component of the sale of dirt, not its transportation after sale.

Finally, Paramount asks us to attribute the majority of the costs to hauling on the basis of the conventional wisdom that "dirt is cheap." We decline this invitation. Dirt might well be cheap, but we have no reason to believe that it is free and no basis for knowing just how cheap it is. We are not prepared to speculate that the commercial value of such dirt is negligible, much less to reverse a judgment entered on a jury verdict based on such speculation.

[Judgment affirmed.]

QUESTIONS

1. Why is it important that DPS was not doing anything else at the airport site other than delivering the dirt?
2. Why is the concept of predominant importance important in determining UCC vs. common law contracts?
3. Is the cost of the backhoes needed to remove the dirt considered by the court as part of the services vs. goods cost component of the contract? Why or why not?

One of the critical issues under Article 2 that has resulted from technological advances is whether Article 2 covers computer software included with the sale of a computer, thus subjecting software manufacturers to warranty liability and the damage provisions of the UCC.[9] Whether software would be covered under Article 2 was the most spirited debate in the 2003 revision process.[10] Under the final draft, Revised Article 2 does not cover "information," but information is not defined. Several state legislatures have addressed this issue by modifying their versions of the UCC with a section that establishes that "goods" does not cover the sale of "information" not associated with "goods."[11]

CPA 3. Formation of Sales Contracts

(A) Necessary Detail for Formation. To streamline business transactions, Article 2 of the UCC does not have standards as rigid as the formation standards of common law contracts.

Under the UCC, a contract can be formed even though one or more terms are left open so long as the parties clearly intend to contract.[12] The minimum

[9] *Multi-Tech Systems, Inc. v. Floreat, Inc.*, 47 UCC Rep. Serv. 2d 924 (D. Minn. 2002).

[10] Section 2-103(1)(k) of Revised Article 2 defines goods as follows: *all things movable at the time of identification to a contract for sale. The term includes future goods, specially manufactured goods, the unborn young of animals, growing crops, and other identified things attached to realty as described in §2-107. The term does not include information, the money in which the price is to be paid, investment securities under Article 8, the subject matter of foreign exchange transactions and choses in action.*

[11] Up through 2002, the UCC revisions included provisions on computer information. However, the original amendments to Section 2-102 (4) and (5) never made their way into the final version of UCC 2-102. We are left only with the comment partially quoted here. The comment basically says "it depends" as to whether Article 2 applies, with the dependency on the nature of the contract.

[12] 5 UCC §2-204(3); *Cargill v. Jorgenson Farms*, 719 N.W.2d 226 (Minn. App. 2006). This provision on formation assumes that the agreement the parties do have provides "a reasonably certain basis for giving an appropriate remedy." Price quotations are not considered offers. *Ace American Ins. Co. v. Wendt, LLP*, 724 F. Supp. 2d 899 (N.D. Ill. 2010).

terms required for formation of an agreement under the UCC are the subject matter and quantity (if there is more than one).[13] **For Example,** an agreement that described "the sale of my white Scion" would be sufficient, but an agreement to purchase "some white Scions" would require a quantity in order to qualify for formation.[14] Other provisions under Article 2 can cover any missing terms so long as the parties are clear on their intent to contract. Article 2 has provisions that cover price, delivery, time for performance, payment, and other details of performance in the event the parties agree to a sale but have not discussed or reduced to writing their desires in these areas.[15]

(B) The Merchant versus Nonmerchant Parties. Because Article 2 applies to all transactions in goods, it is applicable to sales by both **merchants** and nonmerchants,[16] including consumers. In most instances, the UCC treats all buyers and sellers alike. However, some sections in Article 2 are applicable only to merchants, and as a result, there are circumstances in which merchants are subject to different standards and rules. Generally, these areas of different treatment reflect the UCC's recognition that merchants are experienced, have special knowledge of the relevant commercial practices, and often need to have greater flexibility and speed in their transactions. The sections that have different rules for merchants and nonmerchants are noted throughout Chapters 24–27.

CPA **(C) Offer.** Just as in common law, the **offer** is the first step in formation of a sales contract under Article 2.[17] The common law contract rules on offers are generally applicable in sales contract formation with the exception of the **firm offer**[18] provision, which is a special rule on offers applicable only to merchants: A firm offer by a merchant cannot be revoked if the offer (1) expresses an intention that it will be kept open, (2) is in a writing, and (3) is signed by the merchant.[19]

The period of irrevocability in a merchant's firm offer cannot exceed three months. If no specific time is given in the merchant's firm offer for its duration, it remains irrevocable only for a reasonable time. A firm offer need not have consideration to be irrevocable for a period of three months. **For Example,** a rain check given by a store on advertised merchandise is a merchant's firm offer. The rain check guarantees that you will be able to purchase two bottles of Windex at $1.99 each for a period specified in the rain check.

For nonmerchants' offers and offers in which the parties want firm offer periods that exceed three months, there must be consideration. In these situations, the parties must create an option contract just like those used in common law contracts (see Chapters 12 and 13).

(D) Acceptance—Manner. Unlike the common law rules on acceptance, which control with great detail the method of **acceptance**, the UCC rules on acceptance are much more flexible. Under Article 2, an acceptance of an offer may be in any manner and by any medium that is reasonable under the circumstances.[20] Acceptance can occur through written communication or through performance, as when a seller accepts an offer for prompt shipment of goods by simply shipping the goods.[21] However, just as under common law, Article 2 requires that if the offer specifies the manner or medium of acceptance, the offer can be accepted only in that manner.

CPA **(E) Acceptance—Timing.** The timing rules of the common law for determining when a contract has been formed are used to determine the formation of a contract under Article 2 with one slight modification. The **mailbox rule** applies under the UCC not just for the use of the same method of communication as that used by the offeror, but also applies when the offeree uses any reasonable method of communication. Under the common law, the offeree had to use the same method of communication in order to have the mailbox rule of acceptance apply. However, a UCC offeree can use any reasonable method for communicating acceptance and still enjoy the priority timing of the

[13] See also, *H.P.B.C., Inc. v. Nor-Tech Powerboats, Inc.*, 946 So.2d 1108 (Fla. App. 2006).

[14] *Griffith v. Clear Lakes Trout Co., Inc.*, 200 P.3d 1162, 67 UCC Rep. Ser. 2d 883 (Idaho 2009).

[15] For information on terms, see UCC §§2-305 (price), 2-307 to 2-308 (delivery), 2-310 (payment), and 2-311 (performance).

[16] *Merchant* is defined in UCC §2-104(1). An operator of a turkey farm is not a merchant with regard to heaters used on turkey farms, only for the turkeys themselves. *Jennie-O-Foods, Inc. v. Safe-Glo Prods. Corp.*, 582 N.W.2d 576 (Minn. App. 1998).

[17] A purchase order is generally considered an offer, but it must have enough information to meet the minimum standards for an offer. *Biotech Pharmacal, Inc. v. International Business Connections, LLC*, 184 S.W.3d 447 (Ark. Ct. App. 2004). *Westlaw E.C. Styberg Engineering Co. v. Eaton Corp.*, 492 F.3d 912 (7th Cir. 2007).

[18] Firm offers are covered in UCC §2-205.

[19] A quotation is a firm offer. *Rich Products Corp. v. Kemutec, Inc.*, 66 F. Supp. 2d 937 (E.D. Wis. 1999), but *see Boydstun Metal Works, Inc. v. Cottrell, Inc.*, 519 F. Supp. 2d 1119 (D. Or. 2007).

[20] UCC §2-206(1). Governs acceptance methods. See *Ardus Medical, Inc. v. Emanuel County Hospital Authority*, 558 F. Supp. 2d 1301 (D. Ga. 2008).

[21] UCC §2-206(1)(b). Shipment of coal in response to an offer is acceptance. *Central Illinois Public Service Co. v. Atlas Minerals, Inc.*, 146 F.3d 448 (7th Cir. 1998). When the buyer and the seller have exchanged two purchase orders and three invoices that set forth price per pound of resin, quantity of resin, place and time of shipment, delivery charges, and the buyer's obligation to pay interest, they have formed a contract. *Bro-Tech Corp. v. Purity Water Co. of San Antonio, Inc.*, 681 F. Supp. 2d 791 (W.D. Tex. 2010).

Ethics & the Law

Restocking at Overstock

Cynthia Hines purchased an ElectroluxOxygen 3 Ultra Canister vacuum from Overstock.com, an online retailer that sells closeout goods. Ms. Hines returned the vacuum and was refunded her full amount, less a $30 restocking fee. She filed suit for breach of contract because she said that Overstock.com advertises that you can return merchandise at no cost and that Overstock.com did not disclose the restocking fee.

However, Overstock.com states that its Web site includes the following, "All retail purchases from Overstock are conducted through Overstock's Internet website. When an individual accesses the website, he or she accepts Overstock's terms, conditions and policies, which govern all of Overstock's customer purchases."

However, users were not required to click on the terms and conditions or to scroll all the way through the terms and conditions in order to use the site. It was possible, then, for a user to miss all the terms, such as a restocking fee.

Evaluate whether the restocking fee was part of the contract. Was it ethical for Overstock.com to impose the terms without users being aware of those terms? Discuss whether Overstock.com should have done more to disclose the restocking charge or put the notice in a different place.*

*Hines v. Overstock.com, Inc., 668 F. Supp. 2d 362 (E.D.N.Y. 2009)

mailbox rule, something that makes an acceptance effective when it is sent. **For Example,** suppose that Feather-Light Brownies sent a letter offer to Cane Sugar Suppliers offering to buy 500 pounds of confectioner's sugar at $1 per pound. Cane Sugar Suppliers faxes back an acceptance of the letter offer. Cane Sugar Suppliers' acceptance is effective when it sends the fax.

CPA (F) ACCEPTANCE—LANGUAGE. Under the common law, the **mirror image rule** applies to acceptances. To be valid acceptances under common law, the language of the acceptance must be absolute, unconditional, and unequivocal; that is, the acceptance under common law must be the mirror image of the offer in order for a contract to be formed. However, the UCC has liberalized this rigid rule and permits formation even in circumstances when the acceptance includes terms that vary from the offer. The following sections explain the UCC rules on differing terms in acceptances. These rules for additional terms in acceptance were eliminated under Revised Article 2.[22]

(1) Additional Terms in Acceptance—Nonmerchants.

Under Article 2, unless an offer expressly specifies that an offer to buy or sell goods must be accepted exactly as made, the offeree may accept an offer and at the same time propose an additional term or terms. The additional term or terms in the acceptance does not result in a rejection as it would under common law. A contract is formed with the terms of the original offer. The additional terms are proposals for addition to the contract and may or may not be accepted by the other party.[23] **For Example,** Joe tells Susan, "I'll sell you my X-box for $150," and Susan responds, "I'll take it. The 'Call of Duty' game is included." Susan has added an additional term in her acceptance. At this point, Joe and Susan have a contract for the sale of the X-box for $150. Whether the "Call of Duty" game is included is up to Joe; Joe is free to accept Susan's proposal or reject it, but his decision does not control whether he has a contract. There is a contract because Susan has made a definite statement of acceptance. To avoid being bound by a contract before she is clear on the terms, Susan should make an inquiry before using the language of acceptance, such as "Would you include the 'Call of Duty' game as part of the sale?" Susan's inquiry is not an acceptance and leaves the original offer still outstanding, which she is free to accept or reject.

(2) Additional Terms in Acceptance—Merchants.

Under Article 2, the use of additional terms in acceptances by merchants is treated slightly differently. The different treatment of merchants in acceptances is the result of a commercial practice known as the **battle of the forms**, which results because a buyer sends a seller a purchase order for the purchase of goods. The seller sends back an invoice to the buyer. Although the buyer and seller may agree on the front of their documents that the subject matter of their contracts is 500 treadmills, the backs of their forms have details on the contracts, often

[22] However, Revised Article 2 has not been adopted widely by the states.

[23] See the Ethics & Law feature on restocking and Overstock.com.

called *boilerplate language*, that will never match. Suppose, for example, that the seller's invoice adds a payment term of "10 days same as cash." Is the payment term now a part of the parties' agreement? The parties have a meeting of the minds on the subject matter of the contract but now have a slight difference in performance terms.

Under Article 2, in a transaction between merchants, the additional term or terms sent back in an acceptance become part of the contract if the additional term or terms do not materially alter the offer and the offeror does not object in a timely fashion.[24] **For Example,** returning to the Joe and Susan example, suppose that they are both now secondary market video game merchants negotiating for the sale and purchase of a used X-box. They would have a contract, and the "Call of Duty" game would be included as part of the sale. Joe could, however, avoid the problem by adding a limitation to his offer, such as "This offer is limited to these terms." With that limitation, Susan would have a contract, but the contract would not include the "Call of Duty" game. Joe could also object immediately to Susan's proposal for the "Call of Duty" game and still have a contract without this additional term.[25]

If the proposed additional term in the acceptance is material, a contract is formed, but the material additional term does not become a part of the contract.[26] **For Example,** if Susan added to her acceptance the statement, "Game system carries one-year warranty," she has probably added a material term because the one-year warranty for a used game system would be unusual in the secondary market and costly for Joe.[27] Again, Joe can avoid this problem by limiting his offer so as to strike any additional terms, whether material or immaterial.

The most significant changes under Revised Article 2 deal with §2-207. Because there were so many confusing circumstances with additional terms, the effect of the new §2-207 is to leave the issues of what is or is not included in a contract to the courts. However, because so many businesses and individuals are using the Internet to contract, they are working out their terms through ongoing and immediate exchanges and questions. The result has been a significant reduction in the number of §2-207 cases.[28]

Figure 23-1 is a graphic picture of the rules on acceptance and contract terms under current Article 2 when additional terms are proposed.

FIGURE 23-1 *Terms in Contracts under UCC Article §2-207*

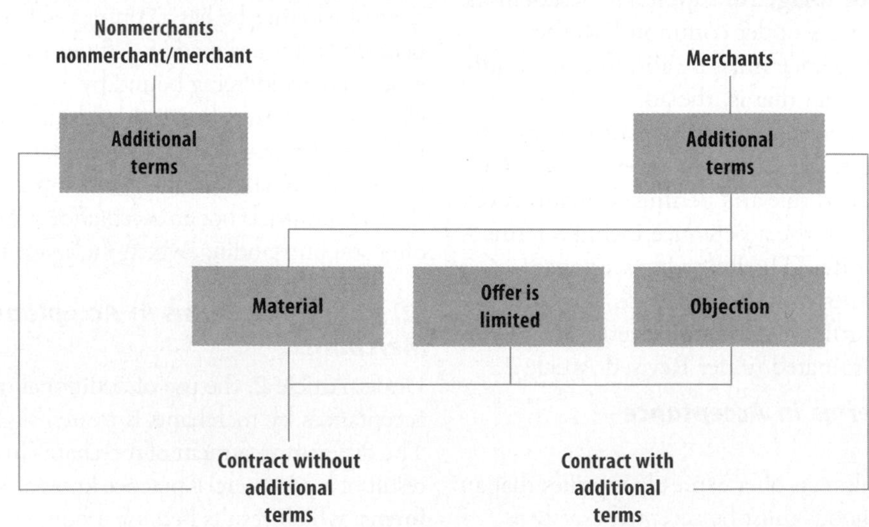

[24] UCC §2-207(2).

[25] *Oakley Fertilizer, Inc. v. Continental Ins. Co.*, 276 S.W.3d 342 (Mo. App. 2009). Revised UCC Article 2 makes changes in the way these additional terms operate. When there is a record of an agreement, with no objection, the terms in the record are the terms of the contract.

[26] Damage limitations clauses are considered material. *Belden Inc. v. American Electronic Components, Inc.*, 885 N.E.2d 751 (Ind. App. 2008). Forum selection clauses are also material. *Hugo Boss Fashions, Inc. v. Sam's European Tailoring, Inc.*, 742 N.Y.S.2d 1 (2002).

[27] A statute of limitations of one year added to the acceptance of an offer is considered a material change because it limits so severely the amount of time for bringing suit on the contract. *American Tempering, Inc. v. Craft Architectural Metals Corp.*, 483 N.Y.S.2d 304 (1985).

[28] Francis J. Mootz III, "After the Battle of the Forms: Commercial Contracting in the Electronic Age," 4 *Journal of Law & Policy for the Information Society* 271, Summer, 2008.

Even without all the UCC provisions on contract terms, an offeror may expressly or by conduct agree to a term added by the offeree to its acceptance of the offer. The offeror may agree orally or in writing to the additional term. There can be acceptance of the additional term by conduct of the parties if the parties just perform their obligations under the contract with knowledge that the term has been added by the offeree.[29]

(3) Conflicting Terms in Acceptance.

In some situations, the offeree has not added a different term from the original offer but has instead proposed terms that contradict the terms of the offer. **For Example,** a buyer's purchase order may require the seller to offer full warranty protection, whereas the seller's invoice may include a disclaimer of all warranties. The buyer's purchase order may include a clause that provides "payment in 30 days same as cash," whereas the seller's invoice may include a term that has "10 days same as cash." Once again, it is clear that the parties intended to enter into a contract, and the subject matter is also clear. The task for Article 2 becomes one of establishing the rules that determine the terms of a contract when both sides have used different forms. However, if there are conflicting terms on the basic requirements (such as price) for formation, the courts may conclude that the parties have not met minds.[30]

When a term of an acceptance conflicts with a term of an offer but it is clear that the parties intended to be bound by a contract, the UCC still recognizes the formation of a contract. The terms that are conflicting cancel each other and are ignored. The contract then consists of the terms of the offer and acceptance that agree. **For Example,** if one party's contract form provided for full warranty protection and the other party's form provided for no warranty protection, the terms cancel each other out, and the parties' contract includes only those warranties provided under Article 2 (see Chapter 25 for a discussion of those warranties). The *C9 Ventures v. SVC-West L.P.* case deals with an issue of acceptance of additional terms as well as other wrinkles and issues in applying the UCC to contracts.

C9 Ventures v. SVC-West, L.P., 202 Cal. App. 4th 1483 136 Cal. Rptr. 3d 550 (Cal. App. 2012)

The Helium That Tanked

SVC–West, L.P. (SVC) did time-share presentations at hotels and ordered helium tanks quite often for balloons. On July 3, 2007, SVC placed a rush order with C9 Ventures (C9) for eight helium-filled tanks used to inflate festive balloons. C9 accepted the order and later that day delivered the tanks.

On the reverse of the invoice was an indemnification provision requiring SVC to indemnify C9 for any loss arising out of the use or possession of the helium-filled tanks. C9 later picked up the tanks, and, weeks later, SVC paid the invoice. SVC had obtained helium-filled tanks from C9 on prior occasions.

The invoice was on a single piece of paper, on the reverse side of which was a section entitled "INDEMNITY/HOLD HARMLESS" (boldface omitted), which stated in part:

> *"Customer agrees to indemnify[,] defend and hold harmless C9 . . . from and against any and all liability, claims, judgments, attorneys fees and cost of . . . every[ ] kind and nature, including, but not limited to injuries or death to persons and damage to property, arising out of the use, maintenance, instruction, operation, possession, ownership or Rental & Decor of the items rented, however cause[d], except claims or litigation arising through the solo [sic] gross negligence or willful misconduct of C9. . . ."*

The reverse side of the invoice also included a section-entitled "LEGAL FEES," which provided, in essence, that in an action to enforce "this Rental & Decor Agreement," the prevailing party would be entitled to recover attorney fees.

Before then, C9 had presented the same or similar invoice to SVC 10 times, but had received the signature of an SVC employee only six times. SVC never attempted to substitute its own form agreement for C9's form.

C9 typically delivered the tanks in the morning when no SVC guests were present, but on July 3, C9's employee, Ernesto Roque, did not arrive at the SVC premises to make the delivery until about 5:00 P.M. Roque asked SVC employee, Zayra Renteria, where to place the eight helium-filled tanks. Renteria, who was expecting the delivery during her shift, instructed Roque

[29] *Panike & Sons Farms, Inc. v. Smith*, 212 P.3d 992 (Idaho 2009).

[30] *Howard Const. Co. v. Jeff-Cole Quarries, Inc.*, 669 S.W.2d 221 (Mo. App. 1984), where the acceptance changed the price, there was not an acceptance but a counteroffer.

Continued

to bring the tanks up to the mezzanine level of the resort, at which point she would inform him where to place them. Roque wrote the following on the invoice, "[N]obody would sign all running around in lobby nobody knew who . . . After accident nobody got signatures." Roque stacked five to seven tanks against the walls next to the service elevator. He was in the process of bringing up another tank when a young boy, whose parents were attending the time-share presentation, ran up to the tanks and hugged one of them, pulling it over. The tank, which was about five feet tall and weighed 130 pounds, fell on the boy's hand. He was hospitalized and underwent surgery for his injuries.

SVC and C9 each paid the boy's family to settle a lawsuit brought to recover for his injuries. C9 filed a cross-complaint against SVC to enforce the indemnification provision on the back ofthe unsigned invoice. The trial court found for C9 and SVC appealed.

JUDICIAL OPINION

FYBEL, Judge.

This case could serve as a question on a law school final examination for a course on the Uniform Commercial Code. As in a law school examination, the facts are undisputed. The question: Is the indemnification provision on the back of the unsigned invoice enforceable against SVC?

The trial court answered the question yes, finding under California Uniform Commercial Code section 2-207, the indemnification provision did not materially alter the contract and therefore became an added term.

We answer the question differently and hold the indemnification provision is not binding on SVC. The summary of our answer is the following. SVC and C9 entered into an oral contract when C9 accepted SVC's telephone order for eight helium-filled tanks. The oral lease was sufficiently definite, although it left open various terms. Under section 2-207, on which the trial court relied, additional terms proposed in an acceptance or confirmation may become terms of the contract in certain situations. Section 2207 is part of division 2 of the California Uniform Commercial Code, and division 2 governs transactions in goods. The oral contract between SVC and C9, however, was a lease of personal property (the helium-filled tanks), and personal property leases are governed by division 10, not division 2, of the California Uniform Commercial Code.

Division 10 of the California Uniform Commercial Code, which governs the oral contract between SVC and C9, does not have an analog to section 2-207. The terms on the back of the unsigned invoice would have become part of the parties' oral contract only if SVC manifested assent to those terms. SVC did not manifest such assent by course of dealing or course of performance, or under basic contract law. SVC did not sign the invoice or otherwise expressly agree to its terms. An unsigned invoice itself is not a contract, and repeated delivery of a particular form does not make the form part of the parties' agreement. Payment of the invoice merely constituted SVC's performance of the obligation under the oral contract to pay for the rental of the helium-filled tanks.

To cover all bases (as one should when answering a law school examination question), we also construe the oral contract between SVC and C9 as if it were a transaction in goods governed by division 2 of the California Uniform Commercial Code and address whether the indemnification provision would have become an additional term under section 2-207, as the trial court found. We conclude it would not. If SVC is not a merchant, the terms of the invoice are considered to be mere proposals for additional terms, which SVC did not accept. If SVC is a merchant, the indemnification provision would not have become part of the contract if the provision materially altered the contract. Because an indemnification provision is deemed a material alteration to an agreement as a matter of law, the indemnification provision on the back of the invoice would not, under section 2-207, become part of the contract between SVC and C9.

We therefore reverse the judgment and remand with directions to enter judgment in SVC's favor. Because we reverse the judgment on which attorney fees were awarded, we also reverse the order awarding attorney fees.

QUESTIONS

1. Why is it important to determine whether the contract involved a sale or lease of goods?
2. Is the indemnification clause material?
3. Would it be important to know if SVC is a merchant? Why?

(g) Defenses to Formation. Article 2 incorporates the common law defenses to formation of contracts by reference to the common law defenses in §1-103 (see Chapter 14 for a full discussion of those defenses). **For Example,** a party to a contract who can establish that the other party engaged in fraud to get the contract formed may cancel the contract and recover for losses that result from any damages for goods already delivered or payment already made.

(1) Unconscionability.

The UCC includes an additional contract defense for parties to a sale contract called *unconscionability*.[31] This section permits a court to refuse to enforce a sales contract that it finds to be **unconscionable**, which is generally defined as grossly unfair.[32] A court may also find a clause or portions of a contract to be unconscionable and refuse to enforce those clauses or sections.[33]

(2) Illegality.

At common law, a contract is void if its subject matter itself is illegal, such as a contract for hire to murder someone. Under the UCC, a contract for the sale of heroin would be void. Likewise, a contract for the sale of a recalled or banned toy would be void.

(3) The Effect of Illegal Sale.

An illegal sale or contract to sell cannot be enforced. As a general rule, courts will not aid either party in recovering money or property transferred under an illegal agreement.

4. Terms in the Formed Contract

As noted earlier, contracts can be formed under Article 2 with terms of performance still missing or open. A contract is formed with just the quantity agreed on, but there are issues that must be resolved if the contract is to be completed. Article 2 has provisions for such missing terms.

CPA **(A) PRICE.** If the price for the goods is not expressly fixed by the contract, the price may be an open term, whereby the parties merely indicate how the price should be determined at a later time. In the absence of any reference to price, the price will be a reasonable price at the time of the delivery of the goods, which is generally the market price.[34]

Parties often use formulas for determining price in sales of goods. The price itself is missing from the contract until the formula is applied at some future time. The so-called **cost plus** formula for determining price has been used a great deal, particularly in commercial contracts. Under this formula, the buyer pays the seller the seller's costs for manufacture or obtaining the goods plus a specified percentage as profit.

The UCC allows contracts that expressly provide that one of the parties may determine the price. In such a case, that party must act in good faith, another requirement under the UCC that applies to merchants and nonmerchants in the formation and performance of their contracts.[35]

CPA **(B) OUTPUT AND REQUIREMENTS CONTRACTS.** The **output contract** and the **requirements contract**[36] do not specify the quantity to be sold or purchased. Instead, the contract amount is what the seller produces or the buyer requires. **For Example,** a homeowner may contract to purchase propane fuel for her winter heating needs. The propane company agrees to sell her the amount of propane she needs, which will vary from year to year according to the winter weather, her time at home, and other factors. Although the open quantity in contracts such as these introduces an element of uncertainty, such sales contracts are valid but subject to two limitations: (1) The parties must act in good faith and (2) the quantity offered or demanded must not be unreasonably disproportionate to prior output or requirements or to a stated estimate. With these restrictions, the homeowner will obtain all of the propane she needs for heating but could not use her particularly beneficial price under her open-quantity contract to purchase additional propane to sell to others.

(C) INDEFINITE DURATION TERM. When the sales contract is a continuing contract, such as one calling for periodic delivery of coal, but no time is set for the life of the contract, the contract runs for a reasonable time. It may be terminated by notice from either party to the other party.

CPA **(D) CHANGES IN TERMS: MODIFICATION OF CONTRACT.** An agreement to modify a contract for the sale of goods is binding even though the modification is not supported by consideration.[37] The modification

[31] UCC §2-302. Teri J. Dobbins, "Losing Faith: Extracting the Implied Covenant of Good Faith from (Some) Contracts", 84 *Oregon Law Rev* 227 (2005). *U.S. Welding, Inc. v. Battelle Energy Alliance, LLC*, 728 F. Supp. 2d 1110 (D.Idaho 2010).

[32] Disparity in bargaining power is an issue but is not controlling. In *Intrastate Piping & Controls, Inc. v. Robert-James Sales, Inc.*, 39 UCC Rep. Serv. 2d 347 (Ill. Cir. Ct. 1999), a clause limiting remedies to replacement of defective pipe with no additional damages was upheld because while the seller was a large, national business and the buyer a small, local business, the contract merely incorporated industry practice in terms of remedies.

[33] An example would be voiding exorbitant interest charges but enforcing the underlying sale.

[34] UCC §2-305(1) provides, "the price is a reasonable price at the time for delivery."

[35] Good faith requires that the party act honestly and, in the case of a merchant, also requires that the party follow reasonable commercial standards of fair dealing that are recognized in the trade. UCC §§1-201(1)(a), 2-103(1)(b).

[36] UCC §2-306; *XTO Energy Inc. v. Smith Production Inc.*, 282 S.W.3d 672 (Tex. App. 2009); *ABC Metals & Recycling Co., Inc. v. Highland Computer Forms, Inc.*, 771 N.W.2d 651(Iowa App. 2009).

[37] UCC §2-209(1); *Horbach v. Kacz Marek*, 934 F. Supp. 981 (N.D. Ill. 1996), aff'd, 388 F.3d 969 (7th Cir. 2002).

is valid so long as the agreement is voluntary. **For Example,** suppose that Chester's Drug Store has agreed to purchase 300 bottles of vitamins from Pro-Life, Inc., at a price of $3.71 per bottle. Pro-Life has experienced substantial cost increases from its suppliers and asks Chester to pay $3.74 per bottle. Chester is not required to agree to such a price increase because it has a valid contract for the lower price. If Chester agrees to the price increase, however, the agreement for the higher price is valid despite the lack of additional consideration on the part of Pro-Life. Chester may agree to the higher price because Pro-Life's price is still much lower than its competitors and Chester has a longstanding relationship with Pro-Life and values its customer service. However, Pro-Life could not threaten to cut off Chester's supply in order to obtain the price increase because that would be a breach of contract and would also be duress that would invalidate Chester's consent to the higher price. (See Chapter 14 for a discussion of duress.)

(E) CONTRADICTING TERMS: PAROL EVIDENCE RULE. The **parol evidence rule** (see Chapter 17 for a complete discussion) applies to the sale of goods, with the slight modification that a writing is not presumed to represent the entire contract of the parties unless the court specifically decides that it does.[38] If the court so decides, parol evidence is not admissible to add to or contradict the terms of the writing. **For Example,** suppose that Ralph Rhodes and Tana Preuss negotiate the sale of Ralph's 1965 Mustang to Tana. During their discussions, Ralph agrees to pay for an inspection and for new upholstery for the car. However, Tana and Ralph sign a simple sales contract that includes only a description of the Mustang and the price. Tana cannot enforce the two provisions because she failed to have them written into their final agreement. The parol evidence rule requires the parties to be certain that everything they want is in their agreement before they sign. The courts cannot referee disputes over collateral agreements the parties fail to put in writing.

If the court decides that the writing was not intended to represent the entire contract, the writing may be supplemented by additional extrinsic evidence, including the proof of additional terms as long as these terms are not inconsistent with the written terms. Parol evidence may also be admitted to interpret contract terms or show what the parties meant by their words. The parol evidence rule also does not prohibit the proof of fraud, misrepresentation, and any other defenses in formation.

(F) INTERPRETING CONTRACT TERMS: COURSE OF DEALING AND USAGE OF TRADE. The patterns of doing business the parties develop through their prior contractual transactions, or **course of dealing**, become part of their contract.[39] These patterns may be used to find what was intended by the express provisions in their contract and to supply otherwise missing terms. **For Example,** if the parties had 10 previous agreements and payment was always made on the 30th day following delivery, that conduct could be used to interpret the meaning of a clause "payment due in 30 days" when the start of the 30 days is not specifically agreed to in the contract.

In addition, the customs of the industry, or **usage of trade**, are adopted by courts in their interpretation of contract terms. **For Example,** suppose that a contract provides for the sale of mohair. There are two types of mohair: adult and kid. Because adult mohair is cheaper and easier to find, industry custom provides that unless the parties specifically place the term *kid* with the term *mohair* in the contract, the contract is one for the sale of adult mohair. Under Article 2, the court need not find that a contract is ambiguous or incomplete in order to examine the parties' pattern of previous conduct as well as industry custom.[40]

5. Bulk Transfers

Bulk transfer law, Article 6 of the UCC, was created to deal with situations in which sellers of businesses fail to pay the creditors of the business and instead use the proceeds of the sale for their own use.

In 1989, the NCCUSL recommended that UCC Article 6 be repealed because it was obsolete and had little value in the modern business world. At the same time, the commissioners adopted a revised version of Article 6 (Alternative B) for adoption by those states that desired to retain the concept for bulk sales. Rather than relying on the bulk sales law, the trend is for suppliers to use UCC Article 9, Secured Transactions, for protection (see Chapter 34).

[38] UCC §2-202.

[39] UCC §2-208. Under Revised Article 2, §2-208 is eliminated for those states that have adopted Revised Article 1 because Revised Article 1 contains the definition for course of performance.

[40] Revised §2-202 provides different rules for the use of extrinsic evidence but still includes "course of performance, course of dealing, or usage of trade" as sources for interpretation of contract terms.

B. Form of Sales Contract

A contract for the sale of goods may be oral or written. However, under the UCC, certain types of contracts must be evidenced by a record or they cannot be enforced in court.

CPA 6. Amount

Whenever the sales price of goods is $500 or more, the sales contract must be evidenced by a record to be enforceable. Under Revised Article 2, this amount has been increased to $5,000.[41] The section of the UCC that establishes this requirement is known as the **statute of frauds**. (For more details on the statute of frauds and its role in common law contracts, see Chapter 17.)

7. Nature of the Writing Required

The requirement for a record for a contract may be satisfied by a complete written contract signed by both parties. Under Article 2, so that the state laws will be consistent with federal laws on electronic signatures (see Chapter 11), the requirement of a writing has been changed to the requirement of a "record." Under Article 2, two merchants can reduce their agreement to a record in much simpler fashion because the detail required under common law is not required to satisfy the UCC standards.

(A) Terms. To satisfy the UCC statute of frauds, the record must indicate that there has been a completed transaction covering certain goods. Specifically, the record must (1) indicate that a sale or contract to sell has been made and (2) state the quantity of goods involved.[42] Any other missing terms may be supplied by reference to Code sections (discussed earlier) or shown by parol evidence.

(B) Signature. The record must be signed or authenticated by the person who is being held to the contract or by the authorized agent of that person. Whatever form of authentication is being used must be put in place in the record with the intention of authenticating the record. The authentication may consist of initials or may be a printed, stamped, electronic, or typewritten signature placed with the intent to authenticate.[43] **For Example,** when you enter into a contract as part of an online transaction, you are generally asked to check a box that states that you understand you are entering into a contract. Once you check that box, a pop-up appears that explains that you are about to charge your credit card or account and that you have agreed to the purchase. These steps are used to authenticate your electronic version of a signature.

The UCC statute of frauds does provide an important exception to the signature requirement for merchants that enables merchants to expedite their transactions. This exception allows merchants to create a confirmation memorandum of their oral agreement as evidence of an agreement. A merchant's *confirmation memorandum* is a letter, memo, or electronic document signed or authenticated by one of the two merchant parties to an oral agreement.[44] This memorandum can be used by either party to enforce the contract. **For Example,** suppose that Ralph has orally agreed to purchase 1,000 pounds of T-bone steak from Jane for $5.79 per pound. Jane sends Ralph a signed memo that reads, "This is to confirm our telephone conversation earlier today. I will sell you 1,000 pounds of T-bone @ $5.79 per pound." Either Ralph or Jane can use the memo to enforce the contract.

A confirming memo, in various forms of communication, sent by one merchant to another results in a binding and enforceable contract that satisfies the statute of frauds. Such a confirmation binds the nonsigning or nonauthenticating merchant, just as if he had signed the letter or a contract. A merchant can object when he receives the confirmation memo, but he must do so immediately because the confirming memo takes effect in 10 days if there is no objection.[45] This confirmation procedure makes it necessary for merchants to watch their communications and all forms of correspondence and to act within 10 days of receiving a confirmation. The *Rosenfeld v. Basquiat* case deals with an issue of whether the writing is sufficient for a contract to be formed.

[41] Under Revised Article 2, the new amount of $5,000 is found at UCC Rev Art 2, §2-201.

[42] *Kelly-Stehney & Assoc., Inc. v. McDonald's Indus. Products, Inc.*, 693 N.W.2d 394 (Mich. 2005).

[43] UCC §§1-201(39), 2-201; *CQ, Inc. v. TXU Min. Co., LP*, 565 F.3d 268 (5th Cir. 2009). Revised Article 2 permits electronic forms and signature and "record" includes e-mail, EDI transmissions, faxes, and printouts of screen pages reflecting transactions.

[44] *Siesta Sol, LLC v. Brooks Pharmacy, Inc.*, 617 F. Supp. 2d 38 (D. R.I. 2007); In re *Sunbelt Grain WKS, LLC*, 406 B.R. 918 (D. Kan. 2009).

[45] A confirmation memo is not effective when there is no underlying agreement or the parties did not agree on the terms. *Cargill Inc. v. Jorgenson Farms*, 719 N.W.2d 226 (Minn.App. 2009).

Rosenfeld v. Basquiat, 78 F.3d 84 (2nd Cir. 1996)

It's Elementary: A Crayon-Scrawled Contract is Good Enough for the Statute of Frauds

Michelle Rosenfeld, an art dealer, alleges she contracted with artist Jean-Michel Basquiat to buy three of his paintings. The works that she claims she contracted to buy were entitled *Separation of the K, Atlas,* and *Untitled Head.* Rosenfeld testified that she went to Basquiat's apartment on October 25, 1982; while she was there, he agreed to sell her three paintings for $4,000 each, and she picked out three. Basquiat asked for a cash deposit of 10 percent; she left his loft and later returned with $1,000 in cash, which she paid him. When she asked for a receipt, he insisted on drawing up a contract and got down on the floor and wrote it out in crayon on a large piece of paper, remarking that some day this contract would be worth money. The handwritten document listed the three paintings, bore Rosenfeld's signature and Basquiat's signature, and stated: "$12,000—$1,000 DEPOSIT = Oct 25 82." Rosenfeld later returned to Basquiat's loft to discuss delivery, but Basquiat convinced her to wait for at least two years so that he could show the paintings at exhibitions. After Basquiat's death, the estate argued that there was no contract because the statute of frauds made the agreement unenforceable. The estate contended that a written contract for the sale of goods must include the date of delivery. From a judgment in favor of the estate, the plaintiff appealed.

JUDICIAL OPINION

CARDAMONE, J.... Because this case involves an alleged contract for the sale of three paintings, any question regarding the Statute of Frauds is governed by the U.C.C. (applicability to "transactions in goods") (contract for $500 or more is unenforceable "unless there is some writing sufficient to indicate that a contract for sale has been made between the parties and signed by the party [charged]"). Under the U.C.C., the only term that *must* appear in the writing is the quantity. See U.C.C. § 2-201.

Beyond that, "[a]ll that is required is that the writing afford a basis for believing that the offered oral evidence rests on a real transaction." The writing supplied by the plaintiff indicated the price, the date, the specific paintings involved, and that Rosenfeld paid a deposit. It also bore the signatures of the buyer and seller. Therefore, the writing satisfied the requirements of § 2-201.

Citing *Berman Stores Co. v Hirsch,* 240 N.Y. 209 (1925), the estate claims that a specific delivery date, if agreed upon, must be in the writing. *Berman Stores* was decided before the enactment of the U.C.C., and was based on the principle that "the note or memorandum... should completely evidence the contract which the parties made." The rule that a specific delivery date is "an essential part of the contract and must be embodied in the memorandum" was rejected by the legislature —at least for sale-of-goods cases—when it enacted the U.C.C. That rule and the statute upon which it was based were repealed to make way for the U.C.C. The U.C.C. "[c]ompletely re-phrased" the provisions of prior legislation and "intended to make it clear that... [t]he required writing need not contain all the material terms."

... Because the writing, allegedly scrawled in crayon by Jean-Michel Basquiat on a large piece of paper, easily satisfied the requirements of § 2-201 of the U.C.C., the estate is not entitled to judgment as a matter of law. It is of no real significance that the jury found Rosenfeld and Basquiat settled on a particular time for delivery and did not commit it to writing.... As a consequence,... the alleged contract is not invalid on Statute of Frauds grounds....

[Judgment reversed]

QUESTIONS

1. Why was the contract required to be in writing?
2. Did the contract comply with the statute of frauds?
3. Does a writing that does not comply with the statute of frauds make the alleged contract void?

(c) Purpose of Execution. A writing or record can satisfy the statute of frauds even though it was not made for that purpose. For example, if a buyer writes to the seller to complain that the goods have not been delivered, there is proof of the contract because the buyer's complaint indicates that there was some kind of understanding or an acknowledgment that there was a sale of those goods

(d) Particular Writings. Formal contracts, bills of sale, letters, and telegrams are common forms of writings that satisfy the record requirement.[46] E-mails, faxes, EDI communications, and verifications through

[46] Contract terms can be pieced together from invoices sent over the period of the agreement and that the buyer paid. *Fleming Companies, Inc. v. Krist Oil Co.,* 324 F. Supp. 2d 933 (W.D. Wi. 2001).

screen printouts will generally satisfy the requirement as to record and authentication so long as they meet minimum formation standards and comply with the requirement of the UCC to specify any quantity. Two or more records grouped together may constitute a record that will be sufficient to satisfy the UCC statute of frauds.[47]

8. Effect of Noncompliance

A sales agreement that does not satisfy the statute of frauds cannot be enforced. However, the oral contract itself is not unlawful and may be voluntarily performed by the parties. The *Home Basket Co. v. Pampered Chef* case deals with issues of formation and writing when the parties communicate by the Internet.

Home Basket Co., LLC v. Pampered Chef, Ltd., 55 UCC Rep. Serv. 2d 792 (D. Kan. 2005)

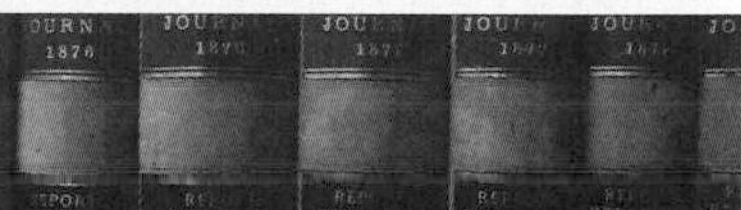

A Real Basket Case

The Greenbrier Basket Company (GBC) (plaintiff) (seller), a goods distributor, entered into a business relationship in October 2003 to sell woven baskets to The Pampered Chef (TPC) (defendant) (buyer). On October 28, 2003, an executive sales agreement was drafted but never signed by the parties. Prior to the October 28, 2003, aborted sales agreement, GBC had accepted purchase orders from TPC.

The ordering process would begin with TPC e-mailing GBC regarding an offer to fill an order. GBC would then go to TPC's Web site and fill out the purchase order using TPC's purchase order management system and would click on the "Accept P.O." button at the end of the terms and conditions field.

Cyndee Pollock (a manager at GBC) would receive offers to purchase goods via e-mail from TPC and would tell an employee, Mark Beal, to accept these purchase orders via TPC's internet site. GBC denies knowing that there were terms and conditions, including a forum selection clause, on the TPC's internet acceptance site. TPC sent Mark Beal an e-mail with an attachment showing him how to use TPC's purchase order management system. The attachment included instructions regarding the use of the purchase order management system, including, in section four, three paragraphs under the title "Accepting and Rejecting Purchase Orders," the relevant portion of which states:

> *Clicking on the Accept P.O. button will cause the terms and conditions of the purchase order to pop-up. The user should review these terms and conditions and click the Accept P.O. button at the bottom of the pop-up screen.... If the purchase order is not acceptable in it's [sic] current form, the user may click on the Reject and Request Changes button. This causes a pop-up window to appear where the user may enter a free-form text describing the reason for rejecting the purchase order and request changes that would make the purchase order acceptable.*

Clause 17 of the Terms and Conditions in TPC's purchase management order system states:

> *This Purchase Order shall be deemed to have been made in Addison, Illinois USA and shall be governed by and construed in accordance with the laws of State of Illinois [sic]. The sole and exclusive jurisdiction for the purpose of resolving any dispute shall be the United States District Court, Northern District of Illinois, Eastern Division.*

When disputes over orders and payments arose, GBC filed suit against TPC in Kansas for breach of contract. TPC moved to dismiss the suit for improper venue.

JUDICIAL OPINION

BROWN, Senior J.... Defendant alleges improper venue because of an allegedly agreed upon forum selection clause. Plaintiff does not dispute that the forum selection clause is valid. Plaintiff instead argues that the forum selection clause was never part of the parties' contract.

TPC's e-mails containing purchase order information constituted an offer to buy baskets. The e-mails consisted of information about the quantity of baskets to be bought, price, shipment information and delivery dates. None of the e-mails had any forum selection clause; however, they did state a specific manner of acceptance:

1. Upon receipt of order, please acknowledge via internet at [website]. By acknowledging this P.O. [purchase order], you also acknowledge the terms and conditions of this P.O.
2. To accept this P.O. via internet, visit [website].

The evidence shows at least nine such e-mail offers. GBC consistently went to the TPC website to accept these offers.

Plaintiff first argues that the e-mail offers are ambiguous because it did not alert GBC to the forum selection clause that had to be accepted on the website. The TPC e-mails state that the way to acknowledge (i.e. accept) the purchase order was to go to the website. The e-mail is not ambiguous as it also

[47] *ReMapp Intern. Corp. v. Comfort Keyboard Co., Inc.*, 560 F.3d 628 (7th Cir. 2009). Letters grouped together satisfy UCC §2-201. *Pepsi-Cola Co. v. Steak 'N Shake, Inc.*, 981 F. Supp. 1149 (S.D. Ind. 1997). Letters and faxes also satisfy the writing requirement. *Den Norske Stats Oljeselskap*, 992 F. Supp. 913 (S.D. Tex. 1998), aff'd, 161 F.3d 8 (5th Cir. 1998).

Continued

alerted GBC that there were terms and conditions associated with acknowledging the P.O. on the website.

GBC next argues that it should not be held to the terms and conditions accepted on the website because plaintiff thought that the e-mails' terms and conditions were all inclusive.

It is a well-established rule of law that contracting parties have a duty to learn the contents of a written contract before signing it, and such duty includes reading the contract and obtaining an explanation of its terms. Therefore, a party who signs a written contract is bound by its provisions regardless of the failure to read or understand the terms, unless the contract was entered into through fraud, undue influence, or mutual mistake.

In determining intent to form a contract, the test is objective, rather than subjective, meaning that the relevant inquiry is the 'manifestation of a party's intention, rather than the actual or real intention.'

This was a website that required action on the part of GBC. Plaintiff objectively agreed to the forum selection clause by scrolling through the terms and conditions and clicking on the "Accept P.O." button. Plaintiff's subjective beliefs that it was the e-mail and not the website terms and conditions that governed the contract are both misplaced and irrelevant. Plaintiff was under a duty to read and understand the terms and conditions prior to clicking the 'Accept P.O.' button as this was the formal acceptance required by TPC's offer to purchase baskets. Failure to read or understand the terms and conditions is not a valid reason to render those provisions nugatory.

Plaintiff next argues that the forum selection clause should not be read into the contract because GBC rejected an Exclusive Sales Agreement containing such a clause. Plaintiff claims that the failure to sign this agreement shows that they did not intend that a forum selection clause be part of the contract. The evidence shows that the Exclusive Sales Agreement was discussed on October 28, 2003. The date of the first e-mail inviting GBC to accept a purchase order was October 7, 2003. Plaintiff's subjective reasons for refusing to sign the Exclusive Sales Agreement are irrelevant as GBC consistently agreed, in an objective manner prior to the Exclusive Sales Agreement, to contracts with the terms and conditions on TPC's website. The Court will not alter the plain terms in the parties' contract because GBC refused to sign the Exclusive Sales Agreement.

Plaintiff also argues that there was no meeting of the minds regarding the forum selection clause on the website. A meeting of the minds requirement is proved when the evidence shows with reasonable definiteness that the minds of the parties met upon the same matter and agreed upon the terms of the contract. Part of clause 17 states 'each shipment received by Buyer from Seller shall be deemed to be only upon the terms and conditions as set forth in this Purchase Order. …' GBC agreed upon these terms and conditions published on TPC's website by clicking the 'Accept P.O.' button and this satisfied the meeting of the minds standard.

The Court holds that the forum selection clause in the terms and conditions on TPC's website are a part of the parties' contract.

The Defendant's Motion to Dismiss due to improper venue is denied. The case is transferred to the United States District Court for Northern District of Illinois, Eastern Division.

QUESTIONS

1. Describe the ordering process between the two parties.
2. Does it matter to the court that neither side ever signed a written agreement?
3. What responsibility does the court impose on those who use Web sites for contracting purposes?

9. Exceptions to Requirement of a Writing

The absence of a writing does not always mean that a sales contract is unenforceable. Article 2 provides some exceptions for the enforceability of certain oral contracts.

CPA **(a) Specially Manufactured Goods.** No record is required when the goods are specially made for the buyer and are of such an unusual nature that they are not suitable forsale in the ordinary course of the seller's business. **For Example,** a manufacturer who builds a stair lift for a two-story home cannot resell the $8,000 device to someone else because it is specially built for the stairs in the buyer's home. The manufacturer could enforce the oral contract against the buyer despite the price being in excess of $500 ($5,000 under Revised Article 2).

For this nonresellable goods exception to apply, the seller must have made a substantial beginning in manufacturing the goods or, if a distributor is the seller, in procuring them before the buyer indicates she will not honor the oral contract.[48]

The stair lift manufacturer, for example, must have progressed to a point beyond simply ordering

[48] *Golden State Porcelain Inc. v. Swid Powell Design Inc.*, 37 UCC Rep. Serv. 2d (N.Y. 1999). Where manufacture has not begun, this exception to the statute of frauds does not apply. *EMSG Sys. Div., Inc. v. Miltope Corp.*, 37 UCC Rep. Serv. 2d 39 (E.D.N.C. 1998).

materials for construction of the lift because those materials could be used for any lift.

CPA **(b) Receipt and Acceptance.** An oral sales contract may be enforced if it can be shown that the goods were delivered by the seller and were both received and accepted by the buyer even if the amount involved is over $500 ($5,000 Revised) and there is no record. The receipt and acceptance of the goods by the buyer makes the contract enforceable despite the statute of frauds issue. The buyer must actually receive and accept the goods. If only part of the goods have been received and accepted, the contract may be enforced only insofar as it relates to those goods received and accepted.[49] **For Example,** suppose that Wayne ordered 700 baseball jackets at a price of $72 each from Pamela. The order was taken over the telephone, and Wayne emphasized urgency. Pamela shipped the 320 jackets she had on hand and assured Wayne the remainder would be finished during the next two weeks. Wayne received the 320 jackets and sold them to a golf tournament sponsor. Wayne refused to pay Pamela because the contract was oral. Wayne must pay for the 320 jackets, but Pamela will not be able to recover for the remaining 380 jackets she manufactured.

CPA **(c) Payment.** An oral contract may be enforced if the buyer has made full payment. In the case of partial payment for divisible units of goods, a contract may be enforced only with respect to the goods for which payment has been made and accepted. In the Pamela and Wayne example, if the circumstances were changed so that Pamela agreed to ship only if Wayne sent payment, then Pamela, upon accepting the payment, would be required to perform the contract for the amount of payment received. If partial payment is made for indivisible goods, such as an automobile, a partial payment avoids the statute of frauds and is sufficient proof to permit enforcement of the entire oral contract.

(d) Admission. An oral contract may be enforced against a party if that party admits in pleadings, testimony, or otherwise in court that a contract for sale was made. The contract, however, is not enforceable beyond the quantity of goods admitted.[50]

Thinking Things Through

Chipping Away at the Contract Terms for Wood Chips

Beginning in the mid-1980s GP and WHI entered into a series of one-year contracts under which WHI supplied wood chips to GP's particle board plant in Gaylord, Michigan. The contract was automatically renewed unless either party gave written notice 60 days before the end of the term. The contracts also permitted either party to terminate a contract at any time with 90 days' notice.

WHI and GP signed a new contract on May 20, 2005 (2005 contract). The contract had a three-year term and a provision for subsequent renewal. It included an early termination clause that permitted either party to terminate the contract after 90 days notice. The contract also contained a clause stating that GP intended to purchase 125,000 tons of wood chips per year but was not required to purchase any minimum quantity.

During the negotiations for the 2005 contract, GP represented that the early termination clause and nonbinding volume clauses were merely generic requirements from GP's legal department and would have no effect on GP's performance. WHI also alleges that both before and after the 2005 contract was signed, GP represented (1) that the early termination clause was subordinate to the clause stating GP's intent to purchase 125,000 tons of wood chips per year, (2) that GP would not exercise the early termination provision during the contract's initial three-year term, and (3) that the contract would be automatically renewed unless WHI defaulted.

In March 2006, GP informed WHI that it was closing the Gaylord plant. It also terminated the 2005 contract and suspended further deliveries of wood chips to the plant. The parties dispute the date on which the decision to close the Gaylord plant was made. WHI alleges that GP knew it would close the plant by October 2004, but repeatedly represented to WHI that there were no plans to close the plant.*

WHI filed suit for breach of contract. GP has responded that the negotiation terms are irrelevant because they were not part of the contract terms and they could not be used as evidence for a breach of contract suit. Who is correct? Is there a breach? Or is there a written contract that does not contain protection for WHI in the event of a plant closure?

**Woodland Harvesting, Inc. v. Georgia Pacific Corporation*, 693 F. Supp. 2f 732 (E.D. Mich. 2010)

[49] *Allied Grape Growers v. Bronco Wine Co.*, 249 Cal.Rptr. 872 (Ct. App. 1988).

[50] *Delta Stat, Inc. v. Michael's Carpet World*, 666 S.E.2d 331 (Va. 2008).

10. Noncode Requirements

In addition to the UCC requirements for contracts that must be evidenced by a record, other statutes may impose requirements. **For Example,** state consumer protection legislation commonly requires that there be a detailed contract and that a copy of it be given to the consumer.

11. Bill of Sale

Regardless of the requirement of the statute of frauds, the parties may wish to execute a writing as evidence or proof of the sale. Through custom, this writing has become known as a **bill of sale**, but it is neither a bill nor a contract. It is merely a receipt orwriting signed by the seller reciting the transfer to the buyer of the title to the described property. A bill of sale can be used as proof of an otherwise oral agreement.

C. Uniform Law for International Sales

The United Nations Convention on **Contracts for the International Sale of Goods (CISG)** applies to contracts between parties in the United States and parties in the other nations that have ratified the convention.[51] The provisions of this convention or international agreement have been strongly influenced by Article 2 of the UCC. The international rules of the convention automatically apply to contracts for the sale of goods if the buyer and seller have places of business in different countries that have ratified the convention. The parties may, however, choose to exclude the convention provisions in their sales contract.

12. Scope of the CISG

The CISG does not govern all contracts between parties in the countries that have ratified it. The CISG does not apply to goods bought for personal, family, or household use.[52] The CISG also does not apply to contracts in which the predominant part of the obligations of the party who furnishes the goods consists of the supply of labor or other services. The CISG has five chapters and 101 articles, and the articles have no titles to them. There is a limited body of case law interpreting the CISG because so many of the decisions under the CISG come through arbitration and other forms of dispute resolution, typical of international commercial arrangements.

D. Leases of Goods

Leases of goods represent a significant part of both contract law and the economy. There are more than $628 billion worth of lease transactions in the United States each year, an amount equal to roughly one-third of all capital investment each year in the United States.[53] One-fourth of all vehicles in the United States are leased. Article 2A of the UCC codifies the law of leases for tangible movable goods. Article 2A applies to any transaction, regardless of form, that creates a lease of personal property or fixtures. Many of the provisions of Article 2 were carried over but changed to reflect differences in style, leasing terminology, or leasing practices.[54] As a practical matter, leases will be of durable goods, such as equipment and vehicles of any kind, computers, boats, airplanes, and household goods and appliances. A **lease** is "a transfer of the right to possession and use of goods for a term in return for consideration."[55]

13. Types of Leases

Article 2A regulates consumer leases, commercial leases, finance leases, nonfinance leases, and subleases. These categories may overlap in some cases, such as when there is a commercial finance lease.

(A) Consumer Lease. A **consumer lease** is made by a merchant lessor regularly engaged in the business of leasing or selling the kinds of goods involved. A consumer lease is made to a natural person (not a corporation) who takes possession of the goods primarily for personal, family, or household use. Each state places a cap on the amount considered a consumer lease. Section 2A-103(f) simply provides that the state should place its own amount in this section with the admonition to place the cap at a level that ensures that

[51] 52 Fed. Reg. 6262 (1987). While the list of adopting countries is always increasing, those countries involved in NAFTA, GATT, and the European Union (EU) (see Chapter 7) have adopted the CISG. For complete text, commentary, and case law on CISG, go to **www.cisg.law.pace.edu**.

[52] The UNIDROIT Principles are often used as guidelines for resolving issues in international consumer contracts. M. J. Bonell, "The CISG, European Contract Law and the Development of a World Contract Law," 56 *American Journal of Comparative Law*, 1–28 (2008).

[53] *Equipment Leasing & Finance Foundation Economic Outlook* (2012).

[54] Forty-nine states (Louisiana has not adopted Article 2A), the District of Columbia, and the Virgin Islands have adopted all or some portions of Article 2A. Not all states have adopted the 1997 version of Article 2A, and some have adopted only selected portions of the 1997 version.

[55] UCC §2A-103(1)(j). The definition of what constitutes a lease is the subject of continuing examination by the UCC Article 2A drafters and the American Law Institute.

vehicle leases will be covered under the law. During the period from 2002 to 2007, there were a number of suits brought by individuals injured in auto accidents against the leasing companies of the drivers who were driving their leased autos at the time they caused an accident. Many states were holding the leasing companies liable for those accidents because they were title holders of the cars. As a result, leasing companies stopped doing business in certain states because of the liability exposure.

In response, the federal government passed legislation that preempted all state laws and limited the liability of vehicle leasing companies to a basic level of liability that was limited to mandatory insurance coverage standards.[56]

(B) Commercial Lease. When a lease does not satisfy the definition of a consumer lease, it may be called a **nonconsumer** or a **commercial lease**. **For Example,** a contractor's one-year rental of a truck to haul materials is a commercial lease.

(C) Finance Lease. A **finance lease** is a three-party transaction involving a lessor, a lessee, and a supplier. Instead of going directly to a supplier for goods, the customer goes to a financier and tells the financier where to obtain the goods and what to obtain. The financier then acquires the goods and either leases or subleases the goods to its customer. The financier-lessor is in effect a paper channel, or conduit, between the supplier and the customer-lessee. The customer-lessee must approve the terms of the transaction between the supplier and the financier-lessor.[57]

14. Form of Lease Contract

The lease must be evidenced by a record if the total of the payments under the lease will be $1,000 or more. The record must be authenticated by the party against whom enforcement is sought. The record must describe the leased goods, state the term of the lease, and indicate that a lease contract has been formed.[58]

15. Warranties

Under Article 2A, the lessor, except in the case of finance leases, makes all usual warranties that are made by a seller in a sale of goods. In a finance lease, however, the real parties in interest are the supplier, who supplies the lessor with the goods, and the lessee, who leases the goods. The lessee looks to the supplier of the goods for warranties. Any warranties, express or implied, made by the supplier to the lessor are passed on to the lessee, who has a direct cause of action on them against the supplier regardless of the lack of privity.[59] **For Example,** if a consumer leased an auto and the auto had a defective steering mechanism that resulted in injury to the consumer, the consumer would have a cause of action against the auto manufacturer.

E-Commerce & Cyberlaw

The Deal with Dell

Dell Computer customers purchased computers through the Dell Web site. There were "Terms and Conditions" on the Web site that included terms and conditions such as the requirement that contract disputes be submitted to arbitration in Illinois and the sales tax provisions related to the purchase of computers and service contracts.

Dell maintains that customers have three separate opportunities to review the terms and conditions agreement: (1) by selecting a hyperlink on the Dell Web site, (2) by reading the terms that were included in the acknowledgment/invoice that was sent to customers after they placed their orders, or (3) by reviewing the copy of the terms Dell included in the packaging of its computer products. The court found that the terms and conditions had to be understood PRIOR to the purchase and that the "Terms and Conditions" tab was not conspicuous on the Dell Web site. From this case and other materials in the chapter, you learn that there are best practices for Internet contracting: (1) Require customers to click on terms and conditions PRIOR to buying; (2) Require customers to physically scroll down through the terms before being allowed to purchase; (3) Notify customers along the way as they are loading their electronic carts that there are terms and conditions and place click points for them to study those terms and conditions; and (4) Posting terms and conditions on your Web site is not enough for those terms and conditions to be part of the contract.

[56] See, e.g., *Oliveira v. Lombardi*, 794 A.2d 453 (R.I. 2002). The federal law did not affect all of the suits that were pending at the time of the passage of the federal law. Those suits were permitted to proceed as long as they had been filed by the end of 2005. Those suits have concluded. Future recovery will be limited to mandatory policy requirements.

[57] UCC §2A-103(1)(g). One of the evolving issues in lease financing is the relationship of the parties, the use of liens, and the role of Article 9 security interests (see Chapter 34). The NCCUSL has created Uniform Certificate of Title Act (UCOTA) that makes the interrelationships of lien laws, Article 2, and Article 9 clear. UCOTA was available for adoption by the states in 2006. As of 2012, only three states had adopted the law.

[58] UCC §2-201(b).

[59] UCC §2A-209.

16. Default

The lease agreement and provisions of Article 2A determine whether the lessor or lessee is in default. If either the lessor or the lessee is in default under the lease contract, the party seeking enforcement may obtain a judgment or otherwise enforce the lease contract by any available judicial or nonjudicial procedure. Neither the lessor nor the lessee is entitled to notice of default or notice of enforcement from the other party. Both the lessor and the lessee have rights and remedies similar to those given to a seller in a sales contract.[60] If the lessee defaults, the lessor is entitled to recover any rent due, future rent, and incidental damages.[61] (See Chapter 27 for more information on remedies.)

LawFlix

Beethoven (1992)(G)

Charles Grodin plays a fussy father who has founded and runs an air freshener company. Part of the plot centers on an investment in the company by some venture capitalists who are interested in using Grodin's company as a supplier. There are contract negotiations as well as issues of warranty and liability.

[60] UCC §§2A-501, 2A-503; *Mitchell v. Ford Motor Credit Co.*, 702 F. Supp. 2d 1356 (M.D. Fla. 2010).
[61] UCC §2A-529.

MAKE THE CONNECTION

SUMMARY

Contracts for services and real estate are governed by the common law. Contracts for the sale of goods are governed by Article 2 of the UCC. *Goods* are defined as anything movable at the time they are identified as the subject of the transaction. Goods physically existing and owned by the seller at the time of the transaction are *existing goods*.

A *sale of goods* is the transfer of title to tangible personal property for a price. A *bailment* is a transfer of possession but not title and is therefore not a sale. A *gift* is not a sale because no price is paid for the gift. A contract for services is an ordinary contract and is not governed by the UCC. If a contract calls for both the rendering of services and the supplying of goods, the contract is classified according to its dominant element.

The common law contract rules for intent to contract apply to the formation of contracts under the UCC. However, several formation rules under the UCC differ from common law contract rules. A merchant's firm offer is irrevocable without the payment of consideration. The UCC rules on additional terms in an acceptance permit the formation of a contract despite the changes. These proposals for new terms are not considered counteroffers under the UCC. The terms that are included are determined by detailed rules. If the transaction is between nonmerchants, a contract is formed without the additional terms, which the original offeror is free to accept or reject. If the transaction is between merchants, the additional terms become part of the contract if those terms do not materially alter the offer and no objection is made to them. There is no distinction between merchant and nonmerchant for additional terms under Revised Article 2 and the terms issues is left to the courts.

The same defenses available to formation under common law are incorporated in Article 2. In addition, the UCC recognizes unconscionability as a defense to formation.

The UCC does not require the parties to agree on every aspect of contract performance for the contract to be valid. Provisions in Article 2 will govern the parties' relationship in the event their agreement does not cover all terms. The price term may be expressly fixed by the parties. The parties may make no provision as to price, or they may indicate how the price should be determined later. In output or requirements contracts, the quantity that is to be sold or purchased is not specified, but such contracts are nevertheless valid. A sales contract can be modified even though the modification is not supported by consideration. The parol evidence rule applies to a sale of goods in much the same manner as to ordinary contracts. However, the UCC permits the introduction of evidence of course of dealing and usage of trade for clarification of contract terms and performance.

The UCC's statute of frauds provides that a sales contract for $500 ($5,000 under Revised Article 2) or more must be evidenced by a record. The UCC's merchant's confirmation memorandum allows two merchants to be bound to an otherwise oral agreement by a memo or letter signed by only one party that stands without objection for 10 days. Several exceptions to the UCC statute of frauds exist: when the goods are specially made or procured for the buyer and are nonresellable in the seller's ordinary market; when the buyer has received and accepted the goods; when the buyer has made either full or partial payment; and when the party against whom enforcement is sought admits in court pleadings or testimony that a contract for sale was made.

Uniform rules for international sales are applicable to contracts for sales between parties in countries that have ratified the CISG. Under the CISG, a contract for the sale of goods need not be in any particular form and can be proven by any means.

Article 2A of the UCC regulates consumer leases, commercial leases, finance leases, nonfinance leases, and subleases of tangible movable goods. A lease subject to Article 2A must be in writing if the lease payments will total $1,000 or more.

LEARNING OUTCOMES

After studying this chapter, you should be able to clearly explain:

A. Nature and Legality

LO.1 Define a sale of goods and explain when UCC Article 2 applies to contracts

See *Paramount Contracting Co. v. DPS Industries, Inc.*, on pp. 428–429.

LO.2 Distinguish between an actual sale of goods and other types of transactions in goods

See footnotes 3 and 4 for examples.

LO.3 Describe how contracts are formed under Article 2, and list the differences in formation standards between the UCC and common law

See the *For Example,* discussion of Joe and Susan's X-box transaction on p. 431.
See the *Greenbrier* basket case on pp. 439–440.
See the *C9 v. SVC* case on pp. 433–434.

B. Form of Sales Contract

LO.4 Explain when a contract for the sale of goods must be in writing

See the *Basquiat* case on p. 438.

LO.5 List and explain the exceptions to the requirement that certain contracts be in writing

See the *For Example,* discussion of Wayne and the baseball jackets on p. 441.

C. Uniform Law for International Sales

LO.6 Discuss the purpose of the United Nations Convention on Contracts for the International Sale of Goods

See the discussion of the CISG on p. 442.

KEY TERMS

acceptance
Article 2
bailee
bailment
battle of the forms
bill of sale
commercial lease
consumer lease
Contracts for the International Sale of Goods (CISG)
cost plus
course of dealing
existing goods
finance lease
firm offer

future goods
gift
goods
lease
mailbox rule
merchants
mirror image rule
nonconsumer lease
offer
output contract
parol evidence rule
requirements contract
statute of frauds
unconscionable
usage of trade

QUESTIONS AND CASE PROBLEMS

1. Triple H Construction Co. contracted with Hunter's Run Stables, Inc., to erect a horse barn and riding arena on Hunter's Run's property in Big Flats, New York. Hunter's Run got a guarantee in its contract with Triple H that "such design with the span so shown will support its weight and will withstand natural forces including but not limited to snow load and wind." Hunter's Run also got the following guarantee from Rigidply, the manufacturer of the rafters: "Rigidply … hereby guarantees that the design to be used for the construction of a horse barn by Triple H … will support the weight of such barn and to snow load and wind as per drawings." The barn was completed in 1983 and collapsed under the weight of snow in 1994. Hunter's Run has sued Triple H for UCC Article2 remedies. Does Article 2 apply? [*Hunter's Run Stables, Inc. v. Triple H, Inc.*, 938F. Supp. 166 (W.D.N.Y.)]

2. R-P Packaging manufactured cellophane wrapping material that was used by Kern's Bakery in packaging its product. Kern's decided to change its system for packaging cookies from a tied bread bag to a tray covered with printed cellophane wrapping. R-P took measurements to determine the appropriate size for the cellophane wrapping and designed the artwork to be printed on the wrapping. After agreeing that the artwork was satisfactory, Kern placed a verbal order for the cellophane at a total cost of $13,000. When the printed wrapping material was received, Kern complained that it was too short for the trays and the art work was not centered. The material, however, conformed exactly to the order placed by Kern. Kern returned the material to R-P by overnight express. R-P sued Kern. Kern claimed that because there was no written contract, the suit was barred by the statute of frauds. What result? [*Flowers Baking Co. v. R-P Packaging, Inc.*, 329 S.E.2d 462 (Va.)]

3. Smythe wrote to Lasco Dealers inquiring about the price of a certain freezer. Lasco wrote her a letter, signed by its credit manager, stating that Smythe could purchase the freezer in question during the next 30 days for $400. Smythe wrote back the next day ordering a freezer at that price. Lasco received Smythe's letter the following day, but Lasco wrote a response letter stating that it had changed the price to $450. Smythe claims that Lasco could not change its price. Is she correct?

4. Mrs. Downing was fitted for dentures by a dentist, Dr. Cook. After she received her dentures, Mrs. Downing began experiencing mouth pain that she attributed to Dr. Cook's manufacture of dentures that did not fit her properly. Mrs. Downing filed suit against Dr. Cook for breach of warranty under Article 2 of the UCC. Dr. Cook defended on the grounds that his denture work was a service and therefore not covered under Article 2 warranties. The trial court found for Mrs. Downing, and Dr. Cook appealed. Is Dr. Cook correct? Are the dentures a contract for services or goods? [*Cook v. Downing*, 891 P.2d 611 (Oka. App.)] Would silicone breast implants be covered by the UCC Article 2 warranties? Does implantation of silicone gel implants constitute a sale of goods by the surgeon? [*In re Breast Implant Product Liability Litigation*, 503 S.E.2d 445 (S.C.)]

5. Meyers was under contract with Henderson to install overhead doors in a factory that Henderson was building. Meyers obtained the disassembled doors from the manufacturer. His contract with

Henderson required Meyers to furnish all labor, materials, tools, and equipment to satisfactorily complete the installation of all overhead doors. Henderson felt the doors were not installed properly and paid less than one-half of the contract price after subtracting his costs for correcting the installation. Because of a business sale and other complications, Meyers did not sue Henderson for the difference in payment until five years later. Henderson raised the defense that because the contract was for the sale of goods, it was barred by the Code's four-year statute of limitations. Meyers claimed that it was a contract for services and that suit could be brought within six years. Who is correct? Why? [*Meyers v. Henderson Construction Co.*, 370 A.2d 547 (N.J.Super.)]

6. Valley Trout Farms ordered fish food from Rangen. Both parties were merchants. The invoice that was sent with the order stated that a specified charge—a percentage common in the industry—would be added to any unpaid bills. Valley Trout Farms did not pay for the food and did not make any objection to the late charge stated in the invoice. When sued by Rangen, Valley Trout Farms claimed that it had never agreed to the late charge and therefore was not required to pay it. Is Valley Trout Farms correct? [*Rangen, Inc. v. Valley Trout Farms, Inc.*, 658 P.2d 955 (Idaho)]

7. LTV Aerospace Corp. manufactured all-terrain vehicles for use in Southeast Asia. LTV made an oral contract with Bateman under which Bateman would supply the packing cases needed for the vehicles' overseas shipment. Bateman made substantial beginnings in the production of packing cases following LTV's specifications. LTV thereafter stopped production of its vehicles and refused to take delivery of any cases. When Bateman sued for breach of contract, LTV argued that the contract could not be enforced because there was no writing that satisfied the statute of frauds. Was this a valid defense? [*LTV Aerospace Corp. v. Bateman*, 492 S.W.2d 703 (Tex. App.)]

8. Syrovy and Alpine Resources, Inc., entered into a "Timber Purchase Agreement." Syrovy agreed to sell and Alpine agreed to buy all of the timber produced during a two-year period. The timber to be sold, purchased, and delivered was to be produced by Alpine from timber on Syrovy's land. Alpine continued harvesting for one year and then stopped after making an initial payment. Syrovy sued Alpine. Alpine alleged there was no contract because the writing to satisfy the statute of frauds must contain a quantity term. Decide. [*Syrovy v. Alpine Resources, Inc.*, 841 P.2d 1279 (Wash. App.)]

9. A subcontractor agreed to remove and dispose of cabinets from a public housing project. When a dispute arose, one party argued that the UCC applied, and the other argued that it was the common law contract. Explain who is correct and why. [*J.O. Hooker's Sons v. Roberts Cabinet*, 683 So. 2d 396]

10. Fastener Corp. sent a letter to Renzo Box Co. that was signed by Ronald Lee, Fastener's sales manager, and read as follows: "We hereby offer you 200 type #14 Fastener bolts at $5 per bolt. This offer will be irrevocable for ten days." On the fifth day, Fastener informed Renzo it was revoking the offer, alleging that there was no consideration for the offer. Could Fastener revoke? Explain.

11. Richard, a retailer of video equipment, telephoned Craft Appliances and ordered a $1,000 videotape recorder for his business. Craft accepted Richard's order and sent him a copy of the purchase memorandum that stated the price, quantity, and model ordered and that was stamped "order accepted by Craft." Richard, however, did not sign or return the purchase memorandum and refused to accept delivery of the recorder when Craft delivered it to him three weeks later. Craft sued Richard, who raised the statute of frauds as a defense. Will Richard prevail? Why or why not?

12. REMC furnished electricity to Helvey's home. The voltage furnished was in excess of 135 volts and caused extensive damage to his 110-volt household appliances. Helvey sued REMC for breach of warranty. Helvey argued that providing electrical energy is not a transaction in goods but a furnishing of services, so that he had six years to sue REMC rather than the UCC's four-year statute of limitations, which had expired. Was it a sale of goods or a sale of services? Identify the ethical principles involved in this case. [*Helvey v. Wabash County REMC*, 278 N.E.2d 608 (Ind. App.)]

13. U.S. Surgical manufactures medical surgical instruments and markets the instruments to hospitals. The packaging for U.S. Surgical's disposable medical instruments is labeled "for single use only." As an example, one label contains the following language: "Unless opened or damaged, contents of package are sterile. DO NOT RESTERILIZE. For multiple use during a SINGLE surgical procedure. DISCARD AFTER USE."

    Orris provides a service to the hospitals that purchase U.S. Surgical's disposable instruments. After the hospitals use or open the instruments, Orris cleans, resterilizes, and/or resharpens the instruments for future use and returns them to the hospitals from which they came.

    U.S. Surgical filed suit asserting that reprocessing, repackaging, and reuse of its disposable instruments constituted a violation of its patent and trademark rights. Orris says that U.S. Surgical did not prohibit hospitals from reusing the instruments and it was not doing anything that violated the contracts U.S. Surgical had with the hospitals. U.S. Surgical says the language on the packaging was an additional term that the hospitals accepted by opening the packages and using the instruments. Who is correct? [*U.S. Surgical Corp. v. Orris, Inc.*, 5 F. Supp. 2d 1201 (D. Kan.); aff'd, 185 F.3d 885 (10th Cir.) and 230 F.3d 1382 (Fed. Cir.)]

14. Flora Hall went to Rent-A-Center in Milwaukee and signed an agreement to make monthly payments of $77.96 for 19 months in exchange for Rent-A-Center's allowing her to have a Rent-A-Center washer and dryer in her home. In addition, the agreement required Hall to pay tax and a liability waiver fee on the washer and dryer. The total amount she would pay under the agreement was $1,643.15. The agreement provided that Hall would return the washer and dryer at the end of the 19 months, or she could, at that time, pay $161.91 and own the washer and dryer as her own. Is this a sales contract? Is this a consumer lease? At the time Hall leased her washer and dryer, she could have purchased a set for about $600. What do you think about the cost of her agreement with Rent-A-Center? Is it unconscionable? Refer to Chapter 33, and determine whether any other consumer laws apply. Must this contract be in writing? [*Rent-A-Center, Inc. v. Hall*, 510 N.W.2d 789 (Wis.)]

15. Click2Boost, Inc. (C2B) entered into an Internet marketing agreement with the New York Times (NYT) on May 10, 2002, for C2B to solicit subscribers for home delivery of the New York Times newspaper through "pop up ads" at Internet Web sites with which C2B maintained "[m]arketing [a]lliances." The agreement required NYT to pay C2B a fee or commission for each home delivery subscription C2B submitted to NYT. NYT paid C2B more than $1.5 million in subscription submission fees from May 2002 to September 2003, but most of the subscriptions were ended, so NYT terminated the C2B agreement on September 16, 2003.

    In October 2003, Wall Street Network (WSN) took over C2B and filed suit for breach of contract against NYT. WSN said that NYT had breached the agreement by terminating it before September 30, 2003, because the contract was one for goods and C2B had furnished those goods. WSN wanted damages under the UCC for breach of a contract because the pop-up ads were sold independently as goods. NYT argued that the contract was one for services for furnishing subscribers, something C2B did not do successfully. WSN countered that the customers generated from the pop-up ads were what was being sold, just like selling a list of names, something that would be considered a good. The trial court granted the NYT summary judgment and WSN appealed. Should WSN win the case? Why or why not? [*Wall Street Network, Ltd. v. New York Times Company*, 164 Cal. App. 4th 1171, 80 Cal. Rptr. 3d 6, 66 UCC Rep. Serv. 2d 261]

CPA QUESTIONS

1. Webstar Corp. orally agreed to sell Northco, Inc., a computer for $20,000. Northco sent a signed purchase order to Webstar confirming the agreement. Webstar received the purchase order and did not respond. Webstar refused to deliver the computer to Northco, claiming that the

purchase order did not satisfy the UCC statute of frauds because it was not signed by Webstar. Northco sells computers to the general public, and Webstar is a computer wholesaler. Under the UCC Sales Article, Webstar's position is:

a. Incorrect, because it failed to object to Northco's purchase order.

b. Incorrect, because only the buyer in a sale-of-goods transaction must sign the contract.

c. Correct, because it was the party against whom enforcement of the contract is being sought.

d. Correct, because the purchase price of the computer exceeded $500.

2. On May 2, Lace Corp., an appliance wholesaler, offered to sell appliances worth $3,000 to Parco, Inc., a household appliances retailer. The offer was signed by Lace's president and provided that it would not be withdrawn before June 1. It also included the shipping terms: "F.O.B.—Parco's warehouse." On May 29, Parco mailed an acceptance of Lace's offer. Lace received the acceptance June 2. Which of the following is correct if Lace sent Parco a telegram revoking its offer and Parco received the telegram on May 25?

a. A contract was formed on May 2.

b. Lace's revocation effectively terminated its offer on May 25.

c. Lace's revocation was ineffective because the offer could not be revoked before June 1.

d. No contract was formed because Lace received Parco's acceptance after June 1.

3. Bond and Spear orally agreed that Bond would buy a car from Spear for $475. Bond paid Spear a $100 deposit. The next day, Spear received an offer of $575, the car's fair market value. Spear immediately notified Bond that Spear would not sell the car to Bond and returned Bond's $100. If Bond sues Spear and Spear defends on the basis of the statute of frauds, Bond will probably:

a. Lose, because the agreement was for less than the fair market value of the car.

b. Win, because the agreement was for less than $500.

c. Lose, because the agreement was not in writing and signed by Spear.

d. Win, because Bond paid a deposit.

4. Cookie Co. offered to sell Distrib Markets 20,000 pounds of cookies at $1.00 per pound, subject to certain specified terms for delivery. Distrib replied in writing as follows: "We accept your offer for 20,000 pounds of cookies at $1.00 per pound, weighing scale to have valid city certificate." Under the UCC:

a. A contract was formed between the parties.

b. A contract will be formed only if Cookie agrees to the weighing scale requirement.

c. No contract was formed because Distrib included the weighing scale requirement in its reply.

d. No contract was formed because Distrib's reply was a counteroffer.

5. Under the Sales Article of the UCC, which of the following requirements must be met for a writing to be an enforceable contract for the sale of goods?

a. The writing must contain a term specifying the price of the goods.

b. The writing must contain a term specifying the quantity of the goods.

c. The writing must contain the signatures of all parties to the writing.

d. The writing must contain the signature of the party seeking to enforce the writing.

6. Card communicated an offer to sell Card's stereo to Bend for $250. Which of the following statements is correct regarding the effect of the communication of the offer?

a. Bend should immediately accept or reject the offer to avoid liability to Card.

b. Card is not obligated to sell the stereo to Bend until Bend accepts the offer.

c. Card is required to mitigate any loss Card would sustain in the event Bend rejects the offer.

d. Bend may not reject the offer for a reasonable period of time.

Title and Risk of Loss

learningoutcomes

After studying this chapter, you should be able to

LO.1 Explain when title and risk of loss pass with respect to goods

LO.2 Determine who bears the risk of loss when goods are damaged or destroyed

LO.3 Explain why it is important to know when risk of loss and title pass in transactions for the sale of goods

LO.4 Describe the passage of title and risk in special situations, such as a bailment, sale or return, or a sale on approval

LO.5 Classify the various circumstances in which title can be passed to a bona fide purchaser

In most sales, the buyer receives the proper goods and makes payment, and the transaction is completed. However, problems may arise during performance that can result in issues of liability. For example, what if the goods are lost in transit? Must the buyer still pay for those lost goods? Can the seller's creditors take goods from the seller's warehouse when they are packed for shipment to buyers? The parties can include provisions in their contract to address these types of problems. If their contract does not cover these types of problems, however, then specific rules under Uniform Commercial Code (UCC) Article 2 apply. These rules are covered in this chapter.

In businesses today, the management of issues of risk and title as goods flow through commerce is called *supply chain management*. Effective managers know the law and the rules of risk of loss and title so that they can negotiate risk-reducing contracts and be certain that they have all necessary arrangements and paperwork to move goods through streams of commerce.

A. Identifying Types of Potential Problems and Transactions

The types of problems that can arise in supply chain management include damage to the goods in transit, claims by creditors of buyers and sellers while the goods are in transit, and questions relating to whose insurance will cover what damage and when such coverage applies.

1. Damage to Goods

One potential problem occurs if the goods are damaged or totally destroyed without any fault of either the buyer or the seller. With no goods and a contract performance still required, the parties have questions: Must the seller bear the loss and supply new goods to the buyer? Or is it the buyer's loss so that the buyer must pay the seller the purchase price even though the goods are damaged or destroyed?[1] What liability does a carrier have when goods in its possession are damaged? The fact that there may be insurance does not avoid this question because the questions of whose insurer is liable and the extent of liability still remain.

CPA 2. Creditors' Claims

Another potential problem that can arise affecting the buyer's and seller's rights occurs when creditors of the seller or buyer seize the goods under the belief that their debtor has title. The buyer's creditors may seize them because they believe them to be the buyer's. The seller's creditors may step in and take goods because they believe the goods still belong to the seller, and the buyer is left with the dilemma of whether it can get the goods back from the creditors. The question of title or ownership is also important in connection with a resale of the goods by the buyer and in determining the parties' liability for, or the computation of, inventory or personal property taxes.

CPA 3. Insurance

Until the buyer has received the goods and the seller has been paid, both the seller and the buyer have an economic interest in the sales transaction. A question that can arise is whether either or both have enough of an interest in the goods to allow them to insure them, in other words, do they have an **insurable interest**? There are certain steps that must take place and timing requirements that must be met before that insurable interest can arise. Once buyers have an insurable interest in goods that are the subject matter of their contracts, they have the right to obtain insurance and can submit claims for losses on the goods.

B. Determining Rights: Identification of Goods

The **identification** of the goods to the contract is a necessary step to provide the buyer an insurable interest. How goods that are the subject matter of a contract are identified depends on the nature of both

[1] UCC §2-509 provides for the allocation of the risk of loss in those situations where the goods are destroyed and neither party has breached the contract.

the contract and the goods themselves.[2] Identification is also the first step for passage of title and risk of loss.

CPA 4. Existing Goods

Existing goods are goods physically in existence at the time of the contract and owned by the seller. When particular goods have been selected by either the buyer or the seller, or both, as being the goods called for by the sales contract, the goods are **identified**. **For Example,** when you go into a store, point to a particular item, and tell the clerk, "I'll take that one," your sales transaction relates to existing goods that are now identified. This step of identification provides you with certain rights in those goods because of your contract as well as Article 2 protections for buyers when goods are identified.[3]

CPA 5. Future Goods

Future goods are those not yet owned by the seller or not yet in existence. **For Example,** suppose that your company is sponsoring a 10-K run and will furnish the t-shirts for the 10,000 runners expected to participate in the race. You have contacted Sporting Tees, Inc., to produce the t-shirts with the name of the race and your company logo on the shirts. The shirts are future goods because you are contracting for goods that will be produced.

Future goods are identified when they are shipped, marked, or otherwise designated by the seller as goods to which the contract refers.[4] The t-shirts cannot be identified until Sporting Tees has manufactured them and designated them for your company. The earliest that the shirts can be identified is when they come off the production line and are designated for your company. Prior to identification of these goods, the buyer has only a future interest at the time of the contract and has few rights with respect to them.[5]

CPA 6. Fungible Goods

Fungible goods are goods that, when mixed together, are indistinguishable. **For Example,** crops such as soybeans and dairy products such as milk are fungible goods. A seller who has 10,000 cases of cling peaches has fungible, unidentified goods. Like future goods, these fungible goods are identified when they are shipped, marked, or otherwise designated for the buyer.[6] The seller's act of tagging, marking, labeling, or in some way indicating to those responsible for shipping the goods that certain goods are associated with a particular contract or order means that identification has occurred.

CPA 7. Effect of Identification

Once goods that are the subject matter of a contract have been identified, the buyer holds an *insurable interest* in them. Once the buyer's economic interest in and the identity of the goods are clear, the buyer's insurance company has an obligation to provide coverage for any mishaps that could occur until the contract is performed completely.

Identification is also significant because the questions surrounding passage of title and risk of loss cannot be resolved until the goods have been identified. Identification is the first step in resolving questions about liability for damaged goods and rights of the parties and third parties, including creditors, in the goods. UCC §2-401(1) provides, "Title to goods cannot pass under a contract for sale prior to their identification to the contract."

C. Determining Rights: Passage of Title

When title to goods passes to the buyer (following identification) depends on whether there is a document of title, whether the seller is required to ship the goods, and what the terms of that shipping agreement are. In the absence of an agreement by the parties as to when title will pass, several Article 2 rules govern the timing for passage of title.

8. Passage of Title Using Documents of Title

A **document of title** is a means whereby the parties can facilitate the transfer of title to the goods without

[2] UCC §2-501(1)(a). *Capital One Financial Corp., and Subsidiaries v. C.I.R.*, 659 F.3d 316 (4th Cir. 2011).
[3] *Duddy v. Government Employees Insurance Co., Inc.*, 23 A.2d 436 (N.J. App. 2011).
[4] UCC §2-501(1)(b). Specially manufactured goods are fully identified when the goods are made.
[5] *In re Highside Pork, LLC*, 450 B.R. 173 (N.D. Iowa 2011).
[6] Farm products, such as corn, are fungible goods. However, contracts for future crops are not contracts for the sale of goods because there are no goods identified as yet for such contracts. *Top of Iowa Co-Op v. Sime Farms, Inc.*, 608 N.W.2d 454 (Iowa 2000).

actually moving them or provide a means for a creditor to take an interest in the goods. The use of a document of title also provides a simple answer to the question of when title to the goods passes from seller to buyer in a sales transaction. Title to the goods passes when the document of title is transferred from the seller to the buyer.[7]

Documents of title are governed under Article 7 of the UCC, the final section of the UCC to undergo major revisions in the last decade of the twentieth century. The purpose of the 2003 revisions to Article 7 was to address the issues that have arisen because of electronic filing of documents of title. Article 7 adoptions have just begun with 40 states passing the new Article 7 by 2011.[8]

Article 7 now addresses the commercial reality of electronic tracking and the use of electronic records as documents of title. Under Article 7, the definition of a document of title now includes electronic documents of title.

The discussion of documents of title here is limited to commercial transactions, transport, and storage. Many forms of documents of title are not covered under Article 7. For example, all states have some form of title system required for the transfer of title to motor vehicles.[9] Those systems govern title passage for automobiles. The two primary forms of documents of title under Article 7 used to pass title to goods are **bills of lading** (issued by a carrier) and **warehouse receipts.**[10] Details on these documents and the rights of the parties are found in Chapter 22.

CPA 9. Passage of Title in Nonshipment Contracts

Unless the parties to the contract agree otherwise, UCC Article 2 does not require that the seller deliver the contracted-for goods to the buyer. In the absence of a provision in the contract, the place of delivery is the seller's place of business or the seller's residence if the seller is not a merchant. When there is no specific agreement for shipment or delivery of the goods and there is no document of title and the goods to the contract have been identified, title passes to the buyer at the time the contract is entered into by the buyer and seller.[11]

10. Passage of Title in Warehouse Arrangements

When the goods to a contract are in a warehouse or the possession of a third party (not the seller), the title to the goods passes from the seller to the buyer when the buyer receives the document of title or, if there is no document of title, any other paperwork required for the third party or warehouse to turn over the goods and the goods are available for the buyer to take. When goods are in the possession of a warehouse, the parties have certain duties and rights. Those rights and duties were covered in Chapter 22.

11. Passage of Title in Bailments and Other Forms of Possession

As a general rule, a seller can sell only what the seller owns. However, some issues of passage of title can arise in specific circumstances. Those circumstances are covered in the following sections.

CPA **(A) Stolen Property.** Neither those who find stolen property nor thieves can pass title to goods. A thief simply cannot pass good title to even a good-faith purchaser. Anyone who has purchased stolen goods must surrender them to the true owner. The fact that the negligence of the owner made the theft possible or contributed to losing the goods does not bar the owner from recovering the goods or money damages from the thief, the finder, or a good-faith purchaser. It does not matter that the thief may have passed the goods along through several purchasers. Title cannot be cleansed by distance between the thief and the good-faith purchaser. The good-faith purchaser always takes the goods subject to the claim by the owner. The public policy reason for this

[7] UCC §2-401(3).

[8] The revisions to Article 7 and their history can be found at **www.uniformlaws.org**. The adopting states are Alabama, Alaska, Arizona, Arkansas, California, Colorado, Connecticut, Delaware, Florida, Georgia, Hawaii, Idaho, Illinois, Indiana, Iowa, Kansas, Louisiana, Maine, Maryland, Minnesota, Mississippi, Montana, Nebraska, Nevada, New Hampshire, New Mexico, North Carolina, North Dakota, Oklahoma, Oregon, Pennsylvania, Rhode Island, South Dakota, Tennessee, Texas, Utah, Virginia, and West Virginia.

[9] Other types of transportation, such as a boat, may not require a title document to be transferred, and title passes at the time of contracting. However, where there are title statutes, they preempt UCC provisions. *Ladd v. NBD Bank*, 550 N.W.2d 826 (Mich. App. 1996). See also *Pierce v. First Nat'l Bank*, 899 S.W.2d 365 (Tex. App. 1995).

[10] UCC §7-202(1) provides, "A warehouse receipt need not be in any particular form. Under Revised Article 7, it can be in electronic form."

[11] *In re Aleris Intern., Inc.*, 456 B.R. 35 (D.Del. 2011).

protection of true owners is to deter theft. Knowing there is no way to sell the goods should deter those who steal and caution those who buy goods to check title and sources. The *Northern Insurance v. 1996 Sea Ray* case deals with an issue of theft and title.

Northern Insurance Company of New York v. 1996 Sea Ray Model 370DA Yacht, 453 F. Supp. 2d 905 (D.S.C 2006)

Fat Boy Hoodwinked by a Yacht Thief

On August 23, 1995, Eric T. Small purchased a 37-foot (37') Sea Ray 370 Sundancer yacht from Gulfwind Marine for $251,000.00. Sea Ray had engraved the vessel's hull identification number ("HIN") into the fiberglass on the vessel's transom. The vessel's HIN was SER4860F596 Sea Ray. Northern issued a Master Mariner yacht policy to Small providing insurance coverage for the Sea Ray yacht for theft or loss for $200,000.00.

On February 27, 2001, Daniel Dey, a Florida resident, stole the Sea Ray yacht while it was moored at her slip at Gulfwind Marina in Venice, Florida. A police report was filed and Northern paid Small a total loss of $200,000.00 for the vessel.

Subsequently, Dey altered the Sea Ray yacht's HIN to SERF3571C298 and made other changes to the vessel to disguise the theft and manufacture date. Dey then advertised a 1998 Sea Ray for sale on an Internet Web site. On August 5, 2002, Dey signed a bill of sale conveying the Sea Ray yacht to Fat Boy, a Delaware limited liability company, for $127,500.00. No boat dealer, retailer, distributor, or seller was involved in the transaction.

Fat Boy gave a ship mortgage on the Sea Ray yacht to Carolina First. Carolina First filed the preferred ship mortgage on the Sea Ray yacht.

George Lee and Paul Degenhart, the lawyer for and principal in Fat Boy, became concerned that the Sea Ray yacht may have been manufactured in 1996, not 1998. Lee and Degenhart confronted Dey about the incorrect model year of the Sea Ray yacht. Dey admitted the alteration to make the boat seem to be a 1998, not 1996, model.

Fat Boy and Lee then attempted to trade the Sea Ray yacht to a vessel dealer for another vessel that Lee wanted to purchase. The dealer determined that the vessel had been stolen and told Small. Small contacted Lee and Fat Boy to get back his yacht, but Lee refused.

In June, 2004, the Sea Ray yacht was seized by the U.S. Marshal Service and Northern filed suit to get the yacht back. Fat Boy and Carolina First also claimed title and interest in the yacht.

JUDICIAL OPINION

WOOTEN, Judge ... This Court finds that the Sea Ray yacht rightfully belongs to Northern. Small did not have knowledge of or consent to Dey's "sale" of the vessel to Fat Boy and/or the alteration of the vessel's HIN. Additionally, as is apparent, Small did not sell the vessel to Fat Boy or Lee. Dey did not have valid title to the Sea Ray yacht when he issued a bill of sale to Fat Boy. The "sale" of the Sea Ray yacht between Dey and Fat Boy was not consummated through a boat dealer, retailer, distributor, or seller of like goods. Dey is not a boat dealer, retailer, distributor, or seller of like goods. Neither Lee nor Fat Boy ever possessed valid title to the Sea Ray yacht.

Since Lee and Fat Boy did not have valid title to the Sea Ray yacht, neither Lee nor Fat Boy could grant a preferred ship mortgage to Carolina First. A preferred ship mortgage can only be granted by the owner of a vessel. Therefore, Lee and Fat Boy did not have authority to grant a preferred ship mortgage on the subject Sea Ray yacht.

The Court further finds that there is insufficient evidence upon which it can be concluded that either Lee or Fat Boy had knowledge that the Sea Ray yacht was stolen prior to their attempted trade-in of the vessel. Dey, a convicted felon sentenced to fifteen (15) years probation in connection with his unlawful conduct in this case, is deemed not credible.

Under Florida law, a purchaser of goods acquires all title which his transferor had or had power to transfer. Florida follows the general rule that one who acquires possession of property by theft cannot confer good title by its sale, even to a bona fide purchaser.

With regards to the rights a purchaser obtains from a thief, "[a]t best, a purchaser in good faith has the title and right to possession of the property against all except the rightful owner." "In Florida a purchaser cannot obtain clear title from a thief to defeat the original owner. The most a bona fide purchaser for value in Florida can obtain from a thief is superior title to everyone except the original owner."

Although Fat Boy possesses a certificate of documentation for the vessel under the incorrect HIN, that is "not conclusive evidence of ownership in a proceeding in which ownership is in issue." In particular, The Fifth Circuit Court of Appeals has noted "federal registration does not, of itself, confer emoluments of title and ownership to a vessel." The certificate of documentation was obtained using an invalid HIN on the application and a bill of sale with the incorrect HIN as well. At the time the application was submitted to the National Vessel Documentation Center and the bill of sale executed, the Sea Ray yacht was already documented by Small under the correct HIN issued by the manufacturer.

Continued

Finally, the parties stipulated prior to trial that the validity of Carolina First's preferred ship's mortgage on the vessel was dependent upon whether Fat Boy or Northern held superior title to the vessel. Because this Court now concludes that Fat Boy does not have superior title to the vessel, and in accordance with the parties' filed stipulation, the Court also concludes that Carolina First has no interest in the vessel.

QUESTIONS

1. What lessons should boat buyers learn from this case?
2. What lessons should lenders learn about the security for their loans?
3. What effect does the change in the identification number have on the UCC rules on thieves in the title?

(B) ESTOPPEL. If an owner has acted in a way that misleads others, the owner of personal property may be prevented, or **estopped**, from asserting ownership. The owner would be barred from denying the right of another person to sell the property. **For Example,** a minor buys a car and puts it in his father's name so that he can obtain lower insurance rates. If the father then sells the car to a good-faith purchaser, the son would be estopped from claiming ownership.

CPA **(C) AUTHORIZATION.** In certain circumstances, persons who just possess someone else's property may sell the property and pass title. Lienholders can sell property when debtors default. **For Example,** if you store your personal property in a storage locker and fail to pay rent, the owner of the storage locker holds a lien on your personal property and could sell it to pay the rent due on your storage unit. Good title passes to the buyer from such a sale. All states have some form of statute giving those who find property the authority to sell the property after certain time periods have passed or when the owner cannot be found.

(D) VOIDABLE TITLE. If the buyer has a **voidable title**—for example, when the goods were obtained by fraud—the seller can rescind the sale. However, if the buyer resells the property to a good-faith purchaser before the seller has rescinded the transaction, the subsequent purchaser acquires valid title. It is immaterial whether the buyer with the voidable title had obtained title by criminal fraud.[12]

(E) BAILMENTS OR SALE BY AN ENTRUSTEE. A bailee can pass good title to a good-faith purchaser even when the sale was not authorized by the owner and the bailee has no title to the goods but is in the business of selling those particular types of goods.[13] **For Example,** if Gunnell's Jewelry sells and repairs watches and Julie has left her watch with Gunnell's for repair, she has created a bailment. If Gunnell's Jewelry sells Julie's watch by mistake (because Gunnell's is both a new and old watch dealer) to David, a good-faith purchaser, David has valid title to the watch. Julie will have a cause of action against Gunnell's for conversion, and in some states, if Gunnell's sold the watch knowing that it belonged to Julie, the sale could constitute a crime, such as larceny. However, all of these legal proceedings will involve Gunnell's, Julie, and possibly a government prosecution, but not David who will take good title to the watch.

In the case of an entrustee who is not a merchant, such as a prospective customer trying out an automobile, there is no transfer of title to the buyer from the entrustee. Similarly, there is no transfer of title when a mere bailee, such as a repairer who is not a seller of goods of that kind, sells the property of a customer.

12. Delivery and Shipment Terms

If delivery is required under the terms of the parties' agreement, the seller is normally required only to make shipment, and the seller's part of the contract is

[12] "Criminal fraud" is the language of Revised Article 2, adopted to increase the scope of the original term *larceny* and intended to encompass all forms of criminal activity that might lead to the possession or entrustment of goods. Revised Article 2 also covers all conduct punishable under criminal law.

[13] *Wells Fargo Bank Northwest, N.A. v. RPK Capital VXI, L.L.C.*, 360 S.W.3d 691 (Tex. App. 2012). *In re Excalibur Machine Co., Inc.*, 404 B.R. 834 (W.D. Pa. 2009).

Thinking Things Through

The Katrina Pillows Donated to Help but Sold for Profit

Tempur-Pedic (TP) manufactures, markets, and distributes mattresses, pillows, cushions, slippers, and other similar products. Mattresses sold in the ordinary course of business by authorized TP distributors are enclosed in a hypo-allergenic cover, sealed in a plastic bag, and packed in cardboard boxes labeled with the TP's registered trademarks. Goods designated for charitable donations are packaged differently.

In 2005, TP decided to make a donation of approximately $15 million in mattress, slipper, and pillow inventory to Gulf Coast residents victimized by Hurricane Katrina. The donation was made to Waste to Charity, Inc. (WTC) with the condition that the donations not be resold, that there were no warranties on the products, that TP be given credit for the donations, and that WTC not portray the TP products in any negative way. If WTC wanted to sell the goods, it had to seek TP's permission.

After the donation, TP was notified by one of its dealers that its products were being sold from a truck in a parking lot in Nashville, TN, and that truckloads of TP mattresses, pillows, and slippers were being sold for $30,000. A TP representative traveled to Nashville and identified the goods as those that had been donated to WTC. The TP representative tried to take the goods, but the owner of the truck said he had purchased the TP products in good faith from WTC and had no way of knowing WTC did not have the authority to sell the products. Who has title to the TP products? Is the good-faith argument relevant? Who will get the mattresses? Does it make a difference if the buyer purchased a TP mattress in a parking lot? **[*Tempur-Pedic Intern., Inc. v. Waste to Charity, Inc.,* 483 F. Supp. 2d 766 (W.D. Ark. 2007).]**

completed by placing the goods in the possession of a carrier for shipment. However, the parties may agree to various shipping provisions that do affect the passage of title under Article 2.[14] Those terms are covered in the following sections, and Figure 24-1 provides a summary.

(A) FOB Place of Shipment. *FOB* is a shipping term that is an acronym for free on board.[15] If a contract contains a delivery term of **FOB place of shipment**, then the seller's obligation under the contract is to deliver the goods to a carrier for shipment. **For Example,** if the contract between a New York

Ethics & the Law

The Fake Seated Woman

David Bakalar was in possession of a drawing by Egon Schiele (the Drawing) as a result of a $670,000 successful bid at an art auction. Although the Drawing was untitled by the artist, one of the descriptive titles by which it is known is "Seated Woman with Bent Left Leg (Torso)." However, Milos Vavra and Leon Fischer, who are heirs to the estate of Franz Friedrich Grunbaum, have documentation showing that the Drawing was part of Grunbaum's estate that was restored to him and his heirs after the fall of Nazi Germany. Records from the Nazi period show that the Drawing and much of Grunbaum's other property was seized by the Nazi government without compensation. Milos and Leon say that the Drawing was, therefore, stolen property and must be returned to its rightful owner. The auction house and Mr. Bakalar claim that they are both bona fide purchasers and had no knowledge of the Drawing's history. Further, they note that a government taking is different from stealing property in that there is legal documentation that accompanied the seizure of the Drawing. Describe how the UCC title provisions would apply in this situation and what the result would be. What are the ethical issues in allowing the Drawing and other art work taken by the Nazis to become part of the commercial art market? What are the ethical issues if the Drawing is given back to the heirs? **[*Bakalar v. Vavra,* 619 F.3d 136 (2nd Cir. 2010)]**

[14] UCC §2-401(2). When a seller simply ships goods in response to a telephone order and there is no paperwork to indicate shipping terms, the contract is one of shipment (FOB place of shipment). *In re Jasper Seating, Inc.,* 967 A.2d 350 (N.J. Super. 2009).

[15] UCC §2-319.

FIGURE 24-1 *Delivery and Shipping Terms*

COD	Cash on delivery (payment term, not shipment term)
CF	Cost plus freight lump sum; price includes cost and freight Risk: buyer on delivery to carrier Title: buyer on delivery to carrier Cost, insurance, and freight expenses: seller pays; includes cost Of freight in contract price
CIF	Lump sum; price includes cost, insurance, and freight Risk: buyer on delivery to carrier Title: buyer on delivery to carrier Expenses: included in contract price (seller buys insurance in Buyer's name and pays freight)
FOB	Free on board
FAS	Free alongside ship (FOB for boats)

buyer and a Los Angeles seller provides for delivery as FOB Los Angeles, then the seller's responsibility is to place the goods in the possession of a Los Angeles carrier and enter into a contract to have the goods shipped to New York.

CPA (B) **FOB PLACE OF DESTINATION.** If a contract contains a delivery term of **FOB place of destination**, then the seller's responsibility is to get the goods to the buyer. **For Example,** if the contract between the New York buyer and the Los Angeles seller is FOB New York, then the seller is responsible for getting the goods to New York. An FOB destination contract holds the seller accountable throughout the journey of the goods across the country.

CPA (C) **FAS. FAS** is a shipping term that means free alongside ship; it is the equivalent of FOB for boat transportation.[16] **For Example,** a contract between a London buyer and a Norfolk, Virginia, seller that is FAS Norfolk requires only that the seller deliver the goods to a ship in Norfolk.

CPA (D) **CF, CIF, AND COD. CF** is an acronym for cost and freight, and **CIF** is an acronym for cost, insurance, and freight.[17] Under a CF contract, the seller gets the goods to a carrier, and the cost of shipping the goods is included in the contract price. Under a CIF contract, the seller must get the goods to a carrier and buy an insurance policy in the buyer's name to cover the goods while in transit. The costs of the freight and the insurance policy are included in the contract price.

Often contracts for the sale of goods provide for **COD**. The acronym stands for cash on delivery. Even though the term includes the word *delivery,* COD is not a shipping term but a payment term that requires the buyer to pay in order to gain physical possession of the goods.

13. Passage of Title in Shipment Contracts

When the parties have shipment and delivery terms in their contract, the type of shipment contract the parties have agreed to controls when title to the goods has passed and, as a result, the rights of creditors of the buyer and seller in those goods.

Revised Article 2 provides for the same results on passage of title in shipment contracts as under Article 2, but the FOB terms are not specifically delineated under the Revised Article 2. (See Figure 24-2.) Revised Article 2 simply uses the generic language of shipment contracts

[16] UCC §2-319.

[17] UCC §§2-320 and 2-321.

FIGURE 24-2 Passage of Title under Article 2 and Revised Article 2

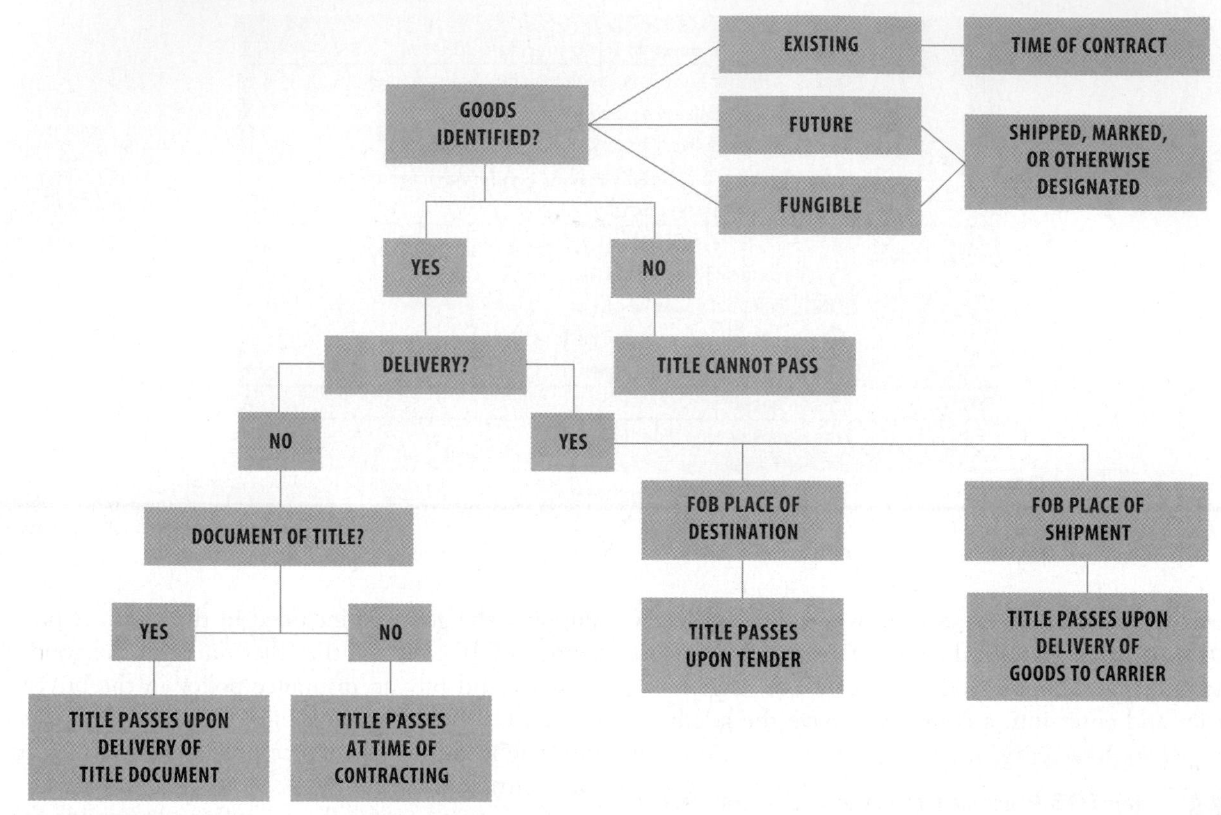

and those shipment contracts in which the seller is required to get the goods to a particular destination.

CPA **(A) Passage of Title in a Shipment-Only Contract (FOB Shipment).** Title to the goods passes from the seller to the buyer in an FOB shipment contract or under a shipment contract for Revised Article 2 when the seller delivers the goods to the carrier.[18] The title to the goods no longer rests with the Los Angeles seller once the goods are delivered to the carrier if the contract is just a shipment contract only (an FOB Los Angeles contract). **For Example,** if the Internal Revenue Service received authorization to collect taxes by seizing the seller's property, it could not take those goods once they were delivered to the carrier. Under a shipment contract (an FOB shipment contract), the buyer owns the goods once they are in the hands of the carrier.

CPA **(B) Passage of Title in a Destination Contract (FOB Place of Destination).** Title to the goods passes from the seller to the buyer in an FOB destination contract when the goods are tendered to the buyer at the destination. **Tender** occurs when the goods have arrived and are available for the buyer to pick up and the buyer has been notified of their availability. **For Example,** when the contract contains an FOB destination provision requiring the seller to deliver to New York, title to the goods passes to the New York buyer when the goods have arrived in New York, they are available for pickup, and the buyer has been notified of their arrival. Thus, the IRS could seize

[18] UCC §2-401(2).

the goods during shipment if the contract is FOB New York because title remains with the seller until actual tender. In the preceding example, the seller's obligation is complete when the goods are at the rail station in New York and the buyer has been notified that she may pick them up at any time during working hours.[19] The *Lite-On Peripherals v. Burlington Air Express* case deals with questions of liability when there is a document of title that is not honored.

Lite-On Peripherals, Inc. v. Burlington Air Express, Inc., 255 F.3d 1189 (9th Cir. 2001)

Taiwan Burlington Express

Burlington Express issued a negotiable bill of lading to the seller of goods (Silitek who assigned the bill of lading to Lite-On) being shipped from Taiwan to the United States. Under the contractual terms of the bill of lading, Burlington Express was not to deliver the goods to the buyer (consignee) until the buyer presented the negotiable bill of lading. Burlington Express delivered the goods to the buyer without having the buyer turn over the negotiable bill of lading. Burlington Express maintained that the shipping contract was FOB Taiwan, which meant that title passed to the buyer upon loading in Taiwan, making the bill of lading irrelevant. The court entered summary judgment for Lite-On for the full value of the goods that Burlington had turned over to the nonpaying buyer, a value of $101,602.80. Burlington appealed.

JUDICIAL OPINION

TROTT, Circuit Judge:

Lite-On contends that this is a straightforward contract case. We agree. Lite-On is the assignee of Silitek's rights under the bill of lading, and is therefore able to enforce that contract as Silitek would. The bill of lading, which Burlington itself issued, contained a "surrender-upon-delivery" clause indicating that the keyboards would not be turned over to the named consignee, unless the consignee produced an endorsed bill of lading. Despite this language, Burlington gave the goods to [the buyer] 1 without first requiring the bill [of lading]. Burlington admits these essential facts, which are the only facts necessary to establish liability under the bill of lading.

We have held in a similar case that where a seller of goods is included within the definition of "Merchant" under a bill of lading, a vessel owner cannot claim that the seller is not entitled to enforce the bill. Moreover, numerous cases have noted that a bill of lading is the basic shipping contract between a seller and carrier of goods.

The documentary sale [evidenced by a bill of lading] enables the distant seller to protect himself from an insolvent or fraudulent foreign buyer by ensuring that the buyer ordinarily cannot take possession of the goods until he has paid for them...Absent a valid agreement to the contrary the carrier, the issuer of the bill of lading, is responsible for releasing the cargo only to the party who presents the original bill of lading.... If the carrier delivers the goods to one other than the authorized holder of the bill of lading, the carrier is liable for misdelivery.

For the foregoing reasons, summary judgment in favor of Lite-On was appropriate. The judgment of the district court is therefore AFFIRMED.

QUESTIONS

1. Does it matter that the bill of lading had been assigned to another party?
2. What lessons should be learned about misdelivery of goods?
3. Why do sellers insist on bills of lading?

CPA D. Determining Rights: Risk of Loss

Identification determines insurability, and title determines rights of such third parties as creditors. **Risk of loss** determines who must pay under a contract in the event the goods that are the subject of the contract are damaged or destroyed during the course of performance.

[19] In re *Sunbelt Grain WKS, LLC, Bkrtcy.*, 406 B.R. 918 (D. Kan. 2009).

E-Commerce & Cyberlaw

Supply Chain and Risk Management

In today's sophisticated supplier and transportation relationships, buyers, sellers, and carriers can pinpoint exactly where goods are and when they have been delivered, and all parties have access to that information online. In many contracts, the parties can avert problems or breaches by monitoring closely the progress of the shipment. The computer interconnection of the supply chain permits faster and better communication among the parties when problems under the contract or in shipment arise. The shipment can be tracked from the time of delivery to the carrier through its route to final signature upon its arrival.

14. Risk of Loss in Nonshipment Contracts

As noted earlier, Article 2 has no provision for delivery in the absence of an agreement. The rules for passage of risk of loss from the seller to the buyer in a nonshipment contract make a distinction between a merchant seller and a nonmerchant seller. If the seller is a merchant, the risk of loss passes to the buyer on actual receipt of the goods from the merchant.[20] If the seller is a nonmerchant, the risk of loss passes when the seller makes the goods available to the buyer or upon tender. **For Example,** if John buys a refrigerator at Kelvinator Appliances and then leaves it there while he goes to borrow a pickup truck, the risk of loss has not yet passed to John. He may have had title at the time he entered into the contract for the existing goods, and the goods are identified, but the risk of loss will not pass to John until he has actually received the refrigerator. His receipt will not occur until the refrigerator is placed in the back of his pickup truck. John is fully protected if anything happens to the refrigerator until then. If John buys the refrigerator from his neighbor at a garage sale, the risk of loss passes at the same time that title passes, or at the time of contracting.

15. Risk of Loss in Shipment Contracts

If the parties have agreed to delivery or shipment terms as part of their contract, the rules for risk of loss are different.[21]

CPA (A) **Contract for Shipment to Buyer (FOB Place of Shipment).** In a contract for shipment only, or FOB place of shipment, the risk of loss passes to the buyer at the same time as title does: when the goods are delivered to the carrier, that is, at the time and place of shipment. After the goods have been delivered to the carrier, the seller has no liability for, or insurable interest in, the goods unless the seller has reserved a security interest in them. **For Example,** if the Los Angeles seller has a shipment contract (an FOB Los Angeles contract), once the goods are in the hands of the carrier, the risk belongs to the buyer or the buyer's insurer. If the goods are hijacked outside Kansas City, the New York buyer must still pay the Los Angeles seller for the goods according to the contract price and terms.

CPA (B) **Contract for Delivery at Destination (FOB Place of Destination).** When the contract requires the seller to deliver the contract goods at a particular destination (FOB place of destination), the risk of loss does not pass to the buyer until the carrier tenders the goods at the destination. **For Example,** if the contract is FOB New York and the goods are hijacked in Kansas City, the seller is required to find substitute goods and perform under the contract because the risk of loss does not pass to the buyer until the goods arrive in New York and are available to the notified buyer.[22]

16. Damage to or Destruction of Goods

In the absence of a contract provision, Article 2 provides for certain rights for the parties in the event of damage to or destruction of goods that are the subject matter in a contract.

[20] UCC §2-509 *Capshaw v. Hickman*, 880 N.E.2d 118 (Oh. App. 2007).
[21] UCC §2-509. *OneBeacon Ins. Co. v. Haas Industries, Inc.*, 634 F.3d 1092 (9th Cir. 2011)
[22] *APL Co. Pte. Ltd. v. UK Aerosols Ltd., Inc.*, 452 F. Supp. 2d 939 (N.D. Cal. 2006).

(A) Damage to Identified Goods Before Risk of Loss Passes. Goods that were identified at the time the contract was made may be damaged or destroyed without the fault of either party before the risk of loss has passed. If so, the UCC provides, "if the loss is total the contract is avoided."[23] The loss may be partial, or the goods may have so deteriorated that they do not conform to the contract. In this case, the buyer has the option, after inspecting the goods, to either avoid the contract or accept the goods subject to an allowance or a deduction from the contract price. There is no breach by the seller, so the purpose of the law is simply to eliminate the legal remedies, allow the buyer to choose to take the goods, and have the insurers involved cover the losses.[24]

(B) Damage to Identified Goods after Risk of Loss Passes. If partial damage or total destruction occurs after the risk of loss has passed to the buyer, it is the buyer's loss. The buyer may be able to recover the amount of the damages from the carrier, an insurer, the person in possession of the goods (such as a warehouse), or any third person causing the loss.[25] However, the carrier is permitted to limit its liability for damages on valuable goods such as artwork. Without special insurance and absent any negligence by the seller in making shipping arrangements, a buyer who holds the risk of loss will still be bound to pay the seller the full amount. The *King Jewelry v. Federal Express* case deals with an issue of the amount of liability when goods are damaged.

King Jewelry Inc. v. Federal Express Corporation, 166 F. Supp. 2d 1280 (C.D. Cal. 2001)

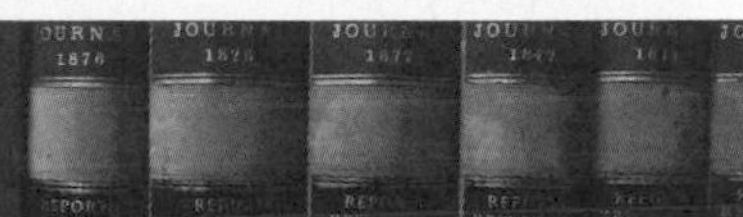

FedEx, Candelabras, and Damages in Shipment

Yehouda Hanasab, president and sole shareholder of King Jewelry, Inc., bought a pair of marble and brass statues with candelabras from Elegant Reflections, a purveyor of jewelry and objets d'art located in Florida, for $37,500.00. Elegant Reflections was to ship the goods to King under FOB place of shipment terms. Elegant Reflections hired Raymond Reppert, a "professional packager and crater" with 12 years experience, to package, crate, and ship the statues and candelabras to King. Reppert packaged and crated the statues with directional markings and signs stating "Fragile—Handle with Care."

Reppert paid FedEx $684.50 (transportation charge in the amount of $485.04, declared value charge in the amount of $185.00, and fuel surcharge in the amount of $14.55) to ship the candelabras. However, both candelabras were broken in transit, something King discovered when they arrived in King's California offices. FedEx's airbill limits damages to $500. King sought recovery from Elegant and/or FedEx and Reppert.

JUDICIAL OPINION

CHAPMAN, United States Magistrate Judge ... Federal Express is a federally certified all-cargo air carrier operating under the authority granted it by the Federal Aviation Administration. "State law regulating the scope of air carrier liability for loss or damage to cargo is preempted by the Airline Deregulation Act of 1978."

As the Ninth Circuit has held:

> *Under established federal common law, if a carrier wishes to enforce a limited liability provision, its contract must offer the shipper (1) reasonable notice of limited liability, and (2) a fair opportunity to purchase higher liability. Limited liability provisions are* prima facie *valid if the face of the contract (or, in this case, air waybill) recites the liability limitation and "the means to avoid it." The burden then shifts to the shipper to prove that it did not have a "fair opportunity" to purchase greater liability coverage.*

The reverse side of the King airbill sets forth the terms and conditions of shipping under the King airbill, and by those terms and conditions, specifically incorporates FedEx's Service Guide. The terms and conditions of the King airbill provide for limitations on FedEx's liability, and specifically limit "items of extraordinary value" to $500.00. Further, "items of extraordinary value" are defined to "include shipments containing such items as artwork, jewelry, furs, precious metals, negotiable instruments, and other items listed in our Service Guide."

It is inconceivable that a professional packager and crater such as Mr. Reppert had not previously shipped with FedEx and was not aware of the terms and conditions of shipment through FedEx. Moreover, since Mr. Reppert was acting as the agent for Elegant Reflections, a purveyor of

[23] UCC §613(a).

[24] *Great Southern Wood Preserving, Inc. v. American Home Assur. Co.*, 505 F. Supp. 2d 1287 (M.D. Ala. 2007). *Design Data Corp. v. Maryland Casualty Co.*, 503 N.W.2d 552 (Neb. 1993).

[25] For a discussion of parties' rights, see *Learning Links, Inc. v. United Parcel Services of America, Inc.* 2006 WL 785274 (S.D.N.Y.), *Spray-Tek, Inc. v. Robbins Motor Transp., Inc.*, 426 F. Supp. 2d 875 (W.D. Wis. 2006), and *Dominion Resource Services, Inc. v. 5K Logistics, Inc.*, 2010 WL 2721355 (E.D. Va.).

Continued

antiques and objets d'art, and he had been informed that shipment of the statues with $37,000.00 insurance was unavailable through two of FedEx's competitors, United Parcel Service and Emery Worldwide, Mr. Reppert's interest should have been piqued about FedEx's terms of shipment, and he should have requested a copy of the Service Guide to expressly read the liability provisions regarding shipments of antiques or *objets d'art.*

Finally, one would have thought that a professional packager and crater such as Mr. Reppert would have known to obtain insurance for the shipment. Thus, the Court finds that the King airbill and Service Guide comply with federal common law requirements, and FedEx's limited liability provisions are enforceable.

King raises several arguments why the limited liability provisions are inapplicable. First, King contends there is a material issue of fact as to whether the statues are "items of extraordinary value" or merely "household items." This is not so. Unfortunately for King, the sales price and declared value of the statues–$37,500.00 make it clear that they are not ordinary household items found in the average American home. Additionally, Elegant Reflections holds itself out as a purveyor of antiques and objets d'art, Finding 1 not household items. In short, based on the evidence presented, this Court concludes, as a matter of law, that the statues are "items of extraordinary value," as defined in the King airbill and FedEx Service Guide.

King also argues that the statues were purchased by Mr. Hanasab for use in his own household, and not for resale, display, or collection. However, Mr. Hanasab's intended use of the statues is of limited relevance Michelangelo's David would be no less an "artwork" if used as a coat rack.

For the foregoing reasons, FedEx's motion for partial summary judgment limiting King to damages of no more than $500.00 is granted.

QUESTIONS

1. How could King have avoided paying the seller and having damaged statues?
2. What important principles does the case set out for interstate shipments?
3. Does it make any difference that the artwork was for personal use and not part of a commercial transaction?

(c) Damage to Unidentified Goods. As long as the goods are unidentified, no risk of loss passes to the buyer. If any goods are damaged or destroyed during this period, the loss is the seller's. The buyer is still entitled to receive the goods described by the contract. The seller is therefore liable for breach of contract if the proper goods are not delivered.

The only exceptions to these general rules on damage or destruction arise when the parties have expressly provided in the contract that the destruction of the seller's inventory, crop, or source of supply releases the seller from liability, or when it is clear that the parties contracted for the purchase and sale of part of the seller's supply to the exclusion of any other possible source of such goods. In these cases, destruction of, or damage to, the seller's supply is a condition subsequent that discharges the contract.

17. Effect of Seller's Breach in Risk of Loss

When the seller breaches the contract by sending the buyer goods that do not conform to the contract and the buyer rejects them, the risk of loss does not pass to the buyer. If there has been a breach, the risk of loss remains with the seller even though the risk, according to the contract terms or the Article 2 rules discussed earlier, would ordinarily have passed to the buyer.

Figures 24-3 and 24-4 provide a summary of all the risk provisions for parties in a sales transaction.

E. Determining Rights: Special Situations

18. Returnable Goods Transactions

The parties may agree that the goods to be transferred under the contract can be returned to the seller. This type of arrangement in which goods may be returned is classified as one of the following: (1) a sale on approval, (2) a sale or return, or (3) a consignment sale. In the first two types of transactions, the buyer is allowed to return the goods as an added inducement to purchase. The consignment sale is used when the seller is actually the owner's agent for the purpose of selling goods.[26]

[26] *Berry v. Lucas*, 150 P.3d 424 (Or. App. 2006).

FIGURE 24-3 *Risk of Loss*

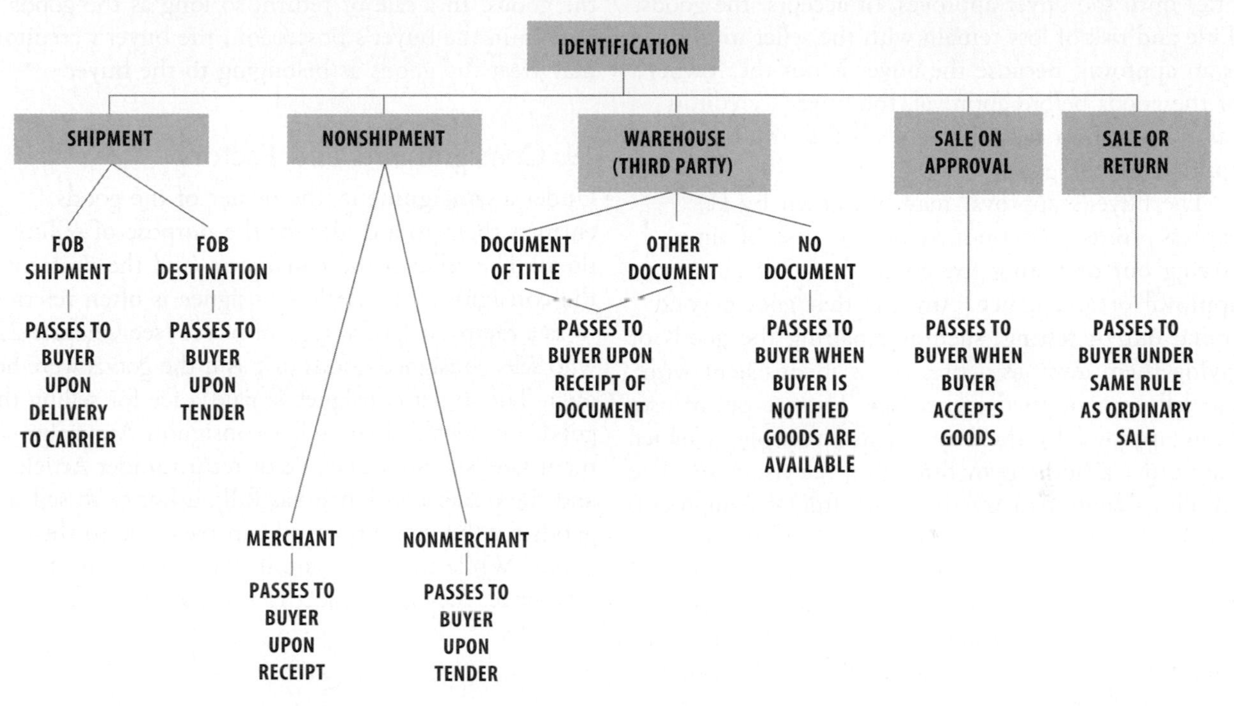

FIGURE 24-4 *Risk of Loss—Revised Article 2*

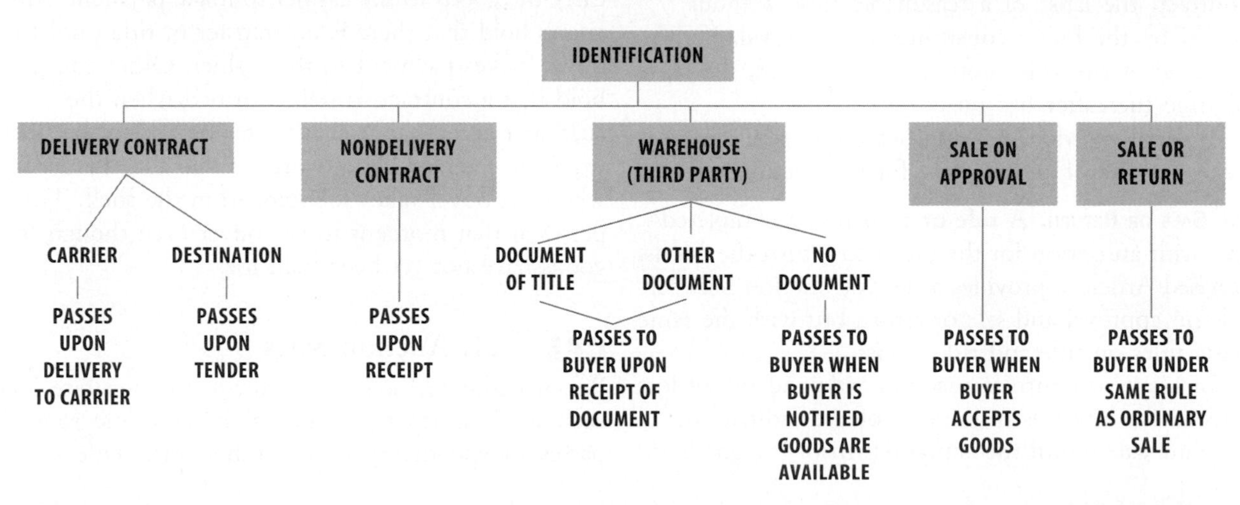

CPA **(A) Sale on Approval.** In a **sale on approval**, no sale takes place (meaning there is no transfer of title) until the buyer approves, or accepts, the goods. Title and risk of loss remain with the seller until there is an approval. Because the buyer is not the "owner" of the goods before approval, the buyer's creditors cannot attach or take the goods before the buyer's approval of the goods.

The buyer's approval may be shown by (1) express words, (2) conduct, or (3) lapse of time. Trying out or testing the goods does not constitute approval or acceptance. Any use that goes beyond trying out or testing, such as repairing the goods or giving them away as a present, is inconsistent with the seller's continued ownership. These types of uses show approval by the buyer. **For Example,** a buyer may order a home gym through a television ad. The ad allows buyers to try the room full of equipment for 30 days and then promises, "If you are not completely satisfied, return the home gym and we'll refund your money." The offer is one for a sale on approval. If the buyer does not return the home gym equipment or contact the seller within 30 days, the sale is complete.

The contract may give the buyer a fixed number of days for approval. The expiration of that period of time, without any action by the buyer, constitutes an approval. Also during this time, the buyer's creditors cannot take the goods pursuant to a judgment or lien. If no time is stated in the contract, the lapse of a reasonable time without action by the buyer constitutes an approval. If the buyer gives the seller notice of disapproval, the lapse of time thereafter has no effect.

If the buyer does not approve the goods, the seller bears the risk of and expense for their return.

(B) Sale or Return. A **sale or return** is a completed sale with an option for the buyer to return the goods. Revised Article 2 provides a new distinction between sale on approval and sale or return but with the same basic rules on title and risk of loss.

In a sale or return transaction, title and risk of loss pass to the buyer as in the case of the ordinary or absolute sale. Until the actual return of the goods is made, title and risk of loss remain with the buyer. The buyer bears the expense for and risk of return of the goods. In a sale or return, so long as the goods remain in the buyer's possession, the buyer's creditors may treat the goods as belonging to the buyer.

19. Consignments and Factors

Under a **consignment**, the owner of the goods entrusts them to a dealer for the purpose of selling them. The seller is the **consignor**, and the dealer is the **consignee**. The dealer-consignee is often referred to as a **factor**, a special type of bailee (see Chapter 22) who sells consigned goods just as if the goods were her own. The dealer-consignee is paid a fee for selling the goods on behalf of the seller-consignor. A consignment sale is treated as a sale or return under Article 2, and the dealer-consignee has full authority to sell the goods for the consignor and can pass title to those goods. While the goods are in the possession of the consignee, they are subject to the claims of the seller's creditors.[27]

20. Self-Service Stores

In the case of goods in a self-service store, the reasonable interpretation of the circumstances is that the store, by its act of putting the goods on display on its shelves, makes an offer to sell such goods for cash and confers on a prospective customer a license to carry the goods to the cashier to make payment. Most courts hold that there is no transfer of title until the buyer makes payment to the cashier. Other courts hold that a contract to sell is formed when the customer accepts the seller's offer by taking the item from the shelf. In other words, a sale actually occurs when the buyer takes the item from the shelf. Title passes at that moment to the buyer even though the goods have not yet been paid for.

CPA 21. Auction Sales

When goods are sold at an auction in separate lots, each lot is a separate transaction, and title to each passes independently of the other lots. Title to

[27] This clarification of creditors' rights in consignments came from Revised Article 9 (see Chapter 34). Revised Article 2 was changed to make the sale or return rights of creditors consistent with Revised Article 9. Prior to these changes, and under current Article 2, whether the seller's creditor could seize the goods depended upon the filing of an Article 9 security interest.

each lot passes when the auctioneer announces by the fall of the hammer or in any other customary manner that the lot in question has been sold to the bidder.

"With reserve" auctions are those that give the auctioneer the right to withdraw the goods from the sale process if the bids are not high enough. If an auction is held "without reserve," the goods must be sold regardless of whether the auctioneer is satisfied with the levels of the bids.

LawFlix

RV (2006)(PG)

Robin Williams leases an RV and drives his family from California to Colorado. Along the way, the RV ends up damaged, in a lake, and generally greatly depreciated in value. The issues of bailment, liability, risk, and title are serious companions to the funny story line of family life and the RV culture.

MAKE THE CONNECTION

SUMMARY

All along the supply chain of a business are issues of risk and title that are often complicated by additional questions about damage to goods in transit, the claims of creditors to goods that are in process under a contract, and insurance. Unless the parties specifically agree otherwise, the solution to these problems depends on the nature of the transaction between the seller and the buyer.

The first issue to be addressed in answering questions of risk, title, and loss is whether the goods are identified. Existing goods are identified at the time the contract is entered into. Future goods, or goods not yet owned by the seller or not yet in existence (as in goods to be manufactured by the seller), are identified when they are shipped, marked, or otherwise designated for the buyer. Without identification, title and risk of loss cannot pass from buyer to seller, nor can the buyer hold an insurable interest.

Once identification has occurred, the issue of title, and hence creditor's rights, can be addressed. If there are identified goods but there is no document of title associated with the goods, then title to the goods passes from the seller to the buyer at the time of the contract.

Sellers can have their goods covered by a document of title. The most common types of documents of title are bills of lading and warehouse receipts. These documents of title, if properly transferred, transfer title to both the document and the underlying goods.

While the seller has no obligation under UCC Article 2 to deliver the goods to the buyer, the parties can agree on delivery as part of their contract. Several common delivery terms are used in supply chain management. *FOB* is "free on board," and its meaning depends on the location that follows the term. *FOB place of shipment* requires the seller to deliver the goods to the carrier. In an FOB place of shipment contract, title to the goods passes from the seller to the buyer when the goods are delivered to the carrier. *FOB place of destination* requires the seller to get the goods to the buyer or a location specified by the buyer and tender the goods there. *FAS* is "free alongside ship," which means free on board for shipment by sea. *CF* is "cost and freight" and requires the seller to deliver the goods to the carrier and make a contract for their shipment. *CIF* is "cost, insurance, and freight" and requires the seller to deliver the goods to the carrier, make a contract for shipment, and purchase insurance for the goods in transit. *COD* means "cash on delivery" and requires the buyer to pay for the goods before taking possession of them.

Ordinarily, sellers cannot pass any title greater than that which they possess. In some cases, however, the law permits a greater title to be transferred even though the transferor may hold voidable title or be in possession of the goods only as in a bailment. These exceptions protect good-faith purchasers.

Risk of loss is an issue for buyers, sellers, and insurers. When risk of loss passes from seller to buyer is controlled, again, by the terms of the contract. In a contract in which there is no agreement on delivery, the risk of loss passes to the buyer upon receipt of the goods if the seller is a merchant and upon tender if the seller is a nonmerchant. Under Revised Article 2, the risk of loss in nonshipment contracts always passes upon receipt, regardless of whether the contract involves a merchant or nonmerchant. If there is an agreement for delivery and the contract provides for shipment only, or FOB place of shipment, then risk of loss passes from seller to buyer when the goods are delivered to the carrier. If the contract provides for delivery to a particular location, or FOB place of destination, then the risk of loss passes from the seller to the buyer when the goods are tendered to the buyer.

Some types of arrangements, such as sales on approval, sales or returns, and consignments or factor arrangements, have specific rules for passage of title and risk of loss. Also, if there is a breach of the contract and the seller ships goods different from those ordered, the breach prevents the risk of loss from passing from the seller to the buyer.

LEARNING OUTCOMES

After studying this chapter, you should be able to clearly explain:

A. Identifying Types of Potential Problems and Transactions

LO.1 Explain when title and risk of loss pass with respect to goods

See *Northern Insurance Company of New York v. 1996 Sea Ray Model 370DA Yacht* on pp. 454–455.

B. Determining Rights: Identification of Goods

LO.2 Determine who bears the risk of loss when goods are damaged or destroyed

See *King Jewelry Inc. v. Federal Express Corporation* on pp. 461–462.

C. Determining Rights: Passage of Title

LO.3 Explain why it is important to know when risk of loss and title pass in transactions for the sale of goods

See *Lite-On Peripherals, Inc. v. Burlington Air Express, Inc.* on p. 459.

D. Determining Rights: Risk of Loss

LO.4 Describe the passage of title and risk in special situations, such as a bailment, sale or return, or a sale on approval

See the *For Example,* discussion of Gunnell's Jewelry on p. 455.

See the *For Example,* discussion of a home gymnasium that is purchased from TV on p. 464.

E. Determining Rights: Special Situations

LO.5 Classify the various circumstances in which title can be passed to a bona fide purchaser

See Thinking Things Through, *Tempur-Pedic Intern., Inc. v. Waste to Charity, Inc.,* on p. 456.

KEY TERMS

bills of lading
CF
CIF
COD
consignee
consignment
consignor
document of title
estoppel
existing goods
factor
FAS
FOB place of destination
FOB place of shipment
fungible goods

future goods	risk of loss	voidable title
identification	sale on approval	warehouse receipts
identified	sale or return	
insurable interest	tender	

QUESTIONS AND CASE PROBLEMS

1. Schock, the buyer, negotiated to purchase a mobile home that was owned by and located on the sellers' property. On April 15, 1985, Schock appeared at the Ronderos' (the sellers') home and paid them the agreed-on purchase price of $3,900. Shock received a bill of sale and an assurance from the Ronderos that the title certificate to the mobile home would be delivered soon. Also on April 15 and with the permission of the sellers, Schock prepared the mobile home for removal. His preparations included the removal of skirting around the mobile home's foundation, the tie-downs, and the foundation blocks, leaving the mobile home to rest on the wheels of its chassis. Schock intended to remove the mobile home from the Ronderos' property a week later, and the Ronderos had no objection to having the mobile home remain on their premises until that time. Two days later, the mobile home was destroyed by high winds as it sat on the Ronderos' property. Schock received a clear certificate of title to the mobile home in the mail. Thereafter, Schock sued the Ronderos for return of his money on the ground that when the mobile home was destroyed, the risk of loss remained with the Ronderos. Who should win the lawsuit? [*Schock v. Ronderos,* 394 N.W.2d 697 (N.D.)]

2. John C. Clark, using the alias Thomas Pecora, rented a 1994 Lexus from Alamo Rent-A-Car on December 21, 1994. Clark did not return the car and, using falsified signatures, obtained a California so-called quick title.

   Clark advertised the car for sale in the *Las Vegas Review Journal.* Terry and Vyonne Mendenhall called the phone number in the ad and reached Clark. He told them that he lived at a country club and could not have people coming to his house to look at the car. He instead drove the car to their house for their inspection the next morning. The car title was in the name of J. C. Clark Enterprises. The Mendenhalls bought the car for $34,000 in cash. They made some improvements on the car and registered it in Utah. On February 24, 1995, Alamo reported the car stolen. On March 21, 1995, the Nevada Department of Motor Vehicles seized the car from the Mendenhalls. The car was returned to Alamo and the Mendenhalls filed suit. The lower court found for the Mendenhalls, and Alamo appealed. Who gets the car and why? [*Alamo Rent-A-Car v. Mendenhall,* 937 P.2d 69 (Nev.)]

3. Felix DeWeldon is a well-known sculptor and art collector. He owned three paintings valued at $26,000 that he displayed in his home in Newport, Rhode Island. In 1991, he declared bankruptcy and DeWeldon, Ltd., purchased all of DeWeldon's personal property from the bankruptcy trustee. Nancy Wardell, the sole shareholder of DeWeldon, Ltd., sold her stock to Byron Preservation Trust, which then sold Felix an option to repurchase the paintings. At all times, the paintings were on display in DeWeldon's home.

   In 1994, DeWeldon's son Byron told Robert McKean that his father was interested in selling the paintings. After viewing them, McKean then purchased the paintings for $50,000. DeWeldon, Ltd., brought suit to have the paintings returned, claiming McKean did not have title because Byron did not have the authority to sell the paintings. Will McKean get the paintings? [*DeWeldon, Ltd. v. McKean,* 125 F.3d 24 (1st Cir)]

4. Helen Thomas contracted to purchase a pool heater from Sunkissed Pools. As part of the $4,000 contract, Sunkissed agreed to install the pool heater, which was delivered to Thomas's home and left in the driveway. The heater was too heavy for Thomas to lift, and she was forced to leave it in the driveway because no one from

Sunkissed responded to her calls about its installation. Subsequently, the heater disappeared from the driveway. Sunkissed maintained that the risk of loss had passed to Thomas. Thomas maintained that the failure to install the heater as promised is a breach of contract. Who should bear the risk for the stolen pool heater? [*In re Thomas,* 182 B.R. 774 (Bankr. S.D. Fla.)]

5. Around June 2005, PPI purchased three pallets of computer wafers from Omneon Video Graphics. PPI requested that Omneon ship the wafers directly to the City University of New York, the end purchaser of the goods. Omneon and PPI agreed that Omneon would ship the wafers FOB Omneon's dock. Somewhere between the loading dock and City University, one pallet of the wafers disappeared. Who bears the loss for the lost pallet and why? [*OneBeacon Ins. Co. v. Hass Industries, Inc.,* 634 F.3d 1092 (9th Cir. 2011)]

6. Using a bad check, B purchased a used automobile from a dealer. B then took the automobile to an auction at which the automobile was sold to a party who had no knowledge of its history. When B's check was dishonored, the dealer brought suit against the party who purchased the automobile at the auction. Was the dealer entitled to reclaim the automobile? [*Greater Louisville Auto Auction, Inc. v. Ogle Buick, Inc.,* 387 S.W.2d 17 (Ky.)]

7. Coppola, who collected coins, joined a coin club, First Coinvestors, Inc. The club would send coins to its members, who were to pay for them or return them within 10 days. What was the nature of the transaction? [*First Coinvestors, Inc. v. Coppola,* 388 N.Y.S.2d 833]

8. Would buying a car from a mechanic who works at a car dealership qualify as purchasing a car in the ordinary course of business? [*Steele v. Ellis,* 961 F. Supp. 1458 (D. Kan.)]

9. Does a pawnbroker who purchases property in good faith acquire good title to that property? Can the pawnbroker pass good title? [*Fly v. Cannon,* 813 S.W.2d 458 (Tenn.App.)]

10. Larsen Jewelers sold a necklace to Conway on a layaway plan. Conway paid a portion of the price and made additional payments from time to time. The necklace was to remain in the possession of Larsen until payment was fully made. The Larsen jewelry store was burglarized, and Conway's necklace and other items were taken. Larsen argued that Conway must bear the risk of loss. Conway sought recovery of the full value of the necklace. Decide. [*Conway v. Larsen Jewelry,* 429 N.Y.S.2d 378]

11. Future Tech International, Inc., is a buyer and distributor of Samsung monitors and other computer products. In 1993, Future Tech determined that brand loyalty was important to customers, and it sought to market its own brand of computer products. Future Tech, a Florida firm, developed its own brand name of MarkVision and entered into a contract in 1994 with Tae II Media, a Korean firm. The contract provided that Tae II Media would be the sole source and manufacturer for the MarkVision line of computer products.

    The course of performance on the contract did not go well. Future Tech alleged that from the time the ink was dry on the contract, Tae II Media had no intention of honoring its commitment to supply computers and computer products to Future Tech. Future Tech alleged that Tae II Media entered into the contract with the purpose of limiting Future Tech's competitive ability because Tae II Media had its own Tech Media brand of computers and computer products.

    Future Tech, through threats and demands, was able to have the first line of MarkVision products completed. Tae II Media delivered the computers to a boat but, while in transit, ordered the shipping line (Maersk Lines) to return the computers. The terms of their contract provided for delivery "FOB Pusan Korea." Future Tech filed suit, claiming that Tae II Media could not take the computer products because title had already passed to Future Tech. Is this interpretation of who has title correct? [*Future Tech Int'l, Inc. v. Tae II Media, Ltd.,* 944 F. Supp. 1538 (S.D. Fla.)]

12. Bakker Brothers of Idaho agreed to buy Charles E. Graff's 1989 onion seed crop. The contract required that the onion seeds have an 85 percent germination rate. Despite careful testing and

advice from experts, Bakker Brothers could not get a germination rate on the seed tested higher than 62 to 69 percent. Bakker Brothers rejected the seed, notified Graff, and awaited instructions. Graff gave no instructions and the seed spoiled. Graff sought to recover the contract price from Bakker Brothers because the risk of loss had passed. The trial court granted summary judgment for Bakker Brothers, and Graff appealed. Was the trial court decision correct? Explain why or why not. [*Graff v. Bakker Brothers of Idaho, Inc.,* 934 P.2d 1228 (Wash. App.)]

13. Without permission, Grissom entered onto land owned by another and then proceeded to cut and sell the timber from the land. On learning that the timber had been sold, the owner of the land brought an action to recover the timber from the purchaser. The purchaser argued that he was a good-faith purchaser who had paid value and therefore was entitled to keep the timber. Decide. [*Baysprings Forest Products, Inc. v. Wade,* 435 So.2d 690 (Miss.)]

14. Brown Sales ordered goods from Eberhard Manufacturing Co. The contract contained no agreement about who would bear the risk of loss. There were no shipping terms. The seller placed the goods on board a common carrier with instructions to deliver the goods to Brown. While in transit, the goods were lost. Which party will bear the loss? Explain. [*Eberhard Manufacturing Co. v. Brown,* 232 N.W.2d 378 (Mich. App.)]

CPA QUESTIONS

1. Bond purchased a painting from Wool, who is not in the business of selling art. Wool tendered delivery of the painting after receiving payment in full from Bond. Bond informed Wool that Bond would be unable to take possession of the painting until later that day. Thieves stole the painting before Bond returned. The risk of loss:
   a. Passed to Bond at Wool's tender of delivery.
   b. Passed to Bond at the time the contract was formed and payment was made.
   c. Remained with Wool, because the parties agreed on a later time of delivery.
   d. Remained with Wool, because Bond had not yet received the painting.

2. Which of the following statements applies to a sale on approval under the UCC Sales Article?
   a. Both the buyer and seller must be merchants.
   b. The buyer must be purchasing the goods for resale.
   c. Risk of loss for the goods passes to the buyer when the goods are accepted after the trial period.
   d. Title to the goods passes to the buyer on delivery of the goods to the buyer.

3. If goods have been delivered to a buyer pursuant to a sale or return contract, the:
   a. Buyer may use the goods but not resell them.
   b. Seller is liable for the expenses incurred by the buyer in returning the goods to the seller.
   c. Title to the goods remains with the seller.
   d. Risk of loss for the goods passes to the buyer.

4. Cey Corp. entered into a contract to sell parts to Deck, Ltd. The contract provided that the goods would be shipped "FOB Cey's warehouse." Cey shipped parts different from those specified in the contract. Deck rejected the parts. A few hours after Deck informed Cey that the parts were rejected, they were destroyed by fire in Deck's warehouse. Cey believed that the parts were conforming to the contract. Which of the following statements is correct?
   a. Regardless of whether the parts were conforming, Deck will bear the loss because the contract was a shipment contract.
   b. If the parts were nonconforming, Deck had the right to reject them, but the risk of loss remains with Deck until Cey takes possession of the parts.

c. If the parts were conforming, risk of loss does not pass to Deck until a reasonable period of time after they are delivered to Deck.

d. If the parts were nonconforming, Cey will bear the risk of loss, even though the contract was a shipment contract.

5. Under the Sales Articles of the UCC, when a contract for the sale of goods stipulates that the seller ship the goods by common carrier "FOB purchaser's loading dock," which of the parties bears the risk of loss during shipment?

a. The purchaser, because risk of loss passes when the goods are delivered to the carrier.

b. The purchaser, because title to the goods passes at the time of shipment.

c. The seller, because risk of loss passes only when the goods reach the purchaser's loading dock.

d. The seller, because risk of loss remains with the seller until the goods are accepted by the purchaser.

6. When do title and risk of loss for conforming goods pass to the buyer under a shipment contract covered by the Sales Article of the UCC?

a. When the goods are identified and designated for shipment.

b. When the goods are given to a common carrier.

c. When the goods arrive at their destination.

d. When the goods are tendered to the buyer at their destination.

CHAPTER 25

© Manuel Gutjahr/iStockphoto.com

Product Liability: Warranties and Torts

learningoutcomes

After studying this chapter, you should be able to

- **LO.1** List the theories of product liability
- **LO.2** Identify who may sue and who may be sued when a defective product causes harm
- **LO.3** Define and give examples of an express warranty
- **LO.4** List and explain the types of implied warranties
- **LO.5** Explain warranty protections under federal law
- **LO.6** State what constitutes a breach of warranty
- **LO.7** Describe the extent and manner in which implied warranties may be disclaimed under the UCC and the CISG

What happens when goods do not work? Who can recover for injury caused by defective goods? What can you do when the goods are not as promised or pictured?

A. General Principles

When defective goods result in damages or injury to the buyer or other parties, the UCC and tort law provide remedies.

1. Theories of Liability

Two centuries ago, a buyer was limited to recovery from a seller for breach of an express guarantee or for negligence or fraud. After the onset of mass production and distribution, however, these remedies had little value. A guarantee was good, but in the ordinary sales transaction no one stopped to get a guarantee. Few customers remembered to ask the manager of the supermarket to give a guarantee that the loaf of bread purchased was fit to eat. Further, negligence and fraud have become difficult to prove in a mass production world. How can one prove there was a problem in the production process for a can of soup prepared months earlier?

To give buyers protection from economic loss and personal injuries, the concept of warranty liability developed. **Warranties** are either express or implied and can be found in the UCC. There have been changes in warranty liability under the Revised UCC, but because of its limited adoption they are mentioned only briefly. Many courts have decided that still broader protection beyond the UCC contract remedies is required and have created the additional concept of **strict tort liability** for defective goods.

There are five theories in law for what is often called *product liability*, or the protection of buyers that also allows them recovery for injury and economic loss: express warranty, implied warranty, negligence, fraud, and strict tort liability. Any statutory remedies under consumer law or employment law are additional means of recovery. The plaintiff does not have a choice of all theories in every case; the facts of the case dictate the choices the plaintiff has available for possible theories of recovery.

2. Nature of Harm

A defective product can cause harm to person, property, or economic interests. **For Example,** the buyer of a truck may be injured when, through a defect, the truck goes out of control and plunges down the side of a hill. Passengers in the truck, bystanders, or the driver of a car hit by the truck may also be injured. The defective truck may cause injury to a total stranger who seeks to rescue one of the victims. Property damage could occur if the buyer's truck careens off the road into a fence or even a house and causes damages. Another driver's car may be damaged. Commercial and economic interests of the buyer are affected by the fact that the truck is defective. Even if there is no physical harm, the defective truck is not as valuable as it would have been. The buyer who has paid for the truck on the basis of its value as it should have been has sustained an economic loss. If the buyer is required to rent a truck from someone else or loses an opportunity to haul freight for compensation, the fact that the truck was defective also causes economic or commercial loss.

CPA 3. Who Is Liable in Product Liability

Until the early part of the twentieth century, only the parties to a sales contract could recover from each other on product liability issues. A seller was liable to the buyer, but the seller was not liable to others because they were not in **privity of contract** with the seller or in a direct contract relationship with the seller. This requirement of privity of contract has now been widely rejected.[1]

(a) Who Can Recover under UCC Warranties. Today, not only the buyer but also customers and employees of the buyer and even third persons or bystanders may recover because of harm caused by a defective product. Most states have abolished the requirement of **privity** when the person injured by a product is a member of the buyer's family or household or is a guest of the buyer and has sustained personal injury

[1] UCC §2-318, Alternative A. The Code gives the states the option of adopting the provision summarized in this chapter or of making a wide abolition of the requirement of privity by adopting Alternative B or C of §2-318. As of October 2012, these states/areas had adopted the versions of §2-318 (not Revised Article 2) as follows: Alternative A adopted in Alaska, Arizona, Arkansas, Connecticut, District of Columbia, Florida, Georgia, Idaho, Illinois, Indiana, Kentucky, Maryland, Michigan, Mississippi, Missouri, Montana, Nebraska, Nevada, New Jersey, New Mexico, North Carolina, Ohio, Oklahoma, Oregon, Pennsylvania, Tennessee, Washington, West Virginia, and Wisconsin. Alternative B adopted in Alabama, Colorado, Delaware, Kansas, South Carolina, South Dakota, Vermont, and Wyoming. Alternative C adopted in Hawaii, Iowa, Minnesota, North Dakota, Vermont, and Utah.

because of the product.[2] A few states require privity of contract, particularly when the plaintiff does not sustain personal injury or property damage and seeks to recover only economic loss.[3]

UCC section 2-318 provides alternatives for who can recover for breach of warranty. Alternative A extends warranty protection to "any individual who is in the family or household of the immediate buyer or the remote purchaser or who is a guest in the home of either…." Alternative B covers "any individual who may reasonably be expected to use, consume, or be affected by the goods." Alternative C covers the same groups as Alternative B but adds that the protections provided cannot be disclaimed.

(b) Who Is Liable under UCC Warranties. Someone who is injured by a defective product can recover from the seller, the manufacturer of the product, and generally even the manufacturer of the component part of the product that caused the harm.[4] **For Example,** when a person is struck by an automobile because the driver has lost control because of the car's defective brakes, the person who was struck and injured may seek recovery from the seller and the manufacturer of the car. The maker of the brake assembly or system that the car manufacturer installed in the car may also be liable.

B. Express Warranties

A warranty may be express or implied. Both express and implied warranties operate as though the defendant had made an express promise or statement of fact. Both express and implied warranties are governed primarily by the UCC.

CPA 4. Definition of Express Warranty

An **express warranty** is a statement of fact or promise of performance relating to the goods that becomes a basis of the buyer's bargain.[5]

"Basis of the bargain" means that the buyer has purchased the goods because of what the seller has stated about those goods. A statement by the seller regarding the quality, capacity, or other characteristic of the goods is an express warranty. **For Example,** express warranties in sellers' statements are "This cloth is all wool," "This paint is for household woodwork," and "This engine can produce 50 horsepower." A representation that an airplane is a 2007 model is an express warranty. "This computer monitor has a glare-proof screen" is another example of an express warranty.

The manufacturer of the goods cannot isolate itself from claims that are communicated through retailers. **For Example,** WorldWide Wholesalers could purchase Pop-Tarts from Kellogg's. Kellogg's makes warranties to WorldWide Wholesalers directly through their contract relationship, one of privity. WorldWide Wholesalers then sells those Pop-Tarts to grocery stores, convenience stores, and perhaps even to commercial food distributors who then sell them to cafeterias in schools and nursing homes. WorldWide's buyers are remote purchasers. The warranty is not lost through the distribution chain.

5. Form of Express Warranty

No particular group of words is necessary to constitute an express warranty. A seller need not state that a warranty is being made or that one is intended. It is sufficient that the seller asserts a fact that becomes a basis of the bargain or transaction between the parties. UCC §2-313(2) provides, "It is not necessary to the creation of an express warranty that the seller use formal words such as 'warrant' or 'guarantee' or that the seller have a specific intention to make a warranty."[6] If a warranty is a critical part of the bargain for the buyer, it cannot be disclaimed.

An express warranty can be written or printed as well as oral. The words on the label of a can and in a newspaper ad for "boned chicken" constitute an express warranty that the can contains chicken that is free of bones.

[2] Lack of privity is not a defense in a suit for breach of warranty. *Hyundai Motor America, Inc. v. Goodin*, 822 N.E.2d 947 (Ind. 2005). Revised Article 2 expands warranty protection (§§2-408 and 2-409).

[3] *Praxair, Inc. v. General Insulation Co.* 611 F. Supp. 2d 318 (W.D.N.Y. 2009).

[4] However, see *Barnett v. Leiserv*, 968 F. Supp. 690 (N.D. Ga. 1997), where the child of the person who bought coffee for a friend could not recover for burns from coffee spilled on her by the friend. The court also noted that a child who spills coffee on himself could not recover either. Where the coffee maker at the retail store where the coffee was purchased is not defective, the case is one in negligence and requires proof of breach of duty but does not require privity. *McMahon v. Bunn-O-Matic Corp.*, 150 F.3d 651 (7th Cir. 1998).

[5] UCC §2-313; *Miles v. Raymond Corp.*, 612 F. Supp. 2d 913 (N.D. Oh. 2005). *Samsung Electronics America, Inc. v. Blu-Ray Class Action Litigation*, 2008 WL 5451024, 67 UCC Rep. Serv.2d 794 (D.N.J. 2008). In the UCC Revised Article 2, the "basis of the bargain" requirement is changed to "become part of the agreement." UCC §2-313(1)(a). Also, §2-404 is the new express warranty section.

[6] UCC §2-313(2).

Descriptions of goods, such as the illustrations in a seller's catalog, are express warranties. The express warranty given is that the goods will conform to the catalog illustrations.

6. Seller's Opinion or Statement of Value

A statement about the value of goods or the seller's opinion or commendation of the goods does not create a warranty.[7] Section 2-313(1)(b) provides, "an affirmation merely of the value of the goods or a statement purporting to be merely the seller's opinion or commendation of goods does not create a warranty."[8] A buyer cannot hold a seller liable for sales talk. **For Example,** sales talk or puffery by a seller that his cloth is "the best piece of cloth on the market" or that her glassware is "as good as anyone else's" is merely an opinion that the buyer cannot ordinarily treat as a warranty. Statements made by a cosmetics seller that its products are "the future of beauty" and are "just the product for [the plaintiff]" are sales talk arising in the ordinary course of merchandising. They do not constitute warranties.

The UCC does permit an exception to the sales talk liability exemption when the circumstances are such that a reasonable person would rely on such a statement. If the buyer has reason to believe that the seller has expert knowledge of the conditions of the market, and the buyer requests the seller's opinion as an expert, the buyer is entitled to accept as a fact the seller's statement of whether a particular good is the best obtainable. The opinion statement could be reasonably regarded as forming part of the basis of the bargain. A statement by a florist that bulbs are of first-grade quality may be a warranty.[9]

7. Warranty of Conformity to Description, Sample, or Model

When the contract is based in part on the understanding that the seller will supply goods according to a particular description or that the goods will be the same as the sample or a model, the seller is bound by an express warranty that the goods conform to the description, sample, or model.[10] Section 2-313 of the UCC provides, "Any sample or model which is made part of the basis of the bargain creates an express warranty that the whole of the goods shall conform to the sample or model."[11] **For Example,** a blender sitting out in a store is a warranty that the blenders in the boxes below are the same. A model of a mobile home is an express warranty that the mobile home being sold contains the same features.

8. Federal Regulation of Express Warranties

A seller who makes a written express warranty for a consumer product costing more than $10 must conform to certain standards imposed by federal statute[12] and by regulations of the Federal Trade Commission (FTC).[13] The seller is not required to make any express warranty. However, if the seller does make an express warranty in a consumer sale, it must be stated in ordinary, understandable language and must be made available for inspection before purchasing so that the consumer may comparison shop.[14]

(A) Full Warranties. If the seller or the label states that a full warranty is made, the seller is obligated to fix or replace a defective product within a reasonable time without cost to the buyer. If the product cannot be fixed or if a reasonable number of repair attempts are unsuccessful, the buyer has the choice of a cash refund or a free replacement. No unreasonable burden may be placed on a buyer seeking to obtain warranty service. **For Example,** a manufacturer offering a full warranty cannot require that the buyer pay the cost of sending the product to or from a warranty service point. A warrantor making a full warranty cannot require the buyer to return the product to a warranty service point if the product weighs over 35 pounds, to return a part for service unless it can be easily removed, or to fill out and return a warranty registration card shortly after purchase to make the warranty effective. If the manufacturer imposes any of these requirements, the warranty is not a "full

[7] Id.; *Giles v. Wyeth, Inc.*, 500 F. Supp. 2d 1063 (S.D. Ill. 2007); *In re Ford Motor Co. E-350 Van Products Liability Litigation*, 2008 WL 4126264, 66 UCC Rep. Serv.2d 726 (D.N.J. 2008).

[8] UCC §2-313(1)(b).

[9] Likewise, a statement by an art gallery owner that a "painting is by Francis Bacon" is an express warranty. *Rogath v. Siebenmann*, 129 F.3d 902 (7th Cir. 1997). See also *Forbes v. General Motors Corp.*, 935 So.2d 869 (Miss. 2006).

[10] *Harlan v. Roadtrek Motorhomes, Inc.*, 2009 WL 928309, 68 UCC Rep. Serv.2d 750 (S.D. Cal. 2009).

[11] UCC §2-313(1)(c).

[12] The Magnuson-Moss Act, or Federal Consumer Product Warranty Law, can be found at 15 U.S.C. §2301 *et seq.*

[13] 16 C.F.R. §700.1 *et seq.*

[14] Federal warranty language rules apply only in consumer sales, or sales for personal or home use, not in business purchases. There are also state laws that can limit express warranties to the first purchaser. *McMahon v. Advance Stores Co. Inc.*, 705 S.E.2d 131 (W. Va. 2010).

warranty" under federal law and must be labeled a *limited warranty*. A **full warranty** runs with the product and lasts for its full term regardless of who owns the product.

(B) Limited Warranties. A **limited warranty** is any warranty that does not meet the requirements for a full warranty. **For Example,** a warranty is limited if the buyer must pay any cost for repair or replacement of a defective product, if only the first buyer is covered by the warranty, or if the warranty covers only part of the product. A limited warranty must be conspicuously described as such by the seller.[15]

(C) International Product Safety Laws in the United States. In 2008, in response to the lead paint discovered in toys imported from China, Congress passed the **Consumer Product Safety Improvement Act (CPSIA)**, which promulgated new standards for product safety.[16] Under CPSIA, the products most affected are those for children under the age of 12. The act provides no discretion for lead levels; it prohibits lead in products for children under 12. Because of the outsourcing issues that resulted in the toys with lead paint making their way into the United States, the CPSIA requires accredited third-party laboratory testing, product tracking, labels, registration, and new warnings in ads and on Web sites about the manufacturing sources of toys. CPSIA increases to $100 million the penalties the Consumer Product Safety Commission can assess.

9. Effect of Breach of Express Warranty

If an express warranty is false, there is a breach of warranty. The warrantor is then liable. It is no defense that the seller or manufacturer who made the express warranty honestly believed that the warranty was true, had exercised due care in manufacturing or handling the product, or had no reason to believe that the warranty was false. The *La Trace v. Webster* case deals with an issue of a descriptive express warranty.

La Trace v. Webster, 17 So. 3d 1210 (Ala. Civ. App. 2008)

Fake Tiffany Lamps for $56,200 and a Disclaimer

Richard W. La Trace attended an auction at B & B Antiques, Auction & Realty, a business owned and operated by Ray Webster, Deborah Webster, Bo Webster, and Laura Webster (collectively "the Websters"). La Trace purchased five lamps that were identified at the auction as "Tiffany" lamps and one lampshade that was also identified at the auction as a "Tiffany" product. La Trace spent a total of $56,200 on the lamps.

La Trace contacted Fontaine's Auction Gallery in Pittsfield, Massachusetts, to inquire about selling the lamps in an auction. Fontaine's sent Dean Lowry, an expert in Tiffany products, to examine La Trace's lamps and Lowry determined that the lamps were not authentic Tiffany products but were, in fact, reproductions. La Trace filed suit against the Websters and B & B for fraudulent suppression, fraudulent misrepresentation, breach of warranty, breach of contract, negligence, and wantonness.[17] The Websters claimed they thought the lamps were authentic and pointed out that their sales brochure and "Conditions of Auction" document contained the following disclaimer:

> *1. All property is sold AS IS WHERE IS, and we make NO guarantees, warranties or representations, expressed or implied, with respect to the property or the correctness of the catalog or other description of authenticity of authorship, physical condition, size, quality, rarity, importance, provenance, exhibitions, literature or historical relevance of the property or otherwise. No statement anywhere, whether oral or written, shall be deemed such a guarantee, warranty or representation.*

On a motion for summary judgment, the court found for the Websters, indicating that La Trace trusted blindly and should not have done so. La Trace appealed.

JUDICIAL OPINION

THOMAS, Judge … La Trace alleged in his complaint that the Websters described the lamps that he bought as "Tiffany" products during the auction. Alabama courts have held that statements by a seller that are mere sales talk or "puffery" do not give rise to express warranties. Examples of puffery include statements describing an item as "in good shape," or "in good condition." On the other hand, as provided in § 7-2-313, representations of fact do give rise to express warranties. This court has held that a statement by a seller of a boat to the

[15] The federal regulations here do not preempt Article 2 warranty coverage. *Wyeth v. Levine,* 555 U.S. 555 (2009). However, FDA regulations can preempt recovery against generic manufacturers of drugs who must use FDA-approved labeling only and not include additional warnings. *PLIVA, Inc. v. Mensing,* 131 S.Ct. 2567 (2011).

[16] 15 U.S.C. §1278a.

[17] B & B was dismissed from the case because it had not yet been properly formed as an LLC. See Chapter 41 for more information on forming a business entity properly.

Continued

effect that the boat was "winterized" was a statement of fact. Similarly, this court has held that a statement by a seller of a trailer that the trailer was a 2000 model-year trailer was a statement of fact.

The Websters do not dispute that the description of the lamps as "Tiffany" products was an affirmation of fact or a "description of the goods." The Websters claim, however, that the description of the lamps as "Tiffany" products did not become part of the basis of the bargain because La Trace signed the conditions of auction before any potential express warranties could be made, effectively rendering such warranties inoperative.... [T]he alleged representations that the lamps were "Tiffany" products took place during the auction and were not accompanied by any qualifying statements indicating that the authenticity of the lamps was in doubt. Although the disclaimers that appeared in the sales brochure and the "Conditions of Auction" document may have been effective to prevent the formation of any express warranties that might otherwise have arisen in those documents, a disclaimer in a document is [not] effective to prevent a seller from making express warranties in the future.

In view of the principle that the whole purpose of the law of warranty is to determine what it is that the seller has in essence agreed to sell, the policy is adopted of those cases which refuse except in unusual circumstances to recognize a material deletion of the seller's obligation. Thus, a contract is normally a contract for a sale of something describable and described. A clause generally disclaiming "all warranties, express or implied" cannot reduce the seller's obligation with respect to such description and therefore cannot be given literal effect.

The foundation of every express warranty provision is the core description. "Toyota," "a pair of shoes," or "a Monet" are all examples of core descriptions. The core description, at base, provides a reference point for the level of performance to which the seller's performance must conform. And, because it is assumed under the Code that the object of every sale regulated by the Code is describable, the core description is nondisclaimable by a seller, being the basic foundation upon which every sales contract is made.

Because the Websters presented no evidence negating La Trace's factual claims and because we have concluded that the Websters' legal arguments in regard to the breach-of-warranty claim are not well founded, we must also conclude that the Websters failed to establish a *prima facie* case that there was no genuine issue of material fact and that they were entitled to a judgment as a matter of law.

[Reversed]

QUESTIONS

1. What is the difference between a core description express warranty and other types of express warranty?
2. Why was the disclaimer in the auction materials ineffective?
3. What lessons should those who sell goods at auctions take from this case?

C. Implied Warranties

Whenever a sale of goods is made, certain warranties are implied unless they are expressly excluded. Implied warranties differ depending on whether the seller is a merchant.

10. Definition of Implied Warranty

An **implied warranty** is one that was not expressly made by the seller but that is implied in certain circumstances by law. An implied warranty arises automatically from the fact that a sale has been made regardless of the seller's conduct.

Express warranties arise because they form part of the basis on which the sale has been made. Implied warranties can exist independent of express warranties. When both express and implied warranties exist, they are interpreted as consistent, if possible. If the warranties cannot be applied together, then the express warranty prevails over any implied warranty except that an implied warranty of fitness for a particular purpose prevails over an express warranty.

11. Implied Warranties of Sellers

Sellers give different types of implied warranties.

CPA **(A) Warranty of Title.** Every seller, by the mere act of selling, makes an implied warranty that the seller's title to the goods is good and that the seller has the right to transfer title to the goods.[18]

The **warranty of title** may be disclaimed either by using the words, "There is no warranty of title," or by

[18] UCC §2-312. The key change in the language in Revised Article 2 is that the seller warrants that the buyer will not be subjected to unreasonable litigation.

certain circumstances.[19] If a buyer has reason to know that the seller does not claim to hold the title or that the seller is limited in what can be promised, the warranty of title is disclaimed. **For Example,** no warranty of title arises when the seller makes the sale in a representative capacity, such as a sheriff, an auctioneer, or an administrator of a decedent's estate. Similarly, no warranty arises when the seller makes the sale as a creditor disposing of a debtor's collateral (security). The damages for warranty of title are often the purchase price because the buyer may have to surrender the goods to their rightful owner.[20]

(B) Warranty against Encumbrances. Every seller makes an implied **warranty against encumbrances**, that is, that the goods will be delivered free from any security interest or any other lien or encumbrance of which the buyer at the time of the sales transaction had no knowledge. If the seller sells an automobile to the buyer and then delivers a car with an outstanding lien on it that was unknown to the buyer at the time of the sale, there is a breach of the warranty against encumbrances.

CPA **(C) Warranty of Fitness for a Particular Purpose.**[21] A buyer may intend to use the goods for a particular or unusual purpose, as contrasted with the ordinary use for which they are customarily sold. If the seller states that the goods will be fit for the buyer's purpose with the buyer relying on the seller's skill or judgment to select or furnish suitable goods, and the seller, at the time of contracting, knows or has reason to know of both the buyer's particular purpose and the buyer's reliance on the seller's judgment, then the seller has created an implied warranty of fitness for a particular purpose.[22] **For Example,** when the seller represents to a buyer that the two hamsters being sold are of the same gender and can safely occupy the same cage with no offspring, an implied warranty of fitness has been given. When the buyer makes the purchase without relying on the seller's skill and judgment, no warranty of fitness for a particular purpose arises.[23]

CPA 12. Additional Implied Warranties of Merchant Sellers

A seller who deals in goods of the kind in question is classified as a merchant by the UCC and is held to a higher degree of responsibility for the product than one who is merely making a casual sale.

(A) Warranty against Infringement. Unless otherwise agreed, every merchant seller warrants that the goods will be delivered free of the rightful claim of any third person by way of patent, copyright, or trademark infringement.

For Example, if a buyer purchases videos from a seller who is later discovered to be a bootlegger of the films on the videos, the buyer has a cause of action against the seller for any damages he experiences for perhaps renting out the bootlegged videos. Under Revised Article 2, the seller can disclaim the warranty against infringement.

E-Commerce & Cyberlaw

"Wii" Were Hurt

Nintendo's "Wii" video game system features games with simulation of tennis and boxing. To play the game, the players use a motion-sensitive controller in their hand. When playing the game, some players, in making the motions necessary for the sport, have lost control of their controllers. The controllers have crashed into other objects, including television sets, and then injured the players. Players who have been so injured brought a class action suit against Nintendo for a defective wrist strap on the controllers, designed to keep the controllers from flying out of control. Although the class action was not certified, the court held that there could be remedies on an individual basis for problems with the design of the physical equipment used with computers. [*Elvig v. Nintendo of America, Inc.*, 696 F. Supp. 2d 1207 (D.Colo. 2010)].

[19] *Quality Components Corp. v. Kel-Keef Enterprises, Inc.*, 738 N.E.2d 524 (Ill. App. 2000).

[20] *Mayberry v. Volkswagen of America, Inc.*, 692 N.W.2d 226 (Wis. 2005).

[21] UCC §2-315. The warranty does not apply when the injury is not caused by any function represented for the product. For example, a buyer could not recover when she hit her head on a wall-mounted fire extinguisher, for the representations were that it would work for home fires, not about mounting it in the home. *Hayes v. Larsen Mfg. Co., Inc.*, 871 F. Supp. 56 (D. Me. 1996).

[22] UCC §2-315. *Nationwide Agribusiness Ins. Co. v. SMA Elevator Const. Inc.*, 816 F. Supp. 2d 631 (N.D. Iowa 2011).

[23] *Berge Helene Ltd. v. GE Oil & Gas, Inc.*, 830 F. Supp. 2d 235 (S.D. Tex. 2011). Manufacturing to buyer's specifications precludes recovery for breach of the warranty of fitness for a particular purpose. *Simmons v. Washing Equipment Technologies* 857 N.Y.S.2d 412 (2008).

(B) WARRANTY OF MERCHANTABILITY OR FITNESS FOR NORMAL USE. A merchant seller makes an **implied warranty of the merchantability** of the goods sold.[24] This warranty is a group of promises, the most important of which is that the goods are fit for the ordinary purposes for which they are sold. This warranty, unless disclaimed, is given in every sale of goods by a merchant. Section 2-314 provides, "Unless excluded or modified, a warranty that the goods shall be merchantable is implied in a contract for their sale if the seller is a merchant with respect to goods of that kind."[25]

Oheka Management, Inc. v. Home Theatre Interiors LLC, 2007 WL 3325861 (N.Y.Supp.)

When the AV Guys Get It Wrong

From February through July 2004, Oheka Management, Inc. (plaintiff) purchased an audiovisual system from Home Theatre Interiors (defendant) for $86,000, which included installation of said audiovisual equipment. The system was required to be operational for an event scheduled for July 18, 2004, at Oheka.

Home Theater Interiors did not properly install or maintain the system. Ohkea was left with no alternative but to hire other technicians to complete the set-up and to repair any improper servicing and installations.

Home Theater Interiors argues that it was Oheka's architect, Richard Diller, who caused the problems with the system and its installation. Additionally, Home Theater maintains that because there was no signed contract for the system, Home Theater could not breach it or any warranties. However, the unsigned contract discussed the variety of audiovisual equipment that Oheka purchased from Home Theatre, as well as the installation that Home Theatre would perform. The unsigned contract contained a warranty for on-site parts and labor for this job which was to run for one year's time from date of purchase.

Oheka moved for summary judgment for breach of warranty and breach of contract.

JUDICIAL OPINION

BUCARIA, Justice

The defendant has not submitted evidence relieving it of the duty of "reasonable care and competence owed generally by practitioners in the particular trade or profession ..." Also, the defendant shows no evidence that demonstrates that the plaintiff's architect was an expert in audiovisual systems and how his design could have led to malfunctioning equipment.

The defendant's last contention that the contract is not for simply a sale of goods but instead is for sale of design and engineering services, with the incidental sale of goods, is incorrect. Under case precedent though, if "there is nothing to indicate that defendant was to perform any services other than installing [the equipment] and making it operational[,]" then it "was a sale of goods, not a service-oriented transaction and therefore it is covered under the contract." As long as the services include installing and ensuring the goods sold are installed and operating properly, the contract is for sale of goods.

Additionally, "[s]ince there was no formal written contract between the parties, only the order bill is available to indicate how the parties saw their transaction." However, the contract discusses the variety of audiovisual equipment that Oheka purchased from Home Theatre, as well as the installation that Home Theatre will perform. Additionally, the defendant guaranteed a warranty for on-site parts and labor for this job was to be one year's time from date of purchase. This purchase date occurred on or about July 12, 2004, when the plaintiffs sent their initial payment to the defendant. The contract therefore covered the improperly installed and malfunctioning equipment at issue.

The defendant does not produce any evidence to show they complied with this contract, except for its unsubstantiated allegations about the malfunctions being the plaintiff's fault.

This court holds plaintiff has met its burden of proof establishing that defendant is liable herein. In return, the defendant has not set forth any material issues of fact that would defeat summary judgment.

[Motion for summary judgment granted*]*

QUESTIONS

1. How does the presence of the service component in the contract affect whether the transaction is governed by UCC or common law?
2. What proof did the defendant (Home Theater) fail to present?

[24] UCC §2-314; *Lawson v. Hale*, 902 N.E.2d 267 (Ind. App. 2009); *Trujillo v. Apple Computer, Inc.*, 581 F. Supp. 2d 935 (N.D. Ill. 2008); limited battery life is not a breach of the implied warranty of merchantability.

[25] UCC §2-314. Revised Article 2 makes only one change as follows: "(c) are fit for the ordinary purposes for which [deleted word *such* here] goods [added following phrase] *of that description* are used... ." The comment explains the change: "The phrase 'goods of that description' rather than 'for which such goods are used' is used in subsection (2)(c). This emphasizes the importance of the agreed description in determining fitness for ordinary purposes."

13. Implied Warranties in Particular Sales

Particular types of sales may involve special considerations in terms of the seller's liability and the buyer's rights.

(A) Sale on Buyer's Specifications. When the buyer furnishes the seller with exact specifications for the preparation or manufacture of goods, the same warranties arise as in the case of any other sale of such goods by the particular seller. No warranty of fitness for a particular purpose can arise, however. It is clear that the buyer is purchasing on the basis of the buyer's own decision and is not relying on the seller's skill and judgment. Similarly, the manufacturer is not liable for loss caused by a design defect.[26]

(B) Sale of Secondhand or Used Goods. Under the UCC, there is a warranty of merchantability in the sale of both new and used goods unless it is specifically disclaimed. However, with respect to used goods, what is considered "fit for normal use" under the warranty of merchantability will be a lower standard. Some courts still follow their pre-Code law under which no warranties of fitness arise in the sale of used goods.

CPA **(C) Sale of Food or Drink.** The implied warranty of merchantability also applies to the purchase of food in grocery stores and restaurants. The food sold must be of average quality and fit for its ordinary purpose, which is consumption by humans.[27] **For Example,** the types of restaurant and grocery store cases brought under the warranty of merchantability include those in which the buyer or customer finds foreign substances such as grasshoppers in a can of baked beans.[28]

The application of this warranty to food cases becomes more complex when it is not a nail in a can of crabmeat, but crab shell in a can of crabmeat, or a cherry pit in the cherries of a McDonald's cherry pie. Some courts refuse to impose warranty liability if the thing in the food that caused the harm was naturally present, such as crab shell in crabmeat, prune stones in stewed prunes, or bones in canned fish. Other courts reject this foreign substance/natural substance liability test. They hold that there is liability if the seller does not deliver to the buyer goods of the character that the buyer reasonably expected. Under this view, there is a breach of the implied warranty of fitness for normal use if the buyer reasonably expected the food to be free of harm-causing natural things, such as shells and bones that could cause harm.[29] The *Mitchell v. T.G.I. Friday's* case deals with a food liability case.

Mitchell v. T.G.I. Friday's, 748 N.E.2d 89 (Ohio App. 2000)

Digging for Teeth among the Clams

On April 11, 1996, Sandra Mitchell (appellant) was having dinner at T.G.I. Friday's restaurant (hereinafter "Friday's" or appellee). Ms. Mitchell was eating a fried clam strip when she bit into a hard substance that she believed to be a piece of a clam shell. She experienced immediate pain and later sought dental treatment. Some time later, the crown of a tooth came loose. It was determined that the crown could not be reattached and the remaining root of the tooth was extracted.

Ms. Mitchell filed a product liability action against Friday's, which served the meal, and Pro Source Distributing (hereinafter "Pro Source" or appellee), the supplier of the fried clams. Both Friday's and Pro Source filed motions for summary judgment, which the trial court granted without explanation.

Ms. Mitchell appealed.

JUDICIAL OPINION

WAITE, Judge.... Appellant argues that in light of Ohio's product liability legislation, the trial court should have applied the "reasonable-expectation test" to her claim and in doing so the court should not have granted appellees' motions for summary judgment. R.C. 2307.74 provides that "[a] product is defective

[26] *Halldav v. Sturm, Ruger, & Co., Inc.*, 792 A.2d 1145 (Md. App. 2002).

[27] *Summers v. Max & Erma's Restaurant, Inc.*, 2008 WL 3822437, 66 UCC Rep. Serv. 2d 664 (Ohio App. 2008).

[28] *Metty v. Shurfine Central Corporation*, 736 S.W.2d 527 (Mo. 1987).

[29] A new type of test for the food cases is called the "duty risk analysis" rule, in which the court examines the injury in light of the risk that comes from the failure to process the items out of the food and weighs that risk with the cost of the processing. *Porteous v. St. Ann's Cafe´ & Deli*, 713 So.2d 454 (La. 1998). Note that the case is from Louisiana, the nation's non-UCC state.

Continued

[if]... [i]t deviated in a material way from the design specifications, formula, or performance standards of the manufacturer...." R.C. 2307.75(A)(2) provides that a product is defective in design or formulation if "[i]t is more dangerous than an ordinary consumer would expect when used in an intended or reasonably foreseeable manner." According to appellant, by the enactment of these statutes the "reasonable-expectation" test supersedes the traditional "foreign-natural test" applied in cases where injury is caused by substances in food. Appellant asserts that there is a reasonable expectation that clams are completely cleaned of their shells and free of foreign materials.

In the present case, Friday's set forth in its motion for summary judgment appellant's deposition testimony to the effect that while eating a clam strip, she bit down on "a hard, foreign substance." Appellant stated that she assumed it was a piece of a clam shell. Appellant described the size of the object as about a quarter of the size of a small fingernail or about a quarter of an inch or smaller and irregular in shape. Moreover, Friday's attached an affidavit from its manager, Eric Hicks, who immediately responded to appellant's report of the incident. In that affidavit, Hicks confirmed that the object appellant presented to him was indeed a piece of clam shell and that it was approximately one-quarter inch in length and irregularly shaped. In its motion for summary judgment, Pro Source adopted and incorporated the statement of Friday's, appellant's deposition testimony, and the affidavit of Eric Hicks. In her response, appellant set forth no facts to dispute that the object in the clam strip was in fact a piece of clam shell.

There being no factual dispute here, we must decide whether appellees are entitled to judgment as a matter of law. Both Friday's and Pro Source presented essentially the same argument, that regardless of whether the foreign-natural test or reasonable expectation test was applied, appellant has no claim against appellees. Appellant, however, has argued for the application only of the reasonable-expectation test. She argues that Ohio's product liability statute supersedes cases employing the foreign-natural test where deleterious substances are found in food. Appellant contends that what a consumer should reasonably expect to be present in food is a question for the jury to decide.

The basis of appellant's argument for application of the reasonable-expectation test is found in R.C. 2307.75, which provides that a product is defective if it is more dangerous than an ordinary consumer would reasonably suspect. However, appellant has not set forth any case law or analysis that would suggest that food products fall under the purview of the statute. We can find no case that has analyzed a food item in that context. Indeed, the weight of product liability cases deal with synthetic products, for example, a cargo door hinge, a glass bottle, or a prosthetic hip joint. Thus, we see no compelling reason to abandon any established test due to the enactment of Ohio's product liability legislation.

Under the foreign-natural test:

"'Bones which are natural to the type of meat served cannot legitimately be called a foreign substance, and a consumer who eats meat dishes ought to anticipate and be on his guard against the presence of such bones.'"

The reasonable-expectation test states:

"'The test should be what is "reasonably expected" by the consumer in the food as served, not what might be natural to the ingredients of that food prior to preparation. . . . As applied to the action for common-law negligence, the test is related to the foreseeability of harm on the part of the defendant. The defendant is not an insurer but has the duty of ordinary care to eliminate or remove in the preparation of the food he serves such harmful substances as the consumer of the food, as served, would not ordinarily anticipate and guard against.'"

Most courts have adopted the foreign-natural test. However, other courts endorse the reasonable-expectation test. One such case is *Thompson v Lawson Milk Co.*, on which appellant relies for her proposition that what should be reasonably expected is a question for the jury to decide.

"Courts cannot and must not ignore the common experience of life and allow rules to develop that would make sellers of food or other consumer goods insurers of the products they sell."

In the present case, it cannot be disputed that the piece of clam shell that caused appellant's injury was natural to the clam strip she consumed. Turning to the question of whether appellant should have reasonably anticipated the presence of the clam shell, we are reminded that "the possible presence of a piece of oyster shell in or attached to an oyster is so well known to anyone who eats oysters that we can say as a matter of law that one who eats oysters can reasonably anticipate and guard against eating such a piece of shell...." We therefore hold that, as a matter of law, one who eats clams can reasonably anticipate and guard against eating a piece of shell.

As appellant's claim fails under both tests, we overrule her assignment of error and affirm the judgment of the trial court.

[Judgment affirmed]

QUESTIONS

1. What did Ms. Mitchell eat and what were her resulting injuries?
2. What did the lower court do in the case that caused an admonition from the appellate court?
3. What test does Ohio follow—the foreign-natural or the reasonable expectation test?

14. Necessity of Defect

To impose liability for breach of the implied warranty of merchantability, the buyer must show that the product is defective and that defect caused harm. A product may be defective because there is (1) a manufacturing defect, (2) a design defect, (3) inadequate instruction on how to use the product, or (4) inadequate warning against dangers involved in using the product.

For Example, if the manufacturer's blueprint shows that there should be two bolts at a particular place and the factory puts in only one bolt, there is a manufacturing defect. If the two bolts are put in but the product breaks because four bolts are required to provide sufficient strength, there is no manufacturing defect, but there is a design defect. A product that is properly designed and properly manufactured may be dangerous because the user is not given sufficient instructions on how to use the product. Also, a product is defective if there is a danger that is not obvious and there is no warning at all or a warning that does not describe the full danger.[30]

15. Warranties in the International Sale of Goods

The warranties of both merchantability and fitness for a particular purpose exist under the Convention on Contracts for the International Sale of Goods (CISG). In most cases, the provisions are identical to those of the UCC. Sellers, however, can expressly disclaim the convention's warranties without mentioning merchantability or making the disclaimer conspicuous.

CPA D. Disclaimer of Warranties

The seller and the buyer may ordinarily agree that there will be no warranties. In some states, disclaimers of warranties are prohibited for reasons of public policy or consumer protection

16. Validity of Disclaimer

Warranties may be disclaimed by agreement of the parties, subject to the limitation that such a provision must not be unconscionable, must be conspicuous, and in certain cases must use certain language.[31]

(a) Conspicuousness. A disclaimer provision is made conspicuous when it appears in a record under a conspicuous heading that indicates there is an exclusion or modification of warranties. A heading cannot be relied on to make such a provision conspicuous when the heading is misleading and wrongfully gives the impression there is a warranty. **For Example,** the heading "Vehicle Warranty" is misleading if the provision that follows contains a limitation of warranties. A disclaimer that is hidden in a mass of materials or records handed to the buyer

Thinking Things Through

What's Foreign to You …

Based on the discussion and the *T. G. I. Friday's* case, decide which of the following would be considered a breach of the implied warranty of merchantability:

Customer ordered "pecan chicken" from T.G.I. Friday's, described on the menu as chicken with "a breaded mixture of pecans and bread crumbs." He broke a tooth when he bit into a pecan shell that was in the breading. **[*Carlton v. T.G.I. Friday's*, 2006 WL 5129475 (Ohio Com. Pl.)]**

Customer suffered an injury to the throat as a result of a bone in a chicken sandwich getting stuck in his throat. **[*Ruvolo v. Homovich*, 778 N.E.2d 661 (Ohio App. 2002)]**

Customer bit into a Baby Ruth candy bar, manufactured by Standard Brands, that contained a "snake bone (vertebrae)" and the customer experienced severe psychological difficulty. **[*Gates v. Standard Brands Inc.*, 719 P.2d 130 (Wash. App. 1986)]**

Standard Candy manufacturers the Goo Goo Cluster candy bar, featuring peanuts from Jimbo's. James Newton purchased a Goo Goo, and when he bit into it, he bit down on an undeveloped peanut. The result was a broken tooth. **[*Newton v. Standard Candy Co.*, 2008 WL 752599 (D.Neb.)]**

[30] *Red Hill Hosiery Mill, Inc. v. Magnetek, Inc.* 582 S.E.2d 632 (N.C. Ct. App. 2003). Following government standards does not mean a product is without defect.

[31] UCC §2-316; In re *Rafter Seven Ranches LP*, 546 F.3d 1194 (10th Cir. 2008).

is not conspicuous and is not effective to exclude warranties. Similarly, an inconspicuous disclaimer of warranties under a posted notice of "Notice to Retail Buyers" has no effect.

When a disclaimer of warranties fails because it is not conspicuous, the implied warranties apply to the buyer.[32]

(B) Unconscionability and Public Policy. An exclusion of warranties made in the manner specified by the UCC is not unconscionable. In some states, warranty disclaimers are invalid because they are contrary to public policy or because they are prohibited by consumer protection laws.

17. Particular Language for Disclaimers

To waive the warranty of merchantability, the record must contain the following language: "The seller undertakes no responsibility for the quality of the goods except as otherwise provided in this contract."[33] The required language for waiving the warranty of fitness for a particular purpose is as follows: "The seller assumes no responsibility that the goods will be fit for any particular purpose for which you may be buying these goods, except as otherwise provided in the contract."[34]

In consumer contracts, the use of terms such as "as is" can also disclaim both of these warranties, as it does for merchant transactions, but the disclaimers must be in the record and must be conspicuously set forth in that record.

Figure 25-1 provides a summary of the warranties under Article 2 and the methods for making disclaimers.

18. Exclusion of Warranties by Examination of Goods

For an inspection of goods by the buyer to constitute a waiver, the seller must demand that the buyer inspect the goods as part of the contracting process. The seller may not use inspection as a defense to warranty issues if that demand was not made at the time the parties contracted.[35]

19. Post-Sale Disclaimer

Frequently, a statement purporting to exclude or modify warranties appears for the first time in a written contract sent to confirm or memorialize an oral contract made earlier. The exclusion or modification may likewise appear in an invoice, a bill, or an instruction manual delivered to the buyer at or after the time the goods are received. Such postsale disclaimers have no effect on warranties that arose at the time of the sale.

E. Other Theories of Product Liability

In addition to recovery for breach of an express guarantee, an express warranty, or an implied warranty, a plaintiff in a given product liability case may be able to recover for negligence, fraud, or strict tort liability.

CPA 20. Negligence

A person injured because of the defective condition of a product may be entitled to recover from the seller or manufacturer for the damages for **negligence**. The injured person must be able to show that the seller was negligent in the preparation or manufacture of the article or failed to provide proper instructions and warnings of dangers. An action for negligence rests on common law tort principles. Negligence does not require privity of contract.

21. Fraud

The UCC expressly preserves the pre-Code law governing fraud. A person defrauded by a distributor's or manufacturer's false statements about a product generally will be able to recover damages for the harm sustained because of such misrepresentations. False statements are fraudulent if the party who made them did so with knowledge that they were false or with reckless indifference to their truthfulness.

CPA 22. Strict Tort Liability

Strict tort liability exists without regard to whether the person injured is a purchaser, a consumer, or a third person, such as a bystander.[36] It is no defense

[32] A warranty disclaimer written in all caps just below the signature line is conspicuous. *Semitekol v. Monaco Coach Corp.*, 582 F. Supp. 2d 1009 (N.D. Ill. 2008).
[33] UCC §2-316(2). If the seller undertakes to repair the goods after their exclusion, the waiver becomes null. *Sabbath v. Martin*, 2009 WL 3449096 (La. App. 2009).
[34] *Id.*
[35] Revised UCC §2-316(3)(b).
[36] The concept of strict tort liability was judicially declared in *Greenman v. Yuba Power Products*, 377 P.2d 897 (Cal. 1963). This concept has been incorporated in the Restatement (Second) and (Third) of Torts as §402A.

FIGURE 25-1 UCC Warranties

NAME OF WARRANTY	CREATION	RESTRICTION	DISCLAIMER
EXPRESS	AFFIRMATION OF FACT, PROMISE OF PERFORMANCE (INCLUDES SAMPLES, MODELS, DESCRIPTIONS)	MUST BE PART OF THE BASIS OF THE BARGAIN	CANNOT MAKE A DISCLAIMER INCONSISTENT WITH AN EXPRESS WARRANTY
IMPLIED WARRANTY OF MERCHANTABILITY	GIVEN IN EVERY SALE OF GOODS BY A MERCHANT ("FIT FOR ORDINARY PURPOSES")	ONLY GIVEN BY MERCHANTS	MUST USE STATUTORY LANGUAGE DISCLAIMER OF "AS IS" OR "WITH ALL FAULTS"; MUST BE CONSPICUOUS IN THE RECORD
IMPLIED WARRANTY OF FITNESS FOR A PARTICULAR PURPOSE	SELLER KNOWS OF BUYER'S RELIANCE FOR A PARTICULAR USE (BUYER IS IGNORANT)	SELLER MUST HAVE KNOWLEDGE; BUYER MUST RELY ON SELLER	(1) MUST HAVE A RECORD (2) MUST BE CONSPICUOUS (3) ALSO DISCLAIMED WITH "AS IS" OR "WITH ALL FAULTS"
TITLE	GIVEN IN EVERY SALE	DOES NOT APPLY IN CIRCUMSTANCES WHERE APPARENT WARRANTY IS NOT GIVEN	MUST SAY "THERE IS NO WARRANTY OF TITLE"
MAGNUSON-MOSS (FEDERAL CONSUMER PRODUCT WARRANTY LAW)	ONLY CONSUMER PRODUCTS OF $10 OR MORE	MUST LABEL "FULL" OR "LIMITED"	

that privity of contract does not exist between the injured party and the defendant. Likewise, it is no defense that the defect was found in a component part purchased from another manufacturer.[37] **For Example,** defective tires sold on a new car were probably purchased from a tire supplier by the auto manufacturer. However, the manufacturer is not excused from liability.

Strict tort liability requires that the defect in the product exist at the time it left the control of the manufacturer or distributor. The defective condition is defined in the same way as under negligence: defective by manufacturing error or oversight, defective by design, or defective by the failure to warn.[38] There is liability if the product is defective and unreasonably dangerous and has caused harm. It is immaterial whether the seller was negligent or whether the user was contributorily negligent. Knowledge of the defect is not a requirement for liability. The *Smith v. Coleman* case deals with an

[37] *Ford v. Beam Radiator, Inc.*, 708 So.2d 1158 (La. App. 1998).
[38] *Lewis v. Ariens*, 751 N.E.2d 862 (Mass. 2011).

Smith v. Coleman Co., 71 UCC Rep. Serv. 2d 131 (M.D. Ala. 2010)

"Towing" the Line on Warnings

Ginger Smith (plaintiff) was a passenger on a Ronald Smith's boat on West Point Lake, Alabama. Ronald Smith (no relation to Ginger) was operating the boat, which was towing Ms. Smith's son, Shane McClellan, on an inflatable inner tube behind the boat. Shane McClellan weighed 150 pounds at the time and the tube itself weighed 5 to 10 pounds. The inner tube was tied to the boat by a 50-foot Model 51650 polypropylene line that was manufactured by Lehigh Consumer Products, LLC, but carried the label of The Coleman Company (defendants) pursuant to a licensing arrangement, and was purchased at a nearby Wal-Mart store. While Shane McClellan was being towed on the inner tube, the line snapped, and the end connected to the boat flew back toward the boat and hit Ms. Smith in the eye, causing the loss of that eye.

The packaging of the line contained several statements. A paper insert identifies it as a "50 ft x 5/16 in UTILITY LINE." Just below that appears the phrase "Ideal for use on boat or dock." Still farther down the insert, and in an all-caps font smaller than that used in the first statement, appears, divided over two lines, "175 LBS WORKING LOAD LIMIT/STAYS AFLOAT." A longer cautionary message appears at the bottom of the insert. It states:

> *Avoid using a knot, splicing is preferable. Knots reduce the strength of the rope up to 40%. Do not use this product where personal safety could be endangered. Never stand in line with a rope under tension. Such a rope, particularly nylon rope, may recoil (snap back). Misuse can result in serious injury or death.*

There was a warning label printed on the inner tube itself, a portion of which advised boaters to "[u]se a tow rope of at least 1500 lbs average tensile strength for pulling a single person...." The overall size of this warning label is 8" × 9", and its text complies with the warning label recommended by the Water Sports Industry Association for use on inflatable tubes.

Ms. Smith filed suit against Coleman, Wal-Mart, and Ronald Smith. (Wal-Mart and Smith were dismissed from the case.) Coleman moved for summary judgment because of the warnings.

JUDICIAL OPINION

WATKINS, District Judge

It is a defense to a negligent failure to warn claim that there is no evidence "that the allegedly inadequate warning would have been read and heeded and would have kept the accident from occurring." In this case, Defendants point to the deposition testimony of Ronald Smith, who purchased the line and attached it to the boat and inner tube. Mr. Smith's testimony was that he did not recall reading "any other part of the warnings on the package other than the poundage."

Conceding that Mr. Smith did not recall reading the relevant warnings, Plaintiff's argument seems to be that the phrase "warning" has a particular, technical meaning, such that the statements on the package here were not "warnings" for the purposes of the Alabama case law. The contours of this view are not very well fleshed out, but the argument is perhaps that because the statements on the packaging did not actually contain the word "WARNING," with accompanying symbols such as an exclamation mark within a triangle, they were not actually warnings at all, but merely "safety information."

Certainly, the common use of the word "warning" does not limit the concept to statements appearing under the word "WARNING," accompanied by particular symbols, or colored in bright orange. The statements appearing on the utility line's package are cautionary in nature, designed to *warn*, in the ordinary sense of the term, users of the product about potential dangers of usage.

Thus, the court concludes that the statements on the package were warnings for purposes of Alabama law. The only remaining question is whether failure to heed the warnings caused the accident. The court is reluctant to conclude that the warning against uses "where personal safety could be endangered" can suffice for this purpose; it is so vague as to be essentially meaningless. The other two warnings, however, are quite specific, and both were violated by Mr. Smith. Mr. Smith tied knots in the rope in order to attach it to the boat and the inner tube. Both Mr. Smith and Plaintiff were on board the open boat towing the inner tube behind it; in the ordinary use of language, they were both standing "in line with a rope under tension."

Indeed, it is difficult to conceive how the rope could ever be used for towing someone behind an open boat without both the person being towed and persons on board the boat violating the warning against standing in line with a rope under tension.

With respect to the express warranty claim, Plaintiff's claim is that the statement that the line was "ideal for use on boat or dock" constitutes an express warranty. Statements "that are mere sales talk or 'puffery' do not give rise to express warranties," while "representations of fact" may give rise to such warranties. While the word "ideal" seems closer to the description of an item as "in good shape" that Alabama courts have found to constitute "puffery," Summary judgment is due to be granted on this claim.

Continued

The final warranty claim is for breach of an implied warranty of fitness for a particular purpose. Plaintiff has done no more than assert that Defendants had "reason to know" that the line would be used to tow persons behind a boat; regardless, Plaintiff clearly did not "rely on the seller's skill or judgment to select or furnish suitable goods." Rather, Mr. Smith selected and purchased the utility line for himself at a Wal-Mart store. Summary judgment is due to be granted on the warranty claims.

[Summary judgment for Defendants.]

QUESTIONS

1. What is the law with regard to product users who do not read package warnings?
2. What point does the court make about Ms. Smith not actually being the purchaser of the line?
3. What lessons should Coleman take from its experience of being a defendant along with its licensee for the line?

issue of the adequacy of a warning given by a manufacturer about its product. Assumption of risk by the injured party, on the other hand, is a defense available to the seller.[39] However, there can still be issues regarding products even in situations, such as a baseball game, where there are some risks. The *Patch v. Hillerich & Bradsby Co.* case deals with the adequacy of warnings about a baseball bat when everyone at a baseball game assumes some risk of being hit by a baseball.

23. Cumulative Theories of Liability

The theories of product liability are not mutually exclusive. A given set of facts may give rise to two or more theories of liability. **For Example,** suppose that a manufacturer advertises, "Coaches! Protect your players' eyes! Shatterproof sunglasses for baseball." If the glasses shattered and injured a player, an express warranty, implied warranty, implied warranty for a particular purpose, and strict tort liability could apply for recovery.

Patch v. Hillerich & Bradsby Co., 257 P.3d 383 (Mont. 2011)

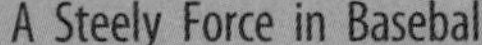

A Steely Force in Baseball

While pitching in an American Legion baseball game on July 25, 2003, eighteen-year-old Brandon Patch was struck in the head by a batted ball that was hit using Hillerich & Bradsby's (H & B) model CB–13 aluminum bat. Tragically, Brandon died from his injuries.

The Patches brought suit against H & B for the wrongful death of their son on the grounds that the CB–13 aluminum bat was in a defective condition because of the enhanced risks associated with its use: It increased the velocity speed of a batted ball when it left the bat, thus decreasing infielders' reaction times, and resulted in a greater number of high energy batted balls in the infield. Some studies note that the average time needed for a pitcher to react to a batted ball is .4 seconds. Analysis of the sound recording from the game confirmed that the reaction time available to Brandon to turn away or defend himself was only .376 of a second.

Before trial, the District Court granted H & B's motion for summary judgment on Patches' manufacturing defect claim, but denied summary judgment on Patches' design defect and failure to warn claims. The trial court excluded H & B's assumption of the risk defense. The jury concluded the model CB–13 aluminum bat was not designed defectively, but determined the bat was in a defective condition due to H & B's failure to warn of the enhanced risks associated with its use and awarded Patches an $850,000 verdict on their failure to warn claim. H & B appealed.

JUDICIAL OPINION

WHEAT, Justice

H & B asserts that only the individual batting (actual user) and the individual who purchased the bat (actual consumer) can assert a failure to warn claim in this case. H & B's narrow interpretation of the terms user and consumer is contrary to the definition of the terms as contained in the *Restatement (Second) of Torts* § 402A.

The realities of the game of baseball support the District Court's decision to submit Patches' failure to warn claim to the

39 *Clark v. Mazda Motor Corp.*, 68 P.3d 207 (Ok. 2003).

Continued

jury. The bat is an indispensible part of the game. The risk of harm accompanying the bat's use extends beyond the player who holds the bat in his or her hands. A warning of the bat's risks to only the batter standing at the plate inadequately communicates the potential risk of harm posed by the bat's increased exit speed. In this context, all of the players, including Brandon, were users or consumers placed at risk by the increased exit speed caused by H & B's bat. H & B is subject to liability to all players in the game, including Brandon, for the physical harm caused by its bat's increased exit speed.

H & B's first argument fails because the "workability" of providing a warning is a jury question. *See Macrie v. SDS Biotech Corp., 267 N.J.Super.* 34, 630 A.2d 805 (N.J.Super.App. Div.1993). In *Macrie,* employees of a produce broker were seriously injured after being exposed to a toxic fungicide while they unpacked produce that had been treated with the fungicide by a farmer who had sold the produce to their employer. The employees brought a failure to warn claim against the manufacturer of the fungicide. As H & B does here, the manufacturer argued that it was not feasible, i.e., "workable," to warn the employees of the risks associated with the fungicide. The *Macrie* court rejected the manufacturer's argument and concluded that the feasibility of providing warnings is a jury question:

> *[W]here a jury could find that plaintiffs foreseeable exposure [to the fungicide] would threaten them with serious physical harm, the jury could also determine that minimizing the danger warranted unusually strenuous efforts to provide them with warnings and instructions.*

H & B's second argument incorrectly limits the scope of the warning by erroneously assuming that placing a warning directly on the bat is the only method to provide a warning. While placing a warning directly on a product is one method of warning, other methods of warning exist, including, but not limited to, issuing oral warnings and placing warnings in advertisements, posters, and media releases. ("[O]ther means of communication such as advertisements, posters, releases to be read and signed … or oral warnings … could easily have been undertaken…."). Such warnings, if issued by H & B in this case, would have communicated to all players the potential risk of harm associated with H & B's bat's increased exit speed. H & B's false assumption fails to establish the absence of genuine issues of material fact.

Because genuine issues of material fact exist regarding the scope of the warning and because the "workability" of providing a warning is a jury question, the District Court properly denied H & B summary judgment on its causation argument.

In a failure to warn case, the plaintiff has the burden of proving (1) the product was sold in a defective condition due to the lack of or an inadequate warning, (2) the defect caused the injury, and (3) the defect is traceable to the defendant. The policy underlying products liability—protecting the consuming public by requiring manufacturers to bear the burden of injuries caused by defective products—requires courts to apply a flexible standard of proof. The nature and quality of evidence used in products liability cases to demonstrate causation varies, and the death or inability of the plaintiff to testify is one of the factors influencing the requisite standard of proof.

The District Court properly allowed the jury to infer that Patches would have heeded a warning had one been given.

In certain situations … where the consequences … are severe, the lack of warning is undisputed, and the person … is dead, the jury may be permitted to infer that a warning would have been heeded and that the failure to warn was a proximate cause of the injury. Not only would it be virtually impossible to prove what the decedent would have done had he been warned, but, as a practical matter, nothing more is added in this case by having a witness merely state that, had the danger been known … he would have acted to avoid the danger.

H & B argues that because Brandon had been hit by batted balls before, he knew he could be hit and, therefore, assumed the risk when he continued playing baseball.

[a] manufacturer [can] assert the affirmative defense of assumption of the risk where "[t]he user or consumer of the product discovered the defect or the defect was open and obvious and the user or consumer unreasonably made use of the product and was injured by it."

Assumption of the risk was not applicable here because there is no evidence that Brandon actually knew he would be seriously injured or killed when pitching to a batter using one of H & B's model CB–13 aluminum bats. In other words, H & B failed to show that Brandon was aware of the enhanced risks associated with the model CB–13 aluminum bat, and, knowing that, he voluntarily proceeded to pitch to a batter using that bat.

The District Court properly denied H & B's motion for summary judgment on Patches' failure to warn claim because H & B is subject to liability to all players, including Brandon, for the physical harm caused by its bat's increased exit speed, and genuine issues of material fact existed regarding the causation element of Patches' claim. A new trial is not warranted.

[Affirmed]

QUESTIONS

1. What does the court say about the argument that it was difficult to warn Brandon about the bat?
2. What does the court say about assumption of risk by Brandon in playing baseball and the fact that he had been hit by baseballs before?
3. Is Brandon a "user" or "consumer" for purposes of strict tort liability?

Ethics & the Law

The Paintball Gun From the Pawn Shop

John Clark purchased a paintball gun at a pawn shop and then participated in a community sport of shooting paintball guns at cars. While John and his friend were riding around their small town with their paintball guns, they spotted Chris and shot his car. Chris Rico then aimed his Brass Eagle paintball gun at the car John was riding in, but instead hit John in the eye. John required surgery on his eye that evening and filed suit against Brass Eagle under a theory of strict tort liability. Brass Eagle responded by stating that its gun was not defective and that the young men had ignored warnings about the need to wear eye protection when using the guns. John said he purchased his gun used and was not given all the packaging and instructions. Brass Eagle says that its gun was not defective and that it functioned as it was supposed to. John says the guns are inherently dangerous. Who should be responsible for the injury? Are paintball guns defective if they can harm individuals? How should the courts allocate the risk and loss on products such as these? **[*Clark v. Brass Eagle, Inc.*, 866 So.2d 456 (Miss. 2004)]**

LawFlix

The Incredible Shrinking Woman (1981) (PG)

Lily Tomlin's exposure to various combinations of products causes her to shrink. Which companies would be liable and how could one go about proving joint and several liability? Discuss privity of contract and whether the interaction with other products would be covered.

Fast Food Nation: The Dark Side of the American Meal (2002)

A look at the harmful effects of too much fast food and an interesting question as to whether the fast-food restaurants should be held liable for those health problems.

MAKE THE CONNECTION

SUMMARY

Five theories protect parties from loss caused by nonconforming goods: (1) express warranty, (2) implied warranty, (3) negligence, (4) fraud, and (5) strict tort liability.

Theories of product liability are not mutually exclusive. A given set of facts may give rise to liability under two or more theories.

The requirement of privity of contract (that is, the parties to the sales contract for warranty liability) has been widely rejected. The law is moving toward the conclusion that persons harmed because of an improper product may recover from anyone who is in any way responsible. The requirement of privity has been abolished by most states, and remote buyers as well as their families, members of their households, and guests are covered under the UCC warranties.

Warranties may be express or implied. The types of implied warranties are the warranty of title, the implied warranty of merchantability, and the implied warranty of fitness for a particular purpose. The warranty of title provides that the transfer is lawful, the title is good, and there are no infringement issues. Under Revised Article 2, the warranty of title also protects the buyer against unreasonable litigation. The warranty of merchantability is given by merchants and warrants that the goods are of average quality and will do what those types of goods commonly can do. The implied warranty of fitness for a particular purpose is given in those circumstances in which the buyer relies on the seller's expertise and the seller is aware of that reliance and offers a recommendation on the types of goods.

Express warranties arise from statements of fact and promises of performance made by the seller to the buyer that become a part of the basis for the buyer contracting. Express warranties arise from samples, models, and descriptions.

Warranties may be disclaimed by agreement of the parties provided the disclaimer is not unconscionable. Merchants can have oral disclaimers, but for consumers, warranty disclaimers must be in a record and must be conspicuous. Also for consumers, certain language must be used to disclaim each type of warranty. However, for both merchants and nonmerchants, the use of terms such as "as is" or "with all faults" can disclaim both the warranty of merchantability and the implied warranty of fitness for a particular purpose (although for consumers, there must still be a record and the language must be conspicuous).

The warranties of merchantability and fitness exist under the CISG. However, disclaimers under the CISG need not mention merchantability, nor must such disclaimers be conspicuous.

The strict tort liability plaintiff must show that there was a defect in the product at the time it left the control of the defendant. No negligence need be established on the part of the defendant, nor is the plaintiff's contributory negligence a defense. If negligence is established, however, knowledge by the seller can result in punitive damages. The defendant may show that the injured party assumed the risk.

LEARNING OUTCOMES

After studying this chapter, you should be able to clearly explain:

A. General Principles

LO.1 List the theories of product liability

See the five theories discussed in the "Theories of Liability" section on p. 472.

LO.2 Identify who may sue and who may be sued when a defective product causes harm

See the discussion of privity on p. 472.

B. Express Warranties

LO.3 Define and give examples of an express warranty

See *La Trace v. Webster* on pp. 475–476.

See *Smith v. Coleman* on pp. 484–485.

C. Implied Warranties

LO.4 List and explain the types of implied warranties

See *Oheka Management, Inc. v. Home Theater Interiors* on p. 478.

See *Mitchell v. T.G.I. Friday's* on pp. 479–480.

LO.5 Explain warranty protections under federal law

See the discussion of the Consumer Product Safety Improvement Act (CPSIA) on p. 475.

LO.6 State what constitutes a breach of warranty

See *Patch v. Hillerich & Bradsby Co.* on pp. 485–486.

D. Disclaimer of Warranties

LO.7 Describe the extent and manner in which implied warranties may be disclaimed under the UCC and the CISG

E. Other Theories of Product Liability

See the *For Example*, discussion of the use of the term "Vehicle Warranty" in the "Conspicuousness" section on pp. 481–482.

See the "Ethics & the Law" discussion of paintball guns on p. 487.

KEY TERMS

Consumer Product Safety Improvement Act (CPSIA)
express warranty
full warranty
implied warranty
implied warranty of the merchantability
limited warranty
negligence
privity
privity of contract
strict tort liability
warranties
warranty against encumbrances
warranty of title

QUESTIONS AND CASE PROBLEMS

1. Maria Gonzalez lived in a rental unit with her sons in Queens, New York. The hot water supplied to their apartment was heated by a Morflo water heater, which had a temperature control device on its exterior manufactured by Robertshaw and sold to Morflo. Maria Garcia, the owner of the Gonzalezes' apartment, had purchased and installed the water heater. The Morflo heater was located in the basement of the apartment house, which was locked and inaccessible to tenants.

   Extensive warnings were on the water heater itself and in the manual given to Garcia at the time of her purchase. The warning on the Robertshaw temperature device read: "CAUTION: Hotter water increases the risk of scald injury." The heater itself contained a picture of hot water coming from a faucet with the word "DANGER" printed above it. In addition, the water heater had a statement on it: "Water temperature over 120 degrees Fahrenheit can cause severe burns instantly or death from scalds. Children, disabled, and elderly are at highest risk of being scalded. Feel water before bathing or showering. Temperature limiting valves are available, see manual."

   In the Morflo manual, the following warning appeared:

   > *DANGER! The thermostat is adjusted to its lowest temperature position when shipped from the factory. Adjusting the thermostat past the 120 degree Fahrenheit bar on the temperature dial will increase the risk of scald injury. The normal position is approximately 120 degrees Fahrenheit.*
   >
   > *DANGER: WARNING: Hot water can produce first degree burns in 3 seconds at 140 degrees Fahrenheit (60 degrees Celsius), in 20 seconds at 130 degrees Fahrenheit (54 degrees Celsius), in 8 minutes at 120 degrees Fahrenheit (49 degrees Celsius).*

   On October 1, 1992, 15-month-old Angel Gonzalez was being bathed by his 15-year-old brother, Daniel. When the telephone rang, Daniel left Angel alone in the bathtub. No one else was at home with the boys, and Daniel left the water running. Angel was scalded by the water that came from the tap. Angel and his mother brought suit against Morflo and Robertshaw, alleging defects in the design of the water heater and the failure to warn. Should they recover? [*Gonzalez v. Morflo Industries, Inc.*, 931 F. Supp. 159 (E.D.N.Y.)]

2. Paul Parrino purchased from Dave's Professional Wheelchair Service a wheelchair manufactured by 21st Century Scientific, Inc. The sales brochure from 21st Century Scientific stated that the wheelchair would "serve [the buyer] well for many years to come." Parrino had problems with the wheelchair within a few years and filed suit against Dave's and 21st Century for breach of express warranty. Both defended on the grounds that the statement on years of service was puffery, not an express warranty. Are they right? [*Parrino v. Sperling,* 648 N.Y.S.2d 702]

3. Jane Jackson purchased a sealed can of Katydids, chocolate-covered pecan caramel candies manufactured by NestlT. Shortly after, Jackson bit into one of the candies and allegedly broke a tooth on

a pecan shell embedded in the candy. She filed a complaint, asserting breach of implied warranty. How would you argue on behalf of the company? How would you argue on behalf of Jackson? In your answer, discuss both the reasonable expectation test and the foreign substance/natural substance test. [*Jackson v. NestlT-Beich, Inc.*, 589 N.E.2d 547 (Ill. App.)]

4. Webster ordered a bowl of fish chowder at the Blue Ship Tea Room. She was injured by a fish bone in the chowder, and she sued the tea room for breach of the implied warranty of merchantability. The evidence at trial showed that when chowder is made, the entire boned fish is cooked. Should she recover? [*Webster v. Blue Ship Tea Room,* 198 N.E.2d 309 (Mass.)]

5. Andy's Sales (owned by Andy Adams) sold a well-built trampoline to Carl and Shirley Wickers. The Wickerses later sold the trampoline to Herbert Bryant. While using the trampoline, Herbert's 14-year-old nephew, Rex, sustained injuries that left him a quadriplegic. Rex's guardian filed suit for breach of express warranty and merchantability. The sales brochure for the round trampoline described it as "safe" because it had a "uniform bounce" and "natural tendency to work the jumper toward the center." The Wickerses had purchased an oval-shaped trampoline. Discuss Rex's ability to recover. Is privity an issue? [*Bryant v. Adams,* 448 S.E.2d 832 (N.C. App.)]

6. Advent purchased ink from Borden. On the labels of the ink drums delivered to Advent, Borden had imprinted in one-sixteenth-inch type in all caps:

   SELLER MAKES NO WARRANTY, EXPRESS OR IMPLIED, CONCERNING THE PRODUCT OR THE MERCHANTABILITY OR FITNESS THEREOF FOR ANY PURPOSE CONCERNING THE ACCURACY OF ANY INFORMATION PROVIDED BY BORDEN.

   This language was printed beneath the following:

   BORDEN PRINTING INKS—"ZERO DEFECTS: THAT'S OUR GOAL"

   All of the printing was in boldface type. The disclaimer was also printed on the sales invoice and on the reverse side of the Borden form, but there was nothing on the front to call attention to the critical nature of the terms on the back because there were simply capital letters reading "SEE REVERSE SIDE." All of the terms on the back were in boldface and although the disclaimer was the first of 19 paragraphs, nothing distinguished it from the other 18 paragraphs of detailed contract terms.

   Advent said that Borden failed to age the black ink that it purchased with the result that the ink separated in Advent's printing machines. Advent refused to pay for the ink and wrote to Borden explaining that it would not tender payment because the ink was defective and demanding that Borden reimburse it for its lost profits from the downtime of printing machines. The trial court held that Borden had disclaimed any and all warranties on the ink and Advent appealed. What would you decide about the disclaimer and why? [*Borden, Inc. v. Advent Ink Co.*, 701 A.2d 255 (Pa. Sup.)]

7. Avery purchased a refrigerator from a retail store. The written contract stated that the refrigerator was sold "as is" and that the warranty of merchantability and all warranties of fitness were excluded. This was stated in large capital letters printed just above the line on which Avery signed her name. The refrigerator worked properly for a few weeks and then stopped. The store refused to do anything about it because of the exclusion of the warranties made by the contract. Avery claimed that this exclusion was not binding because it was unconscionable. Was Avery correct? [*Avery v. Aladdin Products Div., Nat'l Service Industries, Inc.*, 196 S.E.2d 357 (Ga. App.)]

8. James Jelinek purchased Hytest BMR Sorghum Sudan grass seed, which was produced and marketed by Land O'Lakes. Land O'Lakes warranted the seed to be free from defects and expressly warranted that by using normal farming practices and proper maintenance, Mr. Jelinek would obtain yields of 4 1/2 tons per acre. The seed resulted in reduced yields and an inferior quality crop. As a result, Mr. Jelinek was not able

to sell his crop and had significant economic losses. Mr. Jelinek filed suit for breach of express warranty. Is the promise of a crop yield an express warranty? Explain your answer. [*Jelinek v. Land O'Lakes, Inc.*, 797 N.W.2d 289 (Neb. App.)]

9. Brianna Kriefall, a child, died after she ate meat at a Sizzler restaurant that was later found to contain *E. coli.* Her family brought suit against Sizzler USA to recover for the loss of their daughter. Is Sizzler liable for the death? Explain your answer. What would be the liability of Sizzler's meat supplier in the case? [*Estate of Kriefall v. Sizzler USA Franchise, Inc.*, 801 N.W.2d 781 (Wis. App.)]

10. Zogarts manufactured and sold a practice device for beginning golfers. According to statements on the package, the device was completely safe, and a player could never be struck by the device's golf ball. Hauter was hit by the ball while using the device. He sued Zogarts, which denied liability on the ground that the statements were merely matters of opinion, so liability could not be based on them. Was this a valid defense? [*Hauter v. Zogarts,* 534 P.2d 377 (Cal.)]

11. GE Oil & Gas, Inc., is a company that manufactures gas compressors. Berge Helene owns a large barge that it leases to oil companies for purposes of storing and producing petroleum offshore. GE Oil & Gas sold Berge Helene gas compressors that were to be used on the barge. Berge Helene representatives asked GE representatives, as they were negotiating the contract for the compressors, whether the compressors could withstand the movement and vibration that would occur on the front of the barge once it was out in the ocean. GE's representatives assured those from Berge Helene that the compressors were self-stabilizing. Once out in the ocean, the gas compressors on the hull exploded once the vibrations began. Berge Helene brought suit against GE for the resulting crew injuries and damage to the barge. Could Berge Helene recover and, if so, what theory of product liability would apply? [*Berge Helene Ltd. v. GE Oil & Gas, Inc.*, 830 F. Supp. 2d 235 (S.D. Tex.)]

12. After watching a male horse owned by Terry and Manita Darby perform at a horse show, Ashley Sheffield contacted the Darbys about buying him. The Darbys assured her that the horse had no problems and would make a good show horse for use in competition. In the presence of and in consultation with her father (who raised horses for a business), Sheffield rode the horse and decided to purchase him for $8,500.

    Within three weeks, Sheffield and her trainer discerned that the horse was lame. Sheffield sued the Darbys for fraud and for breach of express and implied warranties, and the court entered summary judgment in favor of the Darbys on all claims. Sheffield appealed. Was the court correct in granting summary judgment? Was there a breach of an express warranty? [*Sheffield v. Darby*, 535 S.E.2d 776 (Ga. App.)]

13. On July 27, 2000, Sheldorado Aluminum Products, Inc., installed an aluminum awning on the back of Marie Villette's home for use as a carport. On January 11, 2001, the awning collapsed on top of Ms. Villette's new Mercedes automobile. Ms. Villette brought suit against Sheldorado, seeking recovery of the $3,000 she had paid to them for the awning.

    There was no formal written contract between the parties; the only writing was a one-page order/bill designated a "contract," dated July 11, 2000, and signed by Ms. Villette and apparently by Jack Finklestein, Sheldorado's salesman. No advertising or promotional material was presented by either party. Ms. Villette testified to no express warranty or representation on the transaction, and none appears in the writing. Sheldorado acknowledges that no instructions or warnings were given to Ms. Villette as to care, maintenance, or use of the awning.

    When the awning collapsed, Sheldorado took the position that the cause was an accumulation of snow and high winds and that it bore no responsibility for the loss. Its only response to the incident was to refer Ms. Villette to the insurer on their homeowner's policy.

    Does Ms. Villette have any rights that would allow her to collect damages? Apply the UCC to answer this question. [*Villette v. Sheldorado Aluminum Products, Inc.*, 2001 WL 881055 (N.Y. Supp.), 45 UCC Rep Serv. 2d 470 (N.Y. Ci. Ct.)]

14. Drehman Paving & Flooring Co. installed a brick floor at Cumberland Farms that its salesman promised would be "just like" another floor Cumberland had installed several years earlier. The bricks in the new floor came loose because Drehman had failed to install expansion joints. Expansion joints were not included in the second floor contract but were part of the first. Can Cumberland recover? Under what theory? [*Cumberland Farms, Inc. v. Drehman Paving & Flooring Co.*, 520 N.E.2d 1321 (Mass. Ct. App.)]

15. Brian Felley went to the home of Tom and Cheryl Singleton on June 8 to look at a used car that the Singletons had advertised for sale in the local paper. The car was a 1991 Ford with 126,000 miles on it. Following a test drive and the Singletons' representation that the car was "in good mechanical condition," Felley purchased the car for $5,800. By June 18, 1997, Felley had the car in the shop and had paid $942.76 to have its clutch fixed. By July 9, 1997, Felley also had paid $971.18 for a new brake job. By September 16, 1997, Felley had paid another $429.09 for further brake work.

    Felley brought suit for breach of express warranty. An auto expert testified that the clutch and brakes were defective when Felley bought the car. Was an express warranty breached? Why or why not? [*Felley v. Singleton*, 705 N.E.2d 930 (Ill. App.)]

CPA QUESTIONS

1. Under the UCC Sales Article, the warranty of title may be excluded by:
   a. Merchants or nonmerchants, provided the exclusion is in writing.
   b. Nonmerchant sellers only.
   c. The seller's statement that it is selling only such right or title that it has.
   d. Use of an "as is" disclaimer.

2. Which of the following factors result(s) in an express warranty with respect to a sale of goods?
   I. The seller's description of the goods is part of the basis of the bargain.
   II. The seller selects goods knowing the buyer's intended use.

   a. I only
   b. II only
   c. Both I and II
   d. Neither I nor II

3. Morgan is suing the manufacturer, wholesaler, and retailer for bodily injuries caused by a power saw Morgan purchased. Which of the following statements is correct under the theory of strict liability?
   a. The manufacturer will avoid liability if it can show it followed the custom of the industry.
   b. Morgan may recover even if he cannot show any negligence was involved.
   c. Contributory negligence on Morgan's part will always be a bar to recovery.
   d. Privity will be a bar to recovery insofar as the wholesaler is concerned if the wholesaler did not have a reasonable opportunity to inspect.

4. On May 2, Handy Hardware sent Ram Industries a signed purchase order that stated, in part: "Ship for May 8 delivery 300 Model A-X socket sets at current dealer price. Terms 2/10/net 30." Ram received Handy's purchase order on May 4. On May 5, Ram discovered that it had only 200 Model A-X socket sets and 100 Model W-Z socket sets in stock. Ram shipped the Model A-X and Model W-Z sets to Handy without explanation concerning the shipment. The sockets were received by Handy on May 8. Assuming a contract exists between Handy and Ram, which of the following implied warranties would result?
   I. Implied warranty of merchantability
   II. Implied warranty of fitness for a particular purpose
   III. Implied warranty of title

   a. I only
   b. III only
   c. I and III only
   d. I, II, and III

Chapter 26

© Manuel Gutjahr/iStockphoto.com

Obligations and Performance

learningoutcomes

After studying this chapter, you should be able to

LO.1 List the steps that can be taken when a party to a sales contract feels insecure about the other party's performance

LO.2 Explain the obligations of the seller and the buyer in a sales contract

LO.3 Identify the types of actions and conduct that constitute acceptance

LO.4 Explain the excuses that exist for nonperformance by one party

Contracts for the sale of goods impose both obligations and requirements for performance on the parties.

A. General Principles

Each party to a sales contract is bound to perform according to the terms of the contract. Each is likewise under a duty to exercise **good faith** in the contract's performance and to do nothing that would impair the other party's expectation that the contract will be performed.

CPA 1. Obligation of Good Faith

Every contract or duty within the Uniform Commercial Code (UCC) imposes an obligation of good faith in its performance or enforcement.[1] The UCC defines good faith as "honesty in fact in the conduct or transaction concerned."[2] In the case of a merchant seller or buyer of goods, the UCC carries the concept of good faith further. The UCC imposes the additional requirement that merchants observe "reasonable commercial standards of fair dealing in the trade."[3] Section 1-203 of the UCC provides, "Every contract or duty within this Act imposes an obligation of good faith in its performance or enforcement."[4]

2. Time Requirements of Obligations

In a cash sale that does not require delivery of the goods, the duties of the seller and buyer are concurrent. Each one has the right to demand that the other perform at the same time. That is, as the seller hands over the goods, the buyer hands over the purchase money. If either party refuses to act, the other party has the right to withhold performance. In self-service stores, the performance occurs simultaneously—the buyer pays as the items are bagged at checkout.

In other types of contracts, there may be blocks of time between when the parties enter into an agreement and when performance, either delivery or payment, is due. During those time periods, buyers may become concerned about the ability of a seller experiencing a labor strike to complete production of the goods ordered in the contract. A seller may feel that a buyer who is experiencing credit difficulties may not be able to pay for the goods. Article 2 covers these periods of time and the conduct of the parties after the contract is entered into but before performance is due.

3. Repudiation of the Contract

If the seller or the buyer refuses to perform the contract when the time for performance arises, a **repudiation** of the contract results. Often, before the time for performance arrives, a party to the contract may inform the other that she will not perform the terms of the contract. This repudiation made in advance of the time for performance is called an **anticipatory repudiation**.[5] Under Revised Article 2, repudiation occurs when the party furnishes a *record* (as noted in other chapters, a term that allows for e-mails) including "language that a reasonable party would interpret to mean that the other party will not or cannot make a performance still due under the contract" or when the party exhibits "voluntary, affirmative conduct that would appear to a reasonable party to make a future performance by the other party impossible."[6]

4. Adequate Assurance of Performance

This time between contracting and actual performance may see some developing events that cause the parties concern about the ability of each to perform.[7] **For Example,** if the seller's warehouse is destroyed by fire, the buyer might conclude that the seller might not be able to make a delivery scheduled for the following month. Whenever a party to a sales contract has reasonable grounds to be concerned about the future performance of the other party, a demand may be made in a record for *assurance* that the contract will

[1] UCC §1-201(20); *C & E Services, Inc. v. Ashland Inc.*, 601 F. Supp. 2d 262 (D.D.C. 2009).
[2] UCC §1-202; Selling the goods and then claiming a breach does not constitute good faith. *Rad Concepts, Inc. v. Wilks Precision Instrument Co., Inc.*, 891 A.2d 1148 (Md. App. 2005).
[3] UCC §1-303; *Greenwood Products, Inc. v. Greenwood Forest Products, Inc.*, 273 P.3d 116 (Or. 2012); *Swanson v. Beco Const. Co., Inc.*, 175 P.3d 748 (Idaho 2007).
[4] UCC §1-203.
[5] UCC §2-610; *In re Mayco Plastics, Inc.*, 389 B.R. 7 (Bankr. E.D. Mich. 2008).
[6] UCC §2-610. The loss of a grain dealer's license is an anticipatory repudiation of his contract to sell grains for farmers. *Timmerman v. Grain Exchange, LLC*, 915 N.E.2d 113 (Ill. App. 2009).
[7] UCC §2-609.

be performed.[8] **For Example,** a seller who is concerned about a buyer's ability to pay for goods could demand an updated credit report, financial statement, or even additional security or payment.

(A) Form of Assurance. The person on whom demand for assurance is made must give "such assurance of due performance as is adequate under the circumstances of the particular case."[9] The UCC does not specify the exact form of assurance. If the party on whom demand is made has an established reputation, a reaffirmation of the contract obligation and a statement that it will be performed may be sufficient to assure a reasonable person that it will be performed. In contrast, if the party's reputation or economic position at the time is such that mere words and promises would not give any real assurance, it may be necessary to have a third person (or an insurance company) guarantee performance or to put up property as security for performance.

(B) Failure to Give Assurance. If adequate assurance is not given within 30 days from the time of demand, the demanding party may treat the contract as repudiated. The party demanding assurances may then proceed as if there were a breach and may pursue damage remedies. The nonbreaching party also has the right to enter into a substitute contract with a third person to obtain goods contracted for under the now-broken contract. The *Advanced Bodycare Solutions, LLC v. Thione International, Inc.*, case deals with an issue of assurances and performance.

Advanced Bodycare Solutions, LLC v. Thione International, Inc., 615 F.3d 1352 (11th Cir. 2010)

So, Are We Good on This Contract, or What?

On April 1, 2004, Advanced Body Care Solutions, LLC ("Advanced") and Thione International, Inc. ("Thione") entered into an agreement that required Advanced to make minimum purchases of "Thione Antioxidant Complex," which reduces free radical damage to the body, and Thione's "Free Radical Monitor Test Kit," which is a test kit for at-home use to monitor the body's free radicals. Ampoules are small glass tubes containing a clear liquid reagent, which tests for the presence of free radicals in a urine sample.

In exchange, Advanced received "the license and authority" "to advertise, promote, market, sell and otherwise distribute" the Dietary Supplement and the Test Kit on an exclusive basis. The agreement was to remain in effect for a minimum of five years: April 1, 2004 to March 31, 2009.

On May 26, 2004, Advanced placed an order for 25,000 ampoules, for which it paid $41,250. It received about 20,000 ampoules on September 1. It was immediately apparent that 200–300 of the 20,000 were broken, and about 1,000 were pink, indicating that they were defective. The following day, Dr. Stephen Perry, Advanced's liaison with Thione, sent an email to Dr. Mark Hersh, the CEO and chief scientist of Thione, stating that, "Carl [Pradelli, Advanced's managing member,] received some vials that are pink," and inquiring, "Do we have a production issue?"

As of March 2005, Thione had not yet identified the source of the problem with the first shipment of 20,000 ampoules, and Advanced had placed no subsequent orders. On March 18, Pradelli sent Hersh a summary of Advanced's marketing efforts. Following five pages on that subject was a section of the letter entitled "The Lingering Black Cloud," that stressed that Advanced's "biggest concern" was the defective ampoules and that it could not launch any additional marketing initiatives until satisfied that the problem was permanently solved.

During the summer of 2006, Advanced and Thione attempted to renegotiate the Licensing Agreement. The renegotiation efforts failed.

On September 26, 2006, Advanced filed suit against Thione for damages, claiming that Thione had breached the Licensing Agreement and an implied warranty by providing Advanced with defective ampoules. Thione counterclaimed for breach of the Agreement by Advanced of its minimum purchase obligations and claiming lost profits.

The jury found in favor of Thione on all of Advanced's claims and awarded it $2.5 million on its breach of contract counterclaim.

Advanced appealed.

[8] *GFSI, Inc. v. J-Loong Trading, Ltd.*, 505 F. Supp. 2d 935 (D. Kan. 2007).

[9] UCC §2-609(4).

Continued

JUDICIAL OPINION

TJOFLAT, Circuit Judge...Advanced argues that the jury lacked a legally sufficient evidentiary basis for finding for Thione on Advanced's breach of contract claim and for Thione on its breach of contract counterclaim for two reasons: (1) Thione's inclusion of defective ampoules in the 20,000 ampoule shipment of September 1, 2004, constituted a breach of the contract as a whole; and (2) Thione thereafter repudiated the Licensing Agreement by failing to provide Advanced with adequate assurances. Consequently, Advanced was relieved of its obligation to make further purchases (after the fourth quarter of 2004).

Less than 5,000 of the 25,000 ampoules shipped by the end of 2004 were damaged. Because the Licensing Agreement covered far more than the sale of ampoules, a reasonable jury could find that one order in which less than twenty percent of the goods were impaired did not breach the contract as a whole—especially when the order in question covered only $41,250 of the nearly $9 million contract. Moreover, Advanced never had a problem with the 5,000 ampoules shipped in November 2004 or the 6,700 replacement ampoules shipped in 2005. Given this evidence, the district court properly rejected Advanced's argument that Thione's shipment of the defective ampoules breached the entire Licensing Agreement.

Georgia law provides that "[w]hen reasonable grounds for insecurity arise with respect to the performance of either party the other may in writing demand adequate assurance of due performance and until he receives such assurance may if commercially reasonable suspend any performance for which he has not already received the agreed return." Of course, "[a] party already in breach is not entitled to invoke section 2–609 by demanding assurances."

By January 1, 2005, Advanced was in breach of the Licensing Agreement because it had not met the minimum purchasing requirement of the last quarter of 2004. Therefore, Advanced would have had to make a valid demand for adequate assurances before that date. The only communication that Advanced points to as a demand for adequate assurances made prior to the end of 2004 is Perry's September 2, 2004, email inquiring whether the pink ampoules meant that there was "a production issue." The district court did not err by declining to rule that, as a matter of law, this simple email inquiry constituted a "writing [that] demand[ed] adequate assurance of due performance," for a reasonable jury could have concluded it did not.

[Affirmed]

QUESTIONS

1. What point does the court make about the level of defects in the product?
2. Can a party to a contract use the right to demand assurances after the party is already in breach?
3. What additional information would need to be included in a demand for adequate performance?

B. Duties of the Parties

The obligations of the parties to a sales contract include (1) the seller's duty to deliver the goods, (2) the buyer's duty to accept the goods, and (3) the buyer's duty to pay for the goods.

5. Seller's Duty to Deliver

The seller has the duty to deliver the goods according to the terms of the contract.

(A) Place, Time, and Manner of Delivery. The terms of the contract determine whether the seller is to send the goods or the buyer is to call for them and whether the goods are to be transported from the seller to the buyer or the transaction is to be completed by the delivery of documents without the movement of the goods. In the absence of a provision in the contract or a contrary course of performance or usage of trade, the place of delivery is the seller's place of business if the seller has one; otherwise, it is the seller's residence. (See Chapter 24 for more details on delivery and shipping terms.)[10] However, if the subject matter of the contract consists of identified goods that are known by the parties to be in some other place, that place is the place of delivery. If no time for shipment or delivery is stated, delivery or shipment is required within a reasonable time.

When a method of transportation called for by the contract becomes unavailable or commercially unreasonable, the seller must make delivery by means of a commercially reasonable substitute if available.

(B) Quantity Delivered. The buyer has the right to insist that all the goods be delivered at one time. If the seller delivers a smaller or larger quantity than what is

[10] UCC §2-308.

stipulated in the contract, the buyer may refuse to accept the goods.[11]

6. Buyer's Duty upon Receipt of Goods

The buyer must accept goods that conform to the contract, and the refusal to do so is a breach of the contract. However, the buyer has certain rights prior to acceptance.

CPA **(A) Right to Examine Goods—The Buyer's Right of Inspection.**[12] To determine whether the goods in fact conform to the contract, the buyer has the right to examine the goods when tendered by the seller. An exception to this rule occurs when goods are sent COD. In a COD shipment, the buyer has no right to examine the goods until payment is made.

The buyer's right of inspection includes the right to remove goods from cartons and to conduct tests. **For Example,** a buyer who is purchasing potatoes for use in making potato chips has the right to peel and test a portion of the potatoes to determine whether they are the appropriate type for "chipping."

(B) Right to Refuse or Return the Goods—The Buyer's Right of Rejection.[13] If the goods the seller has tendered do not conform to the contract in any way, the buyer can *reject* the goods. **For Example,** the buyer may reject a mobile home when it does not contain an air conditioner with the capacity specified by the contract. The buyer may reject the goods if they are not perfect.[14] The standard for rejection does not require that the defect in the goods or the breach be material. **For Example,** a small pressure mark on an ottoman is not material; the ottoman will function just as well. However, the buyer still has the right to reject the ottoman because it has a defect.

The buyer has the right to reject the full shipment, accept the full shipment and seek damages for the goods' diminished value (see Chapter 27), or accept any commercial units and reject the remainder. Commercial units are defined by trade and industry according to the customary size of cartons or containers for the goods shipped. Envelopes come in **commercial units** of boxes of 500. Computer CDs often come in packages of 20 or 50. Rejection by a buyer would be not of individual envelopes or disks but of boxes. **For Example,** if Donna purchased a package of 20 CDs and 4 of the 20 CDs were defective, Donna would return the box of 20 CDs for a new box. Rejection and acceptance in commercial units prevent the problems created when a seller has to open other units and mix and match goods in each.

After rejecting the goods, the buyer may not exercise any right of ownership over the goods.

The buyer's rejection must be made within a reasonable time after the delivery or tender of the goods. The buyer must notify the seller of the rejection and, in transactions with merchants particularly, provide the seller with the reason for the rejection.[15]

CPA **(C) Cure of Defective Tender or Delivery.** The buyer's rejection is not an end to the transaction. The seller is given a second chance, or a **right to cure**, to make a proper tender of conforming goods.[16]

This right of cure means that the buyer must give notice of rejection and the reason for that rejection, if the seller has the right, but not necessarily the intent, to cure. That is, the seller has the right to cure if the seller is able to make the cure within the time remaining under the contract. If the time for making delivery under the contract has not expired, the seller need only give the buyer **seasonable** (timely) notice of the intention to make a proper delivery within the time allowed by the contract. Under Revised Article 2, the seller also has the right of cure if the time for making the delivery has expired through the allowance of additional reasonable time in which to make a substitute conforming tender. Such additional time is allowed if (1) the seller so notifies the buyer and (2) the seller had acted reasonably in making the original tender, believing that it would be acceptable to the buyer.[17] Under Revised UCC, installment contracts are also governed under this rule. The *Viking Packaging Technologies, Inc. v. Vassallo Foods, Inc.*, case deals with several issues of performance, cure, and rejection.

[11] UCC §2-307; Failure to deliver right amounts at the right time allows the buyer to repudiate the contract. *Traxys North America, LLC v. Concept Mining, Inc.*, 808 F. Supp. 2d 853 (W.D. Va. 2011).

[12] UCC §2-601.

[13] UCC §2-602; *In re S.M. Acquisition Co.*, 319 B.R. 553 (N.D. Ill. 2005).

[14] *Precision Mirror & Glass v. Nelms*, 797 N.Y.S.2d 720 (2005).

[15] UCC §2-602(1); *Adams v. Wacaster Oil Co., Inc.*, 98 S.W. 3d 832 (Ark. App. 2003).

[16] *Inter-Americas Ins. Corp., Inc. v. Imaging Solutions Co.*, 185 P.3d 963 (Kan. App. 2008).

[17] This right to cure after the time for performance has expired exists in nonconsumer contracts only.

Viking Packaging Technologies, Inc. v. Vassallo Foods, Inc., 804 N.W.2d 507 (Wis. App. 2011)

The Pasta Ties

Country Pasta, located in Polson, Montana, makes noodles. Viking manufactures, fabricates, and services industrial packaging equipment. In 2006, Gary Ivory, the production manager at Country Pasta, contacted Robb Leonhard, one of the owners of Viking, to discuss a quotation for a more automatic pasta bagging system. Country Pasta wanted a system in which the pasta bags would be weighed more accurately and in which the bags would be closed or tied more automatically. Ivory provided Leonhard with a sample of Country Pasta's product in the bag it was using at the time and indicated what he wanted the product to look like. Leonhard then sent Ivory photographs of a bag of Country Pasta's product with a tin-tie on it and stated "this is basically what your look is going to be." Viking included the photographs on the second page of the quotation.

On July 13, 2007, Country Pasta accepted Viking's quotation to purchase a pasta packaging system. The quotation shows photos of the equipment and of Country Pasta bags closed with a tin-tie. The items related to the tin-tie applicator were priced at $47,173. The total purchase price for the product packaging system was $178,074.

The quotation called for a "checkout," or a pre-shipment inspection, by Country Pasta "prior to shipment." In April 2008, Ivory and Scott Knutson went to Viking's facility to perform the checkout of the packaging system. The tin-ties on the finished bags did not regularly close up during this demonstration; however, Viking worked on the packaging system, and told Country Pasta that the system was "working better." Country Pasta approved the shipment and the packaging system was delivered to Country Pasta before June 17, 2008. Ivory helped unpack and set up the equipment; he did not notice any defects.

The contract provided that "if requested by the customer, [Viking] will provide a service technician for installation of the quoted equipment." The contract did not include free installation, but estimated that two days of installation and training for Country Pasta employees would cost $3,373. The contract also provided that "[a]n installation will be considered complete when all systems purchased from [Viking] perform per the Product Performance Specifications."

From June 17, 2008, through June 25, 2008, Viking technician Tim Parrish worked on installing the equipment and training Country Pasta's employees in Montana. During this visit, Parrish discovered that Country Pasta workers would drop or tap bags full of pasta on a table in order to settle the noodles to allow for a twist tie to be applied to the bag. Parrish made adjustments to the machinery, including adding a shelf to assist in the settling of the noodles. Despite these efforts, the tin-tie applicator was not functioning properly at the time he left. Viking and Country Pasta agreed to split the cost of a second visit by Parrish.

Parrish returned to Country Pasta in July 2008 with Steve Almberg, a representative from Weigh Right, the manufacturer of the scale. Parrish and Almberg improved the operation of the scale and bagger by making modifications to Country Pasta's equipment feeding the scale and bagger.

A Country Pasta memorandum regarding a meeting with Parrish on July 10, 2008, notes the improvements with the scale and bagger, but states that "[t]here is no way the current tin-tie system will work with our product." Parrish left Montana and was not asked to return to Montana to continue working on the applicator.

On December 4, 2008, five months after delivery of the packaging system, and four months after Parrish's final visit, Kellogg sent an email to Viking stating that Country Pasta wanted a refund for the tin-tie applicator and the associated conveyor in the amount of $47,173. At that time, Country Pasta had outstanding invoices due to Viking in the amount of $34,110.22. Viking brought suit against Country Pasta, seeking the outstanding amount. Country Pasta counterclaimed, alleging breach of contract.

After a trial to the court, judgment for money damages was entered in favor of Viking. Country Pasta's counterclaim alleging breach of contract by Viking, and alleging Country Pasta's revocation of acceptance of the tin-tie applicator and conveyor were dismissed. Country Pasta appealed.

JUDICIAL OPINION

KESSLER, Judge...Country Pasta contends that Viking breached its contract by failing to complete installation of the entire packaging system because the tin-tie applicator did not consistently put tin-ties on its pasta bags in accordance with the product performance specifications mentioned in the contract. Country Pasta asserts that because the tin-tie applicator would not consistently apply the tin-ties to Country Pasta's product, " a component of the system did not perform according to the product performance specifications." Although Country Pasta makes no complaint about the performance of the bagger, the scale, or their related conveyors, it argues that Viking failed to complete "installation of the entire [p]ackaging [s]ystem " and therefore breached its obligations under the contract.

The contract required Viking to install the packaging system if, and only if, Country Pasta requested that service and agreed to pay for that service at the rates set out in the contract. After Parrish told Country Pasta at the end of his

Continued

second visit in July 2008, that the tin-tie applicator would not work with its product, Kellogg never requested further installation or other work by Viking. Kellogg never asked to have the applicator replaced, nor did he identify any defective or broken parts. All of these alternatives were available to Country Pasta under the contract.

Country Pasta wanted its packaging system to be more automatic. It wanted to have the "bags closed or tied and the bags to be weighed more accurately." Nothing in those photographs, or elsewhere in the contract, establish how quickly the packaging system was required to function. By the end of his second visit to Country Pasta, Parrish testified he was able to give Kellogg a package closed with a tin-tie, but Kellogg was dissatisfied because of the way the tin-tied bag performed during handling. Kellogg himself testified that he thought the bags looked "sloppy." Nothing in the contract even hints at any handling standards the tin-tie must withstand. The record does not explain how the "look" of the bag delivered differed from the photographs attached to the contract. Country Pasta has not established that the packaging system as a whole, or the tin-tie applicator specifically, failed to meet any identifiable "[p]roduct [p]erformance [s]pecifications."

Country Pasta argues that the trial court erred in finding that County Pasta accepted the tin-tie applicator and its related conveyor because without a complete installation, Country Pasta never had a reasonable opportunity to inspect the packaging system. Installation was required under the contract only if requested by Country Pasta. The predominant purpose of the contract was the sale of the packaging system.

Acceptance is the unilateral act of the buyer alone, or of his representative; it requires no action or expression on the part of the seller. Acceptance within the meaning of the statute is an expression of assent by the buyer to become the owner of specific goods as the subject matter of the contract made by him with the seller.

Wisconsin Stat. § 402.606(2) provides that "[a]cceptance of a part of any commercial unit is acceptance of that entire unit."

The purchase of a "packaging system" composed of multiple single machines is very similar in concept to the statutory example of "a suite of furniture or an assortment of sizes." Both the hypothetical suite of furniture and the packaging system would be materially impaired in their value to the user if parts (a chair, a tin-tie applicator) were removed from the whole.

If the contract contemplated separate purchases of distinct machines, delivery of each would complete each "order" and there would be no "remainder" of the order to be considered. Thus, we conclude that the commercial unit here, as understood by the parties in their contract, is the entire integrated packaging system.

The purpose of these various machines, in this contract, is to function as an integrated commercial unit—an automated packaging system. We conclude that Viking quoted, and Country Pasta ordered and received, an integrated packaging system.

By the time Parrish left Montana in July 2008, Country Pasta was dissatisfied only with the performance of the tin-tie applicator. The other machines comprising the packaging system apparently functioned satisfactorily. Country Pasta expressed no intent to return the bagger, the scale, or the other equipment related to the operation of those machines. Earlier, after its "checkout" of the system and knowledge that there had been problems with the tin-tie applicator, Country Pasta approved of the shipment of the packaging system. No defective or broken parts were identified when Country Pasta unpacked and set up the machines. Ultimately, Kellogg was informed that the tin-tie applicator would not work with Country Pasta's product, yet he retained the applicator for an additional four or five months before making a complaint. Country Pasta had a reasonable opportunity to inspect the system. It accepted the system as a whole, as it did not wish to return any equipment other than the tin-tie applicator.

By retaining all of the items in the contract, Country Pasta treated the packaging system in a way that was inconsistent with the seller's ownership. This conduct constitutes acceptance of goods.

The only conduct in this record that might arguably be considered a notice of rejection is an email dated December 4, 2008, from Kellogg to Viking, demanding a refund of the cost of the tin-tie applicator. To reject goods, however, the rejection [must] occur within a reasonable time after delivery, and the rejection only becomes effective when the buyer "seasonably notifies the seller." Kellogg's email was sent four months after Parrish's second visit to Montana, in which Parrish indicated that the tin-tie applicator would not work with Country Pasta's product. Country Pasta never rejected the commercial unit.

Country Pasta finally argues that if it accepted the packaging system, it was done with the assumption that "Viking was continuing to work on a solution to fix the tin-tie applicator" after Parrish left Montana in July 2008. Country Pasta argues that it revoked acceptance upon Kellogg's realization that "Viking was not going to provide a solution."

The revocation must occur "within a reasonable time after the buyer discovers … the ground [for revocation] and … is not effective until the buyer notifies the seller" of the revocation.

Country Pasta knew that Parrish had not been able to fix the problem when he left in June because Country Pasta

Continued

agreed to pay for half of his cost to return and try again. Country Pasta knew in July 2008 that the problem it perceived with the tin-tie applicator continued because Parrish told Country Pasta the machine would not work on Country Pasta's product. Because the seller's agent made repeated repairs to a machine at the buyer's request and the machine still did not work as the contract required, the buyer knew, or should have known that the machine would not do good work, and could not be made to do good work.

Thereafter, Country Pasta "could not reasonably assume that the nonconformity of the machinery would be cured." These findings make revocation unavailable to Country Pasta.

Country Pasta made no effort at any time to revoke its earlier acceptance of the entire package. Instead, four or five months after Country Pasta was told that the tin-tie applicator could not be made to perform to Country Pasta's satisfaction, Country Pasta attempted to revoke its acceptance of only that part of the commercial unit. Such partial revocation of acceptance of a commercial unit is barred. Viking did not breach this contract and Country Pasta's counterclaims were properly dismissed.

[Affirmed]

QUESTIONS

1. Why was the months-long delay important to the court in deciding whether there was revocation of acceptance?
2. Why was the rejection of the bag-tying portion of the machine important to the court's decision?
3. List the steps Country Pasta should have taken to allow it to still have a revocation of acceptance.

7. Buyer's Duty to Accept Goods

Assuming that the buyer has no grounds to reject the goods after inspection, the next step in the performance of the contract is the buyer's **acceptance** of the goods.

CPA **(A) What Constitutes Acceptance of Goods.**[18] Acceptance of goods means that the buyer, pursuant to a contract, has, either expressly or by implication, taken the goods permanently. The buyer's statement of acceptance is an express acceptance. A buyer can accept goods by implication if there is no rejection after a reasonable opportunity to inspect them or within a reasonable time after the buyer has inspected them. Another form of acceptance by implication is conduct by the buyer that is inconsistent with rejection, as when a buyer uses or sells the delivered goods.[19]

A buyer accepts goods by making continued use of them and by not attempting to return them. A buyer also accepts goods by modifying them because such action is inconsistent with a rejection or with the continued ownership of the goods by the seller.[20]

CPA **(B) Revocation of Acceptance.** Even after acceptance of the goods, the performance under the contract may not be finished if the buyer exercises the right to revoke acceptance of the goods.[21] The buyer may revoke acceptance of the goods when they do not conform to the contract, the defect is such that it substantially impairs the value of the contract to the buyer, and either the defect is such that the buyer could not discover the problem or the seller has promised to correct a problem the buyer was aware of and pointed out to the seller prior to acceptance.[22] **For Example,** a buyer who purchased an emergency electric power generator found that the generator produced only about 65 percent of the power called for by the contract. This amount of power was insufficient for the operation of the buyer's electrical equipment. The seller's repeated attempts to improve the generator's output failed. The buyer, despite having used the generator for three months, could revoke his acceptance of it because its value was substantially impaired and he continued to keep it and use it only because of the seller's assurances that it would be repaired.

[18] UCC §2-606; *Stenzel v. Dell, Inc.*, 870 A.2d 133 (Me. 2005).

[19] *Fabrica de Tejidos Imperial v. Brandon Apparel Group, Inc.*, 218 F. Supp. 2d 974 (N.D. Ill. 2002).

[20] UCC §2-606(1)(a), (b), and (c).

[21] UCC §2-608; *Fode v. Capital RV Center, Inc.*, 575 N.W.2d 682 (N.D. 1998); *Barrett v. Brian Bemis Auto World*, 408 F. Supp. 2d 539 (N.D. Ill. 2005).

[22] Repeated requests for service satisfy the requirement for notifying the seller. *Cliffstar Corp. v. Elmar Industries, Inc.*, 678 N.Y.S.2d 222 (1998). But continued use without notification presents problems for establishing rejection. *In re Rafter Seven Ranches*, 546 F.3d 1194 (10th Cir. 2008).

E-Commerce & Cyberlaw

Rejection in Cyberspace

Rejection of computers and software presents novel issues for the UCC provisions on rejection because use of the goods is not so easily defined or distinguished by a bright line. With software, for example, the buyer can use the software as a means of conducting an inspection of the goods. However, fully loading the software constitutes acceptance, and the buyer would then step into the UCC provisions on revocation of acceptance, as opposed to rejection. If the software causes the buyer's computer to "crash" every 10 minutes, the buyer has grounds for either rejection or revocation of acceptance. The buyer could also agree to allow the seller to modify the software to prevent the "crashing" problems. Once the buyer decides to reject the software or revoke acceptance of it, he or she cannot continue to use the software, for such use is inconsistent with the claim that the goods (the software) fail to conform to the contract.*

A buyer is also permitted to test a computer for purposes of inspection and rejection. If, however, the buyer rejects the computer system, it cannot continue to use the system, and allowing third parties to make alterations to the system to help it function better constitutes acceptance.**

**Cooperative Resources, Inc. v. Dynasty Software, Inc.*, 39 UCC Rep. Serv.2d 101 (N.H. Dist. Ct. 1998).
***Softa Group, Inc. v. Scarsdale Development*, 632 N.E.2d 13 (Ill. App. 1993) (using a computer the buyer claims was "defective from inception" is inconsistent with rejection and the required basis for a rejection). *Licitra v. Gateway, Inc.*, 734 N.Y.S.2d 389 (2001). Online retailers have their own rules for rejection. For example, Zappo's offers free returns, but the buyer must comply with the online return processes. There are also time limits placed on revocation of acceptance, such as on Amazon. All goods must be returned within six months of purchase. The online retailers have spelled out the time limits to make rejection and revocation of acceptance requirements clear and not subject to UCC interpretation of reasonableness.

Substantial impairment is a higher standard than the one of "fails to conform in any respect" for rejection. Substantial impairment requires proof of more than the mere fact that the goods do not conform to the contract. The buyer is not required to show that the goods are worthless but must prove that their use to the buyer is substantially different from what the contract promised.

A revocation of acceptance is not a cancellation of the contract with the seller. After revocation of acceptance, the buyer can choose from the remedies available for breach of contract or demand that the seller deliver conforming goods. (See Chapter 27 for more information on remedies for breach.)

(c) Notification of Revocation of Acceptance. To revoke acceptance properly, the buyer must take certain steps. The buyer must give the seller notice of revocation. The revocation of acceptance is effective when the buyer notifies the seller. The buyer need not actually return the goods to make the notification or the revocation effective. The *Jackson Hole Traders v. Joseph* case deals with an issue of revocation of acceptance.

Jackson Hole Traders, Inc. v. Joseph, 931 P.2d 244 (Wyo. 1997)

Jackson Hole Traders: The Retailer Looking for a Loophole

Catherine Joseph, who does business as Metro Classics (appellee), sold clothing to Jackson Hole Traders, Inc., a corporation owned by David and Elizabeth Speaks (appellants). Jackson Hole Traders is located in Jackson, Wyoming, and sells clothing for men and women through a retail store and mail-order catalog business. The clothing Joseph sold was specially manufactured for Jackson Hole Traders and had a total contract price of $50,000, with terms being net 30.

When the clothing items were shipped between July and September 1994, approximately 900 items were sent. Elizabeth Speaks complained about the quality on some of the clothing items when they arrived and was given a credit of $1,096 for returned merchandise. However, Jackson Hole Traders did not pay $32,000 of the total Joseph bill despite it being well past the net-30-day period for payment. When Joseph demanded payment, Elizabeth Speaks boxed up approximately 350 items of the clothing and sent them back, demanding a credit for revocation of acceptance. Joseph filed suit for payment alleging that it was too late for revocation of acceptance. The trial court found for Joseph, and the Speakses appealed.

Continued

JUDICIAL OPINION

MACY, J.… Appellants claim that the trial court improperly concluded that the Uniform Commercial Code governed the parties' transaction, arguing that this transaction was principally one for labor and services. Appellee counters that the trial court appropriately applied the Uniform Commercial Code to this transaction because it was for the sale of goods.

For support of their proposition that this transaction was one for services rather than for goods, Appellants rely on *Wells v 10-X Manufacturing Company,* 609 F.2d 248 (6th Cir.1979). That case, however, differs from the case at bar because the buyer in ***Wells*** furnished the manufacturer with virtually everything but the labor.

Although Appellants purchased and supplied the outer fabric for some of the garments produced by Appellee, Appellee supplied all the other materials which were used to manufacture the garments; i.e., buttons, linings, interfacing, special care labels, as well as the outer fabric for the remaining garments. Some garments were patterned from Appellee's own designs. Even for those styles which utilized a design provided by Appellants, Appellee and her pattern maker had to restyle them because of various changes which were requested by Appellants. Each pattern was then graded into the particular sizes to be used for that garment. Under the facts of this case, the trial court correctly applied the Uniform Commercial Code as this transaction was one for the sale of goods even though labor was involved in producing the goods.

David Speaks gave the following testimony:

[APPELLEE'S ATTORNEY:] *Now, I sent you a letter dated December 9 asking for thirty-two thousand dollars for [Appellee], did I not?*

A. Yes, you did.

Q. And your response was to pack up 350 garments that she had manufactured at your request and ship them back in bulk to her, wasn't it?

A. That's what we did, yes.

....

[Q.] Now, the goods that you shipped back to [Appellee], you instructed—either you or Ms. Speaks instructed someone working for you to take the goods off of the showroom floor and box them up and send them back. Some of the goods that were returned to [Appellee] were pulled off the showroom floor, weren't they?

A. Most likely, yes. I'm almost positive, yeah.

Q. And some of those items were pulled off the shelves where they had been stored for several months, weren't they?

A. You're talking about in the warehouse?

Q. Yes.

A. Yes, they were.

....

Q. If you don't think the goods got there on time and you think that you have been put in a bad way as a result of that, you can refuse the shipment, can't you?

A. You can refuse the shipment, yes, you can. That is one option.

Q. And you could have done that, couldn't you?

A. That's an option, yes.

Q. But you didn't refuse the shipment, did you?

A. No, we did not.

Q. And you put the goods in your warehouse, didn't you?

A. Yes, they were in the warehouse.

Q. And put them on your showroom floor, didn't you?

A. Yes, we did.

Q. And you sold them through your catalog; is that right?

A. Yes, we did.

Q. And you sold many of them in your store, didn't you?

A. Yes, we did.

....

[Q.] When I sent you the letter on December 9th asking for payment of the thirty-two thousand plus dollars owed to [Appellee], your response within 72 hours was to take everything and ship it back to [Appellee]; is that correct?

A. Yes, it was.

Appellants breached the contract when they failed to pay for the garments which had been sent to them and which they had accepted for resale. The trial court properly awarded damages in an amount which would place Appellee in the same position that she would have occupied had the contract been performed.

[Affirmed]

QUESTIONS

1. How long had the goods been with the buyer?
2. Where were the goods when they were packaged to be sent back?
3. Will the seller get her money?

The notice of revocation of acceptance must be given within a reasonable time after the buyer discovers or should have discovered the problems with the goods. The right of revocation is not lost if the buyer gives the seller a longer period of time to correct the defects in the goods.[23] Even the lapse of a year

[23] A buyer who took her pop-up camper in for repairs but was then given a different camper without being told about it was entitled to revoke her acceptance. *Head v. Phillips Camper Sales & Rental, Inc.*, 593 N.W.2d 595 (Mich. Ct. App. 1999).

Thinking Things Through

ICE, Turbines, Iran, and Impracticability

Turbines Ltd. sells and maintains helicopters. Transupport, Inc. sells spare parts and turbine engines. Monarch Aviation contacted Turbines in search of a "First Stage" turbine nozzle. Turbines did not have the nozzle but, in checking with Transupport, discovered that it did. Turbines sent a purchase order to Transupport for the nozzle for $30,000.

Transupport tried to ship the nozzle directly to Turbines' client in Malaysia. However, Customs seized the nozzle because it was on the "United States Munitions List." There was a resulting dispute about the seizure as the parties tried to get it classified as a "dual-use" item.

Immigration and Customs Enforcement (ICE) told Turbines that it was keeping the nozzle because it was likely to end up in Iran. Following this disclosure, Turbines learned that the wife of one of the owners of Transupport was arrested on charges of conspiracy, money laundering, and export of arms and munitions. Turbines eventually returned the nozzle to Transupport. Transupport filed suit for breach of contract. Turbines maintains that it could not perform the contract because of the events that happened after shipment. Is Turbines correct?

Was the standard of commercial impracticability met? [***Turbines Ltd. v. Transupport, Inc.*, 808 N.W.2d 643 (Neb. 2012)**]

will not cost the buyer the right of revocation of acceptance if the seller has been experimenting during that time trying to correct the problems with the goods.

(D) Buyer's Responsibilities upon Revocation of Acceptance. After a revocation of acceptance, the buyer must hold the goods and await instructions from the seller. If the buyer revokes acceptance after having paid the seller in advance, the buyer may retain possession of the goods as security for the refund of the money that has been paid.

8. Buyer's Duty to Pay

The buyer must pay the amount stated in the sales contract for accepted goods.

(A) Time of Payment. The sales contract may require payment in advance or may give the buyer credit by postponing the time for payment.[24]

(B) Form of Payment. Unless otherwise agreed, payment by the buyer requires payment in cash. The seller may accept a check or a promissory note from the buyer. If the check is not paid by the bank, the purchase price remains unpaid. A promissory note payable at a future date gives the buyer credit by postponing the time for payment.

The seller can refuse to accept a check or a promissory note as payment for goods but must give the buyer reasonable time in which to obtain legal tender with which to make payment. The *Magic Valley Foods, Inc. v. Sun Valley Potatoes, Inc.* deals with an issue of payment.

Magic Valley Foods, Inc. v. Sun Valley Potatoes, Inc., 10 P.3d 734 (Idaho. 2000)

Poor Payment Pattern on Potato Contracts

JUDICIAL DECISION

KIDWELL, Justice…Sun Valley Potatoes, Inc. (Sun Valley) is a fresh packer of potatoes. Magic Valley Foods, Inc. (Magic Valley) is a processor of potatoes. Sun Valley and Magic Valley entered into three written contracts wherein Sun Valley agreed to sell and deliver and Magic Valley agreed to purchase potatoes. Sun Valley provided nine weekly invoices, but none of those invoices were paid according to the following term in all of the contracts: "net thirty (30) days on amounts delivered on a weekly basis." As of August 9, 1995, Sun Valley had delivered 108,169 cwt. (at the contract price of $1.13 cwt.) of potatoes to Magic Valley. Magic Valley, on the other hand,

[24] UCC §2-310.

Continued

had withheld payments totaling $236,904.44. Sun Valley ceased its deliveries because it had not been paid for a total of 24 invoices. Magic Valley had to shut down its plant for 14 days and it filed suit against Sun Valley for breach of contract. The district court concluded that because Sun Valley had not insisted on strict compliance with the 30-day payment rule, it could not unilaterally repudiate the contract due to late payments. The district court also ruled that Magic Valley was entitled to offset the $236,904.44 it owed Sun Valley against the $231,660.60 it incurred as a result of its processing plant being down for 14 days and the loss of profits associated therewith. Sun Valley appealed.

DECISION: Magic Valley asserted that its reliance on Sun Valley's waiver of the 30-day payment requirement should be inferred because of Sun Valley's lack of demand for payment. Magic Valley also argues that it detrimentally relied upon Sun Valley's waiver when it made arrangements to purchase cover potatoes from other suppliers. Magic Valley's argument is not logical. The fact that Magic Valley sought cover in case Sun Valley did not deliver enough potatoes does not show that Magic Valley detrimentally relied upon Sun Valley's acceptance of late payments. The fact that Magic Valley sought cover only shows that Magic Valley was concerned that Sun Valley would not deliver all of the potatoes contracted for. Thus, Magic Valley failed to show that it detrimentally relied on Sun Valley's alleged waiver.

Magic Valley was making payments to Sun Valley each month from January to June of 1995. However, the monthly payments during this time were never enough to eradicate the growing balance being carried by Sun Valley. Even with these payments, the balance Sun Valley was carrying grew to $236,904.44 by August 9, 1995. Thus, even if Sun Valley had waived its right to 30-day's payment, it was justified at some point in withholding deliveries due to Magic Valley's failure to bring its account current. The UCC provides that when a buyer under an installment contract makes installments which "substantially impairs the value of the whole contract, there is a breach of the whole."

In an attempt to justify withholding payment, Magic Valley claims that because Sun Valley did not deliver, Magic Valley was forced to enter into contracts for cover. Magic Valley bolsters this claim by arguing that Sun Valley began delivering potatoes to third parties.

In such a situation the UCC provides that "[w]hen reasonable grounds for insecurity arise with respect to the performance of either party the other may in writing demand adequate assurance of due performance and until he receives such assurance may if commercially reasonable suspend any performance for which he has not already received the agreed return."

Magic Valley failed to comply with this statute in two respects. First, Magic Valley did not seek assurances until the end of August 1995, but withheld payment from Sun Valley months prior to that. Thus Magic Valley had already began suspending its performance to pay, months prior to seeking assurances that Sun Valley would deliver. Second, at the time Magic Valley was seeking assurances in August, it had already received the potatoes for which payment was owed. The statute allows suspension of performance only "for which he has not already received the agreed return." Thus, because Magic Valley had already received the potatoes, it was obligated to pay without regards to Sun Valley's assurances of completion of contract 9418.

If Magic Valley was concerned that it was not going to get the potatoes it had contracted for, it should have sought reasonable assurances from Sun Valley when it learned that Sun Valley was shipping to other processors.

In conclusion, Magic Valley breached contract 9418 by unreasonably withholding payment to Sun Valley on contract 9418 and previous contracts. Sun Valley did not anticipatorily breach because it had completed the requirements of the previous contracts and had at least through the month of September to compete contract 9418. Magic Valley had no justifiable reason to withhold payment on either of the previous contracts or 9418. Because Magic Valley breached the contract by not paying Sun Valley's invoices, Sun Valley was justified in withholding the remaining potatoes under contract 9418. The district court erred in holding that Sun Valley breached the contract and that Magic Valley was entitled to offset its damages against the amount owed to Sun Valley. Reversed.

QUESTIONS

1. List the mistakes the parties made in their compliance with UCC requirements for performance.
2. Which party should have demanded assurances and when?
3. Will Magic Valley be able to recover damages for the 14 days it was shut down?

CPA 9. When Duties Are Excused

Under Article 2, the doctrine of commercial impracticability is available as a defense to performance of a contract. The doctrine of **commercial impracticability** is the modern commercial law version of the common law doctrine of impossibility. If a party to a

Ethics & the Law

The Return Season

At Saks Fifth Avenue, they call it the "return season." Return season occurs within the week following a major fundraising formal dance. Women who have purchased formal evening wear return the dresses after the dance. The dresses have been worn, and the tags have been cut, but the women return the dresses with requests for a full refund. Neiman Marcus also experiences the same phenomenon of returns.

Some stores have implemented a policy that formal evening wear may not be returned if the tags are cut from it. Others require a return within a limited period of seven days. Others offer an exchange only after five days.

Are the women covered by a right of rejection under Article 2? What do you think of the conduct of the women? Is it simply revocation of acceptance? Is there good faith on the part of the women?

contract can establish that there has been an occurrence or a contingency not anticipated by the parties and not a basic assumption in their entering into a contract, the party can be excused from performance.

The standard for commercial impracticability is objective, not subjective. Additional cost alone is not grounds for application of commercial impracticability.[25]

For Example, if a farmer has contracted to sell two tons of peanuts to an airline and the crop fails, the farmer is not excused on the grounds of commercial impracticability. So long as peanuts are available for the farmer to buy, even at a higher price, and then sell to the buyer to satisfy their contract terms, the farmer is not excused. Commercial impracticability refers to those circumstances in which peanuts are not available anywhere because the entire peanut harvest was destroyed rather than just the individual farmer's crop. The *Ecology Services Inc. v. GranTurk Equipment, Inc.* case involves an issue of commercial impracticability.

Ecology Services Inc. v. GranTurk Equipment, Inc., 443 F. Supp. 2d 756, 60 UCC. Rep. Serv. 2d 676 (D. Md. 2006)

Just a Bunch of Garbage, Especially When There Are No Dump Trucks

Ecology Services, Inc. (ESI) entered into a contract in late 2002 with Montgomery County, Maryland, for refuse removal services. On a GranTurk "Order Form" dated November 25, 2003, GranTurk agreed to sell the county 12 Split Rear Loaders to be installed on ESI's chassis for a cost of $77,675.13 each. GranTurk subcontracted with G & H for task of installing the loaders on the chassis. G & H agreed to deliver the first (6) units to Granturk on or before April 15 provided the chassis arrived prior to March 15 and the last (6) units on or before May 15 provided the chassis arrive before April 15. G & H agreed to a $100 per day late penalty clause.

There was a steel shortage and ESI and GranTurk had difficulties and additional costs in obtaining the steel necessary for the production of the trucks for the county. Following several delays and no deliveries of the garbage trucks, the county filed suit seeking damages of $500,000. As the suit progressed, ESI delivered nine of the trucks, but, by the time of the trial, three trucks had not yet been delivered. ESI and GranTurk argued that they were excused from timely performance because of the worldwide steel shortage and were only liable for the $100 per day late-fee damages provided for in the contract. The parties moved for summary judgment.

JUDICIAL OPINION

BENNETT, District Judge...In determining if a business should be relieved of its contractual duties for impracticability, a court must consider "[c]ircumstances existing at the contracting date and foreseeability." Furthermore, "where there is an agreed sole source and it is foreseeable that the sole source may fail, the risk of nondelivery is on the seller unless the seller includes exculpatory language thereby expressly transferring the risk to the purchaser." [t]he parties do not dispute that the first prong—that both parties mutually contemplated G & H as the sole source of the truck bodies—

[25] UCC §2-615(a).

Continued

is satisfied. GranTurk asserts in its Motion for Summary Judgment that both parties agreed that G & H would be GranTurk's sole source for the truck bodies at issue in the contract that is the subject of this lawsuit.

This Court cannot, however, conclude on the record before it that there are no material facts in dispute under the second and third prongs of the test. With respect to the second prong—that the failure must not have been foreseeable at the time of the contracting—there is a genuine dispute regarding the foreseeability of the alleged steel shortage that GranTurk cites as the source of G & H's failure to timely supply the truck bodies. GranTurk contends that neither party foresaw the steel shortage, quoting deposition testimony by ESI's CEO, Timothy Osborne, that he did not foresee the national steel shortage. Although the quoted deposition testimony of ESI's CEO shows that he did not foresee the steel shortage, that testimony does not demonstrate that the steel shortage was not foreseeable (by either party) at the time of contracting. GranTurk has provided no documentation to support its contention that the steel shortage that allegedly made GranTurk's performance impracticable was unforeseeable.

Indeed, at least one court has noted that there was a shortage of steel in 2003–2004 but found that the shortage was foreseeable. According to the articles, steel pricing has fluctuated throughout the late 1990's and into 2003. This is simply further evidence that a market shift was foreseeable prior to the parties' agreement [in December of 2003]. As previously noted, the parties in this action entered into the contract at issue precisely during this time frame.

Moreover, to the extent that G & H was unable to procure steel for the truck bodies due to the expense of purchasing steel, rising costs alone is not sufficient to invoke the defense of § 2-615.

Increased cost alone does not excuse performance unless the rise in cost is due to some unforeseen contingency which alters the essential nature of performance. Neither is a rise or a collapse in the market in itself a justification, for that is exactly the business risk which business contracts made at fixed prices are intended to cover.

Any rising cost of steel during the time when the parties entered into their agreement, therefore, is not sufficient for an impracticability defense. Defendant further contends that even if it foresaw the steel shortage, an exculpatory clause in the contract at issue, stating "Delivery promised subject to delay beyond our control," excused GranTurk's delay. In order to overcome the foreseeability issue, an exculpatory clause must "expressly transfer[ ] the risk to the purchaser." This Court cannot conclude at this stage that the clause "Delivery promised subject to delay beyond our control" expressly transfers to ESI the risk that GranTurk's sole supplier will fail. As previously noted, ESI does not concede that GranTurk has established that a steel shortage occurred, nor does it concede that GranTurk has established that G & H was ever affected by any such shortage. GranTurk has provided no documentation of the steel shortage or its effect on G & H beyond deposition testimony. Therefore, GranTurk has failed to show that there are no genuine disputes of material fact with respect to the second prong of the Rockland test.

A severe shortage of raw materials or of supplies due to a contingency such as war, embargo, local crop failure, unforeseen shutdown of major sources of supply or the like, which either causes a marked increase in cost or altogether prevents the seller from securing supplies necessary to his performance is within the contemplation of this section.

Given the lack of documentation supporting GranTurk's contention that a steel shortage precluded it from timely delivering trucks to ESI, this Court determines that genuine disputes of material facts exist and that GranTurk is, therefore, not entitled to summary judgment.

QUESTIONS

1. What are the factors that a court considers when evaluating a defense of commercial impracticability?
2. What types of contract terms might have helped all of the parties in this case?
3. What evidence should GranTurk submit to establish commercial impracticability?

MAKE THE CONNECTION

SUMMARY

Every sales contract imposes an obligation of good faith in its performance. Good faith means honesty in fact in the conduct or transaction concerned. For merchants, the UCC imposes the additional requirement of observing "reasonable commercial standards of fair dealing in the trade."

In the case of a cash sale where no transportation of the goods is required, both the buyer and the seller may demand concurrent performance.

A buyer's or a seller's refusal to perform a contract is called a *repudiation*. A repudiation made in advance of the time for performance is called an *anticipatory repudiation* and is a breach of the contract. If either party to a contract feels insecure about the performance of the other, that party may demand by a record adequate assurance of performance. If that assurance is not given, the demanding party may treat the contract as repudiated.

The seller has a duty to deliver the goods in accordance with the terms of the contract. This duty does not require physical transportation; it requires that the seller permit the transfer of possession of the goods to the buyer.

With the exception of COD contracts, the buyer has the right to inspect the goods upon tender or delivery. Inspection includes the right to open cartons and conduct tests. If the buyer's inspection reveals that the seller has tendered nonconforming goods, the buyer may reject them. Subject to certain limitations, the seller may then offer to replace the goods or cure the problems the buyer has noted.

The buyer has a duty to accept goods that conform to the contract, and refusal to do so is a breach of contract. The buyer is deemed to have accepted goods either expressly or by implication through conduct inconsistent with rejection or by lapse of time. The buyer must pay for accepted goods in accordance with the terms of the contract. The buyer can reject goods in commercial units, accept the goods and collect damages for their problems, or reject the full contract shipment. The buyer must give notice of rejection to the seller and cannot do anything with the goods that would be inconsistent with the seller's ownership rights. The buyer should await instructions from the seller on what to do with the goods.

Even following acceptance, the buyer may revoke that acceptance if the problems with the goods substantially impair their value and the problems were either not easily discoverable or the buyer kept the goods based on the seller's promises to repair them and make them whole. Upon revocation of acceptance, the buyer should await instructions from the seller on what steps to take.

Performance can be excused on the grounds of commercial impracticability, but the seller must show objective difficulties that have created more than cost increases.

LEARNING OUTCOMES

After studying this chapter, you should be able to clearly explain:

A. General Principles

LO.1 List the steps that can be taken when a party to a sales contract feels insecure about the other party's performance

See *Magic Valley Foods, Inc. v. Sun Valley Potatoes, Inc.* on pp. 503–504.

B. Duties of the Parties

LO.2 Explain the obligations of the seller and the buyer in a sales contract

See the *Viking Packaging Technologies* case on pp. 498–500.

LO.3 Identify the types of actions and conduct that constitute acceptance

See *Jackson Hole Traders, Inc. v. Joseph* on pp. 501–502.

See ICE, Turbines, Iran, and Commercial Impracticability on p. 503.

LO.4 Explain the excuses that exist for nonperformance by one party

See *Ecology Services, Inc. v. GranTurk Equipment* on pp. 505–506.

KEY TERMS

acceptance
anticipatory repudiation
commercial impracticability
commercial units
good faith
repudiation
right to cure
seasonable
substantial impairment

QUESTIONS AND CASE PROBLEMS

1. In 1992, Donna Smith telephoned Clark, the manager of Penbridge Farms, in response to an advertisement Clark had placed in the July issue of the *Emu Finder* about the availability for sale of proven breeder pairs. Clark told Smith he had a breeder pair available. Clark sold the pair to Smith for $16,500. Some months later, after Smith had had a chance to inspect the pair, she discovered that Clark had sold her two males. Smith immediately notified Clark and revoked her acceptance of the animals. Clark said the revocation was too late. Was it? [*Smith v. Penbridge Associates, Inc.*, 655 A.2d 1015 (Pa. Super.)]

2. On January 3, 1991, Central District Alarm (CDA) and Hal-Tuc entered into a written sales agreement providing that CDA would sell and install new security equipment described on an equipment list attached to the contract. This list included a Javelin VCR. When the system was installed, CDA installed a used JVC VCR instead of a new Javelin VCR. Hal-Tuc called CDA the day after the installation and complained that the equipment was not the Javelin brand, and that the VCR was a used JVC VCR. CDA told Hal-Tuc that the equipment was not used and that a JVC VCR was better than a Javelin. Hal-Tuc telephoned CDA personnel over a two-week period during which they denied that the equipment was used.

   After two weeks of calls, CDA's installation manager went to the store to see the equipment and admitted that it was used. No one from CDA advised Hal-Tuc in advance that it was installing used equipment temporarily until the right equipment arrived. CDA offered to replace it with a new Javelin VCR as soon as one arrived, which would take one or two months. Hal-Tuc asked CDA to return its deposit and take the equipment back, but CDA refused. Hal-Tuc put all the equipment in boxes and stored it. CDA filed a petition against Hal-Tuc for damages for breach of contract. Hal-Tuc filed a counterclaim, alleging fraud. CDA asserted it had the right to cure by tendering conforming goods after Hal-Tuc rejected the nonconforming goods. Was CDA correct? [*Central District Alarm, Inc. v. Hal-Tuc, Inc.*, 866 S.W.2d 210 (Mo. App.)]

3. Bobby Murray Chevrolet, Inc., submitted a bid to the Alamance County Board of Education to supply 1,200 school bus chassis to the district. Bobby Murray was awarded the contract and contracted with General Motors (GM) to purchase the chassis for the school board.

   Between the time of Bobby Murray's contract with GM and the delivery date, the Environmental Protection Agency (EPA) enacted new emission standards for diesel vehicles, such as school buses. Under the new law, the buses Bobby Murray ordered from GM would be out of compliance, as would the buses Bobby Murray specified in its bid to the school board.

   GM asked for several extensions to manufacture the buses within the new EPA guidelines. The school board was patient and gave several extensions, but then, because of its need for buses, purchased them from another supplier after notifying Bobby Murray of its intent to do so. The school board had to pay an additional $150,152.94 for the buses from its alternative source and sued Bobby Murray for that amount. Bobby Murray claimed it was excused from performance on the grounds of commercial impracticability. Is Bobby Murray correct? Does the defense of commercial impracticability apply in this situation? Be sure to compare this case with other cases and examples in the chapter. [*Alamance County Board of Education v. Bobby Murray Chevrolet, Inc.*, 465 S.E.2d 306 (N.C. App.); rev. denied, 467 S.E.2d 899 (N.C.)]

4. The Home Shopping Club ordered 12,000 Care Bear lamps from Ohio International, Ltd. When the lamps arrived, they had poor painting and staining, elements were improperly glued and could come loose (a danger to the children with the lamps in their rooms), and they overheated very easily (another danger for children and a fire hazard). Home Shopping Network notified International and gave it three months to remedy the problems and provide different lamps. After three months, Home Shopping Network returned all lamps and notified International that it was

pulling out of the contract. Could they do so, or had too much time passed? [*Home Shopping Club, Inc. v. Ohio International, Ltd.*, 27 UCC Rep. Serv. 2d 433 (Fla. Cir. Ct.)]

5. Lafer Enterprises sold Christmas decorations to B. P. Development & Management Corp., the owners and operators of the Osceola Square Mall. The package of decorations was delivered to Osceola Square Mall prior to Thanksgiving 1986 for a total cost of $48,775, which B. P. would pay in three installments. Cathy Trivigno, a manager at B. P. who supervised the installation of the decorations, indicated that she and the Osceola Square Mall merchants were not satisfied with the quality of the decorations, but they needed to be in place for the day after Thanksgiving (the start of the holiday shopping season). B. P. complained to Lafer about the quality of the decorations but had the decorations installed. B. P. paid the first installment to Lafer but then stopped payment on the last two checks. B. P. claimed it had rejected the decorations. Lafer claimed breach for nonpayment because B. P. had used the decorations. Did B. P. accept the decorations? [*B. P. Dev. & Management Corp. v. Lafer Enterprises, Inc.*, 538 So.2d 1379 (Fla. App.)]

6. Westinghouse Electric Corporation entered into uranium supply contracts with 22 electric utilities during the late 1960s. The contract prices ranged from $7 to $10 per pound. The Arab oil embargo and other changes in energy resources caused the price of uranium to climb to between $45 and $75 per pound. Supply tightened because of increased demand.

   In 1973, Westinghouse wrote to the utilities and explained that it was unable to perform on its uranium sales contracts. The utilities needed uranium. Westinghouse did not have sufficient funds to buy the uranium it had agreed to supply, assuming that it could find a supply. One utility executive commented, after totaling up all 22 supply contracts, that Westinghouse could not have supplied the uranium even under the original contract terms. He said, "Westinghouse oversubscribed itself on these contracts. They hoped that not all the utilities would take the full contract amount."

   Westinghouse says it is impossible for it to perform. The utilities say they are owed damages because they must still find uranium somewhere. What damages would the law allow? What ethical issues do you see in the original contracts and in Westinghouse's refusal to deliver? Should we excuse parties from contracts because it is so expensive for them to perform? [*In re Westinghouse Uranium Litigation*, 436 F. Supp. 990 (E.D. Va.)]

7. Steel Industries, Inc., ordered steel from Interlink Metals & Chemicals. The steel was to be delivered from a Russian mill. There were political and other issues in Russia, and the mill was shut down. Interlink did not deliver the steel to Steel Industries, claiming that it was excused from performance because it could not get the steel from the Russian mill. What would Interlink have to establish to show that it was excused from performing under the doctrine of commercial impracticability? [*Steel Industries, Inc. v. Interlink Metals & Chemicals, Inc.*, 969 F. Supp. 1046 (E.D. Mich.)]

8. Spaulding & Kimball Co. ordered from Aetna Chemical Co. 75 cartons of window washers. The buyer received them and sold about a third to its customers but later refused to pay for them, claiming that the quality was poor. The seller sued for the price. Would the seller be entitled to the contract price? Refer to the *Weil v. Murray* case described in problem 12 regarding the Degas painting for some insight. [*Aetna Chemical Co. v. Spaulding & Kimball Co.*, 126 A. 582 (Vt.)]

9. Nuco Plastics, Inc., was developing production molds for Universal Plastics, Inc. During the course of the development of the molds, Universal changed specifications and required the use of different materials. Nuco raised the price from $235 per 1,000 parts to $400 per 1,000 parts. Universal refused to pay the additional amount and ended the contract. Nuco was not paid for the molds it had produced and sued for breach of contract and damages. Universal maintained that Nuco had repudiated the contract by raising the price. Is an attempt to raise the price on a contract a repudiation of the contract? [*Nuco*

Plastics, Inc. v. Universal Plastics, Inc., 601 N.E.2d 152 (Ohio App.)]

10. Economy Forms Corp. sold concrete-forming equipment to Kandy. After using the equipment for more than six months, Kandy notified Economy that the equipment was inadequate. Economy Forms alleged that Kandy had accepted the goods. Kandy denied liability. Was there an acceptance? Why or why not? [*Economy Forms Corp. v. Kandy, Inc.*, 391 F. Supp. 944 (N.D. Ga.)]

11. Hornell Brewing Company is a supplier and marketer of alcoholic and nonalcoholic beverages, including the popular iced tea drink, Arizona. In 1992, Stephen A. Spry and Don Vultaggio, Hornell's chairman of the board, made an oral agreement for Spry to be the exclusive distributor of Arizona products in Canada. The initial arrangement was an oral agreement, and in response to Spry's request for a letter that he needed to secure financing, Hornell provided a letter that confirmed the distributorship.

    During 1993 and 1994, Hornell shipped beverages on 10-day credit terms, but between December 1993 and February 1994, Spry's credit balances grew from $20,000 to $100,000, and a $31,000 check from Spry was returned for insufficient funds.

    In March 1994, Hornell demanded that Spry obtain a line and/or letter of credit to pay for the beverages to place their relationship on a more secure footing. An actual line of credit never came about. Hornell did receive a partial payment by a wire transfer on May 9, 1994. Spry ordered 30 trailer loads of "product" from Hornell at a total purchase price of $390,000 to $450,000. Hornell learned from several sources, including its regional sales manager Baumkel, that Spry's warehouse was empty; that he had no managerial, sales, or office staff; that he had no trucks; and that his operation was a sham.

    On May 10, 1994, Hornell wrote to Spry, telling him that it would extend up to $300,000 of credit to him, net 14 days cash "based on your prior representation that you have secured a $1,500,000 U.S. line of credit." Spry did not respond to this letter. After some months of futile negotiations by counsel, Hornell filed suit. Has there been a breach? What are the parties' rights? [*Hornell Brewing Co., Inc. v. Spry*, 664 N.Y.S.2d 698 (Sup. Ct.)]

12. Mark Murray and Ian Peck are art dealers who own separate art galleries located in New York. Robert and Jean Weil reside in Montgomery, Alabama, and are art collectors. Murray and Sam Lehr, a business acquaintance of his, traveled to Montgomery to see the various paintings in the Weils' collection, including a painting by Edgar Degas titled *Aux Courses*, which Murray examined under ultraviolet light. Murray later telephoned Weil and told him that he had spoken with someone who might be interested in purchasing the Degas.

    On November 3, 1997, the director of Murray's gallery, Stephanie Calman, traveled to the Weils' home in Alabama. Calman, on behalf of Murray, and Robert Weil executed an agreement that provided for consignment of the Degas to Murray's gallery "for a private inspection in New York for a period of a week" from November 3, "to be extended only with the express permission of the consignor." Calman returned to New York with the painting the same day.

    Murray then showed the Degas to Peck. Peck expressed an interest in purchasing the Degas after seeing it, and the price of $1,125,000 was discussed.

    On November 26, 1997, Murray signed an agreement drafted by Weil and retyped on Murray's letterhead. Weil signed the agreement on December 1, 1997.

    Neither Murray nor anyone else ever paid Weil the $1 million. Nonetheless, Murray maintained possession of the Degas from November 3, 1997, through March 25, 1998, when Weil requested its return.

    The Weils filed suit, seeking the price for the painting via summary judgment. Are the Weils entitled to recover? Explain why or why not. [*Weil v. Murray*, 161 F. Supp. 2d 250 (S.D.N.Y.)]

13. Trefalcon (a commercial arm of the government of Ghana) entered into a contract with Supply Commission as a purchaser of residual fuel oil (RFO). Supply Commission agreed, among other

things, to supply Trefalcon with RFO at competitive prices as reserves permitted. Approximately six weeks into the agreement, on May 3, 1974, Supply Commission wrote a letter to Trefalcon proposing a method for pricing the refined fuel it would sell to Trefalcon.

A dispute arose six months later when Supply Commission first began to raise the price of RFO to account for escalations. In an effort to continue the contract, the parties orally agreed to a so-called Standstill Agreement, pursuant to which Ghana temporarily would forgo payment of escalations. By May 12, 1975, Trefalcon had paid only the base price for each of the 26 residual fuel cargoes it had received.

On May 26, 1975, J.V.L. Mensah, a representative of Supply Commission, sent a letter to Trefalcon demanding payment of $7,885,523.12 for escalation charges and declaring that no further oil would be sold until payment in full was made. After receiving the Mensah letter, Trefalcon tendered two payments to Bank of Ghana—one in the amount of $1,617,682.29 (tendered June 10, 1975), the other in the amount of $1,185,000 (tendered June 27, 1975).

With full payment still outstanding in July 1975, Supply Commission canceled the contract and sought damages for breach following the failure to provide assurances. Will Supply Commission recover? [*Reich v. Republic of Ghana*, 2002 WL 142610 (S.D.N.Y.)]

14. Harry Ulmas made a contract to buy a new car from Acey Oldsmobile. He was allowed to keep his old car until the new car was delivered. The sales contract gave him a trade-in value of $650 on the old car but specified that the car would be reappraised when it was actually brought to the dealer. When Ulmas brought the trade-in to the dealer, an Acey employee took it for a test drive and said that the car was worth between $300 and $400. Acey offered Ulmas only $50 for his trade-in. Ulmas refused to buy from Acey and purchased from another dealer, who appraised the trade-in at $400. Ulmas sued for breach of contract on the grounds of violation of good faith. Was he right? [*Ulmas v. Acey Oldsmobile, Inc.*, 310 N.Y.S.2d 147 (N.Y. Civ.)]

15. Cornelia and Ed Kornfeld contracted to sell a signed Picasso print to David Tunick, Inc. The print, entitled *Le Minotauromachie*, was signed "Pablo Picasso." The signature on the print was discovered to be a forgery, and the Kornfelds offered Tunick a substitute Picasso print. Tunick refused the Kornfelds' substituted performance and demanded a return of the contract price. The Kornfelds refused on the grounds that their cure had been refused. Was the substitute print an adequate cure? [*David Tunick, Inc. v. Kornfeld*, 838 F. Supp. 848 (S.D.N.Y.)]

CPA QUESTIONS

1. Under the sales article of the UCC, which of the following statements is correct?
   a. Obligations of the parties to the contract must be performed in good faith.
   b. Merchants and nonmerchants are treated alike.
   c. The contract must involve the sale of goods for a price of more than $500.
   d. None of the provisions of the UCC may be disclaimed by agreement.
2. Rowe Corp. purchased goods from Stair Co. that were shipped COD. Under the sales article of the UCC, which of the following rights does Rowe have?
   a. The right to inspect the goods before paying.
   b. The right to possession of the goods before paying.
   c. The right to reject nonconforming goods.
   d. The right to delay payment for a reasonable period of time.
3. Bibbeon Manufacturing shipped 300 designer navy blue blazers to Custom Clothing Emporium. The blazers arrived on Friday, earlier than Custom had anticipated and on an exceptionally busy day for its receiving department. They were perfunctorily examined and sent to a nearby warehouse for storage until needed. On the

following Monday, upon closer examination, it was discovered that the quality of the blazer linings was inferior to that specified in the sales contract. Which of the following is correct insofar as Custom's rights?

a. Custom can reject the blazers upon subsequent discovery of the defects.
b. Custom must retain the blazers since it accepted them and had an opportunity to inspect them upon delivery.
c. Custom's only course of action is rescission.
d. Custom had no rights if the linings were merchantable quality.

4. Parker ordered 50 cartons of soap from Riddle Wholesale Company. Each carton contained 12 packages of soap. The terms were: $8.00 per carton 2/10, net/30, FOB buyer's delivery platform, delivery June 1. During transit approximately one-half the packages were damaged by the carrier. The delivery was made on May 28. Answer the following with "Yes" or "No."

a. Riddle had the risk of loss during transit.
b. If Parker elects to accept the undamaged part of the shipment, he will be deemed to have accepted the entire shipment.
c. To validly reject the goods, Parker must give timely notice of rejection to Riddle within a reasonable time after delivery.
d. If Riddle were notified of the rejection on May 28, Riddle could cure the defect by promptly notifying Parker of intention to do so and making a second delivery to Parker of conforming goods by June 1.
e. The statute of frauds is inapplicable to the transaction in the facts given.

Remedies for Breach of Sales Contracts

learning outcomes

After studying this chapter, you should be able to

LO.1 List the remedies of the seller when the buyer breaches a sales contract

LO.2 List the remedies of the buyer when the seller breaches a sales contract

LO.3 Determine the validity of clauses limiting damages

If one of the parties to a sale fails to perform the contract, the nonbreaching party has remedies under Article 2 of the Uniform Commercial Code (UCC). In addition, the parties may have included provisions on remedies in their contract.

A. Statute of Limitations

Judicial remedies have time limitations. After the expiration of a particular period of time, the party seeking a remedy can no longer resort to the courts. The UCC **statute of limitations** applies to actions brought for remedies on the breach of a sales contract.[1] When a suit is brought on the basis of a tort theory, such as negligence, fraud, or strict tort liability, other general statutes of limitations apply.

CPA 1. Time Limits for Suits under the UCC

An action for breach of a sales contract must be commenced within four years after the time of the **breach**.[2] The statute of limitations can be reduced between merchants to as little as one year but cannot be reduced in consumer contracts.

When a cause of action arises depends on the nature of the breach. The UCC has three measurements for determining when a breach occurs. The basic rule is that the time begins to run when the breach occurs, but that rule has exceptions that include special timing rules for repudiation, infringement, breach of warranty, and future performance.

A buyer seeking damages because of a breach of the sales contract must give the seller notice of the breach within a reasonable time after the buyer discovers or should have discovered it.[3]

2. Time Limits for Other Suits

When a party seeks recovery on a non-Code theory, such as on the basis of strict tort liability, fraud, or negligence, the UCC statute of limitations does not apply. The action is subject to each state's tort statute of limitations. Tort statutes of limitations are found in individual state statutes, and the time limitations vary by state. However, the tort statutes of limitations tend to be shorter than the UCC statute of limitations.

B. Remedies of the Seller

When the buyer breaches a sales contract, the seller has different remedies available that are designed to afford the seller compensation for the losses caused by the buyer's breach.[4] Revised Article 2 allows the remedies provided to be used together, and although the various remedies may be called out in separate sections, there is no requirement that a party elect only one of the remedies. In many cases of breach, only a combination of the various remedies can make the nonbreaching party whole again.

3. Seller's Lien

In the absence of an agreement for the extension of credit to the buyer for the purchase of goods, and until the buyer pays for the goods or performs whatever actions the contract requires, the seller has the right to retain possession of the goods.[5]

CPA 4. Seller's Remedy of Stopping Shipment

When the buyer has breached the contract prior to the time the goods have arrived at their destination, the seller can stop the goods from coming into the buyer's possession. This remedy is important to sellers because it eliminates the need for sellers to try to recover goods from buyers who have indicated they cannot or will not pay.

A seller has the right to stop shipment if the buyer has received goods on credit and the seller learns that the buyer is insolvent, the buyer has not provided assurances as requested, or the seller has grounds to believe performance by the buyer will not occur.[6] Also, the right to retrieve the goods in the case of a credit buyer's insolvency continues for "a reasonable time after the buyer's receipt of the goods."

[1] UCC §2-703.
[2] The cause of action arises as soon as the breach occurs even if the party is unaware of the breach at that time.
[3] UCC §2-607(3)(a).
[4] Under Revised Article 2 (§2-803), the overall policy change on remedies relates to the parties' expectations. The revision allows courts to deny a remedy if one party thereby benefits to more than a full performance position.
[5] UCC §2-703.
[6] UCC §2-705.

CPA 5. Resale by Seller

When the buyer has breached the contract, the seller may resell any of the goods the seller still holds. After the resale, the seller is not liable to the original buyer on the contract and does not have to surrender any profit obtained on the resale. On the other hand, if the proceeds are less than the contract price, the seller may recover the loss from the original buyer.[7] Under Revised UCC, the failure of the seller to resell the goods does not mean the seller cannot recover under the other remedies available under Article 2.

The seller must give reasonable notice to the breaching buyer of the intention to resell the goods. Such notice need not be given if the goods are perishable or could decline rapidly in value. The seller must conduct any method of resale under standards of commercial reasonableness.[8]

6. Cancellation by Seller

When the buyer materially breaches the contract, the seller may cancel the contract. Such a cancellation ends the contract and discharges all unperformed obligations on both sides. Following cancellation, the seller has any remedy with respect to the breach by the buyer that is still available.

7. Seller's Action for Damages under the Market Price Formula

When the buyer fails to pay for accepted goods, the seller may resell the goods, as discussed earlier, or bring a contract action to recover damages. One formula for a seller's damages is the difference between the market price at the time and place of the tender of the goods and the contract price.[9] Under Revised Article 2, in the case of an anticipatory repudiation, the measurement of damages is the difference between the contract price and the market price "at the expiration of a commercially reasonable time after the seller learned of the repudiation" but not later than the time of tender. Whether the seller chooses to resell or recover the difference between the contract price and the market price is the seller's decision. The flexibility in the remedies under the UCC is provided because certain goods have very high market fluctuations. **For Example,** suppose that Sears has agreed to purchase 10 refrigerators from Whirlpool at a price of $1,000 each, but then Sears notifies Whirlpool that it will not be buying the refrigerators after all. Whirlpool determines the market price at the time of tender to be $850 per refrigerator. The best Whirlpool can find from an alternate buyer after a search is $800. Whirlpool can select the resale remedy ($1,000 – $800, or $200 in damages) to adequately compensate for the change in the market price between the time of tender and the time damages are sought.

CPA 8. Seller's Action for Lost Profits

If the market and resale price measures of damages do not place the seller in the same position in which the seller would have been had the buyer performed, the seller is permitted to recover lost profits.[10] The recovery of lost profits reimburses the seller for costs incurred in gearing up for contract performance.[11] **For Example,** suppose that a buyer has ordered 200 wooden rocking horses from a seller-manufacturer. Before production on the horses begins, the buyer breaches. The seller has nothing to resell, and the goods have not been identified to even permit a market value assessment. Nonetheless, the seller has geared up for production, counted on the contract, and perhaps bypassed other contracts in order to perform. An appropriate remedy for the seller of the rocking horses would be the profits it would have made had the buyer performed.

Some courts also follow the lost volume doctrine that allows sellers to recover for the profits they would have made if the buyer had completed the transaction.[12] **For Example,** suppose that Maytag has a contract to sell 10 washing machines for $600 each to Lakewood Apartment Managers. Lakewood breaches the agreement and refuses to take or pay for the washing machines. Maytag is able to resell them to Suds 'n Duds Laundromat for $600 each. The price is the same, but, the theory of lost volume profits is that Maytag could have sold 20 washers, not just 10, if Lakewood had not breached. Maytag's profit on each machine is $200. Lost volume profits in this situation would be 10 times the $200, or $2,000.

[7] UCC §2-706(1), (6); *In re Circuit City Stores, Inc.*, 441 B.R. 496 (E.D. Va. 2010).
[8] *In re Lakewood Engineering & Mfg. Co., Inc.*, 459 B.R. 306 (N.D. Ill. 2011).
[9] UCC §2-708. *SEC America, LLC v. Marine Elec. Systems, Inc.*, 39 A.3d 1054 (Vt. 2011).
[10] Revised Article 2 greatly expands the availability of lost profits.
[11] UCC §2-709.
[12] *Sunrich v. Pacific Foods of Oregon*, 2004 WL 1124495 (D. Or. 2004); *Collins Entertainment Corp. v. Coats and Coats Rental Amusement*, 629 S.E.2d 635 (S.C. 2006).

CPA 9. Other Types of Damages

So far, the discussion of remedies has focused on the damages that result because the seller did not sell the goods. However, the seller may incur additional expenses because of the breach. Some of those expenses can be recovered as damages. UCC §2-710 provides that the seller can also recover, as **incidental damages**, any commercially reasonable charges, expenses, or commissions incurred[13] in recovering damages.[14] **For Example,** the seller may recover expenses for the transportation, care, and storage of the goods after the buyer's breach, as well as any costs incurred in the return or resale of the goods. Such damages are in addition to any others that may be recovered by the seller.

CPA 10. Seller's Action for the Purchase Price

If goods are specially manufactured and the buyer refuses to take them, it is possible for the seller to recover as damages the full purchase price and keep the goods.[15] **For Example,** a printing company that has printed catalogs for a retail mail-order merchant will not be able to sell the catalogs to anyone else. The remedy for the seller is recovery of the purchase price.[16]

11. Seller's Nonsale Remedies

In addition to the seller's traditional sales remedies, many sellers enter into other transactions that provide protection from buyer breaches. One such protection is afforded when the seller obtains a security interest from the buyer under UCC Article 9. A **secured transaction** is a pledge of property by the buyer-debtor that enables the seller to take possession of the goods if the buyer fails to pay the amount owed. (See Chapter 34.) Figure 27-1 is a summary of the remedies available to the seller under Article 2.

FIGURE 27-1 *Seller's Remedies under Article 2*

REMEDY	STOP DELIVERY	RESALE PRICE	MARKET PRICE	ACTION FOR PRICE	LOST PROFIT
SECTION NUMBER	2–703	2–706 2–710	2–708 2–710	2–709 2–708	2–708(2)
WHEN AVAILABLE	Insolvency Advance breach by buyer	Buyer fails to take goods	Buyer fails to take goods	Specially manufactured goods	Anticipatory repudiation Breach
NATURE OF REMEDY	Stop delivery of any size shipment or recover goods if buyer insolvent	Contract price − Resale price + Incidental damages − Expenses saved + Consequential damages	Contract price − Market price + Incidental damages − Expenses saved + Consequential damages	Contract price + Incidental damages − Expenses saved + Consequential damages	Profits + Incidental damages − Salvage value + Consequential damages

[13] UCC §2-710.
[14] UCC §2-710; *WPS, Inc. v. Expro Americas, LCC*, 369 S.W.3d 384 (Tex. App. 2012).
[15] *Hyosung America, Inc. v. Sumagh Textile Co., Ltd.*, (2nd Cir. 1998). *Barrington Group, Ltd., Inc. v. Classic Cruise Holdings S De RL*, 435 Fed.Appx. 382, 2011 WL 3364383 (5th Cir. 2011).
[16] UCC §2-709(1)(a) and (b).

C. Remedies of the Buyer

When the seller breaches a sales contract, the buyer has a number of remedies under Article 2 of the UCC. Additional remedies based on contract or tort theories of product liability may also be available. (See Chapter 25.)

12. Rejection of Improper Tender

As discussed in Chapter 26, if the goods tendered by the seller do not conform to the contract in some way, the buyer may reject them. However, the rejection is the beginning of the buyer's remedies. Following rejection, the buyer can proceed to recover under the various formulas provided for buyers under the UCC.

13. Revocation of Acceptance

The buyer may revoke acceptance of the goods when they do not conform to the contract, the defect substantially impairs the value of the contract to the buyer, and the buyer either could not discover the problem or kept the goods because of a seller's promise of repair (see Chapter 26). Again, following revocation of acceptance, the buyer has various remedies available under the UCC.

CPA 14. Buyer's Action for Damages for Nondelivery—Market Price Recovery

If the seller fails to deliver the goods as required by the contract or repudiates the contract, the buyer is entitled to collect from the seller damages for breach of contract. Under Revised Article 2, the buyer is entitled to recover the difference between the market price at the time of tender and the contract price; this is a change from the previous Article 2 that measured damages at the time the buyer learned of the breach.[17]

CPA 15. Buyer's Action for Damages for Nondelivery—Cover Price Recovery

A buyer may also choose, as a remedy for the seller's nondelivery of goods that conform to the contract, to purchase substitute goods or cover.[18] If the buyer acts in good faith, the measure of damages for the seller's nondelivery or repudiation is then the difference between the cost of cover and the contract price.[19]

The buyer need only make a reasonable cover purchase as a substitute for the contract goods. The goods purchased need not be identical to the contract goods. **For Example,** if the buyer could secure only 350 five-speed blenders when the contract called for 350 three-speed blenders, the buyer's cover would be reasonable despite the additional expense of the five-speed blenders.

A. L. Schutzman Company, Inc. v. Nutsco, Inc., 2009 WL 5064052 (E.D.Wis. 2009)

Cashing in for the Defective Cashews

Schutzman is a Wisconsin corporation engaged in the business of selling roasted and salted nuts. Nutsco is a New Jersey wholesaler of cashews that imports the nuts from an affiliated Brazilian company and then packs and sells them in the United States.

In 2006, Nutsco used food broker Jim Warner to broker a contract between Nutsco and Schutzman whereby Nutsco promised to deliver twelve 35,000 pound loads of super large, whole, first quality ("SLW-1") cashews. The contract also included an option allowing Schutzman to buy four loads of large, whole, first quality ("LW-1") cashews, if exercised by a certain date.

Though the original contract provided for only 12 loads of SLW-1 cashews, Schutzman later sought to increase that number. Warner amended the contract to add two additional loads. In March 2007, Warner sent a copy of the revised Contract Confirmation adding the two extra loads (loads 13 and 14) to both Nutsco and Schutzman.

Nutsco delivered ten loads of SLW-1 cashews to Schutzman, with the last load being received on November 9, 2007.

---

[17] UCC §2-713.

[18] UCC §2-712; *Irwin Indus. Tool Co. v. Worthington Cylinders Wisconsin, LLC,* 747 F. Supp. 2d 568 (W.D.N.C. 2010). Buyers are also entitled to recover any deposits paid [*Selectouch Corp. v. Perfect Starch, Inc.,* 111 S.W.3d 830, 51 UCC Rep. Serv. 2d 1070 (Tex. App. 2004)].

[19] UCC §2-712(1) and (2). See *New West Charter Middle School v. Los Angeles Unified School Dist.,* 114 Cal. Rptr. 3d 504 (Cal. App. 2010).

Continued

After receiving the tenth load, however, Schutzman roast tested the cashews and determined that they did not qualify as "first quality" under Association of Food Industries, Inc.'s (AFI) specifications because of a high level of scorching. Nutsco represents to the market that if they are going to sell SLW-1 cashews, the cashews will meet AFI standards for SLW-1's.

Schutzman notified Warner that the load was highly scorched and Jim Warner brought the complaint and results of the roast test to Patricio Assis's (at Nutsco) attention. At Warner's request, Schutzman provided six cases of cashews from the tenth load for evaluation by Nutsco. Nutsco did not perform a roast test of the samples, but did conclude after its own analysis that the raw cashews themselves did not meet AFI Specifications for first quality cashews.

Two months after Nutsco delivered the tenth load, in January 2008, Patricio Assis began arguing that the parties' contract only provided for 12 loads of SLW-1 cashews and that Nutsco was not responsible for providing the two additional loads added in March 2007. At this point in time, the market prices for SLW-1 cashews were approximately $2 per pound higher than the price Nutsco was to receive from Schutzman under their contract. (*Id.*). Warner reported to Schutzman that Mr. Assis was arguing that the parties did not have a signed contract covering the additional loads.

Warner acknowledged that Schutzman was within its rights in rejecting the tenth load, but tried to persuade Schutzman to accept the load instead. Schutzman initially agreed to keep the load and pay the contract price, on the condition that Nutsco deliver all remaining loads, including loads 13 and 14. Patricio Assis would not agree to this arrangement. Warner then attempted to circumvent Patricio Assis and contacted Francisco Assis Neto directly. Jim Warner advised Mr. Neto in an email that Schutzman would pay for the scorched tenth load, but wanted delivery of the five loads of cashews remaining under the contract. The communication also stated that the parties would await a reply and not take any action until they received a response. While waiting for a reply, Schutzman stored the tenth load in its refrigerated warehouse.

On May 5, 2008, Jim Warner sent an email to Patricio Assis reminding him that Schutzman was waiting for Nutsco to pick up the rejected tenth load of cashews and advising him to contact Mike Kloth in Schutzman's shipping department. Mr. Assis contacted Mr. Kloth regarding pick-up. Due to confusion with Schutzman's new buyer, Mr. Kloth wrongly informed Mr. Assis that Schutzman did not possess a load of SLW-1 cashews waiting to be picked up by Nutsco. At a July 25, 2008 meeting, Schutzman clarified that it did possess the load of cashews and Nutsco made arrangements to retrieve it from the warehouse. However, Patricio Assis insisted on first personally inspecting the load. Another month passed before Mr. Assis traveled to Wisconsin to conduct his inspection. Mr. Assis finally inspected the load on September 3, 2008, and arranged to have the load picked up on September 10, 2008.

Schutzman did not pay for the rejected tenth load of SLW-1 cashews that Nutsco retrieved in September 2008. Schutzman did pay all invoices for the nine preceding loads it received and accepted. Schutzman paid a reduced price on two of the invoices after Warner agreed that it could apply $1,750 and $1,284 in credit against these invoices.

In addition to the amounts it paid to Nutsco for delivery of the nine accepted loads, Schutzman also paid to purchase loads of SLW-1 cashews from other wholesalers. Schutzman purchased five loads to replace the remaining loads it had expected Nutsco to provide under their contract. Schutzman paid $5.45 per pound for these loads, or $367,850 more for the five loads than it would have paid under the contract with Nutsco. Schutzman filed suit for this amount as its claim of damages.

JUDICIAL OPINION

Stadmueller, District Judge…Schutzman asserts that it contracted with Nutsco for the purchase of 14 loads of SLW-1 cashews and that Nutsco breached this contract by providing only nine loads. Nutsco acknowledges that it never provided the full number of loads required by the contract. However, Nutsco asserts that it was only obligated to provide the number of SLW-1 cashew loads included in the original contract between the parties because it never authorized an amendment to the contract.

Nutsco does not contest that Warner amended the contract between Schutzman and Nutsco to include an additional two loads. Nutsco merely contests that Warner had either the actual or apparent authority to do so. However, Nutsco fails to establish a genuine issue of material fact regarding Warner's authority. Therefore, the revised contract was enforceable and obligated Nutsco to provide 14 loads of SLW-1 cashews.

Schutzman asserts that Warner had actual authority to amend the contract based on Jim Warner's testimony. Schutzman points to Mr. Warner's affidavit testimony stating that Patricio Assis authorized him to make two additional loads available to Schutzman and Mr. Warner's deposition testimony stating that Patricio Assis was happy with the increased order and never informed him that Nutsco objected to an amendment of the contract.

The inclusion of a buyer's option to purchase LW-1 cashews does not explicitly foreclose amendment of the contract to add loads of SLW-1 cashews. Further, the existence of prior, completed contracts is irrelevant. Businesses who engage in ongoing sales relationships need not do so under only one contract. A reasonable fact finder could not determine that Jim Warner did not have authority to add two loads of SLW-1 cashews to a particular contract based solely on the fact that Nutsco and Schutzman had previously executed other contracts.

Continued

Regardless, Warner had apparent authority to amend the contract. A principal may be held liable for the acts of another when the principal had knowledge of those acts and acquiesced in them, causing a third person to reasonably believe that authorized agency existed.

Nearly all of Schutzman's communications and dealings with Nutsco regarding the original contract went directly through Warner and Nutsco held Jim Warner out as its "salesperson."

Nutsco was aware of the amendment Warner made to the contract. Indeed, Nutsco received three contract confirmations that provided for the sale of increased load numbers and increased cashew weights.

Finally, Schutzman has always maintained that it believed Warner's representations that Nutsco would provide it with 14 loads of SLW-1 cashews, and Nutsco does not dispute this fact. Schutzman had no reason to believe otherwise, as it did not receive any word from Nutsco that the two additional loads were unauthorized until January 2008. It was only after Nutsco denied any obligation to provide a thirteenth and fourteenth load that Nutsco purchased loads of cashews from other wholesalers.

Schutzman seeks an award of damages for "cover" expenses it incurred in replacing a load of cashews delivered by Nutsco, but ultimately rejected and returned for not meeting AFI specifications. Nutsco denies that Schutzman is entitled to damages for this "tenth load" because Schutzman does not have a legitimate basis for rejecting the load. Nutsco argues that the AFI specifications for scorching did not apply to its cashews because its contract did not provide for roast testing.

However, the cited language states only that a contractually-required roast test must be conducted in compliance with AFI specifications. It says nothing about the applicability of AFI specifications in the absence of a contract provision for roast testing. Here, the parties understood the AFI specifications to apply.

Even if the cashews did not have to meet AFI specifications for roast cashews, the tenth load failed to meet AFI specifications for raw cashews. Nutsco concedes that it analyzed the raw cashews and confirmed that they did not meet the AFI specifications.

Schutzman argues that it is entitled to summary judgment based on Nutsco's failure to provide promised loads 10 through 14. However, Nutsco argues that Schutzman materially breached the contract by committing the tort of conversion, excusing Nutsco from its contractual obligations to provide the remaining loads. Nutsco asserts that Schutzman converted the tenth load of cashews by holding it for more than eight months. Conversion is the only basis Nutsco asserts as a material breach of the contract.

The tenth load was delivered into Schutzman's possession pursuant to a valid contract. Thus, Schutzman's control over the load was authorized. Even after Schutzman initially complained about the condition of the load, the parties were negotiating for Schutzman's acceptance of the load.

The period of time between Nutsco's delivery of the tenth load and its pick up of that load is insufficient to establish conversion. Nutsco willingly provided the tenth load as part of its contract with Schutzman and the load remained an assumed part of the transaction until Schutzman made the final decision to reject it. Schutzman did not exercise unauthorized control.

Therefore, the only evidence supporting conversion is the misinformation supplied by Schutzman's shipping department employee and Schutzman's control of the load between the time that conversation occurred in June and the time that Nutsco was informed in July that Schutzman did, in fact, have the load in its possession. The court holds that conversion did not occur.

Nutsco next asserts a claim for unjust enrichment arising from Nutsco's payment of inspection and storage fees for shipments of cashews that Schutzman failed to pick up in a timely fashion. Nutsco makes no response to Schutzman's motion for summary judgment on this claim. Additionally, as noted above, Nutsco admits that Schutzman never refused to pick up any load of SLW-1 cashews. The court will grant summary judgment to Schutzman on this claim.

[t]he evidence shows that market prices for SLW-1 cashews remained high even after Nutsco picked up the tenth load. Schutzman paid $5.45 per pound to obtain two loads of cashews from an alternate wholesaler in September 2008, the same period in which Nutsco reclaimed its own load. Therefore, the market price for SLW-1 cashews remained higher than the contract price Nutsco would have received if Schutzman accepted the tenth load instead of rejecting it. Nutsco does not show that it was damaged by offering its cashews for sale on the open market in September 2008, instead of at an earlier time in 2008. Finally, the market price cited by Nutsco is irrelevant if it applies to SLW-1 cashews which conform to AFI specifications. The tenth load that Nutsco reclaimed did not meet these specifications. Consequently, Schutzman is entitled to summary judgment on Nutsco's conversion claim.

Nutsco contracted to provide Schutzman with 14 loads of SLW-1 cashews, but breached the contract by providing only nine. Nutsco's nonperformance is not excused by any material breach on Schutzman's part. Therefore, the court will grant summary judgment in favor of Schutzman on its claim for breach of contract.

QUESTIONS

1. Why does the authority of Warner become an issue in the case?
2. What is the significance of the conversion argument that Nutsco makes? Does it work?
3. What are Schutzman's damages?

Thinking Things Through

The Rolls Royce Engine That Grounded Planes

Qantas Airlines grounded all of its Airbus 380 jetliners after one of those jets experienced an in-air emergency when one of the Rolls Royce engines on the jumbo jet exploded. The jet landed safely, but all of Qantas's fleet was grounded for inspection of the engines. Qantas filed suit against Rolls Royce for the damages resulting from the losses due to the grounded planes. What would be the basis for the suit? What form of damages is Qantas seeking?

Meraiah Foley and Nicola Clark, "Qantas Goes to Court Over A380 Engines, Facing Added Tests," ***New York Times,*** **Dec. 3, 2010, p. B7.**

CPA 16. Other Types of Damages

The buyer is also entitled to collect incidental damages in situations in which he must find substitute goods. Those incidental damages could include additional shipping expenses or perhaps commissions paid to find the goods and purchase them. Buyers often also experience **consequential damages**, which are those damages the buyer experiences with respect to a third party as a result of the seller's breach. Revised UCC provides consequential damages for sellers and buyers. The seller's section provides, "Consequential damages resulting from the buyer's breach include any loss resulting from general or particular requirements and needs of which the buyer at the time of contracting had reason to know and which could not reasonably be prevented by resale or otherwise."[20] **For Example,** a seller's failure to deliver the goods may cause the buyer's production line to come to a halt. The buyer might then breach on its sales and delivery contracts with its buyers. In the case of a government contract, the buyer may have to pay a penalty for being late. These types of damages are consequential ones and can be recovered if the seller knew about the consequences or they were foreseeable. Under Revised Article 2, consequential damages cannot be recovered from a consumer.

17. Action for Breach of Warranty

A remedy available to a buyer when goods are delivered but fail to conform to warranties is an action for breach of warranty.

General Mills Operations, LLC v. Five Star Custom Foods, Ltd, 789 F. Supp. 2d 1148 (D. Minn. 2011)

A Chance of Cloudy Meatballs

General Mills Operations, LLC purchased "Big Meatballs Cooked Italian," used in General Mills' Progresso Italian–Style Wedding Soup, from Five Star Custom Foods, Ltd.

General Mills sent purchase orders to Five Star the face of which states: "This purchase order contract, along with General Mills' standard Purchase Order Terms and Conditions dated [1/29/04] shall govern all terms and conditions of sale.... Shipment of the goods against this order constitutes acceptance of terms and conditions dated [1/29/04]—otherwise do not ship." The Purchase Order Terms and Conditions were on the back of every purchase order, including the meatball orders faxed to Five Star. General Mills also mailed a copy of the 2004 version of its Terms and Conditions to Five Star's Customer Service Manager on February 4, 2004.

The Terms and Conditions included the following:

5. GOODS: The Goods shall conform in all respects to the description on the face of this Order, and/or [General Mills'] then current specifications furnished to [Five Star]. The Goods...shall be new, of first class commercial type...This warranty is in addition to and not in lieu of, any other warranties or guarantees made by [Five Star] or created or implied as a matter of law.

[20] UCC §2-710.

Continued

25. COMPLIANCE WITH LAW: [Five Star]'s performance under this Order shall be in compliance with all applicable federal, state, and local laws, ordinances, regulations, rules and statutes ("Laws").

27. RECALL: [General Mills] shall have the sole right, exercisable in its discretion, to initiate and direct the content and scope of a recall, market withdrawal, stock recovery, product correction and/or advisory safety communication regarding the Goods.

Additionally, the purchase order states that "[t]he goods must conform to all current General Mills' specifications as furnished to Seller." General Mills mailed a copy of the ingredient specifications for its meatballs to Five Star on January 18, 2006. Five Star acknowledges receipt of the specifications, which included the following:

> *The Beef or Beef By–Product in this ingredient must be sourced from countries or regions where USDA recognized BSE controls are in place in accordance with the recommendations of the World Animal Health Organization.*

One of Five Star's beef suppliers was Westland Meat Packing Company. Westland's beef was used in two orders of meatballs supplied to General Mills. In February 2008, the Food Safety Inspection Service (FSIS) issued a Class II recall of all products containing beef produced by Westland between February 1, 2006, and February 15, 2008. The recall was due to Westland's supposed failure to contact FSIS when it identified non-ambulatory disabled, or "downer," cows that became non-ambulatory after passing inspections but before slaughter. In such situations, regulations at the time required the producer to notify FSIS and call a public-health veterinarian to conduct an examination. Westland's alleged failure to consistently do this was deemed noncompliant, and the recall followed. There is no evidence, however, that any of the Westland beef supplied to Five Star or incorporated into General Mills' meatballs came from downer cattle.

When Five Star learned of the recall, it traced the Westland beef that it had incorporated into its products and notified General Mills of the recall on February 8, 2008, and identified two purchase orders of meatballs, totaling 32,460 pounds, which contained Westland beef.

General Mills was required to identify and destroy all soup containing the recalled meatballs in its inventory, as well as soup that it had already sold to grocery stores and other customers. The recall cost General Mills more than one million dollars.

General Mills filed suit in January 2010, asserting claims for breach of contract, breach of express warranties, breach of the implied warranty of merchantability, breach of the implied warranty of fitness for a particular purpose, and negligence. (Five Star filed a Third–Party Complaint asserting claims against Cattleman's Choice, Inc. d/b/a Westland.) Both General Mills and Five Star have moved for summary judgment.

JUDICIAL OPINION

KYLE, Judge...Five Star argues the mere fact its meatballs were recalled does not, as a matter of law, mean they were unfit or defective in any way and thus it did not breach any express or implied warranty.

General Mills responds that the warranties at issue—including that the meatballs were free from defects, of food grade, in compliance with regulations, and met the Specifications—were breached because the meatballs were not in compliance due to the recall. This Court previously [dealt with this issue] in a case involving recalled cribs. *O'Neil v. Simplicity, Inc.*, 553 F.Supp.2d 1110, 1115–16 (D.Minn.2008) aff'd, 574 F.3d 501. Although there had been reports of children being injured, and even dying, as a result of a failure in the crib's drop-side feature, the crib purchased by the O'Neils had not exhibited this problem. The Court dismissed the O'Neils' warranty claims, concluding that the fact the crib had been recalled "does not *ipso facto* mean that the crib has a manifest defect sufficient to permit their claims to proceed." In the Court's view, the same is true here.

General Mills has presented no evidence that the recalled meat was contaminated or defective in any way. At most, it can only claim that Westland's meat may have included meat from downer cattle. In short, there is no evidence of an actual manifestation of any defect in the meatball product to support a claim for breach of an express or implied warranty. Five Star is therefore entitled to summary judgment on the warranty claims.

The contract claim differs in an important way. Unlike warranty claims, evidence of a defect is not an essential element of a breach-of-contract claim.

General Mills argues that the recall does evince a breach, even without any proof of an actual defect, since...[t]he Specifications required the ingredients in the meatballs to comply with the Meat Inspection Act and to "meet or exceed" all USDA stunning, slaughter, and processing requirements. While the fact of the recall may not mean there was anything unsafe about the meatballs, it does mean Five Star failed to fully comply with these regulations as the Specifications required.

Five Star first argues that the reference to the Terms and Conditions on the front of the purchase order is inconspicuous and illegible due to its location and small print. It points to the fact this reference is in the lower left corner of the purchase order and in "extremely small print" that is almost "entirely illegible." While the print is not large, it is only slightly smaller than other information on the purchase order, such as the product, price, and delivery date, and the Court is able to read it without undue strain. Furthermore, the front of the purchase order contains significant blank space, making the type that is present easy to see. In the Court's view, the

Continued

reference to the Terms and Conditions on the purchase order is sufficiently conspicuous.

Similarly, the fact the terms were on the back of the purchase order does not necessarily render them unenforceable where they did not materially alter the parties' agreement. Here, since the same Terms and Conditions had governed the parties' business dealings since 2004, Five Star cannot claim unfair surprise with respect to this particular transaction. In light of the parties' sophistication and ongoing business relationship, the Court finds the Terms and Conditions enforceable despite their location on the back of the purchase order.

Five Star obtained beef from Westland, a U.S. company subject to USDA regulations, yet the meat was later recalled because Westland failed to comply with certain regulations. In the Court's view, it is not unreasonable to apply the provision at issue to Five Star. It is enforceable, and Five Star failed to satisfy it.

Here, because the Court finds that Five Star breached the contract by failing to provide meatballs that fully complied with the Specifications, the contract also requires it to reimburse General Mills for [the costs of the recall of $1,000,000 and] reasonable attorney's fees incurred.

QUESTIONS

1. Why is there no breach of warranty?
2. What breach of contract occurred?
3. Were the terms conspicuous enough to be part of the contract? Explain why.

(A) Notice of Breach. If the buyer has accepted goods that do not conform to the contract or there has been a breach of any warranties given, the buyer must notify the seller of the breach within a reasonable time after the breach is discovered or should have been discovered.[21]

(B) Measure of Damages. If the buyer has given the necessary notice of breach, the buyer may recover damages measured by the loss resulting in the normal course of events from the breach. If suit is brought for breach of warranty, the measure of damages is the difference between the value of the goods as they were at the time of tender and the value that they would have had if they had been as warranted. Under Revised Article 2, the buyer is also entitled to any of the other damage remedies necessary to make the buyer whole.

(C) Notice of Third-Party action against Buyer. When a buyer elects the remedy of resale and sells the contract goods to a third party, that third party has the right of suit against the buyer for breach of warranty. In such a case, it is the buyer's option whether to give the seller notice of the action and request that the seller defend that action.

18. Cancellation by Buyer

The buyer may cancel or rescind the contract if the seller fails to deliver the goods, if the seller has repudiated the contract, or if the goods have been rightfully rejected or their acceptance revoked.[22] A buyer who cancels the contract is entitled to recover as much of the purchase price as has been paid, including the value of any property given as a trade-in as part of the purchase price. The fact that the buyer cancels the contract does not destroy the buyer's cause of action against the seller for breach of that contract. The buyer may recover from the seller not only any payment made on the purchase price but also damages for the breach of the contract. The damages represent the difference between the contract price and the cost of cover.[23] The *Furlong v. Alpha Chi Omega Sorority* case involves an issue of rejection and proper damages.

[21] *Dunleavey v. Paris Ceramics, USA, Inc.*, 819 A.2d 945 (Super. Ct. 2002); *Muehlbauer v. General Motors Corp.*, 431 F. Supp. 2d 847 (N.D. Ill. 2006).
[22] UCC §2-720.
[23] UCC §2-712(1), (2); *GFSI, Inc. v. J-Loong Trading, Ltd.*, 505 F. Supp. 2d 935 (D. Kan. 2007).

Furlong v. Alpha Chi Omega Sorority, 657 N.E. 2d 866 (Ohio. Mun. Ct. 1993)

The Alpha Chi Omega Battle of the Sweaters

Emily Lieberman and Amy Altomondo were members of the Alpha Chi Omega (defendant) sorority at Bowling Green State University. Lieberman and Altomondo negotiated with Johnathan James Furlong (plaintiff) for the purchase of custom-designed sweaters for them and their sorority sisters for a total price of $3,612. Lieberman and Altomondo paid Furlong a $2,000 deposit.

Lieberman and Altomondo had a friend pick up the sweaters in Columbus and deliver them to Bowling Green. Upon opening the boxes, they discovered that Furlong had made color and design alterations in the lettering imprinted on the sweaters as part of their custom design. Altomondo, as president of AXO, called Furlong and told him that the sweaters were unacceptable and offered to return them. Furlong refused, stating that any changes were immaterial. Altomondo refused to pay the balance due and demanded the return of the $2,000 deposit. Furlong filed suit for breach of contract.

JUDICIAL OPINION

BACHMAN, J.... Defendant rejected the sweaters, rather than accepted them, as those terms (***"reject"*** and ***"accept"***) are defined by the law. Defendant's rejection was done within a reasonable time after delivery and was effective because of seasonable notice to plaintiff.

Therefore, plaintiff has breached the contract; defendant has not. Defendant is entitled to cancel the contract, recover so much of the price as has been paid, and hold the sweaters until recovery of that payment. Plaintiff is not entitled to recover the balance of the purchase price, but is entitled to the return of the sweaters upon return of the down payment to defendant.

Furlong was a jobber for Argento Bros., Inc. ("Argento") and had Argento print the sweaters. In doing so, Furlong worked with Argento's artists. Early in the morning of Thursday (October 22, 1992), the artist(s) began to prepare the art work and recommended changes to the design. Furlong authorized the artist(s) to change the design without the knowledge or consent of AXO. Argento spent about eight hours printing the sweaters all day Thursday. Furlong did not phone AXO about the changes until the next day, Friday (October 23), after the sweaters were printed with those changes. Here are the five design changes that he made:

- The ***first change*** was to delete the agreed-upon outline for the letters (namely, the navy blue outline).
- The ***second change*** was to reduce the agreed-upon number of colors for the fronts and the backs (from three colors per side to two colors per side).
- The ***third change*** was to alter one of the agreed-upon colors (from maroon to red).
- The ***fourth change*** was to alter the agreed-upon scheme of colors for the letters on the fronts and the backs (namely, both sides were to have the same two colors of maroon and hunter green; whereas in fact the backs had neither of those colors, and instead had a navy blue color for the letters).
- The ***fifth change*** was to alter the agreed-upon color of the masks (from hunter green to maroon—actually red).

The court specifically finds that the color was *red* (actually, scarlet) and was *not maroon* (like the maroon-colored letters on the Ohio Wesleyan sweater).

Conclusions of law: The sweaters did not conform to the contract (specifically, the express warranty in the contract). Thus (in the words of the statute), the sweaters did "fail in any respect to conform to the contract." Actually, the sweaters failed in at least five respects. Further, not only did they "fail in any respect," they failed in a substantial respect. In either event, they were a nonconforming tender of goods.

As concluded above, the sweaters were nonconforming goods because they "failed in any respect"—actually in many material respects—to conform to the contract (namely, to the express warranty in the contract).

The court rejects Furlong's assertion that he did all that he could do under the circumstances. The obvious answer is that he did not do enough. He should have gotten AXO's prior consent to the changes. He could have done this by providing for more lead time—between the time that Argento prepared the art work and the time that it printed the sweaters. Instead, he had both done at the same time (Thursday morning).

Further, he should have not entered into the contract until Argento had completed the art work and AXO had consented to it. Then, he would not have had to make "an immediate decision" at a time when it "would be difficult if not impossible, to contact [Emily]"—a day before the delivery due date.

Finally, and alternatively, plaintiff should have entered into a contract that gave him discretion to make design changes without AXO's consent. We must remember that "these sweaters," as Furlong himself admits (and describes), were to be "custom-designed" for AXO. Thus, they were to be printed according to AXO's specifications, and not according to Furlong's discretion.

Next, Furlong asserts that AXO—after learning of the changes—should have agreed to his offer of compromise: namely, that he would reduce the unit price of the sweaters in exchange for AXO's keeping them and paying the reduced price. Also, Furlong asserts that AXO should have communicated his compromise offer to AXO's members and pledges. In both respects, the court disagrees: Although the law allowed AXO to do so, it did not require AXO to do so. Instead, AXO

Continued

did exactly what the law allowed: AXO rejected the nonconforming goods in whole.

In regard to the following four types of seller's remedies, Furlong has no legal remedies because AXO did not breach the contract. Thus, he is not entitled to an award for the $1,612 balance that he claims is due on the contract price.

AXO has the following buyer's remedies:

a. Buyer's remedies in general; buyer's security interest in rejected goods (R.C. 1302.85 [UCC § 2-711]).
   - As concluded above, AXO rightfully rejected the sweaters, after having paid part of the purchase price: namely, $2,000. AXO is entitled to cancel the contract and to recover the partial payment of the purchase price (R.C. 1302.85[A] [UCC § 2-711(1)]).
   - Also, as concluded above, AXO still has rightful possession or control of the sweaters. AXO has a security interest in the sweaters in its possession or control for the part payment made on the purchase price—but when reimbursed for that part payment AXO must return the sweaters to Furlong.
   - There is no evidence that AXO has incurred any expenses for their inspection, receipt, transportation, care, and custody. Further, AXO does not claim any such expenses. AXO is not entitled to recover for any such type of expenses.

b. Buyer's damages for breach in regard to accepted goods. As concluded above, AXO never accepted the sweaters, in the legal sense of the word "*acceptance*." Therefore, AXO is not entitled to any damages under this statute.

c. Buyer's incidental and consequential damages. AXO does not claim any of these types of damages, and there was no evidence to justify an award for them. AXO is not entitled to any damages under this statute.

QUESTIONS

1. What was wrong with the sweaters?
2. Did AXO have to accept the sweaters at a reduced price?
3. What are AXO's damages?

The right of the buyer to cancel or rescind the sales contract may be lost by a delay in exercising the right. A buyer who, with full knowledge of the defects in the goods, makes partial payments or performs acts of ownership of the goods inconsistent with the decision to cancel may lose certain remedy provisions or be limited in recovery under Article 2.

19. Buyer's Resale of Goods

When the buyer has possession of the goods after rightfully rejecting them or after rightfully revoking acceptance, the buyer is treated as a seller in possession of goods after default by a buyer. When the seller has breached, the buyer has a security interest in the goods to protect the claim against the seller for breach and may proceed to resell the goods. From the proceeds of the sale, the aggrieved buyer is entitled to deduct any payments made to the seller and any expenses reasonably incurred in the inspection, receipt, transportation, care and custody, and resale of the goods.[24]

CPA 20. Action for Specific Performance

Under Article 2, specific performance is a remedy available only to buyers in those circumstances in which the goods are specially manufactured, unique, or rare, such as antiques or goods with sentimental value for the buyer. **For Example,** a buyer with a contract to buy a chair from Elvis Presley's home would be entitled to a specific performance remedy of delivery of the chair. Distributors have been granted specific performance against suppliers to deliver goods covered by supply contracts because of the unique dependence of the supply chain and the assumed continuous feeding of that chain.

Specific performance will not be granted, however, merely because the price of the goods purchased from the seller has gone up. In such a case, the buyer can still purchase the goods in the open market. The fact that it will cost more to cover can be compensated for by allowing the buyer to recover the cost increase from the seller.

[24] UCC §2-715(1); *Gordon v. Gordon*, 929 So. 2d 981 (Miss. App. 2006).

FIGURE 27-2 Buyer's Remedies under Article 2

REMEDY	SPECIFIC PERFORMANCE (REPLEVIN IDENTIFICATION)	COVER	MARKET PRICE
SECTION NUMBER	2–711	2–712 2–715	2–708 2–710
WHEN AVAILABLE	Rare or unique goods	Seller fails to deliver or goods are defective (rejection) or revocation of acceptance	Seller fails to deliver or goods are defective (rejection or revocation of acceptance)
NATURE OF REMEDY	Buyer gets goods + incidental damages + consequential damages	Cover price – Contract price + Incidental damages + Consequential damages – Expenses saved	Market price – Contract price + Incidental damages + Consequential damages – Expenses saved

21. Nonsale Remedies of the Buyer

In addition to the remedies given the buyer under UCC Article 2, the buyer may have remedies based on contract or tort theories of liability.

The pre-Code law on torts still applies in UCC Article 2 transactions. The seller may therefore be held liable to the buyer for any negligence, fraud, or strict tort liability that occurred in the transaction. (See Chapter 25.)

A defrauded buyer may both avoid the contract and recover damages. The buyer also has the choice of retaining the contract and recovering damages for the losses caused by the fraud.[25]

Figure 27-2 provides a summary of the remedies available to buyers under Article 2.

D. Contract Provisions on Remedies

The parties to a sales contract may modify the remedies provided under Article 2 or limit those remedies.

22. Limitation of Damages

CPA **(a) Liquidated Damages.** The parties may specify the exact amount of damages that may be recovered in case of breach. A **liquidated damages** clause in a contract can be valid if it meets the standards of Article 2. Under Revised Article 2, the enforceability of a liquidated damages clause in a consumer contract is determined by comparing the amount of the liquidated damages specified with the anticipated or actual harm, the difficulties of proof of loss, and the availability of an otherwise adequate remedy. For nonconsumer contracts, the enforceability of a liquidated damages clause depends on whether the amount is reasonable in light of the anticipated or actual harm. The *Rodriguez v. Learjet, Inc.* case discusses an issue related to liquidated damages.

[25] *Sherwin Alumina L.P. v. AluChem, Inc.*, 512 F. Supp. 2d 957 (S.D. Tex. 2007).

Rodriguez v. Learjet, Inc., 946 P.2d 1010 (Kan. App. 1997)

The Cost of Breaching a Jet-Set Contract

On August 21, 1992, Miguel A. Diaz Rodriguez (Diaz) entered into a contract with Learjet to buy a model 60 jet aircraft for $3,000,000 with a $250,000 deposit made on execution of the contract; $750,000 payment on September 18, 1992; $1,000,000 180 days before delivery of the aircraft; and the balance due on delivery of the aircraft. Diaz paid the $250,000 deposit but made no other payments. In fact, near the end of September 1992, Diaz told Alberto Castaneda of Learjet that he was purchasing the aircraft for Alejandro Burillo, his supervisor at Televisa, and that Burillo no longer wanted the aircraft. Diaz asked for the deposit to be returned.

On September 30, 1992, Castaneda sent Diaz a fax requesting payment. Then on October 6, 1992, Castaneda sent Diaz a letter with the following language: "Unless we receive payment from you or your company by October 9, 1992, [Learjet, Inc.,] will consider this agreement terminated and will retain all payments as liquidation damages in accordance with Paragraph C…of Section VII…of said agreement." By letter dated October 20, 1992, Learjet informed Diaz that it considered their contract terminated and that the $250,000 deposit was being retained as liquidated damages.

The contract provides, in part:

Learjet may terminate this Agreement as a result of the Buyer's failure to make any progress payment when due. If this Agreement is terminated by Learjet for any reason stipulated in the previous sentence Learjet shall retain all payments theretofore made by the Buyer as liquidated damages and not as a penalty and the parties shall thenceforth be released from all further obligations hereunder. Such damages include, but are not limited to, loss of profit on this sale, direct and indirect costs incurred as a result of disruption in production, training expense advance and selling expenses in effecting resale of the Airplane.

After Diaz breached the contract, Circus Circus Enterprises, Inc., purchased the Learjet Diaz had ordered with some changes that cost $1,326. Learjet realized a $1,887,464 profit on the sale of the aircraft to Circus Circus, which was a larger profit than Learjet had originally budgeted for the sale to Diaz.

Diaz filed suit seeking to recover the $250,000 deposit. The district court granted summary judgment to Learjet, and Diaz appealed. The case was remanded for a determination of the reasonableness of the liquidated damages. The district court upheld the $250,000 as reasonable damages, and Diaz appealed.

JUDICIAL OPINION

MARQUARDT, Presiding J.…Diaz argues that the district court erred in holding that the liquidated damages clause was reasonable and enforceable. Diaz reasons that the liquidated damages clause was unreasonably large and, therefore, void as a penalty.

A determination concerning the reasonableness and enforceability of a liquidated damages clause is a question of law subject to unlimited review by this court. *Kvassay v Murray,* 15 Kan.App.2d 426, 429, 808 P.2d 896, *rev. denied* 248 Kan. 996 (1991).

K.S.A. 84-2-718 governs liquidated damages in contracts for the sale of goods and provides, in part:

(1) Damages for breach by either party may be liquidated in the agreement but only at an amount which is reasonable in the light of the anticipated or actual harm caused by the breach, the difficulties of proof of loss, and the inconvenience or nonfeasibility of otherwise obtaining an adequate remedy. A term fixing unreasonably large liquidated damages is void as a penalty.

In *Kvassay,* 15 Kan.App.2d at 430, 808 P.2d 896, this court noted that "reasonableness is the only test" for liquidated damages under the Uniform Commercial Code. This court paraphrased the three criteria for measuring the reasonableness of a liquidated damages clause provided in K.S.A. 84-2-718: "(1) anticipated or actual harm caused by breach; (2) difficulty of proving loss; and (3) difficulty of obtaining an adequate remedy." 15 Kan.App.2d at 430, 808 P.2d 896.

A liquidated damages clause that "'fixes damages in an amount grossly disproportionate to the harm actually sustained or likely to be sustained'" is considered a penalty and will not be enforced by the courts. If a liquidated damages clause is invalidated as a penalty, then the nonbreaching party may recover actual damages instead. The burden of proving that a liquidated damages clause is unenforceable rests with the party challenging its enforcement.

Diaz's challenge to the reasonableness of the liquidated damages clause focuses on the first factor of K.S.A. 84-2-718—the anticipated or actual harm caused by the breach. The question of whether a seller qualifies as a lost volume seller is relevant when evaluating whether a liquidated damages clause is reasonable in light of the anticipated or actual harm caused by the breach.

Diaz argues that the district court erred in concluding that Learjet qualifies as a lost volume seller. As a lost volume seller, Learjet's actual damages would include lost profits, notwithstanding that Circus purchased the aircraft which Diaz had contracted to buy and that Learjet made a profit on the Circus sale. The two contracts contained identical base prices, and both contracts had escalation clauses. The evidence indicates that the lost profit from the Diaz contract would have been approximately $1.8 million.

Continued

Whether a seller is a lost volume seller is a question of fact. Awarding lost profits to a lost volume seller serves the general principle that the purpose of awarding damages is to make a party whole by restoring the nonbreaching party to the position that the party occupied prior to the breach—to place a seller in as good a position as if a buyer had performed.

In *Diasonics,* 826 F.2d at 685, the court held that in order to qualify as a lost volume seller and recover for lost profits, a seller must establish three factors: (1) that it possessed the capacity to make an additional sale, (2) that it would have been profitable for it to make an additional sale, and (3) that it probably would have made an additional sale absent the buyer's breach. See also *R.E. Davis Chemical Corp. v Diasonics,* 924 F.2d 709, 711 (7th Cir.1991) (restating rule formulated in prior appeal of case);

Applying the more specific criteria established in *Diasonics,* there is adequate evidence to support the district court's finding. The master scheduler for Learjet testified that Learjet was operating at 60 percent capacity during the relevant time period and that Learjet was able to accelerate its production schedule to produce more of the model 60 planes in any given year. Learjet also presented testimony about its accounting system which indicated that an additional sale would have been profitable to Learjet. Learjet's profit from the Circus transaction and the similarity between the Diaz contract price and the Circus contract price also indicate that the additional sale would have been profitable.

We agree with the district court that Learjet qualifies as a lost volume seller and that the $250,000 in liquidated damages was reasonable in light of the anticipated or actual harm caused by the breach.

Even if we were to conclude that Learjet was not a lost volume seller, there is authority to support the holding that the liquidated damages clause was reasonable. In *Aero Consulting Corp. v Cessna Aircraft Co.,* 867 F.Supp. 1480, 1493–94 (D. Kan, 1994), the court held that a liquidated damages clause in an aircraft purchase agreement was reasonable under Kansas law. The *Aero* court did not consider the lost volume theory. The base price of the aircraft was $3,995,000. The liquidated damages, which were in the form of a deposit that was retained by Cessna after Aero breached, equaled $425,000. The court found that the liquidated damages clause "was reasonable in light of the damages that Cessna could reasonably anticipate would flow from such a cancellation of the contract." The court also noted that "in light of the nature of the production of aircraft and the costs associated with maintaining production, it would not be feasible for Cessna to otherwise obtain an adequate remedy for breach." Under both analyses, the liquidated damages claimed by Learjet were reasonable.

[Affirmed]

QUESTIONS

1. Does it matter that Learjet resold the Diaz plane?
2. Is the $250,000 reasonable?
3. Of what relevance is the fact that Learjet is a volume seller of goods?

(B) Exclusion of Damages. The sales contract may provide that in case of breach, no damages may be recovered or no consequential damages may be recovered. When goods are sold for consumer use and personal injuries are sustained, such total exclusions are unconscionable and unenforceable. Such a contract limitation is not enforceable in other types of contracts (nonconsumer) unless the party seeking to enforce it is able to prove that the limitation of liability was commercially reasonable and fair rather than oppressive and surprising. As discussed in Chapter 25, limitations on damages for personal injuries resulting from breaches of warranty are not enforceable.

CPA 23. Down Payments and Deposits

A buyer can make a deposit with the seller or an initial or down payment at the time of making the contract. If the contract contains a valid provision for liquidation of damages and the buyer defaults, the seller must return any part of the down payment or deposit in excess of the amount specified by the liquidated damages clause. In the absence of such a liquidated damages clause and in the absence of proof of greater damages, the seller's damages are computed as 20 percent of the purchase price or $500, whichever is smaller.

24. Limitation of Remedies

The parties may limit the remedies that are provided by the Code in the case of breach of contract. A seller may specify that the only remedy of the buyer for breach of warranty will be the repair or replacement of the goods or that the buyer will be limited to returning the goods and obtaining a refund of the purchase price, subject to the restrictions discussed in Chapter 25.

Thinking Things Through

The Gun-Totin' Harley Buyer and His Damages

Wiley Sharbino purchased a 2003 Harley Davidson motorcycle from Cooke Family Enterprises, LLC., d/b/a Renegade Harley-Davidson. He gave a gun as a down payment and financed the remaining amount of the purchase price. Within two days of purchase, the motorcycle sustained a broken drive belt. When Sharbino took the motorcycle back, Renegade told him that "the drive sprockets on the transmission and the rear wheel of the motorcycle were mismatched, causing the drive belt to break." The problem could not be fixed without changing the appearance of the motorcycle. Sharbino said he would not have purchased the motorcycle if he had known of the problem.

Renegade took back the motorcycle and told Sharbino to pick up his gun at the office where the dealership had kept it in a safe. Sharbino still filed suit seeking as damages the sales price plus interest, reasonable expenses related to the sale and preservation of the motorcycle, and attorney fees. Renegade said that the rescission of the agreement and return of Sharbino's "down payment" made him whole and that he had no other damages. Who is correct? Is rescission and the restoring of the party to his original position enough to compensate for a breach? [***Sharbino v. Cooke Family Enterprises, Inc.*, 6 So. 3d 1026 (La. App. 3d Cir. 2009)**]

25. Waiver of Defenses

A buyer can be barred from claiming a breach of the contract by the seller if the sales contract expressly states that the buyer will not assert any defenses against the seller.

26. Preservation of Defenses

Consumer protection law prohibits the waiver of defenses in consumer contracts.

(A) Preservation Notice. Consumer defenses are preserved by a Federal Trade Commission (FTC) regulation. This regulation requires that the papers signed by a consumer contain a provision that expressly states that the consumer reserves any defense arising from the transaction.[26] A defense of the consumer arising from the original transaction may be asserted against any third person who acquires rights by assignment in the contract (see Chapter 33).

(B) Prohibition of Waiver. When the FTC preservation notice is included in the contract that is obtained by, or transferred to, a third party, a waiver of defenses cannot be made. If the preservation notice is not included, the seller has committed an unfair trade practice.

E. Remedies in the International Sale of Goods

The United Nations Convention on Contracts for the International Sale of Goods (CISG) provides remedies for breach of a sales contract between parties from nations that have approved the CISG.

27. Remedies of the Seller

Under the CISG, if the buyer fails to perform any obligations under the contract, the seller may require the buyer to pay the price, take delivery, and perform other obligations under the contract. The seller may

Ethics & the Law

Don't Stop Believing

What are the ethical obligations of sales people who are out selling their companies' products when they know that their companies are in trouble financially? Or that their companies are going to stop making a particular product? Is there a duty to disclose this information or are these risks that are inherent in business and contracts? [***NutraSoya Foods, Inc. v. Sunrich, LLC*, 641 F.3d 282 (8th Cir. 2010)**]

[26] 316 C.F.R. §433.1: It is an unfair or deceptive trade practice to take or receive a consumer credit contract that fails to contain such a preservation notice.

E-Commerce & Cyberlaw

Consequential Damages and Software

Computer systems and software often do not function as intended or have some glitches when installed at a company. For example, suppose that a software company sold to a utility a software package that was represented as one that would simplify the utility's billing processes. The program is installed and tested, and some changes are made as a result of trial runs. When the program is fully implemented and all customers and bills are run through the new system, there is a complete breakdown. The bills cannot be produced or sent to customers, and the utility company is without cash flow. Without bills going out, no payments are coming in, and the utility must borrow from a high-interest line of credit at an interest cost of $400,000 per month. What damages could the utility collect? Could the software manufacturer limit its liability?

also declare the contract void if the failure of the buyer to perform obligations under the contract amounts to a fundamental breach of contract.

28. Remedies of the Buyer

Under the CISG, a buyer may reject goods only if the tender is a fundamental breach of the contract. This standard of materiality of rejection is in contrast to the UCC requirement of perfect tender. Under the CISG, a buyer may also reduce the price when nonconforming goods are delivered even though no notice of nonconformity is given. However, the buyer must have a reasonable cause for failure to give notice about the nonconformity.

MAKE THE CONNECTION

SUMMARY

The law provides a number of remedies for the breach of a sales contract. Remedies based on UCC theories generally are subject to a four-year statute of limitations, with Revised UCC adding an extension of one additional year (making it five years) in cases in which the breach is discovered in year four. If the remedy sought is based on a non-UCC theory, a tort or contract statute of limitations established by state statute will apply.

Remedies of the seller may include (1) a lien on the goods until the seller is paid, (2) the right to resell the goods, (3) the right to cancel the sales contract, (4) the right to recover the goods from the carrier and the buyer, and (5) the right to bring an action for damages or, in some cases, for the purchase price. The seller may also have remedies because of secured transactions.

Remedies of the buyer may include (1) the rejection of nonconforming goods, (2) the revocation of acceptance, (3) an action for damages for nondelivery of conforming goods, (4) an action for breach of warranty, (5) the cancellation of the sales contract, (6) the right to resell the goods, (7) the right to bring an action for conversion, recovery of goods, or specific performance, and (8) the right to sue for damages and cancel if the seller has made a material breach of the contract.

The parties may modify their remedies by a contractual provision for liquidated damages, for limitations on statutory remedies, or for waiver of defenses. When consumers are involved, this freedom of contract is to some extent limited for their protection.

Under the CISG, the seller may require the buyer to pay the price, take delivery, and perform obligations under the contract, or the seller may avoid the contract if there is a fundamental breach.

A buyer may reject goods under the CISG only if there is a fundamental breach of contract. The buyer may also reduce the price of nonconforming goods.

LEARNING OUTCOMES

After studying this chapter, you should be able to clearly explain:

A. Statute of Limitations

B. Remedies of the Seller

LO.1 List the remedies of the seller when the buyer breaches a sales contract

See the *For Example,* discussion of the Whirlpool refrigerators on p. 515.

C. Remedies of the Buyer

LO.2 List the remedies of the buyer when the seller breaches a sales contract

See the Thinking Things Through discussion of the Qantas airline suit for recovery for the losses from its grounded fleet on p. 520.

See *Furlong v. Alpha Chi Omega Sorority* on pp. 523–524.

D. Contract Provisions on Remedies

LO.3 Determine the validity of clauses limiting damages

See *Rodriguez v. Learjet, Inc.* on pp. 526–527.
See *Schutzman v. Nutsco* case on pp. 517–519.

See the E-Commerce & Cyberlaw discussion of software damages on p. 529.

See *General Mills Operations, LLC v. Five Star Custom Foods, LTD* on pp. 520–522.

E. Remedies in the International Sale of Goods

KEY TERMS

breach
consequential damages
incidental damages
liquidated damages
secured transaction
statute of limitations

QUESTIONS AND CASE PROBLEMS

1. Firwood Manufacturing Co. had a contract to sell General Tire 55 model 1225 postcure inflators (PCIs). PCIs are $30,000 machines used by General Tire in its manufacturing process. The contract was entered into in 1989, and by April 1990 General Tire had purchased 22 PCIs from Firwood. However, General Tire then closed its Barrie, Michigan, plant. Firwood reminded General Tire that it still had the obligation to purchase the 33 remaining PCIs. General Tire communicated to Firwood that it would not be purchasing the remaining ones. Firwood then was able, over a period of three years, to sell the remaining PCIs. Some of the PCIs were sold as units, and others were broken down and sold to buyers who needed parts. Firwood's sales of the remaining 33 units brought in $187,513 less than the General Tire contract provided, and Firwood filed suit to collect the resale price difference plus interest. Can Firwood recover? Why or why not? [*Firwood Manufacturing Co., Inc. v. General Tire, Inc.*, 96 F.3d 163 (6th Cir.)]

2. Soon after Gast purchased a used auto from a Chevrolet dealer, he experienced a series of mechanical problems with the car. Gast refused to make further payments on the bank note that had financed the purchase. The bank took possession of the automobile and sold it. Gast then brought an action against the dealer, alleging that he had revoked his acceptance. Was Gast correct? Explain your answer. [*Gast v. Rodgers-Dingus Chevrolet*, 585 So.2d 725 (Miss.)]

3. Formetal Engineering submitted to Presto a sample and specifications for precut polyurethane pads to be used in making air-conditioning units. Formetal paid for the goods as soon as they were delivered but subsequently discovered that the pads did not conform to the sample and specifications in that there were incomplete cuts,

color variances, and faulty adherence to the pad's paper backing. Formetal then informed Presto of the defects and notified Presto that it would reject the pads and return them to Presto, but they were not returned for 125 days. Presto argued that it was denied the right to cure because the goods were not returned until some 125 days after Formetal promised to do so. Was there a breach of the contract? Did the buyer (Formetal) do anything wrong in seeking its remedies? [*Presto Mfg. Co. v. Formetal Engineering Co.*, 360 N.E.2d 510 (Ill. App.)]

4. Lam entered into contracts with Dallas Semiconductor to build six machines, referred to in its contracts as Tools A-F.

   The contracts were entered into in 2000 and in 2001, but Maxim Integrated acquired Dallas Semiconductor in 2001. The employees at Dallas who were in charge of the contracts continued to assure Lam that everything was on track. Lam representatives also had meetings with Maxim representatives. However, those discussions broke down and after Lam issued a demand letter for which there was no response, he filed suit for breach of contract. Lam was able to sell the machines to other customers for an equal or greater price. Lam asked for total damages in the amount of $13,860,847, representing lost profits on all six tools, plus lost profits on the extended warranties and training packages for the tools. Is Lam entitled to such recovery? [*Lam Research Corp. v. Dallas Semiconductor Corp.*, 2006 WL 1000573, 59 UCC Rep.2d 716 (Cal. App.)]

5. McNeely entered into a contract with Wagner to pay $250,000 as a lump sum for all timber present in a given area that Wagner would remove for McNeely. The contract estimated that the volume in the area would be 780,000 board feet. Wagner also had provisions in the contract that made no warranties as to the amount of lumber and that he would keep whatever timber was not harvested if McNeely ended the contract before the harvesting was complete. The $250,000 was to be paid in three advances. McNeely paid two of the three advances but withheld the third payment and ended the contract because he said there was not enough timber. Wagner filed suit for the remaining one-third of the payment. McNeely said Wagner could not have the remaining one-third of the payment as well as the transfer; he had to choose between the two remedies. Is he correct? [*Wagner v. McNeely*, 38 UCC 2d 1176 (Or)]

6. Brown Machine Company, a division of Kvaerner U.S., Inc., entered into a contract to supply a machine and tools to Hakim Plast, a food container–producing company based in Cairo, Egypt, to enable Hakim to meet its growing demand for plastic containers. The plastic containers were for customers to use in the ice cream distribution industry. It was understood that the equipment would be ready for delivery before the busy summer ice cream season. Brown Machine was not able to meet the twice extended deadline. It attempted to obtain another extension, but Hakim Plast refused without additional consideration. Brown refused to provide the requested consideration. Hakim Plast declared the contract breached on September 25, 1994. Brown then sold the equipment and brought suit for breach of contract, requesting damages for the loss of the sale. Hakim Plast countersued for Brown's breach seeking out-of-pocket expenses and consequential damages for loss of business. Discuss who breached the contract and determine what possible damages might be recovered. [*Kvaerner U.S., Inc. v. Hakim Plast Co.*, 74 F. Supp. 2d (E.D. Mich.)]

7. Sonya Kaminski purchased from Billy Cain's Cornelia dealership a truck that was represented to her to be a 1989 Chevrolet Silverado pickup. However, subsequent incidents involving repair of the truck and its parts, as well as a title history, revealed that the truck was a GMC rather than a Chevrolet. Sales agents at the Cornelia dealership misrepresented the truck's character and sold the truck to Kaminski as a Chevrolet.

   Kaminski filed suit for intentional fraud and deceit under the Georgia Fair Business Practices Act (FBPA) and for breach of express warranty. The jury awarded Kaminski $2,823.70 for breach of express warranty and $50,000 punitive (exemplary) damages. The judge added damages under the FBPA of $10,913.29 in actual damages and $9,295 in attorney fees and court costs. The dealership appealed. Must the dealership pay the damages?

Why or why not? [*Billy Cain Ford Lincoln Mercury, Inc. v. Kaminski*, 496 SE2d 521 (Ga App)]

8. Mrs. Kirby purchased a wheelchair from NMC/Continue Care. The wheelchair was customized for her and her home. When the wheelchair arrived, it was too wide to fit through the doorways in her home. What options does Mrs. Kirby have? [*Kirby v. NMC Continue Care*, 993 P.2d 951 (Wyo)]

9. Wolosin purchased a vegetable and dairy refrigerator case from Evans Manufacturing Corp. When Evans sued Wolosin for the purchase price, Wolosin claimed damages for breach of warranty. The sales contract provided that Evans would replace defective parts free of charge for one year; it also stated, "This warranty is in lieu of any and all other warranties stated or inferred, and of all other obligations on the part of the manufacturer, which neither assumes nor authorizes anyone to assume for it any other obligations or liability in connection with the sale of its products." Evans claimed that it was liable only for replacement of parts. Wolosin claimed that the quoted clause was not sufficiently specific to satisfy the limitation-of-remedies requirement of UCC §2-719. Provide some insight on this issue for the parties by discussing damage limitation clauses under the UCC. [*Evans Mfg. Corp. v. Wolosin*, 47 Luzerne County Leg. Reg. 238 (Pa)]

10. McInnis purchased a tractor and scraper as new equipment of the current model year from Western Tractor & Equipment Co. The written contract stated that the seller disclaimed all warranties and that no warranties existed except those stated in the contract. Actually, the equipment was not the current model but that of the prior year. The equipment was not new but had been used for 68 hours as a demonstrator model, after which the hour meter had been reset to zero. The buyer sued the seller for damages. The seller's defense was based on the ground that all liability for warranties had been disclaimed. Was this defense valid? [*McInnis v. Western Tractor & Equipment Co.*, 388 P.2d 562 (Wash)]

11. Elmore purchased a car from Doenges Brothers Ford. The car had been placed with the dealership by a dealership employee as part of a consignment arrangement. Elmore was unable to obtain title to the car because the Environmental Protection Agency had issues with the car's compliance with emissions equipment requirements. Elmore was unable to drive the car. He brought suit because he was forced to sell the car for $10,300 less than he paid because of the title defect, and the fact that only a salvage dealer would purchase it. Because he lost his transportation, he was out of work for eight months and experienced a $20,000 decline in income. What damages could Elmore recover under the UCC? [*Elmore v. Doenges Bros. Ford, Inc.*, 21 P.3d 65 (Okla. App.)]

12. Stock Solution is a "stock photo agency" that leases photographic transparencies produced by professional photographers for use in media advertising. Between October 1, 1994, and May 31, 1995, Stock Solution delivered Axiom 107 color transparencies to be used in Axiom's advertising. The contracts provided that in the event the transparencies were not returned by the specified "return date," Axiom would pay the following fees: (1) an initial "service charge" of $30, (2) "holding fee[s]" in the amount of "$5.00 per week per transparency," (3) "service fees" at a rate of "one and one-half percent per month" on unpaid balances of invoices beginning 30 days after invoice date, and (4) reimbursement for loss or damage of each "original transparency" in the amount of $1,500.

    Axiom failed to return 37 of the 107 transparencies in breach of the contracts. Of the 37 missing transparencies, 36 were original color transparencies and 1 was a duplicate color transparency. Stock Solution filed suit seeking damages (1) for the 36 missing original color transparencies, the agreed liquidated value of $54,000 plus sales tax of $3,294; (2) for the 1 missing duplicate color transparency, $1 plus sales tax of $0.06; (3) holding fees on the 37 missing transparencies in the amount of $23,914.83; (4) service fees and charges as provided for in the contracts; and (5) attorney fees.

    Discuss whether the liquidated damage clause was enforceable under the law. [*Bair v. Axiom Design, LLC*, 20 P.3d 388 (Utah)]

13. Ramtreat Metal Technology provided for a "double your money back" remedy in its

contracts for the sale of its metal drilling assemblies. A buyer filed suit seeking consequential damages and cost of replacement. Ramtreat said that its clause was a limitation of remedies. Could Ramtreat limit its remedies to "double your money back"? [*Adcock v. Ramtreat Metal Technology, Inc.*, 44 UCC Rep. Serv. 2d 1026 (Wash App)]

14. Joseph Perna purchased a 1981 Oldsmobile at a traffic auction conducted by Locascio. The car had been seized pursuant to action taken by the New York City Parking Violation Bureau against Jose Cruz. Perna purchased the car for $1,800 plus tax and towing fees "subject to the terms and conditions of any and all chattel mortgages, rental agreements, liens, conditional bills of sale, and encumbrances that may be on the motor vehicle of the above judgment debtor." The Olds had 58,103 miles on it at the time of Perna's purchase. On May 7, 1993, Perna sold the car to Elio Marino, a coworker, for $1,200. The vehicle had about 65,000 miles on it at the time of this sale.

    During his period of ownership, Marino replaced the radiator ($270), repaired the power steering and valve cover gasket ($117), and replaced a door lock ($97.45). He registered and insured the vehicle. In February 1994, Marino's son was stopped by the police and arrested for driving a stolen vehicle. The son was kept in jail until his arraignment, but the charges were eventually dropped. The Oldsmobile was never returned to Marino, who filed suit for breach of contract because he had been given a car with a defective title. He asked for damages that included the costs of getting his son out of jail and having the theft charges dropped. Is he entitled to those damages? [*Marino v. Perna*, 629 N.Y.S. 2d 669 (N.Y. Cir.)]

15. Stephan's Machine & Tool, Inc., purchased a boring mill from D&H Machinery Consultants. The mill was a specialized type of equipment and was essential to the operation of Stephan's plant. The purchase price was $96,000, and Stephan's had to borrow this amount from a bank to finance the sale. The loan exhausted Stephan's borrowing capacity. The mill was unfit, and D&H agreed to replace it with another one. D&H did not keep its promise, and Stephan's sued it for specific performance of the contract as modified by the replacement agreement. Is specific performance an appropriate remedy? Discuss. [*Stephan's Machine & Tool, Inc. v. D&H Machinery Consultants, Inc.*, 417 N.E.2d 579 (Ohio App.)]

CPA QUESTIONS

1. On April 5, 1987, Anker, Inc., furnished Bold Corp. with Anker's financial statements dated March 31, 1987. The financial statements contained misrepresentations that indicated that Anker was solvent when in fact it was insolvent. Based on Anker's financial statements, Bold agreed to sell Anker 90 computers, "F.O.B.—Bold's loading dock." On April 14, Anker received 60 of the computers. The remaining 30 computers were in the possession of the common carrier and in transit to Anker. If, on April 28, Bold discovered that Anker was insolvent, then with respect to the computers delivered to Anker on April 14, Bold may:
    a. Reclaim the computers upon making a demand.
    b. Reclaim the computers irrespective of the rights of any third party.
    c. Not reclaim the computers since 10 days have elapsed from their delivery.
    d. Not reclaim the computers since it is entitled to recover the price of the computers.

2. On February 15, Mazur Corp. contracted to sell 1,000 bushels of wheat to Good Bread, Inc., at $6.00 per bushel with delivery to be made on June 23. On June 1, Good advised Mazur that it would not accept or pay for the wheat. On June 2, Mazur sold the wheat to another customer at the market price of $5.00 per bushel. Mazur had advised Good that it intended to resell the wheat. Which of the following statements is correct?

a. Mazur can successfully sue Good for the difference between the resale price and the contract price.

b. Mazur can resell the wheat only after June 23.

c. Good can retract its anticipatory breach at any time before June 23.

d. Good can successfully sue Mazur for specific performance.

3. Lazur Corp. entered into a contract with Baker Suppliers, Inc., to purchase a used word processor from Baker. Lazur is engaged in the business of selling new and used word processors to the general public. The contract required Baker to ship the goods to Lazur by common carrier pursuant to the following provision in the contract: "FOB Baker Suppliers, Inc., loading dock." Baker also represented in the contract that the word processor had been used for only 10 hours by its previous owner. The contract included the provision that the word processor was being sold "as is," and this provision was in a larger and different type style than the remainder of the contract. Assume that Lazur refused to accept the word processor even though it was in all respects conforming to the contract and that the contract is otherwise silent. Under the UCC Sales Article:

a. Baker can successfully sue for specific performance and make Lazur accept and pay for the word processor.

b. Baker may resell the word processor to another buyer.

c. Baker must sue for the difference between the market value of the word processor and the contract price plus its incidental damages.

d. Baker cannot successfully sue for consequential damages unless it attempts to resell the word processor.

PART 4

Negotiable Instruments

© Manuel Gutjahr/iStockphoto.com

CHAPTER 28

© Manuel Gutjahr/iStockphoto.com

Kinds of Instruments, Parties, and Negotiability

learningoutcomes

After studying this chapter, you should be able to

LO.1 Explain the importance and function of negotiable instruments

LO.2 Name the parties to negotiable instruments

LO.3 Describe the concept of negotiability and distinguish it from assignability

LO.4 List the requirements for a negotiable instrument

For convenience and as a way to facilitate transactions, businesses began to accept certain kinds of paper called **commercial paper** or negotiable instruments as substitutes for money or as a means of offering credit. Negotiable commercial paper is special paper created for the special purpose of facilitating transfer of funds and payment. In addition, the use of this special paper for special purposes can create additional rights in a special person status known as a *holder in due course.* Although the details on holders in due course are covered in Chapters 29 and 30, it is important to understand that one of the purposes of the use of special paper is to allow parties to achieve the special status of holder in due course and its protections and rights. Taking each component of negotiable instruments in step-by-step sequences, from their creation to the rights associated with each, and to their transfer, helps in understanding how commercial paper is used for special purposes in order to create rights for special persons.

A. Types of Negotiable Instruments and Parties

Article 3 of the Uniform Commercial Code (UCC) defines the types of negotiable instruments and the parties for each.[1] Article 3 of the UCC was last amended in 2002 with those reforms adopted in some states and under consideration in others.[2] Those changes are explained in each of the relevant sections.

1. Definition

Section 3-104(a)(1) and (2) of the UCC defines a **negotiable instrument** as "an unconditional promise or order to pay a fixed amount of money, … if it (1) is payable to bearer or order…; (2) is payable on demand or at a definite time; and (3) does not state any other undertaking or instruction … to do any act in addition to the payment of money…."[3] A *negotiable instrument* is a record of a signed promise or order to pay a specified sum of money.[4] The former requirement that the instrument be in writing to be valid has been changed to incorporate requirements of UETA (Uniform Electronic Transactions Act) and E-Sign (Electronic Signatures in Global and National Commerce Act of 2000). Many lenders now use electronic promissory notes.[5] In addition, we now have electronic checks, or those check withdrawals from your account that you authorize over the phone or via the Internet.

Instruments are negotiable when they contain certain elements required by the UCC. These elements are listed and explained in Section 5 of this chapter. However, even those instruments that do not meet the requirements for negotiability may still be referred to by their UCC names or classifications.

CPA 2. Kinds of Instruments

There are two categories of negotiable instruments: (1) promises to pay, which include promissory notes and certificates of deposit,[6] and (2) orders to pay, including drafts and checks.

(A) Promissory Notes. A **promissory note** is a written promise made and signed by the maker to pay a *sum certain* in money to the holder of the instrument.[7] (See Figure 28-1.)

(B) Certificates of Deposit. A **certificate of deposit (CD)** is a promise to pay issued by a bank.[8] Through a CD, a bank acknowledges the customer's deposit of a specific sum of money and promises to pay the customer that amount plus interest when the certificate is surrendered.

(C) Drafts. A **draft, or bill of exchange**, is an order by one party to pay a sum of money to a second

[1] The law covering negotiable instruments has been evolving and changing. The latest version of Article 3 was adopted in 1990. The 1990 version of Article 3 had been adopted in all 50 states by August 1999. States with variations are Alabama, Georgia, Montana, Ohio, South Dakota, and Wisconsin. The earlier version was called UCC-Commercial Paper, and the 1990 version is called UCC-Negotiable Instruments.

[2] As of April 2012, 49 states and the District of Columbia had adopted the 2002 changes to Article 3.

[3] UCC §3-104(a)(1) and (2).

[4] See UCC §3-104.

[5] Electronic Signatures in Global and National Commerce Act, 15 U.S.C. §7001 (Supp. 2011).

[6] UCC §3-104(j).

[7] *IFC Credit Corp. v. Specialty Optical Systems, Inc.*, 252 S.W.3d 761 (Tex. App. 2008).

[8] UCC §3-104(j).

FIGURE 28-1 ***Promissory Note***

MARCH 31, 2013

Six months after date debtor undersigned hereby promises to pay to the order of Galactic Games, Inc., three thousand six hundred dollars with interest at the rate of 5.9%. This note is secured by the Video Arcade game purchased with its funds.

In the event of default, all sums due hereunder may be collected. Debtor agrees to pay all costs of collection including, but not limited to, attorney fees, costs of repossession, and costs of litigation.

/s/ JOHN R. HALDEHAND

VIDEO ARCADE, INC.

party. (See Figure 28-2.) The party who gives the order is called the *drawer*, and the party on whom the order to pay is drawn is the *drawee*.[9] The party to whom payment is to be made is the *payee*. The drawer may also be named as the payee, as when a seller draws a draft naming a buyer as the drawee. The draft is then used as a means to obtain payment for goods delivered to that buyer. A drawee is not bound to pay a draft simply because the drawer has placed his name on it. However, the drawee may agree to pay the draft by accepting it, which then attaches the drawee's liability for payment.

(D) CHECKS. Under UCC §3-104(f), *check* means "a draft, other than a documentary draft, payable on demand and drawn on a bank."[10] A **check** is an order by a depositor (the drawer) on a bank or credit union (the drawee) to pay a sum of money to the order of another party (the payee).[11]

In addition to the ordinary checks just described, there are also cashier's checks, teller's checks, traveler's checks, and bank money orders. A **cashier's check** is a draft drawn by a bank on itself. UCC §3-104(g) defines a cashier's check as "a draft with respect to which the drawer and drawee are the same bank or branches of the same bank."[12] A **teller's check** is a

FIGURE 28-2 ***Draft***

March 17, 2013

TO: Topa Fabrics, Inc.
1700 W. Lincoln
Marina Del Rey, CA

Thirty days from date PAY TO THE ORDER OF
Malden Mills, Inc.

THE SUM OF sixteen thousand and no/100 DOLLARS

ACCEPTED BY:

DATE

Aaron Johnson
Malden Mills, Inc.

[9] UCC §3-103(a)(2)–(3).
[10] UCC §3-104(f).
[11] *Id.*
[12] UCC §3-104(g).

draft drawn by a bank on another bank in which it has an account.[13] A **traveler's check** is a check that is payable on demand, provided it is countersigned by the person whose signature was placed on the check at the time the check was purchased.[14] Money orders are issued by both banks and nonbanks. A **money order** drawn by a bank is also a check.[15]

3. Parties to Instruments

A note has two original parties: the *maker* and the *payee*.[16] A draft or a check has three original parties: the *drawer*, the *drawee*, and the *payee*. The names given to the parties to these instruments are important because the liability of the parties varies depending on the parties' roles. The rights and liabilities of the various parties to negotiable instruments are covered in Chapters 29 and 30.

A **party** to an instrument may be a natural person, an artificial person such as a corporation, or an unincorporated enterprise such as a government agency.

(A) MAKER. The **maker** is the party who writes or creates a promissory note, thereby promising to pay the amount specified in the note.

(B) DRAWER. The **drawer** is the party who writes or creates a draft or check.

(C) DRAWEE. The **drawee** is the party to whom the draft is addressed and who is ordered to pay the amount of money specified in the draft. The bank is the drawee on a check, and the credit union is the drawee on a share draft. Again, a drawee on a draft has no responsibility under the draft until it has accepted that instrument.

(D) PAYEE. The **payee** is the person named in the instrument to receive payment. **For Example,** on a check with the words "Pay to the order of John Jones," the named person, John Jones, is the payee.

The payee has no rights in the instrument until the drawer or the maker has delivered it to the payee. Likewise, the payee is not liable on the instrument in any way until the payee transfers the instrument to someone else.

(E) ACCEPTOR. When the drawee of a draft has indicated by writing or record a willingness to pay the amount specified in the draft, the drawee has accepted liability and is called the **acceptor**.[17]

(F) SECONDARY OBLIGOR (ACCOMMODATION PARTY). When a party who is not originally named in an instrument allows her name to be added to it for the benefit of another party in order to add strength to the collectability of the instrument, that party becomes a secondary obligor (formerly called an **accommodation party**) and assumes a liability role.[18] Revised Article 3 now refers to drawer, indorsers, and accommodation parties as "secondary obligors."[19]

CPA B. NEGOTIABILITY

An instrument is a form of contract that, if negotiable, affords certain rights and protections for the parties. **Negotiability** is the characteristic that distinguishes commercial paper and instruments from ordinary contracts or what makes such paper and instruments special paper.[20] That an instrument is negotiable means that certain rights and protections may be available to the parties to the instrument under Article 3. A **nonnegotiable instrument's** terms are enforceable, but the instrument is treated simply as a contract governed by contract law.[21]

4. Definition of Negotiability

If an instrument is negotiable, it is governed by Article 3 of the UCC, and it may be transferred by negotiation. This form of transfer permits the

[13] UCC §3-104(h).

[14] UCC §3-104(i).

[15] *Com. v. Pantalion*, 957 A.2d 1267 (Pa. Super. 2008). Some items are held to be checks for purposes other than Article 3 negotiability. For example, in *In re Armstrong* 291 F.3d 517 (8th Cir. 2002), the court held that gambling markers were checks for purposes of the state's "bad check" law.

[16] UCC §3-103(a)(5).

[17] UCC §3-103(a)(1).

[18] UCC §3-419; *In re TML, Inc.*, 291 B.R. 400, 50 UCC Rep. Serv.2d 511 (W.D. Mich. 2003).

[19] Revised Article 3, §3-103(12), has the following definition of a secondary obligor on an instrument: "an indorser, a drawer, an accommodation party, or any other party to the instrument that has a right of recourse against another party to the instrument…." This definition was changed to be consistent with the Restatement of Surety.

[20] UCC §3-104.

[21] Loan-and-supply contract is not a negotiable instrument. *Quality Oil, Inc. v. Kelley Partners, Inc.*, 657 F.3d 609 (7th Cir. 2011). A note payable when "lessee is granted possession of the premises" is not a negotiable instrument, but it is an enforceable contract. *Schiffer v. United Grocers, Inc.*, 989 P.2d 10 (Or. 1999). A deed of trust is not a negotiable instrument. *Arnold v. Palmer*, 686 S.E.2d 725 (W.Va. 2009).

E-Commerce & Cyberlaw

The Check Is in the Internet

The Check Clearing for the 21st Century Act ("Check 21") allows banks to use electronic images of checks as full and complete records of transactions, the same status formerly used only for paper checks that had been canceled. You can also pay your monthly credit card bills by preauthorizing your credit card company to withdraw the amount you specify from your account. With the bank's routing number and your account number, the company can obtain payment on the due date or any date you authorize. PayPal allows you to do the same with your bank account when you purchase items on the Internet. Paperless payment is on the increase.

transferee to acquire rights greater than those afforded assignees of contracts under contract law. The quality of negotiability in instruments creates opportunities for transfers and financings that streamline payments in commerce. Transfers can be made with assurance of payment without the need for investigation of the underlying contract. The process of negotiation is covered in Chapter 29. For more information on the rights of assignees of contracts, refer to Chapter 18.

CPA 5. Requirements of Negotiability

To be negotiable, an instrument (1) must be evidenced by a record[22] and (2) must be signed (authenticated under Revised Article 3) by the maker or the drawer, (3) must contain an unconditional promise or order to pay, (4) must pay a sum certain, (5) must be payable in money, (6) must be payable on demand or at a definite time, and (7) must be payable to order or bearer, using what are known as words of negotiability.[23]

(A) A Record (Writing). A negotiable instrument must be evidenced by a record. The requirement of a *record*, under Revised Article 3, is satisfied by handwriting, typing, printing, electronic record, and any other method of making a record. A negotiable instrument may be partly printed and partly typewritten. No particular form is required for an instrument to satisfy the record requirement, although customers of banks may agree to use the banks' forms as part of their contractual agreement with their banks. Telephonic checks are a complete record for purposes of Article 3 rights and obligations.

(B) Authenticated (Signed) by the Maker or Drawer. The instrument must be authenticated (signed under old Article 3) by the maker or the drawer. When a signature is used as authentication, it usually appears at the lower right-hand corner of the face of the instrument, but there is no requirement for where the signature must be placed on the instrument.[24]

The authentication may consist of the full name or of any symbol placed with the intent to authenticate the instrument. Other means of authentication that are valid as signatures include initials, figures, and marks. Electronic security devices can be used as a means of authentication for electronic records. A person signing a trade name or an assumed name is liable just as if the signer's own name had been used.

(1) Agent.

An authentication may be made by the drawer or the maker or by his or her authorized agent. **For Example,** Eileen Smith, the treasurer of Mills Company, could sign a note for her company as an agent. No particular form of authorization for an agent to authenticate an instrument is required. An authenticating agent should disclose on the instrument (1) the identity of the principal and (2) the fact that the authentication was done in a representative capacity. When this information appears on the face of the instrument, an authorized agent is not liable on it.

[22] Revised Article 3. Existing Article 3 requires a writing, but the revisions reflect electronic transactions and the federal mandate for recognizing electronic transactions as valid and on equal footing with paper transactions. The definition of a record is found in Revised UCC §3-103(a)(14), which provides that *record* "means information that is inscribed on a tangible medium or which is stored in an electronic or other medium and is retrievable in perceivable form."

[23] UCC §3-104.

[24] According to Revised UCC §3-103, *authenticate* means (a) to sign or (b) to execute or otherwise adopt a symbol, or encrypt or similarly process a record in whole or in part, with the present intent of the authenticating person to identify the person and adopt or accept a record.

The representative capacity of an officer of an organization can be shown by the authentication of the officer along with the title of the office and the organization's name.[25] **For Example,** a signature of "James Shelton, Treasurer, NorWest Utilities, Inc.," or "NorWest Utilities, Inc., by James Shelton, Treasurer," on a note is enough to show Shelton's representative capacity. NorWest Utilities, not Shelton, would be liable on the note.

(2) Absence of Representative Capacity or Identification of Principal.

If an instrument fails to show the **representative capacity** of the person who is authenticating or fails to identify the person, then the individual who authenticates the instrument is personally liable on the instrument to anyone who acquires superior rights, such as the rights of a holder in due course (see Chapter 30). Because the instrument is a final agreement, the parol evidence rule applies, and the party who authenticated is not permitted to introduce extrinsic evidence that might clarify his or her representative capacity. The party who authenticated, in order to avoid personal liability, must indicate on the face of the instrument his or her role in the principal, such as president or vice president. (For more information about the parol evidence rule, see Chapter 17.)

However, an agent is not personally liable on a check that is drawn on the bank account of the principal and authenticated by him or her, even though the agent failed to disclose his or her representative capacity on the check. **For Example,** a check that is already imprinted with the employer's name is not the check of the employee, regardless of whether the employee only authenticates with his or her name or also adds a title such as "Payroll Clerk" or "Treasurer" near the signature. The *Major Products Co., Inc. v. Northwest Harvest Products, Inc.* case deals with an issue of signature liability.

Major Products Co., Inc. v. Northwest Harvest Products, Inc., 979 P.2d 905 (Wash. App. 1999)

The Sticky Note That Was a Reminder of Personal Liability

Northwest Harvest Products, Inc. fell behind on payments on its account with Major Products Company, Inc. Major requested a note for the debt, and Northwest sent a $79,000 corporate note. The balance on the note was incorrect, and Northwest sent a second corporate note for $79,361.89. After further discussion, Major sent yet another note for $78,445.24. The Chief Executive Officer of Northwest at that time signed the note "Donald H Eoll CEO," attached a Post-It™ fax transmittal memo indicating that the note came from Donald Eoll at Northwest, and sent the note via facsimile. The note was not paid, and Major sued both Eoll and Northwest for the debt. Only the facsimile copy of the note was presented at trial, and the trial court found that the writing on the Post-It note, coupled with the signature, identified Northwest as the principal on the note. The trial court held that Eoll was not personally liable for the debt because he signed the note as an agent for Northwest. Major appealed.

JUDICIAL OPINION

BAKER, J.... Major appeals, contending that the Post-It brand fax transmittal memo served as a mere convenience for Eoll's transmission of the note and thus Eoll's signature did not identify Northwest as the principal on the note. We agree with Major that the writing on a Post-It brand fax transmittal memo is independent of an underlying document. Thus Eoll's signature did not identify Northwest as the principal on the note and it is not apparent from the body of the note that he signed as an agent for Northwest. Eoll bore the burden of rebutting a presumption of personal liability. Because Eoll did not provide evidence or testimony that rebutted that presumption, he is personally liable on the note.

Unless the instrument clearly indicates that a signature is made in some other capacity it is an indorsement.

Major contends that the Post-It brand memo was merely a convenience for Eoll to facilitate the transmission of the agreement from one facsimile machine to another and did not form an integral part of the parties' agreement. The legal effect of such a memo presents an issue of first impression in this state. In *Birenbaum v Option Care, Inc.*, 971 S.W.2d 497 (Tex. App.1997), a Post-It brand fax transmittal memo with writing and a signature was attached to a document prior to its transmission. The court found that a signature on a Post-It

[25] UCC §3-402. *In re Bedrock Marketing, LLC,* 404 B.R. 939 (D.Utah 2009) and *Arntz v. Valdez,* 2011 WL 3433018, 163 Wash. App. 1003 (Wash. App. 2011).

Continued

brand memo is not evidence from which the trial court could infer an intent to sign the underlying document. Instead, the information and signature on the Post-It brand memo were independent of the underlying document and were not operative on that document in the same manner as a signature on the underlying document would have been.

We think that *Birenbaum* sets forth a sound approach for dealing with Post-It brand fax transmittal memos and the like. We hold that such writings are independent of an underlying document and do not have the same legal effect as writing on the face of a document. Although extrinsic evidence may sometimes show that such writings form an integral part of an agreement, our holding furthers contract law's objective of protecting the justified expectations of parties by promoting certainty in business dealings. The transmission of documents via facsimile is a technological advance that should reinforce the justified expectations of parties by improving transactional communications, and we reject Eoll's arguments that attempt to introduce legal uncertainty into business dealings that are assisted by such advances. If a party wishes to include information or make a modification on the face of a document transmitted via facsimile, such information or modification should be made in writing on the document directly, not by means of a writing that is easily detached or separated from the original.

Because the Post-It brand fax transmittal memo here is independent of the note, the signature on the parties' agreement reads only "Donald H Eoll CEO." Thus for purposes of former RCW 62A.3-403(2)(b), the note does not name the person represented (Northwest), but does show that Eoll signed in a representative capacity. That signature might indicate that the parties intended Eoll would be personally bound by the note or that Eoll would not be personally bound by the note, and thus further inquiry into the parties' intent is warranted.

The indication that the signature is made in another capacity must be clear without reference to anything but the instrument. It may be found in the language used. Thus if John Doe signs after "I, John Doe, promise to pay," he is clearly a maker; and "John Doe, witness" is not liable at all. The capacity may be found in any clearly evidenced purpose of the signature, as where a drawee signing in an unusual place on the paper has no visible reason to sign at all unless he is an acceptor. It may be found in usage or custom. Thus by long established practice judicially noticed or otherwise established a signature in the lower right hand corner of an instrument indicates an intent to sign as the maker of a note or the drawer of a draft. Any similar clear indication of an intent to sign in some other capacity may be enough to remove the signature from the application of this section.

Although extrinsic evidence was admissible as an aid to show these parties' intent, ... Eoll failed to present extrinsic evidence which would rebut a presumption of personal liability. Eoll is personally liable on this note.

[Reversed].

QUESTIONS

1. Without the Post-it, what information was on the promissory note?
2. Why does the court believe that we should not include what is written on Post-it notes as part of a document?
3. Would the court have allowed extrinsic evidence to show who was liable?

(c) Promise or Order to Pay. A promissory note must contain a promise to pay money. A mere acknowledgment of a debt, such as a record stating "I.O.U.," is not a promise. A draft or check must contain an order or command to pay money.

(d) Unconditional Promise or Order. For an instrument to be negotiable, the promise or order to pay must be unconditional.[26]

For Example, when an instrument makes the duty to pay dependent on the completion of the construction of a building, the promise is conditional and the instrument is nonnegotiable. The instrument is enforceable as a contract, but it is not a negotiable instrument given all the rights and protections afforded under Article 3.

An order for the payment of money out of a particular fund is negotiable. The instrument can refer to a particular account or merely indicate a source of reimbursement for the drawee, such as "Charge my expense account." Nor is an instrument conditional when payment is to be made only from an identified fund if the issuer is a government or governmental unit or agency, or when payment is to

[26] UCC §3-109(c).

be made from the assets of a partnership, unincorporated association, trust, or estate.[27] However, the fund noted must in fact exist because payment from a fund to be created by a future event would be conditional. **For Example,** making an instrument "payable from the account I'll establish when the sale of my house occurs" is conditional because the fund's creation is tied to an event whose time of occurrence is unknown.

The standards for negotiability do not require that the issuer of the instrument be personally obligated to pay it.[28] An instrument's negotiability is not destroyed by a reference to a related document. Section 3-106(b) provides, "A promise or order is not made conditional (i) by a reference to another writing for a statement of rights with respect to collateral, prepayment, or acceleration."[29] **For Example,** if a note includes the following phrase, "This note is secured by a mortgage on the property located at Hilding Lane," the note is still negotiable.[30]

(E) PAYMENT IN MONEY. A negotiable instrument must be payable in money. **Money** is defined to include any medium of exchange adopted or authorized by the United States, a foreign government, or an intergovernmental organization. The parties to an instrument are free to decide which currency will be used for payment even though their transaction may occur in a different country.[31] **For Example,** two parties in the United States are free to agree that their note will be paid in pesos.

If the order or promise is not for money, the instrument is not negotiable. **For Example,** an instrument that requires the holder to take stock or goods in place of money is nonnegotiable. The instrument is enforceable as a contract, but it cannot qualify as a negotiable instrument for purposes of Article 3 rights.

(F) SUM CERTAIN. Negotiable instruments must include a statement of a **sum certain**, or an exact amount of money. Without a definite statement as to how much is

Thinking Things Through

When Your John Hancock Is Enough

Work through the following examples of signatures on negotiable instruments and capacity, and determine whether there would be personal liability on the part of the company executives signing the instruments.

1. Donald Schaffer owned and operated Grafton Janitorial Service, Inc. On October 6, 1998, Mr. Schaffer obtained a $25,000 line of credit for his company from First Merit Bank by executing a promissory note, which he signed both as "Donald J. Schaffer, President" and "Donald J. Schaffer, Cosigner." The note contains no guarantee provision, and Mr. Schaffer did not sign the note in the capacity as a guarantor. **[*Schaffer v. First Merit Bank, N.A.*, 927 N.E.2d 15 (Ohio App. 2009)]**

2. A corporate guaranty was signed as follows:

   THE PRODUCERS GROUP OF FLA., INC. a Florida corporation, by the following officers solely on behalf of the corporation:

   /s/ Eddie Beverly, as its President

   CORPORATE PRESIDENT Eddie Beverly

   /s/ Stephen Edman, as its Secretary

   CORPORATE SECRETARY Steve Edman

   /s/ John Bauder, as its Treasurer

   CORPORATE TREASURER John Bauder

   Are the officers personally liable on the guaranty? **[*Tampa Bay Economic Development Corp. v. Edman*, 598 So.2d 172 (Fla. App. 1992)]**

[27] A check issued by a debtor in bankruptcy for payment of court-ordered obligations is not conditional because of the involvement of the court or ongoing conditions on debtor's payments. *In re Blasco*, 352 B.R. 888 (Bankr. N.D. Ala. Div. 2006).

[28] UCC §3-110(c)(1)–(2) (1990); *Ocwen Loan Servicing, LLC v. Branaman*, 554 F. Supp. 2d 645 (N.D. Miss. 2008).

[29] UCC §3-106(b).

[30] Reference to a bill of lading does not affect negotiability. *Regent Corp., U.S.A. v. Azmat Bangladesh, Ltd.*, 686 N.Y.S.2d 24 (1999). However, a reference to a standby agreement does affect negotiability. *In re Sabertooth, LLC*, 443 B.R. 671 (E.D. Pa. 2011).

[31] UCC §3-107. *Means v. Clardy*, 735 S.W.2d 6 (Mo. App. 1987) (payment in cabinets makes a note nonnegotiable).

to be paid under the terms of the instrument, there is no way to determine how much the instrument is worth.

There are some minor variations from sum certain requirement. **For Example,** an instrument is not nonnegotiable because its interest rate provisions include changes in the rate at maturity or because it provides for certain costs and attorney fees to be recovered by the holder in the event of enforcement action or litigation.[32]

In most states, the sum payable under an instrument is certain even though it calls for the payment of a floating or variable interest rate.[33] An instrument is negotiable even though it provides for an interest rate of 1 percent above the prime rate of a named bank. It is immaterial that the exact amount of interest that will be paid cannot be determined at the time the paper is issued because the rate may later change. It is also immaterial that the amount due on the instrument cannot be determined without looking at records outside of the face of the instrument.[34]

(G) Time of Payment. A negotiable instrument must be payable on demand or at a definite time.[35] If an instrument is payable "when convenient," it is nonnegotiable because the day of payment may never arrive. An instrument payable only upon the happening of a particular event that may or may not happen is not negotiable. **For Example,** a provision in a note to pay the sum certain when a person marries is not payable at a definite time because that particular event may never occur. It is immaterial whether the contingency in fact has happened because from an examination of the instrument alone, it still appears to be subject to a condition that might not occur.

(1) Demand.

An instrument is *payable on demand* when it expressly states that it is payable "on demand," at sight, or on presentation. UCC §3-108(a) provides "A promise or order is 'payable on demand' if (i) it states that it is payable on demand or at sight, or otherwise indicates that it is payable at the will of the holder, or (ii) it does not state any time of payment."[36] Presentation occurs when a holder demands payment. Commercial paper is deemed to be payable on demand when no time for payment is stated in the instrument.[37]

(2) Definite Time.

The time of payment is a **definite time** if an exact time or times are specified or if the instrument is payable at a fixed time after sight or acceptance or at a time that is readily ascertainable. The time of payment is definite even though the instrument provides for prepayment, for acceleration, or for extensions at the option of a party or automatically on the occurrence of a specified contingency. The *Smith v. Vaughn* case involves an issue of whether a note is payable at a definite time.

Smith v. Vaughn, 882 N.E.2d 941, 64 UCC Rep. Serv. 2d 757 (Ohio. App. 2007)

Whenever ... Paying When You Can Does Not a Negotiable Instrument Make

Gary Vaughn signed a document stating that Fred and Martha Smith were loaning him $9,900. As to when the loan was to be repaid, the document stated, "when you can." Approximately 18 months later, the Smiths sued Vaughn for the entire amount, claiming default on the note as well as unjust enrichment. The Smiths moved for summary judgment. They contended that Vaughn was immediately liable for the entire amount but that they were willing to work out a repayment schedule. Vaughn also moved for summary judgment, arguing that he did not have to repay the Smiths because he did not have the ability to do so. The trial court denied the Smiths' motion and granted Vaughn's. The Smiths appealed.

[32] UCC §3-106. *In re MCB Financial Group, Inc.*, 461 B.R. 914 (N.D. Ga. 2011).

[33] While revised Article 3 permits variable and market rates, notes entered into before the revised act was adopted will be governed under old Article 3; *YYY Corp. v. Gazda*, 761 A.2d 395 (N.H. 2000), *Barnsley v. Empire Mortgage, Ltd. Partnership*, 720 A.2d 63 (N.H. 1998), but see *Bankers Trust (Delaware) v. 236 Beltway Inv.*, 865 F. Supp. 1186 (E.D. Va. 1994).

[34] *SCADIF, S.A. v. First Union Nat. Bank*, 208 F. Supp. 2d 1352 (S.D. Fla. 2002), aff'd, 344 F.3d 1123 (11th Cir. 2003). See also *Bankers Trust v. 236 Beltway Investment*, 865 F. Supp. 1186 (E.D. Va. 1994).

[35] UCC §3-108.

[36] UCC §3-108(a).

[37] UCC §3-112; *Universal Premium Acceptance Corp. v. York Bank's Trust Co.*, 69 F.3d 695 (3d Cir. 1995); *State v. McWilliams*, 178 P. 3d 121 (Mont. 2008).

Continued

JUDICIAL OPINION

SYLVIA SIEVE HENDON, Judge ... The Smiths and Vaughn agree that the terms of the promissory note control in this case. They argue, however, over what law applies to determine the meaning of the phrase "when you can." The Smiths contend that the note was payable on demand and that it was a negotiable instrument. It was neither. An instrument is payable on demand if it states that it is, or if no time is specified for repayment. Here, "when you can" was when payment was due. This was not the equivalent of completely failing to identify a repayment date. And this conditional term of repayment destroyed negotiability. This argument has no merit.

Vaughn, in turn, argues that he had to repay the Smiths only if they could demonstrate that he had the ability to pay. The Tenth Appellate District has determined that a reasonable amount of time "is not measured by hours, days, weeks, months, or years." Instead, the trier of fact "should ascertain the parties' original expectations and the circumstances surrounding the execution of the agreement." In addition to these considerations, the Seventh Appellate District has stated that the trier of fact should examine all factors "ordinary and extraordinary." We find these cases to be persuasive. And we add that an obligor's ability to pay must also be a part of the court's determination of reasonableness, since the ability to pay is part of "all the circumstances."

Applying the law to the facts of this case, we uphold the court's denial of the Smiths' motion for summary judgment. The Smiths did not support their motion with evidentiary materials concerning the totality of the circumstances.

But we are compelled as a matter of law to reverse the trial court's judgment in favor of Vaughn. In support of his motion, Vaughn attached only his own affidavit stating that he had encountered some financial difficulties in the past, was presently employed, and had attempted to repay the Smiths a small fraction of what he owed. Considering the very broad test for "reasonableness," we hold that Vaughn had failed to establish the absence of a genuine issue of fact concerning whether it was reasonable for him to repay the Smiths.

[We reverse].

QUESTIONS

1. Does "when you can" mean that the instrument is payable on demand?
2. How does the requirement of looking at the debtor's circumstances affect negotiability?
3. What language could have made the "when you can" clause not as critical for negotiability?

(3) Missing Date.

An instrument that is not dated is deemed dated on the day it is issued to the payee. Any holder may add the correct date to the instrument.

(4) Effect of Date on a Demand Instrument.

The date on a demand instrument controls the time of payment, and the paper is not due before its date. Consequently, a check that is postdated ceases to be demand paper and is not properly payable before the date on the check. A bank making earlier payment does not incur any liability for doing so unless the drawer has given the bank a postdated check notice.

(H) Words of Negotiability: Payable to Order or Bearer. An instrument that is not a check must be **payable to order** or **bearer**.[38] This requirement is met by such phrases as "Pay to the order of John Jones," "Pay to John Jones or order," "Pay to bearer," and "Pay to John Jones or bearer." The use of the phrase "to the order of John Jones" or "to John Jones or order" shows that the person executing the instrument had no intention of restricting payment of the instrument to John Jones. These phrases indicate that there is no objection to paying anyone to whom John Jones orders the paper to be paid. Similarly, if the person executing the instrument originally wrote that it will be paid "to bearer" or "to John Jones or bearer," there is no restriction on the payment of the paper to the original payee. However, if the instrument is not a check and it is payable on its face "to John Jones," the instrument is not negotiable.[39] Whether an instrument is bearer or order paper is important because the two instruments are transferred in different ways and because the liability of the transferors can be different. The *Whitaker v. Limeco Corp.* case determines whether loans and liens qualify as negotiable instruments.

[38] *Unlimited Adjusting Group, Inc. v. Wells Fargo Bank*, 94 Cal. Rptr.3d 672 (Cal. App. 2009).
[39] UCC §3-108.

Whitaker v. Limeco Corp., 32 So.3d 429 (Miss. 2010)

The Goal Was a Hockey Team AND a Negotiable Instrument

William Kidd served as managing director of Limeco Corporation. Beginning in 2001, negotiations began between Kidd/Limeco (defendants) and R.W. Whitaker and Monty Fletcher (plaintiffs), the in connection with what later became a failed effort to purchase a hockey team in Tupelo. Whitaker and Fletcher loaned Limeco $750,000. Whitaker and Fletcher claim that Kidd concealed the fact that Limeco had no assets. Whitaker also loaned Kidd an additional $100,000, with the understanding that Kidd and Limeco would be responsible for paying back the loan Whitaker had taken out from the Peoples Bank & Trust Company in Tupelo in order to make the loan to Kidd.

On July 1, 2002, the parties entered into what they referred to as promissory notes (referred to as the "Fletcher note" and the "Whitaker note") to memorialize the terms of the loan agreements they had made in early 2002. Both Fletcher and Whitaker, in an effort to secure what they thought were promissory notes, were granted a continuing lien on Limeco's monies, securities, and/or other property for the entire amount of the promissory notes (each in the amount of $375,000).

On December 11, 2003, Whitaker and Fletcher filed separate complaints against Limeco and Kidd for recovery of the more than $850,000 that had never been repaid. The trial court found that, because the the suit was brought after the contracts statute of limitations had expired that it had to be dismissed. Whitaker and Fletcher argued that the notes were negotiable instruments and their fraud claim was valid because of the six-year statute of limitations that applied with regard to negotiable instruments.

JUDICIAL OPINION

CARLSON, Justice

The Plaintiffs argue that the notes entered into by Kidd, each in the amount of $375,000, met all of the statutory requirements for negotiable instruments pursuant to Mississippi Code Section 75-3-104 (Rev.2002); thus, the complaint was timely filed within the six-year statute of limitations pursuant to Section 75-3-118(b).

The trial court dismissed the Plaintiffs' complaint on the basis that neither of the promissory notes, each in the amount of $375,000, was a negotiable instrument under Section 75-3-104 because neither of the notes contained the required "words of negotiability." As a result, the trial court found that the notes were not subject to the six-year statute of limitations applicable to negotiable instruments under Section 75-3-118(b). Instead, according to the trial court, the notes were subject to the three-year statute of limitations for breach-of-contract claims.

What the Plaintiffs identify as the "Whitaker note" reads as follows: "On demand, for value received, I promise to pay to R.W. Whitaker ... the sum of Three Hundred, Seventy-five Thousand Dollars ($375,000)." The written agreement identified as the "Fletcher note" contains identical language. The Plaintiffs argue that this meets the statutory definition of "payable to order" and urge this Court to interpret Section 75-3-109(b) as defining "payable to order" as follows: payable "to the order of an identified payee," payable to an identified payee, or payable "to order." In support of their argument, the Plaintiffs cite the canon of statutory construction that statutes written in the disjunctive set forth separate and distinct alternatives.

However, interpreting Section 75-3-109(b)(ii) as defining "payable to order" as payable to an identified payee or payable to order is contrary to how the majority of jurisdictions interpret the Uniform Commercial Code's statutory requirements for negotiable instruments. In order to meet the requirements of a negotiable instrument:

> [A] paper or instrument generally must be payable to order or to bearer at the time it is issued or comes into the possession of a holder. This means that notes payable simply to a specific payee, and not to the order of the payee or to the payee or order, are not negotiable.

Thus, the words "payable to the order of" or payable "to [identified payee] or order" must appear within the instrument in order to qualify it as a negotiable instrument, and since the promissory notes in today's case do not contain this language, they cannot be deemed to be negotiable instruments.

Arguing that the agreements met the statutory definition of negotiable instruments, the Plaintiffs contend that the six-year statute of limitations for negotiable instruments under Section 75-3-118 applies in this case and that the statute of limitations would not have expired until July 1, 2008, six years after the Whitaker and Fletcher notes were signed. However, having already found no error on the part of the trial court in declining to find that either of the notes met the statutory requirements for negotiable instruments, we find no error on the part of the trial court in applying the three-year statute of limitations. Accordingly, there was no error on the part of the trial court in dismissing the breach-of-promissory-notes claim as time-barred.

[Affirmed in part, reversed in part (on other issues), and remanded.]

QUESTIONS

1. What was the problem with the words of negotiability?
2. What was the difference for Whitaker and Fletcher if there was negotiability vs. not having negotiability?
3. What advice would you give to business people who are drafting notes for repayment?

Ethics & the Law

Medicaid Eligibility and Article 3 Negotiability

Kenneth Wilson was hospitalized from January 7, 2007, until his death on February 22, 2007. During the hospitalization, Kenneth's wife, Doris, sold her 100% stock ownership in the Brothers Delivery Service (her husband's company) to her son. The agreement provided that Kenneth, Jr. would pay $62,531 in 60 installments of $1.041.82, starting March 1, 2007. Kenneth Jr. did not sign the promissory note for these terms. Doris never signed the purchase agreement. Doris then applied for Medicaid benefits in order to cover the costs of her husband's hospitalization. Eligibility for Medicaid requires a determination that there are insufficient personal assets to pay the bill. The Division of Social Services concluded that Doris was the owner of a promissory note, a liquid asset, that could be sold to pay the medical bills. Coverage was denied due to excessive resources. Doris argues that there is no negotiable note because the requirements for negotiability are not met. The appellate court agreed because the underlying contract had not been signed by Doris and because there was not, as yet, a promissory note. The purchase agreement did not have words of negotiability and there was no definite time for payment because the note did not yet exist. Discuss whether Doris attained Medicaid eligibility through a legal loophole. Does she actually have assets that could be used to pay at least part of the debt? Should legal definitions allow us to escape an obligation to pay? **[*Estate of Wilson v. Division of Social Services*, 685 S.E.2d 135 (N.C. App. 2009)]**

(1) Order Paper.

An instrument is payable to order, or **order paper**, when by its terms it is payable to the order of any person described in it ("Pay to the order of K. Read") or to a person or order ("Pay to K. Read or order").

(2) Bearer Paper.

An instrument is payable to bearer, or **bearer paper**, when it is payable (1) to bearer or the order of bearer, (2) to a specified person or bearer, or (3) to "cash," "the order of cash," or any other designation that does not purport to identify a person or when (4) the last or only indorsement is a blank indorsement (an indorsement that does not name the person to whom the instrument is negotiated). An instrument that does not identify any payee is payable to bearer.[40]

Whether an instrument is bearer or order paper is important for determining how the instrument is transferred (see Chapter 28) and what the liability of the parties under the instrument is. Review Figure 28-3 for more background. The *New Mexico v. Herrera* case decision turns on whether an instrument is bearer or order paper.

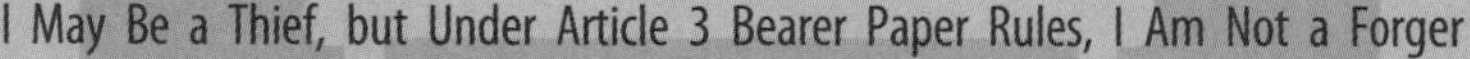

New Mexico v. Herrera, 20 P.3d 810 (N.M. App. 2001)

I May Be a Thief, but Under Article 3 Bearer Paper Rules, I Am Not a Forger

Joshua Herrera (defendant) found a purse in a dumpster near San Pedro and Kathryn Streets in Albuquerque. Herrera took the purse with him to a friend's house. Either Herrera or his friend called the owner of the purse and the owner retrieved the purse at some point. After the purse was returned to the owner, he returned to the dumpster where he found a check and some other items. The check Herrera found was written out to "Cash" and that he thought this meant that he "could get money for [the] check."

When he presented the check to the teller at a credit union to cash it, the teller instructed him to put his name on the payee line next to "Cash." Herrera added "to Joshua Herrera" next to the word "Cash" on the payee line of the check and indorsed the check.

Herrera had pleaded guilty to one count of forgery in violation of NMSA 1978, § 30-16-10 (1963) but moved to have the indictment dismissed on the grounds that adding his name to a bearer instrument was not forgery. He appealed the denial of the motion to dismiss the indictment.

[40] UCC §3-104(d).

Continued

JUDICIAL OPINION

WECHSLER, Judge.… Under Section 30-16-10(B) the State must prove that the defendant gave or delivered a document to a victim with the intent to injure, deceive or cheat the victim or another, knowing that the document (1) was a false document; (2) contained a false signature; (3) had a false indorsement; or (4) was changed so that its effect was different from the original.

Defendant did not make a false signature or offer a false indorsement. Defendant could only have committed forgery by changing the legal effect of the check. If Defendant did change the legal effect of the check, he could have committed forgery under Section 30-16-10(A) and if he transferred the forged check he could have committed forgery under Section 30-16-10(B). Under either subsection of Section 30-16-10, the State must prove that Defendant changed the legal effect of the check. Therefore, whether Defendant changed the legal effect of the check is the dispositive question in this case. Defendant argues that the act of adding his name to the payee line next to the word "Cash" failed to alter the legal effect of the check. We look to the Uniform Commercial Code to determine whether Defendant is correct.

When a negotiable instrument is made payable to "Cash," it is a bearer instrument. A bearer instrument refers to an instrument that is payable to anyone possessing the instrument and is negotiable by transfer alone.

In contrast, an instrument payable to an identified person is considered an order instrument. An order instrument requires the indorsement of the identified person before it can be negotiated. See 55-3- 201(b). The legal effect of an order instrument is different from a bearer instrument because each type of instrument has different negotiability requirements:

[W]hether an instrument is an order instrument or a bearer instrument is important in determining how an instrument is negotiated. If the instrument is payable to bearer, it can be negotiated by delivery alone. If it is payable to the order of an identified person it cannot be negotiated without the indorsement of that person.

At the time Defendant presented the check to the credit union teller, he possessed a bearer instrument because the check was written out to "Cash." At the direction of the teller, however, Defendant added the words "to Joshua Herrera" to the payee line after the word "Cash." By doing so, Defendant added a specific payee to what was otherwise a bearer instrument. We analyze whether Defendant changed the legal effect of the check by adding his name on the payee line of the check.

The words "Cash" and "Bearer" have distinct legal meanings. Their presence upon the face of an instrument signifies the particular legal status of that instrument; namely, that the instrument is payable to anyone bearing it. Similarly, the presence of an identified payee such as "Joshua Herrera" on the face of an instrument signifies that the instrument is payable only to Joshua Herrera.

In this circumstance, with the check payable "to the order of Cash to Joshua Herrera," one who received it could reasonably be confused because it contains both bearer and order instructions. The Uniform Commercial Code resolves such confusion by making the bearer term prevail. We do not view the conjunction "to" in this case as sufficient to avoid confusion from the conflicting terms so as to preclude application of the principles of the commentary.

Indeed, under specific circumstances, a bearer instrument can be transformed to an order instrument. Section 55-3-109(c) provides that when a bearer instrument is specially indorsed, it can be transformed to an order instrument. A special indorsement is one that "identifies a person to whom it makes the instrument payable." Defendant's indorsement in this case included only his name and did not include language making the check payable to an identified person. See § 55-3- 205(c). Thus, the indorsement was not a special indorsement and was not sufficient to transform the legal effect of the check from bearer to order. Instead, because Defendant's indorsement included only his signature, the indorsement qualified as an indorsement in blank. See § 55-3-205(b). Section 55-3-205(b) states that when an instrument is indorsed in blank, "the instrument 'becomes payable to bearer and may be negotiated by transfer of possession alone.'" Consequently, Defendant's indorsement did not change the legal effect of the check from a bearer instrument into an order instrument under Section 55-3-109.

Because Defendant did not change the legal effect of the check when he added his name to the payee line or when he indorsed it, Defendant did not commit the crime of forgery.

Defendant did not commit the crime of forgery. We reverse the district court's denial of Defendant's motion to dismiss the indictment.

[Reversed and remanded]

QUESTIONS

1. What type of instrument was the check when Herrera found it?
2. What type of instrument was the check when Herrera added his name to the "Pay to" line?
3. Could Herrera be charged with forgery?

FIGURE 28-3 Bearer versus Order Paper

"Pay to the order of ABC Corp."	ORDER
"Pay to the order of Bearer"	BEARER
"Pay to the order of ABC Corp. or Bearer"	BEARER
"Pay to the order of ABC Corp., Bearer"	ORDER
"Pay to the order of John Jones" (note)	ORDER
"Pay to the order of John Jones" (check)	ORDER
"Pay to John Jones" (note)	NONNEGOTIABLE
"Pay to John Jones" (check)	NEGOTIABLE/ORDER
"Pay to the order of John Jones or Bearer"	BEARER
"Pay to cash"	BEARER
"Pay to the order of cash"	BEARER

6. Factors Not Affecting Negotiability

Omitting a date of execution or antedating or **postdating** an instrument has no effect on its negotiability.

Provisions relating to **collateral**, such as specifying the collateral as security for the debt or a promise to maintain, protect, or give additional collateral, do not affect negotiability. **For Example,** the phrase "This note is secured by a first mortgage" does not affect negotiability.

7. Ambiguous Language

The following rules are applied when **ambiguous** language exists in words or descriptions:

1. Words control figures where conflict exists.
2. Handwriting supersedes conflicting typewritten and printed terms.
3. Typewritten terms supersede preprinted terms.
4. If there is a failure to provide for the payment of interest or if there is a provision for the payment of interest but no rate is mentioned, the judgment rate at the place of payment applies from the date of the instrument.[41]

8. Statute of Limitations

Article 3 of the UCC establishes a three-year statute of limitations for most actions involving negotiable instruments. This limitation also applies to actions for the conversion of such instruments and for breach of warranty. There is a six-year statute of limitations for suits on certificates of deposit and accepted drafts.

[41] *In re Blasco*, 352 B.R. 888 (N.D. Ala. 2006).

MAKE THE CONNECTION

SUMMARY

An instrument or piece of commercial paper is a transferable, signed promise or order to pay a specified sum of money that is evidenced by a record. An instrument is negotiable when it contains the terms required by the UCC.

Negotiable instruments have two categories: (1) promises to pay and (2) orders to pay. Checks and drafts are orders to pay. Notes and certificates of deposits are promises to pay. In addition to ordinary checks, there are cashier's checks and teller's checks. A bank money order is a check even though it bears the words *money order.*

The original parties to a note are the maker and the payee. The original parties to a draft are the drawer, the drawee, and the payee. The term *party* may refer to a natural person or to an artificial person, such as a corporation. Indorsers and accommodation parties are considered secondary obligors.

The requirements of negotiability are that the instrument (1) be evidenced by a record, (2) be signed (authenticated) by the maker or the drawer, and (3) contain a promise or order (4) of an unconditional character (5) to pay in money (6) a sum certain (7) on demand or at a definite time (8) to order or bearer. A check may be negotiable without being payable to order or bearer.

If an instrument meets the requirements of negotiability, the parties have the rights and protections of Article 3. If it does not meet the requirements of negotiability, the rights of the parties are governed under contract law.

LEARNING OUTCOMES

After studying this chapter, you should be able to clearly explain:

A. Types of Negotiable Instruments and Parties

LO.1 Explain the importance and function of negotiable instruments

See the discussion of negotiability on p. 540.

See *New Mexico v. Herrera* on pp. 548–549.

LO.2 Name the parties to negotiable instruments

See the list of parties to instruments starting on p. 540.

B. Negotiability

LO.3 Describe the concept of negotiability and distinguish it from assignability

See *Whitaker v. Limeco Corp.* on p. 547 for what can happen if an instrument is not negotiable.

LO.4 List the requirements for a negotiable instrument

See the list of negotiability requirements on p. 541.

See *Smith v. Vaughn* on pp. 545–546.

KEY TERMS

acceptor
accommodation party
ambiguous
bearer
bearer paper
cashier's check
certificate of deposit (CD)
check
collateral
commercial paper
definite time
draft, or bill of exchange
drawee
drawer
maker
money
money order
negotiability
negotiable instrument
nonnegotiable instrument
order paper
party
payable to order
payee
postdating
promissory note
representative capacity
sum certain
teller's check
traveler's check

QUESTIONS AND CASE PROBLEMS

1. Harold H. Heidingsfelder signed a credit agreement as vice president of J. O. H. Construction Co. for a line of credit with Pelican Plumbing Co. The credit agreement contained the following language:

In consideration of an open account privilege, I hereby understand and agree to the above terms. Should it become necessary to place this account for collection I shall personally obligate myself and my corporation, if any, to pay the entire amount due including service charges (as outlined above terms) thirty-three and one-third ($33^1/_3$%) attorney's fees, and all costs of collection, including court costs.

Signed [Harold H. Heidingsfelder]
Company J. O. H. Construction Co., Inc.

When J. O. H. Construction failed to make payment, Pelican, claiming it was a holder of a negotiable instrument, sued Heidingsfelder to hold him personally liable for his failure to indicate a representative capacity on the credit agreement. He claims that a credit application is not a negotiable instrument and that he could not be held personally liable. Is he right? [*Pelican Plumbing Supply, Inc. v. J. O. H. Construction Co., Inc.*, 653 So.2d 699 (La.)]

2. Abby Novel signed a note with the following on it: "Glen Gallwitz 1-8-2002 loaned me $5,000 at 6% interest a total of $10,000.00." The note did not contain a payment schedule or a time for repayment.

   Abby used the $10,000 as start-up money for her business and says that she orally agreed to repay the loan out of the proceeds from her first 1,000-product sales. Abby did not make any payments. Glen passed away and his son, as executor of his estate, demanded that Abby repay the $10,000 plus 6% interest for a total of $14,958 (the amount due as of April 2010). The trial court granted judgment for the estate. Abby has appealed, alleging that she repaid the note through the care she gave for Glen. The estate maintains that the instrument was a negotiable promissory note and that it is entitled to collect the amount due in cash. Who is correct and why? [*Gallwitz v. Novel*, 2011 WL 303253 (Ohio App.)]

3. Charter Bank of Gainesville had in its possession a note containing the following provision: "This note with interest is secured by a mortgage on real estate, of even date herewith, made by the maker hereof in favor of said payee…. The terms of said mortgage are by this reference made a part hereof." When the bank sued on the note, it said it was a holder of a negotiable instrument. Is this instrument negotiable? [*Holly Hill Acres, Ltd. v. Charter Bank of Gainesville*, 314 So.2d 209 (Fla. App.)]

4. On October 14, 1980, United American Bank of Knoxville made a $1,700,000 loan to Frederic B. Ingram. William F. Earthman, the president of the bank and a beneficiary of the loan, had arranged for the loan and prepared the loan documents. Mr. Ingram and Mr. Earthman were old friends, and Mr. Ingram had loaned Mr. Earthman money in the past. Mr. Ingram was in jail at the time of this loan and was unable tocomplete the documents for the loan. Mr. Earthman says that Mr. Ingram authorized him to do the loan so long as it did not cost him anything to do it.

   Also on October 14, 1980, Mr. Earthman prepared and executed a personal $1,700,000 note to Mr. Ingram, using a standard Commerce Union Bank note form. Mr. Earthman wrote "Frederic B. Ingram" in the space for identifying the lending bank and also filled in another blank stating that the note would be due "Eighteen Months after Date." With regard to the interest, Mr. Earthman checked a box signifying that the interest would be "At the Bank's 'Prime Rate' plus % per year."

   Mr. Earthman then sold both of the notes, which ended up in the hands of third parties (holders in due course) who demanded payment. Mr. Ingram raised the defense that he had not authorized Mr. Earthman to handle the transactions. The third parties said the notes were negotiable instruments and they were entitled to payment without listening to Mr. Ingram's defenses. Mr. Earthman said his note to Mr. Ingram as well as the bank note from Mr. Ingram were not negotiable and that they could both raise defenses to the third parties seeking payment.

   Who is correct? What do you think of Mr. Earthman's banking processes and procedures? What ethical issues do you see in these loan transactions? [*Ingram v. Earthman*, 993 S.W.2d 611 (Tenn.)]

5. The state of Alaska was a tenant in a large office building owned by Univentures, a partnership. The state made a lease payment of $28,143.47 to Univentures with state treasury warrant No. 21045102. Charles LeViege, the managing partner of Univentures, assigned the warrant to Lee Garcia. A dispute then arose among the Univentures partners, and the company notified the state that it should no longer pay LeViege the rent. The state placed a stop payment order on the warrant. Garcia claimed that he was a holder

of a negotiable instrument and that the state owed him the money. The state claimed that a warrant did not qualify as a negotiable instrument. The warrant was in writing, was signed by the governor of the state, provided a definite sum of $28,143.47, and stated that "it will be deemed paid unless redeemed within two years after the date of issue." The warrant stated that it was "payable to the order of Univentures." Does the warrant meet the requirements for a negotiable instrument? [*National Bank v. Univentures*, 824 P.2d 1377 (Alaska)]

6. Nation-Wide Check Corp. sold money orders through local agents. A customer would purchase a money order by paying an agent the amount of the desired money order plus a fee. The customer would then sign the money order as the remitter or sender and would fill in the name of the person who was to receive the money following the printed words "Payable to." In a lawsuit between Nation-Wide and Banks, a payee on some of these orders, the question was raised as to whether these money orders were checks and could be negotiable even though not payable to order or to bearer. Are the money orders negotiable instruments? [*Nation-Wide Check Corp. v. Banks*, 260 A.2d 367 (D.C.)]

7. George S. Avery signed a letter regarding the unpaid balance on a $20,000 promissory note owed to Jim Whitworth in the form of a letter addressed to Whitworth stating: "This is your note for $45,000.00, secured individually and by our Company for your security, due February 7, 1984." The letter was signed: "Your friend, George S. Avery." It was typed on stationery with the name of Avery's employer, V & L Manufacturing Co., Inc., printed at the bottom and the words "George Avery, President" printed at the top. Avery says he is not personally liable on the note. The court granted summary judgment for Whitworth and Avery appealed. Who is liable? [*Avery v. Whitworth*, 414 S.E.2d 725 (Ga. App.)]

8. Bellino made a promissory note that was payable in installments and contained the provision that on default of the payment of any installment, the holder had the option to declare the entire balance due and payable on demand. The note was negotiated to Cassiani, who sued Bellino for the full debt when there was a default on the installment. Is a note with an acceleration clause still negotiable? [*Cassiani v. Bellino*, 157 N.E.2d 409 (Mass.)]

9. Atlas Capital, LLC's sole member and manager was Weston Wade Sleater. Mr. Sleater signed two promissory notes totaling $4,000,000 as the maker of the notes. The signature blocks of the notes read, "Weston Wade Sleater & Atlas Marketing Group, L.C.," but the signature was only that of Mr. Sleater. Mr. Sleater is referred to as the maker of the note. Mr. Sleater failed to pay the notes and a bankruptcy trustee brought suit to collect the remaining amount due. Mr. Sleater maintains that the notes are not his, but those of Atlas Capital. Is he correct? Is Mr. Sleater liable on the notes? Discuss the ambiguity issues as well as the way the notes were signed. [*In re Bedrock Marketing*, LLC, 404 B.R. 929 (D. Utah)]

10. Lloyd and Mario Spaulding entered into a contract to purchase property from Richard and Robert Krajcir. The two Spaulding brothers signed a promissory note to the Krajcir brothers with the following language: "The amount of $10,000 [is] to be paid sellers at the time of the initial closing [delivery of the deed]; plus, the principal amount payable to sellers at the time of the final indorsement of the subject H.U.D. loan." In litigation over the note, the Spauldings said it was not a negotiable instrument. The lower court found it to be a negotiable promissory note and the Spaulding partners appealed. Is the note negotiable? [*Krajcir v. Egid*, 712 N.E.2d 917 (Ill. App.)]

11. Is the following instrument negotiable?

    I, Richard Bell, hereby promise to pay to the order of Lorry Motors Ten Thousand Dollars ($10,000) upon the receipt of the final distribution from the estate of my deceased aunt, Rita Dorn. This negotiable instrument is given by me as the down payment on my purchase of a 1986 Buick to be delivered in three weeks.

    Richard Bell (signature).

12. Smith has in his possession the following instrument:

    September 1, 2003

    I, Selma Ray, hereby promise to pay Helen Savit One Thousand Dollars ($1,000) one year after *date. This instrument was given for the purchase of Two Hundred (200) shares of Redding Mining Corporation, Interest 6%.*

Selma Ray (signature).

What is this instrument? Is it negotiable?

13. Master Homecraft Co. received a promissory note with a stated face value from Sally and Tom Zimmerman. The note was payment for remodeling their home and contained unused blanks for installment payments but contained no maturity date. When Master Homecraft sued the Zimmermans on the note, the couple argued that they should not be liable on the note because it is impossible to determine from its face the amount due or the date of maturity. Decide. [*Master Homecraft Co. v. Zimmerman*, 22 A.2d 440 (Pa.)]

14. A note from Mark Johnson with HealthCo International as payee for $28,979.15 included the following language:

    [p]ayable in ________, Successive Monthly Installments of $ Each, and in 11 Successive Monthly Installments of $2,414.92 Each thereafter, and in a final payment of $2,415.03 thereafter. The first installment being payable on the ________ day of ______ 20 ______, and the remaining installments on the same date of each month thereafter until paid.

    Johnson signed the note. Is it negotiable? [*Barclays Bank, P.L.C. v. Johnson*, 499 S.E.2d 769 (N.C. App.)]

15. The text of a handwritten note stated simply that "'I Robert Harrison owe Peter Jacob $25,000 …,' /s/ Robert Harrison." Peter Jacob sought to use the handwritten note as a negotiable promissory note. Can he? [*Jacob v. Harrison*, 49 UCC Rep. Serv. 2d 554 (Del. Super.)]

CPA QUESTIONS

1. A company has in its possession the following instrument:

> $500.00 — Dayton, Ohio, October 2, 1987
>
> Sixty days after the date I promise to pay to the order of
>
> Cash
>
> Five Hundred Dollars
>
> at Miami, Florida
>
> Value received with interest at the rate of nine percent. This instrument is secured by a conditional sales contract.
>
> No. 11 Due Dec. 1, 1987
>
> Craig Burk
>
> Craig Burk

This instrument is:

a. Not negotiable until December 1, 1987.

b. A negotiable bearer note.

c. A negotiable time draft.

d. A nonnegotiable note because it states that it is secured by a conditional sales contract.

2. The instrument shown here is a:

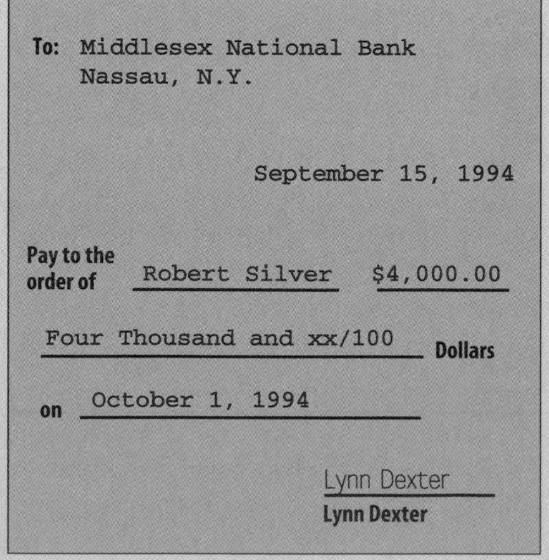

To: Middlesex National Bank
Nassau, N.Y.

September 15, 1994

Pay to the order of Robert Silver $4,000.00

Four Thousand and xx/100 Dollars

on October 1, 1994

Lynn Dexter

Lynn Dexter

a. Draft
b. Postdated check
c. Trade acceptance
d. Promissory note

3. Under the commercial paper article of the UCC, for an instrument to be negotiable, it must:
   a. Be payable to order or to bearer.
   b. Be signed to the payee.
   c. Contain references to all agreements between the parties.
   d. Contain necessary conditions of payment.

4. An instrument reads as follows:

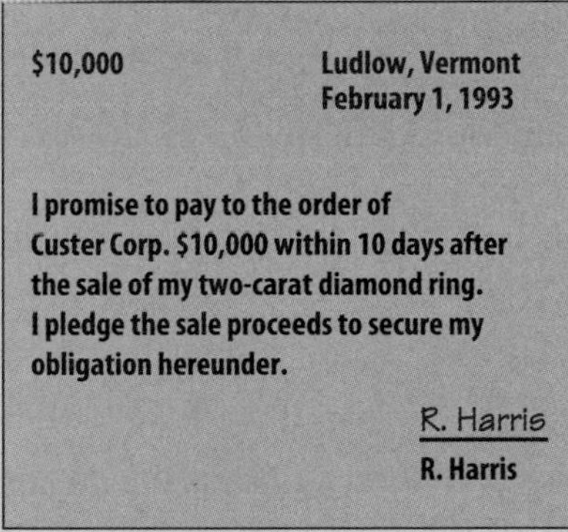

$10,000 Ludlow, Vermont
February 1, 1993

I promise to pay to the order of Custer Corp. $10,000 within 10 days after the sale of my two-carat diamond ring. I pledge the sale proceeds to secure my obligation hereunder.

R. Harris
R. Harris

   Which of the following statements correctly describes this instrument?
   a. The instrument is nonnegotiable because it is not payable at a definite time.
   b. The instrument is nonnegotiable because it is secured by the proceeds of the sale of the ring.
   c. The instrument is a negotiable promissory note.
   d. The instrument is a negotiable sight draft payable on demand.

5. Which of the following instruments is subject to the provisions of the Negotiable Instruments Article of the UCC?
   a. A bill of lading
   b. A warehouse receipt
   c. A certificate of deposit
   d. An investment security

6. Under the Negotiable Instruments Article of the UCC, which of the following statements is correct regarding a check?
   a. A check is a promise to pay money.
   b. A check is an order to pay money.
   c. A check does not need to be payable on demand.
   d. A check does not need to be drawn on a bank.

Transfers of Negotiable Instruments and Warranties of Parties

learningoutcomes

After studying this chapter, you should be able to

LO.1 Explain the difference between negotiation of order paper and negotiation of bearer paper

LO.2 List the types of indorsements and describe their uses

LO.3 Determine the legal effect of forged and unauthorized indorsements

LO.4 Be familiar with the forged payee impostor exceptions

LO.5 List the indorser's warranties and describe their significance

Much of the commercial importance of negotiable instruments lies in the ease with which they can be transferred. This chapter covers the requirements for, and issues in, the transfer or negotiation of negotiable instruments.

CPA A. Transfer of Negotiable Instruments

Negotiable instruments are transferred by a process known as *negotiation.*

1. Effect of Transfer

When a contract is assigned, the transferee has the rights of the transferor. The transferee is entitled to enforce the contract but, as assignee, has no greater rights than the assignor. The assignee is in the same position as the original party to the contract and is subject to any defense that could be raised in a suit on an assigned contract.

When a negotiable instrument is transferred by negotiation, the transferee becomes the *holder of the paper.* A holder who meets certain additional requirements may also be a **holder in due course.** The status of holder in due course gives immunity from certain defenses that might have been asserted against the transferor (see Chapter 30 for a discussion of the rights and role of a holder in due course).

2. Definition of Negotiation

Under UCC §3-201(a), **negotiation** means "a transfer of possession . . . of an instrument by a person other than the issuer to a person who thereby becomes a holder."[1] Negotiation, then, is simply the transfer of a negotiable instrument in such a way that the transferee becomes a holder.[2] A **holder** is different from a possessor or an assignee of the paper. A holder is a transferee in possession of an instrument that runs to her. An instrument runs to a party if it is payable to her order, is indorsed to her, or is bearer paper.

3. How Negotiation Occurs: The Order or Bearer Character of an Instrument

The order or bearer character of the paper determines how it may be negotiated. The order or bearer character of an instrument is determined according to the words of negotiability used (see Chapter 28 for a complete discussion of order and bearer words of negotiation and more examples of bearer versus order instruments). The types of instruments that qualify as bearer paper include those payable to bearer as well as those payable to the order of "Cash" or payable in blank. The character of an instrument is determined as of the time negotiation takes place even though its character originally or at the time of prior transfers may have been different.

CPA B. How Negotiation Occurs: Bearer Instruments

UCC §3-201(b) provides, "If an instrument is payable to bearer, it may be negotiated by transfer of possession alone."[3] If an instrument qualifies for bearer status, then it is negotiated by **delivery** to another.[4] Delivery can be accomplished by actual transfer of possession wherein the transferee has possession of the instrument, or constructive transfer, whereby the transferee has exclusive access. **For Example,** when mortgage lenders finance a home mortgage, they often transfer the underlying promissory note on the mortgage several times through financial streams. Many of the underlying problems in the financial market's collapse in 2008 were the large bundles of the promissory notes tied to home mortgages that were in amounts above the value of the mortgaged properties. Who held the bearer promissory notes became a critical issue in foreclosures. Bearer paper is negotiated to a person taking possession of it without regard to whether such possession is lawful. Because delivery of a bearer instrument is effective negotiation, it is possible for a thief or an embezzling officer to transfer title to a bearer instrument. Such a person's presence in the chain of transfer does not affect the rights of those who have taken the bearer instrument in good faith.[5] The *Emmons v. Capital One* case deals with an indorsement issue and foreclosure rights.

[1] Revised UCC §3-201(a).

[2] Revised UCC §3-201; *In re Kang Jin Hwang,* 396 B.R. 757 (Bkrtcy C.D. Cal. 2008); *In re Miller,* 666 F.3d 1255 (10th Cir. 2012).

[3] Revised UCC §3-201(b).

[4] If no payee is named, the instrument is bearer paper and is negotiated by delivery. *DCM Ltd. Partnership v. Wang,* 555 F. Supp. 2d 808 (E.D. Mich. 2008); *Waldron v. Delffs,* 988, S.W.2d 182 (Tenn. App. 1999).

[5] Revised UCC §§3-202 and 3-204; *Knight Pub. Co., Inc. v. Chase Manhattan Bank, N.A.,* 479 S.E.2d 478 (N.C. App. 1997); review denied 487 S.E.2d 548 (N.C. 1997); *In re Federal-Nogul Global, Inc.,* 319 B.R. 363 (D.Del. 2005).

Emmons v. Capital One, 2012 WL 773288 (S.D. Miss. 2012)

The Blank Indorsement Draws a Blank on Wrongful Foreclosure

On September 22, 2006, Richard and Sabrina Emmons (plaintiffs) signed an adjustable rate promissory note and deed of trust with Chevy Chase Bank (now known as Capital One) for a property located in Vancleave, Mississippi. The note indicates that "[t]he Lender or anyone who takes this Note by Transfer and who is entitled to receive payments under this Note is called the 'Note Holder.'" According to the terms of the deed of trust, "MERS (Mortgage Electronic Recording System) is the beneficiary under this Security Instrument." Based on the assignment of deed of trust, executed on April 9, 2010, MERS then assigned the Emmons' deed of trust to U.S. Bank as trustee.

The deed of trust listed MERS and MERS' successors and assigns as beneficiary and nominee. On April 9, 2010, MERS assigned the deed of trust to U.S. Bank. The Emmons defaulted on their payments. The deed of trust provides for a power of sale in the event of the borrowers' default—a right which U.S. Bank then proceeded with through a non-judicial foreclosure (power of sale). The Emmons then filed suit alleging, among other things, wrongful foreclosure because they claimed U.S. Bank was not a holder of the promissory note.

JUDICIAL OPINION

WALKER, Judge…Plaintiffs' primary contention is that U.S. Bank did not have standing to conduct a non-judicial foreclosure based on ambiguities regarding U.S. Bank's status as holder of the note. Plaintiffs assert that only the holder of the note can conduct a foreclosure and that a note indorsed in-blank, such as occurred in this case, is not sufficient to demonstrate that U.S. Bank was the holder of Plaintiffs' note. Consequently, U.S. Bank did not have standing to conduct the judicial foreclosure.

The Mississippi Code distinguishes between a special indorsement and a blank indorsement. If an indorsement is made by the holder of an instrument, whether payable to an identified person or payable to bearer, and the indorsement identifies a person to whom it makes the instrument payable, it is a "special indorsement." When specially indorsed, an instrument becomes payable to the identified person and may be negotiated only by the indorsement of that person.

If an indorsement is made by the holder of an instrument and it is not a special indorsement, it is a "blank indorsement." When indorsed in blank, an instrument becomes payable to bearer and may be negotiated by transfer of possession alone until specially indorsed.

Plaintiffs apparently concede that the note is indorsed in-blank, but argue that an in-blank indorsement does not prove U.S. Bank's holder status of the note and does not confer legal standing on U.S. Bank to conduct a non-judicial foreclosure.

Contrary to Plaintiffs' assertion, U.S. Bank's status as holder of the note indorsed in-blank is sufficient for U.S. Bank to enforce the provisions of the note. The holder of a negotiable paper is presumed prima facie to be a holder in due course. Likewise, the holder of a note indorsed in-blank is presumed prima facie to be the bona fide owner of it. Title to such a note passes by a delivery of the note. The law of Mississippi "does not require that a holder must present an original wet-ink contract in order to be the holder in due course" for purposes of initiating a non-judicial foreclosure. A negotiable instrument indorsed in-blank does not prevent the bearer of the instrument from enforcing its provisions. The burden to prove that the holder is not entitled to recover upon the note is cast on the party seeking to escape its provisions.

Plaintiffs contend that Defendants needed to show more than mere assignment of the deed of trust to prove U.S. Bank's status as holder. To the extent that Plaintiffs argue that U.S. Bank lacked standing to conduct a nonjudicial foreclosure based on a failure to provide conclusive proof that they were holders of the note, courts have routinely rejected this type of "show me the note" theory.

Plaintiffs also assert that pursuant to the Miss.Code Ann. §§ 75–3–201 and 75–3–302, Defendants must demonstrate that the current holder and any prior holders took title in good faith, for consideration, and not while in default. Plaintiffs' interpretation of Mississippi statutory law is incorrect. Section 201(b) indicates that "[i]f an instrument is payable to bearer, it may be negotiated by transfer of possession alone." The parties agree that the note was indorsed in-blank and therefore would be payable to the bearer of the instrument. Section 205(b) specifically provides that an instrument indorsed in-blank "may be negotiated by transfer of possession alone." Pursuant to Miss.Code § 75–3–301 a "'[p]erson entitled to enforce' an instrument means (i) the holder of the instrument". The provisions of Miss.Code Ann. 75–3–302(a) cited by Plaintiffs would be relevant only if Plaintiffs asserted a defense such as fraud or duress to the enforcement of the note.

The chain of events in this case, as demonstrated by the pleadings and attached documents, is rather straightforward. The assignment of the deed of trust from MERS to U.S. Bank demonstrates U.S. Bank's status as holder of the note. In other words, Plaintiffs owed the debt to U.S. Bank by way of transfer of the indorsed in-blank note and the assignment of the deed of trust from MERS to U.S. Bank. Hence, U.S. Bank was entitled to enforce the provisions of the documents, including the initiation of a non-judicial foreclosure, after Plaintiffs defaulted on the note. Based on the allegations in the pleadings examined in conjunction with the terms of the underlying note, deed of trust, and assignment of deed of trust, the Court concludes that U.S. Bank was the holder of the note and entitled to enforce its provisions. Therefore, as a matter of law, U.S. Bank did not wrongfully foreclose on Plaintiffs' property.

[The case is dismissed.]

Continued

QUESTIONS

1. If U.S. Bank was not the note holder, what would happen to the foreclosure/power of sale processes on the properties of those who are in default?
2. What was required for negotiation of the Emmons note?
3. What role does the deed of trust have with respect to the promissory note?

Ethics & the Law

Having Your Mortgage Set Aside

In cases such as the *Emmons v. Capital One* case, the borrowers bring suit seeking to have their mortgage obligations set aside on the basis of technicalities in the paperwork or the separation of the paperwork. Generally, these borrowers owe far more on their mortgages than their homes are worth. In some cases, the mortgages have been deemed invalid or the courts have held there was no authority for foreclosure because of the problems with note transfers and the right of foreclosure. Evaluate the ethics of the borrowers in seeking to have their mortgages set aside.

Even though a bearer instrument may be negotiated by a mere transfer of possession, the one to whom the instrument is delivered may require the bearer to indorse the instrument. This situation most commonly arises when a check payable to "Cash" is presented to a bank for payment. The reason a transferee of bearer paper would want an indorsement is to obtain the protection of an indorser's warranties from the bearer.[6] The bank wants an indorsement on a check made payable to "Cash" so that it can turn to the check casher in the event payment issues arise.

CPA C. How Negotiation Occurs: Order Instruments

UCC §3-201(b) provides, "if an instrument is payable to an identified person, negotiation requires transfer of possession of the instrument and its indorsement by the holder."[7] A negotiable instrument that is payable to the order of a specific party is *order paper,* which can be negotiated only through indorsement and transfer of possession of the paper.[8] **Indorsement** and transfer of possession can be made by the person to whom the instrument is then payable or by an authorized agent of that person.[9] The *Town of Freeport v. Ring* case shows how critical indorsements are.

Town of Freeport v. Ring, 727 A.2d 901 (Me. 1999)

The Tax Man Cometh, but He Can't Provide Your Indorsement

Thorton Ring was behind on his property taxes for his property in Freeport, Maine. When he received a check payable to his order from Advest, Inc., in the amount of $11,347.09, he wrote the following on the back of the check: "Payable to Town of Freeport Property Taxes 2 Main St."; he sent it along with a letter to the town offices. The letter included the following: "I have paid $11,347.09 of real estate taxes and request the appropriate action to redeem the corresponding property." Ring did nothing further and his property was then liened by the tax clerk. Ring objected

[6] The Uniform Electronic Transactions Act (UETA), promulgated by the National Conference of Commissioners on Uniform State Laws in July 1999 and enacted in 46 states, provides that the transfer of a note by electronic record affords the transferee the same rights as a tangible written note.

[7] Revised UCC §3-201(b). Although the modern spelling is "endorsement," the UCC has retained the British spelling of "indorsement."

[8] Revised UCC §3-204; *Unlimited Adjusting Group, Inc. v. Wells Fargo Bank, N.A.,* 94 Cal. Rptr. 3d 672 (Ca. App. 2009).

[9] Revised UCC §3-204. The UCC spellings are "indorse" and "indorser," the spellings used in this text. However, courts (including in some cases in this text) use the modern "endorse" and "endorser." *Jenkins v. Wachovia Bank,* 711 S. E.2d 80 (Ga. App. 2011).

Continued

because he had paid the taxes. The town argued that the check was not indorsed, and Ring thus had not paid the taxes in time to avoid the lien. The lower court found for the town and Ring appealed.

JUDICIAL OPINION

CLIFFORD, J.... The filing of a tax lien certificate with a registry of deeds by a town creates a tax lien mortgage to secure the payment of outstanding taxes. The tax lien mortgage continues to exist until the taxes are paid or until the lien is terminated by operation of law. A taxpayer has an eighteen month period following the filing of the tax lien certificate to redeem the property by paying the outstanding taxes, plus interest and fees. If the taxes, interest, and fees are not paid within eighteen months after the date of filing, the tax lien mortgage is deemed to have been foreclosed. Because the Town filed the tax lien certificate with the registry of deeds on September 7, 1995, Ring had to redeem his property by March 7, 1997. Ring delivered a check to the Town in January of 1997. The Superior Court, however, concluded that the check did not constitute payment of the outstanding taxes:

With an endorsement, Freeport would have been able to cash the check; without the endorsement, it is doubtful that Freeport could have cashed it. The Court concludes that the unendorsed check delivered by Thornton Ring to Freeport was not a tender of payment, and Freeport was not required to accept it as payment of any of the outstanding taxes.

With respect to a check that is made payable to the order of a specific person, negotiation occurs, and the person receiving the check becomes a holder of a negotiable instrument, if possession of the check is transferred and the check is indorsed by the transferor.

An indorsement is a signature of someone other than the maker, or some other designation identifying the indorser, that is made on an instrument for the purpose of negotiating the instrument.

The check Ring sent to the Town was issued by Advest, Inc., payable to the order of Thornton D. Ring. Because it was payable to Ring's order, the check could only be negotiated by Ring through indorsement and transfer of possession. Ring's signature, however, does not appear on the back of the check. The words that do appear on the back of the check—"Payable To Town of Freeport[/] Property Taxes[/]2 Main st[.]" —do not identify Ring. The words only indicate to whom the instrument should have been payable had the check been properly indorsed. Thus, the writing is an incomplete attempt to create a special indorsement. A special indorsement is an indorsement that identifies a person to whom the indorser is making the check payable. See *id.* The special indorsement still must be signed or otherwise indorsed by the person to whom the check was originally payable. Although Ring could attempt to prove that the words were intended to indorse the instrument in a judicial proceeding brought by the Town to gain payment of the check, payment for purposes of redemption in tax lien cases cannot be contingent upon proof at a judicial proceeding.

Ring contends that the signature of Advest, Inc. is a signature that constitutes a proper indorsement of the check. The statute explicitly states, however, that an indorsement is a signature of anyone other than the maker or issuer of the instrument. Advest, Inc. is the issuer of the check. Alternatively, Ring cites to section 3-1401's description of a signature in support of its position that the check was properly indorsed. That section, however, refers to the means through which indorsers can become liable on the instrument, so-called indorser's liability. That section is not applicable in the determination of whether an instrument is properly indorsed for purposes of receiving payment.

The statement included within the letter accompanying the check does not serve as a valid indorsement either. In determining whether an instrument is properly indorsed, any papers affixed to the instrument are considered part of the instrument. This language specifically references only "affixed" documents. Courts interpreting this language have concluded that a signature on a separate, unattached piece of paper is not an indorsement of the instrument. Ring does not dispute that there is no evidence on record to suggest that the letter was physically attached to the check. (An indorsement on a separate sheet of paper is technically called an allonge.) Many courts have held that signatures included on an allonge are only effective as an indorsement of an instrument if there is no room on the instrument itself for an indorsement.

Ring also contends that even in the absence of an indorsement, the check should have been accepted as payment of his outstanding taxes because the Town (1) had a statutory right to demand an indorsement of the check, or (2) was entitled to enforce the instrument without the indorsement. Title 11 M.R.S.A. § 3-1203(3) provides that "if an instrument is transferred for value and the transferee does not become a holder because of lack of indorsement by the transferor, the transferee has a specifically enforceable right to the unqualified indorsement of the transferor...." Section 3-1203(2) provides, "Transfer of an instrument, whether or not the transfer is a negotiation, vests in the transferee any right of the transferor to enforce the instrument...."

Even if the Town could demand an indorsement pursuant to § 3-1203(3), negotiation does not occur until the indorsement is made. Thus, at the time the check was received, the Town had a right to demand an indorsement, but could not go to the bank to demand payment of the check. Pursuant to 11 M.R.S.A. § 3-1203(2), the bank also had the right to enforce the instrument as the transferee of an instrument from a

Continued

holder. That right, however, could be enforced only through a judicial proceeding. Such contingent rights to receive payment are not sufficient to redeem property subject to a municipal tax lien. Checks are meant to be the functional equivalent of cash when they are properly issued and negotiated. If the Town has to institute a judicial proceeding to receive the cash equivalent of the check, the check has not served its purpose. The unindorsed check presented to the Town is not the type of payment the redemption option of the tax lien statute contemplates.

Because there is no genuine issue of material fact and the $11,347.09 check Ring sent to the Town does not constitute payment of the outstanding taxes as a matter of law, the tax lien certificate for the 1995 real estate taxes is deemed to have foreclosed on March 7, 1997 and the entry of the summary judgment in favor of the Town was proper.

[Judgment affirmed]

QUESTIONS

1. Why did Ring need to have the check delivered to the town within a certain time frame?
2. Was the signature of the issuer enough for the transfer of the check?
3. Was the check indorsed and payment made to the town?

4. Blank Indorsement

When the indorser merely signs a negotiable instrument, the indorsement is called a **blank indorsement** (see Figure 29-1). A blank indorsement does not indicate the person to whom the instrument is to be paid, that is, the transferee. A blank indorsement turns an order instrument into a bearer instrument. A person who possesses an instrument on which the last indorsement is blank is the holder.[10] **For Example,** if a check is payable to the order of Jill Barnes and Ms. Barnes indorses the check on the back "Jill Barnes," then the check that was originally an order instrument is now a bearer instrument. The check can now be transferred as bearer paper, which requires only delivery of possession. Once Jill Barnes's signature appears as a blank indorsement on the back, the check becomes transferrable simply by delivery of possession to another party.

5. Special Indorsement

A **special indorsement** consists of the signature of the indorser and words specifying the person to whom the indorser makes the instrument payable, that is, the **indorsee** (see Figure 29-2).[11] **For Example,** if Jill Barnes wrote on the back of the check payable to her "Pay to Jack Barnes, /s/ Jill Barnes," the check could be negotiated further only through the signature and possession of Jack Barnes. A special indorsement in this case continues an order instrument as an order

FIGURE 29-1 ***Blank Indorsement***

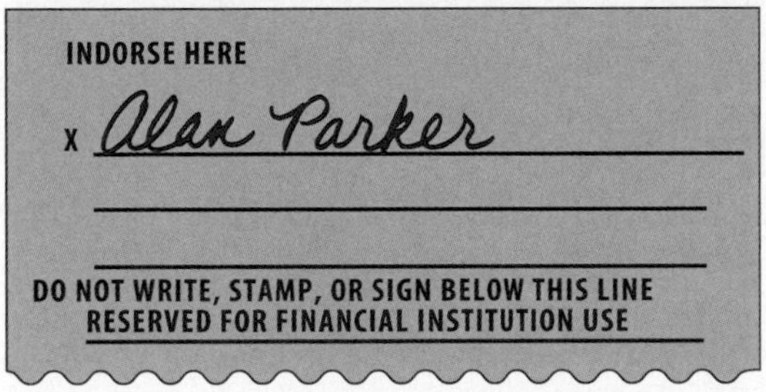

INDORSE HERE

x Alan Parker

DO NOT WRITE, STAMP, OR SIGN BELOW THIS LINE
RESERVED FOR FINANCIAL INSTITUTION USE

[10] *Farmers Bank of Maryland v. Chicago Title Ins. Co.,* 877 A.2d 1145, aff'd 905 A.2d 366 (Md. 2005).

[11] Revised UCC §3-205; *Chicago Title Ins. Co. v. Allfirst Bank,* 905 A.2d 366, 60 UCC Rep. Serv. 2d 864 (Md. 2006).

E-Commerce & Cyberlaw

New Flexibility for Cyberspace Commercial Paper

The Check Clearing for the 21st Century Act (sometimes called "Check 21") allows banks to use images of checks as a substitute for paper checks. The substitute check is the legal equivalent of the paper check that has, for so long, dominated U.S. commerce. Under Check 21, the bank is also able to send you electronic copies of your canceled checks. Even if you still opt for paper summaries of your account activity each month, the bank need not return physical checks and can send small reproductions of your checks grouped together on the statement. Recently, you have been able to secure faster credits to your accounts for deposited checks because ATMs scan the checks in, checks that are recognized immediately as deposits. All the new regulations on check substitutes are known as Regulation CC and can be found at Regulation CC, 12 C.F.R. §229.2(zz)(2).

instrument. If, after receiving the check, Jack Barnes simply signed it on the back, the check would become bearer paper and could be transferred through possession only.

Although words of negotiability are required on the front of negotiable instruments, it is not necessary that indorsements contain the word *order* or *bearer*. Consequently, the paper indorsed as shown in Figure 29-2 continues to be negotiable and may be negotiated further.[12]

An indorsement of "Pay to account [number]" is a special indorsement. In contrast, the inclusion of a notation indicating the debt to be paid is not a special indorsement.

6. Qualified Indorsement

A **qualified indorsement** is one that qualifies the effect of a blank or a special indorsement by disclaiming certain liability of the indorser to a maker or a drawee. This disclaimer is given by using the phrase "Without recourse" as part of the indorsement (see Figure 29-3). Any other words that indicate an intent to limit the indorser's secondary liability in the event the maker or the drawee does not pay on the instrument can also be used.[13]

The qualification of an indorsement does not affect the passage of title or the negotiable character of the instrument. It merely disclaims certain of the indorser's secondary liabilities for payment

FIGURE 29-2 *Special Indorsement*

[12] Only a check may use the phrase "Pay to" on its face and remain negotiable. All other instruments require words of negotiability on their face. Indorsements, on all instruments, need only "Pay to." UCC §3-110.
[13] *Antaeus Enterprises, Inc. v. SD-Barn Real Estate, LLC*, 480 F. Supp. 2d 734 (S.D.N.Y. 2007).

FIGURE 29-3 *Qualified Indorsement*

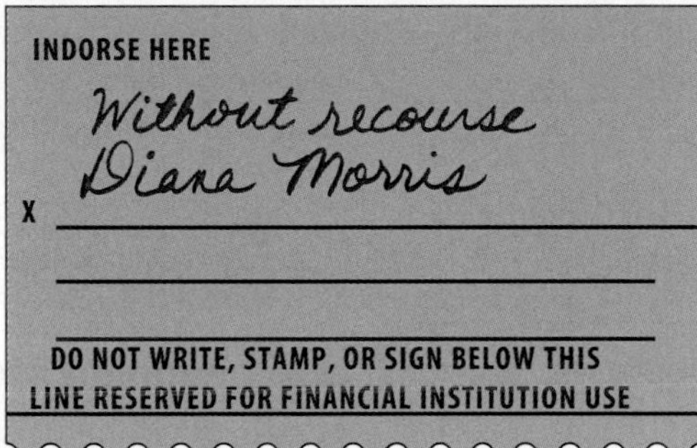

© Cengage Learning

of the instrument in the event the original parties do not pay as the instrument provides.

This qualified form of indorsement is most commonly used when the indorser is a person who has no personal interest in the transaction. **For Example,** an agent or an attorney who is merely indorsing a check of a third person to a client might make a qualified indorsement because he is not actually a party to the transaction.

7. Restrictive Indorsement

A **restrictive indorsement** specifies the purpose of the indorsement or the use to be made of the instrument (see Figure 29-4).[14] An indorsement is restrictive when it includes words showing that the instrument is to be deposited (such as "For deposit only"), when it is negotiated for collection or to an agent or a trustee, or when the negotiation is conditional.[15]

A restrictive indorsement does not prevent transfer or negotiation of the instrument once the initial restriction is honored. The indorsement "For deposit only" requires only that the first party who receives the instrument after the restriction is placed on it comply with that restriction. The indorsement "For deposit only" makes an instrument a bearer instrument for any bank. If the indorser's account number is added to a "For deposit only" indorsement, then

FIGURE 29-4 *Restrictive Indorsement*

INDORSE HERE
For deposit only
E.L. Martin
X
DO NOT WRITE, STAMP, OR SIGN BELOW THIS LINE
RESERVED FOR FINANCIAL INSTITUTION USE

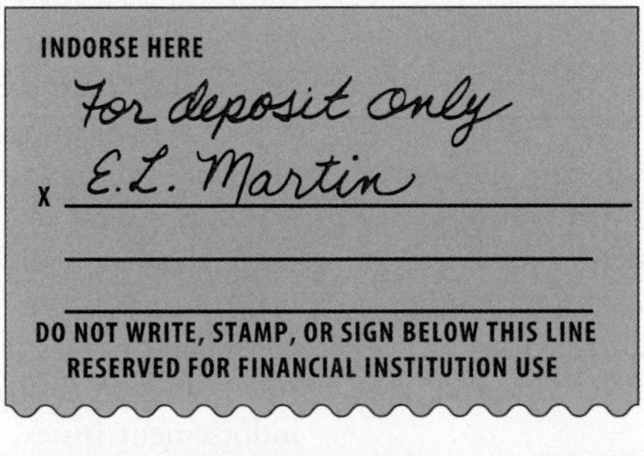

© Cengage Learning

[14] Revised UCC §3-206.

[15] *Id. Travelers Cas. and Sur. Co. of America v. Bank of America*, 2009 WL 5176769 (Sup. Ct. N.Y.).

the only party who can take the instrument after this restrictive indorsement is a bank with that account number. A restrictive indorsement reduces the risk of theft or unauthorized transfer by eliminating the bearer quality of a blank indorsement.

8. Correction of Name by Indorsement

Sometimes the name of the payee or the indorsee of an instrument is spelled improperly. **For Example,** H. A. Price may receive a paycheck that is payable to the order of "H. O. Price." If this error in Price's name was a clerical one and the check is indeed intended for H. A. Price, the employee may ask the employer to write a new check payable to the proper name. However, under Article 3, a much simpler solution allows the payee or indorsee whose name is misspelled to indorse the wrong name, the correct name, or both. The person giving or paying value or taking it for collection for the instrument may require both forms of the signature.[16]

This correction of name by indorsement may be used only when it was intended that the instrument should be payable to the person making the corrective indorsement. If there were in fact two employees, one named H. A. Price and the other H. O. Price, it would be forgery for one to take the check intended for the other and, by indorsing it, obtain the benefit of the proceeds of the check.[17]

A fictitious, assumed, or trade name is treated the same as a wrong name. The same procedure for correction of a misspelled name with indorsement of both names applies to these forms of payee identification as well.[18]

9. Bank Indorsement

To simplify the transfer and collection of negotiable instruments from one bank to another, "any agreed method which identifies the transferor bank is sufficient for the item's further transfer to another bank."[19] A bank could simply indorse with its Federal Reserve System number instead of using its name.

Likewise, when a customer has deposited an instrument with a bank but has failed to indorse it, the bank may make an indorsement for the customer unless the instrument expressly requires the payee's personal indorsement. Furthermore, the mere stamping or marking on the item of any notation showing that it was deposited by the customer or credited to the customer's account is effective as an indorsement by the customer.

10. Multiple Payees and Indorsements

Ordinarily, one person is named as the payee in the instrument, but two or more payees may be named. In that case, the instrument may specify that it is payable to any one or more of them or that it is payable to all jointly. **For Example,** if the instrument is made payable "to the order of Ferns and Piercy," then Ferns and Piercy are joint payees. The indorsements of both Ferns and Piercy are required to negotiate the instrument.

If the instrument is payable to **alternative payees** or if it has been negotiated to alternative indorsees, such as "Stahl or Glass" or "Stahl/Glass," it may be indorsed and delivered by either of them.

Under old Article 3, if the instrument was not clear on the relationship or types of multiple payees or indorsees, they were to be considered joint, and the signatures of all parties were required. Under Revised Article 3, when a court is faced with two or more payees who are separated by a comma or other symbol, for example, "Pay to the order of Jeff Bridges–Susan Sarandon," the court must first determine whether the symbols or separating marks are sufficiently clear to make the instrument payable jointly. If the court concludes that the instrument is ambiguous, then the preference is for alternative payees, which means that either Jeff or Susan could negotiate the instrument with one signature; they would not have to have the other's indorsement for negotiation. Under Revised Article 3, if the instrument is ambiguous, the payees or indorsees are considered payees in the alternative. The *Check City, Inc. v. L & T Enterprises* case deals with proper indorsement issues.

16 Revised UCC §3-204(d).
17 If a check is made payable to an individual "as guardian" for another, it cannot be negotiated until that individual is actually appointed as guardian. *Citibank v. Bank of Salem,* 35 UCC 2d 173 (W.D.N.Y. 1998).
18 *DCM Ltd. Partnership v. Wang,* 555 F. Supp. 2d (E.D. Mich. 2008).
19 Revised UCC §4-103.

Check City, Inc. v. L & T Enterprises, 237 P.3d 910 (Utah App. 2010)

Checking Indorsements at Check City

L & T Enterprises issued checks to one of L & T's subcontractors and one of that subcontractor's suppliers. Check City cashed the checks, but did so with the indorsement of only the subcontractor, not the supplier. The subcontractor had a long, positive history with Check City. Although the reverse side of the checks contained what at cursory glance might appear to be two signatures, even minimal attention to those signatures shows they are the subcontractor's business name and the signature of a presumably authorized employee, albeit in an order that is the opposite of what is customary. Both entries are in the same handwriting, and a prudent person cashing the checks could not possibly have mistaken the two entries for proper indorsements by both the subcontractor and the subcontractor's supplier.

Check City filed suit against L & T for negligence. The trial court held that L & T owed Check City a duty and that L & T breached that duty by failing to exercise ordinary care and substantially contributing to an alteration of an instrument or forged signature. L & T appealed.

JUDICIAL OPINION

ORME, Judge...Articles 3 and 4 of the U.C.C. outline a scheme for allocating the loss resulting from an altered [or forged] check among the parties involved in the check processing system...[through] a burden-shifting framework. The UCC differentiates between forged indorsements and missing indorsements.

Here, the district court based its ultimate ruling on UCC 3-406, which precludes a party that substantially contributes to an *altered or forged* instrument from asserting a claim against a party who accepts the instrument in good faith. However, the checks in this case were not altered or forged, but, instead, the indorsement of one of the joint payees was missing. Thus, the court based L & T's liability on an inapplicable section of the UCC, even though the action was based on common law negligence.

On the facts of this case, UCC 3-406 simply did not impose any duty in favor of Check City on L & T, and Check City bears the loss for cashing L & T's checks made payable to two payees when only one payee had indorsed them.

[The judgment in favor of Check City is reversed.]

QUESTIONS

1. What is the difference between a forged indorsement and a missing indorsement in terms of the liability of the parties?
2. What advice would you give to those who cash checks from contractors to subcontractors?

11. Agent or Officer Indorsement

An instrument may be made payable to the order of an officeholder. **For Example,** a check may read "Pay to the order of Receiver of Taxes." Such a check may be received and negotiated by the person who at the time is the receiver of taxes. This general identification of a payee is a matter of convenience, and the drawer of the check is not required to find out the actual name of the receiver of taxes at that time.

If an instrument is drawn in favor of an officer of a named corporation, the instrument is payable to the corporation, the officer, or any successor to such officer. Any of these parties in possession of the instrument is the holder and may negotiate the instrument.[20]

12. Missing Indorsement

When the parties intend to negotiate an order instrument but for some reason the holder fails to indorse it, there is no negotiation. The transfer without indorsement has only the effect of a contract assignment.[21] If the transferee gave value for the instrument (see Chapter 30 for more information on what constitutes giving value), the transferee has the right to require that the transferor indorse the instrument unqualifiedly and thereby negotiate the instrument.

[20] Revised UCC §3-110(cc)(2)(Ii).

[21] Revised UCC §3-204(d).

Thinking Things Through

The Minor with an Embezzling Conservator

Steven Powell died in a tragic accident at work, entitling his minor son, Cody, to approximately $252,000 in life insurance proceeds. Karen Unrue, Steven's sister, approached Elizabeth Powell, Steven's widow, and offered to manage the insurance proceeds for Cody.

The probate court appointed Karen Unrue and Travis Powell (Steven's brother) as co-conservators. The probate court also waived the bond requirement and ordered "that the funds of the minor child, [Cody], be deposited in a restricted account and that no funds be withdrawn or transferred from such account without written [o]rder of [the probate court]." The certificate of appointment and fiduciary letter included the following restriction: "No withdrawals without court order."

On Cody's behalf, Unrue received seven checks totaling $252,447.51. Three of the checks were made payable to her and Travis jointly and included the designation "Co-conservators For [Cody], A Minor" or "Co–Cn For Minor, [Cody]." The other four checks were made payable to Unrue and included the designation "As Conservator Of [Cody], A Minor." Unrue endorsed the checks without including her title as co-conservator. Unbeknownst to Travis, Unrue forged his name on the three checks made payable to her and Travis as co-conservators and took all the checks to the Pawleys Island Bank of America (BOA). Unrue had Lee Ann Yourko, a personal banker, open a certificate of deposit (CD) account titled "Karen M. Unrue Guardian [Cody]." Yourko collected the checks and took them to a teller, who processed the checks and deposited the proceeds into the CD account. Neither Yourko nor the teller questioned the conservator designation in the payee line of the checks.

A few days later, Unrue returned to the Pawleys Island BOA with a single check for $253.67 made payable to her "As Conservator For Cody A Minor." Unrue requested Meredith Lawrence, the branch manager, to open a Uniform Gift to Minors Act (UGMA) account titled, "Karen M. Unrue—cust [Cody]—UMGA [sic]." Lawrence did not question the conservator title on the payee line of the check. Lawrence also failed to notice that Unrue endorsed the check without including her title.

Approximately a month later, after the CD matured, Unrue withdrew 100% of the funds, $253,991.50, from the CD account. Unrue took the funds to the Pawleys Island BOA and deposited them in the UGMA savings account. Over the next several months, Unrue made seven online transfers totaling $258,500 from the UGMA savings account to her personal checking account.

Mrs. Powell brought suit against BOA for its negligence in managing the accounts and failing to notice the indorsement requirements and restrictions imposed on the conservator. Would Bank of America be liable? Be sure to discuss what you know about indorsement requirements and restrictive indorsements in formulating your answer. **[*Cody P. v. Bank of America, N.A.*, 720 S.E.2d 473 (S.C. App. 2011)]**

CPA D. Problems in Negotiation of Instruments

The issues of signatures and requirements for negotiation can become quite complex when issues such as forgery, employee misconduct, and embezzlement arise.

13. Forged and Unauthorized Indorsements

A **forged** or **unauthorized indorsement** is not a valid indorsement.[22] Accordingly, anyone who has possession of a forged instrument is not a holder because the indorsement of the person whose signature was forged was necessary for effective negotiation of the instrument to the possessor. However, proof of forgery requires expert testimony and a split from a pattern of payments is helpful.[23]

If payment of an instrument is made to one claiming under or through a forged indorsement, the payor ordinarily remains liable to the person who is the rightful owner of the paper. However, if the rightful owner has been negligent and contributed to the forgery or unauthorized signature

[22] Revised UCC §3-403(2); Steven B. Dow, "Imposter Rule and the Problem of Agency under the Revised Uniform Commercial Code: New Risks for Bank Customers?" 16 Comm. L.J. 199 (2001); *Bloom v. G.P.F.*, 588 So.2d 607 (Fla. App. 1991).

[23] *Wagner v. Bank of America*, 51 UCC Rep. Serv. 2d 781 (Cal. App. 2003).

problem, there are exceptions to these general rules on liability for forged indorsements (see Chapter 30 for more information on the rights and liabilities of the parties). *The B.D.G.S., Inc. v. Balio* case deals with the issue of verification of checks by the first party to accept them.

B.D.G.S., Inc. v. Balio, 861 N.E.2d 813, 829 N.Y.S.2d 449, 61 UCC Rep. Serv. 2d 530 (2006)

The Great Rite-Aid Heist

B.D.G.S., Inc., a New York corporation with headquarters in Washington owns a warehouse in Utica, New York. In 1991, B.D.G.S. entered into an oral agreement with two local men, Anthony Balio and his employee, Peter Duniec, to manage the warehouse. Their responsibilities included finding tenants and collecting rent, which was then to be forwarded to B.D.G.S. and deposited into its bank account in Washington. Balio and Duniec formed the Beechgrove Warehouse Corporation and maintained a business account in that name at Savings Bank of Utica (SBU).

Between 1996 and 2000, B.D.G.S. believed that one of its tenants, Rite-Aid, had been falling behind and failing to make its rent payments. B.D.G.S. later discovered that Rite-Aid had been making the payments, but 16 checks had been indorsed to Beechgrove Warehouse and deposited into Beechgrove's own SBU account. The checks had been made payable to DBGS (an apparent typographical error). With minor variations, there was a handwritten indorsement on the back of each check stating:

> *DBGS, Inc.*
> *Pay to the order of Beechgrove Warehouse*
> *For Deposit [followed by Beechgrove's SBU account number]*

A substantial refund check from Niagara Mohawk in the amount of $427,781.82 had similarly been indorsed and deposited in the SBU account. B.D.G.S. filed suit against Balio, Duniec, Beechgrove Warehouse, and B. & R. Motor Express, Inc. (another corporation allegedly owned by Balio). B.D.G.S. also brought a claim against SBU. The jury found that SBU had not acted in accordance with reasonable commercial standards by accepting the checks for deposit. The appellate court affirmed and SBU appealed.

JUDICIAL OPINION

CIPARICK, Justice... Section 3-419(3) limits the liability of representatives—including, as relevant here, depositary banks. As long as the bank complies with any restrictive indorsements and acts in good faith and in accordance with reasonable commercial standards, its liability will be limited to "the amount of any proceeds remaining in [its] hands" (UCC 3-419[3]). Since the statute provides that the bank will not be "liable in conversion or otherwise," the defense applies to a claim for money had and received.

SBU argues that compliance with the restrictive indorsements is tantamount to acting in accordance with reasonable commercial standards under the statute. In support of this argument, SBU relies on *Spielman v Manufacturers Hanover Trust Co.*, 60 N.Y.2d 221, 469 N.Y.S.2d 69, 456 N.E.2d 1192 (1983). In that case, an attorney forged the payee's indorsement on a settlement check made out to a law firm, and the drawer of the check commenced an action against the depositary bank.

Spielman is inapposite. Most notably, the party bringing suit in *Spielman* was the drawer of the check, rather than—as here—the payee. The Court observed that a drawer generally will not have a cause of action against a depositary bank; "either the forgery is effective to transfer the instrument... [or] the depositary has received nothing of the drawer for which the drawer may recover" (*Spielman*, 60 N.Y.2d at 224, 469 N.Y.S.2d 69, 456 N.E.2d 1192). In those situations, the drawer's cause of action is against the drawee. However, the drawer will be permitted to recover from the depositary bank in the limited circumstances "when the depositary has acted wrongfully and yet the drawee has acted properly in honoring the check because the forgery is effective." There are no such limitations placed on a payee's ability to sue the depositary.

SBU places great emphasis on *Spielman's* holding that "[i]t is the direction to deposit to the account of the customer and the bank's action in honoring that direction which... establishes that the bank's action accorded with reasonable business practice for there are many instances in which a family member or a business may indorse for deposit funds to the *113 credit of another and a depositary is not on notice of chicanery because of it nor is it liable if it faithfully follows such a direction" (*Spielman*, 60 N.Y.2d at 228, 469 N.Y.S.2d 69, 456 N.E.2d 1192).

However, *Spielman* did not deal with section 3-419(3). In addition, it did not hold that, in all cases, compliance with restrictive indorsements is commercially reasonable. Plainly, there are situations where following the indorsements would not be reasonable. For example, it would not be reasonable for a bank to deposit a check according to restrictive indorsements that it had good cause to know were forged. Thus, compliance with such indorsements cannot be considered commercially reasonable as a matter of law under all circumstances.

Continued

In this case, the record supports the affirmed findings that SBU's actions were not commercially reasonable. There was expert testimony concerning aspects of the transactions at issue that should have raised red flags for SBU. Further, there was testimony indicating that the bank did not comply with its own procedures for handling business checks. As a result, the Appellate Division properly determined that SBU did not act in accordance with reasonable commercial standards.

[Affirmed].

QUESTIONS

1. What is the difference between a drawer action against a bank and a payee action?
2. Why is SBU liable when it did in fact deposit the checks?
3. What should SBU do in the future?

14. Quasi Forgeries: The Impostor Rule

The **impostor rule** provides three exceptions to the rule that a forged indorsement is not effective to validly negotiate an instrument. If one of the three impostor exceptions applies, the instrument is still effectively negotiated, even though there may have been a forgery of an indorsement.

(A) When the Impostor Rule Applies. The impostor rule applies in cases where an indorser is impersonating a payee and in two cases where the indorser is a dummy payee.[24]

(1) Impersonating Payee.

The impersonation of a payee in the impostor rule exception includes impersonation of the agent of the person who is named as payee. **For Example,** if Jones pretends to be the agent of Brown Corporation and thereby obtains a check payable to the order of the corporation, the impostor exception applies.

(2) Dummy Payee.

Another impostor scenario arises when the preparer of the instrument intends that the named payee will never benefit from the instrument. Such a "dummy" payee may be an actual or a fictitious person. This situation arises when the owner of a checking account wishes to conceal the true purpose of taking money from the account at the bank. The account owner makes out a check purportedly in payment of a debt that in fact does not exist.[25]

(3) Dummy Payee Supplied by Employee.

The third impostor situation arises when an agent or employee of the maker or the drawer has supplied the name to be used for the payee, intending that the payee should not have any interest in the paper.[26] This last situation occurs when an employee fraudulently causes an employer to sign a check made to a customer or another person, whether existing or not. The employee does not intend to send it to that person but rather intends to forge the latter's indorsement, cash the check, and keep the money. This exception to the impostor rule imposes responsibility on employers to have adequate internal controls to prevent employees from taking advantage of an accounting system with loopholes so that others are not required to bear the cost of the employer's lack of appropriate precautions.

(B) Effect of Impostor Rule. When the impostor rule is applicable, any person may indorse the name of the payee. This indorsement is treated as a genuine indorsement by the payee and cannot be attacked on the ground that it is a forgery. This recognition of the fictitious payee's signature as valid applies even though the dummy payee of the paper is a fictitious person.[27]

(C) Limitations on Impostor Rule. The impostor rule does not apply when there is a valid check to an actual creditor for a correct amount owed by the drawer and someone later forges the payee's name. The impostor

[24] Revised UCC §3-405; *Mills v. U.S. Bank*, 83 Cal. Rptr. 146 (Cal. App. 2008).

[25] *State Sec. Check Cashing, Inc. v. American General Financial Services (DE)*, 972 A.2d 882 (Md. 2009).

[26] *Advocate Health and Hospitals Corp. v. Bank One*, 810 N.E.2d 962 (Ill. App. 2004).

[27] *Bank of Nichols Hills v. Bank of Oklahoma*, 196 P.3d 984 (Okla. App. 2008). *Bank of Glen Burnie v. Elkridge Bank*, 707 A.2d 438 (Md. App. 1988), *State Sec. Check Cashing, Inc. v. American General Financial Services*, 972 A.2d 882 (Md. 2009).

rule does not apply in this situation even if the forger is an employee of the drawer.

Even when the unauthorized indorsement of the payee's name is effective by virtue of the impostor rule, a person forging the payee's name is subject to civil and criminal liability for making such an indorsement.

For the impostor rule to apply, the holders or the takers of the instrument must show that they took the instrument (1) in good faith and (2) for payment or collection. The *Unlimited Adjusting Group Inc. v. Wells Fargo Bank* explains what happens when there is underlying fraud, but the check is genuine and authorized.

Unlimited Adjusting Group Inc. v. Wells Fargo Bank, 94 Cal. Rptr. 3d. 672 (2009)

Sorry, Charlie Walks Away with the $6.3 Million

Won Charlie Yi solicited money from investors in the Korean–American community (plaintiffs) by representing that he would invest their money in brokerage accounts at Carlin Equities Corporation, a nationally recognized broker-dealer based in New York. Yi, however, did not invest the money he received from the plaintiffs at all. Instead, Yi registered the name "Carlin Co." as a fictitious name under which he did business. He opened a bank account at Wells Fargo in the name of "Won Charlie Yi dba Carlin Co." Between January and September of 2003, Yi received eight checks, totaling $6.3 million, payable to "Carlin Co.," "Carlin Corp." or "Carlin Corporation." Yi deposited the checks into his Wells Fargo account and absconded with plaintiffs' money. He was later apprehended by federal authorities and convicted of a variety of criminal fraud charges.

The defrauded investors filed suit against Wells Fargo to recover their losses for the bank's lack of ordinary care in being certain that the checks deposited were deposited with the intended payee. A jury found in favor of Wells Fargo and the investors appealed.

JUDICIAL OPINION

MOSK, Judge...The evidence at trial was undisputed that (1) plaintiffs issued checks payable to "Carlin Co.," "Carlin Corp." and "Carlin Corporation"; (2) plaintiffs intended those designations to refer to Carlin Equities Corporation; and (3) Carlin Equities Corporation was the intended payee of the checks.

The identity of the payee is not determined by the name written on the check. Rather, the payee is determined by the intent of the person who signs the check as, or on behalf of, the drawer—that is, the signer. This rule is of particular importance when it is unclear from the face of the check to whom the check is payable. For example, if a check is made payable to "John Smith" and two or more people share that name, the intent of the signer will determine which John Smith is the payee. Similarly, if the signer intended that John Smith would be the payee but misidentified John Smith as "John Jones" on the check, the payee is nevertheless John Smith, not some other person named John Jones.

The intended payee may negotiate a check by indorsing it and depositing it in his or her bank account. Some provisions of Articles 3 and 4 serve to allocate losses due to the payment of unauthorized or fraudulent checks. In general, those provisions place the burden of loss on the party best able to prevent or to insure against the loss. That section allocates to the drawer losses in certain circumstances in which it is presumed the drawer failed to exercise due care to avoid the loss.

Relevant here is section 3404, subdivision (b)(i). In effect, subdivision (b)(i) shields a bank from liability for negotiating an unauthorized or fraudulent check by deeming an indorsement to be effective if (1) the signer of the check did not intend that the named payee would have an interest in the check—that is, the named payee was not the intended payee; and (2) the check was either indorsed in a name substantially similar to that of the named payee, or deposited to an account in a name substantially similar to that of the named payee."In applying section 3–404(b), the key issue is whether the person signing as or on behalf of the drawer ... intended that the [named] payee have no interest in the [check]....[T]he section applies where the ... drawer issues an instrument intending that the named payee have no interest in the instrument. Because the drawer ... knows that there will not be a proper indorsement, ... it is unfair to shift the loss to a subsequent purchaser or payer whose fault is minimal."

By way of example, in a typical case in which section 3404, subdivision (b)(i) would apply, an employee of a company makes out a check on the employer's account to a supplier of the employer. The employee intends when he signs the check that it will never be paid to the supplier. Instead, the employee intends to forge an indorsement in the supplier's name and deposit the check to his or her own account, or to another account controlled by the employee or a confederate.

Continued

In such a case, the employee never intended the supplier to have an interest in the check.

As this example illustrates, the typical case under section 3404, subdivision (b)(i) involves a situation in which the signer issues the check with fraudulent or other wrongful intent.

In the usual case, section 3404 is asserted by a bank as a *defense* against a drawer's claim of improper payment, rather than—as in this case—by the drawer as an affirmative basis for relief against the bank. This is because a drawer typically will seek compensation for payment of an unauthorized or fraudulent check from his or her own bank—that is, the payor bank—on the theory that the check was not properly payable. The payor bank may then seek compensation from the depositary bank (or other collecting bank) on the theory that the depositary bank breached its warranties as the transferor or presentor of the check.

In some cases the person taking the check might have detected the fraud and thus have prevented the loss by the exercise of ordinary care. In those cases, if that person failed to exercise ordinary care, it is reasonable that the person bear loss to the extent the failure contributed to the loss.... [T]he most likely defendant is the depositary bank that took the check and failed to exercise ordinary care.

The undisputed evidence at trial was that plaintiffs issued the checks at Park's direction and that Park was, in effect, the signer—that is, "the person whose intent determines to whom the instrument is payable." In the circumstances of this case, section 3034, subdivision (b)(i) would apply only if Park did not intend the named payee ("Carlin Co." or "Carlin Corp." or "Carlin Corporation") to be the intended payee ("Carlin Equities Corporation"). If this were so, then plaintiffs could try to prove that Wells Fargo was negligent under section 3404, subdivision (d). The undisputed evidence at trial, however, established the contrary. Thus, plaintiffs cannot recover under section 3404.

Plaintiffs' argument that section 3404, subdivision (b)(i) applies to this case is premised on Park's omission of the word "Equities" from the payee designation on the checks. But to accept plaintiffs' argument would mean that section 3404, subdivision (b)(i) applies in *every* case in which a drawer unknowingly or mistakenly misidentifies a payee—even when, as here, the variance between the payee's actual name and the designation on the check is not substantial.

In this case, the signer believes the named payee and the intended payee are the same person or entity. Yi presented to and plaintiffs signed, among other documents, limited powers of attorney in favor of Carlin Equities Corporation and agreements entitled "Carlin Equities Corporation Professional Trader Supplemental Agreement." The investors all "agree[d] to invest the moneys through Carlin Equities Corp."

[The judgment is affirmed].

QUESTIONS

1. What is different about this situation and the fictitious payee exception?
2. Evaluate this statement, "UCC Article 3 does not provide protection for checks written to bad fund managers." Is it true or false? Explain.
3. How would you have advised the investors to make their payments to Charlie in order to avoid this embezzlement?

(D) Negligence of Drawee not Required. The impostor rule applies without regard to whether the drawee bank acted with reasonable care.

15. Effect of Incapacity or Misconduct on Negotiation

A negotiation is effective even though (1) it was made by a minor or any other person lacking capacity; (2) it was an act beyond the powers of a corporation; (3) it was obtained by fraud, duress, or a mistake of any kind; or (4) the negotiation was part of an illegal transaction or was made in breach of duty. The rights of the parties in these types of negotiations depends on who holds the instrument (see Chapter 30).

16. Lost Instruments

The liability on lost instruments depends on who is demanding payment from whom and on whether the instrument was order or bearer paper when it was lost.

(A) Order Instruments. If the lost instrument is order paper, the finder does not become the holder because the instrument has not been indorsed and delivered by the person to whom it was then payable. The former holder who lost it is still the rightful owner of the instrument.

(B) Bearer Instruments. If the lost instrument is in bearer form when it is lost, the finder, as the possessor of a bearer instrument, is the holder and is entitled to enforce payment.

CPA E. Warranties in Negotiation

When a negotiable instrument is transferred by negotiation, the transferors give certain implied warranties.

17. Warranties of Unqualified Indorser

When the transferor receives consideration for the indorsement and makes an unqualified indorsement, the warranties stated in this section are given by the transferor by implication. No distinction is made between an unqualified blank indorsement and an unqualified special indorsement.

(A) Scope of Warranties. The warranties of the unqualified indorser are found in §3-416 of the Revised UCC and provide that the warrantor is a person entitled to enforce the instrument; that all signatures on the instrument are authentic and authorized; that the instrument has not been altered; that the instrument is not subject to a defense or claim; that the drawer of the draft has authorized the issuance of the item in the amount for which the item is drawn; and that the warrantor has no knowledge of any insolvency proceeding with respect to the maker or acceptor.[28]

Those who present an instrument for payment (see Chapter 30), or the last party in line before the payor, make three warranties: that the warrantor is entitled to enforce the draft or authorized to obtain payment or acceptance of the draft; that the draft has not been altered; and that the warrantor has no knowledge that the signature of the drawer of the draft is unauthorized.[29]

If a forged indorsement has appeared during the transfer of the instrument, and there is a refusal to pay because of that problem, the last party who is a holder may turn to her transferor to recover on the basis of these implied warranties. These warranties give those who have transferred and held the instrument recourse against those parties who were involved in the transfer of the instrument, although they were not parties to the original instrument.

(B) What Is not Warranted. The implied warranties stated here do not guarantee that payment of the instrument will be made. Similarly, the holder's indorsement of a check does not give any warranty that the account of the drawer in the drawee bank contains funds sufficient to cover the check. However, implied warranties do, for example, promise that the signatures on the instrument are not forged. Likewise, they promise that no one has altered the amount on the instrument. The warranties are not warranties of payment or solvency. They are simply warranties about the nature of the instrument. A holder may not be paid the amount due on the instrument, but if the lack of payment results from a forgery, the holder has rights against those who transferred the instrument with a forged signature.

(C) Beneficiary of Implied Warranties. The implied warranties of the unqualified indorser pass to the transferee and any subsequent transferees. There is no requirement that subsequent transferees take the instrument in good faith to be entitled to the warranties. Likewise, the transferee need not be a holder to enjoy warranty protections.

(D) Disclaimer of Warranties. Warranties may be disclaimed when the instrument is not a check. A disclaimer of warranties is ordinarily made by adding "Without warranties" to the indorsement.

(E) Notice of Breach of Warranty. To enforce an implied warranty of an indorser, the party claiming under the warranty must give the indorser notice of the breach. This notice must be given within 30 days after the claimant learns or has reason to know of the breach and the identity of the indorser. If proper notice is not given, the warranty claim is reduced by the amount of the loss that could have been avoided had timely notice been given.

18. Warranties of Other Parties

Warranties are also made by the indorser who indorses "Without recourse" and by one who transfers by delivery only.

(A) Qualified Indorser. The warranty liability of a qualified indorser is the same as that of an unqualified indorser.[30] A qualified indorsement means that the indorser does not assume liability for the payment of

[28] Revised UCC §3-416 (1990).

[29] Revised UCC §3-417. These warranties are for consumer accounts.

[30] Revised UCC §3-416(a).

the instrument as written. (See §3-416(4).) However, a qualified indorsement does not eliminate the implied warranties an indorser makes as a transferor of an instrument. The implied warranty that is waived by a qualified indorsement is the fourth warranty on defenses. A qualified indorser still makes the other warranties on signatures and alteration but waives the warranty on defenses.

(B) TRANSFER BY DELIVERY. When the negotiable instrument is negotiated by delivery without indorsement, the warranty liability of the transferor runs only to the immediate transferee. In all other respects, the warranty liability is the same as in the case of the unqualified indorser. **For Example,** Thomas, a minor, gives Craig his note payable to bearer. Craig transfers the note for value and by delivery only to Walsh, who negotiates it to Hall. Payment is then refused by Thomas, who chooses to disaffirm his contract. Hall cannot hold Craig liable. Craig, having negotiated the instrument by delivery only, is liable on his implied warranties only to his immediate transferee, Walsh. Likewise, because Craig did not indorse the note, he is not secondarily liable for payment of the note.

MAKE THE CONNECTION

SUMMARY

Negotiation is the transferring of a negotiable instrument in such a way as to make the transferee the holder. When a negotiable instrument is transferred by negotiation, the transferee becomes the holder of the instrument. If such a holder becomes a holder in due course, the holder will be immune to certain defenses.

An *order instrument* is negotiated by an indorsement and delivery by the person to whom it is then payable. A bearer instrument is negotiated by delivery alone. The order or bearer character of an instrument is determined by the face of the instrument as long as the instrument is not indorsed. If the instrument has been indorsed, the character is determined by the last indorsement.

A number of different kinds of indorsements can be made on negotiable instruments. When an indorser merely authenticates the instrument, the indorsement is called a *blank indorsement.* If the last indorsement is a blank indorsement, the instrument is bearer paper, which may be negotiated by change of possession alone. A special indorsement consists of the authentication by the indorser and words specifying the person to whom the indorser makes the instrument payable. If the last indorsement is a special indorsement, the instrument is order paper and may be negotiated only by an indorsement and delivery. A qualified indorsement eliminates the liability of the indorser to answer for dishonor of the paper by the maker or the drawee. A restrictive indorsement specifies the purpose of the instrument or its use.

A forged or unauthorized indorsement is no indorsement, and the possessor of the instrument cannot be a holder. The impostor rule makes three exceptions to this rule: dummy payee; employee fraud; and impersonating a payee.

A negotiation is effective even though (1) it is made by a minor, (2) it is an act beyond the powers of a corporation, (3) it is obtained by fraud, or (4) the negotiation is part of an illegal transaction. However, the transferor may be able to set aside the negotiation under general legal principles apart from the UCC. The negotiation cannot be set aside if the instrument is held by a person paying it in good faith and without knowledge of the facts on which the rescission claim is based.

The warranties of the unqualified indorser are as follows: (1) the warrantor is a person entitled to enforce the instrument; (2) all signatures on the instrument are authentic and authorized; (3) the instrument has not been altered; (4) the instrument is not subject to a defense or claim in recoupment of any party that can be asserted against the warrantor; with respect to any item drawn on a consumer account, which does not bear a handwritten signature purporting to be the signature of the drawer, that the purported drawer of the draft has authorized the issuance of the item in the amount for which the item is drawn; and (5) the warrantor has no knowledge of any insolvency proceeding commenced with respect to the maker or acceptor or, in the case of an unaccepted draft, the drawer.

LEARNING OUTCOMES

After studying this chapter, you should be able to clearly explain:

A. Transfer of Negotiable Instruments

B. How Negotiation Occurs: Bearer Instruments

C. How Negotiation Occurs: Order Instruments

LO.1 Explain the difference between negotiation of order paper and negotiation of bearer paper

See *Emmons v. Capital One* on pp. 558–559.

LO.2 List the types of indorsements and describe their uses

See *Check City v. L & T Enterprises* on p. 565.

D. Problems in Negotiation of Instruments

LO.3 Determine the legal effect of forged and unauthorized indorsements

See Thinking Things Through on p. 566.

LO.4 Be familiar with the forged payee impostor exceptions

See *B.D.G.S., Inc. v. Balio* on pp. 567–568.
See *Unlimited Adjusting Group, Inc. v. Wells Fargo Bank* on pp. 569–570.

E. Warranties in Negotiation

LO.5 List the indorser's warranties and describe their significance

See the discussion of warranties on p. 571.

KEY TERMS

alternative payees
blank indorsement
delivery
forged or unauthorized indorsement
holder
holder in due course
impostor rule
indorsee
indorsement
negotiation
qualified indorsement
restrictive indorsement
special indorsement

QUESTIONS AND CASE PROBLEMS

1. Corey Brandon Bumgarner, who was separated from his wife, Crystal, had an accident caused by Donald Wood that resulted in $2,164.46 in damages to Corey's vehicle. Wood's insurance carrier mailed a draft in the amount of $2,164.46 drawn on Fleet Bank of Hartford, Connecticut, payable to Corey, to his box at P.O. Box 153, Hillsboro, North Carolina. The draft was negotiated at Community Bank and Trust, and the name, "Crystal Bumgarner," was handwritten on the back of the draft. Corey's name was written below Crystal Bumgarner's name. Crystal Bumgarner's driver's license number was handwritten on the front of the draft.

   Corey Bumgarner filed suit to have the insurer pay him the $2,164.46. The insurer indicated that it had sent order paper, that it had been delivered, and that there was, therefore, no claim against it or Wood. The trial court found that there had been no delivery and that Bumgarner was entitled to another check. Wood and his insurer appealed. Who is correct about delivery and why? [*Bumgarner v. Wood*, 563 S.E.2d 309, 47 UCC Rep. Serv. 2d 1099 (N.C. App.)]

2. How could a check made out to "Joseph Klimas and his Attorney Fritzshall & Gleason & Blue Cross Blue Shield Company and Carpenters Welfare Fund" be negotiated further? What would be required? [*Chicago District Council of Carpenters Welfare Fund v. Gleason's Fritzshall*, 693 N.E.2d 412 (Ill. App.)]

3. An insurer issued a settlement check on a claim brought by an injured minor that was payable to "Trudy Avants attorney for minor child Joseph Walton, mother Dolores Carpenter 11762 S. Harrells Ferry Road #E Baton Rouge LA 70816." The lawyer indorsed the check. Two unknown individuals forged indorsements for the other two names and obtained payment of the check. The insurer sued the payor bank claiming the instruments were not properly payable because of the forged indorsements. The court is unclear whether the indorsement required is one for an either/or payee or joint payee. What advice can you offer the court as it faces this issue? [*Coregis Insurance Co. v. Fleet National Bank*, 793 A.2d 254 (Conn. App.)]

4. ABCO (Abbott Development Company) made a note payable to Western State Bank of Midland. The FDIC took over Western State's operations after it failed. ABCO had defaulted on the note, after which the FDIC permitted ABCO Homes to refinance the note, making its refinancing note payable to the FDIC. The FDIC indorsed its note to SMS Financial and inadvertently sent it to SMS as part of a large batch of documents. When litigation resulted on the note, SMS claimed it was the holder. Others challenged its status, saying that SMS never had the instrument delivered to it. The lower court held SMS was not a holder and SMS appealed. Is SMS a holder? Why or why not? [*SMS Financial, L.L.C. v. ABCO Homes, Inc.*, 167 F.3d 235 (5th Cir.)]

5. Jerry O. Peavy, Jr., who did not have a bank account of his own, received a draft from CNL Insurance America in the amount of $5,323.60. The draft was drawn on CNL's account at Bank South, N.A., and was "payable to the order of Jerry Peavy and Trust Company Bank." Jerry O. Peavy, Sr., allowed his son Peavy, Jr., to deposit the draft in his account at Bank South, N.A. Bank South accepted the draft and deposited it on December 29, 1992, with only the signature of Jerry Peavy, Jr. Both Mr. and Mrs. Peavy, Sr., then wrote checks on the amount of the draft using the full amount to benefit their son.

   On March 30, 1993, Bank South realized that it had improperly deposited the draft because it was lacking an indorsement from Trust Company Bank and reversed the transaction by debiting Mr. and Mrs. Peavy's account for the full amount of the draft. A bank officer then called Mr. and Mrs. Peavy, told them what had happened with the draft, and "threatened to send them to jail if they did not immediately deposit the sum of $5,323.60." The Peavys deposited that amount from the sale of some stock they owned and then filed suit against Bank South for its conversion of their son's draft and funds. Do the Peavys have a case? [*Peavy v. Bank South*, 474 S.E. 2d 690 (Ga. App.)]

6. Getty Petroleum distributes gasoline through dealer-owned stations. Customers who buy gas at a Getty station can pay by cash or credit card. When a customer uses a credit card, Getty processes the transactions, receives payment from the credit card company, and then issues computer-generated checks payable to dealers to reimburse them for their credit card sales. Many checks, however, are not intended for negotiation and are never delivered to the payees. Instead, Getty uses these checks for bookkeeping purposes, voiding them and then crediting the check amount toward the dealer's future purchases of gasoline from Getty.

   Lorna Lewis, a supervisor in Getty's credit processing department, stole over 130 checks, forged the indorsements of the payees by hand or rubber stamp, and then submitted the checks to American Express and other credit card companies to pay her own debts. The credit card companies then forwarded the checks through ordinary banking channels to Chemical Bank, where Getty had its checking account. Chemical Bank honored the checks Lewis had forged.

   Getty, on discovering the larceny of Lewis, sought recovery of the amounts from the credit card companies. Getty sought payment on 31 of the checks from American Express (which had been paid by Chemical Bank). At trial, a judge held American Express liable to Getty for $58,841.60. The appeals court found that American Express was grossly negligent in taking and cashing the checks and also held it liable. American Express appealed. Who wins and why? [*Getty Petroleum Corp. v. American Exp. Travel Related Services Co., Inc.*, 683 N.E.2d 311 (N.Y.)]

7. Snug Harbor Realty Co. had a checking account in First National Bank. When construction work was obtained by Snug Harbor, its superintendent, Magee, would examine the bills submitted for labor and materials. He would instruct the bookkeeper which bills were approved, and the bookkeeper then prepared the checks in accordance with his instructions. After the checks were signed by the proper official of Snug Harbor, Magee picked them up for delivery. Instead of delivering certain checks, he forged the signatures of the respective payees as indorsers and cashed the checks. The drawee bank then debited the Snug Harbor account with the amount of the checks. Snug Harbor claimed this was improper and sued the bank for the amount of the checks. The bank claimed it was protected by the impostor rule. Will the bank be successful? Explain. [*Snug Harbor Realty Co. v. First National Bank*, 253 A.2d 581 (N.J. Super.)]

8. Benton, as agent for Savidge, received an insurance settlement check from Metropolitan Life Insurance Co. He indorsed it "For deposit" and deposited it in Bryn Mawr Trust Co. in Savidge's account. What were the nature and effect of this indorsement? [*Savidge v. Metropolitan Life Ins. Co.*, 110 A.2d 730 (Pa.)]

9. Allstate Insurance Company issued a check payable to "Chuk N. Tang & Rosa C. Tang HWJT" with "Bank of America" on the second line and the following explanation on the front of the check: "Settlement of our rental dwelling loss caused by fire on 11/21/93." The Tangs indorsed the check and forged the indorsement of Bank of America. When Bank of America objected, the Tangs claimed that only they needed to sign the instrument for further negotiations. The check was intended as a joint payment for Bank of America as the mortgagee on the Tangs' rental property because the insurance policy required that the mortgagee be paid first before any proceeds went to the property owners. Bank of America sued Allstate. Is Bank of America entitled to recover for the lack of its indorsement? Was its indorsement necessary for further negotiation? [*Bank of America Nat'l Trust & Savings Ass'n v. Allstate Insurance Co.*, 29 F. Supp. 2d 1129 (C.D. Cal.)]

10. When claims filed with an insurance company were approved for payment, they were given to the claims clerk, who would prepare checks to pay those claims and then give the checks to the treasurer to sign. The claims clerk of the insurance company made a number of checks payable to persons who did not have any claims and gave them to the treasurer with the checks for valid claims, and the treasurer signed all of the checks. The claims clerk then removed the false checks, indorsed them with the names of their respective payees, and cashed them at the bank where the insurance company had its account. The bank debited the account of the insurance company with the amount of these checks. The insurance company claimed that the bank could not do this because the indorsements on the checks were forgeries. Was the insurance company correct? [*General Accident Fire & Life Assur. Corp. v. Citizens Fidelity Bank & Trust Co.*, 519 S.W. 2d 817 (Ky.)]

11. Eutsler forged his brother Richard's indorsement on certified checks and cashed them at First National Bank. When Richard sought to recover the funds from the bank, the bank stated that it would press criminal charges against Eutsler. Richard asked the bank to delay prosecution to give him time to collect directly from his brother. His brother promised to repay him the money but vanished some six months later without having paid any money. Richard sued the bank. What result? [*Eutsler v. First Nat'l Bank, Pawhuska*, 639 P.2d 1245 (Okal.)]

12. Michael Sykes, the president of Sykes Corp., hired Richard Amelung to handle the company's bookkeeping and deal with all of its vendors.

Amelung entered into an agreement with Eastern Metal Supply to help reduce Sykes's debt to Eastern. Whenever Sykes received a check, Amelung would sign it over to Eastern and allow it to keep 30 percent of the check amount. On 28 checks that totaled $200,000, Amelung indorsed the back as follows: "Sykes & Associates or Sykes Corporation, Richard Amelung." Amelung then turned the checks over to Eastern, and Eastern deposited them into its account at Barnett Bank. Eastern would then write one of its checks to Sykes Corp. for the 70 percent remaining from the checks. When Michael Sykes learned of the arrangement, he demanded the return of the 30 percent from Barnett Bank, claiming that it had paid over an unauthorized signature and that the indorsement was restricted and had been violated by the deposit into Eastern's account. What type of indorsement did Amelung make? Did he have the authority to do so? Should Sykes be reimbursed by Barnett? [*Sykes Corp. v. Eastern Metal Supply, Inc.*, 659 So. 2d 475 (Fla. App.)]

13. In January 1998, Allied Capital Partners, L.P. and American Factors Corporation were in the business of factoring accounts receivable for third-party clients. Allied assigned its factoring contract with Complete Design, Inc. to American but retained an interest in the factoring of Complete Design's invoices. On January 25, 1998, in payment of invoices issued by Complete Design, Clark Wilson Homes, Inc., issued a check for $6,823.15. The check was payable to:

    Complete Design
    Allied Capital Partners, L.P.
    2340 E. Trinity Mills Ste. 300
    Carrollton, Texas 75006

    On February 10, 1998, Clark Wilson issued another check for $26,329.32 made payable to:

    Complete Design
    Allied Capital Partners, L.P.
    2340 E. Trinity Mills Ste. 300
    Carrollton, Texas 75006

    Complete Design deposited both checks in its account at Bank One. However, Allied and American received none of the proceeds of the checks.

    Complete Design subsequently declared bankruptcy, and Allied and American made demand on Bank One for damages resulting from Bank One's conversion of the two checks. Bank One denied all liability for conversion of the checks. Allied and American subsequently sued Bank One, asserting conversion. Bank One filed a motion for summary judgment asserting that, because it was ambiguous to whom the checks at issue were payable, they were payable upon a single indorsement. The trial court granted Bank One's motion. Allied and American appealed. Who is correct here? Were both signatures necessary for a proper indorsement, or will one do? [*Allied Capital Partners, L.P. v. Bank One, Texas, N.A.*, 68 S.W. 3d 51 (Tex. App.)]

14. Would a bank be liable to a customer who indorsed a check "For deposit only into account #071698570" if that check were deposited into the wrong account? What if the customer's indorsement was "For deposit only"? Would any account qualify? Would any bank qualify? [*Qatar v. First American Bank of Virginia*, 885 F. Supp. 849 (E.D. Va.)]

15. Two employees of the state of New Mexico fraudulently procured and indorsed a warrant (a draft drawn against funds of the state) made out to the Greater Mesilla Valley Sanitation District. There was no such sanitation district. The employees obtained payment from Citizens Bank. Western Casualty, the state's insurer, reimbursed the state for its loss and then brought suit against the bank for negligently paying the warrant. Is the bank liable for its payment? Discuss your answer. [*Western Casualty & Surety Co. v. Citizens Bank of Las Cruces*, 676 F.2d 1344 (10th Cir.)]

CPA QUESTIONS

1. Hand executed and delivered to Rex a $1,000 negotiable note payable to Rex or bearer. Rex then negotiated it to Ford and indorsed it on the back by merely signing his name. Which of the following is a correct statement?
   a. Rex's indorsement was a special indorsement.
   b. Rex's indorsement was necessary to Ford's qualification as a holder.
   c. The instrument initially being bearer paper cannot be converted to order paper.
   d. The instrument is bearer paper, and Ford can convert it to order paper by writing "pay to the order of Ford" above Rex's signature.

2. Jane Lane, a sole proprietor, has in her possession several checks that she received from her customers. Lane is concerned about the safety of the checks since she believes that many of them are bearer paper that may be cashed without endorsement. The checks in Lane's possession will be considered order paper rather than bearer paper if they were made payable (in the drawer's handwriting) to the order of:
   a. Cash
   b. Ted Tint, and indorsed by Ted Tint in blank
   c. Bearer, and indorsed by Ken Kent making them payable to Jane Lane
   d. Bearer, and indorsed by Sam Sole in blank

3. West Corp. received a check that was originally made payable to the order of one of its customers, Ted Burns. The following indorsement was written on the back of the check:

   Ted Burns, without recourse, for collection only

   Which of the following describes the indorsement?

	Special	*Restrictive*
a.	Yes	Yes
b.	No	No
c.	No	Yes
d.	Yes	No

4. An instrument reads as follows:

   $250.00 Chicago, Illinois April 1, 1992
   Thirty days after date I promise to pay to the
   order of Cash
   Two hundred and fifty Dollars at
   New York City
   Value received with interest at the rate of six percent per annum. This agreement arises out of a separate agreement.
   No. 20 Due May 1, 1992 **Robert Smith**

   Answer "Yes" or "No" for the following questions about the previous item.
   a. The instrument is a draft.
   b. The instrument is order paper.
   c. This is a negotiable instrument.
   d. Robert Smith is the maker.
   e. The instrument may be negotiated without indorsement.

5. Ashley needs to endorse a check that had been endorsed by two other individuals prior to Ashley's receipt of the check. Ashley does not want to have surety liability, so Ashley endorses the check "without recourse." Under the Negotiable Instruments Article of the UCC, which of the following types of endorsement did Ashley make?
   a. Blank
   b. Special
   c. Qualified
   d. Restrictive

Continued

Regent introduced PLS's manual into evidence. The manual emphasizes that PLS earns its fees by cashing checks, so the employee should "[s]pend * * * time proving that the check can be cashed and not looking for excuses not to cash it." The manual identifies several signs that a check might not be valid, including several of the factors present in this case. According to the manual, the employee should "verify that the check is good" by "phoning the maker."

Police arrested Pearson, charging her with check fraud. Two days later, police arrested Tatiana Auson, an employee of Regent, on the same charge. Regent had hired Auson to work as a funder, meaning that Regent authorized Auson to cut checks for the parties to real estate transactions. According to Regent's investigator, Auson cancelled checks intended for parties to real estate transactions, then issued new checks to different payees for the amounts of the original checks. Pearson admitted that Auson gave her the three checks that New Randolph cashed for Pearson. Pearson kept about $5,000 of the proceeds from the checks, and she gave the remainder to Auson. All three checks appeared to bear the signature of Karen Hendricks, who had authority to sign checks on behalf of Regent.

Regent told its bank to stop payment on the check. New Randolph sued Regent for payment of the check, claiming that its status as a holder in due course entitled it to payment, despite the evidence that Auson and Pearson conspired to defraud Regent.

New Randolph appealed.

JUDICIAL OPINION

NEVILLE, Judge...The trial court awarded the judgment based on its finding of fact that New Randolph did not qualify as a holder in due course of the check because the check at issue was "so irregular * * * as to call into question its authenticity." However, grounds for suspicion about a check will not always prevent one from taking the check as a holder in due course. Where all of the evidence available to the holder shows that it lacked notice of a defense, it becomes a holder in due course. 'To defeat the rights of one dealing with negotiable securities it is not enough to show that he took them under circumstances which ought to excite the suspicion of a prudent man and cause him to make inquiry, but that he had actual knowledge of an infirmity or defect, or of such facts that his failure to make further inquiry would indicate a deliberate desire on his part to evade knowledge because of a belief or fear that investigation would disclose a vice in the transaction.'

A federal case involved a similar issue. In *McCook County National Bank v. Compton*, 558 F.2d 871 (8th Cir.1977), McCook cashed a check despite several irregularities, including a discrepancy in the amount of the check. McCook contacted Northwestern, the bank on which the payor drew the check, and Northwestern confirmed the correct amount and assured McCook the check was "'okay to cash.'" The trial court held that McCook did not qualify as a holder in due course.

McCook bank was presented with a check that had an obvious $10,000 discrepancy on its face. As any prudent bank would, McCook contacted the Northwestern bank to ascertain the correct amount and whether adequate funds existed to cover the check. Assured by the bank and indirectly by Compton, who issued the check, that the check was "okay", McCook proceeded to cash the check and issue money orders. There were no remaining irregularities in the instrument itself. Since this court has found no actual notice and insufficient constructive notice from the reporting service, and no other notice at the time the check was cashed, we can find no bad faith or dishonesty on the part of McCook bank in cashing the check. In sum, while a better judgment concerning the negotiability of the check might have been made we can not find the requisite notice or bad faith that would deprive McCook bank of its status as holder in due course.

Here, New Randolph had some grounds for suspecting that the check could be invalid. Regent misspelled Pearson's name, the purpose stated on the check did not match the purpose Pearson described, the check greatly exceeded the amount of prior checks made out to Pearson, and Pearson had only recently renewed her state identification card. However, when it cashed the check, New Randolph also knew that Regent had issued two other checks to Pearson, and those checks had cleared. Most significantly, Arizaga and Keys called Regent and Regent directly confirmed that it issued the check to Pearson for the stated amount.

We agree with the trial court's finding that irregularities involving the check called its authenticity into question. But New Randolph investigated those irregularities in a commercially reasonable manner by calling Regent to verify the check. In this case, unlike *McCook,* the holder did not rely on an indirect verification from the payor. New Randolph contacted Regent directly, as well as American Chartered Bank. New Randolph might have acted more cautiously and asked more questions of the person who spoke to them when they called Regent. But that person's verification of the check made the decision to cash the check commercially reasonable. We find that the trial court committed clear error when it found that New Randolph was not a holder in due course of check number 22221. Therefore, we reverse the judgment.

QUESTIONS

1. Does suspicion cause a holder to lose holder-in-due-course status?
2. What is the impact of the phone call and verification being sought?
3. What advice would you give to check cashing companies on dealing with employees cashing checks?

(3) Ignorance of the Instrument's Being Overdue or Dishonored.

An instrument can be negotiated even though it has been dishonored, it is overdue,[11] or it is demand paper, such as a check, that has been outstanding for more than a reasonable time.[12] These instruments can still be transferred and the transferee is still a holder. However, the fact that the instrument is circulating at a late date or after it has been dishonored is suspicious and results in notice from the circumstances that there may be some adverse claim or defense. A person who acquires title to the instrument under such circumstances can be a holder but cannot be a holder in due course. **For Example,** buying a discounted note after its due date is notice that something may be wrong with the instrument.

(4) Ignorance of Defenses and Adverse Claims.

Prior parties on an instrument may have defenses that entitle them to withhold payment from a holder of an instrument. **For Example,** the drawer of a check, upon demand for payment by the payee, could assert as a defense to payment that the merchandise the payee delivered under the terms of their underlying contract was defective. A person who acquires an instrument with notice or knowledge that there is a defense that a party may have or that there are claims of ownership of the instrument from different parties cannot be an HDC. In general, transferees who are aware of facts that would make a reasonable person ask questions are deemed to know what they would have learned if they had asked questions.[13] Such knowledge and the failure to ask questions will cost them their special status of holder in due course; they remain simply holders.

Knowledge acquired by a holder after the instrument was acquired does not prevent the holder from being a holder in due course. The fact that a holder, after acquiring the instrument, learns of a defense does not work retroactively to destroy the holder's character as an HDC. The *Triffin v. Liccardi Ford, Inc.,* case involves an issue of HDC knowledge and status.

Triffin v. Liccardi Ford, Inc., 10 A.3d 227 (N.J. Super. 2011)

Cashing a Postdated Check from an Embezzler: HDC?

A check dated August 10, 2007, was made payable to one of Liccardi's employees, Charles Stallone, Jr. Liccardi withheld the check from Stallone because he suspected him of embezzlement. However, the check still disappeared from the company offices, and when the disappearance was discovered, Liccardi immediately placed a stop payment on the check.

JCNB Check Cashing, Inc. (JCNB), cashed the check for Stallone before the issue date (the check was postdated) and JCNB then deposited the check in its own bank account on August 9, 2007. However, the issuing bank refused to honor the check. On February 11, 2009, Robert Triffin acquired the dishonored payroll check from JCNB and sued Liccardi and Stallone for the amount of the check plus interest. Triffin's business is buying dishonored checks and attempting to collect on them.

The trial court dismissed Triffin's complaint on the grounds that he was not a holder in due course. Triffin appealed.

JUDICIAL OPINION

REISNER, Judge...Under the New Jersey Uniform Commercial Code, to be a holder in due course one must take "an instrument for value, in good faith, and without notice of dishonor or any defense against or claim to it on the part of any person." *Triffin v. Quality Urban Hous. Partners*, 352 N.J. Super. at 541, 800 A.2d 905. "Good faith" includes "the observance of reasonable commercial standards of fair dealing." Further, the document must not be "so irregular or incomplete as to call into question its authenticity." *Triffin v. Pomerantz Staffing Servs.*, LLC, 851 A.2d 100 (App. Div.2004).

Triffin did not take the Liccardi check as a holder in due course, because he purchased the instrument with notice that it had been dishonored. However, if JCNB was a holder in due course when it obtained the check from Stallone, it could assign its interest in the check to Triffin and he in turn could enforce JCNB's rights as its assignee.

[11] *St. Bernard Savings & Loan Ass'n v. Cella,* 826 F. Supp. 985 (E.D. La. 1993); *Cadle Co. v. DeVincent,* 781 N.E.2d 817 (Mass. App. 2003); *Interim Capital LLC v. Herr Law Group, Ltd.,* 2011 WL 7047062 (D. Nev. 2011).

[12] *Max Duncan Family Investments, Ltd. v. NTFN Inc.,* 267 S.W.3d 447 (Tex. 2008).

[13] *Unr-Rohn, Inc. v. Summit Bank,* 687 N.E.2d 235 (Ind. App. 1997); but see contra view, *Pero's Steak and Spaghetti House v. Lee,* 90 S.W.3d 614 (Tenn. 2002).

Continued

There is no basis on this record to dispute that Stallone stole the check from his employer and induced JCNB to cash it before the issue date on the check. If Stallone attempted to collect on the check from the obligor, he would be subject to Liccardi's defenses. Therefore, the critical question is whether JCNB took the check as a holder in due course and can thereby avoid the defenses to enforcement that Liccardi has against Stallone.

We have previously held that "a holder in due course must satisfy both a subjective and an objective test of good faith, requiring a consideration of the holder's honesty in fact and observance of reasonable commercial standards." *Triffin v. Pomerantz Staffing Servs.*, 370 N.J.Super. at 308, 851 A.2d 100. "A party who fails to make an inquiry, reasonably required by the circumstances of the transaction, so as to remain ignorant of facts that might disclose a defect cannot claim to be a holder in due course." In *Pomerantz*, we denied holder in due course status to an assignor who failed to comply with instructions on the face of the check to test whether the ink on the check was heat-sensitive. We concluded that a check casher must inquire into the authenticity of checks when presented with "evidence that they were not authentic."

It is reasonable, in considering whether the instruments were received in good faith and whether the holder comported with reasonable commercial standards, that the holder be expected to fully examine the front and back of the instrument and, where the instrument purports to contain a method by which its authenticity may be tested, that the holder actually utilize that method.

Similarly, in *Triffin v. Travelers Express Co.*, 370 N.J. Super. 399, 851 A.2d 667 (App.Div.2004), we held that an assignor could not qualify as a holder in due course of money orders that contained "telltale unmatching serial numbers," because the apparent defect "should have caused [the] assignors[ ] to be suspicious about their legitimacy, and should have prompted them to seek information from [the maker]." We concluded that the "assignors, especially because they are in the business of making a profit by cashing such instruments, cannot claim holder in due course status by blithely and blindly cashing such instruments."

Under the express terms of the Check Cashers Regulatory Act of 1993, a check cashing service is prohibited from "cash[ing] or advanc[ing] any money on a postdated check." N.J.S.A. 17:15A–47c. Therefore, the Act requires that a licensee, such as JCNB, examine the face of a check and refrain from cashing it if the check is postdated. We conclude that in this case the Act defined the "reasonable commercial standards" that JCNB was required to follow, and having failed to follow those standards, JCNB was not a holder in due course.

Triffin's reliance on section 113 of the UCC is misplaced. N.J.S.A. 12A:3–113a provides that "[a]n instrument may be antedated or postdated." However, it also defines when an instrument is payable: "Except as provided in subsection c. of 12A:4–401 [permitting banks to make payment on postdated checks], an instrument payable on demand is not payable before the date of the instrument." As we have recognized, "[a] check…is a demand instrument." Therefore, we find no inconsistency between the UCC and the Check Cashers Regulatory Act, which prohibits check cashing services from making payment on postdated checks.

JCNB clearly violated a provision of the Act and, therefore, failed to observe reasonable commercial standards of the check cashing industry as established by the Act. Ibid. Thus, JCNB cannot qualify as a holder in due course.

Triffin's reliance on *Triffin v. Bank of America*, 391 N.J. Super. 83, 917 A.2d 257 (App.Div.2007), is equally unpersuasive. In that case, Triffin sued a bank to collect on a dishonored, overdrawn check. In turn, the bank claimed that the check cashing service from which Triffin bought the check had violated section 48 of the Act, N.J.S.A. 17:15A–48a(5), by dealing with Triffin a person previously found liable for civil fraud. In rejecting the bank's argument, we reasoned that the Act did not necessarily prohibit a check casher from selling checks to such a person.

By contrast, the case before us concerns JCNB's clear violation of a "per se bar" against cashing postdated checks. Moreover, as a practical matter, a check casher may not necessarily know that a person who seeks to buy its checks has been convicted of fraud. On the other hand, a simple perusal of the face of the check will reveal whether it is postdated.

Because the check cashing service from which Triffin bought the Liccardi check violated the Act by paying on a postdated check, Triffin could not, by taking an assignment of the check, assert the rights of a holder in due course. His complaint was properly dismissed.

[Affirmed]

QUESTIONS

1. Why are there so many cases cited in which Triffin is a party?
2. Why is it important to know whether JCNB is a holder in due course?
3. What effect does the postdate on the check have on the decision in the case?

Ethics & the Law

The Corner Check Cashing Company and Good Faith

Some public policy experts have argued that no check cashing company, defined as one that takes a portion of the amount of the check as a fee for cashing checks for individuals who cannot get them cashed at banks and credit unions, should ever be allowed holder in due course status. Do you agree with this argument? Are check cashing companies ethical in their behavior? Do you believe that the state laws on check cashing firms are a means of mandating ethical conduct?

CPA **(B) Holder Through a Holder in Due Course.** Those persons who become holders of the instrument after an HDC has held it are given the same protection as the HDC, provided they are not parties to any fraud or illegality that affects the instrument. This status of **holder through a holder in due course** is given in these circumstances even if the transferee from a holder in due course does not satisfy the requirements for holder-in-due-course status. This elevated or protected status is called Article 3's "shelter rule," and it allows a person who is not an HDC to hide under the "umbrella" with a holder in due course and be sheltered from claims and defenses as if actually being an HDC. **For Example,** a person who acquires an instrument as an inheritance from an estate does not give value and is missing one of the requirements for being a holder in due course. However, if the estate was an HDC, that status does transfer to the heir. Furthermore, suppose that Avery is a holder in due course of a $5,000 promissory note due May 31, 2012. Avery gives the note to his nephew Aaron for Aaron's birthday on June 1, 2012. Aaron did not give value because the note was a gift, and he has taken the note as a holder after it has already become due. Nonetheless, because Avery was a holder in due course, Aaron assumes that status under Article 3's shelter provision.

B. Defenses to Payment of a Negotiable Instrument

One of the key reasons for attaining HDC status is to be able to obtain payment on the negotiable instrument free of any underlying problems between the original parties to the instrument. An HDC takes an instrument free from certain types of defenses to payment. Whether a defense may be raised against an HDC claiming under a negotiable instrument depends on the nature of the defense.

CPA 4. Classification of Defenses

The importance of being a holder in due course or a holder through an HDC is that such holders are not subject to certain defenses called *limited defenses.* Another class of defenses, *universal defenses,* may be asserted against any party, whether an assignee, an ordinary holder, an HDC, or a holder through an HDC.[14]

5. Defenses against Assignee or Ordinary Holder

Assignees of negotiable instruments are subject to every defense raised. Similarly, a holder who does not become an HDC is subject to every payment defense just as though the instrument were not negotiable.

6. Limited Defenses Not Available against a Holder in Due Course

HDCs are not subject to any of the following defenses.

CPA **(A) Ordinary Contract Defenses.** In general terms, the defenses that could be raised in a breach of contract claim cannot be raised against an HDC. The defenses of lack, failure, or illegality of consideration with respect to the instrument's underlying transaction cannot be asserted against the holder in due course. Misrepresentation about the goods underlying the contract is also not a defense.

[14] Under the pre-Code law and under the 1952 Code, the universal defense was called a *real defense*, and the limited defense was called a *personal defense*. These terms have now been abandoned, but some licensing and CPA examinations may continue to use these pre-Code terms.

For Example, a businessperson cannot refuse to pay a holder in due course on the note used to pay for her copy machine just because her copy machine does not have the speed she was promised.

(B) Incapacity of Maker or Drawer. Ordinarily, the maker's or drawer's lack of capacity (except minors) may not be raised as a defense to payment to a holder in due course. Such incapacity is a defense, however, if the incapacity is at a legal level that makes the instrument a nullity. **For Example,** a promissory note made by an insane person for whom a court has appointed a guardian is void. In the case of a claim on the note by an HDC, the incapacity of the maker would be a defense.

CPA **(C) Fraud in the Inducement.** If a person is persuaded or induced to execute the instrument because of fraudulent statements, such **fraud in the inducement** cannot be raised against a party with holder-in-due-course status. **For Example,** suppose Mills is persuaded to purchase an automobile because of Pagan's statements that the car was a demonstrator for the dealership and in good mechanical condition with a certification from the dealership's head mechanic. Mills, a car dealer, gives Pagan a note, which is negotiated until it reaches Han, who is a holder in due course. Mills meanwhile learns that the car has been in an accident and has a cracked engine block, that the head mechanic was paid to sign the certification, and that Pagan's statements were fraudulent. When Han demands payment of the note, Mills cannot refuse to pay on the ground of Pagan's fraud. Mills must pay the note because Han, as an HDC, does not take the note subject to any fraud or misrepresentation in the underlying transaction. Mills is left with the remedy of recovering from Pagan for misrepresentation or fraud.

(D) Miscellaneous Defenses.[15] The limited defenses listed in the preceding three subsections are those most commonly raised against demands by holders in due course for payment. The following are additional limited defenses that may be asserted: (1) prior payment or cancellation of the instrument, (2) nondelivery, (3) conditional or special-purpose delivery, (4) breach of warranty, (5) duress consisting of threats, (6) unauthorized completion, and (7) theft of a bearer instrument. These defenses, however, have a very limited effect in defending against an HDC's demand for payment.

7. Universal Defenses Available against All Holders

Certain defenses are regarded as so basic that the social interest in preserving them outweighs the social interest of giving negotiable instruments the freely transferable qualities of money. Accordingly, such defenses are given universal effect and may be raised against all holders, whether ordinary holders, HDCs, or holders through a holder in due course. These defenses are called **universal defenses.**[16]

CPA **(A) Fraud as to the Nature or Essential Terms of the Instrument.** The fact that a person signs an instrument because the person is fraudulently deceived as to its nature or essential terms is a defense available against all holders.[17] When one person induces another to sign a note by falsely representing that, for example, it is a contract for repairs or that it is a character reference, the note is invalid, and the defense of the misrepresentation of the character of the instrument can be used against a holder in due course. **For Example,** suppose that two homeowners are asked to sign a statement for a sales person that he was in their home and did a demonstration of a new solar water heater. Just as the homeowners are about to sign the verification statement, the salesman distracts them and then switches the verification for a purchase contract and promissory note for a $5,000 solar water heating system that the owners declined to purchase. The owners would have a defense of fraud in factum against a holder in due course of this note. The difference between fraud in the inducement—a personal defense—and fraud in factum—a universal defense—is that fraud in factum involves deception as to the documents themselves, not as to the underlying goods, services, or property.

CPA **(B) Forgery or Lack of Authority.** The defense that a signature was forged or signed without authority can be raised by a drawer or maker against

15 Revised UCC.§3-305.

16 *City Rentals, Inc. v. Kessler*, 946 N.E. 2d 785 (Ohio App. 2010).

17 Revised UCC.§3-305(a)(1)(iii).

any HDC unless the drawer or maker whose name was signed has ratified it or is estopped by conduct or negligence from denying it.[18] The fact that the negligence of the drawer helped the wrongdoer does not prevent the drawee from raising the defense of forgery. (See Chapters 29 and 31 for more discussion of the impact of forgery on liability.)

(C) Duress Depriving Control. A party may execute or indorse a negotiable instrument in response to a force of such a nature that, under general principles of law, duress makes the transaction void rather than merely voidable. Duress of this type and level may be raised as a defense against any holder. Economic duress, in the form of a reluctance to enter into a financially demanding instrument, is not a universal defense.[19] Duress that is attempted murder is a universal defense.

(D) Incapacity. The fact that the defendant is a minor who under general principles of contract law may avoid the obligation is a matter that may be raised against any kind of holder. Other kinds of incapacity may be raised as a defense if the effect of the incapacity is to make the instrument void, as when there has been a formal declaration of insanity.[20]

(E) Illegality. If an instrument is void by law when executed in connection with certain conduct, such as a note for gambling or one that involves usury, such defenses may be raised against an HDC.

CPA **(F) Alteration.** An **alteration** is an unauthorized change or completion of a negotiable instrument designed to modify the obligation of a party to the instrument.[21] **For Example,** changing the amount of an instrument from $150 to $450 is an alteration.[22]

(1) Person Making Alteration.

An alteration is a change made by a party to the instrument. Recovery on the instrument is still possible under the terms of the instrument as it originally existed, if proof of the original terms is possible.

(2) Effect of Alteration.

If the alteration to the instrument was made fraudulently, the person whose obligations under the instrument are affected by that alteration is discharged from liability on the instrument. The instrument, however, can be enforced according to its original terms or its terms as completed. This right of enforcement is given to holders in due course who had no notice of such alteration.[23] While a holder in due course would come within the protected class on alteration, such status is not required for this recovery provision in the event of alteration. **For Example,** Ryan signed a negotiable demand note for $100 made payable to Long. A subsequent holder changed the amount from $100 to $700. A later holder in due course presented the note to Ryan for payment. Ryan would still be liable for the original amount of $100.

A summary of the universal and limited defenses is presented in Figure 30-2.

8. Denial of Holder-in-Due-Course Protection

In certain situations, the taker of a negotiable instrument is denied the status and protections of an HDC.

(A) Participating Transferee. When the transferee is working with the lender or seller to obtain a negotiable instrument from the buyer/borrower, the transferee's holder-in-due-course status comes into question. This close-connection doctrine (discussed earlier in this chapter as an issue in the good-faith requirement for becoming a holder in due course) prevents a transferee with intimate knowledge of the transferor's business practices from becoming an HDC.[24]

(B) The Federal Trade Commission Rule. In 1976, the Federal Trade Commission (FTC) adopted a rule that limits the rights of a holder in due course in a consumer credit transaction. The rule protects

[18] *Bank of Hoven v. Rausch,* 382 N.W.2d 39 (S.D. 1986); for general discussion of estoppel and ratification, see *Ziegler Furniture and Funeral Home, Inc. v. Cicmanec,* 209 N.W.2d 350 (S.D. 2006).

[19] *Miller v. Calhoun/Johnson Co.,* 497 S.E.2d 397 (Ga. App. 1998); *Smith v. Gordon,* 598 S.E.2d 92 (Ga. App. 2004).

[20] Revised UCC.§3-305(a)(1)(ii). *Erkins v. Alaska Trustee LLC,* 265 P.3d 292 (Alaska 2011).

[21] Revised UCC.§3-407(a); *Stahl v. St. Elizabeth Medical Center,* 948 S.W.2d 419 (Ky. App. 1997). *Farmers Deposit Bank v. Bank One,* 2005 WL 3453979 (E.D. Ky. 2005). A material alteration made based on the parties' negotiations (a 13 percent versus an 18 percent interest rate) is not fraudulent. *Darnall v. Petersen,* 592 N.W.2d 505 (Neb. App. 1999); *Knoefler v. Wojtalewicz,* 2003 WL 21496933 (Neb App 2003) (difference between bank interest rate and judgment interest rate is not material).

[22] However, if an instrument, such as a note, has been altered and the maker continues to pay without objection to the alteration, the alteration does not discharge the maker's liability. *Stahl v. St. Elizabeth Medical Center,* 948 S.W.2d 419 (Ky. App. 1997); again, for a general discussion of continuing payment as estoppel, see *Ziegler Furniture and Funeral Home, Inc. v. Cicmanec,* 709 N.W.2d 350 (S.D. 2006).

[23] Revised UCC.§3-407(b), (c).

[24] *In re Neals,* 459 B.R. 612 (D.S.C. 2011). *AIG Global Securities Lending Corp. v. Banc of America Securities LLC,* 2006 WL 1206333 (S.D.N.Y. 2006).

FIGURE 30-2 Defenses to Payment of Negotiable Instrument

UNIVERSAL (AVAILABLE AGAINST ASSIGNEES, HOLDERS, AND HOLDERS IN DUE COURSE)(REAL)	LIMITED (AVAILABLE AGAINST ASSIGNEES AND HOLDERS BUT NOT AGAINST HOLDERS IN DUE COURSE) (PERSONAL)	MIXED (CIRCUMSTANCES VARY THE AVAILABILITY OF THESE DEFENSES)
FRAUD AS TO THE NATURE OF THE INSTRUMENT (FRAUD IN FACTUM) FORGERY UNAUTHORIZED SIGNATURE INCAPACITY (DECLARATION) ILLEGALITY ALTERATION CONSUMER CREDIT CONTRACTS WITH FTC NOTICE	FRAUD IN THE INDUCEMENT MISREPRESENTATION LACK OF CONSIDERATION BREACH OF WARRANTY CANCELLATION FAILURE OF DELIVERY UNAUTHORIZED COMPLETION ALL ORDINARY CONTRACT DEFENSES	DURESS INCAPACITY

consumers who purchase goods or services for personal, family, or household use on credit.[25] When the note the buyer gave the seller as payment for the consumer goods is transferred to even a holder in due course, the consumer buyer may raise any defense that could have been raised against the seller. The FTC regulation requires that the following notice be included in boldface type at least 10 points in size in consumer credit contracts covered under the rule:

> *Notice*
> *Any holder of this consumer credit contract is subject to all claims and defenses which the debtor could assert against the seller of goods or services obtained with the proceeds hereof. Recovery hereunder by the debtor shall not exceed amounts paid by the debtor hereunder.*[26]

When a notice preserving consumer defenses is included in a negotiable instrument, no subsequent person can be a holder in due course of the instrument.[27]

C. Liability Issues: How Payment Rights Arise and Defenses Are Used

In this chapter and in Chapters 28 and 29, issues surrounding the types of instruments, transfers, holders, and holders in due course have been covered. However, there are procedures under Article 3 for bringing together all of the parties, instruments, and defenses so that ultimate liability and, hopefully, payment can be determined and achieved.

[25] The regulation does not cover purchases of real estate, securities, or consumer goods or services for which the purchase price is more than $25,000. *Fifth Third Bank v. Jones*, 168 P.3d 1 (Colo. App. 2007).

[26] One of the controversial changes to Article 3 is found in subsections 3-305(e) and (f). This change provides that if the Federal Trade Commission requires a notice to be included, but it is not, the instrument is deemed to have included it implicitly.

[27] Revised UCC.§3-106(d). This goes beyond the scope of the FTC regulation. The latter merely preserves the defenses of the consumer but does not bar holder-in-due-course protection for other parties, such as an accommodation party to a consumer's note. Also, the FTC regulation does not change the common law and permits the maker to bring contract actions against the holder of the note for contract breaches committed by the maker's original contract party. The rule changes the status of the parties as holders in due course. It does not change contract rights. *Pennsylvania Dept. of Banking v. NCAS of Delaware, LLC*, 931 A.2d 771 (Pa. 2007).

CPA 9. The Roles of Parties and Liability

Every instrument has primary and secondary parties. The **primary party** is the party to whom the holder or holder in due course must turn first to obtain payment. The primary party on a note or certificate of deposit is the **maker**. The primary party on a draft is the **drawee**, assuming that the drawee has accepted the draft. Although a check must first be presented to the drawee bank for payment, the bank is not primarily liable on the instrument because the bank has the right to refuse to pay the check (see following and Chapter 31). The drawee bank on a check is the party to whom a holder or holder in due course turns first for payment despite the lack of primary-party status on the part of that drawee bank. The maker of a note is the party to whom holders and holders in due course must turn first for payment.

The **secondary parties** (or *secondary obligors,* as they are now called under Revised Article 3) to an instrument are those to whom holders turn when the primary party, for whatever reason, fails to pay the instrument. Secondary parties on notes are **indorsers**, and secondary parties on checks and drafts are **drawers** and **indorsers**.

CPA 10. Attaching Liability of the Primary Parties: Presentment

Presentment occurs when the holder or HDC of an instrument orally, in writing, or by electronic communication to the primary party requests that the instrument be paid according to its terms. The primary party has the right to require that the presentment be made in a "commercially reasonable manner," which would include reasonable times for presentment, such as during business hours. The primary party can also require identification, authorization, and even a signature of receipt of the funds due under the instrument. In addition, the primary party can demand a valid indorsement on the instrument prior to making payment. Upon presentment, the primary party is required to pay according to the terms of the instrument unless there are defenses such as forgery, any of the other universal defenses for HDCs, or any defenses for holders.

If the primary party refuses to pay the instrument according to its terms, there has been a *dishonor,* and the holder is then left to turn to the secondary parties.

CPA 11. Dishonor and Notice of Dishonor

Dishonor occurs when the primary party refuses to pay the instrument according to its terms. The primary party is required to give **notice of dishonor**. The notice that the instrument has been dishonored can be oral, written, or electronic. That notice is subject to time limitations. **For Example,** a bank must give notice of dishonor by midnight of the next banking day. Nonbank primary parties must give notice of dishonor within 30 days following their receipt of notice of dishonor. Returning the dishonored check is sufficient notice of dishonor. (See Chapter 31 for more discussion of liability issues on dishonor of checks.) Upon dishonor, the holder must then turn to the secondary parties for payment.

E-Commerce & Cyberlaw

Electronic Presentment: One Fell Swoop, All Rights, All Payments, New Laws

Because we now use debit cards, some of the UCC Article 3 provisions on checks are used far less, and the rights of the merchants and the buyers are covered under various federal and state laws on electronic funds transfers (covered in Chapter 31). Issues continue to evolve, such as the protections on debit cards, including the use of personal identification numbers (PINs) as a way of ensuring identity. Electronic technology requires that we change laws and grow into the new systems.

Thinking Things Through

The Corner Check Cashing Company and Thieves—Who Wins?

Now is an ideal time to bring together all of the concepts you have learned in Chapters 27, 28, and 29. Analyzing this problem will help you integrate your knowledge about negotiable instruments. Sid's Salmon has purchased salmon from Fred's Fisheries. Sid wrote a check for $22,000 to Fred's. A thief broke into Fred's offices and took the cash on hand as well as the unindorsed check from Sid's. The thief took the check to the Corner Check Cashing Company (CCCC) and received $22,000 less the cashing fee of $2,000. Fred notified Sid who then notified First Commerce Bank, the drawee of the check, of the theft. CCCC has presented the check for payment, and First Commerce refuses to pay. CCCC says it is a holder in due course. Are you able to help First Commerce Bank develop its response to CCCC?

Suppose that Fred had already indorsed the check when the thief stole it. Would CCCC be a holder in due course?

The obligation of the secondary parties in these situations is to pay according to the terms of the instrument. These secondary parties will have **limited defenses** if the presenting party is a holder in due course. **For Example,** suppose that a check drawn on First Interstate Bank is written by Ben Paltrow to Julia Sutherland as payment for Julia's Bentley auto that Ben purchased. Julia deposits Ben's check into her account at AmeriBank, and AmeriBank sends the check to First Interstate to present it for payment. First Interstate finds that Ben's account has insufficient funds and dishonors the check. AmeriBank must notify First Interstate by midnight of the next banking day that the check has been dishonored, and then First Interstate must notify Julia by midnight of the next banking day that Ben's check was dishonored. Julia then has 30 days to notify Ben and turn to him as a drawer, or secondary party, for payment on the check.

LawFlix

Ghost (1990) PG 13

Whoppi Goldberg plays a psychic who is asked by a deceased (the late Patrick Swayze) to help get back at his murderer (a co-worker at his finance firm) by posing as a character to obtain a check made payable to her, a fictitious character, who uses a bank account created through computer hacking. The check-cashing scenes are priceless, and, legally, far foreign to normal bank practices employed to prevent forgery.

MAKE THE CONNECTION

SUMMARY

A holder of a negotiable instrument can be either an ordinary holder or an HDC. The ordinary holder has the same rights that an assignee would have. Holders in due course and holders through an HDC are protected from certain defenses. To be an HDC, a person must first be a holder—that is, the person must have acquired the instrument by a proper negotiation. The holder must then also take for value, in good faith, without notice that the paper is overdue or dishonored, and without notice of defenses and adverse claims. Those persons who become holders of the instrument after an HDC are given the same protection as the HDC through the shelter provision, provided they are not parties to any fraud or illegality affecting the instrument.

The importance of being an HDC is that those holders are not being subject to certain defenses when demand for payment is made. These defenses are limited defenses and include ordinary contract defenses, incapacity unless it makes the instrument void, fraud in the inducement, prior payment or cancellation, nondelivery of an instrument, conditional delivery, duress consisting of threats, unauthorized completion, and theft of a bearer instrument. Universal defenses may be asserted against any assignee, an ordinary holder, or HDC. Universal defenses include fraud as to the nature or essential terms of the paper, forgery or lack of authority, duress depriving control, incapacity, illegality that makes the instrument void, and alteration. Alteration is only a partial defense; an HDC may enforce the instrument according to its original terms.

The Federal Trade Commission rule on consumer credit contracts limits the immunity of an HDC from defenses of consumer buyers against their sellers. Immunity is limited in consumer credit transactions if the notice specified by the FTC regulation is included in the sales contract. When a notice preserving consumer defenses is stated in a negotiable instrument, no subsequent person can be an HDC.

Holders and HDCs are required to present instruments for payment to primary parties. Primary parties are makers and drawees. If the primary party refuses to pay, or dishonors, the instrument, it must give notice of dishonor in a timely fashion. The holder can then turn to secondary parties, drawers, and indorsers (secondary obligors) for payment.

LEARNING OUTCOMES

After studying this chapter, you should be able to clearly explain:

A. Parties to Negotiable Instruments: Rights and Liabilities

LO.1 Distinguish between an ordinary holder and a holder in due course

See Sections 2 and 3 on p. 579 for examples of distinction.

LO.2 List the requirements for becoming a holder in due course

See *Triffin v. Liccardi Ford, Inc.* on pp. 583–584.

B. Defenses to Payment of a Negotiable Instrument

LO.3 Explain the rights of a holder through a holder in due course

See *New Randolph Halsted Currency Exchange, Inc. v. Regent Title Insurance Co.* on pp. 581–582.

LO.4 List and explain the limited defenses not available against a holder in due course

See the list of defenses in Figure 30-2 on p. 588.

LO.5 List and explain the universal defenses available against all holders

See the Thinking Things Through discussion of the Corner Check Cashing Company on p. 590.

C. Liability Issues: How Payment Rights Arise and Defenses Are Used

LO.6 Describe how the rights of a holder in due course have been limited by the Federal Trade Commission

See the language of the rule on p. 589.

KEY TERMS

alteration
assignees
close-connection doctrine
dishonor
drawee
drawers
fraud in the inducement
good faith
holders
holder in due course
holder through a holder in due course
indorsers
limited defenses
maker
notice of dishonor
presentment
primary party
secondary parties
universal defenses
value

QUESTIONS AND CASE PROBLEMS

1. Randy Bocian had a bank account with First of America-Bank (FAB). On October 8, Bocian received a check for $28,800 from Eric Christenson as payment for constructing a pole barn on Christenson's property. Bocian deposited the check at FAB on October 9 and was permitted to draw on the funds through October 12. Bocian wrote checks totaling $12,334.21, which FAB cleared. On October 12, Christenson stopped payment on the check as the result of a contract dispute over the pole barn. Bocian's account was then overdrawn once the check was denied clearance by Christenson's bank. FAB brought suit against both Bocian and Christenson to collect its loss. Christenson counterclaimed against Bocian for his contract breach claims on the pole barn construction. FAB maintained that it had given value and was a holder in due course and that, as such, it was not required to be subject to the pole barn issues or the stop payment order. Is FAB right? [*First of America-Bank Northeast Illinois v. Bocian*, 614 N.E.2d 890 (Ill. App.)]

2. Cronin, an employee of Epicycle, cashed his final paycheck at Money Mart Check Cashing Center. Epicycle had issued a stop payment order on the check. Money Mart deposited the check through normal banking channels. The check was returned to Money Mart marked "Payment Stopped." Money Mart brought an action against Epicycle, claiming that, as a holder in due course, it was entitled to recover against Epicycle. Epicycle argued that Money Mart could not be a holder in due course because it failed to verify the check as good prior to cashing it. Is Money Mart a holder in due course? [*Money Mart Check Cashing Center, Inc. v. Epicycle Corp.*, 667 P.2d 1372 (Colo.)]

3. Halleck executed a promissory note payable to the order of Leopold. Halleck did not pay the note when due, and Leopold brought suit on the note, producing it in court. Halleck admitted that he had signed the note but claimed plaintiff Leopold was required to prove that the note had been issued for consideration and that the plaintiff was in fact the holder. Are these elements of proof required as part of the case? [*Leopold v. Halleck*, 436 N.E.2d 29 (Ill. App.)]

4. Calhoun/Johnson Company d/b/a Williams Lumber Company (Williams) sold building materials to Donald Miller d/b/a Millercraft Construction Company (Millercraft) on credit. Miller had signed a personal guaranty for the materials. Miller requested lien waivers from Williams for four of his projects and asked for them from Fabian Boudreau, Williams's credit manager. Fabian refused to grant the waivers because Miller was $28,000 delinquent on his account. Miller agreed to bring his account current with the exception of $11,000 for which he signed a no-interest promissory note. Miller obtained the lien waivers and then defaulted on the note. Williams brought suit for payment, and Williams said there was lack of consideration and that the note was not valid. He said he must give value to be able to recover on the note. Was he correct? [*Miller v. Calhoun/Johnson Co.*, 497 S.E.2d 397 (Ga. App.)]

5. Statham drew a check. The payee indorsed it to Kemp Motor Sales. Statham then stopped payment on the check on the grounds that there was a failure of consideration for the check. Kemp sued Statham on the check. When Statham raised the defense of failure of consideration, Kemp replied that he was a holder in due course. Statham claimed that Kemp could not recover because Statham learned of his defense before Kemp deposited the check in its bank account. Discuss the parties' arguments and rights in this situation. [*Kemp Motor Sales v. Statham*, 171 S.E.2d 389 (Ga. App.)]

6. Can check cashing companies be holders in due course? What arguments can you make for and against their holder-in-due-course status? [*Dal-Tile Corp. v. Cash N' Go*, 487 S.E.2d 529 (Ga. App.)]

7. Jones, wishing to retire from a business enterprise that he had been conducting for a number of years, sold all of the assets of the business to Jackson Corp. Included in the assets were a number of promissory notes payable to the order

of Jones that he had taken from his customers. Upon the maturity of one of the notes, the maker refused to pay because there was a failure of consideration. Jackson Corp. sued the maker of the note. Who should succeed? Explain.

8. Elliot, an officer of Impact Marketing, drew six postdated checks on Impact's account. The checks were payable to Bell for legal services to be subsequently performed for Impact. Financial Associates purchased them from Bell and collected on four of the checks. Payment was stopped on the last two when Bell's services were terminated. Financial argued that it was a holder in due course and had the right to collect on the checks. Impact claimed that because the checks were postdated and issued for an executory promise, Financial could not be a holder in due course. Who was correct? Why? [*Financial Associates v. Impact Marketing,* 394 N.Y.S.2d 814]

9. *D* drew a check to the order of *P*. *P* took the check postdated. *P* knew that *D* was having financial difficulties and that the particular checking account on which this check was drawn had been frequently overdrawn. Do these circumstances prevent *P* from being a holder in due course? [*Citizens Bank, Booneville v. National Bank of Commerce,* 334 F.2d 257 (10th Cir.); *Franklin National Bank v. Sidney Gotowner,* 4 UCC. Rep. Serv. 953 (N.Y. Supp.)]

10. Daniel, Joel, and Claire Guerrette are the adult children of Elden Guerrette, who died on September 24, 1995. Before his death, Elden purchased a life insurance policy from Sun Life Assurance Company of Canada through a Sun Life agent, Steven Hall, and named his children as his beneficiaries. Upon his death, Sun Life issued three checks, each in the amount of $40,759.35, to each of Elden's children. The checks were drawn on Sun Life's account at Chase Manhattan Bank in Syracuse, New York. The checks were given to Hall for delivery to the Guerrettes. Hall and an associate, Paul Richard, then fraudulently induced the Guerrettes to indorse the checks in blank and to transfer them to Hall and Richard, purportedly to be invested in HER, Inc., a corporation formed by Hall and Richard. Hall took the checks from the Guerrettes and turned them over to Richard, who deposited them in his account at the Credit Union on October 26, 1995. The Credit Union immediately made the funds available to Richard.

    The Guerrettes quickly regretted having negotiated their checks to Hall and Richard, and they contacted Sun Life the next day to request that Sun Life stop payment on the checks. Sun Life immediately ordered Chase Manhattan to stop payment on the checks. When the checks were ultimately presented to Chase Manhattan for payment, Chase refused to pay the checks, and they were returned to the Credit Union. The Credit Union received notice that the checks had been dishonored on November 3, 1995, the sixth business day following their deposit. By the time the Credit Union received notice, however, Richard had withdrawn from his account all of the funds represented by the three checks. The Credit Union was able to recover almost $80,000 from Richard, but there remained an unpaid balance of $42,366.56.

    The Credit Union filed suit against Sun Life, and all of the parties became engulfed in litigation. The Credit Union indicated it was a holder in due course and was entitled to payment on the instrument. Sun Life alleged fraud. Is the Credit Union a holder in due course? Can the parties allege the fraud defense against it? [*Maine Family Federal Credit Union v. Sun Life Assur. Co. of Canada,* 727 A.2d 335 (Maine)]

11. G.C. Vincent was an employee of Porter County Development Corporation (PCDC). Vincent had three personal credit cards through Citibank. Vincent diverted checks to the PCDC, deposited them into his personal checking account, and issued checks drawn upon that personal account to pay part of the outstanding balance of his three Citibank-held credit card accounts. Citibank was unaware that Vincent used misappropriated funds to pay his credit card balance. PCDC filed suit to have Citibank return the embezzled funds. Citibank moved for summary judgment on the grounds that it was an HDC. The trial court granted summary judgment and PCDC appealed.

Who should prevail on appeal and why? [*Porter County Development Corp. v. Citibank (South Dakota)*, N.A., 855 N.E. 2d 306 (Ind. App.)]

12. Sanders gave Clary a check but left the amount incomplete. The check was given as advance payment on the purchase of 100 LT speakers. The amount was left blank because Clary had the right to substitute other LT speakers if they became available and the substitution would change the price. It was agreed that in no event would the purchase price exceed $5,000. Desperate for cash, Clary wrongfully substituted much more expensive LT speakers, thereby increasing the price to $5,700. Clary then negotiated the check to Lawrence, one of his suppliers. Clary filled in the $5,700 in Lawrence's presence, showing him the shipping order and the invoice applicable to the sale to Sanders. Lawrence accepted the check in payment of $5,000 worth of overdue debts and $700 in cash. Can Lawrence recover the full amount? Why or why not?

13. GRAS is a Michigan corporation engaged in the business of buying and selling cars. Between 1997 and 2000, Katrina Stewart was employed as a manager by GRAS. During that period, Stewart wrote checks, without authority, on GRAS's corporate account payable to MBNA and sent them to MBNA for payment of her husband's MBNA credit card account. MBNA accepted the checks and credited the proceeds to Stewart's husband's credit card debt. MBNA accepted and processed the GRAS checks in its normal manner through electronic processing. When MBNA receives a check for a credit card payment, the envelope containing the check and the payment slip is opened by machine and the check and the payment slip are electronically processed and credited to the cardholder's account balance. MBNA does not normally review checks for credit card payments. After crediting a payment check to the cardholder's account, MBNA transfers it to the bank on which it is written for collection. Pursuant to its standard practice, MBNA did not review the checks it received from Stewart. GRAS did not have a customer relationship with MBNA during the relevant time period.

    GRAS sought a refund of the amounts Stewart embezzled via the MBNA application of the checks to Stewart's husband's credit card account. MBNA said it was a holder in due course. Was MBNA a holder in due course? Was MBNA subject to GRAS's defense of unauthorized instruments? [*Grand Rapids Auto Sales, Inc. v. MBNA America Bank*, 227 F. Supp. 2d 721 (W.D. Mich.)]

14. William Potts was employed by Jemoli Holdings, Inc., to liquidate assets of defunct companies. Potts had the authority to sign checks for Jemoli. Potts had a personal investment account with Raymond James Financial Services. When the stock market had its 2000 crash due to the dot-com bubble, Potts had difficulty meeting his margin calls. He began giving checks from Jemoli to Raymond James to cover the margin calls. When a representative questioned Mr. Potts about the Jemoli checks, he assured the representative that Jemoli was him, and that it was his firm. Over four months, Potts wrote checks totaling $1.5 million to Raymond James to cover loans and to make more investments. When Jemoli's principals discovered the embezzlement they brought suit to recover the funds from Raymond James. Raymond James says it was an HDC of the checks and not subject to Jemoli's claims for breach of fiduciary duty by its agent, Potts. Who is correct about the HDC status of Raymond James and why? [*Jemoli Holding, Inc. v. Raymond James Financial, Inc.*, 470 F.3d 14 (1st Cir.)]

15. Omni Trading issued two checks totaling $75,000 to Country Grain Elevators for grain it had purchased. Country Grain indorsed the checks over to the law firm of Carter & Grimsley as a retainer. Country Grain then collapsed as a business, and Omni stopped payment on the checks because all of its grain had not been delivered. Carter & Grimsley claimed it was a holder in due course and entitled to payment. However, the Department of Agriculture claimed its interest in the checks for liens and maintained that Carter & Grimsley was not a holder in due course because it had not given value. The trial court granted summary judgment for the Department of Agriculture because the checks were indorsed as a retainer for future legal work and Carter & Grimsley had not given value. Is Carter & Grimsley a holder in due course? [*Carter & Grimsley v. Omni Trading, Inc.*, 716 N.E.2d 320 (Ill. App.)]

CPA QUESTIONS

1. Under the Commercial Paper Article of the UCC, which of the following requirements must be met for a person to be a holder in due course of a promissory note?
   a. The note must be payable to bearer.
   b. The note must be negotiable.
   c. All prior holders must have been holders in due course.
   d. The holder must be the payee of the note.
2. A maker of a note will have a real defense against a holder in due course as a result of any of the following conditions except:
   a. Discharge in bankruptcy
   b. Forgery
   c. Fraud in the execution
   d. Lack of consideration
3. Under the commercial paper article of the UCC, in a nonconsumer transaction, which of the following are real (universal) defenses available against a holder in due course?

Material Alteration	Discharge in Bankruptcy	Discharge in Bankruptcy
a. No	Yes	Yes
b. Yes	Yes	No
c. No	No	Yes
d. Yes	No	No

4. A holder in due course will take free of which of the following defenses?
   a. Infancy, to the extent that it is a defense to a simple contract
   b. Discharge of the maker in bankruptcy
   c. A wrongful filling-in of the amount payable that was omitted from the instrument
   d. Duress of a nature that renders the obligation of the party a nullity
5. Mask stole one of Bloom's checks. The check was already signed by Bloom and made payable to Duval. The check was drawn on United Trust Company. Mask forged Duval's signature on the back of the check at the Corner Check Cashing Company, which in turn deposited it with its bank, Town National Bank of Toka. Town National proceeded to collect on the check from United. None of the parties mentioned were negligent. Who will bear the loss, assuming the amount cannot be recovered from Mask?
   a. Bloom
   b. Duval
   c. United Trust Company
   d. Corner Check Cashing Company
6. Robb stole one of Markum's blank checks, made it payable to himself, and forged Markum's signature to it. The check was drawn on the Unity Trust Company. Robb cashed the check at the Friendly Check Cashing Company, which in turn deposited it with its bank, Farmer's National. Farmer's National proceeded to collect on the check from Unity Trust. The theft and forgery were quickly discovered by Markum, who promptly notified Unity. None of the parties mentioned were negligent. Who will bear the loss, assuming the amount cannot be recovered from Robb?
   a. Markum
   b. Unity Trust Company
   c. Friendly Check Cashing Company
   d. Farmer's National
7. For a person to be holder in due course of a promissory note:
   a. The note must be payable in U.S. currency to the holder.
   b. The holder must be the payee of the note.
   c. The note must be negotiable.
   d. All prior holders must have been holders in due course.

Checks and Funds Transfers

learningoutcomes

After studying this chapter, you should be able to

LO.1 List and explain the duties of the drawee bank

LO.2 Explain the methods for, and legal effect of, stopping payment

LO.3 Describe the liability of a bank for improper payment and collection

LO.4 Discuss the legal effect of forgeries and material alterations

LO.5 Specify the time limitations for reporting forgeries and alterations

LO.6 Describe the electronic transfer of funds and laws governing it

The three previous chapters have focused on the characteristics, parties, and transfer of all negotiable instruments. This chapter covers checks as negotiable instruments, the issues related to their transfer and payment because of the involvement of banks, and special rules applicable to banks as drawees. New technology has enhanced the ability of banks and consumers to make rapid commercial transactions through the use of electronic funds transfers. Special rules and rights have developed to govern these forms of payment that serve to facilitate everything from a consumer's withdrawing money from an automated teller machine to a buyer's wiring money to a seller whose business is located continents away.

CPA A. CHECKS

As discussed in Chapter 28, a **check** is, under Uniform Commercial Code (UCC) §3-104(f), "(i) a draft…payable on demand and drawn on a bank or (ii) a cashier's check or teller's check. An instrument may be a check even though it is described on its face by another term, such as 'money order.'"[1] The distinguishing characteristics of checks[2] and drafts are summarized in Figure 31-1. Under Revised Article 4, the change in consumer payment patterns away from formal, signed checks is reflected with the addition of "remotely-created consumer item," which are items directing payment that are drawn on a consumer account but do not carry a handwritten signature of the drawer.[3] Consumer account is defined as a bank account used for household, family, or personal purposes.[4] These types of payments include PayPal authorizations to pay from consumer checking accounts and automatic bill payments that consumers direct remotely.

1. Nature of a Check

(A) SUFFICIENT FUNDS ON DEPOSIT. As a practical matter, a check is drawn on the assumption that the bank has on deposit in the drawer's account an amount sufficient to pay the check. In the case of other drafts, there is no assumption that the drawee has any of the drawer's money with which to pay the instrument. In international transactions, sellers may require buyers not only to accept a draft agreeing to pay but also to back up that draft with a line of credit from the buyer's bank. That line of credit is the backup should the funds for the draft not be forthcoming from the buyer.

If a draft is dishonored, the drawer is civilly liable. If a check is drawn with intent to defraud the person to whom it is delivered, the drawer is also subject to criminal prosecution in most states. The laws under which such drawers are prosecuted are known as **bad check laws**. Most states provide that if the check is not made good within a stated period, such as 10 days, there is a presumption that the drawer originally issued the check with the intent to defraud.

CPA **(B) DEMAND PAPER.** A draft may be payable either on demand or at a future date. A check is a form of **demand draft**. The standard form of check does not specify when it is payable, and it is therefore automatically payable on demand.

One exception arises when a check is **postdated**—that is, when the check shows a date later than the actual date of execution. Postdating a check means that the check is not payable until the date arrives, and it changes the check from a demand draft to a **time draft**.[5] However, banks are not obligated to hold a postdated check until the time used on the check unless the drawer has filed the appropriate paperwork with the bank for such a delay. Because of electronic processing, banks are not required to examine each instrument and honor postdated instrument requests unless the hold is placed into the bank's processing system by the customer.

[1] Revised UCC §3-104(f).

[2] Checks are governed by both Article 3 of the UCC and Article 4 governing bank deposits and collections. The 2001 and 2002 versions of Article 4 are covered in this chapter, along with notations of the changes since the 1990 version. The new versions of Article 4 incorporate provisions in the American Bankers Association Bank Collection Code, enacted in 18 states, and followed in many other states. The purpose of the code was to introduce clarity into the processing of millions of electronic and paper transactions that banks must handle and to recognize the reality of electronic payments.

[3] Revised UCC §3-104(16).

[4] Revised UCC §3-104(2).

[5] A bank is required to comply with a postdate on a check only if it is notified of the postdate in the same way the customer issues a stop payment order.

FIGURE 31-1 *Differences between a Check and a Draft*

Check	Draft
1. Drawee is always a bank. 2. Check is drawn on assumption money is in bank to cover check. 3. Check is payable on demand. 4. Drawee bank only accepts check through certification.	1. Drawee is not necessarily a bank. 2. No assumption drawee has any of drawer's money to pay instrument. 3. Draft may be payable on demand or at future date. 4. Acceptance is required for liability of drawee.

(c) Form of the Check. A check can be in any form of writing.[6] However, bank customers may agree, as part of the contract with their bank, to use certain forms for check writing. A remotely created consumer item need only be evidenced by a *record,* not by a written document. Under Revised UCC §3-104(a)(14), a *record* is defined as "information that is inscribed on a tangible medium or which is stored in an electronic or other medium and is retrievable in perceivable form."[7]

(d) Delivery Not Assignment. The delivery of a check is not an assignment of the money on deposit, so it does not automatically transfer the rights of the depositor against the bank to the holder of the check. A check written by a drawer on his drawee bank does not result in a duty on the part of the drawee bank to the holder to pay the holder the amount of the check.[8] An ordinary check drawn on a customer's account is direction from a customer to the bank for payment, but it does not impose absolute primary liability on the bank at the time the check is written.

Banks assume more responsibility for some types of checks than for the ordinary customer's check. **For Example,** a bank **money order** payable to John Jones is a check and has the bank as both the drawer and the drawee.[9] UCC §3-104(g) defines a cashier's check as "a draft with respect to which the drawer and drawee are the same bank or branches of the same bank."[10] In other words, a **cashier's check** is a check or draft drawn by a bank again on itself. If a cashier's check is drawn on another bank in which the drawer bank has an account, it is a **teller's check**. Although the drawer and drawee may be the same on a money order or a cashier's check, the instrument does not lose its three-party character or its status as a check.

Under new federal laws that Revised Article 4 recognizes, there is the new term **substitute check**, which is an electronic image or paper printout of an electronic image of a check. A substitute check has the same legal effect as a paper check. The bank that converts the paper check into electronic form, called the *reconverting bank*, has certain duties imposed by federal regulations to be certain that the electronic version or substitute check has all of the necessary legal information such as visible indorsements, magnetic bank code strip, payee, and signature of drawer.

2. Certified Checks

The drawee bank may *certify* or accept a check drawn on it. Under UCC §3-409(d), a certified check is "a check accepted by the bank on which it is drawn."[11] While a bank is under no obligation to certify a check, if it does so, the certification has the effect of

[6] Although not required for negotiation or presentment, a printed bank check, when the customer is using a written form, is preferable because it generally carries magnetic ink figures that facilitate sorting and posting.
[7] *Smith v. Farmers Union Mut. Ins. Co.* 260 P.3d 163 (Mont. 2011).
[8] *Crawford v. J.P. Morgan Chase Bank, NA,* 425 Fed. Appx. 445 (6th Cir. 2011).
[9] Revised UCC §3-104(f).
[10] Revised UCC §3-104(g). *Lerner v. First Commerce Bank,* 302 S.W.2d 16 (Tex. App. 2009).
[11] Revised UCC §3-409(d).

the bank accepting primary liability on the instrument. Check certification requires that the actual certification be written on the check and authenticated by the signature of an authorized representative of the bank.[12] Upon certification, the bank must set aside, in a special account maintained by the bank, the amount of the certified check taken from the drawer's account. The certification is a promise by the bank that when the check is presented for payment, the bank will make payment according to the terms of the check. Payment is made regardless of the status of the drawer's account at that time.

A holder or drawer may request that a check be certified by a bank. When certification is at the request of the holder, all prior indorsers and the drawer are released from liability. When certification is at the request of the drawer, the indorsers and drawer, as secondary parties, are not released. Unless otherwise agreed, the delivery of a certified check, a cashier's check, or a teller's check discharges the debt for which the check is given, up to the amount of that check.[13]

The *South Central Bank of Daviess County v. Lynnville Nat. Bank* case involves an issue of trying to cancel a cashier's check.

South Central Bank of Daviess County v. Lynnville Nat. Bank, 901 N.E.2d 576 (Ind. App. 2009)

A Double-Wide, a Cashier's Check, and a Little Fraud

On May 7, 2004, Bryan K. and Lisa C. Fisher purchased a manufactured home at the sales lot of the Landmark Housing Center, Inc. Landmark was a registered dealer for a Texas company called Patriot Homes, Inc. until May 20, 2004.

On June 1, 2004, the Fishers borrowed $31,917.55 from Lynnville National Bank to make a down payment of one-half of the home's purchase price to Landmark. Lynnville issued a cashier's check made payable to Landmark. The same day, the Fishers delivered the cashier's check to Landmark and Landmark deposited the cashier's check into its business checking account with South Central Bank and requested immediate funds.

South Central's branch manager telephoned Lynnville and confirmed the date, amount, and payee of the cashier's check. The Lynnville employee explained that the funds were for the purchase of a manufactured home. South Central's branch manager later attested that the Lynnville employee said that the cashier's check was "good" or "fine," but the employee denied making such a statement. On the same day—June 1, 2004—South Central gave unfettered and immediate cash and credit to Landmark after the cashier's check was deposited into Landmark's account.

On June 3, 2004, an employee of Patriot called the Fishers and informed them that Landmark was no longer a dealer for Patriot. Lisa Fisher then called Lynnville to report that Landmark could not fulfill its contract and that it had misrepresented itself as a dealer for Patriot. Lynnville confirmed with Patriot that Landmark was not an authorized dealer. The Fishers directed Lynnville to inform South Central of Landmark's suspected fraud and to stop or refuse payment on the cashier's check.

At approximately 10:00 a.m. on June 3, 2004, South Central paid a check for $24,000, which was written to South Central in exchange for a $24,000 cashier's check made payable to James Rice, a Landmark principal. South Central received the phone call from Lynnville regarding Landmark's suspected fraud and Lynnville's refusal to honor the Fishers' cashier's check at approximately 1:45 p.m., after the proceeds of the Fishers' check had already been paid out of Landmark's account. After notification of Lynnville's refusal to pay, South Central took no steps to retrieve or halt the withdrawal of any funds by Landmark. The following day, on June 4, 2004, South Central paid the $24,000 cashier's check upon presentment by Rice. South Central said it cleared the $24,000.00 cashier's check it issued after Lynnville's notice.

At some point, Rice and Landmark declared bankruptcy. With few alternatives as a result, South Central filed suit against Lynnville, alleging that Lynnville had wrongfully refused payment on the $31,917.35 cashier's check payable to Landmark, and sought to recover the amount of the check plus prejudgment interest, attorney fees, and costs. The trial court found for Lynnville and South Central appealed.

JUDICIAL OPINION

BAKER, Chief Judge...This appeal presents an issue of first impression in Indiana, namely, under what circumstances—if

[12] Many courts treat cashier's checks and certified checks as the same because of their uniform commercial acceptability. See *Jones v. Wells Fargo Bank, N.A.*, 666 F.3d 955 (5th Cir. 2012). However, the rights of the parties are different because certification discharges all other parties to the instrument. A cashier's check does not result in the discharge of other parties on the instrument.

[13] Revised UCC §3-104(h) defines a traveler's check as "a draft drawn by a bank (i) on another bank, or (ii) payable at or through a bank."

Continued

any—an issuing bank may properly refuse to pay a cashier's check. A cashier's check is "[a] check drawn by a bank on itself, payable to another person, and evidencing the payee's authorization to receive from the bank the amount of money represented by the check; a draft for which the drawer and drawee are the same bank, or different branches of the same bank." Among other courts, the Seventh Circuit has held that cashier's checks are somewhat akin to cash: "[b]y definition a cashier's check is a bill of exchange drawn by a bank upon itself and accepted in advance by the act of issuance." Th[e] [Indiana] statute is the model version of Article 3 of the Uniform Commercial Code (UCC). The comments to this section of the UCC clarify the purpose of the section. The language of the statute and the Comment could not be clearer. Only under certain, very specific circumstances is a bank entitled to stop payment on a cashier's check: first, if the bank suspends payments—becomes insolvent; second, if the bank has its own defense—as distinguished from its customer's defense—against the person entitled to enforce the instrument; third, if the bank has a reasonable doubt about the identity of the person demanding payment; and finally, if the payment is prohibited by law. None of those circumstances occurred in this case. Lynnville's obligation to pay was clear and it was able to pay, but it refused payment on the check as an accommodation to the Fishers, who had no right to make that request.

Lynnville relies on the defense of fraud as its basis for stopping payment on the cashier's check. But we agree with South Central that "Lynnville cannot maintain an action of its own against Landmark for fraud. Lynnville was never a victim of fraud. Rather, it is Lynnville's customers who claim a fraud was perpetrated upon them by their seller, Landmark." No interaction occurred between Lynnville and Landmark such that Lynnville can assert its own defense of fraud.

Moreover, South Central argues that it was a holder in due course (HDC) of the cashier's check, which would further limit the defenses available to Lynnville. On June 1, when a Landmark representative presented the cashier's check to South Central, South Central took the instrument for value and in good faith. That Landmark had a spotty history as a customer of the bank does not mean that South Central acted in bad faith by depositing the check. Acting with an abundance of caution, South Central telephoned Lynnville to confirm the date, amount, and payee of the check. Although South Central was not required to do so—and, to be clear, we do not intend to imply that the holder of a cashier's check is required to make such a phone call—that act certainly means that South Central was without notice of any problems with the instrument. Indeed, at that time, Lynnville was without notice of any problems with the instrument. Therefore, when South Central accepted the cashier's check on June 1, it became an HDC. The events that occurred after June 1 are irrelevant to the validity of the cashier's check on June 1 and South Central's status as an HDC. The clock stopped following presentment and acceptance.

Because South Central is an HDC, the only defenses that could be raised by Lynnville are the "real" defenses.

Landmark's fraud on the Fishers does not automatically spill over to South Central who had absolutely no knowledge of what Landmark did or did not promise the Fishers.... There is absolutely nothing in the cashier's check that in any way indicated what type of transaction was involved or what, if anything, had been promised to the Fishers.

Given that Lynnville wrongfully refused to pay the cashier's check, South Central "is entitled to compensation for expenses and loss of interest resulting from the nonpayment and may recover consequential damages...." I.C. § 26-1-3.1-411(b). Lynnville argues, however, that South Central failed to mitigate its damages. Lynnville argues that South Central failed to abide by its own policy providing for a delay in payment to its customers. South Central's "Funds Availability Policy" provides as follows:

> *Our general policy is to allow you to withdraw funds deposited in your account on the next business day after the day we receive your deposit. In some cases, we may delay your ability to withdraw funds beyond the next...business day. The funds will generally be available by the fifth business day after the day of deposit.*

Lynnville argues that, given Landmark's history of unreliability as a South Central customer and its request for immediate funds, South Central failed to exercise ordinary care by giving Landmark immediate access to the deposited funds. We cannot agree. Even if the policy had been followed, Landmark would have had access to the funds on the next business day following deposit, which would have been June 2. But it was not until June 3 that Lynnville notified South Central of Landmark's alleged fraud. Thus, in either scenario, South Central would have already given Landmark access to the funds by the time Lynnville picked up the telephone. The Funds Availability Policy, therefore, is of no help to Lynnville.

While Landmark may have been an unreliable customer of South Central, nothing in these facts, the law, or South Central's policy leads us to conclude that its decision to give immediate credit to South Central was an action taken without ordinary care. Finally, Lynnville directs our attention to the Federal Expedited Funds Availability Act and Federal Regulation CC, which directs banks to formulate and provide a funds availability policy that provides a schedule for withdrawals and declares that funds will not be available until a later date. 12 C.F.R. § 229.15.

Continued

South Central's failure to "tak[e] advantage of the protections of Regulation CC is another breach of ordinary care," according to Lynnville, because "South Central had the right to protect itself but chose not to do so." South Central, on the other hand, notes that "the whole purpose of a cashier's check and Regulation CC is to speed funds availability, not slow it down." We agree.

The judgment of the trial court is reversed.

QUESTIONS

1. Why is the fraud of the mobile home seller not an issue for South Central?
2. What point does Lynnville try to make with the Federal Expedited Funds Availability Act?
3. Is South Central a holder in due course?

E-Commerce & Cyberlaw

The Nigerian "I Need Your Help" E-Mails

They are quite common, those e-mails that come into our accounts asking for help in transferring funds in exchange for a percentage of those funds. They only ask that they be able to use our bank accounts in the United States so that they are able to collect the money owed to them, with your 12 to 15 percent service fee for use of your account deducted.

These are scams, accomplished by simple means. The scammers do indeed have their alleged creditors furnish large checks initially to be deposited in your account. Those checks do seem to clear. They then have you write checks in the amount deposited (less your percentage fee) to them. However, subsequent problems develop with those initially deposited checks and your bank wants you to now cover the overdraft created by the scammers cashing your check. You end up owing the money to your bank. You have no claim based on forgery because it was your check. In short, the Nigerians win. There is no remedy under Article 3 or 4 for you. Fraud is the answer, but finding the scammers is a tall order. The federal government works tirelessly to alert people to the scams because it is nearly impossible for them to locate the scammers. Beware of e-mails coming your way from folks from Nigeria, Malaysia, and, well, any other country who wish to use your bank account for processing their payments. **[*Chino Commercial Bank, N.A., v. Peters, 118 Cal. Rptr. 3d 866 (Cal. App. 2010)*]**

CPA 3. Presentment for Obtaining Payment on a Check

A holder of a check must take required steps to obtain payment. As discussed in Chapter 30, there are primary and secondary parties for every negotiable instrument. Primary parties are makers and drawees. Under Revised Article 3, secondary parties are referred to as *secondary obligors* and are defined to include "an indorser, a drawer, an accommodation party, or any other party to the instrument that has a right of recourse against another party to the instrument."[14]

The process for a holder to be paid on an instrument involves mandatory steps with time limitations. The holder must first seek payment from the drawee through **presentment**. No secondary obligor is liable on an instrument until presentment has been made. Presentment is required for checks, and presentment is made first to the drawee bank.[15]

(A) Presentment Requirements. Presentment occurs when the holder of a check or other consumer transaction authorization demands payment.[16] Under Revised Article 3, the party presents either the check or a record for payment. If the presentment is done in person, the party to whom presentment is made can require that the presenter exhibit identification. The holder who is presenting the instrument must present the check or record for payment in a commercially

[14] Revised UCC §3-104(12).

[15] It is important to note that the bank is unique as a drawee because its contract as a primary party is limited by its right to dishonor a check and its right to give only provisional credit.

[16] In addition to the UCC restrictions on times for presentment, banks must comply with federally imposed time constraints. Under the Expedited Funds Availability Act, 12 U.S.C. §4001 *et seq.*, banks are required to lift provisional credits on customer accounts.

reasonable manner; banks can treat the transaction as having occurred the following day when presentment is made after *the close of the business day.*[17] In the case of electronic banking, banks are permitted to impose times after which posting will occur the next day. If a check is presented to the drawee bank for payment and paid, the drawer has no liability because payment has been made. (For more details on presentment, generally, of instruments, see Chapter 30.)

CPA **(B) Time for Presentment of a Check for Payment.**[18] Under the UCC, presentment must be made within a reasonable time after the drawers and indorsers have signed the check. What constitutes a reasonable time is determined by the nature of the instrument, by commercial usage, and by the facts of the particular case.

Failure to make timely presentment discharges all secondary obligors (prior indorsers) of the instrument. It also discharges the drawer to the extent that the drawer has lost, through the bank's failure, money that was on deposit at the bank to make the payment due under the check.[19]

The UCC establishes two presumptions as to what is a reasonable time for presentment of checks. If the check is not certified and is both drawn and payable within the United States, it is presumed that 90 days after the date of the check or the date of its issuance, whichever is later, is the reasonable period in which to make presentment for payment in order to attach secondary liability to the drawer.[20] With respect to attachment of the liability of an indorser, 30 days after indorsement is the presumed reasonable time.[21]

If a check is dated with the date of issue, it may be presented immediately for payment. If it is postdated, ordinarily it may not be presented until that date arrives. However, as noted earlier, the bank need not honor the date on the postdated instrument. If the holder delays in making presentment, the delay discharges the drawer if the bank itself fails during such delay.[22] If the holder of the check does not present it for payment or collection within 90 days after an indorsement was made, the secondary obligors (indorsers) are discharged from liability to the extent that the drawer has lost, through the bank's failure, money that was on deposit at the bank to meet the payment under the check.

Under Revised Articles 3 and 4, agreeing to honor an instrument beyond this time limit changes the obligation of the primary obligor and, as a result, changes the obligation of the secondary obligors. Such changes in the terms and conditions of payment serve to discharge the secondary obligors, a change that brings UCC Articles 3 and 4 in line with the principles of surety law (see Chapter 33).

A bank may continue to honor checks presented for payment after the 90-day period, but it does so with understanding of the discharge of liability for the primary and secondary obligors. A bank honoring a check that is overdue subjects the bank to questions about whether it exercised good faith and reasonable care in honoring it.[23]

4. Dishonor of a Check

If the bank refuses to make payment, the drawer is then subject to the same secondary liability as the drawer of an ordinary draft.[24] To be able to attach that secondary liability, the holder of the instrument must notify the drawer of the dishonor by the drawee. The notice of dishonor may be oral, written, or electronic.

CPA **(A) Time for Notice of Dishonor.** Banks in the chain of collection for a check must give notice of dishonor by midnight of the next banking day. Others, including the payee or holder of the check, must give notice of dishonor within 30 days after learning that the instrument has been dishonored.[25] If proper notice of dishonor is not given to the drawer of

[17] Revised UCC §4-107(1). *Rogers v. Bank of America, N.A.*, 73 UCC Rep. Serv. 2d 47 (S.D. Ill. 2010).
[18] Revised UCC §3-501. *Whooping Creek Const., LLC v. Bartow County Bank*, 713 S.E.2d 871 (Ga. App. 2011).
[19] Revised UCC §3-605.
[20] Under the previous versions of Articles 3 and 4, the time was six months.
[21] Revised UCC §3-304.
[22] Revised UCC §4-208(c).
[23] Revised Article 3 changed the "negligence" of the bank to the "failure to exercise ordinary care" in §3-406. A bank need not pay a check that is presented to it after six months from the date of issue (except for certified checks), but it can honor such a check and charge the customer's account if it does so in good faith.
[24] Revised UCC §3-414. PayPal is not considered a bank for purposes of Articles 3 and 4. *Zepeda v. PayPal, Inc.*, 777 F. Supp. 2d 1215 (N.D. Cal. 2011).
[25] The former time frame for nonbanks was midnight of the third business day.

Ethics & the Law

Getting Hit For SOOO Many Overdraft Fees

On August 28, 2008, Cortney Hassler had a balance of $112.35 in his checking account. He made a $39.58 payment in the morning and a $140.00 debit in the afternoon. Sovereign Bank did not post the transactions in the order that they occurred but, rather, rearranged the debits so that Cortney had to pay two $33 overdraft fees on his account. A provision in his checking account agreement indicated that Sovereign had the right to pay the withdrawals in any order. Cortney filed a class action suit against the bank for unfair trade practices and unjust enrichment. Evaluate the legal rights of the bank to post the transactions as it did. Evaluate the ethical issues in the changes in posting order so as to maximize the overdraft fees. **[*Hassler v. Sovereign Bank,* 374 Fed. Appx. 341 (3rd Cir. 2010)**. See also ***In re Checking Account Overdraft Litigation,* 694 F. Supp. 2d 1032 (S.D. Fla. 2010).]**

the check, the drawer will be discharged from liability to the same extent as the drawer of an ordinary draft.[26]

CPA **(B) Overdraft.** If the bank pays the check but the funds in the account are not sufficient to cover the amount, the excess of the payment over the amount on deposit is an **overdraft**. This overdraft is treated as a loan from the bank to the customer, and the customer must repay that amount to the bank.

If the bank account from which the check is drawn is one held by two or more persons, the joint account holder who does not sign the check that creates an overdraft is not liable for the amount of the overdraft if she received no benefit from the proceeds of that check.[27] Additional issues on overdrafts and dishonor of checks are covered in Section 5.

5. The Customer-Bank Relationship

The relationship between banks and customers is governed by Articles 3 and 4 of the UCC as well as by several federal statutes. These laws impose duties and liabilities on both banks and customers.

(A) Privacy. The bank owes its customer the duty of maintaining the privacy of the information that the bank acquires in connection with its relationship with the customer. Law enforcement officers and administrative agencies cannot require the disclosure of information relating to a customer's account without first obtaining the customer's consent or a search warrant or without following the statutory procedures designed to protect customers from unreasonable invasions of privacy.[28] The **USA Patriot Act** does impose certain reporting requirements on banks, financial institutions, and businesses with regard to deposits of cash and large cash payments. These reporting requirements were imposed to be able to track money laundering efforts as well as possible funding of terrorist activities.[29] For example, checks that involve amounts of more than $10,000 generally trigger the bank reporting systems under the USA Patriot Act.

With the advent of the Internet and other electronic exchanges of information, it has become much easier for businesses, including banks, to exchange information about customers. All businesses are subject to federal constraints on the use of customer information. (See Chapter 33 for more information.)

(B) Payment. A bank is under a general contractual duty to its customers to pay on demand all checks to the extent of the funds in a depositor's account.

CPA ***(1) Stale Checks.***

A bank acting in good faith may pay a check presented more than six months after its date

[26] Revised UCC §4-213. Under Federal Reserve regulations, notice of dishonor may be given by telephone. *Security Bank and Trust Co. v. Federal Nat'l Bank,* 554 P.2d 119 (Okla. Ct. App. 1976). But see *City Check Cashing, Inc. v. Manufacturers Hanover Trust Co.,* 764 A.2d 411, 43 UCC Rep. Serv. 2d 768 (N.J. 2001). See also *JP Morgan Chase Bank, N.A. v. Cohen,* 907 N.Y.S.2d 101 (N.Y. Sup. 2009).

[27] Revised UCC §§4-214 and 4-401(b).

[28] Right to Financial Privacy Act of 1978, 12 U.S.C. §3401 *et seq.*

[29] 12 U.S.C. §5311 *et seq.* 2001.

(commonly known as a **stale check**), but unless the check is certified, the bank is not required to do so.[30] The fact that a bank may refuse to pay a check that is more than six months old does not mean that it must pay a check that is less than six months old or that it is not required to exercise reasonable care in making payment on any check.

(2) Payment after Depositor's Death.

From the time of death, the bank can continue paying items until it actually knows of the customer's death.[31] The bank has the right, even with notice of the death, to continue to pay items for 10 days unless, for example, an heir or a government agency halts the payments.[32]

CPA 6. Stopping Payment of a Check

A drawer may stop payment of a check by notifying the drawee bank in the required manner.[33] **Stop payment orders** are often used when a check is lost or mislaid. The drawer can always write a duplicate check but wants assurance that the original lost or misplaced check will not then also be presented for payment. The drawer can stop payment on the first check to prevent double-dipping. A drawer can also use a stop payment order on a check if the payee has not kept his end of the contract or has failed to provide assurances (see Chapter 26). However, the drawer must keep in mind that if a holder in due course has the check, the holder in due course can demand payment because she would not be subject to the personal defenses of breach of contract or nonperformance of contract. (See Chapter 30 and the rights of holders in due course.)

Stop payment orders are invalid for some forms of checks even when properly executed. Neither the drawer nor a bank customer can stop payment of a **certified check**. A bank customer cannot stop payment of a cashier's check.

CPA **(A) Form of Stop Payment Order.** The stop payment order may be either oral or by record (written or evidence of electronic order). If oral, however, the order is binding on the bank for only 14 calendar days unless confirmed in writing within that time. A record of the stop payment order or confirmation is effective for six months. A stop payment order can be renewed for an additional six months if the customer provides the bank a written extension.

(B) Liability to Holder for Stopping Payment. The act of stopping payment may in some cases make the drawer liable to the holder of the check. If the drawer has no proper ground for stopping payment, the drawer is liable to the holder of the check. In any case, the drawer is liable for stopping payment with respect to any holder in due course or any other party having the rights of a holder in due course unless payment was stopped for a reason that may be asserted as a defense against a holder in due course (see Chapter 30). The fact that payment of a check has been stopped does not affect its negotiable character.[34]

7. Wrongful Dishonor of a Check

A check is **wrongfully dishonored** by the drawee bank if the bank refuses to pay the amount of the check although (1) it is properly payable and (2) the account on which it is drawn is sufficient to pay the item. Dishonor for lack of funds can be a breach of contract if the customer has an agreement with the bank that it will pay overdraft items.

CPA **(A) Bank's Liability to Drawer of Check.** If the bank improperly refuses to make payment, it is liable to the drawer for damages sustained by the drawer as a consequence of such dishonor.

(B) Bank's Liability to Holder. If a check has not been certified, the holder has no claim against the bank for the dishonor of the check regardless of the fact that the bank was wrong in its dishonor. The bank that certifies a check is liable to the holder when it dishonors the check.

(C) Holder's Notice of Dishonor of Check. When a check is dishonored by nonpayment, the holder must follow the procedure for notice to the secondary parties. Notice of dishonor need not be given to the drawer who has stopped payment on a check or to drawers and indorsers who are aware that there are

[30] Revised UCC §§3-304 and 4-404; *Commerce Bank, N.A. v. Rickett*, 748 A.2d 111 (N.J. Super. 2000).
[31] Revised UCC §4-405(2).
[32] Revised UCC §4-405(b); *Hieber v. Uptown Nat'l Bank of Chicago*, 557 N.E.2d 408 (Ill. App. 1990).
[33] Revised UCC §4-403.
[34] *Seigel v. Merrill Lynch, Pierce, Fenner & Smith*, 745 A.2d 301 (D.C. 2000).

insufficient funds on deposit to cover the check. In those circumstances, no party has reason to expect that the check will be paid by the bank.

8. Agency Status of Collecting Bank

When a customer deposits negotiable instruments in a bank, the bank is regarded as being merely an **agent**, even though the customer may be given the right to make immediate withdrawals against the deposited item. Because of the bank's **agency** status, the customer remains the owner of the item and is subject to the risks of ownership involved in its collection.

When a bank cashes a check deposited by its customer or cashes a check drawn by its customer based on an amount from a deposited check, it is a holder of the check deposited by its customer. The bank may still collect from the parties on the check even though the bank is an agent for collection and has the right to charge back the amount of the deposited check if it cannot be collected.

9. Bank's Duty of Care

A bank is required to exercise ordinary care in the handling of items. The liability of a bank is determined by the law of the state where the bank, branch, or separate office involved is located.

CPA **(A) Modification of Bank Duties.** The parties in the bank collection process may modify their rights and duties by agreement. However, a bank cannot disclaim liability for lack of good faith or failure to exercise ordinary care, nor can it limit the measure of damages for such lack of care.

When a bank handles checks by automated processes, the standard of ordinary care does not require the bank to make a physical examination of each item. Banks must use the ordinary care standard of the industry.

(B) Encoding Warranty and Electronic Presentment. In addition to transfer and presentment warranties, an **encoding warranty** is also given by those who transfer instruments. Under this warranty, anyone placing information on an item or transmitting the information electronically warrants that the information is correct. When there is an agreement for electronic presentment, the presenter warrants that the transfer is made properly for transmissions.[35]

(C) Counterfeit Checks. One of the problems that banks now experience is the use of counterfeit checks. Because of automated processing, these checks can sail through bank systems and seemingly are cleared. Customers, in reliance on the check clearing, use those funds only to be told later that the check was a counterfeit and the funds credited to their account are then debited. The liability for the losses resulting from counterfeit checks will depend on whether the bank acted reasonably in its processing systems in clearing checks (particularly those for large amounts) and whether it complied with the time requirements for notifying customers of a dishonor of a deposited counterfeit check.

The *Greenberg, Trager & Herbst, LLP v. HSBC Bank USA* case shows the risks of counterfeit checks.

Greenberg Trager & Herbst, LLP v. HSBC Bank USA, 934 N.Y.S.2d 43, 75 UCC Rep.Serv.2d 775 (Sup. Ct. 2011)

The Lawyers Who Got Taken by Their Counterfeit Clients

Greenberg, Trager & Herbst, LLP (GTH), is a law firm specializing in construction litigation law. In September 2007, a partner at GTH received an e-mail from a representative of Northlink Industrial Limited, a Hong Kong company. Northlink was looking for legal representation to assist it in the collection of debts owed by its North American customers. Through a series of e-mails GTH agreed to represent Northlink and requested a $10,000 retainer. GTH then received a Citibank check for $197,750 from a Northlink customer and was told that it could take its retainer from those funds. On Friday, September 21, 2007, GTH deposited the check into its account at HSBC.

The next business day, Monday, September 24, HSBC processed the check through the Federal Reserve Bank of

[35] Revised UCC §§4-207 to 4-209.

Continued

Philadelphia (FRBP) and because of the federal funds availability law, provisionally credited GTH's account for $197,750. FRBP presented an image replacement document (IRD) of the check to Citibank that same day.

Because the routing number was not recognized by Citi's processing system, the automated sorting system directed the IRD to the reject pocket.

HSBC received the IRD with the notation "sent wrong" the next day, September 25, 2007. Because the check was marked "sent wrong," HSBC assumed that there was a problem with the routing number that required sending the check to a different Federal Reserve bank. On September 26, 2007, HSBC sent the check to the Federal Reserve Bank, San Francisco (FRBS). HSBC never informed GTH of the "administrative return" of the check.

On September 27, 2007, a GTH partner called HSBC to determine whether the check had "cleared" and if the funds were available for disbursement. GTH was informed that the funds were available. Later that day, GTH wired $187,750 from its account to Hong Kong as Northlink instructed.

On October 2, 2007, HSBC received Citibank's notice that the check was being dishonored as "RTM [return to maker] Suspect Counterfeit." HSBC contacted GTH to inform them that the check had been dishonored. HSBC then revoked its provisional settlement and charged back GTH's account.

GTH filed suit against HSBC and Citibank for failure to inform GTH that the check had been returned and dishonored on September 25, and for informing GTH over the phone that the funds had "cleared" and were available for disbursement. HSBC and Citibank moved for summary judgment. The trial court found that HSBC had no duty under the UCC to inform GTH that the check had been returned "sent wrong" on September 25, but rather that the dishonor actually took place when HSBC discovered that the check was "Suspect Counterfeit" and dismissed the complaint.

JUDICIAL OPINION

CIPARICK, Judge...Pursuant to the Expedited Funds Availability Act (12 USC § 4001 et seq.), banks are required to make funds from a deposited check available for the depositor's withdrawal within certain short time periods. Funds availability is provisional and the collecting bank has the right to charge back the amount if the check is dishonored or the bank fails to receive a settlement for the check (see UCC 4–212).

GTH claims that Citibank was negligent in breaching its obligation to implement effective procedures for detecting counterfeit checks in that it failed to detect that the item was fraudulent when Citibank processed the check. GTH notes the uncontroverted fact that on September 24, 2007, the day Citibank returned the check in question to the FRBP, Citibank returned at least six other checks, each in the identical amount of $197,750, which should have put Citibank on notice that something was amiss. Additionally, Citibank admits that the personnel who reviewed checks after being sent to the reject packet were not trained to determine if they were counterfeit. In short, it is clear that Citibank did nothing to determine if the check was counterfeit prior to returning it to FRBP.

The duty of a payor bank (in this case Citibank) to a non-customer depositor of a check is derived solely from UCC 4–301 and 4–302. UCC 4–302(a) provides that a payor bank is liable for an item received by the payor bank if it "does not pay or return the item or send notice of dishonor until after its midnight deadline." In this case, it is uncontroverted that Citibank returned the check to FRBP within its midnight deadline.

GTH is not a customer of Citibank and the duties codified in UCC 4–406(3) are not applicable here. Moreover, there was never any payment made by Citibank on the check. In short, the only duty Citibank owed GTH was to pay the check, return the check or send notice of dishonor of the check by midnight of the next banking day after receiving the check. It is uncontroverted that Citibank returned the check within its midnight deadline. Because GTH cannot establish any duty owing from Citibank that was breached, GTH's claims against Citibank were properly dismissed.

As against HSBC, GTH alleges negligent misrepresentation as a result of HSBC informing GTH that the check had "cleared" and the funds were available for transfer. Second, it alleges negligence for failing to inform GTH and charge back the check on September 26th, when it was originally returned on September 25th by Citibank via FRBP.

We note that GTH, in its own words, asked HSBC if the check had "cleared." "The term 'cleared' is not employed in the UCC and, as commonly used, is not the equivalent of 'final settlement.'"

GTH argues that, pursuant to UCC 4–201, HSBC was an agent of GTH during the period that HSBC was acting as a collecting bank for plaintiff. GTH claims that pursuant to this agency relationship, HSBC owed a fiduciary duty to GTH. HSBC claims that it owed no fiduciary duty, and also relies on a waiver contained in the contract between GTH and HSBC with the following provision:

> *BALANCE INFORMATION*
>
> *Balances may change frequently throughout a business day. You hereby waive any claim against the Bank based on representations made by the Bank, either orally or in writing to you, or your authorized person, or to any other party, regarding balance information.*

Continued

GTH's claim is based on the alleged oral statement by the HSBC representative that the check had "cleared"—an ambiguous remark that may have been intended to mean only that the amount of the check was available (as indeed it was) in GTH's account. Reliance on this statement as assurance that final settlement had occurred was, under the circumstances here, unreasonable as a matter of law.

GTH argues that the return of the check was a dishonor of the check, thereby triggering HSBC's duty to inform GTH and charge back its account by the midnight deadline (i.e., September 26th, the day before GTH wired the funds).

HSBC argues that when the check was returned "sent wrong," it was, what is known in the banking industry, an "administrative return." An "administrative return" occurs when the routing number on the check is damaged or unreadable. When such a return occurs, the bank will do more research, repair the routing number and resubmit the check, which is what happened here. According to HSBC, this type of return is not a dishonor of the check. The check was, in HSBC's view, still being processed.

Since GTH cannot establish that [the banks] breached any duty owed, the courts below have correctly determined that no triable issues of fact exist and properly awarded summary judgment in favor of the defendant banks.

PIGOTT, J. (dissenting in part).

In this case, GTH alleges that on September 27, 2007, David A. Trager, a partner at GTH, telephoned his contact at HSBC, Frances Scott, to inquire about the status of the Citibank check. Trager and Scott had a five-year banking relationship, whereby Trager would call Scott to confirm that checks deposited into GTH's trust account had cleared and were available for disbursement. Scott informed Trager that the Citibank check had "cleared" and that the funds were available to be wired to another account. Relying in good faith on that statement, Trager asked Scott to wire proceeds of the check, which she did.

HSBC makes much of the fact that the word "cleared" is not found in the UCC and the majority finds it to be ambiguous. However, UCC 1–205 entitled "course of dealing and usage of trade," defines "usage of trade" as encompassing "any practice or method of dealing having such regularity of observance in a place, vocation or trade as to justify an expectation that it will be observed with respect to the transaction in question" (*584 UCC 1–205[2]). The term "cleared" is used liberally in the banking business. Indeed, the Federal Trade Commission in a bulletin addressed to consumers states that "[i]t's best not to rely on money from any type of check ... unless you know and trust the person you're dealing with or, better yet—until the bank confirms that the check has cleared." Therefore, I disagree with the majority's position that relying on this statement was unreasonable as a matter of law. I suspect many business professionals would have done the same thing as Trager.

GTH raises questions of fact as to whether HSBC failed to exercise ordinary care when Scott misrepresented the status of the check to Trager.

Counterfeit check scams are pervasive. That Citibank could not recognize one of its own checks as counterfeit is testament to the seriousness of this problem within the banking industry. It is no answer that Citibank and HSBC seemed to stumble along over a period of 10 days resulting in one of their customers being bilked out of $187,750. This problem has long been known to the banks and a mere recitation of their normal practices does not, in my view, establish the appropriate standard of care in this day and age and certainly not their entitlement to summary judgment.

QUESTIONS

1. When was there a dishonor of the check? What is the significance of that time?
2. Why does the dissenting judge disagree with the majority's decision?
3. What do you learn about cautions that customers should take to be sure they have no losses from counterfeit checks?

CPA B. Liability of a Bank

Banks can make mistakes in the payment and collection of items presented to them by their customers. **For Example,** a check may slip through and be cashed over a customer's properly executed stop payment order. The bank would be liable for this improper payment and may also be liable for improperly collecting, paying, or refusing to pay a check.

10. Premature Payment of a Postdated Check

A check may be postdated, but the bank is not liable for making payments on the check before the date stated unless the drawer has given the bank prior notice. Such a notice is similar to a stop payment order; it must provide sufficient information so that the bank is moved to action by the trigger that comes from the orderly processing of the check as it flows through its electronic processing system.[36]

11. Payment Over a Stop Payment Order

A bank must be given a reasonable time in which to put a stop payment order into effect. However, if the bank makes payment of a check after it has been properly notified to stop payment, and there has been sufficient time for the order to be put into the system, the bank is liable to the drawer (customer) for the loss the drawer sustains in the absence of a valid limitation of the bank's liability.[37] The bank must have complete information on a stop payment order, such as the payee, check number, and amount, to be held responsible for the failure to stop payment.

Rovell v. American National Bank, 194 F.3d 867 (7th Cir. 1999)

The Double-Dipping Detective Agency: No Stopping Payment without Details

Michael Rovell, a lawyer (Rovell or Debtor), practiced law in his own firm in Chicago, but his work took him on occasion to Arizona and California, where he engaged the services of an Arizona private investigator, Patricia O'Connor, and her firm, Pretty Eyes Detective Agency. On August 30, 1994, pursuant to a fee agreement between Rovell and O'Connor, Rovell's firm wrote a check to O'Connor for her services. The check in the amount of $38,250 was not immediately cashed. About three weeks later on September 19, Rovell discovered that the firm had overpaid O'Connor by more than $10,000. Wishing to correct the mistake, Rovell directed his associate, attorney Lisa I. Fair, to contact their banker, ANB in Chicago, and inquire whether the check had been cashed. Fair called the firm's account representative at ANB, Linda Williams, to request a stop-payment order.

Fair asserted that she called Williams and asked if the check had been cashed. Because she did not know the check number, she could only supply the account number, check amount, and payee. Fair added that it might be in the range of six checks beginning with number 1084, but that she could not be sure because no record had been kept of the check number. Fair said that Williams put her on hold and then returned to report that the check had not cleared. Fair testified that she then asked for a stop-payment order to be issued and contended that Williams never told her that the bank could not stop payment without a check number. Fair also denied that Williams advised her to wait before writing a replacement check. The correct number for the first check written to Pretty Eyes turned out to be 1105.

Williams recalled the conversation differently. She remembered Fair calling and not knowing the check number, but requesting a stop payment on checks numbered 1084 and 1086, neither of which had cleared the bank yet. Williams processed the stop-payment order on those two checks and said she cautioned Fair to wait a few days before writing the replacement. Williams, who had 26 years of banking experience, said she routinely cautioned customers not to write checks immediately after a stop-payment order had been issued but did not recall specifically telling Fair that a check number was necessary for a stop-payment order.

Williams processed the stop-payment order that day for checks 1084 and 1086, and the order took effect at the start of business the next day. Between the time Williams ended her conversation with Fair and the close of business that day, the check for $38,250 was presented for payment and cashed. Two days later, without waiting for the stop-payment confirmation order to arrive and without calling back to check on the status of the account, Fair wrote a replacement check for $27,284.50 and mailed it by overnight express mail to Arizona. That check also was cashed, causing Rovell to overdraw his account the following December. Despite the uncertainty surrounding the stop-payment order, Rovell never read or responded to the stop-payment confirmation orders and failed to open his monthly account statements for many weeks. Only when he realized that he had overdrawn his account and incurred penalties did Rovell become a dutiful and prolific correspondent with the bank.

In October 1995, Rovell initiated a voluntary bankruptcy under Chapter 11 of the Bankruptcy Code. ANB presented a claim on a secured line of credit for $50,081.25, the validity of which is undisputed.

Rovell, however, filed an objection seeking to reduce the claim by the amount he lost due to the overpayment to Pretty Eyes. He asserted claims under Illinois law for breach of contract on the ground that ANB had promised to stop payment on the first check and negligent misrepresentation based on the bank's alleged "assurance that the check had not cleared and could be stopped."

The bankruptcy court denied both claims. The district court, based on the bankruptcy court's findings of fact, agreed

[36] Note that a "postdated check" is not a check but a time draft. UCC §§4-401 to 4-402.

[37] Revised UCC §4-403(c); *Lombino v. Bank of America, N.A.*, 797 F. Supp. 2d 1078 (D. Nev. 2011).

Continued

that Rovell's reliance on the alleged misrepresentation was unreasonable and therefore not compensable. Rovell appealed.

JUDICIAL OPINION

KANNE, Circuit Judge.... When a law firm plagued by sloppy bookkeeping mistakenly writes a check that results in an overpayment to a private investigator who then decides to pocket the money, should the law firm's bank ultimately bear the loss?

We cannot say that the bankruptcy court's determination that Rovell could not reasonably rely on Williams' advice that a check could be stopped immediately, even without a check number, constituted clear error. Accepting, as we must, the bankruptcy judge's finding that both Fair and Williams presented credible testimony, we are faced with a probability that the conversation between Fair and Williams occurred as Fair recalled it equal to the probability that it occurred as Williams recalled it.

According to Fair's recollection, Fair gave Williams the amount of the check, Rovell's account number and the name of the payee. She could not tell her the check number, but instead provided her with a general range of possible check numbers, which it turned out, was far from the actual check number. Fair then testified that based on this sketchy information, Williams definitively told her the check had not been presented for payment but failed to warn her that she should wait until the stop-payment order could be processed before writing a replacement check.

Williams then remembered Fair saying she wanted to send a replacement check to Pretty Eyes, to which she responded, "Well, Lisa, you should wait a few days." When Fair said she would send a letter explaining that the first check was for the wrong amount, Williams questioned whether the payee could be trusted not to cash both checks.

Taking both memories of the conversation as credible, it appears therefore that this is a case of two honestly held, but differing, memories of a conversation. The question, however, is whether a reasonable person would rely on either version of this exchange, and it seemed clear to both the bankruptcy judge and district judge that they would not.

A reasonable person certainly would not immediately send a replacement check based on the conversation remembered by Williams with an explicit warning to wait a few days. Furthermore, the fact that Williams remembered expressing concerns to Fair about whether the payee was "reputable," would have put a reasonable person on notice that the situation presented a potential for danger.

Even accepting Fair's recollection of the conversation, it seems unreasonable to issue a replacement check before receiving any written confirmation that the check had been effectively stopped. Fair knew that the information she provided Williams for the stop-payment order was incomplete at best, lacking a vital piece of identifying information—the exact check number. One does not need to be a banker or versed in banking law to know that this is a vital piece of information for locating or stopping a check. It is, as the courts below noted, a matter of common sense.

Had Rovell waited until he received the confirmation orders, he would have seen that the stop-payment order covered specific check numbers, alerting him to the strong possibility that the order would not be effective for other check numbers. In fact, Rovell, who often failed to review his monthly bank statements, cannot recall receiving the confirmation orders and apparently did not know they were in his own files until ANB asked for them during discovery. This hardly suggests reasonableness. Finally, we cannot say why Rovell was so anxious to resend a check to a payee who apparently had not been anxious to cash the much larger check sent three weeks earlier, but there certainly seems to be no evidence of a need so pressing that would make Rovell's unexplained haste more reasonable under the circumstances.

Because the record supports the finding of no reasonable reliance, we cannot find that the bankruptcy court committed clear error in denying Rovell's negligent misrepresentation claim. The decision of the district court is

[Affirmed]

QUESTIONS

1. Make a list of the things Mr. Rovell did that the court labels unreasonable.
2. What does a bank need for a valid stop payment order?
3. What does the court say about the differing recollections of the conversation about the stop order?

CPA 12. Payment on a Forged Signature of Drawer

A forgery of the signature of the drawer occurs when the name of the drawer has been signed by another person without authority to do so with the intent to defraud by making it appear that the drawer signed the check. The bank is liable to the drawer if it pays a check on which the drawer's signature has been forged because a forgery ordinarily has no effect as a signature. The risk of loss caused by the forged signature of the drawer is placed on the bank without regard to whether the bank could have detected the forgery.[38] The reasoning behind the bank's liability for a forged drawer's signature is that the bank is presumed to know its own customers' signatures even if it does not regularly review checks for authenticity of the signature.

A bank's customer whose signature has been forged may be barred from holding the bank liable if the customer's negligence substantially contributed to the making of the forgery. This preclusion rule prevents or precludes the customer from making a forgery claim against the bank. However, to enjoy the protection of the preclusion rule, the bank, if negligent in its failure to detect the forgery or alteration, must have cashed the check in good faith or have taken it for value or collection.[39]

Article 4 of the UCC extends forgery protections and rights to alterations and unauthorized signings. When an officer with authority limited to signing $5,000 checks signs a check for $7,500, the signature is unauthorized. If the principal for the drawer account is an organization and has a requirement that two or more designated persons sign negotiable instruments on its behalf, signatures by fewer than the specified number are also classified as unauthorized signatures.

CPA 13. Payment on a Forged or Missing Indorsement

A drawee bank that honors a customer's check bearing a forged indorsement must recredit the customer's account upon the drawer's discovery of the forgery and notification to the bank. A drawee bank is liable for the loss when it pays a check that lacks an essential indorsement.[40] In such a case, the instrument is not properly payable. Without proper indorsements for an order instrument and special indorsements, the person presenting the check for payment is not the holder of the instrument and is not entitled to demand or receive payment. However, the bank can then turn to the indorsers and transferors of the instrument for breach of warranty liability in that all signatures were not genuine or authorized and they did not have title. All transferors can turn to their previous transferor until liability ultimately rests with the party who first accepted the forged indorsement. This party had face-to-face contact and could have verified signatures.

When a customer deposits a check but does not indorse it, the customer's bank may make an indorsement on behalf of the depositor unless the check expressly requires the customer's indorsement. A bank cannot add the missing indorsement of a person who is not its customer when an item payable is deposited in a customer's bank account.[41]

14. Alteration of a Check

If the face of a check has been altered so that the amount to be paid has been increased, the bank is liable to the drawer for the amount of the increase when it makes payment of the greater amount.

The drawer may be barred from claiming that there was an alteration if there was negligence in writing the check or reporting its alteration. A drawer is barred from claiming alteration if the check was written negligently, the negligence substantially contributed to the making of the material alteration, and the bank honored the check in good faith and observed reasonable commercial standards in doing so. **For Example,** the drawer is barred from claiming alteration when the check was written with blank spaces that readily permitted a change of "four" to "four hundred" and the drawee bank paid out the latter sum because the alteration was not obvious. A careful drawer will write figures and words close together and run a line through or cross out any blank spaces.

15. Unauthorized Collection of a Check

A collecting bank, or a bank simply collecting an item for a customer, is protected from liability when it follows its customer's instructions. It is not required to inquire or verify that the customer had the authority to give such instructions. In contrast, instructions do not protect a payor bank. It has an absolute duty to make proper payment. If it does not do so, it is liable unless it is protected by estoppel or by the preclusion rule. The person giving wrongful instructions is liable for the loss caused by those instructions.

The *Burns v. Neiman Marcus Group, Inc.* case involves an issue of a bank's duty of inquiry.

[38] *Lynch v. Bank of America, N.A.*, 493 F. Supp. 2d 265 (D.R.I. 2007). Some states allow for an action for conversion of funds by the customer. *300 Broadway Healthcare Center, LLC v. Wachovia Bank, N.A.*, 39 A.3d 248 (N.J. App. 2012).
[39] Revised UCC §4-406(e); *Bucci v. Wachovia Bank, N.A.*, 591 F. Supp. 2d 773 (E.D. Pa. 2008); *Rodgeres v. Bank of America, N.A.*, 73 UCC Rep. Serv. 2d 47 (S.D. Ill. 2011).
[40] *Bank of Nichols Hills v. Bank of Oklahoma*, 196 P.3d 984 (Ok. App. 2008); *VIP Mortg. Corp. v. Bank of America, N.A.*, 769 F. Supp. 2d 20 (D. Mass. 2011).
[41] *Smith v. Farmers Union Mut. Ins. Co.*, 260 P.3d 163 (Mont. 2011).

Burns v. Neiman Marcus Group, Inc., 93 Cal. Rptr. 3d 130 (Cal. App. 2009)

The Devil Shops at Neiman Marcus Using Her Boss's Checks

Carol Young was employed as Brian P. Burns's secretary at a salary that never exceeded $75,000. Between 1995 and 2000, Young opened several credit card accounts with Neiman Marcus. In the three-year period prior to 2006, Young spent approximately $1 million at Neiman Marcus, and "the balance on [one] credit card, as of January 10, 2006, was in excess of $242,000." Young was offered entrée into Neiman Marcus's exclusive INCIRCLE® rewards program—a loyalty incentive program offered only to Neiman Marcus's most frequent and highest-spending customers. Young was also provided a designated sales associate, or a personal shopper, whose compensation was tied to the volume and price of the merchandise purchased by her clients. Young's personal shopper knew of her annual salary of less than $75,000. However, the personal shopper repeatedly contacted and encouraged Young to make excessive purchases with her various Neiman Marcus cards.

Young would personally deliver on a regular basis fraudulent and forged checks drawn on Burns's Union Bank of California checking account to pay down her various [Neiman Marcus] credit card bills at the Customer Service Center in Neiman's San Francisco store. Young used three different methods for presenting Burns's checks: (a) stealing checks and forging Burns's signature; (b) stealing checks with no signature whatsoever; and (c) stealing checks with Burns's signature—checks that Burns presumed were for payments towards his own Neiman Marcus credit card account, but which were diverted to Young's credit card accounts.

Because Young managed all of Burns's accounts, the reconciliations she made had fake ledger entries for payment to third parties to cover those payments to Neiman Marcus for her own accounts. Burns did not detect Young's activities for three years because he did not see the bank statements, only Young did. A serendipitous examination of the ledger and canceled checks resulted in the discovery. Burns recovered what he could from his bank, an amount limited by UCC Article 4. Burns filed suit against Neiman Marcus, seeking to recover the funds paid on the checks and claiming that Neiman Marcus was subject to the defenses of forgery and unauthorized payments. The trial court granted Neiman Marcus's motion for demurrer and Burns appealed.

JUDICIAL OPINION

JENKINS, Judge…Section 3407 allows a person who pays a fraudulently altered or forged instrument or takes such an instrument for value, in good faith and without notice of the alteration or forgery, to enforce the instrument according to the instrument's original terms. "If negligence of a obligor on the instrument substantially contributes to the alteration or the forgery, then section 3406 gives the holder…the alternative right to treat the altered or forged instrument as though it had been issued in the altered form." Thus, section 3406, together with 3407, outline the rights to enforce and collect on altered or forged checks while precluding the obligor, whose negligence contributed to the alteration or forgery, from asserting the alteration or forgery as a defense to payment.

[T]his Court cannot supply the language that would have created an affirmative cause of action under the circumstances of this case. "Courts are not permitted to rewrite statutes. This is a legislative function. The manifest intention of the legislature, clearly disclosed by its language, must be applied…." Second, Official Comment 1 to [the Uniform Commercial] Code… states that subsection (a) [of section 3-406] "adopts the doctrine" that a "drawer who so negligently draws an instrument as to facilitate its material alteration [or its forgery] is liable to a drawee who pays the altered [or forged] instrument in good faith." But statutory language making a drawer liable to a drawee cannot possibly be taken as showing an intention to create a cause of action in favor of a drawer against a depositary bank…. Third, Official Comment 1 further states: "Section 3-406 does not make the negligent party liable in tort for damages resulting from the alteration. If the negligent party is estopped from asserting the alteration the person taking the instrument is fully protected because the taker can treat the instrument as having been issued in the altered form."

We conclude by noting that we are mindful that plaintiff has sustained substantial losses as a consequence of the fraud by his employee over a number of years. But, we must reject the arguments of plaintiff and our dissenting colleague to impose a duty of inquiry and the resulting liability for breach on Neiman Marcus in this case. As we have stated, the scope of this proposed—yet ill-defined—duty of inquiry is boundless, and would impose a significant and unwarranted burden on retail merchants to ascertain the veracity of third-party checks received for payment of goods and services, which burden would far outweigh any resulting benefit in detecting the isolated instance of fraud.

QUESTIONS

1. Determine who is the drawee, the drawer, and the third party in the court's discussion.
2. What public policy issues is the court balancing?
3. What would happen if nonbank third parties were held liable for negligence with regard to conduct such as that of Young in this case?

16. Time Limitations

The liability of the bank to its depositor is subject to certain time limitations.

CPA **(A) Forgery and Alteration Reporting Time.** A customer must examine with reasonable care and promptness a bank statement and relevant checks that are paid in good faith and sent to the customer by the bank and must try to discover any unauthorized signature or alteration on the checks. The customer must notify the bank promptly after discovering either a forgery or an alteration. If the bank exercises ordinary care in paying a forged or an altered check and suffers a loss because the customer fails to discover and notify the bank of the forgery or alteration, the customer cannot assert the unauthorized signature or alteration against the bank.[42]

Under the Check Truncation Act (CTA—which is part of the Check 21 statute covered in Chapter 28), banks now have the right to substitute electronic images of checks for customer billing statements. The CTA is largely implemented through Federal Reserve Board regulations found at 12 CFR §229.2. Banks do not need to provide the original check to their customers and can simply send copies of electronic images so long as the image provides enough clarity for the customer to see payee, encoding, indorsements, and so on.

With the use of substituted checks and online banking, consumers now have additional rights and time limits with substituted checks. Under the Check 21 statute, consumers have a new right to an expedited recredit to their account if a substitute check was charged improperly to their account. They have the right to see the original check if they can explain why it is necessary and that they are suffering a loss as a result of the improper charge of a substitute check to their account. Consumers have 40 calendar days from whichever of the following is later: (1) the delivery of their monthly bank statements or (2) that date on which the substitute check was made available to them for examination and/or review. If a consumer has been traveling or been ill, the rules permit the extension of the deadline for purposes of challenging a substitute check. Consumers can even call their bank and challenge a payment, but they will not then get the benefit of all the rights and protections under Check 21 and its regulations if they choose to proceed without a written demand on a substitute check.[43] Once the demand is made, the bank must either recredit the consumer's account within one business day or explain why it believes the substitute check was charged properly to the consumer's account. The oral demand does not start this clock running for the consumer's protection. There are also fines and overdraft protections provided while the substitute check issue is in the dispute/investigation stage.

Some cases of forgery are the result of a customer's lack of care, such as when an employee is given too much authority and internal controls are lacking with the result that the employee is able to forge checks on a regular basis not easily detected by the bank. Referred to as the *fictitious payee and impostor exceptions*, this issue was covered in Chapter 29.

Customers are precluded from asserting unauthorized signatures or alterations if they do not report them within one year from the time the bank statement is received.[44] A forged indorsement must be reported within three years.

(B) Unauthorized Signature or Alteration by Same Wrongdoer. If there is a series of improperly paid items and the same wrongdoer is involved, the customer is protected only as to those items that were paid by the bank before it received notification from the customer and during that reasonable amount of time that the customer has to examine items or statements and to notify the bank. If the customer failed to exercise reasonable promptness and failed to notify the bank but the customer can show that the bank failed to exercise ordinary care in paying the items, the loss will be allocated between the customer and the bank.[45]

(C) Statute of Limitations. An action to enforce a liability imposed by Article 4 must be commenced within three years after the cause of action accrued.

[42] *Quilling v. National City Bank of Michigan/Illinois*. Not reported in F. Supp. 2d 2001, 2001 WL 1516732 (N.D. Ill.), 46 UCC Rep. Serv. 2d 207 (N.D. Ill. 2001).
[43] 12 C.F.R. 229.54(b)(1)(iii).
[44] Revised UCC §4-406.
[45] Revised UCC §4-406 (2002); *J. Walter Thompson, U.S.A., Inc. v. First BankAmericano*, 518 F.3d 128 (2nd Cir. 2008), and *Dean v. Commonwealth Bank & Trust Co.*, 2012 WL 1137907 (Ky. App. 2012).

Thinking Things Through

The Embezzling Home Health Care Worker Helped Along by Bank of America

Nancy Z. Paley opened a money market bank account in 1977 at a bank that subsequently was acquired by Bank of America (BOA). BOA was unable to locate Mrs. Paley's signature card, but never told Mrs. Paley to come in and sign a new card. At the time of the BOA acquisition, Mrs. Paley had $45,000 in her interest-bearing, money market account. Mrs. Paley rarely wrote checks on the account because of the restrictions on the number of checks allowed each month.

After losing a leg to diabetes at age 74 in 2002, Mrs. Paley hired Angela Sentore, a home health aide. In 2005, Mrs. Paley wrote a check to her husband that bounced due to insufficient funds. Puzzled because of the small amount of the check, Mrs. Paley checked the account and discovered that Ms. Sentore had negotiated 188 checks from the account, totaling $48,931.83, either by making them payable to herself, or by making them payable to third parties. Sixty-two of the checks were presented in person by Sentore to a teller at a BOA branch office.

Mrs. Paley demanded that BOA credit her account for the amount that had been paid over a forged signature. BOA pointed out that the time for claiming forgeries on the account had expired in 2002 and refused to credit the account.

Mrs. Paley had never received the bank statements and had called once to ask that the statements be sent, but, again, she never received them. Mrs. Paley acknowledged that Ms. Sentore intercepted all of her mail and that the statements could have been destroyed by her.

BOA never questioned Sentore and the checks because they were for such small amounts that it was not bank policy to compare signatures. BOA followed reasonable commercial standards in its signature comparison practices and used automated processing that would only raise questions for checks written for amounts over $500, the BOA trigger for a signature comparison.

Mrs. Paley claimed that the bank should have known because of the differences in her signature. She always signed her checks with the middle initial "Z" in her name. None of the forged checks had the "Z" in the signature.

Mrs. Paley (who passed away before the case was decided) brought suit against BOA for payment over a forged signature as well as violation of New Jersey's consumer fraud statute. BOA defended on the grounds that Mrs. Paley's rights to claim the funds back ended when she did not check her statements. Analyze the claims of both sides and determine whether Mrs. Paley's estate should recover the embezzled funds. **[*Estate of Paley v. Bank of America,* 18 A.3d 1033 (N.J. App. 2011)]**

C. Consumer Funds Transfers

Consumers are using electronic methods of payment at an increasing rate. From the swipe of the card at the grocery store checkout to the retrieval of funds from the local automated teller machine, *electronic funds transfers* represent a way of life for many consumers. A federal statute protects consumers making electronic funds transfers.

17. Electronic Funds Transfer Act

Congress passed the **Electronic Funds Transfer Act (EFTA)** to protect consumers making electronic transfers of funds.[46] **Electronic funds transfer (EFT)** means any transfer of funds (other than a transaction originated by check, draft, or similar paper instrument) that is initiated through an electronic terminal, telephone, computer, or magnetic tape that authorizes a financial institution to debit or credit an account. The service available from an automated teller machine is a common form of EFT.

18. Types of Electronic Funds Transfer Systems

Currently, five common types of EFT systems are in use. In some of these systems, the consumer has a card to access a machine. The consumer usually has a private code that prevents others who wrongfully obtain the card from using it.

(a) Automated Teller Machine. The *automated teller machine (ATM)* performs many of the tasks once performed exclusively by bank employees. Once a user activates an ATM, he can deposit and withdraw funds from his account, transfer funds between

[46] 15 U.S.C. §1693 *et seq.*

accounts, make payments on loan accounts, and obtain cash advances from bank credit cards.

(B) Pay-by-Phone System. This system facilitates paying telephone, mortgage, utility, and other bills without writing checks. The consumer calls the bank and directs the transfer of funds to a designated third party.

(C) Direct Deposit and Withdrawal. Employees may authorize their employers to deposit wages directly to their accounts. A consumer who has just purchased an automobile on credit may elect to have monthly payments withdrawn from a bank account to be paid directly to the seller.

(D) Point-of-Sale Terminal. The *point-of-sale terminal* allows a business with such a terminal to transfer funds from a consumer's account to the store's account. The consumer must be furnished in advance with the terms and conditions of all EFT services and must be given periodic statements covering account activity. Any automatic EFT from an individual's account must be authorized in writing in advance.

Financial institutions are liable to consumers for all damages proximately caused by the failure to make an EFT in accordance with the terms and conditions of an account. Exceptions include insufficient funds, funds subject to legal process, exceeding an established credit limit, or insufficient cash is available in an ATM.

(E) Internet Banking. Internet banking is the customer use of computer access to bank systems to pay bills, balance accounts, transfer funds, and even obtain loans. Increasing in popularity, this form of banking still suffers from concerns about privacy and security. However, the revisions to Articles 3 and 4 recognize electronic records as valid proof of payment.

CPA 19. Consumer Liability

A consumer who notifies the issuer of an EFT card within two days after learning of a loss or theft of the card can be held to a maximum liability of $50 for unauthorized use of the card. Failure to notify within this time will increase the consumer's liability for losses to a maximum of $500.

Consumers have the responsibility to examine periodic statements provided by their financial institution. If a loss would not have occurred but for the failure of a consumer to report within 60 days of the transmittal of the statement any unauthorized transfer, then the loss is borne by the consumer.

CPA D. Funds Transfers

The funds transfers made by businesses are governed by the UCC and Federal Reserve regulations.

20. What Law Governs?

In states that have adopted Article 4A of the Uniform Commercial Code, that article governs funds transfers.[47] In addition, whenever a Federal Reserve Bank is involved, the provisions of Article 4A apply by virtue of Federal Reserve regulations.

21. Characteristics of Funds Transfers

The transfers regulated by Article 4A are characteristically made between highly sophisticated parties dealing with large sums of money. Speed of transfer is often an essential ingredient. An individual transfer may involve many millions of dollars, and the national total of such transfers on a business day can amount to trillions of dollars.

22. Pattern of Funds Transfers

In the simplest form of funds transfer, both the debtor and the creditor have separate accounts in the same bank.[48] In this situation, the debtor can instruct the bank to pay the creditor a specified sum of money by subtracting that amount from the debtor's account and adding it to the creditor's account. As a practical matter, the debtor merely instructs the bank to make the transfer.

A more complex situation is involved if each party has an account in a different bank. In that case, the funds transfer could involve only these two banks and no clearinghouse. The buyer can instruct the buyer's bank to direct the seller's bank to make payment to

[47] The majority of the states have adopted the 1990 version of Article 4A.

[48] The text refers to *debtor* and *creditor* in the interest of simplicity and because that situation is the most common in the business world. However, a gift may be made by a funds transfer. Likewise, a person having separate accounts in two different banks may transfer funds from one bank to another.

the seller. There is direct communication between the two banks. In a more complex situation, the buyer's bank may relay the payment order to another bank, called an **intermediary bank**, and that bank, in turn, transmits the payment order to the seller's bank. Such transactions become even more complex when two or more intermediary banks or a clearinghouse is involved.

23. Scope of UCC Article 4A

Article 4A applies to all funds transfers except as expressly excluded because of their nature or because of the parties involved.

(A) EFTA AND CONSUMER TRANSACTIONS. Article 4A does not apply to consumer transaction payments to which the EFTA applies. If any part of the funds transfer is subject to the EFTA, the entire transfer is expressly excluded from the scope of UCC Article 4A.[49]

(B) CREDIT AND DEBIT TRANSFERS. When the person making payment, such as the buyer, requests that payment be made to the beneficiary's bank, the transaction is called a **credit transfer**. If the beneficiary entitled to money goes to the bank according to a prior agreement and requests payment, the transaction is called a **debit transfer**. The latter transfer type is not regulated by Article 4A. Article 4A applies only to transfers begun by the person authorizing payment to another.

24. Definitions

Article 4A employs terms that are peculiar to that article or are used in a very different context from the contexts in which they appear elsewhere.

(A) FUNDS TRANSFER. A **funds transfer** is more accurately described as a communication of instructions or a request to pay a specific sum of money to, or to the credit of, a specified account or person. There is no actual physical transfer or passing of money.

(B) ORIGINATOR. The person starting the funds transfer is called the **originator** of the funds transfer.[50]

(C) BENEFICIARY. The **beneficiary** is the ultimate recipient of the benefit of the funds transfer. Whether the recipient is the beneficiary personally, an account owned by the beneficiary, or a third person to whom the beneficiary owes money is determined by the payment order.

(D) BENEFICIARY'S BANK. The **beneficiary's bank** is the final bank in the chain of transfer that carries out the transfer by making payment or application as directed by the payment order.

(E) PAYMENT ORDER. The **payment order** is the direction the originator gives to the originator's bank or by any bank to a subsequent bank to make the specified funds transfer. Although called a *payment order*, it is in fact a request. No bank is required or obligated to accept a payment order unless it is so bound by a contract or a clearinghouse rule that operates independently of Article 4A.

25. Manner of Transmitting Payment Order

Article 4A makes no provisions for the manner of transmitting a payment order. As a practical matter, most funds transfers under Article 4A are controlled by computers, and payment orders are electronically transmitted. Article 4A, however, applies to any funds transfer payment order even if made orally, such as by telephone, or in writing. Also, the agreement of the parties or the clearinghouse and funds transfer system rules may impose some restrictions on the methods for communicating orders.

26. Regulation by Agreement and Funds Transfer System Rules

Article 4A, with minor limitations, permits the parties to make agreements that modify or change the provisions of Article 4A that would otherwise govern. Likewise, the rules of a clearinghouse or a funds transfer system through which the banks operate may change the provisions of the Code.

(A) CHOICE OF LAW. When the parties enter into an agreement for a funds transfer, they may designate the law that is to apply in interpreting the agreement.

(B) CLEARINGHOUSE RULES. The banks involved in a particular funds transfer may be members of the same clearinghouse. In such a case, they will be bound by the lawful rules and regulations of the house.

[49] UCC §4A-108 (1990). This exclusion applies when any part of the transaction is subject to Regulation E adopted under the authority of that statute.
[50] UCC §4A-201.

The rights of the parties involved in a funds transfer may be determined by the rules of FedWire, a clearinghouse system operated by the Federal Reserve System, or by CHIPS, which is a similar system operated by the New York clearinghouse.

27. Reimbursement of the Bank

After the beneficiary's bank accepts the payment order, it and every bank ahead of it in the funds transfer chain is entitled to reimbursement of the amount paid to or for the beneficiary. This reimbursement is due from the preceding bank. By going back along the funds transfer chain, the originator's bank, and ultimately the originator, makes payment of this reimbursement amount.

28. Error in Funds Transfer

There may be an error in a payment order. The effect of an error depends on its nature.

(A) Type of Error. The error in a payment order may consist of a wrong identification or a wrong amount.

(1) Wrong Beneficiary or Account Number.

The payment order received by the beneficiary's bank may contain an error in the designation of the beneficiary or in the account number. This error may result in payment being made to or for the wrong person or account.

(2) Excessive Amount.

The payment order may call for the payment of an amount that is larger than it should be. For example, the order may wrongly add an additional zero to the specified amount.

(3) Duplicating Amount.

The payment order may be issued after a similar payment order has already been transferred, so that the second order duplicates the first. This duplication would result in doubling the proper amount paid by the beneficiary's bank.

(4) Underpayment.

The payment order may call for the payment of a smaller sum than was ordered. For example, the order may drop off one of the zeros from the amount ordered by the originator.

(B) Effect of Error. When the error falls under one of the first three classes just discussed, the bank committing the error bears the loss because it caused the item to be wrongfully paid. In contrast, when the error is merely underpayment, the bank making the mistake can cure the fault by making a supplementary order for the amount of the underpayment. If verification by the agreed-upon security procedure would disclose an error in the payment order, a bank is liable for any loss caused by the error if it failed to verify the payment order by such a procedure. In contrast, if the security procedure followed did not reveal any error, there is no liability for accepting the payment order.

When an error of any kind is made, there may be liability under a collateral agreement of the parties, a clearinghouse or funds transfer system rule, or general principles of contract law. However, these rights may be lost in certain cases by failure to notify the involved bank that the mistake has been made.

29. Liability for Loss

Unless otherwise regulated by agreement or clearinghouse rule, banks have little or no liability in the funds transfer chain if they have followed the agreed-upon security procedure.

(A) Unauthorized Order. If a bank executes or accepts an unauthorized payment order, it is liable to any prior party in the transfer chain for the loss caused. If a bank acts on the basis of an unauthorized order that nevertheless is verified by the security procedure, the bank is not liable for the loss that is caused.

(B) Failure to Act. A bank that fails to carry out a payment order is usually liable, at the most, for interest loss and expenses. There is no liability for the loss sustained by the originator or for consequential damages suffered because payment was not made to satisfy the originator's obligation to the beneficiary.

LawFlix

French Kiss (1995)(PG-13)

Meg Ryan is able to have funds transferred from her account in Canada to an account in France to Cartier (the jewelers) so that Cartier can issue a check to her friend. The set-up as well as the execution involve both paper and wire transactions.

MAKE THE CONNECTION

SUMMARY

A *check* is a particular kind of draft; it is drawn on a bank and is payable on demand. A delivery of a check is not an assignment of money on deposit with the bank on which it is drawn. A check does not automatically transfer the rights of the depositor against the bank to the holder of the check, and there is no duty on the part of the drawee bank to the holder to pay the holder the amount of the check.

A check may be an *ordinary check,* a *cashier's check*, or a *teller's check.* The name on the paper is not controlling. Unless otherwise agreed, the delivery of a certified check, a cashier's check, or a teller's check discharges the debt for which it is given, up to the amount of the check.

Certification of a check by the bank is the acceptance of the check—the bank becomes the primary party. Certification may be at the request of the drawee or the holder. Certification by the holder releases all prior indorsers and the drawer from liability.

Notice of nonpayment of a check must be given to the drawer of a check. If no notice is given, the drawer is discharged from liability to the same extent as the drawer of an ordinary draft.

A depositor may stop payment on a check. However, the depositor is liable to a holder in due course unless the stop payment order was for a reason that may be raised against a holder in due course. The stop payment order may be made orally (binding for 14 calendar days) or with a record (effective for six months).

The depository bank is the agent of the depositor for the purpose of collecting a deposited item. The bank may become liable when it pays a check contrary to a stop payment order or when there has been a forgery or an alteration. The bank is not liable, however, if the drawer's negligence has substantially contributed to the forgery. A bank that pays on a forged instrument must recredit the drawer's account. A depositor is subject to certain time limitations to enforce liability of the bank. Banks are subject to reporting requirements under the USA Patriot Act.

A customer and a bank may agree that the bank should retain canceled checks and simply provide the customer with a list of paid items. The customer must examine canceled checks (or their electronic images) or paid items to see whether any were improperly paid.

An *electronic funds transfer (EFT)* is a transfer of funds (other than a transaction originated by check, draft, or other commercial paper) that is initiated through an electronic terminal, telephone, computer, or magnetic tape to authorize a financial institution to debit or credit an account. The Electronic Funds Transfer Act requires that a financial institution furnish consumers with specific information containing all the terms and conditions of all EFT services. Under certain conditions, the financial institution will bear the loss for unauthorized transfers. Under other circumstances, the consumer will bear the loss.

Funds transfers regulated by UCC Article 4A are those made between highly sophisticated parties that deal with large sums of money. If any part of the funds transfer is subject to the EFTA, such as consumer transactions, the entire transfer is expressly excluded from the scope of Article 4A. A funds transfer is simply a request or an instruction to pay a specific sum of money to, or to the credit of, a specified person.

LEARNING OUTCOMES

After studying this chapter, you should be able to clearly explain:

A. Checks

LO.1 List and explain the duties of the drawee bank

See the discussion of duties beginning on p. 601 and Ethics & the Law on overdrafts on p. 603.

LO.2 Explain the methods for, and legal effect of, stopping payment

See *South Central Bank of Daviess County v. Lynnville Nat. Bank* on pp. 599–601.

B. Liability of a Bank

LO.3 Describe the liability of a bank for improper payment and collection

See Thinking Things Through on p. 613.

See Ethics & the Law on p. 603 for a discussion of overdraft fees issues.

LO.4 Discuss the legal effect of forgeries and material alterations

See *Rovell v. American Nat'l Bank* on pp. 608–609.

See *Greenberg, Trager & Herbst v. HSBC Bank USA* on pp. 605–607.

LO.5 Specify the time limitations for reporting forgeries and alterations

See *Burns v. Neiman Marcus* on p. 611.

C. Consumer Funds Transfers

See the EFTA discussion on p. 613.

D. Funds Transfers

LO.6 Describe the electronic transfer of funds and laws governing it

See the discussion of Article 4A on p. 615.

KEY TERMS

agency
agent
bad check laws
beneficiary
beneficiary's bank
cashier's check
certified check
check
credit transfer
debit transfer
demand draft
Electronic Funds Transfer Act (EFTA)
electronic funds transfer (EFT)
encoding warranty
funds transfer
intermediary bank
money order
originator
overdraft
payment order
postdated
presentment
stale check
stop payment orders
substitute check
teller's check
time draft
USA Patriot Act
wrongfully dishonored

QUESTIONS AND CASE PROBLEMS

1. William Elias was the former owner of Direct Lending, a subprime mortgage company purchased by EA Management. Sometime after the sale, Elias went to Chase Bank and had three cashier's checks drawn to third parties and payable out of Direct Lending accounts in the amount of $191,251.31. When the new owners of Direct Lending checked their account balances online, they discovered the withdrawal for the three cashier's checks. The treasurer went to the bank and stopped payment on all three cashier's checks. Elias brought suit against the bank for wrongful dishonor and consequential damages to his businesses as a result of the dishonor. Can Elias recover? Be sure to explain which Article 4 provisions apply and why. [*EA Management v. JP Morgan Chase, N.A.*, 655 F.3d 573 (6th Cir.)]

2. Helen was a very forgetful person, so she had placed her bank code (PIN number) on the back of her debit card. A thief stole Helen's card and was able to take $100 from an ATM on the day of the theft. That same day, Helen realized that the card was gone and phoned her bank. The following morning, the thief withdrew another $100. For how much, if anything, is Helen responsible? Why?

3. Adam Paul Strege (APS) opened a checking account at U.S. Bank. Just below his signature card for the account, he wrote, "Call if I bounce a check." APS bounced several checks and each time U.S. Bank covered those checks, but it did not notify APS of the bounced check status. The result was that APS continued to write checks and U.S. Bank had to request funds from him to cover the overdrafts in his account. APS refused

to pay the amount due because he argued that U.S. Bank had breached its agreement with him to report all bounced checks. Discuss whether U.S. Bank had the obligation to notify APS of the bounced checks. [*APS v. U.S. Bank*, 2009 WL 4723311 (D. Minn.)]

4. Arthur Odgers died, and his widow, Elizabeth Odgers (Elizabeth Salsman by remarriage), retained Breslow as the attorney for her husband's estate. She received a check payable to her drawn on First National City Bank. Breslow told her to deposit it in her husband's estate. She signed an indorsement "Pay to the order of Estate of Arthur J. Odgers." Breslow deposited this check in his trustee account in National Community Bank, which collected the amount of the check from the drawee, First City National Bank. Thereafter, Elizabeth, as administratrix of the estate of Arthur J. Odgers, sued National Community Bank for collecting this check and crediting Breslow's trustee account with the proceeds. Was National Community Bank liable? Explain. [*Salsman v. National Community Bank*, 246 A.2d 162 (N.J. Super.)]

5. Shipper was ill for 14 months. His wife did not take care of his affairs carefully, nor did she examine his bank statements as they arrived each month. One of Shipper's acquaintances had forged his name to a check in favor of himself for $10,000. The drawee bank paid the check and charged Shipper's account. Shipper's wife did not notify the bank for 13 months after she received the statement and the forged check. Can she compel the bank to reverse the charge? Why or why not?

6. Ann Weldon maintained an account at Trust Company Bank. James Weldon, her son and a garment broker, purchased textile goods from Sportswear Services for resale to another corporation known as Thicket Textiles. Sportswear demanded certified funds from James Weldon before it would ship the goods. When James Weldon requested a certified check from Trust Company, Trust Company officer Sweat informed James that if it issued a certified check, payment could not be stopped even if the merchandise delivered was not as promised under the terms of the contract.

   Ann Weldon then obtained a $16,319.29 cashier's check drawn on her account and payable to Sportswear. James had deposited his funds into her account to cover the check. The check was delivered to Sportswear, and the goods were shipped the next day, but they were defective.

   Ann Weldon went to Trust Company Bank to issue a stop payment order, and the bank, believing that the check had not yet been delivered to Sportswear, did so for $25. James Weldon then notified Sportswear of the stop payment order. After Trust Company dishonored the cashier's check, Sportswear's bank was in contact with the bank and informed it that the check had already been delivered to Sportswear. Trust Company honored the check and credited Ann Weldon's account with the $25 stop payment fee. Ann filed suit because Trust Company did not stop payment. Should payment have been stopped? Why or why not? [*Weldon v. Trust Co. Bank of Columbus*, 499 S.E.2d 393 (Ga. App.)]

7. Gloria maintains a checking account at First Bank. On the third day of January, the bank sent her a statement of her account for December accompanied by the checks that the bank had paid. One of the checks had her forged signature, which Gloria discovered on the 25th of the month when she prepared a bank reconciliation. On discovering this, Gloria immediately notified the bank. On January 21, the bank had paid another check forged by the same party who had forged the December item. Who must bear the loss on the forged January check?

8. Dean bought a car from Cannon. As payment, Dean gave him a check drawn on South Dorchester Bank of Eastern Shore Trust Co. Cannon cashed the check at the Cambridge Bank of Eastern Shore Trust Co. The drawee bank refused payment when the check was presented on the ground that Dean had stopped payment because of certain misrepresentations made by Cannon. Will Eastern Shore Trust Co. succeed in an action against Dean for payment? [*Dean v. Eastern Shore Trust Co.*, 150 A. 797 (Md.)]

9. A depositor drew a check and delivered it to the payee. Fourteen months later, the check was presented to the drawee bank for payment. The bank had no knowledge that anything was wrong and paid the check. The depositor then sued the person receiving the money and the bank. The depositor claimed that the bank could not pay a stale check without asking the depositor whether payment should be made. Was the depositor correct? [*Advanced Alloys, Inc. v. Sergeant Steel Corp.*, 340 N.Y.S.2d 266 (Queens Co. Civ. Ct.)]

10. John G. Vowell and his wife, now deceased, had a checking account and a savings/money-market account with Mercantile Bank of Arkansas. In June 1997, Dr. Vowell and his wife allowed their daughter, Suzan Vowell, now also deceased, and her boyfriend to move in with them at their home. At that time, they knew that Suzan and her boyfriend had been involved with drugs, alcohol, writing bad checks, and stealing. They also knew that Suzan had stolen checks from them in the past and forged either Dr. Vowell's or his wife's signatures. They took precautions by hiding Mrs. Vowell's purse, which contained their checkbook, under the kitchen sink.

    Beginning in June 1997, Suzan forged Mrs. Vowell's signature on 42 checks, drawn on both accounts, and committed nine unauthorized ATM withdrawals in the aggregate amount of $12,028.75. Suzan found her mother's purse hidden under the kitchen sink and stole the checkbooks and ATM card from the purse. She apparently had access to the personal identification number (PIN) for the accounts because the number was identical to the home security system code.

    The Vowells received the following statements from the bank for the checking and savings accounts:

Date of Transaction	*Amount*	*Statement date covering*
July 9, 1997	$230.00	June 6–July 7, 1997
August 8, 1997	$1,235.25	July 8–August 6, 1997
August 23, 1997	$5,140.00	July 23–Aug 21, 1997
September 9, 1997	$1,423.50	Aug 7–Sept 7, 1997
September 26, 1997	$4,000.00	Aug 22–Sept 22, 1997

    On September 15, 1997, Dr. Vowell had Mercantile freeze their accounts and begin investigating the alleged forgeries and other unauthorized transactions pursuant to its policy. Suzan was arrested subsequently when she tried to use the ATM card again.

    The bank refused to credit the Vowells' account because it maintained that their negligence in handling their daughter caused the losses. The court found that the bank was liable for only $6,014.38, one-half of the entire sum of Suzan Vowell's unauthorized bank transactions and forgeries. The bank appealed. Can the Vowells recover? How much and why? [*Mercantile Bank of Arkansas v. Vowell*, 117 S.W.3d 603 (Ark. App.)]

11. Bogash drew a check on National Safety Bank and Trust Co. payable to the order of Fiss Corp. At the request of Fiss Corp., the bank certified the check. The bank later refused to make payment on the check because of a dispute between Bogash and the corporation over the amount due the corporation. Fiss sued the bank on the check. Can Fiss recover? [*Fiss Corp. v. National Safety Bank and Trust Co.*, 77 So.2d 293 (N.Y. City Ct.)]

12. David Marx was a gentleman in his 90s and a longtime customer of Whitney National Bank. His account had been in his name only until April 24, 1995, when he added his son, Stanley Marx, and his daughter, Maxine Marx Goodman, as joint owners and signatories on the account. The account names read: "David Marx or Maxine M. Goodman or Stanley B. Marx." At that time, the bank began sending the statements to Stanley Marx.

    Joel Goodman, David Marx's grandson, visited his grandfather often and had access to his grandfather's checkbook. Joel forged 22 checks on his grandfather's account for a total of $22,834. The first 10 checks went unnoticed because they were cleared and the bank statement David Marx received during this time was never reviewed. The last five checks, which appeared on the May 16, 1995, bank statement, were discovered when Stanley Marx reviewed the statement. David and Stanley notified the bank and completed the appropriate forms for the five checks, which totaled $10,000. Whitney National Bank refused to pay the $10,000, and David and Stanley filed suit. The trial court granted summary judgment for David and Stanley, and Whitney appealed. Who is liable on the checks? Did David and Stanley wait too long or are they protected because they let the bank know when they did? [*Marx v. Whitney National Bank*, 713 So.2d 1142 (La.)]

13. Norris, who was ill in the hospital, was visited by his sister during his last days. Norris was very fond of his sister and wrote a check to her that she deposited in her bank account. Before the check cleared, Norris died. Could the sister collect on the check even though the bank knew of the depositor's death? Explain. [*In re Estate of Norris*, 532 P.2d 981 (Colo.)]

14. Scott D. Leibling gave his bank, Mellon Bank, an oral stop payment order. Nineteen months later, the check emerged and Mellon Bank honored it. Leibling has filed suit against Mellon Bank for acting unreasonably under the circumstances. Is Mellon Bank liable to Leibling for paying the 19-month-old check when there was an oral stop payment order? Discuss your reasons for your answer. [*Leibling, P.C. v. Mellon, PSFS (NJ) N.A.*, 710 A.2d 1067, 35 UCC 2d 590 (N.J. Super.)]

15. Hixson paid Galyen Petroleum Co. money he owed by issuing three checks to Galyen. The bank refused to cash the three checks because of insufficient funds in the Hixson account to pay all three. Galyen sued the bank. What was the result? Why? [*Galyen Petroleum Co. v. Hixson*, 331 N.W.2d 1 (Neb)]

CPA QUESTIONS

1. A check has the following endorsements on the back:
   1. Paul Frank **"without recourse"**
   2. George Hopkins **"payment guaranteed"**
   3. Ann Quarry **"collection guaranteed"**
   4. Rachell Ott

   Which of the following conditions occurring subsequent to the endorsements would discharge all of the endorsers?

   a. Lack of notice of dishonor

   b. Late presentment

   c. Insolvency of the maker

   d. Certification of the check

2. Blare bought a house and provided the required funds in the form of a certified check from a bank. Which of the following statements correctly describes the legal liability of Blare and the bank?

   a. The bank has accepted; therefore, Blare is without liability.

   b. The bank has not accepted; therefore, Blare has primary liability.

   c. The bank has accepted, but Blare has secondary liability.

   d. The bank has not accepted, but Blare has secondary liability.

3. In general, which of the following statements is correct concerning the priority among checks drawn on a particular account and presented to the drawee bank on a particular day?

   a. The checks may be charged to the account in any order convenient to the bank.

   b. The checks may be charged to the account in any order provided no charge creates an overdraft.

   c. The checks must be charged to the account in the order in which the checks were dated.

   d. The checks must be charged to the account in the order of lowest amount to highest amount to minimize the number of dishonored checks.

PART 5

Debtor-Creditor Relationships

© Manuel Gutjahr/iStockphoto.com

Chapter 32

© Manuel Gutjahr/iStockphoto.com

Nature of the Debtor-Creditor Relationship

learningoutcomes

After studying this chapter, you should be able to

LO.1 Distinguish a contract of suretyship from a contract of guaranty

LO.2 Define the parties to a contract of suretyship and a contract of guaranty

LO.3 List and explain the rights of sureties to protect themselves from loss

LO.4 Explain the defenses available to sureties

LO.5 Explain the nature of a letter of credit and the liabilities of the various parties to a letter of credit

This section of the book deals with all aspects of debt: the creation of the debtor-creditor relationship, the statutory requirements for disclosure in those credit contracts, the means by which creditors can secure repayment of debt, and finally, what happens when debtors are unable to repay their debts. This chapter covers the creation of the debtor-creditor relationship, as well as two means of ensuring payment: the use of a surety or guarantor and the creation of a line of credit.

A. Creation of the Credit Relationship

A debtor-creditor relationship consists of a contract that provides for the creditor to advance funds to the debtor and requires the debtor to repay that principal amount with specified interest over an agreed-upon time. The credit contract, so long as it complies with all the requirements for formation and validity covered in Chapters 12 through 17, is enforceable just like any other contract. However, credit contracts often have additional statutory obligations and relationships that provide assurances on rights and collection for both the debtor and the creditor. Chapter 33 covers the rights of both debtors and creditors in consumer credit relationships. Chapter 34 covers the additional protection that creditors enjoy when debtors offer security interests in collateral. This chapter covers the additional relationships for securing repayment of debt known as *suretyships* and *lines of credit.*

CPA B. Suretyship and Guaranty

A debtor can make a separate contract with a third party that requires the third party to pay the debtor's creditor if the debtor does not pay or defaults in the performance of an obligation. This relationship, in which a third party agrees to be responsible for the debt or other obligation, is used most commonly to ensure that a debt will be paid or that a contractor will perform the work called for by a contract. **For Example,** a third-party arrangement occurs when a corporate officer agrees to be personally liable if his corporation does not repay funds received through a corporate note. Contractors are generally required to obtain a surety bond in which a third party agrees to pay damages or complete performance of the construction project in the event the contractor fails to perform in a timely manner or according to the contract terms.

CPA 1. Definitions

One type of agreement to answer for the debt or default of another is called a **suretyship**. The **obligor** or third party who makes good on a debtor's obligation is called a **surety**. The other kind of agreement is called a **guaranty**, and the obligor is called a **guarantor**. In both cases, the person who owes the money or is under the original obligation to pay or perform is called the **principal**, **principal debtor**, or **debtor**.[1] The person to whom the debt or obligation is owed is the **obligee** or **creditor**.

As discussed in Chapters 28 and 31, the revisions to Articles 3 and 4 put accommodation parties (now secondary obligors) in the same legal status as those in a surety/guarantor relationship. The revisions place secondary obligors in the position of a surety.

Suretyship and guaranty undertakings have the common feature of a promise to answer for the debt or default of another. The terms are often used interchangeably. However, certain forms of guaranty are qualified by one distinction. A surety is liable from the moment the principal is in default. The creditor or obligee can demand performance or payment from the surety without first proceeding against the principal debtor. A **guaranty of collection** is one in which the creditor generally cannot proceed directly against the guarantor and must first attempt to collect from the principal debtor. An exception is an **absolute guaranty**, which creates the same obligation as a suretyship. A **guaranty of payment** creates an absolute guaranty and requires the guarantor to pay upon default by the principal debtor.

CPA 2. Indemnity Contract Distinguished

Both suretyship and guaranty differ from an **indemnity contract**. An indemnity contract is an undertaking by one person, for a consideration, to pay another person a sum of money in the event that the other person sustains a specified loss. **For Example,** a

[1] Unless otherwise stated, *surety* as used in the text includes guarantor as well as surety. Often, the term *guarantee* is used for guaranty. In law, guarantee is actually one who benefits from the guaranty.

fire insurance policy is an indemnity contract. The insurance you obtain when you use a rental car is also an example of an indemnity contract.

3. Creation of the Relationship

Suretyship, guaranty, and indemnity relationships are based on contract. The principles relating to capacity, formation, validity, and interpretation of contracts are applicable. Generally, the ordinary rules of offer and acceptance apply. Notice of acceptance usually must be given by the obligee to the guarantor.

In most states, the statute of frauds requires that contracts of suretyship and guaranty be evidenced by a record to be enforceable. No record is required when the promise is made primarily for the promisor's benefit.

When the suretyship or guaranty is created at the same time as the original transaction, the consideration for the original promise that is covered by the guaranty is also consideration for the promise of the guarantor. When the suretyship or guaranty contract is entered into after and separate from the original transaction, there must be new consideration for the promise of the guarantor.

The *Feigenbaum v. Guaracini* case involves a question of whether there is a surety relationship.

Feigenbaum v. Guaracini, 952 A.2d 511 (N.J. Super. 2008)

Are You Sure You're My Surety?

James Feigenbaum, Sam Feigenbaum, and the Syma Feigenbaum Testamentary Trust own Lincoln Shopping Center. In 1996, the Feigenbaums leased 25,500 square feet in the Center to Guaracini Supermarkets, Inc. (GSI) for 10 years at a fixed rent of $7,500 per month and taxes, maintenance costs, and insurance. The lease did not impose an obligation on GSI to pay the Feigenbaums' legal expenses and costs if legal proceedings resulted.

The Guaracinis unconditionally guaranteed to the Feigenbaums GSI's performance under the lease (the guaranty) for the full term of the lease.

In 1998, GSI assigned the lease to Wakefern. Wakefern agreed to indemnify GSI against any claims or damages, including "reasonable legal fees and disbursements," arising from its default under the lease; however, Wakefern did not agree to indemnify the Guaracinis personally. Later in 1998, with the consent of the Feigenbaums, Wakefern reassigned the lease to Vineland Supermarket, Inc. Under the assignment, Vineland agreed to indemnify Wakefern and GSI from and against any claims or damages, including reasonable legal fees and disbursements, arising from Vineland's failure to perform under the lease. Vineland became insolvent.

In July 2003, Vineland failed to pay the monthly rent. The Feigenbaums filed suit claiming that the Guaracinis were primarily liable as guarantors of the lease, and Wakefern was liable as assignee of the lease from GSI (GSI had failed financially). The Feigenbaums' damages through August 31, 2006 were $616,815.66, which included attorneys' fees and costs. The trial court held the Guaracinis liable to the Feigenbaums and Wakefern liable to the Guaracinis. An appeal followed.

JUDICIAL OPINION

GILROY, Judge…Wakefern entered into an assignment of lease for the property with GSI, and assumed all of the rights and duties of GSI under the lease. The assignment contained a provision whereby Wakefern agreed to indemnify and hold GSI harmless from and against any damages that GSI only may suffer as a consequence of Wakefern's breach of the lease. Because Wakefern's obligation ran only to GSI, not to the Feigenbaums or the Guaracinis, and because Wakefern undertook to protect GSI only against loss or liability to a third person, Wakefern's obligation was that of an indemnitor. The issue remains whether these relationships permit the Guaracinis to recover from Wakefern under the doctrine of equitable subrogation.

We conclude that the trial judge mistakenly granted the Guaracinis the right of equitable subrogation against Wakefern for several reasons. First, the record does not contain evidence that Wakefern knew of the Guaracinis' guaranty to the Feigenbaums when Wakefern contracted with GSI to accept the assignment of the lease. The lease assignment only bound Wakefern to indemnify GSI for damages caused by a default under the lease. The Guaracinis, the owners of GSI, had the opportunity to negotiate from Wakefern a promise to indemnify them from any demand by the Feigenbaums on their personal guaranty, including the obligation to pay attorneys' fees and costs. Yet, they failed to do so.

That failure, together with the absence of proof of Wakefern's awareness of the Guaracinis' guaranty to the Feigenbaums, precludes the Guaracinis from seeking reimbursement of monies paid in settlement under the principle of equitable subrogation. Because Wakefern only assumed a duty to GSI and there is no

Continued

evidence that it was aware of the Guaracinis' guaranty, we conclude that it would be contrary to fundamental fairness to compel Wakefern to reimburse the Guaracinis.

Here, Vineland was the primary defaulting party, and as such, was the party who ought to have paid. Unfortunately, Vineland is no longer a viable entity.

The Guaracinis argue that Wakefern's acceptance of the lease assignment dissolved the Guaracinis' relationship with GSI and created in its place a new relationship among the Feigenbaums, the Guaracinis, and Wakefern. The Guaracinis contend that under this new relationship the Feigenbaums remained the obligee; Wakefern became the principal obligor; and they became the secondary obligors.

Even assuming the validity of the Guaracinis' argument that Wakefern's assumption of the lease placed Wakefern in the same position as GSI to the Guaracinis, a primary obligor [is not] liable to a secondary obligor, unless the primary obligor has notice of the secondary obligation. Here, the record is devoid of any evidence that Wakefern had actual notice of the Guaracinis' guaranty to the Feigenbaums. Because there is no evidence of such notice, Wakefern does not have a duty to reimburse the Guaracinis.

We conclude that the trial court mistakenly exercised its discretion in applying equitable subrogation to hold Wakefern liable to the Guaracinis.

[Accordingly, we reverse.]

QUESTIONS

1. Diagram the parties' relationships.
2. What should the parties have done differently to clarify the surety relationships?

4. Rights of Sureties

Sureties have a number of rights to protect them from loss, to obtain their discharge because of the conduct of others that would be harmful to them, or to recover money that they were required to pay because of the debtor's breach.

CPA **(A) Exoneration.** A surety can be exonerated from liability, a means of discharging or relieving liability, if the creditor could have taken steps to stop or limit the surety's exposure for the debt. **For Example,** suppose that the surety learns that a debtor is about to leave the state, an act that makes it more difficult to collect debts. The surety may call on the creditor to take action against the debtor to provide a literal and figurative roadblock to the debtor's planned departure. If the creditor could proceed against the debtor who is about to leave and thereby protect the repayment and fails to do so, the surety is released or **exonerated** from liability to the extent that the surety has been harmed by such failure.

CPA **(B) Subrogation.** When a surety pays a claim that it is obligated to pay, it automatically acquires the claim and the rights of the creditor. This stepping into the shoes or position of another is known as **subrogation**.[2] That is, once the creditor is paid in full, the surety stands in the same position as the creditor and may collect from the debtor or enforce any rights the creditor had against the debtor to recover the amount it has paid. The effect is the same as if the creditor, on being paid, made an express assignment of all rights to the surety. Likewise, the surety acquires any rights the debtor has against the creditor. **For Example,** if the creditor has not complied with statutory requirements, the surety can enforce those rights against the creditor just as the original debtor could. The *Man-Data, Inc. v. B & A Automotive, Inc.* case deals with an issue of defenses.

Man-Data, Inc. v. B & A Automotive, Inc., 270 P. 3d 318 (Or. App. 2011)

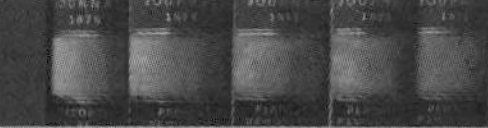

The Dead-Beat Automotive Shop and the Owners' Guaranty

Man-Data is a collection agency that sued Cheryl Mulhall and Robert Gonzales (defendants) to recover legal fees charged pursuant to a fee agreement between defendant B & A Automotive, Inc., and its former attorney, Scott Bassinger. Gonzales and Mulhall, both of whom were associated with B & A, signed a guaranty that they, in their individual

[2] *Middlesex Mut. Assur. Co. v. Vaszil*, 873 A.2d 1030 (Conn. App. 2005); insurer had right of subrogration where guarantor had signed for tenant's liability for causing damage to the landlord's property once the insurer had paid the landlord.

Continued

capacities, would pay legal fees incurred by B & A. Bassinger was not paid and assigned his claim to Man-Data (plaintiff) for collection. Man-Data filed this suit and B & A failed to appear in the case; a bench trial resulted in a judgment against the defendants. The court prevented the individual defendants from attacking the validity of the fees charged under the fee agreement. The defendants appealed.

JUDICIAL OPINION

ORTEGA, Presiding Judge...We begin our analysis by labeling the parties in this case with the nomenclature of surety and guaranty law. Plaintiff here, pursuant to B & A's obligations in the fee agreement and Bassinger's assignment of his claim, is the obligee. B & A, by way of the underlying obligation in the fee agreement, is the principal obligor. The individual defendants, through their guaranty, are the secondary obligors or sureties.

Initially, we note that the cases relied on by plaintiff do not directly address the issue presented by the trial court's ruling as we understand it—that is, whether the individual defendants, as sureties, were properly precluded from defending against the fees charged.

The legal question here is whether the law precludes the individual defendants from challenging the amount of the obligation incurred by B & A. As a general rule, with exceptions that do not apply to this case, "the secondary obligor may raise as a defense to the secondary obligation any defense of the principal obligor to the underlying obligation[.]" As applicable here, that rule indicates that the individual defendants, as sureties, may raise defenses available to B & A in an action seeking to hold the individual defendants liable as sureties. The general rule is that the surety is not liable to the creditor unless the principal obligor is liable; thus, the surety may plead the defenses that are available to the principal." That is so even though a default order was entered against B & A.

Both plaintiff and the trial court appeared to place some significance on the fact that Bassinger assigned his claim to plaintiff. However, plaintiff has not pointed to any authority, nor are we aware of any, that the assignment of a claim to a collection agency affects the general rule stated above. That is, the individual defendants' ability to defend against B & A's obligation is not limited by the assignment of the claim to plaintiff. Consequently, the trial court erred in limiting the individual defendants' ability to defend against the fees charged by Bassinger.

Plaintiff, however, appears to argue that its own offer of proof somehow defeats defendants' first assignment of error. As noted, Bassinger testified during the offer of proof that the fees were reasonable, and defendants were given the opportunity to cross-examine him on that point. However, plaintiff has not presented any cogent argument as to why an offer of proof in this manner would allow us to affirm the trial court's decision to preclude the individual defendants from presenting their own evidence challenging the amount of the fees.

[Reversed and remanded.]

QUESTIONS

1. Is there any problem that arises because the creditor (Bassinger) assigned his claim to Man-Data?
2. Why was cross-examination of Bassinger not enough for the defendants' rights?
3. What does the right of subrogation provide for in this case?

CPA (c) **Indemnity.** A surety that has made payment of a claim for which it was liable as surety is entitled to **indemnity** from the principal debtor; that is, it is entitled to demand from the principal reimbursement of the amount that it has paid.

CPA (d) **Contribution.** If there are two or more sureties (known as co-sureties), each is liable to the creditor or claimant for the full amount of the debt until the claim or debt has been paid in full. Between themselves, however, each co-surety is liable only for a proportionate share of the debt. Accordingly, if a surety has paid more than its share of the debt, it is entitled to demand **contribution** from its **co-sureties**. In the absence of a contrary agreement, co-sureties must share the debt repayment on a *pro rata* basis. **For Example,** Aaron and Bobette are co-sureties of $40,000 and $60,000, respectively, for Christi's $60,000 loan. If Christi defaults, Aaron owes $24,000 and Bobette owes $36,000.

5. Defenses of Sureties

The surety's defenses include those that may be raised by a party to any contract and special defenses that are peculiar to the suretyship relationship.

Thinking Things Through

Pro Rata Shares for Co-Sureties

AFC Corporation borrowed $90,000 from First Bank and demanded three sureties for the loan. Anna Flynn agreed to be a surety for $45,000 for AFC's debt. Frank Conlan agreed to be a surety for $60,000, and Charles Aspen agreed to be a surety for $75,000. When AFC owed $64,000, it defaulted on the loan and demanded payment from the co-sureties. However, Frank Conlan was in bankruptcy. How much would Anna and Charles have to pay to First Bank?

CPA **(A) Ordinary Contract Defenses.** Because the relationship of suretyship is based on a contract, the surety may raise any defense that a party to an ordinary contract may raise. For example, a surety may raise the defense of lack of capacity of parties, absence of consideration, fraud, or mistake.

Fraud and **concealment** are common defenses. Fraud on the part of the principal that is unknown to the creditor and in which the creditor has not taken part does not ordinarily release the surety.

Because the risk of the principal debtor's default is thrown on the surety, it is unfair for a creditor to conceal from the surety facts that are material to the surety's risk. Under common law, the creditor was not required to volunteer information to the surety and was not required to disclose that the principal was insolvent. A modern view that is receiving increased support is that the creditor should be required to inform the surety of matters material to the risk when the creditor has reason to believe that the surety does not possess such information.

CPA **(B) Suretyship Defenses.** Perhaps the most important thing for a surety to understand is the type of defense that does not result in a discharge of her obligation in the suretyship. The insolvency or bankruptcy of the principal debtor does not discharge the surety. The financial risk of the principal debtor is the reason that a surety was obtained from the outset. The lack of enforcement of the debt by the creditor is not a defense to the surety's obligation or a discharge. The creditor's failure to give the surety notice of default is not a defense. The creditor's right, without a specific guaranty of collection, is simply to turn to the surety for payment.[3]

In some cases, the creditor may have also taken a **pledge** of collateral for the debt in addition to the commitment of a surety. It is the creditor's choice as to whether to proceed against the collateral or the surety. If, however, the creditor proceeds first against the surety, the surety then has the right of exoneration and can step into the shoes of the creditor and repossess that collateral.

Changes in the terms of the loan agreement do not discharge a compensated surety. A surety who is acting gratuitously, however, would be discharged in the event of such changes. Changes in the loan terms that would discharge a gratuitous surety's obligation include extension of the loan terms and acceptance of late payments.[4]

A surety is discharged when the principal debtor performs his obligations under the original debt contract. If a creditor refuses to accept payment from a debtor, a surety is discharged.

A surety is also discharged, to the extent of the value of the collateral, if a creditor releases back to the debtor any collateral in the creditor's possession. **For Example,** suppose that Bank One has in its possession $10,000 in gold coins as collateral for a loan to Janice in the amount of $25,000. Albert has agreed to serve as a surety for the loan to Janice in the amount of $25,000. If a Bank One manager returns the $10,000 in coins to Janice, then Albert is discharged on his suretyship obligation to the extent of that $10,000. Following the release of the collateral, the most that Albert could be held liable for in the event of Janice's default is $15,000.

A surety is also discharged from her obligation if the creditor substitutes a different debtor. A surety and a guarantor make a promise that is personal to a

[3] *Rossa v. D.L. Falk Const., Inc.*, 266 P.3d 1022 (Cal. 2012).

[4] *In re Chemtura Corp.*, 448 B.R. 635 (S.D.N.Y. 2011).

FIGURE 32-1 *No Release of Surety*

1. Fraud by debtor
2. Misrepresentation by debtor
3. Changes in loan terms (e.g., Extension of payment)—compensated surety only
4. Release of principal debtor
5. Bankruptcy of principal debtor
6. Insolvency of principal debtor
7. Death of principal debtor
8. Incapacity of principal debtor
9. Lack of enforcement by creditor
10. Creditor's failure to give notice of default
11. Failure of creditor to resort to collateral

specific debtor and do not agree to assume the risk of an assignment or a delegation of that responsibility to another debtor. A surety also enjoys the discharge rights afforded all parties to contracts, such as the statute of limitations. If the creditor does not enforce the suretyship agreement within the time limits provided for such contract enforcement in the surety's jurisdiction, the obligation is forever discharged.[5]

Figures 32-1 and 32-2 provide summaries of the defenses and release issues surrounding suretyship and guaranty relationships.

C. Letters of Credit

A **letter of credit** is a three-party arrangement with a payor, a beneficiary, and a party on whom the letter of credit is drawn, or **issuer**. A letter of credit is an agreement that the issuer of the letter will pay drafts drawn by the beneficiary of the letter. Letters of credit are a form of advance arrangement for financing. Sellers of goods, for example, know in advance how much money may be obtained from the issuer of the letter. A letter of credit may also be used by a creditor as a

FIGURE 32-2 *Release of Surety*

1. Proper performance by debtor
2. Release, surrender, or destruction of collateral (to extent of value of collateral)
3. Substitution of debtor
4. Fraud/misrepresentation by creditor
5. Refusal by creditor to accept payment from debtor
6. Change in loan terms—uncompensated surety only
7. Statute of frauds
8. Statute of limitations

[5] *The Clark Const. Group, Inc. v. Wentworth Plastering of Boca Raton, Inc.*, 840 So.2d 357 (Fla. App. 2002); *The Clark Const. Group, Inc. v. Wentworth*, 840 So.2d 357 (Fla. App. 2003).

security device because the creditor knows that the drafts that the creditor draws will be accepted or paid by the issuer of the letter.[6]

The use of letters of credit arose in international trade. While international trade continues to be the primary area of use, there is a growing use of letters in domestic sales and in transactions in which the letter of credit takes the place of a surety bond. A letter of credit has been used to ensure that a borrower would repay a loan, that a tenant would pay the rent due under a lease, and that a contractor would properly perform a construction contract. This kind of letter of credit is known as a **standby letter**.

There are few formal requirements for creating a letter of credit. Although banks often use a standardized form for convenience, they may draw up individualized letters of credit for particular situations (see Figure 32-3).

In international letters of credit, there are several sources of recognized standards that businesses use for the creation and execution of letters of credit. Along with the UCC, there is the Uniform Customs and Practice for Documentary Credits (or UCP), something that reflects ordinary international banking operational practices on letters of credit. The UCP is revised, generally, about every 10 years by the International Chamber of Commerce (ICC, see Chapter 7).

6. Definition

A letter of credit is an engagement by its issuer that it will pay or accept drafts when the conditions specified in the letter are satisfied. The issuer is usually a bank.

Three contracts are involved in letter-of-credit transactions: (1) the contract between the issuer and the customer of the issuer, (2) the letter of credit itself, and (3) the underlying agreement, often a contract of sale, between the beneficiary and the customer of the issuer of the letter of credit (see Figure 32-4).

FIGURE 32-3 *Letter of Credit*

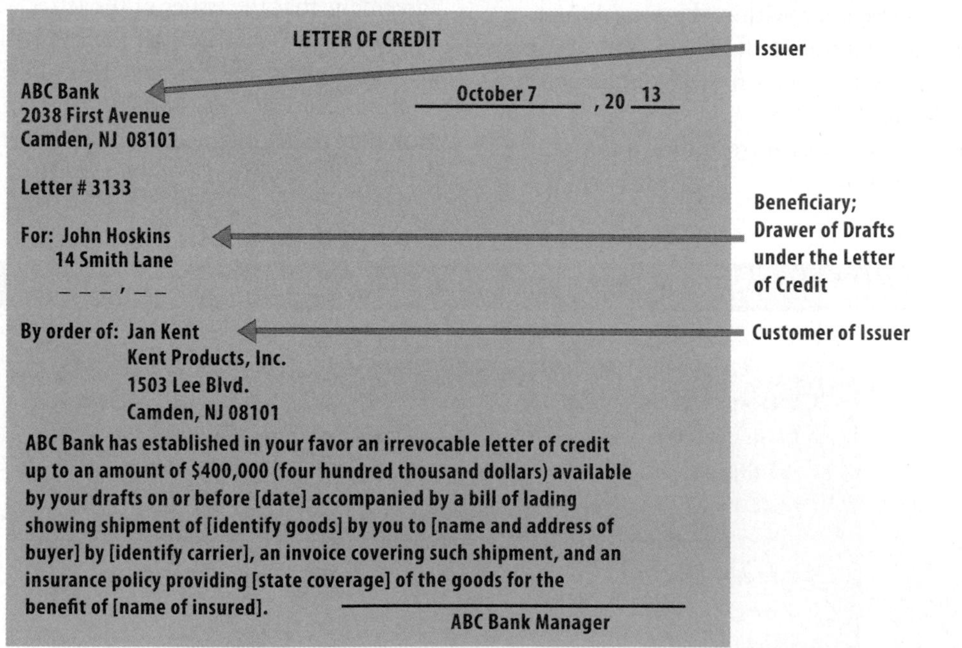
LETTER OF CREDIT

ABC Bank
2038 First Avenue
Camden, NJ 08101

October 7, 20 13

Letter # 3133

For: John Hoskins
14 Smith Lane
___, __

By order of: Jan Kent
Kent Products, Inc.
1503 Lee Blvd.
Camden, NJ 08101

ABC Bank has established in your favor an irrevocable letter of credit up to an amount of $400,000 (four hundred thousand dollars) available by your drafts on or before [date] accompanied by a bill of lading showing shipment of [identify goods] by you to [name and address of buyer] by [identify carrier], an invoice covering such shipment, and an insurance policy providing [state coverage] of the goods for the benefit of [name of insured].

ABC Bank Manager

[6] *U.S. Material Supply, Inc. v. Korea Exchange Bank*, 417 F. Supp. 2d 652 (D.N.J. 2006), discussing the character and purpose of letters of credit. See also *City of Maple Grove v. Marketline Const. Capital, LLC*, 802 N.W. 2d 809 (Minn. App. 2011) for discussion of fact that a document is not a letter of credit if it requires verification of an outside event, as opposed to submission of documents.

FIGURE 32-4 *The Contracts Involved in Letter-of-Credit Transactions*

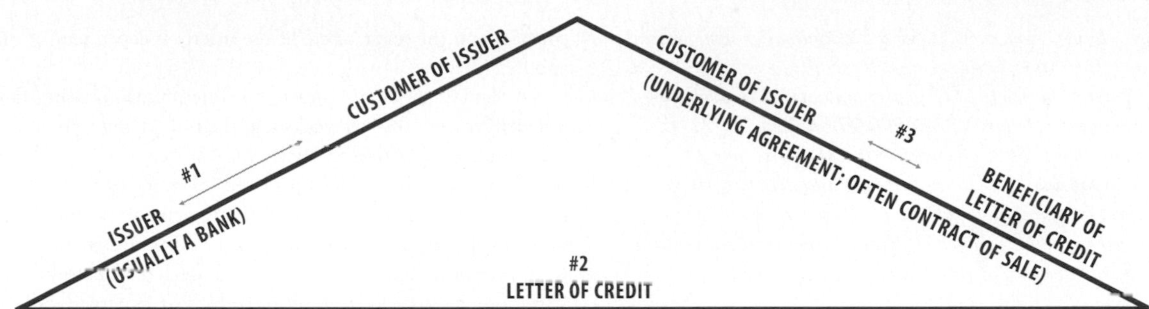

The letter of credit is completely independent from the other two contracts. Consideration is not required to establish or modify a letter of credit.

The issuer of the letter of credit is, in effect, the obligor on a third-party-beneficiary contract made for the benefit of the beneficiary of the letter. The key to the commercial success of letters of credit is their independence. **For Example,** a bank obligated to issue payment under a letter of credit "when the goods are delivered" must honor that obligation even if the buyer has complaints about the goods. It is the terms of the letter of credit that control the payment, not the relationship, contract, or problems of the beneficiary or issuer of the letter of credit.

The key to the commercial vitality and function of a letter of credit is that the issuing bank's promise is independent of the underlying contracts and the bank should not resort to them in interpreting a letter of credit. Sometimes called *the strict compliance rule,* banks must honor the letter of credit terms using strict interpretation. The respective parties are protected by a careful description of the documents that will trigger payment. The claim of a beneficiary of a letter of credit is not subject to defenses normally applicable to third-party contracts. Known as the *independence rule,* banks cannot, except in limited circumstances, delve into the underlying contract issues; the focus of the bank is only on the terms of the letter of credit.

The *Louisville Mall Associates, LP v. Wood Center Properties, LLC* case deals with an issue of when a letter of credit must be paid.

Louisville Mall Associates, LP v. Wood Center Properties, LLC, 361 S.W.3d 323 (Ky. App. 2012)

The Letter of Credit and the Shoddy Mall

In 2007, Wood Center Properties (WCP) entered into a Purchase and Sale Agreement to buy five shopping centers from Robert B. Greene (Greene) and Louisville Mall Associates, LP, and several other mall property groups (collectively, the "Mall Appellants"). While performing its due diligence, WCP discovered environmental contamination at the Crestwood Shopping Center, one of the shopping centers it intended to purchase. A prior shopping center tenant, Crestwood Coin Laundry (Tenant), spilled hazardous chemicals used in its dry cleaning business. As a result of the contamination, WCP chose not to purchase Crestwood Shopping Center, and the parties amended the Purchase and Sale Agreement to reflect WCP's decision.

Shortly thereafter, Greene offered to provide WCP with an irrevocable Letter of Credit, issued by M & T Bank, in the amount of $200,000.00. The Letter of Credit's purpose was to insulate WCP from liability and fund the environmental cleanup if the Tenant failed to do so. With that inducement, Crestwood Shopping Center was put back in the contract as one of the properties being purchased by WCP. Paragraph two of the amended contract provided:

Continued

> *At closing, Robert M. Greene, individually, shall deliver an irrevocable letter of credit for the benefit of Wood Center Properties, LLC in the amount of Two Hundred Thousand Dollars ($200,000.00) drawn on M & T Bank. This letter of credit shall extend for one (1) year from the date of Closing, and shall automatically renew for one (1) additional year unless Notice of non-renewal is given to [WCP] at least 60 days prior to the expiration date on the face of the Greene Letter of Credit.*

On June 13, 2007, M & T Bank issued the Letter of Credit for the benefit of WCP. The Letter of Credit contained an original expiration date of June 12, 2008 that provided:

> *It is a condition of this credit that it shall be deemed automatically extended without amendment for one (1) year from the expiration date hereof, or any future expiration date [emphasis added], unless sixty (60) days prior to any expiration date M & T Bank notifies [WCP] in writing that M & T Bank elects not to consider this credit renewed for any such additional period.*

On April 7, 2008, M & T Bank automatically renewed the Letter of Credit for a second year and provided WCP and Greene with a letter of renewal, notifying them that the Letter of Credit's new expiration date was June 12, 2009. On March 6, 2009, M & T Bank sent a second renewal letter to WCP and Greene, again giving notice that it was automatically extending the Letter of Credit for a third year and its new expiration date was June 12, 2010.

After receiving M & T Bank's March 6, 2009, letter, Greene told M & T Bank his view that the Letter of Credit was only valid for two years and should expire on June 12, 2009. Greene requested that M & T Bank not renew the credit. Despite Greene's request, M & T Bank did not send a nonrenewal notification to WCP. WCP sought payment under the Letter of Credit and submitted the documents to M & T that were necessary for payment.

On July 27, 2009, Greene contacted WCP claiming the Letter of Credit had expired on June 12, 2009, and requested that it be returned. WCP filed a declaratory judgment action seeking the court's ruling that WCP was entitled to draw on the Letter of Credit. The court entered summary declaratory judgment in WCP's favor. Greene appealed.

JUDICIAL OPINION

ACREE, Judge…A standby letter of credit is intended to ensure a party to a contract fulfills his or her obligations, including non-monetary obligations. Here, M & T Bank, the issuer, at the request of Greene, the applicant, issued a standby Letter of Credit in the amount of $200,000.00 to WCP, the beneficiary.

The "independence principle," one of the key principles underlying letter of credit law, provides that the underlying contract and the letter of credit are utterly independent of one another.

A letter of credit must be interpreted on its face, independent of other contracts and the underlying transaction. The underlying contract between the customer and the beneficiary should not be considered in interpreting the letter of credit, and should not be used to supplement or amplify the terms of the letter of credit or to add obligations thereto.

Further, in the case *sub judice* [under consideration], the Letter of Credit itself expressly provides that its terms shall not be amplified or interpreted by reference to any outside document.

Here, the Letter of Credit expressly stated that it automatically extended without amendment for one (1) year from the expiration date set forth in the Letter of Credit, or any future expiration date, unless M & T Bank notified WCP, in writing, that it was electing not to renew the credit. We believe this provision creat[ed] a continuously renewing expiration date until M & T Bank notified WCP otherwise.

The issuing bank can assume no liability for the performance of the underlying contract because it has no control over making the underlying contract or over selection of the beneficiary. Second, the letter of credit would lose its commercial vitality if, before honoring drafts, the issuing bank were obligated to look beyond the terms of the letter of credit to the underlying contractual controversy between its customer and the beneficiary.

Instead, in letter of credit transactions, the issuer deals solely in documents. Accordingly, an issuer is duty-bound to pay when the beneficiary presents the documents specified in the letter of credit, not when the beneficiary complies with the underlying agreement. To state more simply:

In essence, the letter of credit issuer is saying "if you give me the following pieces of paper that say the following things then I will pay you the stated amount without regard to the terms of my agreements with the applicant or your agreements with the applicant." The issuer is neither expected nor entitled to look beyond the pieces of paper to determine whether the statements they contain are true, or to determine whether under its agreement with the applicant, the beneficiary has the right to make demand under the letter of credit.

In the present case, to obtain payment under the Letter of Credit, WCP was required to present to M & T Bank a draft that included the name of the issuing bank and identified the specific letter of credit. Also, the Letter of Credit required WCP to present the following documents with the draft: an original copy of the Letter of Credit, and a certificate on WCP's letterhead signed by an authorized official or representative (Certification). Further, the Certification had to include the following statements: "(a) I [the undersigned] am a duly authorized official of [WCP]; (b) This draw is being presented in accordance with the draw terms outlined in paragraph 2 of the Third Amendment to the Purchase and Sale Agreement dated June 11, 2007 between

Continued

[WCP and the Mall Appellants]; and (c) Beneficiary is hence entitled to and is making a drawing under the credit in the amount of U.S. [$200,000.00]."

WCP complied with the Letter of Credit's draw terms by submitting to M & T Bank a signed draft, the original Letter of Credit, and a proper Certification containing the precise information requested. M & T Bank was only required to examine the documents presented by WCP to determine if they complied with the terms and conditions of the Letter of Credit; M & T Bank was not required to look beyond the documents to determine whether WCP's statement that it complied with [the contract] was, in fact, accurate.

[We find court properly awarded WCP summary declaratory judgment.]

QUESTIONS

1. Explain why the independence principle was critical in the decision in this case.
2. What advice would you offer parties in terms of drafting a letter of credit?
3. What is the effect of a beneficiary of a letter of credit submitting all the required documentation under a letter of credit?

7. Parties

The parties to a letter of credit are (1) the issuer; (2) the customer who makes the arrangements with the issuer; and (3) the beneficiary, who will be the drawer of the drafts that will be drawn under the letter of credit. There may also be (4) an **advising bank**[7] if the local issuer of the letter of credit requests its **correspondent bank**, where the beneficiary is located, to notify or advise the beneficiary that the letter has been issued. **For Example,** a U.S. merchant may want to buy goods from a Spanish merchant. There may have been prior dealings between the parties so that the seller is willing to take the buyer's commercial paper as payment or to take trade acceptances drawn on the buyer. If the foreign seller is not willing to do this, the U.S. buyer, as customer, may go to a bank, the issuer, and obtain a letter of credit naming the Spanish seller as beneficiary. The U.S. bank's correspondent or advising bank in Spain will notify the Spanish seller that this has been done. The Spanish seller will then draw drafts on the U.S. buyer. Under the letter of credit, the issuer is required to accept or pay these drafts.

8. Duration

A letter of credit continues for any length of time it specifies. Generally, a maximum money amount is stated in the letter, so that the letter is exhausted or used up when the issuer has accepted or paid drafts aggregating that maximum. A letter of credit may be used in installments as the beneficiary chooses. The issuer or the customer cannot revoke or modify a letter of credit without the consent of the beneficiary unless that right is expressly reserved in the letter.

9. Form

A letter of credit must be in writing and signed by the issuer. If the credit is issued by a bank and requires a documentary draft or a documentary demand for payment[8] or if the credit is issued by a nonbank and requires that the draft or demand for payment be accompanied by a document of title, the instrument is presumed to be a letter of credit (rather than a contract of guaranty). Otherwise, the instrument must conspicuously state that it is a letter of credit.

10. Duty of Issuer

The issuer is obligated to honor drafts drawn under the letter of credit if the conditions specified in the letter have been satisfied. The issuer takes the risk that the papers submitted are the ones required by the letter. If they are not, the issuer cannot obtain reimbursement for payment made in reliance on such documents. The issuer has no duty to verify that the papers are properly supported by facts or that the underlying transaction has been performed. It is immaterial that the goods sold by the seller in fact do not conform to the contract so long as the seller tenders the documents specified by the

[7] See UCC §5-107; *Speedway Motorsports Intern. Ltd. v. Bronwen Energy Trading, Ltd.*, 706 S.E.2d 262 (N.C. 2011).

[8] A *documentary draft* or a *documentary demand for payment* is one for which honor is conditioned on the presentation of one or more documents. A document could be a document of title, security, invoice, certificate, notice of default, or other similar paper. UCC §5-103(1)(b).

Ethics & the Law

When the Creditors Rule the Debtor

Very often the creditors of a business can exercise a great deal of authority over the operation of the business when it has missed a payment on its debt or has experienced some business or market setbacks. Without owning any stock in a corporation, creditors will, in more than 50 percent of all cases in which they express concern about repayment, succeed in having both boards and officers replaced in part or in toto. For Example, Worlds of Wonder, Inc., a creative and innovative toy manufacturer that was responsible for the first talking toy, Teddy Ruxpin, was required by demands from its secured and unsecured creditors to obtain the resignation of its founder and CEO, Donald Kingsborough. Kingsborough was paid $212,500 at his departure for "emotional distress."* For example, in 2009, the federal government, as a lender, required that the CEO of General Motors resign as a condition to receiving additional funds from the government to cover debt payments. In addition, the federal government negotiated the positions of union workers, investors, and hedge funds in the Chrysler Corporation restructuring as a condition of its receipt of federal funds.

Studies show** that creditors also have input on the following corporate actions:

Type of Decision	*Percentage of Creditors with Vote*
Declaration of dividends	48
Increased security	73
Restructuring of debt	55
Cap on borrowing	50
Cap on capital expenses	25
Restrictions on investment	23

Is it fair to have creditors control corporate governance? What are the risks for shareholders when creditors control the management of a company?

*"Toymaker Has Financing Pact," *New York Times*, April 2, 1988, C1 (Reuters item).

See Tim Reason, "Keeping Skin in the Game," *CFO Magazine*, February 1, 2005, **www.cfo.com, for a discussion of why creditors are involved and what they can do to help manage a debtor.

letter of credit. If the issuer dishonors a draft without justification, it is liable to its customer for breach of contract.[9]

11. Reimbursement of Issuer

When the issuer of a letter of credit makes proper payment of drafts drawn under the letter of credit, it may obtain reimbursement from its customer for such payment. Examples of improper payment include payment made after the letter has expired or a payment that is in excess of the amount authorized by the letter. No reimbursement is possible if the payment is made without the proper presentation of required documents or if the payment is made in violation of a court injunction against payment.

[9] *CRM Collateral II, Inc. v. TriCounty Metropolitan Transp. Dist of Oregon*, 669 F.3d 963 (9th Cir. 2012). In some cases, letters of credit are so poorly drafted that payment must be made despite evolving concerns by the parties. *Nissho Iwai Europe PLC v. Korea First Bank*, 782 N.E.2d 55 (N.Y. 2002).

MAKE THE CONNECTION

SUMMARY

Suretyship and guaranty undertakings have the common feature of a promise to answer for the debt or default of another. The terms are used interchangeably, but a guarantor of collection is ordinarily only secondarily liable, which means that the guarantor does not pay until the creditor has exhausted all avenues of recovery. If the guarantor has made an absolute guaranty, then its status is the same as that of a surety, which means that both are liable for the debt in the event the debtor defaults, regardless of what avenues of collection, if any, the creditor has pursued.

Surety and guaranty relationships are based on contract. Sureties have a number of rights to protect them. They are exoneration, subrogation, indemnity, and contribution. In addition to those rights, sureties also have certain defenses. They include ordinary contract defenses as well as some defenses peculiar to the suretyship relationship, such as release of collateral, change in loan terms, substitution of debtor, and fraud by the creditor.

A letter of credit is an agreement that the issuer of the letter will pay drafts drawn on the issuer by the beneficiary of the letter. The issuer of the letter of credit is usually a bank. There are three contracts involved in letter-of-credit transactions: (1) the contract between the issuer and the customer of the issuer, (2) the letter of credit itself, and (3) the underlying agreement between the beneficiary and the customer of the issuer of the letter of credit.

The parties to a letter of credit are the issuer, the customer who makes the arrangement with the issuer, and the beneficiary who will be the drawer of the drafts to be drawn under the letter of credit. The letter of credit continues for any time it specifies. The letter of credit must be in writing and signed by the issuer. Consideration is not required to establish or modify a letter of credit. If the conditions in the letter of credit have been complied with, the issuer is obligated to honor drafts drawn under the letter of credit.

LEARNING OUTCOMES

After studying this chapter, you should be able to clearly explain:

A. Creation of the Credit Relationship

B. Suretyship and Guaranty

LO.1 Distinguish a contract of suretyship from a contract of guaranty

See the definitions on p. 626 and discussion of the terms related to surety and guaranty on p. 626.

LO.2 Define the parties to a contract of suretyship and a contract of guaranty

See the example on corporate officers and their relationship with company debt on p. 626.

LO.3 List and explain the rights of sureties to protect themselves from loss

See the *Feigenbaum v. Guaracini* case on pp. 627–628.

See *Man-Data, Inc. v. B & A Automotive, Inc.*, on pp. 628–629.

LO.4 Explain the defenses available to sureties

C. Letters of Credit

LO.5 Explain the nature of a letter of credit and the liabilities of the various parties to a letter of credit

See *Louisville Mall Associates, LP v. Wood Center Properties, LLC,* on pp. 633–635.

KEY TERMS

absolute guaranty
advising bank
concealment
contribution
correspondent bank
co-sureties
creditor
debtor
exoneration
fraud
guarantor
guaranty
guaranty of collection
guaranty of payment
indemnity
indemnity contract
issuer
letter of credit

obligee
obligor
pledge
principal
principal debtor
standby letter
subrogation
surety
suretyship

QUESTIONS AND CASE PROBLEMS

1. First Interstate Bank issued a letter of credit in favor of Comdata Network. Comdata is engaged in money transfer services. It provides money to truckers on the road by way of cash advances through form checks written by truckers. When Comdata enters into a business relationship with a trucking company, it requires a letter of credit. This requirement is to secure advances made on behalf of the trucking company. One of the trucking companies defrauded the bank that issued the letter of credit. Comdata demanded that the bank make payment to it under the letter of credit for cash advances that the trucking company had not repaid. The bank, alleging fraud by the trucking company, refused. Comdata filed suit. Can Comdata force payment? [*Comdata Network, Inc. v. First Interstate Bank of Fort Dodge*, 497 N.W.2d 807 (Iowa App.)]

2. LaBarge Pipe & Steel Company agreed to sell PVF $143,613.40 of 30-inch pipe provided that PVF obtain a letter of credit for $144,000, with the letter of credit entitling LaBarge to payment if PVF did not pay for the pipe within 30 days of invoice. PVF obtained the letter of credit from First Bank but received only a facsimile copy of it. The letter of credit required LaBarge to submit the original of the letter of credit for a demand of payment.

   PVF did not pay within 30 days and LaBarge submitted a facsimile copy of the letter of credit and requested payment. First Bank denied the request for payment and LaBarge filed suit against First Bank for failure to pay. LaBarge argued that it was not disputed that PVF had not paid on the contract and First Bank was required to pay on the letter of credit. How would you explain First Bank's rights to LaBarge? [*LaBarge Pipe & Steel Co. v. First Bank*, 550 F.3d 442 (5th Cir.)]

3. On August 1, 1987, Dori Leeds signed a "guarantee of credit" with Sun Control Systems, which guaranteed "the prompt payment, when due, of every claim of [Sun Control Systems] against [Dori Leeds dba 'Blind Ambitions']." At the time she signed the guarantee of credit, Blind Ambitions was in the business of installing window treatments and installed only Faber-brand blinds, which were purchased from Sun Control Systems. In 1991, Sun Control Systems sold and assigned all of its assets to Faber. Shortly thereafter, Dori assigned her interest in Blind Ambitions to David and Judith Leeds, who continued to do business as Blind Ambitions. In 1994 and 1995, Blind Ambitions made credit purchases from Faber and did not pay under the terms of those contracts. Faber brought suit against Dori Leeds as the guarantor of credit for Blind Ambitions. Dori refused to pay on the grounds that she was acting as a personal guarantor for her business, not for Blind Ambitions. Is she correct? [*Faber Industries, Ltd. v. Dori Leeds Witek*, 483 S.E.2d 443 (N.C. App.)]

4. Fern Schimke's husband, Norbert, was obligated on two promissory notes in favor of Union National Bank. Some time prior to his death, Union National Bank prepared a guaranty contract that was given to Norbert for his wife to sign. She signed the guaranty at the request of her husband without any discussion with him about the provisions of the document she was signing. On Norbert's death, the bank brought suit against Fern on the basis of the guaranty. Fern argued that because there was no consideration for the guaranty, she could not be liable. Is Fern correct? Must there be consideration for a guarantor to be responsible for payment? [*Union Nat'l Bank v. Fern Schimke*, 210 N.W.2d 176 (N.D.)]

5. In May 1989, Alma Equities Corp., owned by its sole shareholder and president, Lewis Futterman, purchased a hotel and restaurant in Vail, Colorado, from Alien for $3,900,000. Alma paid

$600,000 in cash to Alien, and Alien provided a purchase money loan to Alma for the remaining amount of the sale price, with the loan secured by a deed of trust on the hotel and restaurant. The hotel and restaurant did not do well, and Futterman negotiated a friendly foreclosure on the property in 1991, whereby Alma would continue to operate the hotel and restaurant on a lease basis, with Futterman providing a personal guaranty for the lease. Alma failed to make the lease payments for the months of November and December 1991 and, following an unlawful detainer action filed by Alien for possession of the hotel and restaurant, was forced into bankruptcy. Alien turned to Futterman for satisfaction on the lease payments. Futterman said he should not have been forced to pay because Alien's unlawful detainer forced Alma into bankruptcy. Was Futterman correct? Did he have a defense? [*Alien, Inc. v. Futterman*, 924 P.2d 1063 (Colo.)]

6. Charles Fontaine completed a form for Gordon Contractors in which he signed that portion of the form labeled "Name of Guarantor." His signature followed immediately after a paragraph beginning, "[I]n consideration of the extension of credit by Gordon Building Supply Inc. the undersigned customer hereby agrees that the terms and conditions of all sales are as follows." There was also a blank following this paragraph for "Customer Name," and it was signed by a Robert Schlaefli, although it is unclear whether he signed it individually or as an agent. At the beginning of the application, the blank for "Name of Individual Applying" was filled in with both Fontaine's and Schlaefli's names, and the blank for "Name of Company or Business" bore the words "McIntyre Development, Inc." Finally, the blank for "Names of People Authorized to Purchase" was filled in with Schlaefli's name and that of a Glen Bush.

   Upon default of the debtor (never clearly identified in the agreement), Gordon Contractors filed suit to collect from Fontaine as a guarantor. Fontaine moved for summary judgment because he was not identified on the contract as a guarantor. The trial court granted Gordon Contractors a summary judgment against Fontaine, and Fontaine appealed. Determine the parties' relationships and who is liable to whom. [*Fontaine v. Gordon Contractors Building Supply, Inc.*, 567 S.E.2d 324 (Ga. App.)]

7. Tri County Truck & Diesel borrowed $165,000 from Security State Bank and pledged its inventory as security for the loan. In addition, Fred and Randelle Burk agreed to act as sureties for the loan. Tri County defaulted on the loan and Security Bank repossessed the collateral. The inventory was damaged while Security Bank held it, and as a result, the sale of the inventory brought only $5,257.50 at a public auction. The Burks raised the defense of the damages as a setoff to their surety amount for the remainder of the loan. Security Bank said the Burks could not raise the damages as a defense because the Burks were sureties and had guaranteed the full amount of the loan. The trial court granted summary judgment for Security Bank, and the Burks appealed. What should the court do? [*Security State Bank v. Burk*, 995 P.2d 1272 (Wash App.)]

8. UPS Capital Business Credit agreed to loan Ashford International, Inc, an American company based in Atlanta, Georgia, for the sale of computers to the Ministry of Education in Jordan. Ashford was required to obtain a letter of credit from United California Discount Corporation (UCDC) for the loan. Ashford filed for bankruptcy and UPS submitted documentation for payment on the letter of credit. UCDC responded to the payment demand with a list of requirements for compliance with the letter of credit demands. UPS satisfied all the demands and UCDC then refused to pay because UPS did not submit original documents as required by the letter of credit. UPS maintains that UCDC waived that requirement by not listing it in its demands. Who is correct and why? [*Export-Import Bank of the U.S. v. United Cal. Discount Corp.*, 738 F. Supp. 2d 1047 (C.D. Cal. 2010)]

9. Ribaldgo Argo Consultores entered into a contract with R. M. Wade & Co. for the purchase of irrigation equipment. Ribaldgo obtained a letter

of credit from Banco General, a bank with its principal place of business in Quito, Ecuador. The letter of credit required that Wade submit certain documents to obtain payment. The documents were submitted through Citibank as correspondent bank for Banco General. However, the documents were incomplete, and Citibank demanded additional information as required under the letter of credit. By the time Wade got the documents to Citibank, more than 15 days had expired, and the letter of credit required that Wade submit all documentation within 15 days of shipping the goods to obtain payment. Citibank refused to authorize the payment. Wade filed suit. Must Citibank pay? Why or why not? [*Banco General Runinahui, S.A. v. Citibank International*, 97 F.3d 480 (11th Cir.)]

10. Hugill agreed to deliver shingles to W. I. Carpenter Lumber Co. and furnished a surety bond to secure the faithful performance of the contract on his part. After a breach of the contract by Hugill, the lumber company brought an action to recover its loss from the surety, Fidelity & Deposit Co. of Maryland. The surety denied liability on the grounds that there was concealment of (a) the price to be paid for the shingles and (b) the fact that a material advance had been made to the contractor equal to the amount of the profit that he would make by performing the contract. Decide. [*W. I. Carpenter Lumber Co. v. Hugill*, 270 P.94 (Wash.)]

11. Donaldson sold plumbing supplies. The St. Paul-Mercury Indemnity Co., as surety for him, executed and delivered a bond to the state of California for the payment of all sales taxes. Donaldson failed to pay, and the surety paid the taxes that he owed and then sued him for the taxes. What was the result? [*St. Paul-Mercury Indemnity Co. v. Donaldson*, 83 S.E.2d 159 (S.C.)]

12. Paul owed Charles a $1,000 debt due September 1. On August 15, George, for consideration, orally promised Charles to pay the debt if Paul did not. On September 1, Paul did not pay, so Charles demanded $1,000 from George. Is George liable? Why or why not?

13. First National Bank hired Longdon as a secretary and obtained a surety bond from Belton covering the bank against losses up to $100,000 resulting from Longdon's improper conduct in the performance of his duties. Both Longdon and the bank signed the application for the bond. After one year of service, Longdon was promoted to teller, and the original bond remained in effect. Shortly after Longdon's promotion, examination showed that Longdon had taken advantage of his new position and stolen $50,000. He was arrested and charged with embezzlement. Longdon had only $5,000 in assets at the time of his arrest. (a) If the bank demands a payment of $50,000 from Belton, what defense, if any, might Belton raise to deny any obligation to the bank? (b) If Belton fully reimburses the bank for its loss, under what theory or theories, if any, may Belton attempt to recover from Longdon?

14. Jack Smith was required by his bank to obtain two sureties for his line of credit of $100,000. Ellen Weiss has agreed to act as a surety for $50,000, and Allen Fox has agreed to act as a surety for $75,000. Smith has used the full $100,000 in the line of credit and is now in bankruptcy. What is the maximum liability of Weiss and Fox if the bank chooses to collect from them for Smith's default? How should the $100,000 be allocated between Weiss and Fox?

15. Industrial Mechanical had a contract with Free Flow Cooling, Ltd., a British company. Free Flow owed Industrial $171,974.44 for work Industrial had performed on a construction project in Texas. Free Flow did not pay Industrial, and Industrial filed suit against Siemens Energy & Automation as a guarantor or surety on the debt. Industrial alleges that Siemens is a surety based on a fax it received from Siemens on January 27, 1994. The fax is handwritten and states: "We have received preliminary notices and we like [*sic*] to point out that the contract we have signed does not allow for such action to recourse [*sic*] with the customer. Please advise all subcontractors and suppliers that the only recourse that they will have is against Siemens." The fax was signed "kind regards" by Arnold Schultz,

Siemens's senior project manager for the Texas construction project. Nowhere in the fax did Siemens guarantee the debt of any specified entity or state that Siemens was agreeing to indemnify anyone or pay the obligations on behalf of anyone else. The fax failed to identify the principal debtor whom Siemens purportedly agreed to indemnify and failed to state that Siemens agreed to answer for that entity's debt. Can Industrial collect the amount of Free Flow's debt from Siemens? Why or why not? [*Industrial Mechanical, Inc. v. Siemens Energy & Automation, Inc.*, 495 S.E.2d 103 (Ga. App.)]

CPA QUESTIONS

1. Marbury Surety, Inc., agreed to act as a guarantor of collection of Madison's trade accounts for one year beginning on April 30, 1980, and was compensated for same. Madison's trade debtors are in default in payment of $3,853 as of May 1, 1981. As a result:
   a. Marbury is liable to Madison without any action on Madison's part to collect the amounts due.
   b. Madison can enforce the guaranty even if it is not in writing because Marbury is a del credere agent.
   c. The relationship between the parties must be filed in the appropriate county office because it is a continuing security transaction.
   d. Marbury is liable for those debts for which a judgment is obtained and returned unsatisfied.
2. Queen paid Pax and Co. to become the surety on a loan that Queen obtained from Squire. The loan is due, and Pax wishes to compel Queen to pay Squire. Pax has not made any payments to Squire in its capacity as Queen's surety. Pax will be most successful if it exercises its right to
   a. Reimbursement (indemnification)
   b. Contribution
   c. Exoneration
   d. Subrogation
3. Which of the following defenses by a surety will be effective to avoid liability?
   a. Lack of consideration to support the surety undertaking
   b. Insolvency in the bankruptcy sense of the debtor
   c. Incompetency of the debtor to make the contract in question
   d. Fraudulent statements by the principal debtor that induced the surety to assume the obligation and that were unknown to the creditor
4. For each of the numbered words or phrases, select the one best phrase from the list a through j. Each response may be used only once.
   (1) Indemnity contract
   (2) Suretyship contract
   (3) Surety
   (4) Third-party beneficiary
   (5) Co-surety
   (6) Statute of frauds
   (7) Right of contribution
   (8) Reimbursement
   (9) Subrogation
   (10) Exoneration

   a. Relationship whereby one person agrees to answer for the debt or default of another
   b. Requires certain contracts to be in writing to be enforceable
   c. Jointly and severally liable to creditor
   d. Promises to pay debt on default of principal debtor
   e. One party promises to reimburse debtor for payment of debt or loss if it arises
   f. Receives intended benefits of a contract
   g. Right of surety to require the debtor to pay before surety pays
   h. Upon payment of more than his/her proportionate share, each co-surety may compel other co-sureties to pay their shares

i. Upon payment of debt, surety may recover payment from debtor

j. Upon payment, surety obtains same rights against debtor that creditor had

5. When a principal debtor defaults and a surety pays the creditor the entire obligation, which of the following remedies gives the surety the best method of collecting from the debtor?

   a. Exoneration

   b. Contribution

   c. Subrogation

   d. Attachment

6. Which of the following bonds are an obligation of a surety?

   a. Convertible bonds.

   b. Debenture bonds.

   c. Municipal bonds.

   d. Official bonds.

Chapter 33

© Manuel Gutjahr/iStockphoto.com

Consumer Protection

learningoutcomes

After studying this chapter, you should be able to

LO.1 Explain what consumer protection laws do

LO.2 List the rights and protections consumer debtors have when a collector contacts them

LO.3 Give a summary of the rights of consumers with regard to credit reports

LO.4 Describe the types of protections available for consumers who have credit cards

The consumer protection movement, which began in the 1960s, continues to expand with rights for consumers in everything from ads to credit collection. These statutory protections exist at both the state and federal level.

A. General Principles

Consumer protection began with the goal of protecting persons of limited means and limited knowledge. One writer described consumer protection statutes as laws that protect "the little guy."[1] Over the past 20 years, however, that protection has expanded considerably in both who is protected and the types of activities that are regulated or provide consumers with statutory remedies.

1. Expansion of Consumer Protection

Some statutes are worded so that consumer protections apply only to natural persons. Some statutes are interpreted to apply only to consumer transactions, not to commercial transactions. However, many consumer protection statutes, once limited to individuals, now include partnerships, corporations, banks, or government entities that use goods or services as consumers. The statutes thus go beyond providing protection only for the unsophisticated and uneducated.[2] **For Example,** in defining **consumer**, courts have held that a collector paying nearly $100,000 for jade art objects, a glass manufacturer purchasing 3 million gallons of diesel oil fuel, and the city of Boston purchasing insurance are all consumers for purposes of statutory protections. Some states, such as Arizona, Arkansas, Delaware, Illinois, Iowa, Missouri, and New Jersey, even have two separate statutes, one for the protection of individual consumers and another for the protection of businesses. In addition, the protected consumer may be a firm of attorneys.[3]

Today, all 50 states and the District of Columbia have some version of what are called "Little FTC Acts" (the Federal Trade Commission Act [which created the FTC] discussed later in the chapter is the federal consumer protection statute that prohibits unfair or deceptive practices) or "unfair or deceptive acts or practices" ("UDAP") statutes. Although there are 51 versions of consumer protection statutes, they have several common threads. First, consumer protection statutes provide faster remedies for consumers. Statutory remedies under consumer protection statutes often mean that consumers need not establish that a tort has been committed or establish actual damage levels because the statute provides for both the elements for recovery and perhaps even a formula for recovery of damages. Second, the harms addressed by consumer statutes tend to affect the public generally and involve more than just one contract or even one seller. **For Example,** one area of consumer protection provides consumers control over both the release and content of their credit report information. The use of credit information, the granting of credit, and the use of credit to make purchases all have a profound impact on buyers, sellers, and national, state, and local economies. These protections provide a statutory formula for consumer damages when credit information is misused or is incorrect.

2. Who Is a Consumer?

A consumer claiming a violation of the consumer protection statute has the burden of proving that the statutory definition of consumer has been satisfied. The business accused of unfair or deceptive trade practices then has the burden of showing that the statute does *not* apply, as well as establishing exceptions and exemptions. **For Example,** some consumer protection statutes do not apply when a buyer is purchasing goods for resale.

3. Who Is Liable under Consumer Protection Statutes?

Those who are liable for violations of consumer protection situations are persons or enterprises that regularly enter into the type of transaction in which the injured consumer was involved. **For Example,** the merchant seller, the finance company, the bank, the leasing company, the home contractor, and any others who regularly enter into transactions with consumers

[1] Olha N. M. Rybakoff, "An Overview of Consumer Protection and Fair Trade Regulation in Delaware," 8 *Delaware L. Rev.* 63) (2005). This article provides a good history and summary of consumer protection laws.

[2] *Lee v. First Union Nat. Bank*, 971 A.2d 1054 (N.J. 2009).

[3] Statutes that broaden the protected group to protect buyers of goods and services are often called *deceptive trade practices statutes* instead of being referred to by the earlier term, *consumer protection statutes.*

are subject to the statutes. Some consumer protection statutes apply only to specific types of merchants and service providers such as auto repair and sale statutes, funeral home disclosure statutes and regulations, and swimming pool contractors.

4. When Is There Liability under Consumer Protection Statutes?

Consumer protection laws typically list the types of conduct that are prohibited as well as failures to act properly that are harmful to consumers. For example, the failure to disclose all of the charges related to a consumer loan or a credit purchase made by a consumer would be an omission that carries rights for the consumers and penalties for the business. *Deceptive advertising* is an act that is prohibited by consumer protection statutes that provide remedies for consumers who were deceived or misled by the ads. Deceptive advertising that is listed and described in detail in the consumer protection statutes is often easier for consumers to prove than a common law case of fraud. Consumer protection statutes do not require proof of intent. An ad might not have seemed deceptive to the merchant selling computers when he reviewed the ad copy for the newspaper. However, a consumer without the merchant's sophistication could be misled. **For Example,** suppose that a consumer sees the ad for a 19-inch flat-screen computer monitor for $158 after rebate that reads, "Compare this price with any 19-inch flat-screen monitor, and you will see we cannot be matched." The average consumer might not understand that speakers are not included with such monitors. The computer store, on the other hand, might have assumed that everyone understands that flat-screen monitors with speakers are in a different price category. Adding "no speakers" or "speakers not included" would have allowed the consumer the information needed to shop and compare.

Consumers enjoy a great deal of protection when there are omissions of material information or they are given misleading information, but consumer protection does not protect consumers from their own negligence. Consumers who sign contracts without reading or understanding what is in them are still bound. Moreover, when the contract signed by the consumer clearly states one thing, the consumer cannot introduce evidence about statements the merchant made if the contract terms are clear. Consumers must exercise reasonable care and cannot blindly trust consumer protection law to rescue them from their own blunders.

One of the areas where there have been many new consumer protections is in the area of mortgage lending and mortgage foreclosure. In the subprime lending market, which includes "do-or-die" loans such as car title loans and home title loans as well as payday loans, there are now extensive disclosure requirements on interest rates, payments, and the effects of default. In addition, these laws have imposed stringent requirements on lenders who seek to foreclose on properties that secure those loans.

The *Gonzalez v. Wilshire Credit Corp.* case deals with an issue of consumer fairness in lending.

Gonzalez v. Wilshire Credit Corp., 25 A.3d 1103 (N.J. 2011)

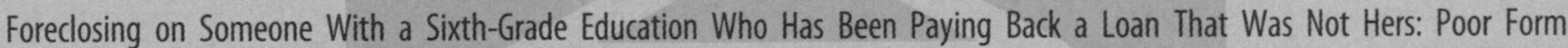

Foreclosing on Someone With a Sixth-Grade Education Who Has Been Paying Back a Loan That Was Not Hers: Poor Form

In 1994, plaintiff Blanca Gonzalez and Monserate Diaz purchased a home in Perth Amboy. In February 1997, Diaz borrowed $72,000 from Cityscape Mortgage Corporation and executed a Fixed Rate Balloon Note with an annual interest rate of 11.250 percent. In the note, Diaz agreed to make monthly payments of $699.31 until the loan's maturity date, March 3, 2012, when a final balloon payment of $61,384.17 would be due. Blanca did not sign the note. As security for the loan, Blanca and Diaz pledged both of their interests in the property by executing a mortgage in favor of Cityscape. The mortgage agreement listed Blanca and Diaz as "borrower[s]."

In March 1997, Cityscape assigned the note and mortgage to U.S. Bank. Wilshire Credit Corporation was U.S. Bank's servicing agent.

In 1999, Diaz died intestate. Blanca continued to live in the home and make payments on the loan. In 2001, Blanca was laid off from her factory job at Mayfair Company, where she had been employed for 17 years. After the layoff, she suffered a heart attack and other health difficulties, and in 2003 was approved for Social Security disability benefits.

Over time, Blanca fell behind on the loan payments. At some point, Wilshire refused to accept further payments.

Continued

In March 2003, U.S. Bank filed a foreclosure. In September 2003, the bank notified Blanca of the foreclosure.

In April 2004, the court entered judgment in favor of U.S. Bank in the amount of $80,454.71 plus interest and costs, including $954.55 in attorneys' fees, on the defaulted loan. The court also ordered that the property be sold to satisfy the judgment. A sheriff's sale was scheduled for the next month.

Before the sheriff's sale, Blanca entered into a written agreement with Wilshire, with Wilshire agreeing to forbear pursuing the sheriff's sale contingent on Blanca paying arrears, including foreclosure fees and costs, of $17,612.84. Blanca agreed to make a lump sum payment of $11,000 and then monthly payments of $1,150 through January 20, 2006. Gail Chester, a lawyer for Central Jersey Legal Services, represented Blanca in the negotiations with Wilshire.

By the end of September 2005, Blanca had made payments totaling $24,800 under the agreement—the $11,000 lump sum payment and 12 monthly payments of $1,150. However, Blanca missed four payments during this period, leaving her $6,461.89 in arrears. A sheriff's sale was scheduled but canceled because the parties entered into a new written agreement that Blanca negotiated without Ms. Chester being present.

In negotiating this second agreement, which was entirely in English, Wilshire dealt solely with Blanca, who did not speak or read English (Spanish is her native language) and who only had a sixth-grade education. Wilshire's own notes indicate that "borrower does not speak English[;] negotiating has been difficult," that Blanca was disabled and on a fixed income of $600 per month, and that Blanca did not want to sell the property because it had been in the family for many years.

In this second agreement signed by Blanca, arrearages, including foreclosure fees and costs, were fixed at $10,858.18. The arrearages in this agreement were $4,396.29 more than that calculated earlier by the trial court. Blanca agreed to make a lump sum payment of $2,200 and then monthly payments of $1,000 through October 2006. As in the first agreement, Wilshire agreed to discharge the foreclosure action when the mortgage payments became current.

In September 2006, the attorney for U.S. Bank copied Blanca on a letter stating that the previously scheduled sheriff's sale had been adjourned to October 4, 2006. Yet Blanca had not missed a single payment required by the 2005 agreement. Indeed, Blanca had made not only all required payments through October 2006 but also additional payments.

Blanca took the letter from U.S. Bank's attorney to Ms. Chester of Legal Services. Having no knowledge of the second agreement, Ms. Chester wrote to the bank's attorney that Blanca had paid $20,569.32 in excess of her regular monthly payment, $699.31, since the May 2004 agreement (the first agreement). Ms. Chester suggested that it was time to return Blanca to the monthly payment schedule of $699.31. The bank's attorney did not respond. Rather, in October 2006, Wilshire sent a letter to Blanca noting that the second agreement was about to expire and that a new agreement needed to be negotiated; otherwise it would resume foreclosure on her property. Ms. Chester contacted the Wilshire Workout Department. Wilshire then forwarded to Ms. Chester the second agreement. Wilshire could not explain how it had come to the $10,858.18 arrears set in the October 2005 agreement, nor could it explain why Blanca was not deemed current on the loan.

In July 2007, Blanca filed suit against Wilshire and U.S. Bank (defendants) for deceptive and unconscionable practices in violation of the Consumer Fraud Act (CFA). The trial court granted summary judgment in favor of defendants. The Appellate Division reversed and reinstated Blanca's CFA claim.

JUDICIAL OPINION

ALBIN, Justice...We must determine whether the manner in which Wilshire secured and executed the post-foreclosure-judgment agreements, as described by plaintiff, constitutes an unconscionable practice prohibited by the CFA.

The broad language of these [CFA] provisions encompasses "the offering, sale, or provision of consumer credit." Indeed, the term "advertisement" includes within its breadth "the attempt ... to induce ... any person ... to make any loan." Accordingly, collecting or enforcing a loan, whether by the lender or its assignee, constitutes the "subsequent performance" of a loan, an activity falling within the coverage of the CFA.

Clearly, Cityscape's loan to Diaz was contingent on plaintiff signing the mortgage papers, which listed both as borrowers. Although in any technical sense plaintiff was not a borrower, she was still in a very real sense indebted to Cityscape. The terms of the mortgage obligated plaintiff to surrender her one-half interest in her home in the event of a default and later foreclosure judgment. Plaintiff may not have been personally obligated to pay the loan, but she would not have had a roof over her head unless she did so.

Unquestionably, U.S. Bank had the right to proceed with a sheriff's sale to satisfy its judgment. Had it done so, plaintiff admittedly would have had no reason to complain. But U.S. Bank and its servicing agent, Wilshire, chose a different path. They decided to give plaintiff the opportunity to reclaim her home conditioned on her satisfying the terms of signed agreements with Wilshire.

We are in the midst of an unprecedented foreclosure crisis in which thousands of our citizens stand to lose their homes, and in desperation enter into agreements that extend credit—post-judgment—in the hope of retaining homeownership. Defendants would have us declare this seemingly unregulated

Continued

area as a free-for-all zone, where predatory-lending practices are unchecked and beyond the reach of the CFA.

The victims of these unsavory practices are most often the poor and the uneducated, and in many circumstances those with little understanding of English, and therefore the "need" for the protections of the CFA is "most acute" in such cases.

Threatening a sheriff's sale of her home, Wilshire inexplicably negotiated a new agreement directly with the unrepresented plaintiff, who could neither read nor speak English, who had only a sixth-grade education, and who was disabled and on a fixed income. The chancery court had calculated plaintiff's arrearages as $6,461.89 as of October 2005, and yet defendants had plaintiff sign an agreement setting the arrearages at $10,858.18. Even though plaintiff had made every payment and was current under that second agreement, defendants nevertheless threatened another sheriff's sale in October 2006. At this time, plaintiff contacted her Legal Services attorney, Ms. Chester, who asked Wilshire to answer a few simple questions. Wilshire could not explain how it had arrived at the $10,858.18 arrearages figure in the October 2005 agreement. It also could not explain how plaintiff's loan was not current, given that plaintiff had paid $20,569.32 in excess of the regular monthly payments since May 2004.

Lending institutions and their servicing agents are not immune from the CFA; they cannot prey on the unsophisticated, those with no bargaining power, those bowed down by a foreclosure judgment and desperate to keep their homes under seemingly any circumstances.

Moreover, Legal Services is only capable of representing a fraction of those low-income consumers who are similarly situated to Blanca Gonzalez, and the Attorney General has limited resources. The CFA was intended to fill that vacuum.

This case *in no way* suggests that settlement agreements in general are now subject to the CFA. Here, we are dealing with forbearance agreements. This case addresses only the narrow issue before us: the applicability of the CFA to a post-foreclosure-judgment agreement involving a stand-alone extension of credit. We hold only that, in fashioning and collecting on such a loan—as with any other loan—a lender or its servicing agent cannot use unconscionable practices in violation of the CFA.

[We affirm the judgment of the Appellate Division vacating the dismissal of plaintiff's complaint. We therefore reinstate plaintiff's cause of action under the CFA.]

QUESTIONS

1. What should lenders and servicing agents learn from this case about settlement agreements?
2. Why is the use of Legal Aid not a defense to unconscionability in this case?
3. What does the phrase, "prey on the unsophisticated, those with no bargaining power" mean in terms of consumer protection and contracts?

5. What Remedies Do Consumers Have?

Although consumers have the theoretical right to bring suit for defenses to contracts or enforcement when the other party does not perform, the right to prove fraud, misrepresentation, duress, or breach is often of little practical value to consumers because both the costs of litigation and the burden of proof are high. The amount that the consumer has lost may be too small to be worth pursuing when compared with the cost of litigation. Consumer protection legislation provides special remedies for consumers so that pursuing their rights in court is cost beneficial. Class action suits provide groups of consumers options for pursuing remedies that they might not be able to pursue (due to the cost) if they were acting alone. **For Example,** some federal statutes permit debtors to bring class action suits, and their recovery is a statutory percentage of the net worth of the company that has violated their rights.

In addition, consumer statutes often provide initial or alternative means for consumers to enforce their rights. Consumer statutes provide procedural steps for consumers to use to try to resolve their problems with the businesses involved and to document what has happened in their contract or relationship. **For Example,** some statutes require consumers to give the business involved written notice of the consumer's complaint. Having this notice then provides the business an opportunity to examine the consumer's complaint or concerns and possibly work out a solution.[4]

[4] *Rutledge v. High Point Regional Health System,* 558 F. Supp. 2d 611 (M.D.N.C. 2008).

In addition to procedural remedies other than litigation, consumer protection statutes provide other ways for consumers to seek their remedies, sometimes with the help of others who are more experienced in resolving consumer protection statutory violations.

(A) Government Agency Action. At both the federal and state levels, administrative agencies that are responsible for the enforcement of laws and regulations also have the power to take steps to obtain relief for consumers. **For Example,** the Federal Trade Commission (FTC) can file a complaint against a company for false advertising. In settling the complaint with the company that had the false ads, the FTC could require the company to refund to the consumers affected by the ads the price of the product featured in the ad. The new Bureau of Consumer Financial Protection (BCFP) (see p. 655) has the same authority to bring such complaints.

(B) Action by Attorney General. A number of states allow their state attorneys general to bring actions on behalf of consumers who are victims of fraud or other unfair conduct. In these actions, the attorney general can request that consumers' contracts be canceled and that they be given restitution of whatever they paid. These suits by attorneys general are not criminal actions; they are civil suits in which the standard of proof is a preponderance of the evidence, not proof beyond a reasonable doubt. **For Example,** the litigation brought by state attorneys general for alleged deception by tobacco companies on the health harms of using tobacco resulted in settlements by those companies. The funds were used to compensate the states for health care costs for individuals with tobacco-related illnesses for whom the state was caring. The funds were also used to pay for educational programs and ads that caution young people not to smoke and warn them about the health hazards of using tobacco.

Many states also permit their attorneys general to bring actions for an injunction against violations of the consumer protection statute. These statutes commonly give the attorney general the authority to obtain a voluntary cease-and-desist consent decree (see Chapter 6) for improper practices before seeking an injunction from a court. The attorney general, like the agency, can impose a penalty for a violation.

(C) Action by Consumer. Consumer protection statutes can also provide that a consumer who has been harmed by a violation of the statutes may recover by his own suit against the business that acted improperly.[5] The consumer may either seek to recover a penalty provided for in the consumer protection statute or bring an action on behalf of consumers as a class. Consumer protection statutes are often designed to rely on private litigation as an aid to enforcement of the statutory provisions. The Consumer Product Safety Act of 1972 authorizes "any interested person" to bring a civil action to enforce a consumer product safety rule and certain orders of the Consumer Product Safety Commission.[6]

(D) Replacement or Refund. Some state consumer protection statutes require that the consumer be made whole by the replacement of the good, the refund of the purchase price, or the repair of the item within a reasonable time.[7]

(E) Invalidation of Consumer's Contract. Other consumer protection statutes provide that when the contract made by a consumer violates the statute, the consumer's contract is void. In such a case, the seller cannot recover from the consumer buyer for any unpaid balance. Likewise, the seller cannot repossess the goods for nonpayment. The consumer keeps the goods without making any further payment.[8]

6. What Are the Civil and Criminal Penalties under Consumer Protection Statutes?

Only certain government agencies and attorneys general can seek criminal and civil penalties against those who violate consumer protection statutes. The agency or attorney general may use those penalties to provide compensation to consumers who have been victims of the violations. When consumers successfully bring individual or class action suits against those who violate their rights as consumers, they recover damages. Some consumer protection statutes authorize the recovery of **compensatory damages** to compensate the consumer for the loss. These types of

[5] *Service Corp. Intern. v. Aragon*, 268 S.W.2d 112 (Tex. App. 2008).
[6] 15 U.S.C. §2051 *et seq.*
[7] Note that apart from these statutes, the buyer may have protection under a warranty to repair or replace. Likewise, a revocation of acceptance under the UCC would give the right to a refund of the purchase price.
[8] *Pennsylvania Dept. of Banking v. NCAS of Delaware*, LLC, 931 A.2d 771 (Pa. App. 2007).

statutes are designed to put the customer in as good a position as he would have been in had there not been a deception, breach, or violation of other requirements under the consumer protection statute. Other statutes authorize the recovery of **punitive damages**,[9] which are additional damages beyond compensatory damages and may be a percentage of the company's net worth. Under antitrust statutes that prohibit anticompetitive behavior, consumers can collect treble punitive damages for a violation. Consumers cannot claim both treble damages authorized by a statute and also punitive damages under the common law. Such double recovery would be duplicative remedies for the same wrong.

B. Areas of Consumer Protection

The following sections discuss important areas of consumer protection. Figure 33-1 provides an overview of these areas.

7. Advertising

Statutes commonly prohibit fraudulent advertising. Most advertising regulations are entrusted to an administrative agency, such as the FTC, which is authorized to issue orders to stop false or misleading advertising. Statutes prohibiting false advertising are liberally interpreted.

A store is liable for false advertising when it advertises a reduced price sale of a particular item that is out of stock when the sale begins. It is no defense that the presale demand was greater than usual.

(a) Deception. Under consumer protection statutes, *deception* rather than *fraud* is the significant element.[10] A breach of these statutes occurs even without proof that the wrongdoer intended to defraud or deceive anyone.

The deception statutes and regulations represent a shift in the law and public policy. These regulations are not laws based on fault; rather, they are based on

FIGURE 33-1 *The Legal Environment of the Consumer*

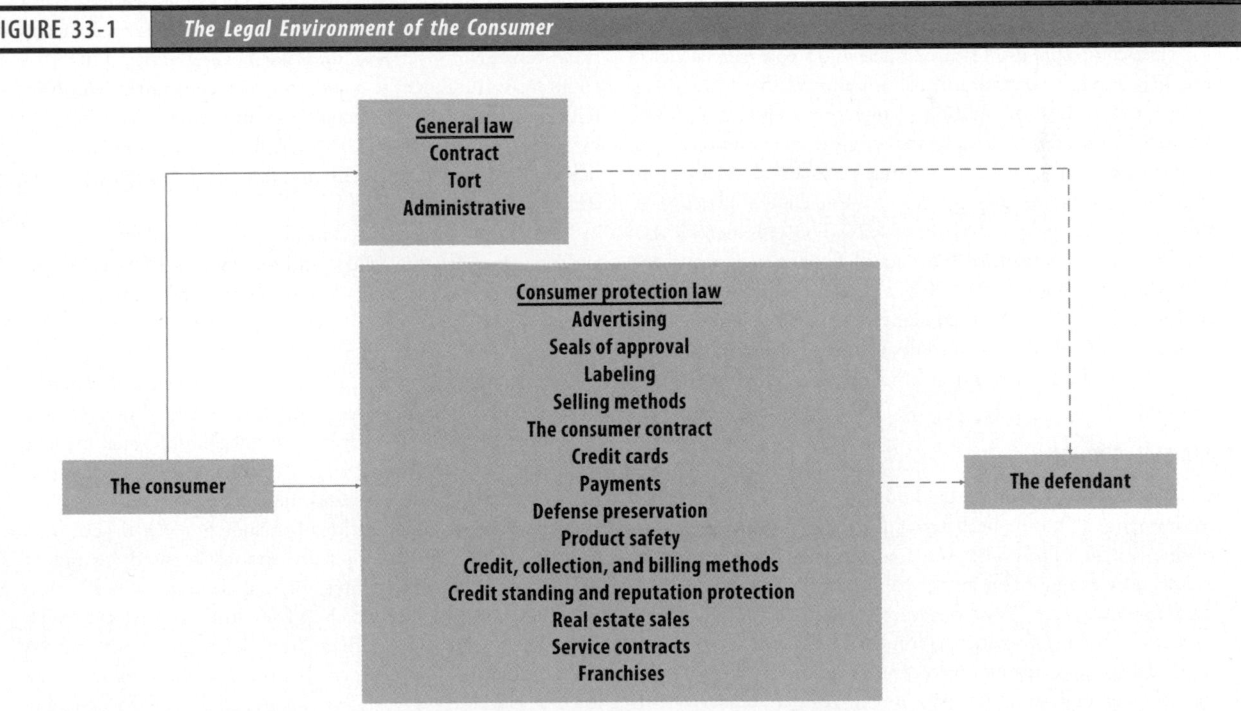

[9] *Adams v. National Engineering Service Corp.*, 620 F. Supp. 2d 319 (D. Conn. 2009).
[10] *Michael v. Mosquera-Lacy*, 200 P.3d 695 (Wash. 2000).

the question of whether a buyer is likely to be misled by the ad. The good faith of an advertiser or the absence of intent to deceive is immaterial. False advertising regulation protects *consumers* regardless of the advertiser's motives.

The FTC requires advertisers to maintain records of the data used as support for statements made in ads that deal with the safety, performance, efficacy, quality, or comparative price of an advertised product. The FTC can require the advertiser to produce these data and backup material. If it is in the interest of the consumer, the FTC can make this information public except to the extent that it contains trade secrets or privileged material.

(B) Corrective Advertising. When an enterprise has made false and deceptive statements in advertising, the FTC may require new advertising to correct the former statements so that consumers are aware of the truth. This corrective advertising required by the FTC is also called *retractive advertising*. The FTC can also halt ads that it finds to be deceptive.

The *McNeil-PPC, Inc. v. Pfizer Inc.* case discusses the remedies for misleading ads by competitors.

McNeil-PPC, Inc. v. Pfizer Inc., 351 F. Supp. 2d 226 (S.D.N.Y. 2005)

Stringing Buyers Along with Floss

In June 2004, Pfizer Inc. ("Pfizer") launched a consumer advertising campaign for its mouthwash, Listerine Antiseptic Mouthrinse. Print ads and hang tags on the bottles in the stores featured an image of a Listerine bottle balanced on a scale against a white container of dental floss.

The campaign also featured a television commercial called the "Big Bang." The commercial announced that "Listerine's as effective as floss at fighting plaque and gingivitis. Clinical studies prove it." Although the commercial cautions that "[t]here's no replacement for flossing," the commercial repeats two more times the message that Listerine is "as effective as flossing against plaque and gingivitis." The commercial also shows a narrow stream of blue liquid flowing out of a Cool Mint Listerine bottle, then tracks a piece of dental floss being pulled from a white floss container and swirled around and between teeth—bringing to mind an image of liquid floss.

PPC filed a motion for an injunction to stop Pfizer from running the ads.

JUDICIAL OPINION

CHIN, District Judge...Traditionally, the "most widely recommended" mechanical device for removing interproximal plaque is dental floss. The ADA recommends "brushing twice a day and cleaning between the teeth with floss or interdental cleaners once each day to remove plaque from all tooth surfaces." Flossing provides a number of benefits. It removes food debris and plaque interdentally and it also removes plaque subgingivally. As part of a regular oral hygiene program, flossing helps reduce and prevent not only gingivitis but also periodontitis and caries. Some 87 percent of consumers, however, floss either infrequently or not at all. Although dentists and dental hygienists regularly tell their patients to floss, many consumers do not floss or rarely floss because it is a difficult and time-consuming process.

As a consequence, a large consumer market exists to be tapped. If the 87 percent of consumers who never or rarely floss can be persuaded to floss more regularly, sales of floss would increase dramatically. PPC has endeavored, with products such as the RADF and the Power Flosser, to reach these consumers by trying to make flossing easier. Pfizer has come to realize that if it could convince consumers who were reluctant flossers that they could obtain the benefits of flossing by rinsing with Listerine, it would be in a position to see its sales of Listerine increase dramatically.... [T]herefore, Pfizer and PPC are competitors.

Pfizer sponsored two clinical studies involving Listerine and floss: the "Sharma Study" and the "Bauroth Study." These studies purported to compare the efficacy of Listerine against dental floss in controlling plaque and gingivitis in subjects with mild to moderate gingivitis.

The authors (of the Sharma study) concluded that the study provided "additional support for the use of the essential oil mouth rinse as an adjunct to mechanical oral hygiene regimens." They cautioned that "[p]rofessional recommendations to floss daily should continue to be reinforced."

The Bauroth Study authors concluded: "[W]e do not wish to suggest that the mouth rinse should be used instead of dental floss or any other interproximal cleaning device."

The ADA reported on the Pfizer studies in its own Web site. The ADA wrote that "[w]hile some study results [referencing the Sharma and Bauroth Studies] indicate the use of a mouth rinse can be as effective as flossing for reducing plaque between the teeth," it continued to recommend "brushing twice a day and cleaning between the teeth with floss or interdental cleaners once each day."

A number of individual dentists and hygienists complained directly to Pfizer that consumers would get the wrong message [and]...noted specifically that "advertising that shows a bottle

Continued

of Listerine on a scale opposite a package of floss leaves [the] impression" that Listerine is an alternative to floss, "[a]s does the sound bite: 'Listerine is as effective as floss.'"

From the time Pfizer launched its advertising campaign, sales of both the RADF and the Power Flosser have taken a steep decline. Consumers who use the RADF and Power Flosser...are predominantly "folks who don't like to floss," who "would love to have a replacement for flossing." These consumers "would be more susceptible to a message like the Listerine advertising campaign."

Pfizer and PPC are in head-to-head competition for the same market—non-flossers or reluctant flossers. These individuals would be easily enticed by the notion that they could obtain the benefits of flossing by rinsing with Listerine. Moreover, there may very well be a future impact on regular flossers as well.

The literal claim in Pfizer's advertisements is overly broad, for the studies did not purport to prove that Listerine is as effective as floss "against plaque and gingivitis," but only against plaque and gingivitis in individuals with mild to moderate gingivitis. What the two studies showed was that Listerine is as effective as floss when flossing is not done properly.

Pfizer's false and misleading advertising also poses a public health risk, as the advertisements present a danger of undermining the efforts of dental professionals—and the ADA—to convince consumers to floss on a daily basis.

[Injunction granted.]

QUESTIONS

1. What are the limitations of the studies on which Pfizer relied?
2. Why are mouthwash and floss competitors?
3. Describe the standards the court uses for stopping a misleading or false ad.
4. Comment on Pfizer's social responsibility, its competitive strategies, and its ethics in this ad campaign.

Thinking Things Through

Those Service Agreements End with Replacements, You Know

In December 2008, Corey and Jamie Baker purchased a TV from Best Buy as well as a four-year service contract for the TV. In November 2010, Best Buy determined that the problems the Bakers were having with the TV could not be fixed, so Best Buy replaced the TV with a comparable model. Best Buy told the Bakers that if they wanted the full protection on the replacement TV, they would need to buy a new four-year policy. The Bakers and others filed suit against Best Buy for consumer fraud and false statements in advertisements because the Bakers felt that the ads depicted the service agreement as being one of full protection for four years. Under the terms of the service contract purchased by the appellants, coverage under the plan was effective from the date the product was purchased and would expire four years from the effective date. But the next paragraph of the service contract adds that "[o]ur obligations under this Plan will be fulfilled in their entirety if we replace your product." The contract further stated "Limits of Liability," defining a limit of the lesser of repair or replacements and finally stating that "[i]n the event...we replace the product, we shall have satisfied all obligations under the Plan." What should the court decide? Was there deception, or is the contract clear enough for buyers? Discuss the factors the court will consider in deciding whether there has been consumer fraud. **[*Baker v. Best Buy Stores, LP,* 812 812 N.W.2d 177 (Minn. App. 2012)]**

8. Labeling

Closely related to the regulation of advertising is the regulation of labeling and marking products. Various federal statutes are designed to give consumers accurate information about a product, whereas others require warnings about dangers of use or misuse. Consumer protection regulations prohibit labeling or marking products with such terms as *jumbo, giant,* and *full,* which tend to exaggerate and mislead. **For Example,** the health foods store Eating Well sold a number of foods with the label "Fat Free." This label was false, and Eating Well knew that the foods were ordinary foods not free of fat. Eating Well violated consumer protection statutes that prohibit false labeling. Sales made on the basis of the false labels meant that Eating Well committed the tort of fraud and the crime of obtaining money by false pretenses.

9. Selling Methods

In addition to regulating ads, consumer protection statutes regulate the methods used to sell goods and services.

(A) Home-Solicited Sales. A sale of goods or services for $25 or more made to a buyer at home may be set aside within three business days. This consumer right of rescission may be exercised merely because the buyer does not want to go through with the contract. There is no requirement that the buyer prove any seller misconduct or defect in the goods or services.[11]

When the buyer has made an oral agreement to purchase and the seller then comes to the buyer's home to work out the details, the transaction is not a

Sports & Entertainment Law

Daisy Duke and Captain Kirk on DirectTV

Jessica Simpson, playing the character of Daisy Duke that she portrayed in the movie *The Dukes of Hazzard,* did an ad for DirectTV in which she said: "Hey, 253 straight days at the gym to get this body and you're not going to watch me on DirectTV HD? You're just not going to get the best picture out of some fancy big-screen TV without DirectTV. It's broadcast in 1080i. I totally don't know what that means but I want it." A narrator's voice then concluded, "For picture quality that beats cable, you've got to get DirectTV." In another DirectTV commercial, William Shatner played Captain James T. Kirk, the character that he portrayed in the *Star Trek* television series and movies. In the ad, Shatner said, "I wish he'd just relax and enjoy the amazing picture clarity of the DirectTV HD we just hooked up. With what Starfleet just ponied up for this big screen TV, settling for cable would be illogical." A narrator's voice concluded, "For picture quality that beats cable, you've got to get DirectTV." The ads depicted an image of cable television showing a fuzzy, distorted picture.

Time Warner Cable said that the ads, particularly with their distorted depiction of cable programming, are deceptive and misleading for consumers and are deceptive advertising. Is Time Warner correct? Could celebrities who appear in ads that are deceptive and who are aware of the deception also be held liable for any damages? **[*Time Warner Cable, Inc. v. Directv, Inc.,* 494 F.3d 144 (2nd Cir. 2007)]**

E-Commerce & Cyberlaw

Apple, Safari, and Google

In February 2012, the *Wall Street Journal* (WSJ) reported that Google was bypassing the built-in security that Apple put on its Safari browser in order to protect users. Google used a secret code to bypass the default protection setting. The result was that millions of Safari users were being tracked by Google for months without their knowledge. When the WSJ story broke, Google had several class action consumer protection lawsuits filed against it and the FTC announced an investigation into the issue. Google was fined $25,000 for impeding the FTC investigation. Google was already under a consent decree entered into in 2011 for continuing to track users from its "Buzz" social network without their knowledge. Google was to report to the FTC any potential violations of the terms of the consent decree, which included a promise to not violate the privacy of consumers and to obtain permission before tracking.

The issue of tracking is one that is the focus of FTC actions. There are three simple rules for staying in compliance with FTC consumer protection regulations on tracking consumers: (1) Always obtain permission; (2) report when you have a breach of privacy; and (3) then fix it so that the breaches do not continue to occur.

[11] Federal Trade Commission Regulation, 16 CFR §429:1.

home-solicited sale and cannot be rescinded under the federal regulation.[12] A sale was also not home-solicited when the seller phoned the consumer at his or her home for permission to mail the consumer a promotional brochure, and thereafter the consumer went to the seller's place of business where the contract was made.[13]

(B) Telemarketing Fraud. High-pressure selling by telephone has attracted sham businesses and resulted in consumer contracts that are often unconscionable. The Telephone Consumer Protection Act (TCPA) gave the FTC authority to promulgate rules that restrict telemarketing.[14] The TCPA outlaws automated marketing calls without the prior express consent of the called party and prohibits calls to emergency telephone lines or patient rooms in hospitals, health care facilities, or elderly homes. The FTC has added rules that prohibit unsolicited transmissions to fax machines as well as telemarketing calls before 8 A.M. or after 9 P.M. States have additional regulations on telemarketing, including systems that require telemarketers to register with the state.[15]

In 2003 the scope of the TCPA was expanded to increase consumer protection significantly with its new provisions for the FTC to create a National Do Not Call Registry.[16] The FTC rules created a means for consumers to register to opt out of any telemarketing, except for political and charitable calls. Consumers who voluntarily give their phone numbers to merchants can also be contacted by those merchants. The constitutionality of the Do Not Call Registry was challenged in court but upheld.[17]

However, consumer frustration with the need to re-register every three years resulted in Congress passing the Do-Not-Call Improvement Act of 2007, a law that makes consumer do-not-call registration permanent.

10. The Consumer Contract

Consumer contracts are regulated in different ways.

(A) Form of Contract. Consumer protection laws commonly regulate the form of the contract, requiring that certain items be specifically listed, that payments under the contract be itemized, and that finance charges be clear (see Chapter 34). Generally, consumer protections require that certain portions of the contract be printed in a certain font size, and that a copy of the contract be furnished the consumer.

(B) Contracts Printed on Two Sides. To be sure that consumers see all contract disclosures required by law, contracts that have their terms printed on both the front and the back of the contract must carry the warning "NOTICE: see other side for important information." Consumers must sign the back side of each sheet.

(C) Particular Sales and Leases. The Motor Vehicle Information and Cost Savings Act requires dealers to make certain disclosure to buyers. In addition, the act prohibits selling an automobile without informing the buyer that the odometer has been reset below the true mileage. For example, if a seller knows that the real mileage on a car is 120,073 miles, but rolls the odometer back to 20,073 miles, the seller has committed odometer fraud, a violation that allows the buyer to recover three times the actual loss or $1,500, whichever amount is higher.[18] This federal odometer law imposes a higher standard on auto dealers. An auto dealer who may not actually know of a roll-back cannot claim lack of knowledge that the odometer was false when that conclusion was reasonably apparent from the condition of the car.[19]

The federal government has also passed laws regulating particular types of leases of goods. For example, under the Consumer Leasing Act of 1976, leases of autos and other durable goods require

[12] *Gray v. First Century Bank*, 547 F. Supp. 2d 815 (E.D. Tenn. 2008).
[13] *United Consumers Club v. Griffin*, 619 N.E.2d 489 (Ohio App. 1993).
[14] 47 U.S.C. §227.
[15] *Blitz v. Agean, Inc.*, 677 S.E.2d 19 (N.C. 2009).
[16] 16 C.F.R. §310.8.
[17] The national list supplements the law in 28 states that already had some form of do-not-call registers. However, constitutional issues (see Chapter 5) limited those protections across state lines so that the national regulation was necessary.
[18] 15 U.S.C. §1901 *et seq.*, as amended; recodified as 49 U.S.C. §§32701–32711.
[19] *State ex rel. Cordray v. Midway Motor Sales, Inc.*, 910 N.E.2d 432 (Ohio 2009).

specific contract details and disclosures such as the number of lease payments as well as the amount due at the end of the lease for the consumer to purchase the leased goods.[20]

(D) Contract Terms. Consumer protection legislation does not ordinarily affect the right of the parties to make a contract on whatever terms they choose. It is customary, however, to prohibit the use of certain clauses that are harsh for the consumer or that have too great a potential for exploitive abuse by a creditor, such as waiving a warranty limitations disclosure. The Warranty Disclosure Act requires sellers to specify whether the provided warranty protection is full or limited, a standard defined in the act itself.

Credit transactions, covered in the next section, carry significant requirements for disclosure.

(E) Limitations on Credit. Consumer debt in the United States, including installment loans and credit card debt, had grown to more than $2.5 trillion dollars as of the first quarter of 2009, a figure that had grown by $500 billion since 2007. From 1998–2008, credit card debt grew by 25 percent. With the economic crisis of 2008, the federal government passed significant reforms in credit contracts (see discussion below in Section 11). Part of the reforms focused on the **subprime lending market**. This credit market makes loans to consumers who have bankruptcies, no credit history, low-to-moderate incomes, or a poor credit history. Because of the higher risk of these types of loans, these credit contracts involve lower loan amounts; higher origination costs, brokers' fees, credit insurance fees; higher interest rates; significant collateral pledges; large prepayment penalties (meaning that the consumer debtor is locked into the high interest rate); and faster repayment requirements. Subprime loans have had notoriously difficult-to-read contracts. Determining all of the charges and fees from the contract was a tall order. Regulations and laws at the state and federal level have changed and simplified contract disclosures for subprime loans.

Part of the subprime lending market includes lenders who take advantage of less sophisticated consumers or even consumers who are just desperate for funds. These lenders use their superior bargaining positions to obtain credit terms that go well beyond compensating them for their risk. For example, title loans (loans made in exchange for title to a car or house if the borrower defaults) have been widely used in subprime markets. These types of loans, sometimes called **predatory lending**, are now highly regulated by both the states and the federal government.[21] The new wave of consumer protection on subprime loans includes limitations on interest rates, 10-day rescission periods, additional contract disclosures requirements, and the requirement of credit counseling before consumers may sign for certain types of subprime loans.

(F) Unconscionability. The UCC has a longstanding form of consumer protection through its prohibition on "unconscionability" in contracts. The types of provisions that make contracts unconscionable include clauses that award excessive damages or the application of credit payments across purchases over time so that the consumer is never able to pay off any goods.[22]

Some specific state statutes are aimed at activities deemed unconscionable—for example, price gouging on consumer goods or services for which the demand is abnormally greater than the supply. **For Example,** New York's statute provides: "During any abnormal disruption of the market for consumer goods and services vital and necessary for the health, safety, and welfare of consumers, resulting from stress of weather, convulsion of nature, failure or shortage of electric power or other source of energy…no merchant shall sell or offer to sell any such consumer goods or services for an amount which represents an unconscionably excessive price." Such a statute protects, for example, purchasers of electric generators for home use during a hurricane-caused blackout. During floods and other natural disasters, these statutes limit what sellers can charge for water and other staples.

11. Credit Disclosures

While general consumer statutes prohibit deception in ads and sales practices, specific federal laws require the disclosure of all interest charges, points, and fees for all types of loans and credit contracts. These laws

[20] 15 U.S.C. §1667.

[21] N.J. Stat. Ann. §46:10B-22 (West 2006); 2003 Ark. Acts 2598; Cal. Fin. Code §§4970-4979.7 (West 2006); Ga. Code Ann. §7-6A-1-13 (2006); 2003 Ill. Laws 93-561; 2003 N.M. Laws 436; 2001 N.Y. Laws 11856; N.C. Gen. Stat. §24-1.1e (2006); 2003 S.C. Acts 42; 2003 N.C. Sess. Laws 24-10.2.

[22] *Guerra v. Hertz Corp.*, 504 F. Supp. 2d 1014 (D. Nev. 2007).

require disclosure of an annual percentage rate (APR) so that the consumer can see just how much the transaction costs per year and can compare alternatives.[23] The Truth in Lending Act (TILA) provides the requirements for disclosures in credit contracts and consumer rights when full disclosure is not made. When a consumer sale or contract provides for payment in more than four installments, it is subject to the TILA. The application of the TILA is required even when there is no service or finance charge for the installment payments. There are additional obligations of disclosure under the Fair Credit and Charge Card Disclosure Act,[24] the Home Equity Loan Consumer Protection Act,[25] and the Credit Card Accountability, Responsibility and Disclosure (CARD) Act of 2009.[26] In 2009, the Federal Reserve promulgated regulations that expanded consumer protection provisions. The CARD Act applies to all credit cards. All of these statutes and regulations, discussed in the following sections, require advance disclosures and timing mandates.

The Federal Reserve Board was originally delegated the responsibility for enforcing TILA and has promulgated regulations to carry out the details of disclosure, but the new **Bureau of Consumer Financial Protection** (BCFP or Bureau), created under the **Dodd-Frank Wall Street Reform and Consumer Protection Act** (DFCPA), also known as the Wall Street Reform and Consumer Financial Protection Act or the Consumer Financial Protection Act (CFPA), will now assume that enforcement role. Housed within the Federal Reserve, the BCFP now serves the combined roles that the Federal Reserve as well as the FTC and other federal agencies played in dealing with consumer credit laws, regulations, and issues.

12. Credit Cards

Credit cards and credit arrangements are so readily available that consumers tell of receiving credit cards when they apply in the name of their Labrador retrievers. Because of the extensive availability of credit cards and the ease with which they are issued, there are extensive federal regulations of credit card use and the rights of consumers with credit cards.[27]

(A) Unsolicited Credit Cards. Federal regulations prohibit the unsolicited distribution of credit cards to persons who have not applied for them. The practice of simply sending credit cards through the mail to consumers is now illegal. The problems with rising identity theft have made this protection especially important to consumers because identity thieves were able to intercept the mail and seize the unsolicited credit cards.

(B) Credit Cards for Those Under the Age of 21. The CARD Act substantially restricts the solicitation of credit card accounts from those under the age of 21. Credit card companies must have a written

E-Commerce & Cyberlaw

The Sneaky Hotel Bill

Travelocity automatically assessed a "Taxes and Fees" charge to customers who had booked hotel rooms on its Web site. The "Taxes and Fees" charged are neither required by nor paid to state or local authorities. The "Taxes and Fees" do, however, represent a steady stream of revenue for Travelocity. These "Taxes and Fees" are not part of what Travelocity actually pays for the rooms. There are several class action suits pending around the country to allow those who booked rooms to recover for the deception in their charges. If a vendor labels a fee as "taxes," then it must actually be paying those taxes to a government authority. **[*Okland v. Travelocity.com, Inc.*, 2009 WL 1740076 (Tex. App. 2009)]**

[23] Consumer Credit Protection Act (CCPA), 15 U.S.C. §§1605, 1606, & 1636; Regulation Z adopted by the Federal Reserve, 12 C.F.R. §226.5.

[24] 15 U.S.C. §1601 *et seq.*

[25] *Id.*

[26] HR 627; passed May 20, 2009.

[27] Heidi Mandanis Schooner, "Consuming Debt: Structuring the Federal Response to Abuses in Consumer Credit," 18 *Loyola Consumer L. Rev.* 43 (2005).

application in hand from those under 21 and those applications must carry the signature of a parent, guardian, or someone over the age of 21 who has the means to repay debt. The line of credit on a co-signed card for someone under the age of 21 cannot be increased without the co-signer's permission. Colleges and universities are now restricted in their partnering with credit card companies, arrangements that allowed the colleges and universities and their alumni associations to receive funds from the credit card companies in exchange for access to their students and alumni. The CARD Act limits locations for college student credit card solicitations, requires colleges and universities to disclose their financial relationships with such credit card companies, and also requires colleges and universities to provide debt counseling for their students.

(c) Surcharge Prohibited. Under some statutes, a seller cannot add any charge to the purchase price because the buyer uses a credit card instead of paying with cash or a check.[28]

(d) Unauthorized Use. A cardholder is not liable for more than $50 for the unauthorized use of a credit card. To even recover the $50 amount, the credit card issuer must show that (1) the credit card was an accepted card,[29] (2) the issuer gave the holder adequate notice of possible liability in such a case, (3) the issuer furnished the holder with notification means in the event of loss or theft of the credit card, (4) the issuer provided a method by which the user of the card could be identified as the person authorized to use it,[30] and (5) unauthorized use of the card had occurred or might occur as a result of loss, theft, or some other event.

The burden of proof is on the card issuer to show that the use of the card was authorized or that the holder is liable for its unauthorized use.[31]

(e) Unauthorized Purpose Distinguished. Unauthorized use of a credit card occurs only when it is used without the permission or approval of the cardholder. The holder may authorize use by another, but only for a limited purpose, such as purchasing office supplies or a new fax machine. If the person uses the card for any item other than the purpose specified, the use remains authorized because merchants cannot know these private restrictions.[32] The same rule is applied when an employer has cards issued to employees for making employment-related purchases but that employees use for personal purposes.

(f) Late Payment Fee. The contract between a credit card issuer and a holder may require the holder to pay a late payment fee. The CARD Act of 2009 changed substantially the law on late payments because of so much abuse by credit card companies with regard to late fees. Under CARD, all credit card companies must have bills in consumers' hands not less than 21 days before the bill is due. In addition, the CARD Act requires conspicuous disclosures about the amount of late fees as well as the impact of a late payment on the consumer's rate of interest.

(g) Credit Card Balance Transfers. Credit card debt grew greatly during the 1997–2007 period because of the wide availability of the balance transfer mechanism. Consumers received offers from credit card companies to transfer their balances from existing cards to what seemed to be lower-interest-rate credit cards. Very often, however, the real costs of the transfer were not disclosed or not disclosed in a conspicuous manner or were later modified through a credit card company's new terms. The CARD Act has now changed everything from the maximum fees allowed with these transfers to how quickly credit card companies can change the advertised terms of the transfer. New disclosure requirements mandate the upfront disclosure of transfer fees as well as potential changes in the APR once the transfer has occurred. The CARD Act also places limits on how often companies can change a credit card holder's interest rate.

[28] In contrast, the Truth in Lending Act Amendment of 1976, 15 U.S.C. §1666f, permits a merchant to offer a discount to cash-paying customers but not to customers using a credit card.

[29] A credit card is accepted when the cardholder has requested and received or has signed, used, or authorized another to use the card for the purpose of obtaining money, property, labor, or services on credit.

[30] Regulation Z of the Board of Governors of the Federal Reserve, 12 C.F.R. §226.13(d), as amended, provides that the identification may be by signature, photograph, or fingerprint on the credit card or by electronic or mechanical confirmation.

[31] The Fair and Accurate Credit Transactions Act (FACTA), 15 U.S.C. §1681, requires merchants to use only the last few digits of a credit card on their receipts (a truncated number) so as to reduce the likelihood of a thief finding the receipt and using the full credit card number. *Van Straaten v. Shell Oil Products., LLC*, 678 F.3d 486 (7th Cir. 2012).

[32] *Asher v. Chase Bank USA, N.A.*, 310 Fed. Appx. 912 (7th Cir. 2009).

13. Gift Cards

Gift cards have become increasingly popular since 2002. Many retailers' gift card revenues for holiday seasons 2010 and 2011 equaled their actual sales of merchandise. However, many retailers imposed expiration dates on those gifts cards or charged inactivity fees that slowly decreased the value of the cards. Under the CARD Act, a gift card cannot have an expiration date any earlier than five years from the time it is issued and there must be a conspicuous disclosure notice about that expiration date. Inactivity fees on gift cards and cards that-decline-in-value cards are now regulated under CARD. There are now controls on those declining value fees, such as when they can be charged and what must be disclosed up front.

14. Payments

Under the CARD Act, consumer payments on their credit cards are now regulated extensively. First, the due date must specify that the time is 5:00 P.M. on that date. This change corrected creditor abuses that resulted when they made 9:00 A.M. the cut-off time for payments, thus depriving the debtors of the possibility that their mailed bills could get in for posting by the due date. Second, how consumer payments are applied to existing balances is now also regulated. When consumers make payments in excess of the minimum payment due on their credit card bills, the creditor must apply that extra amount to that portion of the account that carries the highest interest rate.

There are now new and detailed federal limitations on balance transfers, interest rates, increases in interest rates, and limitations on when and how long an increase in interest rates can be applied to consumers who have been late on payments or who have exceeded their credit limits. In addition, when and how consumers can exceed their credit limits are subject to new detailed disclosures and regulations. These rules all affect the amount of the minimum payment and how long the additional interest and fees can apply when a consumer has been tardy on payments or is delinquent on the credit card account.

15. Preservation of Consumer Defenses

Consumer protection laws generally prohibit a consumer from waiving or giving up any defense provided by law. In an ordinary contract situation, when goods or services purchased or leased by a consumer are not proper or are defective, the consumer is not required to pay for the goods or services or is required to pay only a reduced amount. With the modern expansion of credit transactions, sellers and lessors have used several techniques for getting paid without regard to whether the consumer had any complaint against them. To prevent this, the FTC has adopted a regulation requiring that in every sale or lease of goods or services to a consumer, there must be a contract that gives the consumer the right to assert defenses. This notice can be found in the discussion of negotiable instruments and the rights of the parties in Chapter 29. A good deal of consumer credit issues will no longer be handled by the FTC but rather by the BCFP (see p. 655). Located within the Federal Reserve, this agency will now assume all regulatory responsibility for credit and consumer issues.

16. Product Safety

A variety of statutes and rules of law protects the health and well-being of consumers. Most states have laws governing the manufacture of various products and establishing product safety standards. The federal Consumer Product Safety Act provides for research and setting uniform standards for products to reduce health hazards. This act also establishes civil and criminal penalties for the distribution of unsafe products, recognizes the right of an aggrieved person to recover damages and to obtain an injunction against the distribution of unsafe products, and creates a Consumer Product Safety Commission to administer the act.[33] (See Chapters 9 and 24.)

17. Credit, Collection, and Billing Methods

Various laws and regulations protect consumers from discriminatory and improper credit and collection practices.

[33] 15 U.S.C. §§2051–2081.

CPA **(A) Equal Credit Opportunity Act: Credit Discrimination.** Under the Equal Credit Opportunity Act (ECOA), it is unlawful to discriminate against an applicant for credit on the basis of race, color, religion, national origin, gender, marital status, or age; because all or part of the applicant's income is obtained from a public assistance program; or because the applicant has in good faith exercised any right under the Consumer Credit Protection Act (CCPA). When a credit application is refused, the applicant must be furnished a written explanation.

For Example, when Robert applied for a loan at Tradesman Bank, he was told on the phone that the loan would not be made to him because of his criminal record. Tradesman must furnish Robert with the specifics regarding that denial. Using Robert's race to decline the loan would be an ECOA violation. However, denial based on a criminal record is permitted.[34]

(B) Fair Credit Billing Act: Correction of Errors. When a consumer believes that a credit card issuer has made a billing error, the consumer should send the creditor a written statement and explanation of the error. The creditor or card issuer must investigate and make a prompt written reply to the consumer.[35] Many credit card companies now permit consumers to file these disputes online.

(C) Improper Collection Methods. Unreasonable methods of debt collection are often expressly prohibited by statute or are held by courts to constitute an unreasonable invasion of privacy.[36] A creditor is liable for unreasonably attempting to collect a bill that in fact has been paid. This liability can arise under general principles of tort law as well as under special consumer protection legislation.

(1) Fault of Agent or Employee.

When improper collection methods are used, it is no defense to the creditor that the improper acts were performed by an agent, an employee, or any other person acting on behalf of the creditor. Under general principles of agency law, a creditor hiring an individual or an agency to collect a debt is liable to the debtor for damages for unlawful conduct by the collector.

CPA *(2) Fair Debt Collection Practices Act (FDCPA).*

The federal FDCPA prohibits improper practices in the collection by third parties of debts incurred primarily for personal, family, or household purposes. For purposes of the FDCPA, collectors are defined to include attorneys who are collecting for clients as well as those who are collecting from consumers for bad checks but does not cover original creditors who are collecting from their original debtors.[37]

(i) Collection Letters. Under the FDCPA, collectors must comply with restrictions on correspondence with debtors. The collector must not misrepresent its status in the letterhead, for example, by stating that the collector is a law firm or lawyer.[38] A letter from a collection agency to a consumer that gives the impression a lawsuit is about to be brought against the consumer when in fact it will not be brought is also a violation of the FDCPA.[39]

A debt collection letter sent to the debtor's place of employment that reveals the nature of the correspondence is a violation of FDCPA. For example, if the words "final demand for payment" can be read through the envelope sent to the place of employment, then the collector has violated the debtor's privacy. Postcards that revealed the purpose of the collector's contact or identity would also be FDCPA violations.

(ii) What Is Not a Defense. When a collection agency violates the FDCPA, it is liable to the debtor for damages. It is no defense that the debtor owed the money that the agency was seeking to collect. When a creditor uses improper collection methods, it is no defense that the improper acts were performed by an agent, employee, or any other person acting on behalf of the creditor.

(iii) Federal Preemption. In a conflict between collection practices under federal law and a state

[34] *A.B. & S. Auto Service, Inc. v. South Shore Bank of Chicago*, 962 F. Supp. 1056 (N.D. Ill. 1997).
[35] Fair Credit Billing Act, 15 U.S.C. §1601.
[36] Fair Debt Collection Practices Act, 15 U.S.C. §1692 *et seq.*; Federal Trade Commission Regulation, 16 C.F.R. §237.
[37] *Payday Today, Inc. v. Hamilton*, 911 N.E.2d 26 (Ind. App. 2009).
[38] *Gonzalez v. Kay*, 577 F.3d 600 (5th Cir. 2009).
[39] *Ruth v. Triumph Partnerships*, 577 F.3d 790 (7th Cir. 2009).

Ethics & the Law

Widowed, Broke, Sick, and in Debt to a Hospital with No Cash

Jeanette White was treated at Yale–New Haven Hospital for cancer. She died there in 1993 after almost 20 years of treatment. The hospital added interest of 10 percent per annum to the bill and the amount ultimately due was about $40,000. The hospital tried to collect the bill from her husband Quinton White, who was 77 and suffering from heart and kidney ailments.

Mr. White became a cause célèbre when the *Wall Street Journal* ran a top-fold B1 color-picture story on his plight. Yale–New Haven explained that while it was operating in the black, it had $52 million in bad debt and uncompensated care for 2002. The hospital itself does not charge interest, but when the debts are assigned to third parties, such as lawyers, for collection, they are permitted to charge interest.

Mr. White had missed only 17 payments to the hospital since he began making payments for his wife's treatment almost 20 years earlier. However, the hospital was aggressive through its law firm in pursuing the Whites' assets whenever a payment was missed. The first suit resulted in a judgment for the hospital that was reduced to a lien on the White's house in 1982. If and when the house were sold, proceeds would go first to the mortgage company and then to the hospital. The Whites had offered to pay $25 per month on the bill, but the hospital declined and used the court proceedings. The judge ordered payments of $5 per week, which was tripled to $15 per week after Mrs. White died. Most of the 17 missed payments occurred during 2002 when Mr. White began experiencing his health problems. The hospital's law firm went back to court and received a judgment for Mr. White's bank account, a judgment that was halted when Mr. White established that all of the funds in the account were his Social Security payments.

When Mr. White's story was published, students at the free clinic at Yale Law School undertook representation of Mr. White. A plethora of stories about hospital bills, hospital collections, and excessive charges followed along with class action suits challenging everything from hospital billing policies to collection practices.

What ethical issues arise for the hospitals on uncompensated care? What property does a judgment cover? Who has priority on the Whites' house? Why does a judgment last nearly 20 years?

Source: Lucette Lagnado, "Twenty Years and Still Paying," *Wall Street Journal*, March 13, 2003, B1, B2; "Dunned for Old Bills, Poor Find Some Hospitals Never Forget," *Wall Street Journal*, June 8, 2004, A1, A6; and "Anatomy of a Hospital Bill," *Wall Street Journal*, Sept. 21, 2004, B1, B4.

consumer protection statute, federal law preempts or displaces state law.[40]

CPA 18. Protection of Credit Standing and Reputation

When a person purchases on credit or applies for a loan, a job, or an insurance policy, those who will extend these benefits often wish to know more about the applicant. Credit reporting agencies gather such information on borrowers, buyers, and applicants and sell the information to interested persons.

The Fair Credit Reporting Act (FCRA)[41] protects consumers from various abuses that may arise as this information is recorded and revealed. This statute governs credit reporting agencies, sometimes called *credit bureaus.*

The FCRA applies only to **consumer credit**, which is defined as credit for "personal, family, and household" use; it does not apply to business or commercial transactions. The act does not apply to the investigation report made by an insurance company of a policy claim.[42]

(A) Privacy. Credit reporting agencies are not permitted to disclose information to persons not having a legitimate use for it. It is a federal crime to obtain or to furnish a credit report for an improper purpose.

On request, a credit reporting agency must tell a consumer the names and addresses of persons to whom it has made a credit report during the previous six months. It must also tell, when requested, which employers were given such a report during the previous two years.

[40] *Fischer v. Unipac Service Corp.*, 519 N.W.2d 793 (Iowa 1994).

[41] 15 U.S.C. §1681 *et seq.*

[42] *Reynolds v. Hartford Financial Services Group, Inc.*, 416 F.3d 1097 (9th Cir. 2005). The FCRA does apply, however, to insurers using credit reports to determine policy rates.

A store may not publicly display a list of named customers from whom it will not accept checks; such action is an invasion of the privacy of those persons.

(B) Protection from False Information. Much of the information obtained by credit bureaus is based on statements made by persons, such as neighbors, when interviewed by the bureau's investigator. Sometimes the statements are incorrect. Quite often they are **hearsay evidence** and would not be admissible in a legal proceeding. Nevertheless, such statements may go on credit records without further verification and be furnished to a client of the agency, who will tend to regard them as accurate and true.

A person has a limited right to request that a credit bureau disclose the nature and substance of the information it possesses. The right to know, however, does not extend to medical information. The bureau is also not required to identify the persons giving information to its investigators, nor is it required to give the applicant a copy of, or to permit the applicant to see, any file. The *Phillips v. Grendahl* case involves a right-to-know issue.

Phillips v. Grendahl, 312 F.3d 357 (8th Cir. 2002)

Trouble with the Future In-Laws and the FCRA

Mary Grendahl's daughter Sarah became engaged to marry Lavon Phillips and moved in with him. Mary Grendahl (defendant) became suspicious that Phillips was not telling the truth about his past, particularly about whether he was an attorney and whether he had done legal work in Washington, D.C. She also was confused about who his ex-wives and girlfriends were and where they lived. She contacted Kevin Fitzgerald (defendant), a family friend who worked for McDowell (defendant), a private investigation agency. She asked Fitzgerald to do a "background check" on Phillips, and she gave him the name of the woman Phillips had lived with before he began living with Sarah Grendahl.

Fitzgerald began his search by obtaining Phillips's Social Security number from a computer database. He searched public records in Minnesota and Alabama, where Phillips had lived earlier. He discovered one suit against Phillips for delinquent child support in Alabama, a suit to establish child support for two children in Minnesota, and one misdemeanor conviction for writing dishonored checks.

Fitzgerald then supplied the Social Security information to Econ Control and asked for "Finder's Reports" on Phillips and the former girlfriend. Econ Control was in the business of furnishing credit reports, Finder's Reports, and credit scoring for credit grantors and for private investigators. Robert McDowell, on behalf of McDowell Agency, had signed an Econ Control registration agreement, titled "Agreement for Consumer Credit Services." One clause of the registration agreement stated:

> *3. I certify that I will order consumer reports, as defined by the Fair Credit Reporting Act, only when they are intended to be used as a factor in establishing a consumer's eligibility for new or continued credit, collections of an account, insurance, licensing, employment purposes, or otherwise in connection with a legitimate business transaction involving the consumer. Such reports will be used for no other purpose. Each time I request a report I intend to use for employment purposes, I will specifically identify it to [Econ Control] at the time I request the report.*

Econ Control did not ask why McDowell wanted the report, and McDowell did not tell them. Econ Control obtained a report from Computer Science Corporation on Phillips and passed it onto McDowell.

Fitzgerald met with Mary Grendahl and gave her the results of his investigation, including the Finder's Report. Phillips eventually found out about the background check and became angry, as did Sarah. Mary Grendahl then telephoned and left the following voicemail for Sarah: "Sarah, this is Mom. I didn't directly do a credit report. I hired a PI, and they have every right to do that." Phillips brought suit against Mary Grendahl, McDowell Agency, and Econ Control, alleging violations of the Fair Credit Reporting Act. Phillips appealed the lower court's summary judgment for Grendahl and the others on the grounds that what they had obtained was not a consumer report in violation of the FCRA.

JUDICIAL OPINION

GIBSON, Circuit Judge....The first step in establishing liability under section 1681n(a) or section 1681o for obtaining a consumer report without a permissible purpose is to show that the document at issue was a "consumer report." The statutory definition is complex. Section 1681a(d) defines a consumer report as (1) any written, oral, or other communication of information (2) by a consumer reporting agency (3) bearing on a consumer's credit worthiness, credit standing, credit capacity, character, general reputation, personal characteristics, or mode of living (4) which is used or expected to be used or collected in whole or in part for the purpose of serving as a factor in establishing the consumer's eligibility for (A) credit or insurance to be used primarily for personal,

Continued

family, or household purposes; (B) employment purposes; or (C) any other purposes authorized under section 1681b.

In this case, there is no dispute that the Finder's Report was (1) a written communication (2) by a consumer reporting agency, Computer Science Corporation. The two issues in dispute pertaining to whether the Finder's Report is a consumer report are (3) whether it contained the sort of personal information that would bring it within the definition and (4) whether anyone "expected" the Finder's Report or the information in it to be used for one of the purposes listed in the definition or "collected" the information in it for that purpose.

A consumer report must contain information "bearing on a consumer's credit worthiness, credit standing, credit capacity, character, general reputation, personal characteristics, or mode of living." 15 U.S.C. §1681a(d). The Finder's Report listed "Trade line Information," consisting of the names of several creditors with whom Phillips had credit accounts and the existence of a child support obligation, with dates for "last activity," but no other details such as amount of obligation or payment history. The Finder's Report also lists Phillips's former employers, which also would bear on his mode of living by showing that he has been employed. We conclude that the Finder's Report contains the kind of personal information required by the definition of consumer report.

The second question, whether the putative consumer report or the information in it was "used or expected to be used" or "collected for" one of the listed purposes, such as use in a credit or employment decision, §1681a(d), is more difficult. Three statutory ambiguities in this clause could affect what communications are covered by the clause: the statutory language does not specify who must do the using, collecting or expecting; whether those verbs describe a specific or habitual action; or whether those actions must be done with regard to "information" or with regard to the consumer report itself. McDowell Agency essentially argues the clause requires that either the credit agency prepared the Finder's Report in the expectation that it would be used for a statutory purpose or that the requestors did so use it. McDowell Agency contends that the Finder's Report was too incomplete to enable anyone to base a credit decision on it, so neither the requestors nor the credit agency could have expected the report to be used in a credit decision. Phillips, on the other hand, focuses on the information in the report, rather than the report itself. He argues that some of the information was of a type habitually "used" by people within the credit industry for the purposes covered by the statute and that therefore no showing about anyone's actual intent with regard to the Finder's Report was necessary to make it a consumer report.

The record demonstrates that the Finder's Report, not just the information in it, was actually intended by the credit reporting agency that prepared it to be used for a statutory purpose. The sample Finder's Report supplied by Econ Control to McDowell Agency states: "FINDERS delivers skip-locate power in a cost-effective, easy-to-use format. This remarkable product was designed by and for collections professionals who need timely debt-recovery support at an economical price." It therefore appears that the Finder's Report was prepared by Computer Science Corporation with the expectation that it would be used for a statutory purpose. That being the case, the Finder's Report is a consumer report even though the requestor never used or intended to use it for a statutory purpose.

We next determine whether each of the defendants "obtained or used" the consumer report. There is no dispute that McDowell Agency and Econ Control obtained a consumer report, for each of them requested a Finder's Report.

Mary Grendahl, on the other hand, testified that she did not request the release of any credit information on Phillips. Mere passive receipt of the report would not be enough to satisfy the statutory element that she "use or obtain" a consumer report. However, Phillips argues that the phone machine message Grendahl left for Sarah is evidence that she asked Fitzgerald to obtain credit information: "Sarah, this is mom. I didn't directly do a credit report. I hired a PI and they have every right to do that." This evidence is ambiguous. On the one hand, it could mean that Grendahl hired a private investigator because she thought he was entitled to do a credit report. On the other hand, it could mean that she simply hired a private investigator who ordered a credit report on his own initiative, which she now understood he was entitled to do. Because this case was disposed of on summary judgment, we must resolve any ambiguities in the evidence in favor of Phillips. In this procedural posture, the ambiguous telephone message is sufficient to create a genuine issue of fact as to whether Mary Grendahl asked Fitzgerald to obtain a consumer report on Phillips.

The next inquiry is whether any of the defendants had a permissible statutory purpose for obtaining the consumer report. The only purpose for obtaining the report was to obtain information on Mary Grendahl's prospective son-in-law. Investigating a person because he wants to marry one's daughter is not a statutory consumer purpose under section 1681b(a). Even if getting married can be characterized as a consumer transaction under section 1681b(a)(3), it was not Mary Grendahl, but her daughter, whom Phillips was engaged to marry. He had no business transaction pending with Mary Grendahl. There was no permissible purpose for obtaining or using a consumer report.

The element of culpability varies according to whether the cause arises under section 1681n generally, section 1681n(a), or section 1681o. Section 1681n(a) provides civil liability for willful noncompliance with any requirement of the Fair Credit Reporting Act.

Continued

Fitzgerald testified, "To the best of my knowledge, a finder's report is not considered a credit history." He also testified: "I did not do anything that I know to be illegal, unethical, or outside the standard practice of private investigators." Mary Grendahl testified that she only asked Fitzgerald to look into Phillips's background and that she gave him no instructions on how to do the investigation. She stated: "At no time did I ask Mr. Fitzgerald to try to obtain credit information or a credit report, and it is my understanding that he did not do so."

On the other hand, there is also evidence that each defendant had some experience in dealing with credit reports and either knew of the Fair Credit Reporting Act or at least knew that such reports can only be obtained legally under certain circumstances. This kind of experience can support an inference that the defendants knew that their actions were impermissible. There is also the telephone message that could be interpreted to mean that Mary Grendahl directed Fitzgerald to obtain a credit report. Additionally, someone wrote on the Phillips Finder's Report: "Credit Inquiry Report & Employment Trace." These facts are sufficient to create a genuine issue of material fact as to whether defendants acted knowingly and with conscious disregard for Phillips's legal rights.

Section 1681o provides a private cause of action for negligent failure to comply with the Fair Credit Reporting Act. Since Phillips has raised factual issues sufficient to require trial on whether defendants willfully violated his rights under the Act, it follows that he has also made a submissible case as to negligent violation of those same rights.

We reverse the entry of summary judgment on Phillips's Fair Credit Reporting Act. We remand for further proceedings in accordance with this opinion.

QUESTIONS

1. What evidence does the court point to to show that the defendants knew they might be violating the FCRA?
2. What evidence does the court use to show that when the report was prepared there was an awareness that it was going to be used for purpose that made its use covered by the statutory requirements?
3. What kind of personal information was in the report?

When a person claims that report information is erroneous, the credit bureau must take steps within a reasonable time to determine the accuracy of the disputed item.

Adverse information obtained by investigation cannot be given to a client after three months unless it is verified to determine that it is still valid. Most legal proceedings cannot be reported by a bureau after seven years, although a bankruptcy proceeding can be reported for ten years.

(c) Credit Repair Organizations. These organizations, some nonprofit and others for-profit, advertise their ability to help consumers work their way out of debt and eliminate negative credit information. Congress began regulating these groups with the Credit Repair Organization Act of 1996. Both the bankruptcy reforms (see Chapter 35) and state laws have established standards and procedures to ensure that consumers are not absorbing higher costs for services that they could do for themselves.

19. Other Consumer Protections

Various laws aimed at protecting purchasers of real estate, buyers of services, and prospective franchisees have been adopted in the states and at the federal level.

(a) Real Estate Development Sales: Interstate Land Sales Full Disclosure Act. Anyone promoting the sale of a real estate development that is divided into 50 or more parcels of less than 5 acres each must file a **development statement** with the secretary of Housing and Urban Development (HUD). This statement must set forth significant details of the development as required by the federal Interstate Land Sales Full Disclosure Act (ILSFDA).[43]

Anyone buying or renting one of the parcels in the subdivision must be given a **property report**, which is a condensed version of the development statement filed with the secretary of HUD. This report must be given to the prospective customer at least 48 hours before the signing of the contract to buy or lease.

[43] 15 U.S.C. §1701 *et seq.*

State statutes complement the ILSFDA and frequently require that particular enterprises selling property disclose certain information to prospective buyers. Some state statutes provide protection for sales of real property interests such as time-sharing condominiums that are not covered under the ILSFDA.[44]

(B) SERVICE CONTRACTS. The UCCC treats a consumer service contract the same as a consumer sale of goods if (1) payment is made in installments or a credit charge is made and (2) the amount financed does not exceed $25,000. The UCCC defines *services* broadly as embracing transportation, hotel and restaurant accommodations, education, entertainment, recreation, physical culture (such as athletic clubs or bodybuilding schools), hospital accommodations, funerals, and cemetery accommodations.

In some states, it is unlawful for a repair shop to make unauthorized repairs to an automobile and then refuse to return the automobile to the customer until the customer has paid for the repairs. In some states, a consumer protection statute imposes multiple damages on a repair shop that delays unreasonably in performing a contract to repair property of the consumer.[45]

(C) FRANCHISES. To protect prospective **franchisees** from deception by **franchisors** that seek to sell interests, an FTC regulation requires that the franchisor give a prospective franchisee a disclosure statement 10 days before the franchisee signs a contract or pays any money for a **franchise**. The disclosure statement provides detailed information relating to the franchisor's finances, experience, size of operation, and involvement in litigation. The FTC enforces these disclosure requirements and can impose fines.

(D) AUTOMOBILE LEMON LAWS. All states have adopted special laws for the protection of consumers buying automobiles that develop numerous defects or defects that cannot be corrected. These statutes protect only persons buying automobiles for personal, family, or household use. They generally classify an automobile as a *lemon* if it cannot be put in proper or warranted condition within a specified period of time or after a specified number of repair attempts. In general, they give the buyer greater protection than is given to other buyers by the UCC or other consumer protection statutes (see Chapter 24). In some states, the seller of a car that turns out to be a lemon is required to give the buyer a brand-new replacement car. In some states, certain agencies may also bring an action to collect civil penalties from the seller of a lemon car.

Lemon laws in most states are designed to increase the prelitigation bargaining power of consumers and reduce the greater power of manufacturers to resist complaints or suits by consumers.[46] **For Example,** Abdul, who owned a paint store, purchased two automobiles from Prime Motors, one for delivering paint to his customers and the second for his wife to use for shopping and taking their children to school. Both cars were defective and in need of constant repair. Abdul claimed that he was entitled to remedies provided by the local automobile lemon law. He was wrong with respect to the store's delivery car because lemon laws do not cover cars purchased for commercial use, but the other car was protected by the lemon law because it was clearly a family car.

[44] *Sun Kyung Ahn v. Merrifield Town Center Ltd. Partnership*, 584 F. Supp. 2d 848 (E.D. Va. 2008) (condominium units sold for 14-day time sharing rights not covered under ILSFDA).
[45] *Vader v. Fleetwood Enterprises, Inc.*, 201 P. 3d 139 (Mont. 2009).
[46] *Tague v. Autobarn Motors, Ltd.*, 2009 WL 723403 (Ill. App.).

MAKE THE CONNECTION

SUMMARY

Modern methods of marketing, packaging, and financing have reduced the ordinary consumer to a subordinate position. To protect the consumer from the hardship, fraud, and oppression that could result from being in such an inferior position, consumer protection laws, at both the state and federal levels, afford rights to consumers and impose requirements on those who deal with consumers.

When a consumer protection statute is violated, an action may sometimes be brought by the consumer against the wrongdoer. More commonly, an action is brought by an administrative agency or by the state attorney general.

Consumer protection laws are directed at false and misleading advertising; misleading or false use of labels; the methods of selling, with specific requirements on the disclosure of terms and the permitting of consumer cancellation of home-solicited sales; and types of credit arrangements. The consumer is protected in a contract agreement by regulation of its form, prohibition of unconscionable terms, and limitation of the credit that can be extended to a consumer. Credit card protections include prohibition of the unauthorized distribution of credit cards and limited liability of the cardholder for the unauthorized use of a credit card. Included in consumer protection laws are the application of payments; the preservation of consumer defenses as against a transferee of the consumer's contract; product safety; the protection of credit standing and reputation; and (to some extent) real estate development sales, franchises, and service contracts. Lemon laws provide special protection to buyers of automobiles for personal, household, or family use.

LEARNING OUTCOMES

After studying this chapter, you should be able to clearly explain:

A. General Principles

LO.1 Explain what consumer protection laws do

See the list of headings in this chapter to determine areas of consumer protection.

See the discussion of Jessica Simpson and William Shatner in the Sports & Entertainment Law box on p. 652.

See the Travelocity "Taxes and Fees" discussion on p. 655.

B. Areas of Consumer Protection

LO.2 List the rights and protections consumer debtors have when a collector contacts them

See Ethics & the Law on p. 659.

See Federal Debt Collections Practices Act on p. 658.

LO.3 Give a summary of the rights of consumers with regard to credit reports

See the *Phillips v. Grendahl* case on pp. 660–662.

LO.4 Describe the types of protections available for consumers who have credit cards

See the discussion of the CARD Act on pp. 655–657.

See E-Commerce & Cyberlaw on p. 655.

See the *Gonzalez v. Wilshire Credit Corp.* case on pp. 645–647.

KEY TERMS

Bureau of Consumer Financial Protection
compensatory damages
consumer
consumer credit
development statement
Dodd-Frank Wall Street Reform and Consumer Protection Act
franchise
franchisees
franchisors
hearsay evidence
predatory lending
property report
punitive damages
subprime lending market

QUESTIONS AND CASE PROBLEMS

1. The San Antonio Retail Merchants Association (SARMA) was a credit reporting agency. It was asked by one of its members to furnish information on William Douglas Thompson III. It supplied information from a file that contained data on William III and on William Daniel Thompson Jr. The agency had incorporated information related to William Jr. into the file

relating to William III so that all information appeared to relate to William III. This was a negligent mistake because each William had a different Social Security number, which should have raised a suspicion that there was a mistake. In addition, SARMA should have used a number of checkpoints to ensure that incoming information would be put into the proper file. William Jr. had bad credit standing. Because of its mistake, SARMA gave a bad report on William III, who was denied credit by several enterprises. The federal Fair Credit Reporting Act makes a credit reporting agency liable to any consumer about whom it furnishes a consumer report without following reasonable procedures to ensure maximum possible accuracy of information. William III sued SARMA for its negligence in confusing him with William Jr. Is SARMA liable? [*Thompson v. San Antonio Retail Merchants Ass'n*, 682 F.2d 509 (5th Cir.)]

2. Colgate-Palmolive Co. ran a television commercial to show that its shaving cream, Rapid Shave, could soften even the toughness of sandpaper. The commercial showed what was described as the sandpaper test. Actually, what was used was a sheet of Plexiglas on which sand had been sprinkled. The FTC claimed that this was a deceptive practice. The advertiser contended that actual sandpaper would merely look like ordinary colored paper and that Plexiglas had been used to give the viewer an accurate visual representation of the test. Could the FTC prohibit the use of this commercial? [*Federal Trade Commission v. Colgate-Palmolive Co.*, 380 U.S. 374]

3. Sharolyn Charles wrote a check for $17.93 to a Poncho's Restaurant on July 4, 1996, as payment for a meal she had there. The check was returned for insufficient funds. Poncho's forwarded the check to Check Rite for collection.

   On July 19, Check Rite sent a letter to Charles, stating that "[t]his is an attempt to collect a debt" and requesting total payment of $42.93—the amount of the check plus a service charge of $25. On August 7, Check Rite sent a second letter, requesting payment of $42.93 and advising Charles that failure to pay the total amount due might result in additional liability for damages and attorneys' fees, estimated at $242.93.

   Check Rite subsequently referred the matter to the law firm of Lundgren & Associates for collection. On September 8, Lundgren sent a letter to Charles offering to settle within 10 days for a total amount of $127.93—the amount of the check plus a settlement amount of $110. Lundgren further advised that it had made no decision to file suit, that it could later decide to do so, and that Charles's potential liability was $317.93. Charles immediately sent to Lundgren a money order in the amount of $17.93. On September 13, Lundgren sent a second letter, repeating the settlement offer made in the September 8 letter. Lundgren then returned Charles's payment on September 14, declining to accept it as payment in full and repeating the settlement offer. On September 19, Lundgren sent a fourth letter to Charles, repeating the settlement offer.

   On October 15, 1996, Charles filed suit in federal district court alleging violations of the Fair Debt Collections Practices Act (FDCPA). Lundgren & Associates moved to dismiss the case on grounds that an attempt to collect on a check is not a "debt" governed by FDCPA. The district court dismissed the case; Charles appealed. Should Charles win? Is she protected under the FDCPA? [*Charles v. Lundgren & Associates, P.C.*, 119 F.3d 739 (9th Cir.)]

4. Thomas was sent a credit card through the mail by a company that had taken his name and address from the telephone book. Because he never requested the card, Thomas left the card lying on his desk. A thief stole the card and used it to purchase merchandise in several stores in Thomas's name. The issuer of the credit card claimed that Thomas was liable for the total amount of the purchases made by the thief. Thomas claimed he was not liable for any amount. The court decided Thomas was liable for $50. Who is correct? Why?

5. On May 16, 2003, Sari Smith filed a class action lawsuit in Cook County, Illinois, against J.M. Smucker Co. on behalf of "[a]ll purchasers in the United States of America of spreadable fruit products labeled 'Simply 100% Fruit'

manufactured, produced, and sold by J.M. Smucker Co. excluding its directors, officers and employees" for consumer fraud, deceptive business practices, unjust enrichment, and breach of warranty, alleging that Smucker's Simply 100% Fruit products do not contain 100 percent fruit. The premium jam's label indicates that, for example, its Strawberry jam also contains "fruit syrup, lemon juice concentrate, fruit pectin, red grape juice concentrate and natural flavors." Is the label a form of deceptive advertising?

If you were a Smuckers executive, what would you argue in the case on deceptive ads? [*J.M. Smucker Co. v. Rudge*, 877 So.2d 820 (Fla. App.)]

6. International Yogurt Co. (IYC) developed a unique mix for making frozen yogurt and related products. Morris and his wife purchased a franchise from the company but were not told that a franchise was not a requirement for obtaining the mix—that the company would sell its yogurt mix to anyone. The Morrises' franchise business was a failure, and they sold it at a loss after three years. They then sued the company for fraud and for violation of the state Franchise Investment Protection Act and the state Consumer Protection Act for failing to inform them that the mix could be obtained without a franchise. IYC claimed that no liability could be imposed for failing to make the disclosure. Was it correct? [*Morris v. International Yogurt Co.*, 729 P.2d 33 (Wash.)]

7. General Steel retained Ty Cobb and his law firm, Hogan & Hartson, to defend it in an action brought against it by the Colorado Attorney General. General Steel based its decision to retain Ty Cobb based on a profile that appeared in the *Denver Post*, a profile that depicted Cobb as someone who could make the least sympathetic defendants look great. The retention agreement said that Ty Cobb would have "primary responsibility" for handling General Steel's case. Two months after General Steel retained Ty Cobb and his firm, Cobb moved to the Washington, D.C., office of the firm. General Steel brought suit for "bait and switch" under the Colorado Consumer Protection Act. Will General Steel have rights to recover under that state's consumer protection law? Discuss the issues involved. [*General Steel Domestic Sales, LLC v. Hogan & Hartson*, 230 P.3d 1275 (Colo. App.)]

8. The town of Newport obtained a corporate MasterCard that was given to the town clerk for purchasing fuel for the town hall. The town clerk used the card for personal restaurant, hotel, and gift shop debts. The town refused to pay the card charges on the grounds that they were unauthorized. Was the town correct? [*MasterCard v. Town of Newport*, 396 N.W.2d 345 (Wis. App.)]

9. Stevens purchased a pair of softball shoes manufactured by Hyde Athletic Industries. Because of a defect in the shoes, she fell and broke an ankle. She sued Hyde under the state consumer protection act, which provided that "any person who is injured in...business or property...could sue for damages sustained." Hyde claimed that the act did not cover personal injuries. Stevens claimed that she was injured in her "property" because of the money that she had to spend for medical treatment and subsequent care. Decide. [*Stevens v. Hyde Athletic Industries, Inc.*, 773 P.2d 87 (Wash. App.)]

10. A consumer made a purchase on a credit card. The card issuer refused to accept the charge, and an attorney then sued the consumer for the amount due. In the complaint filed in the lawsuit, the attorney wrongly stated that interest was owed at 18 percent per annum. This statement was later corrected by an amendment of the complaint to 5 percent. The case against the consumer was ultimately settled, but the consumer then sued the attorney for penalties under the Fair Debt Collection Practices Act, claiming that the overstatement of the interest due in the original complaint was a violation of that act. The attorney defended on the ground that the act did not apply. Did it? [*Green v. Hocking*, 9 F.3d 18 (6th Cir.)]

11. Classify each of the following activities as proper or prohibited under the various consumer statutes you have studied.
    a. Calling a hospital room to talk to a debtor who is a patient there.

b. Calling a hospital room to sell surgical stockings.

c. Rolling back the odometer on one's car before selling it privately.

d. No TILA disclosures on an instant tax refund program in which the lender takes 40 percent of the tax refund as a fee for advancing the money when the taxpayer files the tax return.

12. Alpha University has an arrangement with a Axis Credit Card Company to collect 1 percent on all credit card charges made by students who obtain their cards through booths on the Alpha campus. Do any consumer protection statutes apply to this relationship?

13. List three areas in consumer credit cards affected by the CARD Act.

CHAPTER 34

© Manuel Gutjahr/iStockphoto.com

Secured Transactions in Personal Property

learningoutcomes

After studying this chapter, you should be able to

LO.1 Explain the requirements for creating a valid security interest

LO.2 List the major types of collateral

LO.3 Define perfection and explain its significance in secured transactions

LO.4 Discuss the priorities of parties with conflicting interests in collateral when default occurs

LO.5 State the rights of the parties on the debtor's default

Creditors can have some additional assurance of payment if the debtor pledges property as security for the loan. If the debtor does not pay, the creditor can then turn to the property and sell it or keep it as a means of satisfying the obligation.

CPA A. Creation of Secured Transactions

A *secured transaction* is one means by which personal property is used to provide a backup plan or security for the creditor in the event the borrower does not pay. Secured transactions are governed by Article 9 of the Uniform Commercial Code (UCC). Article 9 was formally revised in 2001, and the revisions to it have been adopted in some form by all states and the District of Columbia.[1]

1. Definitions

A **secured transaction** in personal property is created by giving the creditor a security interest in that property. A **security interest** is like a lien in personal property; it is a property right that enables the creditor to take possession of the property if the debtor does not pay the amount owed. **For Example,** if you borrow money from a bank to buy a car, the bank takes a security interest in the car. If you do not repay the loan, the bank can repossess the car and sell it to recover the money the bank has loaned you. If you purchase a side-by-side refrigerator from Kelvin's Appliances on credit, Kelvin's takes a security interest in the refrigerator. If you do not repay Kelvin's, Kelvin's can repossess the refrigerator and sell it to cover the amount you still owe.

The property that is subject to the security interest is called **collateral**. In the preceding examples, the car was the bank's collateral for the loan, and the refrigerator was Kelvin's collateral.

(A) Parties. The person to whom the money is owed, whether a seller or a lender, is called the **creditor** or **secured party**. The buyer on credit or the borrower is called the **debtor**.

(B) Nature of Creditor's Interest. The creditor does not own the collateral, but the security interest is a property right. That property right can ripen into possession and the right to transfer title by sale.

A creditor who has possession of the collateral as a means of security has a duty of care imposed under the UCC. Under the UCC, the creditor in possession must exercise reasonable care to preserve the property. The creditor is liable for any damage that results from falling short of that standard.

(C) Nature of Debtor's Interest. A debtor who is a borrower ordinarily owns the collateral.[2] As such, the debtor has all rights of any property owner to recover damages for the loss or improper seizure of, or damage to, the collateral.[3]

CPA 2. Creation of a Security Interest

The attachment, or the creation of a valid security interest, occurs when the following three conditions are satisfied: There is (1) a security agreement, (2) value has been given, and (3) the debtor has rights in the collateral. These three conditions can occur in any order. A security interest will attach when the last of these conditions has been met.[4] When the security interest attaches, it is then enforceable against the debtor and the collateral.

CPA **(A) Agreement.** The **security agreement** is the contract between creditor and debtor for the security interest. This required agreement must identify the parties, contain a reasonable description of the collateral,[5] indicate the parties' intent that the creditor have a security interest in it, describe the debt or the performance that is secured thereby, and be authenticated by the debtor.

Revised Article 9 eliminated the signature requirement to permit electronic authentication by debtors.

[1] All 50 states, including Louisiana, have some version of Article 9 as law. The latest version of Article 9 (Revised Article 9) was adopted in 1999 and took effect on July 1, 2001. This newest version, adopted as modified in 2000, is referred to as either "New Article 9" or "Revised Article 9." Not all states, however, have adopted verbatim versions. For example, the application of Article 9 to governmental units varies significantly among the states. See "UCC Article 9: Personal Property Secured Transactions," 60 *Bus. Lawyer* 1725 (2005).

[2] *Helms v. Certified Packaging Corp.*, 551 F.3d 675 (7th Cir. 2008), but see *In re Omega Door Co., Inc.*, 399 B.R. 295 (Ohio 2009).

[3] Article 9 does cover consignment arrangements. The consignor continues to own the goods, and the consignee is treated as a secured creditor with a purchase money security interest in the consigned goods.

[4] UCC §9-203 (Revised Article 9, §9-203); *Joseph Stephens & Co., Inc. v. Cikanek*, 588 F. Supp. 2d 870 (N.D. Ill. 2008). Because Revised Article 9 now includes bank accounts as a form of security, the security interest attaches when the creditor has "control" of the account (Revised Article 9, §9-104) and there is a security agreement. "Control" is defined later in the chapter under "Perfection by Control." (p. 723) See also *In re Franchise Pictures LLC*, 389 B.R. 131 (C.D. Cal. 2008).

[5] UCC §§9-201 (Revised Article 9, §9-203), 9-110 (Revised Article 9, §9-108); *In re The Holladay House, Inc.*, 387 B.R. 689 (E.D. Va. 2008). In *In re Cottage Grove Hospital*, 38 UCC 2d 683 (D. Or. 1999), the court held that "All Debtor's Income" was an insufficient description.

The standard is now not a signature but an authenticated document; authentication can come from the debtor's actions that indicate an understanding of a credit and secured debt agreement.[6] Also under Revised Article 9, a description is valid if it "reasonably identifies what is described."[7] Examples of reasonable identification include a specific listing, category,[8] quantity, and computational or allocational formula. "Supergeneric descriptions"[9] such as "all the debtor's personal property" are insufficient,[10] but "livestock" is a sufficient description.[11] The requirement for description of consumer goods as collateral is more stringent than for other types of collateral.[12]

If the creditor has possession of the collateral, the security agreement may be oral regardless of the amount involved.[13] **For Example,** if you pledge your stereo system to a friend as security for the loan and the friend will keep it at his home until you have repaid him, your friend has possession of the collateral, and your oral security agreement is valid and enforceable by your friend. If the creditor does not have possession of the collateral, as in the case of credit sales and most secured loans, the security agreement must be evidenced by a record that meets all requirements.

Field warehousing, covered in Chapter 22, is another form of possession of goods that permits an oral security agreement. Credit unions and banks can possess an account pledged as security if the funds cannot be used by the account holder without permission and clearance from a bank officer.

(B) VALUE. The creditor gives **value** either by lending money to the debtor or by delivering goods on credit. The value may be part of a contemporaneous exchange or given previously as a loan. **For Example,** a debtor who already owes a creditor $5,000 could later pledge a water scooter as collateral for that loan and give the debtor a security interest in the scooter. In fact, creditors who become nervous about repayment often request collateral later during the course of performance of a previously unsecured loan.

(C) RIGHTS IN THE COLLATERAL. The debtor must have rights in the collateral for a security interest to attach. For example, when goods are sent "FOB place of shipment" to a debtor, the debtor has title at the time those goods are delivered to the carrier by the seller See Chapter 24 for more information. The buyer has rights in the collateral that allow for the collateral to be subject to the creditor's security interest.[14]

CPA 3. Purchase Money Security Interest

When a seller sells on credit and is given a security interest in the goods sold, that interest is called a **purchase money security interest (PMSI)**. If the buyer borrows money from a third person so that the purchase can be made for cash, a security interest given in those goods to that lender is also called a purchase money security interest.[15] Certain special priority rights (covered on pp. 673 and 681) are given in some circumstances to creditors who hold a PMSI.

CPA 4. The Nature and Classification of Collateral

The nature of the collateral in a credit transaction, as well as its classification under Article 9, affect the procedural obligations and rights of creditors. Revised Article 9 contains an extensive list of the types of collateral, including the traditional types such as consumer goods, equipment, inventory, general intangibles, farm products, and fixtures,[16] but also accounts, accounts receivable, accounts receivable held because of credit card transactions or license fees, energy contracts, insurance policy proceeds, amounts due for services rendered, amounts earned from chartering a vessel, winnings in the state lottery, and health care insurance receivables. The general category of "account" does not include commercial

[6] Revised Article 9, §9-102(a)(69) defines "record," the new substitute for "signed agreement" of old Article 9, as "information that is inscribed on a tangible medium and is retrievable in perceivable form." Authentication need not be a signature. One court held that a debtor using the proceeds from the loan that was the basis for the security interest constituted authentication, *Barlow Lane Holdings Ltd. v. Applied Carbon Technology (America), Inc.*, 2004 WL 1792456 (W.D.N.Y. 2004); See also 2004 WL 2110733 (W.D.N.Y. 2004).

[7] UCC §9-110.

[8] Commercial tort claims and consumer transactions cannot be sufficiently described by type of collateral. The security agreement must give more specifics. §9-108(e)(1) and (2).

[9] UCC §9-108(c).

[10] The comments to §9-108 indicate that serial numbers are not necessarily required, but an outsider must be able to tell from the description what property is or is not included under the security agreement. Official Comment, §9-108, 2.

[11] *Baldwin v. Castro County Feeders I, Ltd.*, 678 N.W.2d 796 (S.D. 2004).

[12] Under §9-108, in consumer transactions and goods, description by "type of collateral" is insufficient.

[13] UCC §9-207; *In re Rowe*, 369 B.R. 73 (Mass. 2007). If there is no written security agreement ("record" under Revised Article 9), the security interest itself is destroyed when the collateral is surrendered.

[14] UCC §9-112 (Revised Article 9, §9-202).

[15] UCC §9-107 (Revised Article 9, §9-103); *In re Price*, 562 F.3d 618 (9th Cir. 2009).

[16] UCC §§9-106, 9-109. See Revised Article 9, §9-102.

tort claims, deposit accounts,[17] investment property, or letters of credit but does include insurance claims, lottery winnings, and property proceeds.[18]

(A) CONSUMER GOODS. Collateral that is classified as a **consumer good** results in different rights and obligations under Article 9, regardless of the type of property it is. Collateral is considered a consumer good if it is "used or bought for use primarily for personal, family, or household purposes."[19] The use of the good, and not its properties, controls its classification. **For Example,** a computer purchased by an architect for her office is not a consumer good. That same computer purchased by the same architect for use by her children at their home is a consumer good. A refrigerator purchased for the kitchen near an office conference center is not a consumer good. That same model refrigerator purchased for a home is a consumer good. The use of the goods controls the label that is applied to the collateral.

CPA **(B) AFTER-ACQUIRED COLLATERAL AND ONGOING CREDIT.** A creditor's rights can be expanded to include coverage of all future loans and funds advances as well as future acquisitions of collateral. If the security agreement so provides, the security interest attaches to **after-acquired goods** and applies to all loans to the debtor.[20] **For Example,** a security interest can cover the current inventory of the debtor and any future replenishments if a clause in the security agreement adds "after-acquired property" to the description of the inventory. Referred to in lay terms as a **floating lien**, the creditor's security interest covers the inventory regardless of its form or time of arrival in relation to attachment of the security interest.

After-acquired clauses in consumer credit contracts are restricted. An after-acquired property clause in a consumer security agreement can cover only goods acquired by the debtor within 10 days after the creditor gave value to the debtor.

(C) PROCEEDS. The UCC defines proceeds as "whatever is received upon the sale, exchange, collection, or other disposition of collateral."[21] Collateral may change its form and character during the course of the security agreement. **For Example,** a debtor who has pledged its inventory of cars as collateral will be selling those cars. However, the buyers will sign credit contracts for the purchase of those cars. Article 9 considers the credit contracts and the right to payment under those contracts as proceeds. If the collateral has been insured and is damaged or destroyed, the debtor will receive money, another form of proceeds, from the insurance company. Proceeds are automatically subject to the creditor's security interest unless the security agreement provides to the contrary. The proceeds may be in any form, such as cash, checks, promissory notes, or other property.

(D) ELECTRONIC CHATTEL PAPER. "Electronic chattel paper" is a record of a right to funds, payment, or property that is stored in an electronic medium. **For Example,** it is possible to pledge the funds you have available in your Internet shopping account as an Article 9 security interest.[22]

In re Lull, 386 B.R. 261, 65 UCC Rep. Serv. 2d 194 (D. Haw. 2008)

Numismatic Nuance: Coins Are Not Money under Article 9

On April 18, 2006, James W. Lull entered into a consignment agreement with Bowers and Merena for auction of his Standing Liberty quarter-dollar collection. On April 21, 2006, Bowers and Merena also agreed to loan to Lull $700,000, with the loan to be repaid from the auction proceeds.

The collection sold at auction for $1,119,750. After repayment of its loan to Lull and expenses of sale, Bowers held net proceeds of $455,046.11. However, Gardiner, Kapaa 382, and Yamaguchi went to Bowers and Merena and tried to claim the auction proceeds.

[17] Deposit accounts are not considered "general intangibles" under Article 9 because of new, specific provisions on accounts. UCC §§9-102(a)(29), 9-104, 9-109(d)(13), 9-312(b)(1), and §9-314. *In re Cohen*, 305 B.R. 886, 53 UCC Rep. Serv. 2d 148 (9th Cir. 2004).

[18] UCC §§9-102(2)(a)(5), 9-102(72), & 9-109(a)(2). A membership in a golf club can be pledged as security for a loan used to purchase the membership. *Bonem v. Golf Club of Georgia*, 591 S.E.2d 462, 52 U.C.C. Rep. Serv. 2d (West) 280 (Ga. Ct. App. 2003).

[19] UCC §9-109(1).

[20] UCC §9-109 (Revised Article 9, §9-204).

[21] UCC §9-306(1).

[22] UCC §9-105.

Continued

Gardiner's claim resulted from a March 1, 2005, loan to Lull for $3.8 million. Lull was unable to repay the loan when it became due, on February 28, 2006, so in July, 2006, Gardiner agreed not to take legal action to enforce the note after Lull executed a security agreement on July 19, 2006, which granted Gardiner a security interest in "all personal property and other assets" of Lull and specifically listed all commonly known categories of personal property, including goods, accounts, money, chattel paper, general intangibles, instruments, and the proceeds thereof.

Gardiner recorded a financing statement in the Bureau of Conveyances of the State of Hawaii on July 20, 2006. The financing statement described Gardiner's collateral as "All assets and all personal property of the Debtor (including, without limitations, fixtures), whether now owned or hereafter acquired or arising, and wherever located, and all proceeds and products thereof."

Kapaa 382 made short-term loans to Lull on September 20, 2005, for $933,000; on December 5, 2005, for $471,566.82; on December 15, 2005, for $165,000; and on December 19, 2005, for $400,000. On July 26, 2006, Lull executed a "Partial Settlement Agreement" in which he agreed, among other things, to "convey and transfer to [Kapaa 382] title to the Coin Collection currently consigned to Bowers and Merena Auctions, LLC for auction scheduled to occur in August 2006, by Bill of Sale[.]"

Kapaa 382 filed a financing statement with the California Secretary of State on August 22, 2006, but the financing statement listed Kapaa 382 as both the debtor and the secured party and did not mention Lull.

On July 11, 2006, Lull executed an assignment of the proceeds of the coin auction to Yamaguchi, for an unpaid promissory note, dated May 16, 2006, in the amount of $700,000. The assignment was not recorded.

On December 8, 2006, Lull filed a voluntary chapter 7 petition. Claims in the bankruptcy case exceeded $55 million, including unsecured claims of nearly $42 million. The parties involved with the coins all claimed priority.

JUDICIAL OPINION

KING, Bankruptcy Judge...Kapaa 382 argues in opposition to the motion that Gardiner does not have a properly perfected security interest because the auctioned coins are "money" and the filing of a financing statement is insufficient to perfect a security interest in money under the Uniform Commercial Code ("UCC").

Kapaa 382 argues that the filing of Gardiner's financing statement did not perfect a security interest in the coins because the coins are "money," and, under Haw.Rev.Stat. § 490:9-312(b)(3), "a security interest in money may be perfected only by the secured party's taking possession[.]" Kapaa 382 has not had actual possession of the coins. Kapaa 382's argument that the auctioned coins constitute "money" under Article 9 is not persuasive. Coins are not merely "money" where their market value far exceeds their face value.

UCC Article 9 does not define "money," but Article 2, concerning sales, recognizes that "money" can be transformed into "goods" under certain circumstances. The Official Comment to UCC section 2-105 states that "Goods is intended to cover the sale of money, when money is being treated as a commodity, but not to include it when money is the medium of payment." Although the drafters appeared to have had in mind sales of foreign currency in offering this clarification, the same reasoning applies to sales of numismatic coins where "money is being treated as a commodity[.]"

The definition of "goods" in Article 9 specifically excludes money. Haw.Rev.Stat. § 490:9-102. However, it makes little sense to take the narrow view that coins of numismatic value are always money and never goods under Article 9. For example, the old quarter-dollar coins sold at auction by Plaintiff are no longer money that could be used at face value for the purchase of goods.

There is little case law on this issue. However, the cases take the commonsense approach that coins worth more than face value are not merely "money." For example, in *Cordner v U.S.*, 671 F.2d 367 (9th Cir.1982), a corporation paid a dividend to shareholders in the form of collectible coins, $20 U.S. gold Double Eagles. The face value was $5,500. The market value was $70,936. The issue was whether, for tax purposes, the dividend was taxable at the face value or at the market value of the coins. The Court of Appeals held that the taxable dividend was the market value, not the face value, of the coins, observing that, "[w]hen legal tender, by reason of its value to collectors or the intrinsic worth of its contents, has a fair market value in excess of its face value or tender, then it should be deemed property other than money...."

In *In re Midas Coin Co.*, 264 F.Supp. 193 (E.D. Mo.1967), the court found that coins that had numismatic value were "goods" within the Missouri statute authorizing a secured party to perfect a security interest in goods by taking possession of the collateral without filing a financing statement. In that case, the coins were used in the debtor-coin dealer's business and were pledged as collateral for a bank loan. As the court noted, "The law favors a construction which harmonizes with reason and which tends to avoid absurd or unreasonable results."

Kapaa 382 contends that *McKee v State Farm Fire and Casualty Co.*, 145 Cal.App.3d 772, 193 Cal.Rptr. 745 (1983), compels a different result. In McKee, a homeowner sued his insurance company for breach of contract and bad faith after the insurer determined that a valuable silver coin collection stolen from the plaintiff's home was subject to a policy

Continued

exclusion limiting the insurer's liability for "money, bullion, numismatic property and bank notes" to $100. The California Court of Appeals held that a commonsense reading of the exclusion compelled a determination that the coins fell within the categories of "money" and "numismatic property." The court stated that, "Limiting the reasonable meaning of 'money' to only that which is actually circulating as part of the currency is not reasonable."

McKee is distinguishable because the policy exclusion at issue specifically referred to numismatic property. Moreover, McKee does not stand for the proposition that collectible coins must always be "money" and can never be "goods" in commercial transactions; it merely observed, in the context of an insurance policy exclusion that covered numismatic coins, that "money" includes noncirculating, collectible coins. Following the commonsense approach of *Cordner* and *Midas,* it will be held that the valuable coins consigned by Lull to Bowers and Merena for auction are "goods."

QUESTIONS

1. If the coins are not classified as "goods," what happens to the creditors' rights?
2. What is the standard for determining when coins are goods?

CPA B. Perfection of Secured Transactions

The attachment of a security interest gives the creditor the important rights of enforcement of the debt through repossession of the collateral (see Section 23 for more discussion of enforcement and repossession). *Attachment* allows the secured party to resort to the collateral to collect the debt when the debtor defaults. However, more than one creditor may hold an attached security interest in the same collateral. A creditor who obtains a **perfected security interest** enjoys priority over unperfected interests and may in some cases enjoy priority over other perfected interests. A security interest is valid against the debtor even though it is not perfected. However, perfection provides creditors with rights superior to those of other creditors with unperfected interests. Attachment provides creditors with rights; perfection gives them priority, and a creditor can obtain perfection in collateral in several ways.

CPA 5. Perfection by Creditor's Possession

If the creditor has possession of the collateral, the security interest in the possessed goods is perfected.[23] It remains perfected until that possession is surrendered. **For Example,** when a creditor has taken a security interest in 50 gold coins and has those gold coins in his vault, his possession of the coins is perfection.

A more complex example of possession as a means of perfection is found in the commercial tool of **field warehousing**. (See Chapter 22.) In this arrangement, a creditor actually has an agent on site at a buyer's place of business, and the creditor's agent controls the buyer's access to, use of, and transfer of the collateral. **For Example,** an aircraft manufacturer may have an agent on site at an aircraft dealership. That agent decides when the planes can be released to buyers and who will receive the buyers' payments or notes.[24]

CPA 6. Perfection for Consumer Goods

A purchase money security interest in consumer goods is perfected from the moment it attaches.[25] Known as **automatic perfection**, no other action is required for perfection as against other creditors. Because so many consumer purchases are made on credit, the UCC simplifies perfection so that creditors who are merchant sellers are not overly burdened with paperwork. However, as discussed later in this chapter in the section on priorities, the automatic perfection of a PMSI in consumer goods has some limitations. It may be destroyed by the debtor consumer's resale of the

[23] UCC §9-305; *In re Commercial Money Center, Inc.,* 392 B.R. 814 (Ca. 2009).

[24] Revised Article 9, §9-312.

[25] UCC §9-302 (Revised Article 9, §§9-301, & 9-304); *In re T & R Flagg Logging, Inc.,* 399 B.R. 334 (Me. 2009).

goods to a consumer who does not know of the security interest.

7. Perfection for Health Care Insurance Receivables

Revised Article 9 created a new form of collateral known as *health care insurance receivables.* This form of collateral has a unique method of perfection. When a consumer gives a creditor a security interest in health insurance proceeds that are forthcoming, the creditor need not make any filing or take any further steps to have a perfected security interest in those proceeds. The perfection is automatic.[26]

8. Automatic Perfection

A creditor attains automatic perfection in certain circumstances under Article 9. **For Example,** a creditor has an automatic PMSI in software that is sold with a computer that is subject to a creditor's PMSI. If you buy an IBM ThinkPad® from Best Buy on credit and get Microsoft Office software as part of your package deal, Best Buy has an automatically perfected security interest not only in the consumer goods (your new computer) but also in the software sold with it.[27] The perfection for consumer purchase money security interests that occurs when the security interest attaches is also a form of automatic perfection.

In re Bucala, 464 B.R. 626 (S.D. N.Y. 2012)

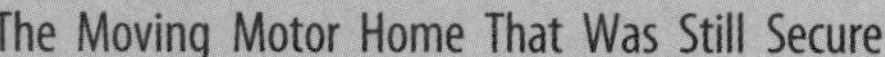

The Moving Motor Home That Was Still Secure

On August 3, 2005, the Bucalas (Defendants/Debtors) purchased a 2005 Skyline Doublewide Ranch manufactured/mobile home from Ultimore, Inc., for $151,258.25. The Bucalas paid $131,158.25 at closing, which was held at the office of their attorney. According to the contract, the Seller was to "hold a note for the $20,000.00 remainder for a period of 20 years (240 months) at 9% interest, which will be a monthly payment of $179.95, and amortized with a Promissory Note to compliment this Contract, as an addendum to the Contract." The Promissory Note provides that "a motor vehicle lien may be filled [sic] against the title of the home" by Ultimore and that Ultimore may repossess the home in the event of the Defendants' default.

On April 15, 2011 (after they had filed for bankruptcy), the Bucalas contracted to sell the mobile home to Mr. and Mrs. Gunning for $100,000. The sale took place in August 2011. On August 26, 2011, the Bucalas removed Ultimore as a secured creditor from bankruptcy schedule D and added Ultimore as an unsecured creditor to bankruptcy schedule F.

The sale was finalized before the bankruptcy discharge was granted and part of the sale terms include the payment of $7,000 to a real estate broker, Century 21, without permission of the bankruptcy court.

Ultimore filed on September 27, 2011, seeking a declaratory judgment that it maintains a security interest in the manufactured home and moved for summary judgment.

JUDICIAL OPINION

MORRIS, Bankruptcy Judge…Pursuant to New York's Uniform Commercial Code, a "[s]ecured party" is "a person in whose favor a security interest is created or provided for under a security agreement, whether or not any obligation to be secured is outstanding…."

Section 9–203 does not require that a security agreement be signed by both parties to be enforceable. The fact that the Defendants signed both the Promissory Note and the Contract is enough to satisfy the authentication requirement.

Pursuant to section 9–108(a), "a description of personal or real property is sufficient, whether or not it is specific, if it reasonably identifies what is described."

The Promissory Note describes the collateral as "a 28′ × 60′ 2006 [sic] Skyline Manufactured Home, model 4911–0179–U–A & B." The Defendants argue that this description is incorrect and that the collateral is "a 2005 Skyline Manufactured Home, Title and Identification No. 49110179UAB."

The Contract identifies the manufactured home as a "2005 Skyline 60′ x 28′ NEW Doublewide ranch Three bedrooms, 2 baths, Birchfield # 8696CT Serial # 4911–0179–UBA [sic] Color: Gold vinyl sided, fuly [sic] skirted, white vinyl." The Contract refers to the existence of the Promissory Note in paragraph 4b. A court may look to multiple documents to determine whether a valid and enforceable security agreement exists.

[26] Revised Article 9, §9-309.

[27] Revised Article 9, §§9-102 & 9-103; *Okefenokee Aircraft, Inc. v. Primesouth Bank* 676 S.E.2d 394 (Ga. App. 2009).

Continued

Despite the fact that both the Contract and the Promissory Note are not identical, when the documents are read together, it is obvious that two documents describe the same collateral. The fact that the Contract describes the collateral with the accurate year and refers to the Promissory Note, which contains a description of the collateral with a different year, is enough to satisfy the requirement that a security agreement contain a description of collateral. To deny secured status to Ultimore based upon a typographical error in the description of the collateral "would represent a warrantless reliance on formalism and violate the general rule that the UCC be 'liberally construed and applied to promote its underlying purposes and policies.'" The description is sufficient.

For there to be a valid and enforceable security agreement, a formal and separately signed document labeled "security agreement" is not necessary. Almost any combination of documents can be used to prove the existence of a security agreement so long as the documents embody the intention of the parties to create a security interest.

In this case, the Defendants signed a "Promissory Note," which includes an indented paragraph numbered 1 and entitled in bold as "Lien" under a section labeled "Additional Promises and Agreements of the [B]orrower."

The Defendants argue that this language does not demonstrate an intent to grant a "present security interest" in the collateral because of the use of the word may. The Promissory Note is replete with references to Ultimore's status as a secured creditor and when read in full, rather than paragraph by paragraph, the Promissory Note clearly demonstrates the Defendants' intent to grant Ultimore a security interest in the manufactured home.

The lien is specifically mentioned in two additional paragraphs in the Promissory Note.

The Promissory Note also requires that the Borrowers maintain home insurance and assign and deliver the policies to Ultimore, and prohibits the Defendants from significantly devaluing the property in anyway. Most significantly, paragraph 8 states that "[i]f Borrower defaults under this Note the Home may be repossessed as provided by law."

Only a secured party may take possession of collateral. The Promissory Note clearly grants Ultimore permission to repossess the Defendants' manufactured home in the event of default. The Promissory Note and Contract create a security agreement that provides the manufactured home as collateral for Ultimore's loan.

The Defendants argue that Ultimore's failure to file a motor vehicle lien or any other perfection document, such as a U.C.C. financing statement, demonstrates that Ultimore never had an interest to protect. The recording of a lien has no effect on the granting of a security interest. Section 9–201(a) of New York's U.C.C. provides that "[e]xcept as otherwise provided in this chapter, a security agreement is effective according to its terms between the parties, against purchasers of the collateral, and against creditors."

The purpose of filing a financing statement is "to put third parties on notice that the secured party who has filed it may have a perfected security interest in the collateral described." A motor vehicle lien serves a similar purpose. A secured party's failure to record a lien does not invalidate the security agreement.

Pursuant to section 9–103(b)(1), "[a] security interest in goods is a purchase-money security interest…to the extent that the goods are purchase-money collateral with respect to that security interest."

Having already determined that Contract and Promissory Note granted Ultimore a security interest in the manufactured home, the Court now finds that Ultimore holds a purchase-money security interest in that home. Failure to perfect that interest does not result in a loss of its secured status.

The Defendants allege that they presented documents of sale to the trustee during the 341 meeting and the chapter 7 trustee allegedly advised them that he did not believe that Ultimore was secured. The Defendants "discussed this advice with [their] attorneys, and in reliance thereon, [they] amended the petition to list Ultimore as an unsecured creditor." It was only after these conversations that the Debtors amended their schedules and changed Ultimore's status from secured to unsecured.

Anything that the trustee told the Defendants is hearsay and cannot be used as evidence in the summary judgment proceeding. Be that as it may, it is for the Court, not the trustee, to determine whether a creditor is secured.

Summary judgment is granted in favor of Ultimore. Ultimore is a secured creditor for purposes of this chapter 7.

QUESTIONS

1. What does the court conclude about inconsistent descriptions in different documents?
2. What is the effect of Ultimore not filing a financing statement or a motor vehicle lien?
3. Who has the authority to change the status of a creditor from secured to unsecured?

CPA 9. Temporary Perfection

Some creditors are given **temporary perfection** for the collateral.[28] **For Example,** a creditor is generally given four months to refile its financing statement in a state to which a debtor has relocated. During that four-month period, the interest of the creditor is temporarily perfected in the new state despite no filing of a financing statement in that state's public records. Most creditors' agreements provide that the failure of the debtor to notify the creditor of a move constitutes a default under the credit agreement. Creditors need to know of the move so that they can refile in the debtor's new state.[29] Creditors enjoy a 20-day temporary perfection in negotiable instruments taken as collateral. Following the expiration of the 20-day period, measured from the time their security interest attaches, creditors must perfect in another way, such as by filing a financing statement or by possession.

CPA 10. Perfection by Control

Control is a form of possession under Article 9;[30] it occurs when a bank or creditor is able to require the debtor account holder to clear all transactions in that account with the bank or creditor. The debtor cannot use the funds that have been pledged as collateral without permission from the party holding the control. **For Example,** a credit union member could secure a loan with the credit union by giving the credit union a security interest in her savings account. The credit union then has control of the account and is perfected by the ability to dictate what the credit union member can do with those funds.

11. Perfection for Motor Vehicles

In most states, a non-Code statute provides that a security interest in a noninventory motor vehicle must be noted on the vehicle title registration. When so noted, the interest is perfected.[31] States that do not have a separate motor vehicle perfection system require financing statements, as described in the next section.

CPA 12. Perfection by Filing a Financing Statement

The **financing statement** (known as a *UCC-1*) is an authenticated record statement that gives sufficient information to alert third persons that a particular creditor may have a security interest in the collateral described (see Figure 34-1). Under previous Article 9, the financing statement had to be in writing and signed by the debtor. Under Revised Article 9, the creditor must simply be able to show that the documents filed were "authorized" and an "authenticated record."[32] In other words, the debtor's signature is not required for the financing statement to be valid. Revised Article 9 gives three ways for the debtor to authorize a financing statement:

1. By authenticating a security agreement.[33]
2. By becoming bound under a security agreement, the debtor agrees to allow financing statements to be filed on the collateral in the security agreement.
3. By acquiring collateral subject to a security agreement.

An unauthorized financing statement filed without meeting one of these requirements does not provide the creditor perfected creditor status.[34]

(A) The Content of the Financing Statement. A financing statement must provide "the name of the debtor…the name of the secured party or representative of the secured party…[and an indication of] the collateral covered by the financing statement."[35] The form provided by Revised Article 9 drafters (see Figure 34-1) includes much more information. Under §9-516, additional requirements are imposed for initial financing statements that include "a mailing address for the debtor [and]…whether the debtor is an individual or organization."[36] Furthermore, §9-511 requires that the secured party of record provide an

[28] UCC §9-304 (Revised Article 9, §9-312).
[29] UCC §9-316(a).
[30] UCC §9-104.
[31] Revised Article 9 does not change this principle.
[32] The sample financing form included with Revised Article 9, §9-521 does not even have a place for the debtor's signature. While a signed security agreement and signed financing statement are valid for both the security agreement and financing statement, the revisions also make it clear that such formalities are no longer necessary.
[33] Revised Article 9, §9-509 permits the debtor and creditor to agree otherwise. For example, a debtor can place a requirement in the security agreement that the creditor obtain his or her signature before filing a financing statement.
[34] Revised Article 9, §9-510.
[35] UCC §9-502(a).
[36] UCC §9-516(b)(5).

FIGURE 34-1 ***Sample Financing Statement***

UCC FINANCING STATEMENT

FOLLOW INSTRUCTIONS (front and back) CAREFULLY

A. NAME & PHONE OF CONTACT AT FILER [optional]

B. SEND ACKNOWLEDGEMENT TO: (Name and Address)

THE ABOVE SPACE IS FOR FILING OFFICE USE ONLY

1. DEBTOR'S EXACT FULL LEGAL NAME—Insert only one debtor name (1a or 1b)—do not abbreviate or combine

1a. ORGANIZATION'S NAME			
OR 1b. INDIVIDUAL'S LAST NAME	FIRST NAME	MIDDLE NAME	SUFFIX
1c. MAILING ADDRESS	CITY	STATE / POSTAL CODE	COUNTRY

1d. TAX ID# SSN OR EIN	ADD'L INFO RE ORGANIZATION DEBTOR	1e. TYPE OF ORGANIZATION	1f. JURISDICTION OF ORGANIZATION	1g. ORGANIZATION ID #, if any ☐ NONE

2. ADDITIONAL DEBTOR'S EXACT FULL LEGAL NAME—Insert only one debtor name (2a or 2b)—do not abbreviate or combine names

2a. ORGANIZATION'S NAME			
OR 2b. INDIVIDUAL'S LAST NAME	FIRST NAME	MIDDLE NAME	SUFFIX
2c. MAILING ADDRESS	CITY	STATE / POSTAL CODE	COUNTRY

2d. TAX ID# SSN OR EIN	ADD'L INFO RE ORGANIZATION DEBTOR	2e. TYPE OF ORGANIZATION	2f. JURISDICTION OF ORGANIZATION	2g. ORGANIZATION ID #, If any ☐ NONE

3. SECURED PARTY'S NAME (or NAME of TOTAL ASSIGNEE of ASSIGNOR S/P)—Insert only one secured party name (3a or 3b)

3a. ORGANIZATION'S NAME			
OR 3b. INDIVIDUAL'S LAST NAME	FIRST NAME	MIDDLE NAME	SUFFIX
3c. MAILING ADDRESS	CITY	STATE / POSTAL CODE	COUNTRY

4. This FINANCING STATEMENT covers the following collateral:

5. ALTERNATIVE DESIGNATION (if applicable) ☐ LESSEE/LESSOR ☐ CONSIGNEE/CONSIGNOR ☐ BAILEE/BAILOR ☐ SELLER/BUYER ☐ AG. LIEN ☐ NON-UCC FILING

6. ☐ This FINANCING STATEMENT is to be filed [for record] (or recorded) in the REAL ESTATE RECORDS. Attach Addendum [if applicable]

7. Check to REQUEST SEARCH REPORT(s) on DEBTOR(s) [ADDITIONAL FEE] [optional] ☐ All Debtors ☐ Debtor 1 ☐ Debtor 2

8. OPTIONAL FILER REFERENCE DATA

NATIONAL UCC FINANCING STATEMENT (FORM UCC 1) (REV. 07/29/98)

address so that there is an address for mailing notices required under other sections.

Because the filings for Article 9 perfection became electronic in 2006, the precise identification of the debtor has become critical. With electronic filings, those who will be doing searches on debtors will not find matches when the name of the debtor has not been properly entered on the financing statement. With computer technology, additional precision in debtors' names is necessary or searches are thwarted. The effect under the Revised Article 9 is to increase the consequences for misspelling a consumer's name, which will be a loss of priority by perfection because the electronic search in the state did not uncover prior interests. Courts continue their balancing of rights, notice, and technology in dealing with proper filing and priorities that result.[37]

The *ProGrowth Bank, Inc. v. Wells Fargo Bank, N.A.* case involves a discussion of the adequacy of the description.

ProGrowth Bank, Inc. v. Wells Fargo Bank, N.A., 558 F.3d 809 (8th Cir. 2008)

The Misplaced "9" Under Article 9

On September 8, 2005, Wells Fargo (Defendants) and the Christopher Hanson Insurance Agency entered into a promissory note and a security agreement for one million dollars. As security for the loan, Hanson assigned his interests in two separate annuity contracts, both issued by Fidelity & Guaranty Life Insurance Company ("Fidelity & Guaranty"). The two annuity contracts were valued at one million dollars, and they were identified as "L9E00015" and "L9E00016," respectively.

That same day, Wells Fargo filed a financing statement with the Secretary of State of Missouri. The financing statement identified the "Debtor" as "Christopher J. Hanson," and it describes the collateral as follows:

> *All of Debtor's right, title, and interest in and to, assets and rights of Debtor, wherever located and whether now owned or hereafter acquired or arising, and all proceeds and products in that certain Annuity Contract No.: LE900015 issued by Lincoln Benefit Life in the name of Debtor....*

The financing statement identified the contract number as "LE900015" instead of "L9E00015," and it identified the issuer as "Lincoln Benefit Life" instead of Fidelity & Guaranty. On September 16, 2005, Wells Fargo filed an additional financing statement that correctly identified the contract number, but once again mistakenly referred to the issuer of this contract as "Lincoln Benefit Life" instead of Fidelity & Guaranty.

On February 9, 2006, Hanson obtained a loan from ProGrowth Bank, Inc. As security for the loan, Hanson assigned his interests in the Fidelity & Guaranty annuity contracts to ProGrowth. On February 14, 2006, ProGrowth filed two financing statements with the Secretary of State of Missouri that identified Hanson and the Agency as the debtor, and accurately described the collateral as: "Fidelity and Guaranty Life Insurance Annuity Contracts Number L9E00015 and Number L9E00016[.]"

ProGrowth filed suit seeking a declaration that Wells Fargo and Global One were not perfected secured creditors and that it had priority to the annuity funds. The district court granted summary judgment in favor of ProGrowth Bank, Inc. Wells Fargo appealed.

JUDICIAL OPINION

BYE, Circuit Judge...[W]e view the validity of the financing statement in terms of whether "it provides notice that a person may have a security interest in the collateral claimed." The UCC allows for imperfect financing statements, and it recognizes that sometimes "[f]urther inquiry from the parties concerned will be necessary to disclose the complete state of affairs." Therefore, errors or omissions in the description of collateral do not render financing statements ineffective unless they are seriously misleading, which "is designed to discourage the fanatical and impossibly refined reading of statutory requirements in which courts have occasionally indulged themselves."

ProGrowth argues the Defendants' financing statements are seriously misleading because they identify the annuity contracts as issued by Lincoln Benefit Life instead of Fidelity & Guaranty, and because contract no. L9E00015 is identified as no. LE900015. Were this the only language contained in the Defendants' financing statements, we may be inclined to agree. These provisions of the financing statements, however, cannot be read in isolation.

It is necessary to analyze the financing statements in their entirety because, under the Missouri UCC, a financing statement sufficiently identifies the collateral it covers if it provides an "indication that the financing statement covers all assets or all personal property." By identifying the collateral as all assets or all

[37] UCC §9-506(a). *In re PTM Technologies, Inc.,* 452 B.R. 165 (M.D.N.C. 2011).

Continued

personal property, the filer ensures that if "the property in question belongs to the debtor and is personal property, any searcher will know that the property is covered by the financing statement." While such a broad, generic description is insufficient to describe collateral in a security agreement, it is sufficient to describe collateral in a financing statement because it puts subsequent searchers on notice that any item of collateral owned by the debtor may be encumbered, which is the purpose of the filing system. When faced with a financing statement purporting to cover "all assets" of a debtor, it is then incumbent upon the subsequent creditor to investigate whether the collateral at issue is in fact covered by a security agreement.

We conclude the Defendants' financing statements satisfy the filing provisions of the Missouri UCC because they indicate coverage over all of Hanson's assets.... [A]ny inaccuracies in describing the specific annuity contracts at issue are immaterial and do not render the statements seriously misleading.

[Reversed.]

QUESTIONS

1. Explain the mistakes Wells Fargo made in its financing statements.
2. What does the court explain is the standard for determining whether a financing statement is sufficient for perfection?
3. What would happen if the court found that Wells Fargo's financing statements did not have sufficient and accurate descriptions?

Like the security agreement changes under Revised Article 9, the requirements for description of the collateral in the financing statements are now more general.[38] A security agreement can be filed as a financing statement if it contains all of the aforementioned required information.

Because the financing statement is intended as notice to third parties, it must be filed in a public place.[39] Revised Article 9 simplifies the formerly complex issues of filing location as a means of encouraging electronic systems that will be statewide, accessible across state lines, and organized simply by name in any index. Revised Article 9's general rule is central filing for financing statements for all types of collateral. Filings for fixtures and other property-related interests have also been simplified with Revised Article 9 deferring to state laws on the proper filing location.[40]

CPA **(B) Defective Filing.** When the filing of the financing statement is defective either because the statement is so erroneous or incomplete that it is seriously misleading or the filing is made in a wrong county or office, the filing fails to perfect the security interest. The idea of perfection by filing is to give public notice of a creditor's interest. To the extent that the notice cannot be located or does not give sufficient information, the creditor then cannot rely on it to obtain the superior position of perfection.

13. Loss of Perfection

The perfection of the security interest can be lost if the creditor does not comply with the Article 9 requirements for continuing perfection.

(A) Possession of Collateral. When perfection is obtained because the creditor takes possession of the collateral, that perfection is lost if the creditor voluntarily surrenders the collateral to the debtor without any restrictions.

(B) Consumer Goods. The perfection obtained by the automatic status of a PMSI is lost in some cases by removal of the goods to another state. The security interest may also be destroyed by resale of the goods to a consumer. To protect against these types of losses of protection, the creditor needs to file a financing statement. In the case of a PMSI, the perfection is good against other creditors but is not superior when it comes to buyers of the goods.

(C) Lapse of Time. The perfection obtained by filing a financing statement lasts five years. The perfection may be continued for successive five-year periods by filing a continuation statement within six months before the end of each five-year period.[41] Revised Article 9 permits a "manufactured home" exception

[38] However, the sample financing form included with Revised Article 9, §9-521 includes boxes for all of the same information required under existing Article 9. The sample form in Figure 34-1 would meet the requirements for Revised Article 9.

[39] UCC §9-401; *In re Ocean Place Development*, LLC, 447 B.R. 726 (D. N.J. 2011) (9th Cir. 2002). *Helms v. Certified Packaging Corp.*, 551 F.3d 675 (7th Cir. 2008).

[40] Revised Article 9, §9-501.

[41] UCC §9-403 (Revised Article 9, §9-516). Failure to file with the secretary of state was fatal for a priority of secured creditor when a central filing was required, despite the filing at the county level. *In re Borden*, 361 B.R. 489 (Neb. 2007).

E-Commerce & Cyberlaw

Engines Are from Mars; Priorities Are from Financing Statements

In 2001, the International Association of Corporate Administrators promulgated Model Administrative Rules (MARS), a set of rules for the standards for search engines for court system, land, tax, and lien records. State and local governments will have different technology and standards that range from a liberal search engine to a strict search engine. A *liberal search engine* is similar to Google, which kicks back a corrected term and says, "Did you mean ___?" when you type in a name or word that is misspelled. A *strict search engine*, such as the simple one in Microsoft Word, will not find a word or phrase in a document unless you have spelled the search item exactly the way it appears in the document.

The MARS standards migrate toward the strict search engine. However, states have adopted different standards, and the result is that the electronic searches for debtors in various states can be very different. If there is a strict search engine in a state and the person doing the search types in "Ann Smythe," the correct spelling of the debtor's name, the financing statement against "Smythe" that was filed as "Ann Smith" will not be a match and the electronic system will kick out a "NO MATCH FOUND." Likewise, a creditor who files under the name "House, Roger" when the debtor's actual name is "Roger House" has not perfected.* The same would be true of a financing statement filed under "Terry J. Kinderknecht" when the debtor's actual legal name is "Terrance Joseph Kinderknecht."**

Revised Article 9 created standard rules for search logic that tend toward the "strict" end of the spectrum. The majority of states have now adopted some version of MARS, although many states have modified the rules in some respect (which has resulted in a great deal of inconsistency; furthermore, some states have not adopted any rule on search logic at all). Creditors should be cautious in their searches.

**Pankratz Implement Company v. Citizens National Bank*, 102 P.3d 1165 (Kan. App. 2004).

**These examples would result in a "NO MATCH FOUND" and emphasize the importance of using both the debtor's legal name and correct spelling. Furthermore, the courts in all three cases, which are Revised Article 9 cases, did not honor the financing statement as perfection because the names were misleading. The person doing the search is permitted to assume that the debtor has no other secured creditors. See *In re Jim Ross Tires, Inc.*, 379 B.R. 670 (S.D. Tex. 2007).

allowing financing statements on mobile homes to be effective for 30 years.[42]

(D) Removal from State. In most cases, the perfection of a security interest lapses when the collateral is taken by the debtor to another state unless, as noted earlier, the creditor makes a filing in that second state within the four-month period of temporary perfection.

(E) Motor Vehicles. If the security interest is governed by a non-Code statute creating perfection by title certificate notation, the interest, if so noted, remains perfected without regard to lapse of time or removal to another state. The perfection is lost only if a state issues a new title without the security interest notation.

CPA C. Rights of Parties before Default

The rights of parties to a secured transaction are different in the time preceding the debtor's default from those in the time following the default.

14. Statement of Account

To keep the record straight, the debtor may send the creditor a written statement of the amount the debtor thinks is due and an itemization of the collateral together with a request that the creditor approve the statement as submitted or correct and return the statement. Within two weeks after receiving the debtor's statement, the creditor must send the debtor a written approval or correction. If the secured creditor has assigned the secured claim, the creditor's reply must state the name and address of the assignee.

15. Termination Statements

A debtor who has paid his debt in full may make a written demand on the secured creditor, or the latter's assignee if the security interest has been assigned, to send the debtor a **termination statement**,[43] which states that a security interest is no longer claimed under the specified financing statement. The debtor may present this statement to the

[42] Revised Article 9, §9-515.

[43] UCC §9-404 (Revised Article 9, §9-513); *McDaniel v. 162 Columbia Heights Housing Corporations*, 863 N.Y.S. 2d 346 (N.Y. Supp. 2008), but see *Mac'Kie v. Wal-Mart Stores, Inc.*, 127 F.3d 1102 (6th Cir. 1997), and *In re Calumet Farms, Inc.*, 2003 WL 24087895 (E.D. Ky. 2003).

filing officer, who marks the record terminated and returns the various papers that were filed to the secured party. The termination statement clears the debtor's record so subsequent buyers or lenders will not be subject to the now-satisfied security interest. The creditor has 20 days from receipt of a demand for a termination statement from a debtor to file a termination statement (one month for consumer goods).[44]

16. Correction Statements

Because Revised Article 9 permits creditors and others to simply file "authorized" financing statements, debtors are given protection for abusive filings of Article 9 interests. Under Revised Article 9, debtors are permitted to protest filed financing statements with a filing of their own correction statements. While the security interest is not abolished by such a filing, its content does provide public notice of an underlying dispute. A debtor can also file a correction statement when a creditor fails to provide a termination statement.[45]

D. Priorities

Two or more parties may have conflicting interests in the same collateral. This section discusses the rights of creditors and buyers with respect to each other and to collateral that carries a secured interest or perfected secured interest.

CPA 17. Unsecured Party versus Unsecured Party

When creditors are unsecured, they have equal priority. In the event of insolvency or bankruptcy of the debtor, all the unsecured creditors stand at the end of the line in terms of repayment of their debts (see Chapter 35 for more details on bankruptcy priorities). If the assets of the debtor are insufficient to satisfy all unsecured debtors, the unsecured debtors simply receive a **pro rata** share of their debts.

CPA 18. Secured Party versus Unsecured Party

A secured creditor has a right superior to that of an unsecured creditor because the secured creditor can take back the collateral from the debtor's assets, while an unsecured creditor simply waits for the leftovers once all secured creditors have taken back their collateral. If the collateral is insufficient to satisfy the secured creditor's debt, the secured debtor can still stand in line with the unsecured creditors and collect any additional amount not satisfied by the collateral or a pro rata share. **For Example,** suppose that Linens Galore has a security interest in Linens R Us's inventory. Linens Galore has the right to repossess the inventory and sell it to satisfy the debt Linens R Us owes. Suppose that Linens R Us owes Linens Galore $22,000, and the sale of the inventory brings $15,000. Linens Galore still has a claim as an unsecured creditor for the remaining $7,000 due.

CPA 19. Secured Party versus Secured Party

If two creditors have a security interest in the same collateral, their priority is determined according to the **first-in-time provision**; that is, the creditor whose interest attached first has priority in the collateral.[46] The secured party whose interest was last to attach must then proceed against the debtor as an unsecured creditor because the collateral was given to the creditor whose interest attached first. **For Example,** if Bob pledged his antique sign collection to Bill on January 15, 2013, with a signed security agreement in exchange for a $5,000 loan, and then pledged the same collection to Jane on February 20, 2013, with a signed security agreement, Bill has priority because his security agreement attached first.

CPA 20. Perfected Secured Party versus Secured Party

The perfected secured creditor takes priority over the unperfected secured creditor and is entitled to take the collateral. The unperfected secured party is

[44] UCC §9-513(b) and (c).
[45] Revised Article 9, §9-518.
[46] UCC §9-312 (Revised Article 9, §9-313); *Arvest Bank v. SpiritBank, N.A.*, 191 P.3d 1228 (Ok. App. 2008), and *Fifth Third Bank v. Peoples Nat. Bank*, 929 N.E.2d 210 (Ind. App. 2010).

then left to seek remedies as an unsecured creditor because the collateral has been given to the perfected creditor. **For Example,** with respect to Bob's sign collection, if Jane filed a financing statement on February 21, 2013, she would have priority over Bill because her perfected interest would be superior to Bill's unperfected interest even though Bill's interest attached before Jane's.

The *General Motors Acceptance Corp. v. Lincoln Nat'l Bank* case involves an issue of a secured, perfected creditor's rights with regard to a bank's rights when a customer is overdrawn.

General Motors Acceptance Corp. v. Lincoln National Bank, 18 S.W. 3d 337, 40 UCC Rep. Serv. 2D 610, 42 UCC Rep. Serv. 2D 834 (Ky 2000)

The Bank Doesn't Win: When Secured Parties Take Priority over Overdrafts

General Motors Acceptance Corporation (GMAC) financed the inventory of Donohue Ferrill Motor Company, Inc., which gave GMAC a security interest in its vehicle inventory and all the proceeds of that inventory. The security agreement and financing statements were executed, and GMAC properly filed the financing statements.

Shortly before Donohue Ferrill's business failed, it sold six trucks and then deposited the proceeds of $124,610.80 from the sale of those trucks into its account at Lincoln National Bank. Lincoln took the deposited funds and applied them to account overdrafts that Donohue Ferrill had. For 38 of the 62 business days of September, October, and November 1991, Donohue Ferrill's account was overdrawn. Lincoln National honored 133 overdrafts during these three months and charged Donohue Ferrill a total of $1,995 in fees. The total amount of the overdrawn balances for those 38 days was $1,943,306.25.

GMAC objected, saying that it had priority in those funds. The trial court and court of appeals found for the bank and GMAC appealed.

JUDICIAL OPINION

LAMBERT, Chief Justice. . . .The issue presented is whether a bank may apply the cash proceeds of collateral to overdrafts allowed a depositor, thereby defeating established priorities.

GMAC based its claim upon KRS 355.9-306(2), which states

> *Except where this article otherwise provides, a security interest continues in collateral notwithstanding sale, exchange or other disposition thereof unless the disposition was authorized by the secured party in the security agreement or otherwise, and also continues in any identifiable proceeds including collections received by the debtor.*

Where cash proceeds are covered into the debtor's checking account and paid out in the operation of the debtor's business, recipients of the funds of course take free of any claim which the secured party may have in them as proceeds. What has been said relates to payments and transfers in ordinary course. The law of fraudulent conveyances would no doubt in appropriate cases support recovery of proceeds by a secured party from a transferee out of ordinary course or otherwise in collusion with the debtor to defraud the secured party.

Payment of an overdraft by a bank is of the nature of a loan to the account owner and is premised upon the condition of repayment. Thus, Lincoln National made loans to Donohue Ferrill in the amount of the overdrafts paid. Since the bank had no security for such loans, it was an unsecured creditor of Donohue Ferrill. Thus, as an unsecured creditor, Lincoln National was without any right to take or retain assets of Donohue Ferrill that were subject to the perfected security interest of other secured creditors.

The trial court and the Court of Appeals found such an exception in Official Comment 2(c) to the UCC § 9-306 (KRS 355.9-306), holding that the proceeds of the collateral used to cover prior overdrafts were transferred out of Donohue Ferrill's account in the ordinary course of business. We disagree with this interpretation. Although the commentary provides an exception for proceeds from the debtor's checking account and paid in the ordinary course of the operation of the debtor's business, this exception does not apply when a bank seizes funds deposited in a customer's account and applies such funds to payment of overdrafts or antecedent debts. Such an interpretation would eviscerate the security interest in proceeds of collateral contrary to KRS 355.9-306(2) and permit a bank that had made an unsecured loan to leapfrog secured creditors.

Our conclusion here…is that a secured party's right to proceeds of collateral deposited to the debtor's bank account is superior to the bank's right to a setoff of the same proceeds against amounts the debtor owes the bank.

For the foregoing reasons, the decision of the Court of Appeals is reversed, and this cause is remanded to the trial court for entry of judgment consistent herewith.

QUESTIONS

1. What did the bank do to the debtor's account?
2. What would happen if banks were permitted to take proceeds deposited by creditors into their accounts?
3. Who has priority in the funds, the bank or GMAC?

The perfected secured party's interest as against other types of creditors, such as lienors, mortgagees, and judgment creditors, is also determined on a **first-to-perfect basis**. If the secured party perfects before a judgment lien or mortgage is recorded, the perfected secured creditor has priority.[47] The perfected party takes priority over the secured party even when the perfected secured party is aware of the security interest prior to perfection.[48]

CPA 21. Perfected Secured Party versus Perfected Secured Party

The general rule for priority among two perfected secured creditors in the same collateral is also a first-in-time rule: The creditor who perfected first is given priority. **For Example,** again with respect to Bob's sign collection, if Bill filed a financing statement on February 22, 2013, Jane would still have priority because she perfected her interest first. If, however, Bill filed a financing statement on January 31, 2013, he would have priority over Jane. There are, however, three exceptions to this rule of first-in-time, first-in-right for perfected secured creditors.

CPA **(A) The Purchase Money Security Interest in Inventory.**[49] If the collateral is inventory, the purchase money secured creditor must do two things to prevail even over prior perfected secured creditors. The creditor must (1) perfect before the debtor receives possession of the goods that will be inventory and (2) give notice to any other secured party who has previously filed a financing statement with respect to that inventory.[50] The other secured parties must receive this notice before the debtor receives possession of the goods covered by the purchase money security interest. Compliance with these notice requirements gives the last creditor to extend credit for the inventory the priority position, which is a rule of law based on the practical notion that a debtor must be able to replenish its inventory to stay in business and keep creditors paid in a timely fashion. With this priority for subsequently perfected creditors, debtors have the opportunity to replenish inventory. **For Example,** suppose that First Bank has financed the inventory for Roberta's Exotic Pets, taken a security interest in the inventory, and filed a financing statement covering Roberta's inventory. Two months later, Animal Producers sells reptiles on credit to Roberta, taking a security interest in Roberta's inventory. To take priority over First Bank, Animal Producers would have to file the financing statement on the inventory before Roberta receives the reptiles and notify First Bank at the same time. The commercial rationale for this priority exception is to permit businesses to replenish their inventories by giving new suppliers a higher priority.

(B) Purchase Money Security Interest—Noninventory Collateral. If the collateral is *noninventory collateral,* such as equipment, the purchase money secured creditor prevails over all others as to the same collateral if that creditor files a financing statement within 20 days after the debtor takes possession of the collateral. **For Example,** First Bank loans money to debtor Kwik Copy and properly files a financing statement covering all of Kwik Copy's present and subsequently acquired copying equipment. Second Bank then loans money to Kwik Copy for the purchase of a new copier. Second Bank's interest in the copier will be superior to First Bank's interest if Second Bank perfects its interest by filing either before the debtor receives the copier or within 20 days thereafter.

(C) Status of Repair or Storage Lien. What happens when the debtor does not pay for the repair or storage of the collateral? In most states, a person repairing or storing goods has a lien or right to keep possession of the goods until paid for such services. The repairer or storer also has the right to sell the goods to obtain payment if the customer fails to pay and if proper notice is given.[51] Article 9 makes a statutory lien for repairs or storage superior to a perfected security interest in the same collateral.

[47] *Banner Bank v. First Community Bank,* 854 F. Supp. 2d 846 (D. Mont. 2012).

[48] *Farm Credit of Northwest Florida, ACA v. Easom Peanut Co.,* 718 S.E.2d 590 (Ga. App. 2011).

[49] Revised Article 9, §9-103 expands the definition of a PMSI in inventory. Consignments are treated as PMSIs in inventory.

[50] Revised Article 9, §9-324.

[51] UCC §9-310 (Revised Article 9, §9-333); In re *James,* 463 B.R. 719 (M.D. Pa. 2011).

Tolbert v. Automotive Finance Corp., 341 S.W.3d 195 (Mo. App. 2011)

Stephen Tolbert and His Inconsistent Tales: A BFP of a Corvette?

In 2003, Automotive Finance Corporation ("AFC") executed a contract to provide "floorplan financing" to R American Auto, Inc., a used car dealership, for the purchase of inventory. As collateral for the financing, AFC took a security interest in all of R American's present and future inventory. AFC filed a UCC Financing Statement to record the security interest on December 16, 2003.

On August 24, 2006, R American purchased a white 2006 Corvette for its inventory. AFC took possession of the Corvette's certificate of title. On January 31, 2007, Kip Rowley, the owner of R American, gave AFC a business check for $43,220 as payment in full for the Corvette, and AFC provided Rowley with the certificate of title to the Corvette. The check was dishonored because R American's bank account had been closed. An agent of AFC went to R American's car lot to secure possession of the Corvette and discovered that it was not on the lot. AFC filed a lien on the missing vehicle.

On March 4, 2008, Steven Tolbert filed a petition seeking a release of AFC's lien on the Corvette because he claimed to be a "*bona fide* purchaser" of the Corvette from Ultimate Motor Cars, LLC, on January 21, 2007. AFC filed an answer to the petition and a counterclaim against Tolbert for conversion, seeking damages for the value of the Corvette.

Tolbert testified that he paid $52,000 to Kip Rowley on November 2, 2006, and immediately took possession of the Corvette. He gave Rowley a check made out to "R American" for $50,900 and also paid $1,100 in cash. Tolbert did not receive a bill of sale and the certificate of title to the Corvette until nearly three months later on January 21, 2007. The bill of sale, issued by "Ultimate Motor Cars, Inc.," indicated that the sale was completed on January 21, 2007, and that the purchase price was $52,099. The certificate of title indicated that R American acquired the Corvette on August 24, 2006, and then transferred the Corvette to Ultimate Motor Cars on October 20, 2006. Tolbert's name was listed both as the seller of the Corvette as agent for R American and as the buyer of the Corvette as agent for Ultimate Motor Cars. Tolbert testified that he inadvertently signed in the wrong spot as seller on the Corvette's certificate of title. Nevertheless, Tolbert was not concerned with these discrepancies because he believed Rowley did business as both R American and Ultimate Motor Cars. Tolbert said he was unaware of AFC's security interest until February 2007, when he attempted to have the Corvette titled in his name and learned about the lien.

Jason Yount, branch manager for AFC, testified that on September 7, 2006, R American paid AFC for the Corvette, and that AFC gave R American the certificate of title to the Corvette. On December 12, 2006, R American gave the certificate of title back to AFC, AFC advanced R American credit for the Corvette, and R American "refloored" the Corvette. Before reclaiming the title, on December 12, 2006, an agent of AFC physically inspected the Corvette on R American's lot, verified the Corvette's VIN, and ensured that the Corvette's certificate of title indicated that R American owned the Corvette. Yount explained that AFC would not have advanced credit to R American and accepted the Corvette's certificate of title on December 12, 2006, if at that time the certificate of title indicated that R American had transferred the Corvette to Ultimate Motor Cars on October 20, 2006.

The court issued a judgment awarding AFC $53,904.41. Tolbert appealed the judgment.

JUDICIAL OPINION

HARDWICK, Chief Judge…A *bona fide* purchaser is one who pays valuable consideration, has no notice of outstanding rights of others, and acts in good faith. A party claiming to be a *bona fide* purchaser has the burden of proving those elements by a preponderance of the evidence. "Even if the prior transactions were fraudulent, [a buyer] takes good title if he is a *bona fide* purchaser."

However, "[a] buyer will not be protected where he is put on notice of the irregularities in a seller's title either by defects in the face of the certificate or by other circumstances." "The requisite notice 'may be imparted to a prospective purchaser by actual or constructive notice of facts which would place a reasonably prudent person upon inquiry as to the title he is about to purchase.'"

In this case, the record indicates Tolbert was aware of unusual circumstances throughout the transaction that would have caused a reasonably prudent person to question whether he obtained good title *200 to the Corvette. Tolbert claims to have paid for and taken possession of the Corvette from R American on November 2, 2006, without examining the Corvette's certificate of title or even receiving a bill of sale. Tolbert admits he did not receive a bill of sale and the certificate of title to the Corvette until nearly three months later. The bill of sale indicates the Corvette was sold to him by Ultimate Motor Cars on January 21, 2007, which is inconsistent with Tolbert's assertion that he purchased the Corvette with a check dated November 2, 2006, made out to R American. The certificate of title also indicates that Tolbert operated as the seller of the Corvette for R American and the buyer of the Corvette for Ultimate Motor Cars. As a representative of R American, Tolbert would have known about AFC's floorplan financing agreement and its security interest in the Corvette.

Continued

Jason Yount's testimony contradicted Tolbert's account of the purchase transaction. Yount testified that on December 12, 2006, an agent of AFC physically inspected the Corvette on R American's lot and verified that the Corvette's certificate of title indicated that R American was owner. Yount also testified that AFC had possession of the certificate of title until January 31, 2007, when it received the check from Rowley that was later dishonored. Thus, Yount's testimony supports an inference that Tolbert could not have had possession of the Corvette until after December 12, 2006, and possession of the certificate of title until after January 31, 2007. This testimony rebutted Tolbert's allegations that he acted in good faith.

Tolbert failed to meet his burden of proving that he was a *bona fide* purchaser of the Corvette. Based on the circumstances surrounding his alleged purchase of the vehicle, Tolbert had actual or constructive notice of facts that cast doubt on the validity of his ownership interest. The evidence, viewed in a light most favorable to the judgment, did not establish that Tolbert acted in good faith or that he was unaware of AFC's lien on the Corvette. Because Tolbert failed to prove he was a *bona fide* purchaser of the vehicle, the court did not err in granting AFC's claim for conversion.

[Affirmed].

QUESTIONS

1. What was odd about the Tolbert purchase of the Corvette?
2. What is the impact of the court's decision on Tolbert? Does he end up paying twice for the car?
3. What lessons do you learn from this case about buying a car?

Figure 34-2 provides a summary of the priorities of various parties with respect to secured and unsecured creditor interests.

22. Secured Party versus Buyer of Collateral from Debtor

The debtor may sell the collateral to a third person. How does this sale affect the secured creditor?

CPA **(A) Sales in the Ordinary Course of Business.** A buyer who buys goods from the debtor in the ordinary course of business is not subject to any creditor's security interest regardless of whether the interest was perfected or unperfected and regardless of whether the buyer had actual knowledge of the security interest. The reason for this protection of buyers in the ordinary course of business is that subjecting buyers to a creditor's reclaim of goods would cause great delay and hesitation in commercial and consumer sales transactions.[52]

CPA **(B) Sales not in the Ordinary Course of Business: The Unperfected Security Interest.** A sale not in the ordinary course of business is one in which the seller is not usually a seller of such merchandise. **For Example,** if a buyer purchases a computer desk from an office supply store, the sale is in the ordinary course of business. If that same buyer purchases that same computer desk from a law firm that is going out of business, that buyer is not purchasing in the ordinary course of business. If a buyer is purchasing collateral and such purchase is not in the ordinary course of business but the security interest is unperfected, such a security interest has no effect against a buyer who gives value and buys in good faith, that is, not knowing of the security interest. A buyer who does not satisfy these conditions is subject to the security interest.

CPA **(C) Sales not in the Ordinary Course of Business: The Perfected Security Interest.** If the security interest was perfected, the buyer of the collateral is ordinarily subject to the security interest unless the creditor consented to the sale.[53]

CPA **(D) Sales not in the Ordinary Course of Business: The Consumer Debtor's Resale of Consumer Goods.** When the collateral constitutes consumer goods in the hands of the debtor, a resale of the goods to another consumer destroys the automatically perfected PMSI of the consumer debtor's creditor. Assuming that the buyer who purchases from the consumer debtor has no knowledge of a security interest, she will take the collateral free and clear from the creditor's security interest even though there was

[52] Revised Article 9, §9-320 covers the rights of buyers of goods.

[53] In Revised Article 9, §1-201(9) adds that a purchase from a pawnbroker will not be considered a sale in the ordinary course of business.

FIGURE 34-2 *Priority of Secured Interest under Article 9*

CONFLICT	PRIORITY
Secured party versus secured party	First to attach
Unsecured party versus secured party	Secured party
Perfected secured party versus secured party	Perfected secured party
Perfected secured party versus perfected secured party	Party who is first to perfect
Perfected secured party versus lienor	Party who filed (financing statement or lien) first [§ 9-307(2)] (rev. § 9-317)
EXCEPTIONS	
PMSI in fixtures versus perfected secured party	PMSI creditor if perfected before annexation or within 20 days after annexation (PMSI will have priority even over prior perfected secured party) (§ 9-313, § 9-314) (rev. § 9-317)
PMSI in equipment versus perfected secured party	PMSI is perfected within 20 days after delivery [§ 9-301(2), § 9-312(4)] (rev. § 9-317)
PMSI in inventory versus perfected secured party	PMSI is perfected before delivery and if perfected secured party given notice before delivery [§ 9-312(3)] (rev. § 9-317)
PMSI in consumer goods versus buyer	Buyer unless perfection is by filing before purchase [§ 9-302(1)(d)] (rev. § 9-317)
Perfected secured party versus buyer	Buyer in ordinary course wins even with knowledge [§ 9-306(1)(d)] (rev. § 9-320)

perfection by that creditor. Thus, the perfection without filing option afforded consumer PMSI creditors has a flaw in its coverage when it comes to a consumer debtor selling his refrigerator to a neighbor. Without a filed financing statement, the neighbor buyer takes the refrigerator free and clear of the creditor's security interest in it. However, consumer creditors can avoid the loss of this perfected interest by perfecting through filing. With filing, consumer PMSI creditors enjoy continuation of their interests even when the neighbor has paid the consumer debtor for the refrigerator.

Figure 34-3 offers a summary of the rights of buyers of collateral with respect to the creditors who hold security interests in that collateral. The *Dawson v. Fifth Third Bank* case illustrates how careful buyers must be when it comes to security interests.

Dawson v. Fifth Third Bank, 965 N.E.2d 730 (Ind. App. 2012)

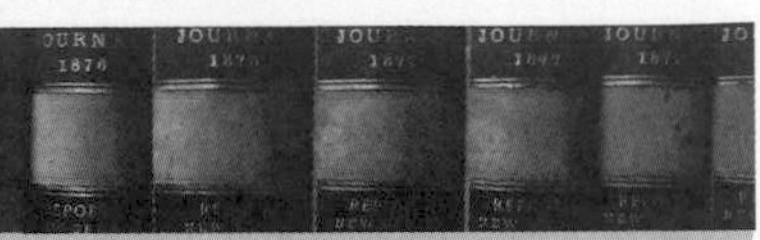

The Craigslist Seller with the Fake Title

In May 2006, Jacob J. Magish agreed to purchase a certain 2001 Harley–Davidson Motorcycle from Christine and Larry Logsdon for $14,635. Magish took out a loan at a Fifth Third Bank branch in Indianapolis with a security interest in the Motorcycle favor of Fifth Third in order to borrow $15,000 for the purchase. Magish presented to Fifth Third the Logsdons' original certificate of title. As part of the transaction, Magish executed, among other documents, an Application for Certificate of Title and a Power of Attorney. Fifth Third's Closing Representative, John Wargel, copied the Logsdon Original Title and then gave the Logsdon Original Title back to Magish. Wargel instructed Magish to apply for a new title at the Indiana Bureau of Motor Vehicles ("BMV"). Wargel kept the May 31 application and the Magish file in the loan file.

Shortly after the transaction, Magish, using deception, approached the Logsdons and requested that they sign paperwork to obtain a duplicate title. The Logsdons, who had no knowledge that Magish had financed the purchase of the Motorcycle through Fifth Third, unwittingly signed an application to obtain a duplicate title and gave the application to Magish.

Magish obtained a duplicate title from the BMV in the name of the Logsdons. The Logsdons signed the Logsdon Duplicate Title as Sellers. The Logsdon Duplicate Title inactivated the Logsdon Original Title in the BMV records.

Magish, using the Logsdon Duplicate Title, submitted an application to the BMV for a new title in his name. Magish intentionally omitted Fifth Third from the June 20 application and did not list a lienholder. Magish concurrently tendered the Logsdon Duplicate Title to the BMV and failed to notate Fifth Third as lienholder. On June 28, 2006, the BMV issued a new title in Magish's name. There was no lien notated on the First Magish Title.

On October 16, 2006, Fifth Third submitted an application for an amended title to the BMV ... Fifth Third did not have the Logsdon Original Title nor the First Magish Title in its possession and so did not tender to the BMV either with the Fifth Third application.

On October 18, 2006, the BMV issued a new title listing Magish as owner and Fifth Third as lienholder. The Second Magish Title inactivated the First Magish Title in the BMV records. The whereabouts of the Second Magish Title are unknown and Fifth Third has no record of receiving it.

In 2009, the Dawsons responded to a Magish posting on Craigslist for the sale of the Motorcycle. On June 18, 2009, Magish sold and delivered the Motorcycle to the Dawsons for $13,050.00. Magish, who was terminally ill and died in August 2009, had defaulted on the loan in 2008. Magish gave the Dawsons the certificate of title that showed it was free of any lienholders. After the sale, the Dawsons submitted an application for a new title to the Motorcycle to the BMV. The BMV advised the Dawsons that, according to the BMV records, the title the Dawsons had was not the most current title. For privacy reasons the BMV would not tell the Dawsons exactly what the issue was, but said it was either there was a duplicate title or a lienholder on the title. After discussions with Magish and his wife, the Dawsons determined that Fifth Third was a lienholder. The BMV refused to issue a new title to the Motorcycle to the Dawsons.

The Dawsons filed suit against Fifth Third, arguing that Fifth Third's lien against the Motorcycle should be unenforceable because, under a theory of equitable estoppel, Fifth Third should bear the loss of Magish's fraud on the Dawsons because Fifth Third's acts and omissions made the loss possible. Fifth Third filed a counterclaim, seeking replevin of the Motorcycle.

The trial court denied the Dawsons' summary judgment motion, granted Fifth Third's summary judgment motion, awarded permanent possession of the Motorcycle to Fifth Third, and ordered that the Dawsons maintain possession of the Motorcycle pending their appeal.

JUDICIAL OPINION

DARDEN, Judge...The stipulated facts show that Fifth Third obtained a security interest in the Motorcycle in 2006 after Magish signed the Simple Interest Note and Security Agreement and pledged the Motorcycle as collateral for his loan with Fifth Third. The stipulated facts also indicate that the most current certificate of title to the Motorcycle that was issued by and on file with the BMV reflects that security interest, and it indicates that Fifth Third is a lienholder on the Motorcycle. The Dawsons acknowledge that, pursuant to the terms of the Security Agreement, Fifth Third has a right to repossess the Motorcycle upon default by Magish, and the parties stipulated to the fact that Magish defaulted on the

Continued

Security Agreement in 2008 when he failed to make payments to Fifth Third. The parties do not dispute that Fifth Third has not released its lien on the Motorcycle. At the time the Dawsons purchased the Motorcycle, they did not check with the BMV to verify that the certificate of title that Magish gave them was the most recent one; thus, they were unaware of Fifth Third's lien on the Motorcycle. However, after learning that Fifth Third was a lienholder on the Motorcycle, the Dawsons have not paid Fifth Third to release the lien but have retained possession of the Motorcycle.

"It is black letter law that, upon default, a secured creditor has the right to take possession of the collateral securing its claim and the rights set forth in the agreement with the defaulting party." Therefore, when Magish defaulted on his loan, Fifth Third, as the secured party, had a right to take possession of the Motorcycle.

The Dawsons do not dispute the fact that Fifth Third had a right to possession of the Motorcycle based on its security interest and lien on the Motorcycle. Instead, they contend that their purchase, and resulting ownership, of the Motorcycle, precludes Fifth Third from being able to prove that the Dawsons wrongfully held possession of the Motorcycle. Fifth Third does not contest the Dawsons' ownership of the Motorcycle but contends that such ownership is subject to Fifth Third's lien, which upon Magish's default, entitles Fifth Third to replevin the Motorcycle.

A security agreement is effective against purchasers of the collateral. The stipulated facts show that Magish pledged the Motorcycle as collateral for his loan with Fifth Third; that the certificate of title, which had been on file with the BMV since October 18, 2006 and was on file when the Dawsons purchased the Motorcycle on June 18, 2009, reflected Fifth Third as lienholder; that Magish defaulted on the loan; and that the lien has not been released. Despite subsequently learning of Fifth Third's lien and acknowledging its right to repossess the Motorcycle, the Dawsons have maintained possession of the Motorcycle. While the Dawsons had an interest in the Motorcycle as purchasers of the collateral, their interest was not superior to Fifth Third's perfected security interest in the Motorcycle. Accordingly, we conclude that the trial court did not err by concluding that Fifth Third, as lienholder of the Motorcycle, had a right to replevin of the Motorcycle from the Dawsons. Thus, we affirm the trial court's grant of summary judgment to Fifth Third on its counterclaim for replevin.

We next turn to the Dawsons' argument that the trial court erred by denying their summary judgment motion on their claim for equitable estoppel. The Dawsons argue that, despite Fifth Third's lien, they are entitled to own the Motorcycle free and clear of such lien based on equitable principles. Specifically, the Dawsons assert that the following equitable principles should apply: (1) when one of two innocent parties must suffer a loss, that loss must be borne by the party whose act or omission made the loss possible; and (2) equity aids the vigilant, not those who slumber on their rights. In other words, the Dawsons contend that Fifth Third should bear the loss of the fraud Magish perpetrated on them because Fifth Third's acts or omissions allowed Magish to obtain a certificate of title that did not reflect Fifth Third's lien and thereafter allowed him to sell the Motorcycle to the Dawsons without their knowledge of Fifth Third's lien. In so arguing, the Dawsons list various things that they contend Fifth Third did or did not do—such as returning the original certificate of title (or the Original Logsdon Title) to Magish so that he could apply for a certificate of title and failing in its duty to protect its own interests in the lien—and argue that Fifth Third could have prevented the Dawsons' loss.

The record reveals that the Dawsons purchased the Motorcycle after seeing Magish's post on Craigslist, and there is no evidence presented that they knew Magish or had any previous dealings or interactions with him. Despite this apparent lack of familiarity with Magish, the Dawsons did not check the BMV to verify the status of the certificate of title that Magish presented to them. Indeed, there would have been little effort on their part to do so, and the record suggests that the Dawsons were in a better position to protect themselves from a loss. "As a general rule, we find that it is unreasonable to rely on the statements of third parties—or the debtor—about the current status of security interests."

[Affirmed].

QUESTIONS

1. How did Magish manage to get a clean title?
2. Was this a sale in the ordinary course of business? Why or why not?
3. What advice would you give to someone buying a vehicle through Craigslist?

E. Rights of Parties after Default

When a debtor defaults on an obligation in a secured transaction, the secured creditor has the option to sue the debtor to enforce the debt or of proceeding against the collateral.

FIGURE 34-3 *Priorities in Transfer of Collateral by Sale*

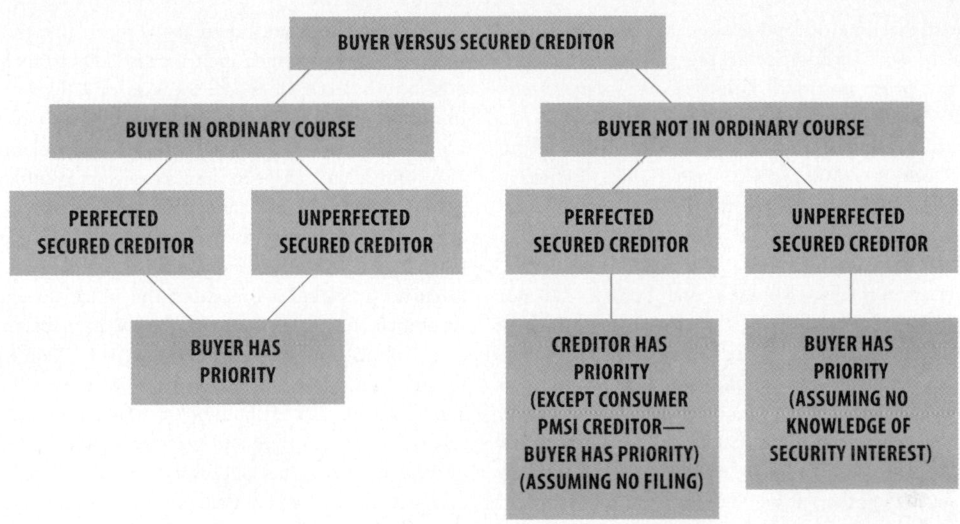

CPA 23. Creditor's Possession and Disposition of Collateral

Upon the debtor's default, the secured party is entitled to take the collateral from the debtor.[54] **Self-help repossession** is allowed if this can be done without causing a **breach of the peace**. If a breach of the peace might occur, the seller must use court action to obtain the collateral. Breaking and entering a debtor's property is a breach of the peace.[55]

The *Chrysler Credit v. Koontz* case answers a question about breach of the peace.

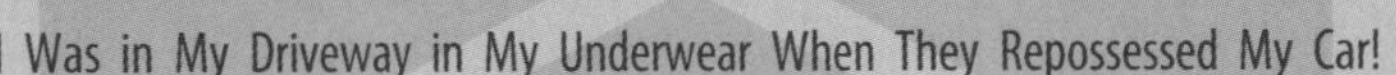

Chrysler Credit v. Koontz, 661 N.E.2d 1171 (Ill. App. Ct. 1996)

I Was in My Driveway in My Underwear When They Repossessed My Car!

Koontz entered into an agreement with Chrysler to purchase a 1988 Sundance in exchange for 60 monthly payments of $185.92. When Koontz defaulted on the contract in early 1991, Chrysler notified him that it would repossess the vehicle if he did not make up the missed payments. Koontz notified Chrysler that he would make every effort to catch up on the payments, that he did not want the vehicle to be repossessed, and that Chrysler was not to enter his private property to repossess the car. Chrysler repossessed the car, however, according to the self-help repossession statute of the UCC.

When Koontz heard the repossession in progress, he rushed outside in his underwear and hollered, "Don't take it," to the repossessor. The repossessor did not respond and proceeded to take the vehicle. Chrysler sold the car and filed a complaint against Koontz seeking a deficiency judgment for the balance due on the loan. Koontz alleged that the repossession was a breach of the peace. From a judgment in favor of Chrysler, Koontz appealed.

JUDICIAL OPINION

KUEHN, J.... Koontz raises only a single issue on appeal. He contends that the trial court erred in finding that Chrysler's repossession did not breach the peace because there was evidence that Koontz made an unequivocal oral protest to the repossession

[54] UCC §9-503 (Revised Article 9, §9-607). Repossession on private property where a creditor cut a lock was not a breach of the peace when security agreement authorized such trespass for repossession. *Wombles Charters, Inc. v. Orix Credit Alliance, Inc.*, 39 UCC 2d 599 (S.D.N.Y. 1999).

[55] *Williams v. Republic Recovery Service, Inc.*, 2010 WL 3732107 (N.D. Ill.).

Continued

of his vehicle at the time of repossession. Koontz argues that when the vehicle was taken despite his protest, "Don't take it," a breach of the peace occurred, citing *Dixon v Ford Motor Credit Co. (1979)* 72 Ill. App.3d 983, 391 N.E.2d 493. In *Dixon,* the court, relying upon White and Summers, Uniform Commercial Code § 26-6, at 972, stated that "[w]hen a creditor repossesses in disregard of the debtor's unequivocal oral protest, the repossession may be found to be in breach of the peace."

Chrysler contends that Koontz's oral protest did not breach the peace because "none of the elements of violence indicated in the decisions cited by the Defendant exists [*sic*] in this case." Chrysler argues by implication that without an element of violence there can be no breach of the peace. Chrysler also argues that if we find that an oral protest without an element of violence constitutes a breach of the peace, then we would be narrowing the self-help repossession statute to the point that it would be useless to a secured creditor.

We recognize that the self-help repossession statute extends a conditional self-help privilege to secured parties; however, we must apply the statute in a way that reduces the risk to the public associated with extrajudicial conflict resolution. It is apparent that the self-help remedy is efficient for secured creditors and results in reduced costs for both creditors and debtors. Efficiency and reduced litigation costs are desirable. Still, a debtor's private property interests and society's interest in tranquility must also be protected.

Because self-help repossession is statutory, we look to the language of § 9-503 to establish the parameters of the remedy that the statute offers to secured parties who seek to repossess collateral without judicial process. The statute provides in pertinent part: "Unless otherwise agreed a secured party has on default the right to take possession of the collateral. In taking possession a secured party may proceed without judicial process if this can be done without breach of the peace or may proceed by action."...The key to whether a self-help repossession is permissible depends on whether the peace has been or is likely to be breached.

Section 9-503 does not define breach of the peace, and the phrase "breach of the peace" has never had a precise meaning in relation to specific conduct. The phrase has been construed on several occasions. In *Cantwell v State of Connecticut (1940)* 310 U.S. 296, 308, 84 L. Ed. 1213, 60 S. Ct. 900, 905, the court stated: "The offense known as breach of the public peace embraces a great variety of conduct destroying or menacing public order and tranquility. It includes not only violent acts but acts and words likely to produce violence in others." In *Leavitt v Charles R. Hearn, Inc. (1974)* 19 Ill. App. 3d 980, 312 N.E.2d 806, we noted that implied force may also constitute a breach of the peace. Threats and epithets directed at another may or may not constitute a breach of the peace, depending upon the likelihood that a disturbance will follow.

We therefore conclude that the term "breach of the peace" connotes conduct which incites or is likely to incite immediate public turbulence, or which leads to or is likely to lead to an immediate loss of public order and tranquility. Violent conduct is not a necessary element. The probability of violence at the time of or immediately prior to the repossession is sufficient.

After a thorough examination of the record, we find no abuse of discretion on the part of the trial court in ruling that Chrysler's repossession did not breach the peace. Whether a given act provokes a breach of the peace depends upon the accompanying circumstances of each particular case. In this case, Koontz testified that he only yelled, "Don't take it," and that the repossessor made no verbal or physical response. He also testified that although he was close enough to the repossessor to run over and get into a fight, he elected not to because he was in his underwear. Furthermore, there was no evidence in the record that Koontz implied violence at the time of or immediately prior to the repossession by holding a weapon, clenching a fist, or even vehemently arguing toe-to-toe with the repossessor so that a reasonable repossessor would understand that violence was likely to ensue if he continued with the vehicle repossession. We think that the evidence, viewed as a whole, could lead a reasonable fact finder to determine that the circumstances of the repossession did not amount to a breach of the peace.

We note that to rule otherwise would be to invite the ridiculous situation whereby a debtor could avoid a deficiency judgment by merely stepping out of his house and yelling once at a nonresponsive repossessor. Such a narrow definition of the conduct necessary to breach the peace would, we think, render the self-help repossession statute useless. Therefore, we reject Koontz's invitation to define "an unequivocal oral protest," without more, as a breach of the peace....

In this case, Koontz testified that he notified Chrysler prior to the repossession that it was not permitted to enter onto his property. He also testified that he pulled his vehicle into his front yard so that he could see it by the light of the front porch. This testimony was uncontroverted. There was no testimony, however, that Chrysler entered through any barricade or did anything other than simply enter onto the property and drive the car away. Viewing this evidence in the light most favorable to the prevailing party, we believe that Chrysler's entry upon the private real property of Koontz and taking possession of the secured collateral, without more, did not constitute a breach of the peace. Chrysler enjoyed a limited privilege to enter Koontz's property for the sole and exclusive purpose of effecting the repossession. So long as the entry was limited in purpose (repossession), and so long as no gates, barricades, doors, enclosures, buildings, or chains were breached or cut, no breach of the peace occurred by virtue of the entry onto his property....

[Affirmed]

Continued

QUESTIONS

1. What was the basis for Koontz arguing that there was a breach of the peace?
2. Did Chrysler have a right to repossess the car?
3. What determines the rights of the parties after default?
4. How did the court define a breach of the peace?

The secured creditor may sell, lease, or otherwise dispose of the collateral to pay the defaulted debt.[56] The sale may be private or public, at any time and place, and on any terms provided that the sale is done in a manner that is commercially reasonable. The creditor's sale eliminates all of the debtor's interest in the collateral.

24. Creditor's Retention of Collateral

Instead of selling the collateral, the creditor may wish to keep it and cancel the debt owed.[57]

(A) Notice of Intention. To retain the collateral in satisfaction of the debt, the creditor must send the debtor written notice of this intent.[58]

CPA **(B) Compulsory Disposition of Collateral.** In two situations, the creditor must dispose of the collateral. A creditor must sell the collateral if the debtor makes a written objection to retention within 21 days after the retention notice was sent. The creditor must also dispose of the collateral if it consists of consumer goods and the debtor has paid 60 percent or more of the cash price or of the loan secured by the security interest. The sale must be held within 90 days of the repossession. However, the debtor, after default, surrenders the right to require the resale.[59]

A creditor who fails to dispose of the collateral when required to do so is liable to the debtor for conversion of the collateral or for the penalty imposed by the Code for violation of Article 9.[60]

25. Debtor's Right of Redemption

The debtor may redeem the collateral at any time prior to the time the secured party has disposed of the collateral or entered into a binding contract for resale. To redeem, the debtor must tender the entire obligation that is owed plus any legal costs and expenses incurred by the secured party.[61]

Thinking Things Through

Repossessing and Replacing Tires

Les Schwab sold Mr. Reed four tires for $509.82 on credit. Between January 2008 and May 2008, Mr. Reed failed to make any payments. After notifying Mr. Reed of his default, Jacob Schreiber, a Les Schwab manager, went to Mr. Reed's residence. Mr. Reed's vehicle was parked in the driveway while Mr. Reed was at work. Mr. Schreiber, after consultation with two other members of the management team, removed the tires and wheels from the vehicle. They removed the tires from the wheels at the store and then returned the wheels to Mr. Reed's vehicle the next day. The purpose of removing the tires at the store was to prevent damage to the wheels by using the store's machine for the removal process.

Mr. Reed filed suit against Les Schwab for breach of the peace because his wheels were taken and they were owned by him. Only the tires were subject to repossession. Mr. Reed claimed damages from having his car immobilized and not being able to go to work because of the conversion of his property by Les Schwab employees. Is Mr. Reed correct? Was this a breach of the peace? Explain your answer. ***[Reed v. Les Schwab Tire Centers, Inc.*, 160 Wash. App. 1020 (Wash. App. 2011)]**

[56] Revised Article 9, §9-611 requires the secured party to notify all other secured parties and lienholders who have filed or recorded interests in the collateral of its intent to sell the collateral. *Coxall v. Clover Commercial Corp.*, 781 N.Y.S.2d 567 (Civ. Ct. 2004).
[57] UCC §9-505 (Revised Article 9, §§9-620, 9-621, & 9-624).
[58] Revised Article 9, §§9-620 through 9-622. If there has been no notice, repossession is a breach of the peace. *Buzzell v. Citizens Auto Finance, Inc.*, 802 F. Supp. 2d 1014 (D. Minn. 2011).
[59] Revised Article 9, §9-620.
[60] UCC §9-507 (Revised Article 9, §§9-625 through 9-627).
[61] UCC §9-506 (Revised Article 9, §9-623).

Ethics & the Law

Women, Children, and the Repo Guys

Repossessions of autos financed on credit are at an all-time high. Lenders explain that the growth period of the past decade inspired many to overextend themselves with credit purchases, and now the repossessions are taking place.

According to the "repo industry," about 15 percent of debtors surrender their cars voluntarily. Confrontations occur about 10 percent of the time during repossession. Many debtors change the color of their cars, change the tires and rims, or cover the vehicle identification number to foil repossession companies' efforts. One auto dealer, trying to repossess a woman's car, had two male employees scale the fence of the Murfeesboro, Tennessee Domestic Violence Program Shelter. The shelter's security cameras spotted the men and after police were notified, they were ordered off the premises. The woman who owned the car left the shelter to make the necessary payments to bring her obligations current. The shelter director said that if the men had come through the proper administrative channels at the shelter, the shelter would have cooperated with them. The shelter director called the men's scaling of the fence at a shelter for women and children "irresponsible." Do you think it is ethical for the debtors to do these things? Should debtors surrender their cars voluntarily?

In two incidents in 2006, cars that were repossessed had children sleeping in them. The cars were hooked to the tow vehicle and the children were transported to the tow yards. An industry spokesman said that "repo guys" have to get in and hook the cars up as quickly as possible; they do not have time to check the inside of the vehicle.

Source: Rich Beattie, "Boom Times for Repo Guys," *New York Times*, April 18, 2003, D1, D8.

26. Disposition of Collateral

Upon the debtor's default, the creditor may sell the collateral at a public or private sale or may lease it to a third party. The creditor must give any required notice and act in a commercially reasonable manner. Revised Article 9 imposes specific notice requirements and provides a form that, if used by the creditor, is deemed adequate notice of sale. There are different notice forms for consumer and other transactions, but the basic information required is the day, time, location for the sale, and a contact number for questions the debtor and other secured parties might have. The notice must be sent to the debtor and any other creditors with an interest in the property.[62]

(A) Distribution of Surplus. If there is any money remaining, the surplus is paid to the debtor.[64]

(B) Liability for Deficit. If the proceeds of the disposition are not sufficient to pay the costs and the debt of the disposing creditor, the debtor is liable for the deficiency. However, the disposition of the collateral must have been conducted in the manner required by the UCC. This means that proper notice must have been given, if required, and that the disposition must have been made in a commercially reasonable manner. Factors that determine commercial reasonableness include notice, the difference between the sale price and the value of the goods, and public versus private sale according to industry practice.[65]

CPA 27. Postdisposition Accounting

When the creditor disposes of the collateral, the proceeds are applied in the following order. Proceeds are first used to pay the expenses of disposing of the collateral. Next, proceeds are applied to the debt owed the secured creditor making the disposition. Remaining proceeds are applied to any debts owed other creditors holding security interests in the same collateral that are subordinate to the interest of the disposing creditor.[63]

LawFlix

Fun with Dick and Jane (1977) (PG)

Jane Fonda and George Segal play a married couple in financial distress. When Segal loses his job, creditors appear to reclaim purchases, including landscapers who repossess the lawn by rolling up the sod. What form of collateral is the sod? Is the repossession appropriate?

[62] UCC §§9-613 and 9-614. *Wilder v. Toyota Financial Services Americas Corp.*, 764 F. Supp. 2d 249 (D. Mass. 2011).

[63] Revised Article 9, §9-615.

[64] Revised Article 9, §9-616. The distribution of proceeds remains substantially unchanged under Revised Article 9.

[65] *Arvelo v. Park Finance of Broward, Inc.*, 15 So.3d 660 (Fla. App. 2009).

MAKE THE CONNECTION

SUMMARY

A security interest is an interest in personal property or fixtures that secures payment or performance of an obligation. The property that is subject to the interest is called the *collateral,* and the party holding the interest is called the *secured party. Attachment* is the creation of a security interest. To secure protection against third parties' claims to the collateral, the secured party must perfect the security interest. *Tangible collateral* is divided into classes: consumer goods, equipment, inventory, general intangibles, farm products, and fixtures. Under Revised Article 9, intangibles have been expanded to include bank accounts, checks, notes, and health care insurance receivables.

Perfection of a security interest is not required for its validity, but it does provide the creditor certain superior rights and priorities over other types of creditors and creditors with an interest in the same collateral. Perfection can be obtained through possession, filing, automatically (as in the case of a PMSI in consumer goods), by control for accounts under Revised Article 9, or temporarily when statutory protections are provided for creditors for limited periods of time.

Priority among creditors is determined according to their status. Unperfected, unsecured creditors simply wait to see whether there will be sufficient assets remaining after priority creditors are paid. Secured creditors have the right to take the collateral on a priority basis. As between secured creditors, the first creditor's interest to attach takes priority in the event the creditors hold security interests in the same collateral. A perfected secured creditor takes priority over an unperfected secured creditor. Perfected secured creditors with interests in the same collateral take priority generally on a first-to-perfect basis. Exceptions include PMSI inventory creditors who file a financing statement before delivery and notify all existing creditors, and equipment creditors who perfect within 20 days of attachment of their interests.

A buyer in the ordinary course of business always takes priority, even over perfected secured creditors who have knowledge of the creditor's interest. A buyer not in the ordinary course of business loses out to a perfected secured creditor but extinguishes the rights of a secured creditor unless the buyer had knowledge of the security interest. A buyer from a consumer debtor takes free and clear of the debtor's creditor's perfected security interest unless the creditor has filed a financing statement and perfected beyond just the automatic PMSI consumer goods perfection.

Upon default, a secured party may repossess the collateral from the buyer if this can be done without a breach of the peace. If a breach of the peace could occur, the secured party must use court action to regain the collateral. If the buyer has paid 60 percent or more of the cash price of the consumer goods, the seller must resell them within 90 days after repossession unless the buyer, after default, has waived this right in writing. Notice to the debtor of the sale of the collateral is usually required. A debtor may redeem the collateral prior to the time the secured party disposes of it or contracts to resell it.

LEARNING OUTCOMES

After studying this chapter, you should be able to clearly explain:

A. Creation of Secured Transactions

LO.1 Explain the requirements for creating a valid security interest

See *ProGrowth Bank, Inc. v. Wells Fargo Bank, N.A.* on pp. 678–679.

See *In re Bucala* on pp. 674–675.

See *Dawson v. Fifth Third Bank* on pp. 687–688.

LO.2 List the major types of collateral

See *In re Lull* on pp. 671–673.

B. Perfection of Secured Transactions

LO.3 Define perfection and explain its significance in secured transactions

See E-Commerce & Cyberlaw, "Engines Are from Mars; Priorities Are from Financing Statements," p. 680.

C. Rights of Parties before Default

D. Priorities

LO.4 Discuss the priorities of parties with conflicting interests in collateral when default occurs

See *General Motors Acceptance Corp. v. Lincoln* on p. 682.

See *Tolbert v. Automotive Finance Corp.* on pp. 684–685 for priorities of buyers and secured parties.

E. Rights of Parties after Default

LO.5 State the rights of the parties on the debtor's default

See *Chrysler Credit v. Koontz* on pp. 689–691.

See Thinking Things Through on repossession of tires on p. 691.

See Ethics & the Law, "Women, Children, and the Repo Guys," p. 692.

KEY TERMS

after-acquired goods
automatic perfection
breach of the peace
collateral
consumer good
creditor
debtor
field warehousing
financing statement
first-in-time provision
first-to-perfect basis
floating lien
perfected security interest
pro rata
purchase money security interest (PMSI)
secured party
secured transaction
security agreement
security interest
self-help repossession
temporary perfection
termination statement
value

QUESTIONS AND CASE PROBLEMS

1. On October 22, 2001, Benjamin Ritchie executed a promissory note and mortgage in consideration for a $47,000 loan from WaMu. The mortgage covered both real estate located at 1790 Mount Mariah Road, Carlisle, Kentucky, and a manufactured home to be situated on the real property. The mortgage was properly filed in the Nicholas County Clerk's Office on October 31, 2001.

   Ritchie used the proceeds of the loan to purchase a manufactured home, which was subsequently rendered a total loss as a result of heavy fire damage. As the named loss payee on the insurance policy for the home, WaMu received and released the insurance proceeds to the Debtor to purchase a replacement manufactured home. WaMu failed, however, to record its lien on the certificate of title to the replacement manufactured home.

   On January 20, 2006, WaMu initiated a foreclosure action on the property. Ritchie raised the defense that WaMu no longer had a valid lien on the manufactured home. Is Ritchie correct? Explain your answer. [*In re Ritchie*, 416 B.R. 638 (6th Cir.)]

2. In 1983, Carpet Contracts owned a commercial lot and building, which it operated as a retail carpet outlet. In April of 1983, Carpet Contracts entered into a credit sales agreement with Young Electric Sign Corp. (Yesco) for the purchase of a large electronic sign for the store. The cost of the sign was $113,000, with a down payment of $25,000 and 60 monthly payments of $2,100 each.

   In August 1985, Carpet Contracts agreed to sell the property to Interstate. As part of the sale, Carpet Contracts gave Interstate an itemized list showing that $64,522 of the proceeds from the sale would be used to pay for the "Electronic Sign." The property was transferred to Interstate, and the Carpet Contracts store continued to operate there, but now it paid rent to Interstate. In June 1986, Carpet Contracts asked Yesco to renegotiate the terms of the sign contract. Yesco reduced Carpet Contracts' monthly payments and filed a financing statement on the sign at the Utah Division of Corporations and Commercial Code.

In December 1986, Interstate agreed to sell the property and the sign to the Webbs, who conducted a title search on the property, which revealed no interest with respect to the electronic sign. Interstate conveyed the property to the Webbs. Carpet Contracts continued its operation but was struggling financially and had not made its payments to Yesco for some time. By 1989, Yesco declared the sign contract in default and contacted the Webbs, demanding the balance due of $26,100. The Webbs then filed suit, claiming Yesco had no priority as a creditor because its financing statement was not filed in the real property records where the Webbs had done their title search before purchasing the land. Was the financing statement filed properly for perfection? [*Webb v. Interstate Land Corp.*, 920 P.2d 1187 (Utah)]

3. McLeod purchased several items from Sears, Roebuck & Co. on credit. The description of the items, in which Sears took a purchase money security interest, was as follows: "MITER SAW; LXITVRACDC [a television, videocassette recorder, and compact disc spinner]; 25″ UPRIGHT, 28″ UPRIGHT [two pieces of luggage]; BRACELET, DIA STUDS, RING; 14K EARR, P, EARRINGS, P [diamond bracelet, ring, and earrings]; and 9-INCH E-Z-LIFT [an outdoor umbrella]." In a dispute over creditors' priorities in McLeod's bankruptcy, one creditor argued that the description of the goods was insufficient to give Sears a security interest. Does the description meet Article 9 standards? [*McLeod v. Sears, Roebuck & Co.*, 41 UCC 2d (Bankr E.D. Mich.)]

4. When Johnson Hardware Shop borrowed $20,000 from First Bank, it used its inventory as collateral for the loan. First Bank perfected its security interest by filing a financing statement. The inventory was subsequently damaged by fire, Flanders Insurance paid Johnson Hardware $5,000 for the loss, but First Bank claimed the proceeds of the insurance. Was First Bank correct? Why or why not?

5. Consider the following cases and determine whether the financing statements as filed would be valid under Article 9. Be sure to consider the standard of "seriously misleading" under Revised Article 9.

    a. *In re Thriftway Auto Supply, Inc.*, 159 B.R. 948, 22 UCC Rep. Serv. 2d 605 (W.D. Okla.). The creditor used the debtor's corporate trade name, "Thriftway Auto Stores," not its legal name, "Thriftway Auto Supply, Inc."

    b. *In re Mines Tire Co., Inc.,* 194 B.R. 23, 29 UCC 2d 617 (Bankr. W.D.N.Y.). The creditor used the name "Mines Company Inc." instead of "Mines Tire Company, Inc."

    c. *Mountain Farm Credit Service, ACA v. Purina Mills, Inc.*, 459 S.E.2d 75 (N.C. App.). The creditor filed the financing statement under "Warren Killian and Robert Hetherington dba Grey Daw Farms" in a situation in which the two individuals were partners running Grey Daw Farms as a partnership.

    d. *B.T. Lazarus & Co. v. Christofides*, 662 N.E.2d 41 (Ohio App.). The creditor filed a financing statement in the debtor's old name when, prior to filing, the debtor had changed its name from B.T.L., Inc., to Alma Manufacturing, Inc.

    e. *In re SpecialCare, Inc.*, 209 B.R. 13, 34 UCC 2d 857 (N.D. Ga). The creditor failed to refile an amended financing statement to reflect debtor's name change from "Davidson Therapeutic Services, Inc." to "SpecialCare, Inc."

    f. *Industrial Machinery & Equipment Co. Inc. v. Lapeer County Bank & Trust Co.*, 540 N.W.2d 781 (Mich. App.). The creditor filed the financing statement under the company's trade name, KMI, Inc., instead of its legal name, Koehler Machine, Inc.

    g. *First Nat'l Bank of Lacon v. Strong*, 663 N.E.2d 432 (Ill. App.). Creditor filed the financing statement using the trade name "Strong Oil Co." instead of the legal name "E. Strong Oil Company."

6. First Union Bank of Florida loaned money to Dale and Lynn Rix for their purchase of Ann's Hallmark, a Florida corporation. First Union took a security interest in the store's equipment, fixtures, and inventory and filed the financing statement under the names of Dale and Lynn Rix.

Subsequently, the Rixes incorporated their newly acquired business as Michelle's Hallmark Cards & Gifts, Inc. When Michelle's went into bankruptcy, First Union claimed it had priority as a secured creditor because it had filed its financing statement first. Other creditors said First Union had priority against the Rixes but not against the corporation. Who was correct? What was the correct name for filing the financing statement? [*In re Michelle's Hallmark Cards & Gifts, Inc.*, 36 UCC 2d 225 (Bankr. M.D. Fla.)]

7. Rawlings purchased a typewriter from Kroll Typewriter Co. for $600. At the time of the purchase, he made an initial payment of $75 and agreed to pay the balance in monthly installments. A security agreement that complied with the UCC was prepared, but no financing statement was ever filed for the transaction. Rawlings, at a time when he still owed a balance on the typewriter and without the consent of Kroll, sold the typewriter to a neighbor. The neighbor, who had no knowledge of the security interest, used the typewriter in her home. Could Kroll repossess the typewriter from the neighbor?

8. Kim purchased on credit a $1,000 freezer from Silas Household Appliance Store. After she had paid approximately $700, Kim missed the next monthly installment payment. Silas repossessed the freezer and billed Kim for the balance of the purchase price, $300. Kim claimed that the freezer, now in the possession of Silas, was worth much more than the balance due and requested that Silas sell the freezer to wipe out the balance of the debt and to leave something for her. Silas claimed that because Kim had broken her contract to pay the purchase price, she had no right to say what should be done with the freezer. Was Silas correct? Explain.

9. Benson purchased a new Ford Thunderbird automobile. She traded in her old car and used the Magnavox Employees Credit Union to finance the balance. The credit union took a security interest in the Ford. Subsequently, the Ford was involved in a number of accidents and was taken to a dealer for repairs. Benson was unable to pay for the work done. The dealer claimed a lien on the car for services and materials furnished. The Magnavox Employees Credit Union claimed priority. Which claim had priority? [*Magnavox Employees Credit Union v. Benson*, 331 N.E. 2d 46 (Ind. App.)]

10. Lockovich borrowed money from a bank to purchase a motorboat. The bank took a security interest in it but never filed a financing statement. A subsequent default on the loan occurred, and the debtor was declared bankrupt. The bank claimed priority in the boat, alleging that no financing statement had to be filed. Do you agree? Why? [*In re Lockovich*, 124 B.R. 660 (W.D. Pa.)]

11. In 1987, the Muirs bought a motor home. In 1988, the Muirs created and Bank of the West acquired and perfected a security interest in the motor home. In 1992, the Muirs entered into an agreement with Gateleys Fairway Motors by which Gateleys would sell the motor home by consignment. Gateleys sold the motor home to Howard and Ann Schultz. The Schultzes did not know of the consignment arrangement or of the security interest of the bank. Gateleys failed to give the sales money to the Muirs and then filed for bankruptcy.

    The Schultzes brought suit seeking a declaration that they owned the motor home free of the bank's security interest. The trial court granted the Schultzes summary judgment. Who has title to the motor home and why? [*Schultz v. Bank of the West, C.B.C.*, 934 P.2d 421 (Or.)]

12. On April 18, 2000, Philip Purkett parked his car, on which he owed $213 in payments, in his garage and locked the garage. Later that night, TWAS, Inc., a vehicle repossession company, broke into the garage and repossessed the car without notice to Purkett. To get the car back, Purkett paid a $140 storage fee and signed a document stating that he would not hold TWAS liable for any damages. Did TWAS and Key Bank violate Article 9 requirements on repossession? [*Purkett v. Key Bank USA, Inc.*, 2001 WL 503050, 45 UCC Rep. Serv. 2d 1201 (N.D. Ill.)]

13. *A* borrowed money from *B* and orally agreed that *B* had a security interest in equipment that was standing in *A*'s yard. Nothing was in writing, and no filing of any kind was made. Nine days later,

B took possession of the equipment. What kind of interest did *B* have in the equipment after taking possession of it? [*Transport Equipment Co. v. Guaranty State Bank*, 518 F.2d 373 (10th Cir.)]

14. Cook sold Martin a new tractor truck for approximately $13,000, with a down payment of approximately $3,000 and the balance to be paid in 30 monthly installments. The sales agreement provided that "on default in any payment, Cook [could] take immediate possession of the property…without notice or demand. For this purpose vendor may enter upon any premises on which the property may be." Martin failed to pay the installments when due, and Cook notified him that the truck would be repossessed. Martin left the tractor truck attached to a loaded trailer and locked on the premises of a company in Memphis. Martin intended to drive to the West Coast with the trailer. When Cook located the tractor truck, no one was around. To disconnect the trailer from the truck (because he had no right to the trailer), Cook removed the wire screen over a ventilator hole by unscrewing it from the outside with his penknife. He next reached through the ventilator hole with a stick and unlocked the door of the tractor truck. He then disconnected the trailer and had the truck towed away. Martin sued Cook for unlawfully repossessing the truck by committing a breach of the peace. Decide. [*Martin v. Cook*, 114 So.2d 669 (Miss.)]

15. Muska borrowed money from the Bank of California and secured the loan by giving the bank a security interest in equipment and machinery at his place of business. To perfect the interest, the bank filed a financing statement that did not contain Muska's address. Muska later filed for bankruptcy. The trustee in bankruptcy claimed that the security interest of the bank was not perfected because the omission of the residence address from the financing statement made it defective. Was the financing statement valid? [*Lines v. Bank of California*, 467 F.2d 1274 (9th Cir.)]

16. Kimbrell's Furniture Co. sold a new television set and tape player to Charlie O'Neil and his wife. Each purchase was on credit, and in each instance, a security agreement was executed. Later on the same day of purchase, O'Neil carried the items to Bonded Loan, a pawnbroker, and pledged the television and tape deck as security for a loan. Bonded Loan held possession of the television set and tape player as security for its loan and contended that its lien had priority over the unrecorded security interest of Kimbrell. Who had priority? [*Kimbrell's Furniture Co. v. Sig Friedman, d/b/a Bonded Loan*, 198 S.E.2d 803 (S.C.)]

CPA QUESTIONS

1. On March 1, Green went to Easy Car Sales to buy a car. Green spoke to a salesperson and agreed to buy a car that Easy had in its showroom. On March 5, Green made a $500 down payment and signed a security agreement to secure the payment of the balance of the purchase price. On March 10, Green picked up the car. On March 15, Easy filed the security agreement. On what date did Easy's security interest attach?
   a. March 1
   b. March 5
   c. March 10
   d. March 15

2. Carr Corp. sells VCRs and videotapes to the public. Carr sold and delivered a VCR to Sutter on credit. Sutter executed and delivered to Carr a promissory note for the purchase price and a security agreement covering the VCR. Sutter purchased the VCR for personal use. Carr did not file a financing statement. Is Carr's security interest perfected?
   a. No, because the VCR was a consumer good.
   b. No, because Carr failed to file a financing statement.
   c. Yes, because Carr retained ownership of the VCR.
   d. Yes, because it was perfected at the time of attachment.

3. On July 8, Ace, a refrigerator wholesaler, purchased 50 refrigerators. This comprised Ace's entire inventory and was financed under an agreement with Rome Bank that gave Rome a security interest in all refrigerators on Ace's premises, all future-acquired refrigerators, and the proceeds of sales. On July 12, Rome filed a financing statement that adequately identified the collateral. On August 15, Ace sold one refrigerator to Cray for personal use and four refrigerators to Zone Co. for its business. Which of the following statements is correct?
   a. The refrigerators sold to Zone will be subject to Rome's security interest.
   b. The refrigerators sold to Zone will not be subject to Rome's security interest.
   c. The security interest does not include the proceeds from the sale of the refrigerators to Zone.
   d. The security interest may not cover after-acquired property even if the parties agree.

4. Fogel purchased a television set for $900 from Hamilton Appliance. Hamilton took a promissory note signed by Fogel and a security interest for the $800 balance due on the set. It was Hamilton's policy not to file a financing statement until the purchaser defaulted. Fogel obtained a loan of $500 from Reliable Finance, which took and recorded a security interest in the set. A month later, Fogel defaulted on several loans and one of his creditors, Harp, obtained a judgment against Fogel, which was properly recorded. After making several payments, Fogel defaulted on a payment due to Hamilton, who then recorded a financing statement subsequent to Reliable's filing and the entry of the Harp judgment. Subsequently, at a garage sale, Fogel sold the set for $300 to Mobray. Which of the parties has the priority claim to the set?
   a. Reliable
   b. Hamilton
   c. Harp
   d. Mobray

5. Under the Secured Transactions Article of the UCC, which of the following items can usually be excluded from a filed original financing statement?
   a. The name of the debtor.
   b. The address of the debtor.
   c. A description of the collateral.
   d. The amount of the obligation secured.

6. Under the Secured Transactions Article of the UCC, which of the following security agreements does not need to be in writing to be enforceable?
   a. A security agreement collateralizing a debt of less than $500.
   b. A security agreement where the collateral is highly perishable or subject to wide price fluctuations.
   c. A security agreement where the collateral is in the possession of the secured party.
   d. A security agreement involving a purchase money security interest.

CHAPTER 35

© Manuel Gutjahr/iStockphoto.com

Bankruptcy

learningoutcomes

After studying this chapter, you should be able to

LO.1 List the requirements for the commencement of a voluntary bankruptcy case and an involuntary bankruptcy case

LO.2 Explain the procedure for the administration of a debtor's estate

LO.3 List a debtor's duties and exemptions

LO.4 Explain the significance of a discharge in bankruptcy

LO.5 Explain when a business reorganization plan or an extended-time payment plan might be used

What can a person or business do when overwhelmed by debts? Bankruptcy proceedings can provide temporary and sometimes permanent relief from those debts.

A. Bankruptcy Law

Bankruptcy is a statutory proceeding with detailed procedures and requirements.

1. The Federal Law

Bankruptcy law is based on federal statutes that have been refined over the years. In October 2005, the Bankruptcy Abuse Prevention and Consumer Protection Act of 2005 (BAPCPA) took effect.[1] The BAPCPA was passed more than 10 years after the Bankruptcy Reform Commission was created, and the changes in bankruptcy law reflect an expressed congressional desire to curb a 15-year trend of increases in the number of bankruptcies.

Jurisdiction over bankruptcy proceedings is vested in the federal district courts. The district courts have the authority to transfer such matters to courts of special jurisdiction called **bankruptcy courts.**

2. Types of Bankruptcy Proceedings

The three types of bankruptcy proceedings that existed before the 2005 reforms are still available to individuals and businesses.

CPA **(A) Liquidation or Chapter 7 Bankruptcy.** A **Chapter 7 bankruptcy** is one in which all of the debtor's assets (with some exemptions) will be **liquidated** to pay debts. Those debts that remain unpaid or are paid only partially are discharged, with some exceptions. The debtor who declares Chapter 7 bankruptcy begins again with a nearly clean slate.

Chapter 7 bankruptcy is available to individuals, partnerships, and corporations. However, farmers, insurance companies, savings and loans, municipalities, Small Business Administration companies, and railroads are not entitled to declare Chapter 7

Ethics & the Law

Bankruptcy Records

According to **www.bankruptcydata.com**, the following are the largest bankruptcies in the history of the United States:

Company	*Date*	*Amount*
Lehman Brothers	09/15/2008	$691,000,000 billion
Washington Mutual (WaMu)	09/26/2008	$327,900,000 billion
WorldCom	07/21/2002	$103,900,000 billion
General Motors	06/01/2009	$91,000,000 billion
CIT	11/01/2009	$80,400,000 billion
Enron	12/02/2001	$65,500,000 billion
Conseco	12/02/2002	$61,300,000 billion
MF Global	10/31/2011	$40,500,000 billion
Chrysler	04/20/2009	$39,300,000 billion
Thornburg Mortgage	05/05/2009	$36,500,000 billion

Total bankruptcy filings in the United States from 2005 to 2011 were as follows. Note the significant drop following the 2005 reforms, followed by the spike in 2008 because of the economic crisis.

Year	*Total*	*Nonbusiness*	*Business*
2011	1,410,653	1,362,847	47,806
2010	1,593,081	1,536,799	56,282
2009	1,473,675	1,412,838	60,837
2008	1,117,641	1,074,108	43,533
2007	850,912	822,590	28,322
2006	617,660	597,965	19,695
2005	2,078,415	2,039,214	39,201

Is there an ethical component to declaring bankruptcy? For example, actor Gary Busey's agent referred to bankruptcy as a business strategy. What are the risks of using bankruptcy as a business strategy?

[1] Pub. L. No. 109-8, 119 Stat. 23 (2005); the act is codified at 11 U.S.C. §101 *et seq.*

bankruptcy because they are specifically governed by other statutes or specialized sections of the Bankruptcy Code.[2]

Under the BAPCPA, consumers generally cannot go directly to a Chapter 7 liquidation bankruptcy because they must demonstrate that they do not have the means to repay the debts before they can do a Chapter 7 liquidation.[3] The means test, which is discussed later, considers the disposable income that is available after the bankruptcy court has deducted allowable expenses that are listed as part of the means section of the BAPCPA, including items such as health insurance and child support.

CPA (B) REORGANIZATION OR CHAPTER 11 BANKRUPTCY. **Chapter 11 bankruptcy** is a way for a debtor to reorganize and continue a business with protection from overwhelming debts and without the requirement of liquidation. Chrysler, General Motors, United Airlines, and Delta are all examples of companies that have gone through Chapter 11 bankruptcies. Stockbrokers, however, are not eligible for Chapter 11 bankruptcy.

CPA (C) CHAPTER 13 BANKRUPTCY OR PAYMENT PLANS OR CONSUMER DEBT ADJUSTMENT PLANS. Chapter 13 of the federal Bankruptcy Code provides consumers an individual form of reorganization. Chapter 13 works with consumer debtors to develop a plan to repay debt. To be eligible for **Chapter 13 bankruptcy**, the individual must owe unsecured debts of less than $360,475 and secured debts of less than $1,081,400 and have regular income.[4] Chapter 13 plays an expanded role in bankruptcy because reforms require debtors with the means to pay their debts to go first into Chapter 13 bankruptcy rather than automatically declaring Chapter 7 bankruptcy.

B. How Bankruptcy Is Declared

Bankruptcy can be declared in different ways. The federal Bankruptcy Code spells out the requirements and process for declaration.

CPA 3. Declaration of Voluntary Bankruptcy

A **voluntary bankruptcy** is begun when the debtor files a petition with the bankruptcy court. A joint petition may be filed by a husband and wife. When a voluntary case is begun, the debtor must file a schedule of current income and current expenditures unless the court excuses this filing.

Under the 2005 reforms, a court can dismiss an individual debtor's (consumer's) petition for abuse if the debtor does not satisfy the **means test**, which measures the debtor's ability to pay by computing the debtor's disposable income. Only those debtors who fall below their state's median disposable income will be able to continue in a Chapter 7 proceeding. Individual debtors who meet the means test are required to go into Chapter 13 bankruptcy because they have not qualified for Chapter 7 bankruptcy. The formula for applying the means test is as follows:

Debtor's current monthly income less
Allowable expenses under the Bankruptcy
Code = Disposable income
Disposable income × 60

The debtor commits bankruptcy abuse if this number is not less than the lower of the following:

- 25 percent of the debtor's unsecured claims or $7,025, whichever is greater; or
- $11,725

A finding of abuse means that the debtor's Chapter 7 voluntary petition is dismissed. Previously, the law required the judge to find "substantial abuse" before dismissing the petition; now the standard reads only "abuse."[5]

Under the BAPCPA, the bankruptcy judge also has the discretion to order the debtor's lawyer to reimburse the trustee for costs and attorney's fees and to assess a civil penalty against the lawyer if the court finds that the lawyer has not acted in good faith in filing the debtor's bankruptcy petition.[6] As part of this change,

[2] For example, the Small Business Investment Act governs the insolvency of small business investment companies, 11 U.S.C. §109(b). Municipalities' bankruptcies are governed by Chapter 9 of the Bankruptcy Code, and farmers' bankruptcies are covered under Chapter 12. Following the 2008 market collapse, there were a series of municipal bankruptcies because of excessive debt and pension obligations.

[3] 11 U.S.C. §707(C)(2)(a). There are exceptions to the requirements of establishing no means, such as those who incurred their debts while on active military service.

[4] 11 U.S.C. §109(e).

[5] 11 U.S.C. §707(b). *In re Lapke*, 428 B.R. 839 (8th Cir. 2010). A debtor who increased his federal income tax withholding to 85% prior to filing bankruptcy and earned over $200,000 per year as a pathologist was guilty of bad faith. *In re Laine*, 383 B.R. 166 (D. Kan. 2008).

[6] 11 U.S.C. §707(b)(4).

lawyers must declare themselves (in public ads as well as in any individual meetings with clients) to be "debt relief agencies" or state that they "help people file for relief under the Bankruptcy Code." The Code now requires those who help consumers deal with their creditors to disclose that part of the assistance could include filing for bankruptcy. Lawyers who advertise their credit/bankruptcy expertise are subject to the laws and regulations that apply to debt relief agencies. If the agency/lawyer advises them to do something that causes the court to declare that there has been bankruptcy abuse, the lawyer/debt relief agency is responsible as well. As part of their role as debt counselors, lawyers are prohibited under the changes in the law from advising clients to undertake more debt in contemplation of filing bankruptcy.[7]

Debtors are required to undergo credit counseling (from an approved nonprofit credit counseling agency) within the 180 days prior to declaring a bankruptcy. In addition, the court applies the means test described earlier to determine whether the debtor qualifies for bankruptcy.[8]

There is significant disagreement among the bankruptcy courts about the meaning of "projected income." The disagreement results from the differing situations of the debtors. **For Example,** how do courts deal with debtors who are about to experience a large drop in disposable income? And do courts then consider what happens when debtors' incomes are expected to go up? If the projected income test used is applied, the bankruptcy could be dismissed. Debtors and creditors take different positions depending on which way the income goes, and the courts continue to debate the definition of projected income.[9]

The *In re Jass* case is one of many decisions on this income question.

In re Jass, 340 B.R. 411 (Utah 2006)

Disposable Income and Predisposed Not to Pay

The Jasses filed for chapter 13 bankruptcy relief. Their Form B22C indicated that their yearly household aggregate income was $143,403.96 based on income they received during the six-month period before filing. After deducting allowed expenses and deductions from their income, the Jasses' Statement of Current Monthly Income shows a "disposable income" of $3,625.63 per month.

The Jasses filed a chapter 13 plan which proposed to return $790.00 to unsecured creditors. At the hearing, the Trustee objected to confirmation because the Jasses' "disposable income," as calculated on their Form B22C, is $3,625.63, and they proposed to pay only $790.00 to unsecured creditors. The Trustee argued that because the Jasses were not proposing to pay their full disposable income of $3,625.63 to unsecured creditors, their plan did not comply with this "disposable income test."

The Jasses argued that the word "projected" modifies the definition of "disposable income." Mrs. Jass testified that beginning in December, 2005 her husband experienced serious medical problems involving injuries to his intestines. She testified that her family incurred $12,000 in medical expenses. In light of these expenses, the Jasses argued that their income in the future will not be commensurate with the "disposable income" shown on Form B22C. They argued that the changes under the BAPCPA do not require them to pay unsecured creditors the amount resulting from their Form B22C, so long as they can show that the income and expenses reported on the Form are inadequate representations of their future budget.

JUDICIAL OPINION

THURMAN, Bankruptcy Judge.…[t]he Court is called upon to determine whether the Jasses' "disposable income" as determined by their Form B22C is the same as "projected disposable income." This matter presents an issue of first impression in light of the Bankruptcy Abuse Prevention and Consumer Protection Act ("BAPCPA"). The Court determines that "disposable income" as calculated by Form B22C is not the same as "projected disposable income."

"Current monthly income" is defined in § 101(10A) as the debtor's income for the six-month period preceding bankruptcy.

The Court believes that the language of § 1325(b)(1)(B) [of the bankruptcy code] is clear and unambiguous— section 1325(b)(1)(B)'s requirement that a plan propose to pay "projected disposable income" means that the number

[7] 11 U.S.C. §§526–528. *Milavetz, Gallop & Milavetz, P.A. v. U.S.*, 130 S.Ct. 1324 (2010).

[8] 11 U.S.C. §109(h)(2). There are exceptions to the counseling requirements; for example, active military duty, disability, and emergencies. 11 U.S.C. 111(a) is the counseling provision. The counseling must be completed prior to filing for bankruptcy or the petition can be dismissed, *In re Ingram*, 460 B.R. 904 (6th Cir. 2011).

[9] *In re Turner*, 425 B.R. 918 (S.D. Ga. 2010); *In re Hilton*, 395 B.R. 433 (E.D. Wis. 2008); *In re Anstett*, 383 B.R. 380 (D.S.C. 2008); *In re Colclasure*, 383 B.R. 463 (E.D. Ark. 2008); and *In re Justice*, 418 B.R. 342 (W.D. Mo. 2009).

Continued

resulting from Form B22C is a starting point for the Court's inquiry only. Section 1325(b)(2) defines "disposable income" but § 1325(b)(1)(B) requires that a debtor propose a plan paying "projected disposable income." The Court must give meaning to the word "projected," as it obviously has independent significance. The word "projected" means "[t]o calculate, estimate, or predict (something in the future), based on present data or trends." Thus, the word "projected" is future-oriented. By definition under § 1325(b)(2), the term "disposable income" is oriented in historical numbers. By placing the word "projected" next to "disposable income" in § 1325(b)(1)(B), Congress modified the import of "disposable income." The significance of the word "projected" is that it requires the Court to consider both future and historical finances of a debtor.

To require all debtors to propose plans paying the number resulting from Form B22C would essentially ignore the word "projected" and give meaning only to the term "disposable income." The only way for the word "projected" to have independent significance is if the word modifies the term "disposable income."

Under the clear meaning of the statute, a debtor must propose to pay unsecured creditors the number resulting from Form B22C, unless the debtor can show that this number does not adequately represent the debtor's budget projected into the future.

The changes under the BAPCPA merely served to change the definition of "disposable income." Pre-BAPCPA cases interpreting the dichotomy between "projected disposable income" and "disposable income" held as the Court does today—that the definition of "disposable income" under § 1325(b)(2) was merely a starting point for the Court's inquiry into whether the debtor was proposing to pay "projected disposable income."

The overarching policy of the Bankruptcy Code is to afford a debtor a "fresh start." Although the changes to the Code under the BAPCPA serve to benefit creditors, the changes are not so broad as to undermine the "fresh start" policy of the Code.

If § 1325(b)(1)(B) required a debtor to always pay the calculated disposable income amount resulting from Form B22C, the Court would essentially foreclose the potential for bankruptcy relief from a group of chapter 13 debtors who are otherwise eligible for relief.

The facts of this case serve as a good example. The Jasses argue that they have recently experienced a change in circumstances, such that their future income will not be commensurate with the income they received six months before filing. If the Court were to require the Jasses to pay the disposable income amount resulting from Form B22C, any plan they propose would not be feasible. Because people are frequently forced to file for bankruptcy relief as a result of sudden life-altering events, the Jasses are exemplary of numerous debtors who would be foreclosed from seeking bankruptcy protections. This result is clearly at odds with the overarching policy that debtors who are eligible for bankruptcy relief be afforded an opportunity for a "fresh start."

The Statement of Current Monthly Income filed by the Jasses would require them to propose a plan paying unsecured creditors $3,625.63 per month. The Court presumes that this number is the "projected disposable income" required in the Jasses' case unless they can present evidence to show a substantial change in circumstances. Because the Jasses have not yet presented evidence addressing the inadequacy of figures contained in their Statement of Current Monthly Income, the Court finds that the Jasses have not carried their burden to rebut the presumption that their "projected disposable income" is the number resulting from Form B22C. The Court may reevaluate this determination if the Jasses present additional evidence at the continued hearing on this matter.

The hearing on confirmation of the Jasses' proposed chapter 13 plan is CONTINUED to address remaining issues in the Jasses' case.

QUESTIONS

1. What interpretation has this court given to the disposable income test that will be used for the means test in bankruptcy?
2. Why does the court make this interpretation?
3. What evidence will now be part of the determination of disposable income?

CPA 4. Declaration of Involuntary Bankruptcy

(A) Eligibility. An **involuntary bankruptcy** is begun when creditors file a petition with the bankruptcy court. An involuntary case may be commenced against any individual, partnership, or corporation, except those excluded from filing voluntary petitions. Nonprofit corporations are also exempt from involuntary proceedings.[10]

[10] 11 U.S.C. §303(a). *In re C.W. Min. Co.*, 431 B.R. 307 (Utah 2009). These amounts are adjusted periodically by statutory formulas.

Thinking Things Through

Means Test Justifying the End of Debt

The following excerpt is a hypothetical case an experienced bankruptcy attorney worked through to illustrate the application of the means test.

The Brokes, a married couple in their early 40s, have two children in private schools. They are residents of Memphis, Shelby County, Tennessee; their annual gross income is $86,496. Like many debtors, the Brokes lost their home following an unsuccessful Chapter 13 case three years ago. They now rent a house for $2,000 a month. They owe back federal taxes in the amount of $9,000. They have secured debt on two cars with remaining balances of $10,000 and $6,000 and unsecured, consumer debt totaling $28,000. They desire to seek relief under Chapter 7 of the Bankruptcy Code.

The Brokes' gross monthly income is $7,208. After deducting taxes and other mandatory payroll deductions of $1,509, the couple has $5,699 in monthly income. The means test requires several additional deductions from the Brokes' gross monthly income. Section 707(b)(A)(2)(ii) provides a deduction for living and housing expenses using National Standards and Local Standards and additional Internal Revenue Service (IRS) figures. Allowable living expenses for a family of four in Ura and Ima Brokes' income bracket, based on national standards, total $1,564, while housing and utility figures for Shelby County, Tennessee, allow $1,354. In addition, there are allowable expenses for transportation. Based on IRS figures, the Brokes can subtract national ownership costs of $475 for the first car and $338 for the second, as well as regional operating and public transportation costs of $242 and $336, respectively. They can also deduct their reasonably necessary health insurance costs, here the sum of $600, and $250 a month for private school tuition. Subtracting all of these figures from the Brokes' monthly income leaves $540.

Under §707(b)(2)(A)(iii), the Brokes can subtract payments on secured debt. The amount contractually due on their two automobiles over the next 60 months is $16,000. After dividing this total by 60 and rounding to the nearest dollar, the monthly allowable deduction for secured debt is $267. Subtracting this amount from $540 leaves $273.

Next come priority claim deductions. The Brokes are not subject to any child support or alimony claims, but they do owe $9,000 in back taxes. Again, dividing this amount by 60 yields a deductible amount of $150. Subtracting this from $273 leaves $123 in disposable monthly income. This figure would be multiplied by 60, amounting to a total of $7,380 in disposable income over the five-year period. Abuse is thus statutorily presumed because the debtors' current monthly income reduced by allowable amounts is not less than either $7,000 (25 percent of their nonpriority unsecured claims of $28,000) or $6,000. The Brokes' Chapter 7 case will therefore be dismissed (or they will be allowed voluntarily to convert their Chapter 7 case to a case under Chapter 13).

Does the means test make it more difficult for debtors to declare bankruptcy?*

*Robert J. Landry III and Nancy Hisey Mardis, "Consumer Bankruptcy Reform: Debtors' Prison without Bars or 'Just Desserts' for Deadbeats?" 36 *Golden Gate U. L. Rev.* 91 (2006). Reprinted with permission.

CPA **(b) Number and Claims of Petitioning Creditors.** If there are 12 or more creditors, at least 3 of those creditors whose unsecured and undisputed claims total $14,425 or more must sign the involuntary petition.[11] If there are fewer than 12 creditors, excluding employees or insiders (that is, the debtor's relatives, partners, directors, and controlling persons), any creditor whose unsecured claim is at least $14,425 may sign the petition. In the case of involuntary consumer petitions, there is disagreement as to whether the debtor will still be required to complete the credit counseling requirement prior to the granting of the automatic stay.

If a creditor holds security for a claim, only the amount of the claim in excess of the value of the security is counted. The holder of a claim that is the subject of a **bona fide** dispute may not be counted as a petitioning creditor.[12] **For Example,** David, a CPA, is an unsecured creditor of Arco Company for $15,000. Arco has a total of 10 creditors, all of whom are unsecured. Arco has not paid any of the creditors for three months. The debtor has fewer than 12 creditors. Any one of the creditors may file the petition if the unsecured portion of the amount due that creditor is at least $14,425.[13] Because David is owed $15,000 in unsecured debts, he may file the petition alone.

[11] 11 U.S.C. §303. The term "undisputed" was added to this section. *In re Memorial Medical Center, Inc.*, 337 B.R. 388 (D.N.M. 2005).

[12] 11 U.S.C. §303(b)(1). *In re Ballato*, 252 B.R. 553 (M.D. Fla. 2000).

[13] The amount was $10,000 originally, but the bankruptcy reforms had a built-in clause for increases in this figure.

CPA (c) Grounds for Relief for Involuntary Case. The mere filing of an involuntary case petition does not result in an order of relief. The debtor may contest the bankruptcy petition. If the debtor does not contest the petition, the court will enter an order of relief if at least one of the following grounds exists: (1) The debtor is generally not paying debts as they become due or (2) within 120 days before the filing of the petition, a custodian has been appointed for the debtor's property.

CPA 5. Automatic Stay

Just the filing of either a voluntary or an involuntary petition operates as an **automatic stay**, which prevents creditors from taking action, such as filing suits or foreclosure actions, against the debtor.[14] The stay freezes all creditors in their filing date positions so that no one creditor gains an advantage over other creditors. This automatic stay ends when the bankruptcy case is closed or dismissed (for example, on a finding of abuse by the debtor who has failed to survive the means-to-pay test) or when the debtor is granted a discharge. An automatic stay means that all activity by creditors with respect to collection must stop, with some exceptions incorporated for child support and other family support issues under the 2005 reforms. All litigation with the debtor is halted, and any judgments in place cannot be executed.[15]

6. If the Creditors Are Wrong: Rights of Debtor in an Involuntary Bankruptcy

If an involuntary petition is dismissed other than by consent of all petitioning creditors and the debtor, the court may award costs, reasonable attorney fees, or damages to the debtor. The damages are those that were caused by taking possession of the debtor's property. The debtor may also recover damages against any creditor who filed the petition in bad faith.[16]

Figure 35-1 provides a summary of the requirements for declaration of bankruptcy and the standards for relief.

FIGURE 35-1 *Declaration of Bankruptcy*

	Chapter 7	Chapter 11	Chapter 13
Trustee	Yes	No	Yes
Eligible persons: Individuals Partnerships Corporations	 Yes (consumer restrictions) Yes Yes	 Yes (individual restrictions) Yes Yes	 Yes (consumer restrictions) No No
Voluntary	Yes	Yes	Yes
Involuntary	Yes, except for farmers and nonprofits**	Yes, except for farmers and nonprofits	No
Exemptions	S & L's, credit unions, SBA, railroads, municipalities	Same as chapter 7 plus stockbrokers*	Only individuals allowed
Requirements-Voluntary	Debts; means test applies to consumers	Debts; means test applies to consumers	Income plus <$360,475 unsecured debt; <$1,081,400 secured debt
Requirements-Involuntary	<12 = 1/$14,425 ≥12 = 3/$14,425	<12 = 1/$14,425 ≥12 = 3/$14,425	N/A

*Railroads are eligible
**Chapter 9 — Municipalities; Chapter 12 — Farmers

[14] 11 U.S.C. §362. *In re Webb*, 2012 WL 1150139 (Ohio) and *In re Wolverine Fire Apparatus Co. of Sherwood Michigan*, 465 B.R. 808 (E.D. Wis. 2012). Proceeding with the foreclosure on a home after a stay is entered is a violation of the stay order. *In re Gonzalez*, 456 B.R. 429 (C.D. Cal. 2011).

[15] The reforms exempt dissolution, custody, child support, and other related litigation from the stay.

[16] *Arizona Public Service v. Apache County*, 857 P. 2d 1339 (Ariz. App. 1993).

C. Administration of the Bankruptcy Estate

The administration of the bankruptcy estate varies according to the type of bankruptcy declared. This section of the chapter focuses on the process for liquidation or Chapter 7 bankruptcy. Figure 35-2 provides a flowchart view of the Chapter 7 liquidation process.

7. The Order of Relief

The **order of relief** is granted by the bankruptcy court and is the procedural step required for the case to proceed in bankruptcy court.[17] An order of relief is entered automatically in a voluntary case and in an involuntary case when those filing the petition have established that the debtor is unable to pay his, her, or its debts as they become due. In consumer cases and Chapter 11 cases that involve an individual, the bankruptcy court must apply the means test to determine whether the individual is eligible for declaring bankruptcy or whether there has been an abuse of the bankruptcy court and system.

Sports & Entertainment Law

From Millions to Nada: Celebrity Bankruptcies

- Michael Vick, who was one of the highest paid NFL players, filed for bankruptcy in 2008, from prison. Mr. Vick could not afford to pay his bills as well as the fines that were imposed when he entered a guilty plea on charges related to a dog-fighting operation. The former Atlanta Falcons player would not have the fines discharged in bankruptcy, but he was relieved of his other debts related to his personal property.
- MC Hammer, the "Hammer Time" mega star of the early 1990s declared bankruptcy in 1996 with $9.6 million in assets and $13.7 million in debts. Mr. Hammer's problem was that he had salary costs of $500,000 per month in order to maintain his entourage.
- Mike Tyson, the champ, facing sexual harassment charges, and the lawyer fees that go with them, declared bankruptcy in 2003. Today, Mr. Tyson says that he is broke but happy.
- Willie Nelson, Country Western singer, declared bankruptcy in 1990, a necessary result of his owing $16.7 million in taxes because the IRS won its case on Nelson's tax shelters, which were fraudulent. Mr. Nelson also said that he had too many hangers-on that he was supporting. Mr. Nelson was not able to get all of his tax debt discharged because the last three years survive bankruptcy. That is, not all tax debts are fully dischargeable and there is no discharge allowed for tax debts that resulted from fraud.
- Walt Disney, the founder of Disney Films, Disneyland, Disney World, and Disney Entertainment, declared bankruptcy in Kansas City before he moved to Hollywood. Mr. Disney ran a small animation studio there and when his only customer went bankrupt, Mr. Disney tried to continue on, living in his office and eating only canned beans. He eventually gave up, declared bankruptcy, and moved to Hollywood, where his animation skills were welcomed and, as a result, he founded an empire.
- Sir Elton John is the quintessential profligate spender whose purchases landed him in bankruptcy. By the time he declared bankruptcy in 2002, Sir Elton had credit card charges of $400,000 per month. His total debt per month was $2,000,000. He was discharged from most of his credit card and contract debt.
- Sinbad, the comedian, failed to pay taxes on his earnings from *Jingle All the Way*. California's Department of Revenue filed a $2.5 million lien on his home and he and his wife declared bankruptcy shortly after in 2009. Again, California will be paid, but the comedian and his spouse are relieved of other debts.
- Gary Coleman, the 4'8" comedian/actor, simply could not pay all the medical bills related to his various health problems. He was once worth $7,000,000 but declared bankruptcy with $72,000 in debt and no assets. The actor passed away in 2010 and there is an ongoing dispute among relatives over his estate, which grew after his bankruptcy.

What are the causes of bankruptcy? What advice would you give to celebrities and athletes about management of their income and bills?

[17] 11 U.S.C. §301.

8. List of Creditors

It is the debtor's responsibility to furnish the bankruptcy court with a list of creditors. Although imposing the responsibility for disclosing debts on the debtor may not seem to be effective, the debtor has an incentive for full disclosure. Those debts not disclosed by the debtor will not be discharged in bankruptcy.

9. Trustee in Bankruptcy

The **trustee in bankruptcy** is elected by the creditors. The court or the U.S. trustee will appoint an interim trustee if the creditors do not elect a trustee.

The trustee is the successor to the property rights of the debtor. By operation of law, the trustee automatically becomes the owner of all of the debtor's property in excess of the property to which the debtor

FIGURE 35-2 *Anatomy of Bankruptcy Case*

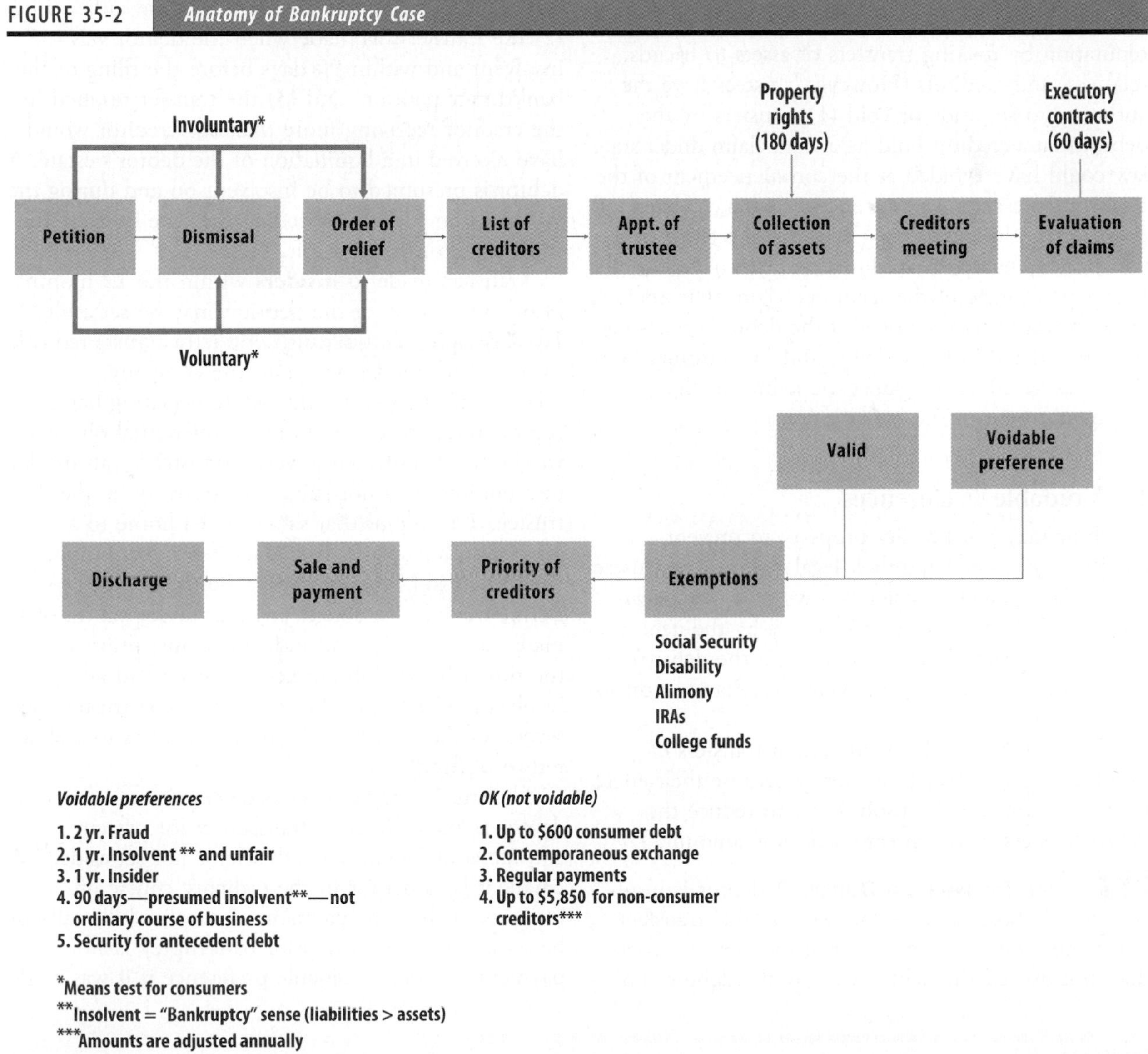

is entitled under exemption laws. The trustee holds all of the rights formerly owned by the debtor.

CPA 10. The Bankrupt's Estate

All of the debtor's property, with certain exceptions discussed later, is included in the *bankrupt's estate.* Property inherited by the debtor within six months after the filing of the petition also passes to the trustee.

In many cases, when a debtor knows that insolvency is a problem and bankruptcy is imminent, the debtor attempts to hang onto property or reputation by making transfers of assets to friends, relatives, and creditors. However, trustees have the authority to set aside or void (1) transfers by the debtor that a creditor holding a valid claim under state law could have avoided at the commencement of the bankruptcy case, (2) **preferences**, that is, transfers of property by the debtor to a creditor, the effect of which is to enable the creditor to obtain payment of a higher percentage of the creditor's claim than the creditor would have received if the debtor's assets had been liquidated in bankruptcy, and (3) statutory liens that became effective against the debtor at the commencement of the bankruptcy.

11. Voidable Preferences

A debtor may not transfer property to prevent creditors from satisfying their legal claims. The trustee may void any such transfer, known as a *fraudulent transfer,* made or obligation incurred by the debtor within two years of bankruptcy when the debtor's actual intent was to hinder, delay, or defraud creditors by doing so.[18]

The trustee may also void certain transfers of property made by a debtor merely because their effect is to make the debtor insolvent or to reduce the debtor's assets to an unreasonably low amount.[19]

CPA **(A) The Insolvent Debtor.** A debtor is insolvent for purposes of determining voidable transfers when the total fair value of all of the debtor's assets does not exceed the debts owed by the debtor. This test for **insolvency** under voidable transfers is commonly called the **balance sheet test** because it is merely a comparison of assets to liabilities without considering whether the debtor will be able to meet future obligations as they become due. The debtor is presumed to be insolvent in the 90 days prior to declaration of bankruptcy.

(B) Preferential Transfers. A transfer of property by the debtor to a creditor may be set aside as **preferential transfers** and the property recovered by the debtor's trustee in bankruptcy if (1) the transfer was made to pay a debt incurred at some earlier time, (2) the transfer was made when the debtor was insolvent and within 90 days before the filing of the bankruptcy petition, and (3) the transfer resulted in the creditor receiving more than the creditor would have received in a liquidation of the debtor's estate. A debtor is presumed to be insolvent on and during the 90 days immediately preceding the date of the filing of the bankruptcy petition.[20]

Transfers made to **insiders** within the 12 months prior to the filing of the petition may be set aside.[21] **For Example,** if a building contractor transferred title to one of his model homes to the company accountant just six months before declaring bankruptcy, the transfer would be a preferential one that would be set aside. However, a transfer by an insider to a noninsider is not subject to recovery by the trustee. The sale of that same model home to a good faith buyer just three days before bankruptcy would be valid. **For Example,** the trustee in the Bernie Madoff case sought to set aside several transfers made to companies and individuals just prior to the time Mr. Madoff admitted that he had an insolvent, $50-billion Ponzi scheme. The trustee used several of the voidable preferences theories to seek a return of funds.

The trustee may not set aside certain transfers by a debtor as preferences. A transaction for present consideration, such as a cash sale, is not set aside.[22] A payment by a debtor in the ordinary course of business, such as the payment of a utility bill, will not be set aside. Under the prior bankruptcy law, a payment was not a voidable preference if it was made

[18] Prior to the reforms, the time period for fraudulent transfers was one year. *Grochocinski v. Schlossberg*, 402 B.R. 825 (N.D. Ill. 2009).

[19] 11 U.S.C. §548.

[20] 11 U.S.C. §547(f).

[21] 11 U.S.C. §547(b)(4)(B). *In re Manhattan Inv. Fund Ltd.*, 421 B.R. 613 (S.D.N.Y. 2009).

[22] *In re Smith Min. and Material, LLC*, 405 B.R. 589 (W.D. Ky. 2009).

in the ordinary course of business and it was made according to industry terms and practices. Under the 2005 reforms, the *and* is changed to *or,* and it is now easier for creditors to show that they were not the recipients of a voidable preference. Also under the 2005 reforms, nonconsumer debt payments that have a value of less than $5,850 are not subject to the voidable preference standards. The expectation is that the time and effort spent by bankruptcy trustees and courts will be reduced because of the minimum amount required before a challenge can be made. In nonconsumer debts, transfers of less than $5,850 within the voidable preference period are not considered voidable preferences.

The In *re Ames Dept. Stores* case deals with a voidable preference question.

In re Ames Dept. Stores, Inc., 450 B.R. 24 (S.D.N.Y. 2011)

Favoring Friends and Paying Early and Often

Ames Department Stores operated over 400 retail stores throughout the northeastern United States. Promotions and advertising were crucial to Ames' business strategy, and Ames attributed over 50 percent of store revenue to advertised sales. Cellmark was Ames' principal paper supplier for all of these circulars, including the Home Book. Ames was also one of Cellmark's largest customers and top credit exposures.

Between June 1, 2000, and the beginning of the preference period (the "Preference Period")—90 days before Ames filed for Chapter 11 bankruptcy on August 20, 2001,—Ames employed an automated accounts payable system created by Oracle to track orders and generate payments to all of its domestic merchandise vendors. During that same period, Ames paid invoices in full at or around the invoice due date, because its computerized payables system automatically printed checks according to payment due date without regard to the identity of the vendor. The computer-generated checks were routinely mailed to vendors within a day or two of being printed. In the three years of the parties' prior dealings, Cellmark issued approximately 300 invoices to Ames.

In May 2001, as Ames' cash was becoming increasingly tight, Ames executives, including CFO Rolando de Aguiar, began holding regular meetings to decide which vendors should be paid. The decisions were based on the identity of the vendor and the needs of Ames' business. By August 2001, in the last three weeks before Ames' Chapter 11 filing, Ames was not issuing any checks to its creditors through a general check run. Instead, Ames issued checks only to pay invoices specifically selected out of the Oracle database and based on specific requests.

Eugene Bankers, Ames' Senior Vice President of Marketing and Advertising, or someone acting on his behalf, repeatedly inquired about the status of payments to Cellmark.

Bankers communicated to others at Ames that if Ames did not send payment to Cellmark, Ames would not get the circular out, and it would go out of business. Bankers told Cellmark CEO Joe Hoffman that he was "aggressive with [Ames'] finance department to make sure that checks sent were being sent on a continuity [sic] basis to them."

The bankruptcy trustee sought to recover approximately $1.9 million that Ames had made by three checks to Cellmark for four invoices in the two weeks before filing for bankruptcy:

1. a check for $700,000.00 (the "$700,000 Check"), issued on August 6, 2001, that cleared on August 10, 2001;
2. a check for $690,690.52 (the "$691,000 Check"), issued on August 9, 2001, that cleared on August 13, 2001; and
3. a check for $764,918.81 (the "$765,000 Check"), issued on August 13, 2001, that cleared on August 15, 2001.

As of the Petition Date, Ames did not owe Cellmark anything.

JUDICIAL OPINION

GERBER, Bankruptcy Judge…Preferential transfers, referred to colloquially as "preferences," are recoverable because they run contrary to the goal of equality of treatment amongst creditors—one of the longest standing, and fundamental, principles of American bankruptcy law. It is not unlawful or otherwise improper to receive a preference, but when the requirements of the Code are satisfied, and no applicable defense is available, preferences must be returned to the estate, so they then may be made available for the entirety of the unsecured creditor community.

To establish the avoidability of a preferential transfer, section 547(b) of the Code requires the Debtor to demonstrate by a preponderance of the evidence that the transfer was:

1. to or for the benefit of a creditor;
2. for or on account of an antecedent debt owed by the debtor before such transfer was made;
3. made while the debtor was insolvent;

Continued

4. made [during the Preference Period]...; and
5. ...[enabled the creditor] to receive more than such creditor would receive [if the creditor received payment on the debt in a chapter 7 liquidation, rather than through the transfer]....

Here the parties have stipulated that the first, second, fourth and fifth of the above-listed requirements are satisfied.

Cellmark defends this action by challenging insolvency (the third of the requirements listed above), and by alleging that the payments were received in the ordinary course.

The definition of "insolvent" appears in section 101(32) [and] defines the term "insolvent," in the context of a corporate business debtor, to mean "financial condition such that the sum of such entity's debts is greater than all of such entity's property, at a fair valuation...."

Under section 547(f) of the Code, the debtor is presumed to have been insolvent on and for the 90 days preceding the bankruptcy filing.

Cellmark's assertions that omissions in Ames' financial statements support Ames' solvency are without merit. Cellmark misses the point that Ames' statements do not include $200 million of bond debt that Ames guaranteed to its corporate parent. But apart from that, Cellmark's reliance only on statements of assets and liabilities was insufficient to rebut the presumption of insolvency. Cellmark offered no evidence of the fair market value of Ames' merchandise inventory, or other, less valuable, assets.

To prevail on the ordinary course of business defense, in this pre–2005 chapter 11 case, Cellmark needs to establish that the debt was incurred by Ames in the ordinary course of its business.

The baseline of 300 invoices and payments between Ames and Cellmark revealed that prior to the Preference Period, Ames paid Cellmark invoices in full and shortly after the due date. In the entire relationship with Cellmark, there were no instances where Ames made partial payment on an invoice; no instances where Ames issued a lump sum check; no instances where Ames paid a manually generated invoice; and no instances in the year before the Preference Period that Ames paid an invoice early. In each of these respects, the payments to Cellmark at issue here were different.

Cellmark observes that here the payments at issue were not made in response to any communications or pressure from Cellmark, and argues that this means that the payments were made in the ordinary course of business between Ames and Cellmark. The Court cannot agree.

First, Invoice 70 was out-of-sequence and manually prepared. A manually prepared invoice was unprecedented in the three-year relationship between Ames and Cellmark.

Second, Invoice 70 was paid in two partial payments. While a split payment is not necessarily outside of the ordinary course, it may be atypical for the parties. Here it was the first time that a split payment had been made in Cellmark and Ames' relationship.

Third, Invoice 70 was sent out earlier than corresponding Home Book invoices from the previous two years. Invoice 70's due date was August 2, 2001, which is about three weeks earlier than payment on account of a Home Book invoice had been due in the two years before the Preference Period.

Though there is no evidence of Cellmark directly communicating with Ames and coercing Ames to make an earlier payment, Ames understood, that payment to Cellmark was necessary to keep the business going. This is not to say that either Cellmark acted wrongfully in this regard. It is merely to say that the payments to Cellmark at this time were no longer ordinary, and cannot be found to have been in the ordinary course.

Similarly, in material respects, the third payment—the $765,000 Check on account of invoices # 15993 and # 16131—was made before the payment was due. Cellmark offered no discount for early payment. The early payment of two invoices was without any incentive to do so, and had never been done in the year before the Preference Period. Ames' computer system would have ordinarily not cut the check until the pay date, and an override of the system was necessary to make these payments. Also, of course, the third payment was made in the same context of the first two payments—Ames' perception that Cellmark, above other creditors, had to be paid to achieve critical marketing needs.

[Thus the Court finds, as mixed question of fact and law, that the transfers were not in the ordinary course, and that Cellmark has failed to establish this defense.]

[The Court determines that each of the three Ames payments in question was made while Ames was insolvent, and finds the ordinary course defense to be inapplicable.]

QUESTIONS

1. What does this decision teach us about regularity of payments and patterns of invoicing and payment?
2. Why does Cellmark lose the argument on solvency?
3. What did Ames officials do that resulted in a problem with ordinary course findings?

(c) Self-Settled Trust. Under the Reform Act, the trustee has the ability to set aside the transfer of property into a "self-settled" (a self-created personal trust) any time within the past 10 years if the trustee can establish that the trust was created with actual intent to hinder, delay, or defraud existing or future creditors.[23] This section was added to address the problem of the many assets of individuals being in personal trusts for which those individuals serve as trustees.

12. Proof of Claim

Bankruptcy law regulates the manner in which creditors present their claims and the way in which the debtor's assets are distributed in payment of these claims.

After the debtor has filed a list of creditors, the court then sends a notice of the bankruptcy proceedings to listed creditors. The creditors who wish to participate in the distribution of the proceeds of the liquidation of the debtor's estate must file a proof of claim. A **claim** is a right to payment, whether liquidated (certain and not disputed), unliquidated, contingent, unmatured, disputed, legal, or equitable. A **proof of claim** is a written statement, signed by the creditor or an authorized representative, setting forth any claim made against the debtor and the basis for it. It must ordinarily be filed within 90 days after the first meeting of creditors.[24] A creditor must file within that time even though the trustee in bankruptcy in fact knows of the existence of the creditor's claim.

CPA 13. Priority of Claims

Creditors who hold security for payment, such as a lien or a mortgage on the debtor's property, are less affected by the debtor's bankruptcy. Secured creditors may enforce their security interest to obtain payment of their claims up to the value of their security, the collateral in which they hold an interest. **For Example,** suppose that First Bank holds a mortgage on a company's office building. The mortgage amount is $750,000. The building is sold for $700,000. First Bank is entitled to the $700,000 from the sale. For the remaining portion of the debt, First Bank drops down in priority to wait with the other unsecured creditors for its remaining $50,000. Unsecured creditors with unsecured debts have a statutory order of priority following the secured creditors' rights in their collateral as outlined in the list that appears below.[25] Once the bottom of the priority list is reached, any remaining unsecured creditors share on a *pro rata* basis any remaining assets of the debtor. Any balance remaining after all creditors have been paid goes to the debtor. However, in 98 to 99 percent of all bankruptcies, no unsecured creditors receive any payments, so it is highly unlikely that the debtor would ever receive anything from the bankruptcy litigation of the debtor's property and funds.

The list below is the statutory one for priorities of the unsecured creditors following the payment to any secured creditors from the debtors' pledged property:[26]

1. Allowed claims for debts to a spouse, former spouse, or child of the debtor and for alimony to, maintenance for, or support of such spouse or child (that were obligations at the time of the filing of the bankruptcy petition).
2. Costs and expenses of administration of the bankruptcy case, including fees to trustees, attorneys, and accountants, and the reasonable expenses of creditors in recovering property transferred or concealed by the debtor.
3. Claims arising in the ordinary course of a debtor's business or financial affairs after the commencement of the case but before the order of relief (involuntary).
4. Claims for wages, salaries, or commissions, including vacation, severance, or sick leave pay earned within 180 days before the filing of the petition or the date of cessation of the debtor's business, whichever occurred first, limited, however, to $11,725 for each person.[27]

[23] 11 U.S.C. §548(e).

[24] 11 U.S.C. §302(c).

[25] 11 U.S.C. §507(1)–(6). Secured creditors' priority is determined by the priority rules related to Article 9, liens, and mortgages. *In re Black Angus Holdings, LLC*, 434 B.R. 612 (D. Kan. 2010).

[26] 11 U.S.C. §507. *In re Penaran*, 424 B.R. 868 (D. Kan. 2010). Debts owed to government agencies for unlawful receipt of food stamps are grouped in with alimony and support payments. *Wisconsin Dept. of Workforce Development v. Ratliff*, 390 B.R. 607 (E.D. Wis. 2008).

[27] Claims involving wage disputes or discrimination are treated as the claims of unsecured creditors. *In re Trans World Airlines, Inc.*, 322 F.3d 283 (3rd Cir. 2003).

5. Claims arising for contributions to employee benefit plans, based on services rendered within 180 days before the filing of the petition or when the debtor ceased doing business, whichever occurred first; the maximum amount is $11,725. Under the 2005 reforms (especially in Chapter 11 reorganizations), payments of key-employee retention plans are not permitted unless the plans are "essential" to keeping the key employee at the company that is in bankruptcy. Proving that they are essential requires the key employee actually to have a "bona fide" offer of employment from another company. In addition, there are limits on how much can be paid under key-employee retention plans.
6. Farm producers (up to $5,775) and fishers against debtors who operate grain storage facilities or fish storage or processing facilities, up to $5,775 per claim.
7. Claims by consumer creditors, not to exceed $2,600 for each claimant, arising from the purchase of consumer goods or services when such property or services were not delivered or provided.
8. Certain taxes and penalties due government, such as income and property taxes (there are time limits, for example, three years is the general time limit, with exceptions for fraud).
9. All other unsecured creditors.
10. Tort claims for death or personal injury resulting from operation of a vehicle or vessel while intoxicated from alcohol, drug, and other substances.
11. Remainder (if any) to debtor.

Each claim must be paid in full before any lower claim is paid anything. If a class of claims cannot be paid in full, the claims in that case are paid on a *pro rata* basis. **For Example,** suppose that following the payment of all secured creditors, $10,000 is left to be distributed. The accountants who performed work on the bankruptcy are owed $15,000, and the lawyers who worked on it are owed $10,000. Because there is not enough to pay two parties in the same priority ranking, the $10,000 is split proportionately. The accountants will receive 15/25, or 3/5, of the $10,000, or $6,000, and the lawyers will receive 10/25, or 2/5, of the $10,000, or $4,000.

D. Debtor's Duties and Exemptions

Bankruptcy law imposes certain duties on the debtor and provides for specific exemptions of some of the debtor's estate from the claims of creditors.

14. Debtor's Duties

A debtor must file with the court a list of creditors, a schedule of assets and liabilities, and a statement of her financial affairs. The debtor must also appear for examination under oath at the first meeting of creditors.

CPA 15. Debtor's Exemptions

A debtor is permitted to claim certain property of the estate in the trustee's possession and keep it free from claims of creditors. Exemptions are provided under federal law, but state laws also provide for exemptions. In 14 states (examples are Massachusetts, New Jersey, Pennsylvania, and Connecticut), debtors can elect either federal or state exemption. In the other states (New York, California, Florida, and Delaware are examples), debtors are permitted to use only the state exemptions.[28] Examples of exempt property from the federal code include wedding rings, property used to earn a living, one VCR, and one car. New York exemptions include "all stoves in the home, one sewing machine, the family Bible, a pew in a public house of worship, enough food for sixty days, a wedding ring, and a watch not exceeding thirty-five dollars in value."[29] California exempts tools of the trade and the family cemetery plot.[30]

The principal exemptions provided by the Bankruptcy Code are the debtor's interest in real or personal property used as a residence.[31] The Reform Act has greatly limited the homestead exemption

[28] 11 U.S.C. §522.

[29] N.Y. C.P.L.R. §5205 (2010).

[30] Cal. Civ. Proc. Code §704.010-704.210 (2009).

[31] A married couple gets a single homestead exemption. Gay couples who have registered under state domestic partner rights statutes are also entitled to only one homestead exemption. *In re Rabin*, 359 B.R. 242 (2007).

and, in effect, preempts state law on this debtor exemption. Debtors are required to have lived in the home for two years prior to bankruptcy, and the amount of the homestead exemption would be limited to $146,450.[32] To be able to use a higher state homestead exemption, the debtor must have lived in the home for 1215 days (40 months).[33] Labeled as the most flagrant abuse of the existing bankruptcy system, debtors have used the homestead exemption to shift their assets into expensive homes to shield everything from bankruptcy. Known as the "mansion loophole," the changes in the Reform Act related to the homestead exemption were among the most debated and the most dramatic.[34] **For Example,** prior to the reforms actor Burt Reynolds declared bankruptcy in Florida and was relieved of millions in debt, but he was able to keep his $2.5 million Valhalla estate there. Corporate raider Paul Bilzerian, who was convicted of securities fraud, also declared bankruptcy in Florida but kept his mansion, the largest home in Hillsborough County, Florida. Former WorldCom CFO Scott Sullivan (who entered a guilty plea to fraud and other charges and is serving a five-year sentence) built a multimillion-dollar home in Florida to gain homestead protections. Wendy Gramm, who sat on Enron's board, purchased 200 acres of land in Texas and constructed a large home with her husband, former senator Phil Gramm, to take advantage of homestead exemptions then available in Texas. However, the Reform Act closed this corporate executive loophole by requiring that the $146,450 exemption apply to debtors who are convicted of securities fraud or bankruptcy fraud.[35]

Other exemptions include payments under a life insurance contract, alimony and child support payments, and awards from personal injury litigation.[36] Under the Reform Act, college savings accounts and IRAs are exempt property under the federal exemptions and can be used even by those debtors who are using state exemptions. The IRA exemption is limited to $1,171,650.[37]

The *In re Werth* case involves a question of savings made just prior to declaring bankruptcy.

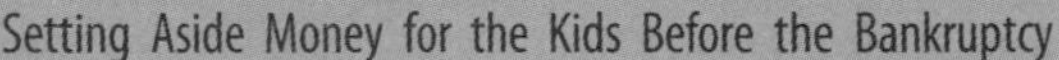

In re Werth, 468 B.R. 412 (D.Kan. 2012)

Setting Aside Money for the Kids Before the Bankruptcy

Michael and Alice Werth (debtors) filed a Chapter 7 petition on April 14, 2011, and received a discharge on January 23, 2012. On December 2, 2010, the Werths had opened two 529 accounts for the benefit of Michael Werth's two children by a previous marriage. They deposited $6,000.00 into each account. The accounts are owned by Alice Werth. By the petition date, the accounts held $12,197.12.

Michael Werth is responsible for one-half of the post-secondary educational expenses for his two children pursuant to a 2002 Separation Agreement, subject to certain limitations. As of the petition date, neither of Werth's children had yet graduated from high school.

The bankruptcy trustee moved for an order directing the debtors to turn over the balances in the two 529 education savings accounts.

JUDICIAL OPINION

BERGER, Bankruptcy Judge....The 529 accounts are property of the estate because Alice Werth owns the accounts, and the contributions were made within the year preceding bankruptcy. The accounts do not fall into either a state or federal exemption. Both the Kansas Legislature and Congress excluded 529 account contributions made within one year preceding a bankruptcy filing from a general exemption for post-secondary education savings accounts. Thus, both the state and federal statutes exempt long-term planning and savings for post-secondary education expenses, but neither provide for 529 accounts to be a pre-bankruptcy planning safe haven for assets otherwise available to pay creditors.

[32] The time requirement is at 11 U.S.C. §522(b)(3)(A), and the amount limitation is at 11 U.S.C. §522(o)(1). This amount refers to those who elect state exemptions. In the absence of state exemptions, the federal maximum is $21,625.

[33] 11 U.S.C. §522(p)(2)(B).

[34] 11 U.S.C. §522(p).

[35] 11 U.S.C. §522(q).

[36] 11 U.S.C. §522(d) (including automatic adjustments).

[37] 11 U.S.C. §522(n). There are time requirements on college savings (529) accounts in order to obtain the exemption.

Continued

The Bankruptcy Code provides special treatment for domestic support obligations; however, such treatment does not include earmarking pre-petition assets for post-petition obligations. Only a pre-petition support obligation can be a claim against the estate. Post-petition support obligations are to be paid out of the debtor's post-petition income, not from estate property. In *Coggin,* 30 F.3d 1443, 1452 (11th Cir.1994), a debtor-father attempted to pre-pay his son's college expenses prior to bankruptcy and pursuant to a divorce decree. But Coggin made the payment with pre-petition assets while insolvent and while there were many existing creditors. The *Coggin* trustee recovered the money as a fraudulent transfer even though Coggin argued the payment satisfied his obligation under the divorce to provide for his son's college education. The court found the son could not have a claim against the estate for post-petition support even though the child support obligation would not be dischargeable through Coggin's bankruptcy. The court summarized the overall plan and concept of bankruptcy are for estate assets to pay only the legitimate claims of the creditors in existence on the petition date. The future support owed to the son was not a matured debt and, thus, § 502(b)(5) would prevent the payment of such claim from estate assets. For this reason, Coggin could not be permitted to pay post-petition support from pre-petition assets before he filed for bankruptcy protection from his creditors. The Eleventh Circuit's summary of the overall plan and concept of bankruptcy regarding pre-petition assets and post-petition domestic support obligations is more persuasive than Debtors' arguments in this case.

The accounts are nonexempt estate property, and the Trustee is entitled to the turnover of the funds so he may distribute them to creditors.

QUESTIONS

1. What is the rule on 529 college accounts and bankruptcy exemptions?
2. Does it make a difference if the debtor is required to pay or save for college for his or her children pursuant to a divorce decree? Explain why or why not.
3. What advice would you give to parents in terms of college account savings surviving bankruptcy?

Businesses that declare bankruptcy would not have employee pension plan contributions included in their bankruptcy estates. Those contributions would be returned to the employees. The proposed changes are the result of the numerous large corporate bankruptcies, such as the one involving United Airlines and the pensions of its employees.[38]

16. Debtor's Protection against Discrimination

Federal, state, and local law may not discriminate against anyone on the basis of a discharge in bankruptcy. For example, a state cannot refuse to issue a new license to an individual if the license fees on a previous one have been discharged as a debt in the individual's declaration of bankruptcy.

E. Discharge in Bankruptcy

The main objectives of a bankruptcy proceeding are to collect and distribute the debtor's assets and then issue a **discharge in bankruptcy** of the debtor from obligations. The decree terminating the bankruptcy proceeding is generally a discharge that releases the debtor from most debts. Under the BAPCPA, a discharge is available only once every eight years.

17. Denial of Discharge

The court will refuse to grant a discharge if the debtor has (1) within one year of the filing of the petition fraudulently transferred or concealed property with intent to hinder, delay, or defraud creditors, (2) failed to keep proper financial records, (3) made a false oath or account,[39] (4) failed to explain satisfactorily any

[38] 11 U.S.C. §541(b).

[39] The debtor must actually make a false statement. In *In re Mercer*, 211 F.3d 214 (5th Cir. 2000), the debtor ran up $3,186.82 on a credit card she was given by AT&T with a $3,000 credit limit. The credit card was issued to the debtor on a preapproved basis, so there was no fraud, just a great deal of spending. See also *In re Carver*, 418 B.R. 734 (C.D. Ill. 2009) that did not punish a debtor because he was mixed up when he began paying his attorney.

Ethics & the Law

The Skies Are Not So Friendly to Employee Pensions

As part of its Chapter 11 bankruptcy, United Airlines was relieved of its pension liabilities. Employees and unions wonder how a company can be permitted to renege on those benefits when so many protections were built into the law under ERISA. Congressional hearings now reveal that there were loopholes in the accounting processes for pension fund reporting that permitted United, and many others, to report pension numbers that made the pension funds look healthy when they really were not. The loopholes were Enronesque in nature. Companies could spin the pension obligations off the books so that the existing levels of obligations of the plan looked small and the assets very rich. Because of United's pension bailout, Congress changed the accounting for pension plans to avoid the problem of the rosy picture when the funds really need further funding. One interesting approach to protecting pension plans is to require companies to fund the pension plans according to the numbers they have reported to the SEC in their financials. The numbers reported to the SEC for company pensions are accurate whereas the numbers reported for ERISA purposes are inflated. If United had funded its plans when its SEC numbers indicated it needed to (e.g., in 1998), the plan would have been sufficiently funded. Under ERISA guidelines, it was not required to kick in funds until 2002 when it was grossly underfunded.

Were companies acting ethically on their pension accounting? Were they acting legally?*

*Marry Williams Walsh, "Pension Law Loopholes Helped United Hide Its Troubles," *New York Times*, June 7, 2005, C1.

loss of assets, (5) refused to obey any lawful order of the court or refused to testify after having been granted immunity, (6) obtained a discharge within the last eight years,[40] (7) filed a written waiver of discharge that is approved by the court,[41] or (8) in the case of a consumer debtor, has failed to complete a personal financial management instructional course.[42]

A discharge releases the debtor from the unpaid balance of most debts except for taxes, customs duties, child support obligations, and tax penalties.[43] Student loan obligations are not discharged in bankruptcy unless the loan first became due more than seven years before bankruptcy or unless not allowing a discharge would impose undue hardship on the debtor.

In *re Looper* addresses an interesting excuse for not repaying student loans.

In re Looper, 2007 WL 1231700 (B. E.D. Tenn. 2007)

Your Living Expenses Are Fairly Minimal in Maximum Security

Bryan Anthony Looper (debtor) had over $300,000 in student loans that were used to finance his education at Mercer University where he obtained an A.B., an M.B.A, and another unspecified graduate degree as well as a large number of courses toward his J.D. degree. He did not make payments on these student loans.

In 1996, he was elected assessor for Putnam County, Tennessee, a position he held for two years and four months. He was then convicted of the first-degree murder of state senator Tommy Burks. He exhausted all of his appeals and is currently serving a life sentence without the possibility of parole. The debtor has one dependent, a son born in August 1998. The circuit court for Putnam County, Tennessee, ordered Looper to pay child support of $161.00 per month plus $7,254.20 in medical expenses. Looper did not make any of the court-ordered child support payments and was in arrears by more than $23,515.00.

Looper asked to have his student loans discharged on the basis of his hardship.

[40] 11 U.S.C. §727(a)(8).

[41] 11 U.S.C. §523.

[42] 11 U.S.C. §727(a)(11). The financial management course requirement applies to both Chapter 7 and Chapter 13 consumer bankruptcies.

[43] Child support obligations enjoy additional protections and priorities in bankruptcy. 11 U.S.C. §507(a).

Continued

JUDICIAL OPINION

STAIR, Bankruptcy Judge...The first factor before the court requires the court to assess the Debtor's standard of living and determine whether he can afford to repay his loans. "The essence of the minimal standard of living requirement" is that a debtor, after providing for his or her basic needs, may not allocate any of his or her financial resources to the detriment of...student loan creditor(s). In order to meet the minimal standard of living factor, debtors are required to "make some major sacrifices, both personal and financial, with respect to their current style of living." This does not mean, however, that debtors must "live in abject poverty." A debtor earning a modest income and living on an unbalanced budget with no unnecessary or frivolous expenses may be discharged based upon an undue hardship.

The proof shows that the Debtor has earned $1,321.60 since being incarcerated in 2000, an average of $188.80 per year. Nevertheless, the proof also shows that the Debtor does not have actual living expenses. His meals, clothing, shelter, basic medical care, dental care, and eye care are provided by the State of Tennessee. The Debtor asserts that the Tennessee Department of Corrections can assess him tens of thousands of dollars every year for health care costs, housing, board, and medical costs. However, these "facts" were disputed by ECMC, and the Debtor failed to offer into evidence any proof of their validity, and the court considers these statements to be unsubstantiated argument. Moreover, while the Debtor submitted evidence that commissary items must be purchased and argues that he requires many of these items in order to alleviate his various medical conditions, these items appear to be "extras" rather than "essentials."

The Debtor also argues that he has substantial litigation and copy expenses, requiring approximately $3,300.00 per month for his expert witness, legal copies, postage, notary fees, deposition expenses, attorneys, legal books, and research and support services. The question is whether the Debtor can meet a minimal standard of living, which includes only those expenses that are necessary for meeting the Debtor's basic needs. Based upon the proof presented, the court finds that the Debtor maintains a minimal standard of living. He earns minimal funds; however, his basic living needs are furnished by the State of Tennessee.

The second factor to be considered is the existence of "additional circumstances" to indicate that the Debtor's current financial circumstances are beyond his control and will continue into the future. The Bankruptcy Code does not provide a specific list of "additional circumstances" to be considered to indicate the persistence of a debtor's state of affairs. "Such circumstances must be indicative of a 'certainty of hopelessness, not merely a present inability to fulfill financial commitment.' They may include illness, disability, a lack of useable job skills, or the existence of a large number of dependents. And, most importantly, they must be beyond the debtor's control, not borne of free choice. Choosing a low-paying job cannot merit undue hardship relief." The Debtor must establish that his distressed state of financial affairs [is] the result of events which are clearly out of the debtor's control;...that [he has] done everything within [his] power to improve [his] financial situation [, and] that the hardship [he] is experiencing is actually "undue," as opposed to the garden variety financial hardship experienced by all debtors who file for bankruptcy relief.

The Debtor argues that he suffers from severe health problems, including (1) chronic sinus troubles; (2) fluid/congestion in his ears; (3) dry eyes; (4) dizziness; (5) heart problems; (6) chronic enlarged veins/arteries in his chest, neck, and left arm; (7) hemorrhoids; (8) irritable bowel syndrome; (9) gastrointestinal problems; and (10) chronic knee and shoulder problems. He does not claim that these health issues are the reason for his inability to earn additional income, but he does maintain that due to these health problems, his limited funds are necessarily spent on remedies.

The Department of Education and ECMC argue that the Debtor cannot meet this prong because his circumstances are self-imposed, and the court agrees. Prior to his conviction and incarceration, the Debtor had been elected to the position of Property Assessor for Putnam County, Tennessee. He has three college degrees and has completed course work toward obtaining a law degree. It is the Debtor's own actions that led to his conviction and incarceration. While the Debtor's earning potential is decidedly limited by his incarceration, his current and future state of financial affairs is directly attributable to his actions, and he cannot escape the responsibility therefor.

Finally, under the third factor of the *Brunner/Oyler* test, the court focuses on whether the Debtor has made a good faith effort to repay the loans. Under the *Brunner/Oyler* test, the Debtor should explore payment alternatives, such as the William D. Ford Direct Loan program. Here, the Debtor did not apply for this program, stating that he did not qualify because his low income would not cover even the interest payments. The Debtor states that he did request a deferment/forbearance from Mercer University in February 1999, which it declined, and that he requested and was granted a deferment/forbearance from his other lenders, so that he did not default upon them until after his August 2000 trial. The Debtor also inquired as to loan consolidation; however, he was advised by the Office of the Ombudsman for the Department of Education that, under federal regulations, incarcerated persons in a federal or state penal institution are ineligible to participate in any of the federal financial aid program loans.

Continued

The Debtor does not dispute that he received a benefit, in the form of three degrees, from his student loans. There is also no dispute that the Debtor has never made any payments on his loan obligations to [any of his lenders]. Although the Debtor remained in school at least part-time until May 1998, thus entitling him to a deferral through November 1998, he never made a single payment on his student loan obligations following the end of his deferral period and/or any of the deferment/forbearance periods granted him.

Based upon these facts, it does not appear to the court that the Debtor has made any real effort, much less a good faith one, to repay his student loans. The Debtor never made any payments to any entity to which he owed or owes his student loan obligations, from which he has acknowledged receiving a direct benefit in the form of three degrees. His lack of earning potential and subsequent failure to repay are a direct result of his own actions. Finally, the Debtor has received a discharge of his pre-petition debts other than his student loan obligations.

[T]he court finds the Debtor can, based upon his current income and expenses, maintain a minimal standard of living for himself. [The debts are not discharged.]

QUESTIONS

1. Discuss the three factors the court examines to determine whether to discharge the student loans.

In addition, the following debts are not discharged by bankruptcy: (1) loans obtained by use of a false financial statement made with intent to deceive and on which the creditor reasonably relied, (2) debts not scheduled or listed with the court in time for allowance, (3) debts arising from fraud while the debtor was acting in a fiduciary capacity or by reason of embezzlement or larceny, (4) alimony and child support, (5) a judgment for willful and malicious injury, (6) a consumer debt to a single creditor totaling more than $5,775 for luxury goods or services (within 90 days of the order of relief) and cash advances exceeding $825 based on consumer open-end credit, such as a credit card (within 70 days of

FIGURE 35-3 ***Nondischargeable Debts in Bankruptcy***

1. Taxes within three years of filing bankruptcy petition
2. Liability for obtaining money or property by false pretenses
3. Willful and malicious injuries
4. Debts incurred by driving DWI*
5. Alimony, maintenance, or child support
6. Unscheduled debts (unless actual notice)
7. Debts resulting from fraud as a fiduciary (embezzlement)
8. Government fines or penalties imposed within three years prior
9. Educational loans due within seven prior years (unless hardship)
10. Prior bankruptcy debts in which debtor waived discharge
11. Presumption on luxury goods: $550 goods; $825 cash
12. Reaffirmation agreements
    - Writing
    - Filed with court
    - Not rescinded prior to discharge

*Includes vessels and aircraft

the order of relief),[44] (7) damages arising from drunk driving or the operation of vessels and aircrafts by people who are inebriated,[45] (8) loans used to pay taxes (including credit cards),[46] (9) taxes not paid as a result of a fraudulent return, although other unpaid taxes beyond the past three years can be discharged,[47] (10) prebankruptcy fees and assessments owed to homeowners associations, and (11) debts owed to tax-qualified retirement plans. **For Example,** in regard to (5), the finding of malice in *Goldman v. O. J. Simpson* precluded the discharge by bankruptcy of the $8.5 million damage award from Simpson to the families of his murder victims, the Goldmans and Browns. Figure 35-3 has a listing of nondischargeable debts.

F. Reorganization Plans under Chapter 11

In addition to liquidation under Chapter 7, the Bankruptcy Code permits debtors to restructure the organization and finances of their businesses so that they may continue to operate. In these rehabilitation plans, the debtor keeps all of the assets (exempt and nonexempt), continues to operate the business, and makes a settlement that is acceptable to the majority of the creditors. This settlement is binding on the minority creditors.

Individuals, partnerships, and corporations in business may all be reorganized under the Bankruptcy Code. The first step is to file a plan for the debtor's reorganization. This plan may be filed by the debtor, any party in interest, or a committee of creditors. If the debtor wishes to move from a Chapter 11 proceeding (in the case of an individual debtor), the debtor must survive the means test that is now a requirement for determining eligibility for bankruptcy.

18. Contents of the Plan

The plan divides ownership interests and debts into those that will be affected by the adoption of the plan and those that will not be. It then specifies what will be done to those interests and claims that are affected. **For Example,** when mortgage payments are too high for the income of a corporation, a possible plan would be to reduce the mortgage payments and give the mortgage holder preferred stock to compensate for the loss sustained.

All creditors, shareholders, and other interest holders within a particular class must be treated the same way. **For Example,** the holders of first mortgage bonds must all be treated similarly. The treatment of the bondholders in the Chrysler and GM bankruptcies was a point of contention and negotiation in those reorganizations.

A plan can also provide for the assumption, rejection, or assignment of executory contracts. The trustee or debtor can, under certain circumstances, suspend performance of a contract not yet fully performed. **For Example,** collective bargaining agreements may be rejected with the approval of the bankruptcy court.[48]

19. Confirmation of the Plan

After the plan is prepared, the court must approve or confirm it. A plan will be confirmed if it has been submitted in good faith and if its provisions are reasonable.[49] After the plan is confirmed, the owners and creditors of the enterprise have only the rights that are specified in the plan. They cannot go back to their original contract positions.

CPA G. Payment Plans under Chapter 13

The Bankruptcy Code also provides for the adoption of extended-time payment plans for individual debtors who have regular income. These debtors must owe unsecured debts of less than $360,475 and secured debts of less than $1,081,400.

An individual debtor who has a regular income may submit a plan for the installment payment of outstanding debts. If the court approves it, the debtor may then pay the debts in the installments specified

[44] 11 U.S.C. §523(a)(2)(c)(i). (Amounts are adjusted each year).
[45] 11 U.S.C. §523(a)(9).
[46] 11 U.S.C. §523(a)(14A),(14B).
[47] 11 U.S.C. §§1129(a)(9)(c), (D), 1129(b)(2)(B), 1141(d)(6)(B).
[48] 11 U.S.C. §1113.
[49] 11 U.S.C. §1129.

by the plan even if the creditors had not originally agreed to such installment payments.

20. Contents of the Plan

The individual debtor plan is, in effect, a budget of the debtor's future income with respect to outstanding debts. The plan must provide for the eventual payment in full of all claims entitled to priority under the Bankruptcy Code. All creditors holding the same kind or class of claim must be treated the same way.

21. Confirmation of the Plan

The plan has no effect until the court approves or confirms it. A plan will be confirmed if it was submitted in good faith and is in the best interests of the creditors.[50] When the plan is confirmed, debts are payable in the manner specified in the plan.

22. Discharge of the Debtor

After all of the payments called for by the plan have been made, the debtor is given a discharge. The discharge releases the debtor from liability for all debts except those that would not be discharged by an ordinary bankruptcy discharge.[51] Under the bankruptcy reforms, the court cannot grant a discharge until the debtor has completed an instructional course concerning personal financial management.[52] If the debtor does not perform under the plan, the creditors can move to transfer the debtor's case to a Chapter 7 proceeding, but they would still face the means test in qualifying for this move to Chapter 7.

[50] 11 U.S.C. §1325.
[51] 11 U.S.C. §1328.
[52] 11 U.S.C. §1328(g)(1).

MAKE THE CONNECTION

SUMMARY

Jurisdiction over bankruptcy cases is in U.S. district courts, which may refer all cases and related proceedings to adjunct bankruptcy courts.

Three bankruptcy proceedings are available: liquidation (Chapter 7), reorganization (Chapter 11), and extended-time payment (Chapter 13). A liquidation proceeding under Chapter 7 may be either voluntary or involuntary.

A *voluntary case* is commenced by the debtor's filing a petition with the bankruptcy court. A voluntary petition is subject to the means test to determine if the debtor meets the standard for declaring bankruptcy. An involuntary case is commenced by the creditors' filing a petition with the bankruptcy court. If there are 12 or more creditors, at least 3 whose unsecured claims total $14,425 or more must sign the involuntary petition. If there are fewer than 12 creditors, any creditor whose unsecured claim is at least $14,425 may sign the petition. If the debtor contests the bankruptcy petition, it must be shown that the debtor is not paying debts as they become due.

Eligibility for Chapters 7 and 11 bankruptcy excludes railroads, municipalities, and Small Business Administration companies. Individual debtors are restricted on Chapters 7 and 11 filings by their ability to repay. If found to have the means to pay, they go into a Chapter 13 proceeding. Chapter 13 eligibility is limited to consumers with $360,475 in unsecured debt and $1,081,400 in secured debt.

An automatic stay prevents creditors from taking legal action against the debtor after a bankruptcy petition is filed. The trustee in bankruptcy is elected by the creditors and is the successor to, and acquires the rights of, the debtor. In certain cases, the trustee can avoid transfers of property to prevent creditors from satisfying their claims. Preferential transfers may be set aside. A transfer for a present consideration, such as a cash sale, is not a preference.

Bankruptcy law regulates the way creditors present their claims and how the assets of the debtor are to be distributed in payment of the claims. Some assets of the debtor are exempt from the bankruptcy estate, such as a portion of the value of the debtor's home.

Secured claims are not affected by the debtor's bankruptcy. Unsecured claims are paid in the following order of priority:

1. Support or maintenance for a spouse, former spouse, or child.
2. Costs and expenses of administration of the bankruptcy case.
3. Claims arising in the ordinary course of a debtor's business or financial affairs after the commencement of the case but before the order of relief (involuntary).
4. Claims for wages, salaries, or commissions, including vacation, severance, or sick leave pay earned within 180 days before the filing of the petition or the date of cessation of the debtor's business, limited to $11,725 for each person.
5. Claims arising for contributions (up to $5,850) to employee benefit plans based on services rendered within 180 days before the filing of the petition or when the debtor ceased doing business.
6. Farm producers (up to $5,775) and fishers against debtors who operate grain storage facilities or fish produce storage or processing facilities, up to $5,775 per claim.
7. Claims by consumer creditors, not to exceed $2,600 for each claimant.
8. Certain taxes and penalties due government units, such as income and property taxes.
9. All other unsecured creditors.
10. Remainder (if any) to debtor.

The decree terminating bankruptcy proceedings is generally a discharge that releases the debtor from most debts. Certain debts, such as income taxes, student loans, loans obtained by use of a false financial statement, alimony, and debts not listed by the debtor, are not discharged.

Under Chapter 11 bankruptcy, individuals, partnerships, and corporations in business may be reorganized so that the business can continue to operate. A plan for reorganization must be approved by the court. Under a Chapter 13 bankruptcy proceeding, individual debtors with a regular income may adopt extended-time payment plans for the payment of debts. A plan for extended-time payment must also be confirmed by the court. Federal, state, and local law may not discriminate against anyone on the basis of a discharge in bankruptcy.

LEARNING OUTCOMES

After studying this chapter, you should be able to clearly explain:

A. Bankruptcy Law

B. How Bankruptcy Is Declared

LO.1 List the requirements for the commencement of a voluntary bankruptcy case and an involuntary bankruptcy case

See the Sports & Entertainment Law discussion of celebrity bankruptcies on p. 706.

See discussion of Chapters 7, 11, and 13 on pp. 700–701 and chart on p. 705.

C. Administration of the Bankruptcy Estate

LO.2 Explain the procedure for the administration of a debtor's estate

See the list of priorities on p. 711.

See *In re Ames Dept. Stores* on pp. 709–710.

D. Debtor's Duties and Exemptions

LO.3 List a debtor's duties and exemptions

See the discussion of the homestead exemptions on p. 712.

See *In re Werth* case on pp. 713–714.

E. Discharge in Bankruptcy

LO.4 Explain the significance of a discharge in bankruptcy

See *In re Looper* on pp. 715–717.

F. Reorganization Plans under Chapter 11

See Ethics & the Law, The Skies Are Not So Friendly on p. 715.

G. Payment Plans under Chapter 13

LO.5 Explain when a business reorganization plan or an extended-time payment plan might be used

See the Ethics & the Law discussion of United Airlines on p. 715.

See the discussion of Chrysler and GM on p. 718.

KEY TERMS

automatic stay
balance sheet test
bankruptcy courts
bona fide
Chapter 7 bankruptcy
Chapter 11 bankruptcy
Chapter 13 bankruptcy
claim
discharge in bankruptcy
insiders
insolvency
involuntary bankruptcy
liquidated
means test
order of relief
preferences
preferential transfers
proof of claim
trustee in bankruptcy
voluntary bankruptcy

QUESTIONS AND CASE PROBLEMS

1. Hall-Mark regularly supplied electronic parts to Peter Lee. On September 11, 1992, Lee gave Hall-Mark a $100,000 check for parts it had received. Hall-Mark continued to ship parts to Lee. On September 23, 1992, Lee's check was dishonored by the bank. On September 25, 1992, Lee delivered to Hall-Mark a cashier's check for $100,000. Hall-Mark shipped nothing more to Lee after receipt of the cashier's check. On December 24, 1992, Lee filed a voluntary petition for bankruptcy. The trustee filed a complaint to have the $100,000 payment to Hall-Mark set aside as a voidable preference. Hall-Mark said it was entitled to the payment because it gave value to Lee. The trustee said that the payment was not actually made until the cashier's check was delivered on September 25, 1992, and that Hall-Mark gave no further value to Lee after that check was paid. Who was correct? [*In re Lee*, 108 F.3d 239 (9th Cir.)]

2. Orso, who had declared bankruptcy, received a structured tort settlement in a personal injury claim he had pending. The settlement would pay him an annuity each year for 30 years because the claim was the result of an auto accident that left him permanently and severely brain damaged with an IQ of about 70. His ex-wife had a pending claim for $48,000 in arrearages on Orso's $1,000 per month child support payments. His ex-wife wanted the annuity included in the bankruptcy estate. Would this property have been included in Orso's bankruptcy estate? [*In re Orso*, 214 F.3d 637 (5th Cir.)]

3. Harold McClellan sold ice-making machinery to Bobbie Cantrell's brother for $200,000 to be paid in installment payments. McClellan took a security interest in the ice machine but did not perfect it by filing a financing statement. The brother defaulted when he owed $100,000, and McClellan brought suit. With the suit pending, the brother "sold" the ice machine to Bobbie Cantrell for $10. Bobbie then sold the machine to someone for $160,000 and refused to explain what happened to that money. McClellan added Bobbie as a defendant in his suit against her brother. Bobbie then declared bankruptcy. McClellan sought to have the various transfers set aside. The trial court refused to do so, and McClellan appealed. Should the transfers be set aside? Why or why not? [*McClellan v. Cantrell*, 217 F.3d 890 (7th Cir.)]

4. Okamoto owed money to Hornblower & Weeks-Hemphill, Noyes (a law firm and hereafter Hornblower). Hornblower filed an involuntary bankruptcy petition against Okamoto, who moved to dismiss the petition on the ground that he had more than 12 creditors and the petition

could not be filed by only one creditor. Hornblower replied that the other creditors' claims were too small to count and, therefore, the petition could be filed by one creditor. Decide. [*In re Okamoto*, 491 F.2d 496 (9th Cir.)]

5. Jane Leeves declared voluntary Chapter 7 bankruptcy. The trustee included the following property in her bankruptcy estate:
   - Jane's wedding ring
   - Jane's computer for her consulting business that she operated from her home
   - Jane's car payment from a client in the amount of $5,000 that was received 91 days after Jane filed bankruptcy

   After collecting all of Jane's assets, the bankruptcy trustee was trying to decide how to distribute the assets. Jane had the following creditors:
   - Mortgage company—owed $187,000 (the trustee sold Jane's house for $190,000)
   - Expenses of the bankruptcy—$3,000
   - Federal income taxes—$11,000
   - Utility bills—$1,000
   - Office supply store open account—$1,000

   The trustee had $11,500 in cash, including the $3,000 additional cash left from the sale of the house after the mortgage company was paid. How should the trustee distribute this money? What if the amount were $14,500; how should that be distributed?

6. Kentile sold goods over an extended period of time to Winham. The credit relationship began without Winham's being required to furnish a financial statement. After a time, payments were not made regularly, and Kentile requested a financial statement. Winham submitted a statement for the year just ended. Kentile requested a second statement. The second statement was false. Kentile objected to Winham's discharge in bankruptcy because of the false financial statement. Should the discharge be granted? Why or why not?

7. D. Erik Von Kiel obtained loans from the U.S. Department of Health & Human Services so that he could complete his education as an osteopathic physician. He works at the International Academy of Life (IAL) in Orem, Utah, for no salary but receives gifts from IAL that total $150,000 per year, or about $12,787 per month. He pays no taxes on these "gifts" and has received them since 2005. Dr. Von Kiel pays all but $1,000 to his ex-wife and nine children for their support. He has given up his practice, taken a vow of poverty, and works at IAL to concentrate on alternative medicine. He has signed over full authority for the management of his financial affairs to two individuals, who apparently failed to manage wisely. As a result, Dr. Von Kiel filed for bankruptcy in order to be discharged from his HHS loans. HHS says that Dr. Von Kiel should not be discharged because of bad faith. Who is correct and why? [*In re Von Kiel*, 461 B.R. 323 (E.D. Pa.)]

8. Sonia, a retailer, has the following assets: a factory worth $1 million; accounts receivable amounting to $750,000, which fall due in four to six months; and $20,000 cash in the bank. Sonia's sole liability is a $200,000 note falling due today, which she is unable to pay. Can Sonia be forced into involuntary bankruptcy under the Bankruptcy Code?

9. Samson Industries ceased doing business and is in bankruptcy proceedings. Among the creditors are five employees seeking unpaid wages. Three of the employees are owed $3,500 each, and two are owed $1,500 each. These amounts became due within 90 days preceding the filing of the petition. Where, in the priority of claims, will the employees' wage claims fall?

10. Carol Cott, doing business as Carol Cott Fashions, is worried about an involuntary bankruptcy proceeding being filed by her creditors. Her net worth, using a balance sheet approach, is $8,000 ($108,000 in assets minus $100,000 in liabilities). However, her cash flow is negative, and she has been hard pressed to meet current obligations as they mature. She is in fact some $12,500 in arrears in payments to her creditors on bills submitted during the past two months. Will the fact that Cott is solvent in the balance-sheet sense result in the court's dismissing the creditors' petition if Cott objects to the petition? Explain.

11. On July 1, Roger Walsh, a sole proprietor operating a grocery, was involuntarily petitioned into bankruptcy by his creditors. At that time, and for at least 90 days prior to that time, Walsh was unable to pay current obligations. On June 16, Walsh paid the May electric bill for his business. The trustee in bankruptcy claimed that this payment was a voidable preference. Was the trustee correct? Explain.

12. Steven and Teresa Hornsby are married and have three young children. On May 25, 1993, the Hornsbys filed a voluntary Chapter 7 petition. They had by that date accumulated more than $30,000 in debt, stemming almost entirely from student loans. They wanted a discharge of their student loans on grounds of undue hardship. The Hornsbys attended a succession of small Tennessee state colleges. Both studied business and computers, but neither graduated. Although they received several deferments and forbearances on the loans, they ultimately defaulted before making any payments. Interest had accumulated on the loans to the extent that Steven was indebted to the Tennessee Student Assistance Corporation (TSAC) for $15,058.52, and Teresa was indebted to TSAC for $18,329.15.

    Steven was working for AT&T in Dallas, Texas; he made $6.53 per hour, occasionally working limited overtime hours. Teresa was employed by KinderCare Learning Center. Although she had begun work in Tennessee, she had transferred to become the director of a child care facility in Dallas. Teresa was earning $17,500 per year with medical benefits at the time of the hearing. In monthly net income, Steven earned approximately $1,083.33, and Teresa earned $1,473.33, amounting to $2,556.66 of disposable income per month. The Hornsbys' reported monthly expenses came to $2,364.90. They operated with a monthly surplus of $191.76 to $280.43, depending on whether Steven earned overtime for a particular month. Under the federal bankruptcy laws, are the Hornsbys entitled to a discharge on their student loans? Explain your answer. [*In re Hornsby*, 144 F.3d 433 (6th Cir.)]

13. TLC was an Atlanta rhythm, blues, and hip-hop band that performed at clubs in 1991. The three-woman group signed a recording contract with LaFace Records. The group's first album that LaFace produced, *Ooooooohhh on the TLC Tip*, sold almost 3 million albums in 1992. The group's second album, *Crazysexycool*, also produced by LaFace, sold 5 million albums through June 1996. The two albums together had six top-of-the-chart singles.

    LaFace had the right to renew TLC's contract in 1996 following renegotiation of the contract terms. In the industry, royalty rates for unknown groups, as TLC was in 1991, are generally 7 percent of the revenues for the first 500,000 albums and 8 percent for sales on platinum albums (albums that sell over 1 million copies). The royalty rate increases to 9.5 percent for all sales on an eighth album. Established artists in the industry who renegotiate often have royalty rates of 13 percent, and artists with two platinum albums can command an even higher royalty.

    The three women in TLC—Tionne Watkins (T-Boz), Lisa Lopes (Left-Eye, who has since died), and Rozonda Thomas (Chili)—declared bankruptcy in July 1995. All three listed debts that exceeded their assets, which included sums owed to creditors for their cars and to Zale's and The Limited for credit purchases. Lopes was being sued by Lloyd's of London, which claimed she owed it $1.3 million it had paid on a policy held by her boyfriend on his home that was destroyed by fire. Lopes pleaded guilty to one count of arson in the destruction of the home but denied that she intended to destroy it. She was sentenced to five years probation and treatment at a halfway house.

    Lopes asked that the Lloyd's claim be discharged in her bankruptcy. All three members of TLC asked that their contract with LaFace be discharged in bankruptcy because being bound to their old contract could impede their fresh financial starts.

    Did the three women meet the standards for declaring bankruptcy? Evaluate whether Lopes's Lloyd's claim should be discharged. Determine whether the record contract should be discharged.

14. Place the following in order for a bankruptcy proceeding:
    a. Order of relief
    b. Collection of bankrupt's estate
    c. List of creditors
    d. Petition
    e. Evaluation of claims
    f. Voidable preferences
    g. Discharge

15. Three general unsecured creditors are owed $45,000 as follows: *A,* $15,000; *B,* $5,000; and *C,* $25,000. After all other creditors were paid, the amount left for distribution to general unsecured creditors was $9,000. How will the $9,000 be distributed?

CPA QUESTIONS

1. Which of the following statements is correct concerning the voluntary filing of a petition of bankruptcy?
    a. If the debtor has 12 or more creditors, the unsecured claims must total at least $13,475.
    b. The debtor must be solvent.
    c. If the debtor has less than 12 creditors, the unsecured claims must total at least $13,475.
    d. The petition may be filed jointly by spouses (AICPA adapted).

2. On February 28, Master, Inc., had total assets with a fair market value of $1,200,000 and total liabilities of $990,000. On January 15, Master made a monthly installment note payment to Acme Distributors Corp., a creditor holding a properly perfected security interest in equipment having a fair market value greater than the balance due on the note. On March 15, Master voluntarily filed a petition in bankruptcy under the liquidation provisions of Chapter 7 of the federal Bankruptcy Code. One year later, the equipment was sold for less than the balance due on the note to Acme.

    If a creditor challenged Master's right to file, the petition would be dismissed:
    a. If Master had less than 12 creditors at the time of filing.
    b. Unless Master can show that a reorganization under Chapter 11 of the federal Bankruptcy Code would have been unsuccessful.
    c. Unless Master can show that it is unable to pay its debts in the ordinary course of business or as they come due.
    d. If Master is an insurance company.

3. A voluntary petition filed under the liquidation provisions of Chapter 7 of the federal Bankruptcy Code:
    a. Is not available to a corporation unless it has previously filed a petition under the reorganization provisions of Chapter 11 of the federal Bankruptcy Code.
    b. Automatically stays collection actions against the debtor except by secured creditors for collateral only.
    c. Will be dismissed unless the debtor has 12 or more unsecured creditors whose claims total at least $13,475.
    d. Does not require the debtor to show that the debtor's liabilities exceed the fair market value of assets.

4. Which following conditions, if any, must a debtor meet to file a voluntary bankruptcy petition under Chapter 7 of the federal Bankruptcy Code?

	Insolvency	*Three or More Creditors*
a.	Yes	Yes
b.	Yes	No
c.	No	Yes
d.	No	No

5. On July 15, 1988, White, a sole proprietor, was involuntarily petitioned into bankruptcy under the liquidation provisions of the Bankruptcy Code. White's nonexempt property has been converted to $13,000 cash, which is available to satisfy the following claims:

Unsecured claim for 1986 state income tax	$10,000
Fee owed to Best & Co., CPAs, for services rendered from April 1, 1988, through June 30, 1988	$6,000
Unsecured claim by Stieb for wages earned as an employee of White during March 1988	$3,000

There are no other claims.

What is the maximum amount that will be distributed for the payment of the 1986 state income tax?

a. $4,000
b. $5,000
c. $7,000
d. $10,000

6. On May 1, 1997, two months after becoming insolvent, Quick Corp., an appliance wholesaler, filed a voluntary petition for bankruptcy under the provisions of Chapter 7 of the federal Bankruptcy Code. On October 15, 1996, Quick's board of directors had authorized and paid Erly $50,000 to repay Erly's April 1, 1996, loan to the corporation. Erly is a sibling of Quick's president. On March 15, 1996, Quick paid Kray $100,000 for inventory delivered that day. Which of the following is not relevant in determining whether the repayment of Erly's loan is a voidable preferential transfer?

a. That Erly is an insider.
b. That Quick's payment to Erly was made on account of an antecedent debt.
c. Quick's solvency when the loan was made by Erly.
d. That Quick's payment to Erly was made within one year of the filing of the bankruptcy petition.

Insurance

learningoutcomes

After studying this chapter, you should be able to

LO.1 Explain the necessity of having an insurable interest to obtain an insurance policy

LO.2 Recognize that the formation of a contract is governed by the general principles of contract law

LO.3 Explain why courts strictly construe insurance policies against insurance companies

LO.4 List and explain the five major categories of insurance

LO.5 Explain coinsurance and its purpose

LO.6 Explain incontestability clauses

By means of insurance, protection from loss and liability may be obtained.

A. The Insurance Contract

Insurance is a contract by which one party for a stipulated consideration promises to pay another party a sum of money on the destruction of, loss of, or injury to something in which the other party has an interest or to indemnify that party for any loss or liability to which that party is subjected.

1. The Parties

The promisor in an insurance contract is called the **insurer** or **underwriter**. The person to whom the promise is made is the **insured** or the policyholder. The promise of the insurer is generally set forth in a written contract called a **policy**.

Insurance contracts are ordinarily made through an agent or broker. The **insurance agent** is an agent of the insurance company, often working exclusively for one company. For the most part, the ordinary rules of agency law govern the dealings between this agent and the applicant for insurance.[1]

An **insurance broker** is generally an independent contractor who is not employed by any one insurance company. When a broker obtains a policy for a customer, the broker is the agent of the customer for the purpose of that transaction. Under some statutes, the broker is made an agent of the insurer with respect to transmitting the applicant's payments to the insurer.

2. Insurable Interest

A person obtaining insurance must have an insurable interest in the subject matter insured. If not, the insurance contract cannot be enforced.

(A) Insurable Interest in Property. A person has an insurable interest in property whenever the destruction of the property will cause a direct pecuniary loss to that person.[2]

It is immaterial whether the insured is the owner of the legal or equitable title, a lienholder, or merely a person in possession of the property.[3] **For Example,** Vin Harrington, a builder, maintained fire insurance on a building he was remodeling under a contract with its owner, Chestnut Hill Properties. The building was destroyed by fire before renovations were completed. Harrington had an insurable interest in the property to the extent of the amount owed him under the renovation contract.

To collect on property insurance, the insured must have an insurable interest at the time the loss occurs.

(B) Insurable Interest in Life. A person who purchases life insurance can name anyone as beneficiary regardless of whether that beneficiary has an insurable interest in the life of the insured. A beneficiary who purchases a policy, however, must have an insurable interest in the life of the insured. Such an interest exists if the beneficiary can reasonably expect to receive pecuniary gain from the continued life of the other person and, conversely, would suffer financial loss from the latter's death. Thus, a creditor has an insurable interest in the life of the debtor because he may not be paid the amount owed upon the death of the debtor.

A partner or partnership has an insurable interest in the life of each of the partners because the death of any one of them will dissolve the firm and cause some degree of loss to the partnership. A business enterprise has an insurable interest in the life of an executive or a key employee because that person's death would inflict a financial loss on the business to the extent that a replacement might not be readily available or could not be found.

In the case of life insurance, the insurable interest must exist at the time the policy is obtained. It is immaterial that the interest no longer exists when the loss is actually sustained.[4] Thus, the fact that a husband (insured) and wife (beneficiary) are divorced after the life insurance policy was procured does not affect the validity of the policy. Also, the fact that a

[1] *Tidelands Life Ins. Co. v. France*, 711 So.2d 728 (Tex. App. 1986).

[2] *Plaisance v. Scottsdale Insurance Co.*, 2008 WL 4372888 (E.D. La. Sept. 22, 2008).

[3] *Gorman v. Farm Bureau Town & Country Insurance Co.*, 977 S.W.2d 519 (Mo. App. 1998).

[4] One who obtains insurance on his own life may legally name a beneficiary without an insurable interest or later assign the policy to one without an insurable interest. Stranger-owned life insurance policies, or "STOLI" plans, are a growing concern for insurers in the life insurance industry. Under STOLI schemes elderly individuals are able to obtain third-party financing to purchase a life insurance policy and to fund the premiums owed under that policy, with some understanding or expectation that the policy will be assigned to an individual lacking an insurable interest, following the expiration of the policy's two-year contestability period. And, these policies may be sold on the Secondary Life Insurance Market. Although an insured may generally purchase life insurance in good faith, intending to keep it for himself and later assign it to a third party, regardless of whether the third party has an insurable interest, where a person who has an interest "lends himself to one without any, as a cloak to what is, in its inception, a wager" then the contract is void as against public policy. See *Carton v. B&B Equities Group, LLC*, 827 F. Supp. 2d 1235 (D. Nev. 2011). STOLI arrangements are in violation of public policy in most states that have addressed the issue.

partnership is terminated after a life insurance policy is obtained by one partner on another does not invalidate the policy. In the *Graves* case, the court was faced with two questions: (1) Does a partner have an insurable interest in the life of another partner? (2) Was the surviving partner required to remit the insurance proceeds to the estate of the deceased partner?

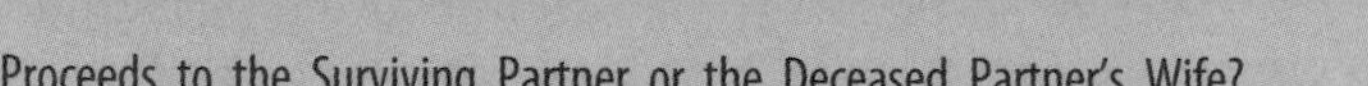

Graves v. Norred, 510 So.2d 816 (Ala. 1987)

Proceeds to the Surviving Partner or the Deceased Partner's Wife?

Jewell Norred's husband, James Norred, was the business partner of Clyde Graves for about 10 years. On May 7, 1979, Graves and Norred took out term life insurance policies, with Graves being the beneficiary of Norred's policy and Norred being the beneficiary of Graves's policy. Premiums were paid out of partnership funds. On February 28, 1983, Graves and Norred divided the partnership assets but did not perform the customary steps of dissolving the partnership.

Graves became the sole owner of the business and continued to pay the premiums on both insurance policies until James Norred died on December 5, 1983. Jewell Norred sued Graves to obtain the proceeds of the insurance policy for herself, alleging that Graves had no insurable interest in the life of James Norred at the time of his death. She also contended that the proceeds should go to the estate as a payment for Norred's interest in the partnership. From a judgment on behalf of the estate, Graves appealed.

JUDICIAL OPINION

ADAMS, J.... Jewell Norred argues that she should receive the benefits of the insurance policy because she alone had an insurable interest in the insurance contract.... The prevailing rule among the states is that a partner or partnership has an insurable interest in the life of one of the partners. ... It is not the mere existence of the partnership which provides the basis for the insurable interest. It is the insuring partner's "reasonable expectation of pecuniary benefit from the continuance of the insured's life."... This interest continues even if the partnership is discontinued prior to death of one of the partners....

In the instant case each partner took out a life insurance policy on the other. Both sides testified that the purpose was to provide for one partner at the other partner's death....There is not legal uncertainty that both partners had an insurable interest in the life of the other partner.

We next turn our analysis to the designation of the beneficiary in order to determine who should be entitled to the proceeds of the life insurance policy. In the case of *Williams v Williams,* 438 So. 2d 735 (Ala. 1983), a partner designated the other partners (his brothers) as the beneficiaries of his life insurance policy. Pursuant to the partnership's dissolution agreement, the surviving partners were to receive the insurance proceeds and then use those proceeds to purchase the deceased partner's interest.... Unlike the present case, in *Williams* a written partnership agreement and a dissolution agreement existed. However, both agreements involved the designation of the partners as beneficiaries instead of the spouse or estate. As stated by Chief Justice Torbert, "The fact that the decedent selected his partners, as opposed to his spouse or estate, as beneficiaries of the life insurance ... is unquestionably permissible. Partners continue to be free to select whomever they wish to benefit from insurance on their lives." *Williams,* 438 So. 2d at 739. In this case, the plaintiff's evidence that the decedent intended for the proceeds to go to his estate consisted solely of oral testimony from the plaintiff's brother (the insurance agent) and an ambiguous statement from a mutual friend of both partners. No ambiguity existed in the designation of the beneficiary. There was no written agreement like the dissolution agreement in *Williams,* supra, which provided that the surviving partners were to use the proceeds to purchase the deceased partner's interest. We require more than oral testimony, like the testimony presented here, in order to show that it was not the intention of the decedent that the designated beneficiary retain the proceeds. Therefore, we reverse the trial court's judgment designating Norred's estate as the rightful recipient of the proceeds instead of the designated beneficiary.

[Reversed and remanded]

QUESTIONS

1. Did Graves have an insurable interest in the life of Norred following the discontinuance of the partnership?
2. Was Graves required to remit the proceeds of the insurance to Norred's estate?
3. Can an individual select his or her business partner, as opposed to his or her spouse or estate, as beneficiary under a life insurance policy?

E-Commerce & Cyberlaw

Insurance Contracts & E-Sign

The Electronic Signatures in Global and National Commerce Act (E-Sign) applies broadly to the insurance business.* Thus, with consent of the consumer, contracts may be executed with electronic signatures and documents may be delivered by electronic means. E-Sign also provides protections for insurance agents against liability resulting from any deficiencies in the electronic procedures set forth in an electronic contract, provided the agent did not engage in tortious conduct and was not involved in the establishment of the electronic procedures.

Insurance providers are precluded from canceling health insurance or life insurance protection by means of electronic notices.

*15 U.S.C. §7001(i).

3. The Contract

The formation of a contract of insurance is governed by the general principles applicable to contracts. By statute, an insurance policy must be written. To avoid deception, many state statutes also specify the content of certain policies, in whole or in part. Some statutes specify the size and style of type to be used in printing the policies. Provisions in a policy that conflict with statutory requirements are generally void.

(A) The Application as Part of the Contract. The application for insurance is generally attached to the policy when issued and is made part of the contract of insurance by express stipulation of the policy.

The insured is bound by all material statements in the attached application. **For Example,** insurers seek to stop the issuance of stranger-owned life insurance policies or "STOLI" plans by amending their application process to require all applicants and their brokers to fill out Policy Owner Intent Forms, requiring disclosures that, if answered honestly, will indicate a STOLI scheme and rejection of the application. And, if not answered honestly, the policy can be voided during the two-year contestability period because of the material misrepresentations.[5]

(B) Statutory Provisions as Part of the Contract. When a statute requires that insurance contracts contain certain provisions or cover certain specified losses, a contract of insurance that does not comply with the statute will be interpreted as though it contained all the provisions required by the statute. **For Example,** Louisiana law clearly requires liability insurance coverage on all rental vehicles to protect the victims injured due to the fault of the drivers of the rental vehicles. Avis did provide liability protection for the vehicle it rented to White. However, the terms of the car rental agreement provided for termination of liability coverage in wide-ranging circumstances. White injured Terence Czop while driving intoxicated, one of the causes set forth in the rental agreement for termination of liability coverage. Because state law requires coverage on rental vehicles, the court determined that to allow termination of coverage based on a violation of the rental agreement is against public policy.[6]

4. Antilapse and Cancellation Statutes and Provisions

If the premiums are not paid on time, the policy under ordinary contract law would lapse because of nonpayment. However, with life insurance policies, by either policy provision or statute, the insured is allowed a grace period of 30 or 31 days in which to make payment of the premium due. When there is a default in the payment of a premium by the insured, the insurer may be required by statute to (1) issue a paid-up policy in a smaller amount, (2) provide extended insurance for a period of time, or (3) pay the cash surrender value of the policy.

The contract of insurance may expressly declare that it may or may not be canceled by the insurer's unilateral act. By statute or policy provision, the

[5] See *Principal Life Insurance Co. v. DeRose*, 2011 WL 4738114 (M.D. Pa. Oct. 5, 2011).

[6] *Czop v. White*, 80 So.3d 1255 (La. App. 2011).

insurer is commonly required to give a specific number of days' written notice of cancellation.[7]

5. Modification of Contract

As is the case with most contracts, a contract of insurance can be modified if both insurer and insured agree to the change. The insurer cannot modify the contract without the consent of the insured when the right to do so is not reserved in the insurance contract.

To make changes or corrections to the policy, it is not necessary to issue a new policy. An endorsement on the policy or the execution of a separate rider is effective for the purpose of changing the policy. When a provision of an endorsement conflicts with a provision of the policy, the endorsement controls because it is the later document.

6. Interpretation of Contract

A contract of insurance is interpreted by the same rules that govern the interpretation of ordinary contracts. Words are to be given their plain and ordinary meaning and interpreted in light of the nature of the coverage intended. However, an insurance policy is construed strictly against the insurer, who chooses the language of the policy, and if a reasonable construction may be given that would justify recovery, a court will do so. **For Example,** Dr. Kolb consented to an elective surgical procedure on his right eye after which "something happened that caused the wound to start leaking" and resulted in loss of vision in his eye. This forced him to retire as an orthopedic surgeon. His Paul Revere Life Insurance disability income insurance policy provided income for life for a disability due to "accidental bodily injury." The policy provided benefits for a shorter duration if the disability was caused by "sickness." Dr. Kolb's vision loss was not expected and proceeded from an unidentified postsurgical cause. Applying the plain and ordinary meaning of "accidental" and "injury," the court decided that Dr. Kolb was entitled to income for life under the "injury" provision of the policy.[8]

If there is an ambiguity in the policy, the provision is interpreted against the insurer.[9] **For Example,** on August 29, 2005, the Buentes' residence in Gulfport, Mississippi, was damaged during Hurricane Katrina. Allstate tendered a check for $2,600.35 net after the deductible, under its Deluxe Homeowner's Policy. The Buentes contend their covered losses are between $50,000 and $100,000. They brought suit against Allstate. The trial judge denied Allstate's motion to dismiss, finding the two provisions of the policy that purport to exclude coverage for wind and rain damage were ambiguous in light of other policy provisions granting coverage for wind and rain damage and in light of the inclusion of a "hurricane deductible" as part of the policy. The court found that because the policy was ambiguous, its weather exclusion was unenforceable in the context of losses attributable to wind and rain that occur in a hurricane.[10]

7. Burden of Proof

When an insurance claim is disputed by the insurer, the person bringing suit has the burden of proving that there was a loss, that it occurred while the policy was in force, and that the loss was of a kind that was within the coverage or scope of the policy.[11]

A policy will contain exceptions to the coverage. This means that the policy is not applicable when an exception applies to the situation. Exceptions to coverage are generally strictly interpreted against the insurer. However, insurance policies are contracts and the plain and unambiguous language of the contract will apply. **For Example,** Aroa Marketing, Inc., purchased a commercial general liability (CGL) policy from Hartford Midwest Insurance Co. The policy covered any damages that Aroa became legally obligated to pay because of "bodily injury," "property damage," or "personal and advertising injury" arising out of Aroa's business. Coverage was excluded, however, for "personal and advertising injury" arising out of "any violation of any intellectual property rights, such as copyright, patent, trademark, trade name, trade secret, service mark, or other destination of origin or authenticity." Aroa hired Tara Radcliffe to appear in and film an exercise video for its business to

[7] *Transamerican Ins. Co. v. Tab Transportation*, 906 P.2d 1341 (Cal. 1995).
[8] *Kolb v. Paul Revere Life Insurance Co.*, 355 F.3d 1132 (8th. Cir. 2004).
[9] See *Arrowood Indemnity Co. v. King*, 39 A.3d 712 (Conn. 2012); *Koziol v. Peerless Insurance Co.*, 41 A.3d 647 (R.I. 2012).
[10] *Buente v. Allstate Ins. Co.*, 422 F. Supp. 2d 690 (S.D. Miss. 2006).
[11] *Koslik v. Gulf Insurance Co.*, 673 N.W.2d 343 (Wis. App. 2003).

be used at a consumer electronics show and on a client's Internet site. Aroa used her images to sell other products, and she sued for misappropriation of her image and violation of her right of publicity. The court found that Hartford had no duty to defend or indemnify Aroa because the model's claim fell within the intellectual property exclusion.[12]

8. Insurer Bad Faith

As is required in the case of all contracts, an insurer must act in good faith in processing and paying claims under its policy. In some states, laws have been enacted making an insurer liable for a statutory penalty and attorney fees in case of a bad-faith failure or delay in paying a valid claim within a specified period of time. A bad-faith refusal is generally considered to be any frivolous or unfounded refusal to comply with the demand of a policyholder to pay according to the policy.[13]

The *Leland v. Lafayette Insurance Co.* case deals with an insurer's lack of good faith and fair dealing in its settlement practices and the resulting damages and penalties assessed it for the harm caused the insured.

Leland v. Lafayette Insurance Co., 77 So.3d 1078 (La. App. 2011)

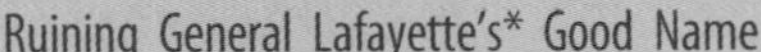

Ruining General Lafayette's* Good Name

Don and Myna Leland owned rental property in Lake Charles, Louisiana, that was damaged by a tree falling into the building, shearing off a portion of the facade during Hurricane Rita in September 2005. By October 7, 2005, they notified their insurer, Lafayette Insurance Co., of the damages to this property. In September 2007, two years after the hurricane, the Lelands filed a lawsuit against the issuer for breach of the insurer's duty of good faith and fair dealing in adjusting losses associated with the hurricane. The jury found in favor of the Lelands, concluding that the plaintiffs sustained losses in excess of the amount paid under the defendant's policy in the amount of $144,800.00. Further, the jury concluded that the defendant: (1) failed to initiate a loss adjustment to the property within 30 days after notification of loss; (2) was arbitrary, capricious, or without probable cause in failing to pay any claim due within 60 days after receipt of satisfactory proof of loss; (3) failed to make an offer to settle the property damage within 30 days of receipt of satisfactory proof of loss; and (4) misrepresented pertinent facts or insurance policy provisions related to coverage at issue. From a judgment for the Lelands, Lafayette appealed.

JUDICIAL OPINION

AMY, J.... [The court of appeals affirmed the trial court's damages as amended as follows: $5,000 for loss of rental income, $53,000 for loss of personal income, $30,000 in interest and $45,000 each for the Lelands for mental anguish and emotional distress for a total of $178,000 in damages attributable to the insurer's breach of its duties. State law added a penalty of two times these damages or $356,000. The insurer was also obligated to pay $144,800 in contractual damages for repairs owed under the insurance contract, and $226,266 in attorneys fees. The court responded to Lafayette's contention that the evidence did not support the mental anguish awards to the Lelands.]

Mental Anguish

...Lafayette does not question the availability of mental anguish damages following a violation of La.R.S. 22:1220, now La.R.S. 22:1973. Instead, it asserts that the plaintiffs did not present sufficient evidence to support the individual awards of $45,000.00 to each of them. Primarily, Lafayette asserts that the figure is not supported as they did not present medical support for their claims.

We do not disturb the jury's award in this regard, finding adequate support in the record. Both plaintiffs offered testimony on this element of recovery. Mr. Leland testified extensively regarding the frustrations encountered in pursuing this multi-year claim and in making little progress toward a satisfactory conclusion. The record is replete with repeated and persistent inquiries and demands regarding his property, which remained unrepaired by him in light of the insurer's actions and the financial commitment required. The stressful circumstances created by the situation are evident from the documentary evidence and from his testimony. Additionally, he testified that this property and its rental income were intended to serve as a retirement investment for the couple. Rather than being able to rely on that investment, they were

*Check him out online.

[12] *Aroa Marketing, Inc. v. Hartford Insurance Co.*, 130 Cal. Rptr.3d 466 (Cal. App. 2011).

[13] *Uberti v. Lincoln National Life Ins. Co.*, 144 F. Supp. 2d 90 (D. Conn. 2001).

Continued

without rental income for years and had to, eventually, borrow more than $142,000.00 for the repairs in order to avoid having it destroyed by the City. He explained that this process was particularly difficult for his wife, who was reluctant to accept the debt. Mrs. Leland testified regarding the "constant worry of that burden."

Both plaintiffs testified regarding the negative impact that the events had on their relationship. Mr. Leland explained that they had both gained weight and that they "don't sleep." He further stated that "[t]he lack of sleep is one of the hard things because when you don't sleep you don't feel good, and when you don't feel good you fight." Mrs. Leland explained that her husband did not talk as much as he used to and that he no longer golfed or fished as he once had. She stated that: "The marriage will make it because we made a commitment 40 years ago, but it is not the marriage we had. It's not the marriage we thought we would have at this point in life. He doesn't talk very much, he doesn't talk to me."

In light of this testimony and the evidence in the record regarding the plaintiffs' pursuit of their insurer in having their claims satisfied, the jury's award is supported by the record.

[Affirmed as Amended]

QUESTIONS

1. Did the Lelands present sufficient evidence to support damages for mental anguish in this case?
2. What purpose is served by the state statute that provided for a penalty of two times the actual damages attributable to the insurer's breach of its duty of good faith and fair dealing in servicing the Leland's claims?

When it is a liability insurer's duty to defend the insured and the insurer wrongfully refuses to do so, the insurer is guilty of breach of contract and is liable for all consequential damages resulting from the breach. In some jurisdictions, an insured can recover for an excess judgment rendered against the insured when it is proven that the insurer was guilty of negligence or bad faith in failing to defend the action or settle the matter within policy limits.

If there is a reasonable basis for the insurer's belief that a claim is not covered by its policy, its refusal to pay the claim does not subject it to liability for a breach of good faith or for a statutory penalty.[14] This is so even though the court holds that the insurer is liable for the claim.

For Example, the following illustrates an insurer's bad-faith failure to pay a claim, as opposed to an insurer's reasonable basis for failure to pay. Carmela Garza's home and possessions were destroyed in a fire set by an arsonist on August 19. Carmela's husband, Raul, who was no longer living at the home, had a criminal record. An investigator for the insurer stated that while he had no specific information to implicate the Garzas in the arson, Carmela may have wanted the proceeds to finance relocation to another city. By October, however, Aetna's investigators ruled out the possibility that Garza had the motive or the opportunity to set the fire. The insurer thus no longer had a reasonable basis to refuse to pay the claim after this date. Yet it took over a year and a half and court intervention for Aetna to allow Carmela to see a copy of her policy, which had been destroyed in the fire. Two years after the fire, Aetna paid only $28,624.55 for structural damage to the fire-gutted home, which was insured for $111,000. The court held that Aetna's actions constituted a bad-faith failure to pay by the insurer.[15]

9. Time Limitations on Insured

The insured must comply with a number of time limitations in making a claim. For example, the insured must promptly notify the insurer of any claim that may arise, submit a proof-of-loss statement within the time set forth in the policy, and bring any court action based on the policy within a specified time period.[16]

[14] *Shipes v. Hanover Ins. Co.*, 884 F.2d 1357 (11th Cir. 1989).

[15] See *Aetna Casualty & Surety Co. v. Garza*, 906 S.W.2d 543 (Tex. App. 1995).

[16] But see *Seeman v. Sterling Ins. Co.*, 699 N.Y.S.2d 542 (A.D. 1999), where the insured's four-month delay in notifying the insurer was excused because of his belief that only on-premises injuries were covered by his homeowners insurance policy and thus the policy would not cover an injury in which a paintball he fired at work struck his coworker in the eye.

10. Subrogation of Insurer

In some instances, the insured has a claim against a third person for the harm covered by the insurance policy. **For Example,** *A* sells an automobile insurance policy that provides collision coverage to *B*. *C* "rear-ends" *B*'s car at a traffic rotary in the city. *A* pays *B* the full amount of the property damage repair costs. *A* is then **subrogated** to *B*'s claim against *C*, the person who caused the harm. See Figure 36-1. When the insurer is subrogated to the insured's claim, the insurer may enforce that claim against the third person.[17]

B. Kinds of Insurance

Businesses today have specialized **risk** managers who identify the risks to which individual businesses are exposed, measure those risks, and purchase insurance to cover those risks (or decide to self-insure in whole or in part).

FIGURE 36-1 *Subrogation*

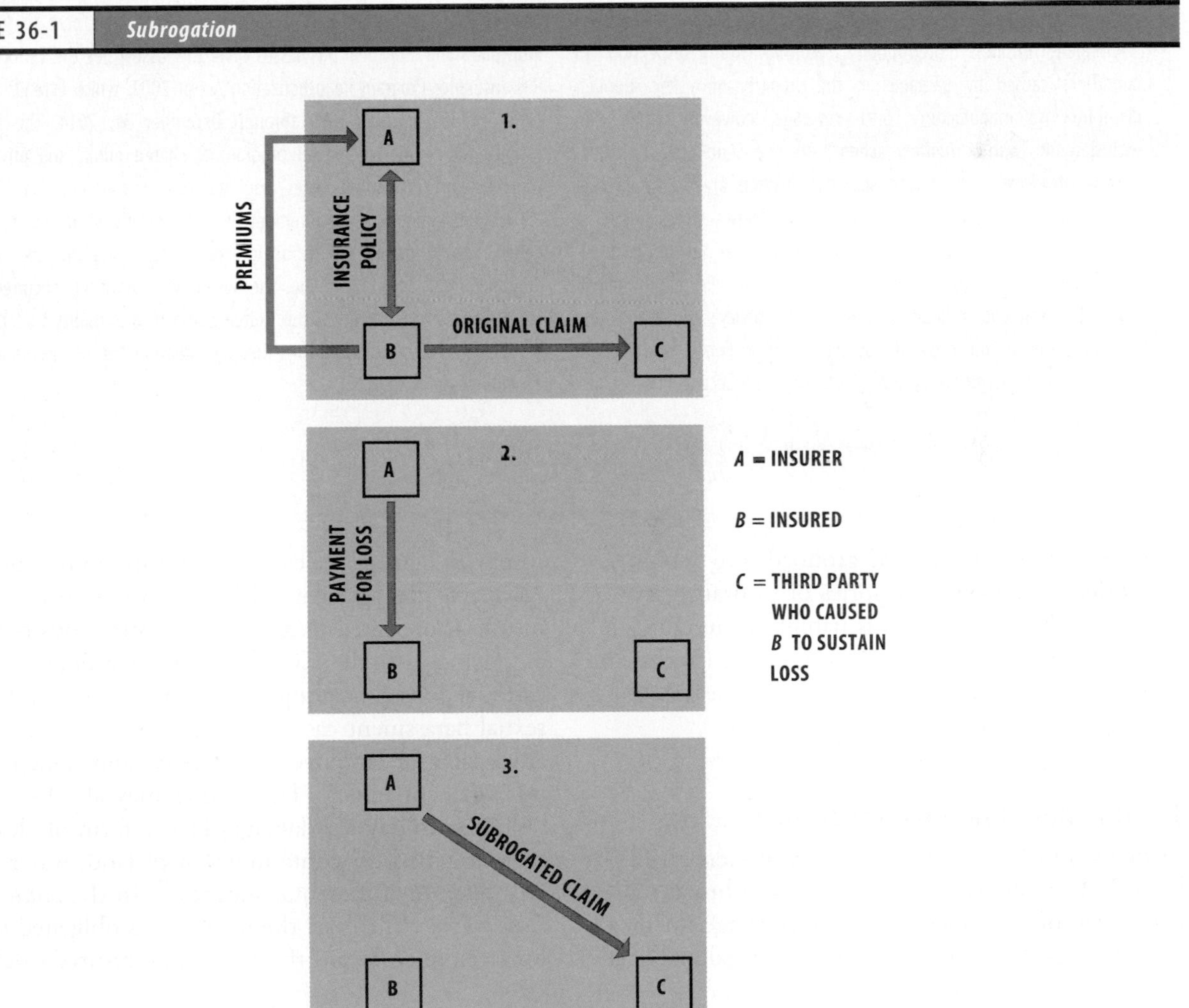

[17] *Stratus Services Group, Inc. v. Kash 'N Gold Ltd.*, 935 N.Y.S.2d 302 (A.D. 2011).

Ethics & the Law

On September 11, 2001, terrorist attacks killed 3,119 persons, devastated the U.S. airline industry, and had a severe impact on the U.S. insurance industry. In New York City, several office buildings, including One and Two World Trade Center, were destroyed, and other businesses in lower Manhattan were forced to shut down.

Business interruption insurance coverage is usually written as part of a company's commercial property insurance package. It not only covers policyholders for their lost profits and fixed charges and expenses for interruption to their business caused by physical damage or destruction to the insured's own property, but it may also cover "contingent business interruption" resulting from suspension of operations caused by damages to the property of a key supplier, distributor, or manufacturer. Such coverage, however, contains an exclusion for "war or military action." Are the September 11, 2001, terrorist attacks an "act of war" such that insurers are not responsible for business interruption claims? Can the president's words regarding war with al Qaeda be used to prove an "act of war" exclusion?

A court called upon to interpret an "act of war" exclusion will apply the plain and ordinary meaning of the policy's terms, and any ambiguity will be construed against the insurer. In *Pan American World Airways, Inc., v. Aetna Casualty & Surety Co.,** the Second Circuit Court of Appeals held that an air carrier was entitled to recover for the destruction of its plane by terrorists in Cairo, Egypt, and the damage was not excluded under the policy's "act of war" exclusion. The court reasoned in part that there was no existing "war" between recognized sovereign states.

Pressured by historic losses as a result of 9/11, insurance companies in certain areas excluded perils resulting from "terrorism" in new commercial property insurance policies. Is it fair for insurers to exclude coverage altogether for losses due to acts of terrorism? Is it best to have the community absorb the losses? Is it best to have individuals and individual businesses cover the losses? See the Terrorism Risk Insurance Program Reauthorization Act of 2007, which extends the Terrorism Risk Insurance Act through December 31, 2014. The law extends the temporary federal program of shared public and private compensation for insured losses resulting from acts of terrorism. The 2007 law eliminates the requirement that the terrorist(s) are acting on behalf of any foreign person or foreign interest, and increases the program trigger to $110 million. The Secretary of State, in concurrence with the Attorney General of the United States, has authority to certify an event as an act of terrorism, thereby initiating the provisions and benefits of the act.

*See *Pan American World Airways, Inc. v. Aetna Casualty & Surety Co.*, 505 F.2d 989 (2d Cir. 1974).

Insurance policies can be grouped into certain categories. Five major categories of insurance are considered here: (1) business liability insurance, (2) marine and inland marine insurance, (3) fire and homeowners insurance, (4) automobile insurance, and (5) life insurance.

11. Business Liability Insurance

Businesses may purchase Commercial General Liability (CGL) policies. This insurance is a broad, "all-risk" form of insurance providing coverage for mostly all sums that the insured may become legally obligated to pay as damages because of "bodily injury" or "property damage" caused by an "occurrence." The insurer is obligated to defend the insured business and pay damages under CGL policies for product liability cases, actions for wrongful termination of employees, sexual harassment cases, damages caused by business advertising or employee dishonesty, and trademark infringement suits.[18] The insurer may also be obligated to pay for damages in the form of cleanup costs imposed for contamination of land, water, and air under environmental statutes.[19] In the *Anderson Development Co.* case, the insurer was obligated to pay for cleanup costs and the cost of the insured's defense.

[18] *Charter Oak Fire Ins. Co. v. Heedon & Cos.*, 280 F.3d 730 (7th Cir. 2002).

[19] *Chemical Leaman Tank Lines, Inc. v. Aetna Casualty Co.*, 788 F. Supp. 846 (D.N.J. 1992); *United States v. Pepper's Steel, Inc.*, 823 F. Supp. 1574 (S.D. Fla. 1993). But see *Northville Industries v. National Union Fire and Ins. Co.*, 636 N.Y.S.2d 359 (A.D. 1995); *Aydin Corp. v. First State Ins. Co.*, 62 Cal. Rptr. 2d 825 (A.D. 1997).

Anderson Development Co. v. Travelers Indemnity Co., 49 F.3d 1128 (6th Cir. 1995)

EPA's PRP Suits the Court Just Fine

Anderson Development Co. (ADC) manufactures and sells specialty organic materials in Adrian, Michigan. It built a lagoon to handle the occasional accidental discharge of Curene 442 process water, believing it to be insoluble in water. Curene 442, which it manufactured between 1970 and 1979, was a known animal carcinogen, and it turned out to be soluble. The lagoon's discharge piping was connected to the sewer system and found its way to the city's sewage treatment plant.

In 1985, the Environmental Protection Agency (EPA) sent ADC a formal notification that it was considered a "potentially responsible party" (PRP) for the release of hazardous substances into the soil and groundwater. This notice was called a "PRP" letter. ADC notified Travelers Indemnity Co., its insurer, of the letter, and Travelers contended that it was not prepared to defend or cover ADC in the matter. ADC did a study that revealed contamination on its property. The EPA and ADC entered a consent decree wherein ADC agreed to the cleanup activities required by the EPA, spending over $6 million on the cleanup. ADC brought an action against its insurer seeking coverage under its general liability insurance policies for the cost of its defense and the cost of the cleanup. Travelers alleged that it was not liable under the policies.

JUDICIAL OPINION

BROWN, C. J. … Travelers and ADC entered into a series of general liability and umbrella insurance contracts spanning a period of 1974 to 1980. The contracts covering the Adrian facility provided in pertinent part that:

> *The Travelers will pay on behalf of the Insured all sums which the Insured shall become legally obligated to pay as damages because of body injury or property damage to which this insurance applies, caused by an occurrence.*

As to Travelers' duty to defend, the policies further provided that:

> *Travelers shall have the right and duty to defend any suit against the Insured seeking damages on account of such bodily injury or property damage….*

…The district court determined that the issuance of the PRP letter and other actions taken by the EPA did not constitute a "suit" triggering Travelers' duty to defend ADC. …

The Michigan Supreme Court, however, recently having had the opportunity to rule on this exact issue, … held that a PRP letter issued by the EPA is the functional equivalent of a "suit" brought in a court of law. *Michigan Miller Mut. Ins. Co. v Bronson Plating Co.,*445 Mich. 558, 519 N.W.2d 864, 870 (1994). Factually, *Bronson Plating* is also substantially similar to our case: The insurer brought an action against its insured seeking a declaration that it had no duty to defend or indemnify the insured with respect to EPA administrative actions (PRP letter) regarding environmental contamination of the insured's operation site. Moreover, the insurance policy provisions with respect to the insurer's duty to defend and indemnify, as well as the relevant portions of the PRP letter, were essentially identical to those in our case. The court first noted that the term "suit" is ambiguous and capable of application to nontraditional legal actions that are the functional equivalent of a suit brought in a court of law. Under this definition, the court concluded, a PRP letter constitutes the initiation of a suit that the insurers are obligated to defend. The court reasoned that "[t]he significant authority given to the EPA in such matters allows it essentially to usurp the traditional role of a court in determining and apportioning liability," and may be viewed as "coercing the voluntary participation of PRP's." *Id.* 519 N.W.2d at 871–72.

In light of the *Bronson Plating* decision, we reverse the district court as to the first issue and hold that the PRP letter received by ADC constituted the initiation of a suit triggering Travelers' duty to defend.

We now turn to the issue of whether environmental response and clean-up costs mandated by the EPA are "damages" within the meaning of the insurance contract, thereby triggering Travelers' duty to indemnify. Travelers notes that these costs are equitable in nature. Likewise, Travelers contends that the word "damages" is clear and unambiguous, and that it refers to legal and not equitable relief. Hence, Travelers maintains that the district court correctly held that the term "damages" does not contemplate the relief sought here.…

In *United States Aviex Co. v Travelers Ins. Co.,*125 Mich. App. 579, 336 N.W.2d 838 (1983), the Michigan Court of Appeals specifically addressed the question whether environmental clean-up costs constituted damages under the insurance policies at issue. In that case, the Michigan Department of Natural Resources notified the insured that the insured had the obligation to conduct an investigation regarding the extent of on-site contamination and to correct the same. The Department threatened legal action if the insured did not comply. The insured later brought an action against its insurer, Travelers, for a declaratory judgment seeking coverage under the insurance contract for costs incurred in determining and correcting the contamination.…

Continued

...We construe the Michigan appellate court cases to hold that response and environmental clean-up costs mandated by the EPA constitute damages. The fact that the insured cooperates and assumes the obligation to conduct the clean-up, rather than forcing the EPA to incur the expenses of a clean-up and then bring a coercive suit, does not change the bottom line that a legal obligation exists. Accordingly, we reverse the district court as to the second issue and hold that, under Michigan law, government imposed environmental clean-up costs constitute "damages."...

We therefore reverse the district court's grant of summary judgment for the Defendant/Appellee, Travelers, affirm the grant of summary judgment on behalf of the Plaintiff/Appellant, ADC, and remand to the district court for further proceedings in accordance with this opinion.

QUESTIONS

1. Was Travelers obligated under its insurance policies with ADC to defend ADC in its dealings with the EPA?
2. Was Travelers obligated to pay for the clean-up costs under the insurance policies with ADC?
3. Assess the business judgment of Travelers in refusing to defend ADC and refusing to pay the cleanup costs.

The insurer must defend when coverage is a "close issue" regarding whether the policy would provide indemnity. The duty to defend does not depend on the truth or falsity of the allegations made against the insured by a third party; rather, the factual allegations in the complaint that potentially support a covered claim are all that is needed to invoke the insurer's duty to defend.[20] It is common for the insurer to seek a declaratory judgment if it believes the policy does not call for either a defense or indemnity. **For Example,** State Automobile Mutual Insurance Co. brought an action for declaratory judgment that it had no duty to defend and indemnify Flexdar, Inc., for the cost of cleanup of a chemical solvent discovered in the soil of Fexdar's manufacturing site, referencing its "pollution exclusion" language in its policies. The court found the language in the CGL policy in question was ambiguous, and thus ruled against the insurer.[21]

Businesses may purchase policies providing liability insurance for their directors and officers. Manufacturers and sellers may purchase product liability insurance. Professional persons, such as accountants, physicians, lawyers, architects, and engineers, may obtain liability insurance protection against malpractice suits. **For Example,** the architects of the MCI Center, a sports arena in Washington, D.C., were entitled under their professional liability insurance coverage to be defended by their insurer in a lawsuit seeking only injunctive relief for the firm's alleged failure to comply with the Americans with Disabilities Act's enhanced sightline requirements.[22]

12. Marine Insurance

Marine insurance policies cover perils relating to the transportation of goods. **Ocean marine** insurance policies cover the transportation of goods in vessels in international and coastal trade. **Inland marine** insurance principally covers domestic shipments of goods over land and inland waterways.

(A) Ocean Marine. Ocean marine insurance is a form of insurance that covers ships and their cargoes against "perils of the sea." Four classes of ocean marine insurance are generally available: (1) hull, (2) cargo, (3) liability, and (4) freight. **Hull insurance** covers physical damage to the vessel.[23] **Cargo insurance** protects the cargo owner against financial loss if the goods being shipped are lost or damaged at sea.[24]

Cargo insurance does not cover risks prior to the loading of the insured cargo on board the vessel. An additional warehouse coverage endorsement is needed

[20] *Mid Continent Casualty Co. v. JHP Development Inc.*, 557 F.3d 207 (6th Cir. 2009).

[21] *State Automobile Mutual Insurance Co. v. Flexdar, Inc.*, 964 N.E.2d 845 (Ind. 2012). The court majority stated:

> After all, "[t]he insurance companies write the policies; we buy their forms or we do not buy their insurance." By more careful drafting State Auto has the ability to resolve any question of ambiguity. And in fact it has done so. In 2005 State Auto revised its policies to add an "Indiana Changes—Pollution Exclusion" endorsement. Id. At 852.

[22] *Washington Sports and Entertainment, Inc. v. United Coastal Ins.*, 7 F. Supp. 2d 1 (D.D.C. 1998).

[23] *Lloyd's v. Labarca*, 260 F.3d 3 (1st Cir. 2001).

[24] *Kimta, A. S. v. Royal Insurance Co., Inc.*, 9 P.3d 239 (Wash. App. 2001).

to insure merchandise held in a warehouse prior to import or export voyages.

Liability insurance covers the shipowner's liability if the ship causes damage to another ship or its cargo. **Freight insurance** ensures that the shipowner will receive payment for the transportation charges. "All-risk" policies consolidate coverage of all four classes of ocean marine insurance into one policy.[25]

(B) INLAND MARINE. Inland marine insurance evolved from marine insurance. It protects goods in transit over land; by air; or on rivers, lakes, and coastal waters. Inland marine insurance can be used to insure property held by a bailee. Moreover, it is common for institutions financing automobile dealers' new car inventories to purchase inland marine insurance policies to insure against damage to the automobiles while in inventory.

13. Fire and Homeowners Insurance

A **fire insurance policy** is a contract to indemnify the insured for property destruction or damage caused by fire. In almost every state, the New York standard fire insurance form is the standard policy. A **homeowners insurance policy** is a combination of the standard fire insurance policy and comprehensive personal liability insurance. It thus provides fire, theft, and certain liability protection in a single insurance contract.

(A) FIRE INSURANCE. For fire insurance to cover fire loss, there must be an actual hostile fire that is the immediate cause of the loss. A *hostile fire* is one that becomes uncontrollable, burns with excessive heat, or escapes from the place where it is intended to be. To illustrate, when soot is ignited and causes a fire in the chimney, the fire is hostile. On the other hand, if a loss is caused by the smoke or heat of a fire that has not broken out of its ordinary container or become uncontrollable, the loss results from a friendly fire. The policy does not cover damage from a friendly fire.

By policy endorsement, however, the coverage may be extended to include loss by a friendly fire.

(1) Coinsurance.

The insurer is liable for the actual amount of the loss sustained up to the maximum amount stated in the policy. An exception exists when the policy contains a coinsurance clause. A **coinsurance clause** requires the insured to maintain insurance on the covered property up to a certain amount or a certain percentage of the value (generally 80 percent). Under such a provision, if the policyholder insures the property for less than the required amount, the insurer is liable only for the proportionate share of the amount of insurance required to be carried. **For Example,** suppose that the owner of a building with a value of $400,000 insures it against loss to the extent of $240,000. The policy contains a coinsurance clause requiring that insurance of 80 percent of the value of the property be carried (in this case, $320,000). Assume that a $160,000 loss is then sustained. The insured would receive not $160,000 from the insurer but only three-fourths of that amount, which is $120,000, because the amount of the insurance carried ($240,000) is only three-fourths of the amount required ($360,000).

Some states prohibit the use of a coinsurance clause.

(2) Assignment.

Fire insurance is a personal contract, and in the absence of statute or contractual authorization, it cannot be assigned without the consent of the insurer.

(3) Occupancy.

Provisions in a policy of fire insurance relating to the use and occupancy of the property are generally strictly construed because they relate to the hazards involved.

(B) HOMEOWNERS INSURANCE. In addition to providing protection against losses resulting from fire, the homeowners policy provides liability coverage for accidents or injuries that occur on the premises of the insured. Moreover, the liability provisions provide coverage for unintentional injuries to others away from home for which the insured or any member of the resident family is held responsible, such as injuries caused to others by golfing, hunting, or fishing accidents.[26] Generally, motor vehicles, including mopeds and recreational vehicles, are excluded from such personal liability coverage.

A homeowners policy also provides protection from losses caused by theft. In addition, it provides

[25] *Transamerican Leasing, Inc. v. Institute of London Underwriters*, 7 F. Supp. 2d 1340 (S.D. Fla. 1998).

[26] *American Concept Ins. Co. v. Lloyds of London*, 467 N.W.2d 480 (S.D. 1991).

protection for all permanent residents of the household, including all family members living with the insured. Thus, a child of the insured who lives at home is protected under the homeowners policy for the value of personal property lost when the home is destroyed by fire.

14. Automobile Insurance

Associations of insurers, such as the National Bureau of Casualty Underwriters and the National Automobile Underwriters Association, have proposed standard forms of automobile insurance policies. These forms have been approved by the association members in virtually all states. The form used today by most insurers is the Personal Auto Policy (PAP).

(A) Perils Covered. Part A of the policy provides liability coverage that protects the insured driver or owner from the claims of others for bodily injuries or damage to their property. Part B of the policy provides coverage for medical expenses sustained by a covered person or persons in an accident. Part C of the PAP provides coverage for damages the insured is entitled to recover from an *uninsured motorist.*[27] Part D provides coverage for loss or damage to the covered automobile. Coverage under Part D includes collision coverage and coverage of "other than collision" losses, such as fire and theft.

(B) Covered Persons. Covered persons include the named insured or any family member (a person related by blood, marriage, or adoption or a ward or foster child who is a resident of the household). If an individual is driving with the permission of the insured, that individual is also covered.

(C) Use and Operation. The coverage of the PAP policy is limited to claims arising from the "use and operation" of an automobile. The term *use and operation* does not require that the automobile be in motion. Thus, the term embraces loading and unloading as well as actual travel.[28]

(D) Notice and Cooperation. The insured is under a duty to give notice of claims, to inform, and to cooperate with the insurer. Notice and cooperation are conditions precedent to the liability of the insurer.

(E) No-Fault Insurance. Traditional tort law (negligence law) placed the economic losses resulting from an automobile accident on the one at fault. The purpose of automobile liability insurance is to relieve the wrongdoer from the consequences of a negligent act by paying defense costs and the damages assessed. Under no-fault laws, injured persons are barred from suing the party at fault for ordinary claims. When the insured is injured while using the insured automobile, the insurer will make a payment without regard to whose fault caused the harm. However, if the automobile collision results in a permanent serious disablement or disfigurement, or death, or if the medical bills and lost wages of the plaintiff exceed a specified amount, suit may be brought against the party who was at fault.

15. Life Insurance

There are three basic types of life insurance: term insurance, whole life insurance, and endowment insurance.

Term insurance is written for a specified number of years and terminates at the end of that period. If the insured dies within the time period covered by the policy, the face amount is paid to the beneficiary. If the insured is still alive at the end of the time period, the contract expires, and the insurer has no further obligation. Term policies have little or no cash surrender value.

Whole life insurance (or ordinary life insurance) provides lifetime insurance protection. It also has an investment element.

Part of every premium covers the cost of insurance, and the remainder of the premium builds up a **cash surrender value** of the policy.

An **endowment insurance** policy is one that pays the face amount of the policy if the insured dies within the policy period. If the insured lives to the end of the policy period, the face amount is paid to the insured at the end of the period.

Many life insurance companies pay double the amount of the policy, called **double indemnity**, if death is caused by an accident and death occurs within 90 days afterward. A comparatively small additional premium is charged for this special protection.

[27] *Montano v. Allstate Indemnity*, 211 F.3d 1278 (10th Cir. 2002).

[28] See *American Home Insurance Co. v. First Speciality Insurance Corp.*, 894 N.E.2d 1167 (Mass. App. 2008).

In consideration of an additional premium, many life insurance companies also provide insurance against total permanent disability of the insured. **Disability** is usually defined in a life insurance policy as any "incapacity resulting from bodily injury or disease to engage in any occupation for remuneration or profit."

(A) Exclusions. Life insurance policies frequently provide that death is not within the protection of the policy and that a double indemnity provision is not applicable when death is caused by (1) suicide,[29] (2) narcotics, (3) the intentional act of another, (4) execution for a crime, (5) war activities, or (6) operation of aircraft.

(B) The Beneficiary. The recipient of life insurance policy proceeds that are payable upon the death of the insured is called the **beneficiary**. The beneficiary may be a third person or the estate of the insured, and there may be more than one beneficiary.

The beneficiary named in a policy may be barred from claiming the proceeds of the policy. It is generally provided by statute or stated by court decision that a beneficiary who has feloniously killed the insured is not entitled to receive the proceeds of the policy.

The customary policy provides that the insured reserves the right to change the beneficiary without the latter's consent. When the policy contains such a provision, the beneficiary cannot object to a change that destroys all of that beneficiary's rights under the policy and that names another person as beneficiary.

An insurance policy will ordinarily state that to change the beneficiary, the insurer must be so instructed in writing by the insured and the policy must then be endorsed by the company with the change of the beneficiary. These provisions are construed liberally. If the insured has notified the insurer but dies before the endorsement of the change by the company, the change of beneficiary is effective.[30] However, if the insured has not taken any steps to comply with the policy requirements, a change of beneficiary is not effective even though a change was intended.

(C) Incontestability Clause. Statutes commonly require the inclusion of an **incontestability clause** in life insurance policies. Ordinarily, this clause states that after the lapse of two years, the policy cannot be contested by the insurance company.[31] The insurer is free to contest the validity of the policy at any time during the contestability period. Once the period has expired, the insurer must pay the stipulated sum upon the death of the insured and cannot claim that in obtaining the policy, the insured had been guilty of misrepresentation, fraud, or any other conduct that would entitle it to avoid the contract of insurance.[32]

Courts and legislatures have addressed the issue of "imposter fraud." In *Amex Life Assurance Co. v. Superior Court,* the California Supreme Court concluded that after the contestability period had expired, an insurer may not assert the defense that an imposter took the medical examination. Jose Morales had applied for a life insurance policy from Amex. A paramedic working for Amex met a man claiming to be Morales and took blood and urine samples, listing him as 5′10″ and weighing 172 pounds. His blood sample was HIV negative. The individual did not provide identification. Some two years later, Morales died of AIDS–related causes. Morales had listed his height as 5′6″ and his weight as 142 on his insurance application. The California Supreme Court stated that Amex, which had done nothing to protect its interest but collect premiums, could not challenge coverage based on the imposter defense.[33] Subsequent to the court's decision, the California legislature amended state insurance law to provide for an "imposter defense" in that state. As set forth in the *Miller* case, Florida does not recognize an imposter defense to incontestability. The legislative purpose of such clauses is to protect beneficiaries from an insurer's refusal to honor policies by asserting pre-existing conditions, leaving beneficiaries in the untenable position of having to battle with powerful insurance companies in court.

[29] *Mirza v. Maccabees Life and Annuity Co.,* 466 N.W.2d 340 (Mich. App. 1991).

[30] *Zeigler v. Cardona,* 830 F. Supp. 1395 (M.D. Ala. 1993).

[31] The two-year period runs from the policy's date of issue to the date the suit is filed in court. See *PHL Variable Insurance Co. v. The Sheldon Hathaway Family Insurance Trust,* 2011 WL 703839 (D. Utah Feb. 20, 2011).

[32] *Amica Life Insurance Co. v. Barbor,* 488 F. Supp. 2d 750 (N.D. Ill. 2007).

[33] *Amex Life Assurance Co. v. Superior Court,* 930 P.2d 1264 (Cal. 1997).

Allstate Life Ins. Co. v. Miller, 424 F.3d 1113 (11th Cir. 2005)

The Allstate life insurance policy on which this case centers went into effect on September 20, 2000, insuring the life of John Miller. The policy stated that if the insured died while the policy was in force, Allstate would pay a death benefit to the policy beneficiaries upon receiving proof of death. As required by Fla. Stat. § 627.455, the policy further provided that it would become incontestable after remaining in force during the lifetime of the insured for a period of two years from its effective date. John Miller died on April 20, 2003—more than two years after the policy went into effect. The beneficiaries accordingly filed statements seeking to collect benefits under the policy. Rather than disburse the benefits, Allstate sought a declaratory judgment that the policy was void alleging that the application was completed using fraudulent information and that an imposter had appeared at the medical exam in place of John Miller. The beneficiaries counterclaimed, alleging breach of contract based on Allstate's failure to pay benefits upon proof of death in accordance with the insurance policy's terms. From a judgment in favor of the beneficiaries Allstate appealed.

JUDICIAL OPINION

BARKETT, C. J.… Florida law requires that "[e]very insurance contract shall provide that the policy shall be incontestable after it has been in force during the lifetime of the insured for a period of 2 years from its date of issue. …" Fla. Stat. § 627.455.…

The Florida Supreme Court has explained that incontestability clauses, such as the one contained in § 627.455, are "in the nature of, and serve[ ] a similar purpose as, a statute of limitations." *Prudential Ins. Co. of Am. v Prescott,* 130 Fla. 11, 176 So. 875, 878 (1937). As such, while incontestability clauses "recognize[ ] fraud and all other defenses, [they] provide[ ] a reasonable time in which they may be, but beyond which they cannot be, established." *Id.* The incontestability clause thus works to the mutual advantage of the insurer and the insured, "giv[ing] the insured a guaranty against expensive litigation to defeat his policy after the lapse of the time specified, and at the same time giv[ing] the company a reasonable time and opportunity to ascertain whether the [insurance] contract should remain in force." *Id.*

Accordingly, just as Florida courts would dismiss an otherwise-valid action once the statute of limitations on that claim had run, Florida's appellate courts have uniformly held that once the incontestability clause becomes effective, insurers are barred from attempting to rescind or cancel the insurance policy based on allegations that the insured engaged in fraud or misrepresentation.…

…Allstate relies on the "weight of authority in other jurisdictions" to argue that we should recognize an imposter exception to the incontestability period.…

As discussed above, the Florida appellate courts have uniformly and expressly held that the § 627.455 incontestability clause bars an insurer from rescinding or contesting the policy based on alleged fraudulent misrepresentations the insured made in the policy application. We can discern no indication that the Florida Supreme Court would disagree. While Allstate argues that its so-called "imposter defense" is different in kind from the sorts of fraud and misrepresentation that Florida's appellate courts have rejected as a basis for obviating the statutory incontestability clause, we agree with the district court that the "imposter defense" is merely a species of fraud, indistinguishable from the use of an imposter for incontestability purposes.

[Affirmed]

QUESTIONS

1. Why are incontestability clauses placed in life insurance contracts?
2. Do incontestability clauses work to the mutual advantage of the insurer and the insured?
3. Express your opinion on whether or not there should be an imposter defense to incontestability clauses.

LawFlix

Double Indemnity (1944)

In this Billy Wilder film, Fred MacMurray is an insurance salesman coerced into a murder plot. The movie provides good coverage of insurable interest in life.

MAKE THE CONNECTION

SUMMARY

Insurance is a contract called a *policy*. Under an insurance policy, the insurer provides in consideration of premium payments, to pay the insured or beneficiary a sum of money if the insured sustains a specified loss or is subjected to a specified liability. These contracts are made through an insurance agent, who is an agent for the insurance company, or through an insurance broker, who is the agent of the insured when obtaining a policy for the latter.

The person purchasing an insurance contract must have an insurable interest in the insured's life or property. An insurable interest in property exists when the damage or destruction of the property will cause a direct monetary loss to the insured. In the case of property insurance, the insured must have an insurable interest at the time of loss. An insurable interest in the life of the insured exists if the purchaser would suffer a financial loss from the insured's death. This interest must exist as of the time the policy is obtained.

Ocean marine policies insure ships and their cargoes against the perils of the sea. Inland marine policies insure goods being transported by land, by air, or on inland and coastal waterways.

For fire insurance to cover a fire loss, there must be an actual hostile fire that is the immediate cause of the loss. The insurer is liable for the actual amount of the loss sustained up to the maximum amount stated in the policy. An exception exists when the policy contains a coinsurance clause requiring the insured to maintain insurance up to a certain percentage of the value of the property. To the extent this is not done, the insured is deemed a coinsurer with the insurer, and the insurer is liable for only its proportional share of the amount of insurance required to be carried. A homeowners insurance policy provides fire, theft, and liability protection in a single contract.

Automobile insurance may provide protection for collision damage to the insured's property and injury to persons. It may also cover liability to third persons for injury and property damage as well as loss by fire or theft.

A life insurance policy requires the insurer to pay a stated sum of money to a named beneficiary upon the death of the insured. It may be a term insurance policy, a whole life policy, or an endowment policy. State law commonly requires the inclusion of an incontestability clause, whereby at the conclusion of the contestability period, the insurer cannot contest the validity of the policy.

LEARNING OUTCOMES

After studying this chapter, you should be able to clearly explain:

A. The Insurance Contract

LO.1 Explain the necessity of having an insurable interest to obtain an insurance policy

See the Vin Harrington example of insurable interest in property, p. 727.

See the discussion of a creditor's insurable interest in the life of a debtor, p. 727.

LO.2 Recognize that the formation of a contract is governed by the general principles of contract law

See how insurers stop "STOLI" schemes through the application process where false answers to material questions make the insurance contract voidable by insurer, p. 729.

LO.3 Explain why courts strictly construe insurance policies against insurance companies

See the discussion and examples in which the courts awarded coverage for the insured because the insurers chose the ambiguous language of the policies, p. 730.

B. Kinds of Insurance

LO.4 List and explain the five major categories of insurance

See the description on business liability insurance, marine and inland insurance, fire and homeowners insurance, automobile insurance, and life insurance, beginning on p. 734.

LO.5 Explain coinsurance and its purpose

See the example of the homeowner who underinsured his property, resulting in the insurer paying a claim at a proportionate share of the amount of insurance required, p. 737.

LO.6 Explain incontestability clauses

See the example of the handling of imposter fraud after the incontestability period has run out, p. 739.

KEY TERMS

beneficiary
cargo insurance
cash surrender value
coinsurance clause
disability
double indemnity
endowment insurance
fire insurance policy
freight insurance
homeowners insurance policy
hull insurance
incontestability clause
inland marine
insurance
insurance agent
insurance broker
insured
insurer
liability insurance
marine insurance
ocean marine
policy
risk
subrogated
term insurance
underwriter
whole life insurance

QUESTIONS AND CASE PROBLEMS

1. Mr. Keyes was injured on April 30, 2010, when he fell off Ms. Thibodeaux's roof. Mr. Keyes was cleaning and measuring the roof in preparation for painting when, unbeknownst to him, Ms. Thibodeaux sprayed a section of the metal roof with water. Mr. Keyes slipped on the wet roof and fell, seriously injuring himself. He filed the lawsuit under Ms. Thibodeaux's homeowner's policy against Lighthouse Property Insurance. Mr. Keyes and Ms. Thibodeaux married in August of 2008 but physically separated four months into the marriage. Mr. Keyes and Ms. Thibodeaux have not divorced. Mr. Keyes testified that he lives in a home he owns with his grandmother and aunt. He stated that he lived in that house prior to marrying Ms. Thibodeaux and returned there after he was kicked out of her home 15 months prior to the accident. The homeowners policy precluded coverage for bodily injury to the named insured and relatives "who are residents of the insured's household." The definitions section of the policy states that the spouse of the name insured is treated as the named insured, if a resident of the same household. Lighthouse has refused coverage for Keyes under its reading of the policy. Keyes disagrees. Decide. [*Keyes v. Thibodeaux*, 85 So.3d 1284 (La. App.)]

2. Cecil Usher owned Belize NY, Inc. (Belize), a small construction company doing business in New York City. Belize purchased a commercial general liability insurance policy from Mount Vernon Fire Insurance Co. The policy's first page, entitled "Policy Declarations," describes the insured as "Belize N.Y., Inc."; it classifies the "Form of Business" as "Corporation," the "Business Description" as "Carpentry," and indicates that Belize was afforded commercial liability insurance in the amount of $1,000,000 per occurrence and $2,000,000 in the aggregate for the period June 1, 1995, to June 1, 1996. Two classifications are listed under "Premium Computation" on the Declarations page: "Carpentry—Interior—001"

and "Carpentry—001." The policy makes no further mention of these two terms. Belize performed some $60,000 of demolition work on the United House of Prayer's renovation project on 272 West 125th Street in New York City. Belize was thereafter hired to supervise subcontractors working on the job. During that period of time, a person entered the building, shot several people with a firearm, and started a fire. Seven people died and several others were injured. The estates of the victims sued Belize, Inc., for "negligence, carelessness and recklessness" regarding the fire, and Belize notified Mount Vernon of the lawsuit. Mount Vernon refused to defend or indemnify Belize because Belize was not engaging in its carpentry operations in the building at the time of the incident. It asserted that its risk is limited to carpentry operations in accordance with the classifications set forth in the policy. Belize contended that the language of the policy did not provide that the classification "Carpentry" defined covered risks, and exclusions should have been stated in the contract. Decide. [*Mount Vernon Fire Insurance Co. v. Belize NY, Inc.*, 227 F.3d 232 (2d Cir.)]

3. On April 6, 1988, Luis Serrano purchased for $75,000 a 26′8″–long Carrera speedboat named *Hot Shot.* First Federal Savings Bank provided $65,000 financing for this purchase. Serrano obtained a marine yacht policy for hull insurance on the boat for $75,000 from El Fenix, with First Federal being named as payee under the policy.

   On May 2, 1988, Serrano sold the boat to Reinaldo Polito, and Serrano furnished First Federal with documents evidencing the sale. Polito assumed the obligation to pay off the balance due First Federal. On October 6, 1989, Serrano again applied to El Fenix for a new yacht policy, covering the period from October 6, 1989, through October 6, 1990, and the coverage extended to peril of confiscation by a governmental agency. Serrano did not have ownership or possession of the boat on October 6, 1989. First Federal, the named payee, had not perfected or recorded a mortgage on *Hot Shot* until July 5, 1990.

   On November 13, 1989, in the waters off Cooper Island in the British Virgin Islands (BVI), *Hot Shot* was found abandoned after a chase by governmental officials. A large shipment of cocaine was recovered, although no one was arrested. When Serrano and First Federal were informed that *Hot Shot* was subject to mandatory forfeiture under BVI law, they both filed claims under the October 6, 1989, insurance policy. What defenses would you raise on behalf of the insurer in this case? Decide. [*El Fenix v. Serrano Gutierrez*, 786 F. Supp. 1065 (D.P.R.)]

4. From the United Insurance Co., Rebecca Foster obtained a policy insuring the life of Lucille McClurkin and naming herself as beneficiary. McClurkin did not live with Foster, and Foster did not inform McClurkin of the existence of the policy. Foster paid the premiums on the policy and upon the death of McClurkin sued the United Insurance Co. for the amount of the insurance. At the trial, Foster testified vaguely that her father had told her that McClurkin was her second cousin on his side of the family. Was Foster entitled to recover on the policy? [*Foster v. United Ins. Co.*, 158 S.E.2d 201 (S.C.)]

5. Dr. George Allard and his brother-in-law, Tom Rowland, did not get along after family land that was once used solely by Rowland was partitioned among family members after the death of Rowland's father. Rowland had a reputation in the community as a bully and a violent person. On December 17, Allard was moving cattle down a dirt road by "trolling" (leading the cattle with a bucket of feed, causing them to follow him). When he saw a forestry truck coming along the road, he led the cattle off the road onto Rowland's land to prevent frightening the cattle. When Rowland saw Allard, Rowland ran toward him screaming at him for being on his land. Allard, a small older man, retreated to his truck and obtained a 12-gauge shotgun. He pointed the gun toward the ground about an inch in front of Rowland's left foot and fired it. He stated that he fired the shot in this fashion to bring Rowland to his senses and that Rowland stepped forward into the line of fire. Allard claimed that if Rowland had not stepped forward, he would not have been hit and injured. Allard was insured by Farm Bureau homeowners and general liability policies, which did not cover liability resulting from

intentional acts by the insured. Applying the policy exclusion to the facts of this case, was Farm Bureau obligated to pay the $100,000 judgment against Allard? [*Southern Farm Bureau Casualty Co. v. Allard*, 611 So.2d 966 (Miss.)]

6. Arthur Katz testified for the U.S. government in a stock manipulation case. He also pled guilty and testified against three of his law partners in an insurance fraud case. He received a six-month sentence in a halfway house and a $5,000 fine. Katz was placed in the Federal Witness Protection Program. He and his wife changed their names to Kane and moved to Florida under the program. Both he and his wife obtained new driver's licenses and Social Security numbers. Using his new identity, "Kane" obtained two life insurance policies totaling $1.5 million. He named his wife beneficiary. A routine criminal background check on Kane found no criminal history.

   From 1984 to 1987, Kane invested heavily in the stock market. On October 17, 1987, the day the stock market crashed, Kane shot and wounded his stockbroker, shot and killed the office manager, and then committed suicide. The insurers refused to pay on the policies, claiming that they never insure persons with criminal records. Mrs. Kane contended that the policies were incontestable after they had been in effect for two years. Decide. [*Bankers Security Life Ins. Society v. Kane*, 885 F.2d 820 (11th Cir.)]

7. Linda Filasky held policies issued by Preferred Risk Mutual Insurance Co. Following an injury in an automobile accident and storm damage to the roof of her home, Filasky sustained loss of income, theft of property, and water damage to her home. These three kinds of losses were covered by the policies with Preferred, but the insurer delayed unreasonably in processing her claims and raised numerous groundless objections to them. Finally, the insurer paid the claims in full. Filasky then sued the insurer for the emotional distress caused by the bad-faith delay and obstructive tactics of the insurer. The insurer defended that it had paid the claims in full and that nothing was owed Filasky. Decide. [*Filasky v. Preferred Risk Mut. Ins. Co.*, 734 P.2d 76 (Ariz.)]

8. Baurer purchased a White Freightliner tractor and agreed that his son-in-law, Britton, could use it in the trucking business. In return, Britton agreed to haul Baurer's hay and cattle, thus saving Baurer approximately $30,000 per year. Baurer insured the vehicle with Mountain West Farm Bureau Insurance Company. The policy contained an exclusionary clause that provided: "We don't insure your [truck] while it is rented or leased to others.… This does not apply to the use of your [truck] on a share expense basis." When the vehicle was destroyed, Mountain West refused to pay on the policy, contending that the arrangement between Baurer and Britton was a lease of the vehicle, which was excluded under the policy. Baurer sued, contending that it was a "share expense basis" allowed under the policy. Is the insurance policy ambiguous? What rule of contract construction applies in this case? Decide. [*Baurer v. Mountain West Farm Bureau Ins.*, 695 P.2d 1307 (Mont.)]

9. Collins obtained from South Carolina Insurance Co. a liability policy covering a Piper Colt airplane he owned. The policy provided that it did not cover loss sustained while the plane was being piloted by a person who did not have a valid pilot's certificate and a valid medical examination certificate. Collins held a valid pilot's certificate, but his medical examination certificate had expired three months before. Collins was piloting the plane when it crashed, and he was killed. The insurer denied liability because Collins did not have a valid medical certificate. It was stipulated by both parties that the crash was in no way caused by the absence of the medical certificate. Decide. [*South Carolina Ins. Co. v. Collins*, 237 S.E.2d 358 (S.C.)]

10. Marshall Produce Co. had insured its milk- and egg-processing plant against fire. When smoke from a fire near its plant permeated the environment and was absorbed into the company's egg powder products, cans of powder delivered to the U.S. government were rejected as contaminated. Marshall Produce sued the insurance company for a total loss, but the insurer contended there had been no fire involving the insured property and no total loss. Decide. [*Marshall Produce Co. v.*

St. Paul Fire & Marine Ins. Co., 98 N.W.2d 280 (Minn.)]

11. Amador Pena, who had three insurance policies on his life, wrote a will in which he specified that the proceeds from the insurance policies should go to his children instead of to Leticia Pena Salinas and other beneficiaries named in the policies. He died the day after writing the will. The insurance companies paid the proceeds of the policies to the named beneficiaries. The executor of Pena's estate sued Salinas and the other beneficiaries for the insurance money. Decide. [*Pena v. Salinas*, 536 S.W.2d 671 (Tex. App.)]

12. Spector owned a small automobile repair garage in rural Kansas that was valued at $80,000. He purchased fire insurance coverage against loss to the extent of $48,000. The policy contained an 80 percent coinsurance clause. A fire destroyed a portion of his parts room, causing a loss of $32,000. Spector believes he is entitled to be fully compensated for this loss, as it is less than the $48,000 of fire protection that he purchased and paid for. Is Spector correct?

13. Carman Tool & Abrasives, Inc., purchased two milling machines, FOB Taiwan, from the Dah Lih Machinery Co. Carman obtained ocean marine cargo insurance on the machines from St. Paul Fire and Marine Insurance Co. and authorized Dah Lih to arrange for the shipment of the two machines to Los Angeles, using the services of Evergreen Lines. Dah Lih booked the machinery for shipment onboard Evergreen's container ship, the *M/V Ever Giant;* arranged for the delivery of the cargo to the ship; provided all of the shipping information for the bill of lading; and was the party to whom the bill was issued. Dah Lih then delivered the bill of lading to its bank, which in turn negotiated it to Carman's bank to authorize payment to Dah Lih. After the cargo was removed from the vessel in Los Angeles but before it was delivered to Carman, the milling machines were damaged to the extent of $115,000. Is the insurer liable to Carman? Can the insurer recover from Evergreen? [*Carman Tool & Abrasives, Inc. v. Evergreen Lines*, 871 F.2d 897 (9th Cir.)]

14. Vallot was driving his farm tractor on the highway. It was struck from the rear by a truck, overturned, exploded, and burned. Vallot was killed, and a death claim was made against All American Insurance Co. The death of Vallot was covered by the company's policy if Vallot had died from "being struck or run over by" the truck. The insurance company claimed that the policy was not applicable because Vallot had not been struck; the farm tractor had been struck, and Vallot's death occurred when the overturned tractor exploded and burned. The insurance company also claimed that it was necessary that the insured be both struck and run over by another vehicle. Decide. [*Vallot v. All American Ins. Co.*, 302 So.2d 625 (La. App.)]

15. When Jorge de Guerrero applied for a $200,000 life insurance policy with John Hancock Mutual Life Insurance Co., he stated on the insurance application that he had not seen a physician within the past five years. In fact, he had had several consultations with his physician, who three weeks prior to the application had diagnosed him as overweight and suffering from goiter. His response to the question on drug and alcohol use was that he was not an alcoholic or user of drugs. In fact, he had been an active alcoholic since age 16 and was a marijuana user. De Guerrero died within the two-year contestability period included in the policy, and John Hancock refused to pay. The beneficiary contended that all premiums were fully paid on the policy and that any misstatements in the application were unintentional. John Hancock contended that if the deceased had given the facts, the policy would not have been issued. Decide. [*de Guerrero v. John Hancock Mutual Life Ins. Co.*, 522 So.2d 1032 (Fla. App.)]

PART 6

Agency and Employment

© Manuel Gutjahr/iStockphoto.com

Chapter 37

© Manuel Gutjahr/iStockphoto.com

Agency

learningoutcomes

After studying this chapter, you should be able to

LO.1 Explain the difference between an agent and an independent contractor

LO.2 Explain three methods of creating an agency relationship

LO.3 Recognize that third persons who deal with an agent are required to take notice of acts contrary to the interests of the principal

LO.4 List and explain the duties an agent owes the principal

LO.5 Explain how the Uniform Durable Power of Attorney Act changes the common law rule on incapacity of the principal

One of the most common business relationships is that of agency. By virtue of the agency device, one person can make contracts at numerous places with many different parties at the same time.

A. Nature of the Agency Relationship

Agency is ordinarily based on the consent of the parties, and for that reason is called a *consensual relationship*. However, the law sometimes imposes an agency relationship. If consideration is present, the agency relationship is contractual.

1. Definitions and Distinctions

Agency is a relationship based on an express or implied agreement by which one person, the **agent**, is authorized to act under the control of and for another, the **principal**, in negotiating and making contracts with third persons.[1] The acts of the agent obligate the principal to third persons and give the principal rights against third persons. (See Figure 37-1.)

The term *agency* is frequently used with other meanings. It is sometimes used to denote the fact that one has the right to sell certain products, such as when a dealer is said to possess an automobile agency. In other instances, the term is used to mean an exclusive right to sell certain articles within a given territory. In these cases, however, the dealer is not an agent in the sense of representing the manufacturer.

It is important to be able to distinguish agencies from other relationships because certain rights and duties in agencies are not present in other relationships.

(A) Employees and Independent Contractors. Control and authority are characteristics that distinguish ordinary employees and independent contractors from agents.

(1) Employees.

An agent is distinguished from an ordinary employee who is not hired to represent the employer in making contracts with third persons. It is possible, however, for the same person to be both an agent and an employee. **For Example,** the driver for a spring water delivery service is an agent in making contracts between the company and its customers but is an employee with respect to the work of delivering products.

(2) Independent Contractors.

An **independent contractor** is bound by a contract to produce a certain result—for example, to build a house. The actual performance of the work is controlled by the contractor, not the owner. An agent or employee differs from an independent contractor in that the principal or employer has the right to control the agent or employee, but not the contractor, in the performance of the work. **For Example,** Ned and Tracy Seizer contract with Fox Building Company to build a new home on Hilton Head Island, South Carolina, according to referenced plans and specifications. Individuals hired by Fox to work on the home are subject to the authority and control of Fox, the independent contractor, not the Seizers. However, Ned and Tracy could decide to build the home themselves, hiring two individuals from nearby Beaufort, Ted Chase and Marty Bromley, to do the work the Seizers will direct each day. Because Ted and Marty would be employees of the Seizers, the Seizers would be held responsible for any wrongs committed by these employees within the scope of their employment. As a general rule, on the other hand, the Seizers are not responsible for the torts of Fox, the independent contractor, and the contractor's employees. A "right to control" test determines whether an individual is an agent, an employee, or an independent contractor.[2]

A person who appears to be an independent contractor may in fact be so controlled by the other party that the contractor is regarded as an agent of, or employee of, the controlling person. **For Example,** Pierce, who was under contract to Brookville Carriers, Inc., was involved in a tractor-trailer/car collision with Rich and others. Pierce owned the tractor involved in the accident on a lease from Brookville but could use it only to haul freight for Brookville; he had no authority to carry freight on his own, and all of his

[1] Restatement (Second) of Agency §1; *Union Miniere, S.A. v. Parday Corp.*, 521 N.E.2d 700 (Ind. App. 1988).

[2] *NE Ohio College of Massotherapy v. Burek*, 759 N.E.2d 869 (Ohio App. 2001).

FIGURE 37-1 Agency Relationships

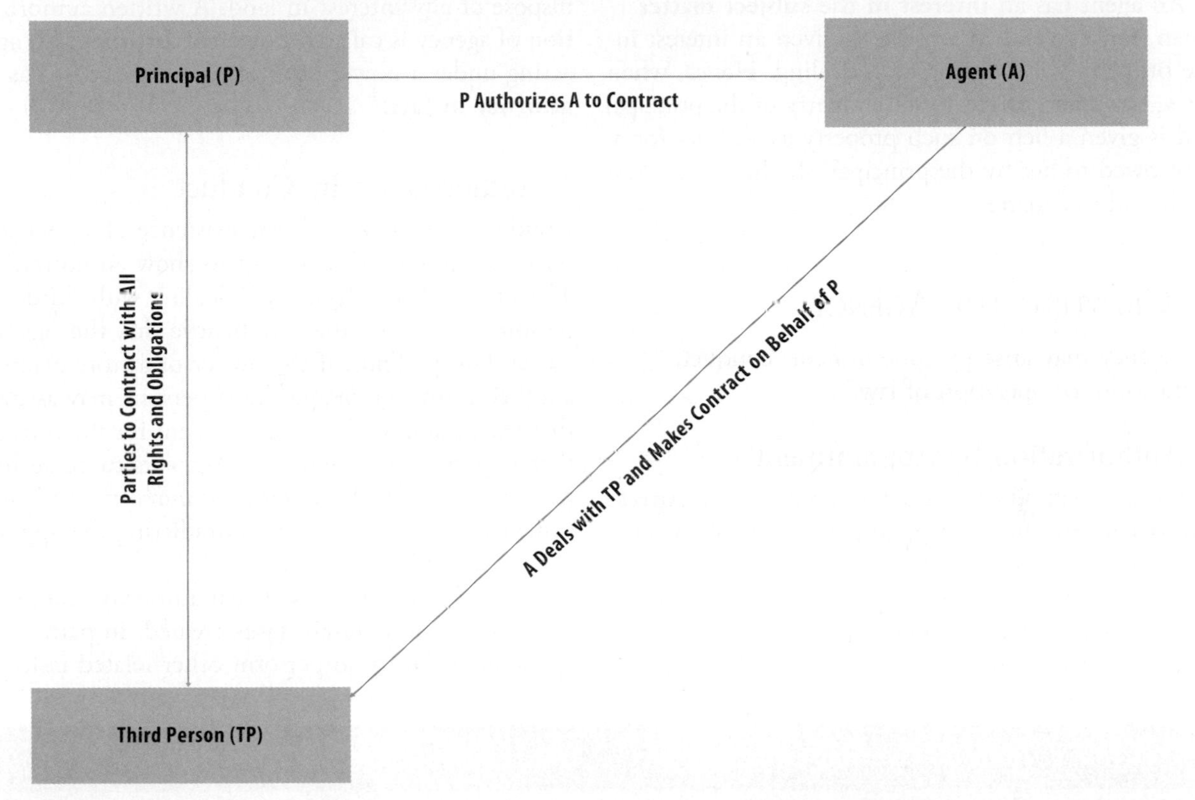

operating authority belonged to Brookville. The "owner/operator" was deemed an employee rather than independent contractor for purposes of assessing the liability of the employer.[3] The separate identity of an independent contractor may be concealed so that the public believes that it is dealing with the principal. When this situation occurs, the principal is liable as though the contractor were an agent or employee.

2. Classification of Agents

A **special agent** is authorized by the principal to handle a definite business transaction or to do a specific act. One who is authorized by another to purchase a particular house is a special agent.

A **general agent** is authorized by the principal to transact all affairs in connection with a particular type of business or trade or to transact all business at a certain place. To illustrate, a person who is appointed as manager by the owner of a store is a general agent.

A **universal agent** is authorized by the principal to do all acts that can be delegated lawfully to a representative. This form of agency arises when a person absent because of being in the military service gives another person a blanket power of attorney to do anything that must be done during such absence.

CPA 3. Agency Coupled with an Interest

An agent has an **interest in the authority** when consideration has been given or paid for the right to exercise the authority. To illustrate, when a lender, in return for making a loan of money, is given, as security, authority to collect rents due the borrower and to apply those rents to the payment of the debt,

[3] *Rich v. Brookville Carriers, Inc.*, 256 F. Supp. 2d 26 (D. Me. 2003).

the lender becomes the borrower's agent with an interest in the authority given to collect the rents.

An agent has an **interest in the subject matter** when, for a consideration, she is given an interest in the property with which she is dealing. Hence, when the agent is authorized to sell property of the principal and is given a lien on such property as security for a debt owed to her by the principal, she has an interest in the subject matter.

B. Creating the Agency

An agency may arise by appointment, conduct, ratification, or operation of law.

4. Authorization by Appointment

The usual method of creating an agency is by **express authorization**; that is, a person is appointed to act for, or on behalf of, another.

In most instances, the authorization of the agent may be oral. However, some appointments must be made in a particular way. A majority of the states, by statute, require the appointment of an agent to be in writing when the agency is created to acquire or dispose of any interest in land. A written authorization of agency is called a **power of attorney**. An agent acting under a power of attorney is referred to as an **attorney in fact**.[4]

5. Authorization by Conduct

Conduct consistent with the existence of an agency relationship may be sufficient to show authorization. The principal may have such dealing with third persons as to cause them to believe that the "agent" has authority. Thus, if the owner of a store places another person in charge, third persons may assume that the person in charge is the agent for the owner in that respect. The "agent" then appears to be authorized and is said to have *apparent authority*, and the principal is estopped from contradicting the appearance that has been created.[5]

In the *Taylor* case, the actual authority granted an agent to perform certain tasks created, in part, apparent authority to perform other related tasks.

Taylor v. Ramsay-Gerding Construction Co., 196 P.3d 532 (Or. 2008)

The "Bulletproof Against Rust" Case. Oops. Now What?

While constructing a hotel in Lincoln City, Oregon, the owner, Todd Taylor, became concerned about possible rusting in the exterior stucco system manufactured by ChemRex that was being installed at the hotel. The general contractor Ramsay-Gerding arranged a meeting with the owner, the installer, and ChemRex's territory manager for Oregon, Mike McDonald, to discuss Mr. Taylor's concerns. McDonald told those present that the SonoWall system was "bulletproof against rust," and stated that "you're getting a five year warranty." He followed up with a letter confirming the five-year warranty on parts and labor. A year later rust discoloration appeared, and no one from ChemRex ever fixed the problem. Taylor sued ChemRex for breach of warranty. ChemRex defended that McDonald did not have actual or apparent authority to declare such a warranty.

JUDICIAL OPINION

BALMER, J.... A principal can create the appearance of authority "by written or spoken words or any other conduct * * *." *Restatement* at § 27. For example, when a principal clothes an agent with actual authority to perform certain tasks, the principal might create apparent authority to perform other, related tasks....

Similarly, when a distant principal places an agent "in charge of a geographically distinct unit or branch[,]" that may lend weight to a finding of apparent authority, depending on the circumstances. *Restatement (Third) of Agency* § 3.03 comment d (2006). For example, if the principal structures its organization so that the "branch manager"—or territory manager—"makes decisions and directs activity without checking elsewhere in the organization[,]" that may create apparent authority to commit the principal to similar transactions. *Id.*

We turn to the application of those principles to the actions of ChemRex at issue here. Using the standards discussed above, we conclude that there is sufficient evidence in the record to support the jury's finding that McDonald acted with apparent authority when he warranted the stucco system to plaintiffs. The first issue is whether ChemRex took

[4] *Lamb v. Scott*, 643 So.2d 972 (Ala. 1994).
[5] *Intersparex Leddin KG v. AL-Haddad*, 852 S.W.2d 245 (Tenn. App. 1992).

Continued

sufficient steps to create the apparent authority to provide a warranty. Significantly, ChemRex gave McDonald actual authority to help in processing warranties and to communicate with customers—about warranties—using ChemRex letterhead. Indeed, McDonald used that authority to confirm, in his July 1999 letter, that plaintiffs had a five-year warranty. Furthermore, ChemRex clothed McDonald with the title of "territory manager" and gave him the actual authority to visit job sites and to solve problems, such as plaintiffs' rust problem, that he found there. McDonald also had the authority to sell an additional product intended to address the very performance at issue here and to answer plaintiffs' questions about the system, which he did in response to plaintiffs' stated concerns.

The next issue is whether there was evidence form which the jury could have concluded that those actions by ChemRex reasonably led plaintiffs to believe that McDonald was authorized to provide the warranty....Taylor testified that he believed that McDonald "was the person that was in charge of or supervising this area, the coastal area. He was the guy that you had to get your answers from." He also stated that he knew that McDonald "represented" ChemRex. It is not necessary that plaintiffs knew McDonald's exact title; they knew generally that McDonald was in charge of the geographical area in which their project was located and that he represented ChemRex. In any event, McDonald used his title of territory manager for Oregon when signing the July 1999 letter confirming the five-year warranty. Because...the jury was permitted to find that plaintiffs relied on the letter, it is further evidence that plaintiffs knew of McDonald's position.

...Because of McDonald's position and his actual authority to help allay plaintiffs' concerns about rust, it was reasonable for plaintiffs to infer that one of the ways in which McDonald had authority to allay their concerns was by warranting the system for five years....

In sum, plaintiffs presented sufficient evidence for the jury to find that McDonald had apparent authority to provide the warranty on ChemRex's behalf. We therefore reverse the Court of Appeals decision on that issue....

[Remanded]

QUESTIONS

1. Did Mike McDonald have the title "territory manager" and have actual authority to visit job sites and resolve problems?
2. Did Mike McDonald have actual authority to provide a purchaser with a five-year warranty on parts and labor?
3. Did the court find that ChemRex had provided Mr. McDonald sufficient actual authority to perform certain tasks, so as to create apparent authority to issue the five-year warranty on parts and labor to resolve the job site problem in this case?

The term *apparent authority* is used when there is only the appearance of authority but no actual authority, and that appearance of authority was created by the principal. The test for the existence of apparent authority is an objective test determined by the principal's outward manifestations through words or conduct that lead a third person reasonably to believe that the "agent" has authority. A principal's express restriction on authority not made known to a third person is no defense.

Apparent authority extends to all acts that a person of ordinary prudence, familiar with business usages and the particular business, would be justified in believing that the agent has authority to perform. It is essential to the concept of apparent authority that the third person reasonably believe that the agent has authority. The mere placing of property in the possession of another does not give that person either actual or apparent authority to sell the property.

CPA 6. Agency by Ratification

An agent may attempt, on behalf of the principal, to do an act that was not authorized, or a person who is not the agent of another may attempt to act as such an agent. Very generally, notification may be express, where the principal explicitly approves the contract, or implied, where the principal does not object to the contract and accepts the contract's benefits. **For Example,** homeowners Schafstall and Alexander went to Lowe's Home Center to purchase a water system. Schafstall completed the purchase and signed the warranty contract for the installation service. The installation failed and resulted in over $100,000 in water damages to the property. Lowe's warranty limited its liability to just the cost of the reinstallation and repair parts for the system. Not only was Schafstall bound by the terms of the contract with its warranty, but Alexander ratified the contract by his presence at the transaction and is thus bound by its terms.[6]

(A) Intention to Ratify. Initially, ratification is a question of intention. Just as in the case of authorization, when there is a question of whether the principal authorized the agent, there is a question of whether the principal intended to approve or ratify the action of the unauthorized agent.

The intention to ratify may be expressed in words, or it may be found in conduct indicating an intention to ratify. **For Example,** James Reiner signed a five-year lease of commercial space on 320 West Main Street in Avon, Connecticut, because his father Calvin was away on vacation, and the owner, Robert Udolf, told James that if he did not come in and sign the lease, his father would lose the opportunity to rent the space in question. James was aware that his father had an interest in the space, and while telling Robert several times that he had no authority, James did sign his name to the lease. In fact, his father took occupancy of the space and paid rent for three years and then abandoned the space. James is not liable on the remainder of the lease because the owner knew at the time of signing that James did not have authority to act. Although he did not sign the lease, Calvin ratified the lease signed by James by his conduct of moving into the space and doing business there for three years with full knowledge of all material facts relating to the transaction. The owner, therefore, had to bring suit against Calvin, not James.[7]

CPA **(B) Conditions for Ratification.** In addition to the intent to ratify, expressed in some instances with a certain formality, the following conditions must be satisfied for the intention to take effect as a ratification:

1. The agent must have purported to act on behalf of or as agent for the identified principal.
2. The principal must have been capable of authorizing the act both at the time of the act and at the time it was ratified.
3. The principal must have full knowledge of all material facts.

It is not always necessary, however, to show that the principal had actual knowledge. Knowledge will be imputed if a principal knows of other facts that would lead a prudent person to make inquiries or if that knowledge can be inferred from the knowledge of other facts or from a course of business. **For Example,** Stacey, without authorization but knowing that William needed money, contracted to sell one of William's paintings to Courtney for $298. Stacey told William about the contract that evening; William said nothing and helped her wrap the painting in a protective plastic wrap for delivery. A favorable newspaper article about William's art appeared the following morning and dramatically increased the value of all of his paintings. William cannot recover the painting from Courtney on the theory that he never authorized the sale because he ratified the unauthorized contract made by Stacey by his conduct in helping her wrap the painting with full knowledge of the terms of the sale. The effect is a legally binding contract between William and Courtney.

(C) Effect of Ratification. When an unauthorized act is ratified, the effect is the same as though the act had been originally authorized. Ordinarily, this means that the principal and the third party are bound by the contract made by the agent.[8] When the principal ratifies the act of the unauthorized person, such ratification releases that person from the liability that would otherwise be imposed for having acted without authority.

CPA 7. Proving the Agency Relationship

The burden of proving the existence of an agency relationship rests on the person who seeks to benefit by such proof. The third person who desires to bind the principal because of the act of an alleged agent has the burden of proving that the latter person was in fact the authorized agent of the principal and possessed the authority to do the act in question.[9]

[6] *Guideone Insurance Co. v. U.S. Water Systems, Inc. and Lowe's Home Centers*, 950 N.E.2d 1236 (Ind. App. 2011).
[7] *Udolf v. Reiner*, 2000 WL 726953 (Conn. Super. May 19, 2000).
[8] *Bill McCurley Chevrolet v. Rutz*, 808 P.2d 1167 (Wash. App. 1991).
[9] *Cummings, Inc. v. Nelson*, 115 P.3d 536 (Alaska 2005).

C. Agent's Authority

When there is an agent, it is necessary to determine the scope of the agent's authority.

8. Scope of Agent's Authority

The scope of an agent's authority may be determined from the express words of the principal to the agent or it may be implied from the principal's words or conduct or from the customs of the trade or business.

(A) Express Authority. If the principal tells the agent to perform a certain act, the agent has express authority to do so. Express authority can be given orally or in writing.

(B) Incidental Authority. An agent has implied **incidental authority** to perform any act reasonably necessary to execute the express authority given to the agent. **For Example,** if the principal authorizes the agent to purchase goods without furnishing funds to the agent to pay for them, the agent has the implied incidental authority to purchase the goods on credit.[10]

(C) Customary Authority. An agent has implied **customary authority** to do any act that, according to the custom of the community, usually accompanies the transaction for which the agent is authorized to act. An agent who has express authority to receive payments from third persons, for example, has the implied customary authority to issue receipts.

(D) Apparent Authority. A person has **apparent authority** as an agent when the principal's words or conduct leads a third person to reasonably believe that the person has that authority and the third person relies on that appearance.[11]

In the *CSX* case, the court considered whether a business clothed an individual with apparent authority solely by allowing him to use its e-mail domain name.

CSX Transportation, Inc. v. Recovery Express, Inc., 415 F. Supp. 2d 6 (D. Mass. 2006)

CSX Gets Railroaded by Albert Arillotta

Recovery Express and Interstate Demolition (IDEC) are two separate corporations located at the same business address in Boston. On August 22, 2003, Albert Arillotta, a "partner" at IDEC sent an e-mail to Len Whitehead Jr. of CSX Transportation expressing an interest in buying "rail cars as scrap." Arillotta represented himself to be "from interstate demolition and recovery express" in the e-mail. And the e-mail address from which he sent his inquiry was "albert@recoveryxpress.com." Arillotta went to CSX rail yard, disassembled the cars and transported them away. Thereafter CSX sent invoices for payment for the scrap railcars totaling $115,757.36 addressed to IDEC at its Boston office shared with Recovery Express. Whitehead believed Arillotta was authorized to act for Recovery Express, based on the e-mail's domain name—"recoveryexpress.com" Recovery claims that Arillotta never worked for it. Recovery's president Thomas Trafton allowed the "fledgling" company to use telephone, fax, and e-mail services at its offices, but never shared anything with IDEC—assets, funds, books of business, or financials. CSX sued Recovery for the invoice amount on the doctrine of "apparent authority." IDEC is now defunct. Recovery claims that Arillotta never worked for it, and it is not liable.

JUDICIAL OPINION

YOUNG, D.J.…The Case, then, rests on the doctrine of apparent authority. "Apparent authority is the power held by an agent or other actor to affect a principal's legal relations with third parties when a third party reasonably believes the actor has authority to act on behalf of the principal and that belief is traceable to the principal's manifestations." Restatement at § 2.03. It "is not established by the putative agent's words or conduct, but by those of the principal."… Moreover, apparent authority "may exist only when the plaintiff *reasonably* may believe as a result of the principal's words or conduct that the agent is authorized to act on its behalf."…

In what looks to be an issue of first impression, the facts of this case set up the question whether an e-mail domain name, by itself, cloaks a purported agent with authority sufficient as matter of law to be called "apparent." Because

[10] *Badger v. Paulson Investment Co.*, 803 P.2d 1178 (Or. 1991).

[11] *Alexander v. Chandler*, 179 S.W.2d 385 (Mo. App. 2005).

Continued

apparent authority depends on the knowledge held by Whitehead and CSX of Arillotta's authority, which knowledge was derived from actions of Recovery, the only relevant conduct by Recovery is that it issued Arillotta an e-mail address with its domain name. Such associations as Recovery having the same offices, mailing address, phone number, or fax number are red herrings; these facts—if Whitehead even possessed them prior to entering the contract—emanated from Arillotta by way of his e-mail signature or telephone representations. There is no evidence of the manifestation of those facts by Recovery to Whitehead and CSX (i.e., by way of its website, as CSX asserted at oral argument) until after the contract was entered and collection efforts had begun.

The only act taken by Recovery known to Whitehead and CSX prior to entering the contract and upon which Whitehead could rely, was its issuance to Arillotta of an e-mail address sporting Recovery's domain name (@recoveryexpress.com). The Court holds that Whitehead and CSX were unreasonable, as matter of law, in their reliance solely on an e-mail domain name. Such a manifestation by Recovery cannot be sufficient to sustain a claim of apparent authority. Granting an e-mail domain name, by itself, does not cloak the recipient with carte blanche authority to act on behalf the grantee. Were this so, every subordinate employee with a company e-mail address—down to the night watchman—could bind a company to the same contracts as the president. This is not the law.

Though e-mail communication may be relatively new to staid legal institutions, the results in analogous low-tech situations confirm this conclusion. The Court could find no cases where, for example, giving someone a business card with the company name or logo, access to a company car, or company stationery, *by themselves,* created sufficient indicia of apparent authority....

An e-mail domain name is sufficiently analogous to business cards, company vehicles, and letterhead for these cases to be persuasive. Those indicia of apparent authority all convey some degree of association between the purported principal and agent. By themselves, however, no reasonable person could conclude that apparent authority was present. The same is true with e-mail domain names.

In the end, CSX and Whitehead should have been more suspicious of an unsolicited, poorly written e-mail that arrived late one Friday afternoon. There are means by which CSX could have protected itself (e.g., requiring a purchase order form from IDEC or Recovery).* Before delivering goods worth over $115,000 to a stranger, one reasonably should be expected to inquire as to the authority of the person to have made such a deal. Given the anonymity of the Internet, this case illustrates the potential consequences of operating—even in today's fast-paced business world—as did CSX.

[Judgment for Recovery]

QUESTION

1. Appraise the correctness of the following statement: "Apparent authority comes from the actions of a principal, not the statements of an individual who claims to be an agent."

*"Parties can feel confident that they have formed binding contracts while communicating over open networks only if they use reliable authentication procedures." Jane Kaufman Winn, *Open System, Free Markets, and Regulation of Internet Commerce,* 72 Tulane L. Rev 1177, 1180 (1998) (discussing potential legal problems and technical solutions in Internet commerce).

9. Effect of Proper Exercise of Authority

When an agent with authority properly makes a contract with a third person that purports to bind the principal, there is by definition a binding contract between the principal and the third person. The agent is not a party to this contract. Consequently, when the owner of goods is the principal, the owner's agent is not liable for breach of warranty with respect to the goods "sold" by the agent. The owner-principal, not the agent, was the "seller" in the sales transaction.

CPA 10. Duty to Ascertain Extent of Agent's Authority

A third person who deals with a person claiming to be an agent cannot rely on the statements made by the agent concerning the extent of authority.[12] If the agent is not authorized to perform the act or is not even the agent of the principal, the transaction between the alleged agent and the third person will have no legal effect between the principal and the third person.

[12] *Breed v. Hughes Aircraft Col.,* 35 Fed. App. 864 (Fed. Cir. 2002).

Third persons who deal with an agent whose authority is limited to a special purpose are bound at their peril to find out the extent of the agent's authority. An attorney is such an agent. Unless the client holds the attorney out as having greater authority than usual, the attorney has no authority to settle a claim without approval from the client.

(A) Agent's Acts Adverse to Principal. The third person who deals with an agent is required to take notice of any acts that are clearly adverse to the interest of the principal. Thus, if the agent is obviously using funds of the principal for the agent's personal benefit, persons dealing with the agent should recognize that the agent may be acting without authority and that they are dealing with the agent at their peril.

The only certain way that third persons can protect themselves is to inquire of the principal whether the agent is in fact the agent of the principal and has the necessary authority. **For Example,** Ron Fahd negotiated the sale of a fire truck to the Edinburg Volunteer Fire Company, on behalf of the manufacturer, Danko Company, at a price of $158,000. On Danko forms and letterhead Fahd drafted a "Proposal for Fire Apparatus" and it was signed by the president of the Fire Company and Fahd, as a dealer for Danko. Fahd gave a special $2,000 discount for prepayment of the cost of the chassis. Fahd directed that the prepayment check of $55,000 be made payable to "Ron Fahd Sales" in order to obtain the discount. The Fire Company's treasurer inquired of Fahd why the prepayment check was being made out to Fahd rather than Danko, and he accepted Fahd's answer without contacting Danko to confirm this unusual arrangement. Fahd absconded with the proceeds of the check. The Fire Company sued Danko claiming Fahd had apparent authority to receive the prepayment. While there was some indicia of agency, the court found that the Fire Company had failed to make reasonable inquiry with Danko to verify Fahd's authority to receive the prepayment in Fahd's name, and it rejected the claim that Fahd had apparent authority to accept the prepayment check made out to Fahd as opposed to Danko.[13]

11. Limitations on Agent's Authority

A person who has knowledge of a limitation on the agent's authority cannot ignore that limitation. When the third person knows that the authority of the agent depends on whether financing has been obtained, the principal is not bound by the act of the agent if the financing in fact was not obtained. If the authority of the agent is based on a writing and the third person knows that there is such a writing, the third person is charged with knowledge of limitations contained in it.

(A) "Obvious" Limitations. In some situations, it may be obvious to third persons that they are dealing with an agent whose authority is limited. When third persons know that they are dealing with a representative of a government agency, they should recognize that such a person will ordinarily have limited authority. Third persons should recognize that a contract made with such an officer or representative may not be binding unless ratified by the principal.

The federal government places the risk on any individual making arrangements with the government to accurately ascertain that the government agent is within the bounds of his or her authority, as set forth in the *Humlen* case.

Humlen v. United States, 49 Fed. Cl. 497 (2001)

Humlen Was Had?

In 1993, the U.S. Customs Service contacted Peder Humlen on numerous occasions regarding an ongoing investigation of Colombian cartel leader John Jairo Montoya's drug trafficking activities. In early 1994, FBI Special Agents Craig Howland and Ralph Hope sought Humlen's assistance in an FBI attempt to secure Montoya's conviction. Humlen was formally "opened" as an FBI cooperative witness and agreed to wear equipment to record conversations with the subjects of an FBI criminal investigation known as Steelwind. He alleges that Special Agents Hope and Howland promised to reimburse him for his reasonable

[13] *Edinburg Volunteer Fire Company v. Danko,* 867 N.Y.S.2d 547 (A.D. 2008).

Continued

expenses and compensate him up to $2,000 per month. In addition, Humlen claims that the FBI, through Special Agents Hope and Howland, promised to pay him 25 percent of any monies recovered from property or money forfeiture, $500 for every kilogram of cocaine seized, and a lump-sum award of up to $250,000 at the conclusion of the investigation.

On January 20, 1994, Humlen executed a "Non-Personal Services Agreement" with the FBI to formalize his status as a confidential informant. This agreement was reviewed by the FBI Contracts Unit at FBI Headquarters and signed by the FBI Supervisory Special Agent James Dietz. Under the terms of the agreement, Humlen would provide the FBI with information regarding Montoya's drug trafficking activities in exchange for a monthly compensation of, at most, $2,000. In addition,

> *The FBI may, at its sole option and choice, elect to furnish Humlen with an award of money upon the completion of the investigation. The amount of any award is at the complete and total discretion of the FBI and/or the Attorney General of the United States and, as stated in 28 U.S.C. § 524 [(1994)], any award for information or assistance leading to a civil or criminal forfeiture is at the complete and full discretion of the Attorney General and shall not exceed the lesser of $250,000 or one-fourth of the amount realized by the United States from the property forfeited.*

In addressing the scope of the agreement, the document expressly stated:

> *This document constitutes the full and complete agreement between Humlen and the FBI. Modifications to this agreement will have no force and effect unless and until such modifications are reduced to writing and signed by all parties thereto.*

The agreement also provided that Special Agent Hope is the "designated representative for the FBI Contracting Officer."

Humlen asserts that when FBI Special Agents Howland and/or Hope presented the agreement for his signature, he asked the agents why the written contract differed form the oral promises they had made to him regarding the 25 percent reward, the $500 per kilogram of cocaine seized, and the "up to $250,000 lump-sum." In response, the agents allegedly explained that the agreement had to be "couched" in that way because it was a discoverable document in any future criminal prosecution and thus could be used to discredit the plaintiff's reliability and credibility. The plaintiff maintains that the agents assured him that despite the wording of the contract, he would receive 25 percent of all forfeited money and property, as well as $500 per kilogram of cocaine seized.

Based in part on information provided by the plaintiff, Montoya was arrested and pleaded guilty on November 27, 1995, to Interstate Travel and Transportation in Aid of a Racketeering Enterprise, among other charges. In addition, Humlen claims his information led to the arrest of three of Montoya's colleagues, the seizure of 428 kilograms of cocaine, the seizure and eventual forfeiture of $754,000, a residence on Allesandro Street in Los Angeles, a Nissan pickup truck, two Ford Aerostar vans, and a 1990 Blue Camaro. The government, on the other hand, maintains that the plaintiff's information supplied to the FBI in the Steelwind Investigation led to the arrest of Montoya's colleagues, and the seizure of over 230 kilograms of cocaine, and approximately $50,000.

During the course of the FBI Steelwind Investigation, Humlen's handling agents changed due to transfer assignments. Humlen maintains that throughout the investigations, FBI Special Agents Howland, Hope, Embry, and Sierra, and USCS Agent O'Shaughnessy repeatedly assured him that he would receive his anticipated remuneration for continued cooperation in the investigative effort as Special Agents Hope and Howland had originally promised.

Form the time Humlen executed the agreement through the prosecutoral phase of the FBI steelwind investigation, the FBI remitted to the plaintiff monthly payments of up to $2,000. Also in accordance with the agreement, he was reimbursed for the reasonable expenses he incurred in furtherance of the criminal investigation and offered sponsorship into the Federal Witness Protection Program. The DEA also remitted to him a one-time lump-sum $5,000 payment to relocate himself and his family. A final $2,000 payment request was made on January 1996, and when no additional payment was forthcoming, Humlen sued the U.S. Government in the Court of Federal Claims.

JUDICIAL OPINION

MARGOLIS, S. J.…On January 25, 1996, Agent Sierra prepared a request for a final $2,000 payment to plaintiff and noted that "this will be the final payment to the source from case funds; however, 'Sara 5' is preparing a request for lump sum payment which will be forwarded via separate cover *for approval."*…On or about March 27, 1996, Agent Sierra prepared a formal request for a $50,000 one-time lump-sum award payment for plaintiff's "services" as a cooperative witness during the FBI Steelwind Investigation. Ultimately intended for review and possible approval by FBI Headquarters, Agent Sierra's request was forwarded to her immediate supervisor [Linas] Danilevicius and then, to his immediate supervisor, Steinhauser. On April 10, 1996, Steinhauser returned the awarded request to Danilevicius with a note stating:

> *Linas—the [cooperative witness] is credited with 232 kilos of coke, $50K cash sized, 3 arrests and convictions. For this, he has been paid $50,000 on a personal services agreement during 1/20/94 to 2/12/96. We are now asking for a lump sum of $50,000 for the same information and*

Continued

accomplishment, for the same period of time! I must be missing something here!

Please shed some light and provide justification; I have reviewed the file and I don't see it.

No further action was taken on this request. Agent Sierra informed [Peder Humlen] that the requested $50,000 had been denied. On May 23, 1996, the FBI officially "closed" plaintiff as a cooperative witness.

DISCUSSION

...The Government, unlike private parties, cannot be bound by the apparent authority of its agents. See *Roy v United States, 38 Fed. Cl. 184, 187, (1997)*. Thus, the Court must determine "whether plaintiff has submitted sufficient evidence to establish a disputed issue of fact as to whether the FBI [Special Agents] with whom he allegedly dealt had [actual] authority contractually to obligate the Government." The general rule regarding the authority of government agents to bind the government is set forth in *Federal Crop Insurance Corp. v Merrill, 332 U.S. 380, 92 L. Ed. 10, 68 S. Ct. 1 (1947)*: "Anyone entering into an arrangement with the Government takes the risk of having accurately ascertained that he who purports to act for the Government stays within the bounds of his authority...this is so even though...the agent may have been unaware of the limitations upon his authority." *Federal Crop Insurance, 332 U.S at 384.* When an agent exceeds his authority, the government can "disavow the [agent's] words and is not bound by an implied contract."

Implied actual authority, like express actual authority, also can bind the Government for the acts of its agents. See *H. Landau & Co., 886 F.2d at 324.* Authority is "generally implied when such authority is considered to be an integral part of the duties assigned to that Government employee." As a general rule, DEA Field Agents and FBI Special Agents lack the requisite actual authority—either expressed or implied—to contractually bind the United States to remit rewards to confidential informants/cooperative witnesses. This is so because contractual duty is not considered to be an integral part of their duties. See *Roy, 38 Fed. Cl. At 188-91* (contracting authority is not essential or necessary for FBI Special Agents to effectively perform their tasks of developing, controlling and supervising confidential informants);...In *Roy* the court held that the doctrine of implied actual authority was inapplicable because "contracting authority is not integral to FBI [Special Agents'] informant responsibilities." Accordingly, this court holds that any promises that Special Agents Howland, Hope, Embry and Sierra might have made to the plaintiff cannot bind the government because the Special Agents lack the requisite authority....

CONCLUSION

...Defendant's motion for summary judgment is granted.

QUESTIONS

1. State the rule of law applicable to third persons dealing with representatives of the U.S. government. Does an apparent authority rule bind the government? May the government "disavow" the promises made by their agents beyond their authority?
2. Was it "okay" for the government agents to explain away the terms of the written agreement as being "couched" for discovery purposes, and to assure Humlen that he would get the anticipated remuneration promised?

(B) Secret Limitations. If the principal has clothed an agent with authority to perform certain acts but the principal gives secret instructions that limit the agent's authority, the third person is allowed to take the authority of the agent at its face value. The third person is not bound by the secret limitations of which the third person has no knowledge.

D. Duties and Liabilities of Principal and Agent

The creation of the principal-agent relationship gives rise to duties and liabilities.

12. Duties and Liabilities of Agent during Agency

While the agency relationship exists, the agent owes certain duties to the principal.

(A) Loyalty. An agent must be loyal or faithful to the principal.[14] The agent must not obtain any secret benefit from the agency. If the principal is seeking to buy or rent property, the agent cannot secretly obtain the property and then sell or lease it to the principal at a profit.

An agent who owns property cannot sell it to the principal without disclosing that ownership to the principal. If disclosure is not made, the principal may

[14] *Patterson Custom Homes v. Bach*, 536 F. Supp. 2d 1026 (E.D. Ill. 2008).

avoid the contract even if the agent's conduct did not cause the principal any financial loss. Alternatively, the principal can approve the transaction and sue the agent for any secret profit obtained by the agent.

A contract is voidable by the principal if the agent who was employed to sell the property purchases the property, either directly or indirectly, without full disclosure to the principal.

An agent cannot act as agent for both parties to a transaction unless both know of the dual capacity and agree to it. If the agent does act in this capacity without the consent of both parties, any principal who did not know of the agent's double status can avoid the transaction.

An agent must not accept secret gifts or commissions from third persons in connection with the agency. If the agent does so, the principal may sue the agent for those gifts or commissions. Such practices are condemned because the judgment of the agent may be influenced by the receipt of gifts or commissions.

It is a violation of an agent's duty of loyalty to make and retain secret profits.

In the *Ellison* case, the agent took additional secret compensation for himself.

Ellison v. Alley 842 S.W.2d 605 (Tenn. 1992)

This "Option" Quarterback Is Out of Bounds!

Real estate broker Donald Alley Sr. had a listing contract that gave him the exclusive right to sell wayman Ellison's farm for at least $200,000. Ellison was told that a buyer was found. The buyer, Cora Myers, who had been paid $585,000 for her small farm because the land was needed for a commercial development, agreed to pay $380,000 for the large Ellison farm. Alley told Ellison that the sales price was $200,000. The buyer paid $380,000, however, and Alley kept the difference. When Ellison later learned of these details, he sued Alley for the $180,000. From a judgment for Ellison, Alley appealed, seeking at least his commission on the sale.

JUDICIAL OPINION

O'BRIEN, J....We are in agreement with the finding of breach of fiduciary duty and the award to the plaintiff of the defendant's profits. But, on the narrow issue upon which this appeal was granted, we find that the defendant [is] not entitled to a commission on the sale of the Ellison property. It is apparent that the defendant manipulated [the] transactions in such a manner as to willfully, and wrongfully, conceal [his] true role and [his] intention to reap a $180,000 ill-gained profit from the sale of the property.

It is well settled that the real estate agent acts as a fiduciary to the client. In any transaction or dealing related to such relationship, "the agent can in no way and under no circumstances act for himself or for any other than the principal without first making full and complete disclosure of the facts to the principal. He cannot profit by his failure to make such disclosure."...When a broker procures legal title to property, in violation of a fiduciary duty owed to the owner, equity constructs a trust out of the transaction. In such a case, the property owner is entitled to the profits wrongfully received by the broker in the transaction....The construction of such a trust is without regard to whether the principal received a fair price for the conveyance of the property....

Likewise, "where a broker's actions in a sale transaction amounts to bad faith or misconduct, the broker is not entitled to a commission on the sale."...It is undeniable that the defendant acted in these transactions with bad faith and beyond the bounds of ethical conduct. To permit the defendant credit for a reasonable commission on the sale of the Ellison property would be no more than offering an undeserved reward for avarice....

[Judgment affirmed]

QUESTIONS

1. Is the seller's right to a remedy not defeated by the fact that the seller received the net price he sought?
2. May an agent ever buy a principal's property?
3. Did Alley act contrary to any ethical principles?
4. Since Alley did find a ready, willing, and able buyer, is he not at least entitled to his commission?

An agent is, of course, prohibited from aiding the competitors of a principal or disclosing to them information relating to the business of the principal. It is also a breach of duty for the agent to knowingly deceive a principal.[15]

(B) Obedience and Performance. An agent is under a duty to obey all lawful instructions.[16] The agent is required to perform the services specified for the period and in the way specified. An agent who does not do so is liable to the principal for any harm caused. For example, if an agent is instructed to take cash payments only but accepts a check in payment, the agent is liable for the loss caused the principal if a check is dishonored by nonpayment.

(C) Reasonable Care. It is the duty of an agent to act with the care that a reasonable person would exercise under the circumstances. **For Example,** Ethel Wilson applied for fire insurance for her house with St. Paul Reinsurance Co., Ltd., through her agent Club Services Corp. She thought she was fully covered. Unbeknownst to her, however, St. Paul had refused coverage and returned her premium to Club Services, who did not refund it to Ms. Wilson or inform her that coverage had been denied. Fire destroyed her garage and St. Paul denied coverage. Litigation resulted, and St. Paul ended up expending $305,406 to settle the Wilson matter. Thereafter, St. Paul successfully sued Club Services Corp. under basic agency law principles that an agent (Club Services) is liable to its principal for all damages resulting from the agent's failure to discharge its duties.[17] In addition, if the agent possesses a special skill, as in the case of a broker or an attorney, the agent must exercise that skill.

(D) Accounting. An agent must account to the principal for all property or money belonging to the principal that comes into the agent's possession. The agent must, within a reasonable time, give notice of collections made and render an accurate account of all receipts and expenditures. The agency agreement may state at what intervals or on what dates such accountings are to be made. An agent must keep the principal's property and money separate and distinct from that of the agent.

(E) Information. It is the duty of an agent to keep the principal informed of all facts relating to the agency that are relevant to protecting the principal's interests.[18]

13. Duties and Liabilities of Agent after Termination of Agency

When the agency relationship ends, the duties of the agent continue only to the extent necessary to perform prior obligations. For example, the agent must return to the former principal any property that had been entrusted to the agent for the purpose of the agency. With the exception of such "winding-up" duties, the agency relationship is terminated, and the former agent can deal with the principal as freely as with a stranger.[19]

14. Duties and Liabilities of Principal to Agent

The principal must perform the contract, compensate the agent for services, make reimbursement for proper expenditures and, under certain circumstances, must indemnify the agent for loss.

(A) Employment According to Terms of Contract. When the contract is for a specified time, the principal is obligated to permit the agent to act as agent for the term of the contract. Exceptions are made for just cause or contract provisions that permit the principal to terminate the agency sooner. If the principal gives the agent an exclusive right to act in that capacity, the principal cannot give anyone else the authority to act as agent, nor may the principal do the act to which the exclusive agent's authority relates. **For Example,** if Jill Baker gives Brett Stamos the exclusive right for six months to sell her house, she cannot give another real estate agent the right to sell it during the six-month period or undertake to sell the house herself. If the principal or another agent sells the house, the exclusive agent is entitled to full compensation just as though the act had been performed by the exclusive agent.

[15] *Koontz v. Rosener*, 787 P.2d 192 (Colo. App. 1990).
[16] *Stanford v. Neiderer*, 341 S.E.2d 892 (Ga. App. 1986).
[17] *St. Paul Reinsurance Co., Ltd. v. Club Services Corp.*, 30 Fed. Appx. 834 (10th Cir. 2002).
[18] Restatement (Second) of Agency §381; *Lumberman's Mutual Ins. Co. v. Franey Muha Alliant Ins.*, 388 F. Supp. 2d 292 (S.D.N.Y. 2005).
[19] *Corron & Black of Illinois, Inc. v. Magner*, 494 N.E.2d 785 (Ill. App. 1986).

(B) Compensation. The principal must pay the agent the agreed compensation.[20] If the parties have not fixed the amount of the compensation by their agreement but intended that the agent should be paid, the agent may recover the customary compensation for such services. If there is no established compensation, the agent may recover the reasonable value of the services rendered.

(1) Repeating Transactions.

In certain industries, third persons make repeated transactions with the principal. In these cases, the agent who made the original contract with the third person commonly receives a certain compensation or percentage of commissions on all subsequent renewal or additional contracts. In the insurance business, for example, the insurance agent obtaining the policyholder for the insurer receives a substantial portion of the first year's premiums and then receives a smaller percentage of the premiums paid by the policyholder in subsequent years.

(2) Postagency Transactions.

An agent is not ordinarily entitled to compensation in connection with transactions, such as sales or renewals of insurance policies, occurring after the termination of the agency even if the postagency transactions are the result of the agent's former activities. However, if the parties' employment contract calls for such compensation, it must be paid. **For Example,** real estate agent Laura McLane's contract called for her to receive $1.50 for every square foot the Atlanta Committee for the Olympic Games, Inc. (ACOG), leased at an Atlanta building; and even though she had been terminated at the time ACOG executed a lease amendment for 164,412 additional square feet, she was contractually entitled to a $246,618 commission.[21]

E. Termination of Agency

An agency may be terminated by the act of one or both of the parties to the agency agreement or by operation of law. When the authority of an agent is terminated, the agent loses all right to act for the principal.

15. Termination by Act of Parties

The duration of the agency relationship is commonly stated in the contract creating the relationship. In most cases, either party has the power to terminate the agency relationship at any time. However, the terminating party may be liable for damages to the other if the termination is in violation of the agency contract.

When a principal terminates an agent's authority, it is not effective until the agent receives the notice. Because a known agent will have the appearance of still being an agent, notice must be given to third persons of the termination, and the agent may have the power to bind the principal and third persons until this notice is given.

16. Termination by Operation of Law

The agency relationship is a personal one, and anything that renders one of the parties incapable of performing will result in the termination of the relationship by operation of law. The death of either the principal or the agent ordinarily terminates the authority of an agent automatically even if the death is unknown to the other.[22]

An agency is also terminated by operation of law on the (1) insanity of the principal or agent, (2) bankruptcy of the principal or agent, (3) impossibility of performance, such as the destruction of the subject matter, or (4) when the country of the principal is at war with that of the agent.

17. Disability of the Principal under the UDPAA

The Uniform Durable Power of Attorney Act (UDPAA) permits the creation of an agency by specifying that "this power of attorney shall not be affected by subsequent disability or incapacity of the principal." Alternatively, the UDPAA permits the agency to come into existence upon the disability or incapacity of the principal. For this to be effective, the principal must designate the attorney in fact in writing. The writing must contain words showing the intent of the principal that the authority conferred

[20] *American Chocolates, Inc. v. Mascot Pecan Co., Inc.*, 592 So.2d 93 (Miss. 1992).
[21] *McLane v. Atlanta Market Center Management Co.*, 486 S.E.2d 30 (Ga. App. 1997).
[22] *New York Life Ins. Co. v. Estate of Haelen*, 521 N.Y.S.2d 970 (N.Y. Civ. Ct.1987).

shall continue notwithstanding the disability or incapacity of the principal. The UDPAA, which has been adopted by most states,[23] changes the common law and the general rule that insanity of the principal terminates the agent's authority to act for the principal. Society today recognizes that it may be in the best interest of a principal and good for the business environment for a principal to designate another as an attorney in fact to act for the principal when the principal becomes incapacitated.[24] It may be prudent to grant durable powers of attorney to different persons for property matters and for health care decisions.

Durable powers of attorney grant only those powers that are specified in the instrument. A durable power of attorney may be terminated by revocation by a competent principal and by the death of the principal.

The *Estate of Graham* case deals with issues related to the utilization of a durable power of attorney.

Estate of Graham v. Morrison, 607 S.E.2d 295 (N.C. App. 2005)

Broad Powers...But There Is a Limit, Lucille

On May 31, 2001, Thomas Graham made his niece Lucille Morrison his attorney in fact by executing a durable power of attorney. It was notarized and filed at the Registry of Deeds. The power of attorney granted Lucille broad powers and discretion in Graham's affairs. However, it did not contain express authority to make gifts. On October 26, 2000, Lucille conveyed 11.92 acres of property valued at between $400,000 and $700,000 to herself based upon consideration of services rendered to the principal, Thomas Graham. On June 5, 2001, Lucille, as attorney in fact for Graham, conveyed Graham's house in Charlotte to her son Ladd Morrison. And, on June 20, 2001, she conveyed Graham's oakview Terrace property to her brother John Hallman for $3,000 to pay for an attorney to defend Graham in a competency proceeding. Graham died on August 7, 2001, and the estate of Thomas Graham sued to set aside the deeds alleging Lucille's breach of fiduciary duties. After a judgment for the defendants, the estate appealed.

JUDICIAL OPINION

HUNTER, J.…[W]e hold that in situations where an attorney-in-fact conveys the principal's property to herself base upon a consideration of alleged services rendered to the principal, the valuable consideration must reflect a fair and reasonable price when compared to the fair market value of the property.…

Although Lucille took care of Graham and his wife during their illnesses and helped handle their business affairs,… Graham did not execute the deed to Lucille. Rather, Lucille utilized her power of attorney to execute the deed to herself. Given that during the time the deed was drafted, Graham was trying to sell the property, and that Lucille testified the deed was drafted to help finalize the sale of Graham's property, the testimony tends to indicate that the land was not conveyed to Lucille as compensation for her past services. Moreover, there was no testimony indicating the value of Lucille's services were comparable to the value of the real property, between $400,000.00 and $700,000.00. Accordingly, we conclude the trial court erroneously denied plaintiffs' motion for judgment not-withstanding the verdict.

Plaintiff has also challenged a conveyance of Graham's home on Coronet Way in Charlotte, North Carolina, to Ladd Morrison, the son of Lucille Morrison.…Lucille testified that Ladd had spent over $12,000.00 to improve the condition of the house so Graham could live in it. Ladd paid for windows, paint, supplies, a furnace, and labor. Ladd testified, however, that "[he] was just taking care of [his] family" and that he never expected to get the money back. According to Lucille, Graham told her to give Ladd the property on Coronet Way and she indicated that she was following his instructions. However, there was no indication in the testimony that the conveyance was intended to be payment for services. Thus, this deed must be set aside because this Court has already determined that the power of attorney held by Lucille over Graham's affairs did not give her the power to make gifts.…

Plaintiffs contend Lucille sold property owned by Graham to her brother, John to secure an attorney for herself. However, Lucille testified that the money was used to retain an attorney to represent Graham in an incompetency proceeding. According to the testimony, on 6 June 2001, Graham was admitted to the hospital. The next day, on 7 June 2001, his daughter filed a petition to have Graham declared incompetent. Upon learning of the petition, Lucille testified she sold the property and retained an attorney to represent

[23] The Uniform Durable Power of Attorney Act has been adopted in some fashion in all states except Connecticut, Florida, Georgia, Illinois, Indiana, Kansas, Louisiana, and Missouri.

[24] The Uniform Probate Code and the Uniform Durable Power of Attorney Act provide for the coexistence of durable powers and guardians or conservators. These acts allow the attorney in fact to continue to manage the principal's financial affairs while the court-appointed fiduciary takes the place of the principal in overseeing the actions of the attorney in fact. See *Rice v. Flood*, 768 S.W.2d 57 (Ky. 1989).

Continued

herself and Graham at the hearing. The power of attorney granted Lucille the power to sell Graham's real estate and to "perform all and every act or thing, whatsoever requisite or necessary to be done for [Graham's] upkeep, care, and maintenance, and for the management of any property owned by me, as fully, and to all intents and purposes as I might or could do if I were personally present and acting...." The power of attorney also granted Lucille the authority to make contracts, including selling real property for adequate consideration, on Graham's behalf. As Lucille testified that she hired the attorney to represent Graham in the competency hearing, and the power of attorney granted Lucille the authority to take such actions, we conclude the trial court properly denied plaintiff's motion for judgment notwithstanding the verdict on this particular conversion allegation....

...Lucille did not have authority under the power of attorney to give Graham's property to herself or her son. Therefore, she breached the fiduciary duty owed to Graham. ...

[Affirmed in part, reversed and remanded in part]

Judges WYNN and THORNBURG concur.

Judge THORNBURG concurred in this opinion prior to 31 December 2004.

QUESTIONS

1. Can an attorney in fact convey property to herself based on consideration of services rendered to the principal?
2. Can an attorney in fact sell a principal's property to obtain funds to pay an attorney to represent the principal?
3. Was the conveyance of the home in Charlotte to Ladd Morrison allowable under the power of attorney?

18. Termination of Agency Coupled with an Interest

An agency coupled with an interest is an exception to the general rule as to the termination of an agency. Such an agency cannot be revoked by the principal before the expiration of the interest. It is not terminated by the death or insanity of either the principal or the agent.

19. Protection of Agent from Termination of Authority

The modern world of business has developed several methods of protecting an agent from the termination of authority for any reason.[25]

These methods include the use of an exclusive agency contract, a secured transaction, an escrow deposit, a standby letter of agreement, or a guarantee agreement.

20. Effect of Termination of Authority

If the principal revokes the agency, the authority to act for the principal is not terminated until the agent receives notice of revocation. As between the principal and the agent, the right of the agent to bind the principal to third persons generally ends immediately upon the termination of the agent's authority. This termination is effective without giving notice to third persons.

When the agency is terminated by the act of the principal, notice must be given to third persons. If this notice is not given, the agent may have the power to make contracts that will bind the principal and third persons. This rule is predicated on the theory that a known agent will have the appearance of still being the agent unless notice to the contrary is given to third persons.[26] **For Example,** Seltzer owns property in Boca Raton that he uses for the month of February and leases the remainder of the year. O'Neil has been Seltzer's rental agent for the past seven years, renting to individuals like Ed Tucker under a power of attorney that gives him authority to lease the property for set seasonal and off-season rates. O'Neil's right to bind Seltzer on a rental agreement ended when Seltzer faxed O'Neil a revocation of the power of attorney on March 1. A rental contract with Ed Tucker signed by O'Neil on behalf of Seltzer on

[25] These methods generally replace the concept of an agency coupled with an interest because of the greater protection given to the agent. Typically, the rights of the agent under these modern devices cannot be defeated by the principal, by operation of law, or by claims of other creditors.

[26] See *Stout Street Funding, LLC v. Johnson*, 2012 WL 1994800 (E.D. Pa. June 1, 2012). TRGC terminated its contract with Mabstract to serve as TRGC's closing agent on July 12, 2010, and obtained a court injunction barring Mabstract from engaging in any business on behalf of TRGC on July 15. Stout asserts that it had no actual notice of Mabstract's termination nor were there any red flags when it transmitted $480,000 into an escrow account held by Mabstract for a July 19 real estate transaction, which funds were misappropriated by Mabstract. It asserts that apparent authority lasts until a third party has actual notice of an agent's termination or until the third party has enough information to put that individual on inquiry.

March 2 will bind Seltzer, however, because O'Neil still appeared to be Seltzer's agent and Tucker had no notice to the contrary.

When the law requires giving notice in order to end the power of the agent to bind the principal, individual notice must be given or mailed to all persons who had prior dealings with the agent. In addition, notice to the general public can be given by publishing in a newspaper of general circulation in the affected geographic area a statement that the agency has been terminated.

If a notice is actually received, the power of the agent is terminated without regard to whether the method of giving notice was proper. Conversely, if proper notice is given, it is immaterial that it does not actually come to the attention of the party notified. Thus, a member of the general public cannot claim that the principal is bound on the ground that the third person did not see the newspaper notice stating that the agent's authority had been terminated.

MAKE THE CONNECTION

SUMMARY

An agency relationship is created by an express or implied agreement by which one person, the agent, is authorized to make contracts with third persons on behalf of, and subject to, the control of another person, the principal. An agent differs from an independent contractor in that the principal, who controls the acts of an agent, does not have control over the details of performance of work by the independent contractor. Likewise, an independent contractor does not have authority to act on behalf of the other contracting party.

A special agent is authorized by the principal to handle a specific business transaction. A general agent is authorized by the principal to transact all business affairs of the principal at a certain place. A universal agent is authorized to perform all acts that can be lawfully delegated to a representative.

The usual method of creating an agency is by express authorization. However, an agency relationship may be found to exist when the principal causes or permits a third person to reasonably believe that an agency relationship exists. In such a case, the "agent" appears to be authorized and is said to have apparent authority.

An unauthorized transaction by an agent for a principal may be ratified by the principal.

An agent acting with authority has the power to bind the principal. The scope of an agent's authority may be determined from the express words of the principal to the agent; this is called express authority. An agent has incidental authority to perform any act reasonably necessary to execute the authority given the agent. An agent's authority may be implied so as to enable the agent to perform any act in accordance with the general customs or usages in a business or an industry. This authority is often referred to as customary authority.

The effect of a proper exercise of authority by an agent is to bind the principal and third person to a contract. The agent, not being a party to the contract, is not liable in any respect under the contract. A third person dealing with a person claiming to be an agent has a duty to ascertain the extent of the agent's authority and a duty to take notice of any acts that are clearly adverse to the principal's interests. The third person cannot claim that apparent authority existed when that person has notice that the agent's conduct is adverse to the interests of the principal. A third person who has knowledge of limitations on an agent's authority is bound by those limitations. A third person is not bound by secret limitations.

While the agency relationship exists, the agent owes the principal the duties of (1) being loyal, (2) obeying all lawful instructions, (3) exercising reasonable care, (4) accounting for all property or money belonging to the principal, and (5) informing the principal of all facts relating to the agency that are relevant to the principal's interests. An agency relationship can be terminated by act of either the principal or the agent. However, the terminating party may be liable for damages to the other if the termination is in violation of the agency contract.

Because a known agent will have the appearance of still being an agent, notice must be given to third persons of the termination, and the agent may have the power to bind the principal and third persons until this notice is given.

An agency is terminated by operation of law upon (1) the death of the principal or agent, (2) insanity of the principal or agent, (3) bankruptcy of the principal or agent, (4) impossibility of performance, caused, for example, by the destruction of the subject matter, or (5) war.

In states that have adopted the Uniform Durable Power of Attorney Act (UDPAA), an agency may be created that is not affected by subsequent disability or incapacity of the principal. In UDPAA states, the agency may also come into existence upon the "disability or incapacity of the principal." The designation of an attorney in fact under the UDPAA must be in writing.

LEARNING OUTCOMES

After studying this chapter, you should be able to clearly explain:

A. Nature of the Agency Relationship

LO.1 Explain the difference between an agent and an independent contractor

See the Ned and Tracy Seizer example and the "right to control" test, beginning on p. 750.

B. Creating the Agency

LO.2 Explain three methods of creating an agency relationship

See the discussion on the usual method of creating an agency (which is by express authorization), p. 752.

See the *Taylor* case where actual authority to perform some tasks created apparent authority to perform other related tasks, pp. 752–753.

See the agency by ratification example of James and Calvin Reiner on p. 754.

C. Agent's Authority

LO.3 Recognize that third persons who deal with an agent are required to take notice of acts contrary to the interests of the principal

See the example of the Fire Company that failed to verify with the principal an agent's authority to receive a prepayment check of $55,000 made out in the agent's name, p. 757.

D. Duties and Liabilities of Principal and Agent

LO.4 List and explain the duties an agent owes the principal

See the discussion concerning an agent's duty of loyalty, obedience, reasonable care, accounting, and information beginning on p. 759.

E. Termination of Agency

LO.5 Explain how the Uniform Durable Power of Attorney Act changes the common law rule on incapacity of the principal

See the *Estate of Graham* case on the limits of a durable power of attorney, pp. 763–764.

KEY TERMS

agency
agent
apparent authority
attorney in fact
customary authority
express authorization
general agent
incidental authority
independent contractor
interest in the authority
interest in the subject matter
power of attorney
principal
special agent
universal agent

QUESTIONS AND CASE PROBLEMS

1. How does an agent differ from an independent contractor?

2. Compare authorization of an agent by (a) appointment and (b) ratification.

3. Ernest A. Kotsch executed a durable power of attorney when he was 85 years old, giving his son, Ernie, the power to manage and sell his real estate and personal property "and to do all acts necessary for maintaining and caring for [the father] during his lifetime." Thereafter, Kotsch began "keeping company" with a widow, Margaret Gradl. Ernie believed that the widow was attempting to alienate his father from him, and he observed that she was exerting a great deal of influence over his father. Acting under the durable power of attorney and without informing his father, Ernie created the "Kotsch Family Irrevocable Trust," to which he transferred $700,000, the bulk of his father's liquid assets, with the father as grantor and initial beneficiary and Ernie's three children as additional beneficiaries. Ernie named himself trustee. His father sued to avoid the trust. Ernie defended his action on the ground that he had authority to create the trust under the durable power of attorney. Decide. [*Kotsch v. Kotsch*, 608 So.2d 879 (Fla. App.)]

4. Ken Jones, the number-one-ranked prizefighter in his weight class, signed a two-year contract with Howard Stayword. The contract obligated Stayword to represent and promote Jones in all business and professional matters, including the arrangement of fights. For these services, Jones was to pay Stayword 10 percent of gross earnings. After a year, when Stayword proved unsuccessful in arranging a title match with the champion, Jones fired Stayword. During the following year, Jones earned $4 million. Stayword sued Jones for $400,000. Jones defended himself on the basis that a principal has the absolute power at any time to terminate an agency relationship by discharging the agent, so he was not liable to Stayword. Was Jones correct?

5. Paul Strich did business as an optician in Duluth, Minnesota. Paul used only the products of the Plymouth Optical Co., a national manufacturer of optical products and supplies with numerous retail outlets and some franchise arrangements in areas other than Duluth. To increase business, Paul renovated his office and changed the sign on it to read "Plymouth Optical Co." Paul did business this way for more than three years—advertised under that name, paid bills with checks bearing the name of Plymouth Optical Co., and listed himself in the telephone and city directories by that name. Plymouth immediately became aware of what Paul was doing. However, because Paul used only Plymouth products and Plymouth did not have a franchise in Duluth, it saw no advantage at that time in prohibiting Paul from using the name and losing him as a customer. Paul contracted with the *Duluth Tribune* for advertising, making the contract in the name of Plymouth Optical Co. When the advertising bill was not paid, the *Duluth Tribune* sued Plymouth Optical Co. for payment. Plymouth's defense was that it never authorized Paul to do business under the name, nor authorized him to make a contract with the newspaper. Decide.

6. Record owned a farm that was managed by his agent, Berry, who lived on the farm. Berry hired Wagner to bale the hay and told him to bill Record for this work. Wagner did so and was paid by Record. By the summer of the following year, the agency had been terminated by Record, but Berry remained in possession as tenant of the farm and nothing appeared changed. Late in the summer, Berry asked Wagner to bale the hay as he had done the previous year and bill Record for the work. He did so, but Record refused to pay on the ground that Berry was not then his agent. Wagner sued him. Decide. [*Record v. Wagner*, 128 A.2d 921 (N.H.)]

7. Gilbert Church owned Church Farms, Inc., in Manteno, Illinois. Church advertised its well-bred stallion Imperial Guard for breeding rights at $50,000, directing all inquiries to "Herb Bagley, Manager." Herb Bagley lived at Church Farms and was the only person available to visitors. Vern Lundberg answered the ad, and after discussions in which Bagley stated that Imperial Guard would

remain in Illinois for at least a two-year period, Lundberg and Bagley executed a two-year breeding rights contract. The contract was signed by Lundberg and by Bagley as "Church Farms, Inc., H. Bagley, Mgr." When Gil Church moved Imperial Guard to Oklahoma prior to the second year of the contract, Lundberg brought suit for breach of contract. Church testified that Bagley had no authority to sign contracts for Church Farms. Decide. [*Lundberg v. Church Farms, Inc.*, 502 N.E.2d 806 (Ill.)]

8. The Holzmans signed an exclusive listing agreement with the Blum real estate brokerage firm. The contract provided that the Holzmans had an obligation to pay a commission "if they enter into a written agreement to sell the property to any person during the term of this exclusive listing agreement." The Holzmans entered into a written agreement to sell their house for $715,000 to the Noravians. On the advice of their attorney, the Holzmans included a default provision in this contract stating that in the event of default by the Holzmans, the Noravians' only remedy would be a refund of their deposit. Subsequently, the Sterns offered $850,000 for the property and the Holzmans canceled their contract with the Noravians and returned their deposit. After the exclusive listing period expired, the Holzmans executed a contract to sell their property to the Sterns at the offered price of $850,000—with the contract calling for the Holzmans to pay half the real estate fee to Blum and half to a cooperating broker. Blum was paid this fee of $21,500. Blum brought suit against the Holzmans seeking the full commission for the Noravian contract under the exclusive listing agreement. Did Blum have a legal obligation or ethical duty to advise the Holzmans when considering the Sterns' offer that he believed they were obligated to him for the full commission under the Novarian contract? Decide. [*Holzman v. Blum*, 726 A.2d 818 (Md. App.)]

9. Tillie Flinn properly executed a durable power of attorney designating her nephew James C. Flanders and/or Martha E. Flanders, his wife, as her attorney in fact. Seven months later, Martha Flanders went to the Capitol Federal Savings and Loan Association office. She had the durable power of attorney instrument, five certificates of deposit, and a hand-printed letter identifying Martha as an attorney in fact and stating that Tillie wished to cash her five CDs that Martha had with her. At approximately 10:31 A.M., five checks were given to Martha in the aggregate amount of $135,791.34, representing the funds in the five CDs less penalties for early withdrawal. Some of the checks were drawn to the order of Martha individually and some to the order of James and Martha, as individuals. Tillie was found dead of heart disease later that day. The time of death stated on her death certificate was 11:30 A.M. The Flanderses spent the money on themselves. Bank IV, as administrator of Tillie's estate, sued Capitol Federal to recover the amount of the funds paid to the Flanderses. It contended that Capitol Federal breached its duty to investigate before issuing the checks. Capitol Federal contended that it did all that it had a duty to do. Decide. [*Bank IV v. Capitol Federal Savings and Loan Ass'n*, 828 P.2d 355 (Kan.)]

10. Lew owns a store on Canal Street in New Orleans. He paid a person named Mike and other individuals commissions for customers brought into the store. Lew testified that he had known Mike for less than a week. Boulos and Durso, partners in a wholesale jewelry business, were visiting New Orleans on a business trip when Mike brought them into the store to buy a stereo. While Durso finalized the stereo transaction with the store's manager, Boulos and Mike negotiated to buy 2 cameras, 3 videos, and 20 gold Dupont lighters. Unknown to the store's manager, Mike was given $8,250 in cash and was to deliver the merchandise later that evening to the Marriott Hotel, where Boulos and Durso were staying. Mike gave a receipt for the cash, but it showed no sales tax or indication that the goods were to be delivered. Boulos testified that he believed Mike was the store owner. Mike never delivered the merchandise and disappeared. Boulos and Durso contended that Lew is liable for the acts of his agent, Mike. Lew denied that Mike was his agent, and the testimony showed that Mike had no actual authority to make a sale, to use a cash register, or even to go behind a sales counter. What ethical principle applies to the conduct

of Boulos and Durso? Decide. [*Boulos v. Morrison*, 503 So.2d 1(La.)]

11. Martha Christiansen owns women's apparel stores bearing her name in New Seabury, Massachusetts; Lake Placid, New York; Palm Beach, Florida; and Palm Springs, California. At a meeting with her four store managers, she discussed styles she thought appropriate for the forthcoming season, advised them as always to use their best judgment in the goods they purchased for each of their respective stores, and cautioned "but no blue jeans." Later, Jane Farley, the manager of the Lake Placid store, purchased a line of high-quality blue denim outfits (designer jeans with jacket and vest options) from Women's Wear, Inc., for the summer season. The outfits did not sell. Martha refused to pay for them, contending that she had told all of her managers "no blue jeans" and that if it came to a lawsuit, she would fly in three managers to testify that Jane Farley had absolutely no authority to purchase denim outfits and was, in fact, expressly forbidden to do so. Women's Wear sued Martha, and the three managers testified for her. Is the fact that Martha had explicitly forbidden Farley to purchase the outfits in question sufficient to protect her from liability for the purchases made by Farley?

12. Fred Schilling, the president and administrator of Florence General Hospital, made a contract, dated August 16, 1989, on behalf of the hospital with CMK Associates to transfer the capacity to utilize 25 beds from the hospital to the Faith Nursing Home. Schilling, on behalf of the hospital, had previously made a contract with CMK Associates on May 4, 1987. Schilling had been specifically authorized by the hospital board to make the 1987 contract. The hospital refused to honor the 1989 contract because the board had not authorized it. CMK contended that Schilling had apparent authority to bind the hospital because he was president and administrator of the hospital and he had been the person who negotiated and signed a contract with CMK in 1987. Thus, according to CMK, the hospital had held out Schilling as having apparent authority to make the contract. The hospital disagreed. Decide. [*Pee Dee Nursing Home v. Florence General Hospital*, 419 S.E.2d 843 (S.C. App.)]

13. Barbara Fox was the agent of Burt Hollander, a well-known athlete. She discovered that Tom Lanceford owned a 1957 Chevrolet convertible, which had been stored in a garage for the past 15 years. After demonstrating to Lanceford that she was the authorized agent of Hollander, she made a contract with Lanceford on behalf of Hollander to purchase the Chevrolet. Lanceford later discovered that the car was much more valuable than he originally believed, and he refused to deliver the car to Fox. Fox sued Lanceford for breach of contract. Can she recover?

14. Francis Gagnon, an elderly gentleman, signed a power of attorney authorizing his daughter, Joan, "to sell any of my real estate and to execute any document needed to carry out the sale…and to add property to a trust of which I am grantor or beneficiary." This power was given in case Gagnon was not available to take care of matters personally because he was traveling. When Joan learned that Gagnon intended to sell his Shelburne property to Cosby for $750,000, she created an irrevocable trust naming Gagnon as beneficiary and herself as trustee. Acting then on the basis of the authority set forth in the power of attorney, she conveyed the Shelburne property to herself as trustee of the irrevocable trust, thus blocking the sale to Cosby. When Gagnon learned of this, he demanded that Joan return the Shelburne property to him, but she refused, saying she had acted within the authority set forth in the power of attorney. Did Joan violate any duty owed to Gagnon? Must she reconvey the property to Gagnon? [*Gagnon v. Coombs*, 654 N.E.2d 54 (Mass. App.)]

15. Daniels and Julian were employed by the Marriott Hotel in New Orleans and were close personal friends. One day after work, Daniels and Julian went to Werlein's music store to open a credit account. Julian, with Daniels's authorization and in her presence, applied for credit using Daniels's name and credit history. Later, Julian went to Werlein's without Daniels and charged the purchase of a television set to Daniels's account, executing a retail installment contract by signing Daniels's name. Daniels saw the new television in Julian's home and was informed that it was charged to the Werlein's account. Daniels

told Julian to continue making payments. When Werlein's credit manager first contacted Daniels to inform her that her account was delinquent, she claimed that a money order for the television was in the mail. On the second call, she asked for a "payment balance." Some four months after the purchase, she informed Werlein's that she had not authorized the purchase of the television nor ratified the purchase. Werlein's sued Daniels for the unpaid balance. Decide. [*Philip Werlein, Ltd. v. Daniels*, 536 So.2d 722 (La. App.)]

CPA QUESTIONS

1. Generally, an agency relationship is terminated by operation of law in all of the following situations except the:
   a. Principal's death
   b. Principal's incapacity
   c. Agent's renunciation of the agency
   d. Agent's failure to acquire a necessary business license
2. Able, on behalf of Pix Corp., entered into a contract with Sky Corp., by which Sky agreed to sell computer equipment to Pix. Able disclosed to Sky that she was acting on behalf of Pix. However, Able had exceeded her actual authority by entering into the contract with Sky. If Pix wishes to ratify the contract with Sky, which of the following statements is correct?
   a. Pix must notify Sky that Pix intends to ratify the contract.
   b. Able must have acted reasonably and in Pix's best interest.
   c. Able must be a general agent of Pix.
   d. Pix must have knowledge of all material facts relating to the contract at the time it is ratified.
3. Which of the following actions requires an agent for a corporation to have a written agency agreement?
   a. Purchasing office supplies for the principal's business
   b. Purchasing an interest in undeveloped land for the principal
   c. Hiring an independent general contractor to renovate the principal's office building
   d. Retaining an attorney to collect a business debt owed the principal
4. Simmons, an agent for Jensen, has the express authority to sell Jensen's goods. Simmons also has the express authority to grant discounts of up to 5 percent of list price. Simmons sold Hemple a 10 percent discount. Hemple had not previously dealt with either Simmons or Jensen. Which of the following courses of action may Jensen properly take?
   a. Seek to void the sale to Hemple
   b. Seek recovery of $50 from Hemple only
   c. Seek recovery of $50 from Simmons only
   d. Seek recovery of $50 from either Hemple or Simmons
5. Ogden Corp. hired Thorp as a sales representative for nine months at a salary of $3,000 per month plus 4 percent of sales. Which of the following statements is correct?
   a. Thorp is obligated to act solely in Ogden's interest in matters concerning Ogden's business.
   b. The agreement between Ogden and Thorp formed an agency coupled with an interest.
   c. Ogden does not have the power to dismiss Thorp during the nine-month period without cause.
   d. The agreement between Ogden and Thorp is not enforceable unless it is in writing and signed by Thorp.
6. Frost's accountant and business manager has the authority to:
   a. Mortgage Frost's business property
   b. Obtain bank loans for Frost
   c. Insure Frost's property against fire loss
   d. Sell Frost's business

Third Persons in Agency

learningoutcomes

After studying this chapter, you should be able to

LO.1 Explain when an agent is and is not liable to a third person as a party to a contract

LO.2 Describe how to execute a contract as an agent on behalf of a principal

LO.3 Explain the legal effect of a payment made by a third person to an authorized agent

LO.4 Explain the doctrine of *respondeat superior*

LO.5 Distinguish between the authority of a soliciting agent and that of a contracting agent

The rights and liabilities of the principal, the agent, and the third person with whom the agent deals are generally determined by contract law. In some cases, tort or criminal law may be applicable.

A. Liability of Agent to Third Person

The liability of the agent to the third person depends on the existence of authority and the manner of executing the contract.

1. Action of Authorized Agent of Disclosed Principal

If an agent makes a contract with a third person on behalf of a disclosed principal and has proper authority to do so and if the contract is executed properly, the agent has no personal liability on the contract. Whether the principal performs the contract or not, the agent cannot be held liable by the third party. **For Example,** Lincoln Apartment Management, LP, required a vendor to sign a form before commencing work renovating Woodchase Village Apartments, which stated:

> *Vendor understands and agrees that the legal Owner of the community is responsible for the payments of any services or materials performed or delivered, and not Lincoln, which is the property management company and Agent for the Owner of the community.*

The contractor's field manager, Jane Yang, signed the form before commencing work. After the work was performed the apartment complex was foreclosed, with the contractor still owed $59,758 for unpaid services. In a lawsuit against Lincoln by the contractor, the court determined that the owner, not the property manager, was solely liable for the debt.[1]

In speaking of an agent's action as authorized or unauthorized, it must be remembered that *authorized* includes action that, though originally *unauthorized*, was subsequently ratified by the principal. Once there is an effective ratification, the original action of the agent is no longer treated as unauthorized.

2. Unauthorized Action

If a person makes a contract as agent for another but lacks authority to do so, the contract does not bind the principal. When a person purports to act as agent for a principal, an implied warranty arises that that person has authority to do so. If the agent lacks authority, there is a breach of this warranty.

If the agent's act causes loss to the third person, that third person may generally hold the agent liable for the loss.

It is no defense for the agent in such a case that she acted in good faith or misunderstood the scope of authority. The purported agent is not liable for conduct in excess of authority when the third person knows that she is acting beyond the authority given by the principal.

An agent with a written authorization may avoid liability on the implied warranty of authority by showing the written authorization to the third person and permitting the third person to determine the scope of the agent's authority.

3. Disclosure of Principal

There are three degrees to which the existence and identity of the principal may be disclosed or not disclosed. An agent's liability as a party to a contract with a third person is affected by the degree of disclosure.

(a) Disclosed Principal. When the agent makes known the identity of the principal and the fact that the agent is acting on behalf of that principal, the principal is called a **disclosed principal**. The third person dealing with an agent of a disclosed principal ordinarily intends to make a contract with the principal, not the agent. Consequently, the agent is not a party to, and is not bound by, the contract that is made.[2] **For Example,** Biefeld Jewelers was the trade name of Bie-Jewel Corp.,

[1] *Grand Master Contracting, LLC v. Lincoln Apartment Management, LP*, 724 S.E.2d 456 (Ga. App. 2012).
[2] *Stinchfield v. Weinreb*, 797 N.Y.S.2d 521 (A. D. 2005).

a closely held corporation of which Margie Biefeld was one of several employees. The plaintiff sought to hold her personally liable on a contract for advertising services. While Ms. Biefeld signed a contract for advertising services without reference to holding a corporate office, the plain language of the agreement established that she was acting as an agent for a disclosed principal and that the plaintiff had notice of her status.[3]

(B) Partially Disclosed Principal. When the agent makes known the existence of a principal but not the principal's identity, the principal is a **partially disclosed principal**. Because the third party does not know the identity of the principal, the third person is making the contract with the agent, and the agent is therefore a party to the contract.

(C) Undisclosed Principal. When the third person is not told or does not know that the agent is acting as an agent for anyone else, the unknown principal is called an **undisclosed principal**.[4] In this case, the third person is making the contract with the agent, and the agent is a party to that contract.

In the *ICG Link Inc.* case the court was faced with deciding whether a managing member of a limited liability company was personally liable for services performed where he identified himself as the "Executive" of "Nashville Sports Leagues."

ICG Link, Inc. v. Steen, 363 S.W.3d 533 (Tenn. App. 2011)

You've Got to Tell Them You're Contracting on Behalf of the Named Principal, Silly

In 2003, Philip Steen formed Nashville Sports Leagues, LLC, for the purpose of providing a recreational sports league for a growing demographic of active adults in Middle Tennessee. Mr. Steen served as the managing member of Nashville Sports until the LLC was administratively dissolved in 2004. Three years later, in January 2007, Mr. Steen registered TN Sports, LLC, with the Tennessee Secretary of State. TN Sports performed the same functions as Nashville Sports, and Mr. Steen continued to serve as the managing member. Mr. Steen also continued to do business under the name "Nashville Sports Leagues." In correspondence, he identified himself as an executive of Nashville Sports Leagues and used an "@nashvillesports.com" e-mail address. By spring 2007, the popularity of TN Sports had grown considerably with 11,000 members on more than 175 teams. Players had their choice of six different sports with options year-round. The success of TN Sports was due at least in part to the ease of finding willing players and forming teams on the TN Sports Web site. In addition to its essential networking function, the Web site provided users with game schedules and venue information, among other details about leagues and events. In the spring of 2007, Mr. Steen moved his TN Sports Web site to ICG Link, Inc., and it recommended that Mr. Steen build a new Web site to improve functionality. However, problems existed with the new Web site. Mr. Steen had not paid invoices from March to October, and ICG employees were instructed to "slow walk" the TN Sports Web site. The parties were unable to resolve their differences, and ICG Link filed a lawsuit against the LLC, and Mr. Steen personally, for breach of contract. The trial court found there was quasi-contract liability, less the cost to repair defects, in the new Web site. It found Mr. Steen personally liable for the judgment.

JUDICIAL OPINION

CLEMENT, J.... ICG contends that Mr. Steen should be held personally liable for the obligations of TN Sports; Mr. Steen insists he is not liable. We have determined that Philip Steen is personally liable for the obligations of TN Sports because he failed to disclose the identity of his principal.

It is a well-settled principle of law that, in order for an agent to avoid personal liability on a contract negotiated on behalf of the agent's principal, "the agent must disclose not only the fact of the agency, but also the identity of the principal." (citations omitted)

Although it is clear from the proof that Mr. Steen intended to bind TN Sports, LLC, when he was doing business with ICG in 2007 and 2008, Mr. Steen conducted

[3] *CBS Outdoor Group, Inc. v. Biefeld*, 836 N.Y.S.2d 497 (Civ. Ct. 2007).

[4] See *Castle Cheese Inc. v. MS Produce Inc.*, 2008 WL 4372856 (W.D. Pa. Sept. 19, 2008), where the court held that an agent must disclose both the identity of the principal and the fact of the agency relationship to avoid liability under a contract. One of the defendants, CVS Foods, did not establish that it had disclosed the fact it was acting as an agent, and it was held liable for breach of contract.

Continued

business under the name of "Nashville Sports Leagues," not TN Sports. Although Nashville Sports Leagues, LLC, was properly organized, it was administratively dissolved in 2004, long before ICG came into the picture and it was never reinstated. As the trial court found, Mr. Steen identified himself as, "Executive, Nashville Sports Leagues" in his transactions with ICG, his email address was "psteen@nashvillesportsleagues.com," and the web address of the website was "www.nashvillesportsleagues.com." Moreover, all of ICG's invoices identify Nashville Sports Leagues as the business Mr. Steen represented.

The only document showing "TN Sports, LLC" as the relevant entity is a payment "voucher," which Mr. Steen testified was a check payable to ICG on the bank account of "TN Sports, LLC." Mr. Massari, however, testified it is common for ICG to accept payment from entities other than the actual client. Considering the totality of the circumstances, we find the voucher insufficient to constitute "disclosure" of Mr. Steen's principal.

We also find no merit to Mr. Steen's assertion that "Nashville Sports Leagues" was a marketing moniker, or "d/b/a" name for TN Sports:...

We, therefore, affirm the trial court's finding that Mr. Steen failed to disclose the identity of his principal, TN Sports, LLC; thus, he is personally liable on the judgment in this action.

[Affirmed as modified.]

QUESTIONS

1. Did Mr. Steen have an obligation to disclose to ICG that he was acting in a representative capacity as an agent for TN Sports, LLC, his principal?
2. Would Mr. Steen be correct in asserting that, in this day and age, listing himself as executive of Nashville Sports Leagues with an appropriate e-mail address and a thriving Web site, that state law should not allow businesses like ICG Link Inc. to feign ignorance of his limited liability business structure?

4. Assumption of Liability

Agents may intentionally make themselves liable on contracts with third persons.[5] This situation frequently occurs when the agent is a well-established local brokerage house or other agency and when the principal is located out of town and is not known locally.

In some situations, the agent makes a contract that will be personally binding. If the principal is not disclosed, the agent is necessarily the other contracting party and is bound by the contract. Even when the principal is disclosed, the agent may be personally bound if it was the intention of the parties that the agent assume a personal obligation even though this was done to further the principal's business.[6]

5. Execution of Contract

A simple contract that would appear to be the contract of the agent can be shown by other evidence, if believed, to have been intended as a contract between the principal and the third party. The *Walton* case raised the question of whether a daughter was responsible for her mother's unpaid medical bills because she had signed nursing home admission papers.

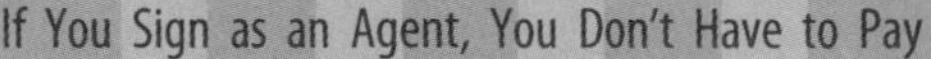

Walton v. Mariner Health, 894 A.2d 584 (Md. 2006)

If You Sign as an Agent, You Don't Have to Pay

Audrey Walton was transferred from a hospital to Mariner Health Nursing Home on January 26, 2001. Her daughter, Patricia Walton signed a 30-page document entitled "Resident's Agent Financial Agreement." Patricia indicated in that agreement that the only method of payment would be Medicare or Medical Assistance. Medicare assistance stopped in February 2001. On January 10, 2003, Mariner Health sued both Audrey and Patricia for unpaid monthly bills amounting to $86,235. From a judgment for Mariner Health against both the patient and her daughter, Patricia appealed.

[5] *Fairchild Publications v. Rosston*, 584 N.Y.S.2d 389 (N.Y. County Sup. 1992).
[6] See *Boros v. Carter*, 537 So.2d 1134 (Fla. App. 1989).

Continued

JUDICIAL OPINION

GREENE, J.…If the contract is to benefit the principal only, the agent is immune from personal liability for breach of that contract. ("It is also a universal principle of the law of agency that the powers of the agent are to be exercised for the benefit of the principal only, and not for the agent or third parties."); ("It is a well settled principle of agency law that an agent acting within the scope of his authority for a disclosed principal is not bound on a contract made in the principal's name.")….

Patricia, as an agent, had a primary duty to Audrey, the principal, and Patricia's duty to Mariner Health, a third party, was limited. Agency law precludes a finding against Patricia for damages. As an agent, Patricia entered into the contract only for the benefit of Audrey and is personally insulated from liability by virtue of her station as an agent….

In 1988, the General Assembly passed House Bill 683 which amended § 19–344 of the Health–General Article and prescribed in subsection 19–344(c) the rights and responsibilities of an "agent." The legislature intended to limit an agent's personal liability. That intent was evidenced by the bill summary, which states: "…the legislative rationale for the amendment was that the circumstances surrounding admission to a nursing home are highly stressful for applicants and their families. Most people are not in a position to carefully read and negotiate a contract at this time. It is vital that the contracts be screened to assure that they conform to existing law and are clear and understandable…."

Supra at 2.

In summary, an agent's responsibility is limited to the administration and management of the resident's funds. An agent is not personally liable for the resident's nursing home care costs, unless the agent, voluntarily and knowingly agrees to pay for the resident's care with the agent's own funds….

QUESTIONS

1. What defense did Patricia Walton raise in the lawsuit against her by the nursing home for payment of her mother's nursing home bills?
2. How did the court decide this case?
3. Speculate on why the state enacted a Nursing Home Bill of Rights Law.

To avoid any question of interpretation, an agent should execute an instrument by signing the principal's name and either *by* or *per* and the agent's name. **For Example,** if Jane R. Craig is an agent for B. G. Gray, Craig should execute instruments by signing either "B.G. Gray, by Jane R. Craig" or "B. G. Gray, per Jane R. Craig." Such a signing is in law a signing by Gray, and the agent is therefore not a party to the contract. The signing of the principal's name by an authorized agent without indicating the agent's name or identity is likewise in law the signature of the principal.

If the instrument is ambiguous as to whether the agent has signed in a representative or an individual capacity, parol evidence is admissible as between the original parties to the transaction for establishing the character in which the agent was acting.

6. Torts and Crimes

Agents are liable for harm caused third persons by the agents' fraudulent, intentional, or negligent acts.[7] The fact that persons were acting as agents at the time or that they acted in good faith under the directions of a principal does not relieve them of liability if their conduct would impose liability on them when acting for themselves.

If an agent commits a crime, such as stealing from a third person or shooting a third person, the agent is liable for the crime without regard to the fact of acting as an agent. The agent is liable without regard to whether the agent acted in self-interest or sought to advance the interest of the principal.

B. Liability of Principal to Third Person

The principal is liable to the third person for the properly authorized and executed contracts of the agent and, in certain circumstances, for the agent's unauthorized contracts.

[7] *Mannish v. Lacayo*, 496 So.2d 242 (Fla. App. 1986).

Ethics & the Law

Some time ago, dairy farmers owned large tracts of land in south Tempe, Arizona. The farmers used the land for grazing animals. Economic growth in this suburb of Phoenix was limited because of the state's inability at that time to attract large businesses to the area for relocation or location of new facilities.

In 1973, three farmers who owned adjoining parcels of land in the south Tempe area were approached by a local real estate agent with an offer for the purchase of their property. The amount of the offer was approximately 10 percent above the property's appraised value. The three farmers discussed the offer and concluded that with their need to retire, it was best to accept the offer and sell the land. All three signed contracts for the sale of their land.

After the contracts were entered into but before the transactions had closed, the three farmers learned that the land was being purchased by a real estate development firm from southern California. The development firm had planned, and would be proposing to the Tempe City Council, a residential community, the Lakes. The Lakes would consist of upper-end homes in a community laced with parks, lakes, and ponds, with each house in the developed area backing up to its own dock and water recreation. The development firm had begun the project because it had learned of the plans of American Express, Rubbermaid, and Dial to locate major facilities in the Phoenix area.

The three farmers objected to the sale of their land when they learned the identity of the buyer. "If we had known who was coming in here and why, we never would have sold for such a low price." Were the farmers' contracts binding?

Is it ethical to use the strategy of an undisclosed principal? What is the role of an agent in a situation in which the third party is making a decision not as beneficial to him or her as it could or should be? Can the agent say anything?

7. Agent's Contracts

The liability of a principal to a third person on a contract made by an agent depends on the extent of disclosure of the principal and the form of the contract that is executed.

CPA **(A) Simple Contract with Principal Disclosed.** When a disclosed principal with contractual capacity authorizes or ratifies an agent's transaction with a third person and when the agent properly executes a contract with the third person, a binding contract exists between the principal and the third person. The principal and the third person may each sue the other in the event of a breach of the contract. The agent is not a party to the contract, is not liable for its performance, and cannot sue for its breach.[8]

The liability of a disclosed principal to a third person is not discharged by the fact that the principal gives the agent money with which to pay the third person. Consequently, the liability of a buyer for the purchase price of goods is not terminated by the fact that the buyer gave the buyer's agent the purchase price to remit to the seller.

(B) Simple Contract with Principal Partially Disclosed. A partially disclosed principal is liable for a simple contract made by an authorized agent. The third person may recover from either the agent or the principal.

(C) Simple Contract with Principal Undisclosed. An undisclosed principal is liable for a simple contract made by an authorized agent. Although the third person initially contracted with the agent alone, the third person, on learning of the existence of the undisclosed principal, may sue that principal.[9] In most jurisdictions, third persons can sue and collect judgments from the agent or principal, or both, until the judgment is fully satisfied (joint and several liability).[10]

8. Payment to Agent

When the third person makes payment to an authorized agent, the payment is deemed made to the principal. Even if the agent never remits or delivers

[8] *Levy v. Gold & Co., Inc.*, 529 N.Y.S.2d 133 (A.D. 1988).
[9] *McDaniel v. Hensons, Inc.*, 493 S.E.2d 529 (Ga. App. 1997).
[10] *Crown Controls, Inc. v. Smiley*, 756 P.2d 717 (Wash. 1988).

the payment to the principal, the principal must give the third person full credit for the payment so long as the third person made the payment in good faith and had no reason to know that the agent would be guilty of misconduct.[11]

Because apparent authority has the same legal effect as actual authority, a payment made to a person with apparent authority to receive the payment is deemed a payment to the apparent principal.

When a debtor makes payment to a person who is not the actual or apparent agent of the creditor, such a payment does not discharge the debt unless that person in fact pays the money to the creditor.

9. Agent's Statements

A principal is bound by a statement made by an agent while transacting business within the scope of authority. This means that the principal cannot later contradict the statement of the agent and show that it is not true. Statements or declarations of an agent, in order to bind the principal, must be made at the time of performing the act to which they relate or shortly thereafter.

10. Agent's Knowledge

The principal is bound by knowledge or notice of any fact that is acquired by an agent while acting within the scope of actual or apparent authority. When a fact is known to the agent of the seller, the sale is deemed made by the seller with knowledge of that fact.

The rule that the agent's knowledge is imputed to the principal is extended in some cases to knowledge gained prior to the creation of the agency relationship. The notice and knowledge in any case must be based on reliable information. Thus, when the agent hears only rumors, the principal is not charged with notice.

If the subject matter is outside the scope of the agent's authority, the agent is under no duty to inform the principal of the knowledge, and the principal is not bound by it. The principal is not charged with knowledge of an agent when (1) the agent is acting adversely to the principal's interest or (2) the third party acts in collusion with the agent for the purpose of cheating the principal.

C. Liability of Principal for Torts and Crimes of Agent

Under certain circumstances, the principal may be liable for the torts or crimes of the agent or the employee.

CPA 11. Vicarious Liability for Torts and Crimes

Assume that an agent or an employee causes harm to a third person. Is the principal or the employer liable for this conduct? If the conduct constitutes a crime, can the principal or the employer be criminally prosecuted? The answer is that in many instances, the principal or the employer is liable civilly and may also be prosecuted criminally. That is, the principal or the employer is liable although personally free from fault and not guilty of any wrong. This concept of imposing liability for the fault of another is known as **vicarious liability**.

This situation arises both when an employer's employee or a principal's agent commits the wrong. The rules of law governing the vicarious liability of the principal and the employer are the same. In the interest of simplicity, this section is stated in terms of employees acting in the course of employment. Remember that these rules are equally applicable to agents acting within the scope of their authority. As a practical matter, some situations will arise only with agents. **For Example,** the vicarious liability of a seller for the misrepresentations made by a salesperson arise only when the seller appointed an agent to sell. In contrast, both the employee hired to drive a truck and an agent driving to visit a customer could negligently injure a third person with their vehicles. In many situations, a person employed by another is both an employee and an agent, and the tort is committed within the phase of "employee work."

The rule of law imposing vicarious liability on an innocent employer for the wrong of an employee is also known as the doctrine of ***respondeat superior***. In modern times, this doctrine can be justified on the grounds that the business should pay for the harm caused in the doing of the business, that the employer will be more careful in the selection of employees if made responsible for their actions, and that the

[11] This general rule of law is restated in some states by Section 2 of the Uniform Fiduciaries Act, which is expressly extended by Section 1 of the act to agents, partners, and corporate officers. Similar statutory provisions are found in a number of other states.

employer may obtain liability insurance to protect against claims of third persons.

(A) NATURE OF ACT. The wrongful act committed by an employee may be a negligent act, an intentional act, a fraudulent act, or a violation of a government regulation. It may give rise only to civil liability of the employer, or it may also subject the employer to prosecution for crime.

(1) Negligent Act.

Historically, the act for which liability would be imposed under the doctrine of *respondeat superior* was a negligent act committed within the scope of employment.

(2) Intentional Act.

Under the common law, a master was not liable for an intentional tort committed by a servant. The modern law holds that an employer is liable for an intentional tort committed by an employee for the purpose of furthering the employer's business.[12] **For Example,** Crane Brothers, Inc., drilled a well for Stephen May. When May did not pay his bill, two Crane Brothers' employees went to May's workplace, and an altercation ensued in which May was injured. Crane Brothers, Inc., was held vicariously liable for the torts of the employees, not because the employer itself committed the wrongful acts but because it was answerable for the manner in which its agents, the two employees, conducted themselves in doing the business of the employer.[13]

(3) Fraud.

Modern decisions hold the employer liable for fraudulent acts or misrepresentations. The rule is commonly applied to a principal-agent relationship. To illustrate, when an agent makes fraudulent statements in selling stock, the principal is liable for the buyer's loss. In states that follow the common law rule of no liability for intentional torts, the principal is not liable for the agent's fraud when the principal did not authorize or know of the agent's fraud.

(4) Government Regulation.

The employer may be liable because of the employee's violation of a government regulation. These regulations are most common in the areas of business and of protection of the environment. In such cases, the employer may be held liable for a penalty imposed by the government. In some cases, the breach of the regulation will impose liability on the employer in favor of a third person who is injured as a consequence of the violation.

(B) COURSE OF EMPLOYMENT. The mere fact that a tort or crime is committed by an employee does not necessarily impose vicarious liability on the employer. It must also be shown that the individual was acting within the scope of authority if an agent or in the course of employment if an employee. If an employee was not acting within the scope of employment, there is no vicarious liability.[14] **For Example,** after Rev. Joel Thomford accidentally shot and killed his parishioner during a deer hunting trip, the parishioner's wife brought a wrongful death action against the pastor and the church. Because the accident occurred on the pastor's day off and the trip was not sponsored by the church, the pastor was not acting within the course of his employment at the time of the accident, and the church was not liable.[15] The *Studebaker* case raised questions of whether the tortfeasor was an employee of the defendant and had acted in furthering the employer's business.

Studebaker v. Nettie's Flower Garden Inc., 842 S.W.2d 227 (Mo. App. 1992)

He Was Back to Nettie's Business When He Hit the Studebaker

Judith Studebaker was injured when a van driven by James Ferry collided with her vehicle. She brought an action against Nettie's Flower Garden, Inc. (Nettie's), under a *respondeat superior* theory in the belief that Ferry was Nettie's employee at the time of the accident. Nettie's maintained that Ferry was an independent contractor, not an employee. From a

[12] Restatement (Second) of Agency §231.

[13] *Crane Brothers, Inc. v. May*, 556 S.E.2d 865 (Ga. App. 2001).

[14] *Young v. Taylor-White LLC*, 181 S.W.2d 324 (Tenn. 2005).

[15] *Hentges v. Thomford*, 569 N.W.2d 424 (Minn. App. 1997).

Continued

judgment in favor of Studebaker for $125,000, Nettie's appealed.

JUDICIAL OPINION

CRANDALL, P. J.…Ferry delivered flowers for Nettie's from its main shop on Grand Avenue in the City of St. Louis. Ferry was paid, not by the hour, but at a rate of $2.50 to $3.00 per delivery. If there were no deliveries, he was not paid. He delivered only in an area of St. Louis which Nettie's designated as his territory. Nettie's required him to make two runs each day: one in the morning at 9:30 A.M.; one in the afternoon at 1:30 P.M. When he arrived at the shop, he set up his own route based upon the location of the deliveries in his area. He generally got to work at 8:00 A.M. to prepare for the morning run and at 12:00 P.M. to prepare for the afternoon run. Nettie's also required Ferry to stop by its shop in downtown St. Louis at St. Louis Centre before noon each day to pick up items which needed to be transported to the Grand Avenue shop. After this stop, Ferry proceeded to the Grand Avenue shop for his afternoon run. Nettie's paid Ferry $5.00 for this stop, whether or not there was anything for him to take to the Grand Avenue shop.

Ferry used his own van for the deliveries; Nettie's required that it be heated and airconditioned to protect the flowers and plants. Although he did not wear a uniform, Nettie's directed that Ferry be neat in appearance and that he conduct himself in a certain manner when on the job. If his behavior or appearance fell below its standards, Nettie's reprimanded Ferry. Ferry paid his own expenses and received no fringe benefits from Nettie's.

On August 9, 1989, the date of the accident in question, Ferry made his morning run and then his mid-day stop at the downtown shop at about 11:00 A.M. There was nothing for him to transport to the Grand Avenue shop. After Ferry left the downtown shop, he stopped at a pawn shop to conduct personal business. He then proceeded to the Grand Avenue shop to prepare for his afternoon run. On the way to the Grand Avenue shop, at approximately 11:45 A.M., Ferry's van collided with plaintiff's automobile.…

Under the doctrine of respondeat superior an employer is liable for those negligent acts or omissions of his employee which are committed within the scope of his employment.… Liability based on respondeat superior requires some evidence that a master-servant relationship existed between the parties. …The test to determine if respondeat superior applies to a tort is whether the person sought to be charged as master had the right or power to control and direct the physical conduct of the other in the performance of the act.…If there was no right to control there is no liability; for those rendering services but retaining control over their own movements are not servants. …The master-servant relationship arises when the person charged as master has the right to direct the method by which the master's service is performed.…An additional inquiry is whether the person sought to be charged as the servant was engaged in the prosecution of his master's business and not simply whether the accident occurred during the time of employment.…Whether a party is liable under the doctrine of respondeat superior depends on the facts and circumstances in evidence in each particular case and no single test is conclusive of the issue of the party's interest in the activity and his right of control.…

Nettie's first asserts that, when the accident in question occurred, Ferry was not driving his vehicle to serve Nettie's business interests. It argues that Ferry was on his own time, conducting his own business.…

Ferry's slight detour prior to the accident to conduct personal business did not mean that he was using his van exclusively for his independent purposes.…The object of Ferry's trip was not just to go to the pawn shop. At the time of the accident, Ferry was doing Nettie's business because he was returning to the Grand Avenue shop after making his routine mid-day stop at the downtown shop. This stop was so encompassed within his daily routine that it would be difficult to segregate it from his morning and afternoon runs.

There was sufficient evidence for the jury to determine that at the time of the accident, Ferry was engaged primarily in advancing the business interests of Nettie's and thus was acting within the scope of his employment. Nettie's first point is denied.

Nettie's further contends that there was no substantial evidence that Nettie's controlled or had the right to control Ferry at the time of the collision. Whether or not the right of control existed in a particular case is ordinarily a question of fact for the jury.…

In the instant action, Ferry furnished his own means of transportation; but it was mandatory that he have a vehicle to carry out his job responsibilities. Nettie's required that his vehicle be equipped with heating and airconditioning systems. Nettie's also set standards for Ferry's dress and conduct while he was on the job, and monitored his compliance with these standards. In addition, although Ferry mapped out his own route to deliver the flowers, Nettie's gave him the list of customers and determined his territory. Nettie's directed Ferry to make the mid-day stop at its downtown shop on a daily basis and paid him for that stop. Ferry incorporated that stop into his route. The stop usually occurred after his morning run and prior to his return trip to the Grand Avenue shop for his afternoon run. In addition, Nettie's always paid him for this stop, whether or not he transported anything. There was

Continued

substantial evidence from which a jury reasonably could have found that, at the time of the accident in question, Nettie's either controlled or had the right to control the manner in which Ferry performed the duties for which he was employed. Nettie's second point is denied.

[Judgment affirmed]

QUESTIONS

1. Did Nettie's control or have the right to control Ferry at the time of the collision?
2. Is not the fact that Ferry, just prior to the accident, had gone to a pawn shop compelling evidence he was using his van exclusively for his independent purposes and was not acting within the course of his employer's business?
3. Review the ethical principles set forth in Chapter 3 and give your opinion of the ethics of businesses converting employees to independent contractors to reduce or eliminate costs, such as health and retirement benefits, overtime, and maintenance and proper insurance of motor vehicles.

(c) Employee of the United States. The Federal Tort Claims Act (FTCA) declares that the United States shall be liable vicariously whenever a federal employee driving a motor vehicle in the course of employment causes harm under such circumstances that a private employer would be liable. Contrary to the general rule, the statute exempts the employee driver from liability.[16]

12. Negligent Hiring and Retention of Employees

In addition to a complaint against the employer based on the doctrine of *respondeat superior*, a lawsuit may often raise a second theory, that of negligent hiring or retention of an employee.[17] Unlike the *respondeat superior* theory by which the employer may be vicariously liable for the tort of an employee, the negligent hiring theory is based on the negligence of the employer in the hiring process. Under the *respondeat superior* rule, the employer is liable only for those torts committed within the scope of employment or in the furtherance of the employer's interests. The negligent hiring theory has been used to impose liability in cases when an employee commits an intentional tort, almost invariably outside the scope of employment, against a customer or the general public, and the employer knew or should have known that the employee was incompetent, violent, dangerous, or criminal.[18]

(a) Need for Due Care in Hiring. An employer may be liable on a theory of negligent hiring when it is shown that the employer knew, or in the exercise of ordinary care should have known, that the job applicant would

Thinking Things Through

Rule No. 1: Take the Safe Course

The National Safety Council estimates that one quarter of all automobile and truck accidents involve cell phone use or texting. In fatality and injury vehicle accidents, plaintiffs' attorneys subpoena cell phone records, which often form the basis of compelling liability cases against driver-employees *and* their employers. It is a near automatic conclusion by jurors that the operator using a cell phone or texting caused the accident. Thinking Things Through, for the safety of employees and the public, as well as the extraordinary liability risks for employers, it may well be a sound business practice to ban all cell phone usage while driving on company business.

[16] Claims of negligent hiring are not permissible under the FTCA. See *Tonelli v. United States*, 60 F.3d 492 (8th Cir. 1995).

[17] *Medina v. Graham's Cowboys, Inc.*, 827 P.2d 859 (N.M. App. 1992).

[18] *Rockwell v. Sun Harbor Budget Suites*, 925 P.2d 1175 (Nev. 1996).

create an undue risk of harm to others in carrying out job responsibilities. Moreover, it must also be shown that the employer could have reasonably foreseen injury to the third party. Thus, an employer who knows of an employee's preemployment drinking problems and violent behavior may be liable to customers assaulted by that employee.

Employers might protect themselves from liability in a negligent hiring case by having each prospective employee fill out an employment application form and then checking into the applicant's work experience, background, character, and qualifications. This would be evidence of due care in hiring. Generally, the scope of a preemployment investigation should correlate to the degree of opportunity the prospective employee would have to do harm to third persons. A minimum investigation consisting of filling out an application form and conducting a personal interview would be satisfactory for hiring an outside maintenance person, but a full background inquiry would be necessary for hiring a security guard. However, such inquiry does not bar *respondeat superior* liability.

(B) Employees with Criminal Records. The hiring of an individual with a criminal record does not by itself establish the tort of negligent hiring.[19] An employer who knows that an applicant has a criminal record has a duty to investigate to determine whether the nature of the conviction in relationship to the job to be performed creates an unacceptable risk to third persons.

(C) Negligent Retention. Courts assign liability under negligent retention on a basis similar to that of negligent hiring. That is, the employer knew, or should have known, that the employee would create an undue risk of harm to others in carrying out job responsibilities.

A hospital is liable for negligent retention when it continues the staff privileges of a physician that it knew or should have known had sexually assaulted a female patient in the past.[20]

The *Bryant v. Livigni* case involves *respondeat superior* liability as well as negligent retention liability.

Bryant v. Livigni, 619 N.E.2d 550 (Ill. App. 1993)

(1) Alcohol, (2) Battery, and (3) Negligent Retention: Three Strikes and You're Out!

Mark Livigni was manager of the National Super Markets, Inc., store in Cahokia, Illinois. After drinking alcoholic beverages one evening, he stopped by the store to check the premises when he observed a 10-year-old boy's unacceptable behavior outside the store. Livigni chased the boy to a car, where he pulled another child, a 4-year-old named Farris Bryant, from the car and threw him through the air. A multicount lawsuit was brought against National and Livigni. A verdict was rendered against National for $20,000 under a *respondeat superior* theory of the battery of Farris Bryant. A verdict was also rendered against National for $15,000 in negligent retention of Livigni and for $115,000 punitive damages for willful and wanton retention. National appealed the trial court's denial of its motions for directed verdicts on these counts.

JUDICIAL OPINION

MAAG, J.…On March 18, 1987, while off duty, Livigni stopped by the Cahokia National store. As manager, he was authorized to check and supervise the operation of the store even during off-duty hours. He was intoxicated at the time of this visit, which was a violation of National rules.…Livigni observed a young man urinating on the store wall outside the east exit doors. He hollered at the young man and followed the fleeing youth to the parked vehicle of Diana Bryant.

Livigni pulled four-year-old Farris Bryant from the automobile,…throwing the child through the air.

Farris was taken to Centreville Township Hospital's emergency room for medical treatment. Farris was admitted to the hospital and was released after four days. He was released from all medical treatment approximately one month after the battery.…

At trial, Livigni's supervisor testified that during Livigni's 17-year tenure with National, Livigni had been a good employee. This supervisor never received any reports from customers or employees that Livigni had "violent-related" problems, although he was aware of a report that Livigni threw an empty milk crate which struck a coworker.

[19] *Connes v. Molalla Transportation Systems*, 831 P.2d 1316 (Colo. 1992).

[20] *Capithorne v. Framingham Union Hospital*, 520 N.E.2d 139 (Mass. 1988). A hospital may also be vicariously liable for the negligent credentialing of its physicians, as determined in *Larson v. Wasemiller*, 738 N.W.2d 300 (Minn. 2007).

Continued

Evidence was offered of two batteries committed by Livigni prior to his attack of Farris. In 1980, Livigni had a disagreement with a subordinate employee resulting in Livigni throwing an empty milk crate at the employee striking him on the arm and necessitating medical treatment. At the time of this battery, Livigni was an assistant store manager. A workers' compensation claim was filed against National by the injured employee. A short time after the workers' compensation claim was resolved, Livigni was promoted to store manager by National in spite of this incident.

The second battery occurred in 1985 when Livigni, while disciplining his 13-year-old son, threw the boy into a bed causing the boy to sustain a broken collar bone. In June 1986 Livigni pleaded guilty to aggravated battery to a child and was sentenced to two years' probation. He was still on probation at the time he attacked Farris.

Livigni testified at trial that he had not told any of his supervisors at National about the battery of his son. He admitted to telling employees of equal or lesser positions than himself about the battery. He considered these people to be his friends....

According to National, there was no evidence that it knew or had reason to know that Livigni was anything other than "an excellent store manager, fit for his position." To support this argument, National claims that there was conflicting evidence regarding the 1980 incident where Livigni threw a milk crate at a coworker causing injury. It argues that the 1980 incident was of uncertain origin since differing versions of the incident and its cause were presented in the evidence. It asserts that due to this conflicting evidence the incident could not form the basis for a negligent retention claim....

Rather than disciplining Livigni after he injured a subordinate employee in an unprovoked attack, National promoted him following the resolution of the injured employee's workers' compensation claim.

National further argues that it had no knowledge of the incident involving Livigni's son that resulted in Livigni's felony conviction for aggravated battery of a child. Relying upon *Campen v Executive House Hotel, Inc.*(1982), 105 Ill. App.3d 576, 61 Ill.Dec. 358, National points to the general rule which states that to impute knowledge of this occurrence to National a showing was required that an agent or employee of National had notice or knowledge of the incident and that the knowledge concerned a matter within the scope of the agent's authority. According to National, evidence of such knowledge was lacking....

National first admits that Livigni told employees of equal or lesser rank within the corporation about the battery involving his son. However, it claims that this is insufficient notice to the corporation. It argues that the people Livigni told were his "friends" and that as mere "coworkers" of equal or subordinate position no notice could legally be imputed to National. We disagree....

...Viewing the evidence in the light most favorable to the plaintiff (Pedrick), we believe that a reasonable jury could have concluded that the information concerning the battery of Livigni's son, learned by these coworkers, was within the scope of their authority to act upon. Whether reported to higher authorities or not, the information still constitutes "corporate knowledge." (*Campen,* 105 Ill. App.3d at 586.) In such a case, their knowledge is chargeable to National....

We conclude that the circuit court did not err in denying National's motion for a directed verdict, nor did it err in refusing to grant a judgment *n.o.v.* on plaintiff's claim of negligent retention. Viewing the evidence in the light most favorable to the plaintiff, we cannot state that the evidence so overwhelmingly favored National that this verdict cannot stand.

National next claims that the circuit court should have directed a verdict in its favor or granted a judgment *n.o.v.* on the plaintiff's punitive damages claim. This count alleged that National's retention of Mark Livigni as a management employee constituted willful and wanton misconduct....

The Restatement (Second) of Torts, section 909, at 467 (1977) provides:

> *"Punitive damages can properly be awarded against a master or other principal because of an act by an agent if, but only if,*
>
> * * * * * *
>
> *(b) the agent was unfit and the principal or a managerial agent was reckless in * * * retaining him."*

This count did not seek to impose liability upon the defendant vicariously. Rather, the plaintiff's cause of action alleged wrongful conduct on the part of National itself. Section 909(b) of the Restatement (Second) of Torts speaks directly to the issue under discussion. So too does the case of *Easley v Apollo Detective Agency, Inc.*(1979), 69 Ill.App.3d 920.

Easley recognized that it is settled law that a cause of action exists in Illinois for negligent hiring of an employee, and that if the defendant's conduct could properly be characterized as willful and wanton then punitive damages are recoverable. We see little difference between a punitive damages claim for willfully and wantonly hiring an employee in the first instance and a claim for willfully and wantonly retaining an unfit employee after hiring. In both instances, the interest to be protected is the same. Employers that wrongfully (whether negligently or willfully and wantonly) hire or retain unfit employees expose the public to the acts of these employees. In such cases it is not unreasonable to hold the

Continued

employer accountable when the employee causes injury or damage to another. The principle at issue is not *respondeat superior,* although that may also be implicated. Rather, the cause of action is premised upon the wrongful conduct of the employer itself....

The jury heard evidence that Livigni attacked a fellow employee in 1980 and was then promoted. He injured his own son, he was convicted of aggravated battery in a criminal proceeding, and members of National's management admittedly knew of that incident. National took no action. Then while a store manager, in an intoxicated state, he attacked a four-year-old child and threw him through the air, resulting in hospitalization. National itself characterizes this attack on young Farris as outrageous. We cannot say the jury was unjustified in concluding the same and also concluding that retaining this man as a managerial employee constituted willful and wanton misconduct....

Finally, National asks that a judgment *n.o.v.* be entered in its favor on the plaintiffs' *respondeat superior* claims....

In order to impose liability upon National, it was not necessary that Livigni be motivated *solely* by a desire to further National's interest. It is sufficient if his actions were prompted only *in part* by a purpose to protect store property or further the employers' business. (*Wilson v Clark Oil & Refining Corp.* (1985), 134 Ill.App.3d 1084, 1089.) The evidence was sufficient to justify such a conclusion by the jury.

Finally, the actions of Livigni in attacking Farris were committed within the constraints of the authorized time and location of his employment, thus bolstering a finding that the battery occurred within the course and scope of his employment. *Sunseri v Puccia* (1981), 97 Ill. App.3d 488....

[Judgment affirmed]

J. WELCH, concurring in part and dissenting in part...I concur with the majority's opinion with respect to, and would affirm the judgment of the circuit court on the jury verdict against National Food Stores on, the *respondeat superior* counts of plaintiffs' complaint. With respect to the majority's opinion concerning the judgment against National on the negligent and willful and wanton retention counts of plaintiffs' complaint, however, I must respectfully dissent....

From a practical standpoint, the majority's opinion sends a message to all employers that in order to insulate themselves from liability for negligent or willful and wanton retention any employee who has ever had an altercation on or off the workplace premises must be fired. Moreover, the majority opinion places an unreasonable investigative burden upon the employer by forcing the employer to discover, retain, and analyze the criminal records of its employees. Is not the majority's opinion then at cross-purposes with the established public policy and laws of Illinois protecting the privacy of citizens and promoting the education and rehabilitation of criminal offenders? See Ill.Rev.Stat.1991, ch. 68, par. 2-103 (making it a civil rights violation to ask a job applicant about an arrest record); see also Ill.Rev.Stat.1991, ch. 38, par. 1003-12-1 *et seq.* (concerning correctional employment programs whose function is to teach marketable skills and work habits and responsibility to Illinois prisoners).

I would have granted defendant National Food Stores' motion for judgment *non obstante veredicto*....

QUESTIONS

1. Was there *respondeat superior* liability in this case?
2. Should National have reasonably known about Livigni's violence-related problems? If so, did it act negligently in retaining him as an employee?
3. From Judge Welch's dissent, will the *Livigni* case hurt the employment prospects of other individuals who have criminal records involving violence?

13. Negligent Supervision and Training

A separate theory of liability in addition to the doctrine of *respondeat superior* is that of negligent supervision and training, that holds the principal directly liable for its negligence in regard to training and supervision of its employees and agents. **For Example,** Monadnock Training Council, Inc., certified Robert Hebert as an "authorized Monadnock instructor" and granted him actual authority to market and promote its PR-24 police baton. In a training session run by Hebert at the Chesire County House of Corrections in New Hampshire, Charles Herman suffered severe head trauma when training with Hebert without protective headgear in a room with unpadded cement walls. Monadnock was held directly liable for Herman's injuries based on its negligent supervision and training of Hebert.[21]

[21] *Herman v. Monadnock PR-24 Training Council, Inc.,* 802 A.2d 1187 (N.H. 2002).

FIGURE 38-1 Liability for Torts of Agent or Employee

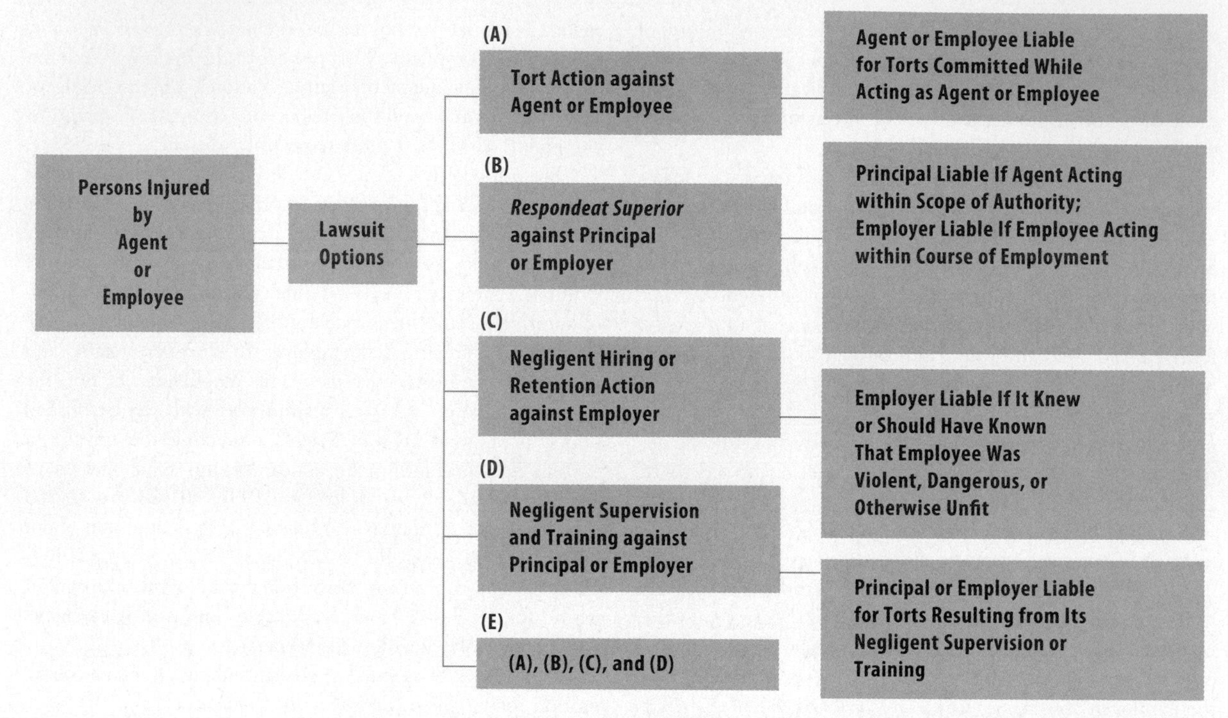

14. Agent's Crimes

A principal is liable for the crimes of an agent committed at the principal's direction. When not authorized, however, the principal is ordinarily not liable for an agent's crime merely because it was committed while the agent was otherwise acting within the scope of the latter's authority or employment. **For Example,** the owner of the Main Tower Cafe in Hartford, Connecticut, was not vicariously liable for injuries sustained by a patron who was shot by a bouncer while attempting to enter the bar because the bouncer's intentional and willful act was motivated by his own spleen and malevolence against the victim in clear departure from his employment.[22] As an exception to the rule of nonliability just stated, courts now hold an employer criminally liable when the employee has in the course of employment violated environmental protection laws, liquor sales laws, pure food laws, or laws regulating prices or prohibiting false weights. **For Example,** an employer may be held criminally responsible for an employee's sale of liquor to a minor in violation of the liquor law even though the sale was not known to the employer and violated instructions given to the employee.

15. Owner's Liability for Acts of an Independent Contractor

If work is done by an independent contractor rather than by an employee, the owner is not liable for harm caused by the contractor to third persons or their property. Likewise, the owner is not bound by the contracts made by the independent contractor. The owner is ordinarily not liable for harm caused to third persons by the negligence of the employees of the independent contractor.[23] As is shown in the *McLaurin* case, the owner is not liable for harm caused to a contractor's employee who is working under the control of the contractor.

[22] *Pruitt v. Main & Tower, Inc.*, 2002 WL 532467 (Conn. Super. March 14, 2002); see also *Burgess v. Lee Acceptance Corp.*, 2008 WL 5111905 (E.D. Mich. Dec. 4, 2008).

[23] *King v. Lens Creek, Ltd., Partnership*, 483 S.E.2d 265 (W. Va. 1996).

McLaurin v. Noble Drilling Inc., 2009 WL 367401 (S.D. Miss. Feb. 10, 2009)

Plaintiffs' Attorneys Whine, "Why Do Courts Keep on Applying the 'Right to Control Test'?"

Mark McLaurin was employed as a carpenter by Friede Goldman Offshore, Inc. Noble Drilling, Inc., contracted with Friede Goldman (FG) to refit one of its offshore drilling rigs, the "Noble Clyde Boudreaux," at FG's Jackson Country, Mississippi, facility. On July 30 and 31, 2002, McLaurin was assigned by Friede Goldman to construct scaffolding inside one of the pontoon extensions. A crane, operated by Friede Goldman employees, was in the process of lowering the roof structure of the pontoon for final placement. McLaurin was injured when he placed his hand in a "pinch point"—a space between two objects—while the roof was being lowered. McLaurin suffered a severely crushed left hand and arm. He received medical benefits and disability compensation from FG under the Longshore Harbor Workers' Compensation Act. Maritime workers are also allowed to pursue separate claims against third parties responsible for their injuries, and McLaurin sued Noble Drilling for negligence. Noble Drilling sought the dismissal of the case asserting that it was not responsible for the negligence of the employees of an independent contractor.

JUDICIAL OPINION

GUIROLA, J.…McLaurin's supervisor testified that Noble never told any members of his crew what to do and that he had "total control over my crew." McLaurin himself testified that no one from Noble instructed him to perform his work, and it was one of his Friede Goldman supervisors who told him to work inside the pontoon extension.

Reviewing all of this evidence, the Court finds that it is insufficient to create a jury question as to whether Noble had substantial de facto control over the work performed on the pontoon extension. Although Noble and Friede Goldman cooperated in planning and completing the project, it is clear that Friede Goldman retained ultimate decision-making authority to direct the day-to-day work and activities of its own employees. It was Friede Goldman that established the procedure to complete the pontoon extension work, and Friede Goldman had responsibility for the manner of completion of the work. Only Friede Goldman employees were involved in fitting the shelf on the pontoon extension at the time of McLaurin's injury. The mere fact that Noble could observe, inspect and make recommendations does not establish that it had substantial de facto control over this operation.…

The testimony noted by the Court above tends to show that Noble was neither expected nor allowed to direct the work of Friede Goldman's employees. Furthermore, there is no evidence that a Noble employee was present to observe the unsafe placement of McLaurin's hand in the pontoon extension.…

[Judgment for Noble Drilling Inc.]

QUESTIONS

1. Is the owner liable for harm caused to a third person by the negligence of the employees of an independent contractor when the owner retains control over the performance of the work that has given rise to the injury?
2. Did Noble Drilling retain control over the performance of the work that gave rise to Mark McLaurin's injury?

(A) Exceptions to Owner's Immunity. There is a trend toward imposing liability on the owner when work undertaken by an independent contractor is inherently dangerous.[24] That is, the law is taking the position that if the owner wishes to engage in a particular activity, the owner must be responsible for the harm it causes. The owner cannot be insulated from such liability by the device of hiring an independent contractor to do the work.

Regardless of the nature of the activity, the owner may be liable for the torts and contracts of the independent contractor when the owner controls the conduct of the independent contractor.

In certain circumstances, such as providing security for a business, collecting bills, and repossessing collateral, there is an increased risk that torts may be committed by the individuals performing such duties. The trend of the law is to refuse to allow the use of an independent contractor for such work to insulate the employer.

[24] *Hinger v. Parker & Parsley Petroleum Co.*, 902 P.2d 1033 (N.M. App. 1995).

(B) Undisclosed Independent Contractor. In some situations, the owner appears to be doing the act in question because the existence of the independent contractor is not disclosed or apparent. This situation occurs most commonly when a franchisee does business under the name of the franchisor; when a concessionaire, such as a restaurant in a hotel, appears to be the hotel restaurant, although in fact it is operated by an independent concessionaire; or when the buyer of a business continues to run the business in the seller's name. In such cases of an undisclosed independent contractor, it is generally held that the apparent owner (that is, the franchisor, the grantor of the concession, or the seller) is liable for the torts and contracts of the undisclosed independent contractor.

16. Enforcement of Claim by Third Person

A lawsuit may be brought by a third person against the agent or the principal if each is liable. In most states and in the federal courts, the plaintiff may sue either or both in one action when both are liable. If both are sued, the plaintiff may obtain a judgment against both, although the plaintiff is allowed to collect the full amount of the judgment only once.

D. Transactions with Sales Personnel

Many transactions with sales personnel do not result in a contract with the third person with whom the salesperson deals.

17. Soliciting and Contracting Agents

Giving an order to a salesperson often does not give rise to a contract. Ordinarily, a salesperson is a **soliciting agent**, whose authority is limited to soliciting offers from third persons and transmitting them to the principal for acceptance or rejection. Such an agent does not have authority to make a contract that will bind the principal to the third person. The employer of the salesperson is not bound by a contract until the employer accepts the order, and the third person (customer) may withdraw the offer at any time prior to acceptance.

In contrast, if the person with whom the buyer deals is a **contracting agent** with authority to make contracts, by definition a binding contract exists between the principal and the customer from the moment that the agent agrees with the customer. In other words, the contract arises when the agent accepts the customer's order.[25]

[25] But see the complications that developed in *Ferris v. Tennessee Log Homes, Inc.*, 2009 WL 1506724, (W.D. Ky. May 27, 2009), where Tennessee Log Homes (TLH) had a licensing agreement that explicitly granted authority to its "agent" to generate contracts for the sale of log home packages on behalf of TLH.

MAKE THE CONNECTION

SUMMARY

An agent of a disclosed principal who makes a contract with a third person within the scope of authority has no personal liability on the contract. It is the principal and the third person who may each sue the other in the event of a breach. A person purporting to act as an agent for a principal warrants by implication that there is an existing principal with legal capacity and that the principal has authorized the agent to act. The person acting as an agent is liable for any loss caused the third person for breach of these warranties. An agent of a partially disclosed or an undisclosed principal is a party to the contract with the third person. The agent may enforce the contract against the third person and is liable for its breach. To avoid problems of interpretation, an agent should execute a contract "Principal, by Agent." Agents are liable for harm caused third persons by their fraudulent, malicious, or negligent acts.

An undisclosed or a partially disclosed principal is liable to a third person on a simple contract made by an authorized agent. When a third person makes payment to an authorized agent, it is deemed paid to the principal.

A principal or an employer is vicariously liable under the doctrine of *respondeat superior* for the torts of an agent or an employee committed within the scope of authority or the course of employment. The principal or the employer may also be liable for some crimes committed in the course of employment. An owner is not liable for torts caused by an independent contractor to third persons or their property unless the work given to the independent contractor is inherently hazardous.

A salesperson is ordinarily an agent whose authority is limited to soliciting offers (orders) from third persons and transmitting them to the principal. The principal is not bound until he or she accepts the order. The customer may withdraw an offer at any time prior to acceptance.

LEARNING OUTCOMES

After studying this chapter, you should be able to clearly explain:

A. Liability of Agent to Third Person

LO.1 Explain when an agent is and is not liable to a third person as a party to a contract

See the Biefeld Jewelers example in which Margie Biefeld was acting as an agent for a disclosed principal when she signed the contract and was not a party to the contract, pp. 772–773.

LO.2 Describe how to execute a contract as an agent on behalf of a principal

See the "B. G. Gray, by Jane R. Craig" example on p. 775.

Learn from the mistake of Philip Steen's insufficient disclosure of his principal in the *ICG Link case*, pp. 773–774.

B. Liability of Principal to Third Person

LO.3 Explain the legal effect of a payment made by a third person to an authorized agent

See the discussion of a third party's payment to an authorized agent who absconds with the payment, starting on p. 776.

C. Liability of Principal for Torts and Crimes of Agent

LO.4 Explain the doctrine of *respondeat superior*

See the Crane Brothers, Inc. example of employer liability for torts of the employees, p. 778.

See the Rev. Joel Thomford example in which Rev. Thomford's employer, the church, was not liable for the pastor's accidental shooting of a parishioner on a hunting trip not sponsored by the church, p. 778.

D. Transactions with Sales Personnel

LO.5 Distinguish between the authority of a soliciting agent and that of a contracting agent

See the discussion of the soliciting and contracting of agents, p. 786.

KEY TERMS

contracting agent
respondeat superior
disclosed principal
partially disclosed principal
soliciting agent
undisclosed principal
vicarious liability

QUESTIONS AND CASE PROBLEMS

1. Richard Pawlus was an owner of Dutch City Wood Products, Inc., which did business as "Dutch City Marketing." Pawlus purchased merchandise from Rothschild Sunsystems from

April 24 to June 24 using the designation "Richard Pawlus Dutch City Marketing" on orders and correspondence. In October, Rothschild was notified that Pawlus was acting on behalf of the corporation when the merchandise was purchased. Rothschild sued Pawlus for payment for the merchandise. Pawlus contended that he was an agent of the corporation and was thus not personally liable. Decide. [*Rothschild Sunsystems, Inc. v. Pawlus*, 514 N.Y.S.2d 572 (A.D.)]

2. Myles Murphy was appointed by Cy Sinden, a famous developer, to purchase land for a shopping center near the intersection of I-95 and Route 1. Mary Mason, the property owner, contracted with Murphy for the sale of the property. Because of an economic downturn, Sinden was unable to provide the planned behind-the-scenes financing for the venture, and the contract was not performed. Mason's real estate experts determined that she lost $2 million because of the breach of contract. Mason also discovered that Sinden was "behind the deal." If Mason elects to sue Sinden, who turns out to be unable to pay the judgment because of the collapse of his business "empire," can she later bring suit against Murphy?

3. Lowell Shoemaker, an architect, was hired by Affhouse to work on a land development project. In September Shoemaker contacted Central Missouri Professional Services about providing engineering and surveying services for the project. Central submitted a written proposal to Shoemaker in October. About a week later, Shoemaker orally agreed that Central should proceed with the work outlined in the proposal. When the first phase of the work was completed, a bill of $5,864.00 was sent to Shoemaker. Shoemaker called Central and requested that all bills be sent directly to the owner/developer, Affhouse. When the bills were not paid, Central sued Shoemaker and Affhouse. The trial court entered a judgment against Shoemaker for $5,864 and he appealed. Shoemaker acknowledged that he did not disclose the identity of the principal to Central at the time the transaction was conducted, and explained:

   Q. You never told Mike Bates or Central Missouri Professional Services that you were an agent for Affhouse or any other undisclosed principal?
   A. That's correct. I never did.

   Q. Another note I wrote down was that the subject of Affhouse came up in your conversations with Mike Bates of Central Missouri Professional Services after he sent the bill to you?
   A. The early part of the year, yes.

   Shoemaker contends that since he made clear to Central that he was an architect and not the developer, there was no binding oral contract between Central and him. Decide. [*Central Missouri Professional Services v. Shoemaker*, 108 S.W.3d 6 (Mo. App.)]

4. Beverly Baumann accompanied her mother to Memorial Hospital, where her mother was placed in intensive care for heart problems. A nurse asked Baumann to sign various documents, including one that authorized the hospital to release medical information and to receive the mother's insurance benefits directly. This form stated: "I understand I am financially responsible to the hospital for charges not covered by this authorization." Baumann's mother died during the course of her hospitalization. The hospital later sued Baumann to recover $19,013.42 in unpaid hospital charges based on the form she signed, which the hospital called a "guarantee of payment." Baumann contended that she signed the document as an agent for her mother and was thus not personally liable. Decide. [*Memorial Hospital v. Baumann*, 474 N.Y.S.2d 636 (A.D.)]

5. Mills Electric Co. signed a contract with S&S Horticulture Architects, a two-person landscaping partnership operated by Sullivan and Smyth, to maintain the grounds and flowers at the Mills Electric Co. plant in Jacksonville, Florida. Mills checked references of S&S and found the company to be highly reputable. The contract set forth that S&S would select the flowers for each season and would determine when to maintain the lawns so long as they were properly maintained. The contract called for payments to be made to S&S on the first workday of each month, and the contract stipulated that "nothing herein shall make S&S an agent of the company." The contract also required that S&S personnel wear

uniforms identifying them as employees of S&S. S&S had other accounts, but the large Mills Electric plant took up most of its time. While working on a terraced area near the visitors' entrance to the plant, Sullivan lost control of his large commercial mower, and the mower struck Gillespie, a plant visitor, causing her serious injury. A witness heard Sullivan apologizing to Gillespie and saying that "running that mower on the terrace is a two-person job." Gillespie brought suit against Mills Electric Co., contending Mills should be held vicariously liable. Decide.

6. Leo Bongers died intestate. Alfred Bongers and Delores Kuhl, Leo's nephew and niece, were appointed personal representatives of his estate. Leo left more than 120 antique cars, trucks, and motorcycles. The estate hired Bauer-Moravec to sell the vehicles at auction. Auctioneer Russ Moravec suggested that the vehicles be sold at an airstrip auction in May, June, or July. The estate rejected this recommendation and insisted that the sale be conducted in January on a farm owned by the estate. On January 30, the auction took place beginning at 9:30 A.M. with temperatures below freezing and some 800 people jammed into the bid barn. One auctioneer had purchased Putnam hitch balls to be used with mylar-type ropes so that small farm tractors could tow the vehicles into and out of the bid barn. One hour into the auction, Joseph Haag was seriously injured when a hitch ball came loose from the drawbar of the tractor towing an antique Studebaker truck. Haag sued the estate, claiming that Bauer-Moravec was acting as agent for the estate and that its negligence in not properly attaching the hitch ball and in using mylar-type tow rope rather than chains should be imputed to the estate under the doctrine of *respondeat superior*. The estate defended that it was not liable for the torts of the auctioneer and its employees because the auctioneer was an independent contractor. Decide. [*Haag v. Bongers*, 589 N.W.2d 318 (Neb.)]

7. On July 11, 1984, José Padilla was working as a vacation-relief route salesperson for Frito-Lay. He testified that he made a route stop at Sal's Beverage Shop, where he was told by Mrs. Ramos that she was dissatisfied with Frito-Lay service and no longer wanted its products in the store. He asked if there was anything he could do to change her mind. She said no and told him to pick up his merchandise. He took one company-owned merchandise rack to his van and was about to pick up another rack when Mr. Ramos said that the rack had been given to him by the regular route salesperson. Padilla said the route salesperson had no authority to give away Frito-Lay racks. A confrontation occurred over the rack, and Padilla pushed Mr. Ramos against the cash register, injuring Ramos's back. Frito-Lay has a company policy, clearly communicated to all employees, that prohibits them from getting involved in any type of physical confrontation with a customer. Frito-Lay contended that Padilla was not acting within the course and scope of his employment when the pushing incident took place and that the company was therefore not liable to Ramos. Ramos contended that Frito-Lay was responsible for the acts of its employee Padilla. Decide. [*Frito-Lay, Inc. v. Ramos*, 770 S.W.2d 887 (Tex. App.)]

8. Jason Lasseigne, a Little League baseball player, was seriously injured at a practice session when he was struck on the head by a poorly thrown baseball from a team member, Todd Landry. The league was organized by American Legion Post 38. Claude Cassel and Billy Johnson were the volunteer coaches of the practice session. The Lasseignes brought suit on behalf of Jason against Post 38, claiming that the coaching was negligent and that Post 38 was vicariously liable for the harm caused by such negligence. Post 38 contended that it had no right to control the work of the volunteer coaches or the manner in which practices were conducted and as a result should not be held vicariously liable for the actions of the coaches. Decide. [*Lasseigne v. American Legion Post 38*, 543 So.2d 1111 (La. App.)]

9. Moritz, a guest at Pines Hotel, was sitting in the lobby when Brown, a hotel employee, dropped a heavy vacuum cleaner on her knee. When Moritz complained, the employee insulted her and hit

her with his fist, knocking her unconscious. She sued the hotel for damages. Was the hotel liable? [*Moritz v. Pines Hotel, Inc.*, 383 N.Y.S.2d 704 (A.D.)]

10. Steve Diezel, an employee of Island City Flying Service in Key West, Florida, stole a General Electric Credit Corp. (GECC) aircraft and crashed the plane while attempting to take off. GECC brought suit against Island City on the theory that it had negligently hired Diezel as an employee and was therefore legally responsible for Diezel's act of theft. Diezel had a military prison record as a result of a drug offense and had been fired by Island City twice previously but had been immediately reinstated each time. Island City claimed that the evidence was insufficient to establish that it had been negligent in employing Diezel. Decide. [*Island City Flying Service v. General Electric*, 585 So.2d 274 (Fla.)]

11. The Bay State Harness Horse Racing and Breeding Association conducted horse races at a track where music for patrons was supplied by an independent contractor hired by the association. Some of the music played was subject to a copyright held by Famous Music Corp. The playing of that music was a violation of the copyright unless royalties were paid to Famous Music. No royalties were paid, and Famous Music sued the association, which raised the defense that the violation had been committed by an independent contractor specifically instructed not to play Famous Music's copyrighted material. Decide. [*Famous Music Corp. v. Bay State Harness Horse Racing and Breeding Association, Inc.*, 554 F.2d 1213 (1st Cir.)]

12. Steven Trujillo, told by the assistant door manager of Cowboys Bar "to show up to work tonight in case we need you as a doorman," came to the bar that evening wearing a jacket with the bar logo on it. Trujillo "attacked" Rocky Medina in the parking lot of the bar, causing him serious injury. Prior to working for Cowboys, Trujillo was involved in several fights at that bar and in its parking lot, and Cowboys knew of these matters. Medina sued Cowboys on two theories of liability: (1) *respondeat superior* and (2) negligent hiring of Trujillo. Cowboys's defense was that *respondeat superior* theory should be dismissed because the assault was clearly not within the course of Trujillo's employment. Concerning the negligent hiring theory, Cowboys asserted that Trujillo was not on duty that night as a doorman. Decide. [*Medina v. Graham's Cowboys, Inc.*, 827 P.2d 859 (N.M. App.)]

13. Neal Rubin, while driving his car in Chicago, inadvertently blocked the path of a Yellow Cab Co. taxi driven by Robert Ball, causing the taxi to swerve and hit Rubin's car. Angered by Rubin's driving, Ball got out of his cab and hit Rubin on the head and shoulders with a metal pipe. Rubin sued Yellow Cab Co. for the damages caused by this beating, contending that the employer was vicariously liable for the beating under the doctrine of *respondeat superior* because the beating occurred in furtherance of the employer's business, which was to obtain fares without delay. The company argued that Ball's beating of Rubin was not an act undertaken to further the employer's business. Is the employer liable under *respondeat superior*? [*Rubin v. Yellow Cab Co.*, 507 N.E.2d 114 (Ill. App.)]

14. Brazilian & Colombian Co. (B&C), a food broker, ordered 40 barrels of olives from Mawer-Gulden-Annis (MGA). MGA's shipping clerk was later told to make out the bill of lading to B&C's customer Pantry Queen; the olives were shipped directly to Pantry Queen. Eight days after delivery, the president of B&C wrote MGA to give it the name of its principal, Pantry Queen, and advised MGA to bill the principal directly. Pantry Queen was unable to pay for the olives, and MGA sued B&C for payment. B&C contended that it was well known to MGA that B&C was a food broker (agent) and the olives were shipped directly to the principal by MGA. It stated that as an agent, it was not a party to the contract and was thus not liable. Decide. [*Mawer-Gulden-Annis, Inc. v. Brazilian & Colombian Coffee Co.*, 199 N.E.2d 222 (Ill. App.)]

CPA QUESTIONS

1. Frey entered into a contract with Cara Corp. to purchase televisions on behalf of Lux, Inc. Lux authorized Frey to enter into the contract in Frey's name without disclosing that Frey was acting on behalf of Lux. If Cara repudiates the contract, which of the following statements concerning liability on the contract is *not* correct?
   a. Frey may not hold Cara liable and obtain money damages.
   b. Frey may hold Cara liable and obtain specific performance.
   c. Lux may hold Cara liable upon disclosing the agency relationship with Frey.
   d. Cara will be free from liability to Lux if Frey fraudulently stated that he was acting on his own behalf.
2. A principal will *not* be liable to a third party for a tort committed by an agent:
   a. Unless the principal instructed the agent to commit the tort
   b. Unless the tort was committed within the scope of the agency relationship
   c. If the agency agreement limits the principal's liability for the agent's tort
   d. If the tort is also regarded as a criminal act
3. Cox engaged Datz as her agent. It was mutually agreed that Datz would *not* disclose that he was acting as Cox's agent. Instead, he was to deal with prospective customers as if he were a principal acting on his own behalf. This he did and made several contracts for Cox. Assuming Cox, Datz, or the customer seeks to avoid liability on one of the contracts involved, which of the following statements is correct?
   a. Cox must ratify the Datz contracts in order to be held liable.
   b. Datz has *no* liability once he discloses that Cox was the real principal.
   c. The third party can avoid liability because he believed he was dealing with Datz as a principal.
   d. The third party may choose to hold either Datz or Cox liable.
4. Which of the following statements is (are) correct regarding the relationship between an agent and a nondisclosed principal?
   I. The principal is required to indemnify the agent for any contract entered into by the agent within the scope of the agency agreement.
   II. The agent has the same actual authority as if the principal had been disclosed.
   a. I only
   b. II only
   c. Both I and II
   d. Neither I nor II

CHAPTER 39

© Manuel Gutjahr/iStockphoto.com

Regulation of Employment

learningoutcomes

After studying this chapter, you should be able to

LO.1 Explain the contractual nature of the employment relationship

LO.2 Explain how whistleblower protection under Sarbanes-Oxley is limited to conduct in violation of fraud or securities laws

LO.3 Explain how Dodd-Frank expands whistleblower protection to a wide range of financial services employees and provides incentives for whistleblowers

LO.4 Explain how the National Labor Relations Act prohibits employers from firing employees attempting to form a union, and requires employers to bargain with unions in good faith over wages, hours, and working conditions

LO.5 Explain how ERISA protects employee pensions and benefits

LO.6 Explain the essentials of unemployment benefits, family and medical leaves, military leaves, and Social Security benefits

LO.7 Explain how OSHA is designed to ensure workers safe and healthful working conditions

LO.8 Explain the three types of benefits provided by workers' compensation statutes

LO.9 Explain the sources of privacy rights, and applications to telephone, e-mail, text-messaging, and property searches

LO.10 Explain an employer's verification obligations when hiring new employees and discuss special hiring programs allowing aliens to work in the United States

Employment law involves the law of contracts and the law established by lawmakers, courts, and administrative agencies.

A. The Employment Relationship

The relationship of an employer and an employee exists when, pursuant to an express or implied agreement of the parties, one person, the employee, undertakes to perform services or to do work under the direction and control of another, the employer, for compensation. In older cases, this relationship was called the *master-servant relationship*.

1. Characteristics of Relationship

An employee is hired to work under the control of the employer. An employee differs from an agent, who is to negotiate or make contracts with third persons on behalf of, and under the control of, a principal. However, a person may be both an employee and an agent for the other party. An employee also differs from an independent contractor, who is to perform a contract independent of, or free from, control by the other party.[1]

2. Creation of Employment Relationship

The relationship of employer and employee can be created only with the consent of both parties.

(A) Individual Employment Contracts. As in contracts generally, both parties must assent to the terms of an employment contract. Subject to statutory restrictions, the parties are free to make a contract on any terms they wish.

(B) Collective Bargaining Contracts. Collective bargaining contracts govern the rights and obligations of employers and employees in many private and public areas of employment. Under collective bargaining, representatives of the employees bargain with a single employer or a group of employers for an agreement on wages, hours, and working conditions. The agreement worked out by the representatives of the employees, usually union officials, is generally subject to a ratification vote by the employees. Terms usually found in collective bargaining contracts are (1) identification of the work belonging exclusively to designated classes of employees, (2) wage and benefits clauses, (3) promotion and layoff clauses, which are generally tied in part to seniority, (4) a management's rights clause, and (5) a grievance procedure. A grievance procedure provides a means by which persons claiming that the contract was violated or that they were disciplined or discharged without just cause may have their cases decided by impartial labor arbitrators.

3. Duration and Termination of Employment Contract

In many instances, the employment contract does not state any time or duration. In such a case, it may be terminated at any time by either party. In contrast, the employment contract may expressly state that it shall last for a specified period of time; an example would be an individual's contract to work as general manager for five years.

(A) Employment-at-Will Doctrine and Developing Exceptions. Ordinarily, a contract of employment may be terminated in the same manner as any other contract. If it is to run for a definite period of time, the employer cannot terminate the contract at an earlier date without justification. If the employment contract does not have a definite duration, it is terminable at will. Under the **employment-at-will doctrine** the employer has historically been allowed to terminate the employment contract at any time for any reason or for no reason.[2] Gradually, federal and state statutes were enacted to provide certain individual rights to workers, protecting them from workplace exploitation and discrimination by employers. And, in most states, courts have carved out narrow exceptions to the employment-at-will doctrine when the discharge violates an established public policy.[3] **For Example,** home health care nurse Eugene Patterson continued to provide wound care to a patient after he was directed to cease the care by his employer, and he was discharged for insubordination. Patterson did so because the physician's order for the

[1] *Ost v. West Suburban Travelers Limousine, Inc.*, 88 F.3d 435 (7th Cir. 1996).
[2] *Payne v. Western & Atlantic Railroad Co.*, 82 Tenn. 507, 518–519 (1884).
[3] *Patterson v. Gentiva Health Services, Inc.*, 2011 WL 3235466 (D. S.C. July 25, 2011).

care remained in place, and he believed that state law governing the practice of nursing required him to complete the physician-directed care. The court held Patterson could sue his employer Gentiva Health Services for wrongful termination in violation of public policy. Absent statutory protection, or a court-created contract or tort exception, the employment-at-will doctrine is still the basic default rule governing employment in the United States.

Public policy exceptions are often made to the employment-at-will doctrine when an employee is discharged in retaliation for insisting that the employer comply with the state's food and drug act or for filing a workers' compensation claim.[4] In some states, so-called whistleblower laws have been enacted to protect employees who disclose employer practices that endanger public health or safety. Also, a statutory right exists for at-will employees who are terminated in retaliation for cooperating with a federal criminal prosecution or are terminated in violation of the public policy to provide truthful testimony.[5]

The *Adams* case involves the application of a state whistleblower law.

Adams v. Uno Restaurants, Inc., 794 A.2d 489 (R.I. 2002)

Pretext at the Pizzeria

After a jury returned a verdict in favor of the plaintiff, Gerald K. Adams, finding that his employer, the Warwick Rhode Island Pizzaria Uno had wrongfully terminated Adams in violation of the state's Whistleblowers Act,* the trial court set aside the jury's award of $7,500 in damages, and Adams appealed to the state's Supreme Court.

JUDICIAL OPINION

PER CURIAM: On May 20, 1996, the plaintiff, who had been employed by the defendant for several years, arrived for his nighttime line cooking shift at the defendant's Warwick restaurant. Shortly after his shift began, the plaintiff noticed that the kitchen floor was saturated with a foulsmelling liquid coming from drains and backing up water onto the floor. He complained of illness and went home, at which time he contacted the Department of Health about the drainage problem in the restaurant's kitchen. A Department of Health representative visited the restaurant that evening and noticed that the floor drains were backed up and that the floor was wet and slippery. She ordered the kitchen staff to dispose of all the food they had touched with their bare hands and closed the restaurant for the night, leaving instructions to sanitize the kitchen area and clear all the drains. She also inquired about which employee went home sick. The restaurant reopened the next day after sanitizing the kitchen.

*The Rhode Island Whistleblowers' Protection Act, G.L. 1956 28-50-4(a) provides that "A person who alleges a violation of this act may bring a civil action for appropriate injunctive relief, or actual damages, or both within three (3) years after the occurrence of the alleged violation of this chapter."

On May 22, 1996, two days after the incident, the plaintiff, who was not scheduled to work that day, returned to the restaurant curious to determine whether there was any hostility toward him resulting from his having called the Department of Health. The plaintiff testified that he was summarily ordered by David Badot, the restaurant's manager, to come into his office and that Badot proceeded to shout at him while inquiring whether he had contacted the Department of Health. The plaintiff testified that he shouted back at Badot and acknowledged that he had indeed called the Department of Health. Badot then accused the plaintiff of stealing one of the defendant's softball team shirts and of taking a work schedule home. Badot then left his office, and the plaintiff followed him out into the general cooking area, where other employees were present. The shouting match between Badot and the plaintiff continued and in the course thereof, the plaintiff told Badot that he "was going to follow him back to Massachusetts on this, and [he] was going to blow the intelligence out of his head." The plaintiff then left the restaurant. Badot claimed to have perceived the plaintiff's words as threatening and instructed an employee to call the police. When the plaintiff later heard that the police were looking for him, he voluntarily went to the Warwick police station, whereupon he was then charged with disorderly conduct, arraigned, and pled not guilty. No trial on the charge ensued. The charge was later filed. One year later his record of arrest and charge automatically was expunged pursuant to the case filing statute.

Shortly thereafter, the plaintiff commenced this civil action against the defendant alleging therein that he had

[4] *Brigham v. Dillon Companies, Inc.*, 935 P.2d 1054 (Kan. 1997).

[5] *Fitzgerald v. Salsbury Chemical, Inc.*, 613 N.W.2d 275 (Iowa 2000). In *Garcetti v. Ceballos*, 547 U.S. 410 (2006), the U.S. Supreme Court held that when public employees make statements pursuant to their official duties, the First Amendment of the Constitution does not insulate their communications from employer discipline because the employees are not speaking as citizens for First Amendment purposes. In his dissent, Justice Souter argued that a public employee should have constitutional protection when the employee acts as a whistleblower.

Continued

been unlawfully terminated only because he had notified the Department of Health regarding the unsanitary kitchen conditions existing at the defendant's Warwick Pizzeria Uno Restaurant & Bar....

After examining the evidence in the light most favorable to the plaintiff, the trial justice decided that a reasonable jury could have found that Badot's actions in badgering the plaintiff and then having him arrested were a pretext for retaliating against the plaintiff for having called in the Department of Health. The trial justice concluded that a reasonable jury certainly could have found that the confrontation between Badot and the plaintiff was designed by Badot to provoke a reaction from the plaintiff that would serve as Badot's excuse to fire him, even though that was merely a pretext for the real reason—the plaintiff's call to the Department of Health....

Although the plaintiff at trial did not specifically quantify his damages, he did testify that it took him eleven days to find employment after his being terminated by the defendant. In addition to his economic damages, he claimed and testified that he suffered emotional distress and humiliation as a result of the defendant's wrongful conduct in initiating criminal proceedings against him that resulted in the loss of his National Guard security clearance and disqualification from an overseas National Guard mission. He offered no expert medical testimony in support of his claim for emotional distress....

On the particular case facts before us, we do not find the absence of expert medical testimony to support the plaintiff's claim for damages resulting from his alleged emotional distress and humiliation to be fatal to that portion of his claim for damages. Unlike the usual case where a claim for emotional distress and humiliation is oftentimes made without objective facts to substantiate such a claim, expert medical testimony is deemed necessary to assist the factfinder in determining not only the validity but also the casual relationship of any emotional distress. In this case, the trial jury had before it clear objective and uncontroverted evidence concerning the complaint to the Warwick police; his arrest by the Warwick police; the criminal charge for disorderly conduct made against him; his arraignment on that charge; the revocation of his military security clearance and the resulting loss of his opportunity to accompany his National Guard unit in an overseas mission to Germany.** From such objective and uncontradicted evidence, we believe that an ordinary lay person or trial juror would be capable of determining without the aid of expert medical testimony whether emotional distress and humiliation could ordinarily and naturally follow from such events. Trial jurors, we are satisfied, do not leave their common sense in the cloakroom when they come to sit in the courtroom....

In this case, the trial evidence clearly reveals that the plaintiff Adams was particularly troubled over his being arrested for disorderly conduct and the resulting loss of his security clearance as a National Guard reservist. That loss of security clearance subsequently prevented him from participating with his National Guard unit in an overseas mission to Germany. The trial justice apparently noted the significance of those matters upon the plaintiff's emotional well-being, when in overruling defense counsel's objection to the plaintiff's testimony concerning those matters he noted: "I'll allow it. To him it's very important. Whether it is to you or the jury remains to be seen."

In passing upon and granting the defendant's motion to set aside the jury's damages award to the plaintiff, the trial justice pondered whether the proximate cause for any damages the plaintiff would otherwise have been entitled to recover had been interrupted when the plaintiff threatened Badot. However, he later acknowledged that the jury could have reasonably concluded from the plaintiff's testimony that he did suffer actual economic losses and mental anguish from his having been terminated and humiliated by Badot in the presence of the plaintiff's fellow employees as well as from embarrassment stemming from the police visit to his second employer inquiring about the threat made against Badot. He observed also that the jury could reasonably have concluded that the plaintiff's loss of his National Guard security clearance and subsequent inability to participate in overseas missions caused him emotional distress....

Conclusion

For the reasons set out above, the case papers are remanded to the court for entry of an amended final judgment that will include the trial jury's award of damages to the plaintiff in the amount of $7,500.

Questions

1. Is it illegal under state law for an employer to retaliate against an employee for calling the state Health Department about an unsafe or unsanitary kitchen condition?
2. What is a pretext? How did the pretext apply in this case?
3. Was Adams entitled to damages for emotional distress without supportive expert medical testimony?

**The plaintiff aptly summarized the scope of his damages at trial: "So now I'm still fighting through the momentum that they caused on me affecting my civil life, my military career, my standing in the job market."

The contract of employment may be construed to bar a discharge of the employee except for cause. If so construed, good cause would then be required for the discharge of an at-will employee. Written personnel policies used as guidelines for supervisors have also been interpreted as being part of the employment contract. These policies have thus been held to restrict the employer's right to discharge at-will employees without proof of good or just cause. Moreover, employee handbooks that provide for "proper notice and investigation" before termination may bar employers from terminating employees without providing such notice and an investigation.[6]

Other courts still follow the common law at-will rule because they believe that a court should not rewrite the contract of the parties to provide employee protection that was never intended.[7]

(B) Employer Reactions. Employers have revised their personnel manuals and employee handbooks and have issued directives to all employees that no assurance of continued employment exists—that the employers are not obligated to have good cause to terminate employees, just as employees are free to leave their positions with the employers. While simultaneously reserving their at-will termination powers, many employers also may design specific, apparently fair termination procedures and promulgate antiharassment policies and procedures, as seen in the *Semple v. FedEx* decision.

Semple v. Federal Express Corp., 2008 WL 1793481 (D. S.D. April 17, 2008); affirmed 566 F. 3d 788 (8th Cir. 2009)

It's Not Easy to Get Around the Employment-at-Will Doctrine, Mr. Semple

John Semple was terminated from his employment with FedEx for falsification of company documents. He appealed his termination through internal FedEx procedures without success and thereafter sued the employer in federal court, contending that his termination was in violation of the "public policy exception" to the employment-at-will doctrine in that his termination resulted from his filing internal grievances regarding harassment by his superiors and that he was protected by the employee handbook exception to the at-will doctrine. The employer disagreed.

JUDICIAL OPINION

BOGUE, Senior District Judge...Plaintiff was hired by Federal Express Corporation (FedEx) in 1990. At that time, he signed an employment contract that included the following statement:

> *I do hereby agree...(11) That during the time of my employment, which term I understand is indefinite, I will comply with the guidelines set forth in the Company's policies, rules, regulations and procedures...I ALSO AGREE THAT MY EMPLOYMENT AND COMPENSATION CAN BE TERMINATED WITH OR WITHOUT CAUSE AND WITHOUT NOTICE OR LIABILITY WHATSOEVER, AT ANY TIME, AT THE OPTION OF EITHER THE COMPANY OR MYSELF.*

Plaintiff signed this contract below the statement: "I HAVE READ AND UNDERSTAND THIS AGREEMENT."... Regarding the handbook he received in 1990, Plaintiff signed a record of receipt which stated: "I understand [the handbook] is not a contract and the information provided may need to be changed by the company from time to time."...

The handbook...includes Section 4-90 "Termination," which is almost entirely made up of a subsections entitled "Guidelines" and "Employment Termination Chart." Within the Guidelines portion, a subsection labeled "Employment at Will" states the following:

> *The employment relationship between the Company and any employee may be terminated at the will of either party as stated in the employment agreement signed upon application for employment. As described in that agreement, the policies and procedures set forth in this manual provide guidelines for management and employees during employment, but do not create contractual rights regarding termination or otherwise...*

PUBLIC POLICY EXCEPTION

...The Court is not persuaded that a termination in retaliation for an internal complaint of harassment violates a "clear mandate of a substantial public policy," as required for the

[6] *Carlson v. Lake Chelan Community Hospital*, 66 P.3d 1080 (Wash. App. 2003); but see *Trabing v. Kinko's, Inc.*, 57 P.3d 1248 (Wyo. 2002); *Williams v. First Tennessee National Corp.*, 97 S.W.3d 798 (Tex. App. 2003).

[7] See *Texas Farm Bureau Mutual Insurance Co. v. Sears*, 84 S.W.3d 604 (Tex. 2002).

Continued

public policy exception to apply. The primary sources of public policy are constitutions, statues, and judicial decisions. The Court does not believe that the public policy Plaintiff is claiming–anti-retaliation policy borrowed from employment discrimination statutes–is indeed a "clear mandate" but instead can only arise from a distorted interpretation of existing state law. Simply, South Dakota has not outlawed retaliatory firings for filing an internal grievance of general harassment, and this Court refuses to create such a public policy here....

EMPLOYEE HANDBOOK EXCEPTION

Plaintiff also claims that the Court should apply the employee handbook exception to the at-will doctrine and hold that FedEx's handbook created an implied contract that he would only be fired for cause.

The Court does not believe that FedEx's employment manual includes a "a clear intention on the employer's part to surrender its statutory power to terminate its employees at will,"...First, Plaintiff's employment contract includes explicit language that his employment could be terminated "WITH OR WITHOUT CAUSE AND WITHOUT NOTICE OR LIABILITY WHATSOEVER, AT ANY TIME, AT THE OPTION OF EITHER THE COMPANY OR MYSELF." Second, Plaintiff signed a receipt form certifying that he received periodic copies of FedEx's employment manual; that receipt form stated that the handbook is not a contract and that the company reserves the right to change the information within the manual at its discretion. Two of such receipts signed by Plaintiff stated that the handbook should not be read or implied to create a contract and that the handbook "contains guidelines only," stating that "[y]our specific rights as an employee are governed by the Employment Agreement you signed in your employment application." Finally, the employment manual itself in policy 4-90 Termination states:

> *The employment relationship between the Company and employee may be terminated at the will of either party as stated in the employment agreement signed upon application for employment. As described in that agreement, the policies and procedures set forth in this manual provide guidelines for management and employees during employment, but do not create contractual rights regarding termination or otherwise.*

CONCLUSION

As the Court finds that Defendant has not surrendered its statutory right to terminate employees at will through its employment handbook, nor does any public policy prevent FedEx from terminating Plaintiff's employment, Plaintiff is an at-will employee....Thus, Plaintiff does not have a cause of action for wrongful discharge. Accordingly, summary judgment for Defendant is required.

QUESTIONS

1. Did the policies and procedures set forth in the employee handbook provide legally enforceable rights for the covered employees working under the handbook rules?
2. What are the primary sources of public policy under the state's public policy exception to the employment-at-will doctrine? Is a retaliation firing for a general harassment grievance against supervisors a protected public policy under state law?

Most employers have no interest in terminating employees without good and sufficient cause. They have taken steps to ensure that terminations are in fact for good cause and that a solid case exists for each termination should the employee in question sue on an unjust dismissal theory. Employers have standardized their termination methods. Employers often require that every disciplined employee be advised in writing of the infraction, informed of the expected corrective action, and informed of the fact that further misconduct could lead to additional discipline up to and including discharge. When a termination appears to be warranted, most employers require that at least two supervisors be involved and that they take care to ensure that the reasons for the termination are accurate and consistent with the documentation concerning the employee's deficiencies. Moreover, employers should inform the employee of the basis of the proposed termination and give the employee an opportunity to be heard before the dismissal notice is issued.

(c) Justifiable Discharge. An employer may be justified in discharging an employee because of the employee's (1) nonperformance of duties, (2) misrepresentation or fraud in obtaining the employment, (3) disobedience of proper directions, (4) disloyalty, (5) theft or other dishonesty, (6) possession or use of drugs or intoxicants, (7) misconduct, or (8) incompetence.

Employers generally have the right to lay off employees because of economic conditions, including a lack of work. Such actions are sometimes referred to as *reductions in force (RIFs)*.

Employers, however, must be very careful not to make layoffs based on age, for that is a violation of the Age Discrimination in Employment Act.

In some states, a "service letter" statute requires an employer on request to furnish to a discharged employee a letter stating the reason for the discharge.

4. Whistle Blower Protection under the Sarbanes-Oxley and Dodd-Frank Acts

The Sarbanes-Oxley Act (SOX) of 2002 was enacted to restore investor confidence in financial markets following the exposure in 2001–2002 of widespread misconduct by directors and officers of publicly held companies. SOX contains reforms regarding corporate accountability, enhanced disclosure requirements, and enforcement and liability provisions. Title VIII of the Act contains protections for corporate whistleblowers.[8]

(A) Protection Provided. SOX prohibits a publicly traded company or any agent of it from taking an adverse employment action against an employee who provides information, testifies, or "otherwise assists" in proceedings regarding (1) mail, wire, bank, or securities fraud, (2) any violation of an SEC rule or regulation, or (3) any federal law protecting shareholders against fraud. The Act sets forth the types of adverse employment actions that qualify for protection, specifically protecting employees from discharge, demotion, suspension, threats, harassment, failure to hire or rehire, blacklisting, or action otherwise discriminatory against employees in their terms and conditions of employment.

The Act protects employees who provide information or assistance to supervisors, or a federal regulatory or law enforcement agency, or to members of Congress or a congressional committee. The Act does not protect employees who provide information to the world, however. **For Example,** Nicholas Tides and Matthew Neumann were not protected under SOX when they provided a newspaper reporter information and documents about the questionable integrity of Boeing's data storage system and were fired for violating company confidentiality rules.[9]

Case law cautions that SOX whistleblower protection provisions do not provide "whistleblower protection for all employee complaints about how a public company spends its money and pays its bills."[10]

(B) Procedures. An individual who believes that she or he has been subject to an adverse employment action because of whistleblowing activities must file a complaint with the Department of Labor's Occupational Safety and Health Administration (OSHA) within 90 days after the asserted adverse employment action. OSHA administers 13 other federal whistleblower laws and has experienced investigators to facilitate its responsibilities under SOX.

(C) The Dodd-Frank Expansion. The Dodd-Frank Wall Street Reform and Consumer Protection Act of 2010 (Dodd-Frank)[11] expands whistleblower protections to a wide range of financial services employees and provides expanded protections and incentives for whistleblowers.

Dodd-Frank covers almost any employee working in the financial services industry related to the extension of credit, including employees of privately held companies, and protects them from retaliation for disclosing information about fraud or unlawful conduct related to consumer financial products. It covers employees who extend credit, service loans, provide real estate settlement services, and provide financial advice, including credit counseling to consumers.

Dodd-Frank requires the Securities and Exchange Commission to pay whistleblowers bounties of between 10 and 30 percent on monetary sanctions that aggregate to at least $1 million. To recover an award, a whistleblower must provide the SEC (1) voluntarily (2) with original information (3) that leads to a successful enforcement action or actions in

[8] 18 U.S.C. §1514A (2005).

[9] *Tides v. Boeing Co.*, 644 F.3d 809 (9th Cir. 2011).

[10] *Platone v. Flyi, Inc.*, 2006 WL 3246910 (Dept. of Labor Sept. 29, 2006). See also *Welch v. Choa*, 536 F.3d 269 (4th Cir. 2008), in which CFO Welch had refused to certify an SEC quarterly report as required by SOX because of accounting irregularities and thus was fired. The court of appeals held that the conduct in question was not shown to be in violation of any fraud or securities laws listed in SOX; thus, Welch was not protected. However, in *Sylvester v. Parexel International LLC*, 2011 WL 2165854 (DOL Adm. Rev. Bd. May 25, 2011) the DOL's Administrative Review Board subsequently held that its prior ruling in *Platone v. Flyi, Inc.*—that an employee's complaint must "definitely and specifically" relate to the categories of fraud or securities violations listed in Section 806—"has evolved into an inappropriate test and is often applied too strictly."

[11] The whistleblower protection provisions are codified at 15 U.S.C. §78u-6.

federal court or before an agency (4) in which overall recovery totals over $1,000,000.[12]

Dodd-Frank expands on the SOX cause of action as follows:

1. Dodd-Frank expands the SOX statute of limitations from 90 to 180 days. The Dodd-Frank limitations period is six years.
2. Whistleblowers must exhaust administrative remedies under SOX at OSHA and DOL's Administrative Review Board before court review. Dodd-Frank allows an immediate lawsuit in federal district court.
3. SOX provides for actual back pay lost, as part of make whole relief, while Dodd-Frank allows recovery of double back pay as liquidated damages.

Dodd-Frank exempts whistleblower claims from predispute arbitration agreements. And it provides a burden-shifting framework for a private cause of action for employees who are retaliated against for protected activity so that once an employee has shown by a preponderance of the evidence that the protected activity was a contributing factor in an adverse employment action, the employer must show by clear and convincing evidence that it would have taken the same action in the absence of the employee's whistleblowing activities to avoid liability.

5. Duties of the Employee

The duties of an employee are determined primarily by the contract of employment with the employer. The law also implies certain obligations.

(A) Services. Employees are under the duty to perform such services as may be required by the contract of employment.

(B) Trade Secrets. An employee may be given confidential trade secrets by the employer but must not disclose this knowledge to others. An agreement by the employee to refrain from disclosing trade secrets is binding. If the employee violates this obligation, the employer may enjoin the use of the information by the employee and by any person to whom it has been disclosed by the employee.

Former employees who are competing with their former employer may be enjoined from using information about suppliers and customers that they obtained while employees when this information is of vital importance to the employer's business. Injunctive relief is denied, however, if the information is not important or not secret.

(C) Inventions. Employment contracts commonly provide that an employer will own any invention or discovery made by an employee, whether during work hours, after work hours, or for a period of one or two years after leaving the employment. In the absence of an express or implied agreement to the contrary, the inventions of an employee usually belong to the employee. This is true even though the employee used the time and property of the employer in the discovery. In this case, however, the employer has what is known as a **shop right** to use the invention without cost in its operations.

6. Rights of the Employee

The rights of an employee are determined by the contract of employment and by the law as declared by courts, lawmakers, and administrative agencies.

(A) Compensation. The rights of an employee with respect to compensation are governed in general by the same principles that apply to the compensation of an agent. In the absence of an agreement to the contrary, when an employee is discharged, whether for cause or not, the employer must pay wages to the expiration of the last pay period. State statutes commonly authorize employees to sue employers for wages improperly withheld and to recover penalties and attorney fees. In addition to hourly wages, payments due for vacations and certain bonuses are considered "wages" under state statutes.[13] **For Example,** Diane Beard worked for Summit Institute as a licensed practical nurse for 13 months when she walked off the job and terminated her employment. She requested her accrued vacation pay of $432, but Summit refused to pay her, claiming she had abandoned her job and thus forfeited her right to vacation pay under company policy. Accrued vacation qualifies as "wages," and she was entitled to the $432

[12] 17 C.F.R. §240.21F-1, *et seq.* To start an action a whistleblower must file a complaint with the SEC's Office of the Whistleblower, which includes a description of the misconduct, demonstrates eligibility, and declares under penalty of perjury that the information is true and accurate. Whistleblowers may submit a claim anonymously through an attorney.

[13] *Knutson v. Snyder Industries, Inc.*, 436 N.W.2d 496 (Neb. 1989).

vacation pay plus a penalty equal to 90 days' wages at the employee's rate of pay or $9,720, plus $2,400 in attorneys' fees for the trial and an additional $2,600 in attorneys' fees for the appeal. These statutes with their penalty provisions are designed as a coercive means to compel employers to promptly pay their employees.[14]

(B) Federal Wage and Hour Law. Workers at enterprises engaged in interstate commerce are covered by the Fair Labor Standards Act (FLSA),[15] popularly known as the Wage and Hour Act. These workers cannot be paid less than a specified minimum wage.

The FLSA has been amended to cover domestic service workers, including housekeepers, cooks, and nannies. Executive, administrative, and professional employees and outside salespersons are exempt from both the minimum wage and overtime provisions of the law.[16] Students "working" at internships *may* be covered by the FLSA.[17]

(1) Subminimum Wage Provisions.

The FLSA allows for the employment of full-time students at institutions of higher education at wage rates below the statutory minimum. Also, individuals whose productive capacity is impaired by age, physical or mental deficiency, or injury may be employed at less than the minimum wage to prevent the curtailment of work opportunities for these individuals. In these cases, however, a special certificate is needed by the employer from the Department of Labor's (DOL) Wage and Hour Division, which has offices throughout the United States.

(2) Wage Issues.

Deductions made from wages as a result of cash or merchandise shortages and deductions for tools of the trade are not legal if they reduce wages below the minimum wage. An employer's requirement that employees provide uniforms or tools of their own is a violation of the law to the extent that the expenses for these items reduce wages below the minimum wage.[18]

Job-related training generally is compensable under the FLSA. However, an exception exists for voluntary training not directly related to an employee's job when the employee does not perform productive work. **For Example,** Hogar, Inc., operates a nursing home and required new employees to undergo two days of unpaid training before assuming paid duties as nurses' aides, maintenance/laundry workers, and kitchen workers. Little or no instruction was offered to these "trainees," and each individual would perform the regular duties of the position for the two-day period. Hogar's practices did not fall within the training exception because the trainees performed productive work with little or no actual training during a regular shift. In a lawsuit brought by the Secretary of Labor, Hogar was ordered by the court to pay 14 hours' pay (two days' pay) for each employee so "trained," plus liquidated damages of an additional 14 hours pay.[19]

A large Pennsylvania landscape contractor whose cash wages appeared to comply with all applicable laws was found to be in violation of the FLSA because his Guatemalan and Mexican seasonal workers were required to pay employment-related costs, such as point-of-hire transportation costs, visa costs, and recruiter's fees, which reduced their real wages to below the minimum wage.[20]

(3) Overtime Pay.

Overtime must be paid at a rate of one and a half times the employee's regular rate of pay for each hour worked in excess of 40 hours in a workweek.[21]

[14] *Beard v. Summit Institute of Pulmonary Medicine and Rehabilitation, Inc.*, 707 So.2d 1233 (La. 1998); see also *Beckman v. Kansas Dep't. of Human Resources*, 43 P.3d 891 (Kan. App. 2002).

[15] P.L. 75-718, 52 Stat. 1060, 29 U.S.C. §201 *et seq.*

[16] In *Christopher v. SmithKline Beecham Corp.*, 132 S. Ct. 2156 (2012), the U.S. Supreme Court determined that pharmaceutical representatives, whose primary duty is to obtain nonbinding commitments from physicians to prescribe their drugs, are "outside salesmen" excluded from overtime pay requirements of the FLSA.

[17] A developing issue in our society is the utilization of unpaid interns—generally high school or college students—and their coverage, if any, under the FLSA and other employment laws. The FLSA does not define the terms *intern* or *trainee*. The Act broadly defines the word "employee" as "to suffer or permit to work." The DOL utilizes a six-factor test for determining whether an individual is a trainee (intern) or an employee under the FLSA. In *Solis v. Laurelbrook Sanitarium and School, Inc.*, 642 F.3d 518 (6th Cir. 2011), the U.S. Court of Appeals for the Sixth Circuit determined that the DOL's test was overly rigid, and applied a "primary benefit of the relationship test" deciding that the primary benefit in that case ran to the students. Unpaid interns not considered employees are not entitled to the protections of the FLSA and Title VII of the Civil Rights Act of 1964. Practically speaking, it is up to the high schools and colleges to make sure that the internships they arrange are for the primary benefit of their students, and not substitutes for regular, paid employees.

[18] See Gayle Cinqugrani, "Uniform Deductions, Low Commissions Lead to DOL Penalties for FLSA Violations," 107 D.L.R. A-10 (June 6, 2012), where an investigation by the Wage and Hour Division of the DOL between November 2008 and November 2010 found that Vizza Wash LP, doing business as Wash-Tub, made illegal deductions from employees' paychecks for items such as uniforms, insurance claims, and cash register shortages, which caused the employees' pay to fall below the federal minimum wage of $7.25 per hour.

[19] *Herman v. Hogar Praderas De Amor, Inc.*, 130 F. Supp. 2d 257 (S.D. P.R. 2001).

[20] *Rivera v. Brickman Group, Ltd.*, 2008 WL 81570 (E.D. Pa. Jan. 7, 2008).

[21] DOL regulations, referred to as the *white collar exemptions* from the overtime requirements of the FLSA, took effect on August 23, 2004. Generally, executive, administrative, professional, outside sales, computer professional, and certain "highly compensated employees" are exempt from the overtime requirements if they meet the "tests" set forth in the new regulations.

(4) Child Labor Provisions.

The FLSA child labor provisions are designed to protect educational opportunities for minors and prohibit their employment in occupations detrimental to their health and well-being. The FLSA restricts hours of work for minors under 16 and lists hazardous occupations too dangerous for minors to perform.

B. Labor Relations Laws

Even if employers are not presently unionized, they are subject to certain obligations under federal labor relations law. It is important to both unionized and nonunionized employers to know their rights and obligations under the National Labor Relations Act (NLRA).[22] Employee rights and obligations are also set forth in this act. The Labor-Management Reporting and Disclosure Act regulates internal union affairs.[23]

7. The National Labor Relations Act

The National Labor Relations Act (NLRA), passed in 1935, was based on the federal government's power to regulate interstate commerce granted in Article 1, Section 8, of the Constitution. Congress, in enacting this law, explained that its purpose was to remove obstructions to commerce caused by employers who denied their employees the right to join unions and refused to accept collective bargaining.[24] Congress stated that these obstructions resulted in depression of wages, poor working conditions, and diminution of purchasing power.

Section 7 of the amended NLRA is the heart of the act, stating in part that "[e]mployees shall have the right to self-organization…to bargain collectively through representatives of their own choosing and to engage in other concerted activities for the purpose of collective bargaining or other mutual aid or protection…and shall have the right to refrain from such activities…."

Section 8 of the NLRA contains employer and union unfair labor practices, set forth in Figure 39-1, and authorizes the National Labor Relations Board to conduct proceedings to stop such practices.

The act applies to private-sector employers with gross incomes of $500,000 or more. The Railway Labor Act applies to employees of railroad and air carriers.

8. National Labor Relations Board

Administration of the NLRA is entrusted to the five-member National Labor Relations Board (NLRB, or Board) and the general counsel of the Board. The general counsel is responsible for investigating and prosecuting all unfair labor practice cases. The five-member Board's major function is to decide unfair labor practice cases brought before it by the general counsel.

The Board is also responsible for conducting representation and decertification elections. This responsibility is delegated to the regional directors of the 32 regional offices located throughout the United States who (1) determine the appropriateness of each proposed bargaining unit for the purpose of collective bargaining, (2) investigate petitions for the certification or decertification of unions, and (3) conduct elections to determine the choice of the majority of those employees voting in the election. Should a majority of the employees voting select a union, the NLRB will certify that union as the exclusive representative of all employees within the unit for the purpose of bargaining with the employer to obtain a contract with respect to wages, hours, and other conditions of employment.

9. Election Conduct

The Board of the NLRB has promulgated preelection rules restricting electioneering activities so that the election will express the true desire of employees. The NLRA prohibits employer interference or coercion during the preelection period. The act also prohibits during this period employer statements that contain threats of reprisal or promises of benefits.

For Example, it is a violation of section 8(c) of the NLRA for a Southern California manufacturer to make implied threats to relocate its plant to Mexico if the employees choose union representation. Furthermore, when the company announced its intent to move to Mexico one day after the union

[22] 29 U.S.C. §§141–169. Note that in the *Lechmere* and *Transportation Management* cases presented in this section, the employers were not unionized.

[23] 29 U.S.C. §§401–531.

[24] N.L.R.A. §1; 29 U.S.C. §141.

FIGURE 39-1 *Employer and Union Unfair Labor Practices Charge*

UNFAIR LABOR PRACTICES CHARGES AGAINST EMPLOYERS	SECTION OF THE NLRA*
1. Restrain or coerce employees in the exercise of their rights under section 7; threat of reprisals or promise of benefits	8(a)(1); 8(c)
2. Dominate or interfere with the formation or administration of a labor organization or contribute financial or other support to it	8(a)(2)
3. Discriminate in regard to hire or tenure of employment or any term or condition of employment in order to encourage or discourage membership in any labor organization	8(a)(3)
4. Discharge or otherwise discriminate against employees because they have given testimony under the act	8(a)(4)
5. Refuse to bargain collectively with representatives of its employees	8(a)(5)

UNFAIR LABOR PRACTICES CHARGES AGAINST UNIONS	SECTION OF THE NLRA
1. Restrain or coerce employees in the exercise of their rights under section 7	8(b)(1)(A)
2. Restrain or coerce an employer in the selection of its representatives	8(b)(1)(B)
3. Cause or attempt to cause an employer to discriminate against an employee	8(b)(2)
4. Refuse to bargain collectively with the employer	8(b)(3)
5. Require employees to pay excessive fees for membership	8(b)(5)
6. Engage in "featherbed practices" of seeking pay for services not performed	8(b)(6)
7. Use secondary boycotts (banned, except for publicity proviso)	8(b)(4)
8. Allow recognitional and organizational picketing by an uncertified union	8(b)(7)
9. Enter into "hot cargo" agreements, except for construction and garment industries	8(e)

* 29 U.S.C. §151.

won a representation election, the Labor Board obtained an injunction against the move.[25]

The Board prohibits all electioneering activities at polling places and has formulated a "24-hour rule," which prohibits both unions and employers from making speeches to captive audiences within 24 hours of an election. The rationale is to preserve free elections and prevent any party from obtaining undue advantage.

10. Union Activity on Private Property

Although section 7 of the NLRA gives employees the statutory right to self-organization, employers have the undisputed right to make rules to maintain discipline in their establishments. Generally speaking, employers may prohibit union solicitation by employees during work periods. During nonworking time, employers may prohibit activity and communications only for legitimate efficiency and safety reasons and only if the prohibitions are not manifestly intended to impede employees' exercise of their rights under the law. Nonunion employers, moreover, may not refuse to interview or retain union members because of their union membership. And even if a union pays an individual working for a nonunion employer to help organize the company, that individual is still protected under the NLRA.[26]

An employer may validly post its property against all nonemployee solicitations, including distribution of union literature, if reasonable efforts by the union through other available channels of communication would enable it to reach the employees with its message.

10a. Social Media and Section 7: Protected Activity for Union and Nonunion Workers

Section 7 of the NLRA grants all employees—union and nonunion—the right to engage in protected concerted activities pertaining to self-organization, forming, joining, or assisting a union or "for other mutual aid or protection."[27] Under Section 7, employees have a right to discuss their terms and conditions of employment with coworkers. Some employers' Internet and social media policies may be overly broad in that they may tend to chill employees' exercise of their Section 7 rights. **For Example,** American Medical Response of Connecticut (AMR), an ambulance service, terminated an employee in part for posting unfavorable remarks about her supervisor on her Facebook page. The employee, Ms. Souza, had mocked her supervisor on Facebook; when she received supportive comments from some coworkers, she posted additional remarks about the supervisor and was terminated. AMR's company handbook contained several policy provisions about blogging and Internet postings, including prohibiting employees from making "disparaging, discriminatory or defamatory comments when discussing the company or the employee's supervisors, co-workers and/or competitors." The acting Regional Director issued an unfair labor practice complaint against AMR, asserting that AMR enforced an overly broad policy on blogging and Internet posting. The matter settled before the scheduled hearing before the ALJ. Other Facebook firing cases are in the settlement, complaint, or ALJ stages of Board procedures.[28]

Though employees retain the right to talk about working conditions on social media, including discussing treatment by a supervisor in blunt language, case law will develop that not only protects Section 7 rights, but also protects employer rights to make rules to maintain discipline in the workplace and to protect the employer's reputation when a Facebook conversation on a page set to allow access to "friends of friends" involves very offensive, insulting, and disrespectful comments about supervisors or managers. The latter situation is not like a conversation between employees at a water cooler, where there is an expectation of privacy, but is more like calling the boss names on the plant floor in front of multiple employees and the public, as there is no expectation of privacy. This conduct does not involve protected concerted activity.

[25] See *Quadrtech Corp.*, N.L.R.B., No. 21–CA–33997 (settlement Dec. 11, 2000).

[26] *N.L.R.B. v. Town & Country Electric, Inc.*, 516 U.S. 85 (1995).

[27] On June 18, 2012, the NLRB announced that it has launched a Web page describing the rights of employees to engage in concerted activity, even if they do not belong to a union. It is available at **www.nlrb.gov/concerted-activity.**

[28] *See* the ALJ's ruling in *Hispanics United of Buffalo*, 2011 WL 3894520 (N.L.R.B. Div. of Judges Sept. 2, 2011), where the ALJ followed the Board's *Parexel International LLC* "concerted activity" precedent, 356 N.L.R.B. No. 82 (Jan. 28, 2011), finding that the nonunion nonprofit organization unlawfully terminated five employees who had posted comments on Facebook, some of which were profane and sarcastic, in response to a complaint by a coworker, Cruz-Moore, about their job performance. The ALJ stated in part:

> ...The discriminates herein were taking a first step towards taking group action to defend themselves against the accusations they could reasonably believe Cruz-Moore was going to make to management. By discharging the discriminates on October 12, Respondent prevented them from taking any further group action vis-à-vis Cruz-Moore's criticisms. Moreover, the fact that Respondent lumped the discriminates together in terminating them, established that Respondent viewed the five as a group and that their activity was concerted....

Although discussion of grievances in the context of "mutual aid or protection" is protected under Section 7, an individual's personal griping is not.

11. Firing Employees for Union Activity

Although employers and supervisors often feel betrayed by individual employees who take leadership roles in forming organizations, the NLRA prohibits discrimination against such employees because of their union activity.

The NLRB has found evidence of discrimination against active union supporters when the employer

1. Discharges on the strength of past misdeeds that were condoned;
2. Neglects to give customary warnings prior to discharge;
3. Discharges for a rule generally unenforced;
4. Applies disproportionately severe punishment to union supporters; or
5. Effects layoffs in violation of seniority status with disproportionate impact on union supporters.

The NLRA preserves the right of the employer to maintain control over the workforce in the interest of discipline, efficiency, and pleasant and safe customer relations. Employees, on the other hand, have the right to be free from coercive discrimination resulting from union activity.

At times these two rights may collide. For example, an employee may be discharged for apparently two reasons: (1) violation of a valid company rule and (2) union activity. The employer gives the former as the reason for termination; the latter remains unstated on the employer's part, causing the filing of a section 8(a) (3) unfair labor practice charge against the employer. These are known as *dual motive cases.* The general counsel must present on behalf of the dismissed employee a prima facie case that such protected conduct as union activity was a motivating factor in the dismissal. After this showing, the burden shifts to the employer, who must prove that the employee would have been dismissed for legitimate business reasons even absent the protected conduct.

The *Transportation Management* case is a dual motive case.

NLRB v. Transportation Management Corp., 462 U.S. 393 (1983)

The Sam Santillo Story

Prior to his discharge, Sam Santillo was a bus driver for Transportation Management Corp. On March 19, 1979, Santillo talked to officials of the Teamster's Union about organizing the drivers who worked with him. Over the next four days, Santillo discussed with his fellow drivers the possibility of joining the Teamsters and distributed authorization cards. On the night of March 23, George Patterson, who supervised Santillo and the other drivers, told one of the drivers that he had heard of Santillo's activities. Patterson referred to Santillo as two-faced and promised to get even with him. Later that evening, Patterson talked to Ed West, who was also a bus driver for Transportation Management. Patterson asked, "What's with Sam and the Union?" Patterson said that he took Santillo's actions personally, recounted several favors he had done for Santillo, and added that he would remember Santillo's activities when Santillo again asked for a favor. On Monday, March 26, Santillo was discharged. Patterson told Santillo that he was being fired for leaving his keys in the bus and taking unauthorized breaks. Santillo filed charges with the Board, and the General Counsel issued a complaint alleging that Santillo was discharged because of his union activities in distributing authorization cards to fellow employees. The administrative law judge (ALJ) determined that Patterson's disapproval of Santillo's practice of leaving his keys in the bus was clearly a pretext because this practice was commonplace among company employees. The company identified two types of unauthorized breaks: coffee breaks and stops at home. With respect to both coffee breaks and stopping at home, the ALJ found that Santillo was never cautioned or admonished about such behavior and that the employer had not followed its customary practice of issuing three written warnings before discharging a driver. The ALJ also found that taking coffee breaks during work hours was normal practice and that the company tolerated the practice unless the breaks interfered with the driver's duties. The ALJ found that the company had never taken any adverse personnel action against an employee because of such behavior. The Board adopted the ALJ's findings. The U.S. Court of Appeals for the First Circuit refused to enforce the Board's order, and an appeal was taken to the Supreme Court.

Continued

JUDICIAL OPINION

WHITE, J.…The Court of Appeals erred in holding that § 10 (c) forbids placing the burden on the employer to prove that absent the improper motivation he would have acted in the same manner for wholly legitimate reasons.…

The employer is a wrongdoer; he has acted out of a motive that is declared illegitimate by the statute. It is fair that he bear the risk that the influence of legal and illegal motives cannot be separated, because he knowingly created the risk and because the risk was created not by innocent activity but by his own wrongdoing.…

The Board was justified in this case in concluding that Santillo would not have been discharged had the employer not considered his efforts to establish a union. At least two of the transgressions that purportedly would have in any event prompted Santillo's discharge were commonplace, and yet no transgressor had ever before received any kind of discipline. Moreover, the employer departed from its usual practice in dealing with rules infractions; indeed, not only did the employer not warn Santillo that his actions would result in being subjected to discipline, it never even expressed its disapproval of his conduct. In addition, Patterson, the person who made the initial decision to discharge Santillo, was obviously upset with Santillo for engaging in such protected activity. It is thus clear that the Board's finding that Santillo would not have been fired if the employer had not had an anti-union animus was "supported by substantial evidence on the record considered as a whole."…

[Judgment reversed]

QUESTIONS

1. According to the General Counsel, why was Santillo fired by his employer?
2. According to the company, why was Santillo fired?
3. Did the Supreme Court find that the Board was justified in concluding that Santillo would not have been discharged had the employer not considered his efforts to establish a union?

12. Duty of Employer to Bargain Collectively

Once a union wins a representative election, the Board certifies the union as the exclusive bargaining representative of the employees. The employer then has the obligation under the NLRA to bargain with the union in good faith over wages, hours, and working conditions. These matters are *mandatory subjects of bargaining* and include seniority provisions, promotions, layoff and recall provisions, no-strike no-lockout clauses, and grievance procedures. Employers also have an obligation to bargain about the "effects" of the shutdown of a part of a business[29] and may have an obligation to bargain over the decision to relocate bargaining unit work to other plants.[30] Absent clearly expressed consent by a union, an employer violates its duty to bargain by changing a term or condition of employment without first bargaining to impasse with a union. **For Example,** Aramark Educational Services violated the NLRA when it unilaterally implemented a new, strict "Social Security no-match" policy of suspending employees with uncorrected discrepancies in their social security numbers prior to any discussion and impasse in bargaining with UNITE HERE Local 26.[31]

Permissive subjects of bargaining are those over which an employer's refusal to bargain is not a section 8(a)(5) unfair labor practice. Examples are the required use of union labels, internal union affairs, union recognition clauses, and benefits for already retired workers.

13. Right to Work

The NLRA allows states to enact **right-to-work laws**. These laws restrict unions and employers from negotiating clauses in their collective bargaining agreements that make union membership compulsory.[32]

Advocates of such laws contend that compulsory union membership is contrary to the First Amendment right of freedom of association. Unions have attacked these laws as unfair because unions must represent all employees, and in right-to-work states where a majority

[29] *First National Maintenance v. N.L.R.B.*, 452 U.S. 666 (1981).

[30] *Dubuque Packing Co. and UFCWIU, Local 150A*, 303 N.L.R.B. 66 (1991).

[31] *Aramark Educational Services, Inc.*, 335 N.L.R.B. No. 11 (Feb. 18, 2010).

[32] Right-to-work statutes declare unlawful any agreement that denies persons the right to work because of nonmembership in a union or the failure to pay dues to a union as a condition of employment. These laws have been adopted in Alabama, Arizona, Arkansas, Florida, Georgia, Idaho, Indiana Iowa, Kansas, Louisiana, Mississippi, Nebraska, Nevada, North Carolina, North Dakota, Oklahoma, South Carolina, South Dakota, Tennessee, Texas, Utah, Virginia, and Wyoming.

of employees vote for union representation, nonunion employees receive all of the benefits of collective bargaining contracts without paying union dues.

14. Strike and Picketing Activity

If the parties reach an impasse in the negotiation process for a collective bargaining agreement, a union may call a strike and undertake picketing activity to enforce its bargaining demands. Strikers in such a situation are called **economic strikers**. Although the strike activity is legal, the employers may respond by hiring temporary or permanent replacement workers.

(A) Rights of Strikers. Economic strikers who unconditionally apply for reinstatement when their positions are filled by permanent replacements are not entitled to return to work at the end of the economic strike. They are, however, entitled to full reinstatement when positions become available.

Strikers responsible for misconduct while out on strike may be refused reemployment by the employer.

When employees strike to protest an employer's unfair labor practice, such as firing an employee for union-organizing activity, these unfair labor practice strikers have a right to return to their jobs immediately at the end of the strike. This right exists even if the employer has hired permanent replacements.[33]

(B) Picketing. Placing persons outside a business at the site of a labor dispute so that they may, by signs or banners, inform the public of the existence of a labor dispute is called **primary picketing** and is legal. Should the picketing employees mass together in great numbers in front of the gates of the employer's facility to effectively shut down the entrances, such coercion is called **mass picketing**; it is illegal. **Secondary picketing** is picketing an employer with whom a union has no dispute to persuade the employer to stop doing business with a party to the dispute. Secondary picketing is generally illegal under the NLRA. An exception exists for certain product picketing at supermarkets or other multiproduct retail stores provided that it is limited to asking customers not to purchase the struck product at the neutral employer's store.[34]

15. Regulation of Internal Union Affairs

To ensure the honest and democratic administration of unions, Congress passed the Labor-Management Reporting and Disclosure Act (LMRDA).[35] Title IV of the LMRDA establishes democratic standards for all elections for union offices, including

1. Secret ballots in local union elections;
2. Opportunity for members to nominate candidates;
3. Advance notice of elections;
4. Observers at polling and at ballot-counting stations for all candidates;
5. Publication of results and preservation of records for one year;
6. Prohibition of any income from dues or assessments to support candidates for union office; and
7. Advance opportunity for each candidate to inspect the membership name and address lists.

C. Pension Plans and Federal Regulation

The Employee Retirement Income Security Act (ERISA)[36] was adopted in 1974 to protect employee pensions and benefits.

16. ERISA

The act sets forth fiduciary standards and requirements for administration, vesting, funding, and termination insurance.

(A) Administration. Commonly a "benefits claims committee" is set up under the plan to make determinations about coverage issues, and courts will not disturb the finding of a benefits committee unless the determinations are "arbitrary and capricious." **For Example,** Joe Gustafson, who provided chauffeur services for senior executives at NYNEX for a number of years while classified as an independent contractor, sought benefits under ERISA because he asserted he was a common law

[33] *Poly America, Inc. v. N.L.R.B.*, 260 F.3d 465 (5th Cir. 2001).
[34] *N.L.R.B. v. Fruit and Vegetable Packers, Local 760 (Tree Fruits, Inc.)*, 377 U.S. 58 (1964); but see *N.L.R.B. v. Retail Clerks, Local 1001 (Safeco Title Ins. Co.)*, 477 U.S. 607 (1980).
[35] 29 U.S.C. §§401–531.
[36] P.L. 93-406, 88 Stat. 829, 29 U.S.C. §§1001–1381.

employee of NYNEX. While the court determined he was in fact an employee entitled to overtime compensation under the Fair Labor Standards Act, the court was compelled to defer to the benefits committee's determination that Gustafson was not an employee under the NYNEX plan because he was not "on the payroll" as required by the plan guidelines. The court found that such a determination was not arbitrary or capricious.[37] Nevertheless, individuals may successfully challenge determinations of the plan administrators. **For Example,** Bell South denied ERISA-covered benefits to Suzanne Lee under both its Short Term Disability Plan and its Long Term Disability Plan. She suffered from chronic pain syndrome, and the administrator determined that she had failed to submit "objective medical evidence" of her condition. The U.S. Court of Appeals reviewed the extensive medical record of pain care specialists supporting her diagnosis and determined that Bell South had acted arbitrarily and capriciously in denying Lee's claim of benefits.[38]

(B) Fiduciary Standards and Reporting. Persons administering a pension fund must handle it to protect the interest of employees.[39]

The fact that an employer contributed all or part of the money to the pension fund does not entitle it to use the fund as though the employer still owned it. Persons administering pension plans must make detailed reports to the Secretary of Labor.

(C) Vesting. *Vesting* is the right of an employee to pension benefits paid into a pension plan in the employee's name by the employer. Prior to ERISA, many pension plans did not vest accrued benefits until an employee had 20 to 25 years of service. Thus, an employee who was forced to terminate service after 18 years would have no pension rights or benefits. Under ERISA, employees' rights must be fully vested within five or seven years in accordance with the two vesting options available under the law.

In the past, it had been common for pension plans to contain break-in-service clauses, whereby employees who left their employment for a period longer than one year for any reason other than an on-the-job injury lost pension eligibility rights. Under the Retirement Equity Act of 1984,[40] an individual can leave the workforce for up to five consecutive years and still retain eligibility for pension benefits.

(D) Funding. Pension funds may be broadly classified as "defined contribution plans" and "defined benefit plans."

A **defined contribution plan** is one that provides for an individual account for each plan participant and for benefits based solely on the amount contributed to the participant's account. It is also known as an *individual account plan*. These plans include 401(k) plans, employee stock option plans (ESOPs), profit-sharing plans, and stock bonus plans. Commonly, the employer establishes these plans and defines its own contributions to be matched by contributions from plan participants.

A **defined benefit plan** is an employer commitment to make specified future payments to participants upon retirement. The employer establishes a pension fund for this purpose, and the employer is contractually obligated to make those payments even if the assets set aside to finance the plan turn out to be inadequate. ERISA established an insurance plan, called the **Pension Benefit Guaranty Corporation (PBGC)**, to protect employees covered under defined benefit plans should the employer go out of business.

In the case of defined benefit plans, the entire investment risk is on the employer who sponsors the plan. The employer must cover any underfunding that may result from the plan's poor performance. However, if the plan becomes overfunded, the employer may reduce or suspend its contributions.[41]

Defined contribution plans are the ones most frequently offered by employers today, in part because of the employers' risk of underfunding defined benefit plans. Defined contribution plans are not insured by the PBGC.

(E) Enforcement. ERISA authorizes the Secretary of Labor and employees to bring court actions to compel the observance of statutory requirements.

[37] *Gustafson v. Bell Atlantic Corp.*, 171 F. Supp. 2d 311 (S.D.N.Y. 2001).

[38] *Lee v. Bell South Telecommunications Inc.*, 318 Fed. Appx. 829 (11th Cir. 2009).

[39] *John Hancock Mutual Life Ins. Co. v. Harris Trust*, 510 U.S. 86 (1993).

[40] P.L. 98-397, 29 U.S.C. §1001.

[41] *Hughes Aircraft Co. v. Jacobson*, 523 U.S. 1093 (1998).

D. Unemployment Benefits, Family Leaves, and Social Security

Generally, when employees are without work through no fault of their own, they are eligible for unemployment compensation benefits. Twelve-week maternity, paternity, or adoption leaves and family and medical leaves are available for qualifying employees. Social Security provides certain benefits, including retirement and disability benefits.

17. Unemployment Compensation

Unemployment compensation today is provided primarily through a federal-state system under the unemployment insurance provisions of the Social Security Act of 1935.[42] All states have laws that provide similar benefits, and the state agencies are loosely coordinated under the federal act. Agricultural employees, domestic employees, and state and local government employees are not covered by this federal-state system. Federal programs of unemployment compensation exist for federal civilian workers and former military service personnel. A separate federal unemployment program applies to railroad workers.

(A) Eligibility. In most states, an unemployed person must be available for placement in a similar job and willing to take such employment at a comparable rate of pay. Full-time students generally have difficulty proving that they are available for work while they are still going to school.

If an employee quits a job without cause or is fired for misconduct, the employee is ordinarily disqualified from receiving unemployment compensation benefits. **For Example,** stealing property from an employer constitutes misconduct for which benefits will be denied. Moreover, an employee's refusal to complete the aftercare portion of an alcohol treatment program has been found to be misconduct connected with work, disqualifying the employee from receiving benefits.

(B) Funding. Employers are taxed for unemployment benefits based on each employer's "experience rating" account. Thus, employers with a stable workforce with no layoffs, who therefore do not draw on the state unemployment insurance fund, pay lower tax rates. Employers whose experience ratings are higher pay higher rates. Motivated by the desire to avoid higher unemployment taxes, employers commonly challenge the state's payment of unemployment benefits to individuals who they believe are not properly entitled to benefits.

18. Family and Medical Leaves of Absence

The Family and Medical Leave Act of 1993 (FMLA)[43] entitles an eligible employee, whether male or female, to a total of 12 workweeks of unpaid leave during any 12-month period (1) because of the birth or adoption of the employee's son or daughter, (2) to care for the employee's spouse, son, daughter, or parent with a serious health condition, or (3) because of a serious health condition that makes the employee unable to perform the functions of his or her position. Notice should be given by the employer to an employee that the leave he or she is taking will count against FMLA entitlement in order to comply with the Secretary of Labor's regulations.[44] In the case of an employee's serious health condition or that of a covered family member, an employer may require the employee to use any accrued paid vacation, personal, medical, or sick leave toward any part of the 12-week leave provided by the act. When an employee requests leave because of the birth or adoption of a child, the employer may require the employee to use all available paid personal, vacation, and medical leave, but not sick leave, toward any FMLA leave.

To be eligible for FMLA leave, an employee must have been employed by a covered employer for at least 12 months and have worked at least 1,250 hours during the 12-month period preceding the leave. Covered employers are those that employ 50 or more employees.[45] Upon return from FMLA leave, the employee is entitled to be restored to the same or an equivalent position with equivalent pay and benefits. **For Example,** when Magda Brenlla returned to her position at LaSorsa Buick in the Bronx, New York, after quadruple bypass surgery, she was terminated by the owner who told her he had decided to consolidate

[42] 42 U.S.C. §§301–1397e.

[43] 29 U.S.C. §§2601–2654.

[44] See *Ragsdale v. Wolverine World Wide, Inc.*, 535 U.S. 81 (2002).

[45] *Bellum v. PCE Constructors Inc.*, 407 F.3d 734 (5th Cir. 2005). Joint employers are obligated to honor FMLA-qualifying leaves. See *Grace v. USCAR*, 521 F.3d 655 (6th Cir. 2008).

the positions of office manager and controller, even though he had no business plan for restructuring, and soon thereafter had to hire additional help in the office. The judge upheld a jury verdict of $320,000, finding that the jury had ample evidence to conclude that the real reason for her termination was her FMLA leave.[46]

The FMLA provides specific statutory relief for violations of the provisions of the act, including pay to the employee for damages equal to lost wages and benefits or any actual monetary losses, plus interest, plus an equal amount in liquidated damages.[47]

19. Leaves for Military Service under USERRA

The Uniformed Services Employment and Re-Employment Rights Act (USERRA) was enacted in 1994 to encourage noncareer service in the armed services, minimize the disruption experienced in the civilian careers of reservists, and promote prompt reemployment of reservists upon return from military leave.[48] In the context of mobilizing more than 500,000 reservists between September 11, 2001, and the summer of 2006, the USERRA has and will have a broad impact on U.S. employers as it provides reemployment and benefit protection rights for returning military personnel and prohibits discrimination against individuals because of their application for or performance of military service.[49]

(A) Protections. Section 4312 of the USERRA generally requires returning reservists to be "promptly reemployed" and returned to the same or comparable positions of like seniority, status, and pay they would have had if they had not been activated. Moreover, Section 4316(c) provides that persons reemployed under the act shall not be discharged from employment within a year of their reemployment if their period of service was more than 180 days. For service of more than 30 days, the protective period is 180 days. However, the employer may terminate an individual for cause regardless of the duration of service.

Sections 4312(a)(3) and (4) provide protection for those disabled while in the service and requires employers to make reasonable efforts to accommodate each employee's disability so that each individual may return to the same or comparable positions or, if no longer qualified for the position, allow for the transfer to a position the disabled individual can perform closest to the prior position in terms of seniority, status, and pay.

Section 4323 of the act provides a full range of remedies, including back pay for loss of wages and benefits as well as liquidated damages in an amount equal to the actual damages when the employer's failure to comply with the act was willful. The Department of Labor has issued USERRA regulations.[50] The act's enforcement is performed by the U.S. Justice Department's Division of Civil Rights.

The *Serricchio v. Wachovia Securities LLC*, case addressed the issue of whether Michael Serricchio had been offered the same terms by his employer as he had prior to his deployment to Iraq, and whether he was entitled to liquidated damages for a willful violation of the USERRA.

Serricchio v. Wachovia Secrurities LLC, 658 F.3d 169 (2d Cir. 2011)

USERRA—Because It's the Right Thing to Do!

Michael Serricchio, an Air Force reservist, was employed as a financial advisor at Wachovia Securities and called up to active duty in the wake of September 11, 2001. Upon completion of his active duty, he sought to return to Wachovia with comparable earnings potential and opportunity for advancement. In the year prior to his activation for

[46] *Brenlla v. LaSorsa Buick*, 2002 WL 1059117 (S.D.N.Y. May 28, 2002).

[47] See *Arban v. West Publishing Co.*, 345 F.3d 390 (6th Cir. 2003), in which the U.S. Court of Appeals required the doubling of a jury verdict of $130,000 under the FMLA provision providing for liquidated damages unless the employer is able to prove that it acted "in good faith…" and had reasonable grounds to believe it was not in violation of the FMLA. 29 U.S.C. §2617(a)(iii).

[48] 38 U.S.C.§4301 (2005).

[49] 38 U.S.C. §§4312, 4316, and 4317 (2005).

[50] 30 Federal Register Vol. 70 No. 242 (Dec. 19, 2005).

Continued

military duty, Mr. Serricchio was personally responsible for servicing in excess of 200 accounts, was responsible for managing in excess of $9 million dollars with his partner and was earning $6,500 per month based on those assets. If Serricchio accepted Wachovia's reemployment offer, he would have been managing a handful of accounts, generating, according to Wachovia's own documents, a small amount in monthly commissions that had to be repaid to Wachovia to offset his monthly draw. The employer argued that it provided the same draw and commission structure to the plaintiff and this was sufficient to fulfill its reemployment obligations under Section 4316. Serricchio contended that Wachovia's offer did not satisfy its obligation to reemploy him in a position of like pay; and the employer's failure to comply with the USERRA was willful, entitling him to double backpay as liquidated damages.

JUDICIAL OPINION

POLLER, C. J.…The purpose of USERRA is to encourage military service "by eliminating or minimizing the disadvantages to civilian careers"; "to minimize the disruption to the lives" of servicemembers and their employers "by providing for the prompt reemployment" of servicemembers; and "to prohibit discrimination" against servicemembers. 38 U.S.C. § 4301(a).…

Section 4316(a) of USERRA entitles a returning servicemember to "the seniority and other rights and benefits determined by seniority that the person had on the date of the commencement of service in the uniformed services *plus* the additional seniority and rights and benefits that such person would have attained if the person had remained continuously employed." 38 U.S.C. § 4316(a) (emphasis added); 38 U.S.C. § 4313(a)(2)(A) (stating that a servicemember whose period in service exceeds 90 days is entitled to reemployment "in the position of employment in which the person would have been employed if the continuous employment of such person with the employer had not been interrupted by such service, or a position of like seniority, status and pay, the duties of which the person is qualified to perform"). USERRA's regulations explain that this means that "[a]s a general rule, the employee is entitled to reemployment in the job position that he or she would have attained with reasonable certainty if not for the absence due to uniformed service." 20 C.F.R. § 1002.191. This position is referred to as the "escalator position." *Id.*…

In the first instance, we note that Wachovia's failure to reply to Serricchio's letter requesting reinstatement for nearly two months, coupled with the bank's failure to actually reemploy him for nearly four months, created a triable issue of fact regarding whether Wachovia violated USERRA. *See* 20 C.F.R. § 1002.181 ("Absent unusual circumstances, reemployment must occur within *two weeks* of the employee's application for reemployment." (emphasis added)). Indeed, the jury concluded that Wachovia's failure to reemploy Serricchio by December 18, 2003, constituted a violation of Serricchio's rights under USERRA. Wachovia has not appealed this portion of the verdict. Thus, the question of whether Wachovia offered Serricchio suitable reemployment is relevant primarily to the district court's calculation of damages—not to the jury's finding of liability, which was based in part on Wachovia's failure to offer Serricchio *any* position of reemployment by December 18.…

Here, the evidence indicated that prior to his activation, Serricchio was responsible for servicing in excess of 130 accounts, and, along with a partner, was responsible for managing in excess of $9 million dollars. By contrast, Wachovia's offer for reemployment consisted of providing Serricchio with a limited number of small accounts, a modest monthly draw that would be offset by any commissions earned, and opportunities for cold calling clients. As the district court concluded, these facts were sufficient for a reasonable fact finder to conclude that the position Serricchio was offered upon his return to Wachovia did not provide the same opportunities for advancement, working conditions and responsibility that he would have had but for his period of military service.…

USERRA provides that a prevailing party is entitled to a doubling of the backpay award upon a determination that "the employer's failure to comply with the provisions of [USERRA] was willful." 38 U.S.C. § 4323(d)(1)(C). The Supreme Court has explained that where "an employer acts reasonably in determining its legal obligation, its action cannot be deemed willful." *McLaughlin v. Richland Shoe Co.,* 486 U.S. 128, 135 n. 13, 108 S.Ct. 1677, 100 L.Ed.2d 115 (1988). Similarly, where an "employer acts unreasonably, but not recklessly, in determining its legal obligation," then its action should not be "considered willful." *Id.*

Here, the district court concluded that Wachovia had willfully violated USERRA in failing to reemploy Serricchio promptly, in failing to offer him a position comparable to his pre-service position when it did offer Serricchio reemployment, and by constructively discharging him. The district court based its conclusion in large part on the testimony of Nancy Gibbons, the Wachovia manager responsible for the company's military leave policies, who testified that she understood that USERRA required "prompt" reinstatement. In light of the fact that Wachovia made no attempt to reinstate Serricchio "promptly," and the company did not even respond to his request for

Continued

reinstatement for months, the district court concluded that Wachovia's actions were willful. ... The same reasoning applies here. Wachovia offered no evidence to excuse its failure to "promptly" reinstate Serricchio as required by USERRA. Accordingly, we conclude that there was no error in the district court's finding of willfulness as to the prompt reinstatement claim....

[Affirmed.]

QUESTIONS

1. Did Wachovia offer Serricchio reemployment at terms comparable to the terms of his employment before going on military leave?
2. Did the court determine that Wachovia acted willfully and thus was responsible for liquidated damages or double back pay?

(B) Defenses. In addition to an employer's right to terminate a reemployed service-person for cause, employers may be excused from reemploying or continuing employment of persons under §4312(d)(1) of the act when the employer's circumstances have so changed as to make reemployment impossible, unreasonable, or an undue hardship. The burden of proof on the matter is on the employer. **For Example,** Joseph Duarte was called to active duty in the Marine Corps Reserve to serve nine months' active duty from November to July. On his return in July he was given his same pay but diminished status by being assigned a temporary assignment rather than acting as a primary consultant to one of the employer's business groups. Faced with financial need to reduce its payroll, the employer eliminated Duarte's temporary assignment and terminated him four months later for what it believed was economic "cause." Duarte believed that his termination violated the USERRA. The court disagreed with the employer and determined that Duarte was within the act's one-year protective period and had been returned to work in the diminished status of a temporary assignment that was a direct result of his military service. Duarte was awarded back pay of $114,500 and front pay of $324,000, less $55,000 in severance benefits already paid him, for a total of $384,000 in damages.[51] Liquidated damages equal to $384,000 were declined because the employer's actions were not deemed willful.

(C) Discrimination and Retaliation Protection. As opposed to the protections contained in Section 4312, the act's Section 4311 provides separate and distinct statutory protection against discrimination of employees on the basis of military service and retaliation against individuals, whether military or not, who give testimony or statements on behalf of a USERRA claimant. **For Example,** a Section 4311 discrimination violation is made out that bakery driver Robert Mills was terminated by Multigrain Baking Co. because of his need to have time off for reserve duty training after the personnel director, Marsha Coyle, testified on cross-examination, "If we knew Bobby Mills was in the Guard, we would not have hired him. These drivers have to be available to protect their territories or we lose business."

20. Social Security

Employees and employers are required to pay Social Security taxes, which provide employees with four types of insurance protection: retirement benefits, disability benefits, life insurance benefits, and health insurance (Medicare). The federal Social Security Act established a federal program of aid for the aged, the blind, and the disabled. This is called the Supplemental Security Income (SSI) program. Payments are administered directly by the Social Security Administration, which became an independent government agency in 1995.

E. Employees' Health and Safety

The Occupational Safety and Health Act of 1970 (OSHA) was passed to assure every worker, so far as possible, safe and healthful working conditions and to

[51] *Duarte v. Agilent Technologies, Inc.*, 366 F. Supp. 2d 1039 (D. Colo. 2005).

preserve the country's human resources.[52] OSHA provides for (1) the establishment of safety and health standards and (2) effective enforcement of these standards and the other employer duties required by OSHA.

21. Standards

The Secretary of Labor has broad authority under OSHA to promulgate occupational safety and health standards.[53] Except in emergency situations, public hearings and publication in the *Federal Register* are required before the secretary can issue a new standard. Any person adversely affected may then challenge the validity of the standard in a U.S. Court of Appeals. The secretary's standards will be upheld if they are reasonable and supported by substantial evidence. The secretary must demonstrate a need for a new standard by showing that it is reasonably necessary to protect employees against a "significant risk" of material health impairment. The cost of compliance with new standards may run into billions of dollars. The secretary is not required to do a cost-benefit analysis for a new standard but must show that the standard is economically feasible.

22. Employer Duties

Employers have a "general duty" to furnish each employee a place of employment that is free from hazards that are likely to cause death or serious physical injuries.

OSHA requires employers to maintain records of occupational illness and injuries if they result in death, loss of consciousness, or one or more lost workdays or if they require medical treatment other than first aid. Such records have proven to be a valuable aid in recognizing areas of risk. They have been especially helpful in identifying the presence of occupational illnesses.

23. Enforcement

The Occupational Safety and Health Administration (also identified as OSHA) is the agency within the Department of Labor that administers the act. OSHA has authority to conduct inspections and to seek enforcement action when noncompliance has occurred. Worksite inspections are conducted when employer records indicate incidents involving fatalities or serious injuries.[54] These inspections may also result from employee complaints. The act protects employees making complaints from employer retaliation. Employers have the right to require an OSHA inspector to secure a warrant before inspecting the employer's plant.

If OSHA issues a citation for a violation of workplace health or safety standards, the employer may challenge the citation before the Occupational Safety and Health Review Commission (OSHRC). Judicial review of a commission ruling is obtained before a U.S. Court of Appeals. **For Example,** after an accident at Staley Manufacturing Company's Decatur, Illinois, plant in which an employee was fatally asphyxiated, OSHA inspectors issued citations for multiple violations of the OSH Act. The employer challenged the citations before the OSHRC. Upon review by the U.S. Court of Appeals, the court affirmed OSHRC's decision, finding that the company's "plain indifference" to act on the hazards at the workplace and train employees how to handle the hazards was a willful violation of the act, allowing for civil penalty of no more than $70,000 for each violation.[55]

The Occupational Safety and Health Act provides that no employer shall discharge or in any manner discriminate against employees because they filed a complaint with OSHA, testified in any OSHA proceeding, or exercised any right afforded by the act. A regulation issued by the Secretary of Labor under the act provides that if employees with no reasonable alternative refuse in good faith to expose themselves to a dangerous condition, they will be protected against subsequent discrimination. The Secretary of Labor may obtain injunctive and other appropriate relief in a U.S. district court against an employer who discriminates against employees for testifying or exercising any right under the act.

24. State "Right-to-Know" Legislation

Laws that guarantee individual workers the "right to know" if there are hazardous substances in their

[52] 29 U.S.C. §651 *et seq.*
[53] *Martin v. OSHRC*, 499 U.S. 144 (1991).
[54] *Chao v. Mallard Bay Drilling Co.*, 534 U.S. 235 (2002).
[55] *A. E. Staley Manufacturing Co. v. Chao*, 295 F.3d 1341 (D.C. Cir. 2002).

Thinking Things Through

Taking Chances or Shortcuts in Violation of OSHA Standards Is Bad Management

John Carlo, Inc. (JCI) was installing a sewer line down the middle of an existing roadway in Jacksonville, Florida. The new line crossed under an existing gas line that was perpendicular to the proposed sewer line. The JCI crew worked in two stacked trench boxes, laying pipe up to the location where the pipeline crossed the trench for the sewer line. OSHA regulations require protection of employees from cave-ins; trench boxes and sloping of trench walls provide this protection. The following day, the crew removed the top trench box because both boxes would not fit under the perpendicular gas line. The crew pulled the bottom box under the perpendicular gas line and prepared the bottom of the trench to lay one joint of the sewer pipe. Project superintendent Cox had discussed this move with his foreman Jacobs. Jacobs reminded Cox that this move would leave the top portion of the trench unprotected. Cox explained that he realized the problem, but because JCI had bid the project based on 6-foot-wide trenches, they could not slope the trenches. The supervisors anticipated that just 15 minutes was needed to lay the one joint of pipe. Two crew members entered the trench to lay the pipe. The trench walls above the box (approximately 6 feet) were not sloped or otherwise protected. A large clay ball dislodged, fell into the trench, and struck one employee, who eventually died as a result.

Thinking Things Through, was it a reasonable risk for the employer to utilize the two employees in the trench for just 15 minutes to lay one joint of pipe? Of course not! The ALJ found that both supervisors "knowingly and deliberately" violated the OSHA standard because it was "more expedient to place employees in an unprotected trench... than to take the time to adequately shore up or slope the trench to protect the employees." The $50,000 willful violation penalty was upheld by the U.S. Court of Appeals.*

In 1970, the year that OSHA became law, the American population was approximately 204,000,000; over 14,000 workers were killed in industrial accidents. In 2009, with the U.S. population at an estimated 307,000,000, some 4,551 workers were killed in work-related incidents. OSHA has drastically improved the safety and health of workers. OSHA standards are commonly devised as corrective responses to the occurrence of previous fatalities or injuries on often similarly situated work sites. Employees are empowered to refuse to expose themselves to dangerous duties under the *Whirlpool v. Marshall* U.S. Supreme Court decision.** Management and employees must always be encouraged to take the safe course!

**John Carlo, Inc. v. Secretary of Labor*, 2008 CCH OSHD ¶ 32,929.
**445 U.S. 1 (1980).

workplaces have been enacted by many states in recent years. These laws commonly require an employer to make known to an employee's physician the chemical composition of certain workplace substances in connection with the employee's diagnosis and treatment by the physician. Furthermore, local fire and public health officials, as well as local neighborhood residents, are given the right to know if local employers are working with hazardous substances that could pose health or safety problems.

F. Compensation for Employees' Injuries

For most kinds of employment, workers' compensation statutes govern compensation for injuries. These statutes provide that an injured employee is entitled to compensation for accidents occurring in the course of employment from a risk involved in that employment.

25. Common Law Status of Employer

In some employment situations, common law principles apply. Workers' compensation statutes commonly do not apply to employers with fewer than a prescribed minimum number of employees or to agricultural, domestic, or casual employment. When an exempted area of employment is involved, it is necessary to consider the duties and defenses of employers apart from workers' compensation statutes.

(A) Duties. The employer is under the common law duty to furnish an employee with a reasonably safe place in which to work, reasonably safe tools and appliances, and a sufficient number of competent fellow employees for the work involved. The employer is also under the common law duty to warn the employee of any unusual dangers particular to the employer's business.

(B) Defenses. At common law, the employer is not liable to an injured employee if the employee is harmed by the act of a fellow employee. Similarly, an employer is not liable at common law to an employee harmed by an ordinary hazard of the work because the employee assumed such risks. If the employee is guilty of contributory negligence, regardless of the employer's negligence, the employer is not liable at common law to an injured employee.

26. Statutory Changes

The rising incidence of industrial accidents resulting from the increasing use of more powerful machinery and the growth of the industrial labor population led to a demand for statutory modification of common law rules relating to the liability of employers for industrial accidents.

(A) Modification of Employer's Common Law Defenses. One type of change by statute was to modify the defenses that an employer could assert when sued by an employee for damages. **For Example,** under the Federal Employer's Liability Act (FELA), which covers railroad workers, the injured employee must still bring an action in court and prove the negligence of the employer or other employees. However, the burden of proving the case is made lighter by limitations on employers' defenses. Under FELA, contributory negligence is a defense only in mitigation of damages; assumption of the risk is not a defense.[56]

(B) Workers' Compensation. A more sweeping development was made by the adoption of workers' compensation statutes in every state. In addition, civil employees of the U.S. government are covered by the Federal Employees' Compensation Act. When an employee is covered by a workers' compensation statute and the injury is job connected, the employee's remedy is limited to that provided in the workers' compensation statute.[57]

Workers' compensation proceedings are brought before a special administrative agency or workers' compensation board. In contrast, a common law action for damages or an action for damages under an employer's liability statute is brought in a court of law.

For injuries arising within the course of the employee's work from a risk involved in that work, workers' compensation statutes usually provide (1) immediate medical benefits, (2) prompt periodic wage replacement, often computed as a percentage of weekly wages (ranging from 50 percent to 80 percent of the injured employee's wage) for a specified number of weeks, and (3) a death benefit of a limited amount.[58] In such cases, compensation is paid without regard to whether the employer or the employee was negligent. However, no compensation is generally allowed for a willful, self-inflicted injury or one sustained while intoxicated.[59]

There has been a gradual widening of the workers' compensation statutes, so compensation today is generally recoverable for both accident-inflicted injuries and occupational diseases.

G. Employee Privacy

Employers may want to monitor employee telephone conversations in the ordinary course of their business to evaluate employee performance and customer service; to document business transactions between employees and customers; or to meet special security, efficiency, or other needs. Employers may likewise want to monitor e-mail for what they perceive to be sound business reasons. Employers also may seek to test employees for drug use or search employee lockers for illicit drugs. Litigation may result because employees may believe that such activities violate their right to privacy.

27. Source of Privacy Rights

The Bill of Rights contained in the U.S. Constitution, including the Fourth Amendment, which protects against unreasonable search and seizure, provides a philosophical and legal basis for individual privacy rights for federal employees. The Fourteenth Amendment applies this privacy protection to actions taken by state and local governments that affect their employees. The privacy rights of individuals working in the private sector are not directly controlled by the Bill of Rights, however, because challenged employer actions are not government actions. Limited employee

[56] 45 U.S.C. §1 *et seq.*

[57] In *Fu v. Owens*, 622 F.3d 880 (8th Cir. 2010), Helen Fu's injuries, incurred when a coworker assaulted her at work at a Target-owned clinic in Minnesota, occurred because she was at the job, in touch with associations and conditions inseparable from it. The injuries occurred because she was on the job and thus she was subject to the exclusivity provision of the Workers' Compensation Act.

[58] *Union Light & Power Co. v. DC Department of Employment Services*, 796 A.2d 665 (D.C. App. 2002).

[59] See *Beck v. Newt Brown Contractors, LLC*, 72 So.3d 982 (La. App. 2011).

privacy rights in the private sector are provided by statute, case law, and collective bargaining agreements.

28. Monitoring Employee Telephone Conversations

The Federal Wiretapping Act[60] makes it unlawful to intercept oral and electronic communications and provides for both criminal liability and civil damages against the violator. There are two major exceptions, however. The first allows an employer to monitor a firm's telephones in the "ordinary course of business" through the use of extension telephones; a second exception applies when there is prior employee consent to the interception. If employer monitoring results in the interception of a business call, it is within the ordinary-course-of-business exception. Personal calls can be monitored, however, only to the extent necessary to determine that the call is personal, and the employer must then cease listening. **For Example,** Newell Spears taped all phone conversations at his store in trying to find out if an employee was connected to a store theft. He listened to virtually all 22 hours of intercepted and recorded telephone conversations between his employee Sibbie Deal and her boyfriend Calvin Lucas without regard to the conversations' relation to Spears's business interest. While Spears might well have legitimately monitored Deal's calls to the extent necessary to determine that the calls were personal and made or received in violation of store policy, the scope of the interception in this case was well beyond the boundaries of the ordinary-course-of-business exception and in violation of the act.[61]

Employer monitoring of employee phone calls can be accomplished without fear of violating the act if consent is established. Consent may be established by prior written notice to employees of the employer's monitoring policy. It is prudent, as well, for the employer to give customers notice of the policy through a recorded message as part of the employer's phone-answering system.

29. E-Mail Monitoring

Electronic mail (e-mail) is a primary means of communication in many of today's businesses, serving for some employers as an alternative to faxes, telephones, or the U.S. Postal Service. Employers may want to monitor employees' e-mail messages to evaluate the efficiency and effectiveness of their employees or for corporate security purposes, including the protection of trade secrets and other intangible property interests. When employees are disciplined or terminated for alleged wrongful activities discovered as a result of e-mail searches, however, the issue of privacy may be raised. (See Chapter 2 for a discussion of use of e-mail in litigation and discovery.)

The Electronic Communications Privacy Act of 1986 (ECPA)[62] amended the federal wiretap statute and was intended in part to apply to e-mail. However, ordinary-course-of-business and consent exceptions apply to e-mail, and it would appear that employers have broad latitude to monitor employee e-mail use. **For Example,** the e-mails that Gina Holmes sent to her personal attorney on a company-issued computer regarding litigation with the company were not protected by the attorney-client privilege because the company handbook stated that employees were prohibited from using the computer to send or receive personal e-mails. Moreover, the company warned that it would monitor its technology resources for compliance with its computer policy, and that employees "have no rights of privacy" with respect to information on the computers.[63] Very few cases involving e-mail and Web site issues have been adjudicated so far under the ECPA. It has been held that for an employee's secure Web site to be "intercepted" in violation of the wiretap act, the electronic documents acquired must be acquired during transmission, not while in electronic storage.[64]

An employer can place itself within the consent exception of the act by issuing a policy statement to all employees that informs them of the monitoring program and its purposes and justification.

[60] Title III of the Omnibus Crime Control and Safe Streets Act of 1968, 28 U.S.C. §§2510–2520.

[61] *Deal v. Spears*, 580 F.2d 1153 (8th Cir. 1992); *Arias v. Mutual Central Alarm Services, Inc.*, 182 F.R.D. 407 (S.D.N.Y. 1998).

[62] 18 U.S.C. §§2510–2520.

[63] *Holmes v. Petrovich Development Co.*, 191 Cal. App. 4th 1047 (3d Dist. 2011).

[64] *Konop v. Hawaiian Airlines, Inc.*, 302 F.3d 868 (9th Cir. 2002); *Fraser v. Nationwide Mutual Insurance Co.*, 352 F.3d 107 (3d Cir. 2003) (court held that the wiretaps act was not violated because the employer did not "intercept" the e-mail but retrieved it after it had been sent and received).

30. Property Searches

Protected by the Fourth Amendment, public-sector employees have a reasonable expectation of privacy with respect to their desks and file cabinets. However, depending on the fact-specific purpose, justification, and scope of the search, the balance of interest should favor the public employer because its interests in supervision, control, and the efficient operation of the workplace outweigh a public employee's privacy interests.[65] Search of a postal service employee's locker was held not to be a Fourth Amendment violation because well-publicized regulations informed employees that their lockers were subject to search to combat pilferage and stealing. However, the warrantless search of the desk and files of a psychiatrist employed by a state hospital was found to be a Fourth Amendment violation, exceeding the scope of a reasonable work-related search when the search examined his private possessions, including purely personal belongings, and management sought to justify the search on false grounds.[66]

In the private sector, employers may create a reasonable expectation of privacy by providing an employee a locker and allowing the employee to provide his or her own lock. A search of that locker could be an invasion of privacy.[67] If, however, the employer provides a locker and lock but retains a master key and this is known to employees, the lockers may be subject to legitimate reasonable searches by the employer. If a private-sector employer notifies all employees of its policy on lockers, desks, and office searches and the employer complies with its own policy, employees will have no actionable invasion of privacy case.

Many businesses use overt or hidden video cameras as a security method in the workplace to enhance worker safety and to prevent and/or detect theft or other criminal conduct. To avoid state constitutional or statutory claims for invasion of privacy, employers should not set up video cameras in areas where employees have a reasonable expectation of privacy.[68] Utilizing signs to notify employees and members of the public that certain areas are under video surveillance is a common business practice not likely to initiate privacy claims. Additionally, employers should disseminate their written policy on surveillance and obtain a consent form from employees acknowledging that they received this notice to preserve their consent defense.

31. Drug and Alcohol Testing

Drug and alcohol testing is an additional source of privacy concerns for employees. Public-sector employees may see drug and alcohol testing as potentially infringing on their Fourth and Fifth Amendment rights, although they may be subject to this testing on the basis of reasonable suspicion. In ordinary circumstances, however, random drug testing is not permissible in the public sector except for mass transit workers and some safety-sensitive positions. The Federal Omnibus Transportation Employee Testing Act,[69] which covers certain classes of employees working in the airline, railroad, and trucking industries, makes covered employees subject to random drug and alcohol testing. Random drug and alcohol testing of employees working in safety-sensitive positions in the private sector also is permissible, as is the testing of private-sector employees on the basis of reasonable suspicion.

H. Employer-Related Immigration Laws

The Immigration and Naturalization Act (INA), the Immigration Reform and Control Act of 1986 (IRCA), and the Immigration Act of 1990[70] are the principal employer-related immigration laws. Administration of these laws was formerly under the Immigration and Naturalization Service, and is now reorganized under the Department of Homeland Security (DHS) as the United States Bureau of Citizenship and Immigration Services (USCIS).

[65] *O'Connor v. Ortega*, 480 U.S. 709 (1987).

[66] *Ortega v. O'Connor*, 146 F.3d 1149 (9th Cir. 1998).

[67] *Kmart Corp. v. Trotti*, 677 S.W.2d 632 (Tex. App. 1984).

[68] See *Kline v. Security Guards, Inc.*, 386 F.3d 246 (3rd Cir. 2004). Some 370 employees of Dana Corporation's Reading, Pennsylvania, facility sued the corporation and its security guard company after employees learned that a new audio and video surveillance system at the entrance of the facility allowed what was said in the area where employees "punch in" for work to be observed and heard in the guard booth. The Third Circuit Court of Appeals rejected the employer's preemption claims and remanded the matter to the state court to handle the invasion of privacy and other tort claims.

[69] P.L. 102-143, 105 Stat. 952, 49 U.S.C. §1301 nt.

[70] P.L. 101-649, 8 U.S.C. §1101.

32. Employer Liability

The IRCA sets criminal and civil penalties against employers who knowingly hire aliens who have illegally entered the United States. The IRCA was designed to stop illegal immigration by eliminating job opportunities for these aliens.

33. Employer Verification and Special Hiring Programs

Upon hiring a new employee, an employer must verify that the employee is authorized to work in the United States. USCIS has designated Form I-9, Immigration Eligibility Verification Form, as the official verification form to comply with the IRCA.

The prospective employee must complete the initial portion of Form I-9, attesting under the penalty of perjury that he or she is a U.S. citizen or is authorized to work in the United States, and that the verification document(s) presented to the employer are genuine and relate to the signer. The employer must then review the documents that support the individual's right to work in the United States.

In April 2011, USCIS issued a final rule on acceptable identity documents for the I-9 employment eligibility process, divided into three sections.[71] List A documents verify identity and employment authorization and include a U.S. passport, the new U.S. passport card, and the temporary Form I-551 (permanent resident card) or a permanent resident card that includes a machine-readable immigrant visa. List B documents verify only identity; an example is a state-issued driver's license. List C documents, such as a Social Security card or official birth certificate, verify employment authorization. The employer is prohibited from requiring other documentation.[72]

(A) E-Verify. Employers may verify new employee eligibility status through the federal government's mostly voluntary employment verification program called E-Verify. The E-Verify system is an Internet-based voluntary system that electronically compares information on I-9 forms with records at the Social Security Administration and the Department of Homeland Security (DHS). In 2010, DHS instituted a U.S. passport photo matching program by comparing E-Verify data with State Department records. Employers that use E-Verify must notify applicants that they use E-Verify and cannot use the program as a prescreening tool. USCIS statistics for FY 2010 on E-Verify use showed that 98.3 percent of new hires surveyed were confirmed "work authorized" in three to five seconds.

Executive Order 12989 was amended in 2008 to require federal contractors to use E-Verify to confirm the employment eligibility of their workforce.

Under the Legal Arizona Workers Act, upheld by the Supreme Court, all an Arizona employer is required to do to avoid sanctions is to use the I-9 system and E-Verify.[73]

(B) Special Hiring Programs. Congress has provided increases in visas for entrepreneurs and those aliens with the greatest skills who could stimulate the American economy through their employment and job-creating investments.[74] H-1 classification visas allow aliens of "distinguished merit and ability" to enter and work in the United States on a temporary basis. These people include architects, engineers, lawyers, physicians, and teachers. An annual cap of 65,000 visas is applied to the H-1B visa classification (the regular cap). An advanced degree exception (ADE) cap provides for an additional 20,000 annual visas for individuals who have obtained master's degrees or higher at U.S. universities. The hiring employer must attest that it will not lay off an American employee 90 days before or after filing a petition to employ a foreign worker regarding any position to be filled by the foreign worker. H-1B professionals must be paid the higher of the actual or prevailing wage for each position in order to eliminate economic incentives to use this foreign workers' program.

[71] *See Federal Register* (Apr. 15, 2011). USCIS stated that concerns about document fraud were among the most important reasons for this rulemaking.

[72] 8 U.S.C. §1324B (a)(b).

[73] *Chamber of Commerce of the United States v. Whiting*, 131 S. Ct. 624 (2011).

[74] In a report released by the Fiscal Policy Institute of Albany, New York, on November 16, 2007, entitled "Working for A Better Life: A Profile of Immigrants in the New York State Economy," the whole range of immigrants in the state, both documented and undocumented, was studied. The report found that immigrants constitute 37 percent of the population of New York City and 46 percent of its labor force. They make up 25 percent of the city's CEOs; 50 percent of accountants; and 33 percent of clerks, receptionists, and cleaners. In upstate areas, immigrants constitute 5 percent of the population and labor force, 20 percent of professors, 35 percent of physicians, 20 percent of software engineers, and 80 percent of seasonal farm workers. All told, they contributed an estimated $229 billion in economic output in the state in 2006. Basically, there are rich, poor, and middle-class immigrants, like everyone else. See 227 DLR A-9 (Nov. 27, 2007). The Fiscal Policy Institute's 2010 report found that immigrants constituted 37 percent of New York City's population and 48 percent of its workforce. 147 DLR A-9 (Aug. 2, 2010).

L-1 visas allow qualifying multinational businesses to make intracompany transfers of foreign persons to the United States when the individuals are employed in management or have "specialized knowledge." L-1 visas are good for up to seven years for executives and managers. "Specialized knowledge" personnel may stay for five years. There are no annual caps on the number of L-1 visas issued, and the employer is not required to attest that no American worker will be laid off.

Many technology companies are utilizing L-1 visas as an alternative to the H-1B visas. Although the H-1B visa program requires employers to pay foreign workers the prevailing U.S. wage for a particular job, the L-1 visa has no such requirement. **For Example,** an engineer on an L-1 visa from India may be paid the same wage rate as paid in India, rather than the much higher prevailing rate for U.S. engineers. USCIS requires each transferee, or his or her employer, to demonstrate that the transferee's responsibilities are "primarily managerial."

For Example, Brazilian corporation Granite Ebenezer established a U.S.-based affiliate, Brazil Quality Stones, Inc. (BQS), as a California corporation. Eugene dos Santos, a Brazilian citizen, served as President and CEO of both entities and owned 99 percent of the corporation's stock. Citizenship and Immigration Services determined that he was not entitled to an L-1 visa. Although BQS submitted an organizational chart with him at the top supervising five employees, only three had received pay during the quarter. The USCIS determined that BQS had not reached the level of development in which dos Santos could devote his primary attention to managerial duties as opposed to operational ones.[75]

[75] *Brazil Quality Stones, Inc. v. Chertoff*, 531 F.3d 1063 (9th Cir. 2008).

MAKE THE CONNECTION

SUMMARY

The relationship of employer and employee is created by the agreement of the parties and is subject to the principles applicable to contracts. If the employment contract sets forth a specific duration, the employer cannot terminate the contract at an earlier date unless just cause exists. If no definite time period is set forth, the individual is an at-will employee. Under the employment-at-will doctrine, an employer can terminate the contract of an at-will employee at any time for any reason or for no reason. Courts in many jurisdictions, however, have carved out exceptions to this doctrine when the discharge violates public policy or is contrary to good faith and fair dealing in the employment relationship. The Fair Labor Standards Act regulates minimum wages, overtime hours, and child labor.

Under the National Labor Relations Act, employees have the right to form a union to obtain a collective bargaining contract or to refrain from organizational activities. The National Labor Relations Board conducts elections to determine whether employees in an appropriate bargaining unit desire to be represented by a union. The NLRA prohibits employers' and unions' unfair labor practices and authorizes the NLRB to conduct proceedings to stop such practices. Economic strikes have limited reinstatement rights. Federal law sets forth democratic standards for the election of union offices.

The Employees Retirement Income Security Act (ERISA) protects employees' pensions by requiring (1) high standards of those administering the funds, (2) reasonable vesting of benefits, (3) adequate funding, and (4) an insurance program to guarantee payments of earned benefits.

Unemployment compensation benefits are paid to persons for a limited period of time if they are out of work through no fault of their own. Persons receiving unemployment compensation must be available for placement in a job similar in duties and comparable in rate of pay to the job they lost. Twelve-week maternity, paternity, and adoption leaves are available under the Family and Medical Leave Act. Employers and employees pay Social Security taxes to provide retirement benefits, disability benefits, life insurance benefits, and Medicare.

The Occupational Safety and Health Act provides for the (1) establishment of safety and health standards and (2) effective enforcement of these standards. Many states have enacted "right-to-know" laws, which require employers to inform their employees of any hazardous substances present in the workplace.

Workers' compensation laws provide for the prompt payment of compensation and medical benefits to persons injured in the course of employment without regard to fault. An injured employee's remedy is generally limited to the remedy provided by the workers' compensation statute. Most states also provide compensation to workers for occupational diseases.

The Bill of Rights is the source of public-sector employees' privacy rights. Private-sector employees may obtain limited privacy rights from statutes, case law, and collective bargaining agreements. Employers may monitor employee telephone calls, although once it is determined that the call is personal, the employer must stop listening or be in violation of the federal wiretap statute. The ordinary-course-of-business and consent exceptions to the Electronic Communications Privacy Act of 1986 (ECPA) give private employers a great deal of latitude to monitor employee e-mail. Notification to employees of employers' policies on searching lockers, desks, and offices reduces employees' expectations of privacy, and a search conducted in conformity with a known policy is generally not an invasion of privacy. Drug and alcohol testing is generally permissible if it is based on reasonable suspicion; random drug and alcohol testing may also be permissible in safety-sensitive positions.

Immigration laws prohibit the employment of aliens who have illegally entered the United States.

LEARNING OUTCOMES

After studying this chapter, you should be able to clearly explain:

A. The Employment Relationship

LO.1 Explain the contractual nature of the employment relationship

See the *FedEx* case in which the employment contract and the employee handbook both preserved the employer's at-will termination powers, pp. 796–797.

See the example of the public policy exception to the employment-at-will doctrine protecting home health care nurse Eugene Patterson, pp. 793–794.

LO.2 Explain how whistleblower protection under Sarbanes-Oxley is limited to conduct in violation of fraud or securities laws

See the example involving whistleblowers Tides and Neumann who were not protected under SOX because they disclosed information and documents to a newspaper and not a regulatory or law enforcement agency on p. 798.

LO.3 Explain how Dodd-Frank expands whistleblower protection to a wide range of financial services employees and provides incentives for whistleblowers

See what a whistleblower must do to recover a bounty under Dodd-Frank on p. 798.

B. Labor Relations Laws

LO.4 Explain how the National Labor Relations Act prohibits employers from firing employees attempting to form a union, and requires employers to bargain with unions in good faith over wages, hours, and working conditions

See the *Sam Santillo* case on wrongful termination of an employee because of his union activity, pp. 804–805.

See the role that the National Labor Relations Board plays in regulating employers' overly broad social media policies that are in violation of Section 7 of the NLRA, starting on p. 803.

See the discussion of mandatory and permissive subjects of bargaining, p. 805.

C. Pension Plans and Federal Regulation

LO.5 Explain how ERISA protects employee pensions and benefits

See the Bell South example in which Ms. Lee successfully sued for disability benefits, p. 807.

See the discussion of defined contribution plans and defined benefit plans on p. 807.

D. Unemployment Benefits, Family Leaves, and Social Security

LO.6 Explain the essentials of unemployment benefits, family and medical leaves, military leaves, and Social Security benefits

E. Employees' Health and Safety

LO.7 Explain how OSHA is designed to ensure workers safe and healthful working conditions

See the Thinking Things Through discussion for reasons why taking chances or shortcuts in violation of OSHA standards is bad management, p. 813.

F. Compensation for Employees' Injuries

LO.8 Explain the three types of benefits provided by workers' compensation statutes

G. Employee Privacy

LO.9 Explain the sources of privacy rights, and applications to telephone, e-mail, text-messaging, and property searches

H. Employer-Related Immigration Laws

LO.10 Explain an employer's verification obligations when hiring new employees and discuss special hiring programs allowing aliens to work in the United States

See the *Brazilian Quality Stones* example of a CEO who did not meet his burden of proof that his responsibilities were "primarily managerial," p. 818.

KEY TERMS

defined benefit plan
defined contribution plan
economic strikers
employment-at-will doctrine
mass picketing
Pension Benefit Guaranty Corporation (PBGC)
primary picketing
right-to-work laws
secondary picketing
shop right

QUESTIONS AND CASE PROBLEMS

1. What remedies does an employee who has been wrongfully discharged have against an employer?

2. Michael Smyth was an operations manager at Pillsbury Co., and his employment status was that of an employee at will. Smyth received certain e-mail messages at home, and he replied to his supervisor by e-mail. His messages contained some provocative language including the phrase "kill the backstabbing bastards" and a reference to an upcoming company party as the "Jim Jones Koolaid affair." Later, Smyth was given two weeks' notice of his termination, and he was told that his e-mail remarks were inappropriate and unprofessional. Smyth believes that he is the victim of invasion of privacy because the e-mail messages caused his termination, and the company had promised that e-mail communications would not be intercepted and used as a basis for discipline or discharge. The company denies that it intercepted the e-mail messages and points out that Smyth himself sent the unprofessional comments to his supervisor. Is Smyth entitled to reinstatement and back pay because of the invasion of privacy? [*Smyth v. Pillsbury Co.*, 914 F. Supp. 97 (E.D. Pa.)]

3. Michael Hauck claimed that he was discharged by his employer, Sabine Pilot Service, because he refused its direction to perform the illegal act of pumping the bilges of the employer's vessel into the waterways. Hauck was an employee at will, and Sabine contends that it therefore had the right to discharge him without having to show cause. Hauck brought a wrongful discharge action

against Sabine. Decide. [*Sabine Pilot Service, Inc., v. Hauck*, 687 S.W.2d 733 (Tex.)]

4. Jeanne Eenkhoorn worked as a supervisor at a business office for the New York Telephone Co. While at work, she invented a process for terminating the telephone services of delinquent subscribers. The telephone company used the process but refused to compensate her for it, claiming a shop right. Eenkhoorn then sued for damages on a quasi-contract theory. Decide. [*Eenkhoorn v. New York Telephone Co.*, 568 N.Y.S.2d 677]

5. One Monday, a labor organization affiliated with the International Ladies Garment Workers Union began an organizational drive among the employees of Whittal & Son. On the following Monday, six of the employees who were participating in the union drive were discharged. Immediately after the firings, the head of the company gave a speech to the remaining workers in which he made a variety of antiunion statements and threats. The union filed a complaint with the NLRB, alleging that the six employees were fired because they were engaging in organizational activity and were thus discharged in violation of the NLRA. The employer defended its position, arguing that it had a business to run and that it was barely able to survive in the global economy against cheap labor from third-world countries. It asserted that the last thing it needed was "union baloney." Was the NLRA violated?

6. David Stark submitted an application to the maintenance department of Wyman-Gordon Co. Stark was a journeyman millwright with nine years' experience at a neighboring company at the time of his application to Wyman-Gordon. Stark was vice president of the local industrial workers' union. In his preliminary interview with the company, Ms. Peevler asked if Stark was involved in union activity, and Stark detailed his involvement to her. She informed Stark that Wyman-Gordon was a nonunion shop and asked how he felt about this. Peevler's notes from the interview characterize Stark's response to this question as "seems to lean toward third-party intervention." Company officials testified that Stark's qualifications were "exactly what we were looking for," but he was not hired. Stark claimed that he was discriminated against. Wyman-Gordon denied that any discrimination had occurred. Is a job applicant (as opposed to an employee) entitled to protection from antiunion discrimination? On the facts of this case, has any discrimination taken place? [*Wyman-Gordon Co. v. N.L.R. B.*, 108 L.R.R.M. 2085 (1st Cir.)]

7. Armenda Malone and Stephen Krantz were induced to leave other employment and join ABI's CD-ROM division as national account managers in part because of a favorable commission agreement at ABI. Their employment relationship with ABI had no set duration, and as such they were employees at will. For the first two quarters of their employment, their commission reports were approved by the president of the division and paid without incident. Thereafter, a new management team took over the division. When the mid-level manager presented third quarter commission reports based on the prior practice to the new vice president, Bruce Lowry, for approval, he was told, "You got to learn how to f— these people." Lowry then utilized severable variables—some of which the mid-level manager found "ridiculous"—to reduce the commission figures. After much discourse that carried on well into the fourth quarter, Lowry announced that a new model for determining commissions would be implemented. Commissions for both the third and fourth quarters, ending in December, were then calculated based on this model. ABI asserts that because Malone and Krantz were employees at will, the employer had the right to interpret or alter how it pays employees as it sees fit. Krantz and Malone left ABI and have sued for what they believe are the full commissions earned in the third and fourth quarters. Present a legal theory on behalf of Malone and Krantz for the payment of back commissions. Assess the strengths and weaknesses of Lowry's approach to employee relations. How would you decide this case? [*Malone v. American Business Information, Inc.*, 647 N.W.2d 569 (Neb.)]

8. Jane Richards was employed as the sole crane operator of Gale Corp. and held the part-time

union position of shop steward for the plant. On May 15, Richards complained to OSHA concerning what she contended were seven existing violations of the Occupational Safety and Health Act that were brought to her attention by members of the bargaining unit. On May 21, she stated to the company's general manager at a negotiating session: "If we don't have a new contract by the time the present one expires on June 15, we will strike." On May 22, an OSHA inspector arrived at the plant, and Richards told her supervisor, "I blew the whistle." On May 23, the company rented and later purchased two large electric forklifts that were used to do the work previously performed by the crane, and the crane operator's job was abolished. Under the existing collective bargaining contract, the company had the right to lay off for lack of work. The contract also provided for arbitration, and it prohibited discipline or discharge without "just cause." On May 23, Richards was notified that she was being laid off "for lack of work" within her classification of crane operator. She was also advised that the company was not planning on using the crane in the future and that, if she were smart, she would get another job. Richards claimed that her layoff violated the National Labor Relations Act, the Occupational Safety and Health Act, and the collective bargaining agreement. Was she correct?

9. Virgil Deemer and Thomas Cornwell, employees at a Whirlpool Corporation plant, refused to comply with a supervisor's order that they perform maintenance work on certain mesh screens located some 20 feet above the plant floor. Twelve days before a fellow employee had fallen to his death from the screens. Because they refused to do the work assigned them, they were told to punch out and go home; reprimands were placed in their files. Should employees be able to pick and choose what work they will perform? Do Deemer and Cornwell have any recourse? [*Whirlpool v. Marshall*, 445 U.S. 1]

10. In May, the nurses union at Waterbury Hospital went on strike, and the hospital was shut down. In mid-June, the hospital began hiring replacements and gradually opened many units. To induce nurses to take employment during the strike, the hospital guaranteed replacement nurses their choice of positions and shifts. If a preferred position was in a unit that was not open at that time, the hospital guaranteed that the individual would be placed in that position at the end of the strike. The strike ended in October and as the striking workers returned to work, the hospital began opening units that had been closed during the strike. It staffed many of these positions with replacement nurses. The nurses who had the positions prior to the strike and were waiting to return to work believed that they should have been called to fill these positions rather than the junior replacements who had held other positions during the strike. Decide. [*Waterbury Hospital v. NLRB*, 950 F.2d 849 (2d Cir.)]

11. Buffo was employed by the Baltimore & Ohio Railroad. Along with a number of other workers, he was removing old brakes from railroad cars and replacing them with new brakes. In the course of the work, rivet heads and scrap from the brakes accumulated on the tracks under the cars. This debris was removed only occasionally when the workers had time. Buffo, while holding an air hammer in both arms, was crawling under a car when his foot slipped on scrap on the ground, causing him to strike and injure his knee. He sued the railroad for damages under the Federal Employers Liability Act. Decide. [*Buffo v. Baltimore & Ohio Railroad Co.*, 72 A.2d 593 (Pa.)]

12. Mark Phipps was employed as a cashier at a Clark gas station. A customer drove into the station and asked him to pump leaded gasoline into her 1976 Chevrolet, an automobile equipped to receive only unleaded gasoline. The station manager told Phipps to comply with the request, but he refused, believing that his dispensing leaded gasoline into the gas tank was a violation of law. Phipps stated that he was willing to pump unleaded gas into the tank, but the manager immediately fired him. Phipps sued Clark for wrongful termination. Clark contended that it was free to terminate Phipps, an employee at will, for any reason or no reason. Decide. [*Phipps v. Clark Oil & Refining Corp.*, 396 N.W.2d 588 (Minn. App.)]

13. Reno, Nevada, police officers John Bohach and Jon Catalano communicated with each other on the Alphapage computer system, typing messages on a keyboard and sending them to each other by use of

a "send" key. The computer dials a commercial paging company, which receives the message by modem, and the message is then sent to the person paged by radio broadcast. When the system was installed, the police chief warned that every Alphapage message was logged on the network, and he barred messages that were critical of department policy or discriminatory. The two police officers sought to block a department investigation into their messages and prevent disclosure of the messages' content. They claimed that the messages should be treated the same as telephone calls under federal wiretap law. The department contended that the system was essentially a form of e-mail whose messages are by definition stored in a computer, and the storage was itself not part of the communication. Was the federal wiretap law violated? [*Bohach v. City of Reno*, 932 F. Supp. 1232 (D. Nev.)]

14. Michael Kittell was employed at Vermont Weatherboard. While operating a saw at the plant, Kittell was seriously injured when a splinter flew into his eye and penetrated his head. Kittell sued Vermont Weatherboard, seeking damages under a common law theory. His complaint alleged that he suffered severe injuries solely because of the employer's wanton and willful acts and omissions. The complaint stated that he was an inexperienced worker, put to work without instructions or warning on a saw from which the employer had stripped away all safety devices. Vermont Weatherboard made a motion to dismiss the complaint on the ground that the Workers' Compensation Act provided the exclusive remedy for his injury. Decide. [*Kittell v. Vermont Weatherboard, Inc.*, 417 A.2d 926 (Vt.)]

Equal Employment Opportunity Law

learningoutcomes

After studying this chapter, you should be able to

LO.1 Explain the difference between the *disparate treatment* theory of employment discrimination and the *disparate impact* theory of employment discrimination

LO.2 List and explain the categories of individuals protected against unlawful employment discrimination under Title VII

LO.3 Recognize, and know the remedies for, sexual harassment in the workplace

LO.4 Explain the antiretaliation provision of Title VII

LO.5 List and explain the laws protecting equal pay for women and men for equal work, as well as the laws forbidding discrimination on the basis of age and against individuals with disabilities

LO.6 Explain how both Title VII of the Civil Rights Act and the ADA protect from discrimination U.S. citizens working in foreign countries for American-owned and American-controlled businesses

Laws of the United States reflect our society's concern that all Americans, including minorities, women, and persons with disabilities, have equal employment opportunities and that the workplace is free from discrimination and harassment. Title VII of the Civil Rights Act of 1964, as amended in 1972, 1978, and 1991, is the principal law regulating equal employment opportunities in the United States. Other federal laws require equal pay for men and women doing substantially the same work and forbid discrimination because of age or disability.

CPA A. Title VII of the Civil Rights Act of 1964, as Amended

Title VII of the Civil Rights Act of 1964[1] seeks to eliminate employer and union practices that discriminate against employees and job applicants on the basis of race, color, religion, sex, or national origin. The law applies to the hiring process and to discipline, discharge, promotion, and benefits.

1. Theories of Discrimination

The Supreme Court has created, and the Civil Rights Act of 1991 has codified, two principal legal theories under which a plaintiff may prove a case of unlawful employment discrimination: disparate treatment and disparate impact.

A *disparate treatment* claim exists where an employer treats some individuals less favorably than others because of their race, color, religion, sex, or national origin. Proof of the employer's discriminatory motive is essential in a disparate treatment case.[2]

Disparate impact exists when an employer's facially neutral employment practices, such as hiring or promotion examinations, although neutrally applied and making no adverse reference to race, color, religion, sex, or national origin, have a significantly adverse or disparate impact on a protected group. In addition, the employment practice in question is not shown by the employer to be job related and consistent with business necessity. Under the disparate impact theory, it is not a defense for an employer to demonstrate that it did not intend to discriminate. **For Example,** if plant manager Jones is heard telling the personnel director that the vacant welder's position should be filled by a male because "this is man's work," a qualified female applicant turned down for the job would prevail in a *disparate treatment* theory case against the employer because she was not hired because of her gender. Necessary evidence of the employer's discriminatory motive would be satisfied by testimony about the manager's "this is man's work" statement.

If the policy for hiring new pilots at Generic Airlines, Inc., required a minimum height of 5 feet 7 inches, and no adverse reference to gender was stated in this employment policy, nevertheless, the 5-feet-7-inch minimum height policy has an adverse or disparate impact on women because far fewer women than men reach this height. Such an employment policy would be set aside on a *disparate impact* theory, and a minimum height for the position would be established by the court based on evidence of job-relatedness and business necessity. A 5-feet-5-inch height requirement was set by one court for pilots.

The *Griggs v. Duke Power Co.* case is a disparate impact case.

Griggs v. Duke Power Co., 401 U.S. 424 (1971)

Number 1 on the Charts! The Case that Created the Disparate Impact Theory

Griggs and other black employees at Duke Power Company's Dan River Station challenged Duke Power's requirements of a high school diploma and passing standardized general intelligence tests in order to transfer to more desirable "inside jobs." The district court and Court of Appeals found no violation of Title VII because Duke Power did not adopt the

[1] 42 U.S.C. §2000(e) *et seq.*

[2] *Woodson v. Scott Paper Co.*, 109 F.3d 913 (3d Cir. 1997).

Continued

diploma and test requirements with the purpose of intentionally discriminating against black employees. The case was appealed to the Supreme Court.

JUDICIAL OPINION

BURGER, C. J.... The objective of Congress in the enactment of Title VII is plain from the language of the statute. It was to achieve equality of employment opportunities and remove barriers that have operated in the past to favor an identifiable group of white employees over other employees. Under the Act, practices, procedures, or tests neutral on their face, and even neutral in terms of intent, cannot be maintained if they operate to "freeze" the status quo of prior discriminatory employment practices.

...In short, the Act does not command that any person be hired simply because he was formerly the subject of discrimination, or because he is a member of a minority group. Discriminatory preference for any group, minority or majority, is precisely and only what Congress has proscribed. What is required by Congress is the removal of artificial, arbitrary, and unnecessary barriers to employment when the barriers operate invidiously to discriminate on the basis of racial or other impermissible classification.

Congress has now provided that tests or criteria for employment or promotion may not provide equality of opportunity merely in the sense of the fabled offer of milk to the stork and the fox. On the contrary, Congress has now required that the posture and condition of the job-seeker be taken into account. It has—to resort again to the fable—provided that the vessel in which the milk is proffered be one all seekers can use. The Act proscribes not only overt discrimination but also practices that are fair in form, but discriminatory in operation. The touch-stone is business necessity. If an employment practice which operates to exclude Negroes cannot be shown to be related to job performance, the practice is prohibited.

On the record before us, neither the high school completion requirement nor the general intelligence test is shown to bear a demonstrable relationship to successful performance of the jobs for which it was used. Both were adopted, as the Court of Appeals noted, without meaningful study of their relationship to job-performance ability. Rather, a vice president of the Company testified, the requirements were instituted on the Company's judgment that they generally would improve the overall quality of the work force.

The evidence, however, shows that employees who have not completed high school or taken the tests have continued to perform satisfactorily and make progress in departments for which the high school and test criteria are now used....

The Court of Appeals held that the Company had adopted the diploma and test requirements without any "intention to discriminate against Negro employees." We do not suggest that either the District Court or the Court of Appeals erred in examining the employer's intent; but good intent or absence of discriminatory intent does not redeem employment procedures or testing mechanisms that operate as "built-in headwinds" for minority groups and are unrelated to measuring job capability.

The Company's lack of discriminatory intent is suggested by special efforts to help the undereducated employees through Company financing of two-thirds the cost of tuition for high school training. But Congress directed the thrust of the Act to the *consequences* of employment practices, not simply the motivation. More than that, Congress has placed on the employer the burden of showing that any given requirement must have a manifest relationship to the employer in question.

The facts of this case demonstrate the inadequacy of broad and general testing devices as well as the infirmity of using diplomas or degrees as fixed measures of capability. History is filled with examples of men and women who rendered highly effective performance without the conventional badges of accomplishment in terms of certificates, diplomas, or degrees. Diplomas and tests are useful servants, but Congress has mandated the common sense proposition that they are not to become masters of reality.

The Company contends that its general intelligence tests are specifically permitted by Section 703(h) of the Act. That section authorizes the use of "any professionally developed ability test" that is not "designed, intended or *used* to discriminate because of race...." [Emphasis added.]

The Equal Employment Opportunity Commission, having enforcement responsibility, has issued guidelines interpreting Section 703(h) to permit only the use of job-related tests. The administrative interpretation of the Act by the enforcing agency is entitled to great deference.... Since the Act and its legislative history support the Commission's construction, this affords good reason to treat the guidelines as expressing the will of Congress....

Nothing in the Act precludes the use of testing or measuring procedures; obviously they are useful. What Congress has forbidden is giving these devices and mechanisms controlling force unless they are demonstrably a reasonable measure of job performance. Congress has not commanded that the less qualified be preferred over the better qualified simply because of minority origins. Far from disparaging job qualifications as such, Congress has made such qualifications the controlling factor, so that race, religion, nationality, and sex become irrelevant. What Congress has commanded is that any tests used must measure the person for the job and not the person in the abstract....

[Judgment reversed]

Continued

QUESTIONS

1. What was the question before the Supreme Court?
2. What was the objective of Congress in the enactment of Title VII?
3. Would the Court order the case against the employer to be dismissed if it found that the employer had adopted the diploma and test requirements without any intention to discriminate against minority employees?
4. As a result of the *Griggs* decision, may employers insist that both minority and white job applicants meet the applicable job qualifications as determined through the use of testing or measuring procedures?

"Disparate treatment" and "disparate impact" may both be at issue in the same case. **For Example,** as required by the city charter, the city of New Haven used objective examinations to identify those firefighters best qualified for promotion to fill vacant lieutenant and captain positions. On the basis of the examinations' results, no black candidates were eligible for immediate promotion. A rancorous public debate ensued. The city threw out the results based on the statistical racial disparity to avoid potential liability in a lawsuit based on *disparate impact* against the black candidates. White and Hispanic firefighters who passed the exams but were denied a chance for promotion by the city's refusal to certify the test results, sued the city, alleging a *disparate treatment* (intentional discrimination) case—that discarding the test results discriminated against them based on their race in violation of Title VII. The Supreme Court determined that the city rejected the test results because the higher-scoring candidates were white and that without some other justification this express race-based decision making is prohibited. The Court stated that "a strong basis in evidence" standard was necessary before the city could make an employment decision based on fear of liability under Title VII—and the Court held that the city did not meet this standard. The statistical disparity by itself was insufficient to constitute a strong basis in evidence of unlawful disparate impact. The examinations were job related and consistent with business necessity. And there was no strong basis in evidence of an equally valid, less-discriminating testing alternative. Thus, in a 5–4 decision, the U.S. Supreme Court ruled that the city had violated the civil rights of the white and Hispanic firefighters and remanded the case for further proceedings.[3]

2. The Equal Employment Opportunity Commission

The Equal Employment Opportunity Commission (EEOC) is a five-member body appointed by the president to establish equal employment opportunity policy under the laws it administers. The EEOC supervises the agency's conciliation and enforcement efforts.

The EEOC administers Title VII of the Civil Rights Act, the Equal Pay Act (EPA), the Age Discrimination in Employment Act (ADEA), Section 501 of the Rehabilitation Act (which prohibits federal-sector discrimination against persons with disabilities), and Title I (the employment provisions) of the Americans with Disabilities Act (ADA).

(A) Procedure. Where a state or local EEO agency with the power to act on claims of discriminatory practices exists, the charging party must file a complaint with that agency. The charging party must wait 60 days or until the termination of the state proceedings, whichever occurs first, before filing a charge with the EEOC. If no state or local agency exists, a charge may be filed directly with the EEOC so long as it is filed within 180 days of the occurrence of the discriminatory act. The commission conducts an investigation to determine whether reasonable cause exists to believe that the charge is true. If such cause is found to exist, the EEOC attempts to remedy

[3] *Ricci v. DeStefano*, 557 U.S. 557 (2009). Contrary to the extensive presentation in the majority decision of the detailed steps taken to develop and administer the examinations, the dissent asserted that the Court had ignored substantial evidence of multiple flaws in the tests and that the Court had failed to acknowledge that better tests used in other cities have yielded less racially skewed outcomes. The decision, the dissent, and two concurrences provide an insight into the complexities of our judicial process.

the unlawful practice through conciliation. If the EEOC does not resolve the matter to the satisfaction of the parties, it may decide to litigate the case when systemic or unusual circumstances exist, including a "pattern or practice of discrimination." In most instances, however, the EEOC issues the charging party a *right-to-sue letter.* Thereafter, the individual claiming a violation of EEO law has 90 days to file a lawsuit in a federal district court.[4]

(1) Pattern-or-Practice Cases.

Section 707 of Title VII permits the EEOC to sue employers when it has reasonable cause to believe they are engaged in a *pattern or practice* of unlawful employment discrimination. It must establish that intentional discrimination was the defendant employer's "standard operating procedure." A first phase focuses on the employer's policy or practice, not on individual charges. Once the pattern or practice of discrimination is established, the process moves to the individual relief phase, where individual claims may be presented. The purpose of Section 707 is to provide the government with a swift and effective weapon to eliminate unlawful practices.[5]

(2) Systemic "Class Action" Cases.

The EEOC has placed renewed focus on identifying, developing, and litigating discrimination cases involving employment policies affecting large classes of individuals in every statute enforced by the agency. When an individual files a discrimination charge with the EEOC, it now may expand its investigation into that employer's related employment practices involving similarly situated individuals. Possible statutory violations discovered during the course of the investigation of the initial individual charge may lead to the EEOC bringing a "systemic" case on behalf of a number of employees against the employer under Section 706 of the Act. However, before bringing the action to court under Section 706 the EEOC itself must conduct an investigation of each individual charge that is filed and if reasonable cause is found, the agency must provide the employer an opportunity to conciliate each individual case.[6]

(B) DAMAGES. Title VII sets damages available to victims of discrimination (see Figure 40-1).

Section 706(k) of Title VII provides that the court in its discretion allow the prevailing party, other than the EEOC and the United States, a reasonable attorneys' fee. Thus, a court may award a prevailing individual in a Civil Rights Act lawsuit against an employer reasonable attorney fees and costs. It also may award attorneys' fees against the EEOC itself if the agency's lawsuit is without foundation.

For Example, in *EEOC v. Peoplemark,* the federal district court awarded a temporary staffing firm, Peoplemark, the prevailing party in a lawsuit initiated by the EEOC, attorneys' fees, expert witness fees, and other expenses totaling $751,942.48, because the EEOC should have known at a certain point that there was no evidence supporting its complaint that the company maintained a policy adversely affecting a class of African Americans of denying employment to any person with a criminal record.[7]

(C) THE ARBITRATION OPTION. With the exception of transportation employees, employers can craft arbitration agreements that require employees to arbitrate any employment dispute, including statutory discrimination claims, and these mandatory arbitration clauses can be enforced in federal courts under the Federal Arbitration Act.[8] Courts do, however, require that the arbitration clauses be "fair." Moreover, a party agreeing to arbitration does not forgo substantive rights afforded by Title VII or alter federal antidiscrimination statutes. A fair arbitration clause requires adequate discovery, mandates that the arbitrator have authority to apply the same types of relief available from a court, and should not preclude an employee from vindicating statutory rights because of arbitration costs.[9]

[4] An individual who misses the filing deadline of Title VII may be able to bring a race discrimination case under the two-year time limit allowed under Section 1981 of the Civil Rights Act of 1964, codified at 42 U.S.C. §1981, and sometimes called a *Section 1981 lawsuit*. In the *Edelman v. Lynchburg College* decision, 535 U.S. 106 (2002), the U.S. Supreme Court approved an EEOC regulation that allows certain defective charges to be cured, with the cured charge relating back to the date the EEOC first received the initial charge, which was within the 300-day filing period.

[5] See *EEOC v. Mitsubishi Motor Manufacturing of America*, 102 F.3d 869 (7th Cir. 1996).

[6] See *EEOC v. CRST Van Expedited, Inc.*, 679 F.3d 657 (8th Cir. 2012).

[7] *EEOC v. Peoplemark*, 2010 WL 748250 (W.D. Mich. Feb. 26, 2010).

[8] *Circuit City Stores, Inc. v. Adams*, 532 U.S. 105 (2001).

[9] See *Circuit City II*, 279 F.3d 889 (9th Cir. 2002).

FIGURE 40-1 *Unlawful Discrimination under Title VII of the Civil Rights Act of 1964 as Amended by the Civil Rights Act of 1991*

DISCRIMINATORY TREATMENT IN EMPLOYMENT DECISIONS ON THE BASIS OF RACE, COLOR, RELIGION, SEX, OR NATIONAL ORIGIN	
DISPARATE TREATMENT THEORY	**DISPARATE IMPACT THEORY**
NONNEUTRAL PRACTICE OR NONNEUTRAL APPLICATION	FACIALLY NEUTRAL PRACTICE AND NEUTRAL APPLICATION
REQUIRES PROOF OF DISCRIMINATORY INTENT	DOES NOT REQUIRE PROOF OF DISCRIMINATORY INTENT REQUIRES PROOF OF ADVERSE EFFECT ON PROTECTED GROUP AND EMPLOYER IS UNABLE TO SHOW THAT THE CHALLENGED PRACTICE IS JOB RELATED FOR THE POSITION IN QUESTION AND IS CONSISTENT WITH BUSINESS NECESSITY
EITHER PARTY HAS A RIGHT TO REQUIRE A JURY TRIAL WHEN SEEKING COMPENSATORY OR PUNITIVE DAMAGES	NO RIGHT TO A JURY TRIAL
REMEDY REINSTATEMENT, HIRING, OR PROMOTION BACK PAY LESS INTERIM EARNINGS RETROACTIVE SENIORITY ATTORNEY AND EXPERT WITNESS FEES PLUS COMPENSATORY* AND PUNITIVE DAMAGES DAMAGES CAPPED FOR CASES OF SEX AND RELIGIOUS DISCRIMINATION DEPENDING ON SIZE OF EMPLOYER: NUMBER OF EMPLOYEES — DAMAGES CAP 100 OR FEWER — $ 50,000 101 TO 200 — 100,000 201 TO 500 — 200,000 OVER 500 — 300,000 NO CAP ON DAMAGES FOR RACE CASES	**REMEDY** REINSTATEMENT, HIRING, OR PROMOTION BACK PAY LESS INTERIM EARNINGS RETROACTIVE SENIORITY ATTORNEY AND EXPERT WITNESS FEES

* COMPENSATORY DAMAGES INCLUDE FUTURE PECUNIARY LOSSES AND NONPECUNIARY LOSSES SUCH AS EMOTIONAL PAIN AND SUFFERING.

A union may negotiate a provision in a collective bargaining agreement requiring all employment-related discrimination claims to be resolved in arbitration.[10]

[10] For some 35 years it was widely understood that an individual may prospectively waive his or her own statutory right to a judicial forum and be compelled to resolve a statutory discrimination claim in arbitration, but a union may not prospectively waive that right for the individual in a collective bargaining agreement. See *Alexander v. Gardner-Denver Co.*, 485 U.S. 36 (1974) and *Gilmer v. Interstate/Johnson Lane Corp.*, 500 U.S. 20 (1991). In *14 Penn Plaza, LLC v. Pyett*, 556 U.S. 247 (2009), the U.S. Supreme Court, in a 5-4 decision, held that a provision in a collective bargaining agreement (CBA) negotiated under the National Labor Relations Act between a union and employer group that requires union members to arbitrate Age Discrimination in Employment Act (ADEA) claims is enforceable as a matter of federal law. Thus, the petitioner union members were precluded from bringing their ADEA case in federal court and the matter had to be resolved under the arbitration provisions of the CBA.

B. Protected Classes and Exceptions

To successfully pursue a Title VII lawsuit, an individual must belong to a protected class and meet the appropriate burden of proof. Exceptions exist for certain employment practices.

3. Race and Color

The legislative history of Title VII of the Civil Rights Act demonstrates that a primary purpose of the act is to provide fair employment opportunities for black Americans. The protections of the act are applied to blacks based on race or color.

The word *race* as used in the act applies to all members of the four major racial groupings: white, black, Native American, and Asian-Pacific. Native Americans can file charges and receive the protection of the act on the basis of national origin, race, or, in some instances, color. Individuals of Asian-Pacific origin may file discrimination charges based on race, color, or, in some instances, national origin. Whites are also protected against discrimination because of race and color.

For Example, two white professors at a predominately black university were successful in discrimination suits against the university when it was held that the university had discriminated against them on the basis of race and color in tenure decisions.[11]

4. Religion

Title VII requires employers to accommodate their employees' or prospective employees' religious practices. Most cases involving allegations of religious discrimination revolve around the determination of whether an employer has made reasonable efforts to accommodate religious beliefs.

If an employee's religious beliefs prohibit working on Saturday, an employer's obligation under Title VII is to try to find a volunteer to cover for the employee on Saturdays. The employer would not have an obligation to violate a seniority provision of a collective bargaining agreement or call in a substitute worker if such accommodation would require more than a *de minimis* or very small cost.

(a) Garments Worn for Religious Reasons. Ordinarily employers have little reason to be informed or concerned about the religious practices of individual employees. However, because many Muslim women wear special clothing as part of their religious observances, which may conflict with an employer's safety or grooming standards, employers should develop appropriate and justifiable policies for their business and provide training for supervisors on how to properly handle requests for religious accommodations. **For Example,** a federal district court ruled in favor of a Muslim employee who was terminated for refusal to remove her head scarf when dealing with customers, where the employer did not strictly enforce its "company uniform policy" until after September 11, 2001. The court did not accept the employer's argument that allowing an exception for the employee would lead to the need for many other exceptions, making its company uniform policy meaningless.[12]

Safety risks may provide a justifiable basis for a dress code. **For Example,** a court ruled that Kelly Services did not discriminate against a Muslim woman when it decided not to refer her to a client company, Nahan Printing, because she wears a khimar. She had been informed by a Kelly staffing supervisor that "you would have to take your scarf off—you cannot cover your hair," and the applicant replied that she could not remove her khimar because her religion required her to wear it. The EEOC asserted that the employer could have reasonably accommodated her by allowing her to tie her khimar back like people with long hair are allowed to do. However, the Nahan Printing executive explained that hair is permanent; a khimar is different from hair because of the risk that the khimar—like a hat—could fall off into the machinery; and the safety risk would be the worker reaching in and trying to grab it, pulling an individual into a piece of equipment or damaging equipment, or other individuals who are trying to help could potentially be hurt as well.[13]

(b) Body Art Work Rules and Religious Beliefs. Employees have challenged employer bans on body art as religious discrimination, asserting that the employers have not made reasonable efforts to accommodate religious beliefs. EEOC's 1980

[11] *Turgeon v. Howard University*, 571 F. Supp. 679 (D.D.C. 1983).

[12] *EEOC v. Alamo Rent-A-Car*, 432 F. Supp. 2d 1006 (D. Ariz. 2006).

[13] *EEOC v. Kelly Services, Inc.*, 598 F.3d 1022 (8th Cir. 2010).

Guidelines broadly define religion "to include moral or ethical beliefs as to what is right and wrong which are sincerely held with the strength of traditional religious views."[14] The Guidelines do not limit religion to theistic practices or to beliefs professed by organized religions. **For Example,** Kimberly Cloutier was a member of the Church of Body Modification. Costco's grooming policy prohibited any "visible facial or tongue jewelry" in order to present a professional image to its customers. Ms. Cloutier wore an eyebrow ring as a religious practice. Ms. Cloutier rejected Costco's offer to return her to work if she wore a bandage or plastic retainer over the jewelry because it would violate her religious beliefs. The U.S. Court of Appeals determined that her refusal to accept an accommodation short of an exemption was an undue hardship for the employer because an exemption would negatively impact the company's policy of professionalism.[15]

Some courts, however, look for actual proof of harm to the employer in assessing whether undue hardship exists for an employer. **For Example,** the EEOC brought an action against Red Robin Gourmet Burgers, Inc., for failure to provide an exemption from its grooming policy for an employee's religious tattoos surrounding his wrists. The federal district court looked for actual proof of the restaurant's assertion that the tattoos contravened the company's "family-oriented image," such as customer complaints or other evidence, as opposed to the mere assertion. The court concluded that the employer failed to provide sufficient evidence of undue hardship in accommodating an exemption for the employee.[16]

Title VII permits religious societies to grant hiring preferences in favor of members of their religion. It also provides an exemption for educational institutions to hire employees of a particular religion if the institution is owned, controlled, or managed by a particular religious society. The exemption is a broad one and is not restricted to the religious activities of the institution.

5. Sex

Employers who discriminate against female or male employees because of their sex are held to be in violation of Title VII. The EEOC and the courts have determined that the word *sex* as used in Title VII means a person's gender, not the person's sexual orientation. State and local legislation, however, may provide specific protection against discrimination based on sexual orientation.

(A) Height, Weight, and Physical Ability Requirements. Under the *Griggs v. Duke Power* precedent, an employer must be able to show that criteria used to make an employment decision that has a disparate impact on women, such as minimum height and weight requirements, are in fact job related. All candidates for a position requiring physical strength must be given an opportunity to demonstrate their capability to perform the work. Women cannot be precluded from consideration just because they have not traditionally performed such work.

(B) Pregnancy-Related Benefits. Title VII was amended by the Pregnancy Discrimination Act (PDA) in 1978. The amendment prevents employers from treating pregnancy, childbirth, and related medical conditions in a manner different from the manner in which other medical conditions are treated. Thus, women unable to work as a result of pregnancy, childbirth, or related medical conditions must be provided the same benefits as all other workers. These include temporary and long-term disability insurance, sick leave, and other forms of employee benefit programs. An employer who does not provide disability benefits or paid sick leave to other employees is not required to provide them for pregnant workers.[17]

The PDA also protects women from termination or other employment actions because of pregnancy. **For Example,** a catering manager who informed her employer that she would be taking a 12-week leave after childbirth, during the busiest time of the year, and was subsequently fired by her employer for "customer complaints," was able to bring suit against

[14] 29 C.F.R. §1605.1 (1980). The EEOC's definition of religion was derived from early Selective Service cases that moved beyond institutional religions and theistic belief structures in handling exemptions to the draft and military service. See *Welsh v. U.S.*, 398 U.S. 333, 343-44 (1970), which allows for expansion of belief systems to include nonreligious ethical or moral codes.

[15] *Cloutier v. Costco*, 390 F.3d 126 (1st Cir. 2004).

[16] *EEOC v. Red Robin Gourmet Burger, Inc.*, 2005 WL 2090677 (W.D. Wash. Aug. 29, 2005).

[17] In *AT&T Corporation v. Hulteen*, 556 U.S. 701 (2009), the U.S. Supreme Court addressed a current effect of a pre-PDA personnel policy. Prior to the PDA of 1978, AT&T employees on "disability" leave received full-service credit towards retirement benefits for the entire period of absence. Pregnancy at that time was considered a "personal" leave of absence and women on this leave received a maximum service credit of 30 days. Upon retirement, Noreen Hulteen received seven months less service credit for the pre-PDA leave for a pregnancy than she would have had for the same leave time for a disability, and it resulted in a smaller pension benefit. The Court decided against Ms. Hulteen, determining that there was no intent to apply the PDA retroactively, and that AT&T's pre-PDA leave policy was not discriminatory when adopted.

the employer under the PDA, where the employer's reason was a "pretext."[18]

6. Sexual Harassment

Tangible employment action and hostile work environment are two classifications of sexual harassment.

(A) Tangible Employment Action. Sexual harassment classified as *tangible employment action* involves situations in which a supervisor performs an "official act" of the enterprise, such as discharge, demotion, or undesirable reassignment against a subordinate employee because of the employee's refusal to submit to the supervisor's demand for sexual favors. The employer is always vicariously liable for this harassment by a supervisor under the so-called aided-in-the-agency-relation standard. That is, the supervisor is aided in accomplishing the wrongful objective by the existence of the agency relationship. The employer empowered the supervisor as a distinct class of agent to make economic decisions affecting other employees under the supervisor's control. The employer can raise no affirmative defense based on the presence of an employer's antiharassment policy in such a case.

(B) Hostile Work Environment. A second type of sexual harassment classified as *hostile work environment* occurs when a supervisor's conduct does not affect an employee's economic benefits but causes anxiety and "poisons" the work environment for the employee. Such conduct may include unwelcome sexual flirtation, propositions, or other abuses of a sexual nature, including the use of degrading words or the display of sexually explicit pictures.[19] This type of sexual harassment applies to all cases involving supervisors in which the enterprise takes no official act, including constructive discharge cases. The plaintiff must prove severe and pervasive conduct on the supervisor's part to meet the plaintiff's burden of proof.[20] The employer may raise an affirmative defense to liability for damages by proving that (1) it exercised reasonable care to prevent and promptly correct any sexually harassing behavior at its workplace and (2) the plaintiff employee unreasonably failed to take advantage of corrective opportunities provided by the employer. The existence of an employer's sexual harassment policy and notification procedures (see Figure 40-2) will aid the employer in proving the affirmative defense in hostile working environment cases.

(C) Rationale. The "primary objective of Title VII, like that of any statute meant to influence primary conduct, is not to provide redress but to avoid harm."[21] When there is no "official act" of the employer, the employer may raise an affirmative defense. This approach fosters the preventative aspect of Title VII, encouraging employers to exercise reasonable care to prevent and correct sexual harassment while providing damages only when the conduct is clearly attributed to an official action of the enterprise or when the employer has not exercised reasonable care to prevent and correct misconduct. **For Example,** Kim Ellerth alleged that she was subject to constant sexual harassment by her supervisor, Ted Slowik, at Burlington Industries. Slowik made comments about her breasts, told her to "loosen up," and warned, "You know, Kim, I could make your life very hard or very easy at Burlington." When Kim was being considered for promotion, Slowik expressed reservations that she was not "loose enough" and then reached over and rubbed her knee. She received the promotion, however. After other such incidents, she quit and filed charges alleging that she was constructively discharged because of the unendurable working conditions resulting from the hostile work environment created by Slowik. She did not use Burlington's sexual harassment internal complaint procedures. Because she was not a victim of a tangible employment action involving an official act of the enterprise, because she received the promotion sought, the employer will be able to raise an affirmative defense. She will be able to prove severe and pervasive conduct on the part of a supervisor under a hostile work environment theory. However, the employer may defeat liability by proving both

[18] *Newman v. Deer Path Inn*, 1999 WL 1129105 (N.D. Ill. Nov. 7, 1999).

[19] According to EEOC Guidelines §1604.11(f), unwelcome sexual advances, requests for sexual favors, and other verbal or physical conduct of a sexual nature constitute sexual harassment when (1) submission to or rejection of such conduct has the purpose or effect of unreasonably interfering with an individual's work performance or creating an intimidating, hostile, or offensive working environment.

[20] *Oncale v. Sundowner Offshore Services, Inc.*, 523 U.S. 75 (1998). The Supreme Court stated in *Oncale* that it did not intend to turn Title VII into a civility code, and the Court set forth the standard for judging whether the conduct in question amounted to sexual harassment requiring that the conduct be judged from the perspective of a reasonable person in the plaintiff's position, considering all circumstances. The Court warned that "common sense" and "context" must apply in determining whether the conduct was hostile or abusive.

[21] *Faragher v. City of Boca Raton*, 524 U.S. 775, 805 (1998) (citing *Albemale Paper Co. v. Moody*, 422 U.S. 405, 418 (1975)).

FIGURE 40-2 *Employer Procedure—Sexual Harassment*

A. DEVELOP AND IMPLEMENT AN EQUAL EMPLOYMENT POLICY THAT SPECIFICALLY PROHIBITS SEXUAL HARASSMENT AND IMPOSES DISCIPLINE UP TO AND INCLUDING DISCHARGE. SET FORTH SPECIFIC EXAMPLES OF CONDUCT THAT WILL NOT BE TOLERATED SUCH AS:

- UNWELCOME SEXUAL ADVANCES, WHETHER OR NOT THEY INVOLVE PHYSICAL TOUCHING
- SEXUAL EPITHETS AND JOKES; WRITTEN OR ORAL REFERENCES TO SEXUAL CONDUCT; GOSSIP REGARDING ONE'S SEX LIFE; COMMENTS ON AN INDIVIDUAL'S BODY; AND COMMENTS ABOUT AN INDIVIDUAL'S SEXUAL ACTIVITY, DEFICIENCIES, OR PROWESS
- DISPLAY OF SEXUALLY SUGGESTIVE OBJECTS, PICTURES, AND CARTOONS
- UNWELCOME LEERING, WHISTLING, BRUSHING AGAINST THE BODY, SEXUAL GESTURES, AND SUGGESTIVE OR INSULTING COMMENTS
- INQUIRIES INTO ONE'S SEXUAL EXPERIENCES
- DISCUSSION OF ONE'S SEXUAL ACTIVITIES

B. ESTABLISH ONGOING EDUCATIONAL PROGRAMS, INCLUDING ROLE-PLAYING AND FILMS TO DEMONSTRATE UNACCEPTABLE BEHAVIOR.

C. DESIGNATE A RESPONSIBLE SENIOR OFFICIAL TO WHOM COMPLAINTS OF SEXUAL HARASSMENT CAN BE MADE. AVOID ANY PROCEDURE THAT REQUIRES AN EMPLOYEE TO FIRST COMPLAIN TO THE EMPLOYEE'S SUPERVISOR, BECAUSE THAT INDIVIDUAL MAY BE THE OFFENDING PERSON. MAKE CERTAIN COMPLAINANTS KNOW THAT THERE WILL BE NO RETALIATION FOR FILING A COMPLAINT.

D. INVESTIGATE ALL COMPLAINTS PROMPTLY AND THOROUGHLY.

E. KEEP COMPLAINTS AND INVESTIGATIONS AS CONFIDENTIAL AS POSSIBLE AND LIMIT ALL INFORMATION TO ONLY THOSE WHO NEED TO KNOW.

F. IF A COMPLAINT HAS MERIT, IMPOSE APPROPRIATE AND CONSISTENT DISCIPLINE.

that it exercised reasonable care to prevent and correct sexual harassing behavior through its internal company complaint policies and that Kim unreasonably failed to take advantage of the company procedures.[22]

(D) NONSUPERVISORS. An employer is liable for the sexual harassment caused its employees by coworkers or customers only when it knew or should have known of the misconduct and failed to take prompt remedial action.

7. Protection against Retaliation

Section 704(a) sets forth Title VII's antiretaliation provision in the following terms:

> It shall be an unlawful practice for an employer to discriminate against any of his employees or applicants for employment...because he has opposed any practice made an unlawful employment practice by this subchapter [*the opposition clause*], or because he has made a charge, testified, assisted, or participated in any manner

[22] *Burlington Industries, Inc. v. Ellerth*, 524 U.S. 742 (1998); see also *Faragher v. City of Boca Raton*, 524 U.S. 775 (1998). In *Pennsylvania v. Suders*, 542 U.S. 129 (2004), the U.S. Supreme Court reviewed a decision of the Third Circuit Court of Appeals that held that a "constructive discharge," if proved, constituted a "tangible employment action" that renders the employer liable for damages and precludes an affirmative defense. The Supreme Court disagreed with the Third Circuit's reading of its *Ellerth/Faragher* decisions, and made it very clear that "an official act of the enterprise" is necessary for the plaintiff to defeat the employer's right to raise an affirmative defense.

Thinking Things Through

Retaliation—The Number One Risk for Employers

Since the Supreme Court's adoption of a broader definition of retaliation than was used in some judicial circuits prior to the *Burlington* decision, the number of retaliation charges filed with the EEOC has risen dramatically. Management-side employment lawyers see "retaliation as the number one risk for employers today." The litigation costs involved in a single retaliation case are substantial.

The source of unlawful retaliation can emanate from a CEO and other top executives down through middle managers or first-level managers, and it can also originate from organizational tolerance of coworker retaliation. Retaliation occurs in all types and sizes of organizations in all employment sectors of society.

(A) Need for a Comprehensive Program. Employers must develop and implement effective antiretaliation and educational policies and procedures for their top executives, middle managers, and first-level supervisors. Additionally, each organization's highest human resource (HR) officer must have authority to independently investigate and report directly to the CEO, and have authority as well to report to an appropriate board of directors' committee regarding the business justification for proposed or actual employer actions with potential retaliation liability.*

(B) Educational Discussion of Human Nature and the Costs of Retaliation. Employers must recognize that the educational effort is going to be challenging in some cases because of the "human nature" of the controversy. For instance, an employee has gone to a supervisor's supervisor, the HR department, or the EEOC, and has charged his or her supervisor with discrimination based on race, color, religion, sex, national origin, age, or disability. If the complaint is valid, the supervisor should be appropriately disciplined. It may well be that the complaint is perceived by management or coworkers as lacking merit. How can the accused supervisor or coworkers treat the complainant as though nothing has happened? Is it not human nature for the supervisor to want to take materially adverse action against that individual? Would not the ideal solution for the supervisor be to "come up with" a business basis for terminating the complainant?

The adverse economic consequences of such an action to the employer could be severe. For Example, in the Supreme Court's *Crawford v. Metropolitan Government of Nashville*** case, on remand to the district court, the employer contended that it fired Crawford for irregularities in the school system's payroll office for which Crawford was responsible. Crawford testified that she had never previously been disciplined during her 30 years of service with Metro, and local officials did not begin to investigate her job performance until after she disclosed the alleged sexual harassment by the school district's employee relations coordinator. The jury found that the reasons for firing Crawford were pretextual and awarded Crawford $420,000 in compensatory damages, $408,762 in back pay, and $727,496 in front pay, for a total monetary award of approximately $1.56 million.

Thinking Things Through, all employees at all levels should be instructed that because of the adverse impact on the complainant-victim, the potential adverse economic consequence to the employer, and the distraction and disruption to the workforce caused by ongoing litigation, violations of the employer's no-discrimination and no-retaliation policy will been enforced with major discipline—up to and including discharge!

*Some employees with poor records believe that if they have filed complaints with the EEOC, they are immune from all discipline. However, these "protected" employees are not immune from discipline or discharge. The *Burkhart v. American Railcar Industries Inc.* decision, 603 F.3d 472 (8th Cir. 2010), can be used in an educational program for executives, managers, and staff to demonstrate that employees who have engaged in protected activities under Title VII are not immune from discipline or discharge for major performance issues.

**555 U.S. 271 (2009).

> in an investigation, proceeding, or hearing under this subchapter [*the participation clause*].

Some U.S. courts of appeals had held that the retaliation provisions set forth in Section 704(a) of Title VII apply only to retaliation that takes the form of "ultimate employment actions" such as demotions, suspensions, and terminations and do not apply to ministerial matters such as reprimands and poor evaluations. The EEOC believed that the statute prohibits any adverse treatment that is based on a retaliatory motive and is reasonably likely to deter the charging party or others from engaging in protected activity. In *Burlington Northern v. White* (*Burlington*) the Supreme Court held that a plaintiff may pursue a retaliation claim under Title VII if the "employer's challenged action would have been material to a reasonable employee" and likely would have "dissuaded a reasonable worker from making or supporting a charge of discrimination."[23] By focusing

[23] *Burlington Northern Santa Fe Railway Co. v. White*, 548 U.S.133 (2006).

on the materiality of the challenged action and the perspective of a reasonable person, this standard was designed to screen out trivial conduct while capturing those acts that are likely to dissuade employees from complaining or assisting in complaints about discrimination.

Subsequent to the *Burlington* decision, the Supreme Court has settled the broad legal issues regarding retaliation claims under federal antidiscrimination laws, including protection of an employee who speaks out about discrimination not of her own initiative, but in answering questions during an internal investigation into rumors of sexual harassment by her supervisor[24] and also providing a "zone of interest" standard for determining whether third parties' retaliation claims are protected under Title VII.[25]

The EEOC takes the position that claims can be filed for retaliation not only under Title VII but also under the Americans with Disabilities Act, the Age Discrimination in Employment Act, and the Equal Pay Act.

8. National Origin

Title VII protects members of all nationalities from discrimination. The judicial principles that have emerged from cases involving race, color, and gender employment discrimination are generally applicable to cases involving allegations of discrimination related to national origin. Thus, physical standards, such as minimum height requirements, that tend to exclude persons of a particular national origin because of the physical stature of the group have been found unlawful when these standards cannot be justified by business necessity.

Adverse employment action based on an individual's lack of English language skills violates Title VII when the language requirement bears no demonstrable relationship to the successful performance of the job to which it is applied.

In the *Fragrante* case, the court considered whether there was unlawful national origin discrimination when a job applicant with a heavy Filipino accent was not selected for employment.

Fragante v. City and County of Honolulu, 888 F.2d 591 (9th Cir. 1989)

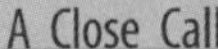

A Close Call

Manuel Fragante applied for a clerk's job with the city and county of Honolulu. Although he placed high enough on a civil service eligibility list to be chosen for the position, he was not selected because of a perceived deficiency in oral communication skills caused by his "heavy Filipino accent." Fragante brought suit, alleging that the defendants had discriminated against him on the basis of his national origin in violation of Title VII of the Civil Rights Act. The district court held that the ability to communicate orally and clearly was a legitimate occupational qualification for the job in question. There was no proof of a discriminatory intent or motive by the defendant. The court dismissed Fragante's complaint. Fragante appealed to the Court of Appeals.

JUDICIAL OPINION

TROTT, C. J.…Preliminarily, we do well to remember that this country was founded and has been built in large measure by people from other lands, many of whom came here—especially after our early beginnings—with a limited knowledge of English. This flow of immigrants has continued and has been encouraged over the years. From its inception, the United States of America has been a dream to many around the world. We hold out promises of freedom, equality, and economic opportunity to many who only know these words as concepts. It would be more than ironic if we followed up our invitation to people such as Manuel Fragante with a closed economic door based on national origin discrimination. It is no surprise that Title VII speaks to this issue and clearly articulates the policy of our nation: unlawful discrimination based on national origin shall not be permitted to exist in the workplace. But, it is also true that there is another important aspect of Title VII: the "preservation of an employer's remaining freedom of choice."…

Accent and national origin are obviously inextricably intertwined in many cases. It would therefore be an easy refuge in this context for an employer unlawfully discriminating against someone based on national origin to state falsely that it was not the person's national origin that caused the employment or promotion problem, but the candidate's

[24] *Crawford v. Metropolitan Government of Nashville*, 555 U.S. 271 (2009).

[25] *Thompson v. North American Stainless, LP*, 131 S.Ct. 863 (2011).

Continued

inability to measure up to the communication skills demanded by the job. We encourage a very searching look by the district courts at such a claim.

An adverse employment decision may be predicated upon an individual's accent when—but only when—it interferes materially with job performance. There is nothing improper about an employer making an *honest* assessment of the oral communication skills of a candidate for a job when such skills are reasonably related to job performance. EEOC Compliance Manual (CCH) 4035 at 3877-78 (1986); *see also Mejia v New York Sheraton Hotel,* 459 F. Supp. 375, 377 (S.D.N.Y. 1978) (Dominican chambermaid properly denied promotion to front desk because of her "inability to articulate clearly or coherently and to make herself adequately understood in...English"); *Carino v University of Oklahoma Board of Regents,* 750 F.2d 815, 819 (10th Cir. 1984) (plaintiff with a "noticeable" Filipino accent was improperly denied a position as supervisor of a dental laboratory where his accent did not interfere with his ability to perform supervisory tasks); *Berke,* 628 F.2d at 981 (employee with "pronounced" Polish accent whose command of English was "well above that of the average adult American" was improperly denied two positions because of her accent)....

...In a letter, dated June 28, 1982, the reasons why [Fragante] was not selected were [stated] as follows:

> *As to the reason for your non-selection we felt the two selected applicants were both superior in their verbal communication ability. As we indicated in your interview, our clerks are constantly dealing with the public and the ability to speak clearly is one of the most important skills required for the position. Therefore, while we were impressed with your educational and employment history, we felt the applicants selected would be better able to work in our office because of their communication skills.*

The interviewers' record discloses that Fragante's third-place ranking was based on his "pronounced accent which is difficult to understand." Indeed, Fragante can point to no facts which indicate that his ranking was based on factors other than his inability to communicate effectively with the public. This view was shared by the district court....

Fragante argues the district court erred in considering "listener prejudice" as a legitimate, nondiscriminatory reason for failure to hire. We find, however, that the district court did not determine defendants refused to hire Fragante on the basis that some listeners would "turn off" a Filipino accent. The district court after trial noted that: "Fragante, in fact, has a difficult manner of pronunciation and the Court further finds as a fact from his general testimony that he would often not respond directly to the questions as propounded."...

In sum, the record conclusively shows that Fragante was passed over because of the deleterious *effect* of his Filipino accent on his ability to communicate orally, not merely because he had such an accent.

[Judgment affirmed]

QUESTIONS

1. Why do courts take a very careful look at nonselection decisions based on foreign accents?
2. Why was Fragante not selected for the clerk's position when he had higher test scores than the two successful candidates?
3. Is it ethical for employers to hire "Americans" over individuals with heavy foreign accents who have the legal credentials to work in the United States?

9. Title VII Exceptions

Section 703 of Title VII defines which employment activities are unlawful. This same section, however, also exempts several key practices from the scope of Title VII enforcement. The most important are the bona fide occupational qualification exception, the testing and educational requirement exception, and the seniority system exception.

(A) Bona Fide Occupational Qualification Exception. It is not an unlawful employment practice for an employer to hire employees on the basis of religion, sex, or national origin in those certain instances where religion, sex, or national origin is a bona fide occupational qualification (BFOQ) reasonably necessary to the normal operation of a particular enterprise. **For Example,** a valid BFOQ is a men's clothing store's policy of hiring only males to do measurements for suit alterations. An airline's policy of hiring only female flight attendants is not a valid BFOQ because such a policy is not reasonably necessary to safely operate an airline.

The Supreme Court, in the *Johnson Controls* case, considered the employer's BFOQ defense to its "fetal-protection policy" to discriminate against women.

UAW v. Johnson Controls, 499 U.S. 187 (1991)

It's a Woman's Choice

Johnson Controls, Inc. (JCI), manufactures batteries. A primary ingredient in the battery manufacturing process is lead. Occupational exposure to lead entails health risks, including the risk of harm to any fetus carried by a female employee.

After eight of its employees became pregnant while maintaining blood lead levels exceeding those set by the Centers for Disease Control (CDC) as dangerous for a worker planning to have a family, JCI announced a new personnel policy. This policy barred all women, except those whose infertility was medically documented, from jobs involving actual or potential lead exposure exceeding OSHA standards. Petitioners brought a class action in the district court, claiming that the policy constituted sex discrimination violative of Title VII of the Civil Rights Act of 1964, as amended. The court granted summary judgment for JCI, and the Court of Appeals affirmed. The case was appealed to Supreme Court.

JUDICIAL OPINION

BLACKMUN, J.…The bias in Johnson Controls' policy is obvious. Fertile men, but not fertile women, are given a choice as to whether they wish to risk their reproductive health for a particular job. Section 703(a) of the Civil Rights Act of 1964, 78 Stat. 255, as amended, 42 U.S.C. § 2000e-2-(a), prohibits sex-biased classifications in terms and conditions of employment, in hiring and discharging decisions, and in other employment decisions that adversely affect an employee's status. Respondent's fetal-protection policy explicitly discriminates against women on the basis of their sex. The policy excludes women with childbearing capacity from lead-exposed jobs and so creates a facial classification based on gender.…

First, Johnson Controls' policy classifies on the basis of gender and childbearing capacity, rather than fertility alone. Respondent does not seek to protect the unconceived children of all its employees. Despite evidence in the record about the debilitating effect of lead exposure on the male reproductive system, Johnson Controls is concerned only with the harms that may befall the unborn offspring of its female employees.…

…We hold that Johnson Controls' fetal-protection policy is sex discrimination forbidden under Title VII unless respondent can establish that sex is a "bona fide occupational qualification."

Under § 703(e)(1) of Title VII, an employer may discriminate on the basis of "religion, sex, or national origin in those certain instances where religion, sex, or national origin is a bona fide occupational qualification reasonably necessary to the normal operation of that particular business or enterprise." We therefore turn to the question whether Johnson Controls' fetal-protection policy is one of those "certain instances" that come within the BFOQ exception.

The BFOQ defense is written narrowly, and this Court has read it narrowly.…Our emphasis on the restrictive scope of the BFOQ defense is grounded on both the language and the legislative history of 703.

The wording of the BFOQ defense contains several terms of restriction that indicate that the exception reaches only special situations. The statute thus limits the situations in which discrimination is permissible to "certain instances" where sex discrimination is "reasonably necessary" to the "normal operation" of the "particular" business. Each one of these terms—certain, normal, particular—prevents the use of general subjective standards and favors an objective, verifiable requirement. But the most telling term is "occupational"; this indicates that these objective, verifiable requirements must concern job-related skills and aptitudes.

Johnson Controls argues that its fetal-protection policy falls within the so-called safety exception to the BFOQ. Our cases have stressed that discrimination on the basis of sex because of safety concerns is allowed only in narrow circumstances. In *Dothard v Rawlinson,* this Court indicated that danger to a woman herself does not justify discrimination. 433 U.S., at 335, 97 S. Ct. at 2729–2730. We there allowed the employer to hire only male guards in contact areas of maximum-security male penitentiaries only because more was at stake than the "individual woman's decision to weigh and accept the risks of employment." *Ibid.* We found sex to be a BFOQ inasmuch as the employment of a female guard would create real risks of safety to others if violence broke out because the guard was a woman. Sex discrimination was tolerated because sex was related to the guard's ability to do the job—maintaining prison security. We also required in *Dothard* a high correlation between sex and ability to perform job functions and refused to allow employers to use sex as a proxy for strength although it might be a fairly accurate one.…

Our case law, therefore, makes clear that the safety exception is limited to instances in which sex or pregnancy actually interferes with the employee's ability to perform the job. This approach is consistent with the language of the BFOQ provision itself, for it suggests that permissible distinctions based on sex must relate to ability to perform the duties of the job. Johnson Controls suggests, however, that we expand the exception to allow fetal-protection policies that mandate particular standards for pregnant or fertile women. We decline to do so. Such an expansion contradicts not only the language of the BFOQ and the narrowness of its exception but the plain language and history of the Pregnancy Discrimination Act.…

Continued

We have no difficulty concluding that Johnson Controls cannot establish a BFOQ. Fertile women, as far as appears in the record, participate in the manufacture of batteries as efficiently as anyone else. Johnson Controls' professed moral and ethical concern about the welfare of the next generation do not suffice to establish a BFOQ of female sterility. Decisions about the welfare of future children must be left to the parents who conceive, bear, support, and raise them rather than to the employers who hire those parents....

A word about tort liability and the increased cost of fertile women in the workplace is perhaps necessary....

More than 40 states currently recognize a right to recover for a prenatal injury based either on negligence or on wrongful death. According to Johnson Controls, however, the company complies with the lead standard developed by OSHA and warns its female employees about the damaging effects of lead. It is worth noting that OSHA gave the problem of lead lengthy consideration and concluded that "there is no basis whatsoever for the claim that women of childbearing age should be excluded from the workplace in order to protect the fetus or the course of pregnancy." Instead, OSHA established a series of mandatory protections which, taken together, "should effectively minimize any risk to the fetus and newborn child."...Without negligence, it would be difficult for a court to find liability on the part of the employer. If, under general tort principles, Title VII bans sex-specific fetal-protection policies, the employer fully informs the woman of the risk, and the employer has not acted negligently; the basis for holding an employer liable seems remote at best....

[Judgment reversed and action remanded]

QUESTIONS

1. Did Johnson Controls' "fetal-protection policy" discriminate against women?
2. JCI's policy was adopted only after eight employees became pregnant but maintained blood lead levels exceeding those set by the CDC as critical. Considering JCI's moral and ethical obligations to the unborn fetuses and its possible extensive liability in future lawsuits, should not the BFOQ defense be available to it?
3. Was JCI's policy within the so-called safety exception to the BFOQ?

(B) Testing and Educational Requirements. Section 703 (h) of the act authorizes the use of "any professionally developed ability test [that is not] designed, intended, or used to discriminate." Employment testing and educational requirements must be "job related"; that is, the employers must prove that the tests and educational requirements bear a relationship to job performance.

Courts will accept prior court-approved validation studies developed for a different employer in a different state or region so long as it is demonstrated that the job for which the test was initially validated is essentially the same job function for which the test is currently being used. **For Example,** a firefighters' test that has been validated in a study in California will be accepted as valid when later used in Virginia. Such application is called *validity generalization.*

The Civil Rights Act of 1991 makes it an unlawful employment practice for an employer to adjust scores or use different cutoff scores or otherwise alter the results of employment tests to favor any race, color, religion, sex, or national origin. This provision addresses the so-called race-norming issue, whereby the results of hiring and promotion tests are adjusted to ensure that a minimum number of minorities are included in application pools.

(C) Seniority System. Section 703(h) provides that differences in employment terms based on a bona fide seniority system are sanctioned so long as the differences do not stem from an intention to discriminate. The term *seniority system* is generally understood to mean a set of rules that ensures that workers with longer years of continuous service for an employer will have a priority claim to a job over others with fewer years of service. Because such rules provide workers with considerable job security, organized labor has continually and successfully fought to secure seniority provisions in collective bargaining agreements.

10. Affirmative Action and Reverse Discrimination

Employers have an interest in affirmative action because it is fundamentally fair to have a diverse and representative workforce. Moreover, affirmative action is an effective means of avoiding litigation costs associated with discrimination cases while at the same time preserving management prerogatives and preserving rights to government contracts. Employers, under **affirmative action plans (AAPs)**, may undertake special recruiting and other efforts to hire and train minorities and women and help them advance within the company. However, the plan may also provide job preferences for minorities and women. Such aspects of affirmative action plans have resulted in numerous lawsuits contending that Title VII of the Civil Rights Act of 1964, the Fourteenth Amendment, or collective bargaining contracts have been violated. The Supreme Court has not been able to settle the many difficult issues before it with a clear and consistent majority. The Court has decided cases narrowly, with individual justices often feeling compelled to speak in concurring or dissenting opinions.

(A) Affirmative Action Programs. In its 1995 *Adarand Constructors, Inc. v. Pena*[26] decision, the Supreme Court placed significant limits on the federal government's authority to implement programs favoring businesses owned by racial minorities over white-owned businesses. The decision reinstated a reverse discrimination challenge to a federal program designed to provide highway construction contracts to "disadvantaged" subcontractors in which race-based presumptions were used to identify such individuals. The Court found the program to be violative of the equal protection component of the Fifth Amendment's due process clause and announced a strict scrutiny standard for evaluating the racial classifications used in the federal government's Disadvantaged Business Enterprise (DBE) program. This standard can be satisfied only by narrowly tailored measures that further compelling governmental interests. The Court stated that programs based on disadvantage rather than race are subject only to the most relaxed judicial scrutiny. Six additional years of litigation ensued before the case involving Adarand Constructors, Inc., was finally concluded on procedural and jurisdictional grounds. *Adarand I*, as it is now called, is now the landmark Supreme Court decision setting forth the legal principles for evaluating affirmative action programs involving race and remedies.

Following the Court's *Adarand I* decision, the EEOC issued a statement on affirmative action, stating, in part:

> *Affirmative action is lawful only when it is designed to respond to a demonstrated and serious imbalance in the workforce, is flexible, is time limited, applies only to qualified workers, and respects the rights of nonminorities and men.*[27]

(B) Reverse Discrimination. When an employer's AAP is not shown to be justified or "unnecessarily trammels" the interests of nonminority employees, it is often called *reverse discrimination.* **For Example,** a city's decision to rescore police promotional tests to achieve specific racial and gender percentages unnecessarily trammeled the interests of nonminority police officers.[28]

(C) Executive Order. Presidential Executive Order 11246 regulates contractors and subcontractors doing business with the federal government. This order forbids discrimination against minorities and women and in certain situations requires affirmative action to be taken to offer better employment opportunities to minorities and women. The Secretary of Labor has established the Office of Federal Contract Compliance Programs (OFCCP) to administer the order.

C. Other Equal Employment Opportunity (EEO) Laws

Major federal laws require equal pay for men and women doing equal work and forbid discrimination against older people and those with disabilities.

11. Equal Pay

The Equal Pay Act prohibits employers from paying employees of one gender a lower wage rate than the rate paid employees of the other gender for equal work, or substantially equal work, in the same establishment for jobs that require substantially equal skill, effort, and responsibility and that are performed under similar working conditions.[29]

[26] 515 U.S. 200 (1995).

[27] *The Steelworkers v. Weber*, 443 U.S. 193 (1979), and *Johnson v. Santa Clara Transportation Agency*, 480 U.S. 617 (1987), are very important U.S. Supreme Court decisions in the developing law on permissible affirmative action plans.

[28] *San Francisco Police Officers Ass'n v. San Francisco*, 812 F.2d 1125 (9th Cir. 1987).

[29] 29 U.S.C. §206 (d)(1).

The Equal Pay Act does not prohibit all variations in wage rates paid men and women but only those variations based solely on gender. The act sets forth four exceptions. Variances in wages are allowed where there is (1) a seniority system, (2) a merit system, (3) a system that measures earnings by quantity or quality of production, or (4) a differential based on any factor other than gender.

12. Age Discrimination

The Age Discrimination in Employment Act (ADEA) forbids discrimination by employers, unions, and employment agencies against persons over 40 years of age.[30] Section 4(a) of the ADEA sets forth the employment practices that are unlawful under the act, including the failure to hire because of age and the discharge of employees because of age. Section 7(b) of the ADEA allows for doubling the damages in cases of willful violations of the act. Consequently, an employer who willfully violates the ADEA is liable not only for back wages and benefits but also for an additional amount as liquidated damages.[31]

The *Rhodes* case deals with an ADEA claim by a discharged employee who was qualified for the job and was within the protected class but was replaced by a younger individual. The employer gave its reasons for the termination, and the jury believed the true reason for the termination was age discrimination.

Rhodes v. Guiberson Oil Tools, 75 F.3d 989 (5th Cir. 1996)

Miffed at Being RIF-ed

Calvin Rhodes began his employment with Dresser Industries in 1955 as an oil industry salesman. In the throes of a severe economic downturn, Rhodes took a job selling oil field equipment at another Dresser company that became Guiberson Oil Tools. After seven months, he was discharged and told the reason was a reduction in force (RIF) but that he would be eligible for rehiring. At that time, he was 56 years old. Within two months, Guiberson hired a 42-year-old salesperson to do the same job. Rhodes sued Guiberson for violating the ADEA. A jury found for plaintiff Rhodes, but a divided panel of the U.S. Court of Appeals for the Fifth Circuit rendered judgment for the employer. The matter was reheard *en banc* before the Court of Appeals.

JUDICIAL OPINION

DAVIS, C. J.…Lee Snyder terminated Rhodes on October 31, 1986. Mr. Snyder told Rhodes he was part of a reduction in force (RIF) because of adverse economic conditions that persisted in the oil field. Snyder told Rhodes, however, that Guiberson would consider him for reemployment. Rhodes' personnel file reflected this same reason for the discharge. It was uncontradicted that Rhodes' position remained unfilled for only 6 weeks and that Guiberson knew at the time of termination or soon after that Rhodes would be replaced.…

Lee Snyder, Rhodes' supervisor, testified via deposition that more than one salesman was clearly needed for the territory. Jack Givens, who had been Snyder's supervisor, testified that he told Snyder to replace Rhodes. Givens also testified that the business required more than one salesman, and that Rick Attaway had been hired to replace Rhodes. James Sewell, Snyder's other supervisor, testified that Rhodes was told that his position was being eliminated and that this statement was not true. The evidence supports a finding that Guiberson did not tell Rhodes the truth about why it was discharging him.

Guiberson Oil's defense at trial was not that Rhodes was RIF'd, but that he was discharged because of his poor work performance. Here, too, Rhodes presented evidence to counter Guiberson's assertion.…

Guiberson officials' testimony…provided support for Rhodes' contention that Guiberson's "productivity" justification of his termination was a pretext for age discrimination. Lee Snyder testified that the memo placed in Rhodes' file explaining that Rhodes lacked technical expertise in downhole operations was substantially true but noted that it was also a "CYA…(cover your _ss)" letter. Snyder testified that Rhodes was a good salesman with strong customer contacts and noted that Jack Givens—Snyder's boss who instructed Snyder to fire Rhodes—once said that he could hire two young salesmen for what some of the older salesmen were costing. Snyder quickly backed away from this statement and said that Givens had said he could hire two *new* salesmen for what some of the *others* were costing him. Givens said he was not aware of telling Snyder this. He also admitted that he had never talked to any of Rhodes' customers about Rhodes' performance as a salesman.

[30] 29 U.S.C. §623.

[31] In *Reeves v. Sanderson Plumbing Products Co., Inc.*, 530 U.S. 133 (2000), the Supreme Court reinstated a $98,490 judgment for Roger Reeves, which included $35,000 in back pay, $35,000 in liquidated damages, and $28,490.80 in front pay, and held that the plaintiff's evidence establishing a prima facie case and showing that the employer's stated reason for the termination was false was sufficient to prove that age was the motivation for the discharge.

Continued

James Sewell, Snyder's other supervisor, testified that he had been very impressed with Rhodes' sales plans and that technical ability was not necessary to sell the product. He also testified that Rhodes had a poor customer base, but admitted that he did not know who Rhodes' customers were, had not talked to any of Rhodes' customers, and had no documentation to support his testimony about Rhodes' poor performance.

Lloyd Allen, the other salesman in the New Orleans office with whom Rhodes was compared, at first testified that his sales were much higher than Rhodes' but clarified on cross-examination that Rhodes' sales during the period in question nearly matched his own. Allen also admitted that the records supporting his testimony may have been incomplete, that Rhodes may have made another sale for which Allen had not credited him, and that another salesman may have been responsible for one of the sales Allen credited to himself....

Based on this evidence, the jury was entitled to find that the reasons given for Rhodes' discharge were pretexts for age discrimination. The jury was entitled to find that Guiberson's stated reason for discharging Rhodes—RIF—was false. Additionally, the reason for discharge that Guiberson Oil proffered in court to meet Rhodes' prima facie case was countered with evidence from which the jury could have found that Rhodes was an excellent salesman who met Guiberson Oil's legitimate productivity expectations. Viewing this evidence in the light most favorable to Rhodes, a reasonable jury could have found that Guiberson Oil discriminated against Rhodes on the basis of his age.

CONCLUSION

After considering all of the evidence in the record under the standard set forth in *Boeing Co. v Shipman,* we are convinced that the district court properly accepted the jury's verdict on liability and willfulness. Guiberson Oil's motion for JNOV was properly denied....

[Judgment affirmed]

QUESTIONS

1. Why did his employer tell Rhodes that he was being terminated because of a RIF, and why did the supervisor Snyder place a memo in Rhodes's file about lacking expertise in downhole operations?
2. Evaluate the statement attributed to Jack Givens, the person who directed that Rhodes be fired, that "I could hire two young salesmen for what some of the older salesmen are costing."
3. Was the jury "entitled" to find that the reasons given by the employer for Rhodes's discharge were merely pretexts for age discrimination?

The Older Workers Benefit Protection Act (OWBPA) of 1990[32] amends the ADEA by prohibiting age discrimination in employee benefits and establishing minimum standards for determining the validity of waivers of age claims. The OWBPA amends the ADEA by adopting an "equal benefit or equal cost" standard, providing that older workers must be given benefits at least equal to those provided for younger workers unless the employer can prove that the cost of providing an equal benefit would be more for an older worker than for a younger one.

Employers commonly require that employees electing to take early retirement packages waive all claims against their employers, including their rights or claims under the ADEA. The OWBPA requires that employees be given a specific period of time to evaluate a proposed package.

Enforcement of the ADEA is the responsibility of the EEOC. Procedures and time limitations for filing and processing ADEA charges are the same as those under Title VII.[33] However, Title VII is materially different from the ADEA with respect to burdens of persuasion, and Supreme Court decisions construing Title VII do not control the construction of the ADEA. Rather, in all cases of disparate treatment, including mixed-motive cases, the plaintiff has to prove, by a preponderance of the evidence, that age was the "but for" cause of the challenged adverse employment action.[34]

[32] 29 U.S.C. §623. This law reverses the Supreme Court's 1989 ruling in *Public Employees Retirement System of Ohio v. Betts*, 492 U.S. 158 (1989), which had the effect of exempting employee benefit programs from the ADEA.

[33] In *Smith v. City of Jackson, Mississippi*, 544 U.S. 228 (2005), the U.S. Supreme Court determined that disparate impact claims of age discrimination are permitted under the ADEA. The Court relied on its Title VII *Griggs v. Duke Power Co.* precedent, which interpreted text identical to that in the ADEA, with the substitution of the word "age" for the words "race, color, religion, sex or national origin," the narrowing of the coverage of the ADEA, which permits employers to take actions that would otherwise be prohibited based on "reasonable factors other than age" (called the *RFOA provision*) and the EEOC regulations permitting disparate impact claims. The dissenting justices asserted that in the nearly four decades since the law's enactment, the Court had never read it to impose liability on an employer without proof of discriminatory intent. The *Smith v. City of Jackson* court decided the disparate impact case before it against the petitioning police officers, finding that the City's larger pay raises to younger employees were based on an RFOA that responded to the City's legitimate goal of retaining its new police officers.

[34] *Gross v. FBL Financial Services, Inc.*, 557 U.S. 167 (2009).

13. Discrimination against Persons with Disabilities

The right of persons with disabilities to enjoy equal employment opportunities was established on the federal level with the enactment of the Rehabilitation Act of 1973.[35]

Although not specifically designed as an employment discrimination measure but as a comprehensive plan to meet many of the needs of persons with disabilities, the act contains three sections that provide guarantees against discrimination in employment. Section 501 is applicable to the federal government itself, Section 503 applies to federal contractors, and Section 504 applies to the recipients of federal funds.

Title I of the Americans with Disabilities Act of 1990 extends employment protection for disabled persons beyond the federal level to state and local governmental agencies and to all private employers with 15 or more employees. The ADA refers to the term *qualified individuals with disabilities* rather than the term *handicapped persons,* which is used in the Rehabilitation Act. In drafting the ADA, Congress relied heavily on the language of the Rehabilitation Act and its regulations. It was anticipated that the body of case law developed under the Rehabilitation Act would provide guidance in the interpretation and application of the ADA. However, protections for individuals were eroded by U.S. Supreme Court decisions in 1999 and 2002. Under these precedents, numerous claims of ADA plaintiffs were extinguished at the threshold stage of proving the plaintiff had a disability. With the cooperation and agreement of both the employer and disability communities, the ADA Amendments Act of 2008 (ADAAA) became law (effective January 1, 2009), effectively overturning the Supreme Court decisions and restoring the original congressional intent of providing broad coverage to protect individuals who face discrimination on the basis of disability.[36] Under Title I of the ADA, an employer may make preemployment inquiries into the ability of a job applicant to perform job-related functions. Under "user-friendly" EEOC guidelines on preemployment inquiries under the ADA, an employer may ask applicants whether they will need reasonable accommodations for the hiring process. If the answer is yes, the employer may ask for reasonable documentation of the disability. In general, the employer may not ask questions about whether an applicant will need reasonable accommodations to do the job. However, the employer may make preemployment inquiries regarding the job applicant's ability to perform job-related functions.

After making a job offer (contingent upon the applicant's passing a medical examination), the employer may rescind the offer if the position in question poses a direct threat to the worker's health or safety. **For Example,** Mario Echazabal was initially offered a job at Chevron's El Segundo, California, oil refinery but the offer was rescinded when the company doctors determined that exposure to chemicals on the job would further damage his already-reduced liver functions (due to hepatitis C) and might potentially kill him. An affirmative defense then exists for employers—not only in cases where hiring an individual poses a direct threat to the health or safety of other employees in the workplace, but also when there is a direct threat to the employee in question. However, the employer must make an individualized medical risk assessment of the employee's condition.[37]

(A) Proving a Case. The Americans with Disabilities Act, as amended in 2008, prohibits employers from discriminating "against a qualified individual on the basis of a disability." A qualified individual with a disability is one "who, with or without reasonable accommodation, can perform the essential functions of the employment position." To establish a viable claim under the act, a plaintiff must prove that (1) he or she has a disability; (2) he or she is qualified for the position; and (3) an employer has discriminated against him or her because of a disability.

The ADAAA defines the term "disability" in a three-pronged definition as follows:

1. *DISABILITY: The term "disability" means, with respect to an individual—*
   - *A. a physical or mental impairment that substantially limits one or more major life activities of such individual;*
   - *B. a record of such an impairment; or*
   - *C. being regarded as having such an impairment.*

[35] 42 U.S.C. §§701–794.

[36] 42 U.S.C. §§12101-12117; P.L. 110-325, S3406 (Sept. 25, 2008).

[37] *Chevron v. Echazabal*, 536 U.S. 73 (2002).

The ADAAA sets forth in unmistakable language that the definition of disability "shall be construed in favor of broad coverage of individuals under this Act" and mandates that the term "substantially limits" be construed accordingly. Moreover, the determination of whether an impairment substantially limits a major life activity must be made without regard to the ameliorative effects of mitigating measures (with the exception that ameliorative effects of ordinary eyeglasses or contact lenses are considered in determinations of whether an impairment substantially limits a major life activity).

The ADAAA includes an expansive compilation of major life activities to confirm the congressional purpose of providing a broad scope of protection to individuals under the ADA.[38]

(B) Reasonable Accommodations under the ADA. Section 101(9) of the ADA defines an employer's obligation to make "reasonable accommodations" for individuals with disabilities to include (1) making existing facilities accessible to and usable by individuals with disabilities and (2) restructuring jobs, providing modified work schedules, and acquiring or modifying equipment or devices.[39] An employer is not obligated under the ADA to make accommodations that would be an "undue hardship" on the employer.

For Example, before passage of the ADA, a supermarket meatcutter unable to carry meat from a refrigerator to a processing area might have been refused clearance to return to work after a back injury until he was able to perform all job functions. Today, under the ADA, it would be the employer's obligation to provide that worker with a cart to assist him in performing the job even if the cart cost $500. However, if the meatcutter was employed by a small business with limited financial resources, an "accommodation" costing $500 might be an undue hardship that the employer could lawfully refuse to make.

Seniority systems provide for a fair and uniform method of treating employees whereby employees with more years of service have a priority over employees with less years of service when it comes to layoffs, job selection, and other benefits such as days off and vacation periods. Seniority rules apply not only under collective bargaining agreements but also to many nonunion job classifications and to nonunion settings. An employer's showing that a requested accommodation conflicts with seniority rules is ordinarily sufficient to show that the requested "accommodation" is not "reasonable." **For Example,** Robert Barnett, a cargo handler for U.S. Airways, Inc., sought a less physically demanding job in the mailroom due to a back injury. Because a senior employee bid the job, U.S. Airways refused Barnett's request to accommodate his disability by allowing him to work the mailroom position. Barnett filed suit under the ADA, and the case progressed to the U.S. Supreme Court, which determined that ordinarily such a requested accommodation is not "reasonable." On remand to the trial court, Barnett was given the opportunity to show that the company allowed exceptions to the seniority rules and he fit within such exceptions.[40]

(C) Failure to Take Action. With courts applying a less-demanding standard for coverage under the amended ADA, employers are finding requests to provide "reasonable accommodations" more common. Employers are liable for failure to take appropriate action regarding requests for reasonable accommodations. **For Example,** Jane Gagliardo had been diagnosed with multiple sclerosis that began affecting her work. The most severe symptom was fatigue, which affected her ability to think, focus, and remember. All of her symptoms were subject to being exacerbated by stress. She sought a "reasonable accommodation" under the ADA of having one major client removed from her job responsibilities. The employer took no action on

[38] Section 3(2) of the act provides:
MAJOR LIFE ACTIVITIES—

A. IN GENERAL.—For purposes of paragraph (1), major life activities include, but are not limited to, caring for oneself; performing manual tasks; seeing, hearing, eating, sleeping, walking, standing, lifting, bending, speaking, breathing, learning, reading, concentrating, thinking, communicating, and working.
B. MAJOR BODILY FUNCTIONS.—For purposes of paragraph (1), a major life activity also includes the operation of major bodily functions, included but not limited to, functions of the immune system; normal cell growth; digestive, bowel, bladder, neurological, brain, respiratory, circulatory, endocrine, and reproductive functions.

[39] A reasonable accommodation may also include "reassignment to a vacant position." In *Duvall v. Georgia-Pacific Consumer Products L.P.*, 607 F.3d 1255 (10th Cir. 2010), the Tenth Circuit Court of Appeals was called upon to decide when a position is "vacant" for the purpose of the ADA. It determined that when a disabled employee seeks the reasonable accommodation of reassignment to a vacant position, positions within the company are "vacant" for the purpose of the ADA when they would be available to similarly suited nondisabled employees to apply for and obtain. Duvall, the employee in question, did not meet his burden of showing that the jobs he sought were available within GP, as they were occupied by a contractor service, and no GP employee had been given a contractor-filled position during the time in question.

[40] *U.S. Airways v. Barnett*, 535 U.S. 391 (2002).

this request. Moreover, while she continued to seek accommodation to no avail, the employer began disciplining her for poor job performance and ultimately fired her. She was awarded $2.3 million in compensation and punitive damages.[41]

Where a disability is obvious and known to the employer, an employee is obligated to engage in an "interactive process" regarding accommodation of a disability, even when a formal request for accommodation is not made. **For Example,** 19-year-old Patrick Brady, who has cerebral palsy, was hired to work as a Wal-Mart pharmacy aide. After "a few days" on the job with no training, he was transferred to the job of collecting shopping carts and garbage in the parking lot. His supervisor, Ms. Chin, regarded Brady as "too slow" and stated that "she knew there was something wrong with him." While Brady did not request reasonable accommodations because his disability was obvious and known to the employer, Wal-Mart was found to be in violation of the ADA, and a judgment of $900,000—including $300,000 in punitive damages—was upheld by the U.S. Court of Appeals.[42]

(D) Exclusions from Coverage of the Act. The act excludes from its coverage employees or applicants who are "currently engaging in the illegal use of drugs." The exclusion does not include an individual who has been successfully rehabilitated from such use or is participating in or has completed supervised drug rehabilitation and is no longer engaging in the illegal use of drugs.

Title V of the act states that behaviors such as transvestitism, transsexualism, pedophilia, exhibitionism, compulsive gambling, kleptomania, pyromania, and psychoactive substance use disorders resulting from current illegal use of drugs are not in and of themselves considered disabilities.

D. Extraterritorial Employment

The Civil Rights Act of 1991 amended both Title VII and the ADA to protect U.S. citizens employed in foreign countries by American-owned or American-controlled companies against discrimination based on race, color, religion, national origin, sex, or disability.[43] The 1991 act contains an exemption if compliance with Title VII or the ADA would cause a company to violate the law of the foreign country in which it is located.

LawFlix

Parenthood (1989) (PG)

A candid movie about raising children that has the added bonus of a scene involving Steve Martin (Gil) and his boss, Dave, in which the two cross quite a few Title VII lines in their discussion about Gil's job and future at the company.

41 *Gagliardo v. Connaught Laboratories, Inc.*, 311 F.3d 565 (3d Cir. 2008). See also *Tobin v. Liberty Mutual Insurance Co.*, 553 F.3d 121 (1st Cir. 2009).
42 *Brady v. Wal-Mart Stores, Inc.*, 531 F.3d 127 (2d Cir. 2008).
43 Section 109 of the Civil Rights Act of 1991, P.L. 102-166, 105 Stat. 1071.

MAKE THE CONNECTION

SUMMARY

Title VII of the Civil Rights Act of 1964, as amended, forbids discrimination on the basis of race, color, religion, sex, or national origin. The EEOC administers the act. Intentional discrimination is unlawful when there is disparate treatment of individuals because of their race, color, religion, gender, or national origin. Also, employment practices that make no reference to race, color, religion, sex, or national origin, but that nevertheless have an adverse or disparate impact on the protected group, are unlawful. In disparate impact cases, the fact that an employer did not intend to discriminate is no defense. The employer must show that there is a job-related business necessity for the disparate impact practice in question. Employers have several defenses they may raise in a Title VII case to explain differences in employment conditions: (1) bona fide occupational qualifications reasonably necessary to the normal operation of the business, (2) job-related professionally developed ability tests, and (3) bona fide seniority systems. If a state EEO agency or the EEOC is not able to resolve the case, the EEOC issues a right-to-sue letter that enables the person claiming a Title VII violation to sue in a federal district court. An affirmative action plan is legal under Title VII provided there is a voluntary "plan" justified as a remedial measure and provided it does not unnecessarily trammel the interests of whites.

Under the Equal Pay Act (EPA), employers must not pay employees of one gender a lower wage rate than the rate paid to employees of the other gender for substantially equal work. Workers over 40 years old are protected from discrimination by the Age Discrimination in Employment Act (ADEA). Employment discrimination against persons with disabilities is prohibited by the Americans with Disabilities Act (ADA). Under the ADA, employers must make reasonable accommodations without undue hardship on them to enable individuals with disabilities to work.

LEARNING OUTCOMES

After studying this chapter, you should be able to clearly explain:

A. Title VII of the Civil Rights Act of 1964, as Amended

LO.1 Explain the difference between the *disparate treatment* theory of employment discrimination and the *disparate impact* theory of employment discrimination

See the discussion of the New Haven Firefighters case in which the city relied on a disparate impact theory and the firefighters asserted disparate treatment, p. 827.

B. Protected Classes and Exceptions

LO.2 List and explain the categories of individuals protected against unlawful employment discrimination under Title VII

See the discussion and examples of protections under Title VII applied to the categories of race and color, religion, sex, and national origin, beginning on p. 830.

LO.3 Recognize, and know the remedies for, sexual harassment in the workplace

See the Ellerth example and the employer's affirmative defense on pp. 832–833.

See Figure 40-2 for a presentation of an employer sexual harassment policy, p. 833.

LO.4 Explain the antiretaliation provision of Title VII

See the *Burlington Northern v. White*, which sets forth the elements of retaliatory discrimination and the remedy provided, pp. 834–835.

See why retaliation is the number one employment liability risk for employers and the antiretaliation actions proposed for employers, p. 834.

C. Other Equal Employment Opportunity (EEO) Laws

LO.5 List and explain the laws protecting equal pay for women and men for equal work, as well as the laws forbidding discrimination on the basis of age and against individuals with disabilities

See the *Rhodes* case with facts and a remedy applicable to age discrimination on pp. 840–841.

See the Patrick Brady example of the attention-getting judgment in a case where the employer failed to recognize its obligation to make a reasonable accommodation, p. 844.

D. Extraterritorial Employment

LO.6 Explain how both Title VII of the Civil Rights Act and the ADA protect from discrimination U.S. citizens working in foreign countries for American-owned and American-controlled businesses

See the discussion of the exemption for employers where compliance would cause a company to violate the law of the country in which it is located, p. 844.

KEY TERMS

affirmative action plans (AAPs)

QUESTIONS AND CASE PROBLEMS

1. List the major federal statutes dealing with the regulation of equal rights in employment.

2. The EEOC notified North American Stainless (NAS) in February 2003 that Miriam Regalado had filed a charge of sex discrimination against the company. Three weeks later NAS fired her coworker Eric Thompson, a person to whom Ms. Regalado was engaged. Thompson had worked for NAS for seven years as a metallurgical engineer. Thompson filed his own charge with the EEOC and a subsequent lawsuit under Title VII of the Civil Rights Act, claiming that NAS fired him to retaliate against Regalado for filing her charge with the EEOC.

   The employer contended that because Thompson did not "engag[e] in any statutorily protected activity, either on his own behalf or on behalf of Miriam Regalado," he is not included in the class of persons for whom Congress created a retaliation cause of action. Thompson argued that the Supreme Court adopted a broad standard in its *Burlington* decision because Title VII's anti-retaliation provision is worded broadly, and that there is no textual basis for making an exception to it for third-party reprisals. Decide. [*Thompson v. North American Stainless Steel, LP*, 131 S.Ct. 863]

3. Dial Corp. implemented a "work tolerance test," which all new employees were required to pass to obtain employment in its Armour Star brand sausage-making department. Of the applicants who passed the test, 97 percent were male and 38 percent were female. The EEOC "demonstrated" that the facially neutral work tolerance test "caused" a disparate impact on women. The defending employer did not deny that the employment practice in question caused the disparate impact. Rather, the employer responded that the test was "job related" and "necessary" to reduce job-related injuries at the plant and submitted evidence that the number of job injuries had been reduced after implementation of the testing program. The evidence showed that the company had initiated numerous other safety initiatives that had an impact on reducing injuries at the plant. After they failed the test, 52 women were denied jobs. Decide this case. [*EEOC v. Dial Corp.*, 2005 WL 2839977 (S.D. Iowa)]

4. Continental Photo, Inc., is a portrait photography company. Alex Riley, a black man, applied for a position as a photographer with Continental. Riley submitted an application and was interviewed. In response to a question on a written application, Riley indicated that he had been convicted for forgery (a felony) six years before the interview, had received a suspended sentence, and was placed on five-year probation. He also stated that he would discuss the matter with his interviewer if necessary. The subject of the forgery conviction was subsequently not mentioned by Continental's personnel director in his interview with Riley. Riley's application for employment was eventually rejected. Riley inquired about the reason for his rejection. The personnel director, Geuther, explained to him that the prior felony conviction on his application was a reason for his rejection. Riley contended that the refusal to hire him because of his conviction record was actually discrimination against him because of his race in violation of Title VII. Riley felt that his successful completion of a five-year probation without incident and his steady work over the years qualified him for the job. Continental maintained that because its photographers handle approximately $10,000 in cash per year, its policy of not hiring applicants whose honesty was questionable was justified. Continental's policy excluded all applicants with felony convictions. Decide. Would the result have been different if Riley had been a convicted murderer? [*Continental Photo, Inc.*, 26 Fair Empl. Prac. Cas. (B.N.A.) 1799 (E.E.O.C.)]

5. Beth Faragher worked part-time and summers as an ocean lifeguard for the Marine Safety Section of the city of Boca Raton, Florida. Bill Terry and David Silverman were her supervisors over the five-year period of her employment. During this period, Terry repeatedly touched the bodies of female employees without invitation and would put his arm around Faragher, with his hand on her buttocks. He made crudely demeaning references to women generally. Silverman once told Faragher, "Date me or clean the toilets for a year." She was not so assigned, however. The city adopted a sexual harassment policy addressed to all employees. The policy was not disseminated to the Marine Safety Section at the beach, however. Faragher resigned and later brought action against the city, claiming a violation of Title VII and seeking nominal damages, costs, and attorneys' fees. The city defended that Terry and Silverman were not acting within the scope of their employment when they engaged in harassing conduct, and the city should not be held liable for their actions. Are part-time employees covered by Title VII? Was Silverman's threat, "Date me or clean toilets for a year," a basis for *quid pro quo* vicarious liability against the city? Decide this case. [*Faragher v. City of Boca Raton*, 524 U.S. 775]

6. Mohen is a member of the Sikh religion whose practice forbids cutting or shaving facial hair and requires wearing a turban that covers the head. In accordance with the dictates of his religion, Mohen wore a long beard. He applied for a position as breakfast cook at the Island Manor Restaurant. He was told that the restaurant's policy was to forbid cooks to wear facial hair for sanitary and good grooming reasons and that he would have to shave his beard or be denied a position. Mohen contended that the restaurant had an obligation to make a reasonable accommodation to his religious beliefs and let him keep his beard. Is he correct?

7. Sylvia Hayes worked as a staff technician in the radiology department of Shelby Memorial Hospital. On October 1, Hayes was told by her physician that she was pregnant. When Hayes informed the doctor of her occupation as an X-ray technician, the doctor advised Hayes that she could continue working until the end of April so long as she followed standard safety precautions. On October 8, Hayes told Gail Nell, the director of radiology at Shelby, that she had discovered she was two months pregnant. On October 14, Hayes was discharged by the hospital. The hospital's reason for terminating Hayes was its concern for the safety of her fetus given the X-ray exposure that occurs during employment as an X-ray technician. Hayes brought an action under Title VII, claiming that her discharge was unlawfully based on her condition of pregnancy. She cited scientific evidence and the practice of other hospitals where pregnant women were allowed to remain in their jobs as X-ray technicians. The hospital claimed that Hayes's discharge was based on business necessity. Moreover, the hospital claimed that the potential for future liability existed if an employee's fetus was damaged by radiation encountered at the workplace. Decide. [*Hayes v. Shelby Memorial Hospital*, 546 F. Supp. 259 (N.D. Ala.)]

8. Overton suffered from depression and was made sleepy at work by medication taken for this condition. Also, because of his medical condition, Overton needed a work area away from public access and substantial supervision to complete his tasks. His employer terminated him because of his routinely sleeping on the job, his inability to maintain contact with the public, and his need for supervision. Overton argued that he is a person with a disability under the ADA and the Rehabilitation Act, fully qualified to perform the essential functions of the job, and that the employer had an obligation to make reasonable accommodations, such as allowing some catnaps as needed and providing some extra supervision. Decide. [*Overton v. Reilly*, 977 F.2d 1190 (7th Cir.)]

9. A teenage female high school student named Salazar was employed part-time at Church's Fried Chicken Restaurant. Salazar was hired and supervised by Simon Garza, the assistant manager of the restaurant. Garza had complete supervisory powers when the restaurant's manager, Garza's roommate, was absent. Salazar claimed that while she worked at the restaurant, Garza would refer to

her and all other females by a Spanish term that she found objectionable. According to Salazar, Garza once made an offensive comment about her body and repeatedly asked her about her personal life. On another occasion, Garza allegedly physically removed eye shadow from Salazar's face because he claimed it was unattractive. Salazar also claimed that one night she was restrained in a back room of the restaurant while Garza and another employee fondled her. Later that night, when Salazar told a customer what had happened, she was fired. Salazar brought suit under Title VII against Garza and Church's Fried Chicken, alleging sexual harassment. Church's, the corporate defendant, maintained that it should not be held liable under Title VII for Garza's harassment. Church's based its argument on the existence of a published fair treatment policy. Decide. [*Salazar v. Church's Fried Chicken, Inc.*, 44 Fair Empl. Prac. Cas. (B.N.A.) 472 (S.D. Tex.)]

10. John Chadbourne was hired by Raytheon on February 4, 1980. His job performance reviews were uniformly high. In December 1983, Chadbourne was hospitalized and diagnosed with AIDS. In January 1984, his physician informed Raytheon that Chadbourne was able to return to work. On January 20, 1984, Chadbourne took a return-to-work physical examination required by Raytheon. The company's doctor wrote the County Communicable Disease Control Director, Dr. Juels, seeking a determination of the appropriateness of Chadbourne's returning to work. Dr. Juels informed the company that "contact of employees to an AIDS patient appears to pose no risk from all evidence accumulated to date." Dr. Juels also visited the plant and advised the company doctor that there would be no medical risk to other employees at the plant if Chadbourne returned to work. Raytheon refused to reinstate Chadbourne to his position until July 19, 1984. Its basis for denying reinstatement was that coworkers might be at risk of contracting AIDS. Was Raytheon entitled to bar Chadbourne from work during the six-month period of January through July? [*Raytheon v. Fair Employment and Housing Commission*, 261 Cal. Rptr. 197 (Ct. App.)]

11. Connie Cunico, a white woman, was employed by the Pueblo, Colorado, School District as a social worker. She and other social workers were laid off in seniority order because of the district's poor financial situation. However, the school board thereafter decided to retain Wayne Hunter, a black social worker with less seniority than Cunico because he was the only black on the administrative staff. No racial imbalance existed in the relevant workforce with black persons constituting 2 percent. Cunico, who was rehired over two years later, claimed that she was the victim of reverse discrimination. She stated that she lost $110,361 in back wages plus $76,000 in attorneys' fees and costs. The school district replied that it was correct in protecting with special consideration the only black administrator in the district under the general principles it set forth in its AAP. Did the employer show that its affirmative action in retaining Hunter was justified as a remedial measure? Decide. [*Cunico v. Pueblo School District No. 6*, 917 F.2d 431 (10th Cir.)]

12. Della Janich was employed as a matron at the Yellowstone County Jail in Montana. The duties of the position of matron resemble those of a parallel male position of jailer. Both employees have the responsibility of booking prisoners, showering and dressing them, and placing them in the appropriate section of the jail depending on the offender's sex. Because 95 percent of the prisoners at the jail were men and 5 percent were women, the matron was assigned more bookkeeping duties than the jailer. At all times during Janich's employment at the jail, her male counterparts received $125 more per month as jailers. Janich brought an action under the Equal Pay Act, alleging discrimination against her in her wages because of her sex. The county sheriff denied the charge. Decide. [*Janich v. Sheriff*, 29 Fair Empl. Prac. Cas. (B.N.A.) 1195 (D. Mont.)]

13. Following a decline in cigarette sales, L & M, Inc., hired J. Gfeller as vice president of sales and charged him to turn around the sales decline. After receiving an analysis of the ages of sales personnel and first-line management, Gfeller and his assistant, T. McMorrow, instituted an intensive program of personnel changes that led to the

termination of many older managers and sales representatives. A top manager who sought to justify keeping an older manager was informed that he was "not getting the message." Gfeller and McMorrow emphasized that they wanted young and aggressive people and that the older people were not able to conform or adapt to new procedures. R. E. Moran, who had been rated a first-rate division manager, was terminated and replaced by a 27-year-old employee. Gfeller and McMorrow made statements about employees with many years' experience: "It was not 20 years' experience, but rather 1 year's experience 20 times." The EEOC brought suit on behalf of the terminated managers and sales representatives. The company vigorously denied any discriminatory attitude with regard to age. Decide. [*EEOC v. Liggett and Meyers, Inc.*, 29 F.E.P. 1611 (E.D.N.C.)]

14. Mazir Coleman had driven a school bus for the Casey County, Kentucky, Board of Education for four years. After that time, Coleman's left leg had to be amputated. Coleman was fitted with an artificial leg and underwent extensive rehabilitation to relearn driving skills. When his driving skills had been sufficiently relearned over the course of four years, Coleman applied to the county board of education for a job as a school bus driver. The board refused to accept Coleman's application, saying that it had no alternative but to deny Coleman a bus-driving job because of a Kentucky administrative regulation. That regulation stated in part: "No person shall drive a school bus who does not possess both of these natural bodily parts: feet, legs, hands, arms, eyes, and ears. The driver shall have normal use of the above named body parts." Coleman brought an action under the Rehabilitation act, claiming discrimination based on his physical handicap. The county board of education denied this charge, claiming that the reason they rejected Coleman was because of the requirement of the state regulation. Could Coleman have maintained an action for employment discrimination in light of the state regulation on natural body parts? Decide. [*Coleman v. Casey County Board of Education*, 510 F. Supp. 301 (N.D. Ky.)]

15. Marcia Saxton worked for Jerry Richardson, a supervisor at AT&T's International Division. Richardson made advances to Saxton on two occasions over a three-week period. Each time Saxton told him she did not appreciate his advances. No further advances were made, but thereafter Saxton felt that Richardson treated her condescendingly and had stopped speaking to her on a social basis at work. Four months later, Saxton filed a formal internal complaint, asserting sexual harassment, and went on "paid leave." AT&T found inconclusive evidence of sexual harassment but determined that the two employees should be separated. Saxton declined a transfer to another department, so AT&T transferred Richardson instead. Saxton still refused to return to work. Thereafter, AT&T terminated Saxton for refusal to return to work. Saxton contended she had been a victim of hostile working environment sexual harassment. AT&T argued that while the supervisor's conduct was inappropriate and unprofessional, it fell short of the type of action necessary for sexual harassment under federal law (the *Harris* case). Decide. [*Saxton v. AT&T Co.*, 10 F.3d 526 (7th Cir.)]

PART 7

Business Organizations

© Manuel Gutjahr/iStockphoto.com

CHAPTER 41

© Manuel Gutjahr/iStockphoto.com

Types of Business Organizations

learningoutcomes

After studying this chapter, you should be able to

LO.1 Explain the advantages and disadvantages of the three principal forms of business organizations

LO.2 Recognize that the rules of law governing the rights and liabilities of joint ventures are substantially the same as those that govern partnerships

LO.3 Evaluate whether a business arrangement is a franchise protected under state or federal law

LO.4 Explain how the rights of the parties to a franchise agreement are determined by their contract

LO.5 Explain why freedom from vicarious liability is a reason for franchisors to use the franchise format

LO.6 Recognize the implications of the misclassifications of employees as franchisee-independent contractors

What form of legal organization should you have for your business? The answer will be found in your needs for money, personnel, control, tax and estate planning, and protection from liability.

A. Principal Forms of Business Organizations

The law of business organizations may be better understood if the advantages and disadvantages of proprietorships, partnerships, and corporations are first considered.

1. Individual Proprietorships

A **sole or individual proprietorship** is a form of business ownership in which one individual owns the business. The owner may be the sole worker of the business or employ as many others as needed to run the concern. Individual proprietorships are commonly used in retail stores, service businesses, and agriculture.

(a) Advantages. The proprietor or owner is not required to expend resources on organizational fees. The proprietor, as the sole owner, controls all decisions and receives all profits. The net earnings of the business are not subject to corporate income taxes but are taxed only as personal income.

(b) Disadvantages. The proprietor is subject to unlimited personal liability for the debts of the business and cannot limit this risk. The investment capital in the business is limited by the resources of the sole proprietor. Because all contracts of the business are made by the owner or in the owner's name by agents of the owner, the authority to make contracts terminates on the death of the owner, and the business is subject to disintegration.

2. Partnerships, LLPs, and LLCs

A **partnership** involves the pooling of capital resources and the business or professional talents of two or more individuals whose goal is making a profit. Law firms, medical associations, and architectural and engineering firms may operate under the partnership form. Today, however, these firms may convert to a **limited liability partnership (LLP)**. A wide range of small manufacturing, retail, and service businesses operate as partnerships. These businesses may operate under the form of organization called **limited liability company (LLC)**, which allows tax treatment as a partnership with limited liability for the owners.

(a) Advantages. The partnership form of business organization allows individuals to pool resources and then initiate and conduct their business without the requirement of a formal organizational structure.

(b) Disadvantages. Major disadvantages of a partnership are the unlimited personal liability of each partner and the uncertain duration of the business because the partnership is dissolved by the death of one partner. Unlimited personal liability is remedied by the LLC form of business organization. Professional partnerships that convert to an LLP shield innocent partners from personal liability beyond their investment in the firm.

3. Corporations

Business **corporations** exist to make a profit and are created by government grant. State statutes regulating the creation of corporations require a corporate structure consisting of shareholders, directors, and officers. The shareholders, as the owners of the business, elect a board of directors, which is responsible for managing the business. The directors employ officers, who serve as the agents of the business and run day-to-day operations. Corporations range in size from incorporated one-owner enterprises to large multinational concerns.

(a) Advantages. The major advantage to the shareholder, or investor, is that the shareholder's risk of loss from the business is limited to the amount of capital she invested in the business or paid for shares. This factor, coupled with the free transferability of corporate shares, makes the corporate form of business organization attractive to investors.

By purchasing shares, a large number of investors may contribute the capital assets needed to finance large business enterprises. As the capital needs of a business expand, the corporate form becomes more attractive.

A corporation is a separate legal entity capable of owning property, contracting, suing, and being sued in its own name. It has perpetual life. In other words, a corporation is not affected by the death of any of its shareholders or the transfer of their shares. In contrast to the case of a partnership or proprietorship, the death of an owner has no legal effect on the corporate entity.

(B) DISADVANTAGES. A corporation is required to pay corporate income taxes. Shareholders are required to pay personal income taxes on the amount received when they receive a distribution of profits from the corporation. This is a form of double taxation.

Incorporation involves the expenditure of funds for organizational expenses. Documents necessary for the formation of a corporation, which are required by state law, must be prepared, and certain filing fees must be paid. State corporation laws may also require filing an annual report and other reports.

B. SPECIALIZED FORMS OF ORGANIZATIONS

CPA 4. Joint Ventures

A **joint venture**, or joint adventure, is a relationship in which two or more persons or entities combine their labor or property for a single business undertaking and share profits and losses equally or as otherwise agreed.[1] **For Example,** Front-Line Promotions and Insights Promotions formed a "joint venture" to produce two events with musical and celebrity talent at the Sugar Mill in New Orleans on February 16 and February 17, 2008, the NBA All-Star Weekend in New Orleans. The entities agreed to split the costs and revenues from the events.[2]

A joint venture is similar in many respects to a partnership. It differs primarily in that the joint venture typically involves the pursuit of a single enterprise or transaction, although its accomplishment may require several years. A partnership is generally a continuing business or activity but may be expressly created for a single transaction. Because the distinction is so insubstantial, most courts hold that joint ventures are subject to the same principles of law as partnerships. **For Example,** the Virginia Uniform Partnership Act was utilized to enable PGI, Inc., to sue Rathe Productions, Inc., for conversion of its share of a settlement agreement with the Smithsonian Institute because PGI/Rathe was involved in a joint venture and the "rules of law governing the rights, duties and liabilities of joint ventures are substantially the same as those which govern partnerships."[3]

Joint ventures may choose to operate their venture in the corporate form without divesting themselves of the rights and obligations of joint venturers, as presented in the *Kurwa v. Kislinger* case.

Kurwa v. Kislinger, 138 Cal. Rptr.3d 610 (Cal. App. 2012)

Unilateral Action: Years of Litigation

Prior to 1992, Drs. Kurwa and Kislinger maintained their own ophthalmologist practices in the San Gabriel Valley. They subsequently agreed to pursue a new business model at that time by creating a joint venture where, under what is called a "capitation agreement," HMOs would pay the joint venture a monthly fee based on the number of members of the HMO in exchange for their ophthalmologist services. They signed a handwritten "Agreement between Bud and Mark" in which they outlined the structure within which they would solicit business and share profits. They agreed to incorporate as a professional medical corporation to operate their joint venture business. Thus, Trans Valley Eye Associates, Inc., was formed. The joint venture had capitation agreements with three HMOs serving some 200,000 patients in the year before its demise and earned revenues of $2 million. Beginning September 26, 2003, Dr. Kurwa was suspended from the practice of medicine for 60 days and placed on five years' probation by the California Medical Board. The doctors also discovered at that time that their corporation did not contain a specific statement in its Articles of Incorporation that it was a

[1] See *Abeles Inc. v. Creekstone Farms Premium Beef*, LLC, 2009 WL 2495802 (E.D.N.Y. March 30, 2009), for an in-depth discussion of the law of joint ventures. The court referenced a precedent, stating: "A joint venture has been described as a nebulous concept whose boundaries are not precisely drawn. Defining a joint venture is easier than identifying it, for each case depends upon its own facts."

[2] Boxer Floyd "Money Mayweather" was to appear at the event on February 17, 2008, and be paid $25,000, but he did not appear. The joint venture sued him for breach of contract and consequential damages. In *Front-Line Inc. v. Mayweather Promotions, LLC*, 2009 U.S. Lexis 27136 (E.D.N.Y. April 2, 2009), the U.S. District Court allowed Front-Line Promotions to pursue its claim against Mayweather Promotions, LLC.

[3] *PGI, Inc. v. Rathe Productions, Inc.*, 576 S.E.2d 438 (Va 2003). See also *Pugliese v. Mandello*, 871 N.Y.S.2d 174 (A.D. 2008).

Continued

professional medical corporation, thus making it an ordinary for-profit corporation. In this setting Dr. Kislinger unilaterally terminated the joint venture and appropriated for himself, without any compensation to Dr. Kurwa, the very successful 11-year venture. Dr. Kislinger contended that Dr. Kurwa had no standing to bring an action against him on behalf of Trans Valley. From adverse decisions in the trial court, Dr. Kurwa appealed.

JUDICIAL OPINION

KRIEGLER, J.... Courts in other states have likewise recognized that joint venturers may choose to operate their venture in the corporate form without divesting themselves of the rights and obligations of joint venturers. (See, e.g., *Richbell Info. Servs. v. Jupiter Partners* (2003) 309 A.D.2d 288, 765 N.Y.S.2d 575, 585; *Yoder v. Hooper* (Colo.App.1984) 695 P.2d 1182, 1187–1188; *Jolin v. Oster* (1969) 44 Wis.2d 623, 172 N.W.2d 12, 17; *Campbell v. Campbell* (1967) 198 Kan. 181, 422 P.2d 932, 941.)

Here, the complaint alleges that Drs. Kurwa and Kislinger formed a joint venture to provide medical services to HMO patients by entering into capitation agreements with local medical groups. The doctors incorporated the joint venture, and issued shares of stock to the two principals. Dr. Kislinger induced the HMOs to terminate their contracts with the corporation and to enter into capitation agreements exclusively with his medical corporation. These facts state a cause of action for breach of fiduciary duty owed by one joint venturer to another.

... Dr. Kurwa did not sue solely in his individual capacity, but derivatively on behalf of Trans Valley. In Trans Valley's cause of action for breach of fiduciary duty, the complaint alleged that Dr. Kislinger misappropriated assets of the corporation in breach of his fiduciary duties as a director. "It is without dispute that in California, corporate directors owe a fiduciary duty to the corporation and its shareholders and now as set out by statute, must serve 'in good faith, in a manner such director believes to be in the best interests of the corporation and its shareholders.' ... Dr. Kurwa maintains that Dr. Kislinger was obliged to correct the formal defects which precluded the corporation from practicing medicine; that is, to amend Trans Valley's Articles of Incorporation to include the statement required by Corporations Code section 13404, and to register the corporation with the California Medical Board, and that his failure to do so damaged Trans Valley. These allegations state a derivative cause of action on behalf of Trans Valley, which Dr. Kurwa is entitled to pursue on behalf of the corporation.

In short, because the factual allegations of the complaint state a cause of action against Dr. Kislinger for breach of fiduciary duty, the trial court erred in dismissing Dr. Kurwa's lawsuit based on the absence of a fiduciary duty on the part of Dr. Kislinger.

Finally, Dr. Kislinger, citing the California Code of Regulations which provides that "Where there are two or more shareholders in a professional corporation and one of the shareholders [¶] ... [¶] [b]ecomes a disqualified person[5] as defined in Section 13401(d) of the Corporations Code [, h]is or her shares shall be sold and transferred to the corporation, its shareholders or other eligible licensed persons on such terms as are agreed upon." contends that, even if he had resolved the defect in Trans Valley's corporate status as Dr. Kurwa contends he had a duty to do, upon the latter's suspension from the practice of medicine in September 2003, Dr. Kurwa was precluded from owning shares in any professional medical corporation during the period of his suspension: "the regs which we cited say he must give up his stock in a medical corporation, [and] has no right to get it back." That may be so, but that does not mean that Dr. Kislinger is not required to account to Dr. Kurwa for the latter's interest in the parties' joint enterprise. Indeed, due to Dr. Kislinger's alleged actions in abandoning the joint venture and appropriating its assets to his own benefit, Dr. Kurwa was deprived of the opportunity to sell his shares in Trans Valley to another eligible licensed person as contemplated by the cited regulation.

[Reversed.]

QUESTIONS

1. Describe the formation of the joint venture between Drs. Kurwa and Kislinger.
2. What is meant by the statement that "Dr. Kislinger unilaterally terminated the joint venture"?
3. Did the two doctors owe a fiduciary duty to each other as joint venturers under the Trans Valley Eye Associates, Inc., business organization?

(A) DURATION OF JOINT VENTURE. A joint venture continues for the time specified in the agreement of the parties. In the absence of a fixed-duration provision, a joint venture is ordinarily terminable at the will of any participant. When the joint venture clearly relates to a particular transaction, such as the construction of a specified bridge, the joint venture ordinarily lasts until the particular transaction or project is completed or becomes impossible to complete.

(B) Liability to Third Persons. The conclusion that persons are joint venturers is important when a suit is brought by or against a third person for personal injuries or property damage. If there is a joint venture, the fault or negligence of one venturer will be imputed to the other venturers.[4]

5. Unincorporated Associations

An **unincorporated association** is a combination of two or more persons for the furtherance of a common purpose.[5] No particular form of organization is required. Any conduct or agreement indicating an attempt to associate or work together for a common purpose is sufficient.[6]

The authority of an unincorporated association over its members is governed by ordinary contract law. Except when otherwise provided by statute, an unincorporated association does not have any legal existence apart from its members. Thus, an unincorporated association cannot sue or be sued in its own name.

Generally, the members of an unincorporated association are not liable for the debts or liabilities of the association by the mere fact that they are members. It must usually be shown that they authorized or ratified the act in question. If either authorization or ratification by a particular member can be shown, that member has unlimited liability for the act.

6. Cooperatives

A **cooperative** consists of a group of two or more independent persons or enterprises that cooperate for a common objective or function. Thus, farmers may pool their farm products and sell them. Consumers may likewise pool their orders and purchase goods in bulk.

(A) Incorporated Cooperatives. Statutes commonly provide for the special incorporation of cooperative enterprises. Such statutes often provide that any excess of payments over the cost of operation shall be refunded to each participant member in direct proportion to the volume of business that the member has done with the cooperative. This contrasts with the payment of a dividend by an ordinary business corporation in which the payment of dividends is proportional to the number of shares held by the shareholder and is unrelated to the extent of the shareholder's business activities with the enterprise.

(B) Antitrust Law Exemption. The agreement by the members of sellers' cooperatives that all products shall be sold at a common price is an agreement to fix prices. Therefore, the sellers' cooperative is basically an agreement in restraint of trade and a violation of antitrust laws. The Capper-Volstead Act of 1922 expressly exempts normal selling activities of farmers' and dairy farmers' cooperatives from the operation of the federal Sherman Antitrust Act so long as the cooperatives do not conspire with outsiders to fix prices.

C. The Franchise Business Format

In individual situations, *franchising* is a *method* of doing business, not a *form* of business organization. A franchisor or franchisee could be a sole proprietor, a partnership, a limited liability company, or a corporation. It is a *business format*, as opposed to a business organization. Franchising relies on contract law to set forth the rights and obligations of the parties. However, the Federal Trade Commission Act and certain state laws require disclosure. Any federal and/or state laws regulating securities, intellectual property, antitrust violations, sales, agency, employment, and tort law apply to franchises.

Section 5 of the Federal Trade Commission Act prohibits deceptive, manipulative, or unfair business practices,[7] and state deceptive trade practices acts similarly prohibit such practice.

As defined by the Federal Trade Commission (FTC) a commercial business arrangement is a **franchise** if it satisfies three definitional elements: the

[4] *Kim v. Chamberlain*, 504 So.2d 1213 (Ala. App. 1987).

[5] The National Conference of Commissioners on Uniform State Laws has adopted a Uniform Unincorporated Nonprofit Association Act. In addition, community associations are being formed, primarily for the purpose of community planning and environmental protection.

[6] Under a policy of minimizing judicial involvement in private organizations, courts ordinarily will refrain from reviewing decisions on the internal-governance issues of unincorporated private associations where the organization's own adjudicatory procedures are followed. In *Tackney v. United States Naval Academy Alumni Association Inc.*, 971 A.2d 309 (Md. App. 2009), involving an incorporated private association, the court found that judicial intervention was not warranted regarding the election of trustees in 2006, because the alumni board's actions were not fraudulent or arbitrary.

[7] 15 U.S.C. §45.

franchisor must (1) promise to provide a trademark or other commercial symbol; (2) promise to exercise significant control or provide significant assistance in the operation of the business; and (3) require a minimum payment of at least $500 during the first six months of operations.[8]

7. Definition and Types of Franchises

The **franchisor** is the party granting the franchise, and the **franchisee** is the person to whom the franchise is granted. There are three principal types of franchises. The first is a *manufacturing* or *processing franchise*, in which the franchisor grants the franchisee authority to manufacture and sell products under the trademark(s) of the franchisor. The franchisor may supply an essential ingredient in a processing franchise, such as the syrup for an independent regional Coca-Cola bottling company. The second type of franchise is a *service franchise*, whereby the franchisee renders a service to customers under the terms of a franchise agreement. The drain-cleaning service provided by Roto-Rooter is an example of a service franchise. The third type is a *distribution franchise*, in which the franchisor's products are sold to a franchisee, who then resells to customers in a geographical area. Exxon Mobil Oil Company's products are often sold to retail customers through independent distribution franchises.

A common issue in litigation under state laws protecting franchisees or dealers is whether the business arrangement is a franchise or dealership under the applicable state law.[9] The *Girl Scouts of Manitou* case dealt with such a question.

Girl Scouts of Manitou v. GSUSA, 549 F.3d 1079 (7th Cir. 2008)

Are Girl Scouts "Dealers"?

The Girl Scouts of the United States of America (GSUSA) is led by the National Council. Local councils are governed by their own independent board of directors, and employ their own officers and professional staff and are responsible for their own financial health. For a nominal fee, GSUSA issues a charter to the local council, which grants to that council "the right to develop, manage, and maintain Girl Scouting throughout the areas of its jurisdiction, including the right to use GSUSA's names and protected marks." Plaintiff Manitou Council is one of GSUSA's local councils. It employs a full-time staff of 17 people. It owns significant real property, including two large Girl Scout camps and a corporate office building. Manitou asserts that nearly 100 percent of its annual revenues derive from the sale of Girl Scout merchandise and services, private donations, and investment income from Manitou's reserve funds. Girl Scout cookie sales alone generate more than $1 million in revenue each year. While the charter was still in effect, Manitou rejected the GSUSA merger directive, and GSUSA sought to unilaterally remove more than half of Manitou's jurisdiction. Manitou sued GSUSA under the Wisconsin Fair Dealership Law (WFDL), seeking a preliminary injunction. From a ruling in favor of GSUSA, Manitou appealed.

JUDICIAL OPINION

KANNE, Circuit J.... The Wisconsin legislature enacted the WFDL to promote "fair business relations between dealers and grantors, ... the continuation of dealerships on a fair basis," and "[t]o protect dealers against unfair treatment by grantors, who inherently have superior economic power and superior bargaining power in the negotiation of dealerships." Specifically, the WFDL makes it illegal for any grantor to "terminate, cancel, fail to renew or substantially change the competitive circumstances of a dealership agreement without good cause." A party properly seeking protection under the WFDL enjoys a statutory presumption of irreparable harm.

The WFDL protects only a "dealer," defined as an organization that is the grantee of a dealership. *Id.* § 135.02 (2). The statute specifies three requirements for a dealership to exist. First, that there be a contract or agreement between the two parties. *Id.* Second, that the agreement provide the grantee the right to do one of three things: (1) sell goods or services; (2) distribute goods or services; or (3) use the grantor's trademarks, names, logos, or other commercial symbols. Third, that there exist a "community of interest" between the parties "in the business of offering, selling or distributing goods or services at wholesale, retail, by lease, agreement or

[8] Many business opportunities are not franchises and are subject to federal and state "business opportunity" laws. Companies that market and sell products to persons to enable them to start a business may be subject to these laws. The FTC issued a new "business opportunity rule" effective March 1, 2012, 12 C.F.R. Part 437. It exempts franchisors covered by the FTC Franchise Rule from the new rule.

[9] *Missouri Beverage Co., Inc. v. Sheldon Brothers, Inc.*, 669 F.3d 873 (8th Cir. 2012).

Continued

otherwise." Applying the facts to these requirements, we conclude that Manitou is a dealer and therefore falls within the purview of the WFDL.

AGREEMENT BETWEEN THE PARTIES

For a dealership to exist, the first requirement is that there be an agreement between the parties. ... GSUSA does not contest the presence of an agreement between GSUSA and Manitou.

SALE OR DISTRIBUTION OF GOODS OR SERVICES; USE OF PROTECTED MARKS

The second requirement for a dealership is that the agreement must grant to Manitou "the right to sell or distribute goods or services, or use a trade name, trademark, service mark, logotype, advertising or other commercial symbol." Although any one of these three functions would suffice to satisfy the requirement, Manitou succeeds on all three grounds.

Manitou sells and distributes goods. Manitou's primary revenue stream derives from its annual sale of Girl Scout cookies, which nets Manitou a yearly profit in excess of $1 million. During this process, Manitou's members both solicit sales and distribute the products....

Manitou distributes services—namely, educational and community services afforded by participation in Girl Scouting....

Manitou makes exhaustive use of GSUSA's names and marks. These names and marks, which are the essence of Manitou's identity, provide Manitou with its entire reason for being....

... GSUSA's argument that the Girl Scouts are not "'dealers' of anything," emphasizing the word "dealer" as if its members are accused of selling drugs on the street corner, is unavailing. It matters not whether we would call the Girl Scouts "dealers" in everyday conversation; what matters is only how the statute defines the term, and the activities of Manitou clearly fall within its definition.

... Finding that Manitou qualifies as a dealer requires no expansion of the WFDL. Manitou is a business. It sells and distributes goods. It distributes services. It makes extensive use of GSUSA's marks and names. These requirements satisfy the statute's plain language, which the Wisconsin Supreme Court has recognized was designed "to encompass an extraordinarily diverse set of business relationships not limited to the traditional franchise....

... Because the balance of irreparable harms, including the public interest, weighs entirely in Manitou's favor, we need not conduct a lengthy examination to quantify the likelihood of Manitou's success on the merits of its claims....

CONCLUSION

For the foregoing reasons, our order of September 11, 2008, REVERSED the decision of the district court and ENJOINED GSUSA "from making any changes to, or interfering with, the current council jurisdiction of appellant Girl Scouts of Manitou Council, Inc., pending final resolution on the merits in the district court."

QUESTIONS

1. What is the purpose of the state Fair Dealership Law?
2. Did the appeals court find that the local council was a dealer under the act?

8. The Franchise Agreement

The relationship between the franchisor and the franchisee is ordinarily an arm's-length relationship between two independent contractors. Their respective rights are determined by the contract existing between them, called the **franchise agreement**.[10] The agreement sets forth the rights of the franchisee to use the **trademarks**, **trade name**, **trade dress**, and **trade secrets** of the franchisor. **For Example,** Burger King Corporation licenses franchisees to use the trademarks Burger King, Whopper, Croissanwich, and Whopper Jr.[11] The franchise agreement commonly requires the franchisor to provide training for the franchisee's employees, including processing or repair training. Thus, a new Chili's Bar and Grill franchise can expect to have its employees taught how to prepare and serve the food on its menu. In a distribution franchise, an Acura dealer can expect the franchisor to train its mechanics to repair the automobiles it sells. The franchise agreement also deals with terms for payment of various fees by the franchisee and sets forth compliance requirements for quality control set by the franchisor.

The duration of a franchise is a critical element of the franchise agreement. The franchise may last for as long as the parties agree. The laws in some states may require advance written notice of cancellation.[12] Franchise

[10] *See American Standard Inc. v. Meehan*, 517 F. Supp. 2d 976 (N.D. Ohio 2007).
[11] *Burger King Corp. v. Hinton, Inc.*, 203 F. Supp. 2d 1357 (S.D. Fla. 2002).
[12] See, for example, Mo. Rev. Stat. §407.405.

contracts generally specify the causes for which the franchisor may terminate the franchise, such as the franchisee's death, bankruptcy, failure to make payments, or failure to meet sales quotas.[13] **For Example,** Burger King Corp. (BKC) instituted a required new item, value meals, "which must be sold in all U.S. restaurants ... and failure to comply will be considered a default under the applicable franchise agreement." After due notice to franchisees Elizabeth and Luan Sadik and no compliance by the Sadiks with regard to the directive to sell the new value meal items, BKC cancelled the franchise, and the courts upheld BKC's action as proper under the franchise contract.[14]

Franchise agreements frequently contain an arbitration provision under which a neutral party is to make a final and binding determination whether there has been a breach of the contract sufficient to justify cancellation of the franchise.[15] The arbitration provision may provide that the franchisor can appoint a trustee to run the business of the franchisee while arbitration proceedings are pending.

9. Special Protections under Federal Laws

Holders of automobile dealership franchises are protected from bad-faith termination of their dealerships by the federal Automobile Dealers' Day in Court Act (ADDCA).[16] **For Example,** Anthony Arciniaga was allowed to proceed with his ADDCA lawsuit against General Motors. The court refused to allow GM to create and apply a corporate structure that evades the ADDCA. Collectively, the court looked to the Dealer Sales and Service Agreement, the Shareholders' Agreement, and other documents that together made up the understanding between Arciniaga and GM, which made it possible for Arciniaga to become an automobile dealer. The court concluded that all of the agreements viewed together constituted a "motor vehicle franchise contract." The court refused to focus on just one document as asserted by GM because doing so would negate the protective features of the ADDCA.[17]

When an automobile manufacturer makes arbitrary and unreasonable demands and then terminates a dealer's franchise for failure to comply with the demands, the manufacturer is liable for the damages caused. The right of a franchisee to transfer its contractual rights in the franchise is protected by the state law subject to notice and approval by the franchisor.[18]

In the *VW Credit, Inc.*, case, the court was faced with a question of whether or not the franchisor unreasonably withheld approval of a transfer, and if so, what should be the remedy.

VW Credit, Inc. v. Coast Automobile Group, Ltd., 787 A.2d 950 (N.J. Super. 2002)

An Associate of Tony and Carmella Soprano? Prove It

After a fire at its Volkswagen-Audi dealership in Tom's River, New Jersey, the owner, Coast Automotive Group, Ltd., agreed to transfer all assets to Aspen Knolls, Ltd., in order to salvage its franchise investment. Volkswagen of America (VOA) and Audi of America (AOA) brought suit to terminate Coast's franchise. Aspen Knolls meanwhile proceeded with the formality of submitting applications to VOA and AOA to transfer the Coast dealership, which were rejected by VOA and AOA. The trial court determined that VOA and AOA unreasonably withheld approval of the transfer and ordered specific performance of the transfer. VOA and AOA appealed.

JUDICIAL OPINION

NEWMAN, J. ... VWOA and AOA assert that the Act does not authorize the relief granted by the trial court. WVOA and AOA argue that the court erred in determining that the consent was unreasonably withheld and, even if it was, the court was limited to awarding damages under *N.J.S.A.* 56: 10–10 for a violation of the Act, and only to a franchisee, not to a potential transferee who is not covered by the Act. ...

The pivotal provision of the Act in terms of the transfer or sale of a franchise is *N.J.S.A.* 56:10–6, which provides:

[13] *Smith's Sports Cycles, Inc. v. American Suzuki*, 82 So.3d 682 (Ala. 2011).
[14] *Burger King Corp. v. E-Z Corporations*, 572 F.3d 1306 (11th Cir. 2009).
[15] *Central New Jersey Freightliner, Inc., v. Freightliner Corp.*, 987 F. Supp. 289 (D.N.J. 1998).
[16] 15 U.S.C. §§1221–1225.
[17] *Arciniaga v. General Motors Corp.*, 418 F. Supp. 2d 374 (S.D.N.Y. 2005).
[18] *KMS Restaurant Corp. v. Wendy's International*, 361 F.3d 1321 (11th Cir. 2004).

Continued

It shall be a violation of this act for any franchisee to transfer, assign or sell a franchise or interest therein to another person unless the franchisee shall first notify the franchisor of such intention by written notice setting forth in the notice of intent the prospective transferee's name, address, statement of financial qualification and business experience during the previous 5 years. The franchisor shall within 60 days after receipt of such notice either approve in writing to the franchisee such sale to proposed transferee or by written notice advise the franchisee of the unacceptability of the proposed transferee setting forth material reasons relating to the character, financial ability or business experience of the proposed transferee. If the franchisor does not reply within the specified 60 days, his approval is deemed granted. No such transfer, assignment or sale hereunder shall be valid unless the transferee agrees in writing to comply with all the requirements of the franchise then in effect.

We have previously interpreted *N.J.S.A.* 56:10–6 to impose a requirement of reasonableness on a franchisor's decision to disapprove a transfer. *Simmons, supra,* 180 *N.J. Super.* at 539, 435 A.2d 1167. The standard of review to determine the reasonableness of withholding consent to transfer of a franchise is an objective test that requires that the decision be supported by substantial evidence showing that the proposed franchisee is materially deficient. *InreVan Ness Auto Plaza, Inc.* 120 *B.R.* 545, 549 (Bankr.N.D.Cal.1990). The burden of presenting credible reasons for the refusal to consent rests on the franchisor. *Ibid.* We agree with the trial judge that VWOA and AOA did not meet this burden.

In support of their determination to withhold consent, VWOA and AOA asserted that Aspen Knolls submitted a deficient application and that there were concerns related to the character of Mazzuoccola, the majority member of Aspen Knolls. The trial court made the following findings regarding the reasons asserted by VWOA and AOA for withholding consent to assignment of the franchise.

As to the issue of business experience, the court found that Reynolds and Rutigliano, both of whom are principals of Aspen Knolls, began to operate an Audi Dealership in Bernardsville in 1995, and within the first year of operation, the dealership was ranked third in the nation in volume and sales. Since its inception, that dealership has maintained a high ranking among the 365 Audi dealerships in the country in terms of sales and volume. There was also testimony that the Bernardsville dealership ranked in the top ten percentiles in customer satisfaction in both the regional area and the nation. The judge also noted that Reynolds and Rutigliano had extensive prior experience as automobile dealers.

Mazzuoccola's experience was not as extensive. However, the judge noted that Mazzuoccola, a race car enthusiast who sponsored a professional racing team, did own a Jeep dealership in Essex County. The judge found that Aspen Knolls, an entity comprising Reynolds, Rutigliano, and Mazzuoccola, demonstrated an ability to operate the Coast dealership.

As to the issue of VWOA and *[sic.]* AOA's concerns regarding Mazzuoccola's character, the judge noted that VWOA and AOA based those concerns upon certain allegations raised in an affidavit filed by Shansab in the litigation between Coast and Aspen Knolls. The affidavit, which had been withdrawn by Shansab, raised issues of whether Mazzuoccola had affiliated or associated with known organized crime figures as well as the propriety of his business practices. The underlying litigation in which the affidavit had been submitted settled. … In this regard, the judge noted that

> *no testimony was produced by either side to address the allegations that related to the character allegations involving Mr.Mazzuoccola. And that Mr. Mazzuoccola, in fact, took the stand and exposed himself to the opportunity for cross examination by the … franchisor's representatives. That the issue of his involvement with any unsavory business activities, or association with undesirable individuals, or people of known criminal connections or histories or even personalities, was just not raised.*
>
> …
>
> *[T]he hearing was … scheduled primarily to address these issues of character.… I continue to be fully satisfied that any purported deficiencies in terms of character have not been proved. And even if raised … [the allegations] have been effectively dispelled through the testimony of the parties. … Character, then, cannot form a basis for the rejection of the proposed franchisees under … these circumstances.…*

We are satisfied that Judge Ford's findings that VWOA and AOA unreasonably withheld their consent to the proposed transfer are supported by adequate, substantial, and credible evidence. *Rova Farms Resort, Inc. v. Investors Ins. Co. of Am.,* 65 *N.J.* 474, 484, 323 A.2d 495 (1974).

VWOA and AOA's contention that the relief granted by the trial court is not authorized, amounts to a claim that under *N.J.S.A.* 56:10–6, the franchisor has a right to reject a proposed transferee and once it does, regardless of the reasonableness of its disapproval, the remedy of specific performance is unavailable. We disagree. …

The order approving Aspen Knolls as the franchise transferee of Coast's Volkswagen and Audi franchises is affirmed. …

[Judgement affirmed]

Continued

QUESTIONS

1. Under Section 6 of the state Franchise Practices Act, on what statutory basis may a franchisor reject a proposed transferee? Which party has the burden of proof?
2. May a franchisor reject a transferee on character grounds because the transferee is a race car enthusiast, sponsors a professional racing team, and is suspected of associating with organized crime figures?

The Petroleum Marketing Practices Act (PMPA) gives gas station franchisees the opportunity to continue in business by purchasing the entire premises used in selling motor fuel when the franchisor decides to sell the property and not renew a lease. In some instances, the franchisor's intentions are unclear and its actions may be perceived as contrary to the PMPA. Litigation may be necessary to resolve the matter. **For Example,** eight independent gas station operators who leased stations from Shell Oil Co. and sold Shell products were successful in their PMPA lawsuit against Shell when Shell phased out rental subsidies provided franchisees under the parties' lease agreements and set the wholesale prices it charged dealers for gasoline so high that the increase would squeeze dealers' profits or force them to raise prices that competition could undercut. The dealers argued this was done to reduce the number of independent gas stations in the region. A jury awarded $3.3 million in compensatory damages.[19]

The PMPA prohibits early termination of a franchise, except when the franchisee's failure to comply with a provision of the franchise is so serious as to undermine the entire relationship.[20]

10. Disclosure

The offer and sale of a franchise requires compliance with both federal and state laws.

(A) Federal Law. Franchisors must comply with the FTC's amended **Franchise Rule**, which supplanted the FTC's Uniform Franchise Offering Circular (UFOC) disclosure format in 2008. The amended Rule updates the UFOC to address utilization of new technologies, like the Internet; requires more disclosure about the nature of the franchisor-franchisee relationship; exempts certain entities like large franchisees; and prohibits certain practices not addressed in the UFOC. The Franchise Rule requires a franchisor to provide each prospective franchisee with a detailed franchise disclosure document ("FDD") at least 14 calendar days before the prospective franchisee signs a binding agreement or makes any payment to the franchisor. This ensures that prospective franchisees have sufficient time in which to review the disclosures. The FDD requires some 23 items of disclosure, including topics such as: (1) the business experience of the franchisor and its brokers, (2) any current and past litigation against the franchisor, (3) any previous bankruptcy, (4) the material terms of the franchise agreement, (5) initial and recurring payments, (6) restrictions on territories, (7) grounds for termination of the franchise, and (8) actual, average, or projected sales, profits, or earnings.[21]

(B) State Laws. Some 35 states allow franchisors who utilize properly prepared FDDs and comply with the FTC's Franchise Rule 14-day reflection period to enter franchise agreements with franchisees. The remaining 15 states have franchising laws of their own, often requiring franchisors to file a franchise offering circular with a state agency. These states, referred to as "registration states," seek to protect citizens from fraudulent schemes and provide recourse in state court if a franchisor violates state laws.[22]

[19] Kimberly Blanton, "Jury Rules for Franchisees in Shell Trial," *Boston Globe*, December 9, 2004, at C-3.

[20] In *Chevron v. El-Khoury*, 285 F.3d 1159 (9th Cir. 2002), the Court of Appeals remanded a franchise termination case for trial on the materiality of a franchisee's failure to pay $15,000 in California sales taxes when the oil company had unsuccessfully attempted to buy out the dealer and, when the last buyout offer was rejected, had selected him to be audited. The dealer eventually paid all taxes due. One of Chevron's executives testified that the failure to pay taxes was between "the dealer and the state" rather than the dealer and Chevron. However, Chevron contended that the failure to pay all taxes when due was a violation of the franchise agreement and tarnished the company's image.

[21] See the Federal Trade Commission, *Franchise Rule Compliance Guide*, 16 C.F.R. Part 436, for details on the other disclosure items required by the FDD. For FTC staff opinions, see **www.ftc.gov/bcp/franchise/netadopin.shtm**.

[22] The registration states are California, Hawaii, Illinois, Indiana, Maryland, Michigan, Minnesota, New York, North Dakota, Oregon, Rhode Island, South Dakota, Virginia, Washington, and Wisconsin.

11. Vicarious Liability Claims against Franchisors

In theory, a franchisor is not liable to a third person dealing with or affected by the franchise holder. This freedom from liability is one of the main reasons franchisors use franchises. If the negligence of the franchisee causes harm to a third person, the franchisor is not liable because the franchisee is an independent contractor. However, franchisors continue to be subject to lawsuits based on the wrongful conduct of their franchisees under the theory of either actual authority or apparent authority.[23]

The *D.L.S. v. Maybin* decision presents both the plaintiffs' and franchisor's views on liability.

D.L.S. v. Maybin, 121 P.3d 1210 (Wash. App. 2005)

Why Franchisors Use Franchises!

William Roberts operated a McDonald's restaurant in Newcastle, Washington, under a franchise agreement with McDonald's Corporation. A thriving drug scene existed among employees and assistant managers at the restaurant. In May of 2000, 15-year-old D.L.S. was hired by the restaurant and within weeks she was part of the drug scene there. Thereafter, she left home to live with an assistant manager and use drugs. Her father, Clifford Street, and D.L.S. sued McDonald's Corp. and Roberts for introducing D.L.S. to drugs and sex. The trial court dismissed the claims against McDonald's Corp. and D.L.S. and her father appealed. Mr. Street testified that "no person in their right mind would believe that McDonald's did not control what happened at the individual restaurants."

JUDICIAL OPINION

KENNEDY, J.... The only question before us is whether McDonald's Corporation has liability as Roberts' principal. The parties' franchise agreement clearly provided that Roberts was not an agent of McDonald's, and the evidence established no control over daily operations. Under these circumstances, McDonald's has no liability as Roberts' actual principal.

Rather, the issue is whether Roberts was McDonald's ostensible agent. Apparent agency occurs, and vicarious liability for the principal follows, where a principal makes objective manifestations leading a third person to believe the wrongdoer is an agent of the principal. Restatement, (Second) of Agency § 267 (1957). The doctrine is intended to protect third parties who justifiably rely upon the belief that another is the agent of a principal.

D.L.S. appears to argue that her parents' permission for her to work was given in reliance upon their belief that she would be working for McDonald's Corporation. We thus turn to her father's claims.

Apparent authority can be inferred only from acts of the principal which cause the third party to "actually, or subjectively, believe that the agent has authority to act for the principal."

Mr. Street and D.L.S.'s stepmother testified that they gave permission for D.L.S. to work at the Newcastle McDonald's in the belief that "a McDonald's is a McDonald's" and would offer a safe, wholesome environment for teenage workers. They contend this belief came from McDonald's marketing and advertising.

Mr. Street described McDonald's ads portraying McDonald's as a "very positive, safe environment with young children getting 'Happy Meals' and playing in McDonald's play areas." He also points to ads emphasizing McDonald's support for the Olympics, successful young athletes, and the Ronald McDonald House. This marketing made McDonald's appear to be a highly organized, well-run corporation that values "good citizenship and youth," in "a uniform, quality, wholesome environment." He points out that McDonald's advertising emphasizes "youth-related themes" and shows "smiling, happy, and friendly young people as their employees." He testified that "[b]ased [on] McDonald's targeting of minors as employees, I believed that McDonald's would take at least ordinary precautions in the hiring and supervising of its employees, especially the teenagers." He declared that McDonald's marketing of its wholesome image "deliberately misleads parents such as myself to think a McDonald's restaurant is a good, safe working environment for our teenage children to try out their first jobs."

D.L.S.'s parents denied any knowledge that the Newcastle McDonald's was a franchise, or that most McDonald's are franchises, and alleged they allowed D.L.S. to work there believing that McDonald's "stands for a uniform, quality, wholesome environment[.]" *Id.* at 309. Mr. Street contended that "[n]o person in their right mind would believe that McDonald's did not control what happened at the individual restaurants." He thus contends a question of fact exists as to whether the Corporation, through its intentional creation of a wholesome image, held out its franchisees as its agents.

[23] *Ketterling v. Burger King Corporation*, 272 P.3d 527 (Idaho 2012).

Continued

More is required of the principal before its acts can create liability under the apparent authority doctrine. ...

Beyond the general impression created by its advertising that McDonald's restaurants offer a wholesome environment, D.L.S.'s father points to no representations or acts by McDonald's upon which he relied in believing that D.L.S. worked for the Corporation or that McDonald's would ensure a safe working environment in its franchise restaurants. Using young people in advertisements, serving Happy Meals, sponsoring the Ronald McDonald house, and supporting Olympic athletes are not enough to create an apparent employment relationship between McDonald's Corporation and its franchisees' employees.

The circumstances of D.L.S.'s employment at the Newcastle McDonald's franchise are deeply regrettable. But the trial court did not err in concluding the theory of liability advanced against McDonald's is unsupported. D.L.S. and her parents must pursue their claims against the tortfeasor and the franchisee.

[Affirmed]

QUESTIONS

1. Was Roberts an actual agent of McDonald's Corporation?
2. Did McDonald's Corporation make objective manifestations leading Mr. Street to reasonably believe that his daughter worked for McDonald's Corporation?
3. Speculate on why the Streets were so intent on suing the corporation when they had the clear right to sue the tortfeasor assistant manager and the franchisee Roberts.

To maintain uniform systems for processing or distributing goods or rendering services, franchisors often place significant controls on their franchisees' businesses. These controls are set forth in franchise agreements and operating manuals. In a lawsuit brought against a franchisor for the wrongful conduct of its franchisee, the franchise agreement and operations manuals may be used as evidence of the franchisor's right to control the franchisee and the existence of an agency relationship rather than an independent contractor relationship.[24]

To avoid negating its franchisees' independent contractor status and being liable for the wrongful conduct of a franchisee, the franchisor should make certain that the franchise agreement minimizes the number and kind of provisions that authorize the franchisor to control the "means" of operating the business. **For Example,** the franchisor should not exercise control over employment-related matters.[25]

Franchisors may also insulate themselves from liability by requiring individual franchisees to take steps to publicly maintain their own individual business identities.

For Example, a gas station may post a sign stating that it is "dealer owned and operated," or a real estate franchise may list on its business sign the franchise name and the name of the local owner, such as Century 21, L & K Realty Co. All invoices, purchase orders, paychecks, and notices to employees should contain notice of the independent ownership and operation of the business. Finally, franchisors should require their franchisees to maintain appropriate comprehensive general liability insurance, workers' compensation insurance, and other appropriate insurance.

12. Franchises and Employee Misclassifications

Whether someone is a franchisee-independent contractor or an employee is determined by the actual relationship between the individual and the business, and not by a label or a franchise agreement. **For Example,** Coverall North American Inc. is one of

[24] *J. M. v. Shell Oil Co.*, 1996 Bus. Franchise Guide (C.C.H.) ¶ 10,817 (Mo. App.).

[25] Consider the degree of control exercised by McDonald's Corp. over its franchises. Only designated food and beverages may be served, and franchisees are required to use prescribed buildings and equipment. The franchisor dictates the level of quality, service, and cleanliness. All franchisees' employees must wear the uniforms designated by the franchisor with McDonald's logos. McDonald's dictates management, advertising, and personnel policies and requires that managers be trained at its "Hamburger University." The Illinois Court of Appeals held that the question of whether a franchise was an apparent agent of McDonald's was an issue of material fact that should go to a jury in a lawsuit involving a customer's slip and fall on ice in the franchised restaurant's bathroom. The court stated that the employees responsible for maintaining the bathroom wore "McDonald's uniforms" and were required to follow McDonald's standards of "quality, service, and cleanliness." *O'Banner v. McDonald's Corp.*, 653 N.E.2d 1267 (Ill. App. 1995). On further appeal to the Supreme Court of Illinois, the Court of Appeals was reversed because in order to recover on an apparent agency theory, the customer had to show that he actually relied on the apparent agency in going to the restaurant where he was injured. The customer failed to do so, thus losing the right to hold McDonald's Corp. liable for his injuries. *O'Banner v. McDonald's Corp.*, 670 N.E.2d 632 (Ill. 1996). See *Husain v. McDonald's Corp.*, 140 Cal. Rptr. 3d 370, 377 (Cal. App. 2012), where the form license agreement between McDonald's and the franchisor explains the essence of the "McDonald's system" is to ensure comprehensive control by McDonald's over every material aspect of the restaurant's operations so the uniformity of the McDonald's customer experience could be assured in every one of its locations.

Thinking Things Through

Don't Finagle the Bagel!

Ken Miyamoto was president and a shareholder of Bixby's Food Systems, Inc. (Bixby's), a franchisor of bagel restaurants. The business is incorporated and provides limited liability to Miyamoto and its other corporate investors. Bixby's hired a lawyer familiar with franchise disclosure laws in Illinois and drafted a franchise offering circular (FOC) in accordance with state laws. Jan and Phillip McKay attended a meeting of existing and prospective franchisees where Miyamoto spoke and said that prospective franchisees had signed and paid for 340 development agreements; a similar statement also appeared in a Bixby's newsletter. The McKays soon thereafter executed a franchise agreement. Based on Miyamoto's view that a lease of larger retail space than recommended in Bixby's circular would bring in larger revenues, the McKays executed the larger-than-recommended lease and spent $400,000 making their restaurant operational, which was a much higher investment than projected in the FOC. When the restaurant opened, sales did not come close to the figures estimated in the FOC. After eight months of operations, Bixby's terminated the McKays' franchise for their inability to pay Bixby's franchise royalty fees. Bixby's sued the McKays for continuing to use its trademark, and the McKays counterclaimed against Bixby's, Inc. and Miyamoto as an individual for violation of the state Franchise Disclosure Act and the state Deceptive Business Practices Act.

Bixby's FOC was not shown to contain material misstatements of fact. However, the McKays listed a number of statements made by Miyamoto that were untrue concerning future events regarding costs, profitability, and financial success, like his encouraging them to rent larger-than-recommended retail space to bring in larger revenues, which did not materialize. The court held that such statements about future events, costs, and profitability are not actionable misrepresentations under the state Franchise Disclosure Act. Corporate executives selling franchises have latitude to take the facts set forth in franchise offering circulars and project a bright future in most respects. That is, they have a legal right to put their "spin" on the facts, just as society does in governmental and personal affairs. Of course, buyers must beware and view assertions about future events, costs, and profitability with critical analysis and informed skepticism.

With his business incorporated and his circulars drafted by competent counsel, was Miyamoto immune from personal liability in this case? The answer is no. When Miyamoto told the group of prospective franchisees that some 340 development agreements had been signed and paid for and later repeated this statement in a newsletter, he was not Thinking Things Through. Through the discovery process that preceded a trial, the McKays' attorney "discovered" that Bixby's had just 15 agreements executed and paid for at the time of Miyamoto's assertion that 340 agreements were executed and paid for. Such a material misstatement of fact was a violation of the state franchising and deceptive practices laws.

The economic resources expended by Bixby's, Inc., to provide limited liability could not shield its shareholder-president from the consequences of his enormous lie. Along with Bixby's, Inc., Miyamoto was held personally liable to the McKays under the state statutes.*

**Bixby's Food Systems, Inc. v. McKay*, 193 F. Supp. 2d 1053 (N.D. Ill. 2002).

the largest global commercial cleaning franchisors in North America, with over 9,000 franchise owners and 50,000 customers. Each individual who purchases a janitorial cleaning franchise must enter a standard unit agreement with Coverall. The agreement gives Coverall the exclusive rights to perform all billing and collection services provided by franchisees and to deduct fees before remitting payments. State law deals with whether an individual who is performing services is an independent contractor or an employee. Under one prong of the Massachusetts law, the burden is placed on Coverall to establish that the individual "is performing services that are part of an independent, separate, and distinct business from that of the employer." Coverall trains its franchisees and provides them with uniforms and identification badges; it contracted with all customers, with limited exceptions, until May 2009; and Coverall is the party billing all customers for cleaning services performed and receives a percentage of the revenues earned on every cleaning service. Accordingly, Coverall sells cleaning services, the same services provided by the "franchisees." Because the franchisees did not perform services outside the usual course of Coverall's business, Coverall failed to establish that franchisees were independent contractors.[26]

[26] *Awauh v. Coverall North America, Inc.* 707 F. Supp. 2d 80 (D. Mass. 2010).

The U.S. Labor Secretary stated that misclassification has saved some employers as much as 20 to 30 percent on their labor costs, which allows them to gain business by underbidding employers that obey the rules and causes a downward pressure on wages and a loss in government revenues.[27]

LawFlix

Good Burger (1997) (PG)

This film is a story of the competition, mass marketing, and secret sauce issues in franchising. The movie provides a look at liability, product quality, and espionage.

[27] Misclassification deprives employees of the protection of wage and hour laws and time-and-one-half rates for overtime work; it also denies them eligibility for unemployment insurance coverage, workers' compensation protection, and other statutory right under the antidiscrimination and labor laws.

Employers who pay workers' compensation and unemployment insurance premiums for their employees as required by law and pay overtime rates under the Fair Labor Standards Act are placed at a competitive disadvantage compared to employers who misclassify their employees. States are deprived of payroll taxes and unemployment and workers' compensation taxes.

MAKE THE CONNECTION

SUMMARY

The three principal forms of Business Organizations are sole proprietorships, partnerships, and corporations. A *sole proprietorship* is a form of business organization in which one person owns the business, controls all decisions, receives all profits, and has unlimited liability for all obligations and liabilities. A *partnership* involves the pooling of capital resources and talents of two or more persons whose goal is making a profit; the partners are subject to unlimited personal liability. However, newly created forms of Business Organizations—the *limited liability company* and the *limited liability partnership*—allow for tax treatment as a partnership with certain limited liability for the owners.

A business *corporation* exists to make a profit. It is created by government grant, and its shareholders elect a board of directors whose members are responsible for managing the business. A shareholder's liability is limited to the capital the shareholder invested in the business or paid for shares. Corporate existence continues without regard to the death of shareholders or the transfer of stock by them.

The selection of the form of organization is determined by the nature of the business, tax considerations, the financial risk involved, the importance of limited liability, and the extent of management control desired.

A *joint venture* exists when two or more persons combine their labor or property for a single business undertaking and share profits and losses as agreed. An unincorporated association is a combination of two or more persons for the pursuit of a common purpose.

A *cooperative* consists of two or more persons or enterprises, such as farmers, who cooperate to achieve a common objective, such as the distribution of farm products.

By a franchise, the owner of a trademark, trade name, or copyright licenses others to use the mark or copyright in selling goods or services. To protect against fraud, the FTC requires that franchisors provide prospective franchisees with a disclosure statement 10 days prior to any transaction. The Automobile Dealers' Day in Court Act and the Petroleum Marketing Practices Act are federal laws that provide covered franchisees with protection from bad-faith terminations. State laws also protect franchisees in a wide range of businesses. A franchisor is not liable to third persons dealing with its franchisees. Liability of the franchisor may, however, be imposed on the ground of the apparent authority of the franchisee or the latter's control by the franchisor. Liability of the franchisor may also arise in cases of product liability.

LEARNING OUTCOMES

After studying this chapter, you should be able to clearly explain:

A. Principal Forms of Business Organizations

LO.1 Explain the advantages and disadvantages of the three principal forms of business organizations

See the discussion on proprietorships, partnerships (LLPs and LLCs), and corporations beginning on p. 854.

B. Specialized Forms of Organizations

LO.2 Recognize that the rules of law governing the rights and liabilities of joint ventures are substantially the same as those that govern partnerships

See the *PGI/Rathe* joint venture remedy on p. 855.

See the *Kurwa* case and the joint venture remedy while operating in the corporate form on pp. 855–856.

C. The Franchise Business Format

LO.3 Evaluate whether a business arrangement is a franchise protected under state or federal law

See the *Girl Scouts of Manitou* case applying a state's fair dealership law, pp. 858–859.

See the example where Mr. Arciniaga was allowed to proceed with his federal ADDCA lawsuit against General Motors on p. 860.

LO.4 Explain how the rights of the parties to a franchise agreement are determined by their contract

See the *Burger King* example involving cancellation of franchises, p. 860.

LO.5 Explain why freedom from vicarious liability is a reason for franchisors to use the franchise format

See the *McDonald's* case in which only the franchisee was liable for the torts to the minor emanating from the McDonald's restaurant, pp. 863–864.

LO.6 Recognize the implications of the misclassifications of employees as franchisee-independent contractors

See the *Coverall* misclassification scheme on pp. 864–8665.

KEY TERMS

cooperative
corporations
franchise
franchise agreement
Franchise Rule
franchisee
franchisor
joint venture
limited liability company (LLC)
limited liability partnership (LLP)
partnership
sole or individual proprietorship
trade dress
trade name
trade secrets
trademarks
unincorporated association

QUESTIONS AND CASE PROBLEMS

1. In July 2008 Miller Brewing Co. and Coors Brewing Co. formed a joint venture to better compete with the dominant beer manufacturer, Anheuser Busch. The venture was named "MillerCoors LLC." Under the joint venture Miller Brewing Co. and Coors Brewing Company have a 50 percent voting interest in the entity, and each appoints half of the directors. Moreover, the CEOs of Miller and Coors resolve disputes, and all revenues are distributed directly to Miller and Coors, with cash returned to meet the operating needs of the joint venture. Ohio law requires just cause for the termination of beer distributors but allows a "successor manufacturer" to terminate existing distributorships without proving just cause so long as the predecessor does not exercise

control over the successor. In accordance with the "successor manufacturer" exception, MillerCoors LLC notified Ohio wholesale beer distributors that it was terminating their distributorships. The distributorships sought injunctive relief. Miller-Coors LLC moved for summary judgment. Decide. [*Beverage Distributors, Inc. v. Miller Brewing Co.*, 803 F. Supp. 2d 765 (S.D. Ohio)]

2. Jerome, Sheila, Gary, and Ella agreed to purchase a tract of land and make it available for use as a free playground for neighborhood children. They called the enterprise Meadowbrook Playground. Jerome and Gary improperly hung one of the playground swings, and a child was injured. Suit was brought against Meadowbrook Playground. Can damages be recovered?

3. Morris Friedman was president of Tiny Doubles International, Inc. He sold business opportunities for Tiny Doubles Studios, which made small photographic statues of people for customers. Friedman was the primary negotiator with prospective buyers of these studio business opportunities. He advised buyers up front that the opportunities were not franchises, and accordingly, he did not provide all of the information set forth in the disclosure rule on franchising, although he did provide full answers to all questions asked. Many businesses closed, however, because of lack of success. The FTC claims Friedman violated its disclosure rule. Friedman disagrees. Decide. [*FTC v. Tiny Doubles Int'l, Inc.*, 1996 Bus. Franchise Guide (C.C.H.) ¶ 10,831]

4. Wolf, King, and others sold business "opportunities" in vending machines by taking out ads in newspapers throughout the country. When individuals responded, telemarketers called "fronters" would tell them of false earnings estimates, and those who could afford $16,000 to $25,000 for vending machines were turned over to "closers" who promised wonderful results. References were provided who were "shills"—they did not own vending machines but were paid to tell "stories" that were monitored by Wolf, King, and other supervisors. None of the individuals was given franchise disclosure documents. King induced one investor to mortgage her house so that she could pay $70,000 for a number of vending machines. In three years Wolf, King, and others took in some $31.3 million. The FTC alleged that the defendants violated the FTC franchise disclosure rule.

Is there a franchise disclosure rule violation if Wolf and King were merely selling vending machines? What if Wolf and King promised exclusive territories for the machines? Why would a franchise disclosure rule be necessary in this case? Decide. [*FTC v. Wolf*, Bus. Franchise Guide ¶ 27,655 (C.C.H. D. Fla.)]

5. Katherine Apostoleres owned the rights to Dunkin Donuts franchises in Brandon and Temple Terrace, Florida. The franchisor offered all its franchisees the right to renew their existing franchise agreements if they agreed to abide by advertising decisions favored by two-thirds of the local franchise owners in a given television market. Apostoleres refused the offer because she did not want to be bound by the two-thirds clause. Soon thereafter, Dunkin Donuts audited her two stores, and using a "yield and usage" analysis, it concluded that gross sales were being underreported. Based on these audits and a subsequent audit, Dunkin Donuts gave notice of immediate termination of Apostoleres's franchises, contending that the franchise agreement had been violated. Apostoleres stated that an implied obligation of good faith exists by operation of law in every contract, and she asserted that the audits were in retaliation for her refusal to accept the renewal agreement. The yield and usage test used in the audit was not specified in the franchise agreement as a measure to be used to enforce the franchisor's rights, and certain accounting experts testified as to the unreliability of this test. Was Dunkin Donuts liable for breach of its implied obligation of good faith in this case? [*Dunkin Donuts of America v. Minerva, Inc.*, 956 F.2d 1566 (11th Cir.)]

6. To establish that a business is a "franchisee" qualifying for protection under the Illinois Franchise Disclosure Act, the business must demonstrate that it paid a franchise fee either directly or indirectly to the "franchisor" to enter the business. To-Am Equipment Company believed it had paid an implied fee in excess of $500 to enter

the forklift business as a dealer for Mitsubishi-Caterpillar Forklift of America (MCFA) when it paid $1,658 for service manuals, which MCFA had commanded it to possess. MCFA denied that it had charged To-Am a franchise fee and asserted that it was not obligated to To-Am under the state Franchise Disclosure Act. Decide. [*To-Am Equipment Co. v. Mitsubishi-Caterpillar Forklift of America*, 853 Supp. 987 (N.D. Ill.)]

7. For a five-year period, Laurie Henry worked for James Doull, the owner of four Taco Bell franchises. During that time, she had an affair with Doull. He was the father of her two illegitimate children. Enraged over a domestic matter, Doull physically assaulted her at the Taco Bell Restaurant and then fired her and ordered her off the premises. Later, on Doull's recommendation, she was hired by a "company store" in an adjoining state. Henry brought suit against Doull, his corporate entity Taco Tia, Inc., and the Taco Bell Corporation (TBC). She did not characterize her suit as a case of sexual harassment. Rather, she contended that TBC was responsible for Doull's actions because he was TBC's agent. She sought damages for the loss of romantic and material satisfactions a person might expect from a traditional courtship and wedding. TBC denied that Doull was its employee or agent. The evidence showed that Henry knew that Doull's stores differed from TBC "company" stores. She insisted, having worked for four years for Doull at stores adorned with Taco-Bell signs, that Taco Bell was responsible for Doull's actions. Decide. [*Henry v. Taco Tia, Inc.*, 606 So.2d 1376 (La. App.)]

8. The Armory Committee was composed of officers from various National Guard units. It organized a New Year's Eve dance at a charge of $2 per person to defray costs. Perry, along with others, was a member of the Armory Committee. Libby was a paying guest at the dance who was injured by slipping on frozen ruts in the immediate approaches to the steps leading to the armory building where the dance was held. He sued Perry, Turner, and the other committee members. The evidence showed that every member of the committee had taken some part in planning or running the dance with the exception of Turner. Was the Armory Committee an unincorporated association or a joint venture? Decide. [*Libby v. Perry*, 311 A.2d 527 (Me.)]

9. The Kawasaki Shop of Aurora, Illinois (dealer), advised Kawasaki Motors Corp. (manufacturer) that it intended to move its Kawasaki franchise from New York Street to Hill Avenue, which was in the same market area. The Hill Avenue location was also the site of a Honda franchise. The manufacturer's sales manager advised the dealer that he did not want the dealer to move in with Honda at the Hill Avenue site. In February, the dealer moved to the Hill Avenue location. Effective May 1, the manufacturer terminated the dealer's franchise. The dealer brought suit against the manufacturer under the state's Motor Vehicle Franchise Act, which made it unlawful to terminate franchises for site control (requiring that the dealer's site be used exclusively as a Kawasaki dealership). The manufacturer argued that it had a right to have its products sold by a dealer who was not affiliated with a competitor. Decide. [*Kawasaki Shop v. Kawasaki Motors Corp.*, 544 N.E.2d 457 (Ill. App.)]

10. Goodward, a newly hired newspaper reporter for the *Cape Cod News*, learned that the local cranberry growers had made an agreement under which they pooled their cranberry crops each year and sold them at what they determined to be a fair price. Goodward believes that such an agreement is in restraint of trade and a violation of the antitrust laws. Is he correct?

11. Food Caterers of East Hartford, Connecticut, obtained a franchise from Chicken Delight to use that name at its store. Food Caterers agreed to the product standards and controls specified by the franchisor. The franchise contract required the franchisee to maintain a free delivery service to deliver hot, freshly prepared food to customers. The franchisee used a delivery truck that bore no sign or name. Its employee Carfiro was driving the truck in making a food delivery when he negligently struck and killed McLaughlin. The victim's estate sued Chicken Delight on the theory that Carfiro was its agent because he was doing work that Chicken Delight required and that benefited Chicken Delight. Was Carfiro the

agent of Chicken Delight? [*McLaughlin's Estate v. Chicken Delight, Inc.*, 321 A.2d 456 (Conn.)]

12. Groseth had the International Harvester (IH) truck franchise in Yankton, South Dakota. The franchise agreement Groseth signed required dealers to "cooperate with the Company by placing orders for goods in accordance with advance ordering programs announced by the Company." IH wanted to terminate Groseth's franchise because he refused to comply with IH's requirement that a computerized "dealer communication network" (DCN) be set up. Under the DCN, each dealer was required to obtain a computer terminal, display screen, and software. The DCN was initially used for ordering parts and allowed IH to reduce the number of employees needed for manual processing of "parts" orders. Groseth refused to set up the DCN because of the expense. Moreover, he contended that the task of ordering parts was easily accomplished by telephone or written orders. Did IH have good cause to terminate Groseth's franchise? [*Groseth International Harvester, Inc. v. International Harvester*, 442 N.W.2d 229 (S.D.)]

13. Brenner was in the scrap iron business. Almost daily, Plitt lent Brenner money with which to purchase scrap iron. The agreement of the parties was that when the scrap was sold, Plitt would be repaid and would receive an additional sum as compensation for making the loans. The loans were to be repaid in any case without regard to whether Brenner made a profit. A dispute arose over the nature of the relationship between the two men. Plitt claimed that it was a joint venture. Decide. [*Brenner v. Plitt*, 34 A.2d 853 (Md.)]

14. Donald Salisbury, William Roberts, and others purchased property from Laurel Chapman, a partner of Chapman Realty, a franchisee of Realty World. The purchasers made payments directly to Laurel Chapman at the Realty World office, and Chapman was to make payments on the property's mortgage. However, Chapman did not make the payments and absconded with the funds. Salisbury and Roberts sued the franchisor, Realty World, claiming that Realty World was liable for the wrongful acts of the apparent agent, Chapman. Realty World and Chapman Realty were parties to a franchise agreement stating that the parties were franchisor and franchisee. The agreement contained a clause that required Chapman to prominently display a certificate in the office setting forth her status as an independent franchisee. Chapman displayed such a sign, but the plaintiffs did not recall seeing it. Chapman Realty hires, supervises, and sets the compensation for all of its employees. The plaintiffs pointed out that Chapman Realty used the service mark Realty World on its signs, both outside and inside its offices. They pointed out that a Realty World manual sets forth the general standards by which franchisees must run their businesses and that this represents clear control over the franchise. They contended that, all things considered, Realty World held out Chapman Realty as having authority to bind Realty World. Realty World disagreed, stating that both were independent businesses. Decide. [*Salisbury v. Chapman and Realty World, Inc.*, 65 N.E.2d 127 (Ill. App.)]

15. H.C. Blackwell Co. held a franchise from Kenworth Truck Co. to sell its trucks. After 12 years, the franchise was nearing expiration. Kenworth notified Blackwell that the franchise would not be renewed unless Blackwell sold more trucks and improved its building and bookkeeping systems within the next 90 days. Blackwell spent $90,000 attempting to meet the demands of Kenworth but could not do so because a year was required to make the specified changes. Kenworth refused to renew the franchise. Blackwell sued Kenworth for damages under the federal Automobile Dealers' Day in Court Act. Blackwell claimed that Kenworth had refused to renew in bad faith. Decide. [*Blackwell v. Kenworth Truck Co.*, 620 F.2d 104 (5th Cir.)]

CPA QUESTIONS

1. A joint venture is a(an):
   a. Association limited to no more than two persons in business for profit
   b. Enterprise of numerous co-owners in a nonprofit undertaking
   c. Corporate enterprise for a single undertaking of limited duration
   d. Association of persons engaged as co-owners in a single undertaking for profit

Partnerships

learningoutcomes

After studying this chapter, you should be able to

LO.1 Explain how partnerships are created by agreement, and understand that only when the partners' partnership agreement does not resolve an issue does partnership law apply

LO.2 Understand that no writing is needed to form a partnership, nor a tax ID number, nor a partnership name. All that is needed is clear evidence that the partners carried on as co-owners of a business for profit

LO.3 Distinguish between express authority and customary authority of a partner to act for a partnership

LO.4 List the duties of partners to one another

LO.5 Explain the nature and extent of a partner's liability on firm contracts and torts

LO.6 Describe how a partnership may be dissolved by the acts of partners, by operation of law, and by order of the court

Partnerships may be created without the formality of even a written partnership agreement when two or more individuals simply operate a business for a profit as co-owners. In July 2008 Paula Balzer was recruited to work for Blue Flame, a firm specializing in the business of marketing and live promotions. As of October 1, 2008, she states she was made a partner. Two firm e-mails reference her as a partner, and she was paid a monthly $15,000 draw. The firm's 2008 and 2009 tax returns listed her as a partner of Blue Flame. In October 2010, the partners had a falling-out with Paula. She disengaged from the firm on November 12, 2010, upon completion of two events she was committed to staging. The partners never executed a written partnership agreement with Paula and as a result did not believe she had partnership rights. When the firm failed to pay her certain money and expenses the court reverted to basic partnership law that a written contract of partnership is not necessary to the formation of a partnership and concluded that a partnership existed on the basis of the facts before the court.[1] Partnership relations are not narrowly governed by partnership law but are governed by the partners' partnership agreement. Only when the partnership agreement does not resolve an issue does partnership law apply. In many instances, individuals do not obtain legal advice in choosing the partnership form of business organization. Properly informed individuals today will probably not choose the partnership form of organization because partners are open to unlimited personal liability; they may choose a limited liability company to insulate the members from personal liability.

A. Nature and Creation

Partnerships are created by agreement. A codification of general partnership law is found in the Uniform Partnership Act (UPA), which has been revised (Revised Uniform Partnership Act, or RUPA). Together, the UPA and the RUPA are in effect in 49 states.[2] Limited partnerships (LPs) and limited liability partnerships (LLPs) differ significantly from general partnerships and are discussed in the next chapter. The 1994 or 1997 versions of the Revised Uniform Partnership Act apply in 38 states.[3] Like the UPA, most of the provisions of the RUPA apply only when the partners do not have partnership agreement language that deals with the matter at issue.[4] Certain features of the RUPA that differ from those of the UPA are identified in the text.

1. Definition

A **partnership** (also called a **general partnership**) is a relationship created by the voluntary "association of two or more persons to carry on as co-owners of a business for profit."[5] The persons so associated are called **partners** or **general partners**. A partner is the agent of the partnership and of each partner with respect to partnership matters. A partner is not an employee of the partnership even when doing work that would ordinarily be done by an employee.

2. Characteristics of a Partnership

A partnership has distinguishing characteristics:

1. A partnership is a voluntary, consensual relationship.
2. A partnership involves partners' contributions of capital, services, or a combination of these.
3. The partners are associated as co-owners to transact the business of the firm for profit.

If profit is not the object, the group will commonly be an **unincorporated association**.

[1] *Balzer v. Millward*, 2011 WL 1547211 (D. Conn. April 21, 2011).

[2] The UPA or the RUPA is in effect in all states except Louisiana.

[3] The RUPA or versions of it have been adopted by Alabama, Alaska, Arizona, Arkansas, California, Colorado, Connecticut, Delaware, District of Columbia, Florida, Hawaii, Idaho, Illinois, Iowa, Kansas, Kentucky, Maine, Maryland, Minnesota, Mississippi, Montana, Nebraska, Nevada, New Jersey, New Mexico, North Dakota, Ohio, Oklahoma, Oregon, Puerto Rico, South Dakota, Tennessee, Texas, Utah, Vermont, Virginia, Washington, West Virginia, and Wyoming. The RUPA was approved in 1992 and amended in 1993, 1994, and 1997. It provides for a transition period after passage, during which only newly created partnerships come under the new law, with all partnerships in the state eventually being governed by the RUPA (see R.U.P.A. §1206(a)).

[4] See *Mission West v. Republic*, 873 A.2d 372 (Md. App. 2005).

[5] U.P.A. §6(1).

The UPA does not make the partnership a separate entity, and, therefore, suit cannot be brought by the firm in its name in the absence of a special statute or procedural rule so providing. However, in RUPA states, partnerships are recognized as "entities."

3. Rights of Partners

The rights of partners are determined by the partnership agreement. If written, this agreement is interpreted by the same rules that govern the interpretation of any other written document. Any matter not covered by the partnership agreement may be covered by a provision of the applicable UPA or RUPA.

4. Partnership Agreement

Because of the complexity of the problems involved, *partnership agreements* are typically written. However, there is no requirement that they be in writing unless compliance with a statute of frauds is required. **For Example,** the world's highest-paid performers in the early 1990s, the New Kids on the Block, who grossed $74.1 million in one year, were a group started by promoter Maurice Starr. He obtained $60,000 from James Martorano, who was connected with organized crime, and $50,000 from businessman Jeffrey Furst to finance the initial recording and promotion of the group. Martorano and Furst testified that ultimately all three agreed with a handshake that 50 percent of the profits from the group would be shared between Martorano as a silent partner and Furst, who would also provide limousine service and security. They testified that Starr would keep half of the profits. Starr denied that a partnership existed because he believed that such an alleged business arrangement would have had to be reduced to writing with great detail. However, based on the evidence, which included damaging testimony that Starr tried to buy some witnesses' silence, a jury decided that a binding oral partnership agreement existed.[6]

To reduce or avoid disputes and litigation, partnership agreements should be in writing. Courts will enforce partnership agreements, under the standards of the law of contracts, according to the agreements' terms.[7] **For Example,** dentist Steven Schwartz was terminated from a three-dentist practice "without cause" by vote of his two other partners. The partnership agreement allowed for termination of a partner as long as either party gave the other 90 days notice. The appeals court interpreted the partnership agreement as written, finding that the provision was entered into by sophisticated and highly educated professionals, and not in violation of public policy.[8]

The formal document that is prepared to evidence the contract of the parties is termed a **partnership agreement**, **articles of partnership**, or **articles of copartnership**. The partnership agreement governs the partnership during its existence and may contain provisions relating to dissolution. (See Figure 42-1.)

CPA 5. Determining the Existence of a Partnership

If the parties agree that the legal relationship between them shall be such that they in fact operate a business for profit as co-owners, a partnership is created even though the parties may not have labeled their new relationship as such.[9] The law is concerned with the substance of what is done rather than the name. Conversely, a partnership does not arise if the parties do not agree to the elements of a partnership even though they call it one.[10]

The *Byker v. Mannes* decision deals with the question of whether individuals have to be aware of their status as "partners" in order to have a legal partnership.

[6] *Boston Globe*, November 13, 1995, 13. For an example of a situation in which no oral partnership was found to exist, see *Prince v. O'Brien*, 683 N.Y.S.2d 504 (A.D. 1998). Marvin Prince and Darren O'Brien met and became friends while living in Toronto. Prince, a Jamaican native, helped O'Brien refine his reggae-singing ability and knowledge of Jamaican dialect, and participated in the coining of O'Brien's stage name "Snow." Before O'Brien became a success with his debut reggae album *12 Inches of Snow*, the friends may have casually discussed splitting their hypothetical profits equally but never agreed to share losses. Later, when Marvin Prince toured with O'Brien, he was designated and paid as an employee of O'Brien's corporation. The court found that Prince failed to prove the existence of an oral partnership agreement.

[7] *Krajacich v. Great Falls Clinic*, 276 P.3d 922 (Mont. 2012).

[8] *Schwartz v. Family Dental Group, P.C.*, 943 A.2d 1122 (Conn. App. 2008).

[9] *Swecker v. Swecker*, 360 S.W.3d 422 (Tenn. App. 2011).

[10] See *Cleland v. Thirion*, 704 N.Y.S.2d 316 (A.D. 2000).

Byker v. Mannes, 641 N.W.2d 210 (Mich. 2002)

The Case of the Absolutely Dumbfounded Investor (Partner)

David Byker, an accountant, and Tom Mannes, an individual with a real estate background, stipulated to the following facts in a lawsuit brought by Byker against Mannes:

[T]he Plaintiff...and Defendant...agreed to engage in an ongoing business enterprise, to furnish capital, labor and/or skill to such enterprise, to raise investment funds and to share equally in the profits, losses and expenses of such enterprise.... In order to facilitate investment of limited partners, Byker and Mannes created separate entities wherein they were general partners or shareholders for the purposes of operating each separate entity.

Over the years, the parties pursued various business enterprises, including five limited partnerships, where they served as general partners or shareholders in order to operate each separate entity. With regard to these entities, they shared equally in commissions, financing fees, and termination costs, and they personally guaranteed loans from financial lenders. A subsequent entity, Pier 1000, Ltd., created by Byker and Mannes to own and manage a marina, was not successful, and they took profits from a prior entity and borrowed money from financial institutions to continue its operations. Mannes subsequently refused to make any additional contributions. Thereafter, the unsuccessful marina venture was returned to its previous owners in exchange for assumption of Byker's and Mannes's direct obligations to that business. The nine-year business relations between Byker and Mannes ceased. Subsequently, Byker approached Mannes for him to share equally in the payments resulting from losses incurred from their various entities. Mannes was in his words "absolutely dumbfounded" by Byker's request for money, and he refused payment. Byker sued, contending that the obligations between him and Mannes were not limited to their formal business relationships established by the individual partnerships and corporate entities, but that there was a "general" partnership underlying all their business affairs. In response, Mannes asserted that he had merely invested in separate business ventures with Byker and that there were no other understandings between them.

The trial court decided in favor of Byker as follows:

> *Having weighed the credibility of the witnesses, principally plaintiff and defendant, we conclude that they began their relationship with a general agreement that they were partners and would share profits and losses equally. Whether understood or not they had a general or super partnership. The evidence supports that both understood it.*

The Court of Appeals reversed, finding that no underlying partnership existed because the parties did not intend to form a partnership. The case was thereafter heard by the state supreme court.

JUDICIAL OPINION

MARKMAN, J....

A. Uniform Partnership Acts

In 1917, the Michigan Legislature drafted the Michigan Uniform Partnership Act. 1917 PA 72. In this act, a partnership was defined as "an association of two [2] or more persons to carry on as co-owners a business for profit...." at §6, codified in 1929 CL 9846. Over the years, the definition has remained essentially constant. At present, partnership is defined as "an association of 2 or more persons, which may consist of husband and wife, to carry on as co-owners a business for profit...." M.C.L. §449.6(1). This definition, as well as its predecessors, was modeled after the definition of partnership set forth in the 1914 UPA. In 1914, the UPA had defined a partnership as "an association of two or more persons to carry on as owners a business for profit." Uniform Partnership Act of 1914, §6. In construing §6, courts had "universal[ly]" determined that a partnership was formed by "the association of persons whose intent is to carry on as co-owners a business for profit, regardless of their subjective intention to be 'partners.'"

In 1994, however, the UPA definition of partnership was amended by the National Conference of Commissioners. The amended definition stated that "the association of two or more persons to carry on as co-owners a business for profit forms a partnership, *whether or not the persons intend to form a partnership.*" Section 202 (emphasis added). Although the commissioners were apparently satisfied with the existing judicial construction of the definition of partnership, the commissioners added the new language "whether or not the persons intend to form a partnership" in order to "codif[y] the universal judicial construction of UPA Section 6(1) that a partnership is created by the association of persons whose intent is to carry on as co-owners a business for profit, regardless of their subjective intention to be 'partners.'" Section 202 (Comment 1). The commissioners emphasized that "[n]o substantive change in the law" was intended by the amendment of §6. To date, Michigan has not adopted the amended definition of partnership.

B. MCL 449.6(1)

Although Michigan has not adopted the amended definition of partnership as set forth in §202 of the Uniform Partnership Act of 1994, we believe nonetheless that M.C.L. §449.6 is consistent with the amendment....

As already noted, a partnership in Michigan is statutorily defined as "an association of 2 or more persons, which may consist of husband and wife, to carry on as co-owners a business for profit...." M.C.L. §449.6(1). That is, if the

Continued

parties associate themselves to "carry on" as co-owners a business for profit, they will be deemed to have formed a partnership relationship regardless of their subjective intent to form such a legal relationship. The statutory language is devoid of any requirement that the individuals have the subjective intent to create a partnership. Stated more plainly, the statute does not require partners to be aware of their status as "partners" in order to have a legal partnership....

When the Legislature initially drafted M.C.L. §449.6(1) the definition of partnership was well established in our common law, and is consistent with the interpretation that we give it today. See *Beecher v Bush* 45 Mich. 188, 193–194, 7 N.W. 785 (1881)....

CONCLUSION

With the language of the statute as our focal point, we conclude that the intent to create a partnership is not required if the acts and conduct of the parties otherwise evidence that the parties carried on as co-owners a business for profit. MCL 449.6, 449.7. Thus, we believe that, to the extent that the Court of Appeals regarded the absence of subjective intent to create a partnership as dispositive regarding whether the parties carried on as co-owners a business for profit, it incorrectly interpreted the statutory (and the common) law of partnership in Michigan.

Pursuant to M.C.L. §449.6(1), in ascertaining the existence of a partnership, the proper focus is on whether the parties intended to, and in fact did, "carry on as co-owners a business for profit" and not on whether the parties subjectively intended to form a partnership....

Accordingly, we remand this matter to the Court of Appeals for analysis under the proper test for determining the existence of a partnership under the Michigan Uniform Partnership Act.

[Reversed and remanded]

QUESTIONS

1. Is it the law that individuals must be aware of their status as "partners" in order to have a legal partnership?
2. In a footnote to the state supreme court's decision, the court reported that the parties stipulated that the alleged partnership was never memorialized in a written partnership agreement, had no formal name, no tax identification number, and no income tax filings. Based on these facts and the other facts of record, is it nevertheless possible for a partnership to exist?
3. Assess the fairness of Mannes's contention that he merely invested in separate business ventures and that no other understanding existed.

A partnership is shown to exist when it is established that the parties have agreed to the formation of a business organization that has the characteristics of a partnership. The burden of proving the existence of a partnership is on the person who claims that one exists.[11]

When the nature of the relationship is not clear, the following rules aid in determining whether the parties have created a partnership.

CPA **(A) Control.** The presence or absence of control of a business enterprise is significant in determining whether there is a partnership and whether a particular person is a partner.

CPA **(B) Sharing Profits and Losses.** The fact that the parties share profits and losses is strong evidence of a partnership.[12]

CPA **(C) Sharing Profits.** An agreement that does not provide for sharing losses but does provide for sharing profits is evidence that the parties are partners. If the partners share profits, it is assumed that they will also share losses. Sharing profits is prima facie evidence of a partnership. However, a partnership is not to be inferred when profits are received in payment (1) of a debt, (2) of wages, (3) of an annuity to a deceased partner's surviving spouse or representative, (4) of interest, or (5) for the goodwill of the business.[13] **For Example,** the fact that one doctor receives one-half of the net income does not establish that doctor as a partner of another doctor when the former was guaranteed a minimum annual amount. Also, federal income tax and Social Security contributions were deducted from the payments to the doctor, thus indicating that the relationship was employer and employee. If there is no evidence of the

[11] *MacArthur v. Stein*, 934 P.2d 214 (Mont. 1997).

[12] *Botsee Gates v. Houston*, 897 N.E.2d 532 (Ind. App. 2008).

[13] U.P.A. §7(4).

FIGURE 42-1 Partnership Agreement

PARTNERSHIP AGREEMENT

THIS IS A PARTNERSHIP AGREEMENT EXECUTED AT CINCINNATI, OHIO, THIS 9TH DAY OF SEPTEMBER, 1998, BY AND AMONG LOUIS K. HALL, SHARON B. YOUNG, AND C. LYNN MUELLER, INDIVIDUALS RESIDING IN CINCINNATI, OHIO, HEREINAFTER SOMETIMES REFERRED TO INDIVIDUALLY AS "PARTNER" AND COLLECTIVELY AS "PARTNERS."

RECITALS

THE PARTNERS TO THIS AGREEMENT DESIRE TO ACQUIRE A CERTAIN PARCEL OF REAL ESTATE AND TO DEVELOP SUCH REAL ESTATE FOR LEASE OR SALE, ALL FOR INVESTMENT PURPOSES. THIS AGREEMENT IS BEING EXECUTED TO DELINEATE THE BASIS OF THEIR RELATIONSHIP.

PROVISIONS

1. NAME; AND PRINCIPAL OFFICES. THE NAME OF THE PARTNERSHIP SHALL BE: HALL, YOUNG AND MUELLER, ASSOCIATES. ITS PRINCIPAL PLACE OF BUSINESS SHALL BE AT: 201 RIVER ROAD, CINCINNATI, OHIO 45238.

2. PURPOSE. THE PURPOSE OF THE PARTNERSHIP SHALL BE TO PURCHASE AND OWN FOR INVESTMENT PURPOSES, A CERTAIN PARCEL OF REAL ESTATE LOCATED AT 602 SIXTH STREET, CINCINNATI, OHIO, AND TO ENGAGE IN ANY OTHER TYPE OF INVESTMENT ACTIVITIES THAT THE PARTNERSHIP MAY FROM TIME TO TIME HEREINAFTER UNANIMOUSLY AGREE UPON.

3. CAPITAL CONTRIBUTIONS. THE CAPITAL OF THE PARTNERSHIP SHALL BE THE AGGREGATE AMOUNT OF CASH AND PROPERTY CONTRIBUTED BY THE PARTNERS. A CAPITAL ACCOUNT SHALL BE MAINTAINED FOR EACH PARTNER.

A. CAPITAL CONTRIBUTIONS. ANY ADDITIONAL CAPITAL WHICH MAY BE REQUIRED BY THE PARTNERSHIP SHALL BE CONTRIBUTED TO THE PARTNERSHIP BY THE PARTNERS IN THE SAME RATIO AS THAT PARTNER'S ORIGINAL CONTRIBUTION TO CAPITAL AS TO THE TOTAL OF ALL ORIGINAL CAPITAL CONTRIBUTIONS TO THE PARTNERSHIP UNLESS OTHERWISE AGREED BY THE PARTNERS.

reason for receiving the profits, a partnership of the parties involved exists.

CPA **(D) Gross Returns.** The sharing of gross returns is itself very slight, if any, evidence of partnership. **For Example,** in a case in which one party owned a show that was exhibited on land owned by another under an agreement to divide the gross proceeds, no partnership was proven. There was no co-ownership or community of interest in the business.

CPA **(E) Contribution of Skill or Labor.** The fact that all persons have not contributed capital to an enterprise does not establish that the enterprise is not a partnership. A partnership may be formed even though some of its members furnish only skill or labor.

CPA **(F) Fixed Payment.** When a person who performs continuing services for another receives a fixed payment that does not depend on the existence of profit and is not affected by losses, that person is not a partner.

CPA 6. Partners as to Third Persons

In some instances, persons who are in fact not partners may be held liable to third persons as though they were partners. This liability arises when they conduct themselves in such a manner that others are reasonably led to believe that they are partners and to act in reliance on that belief to their injury.[14] A person who is held liable as a partner under such circumstances is termed a *nominal partner*, a *partner by estoppel*, or an *ostensible partner*.

Partnership liability may arise by estoppel when a person who in fact is not a partner is described as a partner in a document filed with the government provided the person so described has in some way participated in the filing of the document and the person claiming the benefit of the estoppel had knowledge of that document and relied on the statement. **For Example,** Jean Collins allowed the partnership of Holt and Schwark to use her name to

[14] U.P.A. §16(1); *Andrews v. Elwell*, 367 F. Supp. 2d 35 (D. Mass. 2005).

help the partnership get started. A business name registration certificate filed at city hall and signed by all of the individuals specifies Holt, Schwark, and Collins as partners. If a creditor who sees this registration statement extends credit to the firm in reliance in part on the fact that Collins is a partner, Collins is estopped from denying that she is a partner. She has a partner's liability along with the other partners insofar as that creditor is concerned.

Under the RUPA, an apparent partnership or partnership by estoppel is called a *purported* partnership, and a third person who relies on the partnership's representations that the purported partner had authority to bind the partnership can hold it liable as if the purported partner were an actual partner with authority.[15] Under the RUPA, a partnership can limit potential liability with a publicly recorded statement of partnership authority or limitation on partner authority.[16]

CPA 7. Partnership Property

In general, partnership property consists of all property contributed by the partners or acquired for the firm or with its funds.

There is usually no limitation on the type and amount of property that a partnership may acquire. The firm may own real as well as personal property unless it is prohibited from doing so by statute or by the partnership agreement.

The parties may agree that real estate owned by one of the partners should become partnership property. When this intent exists, the particular property constitutes partnership property even if it is still in the name of the original owner.

Article 2 of the RUPA recognizes that partnerships are "entities" that can acquire and own property in the partnership's name. If a partner desires to retain an interest in property contributed to the partnership in RUPA states, the partner must condition the transfer of the property to the partnership to reflect this interest or set forth the condition in the partnership agreement. Otherwise, the property becomes partnership property under the entity theory, and the contributing partner has no right to get it back, even in liquidation.[17]

8. Tenancy in Partnership

Under the UPA, partners hold title to firm property by **tenancy in partnership.**[18] The characteristics of such a tenancy are as follows:

1. Each partner has an equal right to use firm property for partnership purposes in the absence of a contrary agreement.
2. A partner possesses no divisible interest in any specific item of partnership property that can be voluntarily sold, assigned, or mortgaged by a partner.
3. A creditor of a partner cannot proceed against any specific items of partnership property. The creditor can proceed only against the partner's interest in the partnership. This is done by applying to a court for a **charging order**. By this procedure, the share of any profits that would be paid to the debtor-partner is paid to a receiver on behalf of the creditor, or the court may direct the sale of the interest of the debtor-partner in the partnership.
4. Upon the death of a partner, the partnership property vests in the surviving partners for partnership purposes and is not subject to the rights of the surviving spouse of the deceased partner.

CPA 9. Assignment of a Partner's Interest

Although a partner cannot transfer specific items of partnership property in the absence of authority to so act on behalf of the partnership, a partner's interest in the partnership may be voluntarily assigned by the partner. The assignee does not become a partner without the consent of the other partners. Without this consent, the assignee is entitled to receive only the assignor's share of the profits during the continuance of the partnership and the assignor's interest upon the dissolution of the firm. The assignee has no right to participate in the management of the partnership or to inspect the books of the partnership.

[15] R.U.P.A. §308.
[16] R.U.P.A. §303.
[17] R.U.P.A. §204.
[18] U.P.A. §25(1); *Krause v. Vollmar*, 614 N.E.2d 1136 (Ohio App. 1992).

B. Authority of Partners

The scope of a partner's authority is determined by the partnership agreement and by the nature of the partnership.

10. Authority of Majority of Partners

When there are more than two partners in a firm, the decision of the majority prevails in matters involving how the ordinary functions of the business will be conducted. To illustrate, a majority of the partners of a firm decide to increase the firm's advertising. They subsequently enter into a contract for that purpose. The transaction is valid and binds the firm and all of the partners.

Majority action is not binding if it contravenes the partnership agreement. For such matters, unanimous action is required.[19] Thus, the majority of the members cannot change the nature of the business against the protests of the minority.

When there are an even number of partners, an even division on a matter that requires majority approval is always a possibility. In such a case, the partnership is deadlocked. When the partners are evenly divided on any question, one partner has no authority to act.

If the division is over a basic issue and the partners persist in the deadlock so that it is impossible to continue the business, any one of the partners may petition the court to order the dissolution of the firm.

11. Express Authority of Individual Partners

An individual partner may have **express authority** to perform certain acts either because the partnership agreement provides for this or because a sufficient number of partners have agreed to it.

A partner's authority to act for the firm is similar to that of an agent to act for a principal. Thus, in addition to express authority, a partner has the authority to do those acts that are customary for a member of a partnership conducting the particular business of that partnership.[20] As in the case of an agent, the acts of a partner in excess of authority do not ordinarily bind the partnership.

12. Customary Authority of Individual Partners

A partner, by virtue of being a comanager of the business, customarily has certain powers necessary and proper for carrying out that business. The scope of such powers varies with the nature of the partnership and with the business customs and usages of the area in which the partnership operates.

A partner may make any contract necessary to transact the firm's business.

A partner can sell the firm's goods in the regular course of business, make purchases within the scope of the business, and borrow money for firm purposes. When borrowing money, a partner may execute commercial paper in the firm's name or give security such as a mortgage.[21] A partner may purchase insurance, hire employees, and adjust claims for or against the firm. Notice given to a partner is effective notice to the partnership.[22]

13. Limitations on Authority

The partners may agree to limit the powers of each partner. When a partner, contrary to such an agreement, executes a contract on behalf of the firm with a third person, the firm is bound if the third person was unaware of the limitation. In this case, the partner violating the agreement is liable to the other partners for any loss caused by the breach of the limitation. Under the UPA, if the third person knew of the limitation, the firm would not be bound.[23] Under the RUPA, the term *knew* is confined to actual knowledge,[24] which is cognitive awareness. Under the RUPA, a partnership may file a statement of partnership authority setting forth any restrictions on a general partner's authority.[25] **For Example,** Bernard Roeger was general partner of RNR, with three limited partners. Restrictions were clearly set forth in the partnership agreement limiting Roeger's borrowing

[19] U.P.A. §18(h).
[20] *Ball v. Carlson*, 641 P.2d 303 (Colo. App. 1981).
[21] *U.S. Leather v. H&W Partnership*, 60 F.3d 222 (5th Cir. 1995).
[22] *Cham, Hill, Inc., v. Block & Veatch*, 557 N.W.2d 829 (Wis. App. 1996).
[23] U.P.A. §9(4).
[24] R.U.P.A. §102(a).
[25] R.U.P.A. §303.

authority to no more than $650,000 for the construction of a building on partnership property. Roeger on behalf of RNR entered a construction loan agreement with People's Bank with a note and mortgage in the amount of $990,000, and over an 18-month period, the bank disbursed an aggregate sum of $952,699. The bank did not request a written consent from any of the other partners or review the partnership agreement. When the loan was not paid, the bank foreclosed on the property. RNR defended on behalf of the partnership that the bank negligently failed to investigate and discover the limitation on Roeger's authority to borrow. The case was decided for the bank because it had no actual knowledge or notice of the restriction on the general partner's authority. The court also pointed out that the partnership could have protected itself by filing a statement of partnership authority setting forth the restrictions on the general partner under RUPA section 303.[26]

A third person must not assume that a partner has all of the authority that the partner purports to have. If there is anything that would put a reasonable person on notice that the partner's powers are limited, the third person is bound by that limitation.

The third person must be on the alert for the following prohibited transactions because they warn that the partner with whom the third person deals has either restricted authority or no authority at all. (See Figure 42-2.)

14. Prohibited Transactions

A partner cannot enter into certain transactions on behalf of the partnership unless expressly authorized to do so. A third person entering into such a transaction does so at the risk that the partner has not been authorized. The following are prohibited transactions.

(A) Cessation of Business. A partner cannot bind the firm by a contract that would make it impossible for the firm to conduct its usual business.[27]

(B) Suretyship. A partner has no implied authority to bind the firm by contracts of surety, guarantee, or indemnity for purposes other than firm business.[28]

(C) Arbitration. A partner cannot submit controversies of the firm to arbitration "unless authorized by the

FIGURE 42-2 *Limitations on Authority of Individual Partner to Bind Partnership*

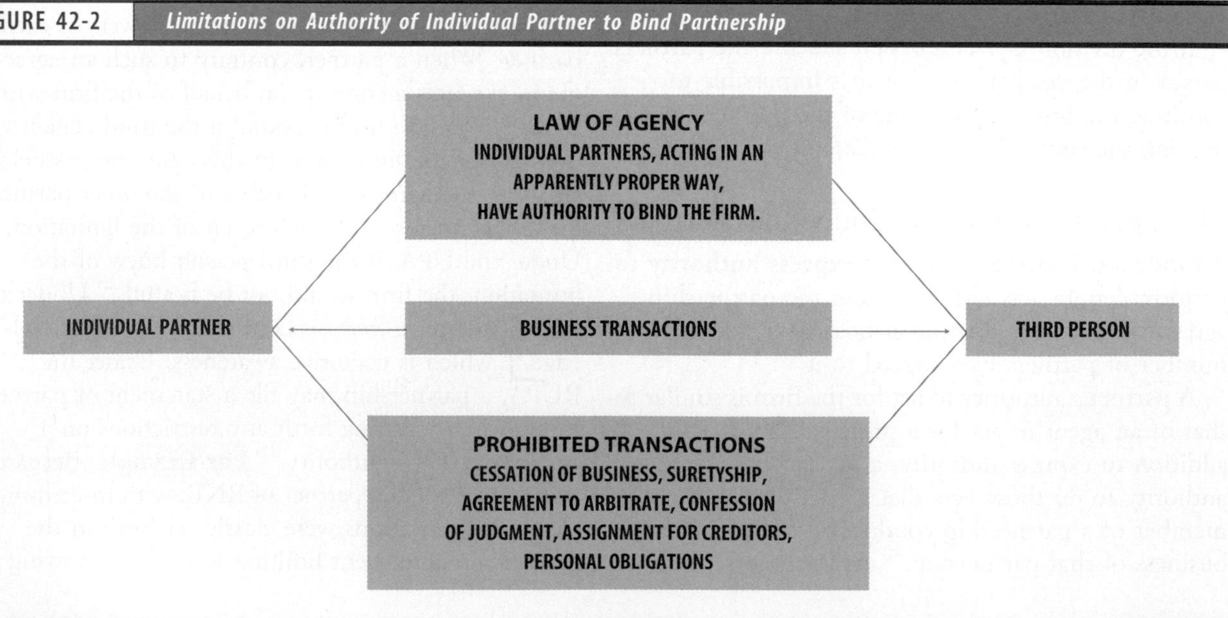

[26] *RNR Investments, Ltd. v. People's First Community Bank*, 812 So.2d 561 (Fla. App. 2002).

[27] *Wales v. Roll*, 769 P.2d 899 (Wyo. 1989).

[28] *First Interstate Bank of Oregon v. Bergendahl*, 723 P.2d 1005 (Or.App. 1986).

other partners or unless they have abandoned the business."[29]

(D) Confession of Judgment. All partners should have an opportunity to defend in court. Because of this, a partner cannot confess judgment against the firm on one of its obligations. Exceptions exist when the other partners consent or when they have abandoned the business.

(E) Assignment for Creditors. A partner cannot make a general assignment of firm property for the benefit of creditors unless authorized by the other partners or unless they have abandoned the business.

(F) Personal Obligations. A partner cannot discharge personal obligations or claims of the firm by interchanging them in any way.

C. Duties, Rights, and Liabilities of Partners

The rights and duties of partners are based on their dual capacity of agent and co-owner.

15. Duties of Partners

In many respects, the duties of a partner are the same as those of an agent.

(A) Loyalty and Good Faith. Each partner must act in good faith toward the partnership. One partner must not take any advantage over the other(s) by the slightest misrepresentation or concealment.[30] Each partner owes a duty of loyalty to the firm. This duty requires a partner's devotion to the firm's business and bars making any secret profit at the expense of the firm.[31]

Moreover, the duty of loyalty bars the use of the firm's property for personal benefit or the exploitation of a business opportunity of the partnership for personal gain. **For Example,** when one partner renewed the lease of the building occupied by the firm but the lease was renewed in the name of that partner alone, that partner was compelled to hold the lease for the firm. The failure to renew the lease in the name of the firm was a breach of the duties of good faith and loyalty owed to the firm.

A partner cannot promote a competing business. A partner who does so is liable for damages sustained by the partnership.

Each partner also owes a fiduciary duty of good faith to all other partners. This duty extends to any transaction connected with the formation, conduct, or liquidation of the partnership

A breach of fiduciary duty requires the complete forfeiture of all compensation during the period of the breach. **For Example,** general partners Michael Morton and Scott DeGraff breached their fiduciary duty to their partners when they did not disclose the parts of a deal they were keeping for themselves relating to a proposed relocation of the partnership's Las Vegas nightclub, Drink. Morton and DeGraff had been paid $833,190 in management fees during the period of time they were found to be in breach of their fiduciary duty to the partnership, and the court ordered them to return these funds to the partnership.[32]

(B) Obedience. Each partner is obligated to perform all duties and to obey all restrictions imposed by the partnership agreement or by the vote of the required number of partners.[33] **For Example,** when the partnership agreement required that each partner in an insurance sales firm give his "entire time" to the business and "not engage in any other business that would work to the disadvantage of the partnership," Richard Levatino's engaging in an insurance-related business outside the firm was a breach of the partnership agreement and was a proper basis for the assessment of punitive damages.[34]

(C) Other Duties. A partner must refrain from engaging in grossly negligent or intentional misconduct in transacting firm business under the RUPA.[35] Partners are accountable as a fiduciary and must hold as trustee for the firm any profits derived by a partner without the consent of the other partners.[36]

[29] U.P.A. §9(3)(e).
[30] *Brosseau v. Ranzau*, 81 S.W.3d 381 (Tex. App. 2002).
[31] Under R.U.P.A. 404(e), partners may pursue their own interests without automatically violating their fiduciary duties to the firm.
[32] *Caparos v. Morton*, 845 N.E.2d 773 (Ill. App. 2006).
[33] *Cobin v. Rice*, 823 F. Supp. 1419 (D. Ind. 1993).
[34] *Gates, Duncan, and VanCamp v. Levatino*, 962 S.W.2d 21 (Tenn. App. 1997).
[35] R.U.P.A. §404(c).
[36] U.P.A. §21; R.U.P.A. §404(b)(1).

CPA 16. Rights of Partners as Owners

Each partner, in the absence of a contrary agreement, has the following rights. These rights stem from the fact that the partner is a co-owner of the partnership business.

CPA **(A) Management.** Each partner has a right to take an equal part in transacting the business of the firm. It is immaterial that one partner contributed more than another or that one contributed only services.

Incidental to the right to manage the partnership, each partner has the right to possession of the partnership property for the purposes of the partnership.

CPA **(B) Inspection of Books.** All partners are equally entitled to inspect the books of the firm. "The partnership books shall be kept, subject to any agreement between the partners, at the principal place of business of the partnership, and every partner shall at all times have access to and may inspect and copy any of them."[37]

CPA **(C) Share of Profits.** Each partner is entitled to a share of the profits. The partners may provide, if they so wish, that profits shall be shared in unequal proportions. In the absence of such a provision in the partnership agreement, each partner is entitled to an equal share of the profits without regard to the amount of capital contributed or services performed for the partnership.

CPA **(D) Compensation.** In the absence of a contrary agreement, a partner is not entitled to compensation for services performed for the partnership. There is no right to compensation even if the services are unusual or more extensive than the services rendered by other partners. Consequently, when one partner becomes seriously ill and the other partners transact all of the firm's business, they are not entitled to compensation for those services. The sickness of a partner is considered a risk assumed in the relationship. No agreement can be inferred that the active partners are to be compensated even though the services rendered by them are such that they would ordinarily be rendered in the expectation of receiving compensation. As an exception, "a surviving partner is entitled to reasonable compensation for services performed in winding up the partnership affairs."[38]

Contrary to the preceding, the partners may agree that one of the partners will devote full time as manager of the business and receive for such services a salary in addition to the managing partner's share of the profits.

(E) Repayment of Loans. A partner is entitled to the return of any money advanced to or for the firm. Such amounts must be separate and distinct from original or additional contributions to the capital of the firm.

CPA **(F) Payment of Interest.** In the absence of an agreement to the contrary, contributions to capital do not draw interest. The theory is that the profits constitute sufficient compensation. Advances by a partner in the form of loans are treated as if they were made by a stranger and bear interest from the date the advance is made. When the partnership business continues after dissolution, a retiring partner is entitled to interest on the value of her interest in the partnership.[39]

CPA **(G) Contribution and Indemnity.** A partner who pays more than a proportionate share of the debts of the firm has a right to contribution from the other partners. Under this principle, if an employee of a partnership negligently injures a third person while acting within the scope of employment and if the injured party collects damages from one partner, the latter may enforce contribution from the other partners to divide the loss proportionately among them.

The partnership must indemnify every partner for payments made and personal liabilities reasonably incurred in the ordinary and proper conduct of its business or for the preservation of its business or property. A partner has no right, however, to indemnity or reimbursement if the partner has (1) acted in bad faith, (2) negligently caused the necessity for payment, or (3) previously agreed to assume the expense alone.[40]

CPA **(H) Distribution of Capital.** After the payment of all creditors and the repayment of loans made to

---

37 U.P.A. §19. See *Smith v. Brown & Jones*, 633 N.Y.S.2d 436 (Sup. Ct. 1995).
38 U.P.A. §18(f).
39 *Lewis v. Edwards*, 554 S.E.2d 17 (N.C. App. 2001).
40 *Gramacy Equities Corp. v. DuMont*, 531 N.E.2d 629 (N.Y. A.D.1988).

the firm by partners, every partner is entitled to receive a share of the firm property upon dissolution. Unless otherwise stated in the partnership agreement, all partners are entitled to the return of their capital contributions.

After such distribution is made, each partner is the sole owner of the fractional part distributed to that partner rather than a co-owner of all the property as during the existence of the partnership.

CPA 17. Liability of Partners and Partnership

The liability of a partnership and of the partners for the acts of individual partners and of employees is governed by the same principles that apply to the liability of an employer or a principal for the acts of an employee or agent.

CPA (A) Nature and Extent of Partner's Liability. Partners are **jointly liable** on all firm contracts. They are **jointly and severally liable** for all torts committed by an employee or one of the partners in the scope of the partnership business.[41] When partners are liable for the wrongful injury caused a third person, the latter may sue all or any of the members of the firm.

Partners who have satisfied a claim against the partnership have the right to contribution from the other partners, whereby the liability is apportioned among all partners. Unlike the UPA, partners under the Revised Uniform Partnership Act (RUPA) are jointly and severally liable for both tort and contract obligations of the firm.[42] However, the RUPA alters the traditional applications of "joint and several" liability by requiring that the creditors and tort victims satisfy their claims against the partnership before pursuing the personal assets of a partner.

As seen in the *PNC Bank* case, when states enact the RUPA, the act does not apply to partnerships formed prior to the enactment of the legislation, with certain exceptions.

PNC Bank N.A. v. Farinacci, 964 N.E. 2d 1124 (Ohio App. 2011)

"Joint Liability" and "Joint and Several Liability": A Big Difference

PNC Bank sued two of the eight general partners of Washington Square Enterprises, Farinacci and Gruttadauria, for the unpaid balance of their partnership's business line of credit. The trial court entered judgment in the amount of $4,190.33 plus interest against each of the two partners. The trial court determined that the eight general partners were jointly liable, not jointly and severally liable, for the debt to PNC. In addition, it issued a separate judgment against Farinacci and Gruttadauria in the amount of one-eighth each of the entire debt of $33,522. PNC appealed, contending that the trial court should have found the partners jointly and severally liable or that the trial court should have apportioned the debt according to the percentages of each partner's ownership interest in the partnership, rather than dividing the debt equally among the eight partners.

JUDICIAL OPINION

COONEY, J.…In the first assignment of error, PNC argues that the trial court erred in applying R.C. 1775.14 instead of R.C. 1776.36 to determine the extent of appellees' liability.

PNC contends that the trial court should have applied R.C. 1776.36 because R.C. 1775.14 was repealed and replaced by R.C. 1776.36, effective January 1, 2010. These changes were made when the Ohio General Assembly passed the Ohio Uniform Partnership Act for the purpose of adopting the Revised Uniform Partnership Act. 2007 Ohio HB 332, 1. As part of this legislation, R.C. 1776.36 provides that "all partners are liable jointly and severally for *all obligations* of the partnership unless otherwise agreed by the claimant or provided by law." (Emphasis added.) Thus, PNC argues, the trial court should have applied R.C. 1776.36 and found the partners jointly and severally liable.

[41] See *Wayne Smith Construction v. Wolman, Durberstein*, 604 N.E.2d 157 (Ohio 1992), where the Ohio Supreme Court described joint liability and joint and several liability as follows: Joint liability apportions responsibility for a contractual debt equally, in the absence of a partnership agreement to the contrary, among the partners and thereby limits the creditor's execution on one individual partner's personal property to a *pro rata* share of the debt. Joint and several liability, on the other hand, allows for disproportionate satisfaction of the partnership obligation by rendering each general partner responsible for the entire amount of the partnership debt.

[42] R.U.P.A. §307(d).

Continued

However, R.C. 1776.95, which was also enacted as part of the Ohio Uniform Partnership Act, states that the act does not apply to partnerships formed prior to January 1, 2009, except under a few enumerated circumstances that are inapplicable here.

Washington Square was formed in 1978 with eight partners. There is no evidence that the partners agreed to be governed by the Ohio Uniform Partnership Act. PNC commenced this action in November 2009. Therefore, R.C. 1776.36 does not apply to Washington Square to extend the partners' liability.

The law in effect at the time the obligation accrued governs the action.…Evidence in the record indicates that Washington Square defaulted on the line of credit in June 2002. Thus, the court properly applied R.C. 1775.14, which was in effect at the time of Washington Square's default. Under R.C. 1775.14, partners are jointly, not jointly and severally liable, for the ordinary debts of the partnership.…

PNC argues that the trial court erroneously failed to consider the partners' ownership interests when determining the extent of appellees' liability. PNC contends that rather than dividing the debt equally among the eight partners, the trial court should have apportioned the debt according to the percentage of each partner's ownership interest in the partnership.

R.C. 1775.17, which was in effect at the time Washington Square defaulted on the line of credit, provides that unless the partners agree otherwise, partners share the partnership losses in the same proportion as they share in the profits. However, the allocation of liability for losses provided in R.C. 1775.17 applies only to the rights and duties of the partners to each other and is not relevant to partnership liability toward third parties…

PNC has offered no evidence showing that the Washington Square partners agreed to apportion liability to third parties according to their ownership shares in the business, much less evidence that it had notice of such an agreement when it extended the line of credit to Washington Square. "Joint liability apportions responsibility for a contractual debt equally, in the absence of a partnership agreement to the contrary." *Wayne Smith Constr. Co.*, 65 Ohio St.3d at 390–391, 604 N.E.2d 157. Therefore, the trial court correctly divided the partnership obligation equally among the eight partners.

[Judgment affirmed.]

QUESTIONS

1. Explain "joint liability" and "joint and several" liability in the context of the facts of this case.
2. Speculate on why PNC Bank was so interested in having the court apply joint and several liability in this case.

CPA **(B) Liability of New Partners.** A person admitted as a partner into an existing partnership has *limited liability* for all obligations of the partnership arising before such admission. This is a limited liability in that the preadmission claim may be satisfied only out of partnership property and does not extend to the individual property of the newly admitted partner.[43] **For Example,** Citizens Bank was unsuccessful in its attempt to satisfy part of a $1.2 million deficiency judgment against the Parkham-Woodman Medical partnership from the individual property of Dr. Hunley, who had joined the practice after the underlying obligation leading to the deficiency judgment was assumed.[44]

(C) Effect of Dissolution on Partner's Liability. A partner remains liable after dissolution of the partnership unless expressly released by the creditors or unless all claims against the partnership have been satisfied. The dissolution of the partnership does not of itself discharge the existing liability of any partner. The individual property of a deceased partner is liable for the obligations of the partnership that were incurred while the deceased partner was alive. However, the individual creditors of the deceased partner have priority over the partnership creditors with respect to such property.[45]

18. Enforcement and Satisfaction of Creditors' Claims

The firm may have been sued in the name of all individual partners doing business as the partnership, as in the case of "*Plaintiff v. A, B, C, doing business as the Ajax Warehouse.*" The partners named are bound by the judgment against the firm if they have been properly served in the suit.

[43] U.P.A. §17; see also U.P.A. §41(1), (7).
[44] *Citizens Bank v. Parkman Woodman Medical Associates*, 874 F. Supp. 705 (D. Mass. 1995).
[45] U.P.A. §36.

If a debt is contractual in origin, common law requires that the partnership's assets be resorted to and exhausted before partnership creditors can reach a partner's individual assets.[46]

Personal creditors of a partner must first pursue the assets of that partner for satisfaction of their claims. After a partner's personal assets are exhausted, the creditor may enforce the unpaid portion of a judgment by obtaining a charging order against the partner's interest in the partnership. Under such an order, a court requires that the partner's share of the profits be paid to the creditor until the debt is discharged.

D. Dissolution and Termination

The end of a partnership's existence is marked by dissolution and termination.

CPA 19. Effect of Dissolution

Dissolution is the "change in the relationship of the partners caused by any partner ceasing to be associated in the carrying on as distinguished from the winding-up of the business."[47] Dissolution does not necessarily mean that the business has ended. If the partnership agreement provides that the business is to be continued by the remaining partner(s), it will continue without a winding up, and the former partner's interest will be bought out according to the partnership agreement. Also, when breach of the partnership agreement causes dissolution, innocent partners may continue the business, provided they pay the breaching partner the value of his or her interest.[48]

If no legal basis exists to continue the business, dissolution ends the right of the partnership to exist as a going concern, but it does not end the existence of the partnership.[49] Dissolution is followed by a winding-up period at the conclusion of which the partnership's legal existence terminates.

Dissolution reduces the authority of the partners. From the moment of dissolution, the partners lose authority to act for the firm "except so far as may be necessary to wind up partnership affairs or to complete transactions begun but not then finished."[50] The vested rights of the partners are not extinguished by dissolving the firm, and the existing liabilities remain.

20. Dissolution by Act of the Parties

A partnership may be dissolved by action of the parties. However, certain acts of the parties do not cause a dissolution.

(a) Agreement. A partnership may be dissolved in accordance with the terms of the original agreement of the parties. This may be by the expiration of the period for which the relationship was to continue or by the performance of the object for which the partnership was organized.[51] The relationship may also be dissolved by subsequent agreement. The partners may agree to dissolve the firm before the lapse of the time specified in the articles of partnership or before the attainment of the object for which the firm was created.

(b) Expulsion. A partnership is dissolved by the expulsion of any partner from the business, whether or not authorized by the partnership agreement.[52]

(c) Alienation of Interest. Neither a voluntary sale of a partner's interest nor an involuntary sale for the benefit of creditors works a dissolution of the partnership.

(d) Withdrawal. A partner has the power to withdraw from the partnership at any time. However, if the withdrawal violates the partnership agreement, the withdrawing partner becomes liable to the copartners for damages for breach of contract.[53] When the relationship is for no definite purpose or time, a partner may withdraw without liability at any time. **For Example,** a partner, Mary Harshman, was able to bring about the dissolution of a family partnership that held and managed 1,879 acres of land in

[46] *McCune & McCune v. Mountain Bell Tel. Co.*, 758 P.2d 914 (Utah 1988).
[47] U.P.A. §29.
[48] U.P.A. §38 (2)(b).
[49] *Sheppard v. Griffin*, 776 S.W.2d 119 (Tenn. App. 1989).
[50] U.P.A. §33.
[51] U.P.A. §31(1)(a).
[52] *Susman v. Cypress Venture*, 543 N.E.2d 184 (Ill. App. 1989).
[53] *BPR Group v. Bendetson*, 906 N.E.2d 956 (Mass. 2009).

New York state and force the distribution of the partnership assets because it was an at-will partnership with no definite term or particular objective to be achieved.[54] Restrictive provisions on later employment are commonly found in professional and marketing partnership agreements.

21. Dissolution by Operation of Law

A partnership is dissolved by **operation of law** in the following instances.

(A) Death. A partnership is dissolved immediately upon the death of any partner. Thus, when the executor of a deceased partner carries on the business with the remaining partner, there is legally a new firm.

(B) Bankruptcy. Bankruptcy of the firm or of one of the partners causes the dissolution of the firm; insolvency alone does not.

(C) Illegality. A partnership is dissolved by an event that makes it unlawful for the business of the partnership to be carried on or for the members to carry it on in partnership. To illustrate, when it is made unlawful by statute for judges to engage in the practice of law, a law firm is dissolved when one of its members becomes a judge.

22. Dissolution by Decree of Court

A court may decree the dissolution of a partnership for proper cause. A court will not order the dissolution for trifling causes or temporary grievances that do not involve a permanent harm or injury to the partnership.

The filing of a complaint seeking a judicial dissolution does not in itself cause a dissolution of the partnership; it is the decree of the court that has that effect.

A partner may obtain a decree of dissolution for any of the following reasons.

(A) Insanity. A partner has been judicially declared insane or of unsound mind.

(B) Incapacity. One of the partners has become incapable of performing the terms of the partnership agreement.

(C) Misconduct. One of the partners has been guilty of conduct that substantially prejudices the continuance of the business. The habitual drunkenness of a partner is a sufficient cause for judicial dissolution.

(D) Impracticability. One of the partners persistently or willfully acts in such a way that it is not reasonably practicable to carry on the partnership business. Dissolution will be granted when dissensions are so serious and persistent that continuance is impracticable or when all confidence and cooperation between the partners have been destroyed.

A court may decree dissociation and dissolution of a partnership for proper cause, as set forth in the *Della Ratta* case.

Della Ratta v. Dyas, 961 A.2d 629 (Md. App. 2008)

Strategy = Squeeze Out Dyas
Ethics (Trust, Fairness, Loyalty, Doing No Harm) = None
Law = Dissociation, Dissolution

Edward Dyas and Joseph Della Ratta were equal owners of two hotels in Ocean City, Maryland. The "old" hotel was completed in 1988 and the "new" hotel was completed in 2006, with both properties owned under the men's Spa Motel General Partnership (Spa). They were also developers and equal owners of the Maresol Condominium project in Ocean City, which was completed in 2004 and held under Dyas's and Della Ratta's Bay View Limited Liability Company (Bay View). Della Ratta owned the construction company that built these projects, "DRI," and he also owned "CMC," the company that managed the two hotels. Dyas believed that Della Ratta was attempting to squeeze him out from Spa and Bay View. Under Dyas's analysis, Della Ratta's strategy in the general partnership, Spa, was to call for a very substantial capital contribution to pay

[54] *Harshman v. Pantaleoni*, 741 N.Y.S.2d 348 (A.D. 2002).

Continued

claims asserted by CMC for alleged advances made by it to pay for operational expenses and to pay claims to DRI for the new hotel's construction costs. Dyas contended those calls were unauthorized because the underlying claims could not be substantiated and the partnership agreement required that the developers first seek a commercial loan.

With respect to Bay View, Dyas's theory of Della Ratta's squeeze-out strategy involved two ploys. First, that Della Ratta sought personally to purchase the loan from Severn Bank and obtain from it an assignment of the security instrument, on which Della Ratta then would foreclose, so that he could buy in at the foreclosure sale. Severn Bank, however, would not assign the loan to Della Ratta. Dyas further alleged that, as an alternate squeeze-out strategy, Della Ratta wrongfully refused to sell condominium units in Maresol. The resulting illiquidity would deprive Bay View of the cash needed to repay Severn Bank, so that Della Ratta could buy Maresol at a foreclosure sale conducted by Severn Bank. After a 10-day trial, the circuit court concluded that Dyas had proven these allegations. The ultimate findings of the trial court were that it was "no longer reasonably practicable to carry on the business" of Spa or of Bay View and that Dyas "had proved to the court's satisfaction facts sufficient for the court to grant a dissolution" of the entities. The court further ordered dissociation of Della Ratta as a partner in Spa. The court supervised the winding up of the general partnership. Della Ratta appealed.

JUDICIAL OPINION

Rodowsky, Judge....

DISSOCIATION

Appellants...contend that the trial court erred (1) by dissociating Della Ratta from Spa and (2) by enjoining his capital calls for Spa....The conduct of Della Ratta, as a partner in Spa, supports the relief.

...Within Spa, the management of the two hotels was entrusted to Della Ratta's wholly owned company, CMC. Under the 1988 contract between Spa and CMC for the management of Sea Bay, CMC was to "utilize [the] latest revised edition, A UNIFORM SYSTEM OF ACCOUNTS FOR HOTELS[.]" There were to be monthly financial statements and, "[a]s additional support...detailed analysis of expenditures and variances to Budget." Instead, Della Ratta's "accounting principle" was "taking money from wherever is necessary." The trial court was referring to Della Ratta's practice of disregarding entities and using cash in one of his holdings to meet a need in some other holding. Thus, CMC would request or issue checks that bore no notation of purpose, or merely noted "loan" or "advance." CMC "utterly failed to comply" with the accounting requirements of its management contract.

Against this background, Della Ratta issued the capital calls of December 10, 2004. Writing to Spa as President of CMC, Della Ratta claimed $1,485,650.04 in cash advances to Spa, including interest, for operating losses and CMC claimed $640,920, including interest, to be due on lease financing for furniture, fixtures, and equipment for the Old Hotel. Writing to Spa as president of DRI, Della Ratta claimed $1,439,110, including interest, for cash advances. Writing to Spa for his own account, Della Ratta claimed $1,967,030.97, including interest, for cash advances. Each claim demanded payment on or before January 14, 2005. Then, writing as general partner of Spa, Della Ratta called for capital by January 14, 2005, of $5,532,711, of which Dyas's share would be $2,766,355.50. This is the "Old Money Call." In addition, Della Ratta claimed on behalf of Spa, payment by Dyas, by January 14, 2005, of $798,047.50, representing fifty percent of $1,596,095, the projected cost overrun on the New Hotel. Dyas was also requested to pay a total of $225,146.50 in monthly payments from December 2004 through April 2005 for projected cash requirements of the two hotels. These two demands are the "New Money Call."

The trial court expressly found that both of those calls "were issued in bad faith."

The trial court also found that, "[by] another improper accounting movement" in Spa, $580,000 was taken "for executive office expenses which was improper[.]"

This partial review of the unchallenged fact-findings relation to Della Ratta's activities while a partner in Spa is sufficient to demonstrate that dissociation from Spa and voiding of the capital calls was not based on Della Ratta's conduct as a member of Bay View. It also demonstrates satisfaction of the grounds for dissociation relied upon by the trial court, *i.e.*, that Della Ratta's conduct relating to Spa's business was such that it was "not reasonably practicable to carry on the business in partnership with [him]." CA § 9A-601(5)(iii)....

QUESTIONS

1. What arguments can you present in defense of Della Ratta's actions in this case?
2. Maryland is an RUPA state. Explain the use of the terms *dissociation, dissolution, and winding up* in this case.

(E) Lack of Success. The partnership cannot continue in business except at a loss.

(F) Equitable Circumstances. A decree of dissolution will be granted under any other circumstances that equitably call for a dissolution. Such a situation exists when one partner was induced by fraud to enter into the partnership.

CPA 23. Dissociation under the RUPA

Under the RUPA and its "entity" concept, a partner can leave the firm and not disrupt the partnership's legal existence. The RUPA uses the term *dissociation* for the departure of a partner[55] and reserves the term *dissolution* for those instances when a partner's departure results in the winding up and termination of the business.[56]

A partner has the absolute power to dissociate at will, just as a partner has the power to withdraw under the UPA, even if it is wrongful.[57] If wrongful, the partner is liable for damages for breach of contract.

A partner's dissociation from a firm ends the individual's right to participate in the management of the business.[58] It also ends the duty of loyalty owed the firm, and the individual may compete with the firm once dissociated.[59] If the partnership business continues after a partner dissociates from a firm, the partnership must buy out the dissociated partner's interest based on his share of the higher of the liquidation value of the firm or the value of the firm's business as a going concern on the date of dissociation, with interest.[60]

The RUPA created "notices" to deal with lingering authority of a dissociated partner based on apparent authority. To avoid liability, notice of lack of authority or liability should be given to customers and creditors regarding the dissociation of a partner. A filing with the Secretary of State limits liability and authority to 90 days after filing.[61] If no notice is given or filed, the partnership may be bound by the acts of a dissociated partner for up to two years after dissociation based on apparent authority.[62]

CPA 24. Notice of Dissolution

Under some circumstances, one partner may continue to possess the power to make a contract that binds the partnership even though the partnership has been dissolved.

(A) Notice to Partners. When the firm is dissolved by the act of a partner, notice must be given to the other partners unless that partner's act clearly shows an intent to withdraw from or to dissolve the firm. If the withdrawing partner acts without notice to the other partners, that partner is bound by contracts created for the firm.

When the dissolution is caused by the act, death, or bankruptcy of a partner, each partner is liable to the copartners for a share of any liability created by any other partner acting for the partnership without knowledge or notice of the act, death, or bankruptcy of the partner who caused the dissolution.

CPA (B) Notice to Third Persons. When dissolution is caused by the act of a partner or of the partners, notice must be given to third parties. A notice should expressly state that the partnership has been dissolved. Circumstances from which a termination may be inferred are generally not sufficient notice.

Thus, the fact that the partnership checks added the abbreviation *Inc.* after the partnership name was not sufficient notice that the partnership did not exist and that the business had been incorporated.

Actual notice of dissolution must be given to persons who have dealt with the firm.

For persons who have had no dealings with the firm, a publication of the fact of dissolution is sufficient. Such notice may be by newspaper publication, by posting a placard in a public place, or by any

[55] R.U.P.A. §601 cmt 1.
[56] R.U.P.A. §801.
[57] R.U.P.A. §601(1), 602(a).
[58] In a two-person partnership, when one partner withdraws, the partnership is dissolved by operation of law because there cannot be a one-person partnership. The buyout rule of RUPA §701(b) does not apply, and the dissolution procedures take over. See *Corrales v. Corrales*, 129 Cal. Rptr. 3d 428 (Cal. App. 2011).
[59] R.U.P.A. §404(2).
[60] R.U.P.A. §701(b). In *Rapport v. Gelfand*, 129 Cal. Rptr. 3d 670, 680 (Cal. App. 2011), the court interprets the term *liquidation value* as used in RUPA §701(b) to mean the sale price of the separate assets based on their market value as determined by a willing and knowledgeable buyer and a willing and knowledgeable seller, neither of whom is under any compulsion to buy or sell. Thus, for purposes of section 701, subdivision (b), "liquidation value" does not incorporate the common definition of "liquidation," which generally implies some urgency for immediate cash.
[61] R.U.P.A. §704.
[62] R.U.P.A. §702.

similar method. Failure to give proper notice continues the power of each partner to bind the others with respect to third persons on contracts within the scope of the business.

When dissolution has been caused by operation of law, notice to third persons is not required. As between the partners, however, the UPA requires knowledge or notice of dissolution by death and bankruptcy.

25. Winding up Partnership Affairs

Most established partnerships deal with the question of how to proceed with the business upon the death of a partner in the written partnership agreement. The agreement may set forth a method for establishing the value of the deceased partner's interest as of the date of death or allow for the remaining partners to purchase the deceased partner's interest. The agreement may also allow for the continuation of the business as usual while the valuation process is completed. However, in the absence of an agreement, either express or implied, permitting the surviving partners to continue the business, the partners must wind up the business and account for the share of the deceased partner.[63]

When dissolution is obtained by court decree, the court may appoint a receiver to conduct the winding up of the partnership business. This may be done in the usual manner, or the receiver may sell the business as a going concern to those partners who wish to continue its operation.

With a few exceptions, all partners have the right to participate in the winding up of the business.[64]

CPA 26. Distribution of Assets

Creditors of the firm have first claim on the assets of the partnership.[65] Difficulty arises when there is a contest between the creditors of the firm and the creditors of the individual partners. The general rule is that firm creditors have first claim on assets of the firm. The individual creditors share in the remaining assets, if any.

After the firm's liabilities to nonpartners have been paid, the assets of the partnership are distributed as follows: (1) each partner is entitled to a refund of advances made to or for the firm, (2) contributions to the capital of the firm are then returned, and (3) the remaining assets, if any, are divided equally as profits among the partners unless there is some other agreement. A partner who contributes only services to the partnership is not considered to have made a capital contribution, absent an agreement to the contrary.

If the partnership has sustained a loss, the partners assume it equally in the absence of a contrary agreement. Distribution of partnership assets must be made on the basis of actual value when it is clear that the book values are merely nominal or arbitrary amounts.

A provision in a partnership agreement that upon the death of a partner the interest of the partner shall pass to that partner's surviving spouse is valid. Such a provision takes effect against the contention that it is not valid because it does not satisfy the requirements applicable to wills.

27. Continuation of Partnership Business

As a practical matter, the business of the partnership is commonly continued after dissolution and winding up. In all cases, however, there is a technical dissolution, winding up, and termination of the life of the original partnership.

If the business continues, either with the surviving partners or with them and additional partners, it is a new partnership. Again, as a practical matter, the liquidation of the old partnership may in effect be merely a matter of bookkeeping entries, with all partners contributing again or relending to the new business any payment to which they would be entitled from the liquidation of the original partnership.

[63] *Chaney v. Burdett*, 560 S.E.2d 21 (Ga. 2002); *King v. Stoddard*, 104 Cal.Rptr. 903 (Cal. App. 1972).
[64] U.P.A. §37.
[65] *Holmes v. Holmes*, 849 P.2d 1140 (Or. App. 1993).

MAKE THE CONNECTION

SUMMARY

A *partnership* is a relationship created by the voluntary association of two or more persons to carry on as co-owners a business for profit.

A partnership agreement governs the partnership during its existence and may also contain provisions relating to dissolution. The partnership agreement will generally be in writing, and this may be required by the statute of frauds. The existence of a partnership may be found from the existence of shared control in the running of the business and the fact that the parties share profits and losses. The sharing of gross returns, as opposed to profits, is slight evidence of a partnership.

Partners hold title to firm property by tenancy in partnership. A creditor of a partner cannot proceed against any specific item of partnership property but must obtain a charging order to seize the debtor-partner's share of the profits. An assignee of a partner's interest does not become a partner without the consent of the other partners and is entitled only to a share of the profits and the assignor's interest upon dissolution.

When there are more than two partners in a firm, the decisions of the majority prevail on ordinary matters relating to the firm's business unless the decisions are contrary to the partnership agreement. A partner's authority to act for the firm is similar to that of an agent to act for a principal. A partner may not bind the firm by a contract that makes it impossible for the firm to conduct its business.

A partner's duties are the same as those of an agent. If there is no contrary agreement, each partner has the right to take an equal part in the management of the business, to inspect the books, to share in the profits, and after payment of all of the firm's debts and the return of capital, to share in the firm's property or surplus upon dissolution.

Partners have unlimited personal liability for partnership liabilities. Partners are jointly liable on all firm contracts. They are jointly and severally liable for all torts committed by one of the partners or by a firm employee within the scope of the partnership's business. A partner remains liable after dissolution unless expressly released by creditors. An incoming partner is not liable for the existing debts of the partnership unless the new partner expressly assumes those debts.

Dissolution ends the right of the partnership to exist as a going concern. Dissolution is followed by a winding-up period and the distribution of assets. A partnership may be dissolved by the parties themselves in accordance with the terms of the partnership agreement, by the expulsion of a partner, by the withdrawal of a partner, or by the bankruptcy of the firm or one of the partners. A court may order dissolution of a partnership upon the petition of a partner because of the insanity, incapacity, or major misconduct of a partner. Dissolution may be decreed because of lack of success, impracticability, or other circumstances that equitably call for dissolution. Notice of dissolution, except dissolution by operation of law, must be given. Actual notice must be given to those who have dealt with the firm as a partnership.

All partners generally have a right to participate in the winding up of the business. After the firm's liabilities to nonpartners have been paid, the assets are distributed among the partners as follows: (1) refund of advances, (2) return of contributions to capital, and (3) division of remaining assets in accordance with the partnership agreement or, if no agreement is stated, division of net assets equally among the partners.

LEARNING OUTCOMES

After studying this chapter, you should be able to clearly explain:

A. Nature and Creation

LO.1 Explain how partnerships are created by agreement, and understand that only when the partners' partnership agreement does not resolve an issue does partnership law apply

See the example of the dentist who was terminated from the three-person dental partnership without cause by majority vote, where the partnership agreement allowed for such a termination, p. 874.

LO.2 Understand that no writing is needed to form a partnership, nor a tax ID number, nor a partnership name. All that is needed is clear evidence that the partners carried on as co-owners of a business for profit

See the *Byker* case where one individual who carried on a business for a profit was dumbfounded to find out that he was, by law, a partner, pp. 875–876.

B. Authority of Partners

LO.3 Distinguish between express authority and customary authority of a partner to act for a partnership

See the discussion on the role of individual partners to act as expressly directed by a majority of partners (express authority) and to act on their own to make ordinary contracts necessary to transact the firm's business (customary authority) beginning on p. 879.

C. Duties, Rights, and Liabilities of Partners

LO.4 List the duties of partners to one another

See the discussion and examples of partners' duties of loyalty, good faith, and obedience, beginning on p. 881.

LO.5 Explain the nature and extent of a partner's liability on firm contracts and torts

See the *PNC Bank* case dealing with the question of joint liability or joint and several liability, on pp. 883–884.

D. Dissolution and Termination

LO.6 Describe how a partnership may be dissolved by the acts of partners, by operation of law, and by order of the court

See the example of withdrawal by a partner, Mary Harshman, without liability because the partnership was at-will, pp. 885–886.

See the *Della Ratta* case involving partnership dissolution by decree of court because of impractability, pp. 886–887.

KEY TERMS

articles of copartnership
articles of partnership
charging order
express authority
general partners
general partnership
jointly and severally liable
jointly liable
operation of law
partners
partnership
partnership agreement
tenancy in partnership
unincorporated association

QUESTIONS AND CASE PROBLEMS

1. Ray, Linda, and Nancy form a partnership. Ray and Linda contribute property and cash. Nancy contributes only services. Linda dies, and the partnership is liquidated. After all debts are paid, the surplus is not sufficient to pay back Linda's estate and Ray for the property and cash originally contributed by Linda and Ray. Nancy claims that the balance should be divided equally among Ray, Linda's estate, and Nancy. Is she correct?

2. Baxter, Bigelow, Owens, and Dailey were partners in a New York City advertising agency. Owens, who was in poor health and wanted to retire, advised the partners that she had assigned her full and complete interest in the partnership to her son, Bartholomew, a highly qualified person with 10 years of experience in the advertising business. Baxter, Bigelow, and Dailey refused to allow Bartholomew to attend management meetings and refused his request to inspect the books. Bartholomew pointed out that his mother had invested as much in the firm as any other partner. He believed, as assignee of his

mother's full and complete partnership interest, that he is entitled to (a) inspect the books as he sees fit and (b) participate fully in the management of the firm. Was Bartholomew correct?

3. Amy Gargulo and Paula Frisken operated as a partnership Kiddies Korner, an infants' and children's clothing store. They operated the business very successfully for three years, with both Paula and Amy doing the buying and Paula keeping the books and paying the bills. Amy and Paula decided to expand the business when an adjoining store became vacant. At the same time, they incorporated the business. Children's Apparel, Inc., was a major supplier to the business before the expansion. After the expansion, business did not increase as anticipated, and when a nationally known manufacturer of children's apparel opened a factory outlet nearby, the business could no longer pay its bills. Children's Apparel, which had supplied most of the store's stock after expansion, sued Amy and Paula as partners for bills due for expansion stock. Children's Apparel did not know that Amy and Paula had incorporated. Amy and Paula contended that the business was incorporated and that they therefore were not liable for business debts occurring after incorporation. Were Amy and Paula correct?

4. Calvin Johnson and Rudi Basecke did business as the Stockton Cheese Co., a partnership, which owned a building and equipment. The partners agreed to dissolve the partnership but never got around to completing the winding-up process. Calvin continued to use the building and to pay insurance on it but removed Rudi's name as an insured on the policy. When the building was later destroyed by fire, Calvin claimed the proceeds of the fire insurance policy because he and his wife were the named insureds on the policy and they had paid the premiums. Rudi claimed that although the partnership was dissolved before the fire, the winding up of the partnership was not completed at the time of the fire. He therefore claimed that he was entitled to half of the net proceeds of the policy. Decide. [*State Casualty v. Johnson*, 766 S.W.2d 113 (Mo. App.)]

5. Samuel Shaw purchased a ticket through Delta Airlines to fly a "Delta Connection" flight on SkyWest Airlines to Elko, Nevada. He was seriously injured when the SkyWest plane crashed near Elko. SkyWest's relationship with Delta was a contractual business referral arrangement, whereby Delta benefits through its charges for issuing tickets to connecting passengers to and from smaller communities, and SkyWest benefits from revenue generated by passengers sent to it by Delta. Both firms make a profit from this arrangement. SkyWest and Delta are often mentioned together by Delta in national print advertisements. Shaw believed that regardless of how the airlines characterize themselves, these airlines are in fact partners because they share profits from their combined efforts. Delta contended that it had no control over SkyWest's airplane operations and that sharing profits as compensation for services does not create a partnership. Decide. [*Shaw v. Delta Airlines, Inc.*, 798 F. Supp. 1453 (D. Nev.)]

6. Larson entered into a Special Manager Incentive Agreement (SMIA) with Tandy Corp. He agreed to manage a Radio Shack store for compensation equal to one-half of the adjusted gross profit of the store as computed by a specific formula and to provide the company with a $20,000 "security deposit" on equipment used to set up the store. The agreement was for a period of two years, automatically renewable annually until either party gave notice of termination 30 days prior to the end of a fiscal year. After some eight and one-half years of operating under renewed agreements, Tandy gave Larson notice of his termination. Larson sued Tandy, claiming that the SMIA was a partnership agreement because there were shared risks, expenses, profits, and losses. He sought an accounting for his reasonable share in the value of the store. Tandy argued that under the SMIA, Larson was an employee-manager, not a partner, and that the ultimate decision making on all matters was Tandy's. Decide. [*Larson v. Tandy Corp*, 371 S.E.2d 663 (Ga. App.)]

7. Two brothers, Eugene and Marlowe Mehl, formed a partnership to operate the family farm. One year, Eugene Mehl withdrew $7,200 from the partnership account and bought the Dagmar

Bar. The warranty deed and the liquor license to the bar were obtained in the names of Eugene Mehl and his wife, Bonnie. In a subsequent lawsuit, Marlowe claimed that the bar was a partnership asset. Decide. [*Mehl v. Mehl*, 786 P.2d 1173 (Mont.)]

8. Daniel Zuckerman, a minor, and Elaine, his mother, brought a medical malpractice action against Dr. Joseph Antenucci and Dr. Jose Pena. Although the summons did not state that the two defendants were partners, the undisputed evidence at the trial established that this was their relationship and that the alleged acts of malpractice were done in the course of partnership business. The jury returned a verdict finding that Dr. Pena was guilty of malpractice but that Dr. Antenucci was not guilty of malpractice. The amount of the verdict was $4 million. Antenucci contended that he cannot be held liable on a partnership theory for the act of his partner. Is he correct? [*Zuckerman v. Antenucci*, 748 N.Y.S.2d 578 (A.D.)]

9. Thomas Bartomeli decided to leave his employment to join his brother Raymond full-time in a small construction company. The brothers each contributed individual assets to the company and worked together to acquire equipment with both signing notes jointly to acquire certain equipment. Thomas considered himself a partner in the company; Raymond often referred to Thomas as his partner. It was the practice of the company to garage the equipment at Thomas's house. In 1983, the company was incorporated, but Thomas never held any shares in the company. On several occasions, Thomas's careless operation of equipment resulted in loss or damage to the company. Raymond became dissatisfied with Thomas's work performance, and on January 17, 1991, Thomas was removed as secretary of the corporation.

   On April 19, 1991, Thomas went to the company office and demanded a blank check from the secretary. Raymond found out about this demand and fired him. On April 20, 1991, Thomas demanded from Raymond either 50 percent of the company or certain equipment owned by the company. On April 22, 1991, Thomas was removed as vice president of the company. Raymond attempted to reach an agreement with Thomas on a division of company assets at that point but was not successful. Thereafter, Thomas sued his brother, alleging that Raymond had breached the brothers' contract of partnership. Because the company was a corporation, is it legally inconsistent for Thomas to contend that there was a contract for partnership in the company? How would you decide this case? [*Bartomeli v. Bartomeli*, 783 A.2d 1050 (Ct. App.)]

10. Friedman, the "O" Street Carpet Shop, Inc., and Langness formed a partnership known as NFL Associates. "O" Street Carpet's net contribution to capital was $5,004; Langness contributed $14,000 in cash; and Friedman contributed his legal services, on which no value was placed by the articles of partnership. The articles stated that Friedman was entitled to 10 percent of the profits and that Langness was to receive payments of $116.66 per month. The partnership's accountant treated the payments to Langness as a return of her capital. Years later, the partnership sold the rental property owned by the partnership, and the partnership was wound up. Friedman claimed that he was entitled to 10 percent of the partnership capital upon dissolution. Langness claimed that Friedman was not entitled to a capital distribution and that the monthly payments to her should not have been treated as a return of capital. Decide. [*Langness v. "O" Street Carpet, Inc.*, 353 N.W.2d 709 (Neb.)]

11. Ross, Marcos, and Albert are partners. Ross and Marcos each contributed $60,000 to the partnership; Albert contributed $30,000. At the end of the fiscal year, distributable profits total $150,000. Ross claims $60,000 as his share of the profits. Is he entitled to this sum?

12. Leland McElmurry was one of three partners of MHS Enterprises, a Michigan partnership. Commonwealth Capital Investment Corp. sued the partnership and obtained a judgment of $1,137,285 against it, but the partnership could not pay the judgment. Commonwealth then sued McElmurry for the entire debt on the theory that, as a partner of MHS, he was liable for its debts. What, if any, is McElmurry's liability?

[*Commonwealth Capital Investment Corp. v. McElmurry*, 302 N.W.2d 222 (Mich. App.)]

13. Thomas Smith and Jackie Lea were partners in the logging business. In January 1981, they joined Gordon Redd and went into business running a sawmill, calling the business Industrial Hardwood Products (IHP). Smith and Lea used their logging equipment at the mill site. Smith hauled 400 loads of gravel, worth some $26,000, from his father's land for the mill yard in the process of getting the mill operational. Smith and Lea received $300 a week compensation for their work, which was reported on federal W-2 forms. They worked up to 65 hours per week and were not paid overtime. All three discussed business decisions. Smith and Lea had the authority to write checks and to hire and fire employees. Lea left the business in 1983 and was paid $20,000 by Redd. The testimony indicated that the three individuals agreed in January 1981 that as soon as the bank was paid off and Redd was paid his investment, Lea and Smith would be given an interest in the mill. No written agreement existed. Redd invested $410,452 in the business and withdrew $500,475 from it. As of December 31, 1986, IHP had sufficient retained earnings to retire the bank debt. In April 1987, Smith petitioned the Chancery Court for dissolution of the "partnership" and an accounting. Redd denied that any partnership agreement was formed and asserted that Smith was an employee because he was paid wages. He offered to pay Smith $50,000 for the gravel and use of his equipment. Decide. [*Smith v. Redd*, 593 So.2d 989 (Miss.)]

14. Mason and Phyllis Ledbetter operated a business in Northbrook, Illinois, as a partnership called Ledbetters' Nurseries that specialized in the sale of garden lilies. The grounds of the nurseries were planted with numerous species of garden lilies, and hundreds of people toured the Ledbetters' gardens every day. After a tour, Sheila Clark offered to buy the facilities at a "top-notch price." Mason felt he could not refuse the high offer, and he signed a contract to sell all the facilities, including all flowers and the business name. When Phyllis refused to go along with the contract, Clark sued the Ledbetters' Nurseries partnership, seeking to obtain specific performance of the sales contract. Decide.

15. St. John Transportation Co., a corporation, made a contract with the partnership of Bilyeu and Herstel, contractors, by which the latter was to construct a ferryboat. Herstel, a member of the firm of contractors, executed a contract in the firm name with Benbow for certain materials and labor in connection with the construction of the ferryboat. In an action brought by Benbow to enforce a lien against the ferryboat, the *James Johns*, it was contended that all members of the firm were bound by the contract made by Herstel. Do you agree? [*Benbow v. The Ferryboat James Johns*, 108 P. 634 (Or.)]

CPA QUESTIONS

1. Acorn and Bean were general partners in a farm machinery business. Acorn contracted, on behalf of the partnership, to purchase 10 tractors from Cobb Corp. Unknown to Cobb, Acorn was not authorized by the partnership to make such contracts. Bean refused to allow the partnership to accept delivery of the tractors, and Cobb sought to enforce the contract. Cobb will:

   a. Lose, because Acorn's action was beyond the scope of Acorn's implied authority.

   b. Prevail, because Acorn had implied authority to bind the partnership.

   c. Prevail, because Acorn had apparent authority to bind the partnership.

   d. Lose, because Acorn's express authority was restricted, in writing, by the partnership agreement.

2. Upon dissolution of a general partnership, distributions will be made on account of:

   I. Partners' capital accounts.

II. Amounts owed partners with respect to profits.

III. Amounts owed partners for loans to the partnership in the following order:

a. III, I, II

b. I, II, III

c. II, III, I

d. III, II, I

3. Which of the following statements is correct with respect to a limited partnership?

a. A limited partner may *not* be an unsecured creditor of the limited partnership.

b. A general partner may *not* also be a limited partner at the same time.

c. A general partner may be a secured creditor of the limited partnership.

d. A limited partnership can be formed with limited liability for all partners.

4. When a partner in a general partnership lacks actual or apparent authority to contract on behalf of the partnership, and the party contracted with is aware of this fact, the partnership will be bound by the contract if the other partners:

	Ratify the Contract	*Amend the Partnership Agreement*
a.	Yes	Yes
b.	Yes	No
c.	No	Yes
d.	No	No

CHAPTER 43

© Manuel Gutjahr/iStockphoto.com

LPs, LLCs, and LLPs

learningoutcomes

After studying this chapter, you should be able to

LO.1 Explain the history of making limited liability available to general partnerships

LO.2 Explain the extent of a founding general partner's liability for the debts of the firm, and how unlimited liability can be avoided by utilization of a corporate general partner

LO.3 Explain the nature and extent of a limited partner's liability for the debts of the firm

LO.4 Explain the advantages of a limited liability company

LO.5 Understand that unless modified in an operating agreement, managers of LLCs owe member-investors the traditional duties of loyalty and care

LO.6 Explain how a limited liability partnership "shields" innocent partners from liability to third parties

A. The Arrival of Partnership Limited Liability

Individuals owning businesses or professional firms are concerned about exposing their personal wealth to liability beyond that invested in their businesses or firms. As discussed previously, limited liability is not a feature of general partnership law. The concept of making limited liability available to general partnerships was considered by the RUPA Drafting Committee when it began its work to revise the Uniform Partnership Act in 1987, but the concept was rejected. A limited partnership form of business organization had existed since 1916 under the Uniform Limited Partnership Act with limited partners (investors) having limited liability, but the firms' general partners were exposed to personal liability for firm debts under this act. The concept of full limited liability for partnerships began to take hold in 1986 when businesses forming limited partnerships under the Revised Uniform Limited Partnership Act utilized corporate general partners, with the general partners avoiding personal liability by the simple expedient of incorporating.

An IRS ruling classifying a Wyoming limited liability company (LLC) as a partnership for tax purposes led to the rapid spread of LLC statutes to every state within six years of the IRS ruling.[1] As part of the limited liability trend established by the swift enactment of LLC laws throughout the country, most states have also enacted limited liability partnership (LLP) acts. Like LLCs, they provide businesses and those offering professional services the benefit of single taxation as a partnership as well as limited liability.

B. Limited Partnership

A limited partnership is a special kind of partnership.

1. Formation of Limited Partnerships

The Uniform Limited Partnership Act (ULPA) was approved by the National Conference of Commissioners on Uniform State Law in 1916. It was revised in 1976 (RULPA), and this RULPA was amended in 1985. All states except Louisiana have adopted a version of the RULPA.

CPA **(A) Members of a Limited Partnership.** In a **limited partnership** certain members contribute capital but have limited liability for firm debts. The most these members can lose is their investment. These members are known as **limited partners**. The partners who manage the business and are personally liable for the firm debts are **general partners.**[2] A limited partnership can be formed by "one or more general partners and one or more limited partners."[3]

CPA **(B) Certificate of Limited Partnership.** Unlike a general partnership, a limited partnership can be created only by executing a certificate of limited partnership.

Under the 1985 amendments to the RULPA, the certificate requires the following information: (1) the limited partnership's name, (2) the address of the partnership's registered office and the name and business address of its agent for service of process, (3) the name and business address of each general partner, (4) the partnership's mailing address, and (5) the latest date on which the limited partnership is to dissolve. The names of the limited partners (the investors) are not required. This allows for the preservation of the confidentiality of the investors' names from competitors. Moreover, new investors may be admitted as limited partners without the significant administrative burden involved in amending the certificate, as was required under the ULPA. The RULPA provides for filing the certificate with the office of the secretary of state, as opposed to the local filing required under the ULPA.

When there is no filing of the limited partnership certificate, all participants have the status and liability of general partners in a general partnership. However, technical defects in the certificate do not prevent formation of a limited partnership if there has been substantial, good-faith compliance with the filing requirements.[4]

[1] Rev. Rul. 88-76, 1988—2 C.B. 360.
[2] *Brooke v. Mt. Hood Meadows, Ltd.*, 725 P.2d 925 (Or. App. 1986).
[3] R.U.L.P.A. §101(7).
[4] R.U.L.P.A. §201(b); *Fabry Partnership v. Christensan*, 794 P.2d 719 (Nev. 1990).

CPA **(c) Limited Partnership Agreement.** The RULPA embodies the policy of freedom of contract and maximum flexibility regarding the limited partnership agreement.[5] Most limited partnership agreements are drafted almost exclusively by their founding general partners, and courts resolve ambiguities against the drafting general partners and in favor of the reasonable expectations of the limited partners. **For Example,** when the general partners of the Nantucket Island Associates Limited Partnership unilaterally amended the limited partnership agreement to add a new class of preferred limited partnership units with superior rights to existing unit holders, ambiguous agreement language was construed against the general partners by the court, and the general partners were found to be in breach of the agreement by adding the new class of units.[6]

2. Characteristics of Limited Partnerships

A limited partnership has the following characteristics.

CPA **(a) Capital Contributions.** Under the ULPA, a limited partner contributed either cash or property but not services. Under the RULPA, however, a limited partner may contribute services.

CPA **(b) Firm Name.** With certain exceptions, a limited partner's name cannot appear in the firm name. Under the RULPA, the words *limited partnership* must appear without abbreviation in the firm name.

CPA **(c) Management and Control of the Firm.** The general partners manage the business and are personally liable for firm debts. However, general partners may avoid personal liability by incorporating. Limited partners (the investors) have the right to a share of the profits and a return of capital upon dissolution and have limited liability. The limitation of liability is lost, however, if they participate in the control of the business, as seen in the *Gilroy, Sims & Associates Ltd.* case.

American National Ins. Co. v. Gilroy, Sims & Associates, Ltd., 874 F. Supp. 971 (E.D. Mo. 1995)

The Problem of Limited Partners in Control

Gilroy, Sims & Associates, Ltd. (Gilroy, Sims), was a limited partnership engaged in real estate development whose original general partners were Richard Gilroy and William Sims. Thomas Green and John Murphy Jr. were listed as limited partners along with certain other individuals on the certificate of limited partnership. Green and Murphy took an active role in the day-to-day operations of the real estate developed by the limited partnership. Financing was obtained to construct the venture's building in St. Louis in 1968, and a mortgage was payable to American National Insurance Co. over 27 years. In 1976, the partnership executed a Restated Agreement, and Green and Murphy became general partners of Gilroy, Sims, agreeing to "unlimited liability for the debts of the partnership." In the fall of 1990, the partnership stopped making mortgage payments. After foreclosure by American National, a deficiency of $1,437,840 was outstanding. Green and Murphy believed that as limited partners when the debt was incurred in 1968, they were absolved from any personal liability beyond the assets of the firm. American National disagreed.

JUDICIAL OPINION

GUNN, D. J.…With respect to defendants Green and Murphy's motion for summary judgment for the remaining deficiency, the Court finds that defendants are liable for the remaining deficiency pursuant to the terms of the Restated Agreement.

Even though the Restated Agreement signed by Green and Murphy provides that "the partners shall have unlimited liability for the debts of the partnership," Green and Murphy contend that as incoming partners they are liable for prior debts only to the extent of partnership property and are absolved of personal liability under § 17 of the Uniform Partnership Act. An incoming partner, however, may by agreement bind himself to personal liability for past debts. See *Resolution Trust Corp v Teem Partnership,* 835 F. Supp. 563, 570 (D.Colo. 1993) (some jurisdictions interpreting parallel statutes have held that UPA § 17 does not apply to incoming partner who expressly assumes pre-existing obligation).

[5] See *Gotham Partners, L.P. v. Hallowood Realty Partners, L.P.,* 817 A.2d 160 (Del. 2002).

[6] *In re Nantucket Island Associates Limited Partnership Unit Holders Litigation,* 810 A.2d 351 (Del. Ch. 2002).

Continued

The dispositive issue before the Court is whether Green and Murphy assumed personal liability for the pre-existing debts and, if so, to what extent. In executing the Restated Agreement, defendants failed to limit the debts or time period of the debts for which they assumed unlimited liability, but instead assumed liability as general partners for all of the debts of the partnership in section 10. Defendants expressly adopted the partnership obligation incurred prior to their execution of the Restated Agreement by their words as well as their actions. Moreover, section 5 of the Restated Agreement describing the duration of the partnership specifically provides that the partnership commenced on November 1, 1968.

Under Missouri law, limited partners are not liable as general partners if they do not take part in the control of the day-to-day business operations of the partnership. *First Wisconsin Nat'l Bank v Towboat Partners, Ltd.*, 630 F. Supp. 171, 176 (E.D.Mo.1986) (limited partners not liable if only possible control was over expenditure of funds from extended line of credit agreed to by limited partners under restructuring agreement to keep partnership afloat). Although Green and Murphy's limited partner status would ordinarily limit their potential liability to creditors, their active roles in taking part in the control of the business subjected them to potential general partner liability.

[Judgment against Green and Murphy]

QUESTIONS

1. Were the incoming general partners, Green and Murphy, personally liable for the pre-existing partnership obligations in this case?
2. Under what circumstances may limited partners be subjected to general partner liability?
3. Were Green and Murphy subject to unlimited personal liability as general partners for the indebtedness that arose while they were limited partners?

The RULPA lists a number of "safe harbor" activities in which limited partners may engage without losing their protection from liability. These activities include

1. Being a contractor for, or an agent or employee of, the limited partnership or of a general partner;
2. Consulting with and advising a general partner regarding the partnership business;
3. Acting as a surety for the limited partnership; and
4. Voting on partnership matters, such as dissolving and winding up the limited partnership or removing a general partner.

(d) Right to Sue. A limited partner may bring a derivative action on behalf of the limited partnership to enforce a claim that the limited partnership possesses against others but that the partnership refuses to enforce.[7] This derivative suit is filed in the name of the limited partner, and the partnership is named as a defendant, with the limited partnership deriving the benefits of the action.

Limited partners may sue their partnership's general partner to protect the limited partners' interest. General partners today are commonly corporations with their own boards of directors and management teams, with the limited partnership format providing investment and tax incentives for investor–limited partners and the general partners reserving to themselves broad authority to act in the general partners' sole discretion and often in the general partners' own best interest. **For Example,** Donald Weedon and others formed a limited partnership under Delaware law to raise capital for the securities broker–dealer business. The partnership agreement, as allowed by Delaware law, gave the corporate general partners and its directors the right to restrict their fiduciary duties in managing the partnership and gave the general partner broad power to act, even in conflicted situations, subject only to very loose constraints of a subjective bad-faith standard. Nonemployee limited partners referred to by the court as the "outside investors" brought suit against the corporate general partners and members of the general partner's board of directors and top management for squeezing out all nonemployee limited partners and paying less than the fair value for their units in violation of fiduciary duties and the partnership agreement. The trial court decided in favor of the plaintiffs, stating in part:

[7] *Garber v. Stevens*, 941 N.Y.S.2d 127 (A.D. 2012).

> *...Even given the wide discretion the partnership agreement gives to the defendants to issue new units without fear of liability, the defendants managed to step out of bounds in one important respect. By deciding to permit the general partner's outside directors to acquire new units at a favorable price and by denying the same opportunity to Outside Investors, the defendants breached their contractual duties. This decision, I find, was not undertaken in good faith but instead as quid pro quo for the outside directors' willing assent to the issuance of a large number of new units to management and employees....*

The plaintiffs received a make-whole remedy from the court with monetary damages tied to fair market values.[8]

(E) Dissolution. The dissolution and winding up of limited partnerships is governed by the same principles applicable to general partnerships.

C. Limited Liability Companies

Limited liability company (LLC) acts were rapidly adopted by state legislatures throughout the country following a favorable tax ruling on this form of organization by the Internal Revenue Service.[9] This corporate-sounding entity is considered in this chapter because it is a form of limited partnership.

CPA 3. Characteristics of LLCs

The IRS has determined that an LLC may qualify for partnership federal tax treatment. Unlike a corporation, an LLC pays no federal taxes on its income as an entity. Instead, the income (or losses, deductions, and credits) flows through to the LLC's owners (called *members*) based on their proportionate interest in the company. The members report the income on their personal tax returns. The LLC combines this tax advantage with the limited liability feature of the corporate form of business organization. The owners and managers are not personally liable for the debts and obligations of the entity, provided that these individuals fulfill their common law duty to disclose that they are acting as agents for the limited liability company.

CPA **(A) Formation.** As set forth previously, general partnerships may be created without the formality of even a written partnership agreement when two individuals simply operate a business for profit as co-owners. LLCs, however, require a formal filing of articles of organization with the secretary of state in a manner similar to a filing of articles of incorporation by a corporation or a certificate of limited partnership for a limited partnership.

The articles for an LLC must contain the name, purpose, duration, registered agent, and principal office of the LLC. An LLC must use the words *limited liability company* or *LLC* in the company's name. The LLC is a legal entity with authority to conduct business in its own name.[10] LLC acts are characterized as "flexible statutes" because they generally permit owners to engage in the private ordering of relationships, with broad freedom of contract to govern these relationships as set forth in their operating agreements.[11]

CPA **(B) Capital Contributions.** An ownership interest in an LLC may be issued for cash, property, or services. The owners of the entity are known as *members*.

Capital contributions must comply with the "operating agreement" as discussed in the following paragraph. **For Example,** William Eichengrun claims his capital contribution to the LLC was in services, not cash, because he was the LLC's managing member. However, in proceedings to dissolve the LLC and distribute its assets, Eichengrun was not allowed to participate in the distribution because the operating agreement required that "initial capital contributions" of members be in cash or the fair market value of property.[12]

[8] *Gelfman v. Weeden Investors, L.P.*, 859 A.2d 89 (Del. Ch. 2004).

[9] IRS Rev. Rul. 88-76. LLCs have been adopted by every state and the District of Columbia. A Uniform Limited Liability Company Act was approved by the National Conference of Commissioners on Uniform State Law.

[10] An individual has a right to appear before a court and represent himself or herself. However, a member of an LLC who as such is not personally liable for the LLC's actions cannot appear before a court on behalf of the LLC entity. The LLC may appear in court only through counsel. Thus, a nonattorney member of an LLC was not allowed to represent the LLC in a court case. *Collier v. Cobalt, LLC*, 2002 WL 726640 (E.D. La. April 22, 2002). See also *Gobe Media Group, LLC v. Cisneros*, 959 A.2d 892 (N.J. Super. 2008).

[11] *Elf Atochem N. America, Inc. v. Jaffari*, 727 A.2d 286 (Del. Super. Ct. 1999).

[12] *KSI Rockville, LLC v. Eichengrun*, 760 N.Y.S.2d 520 (A. D. 2003).

CPA **(c) Management.** Management of an LLC is vested in its members. An *operating agreement*, equivalent to the bylaws of a corporation or a partnership agreement, sets forth the specific management authority of members and managers.

The operating agreement need not be in writing. All amendments must be unanimous unless otherwise agreed to by the members. Oral amendments may modify written terms unless otherwise set forth in the operating agreement. To promote certainty in management, it is recommended that the operating agreement be in writing and that it be changed only by written amendments adopted by a specified percentage or number of members.

The management structure created in the operating agreement may provide for the company to be member managed. However, members commonly delegate authority to run the entity to managers who may or may not be required to be members of the LLC. A member is not entitled to compensation for services performed by an LLC unless it is stipulated in the operating agreement. (Members receive profits and losses according to the terms of the operating agreement.)

In a member-managed company, each member has equal rights in management, with decisions made by a majority vote of the members.[13] In a manager-managed company, nonmanager members have no rights in management except for extraordinary matters, such as amending the operating agreement or consenting to merge with another entity.

Managers have the same fiduciary duties to the entity as corporate officers have to a corporation. LLC acts are characterized as "flexible statutes" allowing broad freedom of contract to govern relationships, as spelled out in detail in operating agreements. The parties are free to waive or modify in their operating agreements the duties of loyalty and care owed by managers to members. Unless modified, however, state LLC acts may apply fiduciary duties to managers who would qualify as fiduciaries under traditional equitable principles.

LLC acts are characterized as "flexible statutes" allowing broad freedom of contract to govern relationships, as spelled out in detail in operating agreements. The parties are free to waive or modify in their operating agreements the duties of loyalty and care owed by managers to members. Unless modified, however, state LLC acts may apply fiduciary duties to managers who would qualify as fiduciaries under traditional equitable principles, as set forth in the *Auriga Capital Corp. v. Gatz Properties* case.

Auriga Capital Corp. v. Gatz Properties, LLC, 40 A.3d 839 (Del. Chancery 2012)

Golf Course Owner Out of Bounds

Minority members in a Delaware limited liability company, Peconic Bay, LLC, brought a breach of fiduciary duty action against the LLC's manager and its majority interest holder regarding the sale of the LLC at an auction, in which the LLC was purchased by the manager. The "manager" is Gatz Properties, LLC, which is managed and partially owned by William Gatz. Peconic Bay, LLC, held a long-term lease on valuable property in New York that allowed the LLC to operate a first-rate Robert Trent Jones, Jr. designed golf course, called Long Island National Golf Course. The golf management company, American Golf, held a sublease on the property after it opened in 1999, never made a profit, and let the course fall into disrepair. Gatz knew in 2004 that American Golf would exercise its early termination option in 2010, yet he did nothing to plan for its exit. Rather, Gatz made a series of decisions that placed Peconic Bay in an economically vulnerable position. Then Gatz decided to put Peconic Bay on the auction block without engaging an experienced broker to market it to golf course managers or owners. Gatz, on behalf of Gatz Properties, was the only bidder to show up. Knowing this fact before formulating his bid, Gatz purchased Peconic Bay for a nominal value over the debt, and merged Peconic Bay into Gatz Properties.

[13] *IIC Holdings, LLC v. HR Software Acquisition Group, Inc.*, 750 N.Y.S.2d 425 (Sup. Ct. 2002).

Continued

JUDICIAL OPINION

STRINE, Ch.... The LLC agreement here does not displace the traditional duties of loyalty and care that are owed by managers of Delaware LLCs to their investors in the absence of a contractual provision waiving or modifying those duties. The Delaware Limited Liability Company Act (the "LLC Act") explicitly applies equity as a default and our Supreme Court, and this court, have consistently held that default fiduciary duties apply to those managers of alternative entities who would qualify as fiduciaries under traditional equitable principles, including managers of LLCs. Here, the LLC agreement makes clear that the manager could only enter into a self-dealing transaction, such as its purchase of the LLC, if it proves that the terms were fair. In other words, the LLC agreement essentially incorporates a core element of the traditional fiduciary duty of loyalty. Not only that, the LLC agreement's exculpatory provision makes clear that the manager is not exculpated for bad faith action, willful misconduct, or even grossly negligent action, *i.e.*, a breach of the duty of care.

The manager's course of conduct here breaches both his contractual and fiduciary duties. Using his control over the LLC, the manager took steps to deliver the LLC to himself and his family on unfair terms. When the LLC had a good cushion of cash from the remaining years of the lease, it was in a good position to take the time needed to responsibly identify another strategic option to generate value for the LLC and all of its investors. Although the economy was weakening, the golf course was well-designed and located in a community that is a good one for the profitable operation of a golf course. With a minimally competent and loyal fiduciary at the helm, the LLC could have charted a course that would have delivered real value to its investors. Had the manager acted properly, for example, the buyer he rebuffed could have entered into a new lease or purchased the LLC on terms that would have at least gotten the LLC's minority investors back what they had put in and some modest return.

The manager himself is the one who has created evidentiary doubt about the LLC's value by failing to pursue any strategic option for the LLC in a timely fashion because he wished to squeeze out the minority investors. The manager's defense that his voting power gave him a license to exploit the minority fundamentally misunderstands Delaware law. The manager was free not to vote his membership interest for a sale. But he was not free to create a situation of distress by failing to cause the LLC to explore its market alternatives and then to buy the LLC for a nominal price. The purpose of the duty of loyalty is in large measure to prevent the exploitation by a fiduciary of his self-interest to the disadvantage of the minority. The fair price requirement of that duty, which is incorporated in the LLC agreement here, makes sure that if the conflicted fiduciary engages in self-dealing, he pays a price that is as much as an arms-length purchaser would pay.

[The court awarded each minority member their full capital contribution of $725,000 plus 10% aggregate return of $72,500.]

QUESTIONS

1. Did the LLC agreement incorporate a core element of the traditional fiduciary duty of loyalty?
2. What is the purpose of the enforcement of a duty of loyalty?
3. Was not the manager free to utilize his voting power to exploit the opportunity for his own best interest?

In some states, members of manager-managed LLCs owe no fiduciary duty to the LCC unless a member exercises some or all of the authority of a manager pursuant to the operating agreement.[14]

CPA **(D) DISTRIBUTIONS.** Profits and losses are shared according to the terms of the operating agreement.

Liquidating distributions must first be applied to return all contributions not previously returned, and the remainder is distributed per capita to members unless members alter these rules in the operating agreement.

Any distribution made when the company is insolvent is unlawful. Each member or manager who votes to make an unlawful distribution is in violation of his or her fiduciary duty to the firm and is personally liable for the amount of distribution improperly paid.[15] However, the individual may

[14] In *Remora Investments, LLC v. Orr*, 673 S.E.2d 845 (Va. 2009), the Virginia Supreme Court held that nothing in the statutory provisions relating to LLCs provides for fiduciary duties between members of an LLC or between a member and a manager of an LLC. The statutory standard of conduct for a manager of an LLC is to discharge duties in accordance with his or her good-faith business judgment of the best interests of the company, rather than by imposing fiduciary duties on members. In contrast, the Uniform Limited Liability Act of 2006, which has been adopted in Idaho, Iowa, Nebraska, Utah, and Wyoming, states that members of an LLC owe each other the fiduciary duties of loyalty and care. See *Bush v. Sage Health Care, LLC*, 203 P.3d 694 (Idaho 2009). See also *Melcher v. Apollo Medical Fund Management*, 208 N.Y.S.2d 207 (A. D. 2006), referencing Delaware Code, Title 6 §18-110(c).

[15] *Florence Cement Co. v. Vitttaino*, 807 N.W.2d 461 (Mich. App. 2011).

compel contribution from all other responsible members and managers.

(E) LLC Property. The LLC is an independent entity separate and distinct from the members. The LLC owns and holds property in its own name.[16]

(F) Assignment. An interest in an LLC is personal property and is generally assignable. However, LLC members cannot transfer the right to participate in management without the consent of the other members of the LLC.

A creditor's right against a member's interest in an LLC is limited to a *charging order*. The creditor with such an order has only the rights of an assignee of an interest in an LLC.

(G) Dissolution. Most LLC statutes provide that an LLC will dissolve by the consent of the members or upon the death, retirement, resignation, expulsion, or bankruptcy of a member. Statutes also provide, however, that the business of the LLC may be continued with the consent of all of the remaining members. With a change in IRS regulations away from its four-factor corporate characteristics test, discussed in the following section, some states have begun to amend LLC laws to give limited liability companies the option of perpetual existence.

Situations in which it is not reasonably practicable to carry on the business in conformity with the operating agreement may arise. The LLC statute commonly permits a court to decree dissolution of the LLC when such a situation occurs.[17] **For Example,** Haley and Talcott each had a 50 percent interest in a real estate LLC. They had a falling out. The operating agreement contained an exit mechanism to buy out Haley's share, but the mechanism could not relieve Haley of his obligation as a personal guarantor for the LLC's mortgage. Because the LLC was deadlocked and the exit mechanism was not an adequate remedy, the court ordered the dissolution of the LLC and the sale of its property.[18]

Upon the winding up of an LLC, the assets are distributed according to the operating agreement. Should the agreement fail to provide for this event, the assets will be distributed according to the state's LLC statute.

(H) Tax Classification. The IRS applied a four-factor corporate characteristics test in determining whether an LLC would be taxed as a partnership or a corporation, allowing no more than two characteristics to exist to qualify for taxation as a partnership. The factors were continuity of life, centralized management, limited liability, and free transferability of interest. The four-factor test became obsolete on the implementation by the IRS of its so-called check-the-box entity classification election procedure available to unincorporated associations that are not publicly traded.[19] Now, if an LLC wants to be classified as a partnership, all it needs to do is make that election by checking the box on the appropriate IRS form.

(I) Disregarding the LLC Entity. Some LLC statutes provide that courts may disregard the LLC entirely and hold the owners personally liable beyond their investments to the same extent as done in corporate law when exceptional circumstances demand.[20]

The *Kaycee Land and Livestock* case involves the issue of piercing the LLC veil.

Kaycee Land and Livestock v. Flahive, 46 P.3d 323 (Wyo. 2002)

Piercing the LLC Veil

Flahive Oil & Gas is a Wyoming Limited Liability Company with no assets at this time. Kaycee Land and Livestock (Kaycee) entered into a contract with Flahive Oil & Gas LLC allowing Flahive Oil & Gas to use the surface of its real property. Roger Flahive is and was the managing member of Flahive Oil & Gas at all relevant times. Kaycee alleges that Flahive Oil & Gas caused environmental contamination to its real property. Kaycee seeks to pierce the LLC veil and

[16] *Northeast Realty, LLC v. Misty Bayou, LLC*, 920 So.2d 938 (La. App. 2006).

[17] *Venture Sales, LLC v. Perkins*, 86 So.3d 910 (Miss. 2012).

[18] *Haley v. Talcott*, 864 A.2d 86 (Del. Ch. 2004).

[19] Treas. Reg. 301.7701 *et seq.*

[20] *Net Jets Aviation, Inc. v. LHC Communications, LLC*, 537 F.3d 168 (2d Cir. 2008); but see *Serio v. Baystate Properties, LLC*, 39 A.3d 131 (Md. App. 2012).

Continued

disregard the LLC entity of Flahive Oil & Gas and hold Roger Flahive individually liable for the contamination. There is no allegation of fraud. The question presented to the Wyoming Supreme Court is whether, in the absence of fraud, the remedy of piercing the veil is available against a company formed under the Wyoming Limited Liability Company Act.

JUDICIAL OPINION

KITE, J.…Wyoming courts, as well as courts across the country, have typically utilized a fact driven inquiry to determine whether circumstances justify a decision to pierce a corporate veil. This case comes to us as a certified question in the abstract with little factual context, and we are asked to broadly pronounce that there are no circumstances under which this court will look through a failed attempt to create a separate LLC entity and prevent injustice. We simply cannot reach that conclusion and believe it is improvident for this court to prohibit this remedy from applying to any unforeseen circumstance that may exist in the future.…

…We note that Wyoming was the first state to enact LLC statutes. Many years passed before the Internal Revenue Service's approval of taxation of LLCs as partnerships led to other states adopting LLC legislation and the broad usage of this form for business organizations. Wyoming's statute is very short and establishes only minimal requirements for creating and operating LLCs. It seems highly unlikely that the Wyoming legislature gave any consideration to whether the common law doctrine of piercing the veil should apply to the liability limitation granted by that fledgling statute.…

…With the dearth of legislative consideration on this issue in Wyoming, we are left to determine whether applying the well established common law to LLCs somehow runs counter to what the legislature would have intended had it considered the issue. In that regard, it is instructive that: "Every state that has enacted LLC piercing legislation has chosen to follow corporate law standards and not develop a separate LLC standard." Philip P. Whynott, *The Limited Liability Company* §11:140 at 11-5 (3d ed. 1999). Statutes which create corporations and LLCs have the same basic purpose—to limit the liability of individual investors with a corresponding benefit to economic development. Statutes created the legal fiction of the corporation being a completely separate entity which could act independently from individual persons. If the corporation were created and operated in conformance with the statutory requirements, the law would treat it as a separate entity and shelter the individual shareholders from any liability caused by corporate action, thereby encouraging investment. However, courts throughout the country have consistently recognized certain unjust circumstances can arise if immunity from liability shelters those who have failed to operate a corporation as a separate entity. Consequently, when corporations fail to follow the statutorily mandated formalities, comingle funds, or ignore the restrictions in their articles of incorporation regarding separate treatment of corporate property, the courts deem it appropriate to disregard the separate identity and do not permit shareholders to be sheltered from liability to third parties for damages caused by the corporations' acts.

We can discern no reason, in either law or policy, to treat LLC's differently than we treat corporations. If the members and officers of an LLC fail to treat it as a separate entity as contemplated by statute, they should not enjoy immunity from individual liability for the LLC's acts that cause damage to third parties. Most, if not all, of the expert LLC commentators have concluded the doctrine of piercing the veil should apply to LLCs.… It also appears that most courts faced with a similar situation—LLC statutes which are silent and facts which suggest the LLC veil should be pierced—have had little trouble concluding the common law should be applied and the factors weighed accordingly.

Certainly, the various factors which would justify piercing an LLC veil would not be identical to the corporate situation for the obvious reason that many of the organizational formalities applicable to corporations do not apply to LLCs. The LLC's operation is intended to be much more flexible than a corporation's. Factors relevant to determining when to pierce the corporate veil have developed over time in a multitude of cases. It would be inadvisable in this case, which lacks a complete factual context, to attempt to articulate all the possible factors to be applied to LLCs in Wyoming in the future. For guidance, we direct attention to commentators who have opined on the appropriate factors to be applied in the LLC context.

CONCLUSION

No reason exists in law or equity for treating an LLC differently than a corporation is treated when considering whether to disregard the legal entity. We conclude the equitable remedy of piercing the veil is an available remedy under the Wyoming Limited Liability Company Act.

QUESTIONS

1. How did this case happen to come to be heard before the state's supreme court?
2. What public policy reason(s), if any, exists to create separate standards for LLC veil piercing versus corporate veil piercing?

FIGURE 43-1 *Comparison of General Partnership, Limited Partnership, Limited Liability Company, and Limited Liability Partnership*

	General Partnership	Limited Partnership	Limited Liability Company (LLC)	Limited Liability Partnership (LLP)
Creation	No formality required.	Filing a certificate of limited partnership with appropriate state office.	Filing articles of organization with secretary of state.	Registration of LLP filed with state government.
Liability	Unlimited liability of each partner for firm debts.	General partners: unlimited liability for firm debts. Limited partners: no liability beyond loss of investment.	All members are liable for LLC debts to the extent of their capital contributions and equity in firm. No personal liability beyond this.	No liability for partners beyond their contributions and equity in firm, except unlimited personal liability for their own wrongful acts and those of persons whom they supervise.
Management	All partners according to their partnership agreement or the UPA or RUPA.	General partners according to their partnership agreement or the UPA or RUPA. Limited partners excluded.	By members of firm, who may delegate authority to managers.	All partners according to partnership agreement or the UPA.
Dissolution	As set forth in the partnership agreement or the UPA or RUPA.	As set forth in the partnership agreement or the ULPA or RULPA.	As set forth in LLC statute or articles of organization.	As set forth in partnership agreement or the UPA or RUPA.

4. LLCs and Other Entities

LLCs are distinguishable from Subchapter S corporations and limited partnerships.

(A) LLC Distinguished from a Subchapter S Corporation. Under a Subchapter S corporation (so named from Subchapter S of the Internal Revenue Code), shareholders of a close corporation may be treated as partners for tax purposes and retain the benefit of limited liability under the corporate form. An S corporation is limited to 75 shareholders who must be U.S. citizens or resident aliens. Although partnerships and corporations may generally not be shareholders, employee stock ownership plans (ESOPs) and nonprofit entities may be. In contrast, an LLC has no limit on the number of owners, and there is no restriction on the types of entities or persons that may own an LLC. Thus, partnerships, corporations, and foreign investors may be owners of an LLC. Because substantial taxes on appreciated assets are payable on the liquidation of an S corporation, it is generally not feasible to convert an existing S corporation to an LLC.

CPA **(B) LLC Distinguished from a Limited Partnership.** Limited partners in a limited partnership have the advantage of limited liability. However, every limited partnership must have a general partner who manages the business, and this partner can be subject to unlimited liability. This structural feature is a major disadvantage of the limited partnership form that does not exist in a limited liability company (LLC). Also, individual limited partners may lose their limited liability if they participate in the control of the business. Under an LLC, the members may actively participate in the control of the business and still receive limited liability protection. As stated previously in this chapter, a general partner may avoid unlimited liability on a sizeable limited partnership project by incorporating.

(C) Usage. It is expected that the LLC will in many instances replace general and limited partnerships as well as close corporations and S corporations. The LLC will not replace the publicly traded corporation, however, because publicly traded partnerships and LLCs must be classified as corporations for tax purposes.[21]

D. Limited Liability Partnerships

As part of the limited liability trend established by the swift enactment of LLC laws throughout the country, most states have recently enacted limited liability partnership (LLP) acts. Like LLCs, they provide businesses and those offering professional services the benefit of single taxation as a partnership as well as limited liability.[22]

CPA 5. Extent of Limited Liability

In a general partnership, partners are jointly liable for partnership debts and jointly and severally liable for partnership torts. LLP statutes were initially drafted to shield innocent partners from vicarious negligence or malpractice liability of their partners. Some states now provide "full shields" for innocent partners that eliminate the vicarious personal liability of these partners for the obligations of the partnership and free them from any obligation to contribute personal assets beyond their investments in the partnership. However, the "liability shield" of a registered limited liability partnership only applies to a partner's liability to third parties and does not shield against breaches of the partnership's or partners' obligations to each other. In every state, however, LLP partners remain fully liable for their own negligence and continue to have unlimited liability for the wrongful acts of those whom they directly supervise and control.

Professional LLPs continue to be subject to professional regulations, and the appropriate regulating boards set the amount and type of malpractice insurance firms must carry to operate as an LLP.

For Example, to illustrate the effects of a change from a general partnership to an LLP, surgeons Jones, Smith, and Gray are partners. Jones inadvertently removed Miller's healthy kidney rather than his diseased kidney, and a jury returned a verdict of $2 million. Smith and Gray, although innocent

[21] See IRS Notice 88-75, 1988, 1988-2 CB 386. The traditional corporation retains many advantages, such as the low corporate income tax on corporate profits, which allows accumulation of capital for expansion or the distribution of all corporate earnings as compensation as well as providing fringe benefits for employee-owners with pretax dollars (IRC §§79, 119, 162).

[22] The 1994 Revised Uniform Partnership Act (RUPA) was amended in 1996 to include two new articles: Article 10, dealing with limited liability partnerships, and Article 11, dealing with foreign limited liability partnerships. Articles 1 through 11 constitute the Uniform Limited Liability Partnership Act.

Ethics & the Law

The S & L Crisis

When the Office of the Special Counsel concluded its work in both civil and criminal litigation against officers, directors, and consultants involved with failed savings and loan institutions in the late 1980s, it released a report on its work. On the civil side, the Office of the Special Counsel had obtained settlements from defendants in civil suits of $2.9 billion in restitution. Accounting firms, along with lawyers and consultants, comprised 71 percent of the defendants.

Because most accounting firms were organized as partnerships, the result was that many partners were required to dig into their personal assets to meet the restitution requirements imposed by the federal government. Since the creation of LLPs, all of the largest accounting firms in the United States have restructured, with most choosing the LLP for conducting business. All forms of restructuring will ensure limited personal liability for their principals.

Was the restructuring undertaken to avoid liability? Does limited liability insulate those who make decisions from liability for those decisions? Financiers attempt to determine what stake the officers in a corporation have in the corporation. Stock ownership and exposure to losses through the value of those shares are seen as a positive influence. Do liability limitations reduce the stake a principal has? Is it good to have decision makers separated from the costs of those decisions?

partners, are jointly and severally liable along with Jones under general partnership law, and their personal assets can be reached to pay the judgment if necessary. Under an LLP, only partnership assets and the personal assets of Jones are available to pay the judgment. Smith's and Gray's personal assets cannot be reached.

CPA 6. Registration and Usage

LLP statutes are designed to permit the conversion of existing general partnerships into limited liability partnerships. The statutes require registration with the secretary of state, and the name of the partnership must contain the term *limited liability partnership* or *LLP*.

Traditional partnership agreements, like those used by many accounting and law firms and other professional partnerships, can be converted into limited liability partnership agreements without major redrafting or renegotiating of the underlying agreements. It is thus expected that many of these professional firms will organize under this new form of partnership.

MAKE THE CONNECTION

SUMMARY

A limited partnership consists of one or more limited partners who contribute cash, property, or services without liability for losses beyond their investment, and one or more general partners, who manage the business and have unlimited personal liability. A limited partner's protection from unlimited liability may be lost if the partner participates in the control of the business. "Safe harbor" activities for limited partners are set forth in the RULPA. General partners may avoid personal liability by incorporating. A certificate of limited partnership must be filed when the partnership is formed for the law to apply. Otherwise, general partnership law applies.

A limited liability company is a hybrid form of business organization that combines the tax advantages of a partnership with the limited liability feature of the corporation. It must be formed in accordance with state law in order to have effect, and the designation LLC must appear with the company's name. Management of an LLC is vested in its members, and members can delegate authority to run the entity to managers, the terms of which are set forth in the company's operating agreement. Members receive profits and losses according to the operating agreement. A member's interest in an LLC is assignable, but consent of the other members is needed for the assignee to participate in the firm's management.

A limited liability partnership is a new form of business organization that allows existing partnerships to convert to this form without major renegotiation of the underlying partnership agreement. Innocent partners in a limited liability partnership are not personally liable for the torts of other partners beyond their investment in the firm.

LEARNING OUTCOMES

After studying this chapter, you should be able to clearly explain:

A. The Arrival of Partnership Limited Liability

LO.1 Explain the history of making limited liability available to general partnerships

See the presentation of the developing law of partnership limited liability on p. 897.

B. Limited Partnership

LO.2 Explain the extent of a founding general partner's liability for the debts of the firm, and how unlimited liability can be avoided by utilization of a corporate general partner

See the discussion of general partners' avoidance of personal liability through incorporation, p. 898.

LO.3 Explain the nature and extent of a limited partner's liability for the debts of the firm

See the *Gilroy* case in which limited partners (investors) lost their limitation of liability by participating in the control of the business, pp. 898–899.

C. Limited Liability Companies

LO.4 Explain the advantages of a limited liability company

See the discussion of the advantages of an LLC, including the tax advantages of treatment as a partnership with the limited liability feature of a corporation, beginning on p. 900.

LO.5 Understand that unless modified in an operating agreement, managers of LLCs owe member-investors the traditional duties of loyalty and care

See the *Gatz* case, where the manager's conduct breached his fiduciary duties to minority members, on pp. 901–902.

D. Limited Liability Partnerships

LO.6 Explain how a limited liability partnership "shields" innocent partners from liability to third parties

See the example involving Dr. Jones's removal of the wrong kidney, with innocent partners Smith's and Grey's personal assets being shielded from liability from a large judgment beyond partnership and Dr. Jones' assets, pp. 906–907.

KEY TERMS

general partners

limited partners

limited partnership

QUESTIONS AND CASE PROBLEMS

1. What is the principal advantage of an LLP over an LLC?

2. Alan Waung, a Hong Kong businessperson, purchased a golf course in Saginaw, Michigan, as an investment. As an avid golfer, Alan anticipates spending several weeks during the year at his "Northern Pines" course. He has been informed that a Subchapter S corporation would allow him and his family-member shareholders to be treated as partners for U.S. tax purposes while retaining the limited liability of the corporate form. Advise Mr. Waung on this matter. What form of business organization would you recommend?

3. Kate Haley, an experienced builder, formed a limited partnership in August 2011, along with two limited partners, Drs. Growbioski and Gailen, who each provided $100,000 to the partnership for initial capital for the construction of a medical office building near Stowe, Vermont. With the bustle of getting building and environmental permits and placating abutters to the property, as well as lining up suppliers and subcontractors and getting the job started, Kate simply did not find an opportunity to take the long drive to file the certificate of limited partnership with the secretary of state's office in Montpelier. A confluence of bad weather, an accident causing serious personal injury, financing disappointments, labor difficulties, design problems, and some personal problems resulted in the project being stopped before completion with some $550,000 in overdue bills. Dr. Growbioski has been approached by several suppliers and craftsmen seeking payment for supplies and work performed. As a limited partner, he believes that he is not liable for firm debts beyond his investment, which was $100,000. Explain to Dr. Growbioski his obligations at this point.

4. Alice Meyers, Monroe Moylan, and Bart Means practice medicine as Bay Area Anesthetics Associates (BAAA), a limited liability partnership. A newly certified nurse anesthesiologist, Mary Noyes, working with Dr. Means and not realizing a patient's allergy condition set forth on her chart, inadvertently administered the wrong anesthesia, which resulted in the patient's death. In a malpractice suit against Bay Area Anesthetics Associates, LLP, is the partnership liable for Mary Noyes's actions if she was employed by the hospital? What if she was employed by the partnership? Explain in detail.

5. Sabastian Hafner joined a start-up business with a business plan focused on making breads without common food allergens, such as wheat, yeast, dairy, and gluten, to be marketed in a major metropolitan area. The five founders of the business, including Sabastian, selected the limited liability company (LLC) as their form of business organization. The Articles of Organization for the limited liability company were duly filed with the secretary of state. The Operating Agreement simply provided that founding member Jillian Lopez would be the sole manager of the firm, and it set a salary for her at $40,000 per year. She hired employees to perform production, delivery, and sales work. Sebastian and the other three members spent time nights and early mornings "pitching in" at the bakery. After two months of diligent work, Sabastian, a second-year MBA student, sought back pay for the 40 hours each week he spent at the bakery during the previous eight weeks. He pointed out to the other members of the LLC that state law authorizes employees to sue for their wages. What are Sabastian's rights regarding pay for the service he performed for the LLC?

6. Hurwitz and Padden practiced law as equal partners for a short period of time before converting to an LLC. Some three years later, Padden informed Hurwitz that he intended to leave the firm. When they could not agree on how to divide $200,000 in fees relating to work acquired before the dissolution of the LLC, Hurwitz filed suit seeking an equal division of the fees under partnership principles. Padden contended that partnership principles should not apply to the dissolution of an LLC even though the state's LLC law incorporated the definition and use of the term *dissolution* from the UPA. Decide. [*Hurwitz v. Padden*, 581 N.W.2d 359 (Minn. App.)]

7. Don Mason and Beth Daley were managers and members of Pacific Beach Developers, LLC (PBD), a start-up real estate development company focusing on rehabilitating older properties for increased rental values and possible resale. Daley made a contract with San Diego Architects Associates (SDAA) to provide plans for the rehabilitation of a 60-unit building on Ingraham Street for $97,000, signing the contract "Beth Daley, manager P.B.D. LLC." Financing for the Ingraham Street property fell through, and PBD's option on the property expired. Although Daley notified SDAA that the "Ingraham Street deal was off," SDAA had nearly completed its work, and SDAA brought suit for the contract price against both the LLC and Beth Daley. At the point the lawsuit was initiated, PBD had no working capital remaining, and Don and Beth had "moved on," having taken jobs as mutual fund salespersons. Advise Beth of her legal obligations to SDAA.

8. John and Amelia have general commitments from a number of individuals to invest in their Sproondrift Cove Club golf course and distinctive residential community in Duval County. John wants to form a limited partnership. He realizes that every limited partnership must have a general partner who manages the business and is subject to unlimited liability for all debts and liabilities of the limited partnership. But he says that is no problem because the general partner can be a corporation and can limit its liability exposure by simply creating a "shell" corporation. John stated to Amelia, "As officers of the corporate general partner, you and I can operate the business without the limited partners interfering…we run the show!" Amelia responded, "John, what you propose seems so very complicated, risky, and expensive. A number of our investors are relatives who may want to be listened to, and some of our investors are professionals who could give us some valuable advice. Maybe a limited liability company would be a better entity for us." Compare the advantages and disadvantages of an LLC with a limited partnership and recommend the most appropriate form of business organization for this venture.

9. Hacienda Farms, Ltd., was organized as a limited partnership with Ricardo de Escamilla as the general partner and James L. Russell and H. W. Andrews as limited partners. The partnership raised vegetables and truck crops that were marketed principally through a produce concern controlled by Andrews. All three individuals decided which crops were to be planted. The general partner had no power to withdraw money from the partnership's two bank accounts without the signature of one of the limited partners. After operating for some seven and one-half months under these procedures, the limited partners demanded that the general partner resign as farm manager, which he did. Six weeks later, the partnership went into bankruptcy. Laurance Holzman, as trustee in bankruptcy, brought an action against Russell and Andrews, claiming that they had become liable to the creditors of the partnership as general partners because they had taken part in the control of the partnership business. How would you decide the case under the ULPA? Would the outcome be different under the RULPA? [*Holzman v. de Escamilla*, 195 P.2d 833 (Cal. App.)]

10. Jerome Micco was a major shareholder and corporate officer of Micco and Co., Inc., which was a limited partner in Harbor Creek, Ltd., a limited partnership formed to build a condominium complex. Hommel, an electrical contractor, was the successful bidder on certain electrical work for the project. For several months, Hommel worked under the direction of the construction supervisor and was paid by the limited partnership for his work. Because of financial difficulties, the supervisor was released. Thereafter, Jerome Micco played a major role in the building of the project, directing what work was to be performed. Hommel submitted payment invoices directly to Micco. When Hommel was not paid, he sued Micco, contending that Micco was a limited partner who ran the operation personally and was personally responsible for the debt. Micco argued that he was an employee or agent of a corporation (Micco and Co., Inc.) and thus could not be held liable for the debt. The evidence reveals that Micco had no occasion to tell Hommel that he was acting as a corporate officer. Is it ethical for a corporate officer and shareholder to seek to avoid individual

liability in this case? How would you decide the case? [*Hommel v. Micco*, 602 N.E.2d 1259 (Ohio App.)]

11. Ralph and Maureen K. Hagan (collectively "Hagan") owned the Stuart Court Apartments in Richmond, Virginia. On April 30, 1994, Hagan executed an agreement with Adams Property Associates, Inc. (Adams), giving Adams the exclusive right to sell the property for $1,600,000. The agreement provided that if the property was "sold or exchanged" within one year, with or without Adams's assistance, Hagan would pay Adams a fee of 6 percent of the "gross sales amount." Seven days before the year expired, Hagan, Roy T. Tepper, and Lynn Parsons formed a limited liability company, Hagan, Parsons, & Tepper, LLC (HPT). By deed dated April 23, 1995, Hagan transferred the property to HPT. Adams contends it is entitled to a commission from Hagan pursuant to the April 1994 agreement. Hagan contends the transaction was just a contribution of capital to a new company, not a sale. Decide. [*Hagan v. Adams Property Associates, Inc.*, 482 S.E.2d 805 (Va. 1997)]

12. Peter Kertesz formed an LLC and operated it in South Florida under the business name "Mourning Flowers." The LLC specialized in the sale of flowers to funeral homes. Although Kertesz was initially the only member and manager, he ultimately granted ownership interests totaling 55 percent of the LLC to six individuals. In mid-2007, the members had a falling out that culminated in the majority removing Kertesz as managing member. Kertesz alleged that shortly after this, the LLC's distributors and clients "threatened to terminate their relationship with the LLC if Kertesz was not brought back into the operations of the LLC." These actions, Kertesz claimed, caused the LLC to suffer irreparable harm. Kertesz sought the judicial dissolution of the LLC on the basis of these circumstances and an alleged deadlock in management of the LLC, and sought the appointment of a receiver to protect the assets and goodwill of the LLC. What relief, if any, is Kertesz entitled to? [*Kertesz v. The Spa Floral, LLC*, 994 So.2d 473 (Fla. App.)]

13. Thomas Banner assigned his voting rights and his right to receive distributions in the Hut at Avon, LLC, to Elizabeth Condo as part of a divorce settlement. When the other members of the Hut Group, Thomas Connors and George Roberts, learned of the unapproved assignment, they contacted Banner and expressed the view that the assignment violated the antiassignment clause of the operating agreement, which required the primary consent of all the members. After some negotiations, Banner agreed to sell his entire rights to Connors and Roberts for $125,000. Condo sued these members in court for the destruction of the value of the assignment. The LLC defended that the assignment was in violation of the operating agreement and thus was void. Decide. [*Condo v. Connors*, 266 P.3d 1110 (Colo. 2011)]

CPA QUESTIONS

1. Which of the following statements is correct with respect to a limited partnership?
   a. A limited partner may *not* be an unsecured creditor of the limited partnership.
   b. A general partner may *not* also be a limited partner at the same time.
   c. A general partner may be a secured creditor of the limited partnership.
   d. A limited partnership can be formed with limited liability for all partners.

Corporation Formation

learningoutcomes

After studying this chapter, you should be able to

LO.1 Recognize that a corporation is a separate legal entity, distinct and apart from its stockholders

LO.2 Explain the wide range of power given to corporations under modern corporate codes

LO.3 Understand that the promoter is personally liable for preincorporation contracts

LO.4 Understand that after a corporate charter has been dissolved the owners and officers may be personally responsible for contracts made in the corporate name if they knew or should have known of the dissolution

LO.5 Explain a stockholder's option when he or she objects to a proposed consolidation or merger of the corporation

LO.6 Recognize that liabilities of predecessor corporations can be imposed on successor corporations when the transaction is a de facto merger or a continuation of the predecessor

The corporation is one of the most important forms of business organization.

A. Nature and Classes

A *corporation* is an artificial person that is created by government action.

1. The Corporation as a Person

A **corporation** is an artificial person created by government action and granted certain powers. It exists in the eyes of the law as a person, separate and distinct from the persons who own the corporation.

The concept that the corporation is a distinct legal person means that the corporation's property is owned not by the persons who own shares in the corporation but by the corporation. Debts of the corporation are debts of this artificial person, not of the persons running the corporation or owning shares of stock in it.[1] The corporation can sue and be sued in its own name, but shareholders cannot be sued or held liable for corporate actions or obligations.[2]

The *Hayes v. Collins* case addresses the issue of personal liability of the sole owner of a corporation for a corporate debt.

Hayes v. Collins, 538 S.E.2d 785 (Ga. App. 2000)

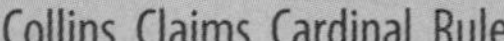

Collins Claims Cardinal Rule

Lisa Hayes sued Jennifer Collins seeking repayment of a loan. Ms. Hayes's late husband, Tony Hayes, loaned Corporate Staffing Solutions, Inc. (the "Corporation"), a total of $33,500 by writing three checks from his home equity line of credit. Mr. Hayes made two of the checks payable to the Corporation and the third payable to himself. The third check was deposited into the Corporation's account. The terms of the loan were not reduced to writing, and Mr. Hayes did not establish any deadlines for repayment. Mr. Hayes died in February 1998. On May 28, 1998, Ms. Hayes and Ms. Collins held a meeting with the executor of the estate. Collins, who is the Corporation's president and sole shareholder, stated that she would attempt to repay the loan made to the Corporation. Ms. Hayes testified that she subsequently discovered that her late husband and Ms. Collins had been engaged in an affair prior to his death. Ms. Hayes filed suit against Collins individually. The complaint alleged that Collins had failed to repay the loan made to the Corporation and sought judgment in the amount of the outstanding corporate debt. Collins filed an answer in which she denied individual liability for the corporate debt. The court entered judgment in favor of Collins and Hayes appealed.

JUDICIAL OPINION

MIKELL, J.... We conclude that the trial court properly entered summary judgment in favor of Collins. It is an undisputed fact that Mr. Hayes made the loan at issue to the Corporation. It is also undisputed that the Corporation has not repaid the loan; however, Collins cannot be held personally liable for corporate debts absent evidence to warrant piercing the corporate veil. "Because the cardinal rule of corporate law is that a corporation possesses a legal existence separate and apart from that of its officers and shareholders, the mere operation of a corporate business does not render one personally liable for corporate acts."

Whether to pierce the corporate veil is normally a question for jury determination. However, in order for the trial court to submit the issue to a jury, the plaintiff must introduce evidence "that the corporate arrangement was a sham, used to defeat justice, to perpetrate fraud, or to evade statutory, contractual or tort responsibility." There is no such evidence in the record. Contrary to the argument of Ms. Hayes, "[s]ole ownership of a corporation by one person...is not a factor, and neither is the fact that the sole owner uses and controls it to promote [her] own ends...."

"One who deals with a corporation as such an entity cannot, in the absence of fraud, deny the legality of the corporate existence for the purpose of holding the owner liable." Because the record is devoid of evidence to warrant piercing the corporate veil, Ms. Hayes cannot recover from Collins individually for repayment of the corporate loan. The trial court properly granted summary judgment to Collins.

[Judgment affirmed]

QUESTIONS

1. Should Ms. Collins as sole owner of Corporate Staffing Solutions, Inc. (CSS, Inc.), be legally obligated to repay a loan to the estate of a friend who loaned money to CSS, Inc., from his home equity line of credit?
2. State the cardinal rule of corporate law set forth in the court's opinion.

[1] *American Truck Lines, Inc. v. Albino*, 424 S.E.2d 367 (Ga. App. 1992).

[2] Also, a corporation does not have standing to pursue a claim on behalf of its sole shareholders. See *Accurate Printers, Inc. v. Stark*, 671 S.E.2d 228 (Ga. App. 2008).

A corporation is formed by obtaining approval of a **certificate of incorporation**, **articles of incorporation**, or a **charter** from the state or national government.[3]

2. Classifications of Corporations

Corporations may be classified in terms of their relationship to the public, the source of their authority, and the nature of their activities.

(A) Public, Private, and Quasi-Public Corporations. A **public corporation** is one established for governmental purposes and for the administration of public affairs. A city is a public or municipal corporation acting under authority granted to it by the state.

A **private corporation** is one organized for charitable and benevolent purposes or for purposes of finance, industry, and commerce. Private corporations are often called *public* in business circles when their stock is sold to the public.

A **quasi-public corporation**, sometimes known as a public service corporation or a public utility, is a private corporation furnishing services on which the public is particularly dependent. An example of a quasi-public corporation is a gas and electric company.

(B) Public Authorities. The public increasingly demands that government perform services. Some of these are performed directly by government. Others are performed by separate corporations or **authorities** created by government. **For Example,** a city parking facility may be organized as a separate municipal parking authority, or a public housing project may be operated as an independent housing authority.

(C) Domestic and Foreign Corporations. A corporation is called a **domestic corporation** with respect to the state under whose law it has been incorporated. Any other corporation going into that state is called a **foreign corporation**. Thus, a corporation holding a Texas charter is a domestic corporation in Texas but a foreign corporation in all other states.[4]

(D) Special Service Corporations. Corporations formed for transportation, banking, insurance, and savings and loan operations and similar specialized functions are subject to separate codes or statutes with regard to their organization. In addition, federal and state laws and administrative agencies regulate in detail the way these businesses are conducted.

(E) Close Corporations. A corporation whose shares are held by a single shareholder or a small group of shareholders is known as a **close corporation**. Its shares are not traded publicly. Many such corporations are small firms that are incorporated to obtain either the advantage of limited liability or a tax benefit, or both.

Many states have statutes that have liberalized corporation law as it applies to close corporations. **For Example,** Nancy Davis Judson and Hall Davis IV are siblings who inherited their parents' stock in a domestic close corporation, Hall's Mortuary, Inc., a prominent and successful funeral home in Port Allen, Louisiana. Nancy was the secretary-treasurer, a director, and shareholder of 50 percent of the corporation's stock. Hall was president, a director, and the shareholder of the other 50 percent of the corporation's stock. The siblings had a falling out. Nancy filed a court action to compel Hall to comply with the bylaws regarding her participation in the management of the business and to allow her access to all corporate records. Hall responded with accusations of his own. Thereafter, Hall alleged that he and Nancy were deadlocked in the management of corporate affairs and petitioned the court for involuntary dissolution and the appointment of a liquidator. Nancy objected and wanted a jury trial on a number of issues. The court applied a statute, nearly identical to a Delaware statute, "designed to obviate a deadlocked vote of two equal shareholders" of a close corporation and ordered the dissolution of the corporation.[5]

[3] *Charter, certificate of incorporation,* and *articles of incorporation* are all terms used to refer to the documents that serve as evidence of a government's grant of corporate existence and powers. Most state incorporation statutes now provide for a certificate of incorporation issued by the secretary of state, but a Revised Model Business Corporation Act (RMBCA) has done away with the certificate of incorporation. Under the RMBCA, corporate existence begins when articles of incorporation are filed with the secretary of state. An endorsed copy of the articles together with a fee, receipt, or acknowledgment replaces the certificate of incorporation. See RMBCA §§1.25 and 2.03 and footnote 8 in this chapter.

[4] Failure of a foreign corporation to obtain a certificate of authority to do intrastate business in the state, under that state's door-closing statute, may mean that the foreign corporation cannot enforce a contract entered into in the state. **For Example,** TradeWinds Environmental Restoration, Inc., a New York–based company, entered into a contract with Alabama contractor BBC to do structural-drying services at a number of coastal condominiums after Hurricane Ivan in 2004. TradeWinds performed the work under the contract valued at $400,000. When TradeWinds sued for the money owed under the contract, the court determined that the "labor" performed is not an article of commerce, nor is the agreement to supply it an act of commerce. And the court determined that TradeWinds' business was intrastate, rather than interstate, and without a certificate of authority to perform the work, TradeWinds could not enforce the contract. *TradeWinds Environmental Restoration, Inc. v. Brown Brothers Construction, LLC*, 999 So.2d 875 (Ala. 2008).

[5] *Judson v. Davis*, 916 So.2d 1106 (La. App. 2005).

CPA **(F) Subchapter S Corporations.** Subchapter S is a subdivision of the Internal Revenue Code. If corporate shareholders meet the requirements of this subdivision, they may elect Subchapter S status, which allows the shareholders to be treated as partners for tax purposes and retain the benefit of limited liability under the corporate form. A Subchapter S corporation is limited to 75 shareholders.

Under the Small Business Job Protection Act of 1996, employee stock ownership plans (ESOPs) and tax-exempt entities may be shareholders subject to certain special taxation rules.[6] Other reforms in this act make it easier for small businesses to comply with S corporation rules.

(G) Professional Corporations. A corporation may be organized for the purpose of conducting a profession. Each officer, director, and shareholder of a professional corporation must be licensed to practice the profession. Professional incorporation does not shield a practitioner from personal liability relating to the professional services rendered.

(H) Nonprofit Corporations. A *nonprofit corporation* (or an **eleemosynary corporation**), is one that is organized for charitable or benevolent purposes. Nonprofit corporations include hospitals, nursing homes, and universities.[7] Special procedures for incorporation are prescribed, and provision is made for a detailed examination of and hearing regarding the purpose, function, and methods of raising money for the enterprise.

3. Corporations and Governments

Problems arise about the power of governments to create and regulate corporations.

(A) Power to Create. Because by definition a corporation is created by government, the right to be a corporation must be obtained from the proper governmental agency. The federal government may create corporations whenever appropriate to carry out the powers granted to it.

Generally, a state by virtue of its **police power** may create any kind of corporation for any purpose. Most states have a **general corporation code**, which lists certain requirements, and anyone who satisfies the requirements and files the necessary papers with the government may automatically become a corporation. In 1950, the American Bar Association (ABA) published a Model Business Corporation Act (MBCA) to assist legislative bodies in the modernization of state corporation laws. An updated version was published in 1969. Statutory language similar to that contained in the 1969 version of the MBCA has been adopted in whole or in part by 35 states. A complete revision of the model act was approved in 1984 (RMBCA).[8] Updates to the model act have been approved subsequent to the scandals involving public corporations in recent years.[9] Jurisdictions following the model act have made numerous modifications to reflect their differing views about balancing the interests of public corporations, shareholders, and management. Caution must therefore be exercised in making generalizations about model act jurisdictions. There is no *uniform* corporation act.

(B) Power to Regulate. Subject to constitutional limitations, corporations may be regulated by statutes.

(1) Protection of the Corporation as a Person.

The Constitution of the United States prohibits the national government and state governments from depriving any person of life, liberty, or property without due process of law. Many state constitutions contain a similar limitation on their respective state governments. A corporation is regarded as a "person" within the meaning of such provisions.

The federal Constitution prohibits a state from denying to any person within its jurisdiction the equal protection of the laws. No such express limitation is placed on the federal government, although the due process clause binding the federal government is liberally interpreted so that it prohibits substantial inequality of treatment.

[6] Pub. L. No. 104-188 (August 20, 1996).

[7] The Committee on Corporate Laws of the American Bar Association has prepared a Model Nonprofit Corporation Act. A revised Model Nonprofit Corporation Act was approved in 1986.

[8] The Revised Model Business Corporation Act (1984) was approved by the Committee on Corporate Laws Section of Business Law of the American Bar Association. The committee approved revisions to sections 6.40 and 8.33 on March 27, 1987, and to section 7.08 on June 16, 1996; changes to Subchapters B and D of Chapter 1 of the model act, which accommodate the use of electronic means for transmitting and filing required corporate documents with the secretary of state, were approved on September 20, 1997. Model act citations are to the 1984 Revised Model Business Corporation Act (RMBCA) unless designated otherwise.

[9] Revisions included in the 2005 edition of the act apply to directors' conflicting interest transactions, provisions relating to directors' involvement with corporate opportunities, and updates on the role and responsibilities of corporate directors and officers.

(2) Protection of the Corporation as a Citizen. For certain purposes, such as determining the right to bring a lawsuit in a federal court, a corporation is a citizen of any state in which it has been incorporated and of the state where it has its principal place of business.

B. Corporate Powers

Except for limitations in the federal Constitution or the state's own constitution, a state legislature may give corporations any lawful powers. The RMBCA contains a general provision on corporate powers granting a corporation "the same powers as an individual to do all things necessary or convenient to carry out its business and affairs."[10]

4. Particular Powers

Modern corporation codes give corporations a wide range of powers.

(a) Perpetual Life. One of the distinctive features of a corporation is its perpetual or continuous life—the power to continue as an entity forever or for a stated period of time regardless of changes in stock ownership or the death of any shareholders.

(b) Corporate Name. A corporation must have a name to identify it. As a general rule, it may select any name for this purpose. Most states require that the corporate name contain some word indicating the corporate character[11] and that the name not be the same as, or deceptively similar to, the name of any other corporation. Some statutes prohibit the use of a name that is likely to mislead the public.

(c) Corporate Seal. A corporation may have a distinctive seal. However, a corporation need not use a seal in the transaction of business unless this is required by statute or a natural person in transacting that business would be required to use a seal.

CPA **(d) Bylaws. Bylaws** are the rules and regulations enacted by a corporation to govern the affairs of the corporation and its shareholders, directors, and officers.

Bylaws are adopted by shareholders, although in some states they may be adopted by the directors of the corporation. Approval by the state or an amendment of the corporate charter is not required to make the bylaws effective.

The bylaws are subordinate to the general law of the state, the statute under which the corporation is formed, and the charter of the corporation.[12] Bylaws that conflict with such superior authority or that are in themselves unreasonable are invalid. Bylaws that are valid are binding on all shareholders regardless of whether they know of the existence of those bylaws or were among the majority that consented to their adoption. Bylaws are not binding on third persons, however, unless they have notice or knowledge of them.

(e) Stock. A corporation may issue certificates representing corporate stock. Under the RMBCA, authorized, but unissued, shares may be issued at the price set by the board of directors. Under UCC Article 8 (1978 and 1994 versions), securities may be "uncertificated," or not represented by an instrument.

(f) Making Contracts. Corporation codes give corporations the power to make contracts.

(g) Borrowing Money. Corporations have the implied power to borrow money in carrying out their authorized business purposes.

(h) Executing Negotiable Instruments. Corporations have the power to issue or indorse negotiable instruments and to accept drafts.

(i) Issuing Bonds. A corporation may exercise its power to borrow money by issuing bonds.

(j) Transferring Property. The corporate property may be leased, assigned for the benefit of creditors, or sold. In many states, however, a solvent corporation may not transfer all of its property without the consent of all or a substantial majority of its shareholders.

A corporation, having power to incur debts, may mortgage or pledge its property as security for those debts. This rule does not apply to public service companies, such as street transit systems and gas and electric companies.

[10] RMBCA §3.02. State statutes generally contain similar broad catchall grants of powers.

[11] RMBCA §4.01(a) declares that the corporate name must contain the word *corporation, company, incorporated,* or *limited* or an abbreviation of one of these words.

[12] *Roach v. Bynum,* 403 So.2d 187 (Ala. 1981).

(K) Acquiring Property. A corporation has the power to acquire and hold such property as is reasonably necessary for carrying out its express powers.

(L) Buying Back Stock. Generally, a corporation may purchase its own stock if it is solvent at the time and the purchase does not impair capital. Stock that is reacquired by the corporation that issued it is commonly called **treasury stock**.

Although treasury stock retains the character of outstanding stock, it has an inactive status while it is held by the corporation.[13] Thus, the treasury shares cannot be voted, nor can dividends be declared on them.

(M) Doing Business in Another State. A corporation has the power to engage in business in other states. However, this does not exempt the corporation from satisfying valid restrictions imposed by the foreign state in which it seeks to do business.

(N) Participating in an Enterprise. Corporations may generally participate in an enterprise to the same extent as individuals. Not only may they enter into joint ventures, but also the modern statutory trend is to permit a corporation to be a member of a partnership, and a corporation may be a limited partner. The RMBCA authorizes a corporation "to be a promoter, partner, member, associate, or manager of any partnership, joint venture, trust, or other entity."[14]

(O) Paying Employee Benefits. The RMBCA empowers a corporation "to pay pensions and establish pension plans, pension trusts, profit-sharing plans, share bonus plans, share option plans, and benefit or incentive plans for any or all of its current or former directors, officers, employees, and agents."[15]

(P) Charitable Contributions. The RMBCA authorizes a corporation, without any limitation, "to make donations for the public welfare or for charitable, scientific, or educational purposes."[16] In some states, a limitation is imposed on the amount that can be donated for charitable purposes.

5. *Ultra Vires* Acts

When a corporation acts in excess of or beyond the scope of its powers, the corporation's act is described as ***ultra vires***. Such an action is improper in the same way that it is improper for an agent to act beyond the scope of the authority given by the principal. It is also improper with respect to shareholders and creditors of the corporation because corporate funds have been diverted to unauthorized uses.

The modern corporation statute will state that every corporation formed under it will have certain powers unless the articles of incorporation expressly exclude some of the listed powers, and then the statute will list every possible power that is needed to run a business. In some states, the legislature makes a blanket grant of all power that a natural person running the business would possess.[17] The net result is that the modern corporation possesses such a broad scope of powers that it is difficult to find an action that is *ultra vires*. If a mining corporation should begin to manufacture television sets, that might be an *ultra vires* transaction, but such an extreme departure rarely happens.

Because nonprofit corporations have a more restricted range of powers than business corporations, actions not authorized by the charters of nonprofit corporations are more likely to be found *ultra vires*.[18]

C. Creation and Termination of the Corporation

All states have general laws governing the creation of corporations.

CPA 6. Promoters

Corporations come into existence as the result of the activities of one or more persons known as **promoters** who bring together persons interested in the enterprise, aid in obtaining subscriptions to stock, and set in motion the machinery that leads to the formation of the corporation itself.

[13] When a corporation reacquires its own shares, it has the choice of retiring them and thus restoring them to the status of authorized, but unissued, shares or of treating them as still issued and available for transfer. The latter are described as treasury shares.

[14] RMBCA §3.02(9).

[15] RMBCA §3.02(12).

[16] RMBCA §3.02(13).

[17] Note the broad powers granted under RMBCA §3.02; see also Cal Corp Code §§202(b), 207, 208 for an all-purpose clause granting all of the powers of a natural person in carrying out business activities. See *MIC v. Battle Mountain Corp.*, 70 P.3d 1176 (Colo. 2003), where Colorado's *ultra vires* statute prohibits claims that a corporation is acting beyond the scope of its powers.

[18] *Lovering v. Seabrook Island Property Owners Ass'n*, 344 S.E.2d 862 (S.C. App. 1986). But see *St. Louis v. Institute of Med. Ed. & Res.*, 786 S.W.2d 885 (Mo. App. 1990).

A corporation is not liable on a contract made by its promoter for its benefit unless the corporation takes some affirmative action to adopt such a contract. This action may be express words of adoption, or it may be acceptance of the contract's benefits. A corporation may also become bound by such contracts through assignment or novation.

The promoter is personally liable for all contracts made on behalf of the corporation before its existence unless the promoter is exempted by the terms of the agreement or by the circumstances surrounding it.[19]

In *Clinton Investors*, a person executing preincorporation lease in the name of a proposed corporation did not believe himself to be a promoter, nor did he think that he could be personally liable for obligations incurred under the lease.

Clinton Investors Co. v. Watkins, 536 N.Y.S.2d 270 (A.D. 1989)

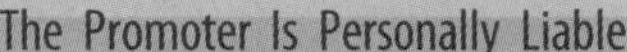

The Promoter Is Personally Liable

Clinton Investors Co. (Clinton), as landlord, entered into a three-year lease with "The Clifton Park Learning Center" (learning center) as tenant. The lease was signed by Berne Watkins as treasurer of the learning center. On May 31, 1984, the day before the lease's term commenced, Watkins signed a rider to the lease. He again signed as treasurer of the tenant but identified the tenant as "the Clifton Park Learning Center, Inc." Watkins had not consulted an attorney regarding the formation of the corporation. He mistook reserving the business name with the secretary of state as a filing of a certificate of incorporation. On February 11, 1985, a certificate of incorporation was filed. By March 1986, the learning center had become delinquent in rental payments and other fees in the amount of $18,103. Clinton sued Watkins and the learning center for the amounts due. The court dismissed the complaint, and Clinton appealed.

JUDICIAL OPINION

VESAWICH, J.…Because no corporation existed when Watkins signed the lease with plaintiff, his legal status was that of a promoter of the learning center.…Generally, a promoter who executes a preincorporation contract in the name of a proposed corporation is himself personally liable on the contract unless the parties have otherwise agreed. Watkins asserts that because the learning center corporation subsequently adopted the lease, he is therefore no longer liable on the lease. However, corporate adoption of a contract "gives rise to corporate liability in addition to any individual liability" (*Universal Inds. Corp. v Lindstrom*, 92 A.D. 2d 150, 152, 459, N.Y.S.2d 492) so that the promoter nevertheless remains obligated unless there has been a novation between the corporation and the plaintiff, which is not the situation here. Nor does the record disclose any explicit or implicit agreement by plaintiff not to hold Watkins personally liable on the lease. . . .

[Judgment reversed and summary judgment entered against Watkins]

QUESTIONS

1. What was Watkins's status when he signed the lease?
2. Is it true that because the learning center corporation subsequently adopted the lease, Watkins was no longer liable on the lease?

A promoter is liable for all torts committed in connection with the promoter's activities. The corporation is not ordinarily liable for the torts of the promoter, but it may become liable by its conduct after incorporation. If a promoter induces making a contract by fraud, the corporation is liable for the fraud if it assumes or ratifies the contract with knowledge or notice of such fraud.

A promoter stands in a fiduciary relation to the corporation and to stock subscribers and cannot make secret profits at their expense. Accordingly, if a promoter makes a secret profit on a sale of land to the corporation, the promoter must surrender the profit to the corporation.

The corporation is not liable in most states for the expenses and services of the promoter unless it subsequently promises to pay for them, or the corporation's charter or a statute imposes such liability on it.

[19] See *GS Petroleum, Inc. v. R and S Fuel, Inc.*, 2009 WL 1554680 (Del. Super. June 4, 2009), where the court found that the promoters were not liable on the preincorporation contract for the sale of a Shell gas station. The court reasoned that the terms of the contract did not intend promoter liability, and the business was incorporated by the buyer before taking possession of the business.

7. Incorporation

One or more natural persons or corporations may act as **incorporators** of a corporation by signing and filing appropriate forms with a designated government official.[20] These papers are filed in duplicate, and a filing fee must be paid. The designated official (usually the secretary of state), after being satisfied that the forms conform to statutory requirements, stamps "Filed" and the date on each copy. The official then retains one copy and returns the other copy, along with a filing fee receipt, to the corporation.[21]

Statutes may require incorporators to give some form of public notice, such as by advertising in a newspaper, of their intention to form a corporation, stating its name, address, and general purpose.

8. Application for Incorporation

In most states, the process of forming a corporation is begun by filing an application for a certificate of incorporation. This application contains or is accompanied by articles of incorporation. The instrument is filed with the secretary of state and sets forth certain information about the new corporation. The articles of incorporation must contain (1) the name of the corporation, (2) the number of shares of stock the corporation is authorized to issue, (3) the street address of the corporation's initial registered office and the name of its initial registered agent, and (4) the name and address of each incorporator.[22] The articles of incorporation may also state the purpose or purposes for which the corporation is organized. If there is no "purpose clause," the corporation automatically has the purpose of engaging in any lawful business.[23] Also, if no reference is made to the duration of the corporation in the articles of incorporation, it will automatically have perpetual duration.[24]

9. The Certificate of Incorporation

Most state incorporation statutes now provide for a certificate of incorporation to be issued by the secretary of state after articles of incorporation that conform to state requirements have been filed. The Revised Model Business Corporation Act (RMBCA) has eliminated the certificate of incorporation in an effort to reduce the volume of paperwork handled by the secretary of state.

Under the RMBCA, corporate existence begins when the articles are filed with the secretary of state.[25] In some states, corporate existence begins when the proper government official issues a certificate of incorporation. In other states, it does not begin until an organizational meeting is held by the new corporation.

10. Proper and Defective Incorporation

If the procedure for incorporation has been followed, the corporation has a legal right to exist. It is then called a **corporation de jure**, meaning that it is a corporation by virtue of law.

Assume that there is some defect in the corporation that is formed. If the defect is not a material one, the law usually overlooks the defect and holds that the corporation is a corporation de jure.

The RMBCA abolishes objections to irregularities and defects in incorporating. It provides that the

> *secretary of state's filing of the articles of incorporation is conclusive proof that the incorporators satisfied all conditions precedent to incorporation....*[26]

Many state statutes follow this pattern. Such an approach is based on the practical consideration that when countless persons are purchasing shares of stock and entering into business transactions with thousands of corporations, it becomes an absurdity to expect that anyone is going to make the detailed search that would be required to determine whether a given corporation is a corporation de jure.[27]

(A) De Facto Corporation. The defect in the incorporation may be so substantial that it cannot be ignored, and the corporation will not be accepted as a corporation de jure, yet compliance may be sufficient

[20] RMBCA §2.01.
[21] RMBCA §1.25.
[22] RMBCA §2.02.
[23] RMBCA §3.01.
[24] RMBCA §3.02.
[25] RMBCA §2.03(a).
[26] RMBCA §2.03(b).
[27] This trend and the reasons for it may be compared to those involved in the concept of the negotiability of commercial paper. Note the similar protection from defenses given to the person purchasing shares of stock for value and without notice. U.C.C. §8–202.

for recognizing that there is a corporation. When this occurs, the association is called a **de facto** corporation.

Although conflict exists among authorities, the traditional elements of a de facto corporation are that (1) a valid law exists under which the corporation could have been properly incorporated, (2) an attempt to organize the corporation has been made in good faith, (3) a genuine attempt to organize in compliance with statutory requirements has been made, and (4) corporate powers have been used.

(B) CORPORATION BY ESTOPPEL. The defect in incorporation may be so great that by law the association cannot be accepted as a de facto corporation. In such a case then, there is no corporation. If the individuals involved proceed to run the business in spite of such irregularity, they may be held personally liable as partners for the business's debts.[28] This rule is sometimes not applied when a person has dealt with the business as though it were a corporation.[29] In such instances, the party is estopped from denying that the "corporation" had legal existence. In effect, there is **corporation by estoppel** with respect to that party.

Several jurisdictions that follow the 1969 MBCA have expressly retained the doctrines of corporation by estoppel and de facto corporations.[30] Other courts interpreting the language of the 1969 MBCA, however, have held that the doctrines of de facto corporation and corporation by estoppel no longer exist.

The language of the 1984 version allows some jurisdictions sufficient room for the de facto and estoppel doctrines to operate through section 2.04 of the MBCA. The *First Community Bank* case applied the corporation by estoppel doctrine in a 1984 MBCA jurisdiction.

First Community Bank, N.A. v. Community Youth Center, 2010 WL 8696179 (Va. Cir. Ct. Dec. 20, 2010)

Corporation by Estoppel Is Still Good Law Under the 1984 MBCA

The Community Youth Center (CYC) corporation failed to pay its annual registration fee in 2000, and was automatically dissolved by the State Corporation Commission. CYC continued to operate and held itself out as a corporation well into 2005 when it obtained a loan from the First Community Bank to finance a swimming pool at its facility. The loan was secured by the CYC property. After the corporation defaulted on its loan payments the bank foreclosed and subsequently purchased the property at a foreclosure sale. CYC contended that the president, vice president, and treasurer of CYC had no standing to make the 2005 loan transaction because CYC's corporate status had been terminated. The bank contended that under the doctrine of corporation by estoppel, CYC continued to exist in 2005, and consequently the officer-directors had authority to borrow money and grant a deed of trust, thereby giving the bank a valid lien on the property.

JUDICIAL OPINION

SHARRETT, J.... A corporation acting and carrying on its corporate business under its corporate name for more than five years after the SCC [State Corporation Commission] automatically terminated its corporate existence should be deemed a corporation by estoppel. CYC may not have been a de jure corporation, but the Court cannot reasonably ignore the actual existence of such a corporation. CYC continued its operations well beyond 2000 to such an extent that it believed the community center would benefit from a new swimming pool. CYC obtained a loan from First Community Bank for that purpose, and made numerous payments towards that loan before ultimately defaulting on the loan. These acts and such dealings are not necessarily legally ineffective for a failure to pay the annual registration fee in 2000.

In order to relieve CYC of its loan obligations, the corporation must have ceased to exist in 2000 both in law and in fact. The Court finds that CYC ceased to exist only in law, not in fact. CYC's directors failed to wind up the corporate business when CYC's corporate existence was automatically terminated, as was their duty under the provisions of Va. Code § 13.1-752. Consequently, they cannot relieve the corporation from liability for acts done in its name and during its actual existence as a corporation by estoppel.

For these reasons, the Court finds that the president, vice president, and treasurer of CYC were capable of entering into an agreement with the Bank on CYC's behalf. The Court also finds the foreclosure sale to be valid. Accordingly, the Court

[28] In a minority of states, a court will not hold individuals liable as partners but will hold liable the person who committed the act on behalf of the business on the theory that that person was an agent who acted without authority and is therefore liable for breach of the implied warranties of the existence of a principal possessing capacity and of proper authorization.

[29] *Am. South Bank v. Holland*, 669 So.2d 151 (Ala. Civ. App. 1994).

[30] See Ga. Bus. Corp Code §22–5103; Minn. Bus Corp Act §301:08. See also *H. Rich Corp. v. Feinberg*, 518 So.2d 377 (Fla. App. 1987).

Continued

hereby grants First Community Bank's Motion, and declares that (1) First Community Bank was granted a valid deed of trust lien on the property to secure the loan pursuant to the deed of trust, and (2) First Community Bank, as purchaser at the foreclosure sale, has fee simple title to the property.

[So ordered.]

QUESTIONS

1. State the Community Youth Center's position before the court.
2. Did the court apply the doctrine of corporation by estoppel in its resolution of the controversy before it?

With respect to preincorporation debts, the 1984 act imposes liability only on persons who act as, or on behalf of, a corporation while knowing that no corporation exists.[31]

11. Insolvency, Bankruptcy, and Reorganization

When a corporation has financial troubles so serious that it is insolvent, the best thing may be to go through bankruptcy or reorganization proceedings. The law with respect to bankruptcy and reorganizations is discussed in Chapter 35.

12. Forfeiture of Charter

In states that have adopted the RMBCA, the secretary of state may commence proceedings to administratively dissolve a corporation if (1) the corporation does not pay franchise taxes within 60 days after they are due, (2) the corporation does not file its annual report within 60 days after it is due, or (3) the corporation is without a registered agent or registered office for 60 days or more.[32] After a corporate charter has been dissolved, the owners and officers of the dissolved corporation are not shielded from personal liability by using the corporate name when making contracts if they knew or should have known of the dissolution. **For Example,** on October 2, 2004, Dinky, Inc., was involuntarily dissolved for failure to file an annual report and pay an annual franchise tax. Elaine Kostopulos, the president and sole shareholder of Dinky, Inc., had incorporated her business in 1989 and regularly purchased products manufactured by Benetton USA, Inc., since that time. During the five years after Dinky was dissolved, she continued to operate as a corporation, ordering and making payments to Benetton through June 7, 2009. Between June and November 2009, Benetton sought payment of over $200,000 owed by Dinky. Ms. Kostopulos claims she was unaware of the dissolution until late 2009, when payment problems arose. Dinky applied for reinstatement at that time. With corporate status reinstated, Ms. Kostopulos contends that she is not personally liable for the debts incurred by the dissolved corporation during the time of its dissolution. The court determined that Ms. Kostopulos cannot escape personal liability by reinstating her corporation, holding that "she should have known" about the dissolution of Dinky, over such a long period of time.[33]

After a corporation is dissolved, a contract made by an officer of the dissolved corporation cannot be enforced against the other party to the contract. **For Example,** a lucrative contract with Florio Entertainment, Inc., was signed "Louis Lofredo, LL Associates as company president" using a letterhead "LL Associates, Inc." In fact, the corporation "LL Associates, Inc." had been dissolved years before the contract was negotiated and signed, and Lofredo had made no effort to reinstate the corporation. LL Associates, Inc., had no legal existence and thus could not be a party to the contract and could not enforce the contract.[34]

A corporation whose powers are suspended for nonpayment of taxes cannot sue or defend a lawsuit while its taxes remain unpaid.[35]

13. Judicial Dissolution

Judicial dissolution of a corporation may be decreed when its management is deadlocked and the

[31] RMBCA §2.04.

[32] RMBCA §14.20.

[33] *Benetton U.S.A. Corp. v. Dinky, Inc.*, 2011 WL 5024549 (N.D. Ill. Oct. 19, 2011). But see section 2.04 of the 1984 RMBCA, which provides that all persons purporting to act for or on behalf of a corporation "knowing that there was no incorporation" under the Act are jointly and severally liable for all liabilities while so acting. There would be no liability for an individual that did not and should not have known of the dissolution.

[34] *Animazing Entertainment, Inc. v. Louis Lofredo Associates, Inc.*, 88 F. Supp. 2d 265 (S.D.N.Y. 2000).

[35] *Kaufman, Inc. v. Performance Plastering, Inc.*, 39 Cal.Rptr. 3d 33 (Cal. App. 2006).

FIGURE 44-1 Consolidation

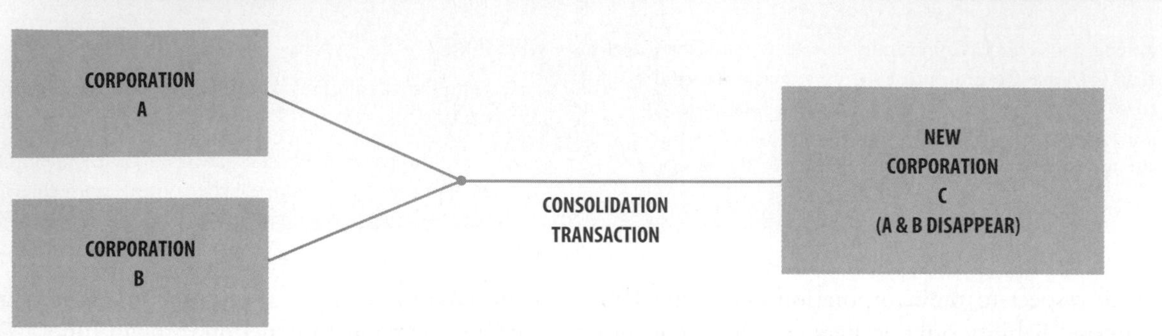

deadlock cannot be broken by the shareholders.[36] In some states, a "custodian" may be appointed for a corporation when the shareholders are unable to break a deadlock in the board of directors and irreparable harm is threatened to, or sustained by, the corporation because of the deadlock.

D. Consolidations, Mergers, and Conglomerates

Two or more corporations may be combined to form a new structure or enterprise.

CPA 14. Definitions

Enterprises may be combined by a consolidation or merger of corporations or by the formation of a conglomerate.

CPA **(a) Consolidation.** In a **consolidation** of two or more corporations, their separate existences cease, and a new corporation with the property and assets of the old corporations comes into being (see Figure 44-1).

When a consolidation occurs, the new corporation ordinarily succeeds to the rights, powers, and immunities of its component parts. However, limitations may be imposed by constitution, statute, or certificate of incorporation.

CPA **(b) Merger.** When two corporations **merge**, one absorbs the other. One corporation retains its original charter and identity and continues to exist; the other disappears, and its corporate existence terminates (see Figure 44-2).

A stockholder who objects to a proposed consolidation or merger or who fails to convert existing

FIGURE 44-2 Merger

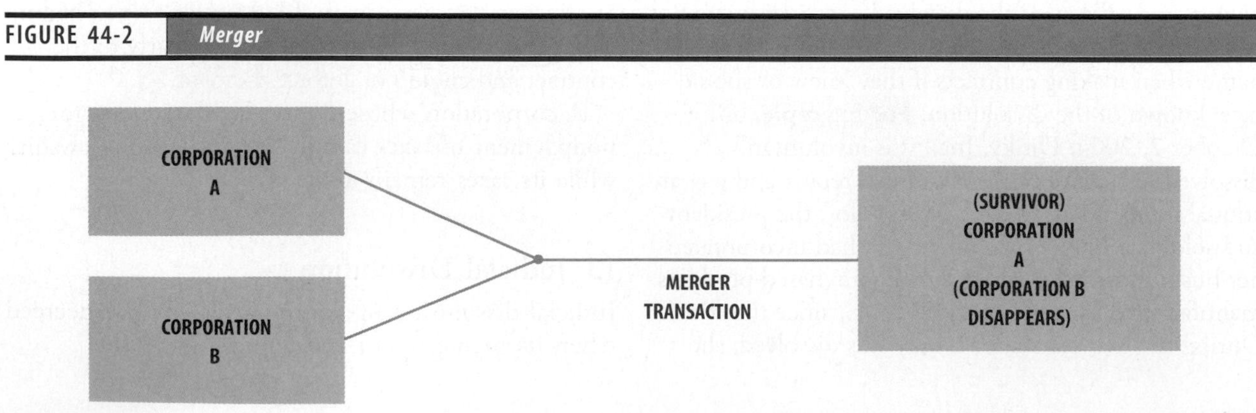

[36] After a shareholder has requested dissolution of a corporation, a state statute may offer an option to the corporation or other existing shareholders to purchase shares owned by the petitioning shareholder(s) for "fair value" in lieu of dissolution. See *Dawkins v. Hickman Family Corp.*, 2010 WL 4683472 (N.D. Miss. Nov. 10, 2010).

shares into stock of the new or continuing corporation may apply to a court to appraise the value of the stock that she holds.[37] Should either party act arbitrarily, vexatiously, or not in good faith in the appraisal process, the courts have the right to assess court costs and attorney fees. The new or continuing corporation is then required to pay the "fair value" of the stock to the stockholder.[38]

In the *Trapp Family Lodge, Inc.*, case, the court was called upon to decide what fair value means and how it applied to dissenting shareholders who objected to a merger into a new corporation.

In Re 75,629 Shares of Common Stock of Trapp Family Lodge, Inc., 725 A.2d 927 (Vt. 1999)

The Sound of Music: $63.44 per Share

The Trapp Family Lodge, Inc. (TFL), was incorporated in 1962 as a holding company for certain assets of the Von Trapp family, including the Trapp Family Lodge, a resort hotel complex located in Stowe, Vermont, and other assets including certain royalty rights related to the family's story as portrayed in a Broadway musical and movie. A majority of TFL shareholders approved a merger with a new corporation in 1994, and the merger took place on January 28, 1995. The dissenting shareholders, holding 75,629 of the corporation's 198,000 outstanding shares, were paid $33.84 per share as fair value by the TFL board of directors. The dissenting shareholders brought suit seeking a higher price as fair value. After the trial court set the fair value of $63.44, TFL appealed.

JUDICIAL OPINION

JOHNSON, J.... Under the statute, a shareholder of a Vermont corporation who dissents from certain enumerated corporate actions, including consummation of a plan of merger, is entitled to obtain from the corporation payment of the "fair value" of his or her shares. Section 13.01(3) defines "fair value" to mean "the value of the shares immediately before the effectuation of the corporate action to which the dissenter objects, excluding any appreciation or depreciation in anticipation of the corporate action unless exclusion would be inequitable." This definition mirrors the definition of "fair value" in the Model Business Corporation Act. See Model Bus. Corp. Act § 13.01 (1978). The official comment to the Model Act indicates that this broad definition "leaves untouched the accumulated case law" on the various methods of determining fair value.

Dissenters' rights statutes were enacted in response to the common-law rule that required unanimous consent from shareholders to make fundamental changes in a corporation. See *Hansen v 75 Ranch Co.*, 957 P.2d 32, 37 (Mont.1998). Under this rule, minority shareholders could block corporate change by refusing to cooperate in hopes of establishing a nuisance value for their shares. In response, legislatures enacted statutes authorizing corporate changes by majority vote. See *Hansen*, 957 P.2d at 37. To protect the interests of minority shareholders, the statutes generally permitted a dissenting minority to recover the appraised value of its shares. Most recent statutes allow dissenting shareholders to demand that the corporation buy back shares at fair value.

The basic concept of fair value under a dissenters' rights statute is that the stockholder is entitled to be paid for his or her "proportionate interest in a going concern." *Weinberger v UOP, Inc.*, 457 A.2d 701, 713 (Del.1983); accord *In re Valuation of Common Stock of McLoon Oil Co.*, 565 A.2d 997, 1004 (Me.1989); *Friedman v Beway Realty Corp.*, 87 N.Y.2d 161, 638 N.Y.S.2d 399, 661 N.E.2d 972, 976 (1995). The focus of the valuation "is not the stock as a commodity, but rather the stock only as it represents a proportionate part of the enterprise as a whole." *McLoon Oil*, 565 A.2d at 1004. Thus, to find fair value, the trial court must determine the best price a single buyer could reasonably be expected to pay for the corporation as an entirety and prorate this value equally among all shares of its common stock. See *id.* Under this method, all shares of the corporation have the same fair value. See *id.*

A dissenting shareholder is not in the position of a willing seller, however, and thus, courts have held that fair value cannot be equated with "fair market value." See, e.g., *McLoon Oil*, 565 A.2d at 1005; *Hansen*, 957 P.2d at 41. Accordingly, methods of stock valuation used in tax, probate or divorce cases to determine fair market value are inapposite to the determination of "fair value" under the dissenters' rights statute. A shareholder who disapproves of a proposed merger gives up the right of veto in exchange for the right to be bought out at "fair value," not at market value. See *Hansen*, 957 P.2d at 41.

Finally, a fair-value determination is "necessarily a fact-specific process."...

[37] *Delaware Open MRI Radiology v. Kessler*, 898 A.2d 290 (Del. Ch. 2006).

[38] See *Spenlinhauer v. Spencer Press Inc.*, 959 N.E.2d 436 (Mass. App. 2011), where a minority shareholder dissented to a proposed merger, and after executing a cash-out merger, the court determined the "fair value" of the minority shares as the pro rata percentage of the net selling price.

Continued

...The dissenters' expert, Gordon, a certified financial analyst, conducted his appraisal using a net-asset-value approach; he used different methods to arrive at the values for individual assets, which were the lodge, the guest house option, the other guest house subsidiary assets, the royalties, and the excess land. Gordon used two methods to determine the value of the lodge. First, he used a discounted-cashflow method; the value of the lodge added to the value of TFL's other assets resulted in a share value of $64.00. Second, Gordon recalculated the net assets value using a prior real estate appraisal by Frank Bredice for the lodge; the Bredice value of the lodge added to the other TFL assets resulted in a share value of $62.67. Averaging these results, Gordon determined that the fair value of TFL was $63.44 per share.

TFL's expert, Haut, a certified public accountant, separated TFL's assets into three separate groups: the lodge facility and related operations, the excess land, and the guest house option...Haut valued TFL in its entirety at $6,700,000, which yields a per share value of $33.84.

The trial court held that the fair value of TFL was $63.44 per share, as established by Gordon. The court rejected Haut's appraisal for several reasons, including (1) Haut's valuation lacked the thoroughness and credibility of Gordon's valuation and the Bredice appraisal, (2) Haut unreasonably assumed TFL's earnings would not grow, (3) Haut valued the lodge operations at $7,300,000 in 1992, $7,000,000 in 1993, but then at only $4,748,000 for 1994, and (4) Haut overstated income taxes reducing after-tax cashflows.

We conclude...that the trial court's finding setting the fair value of TFL's stock at $63.44 is supported by the evidence and is not clearly erroneous....

[Affirmed]

QUESTIONS

1. Why were dissenters' rights statutes enacted?
2. What does "fair value" mean, and how is it determined?
3. Do you believe that TFL's expert attempted to fairly value the stock, or did he simply draft figures to support what the corporation asserted was fair value, $33.84? Is this ethical? How does it square with his oath as a witness to "tell the whole truth"?

(c) Conglomerate. **Conglomerate** describes the relationship of a parent corporation to subsidiary corporations engaged in diversified fields of activity unrelated to the parent corporation's field of activity. **For Example,** a wire-manufacturing corporation that owns all stock of a newspaper corporation and of a drug-manufacturing corporation would be described as a conglomerate. In contrast, if the wire-manufacturing company owned a mill that produced the metal used in making the wire and a mine that produced the ore that was used by the mill, the relationship would probably be described as an *integrated industry* rather than as a conglomerate. This term is merely a matter of usage rather than of legal definition. Likewise, when the parent company is not engaged in production or the rendering of services, it is customary to call it a *holding company*.

Without regard to whether the enterprise is a holding company or whether the group of corporations constitutes a conglomerate or an integrated industry, each part is a distinct corporation to which ordinary corporation law applies. In some instances, additional principles apply because of the nature of the relationships existing among the several corporations involved.

15. Legality

Consolidations, mergers, and asset acquisitions between enterprises are prohibited by federal antitrust legislation when the effect is to lessen competition in interstate commerce. A business corporation may not merge with a charitable corporation because this combination would divert the assets of the respective corporations to purposes not intended by their shareholders.

16. Liability of Successor Corporations

When corporations are combined in any way, the question of who is liable for the debts and obligations of the predecessor corporation arises.

(a) Mergers and Consolidations. Generally, the enterprise engaging in or continuing the business after a merger or consolidation succeeds to all of the rights and property of the predecessor, or disappearing, corporation.[39]

The *Marsh* case involves a school board's refusal to pay a successor corporation for the work of its predecessor corporation.

[39] *Corporate Express Office Products, Inc. v. Phillips*, 847 So.2d 406 (Fla. 2003).

Marsh Advantage America v. Orleans Parish School Board, 995 So.2d 53 (La. App. 2008)

A Marshmallow of a Case for the Plaintiff Marsh USA

The Orleans Parish School Board ("School Board") in New Orleans, Louisiana, hired Johnson & Higgins, Inc. (J&H), in 1996, creating an ongoing insurance consulting agreement between them. The terms of the agreement provided that the School Board would pay J&H, Inc. for its consulting services and would later be reimbursed by the insurance carrier eventually selected by the School Board. Pursuant to their agreement, over the next few years, J&H's Mrs. Ippolito prepared several Requests for Proposals ("RFP") on behalf of the School Board. The School Board paid its fees for this consulting work without complaint. During this time, Johnson & Higgins merged with Marsh McLennan, a company that thereafter merged into Marsh USA, Inc. In 2001, Mrs. Ippolito prepared, at the request of the School Board, two more requests for proposals. Per the terms of the RFPs, Marsh was to receive $70,000 as its consulting fee under NO. 7656 and a $5,000 consulting fee under NO. 7657. Mrs. Ippolito and her staff spent several months working on the project for the School Board. The School Board never paid Marsh for the services and Marsh USA, Inc., sued the School Board for breach of contract, seeking payment of $75,000. The School Board asserted that Marsh USA was not a proper party to the lawsuit and that no contract had existed with it. From a judgment for Marsh USA, Inc., the School Board appealed.

JUDICIAL OPINION

LOMBARD, J.….In its brief, the School Board attempts to make several arguments why it should not have to pay Marsh for the consulting fees it purportedly owes. The School Board's first argument is that the trial court erred in finding that Marsh proved it was the successor corporation to Johnson & Higgins, the party with which it initially contracted for the insurance consulting services. The School Board argues that Marsh failed to produce documents proving that Marsh is the legal successor in interest of Johnson & Higgins, and thus, failed to prove an essential element of its case and that it had a right of action to bring this lawsuit.

The evidence in the record indicates that Marsh is the proper party to bring this lawsuit. Minutes from a 1997 School Board meeting reflect the School Board's awareness of the merger between Johnson & Higgins and Marsh McLennan as well as the School Board's acknowledgement of its continuing consulting contract with Johnson & Higgins/Marsh McLennan. The same minutes also reflect the School Board's acknowledgement that a merger had thereafter occurred whereby Marsh McLennan was acquired by Marsh, USA. Moreover, a review of the Louisiana Secretary of State Corporations database confirms that Johnson & Higgins of Louisiana, Inc. merged into J & H Marsh & McLennan, which then merged into Marsh USA, Inc. As a matter of law, when two corporations merge or consolidate, the new successor corporation acquires all of the assets and rights of the former corporation. LSA-R.S. 12:115; *McCarthy v. Osborn*, 223 LA. 305, 65 So. 2d 776, 779 (La. 1953). Therefore, the School Board's argument that Marsh has no right to bring the instant action is without merit.…

The School Board contracted with Marsh's corporate predecessor for insurance consulting services. Marsh performed the services requested and the School Board accepted the work and used it to select its employee benefit programs. Marsh is entitled to recover the total sum of the fees owed in developing RFPs 7656 and 7657.

[Affirmed]

QUESTIONS

1. Summarize the facts of this case.
2. State the applicable rule of law.

The enterprise continuing the business is also subject to all of the debts and liabilities of the predecessor corporation.[40]

Liabilities of predecessor corporations can be imposed on a successor corporation when the transaction is a de facto merger[41] or the successor is a mere continuation of the predecessor. **For Example,** Steven Stepp manufactured pleasure boats through Thoroughbred Power Boats, Inc., until August 1996 at which time Thoroughbred Power Boats, Inc., ceased manufacturing and selling boats. In August 1996, Velocity Power Boats, Inc., began manufacturing and selling pleasure boats at the same location. Stephen Stepp and his wife were the only officers and board members of both corporations. Finding that Velocity was merely a "new hat" for Thoroughbred Power Boats, Inc., with the same or similar management and ownership, Velocity Power

[40] *Beck v. Roper Whitney, Inc.*, 190 F. Supp. 2d 524 (W.D.N.Y. 2001).

[41] *Ulanet v. D'Artagnan, Inc.*, 170 F. Supp. 2d 356 (E.D.N.Y. 2001); see *Callahan & Sons, Inc. v. Dykeman Electric Co. Inc.*, 266 F. Supp. 2d 208 (D. Mass 2003).

Boats, Inc., was held liable as a successor corporation for damages for a May 6, 1995, boating accident caused by a defective Thoroughbred Power Boats, Inc., manufactured boat.[42]

(B) Asset Sales. In contrast with a merger or consolidation, a corporation may merely purchase the assets of another business. In that case, the purchaser does not become liable for the obligations of the predecessor business. **For Example,** Hull Corporation sold one of its operating divisions to SP Industries, Inc. (SPI) for $6 million under an asset purchase agreement (APA) that stated that the buyer SPI assumed no liability for preclosing claims against Hull. In fact as Hull and SPI were negotiating the APA, Hull was having difficulties regarding engineering and installation work the division had performed in China for Berg Chilling Systems, Inc. Berg Chilling sued SPI under the doctrine of successor liability for the payment of a $1,650,000 arbitration award because of the defective work done by Hull in China. The court held that SPI did not assume Hull's contractual liability to Berg under any exception to the traditional corporate rule of successor nonliability.[43]

Corporations may seek to avoid liability for the obligations of a predecessor corporation by attempting to disguise a consolidation or merger as being merely a sale of assets. Courts will not recognize such a transaction and will impose a successor's liability on the successor corporation.[44] In addition, even when the old corporate entity is not formally dissolved, a finding of a de facto merger resulting in successor liability may occur. **For Example,** "old" Duro Industries, Inc., owed its supplier, Milliken & Co., $8,754,680 for raw materials and Milliken obtained a judgment for this amount from a New York court. Investors and related entities executed a plan acquiring the assets of old Duro, while shedding old Duro's debts to Milliken and establishing "new" Duro Textiles, LLC. New Duro had the same CEO as old Duro, continued to sell the same product line, and employed all of old Duro's employees. The court found successor liability for the Milliken debt against new Duro.[45]

LawFlix

Barbarians at the Gate (1996) (R)

In this movie that focuses on the law and ethics of takeovers, you can see the manipulation that occurs and the impact greed has on the companies themselves.

[42] *Paten v. Thoroughbred Power Boats, Inc.*, 294 F.3d 640 (5th Cir. 2002).
[43] *Berg Chilling Systems Inc. v. Hull Corp.*, 435 F.3d 455 (3d Cir. 2006).
[44] *State v. Westwood Squibb Pharmaceutical Co., Inc.*, 981 F. Supp. 760 (W.D.N.Y. 1997).
[45] *Milliken & Co. v. Duro Textiles, LLC*, 887 N.E.2d 244 (Mass. 2008).

MAKE THE CONNECTION

SUMMARY

A *corporation* is an artificial person created by government action. It exists as a separate and distinct entity possessing certain powers. In most states, the corporation comes into existence when the secretary of state issues a certificate of incorporation. The most common forms of corporations are private business corporations whose stock is sold to the public (publicly held) and close corporations, which are business firms whose shares are not traded publicly. Corporations may be formed for purposes other than conducting a business. For example, there are nonprofit corporations, municipal corporations, and public authorities for governmental purposes.

An *ultra vires* act occurs when a corporation acts beyond the scope of the powers given it. Because states now grant broad powers to corporations, it is unlikely that a modern corporation would act beyond the scope of its powers.

A *promoter* is a person who brings together the persons interested in the enterprise and sets in motion all that must be done to form a corporation. A corporation is not liable on contracts made by its promoter for the corporation unless it adopts the contracts. The promoter is personally liable for contracts made for the corporation before its existence. A promoter stands in a fiduciary relation to the corporation and stockholders.

The procedures for incorporation are set forth in the statutes of each state. In most states, the corporation comes into existence on issuance of the certificate of incorporation. When all requirements have been satisfied, the corporation is a corporation de jure. When there has not been full compliance with all requirements for incorporation, a de facto corporation may be found to exist. Or when sufficient compliance for a de facto corporation does not exist, in some jurisdictions a third person may be estopped from denying the legal existence of the "corporation" with which it did business (corporation by estoppel).

A corporation has the power to continue as an entity forever or for a stated period of time regardless of changes in the ownership of the stock or the death of a shareholder. It may make contracts, issue stocks and bonds, borrow money, execute commercial paper, transfer and acquire property, acquire its own stock if it is solvent and the purchase does not impair capital, and make charitable contributions. Subject to limitations, a corporation has the power to do business in other states. A corporation may also participate in a business enterprise to the same extent as an individual; that is, it may be a partner in a partnership, or it may enter a joint venture or other enterprise. Special service corporations, such as banks, insurance companies, and railroads, are subject to separate statutes governing their organization and powers.

Two or more corporations may be combined to form a new enterprise. This combination may be a consolidation, with a new corporation coming into existence, or a merger, in which one corporation absorbs the other.

LEARNING OUTCOMES

After studying this chapter, you should be able to clearly explain:

A. Nature and Classes

LO.1 Recognize that a corporation is a separate legal entity, distinct and apart from its stockholders

See the *Collins* case in which Ms. Collins was not personally liable for a loan to her corporation, p. 913.

B. Corporate Powers

LO.2 Explain the wide range of power given to corporations under modern corporate codes

See the RMBCA general provision granting corporations "the same powers as an individual to do all things necessary or convenient to carry out its business and affairs," p. 916.

C. Creation and Termination of the Corporation

LO.3 Understand that the promoter is personally liable for preincorporation contracts

See the *Clinton Investors Co.* case in which Watkins, a promoter, was held personally liable for a preincorporation lease, p. 918.

LO.4 Understand that after a corporate charter has been dissolved the owners and officers may be personally responsible for contracts made in the corporate name if they knew or should have known of the dissolution

See the example where Ms. Kostopulos was personally liable for debts incurred during the time of dissolution because she should have known about the dissolution, p. 921.

D. Consolidations, Mergers, and Conglomerates

LO.5 Explain a stockholder's option when he or she objects to a proposed consolidation or merger of the corporation

LO.6 Recognize that liabilities of predecessor corporations can be imposed on successor corporations when the transaction is a de facto merger or a continuation of the predecessor

See the example of Velocity Power Boats, Inc., which became essentially a "new hat" for Thoroughbred Power Boats, Inc., with liability as a corporate successor for a defective Thoroughbred boat, pp. 925–926.

KEY TERMS

articles of incorporation
authorities
bylaws
certificate of incorporation
charter
close corporation
conglomerate
consolidation
corporation
corporation by estoppel
corporation de jure
de facto
domestic corporation
eleemosynary corporation
foreign corporation
general corporation code
incorporators
merge
police power
private corporation
promoters
public corporation
quasi-public corporation
treasury stock
ultra vires

QUESTIONS AND CASE PROBLEMS

1. Edwin Edwards and Karen Davis owned EEE, Inc., which owned three convenience stores, all of which sold gasoline. Reid Ellis delivered to the three convenience stores $26,675.02 worth of gasoline for which he was not paid. Ellis proved that Edwards and Davis owned the business, ran it, and in fact personally ordered the gasoline. He claimed that they were personally liable for the debt owed him by EEE, Inc. Decide. [*Ellis v. Edwards*, 348 S.E.2d 764 (Ga. App.)]

2. Graham and Black were each 50 percent shareholders of a building supply business. When Graham filed a petition to dissolve the corporation under RMBCA §14.30, the court appointed a custodian with full powers to run the corporation's day-to-day operations. Subsequently, the court concluded that Black and Graham functioned as directors, they were deadlocked within the meaning of RMBCA §14.30(2)(1), and adequate grounds existed to dissolve the corporation because of the lack of cooperation between Black and Graham and its probable irreparable harm to the business. The court entered an order directing that within one week of receiving an expected appraisal, each would submit a sealed bid in writing for the other's stock. The custodian was to accept the high bid, and the purchaser was to immediately tender the purchase price. In the event that neither stockholder made a bona fide offer, the custodian would be redesignated the receiver and proceed to dissolve the corporation (RMBCA §14.32 [c]-[e]). The sale was unsuccessful, and by subsequent order, the court converted the custodianship into a receivership, directing that the receiver wind up and liquidate the business affairs of the corporation. Black did not believe that the successful business should be liquidated, and he directed his attorney to appeal. Decide. [*Black v. Graham*, 464 S.E.2d 814 (Ga.)]

3. Compare and contrast consolidations, mergers, and conglomerates.

4. On January 27, 1982, Joe Walker purchased a wheel-loader machine from Thompson & Green Machinery Co. (T&G). Walker signed a promissory note for $37,886.30 on behalf of "Music City Sawmill, Inc., by Joe Walker, President." When Sawmill was unable to make payments on the loader, the machine was returned to T&G. T&G brought suit against Sawmill and

subsequently discovered that Sawmill had not been incorporated on January 27, 1982, when the machine was purchased but had been incorporated the next day. T&G then sued Walker individually. The lawsuit was Walker's first notice that Sawmill was not incorporated on the date of the sale. Walker's defense was that T&G dealt with Sawmill as a corporation and did not intend to bind him personally on the note and therefore was estopped to deny Sawmill's corporate existence. Decide based on the 1969 MBCA. What would be the result if the RMBCA applied? [*Thompson & Green Machinery Co. v. Music City Lumber Co., Inc., Music City Sawmill Co., Inc.*, 683 SW.2d 340 (Tenn. App.)]

5. North Pole, Inc., approved a plan to merge with its subsidiary, Santa's Workshop, Inc. The merger plan provided that certain of Workshop's shareholders would receive $3.50 per share. The highest independent appraisal of the stock was $4.04 per share. Hirschfeld, Inc., a shareholder, claimed the fair value was $16.80 per share. Workshop offered to make its corporate books and records available to Hirschfeld to assess the validity of the $16.80 demand. This offer was declined. Hirschfeld did not attempt to base the $16.80 demand on any recognizable method of stock valuation. Hirschfeld contended it had a right to get the asking price. Refer to RMBCA §§13.02, 13.28, and 13.31. Could Hirschfeld have blocked the merger until Workshop paid the $16.80? Decide. [*Santa's Workshop v. Hirschfeld, Inc.*, 851 P.2d 265 (Colo. App.)]

6. Richard Ramlall was hired by CloseCall (MD) Inc. to negotiate a billing dispute with Verizon involving some $2 million in asserted overcharges. CloseCall (MD) agreed to a contingent fee "bonus" for its negotiators of 10 percent of the refund. The negotiations were successful. However, before he could collect his fee CloseCall (MD) merged with MVCC Acquisition Corp., a wholly owned subsidiary of MobilePro Corp., which was created for the express purpose of merging with CloseCall (MD). MVCC survived and CloseCall (MD) dissolved. MVCC then changed its name to CloseCall (DE). The merger agreement between CloseCall and MVCC referenced the 10 percent bonus due on the Verizon billing dispute. The surviving Delaware corporation created by the merger of CloseCall (MD) into MVCC is CloseCall (DE). Ramlall sued CloseCall (DE) for the bonus as the successor corporation of CloseCall (MD). CloseCall (DE) contends that after the merger CloseCall (DE) did not owe any money to Ramlall. Is CloseCall (DE) a successor corporation? Is it liable to Ramlall for the "bonus fee"? [*Ramlall v. Mobile Pro Corp.*, 30 A.2d 1003 (Md. App.)]

7. Morris Gray leased waterfront property on the Ross Barnett Reservoir to a restaurant, Edgewater Landing, Inc., for a 10-year term. After a year and a half, Edgewater's original shareholder, Billy Stegall, sold all of his shares in the corporation to Tom Bradley and Bradley's bookkeeper, Sandra Martin. Gray visited the property in the ninth year of the lease and found many problems with the condition of the property. He claimed that the lease required the tenant to make necessary repairs. Gray sued Edgewater Landing, Inc., and Tom Bradley and Sandra Martin individually for breach of the lease. Bradley and Martin replied that they were not liable for the debt of the corporation. Decide. [*Gray v. Edgewater Landing, Inc.*, 541 So.2d 1044 (Miss.)]

8. Emmick was a director and shareholder of Colonial Manors, Inc. (CM). He organized another corporation named Oahe Enterprises, Inc. To obtain shares of the Oahe stock, Emmick transferred CM shares arbitrarily valued by him at $19 per share to Oahe. The CM shares had a book value of $.47 per share, but Emmick believed that the stock would increase to a value of $19. The directors of Oahe approved Emmick's payment with the valuation of $19 per share. Golden sued Emmick on the ground that he had fraudulently deceived Oahe Corp. about the value of the CM shares and thus had made a secret profit when he received the Oahe shares that had a much greater value than the CM shares he gave in exchange. Emmick contended that his firm opinion was that the future potential value of CM shares would surely reach $19 per share. Decide. [*Golden v. Oahe Enterprises, Inc.*, 295 N.W.2d 160 (S.D.)]

9. Madison Associates purchased control of the majority of shares of 79 Realty Corp. from the

Kimmelmans and the Zauders, who then resigned as directors. The Alpert group, which owned the remaining 26 percent of 79 Realty refused to sell their shares. Partners of Madison Associates replaced the Kimmelmans and Zauders as directors of 79 Realty Corp., and as controlling directors, they approved a plan to merge 79 Realty Corp. with the Williams Street Corp., which was owned by Madison Associates. A shareholders' meeting was called, and the merger was approved by two-thirds of the shareholders. The Alpert group's shares were then forcibly canceled, with the price paid for these shares determined at their fair market value. The Alpert group brought suit contending the merger was unlawful because the sole purpose was to benefit the Madison Associates. Decide. [*Alpert v. 28 Williams Street Corp.*, 473 N.E.2d 19 (N.Y.)]

10. The Seabrook Island Property Owners Association, Inc., is a nonprofit corporation organized under state law to maintain streets and open spaces owned by property owners of Seabrook Island. Seabrook Island Co. is the developer of Seabrook Island and has majority control of the board of directors of the association. The association's bylaws empower the board of directors to levy an annual maintenance charge. Neither the association's charter nor its bylaws authorize the board to assess any other charges. When the board levied, in addition to the annual maintenance charge, an emergency budget assessment on all members to rebuild certain bridges and to revitalize the beach, the Loverings and other property owners challenged in court the association's power to impose the assessment. Decide. [*Lovering v. Seabrook Island Property Owners Ass'n*, 344 S.E.2d 862 (S.C. App.)]

11. Adams and two other persons were promoters for a new corporation, Aldrehn Theaters Co. The promoters retained Kridelbaugh to perform legal services in connection with the incorporation of the new business and promised to pay him $1,500. Aldrehn was incorporated through Kridelbaugh's services, and the promoters became its only directors. Kridelbaugh attended a meeting of the board of directors at which he was told that he should obtain a permit for the corporation to sell stock because the directors wished to pay him for his previous services. The promoters failed to pay Kridelbaugh, and he sued the corporation. Was the corporation liable? [*Kridelbaugh v. Aldrehn Theaters Co.*, 191 N.W. 803 (Iowa)]

12. On August 19, 1980, Joan Ioviero injured her hand when she slipped and fell while leaving the dining room at the Hotel Excelsior in Venice, Italy. This hotel was owned by an Italian corporation, Cigahotels, S.p.A. (The designation *S.p.A.* stands for *Societa per Azionean*, the Italian term for *corporation*.) In 1973, a firm called Ciga Hotels, Inc., was incorporated in New York. Its certificate of incorporation was amended in 1979, changing the name of the firm to Landia International Services, Inc. This New York corporation was employed by the Italian corporation Cigahotels, S.p.A., to provide sales and promotional services in the United States and Canada. Ioviero sought to hold the New York corporation liable for her hand injury at the Venice hotel. She pointed to the similarity of the first corporate name used by the New York firm to the name Cigahotels, S.p.A., and the fact that the New York firm represented the interests of the Italian firm in the United States as clear evidence that the two firms were the same single legal entity. She asked that the court disregard the separate corporate entities. The New York corporation moved that the case be dismissed because it was duly incorporated in New York and did not own the Excelsior Hotel in which Ioviero was injured. Decide. [*Ioviero v. CigaHotel, Inc., aka Landia I.S., Inc.*, 475 N.Y.S.2d 880 (A.D.)]

13. William Sullivan was ousted from the presidency of the New England Patriots Football Club, Inc. Later, he borrowed $5,348,000 to buy 100 percent control of the voting shares of the corporation. A condition of the loan was that he reorganize the Patriots so that the income from the corporation could be devoted to repayment of the personal loan and the team's assets could be used as collateral. Sullivan, therefore, arranged for a cash freeze-out merger of the holders of the 120,000 shares of nonvoting stock. David Coggins, who owned 10 shares of nonvoting stock and took special pride in the fact that he was an owner of the team, refused the $15-a-share buyout and challenged the merger in court. He contended that the merger was not for a legitimate corporate purpose but to enable

Sullivan to satisfy his personal loan. Sullivan contended that legitimate business purposes were given in the merger proxy statement, such as the National Football League's policy of discouraging public ownership of teams. Coggins responded that before the merger, Sullivan had 100 percent control of the voting stock and thus control of the franchise, and that no legal basis existed to eliminate public ownership. Decide. [*Coggins v. New England Patriots Football Club*, 492 N.E.2d 1112 (Mass.)]

CPA QUESTIONS

1. Which of the following statements is correct concerning the similarities between a limited partnership and a corporation?
   a. Each is created under a statute and must file a copy of its certificate with the proper state authorities.
   b. All corporate stockholders and all partners in a limited partnership have limited liability.
   c. Both are recognized for federal income tax purposes as taxable entities.
   d. Both are allowed statutorily to have perpetual existence.
2. Rice is a promoter of a corporation to be known as Dex Corp. On January 1, 1985, Rice signed a nine-month contract with Roe, a CPA, which provided that Roe would perform certain accounting services for Dex. Rice did not disclose to Roe that Dex had not been formed. Prior to the incorporation of Dex on February 1, 1985, Roe rendered accounting services pursuant to the contract. After rendering accounting services for an additional period of six months pursuant to the contract, Roe was discharged without cause by the board of directors of Dex. In the absence of any agreements to the contrary, who will be liable to Roe for breach of contract?
   a. Both Rice and Dex
   b. Rice only
   c. Dex only
   d. Neither Rice nor Dex
3. In general, which of the following must be contained in articles of incorporation?
   a. The names of the states in which the corporation will be doing business
   b. The name of the state in which the corporation will maintain its principal place of business
   c. The names of the initial officers and their terms of office
   d. The classes of stock authorized for issuance

Shareholder Rights in Corporations

learningoutcomes

After studying this chapter, you should be able to

LO.1 Explain how to calculate the book value of a share of stock

LO.2 Distinguish between stocks and bonds

LO.3 Distinguish between subscriptions for and transfers of stock

LO.4 Explain the rights of shareholders

LO.5 Explain the nature of a shareholder derivative lawsuit

LO.6 Explain the exceptions to the limited liability of shareholders

The two most common instruments used to provide funds for a corporation are stocks and bonds.

A. Corporate Stocks and Bonds

Ownership of a corporation is represented by stock. A *bond* is a corporate debt.

1. Nature of Stock

An interest in a corporation is based on ownership of one or more shares of stock of the corporation. Each share represents a fractional interest in the total property of the corporation. The shareholder does not own or have an interest in any specific property of the corporation; the corporation is the owner of all of its property. The terms *share, stock*, and *share of stock* mean the same thing.

(A) Capital and Capital Stock. *Capital* refers to the net assets of the corporation. Shares that have been issued to holders are said to be **outstanding**. **Capital stock** refers to the value received by the corporation for its outstanding stock.

(B) Valuation of Stock. Corporate stock may have a specified **par value**. This means that the person subscribing to the stock and acquiring it from the corporation must pay that amount.

Shares may be issued with no par value. In that case, no amount is stated in the certificate, and the amount that the subscriber pays the corporation is determined by the board of directors. The Revised Model Business Corporation Act (RMBCA) eliminates the concept of par value, so stock issued by corporations in states following the RMBCA is always no par.

The value found by dividing the value of the net corporate assets by the number of shares outstanding is the **book value** of the shares. **For Example,** Roger Eggett entered a Shareholder Agreement in 1995 with Todd Cusick and Curtis Chisholm, forming the Wasatch Energy Corporation. The terms of the Shareholder Agreement provided that should a shareholder separate from the corporation, the remaining shareholders would have the option to purchase that shareholder's corporate stock. The remaining shareholders, as per the Shareholder Agreement, would either purchase the stock for book value, if the separating shareholder voluntarily left the corporation, or for par value if the shareholder was terminated for cause. The Shareholder Agreement defined *book value* as the shareholder's net equity in the corporation, which would be determined by Wasatch's certified year-end financial statements. The Shareholder Agreement defined *par value* as the original price the shareholder paid for the stock. Egget tendered his resignation two years later, and offered to sell his stock according to the Shareholder Agreement "for the audited book value of the corporation as of June 30, 1997 divided by the number of shares he owned." Wasatch Corp. responded by firing Egget, wrongly asserting the firing was for cause, and tendered him a check for the par value of his stock, $1,217, Eggett's original investment. Eggett sued and was awarded the book value of his shares, $135,671, plus $60,000 in attorney fees.[1] The **market value** of a share of stock is the price at which that stock can be voluntarily bought or sold in the open market.

2. Certificates of Stock and Uncertificated Shares

A corporation ordinarily issues a **certificate of stock** or *share certificate* as evidence of the shareholder's ownership of stock. The issuance of such certificates is not essential either to the existence of a corporation or to the ownership of its stock.

In states that have adopted the 1978 and 1994 amendments to Article 8 of the U.C.C., uncertificated shares may be issued. Uncertificated shares are not represented by instruments. Their ownership and transfer are registered on the books maintained by, or on behalf of, the issuer corporation.[2]

3. Kinds of Stock

The stock of a corporation may be divided into two or more classes.

CPA **(A) Classification by Preferences. Common stock** is ordinary stock that has no preferences. Each share usually entitles the holder to have one vote, to

[1] *Eggett v. Wasatch Energy Corp.*, 29 P.3d 668 (Utah App. 2001).

[2] U.C.C. §8-102(1)(b). The 1978 and 1994 amendments to Article 8 of the U.C.C. have been adopted in all of the states except Alabama.

receive a share of the profits in the form of dividends when declared, and to participate in the distribution of capital upon dissolution of the corporation. **Preferred stock** has a priority over common stock. The priority may be with respect to either dividends or the distribution of capital upon dissolution of the corporation, or both. Preferred stock is ordinarily nonvoting.

CPA ***(1) Cumulative Preferred Stock.*** The right to receive dividends depends on the declaration of dividends by the board of directors for a particular period of time. If there is no fund from which the dividends may be declared or if the directors do not declare them from an available fund, the shareholder has no right to dividends. The fact that a shareholder has not received dividends for the current year does not in itself give the right to accumulate or carry over into the next year a claim for those dividends. However, in the absence of a statement that the right to dividends is noncumulative, courts frequently hold that preferred stock has the right to accumulate dividends for each year in which there was a surplus available for dividend payment but dividends were not declared.

CPA ***(2) Participating Preferred Stock.*** Sometimes the preferred stock is given the right of participation. If it is, then after the common shares receive dividends or a capital distribution is made equal to that first received by the preferred stock, both kinds participate or share equally in the balance.

(B) DURATION OF SHARES. Ordinarily, shares continue to exist for the life of the corporation. However, any kind of share, whether common or preferred, may be made terminable at an earlier date.

(C) FRACTIONAL SHARES. A corporation may issue fractional shares or scrip or certificates representing fractional shares. These can be sold or combined for the acquisition of whole shares.

4. Characteristics of Bonds

A **bond** is an instrument promising to repay a loan of money to a corporation. Typically, the loan is for a relatively long period of time, generally five years or longer. A bond obligates the corporation to pay the bondholder the amount of the loan, called the *principal*, at a stated time, called the **maturity date**, and to pay a fixed amount of *interest* at regular intervals, commonly every six months. The relationship between the bondholder and the issuing corporation is that of creditor and debtor. Unlike dividends, which are discretionary, bond interest must be paid. A bond may be secured by a mortgage or lien on corporate property. A **debenture** is an unsecured bond of the corporation with no specific corporate assets pledged as security for payment.

Bonds are negotiable securities.[3] Bonds held by owners whose names and addresses are registered on the books of the corporation are called **registered bonds.**

5. Terms and Control

The contractual terms of a particular bond issue are set forth in an agreement called a **bond indenture** or **deed**. An **indenture trustee**, usually a commercial banking institution, represents the interests of the bondholders in making sure that the corporation meets the terms and covenants of the bond issue.[4] For example, the terms of the bond indenture may require a **sinking fund**, by which the borrowing corporation is required to set aside a fixed amount of money each year toward the ultimate payment of the bonds. The indenture trustee makes certain that such terms are complied with in accordance with its responsibilities set forth in the bond indenture.

Bondholders do not vote for directors or have the right to vote on matters on which shareholders vote. However, when the debt is risky, it is highly likely that significant restraints on the corporation's freedom of action will be imposed by the terms of the indenture.

B. ACQUISITION OF SHARES

Shares may be acquired from the corporation or from an existing shareholder.

[3] U.C.C. §8-105.

[4] *Lorenc v. CSX Corp.*, CCH Sec. L. Rep. 95298 (W.D. Pa. 1990).

6. Nature of Acquisition

Shares of stock may be acquired (1) from the corporation by subscription, either before or after the corporation is organized, or (2) by transfer of existing shares from a shareholder or from the corporation. The transfer may be voluntary, as by a sale, gift, or bequest by will, or involuntary, as by an execution sale to pay the judgment of a creditor. The transfer may also take place by operation of law—as when the stock of a shareholder passes to the shareholder's trustee in bankruptcy.

7. Statute of Frauds

Under the 1978 version of Article 8, a contract for the sale of corporate shares must be evidenced by a writing, or it cannot be enforced.[5] The 1994 version of Article 8 renders the statute of frauds inapplicable to contracts for the sale or purchase of securities.[6] The commentary notes explain that the 1978 statute's potential for filtering out fraudulent claims is outweighed by the obstacles the statute presents to the development of modern commercial practices in the securities business.

No writing is required for a contract by which a broker agrees with a customer to buy or sell securities for the customer. That is an agency agreement, not a sale made between the customer and the broker.

8. Subscription

A **stock subscription** is a contract or an agreement to buy a specific number and kind of shares when the corporation issues them. As in the case of any other contract, the agreement to subscribe to shares of a corporation may be avoided for fraud.

(a) Subscription before Incorporation. In many states, a preincorporation subscription of shares is an offer to the corporation. According to this view, it is necessary for the corporation to accept the subscription offer either expressly or by conduct. A few states hold that subscriptions automatically become binding contracts when the organization of the corporation has been completed. In some states, the preincorporation subscription is irrevocable for a stated period. The RMBCA provides that "a subscription for shares entered into before incorporation is irrevocable for six months unless the subscription agreement provides a longer or shorter period or all the subscribers agree to revocation."[7]

(b) Subscription after Incorporation. Subscriptions may be made after incorporation. In that event, the transaction is like any other contract with the corporation. The offer of the subscription may come from the subscriber or from the corporation. In either case, there must be an **acceptance**. Upon acceptance, the subscriber immediately becomes a shareholder with all the rights, privileges, and liabilities of a shareholder even though she has not paid any of the purchase price. Moreover, the subscriber is a shareholder even though no share certificate has been issued. In contrast with a contract for immediate subscription to shares, the contract may be one for the future issue of shares. In that case, the contracting party has only a contract and is not a shareholder as of the formation of the contract.

9. Transfer of Shares

In the absence of a valid restriction, a shareholder may transfer shares to anyone.

(a) Restrictions on Transfer. Restrictions on the transfer of stock are valid if they are not unreasonable. It is lawful to require that the corporation or other stockholders be given the first right to purchase stock before a shareholder may sell stock to an outsider.

Such restrictions are widely used, particularly in close corporations, so current shareholders can control the ownership and management of the corporation and prevent outsiders from "invading the business"; also, restrictions serve to maintain parity among shareholders.

A provision giving a corporation the right to purchase a shareholder's shares on the death of the shareholder is valid.[8]

A restriction on the right of a certificate's purchaser to transfer his stock is not valid unless the restriction is conspicuously noted on the certificate or the transferee had actual knowledge of the restriction.

[5] U.C.C. §8-319(a); *Goldfinger v. Brown*, 564 N.Y.S.2d 461 (A.D. 1991).

[6] U.C.C. §8-113.

[7] RMBCA §6.20(a).

[8] See *Puritas Metal Products v. Cook*, 972 N.E2d 615 (Ohio 2012), where a trial court incorrectly determined that the decedent's death resulted in a "transfer" under the corporation's code of regulation. In fact, the decedent's shares were in a marital trust, and upon his death the shares were retained by the trustee of the trust, his wife, to administer and vote as she saw fit.

A restriction on the transfer of stock is strictly interpreted.[9]

When no restrictions exist, the issuer has a duty to register the transfer. **For Example,** Richard Jones purchased 1,000 certificated shares of International Generic Corporation (IGC) from Madison Tucker on March 30, 2013, at fair market value. Tucker properly indorsed the certificates to Jones on that date, and her signatures were duly notarized. On September 15, 2013, Jones presented the securities to IGC to register the transfer of shares and to collect dividends for the second quarter (April 1 through June 30) and the third quarter (July 1 through September 30). IGC refused to register the shares in Jones's name, believing him to be a person of questionable integrity that it did not want as an "owner" of IGC. Under either the 1978 or 1994 version of Article 8 of the U.C.C., it was improper for IGC to fail to register the stock that had been transferred to a bona fide purchaser, Jones.[10] No restrictions existed on the certificate, and IGC had a duty to register the transfer and was liable for its failure to do so. Jones was entitled to the dividends from the date of presentation of the stock for transfer. Prior to that date, the issuer, IGC, was entitled to treat the registered owner, Madison Tucker, as exclusively entitled to exercise the rights of ownership, including the right to dividends.[11] Thus, IGC was not liable to Jones for the second-quarter dividends. However, dividends declared after the date of presentment, which included the third-quarter dividend declared in October 2013 with a record date in October, must be paid to Jones by IGC.

(B) Interest Transferred. The transfer of shares may be absolute; that is, it may divest all ownership and make the transferee the full owner. The transfer may be of only a partial interest in the stock, or the transfer may be for security, such as when stock is pledged to secure the repayment of a loan.

10. Mechanics of Transfer

When stock is represented by a certificate, the ownership of shares is transferred by the delivery of the certificate of stock, indorsed by its owner in blank or to a specified person. Ownership may also be transferred by the delivery of the certificate accompanied by a separate assignment or power of attorney executed by the owner.[12]

A delivery from the owner of the shares directly to the transferee is not required. It can be made to an intermediary. When there is no delivery of the share certificate to anyone, however, there is no transfer of ownership of the shares.

A physical transfer of the certificate without a necessary indorsement is effective as between the parties. Thus, a gift of shares is binding even though no indorsement has been made. An indorsement is required to make the transferee a bona fide purchaser.

11. Effect of Transfer

The transfer of existing shares of stock may raise questions between the parties to the transfer and between them and the corporation.

(A) Validity of Transfer. Because a transfer of shares is a transfer of ownership, the transfer must satisfy the requirements governing any other transfer of property or agreement to transfer property.[13] As between the parties, a transfer may be set aside for any ground that would warrant similar relief under property law. If the transfer has been obtained by duress, the transferor may obtain a rescission of the transfer.

(B) Negotiability. Under common law, the transferee of shares of stock had no greater right than the transferor because the certificate and the shares represented by the certificate were nonnegotiable. By statute, the common law rule has been changed by imparting negotiability to certificated stock. Just as various defenses cannot be asserted against the holder in due course of a commercial paper, statutory law provides that similar defenses cannot be raised against the person acquiring the certificate in good faith and for value. Against such a person, the defense cannot be raised that the transferor did not own the shares or did not have authority to deliver the certificate or that the transfer was made in violation of a restriction on

[9] *Capano v. Wilmington Country Club, Inc.*, 2001 WL 1359254 (Del. Ch. Nov. 1, 2001).

[10] U.C.C. §8-401 (1978); U.C.C. §8-401 (1994).

[11] U.C.C. §8-207(1) (1978); U.C.C. §8-207(a) (1994).

[12] U.C.C. §8-309. See *Kesling v. Kesling*, 967 N.E.2d 66, 68 (Ind. App. 2012), where the corporate bylaws set forth the two methods of transferring stock in TP Orthodontics, Inc.

[13] *Gallant v. Kanterman*, 671 N.Y.S.2d 50 (A.D. 1998).

transfer not known to the person and not noted conspicuously on the certificate.

Statements sent by the issuer identifying the ownership of uncertificated securities are neither certificated securities nor negotiable instruments. Although certificated securities have the quality of negotiability, they are not commercial paper within Article 3 of the U.C.C.

(C) SECURED TRANSACTION. Corporate stock is frequently delivered to a creditor as security for a debt owed by the shareholder. Thus, a debtor borrowing money from a bank may deliver shares of stock to the bank as collateral security for the repayment of the loan. A broker's customer purchasing stock on margin may leave the stock in the possession of the broker as security for the payment of any balance due. The delivery of the security to the creditor is a pledge. This gives rise to a perfected security interest without any filing by the creditor. In itself, the pledge does not make the pledgee of the corporate stock the owner of the stock.

(D) EFFECT OF TRANSFER ON CORPORATION. The corporation is entitled to treat as the owner of shares the person whose name is on the corporation's books as the owner. Therefore, until there is a transfer on its books, the corporation may still treat a transferor of shares as the owner. The corporation may properly refuse to recognize a transferee when the corporation is given notice or has knowledge that the transfer is void or in breach of trust. In such a case, the corporation properly refuses to register a transfer until the rights of the parties have been determined. The corporation may also refuse to register the transfer of shares when the outstanding certificate is not surrendered to it or there is a lack of satisfactory proof that the certificate has been lost, destroyed, or stolen.

12. Lost, Destroyed, and Stolen Share Certificates

The owner of a lost, destroyed, or stolen share certificate is entitled to a replacement if the owner files a sufficient indemnity bond and requests the new certificate within a reasonable time before the issuer has notice that the original certificate has been acquired by a bona fide purchaser. **For Example,** if established by clear and convincing evidence, Linda Rosso would be entitled to the replacement of damaged jointly held stock certificates that her late husband Richard disposed of and never replaced. The court pointed out that there is a distinction between certificates issued a shareholder and the "shares" issued the shareholder. A *share* is the actual property of the shareholder while the *certificate* is merely the authentic evidence of the stockholder's ownership of shares.[14] If, after the new security is issued, a bona fide purchaser appears with the original certificate, the corporation must register a transfer of the security to that person and accept that person as the owner of the shares.

CPA C. RIGHTS OF SHAREHOLDERS

The rights of shareholders stem from their status as owners.

CPA 13. Ownership Rights

Shareholder control over the corporation is indirect. Periodically (ordinarily once a year), the shareholders elect directors and by this means control the corporation. At other times, however, the shareholders have no right or power to control corporate activity so long as it is conducted within lawful channels.

CPA **(A) CERTIFICATES OF STOCK.** A shareholder has the right to have a properly executed certificate as evidence of ownership of shares. An exception is made when the corporation is authorized to issue uncertificated securities.

CPA **(B) TRANSFER OF SHARES.** Unless limited by a valid restriction, a shareholder has the right to transfer her shares. The shareholder may sell the shares at any price or transfer them as a gift. The fact that the seller sells at a price higher than the market price is not unlawful even if the seller is a director or an officer.

In the *Shoaf* case, the court considered whether a shareholder who controlled a majority of the corporation's shares had a duty to refrain from making a profit by selling his controlling stock above the market price.

[14] *Rosso v. Rosso*, 701 N.W.2d 355 (Neb. 2005).

Shoaf v. Warlick, 380 S.E.2d 865 (S.C. App. 1989)

Control of Coke-Anderson, S.C.: It's the Real Thing, Entitled to a Premium

Paul Warlick Jr. was the president, chief executive officer, and a stockholder of Coca-Cola Bottling Co. of Anderson, South Carolina (Coke-Anderson). He controlled 273.5 shares of stock of the total of 480 shares of stock outstanding, including the stock of his mother, uncle, and aunt. Warlick agreed to sell this controlling interest in Coke-Anderson to Coke-Ashville for $4 million, which included a premium (difference between market and sale price) to be paid him for his controlling interest. Wayne Shoaf, a minority shareholder, brought suit against Warlick, contending that Warlick had violated his fiduciary duty to the corporation and had received an unlawful premium for the sale of the majority interest in Coke-Anderson. From a judgment for Warlick, Shoaf appealed.

JUDICIAL OPINION

SHAW, J.... The issues we are asked to consider are whether Warlick had a fiduciary duty owed to the other stockholders and whether he breached this duty, and whether Warlick has a basis to claim appellants are equitably estopped from attacking his premium received for his stock.

South Carolina has long followed the general rule that corporate stock is personal property which the owner may "dispose of ... as he sees fit." ... Concomitantly, when selling stock, stockholders must "necessarily act for themselves, and not as trustees for other stockholders." ... This general rule applies as well to majority shareholders:

> *"A dominant or majority shareholder is generally under no duty to the minority stockholders to refrain from receiving a premium upon the sale of his controlling stock."*

"The law of the marketplace dictates that a shareholder who has a controlling interest in a corporation will likely be able to receive a higher price per share than a minority shareholder. *'As a general rule, nothing in the law of the courthouse prevents a majority shareholder from retaining this "control premium."* ... *This is so even if, as is so frequently the case, the controlling shareholder is an officer or director of the corporation.... A shareholder, irrespective of whether he is also a director, officer, or both, may sell his shares, just as he may sell other kinds of personal property, for whatever price he can obtain, even if his shares constitute a controlling block and the price per share is enhanced by that fact.'* Further, the courts generally hold that neither the selling shareholder nor his purchaser is under an obligation to see that other shareholders are provided opportunities to sell their shares on the same favorable terms as the controlling shareholder or even to inform minority shareholders of the price and other terms of the sale of the controlling interest."

Martin v Martin, 529 So. 2d 1174 (Fla. 3d Dist. Ct. App. 1988)

[Judgment affirmed]

QUESTIONS

1. What did the plaintiff contend?
2. Can a shareholder who is also an officer and director of a corporation lawfully obtain a premium for selling controlling interest in a corporation?
3. State the general rule of law applicable to this case.

CPA 14. Right to Vote

The right to vote means the right to vote at shareholders' meetings for the election of directors and on other special matters that shareholders must vote on. **For Example,** a proposal to change the capital structure of the corporation or a proposal to sell all or substantially all assets of the corporation must be approved by the shareholders.

CPA **(A) WHO MAY VOTE.** Ordinarily, only shareholders of record—those common shareholders in whose name the stock appears on the books of the corporation—are entitled to vote. The board of directors may fix a date for closing the corporate books for this purpose.

CPA **(B) NUMBER OF VOTES.** Unless there is a provision to the contrary, for each share owned, each shareholder is entitled to one vote on each matter to be voted. This procedure is called *straight voting*, and it is the normal method for shareholder voting on corporate matters. However, in the case of voting to elect directors only, **cumulative voting** is mandatory in nearly half of the states. This requirement is imposed by either state constitution or state statute. Cumulative voting is permitted by law in other states when provided for in the articles of incorporation or bylaws.

Cumulative voting is a form of voting that is designed to give proportional representation on the board of directors to minority shareholders. Under a cumulative voting plan, each shareholder has as many votes as the number of shares owned multiplied by the number of directors to be elected. A shareholder may cast all of these votes for one candidate or may divide the votes between two or more candidates. This system enables minority shareholders to cast all of their votes for a candidate who will represent their interests on the board of directors.

Under straight voting, minority shareholders would always be outvoted. **For Example,** assume that minority shareholder Tyler Feldberg owned 400 shares of stock and majority shareholder C. J. Jones controlled the remaining 600 shares. Also assume that five directors are to be elected to the board. If straight voting were used for the election of directors, C. J., with 600 shares, would always outvote Tyler's 400 shares. However, under cumulative voting, Tyler would be allowed 2,000 votes (400 shares times five directors), and C. J. would be allowed 3,000 votes (600 shares times five directors). The five candidates with the highest number of votes will be elected. If Tyler casts 1,000 votes for each of two directors and C. J. casts 1,000 votes for each of three directors, Tyler, who owns 40 percent of the stock, is able to elect two-fifths of the board to represent his interests.

(c) Voting by Proxy. A shareholder has the right to authorize another to vote the shares owned by the shareholder. This procedure is known as **voting by proxy**. In the absence of restrictions to the contrary, any person, even someone who is not a shareholder, may act as a proxy. The authorization from the shareholder may be made by any writing.[15] The authorization is also commonly called a **proxy**.

(d) Voting Agreements and Trusts. Shareholders, as a general rule, are allowed to enter into an agreement by which they concentrate their voting strength for the purpose of electing directors or voting on any other matter.

A **voting trust** is created when by agreement a group of shareholders or all of the shareholders transfer their shares in trust to one or more persons as trustees. The trustees are authorized to vote the stock during the life of the trust agreement.[16] In general, such agreements are upheld if their object is lawful. In some jurisdictions, such trusts cannot run beyond a stated number of years. There are some signs of a relaxation as to time. Several states have abandoned all time limitations, several have extended the time limitation, and many provide for an extension or renewal of the agreement.

CPA 15. Preemptive Offer of Shares

If the capital stock of a corporation is increased, shareholders ordinarily have the **preemptive right** to subscribe to the same percentage of the new shares that their old shares represented of the former total of capital stock. This right is given to enable shareholders to maintain their relative interests in the corporation.

The existence of a preemptive right may make it impossible to conclude a transaction in which the corporation is to transfer a block of stock as consideration. Moreover, practical difficulties arise as to how stock should be allocated among shareholders of different classes.

The RMBCA provides that shareholders do not have preemptive rights unless the articles of incorporation provide for them.

CPA 16. Inspection of Books

A shareholder has the right to inspect the books of the shareholder's corporation. In some states, there are no limitations on this right. In most states, the inspection must be made in good faith, for proper motives, and at a reasonable time and place.[17] In many states, a shareholder must own a certain percentage of the outstanding stock of a corporation (commonly 5 percent) or must own at least one share of stock for a minimum amount of time (commonly six months) to have the right to inspect the books. A shareholder is not relegated to accepting opinions and numbers offered by a company's auditor and may employ an expert accountant of his own to review and analyze the books and records of the corporation.[18]

The purpose of inspection must be reasonably related to the shareholder's interest as a shareholder. **For Example,** minority shareholder Julio Herencia was

[15] RMBCA §7.07.

[16] *Bettner Trust v. Bettner*, 495 N.E.2d 194 (Ind. App. 1986).

[17] RMBCA §16.02(c); *Leary v. Foley*, 884 So.2d 655 (La. App. 2004).

[18] *Missouri v. III Investments, Inc.*, 80 S.W.3d 855 (Mo. App. 2002).

entitled access to corporate books and records and an accounting when the majority shareholders of Centercut Restaurant Corp. did not follow the shareholders agreement's method of valuation for the repurchase of his shares.[19] A shareholder is entitled to inspect the records to determine the financial condition of the corporation, the quality of its management, and any matters relating to rights or interests in the corporate business, such as the value of stock.[20]

The *Security First* case deals with a stockholder's right to inspect books and records when there is some credible basis to believe there is mismanagement, versus management's right to protect the corporation from indiscriminate "fishing expeditions."

Security First v. U.S. Die Casting, Inc., 687 A.2d 563 (Del. Super. 1997)

... No Fury Like a Stockholder Scorned

U.S. Die Casting, Inc., is a closely held Ohio corporation that owns 5 percent of Security First Corporation, a Delaware Corporation, which owns an Ohio savings and loan bank. David Slyman is the president of U.S. Die and its sole stockholder. The defendant, Security First, entered into a merger agreement with Mid Am, Inc., a large regional bank holding company; and after the announcement of the merger, Security First's stock increased significantly. The merger agreement required Security First to pay a termination fee of $2 million plus third-party expenses not to exceed $250,000 contingent on the occurrence of certain events within one year after termination, should Security First pull out of the merger. The merger did not go through, and the market price for Security First stock dropped significantly. Security First gave as a reason for failing to go through with the merger "the realization that Mid Am's management philosophy and direction were fundamentally different from its own." Security First paid Mid Am $275,000 and agreed to pay an additional $2 million if a certain event occurred within a year and one-half after termination. U.S. Die submitted a written demand to Security First persuant to Section 220 to inspect all of its books and records related to the Mid Am merger and its termination. Security First refused to comply. The Court of Chancery granted U.S. Die's demand, and Security First appealed.

JUDICIAL OPINION

VEASEY, C. J. ... Concerning the purpose for the inspection, Slyman testified:

> *I would like to make my own decision as to why the merger was not completed. Telling me that it was a difference of philosophies didn't get me to understand why it was not completed. The philosophy was there prior to it. ...*

Defendant argues that the purpose which Slyman articulated at trial was insufficient and that this insufficiency is fatal. This argument must fail. Slyman's testimony does call into question defendant's purported reason for abrogating the Merger Agreement—namely, that "the realization that Mid Am's management philosophy and direction were fundamentally different from its own." The Court of Chancery found defendant's reason suspect. The Court stated that "[a] reasonable stockholder could conclude prudent management would have researched 'fundamental' similarities and dissimilarities of the merging company before entering the Merger Agreement."...

Defendant maintains that plaintiff failed to produce any evidence of mismanagement. This argument misses the point. In a Section 220 action, a stockholder has the burden of proof to demonstrate a proper purpose, but a stockholder is "not required to prove by a preponderance of the evidence that waste and [mis]management are actually occurring." The threshold for a plaintiff in a Section 220 case is not insubstantial. Mere curiosity or a desire for a fishing expedition will not suffice. But the threshold may be satisfied by a credible showing, through documents, logic, testimony or otherwise, that there are legitimate issues of wrongdoing.

As specific instances of misconduct, plaintiff questions defendant's payment of $275,000 to Mid Am "when Defendant never broke the Merger Agreement." Plaintiff also questions defendant's failure to request documentation from Mid Am of its expenses to justify defendant's expenditure of $275,000, which was $25,000 more than the Merger Agreement stipulated for expenses. On their face, these issues raise questions. The effect of the Vice Chancellor's conclusion after trial is that the questions remain.

Defendant also agreed to pay Mid Am $2 million contingent on the occurrences of certain events of the Termination Agreement. Pursuant to the Merger Agreement, defendant previously had agreed to pay Mid Am $2 million contingent on the same occurrences within one year. As plaintiff's counsel, in a letter dated 1/19/95 to Security First's Chairman and CEO Charles Valentine, stated "This either takes the company 'out of play' or diminishes the amount

19 *Herencia v. Centercut Restaurant Corp.*, 938 N.Y.S.2d 286 (A. D. 2012). See also *Feil v. Greater Lakeside Corp.*, 81 So.3d 178 (La. App. 2011).
20 *Ihrig v. Frontier Equity Exchange*, 128 P.3d 993 (Kan. App. 2006).

Continued

payable to the stockholders if it is sold. In either event, the agreement seems inappropriate and destructive to stockholder values."

Section 220(c) provides that "[t]he Court may, in its discretion, prescribe any limitations or conditions with reference to the inspection." While the trial court has wide latitude in determining the proper scope of inspection, it is the responsibility of the trial court to tailor the inspection to the stockholder's stated purpose. "Undergirding this discretion is a recognition that the interests of the corporation must be harmonized with those of the inspecting stockholder." ...

Section 220 proceedings are an important part of the corporate governance landscape in Delaware. Stockholders have a right to at least a limited inquiry into books and records when they have established some credible basis to believe that there has been wrongdoing. In fact, a Section 220 proceeding may serve a salutary mission as a prelude to a derivative suit. Yet it would invite mischief to open corporate management to indiscriminate fishing expeditions. The trial court must assure that a proper balance is struck.

The judgment of the Court of Chancery granting U.S. Die's entitlement to inspect books and records is **AFFIRMED**. The breadth of the order is **REVERSED** on this record, however. This case is **REMANDED** to the Court of Chancery to open the record and to consider whether the plaintiff has carried its burden of proving that each category of books and records is essential to the accomplishment of the stockholder's articulated purpose for the inspection.

QUESTIONS

1. Why did the president of U.S. Die seek to inspect the books and records?
2. Does a stockholder have the right to demand to review books and records at his or her discretion or must the stockholder prove waste and mismanagement are occurring? Or, is there a different standard for the stockholder?
3. Did U.S. Die make a credible showing that there was a legitimate issue of wrongdoing? Explain.

A shareholder is entitled to inspect the books to obtain information needed for a lawsuit against the corporation or its directors or officers, to organize the other shareholders into an "opposition" party to remove the board of directors at the next election, or to buy the shares of other shareholders.[21]

Inspection has frequently been refused when it was sought merely from idle curiosity or for "speculative purposes." Inspection has sometimes been denied on the ground that it was sought merely to obtain a mailing list of persons who would be solicited to buy products of another enterprise. Inspection has also been refused when the object of the shareholder was to advance political or social beliefs without regard to the welfare of the corporation. Cases that deny the right of inspection do so when it would be harmful to the corporation[22] or is sought only for the purpose of annoying, harassing, or causing vexation or of aiding competitors of the corporation.

(A) Form of Books. There are generally no requirements regarding the form of corporate books and records. The RMBCA recognizes that corporate books and records may be stored in modern data storage systems. "A corporation shall maintain its records in written form or in any other form capable of conversion into written form within a reasonable time."[23]

(B) Financial Statements. The RMBCA requires a corporation to furnish annual financial statements. These statements include a balance sheet as of the end of the fiscal year, an income statement for that year, and a statement of changes in shareholders' equity for that year.[24] A number of state statutes contain similar provisions and set forth a statutory penalty for any officer responsible for providing the financial statements who fails to perform such duties after written request.

[21] See *Kelley Manufacturing Co. v. Martin*, 674 S.E.2d 92 (Ga. App. 2009), where the court determined that two shareholders showed a proper purpose for seeking inspection of books: to enforce the company's bylaws; to ensure proper corporate governance and to determine if corporate waste, mismanagement, and other breaches of fiduciary duty were occurring; to inspect corporate records to protect the shareholders' substantial ownership interest; and to inspect records related to the shareholders' removal as trustees, directors, officers, and employees of the corporation.

[22] *Retail Property Investors, Inc., v. Skeens*, 471 S.E.2d 181 (Va. 1996).

[23] RMBCA §16.01(d).

[24] RMBCA §16.20. See *Troccoli v. Lab Contract Industries, Inc.*, 687 N.Y.S.2d 400 (A.D. 1999).

CPA 17. Dividends

A shareholder has the right to receive a proportion of dividends as they are declared, subject to the relative rights of other shareholders to preferences, accumulation of dividends, and participation. There is no absolute right that dividends be declared, but dividends, when declared, must be paid in the manner indicated.

CPA **(A) FUNDS AVAILABLE FOR DECLARATION OF DIVIDENDS.** Statutes commonly provide that no dividends may be declared unless there is an "earned surplus" for their payment. Earned surplus, also known as *retained earnings*, consists of the accumulated profits earned by the corporation since its formation less prior dividend distributions. Dividend payments are prohibited if the corporation is insolvent or would be rendered insolvent by the payment of the dividend.

As an exception to these rules, a wasting assets corporation may pay dividends out of current net profits without regard to the preservation of the corporate assets. **Wasting assets corporations** are those designed to exhaust or use up the assets of the corporation (for example, by extracting oil, coal, iron, and other ores) as compared with manufacturing plants whose object is to preserve the plant as well as to continue to manufacture. A wasting assets corporation may also be formed for the purpose of buying and liquidating a stock of merchandise from a company that has received a discharge in bankruptcy court.

In some states, statutes provide that dividends may be declared from earned surplus or from current net profits without regard to the existence of a deficit from former years.

CPA **(B) DISCRETION OF DIRECTORS.** Assuming that a fund is available for the declaration of dividends, it is then a matter primarily within the discretion of the board of directors whether a dividend shall be declared. The fact that there is an earned surplus that could be used for dividends does not mean that they must be declared. This rule is not affected by the nature of the shares. Thus, the fact that the shareholders hold cumulative preferred shares does not give them any right to demand a declaration of dividends or to interfere with an honest exercise of discretion by the directors.

Maintaining an adequate cash and working capital position is an important practical consideration in determining whether to declare a cash dividend. In general, courts refuse to substitute their judgment for the judgment of the directors of the corporation and interfere with their decision on dividend declaration only when it is shown that their conduct is harmful to the welfare of the corporation or its shareholders.[25]

(C) FORM OF DIVIDENDS. Customarily, a dividend is paid in money. However, it may be paid in property, such as a product manufactured by the corporation; in shares of other corporations held by the corporation; or in shares of the corporation itself.

(D) EFFECT OF TRANSFER OF SHARES. When a corporation declares a cash or property dividend, the usual practice is for the board of directors to declare a dividend as of a certain date—the *declaration date*—payable to shareholders of record on a stated future date—the *record date*—with a *payment date* following the record date, usually by some 30 days. The person who is the owner of the shares on the record date is entitled to the dividend even if the shares are transferred prior to the payment date.

If the dividend consists of shares in the corporation declaring the dividend, ownership of the dividend is determined by the date of distribution. Whoever is the owner of the shares when the stock dividend is distributed is entitled to the stock dividend. The reason for this variation from the cash dividend rule is that the declaration of a stock dividend has the effect of diluting the existing corporate assets among a larger number of shares. The value of the holding represented by each share is diminished as a result. Unless the person who owns the stock on the distribution date receives a proportionate share of the stock dividend, the net effect will be to lessen that person's holding.

18. Capital Distribution

Upon dissolution of the corporation, shareholders are entitled to receive any balance of the corporate assets that remains after the payment of all creditors. Certain

[25] *Gabelli & Co. v. Liggett Group, Inc.*, 479 A.2d 276 (Del. Super. 1984).

classes of stock may have a preference or priority in this distribution.

CPA 19. Shareholders' Actions

When the corporation has the right to sue its directors, officers, or third persons for damages caused by them to the corporation or for breach of contract, one or more shareholders may bring such action if the corporation refuses to do so. This is a **derivative (secondary) action** in that the shareholder enforces only the cause of action of the corporation and any money recovery is paid into the corporate treasury.

In a derivative action, when a corporation has failed to enforce a right, a shareholder bringing such a suit must show that a demand was made on the directors to enforce the right in question. The shareholder must show (1) that the directors refused to enforce the right[26] or (2) that a demand that the directors enforce the right is excused because the directors are deemed incapable of making an impartial decision regarding the pursuit of the litigation. Additionally, where a special litigation committee (SLC) is formed by the board of directors with full authority to decide what position to take with regard to a derivative lawsuit, demand on the entire board may be excused on a case-by-case basis, as exemplified in the *AIG, Inc.*, case.

AIG, Inc. v. Greenberg, 965 A.2d 763 (Del. Ch. 2009)

"Curb Your Enthusiasm," Defendants Greenberg and Smith Argue

Plaintiff stockholders sued derivatively CEO Maurice Greenberg, CFO Howard Smith, and other former officers who had served on American Insurance Group's (AIG's) board of directors. The plaintiffs took this action on behalf of the corporation for damages the Former officers had caused AIG by having the corporation engage in illegal acts. In one example, it was asserted by the plaintiffs that AIG had created a fictional reinsurance business transaction with General Reinsurance Corp. to inflate loss reserves, thus making AIG appear to be a healthier company than it actually was and inflating AIG's stock price. AIG's board of directors formed a special litigation committee (SLC) to look into the stockholder plaintiffs' allegations, giving full authority to the SLC to address the litigation. The SLC investigated all matters and decided to join this action as a direct plaintiff on behalf of the corporation, asserting breach of fiduciary duty and indemnification claims against former CEO Greenberg and former CFO Smith. The defendants, Greenberg and Smith, contended that the stockholder plaintiffs must make a demand on the full board. Moreover, they asserted that under procedural law, boards of directors should not be lightly bypassed by derivative plaintiffs.

JUDICIAL OPINION

STRINE, Vice Chancellor … Here, the AIG board's primacy in decision making has been fully honored. The AIG board invested complete authority in an SLC to decide what position the corporation would take with regard to this lawsuit. This case was then delayed for a lengthy period during which the SLC evaluated what position to take.

The SLC's task was a complicated one, especially given the reality that the fraudulent schemes pled in the Complaint were ones that exposed AIG itself to liability. Thus, the SLC had to weigh the advantage of having AIG prosecute claims against the defendants with the disadvantage of affirmatively accusing AIG officials of wrongful acts that third-party plaintiffs would impute to AIG itself. In the end, the SLC chose to have AIG sue Greenberg and Smith itself, to seek dismissal of certain defendants, and to otherwise take no position on the Stockholder Plaintiffs' claims. …

Given this reality, the Stockholder Plaintiffs need not make a demand because demand would be futile. The SLC has had a full and fair opportunity to decide whether to prosecute the claims brought by the Stockholder Plaintiffs, seek their dismissal, or take no position and permit the Stockholder Plaintiffs to proceed. Having taken the latter course, the SLC recognized that the Stockholder Plaintiffs would go forward without the demand requirement being a barrier to their claims.…

… The moving defendants seek to avoid this precedent. … The defendants argue that because the SLC chose not to oppose the claims because they feared that taking that route might expose information developed in the SLC's investigation to parties with interests adverse to AIG, the SLC did not endorse the derivative claims, and thus the Stockholder Plaintiffs should be required to make a demand on the full board, which may not have the same concerns about disclosure.

[26] *Marx. v. Akers*, 666 N.E.2d 1034 (N.Y. 1996). But see *Potter v. Hughes*, 546 F.3d 1051 (9th Cir. 2008).

Continued

...The point of Rule 23.1 is to prevent stockholders from usurping the board's right to manage the affairs of the corporation. Here, there is no such concern. AIG's board has decided to give full authority to the SLC to address this litigation, and through its duly empowered SLC, the AIG board has had the chance to assert control over this lawsuit, prosecute some claims and dismiss others. Instead, it chose to take over two claims, seek the dismissal of certain defendants, and take no position on the rest of the litigation. Its decision-making primacy has been honored, and that is all our law requires.

The demand requirement is not, as these defendants would have it, an immunity shield for defendants. It is an assurance that the stockholders' duly elected representatives control the legal rights of the corporation unless there is a basis for excusing their control. In fact, the particularized pleading requirement of Rule 23.1 is expressly designed to ensure that boards are not lightly bypassed by derivative plaintiffs; that is why a plaintiff hoping to avoid demand must plead particularized facts demonstrating the board's inability to impartially respond to a demand on a breach of fiduciary duty claim. The latter method of bypass is related to the first, in the sense that if a plaintiff can satisfy a particularized pleading standard for pleading a fiduciary breach, the intuition is that the board faces a sufficiently real threat of liability that it cannot act objectively on the demand.

When, however, a corporate board has had the chance to consider what position to take regarding a derivative suit and has decided to take no position, the resulting procedural implications are clear. Demand in such a situation is excused, and the derivative plaintiff is free to proceed against the defendants under the procedural rules ordinarily applicable....

[Judgment for the Plaintiffs]

QUESTIONS

1. What is the purpose of Rule 23.1?
2. Did the stockholder plaintiffs usurp the board's right to manage the affairs of the corporation in this case?

A special litigation committee is vested with enormous power to pursue a corporate claim or seek dismissal of a derivative suit. But courts will defer to the business judgment and conclusions of the SLC only if the directors involved possess a disinterested independence and do not have relationships that prevent an unprejudicial exercise of judgment.[27]

Mere allegations that a director and other directors move in the same social circles or are characterized as close friends is not enough to negate a director's independence for presuit demand excusal purposes.

Lawsuits may be brought by minority shareholders against majority shareholders who are oppressive toward minority shareholders. Oppressive conduct may include payment of grossly excessive salaries and fringe benefits to the majority stockholders who are also officers of the corporation. Shareholders may bring a derivative action to obtain a dissolution of the corporation by judicial decree.[28]

D. Liability of Shareholders

A shareholder is ordinarily protected from the liabilities of the corporation. Some exceptions exist, however.

20. Limited Liability

The liability of a shareholder is generally limited. This means that the shareholder is not personally liable for the debts and liabilities of the corporation. The capital contributed by shareholders may be exhausted by the claims of creditors, but there is no personal liability for any unpaid balance.

21. Ignoring the Corporate Entity

Ordinarily a corporation is regarded and treated as a separate legal entity, and the law does not look behind a corporation to see who owns or controls it.

The fact that two corporations have identical shareholders does not justify a court's regarding the two corporations as one. Similarly, the fact that there

[27] *In re Comverse Technology, Inc.*, 766 N.Y.S.2d 10 (A.D. 2008).

[28] *Miller v. Up In Smoke, Inc.*, 738 F. Supp.2d 878 (N.D. Ind. 2010). But see *Whithorn v. Whithorn Farms, Inc.*, 195 P.3d 836 (Mont. 2008).

is a close working relationship between two corporations does not in itself constitute any basis for ignoring their separate corporate entities when they in fact are separately run enterprises.

(A) "PIERCING THE CORPORATE VEIL." A court may disregard the corporate entity, or figuratively "pierce the corporate veil," when exceptional circumstances warrant. The decision whether to disregard the corporate entity is made on a case-by-case basis, weighing all factors before the court. Factors that may lead to piercing the corporate veil and imposing liability on its owners (the shareholders) are (1) the failure to maintain adequate corporate records and the commingling of corporate and other funds,[29] (2) grossly inadequate capitalization,[30] (3) the diversion by shareholders of corporate funds or assets,[31] (4) the formation of the corporation to evade an existing obligation, (5) the formation of the corporation to perpetrate a fraud or conceal illegality, and (6) a determination that injustice and inequitable consequences would result if the corporate entity were recognized.[32]

In the *Inter-Tel* case, the landlord claimed that the corporate entities should be ignored.

Inter-Tel Technologies Inc. v. Linn Station Properties, LLC, 360 S.W.3d 152 (Ky. 2012)

Sometimes "Parents" Have to Pay the Rent in Business, Too

Inter-Tel is an Arizona corporation that designs, manufacturers, and sells telecommunication services primarily to businesses. Inter-Tel Technology Inc. (Technologies) operates Inter-Tel's retail division. On July 2, 1998, Technologies purchased Integrated Telecom Services Corp. (ITS), with Inter-Tel, the Arizona parent, paying for the stock. ITS was Inter-Tel's first retail branch in Kentucky, selling Inter-Tel's products from an office building in Louisville it leased from Linn Station Properties. After ITS was acquired by Technologies, ITS no longer possessed any financial independence. ITS could not maintain a bank account, hold any funds, or pay any bills. All of ITS's regional offices were transformed from independent dealers of communications equipment into direct sales "branches" of Inter-Tel. ITS employees became employees of Inter-Tel and were paid by Inter-Tel from its headquarters in Arizona. When a customer purchased a telecommunications system from ITS the payment went directly into a "lock box" or depository account controlled by Inter-Tel. Once the funds were placed in this account, they belonged to Inter-Tel. Inter-Tel paid all the vendors who provided ITS with goods and services. Inter-Tel paid ITS's rent for the Linn Station Road property from the time Technologies acquired ITS until ITS abandoned the premises in 2002. Linn Properties sued ITS for unpaid rent and failure to maintain the property, and a default judgment was entered against ITS for $332,900. ITS was a defunct corporation without any assets, so Linn Properties brought a breach of corporate veil action against Technologies and Inter-Tel.

JUDICIAL OPINION

Abramson, J....Limited liability for corporate entities is described by some scholars as springing from both democratic and economic principles in the early days of the United States. The "imposition of limited liability was perceived as a means of encouraging the small-scale entrepreneur, and of keeping entry into business markets competitive and democratic," assuring that the corporate world was not dominated by industrialists who had the immense personal wealth to withstand any business risk. Presser, *supra,* at 19. The economic rationale was that the public would benefit from investment by shareholders who would be willing to take risks in industry, manufacturing and general commercial development if personal liability could be avoided should their ventures not succeed. *Id.* at 21. By the twentieth century, deliberate misuse of the corporate form by shareholders who were either individuals or other corporations had led courts to authorize piercing the corporate veil....

[29] *East Market v. Tycorp Pizza IV, Inc.*, 625 S.E.2d 191, 198 (N.C. App. 2006).

[30] In *Trevino v. MERSCORP, Inc.*, 583 F. Supp. 2d 521 (D. Del. 2008), the court determined that a shortage of capital is not per se a reason to pierce the corporate veil; rather, a more relevant inquiry would be "Was the entity established to defraud its creditors?" An example of grossly inadequate capitalization is found in *Klokke Corp. v. Classic Exposition, Inc.*, 912 P.2d 929 (Or. App. 1996), in which Classic's two shareholders invested $1,000 of capital to start a business and immediately took out a $200,000 loan. The business remained undercapitalized until part of it was sold. However, the two shareholders effectively withdrew all of the proceeds of the sale in October 1991, and the business was again without sufficient capital, leaving it unable to meet its financial obligations. The court held that the shareholders were personally liable up to the amount withdrawn in October 1991 after the partial sale of the business.

[31] See *Trustees of the National Elevator Industry Pension Fund v. Lutyk*, 332 F.3d 188 (3d Cir. 2003), in which the Court of Appeals found the equitable remedy of piercing the corporate veil justified. The sole shareholder, Andrew Lutyk, siphoned funds over the final months of the corporation's operations while it was known to be deeply insolvent, used corporate funds to pay entertainment expenses without an identifiable business purpose, and commingled corporate assets with his own. Personal liability was imposed on Lutyk to make unpaid payments to a union's benefit plans.

[32] *Barton v. Moore*, 558 N.W.2d 746 (Minn. 1997).

Continued

....Judge Cardozo noted that "[w]e say at times that the corporate entity will be ignored when the parent corporation operates a business through a subsidiary which is characterized as an 'alias' or 'dummy.' " *Berkey,* 155 N.E. at 61.

In the ensuing years courts have invoked other, often colorful, terms in an attempt to capture the concept of loss of separate corporate existence including "dry shell," "puppet," "stooge," "conduit" and "marionette," among dozens of others. Peter B. Oh, *Veil–Piercing,* 89 Tex. L.Rev. 81, 83 n. 7 (2010). This Court, then the Court of Appeals, joined in the vivid descriptions in one of the Commonwealth's earliest piercing cases, *Veterans Service Club v. Sweeney,* 252 S.W.2d 25 (Ky.1952), a case with somewhat curious facts. Mrs. Sweeney apparently gambled $1,535.00 of family funds in games of chance at the "veterans" club, causing her displeased husband to bring suit under a Kentucky anti-gaming statute that allowed "the loser or his creditor" to recover treble damages against gambling winners. Without extensive discussion, this Court found the Chancellor correctly "swept aside the legal fiction of separate corporate personality" to hold the three individual incorporators of the Veterans Service Club liable for their "unlawful acts." 252 S.W.2d at 27. In so doing, the Court stated:

> *The incorporation was but a cloak or mask devised by the incorporators to cover their illegal acts of gambling and to shield them from the consequences of these acts. In such a case the corporate form will be disregarded to the same extent as if it were nonexistent and liability will be fixed upon those who attempt to employ this type of instrumentality as a protective measure for their unlawful practices. It is a stern but just maxim of law that fraud vitiates everything into which it enters.*

... ITS lost all semblance of separate corporate existence and through the joint acts of Technologies and Inter-Tel was rendered income-less and asset-less. Their diversion of ITS's corporate income and transfer of ITS's corporate assets for their own benefit provides the extra "injustice" discussed in *Sea–Land,* something more than simply a creditor's inability to collect a debt from ITS.....

In any event, where the parent is the wholly-owned subsidiary of the grandparent; the grandparent has provided 100% of the funds for the parent's purchase of the subsidiary; the parent itself has failed to follow corporate formalities; the grandparent pays the subsidiary's employees; the grandparent acts interchangeably with the parent in filing tax returns regarding what is supposedly the subsidiary's business; and the officers of the subsidiary and parent are also officers of the grandparent it is apparent that little, if any, effort has been exerted in maintaining separate corporate identities....

... The equitable doctrine of veil piercing cannot be thwarted by having two entities, rather than one, dominate the subsidiary and dividing the conduct between the two so that each can point the finger to some extent at the other....

Inter-Tel and Technologies, together, exercised complete control and dominion over ITS, causing it to lose any semblance of separate corporate existence. As ITS's parent and grandparent, Technologies and Inter-Tel transferred all of ITS's income and assets to themselves, thus deriving all of the benefits from the business conducted at the Linn Station Road premises while leaving behind a shell entity from which a legitimate creditor could recover nothing. Under these circumstances there was the requisite domination and injustice to justify piercing ITS's corporate veil to hold both Technologies and Inter-Tel responsible for the default judgment previously obtained by Linn Station against ITS....

[Affirmed.]

QUESTIONS

1. What is meant by the remedy of piercing the corporate veil?
2. In the history of the doctrine, what terms have been used to capture the concept of loss of separate corporate existence?
3. How did the court decide this case?

(B) "ALTER EGO" THEORY. Some courts express their reasons for disregarding the corporate entity by stating that the corporation is the "*alter ego*" of the wrongdoer. A corporation is a separate and distinct person from the person or persons who own the corporation. However, when a corporation is so dominated and controlled by a shareholder(s), officer(s), or director(s) that the separate personalities of the individual and the corporation no longer exist and there is a wrongful use of that control, the courts will disregard the corporate entity so as not to sanction a fraud or injustice.[33] **For Example,**

[33] *Dishon v. Ponthie,* 918 So.2d 1132 (La. App. 2005).

V&M Industries, Inc., owned land on which some 40,000 plus used tires caught fire. It took nearly a week to extinguish the fire and caused severe air pollution in the St. Louis area. Vernon Leirer originally owned 99 percent of V&M corporate stock; all corporate officers other than Leirer were nonfunctioning; the corporation was inadequately capitalized; no stock certificates were issued; and corporate records were generally not kept. At a time just before the fire, when Leirer was no longer a shareholder or officer, he exercised total direction and control over the corporation and "ran the show." The court held that to adhere to the fiction of separate corporate existence would sanction fraud. It concluded that V&M, Inc., was the *alter ego* for Leirer, and Leirer was personally responsible for civil penalties under the Environmental Protection Act.[34]

Limited liability is important to our economy because it encourages investors to make investments in high-risk ventures. It should be disregarded only in exceptional circumstances. When fraud or deceit is absent, other circumstances for piercing the corporate veil must be so strong as to clearly indicate that the corporation is the alter ego of the controlling person.

(c) Obtaining Advantages of Corporate Existence. Courts will not go behind the corporate identity merely because the corporation has been formed to obtain tax savings or to obtain limited liability for its shareholders. Similarly, the corporate entity will not be ignored merely because the corporation does not have sufficient assets to pay the claims against it.

One-person, family, and other closely held corporations are permissible and entitled to all of the advantages of corporate existence. The fact that the principal shareholder runs or oversees the day-to-day operations does not justify ignoring the corporate entity.

22. Other Exceptions to Limited Liability

Liability may be imposed on a shareholder as though there were no corporation when the court ignores the corporate entity either because of the particular circumstances of the case or because the corporation is so defectively organized that it is deemed not to exist.

(a) Wage Claims. Statutes sometimes provide that the shareholders shall have unlimited liability for the wage claims of corporate employees. This exception has been abandoned in some states in recent years or has been confined to corporate officers who are active in corporate decision making.[35]

(b) Unpaid Subscriptions. Most states prohibit the issuance of par value shares for less than par or except for "money, labor done, or property actually received." Whenever shares issued by a corporation are not fully paid for, the original subscriber receiving the shares, or any transferee who does not give value or who knows that the shares were not fully paid for, is liable for the unpaid balance if the corporation is insolvent and the money is required to pay its creditors.[36]

If the corporation has issued the shares as fully paid for, has given them as a bonus, or has agreed to release the subscriber for the unpaid balance, the corporation cannot recover that balance. The fact that the corporation is thus barred does not prevent creditors of the corporation from bringing an action to compel payment of the balance. The same rules are applied when stock is issued as fully paid for in return for property or services that were overvalued so that the stock is not actually paid for in full. A conflict of authority exists, however, as to whether the shareholder is liable from the mere fact that the property or service given for the shares was in fact overvalued by the directors or whether it must also be shown that the directors acted in bad faith in making the erroneous valuation. The trend of modern statutes is, in the absence of proof of fraud, to prohibit disputing the valuation placed by the corporation on services or property.

(c) Unauthorized Dividends. If dividends are improperly paid out of capital, shareholders are generally liable to creditors to the extent of such depletion of capital. In some states, the liability of a shareholder depends on whether the corporation was insolvent at the time and whether debts were existing at the time.

23. The Professional Corporation

The extent to which incorporation limits the liability of shareholders of a professional corporation depends

[34] *Illinois v. V&M Industries*, 700 N.E.2d 746 (Ill. App. 1998).

[35] *Cusimano v. Metro Auto, Inc.*, 860 P.2d 532 (Colo. App. 1993).

[36] *Frasier v. Trans-Western Land Corp.*, 316 N.W.2d 612 (Neb. 1982). But see *Brunfield v. Horn*, 547 So.2d 415 (Ala. 1989).

on the interpretation of the statute under which the corporation was formed.

(A) ACT OF SHAREHOLDER IN CREATING LIABILITY. The statutes that authorize the formation of professional corporations usually require that share ownership be limited to duly licensed professionals. If a shareholder in a professional corporation, such as a corporation of physicians, negligently drives the professional corporation's automobile in going to attend a patient or is personally obligated on a contract made for the corporation or is guilty of malpractice, the physician-shareholder is liable without limit for the liability that has been created. This is the same rule of law that applies in the case of the ordinary business corporation.

Professional corporation statutes generally repeat the rule governing malpractice liability by stating that the liability of a shareholder for malpractice is not affected by the fact of incorporation.

(B) MALPRACTICE LIABILITY OF AN ASSOCIATE. The liability of a shareholder in a professional corporation for the malpractice of an associate varies from state to state depending on the language of the professional corporation statute in effect and on the court decisions under the statute.[37]

If the statute provides for limited liability, as in a business corporation, then where doctors *A, B,* and *C* are a professional corporation, *A* and *B* will not be liable for the malpractice of *C* beyond the extent of corporate assets. If the statute provides for vicarious personal liability, as in a partnership, and doctors *A, B,* and *C* are a professional corporation, each will have unlimited liability for any malpractice liability incurred by the others. Often the statutory reference to malpractice liability is not very clear, and the courts are called on to resolve the question of the liability of a professional shareholder for the malpractice of an associate.

LawFlix

Meet Joe Black (1998) (PG-13)

A transfer of corporate control and the role of shareholder control is at the heart of this film about a corporation under takeover fire.

[37] ABA Model Professional Corporation Act Amendments (1984) §34 offers three alternative positions regarding the liability of shareholders: (1) limited liability, as in a business corporation, (2) vicarious personal liability, as in a partnership, and (3) personal liability limited in amount and conditioned on financial responsibility in the form of insurance or a surety bond.

MAKE THE CONNECTION

SUMMARY

The ownership of a corporation is evidenced by a holder's shares of stock that have been issued by the corporation. Common stock is ordinary stock that has no preferences but entitles the holder to (1) participate in the control of the corporation by exercising one vote per share of record, (2) share in the profits in the form of dividends, and (3) participate, upon dissolution, in the distribution of net assets after the satisfaction of all creditors (including bondholders). Other classes of stock exist, such as preferred stock, that have priority over common stock with regard to distribution of dividends and/or assets upon liquidation. Shares may be acquired by subscription of an original issue or by transfer of existing shares.

Bonds are debt securities, and a bondholder is a creditor rather than an owner of the corporation. Bondholders' interests are represented by an indenture trustee who is responsible for ensuring that the corporation complies with the terms of the bond indenture.

Shareholders control the corporation, but this control is indirect. Through their voting rights, they elect directors, and by this means, they can control the corporation. *Preemptive rights,* if they exist, allow shareholders to maintain their voting percentages when the corporation issues additional shares of stock. Shareholders have the right to inspect the books of the corporation unless it would be harmful to the corporation. Shareholders also have the right to receive dividends when declared at the discretion of the directors. Shareholders may bring a derivative action on behalf of the corporation for damages to the corporation. Shareholders are ordinarily protected from liability for the acts of the corporation.

Ordinarily, each corporation is treated as a separate person, and the law does not look beyond the corporate identity merely because the corporation was formed to obtain tax savings or limited liability. The fact that two corporations have the same shareholders does not justify disregarding the separate corporate entities. However, when a corporation is formed to perpetrate a fraud, a court ignores the corporate form, or "pierces the corporate veil." The corporate form is also ignored to prevent injustice or because of the functional reality that the two corporations in question are one.

LEARNING OUTCOMES

After studying this chapter, you should be able to clearly explain:

A. Corporate Stocks and Bonds

LO.1 Explain how to calculate the book value of a share of stock

See the example in which Roger Eggett was awarded the book value of his stock, p. 933.

LO.2 Distinguish between stocks and bonds

See the discussion of stocks as an ownership interest in a corporation and bonds as a corporate debt, beginning on p. 933.

B. Acquisition of Shares

LO.3 Distinguish between subscriptions for and transfers of stock

See the discussion of stock subscriptions for new issues of stock on p. 935.

See the discussion of transfers of shares and the impact of restrictions, beginning on p. 935.

C. Rights of Shareholders

LO.4 Explain the rights of shareholders

See the discussion of shareholder ownership rights, including the right to vote, inspect books and records, and receive dividends when declared, beginning on p. 937.

LO.5 Explain the nature of a shareholder derivative lawsuit

See the *AIG* case, where stockholder plaintiffs were excused from making a demand on the full board, pp. 943–944.

D. Liability of Shareholders

LO.6 Explain the exceptions to the limited liability of shareholders

See the *Inter-Tel* case where "grandparent" and "parent" corporations transferred all income and assets to themselves, and as a result the corporate entities were disregarded to accomplish justice, pp. 945–946.

KEY TERMS

acceptance
bond
bond indenture
book value
capital stock
certificate of stock
common stock
cumulative voting
debenture
deed
derivative (secondary) action
indenture trustee
market value
maturity date

outstanding	proxy	voting by proxy
par value	registered bonds.	voting trust
preemptive right	sinking fund	wasting assets
preferred stock	stock subscription	corporations

QUESTIONS AND CASE PROBLEMS

1. Monica Beam, a shareholder of Martha Stewart Living Omnimedia, Inc. (MSO), filed a derivative action against Martha Stewart and the other MSO board of directors, alleging that Stewart breached her duties to MSO by illegally selling ImClone stock and mishandling media attention, thereby jeopardizing the financial future of MSO. Ms. Beam asserted that it would be a futile act to make a demand on the corporation because a majority of the outside directors were not independent of Stewart. Ms. Beam pleaded the particularized facts that director Darla Moore attended a wedding reception hosted by Stewart's personal lawyer for his daughter and was a longtime friend of Stewart; and that director Naomi Seligman made a phone call to publisher John Wiley, Inc., to express concern over a planned book critical of Stewart. Should Ms. Beam be excused from making a demand on the board of directors to pursue the derivative action because the outside directors were not independent of Stewart? [*Beam v. Stewart*, 845 A.2d 1040 (Del)]

2. Six members of the Weston family, who owned 6.8 percent of the stock of Weston Paper and Manufacturing Company, brought suit against three corporate directors and CFIS, a firm hired by the company to make the annual evaluation of the company's stock for allocating stock options to its employees. The Westons stated that their claims against the defendants were personal claims, alleging that they were injured by CFIS and the three directors who kept the price of the stock low to obtain more shares of stock through the stock option plan. From an adverse ruling on their right to maintain a direct action against the directors, the Westons appealed. How would you decide this case? [*Weston v. Weston Paper and Manufacturing Co.*, 74 Ohio 377]

3. Tomlinson and Hubbard were two of five shareholders in Multimedia Software Distributors, a corporation. The corporation was formed in 1992 and filed for bankruptcy in 1994. In 1996, Tomlinson filed a claim in his own name, alleging that Hubbard had breached his fiduciary duties to Tomlinson by diverting proceeds owned by Multimedia to another business owned by Hubbard. Hubbard contends that Tomlinson is an improper plaintiff. Decide. [*Hubbard v. Tomlinson*, 747 N.E.2d 69 (Ind. App.)]

4. Russell Nugent was involved in the roofing business in Kansas City, incorporating his business as Russell Nugent Roofing, Inc. In 1985, the name was changed to On Top Roofing, Incorporated. On August 27, 1987, On Top, Inc., ceased to exist, and RNR, Inc., was incorporated. RNR, Inc., went out of business in 1988, and RLN Construction, Inc., was incorporated. In 1989, the business was organized as Russell Nugent, Inc. Nugent and his wife had been sole shareholders, officers, and directors of each corporation. When one roofing company was incorporated, the prior roofing company ceased doing business. All of the companies were located at the same business address and used the same telephone number. Nugent paid himself and his wife more than $100,000 in salaries in 1986. In 1986, the corporation paid $99,290 in rent for property that the Nugents owned. Nugent testified that he changed to a new corporation every time he needed to get a "fresh start." The evidence showed that he used the On Top Roofing logo on his trucks and Yellow Pages advertisements throughout the period of the successive corporations. Suppliers who were not paid for materials in 1986 and 1987 by the insolvent corporations sought to pierce the corporate veils and hold Nugent personally liable. Nugent defended that as a shareholder, he had no personal liability. Decide. [*K.C. Roofing Center v. On Top Roofing, Inc.*, 807 S.W.2d 545 (Mo. App.)]

5. The stock of West End Development Co. was subject to a transfer restriction. This restriction required that any shareholder selling shares first offer every other shareholder the right to purchase a proportion of the shares being sold. The proportions were to be the same as the percentages of the outstanding shares that the other shareholders already owned. This restriction was stated in the articles of incorporation but was not stated on the stock certificate of the corporation. The Taylors owned stock in the company and sold their stock to Vroom, an officer of the corporation, without first offering any stock to the other shareholders, as required by the restriction. The other shareholders brought an action against Vroom to recover from him the percentages of the shares they would have been entitled to if the Taylors had followed the transfer restriction. Decide. [*Irwin v. West End Development Co.*, 481 F.2d 34 (10th Cir.)]

6. Siebrecht organized Siebrecht Realty Co., a corporation, and then transferred his building to the corporation in exchange for its stock. The corporation rented different parts of the building to different tenants. Elenkrieg, an employee of one of the tenants, fell and was injured because of the defective condition of a stairway. She sued Siebrecht individually on the ground that the corporation had been formed by him for the purpose of securing limited liability. Decide. [*Elenkrieg v. Siebrecht*, 144 N.E. 519 (N.Y.)]

7. William Carter, a former officer and employee of Wilson Construction Co., Inc., owned 317 shares of stock in Wilson. Carter left Wilson to become part owner and employee of C&L Contracting Co., which was a direct competitor of Wilson. Carter requested access to Wilson's corporate books to determine the value of his shares. Wilson refused, not wanting to divulge its business practices to a direct competitor. Decide. [*Carter v. Wilson Construction Co., Inc.*, 348 S.E.2d 830 (N.C. App.)]

8. Ken and Charlotte Maschmeier were the majority shareholders of Southside Press; each owned 1,300 shares. Marty and Larry Maschmeier, who each owned 1,200 shares of the corporation, had a falling out with Ken and Charlotte and were terminated as employees of the business. Ken and Charlotte started a new corporation, which employed most of the employees of the old corporation and which took most of its former customers. Gross receipts of Southside Press went from $613,258 down to $18,172 two years later. The $18,172 figure was from the lease of equipment. Ken and Charlotte continued to draw from Southside annual salaries of $20,000, which were in excess of the gross receipts of the business. Marty and Larry brought suit against Ken and Charlotte, alleging "oppressive" conduct. Ken and Charlotte stated that they had paid Marty and Larry excellent salaries when they were employed by the corporation. Ken and Charlotte contended they had a right to start a new corporation as they saw fit. Decide. [*Maschmeier v. Southside Press, Inc.*, 435 N.W.2d 377 (Iowa App.)]

9. Gladys Boles and 28 other owners of property at Hidden Valley Lakes Development sued the corporate developer, National Development Co. Inc. (NDC); NDC's parent, Sunstates Corporation; and the individual behind both corporations, Clyde Engle, for breach of contract and fraud. The centerpiece of this development, Crystal Lake, a 30-acre recreational lake, failed to hold water; and it was determined that it could never do so. Instead of having a 30-acre lake as the centerpiece, the plaintiffs had a 30-acre hole in the ground. While the controversy over NDC's breach of contract was pending, Engle made a "proposal" to the CEO of NDC to transfer $2.4 million in receivables to Sunstates in exchange for an unsecured promissory note. Evidence showed that all of Sunstates' assets thereafter were transferred to Engle, making the note NDC held from Sunstates worthless. Sunstates purchased approximately $1.9 million of oriental art, antique jewelry, rare books, and other collectibles, which were maintained in Engle's home in Illinois. Likewise, Sunstates purchased a Rolls Royce from Libco, a corporation in which Engle was the majority shareholder. This automobile also appeared to be in Engle's possession or control. Engles regrets that the lake did not work out, a risk that the developer and the homeowners have to live with, and points out that NDC is a separate legal entity with limited

liability for its shareholders. Engle asserts that he is not personally liable for damages in this case. Decide. [*Boles v. National Development Co., Inc.*, 175 N.W.3d 226 (Tenn. App.)]

10. Ed Klein was the sole shareholder, director, and chief executive officer of The Gun Exchange, Inc., a retail firearms dealership. The inventory of The Gun Exchange had been pledged as security for a $622,500 debt owed to InterFirst Bank. It also owed $231,484.60 to Sporting Goods, Inc.; this debt was unsecured. On May 20, InterFirst Bank notified Klein of its intention to foreclose on the inventory and sell it at public auction. InterFirst Bank further advised Klein that, pursuant to his personal guarantee, he would be responsible for any deficiency following the sale. Klein immediately incorporated The Gun Store, Inc., for the purpose of purchasing the assets of The Gun Exchange at the foreclosure sale. Before the foreclosure sale, Klein obtained a $650,000 line of credit from CharterBank on behalf of The Gun Store. At the sale, Klein purchased the assets of The Gun Exchange for $650,000 even though the highest prior bid was $175,000. (Had the $175,000 bid been accepted, Klein would have been personally liable for the deficiency to InterFirst Bank.)

    After the foreclosure sale, no funds existed to pay the unsecured creditors of The Gun Exchange. Following the sale, The Gun Store began operating as a retail firearms dealer with the inventory purchased from the foreclosure sale. It operated in the same location and with the same personnel as The Gun Exchange. Sporting Goods, Inc., sued Klein individually for the $231,484.60. Klein contended that the corporate form under which he did business insulated him as a shareholder from liability for corporate obligations. Decide. Is it ethical to seek limited liability under the corporate form, as Klein did in this case? [*Klein v. Sporting Goods, Inc.*, 772 S.W.2d 173 (Tex. Civ. App.)]

11. Ibanez owned shares of stock in Farmers Underwriters. He left the stock certificate lying on top of his desk in his office. Many persons continually passed through the office, and one day Ibanez realized that someone had taken the certificate from the top of his desk. Ibanez applied to Farmers Underwriters for a duplicate stock certificate. The corporation refused to issue a duplicate on the ground that it was Ibanez's own fault that the original certificate had been stolen. Ibanez claimed that he was entitled to a new certificate even though he had been at fault. Was he correct? [*Ibanez v. Farmers Underwriters Ass'n*, 534 P.2d 1336 (Cal.)]

12. On March 3, 2002, pursuant to a public offering, First All State Trucking Corp. (FAST) issued securities to investors in denominations of $1,000. The interest rate was 7 percent per year payable semiannually, and the maturity date was March 3, 2010. The rights and obligations of the issuer, FAST, and the holders of the securities were set forth in an indenture agreement. Because the securities were not secured by a mortgage or lien on corporate property, Alec believes they are shares of preferred stock. Is Alec correct? Fully explain the type of security involved, and discuss the extent of the holders' voting rights.

13. Linhart owned shares of stock in First National Bank. She borrowed money from the bank and pledged the stock as security. She later decided to transfer 70 head of cattle and the shares of stock to her son, but she could not deliver the share certificate to him because it was held by the bank. She therefore executed a bill of sale reciting the transfer of the cattle and the stock to the son. She gave him the bill of sale, and he had the bill recorded. After her death, the son brought an action to determine the ownership of the stock. Was the son the owner of the shares?

14. Birt was a hospital patient. The doctor who treated him was a shareholder of a professional corporation organized under the Indiana Medical Professional Corporation Act. Birt claimed that the doctor who treated him was guilty of malpractice, and he sued the doctor. He also sued the professional corporation and all of its officers, directors, and shareholders. These other defendants asserted that they were not liable because the corporate entity shielded them. The plaintiff claimed that the corporation was not a shield because in fact all of the persons were rendering medical services and should be held liable as in a partnership. The statute did not expressly regulate

the matter of limited liability beyond declaring that it did not change the law between a person supplying medical services and the patient. Decide. [*Birt v. St. Mary Mercy Hospital*, 370 N. E.2d 379 (Ind. App.)]

15. Ronald Naquin, an employee of Air Engineered Systems & Services, Inc., owned one-third of its outstanding shares. After six years, he was fired and an offer was made to buy out his interest in Air Engineered at a price that Naquin thought inadequate. He then formed a competing business and made a written request to examine the corporate records of Air Engineered. This request was denied. Naquin filed suit to require Air Engineered to allow him to examine the books. Air Engineered raised the defense that he was a competitor seeking to gain unfair competitive advantage. Decide. [*Naquin v. Air Engineered Systems & Services, Inc.*, 463 So.2d 992 (La. App.)]

CPA QUESTIONS

1. A stockholder's right to inspect books and records of a corporation will be properly denied if the stockholder:
   a. Wants to use corporate stockholder records for a personal business
   b. Employs an agent to inspect the books and records
   c. Intends to commence a stockholder's derivative suit
   d. Is investigating management misconduct
2. The limited liability of a stockholder in a closely held corporation may be challenged successfully if the stockholder:
   a. Undercapitalized the corporation when it was formed
   b. Formed the corporation solely to have limited personal liability
   c. Sold property to the corporation
   d. Was a corporate officer, director, or employee
3. Price owns 2,000 shares of Universal Corp.'s $10 cumulative preferred stock. During its first year of operations, cash dividends of $5 per share were declared on the preferred stock but were never paid. In the second year, dividends on the preferred stock were neither declared nor paid. If Universal is dissolved, which of the following statements is correct?
   a. Universal will be liable to Price as an unsecured creditor for $10,000.
   b. Universal will be liable to Price as a secured creditor for $20,000.
   c. Price will have priority over the claims of Universal's bond owners.
   d. Price will have priority over the claims of Universal's unsecured judgment creditors.
4. Under the Revised Model Business Corporation Act, a dissenting stockholder's appraisal right generally applies to which of the following corporate actions?

	Consolidations	*Shares from mergers*
a.	Yes	Yes
b.	Yes	No
c.	No	Yes
d.	No	No

CHAPTER 46

© Manuel Gutjahr/iStockphoto.com

Securities Regulation

learningoutcomes

After studying this chapter, you should be able to

LO.1 Explain the meaning of state "blue sky laws"

LO.2 Define "security"

LO.3 Compare and distinguish between the Securities Act of 1933 and the Securities Exchange Act of 1934

LO.4 Explain how the 1934 Act's policy of fostering reliance on market integrity is served by Rule 10b-5 private investor lawsuits when injured by material misstatements by the issuer

LO.5 Explain the factors that subject an individual to liability for insider trading

LO.6 Explain how securities firms regulate themselves and provide a process to resolve controversies relating to the sale of securities

Is there anything that protects you when you buy corporate securities?

A. State Regulation

To protect the public from the sale of fraudulent securities, many states have adopted statutes regulating the intrastate sale of securities.

CPA 1. State Blue Sky Laws

State laws regulating securities are called **blue sky laws**. The term *blue sky* is derived from the purpose of such laws, which is to prevent the sale of speculative schemes that have no more value than the blue sky. The state statutes vary in detail. They commonly contain (1) an antifraud provision prohibiting fraudulent practices and imposing criminal penalties for violations, (2) broker-dealer licensing provisions regulating the persons engaged in the securities business, and (3) provisions for the registration of securities, including disclosure requirements, with a designated government official.

A Uniform Securities Act, covering the foregoing three categories of regulations, exists to provide guidance to states in updating their securities laws. This act also contains alternative regulations that can be adopted by states with different regulatory philosophies.

2. National Securities Markets Improvement Act

Congress reallocated responsibility between state and federal security regulators in the National Securities Markets Improvement Act (NSMIA) of 1996,[1] recognizing that the dual system of state and federal regulation of securities resulted in duplicative regulation and expenses. Title I of the act exempts from state review and registration securities offered by mutual funds and stocks listed on the New York Stock Exchange, the NASDAQ National Market system, and other stock exchanges identified by the Securities and Exchange Commission (SEC). The act preserves the states' authority to investigate and bring enforcement actions for fraud or deceit or for unlawful conduct by a broker or dealer in connection with securities transactions.[2] Also, the states may continue to collect filing fees for securities in effect as of October 25, 1996. The act also eliminates duplicative registration requirements for investment advisors by dividing regulatory authority between the SEC, which exclusively regulates investment advisors with assets under management of $25 million or more, and the states, which have the responsibility to regulate all investment advisors managing lower sums of money.[3]

B. Federal Regulation

The stock market crash of 1929 and the Great Depression that followed led to the enactment of federal legislation to regulate the securities industry.

3. Federal Laws Regulating the Securities Industry

Six federal securities regulation laws were passed between 1933 and 1940. The two principal laws that provide the basic framework for the federal regulation of the sale of securities in interstate commerce are the Securities Act of 1933 and the Securities Exchange Act of 1934.

The 1933 act deals with the original distribution of securities by the issuing corporations. It is a disclosure statute designed to secure essential facts for the investor. The 1934 act is concerned with the secondary distribution of securities in the national securities exchanges and in the over-the-counter markets. That is, the 1933 act regulates the issuance of securities by a corporation to the first owner. The 1934 act regulates the sale of securities from one owner to another. Four other federal laws deal with specific aspects of the securities industry.[4] These aspects include holding companies in utility

[1] P.L. 104-290, 110 Stat 3416, 15 U.S.C. §78a nt.

[2] The 1996 Act amends §18(c) of the 1933 Securities Act to accomplish this result.

[3] NSMIA §303(a), which adds a new §203A to the Investment Advisors Act of 1940.

[4] The Public Utility Holding Company Act of 1935 (15 U.S.C. §79 *et seq.*) provides comprehensive regulation of holding companies and their subsidiaries in interstate gas and electric utilities businesses. The Trust Indenture Act of 1939 (15 U.S.C. §§77aaa to 77bbb) was enacted to protect the interests of the holders of bonds and other debt securities offered to the public in interstate commerce by requiring the appointment of independent institutional trustees. The Investment Company Act of 1940 (15 U.S.C. §§80a-1 to 80a-52) provides for the registration and comprehensive regulation of mutual funds and all other investment companies. The Investment Advisors Act of 1940 (15 U.S.C. §§80b-1 to 80b-21) requires registration with the Securities and Exchange Commission of all persons engaged in the business of providing investment advice in interstate commerce. In 1970, the Securities Investors Protection Act was enacted to protect investors from the business failures of brokers and dealers.

businesses, trustees for debt securities, mutual funds, and investment advisors.

The Securities Enforcement Remedies and Penny Stock Reform Act of 1990[5] (Remedies Act) expands the enforcement remedies of the SEC to reduce fraudulent financial reporting and financial fraud. Under the Remedies Act, the SEC may start administrative proceedings against any person or entity, whether regulated by the SEC or not, and may issue a temporary cease-and-desist order prior to notice and a hearing. The SEC may also order an accounting and disgorgement of ill-gotten gains. In addition, the Remedies Act authorizes courts to bar individuals who have engaged in fraudulent activities from serving as officers and directors of public corporations.

The Securities Acts Amendments of 1990[6] authorize sanctions against SEC-regulated persons for violation of foreign laws. The amendments facilitate the ability of the SEC and foreign regulators to exchange information and cooperate in international securities law enforcement.

The Market Reform Act of 1990[7] was enacted to provide the SEC with powers to deal with market volatility. Under the law, the SEC has the power to suspend all trading when markets are excessively volatile. Also, the SEC may require "large traders" to identify themselves and provide information concerning their trading.

The Private Securities Litigation Reform Act (PSLRA) of 1995[8] was passed to alleviate abuses in private securities litigation. The intent of the act is to reduce the number of lawsuits brought against issuers of securities and accounting firms. This law applies only to private securities litigation, and the SEC's enforcement activities are not affected by the act.

The NSMIA, previously referred to in regard to the allocation of responsibility for securities regulation between the states and the federal government, also provides for national standards allowing brokers and dealers to improve their ability to borrow funds to finance market-making and underwriting activities.[9] This act also provides new national standards regulating margin restriction.

The Sarbanes-Oxley Act of 2002[10] contains numerous reforms regarding corporate accountability, enhanced disclosure requirements, auditor- and accounting-related provisions, and enforcement and liability provisions, which will be discussed in this chapter and the subsequent chapter on accountants' liability.

The Dodd-Frank Wall Street Reform and Consumer Protection Act of 2010[11] contains numerous reforms and initiatives to create a sound economic foundation to grow jobs, protect consumers, and reform Wall Street to protect the economy, American consumers, investors, and businesses. To prevent another financial crisis the Act created the Financial Stability Oversight Council to oversee the various government agencies responsible for regulating financial institutions. Many sections of the Act require various studies to be undertaken and mandate or permit rulemaking by the Commodity Futures Trading Commission and the SEC. The impact of

E-Commerce & Cyberlaw

Facilitation of the Use of Electronic Record Keeping

Under the Electronic Signatures in Global and National Commerce Act (E-Sign), brokerage firms and mutual funds may avoid the expense of paper mailings of legally required documents, such as monthly statements, trade confirmations, prospectuses, and financial reports, and deliver these documents or "records" by electronic means. The consumer must, however, consent to receiving these electronic records, and the consumer must consent electronically or confirm the consent electronically. Moreover, firms must inform consumers of their right to receive hard copy documents.

5 P.L. 101-429, 104 Stat. 931, 15 U.S.C. §77g.
6 P.L. 101-550, 104 Stat. 2713, 15 U.S.C. §78a.
7 P.L. 101-432, 104 Stat. 963, 15 U.S.C. §78a.
8 P.L. 104-67, 109 Stat. 737, 15 U.S.C. §78a nt.
9 NSMIA §104 P.L. 104-290, 110 Stat. 3416, 15 U.S.C. §776.
10 P.L. 107-204, 116 Stat. 745.
11 P.L. 111-203, 124 Stat. 1376, 15 U.S.C. §8305 (2012).

this comprehensive law will become increasingly apparent as rulemaking advances.[12]

CPA 4. Definition of Security

For the securities acts to apply, the transaction must involve a "security" within the meaning of the acts.[13] Congress adopted a definition of **security** sufficiently broad to encompass virtually any instrument that might be sold as an investment.

The definition of *security* includes not only investment instruments such as stocks and bonds but also "investment contracts." The definition of an *investment contract*, developed by the Supreme Court, is sufficiently broad to allow the securities acts to apply to a wide range of investment transactions or schemes, including the sale of bottled whiskey, cattle-breeding programs, and a limited liability partnership to operate local telephone companies.[14] Under the Supreme Court's definition, an investment contract exists if the following elements are present: (1) an investment of money, (2) a common enterprise, and (3) an expectation of future profits from the efforts of others. **For Example,** the sale of citrus groves to investors, coupled with the execution of service contracts to plant, harvest, and sell the fruit and the distribution of the profits of the venture to the investors, is an investment contract. An instrument denominated as a "note" may in fact be a "security" subject to regulation under the 1934 act.[15]

In the *Edwards* case, the Supreme Court considered whether a commercial equipment lease can be an "investment contract" subject to the securities laws.

SEC v. Edwards, 540 U.S. 389 (2004)

10,000 Investors Wish They Had Missed This Opportunity

"Opportunity doesn't always knock...sometimes it rings" (ETS Payphones promotional brochure). And sometimes it hangs up. So it did for the 10,000 people who invested a total of $300 million in the payphone sale-and-leaseback arrangements touted by ETS under that slogan. Charles Edwards was the chairman, chief executive officer, and sole shareholder of ETS Payphones, Inc. ETS, acting partly through a subsidiary sold payphones to the public via independent distributors. The payphones were offered packaged with a site lease, a five-year leaseback and management agreement, and a buyback agreement. The purchase price for the payphone packages was approximately $7,000. Under the leaseback and management agreement, purchasers received $82 per month, a 14 percent annual return. Purchasers were not involved in the day-to-day operation of the payphones they owned. ETS selected the site for the phones, installed the equipment, arranged for connection and long distance service, collected coin revenues, and maintained and repaired the phones. Under the buyback agreement, ETS promised to refund the full purchase price of the package at the end of the lease or within 180 days of the purchaser's request. The payphones did not generate enough revenue for ETS to make the payments required by the leaseback agreements, so the company depended on funds from new investors to meet its obligations. In September 2000, ETS filed for bankruptcy protection. The SEC brought this civil enforcement action alleging that Edwards and ETS had violated the registration requirements and antifraud provisions of the 1933 act. The district court concluded the arrangement was an "investment contract" subject to the securities laws. The Eleventh Circuit Court of Appeals reversed the lower court because the scheme offered a contractual entitlement to a fixed rather than a variable return.

JUDICIAL OPINION

O'CONNOR, J...."Congress' purpose in enacting the securities laws was to regulate *investments,* in whatever form they are made and by whatever name they are called." *Reves v. Ernst & Young,* 494 U.S. 56, 61, 110 S.Ct. 945, 108 L.Ed.2d

[12] See, for example, *Statement of General Policy on the Sequencing of the Compliance Dates for Final Rules Applicable to Security-Based Swaps Adopted Pursuant to the Securities Exchange Act of 1934* and the *Dodd-Frank Wall Street Reform and Consumer Protection Act*, 77 F.R. 35625 (June 14, 2012).

Political considerations may also impede the rulemaking process. For example, Sections 1502 and 1504 of the Act required the SEC to produce final rules mandating disclosures relating to conflict minerals and payments made by U.S. oil, gas, and mining companies to foreign government for projects in their countries, such as money for production licenses, taxes, and royalties. Congress required disclosure of payments for conflict minerals being used to finance the war in the Democratic Republic of the Congo or a neighboring country. Moreover, the nontransparent payments weigh on developing nations' growth and are a risk to investors and the public. Major oil companies believe that the proposed rules by the SEC will provide a competitive advantage to Russian and Chinese firms not bound by the Dodd-Frank mandates. The SEC is well past the April 17, 2011, statutory deadline for a final rule.

[13] The Supreme Court has consistently held that the definition of a security set forth in §3(a)(10) of the 1934 Act is identical to the definition set forth in §2(1) of the 1933 Act. The definition of security under these acts is not to be confused with the narrower definition in Article 8 of the Uniform Commercial Code. See *SEC v. Infinity Group Co.*, 993 F. Supp. 321 (E.D. Pa. 1998).

[14] *SEC v. Shiner*, 268 F. Supp. 2d 1333 (S.D. Fla. 2003).

[15] *SEC v. Wallenbrock*, 313 F.3d 532 (9th Cir. 2002).

Continued

47 (1990). To that end, it enacted a broad definition of "security," sufficient "to emcompass virtually any instrument that might be sold as an investment." *Ibid.*...

The test for whether a particular scheme is an investment contract was established in our decision in *SEC v W.J. Howey Co.*, 328 U.S. 293, (1946). We look to "whether the scheme involves an investment of money in a common enterprise with profits to come solely from the efforts of others." *Id.*, at 301. This definition "embodies a flexible rather than a static principle, one that is capable of adaptation to meet the countless and variable schemes devised by those who seek the use of the money of others on the promise of profits." *Id.*, at 299....

...[W]hen we held that "profits" must "come solely from the efforts of others," we were speaking of the profits that investors seek on their investment, not the profits of the scheme in which they invest. We used "profits" in the sense of income or return, to include, for example, dividends, other periodic payments, or the increased value of the investment.

There is no reason to distinguish between promises of fixed returns and promises of variable returns for purposes of the test, so understood. In both cases, the investing public is attracted by representations of investment income, as purchasers were in this case by ETS' invitation to "'watch the profits add up.'" Moreover, investments pitched as low-risk (such as those offering a "guaranteed" fixed return) are particularly attractive to individuals more vulnerable to investment fraud, including older and less sophisticated investors. Under the reading respondent advances, unscrupulous marketers of investments could evade the securities laws by picking a rate of return to promise. We will not read into the securities laws a limitation not compelled by the language that would so undermine the laws' purposes....

The Eleventh Circuit's perfunctory alternative holding, that respondent's scheme falls outside the definition because purchasers had a contractual entitlement to a return, is incorrect and inconsistent with our precedent. We are considering investment *contracts*. The fact that investors have bargained for a return on their investment does not mean that the return is not also expected to come solely from the efforts of others. Any other conclusion would conflict with our holding that an investment contract was offered in *Howey* itself. 328 U.S., at 295–296, 66 S.Ct. 1100 (service contract entitled investors to allocation of net profits).

We hold that an investment scheme promising a fixed rate of return can be an "investment contract" and thus a "security" subject to the federal securities laws. The judgment of the United States Court of Appeals for the Eleventh Circuit is reversed, and the case is remanded for further proceedings consistent with this opinion.

[It is so ordered.]

QUESTIONS

1. ETS argued that the arrangement involved commercial equipment leases, not securities. Did Congress intend to cover the leases under the securities laws?
2. Is it fair to say that investments promising a fixed return are attractive to individuals more vulnerable to investment fraud?
3. State the *Hovey* test for determining whether a particular scheme is an investment contract.

CPA 5. Securities Act of 1933

The 1933 act deals with the original issue of securities. It prohibits the offer or sale of securities to the public in interstate commerce before a registration statement is filed with the SEC. A **registration statement** is a document disclosing specific financial information regarding the security, the issuer, and the underwriter. The seller must also provide a prospectus to each potential purchaser of the securities. The **prospectus** sets forth the key information contained in the registration statement. The object is to provide the interested investor detailed information about the security and the enterprise. The SEC does not approve or disapprove the securities as being good or bad investments but only reviews the form and content of the registration statement and the prospectus to ensure full disclosure. The requirements of advance disclosure to the public through the filing of the registration statement with the SEC and the sending of a prospectus to each potential purchaser are commonly referred to as the **registration requirements** of the 1933 act.

CPA (A) Applicability. The 1933 act applies to (1) stocks, (2) corporate bonds, and (3) any conceivable type of corporate interest or instrument that has the characteristics of an investment security, including convertible securities and variable annuities. The act applies to all such instruments that have investment characteristics.

Thinking Things Through

Problem: Conflicts of Interest—Remedy: Commonsense Rules

Full-service brokerage firms serve both retail and corporate clients. On the retail side, brokers buy and sell stocks and bonds for retail clients from all walks of life. The firms' research analysts perform the very important function of studying the performance of companies listed on the major stock exchanges, and the analysts make recommendations on these companies' securities, such as "buy," "hold," or "sell," for the benefit of their brokers and clients. Brokerage firms also serve corporate clients by underwriting and distributing new issues of stocks and bonds. This is called the INVESTMENT BANKING function of the firm. When a manufacturing or service company issues securities for the first time, the transaction is called an INITIAL PUBLIC OFFERING or IPO. Lucrative fees are earned by brokerage firms from the successful placement of such issues. These securities are sold to retail clients and the public by the brokerage firms, with firm analysts' recommendations being an important element in the success of the placements and the overall profitability of the brokerage firms.

An investigation into Merrill Lynch by the New York Attorney General's Office revealed that while certain Merrill analysts were publicly recommending certain technology companies that were investment banking clients of the firm, internal e-mails indicated that these analysts believed the same companies were "crap" and "junk." One wrote to a colleague questioning his "positive" recommendation of a company whose numbers seemed weak to her, and his response to her was, he had written "pos," in place of [expletive deleted].

The public and retail clients believed that the firm's analysts were independent of the investment banking function of the firm and that the recommendations were made solely with retail clients' interests in mind. The New York Attorney General's Office concluded, however, that analysts and investment bankers were closely involved in each other's work and were not independent; that the analyst department's compensation was tied to the results of the investment banking department's results; and that analysts were negotiating with investment banking clients for ratings.

Now the SEC has rules that eliminate this type of blatant conflict of interest at full-service brokerage firms. These rules are based on management common sense. The rules include the following: (1) Investment banking divisions may not supervise firms' analysts, (2) compensation for analysts may not be linked to specific investment banking transactions, (3) analysts must disclose whether they own shares in a company they recommend and certify that their recommendations are their true opinions, (4) analysts appearing in public forums before the media must disclose whether they have an interest in the company being discussed, and (5) firms must make comprehensive disclosures about their rating systems and the firms they represent as investment banking clients.*

*Section 501(a) of the Sarbanes-Oxley Act required the SEC to adopt rules that address potential conflicts of interest in securities research. Regulation Analyst Certification ("Regulation AC") requires certification of any research report by an analyst that the views expressed accurately reflect the analyst's personal views. Moreover, the written certification requires disclosure of any compensation received by the analyst that was either directly or indirectly paid in relation to the views or recommendations expressed in the report or the views expressed in any public appearance. The SEC has approved National Association of Securities Dealers (NASD) and New York Stock Exchange (NYSE) rule changes relating to research analyst conflicts of interest.

CPA **(B) THE REGISTRATION PROCESS.** Section 5 of the 1933 act provides for the division of the registration process into three time periods: (1) the prefiling period, (2) the waiting period, from the date of filing with the SEC to the date the registration statement becomes effective (a minimum of 20 days but commonly extended for additional 20-day periods after each amendment by the issuer in compliance with SEC requirements for additional information), and (3) the posteffective period. The time divisions allow the public an opportunity to study the information disclosed in the registration process before a sale can be made. Permissible, required, and prohibited activities during these time periods are set forth in Figure 46-1.

CPA **(C) REGULATION A OFFERINGS.** Regulation A provides a simplified registration process for small issues of securities by small businesses. Although technically exempt from the 1933 act registration requirements, a Regulation A offering involves a "mini-registration" with the SEC. Under the SEC's Small Business Initiative, Regulation A applies to the offerings of securities up to $5 million in a 12-month period. Disclosure requirements are simplified by the use of the small corporate offerings registration (SCOR) form, with its question-and-answer, "fill-in-the-blank" format. Also, the financial statements required in a Regulation A offering are less extensive than those required for a registered public offering.

FIGURE 46-1 Registration Periods

	PROHIBITED OR REQUIRED ACTIVITIES	PERMITTED ACTIVITIES
PREFILING PERIOD	ISSUER MUST NOT SELL OR OFFER FOR SALE A SECURITY BEFORE REGISTRATION STATEMENT IS FILED.	ISSUER MAY PLAN WITH UNDERWRITERS THE DISTRIBUTION OF THE SECURITY.
WAITING PERIOD	NO FINAL SALE OF A SECURITY PERMITTED DURING THIS PERIOD.	PRELIMINARY PROSPECTUS* CONTAINING INFORMATION FROM THE REGISTRATION STATEMENT BEING REVIEWED BY THE SEC MAY BE DISTRIBUTED TO INVESTORS, WHO MAY MAKE OFFERS. ADVERTISEMENTS MAY BE PLACED IN FINANCIAL PUBLICATIONS, IDENTIFYING PARTICULARS OF THE SECURITY, FROM WHOM A PROSPECTUS CAN BE OBTAINED, AND BY WHOM ORDERS WILL BE EXECUTED.**
POSTEFFECTIVE PERIOD	MUST PROVIDE A COPY OF FINAL PROSPECTUS WITH EVERY WRITTEN OFFER, CONFIRMATION OF SALE, OR DELIVERY OF SECURITY. MUST UPDATE PROSPECTUS WHENEVER IMPORTANT NEW DEVELOPMENTS OCCUR OR AFTER NINE MONTHS.	SALES OF THE SECURITY MAY BE COMPLETED.

*The preliminary prospectus is commonly called the *red herring* prospectus because of the red ink caption required by the SEC, informing the public that a registration statement has been filed but is not yet effective and that no final sale can be made until after the effective date.

**These advertisements are sometimes called *tombstone ads* because they are commonly framed by a black ink border.

Issuers may broadly solicit indications of interest from prospective investors before filing an *offering statement* with the SEC. This allows the issuer to "test the waters" and explore investor interest before incurring the expenses associated with a Regulation A offering. Solicitation-of-interest documents must be factual and comply with the antifraud provisions of the securities acts. No sales may be made until the SEC qualifies the offering statement and the seller delivers the final-offering circular, including the offering price, to the investor.

CPA **(D) Registration Exemptions.** Certain private and limited offerings of securities are exempt from the registration requirements of the act under SEC Regulation D.

Offerings of securities restricted to residents of the state in which the issuing corporation is organized and doing business are exempt from federal regulation. This intrastate offering exemption is applied very narrowly by the SEC and the courts, and such offerings are subject to state laws.

CPA ***(1) Rule 506 Exemption.***

The most important exemption under Regulation D is SEC Rule 506. This rule provides general permission to offer and sell to a potentially indefinite number of individuals who meet the definition of accredited investor.[16] It is commonly referred to as the *private placement exemption*. There is no limitation on the amount of money that can be raised by the offering.[17] Specific information must be provided to all buyers if any buyers are nonaccredited investors; the number of nonaccredited investors is limited to no more than 35.

CPA ***(2) Rule 505 Exemption.***
SEC Rule 505 of Regulation D exempts from registration offerings of less than $5 million to no more than 35 nonaccredited purchasers over a 12-month period. No limit exists on the number of accredited investors who may participate. No general solicitation or general advertising is permitted under Rule 505. If any prospective investors are nonaccredited, the issuer must furnish all investors specific information on the issuer, its business, and the securities offered for sale.

CPA ***(3) Rule 504 Exemption.***
Under SEC Rule 504 of Regulation D, as amended in 1999, an issuer can offer and sell securities up to $1 million within a 12-month period without registration and without most of the restrictions contained in Rules 505 and 506.

CPA ***(4) Restrictions.***
Securities acquired under Rules 506, 505, and 504 exemptions from registration are considered restricted securities. Their resale may require registration. Rules requiring registration of these Regulation D securities prior to resale ensure that investors purchase these securities as an investment rather than for public distribution. When there is no attempt to make public distributions, investors ordinarily fit within one of several exemptions to registration upon resale. Generally, all restrictions expire after two years.

CPA **(E) Liability.** Issuers, sellers, and "aiders and abettors" may be subject to civil and criminal liability under the 1933 act.

CPA ***(1) Issuer's Civil Liability for False or Misleading Statements.***
The Securities Act of 1933 imposes civil liability under section 11 for making materially false or misleading statements in a registration statement and for omitting any required material fact. An issuing company has virtually no defense if there has been a false statement and a loss.

CPA ***(2) Civil Liability of Sellers of Securities.***
Section 12 of the 1933 act applies to those who "offer or sell" securities and employ any device or scheme to defraud or obtain money by means of untrue statements of material facts. This section makes such persons or firms liable to purchasers for damages sustained.

CPA ***(3) Criminal Liability.***
Section 24 of the 1933 act imposes criminal penalties on anyone who willfully makes untrue statements of material facts or omits required material facts from a registration statement. Section 17 of the act makes it unlawful for any person to employ any device, scheme, or artifice to defraud in the offer or sale of securities.

6. Securities Exchange Act of 1934

The 1934 act deals with the secondary distribution of securities. It was designed to prevent fraudulent and manipulative practices on the security exchanges and in over-the-counter markets. The act requires the disclosure of information to buyers and sellers of the securities. Furthermore, the act controls credit in these markets.

CPA **(A) Registration and Reporting Requirements.** Exchanges, brokers, and dealers who deal in securities traded in interstate commerce or on any national security exchange must register with the SEC unless exempted by it.

Companies whose securities are listed on a national securities exchange and unlisted companies with assets

[16] The term *accredited investor* is defined to include virtually every type of institution that participates in the private placement market such as banks, stock brokerage firms, insurance companies, mutual fund companies, retirement plans with assets in excess of $5 million, and so on as well as individual investors with substantial income or large net worth.
[17] *Kunz v. SEC*, 2003 WL 1605865, 64 Fed. Appx. 659 (10th Cir. 2003).

in excess of $10 million and 500 or more shareholders are subject to the reporting requirements of the act.[18]

CPA (1) Principal Reports.

Form 10-K is the principal annual report form used by commercial and industrial companies required to file under the 1934 act. The reports require nonfinancial information about the registrant's activities during the year, such as the nature of the firm's business, the property or businesses it owns, and a statement concerning legal proceedings by or against the company. The report requires the submission of financial statements with management's analysis of the financial condition of the company as well as a report and analysis of the performance of corporate shares. It requires a listing of all directors and executive officers and disclosure of executive compensation information.

Registrants who are required to file 10-K reports must also file quarterly reports, called *10-Q reports.* The 10-Q reports are principally concerned with financial information relevant to the quarterly period.

The SEC requires that annual shareholder reports be submitted to shareholders in any proxy solicitation on behalf of management. These reports contain essentially the same information as the 10-K.

CPA (2) Certifications and Disclosure Controls.

The Sarbanes-Oxley Act of 2002 requires written certification of the 10-K and 10-Q reports by each company's CEO and CFO, as set forth in section 302 (a) of the act and shown in the following excerpt. A "knowing" misrepresentation in connection with the certification process is punishable by fine up to $1 million and imprisonment of up to 10 years. A "willful" misrepresentation in connection with the certification process is punishable by fine up to $5 million and imprisonment of up to 20 years.[19]

Moreover, under Section 304 of the Act, if an issuer is required to prepare an accounting restatement due to the material noncompliance of the issuer as a result of misconduct concerning any reporting requirement under the Securities laws, the CFO shall reimburse the issuer for any bonus received within a 12-month period. **For Example,** Carl Jasper, the CFO of semiconductor manufacturer Maxim Integrated Products, back-dated stock options granted employees and directors, concealing millions of dollars in expenses from investors. Maxim was required to restate its financial statements for 2002, 2003, 2004, and 2005. In addition to a civil fine, Jasper was ordered in accordance with SOX Section 304 to reimburse Maxim for $1.8 million in bonuses and profits he received from the sale of Maxim stocks.[20]

Section 302(a) of the act requires CEOs and CFOs to certify that:

(1) the signing officer has reviewed the report;
(2) based on the officer's knowledge, the report does not contain any untrue statement of a material fact or omit to state a material fact necessary in order to make the statements made, in light of the circumstances under which such statements were made, not misleading;
(3) based on such officer's knowledge, the financial statements, and other financial information included in the report, fairly present in all material respects the financial condition and results of operations of the issuer as of, and for, the periods presented in the report;
(4) the signing officers—
(A) are responsible for establishing and maintaining internal controls....

The SEC considers information "material" if there is a substantial likelihood that it would have been viewed by a reasonable investor as having significantly altered the total mix of information made available and if a reasonable investor would have considered the fact important in making an investment decision. The SEC has recommended that each company organize key employees into a "disclosure committee" responsible for considering the "materiality" of information and the company's disclosure obligations. For example, any transactions with insiders should be carefully considered for SEC filings.

Before Sarbanes-Oxley, many public companies published pro forma (provided in advance) financial results in press releases before filing their official quarterly reports with the SEC. This approach allowed these companies to cast their "financials" in a favorable light. The SEC financial statements are prepared under a set of accounting conventions called *generally accepted accounting principles*, or GAAP. Pro forma financial

[18] 61 F.R. 21354, 21356 (May 9, 1996).
[19] 18 U.S.C. §1350(c).
[20] *SEC v. Jasper*, 678 F.2d 1116 (9th Cir. 2012).

results are not prepared using GAAP, and they may not provide a true and accurate picture of a company's financial status. Section 401 of the Sarbanes-Oxley Act instructed the SEC to issue rules requiring the presentation of pro forma financial statements in a manner that does not contain material misstatements or omit material facts and can be reconciled with financial results using GAAP. SEC Regulation G imposes a broad range of limitations on the use of pro forma results. If a company issues a press release saying that its pro forma earnings will be $5 million for the quarter when its official GAAP earnings will be just $4 million, the company will have to disclose both figures and explain what expenses were excluded from the pro forma figures and why.

CPA **(B) Antifraud Provision.** Section 10(b) of the 1934 act makes it unlawful for any person to use any manipulative or deceptive device in contravention of SEC rules. Under the authority of Section 10(b) of the 1934 act, the SEC has promulgated *Rule 10b-5*. This rule is the principal antifraud rule relating to the secondary distribution of securities. The rule states:

> *It shall be unlawful for any person, directly or indirectly, by use of any means or instrumentality of interstate commerce, or of the mails or of any facility of any national securities exchange,*
>
> *(a) To employ any device, scheme, or artifice to defraud,*
>
> *(b) To make any untrue statement of a material fact or to omit to state a material fact necessary in order to make the statements made, in the light of the circumstances under which they were made, not misleading, or*
>
> *(c) To engage in any act, practice, or course of business that operates or would operate as a fraud or deceit upon any person, in connection with the purchase or sale of any security.*[21]

CPA ***(1) Private Actions.***

Rule 10b-5 applies to all securities, whether registered or not, as long as use is made of the mail, interstate commerce, or a national stock exchange. Subject to the safe harbor provisions of the Private Securities Litigation Reform Act as discussed in the following section, under Rule 10b-5, a civil action for damages may be brought by any private investor who purchased or sold a security and was injured because of false, misleading, or undisclosed information.[22]

CPA ***(2) Liability for "Material Misstatements or Omissions of Fact."***

Rule 10b-5 prohibits the making of any untrue statement of a "material" fact or the omission of a material fact necessary to render statements made not misleading. In every Rule 10b-5 case, the plaintiff must show "reliance" on the misrepresentation and resulting injury.

In *Basic, Inc. v. Levinson*, the Supreme Court dealt with the question of what should be the standard of "materiality" in merger cases.

Basic, Inc. v. Levinson, 485 U.S. 224 (1988)

Why Silence Is Golden

In December 1978, Combustion Engineering, Inc., and Basic, Inc., agreed to merge. During the preceding two years, representatives of the two companies had held meetings regarding the possibility of a merger. During this time, Basic made three public statements denying that any merger negotiations were taking place or that it knew of any corporate developments that would account for the heavy trading activity in its stock. Sometime later, it was publicly announced that there would be a merger. Certain former shareholders who had sold their Basic stock between Basic's first public denial of merger activity and the public announcement of the merger brought a Section 10(b) and Rule 10b-5 action against Basic and some of its directors, contending that material misrepresentation had been made by Basic in its public statements

[21] 17 C.F.R. §240.10b-5.

[22] *Miller v. Thane International, Inc.*, 519 F.3d 879 (9th Cir. 2008).

Continued

denying merger activity. Basic raised the defense that the alleged misrepresentations were not material and that there was no showing of reliance by the shareholders on Basic's statements. The Court of Appeals reversed the district court's summary judgment for Basic that preliminary merger discussions are not material information. Basic appealed to the U.S. Supreme Court.

JUDICIAL OPINION

BLACKMUN, J.…The 1934 Act was designed to protect investors against manipulation of stock prices.…Underlying the adoption of extensive disclosure requirements was a legislative philosophy: "There cannot be honest markets without honest publicity. Manipulation and dishonest practices of the market place thrive upon mystery and secrecy." H. R. Rep. No. 1383, 73d Cong. 2d Sess., 11 (1934). This Court "repeatedly has described the 'fundamental purpose' of the Act as implementing a 'philosophy of full disclosure.'"…

Pursuant to its authority under § 10(b) of the 1934 Act, 15 U.S.C. § 78j, the Securities and Exchange Commission promulgated Rule 10b-5. Judicial interpretation and application, legislative acquiescence, and the passage of time have removed any doubt that a private cause of action exists for a violation of § 10(b) and Rule 10b-5, and constitutes an essential tool for enforcement of the 1934 Act's requirements ….

The Court previously has addressed various positive and common-law requirements for a violation of § 10(b) or of Rule 10b-5.…The Court also explicitly has defined a standard of materiality under the securities laws; see *TSC Industries, Inc., v Northway, Inc.,* 426 U.S. 438, 96 S. Ct. 2126, 48 L. Ed. 2d 757 (1976), concluding in the proxy-solicitation context that "an omitted fact is material if there is a substantial likelihood that a reasonable shareholder would consider it important in deciding how to vote."…Acknowledging that certain information concerning corporate developments could well be of "dubious significance,"…the Court was careful not to set too low a standard of materiality; it was concerned that a minimal standard might bring an overabundance of information within its reach, and lead management "simply to bury the shareholders in an avalanche of trivial information—a result that is hardly conducive to informed decision making."…It further explained that to fulfill the materiality requirement "there must be a substantial likelihood that the disclosure of the omitted fact would have been viewed by the reasonable investor as having significantly altered the 'total mix' of information made available."…We now expressly adopt the *TSC Industries* standard of materiality for the § 10(b) and Rule 10b-5 context.…

As we clarify today, materiality depends on the significance the reasonable investor would place on the withheld or misrepresented information.…Because the standard of materiality we have adopted differs from that used by both courts below, we remand the case for reconsideration of the question whether a grant of summary judgment is appropriate on this record.

We turn to the question of reliance and the fraud-on-the-market theory. Succinctly put:

> *The fraud-on-the-market theory is based on the hypothesis that, in an open and developed securities market, the price of a company's stock is determined by the available material information regarding the company and its business.…Misleading statements will therefore defraud purchasers of stock even if the purchasers do not directly rely on the misstatements.…The causal connection between the defendants' fraud and the plaintiffs' purchase of stock in such a case is no less significant than in a case of direct reliance on misrepresentations.* Peil v Speiser, *806 F.2d 1154, 160-1161 (CA3 1986).…*

Requiring proof of individualized reliance from each member of the proposed plaintiff class effectively would have prevented respondents from proceeding with a class action, since individual issues then would have overwhelmed the common ones.…

We agree that reliance is an element of a Rule 10b-5 cause of action.…Reliance provides the requisite causal connection between a defendant's misrepresentation and a plaintiff's injury.…Commentators generally have applauded the adoption of one variation or another of the fraud-on-the-market theory. An investor who buys or sells stock at the price set by the market does so in reliance on the integrity of that price. Because most publicly available information is reflected in market price, an investor's reliance on any public material misrepresentations, therefore, may be presumed for purposes of a Rule 10b-5 action.…

In summary:

We specifically adopt, for the § 10(b) and Rule 10b-5 context, the standard of materiality set forth in *TSC Industries, Inc., v Northway, Inc.,* 426 U.S., at 449.…

Materiality in the merger context depends on the probability that the transaction will be consummated, and its significance to the issuer of the securities. Materiality depends on the facts and thus is to be determined on a case-by-case basis.

It is not inappropriate to apply a presumption of reliance supported by the fraud-on-the-market theory.

That presumption, however, is rebuttable.

[Judgment vacated and action remanded]

QUESTIONS

1. What was the legislative philosophy underlying the adoption of the extensive disclosure requirements of the 1934 act?
2. What is the standard of materiality to be applied in a merger-related context?
3. What is the "fraud-on-the-market theory"?

In the pharmaceutical industry "materiality" of adverse event reports is a "fact-specific" inquiry. It requires consideration of the source and content and context of the reports, as set forth in the *Matrixx Initiatives* case.

Matrixx Initiatives, Inc. v. Siracusano, 131 S. Ct. 1309 (2011)

Rule No. 1 for Corporate Finance Executives: Be Very Careful About What You Say

Matrixx develops, manufactures, and markets over-the-counter pharmaceutical products. Its core product, Zicam Cold Remedy, with its active ingredient zinc gluconate, accounted for approximately 70 percent of Matrixx's sales. Individuals who purchased Matrixx securities between October 22, 2003, and February 6, 2004, filed a securities fraud class action against Matrixx under Section 10(b) of the 1934 Act. In October 2003 Matrixx made a statement to the market that Zicam was "poised for growth in the upcoming cold and cough season." It expressed its expectations that revenues would "be up in excess of 50%." In January 2004 it raised its revenue guidance, predicting an 80 percent increase.

On January 30, 2004, Dow Jones Newswires reported that the Food and Drug Administration (FDA) was "'looking into complaints that an over-the-counter common-cold medicine manufactured by a unit of Matrixx Initiatives, Inc. may be causing some users to lose their sense of smell'" in light of at least three product liability lawsuits. Matrixx's stock fell from $13.55 to $11.97 per share after the report. In response, on February 2, Matrixx issued a press release that stated in part:

> *Matrixx believes statements alleging that intranasal Zicam products caused anosmia (loss of smell) are completely unfounded and misleading. In no clinical trial of intranasal zinc gluconate gel products has there been a single report of lost or diminished olfactory function (sense of smell). Rather, the safety and efficacy of zinc gluconate for the treatment of symptoms related to the common cold have been well established....*

The day after Matrixx issued this press release, its stock price bounced back to $13.40 per share. On February 6, 2004, *Good Morning America*, a nationally broadcast morning news program, reported that Dr. Jafek had discovered more than a dozen patients suffering from anosmia after using Zicam. It also noted that four lawsuits had been filed against Matrixx. The price of Matrixx stock plummeted to $9.94 per share that same day. Zicam again issued a press release, largely repeating its February 2 statement.

Prior to these public statements, between October 2003 and February 2004, medical experts had revealed to Matrixx a plausible causal relationship between Zicam Cold Remedy and anosmia. For example, Dr. Linscholen sent abstracts of studies to Matrixx that had confirmed "zinc's toxicity." In September 2003 Matrixx learned of a planned national medical conference presentation by Dr. Jafek of the University of Colorado finding that 10 patients suffered loss of smell after Zicam use. The investors claim that the information the company had about the causal relationship between Zicam and anosmia were material facts necessary in order to make the statements made by Matrixx to the market not misleading. Matrixx defended that the investors had not alleged a statistically significant correlation between the use of Zicam and anosmia so as to make failure to publicly disclose complaints and the University of Colorado study a material omission.

JUDICIAL OPINION

SOTOMAYOR, J.... To prevail on a § 10(b) claim, a plaintiff must show that the defendant made a statement that was "*misleading* as to a *material* fact." *Basic,* 485 U.S., at 238. In *Basic,* we held that this materiality requirement is satisfied when there is "'a substantial likelihood that the disclosure of the omitted fact would have been viewed by the reasonable investor as having significantly altered the "total mix" of information made available.'" *Id.,* at 231–232.

Matrixx urges us to adopt a bright-line rule that reports of adverse events associated with a pharmaceutical company's products cannot be material absent a sufficient number of such reports to establish a statistically significant risk that the product is in fact causing the events. Absent statistical significance, Matrixx argues, adverse event reports provide only "anecdotal" evidence that "the user of a drug experienced an adverse event at some point during or following the use of that drug." Accordingly, it contends, reasonable investors would not consider such reports relevant unless they are statistically significant because only then do they "reflect a scientifically reliable basis for inferring a potential causal link between product use and the adverse event."

As in *Basic,* Matrixx's categorical rule would "artificially exclud[e]" information that "would otherwise be considered significant to the trading decision of a reasonable investor." Matrixx's argument rests on the premise that statistical significance is the only reliable indication of causation. This premise is flawed: As the SEC points out, "medical researchers...consider multiple factors in assessing causation." Statistically significant data are not always available. For example, when an adverse event is subtle or rare, "an inability

Continued

to obtain a data set of appropriate quality or quantity may preclude a finding of statistical significance."

A lack of statistically significant data does not mean that medical experts have no reliable basis for inferring a causal link between a drug and adverse events....

The FDA similarly does not limit the evidence it considers for purposes of assessing causation and taking regulatory action to statistically significant data. In assessing the safety risk posed by a product, the FDA considers factors such as "strength of the association," "temporal relationship of product use and the event," "consistency of findings across available data sources," "evidence of a dose-response for the effect," "biologic plausibility," "seriousness of the event relative to the disease being treated."

Given that medical professionals and regulators act on the basis of evidence of causation that is not statistically significant, it stands to reason that in certain cases reasonable investors would as well.... As a result, assessing the materiality of adverse event reports is a "fact-specific" inquiry, *Basic,* 485 U.S., at 236, that requires consideration of the source, content, and context of the reports. This is not to say that statistical significance (or the lack thereof) is irrelevant—only that it is not dispositive of every case.

Application of *Basic*'s "total mix" standard does not mean that pharmaceutical manufacturers must disclose all reports of adverse events. Adverse event reports are daily events in the pharmaceutical industry; in 2009, the FDA entered nearly 500,000 such reports into its reporting system. The fact that a user of a drug has suffered an adverse event, standing alone, does not mean that the drug caused that event. The question remains whether a *reasonable* investor would have viewed the nondisclosed information 'as having *significantly* altered the "total mix" of information made available.'

...[I]t bears emphasis that § 10(b) and Rule 10b–5(b) do not create an affirmative duty to disclose any and all material information. Disclosure is required under these provisions only when necessary "to make...statements made, in the light of the circumstances under which they were made, not misleading." ("Silence, absent a duty to disclose, is not misleading under Rule 10b–5"). Even with respect to information that a reasonable investor might consider material, companies can control what they have to disclose under these provisions by controlling what they say to the market.

Applying *Basic*'s "total mix" standard in this case, we conclude that respondents have adequately pleaded materiality. This is not a case about a handful of anecdotal reports, as Matrixx suggests.

The information provided to Matrixx by medical experts revealed a plausible causal relationship between Zicam Cold Remedy and anosmia. Consumers likely would have viewed the risk associated with Zicam (possible loss of smell) as substantially outweighing the benefit of using the product (alleviating cold symptoms), particularly in light of the existence of many alternative products on the market. Importantly, Zicam Cold Remedy allegedly accounted for 70 percent of Matrixx's sales. Viewing the allegations of the complaint as a whole, the complaint alleges facts suggesting a significant risk to the commercial viability of Matrixx's leading product.

It is substantially likely that a reasonable investor would have viewed this information "'as having significantly altered the "total mix" of information made available.'" *Basic,* 485 U.S., at 232. Matrixx told the market that revenues were going to rise 50 and then 80 percent. Assuming the complaint's allegations to be true, however, Matrixx had information indicating a significant risk to its leading revenue-generating product. Matrixx also stated that reports indicating that Zicam caused anosmia were "'completely unfounded and misleading'" and that "'the safety and efficacy of zinc gluconate for the treatment of symptoms related to the common cold have been well established.'" Importantly, however, Matrixx had evidence of a biological link between Zicam's key ingredient and anosmia, and it had not conducted any studies of its own to disprove that link....

Assuming the facts to be true, these were material facts "necessary in order to make the statements made, in the light of the circumstances under which they were made, not misleading." 17 CFR § 240.10b–5(b). We therefore affirm the Court of Appeals' holding that respondents adequately pleaded the element of a material misrepresentation or omission....

[Affirmed]

QUESTIONS

1. Assess Matrixx's position that reports of adverse events associated with a pharmaceutical company's products cannot be "material," absent a sufficient number of reports to establish a statistically significant risk.
2. Do Section 10(b) and Rule 10b-5 create an affirmative duty to disclose any and all material information to investors so they can be fully informed about their investment choices?
3. Having evaluated what the company told investors and with knowledge from the record as to the omitted facts asserted in this case, would a reasonable investor believe that the omitted facts would have significantly altered the "total mix" of information—positive, neutral, and negative—needed to make a sound investment decision?

CPA **(c) Litigation Reform Act.** The Private Securities Litigation Reform Act (PSLRA, or the Litigation Reform Act) of 1995 was passed because of (1) congressional concern over an excess of frivolous private securities lawsuits, (2) the financial burdens placed on accountants and other professional advisors by such litigation, and (3) concern that the investors in a class-action lawsuit have their interests fairly represented. Important features of the act are as follows.

CPA ***(1) Safe Harbor Rules.***

Issuers of securities frequently believed that lawsuits against them under Rule 10b-5 occurred simply because the corporation made a projection that failed to materialize. The Litigation Reform Act provides shelter for issuers from private liability for forward-looking statements that were not known to be false when made and that were accompanied by meaningful cautionary statements informing investors of contingencies that could cause results to differ from projected results.

To preserve the protections of the PSLRA, quarterly and annual reports to the SEC (Forms 10-Q and 10-K) and quarterly and annual reports to stockholders, as well as corporate press releases on financial matters, now commonly utilize the expression *forward-looking statements* regarding corporate statements that estimate or project the short-term and long-term outlook for a business. Moreover, these reports typically include a section entitled "Cautionary Statements" or "Risk Factors," and contain a statement such as:

> *Forward-looking statements as contained in this report involve a number of risks, including but not limited to product demand, pricing, market acceptance, supply problems, intellectual property rights and litigation, and risks in product and technology development.*

Corporations do not have to caution against every conceivable factor that may cause results to differ from the issuer's forward-looking statements.

For Example, Ivax Corporation, a drug company, issued a press release including optimistic assumptions about future events. Attached to the release was an italicized warning that stated in specific detail the kinds of misfortunes that could befall Ivax and could cause results to differ from its forward-looking statements. This cautionary statement did not mention that a large goodwill writedown could occur; and when a writedown did occur, Ivax stock declined sharply. Harris, Wolpin, and others brought a Rule 10b-5 fraud suit against Ivax based on the omission of a warning about the writedown risk. The court held that the cautionary statements were sufficient to warn an investor of risks similar to that actually realized and the statements satisfied Ivax's burden to warn under the statute. Ivax was not required to list all risk factors, and the failure to mention one risk that in fact occurred did not "blow Ivax out of the safe harbor."[23]

CPA ***(2) Litigation Reform.***

The Litigation Reform Act places a heightened pleading requirement on plaintiffs attempting to plead fraud in securities cases, and requires not only that the plaintiffs specify each statement alleged to have been false or misleading and the reason for the belief but also that the plaintiffs plead "scienter"—the mental state embracing intent to deceive, manipulate, or defraud.[24] In the *Matrixx Initiatives* case, the Supreme Court held that the investors adequately pleaded scienter, where the allegations give rise to the compelling inference that Matrixx elected not to disclose the reports of adverse events not because it believed they were meaningless, but because it understood their likely effect on the market.[25]

The Litigation Reform Act also provides for *proportionate liability*, as opposed to joint and several liability, for defendants who are found not to have knowingly committed a violation of the security laws. In addition, securities fraud is eliminated as a predicate for private RICO actions absent a prior criminal conviction. Under the act, frivolous private securities lawsuits require payment of the defendant's reasonable attorney fees.

[23] *Harris v. Ivax Corp.*, 182 F.3d 799 (11th Cir. 1999).

[24] In an October 26, 1999, Bloomberg Forum conference call, Lucent Technologies' CEO, McGinn, characterized Lucent as a market "leader" reaping "exceptionally strong growth in…optical networking" and described Lucent as growing at the same rate as the market (40 to 50 percent). After the conference call, Lucent stock moved from $59 per share to $80.62. The following year, however, the stock "tanked" to $2.19 a share, and investors who had purchased stock in 1999 and 2000 sued. In the fall of 1999, management e-mails acknowledged that the optical networking group was in "serious disrepair" and was up against a "revenue wall." The court determined that the plaintiffs were in compliance with the PSLRA and that McGinn's October 26, 1999, statement had not been "forward looking"—and that there were sufficient allegations to demonstrate that his statements had been misleading. Subsequently, the court approved a $610 million settlement of the case. *In re Lucent Technologies Inc., Securities Litigation*, 307 F. Supp. 2d 633 (D. N.J. 2004).

[25] *Matrixx Initiatives, Inc. v. Siracusano*, 131 S. Ct. 1309, 1324 (2011); see also *Frank v. Dana Corp.*, 646 F.3d 954 (6th Cir. 2011).

CPA ***(3) Class-Action Reforms.***
Reforms were necessary to protect against "lawyer-driven lawsuits" in which a class-action counsel would direct a "professional" plaintiff to buy a security to have standing to bring a class-action lawsuit. Thereafter, the class-action counsel would race to the courthouse to file before any other plaintiff and thus be able to claim enhanced standing to represent the class. The Litigation Reform Act provides that the status of lead plaintiff is offered to the person with the largest financial interest in the case, who then selects the lead counsel.

(4) Aiders and Abettors.
In its *Central Bank of Denver*[26] decision, the U.S. Supreme Court ruled that a private investor may not bring an action under Section 10(b) of the 1934 act against "aiders and abettors" such as accountants, lawyers, and investment bankers who provide assistance to the primary violator. In enacting the Litigation Reform Act, Congress did not follow the then–SEC Chairman's recommendation that aiding and abetting liability in private claims be established in the act. Instead, Congress directed the SEC's prosecution of aiders and abettors. Courts, however, have affirmed a private cause of action under Section 10(b) with a rebuttable presumption of reliance on the defendant's deceptive acts (1) where there is an omission of a material fact by one who has a duty to disclose, or (2) under the **fraud-on-the-market** doctrine where reliance is presumed when the statements in question become public.[27] The *Stoneridge Investments*[28] case is an example of "aiding and abetting" and the reluctance of the U.S. Supreme Court to expand the Section 10(b) private right of action where there was no duty to disclose and the deceptive acts were not communicated to the public. In its *Janus Capital Group, Inc.*, decision, the U.S. Supreme Court considered whether a mutual fund investment advisor, Janus Capital Management LLC (JCM), can be held liable in a private cause of action under Section 10(b) for false statements included in its client mutual funds' prospectuses, the client being Janus Investment Fund (JIF), a separate legal entity owned entirely by mutual fund investors. The court majority determined that JCM was not the "maker" of the false statement in the JIF prospectuses, just as one who prepares or publishes a statement on behalf of another is not its maker. It stated that a broader reading of "make," including persons or entities without ultimate control over the content of the statement, would substantially undermine the Court's *Central Bank* decision.[29]

CPA ***(5) Auditor Disclosure.***
The Litigation Reform Act amends the 1934 act by requiring auditors who discover illegal acts to notify management and the board of directors and, in some cases, to notify the SEC if the issuer does not.[30] Auditors are relieved from liability for any such disclosure to the SEC.

CPA ***(6) Lawyer Reporting of Wrongdoing.***
The ABA Model Rules of Professional Conduct, which serve as a basis for most states' ethics rules for lawyers, were revised to free lawyers from their duty of confidentiality to those clients who use the lawyers' advice to commit a crime or fraud.[31] The ABA also revised its Model Rules to allow a lawyer who knows that an officer or employee of a corporation will likely harm the company to refer the matter to higher-up officials of the organization.[32]

7. Trading on Insider Information

Section 10(b) and Rule 10b-5 form a basis for imposing sanctions for trading on **insider information**. The Insider Trading and Securities Fraud Enforcement Act of 1988, which amended the 1934 act, gave the SEC authority to bring an action against an individual purchasing or selling a security while in possession of material inside information. The court may impose a civil penalty of up to three times the profit gained or loss avoided as a result of the unlawful

26 *Central Bank of Denver v. First Interstate Bank of Denver*, 611 U.S. 164 (1994).
27 In *Connecticut Retirement Plans and Trust Funds v. Amgen Inc.*, 660 F.3d 1170 (9th Cir. 2011), the Ninth Circuit held that at the class certification stage of a securities fraud lawsuit, proof of the materiality of an allegedly fraudulent statement or omission is not a precondition to invoking the fraud-on-the-market presumption of reliance. The Supreme Court affirmed the decision. 133 S. Ct. 1184 (2013).
28 *Stoneridge Investment Partners, LLC v. Scientific Atlanta, Inc.*, 552 U.S. 148 (2008).
29 *Janus Capital Group v. First Derivative Traders*, 131 S. Ct. 2296 (2011).
30 P.L. 104-671, 109 Stat. 763, 15 U.S.C. §78j-l nt.
31 Model Rule 1.6, "Confidentiality of Information."
32 Model Rule 1.13, "Organization as Client."

sale. Persons who "aid or abet" in the violation may also be held liable under the act.

Under the 1988 insider trading act, "controlling persons," including employers whose lax supervision may allow employees to commit insider trading violations, are subject to civil penalties.[33] The SEC must prove "knowing" or "reckless" behavior by the controlling person. The 1988 law establishes bounty programs that allow the SEC to reward informants giving information on insider trading activity. The reward is up to 10 percent of any penalty imposed.

(A) TRADING BY INSIDERS AND TIPPEES. An **insider** may be a director or corporate employee. A **temporary insider** is someone retained by the corporation for professional services, such as an attorney, accountant, or investment banker. Insiders and temporary insiders are liable for inside trading when they fail to disclose material nonpublic information before trading on it and thus make a secret profit. A **tippee** is an individual who receives information from an insider or a temporary insider. A tippee is subject to the insider's fiduciary duty to shareholders when the insider has breached the fiduciary duty to shareholders by improperly disclosing the information to the tippee and when the tippee knows or should know there has been a breach.[34] Such a breach occurs when an insider benefits personally from her disclosure. When the insider does not breach a fiduciary duty, a tippee does not violate the securities laws.

In the *Dirks* case, the Supreme Court discussed the factors that subject a tippee to liability.

Dirks v. SEC, 463 U.S. 646 (1983)

No Secrets from Secrist!

On March 6, 1973, Raymond Dirks, an investment analyst, received information from Ronald Secrist, a former officer of Equity Funding of America, alleging that the assets of Equity Funding were vastly overstated as the result of fraudulent corporate practices. Upon investigation, Dirks received only denials from senior management, but certain corporation employees corroborated the charges of fraud. Neither Dirks nor his firm owned or traded any Equity Funding stock, but throughout his investigation, he openly discussed the information he had obtained with a number of clients and investors, causing liquidation of Equity Funding stock in excess of $16 million. Dirks urged the *Wall Street Journal* to publish a story on the fraud allegations. However, it declined because it feared that publishing damaging hearsay might be libelous. Dirks continued his investigation and spread word of Secrist's charges over the next two weeks. During this time, Equity Funding stock fell from $26 per share to less than $15 per share. On March 27, the NYSE halted trading of Equity Funding stock, and a subsequent investigation revealed the vast fraud that had taken place. The SEC, investigating Dirks's role in the exposure of the fraud, found that Dirks had aided and abetted violations of the Securities Act of 1933, the Securities Exchange Act of 1934, and SEC Rule 10b-5 by publicly repeating the allegations of fraud. Upon appeal by Dirks, the decision of the lower court was upheld by the Court of Appeals. An appeal was taken to the Supreme Court.

JUDICIAL OPINION

POWELL, J.…In the seminal case of *In re Cady, Roberts & Co.*, 40 S.E.C. 907 (1961), the SEC recognized that the common law in some jurisdictions imposes on "corporate 'insiders', particularly officers, directors, or controlling stockholders" an "affirmative duty of disclosure…when dealing in securities." The SEC found that not only did breach of this common-law duty also establish the elements of a Rule 10b-5 violation, but that individuals other than corporate insiders could be obligated either to disclose material nonpublic information before trading or to abstain from trading altogether. In *Chiarella* [445 U.S. 222 (1980)], we accepted the two elements set out in *Cady, Roberts* for establishing a Rule 10b-5 violation: "(i) the existence of a relationship affording access to inside information intended to be available only for a corporate purpose, and (ii) the unfairness of allowing a corporate insider to take advantage of that information by trading without disclosure." In examining whether Chiarella had an obligation to disclose or abstain, the Court found that there is no general duty to disclose before trading on material nonpublic information, and held that "a duty to disclose under § 10(b) does not arise from the mere possession of nonpublic market information." Such a duty arises rather from the existence of a fiduciary relationship.

[33] P.L. 100-704, 102 Stat. 4677, 15 U.S.C. §78u-1(a)(2).

[34] *United States v. Chestman*, 974 F.2d 564 (2d Cir. 1991).

Continued

Not "all breaches of fiduciary duty in connection with a securities transaction," however, come within the ambit of Rule 10b-5. There must also be "manipulation or deception." In an inside-trading case this fraud derives from the "inherent unfairness involved where one takes advantage" of "information intended to be available only for a corporate purpose and not for the personal benefit of anyone." Thus, an insider will be liable under Rule 10b-5 for inside trading only where he fails to disclose material nonpublic information before trading on it and thus makes "secret profits."

We were explicit in *Chiarella* in saying that there can be no duty to disclose where the person who has traded on inside information "was not [the corporation's] agent,...was not a fiduciary, [or] was not a person in whom the sellers [of the securities] had placed their trust and confidence." Not to require such a fiduciary relationship, we recognized, would "depart radically from the established doctrine that duty arises from as specific relationship between two parties" and would amount to "recognizing a general duty between all participants in market transactions to forgo actions based on material nonpublic information." This requirement of a specific relationship between the shareholders and the individual trading on inside information has created analytical difficulties for the SEC and courts in policing tippees who trade on inside information. Unlike insiders who have independent fiduciary duties to both the corporation and its shareholders, the typical tippee has no such relationships.* In view of this absence, it has been unclear how a tippee acquires the *Cady, Roberts* duty to refrain from trading on inside information.

The SEC's position, as stated in its opinion in this case, is that a tippee "inherits" the *Cady, Roberts* obligation to shareholders whenever he receives inside information from an insider....

In effect, the SEC's theory of tippee liability...appears rooted in the idea that the antifraud provisions required equal information among all traders. This conflicts with the principle set forth in *Chiarella* that only some persons, under some circumstances, will be bared from trading while in possession of material nonpublic information....

Imposing a duty to disclose or abstain solely because a person knowingly receives material nonpublic information from an insider and trades on it could have an inhibiting influence on the role of market analysts, which the SEC itself recognizes is necessary to the preservation of a healthy market. It is commonplace for analysts to "ferret out and analyze information," and this often is done by meeting with and questioning corporate officers and others who are insiders. And information that the analysts obtain normally may be the basis for judgments as to the market worth of a corporation's securities. The analyst's judgment in this respect is made available in market letters or otherwise to clients of the firm. It is the nature of this type of information, and indeed of the markets themselves, that such information cannot be made simultaneously available to all of the corporation's stockholders or the public generally.

The conclusion that recipients of inside information do not invariably acquire a duty to disclose or abstain does not mean that such tippees always are free to trade on the information. The need for a ban on some tippee trading is clear. Not only are insiders forbidden by their fiduciary relationship from personally using undisclosed corporate information to their advantage, but they may not give such information to an outsider for the same improper purpose of exploiting the information for their personal gain. See 15 USC § 78t(b) (making it unlawful to do indirectly "by means of any other person" any act made unlawful by the federal securities laws). Similarly, the transactions of those who knowingly participate with the fiduciary in such a breach are "as forbidden" as transactions "on behalf of the trustee himself."...

Thus, some tippees must assume an insider's duty to the shareholders not because they receive inside information, but rather because it has been made available to them *improperly*. And for Rule 10b-5 purposes, the insider's disclosure is improper only where it would violate his *Cady, Roberts* duty. Thus, a tippee assumes a fiduciary duty to the shareholders of a corporation not to trade on material nonpublic information only when the insider has breached his fiduciary duty to the shareholders by disclosing the information to the tippee and the tippee knows or should know that there has been a breach.

In determining whether a tippee is under an obligation to disclose or abstain, it thus is necessary to determine whether the insider's "tip" constituted a breach of the insider's fiduciary duty. All disclosures of confidential corporate information are not inconsistent with the duty insiders owe to shareholders.... Thus, the test is whether the insider personally will benefit, directly or indirectly, from his disclosure. Absent some personal gain, there has been no breach of duty to stockholders. And absent a breach by the insider, there is no derivative breach....

Under the inside-trading and tipping rules set forth above, we find that there was no actionable violation by Dirks. It is undisputed that Dirks himself was a stranger to Equity Funding, with no pre-existing fiduciary duty to its shareholders. He took no action, directly or indirectly, that induced

*Under certain circumstances, such as where corporate information is revealed legitimately to an underwriter, accountant, lawyer, or consultant working for the corporation, these outsiders may become fiduciaries of the shareholders. The basis for recognizing this fiduciary duty is not simply that such persons acquired nonpublic corporate information, but rather that they have entered into a special confidential relationship in the conduct of the business of the enterprise and are given access to information solely for corporate purposes....When such a person breaches his fiduciary relationship, he may be treated more properly as a tipper than a tippee....For such a duty to be imposed, however, the corporation must expect the outsider to keep the disclosed nonpublic information confidential, and the relationship at least must imply such a duty.

Continued

the shareholders or officers of Equity Funding to repose trust or confidence in him. There was no expectation by Dirks' sources that he would keep their information in confidence. Nor did Dirks misappropriate or illegally obtain the information about Equity Funding. Unless the insiders breached their *Cady, Roberts* duty to shareholders in disclosing the nonpublic information to Dirks, he breached no duty when he passed it on to investors as well as to the *Wall Street Journal.*

It is clear that neither Secrist nor the other Equity Funding employees violated their *Cady, Roberts* duty to the corporation's shareholders by providing information to Dirks. The tippers received no monetary or personal benefit for revealing Equity Funding's secrets, nor was their purpose to make a gift of valuable information to Dirks. As the facts of this case clearly indicate, the tippers were motivated by a desire to expose the fraud.

[Judgment reversed]

QUESTIONS

1. State the SEC's theory of tippee liability. Would such a theory have an inhibiting influence on the role of market analysts?
2. When is a tippee subject to a fiduciary duty to the shareholders not to trade on material nonpublic information?
3. Does the Court establish a "constructive insider" rule in its footnote?

(B) MISAPPROPRIATORS. Individuals who misappropriate or steal valuable nonpublic information in breach of a fiduciary duty to their employer and trade in securities on that information are guilty of insider trading as "misappropriators." **For Example,** an employee working for a financial printing firm was found guilty of insider trading under section 10(b) and Rule 10b-5.[35] While proofreading a financial document being prepared for a client firm, he figured out the identity of tender offer targets. Soon after that, he traded on this valuable nonpublic information to his advantage.

It is no defense to a section 10(b) and Rule 10b-5 criminal charge of participating in a "scheme to defraud" that the victim of the fraud (an employer) had no economic interest in the securities traded. The convictions of a stockbroker and a columnist for the *Wall Street Journal* were upheld under section 10(b) of the 1934 act. The columnist violated his fiduciary duty to his employer by revealing prepublication information about his column to the stockbroker. The stockbroker then used the information to trade in the securities identified in the column.[36]

Where an individual misappropriates confidential information for security trading purposes in breach of a fiduciary duty owed to the source of the information rather than to the shareholders who sold securities to the individual, that individual may be convicted of security fraud in violation of section 10(b) and Rule 10b-5.

The *O'Hagan* case involves the propriety of criminal liability under Rule 10b-5 under a misappropriation theory.

United States v. O'Hagan, 521 U.S. 657 (1997)

The Case of the Dastardly Misappropriator

James O'Hagan was a partner in the law firm of Dorsey & Whitney in Minneapolis, Minnesota. In July 1988, Grand Metropolitan PLC, a company based in London, England, retained Dorsey & Whitney as local counsel to represent Grand Met regarding a potential tender offer for the common stock of the Pillsbury Company headquartered in Minneapolis. O'Hagan did no work on the Grand Met representation. Dorsey & Whitney withdrew from representing Grand Met

[35] *SEC v. Materia,* 745 F.2d 197 (2d Cir. 1984).
[36] *Carpenter v. United States,* 484 U.S. 19 (1987).

Continued

on September 9, 1988. Less than a month later, on October 4, 1988, Grand Met publicly announced its tender offer for Pillsbury stock. Previously, on August 18, 1988, while Dorsey & Whitney was still representing Grand Met, O'Hagan began purchasing call options for Pillsbury stock. Each option gave him the right to purchase 100 shares of Pillsbury stock by a specified date in September. Later, in August and September, O'Hagan purchased additional Pillsbury call options. By the end of September, he owned 2,500 unexpired Pillsbury options, apparently more than any other individual investor. O'Hagan also purchased, in September 1988, some 5,000 shares of Pillsbury common stock at a price just under $39 per share. When Grand Met announced its tender offer in October, the price of Pillsbury stock rose to nearly $60 per share. O'Hagan then sold his Pillsbury call options and common stock, making a profit of more than $4.3 million. O'Hagan was charged and convicted of securities fraud in violation of Section 10(b) and Rule 10b-5. On appeal, he claimed that he was not a "misappropriator," for he had no fiduciary duty to the Pillsbury shareholders from whom he purchased calls and stock; in fact, he had not even worked on the transaction at the law firm. From the reversal of the conviction by the Eighth Circuit Court of Appeals, the U.S. Supreme Court granted *certiorari.*

JUDICIAL OPINION

GINSBURG, J.... Under the "traditional" or "classical theory" of insider trading liability, § 10(b) and Rule 10b-5 are violated when a corporate insider trades in the securities of his corporation on the basis of material, nonpublic information. Trading on such information qualifies as a "deceptive device" under § 10(b), we have affirmed, because "a relationship of trust and confidence [exists] between the shareholders of a corporation and those insiders who have obtained confidential information by reason of their position with that corporation." *Chiarella v United States,* 445 U.S. 222, 228, (1980). That relationship, we recognized, "gives rise to a duty to disclose [or to abstain from trading] because of the 'necessity of preventing a corporate insider from...tak[ing] unfair advantage of... uninformed...stockholders.'" *Id.,* at 228–229, (citation omitted). The classical theory applies not only to officers, directors, and other permanent insiders of a corporation, but also to attorneys, accountants, consultants, and others who temporarily become fiduciaries of a corporation. See *Dirks v. SEC,* 463 U.S. 646, 655, n. 14, 103 S.Ct. 3255, 3262, 77 L.Ed.2d 911 (1983).

The "misappropriation theory" holds that a person commits fraud "in connection with" a securities transaction, and thereby violates § 10(b) and Rule 10b-5, when he misappropriates confidential information for securities trading purposes, in breach of a duty owed to the source of the information. Under this theory, a fiduciary's undisclosed, self-serving use of a principal's information to purchase or sell securities, in breach of a duty of loyalty and confidentiality, defrauds the principal of the exclusive use of that information. In lieu of premising liability on a fiduciary relationship between company insider and purchaser or seller of the company's stock, the misappropriation theory premises liability on a fiduciary-turned-trader's deception of those who entrusted him with access to confidential information.

The two theories are complementary, each addressing efforts to capitalize on nonpublic information through the purchase or sale of securities. The classical theory targets a corporate insider's breach of duty to shareholders with whom the insider transacts; the misappropriation theory outlaws trading on the basis of nonpublic information by a corporate "outsider" in breach of a duty owed not to a trading party, but to the source of the information. The misappropriation theory is thus designed to "protec[t] the integrity of the securities markets against abuses by 'outsiders' to a corporation who have access to confidential information that will affect th[e] corporation's security price when revealed, but who owe no fiduciary or other duty to that corporation's shareholders." *Ibid.*

In this case, the indictment alleged that O'Hagan, in breach of a duty of trust and confidence he owed to his law firm, Dorsey & Whitney, and to its client, Grand Met, traded on the basis of nonpublic information regarding Grand Met's planned tender offer for Pillsbury common stock. This conduct, the Government charged, constituted a fraudulent device in connection with the purchase and sale of securities.

We agree with the Government that misappropriation, as just defined, satisfies § 10(b)'s requirement that chargeable conduct involve a "deceptive device or contrivance" used "in connection with" the purchase or sale of securities. We observe, first, that misappropriators, as the Government describes them, deal in deception. A fiduciary who "[pretends] loyalty to the principal while secretly converting the principal's information for personal gain," Brief for United States 17, "dupes" or defrauds the principal....

...Because the deception essential to the misappropriation theory involves feigning fidelity to the source of information, if the fiduciary discloses to the source that he plans to trade on the nonpublic information, there is no "deceptive device" and thus no § 10(b) violation—although the fiduciary-turned-trader may remain liable under state law for breach of a duty of loyalty.

We turn next to the § 10(b) requirement that the misappropriator's deceptive use of information be "in connection with the purchase or sale of [a] security." This element is satisfied because the fiduciary's fraud is consummated, not when the fiduciary gains the confidential information, but when, without disclosure to his principal, he uses the

Continued

information to purchase or sell securities. The securities transaction and the breach of duty thus coincide. This is so even though the person or entity defrauded is not the other party to the trade, but is, instead, the source of the nonpublic information.…A misappropriator who trades on the basis of material, nonpublic information, in short, gains his advantageous market position through deception; he deceives the source of the information and simultaneously harms members of the investing public.…

The misappropriation theory comports with § 10(b)'s language, which requires deception "in connection with the purchase or sale of any security," not deception of an identifiable purchaser or seller. The theory is also well-tuned to an animating purpose of the Exchange Act: to insure honest securities markets and thereby promote investor confidence.…

….The misappropriation at issue here was properly made the subject of a § 10(b) charge because it meets the statutory requirement that there be "deceptive" conduct "in connection with" securities transactions.

In sum, the misappropriation theory, as we have examined and explained it in this opinion, is both consistent with the statute and with our precedent.…

[Reversed and remanded]

Justices SCALIA and THOMAS and the Chief Justice concurred in part and dissented in part.

QUESTIONS

1. Identify and explain the two types of insider training liability under Rule 10b-5.
2. Explain how O'Hagen violated Rule 10b-5.
3. What is the purpose behind the "misappropriation theory" of insider trading?

(c) REGULATION FD. The SEC adopted Regulation FD (Fair Disclosure) to end the practice of selective disclosure by issuers of securities to security analysts and selected institutional investors of important nonpublic information, such as advance warnings of negative or positive earnings results, before disclosing the information to the general public. Those privy to the early release of the information had been able to make a profit or avoid a loss at the expense of the uninformed general public. For example, uninformed investors may have watched the price of XYZ Corporation fall from $47 a share to $32 a share over two days only to find out later in a subsequently disseminated general press release by the corporation that "earnings will not meet street estimates." Analysts with prior knowledge of the negative earnings reports were able to take action before the public was informed. Regulation FD requires that any disclosure be a public disclosure by filing Form 8-K or other disclosures to the public, including use of the Internet to broadly disseminate information.[37] **For Example,** when Brian Moynihan, CEO of Bank of America, speaks to a group of investment analysts about his company at a Wall Street meeting, Bank of America may broadcast the talk over the Web and issue a press release summarizing Moynihan's comments to comply with Regulation FD.

(d) REMEDY FOR INVESTORS. Investors who lack the inside information possessed by the insider and sell their stock during the relevant time period may recover damages from any insider who made use of undisclosed information. Recovery is by a civil action based on Rule 10b-5.

8. Disclosure of Ownership and Short-Swing Profits

Corporate directors and officers owning equity securities in their corporation and any shareholder owning more than 10 percent of any class of the corporation's equity securities are statutorily defined as insiders and must file with the SEC a disclosure statement regarding such ownership and all related transactions. This is required under section 16(a) of the 1934 act. Under section 403(a) of the Sarbanes-Oxley Act, these individuals must electronically report transactions in company stock to the SEC by the second business day after the transaction. Moreover, the transaction must be posted on the SEC's and the company's Web sites within one day after the filing date.

[37] 17 C.F.R. §240.10b5-1.

Section 16 is designed to prevent the unfair use of information available to these corporate insiders. This section prevents insiders from participating in short-term trading in their corporation's securities.

If such a person sells at a profit any of these securities less than six months after their purchase, the profit is called a **short-swing profit**. Under section 16(b), the corporation may sue a director, officer, or major stockholder for a short-swing profit.[38] The corporation may recover that profit even without a fraudulent intent in acquiring and selling the securities. However, the corporation must bring the lawsuit within two years after the date the profit was realized.[39]

9. Tender Offers

A corporation or group of investors may seek to acquire control of another corporation by making a general offer to all shareholders of the target corporation to purchase their shares for cash at a specified price. This is called a **cash tender offer**. The offer to purchase is usually contingent on the tender of a fixed number of shares sufficient to ensure takeover. The bid price is ordinarily higher than the prevailing market price. Should more shares be tendered than the offeror is willing to purchase, the tender offeror must purchase shares from each shareholder on a pro rata basis.

The Williams Act, which amended the 1934 act,[40] was passed to ensure that public shareholders who are confronted with a cash tender offer will not be required to act without adequate information. Under section 14(d) of the Williams Act, a person making a tender offer must file appropriate SEC forms. These forms provide information about the background and identity of the person filing, the source of funds used to make stock purchases, the amount of stock beneficially owned, the purpose of the purchases, any plan the purchaser proposes to follow if it gains control over the target corporation, and any contracts or understandings that it has with other persons concerning the target corporation.[41]

Section 14(e) of the Williams Act is the antifraud section. It prohibits fraudulent, deceptive, or manipulative practices. SEC Rule 14e-1 requires any tender offer to remain open for a minimum of 20 business days from the date it is first published or given to security holders. Federal and state legislation, as well as administrative regulation, is aimed at requiring disclosure of information and allowance of a reasonable length of time for consideration of the facts. These requirements are designed to make agreement to takeovers the result of voluntary action based on full knowledge of material facts.

As far as the courts are concerned, takeovers must be regarded with a neutral eye. If there is misrepresentation or other misconduct, the law will interfere. Otherwise, freedom of contract requires that courts not interfere with the judgment of the contracting parties.

10. Regulation of Accountants and Attorneys by the SEC

Accountants play a vital role in financial reporting under the federal securities laws administered by the SEC. Sections 1, 12, 17, and 24 of the 1933 act and section 10(b) of the 1934 act are the sections under which accountants may be subject to liability.

An accountant who prepares any statement, opinion, or other legal paper filed with the SEC with the preparer's consent is deemed to be practicing before the SEC. Because it relies so heavily on accountants, the SEC has promulgated Rule 2(e), which regulates and provides the basis for discipline of accountants, attorneys, and consultants who practice before the SEC.[42] Under Rule 2(e), the SEC may suspend or disbar from practice before it those who are unqualified or unethical or who have violated federal securities laws or SEC rules.[43]

[38] *Levy v. Southbrook International Investments, Ltd.*, 263 F.3d 10 (2d Cir. 2001); *Donaghue v. Natural Microsystems Corp.*, 198 F. Supp. 2d 487 (S.D.N.Y. 2002).

[39] *Credit Suisse Securities (USA) LLC v. Simmons*, 132 S. Ct. 1414 (2012).

[40] P.L. 90-439, 82 Stat. 454, 15 U.S.C. §78m(d), (e).

[41] Section 14(d) requires a filing by any person making a tender offer that, if successful, would result in the acquisition of 5 percent of any class of an equity security required to be registered under the 1934 Act. Section 13(d) of the Act requires disclosure to the issuer, the SEC, and the appropriate stock exchange when a person acquires 5 percent of a class of equity security through stock purchases on exchanges or through private purchases. The person may have acquired the stock for investment purposes, not for control, but must still file disclosure forms under §13(d). See *SEC v. Bilzerian*, 814 F. Supp. 116 (D. D.C. 1993). Section 14(d) applies only to shares to be acquired by tender offer.

[42] 17 C.F.R. §201.2e.

[43] Rule 2(e) provides: "Suspension and disbarment. (1) The Commission may deny, temporarily or permanently, the privilege of appearing or practicing before it in any way to any person who is found by the Commission after notice of an opportunity for hearing in the matter (i) not to possess the requisite qualifications to represent others, or (ii) to be lacking in character or integrity or to have engaged in unethical or improper professional conduct, or (iii) to have willfully violated, or willfully aided and abetted, the violation of any provision of the federal securities laws (15 U.S.C. §§77a to 80B-20), or the rules and regulations thereunder." 17 C.F.R. §201.2e.

E-Commerce & Cyberlaw

Douglas Colt was a second-year law student who developed a way to make money from the Internet. He set up a free Web site promising folks hot tips on stocks. However, Colt bought the stocks himself at low prices before pumping them up at his Web site. Once the shares were pumped up to a high enough price from the users of his Web site buying the shares, he would then sell all of his shares (i.e., dump them). Colt made more than $345,000 using the old tool of "pump-and-dump."

Colt had attracted 9,000 investors to his Web site (Fast-Trades .com). One of his shares, American Education Corporation, climbed 700 percent before he sold his holdings.

Those who participated in the pump-and-dump scam, including Colt's mother, a councilwoman from Colorado, agreed to a consent decree settlement. None will pay a fine and none will repay their profits. They have simply agreed not to violate federal securities laws in the future. Georgetown University, Colt's law school, said there will be no disciplinary action.

Did Colt violate insider trading laws or any federal securities laws? Was Colt's conduct ethical?

Enforcement on insider trading has been on the increase. The SEC has created a new group, called its Cyberforce, to deal specifically with insider trading over the Internet.

Section 307 of the Sarbanes-Oxley Act explicitly requires the SEC to establish minimum standards of professional conduct for attorneys practicing before the SEC in the representation of publicly held companies. The act and SEC rules require that attorneys report evidence of material violations of securities laws, up the chain of command, to the companies' general counsel, CEO, audit committees, or the full board of directors.

CPA C. Industry Self-Regulation

The National Association of Securities Dealers (NASD) is a self-regulatory organization guided by procedural and conduct rules. It seeks to detect misconduct of regulated persons and firms, and may issue appropriate sanctions as a means of protecting investors. The sanctions are subject to SEC review and thereafter review by the U.S. Court of Appeals. **For Example,** PAZ Securities, Inc., and its president, Joseph Mizrachi, repeatedly failed to provide information requested by the NASD under its rules. The SEC affirmed the NASD's default judgment expelling PAZ and also barring Mizrachi from ever associating with an NASD member. The U.S. Court of Appeals ultimately upheld the SEC's sanctions since failure to respond is a significant harm to the self-regulatory system because it undermines the NASD's ability to detect misconduct.[44] Subsequently, the NASD and the New York Stock Exchange merged their member regulation functions into one self-regulatory organization, the Financial Industry Regulatory Authority (FINRA). FINRA is the largest independent regulator for all securities firms doing business in the United States, registering industry participants, enforcing rules, and administering the largest dispute resolution forum for investors and registered firms.[45] It provides a BrokerCheck system, which allows investors to check out the professional and disciplinary backgrounds of firms and brokers online.[46]

11. Arbitration of Securities Disputes

Both NASD and securities firms with seats on the New York Stock Exchange have adopted codes of arbitration that allow customers and members to submit disputes to arbitration. The arbitration rights are contractual and are set forth in writing when opening an account with the securities firms. Investors who have agreed to arbitrate their securities disputes can be compelled to arbitrate, rather than sue, in courts.[47] NASD and NYSE arbitrations are now administered by FINRA. Courts are very reluctant to vacate an arbitration award.

44 *PAZ Securities, Inc. v. SEC*, 566 F.3d 1172 (D.C. Cir. 2009).

45 FINRA oversees some 629,640 registered securities representatives. In 2011, it barred 329 individuals and suspended 475 brokers from association with FINRA-regulated firms, levied fines totaling more than $63 million, and ordered more than $19 million in restitution to harmed investors. See **www.finra.org/ABOUTFINRA**.

46 **www.finra.org/brokercheck**.

47 *99 Commercial Street, Inc. v. Goldberg*, 811 F. Supp. 900 (S.D.N.Y.1992).

LawFlix

Wall Street (1987) (R)

This movie will walk you through not just the evolution of greed but the evolution of a young broker moving from gathering information to stealing it to obtaining it through insiders. The movie chronicles the market's regulations as well as an individual's loss of values.

MAKE THE CONNECTION

SUMMARY

State blue sky laws, which apply only to intrastate transactions, protect the public from the sale of fraudulent securities. The term *security* is defined sufficiently broadly to encompass not only stocks and bonds but also any conceivable type of corporate interest that has investment characteristics.

Two principal laws provide the basic framework for federal regulation of the sale of securities in interstate commerce. The Securities Act of 1933 deals with the issue or original distribution of securities by issuing corporations. The Securities Exchange Act of 1934 regulates the secondary distribution or sale of securities on exchanges. These acts are administered by the Securities and Exchange Commission. Except for certain private and limited offerings, the 1933 act requires that a registration statement be filed with the SEC and that a prospectus be provided to each potential purchaser. Criminal and civil penalties exist for fraudulent statements made in this process. The 1934 act provides reporting requirements for companies whose securities are listed on a national exchange and unlisted companies that have assets in excess of $10 million and 500 or more shareholders.

Rule 10b-5 is the principal antifraud rule under the 1934 act. Trading on "inside information" is unlawful and may subject those involved to a civil penalty of three times the profit made on the improperly disclosed information. Cash tender offers are regulated by the SEC under authority of the Williams Act. The securities industry provides arbitration procedures to resolve disputes between customers and firms.

LEARNING OUTCOMES

After studying this chapter, you should be able to clearly explain:

A. State Regulation

LO.1 Explain the meaning of state "blue sky laws"

See the discussion of the common-content features of state securities laws such as antifraud provisions, licensing provisions, and regulation of securities on p. 955.

B. Federal Regulation

LO.2 Define "security"

See the *Edwards* case as an example of the broad definition of *security* sufficient to encompass virtually any instrument that might be sold as an investment, pp. 957–958.

LO.3 Compare and distinguish between the Securities Act of 1933 and the Securities Exchange Act of 1934

See the discussion regarding the regulation of the original issue of securities, beginning on p. 958.

See the discussion regarding the secondary distribution of securities designed to prevent fraudulent and manipulative practices on the securities exchanges, beginning on p. 961.

LO.4 Explain how the 1934 Act's policy of fostering reliance on market integrity is served by Rule 10b-5 private investor lawsuits when injured by material misstatements by the issuer

See the *Basic Inc.* case on "materiality" in merger cases on pp. 963–964.

See the *Matrixx* case on "materiality" in the pharmaceutical industry on pp. 965–966.

LO.5 Explain the factors that subject an individual to liability for insider trading

See the *Dirks* case that illustrates the rule that when the insider does not breach a fiduciary duty, a tippee does not violate securities laws, pp. 969–971.

See the *O'Hagan* case regarding outsiders who have access to confidential information that will affect a company's stock price, pp. 971–973.

LO.6 Explain how securities firms regulate themselves and provide a process to resolve controversies relating to the sale of securities

See the regulatory functions performed by the Financial Industry Regulatory Authority on p. 975.

See the discussion on the NASD and NYSE regulatory procedures and arbitration codes beginning on p. 975.

KEY TERMS

blue sky laws
cash tender offer
fraud-on-the-market
insider
insider information
prospectus
registration requirements
registration statement
security
short-swing profit
temporary insider
tippee

QUESTIONS AND CASE PROBLEMS

1. Cable operator Charter Communications Inc. arranged to overpay Scientific Atlanta and Motorola $20 for each set-top box it purchased—with the understanding that they would return the overpayment by purchasing cable advertising from Charter. The transactions, it was alleged, had no economic substance; but because Charter would then record the advertising purchases as revenue and capitalize its purchases of the set-top boxes—in violation of generally accepted accounting principles—the transactions would enable Charter to fool its auditor into approving a financial statement showing it met projected Wall Street revenue and operating cash-flow numbers. The suppliers agreed to the arrangement. Charter used the inflated number of $17 million on its financial statements that were filed with the SEC and reported to the public. The suppliers had no role in preparing or disseminating Charter's financial statements, and their own statements booked the transactions as a wash. A private right of action was brought against the cable box suppliers by investors for damages under Section 10(b) of the 1934 Act as "aiders and abettors." Decide. [*Stoneridge Investment Partners, LLC v. Scientific Atlantic, Inc.*, 552 U.S. 148]
2. Corporation A was involved in merger discussions with Corporation B. During this time, Corporation A made public statements denying that any merger negotiations were taking place or that it knew of any corporate developments that would account for heavy trading activity in its stock. A class of former shareholders who sold Corporation A stock after the public denial of merger activity and the announcement of the merger some six weeks later sued Corporation A, contending it made material misrepresentations of fact in denying the merger activity. Corporation A stock

increased 25 percent upon the merger announcement. Corporation A stated that at the time of its denial of merger activity it was just involved in preliminary negotiations and its actions were not material until negotiations reached an agreement in principle. Moreover, it asserted that the shareholders made no showing that they relied on the denial statement. Decide.

3. *Business Week* magazine is sent to a national distributor of magazines, Curtis Circulations Co., which sells the magazines to various wholesalers, including Hudson News. *Business Week* publishes a column entitled "Inside Wall Street," and the evidence shows that stocks discussed favorably in the column tend to increase in value after release to the public. *Business Week* has a strict confidentiality policy prior to release of the magazine to the public applicable to all employees involved in production and distribution. This policy also applies to Hudson News. Gregory Savage, an employee of Hudson News, and the "top person" in the delivery room area, arranged to have the "Inside Wall Street" column faxed to his neighbor, a stockbroker named Larry Strath, prior to the close of the market on Thursday and prior to release to the public that evening. Strath traded on the information and passed it on to Joseph Falcone, who likewise traded on the basis of this information. While Falcone paid Strath $200 for a copy of the column each week, he contends that the information he received was too remote from the *Business Week* confidentiality policy to be actionable by the SEC. What theory do you believe the SEC pursued against Falcone? What are the elements of the theory? How would you decide this case? *[United States v. Falcone.* 257 F.3d 226 (2d Cir.)]

4. Minnesota Prostate Research Labs, Inc. (MPRL), made an initial public offering of its shares in August 1998. It stated in its prospectus that research on laboratory animals indicated that the lab may have discovered a cure for prostate cancer in humans. MPRL pointed out as well that results in animal testing did not necessarily mean that the same positive result would occur in humans. MPRL shares initially traded at $10 per share in 1999 and rose to $18 in August 2001, when the MPRL prostate cancer drug was finally approved for sale to the public. Tuttle reviewed the initial prospectus and analysts' reports on the drug and purchased 10,000 shares at $18 per share on August 18, 2001. In September of 2002, an independent study of the four leading prostate medicines indicated that MPRL's product was as effective as sugar pills in curing prostate cancer and other prostate symptoms. The price of MPRL shares plummeted to $6 per share. Tuttle is contemplating a Rule 10b-5 securities fraud class-action lawsuit against MPRL. Advise him of his chances of success in this lawsuit and any expenses that he would be exposed to other than the cost of his attorney.

5. The following transactions in Heritage Cosmetics Co., Inc., stock took place: On January 21, Jones, the corporation's vice president of marketing, purchased 1,000 shares of stock at $25 per share. On January 24, Sylvan, a local banker and director of Heritage, purchased 500 shares of stock at $26 per share. On January 30, McCarthy, a secretary at Heritage, purchased 300 shares of stock at $26.50. On February 12, Winfried, a rich investor from New England, purchased 25,000 shares at an average price of $26 per share. At that time, Heritage had a total of 200,000 shares of stock outstanding. On June 14, Winfried sold his entire holding in Heritage at an average price of $35 per share. In a local newspaper interview, Winfried was quoted regarding his reasons for selling the stock: "I have not had the pleasure of meeting any person from Heritage, but I have the highest regard for the Heritage Company,...I sold my stock simply because the market has gone too high and in my view is due for a correction." After independently reading Winfried's prediction on the stock market, Jones, Sylvan, and McCarthy sold their shares on June 15 for $33 per share. On June 20, Heritage Co. demanded that Jones, Sylvan, McCarthy, and Winfried pay the corporation the profits made on the sale of the stock. Was the corporation correct in making such a demand on each of these people?

6. Dorozhko hacked into the corporate network of Thomson Financial on October 17, 2007, at 2:15 P.M. and gained access to IMS Health's soon-to-be-released negative earnings

announcement due out at 5:00 P.M. He purchased $41,670 worth of put options. IMS shares were trading at $29.56 at the close on October 17. On October 18, 2007, IMS Health's stock price plunged at the opening of trading to $21.20 per share, on the negative news issued at 5:00 P.M. on October 17. Within six minutes, Dorozhko sold the put options for a net profit of $286,456. Did Dorozhko's "hacking and trading" violate either the traditional or misappropriation theories of "insider trading"?

7. Mary Dale worked in the law office of Emory Stone, an attorney practicing securities law. While proofreading Mary's keying of a document relating to the merger of two computer software companies, Emory joked to her, "If I weren't so ethical, I could make a few bucks on this info. Nomac Software stock prices are going to take off when this news hits 'The Street.'" That evening, Mary told her friend Rick Needleworth, a stockbroker, what her boss had said. Needleworth bought 500 shares of Nomac Software stock the next day and sold it three days later when the news of the merger was made public. He made a profit of $3,500. Did Dale, Stone, or Needleworth violate any securities law(s) or ethical principles with respect to the profit made by Needleworth?

8. International Advertising, Inc. (IA), would like to raise $10 million in new capital to open new offices in eastern Europe. It believes it could raise the capital by selling shares of stock to its directors and executive officers as well as to its bank and a large insurance company whose home office is located near IA's headquarters. Opposition to the financing plan exists because of the trouble, time, and cost involved with registering with the SEC. Advise IA how best to proceed with the registration of the new issue of stock.

9. Dubois sold Hocking a condominium that included an option to participate in a rental pool arrangement. Hocking elected to participate in the arrangement. Under it, the rental pool's agent rented condominiums, pooled the income, and after deducting a management fee, distributed the income to the owners on a pro rata basis. Hocking brought a Rule 10b-5 fraud action against Dubois. Dubois contended that the sale of the condominium was not a security under the securities acts, so Hocking could not bring a securities suit against her. Was Dubois correct? [*Hocking v. Dubois*, 839 F.2d 290 (9th Cir.)]

10. William Rubin, president of Tri-State Mining Co., sought a loan from Bankers Trust Co. To secure the loan, he pledged worthless stock in six companies and represented that the stock was worth $1.7 million. He also arranged for fictitious quotations to appear in an investment reporting service used by the bank to value the pledged securities. The bank loaned Rubin $475,000 and took the securities as pledged collateral. In a criminal action against Rubin under section 17(a) of the 1933 act, Rubin's defense was that the pledging of securities did not constitute an offer or sale of securities under the act. Was Rubin correct? [*Rubin v. United States*, 449 U.S. 424]

11. J. C. Cowdin, a director of Curtis-Wright Co., phoned Robert Gintel, a partner of Cady, Roberts & Co., a stock brokerage house, and advised him that Curtis-Wright's quarterly dividend had been cut. Gintel immediately entered orders selling Curtis-Wright shares for his customers' accounts. The stock was selling at over $40 a share when the orders were executed but fell to $30 soon after the dividend cut was announced to the public. The SEC contended that the firm, Cady, Roberts & Co., and Gintel violated section 10(b) of the 1934 act, Rule 10b-5, and section 17 (a) of the 1933 act. Gintel and Cady, Roberts & Co. disagreed. Decide. [*In re Cady, Roberts & Co.*, 40 SEC 907]

12. In a January 2000 prospectus for its initial public offering of shares, Apex Oil Discovery Co. (AODC) estimated a sizable volume of oil production based on the studies of two geologists and a test well at one of its Oklahoma properties. A cautionary statement advised that the projections were only estimates based on the opinion of the two experts and a test well, and that actual production could vary significantly. Lutz bought 10,000 shares of Apex in May 2000 for $20 per share. By October 2000, 12 of its 15 drilling operations under way that year turned out to be

dry holes. On October 18, 2000, AODC stock fell to $6 per share. Lutz brought a private securities civil action under SEC Rule 10b-5 against AODC, alleging that the AODC oil production estimates that induced him to buy the stock were fraudulent as evidenced by the 80 percent failure rate of its drilling operations. What defense, if any, does AODC have in this case? Decide.

13. Douglas Hansen, Leo Borrell, and Bobby Lawrence were three psychiatrists who recognized the need for an inpatient treatment facility for adolescents and children in their community. They became limited partners in building a for-profit psychiatric facility. Each had a 6.25 percent interest in the partnership. Health-care International, Inc., the general partner with a 75 percent interest, had expertise in hospital construction, management, and operation. Hansen, Borrell, and Lawrence asserted that the managerial control of the partnership was undertaken and operated by the general partner to the exclusion of the limited partners. The doctors claimed that their interest was a security—"an investment contract"—that gave them status to file a securities suit against the general partner under the 1934 act. The general partner disagreed. Decide. [*L & B Hospital Ventures, Inc. v. Health-care International, Inc.*, 894 F.2d 150 (5th Cir.)]

14. Texas International Speedway, Inc. (TIS), filed a registration statement and prospectus with the Securities and Exchange Commission offering a total of $4,398,900 in securities to the public. The proceeds of the sale were to be used to finance the construction of an automobile speedway. The entire issue was sold on the offering date. TIS did not meet with success, and the corporation filed a petition for bankruptcy. Huddleston and Bradley instituted a class-action suit in U.S. district court on behalf of themselves and other purchasers of TIS securities. Their complaint alleged violations of section 10(b) of the 1934 act. The plaintiffs sued most of the participants in the offering, including the accounting firm of Herman & MacLean. Herman & MacLean had issued an opinion concerning certain financial statements and a pro forma balance sheet that were contained in the registration statement and prospectus. The plaintiffs claimed that the defendants had engaged in a fraudulent scheme to misrepresent or conceal material facts regarding the financial condition of TIS, including the costs incurred in building the speedway. Herman & MacLean contended that the case should be dismissed because section 11 of the 1933 act provides an express remedy for a misrepresentation in a registration statement, so an action under section 10(b) of the 1934 act is precluded. Decide. [*Herman & MacLean v. Huddleston*, 459 U.S. 375]

15. Melvin J. Ford, president of International Loan Network, Inc. (ILN), promoted ILN's financial enrichment programs to ILN members and prospective members with evangelical fervor at revival-style "President's Night" gatherings. His basic philosophy was this:

> *The movement of money creates wealth. What we believe is that if you organize people and get money moving, it can actually create wealth.*

One ILN program was the Maximum Consideration Program, which, somewhat like a chain letter, provided $5,000 awards to members who sold $3,000 worth of new memberships called PRAs and made a deposit on the purchases of nonresidential real estate. According to Ford, an individual purchasing $16,000 worth of PRAs could receive an award of up to $80,000 because "all of a sudden the velocity of money increases to such a point, the ability to create wealth expands to such a degree, that we could come back and give somebody an award for up to $80,000." The SEC contended that ILN was selling unregistered investment contracts in violation of the 1933 act. ILN disagreed, contending that the program never guaranteed a return and was thus not an investment contract. Decide. Could ILN have provided full disclosure to investors concerning the program in a prospectus if required by the 1933 act? [*SEC v. ILN, Inc.*, 968 F.2d 1304 (D.C. Cir.)]

CPA QUESTIONS

1. Which of the following is least likely to be considered a security under the Securities Act of 1933?
   a. Stock options
   b. Warrants
   c. General partnership interests
   d. Limited partnership interests

2. Which of the following statements is correct regarding a common stock offering that requires registration under the Securities Act of 1933?
   a. The registration statement is automatically effective when filed with the SEC.
   b. The issuer would act unlawfully if it were to sell the common stock without providing the investor with a prospectus.
   c. The SEC will determine the investment value of the common stock before approving the offering.
   d. The issuer may make sales 10 days after filing the registration statement.

3. Hamilton Corp. is making a $4,500,000 securities offering under Rule 505 of Regulation D of the Securities Act of 1933. Under this regulation, Hamilton is:
   a. Required to provide full financial information to accredited investors only
   b. Allowed to make the offering through a general solicitation
   c. Limited to selling to no more than 35 nonaccredited investors
   d. Allowed to sell to an unlimited number of investors both accredited and nonaccredited

4. Under the liability provisions of Section 11 of the Securities Act of 1933, an auditor may help to establish the defense of due diligence if:
   I. The auditor performed an additional review of the audited statements to ensure that the statements were accurate as of the effective date of a registration statement.
   II. The auditor complied with GAAS.
   a. I only
   b. II only
   c. Both I and II
   d. Neither I nor II

5. Under the Securities Exchange Act of 1934, which of the following conditions generally will allow an issuer of securities to terminate the registration of a class of securities and suspend the duty to file periodic reports?

	The corporation has fewer than 300 shareholders	*The securities are listed on a national securities exchange*
a.	Yes	Yes
b.	Yes	No
c.	No	Yes
d.	No	No

Accountants' Liability and Malpractice

learningoutcomes

After studying this chapter, you should be able to

LO.1 Define *malpractice*

LO.2 Distinguish malpractice liability from breach of contract liability

LO.3 List which third parties may recover for the malpractice liability of accountants and when they may do so

LO.4 Discuss the difference between accounting malpractice and fraud

LO.5 Explain how Sarbanes-Oxley and Dodd-Frank have affected the accounting profession and accountants' liability

When is a professional, such as an accountant, liable for harm caused by improper performance?

A. General Principles of Accountants' Liability

Whether an accountant can be held liable for malpractice requires a look at what constitutes malpractice, the effect of others' conduct on liability, whether there are limitations on such liability, and whether there are damages that resulted from malpractice.

1. What Constitutes Malpractice?

An accountant who makes a contract to perform services has a duty to exercise the skill and care that are common for the accounting profession.[1] If the services are not rendered in accordance with those standards, the result is **malpractice**, as it is commonly called, which is a tort and a form of negligence.

Accountants are not insurers of the content of financial statements they prepare and, unless they agree to do so, are not normally liable for detecting fraud.[2] Changes made under Sarbanes-Oxley (covered later in the chapter) require accountants who perform audit work to undertake the role of certifying the internal controls of companies. This certification requirement was imposed with the hope that adequate internal controls can prevent fraud.[3] An accountant can, however, be held liable for turning a blind eye to suspicious issues and items.[4]

The standards for accountants' professional liability are found in state and federal statutes (see Chapter 46 for a discussion of federal securities issues, liabilities, and standards), court decisions, the actual contract with the client, generally accepted auditing standards (GAAS), and generally accepted accounting practices (GAAP).[5] Following GAAP and GAAS is persuasive but not conclusive evidence of meeting standards for the profession. Customs in any profession are persuasive but not conclusive evidence of professional performance.

Recovery from an accountant for malpractice requires proof of the elements of negligence (see Chapter 9 for more information). The duty and breach of duty elements are determined by the professional performance standards. The breach of professional standards must have caused the losses or damages, which must also be established.

Certified public accountants are liable for damages proximately caused by their negligence, or their failure to observe sound accounting practices. Accountants owe their clients a duty to exercise the degree of care, skill, and competence that reasonably competent members of their profession would exercise under similar circumstances.[6] Accountants are also liable if they fail to call attention to a condition that causes losses if the client could have taken preventive steps following the accountant's warning.[7]

An accountant is liable to the client if the accountant negligently fails to detect or fraudulently conceals signs that an employee of the client is embezzling or the internal audit controls of the client's business are not being observed or are lax. An accountant who prepares tax returns and acts as tax manager for the client will be liable when additional taxes or penalties are assessed against the client as a result of the accountant's negligent advice. For example, a client may recover damages from the accountant when the accountant negligently fails to inform the client of the tax consequences of selling the business.[8] The *O'Bryan v. Ashland* case deals with a question of accountant liability for a mistake in tax advice.

[1] *Thornton, LLP v. Federal Deposit Ins. Corp.*, 435 Fed. Appx. 188 (4th Cir. 2011).
[2] In re *Countrywide Litigation*, 588 F. Supp. 2d 1132 (C.D. Cal. 2009).
[3] Section 404 of Sarbanes-Oxley has become a day-to-day term in business language as companies work to obtain their "404 certifications" from auditors. Securities and Exchange Commission, *Management's Reports on Internal Controls over Financial Reporting and Certification in Exchange Act Periodic Reports*, Securities Act Release No. 33-8283 (June 5, 2003).
[4] In re *MoneyGram Intern., Inc. Securities Litigation*, 626 F. Supp. 2d 947 (W.D. Minn. 2009).
[5] In re *CBI Holding Co.*, 419 B.R. 553 (S.D.N.Y. 2009).
[6] *Greenstein, Logan & Co. v. Burgess Marketing, Inc.*, 744 S.W.2d 170 (Tex. 1987).
[7] *Ronson v. David S. Talesnick, CPA*, 33 F. Supp. 2d 347 (D.N.J. 1999).
[8] *Deloitte, Haskins, & Sells v. Green*, 403 S.E.2d 818 (Ga. 1991).

O'Bryan v. Ashland, 717 S.W.2d 332 (S.D. 2006)

This Is Interesting—You Owe Me

Bruce Ashland is a certified public accountant. He began providing services for Doug O'Bryan Contracting in 1987–1988. From 1979 through the first quarter of 1995, O'Bryan operated as a sole proprietorship. On several occasions over the years, Ashland recommended to O'Bryan that he incorporate. O'Bryan ultimately followed Ashland's advice and incorporated effective April 1, 1995.

For taxation purposes, incorporating in April meant that O'Bryan remained a cash basis taxpayer for the first quarter of the year, January 1, 1995 through March 31, 1995. Then, on incorporation, the business changed to accrual basis accounting for the last three quarters, April 1, 1995 through December 31, 1995. But, when Ashland prepared O'Bryan's 1995 tax return in October 1996, he mistakenly calculated O'Bryan's income for the first quarter using accrual based figures. As a result, Ashland understated, and consequently underreported, the income O'Bryan realized for the first quarter.

Ashland's mistake was discovered by another accountant during O'Bryan's divorce proceedings in 1997. After the accountant informed Ashland, he wrote a letter to O'Bryan disclosing the mistake and the need to correct the tax return. O'Bryan's divorce attorney hired a different accountant to review and amend the mistaken return, and, as of June 28, 1998, O'Bryan had $239,933 in additional tax liability for 1995, together with approximately $50,000 in interest. O'Bryan brought suit against Ashland for malpractice, seeking recovery for the additional expenses he incurred in correcting the erroneous tax returns. He also sought the interest the IRS charged on his unpaid tax liability.

At trial, Ashland admitted negligence and left for the jury the question of damages. The jury held Ashland liable for, among other things, the interest the IRS assessed against O'Bryan.

Based on the jury verdict the court awarded $39,038.83 in interest charges as damages. Ashland appealed.

JUDICIAL OPINION

KONENKAMP, Justice.... In ordinary circumstances, when a tax advisor's negligence leads to an underpayment of tax, the taxpayer cannot recover as damages the tax deficiency itself because the tax liability arose not from the negligent advice, but from the ongoing obligation to pay the tax. An issue never before decided in South Dakota, however, is whether the taxpayer can recover from the negligent advisor the accrued interest the IRS charged on the delinquent tax.

Ashland urges us to follow a line of authority generally holding that recovery of interest payable to the IRS is not allowed because taxpayers have the interim use of the taxes, and therefore they are not damaged by later having to pay interest for the period of that use.

As a matter of settled law, the circuit court ruled that O'Bryan's delinquent tax debt ($239,933) could not be included in his measure of damages because it was solely O'Bryan's obligation, which he would have owed regardless of his accountant's negligence.

While Ashland conceded that under certain situations a negligent accountant should pay interest assessed against the taxpayer, such requirement would apply only to situations where the client had "the money just sitting in their one percent savings account. ..." Here, Ashland argued, the situation was distinguishable because O'Bryan did not have the cash readily available when his 1995 tax return was originally filed in October 1996, and if it would have been correctly filed, O'Bryan would have had to borrow the money to pay the tax at a higher interest rate than the IRS charged. As a result, Ashland contended that the loss O'Bryan sustained should not include the interest assessed by the IRS.

O'Bryan, on the other hand, maintained that he would have been able to fully pay his 1995 tax obligation had it been properly calculated, and thus he would have incurred no interest. Ashland asks us to adopt a categorical rule that interest payable to the IRS is not recoverable as a measure of damages. O'Bryan, on the other hand, asserts that he was damaged by the interest charged against him, and he should be allowed to recover it. These conflicting arguments have divided the courts around the country. Some jurisdictions hold that interest is never recoverable because delinquent taxpayers will have had the interim use of the funds owed to the IRS, and thus they are not damaged by having to pay interest for the period of that use. Other jurisdictions conclude that taxpayers would not have had to pay interest if they had received competent advice, and therefore awarding interest allows them to be restored to the situation they would have been in had they not received the faulty advice.

But what if taxpayers can prove they were truly damaged? Acknowledging this possibility, several courts refuse to adopt an absolute rule barring recovery: whether a taxpayer has been damaged is left to the finder of fact, with the burden of proof on the taxpayer. The courts taking this approach recognize that, under traditional damage principles, if the taxpayer has been injured, recovery should be allowed. These decisions focus on the position the parties would have been in had they not received the negligent advice.

Our own precedent supports the rule that "[i]n a professional negligence action, the appropriate measure of damages is the difference between what the taxpayer would have owed absent the negligence, and what [the taxpayer] paid because of [the]

Continued

accountant's negligence, plus incidental damages." While this standard does not expressly include interest payable to the IRS, it does lay the foundation for such an award.

Having concluded that interest charged by the IRS may be recoverable in the proper circumstance, we now examine the facts of this case. Confronted with O'Bryan's and Ashland's conflicting theories, the trial court allowed them to be evaluated by the jury, and, through special interrogatories, the jury found that O'Bryan was damaged by the interest assessed. There was evidence to support this verdict. He said that he would not have necessarily had to borrow the money from a bank; he may have been able to borrow money from his family as he had done before. Only a trier of fact could adequately assess these claims. We conclude that there was sufficient evidence in the record to support the jury's determination that the interest charged by the IRS was directly related to Ashland's negligence and that O'Bryan suffered a loss as a result. Therefore, the circuit court did not err when it allowed the issue to go to the jury.

[Affirmed]

QUESTIONS

1. What was the malpractice by the accountant?
2. What were the financial consequences to the client?
3. What argument does the accountant make against having to pay the interest charges?

2. Choice of Remedy

In addition to liability under tort law for malpractice, accountants may be held liable for breach of contract for their failure to meet professional standards.

(A) Breach of Contract. An accountant breaches an audit contract if the audit work, for example, was not completed. In such a situation, the client need not pay the accountant's fee. If the work was complete, but there were minor errors, the damages caused by the error can be deducted from the fee.

Remedies for breach of contract are not available to third parties against accountants because they are not ordinarily considered third-party beneficiaries of contracts with accountants.

(B) Tort Liability. A client or third party may be able to recover from an accountant on the basis of negligence, gross negligence, or fraud. These theories are covered in the remaining sections of the chapter.

Because malpractice is both a breach of contract and an independent tort, the client who is harmed has the choice of recovering for breach of contract or for the particular tort that is involved. Generally, the client will bring a tort action because there are higher damages under tort law than those afforded for a breach of contract. The statute of limitations on torts versus contracts may also influence the theory for liability. The statute of limitations begins to run on the tort of malpractice from the date the harm was discovered. The contract statute of limitations runs from the date the contract is breached. This time differential may be very important because in some cases, the client may not realize that there has been any harm until some time after a breach of the contract occurred.

3. The Environment of Accountants' Malpractice Liability

Accountants have moved from being primarily clerical business participants to being essential players in business strategies. In addition, accountants have moved from being employees of one employer to being independent contractors performing accounting services for many clients. Accountants are now employed to produce data that third parties use and rely on in making decisions about loans or investments. **For Example,** accountants prepare statements submitted to banks that will use those statements to determine whether to make a loan or extend a line of credit. Auditors' certifications of financial statements become part of the documents given to potential investors in companies. As these changes in the role of accountants took place, it became natural for courts to allow third parties relying on accountants' work and certifications to recover from the accountants when the accountants' and auditors' malpractice caused damages to them.

At the same time that these changes were taking place in the nature and role of accountants, changes were also taking place in other areas of the law. Manufacturers and parts suppliers were held liable to those who purchased the final products and were injured by defects in them. The rising tide of liability to third parties has naturally influenced the law regulating accountants.[9]

4. Limitation of Liability

Can accountants protect themselves from liability for malpractice claims of clients and third parties? Because the law generally permits any contracting party to limit or disclaim liability for negligence, an accountant may exclude liability for malpractice on a theory of negligence. Influenced by the consumer protection movement and by the law governing product liability, courts will require such disclaimers to be (1) clear and unambiguous and (2) conspicuous. If these requirements are not met, the disclaimers are not enforceable.

(A) Scope of Limitation. Disclaimers are valid in certain limited circumstances.[10] **For Example,** when a client owns land in a foreign country, it is reasonable for the accountant to accept the valuation placed on the land by someone in that foreign country. The accountant should, however, include in the financial statement prepared for the client a statement that the valuation of that land was obtained from an identified person in the foreign country and that the accountant assumes no responsibility for the accuracy of that valuation. If the accountant's work has been so restricted, the accountant is protected from claims of third parties because there has been full disclosure about the accountant's limited information and ability to verify the work of others. **For Example,** when the accountant is restricted from examining accounts receivable and the accountant's certification states that no opinion was expressed as to accounts receivable, the accountant cannot be held liable if the accounts receivable turn out to be overstated.[11]

(B) Limitations on Exculpatory Provisions. A disclaimer based on lack of knowledge does not protect the accountant from liability if the accountant knew or had reason to know that the statements made were false. If the accountant states that he had no personal knowledge, he impliedly represents that he did not have any knowledge or reason to know that the statements were not correct. A disclaimer that is made when the accountant has reason to suspect that underlying information is false would be **misrepresentation** and would result in the accountant's liability.[12]

In some states, a **limitation-of-liability** or **exculpatory clause** protects the accountant from a malpractice suit brought by a client only, not from a suit brought by a third party. In such cases, courts apply the general rule of contract law that only a party to a contract is bound by an exculpatory or limitation-of-liability clause.

B. Accountants' Liability to Third Parties: Beyond Privity

Most accountants' malpractice litigation involves the question of whether third parties may recover from the accountants, not on what standards of conduct accountants should observe. Various issues and factors, covered in both judicial decisions and statutes, determine whether accountants will be held liable to third parties.[13]

5. Status of the Accountant

An accountant may be a full-time employee of a company, an independent contractor doing regular work for a client, or an independent outside auditor. What constitutes negligence is the same for all three types of accountants. The liability of the accountant to the third party, when recognized, is based on the reliance of the third party on the work of the accountant.[14]

[9] The interplay between the various areas of malpractice liability and those of accountants is seen further in the fact that the Restatement (Second) of Torts does not contain a separate provision applicable only to accountants but deals with the subject of malpractice liability of accountants to third parties in a general section (§552). Section 552 provides that

> *[O]ne who in the course of his business, profession or employment, or in any other transaction in which he has a pecuniary interest, supplies false information for the guidance of others in their business transactions, is subject to liability for pecuniary loss caused to them by their justifiable reliance on the information, if he fails to exercise reasonable care or competence in obtaining or communicating the information.*

The section then defines which parties can enforce this liability.

[10] The American Institute of Certified Public Accountants has an ethics rule on liability limitations and indemnifications that took effect on July 1, 2009, and can be found at **www.aicpa.org/download/ethics/EDITED_Adopted_501_8_final.pdf**.

[11] *Stephans Industries, Inc. v. Haskins & Sells*, 438 F.2d 357 (10th Cir. 1971).

[12] However, an accountant can provide financial information on an employee's severance package and disclaim liability by advising the employee to obtain independent tax advice. *Buehner v. IBM Corp.*, 704 N.Y.S.2d 303 (2000).

[13] *Tricontinental Industries, Ltd. v. PricewaterhouseCoopers, LLP*, 475 F.3d 824 (8th Cir. 2007).

[14] *Brown v. KPMG Peat Marwick*, 856 S.W.2d 742 (Tex 1993) but see *Prospect High Income Fund v. Grant Thorton, LLP*, 203 S.W.3d 602 (Tex. App. 2006).

6. Conflicting Theories of Accountants' Third-Party Liability

There are a number of theories that have been developed for third parties to recover for an accountant's negligence. These views may be identified as (1) the privity rule, (2) the contact rule, (3) the known user rule, (4) the foreseeable user rule, and (5) the intended user rule. In addition, some courts follow (6) a flexible rule, deciding each case as it arises. Each of these views is an attempt to draw a boundary line between the interloper and a "proper" plaintiff with sufficient connection to the accountant for recovery for the accountant's negligence. In some states, statutes define when nonprivity plaintiffs may recover for an accountant's negligence.[15]

(A) The Privity Rule. The **privity rule** precludes a negligence malpractice suit by a third party. This rule holds that only the party in privity with the accountant—that is, the accountant's client—may recover from the accountant.[16] When the privity rule is applied, a bank lending money to the accountant's client cannot recover from the accountant for malpractice. The *Citibank, N.A. v. McGladrey and Pullen, LLP* case deals with an issue of liability of an auditor.

Citibank, N.A. v. McGladrey and Pullen, LLP, 953 N.E.2d 38 (Ill. App. 2011)

The Ear, Nose, and Throat Guy Who Took $1.4 Million to the Alps

McGladrey conducted a financial audit of Subspecialty Centers of America, LLC (SCA). SCA is owned by Dr. Mark S. Weinberger, an ear, nose, and throat surgeon. The audit was for the year ending December 31, 2003. McGladrey issued its audit report in March 2004. The audit report indicated that SCA's "balance sheet presents fairly in all material respects to the financial position of SCA in conformity with generally accepted auditing standards." Citibank received the audit report and in June 2004 made a $1.4 million term loan to SCA. The term loan was a modification of a prior term loan that Citibank had made to SCA. Prior to 2004, Citibank had four outstanding loans to SCA: (1) a mortgage loan for its diagnostic surgery center; (2) a mortgage loan for its office condominium; (3) a revolving line of credit; and (4) a term loan. The 2004 term loan was an increase and an extension of the prior term loan.

Dr. Weinberger took the $1.4 million and left for Europe. Dr. Weinberger was subsequently located residing in a tent in the Italian Alps and was brought back to the United States in 2010. Hundreds of malpractice suits were filed against him, and federal prosecutors charged him with multiple counts of health care fraud.

Citibank brought suit to recover money it loaned SCA ($1.4 million term loan) from McGladrey on the grounds that it negligently audited Dr. Weinberger's surgical practice. Citibank claims that it relied on McGladrey's audit in making the $1.4 million term loan to SCA.

The trial court excluded testimony from Edward A. Bartko, an accountant and senior managing director in the corporate finance department of FTI Consulting, Inc., who was engaged by Citibank to offer a professional opinion regarding McGladrey's audit of SCA. Bartko opined that McGladrey's audit was deficient because McGladrey did not use health care specialists who possessed the expertise to analyze the medical files of SCA's patients, and who would have ultimately uncovered any medical fraud. Bartko's report indicated that FTI's team of health care specialists uncovered numerous red flags in SCA's patient files, which should have been discovered by McGladrey's audit.

The jury found for McGladrey and Citibank appealed.

JUDICIAL OPINION

KARNEZIS, Judge … Citibank argues that Bartko should have been permitted to testify as to the specific opinions and conclusions. Citibank argues that although Bartko was not qualified to interpret a patient's medical records, he should have nevertheless been permitted to testify as to the health care specialists' opinions and conclusions that medical fraud was prevalent and obvious in many of SCA's patient files.

Bartko was attempting to testify to the opinions and conclusions of FTI's health care specialists who read and interpreted many of CSA's [sic] patients' medical charts, even though Bartko admitted he was not qualified to read a

[15] See, e.g., *Ark. Code Ann.* §16–114–302 (2012); 225 *Ill. Comp. Stat.* 450/30.1 (2012); *Kan. Stat. Ann.* §1–402 (2012); *La.Rev.Stat. Ann.* §37:91 (2007); *Mich. Comp. Laws* §600.2962 (2012); *N.J.S.A.* 2A:53A–25(b)(2) (2012); *Utah Code Ann.* §58–26a-602 (2012); *Wyo. Stat. Ann.* §33–3–201 (2009).

[16] This rule was originally known as the New York rule, *Ultramares Corp. v. Touche*, 174 N.E. 441 (N.Y. 1931). Although it has been replaced in New York by the contact rule, the privity rule is still the law in many jurisdictions. *Solow v. Heard McElroy & Vestal, LLP*, 7 So.3d 1269 (La. App. 2009).

Continued

patient's medical chart. In other words, Bartko would be testifying to or "parroting" those opinions and conclusions that were beyond his ken, which [is] improper.

Citibank contends the circuit court's order denying Citibank's motion *in limine* to exclude any evidence of Citibank's alleged contributory negligence unrelated to the 2004 term loan to SCA was in error. Citibank argues that it was improper for the court to allow testimony regarding its lending decisions to SCA on all of its loans other than the 2004 term loan.

In denying Citibank's motion *in limine*, the circuit court determined that any evidence relating to Citibank's lending decisions with SCA was relevant to the issue of causation and reliance, and was therefore admissible.

Citibank relies on *Congregation of the Passion, Holy Cross Province v. Touche Ross & Co.*, 224 Ill.App.3d 559, 166 Ill. Dec. 642, 586 N.E.2d 600 (1991), for support. In Congregation of the Passion, the plaintiff sued the defendant accounting firm for its negligent audit of one of its investment advisers, Cranford Newell. Prior to trial, the plaintiff filed a motion *in limine* to exclude any reference to any of its investment accounts other than the accounts managed by Newell. The circuit court granted the motion and this court affirmed on appeal. This court determined that the evidence was properly excluded because it did not bear on the specific issues under consideration, which concerned only the Newell accounts. This court further stated that the fact that the plaintiff may have had problems with other investment advisors had no relevance and was not material to the plaintiff's claims that the defendant negligently failed to properly value the Newell investments.

Citibank argues that, similar to *Congregation of the Passion*, the loans it made to SCA other than the term loan were not relevant in light of the court's order limiting Citibank's damages to the 2004 term loan.

Here, however, all of the loans Citibank made to SCA were relevant to the issue of whether Citibank relied on McGladrey's audit in making the 2004 term loan. Citibank's conduct regarding its prior loans to SCA was relevant to shed light on whether the McGladrey audit caused Citibank to make the 2004 term loan. Unlike in *Congregation of the Passion*, Citibank's motion *in limine* did not go beyond the specific issues under consideration, namely, Citibank's lending relationship with SCA. Although the circuit court limited Citibank's damages to the 2004 term loan, the issue of whether Citibank relied on McGladrey's audit in making the 2004 term loan involved Citibank's entire lending relationship with SCA. We find no abuse of discretion in the circuit court's denial of Citibank's motion *in limine* to exclude any evidence of Citibank's alleged contributory negligence unrelated to the 2004 term loan to SCA.

[Affirmed]

QUESTIONS

1. What was the interrelationship of the Citibank loans to SCA?
2. Why was the expert witness on medical care fraud excluded?
3. Can an auditor predict or detect behavior such as Dr. Weinberger's?

(B) The Contact Rule. In relaxing the privity requirement, New York now allows a third party to recover from a negligent accountant if there was some contact between the third party and the accountant. **For Example,** an accountant may go to a bank to see what information the bank requires for the accountant's client to obtain a loan. In this case, there is a sufficient "link" or "contact" between the bank and the accountant to allow the bank to recover from the accountant if it sustains a loss because of the accountant's negligence.[17] The New York *contact rule* requires that the accountant meet or communicate with the nonprivity party to establish a relationship equivalent to privity. The accountant must also know the purpose of the accounting work and foresee the nonprivity party's reliance on that work.[18]

There must be enough contact with, or dealings between, the third party and the accountant to give the accountant reason to know that the third party was relying for a particular purpose on the financial statements prepared by the accountant.[19]

[17] *Sykes v. RFD Third Ave.*, 938 N.E.2d 325 (N.Y. 2010); *Retirement Programs for Employees of Town of Fairfield v. NEPC, LLC*, 2011 WL 6934794, 53 Conn. L. Rptr. 194 (Conn. Super. 2011). Some courts are strict on the contact rule and describe the contact rule not as a different rule but as requiring "a relationship sufficiently intimate to be equated with privity." *Empire of American v. Arthur Andersen & Co.*, 514 N.Y.S.2d 578 (N.Y. 1987). The contact rule has been adopted by a minority of states. *Idaho Bank & Trust Co. v. First Bankcorp of Idaho*, 772 P.2d 720 (Idaho 1989).

[18] *Travelers Cas. and Sur. Co. of America v. Ernst & Young LLP*, 542 F.3d 475 (5th Cir. 2008).

[19] The contact rule applies to malpractice defendants generally. It is not limited to suits against accountants. *Ossining Union Free School District v. Anderson*, 539 N.E.2d 91 (N.Y. 1989), but see *Indianapolis-Marion County Public Library v. Charlier Clark & Linard, P.C.*, 900 N.E.2d 801 (Ind. App. 2009).

(c) The Known User Rule. Under this rule for nonprivity parties, the accountant is liable to third parties who experience a loss as a result of the accountant's negligence when the accountant knew that the third party would be using the accountant's work product. **For Example,** a shareholder may recover from an accountant for negligently preparing and certifying an annual financial report that was prepared for distribution to shareholders.[20]

Under the known user rule, the fact that the nonprivity party's reliance on a financial statement was foreseeable does not entitle the third party to recover from the accountant for negligent preparation of the statement. The third party must show that the accountant knew the statement would be furnished to that plaintiff. Thus, under this rule, the plaintiff's reliance must thus be actually foreseen and not merely reasonably foreseeable.[21]

Under the known user rule, it is sufficient if the user or third party is a member of a known class even though the identity of the particular user is not known to the accountant. However, some states hold that when the identity of the intended user is known to the accountant, another party coming within the same class cannot recover from the accountant.[22] **For Example,** an accountant prepares a financial statement for a client with the knowledge that the client will take it to First National Bank to obtain a loan. First National Bank may recover from the accountant for negligent loss even though the bank never had any direct contact or dealings (that is, was never in privity) with the accountant. However, no one other than First National may seek recovery from the accountant for negligence.

The fact that the third party was a foreseeable user does not afford a basis for recovery in a "known user" state. When an accountant prepares a financial statement for the client and nothing is said about what further use of the statement will be made, creditors of the client cannot recover from the accountant for negligent preparation of the statement. The client would be the only known user.

If the court follows the privity rule or the contact rule described in the two preceding sections, the known user cannot seek recovery from the accountant for negligent malpractice. Moreover, some courts that follow the known user rule apply it so strictly that a substitute foreseeable user is not permitted to recover. To illustrate, assume that in the example just given, the client was refused the loan by First National Bank. The client might then make an application for a loan to Second National Bank. In known-user states, Second National Bank could not recover from the accountant because it was not a known user.

(d) The Foreseeable User Rule. The accountant may foresee that a particular class of unknown parties will rely on her work. **For Example,** when the accountant prepares a financial statement knowing that the client is going to use it to borrow money from some bank or finance company, the accountant foresees a class of lenders. Similarly, the accountant may know that the financial statement will be used to sell the stock of the client corporation. Here again, there is a foreseeable class consisting of unknown parties.

The *foreseeable user rule* imposes liability on the accountant for negligent malpractice when he can foresee the parties who will rely on his work in the financial statements. The foreseeable user rule allows these third parties to recover for their losses without regard to the lack of privity of contract between them and the accountant.[23] The *Cast Art Industries, LLC v. KPMG LLP* case deals with an issue of auditor liability to those who do business with the audited company.

[20] *Altrust Financial Services, Inc. v. Adams*, 76 So.2d 228 (Ala. 2011).

[21] *Lindner Fund v. Abney*, 770 S.W.2d 437 (Mo. App. 1989). The rule that the nonprivity plaintiff may recover from the accountant for malpractice negligence only if the accountant's statement was furnished to that plaintiff, or the accountant knew that the client who was given the statement would in turn give the statement to the plaintiff, is often identified as "the Restatement rule." This rule is based on Restatement (Second) Torts §482 (1965). There is, however, some uncertainty as to the exact boundaries of the Restatement rule. See *Finderne Management Co. Inc. v. Barrett*, 809 A.2d 857 (N.J. Super. 2002).

[22] *In re Enron Corp. Securities, Derivatives, & ERISA Litigation*, 762 F. Supp. 2d 942 (S.D. Tex. 2010).

[23] *In re Washington Mut., Inc. Securities, Derivative & ERISA Litigation*, 2010 WL 2545415 (W.D. Wash. 2010). See also *Bank of America, N.A. v. BDO Seidman, LLP*, 2012 WL 806007 (Mass. Super. 2012).

Cast Art Industries, LLC v. KPMG LLP, 36 A.3d 1049 (N.J. 2012)

Cast Art Industries* produced and sold collectible figurines and giftware. Papel Giftware was in the same line of business as Cast Art, and in spring 2000 Cast Art explored acquiring Papel. Among the factors that made such Papel attractive to Cast Art were Papel's large number of existing customer accounts, its existing sales force, and its production facilities. Eventually, Cast Art decided on a merger, rather than an acquisition. Cast Art negotiated a loan agreement with PNC Bank for $22 million to fund the venture. PNC's conditions included that it receive audited financial statements and that Cast Art's CEO, Scott Sherman, personally guarantee $3.3 million of the loan.

KPMG (defendant) had audited Papel's financial statements since 1997. KPMG was already in the process of auditing Papel's 1998 and 1999 financial statements when Cast Art and Papel began their merger discussions. In its letter to the chairman of Papel's audit committee dated November 17, 1999, in which it agreed to undertake these audits and report the results, KPMG noted the parameters of its work:

> *An audit is planned and performed to obtain reasonable assurance about whether the financial statements are free of material misstatement, whether caused by error or fraud. Absolute assurance is not attainable because of the nature of audit evidence and the characteristics of fraud. Therefore, there is a risk that material errors, fraud (including fraud that may be an illegal act), and other illegal acts may exist and not be detected by an audit performed in accordance with generally accepted auditing standards. Also, an audit is not designed to detect matters that are immaterial to the financial statements.*

The process of KPMG completing its audits of Papel's financial statements for the years 1998 and 1999 was protracted because of tensions between John Quinn, the KPMG partner responsible for the audit, and Frederick Wasserman, Papel's chief financial officer, resulting from slowness in providing KPMG with records as well as disagreements over adjustments that KPMG concluded had to be made to Papel's financial statements. Eventually, Wasserman agreed to certain adjustments, and KPMG concluded that the remainder were immaterial and waived their inclusion. In September 2000, KPMG delivered to Papel the completed audits for the years 1998 and 1999. KPMG included in its accompanying opinion letter, which again was addressed to the chairman of Papel's audit committee, that Papel "was not in compliance with certain financial covenants" with its lenders, which KPMG characterized as raising "substantial doubt about the Company's ability to continue as a going concern."

Cast Art obtained copies of the completed 1998 and 1999 audits and provided copies to PNC. Three months later, in December 2000, Cast Art and Papel consummated the merger. Shortly after the merger was finalized, Cast Art began to experience difficulty in collecting some of the accounts receivable that it had believed Papel had had outstanding prior to the merger. Cast Art began its own investigation and learned that the 1998 and 1999 financial statements prepared by Papel were inaccurate and that Papel had engaged regularly in accelerating revenue.

Papel did not follow its stated policy to recognize revenue from sales when goods were shipped and invoices sent. Papel routinely booked revenue from goods that had not yet been shipped. For example, testimony at trial established that Papel would pack goods for shipment and book the revenue but then simply place the shipping cartons in trailers on its property and color code the invoices to note when the goods were, in fact, to be shipped and billed. There was also testimony that at certain points Papel would not close out its books at month's end. Rather, it would hold them open and book the improperly extended month revenue that was earned in the following period. There was also testimony that at least one transaction, referred to at trial as the "Bookman" transaction, was a fraudulent entry of a $121,244 sale that never occurred.

Although Cast Art knew at the time of the merger that Papel was carrying a significant amount of debt, it was unaware of those accounting irregularities until after the merger was complete. The surviving corporation was unable to generate sufficient revenue to carry its debt load and produce new goods, and it eventually failed.

Following a lengthy trial for KPMG's malpractice, a jury returned a verdict in favor of Cast Art and awarded damages totaling $31.8 million, which was amended to $38,096,902 by the trial court judge. The Appellate Division upheld the verdict on liability but vacated the damage award and remanded for a new trial on damages. The case was certified to the New Jersey Supreme Court.

JUDICIAL OPINION

WEFING, Justice ... In this litigation, Cast Art alleged that KPMG negligently audited Papel because its audit had not revealed Papel's accounting irregularities and sought to recover for the loss of its business. It contended that if KPMG had performed a proper audit, it would have uncovered the fraudulent accounting activity that was taking place at Papel. Cast Art further maintained that it never would have proceeded with the merger if it had been alerted to this fraud. Thus, Cast Art asserted that its losses were caused by

*The individual plaintiffs, Scott Sherman, Gary Barsellotti, and Frank Colapinto, were Cast Art's shareholders. Because the claims of Cast Art and the individual plaintiffs are inextricably intertwined, the court referred simply to Cast Art and plaintiff in the singular.

Continued

KPMG's negligence, and it argued that KPMG should be responsible to make it whole.

KPMG defended this litigation on several fronts. It argued that because Cast Art had not retained it to audit Papel, Cast Art was not its client, and Cast Art's claim was consequently barred by the Accountant Liability Act, N.J.S.A. 2A:53A–25.

Because an auditor's report may be circulated well beyond the borders of its subject, case law has developed three analytical frameworks within which to consider whether and under what circumstances auditors may be held liable for their negligence in conducting an audit. The earliest cases dealing with the question of an auditor's liability to third parties for negligence required the existence of privity or its equivalence as a necessary precondition to holding an auditor liable.

The leading case standing for the privity principle is *Ultramares v. Touche*, 255 N.Y. 170, 174 N.E. 441 (1931). The New York Court of Appeals held that imposing liability for negligence on an auditor in the absence of privity or an equivalent relationship "may expose accountants to a liability in an indeterminate amount for an indeterminate time to an indeterminate class."

The Restatement (Second) of Torts formulated a somewhat broader test.

One who, in the course of his business, profession or employment ... supplies false information for the guidance of others in their business transactions, is subject to liability for pecuniary loss caused to them by their justifiable reliance upon the information, if he fails to exercise reasonable care or competence in obtaining or communicating the information. [Restatement (Second) of Torts § 552(1) (1977)].

New Jersey rejected those tests. When the independent auditor furnishes an opinion with no limitation in the certificate as to whom the company may disseminate the financial statements, he has a duty to all those whom that auditor should reasonably foresee as recipients from the company of the statements for its proper business purposes, provided that the recipients rely on the statements pursuant to those business purposes... . In those circumstances accounting firms should no longer be permitted to hide within the citadel of privity and avoid liability for their malpractice.

Clearly, KPMG did not know in November 1999, when it agreed to perform this audit, that its work could play a role in a subsequent merger because its agreement predated by several months Cast Art's interest in Papel. Cast Art urges that the statute should not be given such a restrictive interpretation and that the phrase "at the time of the engagement" should be construed to mean "at any time during the period of the engagement." KPMG, on the other hand, contends the phrase means "at the outset of the engagement."

The Appellate Division, in concluding that the phrase "at the time of the engagement" was not limited to the point of Papel's initial hiring of KPMG, referred to the Code of Professional Conduct of the American Institute of Certified Professional Accountants. Under that Code, an accountant's "engagement" spans the entire period of the professional relationship with the client. Cast Art, supra, 416 N.J. Super. at 88–89, 3 A.3d 562. It rejected KPMG's argument that the additional phrase "by the client" indicated a more restrictive meaning to the term "engagement."

We are unable to agree with the Appellate Division's conclusion. An auditor is entitled to know at the outset the scope of the work it is being requested to perform and the concomitant risk it is being asked to assume. We have earlier set forth the pertinent language of KPMG's engagement letter with Papel with respect to those audits, and it is silent as to Cast Art. Thus, at the outset of its engagement with Papel, KPMG was not told that a nonclient would be relying on its work.

Cast Art contends that its cause of action nonetheless fits within that portion of the statute permitting a third party to seek recovery from an accountant if the accountant "agreed with the client after the time of the engagement, that the professional accounting service rendered to the client would be made available to the claimant, who was specifically identified to the accountant in connection with a specified transaction made by the claimant." N.J.S.A. 2A:53A–25(b)(2)(a). It points to Scott Sherman's (Cast Art's CEO) testimony that he had a conference call with an unnamed KPMG representative in which he inquired about the status of the audit and was assured it would be forthcoming. This, Cast Art maintains, satisfies the statutory mandate.

We do not agree. In our judgment, the most that can be said is that Sherman's testimony would support an inference that KPMG was aware that Cast Art required audited financial statements to proceed with the planned merger. The statute, however, requires agreement, not mere awareness, on the part of the accountant to the planned use of his work product. Sherman's testimony is wholly inadequate in that respect.

Because Cast Art failed to establish that KPMG "knew at the time of the engagement by the client" or thereafter agreed that Cast Art could rely on its work in proceeding with this merger, Cast Art failed to satisfy the requisite elements of N.J.S.A. 2A:53A–25(b)(2), and KPMG was entitled to judgment.

[The judgment of the Appellate Division is reversed, and the matter is remanded to the trial court for entry of a judgment of dismissal.]

QUESTIONS

1. Describe the types of accounting irregularities that were going on at Papel.
2. What is the significance of the term "engagement" in the opinion?
3. Where does New Jersey fit with regard to privity and the Restatement rule when it comes to auditor liability to third parties?

Thinking Things Through

How Many Plaintiffs Can There Be in a Class-Action Securities Litigation? How Many Defendants?

With the collapse of companies such as Countrywide, New Century Financial, Lehman Brothers, and other firms affected by or involved in the subprime mortgage market, litigation against all of these firms' auditors is ongoing. The following is a list of all of the types of plaintiffs who have brought suit against auditors:

- Shareholders who purchased stock in the companies
- State pension funds with stock in their portfolios
- Banks and other institutions that lent money
- Banks and other institutions that accepted stock as collateral for loans
- Universities that received stock as endowment gifts
- Companies that contracted with the companies after having requested financial statements

Applying the various standards for accountant liability you have learned, discuss whether each of these groups will be able to recover from the auditors for these firms and why or why not.

(E) THE INTENDED USER RULE. Fear that the foreseeability rule does not sufficiently restrict the number of potential claimants has led some courts to limit recovery to those nonprivity users who were not merely foreseeable but also expected or intended to rely on the work of the accountant in a particular transaction or another similar transaction.[24] In this view, the accountant must have furnished the information directly to the nonprivity user or to the client, knowing that the client would transmit the information to the nonprivity plaintiff.

(F) THE FLEXIBLE RULE. Some courts have rejected the requirement of privity for malpractice against accountants but have not adopted any of the rules discussed in the preceding sections. These courts prefer to keep the question open and to decide each case as it arises.

(G) UNKNOWN USER. When the accountant has no knowledge of, or reason to know of, any third party's use of the accountant's work, the third party is not able to come within any exception to the requirement of privity. Consequently, a nonprivity party cannot recover for the accountant's negligence when the accountant had no knowledge of any use that could affect the party.[25]

7. Nonliability Parties

There are some third parties to whom accountants do not have liability.

(A) INTERLOPERS. No court imposes liability on the accountant to a total stranger who gets possession of the accountant's work and then sustains a loss because of a false statement in the work. This applies regardless of whether the statement was negligent or intentional. **For Example,** assume that a negligently prepared financial statement of a corporation is thrown in the wastepaper basket and is then retrieved by a security guard. If the guard thinks that the statement is a "hot tip" and invests in the stock of the corporation on the basis of the statement, the guard cannot recover from the accountant for negligence in preparing the statement. Accountants are not liable to interlopers, but courts continue to struggle with drawing the line between interlopers and rightful third parties.

(B) PARTIES AFFECTED BY THE DECISION OF ACCOUNTANT'S CLIENT. On the basis of information furnished by the accountant to a client, the client may make a decision that affects a third party. **For Example,** a report by an independent auditor may indicate that a fiscal officer

[24] *Bay Harbour Management LLC v. Carothers*, 282 Fed. Appx. 71, 2008 WL 2566557 (2nd Cir.). Some courts regard this rule as representing the majority view. The foreseeable user rule brings the law with respect to accountants into harmony with the tort law relating to other parties and activities.

[25] *Sundamerican Bank & Trust Co. v. Harrison*, 851 S.W.2d 563 (Mo. App. 1993).

of the client has not handled funds properly. The report may indicate that it is economically unsound to enter into a contract with a third party. Assume that the client relies on the accountant's report and fires the employee or refuses to make a contract with the third party. If the report of the accountant was negligently made and the true facts would not have justified the action taken by the client, most courts hold that third parties harmed in this indirect way have no cause of action.[26]

8. Defenses to Accountants' Liability: Contributory and Comparative Negligence of the Client or Third Party

(A) Contributory Negligence. When an accountant has been negligent, the client's negligence may reduce the accountant's liability. To establish client **contributory negligence**, the accountant must show that the client contributed to the accountant's failure or that the client ignored the accountant's instructions. **For Example,** when the financial statement indicates that it is merely a working examination and is not certified by the accountant, the third party is negligent in relying on the statement and has been contributorily negligent.

If those who are using a financial statement are highly sophisticated and have been warned by their advisers that the corporate assets have been overvalued, the users cannot hold the accountant who prepared the financial statement liable for negligence in overstating the value of the corporate assets. In such a case, the users ares contributorily negligent, something that reduces or eliminates the accountant's liability.[27]

Some states ignore the contributory negligence of clients except in two circumstances. One is if the client interfered with the accountant's audit. Client interference with the accountant's work will excuse the accountant's liability. Another is if the client's negligence contributed to the accountant's negligence, but such contribution is not a bar to recovery by the client. **For Example,** the negligence of the accountant's client in keeping records is not a bar to the accountants' liability to the client because the liability comes from the accountant's failure to discover the true facts.[28] The issue in these circumstances becomes not whether the accountant knew, but whether the accountant should have known.

(B) Comparative Negligence. Some states apply the **comparative negligence** concept and permit proof of the client's negligence.[29] Under comparative negligence standards, the accountant and the client are assessed a percentage of blame for their respective levels of negligence in the use and preparation of the financial statements, and the client's recovery is reduced by its percentage of fault. **For Example,** if a jury finds that the client was responsible for 30 percent of the resulting loss, recovery from the accountant is reduced by 30 percent.

9. Accountants' Fraud Malpractice Liability to Third Parties

Society in general condemns fraud more strongly than it does negligence. There is greater liability of accountants for fraudulent malpractice.

(A) What Constitutes Fraud by Accountants. *Fraud* is defined as a false statement made with knowledge that it was false or with reckless indifference as to whether it was true[30] with the intent that the listener rely on it. A false statement in accounting typically occurs when the client's financial statements make it appear to be in a better financial position than is actually the case. **For Example,** in the case of Bernie Madoff Securities, the auditor signed off for years on financial statements that made the firm seem solvent when in fact the company had lost $50 billion.

At times, falsified financial statements are used as a means to obtain a downgrade on the ratings for the financial condition of a corporation. Such undervaluation then induces shareholders to sell their stock to a dominant group of shareholders. The false financial statement purposely undervalues the corporation's assets to make the shareholders believe their stock has little value and that sale at the low price offered by the dominant group is a good buy.

[26] *Harper v. Inkster Public Schools,* 404 N.W.2d 776 (Mich. App. 1987).
[27] *Scottish Heritable Trust v. Peat Marwick Main & Co.,* 81 F.3d 606 (5th Cir. 1996).
[28] *World Radio Laboratories, Inc. v. Coopers & Lybrand,* 538 N.W.2d 501 (Neb. App. 1995).
[29] *American Nat'l Bank v. Touche Ross & Co.,* 659 N.E.2d 1276 (Ohio 1996).
[30] In re *Dell Securities Litigation,* 591 F. Supp. 2d 877 (W.D. Tex. 2009).

FIGURE 47-1 *Theories of Accountants' Liability to Third Parties*

THEORY	TYPE OF LIABILITY	THIRD PARTY LIABILITY	CLIENT LIABILITY
STATUTORY	1933 SECURITIES ACT—OMISSION OR MISSTATEMENT IN REGISTRATION STATEMENT	PURCHASERS OF SHARES	COMPANY
	1934 SECURITIES EXCHANGE ACT—10b (SEE CHAPTER 46)	SHAREHOLDERS; PURCHASER OF SHARES	
CONTRACT	BREACH OF CONTRACT	NO—NOT CONSIDERED THIRD PARTY BENEFICIARIES	MATERIAL BREACH; MINOR BREACH DAMAGES
TORT	PRIVITY REQUIRED	NO RECOVERY	RECOVERY ALLOWED UNLESS DEFENSES APPLY
	CONTACT RULE REQUIRED	CAN RECOVER IF ACTUAL CONTACT WITH ACCOUNTANT	↓
	KNOWN USER RULE	CAN RECOVER IF ACCOUNTANT KNOWS THIRD PARTY WILL USE FINANCIALS/WORK	↓
	FORESEEABLE USER RULE	CAN RECOVER IF ACCOUNTANT CAN FORESEE UNKNOWN PERSONS RELYING ON FINANCIALS	↓
	INTENDED USER RULE	CAN RECOVER IF ACCOUNTANT KNOWS CLIENT WILL GIVE IT TO ANOTHER	↓
	UNKNOWN USER	NO RECOVERY	↓
FRAUD	KNOWN AND UNKNOWN	RECOVERY	RECOVERY

(B) ACCOUNTANTS' FRAUD LIABILITY TO INTENDED VICTIMS. Fraud by an accountant typically misleads a third party or a class of parties, a group whose identity is known to the accountant. Any such victim, whether an identified party or member of a class of potential victims, may recover from the accountant for loss caused by fraud. Privity (relating to liability for negligence) is not required when the basis of the malpractice suit is fraud. The public policy of preventing fraud overrides the concern of holding accountants liable to third parties.

An accountant might certify a false financial statement for a corporate client with knowledge that it will be used to sell the corporation's securities to third parties.[31] If so, the third parties may recover from the accountant for the damages sustained. **For Example,** an accountant has been held liable for disguising the true character of a hoped-for profit from the sale and resale of real estate. The accountant described the sale and resale as "deferred income," although there was little reason to believe that the transaction could ever be completed because the buyer, who was obligated to pay $5 million for the property, had assets of only $100,000. The financial statement would have shown a loss instead of a substantial profit if the true character of this risky transaction had been disclosed. The *Carlson v. Xerox Corp.* case deals with the issue of auditors giving in to management financial reporting requests.

Carlson v. Xerox Corp., 392 F. Supp. 2d 267 (D. Conn. 2005)

When the Auditor Just Duplicates What Management Wants

Throughout the early and mid-1990s, Xerox financial reports reflected a financially healthy company with revenues rising at a double-digit rate. By the late 1990s, however, Xerox faced increasing competition from Japanese competitors in the digital copier market and it was able to meet Wall Street's earning expectations only by engaging in massive accounting fraud.

An SEC complaint alleged that Xerox reallocated revenues from service to the equipment portion of sales-type leases by assuming an artificial gross margin differential between the two lease components (or an assumed profit margin) that had no basis in economic reality. Equipment margins were in fact falling. Xerox used this method to pull forward $617 million of equipment revenues from 1997–2000. Internally, KPMG referred to this method as "half-baked revenue recognition." By relying on this methodology, from 1997 to 1999, Xerox inflated its pre-tax earnings by a net of $43 million. According to the SEC, in 1996, KPMG objected to this practice as violating GAAP but, after arguments with Xerox senior management, approved its implementation in 1998, while continuing to criticize its use.

In 1999, KPMG informed Xerox that this practice violated GAAP, but Xerox refused to follow this advice. Nevertheless, KPMG certified Xerox's 1999 and 2000 financial statements.

In November of 1999, Xerox senior managers discussed the fact that without their accounting actions, Xerox had essentially no growth through the late 1990s. In 2001, Xerox began issuing a series of earnings restatements that would total $11 billion. In late 2001, Xerox announced that PriceWaterhouse Coopers, LLP ("PwC") was replacing KPMG as the company's new auditor for the 2001 fiscal year. Xerox paid a $10 million fine to the SEC to settle civil charges and also agreed to complete its restatement of earnings for 1997 through 2001.

Investors such as the Florida State pension plan and other individual investors (plaintiffs) brought suit against the executive officers of Xerox as well as KPMG for fraud.

KPMG moved to have the complaint against it dismissed because of its lack of scienter.

JUDICIAL OPINION

THOMPSON, District Judge.... It is not hard to visualize a slippery slope where accounting integrity is degraded in tiny increments in the pursuit of earnings consistency. In the case of Xerox, it is troubling that the company could become so financially distressed in such a short period of time.

The $10 million fine was the largest ever paid by a public company to settle a case brought by the SEC. The SEC stated that the "largest fine ever obtained by the SEC against a public company in a financial fraud case" was called for "because of the fact that Xerox's senior management orchestrated a four-year scheme to disguise the company's true operating performance" and that the size of the fine also reflected, in part, a sanction "for the company's lack of full cooperation in the investigation."

To satisfy the requirement for pleading scienter, as set forth in 15 U.S.C. § 78u-4(b)(2), "a complaint may (1) allege facts that constitute strong circumstantial evidence of conscious misbehavior or recklessness, or (2) allege facts to show that defendants had both motive and opportunity to commit fraud."

[A]llegations of GAAP violations or accounting irregularities, standing alone, are insufficient to state a securities fraud claim.

KPMG contends that the plaintiffs have failed to allege scienter as to it under either the motive and opportunity prong or the conscious misbehavior or recklessness prong of scienter. When the factual allegations in the Complaint are viewed as a whole, the plaintiffs have at a minimum alleged facts

[31] In re *IMAX Securities Litigation*, 587 F. Supp. 2d 471 (S.D.N.Y. 2008).

Continued

constituting strong circumstantial evidence of recklessness on the part of KPMG. The plaintiffs have alleged inter alia,

(i) that Xerox used artificially low interest rate assumptions to artificially inflate the recognized present value of long-term leases, and KPMG expressly approved Xerox's use of such artificially depressed interest rates in countries with extremely high interest rates, such as Mexico and Brazil, for purposes of calculating revenues from leases; and that ROE was a series of top-side adjustments, and KPMG never tested Xerox's claim that the top-side adjustments were necessary, notwithstanding the fact that in 1998 the American Institute of Certified Public Accountants issued an Audit Risk Alert pointing out the increased risk associated with such;

(ii) that KPMG knew that Xerox engaged in "margin normalization," knew this practice violated GAAP, and internally referred to the practice as "half-baked revenue recognition"; and that KPMG expressed concern to Xerox about the frequency with which Xerox's long-term leasing revenue recognition methodology was changing, but took no corrective action and permitted Xerox to recognize the revenue in violation of GAAP;

(iii) that although GAAP prohibits increasing the estimated residual value of leased equipment for any reason after it is first established, Xerox recorded adjustments of at least $95 million as a result of retroactive revisions to residual values, and while KPMG initially objected to this practice as being in violation of GAAP, after "heated debates with Xerox management, KPMG approved its implementation in 1997 and allowed the practice to continue through 1998"

* * *

(iv) that after KPMG informed Xerox in 1999 that Xerox's practice of immediately recognizing revenue from price increases and extensions on leases with existing lease customers violated GAAP, Xerox did not cease this practice but merely reduced the amount of revenue it recognized, and KPMG nonetheless signed off on Xerox's 1999 and 2000 financial statements;

(v) that after the 1999 audit, Xerox "approached KPMG with a plan dubbed 'Project Mozart,' that would have shifted Xerox's big losses from selling copiers to homes and small businesses to an off-balance sheet vehicle," but the plan was scrapped after Ronald Safran, the senior audit engagement partner at KPMG, refused to sign off on the plan, after which Xerox insisted that KPMG replace Safran as the engagement partner and KPMG did so, replacing him with Michael Conway.

In March 2001, Safran was subpoenaed to appear before the SEC and was confronted with evidence of "numerous accounting irregularities engaged in by Xerox" that in March 2001, KPMG and its attorneys confronted Xerox officials with some of the documents shown to KPMG by the SEC, including an anonymous note to Xerox executives alleging "fake transactions" and "illegal revenue recognition," and KPMG interpreted the executive's response as a signal that Xerox had "a culture that didn't recognize that it was not a good thing to be getting anonymous letters about fraud"; that KPMG knew prior to the First Restatement "that the SEC already suspected the massive overstatement of profit from 1997 to 2000 that it detailed in its consent decree with Xerox"; and that it was in the context of all of the foregoing that KPMG required the First Restatement, which represented "only minor restatements of [Xerox's] past financials", and "[i]n fact … Romeril intimidated KPMG into signing off on the Xerox audit despite the improper accounting devices by threatening KPMG that any refusal to sign could trigger debt default and throw [Xerox] into bankruptcy."

Thus, the factual allegations in the Complaint do, in fact, portray KPMG as a "virtual pushover" in its dealings with the Xerox Defendants, which at a minimum went along with accounting practices it knew to be clear violations of GAAP, and which, even after it was clear early in 2001 that there were very serious concerns about Xerox's accounting practices and it was apparent that it was questionable—at best—whether Xerox took seriously its obligation to comply with applicable accounting rules, was intimidated into signing off on a minimal restatement of Xerox's financial statements that accounted for only a small portion of Xerox's overstatements of revenues and pre-tax earnings. The court concludes that the allegations of the Complaint describe conduct on the part of a non-fiduciary accountant that is highly unreasonable and represents an extreme departure from the standards of ordinary care.

[The court denied KPMG's motion to dismiss after concluding that there was enough in the pleadings to give rise to scienter.]

QUESTIONS

1. Give some examples of "turning points" or events when KPMG should have acted differently.
2. Describe the level of accounting errors at Xerox from 1997 through 2001.
3. Why do you think the officers and KPMG auditors acted as they did?

C. Sarbanes-Oxley Auditor and Accounting-Related Provisions

Following the collapses of Enron and WorldCom during 2001–2002, Congress quickly passed sweeping legislation (see Chapter 8 and Chapter 46) designed to increase the liability for securities violations, financial fraud, and obstruction of justice and to impose new responsibility and accountability with regard to financial reporting by companies. Called the *Sarbanes-Oxley Act* (SOX or SarBox), this legislation imposes substantial requirements on auditors and the standards and practices of the audit profession.

10. Auditor Independence

One of the concerns reflected in SOX was that auditors were not exercising sufficient discretion and independence in conducting audits of their clients. The act takes several steps to increase the auditor's independence as it conducts its audits of company financial records.

(A) Public Company Accounting Oversight Board. The first section of SOX created a new Public Company Accounting Oversight Board (PCAOB, often referred to as *Peekaboo*) that is responsible for promoting high professional standards among auditors.[32] The board, which consists of five presidential appointees, is not a governmental body but a nonprofit organization with its own budgeting and staffing authority. No more than two members of the board can be CPAs, and members of the board operate on a full-time basis. The board has the following responsibilities:

- Operating a registration system for public accounting firms that prepare audit reports for companies that issue securities
- Enforcing and refining rules to ensure audit quality, ethics, and independence by auditors
- Conducting inspections of public accounting firms to determine their compliance with Sarbanes-Oxley requirements
- Investigating violations and imposing disciplinary sanctions where necessary for members of the profession
- Encouraging the highest professional standards among public accounting firms and auditors

(B) Registration with the PCAOB. Any public accounting firm that conducts audits for companies that issue securities must file an annual registration statement with PCAOB. That registration requires the accounting firm to disclose all companies for which it has done audits and all the fees paid by those companies—both audit fees and nonaudit fees, commonly referred to

Ethics & the Law

The Bernie Madoff Feeder Firm Auditor

Philip Stevenson's living trust had its assets invested in Greenwich Sentry, an investment advisor. Greenwich Sentry was a feeder fund for Madoff Securities, an investment firm run by Bernie Madoff that turned out to be a $50 billion Ponzi scheme. Mr. Madoff entered a guilty plea to charges of securities fraud and was sentenced to 150 years in prison.

PricewaterhouseCoopers was the auditor for Greenwich Sentry. When Mr. Stephenson first invested his trust's assets in Greenwich, he did very well. For example, in the initial five months, his $60 million investment grew to $62,540,565, despite the fact that the Dow Jones Industrial Average was going down during this period. As we now know, the gains were illusory, and when Madoff revealed his fraud on December 8, 2008, Stephenson learned that his investment was gone, an investment that he has yet to recover.

Stephenson's suit against PricewaterhouseCoopers (PWC) alleged that there were red flags that should have alerted PWC to the fraud such as control problems at Greenwich as well as problems with risk management procedures at the firm. Also, Stephenson argued that the extraordinary returns were, in and of themselves, a red flag. Can PWC be held liable for the losses experienced with another firm? Discuss the ethical obligations of PWC. PWC's literature touts itself as an expert in auditing hedge funds. Does that claim make a difference in your answer? **[*Stephenson v. PricewaterhouseCoopers, LLP*, 768 F. Supp. 2d 562 (S.D.N.Y. 2011)]**

[32] In the financial industry, professionals have translated the acronym for the new board, PCAOB, as *Peekaboo* because of the board's role in shedding light on financial systems and reporting.

as *consulting services*. The accounting firm is also required to disclose any sanctions and pending civil or criminal proceedings against it, along with its policies and procedures for quality control in audits. PCAOB then approves the accounting firm for continued work in the audit of issuers of securities. That approval or denial must be made within 45 days following the accounting firm's annual registration filing.

(c) Maintaining Auditor Independence. In many of the companies that experienced financial collapse prior to SOX, the companies' auditors had conflicts that may have tainted their independent judgment on accounting issues or even on whether the companies were viable entities. **For Example,** many of the audit firms received substantial fees from companies for management consulting services for which they were providing certified statements. Arthur Andersen received $21 million annually for its audit work with Enron and another $29 million for its consulting services. The consulting contract created a conflict that interfered with the audit firm's ability to make honest decisions in its audit work.

To help eliminate conflicts of interest, Sarbanes-Oxley prohibits certain activities by audit firms for their audit clients, including the following:

1. Bookkeeping and other services related to the accounting records or financial statements of the audit client
2. Design and implementation of financial information systems
3. Appraisal and valuation services, fairness opinions, and contribution-in-kind reports
4. Actuarial services
5. Internal audit outsourcing services
6. Management functions and human resources
7. Broker or dealer, investment adviser, and investment banking services
8. Legal services and expert services unrelated to the audit
9. Any other service that the board determines, by regulation, is impermissible[33]

All nonaudit services to be performed by the auditor for an audit client (except those listed above as expressly prohibited) require prior approval by the board.

In addition, to ensure that audit partners do not become entrenched, Sarbanes-Oxley requires audit firms to change audit partners at least once every five years.[34] The rotation of the audit partner in charge of a company account brings a new perspective to the issues in the financial systems and reports and helps to eliminate the bias of close, personal relationships that develop over longstanding working relationships.

SOX also requires accounting firms to set up internal systems for developing and monitoring professional ethics and for the discussion of ethical issues that arise during the course of the audits of clients.

11. Audit Committees

SOX also addresses issues on the corporate side of the interaction between auditors and companies—the audit committee of the company's board. Under the statute, audit committees must be composed of board members who are independent, defined in the statute as directors who do not accept consulting or other fees from the company and who are not affiliated with the company, certain of its employees, or any of its subsidiaries.[35]

Members of audit committees must also be allowed to interact with auditors without management being present and also be permitted to hire independent advisors. At least one member of the audit committee must be a financial expert or someone who understands financial reporting and audit work. The audit committee is now the central point for ensuring that SOX standards are being followed.

Audit committees are required to establish procedures whereby they can be notified of problems with the company's internal controls. Audit committees need to establish the means and mechanisms for monitoring the company's internal control systems so they can verify that financial reports are based on data generated by effective company reporting systems.

[33] 15 U.S.C. §78j-1. *Baena v. KPMG LLP*, 389 F. Supp. 2d 112, affirmed 453 F.3d 1 (D. Mass. 2005).
[34] 15 U.S.C. §78j-1.
[35] 15 U.S.C. §1741.

E-Commerce & Cyberlaw

Destruction of Documents, Destruction of a Career, Destruction of a Firm

The congressional investigation into the Enron collapse uncovered the following e-mails:

- A May 28, 1999, e-mail to David Duncan from Benjamin Neuhausen, a member of Andersen's Professional Standards Group at its Chicago main office, evaluated the wisdom of having Enron's CFO Andrew Fastow as the principal in a company that was off the books and doing trades with Enron: "Setting aside the accounting, idea of a venture entity managed by CFO is terrible from a business point of view. Conflicts galore. Why would any director in his or her right mind ever approve such a scheme?"
- A June 1, 1999, e-mail from David Duncan responded: "[O]n your point 1 (i.e., the whole thing is a bad idea), I really couldn't agree more. Rest assured that I have already communicated and it has been agreed to by Andy that CEO, General [Counsel], and Board discussion and approval will be a requirement, on our part, for acceptance of a venture similar to what we have been discussing."

These e-mails are discoverable and admissible when litigation results from an auditor's work. The only protections are the privilege between lawyer and client, but these e-mails were between auditors who worked for the same audit firm.

12. Records Retention

Accounting firm Arthur Andersen was convicted of one count of obstruction of justice for its destruction of Enron records while SEC investigations were pending. The conviction was later reversed because the court held that although there may have been sufficient evidence about individual Andersen employees' willful destruction of documents, the jury instructions were flawed in attributing that knowledge to the full Andersen firm automatically without proof of actual knowledge (an element required in all criminal cases; see Chapter 8).[36] The statute used for prosecution in that case was not specific enough to tie the firm to individual employee conduct. Furthermore, the penalties, even with such a conviction, were minimal. As discussed in Chapter 8, SOX substantially increased both the scope of and penalties for the obstruction of justice through accountants' and auditors' destruction of records. Under Sarbanes-Oxley, those who destroy, conceal, alter, or mutilate documents when either a civil or criminal investigation is pending are subject to up to 20 years' imprisonment as well as fines.[37]

13. Dodd-Frank and Accountants as Whistleblowers

Under the Dodd-Frank Act (see Chapter 47 for more information), accountants who work for audit firms are not permitted to use information obtained during the court of an audit for purposes of obtaining an award that comes from their reporting information to the SEC that results in an enforcement action. Auditors and audit firm responsibilities are to report any fraud at the company to management and the audit committee. If the board takes no action, the auditor must then go to the SEC. Auditors are only eligible for whistleblower rewards if they report conduct by the company that is intended to thwart an SEC investigation.

LawFlix

Midnight Run (1988) (R)

Charles Grodin plays an accountant who embezzles from his mafia boss but gives the money to charity.

[36] *Andersen, LLP v. U.S.*, 544 U.S. 696 (2005). David Duncan, the partner in charge of the Enron account, withdrew his guilty plea on obstruction when the court reversed the firm's verdict.

[37] 18 U.S.C. §1512. Persuading another to destroy documents is obstruction of justice. *U.S. v. Moyer*, 674 F.3d 192 (3rd Cir. 2012).

MAKE THE CONNECTION

SUMMARY

Professionals who agree to perform services for others must perform those services according to the standards of the profession. Accountants, as professionals, must perform their audit work at the levels and standards of competency and thoroughness established for their profession. If an accountant negligently fails to observe those standards, the accountant could be liable for breach of contract or negligence. This tort of negligent breach of contract constitutes malpractice, and the other party to the contract can recover from the accountant either for breach of contract or for the negligence involved.

In some circumstances, not only are accountants liable to their clients, they may also be liable for malpractice to certain third parties who have used or relied on the financial statement. States and courts differ as to when an accountant is liable to third parties. Some courts do not recognize accountant liability to third parties; these courts require privity between the parties. Most courts hold accountants liable to some third parties but differ as to which third parties and how far to extend the accountant's liability. The various rules that determine accountant liability to third parties are the contact rule, which requires that the third party must have had some contact with the accountant before there can be liability; the known user rule in which the accountant is aware of the third party who will use the accountant's information; the foreseeability rule in which the accountant is held liable if it was possible to foresee that the third party would use the accountant's information; the intended user rule in which the client tells the accountant of the intended use of the audit work; the unknown user rule in which the accountant is not liable to third parties it could not have known would use the information or audit work; and the flexible rule that decides on a case-by-case basis.

Accountants guilty of fraud have liability to all third parties, even those not in privity of contract with the accountant.

To a limited degree, an accountant is protected from malpractice liability by a disclaimer of liability or by the contributory negligence of the plaintiff.

Sarbanes-Oxley (SOX) increases the penalties for accountants who destroy documents when civil or criminal investigations are pending. The act also prohibits conduct by accountants that creates a conflict of interest and requires audit firms to register for authorization to do audit work on public companies. Audit committees of boards are now required to work closely with auditors to make sure that the financial systems in the company and its reports are sound. A federal oversight board reviews the work of audit firms and is authorized to discipline audit firms and accountants for their failure to honor standards or comply with the law.

Dodd-Frank whistleblower provisions do not apply to auditors unless the company is obstructing an investigation.

LEARNING OUTCOMES

After studying this chapter, you should be able to clearly explain:

A. General Principles of Accountants' Liability

LO.1 Define *malpractice*

See Section 1 on p. 983.

LO.2 Distinguish malpractice liability from breach of contract liability

See "Choice of Remedy" on p. 985.

See *Cast Art Industries, LLC v. KPMG LLP* on pp. 990–991.

B. Accountants' Liability to Third Parties: Beyond Privity

LO.3 List which third parties may recover for the malpractice liability of accountants and when they may do so

See *Citibank, N.A. v. McGladrey and Pullen, LLP* on pp. 987–988.

LO.4 Discuss the difference between accounting malpractice and fraud

See *Carlson v. Xerox Corp* on pp. 995–996
See Ethics & the Law on Bernie Madoff feeder fund, p. 997.

C. Sarbanes-Oxley Auditor, Dodd-Frank, and Accounting-Related Provisions

LO.5 Explain how Sarbanes-Oxley has affected the accounting profession and accountants' liability

See E-Commerce & Cyberlaw on p. 999.

KEY TERMS

comparative negligence
contributory negligence
exculpatory clause
limitation-of-liability
malpractice
misrepresentation
privity rule

QUESTIONS AND CASE PROBLEMS

1. The auditing firm of Timm, Schmidt & Co. prepared annual financial statements for Clintonville Fire Apparatus, Inc. (CFA). CFA showed these statements to Citizens State Bank and asked for loans. On the basis of the financial statements, Citizens loaned CFA approximately $380,000. Timm later discovered that the financial statements overvalued CFA by more than $400,000. Citizens demanded repayment of the loans. CFA could not pay the balance, and Citizens sued Timm and its malpractice liability insurer. They raised the defense that the suit was barred by lack of privity and the fact that no one in the Timm firm knew that CFA intended to use the financial statements to obtain loans from anyone. Is the lack of privity a defense? [*Citizens State Bank v. Timm, Schmidt & Co.*, 335 N.W.2d 361 (Wis.)]

2. Parente, Randolph, Orlando & Associates (Parente) is an accounting firm that had done auditing work for Sparkomatic for nearly 20 years. On June 14, 1993, Sparkomatic entered into a Memorandum of Intent with Williams Controls to sell Williams assets from Sparkomatic's Kenco division. The sale price was to be the "audited book value" of the assets, and the book value would be based on the June 30, 1993, balance sheet (which Parente did not prepare). Sparkomatic then engaged Parente to audit the financial statements for December 31, 1990, 1991, and 1992 and to prepare an interim balance sheet for 1993.

   On August 1, 1993, Sparkomatic and Williams Controls entered into an asset purchase agreement, which required that Williams be furnished financials through June 1993 as prepared by "Sparkomatic's independent public accountant." Parente was not identified by name in the agreement. Parente did review the asset purchase agreement with Williams prior to commencing its work and knew that Williams would be using the information Parente prepared.

   Following the closing, additional information came to light indicating that Williams had overpaid for the assets of Kenco, and Williams filed suit against Parente for negligence, negligent misrepresentation, and breach of contract. Parente moved for summary judgment. What should the decision be and why? Discuss several possible theories. [*Williams Controls v. Parente, Randolph, Orlando, & Associates*, 39 F. Supp. 2d 517 (M.D. Pa.)]

3. David S. Talesnick served as the accountant for Kenneth Ronson and his wife as well as for Ronson's company, performing accounting and tax services for all. From 1980 to 1983, Ronson, his wife, and his company invested in the White Rim Oil & Gas, Pine Coal, and Winchester Coal limited partnerships. During those years, the Ronsons and his company were able to report losses on their income tax returns because of these investments. However, the IRS determined that the limited partnerships were not qualified investments under the tax code and disallowed the loss deductions. The Ronsons and his company all owed back taxes, interest, and penalties as a result. The Ronsons disputed the finding and

asked Talesnick how they might appeal the ruling and not have the interest clock ticking on what they owed. Talesnick wrote a letter and advised them to post a bond of $91,300, the amount then due. Talesnick was incorrect in his advice on payment and accrual of interest, and by the time the final determination was made against the Ronsons and Ronson's company, they owed $235,063 with interest. The Ronsons sued Talesnick for malpractice. Could they recover? How much? [*Ronson v. David S. Talesnick, CPA*, 33 F. Supp. 2d 347 (D.N.J.)]

4. The certified public accounting partnership of James, Guinn, and Head prepared a certified audit report of four corporations, known as the Paschal Enterprises, with knowledge that their report would be used to induce Shatterproof Glass Corp. to lend money to those corporations. The report showed the corporations to be solvent when in fact they were insolvent. Shatterproof relied on the audit report, loaned approximately $500,000 to the four corporations, and lost almost all of it because the liabilities of the companies were in excess of their assets. Shatterproof claimed that James and other accountants had been negligent in preparing the report and sued them to recover the loss on the loan. The accountants raised the defense that they had been retained not by Shatterproof but by Paschal. Was this defense valid? [*Shatterproof Glass Corp. v. James*, 466 S.W.2d 873 (Tex. App.)]

5. AUSA Life Insurance Company and others were institutional investors in the securities of JWP, Inc., a company that went belly up, resulting in nearly a 100 percent loss of their investments. Ernst & Young served as auditor for JWP from 1985 to 1992. During most of that period, JWP was in a period of rapid expansion that was financed by private placements of debt securities, and it became increasingly leveraged. By 1991, it was losing an average of $10 million per month. Ernst & Young knew of "accounting irregularities" from at least 1988 through 1991 but did not insist on their correction. Ernst & Young issued unqualified financial opinions for all of those years. One of the irregularities was recording anticipated future tax benefits of net operating loss in violation of GAAP. AUSA and its fellow investors sued Ernst & Young for their losses. The federal district court dismissed the case and AUSA appealed. Should AUSA be able to recover? Explain your answer. [*AUSA Life Insurance Co. v. Ernst & Young*, 206 F.3d 202 (2d Cir. 2000), 119 F. Supp. 2d 394 (S.D.N.Y. 2000), aff'd in unpublished opinion]

6. For almost 13 years, Touche Ross had prepared the annual audit of Buttes Gas and Oil Co. Buttes wanted to obtain a loan from Dimensional Credit Corp. (DCC) and showed DCC its most recent annual audit. DCC made the loan on the basis of what it learned from the audit. The loan was not repaid, and DCC then realized that it had been misled by negligent statements about Buttes's financial condition that appeared in the annual statement prepared by Touche Ross. Would DCC be able to recover against Touche Ross for its negligence in preparing this report?

7. Henry Hatfield, CPA, was hired to prepare audited financial statements for Happy Campers, a nonprofit organization providing summer camp scholarships for inner-city, low-income children. The executive director of Happy Campers was embezzling but falsified records that Hatfield used in his audit. First Bank gave Happy Campers a $100,000 loan based on Hatfield's certified financials. The embezzlement was discovered, and Happy Campers defaulted on the loan. Can First Bank recover its loss from Hatfield?

8. What is the difference between the standards for auditor liability in a civil action by investors against the auditor versus auditor liability for violation of securities laws?

9. Hicks, the president and manager of Intermountain Merchandising, wanted to sell the business to Montana Merchandising, Inc. To provide a basis for the transaction, he retained Bloomgren, an accountant, to conduct an audit of Intermountain. Bloomgren knew that Montana would use the audit report in making the purchase of the business from Intermountain. Bloomgren's audit report showed the Intermountain business as

profitable. Thayer, Montana's president, relied on this report in agreeing to purchase the business of Intermountain and in agreeing to the terms of the purchase. Sometime later, it was discovered that the accountant had made a number of mistakes and that the business that was sold was actually insolvent. Thayer and Montana Merchandising sued Hicks and Bloomgren for damages. The suit claimed that the accountant had negligently misrepresented the facts. The accountant defended on the basis that Thayer was not in privity of contract with him and therefore could not sue him. Was he right? [*Thayer v. Hicks*, 793 P.2d 784 (Mont.)]

10. Audit firm Grant Thornton had prepared financial reports for use by the board of directors of First National Bank of Keystone (Keystone) in response to an investigation by the Office of the Comptroller of the Currency (OCC) that raised questions about the value of Keystone's loan portfolio. Stan Quay, a partner at Grant Thornton, was in charge of the 1998 audit. On March 24, 1999, Quay presented several members and prospective members of Keystone's board and Keystone's shareholders with draft copies of Keystone's 1998 financial statements and told them that Keystone was going to get an unqualified or "clean" audit opinion on its 1998 financial statements.

    In April 1999, and despite the fact that Keystone was in fact insolvent at the end of 1998, Grant Thornton issued a clean audit report for Keystone. The audit report contained the following statement: "This report is intended for the information and use of the Board of Directors and Management of The First National Bank of Keystone and its regulatory agencies and should not be used by third parties for any other purpose."

    Gary Ellis, a president of another bank, was being recruited in early 1999 by the Keystone board to take the president's position at Keystone. Following the Keystone board meeting on March 24, 1999, Ellis met Quay and two other outside directors at a bar at the Fincastle Country Club. Quay spoke with Ellis and the two outside directors because Keystone did not have a chief financial officer, thus making Quay the only person capable of going over the financial statements with the others. At the country club, Quay told Ellis and the two outside directors that Keystone was going to receive a "clean [audit]." Ellis also attended the March 25, 1999, shareholders' meeting at which Quay informed the group that Grant Thornton was going to give Keystone a clean audit opinion for 1998. On March 30, 1999, Ellis visited Keystone. During this visit, Quay told Ellis once again that Keystone would receive a clean audit opinion for 1998.

    Ellis signed a two-year contract at a base salary of $375,000 plus benefits, including the use of a corporate vehicle and a country club membership. He also purchased $49,500 in Keystone stock. By September 1999, Keystone Bank was closed. Ellis filed suit against Grant Thornton. The district court ruled in favor of Ellis on his negligent misrepresentation claim and found that he was entitled to $2,419,233 in damages. Grant Thornton appealed. Is this verdict correct? Explain why or why not Grant Thornton is liable for the loss of the job. [*Ellis v. Grant Thornton LLP*, 530 F.3d 280 (4th Cir. 2008)]

11. Equisure, Inc., was required to file audited financial statements when it applied for a listing on the American Stock Exchange (AMEX). Stirtz, Equisure's auditor, issued a favorable audit opinion used for the AMEX application. Stirtz also issued "clean" opinions on Equisure's required SEC filings, such as its 10k.

    Noram, a securities broker, loaned $900,000 in margin credit to purchasers of Equisure's stock based on the firm's audited financials. AMEX stopped trading on Equisure's stock because of allegations of insider trading and stock manipulation, and Noram was left without collateral for $2.5 million in loans. Stirtz resigned as Equisure's auditor, and Noram filed suit against Stirtz. The trial court granted Stirtz summary judgment. Noram appealed. Who is liable here? Was the court's decision correct? [*Noram Investment Services, Inc. v. Stirtz Bernards Boyden*, 611 N.W.2d 372 (Minn. App.)]

CPA QUESTIONS

1. In general, the third-party (primary) beneficiary rule as applied to a CPA's legal liability in conducting an audit is relevant to which of the following causes of action against a CPA?

	Fraud	*Constructive Fraud*	*Negligence*
a.	Yes	Yes	No
b.	Yes	No	No
c.	No	Yes	Yes
d.	No	No	Yes

2. Beckler & Associates, CPAs, audited and gave an unqualified opinion on the financial statements of Queen Co. The financial statements contained misstatements that resulted in a material overstatement of Queen's net worth. Queen provided the audited financial statements to Mac Bank in connection with a loan made by Mac to Queen. Beckler knew that the financial statements would be provided to Mac. Queen defaulted on the loan. Mac sued Beckler to recover for its losses associated with Queen's default. Which of the following must Mac prove in order to recover?
   I. Beckler was negligent in conducting the audit.
   II. Mac relied on the financial statements.
   a. I only
   b. II only
   c. Both I and II
   d. Neither I nor II

3. In a common law action against an accountant, lack of privity is a viable defense if the plaintiff:
   a. Is the client's creditor who sues the accountant for negligence.
   b. Can prove the presence of gross negligence that amounts to a reckless disregard for the truth.
   c. Is the accountant's client.
   d. Bases the action upon fraud.

4. Cable Corp. orally engaged Drake & Co., CPAs, to audit its financial statements. Cable's management informed Drake that it suspected the accounts receivable were materially overstated. Though the financial statements Drake audited included a materially overstated accounts receivable balance, Drake issued an unqualified opinion. Cable used the financial statements to obtain a loan to expand its operations. Cable defaulted on the loan and incurred a substantial loss.

   If Cable sues Drake for negligence in failing to discover the overstatement, Drake's best defense would be that Drake did *not*
   a. Have privity of contract with Cable.
   b. Sign an engagement letter.
   c. Perform the audit recklessly or with an intent to deceive.
   d. Violate generally accepted auditing standards in performing the audit.

5. Which of the following services is a CPA generally required to perform when conducting a personal financial planning engagement?
   a. Assisting the client to identify tasks that are essential in order to take action on planning decisions.
   b. Assisting the client to take action on planning decisions.
   c. Monitoring progress in achieving goals.
   d. Updating recommendations and revising planning decisions.

6. Which of the following statements is (are) correct regarding the common law elements that must be proven to support a finding of constructive fraud against a CPA misrepresentation?
   I. The plaintiff has justifiably relied on the CPA's misrepresentation.
   II. The CPA has acted in a grossly negligent manner.
   a. I only
   b. II only
   c. Both I and II
   d. Neither I nor II

CHAPTER 48

© Manuel Gutjahr/iStockphoto.com

Management of Corporations

learningoutcomes

After studying this chapter, you should be able to

LO.1 Explain how shareholders, as owners of the corporation, exercise limited control over management by voting at shareholders' meetings to elect directors

LO.2 Explain the qualifications and powers of directors

LO.3 Explain the liability of directors and the meaning of the business judgment rule (BJR)

LO.4 Explain the obligation of officers—who have access to corporate information and agency powers—to not violate their fiduciary duties to the corporation

LO.5 Explain the rationale for the "say-on-pay" provision of the Dodd-Frank Act

LO.6 Explain how directors, officers, and the corporation itself may be criminally liable for regulatory offenses

A corporation is managed, directly or indirectly, by its shareholders, board of directors, and officers.

A. Shareholders

As owners, the shareholders have the right to control the corporation.

1. Extent of Management Control by Shareholders

As a practical matter, control of the shareholders is generally limited to voting at shareholders' meetings to elect directors. In this sense, shareholders indirectly determine the management policies of the business. At shareholders' meetings, they may also vote to amend bylaws, approve shareholder resolutions, or vote on so-called extraordinary corporate matters. *Extraordinary matters* include the sale of corporate assets outside the regular course of the corporation's business or the merger or dissolution of the corporation.

2. Meetings of Shareholders

To have legal effect, action by the shareholders must ordinarily be taken at a regular or special meeting.

(a) Regular Meetings. The time and place of regular or stated meetings are usually prescribed by the articles of incorporation or the bylaws. Notice to shareholders of such meetings is ordinarily not required, but it is usually given as a matter of good business practice. Some statutes require that notice of all meetings be given.

(b) Special Meetings. Generally, notice must be given specifying the subject matter of special meetings. Unless otherwise prescribed, special meetings are called by the directors. It is sometimes provided that a special meeting may be called by a certain percentage of shareholders.[1] Notice of the day, hour, and place of a special meeting must be given to all shareholders. The notice must include a statement of the nature of the business to be transacted, and no other business may be transacted at this meeting.

(c) Quorum. A valid meeting requires the presence of a quorum of the voting shareholders. A **quorum** is the minimum number of persons (shareholders or persons authorized to vote a stated proportion of the voting stock) required to transact business. If a quorum is present, a majority of those present may act on any matter unless there is an express requirement of a higher affirmative vote.

When a meeting opens with a quorum, the quorum is generally not broken if shareholders leave the meeting and those remaining are not sufficient to constitute a quorum.

3. Action without Meeting

A number of statutes provide for corporate action by shareholders without holding a meeting. The Revised Model Business Corporation Act (RMBCA) provides that "action required or permitted by this Act to be taken at a shareholders' meeting may be taken without a meeting if the action is taken by all shareholders entitled to vote on the action."[2] The action must be evidenced by a written consent describing the action taken, signed by all shareholders entitled to vote on the action, and delivered to the corporation for inclusion in the minutes.

B. Directors

The board of directors has oversight responsibility for a company's business affairs, including (1) approving strategic plans, (2) reviewing operating and financial results, (3) approving SEC filings, (4) approving the hiring of executives, (5) evaluating management's performance and approving executive compensation packages, (6) appointing and meeting with auditors, and (7) evaluating and acting on extraordinary matters, such as the merger, acquisition, or sale of the business.

Most states now permit the number of directors to be fixed by the bylaws. Many specify that the board of directors shall consist of not less than three directors; a few authorize one or more.[3] Professional corporation legislation often authorizes or is interpreted as authorizing a one- or two-person board of directors.

[1] N.Y. Bus.Corp. Law §603.
[2] RMBCA §7.04(a).
[3] Del. Code §141(b). See also RMBCA §8.03.

4. Qualifications

Eligibility for membership on a board of directors is determined by statute, articles of incorporation, or bylaws.[4] In the absence of a contrary provision, any person (including a nonresident, a minor, or a person who is not a shareholder) is eligible for membership. Bylaws may require that a director own stock in the corporation although this requirement is not ordinarily imposed.

CPA 5. Powers of Directors

The board of directors has authority to manage the corporation. Courts will not interfere with the board's discretion in the absence of (1) illegal conduct or (2) fraud harming the rights of creditors, shareholders, or the corporation.

The board of directors may enter into any contract or transaction necessary to carry out the business for which the corporation was formed. The board may appoint officers and other agents to act for the company, or it may appoint several of its own members as an executive committee to act for the board between board meetings. (See Figure 48-1.) Broad delegation of authority, however, may involve the risk of being treated as an unlawful abdication of the board's management power.

CPA 6. Conflict of Interest

A director is disqualified from taking part in corporate action involving a matter in which the director has an undisclosed conflicting interest. Because it cannot be known how the other directors would have acted if they had known of the conflict of interest, the corporation generally may avoid any transaction because of a director's secret disqualification.

A number of states provide by statute that a director's conflict of interest does not impair the transaction or contract entered into or authorized by the board of directors if the disqualified director disclosed the interest and if the contract or transaction

FIGURE 48-1 Powers of Directors

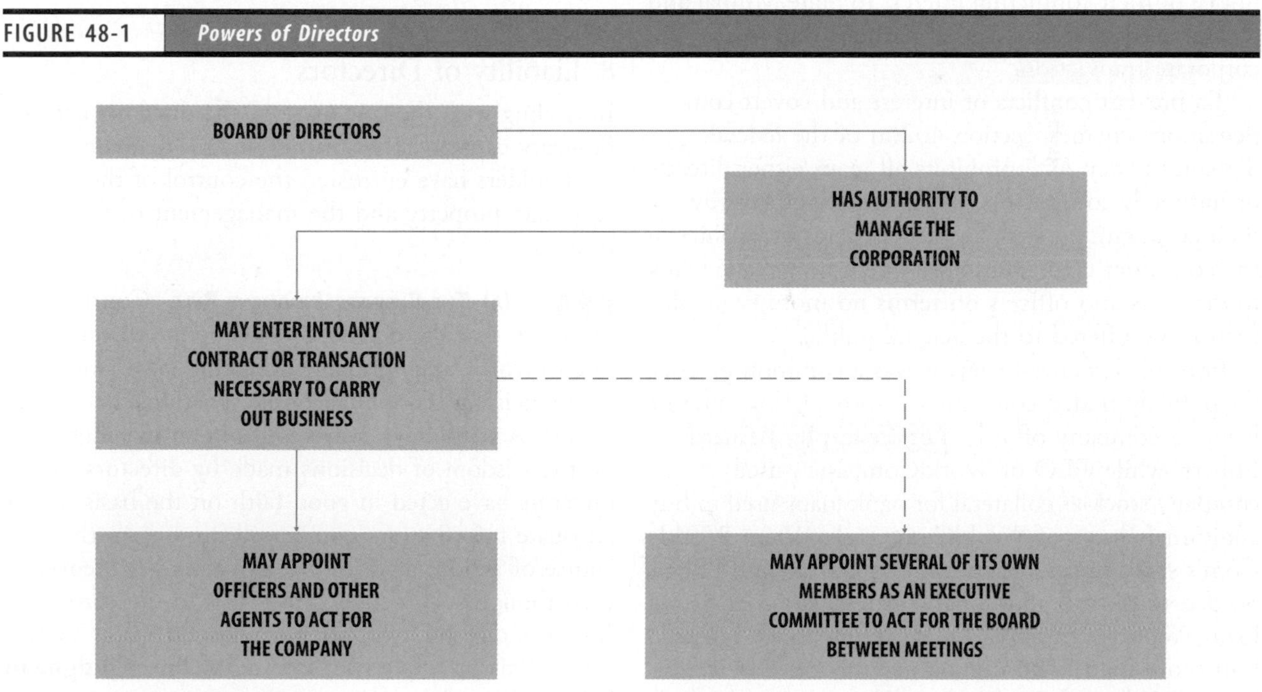

[4] In family-owned businesses, shareholder agreements are often utilized to impose restrictions on the voting of shares and eligibility standards for membership on the board of directors to maintain continuity of management, ownership, and control of a corporation. See *Miniat v. EMI*, 315 F.3d 712 (7th Cir. 2002).

is fair and reasonable with respect to the corporation. Thus, a director may lend money to a corporation if the board of directors is informed of the transaction and the terms approximate the market rate for businesses with similar credit ratings. Some states simply require notice of the conflicting interests and abstaining from all participation in the transaction. **For Example,** Delos Yancey, Jr., and Delos Yancey III were directors of State Mutual Insurance Co. Subsequently, they formed North American Services, Inc., and served as directors of both companies. State Mutual decided to sell one of its companies, Atlas Life Insurance, Inc. North American expressed an interest in purchasing Atlas, and thereafter the Yanceys recused themselves from State Mutual's decision-making process in selling the company. State Mutual sold Atlas to North American at a $5.2 million loss. Some two years later, North American resold Atlas for a $22.6 million gain, and a shareholder derivative suit was brought against the Yanceys. The court decided the case in favor of the Yanceys, holding that they complied with the state's "safe harbor" law by giving notice of their conflicting interest to State Mutual and thereafter abstaining from all participation in the corporate transaction.[5]

To prevent conflicts of interest and covert compensation schemes, section 402(a) of the federal Sarbanes-Oxley Act[6] prohibits all loans either directly or indirectly to directors and executive officers by their corporations, with an exception for companies in the consumer credit business, which may make loans to directors and officers on terms no more favorable than those offered to the general public.

Prior to Sarbanes-Oxley, it was a common practice for publicly traded companies to provide low-interest loans to company officers. **For Example,** Bernard Ebbers, while CEO of WorldCom, Inc., used company stock as collateral for bank loans used to buy additional shares of WorldCom stock. When WorldCom's share prices weakened in late 2000 and Ebbers needed to put up additional collateral to cover his loans, WorldCom's board of directors decided to lend him more than $400 million at just over 2 percent interest with no fixed due date. The company rate was far below the personal loan rate at banks near company headquarters of between 9.75 percent and 16.67 percent, and well below margin loan rates at 5 percent. Business conglomerate Tyco International Ltd. maintained a "key employee loan fund" that was used like a revolving line of credit by Tyco executives Dennis Kozlowski and Martin Swartz to fund their lavish lifestyles. The language of Sarbanes-Oxley is broad and far reaching and prohibits all direct personal loans by public companies, such as relocation loans, tax loans, and loans to purchase securities.

7. Meetings of Directors

Action by directors is ordinarily taken at a meeting of the board of directors. Bylaws sometimes require the meeting to be held at a particular place. Generally, a director is not allowed to vote by proxy.

Most states permit action to be taken by the board of directors without holding an actual meeting. It is required when such action is taken that it be set forth in writing and signed by all directors.

8. Liability of Directors

In dealing with the corporation, the directors act in a fiduciary capacity. It is into their care that the stockholders have entrusted the control of the corporate property and the management of the business.

CPA **(A) THE BUSINESS JUDGMENT RULE.** Courts recognize that the decisions of corporate directors often involve weighing and balancing legal, ethical, commercial, promotional, public relations, and other factors. Accordingly, courts will not sit in judgment on the wisdom of decisions made by directors. If the directors have acted in good faith on the basis of adequate information, courts will not enjoin the course of action taken by the directors.[7] Moreover, even though such action causes loss to the corporation, the directors will not be held personally liable for it. This principle is called the **business judgment rule (BJR)**.

[5] *Fisher v. State Mutual Insurance Co.*, 290 F.3d 1256 (11th Cir. 2002).

[6] P.L. 107-204, 116 Stat. 745.

[7] In discharging their duties, directors are not individually liable if, acting in good faith, they rely upon "the opinion of counsel for the corporation" or "written reports setting forth financial data concerning the corporation and prepared by an independent public accountant or certified public accountant or firm of such accountants"—which opinions or statements turn out to be flawed. *Casey v. Brennan*, 344 N.J. Super.83 (2002).

CPA ***(1) The Traditional Rule.***
Courts apply the business judgment rule as a presumption that in making a business decision, the directors acted (1) on an informed basis, (2) in good faith, and (3) in the honest belief that the action taken was in the best interest of the corporation. The party challenging the directors' actions has the burden of proving that they did not act on an informed basis or in good faith or in the best interest of the corporation.[8]

The *Disney* case illustrates an application of the business judgment rule.

In re Walt Disney Co. Derivitive Litigation, 907 A.2d 693 (Del. Ch. 2005)

Problem: "A Mismatch of Cultures and Styles"
Solution: $140 Million Severance Payment
Shareholders: Not Happy!

Michael Ovitz was a founder of Creative Artists Agency (CAA), an agency in 1995 with 1,400 of Hollywood's top actors, directors, writers, and musicians. Ovitz was considered one of the most powerful figures in Hollywood at that time. Because of the untimely death of Disney's prior president in a helicopter crash, Disney CEO Michael Eisner focused on hiring Ovitz as president. The chairman of Disney's compensation committee, Irwin Russell, in consultation with Eisner, negotiated the Ovitz employment agreement (OEA). As part of the OEA, if Disney fired Ovitz for any reason other than gross negligence or malfeasance, Ovitz would be entitled to a nonfault termination (NFT) package consisting of his remaining salary for the five-year period, bonuses, and the immediate vesting of stock options. Russell met with a compensation expert for advice on the contract, and had telephone conversations with two compensation committee members, Sidney Poitier and Ignatio Lozano. CEO Eisner telephoned each member of the board of directors to inform them of his plan to hire Ovitz. On September 26, 1995, the compensation committee had a one-hour meeting to discuss several topics, including the Ovitz employment contract. Thereafter, the full board of directors met and elected Ovitz president of Disney. After he joined Disney, it soon became apparent that a "mismatch of cultures and styles" ensued and that Ovitz was not succeeding as president. The trial court gave an example as follows:

> *In January 1996, a corporate retreat was held at Walt Disney World in Orlando, Florida. At that retreat, Ovitz failed to integrate himself in the group of executives by declining to participate in group activities, insisting on a limousine, when the other executives, including Eisner, were taking a bus, and making inappropriate demands of the park employees. In short, Ovitz "was a little elitist for the egalitarian Walt Disney World cast members [employees]," and a poor fit with his fellow executives.*

When it became clear that Ovitz was not working out, Eisner considered his options. Sanford Litvak, Disney's general counsel, advised Eisner and other directors that Ovitz had not been shown to have been grossly negligent or malfeasant in his year at Disney, and no cause existed to avoid the NFT payments. Eisner decided it was necessary to terminate Ovitz on a nonfault basis, and notified the board members. The board members supported this decision under the nonfault termination agreement. Ovitz was ultimately paid $140 million in severance pay. Stockholders brought a derivative suit, asserting that Eisner and the board of directors had breached their fiduciary duties in connection with the hiring and termination of Ovitz. Years of litigation cumulated in a 37-day trial that ended on January 19, 2005.

JUDICIAL OPINION

CHANDLER, Ch.…Unlike ideals of corporate governance, a fiduciary's duties do not change over time. How we understand those duties may evolve and become refined, but the duties themselves have not changed, except to the extent that fulfilling a fiduciary duty requires obedience to other positive law. This Court strongly encourages directors and officers to employ best practices, as those practices are understood at the time a corporate decision is taken. But Delaware law does not—indeed, the common law cannot—hold fiduciaries liable for a failure to comply with the aspirational ideal of best practices, any more than a common-law court deciding a medical malpractice dispute can impose a standard of liability based on ideal—rather than competent or standard—medical treatment practices, lest the average medical practitioner be found inevitably derelict.…

…Because this matter, by its very nature, has become something of a public spectacle—commencing as it did with the spectacular hiring of one of the entertainment industry's best-known personalities to help run one of its iconic businesses, and ending with a spectacular failure of that union, with breathtaking amounts of severance pay the consequence—it is, I think, worth noting what the role of this Court must be in evaluating decision-makers' performance with respect to decisions gone awry, spectacularly or otherwise. It is easy, of course, to fault a decision that ends in a failure,

[8] *Huang Group v. LTI*, 760 N.E.2d 14 (Ohio App. 2002).

Continued

once hindsight makes the result of that decision plain to see. But the essence of business is risk—the application of informed belief to contingencies whose outcomes can sometimes be predicted, but never known. The decision makers entrusted by shareholders must act out of loyalty to those shareholders. They must in good faith act to make informed decisions on behalf of the shareholders, untainted by self-interest. Where they fail to do so, this Court stands ready to remedy breaches of fiduciary duty.

Even where decision makers act as faithful servants, however, their ability and the wisdom of their judgments will vary. The redress for failures that arise from faithful management must come from the markets, through the action of shareholders and the free flow of capital, and not from this Court. Should the Court apportion liability based on the ultimate outcome of decisions taken in good faith by faithful directors or officers, those decision makers would necessarily take decisions that minimize risk, not maximize value. The entire advantage of the risk-taking, innovative, wealth-creating engine that is the Delaware corporation would cease to exist, with disastrous results for shareholders and society alike. That is why, under our corporate law, corporate decision makers are held strictly to their fiduciary duties, but within the boundaries of those duties are free to act as their judgment and abilities dictate, free of *post hoc* penalties from a reviewing court using perfect hindsight. Corporate decisions are made, risks are taken, the results become apparent, capital flows accordingly, and shareholder value is increased....

THE BUSINESS JUDGMENT RULE...

Delaware law is clear that the business and affairs of a corporation are managed by or under the direction of its board of directors. The business judgment rule serves to protect and promote the role of the board as the ultimate manager of the corporation. Because courts are ill equipped to engage in *post hoc* substantive review of business decisions, the business judgment rule "operates to preclude a court from imposing itself unreasonably on the business and affairs of a corporation."

The business judgment rule is not actually a substantive rule of law, but instead it is a presumption that "in making a business decision the directors of a corporation acted on an informed basis,...and in the honest belief that the action taken was in the best interests of the company [and its shareholders]." This presumption applies when there is no evidence of "fraud, bad faith, or self-dealing in the usual sense of personal profit or betterment" on the part of the directors. In the absence of this evidence, the board's decision will be upheld unless it cannot be "attributed to any rational business purpose."...

Upon long and careful consideration, I am of the opinion that the concept of *intentional dereliction of duty,* a *conscious disregard for one's responsibilities,* is an appropriate (although not the only) standard for determining whether fiduciaries have acted in good faith. Deliberate indifference and inaction *in the face of a duty to act* is, in my mind, conduct that is clearly disloyal to the corporation. It is the epitome of faithless conduct....

....[P]laintiffs must prove by a preponderance of the evidence that the presumption of the business judgment rule does not apply either because the directors breached their fiduciary duties, acted in bad faith or that the directors made an "unintelligent or unadvised judgment," by failing to inform themselves of all material information reasonably available to them before making a business decision.

If plaintiffs cannot rebut the presumption of the business judgment rule, the defendants will prevail....

By virtue of his Machiavellian (and imperial) nature as CEO, and his control over Ovitz's hiring in particular, Eisner to a large extent is responsible for the failings in process that infected and handicapped the board's decisionmaking abilities. Eisner stacked his (and I intentionally write "his" as opposed to "the Company's") board of directors with friends and other acquaintances who, though not necessarily beholden to him in a legal sense, were certainly more willing to accede to his wishes and support him unconditionally than truly independent directors. On the other hand, I do not believe that the evidence, considered fairly, demonstrates that Eisner actively took steps to defeat or short-circuit a decision-making process that would otherwise have occurred....

...[T]he decision to hire Ovitz and enter into the OEA is one of business judgment, to which the presumptions of the business judgment rule apply. In order to prevail, therefore, plaintiffs must demonstrate by a preponderance of the evidence that Eisner was either grossly negligent or acted in bad faith in connection with Ovitz's hiring and the approval of the OEA.

As I mentioned earlier, Eisner was very much aware of what was going on as the situation developed. In the limited instances where he was not the primary source of information relating to Ovitz, Russell kept Eisner informed of negotiations with Ovitz. Eisner knew Ovitz; he was familiar with the career Ovitz had built at CAA and he knew that the Company was in need of a senior executive....In light of this knowledge, I cannot find that plaintiffs have demonstrated by a preponderance of the evidence that Eisner failed to inform himself of all material information reasonably available or that he acted in a grossly negligent manner.

Notwithstanding the foregoing, Eisner's actions in connection with Ovitz's hiring should not serve as a model for fellow executives and fiduciaries to follow. His lapses were many. He failed to keep the board as informed as he should have. He stretched the outer boundaries of his authority as CEO by acting without specific board direction or involvement. He prematurely issued a press release that placed significant pressure on the board to accept Ovitz and approve his compensation package in accordance with the press release. To my mind, these actions fall far short of what shareholders expect

Continued

and demand from those entrusted with a fiduciary position. Eisner's failure to better involve the board in the process of Ovitz's hiring, usurping that role for himself, although not in violation of law, does not comport with how fiduciaries of Delaware corporations are expected to act.

Despite all of the legitimate criticisms that may be leveled at Eisner, especially at having enthroned himself as the omnipotent and infallible *monarch* of his *personal Magic Kingdom*, I nonetheless conclude, after carefully considering and weighing all the evidence, that Eisner's actions were taken in good faith. That is, Eisner's actions were taken with the subjective belief that those actions were in the best interests of the Company—he believed that his taking charge and acting swiftly and decisively to hire Ovitz would serve the best interests of the Company notwithstanding the high cost of Ovitz's hiring and notwithstanding that two experienced executives who had arguably been passed over for the position (Litvack and Bollenbach) were not completely supportive. Those actions do not represent a knowing violation of law or evidence a conscious and intentional disregard of duty. In conclusion, Eisner acted in good faith and did not breach his fiduciary duty of care because he was not grossly negligent.

[*Authors' Note:* The court found that CEO Eisner acted in accordance with his fiduciary duties and in good faith when he terminated Ovitz. It determined that the chairman of the Compensation Committee and the general counsel acted in good faith in the respective hiring and termination of Ovitz, and that no director had breached a fiduciary duty.]

QUESTIONS

1. Explain the business judgment rule.
2. Did the court approve of CEO Eisner's management practices?
3. When it becomes evident to shareholders that the directors approved the hiring of a president who turned out to be a spectacular failure with the consequence being the payment of a breathtaking amount of severance pay to the failed president, should the directors not be held liable under corporate law for such an error in judgment?

CPA *(2) Application in Corporate Control Transactions.*

When a corporation receives a takeover bid, the target board of directors may tend to take actions that are in their own interest and not in the interest of the shareholders. Courts have recognized the potential for director self-interest in this situation.

In *Smith v. Van Gorkom*, the directors relied on the business judgment rule to shield themselves from individual liability in a lawsuit charging that the directors did not act on an "informed basis" in accepting and recommending a merger.

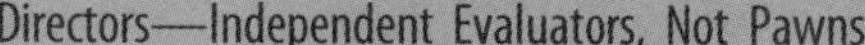

Smith v. Van Gorkom, 488 A.2d 858 (Del. 1985)

Directors—Independent Evaluators, Not Pawns

On September 13, 1980, Jerome Van Gorkom, as chairman and chief executive officer of Trans Union, Inc., a holding company in the railcar leasing business, arranged a meeting with Jay Pritzker, a well-known takeover specialist and social acquaintance, to determine his interest in acquiring Trans Union. On Thursday, September 18, Pritzker made an offer of $55 per share (a price suggested by Van Gorkom), with a decision to be made by the board no later than Sunday, September 21. On Friday, Van Gorkom called a special meeting of the board of directors for noon the following day; no agenda was announced. At the directors' meeting, Van Gorkom made a 20-minute oral analysis of the merger transaction, showed that the company was having difficulty generating sufficient income, and discussed his meeting with Pritzker and the reasons for the meeting. Copies of the proposed merger agreement were delivered too late to be studied before or during the meeting. No consultants or investment advisers were called upon to support the merger price of $55 per share. The merger was approved at the end of the two-hour meeting. Certain shareholders brought a class-action suit against the directors, contending that the board's decision was not the product of informed business judgment. The directors replied that their good-faith decision was shielded by the business judgment rule. From a decision for the directors, the shareholders appealed.

JUDICIAL OPINION

HORSEY, J.... Under Delaware law, the business judgment rule is the offspring of the fundamental principle, codified in 8 *Del. C.* § 141(a), that the business and affairs of a Delaware corporation are managed by or under its board of directors. In carrying out their managerial roles, directors are charged with

Continued

an unyielding fiduciary duty to the corporation and its shareholders. The business judgment rule exists to protect and promote the full and free exercise of the managerial power granted to Delaware directors. The rule itself "is a presumption that in making a business decision, the directors of a corporation acted on an informed basis, in good faith and in the honest belief that the action taken was in the best interests of the company." [*Aronson v Lewis,* Del. Supr., 473 A2d 805, 812]. Thus, the party attacking a board decision as uninformed must rebut the presumption that its business judgment was an informed one.

The determination of whether a business judgment is an informed one turns on whether the directors have informed themselves "prior to making a business decision, of all material information reasonably available to them."…

A director's duty to exercise an informed business judgment is in the nature of a duty of care, as distinguished from a duty of loyalty.…

The standard of care applicable to a director's duty of care has also been recently restated by this Court. In *Aronson, supra,* we stated:

> *While the Delaware cases use a variety of terms to describe the applicable standard of care, our analysis satisfies us that under the business judgment rule director liability is predicated upon concepts of gross negligence.*

473 A2d at 812.

We again confirm that view. We think the concept of gross negligence is also the proper standard for determining whether a business judgment reached by a board of directors was an informed one.

In the specific context of a proposed merger of domestic corporations, a director has a duty under 8 *Del. C.* 251(b), along with his fellow directors, to act in an informed and deliberate manner in determining whether to approve an agreement of merger before submitting the proposal to the stockholders. Certainly in the merger context, a director may not abdicate that duty by leaving to the shareholders alone the decision to approve or disapprove the agreement.…

It is against those standards that the conduct of the directors of Trans Union must be tested…regarding their exercise of an informed business judgment in voting to approve the Pritzker merger proposal.

…The issue of whether the directors reached an informed decision to "sell" the Company on September 20, 1980, must be determined only upon the basis of the information then reasonably available to the directors and relevant to their decision to accept the Pritzker merger proposal.…

On the record before us, we must conclude that the Board of Directors did not reach an informed business judgment on September 20, 1980, in voting to "sell" the Company for $55 per share pursuant to the Pritzker cash-out merger proposal. Our reasons, in summary, are as follows:

The directors (1) did not adequately inform themselves as to Van Gorkom's role in forcing the "sale" of the Company and in establishing the per share purchase price; (2) were uninformed as to the intrinsic value of the Company; and (3) given these circumstances, at a minimum, were grossly negligent in approving the "sale" of the Company upon two hours' consideration, without prior notice, and without the exigency of a crisis or emergency.

As has been noted, the Board based its September 20 decision to approve the cash-out merger primarily on Van Gorkom's representations. None of the directors, other than Van Gorkom and Chelberg, had any prior knowledge that the purpose of the meeting was to propose a cash-out merger of Trans Union. No members of Senior Management were present, other than Chelberg, Romans and Peterson; and the latter two had only learned of the proposed sale an hour earlier. Both general counsel Moore and former general counsel Browder attended the meeting, but were equally uninformed as to the purpose of the meeting and the documents to be acted upon.

Without any documents before them concerning the proposed transaction, the members of the Board were required to rely entirely upon Van Gorkom's 20-minute oral presentation of the proposal. No written summary of the terms of the merger was presented; the directors were given no documentation to support the adequacy of $55 price per share for sale of the Company; and the Board had before it nothing more than Van Gorkom's statement of his understanding of the substance of an agreement which he admittedly had never read, nor which any member of the Board had ever seen.…

We hold, therefore, that the Trial Court committed reversible error in applying the business judgment rule in favor of the director defendants in this case.

On remand, the Court of Chancery shall conduct an evidentiary hearing to determine the fair value of the shares represented by the plaintiffs' class, based on the intrinsic value of Trans Union on September 20, 1980.…Thereafter, an award of damages may be entered to the extent that the fair value of Trans Union exceeds $55 per share.

[Judgment reversed and action remanded]

QUESTIONS

1. Did the court hold that the business judgment rule shielded the directors from personal liability in this case?
2. Upon what facts did the court rely in reaching its decision in this case?
3. State the applicable standard of care for determining whether a board of directors' decision was an informed one.

(3) Protection of Directors.

In the wake of court decisions holding directors personally liable for damages for gross negligence and in the wake of the resulting general reluctance of individuals to serve as directors, states have passed statutes to protect directors. The aim of the various state laws is essentially the same: to reduce the risk of personal liability for directors who act in good faith when their decisions are challenged. The laws permit a corporation, by a stockholder-approved amendment to its charter or certificate of incorporation, to protect its directors from monetary liability for duty-of-care violations (gross negligence) provided they have not acted in bad faith, breached their duty of loyalty, or gained an improper personal benefit.[9] The laws provide for indemnification and advancement of expenses. **For Example,** the certificate of incorporation of Jennifer Convertibles, Inc., a Delaware

Thinking Things Through

Are the Days of the Imperial CEO Over?

Many changes clarifying the role of corporate directors have occurred since the Enron and WorldCom debacles came to light in 2001. The Sarbanes-Oxley Act and its legal reforms followed. The financial crisis of 2008–2009 resulted in the Dodd-Frank Act and its legal reforms. The American Bar Association Committee on Corporate Laws published its *Corporate Director's Guidebook, Sixth Edition,* in 2012, which emphasizes themes arising out of these crises important to all directors. For example, consider this outline of a corporation's "risks" regarding its legal and regulatory compliance profile:

> The board should ensure that employees of the corporation are informed and periodically reminded of corporate policies, including those pertaining to compliance with
>
> (i) codes of business conduct and ethics;
> (ii) anti-discrimination and employment laws;
> (iii) environmental and health and safety laws;
> (iv) anti-bribery laws;
> (v) anti-trust and competition laws;
> (vi) securities laws, particularly those addressing insider trading; and
> (vii) laws and regulations of other countries as applicable.
>
> The major securities markets require their listed companies to adopt codes of business conduct and ethics applicable to all employees, officers, and directors. The corporation should have appropriate controls throughout the organization for monitoring compliance with such laws and codes. Controls may include whistleblower and hotline policies. The corporation also must establish procedures for addressing violations.*

Michael Eisner, considered by many as the Imperial CEO, stacked the board with his friends and expected and received loyalty from them regarding all-important corporate decisions. Is it critical for a board's nominating/corporate governance committee to receive nomination from not only other directors but also institutional investors and other shareholders rather than just the CEO—as was the case at Disney with CEO Eisner?

The chairman of Disney's Compensation Committee hired a highly regarded consultant regarding Ovitz's employment contract and telephoned two members of the committee to inform them of progress. A vote was taken on September 26, after less than an hour of discussion by the committee, and, thereafter, Ovitz was elected president. As a best practice, should the entire compensation committee have been kept in the loop on this significant matter during negotiations by e-mail, executive summaries, and backup documentation? Should the Disney board have been given meaningful documentation on the appointment to study a week before the board meeting? Do you think it would have been good form for a Disney director back then to question "Mr." Eisner regarding the Ovitz appointment: "I don't think we are ready to vote ... give us some more supporting documents"? Do you believe that members of a board of directors today feel entitled to have adequate and timely information and to ask, with civility, the tough questions? Has the private governance of a public corporation like Disney with CEO Eisner been supplanted in part by a layer of government governance of public corporations guided by Sarbanes-Oxley and Dodd-Frank regulations to protect public interests along with the very vital corporate interests?**

*Corporate Director's Guidebook, 7th ed. (ABA April 2012) p. 36, www.abanet.org/abastore.

**See Hillary A. Sale, "The New 'Public' Corporation," 74 *Law and Contemporary Problems* 137 (Winter 2011).

[9] See Del. Code §102(b)(7); N.Y. Bus. Corp. Law §§721–723; Ohio Gen. Corp. Law §1701.59; Ind. Bus. Corp. Law, ch. 35,§1(e); Mo. Gen. Bus. Corp. Law 351.355 §§2, 7.

corporation, includes an exculpatory clause, pursuant to section 102(b)(7) of Delaware's General Corporate Law. The clause protects directors from liability for breach of fiduciary duty except in cases of breach of duty of loyalty, bad faith, knowing violation of the law, or improper personal benefit, as is appropriate under Delaware law.[10]

For Example, to avoid supervision by the Office of Thrift Supervision (OTS), the directors of Oak Tree Savings Bank, a subsidiary of Landmark Land Company, Inc., which had loaned subsidiary land development companies $986 million, placed the bank in bankruptcy. Because of this, director Bernard Ille resigned. In civil proceedings brought against all of the bank directors, Ille successfully defended himself against the OTS charges. He thus would be entitled to mandatory indemnification from the bank. In addition, employees Trapani and Braun, who were subpoenaed and deposed under adversarial circumstances but were not charged, were deemed to have succeeded on the merits in their defense and were entitled to mandatory indemnification for legal expenses under state law. The other directors and employees charged were found not to have acted in good faith and were not entitled to indemnification.[11]

(B) Actions against Directors. Actions against directors should be brought by the corporation. If the corporation fails to act, as is the case when the directors alleged to be liable control the corporation, shareholders may bring the action in a representative capacity for the corporation.[12] **For Example,** Risa Weinberger became concerned that the president and majority shareholder of American Composting Inc., James Willits, was using corporate funds for his own personal benefit. Corporate bank statements showed payments to his ex-wife of $283,068.48, payments to the law firm that represented him in his divorce of $145,789, and a "loans to shareholders" balance that increased from $21,075 in 2004 to $444,642 by September 2011. The court determined that Ms. Weinberger may pursue the shareholder derivative suit on behalf of American Composting Inc. because a demand on the board of directors controlled by Willets would be futile.[13]

(C) Removal of Director. Ordinarily, directors are removed by vote of the shareholders. In some states, the board of directors may remove a director and elect a successor on the ground that the removed director (1) did not accept office, (2) failed to satisfy the qualifications for office, (3) was continually absent from the state without a leave of absence granted by the board, generally for a period of six months or more, (4) was discharged in bankruptcy, (5) was convicted of a felony, (6) was unable to perform the duties of director because of any illness or disability, generally for a period of six months or more, or (7) had been judicially declared of unsound mind.[14]

The RMBCA provides for removal of directors "with or without cause" by a majority vote of the shareholders unless the articles of incorporation provide that directors may be removed only for cause.[15] **For Example,** former Conseco, Inc., director Dennis Murray, Sr., was unsuccessful in his action against the board of directors challenging his removal from the board. The court held that the directors had unlimited authority to remove a fellow director without regard for the reasons why the other directors wished to remove him.[16] Directors may always be voted out of office at a regular meeting of shareholders held for the election of directors.

C. Officers, Agents, and Employees

Corporations generally have a president, at least one vice president, a secretary, a treasurer, and, frequently, a chief executive officer (CEO). The duties of these officers are generally set forth in the corporation's bylaws. The duty of the secretary to keep minutes of the proceedings of shareholders and directors is commonly included. Corporation codes generally expressly permit the same person to be both secretary

[10] *KDW Restructuring & Liquidation Services LLC v. Greenfield*, 2012 WL 2125986 (S.D. N.Y. June 12, 2012). The court found that there was sufficient facts in the complaint against Harley Greenfield, Jennifer's CEO, to support claims for breach of duty of loyalty and breach of the duty to act in good faith regarding a 2009 transaction causing a net loss of $11 million at the end of the 2009 fiscal year.

[11] *In re Landmark Land Co. of California*, 76 F.3d 553 (4th Cir. 1996).

[12] *In re Abbott Laboratories Derivative Shareholder Litigation*, 325 F.3d 795 (7th Cir. 2003).

[13] *Weinberger v. American Composting, Inc.*, 2012 WL 1190970 (E.D. Ark. Apr. 9, 2012).

[14] See California Corp Code §807, recognizing grounds (1), (2), (5), and (7).

[15] RMBCA §8.08(a).

[16] *Murray v. Conseco, Inc.*, 766 N.E.2d 38 (Ind. App. 2002).

and treasurer. In large corporations, there is often a recording secretary and a corresponding secretary.

Sometimes the officers are elected by the shareholders, but usually they are appointed by the board of directors. The RMBCA follows the general pattern of providing for the appointment of officers by the board of directors.[17] Ordinarily, no particular formality is required to make such appointments. Unless prohibited, a director may hold an executive office.

Officers ordinarily hire the employees and agents of the corporation.

9. Powers of Officers

The officers of a corporation are its agents. Consequently, their powers are controlled by the laws of agency.[18] As in the case of any other agency, a third person has the burden of proving that a particular officer had the authority he or she purported to have.

The fact that the officer or employee acting on behalf of the corporation is a major shareholder does not give either any greater agency powers. Moreover, the person dealing with the officer or employee is charged with knowledge of any limitation on authority contained in the recorded corporate charter or articles of incorporation.

When the nature of the transaction is unusual, that unusual nature should alert a third person to the necessity of specific authorization from the corporation.

(A) President. It is sometimes held that, in the absence of some limitation on authority, the president of a corporation has by virtue of that office the authority to act as agent on behalf of the corporation within the scope of the business in which the corporation is empowered to engage. It has also been held, however, that the president has such broad powers only when the president is the general manager of the corporation. In instances in which a corporation has a president and chief executive officer, the CEO has authority to exercise personal judgment and discretion in the administrative and executive functions of the corporation as endowed by its bylaws and the resolutions of the board of directors. When a corporation has both a CEO and a president, the CEO is ordinarily the officer entrusted with the broader decisional powers, whereas the president is the executing officer. The president does not have authority by virtue of that office to make a contract that, because of its unusual character, would require action by the board of directors or shareholders.[19]

The president cannot make a contract to fix long-term or unusual contracts of employment, release a claim of the corporation, promise that the corporation will later repurchase shares issued to a subscriber, or mortgage a corporate property.[20]

It is ordinarily held that the president of a business corporation is not authorized to execute commercial paper in the name of the corporation. However, the president may do so when authorized by the board of directors to borrow money for the corporation.

(B) Other Officers and Employees. The authority of corporate employees and other officers, such as the secretary or treasurer, is generally limited to the duties of their office. However, the authority may be extended by the conduct of the corporation in accordance with the general principles governing apparent authority based on the conduct of the principal. An unauthorized act may, of course, be ratified. The authority of the general manager of the corporation is determined by principles of ordinary agency law.

10. Liability Relating to Fiduciary Duties

The relationship of officers to the corporation, like that of directors, is a fiduciary one. Officers, because of their access to corporate information developed in the pursuit of their daily duties on behalf of the corporation, have an obligation to inform the directors of material information relating to the business. Officers have an obligation not to make any secret financial gain at the expense of the corporation. Because of their level of knowledge of the business, officer-directors have a high fiduciary duty to the corporation.

(A) Corporate Opportunities. If an officer diverts a corporate opportunity, the corporation may recover from the officer the profits of which the corporation has been deprived.

In the *Demoulas* case, the court was faced with multiple issues relating to corporate opportunity.

[17] RMBCA §8.40(a).
[18] *IFC Credit Corp. v. Nuova Pasta Co.*, 815 F. Supp. 268 (N.D. Ill. 1993).
[19] *French v. Chosin Few, Inc.*, 173 F. Supp. 2d 451 (W.D.N.Y. 2001).
[20] *Schmidt v. Farm Credit Services*, 977 F.2d 511 (10th Cir. 1992).

Demoulas v. Demoulas Super Markets, Inc., 677 N.E.2d 159 (Mass. 1997)

Ruling Wisely and Decently?

Demoulas Super Markets, Inc. (DSM), was owned by brothers George and Telemachus Demoulas, each owning an equal number of shares of stock. From 1964 through May 1971, the company grew from 5 stores to a chain of 14 supermarkets, including 2 stores in New Hampshire. George died suddenly on June 27, 1971, and at his death, Telemachus assumed control of DSM under the terms of a voting trust.

Valley Properties, Inc. (Valley), was set up in 1974 to provide real estate for DSM. In 1990, George's son Arthur, age 22 and a shareholder of DSM and Valley, brought shareholder derivative actions on behalf of DSM and Valley, contending that since George's death Telemachus had diverted business opportunities away from DSM into other businesses that were solely owned by Telemachus's branch of the family. The evidence showed that in the 1970s two new corporations were formed and operated supermarkets in New Hampshire; DSM supplied the financing and management, but ownership was held in Telemachus's sister's and daughter's names. By 1986, these stores grew into a single supermarket chain operating under the Market Basket name and entirely owned by members of Telemachus's branch of the family.

The trial court judge determined that Telemachus had diverted these corporate opportunities from DSM, and the court ordered the transfer back to DSM of the assets and liabilities of the new corporations. In her decision, the judge cited lines from *Ulysses,* by Alfred Lord Tennyson, in which Ulysses speaks lovingly of his son Telemachus, expressing the belief that he would rule wisely and decently after his death. Telemachus denied that any acts were improper or gave rise to liability and charged that the judge was not impartial, as evidenced by her quotation from Tennyson's poem. Telemachus appealed.

JUDICIAL OPINION

GREANEY, J.... We reject the various arguments that a new trial is required because the judge was not impartial....

The judge's use of a literary reference from Tennyson's "Ulysses" to begin her findings of fact and rulings of law and the few sharp remarks alluded to by the defendants make no case for bias. The literary reference was the judge's stylistic way of stating the theme of her decision, based on the facts she had found. The trial was long, arduous, and, at times, very bitter. "There might have been, from time to time, a momentary lapse—but, especially in a case as acrimonious as this one proved to be, 'appellate courts must grant the presider some margin of humanity.'"

The j[trial]udge found that DSM and Valley had been injured when "corporate opportunities," namely, potential business ventures that should rightfully have been offered to those corporations, were instead pursued either by the individual defendants or by other companies in which those defendants held ownership interests. The judge found as well that "self-dealing" transactions had occurred in which defendants who had fiduciary duties to DSM and Valley transferred assets from these corporations to other defendant-owned companies, for less than fair value. The requirements that determine the propriety of pursuing corporate opportunities and engaging in self-dealing transactions are similar, and will be referred to here as the "corporate opportunity doctrine." In applying the doctrine to the facts of this case, we agree with the judge's conclusions that the defendants participated in, or benefited from, improper diversions of corporate opportunities and self-dealing transactions, to the detriment of DSM and Valley....

...In the case of a close corporation, which resembles a partnership, duties of loyalty extend to shareholders, who owe one another substantially the same duty of utmost good faith and loyalty in the operation of the enterprise that partners owe to one another, a duty that is even stricter than that required of directors and shareholders in corporations generally....In the often repeated words of then Chief Judge Cardozo of the New York Court of Appeals, "[n]ot honesty alone, but the punctilio of an honor the most sensitive, is then the standard of behavior" that describes this more rigorous duty.

A director or officer is not entirely barred from pursuing a corporate opportunity, but a person holding either position cannot do so unless the opportunity is first offered to the corporation and rejected by it. In this aspect, the corporate opportunity doctrine may be considered to be a rule of disclosure....To satisfy the principle of fairness to the corporation and to meet his duty of loyalty, the fiduciary must fully disclose to the corporation, all material facts concerning the opportunity....

In short, to meet a fiduciary's duty of loyalty, a director or officer who wishes to take advantage of a corporate opportunity or engage in self-dealing must first disclose material details of the venture to the corporation, and then either receive the assent of disinterested directors or shareholders, or otherwise prove that the decision is fair to the corporation. Otherwise, the officer or director acts in violation of his fiduciary duties, and whatever gain or advantage that he acquires may be held for the benefit of the corporation so as to deny him any benefit or profit.

With these principles in mind, we next examine the ventures and transactions that the judge found to have been conducted in violation of the fiduciary duties of DSM's and Valley's directors and officers....

The judge concluded that Market Basket represents a corporate opportunity that rightfully belonged to DSM and

Continued

was diverted from it in a breach of fiduciary duty, and that its assets are derived from that diversion or from additional wrongful self-dealing transactions. She therefore ordered the return of Market Basket's assets and liabilities to DSM. We conclude that the result reached by the judge is supported by her extensive factual findings (which in turn have support in the evidence)....

...The creation of Seabrook Sales and P & P Foods was a breach of Telemachus's fiduciary duty of loyalty, notwithstanding the fact that the companies were initially owned by persons who were not themselves directors or officers of DSM. (As has been mentioned, Telemachus's sister Ann Burliss owned Seabrook, and his daughter Frances owned P & P Foods. In 1981, Frances exercised an option that had been arranged by Telemachus and purchased Seabrook from Burliss.) A fiduciary is liable either where he benefits directly or where profits flow instead to a third party or to another company under the fiduciary's control. It is clear from the judge's findings that these companies were set up at Telemachus's direction and were independent in name only. DSM, which Telemachus fully controlled, managed and financed the operations of these companies. The use of DSM's corporate resources to support these companies indicates that they were wrongfully diverted corporate opportunities.

Seabrook Sales opened its second store in 1975 under the Market Basket name (which had previously been registered by DSM in both Massachusetts and New Hampshire), and changed its corporate name to Market Basket, Inc., in 1979 (with DSM's permission). In 1981, P & P Foods exercised Frances's option and acquired Market Basket, Inc. The latter was a subsidiary of P & P Foods until the two were merged in December, 1983; the next month, P & P changed its name to Market Basket. By this time, the company owned seven stores: six in New Hampshire, and one in Chelsea, Massachusetts (a store whose ownership by Market Basket instead of DSM belies the defendants' argument that Seabrook Sales and P & P Foods were created simply to overcome New Hampshire liquor law restrictions).

Because the entity that is now Market Basket arose from the merger of two diverted corporate opportunities that rightfully belonged to DSM, the relief ordered with respect to the current assets and liabilities of Market Basket could rest on that fact alone....

[*Authors' Note:* With certain technical adjustments, the Supreme Judicial Court of Massachusetts upheld the trial court's order to the Telemachus Branch to transfer back to the original corporations the assets and liabilities of the entities that benefited from the improper diversion of corporate opportunities and resources.]

QUESTIONS

1. Is a director or officer of a corporation totally barred from pursuing corporate opportunities?
2. What, if anything, is wrong with Telemachus setting up his sister Ann as owner of the Seabrook Corporation and his daughter Frances as owner of the P & P Foods Corporation in order to avoid the appearance of violating his fiduciary duty to DSM? Do family members have a right to start their own businesses?
3. What is the remedy in this case?

An opportunity that would be advantageous to the corporation must first be offered to the corporation before an officer or a director, who owes a fiduciary duty to the corporation, can take advantage of the opportunity. Full disclosure is required. Only if the opportunity is rejected by a majority of disinterested directors may the officer then take advantage of the opportunity. **For Example,** Nancy Harris was president of the Northeast Harbor Golf Club, Inc. In her capacity as club president, she learned of an opportunity to purchase the Gilpin property, which adjoined the golf club. Her private purchase of the property constituted the taking of a corporate opportunity and resulted in her liability to the club. Harris believed that her purchase, in a separate transaction, of the Smallidge land, which was adjacent to three of the golf club's holes and could be developed, was not usurpation of a corporate opportunity because she learned of the availability independently of the club. However, this also was a corporate opportunity because it was so closely related to the club's business. She was obligated to disclose the opportunity to the corporation and let it decide whether to pursue it.[21]

[21] *Northeast Harbor Golf Club v. Harris,* 725 A.2d 1018 (Me. 1999); see *Anderson v. Bellino,* 658 N.W.2d 645 (Neb. 2003).

Officers may avail themselves of all opportunities lying outside the field of their duties as officers when business opportunities come to them in an individual capacity.[22]

(B) Secret Profits. Officers are liable to the corporation for secret profits made in connection with, or at the expense of, the business of the corporation.

(C) Duty of Loyalty. A corporate officer, while still employed by his or her firm, may be in breach of the officer's fiduciary duty of loyalty by recruiting key management employees to join a competing company by telling them about the competitor's beneficial compensation, signing bonuses, medical benefits, and superior computer systems. However, an officer may legally make arrangements before leaving the firm to compete in the future. The line separating mere preparation from active competition may be difficult to discern, and, if misjudged, may lead to significant liability for the officer and a competitor aider and abettor, as is evidenced by the *Security Title v. Pope* case.

Security Title Agency, Inc. v. Pope, 200 P.3d 977 (Ariz. App. 2008)

Walkin' with Linda Pope

Linda Pope ran one of the largest and most successful title insurance branches in the title insurance industry for Security Title Insurance. First American Title Insurance sought to regain its top position in title insurance sales through its Talon division by recruiting key people from other companies who had relationships with key customers and other key employees. Talon recruited Pope. While still employed by Security Title, Pope secretly solicited key management employees to join Talon–First American and planned to bring all 40 employees with her. She arranged for a Talon official, over drinks and dinners, to help with the recruiting by telling Security Title employees about Talon's beneficial compensation, signing bonuses, medical benefits, and superior computer system. Security Title asserted that Pope's actions, aided and abetted by Talon, resulted in $12,194,335 in lost profits after 35 employees walked out on October 20, when Security Title "walked her out"— i.e., fired Pope—having discovered her plans to leave. Security Title sued Pope for breach of fiduciary duty of loyalty and sued Talon–First American as an aider and abettor. Pope defended that she was merely making arrangements to compete in the future.

JUDICIAL OPINION

JOHNSEN, P.J.…We conclude that…substantial evidence supports a conclusion that Pope breached her fiduciary duty by improperly recruiting Security Title employees for Talon while she was still employed by Security Title. First American's argument that Pope merely discussed her plans with the other employees and was only preparing to compete with Security Title flies in the face of a wealth of evidence presented to the jury. First American relies on *Motorola, Inc. v Fairchild Camera.,* 366 F Supp 1173 (D Ariz 1973) but the defendant in that case merely discussed with co-workers his plan to join a competing company and gave the competing company's contact information to those who asked for it. Indeed, the defendant in that case refused to discuss with his co-workers their own possible employment at the competing company. 366 F.Supp. at 1177. By contrast, Pope…secretly solicited key managerial employees to join a competitor. She arranged for Clifford [Talon, senior vice president] to help her recruit key Security Title employees and enticed other Branch66 employees to leave Security-Title by telling them about Talon's "beneficial" compensation, signing bonuses, medical benefits and superior computer systern. We conclude the evidence easily supports the conclusion that Pope breached her fiduciary duty by improperly recruiting Security Title's employees for Talon while she was still employed by Security Title.

[Judgment for Security Title affirmed. Punitive damages awarded, $6,100,290.]

QUESTIONS

1. Based on your sense of fair play and justice, does it sound "right" or sensible to think that one officer, while still employed by her employer, could arrange to recruit all 40 of her coworkers to leave for a competitive firm and not be in violation of some law?
2. Assess Pope's defense that she was merely making arrangements to compete in the future.

[22] *Hill v. Southeastern Floor Covering Co.*, 596 So.2d 874 (Miss. 1992).

11. Agents and Employees

The authority, rights, and liabilities of an agent or employee of a corporation are governed by the same rules as those applicable when the principal or employer is a natural person. The authority of corporate employees is also governed by general agency principles. **For Example,** R. Bryan Smith, president of Allstate Building Systems applied for a credit account with 84 Lumber Company. The first sentence of the application stated: "BY SIGNING BELOW I HEREBY CERTIFY THAT I AM THE OWNER, GENERAL PARTNER OR PRESIDENT OF THE ABOVE BUSINESS,…" The instructions on the first page of the contract state, "If the Applicant is a corporation, then President must sign the application." The language is a certification that the individual signing the contract has the authority to sign the contract in a representative capacity for the company. Immediately following this clause is the language, "I DO UNCONDITIONALLY … PERSONALLY GUARANTEE THIS CREDIT ACCOUNT AND PAYMENTS OF ANY AND ALL AMOUNTS DUE BY THE ABOVE BUSINESS." Mr. Smith signed both in a representative capacity and personally guaranteed the contract. He agreed to be personally responsible for the $27,611 owed on the account and the court enforced the agreement as written.[23]

The fact that a person is acting on behalf of a corporation does not serve as a shield from the liability that would be imposed for acts done on behalf of a natural person.

D. Liability

Limited liability is a major reason for incorporating. Management, however, is not free from all civil and criminal liability simply because the corporate form is used.

12. Liability of Management to Third Persons

Officers and managers of a corporation are not liable to third parties for the economic consequences of their advice so long as they acted in good faith to advance the interests of the corporation, even if they cause the corporation to refuse to deal with or break its contract with these third persons.

Ordinarily, the management of a corporation (its directors, officers, and executive employees) is not liable to third persons for the effect of its management or advice. The liability of a director or an officer for misconduct may usually be enforced only by the corporation or by shareholders bringing a derivative action on behalf of the corporation. Ordinarily, directors or officers are not liable to a third person for loss caused by the negligent performance of their duties as directors or officers even if, because of such negligence, the corporation is in turn liable to the third person to whom the corporation owed the duty to use care or was under a contract obligation to render a particular service.

However, in those rare cases when a director or an officer has in some way participated in or directed the tortious act, personal liability will attach. For example, a corporate officer and director may be held personally liable for the tort of fraud in the inducement regarding a false promise to grant an insurance agency an exclusive territory selling viatical settlements, by which life insurance policies of terminally ill people are purchased at a discount in exchange for an immediate cash settlement.[24]

13. Criminal Liability

Officers and directors, as well as the corporation itself, may be criminally accountable for business regulatory offenses.

(a) Active Participation. Officers and directors, as in the case of agents, are personally responsible for any crimes committed by them even when they act on behalf of the corporation.[25] At the local level, they may be criminally responsible for violation of ordinances relating to sanitation, safety, and hours of closing.

At the state level, they may be criminally liable for conducting a business without obtaining necessary licenses or after the corporate certificate of incorporation has been forfeited.

[23] *84 Lumber Co. v. Smith*, 356 S.W.3d 380 (Tenn. 2011); but see *Stamina Products, Inc. v. Zinctec USA Inc.*, 90 A.D.3d 1021 (A.D.2d 2011), where Anthyony Yau signed a contract on behalf of Zinctec, solely as a corporate officer, and did not bind himself individually under the agreement.

[24] *First Financial USA, Inc. v. Steinger*, 760 So.2d 996 (Fla. App. 2000).

[25] *Joy Management Co. v. City of Detroit*, 455 N.W.2d 55 (Mich. App. 1990).

Ethics & the Law

Dodd-Frank "Say-on-Pay"!

For nearly a decade, one of the concerns that shareholders and others have raised about corporate officers is their level of compensation. Former Treasury Secretary Geithner identified executive compensation practices as a contributing factor to the financial crisis of 2008–2009, where incentives for short-term gains overwhelmed the checks and balances meant to mitigate the risk of excessive financial leverage. Some commentators are now identifying excessive executive compensation as the No. 1 problem in corporate governance. While private sector wages rose only 2 percent in 2010, the median compensation for CEOs at Standard & Poor's 500 index companies was up by 18 percent from 2009 to an average of 12 million. It is in this context that Congress passed the Dodd-Frank Wall Street Reform Act and included in it the "say-on-pay provision," whereby publicly traded companies must include a separate shareholder resolution to approve executive compensation in their proxies at least once every three years.* The Act states that the vote shall not be binding on the issuer or construed as overriding a decision of the board of directors. However, while a negative vote does not prove a breach of fiduciary duty, it is a contextual fact where other direct evidence of the directors' conduct may prove a violation of a corporate "pay-for-performance" policy and an abuse of discretion or bad faith.

For Example a pension fund, as shareholders, sued derivatively on behalf of Cincinnati Bell, Inc., the directors of the company for breach of the duty of loyalty and the company's pay-for-performance policy, where the directors granted $4 million in bonuses, on top of $4.5 million in salary and other compensation to CEO Cassidy, in the same year the company incurred a $61.3 million decline in net income, a drop in earnings per share from $.37 to $.09, a reduction in share price from $3.45 to $2.80, and a negative 18.8 percent annual shareholder return. In compliance with Dodd-Frank the board included a shareholder resolution in its March 21, 2011, proxy seeking shareholder approval of the 2010 executive compensation. The board recommended that the shareholders vote in support of the resolution. On May 3, 2011, 66 percent of voting shareholders voted against the 2010 executive compensation. The directors filed a motion to dismiss the lawsuit. Normally, a board of directors is protected by the "business judgment rule" when making decisions about executive compensation, and courts will not inquire into the wisdom of actions taken by directors in the absence of fraud, bad faith, or abuse of discretion. However, the business judgment rule is a presumption that may be rebutted at trial by a plaintiff with factual evidence that board members acted disloyally—that is, not in the best interests of the company or its shareholders. The court determined that the plaintiff had sufficiently pled facts of breach of fiduciary duty and unjust enrichment, and it denied the defendants' motion to dismiss, allowing the case to go to trial. At trial the defendants may offer the affirmative defense of the business judgment rule and the plaintiff will have to prove by clear and convincing evidence that the directors acted with reckless disregard for the best interests of the corporation.**

Most boards that faced "no" votes on compensation packages for their executive officers revised their compensation practices in response. For Example Hewlett-Packard reconstructed the formula that had been used to provide its then CEO, Leo Apotheker, with a $30 million compensation package covering a period when its stock fell by almost half. The following figures are some examples of CEO total annual compensation packages for 2012.***

Company	*CEO*	*Amount*
McKesson	John H. Hammergren	$131,190,000
Ralph Lauren	Ralph Lauren	$66,650,000
Vornado Realty	Michael D. Fascitelli	$64,400,000
Kinder Morgan	Richard D. Kinder	$60,940,000
Honeywell	David M. Cote	$55,790,000
Express Scripts	George Paz	$51,520,000
Priceline.com	Jeffery H. Boyd	$50,180,000
United Health Group	Stephen J. Hemsley	$48,830,000
Marathon Oil	Clarence P. Cazalot Jr.	$43,710,000
Gilead Sciences	John C. Martin	$43,190,000

Is it troubling to shareholders and employees that outsourcing and cost-cutting occur but CEO salaries remain at the same or higher levels? Will the Dodd-Frank Say-on-Pay legislation impact boards of directors' responsiveness to their shareholders?

*15 U.S.C.§78n-1(a) (2010).

***NECA-IBEW Pension Fund v. Cox*, 2011 WL 4383368 (S.D. Ohio, Sept. 20, 2011). But see *Dennis v. Hart*, 2012 WL 33199 (S.D. Cal. Jan. 6, 2012).

***http://forbes.com/lists/2012/12/ceo-compensation-12_rank.html.

At the federal level, officers and directors may be criminally liable for tax and securities law violations as well as egregious environmental protection law and worker safety law violations. International transactions may lead to potential criminal exposure. Under the Foreign Corrupt Practices Act, it is a crime for a U.S. firm to make payments or gifts to a foreign officer to obtain business. Not only is the U.S. corporation subject to a fine but also the officers and individuals involved are subject to fine and imprisonment.

(B) Responsible Corporate Officer Doctrine. Officers and directors may be criminally liable under a number of federal and state statutes for failure to prevent the commission of a crime if they are found to be the "responsible corporate officers." These statutes include the Food, Drug and Cosmetic Act, the Federal Hazardous Substances Act, the Occupational Safety and Health Act, the Federal Water Pollution Act, and, at the state level, the California Corporate Criminal Liability Act. **For Example,** Gary Lundgren was a shareholder and officer of KIE, Inc., which owned and operated a sewage treatment plant on Ketron Island. He knew of the facility's discharge of pollutants into Puget Sound without a permit. As the "responsible corporate officer," he was held personally liable for a $250,000 penalty because he controlled the facility with knowledge of the violations.[26] The California Corporate Criminal Liability Act requires managers in control of corporate operations who have knowledge of "serious concealed dangers" to employees or customers to notify the appropriate regulatory authority or be subject to criminal liability.[27]

(C) Liability of the Corporation Itself. A corporation itself may be convicted of a criminal offense if its agent committed the offense acting within the scope of the agent's authority. **For Example,** Steenberg Homes, Inc., was convicted of negligent criminal homicide in the deaths of two cyclists who were killed when the company's trailer truck, loaded with timber, disengaged from the tractor. If safety chains had been properly attached, the accident would not have happened, and the corporation's failure to establish and enforce safety procedures was a cause of the deaths of the cyclists.[28]

(D) Punishment of Corporations. Under the Organizational Federal Sentencing Guidelines, organizations, including corporations, trusts, pension funds, unions, and nonprofit organizations, are subject to greatly increased fines for criminal convictions. However, corporations and other covered organizations that implement an effective compliance program designed to prevent and detect corporate crimes and voluntarily disclose such crimes to the government will be subject to much lower fines under the guidelines.[29]

14. Indemnification of Officers, Directors, Employees, and Agents

While performing what they believe to be their duty, officers, directors, employees, and agents of corporations may commit acts for which they are later sued or criminally prosecuted. The RMBCA broadly authorizes the corporation to indemnify these persons if they acted in good faith and in a manner reasonably believed to be in, or not opposed to, the interests of the corporation and had no reason to believe that their conduct was unlawful.[30] In some states, statutory provision is made requiring the corporation to indemnify directors and officers for reasonable expenses incurred by them in defending unwarranted suits brought against them by shareholders.

15. Liability for Corporate Debts

Because the corporation is a separate legal person, debts that it owes are ordinarily the obligations of the corporation only. Consequently, neither directors nor officers are individually liable for corporate debts, even though it may have been their acts that gave rise to the debts.

In some states, liability for corporate debts is imposed on the corporation's officers and directors when the corporation improperly engages in business.

16. Protection of Shareholders

Shareholders may obtain protection from misconduct by management and by the majority of the shareholders. Shareholders may protect themselves by voting at the next annual election for new directors and for new officers if the latter are elected. Shareholders may take remedial action at a special meeting

[26] *State Department of Ecology v. Lundgren*, 971 P.2d 948 (Wash. App. 1999).

[27] Cal. Penal Code §387 (West 2006).

[28] *State v. Steenberg Homes, Inc.*, 859 N.W.2d 668 (Wis. App. 1998).

[29] U.S. Sentencing Commission Guidelines Manual §§8C2.5(f), 8C2.6. On April 8, 2004, the Commission adopted amendments to the Guidelines and requires a periodic assessment of the "risk of criminal conduct" by the corporation or organization.

[30] Subchapter 8E, added in 1980 and revised in 1994.

called for that purpose. Objecting shareholders may bring a legal action when the management misconduct complained of constitutes a legal wrong.[31]

17. Civil Liability of the Corporation

A corporation is liable to third persons for the acts of its officers, employees, and agents to the same extent that a natural person is liable for the acts of agents and employees. This means that the ordinary rules of agency law determine the extent to which the corporation is liable to a third person for a contract made or a tort committed by management personnel, employees, and agents.

[31] *Christner v. Anderson, Nietzke & Co.*, 444 N.W.2d 779 (Mich. 1989).

LawFlix

Smartest Guys in the Room (2005)(R)

The story of Enron executives and their ploys that duped creditors, analysts, shareholders, and employees. A look at what happens when a board is asleep at the wheel and the officers have unfettered authority.

MAKE THE CONNECTION

SUMMARY

Ordinarily, stockholder action is taken at a regular or special meeting of the stockholders. The presence of a quorum of the voting shareholders is required.

Management of a corporation is under the control of a board of directors elected by the shareholders. Courts will not interfere with the board's judgment in the absence of unusual conduct such as fraud. A director is disqualified from taking part in corporate action when the director has a conflict of interest. Action by directors is usually taken at a properly called meeting of the board. Directors act in a fiduciary capacity in dealing with the corporation. Directors who act in good faith and have exercised reasonable care are not liable for losses resulting from their management decisions. Ordinarily, directors are removed by shareholders.

Officers of a corporation, including a CEO, president, vice president, secretary, and treasurer, are usually selected and removed by the board of directors. Officers are agents of the corporation, and their powers are governed by the law of agency. Their relations with the corporation are fiduciary in nature, and they are liable for any secret profits and for diverting corporate opportunities to their own advantage.

Directors and officers, as in the case of agents generally, are personally responsible for any torts or crimes they commit even if they act on behalf of the corporation. The corporation itself may be prosecuted for crimes and is subject to fines if convicted. The ordinary rules of agency law determine the extent to which a corporation is liable for a contract made or tort committed by a director, officer, corporate agent, or employee.

LEARNING OUTCOMES

After studying this chapter, you should be able to clearly explain:

A. Shareholders

LO.1 Explain how shareholders, as owners of the corporation, exercise limited control over management by voting at shareholders' meetings to elect directors

See the discussion of shareholder voting and meetings beginning on p. 1006.

B. Directors

LO.2 Explain the qualifications and powers of directors

See the discussion regarding the broad authority of directors to manage the corporation, beginning on p. 1007.

LO.3 Explain the liability of directors and the meaning of the business judgment rule (BJR)

See the *Walt Disney* case in which an unsuccessful action taken by directors was protected by the BJR, pp. 1009–1011.

See the *Van Gorkom* case in which directors were not protected by the BJR, because they were grossly negligent in their judgment, pp. 1011–1012.

See the changes clarifying the role of corporate directors brought about by Sarbanes-Oxley and Dodd-Frank regulations, on p. 1013.

C. Officers, Agents, and Employees

LO.4 Explain the obligation of officers—who have access to corporate information and agency powers—to not violate their fiduciary duties to the corporation

See the *Demoulas Super Markets* case regarding diverting corporate opportunities, pp. 1016–1017.

See the *Security Title v. Pope* case regarding a manager's duty of loyalty, p. 1018.

LO.5 Explain the rationale for the "say-on-pay" provision of the Dodd-Frank Act

See the examples of executive compensation practices leading to the financial crisis of 2008–2009 on p. 1020.

See the *Cincinnati Bell* excessive compensation example on p. 1020.

D. Liability

LO.6 Explain how directors, officers, and the corporation itself may be criminally liable for regulatory offenses

See the Gary Lundgren example in which, as a "responsible corporate officer," Gary was held personably liable for environmental law violations, p. 1021.

KEY TERMS

business judgment rule (BJR)

quorum

QUESTIONS AND CASE PROBLEMS

1. Shareholders of Bear Stearns sued the directors of the corporation for damages for violation of the directors' fiduciary duties in effecting a stock-for-stock merger with J. P. Morgan Chase for an implied value of $10 per share while the company's stock had previously reached a 15-month high of $160. On March 10, 2008, information began leaking into the market that Bear Stearns had a liquidity problem. On March 13, 2008, the company was forced to seek emergency financing from the Federal Reserve and J. P. Morgan Chase. By the weekend of March 14–16, the company could no longer operate without major financing. In an effort to preserve some shareholder value while averting the uncertainty of bankruptcy (where stockholders would likely receive nothing), and represented by teams of legal and financial experts and relying on their financial advisor Lazard Freres & Co.'s opinion that the "exchange ratio is fair, from a financial point of view, to the shareholders," the board of directors approved the initial merger agreement. The shareholder plaintiffs contended that the ultimate $10 share price paid was inadequate and they presented their experts who vigorously dissected the board's decisions. What defense, if any, would you raise on behalf of the Bear Stearns board of directors? [*In re Bear Stearns Litigation*, 870 N.Y.S.2d 709]
2. In 1996, Congress offered national banks the opportunity to become Subchapter S entities. Amboy Bancorporation was a small, highly profitable New Jersey Bank that was overcapitalized. Amboy's president and CEO utilized Bank Advisory Group, Inc. (BAG), to calculate the fair

value of individual shares of Amboy stock. The board of directors approved a merger cash buy-out program designed to reduce the shareholder base to below the 75 qualified shareholders necessary to obtain Subchapter S status. BAG incorrectly applied a minority and marketability discount to its evaluation of the fair value of the stock, bringing it down from $110 per share to $70.13 per share. Casey and other shareholders who cashed out under the plan at $73 per share sued the board of directors individually for damages for approving such a flawed plan. Are directors personally liable when they act in reliance on a report by an outside expert whose advice is flawed? If a public accounting firm or an attorney gave the flawed advice, would the directors be personally liable? [*Casey v. Brennan*, 344 N.J. Super. 83]

3. The majority shareholder and president of Dunaway Drug Stores, Inc., William B. Dunaway, was structuring and executing the sale of virtually all of the corporation's assets to Eckerd Drug Co. While doing this, he negotiated a side noncompete agreement with Eckerd, giving Dunaway $300,000 plus a company car in exchange for a covenant not to compete for three years. He simultaneously amended two corporate leases with Eckerd, thereby decreasing the value of the corporation's leasehold estates. The board of directors approved the asset sale. Minority shareholders brought a derivative action against William Dunaway, claiming breach of his fiduciary duty in negotiating the undisclosed noncompete agreement, which did not require him to perform any service for buyer Eckerd Drug. Did William Dunaway make sufficient disclosure about all of the negotiations of the asset sale to Eckerd Drug? Did William Dunaway violate any fiduciary duty to the corporation? Decide. [*Dunaway v. Parker*, 453 S.E.2d 43 (Ga. App.)]

4. Larry Phillips was hired for a two-year period as executive secretary of the Montana Education Association (MEA). Six months later, he was fired. He then sued MEA for breach of contract and sued the directors and some of the other employees of MEA on the theory that they had caused MEA to break the contract with him and were therefore guilty of the tort of maliciously interfering with his contract with MEA. The evidence showed that the individual defendants, without malice, had induced the corporation to break the contract with Phillips but that this had been done to further the welfare of the corporation. Was MEA liable for breach of contract? Were the individual defendants shielded from personal liability? [*Phillips v. Montana Education Ass'n*, 610 P.2d 154 (Mont.)]

5. Christy Pontiac, a corporation, was indicted for theft by swindle and forgery involving a GM cash rebate program. Hesli, a middle-management employee of Christy Pontiac, had forged the cash rebate applications for two cars so that the rebate money was paid to Christy Pontiac instead of its customers. When confronted by a customer who should have received a rebate, the president of the dealership attempted to negotiate a settlement. The president did not contact GM headquarters until after an investigation was begun by the state attorney general. Christy Pontiac argued that it could not be held responsible for a crime involving specific intent because only natural persons, as opposed to corporations, can form such intent. Decide. [*State v. Christy Pontiac-GMC, Inc.*, 354 N.W.2d 17 (Minn.)]

6. Larry G. Snodgrass and Mark Swinnea owned equal interests in two business entities, ERI Consulting Engineers, Inc. (ERI), and Malmeba Company, Ltd., which they operated together for approximately 10 years. ERI manages asbestos abatement projects for contractors. It leased office space from Malmeba, their partnership that owned the building. Snodgrass and ERI purchased Swinnea's interest in ERI in 2001. ERI paid Swinnea $497,500 to redeem Swinnea's ERI stock, and Snodgrass transferred his half-interest in Malmeba to Swinnea. ERI agreed to employ Swinnea for six years, and Swinnea agreed not to compete with ERI. At the same time, ERI agreed to continue leasing from Malmeba for six years. Unknown to Snodgrass, the wives of Swinnea and Chris Power, an ERI employee, had created a new company called Air Quality Associates a month before Swinnea and Snodgrass executed the buyout agreement. Air Quality Associates was created to perform mold abatement, but later engaged in asbestos abatement as a contractor

even though neither wife had experience in the asbestos abatement field. Swinnea did not disclose the existence of Air Quality Associates to Snodgrass during the ERI buyout negotiations. Over a 33-month period Snodgrass suffered a total loss of profits of $178,000 for business lost to Swinnea. Was Swinnea free to outmaneuver Snodgrass in their buyout agreement as part of the competitive spirit of America? Do owners have a fiduciary duty to each other in negotiating a buyout agreement with a noncompete clause? Are Swinnea's action's so contrary to our public sense of justice and propriety to merit exemplary damages? [*ERI Consulting Engineers, Inc. v. Swinnea*, 318 S.W.3d 867 (Tex.); *Swinnea v. ERI Consulting Engineers*, 364 S.W.3d 421 (Tex. App.)

7. Discuss the power of a corporation president to employ a sales manager and to agree that the manager should be paid a stated amount per year plus a percentage of any increase in the dollar volume of sales that might take place.

8. Richard Grassgreen was executive vice president and then president and chief operating officer of Kinder-Care, Inc., the largest proprietary provider of child care in the country. The company was restructured in 1989 and changed its name to the Enstar Group, Inc. Between 1985 and 1990, while Grassgreen served as the corporation's investment manager, he invested millions of dollars of company money in junk bond deals with Michael Milken, and he secretly retained some $355,000 in commitment fees. When the corporation discovered this, Grassgreen repaid the corporation. It sued him to recover any compensation paid him over the five-year period during which the secret payments were made, some $5,197,663. Grassgreen defended that his conduct caused little, if any, damage to the corporation because the corporation did not lose any money on any of the investments for which he received personal fees. Decide. [*Enstar Group, Inc. v. Grassgreen*, 812 F. Supp. 1562 (M.D. Ala.)]

9. Danny Hill, the general manager of Southeastern Floor Covering Co., Inc. (SE), had full authority to run the business. His responsibilities included preparing and submitting bid proposals to general contractors for floor coverings and ceilings on construction projects. Hill prepared and submitted a bid for a job for Chata Construction Co. for asbestos encapsulation, ceramic tile, ceilings, carpets, and vinyl tile flooring. However, because SE was not licensed by the EPA, the asbestos work was withdrawn. In the past, SE had used Larry Barnes's company, which was EPA licensed, to do asbestos work under a subcontract agreement. Hill did not pursue a subcontract with Barnes for the Chata job. Rather, Hill and Barnes worked up a bid together and submitted it to Chata for the asbestos work. The bid was accepted, and Hill made $90,000 from the Chata job. Two years later, SE found out about Hill's role in the asbestos work done for Chata, and the corporation sued him for the lost profits. Hill argued that SE was not licensed by the EPA to do asbestos work and thus could not claim a lost corporate opportunity when it was not qualified to do the work. Decide. Are any ethical principles applicable to this case? [*Hill v. Southeastern Floor Covering Co.*, 596 So.2d 874 (Miss.)]

10. A director of a corporation cannot lend money to the corporation because that would create the danger of a conflict of interest between the director's status as a director and as a creditor. Appraise this statement.

11. Hamway and other minority shareholders brought an action against majority shareholders of Libbie Rehabilitation Center, Inc., including Frank Giannotti, CEO-director; Alex Grossman, president-director; Henry Miller, vice president–director; Ernest Dervishian, secretary and corporate attorney; and Lewis Cowardin, treasurer-director. The minority shareholders contended that the corporation paid excessive salaries to these director-officers and was wasting corporate assets. Prior to coming to Libbie, Giannotti had been a carpet and tile retailer, Grossman a pharmacist, Miller a real estate developer, Dervishian a lawyer, and Cowardin a jeweler. The evidence showed that the extent of their work for the corporation was very limited. For example, Cowardin, Libbie's finance officer, who was paid $78,121, demonstrated no knowledge of the Medicare and Medicaid programs, the principal source of Libbie's income. Although he claimed to have spent 20 to 25 hours

a week on corporate duties, he reported on the tax return for his jewelry business that he spent 75 percent of his working time in that business. One expert witness of the plaintiff testified that the five men were performing the management functions of one individual. The director-officers contended that the business was making a profit and that all salaries were approved by a board of directors that had extensive business experience. Were the directors within their rights to elect themselves officers and set pay for themselves as they saw fit? Did they violate any legal or ethical duty to their shareholders?

12. Anthony Yee was the president of Waipahu Auto Exchange, a corporation. As part of his corporate duties, he arranged financing for the company. Federal Services Finance Corp. drew 12 checks payable to the order of Waipahu Auto Exchange. These were then indorsed by its president, "Waipahu Auto Exchange, Limited, by Anthony Yee, President," and were cashed at two different banks. Bishop National Bank of Hawaii, on which the checks were drawn, charged its depositor, Federal Services, with the amount of the checks. Federal Services then sued Bishop National Bank to restore to its account the amount of the 12 checks on the ground that Bishop National Bank had improperly made payment on the checks because Anthony Yee had no authority to cash them. Did Yee have authority to indorse and cash the checks? [*Federal Services Finance Corp. v. Bishop Nat'l Bank of Hawaii*, 190 F.2d 442 (9th Cir.)]

13. Klinicki and Lundgren incorporated Berlinair, Inc., a closely held Oregon corporation. Lundgren was president and responsible for developing business. Klinicki served as vice president and director responsible for operations and maintenance. Klinicki owned one-third of the stock, and Lundgren controlled the rest. They both met with BFR, a consortium of Berlin travel agents, about contracting to operate some charter flights. After the initial meeting, all contracts with BFR were made by Lundgren, who learned that there was a good chance that the BFR contract would be available. He incorporated Air Berlin Charter Co. (ABC) and was its sole owner. He presented BFR with a contract proposal, and it awarded the contract to ABC. Although Lundgren was using Berlinair's working time and facilities, he managed to keep the negotiations a secret from Klinicki. When Klinicki discovered Lundgren's actions, he sued him for usurping a corporate opportunity for Berlinair. Lundgren contended that it was not a usurpation of corporate opportunity because Berlinair did not have the financial ability to undertake the contract with BFR. Decide. Are any ethical principles applicable to this case? Consider the applicability of Chief Justice Cardozo's statement in *Meinhard v. Salmon*, 164 N.E. 545 (N.Y. 1928), concerning the level of conduct for fiduciaries: "A trustee is held to something stricter than the morals of the marketplace. Not honesty alone, but the punctillo of an honor the most sensitive is then the standard of behavior…." [*Klinicki v. Lundgren*, 695 P.2d 906 (Or.)]

14. Rudolph Redmont, the president of Abbott Thinlite Corp., left Abbott to run Circle Corp. in competition with his former employer. It was claimed that he diverted contracts from his former employer to his new one, having gained the advantage of specific information about the deals in progress while employed by Abbott. Abbott sued Redmont and Circle Corp. to recover lost profits. Redmont contended that all of the contracts in question were made after he left Abbott, at which time his fiduciary duty to Abbott had ceased. Decide. [*Abbott Thinlite Corp. v. Redmont*, 475 F.2d 85 (2d Cir.)]

15. William Gurtler was president and a board member of Unichem Corp., which produced and sold chemical laundry products. While president of Unichem, he encouraged his plant manager to leave to join a rival business, which Gurtler was going to join in the near future. Moreover, Gurtler sold Unichem products to his son, G. B. Gurtler, at a figure substantially below their normal price and on credit even though G. B. had no credit history. Gurtler made the sales with full knowledge that G. B. was going to start a rival business. Also at that time, Gurtler was aware that his wife was soliciting Unichem employees to join the new Gurtler Chemical Co., and he helped her design Gurtler's label so that it would look like Unichem's. Gurtler guaranteed a

$100,000 bank loan for the new Gurtler Chemical Co. with funds to be disbursed after he left Unichem. One month later, he became president of Gurtler Chemical Co. Unichem sued Gurtler for breach of fiduciary duty and for the loss of profits that resulted. Gurtler contended that his sales to G. B. guaranteed needed revenue to Unichem and constituted a sound business decision that should be applauded and that was protected under the business judgment rule. Decide. Are any ethical principles applicable to this case? [*Unichem Corp. v. Gurtler*, 498 N.E.2d 724 (Ill. App.)]

CPA QUESTIONS

1. Davis, a director of Active Corp., is entitled to:
   a. Serve on the board of a competing business
   b. Take sole advantage of a business opportunity that would benefit Active
   c. Rely on information provided by a corporate officer
   d. Unilaterally grant a corporate loan to one of Active's shareholders
2. Absent a specific provision in its articles of incorporation, a corporation's board of directors has the power to do all of the following *except*:
   a. Repeal the bylaws
   b. Declare dividends
   c. Fix compensation of directors
   d. Amend the articles of incorporation
3. Which of the following statements is correct regarding fiduciary duty?
   a. A director's fiduciary duty to the corporation may be discharged by merely disclosing his or her self-interest.
   b. A director owes a fiduciary duty to the shareholders but *not* to the corporation.
   c. A promoter of a corporation to be formed owes no fiduciary duty to anyone, unless the contract engaging the promoter so provides.
   d. A majority shareholder as such may owe a fiduciary duty to fellow shareholders.

PART 8

Real Property and Estates

© Manuel Gutjahr/iStockphoto.com

Chapter 49

© Manuel Gutjahr/iStockphoto.com

Real Property

learning outcomes

After studying this chapter, you should be able to

LO.1 List the types of real property interests, the rights of the parties and their liabilities

LO.2 Distinguish between liens, licenses, and easements

LO.3 Discuss the nature and form of real property ownership

LO.4 Explain the liability of landowners for injury to others on their property

LO.5 Discuss the forms of co-ownership and parties' rights

LO.6 Describe how deeds convey title to land

LO.7 Describe the characteristics and effect of a mortgage

The law of real property can be highly technical and still relies on vocabulary drawn from the days of feudal lords and castles. This chapter presents a simplified look at the law of real property.

A. Nature of Real Property

Real property has special characteristics of permanence and uniqueness. These characteristics have strongly influenced the rules that society has developed to resolve disputes concerning real property.

1. Land

Land means more than the surface of the earth. It is composed of the soil and all things of a permanent nature affixed to the ground, such as shrubs, grass, trees, and other growing, natural products. The word also includes the waters on the ground and minerals that are embedded beneath the surface.

Technically, land extends downward to the earth's center and upward indefinitely. The general view is that the owner of the land owns the space above that land subject to the right of flying aircraft that do not interfere with the use of the land and are not dangerous to persons or property on the land.

CPA 2. Easements

An **easement** is the right to use another's property, such as the right to cross another's land. Rights in another person's land also include profits, or the right to remove minerals. The easement belongs to the land that is benefited. The benefited land is called the **dominant tenement**, and the land that is subject to the easement is called the **servient tenement**.[1]

(A) Creation of Easement. Because an easement is an interest in land, an oral promise to create an easement is not binding because of the statute of frauds. An oral grant of an easement would be a license (see Section 4). An easement created by agreement is transferred by deed. However, an easement may also be created by implication. An **easement by implication** arises when one conveys a portion the land that has been used as a dominant estate in relation to the part retained. **For Example,** if water pipes or drain pipes run from the part of the land conveyed through the part retained, there is an implied right to continue using the pipes. For an easement to be implied, the use, as in this case with the pipes, must be apparent, continuous, and reasonably necessary.

An easement by implication arises when one subdivides land and sells a portion to which no entry can be made except over the land retained or over the land of a stranger. The grantee's right to use the land retained by the grantor for the purpose of going to and from the land conveyed is known as a **way of necessity**.

An easement may be created by **prescription**. Under prescription, a person acquires an easement by adverse use, or use contrary to the landowner's use, for a statutory period. No easement is acquired by prescription if the use of the land is with the permission of the owner.

(B) Termination of Easement. Once an easement has been granted, it cannot be destroyed by the act of the grantor. A "revocation" attempted without the easement owner's consent has no effect.

An easement may be lost by nonuse when surrounding circumstances show an intent to abandon the easement.[2] **For Example,** when a surface transit system had an easement to maintain trolley tracks but abandoned the easement when the tracks were removed and all surface transportation was discontinued, the easement was lost through abandonment. Likewise, when the owner of the easement planted a flower bed on the land across the end of the path of the easement, the intent to abandon the easement was evident. The *Dianne v. Wingate* case deals with the nature and scope of an easement.

[1] *Gaw v. Seldon*, 85 So.3d 312 (Miss. App. 2012).
[2] *Howard v. U.S.*, 964 N.E.2d 779 (Ind. 2012).

Dianne v. Wingate, 84 So.3d 427 (Fla. App. 2012)

Freddie and Peggy's Speed Bumps on the Easement Get Bumped

Adrian and Charline Wingate (Appellees) own and occupy a home adjoining Gloria Dianne and Freddie L. Wingate's (Appellants) property. On February 1, 1999, Appellant Freddie L. Wingate and his (now deceased) wife, Peggy Ann Wingate (now Peggy Dianne), granted an easement over and across their property, providing ingress and egress to Adrian and Charline, which was recorded. Around October 21, 2009, Freddie and Peggy placed speed bumps across a paved portion of the easement, which is used by Adrian and Charline to gain access to their residence. Freddie and Peggy also placed concrete barriers on either side of the speed bumps to prevent vehicles from going around the speed bumps. The speed bumps have proven dangerous to drivers and their passengers and have damaged vehicles passing over them. Adrian and Charline demanded summary judgment as well as a permanent injunction restraining Freddie and Peggy from keeping the speed bumps across the easement. The court granted summary judgment and ordered the removal of the speed bumps. Peggy and Freddie appealed.

JUDICIAL OPINION

RAY, Judge...Appellants asserted that the passageway sustained heavy traffic, some motorists used excessive speed, and over time, the posted speed limit signs were regularly ignored and ineffective. Appellants deny that the speed bumps are dangerous and/or substantially diminish Appellees' rights.

Under the terms of the easement, the grantors gave, granted, sold, and conveyed to Appellees, as grantees, "a non-exclusive easement or right of way for ingress and egress, over, along, and across a strip or parcel of land," which is legally described in the agreement. The agreement contained no restrictions and reserved no rights to place speed bumps across the easement. Appellees requested the immediate removal of the speed bumps.

Appellees' counsel argued the speed bumps must be removed because, by their very nature, they impede ingress and egress along the easement, have no reflectors or other warning signs, and substantially diminish Appellees' rights established under the easement agreement. Appellees contended that the placement of a fence along the passageway would be a less intrusive means of protecting people from vehicles crossing the easement, without impeding ingress and egress along the passageway.

Appellants' counsel replied that the speed bumps serve a necessary safety function to reduce speeding and are permitted if they do not unreasonably interfere with the ability to cross over the easement. The trial judge, acknowledging that a factual question may arise as to whether the speed bumps are a substantial interference, found it was not reasonable to place the speed bumps across the easement, where the agreement expressly granted Appellees the rights of ingress and egress. The court noted that the presence of large concrete blocks on both sides of the speed bumps prevents drivers from bypassing them. Although an easement is a real property interest in land, it is a right distinct from ownership of the land itself and does not confer title to the land on which the easement is imposed. The easement holder possesses the dominant tenement, while the owner of the land against which the easement exists possesses the servient tenement. The servient estate owner enjoys all rights to the property, except as limited by the easement, and may use the land burdened by the easement in any manner that does not unreasonably interfere with the lawful dominant use.

In the case before us, the parties agree that a valid easement was created and recorded in 1999. The clear, unambiguous language in the agreement gave the dominant estate owners (Appellees) a non-exclusive right-of-way for ingress and egress over and along the parcel of land that is used to access their residence.

Next, in determining the nature and scope of Appellees' rights, we examine the intent of the original parties to the easement, as evidenced by the agreement itself. It is clear that the grantors intended for the grantees to have ingress and egress over the easement property. Where the parties want to keep an easement free of gates, speed bumps, signs, or other obstructions, they can specifically express such intent in their easement agreement. That is not the case with the instant easement agreement, however, which is silent as to whether the servient estate owners (Appellants) have the right to place speed bumps across the easement.

A similar situation existed in *BHB Development, Inc. v. Bonefish Yacht Club Homeowners Ass'n, Inc.*, 691 So.2d 1174 (Fla. 3d DCA 1997), where a homeowners' association obtained a private right-of-way easement for ingress and egress over a portion of BHB Development's property. Subsequently, BHB Development erected a locked gate across the easement for security purposes and offered keys to the homeowners' association members. The issue was whether the easement allowed BHB Development to install the gate. The trial court issued a final judgment in favor of the homeowners' association, directing BHB Development to remove any gates existing across the easement and forbidding the future installation of gates. The Third District Court stated the general rule as follows:

> *[T]he grant of a way without reservation of the right to maintain gates does not necessarily preclude the owner of the land from doing so, and unless it is expressly stipulated that the way shall be an open one, or it appears from the terms of the grant or the circumstances that such was the*

Continued

intention, the owner of the servient estate may erect gates across the way, if they are constructed so as not to interfere unreasonably with the right of passage.

The evidence in *BHB Development* established that having to unlock and open the gate and having to carry a key or have an access code caused inconvenience. The appellate court concluded that the trial court did not err in finding that the locked gate substantially and unreasonably interfered with the homeowners' association's right of passage. The final judgment was affirmed.

As in *BHB Development*, the essential question in this case is whether the speed bumps substantially or unreasonably interfere with the easement holders' right of passage. To conclude as the trial court did, and hold that the speed bumps are impermissible as a matter of law, would effectively grant the easement holders absolute ownership of the easement property contrary to well-established property law.

Whether a particular action by a servient tenement holder constitutes unreasonable interference is ordinarily a question of fact. In resolving the question of reasonableness, significant factors the courts may consider include the number of speed bumps, their height, the spacing between speed bumps, the necessity for their placement in the particular area, and their effect on vehicles and traffic flow. The record reveal[s] the existence of triable issues of fact regarding whether the speed bumps constitute an interference that substantially or unreasonably diminishes Appellees' rights.

[Because genuine issues of material fact remain, we reverse summary judgment and remand for further proceedings.]

QUESTIONS

1. Who owns the dominant easement estate?
2. Who owns the servient easement estate?
3. Explain the precedent on easement barriers and the court's requirements for proof of unreasonable interference with an easement owner's rights.

CPA 3. Profits

Profits are rights to take part of the soil, subsurface materials, or resources or produce from land that belongs to another. **For Example,** profits could include the right to remove coal from the land of another and the right to use the water from another's land.

CPA 4. Licenses

A **license** is a personal, revocable privilege to perform an act or series of acts on the land of another. Unlike an easement, a license is not an interest in land. **For Example,** the person allowed to come into the house to use the telephone has a license. The advertising company that has permission to paint a sign on the side of a building also has a license. A ticket to see a movie is a license.

A license may be terminated at the will of the licensor. It continues only as long as the licensor is the owner of the land.

CPA 5. Liens

Real property may be subject to **liens** that arise by the voluntary act of the owner of the land. **For Example,** the lien of a mortgage is created when the owner borrows money and uses the land as security for repayment of the debt.

Liens may also arise involuntarily, as in the case of **tax liens**, **judgment liens**, and **mechanic's liens**. In the case of taxes and judgments, the liens provide a means for enforcing the obligations of the owner of the land to pay the taxes or the judgment. Mechanic's liens give persons furnishing labor and materials in the improvement of real estate the right to proceed against the real estate for the collection of the amounts due them.

6. Fixtures

Under the laws relating to fixtures, personal property becomes real property.

CPA **(A) DEFINITION.** A **fixture** is personal property that is attached to the earth or placed in a building in such a way or under such circumstances that it is considered part of the real property.

A person may buy a refrigerator, an air conditioner, a furnace, or some other item that is used in a building and then have the item installed. The question of whether such an item is a fixture, and therefore part of a building, can arise in a variety of situations: (1) The real estate tax assessor assesses the

Thinking Things Through

The Dryer Vent That Dumped on the Doc

Danetta Garfink owns a condominium unit at The Cloisters at Charles Condominiums. Garfink purchased her unit (one of the model units) in 1991 during the development and construction phase of the project. The original construction included installed household appliances in each unit, a clothes dryer among them. As originally installed, the clothes dryer was connected and vented into the furnace room, rather than to the outside of the building, contrary to the terms of the construction contract, and in violation of prevailing building codes and regulations.

In 2000, the clothes dryer malfunctioned and Garfink purchased a replacement from Sears, Roebuck & Co. After viewing the existing vent system, however, Sears refused to install the replacement because a "fire hazzard [sic] was identified."

Garfink took it upon herself to have the venting system rerouted. The new system was routed from the dryer through the wall of the laundry room into the adjoining garage, then through the garage and then the exterior wall. Garfink's immediate neighbor, Dr. Oscar Kantt, found that the new vent was within 17 feet of the front door of his residence, and Dr. Kantt complained about the discharge. Garfink says she has an easement for the dryer vent. Analyze whether she does have an easement. Be sure to think through the types of easements. **[*Garfink v. Cloisters at Charles, Inc.*, 897 A.2d 206 (Md. 2006)]**

building and adds in the value of the item on the theory that it is part of the building, (2) the buyer of the item owns and then sells the building, and the new owner of the building claims that the item stays with the building, (3) the buyer places a mortgage on the building, and the mortgagee claims that the item is bound by the mortgage, (4) the buyer is a tenant in the building in which the item is installed, and the landlord claims that the item must stay in the building when the tenant leaves, and (5) the buyer does not pay in full for the item, and the seller of the item has a security interest that the seller wishes to enforce against the buyer or against the landlord of the building in which the buyer installs the item. The seller of the item may also assert a claim against the mortgagee of the building or against the buyer of the building. The determination of the rights of these parties depends on the common law of fixtures, as occasionally modified by statute.

CPA **(B) Tests of a Fixture.** In the absence of an agreement between the parties, the courts apply three tests to determine whether personal property has become a fixture.

(1) Annexation.

Generally, personal property becomes a fixture if it is so attached to the realty that it cannot be removed without materially damaging the real property or destroying the personal property itself. If the property is so affixed as to lose its specific identity, such as bricks in a wall, it becomes part of the realty. When cabinets are attached to kitchen walls so as to be immovable, they are fixtures.

(2) Adaptation.

Personal property especially adapted or suited to the use made of the building may constitute a fixture such as the pipes for a church organ.

(3) Intent.

One controlling test is the intention of the person affixing the property.[3] Intent is considered as of the time the property was affixed. In the absence of direct proof of such intent, courts resort to the nature of the property, the method of its attachment, and all the surrounding circumstances to determine intent.

The fact that machinery installed in a plant would be very difficult and expensive to move or is so delicate that the moving would cause damage is significant in reaching the conclusion that the owner installed the equipment as a permanent addition and intended to make the equipment fixtures. **For Example,** when the floors in a large apartment house are made of concrete and covered with a thin

[3] *Thayer Corp. v. Maine School Administrative Dist. 61*, 38 A.3d 1263 (Me. 2012).

Sports & Entertainment Law

The New England Patriots and Their Season License Holders

In its litigation against StubHub, Inc., over StubHub's listing of its tickets for resale, the New England Patriots alleged that StubHub was engaged in intentional interference with advantageous relations through StubHub's knowing solicitation of ticket holders to violate the terms on which their tickets for access to Patriots home football games are granted (i.e., the license restrictions on transfer of the tickets). Massachusetts' Supreme Court had already held that tickets to entertainment events are revocable licenses, which a venue owner may revoke at any time and for any reason. The Patriots argued that StubHub, by offering season ticket holders' tickets for sale online, was interfering with its license rights. StubHub argued that a ticket was not a license but more like a bearer instrument that could be transferred easily. Not surprisingly, the Patriots continued their winning streak in court. The result is, because 95 percent of the tickets held to a Patriots game are season tickets, there is no open secondary market for ticket sales to Patriots games. Fans have only the license holder options afforded for selling their tickets. **[*Yarde Metals, Inc. v. New England Patriots, L.P.*, 64 Mass. App. Ct. 656 (2005); *New England Patriots, L.P. and NPS LLC, Herman v. Admit One Ticket Agency*, 912 N.E.2d 450 (Mass. 2009)]**

sheet of plywood to which wall-to-wall carpeting is stapled, the carpeting constitutes a fixture that cannot be removed from the building. Removal would probably destroy the carpeting because it was cut to size. In addition, the carpeting is necessary to make the building livable as an apartment.

CPA (c) **Movable Machinery and Equipment.** Machinery and equipment that are movable are ordinarily held not to be fixtures even though, in order to move them, it is necessary to unbolt them from the floor or to disconnect electrical wires or water pipes. **For Example,** refrigerators, freezers, and gas and electric ranges are not fixtures. They do not lose their character as personal property when they are readily removable after disconnecting pipes or unplugging wires. A portable window air conditioner that rests on a rack that is affixed to the windowsill by screws and is connected directly to the building only by an electric cord plug is not a fixture.

The mere fact that an item may be unplugged, however, does not establish that it is not a fixture. **For Example,** a computer and its related hardware constitute fixtures when there is such a mass of wires and cables under the floor that the installation gives the impression of permanence.

CPA (d) **Trade Fixtures.** Equipment that a tenant attaches to a rented building and uses in a trade or business is ordinarily removable by the tenant when the tenant permanently leaves the premises. Such equipment is commonly called a *trade fixture*.[4] The *Kohn v. Darlington Community School District* case deals with issues that turn on whether bleachers are fixtures.

Kohn v. Darlington Community School District, 686 N.W.2d 455 (Wis. 2005)

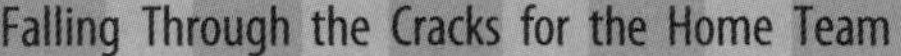

Falling Through the Cracks for the Home Team

On September 29, 2000, Elaine Kohn and her then four-year-old daughter, Lori Kohn, attended the homecoming football game at Darlington High School. At about 2:30 P.M. on a glorious Wisconsin Saturday afternoon, young Lori fell through the space at the foot of her seat in the home bleachers to the ground 15 feet below and was injured. The home bleachers are a huge structure. They are 15 rows tall, over 100 feet long, and contain a 50-inch-wide walkway elevated

[4] *Steel Farms, Inc. v. Croft & Reed, Inc.*, 297 P.3d 222 (Idaho 2012); *Taco Bell of America, Inc. v. Com. Transp. Com'r*, 710 S.E.2d 478 (Va. 2011).

Continued

30 inches above the ground. They can seat nearly 1,500 individuals. They adjoin a rather large press box and incorporate a wheelchair access ramp. While it is unclear whether they are anchored to the ground, they clearly are not readily moveable. The Kohns brought suit in 2001 against Standard Steel Industries, Inc. (Standard was later purchased by Illinois Tool Works [ITW]), a company that sold Darlington the bleachers for $16,167 in 1969, and the insurers. However, the suit was dismissed initially because Wisconsin has a 10-year statute of limitations (statute of repose) on recovery for injuries caused by improvements to real property.

The Wisconsin Court of Appeals reversed the lower court's dismissal because the bleachers were not an improvement to real property because there was no evidence that the bleachers were anchored to the ground. The Court of Appeals held that the Kohns' claims were governed by the three-year statute of limitations on personal injury and product liability actions rather than by the 10-year statute of repose. The Wisconsin Supreme Court then stepped, carefully, as it were, into the fray.

JUDICIAL OPINION

Wilcox, Justice…No one disputes that the installation of the bleachers at Darlington High School was substantially completed in 1969. The question is whether the bleachers constitute an "improvement to real property" under the statute. If they do, then the "exposure period" ended in 1979, and the Kohns' claims against ITW failed to accrue.

The Kohns contend that the bleachers are not an improvement to real property because they are not anchored in the ground and are portable. The Kohns, like the Court of Appeals, rely on the "degree of physical annexation" of the bleachers to support their argument. The Kohns further contend that very little effort or expenditure was required to place the bleachers on the ground. They argue that the bleachers are simply "personal property resting upon the real estate" and are not "integral" to the usefulness of the property. Finally, the Kohns assert that the bleachers are not an improvement to real property because they were not specifically designed or manufactured for use at Darlington High School.

ITW argues that the bleachers are permanent as their permanency is a function of their purpose. ITW emphasizes that in the 30 years since they were erected, the bleachers have not been moved, and there is no evidence that they were ever intended to be moved. ITW also focuses on the size of the bleachers and the fact that they enhance the value and usefulness of the property. ITW states that it is significant that the bleachers are specifically adapted to the purpose for which the property is devoted. ITW also argues that the fact that the bleachers theoretically could be disassembled and moved is not dispositive, as most improvements to real estate, including the Eiffel Tower, can be disassembled and moved.

The Kohns contend that the bleachers are not permanent because they are not anchored into the ground. While there may be a disputed issue of fact as to whether the bleachers are anchored into the ground, we conclude that this fact is not material to the question of whether the bleachers are "permanent" in this case. That is, we conclude that the bleachers here qualify as "permanent" regardless of whether they are anchored into the ground.

We disagree with the Kohns that "the degree of physical annexation" of the alleged improvement is dispositive. While the law of fixtures may focus on the degree of annexation of a chattel to land, courts, applying a commonsense definition to the term "improvement to real property," have "viewed the term 'improvement' as having broader significance than 'fixture' and ha[ve] indicated that the term comprehends all additions and betterments to the freehold, including everything that permanently enhances the value of the premises." Therefore, a given item need not be actually physically annexed to the land in order to constitute a permanent addition to or betterment of property.

We conclude that the bleachers at Darlington High School constitute a "permanent addition to" the Darlington High School stadium and track.

The Kohns focus on the fact that the bleachers can be disassembled and would not require any excavation to be removed. However, while the bleachers could theoretically be disassembled, that is true of almost any addition to property. Almost any structure that is assembled and installed can be dissembled and removed, even, as ITW artfully notes, a structure as large as the Eiffel Tower.

The bleachers…were never intended to be moved or taken apart. As evidence of this, we again note the length of time they have remained at Darlington High School—over 30 years. The fact that Darlington has constructed a large press box adjoining the bleachers is further evidence of the intent that the bleachers be permanent. Moreover, we note that Darlington has made significant improvements to the bleachers themselves, in the form of a wheelchair accessible ramp, new railings, and new footboards. Further evidence of the intended permanency of the bleachers is the fact that the utility of the stadium and track would be seriously diminished were the bleachers removed. In light of the above analysis, we do not find it significant that the bid contract Standard submitted to Darlington labeled the product as "portable bleachers." As such, we are satisfied that the bleachers constitute "a permanent addition to" the property.

Darlington contracted with Standard to provide the materials for the bleachers and supervise their installation at a cost of $16,167. Thus, the installation of the bleachers clearly

Continued

involved the expenditure of labor and a significant amount of money. Further, we conclude that the bleachers increase the capital value of the track and football stadium at Darlington High School and make the property more useful or valuable. It seems patently obvious that a football stadium and track with a set of bleachers is more useful and valuable than an empty field and track. Clearly, the school would not be able to attract as many spectators and charge the same admission fee to see a game or meet if there were no bleachers in the stadium, as far less people would be able to have a clear line of vision to the field. Finally, it cannot seriously be argued that the installation of the bleachers constituted "ordinary repairs."

[W]e hold that the bleachers at Darlington High School constitute an "improvement to real property" for purposes of §893.89. The bleachers qualify as an "improvement to real property" because they are a permanent addition to Darlington's real property that enhance its capital value, involved the expenditure of labor and money, and were which it is used.

[The decision of the Court of Appeals is reversed.]

QUESTIONS

1. Describe the structure, cost, and installation of the bleachers.
2. Why is it important to the Kohns that the bleachers not constitute an improvement to real property?
3. What is the significance of the fact that the contracts for the bleachers described them as "portable"?
4. What is the purpose of statutes of repose?

CPA B. Nature and Form of Real Property Ownership

A person's interest in real property may be defined in terms of the period of time for which the person will remain the owner as (1) a **fee simple estate** or (2) a **life estate**. These estates are termed *freehold estates*, which are interests of uncertain duration. At the time of creation of a freehold estate, a termination date is not known. When a person owns property for a specified period of time, this interest is not regarded as a freehold estate; it is a **leasehold estate**, subject to special rules of law.

CPA 7. Fee Simple Estate

An **estate in fee**, a fee simple, or a fee simple absolute lasts forever. The owner of such a land interest held in fee simple has the absolute and entire interest in the land. The important characteristics of this estate are that (1) it is alienable, or transferable, during life, (2) it is alienable by will, (3) it passes to heirs of the owner if it is not specifically devised (transferred by will), (4) it is subject to rights of the owner's surviving spouse, and (5) it can be attached or used to satisfy debts of the owner before or after death.

There are other forms of the fee simple estate generally used for control of land use. **Fee simple defeasibles** are interests that give the grantee all the rights of a fee simple holder provided that the grantee complies with certain restrictions. **For Example,** the grant "To Ralph Watkins so long as he uses the property for school purposes" is an example of a fee simple defeasible. Watkins will have all the rights of a fee simple holder provided that he uses the property for school purposes. If Watkins ever stops using the property for school purposes, the property reverts back to the grantor.

CPA 8. Life Estate

A *life estate* (or life tenancy), as its name indicates, lasts only during the life of a person (ordinarily its owner). Upon the death of the person by whose life the estate was measured, the owner of the life estate has no interest remaining to pass to heirs or by will. **For Example,** a grant of a life estate would be "To my husband, Nathan Jones, for life, and then to my children." Jones would hold title to the property only for the time he is alive. When Jones dies, he cannot give the property away by will. If Jones conveys the property while he is alive, the grantee for the property holds title to the land only until Jones's death.

CPA 9. Future Interests

In several of the examples given to illustrate fee simple and life estates, interests were created in more than one person. **For Example,** in the preceding life estate example, the children of the grantor are given an interest in the land at the same time that Jones is. However, the interests of the children will not take effect until Jones dies. The children have a future interest in the land. Their interest is referred to as a **remainder interest** because they have the remaining interest in the land once the life estate ends.

In the Watkins fee simple defeasible example, the grantor has a future interest if Watkins violates the restriction. The grantor's interest is called a **possibility of reverter**. It is a future interest because it cannot exist unless Watkins violates the use restriction placed on his present interest.

C. Liability to Third Persons for Condition of Real Property

A person entering the land of another may be injured by the condition of the land. Who is liable for such harm?

CPA 10. Common Law Rule

Under the common law, liability to a person who enters the land of another is controlled by the status of the injured person—that is, whether the person injured was a **trespasser**, a **licensee**, or an **invitee**. A different duty is owed by the owner (or occupier, as when a tenant is leasing property) of land to persons in each of these three categories.

(a) Trespassers. For a trespasser, the landowner ordinarily owes the duty of refraining from causing intentional harm only once the presence of the trespasser is known. The landowner is not under any duty to warn of dangers or to make the premises safe to protect the trespasser from harm. The most significant exception to this rule arises in the case of small children. Even when children are trespassers, they are generally afforded greater protection through the **attractive nuisance doctrine**. **For Example,** the owner of a tract of land was held liable for the death of a seven-year-old child who drowned in a creek on that land. Snow had covered the ice on the creek, and children running across the land did not know of the creek's location or the danger of the ice. The landowner had a duty to fence the creek, put up warnings, or control the children's access.[5]

(b) Licensees. *Licensees* are on the premises with the permission of the landowner, who owes the duty of warning of nonobvious dangers that are known to the owner. A host must warn a guest of such dangers. **For Example,** when a sliding glass door is "invisible" if the patio lights are on and the house lights are off, the owner must warn guests of the presence of the glass. The owner is liable if he has not warned guests of the danger and a guest is injured in shattering the glass. An owner, however, owes no duty to a licensee to take any steps to learn of the presence of dangers that are unknown to the owner.

(c) Invitees. *Invitees* are persons who enter another's land by invitation. The entry is connected with the owner's business or with an activity the occupier conducts on the land. Business customers, for example, are invitees.

Owners have a duty to take reasonable steps to discover any danger and a duty to warn the invitee or to correct the danger. **For Example,** a store must make a reasonable inspection of the premises to determine that there is nothing on the floor that would be dangerous, such as a slippery substance that might cause a patron to fall. The store must correct the condition, appropriately rope off the danger area, or give suitable warning. If the owner of the premises fails to take the degree of care required and an invitee is harmed as a result, then the owner is liable for such harm.

In most states, the courts have expanded the concept of invitees beyond the category of customers, or those whose presence will economically benefit the occupier. Invitees now usually include members of the public who are invited onto the premises and who cannot be reasonably expected to make an inspection of the premises before using them and would not be able to make necessary repairs to dangerous conditions. Some courts have also made inroads into the prior law by treating a recurring licensee, such as a letter carrier, as an invitee. For more information on landowner liability, refer to Chapter 9 on torts. The *Double Quick, Inc. v. Moore* case deals with landowner liability for injuries when the injuries are caused by criminal actions of others.

[5] *Foss v. Kincade,* 766 N.W.2d 317 (Minn. 2009).

Double Quick, Inc. v. Moore, 73 So.3d 1162 (Miss. 2011)

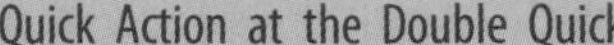

Quick Action at the Double Quick

On May 17, 2008, Wytisha Jackson was an assistant store manager of a Double Quick convenience store in Shelby, Mississippi. At approximately 7:30 P.M., George Ford, accompanied by his young son, entered Double Quick to make a purchase. Shortly afterward, Cassius Gallion entered the store. Ford and Gallion exchanged words. Gallion exited the store first. Then Ford left the store to pump gas into his car. Because she was worried that Ford and Gallion would fight, Jackson accompanied Ford and helped Ford's son into the car. At the gas pumps, Ford and Gallion again exchanged words. Then Mario Moore, who had arrived at the Double Quick but had not yet been inside, approached Ford's car, intervened in the argument, and threw a punch at Ford. Mario missed Ford but struck Jackson, who then returned to the store and called the police. Ford then retrieved a pistol from the trunk of his car and shot Mario. Mario died as a result of his injury.

Dorothy Moore, as administrator of Mario's estate, filed suit against Double Quick. Moore argued that Double Quick had neglected to protect Mario from injury and death while he was on the store's premises. Double Quick filed its motion for summary judgment. The trial court denied summary judgment and Double Quick appealed.

JUDICIAL OPINION

KING, Justice…Double Quick argued that premises-liability law was applicable, and in order for Double Quick to be liable for the failure to protect Mario from the intentional acts of another, Moore must show that the injury was foreseeable. Double Quick argued that Moore had failed to prove foreseeability, which required Moore to establish that Double Quick had actual or constructive knowledge of the assailant's violent nature or actual or constructive knowledge that an atmosphere of violence existed on the premises.

Moore argued that Double Quick and Jackson were negligent, because once Jackson and other employees were aware of the argument, Jackson had failed to call the police immediately or to separate Gallion and Ford by asking Ford to stay inside until the police had arrived.

Double Quick argues that it is entitled to summary judgment under the principles of premises-liability law. "[P]remises liability is a theory of negligence that establishes the duty owed to someone injured on a landowners's premises as a result of 'conditions or activities' on the land."

Moore contends that the instant case is not one of premises liability, but a basic negligence case against Jackson. The only case Moore relies on to support her claim that this is a basic negligence case is *Foradori v. Captain D's, LLC*, 2005 WL 3307102 (N.D.Miss.2005), and its affirmance by the Fifth Circuit in *Foradori v. Harris*, 523 F.3d 477 (5th Cir.2008). In *Foradori*, the plaintiff, a customer, was injured by employees of Captain D's. *Foradori* involved the legal principle of vicarious liability of Captain D's for its manager's negligent failure to control her employees and prevent them from assaulting a customer of the restaurant. The *Foradori* case was not a premises-liability case, and the Fifth Circuit noted that the district court granted summary judgment, dismissing the premises-liability claims.

However, the *Foradori* case is not factually similar to the instance case. In the instant case, Mario was not injured by the Double Quick employees; the Double Quick employees were not even aware of his presence on the premises. Because Mario's injury was the result of an activity that occurred on Double Quick's property, we find that Moore's claim is one of premises liability. Accordingly, the trial court erred in holding that the instant case was not a premises-liability case.

To recover damages in a premises-liability action, Moore must show (a) the duty owed to Mario by Double Quick; (b) a breach of that duty; (c) damages; and (d) a causal connection between the breach and the damages, such that the breach is the proximate cause of Mario's injuries.

Generally, in order to determine the duty owed by the business owner, the status of the injured party must be determined. The injured party should be classified as an invitee, licensee, or trespasser. An invitee is a person who enters the premises of another in response to an "express or implied invitation of the owner or occupant for their mutual advantage." A licensee enters the premises "for his own convenience, pleasure, or benefit pursuant to the license or implied permission[.]" A trespasser enters the premises "without license, invitation, or other right."

Under Mississippi law, a property owner is not the insurer of an invitee's safety. Rather, he owes a duty to the invitee to keep the premises reasonably safe and, when not reasonably safe, to warn only of hidden dangers not in plain and open view. Also, the duty owed to a licensee or trespasser is the same—not to willfully or wantonly injure such person.

The parties disagree on Mario's status, but Mario's classification is irrelevant in determining the outcome of this appeal. The issue is not determinative, because even if Jackson and Double Quick owed Mario a higher duty of care, Moore failed to provide evidence that Jackson's action or inaction was the proximate cause of Mario's death.

Proximate cause is defined as the "cause which in natural and continuous sequence unbroken by any efficient intervening cause produces the injury and without which the result would not have occurred." Generally, "criminal acts can be intervening causes which break the causal connection with the defendant's negligent act, if the criminal act is not within the

Continued

realm of reasonable foreseeability." Thus, in order to establish that Jackson's behavior was the proximate cause of Mario's injury, Moore would have to prove that Mario's injury was reasonably foreseeable.

In premises-liability cases, there are two ways to establish legal causation, or foreseeability, in cases of assault by a third person: the requisite "cause to anticipate" the assault may arise from actual or constructive knowledge of the assailant's violent nature, or actual or constructive knowledge that an atmosphere of violence exists on the premises.

There was no suggestion within the record that Jackson had actual or constructive knowledge of Ford's violent nature. Jackson voluntarily went outside to the gas pumps with Ford. Further, the record does not indicate that an atmosphere of violence existed on the premises of Double Quick. In fact, Moore's attorney conceded during the hearing on the motions for summary judgment that there was no evidence to indicate that Double Quick had a violent atmosphere.

Because Moore failed to prove that the injury was reasonably foreseeable, there is no evidence to suggest that Jackson's behavior was the proximate cause of Mario's injuries. We find that the trial court erred in denying Double Quick's motion for summary judgment.

[Therefore, we reverse the judgment of the trial court and render a judgment of dismissal in favor of Double Quick.]

QUESTIONS

1. What is the difference between a premises-liability case and a negligence case?
2. Why does the court not concern itself with determining whether Mario was an invitee?
3. What would establish proximate cause in this case for purposes of attributing liability to Double Quick?

D. Co-Ownership of Real Property

Real property may be owned by one or several persons, and the method of co-ownership determines the extent of the owners' rights.

11. Multiple Ownership

Several persons may have *concurrent interests* (or interests that exist at the same time) in the same real property. The forms of multiple ownership for real property are the same as those for personal property. Real property can be held by tenants in common, by joint tenants with right of survivorship, by tenants by the entirety, or under community property rights. When co-owners sell property, they hold the proceeds of sale by the same kind of tenancy as that in which they held the original property.

12. Condominiums

A **condominium** is a combination of co-ownership and individual ownership. **For Example,** persons owning an office building or an apartment house by condominium are co-owners of the land and of the halls, lobby, elevators, stairways, exits, surrounding land, incinerator, laundry rooms, and other areas used in common. Each apartment or office in the building, however, is individually owned and is transferred in the same way as other forms of real property.

(a) Control and Expense. In some states, owners of the various units in the condominium have equal voice in its management and share an equal part of its expenses. In others, control and liability for expenses are shared by a unit owner in the same ratio that the value of the unit bears to the value of the entire condominium project. In all states, unit owners have equal rights to use the common areas. An owners' association is created by the condominium owners to operate the common areas of the condominium property and resolve any disputes among owners.

The owner of each condominium unit makes the repairs required by the owner's deed or contract of ownership. The owner is prohibited from making any major change that would impair or damage the safety or value of an adjoining unit.

(b) Collection of Expenses from Unit Owner. When a unit owner fails to pay the owner's share of taxes, operating expenses, and repairs, the owners' association generally has the right to a lien against that owner's unit for the amount due.

(c) Tort Liability. Most condominium projects fail to make provision for the liability of unit owners for a tort occurring in the common areas. A few states expressly provide that when a third person is injured in a common area, a suit may be brought only against the condominium association. Any judgment recovered is a charge against the association to be paid off as a common expense. When the condominium association is incorporated, the same result should be obtained by applying ordinary principles of corporation law. Under principles of corporation law, liability for torts occurring on the premises of the corporation would not be the liability of individual shareholders.

(D) COOPERATIVES DISTINGUISHED. Ownership in a condominium is different from ownership in a **cooperative**. An apartment cooperative is typically a corporation that owns an apartment complex. The "ownership" interests of the apartment occupants are as stockholders of the corporation.

E. TRANSFER OF REAL PROPERTY BY DEED

Although many of the technical limitations of the feudal system and earlier common law on transfer of land have disappeared, much of the law relating to the modern deed originated in those days.

CPA 13. Definitions

A **deed** is an instrument or writing by which an owner or **grantor** transfers or conveys an interest in land to a new owner. The new owner is called a **grantee** or **transferee**. Real property may be either sold or given as a gift. A deed, however, is necessary to transfer title to land, even if it is a gift.

In contrast to the situation with a contract, no consideration is required to make a deed effective. Although consideration is not required to make a deed valid or to transfer title by deed, the absence of consideration may show that the owner makes the transfer to defraud creditors. The creditors may then be able to set aside the fraudulent transfer.

CPA 14. Classification of Deeds

Deeds may be classified according to the interest conveyed as **quitclaim deeds** or **warranty deeds**. A quitclaim deed merely transfers whatever interest, if any, the grantor may have in the property without specifying that interest in any way. A warranty deed transfers a specified interest and warrants or guarantees that such interest is transferred. Figure 49-1 is a sample warranty deed.

CPA 15. Execution of Deeds

Ordinarily, the grantor must sign, by signature or mark, a deed. A deed must be executed and delivered by a person having capacity. A deed may be set aside by the grantor for fraud by the grantee if third persons have not acquired rights in the land in good faith.

CPA 16. Delivery and Acceptance of Deeds

A deed has no effect and title does not pass until the deed has been delivered. Delivery is a matter of intent as shown by words and conduct; no particular form of ceremony is required. The essential intent in delivering a deed is not merely that the grantor intends to hand over physical control and possession of the paper on which the deed is written but also that the grantor intends thereby to transfer the ownership of the property described in the deed. That intent can be shown by handing it to the grantee or placing the deed, addressed to the grantee, in the mail or by giving it to a third person with directions to give it to the grantee.

An effective delivery of a deed may be made symbolically, or constructively, such as by delivering to the grantee the key to a locked box and informing the grantee that the deed to the property is in the box. **For Example,** the delivery of a safe deposit box key has been held to constitute delivery of a deed that was in the box.

Generally, there must be an **acceptance** by the grantee. In all cases, an acceptance is presumed unless the grantee disclaims the transfer.

CPA 17. Recording of Deeds

The owner of land may record the deed in the office of a public official, sometimes called a **recorder** or *commissioner of deeds*. The recording is not required to make the deed effective to pass title, but it is done so that the public will know that the grantee is the present owner and thereby prevent the former owner from making any future transfer or transaction relating to the property.

FIGURE 49-1 ***Form of Warranty Deed***

THIS DEED, made the twentieth day of November, two thousand and . . . between James K. Damron, residing at 132 Spring Street in the Borough of Manhattan, City and State of New York, party of the first part, and Terrence S. Bloemker, residing at 14 Steinway Street in the Borough of Queens, City and State of New York, party of the second part,

WITNESSETH, that the party of the first part, in consideration of the sum of one dollar ($1), lawful money of the United States, and other good and valuable consideration paid by the party of the second part, does hereby grant and release unto the party of the second part, his heirs and assigns forever,

ALL that certain lot, piece, and parcel of land situated in the Borough of Manhattan, City and County of New York, and State of New York, and bounded and described as follows:

Beginning at a point on the northerly side of Spring Street, distant two hundred (200) feet westerly from the corner formed by the intersection of the northerly side of Spring Street with the westerly side of 6th Avenue, running thence northerly parallel with 6th Avenue one hundred (100) feet, thence westerly and parallel with said Spring Street one hundred (100) feet; thence southerly, again parallel with said 6th Avenue one hundred (100) feet to the northerly side of Spring Street, and thence easterly along the said northerly side of Spring Street one hundred (100) feet to the point or place of beginning.

Together with the appurtenances and all the estate and rights of the party of the first part in and to said premises.

TO HAVE AND TO HOLD the premises herein granted unto the party of the second part, his heirs and assigns forever.

AND the party of the first part covenants as follows:

First. That the party of the first part is seised of the said premises in fee simple, and has good right to convey the same;

Second. That the party of the second part shall quietly enjoy the said premises;

Third. That the said premises are free from encumbrances except as expressly stated;

Fourth. That the party of the first part will execute or procure any further necessary assurance of the title to said premises;

IN WITNESS WHEREOF, the party of the first part has hereunto set his hand and seal the day and year first above written.

JAMES K. DAMRON

(L.S.)

In presence of:

DIANA L. REILMAN

State of New York } s.s.:*

County of New York

On the twentieth day of November in the year two thousand and . . . , before me personally came James K. Damron, to me known and known to me to be the individual described in, and who executed, the foregoing instrument, and he acknowledged that he executed the same.

DIANA L. REILMAN
Notary Public, New York County

*Note: Acknowledgment before a notary public is not essential to the effectiveness of a deed, but it is typically required to qualify the deed for recording.

When no document is recorded, states have statutes for determining who obtains title and who will be left to take action against the party that has conveyed the property to more than one person. **For Example,** suppose that Grant conveys a tract of land to Dee. Dee does not record her deed. Grant then conveys the same tract of land to Joe, who also does not record his deed, but Joe is unaware of Dee's acquisition. Then Grant conveys the same property to Larry who knows about Dee and Joe but records his deed. Who will hold title, and who will be left to pursue Grant for remedies? Under **race statutes**, the first party to record the deed holds title, so Larry holds title. Under **notice statutes**, the last good-faith or bona fide purchaser (BFP), someone who does not know about the previous conveyances, takes title. Under notice, Joe holds title because he is the last BFP. Larry knows about the prior transactions and that fact controls title, not the recording of his deed under notice statutes. Under **notice-race** or **race-notice statutes**, the first BFP to record the deed holds title. So, if Dee records first, she holds title. If Joe records first, he will. Larry has recorded but does not meet the second requirement of race-notice, which is that one must be the first BFP to record to take title in a race-notice statute. Suppose that Larry is a BFP, but Joe is not because he is aware of the conveyance to Dee. Under race, Larry holds title. Under notice, Larry holds title. Under race-notice, Larry wins again. If Dee records her deed, all of these issues are moot because recording the deed is complete notice for all subsequent purchasers.

The fact that a deed is recorded provides notice to the world about who holds title. The recording of a deed, however, is only such notice if the deed was properly executed. Likewise, the grantee of land cannot claim any protection by virtue of the recording of a deed when (1) a claim is made by one whose title is superior to that of the owner of record, (2) the grantee had notice or knowledge of the adverse claim when title was acquired, (3) a person acting under a hostile claim was then in possession of the land, (4) the grantee received the land as a gift, or (5) the transfer to the grantee was fraudulent.

18. Additional Protection of Buyers

In addition to the protection given to buyers and third persons by the recorded title to property, a buyer is generally protected by procuring title insurance or an abstract of title. An **abstract of title** is a summarized report of the title to the property as shown by the records, together with a report of all judgments, mortgages, and similar recorded claims against the property. The *Fletcher v. Minton* case shows what can happen when property is conveyed more than once.

Fletcher v. Minton, 217 S.W.3d 755 (Tex. App. 2007)

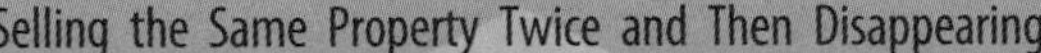

Selling the Same Property Twice and Then Disappearing

Wallace Salls was the recorded owner of a 12.56-acre parcel of real property in Hunt County, Texas. In October 1984, Salls sold two adjoining tracts from the parcel. Tract I, consisting of 3.675 acres, was sold to Paula Malecek and her husband for $14,700. Tract II, consisting of 3.676 acres, was sold to David Minton and his wife for $14,704. Both sales occurred under a contract for deed. Neither contract for deed was recorded but payments under the contract for deed (see Chapter 15) were made.

In September 1994, Salls sold the property again. This sale involved the entire 12.56-acre parcel, including the two tracts previously conveyed to Minton and Malecek. Shannon Cook, the purchaser of the entire parcel, did not record the deed until 1997. In 1999, Cook sold the 12.56-acre parcel to Fletcher. The general warranty deed Fletcher recorded bears the notation "Drafted without Title Examination."

An attorney named Robert Crouch handled all legal matters for both Malecek and Salls, including the drafting of the contract for deed for Tract I. Crouch also drafted the deeds when the property was conveyed to Cook and Fletcher. Crouch is now deceased. Salls filed bankruptcy sometime prior to 1989, and no one has been able to locate him for a number of years.

Fletcher filed a lawsuit against Minton seeking to quiet title to Tracts I and II. Minton denied Fletcher's allegations of ownership. Malecek intervened in the lawsuit and asserted that she was the owner of Tract I. The trial court held that Malecek was the owner of Tract I; Minton was the owner of Tract II;

Continued

and Fletcher was entitled to reimbursement from Malecek for ad valorem taxes paid on Tract I. Fletcher appealed.

JUDICIAL OPINION

RICHTER, Judge…A person who acquires property in good faith, for value, and without notice of any third-party claim or interest is a bona fide purchaser. Status as a bona fide purchaser is an affirmative defense to a title dispute.

Notice will defeat the protection otherwise afforded a bona fide purchaser. Notice may be actual or constructive. Actual notice results from personal information or knowledge, as well as those facts which reasonable inquiry would have disclosed. Constructive notice is notice the law imputes to a person not having personal information or knowledge.

A. *Tract I.*

There is no dispute concerning Fletcher's purchase of the property in good faith and for value. Thus, the bona fide purchaser inquiry centers on whether Fletcher had actual or constructive notice of any of the competing claims to the property. The trial court did not expressly conclude that Fletcher was not a bona fide purchaser. The trial court did find, however, that Fletcher, through her agent, had constructive, if not actual, notice of Minton's claims to both tracts at the time she purchased the property. We agree.

Fletcher testified that although she owns other property near the property at issue in this suit, she claimed that she never noticed mobile homes on the property she purchased. Fletcher further testified that she did not inspect the property prior to her purchase. Fletcher's agent and ex-husband Max also assisted Fletcher with the purchase. Before Fletcher purchased the property, Max visited the property and spoke with Minton on at least one, perhaps two, occasions. Minton lived on the property at the time. Although there is no explanation in the record about why Max visited Minton, it is reasonable to infer that the visit resulted from knowledge or suspicion that Minton occupied or possessed the property. Minton testified that when Max visited him, he told Max that Malecek owned Tract I. Malecek testified that she was on the property when Max was there asking Minton who owned the property. When Max was asked if he knew that Minton occupied Tract II and used Tract I, he admitted that he had seen Minton "go in and out of there." Max also observed that there were two or three mobile homes and some cows on the property.

Max testified that he did see the title search, but it did not reflect that there were any prior owners. The general warranty deed evidencing Fletcher's purchase of the property expressly states that there was no title examination. Based on our review, we cannot conclude that the evidence is insufficient to support the finding that Fletcher, through her agent Max, had constructive, if not actual, notice of a conflicting claim to the property.

Malecek testified that she purchased the property for investment purposes. Because she did not inhabit the property, she told Minton, who resided on the adjoining Tract II, that he could use her property as if it were his own. As a result, from 1990 forward Minton used Tract I for cutting hay, growing watermelons, storing equipment and grazing cattle. Minton also constructed a fence around Tracts I and II. Max testified that he saw Minton going to and from the property, and made no distinction as to whether he observed Minton on Tract I or II. The evidence also shows that Cook, the individual from whom Fletcher purchased the property, was aware of Minton's possession and claimed ownership of the property. In 1997, Cook sent a letter to Minton demanding that he vacate the property. Minton's attorney responded to the letter, and stated that Minton had been the owner of the tract for a number of years. Thus, the trial court's findings support the correct legal theory that Minton's use and occupation of the property was sufficiently open, visible, exclusive, and unequivocal to put Fletcher on notice of a competing claim.

Having concluded that Fletcher is not entitled to the protection of a bona fide purchaser as to Tract I, we examine whether the trial court erred in finding that Malecek is the owner of Tract I.

Initially, Malecek was not aware that the contract for deed had not been filed. Attorney Crouch was supposed to have taken care of everything. When the taxing authority would not allow her to pay the taxes, Malecek attempted to contact both Salls and Crouch to obtain a deed. Salls had disappeared, but Crouch told her that a clear deed would be issued once the property was no longer tied up in Salls' bankruptcy. Malecek testified that she contacted Crouch concerning the deed on numerous occasions. The sale of Tract I to Malecek by contract for deed is also detailed in the amended bankruptcy schedules Salls executed and filed in 1992. We conclude that the evidence is legally and factually sufficient to support the trial court's finding that Malecek is the owner of Tract I.

B. *Tract II.*

There were two competing claims to Tract II: Fletcher, and Minton. Minton signed a contract for deed with Salls in 1984, and has been on Tract II continuously since that time. When Minton was close to the end of his scheduled payments on the property, he asked Salls about "completing the paperwork." He told Salls that he did not know what to do because he had never purchased property before. Salls told Minton he would get back with him on the paperwork, but he never did.

Continued

In addition to Minton's testimony and the contract for deed, Minton's purchase of the property was also supported by an August 16, 1990, letter to Minton from Crouch on behalf of Salls.

Minton testified that he lived on Tract II from 1984 until approximately 2000. He has three mobile homes, two sheds, several vehicles, and a catfish tank on the property. At some point, he also had some chickens and pigs. Minton testified further that he periodically brings materials such as bricks and sheet rock leftover from his construction jobs to store on the property. On one occasion, someone complained about the mess some of the materials made on the property. Minton acknowledged that "things got a little out of hand." An environmental enforcement agency came to the property to show Minton the proper way to clean up the mess, during which time he had several large dumpsters and a front-end loader on the property. Thus, there was not only evidence to suggest that someone occupied the property on a consistent basis, but also extraordinary activity that even a casual observer would be likely to notice. Fletcher owned property nearby, but could not recall if she had called the county to complain about the mess on Minton's property. We conclude that the evidence is sufficient to support the trial court's finding that Minton openly and notoriously occupied Tract II continuously from 1984. The record supports the trial court's finding that Fletcher had notice.

The recordation law in Texas was meant to protect innocent purchasers without prior notice of a transfer from being injured or prejudiced by their lack of knowledge of a competing claim. Fletcher failed to establish that she is the type of innocent purchaser this law seeks to protect. As a result, the trial court properly found that Minton is the owner of Tract II.

[We affirm the judgment of the trial court.]

QUESTIONS

1. Diagram the tracts and ownership rights and transfers.
2. What is the significance of activity on the tracts when it comes to notice statutes?
3. Who ends up with the property and why?

19. Grantor's Warranties

The warranties of the grantor relate to the title transferred by the grantor and to the fitness of the property for use.

CPA **(A) Warranties of Title.** In the common law deed, the grantor may expressly warrant or make certain *covenants* as to the title conveyed. The statutes authorizing a short form of deed provide that, unless otherwise stated in the deed, the grantor is presumed to have made certain **warranties of title**.

The more important of the **covenants (or warranties) of title** that the grantor may make are (1) **covenant of seisin**, or guarantee that the grantor owns the estate conveyed, (2) **covenant of right to convey**, or guarantee that the grantor, if not the owner as in the case of an agent, has the right or authority to make the conveyance, (3) **covenant against encumbrances**, or guarantee that the land is not subject to any right or interest of a third person, such as a lien or an easement, (4) **covenant of quiet enjoyment**, or guarantee by the grantor that the grantee's possession of the land will not be disturbed either by the grantor, in the case of a **limited covenant**, or by the grantor or any person claiming title under the grantor, in the case of a general covenant, and (5) **covenant of further assurances**, or guarantee that the grantor will execute any additional documents that may be required to perfect the title of the grantee.

(B) Fitness for Use. Courts in most states hold that when a builder or real estate developer sells a new house to a home buyer, the buyer gets an implied warranty that the house and foundation are fit for occupancy or use. This warranty arises regardless of whether the house was purchased before, during, or after completion of construction.[6] This first buyer is not responsible for the builder warranty when the house is resold. However, there is authority that the second buyer may recover from the original contractor for breach of the implied warranty even though there is no privity of contract.[7]

[6] *Richards v. Powercraft Homes, Inc.*, 678 P.2d 427 (Ariz. 1984), but see *Long v. Jeb Breithaupt Design Build Inc.*, 4 So.3d 930 (La. App. 2009).

[7] Many states have passed statutes that govern the extent of the implied warranty of habitability. Although the statutes vary, the types of defects covered include defects in construction, design, and appearance. See *Baeza v. Superior Court*, 135 Cal. Rptr. 3d 557 (Cal. App. 2011).

20. Grantee's Covenants

In a deed, the grantee may agree to do or to refrain from doing certain acts. Such an agreement becomes a binding contract between the grantor and the grantee. The grantor may recover from the grantee for its breach.

The right to enforce the covenant also **runs with the land** owned by the grantor to whom the promise was made. **For Example,** a promise not to use a tract of land for a parking lot between two adjoining landowners would be passed (conveyed) to any buyers who subsequently acquire these tracts. For more information on covenants, see Chapter 50, Environmental Law and Land Use Controls.

F. Other Methods of Transferring Real Property

Title to real property can also be acquired by eminent domain and by adverse possession.

CPA 21. Eminent Domain

Under **eminent domain**, property is taken from its private owner for a public purpose. The title is then taken by a government or public authority. There are constitutionally protected rights of property owners under eminent domain. Known as the "takings clause," this portion of the Fifth Amendment to the U.S. Constitution requires compensation when private property is taken for public use. Two important issues arise under the takings clause: (1) whether there is a taking of property and (2) whether the property is taken for a public use. With respect to whether a taking has occurred, it is not necessary that the owner be physically deprived of the property but that normal use of the property has been impaired or lost. Whether there is a public use for the taking is a question that continues to be challenged in court because the definition of public purpose is so broad. **For Example,** property can be taken to build a freeway as well as for the preservation of a historic site. In the eminent domain cases after 2000, much of the litigation centered on whether revitalizations of areas with urban blight were permissible takings. Eminent domain has activated a concerned public as state and local governments take more and more houses and land for purposes of economic development. The *Kelo v. City of New London* case is a landmark decision on eminent domain.

Kelo v. City of New London, 545 U.S. 469 (2005)

Little Pink Houses, for You, but Not for Me...Anymore

In 1978, the city of New London, Connecticut, undertook a redevelopment plan for purposes of creating a redeveloped area in and around the existing park at Fort Trumball. The plan had the goals of achieving all the related ambience a state park should have, including the absence of pink cottages and other architecturally eclectic homes. Part of the redevelopment plan was the city's deal with Pfizer Corporation for the location of its research facility in the area. The preface to the city's development plan stated that it would "*create jobs increase tax and other revenues, encourage public access to and use of the city's waterfront, and eventually 'build momentum' for the revitalization of the rest of the city, including its downtown area.*"

Susette Kelo, and other property owners whose homes would be razed and whose land would be taken to allow for the park, Pfizer's facility, and other redevelopment (15 total owners including Kelo), asked to be permitted to stay in the area. The city refused their request.

Kelo and the other homeowners filed suit challenging New London's legal authority to take their homes. The trial court issued an injunction preventing New London from taking certain of the properties but allowing others to be taken. Those property owners who were held subject to eminent domain appealed.

The appellate court found for New London on all claims; the landowners appealed.

JUDICIAL OPINION

STEVENS, Justice*....[i]t has long been accepted that the sovereign may not take the property of A for the sole purpose of transferring it to another private party B, even though A is paid just compensation. On the other hand, it is equally clear that a State may transfer property from one private party to another if future "use by the public" is the purpose of the taking; the condemnation of land for a railroad with

*The decision in this case was 5-4 with each justice filing either a concurring or dissenting opinion. Justice Rehnquist, in one of his last acts on the bench before his passing, said when he announced the decision and individual opinions on this case, "I didn't know we had that many people on our court." Joan Biskupic, "Rehnquist Leaves Them Laughing—and Guessing," *USA Today*, June 28, 2005, p. 2A.

Continued

common-carrier duties is a familiar example. Neither of these propositions, however, determines the disposition of this case.

As for the first proposition, the City would no doubt be forbidden from taking petitioners' land for the purpose of conferring a private benefit on a particular private party. Nor would the City be allowed to take property under the mere pretext of a public purpose, when its actual purpose was to bestow a private benefit. The takings before us, however, would be executed pursuant to a"carefully considered" development plan.

The disposition of this case therefore turns on the question whether the City's development plan serves a "public purpose." Without exception, our cases have defined that concept broadly, reflecting our longstanding policy of deference to legislative judgments in this field.

In *Berman v. Parker*, 348 U.S. 26, 75 S.Ct. 98, 99 L.Ed. 27 (1954), this Court upheld a redevelopment plan targeting a blighted area of Washington, D.C., in which most of the housing for the area's 5,000 inhabitants was beyond repair. Under the plan, the area would be condemned and part of it utilized for the construction of streets, schools, and other public facilities. The remainder of the land would be leased or sold to private parties for the purpose of redevelopment, including the construction of low-cost housing.

Writing for a unanimous Court, Justice Douglas refused to evaluate this claim in isolation, deferring instead to the legislative and agency judgment that the area "must be planned as a whole" for the plan to be successful.

Those who govern the City were not confronted with the need to remove blight in the Fort Trumbull area, but their determination that the area was sufficiently distressed to justify a program of economic rejuvenation is entitled to our deference. The City has carefully formulated an economic development plan that it believes will provide appreciable benefits to the community, including—but by no means limited to—new jobs and increased tax revenue. As with other exercises in urban planning and development, the City is endeavoring to coordinate a variety of commercial, residential, and recreational uses of land, with the hope that they will form a whole greater than the sum of its parts. Given the comprehensive character of the plan, the thorough deliberation that preceded its adoption, and the limited scope of our review, it is appropriate for us, as it was in *Berman*, to resolve the challenges of the individual owners, not on a piecemeal basis, but rather in light of the entire plan. Because that plan unquestionably serves a public purpose, the takings challenged here satisfy the public use requirement of the Fifth Amendment.

[P]etitioners urge us to adopt a new bright-line rule that economic development does not qualify as a public use. Promoting economic development is a traditional and long accepted function of government. There is, moreover, no principled way of distinguishing economic development from the other public purposes that we have recognized. [I]n *Berman*, we endorsed the purpose of transforming a blighted area into a"well-balanced" community through redevelopment. Clearly, there is no basis for exempting economic development from our traditionally broad understanding of public purpose.

Just as we decline to second-guess the City's considered judgments about the efficacy of its development plan, we also decline to second-guess the City's determinations as to what lands it needs to acquire in order to effectuate the project. "It is not for the courts to oversee the choice of the boundary line nor to sit in review on the size of a particular project area. Once the question of the public purpose has been decided, the amount and character of land to be taken for the project and the need for a particular tract to complete the integrated plan rests in the discretion of the legislative branch."

[The judgment of the Supreme Court of Connecticut is affirmed.]

DISSENTING OPINION

O'CONNOR, Justice, joined by Justices SCALIA, THOMAS and REHNQUIST

Under the banner of economic development, all private property is now vulnerable to being taken and transferred to another private owner, so long as it might be upgraded—i.e., given to an owner who will use it in a way that the legislature deems more beneficial to the public—in the process. To reason, as the Court does, that the incidental public benefits resulting from the subsequent ordinary use of private property render economic development takings "for public use" is to wash out any distinction between private and public use of property—and thereby effectively to delete the words "for public use" from the Takings Clause of the Fifth Amendment. Accordingly I respectfully dissent.

Where is the line between "public" and "private" property use? We give considerable deference to legislatures' determinations about what governmental activities will advantage the public. But were the political branches the sole arbiters of the public-private distinction, the Public Use Clause would amount to little more than hortatory fluff. An external, judicial check on how the public use requirement is interpreted, however limited, is necessary if this constraint on government power is to retain any meaning.

Continued

If it is true that incidental public benefits from new private use are enough to ensure the "public purpose" in a taking, why should it matter, as far as the Fifth Amendment is concerned, what inspired the taking in the first place? How much the government does or does not desire to benefit a favored private party has no bearing on whether an economic development taking will or will not generate secondary benefit for the public. And whatever the reason for a given condemnation, the effect is the same from the constitutional perspective—private property is forcibly relinquished to new private ownership.

QUESTIONS

1. What is different from this case and a case in which property is taken for a freeway?
2. What is the concern of the dissent about the decision?
3. Why does the majority state that the courts should be reluctant to get involved in local government eminent domain activities? [Author's note: Sadly, Pfizer pulled out of the deal. The houses had been razed, but the land remains undeveloped.]

Thinking Things Through

Putting the Brakes on Eminent Domain

Bailey's Brake Service, a bit of an eyesore at a main intersection near a failing downtown area of Mesa, Arizona, was a family-founded, owned, and operated business that had been open in its existing location since 1970. Lenhart's True Value Hardware store was also a longstanding Mesa business with a location south and east of Bailey's and a desire for a better location. The Lenharts had purchased the property abutting Bailey's but felt that the street facing Bailey's property was necessary for its location.

The city did a taking by eminent domain and then "reissued" the property to Lenhart's for its store. The Baileys challenged the city's taking in the Superior Court as unconstitutional, but the court held that the taking was constitutional as part of the city's plan for redevelopment and revitalization of the area. The Baileys appealed the trial court decision. Should the Baileys get their property back? Was this a proper eminent domain taking? **[*Bailey v. Myers*, 76 P.3d 898 (Az. Ct. App. 2003)]**

Ethics & the Law

Hell Hath No Fury Like a NOWMP

The NIMBYs (Not In My Backyard) challenge the placement of everything from power plants to refineries to Wal-Marts. There are also the BANANAs (Build Absolutely Nothing Anywhere Near Anything). Finally, the NOWMPs (Not With My Property) are opposed to eminent domain, the taking of their property for a public use.

Think back to your readings on ethics in Chapter 3. What ethical principles could you apply in favor of the NIMBYs, the BANANAs, and the NOWMPs? What ethical principles could you apply that find that the NIMBYs, the BANANAs, and the NOWMPs are acting unethically?

Source: For more information, see Marianne M. Jennings, "NIMBYs, BANANAs, LULUs, NOPEs, and NOWMPs: The Percolating World of Eminent Domain (The Par Boil Stage or Part I)," 33 *Real Estate Law Journal* (no. 4), 445–457 (2005).

22. Adverse Possession

Title to land may be acquired by possessing it adversely for a statutorily prescribed period of time. A possessor who complies with the requirements for **adverse possession** can gain title. Those who adversely possess property gain title to property even though they had no right to use the property at the beginning of their use or possession.

To acquire title by adverse possession, the possession must be (1) actual, (2) visible and notorious,

(3) exclusive, (4) hostile, and (5) continuous for a required period of time.

State statutes control the required time period, but the typical range is 10 to 20 years. Use or possession of land under a mistaken belief that one is the owner still qualifies for the "hostile" possession required under the fourth element listed.[8]

G. Mortgages

An agreement that creates an interest in real property as security for an obligation until that obligation is repaid is a **mortgage**.

The property owner, whose interest in the property is given as security, is the *mortgagor*.

The person who receives the security is the *mortgagee*.

CPA 23. Characteristics of a Mortgage

A mortgage has three characteristics: (1) the termination of the mortgagee's interest on the performance of the obligation secured by the mortgage, (2) the right of the mortgagee to enforce the mortgage by foreclosure on the mortgagor's failure to perform, and (3) the mortgagor's right to redeem or regain the property.

24. Property Subject to Mortgage

In general, any form of property that may be sold or conveyed may be mortgaged. It is immaterial whether the right is a present right, a future interest, or merely a right in the land of another. It is not necessary that the mortgagor have complete or absolute ownership in the property. Mortgagors may mortgage any type of land interest they own.

CPA 25. Form of Mortgage

Because a mortgage of real property transfers an interest in the property, it must be in writing under the statute of frauds. As a general rule, no particular form of language is required if the language used expresses the intent of the parties to create a mortgage. Many state statutes provide a standardized form for mortgage language that may be used.

26. Creative Forms of Financing

In many situations in which a buyer seeks to purchase property, the conventional methods for obtaining a mortgage are not available because of affordability or qualifications required for a loan. Many creative forms of financing have been developed to help buyers purchase property. **For Example,** residential land buyers, particularly during the real estate boom in 2005–2006, could obtain an **adjustable rate mortgage (ARM)**, in which the lower interest rates applied at the beginning of the mortgage help the buyer qualify for the loan. The ARM changes interest rates along with the market, going up and down, unless the ARM has a fixed minimum rate. Other buyers may have the seller finance their purchase through the use of a land or an installment contract. Some new forms of financing, such as the **reverse mortgage**, permit those who have paid off their mortgages on their property to get the value out of their property by having a mortgage company take a mortgage out on the property and pay them money over time. Many senior citizens are able to obtain the additional monthly income they may need by this form of financing, which permits them to draw on their equity in their land. Because of the collapse of the subprime mortgage market in 2007–2008, these creative forms of financing are now under extensive state and federal regulation. In addition, state and federal reforms (under Dodd-Frank) require additional disclosures about the full cost of financing a real property purchase through a mortgage, especially in the types of mortgages in which payments and interest rates fluctuate. (See Chapter 32 for more information.)

27. Recording or Filing of Mortgage

An unrecorded mortgage is still valid and binding between and among the parties. A mortgage cannot be set aside on the ground that it has not been recorded. However, recording the mortgage does protect the mortgagee in terms of priority as against other creditors. The recording statutes, including the problems with MERS, also apply to mortgages.

[8] The state with the shortest period for adverse possession is Texas, whose adverse possession period can be as short as three years. The state with the longest adverse possession period is Wyoming, with 40 years.

E-Commerce & Cyberlaw

MERS and Problems

Mortgage Electronic Registration Systems, Inc. (MERS), was the system used by most lenders for purposes of recording their mortgages for loans on residential property and, thereby, attaining their secured interest and priority. About one-half of the residential mortgages in the United States were recorded in MERS. The effect was that MERS was listed as the mortgagee on the public records. Debtors wanted to know, "Who is MERS?" The result has been litigation around the country, brought by homeowners facing foreclosure. These suits have alleged that MERS had not perfected its security interest in the mortgaged property because the note was split (and sold off in bundles that were then the foundation of collateralized debt obligations on Wall Street) from the deed of trust or mortgage. And MERS was not their mortgagee. Further, the debtors were unable to fight foreclosure because it became difficult to determine who actually was the mortgagee for purposes of determining default, rights, and redemption. The debtors have argued that their notes were unenforceable without an accompanying mortgage and mortgagee. With the note unenforceable, the debtors argued that they could not be in default because no money was due and owing. The argument has not fared well in deed-of-trust lending, but the litigation continues around the country. Known as the "lost chain of title" cases, the result has been investigations by state attorneys general of how loan and mortgage documents were transferred (including allegations of robo-signing by transferees for transferors). As one writer noted, MERS has had a destructive effect on 400 years of recorded property rights in the United States because the chain of title has been lost in so many cases. **[*Manderville v. Litton Loan Servicing*, 2011 WL 2149105 (D. Nev. 2011)]**

Source: David E. Woolley, "MERS: The Unreported Effects of Lost Chain of Title on Real Property Owners," 8 *Hastings Bus. L. J.*, 365 (2012).

28. Responsibilities of the Parties

The mortgagor and mortgagee have the following duties and liabilities when a mortgage is placed on real property.

CPA **(A) TAXES, ASSESSMENTS, AND INSURANCE.** The duty to pay taxes and assessments rests with the mortgagor. In the absence of an agreement, neither party is under a duty to insure the mortgaged property. Both parties, however, may insure their respective interests. It is common practice for the mortgagor to obtain a single policy of insurance on the property payable to the mortgagee and the mortgagor generally according to the standard mortgagee clause that pays the outstanding loan balance first.

(B) IMPAIRMENT OF SECURITY. The mortgagor is liable to the mortgagee for any damage to the property caused by the mortgagor that impairs the security of the mortgage by materially reducing the value of the property. Both the mortgagor and the mortgagee have a right of action against a third person who wrongfully injures the property.

29. Transfer of Interest

Questions arise as to transfers by the mortgagor and the mortgagee of their respective interests and of the liability of a transferee of the mortgagor.

CPA **(A) TRANSFER BY MORTGAGOR.** The mortgagor may ordinarily transfer the property without the consent of the mortgagee. Such a transfer passes only the interest of the mortgagor and does not divest or impair a properly recorded mortgage.

The transfer of the property by the mortgagor does not affect the liability of the mortgagor to the mortgagee. Unless the mortgagee has agreed to substitute the mortgagor's grantee for the mortgagor, the mortgagor remains liable for the mortgage debt as though no transfer had been made.[9]

CPA **(B) LIABILITY OF THE PARTIES IN A TRANSFER BY A MORTGAGOR.** There are two ways to transfer mortgaged property, and each way has different results in terms of personal liability for the transferee. In the assumption of a mortgage, the transferee agrees to assume liability. In an **assumption**, the mortgagor remains liable, the transferee is liable, and the property is

[9] *Chase Manhattan Mortg. Corp. v. Shelton*, 12 FCDR 580 (Ga. 2012).

subject to foreclosure by the mortgagee in the event the payments are not made. **For Example,** if Bob sold his house with a $175,000 mortgage for $200,000 to Jane, Jane could pay Bob $25,000 cash and then agree to assume Bob's mortgage. Jane may get the benefit of a lower interest rate by assuming Bob's mortgage. Both Bob and Jane are personally liable, and the mortgagee may foreclose on the property if the payments are not made.

The second method of transfer is called a "subject to" transfer. In this type of transfer, the property is subject to foreclosure, but the transferee does not agree to assume the mortgage personally. The mortgagor remains liable in this type of transfer, too.

(c) Transfer by Mortgagee. In most states, a mortgage may be transferred or assigned by the mortgagee.

30. Rights of Mortgagee after Default

Upon the mortgagor's default, the mortgagee in some states is entitled to obtain possession of the property and collect the rents or to have a receiver appointed for that purpose. In all states, the mortgagee may enforce the mortgage by **foreclosure**, a judicial procedure resulting in sale of the mortgaged property.

Generally, upon any default under the terms of the mortgage agreement, the mortgagee has the right to accelerate the debt or declare that the entire mortgage debt is due. The mortgagee generally has this right even though the default related only to paying an installment or to doing some act, such as maintaining insurance on the property or producing receipts for taxes.

A sale resulting from the foreclosure of the mortgage ends the mortgage lien (subject to rights of redemption), and the property passes free of the mortgage to the buyer at the sale. However, the extinction of the mortgage by foreclosure does not destroy the debt that was secured by the mortgage. The mortgagor remains liable for any unpaid balance or deficiency.[10] In many states, the mortgagor is generally given credit for the fair value of the property if it was purchased by the mortgagee.

31. Rights of Mortgagor after Default

After default, the mortgagor may seek to stop or stay foreclosure or to redeem the mortgaged land.

(a) Stay of Foreclosure. In certain cases authorized by statute, a **stay (or delay) of foreclosure** may be obtained by the mortgagor to prevent undue hardship.

CPA **(b) Redemption.** The right of **redemption** is the right of the mortgagor to pay off the mortgage lien and all foreclosure expenses and, by so doing, acquire title to the property. State laws vary, but the right of redemption generally runs from the time of default through to six months after the foreclosure sale.

[10] *M & I Bank, FSB v. Coughlin*, 805 F. Supp. 2d 858 (D. Ariz. 2011).

MAKE THE CONNECTION

SUMMARY

Real property includes land, buildings, fixtures, and rights in the land of another. Some land interests include the right to use the land, such as easements. Easements can be granted or arise by implication or prescription.

The interest held by a person in real property may be defined in terms of the period of time for which the person will remain the owner. The interest may be a fee simple estate, which lasts forever, or a life estate, which lasts for the life of a person. These estates are known as *freehold estates*. If the ownership interest exists for a specified number of days, months, or years, the interest is a leasehold estate.

Personal property may be attached to, or associated with, real property in such a way that it becomes real property. In such a case, it is called a *fixture*. To determine whether property has in fact become a fixture, the courts look to the method of attachment, to how the property is adapted to the realty, and to the intent of the person originally owning the personal property.

Under common law, the liability of a landowner for injury to third persons on the premises depends on the status of the third persons as trespassers, licensees, or invitees. Many jurisdictions, however, are ignoring these common law distinctions in favor of an ordinary negligence standard or are giving licensees the same protection as invitees.

Real property may be the subject of multiple ownership. The forms of multiple ownership are the same as those for personal property. In addition, there are special forms of co-ownership for real property, such as condominiums and cooperatives.

A *deed* is an instrument by which a grantor transfers an interest in land to a grantee. A deed can be a quitclaim deed or a warranty deed. To be effective, a deed must be signed or sealed by the grantor and delivered to the grantee. Recording the deed is not required to make the deed effective to pass title, but recording provides notice to the public that the grantee is the present owner. The warranties of the grantor relate to the title transferred by the grantor and to the fitness of the property for use. In the absence of any express warranty in the deed, no warranty of fitness arises under the common law in the sale or the conveyance of real estate. Most states today hold that when a builder or real estate developer sells a new home to a buyer, an implied warranty of habitability arises. Title to real estate may also be acquired by eminent domain and adverse possession.

An agreement that creates an interest in real property as security for an obligation and that ends upon the performance of the obligation is a mortgage. A mortgage must be in writing under the statute of frauds. If the mortgage is unrecorded, it is valid between the parties. The mortgage should be recorded to put good faith purchasers on notice of the mortgage. A purchaser of the mortgaged property does not become liable for the mortgage debt unless the purchaser assumes the mortgage. The mortgagor still remains liable unless the mortgagee agrees to a substitution of parties. If the mortgagor defaults, the mortgagee may enforce the mortgage by foreclosure. Such foreclosure may be delayed because of undue hardship.

LEARNING OUTCOMES

After studying this chapter, you should be able to clearly explain:

A. Nature of Real Property

LO.1 List the types of real property interests, the rights of the parties and their liabilities

See *Kelo v. City of New London* on pp. 1047–1049.

LO.2 Distinguish between liens, licenses, and easements

See *Dianne v. Wingate* on pp. 1033–1034 for a discussion of easement holder rights.

See the Sports & Entertainment Law discussion of the New England Patriots on p. 1036.

B. Nature and Form of Real Property Ownership

LO.3 Discuss the nature and form of real property ownership

See, *For Example*, on Ralph Watkins on p. 1038.

C. Liability to Third Persons for Condition of Real Property

LO.4 Explain the liability of landowners for injury to others on their property

See the slip-and-fall example on p. 1039.

See *Double Quick, Inc. v. Moore* on pp. 1040–1041.

D. Co-Ownership of Real Property

LO.5 Discuss the forms of co-ownership and parties' rights

See the example on p. 1041 of the rights of condominium owners.

E. Transfer of Real Property by Deed

LO.6 Describe how deeds convey title to land

See *Fletcher v. Minton* on pp. 1044–1046.

F. Other Methods of Transferring Real Property

Explain eminent domain and adverse possession.

See the *Kelo* case on pp. 1047–1049.

G. Mortgages

LO.7 Describe the characteristics and effect of a mortgage

See the *For Example* discussion of Bob and Jane on p. 1052.

KEY TERMS

abstract of title
acceptance
adjustable rate mortgage (ARM)
adverse possession
assumption
attractive nuisance doctrine
condominium
cooperative
covenant against encumbrances
covenant of further assurances
covenant of quiet enjoyment
covenant of right to convey
covenant of seisin
covenants (or warranties) of title
deed
dominant tenement
easement
easement by implication
eminent domain
estate in fee
fee simple defeasibles
fee simple estate
fixture
foreclosure
grantee
grantor
invitee
judgment liens
land
leasehold estate
license
licensee
liens
life estate
limited covenant
mechanic's liens
mortgage
notice statutes
notice-race statute
possibility of reverter
prescription
profits
quitclaim deeds
race statutes
race-notice statute
real property
recorder
redemption
remainder interest
reverse mortgage
runs with the land
servient tenement
stay (or delay) of foreclosure
tax liens
transferee
trespasser
warranties of title
warranty deeds
way of necessity

QUESTIONS AND CASE PROBLEMS

1. In 1972, Donald and Joyce Carnahan purchased a 1-acre lot located on a 22-acre lake. The purchase included a portion of the lake bed. The Carnahans used the lake for recreational activity in both winter and summer, and their activities included motorboats, jet skis, and wave runners. In 1991, the Moriah Property Owners Association, Inc., acquired title to the majority of the lots along the lake and imposed restrictive covenants on the use of the lake, including one that prohibited all motors on the lake except for those powered by 12-volt batteries. The Carnahans filed suit to establish a prescriptive easement in their right to use the lake for all their activities. Do you think the Carnahans acquired an easement by prescription? [*Carnahan v. Moriah Property Owners Association, Inc.*, 716 N.E.2d 437 (Ind.)]

2. Bunn and his wife claimed that they had an easement to enter and use the swimming pool on neighboring land. A contract between the former owners of the Bunns' property and the adjacent apartment complex contained a provision that the use of the apartment complex's swimming pool would be available to the

purchaser and his family. No reference to the pool was made in the contract between the former owners and the Bunns, nor was there any reference to it in the deed conveying the property to the Bunns. Decide. [*Bunn v. Offutt*, 222 S.E.2d 522 (Va.)]

3. After executing the various deeds, J. M. Fernandez Jr. placed them in a closet (with other valuable papers) for safekeeping until they could be physically delivered to the various grantees, including Sylvia Sheppard, when she returned to Key West. This closet was in the home that Fernandez shared with Betty DeMerritt. They were not married but lived together the final 15 years of Fernandez's life. Shortly thereafter, Fernandez was debilitated by a stroke and became a total invalid. He never regained his health and died before Sylvia Sheppard could return to Key West to receive physical delivery of the deed personally from him. When Sylvia Sheppard did arrive in Key West, Betty DeMerritt gave her the deed. This took place two or three days after the death of Fernandez. When questioned as to why she turned the deed over to Sylvia, Betty DeMerritt stated, "I knew he wanted me to do it…because he couldn't do it." She was speaking of Fernandez's physical disability. Does Sylvia have title to the property? Was there delivery? [*Kerr v. Fernandez*, 792 So.2d 685 (Fla.)]

4. Kenneth Corson, 10, lived with his mother, Lynda Lontz, in an apartment building owned by Bruno and Carolyn Kosinski. While playing with other children who lived in the same building, Corson was drawn to a stairwell that provided access to the building's laundry room and roof. Corson and the other children climbed to the roof and discovered an area where they could jump from the roof of their building to that of the building next door. The children engaged in roof-hopping for several days. On the last day, Corson misjudged his jump and fell the three stories to the ground below. Corson and his mother filed suit against the Kosinskis to collect damages for Corson's injuries. What theory might be used to hold the Kosinskis liable? [*Corson by Lontz v. Kosinski*, 801 F. Supp. 75 (N.D. Ill.)]

5. Determine whether the following would be fixtures or personal property.
   a. Refrigerator in a home
   b. Refrigerators in an apartment complex with furnished units
   c. Refrigerators in a restaurant kitchen
   d. Refrigeration/freezer units in a grocery store
   e. Mini-refrigerator in a student dorm

6. What is the relationship between trespass and adverse possession?

7. At approximately 3:00 A.M., on February 3, 2000, Sonya Winchell was driving two of her friends through a Fort Wayne Taco Bell drive-thru. When Winchell arrived in line, there was one car in front of her at the speaker. Winchell noticed that the occupants of the car, Remco Guy and Ariel Graham, were taking a long time placing their order and then got out of their car. At that point, Winchell yelled out her window, "Can we get moving, we are hungry!" Guy approached Winchell's car, stuck his head in the window, and "started cussing everybody out." Guy removed his head from the window, stuck it back in, and asked, "You got an f-ing problem?" Winchell responded by "drill[ing] him in the nose." Guy then pulled a gun out of his pants and shot Winchell. One of Winchell's passengers and others summoned police officers who were in a nearby parking lot. Winchell survived the shooting, and Guy was convicted of attempted murder. Winchell filed a civil action against Guy and Graham, and against Taco Bell, alleging negligence. Is Taco Bell liable for the injuries that occur on its property? [*Winchell v. Guy*, 857 N.E.2d 1024 (Ind.)]

8. Miller executed a deed to real estate, naming Zieg as grantee. He placed the deed in an envelope on which was written "To be filed at my death" and put the envelope and deed in a safe deposit box in the National Bank that had been rented in the names of Miller and Zieg. After Miller's death, Zieg removed the deed from the safe deposit box. Moseley, as executor under Miller's will, brought an action against Zieg to declare the deed void. Decide. [*Moseley v. Zieg*, 146 N.W.2d 72 (Neb.)]

9. Henry Lile owned a house. When the land on which it was situated was condemned for a highway, he moved the house to the land of his daughter, Sarah Crick. In the course of construction work, blasting damaged the house. Sarah Crick sued the contractors, Terry & Wright, who claimed that Lile should be joined in the action as a plaintiff and that Sarah could not sue by herself because it was Lile's house. Were the defendants correct? [*Terry & Wright v. Crick*, 418 S.W.2d 217 (Ky.)]

10. Bradt believed his backyard ran all the way to a fence. Actually, a strip on Bradt's side of the fence belonged to his neighbor Giovannone, but Bradt never intended to take land away from anyone. Bradt later brought an action against Giovannone to determine who owned the strip on Bradt's side of the fence. Who is the owner? Why? [*Bradt v. Giovannone*, 315 N.Y.S.2d 96]

11. Robert E. Long owned land in the City of Hampton that he leased to Adams Outdoor Advertising Limited Partnership. Adams had an advertising billboard placed on the property. On October 6, 1993, Long notified Adams that he was terminating the lease. Adams accepted the termination and told Long that it would have the electrical service disconnected and would schedule demolition of the billboard for the first week in November. Long wanted to use the billboard to advertise his own business and filed suit to enjoin Adams from destroying the billboard. Long maintained the billboard was part of the land and belonged to him. Adams asserted that it owned the billboard as a lessee. The trial court found for Long, and Adams appealed. Decide. [*Adams Outdoor Adv., Ltd., Part. v. Long*, 483 S.E.2d 224 (Va.)]

12. The Friersons have a two-story building in Easley, South Carolina, that shares a common wall with an adjacent two-story building owned by David and Patricia Watson. An outdoor stairway located on the Watsons' property provides access to the second floor of both buildings. A dispute arose when David Watson began to construct apartments on the second floor of his building and proposed to close off a connecting indoor hallway between the two properties at the top of the stairs located inside the building. The Friersons maintained that they had an easement to use both the outdoor stairway and the indoor hallway for access.

    The Friersons' predecessors-in-interest, E. C., E. O., and D. M. Frierson, purchased the building in 1929 from the "Estate of R. F. Smith, Inc." The 1929 deed, dated January 14 and recorded on January 23, expressly conveyed "an easement in a certain four foot stairway in the back of the building, with right of ingress and egress on said stairway to the second story of said building." On January 21, 1929, two days before the deed was recorded, the parties to the sale executed a "Memorandum of Agreement" that granted an easement for the use of the hallway. The memo was not recorded. The Friersons brought suit to stop Watson's construction.

    The Friersons claimed Watson's construction violated their easement by eliminating the hallway, which denied them access to the second floor of their building.

    The circuit court determined that the Friersons had established an easement for use of the hallway by grant and by prescription and granted the Friersons' motion. David Watson appealed. Who is correct on this easement issue? Explain why. [*Frierson v. Watson*, 636 S.E. 2d 872 (S.C. App.)]

13. Martin Manufacturing decided to raise additional long-term capital by mortgaging an industrial park it owned. First National Loan Co. agreed to lend Martin $1 million and to take a note and first mortgage on the land and building. The mortgage was duly recorded. Martin sold the property to Marshall, who took the property and assumed the mortgage debt. Does Marshall have any personal liability on the mortgage debt? Is Martin still liable on the mortgage debt? Explain.

14. Christine and Steve Mallock buried their son in a burial plot purchased at Southern Memorial Park, Inc. Each year the Mallocks conducted a memorial service for their son at his burial plot. On the seventh anniversary of their son's death, the Mallocks went to their son's grave at 11:00 A.M. for the annual service, which generally took 30 minutes. When they arrived, they discovered that a tent and chairs set up for funeral services on the plot next to their son's grave were actually resting on his gravesite. The Mallocks asked

Southern's management if the tent and chairs could be moved until they could conduct their service. The managers refused, and the Mallocks went ahead with their ceremony, cutting it to five minutes, after they moved the chairs and tents by themselves.

Southern's managers called the police and had the Mallocks evicted. Southern claimed the Mallocks had no rights on the property except for the grave and that their deed for the plot did not award an easement for access. Did the Mallocks have the right to access to the gravesite? [*Mallock v. Southern Memorial Park, Inc.*, [561 So.2d 330 (Fla. Ct. App.)]

15. *O* conveys property to *A* on December 1, 2012. *O* conveys the same property to *B* who does not know about *A* and who records his deed on December 2, 2012. *O* then conveys the same property to *C*. Who has title to the property?

CPA QUESTIONS

The topic of insurance has been eliminated from the content outline for the CPA exam as of October 2009. However, the exam lags behind the content change, so this topic may continue to appear on the exam for six to 18 months.

1. Which of the following statements is correct with respect to a real estate mortgage?
   a. It must be signed only by the mortgagor (borrower).
   b. It must be recorded in order to be effective between the mortgagor and the mortgagee.
   c. It does *not* have to be recorded to be effective against third parties without notice if it is a purchase money mortgage.
   d. It is effective even if *not* delivered to the mortgagee.
2. To be enforceable against the mortgagor, a mortgage must meet all the following requirements *except*:
   a. Be delivered to the mortgagee.
   b. Be in writing and signed by the mortgagor.
   c. Be recorded by the mortgagee.
   d. Include a description of the debt and land involved.
3. Ritz owned a building in which there was a duly recorded first mortgage held by Lyn and a recorded second mortgage held by Jay. Ritz sold the building to Nunn. Nunn assumed the Jay mortgage and had no actual knowledge of the Lyn mortgage. Nunn defaulted on the payments to Jay. If both Lyn and Jay foreclosed and the proceeds of the sale were insufficient to pay both Lyn and Jay, then:
   a. Jay would be paid after Lyn was fully paid.
   b. Jay and Lyn would be paid proportionately.
   c. Nunn would be personally liable to Lyn but not to Jay.
   d. Nunn would be personally liable to Lyn and Jay.
4. Which of the following deeds will give a real property purchaser the greatest protection?
   a. Quitclaim
   b. Bargain and sale
   c. Special warranty
   d. General warranty

Environmental Law and Land Use Controls

learningoutcomes

After studying this chapter, you should be able to

LO.1 List and describe the federal statutes that regulate various aspects of the environment

LO.2 Explain how environmental laws are enforced and describe the criminal penalties for violation of environmental laws

LO.3 Define *nuisance* and list the remedies available

LO.4 Explain the role and application of covenants and zoning laws

A. Statutory Environmental Law

As the United States changed from a rural, agricultural society to an urban, industrial one, new laws were needed to prevent the pollution of the environment.

1. Air Pollution Regulation

(a) Legislative History of Air Pollution Regulation. The first legislation that dealt with air pollution, passed in 1955, was the Air Pollution Control Act, which was simply a statutory recognition of a concern about air quality. Even the first statute regulating air pollution, the **Clean Air Act**, passed in 1963, produced no response from the states, which were charged with the responsibility of developing pollution standards and enforcement mechanisms. It was not until the 1970 amendments to the Clean Air Act that the federal law on air pollution got some teeth, for it was in those amendments that Congress established the federal agency responsible for enforcing the law, the Environmental Protection Agency (EPA). The EPA was authorized to establish national air quality standards and see that the states developed plans for the implementation of those standards.

(b) Modern Legislation and Requirements. Under the 1970 Clean Air Act,[1] as well as the 1977 and 1990 amendments to it, states must measure sulfur dioxide, carbon monoxide, and hydrocarbons and then take appropriate steps to bring their air quality within the federal limits established for each of these. States that do not meet federal standards are called **nonattainment areas**, or *dirty areas*, and their plans for implementation are strictly reviewed by the EPA, which can halt federal highway funding in the event the implementation plan is not followed. Those states that do meet the federal standards must still have a plan to remain at that level.

For nonattainment areas, the EPA developed an **emissions offset policy**, which controls whether new factories can be built. For a new plant to obtain a permit to begin operations in a nonattainment area, the business proposing the new plant must be able to show that (1) the plant will have the greatest possible emissions controls, which means having better-than-existing emissions standards, (2) the business has all of its other plants and operations in compliance with federal emissions standards, and (3) the new plant's emissions will be offset by reductions in emissions in other facilities in the area. This last requirement is often referred to as the **bubble concept**, which requires an examination of all emissions from all sources in an area. Before any new operations with emissions can be permitted, the business seeking approval must be able to show that overall emissions in the area will not increase.

The 1990 amendments to the Clean Air Act increased the role of the bubble concept with the ability of businesses to transfer their emissions permits. Those businesses that can reduce their emissions below their allowable amounts or that can eliminate their emissions are free to transfer their permit rights to emit to someone else who can then use them without affecting total emissions in the bubble area. There is a market exchange for emissions permits because the EPA will not, under the 1990 act, issue any additional permits beyond the rights to emission that already exist. Today, approximately 10 percent of all the emissions permit rights are owned by environmental groups.

(c) New Developments in Air Quality: The U.S. Supreme Court and the EPA. In *Environmental Defense v. Duke Energy*, 549 U.S. 561 (2007), the U.S. Supreme Court heard a case in which the EPA had brought suit against Duke Energy for implementing modifications to its coal-fired electricity plants without first filing for approval from the agency. Duke maintained that only major modifications to power plants required EPA approval, a standard the EPA had been following for years. However, the EPA based its expanded permit requirements for even minor modifications under the Prevention of Significant Deterioration (PSD) regulations. The EPA explained its shift because of the need for the prevention of carbon emissions and for addressing the problems stemming from global warming. New conditions, according to the EPA, required more intense and detailed intervention in plant modification in order to carry out its PSD mandate. The utilities challenged the agency's authority to act on greenhouse gases and global warming issues because there was no statutory provision that covered such an expansion. The court

[1] 42 U.S.C. §1857 *et seq.*

held that the EPA could step up its permit requirements and still be within its statutory authority in choosing which modifications to regulate via permit. The standard has now evolved to one that goes beyond best available technology (BAT) to maximum achievable control technology (MACT), a standard that is not controlled by cost alone.

In *Massachusetts v. EPA*, 549 U.S. 497 (2007), the Court held that the Clean Air Act mandated EPA action on greenhouse gases and global warming. Chief Justice Roberts and three other justices dissented because they maintained that redress of the EPA for inaction on global warming lies with Congress and the president, not the federal courts. The justices added that their position was one of jurisdiction and authority and "involves no judgment on whether global warming exists, what causes it, or the extent of the problem." With these decisions and the 2012 re-election, the EPA has been implementing rules that restrict the mining and use of coal and provide incentives for the development of solar and wind energy sources.

2. Water Pollution Regulation

The first meaningful regulation in water pollution began at about the same time as effective air pollution regulation. The first legislation with enforcement power was passed in 1972 as the Federal Water Pollution Control Act and then amended and renamed in 1977 as the **Clean Water Act**.[2] Under the Clean Water Act, the EPA has developed **effluent guidelines**, which are ranges for discharges organized according to industrial groups and for specific plants in each of these groups. The guidelines establish the maximum amounts that can be discharged, and those maximums are coupled with a permit system that requires each plant to obtain a permit from the EPA before discharging anything into any type of pool, pond, river, lake, stream, or ocean.[3] **For Example,** a plant that releases hot water from a steam generator must still have a permit just to release hot water into the stream near the plant. The EPA also has standards for the treatment of water that is used in a plant's production process before that water can be discharged.[4] **For Example,** a plant must still have a permit to discharge water even though that water is cleaner as it is discharged from the plant than it was when it was brought in to be used in production or manufacturing. However, the EPA is permitted to use cost-benefit analysis in setting the standards for the quality of the water that is released back into the river, lake, etc. All discharges into the waterways require a **National Pollutant Discharge Elimination System (NPDES)** permit from the EPA. This type of permit is required only for direct dischargers, or **point sources**, and is not required of plants that discharge into sewer systems (although these secondary dischargers may still be required to pretreat their discharges). Obtaining a permit requires EPA and state approval as well as public hearings.

The permits also impose requirements on the permit holder. If the plant is going to release a conventional pollutant, the EPA can require the plant to pretreat the substance with the **best conventional treatment** (BCT). However, the EPA can also require the **best available treatment** (BAT) standard, which is the highest standard imposed. Until 2009, the standard for requiring BAT was solely the consideration of environmental effects and not the economic effects on the applicant. However, in *Entergy Corporation v. Riverkeeper, Inc.*, 556 U.S. 208 (2009), the U.S. Supreme Court held that the EPA can use cost-benefit analysis to allow variances from those standards. In the case, Entergy's cost of bringing cooling water intake structures to the higher level the EPA requires for new structures would have been nine times the existing costs. The Court held that the additional benefit achieved was too small to justify the cost of bringing the cooling water facilities up to BAT standads.[5]

3. Solid Waste Disposal Regulation

The disposal of solid waste (garbage) has also been regulated since the 1960s, but the initial legislation simply provided money for research by state and local

[2] 33 U.S.C. §1251 *et seq*. The pollution of navigable waters had been regulated by the Rivers and Harbors Act of 1899, which required a permit for discharging into navigable rivers, streams, and lakes.

[3] Even the placement of dirt from adjoining property into a stream can be a CWA violation. *Sackett v. EPA*, 132 S.Ct. 1367 (2012).

[4] In *Coeur Alaska v. Southeast Alaska Conservation*, 557 U.S. 261 (2009), the court held that a project in an Alaskan lake under the supervision of the Army Corps of Engineers did not require an EPA permit process for the operator to obtain permission to dump fill dirt into the lake.

[5] *Entergy Corporation v. Riverkeeper, Inc.*, 556 U.S. 208 (2009). In the case, Entergy's cost of bringing cooling water intake structures to a higher level passed for new structures would be nine times current costs. The court held the additional benefit achieved with new processes and equipment was too small to justify the cost.

governments on how to dispose of solid waste.[6] In 1970, the **Resource Recovery Act** provided federal money for cities and states with recycling programs.

After several major open-dumping problems that produced community-wide illnesses, including those in the Love Canal area near Buffalo, New York, Congress passed the **Toxic Substances Control Act (TOSCA)**, which controls the manufacture, use, and disposal of toxic substances, a list of which the EPA developed. Along with TOSCA, Congress passed the **Resource Conservation and Recovery Act (RCRA)**, which regulates the disposal of potentially harmful substances through a permit system and uses federal grants to encourage the restoration of damaged resources.[7] **For Example,** many strip mine locations were restored due to the RCRA.

In 1980, Congress passed the **Comprehensive Environmental Response, Compensation, and Liability Act (CERCLA)**,[8] which authorizes the U.S. president to issue funds to be used for the cleanup of areas that were once disposal sites for hazardous wastes. The act set up a trust fund for cleanups, to be reimbursed by the company responsible for such hazardous wastes. The funds in the trust are available for government use but are not subject to attachment by private citizens who seek to get an area cleaned up by removing the hazardous waste. Under CERCLA, the EPA has the authority to designate **Superfund sites**, or parcels of land that are deemed to have, or potentially have, hazardous wastes that require cleanup.

The **Superfund Amendment and Reauthorization Act**, passed in 1986, authorizes the EPA to bring suit for the purpose of collecting the costs of cleanup from those who are responsible for the hazardous wastes on the site. The act and its judicial interpretations provide a very broad definition of who is responsible under CERCLA for the costs of cleanup. Four classes of parties can be held liable under CERCLA. "Owners and operators" of contaminated property are liable under the statute. *Owners* include present owners as well as past owners, whether or not they are responsible for the hazardous wastes being dumped on the property. *Operators* include those who are leasing the property, again regardless of whether they are responsible for the hazardous waste being dumped. **For Example,** many gas stations have been designated as Superfund sites because the underground tanks have leaks, causing gas to seep into the soil. Current and past owners of such a station are responsible under CERCLA, as well as an owner who has converted the station into some other use.[9]

Other responsible parties under CERCLA include anyone who transported hazardous waste to a site and anyone who hired another or arranged to transport hazardous waste to the site. Lenders were, at one time, also held liable for cleanup costs in the event they took back property from a debtor. However, the Asset Conservation, Lender Liability, and Deposit Insurance Protection Act of 1996 provides an exclusion for lenders provided the lender does not actually participate in the management or operational affairs of the facility of the debtor.[10] The *Burlington Northern Railway/Shell Oil Co. v. U.S.* deals with an issue of who is liable under CERCLA.

Burlington Northern Railway/Shell Oil Co. v. U.S., 129 S. Ct. 1870 (2009)

Don't Blame Me, I'm Only the Arranger

In 1960, Brown & Bryant, Inc. (B & B), began operating an agricultural chemical distribution business. Using its own equipment, B & B applied its products to customers' farms. B & B opened its business on a 3.8 acre parcel of former farmland in Arvin, California, and in 1975, expanded operations onto an adjacent .9 acre parcel of land owned jointly by the Atchison, Topeka & Santa Fe Railway Company, and the Southern Pacific Transportation Company (Railroads). Waste water and chemical runoff from the facility was allowed to seep into the ground water below.

[6] See the Solid Waste Disposal Act, 42 U.S.C. §3251 *et seq.*, and the Resource Recovery and Policy Act of 1970, 42 U.S.C. §3251 *et seq.*

[7] 42 U.S.C. §6901 *et seq.*

[8] 42 U.S.C. §9601 *et seq.*

[9] Courts do require some proof of causation between a company's conduct and the resulting toxic contamination. *Solutia, Inc. v. McWane, Inc.*, 672 F.3d 1230 (11th Cir. 2012).

[10] "Participating" does not include monitoring or enforcing the security agreement, monitoring or inspecting the premises, providing financial advice, mandating cleanup of hazardous materials, restructuring the loan, foreclosing, or selling or leasing the property.

Continued

During its years of operation, B & B stored and distributed various hazardous chemicals on its property sold by Shell Oil Company (Shell). When B & B purchased chemicals from Shell Oil Company (Shell), Shell would arrange for delivery by common carrier, f.o.b. destination. When the product arrived, it was transferred from tanker trucks to a bulk storage tank located on B & B's primary parcel. During each of these transfers leaks and spills could—and often did—occur. Although the common carrier and B & B used buckets to catch spills from hoses and gaskets connecting the tanker trucks to its bulk storage tank, the buckets sometimes overflowed or were knocked over, causing chemical spills onto the ground during the transfer process.

In the late 1970's Shell took several steps to encourage the safe handling of its products. Shell provided distributors with detailed safety manuals and instituted a voluntary discount program for distributors that made improvements in their bulk handling and safety facilities. Later, Shell required distributors to obtain an inspection by a qualified engineer and provide self-certification of compliance with applicable laws and regulations. B & B's Arvin facility was inspected twice and told Shell that it had made a number of recommended improvements to its facilities. Despite these improvements, B & B remained a " '[s]loppy' [o]perator." The EPA soon discovered significant contamination of soil and ground water.

By 1989, B & B was insolvent and ceased all operations. That same year, the Arvin facility was designated as a Superfund site. By 1998, the Governments had spent more than $8 million in cleanup costs.

In 1991, EPA (Governments) ordered the Railroads to conduct certain cleanup processes. The Railroads did so, incurring expenses of more than $3 million in the process. Seeking to recover at least a portion of these costs, the Railroads brought suit against B & B.

The District Court held that both the Railroads and Shell were potentially responsible parties (PRPs) under CERCLA—the Railroads because they were owners of a portion of the facility, and Shell because it had "arranged for" the disposal of hazardous substances through its sale and delivery of chemicals.

Although the court found the parties liable, it did not impose joint and several liability on Shell and the Railroads for the entire response cost incurred by the Governments. The court apportioned the Railroads' liability as 9% of the Governments' total response cost. Based on estimations of chemicals spills of Shell products, the court held Shell liable for 6% of the total site response cost.

The state and local governments appealed the District Court's apportionment, and Shell cross-appealed the court's finding of liability. Applying a theory of arranger liability, the Ninth Circuit held that Shell arranged for the disposal of a hazardous substance.

The Court of Appeals held Shell and the Railroads jointly and severally liable for the Governments' cost of responding to the contamination of the Arvin facility.

The Railroads and Shell appealed.

JUDICIAL OPINION

STEVENS, Justice...To determine whether Shell may be held liable as an arranger, we begin with the language of the statute. As relevant here, § 9607(a)(3) applies to an entity that "arrange[s] for disposal...of hazardous substances." It is plain from the language of the statute that CERCLA liability would attach under § 9607(a)(3) if an entity were to enter into a transaction for the sole purpose of discarding a used and no longer useful hazardous substance. It is similarly clear that an entity could not be held liable as an arranger merely for selling a new and useful product if the purchaser of that product later, and unbeknownst to the seller, disposed of the product in a way that led to contamination. Less clear is the liability attaching to the many permutations of "arrangements" that fall between these two extremes—cases in which the seller has some knowledge of the buyers' planned disposal or whose motives for the "sale" of a hazardous substance are less than clear. In such cases, courts have concluded that the determination whether an entity is an arranger requires a fact-intensive inquiry.

The Governments do not deny that the statute requires an entity to "arrang[e] for" disposal; however, they interpret that phrase by reference to the statutory term "disposal," which the Act broadly defines as "the discharge, deposit, injection, dumping, spilling, leaking, or placing of any solid waste or hazardous waste into or on any land or water." The Governments assert that by including unintentional acts such as "spilling" and "leaking" in the definition of disposal, Congress intended to impose liability on entities not only when they directly dispose of waste products but also when they engage in legitimate sales of hazardous substances knowing that some disposal may occur as a collateral consequence of the sale itself. The Governments contend that Shell arranged for the disposal of D-D within the meaning of § 9607(a)(3) by shipping D-D to B & B under conditions it knew would result in the spilling of a portion of the hazardous substance by the purchaser or common carrier. Because these spills resulted in wasted D-D, a result Shell anticipated, the Governments insist that Shell was properly found to have arranged for the disposal of D-D.

Shell was aware that minor, accidental spills occurred during the transfer of D-D from the common carrier to

Continued

B & B's bulk storage tanks after the product had arrived at the Arvin facility and had come under B & B's stewardship, the evidence does not support an inference that Shell intended such spills to occur. To the contrary, the evidence revealed that Shell took numerous steps to encourage its distributors to reduce the likelihood of such spills, providing them with detailed safety manuals, requiring them to maintain adequate storage facilities, and providing discounts for those that took safety precautions. Although Shell's efforts were less than wholly successful, given these facts, Shell's mere knowledge that spills and leaks continued to occur is insufficient grounds for concluding that Shell "arranged for" the disposal of D-D within the meaning of § 9607(a)(3). Accordingly, we conclude that Shell was not liable as an arranger for the contamination that occurred at B & B's Arvin facility.

Having concluded that Shell is not liable as an arranger, we need not decide whether the Court of Appeals erred in reversing the District Court's apportionment of Shell's liability for the cost of remediation. We must, however, determine whether the Railroads were properly held jointly and severally liable for the full cost of the Governments' response efforts.

Not all harms are capable of apportionment, however, and CERCLA defendants seeking to avoid joint and several liability bear the burden of proving that a reasonable basis for apportionment exists.

The District Court calculated the Railroads' liability based on three figures. First, the court noted that the Railroad parcel constituted only 19% of the surface area of the Arvin site. Second, the court observed that the Railroads had leased their parcel to B & B for 13 years, which was only 45% of the time B & B operated the Arvin facility. Finally, the court found that the volume of hazardous-substance-releasing activities on the B & B property was at least 10 times greater than the releases that occurred on the Railroad parcel, and it concluded that only spills of two chemicals, Nemagon and dinoseb (not D-D), substantially contributed to the contamination that had originated on the Railroad parcel and that those two chemicals had contributed to two-thirds of the overall site contamination requiring remediation. The court then multiplied .19 by .45 by .66 (two-thirds) and rounded up to determine that the Railroads were responsible for approximately 6% of the remediation costs. "Allowing for calculation errors up to 50%," the court concluded that the Railroads could be held responsible for 9% of the total CERCLA response cost for the Arvin site.

The District Court's detailed findings make it abundantly clear that the primary pollution at the Arvin facility was contained in an unlined sump and an unlined pond in the southeastern portion of the facility most distant from the Railroads' parcel and that the spills of hazardous chemicals that occurred on the Railroad parcel contributed to no more than 10% of the total site contamination, some of which did not require remediation. With those background facts in mind, we are persuaded that it was reasonable for the court to use the size of the leased parcel and the duration of the lease as the starting point for its analysis. Although the Court of Appeals faulted the District Court for relying on the "simplest of considerations: percentages of land area, time of ownership, and types of hazardous products," these were the same factors the court had earlier acknowledged were relevant to the apportionment analysis.

Although the evidence adduced by the parties did not allow the court to calculate precisely the amount of hazardous chemicals contributed by the Railroad parcel to the total site contamination or the exact percentage of harm caused by each chemical, the evidence did show that fewer spills occurred on the Railroad parcel and that of those spills that occurred, not all were carried across the Railroad parcel to the B & B sump and pond from which most of the contamination originated. The fact that no D-D spills on the Railroad parcel required remediation lends strength to the District Court's conclusion that the Railroad parcel contributed only Nemagon and dinoseb in quantities requiring remediation.

The District Court's conclusion that those two chemicals accounted for only two-thirds of the contamination requiring remediation finds less support in the record; however, any miscalculation on that point is harmless in light of the District Court's ultimate allocation of liability, which included a 50% margin of error equal to the 3% reduction in liability the District Court provided based on its assessment of the effect of the Nemagon and dinoseb spills. Had the District Court limited its apportionment calculations to the amount of time the Railroad parcel was in use and the percentage of the facility located on that parcel, it would have assigned the Railroads 9% of the response cost. By including a two-thirds reduction in liability for the Nemagon and dinoseb with a 50% "margin of error," the District Court reached the same result. Because the District Court's ultimate allocation of liability is supported by the evidence and comports with the apportionment principles outlined above, we reverse the Court of Appeals' conclusion that the Railroads are subject to joint and several liability for all response costs arising out of the contamination of the Arvin facility.

For the foregoing reasons, we conclude that the Court of Appeals erred by holding Shell liable as an arranger under CERCLA for the costs of remediating environmental contamination at the Arvin, California facility. Furthermore, we conclude that the District Court reasonably apportioned the Railroads' share of the site remediation costs at 9%.

Continued

[The judgment is reversed, and the cases are remanded for further proceedings consistent with this opinion.]

QUESTIONS

1. Where do you think the term "arranger" fits in the categories of those who are responsible for cleanup costs under CERCLA?
2. What do you think the practical effect of this decision will be on companies who own Superfund sites? Does the complexity of analysis for liability help companies in clean-up cases?
3. What do you think will happen to government agencies in their efforts to seek reimbursement for their cleanup efforts?

CERCLA liability has been extended to those who merge or buy corporations; these parties also buy into CERCLA liability, and liability under CERCLA cannot be avoided by a transfer of ownership. The U.S. Supreme Court has ruled in *United States v. Bestfoods*, 525 U.S. 51 (1998), that a parent corporation is not automatically liable under CERCLA for a subsidiary corporation's conduct but may be responsible if the subsidiary is simply a shell. In other words, CERCLA liability of parent corporations for the actions of their subsidiaries is governed by corporate law on piercing the corporate veil (see Chapter 44 for more information).

One of the new key areas for minimizing CERCLA liability is that of the self-audit, a company's internal investigation of its operations and lands to determine whether any environmental hazards are on its properties. Many companies wanted to know, for the sake of financial planning and minimizing harm, whether they had any Superfund issues. However, they did not want their voluntary investigations and cleanups to work against them. To encourage these types of internal investigations and self-reporting, the EPA developed its Incentives for Self-Policing, Disclosure, Correction, and Prevention of Violations. Under this EPA program, companies can have their penalties reduced and not waive any rights if they follow the procedures and meet the following requirements: (1) the violations were uncovered as part of a self-audit, (2) the violations were uncovered voluntarily, (3) the violations were reported to the EPA within 10 days, (4) the discovery was made independently and disclosed independently, and no one was threatening disclosure, (5) the violations are corrected within 60 days, (6) there is a written agreement that the conduct will not happen again, (7) there is no history of repeat violations, (8) no serious harm came to anyone as a result of the conduct, and (9) the company cooperates completely with the EPA. If these requirements are met, the company is eligible for reductions in fines and penalties of up to 75 percent.

CERCLA has been so effective that designated Superfund sites as of 2010 that remained undeveloped totaled 425,000. Called "**brownfields**," these sites are defined by the EPA as "real property, the expansion, redevelopment, or reuse of which may be complicated by the presence or potential presence of a hazardous substance, pollutant, or contaminant." Brownfields often contribute to urban blight and are barriers to economic development and revitalization. The Small Business Liability Relief and Brownfields Revitalization Act allows 75 federal agencies to work together in the *Federal Partnership Action Agenda* to provide funding for proposals to clean up and use these brownfields (42 U.S.C.A. §9601). EPA rules now provide a process for application to become an "innocent landowner," someone who seeks to develop the brownfield but wants an exemption from CERCLA exposure. That designation then allows the applicant to obtain federal funding for purposes of cleaning up and developing the brownfield.

4. Environmental Quality Regulation

The federal statutes on air, water, and solid waste pollution are directed at private parties in their use of land. However, the federal government also regulates itself in terms of its operations and impact

Thinking Things Through

Wild Horses Cannot Keep Us Away

The Wild Free-Roaming Horses and Burros Act authorized the secretary of the interior with the responsibility of managing wild-roaming horses and burros in order to "achieve and maintain a thriving natural ecological balance on the public lands."

The Bureau of Land Management (the BLM, in the Department of Interior (DOI)) proposed to remove 70 of the 190 wild horses on the Pryor Mountain Wild Horse Range (about 50 miles south of Billings, Montana). The BLM concluded from an environmental assessment that an EIS was not necessary. The BLM did not file an EIS because it read the NEPA as not requiring an EIS for horses. The BLM rounded up the horses and Cloud Foundation filed suit for the failure to file an EIS, something that was necessary given the role of the horses in the ecological balance of the area, including the herd's genetic diversity. The DOI moved to dismiss the case because the horses had already been rounded up. The Cloud Foundation maintains the program is ongoing and needs an EIS. Determine whether an EIS is necessary and why or why not and whether the Cloud Foundation has the right to bring suit. **[*Cloud Foundation, Inc. v. Salazar*, 738 F. Supp. 2d 35 (D.D.C. 2010)]**

on the environment. The **National Environmental Policy Act (NEPA)** requires federal agencies to consider the impact on the environment of their proposed projects.[11] An agency must prepare a report, called an **environmental impact statement (EIS)**, that documents the impact of the proposed federal project on the environment and covers consideration of practical and feasible alternatives with a lesser impact.[12] **For Example,** the federal government has been required to file an EIS for the Alaska oil pipeline, the extermination of wild horses, the construction of a post office, the implementation of a change in national park airport procedures that would permit jets to land, and highway construction.

5. Other Environmental Regulations

In addition to the major categories of environmental laws just covered, several other important statutes regulate specific areas of the environment. The **Noise Control Act** sets standards for noise from low-flying aircraft for the protection of landowners who are in flight paths.[13] The **Endangered Species Act (ESA)** gives the secretary of the interior the responsibility of identifying and protecting endangered terrestrial species, while the secretary of commerce is responsible for endangered marine species.[14] These cabinet-level federal officers have the authority to curtail any development, noise, or other act that threatens those species on their endangered lists.[15] The *Babbitt v. Sweet Home Chapter of Communities for a Great Oregon* case deals with the ESA.

Babbitt v. Sweet Home Chapter of Communities for a Great Oregon, 515 U.S. 687 (1995)

The Loggers and the Naturalists Can't Be Friends: Oregon—Where the Spotted Owl Comes Flying in the Trees

Two U.S. agencies halted logging in the Pacific Northwest because it endangered the habitat of the northern spotted owl and the red-cockaded woodpecker, both endangered species. Sweet Home Chapter (respondents) is a group of landowners, logging companies, and families dependent on the forest products industries in the Pacific Northwest. They brought suit seeking clarification of the authority of the secretary of the interior and the director of the Fish and Wildlife Service

[11] 42 U.S.C. §4321 *et seq.*

[12] For contrasting cases of when an EIS is required, see *Tri-Valley CAREs v. U.S. Dept. of Energy*, 671 F.3d 1113 (9th Cir. 2012), and *Barnes v. U.S. Dept. of Transp.*, 655 F.3d 1124 (9th Cir. 2011).

[13] 42 U.S.C. §4901.

[14] 16 U.S.C. §1530 *et seq.*

[15] The authority to bring suit rests with both landowners and environmentalists. *Bennett v. Spear*, 520 U.S. 154 (1997). See also *American Society for the Prevention of Cruelty to Animals v. Ringling Brothers Barnum & Bailey Circus*, 502 F. Supp. 2d 103 (D.D.C. 2007).

Continued

(petitioners) to include habitation modification as a harm covered by the Endangered Species Act (ESA).

The federal district court found for the secretary and director and held that they had the authority to protect the northern spotted owl through a halt to logging. The court of appeals reversed. Babbitt, the secretary of the interior, appealed.

JUDICIAL OPINION

STEVENS, J.... Section 9(a)(1) of the Endangered Species Act provides the following protection for endangered species:

Except as provided in sections 1535(g) (2) and 1539 of this title, with respect to any endangered species of fish or wildlife listed pursuant to section 1533 of this title it is unlawful for any person subject to the jurisdiction of the United States to—(B) take any such species within the United States or the territorial sea of the United States[.] 16 U.S.C. § 1538(a)(I).

Section 3(19) of the Act defines the statutory term "take":

The term 'take' means to harass, harm, pursue, hunt, shoot, wound, kill, trap, capture, or collect, or to attempt to engage in any such conduct. 16 U.S.C. § 1532(19).

The Act does not further define the terms it uses to define "take." The Interior Department regulations that implement the statute, however, define the statutory term "harm":

Harm in the definition of 'take' in the Act means an act which actually kills or injures wildlife. Such act may include significant habitat modification or degradation where it actually kills or injures wildlife by significantly impairing essential behavioral patterns, including breeding, feeding, or sheltering. 50 CFR § 17.3 (1994).

We assume respondents have no desire to harm either the red-cockaded woodpecker or the spotted owl; they merely wish to continue logging activities that would be entirely proper if not prohibited by the ESA. On the other hand, we must assume *arguendo* that those activities will have the effect, even though unintended, of detrimentally changing the natural habitat of both listed species and that, as a consequence, members of those species will be killed or injured. Under respondents' view of the law, the Secretary's only means of forestalling that grave result—even when the actor knows it is certain to occur—is to use his §5 authority to purchase the lands on which the survival of the species depends. The Secretary, on the other hand, submits that the § 9 prohibition on takings, which Congress defined to include "harm," places on respondents a duty to avoid harm that habitat alteration will cause the birds unless respondents first obtain a permit pursuant to § 10.

The text of the Act provides three reasons for concluding that the Secretary's interpretation is reasonable. First, an ordinary understanding of the word "harm" supports it. The dictionary definition of the verb form of "harm" is "to cause hurt or damage to: injure." Webster's Third New International Dictionary 1034 (1966). In the context of the ESA, that definition naturally encompasses habitat modification that results in actual injury or death to members of an endangered or threatened species.

Respondents argue that the Secretary should have limited the purview of "harm" to direct applications of force against protected species, but the dictionary definition does not include the word "directly" or suggest in any way that only direct or willful action that leads to injury constitutes "harm." Moreover, unless the statutory term "harm" encompasses indirect as well as direct injuries, the word has no meaning that does not duplicate the meaning of other words that § 3 uses to define "take." A reluctance to treat statutory terms as surplusage supports the reasonableness of the Secretary's interpretation.

Second, the broad purpose of the ESA supports the Secretary's decision to extend protection against activities that cause the precise harms Congress enacted the statute to avoid. As stated in § 2 of the Act, among its central purposes is "to provide a means whereby the ecosystems upon which endangered species and threatened species depend may be conserved."

Third, the fact that Congress in 1982 authorized the Secretary to issue permits for takings that § 9(a)(1)(B) would otherwise prohibit, "if such taking is incidental to, and not the purpose of, the carrying out of an otherwise lawful activity," 16 U.S.C. § 1539(a)(1)(B), strongly suggests that Congress understood § 9(a)(1)(B) to prohibit indirect as well as deliberate takings. The permit process requires the applicant to prepare a "conservation plan" that specifies how he intends to "minimize and mitigate" the "impact" of his activity on endangered and threatened species, 16 U.S.C. § 1539(a)(2)(A), making clear that Congress had in mind foreseeable rather than merely accidental effects on listed species.

The Court of Appeals made three errors in asserting that "harm" must refer to a direct application of force because the words around it do. First, the court's premise was flawed. Several of the words that accompany "harm" in the § 3 definition of "take," especially "harass," "pursue," "wound," and "kill," refer to actions or effects that do not require direct applications of force. Second, to the extent the court read a requirement of intent or purpose into the words used to define "take," it ignored § 9's express provision that a "knowing" action is enough to violate the Act. Third, the court employed *noscitur a sociis* to give "harm" essentially the same function as other words in the definition, thereby denying it independent meaning. The canon, to the contrary, counsels that a word "gathers meaning from the words around it." The statutory context of "harm" suggests that Congress meant that term to serve a particular function in the ESA, consistent with but distinct from the functions of the other verbs used to define

Continued

"take." The Secretary's interpretation of "harm" to include indirectly injuring endangered animals through habitat modification permissibly interprets "harm" to have "a character of its own not to be submerged by its association."

The proper interpretation of a term such as "harm" involves a complex policy choice. When Congress has entrusted the Secretary with broad discretion, we are especially reluctant to substitute our views of wise policy for his. In this case, that reluctance accords with our conclusion, based on the text, structure, and legislative history of the ESA, that the Secretary reasonably construed the intent of Congress when he defined "harm" to include "significant habitat modification or degradation that actually kills or injures wildlife."

In the elaboration and enforcement of the ESA, the Secretary and all persons who must comply with the law will confront difficult questions of proximity and degree; for, as all recognize, the Act encompasses a vast range of economic and social enterprises and endeavors. These questions must be addressed in the usual course of the law, through case-by-case resolution and adjudication.

The judgment of the Court of Appeals is reversed.

QUESTIONS

1. Is habitat modification harming endangered species?
2. Does the Court's interpretation mean no intent is required to violate ESA?
3. Did Congress intend to give the secretary authority to shut down an industry?
4. Is logging prevented now?
5. What ethical issues arise from this case?*

*Following this decision, Congress passed a rider to a budget-reduction bill that suspended environmental laws in many national forests in Washington and Oregon. The logging industry, paper products processors, and environmentalists have since worked together to find mutually acceptable solutions to logging and the protection of endangered species. Known as the "Sustainable Forestry Initiative," the goal is ecofriendly logging.

The **Safe Drinking Water Act** requires the EPA to establish national standards for contaminants in drinking water. The **Oil Pollution Act** is a federal law that came about following the oil spill from the *Exxon Valdez* off the coast of Alaska, which resulted in damage to the waters, fish, and birds in that area. Under this law, companies are financially responsible for the cleanup of their spills that occur in U.S. waters. The act also provides for substantial penalties for failure to take action to clean up a spill, and those penalties can be as high as \$25,000 per day or \$3,000 per barrel if the spill is the result of negligence or willful misconduct.[16] Failure to report a spill carries penalties of up to five years in prison and/or \$250,000 per individual and \$500,000 for corporations. In addition, civil penalties for the failure to clean up an oil spill can cost the company up to \$50,000,000 in penalties.

6. State Environmental Regulation

All states have some form of environmental regulation, and their environmental agencies work closely with the EPA on enforcement and standards.[17] All states have some form of hazardous waste controls that define hazardous waste differently and carry a range of penalties for violations. **For Example,** Oregon imposes a fine of \$3,500 per animal killed as a result of hazardous waste dumping. Other states mandate disclosure of the history of property use before that property can be sold, transferred, or mortgaged.

B. Enforcement of Environmental Laws

Federal environmental laws can be enforced through criminal sanctions, penalties, injunctions, and suits by

[16] 33 U.S.C. §2701 *et seq*. The act establishes a cleanup fund for those spills in which the party to blame is unknown or is financially unable to pay the cost of cleanup. The act also requires that boats be double-hulled. After three remands, the damages awarded to those harmed by the spill totaled \$4.5 billion. However, Exxon appealed the award of damages and the U.S. Supreme Court held that the punitive damages were limited to those upper limits in maritime law or about \$500 million (an amount equal to the compensatory damages awarded in the case). *Exxon Shipping Co. v. Baker*, 554 U.S. 471 (2008). Cites of all of the lower court decisions in the Exxon cases can be found referenced in the U.S. Supreme Court decision. In 2012, BP paid a criminal penalty of \$4.5 billion for the spill from its Deepwater Horizon rig in 2010.

[17] *Chico Service Station, Inc. v. Sol Puerto Rico Ltd.*, 633 F.3d 20 (1st Cir. 2011).

Ethics & the Law

Spreading the Manure a Little Too Thick

Mahard Egg Farm, Inc., headquartered in Texas and with operations in Oklahoma, is the country's 17th largest egg producer. Mahard's poultry operations generated significant amounts of manure—estimated to be in excess of 50,000 tons of dry manure per year. Mahard applied poultry manure to its agricultural fields, with the result being that when it rained and the soil washed into creeks and rivers, the waterways also had high levels of nutrients.

In addition, Mahard stored manure on its farms and the manure piles often resulted in what are called "inactive manure lagoons," with the resulting smells and flies as well as seepage of the manure and the nutrients into the groundwater.

Mahard has some NPDES permits for some of its facilities, but it did not for others. In addition, Mahard did not comply with its permit requirements for grass buffers as well as control of soil flow.

Develop a list of possible environmental violations. Does it matter for purposes of EPA discharge regulations that the nutrients came from nature (i.e., the manure)? What are the risks for a business when its operations are not in compliance?

private citizens. In addition to federal enforcement rights, certain common law remedies exist for the protection of property rights, such as the remedies for nuisance.

7. Parties Responsible for Enforcement

The EPA is the primary federal agency responsible for the enforcement of federal environmental laws, including those on air and water pollution, solid waste disposal, toxic substance control, and noise pollution. The EPA establishes emissions standards through regulation and then enforces them with a system of permits and sanctions for violations. The EPA works closely with state environmental agencies in enforcement.

The **Council on Environmental Quality (CEQ)** was established in 1966 as a part of the executive branch to establish national policy on environmental quality and then make recommendations for legislation for the implementation of that policy. Other federal agencies with responsibility for enforcement of federal environmental laws include the Department of Commerce, the Department of the Interior, the U.S. Forest Service, and the Bureau of Land Management.

Private citizens also have the right to enforce federal environmental laws through private litigation. **For Example,** a private citizen can bring a suit to halt the construction of a dam by the federal government if the agency responsible failed to conduct an environmental impact study or if the EIS is inadequate.[18]

8. Criminal Penalties

Most of the federal environmental laws carry criminal penalties for violations. Figure 50-1 provides a summary of those penalties to which both companies and their employees are subject.

9. Civil Remedies

Although criminal remedies are costly to businesses, the EPA also has the authority to have the polluting activity halted through the use of **injunction**. The EPA simply brings suit against a business and shows that it is engaged in unauthorized dumping, the release of emissions in excess of a permit, or discharge without a permit. A court can then order the business to halt the activity that is resulting in the violation. In some cases, the effect of the injunction is to shut down the business. The business is then required to negotiate with the EPA to meet certain standards before the EPA will agree to have the injunction lifted.

Private citizens can also bring suit for injunctions against companies that are in violation of federal law or not in compliance with statutory procedures. **For Example,** private citizens have filed suit against developers to stop construction when there is an issue of possible violation of the Endangered Species Act.

[18] *Rio Silvery Minnow v. Bureau of Reclamation*, 601 F.3d 1096 (10th Cir. 2010).

FIGURE 50-1 *Penalties for Violations of Federal Environmental Laws*

Act	Penalties	Private suit
Clean Air Act	$25,000 per day; up to 1 year of imprisonment; 15 years and/or $1,000,000 for willful or repeat violations; $10,000 rewards	Citizen suits; authorized EPA suit for injunctive relief
Clean Water Act	$25,000 per day, up to 1 year; $50,000 and/or 3 years for violations with knowledge; $100,000 and/or 6 years for subsequent violations	Citizen suits; authorized EPA suit for injunctive relief
Resource Conservation Recovery Act (Solid Waste Disposal Act)	$250,000 and/or 15 years of imprisonment for intentional violations; $1,000,000 for corporations, $50,000 and/or 5 years for others	Citizen and negligence suits (after EPA refuses to handle)
Hazardous Substance/ Response Trust	Fund for cleanup	EPA suit for injunctive relief and reimbursement of trust funds
Oil Pollution Act	$25,000 per day, or $1,000 per barrel; $3,000 per barrel if willful or negligent; $250,000 and/or 5 years for failure to report	Private suits

10. Private Remedies: Nuisance

Conduct that unreasonably interferes with the enjoyment or use of land is a **nuisance**,[19] which may be smoke from a chemical plant that damages the paint on neighboring houses. It may be noise, dirt, or vibration from passing heavy trucks. Some conduct is clearly so great an interference that it is easy to conclude that it constitutes a nuisance, but not every interference is a nuisance. Furthermore, determining whether the interference is sufficiently great to be halted as unreasonable is frequently difficult. The fact that the activity or business is lawful and is conducted in a lawful manner does not mean that it is not a nuisance. The effect on others determines whether there is a nuisance.[20] A neighbor's backyard barbeque pit generating smoke that wafts onto a neighbor's yard is an example of a private nuisance even though no law is broken.[21]

The courts attempt to balance the social utility of the activity with the resulting harm. The mere fact that there is harm does not establish that there is a nuisance. When community welfare outweighs the harm to land and owners, the activity is not a nuisance.[22] **For Example,** courts have held that smoke, fumes, and noise from public utilities and power plants were not nuisances, although they did create harm. The interests of the community in the activity of the public utilities outweighed the interests of those affected.

[19] *Dyer v. Hall*, 928 N.E.2d 273 (Ind. App. 2010).
[20] *U.S. v. EME Homer City Generation L.P.*, 823 F. Supp. 2d 274 (W.D. Pa. 2011).
[21] *Weller v. Blake*, 726 S.E.2d 698 (Ga. App. 2012).
[22] *Natale v. Everflow E., Inc.*, 959 N.E.2d 602 (Ohio App. 2011).

Those affected by a nuisance are entitled to damages for the loss of the use of the land or for harm that is caused by the nuisance. Sometimes, an injunction that stops the conduct is necessary. If the nuisance is permanent, the damages are the loss in value of the land. If the nuisance can be stopped, the measure of damages is the reduction in value of the property during the time of the nuisance.[23]

(A) Private and Public Nuisances. When a nuisance affects only one or a few persons, it is called a **private nuisance**. When it affects the community or public at large, it is called a **public nuisance**. Planting trees or erecting a fence, although otherwise lawful, constitutes a public nuisance when it creates a traffic hazard by obscuring an intersection. However, a landowner did not create a public nuisance by allowing trees to grow tall even though the height of the trees required the neighboring county airport to alter its approach patterns, which, in turn, triggered the Federal Aviation Administration to order the airport to shorten the usable portion of its runways.[24] The existence of a statutory environmental protection procedure may bar or supersede the common law of nuisance.

(B) Remedy for Nuisance. A criminal nuisance may be terminated by abatement or closure by government authority. A civil nuisance may be stopped by an injunction, and the injured person may sue for money damages for the harm caused.

When an injunction is issued, the court must exercise great care to halt the nuisance while avoiding going too far by enjoining conduct that is otherwise lawful.[25] *Spur Industries, Inc. v. Del E. Webb Development Co.* involves a court balancing interests in a nuisance case.

Spur Industries, Inc. v. Del E. Webb Development Co., 494 P.2d 700 (Az. 1972)

Moooving to the Nuisance

Spur Industries operated a cattle feedlot near Youngtown and Sun City, Arizona (communities 14 to 15 miles west of Phoenix). Spur had been operating the feedlot since 1956, and the area had been agricultural since 1911.

In 1959 Del E. Webb began development of the Sun City area, a retirement community. Webb purchased the 20,000 acres of land for about $750 per acre.

In 1960 Spur began an expansion program in which its operating area grew from 5 acres to 115 acres.

At the time of the suit, Spur was feeding between 20,000 and 30,000 head of cattle, which produced 35 to 40 pounds of wet manure per head per day, or over one million pounds per day. And despite the admittedly good feedlot management and good housekeeping practices of Spur, the resulting odor and flies produced an annoying if not unhealthy situation as far as the senior citizens of southern Sun City were concerned. There is no doubt that some of the citizens of Sun City were unable to enjoy the outdoor living which Del Webb had advertised. Del Webb was faced with sales resistance from prospective purchasers as well as strong and persistent complaints from the people who had purchased homes in that area. Nearly 1,300 lots could not be sold. Webb then filed suit alleging Spur's operation was a nuisance because of the flies and odors constantly drifting over Sun City. The trial court enjoined Spur's operations and Spur appealed.

JUDICIAL OPINION

Cameron, Vice Chief Justice...The difference between a private nuisance and a public nuisance is generally one of degree. A private nuisance is one affecting a single individual or a definite small number of persons in the enjoyment of private rights not common to the public, while a public nuisance is one affecting the rights enjoyed by citizens as a part of the public. To constitute a public nuisance, the nuisance must affect a considerable number of people or an entire community or neighborhood.

Where the injury is slight, the remedy for minor inconveniences lies in an action for damages rather than in one for an injunction. Moreover, some courts have held, in the "balancing of conveniences" cases, that damages may be the sole remedy.

Thus, it would appear from the admittedly incomplete record as developed in the trial court, that, at most, residents of Youngtown would be entitled to damages rather than injunctive relief.

[23] *Oglethorpe Power Corp. v. Forrister*, 711 S.E.2d 641 (Ga. 2011).
[24] *County of Westchester v. Town of Greenwich, Connecticut*, 76 F.3d 42 (2d Cir. 1996).
[25] *Barnette v. Grizzly Processing, LLC*, 809 F. Supp. 2d 636 (E.D. Ky. 2011).

Continued

We have no difficulty, however, in agreeing with the conclusion of the trial court that Spur's operation was an enjoinable public nuisance as far as the people in the southern portion of Del Webb's Sun City were concerned.

It is clear that as to the citizens of Sun City, the operation of Spur's feedlot was both a public and a private nuisance. They could have successfully maintained an action to abate the nuisance. Del Webb, having shown a special injury in the loss of sales, had a standing to bring suit to enjoin the nuisance. The judgment of the trial court permanently enjoining the operation of the feedlot is affirmed.

A suit to enjoin a nuisance sounds in equity and the courts have long recognized a special responsibility to the public when acting as a court of equity.

In addition to protecting the public interest, however, courts of equity are concerned with protecting the operator of a lawfully, albeit noxious, business from the result of a knowing and willful encroachment by others near his business.

In the so-called "coming to the nuisance" cases, the courts have held that the residential landowner may not have relief if he knowingly came into a neighborhood reserved for industrial or agricultural endeavors and has been damaged thereby:

Plaintiffs chose to live in an area uncontrolled by zoning laws or restrictive covenants and remote from urban development. In such an area plaintiffs cannot complain that legitimate agricultural pursuits are being carried on in the vicinity, nor can plaintiffs, having chosen to build in an agricultural area, complain that the agricultural pursuits carried on in the area depreciate the value of their homes. The area being primarily agricultural, and opinion reflecting the value of such property must take this factor into account. The standards affecting the value of residence property in an urban setting, subject to zoning controls and controlled planning techniques, cannot be the standards by which agricultural properties are judged.

"People employed in a city who build their homes in suburban areas of the county beyond the limits of a city and zoning regulations do so for a reason. Some do so to avoid the high taxation rate imposed by cities, or to avoid special assessments for street, sewer and water projects. They usually build on improved or hard surface highways, which have been built either at state or county expense and thereby avoid special assessments for these improvements. It may be that they desire to get away from the congestion of traffic, smoke, noise, foul air and the many other annoyances of city life. But with all these advantages in going beyond the area which is zoned and restricted to protect them in their homes, they must be prepared to take the disadvantages." And:

** * * a party cannot justly call upon the law to make that place suitable for his residence which was not so when he selected it. * * *.*

Were Webb the only party injured, we would feel justified in holding that the doctrine of "coming to the nuisance" would have been a bar to the relief asked by Webb, and, on the other hand, had Spur located the feedlot near the outskirts of a city and had the city grown toward the feedlot, Spur would have to suffer the cost of abating the nuisance as to those people locating within the growth pattern of the expanding city.

There was no indication in the instant case at the time Spur and its predecessors located in western Maricopa County that a new city would spring up, full-blown, alongside the feeding operation and that the developer of that city would ask the court to order Spur to move because of the new city. Spur is required to move not because of any wrongdoing on the part of Spur, but because of a proper and legitimate regard of the courts for the rights and interests of the public.

Del Webb, on the other hand, is entitled to the relief prayed for (a permanent injunction), not because Webb is blameless, but because of the damage to the people who have been encouraged to purchase homes in Sun City. It does not equitably or legally follow, however, that Webb, being entitled to the injunction, is then free of any liability to Spur if Webb has in fact been the cause of the damage Spur has sustained. It does not seem harsh to require a developer, who has taken advantage of the lesser land values in a rural area as well as the availability of large tracts of land on which to build and develop a new town or city in the area, to indemnify those who are forced to leave as a result.

Having brought people to the nuisance to the foreseeable detriment of Spur, Webb must indemnify Spur for a reasonable amount of the cost of moving or shutting down. It should be noted that this relief to Spur is limited to a case wherein a developer has, with foreseeability, brought into a previously agricultural or industrial area the population which makes necessary the granting of an injunction against a lawful business and for which the business has no adequate relief.

It is therefore the decision of this court that the matter be remanded to the trial court for a hearing upon the damages sustained by the defendant Spur as a reasonable and direct result of the granting of the permanent injunction. Since the result of the appeal may appear novel and both sides have obtained a measure of relief, it is ordered that each side will bear its own costs.

Affirmed in part, reversed in part, and remanded for further proceedings consistent with this opinion.

QUESTIONS

1. Did Spur create a nuisance?
2. Should it make any difference that Spur was there first?
3. How does the court balance retirement communities and beef production, which are two of Arizona's biggest industries?

E-Commerce & Cyberlaw

EMF and E-Commerce

Because any electrical current sets up a magnetic field, computers and wire transmissions to and from computers set up magnetic fields that might affect electrical equipment in buildings on neighboring land. The stronger the current, the greater the magnetic field.

For example, Meridian Data Processing Center is an independent contractor that performed all of the data processing for many banks and stockbrokers. Because of the large number of computers and direct wire lines to its customers, the Center's operation set up a substantial magnetic field that interfered with some of the electronic display equipment in several neighboring stores. The stores sued to obtain an injunction against the Center for creating a nuisance. However, unless the stores can show some negligence in the maintenance of the Center's equipment that produced unnecessary sparking or a similar cause of electrical disturbance, they have not established a nuisance. Because of the social utility of the Center's business, a court would not condemn this necessary activity as a nuisance. If, however, the stores could suggest a reasonable method of shielding the equipment, it is possible that the court would order the Center to take such protective measures.

(c) The Technological Environment of the Law of Nuisance. As technology changes, new ways of manufacturing, new methods of transportation, and new ways of living develop. As the environment changes, corresponding changes are reflected in the law. **For Example,** the presence of overhead wires and the possibility of electromagnetic field exposure has resulted in courts balancing the interests of utilities and the delivery of power with the safety of homeowners.

11. Private Remedies: Due Diligence

Another method by which problems with land are remedied is through sales transactions in which the buyer demands that a situation or problem on the land be fixed before signing a contract for purchase. **Due diligence** is the process by which the buyer conducts a thorough investigation of the property and its current and former uses to determine whether any problems with respect to environmental law or nuisance exist. Due diligence is conducted through a search of public records, an inspection of the land, and often, when problems appear in these first two steps, some soil testing. This advance determination of problems is a civil means for land cleanup because sellers will be unable to transfer their properties until they meet the buyers' standards, determined by a close examination of the property for violations.

C. Land Use Controls

In addition to environmental laws, other restrictions, both private and public, place controls and limits on how land can be used.

12. Restrictive Covenants in Private Contracts

Real estate developers find that when there are consistent patterns in the appearance of a neighborhood's homes and buildings (for example, similarity of design instead of a hodge-podge look), the property values are enhanced. To make sure this consistency is maintained, developers place **restrictive covenants** on the land that obligate the buyers to honor limitations in their use of their property, the nature of buildings that will be maintained or constructed on the land, and so on. If a restrictive covenant is valid, it binds buyers who had actual notice or knowledge of the restrictions. The notice comes from a notation in the deed about the covenants; the covenants then are said to "run with the land." That is, all owners are subject to them and all owners in that development have the right to stop another owner from violating the covenant.

A restrictive covenant must be clearly stated to be effective. Contract rules apply in interpreting covenants. If any uncertainty exists, the covenant will be construed strictly in favor of the free use of the land. When there is no uncertainty and no reason to depart from the meaning of the words of the covenant, a court will enforce those words.

Because of property rights, courts interpret restrictive covenants narrowly to permit the greatest possible use of the land. However, courts often disagree as to what is permitted by a restrictive covenant. **For Example,** courts have decided differently the issue of the use of a single-family residence for providing day care services when the covenants for that neighborhood prohibit the operation of a business out of a home.[26]

Restrictive covenants that violate laws or constitutional rights are not valid. For example, a restrictive covenant that discriminates against persons with disabilities is void because it violates the Fair Housing Act.[27]

A restrictive covenant that has not been enforced or observed is no longer valid. For example, if houses in a neighborhood have had their roofs replaced with materials that did not comply with the restrictive covenants but no one objects, those new materials become the standard for the neighborhood, not the covenant materials.[28]

13. Public Zoning

By **zoning**, a governmental unit such as a city adopts an ordinance imposing restrictions on the use of the land. The object of zoning is to ensure an orderly physical development of the regulated area. In effect, zoning is the same as restrictive covenants; the difference is in the source of authority. In most cases, zoning is based on an ordinance of a local political subdivision, such as a municipality or a county. Restrictive covenants, on the other hand, are created by agreement of the parties.

The zoning power permits any regulation that is conducive to advancing public health, welfare, and safety. The object of a particular zoning regulation may be to prevent high-density population.

Some zoning ordinances may be conservation inspired. An ordinance may prohibit or regulate the extraction of natural resources from any land within the zoned area. The fact that a zoning restriction limits the owner in the use of a property does not amount to a "taking" of property for which compensation must be made.[29] If, however, the zoning law deprived the owner of use of the land in any fashion, that would be a "taking" that required compensation.

Sports & Entertainment Law

The Star Wars Studio

Quietly over the years, beginning in the 1970s when the money from his films began to roll in, George "Star Wars" Lucas has been acquiring land in Marin County (6,000 acres in total) with the goal of preserving its natural beauty and stopping its development. In fact, 97 percent of the acreage cannot be developed under deed restrictions. Mr. Lucas has planted 8,000 trees on the land and restored pathways for walking and hiking.

However, Mr. Lucas always intended to build a studio complex there, a 269,000-square-foot facility that would be located on a little over 1,000 of the acres. The plan has been 27 years in the making and was canceled last week because of what Mr. Lucas called "regulatory delay" and fierce opposition from the neighborhoods around the planned site. The neighbors (often called NIMBYs for Not in My Back Yard) oppose the facility, known as the Grady Ranch project, because it would employ 463 people and bring too much noise and traffic into the area. Neighbors indicated that regardless of county approval that they would file suits that would delay the project until their concerns were fully litigated. More details on the project can be found at Victoria Baret, "Millionaire NIMBYs 1; Billionaire Filmmaker 0," **www.forbes.com/sites/victoriabarret/2012/04/18/how-star-wars-george-lucas-lost-out-to-a-california-subdivision/** *Forbes*, May 2, 2012, p. 18.

[26] *Nickerson v. Green Valley Recreation, Inc.*, 265 P.3d 1108 (Ariz. App. 2011).

[27] *Villas West II of Willowridge Homeowners Ass'n, Inc. v. McGlothin*, 885 N.E.2d 1274 (Ind. 2008).

[28] *Stuart v. Chawney*, 560 N.W.2d 336 (Mich. App. 1997).

[29] *Cablevision Systems Corp. v. F.C.C.*, 570 F.3d 83 (9th Cir. 2009).

(A) NONCONFORMING USE. When the use of land is in conflict with a zoning ordinance at the time the ordinance goes into effect, such use is described as a **nonconforming use**. **For Example,** when a zoning ordinance that requires a setback of 25 feet from the boundary line is adopted, an existing building that has a 10-foot setback is a nonconforming use.

A nonconforming use has a constitutionally protected right to continue, but if the nonconforming use is discontinued, it cannot be resumed.[30] The right to a nonconforming use may be lost by abandonment. If a garage is a nonconforming use and its owner stops using it as a garage and uses it for storing goods, a return to the use of the property as a garage will be barred by abandonment.

At times, a real estate development or building construction is only partly completed when a zoning ordinance that would prohibit such development or building is adopted. To avoid hardship for the persons involved, it is customary to exempt partly finished projects from the zoning ordinance just as though they were existing nonconforming uses.[31]

(B) VARIANCE. The administrative agency charged with the enforcement of a zoning ordinance may grant a **variance**. This permits the owner of the land to use it in a specified manner that is inconsistent with the zoning ordinance. The *Hold Fast Tattoo, LLC v. City of North Chicago* case deals with a request for a special use permit, a form of a variance.

Hold Fast Tattoo, LLC v. City of North Chicago, 580 F. Supp. 2d 656 (N.D. Ill. 2008)

No Tattoos in My Neighborhood

Hold Fast Tattoo (Plaintiff) wished to open a tattoo studio on North Sheridan Road in the City of North Chicago and obtained a prospective lessor at its desired location. In accordance with North Chicago's zoning ordinance, Hold Fast Tattoo applied for a special use permit to operate a tattoo studio at that location. On June 21, 2007 the Zoning Board of Appeals of North Chicago recommended approval of the permit to its city council. The proposal was discussed at two council meetings, on July 9, 2007, and July 16, 2007, and Hold Fast Tattoo's request for a special use permit was ultimately denied. The city council informed Hold Fast that its special use permit was denied because it was "not the kind of business" the council wanted in North Chicago. Hold Fast filed suit.

JUDICIAL OPINION

MORAN, Senior District Judge…Plaintiff argues that its right to draw tattoos is protected by the First Amendment free speech clause. The nature of the right to draw tattoos is a question that has not been directly addressed by the Seventh Circuit nor the Supreme Court. However, we are persuaded by related authority, as well as the decisions of numerous other courts, that the act of tattooing is not constitutionally protected free speech.

The First Amendment protects speech. It also protects expressive conduct, as long as the conduct is "sufficiently imbued with elements of communication to fall within the scope" of the First Amendment. To determine whether an activity warrants First Amendment protection, the court must determine whether there was intent to convey a particularized message and whether there is a great likelihood that the message would be understood by those who view it.

The act of tattooing fails the first prong of this test because the act itself is not intended to convey a particularized message. The very nature of the tattoo artist is to custom-tailor a different or unique message for each customer to wear on the skin. The act of tattooing is one step removed from actual expressive conduct, which is similar to a sound truck, which enables each customer to express a particularized message, but the sound truck vehicle itself is not expressive. Similarly, the tattoo artist's daily work may be used by customers to convey a message, but it is not protected by the First Amendment in and of itself. Because the act of tattooing fails the first prong of the test for First Amendment protection, there is no "message" to be understood by viewers and tattooing must also fail the second prong. Therefore, this court agrees with other courts that have held the act of tattooing is not an act protected by the First Amendment. Where no fundamental right or suspect class is at issue, "legislation is presumed to be valid and will be sustained if the classification drawn by the statute is rationally related to a legitimate state interest."

[30] *DoMiJo, LCC v. McLain*, 41 A.3d 967 (Pa. Cmwlth. 2012).
[31] See, for example, *Vial v. Provo City*, 210 P.3d 947 (Utah App. 2009).

Continued

Here, Hold Fast Tattoo has not alleged the violation of a suspect class or a fundamental right, so the challenged legislation is presumed valid and will be upheld if the statute's classifications are rationally related to a legitimate state interest.... The special use permit required by North Chicago's zoning ordinance is substantially related to its municipal planning goals. In the motion to dismiss Plaintiff's complaint, Defendant sets forth numerous municipal planning goals that are advanced by the requirement of a special use permit for Plaintiff's business: character, stability, or intended development of the city's central business district; suitability of the location to the proposed use; necessity and desirability of a proposed use in a particular location; and protection of the health and/or safety of the community.... [W]e find defendant's zoning ordinance could be rationally related to a legitimate state interest.

The complaint contains a portion of a sentence that alleges the zoning ordinance "unreasonably requires Plaintiff to submit to controls not imposed on other similarly situated businesses or properties." In order to bring a class of one equal protection claim, a plaintiff must allege that (1) he has been intentionally treated differently from others similarly situated and (2) there is no rational basis for the difference in treatment, or that the differential treatment is due to a "'totally illegitimate animus' toward the plaintiff by the defendant." We cannot conceive of how Hold Fast Tattoo can satisfy the second prong of this test because the grounds for it do not appear in the complaint.

The only deprivation that is alleged in the complaint here is the right to the "use and operation" of Plaintiff's business. Plaintiff does not allege, nor can we find a component of the due process clause or an Illinois state law that gives a legitimate claim of entitlement to perform the act of tattooing. Therefore, since Plaintiff has not alleged the deprivation of a protectable interest, the procedural due process allegation fails before we can reach the second required prong of this claim.

Plaintiff claims that the zoning ordinance enacted by Defendant is an unlawful exercise of the state's police power, both as applied to Plaintiff and on its face. "It is well established that, as an exercise of the police power, a zoning ordinance is presumed to be constitutionally valid." A party challenging the ordinance must show "that the ordinance is clearly arbitrary and unreasonable, having no substantial relation to the public health, safety, morals, or general welfare."

Here, Defendant's zoning ordinance requires a special use permit for certain uses, to meet municipal planning goals that protect the health and/or safety of the community. As discussed above, the zoning ordinance is rationally related to a legitimate state interest.

[Plaintiff's complaint is dismissed.]

QUESTIONS

1. Why is the ordinance not a violation of the First Amendment?
2. What legitimate government interest(s) is/are satisfied with the prohibition on tattoo parlors? Does it matter that 33 percent of the U.S. population now has a tattoo?

Agencies ordinarily are reluctant to permit a variance when neighboring property owners object because, to the extent that variation is permitted, the basic plan of the zoning ordinance is defeated. Likewise, the allowance of an individual variation, or **spot zoning**, may result in such inequality as to be condemned by the courts.[32] In addition, there is a consideration of practical expediency. If variances are readily granted, every property owner will request a variance and flood the agency with these requests.

When the desired use of land is in harmony with the general nature of surrounding areas, a zoning variance is usually granted. A zoning variance is not granted on the ground of hardship, however, when the landowner created the hardship by purchasing land that was subject to a zoning ordinance.

LawFlix

Erin Brockovich (2000) (R)

The movie is the story of ground water pollution and private litigation for recovery.

[32] *Wilson v. Brick Tp. Zoning Bd. of Adjustment*, 963 A.2d 1208 (N.J. Super. 2009).

MAKE THE CONNECTION

SUMMARY

Public and private regulations apply to land use. The public regulations consist of environmental laws and zoning. Environmental laws exist at both the state and the federal levels. At the federal level, regulations govern air pollution through limits on emissions and permits for discharges; water pollution with permit requirements, discharge prohibitions, and treatment standards; solid waste disposal with limitations on dumping and liability for cleanup when hazardous materials are found on property; and environmental quality through the use of advance studies on projects and their impact on the environment. Other federal regulations on the environment protect endangered species, set standards for drinking water, and impose liability for oil spills as well as safety standards for oil tankers.

Environmental laws are primarily enforced at the federal level by the Environmental Protection Agency (EPA), but other federal agencies as well as state agencies work together to enforce these laws, using criminal and civil penalties and injunctions to halt pollution. Private citizens also have the right to bring suit under federal statutes to enforce the requirements imposed.

A *nuisance* is a public or private interference with the use and enjoyment of land, and individuals can bring suit to halt nuisances. Courts perform a balancing test in deciding how to handle concerns about nuisances. They seek to balance the use and enjoyment of land with the economic interests of all involved parties.

Restrictive covenants in deeds are valid land use restrictions that pass from owner to owner and are enforceable as long as they do not violate any constitutional rights. *Zoning* is a public means of regulating land use. Zoning laws are part of an overall plan for development adopted by a governmental entity. Some landowners can obtain variances from zoning laws, and some preexisting uses are permitted to continue with the protection of a nonconforming use.

LEARNING OUTCOMES

After studying this chapter, you should be able to clearly explain:

A. Statutory Environmental Law

LO.1 List and describe the federal statutes that regulate various aspects of the environment

See *Massachusetts v. EPA* discussion on p. 1060.

See the discussion of the air, water, and waste statutes beginning on p. 1059.

Study the Ethics & the Law issue on the egg farm on p. 1068.

B. Enforcement of Environmental Laws

LO.2 Explain how environmental laws are enforced and describe the criminal penalties for violation of environmental laws

See the list of penalties in Figure 50-1.

Study Thinking Things Through on wild horse management on p. 1065.

LO.3 Define *nuisance* and list the remedies available

See *Spur Industries v. Del Webb* on pp. 1070–1071.

C. Land Use Controls

LO.4 Explain the role and application of covenants and zoning laws

See *Hold Fast Tattoo, LLC v. City of North Chicago* on pp. 1074–1073.

KEY TERMS

best available treatment
best conventional treatment
brownfields
bubble concept
Clean Air Act
Clean Water Act
Comprehensive Environmental Response, Compensation, and Liability Act (CERCLA)
Council on Environmental Quality (CEQ)
due diligence
effluent guidelines
emissions offset policy
Endangered Species Act (ESA)
environmental impact statement (EIS)
injunction
National Environmental Policy Act (NEPA)
National Pollutant Discharge Elimination System (NPDES)
Noise Control Act
nonattainment areas
nonconforming use
nuisance
Oil Pollution Act
point sources
private nuisance
public nuisance
Resource Conservation and Recovery Act (RCRA)
Resource Recovery Act
restrictive covenants
Safe Drinking Water Act
spot zoning
Superfund Amendment and Reauthorization Act
Superfund sites
Toxic Substances Control Act (TOSCA)
variance
zoning

QUESTIONS AND CASE PROBLEMS

1. Union Electric wishes to construct a new coal-fired plant in the northeastern corner of Arizona. Union plans to use the maximum achievement technology for the scrubbers on the plant to reduce emissions. Will Union be able to obtain a permit from the EPA to build and operate the new power plant? Discuss the issues that Union faces.

2. Federal Oil Co. was loading a tanker with fuel oil when the loading hose snapped for some unknown reason and about 1,000 gallons of oil poured into the ocean. Federal Oil was prosecuted for this water pollution. It raised the defense that it had exercised due care, was not at fault in any way, and had not intended to pollute the water. What statutes could be used to prosecute Federal Oil? What are the potential penalties?

3. Philip Carey Co. owned a tract of land in Plymouth Township, Pennsylvania, on which it deposited a large pile of manufacturing waste containing asbestos. Carey sold the land to Celotex, and Celotex sold the land to Smith Land & Improvement Corp. The EPA notified Smith that unless it took steps to eliminate the asbestos hazard, the EPA would do the work and pursue reimbursement. Smith cleaned up the land to the EPA's satisfaction at a cost of $218,945.44. Smith asked Celotex and Carey for reimbursement. Which firms have liability for the cleanup costs? [*Smith Land & Improvement Corp. v. Celotex*, 851 F.2d 86 (3d Cir.)]

4. The McConnells bought a home in Sherwood Estates. The land was subject to a restrictive covenant that "no building, fence, or other structure" could be built on the land without the approval of the developer of the property. The McConnells built a dog pen in their yard that consisted of a cement base with fencing surrounding the base. They claimed that approval was not required on the theory that the restrictive covenant did not apply because it showed an intent to restrict only major construction, not minor additions to the landscape. A lawsuit was brought to compel the McConnells to remove the dog pen because prior approval had not been obtained. Are restrictive covenants applied this expansively to homeowners? Must the McConnells have prior approval? [*Sherwood Estates Homes Ass'n, Inc. v. McConnell*, 714 S.W.2d 848 (Mo. App.)]

5. General Automotive operates Grand Auto Parts Stores, which receive used automotive batteries from customers as trade-ins. General's policy in

disposing of these batteries had been to drive a screwdriver through each spent battery and then sell them to a battery-cracking plant operated by Morris P. Kirk & Sons, Inc., which extracted and smelted the lead. After the lead was extracted from the batteries, Kirk washed and crushed the battery casings, loaded them into a dump truck, and then dumped them. Tons of pieces of crushed batteries were dumped onto Catellus Development Corp.'s property. Under CERCLA, Catellus sought to recover from General the costs of cleaning up the hazardous battery parts from its property. General maintained that it was not liable because it sold the batteries to Kirk, and Kirk did the dumping. Was General correct? [*Catellus Development Corp. v. United States*, 34 F.3d 748 (9th Cir.)]

6. A zoning ordinance of the city of Dallas, Texas, prohibited the use of property in a residential district for gasoline filling stations. Lombardo brought an action against the city to test the validity of the ordinance. He contended that the ordinance violated the rights of the owners of property in such districts. Do you agree with this contention? [*Lombardo v. City of Dallas*, 73 S.W.2d 475 (Tex.)]

7. Taback began building a vacation home on a parcel of wooded land. It was to be a three-story house, 31 feet high. This height violated the local zoning ordinance that limited residential homes to two and one-half stories, not exceeding 35 feet. When Taback learned of this violation, he applied for a zoning variance. Because of the delay of the zoning board and because winter was approaching, Taback finished the construction of the building as a three-story house. At a later hearing before the zoning board, he showed that it would be necessary for him to rebuild the third floor to convert the house into a two and one-half story house. The zoning board recognized that Taback's violation could not be seen from neighboring properties. Was Taback entitled to a zoning variance? [*Taback v. Town of Woodstock Zoning Board of Appeals*, 521 N.Y.S.2d 838 (App. Div.)]

8. Bermuda Run Country Club, Inc., developed a tract of land, formed a country club, and sold some of the lots to individual buyers. Following various sales and litigation, an agreement was executed giving the board of governors power to veto club members' assessments. The agreement declared that this was a restrictive covenant that would run with the land and bind subsequent owners. The corporation that later purchased the country club claimed it did not have that effect. Was the provision in question a restrictive covenant that ran with the land? [*Bermuda Run Country Club, Inc. v. Atwell*, 465 S.E.2d 9 (N.C. App.)]

9. The Stallcups lived in a rural section of the state. In front of their house ran a relatively unused, unimproved public county road. Wales Trucking Co. transported concrete pipe from the plant where it was made to a lake where the pipe was used to construct a water line to bring water to a nearby city. In the course of four months, Wales made 825 trips over the road, carrying from 58,000 to 72,000 pounds of pipe per trip and making the same number of empty return trips. Because the heavy use of the road by Wales cut up the dirt and made it like ashes, the Stallcups sued Wales for damages caused by the deposit of dust on their house and for the physical annoyance and discomfort it caused. Wales defended its position on the ground that it had not been negligent and that its use of the road was not unlawful. Decide. [*Wales Trucking Co. v. Stallcup*, 465 S.E.2d 44 (Tex. App.)]

10. Some sections of the city of Manitou Springs have hills of varying degrees of slope. To protect against water drainage and erosion, the city adopted a hillside zoning ordinance that required homes on hillsides to be surrounded by more open land than in the balance of the city. Sellon owned land on a hillside and claimed that the hillside ordinance was unconstitutional because it did not treat all homeowners equally. Was the ordinance valid? [*Sellon v. City of Manitou Springs*, 745 P.2d 229 (Colo.)]

11. Patrick Bossenberry owned a house in a planned community area. Each lot in the area was limited by a restrictive covenant to use for a single-family dwelling. The covenant defined *family* as a blood or marital relationship between most of the occupants. Bossenberry rented his building to Kay-Jan, Inc., which wanted to use the building

as a care home for not more than six adult mentally retarded persons. The neighbors sought to enjoin this use as a breach of the covenant. A number of Michigan statutes had been adopted that advanced the public policy of providing care for mentally retarded persons. Could the neighbors prevent the use of the property as a care home for mentally retarded adults? [*Craig v. Bossenberry*, 351 N.W.2d 596 (Mich. App.)]

12. Kenneth and Mary Norpel purchased a house, and Kenneth attached a 35-foot flagpole to it. He did not obtain the permission of the architectural committee of the Stone Hill Community Association. This consent was required by a restrictive covenant to which the Norpel house was subject. The association objected to the flagpole from which Norpel then flew the American flag. The association brought an action to compel the removal of the pole. Norpel claimed that as a combat veteran of World War II, he had a constitutionally protected right to fly the American flag. Can he be compelled to remove the flagpole?

13. In 1997, Isbell purchased a building in San Diego with the intent to open an adult entertainment establishment there. Because this building was located within 1,000 feet of a residential area, however, a San Diego zoning ordinance precluded him from operating there. Isbell applied for a variance but was unsuccessful. He then filed suit, arguing that the city's ordinance violates the First Amendment, and that its standards for variances violate the equal protection clause. Can the city restrict the operation of this business? What must the city be able to establish? [*Isbell v. City of San Diego*, 258 F.3d 1108 (9th Cir.)]

14. Explain why a company would want to perform a self-audit to determine whether it has any environmental violations.

15. Gregory Mills lives next to Dean Kimbley. Mills kept a journal of Kimbley's activities, and even videotaped a few of the activities, including Kimbley's smoking marijuana and standing drunk in his backyard and yelling, "Hi, neighbor!" Kimbley also threw a snowball into Mills' yard and nearly hit Mills' girlfriend with it. When Mills listed his property for sale because of the issues with Kimbley, Kimbley sent a pizza delivery man to Mills' door and told him to offer $125,000 to buy Mills' home. Kimbley then hired a real estate agent and took a tour of Mills' home with that real estate agent. Kimbley also drove an ATC onto Mills' lawn. Is this a nuisance case? Are these the elements of nuisance? Explain why or why not. [*Mills v. Kimbley*, 909 N.E.2d 1068 (Ind. App.)]

CPA QUESTIONS

1. Which of the following remedies is available against a real property owner to enforce the provisions of federal acts regulating air and water pollution?

	Citizen Suits against the Environmental Protection Agency to Enforce Compliance	*State Suits to Enforce the Laws against Violators*	*Citizen Suits against Violators to Enforce the Laws*
a.	Yes	Yes	Yes
b.	Yes	Yes	No
c.	No	Yes	Yes
d.	Yes	No	Yes

2. Under the Comprehensive Environmental Response, Compensation, and Liability Act (CERCLA), commonly known as Superfund, which of the following parties would be liable to the Environmental Protection Agency (EPA) for the expense of cleaning up a hazardous waste disposal site?
   I. The current owner or operator of the site
   II. The person who transported the wastes to the site
   III. The person who owned or operated the site at the time of the disposal
   a. I and II
   b. I and III
   c. II and III
   d. I, II, and III

3. The National Environment Policy Act was passed to enhance and preserve the environment. Which of the following is not true?
   a. The act applies to all federal agencies.
   b. The act requires that an environmental impact statement be provided if any proposed federal legislation may significantly affect the environment.
   c. Enforcement of the act is primarily accomplished by litigation of persons who decide to challenge federal government decisions.
   d. The act provides generous tax breaks to those companies that help accomplish national environmental policy.

4. Which of the following actions should a business take to qualify for leniency if an environmental violation has been committed?

	Conduct Environmental Audits	*Report Environmental Violations to the Government*
a.	Yes	Yes
b.	Yes	No
c.	No	Yes
d.	No	No

CHAPTER 51

© Manuel Gutjahr/iStockphoto.com

Leases

learningoutcomes

After studying this chapter, you should be able to

LO.1 List the ways in which a lease may be terminated

LO.2 List and explain the rights and duties of the parties to a lease

LO.3 Describe a landlord's liability for a tenant's and a third person's injuries sustained on the premises

LO.4 Define *sublease* and *assignment of a lease* and distinguish between them

If you cannot buy a house or piece of business property, leasing such a property from someone who does own it may be the answer.

A. Creation and Termination

Leases are governed by the common law of property as modified by judicial decisions and statutes.[1]

1. Definition and Nature

A **lease** is the relationship in which one person is in lawful possession of real property owned by another. In common usage, *lease* also refers to the agreement that creates that relationship.

The person who owns the real property and permits the occupation of the premises is known as the **lessor**, or **landlord**. The **lessee**, or **tenant**, is the one who occupies the property. A lease establishes the relationship of landlord and tenant.

2. Creation of the Lease Relationship

The relationship of landlord and tenant is created by an express or implied contract. An oral lease is valid at common law, but statutes in most states require written leases for certain tenancies. Many states provide that a lease for a term exceeding one year must be in writing.

(A) Antidiscrimination. Statutes in many states prohibit an owner who rents property for profit from discriminating against prospective tenants on the basis of race, color, religion, or national origin. Also, the federal *Fair Housing Act* prohibits such discrimination. In addition, landlords are subject to the Americans with Disabilities Act (ADA) and must make reasonable accommodations for tenants with disabilities. **For Example,** a tenant whose physician has prescribed a comfort pet must be allowed to have that pet in his or her apartment even if the complex does not allow pets.[2]

(B) Unconscionability. At common law, the parties to a lease had freedom to include such terms as they chose. However, that freedom has been curbed in some states that require that leases follow the pattern of UCC section 2-302 and not include terms and conditions that are unconscionable.[3] **For Example,** a provision in a residential lease stating that the landlord cutting off heat or water will not constitute an eviction is unconscionable. Such a clause does not prevent the tenant from recovering on the grounds of unconscionability or for breach of the implied warranty of habitability when there has been no heat or water.

3. Classification of Tenancies

Tenancies are classified by duration as tenancies for years, from year to year, at will, and by sufferance.

CPA **(A) Tenancy for Years.** A **tenancy for years** is one under which the tenant has a lease that runs for a definite duration. The expression "for years" is used to describe such a tenancy whether the duration of the tenancy is for only six months or as long as 10 years.

(B) Periodic Tenancy. A **periodic tenancy** is one under which a tenant has a lease that has an indefinite duration and under which the tenant pays annual, monthly, or weekly rent. This tenancy does not terminate at the end of a year, month, or week except with proper notice. Proper notice, in most states, means giving notice for at least one period before ending the lease. **For Example,** on a month-to-month tenancy, the notice must be at least one month prior to ending the lease.

In almost all states, a periodic tenancy is implied if the tenant, with the consent of the landlord, stays in possession of property after a tenancy for years. Consent exists when there is an express statement or by conduct, such as when a landlord continues to accept rent.[4]

CPA **(C) Tenancy at Will.** When a lease runs for an indefinite period, which may be terminated at any time by the landlord or the tenant, a **tenancy at will**

[1] A uniform act, the Uniform Residential Landlord and Tenant Act (URLTA), has been adopted in some form in 21 states. The 21 states are: Alabama, Alaska, Arizona, Connecticut, Florida, Hawaii, Iowa, Kansas, Kentucky, Michigan, Mississippi, Montana, Nebraska, New Mexico, Oklahoma, Oregon, Rhode Island, South Carolina, Tennessee, Virginia, and Washington. URLTA does not apply to dorm rooms, fraternities, homeless shelters, or halfway houses. *Strejac v. YouthCare*, 2009 WL 4066938 (W.D. Wash.).

[2] *Salute v. Stratford Green Apartments*, 136 F.3d 293 (2nd Cir. 1998); and see *Stevens v. Hollywood Towers and Condominium Ass'n*, 836 F. Supp. 2d 800 (N.D. Ill. 2011) for an even broader interpretation of the protections of ADA.

[3] *35 Park Ave. Corp. v. Campagna*, 399 N.E.2d 1144 (N.Y. 1979); URLTA §1.303.

[4] *Bayne v. Smith*, 965 A.2d 265 (Pa. Super. 2009).

exists. A person who possesses land for an indefinite period with the owner's permission but without any agreement as to rent is a tenant at will. Statutes in some states and decisions in others require advance notice of termination of this kind of tenancy.

CPA **(D) Tenancy at Sufferance.** When a tenant remains in possession after the termination of the lease without permission of the landlord, the landlord may treat the tenant as either a trespasser or a tenant. Until the landlord elects to do one or the other, a **tenancy at sufferance** exists. **For Example,** if John's one-year lease expired on January 31, 2013, and John remained in the apartment for a week, he would be a tenant at sufferance during that week. If John's landlord accepted a rental payment at the end of the first week, John would be a *periodic* or *month-to-month tenant*. In this situation, John was a tenant for years, a tenant at sufferance, and then a periodic tenant.

4. Termination of Lease

A lease is generally not terminated by the death, insanity, or bankruptcy of either party except in the case of a tenancy at will. Leases may be terminated in the following ways.

(A) Termination by Notice. Unless prohibited by statute, a lease may give the landlord the power to terminate it by giving notice to the tenant. In states that follow the common law on termination by notice, it is immaterial why the landlord terminates. A provision in a lease giving the landlord the right to terminate the lease by notice is strictly construed against the landlord.

(B) Expiration of Term in a Tenancy for Years. A tenancy for years ends upon the expiration of the term. There is no requirement that one party give the other any notice of termination. However, a lease may require express notice in this type of lease with a specified term except when a statute prohibits the landlord from imposing such a requirement.

(C) Notice in a Periodic Tenancy. In the absence of an agreement of the parties, notice for termination of a periodic tenancy is now usually governed by statute. It is common practice for the parties to require 30 or 60 days' notice to end a tenancy from year to year.

(D) Destruction of Property. By either an express provision in a lease or under a statutory provision, tenants are released from their liability to pay rent if the leased premises are destroyed. Alternatively, the amount of rent may be reduced in proportion to the loss. **For Example,** a tenant may only be able to use one-half of the property, so the rent would be cut in half. Such statutes do not require the landlord to repair or restore the property to its former condition.

When the lease covers rooms or an apartment in a building, a destruction of the leased premises terminates the lease.

(E) Fraud. Because a lease is based on a contract, a lease agreement is subject to the contract defense of fraud. (See Chapter 14.)

(F) Transfer of the Tenant. Residential leases may contain a provision for termination if there is a change in the tenant's circumstances, such as the tenant's being transferred by an employer to another city or on the tenant's being called into active military service. Such provisions are strictly construed against the tenant. Tenants should be certain to request personal circumstances provisions in their leases that are broad enough to cover these types of job events and military duty.

5. Notice of Termination

When notice of termination is required, no particular words are necessary to constitute a sufficient notice so long as the words used clearly indicate the intention of the party. The notice, whether given by the landlord or the tenant, must be definite. Statutes sometimes require that the notice be in writing. In the absence of such a provision, however, oral notice is generally sufficient.

6. Renewal of Lease

When a lease terminates for any reason, the landlord and the tenant ordinarily enter into a new agreement if they wish to extend or renew the lease. The power to renew the lease may be stated in the original lease by declaring that the lease runs indefinitely, as from year to year, subject to being terminated by either party's giving written notice of a specified number of days or months before the termination date. Renewal provisions are strictly construed against the tenant.

The lease may require the tenant to give written notice of intention to renew the lease. In such a case, there is no renewal if the tenant does not give the required notice but merely remains on the premises after the expiration of the original term.[5]

B. Rights and Duties of Parties

The rights and duties of the landlord and tenant are based on principles of real estate law and contract law. There is an increasing tendency to treat the residential lease like any other type of consumer contract and to govern the rights and duties of the parties by general principles of contract law.

7. Possession

The tenant has the right to acquire **possession** of the property and to remain in possession of that property until the term of the lease has expired or he or she is removed according to legal proceedings provided to landlords for removal of tenants in breach of the lease.

(a) Right of Possession. By making a lease, the lessor or landlord agrees to give possession of the premises to the tenant at the time specified in the lease. If the landlord rents a building that is being constructed, there is an implied promise in the contract that the leased premises will be ready for occupancy on the date specified in the lease for the beginning of the lease term.

If the landlord interferes with the tenant's possession, the landlord has breached the lease agreement, and legal remedies are available to the tenant. *Interference* is generally defined to be an eviction that occurs by judicial proceedings or when the landlord prevents access by the tenant, as when the locks are changed and the tenant does not have a key. If the landlord wrongfully deprives the tenant of the use of one room when the tenant is entitled to use an entire apartment or building, there is a partial eviction. An eviction in violation of the lease or law entitles the tenant to collect damages from the landlord for interference with possession of the leased premises.

(b) Covenant of Quiet Enjoyment. Most written leases today contain an express promise by the landlord called a **covenant of quiet enjoyment**. Such a provision protects the tenant from interference with possession by the landlord or the landlord's agent, but it does not impose liability on the landlord for the unlawful acts of third persons.[6]

(c) Constructive Eviction. A **constructive eviction** occurs when some act or omission of the landlord substantially deprives the tenant of the use and enjoyment of the premises.

To establish a constructive eviction, the tenant must show that the condition of the property is such that it is impossible for the tenant to remain in possession. In addition, constructive eviction is not established unless the tenant actually leaves the premises. If the tenant continues to occupy the premises for more than a reasonable time after what is claimed to be a constructive eviction, the tenant waives or loses the right to object to the landlord's conduct. The definition of constructive eviction requires the establishment of conditions so awful that a tenant is forced to leave. The tenant's remaining behind in the leased premises contradicts one of the elements required for establishing constructive eviction.[7] **For Example,** a condition of constructive eviction would be sewage backing up through the bathtub. The tenant could claim the sewage in the apartment constituted constructive eviction, but the tenant would also need to move out of the apartment.

8. Use of Premises

The lease generally specifies those uses authorized for the tenant. In the absence of express or implied restrictions, a tenant is entitled to use the premises for any lawful purpose for which they are adapted or for which they are ordinarily employed or in a manner contemplated by the parties in executing the lease. A provision specifying the use to be made of the property is strictly construed against the tenant.

(a) Change of Use. If the tenant uses the property for any purpose other than the one specified, the landlord has the option to declare the lease terminated.

[5] *Capella III, L.L.C. v. Wilcox*, 940 N.E.2d 1026 (Ohio. App. 2010).

[6] *Haslam-James v. Lawrence*, 35 A.2d 368 (Conn. App. 2012).

[7] Some states prohibit a landlord of residential property from willfully turning off the utilities of a tenant for the purpose of evicting the tenant. *City and County of San Francisco v. Sainez*, 77 Cal. App. 4th 1302, 92 Cal. Rprt. 2d 418 (Cal. App. 2009) (imposing civil penalty of $663,000 for shutting off utilities for 530 days). Such conduct is also a violation of ULTRA §§2.104 and 4.105. *Ervin v. Tsackhouse*, 64 So.3d 666 (Ala. App. 2010).

(B) Continued Use of Property. A tenant is ordinarily required to give the landlord notice of nonuse or vacancy of the premises. This notice is a practical issue; landlords need to be aware when premises are vacant because there is an increased danger of damage to the premises by vandalism or fire. Also, there is commonly a provision in the landlord's fire insurance policy making it void if a vacancy continues for a specified time.

(C) Rules. The modern lease generally contains a blanket agreement by the tenant to abide by the provisions of rules and regulations adopted by the landlord. These rules are generally binding on the tenant whether they exist at the time the lease was made or are adopted afterward.

(D) Prohibition of Pets. A lease restriction prohibiting pet ownership is valid, as are cleaning fees for violations of the restriction.

9. Rent

The tenant is under a duty to pay rent as compensation to the landlord. The amount of rent agreed to by the parties may be subject to government regulation, as when a city or county has enacted rent control laws.[8]

(A) Time of Payment. The time of payment of rent is ordinarily fixed by the lease. However, statutes or custom may require rent to be paid monthly or may require a substantial deposit before the lease begins.

CPA **(B) Assignment.** If the lease is assigned (the tenant's entire interest is transferred to a third person), the assignee is liable to the landlord for the rent. However, the assignment does not in itself discharge the tenant from the duty to pay the rent. If the assignee of the lease does not make the lease payments, the landlord may bring an action for the rent against either the original tenant or the assignee, or both, but is entitled to payment of only what is due under the lease, not a double amount as collected from each party. A **sublessee** (a person to whom part of a tenant's interest is transferred) ordinarily is not liable to the original lessor for rent unless that liability has been expressly assumed or is imposed by statute.

(C) Rent Escalation. When property is rented for a long term, it is common to include some provision for the automatic increase of the rent at periodic intervals. Such a provision is often tied to increases in the cost of living or in the landlord's operating costs and is called an **escalation clause**. There may, however, also be rent controls that would prohibit such rent increases.[9]

10. Repairs and Condition of Premises

In the absence of an agreement to the contrary, the tenant has no duty to make repairs. When the landlord makes repairs, reasonable care must be exercised to make them in a proper manner. The tenant is liable for any damage to the premises caused by his or her willful or negligent acts.

(A) Inspection of Premises. Under the URLTA, the landlord has the right to enter the leased premises for emergency purposes or with notice to the tenant for repairs, evaluations, and estimates.

(B) Housing Laws. Various laws protect tenants by requiring landlords to observe specified safety, health, and fire prevention standards. Some statutes require a landlord who leases a building for dwelling purposes

Thinking Things Through

The Rotting Balcony

Cayetano Giron stepped out onto the balcony of the apartment that he and his wife Robin leased from Jane Bailey. After taking four steps onto the blacony, Cayetano's foot sank into the soft floorboards and he fell toward the railing. He tried to grab the railing, but the railing broke off in his hand and he fell from the balcony to the street below (a two-story fall) and was injured. Robin had notified Mrs. Bailey, shortly after moving into the apartment, that the wooden balcony was "a little lopped." No repair attempts were made. Cayetano brought suit to recover for his injuries. Can he recover from Mrs. Bailey? Why or why not? **[*Giron v. Bailey,* 985 A.2d 1003 (2009)]**

[8] *Fisher v. City of Berkeley, California*, 475 U.S. 260 (1986).
[9] N.Y. Comp. Codes R. & Regs. tit. 9, §2520.1 (2009).

to keep it in a condition fit for habitation. Leases commonly require the tenant to obey local ordinances and laws relating to the care and use of the premises.

Landlords must comply with the ADA. Compliance means that landlords cannot discriminate on the basis of disability in deciding whether to rent to a particular tenant. Also, landlords are required to make reasonable modifications to accommodate tenants with disabilities, which can include everything from making sure that sidewalks on the property are smooth enough for operation of wheelchairs to permitting guide dogs to live with their sight-impaired owners.[10]

One of the developing areas of landlord-tenant law involves landlords' rights with regard to leasing to convicts and those who are registered as sex offenders. About 600,000 inmates are released from prisons each year, and their housing choices generally involve leasing.[11] The federal government requires public housing authorities to screen and evict tenants for drug-related or "safety-threatening" behavior. Public housing authorities that receive federal funds must include a lease clause that requires automatic lease termination for any drug or violent criminal activity, even if the activity does not occur on the landlord's property. The *Department of Housing and Urban Development v. Rucker* case deals with an issue of tenants and criminal activity in public housing.

Department of Housing and Urban Development v. Rucker, 535 U.S. 125 (2002)

But I'm Innocent!!!

Several young men, grandsons of William Lee and Barbara Hill, both of whom were residents on leases of the Oakland Housing Authority (OHA), were caught in the apartment complex parking lot smoking marijuana. The daughter of Pearlie Rucker, who resided with her and was listed on the OHA lease as a resident, was found with cocaine and a crack cocaine pipe three blocks from Rucker's apartment. On three instances within a two-month period, Herman Walker's, another OHA resident, caregiver and two others were found with cocaine in Walker's apartment.

After OHA initiated the eviction proceedings in state court against the Hills, Rucker, and Walker (respondents), they commenced actions against OHA in federal district court, challenging the Department of Housing and Urban Development's (HUD's) interpretation of the federal statute requiring eviction of tenants for criminal activity or the failure to control criminal activity in their apartments. The tenants of OHA argued that the federal statute and HUD regulations result in the eviction of "innocent" tenants and are unconstitutional.

The district court issued a preliminary injunction, enjoining OHA from terminating the leases of the tenants. A panel of the court of appeals reversed, and the full court of appeals reversed the panel and reinstated the district court's injunction. HUD appealed to the U.S. Supreme Court.

JUDICIAL OPINION

REHNQUIST, Chief Justice ... With drug dealers "increasingly imposing a reign of terror on public and other federally assisted low-income housing tenants," Congress passed the Anti-Drug Abuse Act of 1988. § 5122, 102 Stat. 4301, 42 U.S.C. § 11901(3) (1994 ed.). The Act, as later amended, provides that each "public housing agency shall utilize leases which ... provide that any criminal activity that threatens the health, safety, or right to peaceful enjoyment of the premises by other tenants or any drug-related criminal activity on or off such premises, engaged in by a public housing tenant, any member of the tenant's household, or any guest or other person under the tenant's control, shall be cause for termination of tenancy."

42 U.S.C. § 1437d(l)(6) unambiguously requires lease terms that vest local public housing authorities with the discretion to evict tenants for the drug-related activity of household members and guests whether or not the tenant knew, or should have known, about the activity.

That this is so seems evident from the plain language of the statute. It provides that "[e]ach public housing agency shall utilize leases which ... provide that ... any drug-related criminal activity on or off such premises, engaged in by a public housing tenant, any member of the tenant's household, or any guest or other person under the tenant's control, shall be cause for termination of tenancy." Thus, any drug-related

[10] *Brooks Shopping Centers, LLC v. DCHWWC Restaurant, Inc.*, 929 N.Y.S.2d 354 (N.Y. Sup. 2011).

[11] Meghan L. Schneider, "From Criminal Confinement to Social Confinement: Helping Ex-Offenders Obtain Public Housing with a Certificate of Rehabilitation," 36 *New. Eng. J. on Crim. & Civil Confinment*, 335 (2010).

Continued

activity engaged in by the specified persons is grounds for termination, not just drug-related activity that the tenant knew, or should have known, about.

The *en banc* Court of Appeals also thought it possible that "under the tenant's control" modifies not just "other person," but also "member of the tenant's household" and "guest. The court ultimately adopted this reading, concluding that the statute prohibits eviction where the tenant, "for a lack of knowledge or other reason, could not realistically exercise control over the conduct of a household member or guest." But this interpretation runs counter to basic rules of grammar. The disjunctive "or" means that the qualification applies only to "other person." Indeed, the view that "under the tenant's control" modifies everything coming before it in the sentence would result in the nonsensical reading that the statute applies to "a public housing tenant ... under the tenant's control." HUD offers a convincing explanation for the grammatical imperative that "under the tenant's control" modifies only "other person": "by 'control,' the statute means control in the sense that the tenant has permitted access to the premises." Implicit in the terms "household member" or "guest" is that access to the premises has been granted by the tenant. Thus, the plain language of § 1437d(l)(6) requires leases that grant public housing authorities the discretion to terminate tenancy without regard to the tenant's knowledge of the drug-related criminal activity.

And, of course, there is an obvious reason why Congress would have permitted local public housing authorities to conduct no-fault evictions: Regardless of knowledge, a tenant who "cannot control drug crime, or other criminal activities by a household member which threaten health or safety of other residents, is a threat to other residents and the project." With drugs leading to "murders, muggings, and other forms of violence against tenants," and to the "deterioration of the physical environment that requires substantial government expenditures," it was reasonable for Congress to permit no-fault evictions in order to "provide public and other federally assisted low-income housing that is decent, safe, and free from illegal drugs,"

There are, moreover, no "serious constitutional doubts" about Congress' affording local public housing authorities the discretion to conduct no-fault evictions for drug-related crime. *Reno v. Flores,* 507 U.S. 292, 314, n. 9, 113 S.Ct. 1439, 123 L.Ed.2d 1 (1993).

The en banc Court of Appeals held that HUD's interpretation "raise[s] serious questions under the Due Process Clause of the Fourteenth Amendment," because it permits "tenants to be deprived of their property interest without any relationship to individual wrongdoing." The government is not attempting to criminally punish or civilly regulate respondents as members of the general populace. It is instead acting as a landlord of property that it owns, invoking a clause in a lease to which respondents have agreed and which Congress has expressly required.

The Court of Appeals sought to bolster its discussion of constitutional doubt by pointing to the fact that respondents have a property interest in their leasehold interest, citing *Greene v. Lindsey,* 456 U.S. 444, 102 S.Ct. 1874, 72 L.Ed.2d 249 (1982). This is undoubtedly true, and *Greene* held that an effort to deprive a tenant of such a right without proper notice violated the Due Process Clause of the Fourteenth Amendment. But, in the present cases, such deprivation will occur in the state court where OHA brought the unlawful detainer action against respondents. There is no indication that notice has not been given by OHA in the past, or that it will not be given in the future. Any individual factual disputes about whether the lease provision was actually violated can, of course, be resolved in these proceedings.

[Accordingly, the judgment of the Court of Appeals is reversed, and the cases are remanded for further proceedings consistent with this opinion.]

QUESTIONS

1. Why was it important to have landlord eviction rights in public housing regardless of the tenant's knowledge?
2. Why is drug dealing targeted by the statute for automatic eviction?
3. Why are there no constitutional issues here in the automatic eviction?

CPA **(c) Warranty of Habitability.** At common law, a landlord was not bound by any obligation that the premises be fit for use unless the lease contained an express warranty to that effect. Most jurisdictions now reject this view and have created a **warranty of habitability** to protect tenants. The warranty of habitability requires, in most states, that the premises have running water, have heat in winter, and be free from structural defects and infestation. If the landlord breaches a warranty of habitability, the tenant is entitled to damages. These damages may be offset against the rent that is due, or if no rent is due, the tenant may bring an independent lawsuit to recover damages from the landlord.[12] The *Bender v. Green* case deals with the question of bed bugs and habitability.

[12] *Angelo Property Co., LP v. Hafiz,* 274 P.3d 1075 (Wash. App. 2012).

Bender v. Green, 874 N.Y.S.2d 786 (N.Y. Civ. Ct. 2009)

Don't Let the Bedbugs Bite

Geoffrey Green lived in a rent-control apartment in New York City. Bedbugs in his apartment forced him and his partner, Dana Shapiro, to sleep with the lights on, and rotate between sleeping in the bedroom, the kitchen, and the living room. They did not use the bedroom between May and August in 2005 and 2006.

Mr. Green testified that from April 2005 through July 2008, he did not have a single full night's sleep during the summer months. Lack of sleep affected Mr. Green's relationship with Ms. Shapiro and his ability to get to work on time.

Mr. Green withheld rent from October 2005 through January 2007, but only for the prime bedbugs months, i.e., non-winter months, during this period for a total amount of $5,665.84. His landlord (Petitioner) brought a forcible detainer action to have him evicted. Mr. Green counterclaimed for his damages from the bedbugs. Mr. Green offered into evidence two zip-loc bags containing dead bedbugs.

The exterminator for the complex had come to spray the building but said he never saw any live or dead bedbugs in the Green/Shapiro apartment except the specimens that Mr. Green had shown him, in a Ziploc bag. The exterminator believed Green and Shapiro (Respondents) may have brought the bedbugs with them from their previous apartment. Theresa Lonng, a neighbor, testified that she had bedbugs in her apartment, but that she also had them in her apartment in the building next door, where she had lived until moving next to Mr. Green and Ms. Shapiro.

JUDICIAL OPINION

KRAUS, Judge … RPL § 235-b provides that in all residential lease agreements the landlord warrants that the premises leased are "fit for human habitation" and that occupants "shall not be subjected to any conditions which would be dangerous, hazardous or detrimental to their life, health or safety." "[T]he statute places an unqualified obligation on the landlord to keep the premises habitable" throughout the term of the lease, and this obligation may not be waived or delegated. It has been well established that insect infestation is a condition which is considered to adversely impact upon the health and safety of the occupants of a residential premises.

The evidence suggests that the bedbugs were introduced into the Subject Premises, through no fault of the landlord (Petitioner), and in all likelihood by the Respondents themselves. When the Respondents moved into the Subject Premises there were no bedbugs in the premises for at least one year; and no other tenant in the Subject Building made a single complaint about bedbugs during the entire period in which Respondents alleged the Subject Premises were infested with bedbugs; and no violations for bedbugs placed at any point for any apartment in the subject building, including the Subject Premises, during the relevant period; and Respondents admit that they suffered a bedbug infestation in the apartment they lived in, immediately prior to moving into the Subject Premises; and Respondents acknowledge they travel for work-related purposes on a regular basis.

RPL § 235-b provides in pertinent part "[w]hen any such condition has been caused by the misconduct of the tenant or lessee or persons under his direction or control, it shall not constitute a breach of such covenants or warrants."

Petitioner did not establish at trial that the presence of bedbugs was caused by any "misconduct" by Respondents. As one commentator has noted:

> *The world is not only a smaller place for humans, it has become increasingly smaller for bedbugs as well. These opportunistic parasites are known as proficient hitchhikers. They travel from one place to another in luggage and clothing, jumping off at homes and hotels. What is worse is that these resilient pests have been known to survive 500 days without feeding.*

Wenk & Shafer, *Good Night, Sleep Tight, Don't Let the Cimex Lectularis Bite,* N.Y.L.J., Jan. 26, 2006, at 4, co. 4. The same article states that one female is sufficient to lead a local infestation, and that a well-fed female can lay up to 500 eggs in a lifetime, which eggs hatch between six to twenty eight days.

It appears that any individual venturing out into the world today, particularly an individual that travels, risks bringing bedbugs back home.

Petitioners' argument that it has no liability for the bedbugs in the premises is based in part on a recent DHCR ruling, *Matter of 91-31/04 195th St. LLC,* Docket No. WD110043RO. In that case, the tenant had complained about bedbugs and the owner had responded by providing the apartment with extermination services on three occasions. After extermination services were provided, the tenant filed a decrease in services complaint alleging that the apartment remained infested with bedbugs. An onsite inspection ordered by DHCR found "evidence of bedbug infestation in a mattress" and dead bedbugs in the bedroom. The onsite inspection found no evidence of a bedbug infestation in the walls, floors, cabinets, closets and entrance of the apartment. DHCR held that the finding of dead bedbugs by the inspector supported the conclusion that the owner's extermination service was effective, and that the owner could not be held responsible for "an infestation problem that exists solely in the personal property of the tenant's household."

Continued

Thus the Court finds that the presence of bedbugs in the Subject Premises did constitute a breach of the warranty of habitability. The more difficult determination is what, if any, damages Respondents are entitled to as a result of said breach. Once a breach has been established the "parties must come forward with evidence concerning the extensiveness of the breach, the manner in which it impacted upon the health, safety or welfare of the tenants and the measures taken by the landlord to alleviate the violation."

The only bedbugs anyone saw at the Subject Premises were in ziplock [sic] bags, which Respondents had collected, and which were exhibited by Respondent to the Exterminator or Ms. Lonng. Over the three-year period the infestation allegedly took place, Respondents collected approximately twelve bedbugs.

The Court would have expected a three-year unabated bedbug infestation to result in evidence similar to that which Ms. Lonng presented regarding her infestation. Other corroborating evidence could have been photographs of stained sheets, or photographs exhibiting the typical bedbug bites in groups of three.

Moreover, it is not clear to the Court in what manner Petitioners' response to the complaints was deficient. Petitioner made its Exterminator available to Respondents when as Respondents desired his services. Respondents acknowledged that they took no action beyond what Petitioner had done regarding extermination services. Ms. Green testified because she did not believe that hiring a different exterminator would help. What then should the Petitioner have done?

The Court finds it not credible that tenants would suffer for three years with an unabated bedbug infestation, believing that Petitioner's exterminator was inefficient, and take no action on their own, to alleviate the problem. [T]he Court would expect that a tenant might hire their own exterminator, if they believed Petitioner's exterminator was unqualified. Respondents never did.

Moreover, it seems unlikely to the Court that an unabated bedbug infestation in the Subject Premises would not spread, at any point during the three years, to other parts of the Subject Building. The Court finds that Respondents' burden to establish the extent of the condition has not been met, and limits the Court in awarding damages to Respondents.

The Court finds that the period for which Respondents are entitled to be an abatement to cover September 2005 through December 2006. The first documented notification to Petitioner regarding the alleged condition was in September 2005. That was the first documented phone call to the Exterminator, and Respondents withheld their rent in September and October of 2005. Based on the log of bites that was kept by Respondents for January 2007 forward, the Court finds Respondents failed to establish the presence of bedbugs from January 2007 forward, and that the bites documented were in all likelihood other insect bites.

Based on the foregoing the Court finds that Respondents are entitled to a twelve percent abatement in rent, for the period of September 2005 through December 2006, totaling $2724.21. Given the parties' stipulation that there was $5665.84 due at the conclusion of the trial, that leaves $2941.19 remaining due, in unpaid rent, through January 2009. Petitioner is entitled to a final judgment in the amount of $2941.19.

QUESTIONS

1. List the issues that mitigate the landlord's liability even though there is a breach of the warranty of habitability.
2. What lessons should landlords and tenants learn from this case?

(D) Abatement and Escrow Payment of Rent. To protect tenants from unsound living conditions, statutes sometimes provide that a tenant is not required to pay rent as long as the premises are not fit to live in. As a compromise, some statutes require the tenant to continue to pay the rent but require that it be paid into an escrow or agency account. The money in the escrow account is paid to the landlord only upon proof that the necessary repairs have been made to the premises.

11. Improvements

In the absence of a special agreement, neither the tenant nor the landlord is under a duty to make improvements, as contrasted with repairs.[13] Either party may, as a term of the original lease, agree to make improvements, in which case a failure to perform will result in liability in an action for damages for breach of contract brought by the other party. In the absence of an agreement to the contrary, improvements become part of the realty and belong to the landlord.

[13] The Americans with Disabilities Act requires commercial landlords and tenants to comply with legal requirements for access by the disabled. Shopping centers, medical offices, banks, and professional buildings must be in compliance. See *Greer v. Richardson Independent School Dist.*, 471 Fed.Appx. 336, 2012 WL 2141435 (5th Cir. 2012). *Anderson v. Little League Baseball, Inc.*, 794 F. Supp. 342 (D. Ariz. 1992).

12. Taxes and Assessments

In the absence of an agreement to the contrary, the landlord, not the tenant, is usually under a duty to pay taxes and/or assessments. The lease may provide for an increase in rent if taxes on the rented property are increased.[14]

If taxes or assessments are increased because of improvements made by the tenant, the landlord is liable for such increases if the improvements remain with the property. If the improvements can be removed by the tenant, the amount of the increase must be paid by the tenant.

13. Tenant's Deposit

A landlord may require a tenant to make a deposit to protect the landlord from any default on the part of the tenant.[15] There may be statutory limits on the amount of the deposit. Some states provide tenants with protections on these deposits. For example, the landlord may have to hold the deposits in a trust fund or be responsible for paying interest for the period the deposit is held. The landlord may be subject to a penalty if the money is used before the lease would allow for its use.

14. Protection from Retaliation

The URLTA and most state laws protect tenants from retaliation by the landlord for the tenants' exercise of their lawful rights or reporting the landlord for violations of housing and sanitation codes. The types of retaliation from which reporting tenants are protected include refusing to renew a lease and evicting the tenant.

15. Remedies of Landlord

If a tenant fails to pay rent, the landlord may bring an ordinary lawsuit to collect the amount due and in some states may seize and hold the property of the tenant.

(A) Landlord's Lien. In the absence of an agreement or a statute, the landlord does not have a lien on the personal property or crops of the tenant for money due for rent. The parties may create, by express or implied contract, a lien in favor of the landlord for rent and also for advances, taxes, or damages for failure to make repairs. In the absence of a statutory provision, the lien of the landlord is superior to the claims of all other persons except prior lienors and good-faith purchasers.

(B) Suit for Rent. Whether or not the landlord has a lien for unpaid rent, the landlord may collect rent from the tenant as specified in the lease. In some states, the landlord is permitted to bring a combined action against the tenant to recover the possession of the premises and the overdue rent at the same time.

(C) Recovery of Possession. A lease commonly provides that on the breach of any of its provisions by the tenant, such as the failure to pay rent, the lease terminates or the landlord may exercise the option to declare the lease terminated. When the lease is terminated for any reason, the landlord then has the right to evict the tenant and retake possession of the property.

A landlord cannot lock out a tenant for overdue rent. The landlord must employ legal process to regain possession even if the lease expressly gives the landlord the right to self-help.

The landlord may resort to legal process to evict the tenant to enforce the right to possession of the premises. Statutes in many states provide a summary remedy to recover possession that is much more efficient than the slow common law remedies. Often referred to as a **forcible entry and detainer**, this action restores the property to the landlord's possession unless the tenant complies with payment requirements.

(D) Landlord's Duty to Mitigate Damages. If the tenant leaves the premises before the expiration of the lease, is the landlord under any duty to rent the premises again to reduce the rent or damages for which the departing tenant will be liable? By common law and majority rule, a tenant holds a possessory estate in land, and if the tenant abandons it, there is no duty on the landlord to find a new tenant for the premises. But a growing minority view places greater emphasis on the contractual aspects of a lease. Under this view, when the tenant abandons the property, thereby defaulting on the contract, the landlord has a duty to seek to mitigate the damages caused by the tenant's breach and make a reasonable effort to rent the abandoned property.

[14] *Reach Community Development v. Stanley*, 274 P.3d 211 (Or. App. 2012).

[15] URLTA §2.101(a).

C. Liability for Injury on Premises

When the tenant, a member of the tenant's family, or a third person is injured because of the condition of the premises, the question of who is liable for the damages sustained by the injured person arises.

16. Landlord's Liability to Tenant

At common law, in the absence of a covenant to keep the premises in repair, the landlord was not liable for the tenant's personal injuries caused by the defective condition of the premises that, by the lease, are placed under the control of the tenant. Likewise, the landlord was not liable for the harm caused by an obvious condition that was known to the tenant at the time the lease was made.[16] However, recent cases have imposed liability on landlords for their failure to keep leased premises in repair, even when there is no covenant of repair.

(A) Crimes of Third Persons. Ordinarily, the landlord is not liable to the tenant for crimes committed on the premises by third persons, such as when a third person enters the premises and commits larceny or murder. The landlord is not required to establish a security system to protect the tenant from crimes of third persons.

In contrast, when the criminal acts of third persons are reasonably foreseeable, the landlord may be held liable for the harm caused a tenant. **For Example,** when a tenant has repeatedly reported that the deadbolt on the apartment door is broken, the landlord is liable for the tenant's loss when a thief enters through the door because such criminal conduct was foreseeable. Likewise, when the landlord of a large apartment complex does not take reasonable steps to prevent repeated criminal acts, the landlord is liable to the tenant for the harm caused by the foreseeable criminal act of a third person.[17] The *Yu Fang Tan v. Arnel Management Co.* case determines the liability of a landlord for the permanent disability of a tenant due to criminal activity at his apartment complex.

Yu Fang Tan v. Arnel Management Co., 170 Cal. App. 4th 1087, 88 Cal. Rprt. 3d 754 (Cal. App. 2009)

Parking Outside the Gate and Living in a Gated Community: High Risk

Arnel Management Company manages the Pheasant Ridge Apartments. Pheasant Ridge is a 620-unit, multibuilding apartment complex with over 1,000 residents, situated on 20.59 acres in Rowland Heights, California. Before the gated entrance to the complex are two parking lots; one is a visitor lot, and the other is the parking lot for the leasing office, located on the other side of the road. There are two security gates just past the parking lot. The gates are remote-control operated. Most of the property's parking spaces lie behind these gates by the apartments.

Yu Fang Tan and his wife, Chun Kuei Chang, and their child moved into Pheasant Ridge in July 2002 and received one assigned parking space. Tenants could pay an additional fee for a garage, but Tan chose not to rent one. Tenants with a second car could park in unassigned parking spaces located throughout the complex, or in one of the two lots—as long as the car was removed from the leasing office lot before 7:00 A.M.

At around 11:30 P.M. on December 28, 2002, Tan returned home and tried to find an unassigned open parking space because his wife had parked the family's other car in their assigned space. Unable to locate an available space, he parked in the leasing office parking lot outside the gated area.

As Tan was parking his car, an unidentified man approached him and asked for help. When Tan opened his window, the man pointed a gun and told him to get out of the car because the man wanted it. Tan responded, "Okay. Let me park my car first." But then the car rolled a little, and at that point, the assailant shot Tan in the neck. The incident rendered Tan a quadriplegic. Tan and Chang filed suit against Arnel for their negligent management of the complex as well as its policy of not providing sufficient parking inside the gated area and of charging more for such additional spaces. The trial court granted judgment on the pleadings for Arnel, and Tan and Chang appealed.

JUDICIAL OPINION

ALDRICH, J.…At the hearing, plaintiffs' expert, UCLA Sociology Professor Jack Katz, looked at police reports, complaints to the police, property management reports, and records of Pheasant Ridge's security service, PacWest Security

[16] *Georgia Dept. of Transp. v. Smith*, 724 S.E.2d 430 (Ga. App. 2012).

[17] *Santelli v. Rahmatullah*, 966 N.E.2d 661 (Ind. App. 2012).

Continued

Services. Professor Katz found 10 incidents he viewed as being "particularly significant warning signs," of which three involved "prior violent incidents." All of the incidents involved a sudden attack without warning, late at night, by a stranger on someone who was on the ungated portion of the premises.

The first example of a violent incident occurred just under two years before Plaintiff's attack and involved an assault with a deadly weapon. A guard, who was patrolling on his bicycle around 1:30 A.M., saw someone standing by the maintenance garage. The guard approached the subject and asked him what he was doing. The subject replied he was waiting for a friend. When the guard asked for identification, the subject retrieved an unknown object from his pocket and swung it at the guard. The guard raised his arm in self-protection and received an 1.5-inch slash on his forearm.

The second example occurred about a year before plaintiff's attack and before the existing gates at the back of the entrance road were installed. The assailants carjacked a car in Santa Monica with what the victim perceived to be a gun. Finding Pheasant Ridge "a good place to rob somebody" because there was no gate to impede their escape, as they told police later, the assailants came onto the property and robbed a tenant at his parking spot. The assailants committed the robbery by blocking the tenant's car, smashing him on the head, and demanding his valuables. They took the tenant's cell phone and other property.

The third violent incident occurred at 3:55 A.M., nine months before the attack on plaintiff. The incident was "also a violent attack, apparently, by strangers in late nighttime in a parking lot," and may have actually been in the leasing office lot. The assailant suddenly and viciously attacked the tenant in the face causing profuse bleeding. Professor Katz explained that these three prior incidents all involved "strangers coming in late night, suddenly becoming violent against people they don't know in ungated parking areas." Professor Katz opined that these three incidents "show that the probability is foreseeable here that people on this property will be attacked at some point by a stranger in open parking areas late at night."

Plaintiffs also presented nearly 80 examples of thefts from garages or cars or thefts of cars occurring on the Pheasant Ridge property. The trial court excluded the evidence of these thefts because they did not involve robberies or violent attacks on people.

"First, the court must determine the specific measures the plaintiff asserts the defendant should have taken to prevent the harm. Second, the court must analyze how financially and socially burdensome these proposed measures would be to a landlord, which measures could range from minimally burdensome to significantly burdensome under the facts of the case. Third, the court must identify the nature of the third party conduct that the plaintiff claims could have been prevented had the landlord taken the proposed measures, and assess how foreseeable (on a continuum from a mere possibility to a reasonable probability) it was that this conduct would occur. Once the burden and foreseeability have been independently assessed, they can be compared in determining the scope of the duty the court imposes on a given defendant. The more certain the likelihood of harm, the higher the burden a court will impose on a landlord to prevent it; the less foreseeable the harm, the lower the burden a court will place on a landlord."

Referring to the first step of the analysis, i.e., the specific security measures that plaintiffs proposed defendants should have taken, the record shows that plaintiffs requested minimal changes: Professor Katz recommended (1) moving the existing security gates from the back of the access road, or (2) installing "very similar" gates before the visitor and leasing office parking lots. An additional gate could be "any gate ... that would not necessarily impede climbing over it. It wouldn't have spikes or be unusually high. It would just define a property boundary..." "[v]ery similar to the gates they have...". Indeed, Professor Katz did not reject swing-arm gates. Any gate could remain open during the day to allow business in the leasing office. Plaintiffs clearly stated they were not asking for the hiring of a guard or for any form of ongoing surveillance or monitoring. Furthermore, because existing fencing extends around almost the entire perimeter of the property, only a "very minor" extension over a "very small area" would be necessary to close the fencing gap, Professor Katz testified, and could be achieved by merely mounding dirt.

Turning then to the heart of this case, the third element of foreseeability, plaintiffs demonstrated three prior incidents of sudden, unprovoked, increasingly violent assaults on people in ungated parking areas on the Pheasant Ridge premises by a stranger in the middle of the night, causing great bodily injury. Professor Katz opined, based on the three incidents, that "the probability is foreseeable here" of plaintiff's attack because in his experience, "you don't get more than this." The evidence of three vicious criminal assaults in the common areas within two years of plaintiff's attack here is more similar and compelling than the evidence in *Ann M.,* 25 Cal Rptr 2d 137, 863 P2d 207 [no evidence landlord had notice of crime on the property], or *Sharon P. v Arman, Ltd.,* 91 Cal Rptr 2d 35, 989 P2d 121 [no assaults in 10 years on the premises]. We conclude that plaintiffs presented substantial evidence of prior similar incidents or other indications of a reasonably foreseeable risk of violent criminal assaults on the property so as to impose on defendants a duty to provide the comparatively minimal security measures plaintiffs described.

[Reversed]

Continued

QUESTIONS

1. List the three areas a court must review before imposing liability on a landlord for a criminal act by a third party on a tenant.
2. What lessons on security precautions should landlords take away from the decision in this case?

(B) LIMITATION OF LIABILITY. A number of courts, however, have restricted the landlord's power to limit liability in the case of residential, as distinguished from commercial, leasing. A provision in a residential lease excusing a landlord from liability for damage caused by water, snow, or ice is void.

Third persons on the premises, even with the consent of the tenant, are generally not bound by a clause exonerating the landlord. Such third persons may generally recover from the landlord when they sustain injuries.

(C) INDEMNIFICATION OF LANDLORD. The modern lease commonly contains a provision declaring that the tenant will indemnify the landlord for any liability of the landlord to a third person that arises from the tenant's use of the rented premises.

17. Landlord's Liability to Third Persons

A landlord is ordinarily not liable to third persons injured because of the condition of any part of the rented premises that is in the possession of a tenant by virtue of a lease. If the landlord retains control over a portion of the premises, such as hallways or stairways, however, a landlord's liability exists for injuries to third persons caused by failure to exercise proper care in connection with that part of the premises. Most courts impose liability on the landlord for harm caused to a third person when the landlord was obligated, under a contract with the tenant, to correct the condition that caused the harm or to keep the premises in repair.

CPA 18. Tenant's Liability to Third Persons

A tenant in possession has control of the property and is liable when his or her failure to use due care under the circumstances causes harm to (1) licensees, such as a person allowed to use a telephone, and (2) invitees, such as customers entering a store. For both classes, the liability is the same as that of an owner in possession of

Sports & Entertainment Law

The Quarter Pipe 360 Liability Issue

Timothy Lucier, two days shy of his thirteenth birthday, went with his father and several of his friends to Impact (a commercial skate park located in East Providence, Rhode Island) to skateboard to celebrate his birthday. At the skate park, Timothy's father signed the waiver that was required of all who used the park. Timothy donned a helmet, kneepads, and elbow pads, and then he and his friends used the skate park half pipes and quarter pipes. At one point, Timothy climbed on top of the quarter pipe, and as he pushed forward to go down the ramp, the front wheel of his skateboard caught inside a "nub" or "little tiny hole" in the ramp, causing the tail of his skateboard to swing around in a clockwise direction. Timothy twisted off the skateboard and fell on his right leg, causing a spiral fracture in his right leg. Timothy said that after he fell, he looked back at the ramp and saw that there was a split in the wood covering the ramp.

Timothy's parents filed suit against Impact Recreation, Ltd., the operator of the skateboard facility, and Eugene Voll, Impact's landlord. They alleged that there had been a failure by the landlord to ensure that the commercial tenant was not engaging in an activity that was inherently dangerous to the public at large.

Voll required Impact to have insurance, obtain signed waivers from all participants, and obtain his approval prior to the installation of any equipment. Do you believe the landlord is liable to the Luciers? Why or why not? **[*Lucier v. Impact Recreation, LTD.*, 864 A.2d 635 (R.I. 2005)]**

property. It is likewise immaterial whether the property is used for residential or business purposes.

The liability of the tenant to third persons is not affected by the fact that the landlord may have contracted in the lease to make repairs that, if made, would have avoided the injury. The tenant can be protected, however, in the same manner that the landlord can be protected: by procuring liability insurance for indemnity against loss from claims of third persons.

D. Transfer of Rights

Both the landlord and the tenant have property and contract rights with respect to the lease. Can they be transferred or assigned? A landlord who sells his property transfers the rights in the leased premises to the buyer. The tenant also has transfer rights that are covered below.

CPA 19. Tenant's Assignment of Lease and Sublease

An **assignment** of a lease is a transfer by the tenant of the tenant's entire interest in the premises to a third person. A tenancy for years may be assigned by the tenant unless the tenant is restricted from making such an assignment by the terms of the lease or by a statute. A **sublease** is a transfer to a third person, the *sublessee*, of less than the tenant's entire interest, or full lease term.

(A) Limitations on Rights. The lease may contain provisions denying or limiting the right to assign or sublet. Such restrictions protect the landlord from new tenants who might damage the property or be financially irresponsible.

Restrictions in the lease are construed liberally in favor of the tenant. No violation of a provision prohibiting assignment or subleasing occurs when the tenant merely permits someone else to use the premises.

(B) Effect of Assignment or Sublease. An assignee or a sublessee has no greater rights than the original lessee.[18] An assignee becomes bound by the obligations of the lease by the act of taking possession of the premises.

Neither the act of subletting nor the landlord's agreement to it releases the original tenant from liability under the terms of the original lease. When a lease is assigned, the original tenant remains liable for the rent that becomes due thereafter.

The tenant should require the sublessee to perform all obligations under the original lease and to indemnify the tenant for any loss caused if the sublessee defaults. Such liability on the part of the sublessee requires an express covenant. The fact that the sublease is made "subject to" the terms of the original lease merely recognizes the superiority of the original lease but does not impose any duty on the sublessee to perform the tenant's obligation under the original lease. If the sublessee promises to assume the obligations of the original lease, the landlord, as a third-party beneficiary, may recover from the sublessee for breach of the provisions of the original lease.

LawFlix

Barefoot in the Park (1967) (PG)

The movie is a study about Manhattan newlyweds in which you can see many issues about habitability and constructive eviction. Discuss the options the couple has for remedies.

[18] *First Hudson Capital, LLC v. Seaborn*, 862 N.Y.S.2d 501 (N.Y.A.D. 2008).

MAKE THE CONNECTION

SUMMARY

The agreement between a lessor and a lessee by which the latter holds possession of real property owned by the former is a lease. Statutes in many states prohibit discrimination by an owner who rents property. Statutes in some states require that the lease not be unconscionable. Tenancies are classified according to duration as tenancies for years, from year to year, at will, and at sufferance.

A lease is generally not terminated by the death, insanity, or bankruptcy of either party except for a tenancy at will. Leases are usually terminated by the expiration of the specified term, notice, surrender, forfeiture, or destruction of the property or because of fraud. A tenant has the right to acquire possession at the beginning of the lease and has the right to retain possession until the lease is ended. Evictions may be either actual or constructive. The tenant is under a duty to pay rent as compensation to the landlord.

An assignment of a lease by the tenant is a transfer of the tenant's entire interest in the property to a third person; a sublease is a transfer of less than an entire interest—in either space or time. A lease may prohibit both an assignment and a sublease. If the lease is assigned, the assignee is liable to the landlord for the rent. Such an assignment, however, does not discharge the tenant from the duty to pay rent. In a sublease, the sublessee is not liable to the original lessor for rent unless that liability has been assumed or is imposed by statute.

The tenant need not make repairs to the premises, absent an agreement to the contrary. A warranty of habitability was not implied at common law, but most states now reject this view and imply in residential leases a warranty that the premises are fit for habitation.

A landlord is usually liable to the tenant only for injuries caused by latent defects or by defects that are not apparent but of which the landlord had knowledge. The landlord is not liable to the tenant for crimes of third persons unless they are reasonably foreseeable.

LEARNING OUTCOMES

After studying this chapter, you should be able to clearly explain:

A. Creation and Termination

LO.1 List the ways in which a lease may be terminated

See the discussion of the types of tenancies on p. 1082.

B. Rights and Duties of Parties

LO.2 List and explain the rights and duties of the parties to a lease

See *Bender v. Green* on pp. 1088–1089.

See Thinking Things Through on p. 1085.

C. Liability for Injury on Premises

LO.3 Describe a landlord's liability for a tenant's and a third person's injuries sustained on the premises

See *Yu Fang Tan v. Arnel Management Co.* on pp. 1091–1093.

See the Sports & Entertainment Law discussion of the quarter pipe on p. 1093.

D. Transfer of Rights

LO.4 Define *sublease* and *assignment of a lease* and distinguish between them

See the discussion of transfer of rights on p. 1094.

KEY TERMS

assignment
constructive eviction
covenant of quiet enjoyment
escalation clause
forcible entry and detainer
landlord
lease
lessee
lessor
periodic tenancy
possession
sublease
sublessee
tenancy at sufferance
tenancy at will
tenancy for years
tenant
warranty of habitability

QUESTIONS AND CASE PROBLEMS

1. Johnny C. Carpenter and Harvey E. Hill died of asphyxiation when a fire broke out in their Hattiesburg, Mississippi, apartment on the morning of February 20, 1983. There were no smoke detectors in the apartment at the time of the fire, as required under Hattiesburg City Ordinance 2021. The administrators of the estates of Carpenter and Hill filed suit against London, Stetelman, and Kirkwood, the owners and managers of the apartment complex. Who is liable? [*Hill v. London, Stetelman, and Kirkwood, Inc.*, 906 F.2d 204 (5th Cir.)]

2. Petra Valoma and her three roommates rented an apartment in New York City with a security deposit of $2,850, two months of rent for $5,700, and a property loss payment of $800. Less than a month after the group of four took possession of the property, they found bedbugs. The manager sent an exterminator each week for six weeks, with no effective results. The four had to move out and lost most of their furniture because it was infected with bedbugs. The four sought to recover the rent that they had paid as well as damages for their lost furniture. What can they recover? [*Valoma v. G-Way Management, LLC*, 918 N.Y.S.2d 401 (N.Y. Cir. Ct. 2010)]

3. Rod had a five-year lease in a building owned by Darwood and had agreed to pay $800 a month rent. After two years, Rod assigned his rights under the lease to Kelly. Kelly moved in and paid the rent for a year and then, owing two months' rent, moved out without Darwood's knowledge or consent. Darwood demanded that Rod pay him the past-due rent. Must Rod do so? Why or why not?

4. Sue A. Merrill injured her right shoulder when she fell as she was ascending the front steps leading to the porch and front door of the mobile home that her daughter, Sherri Pritchard, rented from Alvina Jansma. The step became loose during the time Ms. Pritchard rented the home. Prior to the fall, Ms. Pritchard had attempted to repair the step by securing it with nails. When that failed, she informed the manager of the property that the step was loose. The manager suggested Ms. Pritchard try using screws to secure the step. Ms. Pritchard told the manager she did not have a screw gun. The manager had one and said she would screw the step into place. Subsequently, and without Ms. Pritchard's knowledge, the manager attempted to repair the step. Apparently, that effort was unsuccessful and Ms. Merrill fell when the step separated from the porch as she stepped on it. Ms. Merrill filed a negligence claim against Ms. Jansma to recover for her medical expenses, lost wages, and damages for emotional distress and pain and suffering. Could Ms. Merrill recover? [*Merrill v. Jansma*, 86 P.3d 270 (Wyo.)]

5. Alexis Gale was shot and killed while working in the rented business offices of her employer, Mon Ami International. Gale's husband sued the property owners and managers of the office complex where Mon Ami's rented offices were located, claiming the landlord had breached a duty to provide adequate security at the complex. The lease provided that the landlord would provide security services in the common areas of the complex and that the lessee was given exclusive control of the portion of the premises rented as office space.

   Gale was shot and killed by a coworker, not in a common area over which the landlord had control but in the Mon Ami office space over which the lessee had exclusive control and in which the landlord had no duty to provide security.

   Gale's husband also alleged that the landlord knew an attack was about to take place because of some strange happenings that had taken place earlier that day. That morning, a maintenance worker noticed a man opening the back door of the Mon Ami office from the inside. This man appeared to be acting strangely: He took a handkerchief out of his suit pocket and picked up a briefcase sitting outside the door. He was wearing what the worker described as a costume-type wig on his head but looked vaguely familiar.

   Later that day, Gale's body was discovered. The maintenance worker reported what he had seen to the landlord and to the police. It was eventually determined that this was the coworker who had shot Gale, and it was also determined that the landlord knew of numerous arguments between Gale and the coworker. Gale's spouse alleged that the landlord had a duty to prevent the shooting. Did such a duty exist? [*Gale v. North Meadow Associates*, 466 S.E.2d 648 (Ga. App.)]

6. On June 21, 1997, Julio Ramos was helping his cousin move out of a second-floor apartment. He positioned himself on the outer side of the second-floor balcony railing, his feet between its spindles, to pass furniture to a friend on the ground below. While perched in this precarious position, Ramos held onto the railing with one hand and used his other hand to move the furniture. The reason for this method of removing the furniture was that many pieces were too large to be taken down the stairs. After approximately an hour of moving furniture in this manner, Ramos heard some cracking and felt the railing giving way. He released the furniture and attempted to grab onto the railing with both hands, but the spindles broke, and Ramos fell to the ground.

   Ramos brought suit against the landlord to recover for his injuries. How does this case compare to the *Tan* case? Should the landlord in this case be held liable? [*Ramos v. Granajo*, 822 A.2d 936 (R.I.)]

7. A tenant leased an apartment in which so much noise emanated from surrounding apartments late at night and in the wee hours of the morning that he could not get much sleep. The tenant brought suit against the landlord, alleging that the landlord had breached the implied warranty of habitability. Is the tenant correct? Can noise be a breach of the warranty of habitability? [*Nostrand Gardens Co-op v. Howard*, 634 N.Y.S.2d 505]

8. James Santelli was staying at a motel owned by Abu Rahmatullah for several months as he worked at a nearby construction project.

   Joseph Pryor had been previously employed at the motel as a general maintenance man. There was no criminal background check done on Pryor. Pryor had a prior conviction and was wanted at the time he was hired for probation violations. When he left his job at the motel, Pryor kept his master keycard. Pryor used the keycard to enter Santelli's room and later confessed to robbing and killing him, with a resulting sentence of 85 years. Mr. Santelli's widow brought suit against Rahmatullah for his negligence in hiring Pryor. Can Rahmatullah be held liable for Mr. Santelli's death? [*Santelli v. Rahmatullah*, [966 N.E.2d 661 (Ind. App.)]

9. During the remodeling of an apartment building, tenants had so much dust from the construction settle in their apartment that they experienced damage to their expensive sound and recording equipment. They had rented the very specialized and large apartment because it was suitable to use as a recording studio. Would the presence of the dust be grounds for constructive eviction? Would it be a breach of the warranty of habitability? [*Minjak Co. v. Rudolph*, 528 N.Y. S.2d 554]

10. Cantanese leased a building for the operation of his drugstore from Saputa. He moved his drugstore from Saputa's building to another location but continued to pay rent to Saputa. Saputa, fearing that he was losing his tenant, entered the premises without Cantanese's permission and made extensive alterations to the premises to suit two physicians who had agreed to rent the premises from Saputa. Cantanese informed Saputa that he regarded the making of the unauthorized repairs as grounds for canceling the lease. Saputa then claimed that Cantanese was liable for the difference between the rent that Cantanese had agreed to pay and the rent that the doctors would pay for the remainder of the term of the Cantanese lease. Was Cantanese liable for such rent? [*Saputa v. Cantanese*, 182 So.2d 826 (La. App.)]

11. Sargent rented a second-floor apartment in a building owned by Ross. Anna, Sargent's four-year-old daughter, fell from an outdoor stairway and was killed. Sargent brought suit against Ross for her daughter's death. Ross contended that she did not have control over the stairway and therefore was not liable for its condition. Was this defense valid? [*Sargent v. Ross*, 308 A.2d 528 (N.H.)]

12. Charles leased a house from Donald for four years. The rent agreed on was $850 per month. After two years, Charles assigned his rights under the lease to Smith, who moved in and paid rent regularly for a year. Owing rent, Smith moved out sometime later without Donald's knowledge or consent. Donald demanded that Charles pay the rent. Is Charles liable?

13. Green rented an apartment from Stockton Realty. The three-story building had a washroom and clothesline on the roof for use by the tenants. The clothesline ran very near the skylight, and there was no guard rail between the clothesline and the skylight. Green's friend, who was 14 years old, was helping Green remove clothes from the line when she tripped on an object and fell against the skylight. The glass was too weak to support her weight, and she fell to the floor below, sustaining serious injuries. Is the landlord responsible for damages for the injury sustained? Decide. [*Reiman v. Moore*, 180 P.2d 452 (Cal.)]

14. Suzanne Andres was injured when she fell from the balcony of her second-floor apartment in the Roswell-Windsor Village Apartments. Andres was leaning against the railing on the balcony when it gave out, and she and the railing fell to the ground. Andres filed suit against Roswell-Windsor for its failure to maintain the railing. Roswell-Windsor maintains that the railing was not in a common area and was in Andres's exclusive possession and that she was responsible for its maintenance or at least letting the manager know the railing needed repairs. Should Andres recover from the landlord for her injuries? [*Andres v. Roswell-Windsor Village Apartments*, 777 F.2d 671 (11th Cir.)]

15. Williams, an elderly man who was sensitive to heat, rented an apartment in the Parker House. His apartment was fully air-conditioned, which enabled him to stand the otherwise unbearable heat of the summer. The landlord was dissatisfied with the current rent, and although the lease had a year to run, insisted that Williams agree to an increase. Williams refused. The landlord attempted to force Williams to pay the increase by turning off the electricity and thereby stopping the apartment's air conditioners. He also sent up heat on the hot days. After one week of such treatment, Williams, claiming that he had been evicted, moved out. Has there been an eviction? Explain.

CPA QUESTIONS

1. Which of the following provisions must be included to have an enforceable written residential lease?

	A Description of the Leased Premises	*A Due Date for the Payment of Rent*
a.	Yes	Yes
b.	Yes	No
c.	No	Yes
d.	No	No

2. Bronson is a residential tenant with a 10-year written lease. In the absence of specific provisions in the lease to the contrary, which of the following statements is correct?
   a. The premises may not be sublet for less than the full remaining term.
   b. Bronson may not assign the lease.
   c. The landlord's death will automatically terminate the lease.
   d. Bronson's purchase of the property will terminate the lease.

3. Which of the following provisions must be included in a residential lease agreement?
   a. A description of the leased premises
   b. The due date for payment of rent
   c. A requirement that the tenant have public liability insurance
   d. A requirement that the landlord will perform all structural repairs to the property

CHAPTER 52

© Manuel Gutjahr/iStockphoto.com

Decedents' Estates and Trusts

learningoutcomes

After studying this chapter, you should be able to

LO.1 Define *testamentary capacity* and *testamentary intent*

LO.2 Discuss how a valid will is created

LO.3 Explain how a will may be modified or revoked

LO.4 Describe briefly the probate and contest of a will

LO.5 Describe the ordinary pattern of distribution by intestacy

LO.6 Explain the nature of a trust

What happens to your property after you die? Public policy dictates that your debts be settled, that property owned at the time of your death be applied to the payment of estate administration expenses and your debts, and that any remainder be distributed among those entitled to receive it.

The law of decedents' estates is governed by state statutes and court decisions. There is wide variation in state law and only 17 states have adopted the **Uniform Probate Code (UPC)**.[1]

A. Wills

When a **decedent** has died with a valid will, he or she is said to have died **testate**, and the will determines who is entitled to receive the estate property after creditors have been paid. If the decedent did not make a valid will, laws for **intestate** distribution determine the distribution.

1. Definitions

Testate distribution describes the distribution that is made when the decedent leaves a valid will. A **will** is ordinarily a writing that provides for a distribution of property upon death but that confers no rights prior to that time. A man who makes a will is called a **testator**; a woman, a **testatrix**.

A gift of personal property by will is a **legacy** or **bequest**, in which case the beneficiary may also be called a **legatee**. A gift of real property by will is a **devise**, and the beneficiary may be called a **devisee**.

2. Parties to Will

Each state has variations on the qualifications of persons who wish to make a will. The following requirements are typical.

(A) Testator. Generally, the right to make a will is limited to persons 18 or older. The testator must have **testamentary capacity**,[2] which means that a person must have sufficient mental capacity to understand that the writing that is being executed is a will—that is, that it disposes of the person's property after death. The testator must also have a reasonable appreciation of who the beneficiaries of his will are as well as a grasp of the identity of relatives and friends and the nature and extent of the property that will be given and to whom upon death.

Testamentary capacity is challenged by surviving relatives quite often. Eccentric behavior does not mean that the individual lacks capacity. The excessive and continued use of alcohol or multiple medications, producing mental deterioration, may be sufficient to justify the conclusion that the decedent lacked testamentary capacity. However, there can be lucid periods even among those who suffer from addictions. Expert testimony, the observations of friends and relatives, and the conduct of the decedent prior to death are all relevant factors in determining whether there was testamentary capacity.[3] The *Maimonides School v. Coles* case deals with a capacity issue.

Maimonides School v. Coles, 881 N.E.2d 778 (Mass. App. 2008)

Just Because You Don't Understand Contracts Doesn't Mean You Lack Capacity

After an 11-month struggle with esophageal cancer, Leonard R. Brener died on December 8, 2001, at age 85. He had never married. He had no children. He had a long and successful career as a stockbroker. The value of his estate approximated $8 million. Several nieces and nephews survived him. He had originally left nearly all of his estate to the Carroll Center for the Blind, the Perkins School for the Blind, and Beth Israel Deaconess Medical Center, Inc. The gifts to these nonprofit organizations during Brener's life and through his will were made through detailed living, testamentary, and pour-over

[1] The Uniform Probate Code has been adopted in Alaska, Arizona, Colorado, Florida, Hawaii, Idaho, Maine, Massachusetts, Michigan, Minnesota, Montana, Nebraska, New Mexico, North Dakota, South Carolina, South Dakota, and Utah. Twenty other states have adopted portions of the UPC: Arkansas, California, Georgia, Illinois, Indiana, Kansas, Kentucky, Maryland, Missouri, New Jersey, Ohio, Oklahoma, Oregon, Pennsylvania, Texas, Virginia, Washington, West Virginia, Wisconsin, and Wyoming. The predominant form of the UPC continues to be the 1969 version, but the 1990 and 2003 versions have been integrated into existing UPC states' statutes.

[2] *Andersen v. Hunt*, 126 Cal. Rptr. 3d 736 (Cal. App. 2011).

[3] *Parish v. Parish*, 704 S.E.2d 99 (Va. 2011).

Continued

trusts. Brener said he did not understand all aspects of the trusts. During the last five weeks of his life he was hospitalized and drafted and executed the final version of his will, which made one niece and her husband the primary beneficiaries of his estate. The nonprofit organizations sought to have the will set aside for lack of testamentary capacity.

During those five weeks of terminal illness, Brener spoke of suicide by jumping out of the window, complained of depression, and often complained to his lawyer that he did not understand all the estate planning tools that were being used in his will. The staff at the hospital testified that Brener did not seem confused and was aware that he was dying and wanted to be sure his affairs were in order.

The lower court held that there is a presumption of mental capacity that the nonprofits were not able to overcome with testimony from either a doctor or those who had daily contact with Brener. The nonprofit organizations appealed.

JUDICIAL OPINION

SIKORA, Judge…The motion judge correctly applied the standard for testamentary capacity and not the more demanding test for contractual capacity. First, Brener's trust instruments were not complex, even though they disposed of property worth millions of dollars. They did not require contractual capacity for their intelligent creation and execution.

The record shows that Brener suffered severe depression accompanied by thoughts of suicide in February of 2001. The contestants do not dispute that Brener had the requisite mental capacity to name them beneficiaries in the first trust amendment on March 14, 2001. No evidence appears that Brener was senile or delusional or that he did not recognize his family and friends. Dr. Welch's promise to expand on his affidavit at trial could not forestall a motion for summary judgment.

On October 28, 2001, a nurse wrote in her report that Brener was "alert and oriented, but depressed." He complained that he was not going to last long and should jump out of the window. During her deposition, a social worker testified that Brener had been mentally alert and not confused about the identity of his family members. Acknowledging that she had mentioned that Brener was confused, she explained that she had meant that Brener was a sick man moving from one setting to another with insufficient time to get used to his new surroundings and without the knowledge of next events. She spoke to Brener after he had made the statements about death and jumping out of the window and attributed the statements to depression.

On October 26, 2001, Brener told the attending physician that he wanted to be "full code," meaning that he wished to be resuscitated in the event the procedure was necessary to maintain, or bring him back to, life. There is no evidence that Brener ever attempted to commit suicide or that any physician or caretaker ever put him on any suicide watch.

The record shows that Brener suffered severe depression accompanied by thoughts of suicide in February of 2001. The contestants do not dispute that Brener had the requisite mental capacity to name them beneficiaries in the first trust amendment on March 14, 2001. No evidence appears that Brener was senile or delusional or that he did not recognize his family and friends.

In sum, the contestants' evidence is insufficient to defeat the presumption that Brener had the requisite mental capacity to execute the second trust amendment.

QUESTIONS

1. Why was this case so important to the nonprofit organizations?
2. Can a will be valid if the person executing the will is depressed?
3. What types of behaviors would result in a finding of no testamentary capacity?

(B) Beneficiary. Generally, the capacity of the **beneficiary** is not an issue. However, when part of a decedent's estate passes to a minor, a guardian may be appointed to administer that interest for the minor. If a will directs that any share payable to a minor be held by a particular person as trustee for the minor, the minor's interest will be so held, and a guardian is not required. Statutes often provide that if the estate or interest of the minor is not large, it may be paid directly to the minor or to the parent or person by whom the minor is maintained.

3. Testamentary Intent

To execute a valid will, testators must demonstrate an intent to transfer property upon their deaths. This mental state is called **testamentary intent.**[4] This is the testator's intent that certain persons become the owners of certain property upon his or her death. However, there is still testamentary intent when the

[4] *Hampton Roads Seventh-Day Adventist Church v. Stevens*, 657 S.E.2d 80 (Va. 2008).

testator designates an executor only and does not make any disposition of property.

4. Form

Because the privilege of disposing of property by will is purely statutory, the will must be executed in the manner required by state statutes. Unless statutory requirements are met, the will is invalid, and the testator is considered to have died intestate. In such a case, the decedent's property will be distributed according to the laws of intestacy of the particular state.

(A) Writing. Ordinarily, a will must be in writing. Some state statutes, however, permit oral wills in limited circumstances, and the use of videotaped wills is gaining some legal ground.

(B) Signature. A written will must be signed by the testator. In case of physical incapacity, the testator may be assisted in signing the will.[5] Witnesses to the will can then verify that simple marks were indeed made by the testator while experiencing a physically debilitating condition.

Generally, a will must be signed at the bottom or end. The purpose of this requirement is to prevent unscrupulous persons from taking a will that has been validly signed and writing or typing additional provisions in the space below the signature.

(C) Attestation. Attestation is the act of witnessing the execution of a will. Generally, attestation consists of a witness signing the will following a clause that declares that the witness either saw the testator sign the will or that the testator told the witness that he or she did indeed sign the will. The clause that describes what the witness saw or knows is called an **attestation clause**. Statutes often require that attestation be made by the witnesses in the presence of the testator and in the presence of each other. Most states and the Uniform Probate Code (UPC) require two witnesses; a few states require three.

Self-proved wills are wills that carry a presumption that they are valid if executed according to the requirements set forth by statute. The UPC recognizes self-proved wills. A will may be simultaneously executed, attested, and made self-proving by acknowledgment by the testator and by affidavits of the witnesses.

The **acknowledgment** and **affidavits** must each be made before an officer authorized to administer oaths under state law, such as a notary. The acknowledgement and affidavits must carry an official seal, such as a notary's seal, which must be evidenced by the officer's certificate under official seal.

The self-proving provisions attached to the will are not a part of the will. Self-proving provisions allow a will to be admitted to probate without requiring the testimony of the witnesses to the will. The will itself must still meet the requirements of the law. The execution of a valid will is a condition precedent to use of the self-proving provisions.

In some states, a witness cannot be a beneficiary under the will. In those states, use of a beneficiary as a witness will not affect the will, but the witness's share is limited to whatever his or her intestate share would have been if there had been no will. Under the UPC, a will can be validly witnessed by an interested person.

E-Commerce & Cyberlaw

Where There's a Video, Is There a Will?

With technology, wills are no longer always just written but may be supplemented with electronic verification. The American Bar Association's Web site (**www.abanet.org**) offers the following thoughts on the new trend in video wills:

More and more people are preparing a video in which they read the will and explain why certain gifts were made and others not made. The video recording might also show the execution of the will. Should a disgruntled relative decide to challenge the will, the video can provide compelling proof that the person making the will was mentally competent and observed the formalities of execution.

Keep in mind that videos do not last forever and are subject to damage. You should consult a lawyer before making such a video to find out about your state's laws on video wills. Generally, such a video would supplement the will and is not always a substitute for a validly executed will.

[5] *Strong v. Holden*, 697 S.E.2d 189 (Ga. 2010).

(D) Date. There is generally no requirement that a testator date a will, but a dated will does reduce confusion. When there are several wills, the most recent one will control when there are conflicting provisions between and among the wills.

5. Modification of Will

A will may be modified by executing a *codicil*, a separate writing that amends a will. The will, except as changed by the codicil, remains the same. The effect is that the provisions of the codicil are substituted for those provisions of the will that are inconsistent with the codicil. A codicil must be executed with all the formality of a will and is treated in all other respects the same as a will.

A will cannot be modified merely by crossing out a clause and writing in what the testator wishes. Such an **interlineation** is not operative unless it is executed with the same formality required of a will or, in some states, unless the will is republished in its interlineated form.

6. Revocation of Will

At any time during the testator's life, the testator may **revoke** the will made or make changes in its terms. It may be revoked by act of the testator or by operation of law. A testator must have the same degree of mental capacity to revoke a will as is required to make one.

(A) Revocation by Act of Testator. A will or a codicil is revoked when the testator destroys, burns, or tears it or crosses out the provisions of the will or codicil with the intention to revoke them. The revocation may be in whole or in part.[6] The *In re Estate of Speers* case deals with a revocation issue.

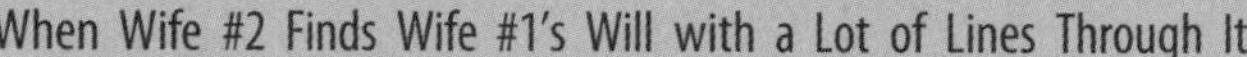

In re Estate of Speers, 179 P.3d 1265 (Okl. 2008)

When Wife #2 Finds Wife #1's Will with a Lot of Lines Through It

On June 15, 1982, Shirley Joyce Speers signed a "Last Will and Testament." It named her husband, Ralph Speers, as her executor. It also gave her daughter, Sherr Arlene Ross, her household furnishings and appliances, and her son, Daniel Eugene Speers, her livestock. Her husband was named the beneficiary of the rest of the estate, provided he paid the estate's expenses. If he failed to do so, his share went to their children and grandsons. The will was probably witnessed and signed, but not notarized. The witnesses did not see any lines or strikeouts in the will when they signed it. Shirley died on April 20, 1997, and the will was not probated at the time of her death.

After his wife's death, Ralph married Ann Speers. Ralph died some time before June of 2005, and Ann then discovered a copy of Shirley's will with lines through it and cross-outs. She filed a petition seeking to admit the will to probate. The will she submitted contained several handwritten strikeouts and interlineations. Shirley's children objected to the admission of the will, arguing that it was invalid because the original will was destroyed. The court found for Ann and the children appealed. The Court of Appeals reversed and Ann appealed.

JUDICIAL OPINION

KAUGER, Justice...This Court has held that where the attestation clause recites due execution of a will, it creates a *prima facie* case of due execution of the instrument, which can be overcome only by clear and convincing evidence. In proceedings for the probate of an instrument as a will where it appears to have been duly executed, and the attestation is established by proof of the handwriting of the witnesses or otherwise, although their testimony is not available, or they do not remember the transaction, it will be presumed, in the absence of evidence to the contrary, that the will was executed in compliance with all the requirements of law.

Several other jurisdictions also permit the execution of will to be established without the testimony of one or both of the subscribing witnesses, but most require the proponent to establish execution by some other method of proof.

Here, there was no evidence offered by the appellee establishing the attestation clause either by handwriting analysis, or any other form of proof. This is not sufficient to create a *prima facie* showing of due execution of the instrument, and therefore the instrument should not have been admitted to probate.

The formalities to be observed in the execution of wills are simple and calculated to prevent fraud and uncertainty in the testamentary dispositions of property. Here, because of the absence of a notary seal, the will presented for probate was not self-proving. The evidence reflects that there was only one

[6] *Horst v. Horst*, 920 N.E.2d 441 (Ohio App. 2009).

Continued

subscribing witness. A determination that there were two subscribing witnesses based solely on one witness's testimony that he couldn't recall the other witness, that he had been told she was deceased, and that he wasn't sure she was present when he signed the will is clearly contrary to the weight of the evidence. The evidence does not establish that the testatrix substantially complied with the statutory requirements for execution and publication. The proponent of the will neglected to make a proper showing that the will was suitable for probate. Therefore, we reverse the trial court and remand with instructions that the will not be admitted to probate.

DISSENTING OPINION

REIF, Justice (Dissenting)…It is important to keep in mind that Mr. Durbin's (a witness to Shirley's will) testimony was given with reference to the copy of the will that was offered for probate. He testified that he *did remember* signing the original and seeing Mrs. Speers sign the original. On cross-examination by contestants' counsel, Mr. Durbin testified without objection that he presumed Sadie Walton and notary Vicky Thomas were present by virtue of their signatures on the will. This commonsense connection made by Mr. Durbin reflects an inference that could certainly be drawn by the trial court as well. In the final analysis, there is simply nothing in the record to suggest that will was not duly executed as it appears to have been.

The copy of the will offered for probate does contain certain handwritten changes in some contingent bequests. To be sure, the presence of handwritten changes on a will or copy of a will can cast doubt on the due execution of the will. However, in the case at hand, the handwritten changes have no bearing on the issue of due execution in light of Mr. Durbin's testimony that the original will "was a three-page typewritten document when she brought it to me … [w]ith no markings on it." Even assuming that Mrs. Speers later tried to indicate a different testamentary intent with respect to the *contingent* bequests, the handwritten changes did not purport to revoke or otherwise affect her *general testamentary intent* that Ralph Speers receive *all* of her estate. More importantly, the handwritten changes were not sufficient to revoke the will.

QUESTIONS

1. Applying the laws of intestacy and wills, why do you think Ann wanted the will admitted to probate?
2. What lessons does this case provide on the importance of witnesses to a will? Of the notarized signatures?
3. Do you think the court would have concluded differently if the copy of the will had not had lines through it?

(B) Revocation by Operation of Law. In certain instances, statutes provide that a change of circumstances has the effect of a revocation. **For Example,** when a person marries after executing a will, the will is revoked or is presumed revoked unless it was made in contemplation of marriage or unless it provided for the future spouse. In some states, the revocation is not total but is effective only to the extent of allowing the spouse to take such share of the estate as that to which the spouse would have been entitled had there been no will.

The birth or adoption of a child after the execution of a will commonly works a revocation or partial revocation of the will as to that child. In the case of a partial revocation, the child is entitled to receive the same share as if the testator had died intestate.

The divorce of the testator does not in itself work a revocation. However, the majority of courts hold that if a property settlement is carried out on the basis of the divorce, a prior will of the testator is revoked, at least to the extent of the legacy given to the divorced spouse.

7. Election to Take against the Will

To protect the husband or wife of a testator, the surviving spouse may generally ignore the provisions of a will and elect to take against the will. In such a case, the surviving spouse receives the share of the estate he or she would have received had the testator died without leaving a will or receives a fractional share specified by statute.

The right to take against the will is generally barred by certain kinds of misconduct by the surviving spouse. If a spouse is guilty of desertion or nonsupport that would have justified the decedent's obtaining a divorce, the surviving spouse usually cannot elect to take against the will.

Sports & Entertainment Law

Not Every Dog Has This Kind of Day

Leona Helmsley, a billionaire hotel magnate who spent time in federal prison for tax evasion, left the bulk of her estate to a foundation for the care of dogs. However, Mrs. Helmsley also left $12,000,000 to her Maltese, Trouble, and left out two grandsons from her will. Her will requested that her brother care for Trouble, but when he refused, Trouble was sent to Florida and cared for by the manager of the Helmsley Sandcastle Hotel, until Trouble died in December 2010.

In 2008, the two grandsons convinced a New York court that Mrs. Helmsley lacked mental capacity at the time she made out her will. The judge reduced Trouble's inheritance to $2,000,000 and allowed the funds to be used for Trouble's yearly expenses: $60,000 for her caretaker's fee; $8,000 for grooming; $1,200 for food (the caretaker had switched Trouble from crab cakes, creamed cheese, and steamed vegetables to Alpo), and $2,500 to $12,000 for medical expenses (Trouble had kidney problems).

Upon Trouble's death, there were two provisions in the will that were to take effect: (1) She was to be cremated and placed next to Mrs. Helmsley's grave; and (2) the remainder of the inheritance was to be transferred over to the foundation.*

*Cara Buckley, "Trouble, the Cosseted Heir of Leona Helmsley, Dies," *New York Times*, June 10, 2011, p. A18.

8. Disinheritance

With some exceptions, any person may be **disinherited** or excluded from sharing in the estate of a decedent.[7] A person who would inherit if there were no will is excluded from receiving any part of a decedent's estate if the decedent has left a will giving everything to other persons.

9. Special Types of Wills

In certain situations, special types of wills are used.

(A) Holographic Wills. A **holographic will** is an unwitnessed will that is written by the testator entirely by hand. Some states make no distinction between holographic and other wills. Other states apply the general law of wills to holographic wills, with certain variations. Some states require that a holographic will be dated. Under the UPC, a holographic will is valid, whether witnessed or not, if the signatures and the material provisions are in the handwriting of the testator.[8]

(B) Living Wills. **Living wills** are documents individuals use to decide in advance what level of life-sustaining medical treatments that want if they become unable to express their wishes and are in an irreversible, incurable condition (see Figure 52-1). Living wills are legal in most states. Such personal wishes are entitled to constitutional protection as long as they are expressed clearly.

B. Administration of Decedents' Estates

A decedent's estate consists of the assets the decedent owned at death, and the administration of the estate requires a determination of who is entitled to receive that property. If the decedent owed debts, those debts must be paid first. After those payments, any balance must be distributed according to the terms of the will or by the intestate law if the decedent did not leave a valid will.

10. Definitions

The decedent has the privilege of naming the person who will administer the estate. A man named in a will to administer the estate of the decedent is an **executor**; a woman, an **executrix**. If the decedent failed to name an executor or executrix or did not leave a will, the law permits another person, usually a close relative, to be appointed to wind up the estate. This person is an **administrator** or **administratrix**. Administrators and executors are referred to generally under the UPC as **personal representatives** of the decedents because they represent the decedents or stand in their place.

11. Probate of Will

Probate is the act by which the proper court or official accepts a will and declares that the

[7] One exception, for example, is a surviving spouse. A surviving spouse has marital property rights and cannot be disinherited completely.

[8] Determination of the validity of a holographic will requires the court to examine the nature of the document submitted for probate. *Succession of Gourgis*, 1 So.3d 528 (La. App. 2008).

FIGURE 52-1 ***Living Will***

Living Will

INSTRUCTIONS:

This is an important legal document It sets forth your directions regarding medical treatment. You have the right to refuse treatment you do not want. You may make changes in any of these directions, or add to them, to conform them to your personal wishes.

I, John Jones, being of sound mind, make this statement as a directive to be followed if I become permanently unable to participate in decisions regarding my medical care. These instructions reflect my firm and settled commitment to decline medical treatment under the circumstances indicated below:

I direct my attending physician to withhold or withdraw treatment that serves only to prolong the process of my dying, if I should be in an incurable or irreversible mental or physical condition with no reasonable expectation of recovery.

These instructions apply if I am (a) in a terminal condition; (b) permanently unconscious; or (c) if I am conscious but have irreversible brain damage and will never regain the ability to make decisions and express my wishes.

I direct that treatment be limited to measures to keep me comfortable and to relieve pain, including any pain that might occur by withholding or withdrawing treatment.

While I understand that I am not legally required to be specific about future treatments, if I am in the condition(s) described above I feel especially strongly about the following forms of treatment:

I do not want cardiac resuscitation.
I do not want mechanical respiration.
I do not want tube feeding.
I do not want antibiotics.
I do want maximum pain relief.

Other directions (insert personal instructions): NONE

Sign and date here in the presence of two adult witnesses, who should also sign.

These directions express my legal right to refuse treatment, under the law of [name of state]. I intend my instructions to be carried out, unless I have rescinded them in a new writing or by clearly indicating that I have changed my mind.

Signed: John Jones

Witness: Earl Hummel

Address: 7852 Bailey Avenue
Buffalo, New York

Witness: Ramona Valey

Address: 8921 Clinton Street
Buffalo, New York

Keep the signed original with your personal papers at home. Give copies of the signed original to your doctor, family, lawyer, and others who might be involved in your care.

instrument satisfies the statutory requirements as the will of the testator. Until a will is probated, it has no legal effect.

When witnesses have signed a will, generally they must appear and state that they saw the testator sign the will (unless the will is self-proving). If those witnesses cannot be found, have died, or are outside the jurisdiction, the will may be probated nevertheless. When no witnesses are required, it is customary to require two or more persons to identify the signature of the testator at the time of probate.

After the probate witnesses have made their statements under oath, the official or court will ordinarily admit the will to probate in the absence of any circumstances indicating that the writing should not be probated. A certificate or decree that officially declares that the will is the will of the testator and has been admitted to probate is then issued.

Any qualified person who wishes to object to the probate of the will on the ground that it is not a proper will may appear before the official or court prior to the entry of the decree of probate. A person may petition after probate to have the probate of the will set aside.

12. Will Contest

The probate of a will may be refused or set aside on the ground that the will is not the free expression of the intention of the testator. It may be attacked on the ground of (1) a lack of mental capacity to execute a will, (2) undue influence, duress, fraud, or mistake existing at the time of the execution of the will that induced or led to its execution, or (3) forgery.[9] With the exception of mental capacity, these terms consist of the same elements they do in contract law.

If any one of these problems exists, the probate court can refuse to admit the will for probate. The decedent's estate is then distributed as if there had been no will unless an earlier will can be probated. The *Ramsey v. Taylor* case involves a will contest.

Ramsey v. Taylor, 999 P.2d 1178 (Or. App. 2000)

There's a Melody in the Heirs

John C. Ramsey Sr. (Senior) executed a will in the last months of his life that left the bulk of his estate to Melody Taylor, his paramour. Senior's relationships with his son and grandsons were strained, and his will included the following clause:

I have intentionally provided significant, yet smaller amounts for my son and grandsons because they have for several years alienated my affections by being irresponsible, contentious, and constantly seeking financial support from me rather than providing for themselves.

I have made provisions for MELODY J. TAYLOR because MELODY J. TAYLOR provides me care and support.

Senior was suffering from cancer and renal failure, and his pain was extraordinary. His doctors prescribed high doses of morphine that Melody administered. Senior died from an overdose of morphine.

John Ramsey Jr. (Junior), Senior's son, challenged the validity of the will on the grounds of undue influence, as well as felonious killing of a testator by a beneficiary. The trial court found there was undue influence and refused to admit the will to probate. Melody appealed.

JUDICIAL OPINION

MUNZ, Presiding Judge.…The issue is whether Taylor exercised undue influence over Senior in the payment of her mortgage, the assignment of a right of survivorship in his checking account, and the disposition of his estate under his final will and trust.

We agree with the trial court that a confidential relationship existed between Senior and Taylor. Evidence in the record establishes not only that Taylor and Senior spent most of their time together in the last few months of his life but also establishes that Taylor took increasing responsibility over that time in managing all aspects of Senior's day-to-day life, including procuring and administering his medications, arranging and driving him to medical and business appointments, caring for his house and clothes, providing his food, and managing his checkbook.

The evidence also amply demonstrates that Senior made numerous financial decisions in the final months of his life that provided monetary benefits to Taylor. Moreover, evidence that Senior was strong-minded does not directly bear on the question of whether he had a confidential relationship with Taylor; that evidence is more properly considered in conjunction with the "susceptibility to influence" factor discussed below. Given the circumstances, we conclude that a confidential relationship existed between Senior and Taylor.

It is undisputed that the documents that Senior actually signed on August 10 did not reflect the same changes in the disposition of his estate as did the changes that Taylor assisted in preparing. However, it also is undisputed that the documents actually executed on August 10 did, in fact, give a greater amount of Senior's estate to Taylor than did the revision that Taylor helped to prepare.

This factor concerns whether Senior "had the benefit of the independent advice of his own attorney in drawing up the

[9] *Shoaf v. Shoaf*, 727 S.E.2d 301 (N.C. App. 2012).

Continued

new will" that benefitted Taylor. Also relevant to this factor is whether the beneficiary was present during the meeting with the attorneys. That a beneficiary made the appointment and escorted a testator to an attorney's office do not, in themselves, support an inference of undue influence. Evidence in the record establishes that Senior met with his attorneys on two occasions to prepare his final will and trust and that Taylor was not present at those meetings. Although we have found it to be a suspicious circumstance where a testator is taken to a beneficiary's attorney rather than his or her own attorney to prepare a will, it is undisputed that Senior consulted his own attorneys, who had previously prepared a will and trust for him. Moreover, one of the attorneys testified that Senior told him that Taylor had been of no help to him in deciding how to dispose of his estate. Also, the attorneys discussed with Senior his intent to benefit Taylor and the reasons why he was benefitting Taylor to a greater extent than he was benefitting his family. We conclude that no "suspicious circumstance" was present regarding whether Senior received independent advice concerning his last will and trust.

Over the last decade of his life, Senior's various wills and trusts did not reveal any settled intent as to the disposition of his estate. Although all of them, including the last, benefitted family members to some extent, which family members were benefitted varied greatly, apparently based on Senior's most recent dealings with them.

On this record, we feel compelled to honor Senior's wishes as to the disposition of his estate. Although Taylor was on the scene only for a short time, she provided Senior the care and comfort that he wanted and needed during the final stages of a very painful illness.

We therefore conclude that the trial court erred in setting aside the portions of Senior's final will and trust that benefitted Taylor. For essentially the same reasons set forth above, we also conclude that the trial court erred in setting aside Senior's inter vivos gifts to Taylor.

Taylor did not feloniously kill Senior by administering the prescribed morphine. John II argues that, as a matter of "equity and good conscience," Taylor should not be entitled to keep any money that she received from Senior because she "was the person who administered or directed the administration of the morphine." We reject John II's argument. We agree with the trial court's conclusion that Taylor administered the morphine in the amounts prescribed by Senior's physicians. We also agree with its conclusion that that amount of morphine was required to control the excruciating pain that Senior was experiencing during the last days of his life. The record shows that, although it was common medical knowledge that administering such an amount of morphine to a terminal cancer patient suffering from renal failure could lead to the result seen here, physicians are known to use morphine in these circumstances anyway, in order to ease the suffering of dying patients.

We have concluded that Taylor did not exercise undue influence over Senior when she received *inter vivos* gifts from him or when he made her a major beneficiary of his final will and trust. Reversed and remanded on appeal with instructions to administer John C. Ramsey Sr.'s estate in accordance with his final will and trust.

QUESTIONS

1. What was the relationship of the testator to Taylor? What were his family relationships like?
2. What factors are considered when determining whether there was undue influence?
3. What does the court see as the evidence that overcomes the findings of some of the factors of undue influence?

13. When Administration Is Not Necessary

No administration is required when the decedent did not own any property at the time of death. In some states, special statutes provide for a simplified administration when the decedent leaves only a small estate. Likewise, when all property owned by the decedent was owned with another person as joint tenants with right of survivorship, no administration is required.

14. Appointment of Personal Representative

Both executors and administrators must be appointed to their roles by a court or an officer designated by law. The appointment is made by granting to the personal representative **letters testamentary**, in the case of an executor, or **letters of administration**, in the case of an administrator.

15. Proof of Claims against the Estate

State statutes vary widely on how **claims** against a decedent's estate are presented. In very general terms, statutes provide for some form of public notice of the grant of letters testamentary or letters of administration. Creditors are then required to give notice of their claims within a period specified by either statute or a court order (for example, within six months). In most states, failure to present a claim within the specified time bars the claim.

Ethics & the Law

Preparing Your Client's Will When You're the Beneficiary

John Richard Tomlan, an attorney, befriended Katherine Rice, a 90-year-old nursing home resident, shortly after she was admitted to the home in 1993. Ms. Rice, unmarried and childless, had Parkinson's disease as well as dementia. Mr. Tomlan handled several legal items for her, including the sale of her cabin and the necessary legal paperwork for its closing. In 1998, Tomlan prepared a will that left her substantial estate to a niece and nephew, with the remainder of the estate to various philanthropic organizations. Later, Ms. Rice told Mr. Tomlan that she wanted to leave the bulk of her estate to him. He explained that he could not ethically prepare such a will. Ms. Rice never contacted another attorney to make the change in the will. After that point, Mr. Tomlan began transferring Ms. Rice's assets into accounts that were joint and survivorship accounts with him. He was then able to convince her to give him a durable power of attorney so that he had control over all of her assets, including investment accounts, property, and bank accounts. Using that power, he had $1,000,000 in shares of stock transferred solely to him. Mr. Tomlan maintained that everything was a gift that Ms. Rice had directed be given to him. When Ms. Rice died at the age of 99, Mr. Tomlan failed to probate her estate despite questions and demands from Ms. Rice's niece. Eventually, the estate was processed and had just over $200,000 left. However, with the property that had been gifted to Mr. Tomlan, the estate was valued at over $2.1 million. Ms. Rice's niece reported Mr. Tomlan to the state bar of Ohio and he was given an indefinite suspension of his license to practice law. Clients are dependent upon absolute trust and arms-length relationships with their lawyers. When friendship and gifting enter the picture, the power of lawyer over client is one that dissipates estates. **[*Disciplinary Counsel v. Tomlan*, 885 N.E.2d 895 (Ohio 2008)]**

16. Construction of a Will

The will of a decedent is interpreted according to the ordinary or plain meaning evidenced by its words. The court will strive to give effect to every provision of the will to avoid concluding that any part of the decedent's estate was not disposed of by the will.[10]

17. Testate Distribution of an Estate

The last phase of the administration of the estate by the decedent's personal representative is the distribution of property remaining after the payment of all debts and taxes in accordance with the provisions of the will or by intestacy rules if there was no valid will.

There are various types of gifts under a will. A testator can bequeath to named persons certain sums of money called **general legacies**, or gifts in which no particular money is specified. The testator may also bequeath identified property called **specific legacies** or *specific devises*. **For Example,** a testator may give "$1,000 to *A;* $1,000 to *B;* my automobile to *C.*" The first two bequests are general; the third is specific. After such specific bequests, the testator may make a bequest of everything remaining, called a *residuary bequest*, such as "the balance of my estate to *D.*"

(A) Abatement of Legacies. Assume in the preceding example that after all debts are paid, only $1,500 and the automobile remain. What disposition is to be made?

Thinking Things Through

Close Enough for a Will?

Gloria Waterloo had difficulty with her handwriting. When Rabbi Zimmerman and his wife came to visit her at a hospice facility, she asked his wife, Sandie, to take dictation and write out her will, a resulting one-page document that listed five provisions. One of the provisions left $3,000,000 to Rabbi Zimmerman and appointed him guardian of her estate. After the provisions were dictated, Gloria went through and signed them all and then signed her name. No one witnessed the will. Gloria died less than a month later. Her heirs moved to set aside the will. Give a list of the possible theories her heirs could use to challenge the will. **[*In re Estate of Waterloo*, 250 P.3d 558 (Ariz. App. 2011)]**

[10] *In re Estate of Sharek*, 930 A.2d 388 (N.H. 2007).

Legacies **abate** or bear loss in the following order: (1) residuary, (2) general, (3) specific. The law also holds that legacies of the same class abate proportionately. **For Example,** in the hypothetical case, *C*, the specific legatee, would receive the automobile; *A* and *B*, the general legatees, would each receive $750; and *D*, the residuary legatee, would receive nothing.

(B) ADEMPTION OF PROPERTY. When specifically bequeathed property is sold or given away by the testator prior to death, the bequest is considered **adeemed**, or canceled. The specific legatee in this instance is not entitled to receive any property or money. *Ademption* has the same consequence as though the testator had formally canceled the bequest. **For Example,** if Aunt Claire left her 2008 Honda Accord to her niece, Helen, but Aunt Claire sold the Honda Accord in 2011 and died in 2013, Helen receives nothing from Aunt Claire's estate because the bequest of the Honda is adeemed or canceled.

(C) ANTILAPSE STATUTES. If the beneficiary named in the testator's will died before the testator and the testator did not make any alternate provision applicable in such a case, the gift ordinarily does not lapse. **Antilapse statutes** commonly provide that the gift to the deceased beneficiary shall not lapse but that the children or heirs of that beneficiary may take the legacy in the place of the deceased beneficiary. An antilapse statute does not apply if the testator specified a disposition that should be made of the gift if the original legatee had died.

18. Intestate Distribution of an Estate

If the decedent does not effectively dispose of all property by will or does not have a will, the decedent's property is distributed to certain relatives. Because such persons acquire or succeed to the rights of the decedent and because the circumstances under which they do so is the absence of an effective will, it is said that they acquire title by **intestate succession.**

The right of intestate succession or inheritance is not a basic right of the citizen or an inalienable right. It exists only because the state legislature so provides. It is within the power of the state legislature to modify or destroy the right to inherit property.

Although wide variations exist among the statutory provisions of the states, a common pattern of intestate distribution exists.

(A) SPOUSES. The surviving spouse of the decedent, whether husband or wife, shares in the estate. Generally, the amount received is a fraction that varies with the number of children. If no children survive, the spouse is generally entitled to take the entire estate. Otherwise, the surviving spouse ordinarily receives a one-half or one-third share of the estate.

(B) LINEALS. Lineals, or lineal descendants, are blood descendants of the decedent. Lineal descendants include children and grandchildren. That portion of the estate that is not distributed to the surviving spouse is generally distributed to lineals.

(C) PARENTS. If the estate has not been fully distributed by this time, the remainder is commonly distributed to the decedent's parents.

(D) COLLATERAL HEIRS. These are persons who are not descendants of the decedent but are related through a common ancestor. Generally, brothers and sisters and their descendants share any part of the estate that has not already been distributed. Statutes vary as to how far distribution will be made to the descendants of brothers and sisters. Under some statutes, a degree of relationship is specified, such as first cousins, and no person more remotely related to the decedent is permitted to share in the estate.

If the entire estate is not distributed within the permitted degree of relationship, the property that has not been distributed is given to the state government. This right of the state to take the property is the **right of escheat**. Under some statutes, the right of escheat arises only when there is no relative of the decedent, however remotely related.

(E) DISTRIBUTION *PER CAPITA* AND *PER STIRPES*. The fact that different generations of distributees may be entitled to receive the estate creates a problem of determining the proportions in which distribution is to be made (see Figure 52-2). When all the distributees stand in the same degree of relationship to the decedent, distribution is made ***per capita***, each receiving the same share. **For Example,** if the decedent is survived by three children—*A, B*, and *C*—each of them is entitled to receive one-third of the estate.

If the distributees stand in different degrees of relationship, distribution is made in as many equal parts as there are family lines, or ***stirpes***, represented in the nearest generation. Parents take to the

FIGURE 52-2 *Distribution Per Capita and Per Stirpes*

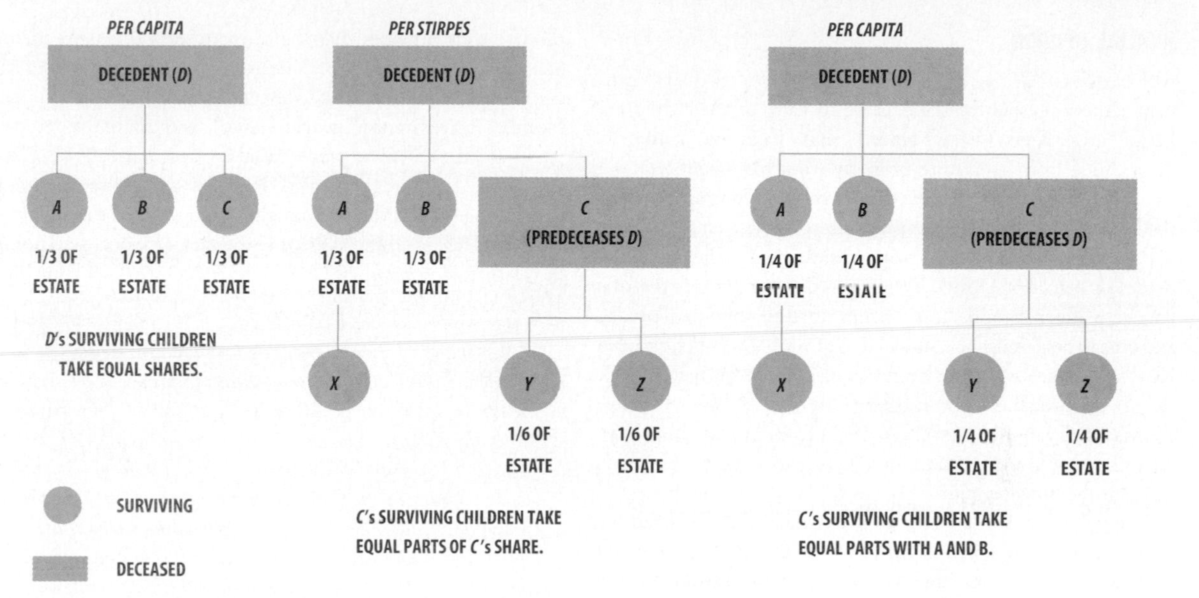

exclusion of their children or subsequent descendants, and when members of the nearest generation have died, their descendants take by way of representation. This is called **distribution *per stirpes***, or *stirpital distribution.* **For Example,** Thomas dies leaving two living children, *A* and *B*, and one child, *C*, who predeceased him but left two children (Thomas's grandchildren, *D* and *E*). *A* and *B* would each take one-third of Thomas's estate, and *D* and *E* would, under a ***per stirpes*** distribution, split a one-third interest, each receiving one-sixth of the estate.

(F) Murder of Decedent. Statutes generally provide that a person who murders the decedent cannot inherit from the victim by intestacy. In the absence of such a statute, courts are divided over whether the heir may inherit. The *In re Estate of Morris P. Van Der Veen* case deals with an inheritance issue when one of the heirs killed the decedent.

In re Estate of Morris P. Van Der Veen, 935 P.2d 1042 (Kan. 1997)

Guilty Father; Innocent Child: Does the Child Inherit as a Grandchild?

On or about April 30, 1993, Kent Van Der Veen murdered his parents, Morris and Deanne Van Der Veen. Kent was 19 years old at the time and had fathered a child two years earlier who had been legally adopted by persons not identified in the court proceedings. Morris and Deanne were not aware of the existence of Kent's child prior to their deaths.

The 1989 joint will of Morris and Deanne Van Der Veen provides for the following distribution of their estate after debts and obligations are paid:

Upon the death of the survivor of us, each of us hereby gives, devises, and bequeaths all of the rest, residue, and remainder of our property of every kind, character, and description, and wherever located, unto our children, Laura Ann Van Der Veen (appellee) and Kent Phillip Van Der Veen, equally and per stirpes.

Kent Van Der Veen was disqualified from inheriting any portion of his parents' estate under Kansas's slayer statute. Kent's child, the biological grandchild of Morris and Deanne, petitioned to inherit one-half of her biological grandparents' estate. The grandchild is identified in the case only as D.B.B. The trial court denied the grandchild any interest in the estate, and the grandchild appealed.

Continued

JUDICIAL OPINION

ALLEGRUCCCI, J.... In their will, the Van Der Veens bequeathed one-half of their estate to each of their children, Laura and Kent. It is agreed that Kent is statutorily disqualified from inheriting property from his parents.

This appeal challenges the district court's determination that the statute prevails over the express terms of the Van Der Veens' will, resulting in D.B.B.'s being disinherited. The argument made on behalf of D.B.B. by her guardian *ad litem* is that the language of her grandparents' bequest to their children, "equally and per stirpes," must be construed to give what would have been Kent's share, if he had not been disqualified, to his heir, D.B.B. D.B.B.'s guardian *ad litem* further argues that D.B.B.'s adoptive status is irrelevant because K.S.A. 59-2118(b) provides that "[a]n adoption shall not terminate the right of the child to inherit ... through the birth parent."

Appellee Laura Van Der Veen counters that the language of 59-2118(b), on which D.B.B. relies, was added in 1993 and became effective after the Van Der Veens' deaths. If the effective date of the amendment does not prevent it from applying in the present case, appellee further argues, the statute should be construed to restrict inheritance "through the birth parent" to instances where the birth parent has died. In other words, it should be interpreted so as to exclude inheritance through a birth parent who is alive but disqualified. In appellee's words, the statute should be interpreted so that the disqualified killer is treated as if he never existed rather than as if he had died.

We first address whether D.B.B.'s adoption affects her right to inherit from her biological grandparents. There is no doubt that the legislature intended that 59-2118(b), at all pertinent times, permitted an adoptee to inherit from and through his or her biological parents.

We find the Court of Appeals' rationale persuasive and conclude that D.B.B.'s adoption would not bar her from inheriting from or through her biological parent.

We next consider whether Kent's being barred from inheriting from his parents prevents the inheritance from passing through him to his child. This was the basis for the trial court's decision and has not been decided by the appellate courts of this state. The question has arisen in other jurisdictions, however, and has been pondered by commentators, scholars, and the National Conference of Commissioners on Uniform State Laws.

In *In re Estate of Benson,* 548 So.2d 775 (Fla.App. 1989), a murderer's minor children were allowed to inherit his share of intestate and testate estates. Margaret Benson, the deceased testator, was the mother of Carol Benson Kendall, Steven Benson, and Scott Benson. Steven had minor children; Scott had no heirs. Steven killed Margaret and Scott. Margaret's will devised her property to her three children in equal shares and per stirpes. Scott died intestate. An intestacy section of Florida's probate code provides that the property of a decedent such as Scott, without parents or lineal descendants, passes to the decedent's siblings and the descendants of deceased siblings. Florida's "slayer statute" provides that "the estate of the decedent passes as if the killer had predeceased the decedent." 548 So.2d at 777. The trial judge applied Florida's anti-lapse statute in concluding that Steven's minor children inherited through him.

With regard to the UPC, the Tennessee Court of Appeals, in *Carter v Hutchison,* 707 S.W.2d 533, 537 n. 10 (Tenn.App. 1985), noted:

> *A vast majority of states enacting the forfeiture statutes have patterned them after the model statute proposed by Dean Wade in 1936, see J. Wade, [Acquisition of Property by Willfully Killing Another—A Statutory Solution, 49 Harv. L.Rev. 715, 753–55 (1936)], or the Uniform Probate Code. Thus, in twenty-nine states there is a statutory presumption that the victim's property passes to his estate as if the slayer had predeceased the decedent. Four states provide for forfeiture but are silent as to distribution. Tennessee is among ten states that provide for forfeiture and for distribution to the decedent's heirs through the laws of intestate succession. The eight remaining states without statutes have forfeiture provisions by court decision.*

It appears that Kansas is one of the few states that does not expressly provide for distribution of the forfeited share.

Turning to the present case, it is clear that under either version of the UPC, appellee would take one-half of the estate of her parents. The other half would be taken by her disqualified brother's minor child.

Kansas' anti-lapse statute, K.S.A. 59-615(a), provides, in part:

> *If a devise or bequest is made to ... any relative by lineal descent ... and such ... relative dies before the testator, leaving issue who survive the testator, such issue shall take the same estate which said devisee or legatee would have taken if he or she had survived, unless a different disposition is made or required by the will.*

The anti-lapse provision is not applicable in the present case. The possibility that one or both of their children would predecease them was taken into account in the Van Der Veens' will by the inclusion of the phrase "per stirpes."

[J]ust treatment of the other beneficiaries does not demand that the slayer's heirs be disqualified or penalized. To illustrate this proposition in the circumstances of the present case, we need only look at appellee's situation. She would take one-half of her parents' estate if they had died from natural causes, and she would take the same if Kent is disqualified for killing their parents and his share passes as if he predeceased them. In contrast, if Kent's child were disqualified because Kent killed his parents, the innocent child would be

Continued

penalized, and appellee would take twice what the testators intended and what she expected.

We conclude that the better rule where the slayer's heir or heirs are wholly innocent would be to dispose of the disqualified slayer's share as if the slayer predeceased the victim(s).

The Van Der Veens intended for their daughter to take one-half of their estate. Their knowledge of Kent's troubled nature is reflected in a provision of the Van Der Veens' will that nominates Laura to serve as Kent's guardian and conservator. Nonetheless, they bequeathed one-half of their estate to him There is nothing in the instrument from which the court could conclude that the Van Der Veens intended for Laura to receive the entire estate in the event of Kent's incapacity or disqualification. By extension, it may reasonably be inferred that they would not have intended for Kent's innocent child to be disqualified in order for Laura to receive the entire estate.

Appellee invites the court to speculate that the Van Der Veens would not have intended for their unknown, illegitimate grandchild to share in their estate. We decline the invitation and note there is no factual support in the record for such a speculation.

[The judgment of the district court is reversed]

QUESTIONS

1. What is a "slayer statute"?
2. What does the court find about adopted children inheriting from their biological parents?
3. What does the court find about grandchildren of murderers inheriting the barred murderer's share of an estate?
4. Is Laura's position different from what it would have been if the inheritance by the grandchild were disallowed?

(G) Death of Distributee after Decedent. The persons entitled to distribution of a decedent's estate are determined as of the date of death. If a distributee dies after that, the rights of the distributee are not lost but pass from the original decedent's estate to the deceased distributee's estate.

(H) Simultaneous Death. The **Uniform Simultaneous Death Act**[11] provides that when survivorship cannot be established, the property of each person shall be disposed of as if he or she had survived the other.

C. Trusts

A **trust** is a legal device by which property, real or personal, is held by one person for the benefit of another. Legal problems in the area of trusts invariably require a determination of the nature of the relationship created by the trust and the rights and obligations of the parties with respect to that relationship.

19. Definitions

The property owner who creates the trust is the **settlor**. (The word *settlor* is taken from the old legal language of "settling the property in trust.") The settlor is sometimes called the **donor** or **trustor**. The person to whom the property is transferred in trust is the **trustee**. The person for whose benefit the trustee holds the property is the beneficiary (or ***cestui que trust***).

Property held in trust is sometimes called the **trust corpus**, *trust fund, trust estate*, or *trust res.* A distinction is made between the **principal**, or the property in trust, and the **income** that is earned by the principal and distributed by the trustee.

If the trust is created to take effect within the lifetime of the settlor, it is a **living trust**, or an *inter vivos trust.* If the trust is provided for in the settlor's will and is to become effective only when the will takes effect after death, the trust is called a **testamentary trust**.

20. Creation of Trusts

The requirements for creating a trust are not uniform, but there are certain typical requirements.

(A) Capacity of Beneficiary. The capacity of the beneficiary of the trust to hold property or to contract

[11] The 1940 version of this act has been adopted in all states except Louisiana and Ohio. The newest version of the act (1993) has been adopted in Alaska, Arizona, Arkansas, Colorado, Hawaii, Kansas, Kentucky, Massachusetts, Montana, New Hampshire, New Mexico, New York, North Carolina, North Dakota, Ohio, Oregon, South Dakota, Utah, Virginia, Washington, and Wisconsin.

is immaterial. Many trusts are created because the beneficiary lacks legal or actual capacity to manage the property. The trustee, as the holder of legal title, must have capacity.

(B) FORMALITY. In creating a trust, it is common practice to execute a writing, called a **trust agreement** or *deed of trust.* No particular form of language is necessary to create a trust as long as the property, the trust purpose, and the beneficiaries are designated. If an *inter vivos* trust relates to an interest in land, the statute of frauds requires that the trust be in writing with the details of the trust included. A writing signed by the trustee and referring to a deed from the trustor can satisfy this requirement. When the trust depends on a transfer of title to land, there must be a valid transfer of the title to the trustee. If a trust is created by the will of the settlor, there must be a writing that meets the requirements of a will.

(C) INTENTION. The settler must express some intention to place property in trust. It is not necessary, however, that the word *trust* or *trustee* be used. The settlor will ordinarily name a trustee, but failure to do so is not fatal to the trust because a trustee will be appointed by the court.

(D) IDENTITY OF BENEFICIARY. Every trust must have a beneficiary. In a private trust, the beneficiaries must be identified by name, description, or designation of the class to which the beneficiaries belong. In a charitable trust, it is sufficient that the beneficiaries be members of the public at large or a general class of the public.

21. Nature of Beneficiary's Interest

When property is transferred to a trust, the trustee has **legal title** and the beneficiary has **equitable title**. The beneficiary may transfer or assign such interest in the trust. The beneficiary's creditors may reach that interest in satisfaction of their claims. However, the trustor can protect beneficiaries from creditors by creating a **spendthrift trust**, which does not allow creditors of the beneficiary to attach the beneficial interest, nor is the beneficiary permitted to assign or pledge that interest.[12]

22. Powers of Trustee

A trustee can exercise only those powers that are given by law or the trust instrument or those that the court will construe as being given by implication. Modern trusts commonly give the trustee discretion to make decisions on matters that could not be foreseen by the settlor. **For Example,** the trustee may be authorized to expend principal as well as income when, in the trustee's opinion, it is necessary for the education or medical care of a beneficiary.

23. Duties of Trustee

The duty of a trustee is to administer the trust. The trustee who accepts the appointment must take all necessary steps to carry out the trust in a proper manner.

(A) PERFORMANCE. A trustee is under a duty to carry out the trust according to its terms and is personally liable for any loss sustained from an unjustified failure to perform such duties. A trustee cannot delegate the performance of personal duties.

(B) DUE CARE. The trustee is under a duty to use reasonable skill, prudence, and diligence in the performance of trust duties. More simply stated, the trustee must use the care that would be exercised by a reasonable person under the circumstances.

(C) LOYALTY. A trustee is entitled to compensation but is not permitted to profit personally from the position of trustee.[13]

(D) POSSESSION AND PRESERVATION OF TRUST PROPERTY. The trustee has a duty to take possession of trust property and to preserve it from loss or damage. If the property includes accounts receivable or outstanding debts, the trustee is responsible for collecting them.

(E) PRODUCTION OF INCOME. By either express or implied direction, the trustee is required to invest the money or property in enterprises or transactions that will yield an income to the estate. A trustee must invest the trust property as a reasonable and prudent investor would.

[12] However, in *In re Marriage of Sharp,* 860 N.E.2d 539 (Ill. App. 2006), the court held that once payments have been made from the trust that they are subject to attachment for back child support.
[13] *Whitman v. Whitman,* 2012 WL 367055 (Ohio App. 2012).

FIGURE 52-3 *Trust Principal/Income Allocation*

PRINCIPAL	PAYABLE FROM PRINCIPAL	INCOME	PAYABLE FROM INCOME
Original trust property	Loans (principal)	Rent	Loans (interest)
Proceeds and gains from sale	Litigation expenses	Interest	Taxes
Insurance payments	Permanent improvements	Cash	Insurance premiums
New property purchased with principal	Costs of purchase	Dividends	Repairs
Stock dividends		Royalties	
Stock splits			

(F) Accounting and Information. A trustee must keep accurate records so that it can be determined whether the trust has been properly administered. On request by a beneficiary, the trustee must furnish information about the trust. Periodically or at certain times, as determined by the law in each state, a trustee must file an account in court. At such time, the court examines the stewardship of the trust.

In some trusts, the trustee must balance the interests of the life beneficiary (the party entitled to the income from the trust while he or she is alive) with those of the eventual recipients of the trust *res*. **For Example,** a testator might put this provision in her will: "To my husband in trust for his life, and upon his death in fee simple to my children." How does the trustee account for rental income? What if the rental properties need repairs? Do the repairs come from the income, or are they taken from principal? There are clear rules for the allocation of income and principal and the expenses of operation of the trust and the trust properties. These rules are summarized in Figure 52-3.

24. Remedies for Breach of Trust

A breach of trust may occur in a variety of ways. The manner in which a trust is breached affects the remedies available. These remedies include the following: (1) A money judgment against the trustee for losses, (2) an injunction, (3) criminal prosecution for misconduct, (4) recovery of trust property, (5) removal of the trustee for misconduct, and (6) recovery from any third parties who participated in a breach of trust.

25. Termination of Trust

A trust may be terminated (1) by its own terms—for example, the trust is an education fund that has a termination date of college graduation, (2) because of the impossibility of attaining the object of the trust—for example, the trust is for the trustor's grandchild and his only child has died before having any children, (3) via revocation by the settlor when allowed by the terms of the trust, but trusts are presumed irrevocable unless the trust document permits revocation, (4) by merger of all interests in the same person (as when there is only one trustee and one beneficiary and they are the same person), or (5) upon the request of all the beneficiaries, as approved by a court, when there is no express purpose that requires continuation of the trust.

LawFlix

Melvin and Howard (1980) (PG)

An interesting look at the difficulty of establishing the validity of an eccentric's will, particularly when the provisions of that will defy conventional notions of proper distribution of one's largesse upon death.

MAKE THE CONNECTION

SUMMARY

A *will* is a writing that provides for a disposition of property to take effect upon death. A man who makes a will is called a *testator;* a woman, a *testatrix.* The person to whom property is left by will is a *beneficiary.* A *legacy* is a gift of personal property by will; a gift of real property by will is a *devise.* A testator must have testamentary capacity to make a will and must manifest some intention that the will is to be effective only upon death. The will must be signed by the testator and be witnessed.

A will may be modified by a codicil or revoked either by the act of the testator or by operation of law.

Probate is the process by which a proper court official accepts a will. Probate may be refused or set aside on grounds that the will is not the free expression of the testator.

A *holographic* will is an unwitnessed will written entirely in the handwriting of the testator. A *self-proved will* may be admitted to probate without the testimony of subscribing witnesses. A *living will* allows a person to make wishes known regarding life-sustaining medical treatment.

If there is a valid will, the last phase of administration of the estate is the distribution of property after the payment of all debts and taxes. *General legacies* are bequests of money, whereas *specific legacies* or *specific devises* are gifts of identified personal or real property. Legacies abate in the following order: residuary, general, and specific. If a beneficiary named in the will has died before the testator and no alternate provision has been made for that beneficiary, antilapse statutes provide that the gift will not lapse. In that event, the children or heirs of the beneficiary may take the legacy in the place of the deceased beneficiary.

If the decedent does not dispose of all property by will or does not have a will, the property will be distributed according to state intestacy statutes. A surviving spouse may generally elect to take the statutory allocation instead of that provided in the will.

The estate of the testator will be administered by the person appointed in the will (the *executor*) or, if there is no will, by a person appointed by the court (an *administrator*). Creditors who have claims against the estate are required to give notice of their claims to the personal representative; otherwise, the claims will be barred.

A *trust* is a legal device by which property is held by one person for the benefit of another. The settlor creates the trust, and the person for whose benefit the trustee holds the property is the beneficiary. Property held in trust is called the *trust corpus, trust fund, trust estate,* or *trust res.*

A trust is usually created by a trust agreement or deed of trust. No particular form or language is required. A trust is not created unless an active duty is placed on the trustee to manage the property in some manner. A trustee's acceptance of duties is presumed.

Legal title to trust property is given to the trustee, and the beneficiary holds equitable title. A beneficiary may transfer an interest in the trust except in the case of a spendthrift trust.

The trustee can exercise only those powers that are given by law or the trust instrument. The trustee must administer the trust and carry out the trust in a proper manner. A trustee is liable for breach of the terms of the trust agreement. A trust comes to an end when its terms so provide or when it becomes impossible to attain the object of the trust.

LEARNING OUTCOMES

After studying this chapter, you should be able to clearly explain:

A. Wills

LO.1 Define *testamentary capacity* and *testamentary intent*

See *Maimonides School v. Coles* on pp. 1100–1101.

See Sports & Entertainment on Leona Helmsley's dog, Trouble, on p. 1105 and the challenge to her capacity.

LO.2 Discuss how a valid will is created

See *Ramsey v. Taylor* on pp. 1107–1108.

LO.3 Explain how a will may be modified or revoked

See *In re Estate of Speers* on pp. 1103–1104.

B. Administration of Decedents' Estates

LO.4 Describe briefly the probate and contest of a will

See the Ethics & the Law discussion of lawyer's duties on p. 1109.

LO.5 Describe the ordinary pattern of distribution by intestacy

See Figure 52-2 on p. 1111.

See In re *Estate of Morris P. Van Der Veen* on pp. 1111–1113.

C. Trusts

LO.6 Explain the nature of a trust

See Sections 20–22 on trust terminology and creation.

KEY TERMS

abate
acknowledgment
adeemed
administrator
administratrix
affidavits
antilapse statutes
attestation clause
beneficiary
bequest
cestui que trust
claims
decedent
devise
devisee
disinherited
distribution *per stirpes*
donor
equitable title
executor
executrix
general legacies
holographic will
income
interlineation
intestate
intestate succession
legacy
legal title
legatee
letters of administration
letters testamentary
lineals
living trust
living wills
per capita
per stirpes
personal representatives
principal
probate
revoke
right of escheat
self-proved wills
settlor
specific legacies
spendthrift trust
stirpes
testamentary capacity
testamentary intent
testamentary trust
testate
testate distribution
testator
testatrix
trust
trust agreement
trust corpus
trustee
trustor
Uniform Probate Code (UPC)
Uniform Simultaneous Death Act
will

QUESTIONS AND CASE PROBLEMS

1. Joseph McKinley Bryan was an elderly, wealthy, and eccentric man. Before his death, he had made provisions for a testamentary trust for his grandchildren and great-grandchildren. Under the terms of the trust, each grandchild who survived him was to receive $500,000, and each great-grandchild who survived him was to receive $100,000. By the time of Bryan's death on April 26, 1995, there had been at least five versions of the trust's provisions. His will was originally dated June 29, 1990, but the trust agreement was originally made in 1985, with two changes in 1988, one in 1990, and another in 1992. In May 1995, NationsBank Corp., the trustee, notified Bryan's grandchildren by letter that they would be receiving only $100,000.

Because the grandchildren had understood that they were to receive $500,000, they asked to see the trust agreements. The trustee refused, contending that there was no duty to share the agreement with the trust beneficiaries. Was the trustee right? [*Taylor v. NationsBank Corp.*, 481 S.E.2d 358 (N.C. App.)]

2. Gerald "Pat" Arrington was diagnosed with a brain tumor. At the time of the diagnosis, he was married to Brenda Arrington, but they were separated pending their divorce. Brenda and Pat had no children, but Pat had five children from a previous marriage. Patricia Daley had lived with Pat since she was born. Pat referred to her as his only "stable" child. After Patricia married David Daley, the two stayed with Pat at his ranch and helped him with the cattle and working the land.

   Pat executed a new will one year before his death and following the brain tumor diagnosis that left everything to Patricia because Pat felt Brenda would just sell his ranch and he did not want it to be sold. After Pat died, Patricia, as executrix of the estate, had the will admitted to probate. Brenda challenged the admission of the will to probate because she said that he gave his property to someone who was not legally his child and that showed he lacked capacity. The will was witnessed by two employees of a bank and both testified that Pat seemed to be his usual self and that he had done business at the bank for 20 years. What should the court do with the will and the challenge to it and why? [In re *Estate of Arrington*, 365 S.W.3d 463 (Tex. App. 2012)]

3. Iona wrote her will. The following year, she wrote another will that expressly revoked the earlier will. Later, while cleaning house, she came across the second will. She mistakenly thought that it was the first will and tore it up because the first will had been revoked. Iona died shortly thereafter. The beneficiaries named in the second will claimed that the second will should be probated. The beneficiaries named in the first will claimed that the second will had been revoked when it was torn up. Had the second will been revoked?

4. Logsdon, who had three children, disliked one of them without any reason. In his will, he left only a small amount to the child he disliked and gave the bulk of his estate to the remaining two. On his death, the disliked child claimed that the will was void and had been obtained by undue influence. Do you agree? [*Logsdon v. Logsdon*, 104 N.E.2d 622 (Ill.)]

5. Field executed a will. On her death, the will was found in her safe deposit box, but the part of it containing the fifth bequest had been torn from the will. This torn fragment was also found in the box. There was no evidence that anyone other than Field had ever opened the box. A proceeding was brought to determine whether the will was entitled to be probated. Had the will been revoked? Was the will still valid with a portion torn from it? [*Flora v. Hughes*, 228 S.W.2d 27 (Ky.)]

6. Miller wrote a will that was 11 pages long and enclosed it in an envelope, which she sealed. She then wrote on the envelope "My last will & testament" and signed her name below this statement. This was the only place where she signed her name on any of the papers. Was this signature sufficient to allow this writing to be admitted to probate as her will? [*Miller's Executor v. Shannon*, 299 S.W.2d 103 (Ky.)]

7. Ms. Lingenfelter's will was offered for probate and was opposed. Ms. Lingenfelter (the testatrix) was sick, highly nervous, and extremely jealous, and she committed suicide a week after executing the will. She had, however, seemed to understand the will when she discussed it with an attorney. The will disinherited her husband because she feared he was not faithful to her despite the fact that he was seriously ill when she wrote the will. He died the day after she executed the will, and she grieved his death terribly for one week before committing suicide. Did she have the capacity to make a will? Should it be admitted to probate? [In re *Lingenfelter's Estate*, 241 P.2d 990 (Cal.)]

8. Copenhaver wrote a will in ink, which was found with her other papers in her bedroom at her death. Pencil lines had been drawn through every provision of the will and the signature. There was no evidence as to the circumstances under which this had been done. Was the will revoked? Why or why not? [*Franklin v. Maclean*, 66 S.E.2d 504 (Va.)]

9. George Baxter executed a will that left the bulk of his estate to the Church of Christ in New Boston, Texas. Two members of the church served as the witnesses for the will. Is the will valid? [In re *Estate of Gordon*, 519 S.W.2d 902 (Tex.)]

10. Jeanette Wall worked for D. J. Sharron for many years. Sharron executed a will, leaving his entire estate to Jeanette. He re-executed the same will sometime thereafter with the same provisions. Sharron's children contested the will, offering evidence that Sharron was a very sick man, physically as well as mentally, and that Wall was active in Sharron's business as well as his personal life. They offered no evidence that Wall had any involvement in the procurement of the original or the re-executed will. Who is entitled to the estate? Why? [*Wall v. Hodges*, 465 So.2d 359 (Ala. App.)]

11. In 1984, Alexander Tolin executed a will under which the residue of his estate was to be devised to his friend Adair Creaig. The will was prepared by Steven Fine, Tolin's attorney, and executed in Fine's office. Fine retained the original will, and gave a blue-backed photocopy to Tolin. In 1989, Tolin executed a codicil to the will that changed the residuary beneficiary from Creaig to Broward Art Guild, Inc. Fine prepared the codicil, and retained the original, giving Tolin a blue-backed photocopy of the original executed codicil.

    Tolin died in 1990. Six months before his death, he told his neighbor Ed Weinstein, who was a retired attorney, that he made a mistake and wished to revoke the codicil and reinstate Creaig as the residuary beneficiary. Weinstein told Tolin he could do this by tearing up the original codicil. Tolin handed Weinstein a blue-backed document that Tolin said was the original codicil. Weinstein looked at the document; it appeared to him to be the original, and gave it back to Tolin. Tolin then tore up and destroyed the document with the intent and for the purpose of revocation.

    Some time after Tolin's death, Weinstein spoke with Fine and found out for the first time that Fine had the original will and codicil. Creaig filed a petition to determine if there had been a revocation of the codicil. From a judgment that Tolin's destruction of a copy of the codicil was not an effective revocation of the codicil, Creaig appealed. Who is correct about the revocation and why? [In re *Estate of Tolin*, 622 So.2d 988 (Fla.)]

12. Valerie and Flora are the beneficiaries of a trust left to them by their mother upon her death. Their mother named Art Casanelli, a family friend, as the trustee. Flora has seen Art driving a new car and has learned that he just purchased a new and rather large home. She is concerned about the trust funds and Art's unfettered access to them. How can she determine whether Art is using trust funds? What happens if she finds that he is?

13. Can a murderer inherit property from his victim? Why or why not?

14. James Horne's will provides that his estate is to be distributed to his heirs *per capita*. Upon his death, two of his three children are surviving and his deceased child left two children (James's grandchildren). His will provides that all his property is to be distributed *per capita* to these children and grandchildren. How will the property be distributed? How would it be distributed if he had provided for a *per stirpes* distribution?

15. Justin Whitman is the adult son of Jeffrey Whitman, an attorney who has served as the trustee for a trust of which Justin is the beneficiary. The trust was established for Justin by his grandfather, Jeffrey's father. Justin asked his father/trustee for an accounting of the principal and income of the trust. Jeffrey asked for the accounting in 2007 and received nothing by 2008 and filed suit for the accounting. Is Jeffrey entitled to receive the accounting? What could a court do in order to obtain the accounting? [*Whitman v. Whitman*, 2012 WL 367055 (Ohio App. 2012)]

Appendix 1

How to Find the Law

In order to determine what the law on a particular question or issue is, it may be necessary to examine (1) compilations of constitutions, treaties, statutes, executive orders, proclamations, and administrative regulations; (2) reports of state and federal court decisions; (3) digests of opinions; (4) treatises on the law; and (5) loose-leaf services. These sources can be either researched traditionally or using fee and/or non-fee-based computerized legal research, accessed through the World Wide Web.

A. Compilations

In the consideration of a legal problem in business it is necessary to determine whether the matter is affected or controlled by a constitution, national or state; by a national treaty; by an Act of Congress, a state legislature, or a city ordinance; by a decree or proclamation of the President of the United States, a governor, or a mayor; or by a regulation of a federal, state, or local administrative agency.

Each body or person that makes laws, regulations, or ordinances usually compiles and publishes at the end of each year or session all of the matter that it has adopted. In addition to the periodical or annual volumes, it is common to compile all the treaties, statutes, regulations, or ordinances in separate volumes. To illustrate, the federal Anti-Injunction Act may be cited as the Act of March 23, 1932, 47 Stat. 70, 29 U.S.C. § 101 et seq. This means that this law was enacted on March 23, 1932, and that it can be found at page 70 in Volume 47 of the reports that contain all of the statutes adopted by the Congress.

The second part of the citation, 29 U.S.C. § 101 et seq., means that in the collection of all of the federal statutes, which is known as the United States Code, the full text of the statute can be found in the sections of the 29th title beginning with Section 101.

B. Court Decisions

For complicated or important legal cases or when an appeal is to be taken, a court will generally write an opinion, which explains why the court made the decision. Appellate courts as a rule write opinions. The great majority of these decisions, particularly in the case of the appellate courts, are collected and printed. In order to avoid confusion, the opinions of each court are ordinarily printed in a separate set of reports, either by official reporters or private publishers.

In the reference "*Pennoyer v. Neff*, 95 U.S. 714, 24 L. Ed. 565," the first part states the names of the parties. It does not necessarily tell who was the plaintiff and who was the defendant. When an action is begun in a lower court, the first name is that of the plaintiff and the second name that of the defendant. When the case is appealed, generally the name of the person taking the appeal appears on the records of the higher court as the first one and that of the adverse party as the second. Sometimes, therefore, the original order of the names of the parties is reversed.

The balance of the reference consists of two citations. The first citation, 95 U.S. 714, means that the opinion which the court filed in the case of *Pennoyer v. Neff* may be found on page 714 of the 95th volume of a series of books in which are printed officially the opinions of the United States Supreme Court. Sometimes the same opinion is printed in two different sets of volumes. In the example, 24 L.Ed. 565 means that in the 24th volume of another set of books, called Lawyer's Edition, of the United States Supreme Court Reports, the same opinion begins on page 565.

In opinions by a state court there may also be two citations, as in the case of *Morrow v. Corbin*, 122 Tex. 553, 62 S.W.2d 641. This means that the opinion in the lawsuit between Morrow and Corbin may be found in the 122nd volume of the reports of the highest court of Texas, beginning on page 553; and also in Volume 62 of the Southwestern Reporter, Second Series, at page 641.

The West Publishing Company publishes a set of sectional reporters covering the entire United States. They are called "sectional" because each reporter, instead of being limited to a particular court or a particular state, covers the decisions of the courts of a particular section of the country. Thus the decisions of the courts of Arkansas, Kentucky, Missouri, Tennessee, and Texas are printed by the West Publishing company as a group in a sectional reporter called the Southwestern Reporter.[1] Because of the large number of decisions involved, generally only the opinions of the state appellate courts are printed. A number of states[2] have discontinued publication of the opinions of their courts, and those opinions are now found only in the West reporters.

The reason for the "Second Series" in the Southwestern citation is that when there were 300 volumes in the original series, instead of calling the next volume 301, the publisher called it Volume 1, Second Series. Thus 62 S. W.2d Series really means the 362nd volume of the Southwestern Reporter. Six to eight volumes appear in a year for each geographic section.

In addition to these state reporters, the West Publishing Company publishes a Federal Supplement, which primarily reports the opinions of the Federal District Courts; the Federal Reporter, which primarily reports the decisions of the United States Courts of Appeals; and the Supreme Court Reporter, which reports the decisions of the United States Supreme Court. The Supreme Court decisions are also reported in a separate set called the Lawyers' Edition, published by the Lawyers Cooperative Publishing Company.

The reports published by the West Publishing Company and Lawyers Cooperative Publishing Company are unofficial reports, while those bearing the name or abbreviation of the United States or of a state, such as "95 U.S. 714" or "122 Tex. 553" are official reports. This means that in the case of the latter, the particular court, such as the United States Supreme Court, has officially authorized that its decisions be printed and that by federal statute such official printing is made. In the case of the unofficial reporters, the publisher prints the decisions of a court on its own initiative. Such opinions are part of the public domain and not subject to any copyright or similar restriction.

C. Digests of Opinions

The reports of court decisions are useful only if one has the citation, that is, the name and volume number of the book and the page number of the opinion one is seeking. For this reason, digests of the decisions have been prepared. These digests organize the entire field of law under major headings, which are then arranged in alphabetical order. Under each heading, such as "Contracts," the subject is divided into the different questions that can arise with respect to that field. A master outline is thus created on the subject. This outline includes short paragraphs describing what each case holds and giving its citation.

D. Treatises and Restatements

Very helpful in finding a case or a statute are the treatises on the law. These may be special books, each written by an author on a particular subject, such as Williston on Contracts, Bogert on Trusts, Fletcher on Corporations, or they may be general encyclopedias, as in the case of *American Jurisprudence, American Jurisprudence, Second,* and *Corpus Juris Secundum.*

Another type of treatise is found in the restatements of the law prepared by the American Law Institute. Each restatement consists of one or more volumes devoted to a particular phase of the law, such as the Restatement of the Law of Contracts, Restatement of the Law of Agency, and Restatement of the Law of Property. In each restatement, the American Law Institute, acting through special committees of judges, lawyers, and professors of law, has set forth what the law is; and in many areas where there is no law or the present rule is regarded as unsatisfactory, the restatement specifies what the Institute deems to be the desirable rule.

E. Loose-Leaf Services

A number of private publishers, notably Commerce Clearing House and Prentice-Hall, publish loose-leaf books devoted to particular branches of the law. Periodically, the publisher sends to the purchaser a number of pages that set forth any decision, regulation, or statute made or adopted since the prior set of pages was prepared. Such services are unofficial.

F. Computerized Legal Research

National and local computer services are providing constantly widening assistance for legal research. The database in such a system may be opinions, statutes, or administrative regulations stored word for word; or the later history of a particular case giving its full citation and showing whether the case has been followed by other

[1] The sectional reporters are: Atlantic—A. (Connecticut, Delaware, District of Columbia, Maine, Maryland, New Hampshire, New Jersey, Pennsylvania, Rhode Island, Vermont); Northeastern—N.E. (Illinois, Indiana, Massachusetts, New York, Ohio); N.W. (Iowa, Michigan, Minnesota, Nebraska, North Dakota, South Dakota, Wisconsin); Pacific—P. (Alaska, Arizona, California, Colorado, Hawaii, Idaho, Kansas, Montana, Nevada, New Mexico, Oklahoma, Oregon, Utah, Washington, Wyoming); Southeastern—S.E. (Georgia, North Carolina, South Carolina, Virginia, West Virginia); Southwestern— S.W. (Arkansas, Kentucky, Missouri, Tennessee, Texas); and Southern—So. (Alabama, Florida, Louisiana, Mississippi). There is also a special New York State reporter known as the New York Supplement and a special California State reporter known as the California Reporter.

[2] See, for example, Alaska, Florida, Iowa, Kentucky, Louisiana, Maine, Mississippi, Missouri, North Dakota, Oklahoma, Texas, and Wyoming.

courts; or the text of forms and documents. By means of a terminal connected to the system, the user can retrieve the legal information at a great saving of time and with the assurance that it is up-to-date.

There are two leading, fee-based systems for computer-aided research. Listed alphabetically, they are LEXIS and WESTLAW.

A specialized service of legal forms for business is provided by Shepard's BUSINESS LAW CASE MANAGEMENT SYSTEM. A monthly fee is required for usage.

Numerous free, private sites offer a lot of legal resources. The federal government offers a variety of case law, regulations, and code enactments, either pending or newly promulgated. To find the most comprehensive source of government-maintained legal information, go to **www.house.gov**. The United States Supreme Court has information about both its current term and past terms at **www.supremecourt.gov**. Another website that provides excellent information about current controversies that reach the United States Supreme Court is **www.scotusblog.com**.

State governments provide access to regulations and codes online. As an example, go to the State of California's site, **www.leginfo.legislation.ca.gov**. You can access an array of information about both state and federal government through links at **www.USA.gov**.

Appendix 2

The Constitution of the United States

We the people of the United States of America, in order to form a more perfect union, establish justice, insure domestic tranquility, provide for the common defense, promote the general welfare, and secure the blessings of liberty to ourselves and our posterity, do ordain and establish this Constitution for the United States of America.

Article I

SECTION 1

All legislative powers herein granted shall be vested in a Congress of the United States, which shall consist of a Senate and House of Representatives.

SECTION 2

1. The House of Representatives shall be composed of members chosen every second year by the people of the several States, and the electors in each State shall have the qualifications requisite for electors of the most numerous branch of the State legislature.

2. No person shall be a representative who shall not have attained to the age of twenty-five years, and been seven years a citizen of the United States, and who shall not, when elected, be an inhabitant of that State in which he shall be chosen.

3. Representatives and direct taxes shall be apportioned among the several States which may be included within this Union, according to their respective numbers, which shall be determined by adding to the whole number of free persons, including those bound to service for a term of years, and excluding Indians not taxed, three fifths of all other persons.[1] The actual enumeration shall be made within three years after the first meeting of the Congress of the United States, and within every subsequent term of ten years, in such manner as they shall by law direct. The number of representatives shall not exceed one for every thirty thousand, but each State shall have at least one representative; and until such enumeration shall be made, the State of New Hampshire shall be entitled to choose three, Massachusetts eight, Rhode Island and Providence Plantations one, Connecticut five, New York six, New Jersey four, Pennsylvania eight, Delaware one, Maryland six, Virginia ten, North Carolina five, South Carolina five, and Georgia three.

4. When vacancies happen in the representation from any State, the executive authority thereof shall issue writs of election to fill such vacancies.

5. The House of Representatives shall choose their speaker and other officers; and shall have the sole power of impeachment.

SECTION 3

1. The Senate of the United States shall be composed of two senators from each State, chosen by the legislature thereof, for six years; and each senator shall have one vote.

2. Immediately after they shall be assembled in consequence of the first election, they shall be divided as equally as may be into three classes. The seats of the senators of the first class shall be vacated at the expiration of the second year, of the second class at the expiration of the fourth year, and of the third class at the expiration of the sixth year, so that one third may be chosen every second year; and if vacancies happen by resignation, or otherwise, during the recess of the legislature of any State, the executive thereof may make temporary appointments until the next meeting of the legislature, which shall then fill such vacancies.[2]

3. No person shall be a senator who shall not have attained to the age of thirty years, and been nine years a citizen of the United States, and who shall not, when elected, be an inhabitant of that State for which he shall be chosen.

4. The Vice President of the United States shall be President of the Senate, but shall have no vote, unless they be equally divided.

5. The Senate shall choose their other officers, and also a president pro tempore, in the absence of the Vice President, or when he shall exercise the office of the President of the United States.

6. The Senate shall have the sole power to try all impeachments. When sitting for that purpose, they shall

[1] See the 14th Amendment.
[2] See the 17th Amendment.

be on oath or affirmation. When the President of the United States is tried, the chief justice shall preside: and no person shall be convicted without the concurrence of two thirds of the members present.

7. Judgment in cases of impeachment shall not extend further than to removal from office, and disqualification to hold and enjoy any office of honor, trust or profit under the United States: but the party convicted shall nevertheless be liable and subject to indictment, trial, judgment and punishment, according to law.

SECTION 4

1. The times, places, and manner of holding elections for senators and representatives, shall be prescribed in each State by the legislature thereof; but the Congress may at any time by law make or alter such regulations, except as to the places of choosing senators.

2. The Congress shall assemble at least once in every year, and such meeting shall be on the first Monday in December, unless they shall by law appoint a different day.

SECTION 5

1. Each House shall be the judge of the elections, returns and qualifications of its own members, and a majority of each shall constitute a quorum to do business; but a smaller number may adjourn from day to day, and may be authorized to compel the attendance of absent members, in such manner, and under such penalties as each House may provide.

2. Each House may determine the rules of its proceedings, punish its members for disorderly behavior, and, with the concurrence of two thirds, expel a member.

3. Each House shall keep a journal of its proceedings, and from time to time publish the same, excepting such parts as may in their judgment require secrecy; and the yeas and nays of the members of either House on any question shall, at the desire of one fifth of those present, be entered on the journal.

4. Neither House, during the session of Congress, shall, without the consent of the other, adjourn for more than three days, nor to any other place than that in which the two Houses shall be sitting.

SECTION 6

1. The senators and representatives shall receive a compensation for their services, to be ascertained by law, and paid out of the Treasury of the United States. They shall in all cases, except treason, felony, and breach of the peace, be privileged from arrest during their attendance at the session of their respective Houses, and in going to and returning from the same; and for any speech or debate in either House, they shall not be questioned in any other place.

2. No senator or representative shall, during the time for which he was elected, be appointed to any civil office under the authority of the United States, which shall have been created, or the emoluments whereof shall have been increased during such time; and no person holding any office under the United States shall be a member of either House during his continuance in office.

SECTION 7

1. All bills for raising revenue shall originate in the House of Representatives; but the Senate may propose or concur with amendments as on other bills.

2. Every bill which shall have passed the House of Representatives and the Senate, shall, before it becomes a law, be presented to the President of the United States; if he approves he shall sign it, but if not he shall return it, with his objections to that House in which it shall have originated, who shall enter the objections at large on their journal, and proceed to reconsider it. If after such reconsideration two thirds of that House shall agree to pass the bill, it shall be sent, together with the objections, to the other House, by which it shall likewise be reconsidered, and if approved by two thirds of that House, it shall become a law. But in all such cases the votes of both Houses shall be determined by yeas and nays, and the names of the persons voting for and against the bill shall be entered on the journal of each House respectively. If any bill shall not be returned by the President within ten days (Sundays excepted) after it shall have been presented to him, the same shall be a law, in like manner as if he had signed it, unless the Congress by their adjournment prevent its return, in which case it shall not be a law.

3. Every order, resolution, or vote to which the concurrence of the Senate and the House of Representatives may be necessary (except on a question of adjournment) shall be presented to the President of the United States; and before the same shall take effect, shall be approved by him, or being disapproved by him, shall be repassed by two thirds of the Senate and House of Representatives, according to the rules and limitations prescribed in the case of a bill.

SECTION 8

The Congress shall have the power

1. To lay and collect taxes, duties, imposts, and excises, to pay the debts and provide for the common defense and general welfare of the United States; but all duties, imposts, and excises shall be uniform throughout the United States;

2. To borrow money on the credit of the United States;

3. To regulate commerce with foreign nations, and among the several States, and with the Indian tribes;

4. To establish a uniform rule of naturalization, and uniform laws on the subject of bankruptcies throughout the United States;

5. To coin money, regulate the value thereof, and of foreign coin, and fix the standard of weights and measures;

6. To provide for the punishment of counterfeiting the securities and current coin of the United States;

7. To establish post offices and post roads;

8. To promote the progress of science and useful arts, by securing for limited times to authors and inventors the exclusive rights to their respective writings and discoveries;

9. To constitute tribunals inferior to the Supreme Court;

10. To define and punish piracies and felonies committed on the high seas, and offenses against the law of nations;

11. To declare war, grant letters of marque and reprisal, and make rules concerning captures on land and water;

12. To raise and support armies, but no appropriation of money to that use shall be for a longer term than two years;

13. To provide and maintain a navy;

14. To make rules for the government and regulation of the land and naval forces;

15. To provide for calling forth the militia to execute the laws of the Union, suppress insurrections and repel invasions;

16. To provide for organizing, arming, and disciplining the militia, and for governing such part of them as may be employed in the service of the United States, reserving to the States respectively, the appointment of the officers, and the authority of training the militia according to the discipline prescribed by Congress;

17. To exercise exclusive legislation in all cases whatsoever, over such district (not exceeding ten miles square) as may, by cession of particular States, and the acceptance of Congress, become the seat of the government of the United States, and to exercise like authority over all places purchased by the consent of the legislature of the State in which the same shall be, for the erection of forts, magazines, arsenals, dockyards, and other needful buildings; and

18. To make all laws which shall be necessary and proper for carrying into execution the foregoing powers, and all other powers vested by this Constitution in the government of the United States, or in any department or officer thereof.

SECTION 9

1. The migration or importation of such persons as any of the States now existing shall think proper to admit, shall not be prohibited by the Congress prior to the year one thousand eight hundred and eight, but a tax or duty may be imposed on such importation, not exceeding ten dollars for each person.

2. The privilege of the writ of habeas corpus shall not be suspended, unless when in cases of rebellion or invasion the public safety may require it.

3. No bill of attainder or ex post facto law shall be passed.

4. No capitation, or other direct, tax shall be laid, unless in proportion to the census or enumeration hereinbefore directed to be taken.[3]

5. No tax or duty shall be laid on articles exported from any State.

6. No preference shall be given by any regulation of commerce or revenue to the ports of one State over those of another: nor shall vessels bound to, or from, one State be obliged to enter, clear, or pay duties in another.

7. No money shall be drawn from the treasury, but in consequence of appropriations made by law; and a regular statement and account of the receipts and expenditures of all public money shall be published from time to time.

8. No title of nobility shall be granted by the United States: and no person holding any office of profit or trust under them, shall, without the consent of the Congress, accept of any present, emolument, office, or title, of any kind whatever, from any king, prince, or foreign State.

SECTION 10

1. No State shall enter into any treaty, alliance, or confederation; grant letters of marque and reprisal; coin money; emit bills of credit; make anything but gold and silver coin a tender in payment of debts; pass any bill of attainder, ex post facto law, or law impairing the obligation of contracts, or grant any title of nobility.

2. No State shall, without the consent of the Congress, lay any imposts or duties on imports or exports, except what may be absolutely necessary for executing its inspection laws: and the net produce of all duties and imposts laid by any State on imports or exports, shall be for the use of the treasury of the United States; and all such laws shall be subject to the revision and control of the Congress.

3. No State shall, without the consent of the Congress, lay any duty of tonnage, keep troops, or ships of war in time of peace, enter into any agreement or compact with another State, or with a foreign power, or engage in war, unless actually invaded, or in such imminent danger as will not admit of delay.

Article II

SECTION 1

1. The executive power shall be vested in a President of the United States of America. He shall hold his office during the term of four years, and, together with the Vice President, chosen for the same term, be elected as follows:

2. Each State shall appoint, in such manner as the legislature thereof may direct, a number of electors, equal

[3] See the 16th Amendment.

to the whole number of senators and representatives to which the State may be entitled in the Congress: but no senator or representative, or person holding an office of trust or profit under the United States, shall be appointed an elector.

The electors shall meet in their respective States, and vote by ballot for two persons, of whom one at least shall not be an inhabitant of the same State with themselves. And they shall make a list of all the persons voted for, and of the number of votes for each; which list they shall sign and certify, and transmit sealed to the seat of the government of the United States, directed to the president of the Senate. The president of the Senate shall, in the presence of the Senate and House of Representatives, open all the certificates, and the votes shall then be counted. The person having the greatest number of votes shall be the President, if such number be a majority of the whole number of electors appointed; and if there be more than one who have such majority, and have an equal number of votes, then the House of Representatives shall immediately choose by ballot one of them for President; and if no person have a majority, then from the five highest on the list the said House shall in like manner choose the President. But in choosing the President, the votes shall be taken by States, the representation from each State having one vote; a quorum for this purpose shall consist of a member or members from two thirds of the States, and a majority of all the States shall be necessary to a choice. In every case, after the choice of the President, the person having the greatest number of votes of the electors shall be the Vice President. But if there should remain two or more who have equal votes, the Senate shall choose from them by ballot the Vice President.[4]

3. The Congress may determine the time of choosing the electors, and the day on which they shall give their votes; which day shall be the same throughout the United States.

4. No person except a natural born citizen, or a citizen of the United States, at the time of the adoption of this Constitution, shall be eligible to the office of President; neither shall any person be eligible to that office who shall not have attained to the age of thirty-five years, and been fourteen years a resident within the United States.

5. In the case of removal of the President from office, or of his death, resignation, or inability to discharge the powers and duties of the said office, the same shall devolve on the Vice President, and the Congress may by law provide for the case of removal, death, resignation, or inability, both of the President and Vice President, declaring what officer shall then act as President, and such officer shall act accordingly, until the disability be removed, or a President shall be elected.

6. The President shall, at stated times, receive for his services a compensation, which shall neither be increased nor diminished during the period for which he shall have been elected, and he shall not receive within that period any other emolument from the United States, or any of them.

7. Before he enter on the execution of his office, he shall take the following oath or affirmation:—"I do solemnly swear (or affirm) that I will faithfully execute the office of President of the United States, and will to the best of my ability, preserve, protect and defend the Constitution of the United States."

SECTION 2

1. The President shall be commander in chief of the army and navy of the United States, and of the militia of the several States, when called into the actual service of the United States; he may require the opinion, in writing, of the principal officer in each of the executive departments, upon any subject relating to the duties of their respective office, and he shall have power to grant reprieves and pardons for offenses against the United States, except in cases of impeachment.

2. He shall have power, by and with the advice and consent of the Senate, to make treaties, provided two thirds of the senators present concur; and he shall nominate, and by and with the advice and consent of the Senate, shall appoint ambassadors, other public ministers and consuls, judges of the Supreme Court, and all other officers of the United States, whose appointments are not herein otherwise provided for, and which shall be established by law: but the Congress may by law vest the appointment of such inferior officers, as they think proper, in the President alone, in the courts of law, or in the heads of departments.

3. The President shall have power to fill up all vacancies that may happen during the recess of the Senate, by granting commissions which shall expire at the end of their next session.

SECTION 3

He shall from time to time give to the Congress information of the state of the Union, and recommend to their consideration such measures as he shall judge necessary and expedient; he may, on extraordinary occasions, convene both Houses, or either of them, and in case of disagreement between them with respect to the time of adjournment, he may adjourn them to such time as he shall think proper; he shall receive ambassadors and other public ministers; he shall take care that the laws be faithfully executed, and shall commission all the officers of the United States.

[4] Superseded by the 12th Amendment.

SECTION 4

The President, Vice President, and all civil officers of the United States, shall be removed from office on impeachment for, and conviction of, treason, bribery, or other high crimes and misdemeanors.

Article III

SECTION 1

The judicial power of the United States shall be vested in one Supreme Court, and in such inferior courts as the Congress may from time to time ordain and establish. The judges, both of the Supreme and inferior courts, shall hold their offices during good behavior, and shall, at stated times, receive for their services, a compensation, which shall not be diminished during their continuance in office.

SECTION 2

1. The judicial power shall extend to all cases, in law and equity, arising under this Constitution, the laws of the United States, and treaties made, or which shall be made, under their authority;—to all cases affecting ambassadors, other public ministers and consuls;—to all cases of admiralty and maritime jurisdiction;—to controversies to which the United States shall be a party;—to controversies between two or more States; between a State and citizens of another State;[5]—between citizens of different States;—between citizens of the same State claiming lands under grants of different States, and between a State, or the citizens thereof, and foreign States, citizens or subjects.

2. In all cases affecting ambassadors, other public ministers and consuls, and those in which a State shall be party, the Supreme Court shall have original jurisdiction. In all the other cases before mentioned, the Supreme Court shall have appellate jurisdiction, both as to law and to fact, with such exceptions, and under such regulations as the Congress shall make.

3. The trial of all crimes, except in cases of impeachment, shall be by jury; and such trial shall be held in the State where the said crimes shall have been committed; but when not committed within any State, the trial shall be at such place or places as the Congress may by law have directed.

SECTION 3

1. Treason against the United States shall consist only in levying war against them, or in adhering to their enemies, giving them aid and comfort. No person shall be convicted of treason unless on the testimony of two witnesses to the same overt act, or on confession in open court.

2. The Congress shall have power to declare the punishment of treason, but no attainder of treason shall work corruption of blood, or forfeiture except during the life of the person attainted.

Article IV

SECTION 1

Full faith and credit shall be given in each State to the public acts, records, and judicial proceedings of every other State. And the Congress may by general laws prescribe the manner in which such acts, records and proceedings shall be proved, and the effect thereof.

SECTION 2

1. The citizens of each State shall be entitled to all privileges and immunities of citizens in the several States.[6]

2. A person charged in any State with treason, felony, or other crime, who shall flee from justice, and be found in another State, shall on demand of the executive authority of the State from which he fled, be delivered up to be removed to the State having jurisdiction of the crime.

3. No person held to service or labor in one State under the laws thereof, escaping into another, shall in consequence of any law or regulation therein, be discharged from such service or labor, but shall be delivered up on claim of the party to whom such service or labor may be due.[7]

SECTION 3

1. New States may be admitted by the Congress into this Union; but no new State shall be formed or erected within the jurisdiction of any other State, nor any State be formed by the junction of two or more States, or parts of States, without the consent of the legislatures of the States concerned as well as of the Congress.

2. The Congress shall have power to dispose of and make all needful rules and regulations respecting the territory or other property belonging to the United States; and nothing in this Constitution shall be so construed as to prejudice any claims of the United States, or of any particular State.

SECTION 4

The United States shall guarantee to every State in this Union a republican form of government, and shall protect each of them against invasion; and on application of the legislature, or of the executive (when the legislature cannot be convened) against domestic violence.

[5] See the 11th Amendment.
[6] See the 14th Amendment, Sec. 1.
[7] See the 13th Amendment.

Article V

The Congress, whenever two thirds of both Houses shall deem it necessary, shall propose amendments to this Constitution, or, on the application of the legislature of two thirds of the several States, shall call a convention for proposing amendments, which in either case, shall be valid to all intents and purposes, as part of this Constitution when ratified by the legislatures of three fourths of the several States, or by conventions in three fourths thereof, as the one or the other mode of ratification may be proposed by the Congress; provided that no amendment which may be made prior to the year one thousand eight hundred and eight shall in any manner affect the first and fourth clauses in the ninth section of the first article; and that no State, without its consent, shall be deprived of its equal suffrage in the Senate.

Article VI

1. All debts contracted and engagements entered into, before the adoption of this Constitution, shall be as valid against the United States under this Constitution, as under the Confederation.[8]

2. This Constitution, and the laws of the United States which shall be made in pursuance thereof; and all treaties made, or which shall be made, under the authority of the United States, shall be the supreme law of the land; and the judges in every State shall be bound thereby, anything in the Constitution or laws of any State to the contrary notwithstanding.

3. The senators and representatives before mentioned, and the members of the several State legislatures, and all executive and judicial officers, both of the United States and of the several States, shall be bound by oath or affirmation to support this Constitution; but no religious test shall ever be required as a qualification to any office or public trust under the United States.

Article VII

The ratification of the conventions of nine States shall be sufficient for the establishment of this Constitution between the States so ratifying the same.

Done in Convention by the unanimous consent of the States present the seventeenth day of September in the year of our Lord one thousand seven hundred and eighty-seven, and of the independence of the United States of America the twelfth. In witness whereof we have hereunto subscribed our names.

[8] See the 14th Amendment, Sec. 4.

A. Amendments

First Ten Amendments passed by Congress Sept. 25, 1789.

Ratified by three-fourths of the States December 15, 1791.

Amendment I

Congress shall make no law respecting an establishment of religion, or prohibiting the free exercise thereof; or abridging the freedom of speech, or of the press; or the right of the people peaceably to assemble, and to petition the government for a redress of grievances.

Amendment II

A well regulated militia, being necessary to the security of a free State, the right of the people to keep and bear arms, shall not be infringed.

Amendment III

No soldier shall, in time of peace be quartered in any house, without the consent of the owner, nor in time of war, but in a manner to be prescribed by law.

Amendment IV

The right of the people to be secure in their persons, houses, papers, and effects, against unreasonable searches and seizures, shall not be violated, and no warrants shall issue, but upon probable cause, supported by oath or affirmation, and particularly describing the place to be searched, and the person or things to be seized.

Amendment V

No person shall be held to answer for a capital, or otherwise infamous crime, unless on a presentment or indictment of a grand jury, except in cases arising in the land or naval forces, or in the militia, when in actual service in time of war or public danger; nor shall any person be subject for the same offense to be twice put in jeopardy of life or limb; nor shall be compelled in any criminal case to be a witness against himself, nor be deprived of life, liberty, or property, without due process of law; nor shall private property be taken for public use without just compensation.

Amendment VI

In all criminal prosecutions, the accused shall enjoy the right to a speedy and public trial, by an impartial jury of the State and district wherein the crime shall have been committed, which district shall have been previously ascertained by law, and to be informed of the nature and cause of the accusation; to be confronted with the witnesses against him; to have compulsory process for obtaining witnesses in his favor, and to have the assistance of counsel for his defense.

Amendment VII

In suits at common law, where the value in controversy shall exceed twenty dollars, the right of trial by jury shall be preserved, and no fact tried by a jury shall be otherwise reexamined in any court of the United States, then according to the rules of the common law.

Amendment VIII

Excessive bail shall not be required, nor excessive fines imposed, nor cruel and unusual punishments inflicted.

Amendment IX

The enumeration in the Constitution of certain rights shall not be construed to deny or disparage others retained by the people.

Amendment X

The powers not delegated to the United States by the Constitution, nor prohibited by it to the States, are reserved to the States respectively, or to the people.

Amendment XI

Passed by Congress March 5, 1794. Ratified January 8, 1798.

The judicial power of the United States shall not be construed to extend to any suit in law or equity, commenced or prosecuted against one of the United States by citizens of another State, or by citizens or subjects of any foreign State.

Amendment XII

Passed by Congress December 12, 1803. Ratified September 25, 1804.

The electors shall meet in their respective States, and vote by ballot for President and Vice President, one of whom, at least, shall not be an inhabitant of the same State with themselves; they shall name in their ballots the person voted for as President, and in distinct ballots, the person voted for as Vice President, and they shall make distinct lists of all persons voted for as President and of all persons voted for as Vice President, and of the number of votes for each, which lists they shall sign and certify, and transmit sealed to the seat of the government of the United States, directed to the President of the Senate;—The President of the Senate shall, in the presence of the Senate and House of Representatives, open all the certificates and the votes shall then be counted;—The person having the greatest number of votes for President, shall be the President, if such number be a majority of the whole number of electors appointed; and if no person have such majority, then from the persons having the highest numbers not exceeding three on the list of those voted for as President, the House of Representatives shall choose immediately, by ballot, the President. But in choosing the President, the votes shall be taken by States, the representation from each State having one vote; a quorum for this purpose shall consist of a member or members from two thirds of the States, and a majority of all the States shall be necessary to a choice. And if the House of Representatives shall not choose a President whenever the right of choice shall devolve upon them, before the fourth day of March next following, then the Vice President shall act as President, as in the case of the death or other constitutional disability of the President. The person having the greatest number of votes as Vice President shall be the Vice President, if such number be a majority of the whole number of electors appointed, and if no person have a majority, then from the two highest numbers on the list, the Senate shall choose the Vice President; a quorum for the purpose shall consist of two thirds of the whole number of Senators, and a majority of the whole number shall be necessary to a choice. But no person constitutionally ineligible to the office of President shall be eligible to that of Vice President of the United States.

Amendment XIII

Passed by Congress February 1, 1865. Ratified December 18, 1865.

SECTION 1

Neither slavery nor involuntary servitude, except as punishment for crime whereof the party shall have been duly convicted, shall exist within the United States, or any place subject to their jurisdiction.

SECTION 2

Congress shall have power to enforce this article by appropriate legislation.

Amendment XIV

Passed by Congress June 16, 1866. Ratified July 23, 1868.

SECTION 1

All persons born or naturalized in the United States, and subject to the jurisdiction thereof, are citizens of the United States and of the State wherein they reside. No State shall make or enforce any law which shall abridge the privileges or immunities of citizens of the United States; nor shall any State deprive any person of life, liberty, or property, without due process of law; nor deny to any person within its jurisdiction the equal protection of the laws.

SECTION 2

Representatives shall be apportioned among the several States according to their respective numbers, counting the whole number of persons in each State, excluding Indians not taxed. But when the right to vote at any election for the choice of electors for President and Vice President of the United States, representatives in Congress, the executive and judicial officers of a State, or the members of the legislature thereof, is denied to any of the male inhabitants of such State, being twenty-one years of age, and citizens of the United States, or in any way abridged, except for participation in rebellion, or other crime, the basis of representation therein shall be reduced in the proportion which the number of such male citizens shall bear to the whole number of male citizens twenty-one years of age in such State.

SECTION 3

No person shall be a senator or representative in Congress, or elector of President and Vice President, or hold any office, civil or military, under the United States, or under any State, who having previously taken an oath, as a member of Congress, or as an officer of the United States, or as a member of any State legislature, or as an executive or judicial officer of any State, to support the Constitution of the United States, shall have engaged in insurrection or rebellion against the same, or given aid or comfort to the enemies thereof. But Congress may by a vote of two thirds of each House, remove such disability.

SECTION 4

The validity of the public debt of the United States, authorized by law, including debts incurred for payment of pensions and bounties for services in suppressing insurrection or rebellion, shall not be questioned. But neither the United States nor any State shall assume or pay any debt or obligation incurred in aid of insurrection or rebellion against the United States, or any claim for the loss or emancipation of any slave; but all such debts, obligations, and claims shall be held illegal and void.

SECTION 5

The Congress shall have power to enforce, by appropriate legislation, the provisions of this article.

Amendment XV

Passed by Congress February 27, 1869. Ratified March 30, 1870.

SECTION 1

The right of citizens of the United States to vote shall not be denied or abridged by the United States or by any State on account of race, color, or previous condition of servitude.

SECTION 2

The Congress shall have power to enforce this article by appropriate legislation.

Amendment XVI

Passed by Congress July 12, 1909. Ratified February 25, 1913.

The Congress shall have power to lay and collect taxes on incomes, from whatever source derived, without apportionment among the several States, and without regard to any census or enumeration.

Amendment XVII

Passed by Congress May 16, 1912. Ratified May 31, 1913.

The Senate of the United States shall be composed of two senators from each State, elected by the people thereof, for six years; and each senator shall have one vote. The electors in each State shall have the qualifications requisite for electors of the most numerous branch of the State legislature.

When vacancies happen in the representation of any State in the Senate, the executive authority of such State shall issue writs of election to fill such vacancies: Provided, That the legislature of any State may empower the executive thereof to make temporary appointments until the people fill the vacancies by election as the legislature may direct.

This amendment shall not be so construed as to affect the election or term of any senator chosen before it becomes valid as part of the Constitution.

Amendment XVIII

Passed by Congress December 17, 1917. Ratified January 29, 1919.

After one year from the ratification of this article, the manufacture, sale, or transportation of intoxicating liquors within, the importation thereof into, or the exportation thereof from the United States and all territory subject to the jurisdiction thereof for beverage purposes is hereby prohibited.

The Congress and the several States shall have concurrent power to enforce this article by appropriate legislation.

This article shall be inoperative unless it shall have been ratified as an amendment to the Constitution by the legislatures of the several States, as provided in the Constitution, within seven years from the date of the submission hereof to the States by Congress.

Amendment XIX

Passed by Congress June 5, 1919. Ratified August 26, 1920.

The right of citizens of the United States to vote shall not be denied or abridged by the United States or by any State on account of sex.

The Congress shall have power by appropriate legislation to enforce the provisions of this article.

Amendment XX

Passed by Congress March 3, 1932. Ratified January 23, 1933.

SECTION 1

The terms of the President and Vice President shall end at noon on the 20th day of January, and the terms of Senators and Representatives at noon on the 3d day of January, of the years in which such terms would have ended if this article had not been ratified; and the terms of their successors shall then begin.

SECTION 2

The Congress shall assemble at least once in every year, and such meeting shall begin at noon on the 3d day of January, unless they shall by law appoint a different day.

SECTION 3

If, at the time fixed for the beginning of the term of the President, the President-elect shall have died, the Vice President-elect shall become President. If a President shall not have been chosen before the time fixed for the beginning of his term, or if the President-elect shall have failed to qualify, then the Vice President-elect shall act as President until a President shall have qualified; and the Congress may by law provide for the case wherein neither a President-elect nor a Vice President-elect shall have qualified, declaring who shall then act as President, or the manner in which one who is to act shall be selected, and such person shall act accordingly until a President or Vice President shall have qualified.

SECTION 4

The Congress may by law provide for the case of the death of any of the persons from whom the House of Representatives may choose a President whenever the right of choice shall have devolved upon them, and for the case of the death of any of the persons from whom the Senate may choose a Vice President whenever the right of choice shall have devolved upon them.

SECTION 5

Sections 1 and 2 shall take effect on the 15th day of October following the ratification of this article.

SECTION 6

This article shall be inoperative unless it shall have been ratified as an amendment to the Constitution by the legislatures of three-fourths of the several States within seven years from the date of its submission.

Amendment XXI

Passed by Congress February 20, 1933. Ratified December 5, 1933.

SECTION 1

The eighteenth article of amendment to the Constitution of the United States is hereby repealed.

SECTION 2

The transportation or importation into any State, Territory, or possession of the United States for delivery or use therein of intoxicating liquors in violation of the laws thereof, is hereby prohibited.

SECTION 3

This article shall be inoperative unless it shall have been ratified as an amendment to the Constitution by conventions in the several States, as provided in the Constitution, within seven years from the date of the submission thereof to the States by the Congress.

Amendment XXII

Passed by Congress March 24, 1947. Ratified February 26, 1951.

SECTION 1

No person shall be elected to the office of the President more than twice, and no person who has held the office of President, or acted as President, for more than two years of a term to which some other person was elected President shall be elected to the office of the President more than once. But this article shall not apply to any person holding the office of President when this article was proposed by the Congress, and shall not prevent any person who may be holding the office of President, or acting as President, during the term within which this article becomes operative from holding the office of President or acting as President during the remainder of such term.

SECTION 2

This article shall be inoperative unless it shall have been ratified as an amendment to the Constitution by the legislatures of three-fourths of the several States within seven years from the date of its submission to the States by the Congress.

Amendment XXIII

Passed by Congress June 16, 1960. Ratified April 3, 1961.

SECTION 1

The District constituting the seat of Government of the United States shall appoint in such manner as the Congress may direct:

A number of electors of President and Vice President equal to the whole number of Senators and Representatives in Congress to which the District would be entitled if it were a State, but in no event more than the least populous State; they shall be in addition to those appointed by the States, but they shall be considered, for the purposes of the election of President and Vice President, to be electors appointed by a State; and they shall meet in the District and perform such duties as provided by the twelfth article of amendment.

SECTION 2

The Congress shall have power to enforce this article by appropriate legislation.

Amendment XXIV

Passed by Congress August 27, 1962. Ratified February 4, 1964.

SECTION 1

The right of citizens of the United States to vote in any primary or other election for President or Vice President, for electors for President or Vice President, or for Senator or Representative in Congress, shall not be denied or abridged by the United States or any State by reason of failure to pay any poll tax or other tax.

SECTION 2

The Congress shall have power to enforce this article by appropriate legislation.

Amendment XXV

Passed by Congress July 6, 1965. Ratified February 23, 1967.

SECTION 1

In case of the removal of the President from office or of his death or resignation, the Vice President shall become President.

SECTION 2

Whenever there is a vacancy in the office of the Vice President, the President shall nominate a Vice President who shall take office upon confirmation by a majority vote of both Houses of Congress.

SECTION 3

Whenever the President transmits to the President pro tempore of the Senate and the Speaker of the House of Representatives his written declaration that he is unable to discharge the powers and duties of his office, and until he transmits to them a written declaration to the contrary, such powers and duties shall be discharged by the Vice President as Acting President.

SECTION 4

Whenever the Vice President and a majority of either the principal officers of the executive departments or of such other body as Congress may by law provide, transmit to the President pro tempore of the Senate and the Speaker of the House of Representatives their written declaration that the President is unable to discharge the powers and duties of his office, the Vice President shall immediately assume the powers and duties of the office as Acting President.

Thereafter, when the President transmits to the President pro tempore of the Senate and the Speaker of the House of Representatives his written declaration that no inability exists, he shall resume the powers and duties of his office unless the Vice President and a majority of either the principal officers of the executive department or of such other body as Congress may by law provide, transmit within four days to the President pro tempore of the Senate and the Speaker of the House of Representatives their written declaration that the President is unable to discharge the powers and duties of his office. Thereupon Congress shall decide the issue, assembling within forty-eight hours for that purpose if not in session. If the Congress, within twenty-one days after receipt of the latter written declaration, or, if Congress is not in session, within twenty-one days after Congress is required to assemble, determines by two-thirds vote of both Houses that the President is unable to discharge the powers and duties of his office, the Vice President shall continue to discharge the same as Acting President; otherwise, the President shall resume the powers and duties of his office.

Amendment XXVI

Passed by Congress March 23, 1971. Ratified July 5, 1971.

SECTION 1

The right of citizens of the United States, who are eighteen years of age or older, to vote shall not be denied or abridged by the United States or by any State on account of age.

Amendment XXVII

Passed by Congress September 25, 1789. Ratified May 18, 1992.

No law, varying the compensation for the services of the Senators and Representatives, shall take effect, until an election of Representatives shall have intervened.

Appendix 3

Uniform Commercial Code (Selected Sections)

(Adopted in fifty-two jurisdictions; all fifty States, although Louisiana has adopted only Articles 1, 3, 4, 7, 8, and 9; the District of Columbia; and the Virgin Islands.)

Articles

1. General Provisions
2. Sales
   2A. Leases
3. Negotiable Instruments
4. Bank Deposits and Collections
   4A. Funds Transfers
5. Letters of Credit
6. Repealer of Article 6—Bulk Transfers and [Revised] Article 6—Bulk Sales
7. Warehouse Receipts, Bills of Lading and Other Documents of Title
8. Investment Securities
9. Secured Transactions

Article 1 General Provisions

Part 1 Short Title, Construction, Application and Subject Matter of the Act

* * * *

§1—103. SUPPLEMENTARY GENERAL PRINCIPLES OF LAW APPLICABLE

Unless displaced by the particular provisions of this Act, the principles of law and equity, including the law merchant and the law relative to capacity to contract, principal and agent, estoppel, fraud, misrepresentation, duress, coercion, mistake, bankruptcy, or other validating or invalidating cause shall supplement its provisions.

* * * *

§1—201. GENERAL DEFINITIONS

* * * *

(3) "Agreement" means the bargain of the parties in fact as found in their language or by implication from other circumstances including course of dealing or usage of trade or course of performance as provided in this Act (Sections 1—205 and 2—208). Whether an agreement has legal consequences is determined by the provisions of this Act, if applicable; otherwise by the law of contracts (Section 1—103). (Compare "Contract".)

(4) "Bank" means any person engaged in the business of banking.

(5) "Bearer" means the person in possession of an instrument, document of title, or certificated security payable to bearer or indorsed in blank.

(6) "Bill of lading" means a document evidencing the receipt of goods for shipment issued by a person engaged in the business of transporting or forwarding goods, and includes an airbill. "Airbill" means a document serving for air transportation as a bill of lading does for marine or rail transportation, and includes an air consignment note or air waybill.

* * * *

(9) "Buyer in ordinary course of business" means a person that buys goods in good faith, without knowledge that the sale violates the rights of another person in the goods, and in the ordinary course from a person, other than a pawnbroker, in the business of selling goods of that kind. A person buys goods in the ordinary course if the sale to the person comports with the usual or customary practices in the kind of business in which the seller is engaged or with the seller's own usual or customary practices. A person that sells oil, gas, or other minerals at the wellhead or minehead is a person in the business of selling goods of that kind. A buyer in ordinary course of business may buy for cash, by exchange of other property, or on secured or unsecured credit, and may acquire goods or documents of title under a pre-existing contract for sale. Only a buyer that takes possession of the goods or has a right to recover the goods from the seller under Article 2 may be a buyer in ordinary course of business. A person that acquires goods in a transfer in bulk or as security for or in total or partial satisfaction of a money debt is not a buyer in ordinary course of business.

(10) "Conspicuous": A term or clause is conspicuous when it is so written that a reasonable person against whom it is

to operate ought to have noticed it. A printed heading in capitals (as: NON-NEGOTIABLE BILL OF LADING) is conspicuous. Language in the body of a form is "conspicuous" if it is in larger or other contrasting type or color. But in a telegram any stated term is "conspicuous". Whether a term or clause is "conspicuous" or not is for decision by the court.

(11) "Contract" means the total legal obligation which results from the parties' agreement as affected by this Act and any other applicable rules of law. (Compare "Agreement".)

* * * *

(15) "Document of title" includes bill of lading, dock warrant, dock receipt, warehouse receipt or order for the delivery of goods, and also any other document which in the regular course of business or financing is treated as adequately evidencing that the person in possession of it is entitled to receive, hold and dispose of the document and the goods it covers. To be a document of title a document must purport to be issued by or addressed to a bailee and purport to cover goods in the bailee's possession which are either identified or are fungible portions of an identified mass.

* * * *

(17) "Fungible" with respect to goods or securities means goods or securities of which any unit is, by nature or usage of trade, the equivalent of any other like unit. Goods which are not fungible shall be deemed fungible for the purposes of this Act to the extent that under a particular agreement or document unlike units are treated as equivalents.

* * * *

(19) "Good faith" means honesty in fact in the conduct or transaction concerned.

(20) "Holder" with respect to a negotiable instrument, means the person in possession if the instrument is payable to bearer or, in the cases of an instrument payable to an identified person, if the identified person is in possession. "Holder" with respect to a document of title means the person in possession if the goods are deliverable to bearer or to the order of the person in possession.

* * * *

(23) A person is "insolvent" who either has ceased to pay his debts in the ordinary course of business or cannot pay his debts as they become due or is insolvent within the meaning of the federal bankruptcy law.

(24) "Money" means a medium of exchange authorized or adopted by a domestic or foreign government and includes a monetary unit of account established by an intergovernmental organization or by agreement between two or more nations.

(25) A person has "notice" of a fact when

(a) he has actual knowledge of it; or

(b) he has received a notice or notification of it; or

(c) from all the facts and circumstances known to him at the time in question he has reason to know that it exists.

* * * *

(37) "Security interest" means an interest in personal property or fixtures which secures payment or performance of an obligation. The term also includes any interest of a consignor and a buyer of accounts, chattel paper, a payment intangible, or a promissory note in a transaction that is subject to Article 9. The special property interest of a buyer of goods on identification of those goods to a contract for sale under Section 2—401 is not a "security interest", but a buyer may also acquire a "security interest" by complying with Article 9. Except as otherwise provided in Section 2—505, the right of a seller or lessor of goods under Article 2 or 2A to retain or acquire possession of the goods is not a "security interest", but a seller or lessor may also acquire a "security interest" by complying with Article 9. The retention or reservation of title by a seller of goods notwithstanding shipment or delivery to the buyer (Section 2—401) is limited in effect to a reservation of a "security interest".

Whether a transaction creates a lease or security interest is determined by the facts of each case; however, a transaction creates a security interest if the consideration the lessee is to pay the lessor for the right to possession and use of the goods is an obligation for the term of the lease not subject to termination by the lessee, and

(a) the original term of the lease is equal to or greater than the remaining economic life of the goods,

(b) the lessee is bound to renew the lease for the remaining economic life of the goods or is bound to become the owner of the goods,

(c) the lessee has an option to renew the lease for the remaining economic life of the goods for no additional consideration or nominal additional consideration upon compliance with the lease agreement, or

(d) the lessee has an option to become the owner of the goods for no additional consideration or nominal additional consideration upon compliance with the lease agreement.

A transaction does not create a security interest merely because it provides that

(a) the present value of the consideration the lessee is obligated to pay the lessor for the right to possession and use of the goods is substantially equal to or is greater than the fair market value of the goods at the time the lease is entered into,

(b) the lessee assumes risk of loss of the goods, or agrees to pay taxes, insurance, filing, recording, or registration fees, or service or maintenance costs with respect to the goods,

(c) the lessee has an option to renew the lease or to become the owner of the goods,

(d) the lessee has an option to renew the lease for a fixed rent that is equal to or greater than the reasonably predictable fair market rent for the use of the goods for the term of the renewal at the time the option is to be performed, or

(e) the lessee has an option to become the owner of the goods for a fixed price that is equal to or greater than the reasonably predictable fair market value of the goods at the time the option is to be performed.

* * * *

(39) "Signed" includes any symbol executed or adopted by a party with present intention to authenticate a writing.

(40) "Surety" includes guarantor.

* * * *

(43) "Unauthorized" signature means one made without actual, implied or apparent authority and includes a forgery.

(44) "Value". Except as otherwise provided with respect to negotiable instruments and bank collections (Sections 3—303, 4—210 and 4—211) a person gives "value" for rights if he acquires them

(a) in return for a binding commitment to extend credit or for the extension of immediately available credit whether or not drawn upon and whether or not a chargeback is provided for in the event of difficulties in collection; or

(b) as security for or in total or partial satisfaction of a pre-existing claim; or

(c) by accepting delivery pursuant to a preexisting contract for purchase; or

(d) generally, in return for any consideration sufficient to support a simple contract.

(45) "Warehouse receipt" means a receipt issued by a person engaged in the business of storing goods for hire.

(46) "Written" or "writing" includes printing, typewriting or any other intentional reduction to tangible form.

* * * *

§1—203. OBLIGATION OF GOOD FAITH

Every contract or duty within this Act imposes an obligation of good faith in its performance or enforcement.

§1—204. TIME; REASONABLE TIME; "SEASONABLY"

(1) Whenever this Act requires any action to be taken within a reasonable time, any time which is not manifestly unreasonable may be fixed by agreement.

(2) What is a reasonable time for taking any action depends on the nature, purpose and circumstances of such action.

(3) An action is taken "seasonably" when it is taken at or within the time agreed or if no time is agreed at or within a reasonable time.

§1—205. COURSE OF DEALING AND USAGE OF TRADE

(1) A course of dealing is a sequence of previous conduct between the parties to a particular transaction which is fairly to be regarded as establishing a common basis of understanding for interpreting their expressions and other conduct.

(2) A usage of trade is any practice or method of dealing having such regularity of observance in a place, vocation or trade as to justify an expectation that it will be observed with respect to the transaction in question. The existence and scope of such a usage are to be proved as facts. If it is established that such a usage is embodied in a written trade code or similar writing the interpretation of the writing is for the court.

(3) A course of dealing between parties and any usage of trade in the vocation or trade in which they are engaged or of which they are or should be aware give particular meaning to and supplement or qualify terms of an agreement.

(4) The express terms of an agreement and an applicable course of dealing or usage of trade shall be construed wherever reasonable as consistent with each other; but when such construction is unreasonable express terms control both course of dealing and usage of trade and course of dealing controls usage trade.

(5) An applicable usage of trade in the place where any part of performance is to occur shall be used in interpreting the agreement as to that part of the performance.

(6) Evidence of a relevant usage of trade offered by one party is not admissible unless and until he has given the other party such notice as the court finds sufficient to prevent unfair surprise to the latter.

* * * *

ARTICLE 2 SALES

§2—102. SCOPE; CERTAIN SECURITY AND OTHER TRANSACTIONS EXCLUDED FROM THIS ARTICLE

Unless the context otherwise requires, this Article applies to transactions in goods; it does not apply to any transaction which although in the form of an unconditional contract to sell or present sale is intended to operate only as a security transaction nor does this Article impair or repeal any statute regulating sales to consumers, farmers or other specified classes of buyers.

§2—103. DEFINITIONS AND INDEX OF DEFINITIONS

(1) In this Article unless the context otherwise requires

(a) "Buyer" means a person who buys or contracts to buy goods.

(b) "Good faith" in the case of a merchant means honesty in fact and the observance of reasonable commercial standards of fair dealing in the trade.

(c) "Receipt" of goods means taking physical possession of them.

(d) "Seller" means a person who sells or contracts to sell goods.

§2—104. DEFINITIONS: "MERCHANT"; "BETWEEN MERCHANTS"; "FINANCING AGENCY"

(1) "Merchant" means a person who deals in goods of the kind or otherwise by his occupation holds himself out as having knowledge or skill peculiar to the practices or goods involved in the transaction or to whom such knowledge or skill may be attributed by his employment of an agent or broker or other intermediary who by his occupation holds himself out as having such knowledge or skill.

§2—105. DEFINITIONS: TRANSFERABILITY; "GOODS"; "FUTURE" GOODS; "LOT"; "COMMERCIAL UNIT"

(1) "Goods" means all things (including specially manufactured goods) which are movable at the time of identification to the contract for sale other than the money in which the price is to be paid, investment securities (Article 8) and things in action. "Goods" also includes the unborn young of animals and growing crops and other identified things attached to realty as described in the section on goods to be severed from realty (Section 2—107).

(2) Goods must be both existing and identified before any interest in them can pass. Goods which are not both existing and identified are "future" goods. A purported present sale of future goods or of any interest therein operates as a contract to sell.

(3) There may be a sale of a part interest in existing identified goods.

(4) An undivided share in an identified bulk of fungible goods is sufficiently identified to be sold although the quantity of the bulk is not determined. Any agreed proportion of such a bulk or any quantity thereof agreed upon by number, weight or other measure may to the extent of the seller's interest in the bulk be sold to the buyer who then becomes an owner in common.

(5) "Lot" means a parcel or a single article which is the subject matter of a separate sale or delivery, whether or not it is sufficient to perform the contract.

(6) "Commercial unit" means such a unit of goods as by commercial usage is a single whole for purposes of sale and division of which materially impairs its character or value on the market or in use. A commercial unit may be a single article (as a machine) or a set of articles (as a suite of furniture or an assortment of sizes) or a quantity (as a bale, gross, or carload) or any other unit treated in use or in the relevant market as a single whole.

* * * *

§2—107. GOODS TO BE SEVERED FROM REALTY: RECORDING

(1) A contract for the sale of minerals or the like (including oil and gas) or a structure or its materials to be removed from realty is a contract for the sale of goods within this Article if they are to be severed by the seller but until severance a purported present sale thereof which is not effective as a transfer of an interest in land is effective only as a contract to sell.

(2) A contract for the sale apart from the land of growing crops or other things attached to realty and capable of severance without material harm thereto but not described in subsection (1) or of timber to be cut is a contract for the sale of goods within this Article whether the subject matter is to be severed by the buyer or by the seller even though it forms part of the realty at the time of contracting, and the parties can by identification effect a present sale before severance.

(3) The provisions of this section are subject to any third party rights provided by the law relating to realty records, and the contract for sale may be executed and recorded as a document transferring an interest in land and shall then constitute notice to third parties of the buyer's rights under the contract for sale.

§2—201. FORMAL REQUIREMENTS; STATUTE OF FRAUDS

(1) Except as otherwise provided in this section a contract for the sale of goods for the price of $500 [some states have increased this amount to $5,000] or more is not enforceable by way of action or defense unless there is some writing sufficient to indicate that a contract for sale has been made between the parties and signed by the party against whom enforcement is sought or by his authorized agent or broker. A writing is not insufficient because it omits or incorrectly states a term agreed upon but the contract is not enforceable under this paragraph beyond the quantity of goods shown in such writing.

(2) Between merchants if within a reasonable time a writing in confirmation of the contract and sufficient against the sender is received and the party receiving it has reason to know its contents, it satisfies the requirements of subsection (1) against such party unless written notice of objection to its contents is given within ten days after it is received.

(3) A contract which does not satisfy the requirements of subsection (1) but which is valid in other respects is enforceable

(a) if the goods are to be specially manufactured for the buyer and are not suitable for sale to others in the ordinary course of the seller's business and the seller, before notice of repudiation is received and under circumstances which reasonably indicate that the goods are for the buyer, has made either a substantial beginning of their manufacture or commitments for their procurement; or

(b) if the party against whom enforcement is sought admits in his pleading, testimony or otherwise in court that a contract for sale was made, but the contract is not enforceable under this provision beyond the quantity of goods admitted; or

(c) with respect to goods for which payment has been made and accepted or which have been received and accepted (Sec. 2—606).

§2—202. FINAL WRITTEN EXPRESSION: PAROL OR EXTRINSIC EVIDENCE

Terms with respect to which the confirmatory memoranda of the parties agree or which are otherwise set forth in a writing intended by the parties as a final expression of their agreement with respect to such terms as are included therein may not be contradicted by evidence of any prior agreement or of a contemporaneous oral agreement but may be explained or supplemented

(a) by course of dealing or usage of trade (Section 1—205) or by course of performance (Section 2—208); and

(b) by evidence of consistent additional terms unless the court finds the writing to have been intended also as a complete and exclusive statement of the terms of the agreement.

* * * *

§2—204. FORMATION IN GENERAL

(1) A contract for sale of goods may be made in any manner sufficient to show agreement, including conduct by both parties which recognizes the existence of such a contract.

(2) An agreement sufficient to constitute a contract for sale may be found even though the moment of its making is undetermined.

(3) Even though one or more terms are left open a contract for sale does not fail for indefiniteness if the parties have intended to make a contract and there is a reasonably certain basis for giving an appropriate remedy.

§2—205. FIRM OFFERS

An offer by a merchant to buy or sell goods in a signed writing which by its terms gives assurance that it will be held open is not revocable, for lack of consideration, during the time stated or if no time is stated for a reasonable time, but in no event may such period of irrevocability exceed three months; but any such term of assurance on a form supplied by the offeree must be separately signed by the offeror.

§2—206. OFFER AND ACCEPTANCE IN FORMATION OF CONTRACT

(1) Unless other unambiguously indicated by the language or circumstances

(a) an offer to make a contract shall be construed as inviting acceptance in any manner and by any medium reasonable in the circumstances;

(b) an order or other offer to buy goods for prompt or current shipment shall be construed as inviting acceptance either by a prompt promise to ship or by the prompt or current shipment of conforming or non-conforming goods, but such a shipment of non-conforming goods does not constitute an acceptance if the seller seasonably notifies the buyer that the shipment is offered only as an accommodation to the buyer.

(2) Where the beginning of a requested performance is a reasonable mode of acceptance an offeror who is not notified of acceptance within a reasonable time may treat the offer as having lapsed before acceptance.

§2—207. ADDITIONAL TERMS IN ACCEPTANCE OR CONFIRMATION

(1) A definite and seasonable expression of acceptance or a written confirmation which is sent within a reasonable time operates as an acceptance even though it states terms additional to or different from those offered or agreed upon, unless acceptance is expressly made conditional on assent to the additional or different terms.

(2) The additional terms are to be construed as proposals for addition to the contract. Between merchants such terms become part of the contract unless:

(a) the offer expressly limits acceptance to the terms of the offer;

(b) they materially alter it; or

(c) notification of objection to them has already been given or is given within a reasonable time after notice of them is received.

(3) Conduct by both parties which recognizes the existence of a contract is sufficient to establish a contract for sale although the writings of the parties do not otherwise establish a contract. In such case the terms of the particular contract consist of those terms on which the writings of the parties agree, together with any supplementary terms incorporated under any other provisions of this Act.

§2—208. COURSE OF PERFORMANCE OR PRACTICAL CONSTRUCTION

(1) Where the contract for sale involves repeated occasions for performance by either party with knowledge of the nature of the performance and opportunity for objection to it by the other, any course of performance accepted or acquiesced in without objection shall be relevant to determine the meaning of the agreement.

(2) The express terms of the agreement and any such course of performance, as well as any course of dealing and usage of trade, shall be construed whenever reasonable as consistent with each other; but when such construction is unreasonable, express terms shall control course of

performance and course of performance shall control both course of dealing and usage of trade (Section 1—205).

(3) Subject to the provisions of the next section on modification and waiver, such course of performance shall be relevant to show a waiver or modification of any term inconsistent with such course of performance.

§2—209. MODIFICATION, RESCISSION AND WAIVER

(1) An agreement modifying a contract within this Article needs no consideration to be binding.

(2) A signed agreement which excludes modification or rescission except by a signed writing cannot be otherwise modified or rescinded, but except as between merchants such a requirement on a form supplied by the merchant must be separately signed by the other party.

(3) The requirements of the statute of frauds section of this Article (Section 2—201) must be satisfied if the contract as modified is within its provisions.

(4) Although an attempt at modification or rescission does not satisfy the requirements of subsection (2) or (3) it can operate as a waiver.

(5) A party who has made a waiver affecting an executory portion of the contract may retract the waiver by reasonable notification received by the other party that strict performance will be required of any term waived, unless the retraction would be unjust in view of a material change of position in reliance on the waiver.

§2—210. DELEGATION OF PERFORMANCE; ASSIGNMENT OF RIGHTS

* * * *

(5) An assignment of "the contract" or of "all my rights under the contract" or an assignment in similar general terms is an assignment of rights and unless the language or the circumstances (as in an assignment for security) indicate the contrary, it is a delegation of performance of the duties of the assignor and its acceptance by the assignee constitutes a promise by him to perform those duties. This promise is enforceable by either the assignor or the other party to the original contract.

§2—301. GENERAL OBLIGATIONS OF PARTIES

The obligation of the seller is to transfer and deliver and that of the buyer is to accept and pay in accordance with the contract.

§2—302. UNCONSCIONABLE CONTRACT OR CLAUSE

(1) If the court as a matter of law finds the contract or any clause of the contract to have been unconscionable at the time it was made the court may refuse to enforce the contract, or it may enforce the remainder of the contract without the unconscionable clause, or it may so limit the application of any unconscionable clause as to avoid any unconscionable result.

(2) When it is claimed or appears to the court that the contract or any clause thereof may be unconscionable the parties shall be afforded a reasonable opportunity to present evidence as to its commercial setting, purpose and effect to aid the court in making the determination.

§2—303. ALLOCATIONS OR DIVISION OF RISKS

Where this Article allocates a risk or a burden as between the parties "unless otherwise agreed", the agreement may not only shift the allocation but may also divide the risk or burden.

§2—304. PRICE PAYABLE IN MONEY, GOODS, REALTY, OR OTHERWISE

(1) The price can be made payable in money or otherwise. If it is payable in whole or in part in goods each party is a seller of the goods which he is to transfer.

(2) Even though all or part of the price is payable in an interest in realty the transfer of the goods and the seller's obligations with reference to them are subject to this Article, but not the transfer of the interest in realty or the transferor's obligations in connection therewith.

§2—305. OPEN PRICE TERM

(1) The parties if they so intend can conclude a contract for sale even though the price is not settled. In such a case the price is a reasonable price at the time for delivery if

(a) nothing is said as to price; or

(b) the price is left to be agreed by the parties and they fail to agree; or

(c) the price is to be fixed in terms of some agreed market or other standard as set or recorded by a third person or agency and it is not so set or recorded.

(2) A price to be fixed by the seller or by the buyer means a price for him to fix in good faith.

(3) When a price left to be fixed otherwise than by agreement of the parties fails to be fixed through fault of one party the other may at his option treat the contract as cancelled or himself fix a reasonable price.

(4) Where, however, the parties intend not to be bound unless the price be fixed or agreed and it is not fixed or agreed there is no contract. In such a case the buyer must return any goods already received or if unable so to do must pay their reasonable value at the time of delivery and the seller must return any portion of the price paid on account.

§2—306. OUTPUT, REQUIREMENTS AND EXCLUSIVE DEALINGS

(1) A term which measures the quantity by the output of the seller or the requirements of the buyer means such actual output or requirements as may occur in good faith, except that no quantity unreasonably disproportionate to any stated estimate or in the absence of a stated estimate to

any normal or otherwise comparable prior output or requirements may be tendered or demanded.

(2) A lawful agreement by either the seller or the buyer for exclusive dealing in the kind of goods concerned imposes unless otherwise agreed an obligation by the seller to use best efforts to supply the goods and by the buyer to use best efforts to promote their sale.

§2—307. DELIVERY IN SINGLE LOT OR SEVERAL LOTS

Unless otherwise agreed all goods called for by a contract for sale must be tendered in a single delivery and payment is due only on such tender but where the circumstances give either party the right to make or demand delivery in lots the price if it can be apportioned may be demanded for each lot.

§2—308. ABSENCE OF SPECIFIED PLACE FOR DELIVERY

Unless otherwise agreed

(a) the place for delivery of goods is the seller's place of business or if he has none his residence; but

(b) in a contract for sale of identified goods which to the knowledge of the parties at the time of contracting are in some other place, that place is the place for their delivery; and

(c) documents of title may be delivered through customary banking channels.

§2—309. ABSENCE OF SPECIFIC TIME PROVISIONS; NOTICE OF TERMINATION

(1) The time for shipment or delivery or any other action under a contract if not provided in this Article or agreed upon shall be a reasonable time.

§2—310. OPEN TIME FOR PAYMENT OR RUNNING OF CREDIT; AUTHORITY TO SHIP UNDER RESERVATION

Unless otherwise agreed

(a) payment is due at the time and place at which the buyer is to receive the goods even though the place of shipment is the place of delivery; and

(b) if the seller is authorized to send the goods he may ship them under reservation, and may tender the documents of title, but the buyer may inspect the goods after their arrival before payment is due unless such inspection is inconsistent with the terms of the contract (Section 2—513).

* * * *

§2—312. WARRANTY OF TITLE AND AGAINST INFRINGEMENT; BUYER'S OBLIGATION AGAINST INFRINGEMENT

(1) Subject to subsection (2) there is in a contract for sale a warranty by the seller that

(a) the title conveyed shall be good, and its transfer rightful; and

(b) the goods shall be delivered free from any security interest or other lien or encumbrance of which the buyer at the time of contracting has no knowledge.

(2) A warranty under subsection (1) will be excluded or modified only by specific language or by circumstances which give the buyer reason to know that the person selling does not claim title in himself or that he is purporting to sell only such right or title as he or a third person may have.

(3) Unless otherwise agreed a seller who is a merchant regularly dealing in goods of the kind warrants that the goods shall be delivered free of the rightful claim of any third person by way of infringement or the like but a buyer who furnishes specifications to the seller must hold the seller harmless against any such claim which arises out of compliance with the specifications.

§2—313. EXPRESS WARRANTIES BY AFFIRMATION, PROMISE, DESCRIPTION, SAMPLE

(1) Express warranties by the seller are created as follows:

(a) Any affirmation of fact or promise made by the seller to the buyer which relates to the goods and becomes part of the basis of the bargain creates an express warranty that the goods shall conform to the affirmation or promise.

(b) Any description of the goods which is made part of the basis of the bargain creates an express warranty that the goods shall conform to the description.

(c) Any sample or model which is made part of the basis of the bargain creates an express warranty that the whole of the goods shall conform to the sample or model.

(2) It is not necessary to the creation of an express warranty that the seller use formal words such as "warrant" or "guarantee" or that he have a specific intention to make a warranty, but an affirmation merely of the value of the goods or a statement purporting to be merely the seller's opinion or commendation of the goods does not create a warranty.

§2—314. IMPLIED WARRANTY: MERCHANTABILITY; USAGE OF TRADE

(1) Unless excluded or modified (Section 2—316), a warranty that the goods shall be merchantable is implied in a contract for their sale if the seller is a merchant with respect to goods of that kind. Under this section the serving for value of food or drink to be consumed either on the premises or elsewhere is a sale.

(2) Goods to be merchantable must be at least such as

(a) pass without objection in the trade under the contract description; and

(b) in the case of fungible goods, are of fair average quality within the description; and

(c) are fit for the ordinary purposes for which such goods are used; and

(d) run, within the variations permitted by the agreement, of even kind, quality and quantity within each unit and among all units involved; and

(e) are adequately contained, packaged, and labeled as the agreement may require; and

(f) conform to the promises or affirmations of fact made on the container or label if any.

(3) Unless excluded or modified (Section 2—316) other implied warranties may arise from course of dealing or usage of trade.

§2—315. IMPLIED WARRANTY: FITNESS FOR PARTICULAR PURPOSE

Where the seller at the time of contracting has reason to know any particular purpose for which the goods are required and that the buyer is relying on the seller's skill or judgment to select or furnish suitable goods, there is unless excluded or modified under the next section an implied warranty that the goods shall be fit for such purpose.

§2—316. EXCLUSION OR MODIFICATION OF WARRANTIES

(1) Words or conduct relevant to the creation of an express warranty and words or conduct tending to negate or limit warranty shall be construed wherever reasonable as consistent with each other; but subject to the provisions of this Article on parol or extrinsic evidence (Section 2—202) negation or limitation is inoperative to the extent that such construction is unreasonable.

(2) Subject to subsection (3), to exclude or modify the implied warranty of merchantability or any part of it the language must mention merchantability and in case of a writing must be conspicuous, and to exclude or modify any implied warranty of fitness the exclusion must be by a writing and conspicuous. Language to exclude all implied warranties of fitness is sufficient if it states, for example, that "There are no warranties which extend beyond the description on the face hereof."

(3) Notwithstanding subsection (2)

(a) unless the circumstances indicate otherwise, all implied warranties are excluded by expressions like "as is", "with all faults" or other language which in common understanding calls the buyer's attention to the exclusion of warranties and makes plain that there is no implied warranty; and

(b) when the buyer before entering into the contract has examined the goods or the sample or model as fully as he desired or has refused to examine the goods there is no implied warranty with regard to defects which an examination ought in the circumstances to have revealed to him; and

(c) an implied warranty can also be excluded or modified by course of dealing or course of performance or usage of trade.

(4) Remedies for breach of warranty can be limited in accordance with the provisions of this Article on liquidation or limitation of damages and on contractual modification of remedy (Sections 2—718 and 2—719).

§2—317. CUMULATION AND CONFLICT OF WARRANTIES EXPRESS OR IMPLIED

Warranties whether express or implied shall be construed as consistent with each other and as cumulative, but if such construction is unreasonable the intention of the parties shall determine which warranty is dominant. In ascertaining that intention the following rules apply:

(a) Exact or technical specifications displace an inconsistent sample or model or general language of description.

(b) A sample from an existing bulk displaces inconsistent general language of description.

(c) Express warranties displace inconsistent implied warranties other than an implied warranty of fitness for a particular purpose.

§2—318. THIRD PARTY BENEFICIARIES OF WARRANTIES EXPRESS OR IMPLIED

Note: If this Act is introduced in the Congress of the United States this section should be omitted. (States to select one alternative.)

Alternative A

A seller's warranty whether express or implied extends to any natural person who is in the family or household of his buyer or who is a guest in his home if it is reasonable to expect that such person may use, consume or be affected by the goods and who is injured in person by breach of the warranty. A seller may not exclude or limit the operation of this section.

Alternative B

A seller's warranty whether express or implied extends to any natural person who may reasonably be expected to use, consume or be affected by the goods and who is injured in person by breach of the warranty. A seller may not exclude or limit the operation of this section.

Alternative C

A seller's warranty whether express or implied extends to any person who may reasonably be expected to use, consume or be affected by the goods and who is injured by breach of the warranty. A seller may not exclude or limit the operation of this section with respect to injury to the person of an individual to whom the warranty extends.

§2—319. F.O.B. AND F.A.S. TERMS

(1) Unless otherwise agreed the term F.O.B. (which means "free on board") at a named place, even though used only in connection with the stated price, is a delivery term under which

(a) when the term is F.O.B. the place of shipment, the seller must at that place ship the goods in the manner provided in this Article (Section 2—504) and bear the expense and risk of putting them into the possession of the carrier; or

(b) when the term is F.O.B. the place of destination, the seller must at his own expense and risk transport the goods to that place and there tender delivery of them in the manner provided in this Article (Section 2—503);

(c) when under either (a) or (b) the term is also F.O.B. vessel, car or other vehicle, the seller must in addition at his own expense and risk load the goods on board. If the term is F.O.B. vessel the buyer must name the vessel and in an appropriate case the seller must comply with the provisions of this Article on the form of bill of lading (Section 2—323).

(2) Unless otherwise agreed the term F.A.S. vessel (which means "free alongside") at a named port, even though used only in connection with the stated price, is a delivery term under which the seller must

(a) at his own expense and risk deliver the goods alongside the vessel in the manner usual in that port or on a dock designated and provided by the buyer; and

(b) obtain and tender a receipt for the goods in exchange for which the carrier is under a duty to issue a bill of lading.

(3) Unless otherwise agreed in any case falling within subsection (1)(a) or (c) or subsection (2) the buyer must seasonably give any needed instructions for making delivery, including when the term is F.A.S. or F.O.B. the loading berth of the vessel and in an appropriate case its name and sailing date. The seller may treat the failure of needed instructions as a failure of cooperation under this Article (Section 2—311). He may also at his option move the goods in any reasonable manner preparatory to delivery or shipment.

(4) Under the term F.O.B. vessel or F.A.S. unless otherwise agreed the buyer must make payment against tender of the required documents and the seller may not tender nor the buyer demand delivery of the goods in substitution for the documents.

§2—320. C.I.F. AND C. & F. TERMS

(1) The term C.I.F. means that the price includes in a lump sum the cost of the goods and the insurance and freight to the named destination. The term C. & F. or C.F. means that the price so includes cost and freight to the named destination.

(2) Unless otherwise agreed and even though used only in connection with the stated price and destination, the term C.I.F. destination or its equivalent requires the seller at his own expense and risk to

(a) put the goods into the possession of a carrier at the port for shipment and obtain a negotiable bill or bills of lading covering the entire transportation to the named destination; and

(b) load the goods and obtain a receipt from the carrier (which may be contained in the bill of lading) showing that the freight has been paid or provided for; and

(c) obtain a policy or certificate of insurance, including any war risk insurance, of a kind and on terms then current at the port of shipment in the usual amount, in the currency of the contract, shown to cover the same goods covered by the bill of lading and providing for payment of loss to the order of the buyer or for the account of whom it may concern; but the seller may add to the price the amount of the premium for any such war risk insurance; and

(d) prepare an invoice of the goods and procure any other documents required to effect shipment or to comply with the contract; and

(e) forward and tender with commercial promptness all the documents in due form and with any indorsement necessary to perfect the buyer's rights.

(3) Unless otherwise agreed the term C. & F. or its equivalent has the same effect and imposes upon the seller the same obligations and risks as a C.I.F. term except the obligation as to insurance.

(4) Under the term C.I.F. or C. & F. unless otherwise agreed the buyer must make payment against tender of the required documents and the seller may not tender nor the buyer demand delivery of the goods in substitution for the documents.

* * * *

§2—322. DELIVERY "EX-SHIP"

(1) Unless otherwise agreed a term for delivery of goods "ex-ship" (which means from the carrying vessel) or in equivalent language is not restricted to a particular ship and requires delivery from a ship which has reached a place at the named port of destination where goods of the kind are usually discharged.

(2) Under such a term unless otherwise agreed

(a) the seller must discharge all liens arising out of the carriage and furnish the buyer with a direction which puts the carrier under a duty to deliver the goods; and

(b) the risk of loss does not pass to the buyer until the goods leave the ship's tackle or are otherwise properly unloaded.

* * * *

§2—324. "NO ARRIVAL, NO SALE" TERM

Under a term "no arrival, no sale" or terms of like meaning, unless otherwise agreed,

(a) the seller must properly ship conforming goods and if they arrive by any means he must tender them on arrival but he assumes no obligation that the goods will arrive unless he has caused the non-arrival; and

(b) where without fault of the seller the goods are in part lost or have so deteriorated as no longer to conform to the contract or arrive after the contract time, the buyer may proceed as if there had been casualty to identified goods (Section 2—613).

* * * *

§2—326. SALE ON APPROVAL AND SALE OR RETURN; RIGHTS OF CREDITORS

(1) Unless otherwise agreed, if delivered goods may be returned by the buyer even though they conform to the contract, the transaction is

(a) a "sale on approval" if the goods are delivered primarily for use, and

(b) a "sale or return" if the goods are delivered primarily for resale.

(2) Goods held on approval are not subject to the claims of the buyer's creditors until acceptance; goods held on sale or return are subject to such claims while in the buyer's possession.

(3) Any "or return" term of a contract for sale is to be treated as a separate contract for sale within the statute of frauds section of this Article (Section 2—201) and as contradicting the sale aspect of the contract within the provisions of this Article or on parol or extrinsic evidence (Section 2—202).

§2—327. SPECIAL INCIDENTS OF SALE ON APPROVAL AND SALE OR RETURN

(1) Under a sale on approval unless otherwise agreed

(a) although the goods are identified to the contract the risk of loss and the title do not pass to the buyer until acceptance; and

(b) use of the goods consistent with the purpose of trial is not acceptance but failure seasonably to notify the seller of election to return the goods is acceptance, and if the goods conform to the contract acceptance of any part is acceptance of the whole; and

(c) after due notification of election to return, the return is at the seller's risk and expense but a merchant buyer must follow any reasonable instructions.

(2) Under a sale or return unless otherwise agreed

(a) the option to return extends to the whole or any commercial unit of the goods while in substantially their original condition, but must be exercised seasonably; and

(b) the return is at the buyer's risk and expense.

§2—328. SALE BY AUCTION

(1) In a sale by auction if goods are put up in lots each lot is the subject of a separate sale.

(2) A sale by auction is complete when the auctioneer so announces by the fall of the hammer or in other customary manner. Where a bid is made while the hammer is falling in acceptance of a prior bid the auctioneer may in his discretion reopen the bidding or declare the goods sold under the bid on which the hammer was falling.

(3) Such a sale is with reserve unless the goods are in explicit terms put up without reserve. In an auction with reserve the auctioneer may withdraw the goods at any time until he announces completion of the sale. In an auction without reserve, after the auctioneer calls for bids on an article or lot, that article or lot cannot be withdrawn unless no bid is made within a reasonable time. In either case a bidder may retract his bid until the auctioneer's announcement of completion of the sale, but a bidder's retraction does not revive any previous bid.

(4) If the auctioneer knowingly receives a bid on the seller's behalf or the seller makes or procures such a bid, and notice has not been given that liberty for such bidding is reserved, the buyer may at his option avoid the sale or take the goods at the price of the last good faith bid prior to the completion of the sale. This subsection shall not apply to any bid at a forced sale.

§2—401. PASSING OF TITLE; RESERVATION FOR SECURITY; LIMITED APPLICATION OF THIS SECTION

Each provision of this Article with regard to the rights, obligations and remedies of the seller, the buyer, purchasers or other third parties applies irrespective of title to the goods except where the provision refers to such title. Insofar as situations are not covered by the other provisions of this Article and matters concerning title became material the following rules apply:

(1) Title to goods cannot pass under a contract for sale prior to their identification to the contract (Section 2—501), and unless otherwise explicitly agreed the buyer acquires by their identification a special property as limited by this Act. Any retention or reservation by the seller of the title (property) in goods shipped or delivered to the buyer is limited in effect to a reservation of a security interest. Subject to these provisions and to the provisions of the Article on Secured Transactions (Article 9), title to goods passes from the seller to the buyer in any manner and on any conditions explicitly agreed on by the parties.

(2) Unless otherwise explicitly agreed title passes to the buyer at the time and place at which the seller completes his performance with reference to the physical delivery of the goods, despite any reservation of a security interest and even though a document of title is to be delivered at a different time or place; and in particular and despite any reservation of a security interest by the bill of lading

(a) if the contract requires or authorizes the seller to send the goods to the buyer but does not require him to deliver them at destination, title passes to the buyer at the time and place of shipment; but

(b) if the contract requires delivery at destination, title passes on tender there.

(3) Unless otherwise explicitly agreed where delivery is to be made without moving the goods,

(a) if the seller is to deliver a document of title, title passes at the time when and the place where he delivers such documents; or

(b) if the goods are at the time of contracting already identified and no documents are to be delivered, title passes at the time and place of contracting.

(4) A rejection or other refusal by the buyer to receive or retain the goods, whether or not justified, or a justified revocation of acceptance revests title to the goods in the seller. Such revesting occurs by operation of law and is not a "sale".

* * * *

§2—403. POWER TO TRANSFER; GOOD FAITH PURCHASE OF GOODS; "ENTRUSTING"

(1) A purchaser of goods acquires all title which his transferor had or had power to transfer except that a purchaser of a limited interest acquires rights only to the extent of the interest purchased. A person with voidable title has power to transfer a good title to a good faith purchaser for value. When goods have been delivered under a transaction of purchase the purchaser has such power even though

(a) the transferor was deceived as to the identity of the purchaser, or

(b) the delivery was in exchange for a check which is later dishonored, or

(c) it was agreed that the transaction was to be a "cash sale", or

(d) the delivery was procured through fraud punishable as larcenous under the criminal law.

(2) Any entrusting of possession of goods to a merchant who deals in goods of that kind gives him power to transfer all rights of the entruster to a buyer in ordinary course of business.

(3) "Entrusting" includes any delivery and any acquiescence in retention of possession regardless of any condition expressed between the parties to the delivery or acquiescence and regardless of whether the procurement of the entrusting or the possessor's disposition of the goods have been such as to be larcenous under the criminal law.

(4) The rights of other purchasers of goods and of lien creditors are governed by the Articles on Secured Transactions (Article 9), Bulk Transfers (Article 6) and Documents of Title (Article 7).

§2—501. INSURABLE INTEREST IN GOODS; MANNER OF IDENTIFICATION OF GOODS

(1) The buyer obtains a special property and an insurable interest in goods by identification of existing goods as goods to which the contract refers even though the goods so identified are non-conforming and he has an option to return or reject them. Such identification can be made at any time and in any manner explicitly agreed to by the parties. In the absence of explicit agreement identification occurs

(a) when the contract is made if it is for the sale of goods already existing and identified;

(b) if the contract is for the sale of future goods other than those described in paragraph (c), when goods are shipped, marked or otherwise designated by the seller as goods to which the contract refers;

(c) when the crops are planted or otherwise become growing crops or the young are conceived if the contract is for the sale of unborn young to be born within twelve months after contracting or for the sale of crops to be harvested within twelve months or the next normal harvest season after contracting whichever is longer.

(2) The seller retains an insurable interest in goods so long as title to or any security interest in the goods remains in him and where the identification is by the seller alone he may until default or insolvency or notification to the buyer that the identification is final substitute other goods for those identified.

(3) Nothing in this section impairs any insurable interest recognized under any other statute or rule of law.

§2—502. BUYER'S RIGHT TO GOODS ON SELLER'S INSOLVENCY

(1) Subject to subsections (2) and (3) and even though the goods have not been shipped a buyer who has paid a part or all of the price of goods in which he has a special property under the provisions of the immediately preceding section may on making and keeping good a tender of any unpaid portion of their price recover them from the seller if:

(a) in the case of goods bought for personal, family, or household purposes, the seller repudiates or fails to deliver as required by the contract; or

(b) in all cases, the seller becomes insolvent within ten days after receipt of the first installment on their price.

(2) The buyer's right to recover the goods under subsection (1)(a) vests upon acquisition of a special property, even if the seller had not then repudiated or failed to deliver.

(3) If the identification creating his special property has been made by the buyer he acquires the right to recover the goods only if they conform to the contract for sale.

As amended in 1999.

§2—503. MANNER OF SELLER'S TENDER OF DELIVERY

(1) Tender of delivery requires that the seller put and hold conforming goods at the buyer's disposition and give the buyer any notification reasonably necessary to enable him to take delivery. The manner, time and place for tender are determined by the agreement and this Article, and in particular

(a) tender must be at a reasonable hour, and if it is of goods they must be kept available for the period reasonably necessary to enable the buyer to take possession; but

(b) unless otherwise agreed the buyer must furnish facilities reasonably suited to the receipt of the goods.

(2) Where the case is within the next section respecting shipment tender requires that the seller comply with its provisions.

(3) Where the seller is required to deliver at a particular destination tender requires that he comply with subsection (1) and also in any appropriate case tender documents as described in subsections (4) and (5) of this section.

(4) Where goods are in the possession of a bailee and are to be delivered without being moved

(a) tender requires that the seller either tender a negotiable document of title covering such goods or procure acknowledgment by the bailee of the buyer's right to possession of the goods; but

(b) tender to the buyer of a non-negotiable document of title or of a written direction to the bailee to deliver is sufficient tender unless the buyer seasonably objects, and receipt by the bailee of notification of the buyer's rights fixes those rights as against the bailee and all third persons; but risk of loss of the goods and of any failure by the bailee to honor the non-negotiable document of title or to obey the direction remains on the seller until the buyer has had a reasonable time to present the document or direction, and a refusal by the bailee to honor the document or to obey the direction defeats the tender.

(5) Where the contract requires the seller to deliver documents

(a) he must tender all such documents in correct form, except as provided in this Article with respect to bills of lading in a set (subsection (2) of Section 2—323); and

(b) tender through customary banking channels is sufficient and dishonor of a draft accompanying the documents constitutes non-acceptance or rejection.

§2—504. SHIPMENT BY SELLER

Where the seller is required or authorized to send the goods to the buyer and the contract does not require him to deliver them at a particular destination, then unless otherwise agreed he must

(a) put the goods in the possession of such a carrier and make such a contract for their transportation as may be reasonable having regard to the nature of the goods and other circumstances of the case; and

(b) obtain and promptly deliver or tender in due form any document necessary to enable the buyer to obtain possession of the goods or otherwise required by the agreement or by usage of trade; and

(c) promptly notify the buyer of the shipment. Failure to notify the buyer under paragraph (c) or to make a proper contract under paragraph (a) is a ground for rejection only if material delay or loss ensues.

* * * *

§2—506. RIGHTS OF FINANCING AGENCY

(1) A financing agency by paying or purchasing for value a draft which relates to a shipment of goods acquires to the extent of the payment or purchase and in addition to its own rights under the draft and any document of title securing it any rights of the shipper in the goods including the right to stop delivery and the shipper's right to have the draft honored by the buyer.

(2) The right to reimbursement of a financing agency which has in good faith honored or purchased the draft under commitment to or authority from the buyer is not impaired by subsequent discovery of defects with reference to any relevant document which was apparently regular on its face.

§2—507. EFFECT OF SELLER'S TENDER; DELIVERY ON CONDITION

(1) Tender of delivery is a condition to the buyer's duty to accept the goods and, unless otherwise agreed, to his duty to pay for them. Tender entitles the seller to acceptance of the goods and to payment according to the contract.

(2) Where payment is due and demanded on the delivery to the buyer of goods or documents of title, his right as against the seller to retain or dispose of them is conditional upon his making the payment due.

§2—508. CURE BY SELLER OF IMPROPER TENDER OR DELIVERY; REPLACEMENT

(1) Where any tender or delivery by the seller is rejected because non-conforming and the time for performance has

not yet expired, the seller may seasonably notify the buyer of his intention to cure and may then within the contract time make a conforming delivery.

(2) Where the buyer rejects a non-conforming tender which the seller had reasonable grounds to believe would be acceptable with or without money allowance the seller may if he seasonably notifies the buyer have a further reasonable time to substitute a conforming tender.

§2—509. RISK OF LOSS IN THE ABSENCE OF BREACH

(1) Where the contract requires or authorizes the seller to ship the goods by carrier

(a) if it does not require him to deliver them at a particular destination, the risk of loss passes to the buyer when the goods are duly delivered to the carrier even though the shipment is under reservation (Section 2—505); but

(b) if it does require him to deliver them at a particular destination and the goods are there duly tendered while in the possession of the carrier, the risk of loss passes to the buyer when the goods are there duly so tendered as to enable the buyer to take delivery.

(2) Where the goods are held by a bailee to be delivered without being moved, the risk of loss passes to the buyer

(a) on his receipt of a negotiable document of title covering the goods; or

(b) on acknowledgment by the bailee of the buyer's right to possession of the goods; or

(c) after his receipt of a non-negotiable document of title or other written direction to deliver, as provided in subsection (4)(b) of Section 2—503.

(3) In any case not within subsection (1) or (2), the risk of loss passes to the buyer on his receipt of the goods if the seller is a merchant; otherwise the risk passes to the buyer on tender of delivery.

(4) The provisions of this section are subject to contrary agreement of the parties and to the provisions of this Article on sale on approval (Section 2—327) and on effect of breach on risk of loss (Section 2—510).

§2—510. EFFECT OF BREACH ON RISK OF LOSS

(1) Where a tender or delivery of goods so fails to conform to the contract as to give a right of rejection the risk of their loss remains on the seller until cure or acceptance.

(2) Where the buyer rightfully revokes acceptance he may to the extent of any deficiency in his effective insurance coverage treat the risk of loss as having rested on the seller from the beginning.

(3) Where the buyer as to conforming goods already identified to the contract for sale repudiates or is otherwise in breach before risk of their loss has passed to him, the seller may to the extent of any deficiency in his effective insurance coverage treat the risk of loss as resting on the buyer for a commercially reasonable time.

§2—511. TENDER OF PAYMENT BY BUYER; PAYMENT BY CHECK

(1) Unless otherwise agreed tender of payment is a condition to the seller's duty to tender and complete any delivery.

(2) Tender of payment is sufficient when made by any means or in any manner current in the ordinary course of business unless the seller demands payment in legal tender and gives any extension of time reasonably necessary to procure it.

(3) Subject to the provisions of this Act on the effect of an instrument on an obligation (Section 3—310), payment by check is conditional and is defeated as between the parties by dishonor of the check on due presentment.

As amended in 1994.

§2—512. PAYMENT BY BUYER BEFORE INSPECTION

(1) Where the contract requires payment before inspection non-conformity of the goods does not excuse the buyer from so making payment unless

(a) the non-conformity appears without inspection; or

(b) despite tender of the required documents the circumstances would justify injunction against honor under this Act (Section 5—109(b)).

(2) Payment pursuant to subsection (1) does not constitute an acceptance of goods or impair the buyer's right to inspect or any of his remedies.

§2—513. BUYER'S RIGHT TO INSPECTION OF GOODS

(1) Unless otherwise agreed and subject to subsection (3), where goods are tendered or delivered or identified to the contract for sale, the buyer has a right before payment or acceptance to inspect them at any reasonable place and time and in any reasonable manner. When the seller is required or authorized to send the goods to the buyer, the inspection may be after their arrival.

(2) Expenses of inspection must be borne by the buyer but may be recovered from the seller if the goods do not conform and are rejected.

(3) Unless otherwise agreed and subject to the provisions of this Article on C.I.F. contracts (subsection (3) of Section 2—321), the buyer is not entitled to inspect the goods before payment of the price when the contract provides

(a) for delivery "C.O.D." or on other like terms; or

(b) for payment against documents of title, except where such payment is due only after the goods are to become available for inspection.

(4) A place or method of inspection fixed by the parties is presumed to be exclusive but unless otherwise expressly

agreed it does not postpone identification or shift the place for delivery or for passing the risk of loss. If compliance becomes impossible, inspection shall be as provided in this section unless the place or method fixed was clearly intended as an indispensable condition failure of which avoids the contract.

* * * *

§2—601. BUYER'S RIGHTS ON IMPROPER DELIVERY

Subject to the provisions of this Article on breach in installment contracts (Section 2—612) and unless otherwise agreed under the sections on contractual limitations of remedy (Sections 2—718 and 2—719), if the goods or the tender of delivery fail in any respect to conform to the contract, the buyer may

(a) reject the whole; or

(b) accept the whole; or

(c) accept any commercial unit or units and reject the rest.

§2—602. MANNER AND EFFECT OF RIGHTFUL REJECTION

(1) Rejection of goods must be within a reasonable time after their delivery or tender. It is ineffective unless the buyer seasonably notifies the seller.

(2) Subject to the provisions of the two following sections on rejected goods (Sections 2—603 and 2—604),

(a) after rejection any exercise of ownership by the buyer with respect to any commercial unit is wrongful as against the seller; and

(b) if the buyer has before rejection taken physical possession of goods in which he does not have a security interest under the provisions of this Article (subsection (3) of Section 2—711), he is under a duty after rejection to hold them with reasonable care at the seller's disposition for a time sufficient to permit the seller to remove them; but

(c) the buyer has no further obligations with regard to goods rightfully rejected.

(3) The seller's rights with respect to goods wrongfully rejected are governed by the provisions of this Article on Seller's remedies in general (Section 2—703).

§2—603. MERCHANT BUYER'S DUTIES AS TO RIGHTFULLY REJECTED GOODS

(1) Subject to any security interest in the buyer (subsection (3) of Section 2—711), when the seller has no agent or place of business at the market of rejection a merchant buyer is under a duty after rejection of goods in his possession or control to follow any reasonable instructions received from the seller with respect to the goods and in the absence of such instructions to make reasonable efforts to sell them for the seller's account if they are perishable or threaten to decline in value speedily. Instructions are not reasonable if on demand indemnity for expenses is not forthcoming.

(2) When the buyer sells goods under subsection (1), he is entitled to reimbursement from the seller or out of the proceeds for reasonable expenses of caring for and selling them, and if the expenses include no selling commission then to such commission as is usual in the trade or if there is none to a reasonable sum not exceeding ten per cent on the gross proceeds.

(3) In complying with this section the buyer is held only to good faith and good faith conduct hereunder is neither acceptance nor conversion nor the basis of an action for damages.

§2—604. BUYER'S OPTIONS AS TO SALVAGE OF RIGHTFULLY REJECTED GOODS

Subject to the provisions of the immediately preceding section on perishables if the seller gives no instructions within a reasonable time after notification of rejection the buyer may store the rejected goods for the seller's account or reship them to him or resell them for the seller's account with reimbursement as provided in the preceding section. Such action is not acceptance or conversion.

§2—605. WAIVER OF BUYER'S OBJECTIONS BY FAILURE TO PARTICULARIZE

(1) The buyer's failure to state in connection with rejection a particular defect which is ascertainable by reasonable inspection precludes him from relying on the unstated defect to justify rejection or to establish breach

(a) where the seller could have cured it if stated seasonably; or

(b) between merchants when the seller has after rejection made a request in writing for a full and final written statement of all defects on which the buyer proposes to rely.

(2) Payment against documents made without reservation of rights precludes recovery of the payment for defects apparent on the face of the documents.

§2—606. WHAT CONSTITUTES ACCEPTANCE OF GOODS

(1) Acceptance of goods occurs when the buyer

(a) after a reasonable opportunity to inspect the goods signifies to the seller that the goods are conforming or that he will take or retain them in spite of their non-conformity; or

(b) fails to make an effective rejection (subsection (1) of Section 2—602), but such acceptance does not occur until the buyer has had a reasonable opportunity to inspect them; or

(c) does any act inconsistent with the seller's ownership; but if such act is wrongful as against the seller it is an acceptance only if ratified by him.

(2) Acceptance of a part of any commercial unit is acceptance of that entire unit.

§2—607. EFFECT OF ACCEPTANCE; NOTICE OF BREACH; BURDEN OF ESTABLISHING BREACH AFTER ACCEPTANCE; NOTICE OF CLAIM OR LITIGATION TO PERSON ANSWERABLE OVER

(1) The buyer must pay at the contract rate for any goods accepted.

(2) Acceptance of goods by the buyer precludes rejection of the goods accepted and if made with knowledge of a non-conformity cannot be revoked because of it unless the acceptance was on the reasonable assumption that the non-conformity would be seasonably cured but acceptance does not of itself impair any other remedy provided by this Article for non-conformity.

(3) Where a tender has been accepted

(a) the buyer must within a reasonable time after he discovers or should have discovered any breach notify the seller of breach or be barred from any remedy; and

(b) if the claim is one for infringement or the like (subsection (3) of Section 2—312) and the buyer is sued as a result of such a breach he must so notify the seller within a reasonable time after he receives notice of the litigation or be barred from any remedy over for liability established by the litigation.

(4) The burden is on the buyer to establish any breach with respect to the goods accepted.

(5) Where the buyer is sued for breach of a warranty or other obligation for which his seller is answerable over

(a) he may give his seller written notice of the litigation. If the notice states that the seller may come in and defend and that if the seller does not do so he will be bound in any action against him by his buyer by any determination of fact common to the two litigations, then unless the seller after seasonable receipt of the notice does come in and defend he is so bound.

(b) if the claim is one for infringement or the like (subsection (3) of Section 2—312) the original seller may demand in writing that his buyer turn over to him control of the litigation including settlement or else be barred from any remedy over and if he also agrees to bear all expense and to satisfy any adverse judgment, then unless the buyer after seasonable receipt of the demand does turn over control the buyer is so barred.

(6) The provisions of subsections (3), (4) and (5) apply to any obligation of a buyer to hold the seller harmless against infringement or the like (subsection (3) of Section 2—312).

§2—608. REVOCATION OF ACCEPTANCE IN WHOLE OR IN PART

(1) The buyer may revoke his acceptance of a lot or commercial unit whose non-conformity substantially impairs its value to him if he has accepted it

(a) on the reasonable assumption that its non-conformity would be cured and it has not been seasonably cured; or

(b) without discovery of such non-conformity if his acceptance was reasonably induced either by the difficulty of discovery before acceptance or by the seller's assurances.

(2) Revocation of acceptance must occur within a reasonable time after the buyer discovers or should have discovered the ground for it and before any substantial change in condition of the goods which is not caused by their own defects. It is not effective until the buyer notifies the seller of it.

(3) A buyer who so revokes has the same rights and duties with regard to the goods involved as if he had rejected them.

§2—609. RIGHT TO ADEQUATE ASSURANCE OF PERFORMANCE

(1) A contract for sale imposes an obligation on each party that the other's expectation of receiving due performance will not be impaired. When reasonable grounds for insecurity arise with respect to the performance of either party the other may in writing demand adequate assurance of due performance and until he receives such assurance may if commercially reasonable suspend any performance for which he has not already received the agreed return.

(2) Between merchants the reasonableness of grounds for insecurity and the adequacy of any assurance offered shall be determined according to commercial standards.

(3) Acceptance of any improper delivery or payment does not prejudice the party's right to demand adequate assurance of future performance.

(4) After receipt of a justified demand failure to provide within a reasonable time not exceeding thirty days such assurance of due performance as is adequate under the circumstances of the particular case is a repudiation of the contract.

§2—610. ANTICIPATORY REPUDIATION

When either party repudiates the contract with respect to a performance not yet due the loss of which will substantially impair the value of the contract to the other, the aggrieved party may

(a) for a commercially reasonable time await performance by the repudiating party; or

(b) resort to any remedy for breach (Section 2—703 or Section 2—711), even though he has notified the repudiating party that he would await the latter's performance and has urged retraction; and

(c) in either case suspend his own performance or proceed in accordance with the provisions of this Article on the seller's right to identify goods to the contract notwithstanding breach or to salvage unfinished goods (Section 2—704).

§2—611. RETRACTION OF ANTICIPATORY REPUDIATION

(1) Until the repudiating party's next performance is due he can retract his repudiation unless the aggrieved party has since the repudiation cancelled or materially changed his position or otherwise indicated that he considers the repudiation final.

(2) Retraction may be by any method which clearly indicates to the aggrieved party that the repudiating party intends to perform, but must include any assurance justifiably demanded under the provisions of this Article (Section 2—609).

(3) Retraction reinstates the repudiating party's rights under the contract with due excuse and allowance to the aggrieved party for any delay occasioned by the repudiation.

§2—612. "INSTALLMENT CONTRACT"; BREACH

(1) An "installment contract" is one which requires or authorizes the delivery of goods in separate lots to be separately accepted, even though the contract contains a clause "each delivery is a separate contract" or its equivalent.

(2) The buyer may reject any installment which is non-conforming if the non-conformity substantially impairs the value of that installment and cannot be cured or if the non-conformity is a defect in the required documents; but if the non-conformity does not fall within subsection (3) and the seller gives adequate assurance of its cure the buyer must accept that installment.

(3) Whenever non-conformity or default with respect to one or more installments substantially impairs the value of the whole contract there is a breach of the whole. But the aggrieved party reinstates the contract if he accepts a non-conforming installment without seasonably notifying of cancellation or if he brings an action with respect only to past installments or demands performance as to future installments.

§2—613. CASUALTY TO IDENTIFIED GOODS

Where the contract requires for its performance goods identified when the contract is made, and the goods suffer casualty without fault of either party before the risk of loss passes to the buyer, or in a proper case under a "no arrival, no sale" term (Section 2—324) then

(a) if the loss is total the contract is avoided; and

(b) if the loss is partial or the goods have so deteriorated as no longer to conform to the contract the buyer may nevertheless demand inspection and at his option either treat the contract as voided or accept the goods with due allowance from the contract price for the deterioration or the deficiency in quantity but without further right against the seller.

§2—614. SUBSTITUTED PERFORMANCE

(1) Where without fault of either party the agreed berthing, loading, or unloading facilities fail or an agreed type of carrier becomes unavailable or the agreed manner of delivery otherwise becomes commercially impracticable but a commercially reasonable substitute is available, such substitute performance must be tendered and accepted.

(2) If the agreed means or manner of payment fails because of domestic or foreign governmental regulation, the seller may withhold or stop delivery unless the buyer provides a means or manner of payment which is commercially a substantial equivalent. If delivery has already been taken, payment by the means or in the manner provided by the regulation discharges the buyer's obligation unless the regulation is discriminatory, oppressive or predatory.

§2—615. EXCUSE BY FAILURE OF PRESUPPOSED CONDITIONS

Except so far as a seller may have assumed a greater obligation and subject to the preceding section on substituted performance:

(a) Delay in delivery or non-delivery in whole or in part by a seller who complies with paragraphs (b) and (c) is not a breach of his duty under a contract for sale if performance as agreed has been made impracticable by the occurrence of a contingency the nonoccurrence of which was a basic assumption on which the contract was made or by compliance in good faith with any applicable foreign or domestic governmental regulation or order whether or not it later proves to be invalid.

(b) Where the causes mentioned in paragraph (a) affect only a part of the seller's capacity to perform, he must allocate production and deliveries among his customers but may at his option include regular customers not then under contract as well as his own requirements for further manufacture. He may so allocate in any manner which is fair and reasonable.

(c) The seller must notify the buyer seasonably that there will be delay or non-delivery and, when allocation is required under paragraph (b), of the estimated quota thus made available for the buyer.

* * * *

§2—702. SELLER'S REMEDIES ON DISCOVERY OF BUYER'S INSOLVENCY

(1) Where the seller discovers the buyer to be insolvent he may refuse delivery except for cash including payment for all goods theretofore delivered under the contract, and stop delivery under this Article (Section 2—705).

(2) Where the seller discovers that the buyer has received goods on credit while insolvent he may reclaim the goods upon demand made within ten days after the receipt, but if misrepresentation of solvency has been made to the particular seller in writing within three months before delivery the ten day limitation does not apply. Except as provided in this subsection the seller may not base a right to reclaim goods on the buyer's fraudulent or innocent misrepresentation of solvency or of intent to pay.

(3) The seller's right to reclaim under subsection (2) is subject to the rights of a buyer in ordinary course or other good faith purchaser under this Article (Section 2—403). Successful reclamation of goods excludes all other remedies with respect to them.

§2—703. SELLER'S REMEDIES IN GENERAL

Where the buyer wrongfully rejects or revokes acceptance of goods or fails to make a payment due on or before delivery or repudiates with respect to a part or the whole, then with respect to any goods directly affected and, if the breach is of the whole contract (Section 2—612), then also with respect to the whole undelivered balance, the aggrieved seller may

(a) withhold delivery of such goods;

(b) stop delivery by any bailee as hereafter provided (Section 2—705);

(c) proceed under the next section respecting goods still unidentified to the contract;

(d) resell and recover damages as hereafter provided (Section 2—706);

(e) recover damages for non-acceptance (Section 2—708) or in a proper case the price (Section 2—709);

(f) cancel.

§2—704. SELLER'S RIGHT TO IDENTIFY GOODS TO THE CONTRACT NOTWITHSTANDING BREACH OR TO SALVAGE UNFINISHED GOODS

(1) An aggrieved seller under the preceding section may

(a) identify to the contract conforming goods not already identified if at the time he learned of the breach they are in his possession or control;

(b) treat as the subject of resale goods which have demonstrably been intended for the particular contract even though those goods are unfinished.

(2) Where the goods are unfinished an aggrieved seller may in the exercise of reasonable commercial judgment for the purposes of avoiding loss and of effective realization either complete the manufacture and wholly identify the goods to the contract or cease manufacture and resell for scrap or salvage value or proceed in any other reasonable manner.

§2—705. SELLER'S STOPPAGE OF DELIVERY IN TRANSIT OR OTHERWISE

(1) The seller may stop delivery of goods in the possession of a carrier or other bailee when he discovers the buyer to be insolvent (Section 2—702) and may stop delivery of carload, truckload, planeload or larger shipments of express or freight when the buyer repudiates or fails to make a payment due before delivery or if for any other reason the seller has a right to withhold or reclaim the goods.

(2) As against such buyer the seller may stop delivery until

(a) receipt of the goods by the buyer; or

(b) acknowledgment to the buyer by any bailee of the goods except a carrier that the bailee holds the goods for the buyer; or

(c) such acknowledgment to the buyer by a carrier by reshipment or as warehouseman; or

(d) negotiation to the buyer of any negotiable document of title covering the goods.

(3) ****

(a) To stop delivery the seller must so notify as to enable the bailee by reasonable diligence to prevent delivery of the goods.

(b) After such notification the bailee must hold and deliver the goods according to the directions of the seller but the seller is liable to the bailee for any ensuing charges or damages.

(c) If a negotiable document of title has been issued for goods the bailee is not obliged to obey a notification to stop until surrender of the document.

(d) A carrier who has issued a non-negotiable bill of lading is not obliged to obey a notification to stop received from a person other than the consignor.

§2—706. SELLER'S RESALE INCLUDING CONTRACT FOR RESALE

(1) Under the conditions stated in Section 2—703 on seller's remedies, the seller may resell the goods concerned or the undelivered balance thereof. Where the resale is made in good faith and in a commercially reasonable manner the seller may recover the difference between the resale price and the contract price together with any incidental damages allowed under the provisions of this Article (Section 2—710), but less expenses saved in consequence of the buyer's breach.

(2) Except as otherwise provided in subsection (3) or unless otherwise agreed resale may be at public or private sale including sale by way of one or more contracts to sell or of identification to an existing contract of the seller. Sale may be as a unit or in parcels and at any time and place and on any terms but every aspect of the sale including the method, manner, time, place and terms must be commercially reasonable. The resale must be reasonably identified as referring to the broken contract, but it is not necessary

that the goods be in existence or that any or all of them have been identified to the contract before the breach.

(3) Where the resale is at private sale the seller must give the buyer reasonable notification of his intention to resell.

(4) Where the resale is at public sale

(a) only identified goods can be sold except where there is a recognized market for a public sale of futures in goods of the kind; and

(b) it must be made at a usual place or market for public sale if one is reasonably available and except in the case of goods which are perishable or threaten to decline in value speedily the seller must give the buyer reasonable notice of the time and place of the resale; and

(c) if the goods are not to be within the view of those attending the sale the notification of sale must state the place where the goods are located and provide for their reasonable inspection by prospective bidders; and

(d) the seller may buy.

(5) A purchaser who buys in good faith at a resale takes the goods free of any rights of the original buyer even though the seller fails to comply with one or more of the requirements of this section.

(6) The seller is not accountable to the buyer for any profit made on any resale. A person in the position of a seller (Section 2—707) or a buyer who has rightfully rejected or justifiably revoked acceptance must account for any excess over the amount of his security interest, as hereinafter defined (subsection (3) of Section 2—711).

* * * *

§2—708. SELLER'S DAMAGES FOR NON-ACCEPTANCE OR REPUDIATION

(1) Subject to subsection (2) and to the provisions of this Article with respect to proof of market price (Section 2—723), the measure of damages for non-acceptance or repudiation by the buyer is the difference between the market price at the time and place for tender and the unpaid contract price together with any incidental damages provided in this Article (Section 2—710), but less expenses saved in consequence of the buyer's breach.

(2) If the measure of damages provided in subsection (1) is inadequate to put the seller in as good a position as performance would have done then the measure of damages is the profit (including reasonable overhead) which the seller would have made from full performance by the buyer, together with any incidental damages provided in this Article (Section 2—710), due allowance for costs reasonably incurred and due credit for payments or proceeds of resale.

§2—709. ACTION FOR THE PRICE

(1) When the buyer fails to pay the price as it becomes due the seller may recover, together with any incidental damages under the next section, the price

(a) of goods accepted or of conforming goods lost or damaged within a commercially reasonable time after risk of their loss has passed to the buyer; and

(b) of goods identified to the contract if the seller is unable after reasonable effort to resell them at a reasonable price or the circumstances reasonably indicate that such effort will be unavailing.

(2) Where the seller sues for the price he must hold for the buyer any goods which have been identified to the contract and are still in his control except that if resale becomes possible he may resell them at any time prior to the collection of the judgment. The net proceeds of any such resale must be credited to the buyer and payment of the judgment entitles him to any goods not resold.

(3) After the buyer has wrongfully rejected or revoked acceptance of the goods or has failed to make a payment due or has repudiated (Section 2—610), a seller who is held not entitled to the price under this section shall nevertheless be awarded damages for non-acceptance under the preceding section.

§2—710. SELLER'S INCIDENTAL DAMAGES

Incidental damages to an aggrieved seller include any commercially reasonable charges, expenses or commissions incurred in stopping delivery, in the transportation, care and custody of goods after the buyer's breach, in connection with return or resale of the goods or otherwise resulting from the breach.

§2—711. BUYER'S REMEDIES IN GENERAL; BUYER'S SECURITY INTEREST IN REJECTED GOODS

(1) Where the seller fails to make delivery or repudiates or the buyer rightfully rejects or justifiably revokes acceptance then with respect to any goods involved, and with respect to the whole if the breach goes to the whole contract (Section 2—612), the buyer may cancel and whether or not he has done so may in addition to recovering so much of the price as has been paid

(a) "cover" and have damages under the next section as to all the goods affected whether or not they have been identified to the contract; or

(b) recover damages for non-delivery as provided in this Article (Section 2—713).

(2) Where the seller fails to deliver or repudiates the buyer may also

(a) if the goods have been identified recover them as provided in this Article (Section 2—502); or

(b) in a proper case obtain specific performance or replevy the goods as provided in this Article (Section 2—716).

(3) On rightful rejection or justifiable revocation of acceptance a buyer has a security interest in goods in his

possession or control for any payments made on their price and any expenses reasonably incurred in their inspection, receipt, transportation, care and custody and may hold such goods and resell them in like manner as an aggrieved seller (Section 2—706).

§2—712. "COVER"; BUYER'S PROCUREMENT OF SUBSTITUTE GOODS

(1) After a breach within the preceding section the buyer may "cover" by making in good faith and without unreasonable delay any reasonable purchase of or contract to purchase goods in substitution for those due from the seller.

(2) The buyer may recover from the seller as damages the difference between the cost of cover and the contract price together with any incidental or consequential damages as hereinafter defined (Section 2—715), but less expenses saved in consequence of the seller's breach.

(3) Failure of the buyer to effect cover within this section does not bar him from any other remedy.

§2—713. BUYER'S DAMAGES FOR NON-DELIVERY OR REPUDIATION

(1) Subject to the provisions of this Article with respect to proof of market price (Section 2—723), the measure of damages for non-delivery or repudiation by the seller is the difference between the market price at the time when the buyer learned of the breach and the contract price together with any incidental and consequential damages provided in this Article (Section 2—715), but less expenses saved in consequence of the seller's breach.

(2) Market price is to be determined as of the place for tender or, in cases of rejection after arrival or revocation of acceptance, as of the place of arrival.

§2—714. BUYER'S DAMAGES FOR BREACH IN REGARD TO ACCEPTED GOODS

(1) Where the buyer has accepted goods and given notification (subsection (3) of Section 2—607) he may recover as damages for any non-conformity of tender the loss resulting in the ordinary course of events from the seller's breach as determined in any manner which is reasonable.

(2) The measure of damages for breach of warranty is the difference at the time and place of acceptance between the value of the goods accepted and the value they would have had if they had been as warranted, unless special circumstances show proximate damages of a different amount.

(3) In a proper case any incidental and consequential damages under the next section may also be recovered.

§2—715. BUYER'S INCIDENTAL AND CONSEQUENTIAL DAMAGES

(1) Incidental damages resulting from the seller's breach include expenses reasonably incurred in inspection, receipt, transportation and care and custody of goods rightfully rejected, any commercially reasonable charges, expenses or commissions in connection with effecting cover and any other reasonable expense incident to the delay or other breach.

(2) Consequential damages resulting from the seller's breach include

(a) any loss resulting from general or particular requirements and needs of which the seller at the time of contracting had reason to know and which could not reasonably be prevented by cover or otherwise; and

(b) injury to person or property proximately resulting from any breach of warranty.

§2—716. BUYER'S RIGHT TO SPECIFIC PERFORMANCE OR REPLEVIN

(1) Specific performance may be decreed where the goods are unique or in other proper circumstances.

(2) The decree for specific performance may include such terms and conditions as to payment of the price, damages, or other relief as the court may deem just.

(3) The buyer has a right of replevin for goods identified to the contract if after reasonable effort he is unable to effect cover for such goods or the circumstances reasonably indicate that such effort will be unavailing or if the goods have been shipped under reservation and satisfaction of the security interest in them has been made or tendered. In the case of goods bought for personal, family, or household purposes, the buyer's right of replevin vests upon acquisition of a special property, even if the seller had not then repudiated or failed to deliver.

§2—717. DEDUCTION OF DAMAGES FROM THE PRICE

The buyer on notifying the seller of his intention to do so may deduct all or any part of the damages resulting from any breach of the contract from any part of the price still due under the same contract.

§2—718. LIQUIDATION OR LIMITATION OF DAMAGES; DEPOSITS

(1) Damages for breach by either party may be liquidated in the agreement but only at an amount which is reasonable in the light of the anticipated or actual harm caused by the breach, the difficulties of proof of loss, and the inconvenience or nonfeasibility of otherwise obtaining an adequate remedy. A term fixing unreasonably large liquidated damages is void as a penalty.

(2) Where the seller justifiably withholds delivery of goods because of the buyer's breach, the buyer is entitled to restitution of any amount by which the sum of his payments exceeds

(a) the amount to which the seller is entitled by virtue of terms liquidating the seller's damages in accordance with subsection (1), or

(b) in the absence of such terms, twenty per cent of the value of the total performance for which the buyer is obligated under the contract or $500, whichever is smaller.

(3) The buyer's right to restitution under subsection (2) is subject to offset to the extent that the seller establishes

(a) a right to recover damages under the provisions of this Article other than subsection (1), and

(b) the amount or value of any benefits received by the buyer directly or indirectly by reason of the contract.

(4) Where a seller has received payment in goods their reasonable value or the proceeds of their resale shall be treated as payments for the purposes of subsection (2); but if the seller has notice of the buyer's breach before reselling goods received in part performance, his resale is subject to the conditions laid down in this Article on resale by an aggrieved seller (Section 2—706).

§2—719. CONTRACTUAL MODIFICATION OR LIMITATION OF REMEDY

(1) Subject to the provisions of subsections (2) and (3) of this section and of the preceding section on liquidation and limitation of damages,

(a) the agreement may provide for remedies in addition to or in substitution for those provided in this Article and may limit or alter the measure of damages recoverable under this Article, as by limiting the buyer's remedies to return of the goods and repayment of the price or to repair and replacement of non-conforming goods or parts; and

(b) resort to a remedy as provided is optional unless the remedy is expressly agreed to be exclusive, in which case it is the sole remedy.

(2) Where circumstances cause an exclusive or limited remedy to fail of its essential purpose, remedy may be had as provided in this Act.

(3) Consequential damages may be limited or excluded unless the limitation or exclusion is unconscionable. Limitation of consequential damages for injury to the person in the case of consumer goods is prima facie unconscionable but limitation of damages where the loss is commercial is not.

§2—720. EFFECT OF "CANCELLATION" OR "RESCISSION" ON CLAIMS FOR ANTECEDENT BREACH

Unless the contrary intention clearly appears, expressions of "cancellation" or "rescission" of the contract or the like shall not be construed as a renunciation or discharge of any claim in damages for an antecedent breach.

§2—721. REMEDIES FOR FRAUD

Remedies for material misrepresentation or fraud include all remedies available under this Article for non-fraudulent breach. Neither rescission or a claim for rescission of the contract for sale nor rejection or return of the goods shall bar or be deemed inconsistent with a claim for damages or other remedy.

§2—722. WHO CAN SUE THIRD PARTIES FOR INJURY TO GOODS

Where a third party so deals with goods which have been identified to a contract for sale as to cause actionable injury to a party to that contract

(a) a right of action against the third party is in either party to the contract for sale who has title to or a security interest or a special property or an insurable interest in the goods; and if the goods have been destroyed or converted a right of action is also in the party who either bore the risk of loss under the contract for sale or has since the injury assumed that risk as against the other;

(b) if at the time of the injury the party plaintiff did not bear the risk of loss as against the other party to the contract for sale and there is no arrangement between them for disposition of the recovery, his suit or settlement is, subject to his own interest, as a fiduciary for the other party to the contract;

(c) either party may with the consent of the other sue for the benefit of whom it may concern.

§2—723. PROOF OF MARKET PRICE: TIME AND PLACE

(1) If an action based on anticipatory repudiation comes to trial before the time for performance with respect to some or all of the goods, any damages based on market price (Section 2—708 or Section 2—713) shall be determined according to the price of such goods prevailing at the time when the aggrieved party learned of the repudiation.

(2) If evidence of a price prevailing at the times or places described in this Article is not readily available the price prevailing within any reasonable time before or after the time described or at any other place which in commercial judgment or under usage of trade would serve as a reasonable substitute for the one described may be used, making any proper allowance for the cost of transporting the goods to or from such other place.

(3) Evidence of a relevant price prevailing at a time or place other than the one described in this Article offered by one party is not admissible unless and until he has given the other party such notice as the court finds sufficient to prevent unfair surprise.

§2—724. ADMISSIBILITY OF MARKET QUOTATIONS

Whenever the prevailing price or value of any goods regularly bought and sold in any established commodity market is in issue, reports in official publications or trade journals or in newspapers or periodicals of general circulation published as the reports of such market shall be admissible in evidence. The circumstances of the preparation of such a report may be shown to affect its weight but not its admissibility.

§2—725. STATUTE OF LIMITATIONS IN CONTRACTS FOR SALE

(1) An action for breach of any contract for sale must be commenced within four years after the cause of action has accrued. By the original agreement the parties may reduce the period of limitation to not less than one year but may not extend it.

(2) A cause of action accrues when the breach occurs, regardless of the aggrieved party's lack of knowledge of the breach. A breach of warranty occurs when tender of delivery is made, except that where a warranty explicitly extends to future performance of the goods and discovery of the breach must await the time of such performance the cause of action accrues when the breach is or should have been discovered.

(3) Where an action commenced within the time limited by subsection (1) is so terminated as to leave available a remedy by another action for the same breach such other action may be commenced after the expiration of the time limited and within six months after the termination of the first action unless the termination resulted from voluntary discontinuance or from dismissal for failure or neglect to prosecute.

(4) This section does not alter the law on tolling of the statute of limitations nor does it apply to causes of action which have accrued before this Act becomes effective.

Article 2 Amendments (Excerpts)

Part 1 Short Title, General Construction and Subject Matter

* * * *

§2—103. DEFINITIONS AND INDEX OF DEFINITIONS

(1) In this article unless the context otherwise requires

* * * *

(b) "Conspicuous", with reference to a term, means so written, displayed, or presented that a reasonable person against which it is to operate ought to have noticed it. A term in an electronic record intended to evoke a response by an electronic agent is conspicuous if it is presented in a form that would enable a reasonably configured electronic agent to take it into account or react to it without review of the record by an individual. Whether a term is "conspicuous" or not is a decision for the court. Conspicuous terms include the following:

(i) for a person:

(A) a heading in capitals equal to or greater in size than the surrounding text, or in contrasting type, font, or color to the surrounding text of the same or lesser size;

(B) language in the body of a record or display in larger type than the surrounding text, or in contrasting type, font, or color to the surrounding text of the same size, or set off from surrounding text of the same size by symbols or other marks that call attention to the language; and

(ii) for a person or an electronic agent, a term that is so placed in a record or display that the person or electronic agent cannot proceed without taking action with respect to the particular term.

(c) "Consumer" means an individual who buys or contracts to buy goods that, at the time of contracting, are intended by the individual to be used primarily for personal, family, or household purposes.

(d) "Consumer contract" means a contract between a merchant seller and a consumer.

* * * *

(j) "Good faith" means honesty in fact and the observance of reasonable commercial standards of fair dealing.

(k) "Goods" means all things that are movable at the time of identification to a contract for sale. The term includes future goods, specially manufactured goods, the unborn young of animals, growing crops, and other identified things attached to realty as described in Section 2—107. The term does not include information, the money in which the price is to be paid, investment securities under Article 8, the subject matter of foreign exchange transactions, and choses in action.

* * * *

(m) "Record" means information that is inscribed on a tangible medium or that is stored in an electronic or other medium and is retrievable in perceivable form.

(n) "Remedial promise" means a promise by the seller to repair or replace the goods or to refund all or part of the price upon the happening of a specified event.

* * * *

(p) "Sign" means, with present intent to authenticate or adopt a record,

(i) to execute or adopt a tangible symbol; or

(ii) to attach to or logically associate with the record an electronic sound, symbol, or process.

* * * *

Part 2 Form, Formation, Terms and Readjustment of Contract; Electronic Contracting

§2—201. FORMAL REQUIREMENTS; STATUTE OF FRAUDS

(1) A contract for the sale of goods for the price of $5,000 or more is not enforceable by way of action or defense unless there is some record sufficient to indicate that a

contract for sale has been made between the parties and signed by the party against whom which enforcement is sought or by the party's authorized agent or broker. A record is not insufficient because it omits or incorrectly states a term agreed upon but the contract is not enforceable under this subsection beyond the quantity of goods shown in the record.

(2) Between merchants if within a reasonable time a record in confirmation of the contract and sufficient against the sender is received and the party receiving it has reason to know its contents, it satisfies the requirements of subsection (1) against such party the recipient unless notice of objection to its contents is given in a record within 10 days after it is received.

(3) A contract which does not satisfy the requirements of subsection (1) but which is valid in other respects is enforceable

(a) if the goods are to be specially manufactured for the buyer and are not suitable for sale to others in the ordinary course of the seller's business and the seller, before notice of repudiation is received and under circumstances which reasonably indicate that the goods are for the buyer, has made either a substantial beginning of their manufacture or commitments for their procurement; or

(b) if the party against whom which enforcement is sought admits in the party's pleading, or in the party's testimony or otherwise under oath that a contract for sale was made, but the contract is not enforceable under this paragraph beyond the quantity of goods admitted; or

(c) with respect to goods for which payment has been made and accepted or which have been received and accepted (Sec. 2—606).

(4) A contract that is enforceable under this section is not rendered unenforceable merely because it is not capable of being performed within one year or any other applicable period after its making.

* * * *

§2—207. TERMS OF CONTRACT; EFFECT OF CONFIRMATION

If (i) conduct by both parties recognizes the existence of a contract although their records do not otherwise establish a contract, (ii) a contract is formed by an offer and acceptance, or (iii) a contract formed in any manner is confirmed by a record that contains terms additional to or different from those in the contract being confirmed, the terms of the contract, subject to Section 2—202, are:

(a) terms that appear in the records of both parties;

(b) terms, whether in a record or not, to which both parties agree; and

(c) terms supplied or incorporated under any provision of this Act.

* * * *

Part 3 General Obligation and Construction of Contract

* * * *

§2—312. WARRANTY OF TITLE AND AGAINST INFRINGEMENT; BUYER'S OBLIGATION AGAINST INFRINGEMENT

(1) Subject to subsection (2) there is in a contract for sale a warranty by the seller that

(a) the title conveyed shall be good, good and its transfer rightful and shall not, because of any colorable claim to or interest in the goods, unreasonably expose the buyer to litigation; and

(b) the goods shall be delivered free from any security interest or other lien or encumbrance of which the buyer at the time of contracting has no knowledge.

(2) Unless otherwise agreed a seller that is a merchant regularly dealing in goods of the kind warrants that the goods shall be delivered free of the rightful claim of any third person by way of infringement or the like but a buyer that furnishes specifications to the seller must hold the seller harmless against any such claim that arises out of compliance with the specifications.

(3) A warranty under this section may be disclaimed or modified only by specific language or by circumstances that give the buyer reason to know that the seller does not claim title, that the seller is purporting to sell only the right or title as the seller or a third person may have, or that the seller is selling subject to any claims of infringement or the like.

§2—313. EXPRESS WARRANTIES BY AFFIRMATION, PROMISE, DESCRIPTION, SAMPLE; REMEDIAL PROMISE

(1) In this section, "immediate buyer" means a buyer that enters into a contract with the seller.

* * * *

(4) Any remedial promise made by the seller to the immediate buyer creates an obligation that the promise will be performed upon the happening of the specified event.

§2—313A. OBLIGATION TO REMOTE PURCHASER CREATED BY RECORD PACKAGED WITH OR ACCOMPANYING GOODS

(1) This section applies only to new goods and goods sold or leased as new goods in a transaction of purchase in the normal chain of distribution. In this section:

(a) "Immediate buyer" means a buyer that enters into a contract with the seller.

(b) "Remote purchaser" means a person that buys or leases goods from an immediate buyer or other person in the normal chain of distribution.

(2) If a seller in a record packaged with or accompanying the goods makes an affirmation of fact or promise that

relates to the goods, provides a description that relates to the goods, or makes a remedial promise, and the seller reasonably expects the record to be, and the record is, furnished to the remote purchaser, the seller has an obligation to the remote purchaser that:

(a) the goods will conform to the affirmation of fact, promise or description unless a reasonable person in the position of the remote purchaser would not believe that the affirmation of fact, promise or description created an obligation; and

(b) the seller will perform the remedial promise.

(3) It is not necessary to the creation of an obligation under this section that the seller use formal words such as "warrant" or "guarantee" or that the seller have a specific intention to undertake an obligation, but an affirmation merely of the value of the goods or a statement purporting to be merely the seller's opinion or commendation of the goods does not create an obligation.

(4) The following rules apply to the remedies for breach of an obligation created under this section:

(a) The seller may modify or limit the remedies available to the remote purchaser if the modification or limitation is furnished to the remote purchaser no later than the time of purchase or if the modification or limitation is contained in the record that contains the affirmation of fact, promise or description.

(b) Subject to a modification or limitation of remedy, a seller in breach is liable for incidental or consequential damages under Section 2—715, but the seller is not liable for lost profits.

(c) The remote purchaser may recover as damages for breach of a seller's obligation arising under subsection (2) the loss resulting in the ordinary course of events as determined in any manner that is reasonable.

(5) An obligation that is not a remedial promise is breached if the goods did not conform to the affirmation of fact, promise or description creating the obligation when the goods left the seller's control.

§2—313B. OBLIGATION TO REMOTE PURCHASER CREATED BY COMMUNICATION TO THE PUBLIC

(1) This section applies only to new goods and goods sold or leased as new goods in a transaction of purchase in the normal chain of distribution. In this section:

(a) "Immediate buyer" means a buyer that enters into a contract with the seller.

(b) "Remote purchaser" means a person that buys or leases goods from an immediate buyer or other person in the normal chain of distribution.

(2) If a seller in advertising or a similar communication to the public makes an affirmation of fact or promise that relates to the goods, provides a description that relates to the goods, or makes a remedial promise, and the remote purchaser enters into a transaction of purchase with knowledge of and with the expectation that the goods will conform to the affirmation of fact, promise, or description, or that the seller will perform the remedial promise, the seller has an obligation to the remote purchaser that:

(a) the goods will conform to the affirmation of fact, promise or description unless a reasonable person in the position of the remote purchaser would not believe that the affirmation of fact, promise or description created an obligation; and

(b) the seller will perform the remedial promise.

(3) It is not necessary to the creation of an obligation under this section that the seller use formal words such as "warrant" or "guarantee" or that the seller have a specific intention to undertake an obligation, but an affirmation merely of the value of the goods or a statement purporting to be merely the seller's opinion or commendation of the goods does not create an obligation.

(4) The following rules apply to the remedies for breach of an obligation created under this section:

(a) The seller may modify or limit the remedies available to the remote purchaser if the modification or limitation is furnished to the remote purchaser no later than the time of purchase. The modification or limitation may be furnished as part of the communication that contains the affirmation of fact, promise or description.

(b) Subject to a modification or limitation of remedy, a seller in breach is liable for incidental or consequential damages under Section 2—715, but the seller is not liable for lost profits.

(c) The remote purchaser may recover as damages for breach of a seller's obligation arising under subsection (2) the loss resulting in the ordinary course of events as determined in any manner that is reasonable.

(5) An obligation that is not a remedial promise is breached if the goods did not conform to the affirmation of fact, promise or description creating the obligation when the goods left the seller's control.

* * * *

§2—316. EXCLUSION OR MODIFICATION OF WARRANTIES.

* * * *

(2) Subject to subsection (3), to exclude or modify the implied warranty of merchantability or any part of it in a consumer contract the language must be in a record, be conspicuous and state "The seller undertakes no responsibility for the quality of the goods except as otherwise provided in this contract," and in any other contract the language must mention merchantability and in case of a

record must be conspicuous. Subject to subsection (3), to exclude or modify the implied warranty of fitness the exclusion must be in a record and be conspicuous. Language to exclude all implied warranties of fitness in a consumer contract must state "The seller assumes no responsibility that the goods will be fit for any particular purpose for which you may be buying these goods, except as otherwise provided in the contract," and in any other contract the language is sufficient if it states, for example, that "There are no warranties which extend beyond the description on the face hereof." Language that satisfies the requirements of this subsection for the exclusion and modification of a warranty in a consumer contract also satisfies the requirements for any other contract.

(3) Notwithstanding subsection (2):

(a) unless the circumstances indicate otherwise, all implied warranties are excluded by expressions like "as is", "with all faults" or other language which in common understanding calls the buyer's attention to the exclusion of warranties, makes plain that there is no implied warranty, and in a consumer contract evidenced by a record is set forth conspicuously in the record; and

(b) when the buyer before entering into the contract has examined the goods or the sample or model as fully as desired or has refused to examine the goods after a demand by the seller there is no implied warranty with regard to defects which an examination ought in the circumstances to have revealed to the buyer; and

(c) an implied warranty can also be excluded or modified by course of dealing or course of performance or usage of trade.

* * * *

§2—318. THIRD PARTY BENEFICIARIES OF WARRANTIES EXPRESS OR IMPLIED

(1) In this section:

(a) "Immediate buyer" means a buyer that enters into a contract with the seller.

(b) "Remote purchaser" means a person that buys or leases goods from an immediate buyer or other person in the normal chain of distribution.

Alternative A to subsection (2)

(2) A seller's warranty whether express or implied to an immediate buyer, a seller's remedial promise to an immediate buyer, or a seller's obligation to a remote purchaser under Section 2—313A or 2—313B extends to any natural person who is in the family or household of the immediate buyer or the remote purchaser or who is a guest in the home of either if it is reasonable to expect that the person may use, consume or be affected by the goods and who is injured in person by breach of the warranty, remedial promise or obligation. A seller may not exclude or limit the operation of this section.

Alternative B to subsection (2)

(2) A seller's warranty whether express or implied to an immediate buyer, a seller's remedial promise to an immediate buyer, or a seller's obligation to a remote purchaser under Section 2—313A or 2—313B extends to any natural person who may reasonably be expected to use, consume or be affected by the goods and who is injured in person by breach of the warranty, remedial promise or obligation. A seller may not exclude or limit the operation of this section.

Alternative C to subsection (2)

(2) A seller's warranty whether express or implied to an immediate buyer, a seller's remedial promise to an immediate buyer, or a seller's obligation to a remote purchaser under Section 2—313A or 2—313B extends to any person that may reasonably be expected to use, consume or be affected by the goods and that is injured by breach of the warranty, remedial promise or obligation. A seller may not exclude or limit the operation of this section with respect to injury to the person of an individual to whom the warranty, remedial promise or obligation extends.

* * * *

Part 5 Performance

* * * *

§2—502. BUYER'S RIGHT TO GOODS ON SELLER'S INSOLVENCY

(1) Subject to subsections (2) and (3) and even though the goods have not been shipped a buyer who that has paid a part or all of the price of goods in which the buyer has a special property under the provisions of the immediately preceding section may on making and keeping good a tender of any unpaid portion of their price recover them from the seller if:

(a) in the case of goods bought by a consumer, the seller repudiates or fails to deliver as required by the contract; or

(b) in all cases, the seller becomes insolvent within ten days after receipt of the first installment on their price.

(2) The buyer's right to recover the goods under subsection (1) vests upon acquisition of a special property, even if the seller had not then repudiated or failed to deliver.

(3) If the identification creating the special property has been made by the buyer, the buyer acquires the right to recover the goods only if they conform to the contract for sale.

* * * *

§2—508. CURE BY SELLER OF IMPROPER TENDER OR DELIVERY; REPLACEMENT

(1) Where the buyer rejects goods or a tender of delivery under Section 2—601 or 2—612 or except in a consumer contract justifiably revokes acceptance under Section 2—608(1)(b) and the agreed time for performance has not expired, a seller that has performed in good faith, upon seasonable notice to the buyer and at the seller's own expense, may cure the breach of contract by making a conforming tender of delivery within the agreed time. The seller shall compensate the buyer for all of the buyer's reasonable expenses caused by the seller's breach of contract and subsequent cure.

(2) Where the buyer rejects goods or a tender of delivery under Section 2—601 or 2—612 or except in a consumer contract justifiably revokes acceptance under Section 2—608(1)(b) and the agreed time for performance has expired, a seller that has performed in good faith, upon seasonable notice to the buyer and at the seller's own expense, may cure the breach of contract, if the cure is appropriate and timely under the circumstances, by making a tender of conforming goods. The seller shall compensate the buyer for all of the buyer's reasonable expenses caused by the seller's breach of contract and subsequent cure.

§2—509. RISK OF LOSS IN THE ABSENCE OF BREACH

(1) Where the contract requires or authorizes the seller to ship the goods by carrier

(a) if it does not require the seller to deliver them at a particular destination, the risk of loss passes to the buyer when the goods are delivered to the carrier even though the shipment is under reservation (Section 2—505); but

(b) if it does require the seller to deliver them at a particular destination and the goods are there tendered while in the possession of the carrier, the risk of loss passes to the buyer when the goods are there so tendered as to enable the buyer to take delivery.

(2) Where the goods are held by a bailee to be delivered without being moved, the risk of loss passes to the buyer

(a) on the buyer's receipt of a negotiable document of title covering the goods; or

(b) on acknowledgment by the bailee to the buyer of the buyer's right to possession of the goods; or

(c) after the buyer's receipt of a non-negotiable document of title or other direction to deliver in a record, as provided in subsection (4)(b) of Section 2—503.

(3) In any case not within subsection (1) or (2), the risk of loss passes to the buyer on the buyer's receipt of the goods.

* * * *

§2—513. BUYER'S RIGHT TO INSPECTION OF GOODS

* * * *

(3) Unless otherwise agreed, the buyer is not entitled to inspect the goods before payment of the price when the contract provides

(a) for delivery on terms that under applicable course of performance, course of dealing, or usage of trade are interpreted to preclude inspection before payment; or

(b) for payment against documents of title, except where such payment is due only after the goods are to become available for inspection.

* * * *

Part 6 Breach, Repudiation and Excuse

* * * *

§2—605. WAIVER OF BUYER'S OBJECTIONS BY FAILURE TO PARTICULARIZE

(1) The buyer's failure to state in connection with rejection a particular defect or in connection with revocation of acceptance a defect that justifies revocation precludes the buyer from relying on the unstated defect to justify rejection or revocation of acceptance if the defect is ascertainable by reasonable inspection

(a) where the seller had a right to cure the defect and could have cured it if stated seasonably; or

(b) between merchants when the seller has after rejection made a request in a record for a full and final statement in record form of all defects on which the buyer proposes to rely.

(2) A buyer's payment against documents tendered to the buyer made without reservation of rights precludes recovery of the payment for defects apparent on the face of the documents.

* * * *

§2—607. EFFECT OF ACCEPTANCE; NOTICE OF BREACH; BURDEN OF ESTABLISHING BREACH AFTER ACCEPTANCE; NOTICE OF CLAIM OR LITIGATION TO PERSON ANSWERABLE OVER

* * * *

(3) Where a tender has been accepted

(a) the buyer must within a reasonable time after the buyer discovers or should have discovered any breach notify the seller; however, failure to give timely notice bars the buyer from a remedy only to the extent that the seller is prejudiced by the failure and

(b) if the claim is one for infringement or the like (subsection (3) of Section 2—312) and the buyer is sued as a result of such a breach the buyer must so notify the seller within a reasonable time after the buyer receives notice of the litigation or be barred from any remedy over for liability established by the litigation.

* * * *

§2—608. REVOCATION OF ACCEPTANCE IN WHOLE OR IN PART

* * * *

(4) If a buyer uses the goods after a rightful rejection or justifiable revocation of acceptance, the following rules apply:

(a) Any use by the buyer that is unreasonable under the circumstances is wrongful as against the seller and is an acceptance only if ratified by the seller.

(b) Any use of the goods that is reasonable under the circumstances is not wrongful as against the seller and is not an acceptance, but in an appropriate case the buyer shall be obligated to the seller for the value of the use to the buyer.

* * * *

§2—612. "INSTALLMENT CONTRACT"; BREACH

* * * *

(2) The buyer may reject any installment which is nonconforming if the non-conformity substantially impairs the value of that installment to the buyer or if the nonconformity is a defect in the required documents; but if the non-conformity does not fall within subsection (3) and the seller gives adequate assurance of its cure the buyer must accept that installment.

(3) Whenever non-conformity or default with respect to one or more installments substantially impairs the value of the whole contract there is a breach of the whole. But the aggrieved party reinstates the contract if the party accepts a non-conforming installment without seasonably notifying of cancellation or if the party brings an action with respect only to past installments or demands performance as to future installments.

* * * *

Part 7 Remedies

§2—702. SELLER'S REMEDIES ON DISCOVERY OF BUYER'S INSOLVENCY

* * * *

(2) Where the seller discovers that the buyer has received goods on credit while insolvent the seller may reclaim the goods upon demand made within a reasonable time after the buyer's receipt of the goods. Except as provided in this subsection the seller may not base a right to reclaim goods on the buyer's fraudulent or innocent misrepresentation of solvency or of intent to pay.

* * * *

§2—705. SELLER'S STOPPAGE OF DELIVERY IN TRANSIT OR OTHERWISE

(1) The seller may stop delivery of goods in the possession of a carrier or other bailee when the seller discovers the buyer to be insolvent (Section 2—702) or when the buyer repudiates or fails to make a payment due before delivery or if for any other reason the seller has a right to withhold or reclaim the goods.

* * * *

§2—706. SELLER'S RESALE INCLUDING CONTRACT FOR RESALE

In an appropriate case involving breach by the buyer, the seller may resell the goods concerned or the undelivered balance thereof. Where the resale is made in good faith and in a commercially reasonable manner the seller may recover the difference between the contract price and the resale price together with any incidental or consequential damages allowed under the provisions of this Article (Section 2—710), but less expenses saved in consequence of the buyer's breach.

* * * *

§2—708. SELLER'S DAMAGES FOR NON-ACCEPTANCE OR REPUDIATION

(1) Subject to subsection (2) and to the provisions of this Article with respect to proof of market price (Section 2—723)

(a) the measure of damages for non-acceptance by the buyer is the difference between the contract price and the market price at the time and place for tender together with any incidental or consequential damages provided in this Article (Section 2—710), but less expenses saved in consequence of the buyer's breach; and

(b) the measure of damages for repudiation by the buyer is the difference between the contract price and the market price at the place for tender at the expiration of a commercially reasonable time after the seller learned of the repudiation, but no later than the time stated in paragraph (a), together with any incidental or consequential damages provided in this Article (Section 2—710), but less expenses saved in consequence of the buyer's breach.

(2) If the measure of damages provided in subsection (1) or in Section 2—706 is inadequate to put the seller in as good a position as performance would have done then the measure of damages is the profit (including reasonable overhead) which the seller would have made from full performance by the buyer, together with any incidental or consequential damages provided in this Article (Section 2—710).

§2—709. ACTION FOR THE PRICE

(1) When the buyer fails to pay the price as it becomes due the seller may recover, together with any incidental or consequential damages under the next section, the price

(a) of goods accepted or of conforming goods lost or damaged within a commercially reasonable time after risk of their loss has passed to the buyer; and

(b) of goods identified to the contract if the seller is unable after reasonable effort to resell them at a reasonable price or the circumstances reasonably indicate that such effort will be unavailing.

* * * *

§2—710. SELLER'S INCIDENTAL AND CONSEQUENTIAL DAMAGES

(1) Incidental damages to an aggrieved seller include any commercially reasonable charges, expenses or commissions incurred in stopping delivery, in the transportation, care and custody of goods after the buyer's breach, in connection with return or resale of the goods or otherwise resulting from the breach.

(2) Consequential damages resulting from the buyer's breach include any loss resulting from general or particular requirements and needs of which the buyer at the time of contracting had reason to know and which could not reasonably be prevented by resale or otherwise.

(3) In a consumer contract, a seller may not recover consequential damages from a consumer.

* * * *

§2—713. BUYER'S DAMAGES FOR NON-DELIVERY OR REPUDIATION

(1) Subject to the provisions of this Article with respect to proof of market price (Section 2—723), if the seller wrongfully fails to deliver or repudiates or the buyer rightfully rejects or justifiably revokes acceptance

(a) the measure of damages in the case of wrongful failure to deliver by the seller or rightful rejection or justifiable revocation of acceptance by the buyer is the difference between the market price at the time for tender under the contract and the contract price together with any incidental or consequential damages provided in this Article (Section 2—715), but less expenses saved in consequence of the seller's breach; and

(b) the measure of damages for repudiation by the seller is the difference between the market price at the expiration of a commercially reasonable time after the buyer learned of the repudiation, but no later than the time stated in paragraph (a), and the contract price together with any incidental or consequential damages provided in this Article (Section 2—715), but less expenses saved in consequence of the seller's breach.

* * * *

§2—725. STATUTE OF LIMITATIONS IN CONTRACTS FOR SALE

(1) Except as otherwise provided in this section, an action for breach of any contract for sale must be commenced within the later of four years after the right of action has accrued under subsection (2) or (3) or one year after the breach was or should have been discovered, but no longer than five years after the right of action accrued. By the original agreement the parties may reduce the period of limitation to not less than one year but may not extend it; however, in a consumer contract, the period of limitation may not be reduced.

(2) Except as otherwise provided in subsection (3), the following rules apply:

(a) Except as otherwise provided in this subsection, a right of action for breach of a contract accrues when the breach occurs, even if the aggrieved party did not have knowledge of the breach.

(b) For breach of a contract by repudiation, a right of action accrues at the earlier of when the aggrieved party elects to treat the repudiation as a breach or when a commercially reasonable time for awaiting performance has expired.

* * * *

ARTICLE 2A LEASES

§2A—102. SCOPE

This Article applies to any transaction, regardless of form, that creates a lease.

§2A—103. DEFINITIONS AND INDEX OF DEFINITIONS

* * * *

(e) "Consumer lease" means a lease that a lessor regularly engaged in the business of leasing or selling makes to a lessee who is an individual and who takes under the lease primarily for a personal, family, or household purpose [, if the total payments to be made under the lease contract, excluding payments for options to renew or buy, do not exceed $___].

* * * *

(g) "Finance lease" means a lease with respect to which:

(i) the lessor does not select, manufacture or supply the goods;

(ii) the lessor acquires the goods or the right to possession and use of the goods in connection with the lease; and

(iii) one of the following occurs:

(A) the lessee receives a copy of the contract by which the lessor acquired the goods or the right to possession and use of the goods before signing the lease contract;

(B) the lessee's approval of the contract by which the lessor acquired the goods or the right to possession and use of the goods is a condition to effectiveness of the lease contract;

(C) the lessee, before signing the lease contract, receives an accurate and complete statement designating the promises and warranties, and any disclaimers of warranties, limitations or modifications of remedies, or liquidated damages, including those of a third party, such as the manufacturer of the goods, provided to the lessor by the person supplying the goods in connection with or as part of the contract by which the lessor acquired the goods or the right to possession and use of the goods; or

(D) if the lease is not a consumer lease, the lessor, before the lessee signs the lease contract, informs the lessee in writing (a) of the identity of the person supplying the goods to the lessor, unless the lessee has selected that person and directed the lessor to acquire the goods or the right to possession and use of the goods from that person, (b) that the lessee is entitled under this Article to any promises and warranties, including those of any third party, provided to the lessor by the person supplying the goods in connection with or as part of the contract by which the lessor acquired the goods or the right to possession and use of the goods, and (c) that the lessee may communicate with the person supplying the goods to the lessor and receive an accurate and complete statement of those promises and warranties, including any disclaimers and limitations of them or of remedies.

* * * *

(h) "Goods" means all things that are movable at the time of identification to the lease contract, or are fixtures (Section 2A—309), but the term does not include money, documents, instruments, accounts, chattel paper, general intangibles, or minerals or the like, including oil and gas, before extraction. The term also includes the unborn young of animals.

(i) "Installment lease contract" means a lease contract that authorizes or requires the delivery of goods in separate lots to be separately accepted, even though the lease contract contains a clause "each delivery is a separate lease" or its equivalent.

(j) "Lease" means a transfer of the right to possession and use of goods for a term in return for consideration, but a sale, including a sale on approval or a sale or return, or retention or creation of a security interest is not a lease. Unless the context clearly indicates otherwise, the term includes a sublease.

(k) "Lease agreement" means the bargain, with respect to the lease, of the lessor and the lessee in fact as found in their language or by implication from other circumstances including course of dealing or usage of trade or course of performance as provided in this Article. Unless the context clearly indicates otherwise, the term includes a sublease agreement.

(l) "Lease contract" means the total legal obligation that results from the lease agreement as affected by this Article and any other applicable rules of law. Unless the context clearly indicates otherwise, the term includes a sublease contract.

* * * *

(o) "Lessee in ordinary course of business" means a person who in good faith and without knowledge that the lease to him [or her] is in violation of the ownership rights or security interest or leasehold interest of a third party in the goods, leases in ordinary course from a person in the business of selling or leasing goods of that kind but does not include a pawnbroker. "Leasing" may be for cash or by exchange of other property or on secured or unsecured credit and includes receiving goods or documents of title under a pre-existing lease contract but does not include a transfer in bulk or as security for or in total or partial satisfaction of a money debt.

(p) "Lessor" means a person who transfers the right to possession and use of goods under a lease. Unless the context clearly indicates otherwise, the term includes a sublessor.

(q) "Lessor's residual interest" means the lessor's interest in the goods after expiration, termination, or cancellation of the lease contract.

* * * *

§2A—104. LEASES SUBJECT TO OTHER LAW

(1) A lease, although subject to this Article, is also subject to any applicable:

(a) certificate of title statute of this State: (list any certificate of title statutes covering automobiles, trailers, mobile homes, boats, farm tractors, and the like);

(b) certificate of title statute of another jurisdiction (Section 2A—105); or

(c) consumer protection statute of this State, or final consumer protection decision of a court of this State existing on the effective date of this Article.

§2A—105. TERRITORIAL APPLICATION OF ARTICLE TO GOODS COVERED BY CERTIFICATE OF TITLE

Subject to the provisions of Sections 2A—304(3) and 2A—305(3), with respect to goods covered by a certificate of title issued under a statute of this State or of another jurisdiction, compliance and the effect of compliance or noncompliance with a certificate of title statute are governed by the law (including the conflict of laws rules) of the jurisdiction issuing the certificate until the earlier of (a) surrender of the certificate, or (b) four months after the goods are removed from that jurisdiction and thereafter until a new certificate of title is issued by another jurisdiction.

* * * *

§2A—108. UNCONSCIONABILITY

(1) If the court as a matter of law finds a lease contract or any clause of a lease contract to have been unconscionable at the time it was made the court may refuse to enforce the lease contract, or it may enforce the remainder of the lease contract without the unconscionable clause, or it may so

limit the application of any unconscionable clause as to avoid any unconscionable result.

(2) With respect to a consumer lease, if the court as a matter of law finds that a lease contract or any clause of a lease contract has been induced by unconscionable conduct or that unconscionable conduct has occurred in the collection of a claim arising from a lease contract, the court may grant appropriate relief.

(3) Before making a finding of unconscionability under subsection (1) or (2), the court, on its own motion or that of a party, shall afford the parties a reasonable opportunity to present evidence as to the setting, purpose, and effect of the lease contract or clause thereof, or of the conduct.

(4) In an action in which the lessee claims unconscionability with respect to a consumer lease:

(a) If the court finds unconscionability under subsection (1) or (2), the court shall award reasonable attorney's fees to the lessee.

(b) If the court does not find unconscionability and the lessee claiming unconscionability has brought or maintained an action he [or she] knew to be groundless, the court shall award reasonable attorney's fees to the party against whom the claim is made.

(c) In determining attorney's fees, the amount of the recovery on behalf of the claimant under subsections (1) and (2) is not controlling.

§2A—109. OPTION TO ACCELERATE AT WILL

(1) A term providing that one party or his [or her] successor in interest may accelerate payment or performance or require collateral or additional collateral "at will" or "when he [or she] deems himself [or herself] insecure" or in words of similar import must be construed to mean that he [or she] has power to do so only if he [or she] in good faith believes that the prospect of payment or performance is impaired.

(2) With respect to a consumer lease, the burden of establishing good faith under subsection (1) is on the party who exercised the power; otherwise the burden of establishing lack of good faith is on the party against whom the power has been exercised.

Part 2 Formation and Construction of Lease Contract

§2A—201. STATUTE OF FRAUDS

(1) A lease contract is not enforceable by way of action or defense unless:

(a) the total payments to be made under the lease contract, excluding payments for options to renew or buy, are less than $1,000; or

(b) there is a writing, signed by the party against whom enforcement is sought or by that party's authorized agent, sufficient to indicate that a lease contract has been made between the parties and to describe the goods leased and the lease term.

(2) Any description of leased goods or of the lease term is sufficient and satisfies subsection (1)(b), whether or not it is specific, if it reasonably identifies what is described.

(3) A writing is not insufficient because it omits or incorrectly states a term agreed upon, but the lease contract is not enforceable under subsection (1)(b) beyond the lease term and the quantity of goods shown in the writing.

(4) A lease contract that does not satisfy the requirements of subsection (1), but which is valid in other respects, is enforceable:

(a) if the goods are to be specially manufactured or obtained for the lessee and are not suitable for lease or sale to others in the ordinary course of the lessor's business, and the lessor, before notice of repudiation is received and under circumstances that reasonably indicate that the goods are for the lessee, has made either a substantial beginning of their manufacture or commitments for their procurement;

(b) if the party against whom enforcement is sought admits in that party's pleading, testimony or otherwise in court that a lease contract was made, but the lease contract is not enforceable under this provision beyond the quantity of goods admitted; or

(c) with respect to goods that have been received and accepted by the lessee.

(5) The lease term under a lease contract referred to in subsection (4) is:

(a) if there is a writing signed by the party against whom enforcement is sought or by that party's authorized agent specifying the lease term, the term so specified;

(b) if the party against whom enforcement is sought admits in that party's pleading, testimony, or otherwise in court a lease term, the term so admitted; or

(c) a reasonable lease term.

§2A—202. FINAL WRITTEN EXPRESSION: PAROL OR EXTRINSIC EVIDENCE

Terms with respect to which the confirmatory memoranda of the parties agree or which are otherwise set forth in a writing intended by the parties as a final expression of their agreement with respect to such terms as are included therein may not be contradicted by evidence of any prior agreement or of a contemporaneous oral agreement but may be explained or supplemented:

(a) by course of dealing or usage of trade or by course of performance; and

(b) by evidence of consistent additional terms unless the court finds the writing to have been intended also as a complete and exclusive statement of the terms of the agreement.

* * * *

§2A—205. FIRM OFFERS

An offer by a merchant to lease goods to or from another person in a signed writing that by its terms gives assurance it will be held open is not revocable, for lack of consideration, during the time stated or, if no time is stated, for a reasonable time, but in no event may the period of irrevocability exceed 3 months. Any such term of assurance on a form supplied by the offeree must be separately signed by the offeror.

§2A—206. OFFER AND ACCEPTANCE IN FORMATION OF LEASE CONTRACT

(1) Unless otherwise unambiguously indicated by the language or circumstances, an offer to make a lease contract must be construed as inviting acceptance in any manner and by any medium reasonable in the circumstances.

(2) If the beginning of a requested performance is a reasonable mode of acceptance, an offeror who is not notified of acceptance within a reasonable time may treat the offer as having lapsed before acceptance.

§2A—207. COURSE OF PERFORMANCE OR PRACTICAL CONSTRUCTION

(1) If a lease contract involves repeated occasions for performance by either party with knowledge of the nature of the performance and opportunity for objection to it by the other, any course of performance accepted or acquiesced in without objection is relevant to determine the meaning of the lease agreement.

(2) The express terms of a lease agreement and any course of performance, as well as any course of dealing and usage of trade, must be construed whenever reasonable as consistent with each other; but if that construction is unreasonable, express terms control course of performance, course of performance controls both course of dealing and usage of trade, and course of dealing controls usage of trade.

(3) Subject to the provisions of Section 2A—208 on modification and waiver, course of performance is relevant to show a waiver or modification of any term inconsistent with the course of performance.

§2A—208. MODIFICATION, RESCISSION AND WAIVER

(1) An agreement modifying a lease contract needs no consideration to be binding.

(2) A signed lease agreement that excludes modification or rescission except by a signed writing may not be otherwise modified or rescinded, but, except as between merchants, such a requirement on a form supplied by a merchant must be separately signed by the other party.

(3) Although an attempt at modification or rescission does not satisfy the requirements of subsection (2), it may operate as a waiver.

(4) A party who has made a waiver affecting an executory portion of a lease contract may retract the waiver by reasonable notification received by the other party that strict performance will be required of any term waived, unless the retraction would be unjust in view of a material change of position in reliance on the waiver.

* * * *

§2A—216. THIRD-PARTY BENEFICIARIES OF EXPRESS AND IMPLIED WARRANTIES

Alternative A

A warranty to or for the benefit of a lessee under this Article, whether express or implied, extends to any natural person who is in the family or household of the lessee or who is a guest in the lessee's home if it is reasonable to expect that such person may use, consume, or be affected by the goods and who is injured in person by breach of the warranty. This section does not displace principles of law and equity that extend a warranty to or for the benefit of a lessee to other persons. The operation of this section may not be excluded, modified, or limited, but an exclusion, modification, or limitation of the warranty, including any with respect to rights and remedies, effective against the lessee is also effective against any beneficiary designated under this section.

Alternative B

A warranty to or for the benefit of a lessee under this Article, whether express or implied, extends to any natural person who may reasonably be expected to use, consume, or be affected by the goods and who is injured in person by breach of the warranty. This section does not displace principles of law and equity that extend a warranty to or for the benefit of a lessee to other persons. The operation of this section may not be excluded, modified, or limited, but an exclusion, modification, or limitation of the warranty, including any with respect to rights and remedies, effective against the lessee is also effective against the beneficiary designated under this section.

Alternative C

A warranty to or for the benefit of a lessee under this Article, whether express or implied, extends to any person who may reasonably be expected to use, consume, or be affected by the goods and who is injured by breach of the warranty. The operation of this section may not be excluded, modified, or limited with respect to injury to the person of an individual to whom the warranty extends, but an exclusion, modification, or limitation of the warranty, including any with respect to rights and remedies, effective against the lessee is also effective against the beneficiary designated under this section.

* * * *

§2A—219. RISK OF LOSS

(1) Except in the case of a finance lease, risk of loss is retained by the lessor and does not pass to the lessee. In the case of a finance lease, risk of loss passes to the lessee.

(2) Subject to the provisions of this Article on the effect of default on risk of loss (Section 2A—220), if risk of loss is to pass to the lessee and the time of passage is not stated, the following rules apply:

(a) If the lease contract requires or authorizes the goods to be shipped by carrier

(i) and it does not require delivery at a particular destination, the risk of loss passes to the lessee when the goods are duly delivered to the carrier; but

(ii) if it does require delivery at a particular destination and the goods are there duly tendered while in the possession of the carrier, the risk of loss passes to the lessee when the goods are there duly so tendered as to enable the lessee to take delivery.

(b) If the goods are held by a bailee to be delivered without being moved, the risk of loss passes to the lessee on acknowledgment by the bailee of the lessee's right to possession of the goods.

(c) In any case not within subsection (a) or (b), the risk of loss passes to the lessee on the lessee's receipt of the goods if the lessor, or, in the case of a finance lease, the supplier, is a merchant; otherwise the risk passes to the lessee on tender of delivery.

§2A—220. EFFECT OF DEFAULT ON RISK OF LOSS

(1) Where risk of loss is to pass to the lessee and the time of passage is not stated:

(a) If a tender or delivery of goods so fails to conform to the lease contract as to give a right of rejection, the risk of their loss remains with the lessor, or, in the case of a finance lease, the supplier, until cure or acceptance.

(b) If the lessee rightfully revokes acceptance, he [or she], to the extent of any deficiency in his [or her] effective insurance coverage, may treat the risk of loss as having remained with the lessor from the beginning.

(2) Whether or not risk of loss is to pass to the lessee, if the lessee as to conforming goods already identified to a lease contract repudiates or is otherwise in default under the lease contract, the lessor, or, in the case of a finance lease, the supplier, to the extent of any deficiency in his [or her] effective insurance coverage may treat the risk of loss as resting on the lessee for a commercially reasonable time.

* * * *

§2A—304. SUBSEQUENT LEASE OF GOODS BY LESSOR

(1) Subject to Section 2A—303, a subsequent lessee from a lessor of goods under an existing lease contract obtains, to the extent of the leasehold interest transferred, the leasehold interest in the goods that the lessor had or had power to transfer, and except as provided in subsection (2) and Section 2A—527(4), takes subject to the existing lease contract. A lessor with voidable title has power to transfer a good leasehold interest to a good faith subsequent lessee for value, but only to the extent set forth in the preceding sentence. If goods have been delivered under a transaction of purchase the lessor has that power even though:

(a) the lessor's transferor was deceived as to the identity of the lessor;

(b) the delivery was in exchange for a check which is later dishonored;

(c) it was agreed that the transaction was to be a "cash sale"; or

(d) the delivery was procured through fraud punishable as larcenous under the criminal law.

(2) A subsequent lessee in the ordinary course of business from a lessor who is a merchant dealing in goods of that kind to whom the goods were entrusted by the existing lessee of that lessor before the interest of the subsequent lessee became enforceable against that lessor obtains, to the extent of the leasehold interest transferred, all of that lessor's and the existing lessee's rights to the goods, and takes free of the existing lease contract.

(3) A subsequent lessee from the lessor of goods that are subject to an existing lease contract and are covered by a certificate of title issued under a statute of this State or of another jurisdiction takes no greater rights than those provided both by this section and by the certificate of title statute.

§2A—305. SALE OR SUBLEASE OF GOODS BY LESSEE

(1) Subject to the provisions of Section 2A—303, a buyer or sublessee from the lessee of goods under an existing lease contract obtains, to the extent of the interest transferred, the leasehold interest in the goods that the lessee had or had power to transfer, and except as provided in subsection (2) and Section 2A—511(4), takes subject to the existing lease contract. A lessee with a voidable leasehold interest has power to transfer a good leasehold interest to a good faith buyer for value or a good faith sublessee for value, but

only to the extent set forth in the preceding sentence. When goods have been delivered under a transaction of lease the lessee has that power even though:

(a) the lessor was deceived as to the identity of the lessee;

(b) the delivery was in exchange for a check which is later dishonored; or

(c) the delivery was procured through fraud punishable as larcenous under the criminal law.

(2) A buyer in the ordinary course of business or a sublessee in the ordinary course of business from a lessee who is a merchant dealing in goods of that kind to whom the goods were entrusted by the lessor obtains, to the extent of the interest transferred, all of the lessor's and lessee's rights to the goods, and takes free of the existing lease contract.

(3) A buyer or sublessee from the lessee of goods that are subject to an existing lease contract and are covered by a certificate of title issued under a statute of this State or of another jurisdiction takes no greater rights than those provided both by this section and by the certificate of title statute.

* * * *

§2A—501. DEFAULT: PROCEDURE

(1) Whether the lessor or the lessee is in default under a lease contract is determined by the lease agreement and this Article.

(2) If the lessor or the lessee is in default under the lease contract, the party seeking enforcement has rights and remedies as provided in this Article and, except as limited by this Article, as provided in the lease agreement.

(3) If the lessor or the lessee is in default under the lease contract, the party seeking enforcement may reduce the party's claim to judgment, or otherwise enforce the lease contract by self-help or any available judicial procedure or nonjudicial procedure, including administrative proceeding, arbitration, or the like, in accordance with this Article.

(4) Except as otherwise provided in Section 1—106 (1) or this Article or the lease agreement, the rights and remedies referred to in subsections (2) and (3) are cumulative.

(5) If the lease agreement covers both real property and goods, the party seeking enforcement may proceed under this Part as to the goods, or under other applicable law as to both the real property and the goods in accordance with that party's rights and remedies in respect of the real property, in which case this Part does not apply.

§2A—502. NOTICE AFTER DEFAULT

Except as otherwise provided in this Article or the lease agreement, the lessor or lessee in default under the lease contract is not entitled to notice of default or notice of enforcement from the other party to the lease agreement.

§2A—503. MODIFICATION OR IMPAIRMENT OF RIGHTS AND REMEDIES

(1) Except as otherwise provided in this Article, the lease agreement may include rights and remedies for default in addition to or in substitution for those provided in this Article and may limit or alter the measure of damages recoverable under this Article.

(2) Resort to a remedy provided under this Article or in the lease agreement is optional unless the remedy is expressly agreed to be exclusive. If circumstances cause an exclusive or limited remedy to fail of its essential purpose, or provision for an exclusive remedy is unconscionable, remedy may be had as provided in this Article.

(3) Consequential damages may be liquidated under Section 2A—504, or may otherwise be limited, altered, or excluded unless the limitation, alteration, or exclusion is unconscionable. Limitation, alteration, or exclusion of consequential damages for injury to the person in the case of consumer goods is prima facie unconscionable but limitation, alteration, or exclusion of damages where the loss is commercial is not prima facie unconscionable.

(4) Rights and remedies on default by the lessor or the lessee with respect to any obligation or promise collateral or ancillary to the lease contract are not impaired by this Article.

As amended in 1990.

§2A—504. LIQUIDATION OF DAMAGES

(1) Damages payable by either party for default, or any other act or omission, including indemnity for loss or diminution of anticipated tax benefits or loss or damage to lessor's residual interest, may be liquidated in the lease agreement but only at an amount or by a formula that is reasonable in light of the then anticipated harm caused by the default or other act or omission.

(2) If the lease agreement provides for liquidation of damages, and such provision does not comply with subsection (1), or such provision is an exclusive or limited remedy that circumstances cause to fail of its essential purpose, remedy may be had as provided in this Article.

(3) If the lessor justifiably withholds or stops delivery of goods because of the lessee's default or insolvency (Section 2A—525 or 2A—526), the lessee is entitled to restitution of any amount by which the sum of his [or her] payments exceeds:

(a) the amount to which the lessor is entitled by virtue of terms liquidating the lessor's damages in accordance with subsection (1); or

(b) in the absence of those terms, 20 percent of the then present value of the total rent the lessee was obligated to pay for the balance of the lease term, or, in the case of a consumer lease, the lesser of such amount or $500.

(4) A lessee's right to restitution under subsection (3) is subject to offset to the extent the lessor establishes:

(a) a right to recover damages under the provisions of this Article other than subsection (1); and

(b) the amount or value of any benefits received by the lessee directly or indirectly by reason of the lease contract.

§2A—505. CANCELLATION AND TERMINATION AND EFFECT OF CANCELLATION, TERMINATION, RESCISSION, OR FRAUD ON RIGHTS AND REMEDIES

(1) On cancellation of the lease contract, all obligations that are still executory on both sides are discharged, but any right based on prior default or performance survives, and the cancelling party also retains any remedy for default of the whole lease contract or any unperformed balance.

(2) On termination of the lease contract, all obligations that are still executory on both sides are discharged but any right based on prior default or performance survives.

(3) Unless the contrary intention clearly appears, expressions of "cancellation," "rescission," or the like of the lease contract may not be construed as a renunciation or discharge of any claim in damages for an antecedent default.

(4) Rights and remedies for material misrepresentation or fraud include all rights and remedies available under this Article for default.

(5) Neither rescission nor a claim for rescission of the lease contract nor rejection or return of the goods may bar or be deemed inconsistent with a claim for damages or other right or remedy.

§2A—506. STATUTE OF LIMITATIONS

(1) An action for default under a lease contract, including breach of warranty or indemnity, must be commenced within 4 years after the cause of action accrued. By the original lease contract the parties may reduce the period of limitation to not less than one year.

(2) A cause of action for default accrues when the act or omission on which the default or breach of warranty is based is or should have been discovered by the aggrieved party, or when the default occurs, whichever is later. A cause of action for indemnity accrues when the act or omission on which the claim for indemnity is based is or should have been discovered by the indemnified party, whichever is later.

(3) If an action commenced within the time limited by subsection (1) is so terminated as to leave available a remedy by another action for the same default or breach of warranty or indemnity, the other action may be commenced after the expiration of the time limited and within 6 months after the termination of the first action unless the termination resulted from voluntary discontinuance or from dismissal for failure or neglect to prosecute.

(4) This section does not alter the law on tolling of the statute of limitations nor does it apply to causes of action that have accrued before this Article becomes effective.

* * * *

§2A—508. LESSEE'S REMEDIES

(1) If a lessor fails to deliver the goods in conformity to the lease contract (Section 2A—509) or repudiates the lease contract (Section 2A—402), or a lessee rightfully rejects the goods (Section 2A—509) or justifiably revokes acceptance of the goods (Section 2A—517), then with respect to any goods involved, and with respect to all of the goods if under an installment lease contract the value of the whole lease contract is substantially impaired (Section 2A—510), the lessor is in default under the lease contract and the lessee may:

(a) cancel the lease contract (Section 2A—505(1));

(b) recover so much of the rent and security as has been paid and is just under the circumstances;

(c) cover and recover damages as to all goods affected whether or not they have been identified to the lease contract (Sections 2A—518 and 2A—520), or recover damages for nondelivery (Sections 2A—519 and 2A—520);

(d) exercise any other rights or pursue any other remedies provided in the lease contract.

(2) If a lessor fails to deliver the goods in conformity to the lease contract or repudiates the lease contract, the lessee may also:

(a) if the goods have been identified, recover them (Section 2A—522); or

(b) in a proper case, obtain specific performance or replevy the goods (Section 2A—521).

(3) If a lessor is otherwise in default under a lease contract, the lessee may exercise the rights and pursue the remedies provided in the lease contract, which may include a right to cancel the lease, and in Section 2A—519(3).

(4) If a lessor has breached a warranty, whether express or implied, the lessee may recover damages (Section 2A—519(4)).

(5) On rightful rejection or justifiable revocation of acceptance, a lessee has a security interest in goods in the lessee's possession or control for any rent and security that has been paid and any expenses reasonably incurred in their inspection, receipt, transportation, and care and custody and may hold those goods and dispose of them in good faith and in a commercially reasonable manner, subject to Section 2A—527(5).

(6) Subject to the provisions of Section 2A—407, a lessee, on notifying the lessor of the lessee's intention to do so,

may deduct all or any part of the damages resulting from any default under the lease contract from any part of the rent still due under the same lease contract.

§2A—509. LESSEE'S RIGHTS ON IMPROPER DELIVERY; RIGHTFUL REJECTION

(1) Subject to the provisions of Section 2A—510 on default in installment lease contracts, if the goods or the tender or delivery fail in any respect to conform to the lease contract, the lessee may reject or accept the goods or accept any commercial unit or units and reject the rest of the goods.

(2) Rejection of goods is ineffective unless it is within a reasonable time after tender or delivery of the goods and the lessee seasonably notifies the lessor.

* * * *

§2A—512. LESSEE'S DUTIES AS TO RIGHTFULLY REJECTED GOODS

(1) Except as otherwise provided with respect to goods that threaten to decline in value speedily (Section 2A—511) and subject to any security interest of a lessee (Section 2A—508(5)):

(a) the lessee, after rejection of goods in the lessee's possession, shall hold them with reasonable care at the lessor's or the supplier's disposition for a reasonable time after the lessee's seasonable notification of rejection;

(b) if the lessor or the supplier gives no instructions within a reasonable time after notification of rejection, the lessee may store the rejected goods for the lessor's or the supplier's account or ship them to the lessor or the supplier or dispose of them for the lessor's or the supplier's account with reimbursement in the manner provided in Section 2A—511; but

(c) the lessee has no further obligations with regard to goods rightfully rejected.

(2) Action by the lessee pursuant to subsection (1) is not acceptance or conversion.

§2A—513. CURE BY LESSOR OF IMPROPER TENDER OR DELIVERY; REPLACEMENT

(1) If any tender or delivery by the lessor or the supplier is rejected because nonconforming and the time for performance has not yet expired, the lessor or the supplier may seasonably notify the lessee of the lessor's or the supplier's intention to cure and may then make a conforming delivery within the time provided in the lease contract.

(2) If the lessee rejects a nonconforming tender that the lessor or the supplier had reasonable grounds to believe would be acceptable with or without money allowance, the lessor or the supplier may have a further reasonable time to substitute a conforming tender if he [or she] seasonably notifies the lessee.

* * * *

Revised Article 3 Negotiable Instruments

Part 1 General Provisions and Definitions

§3—102. SUBJECT MATTER

(a) This Article applies to negotiable instruments. It does not apply to money, to payment orders governed by Article 4A, or to securities governed by Article 8.

(b) If there is conflict between this Article and Article 4 or 9, Articles 4 and 9 govern.

(c) Regulations of the Board of Governors of the Federal Reserve System and operating circulars of the Federal Reserve Banks supersede any inconsistent provision of this Article to the extent of the inconsistency.

§3—103. DEFINITIONS

(a) In this Article:

(1) "Acceptor" means a drawee who has accepted a draft.

(2) "Drawee" means a person ordered in a draft to make payment.

(3) "Drawer" means a person who signs or is identified in a draft as a person ordering payment.

(4) "Good faith" means honesty in fact and the observance of reasonable commercial standards of fair dealing.

(5) "Maker" means a person who signs or is identified in a note as a person undertaking to pay.

(6) "Order" means a written instruction to pay money signed by the person giving the instruction. The instruction may be addressed to any person, including the person giving the instruction, or to one or more persons jointly or in the alternative but not in succession. An authorization to pay is not an order unless the person authorized to pay is also instructed to pay.

(7) "Ordinary care" in the case of a person engaged in business means observance of reasonable commercial standards, prevailing in the area in which the person is located, with respect to the business in which the person is engaged. In the case of a bank that takes an instrument for processing for collection or payment by automated means, reasonable commercial standards do not require the bank to examine the instrument if the failure to examine does not violate the bank's prescribed procedures and the bank's procedures do not vary unreasonably from general banking usage not disapproved by this Article or Article 4.

(8) "Party" means a party to an instrument.

§3—104. NEGOTIABLE INSTRUMENT

(a) Except as provided in subsections (c) and (d), "negotiable instrument" means an unconditional promise or order to pay a fixed amount of money, with or without interest or other charges described in the promise or order, if it:

(1) is payable to bearer or to order at the time it is issued or first comes into possession of a holder;

(2) is payable on demand or at a definite time; and

(3) does not state any other undertaking or instruction by the person promising or ordering payment to do any act in addition to the payment of money, but the promise or order may contain (i) an undertaking or power to give, maintain, or protect collateral to secure payment, (ii) an authorization or power to the holder to confess judgment or realize on or dispose of collateral, or (iii) a waiver of the benefit of any law intended for the advantage or protection of an obligor.

(b) "Instrument" means a negotiable instrument.

(c) An order that meets all of the requirements of subsection (a), except paragraph (1), and otherwise falls within the definition of "check" in subsection (f) is a negotiable instrument and a check.

(d) A promise or order other than a check is not an instrument if, at the time it is issued or first comes into possession of a holder, it contains a conspicuous statement, however expressed, to the effect that the promise or order is not negotiable or is not an instrument governed by this Article.

(e) An instrument is a "note" if it is a promise and is a "draft" if it is an order. If an instrument falls within the definition of both "note" and "draft," a person entitled to enforce the instrument may treat it as either.

(f) "Check" means (i) a draft, other than a documentary draft, payable on demand and drawn on a bank or (ii) a cashier's check or teller's check. An instrument may be a check even though it is described on its face by another term, such as "money order."

(g) "Cashier's check" means a draft with respect to which the drawer and drawee are the same bank or branches of the same bank.

(h) "Teller's check" means a draft drawn by a bank (i) on another bank, or (ii) payable at or through a bank.

(i) "Traveler's check" means an instrument that (i) is payable on demand, (ii) is drawn on or payable at or through a bank, (iii) is designated by the term "traveler's check" or by a substantially similar term, and (iv) requires, as a condition to payment, a countersignature by a person whose specimen signature appears on the instrument.

(j) "Certificate of deposit" means an instrument containing an acknowledgment by a bank that a sum of money has been received by the bank and a promise by the bank to repay the sum of money. A certificate of deposit is a note of the bank.

* * * *

§3—106. UNCONDITIONAL PROMISE OR ORDER

(a) Except as provided in this section, for the purposes of Section 3—104(a), a promise or order is unconditional unless it states (i) an express condition to payment, (ii) that the promise or order is subject to or governed by another writing, or (iii) that rights or obligations with respect to the promise or order are stated in another writing. A reference to another writing does not of itself make the promise or order conditional.

(b) A promise or order is not made conditional (i) by a reference to another writing for a statement of rights with respect to collateral, prepayment, or acceleration, or (ii) because payment is limited to resort to a particular fund or source.

(c) If a promise or order requires, as a condition to payment, a countersignature by a person whose specimen signature appears on the promise or order, the condition does not make the promise or order conditional for the purposes of Section 3—104(a). If the person whose specimen signature appears on an instrument fails to countersign the instrument, the failure to countersign is a defense to the obligation of the issuer, but the failure does not prevent a transferee of the instrument from becoming a holder of the instrument.

(d) If a promise or order at the time it is issued or first comes into possession of a holder contains a statement, required by applicable statutory or administrative law, to the effect that the rights of a holder or transferee are subject to claims or defenses that the issuer could assert against the original payee, the promise or order is not thereby made conditional for the purposes of Section 3—104(a); but if the promise or order is an instrument, there cannot be a holder in due course of the instrument.

§3—107. INSTRUMENT PAYABLE IN FOREIGN MONEY

Unless the instrument otherwise provides, an instrument that states the amount payable in foreign money may be paid in the foreign money or in an equivalent amount in dollars calculated by using the current bank-offered spot rate at the place of payment for the purchase of dollars on the day on which the instrument is paid.

§3—108. PAYABLE ON DEMAND OR AT DEFINITE TIME

(a) A promise or order is "payable on demand" if it (i) states that it is payable on demand or at sight, or otherwise indicates that it is payable at the will of the holder, or (ii) does not state any time of payment.

(b) A promise or order is "payable at a definite time" if it is payable on elapse of a definite period of time after sight or acceptance or at a fixed date or dates or at a time or times readily ascertainable at the time the promise or order is issued, subject to rights of (i) prepayment, (ii) acceleration, (iii) extension at the option of the holder, or (iv) extension to a further definite time at the option of the maker or acceptor or automatically upon or after a specified act or event.

(c) If an instrument, payable at a fixed date, is also payable upon demand made before the fixed date, the instrument is payable on demand until the fixed date and, if demand for payment is not made before that date, becomes payable at a definite time on the fixed date.

§3—109. PAYABLE TO BEARER OR TO ORDER

(a) A promise or order is payable to bearer if it:

(1) states that it is payable to bearer or to the order of bearer or otherwise indicates that the person in possession of the promise or order is entitled to payment;

(2) does not state a payee; or

(3) states that it is payable to or to the order of cash or otherwise indicates that it is not payable to an identified person.

(b) A promise or order that is not payable to bearer is payable to order if it is payable (i) to the order of an identified person or (ii) to an identified person or order. A promise or order that is payable to order is payable to the identified person.

(c) An instrument payable to bearer may become payable to an identified person if it is specially indorsed pursuant to Section 3—205(a). An instrument payable to an identified person may become payable to bearer if it is indorsed in blank pursuant to Section 3—205(b).

§3—110. IDENTIFICATION OF PERSON TO WHOM INSTRUMENT IS PAYABLE

(a) The person to whom an instrument is initially payable is determined by the intent of the person, whether or not authorized, signing as, or in the name or behalf of, the issuer of the instrument. The instrument is payable to the person intended by the signer even if that person is identified in the instrument by a name or other identification that is not that of the intended person. If more than one person signs in the name or behalf of the issuer of an instrument and all the signers do not intend the same person as payee, the instrument is payable to any person intended by one or more of the signers.

(b) If the signature of the issuer of an instrument is made by automated means, such as a check-writing machine, the payee of the instrument is determined by the intent of the person who supplied the name or identification of the payee, whether or not authorized to do so.

(c) A person to whom an instrument is payable may be identified in any way, including by name, identifying number, office, or account number.

§3—111. PLACE OF PAYMENT

Except as otherwise provided for items in Article 4, an instrument is payable at the place of payment stated in the instrument. If no place of payment is stated, an instrument is payable at the address of the drawee or maker stated in the instrument. If no address is stated, the place of payment is the place of business of the drawee or maker. If a drawee or maker has more than one place of business, the place of payment is any place of business of the drawee or maker chosen by the person entitled to enforce the instrument. If the drawee or maker has no place of business, the place of payment is the residence of the drawee or maker.

§3—112. INTEREST

(a) Unless otherwise provided in the instrument, (i) an instrument is not payable with interest, and (ii) interest on an interest-bearing instrument is payable from the date of the instrument.

(b) Interest may be stated in an instrument as a fixed or variable amount of money or it may be expressed as a fixed or variable rate or rates. The amount or rate of interest may be stated or described in the instrument in any manner and may require reference to information not contained in the instrument. If an instrument provides for interest, but the amount of interest payable cannot be ascertained from the description, interest is payable at the judgment rate in effect at the place of payment of the instrument and at the time interest first accrues.

§3—113. DATE OF INSTRUMENT

(a) An instrument may be antedated or postdated. The date stated determines the time of payment if the instrument is payable at a fixed period after date. Except as provided in Section 4—401(c), an instrument payable on demand is not payable before the date of the instrument.

(b) If an instrument is undated, its date is the date of its issue or, in the case of an unissued instrument, the date it first comes into possession of a holder.

§3—114. CONTRADICTORY TERMS OF INSTRUMENT

If an instrument contains contradictory terms, typewritten terms prevail over printed terms, handwritten terms prevail over both, and words prevail over numbers.

§3—115. INCOMPLETE INSTRUMENT

(a) "Incomplete instrument" means a signed writing, whether or not issued by the signer, the contents of which show at the time of signing that it is incomplete but that the signer intended it to be completed by the addition of words or numbers.

(b) Subject to subsection (c), if an incomplete instrument is an instrument under Section 3—104, it may be enforced according to its terms if it is not completed, or according to its terms as augmented by completion. If an incomplete instrument is not an instrument under Section 3—104, but, after completion, the requirements of Section 3—104 are met, the instrument may be enforced according to its terms as augmented by completion.

(c) If words or numbers are added to an incomplete instrument without authority of the signer, there is an alteration of the incomplete instrument under Section 3—407.

(d) The burden of establishing that words or numbers were added to an incomplete instrument without authority of the signer is on the person asserting the lack of authority.

§3—116. JOINT AND SEVERAL LIABILITY; CONTRIBUTION

(a) Except as otherwise provided in the instrument, two or more persons who have the same liability on an instrument as makers, drawers, acceptors, indorsers who indorse as joint payees, or anomalous indorsers are jointly and severally liable in the capacity in which they sign.

(b) Except as provided in Section 3—419(e) or by agreement of the affected parties, a party having joint and several liability who pays the instrument is entitled to receive from any party having the same joint and several liability contribution in accordance with applicable law.

(c) Discharge of one party having joint and several liability by a person entitled to enforce the instrument does not affect the right under subsection (b) of a party having the same joint and several liability to receive contribution from the party discharged.

* * * *

§3—118. STATUTE OF LIMITATIONS

(a) Except as provided in subsection (e), an action to enforce the obligation of a party to pay a note payable at a definite time must be commenced within six years after the due date or dates stated in the note or, if a due date is accelerated, within six years after the accelerated due date.

(b) Except as provided in subsection (d) or (e), if demand for payment is made to the maker of a note payable on demand, an action to enforce the obligation of a party to pay the note must be commenced within six years after the demand. If no demand for payment is made to the maker, an action to enforce the note is barred if neither principal nor interest on the note has been paid for a continuous period of 10 years.

(c) Except as provided in subsection (d), an action to enforce the obligation of a party to an unaccepted draft to pay the draft must be commenced within three years after dishonor of the draft or 10 years after the date of the draft, whichever period expires first.

(d) An action to enforce the obligation of the acceptor of a certified check or the issuer of a teller's check, cashier's check, or traveler's check must be commenced within three years after demand for payment is made to the acceptor or issuer, as the case may be.

(e) An action to enforce the obligation of a party to a certificate of deposit to pay the instrument must be commenced within six years after demand for payment is made to the maker, but if the instrument states a due date and the maker is not required to pay before that date, the six-year period begins when a demand for payment is in effect and the due date has passed.

(f) An action to enforce the obligation of a party to pay an accepted draft, other than a certified check, must be commenced (i) within six years after the due date or dates stated in the draft or acceptance if the obligation of the acceptor is payable at a definite time, or (ii) within six years after the date of the acceptance if the obligation of the acceptor is payable on demand.

(g) Unless governed by other law regarding claims for indemnity or contribution, an action (i) for conversion of an instrument, for money had and received, or like action based on conversion, (ii) for breach of warranty, or (iii) to enforce an obligation, duty, or right arising under this Article and not governed by this section must be commenced within three years after the [cause of action] accrues.

* * * *

Part 2 Negotiation, Transfer, and Indorsement

§3—201. NEGOTIATION

(a) "Negotiation" means a transfer of possession, whether voluntary or involuntary, of an instrument by a person other than the issuer to a person who thereby becomes its holder.

(b) Except for negotiation by a remitter, if an instrument is payable to an identified person, negotiation requires transfer of possession of the instrument and its indorsement by the holder. If an instrument is payable to bearer, it may be negotiated by transfer of possession alone.

* * * *

§3—203. TRANSFER OF INSTRUMENT; RIGHTS ACQUIRED BY TRANSFER

(a) An instrument is transferred when it is delivered by a person other than its issuer for the purpose of giving to the person receiving delivery the right to enforce the instrument.

(b) Transfer of an instrument, whether or not the transfer is a negotiation, vests in the transferee any right of the transferor to enforce the instrument, including any right as a holder in due course, but the transferee cannot acquire rights of a holder in due course by a transfer, directly or indirectly, from a holder in due course if the transferee engaged in fraud or illegality affecting the instrument.

(c) Unless otherwise agreed, if an instrument is transferred for value and the transferee does not become a holder because of lack of indorsement by the transferor, the transferee has a specifically enforceable right to the unqualified indorsement of the transferor, but negotiation of the instrument does not occur until the indorsement is made.

(d) If a transferor purports to transfer less than the entire instrument, negotiation of the instrument does not occur. The transferee obtains no rights under this Article and has only the rights of a partial assignee.

§3—204. INDORSEMENT

(a) "Indorsement" means a signature, other than that of a signer as maker, drawer, or acceptor, that alone or accompanied by other words is made on an instrument for the purpose of (i) negotiating the instrument, (ii) restricting payment of the instrument, or (iii) incurring indorser's liability on the instrument, but regardless of the intent of the signer, a signature and its accompanying words is an indorsement unless the accompanying words, terms of the instrument, place of the signature, or other circumstances unambiguously indicate that the signature was made for a purpose other than indorsement. For the purpose of determining whether a signature is made on an instrument, a paper affixed to the instrument is a part of the instrument.

(b) "Indorser" means a person who makes an indorsement.

(c) For the purpose of determining whether the transferee of an instrument is a holder, an indorsement that transfers a security interest in the instrument is effective as an unqualified indorsement of the instrument.

(d) If an instrument is payable to a holder under a name that is not the name of the holder, indorsement may be made by the holder in the name stated in the instrument or in the holder's name or both, but signature in both names may be required by a person paying or taking the instrument for value or collection.

§3—205. SPECIAL INDORSEMENT; BLANK INDORSEMENT; ANOMALOUS INDORSEMENT

(a) If an indorsement is made by the holder of an instrument, whether payable to an identified person or payable to bearer, and the indorsement identifies a person to whom it makes the instrument payable, it is a "special indorsement." When specially indorsed, an instrument becomes payable to the identified person and may be negotiated only by the indorsement of that person. The principles stated in Section 3—110 apply to special indorsements.

(b) If an indorsement is made by the holder of an instrument and it is not a special indorsement, it is a "blank indorsement." When indorsed in blank, an instrument becomes payable to bearer and may be negotiated by transfer of possession alone until specially indorsed.

(c) The holder may convert a blank indorsement that consists only of a signature into a special indorsement by writing, above the signature of the indorser, words identifying the person to whom the instrument is made payable.

(d) "Anomalous indorsement" means an indorsement made by a person who is not the holder of the instrument. An anomalous indorsement does not affect the manner in which the instrument may be negotiated.

§3—206. RESTRICTIVE INDORSEMENT

(a) An indorsement limiting payment to a particular person or otherwise prohibiting further transfer or negotiation of the instrument is not effective to prevent further transfer or negotiation of the instrument.

(b) An indorsement stating a condition to the right of the indorsee to receive payment does not affect the right of the indorsee to enforce the instrument. A person paying the instrument or taking it for value or collection may disregard the condition, and the rights and liabilities of that person are not affected by whether the condition has been fulfilled.

(c) If an instrument bears an indorsement (i) described in Section 4—201(b), or (ii) in blank or to a particular bank using the words "for deposit," "for collection," or other words indicating a purpose of having the instrument collected by a bank for the indorser or for a particular account, the following rules apply:

(1) A person, other than a bank, who purchases the instrument when so indorsed converts the instrument unless the amount paid for the instrument is received by the indorser or applied consistently with the indorsement.

(2) A depositary bank that purchases the instrument or takes it for collection when so indorsed converts the instrument unless the amount paid by the bank with respect to the instrument is received by the indorser or applied consistently with the indorsement.

(3) A payor bank that is also the depositary bank or that takes the instrument for immediate payment over the counter from a person other than a collecting bank converts the instrument unless the proceeds of the instrument are received by the indorser or applied consistently with the indorsement.

(4) Except as otherwise provided in paragraph (3), a payor bank or intermediary bank may disregard the indorsement and is not liable if the proceeds of the instrument are not received by the indorser or applied consistently with the indorsement.

(d) Except for an indorsement covered by subsection (c), if an instrument bears an indorsement using words to the effect that payment is to be made to the indorsee as agent, trustee, or other fiduciary for the benefit of the indorser or another person, the following rules apply:

(1) Unless there is notice of breach of fiduciary duty as provided in Section 3—307, a person who purchases the instrument from the indorsee or takes the instrument from the indorsee for collection or payment may pay the proceeds of payment or the value given for the instrument to the indorsee without regard to whether the indorsee violates a fiduciary duty to the indorser.

(2) A subsequent transferee of the instrument or person who pays the instrument is neither given notice nor otherwise affected by the restriction in the indorsement unless the transferee or payor knows that the fiduciary dealt with the instrument or its proceeds in breach of fiduciary duty.

(e) The presence on an instrument of an indorsement to which this section applies does not prevent a purchaser of the instrument from becoming a holder in due course of the instrument unless the purchaser is a converter under subsection (c) or has notice or knowledge of breach of fiduciary duty as stated in subsection (d).

(f) In an action to enforce the obligation of a party to pay the instrument, the obligor has a defense if payment would violate an indorsement to which this section applies and the payment is not permitted by this section.

§3—207. REACQUISITION

Reacquisition of an instrument occurs if it is transferred to a former holder, by negotiation or otherwise. A former holder who reacquires the instrument may cancel indorsements made after the reacquirer first became a holder of the instrument. If the cancellation causes the instrument to be payable to the reacquirer or to bearer, the reacquirer may negotiate the instrument. An indorser whose indorsement is canceled is discharged, and the discharge is effective against any subsequent holder.

Part 3 Enforcement of Instruments

§3—301. PERSON ENTITLED TO ENFORCE INSTRUMENT

"Person entitled to enforce" an instrument means (i) the holder of the instrument, (ii) a nonholder in possession of the instrument who has the rights of a holder, or (iii) a person not in possession of the instrument who is entitled to enforce the instrument pursuant to Section 3—309 or 3—418(d). A person may be a person entitled to enforce the instrument even though the person is not the owner of the instrument or is in wrongful possession of the instrument.

§3—302. HOLDER IN DUE COURSE

(a) Subject to subsection (c) and Section 3—106(d), "holder in due course" means the holder of an instrument if:

(1) the instrument when issued or negotiated to the holder does not bear such apparent evidence of forgery or alteration or is not otherwise so irregular or incomplete as to call into question its authenticity; and

(2) the holder took the instrument (i) for value, (ii) in good faith, (iii) without notice that the instrument is overdue or has been dishonored or that there is an uncured default with respect to payment of another instrument issued as part of the same series, (iv) without notice that the instrument contains an unauthorized signature or has been altered, (v) without notice of any claim to the instrument described in Section 3—306, and (vi) without notice that any party has a defense or claim in recoupment described in Section 3—305(a).

(b) Notice of discharge of a party, other than discharge in an insolvency proceeding, is not notice of a defense under subsection (a), but discharge is effective against a person who became a holder in due course with notice of the discharge. Public filing or recording of a document does not of itself constitute notice of a defense, claim in recoupment, or claim to the instrument.

(c) Except to the extent a transferor or predecessor in interest has rights as a holder in due course, a person does not acquire rights of a holder in due course of an instrument taken (i) by legal process or by purchase in an execution, bankruptcy, or creditor's sale or similar proceeding, (ii) by purchase as part of a bulk transaction not in ordinary course of business of the transferor, or (iii) as the successor in interest to an estate or other organization.

(d) If, under Section 3—303(a)(1), the promise of performance that is the consideration for an instrument has been partially performed, the holder may assert rights as a holder in due course of the instrument only to the fraction of the amount payable under the instrument equal to the value of the partial performance divided by the value of the promised performance.

(e) If (i) the person entitled to enforce an instrument has only a security interest in the instrument and (ii) the person obliged to pay the instrument has a defense, claim in recoupment, or claim to the instrument that may be asserted against the person who granted the security interest, the person entitled to enforce the instrument may assert rights as a holder in due course only to an amount payable under the instrument which, at the time of enforcement of the instrument, does not exceed the amount of the unpaid obligation secured.

(f) To be effective, notice must be received at a time and in a manner that gives a reasonable opportunity to act on it.

(g) This section is subject to any law limiting status as a holder in due course in particular classes of transactions.

§3—303. VALUE AND CONSIDERATION

(a) An instrument is issued or transferred for value if:

(1) the instrument is issued or transferred for a promise of performance, to the extent the promise has been performed;

(2) the transferee acquires a security interest or other lien in the instrument other than a lien obtained by judicial proceeding;

(3) the instrument is issued or transferred as payment of, or as security for, an antecedent claim against any person, whether or not the claim is due;

(4) the instrument is issued or transferred in exchange for a negotiable instrument; or

(5) the instrument is issued or transferred in exchange for the incurring of an irrevocable obligation to a third party by the person taking the instrument.

(b) "Consideration" means any consideration sufficient to support a simple contract. The drawer or maker of an instrument has a defense if the instrument is issued without consideration. If an instrument is issued for a promise of performance, the issuer has a defense to the extent performance of the promise is due and the promise has not been performed. If an instrument is issued for value as stated in subsection (a), the instrument is also issued for consideration.

§3—304. OVERDUE INSTRUMENT

(a) An instrument payable on demand becomes overdue at the earliest of the following times:

(1) on the day after the day demand for payment is duly made;

(2) if the instrument is a check, 90 days after its date; or

(3) if the instrument is not a check, when the instrument has been outstanding for a period of time after its date which is unreasonably long under the circumstances of the particular case in light of the nature of the instrument and usage of the trade.

(b) With respect to an instrument payable at a definite time the following rules apply:

(1) If the principal is payable in installments and a due date has not been accelerated, the instrument becomes overdue upon default under the instrument for nonpayment of an installment, and the instrument remains overdue until the default is cured.

(2) If the principal is not payable in installments and the due date has not been accelerated, the instrument becomes overdue on the day after the due date.

(3) If a due date with respect to principal has been accelerated, the instrument becomes overdue on the day after the accelerated due date.

(c) Unless the due date of principal has been accelerated, an instrument does not become overdue if there is default in payment of interest but no default in payment of principal.

§3—305. DEFENSES AND CLAIMS IN RECOUPMENT

(a) Except as stated in subsection (b), the right to enforce the obligation of a party to pay an instrument is subject to the following:

(1) a defense of the obligor based on (i) infancy of the obligor to the extent it is a defense to a simple contract, (ii) duress, lack of legal capacity, or illegality of the transaction which, under other law, nullifies the obligation of the obligor, (iii) fraud that induced the obligor to sign the instrument with neither knowledge nor reasonable opportunity to learn of its character or its essential terms, or (iv) discharge of the obligor in insolvency proceedings;

(2) a defense of the obligor stated in another section of this Article or a defense of the obligor that would be available if the person entitled to enforce the instrument were enforcing a right to payment under a simple contract; and

(3) a claim in recoupment of the obligor against the original payee of the instrument if the claim arose from the transaction that gave rise to the instrument; but the claim of the obligor may be asserted against a transferee of the instrument only to reduce the amount owing on the instrument at the time the action is brought.

(b) The right of a holder in due course to enforce the obligation of a party to pay the instrument is subject to defenses of the obligor stated in subsection (a)(1), but is not subject to defenses of the obligor stated in subsection (a)(2) or claims in recoupment stated in subsection (a)(3) against a person other than the holder.

(c) Except as stated in subsection (d), in an action to enforce the obligation of a party to pay the instrument, the obligor may not assert against the person entitled to enforce the instrument a defense, claim in recoupment, or claim to the instrument (Section 3—306) of another person, but the other person's claim to the instrument may be asserted by the obligor if the other person is joined in the action and personally asserts the claim against the person entitled to enforce the instrument. An obligor is not obliged to pay the instrument if the person seeking enforcement of the instrument does not have rights of a holder in due course and the obligor proves that the instrument is a lost or stolen instrument.

(d) In an action to enforce the obligation of an accommodation party to pay an instrument, the accommodation party may assert against the person entitled to enforce the instrument any defense or claim in recoupment under subsection (a) that the accommodated party could assert against the person entitled to enforce the instrument, except the defenses of discharge in insolvency proceedings, infancy, and lack of legal capacity.

§3—306. CLAIMS TO AN INSTRUMENT

A person taking an instrument, other than a person having rights of a holder in due course, is subject to a claim of a property or possessory right in the instrument or its proceeds, including a claim to rescind a negotiation and to recover the instrument or its proceeds. A person having rights of a holder in due course takes free of the claim to the instrument.

§3—307. NOTICE OF BREACH OF FIDUCIARY DUTY

(a) In this section:

(1) "Fiduciary" means an agent, trustee, partner, corporate officer or director, or other representative owing a fiduciary duty with respect to an instrument.

(2) "Represented person" means the principal, beneficiary, partnership, corporation, or other person to whom the duty stated in paragraph (1) is owed.

(b) If (i) an instrument is taken from a fiduciary for payment or collection or for value, (ii) the taker has knowledge of the fiduciary status of the fiduciary, and (iii) the represented person makes a claim to the instrument or its proceeds on the basis that the transaction of the fiduciary is a breach of fiduciary duty, the following rules apply:

(1) Notice of breach of fiduciary duty by the fiduciary is notice of the claim of the represented person.

(2) In the case of an instrument payable to the represented person or the fiduciary as such, the taker has notice of the breach of fiduciary duty if the instrument is (i) taken in payment of or as security for a debt known by the taker to be the personal debt of the fiduciary, (ii) taken in a transaction known by the taker to be for the personal benefit of the fiduciary, or (iii) deposited to an account other than an account of the fiduciary, as such, or an account of the represented person.

(3) If an instrument is issued by the represented person or the fiduciary as such, and made payable to the fiduciary personally, the taker does not have notice of the breach of fiduciary duty unless the taker knows of the breach of fiduciary duty.

(4) If an instrument is issued by the represented person or the fiduciary as such, to the taker as payee, the taker has notice of the breach of fiduciary duty if the instrument is (i) taken in payment of or as security for a debt known by the taker to be the personal debt of the fiduciary, (ii) taken in a transaction known by the taker to be for the personal benefit of the fiduciary, or (iii) deposited to an account other than an account of the fiduciary, as such, or an account of the represented person.

§3—308. PROOF OF SIGNATURES AND STATUS AS HOLDER IN DUE COURSE

(a) In an action with respect to an instrument, the authenticity of, and authority to make, each signature on the instrument is admitted unless specifically denied in the pleadings. If the validity of a signature is denied in the pleadings, the burden of establishing validity is on the person claiming validity, but the signature is presumed to be authentic and authorized unless the action is to enforce the liability of the purported signer and the signer is dead or incompetent at the time of trial of the issue of validity of the signature. If an action to enforce the instrument is brought against a person as the undisclosed principal of a person who signed the instrument as a party to the instrument, the plaintiff has the burden of establishing that the defendant is liable on the instrument as a represented person under Section 3—402(a).

(b) If the validity of signatures is admitted or proved and there is compliance with subsection (a), a plaintiff producing the instrument is entitled to payment if the plaintiff proves entitlement to enforce the instrument under Section 3—301, unless the defendant proves a defense or claim in recoupment. If a defense or claim in recoupment is proved, the right to payment of the plaintiff is subject to the defense or claim, except to the extent the plaintiff proves that the plaintiff has rights of a holder in due course which are not subject to the defense or claim.

§3—309. ENFORCEMENT OF LOST, DESTROYED, OR STOLEN INSTRUMENT

(a) A person not in possession of an instrument is entitled to enforce the instrument if (i) the person was in possession of the instrument and entitled to enforce it when loss of possession occurred, (ii) the loss of possession was not the result of a transfer by the person or a lawful seizure, and (iii) the person cannot reasonably obtain possession of the instrument because the instrument was destroyed, its whereabouts cannot be determined, or it is in the wrongful possession of an unknown person or a person that cannot be found or is not amenable to service of process.

(b) A person seeking enforcement of an instrument under subsection (a) must prove the terms of the instrument and the person's right to enforce the instrument. If that proof is made, Section 3—308 applies to the case as if the person seeking enforcement had produced the instrument. The court may not enter judgment in favor of the person seeking enforcement unless it finds that the person required to pay the instrument is adequately protected against loss that might occur by reason of a claim by another person to enforce the instrument. Adequate protection may be provided by any reasonable means.

§3—310. EFFECT OF INSTRUMENT ON OBLIGATION FOR WHICH TAKEN

(a) Unless otherwise agreed, if a certified check, cashier's check, or teller's check is taken for an obligation, the obligation is discharged to the same extent discharge would result if an amount of money equal to the amount of the instrument were taken in payment of the obligation. Discharge of the obligation does not affect any liability that the obligor may have as an indorser of the instrument.

(b) Unless otherwise agreed and except as provided in subsection (a), if a note or an uncertified check is taken for an obligation, the obligation is suspended to the same extent the obligation would be discharged if an amount of money equal to the amount of the instrument were taken, and the following rules apply:

(1) In the case of an uncertified check, suspension of the obligation continues until dishonor of the check or until it is paid or certified. Payment or certification of the check results in discharge of the obligation to the extent of the amount of the check.

(2) In the case of a note, suspension of the obligation continues until dishonor of the note or until it is paid. Payment of the note results in discharge of the obligation to the extent of the payment.

(3) Except as provided in paragraph (4), if the check or note is dishonored and the obligee of the obligation for which the instrument was taken is the person entitled to enforce the instrument, the obligee may enforce either the instrument or the obligation. In the case of an instrument of a third person which is negotiated to the obligee by the obligor, discharge of the obligor on the instrument also discharges the obligation.

(4) If the person entitled to enforce the instrument taken for an obligation is a person other than the obligee, the obligee may not enforce the obligation to the extent the obligation is suspended. If the obligee is the person entitled to enforce the instrument but no longer has possession of it because it was lost, stolen, or destroyed, the obligation may not be enforced to the extent of the amount payable on the instrument, and to that extent the obligee's rights against the obligor are limited to enforcement of the instrument.

(c) If an instrument other than one described in subsection (a) or (b) is taken for an obligation, the effect is (i) that stated in subsection (a) if the instrument is one on which a bank is liable as maker or acceptor, or (ii) that stated in subsection (b) in any other case.

* * * *

§3—312. LOST, DESTROYED, OR STOLEN CASHIER'S CHECK, TELLER'S CHECK, OR CERTIFIED CHECK.

(1) "Check" means a cashier's check, teller's check, or certified check.

(2) "Claimant" means a person who claims the right to receive the amount of a cashier's check, teller's check, or certified check that was lost, destroyed, or stolen.

(3) "Declaration of loss" means a written statement, made under penalty of perjury, to the effect that (i) the declarer lost possession of a check, (ii) the declarer is the drawer or payee of the check, in the case of a certified check, or the remitter or payee of the check, in the case of a cashier's check or teller's check, (iii) the loss of possession was not the result of a transfer by the declarer or a lawful seizure, and (iv) the declarer cannot reasonably obtain possession of the check because the check was destroyed, its whereabouts cannot be determined, or it is in the wrongful possession of an unknown person or a person that cannot be found or is not amenable to service of process.

(4) "Obligated bank" means the issuer of a cashier's check or teller's check or the acceptor of a certified check.

* * * *

Part 4 Liability of Parties

§3—401. SIGNATURE

(a) A person is not liable on an instrument unless (i) the person signed the instrument, or (ii) the person is represented by an agent or representative who signed the instrument and the signature is binding on the represented person under Section 3—402.

(b) A signature may be made (i) manually or by means of a device or machine, and (ii) by the use of any name, including a trade or assumed name, or by a word, mark, or symbol executed or adopted by a person with present intention to authenticate a writing.

§3—402. SIGNATURE BY REPRESENTATIVE

(a) If a person acting, or purporting to act, as a representative signs an instrument by signing either the name of the represented person or the name of the signer, the represented person is bound by the signature to the same extent the represented person would be bound if the signature were on a simple contract. If the represented person is bound, the signature of the representative is the "authorized signature of the represented person" and the represented person is liable on the instrument, whether or not identified in the instrument.

(b) If a representative signs the name of the representative to an instrument and the signature is an authorized signature of the represented person, the following rules apply:

(1) If the form of the signature shows unambiguously that the signature is made on behalf of the represented person who is identified in the instrument, the representative is not liable on the instrument.

(2) Subject to subsection (c), if (i) the form of the signature does not show unambiguously that the signature is made in a representative capacity or (ii) the represented person is not identified in the instrument, the representative is liable on the instrument to a holder in due course that took the instrument without notice that the representative was not intended to be liable on the instrument. With respect to any other person, the representative is liable on the instrument unless the representative proves that the original parties did not intend the representative to be liable on the instrument.

(c) If a representative signs the name of the representative as drawer of a check without indication of the representative status and the check is payable from an account of the represented person who is identified on the check, the signer is not liable on the check if the signature is an authorized signature of the represented person.

§3—403. UNAUTHORIZED SIGNATURE

(a) Unless otherwise provided in this Article or Article 4, an unauthorized signature is ineffective except as the signature of the unauthorized signer in favor of a person who in good faith pays the instrument or takes it for value. An unauthorized signature may be ratified for all purposes of this Article.

(b) If the signature of more than one person is required to constitute the authorized signature of an organization, the signature of the organization is unauthorized if one of the required signatures is lacking.

(c) The civil or criminal liability of a person who makes an unauthorized signature is not affected by any provision of this Article which makes the unauthorized signature effective for the purposes of this Article.

§3—404. IMPOSTORS; FICTITIOUS PAYEES

(a) If an impostor, by use of the mails or otherwise, induces the issuer of an instrument to issue the instrument to the impostor, or to a person acting in concert with the impostor, by impersonating the payee of the instrument or a person authorized to act for the payee, an indorsement of the instrument by any person in the name of the payee is effective as the indorsement of the payee in favor of a person who, in good faith, pays the instrument or takes it for value or for collection.

(b) If (i) a person whose intent determines to whom an instrument is payable (Section 3—110(a) or (b)) does not intend the person identified as payee to have any interest in the instrument, or (ii) the person identified as payee of an instrument is a fictitious person, the following rules apply until the instrument is negotiated by special indorsement:

(1) Any person in possession of the instrument is its holder.

(2) An indorsement by any person in the name of the payee stated in the instrument is effective as the indorsement of the payee in favor of a person who, in good faith, pays the instrument or takes it for value or for collection.

(c) Under subsection (a) or (b), an indorsement is made in the name of a payee if (i) it is made in a name substantially similar to that of the payee or (ii) the instrument, whether or not indorsed, is deposited in a depositary bank to an account in a name substantially similar to that of the payee.

(d) With respect to an instrument to which subsection (a) or (b) applies, if a person paying the instrument or taking it for value or for collection fails to exercise ordinary care in paying or taking the instrument and that failure substantially contributes to loss resulting from payment of the instrument, the person bearing the loss may recover from the person failing to exercise ordinary care to the extent the failure to exercise ordinary care contributed to the loss.

§3—405. EMPLOYER'S RESPONSIBILITY FOR FRAUDULENT INDORSEMENT BY EMPLOYEE

(a) In this section:

(1) "Employee" includes an independent contractor and employee of an independent contractor retained by the employer.

(2) "Fraudulent indorsement" means (i) in the case of an instrument payable to the employer, a forged indorsement purporting to be that of the employer, or (ii) in the case of an instrument with respect to which the employer is the issuer, a forged indorsement purporting to be that of the person identified as payee.

(3) "Responsibility" with respect to instruments means authority (i) to sign or indorse instruments on behalf of the employer, (ii) to process instruments received by the employer for book-keeping purposes, for deposit to an account, or for other disposition, (iii) to prepare or process instruments for issue in the name of the employer, (iv) to supply information determining the

names or addresses of payees of instruments to be issued in the name of the employer, (v) to control the disposition of instruments to be issued in the name of the employer, or (vi) to act otherwise with respect to instruments in a responsible capacity. "Responsibility" does not include authority that merely allows an employee to have access to instruments or blank or incomplete instrument forms that are being stored or transported or are part of incoming or outgoing mail, or similar access.

(b) For the purpose of determining the rights and liabilities of a person who, in good faith, pays an instrument or takes it for value or for collection, if an employer entrusted an employee with responsibility with respect to the instrument and the employee or a person acting in concert with the employee makes a fraudulent indorsement of the instrument, the indorsement is effective as the indorsement of the person to whom the instrument is payable if it is made in the name of that person. If the person paying the instrument or taking it for value or for collection fails to exercise ordinary care in paying or taking the instrument and that failure substantially contributes to loss resulting from the fraud, the person bearing the loss may recover from the person failing to exercise ordinary care to the extent the failure to exercise ordinary care contributed to the loss.

(c) Under subsection (b), an indorsement is made in the name of the person to whom an instrument is payable if (i) it is made in a name substantially similar to the name of that person or (ii) the instrument, whether or not indorsed, is deposited in a depositary bank to an account in a name substantially similar to the name of that person.

§3—406. NEGLIGENCE CONTRIBUTING TO FORGED SIGNATURE OR ALTERATION OF INSTRUMENT

(a) A person whose failure to exercise ordinary care substantially contributes to an alteration of an instrument or to the making of a forged signature on an instrument is precluded from asserting the alteration or the forgery against a person who, in good faith, pays the instrument or takes it for value or for collection.

(b) Under subsection (a), if the person asserting the preclusion fails to exercise ordinary care in paying or taking the instrument and that failure substantially contributes to loss, the loss is allocated between the person precluded and the person asserting the preclusion according to the extent to which the failure of each to exercise ordinary care contributed to the loss.

(c) Under subsection (a), the burden of proving failure to exercise ordinary care is on the person asserting the preclusion. Under subsection (b), the burden of proving failure to exercise ordinary care is on the person precluded.

§3—407. ALTERATION

(a) "Alteration" means (i) an unauthorized change in an instrument that purports to modify in any respect the obligation of a party, or (ii) an unauthorized addition of words or numbers or other change to an incomplete instrument relating to the obligation of a party.

(b) Except as provided in subsection (c), an alteration fraudulently made discharges a party whose obligation is affected by the alteration unless that party assents or is precluded from asserting the alteration. No other alteration discharges a party, and the instrument may be enforced according to its original terms.

(c) A payor bank or drawee paying a fraudulently altered instrument or a person taking it for value, in good faith and without notice of the alteration, may enforce rights with respect to the instrument (i) according to its original terms, or (ii) in the case of an incomplete instrument altered by unauthorized completion, according to its terms as completed.

§3—408. DRAWEE NOT LIABLE ON UNACCEPTED DRAFT

A check or other draft does not of itself operate as an assignment of funds in the hands of the drawee available for its payment, and the drawee is not liable on the instrument until the drawee accepts it.

§3—409. ACCEPTANCE OF DRAFT; CERTIFIED CHECK

(a) "Acceptance" means the drawee's signed agreement to pay a draft as presented. It must be written on the draft and may consist of the drawee's signature alone. Acceptance may be made at any time and becomes effective when notification pursuant to instructions is given or the accepted draft is delivered for the purpose of giving rights on the acceptance to any person.

(b) A draft may be accepted although it has not been signed by the drawer, is otherwise incomplete, is overdue, or has been dishonored.

(c) If a draft is payable at a fixed period after sight and the acceptor fails to date the acceptance, the holder may complete the acceptance by supplying a date in good faith.

(d) "Certified check" means a check accepted by the bank on which it is drawn. Acceptance may be made as stated in subsection (a) or by a writing on the check which indicates that the check is certified. The drawee of a check has no obligation to certify the check, and refusal to certify is not dishonor of the check.

§3—410. ACCEPTANCE VARYING DRAFT

(a) If the terms of a drawee's acceptance vary from the terms of the draft as presented, the holder may refuse the acceptance and treat the draft as dishonored. In that case, the drawee may cancel the acceptance.

(b) The terms of a draft are not varied by an acceptance to pay at a particular bank or place in the United States, unless the acceptance states that the draft is to be paid only at that bank or place.

(c) If the holder assents to an acceptance varying the terms of a draft, the obligation of each drawer and indorser that does not expressly assent to the acceptance is discharged.

§3—411. REFUSAL TO PAY CASHIER'S CHECKS, TELLER'S CHECKS, AND CERTIFIED CHECKS

(a) In this section, "obligated bank" means the acceptor of a certified check or the issuer of a cashier's check or teller's check bought from the issuer.

(b) If the obligated bank wrongfully (i) refuses to pay a cashier's check or certified check, (ii) stops payment of a teller's check, or (iii) refuses to pay a dishonored teller's check, the person asserting the right to enforce the check is entitled to compensation for expenses and loss of interest resulting from the nonpayment and may recover consequential damages if the obligated bank refuses to pay after receiving notice of particular circumstances giving rise to the damages.

(c) Expenses or consequential damages under subsection (b) are not recoverable if the refusal of the obligated bank to pay occurs because (i) the bank suspends payments, (ii) the obligated bank asserts a claim or defense of the bank that it has reasonable grounds to believe is available against the person entitled to enforce the instrument, (iii) the obligated bank has a reasonable doubt whether the person demanding payment is the person entitled to enforce the instrument, or (iv) payment is prohibited by law.

§3—412. OBLIGATION OF ISSUER OF NOTE OR CASHIER'S CHECK

The issuer of a note or cashier's check or other draft drawn on the drawer is obliged to pay the instrument (i) according to its terms at the time it was issued or, if not issued, at the time it first came into possession of a holder, or (ii) if the issuer signed an incomplete instrument, according to its terms when completed, to the extent stated in Sections 3—115 and 3—407. The obligation is owed to a person entitled to enforce the instrument or to an indorser who paid the instrument under Section 3—415.

§3—413. OBLIGATION OF ACCEPTOR

(a) The acceptor of a draft is obliged to pay the draft (i) according to its terms at the time it was accepted, even though the acceptance states that the draft is payable "as originally drawn" or equivalent terms, (ii) if the acceptance varies the terms of the draft, according to the terms of the draft as varied, or (iii) if the acceptance is of a draft that is an incomplete instrument, according to its terms when completed, to the extent stated in Sections 3—115 and 3—407. The obligation is owed to a person entitled to enforce the draft or to the drawer or an indorser who paid the draft under Section 3—414 or 3—415.

(b) If the certification of a check or other acceptance of a draft states the amount certified or accepted, the obligation of the acceptor is that amount. If (i) the certification or acceptance does not state an amount, (ii) the amount of the instrument is subsequently raised, and (iii) the instrument is then negotiated to a holder in due course, the obligation of the acceptor is the amount of the instrument at the time it was taken by the holder in due course.

§3—414. OBLIGATION OF DRAWER

(a) This section does not apply to cashier's checks or other drafts drawn on the drawer.

(b) If an unaccepted draft is dishonored, the drawer is obliged to pay the draft (i) according to its terms at the time it was issued or, if not issued, at the time it first came into possession of a holder, or (ii) if the drawer signed an incomplete instrument, according to its terms when completed, to the extent stated in Sections 3—115 and 3—407. The obligation is owed to a person entitled to enforce the draft or to an indorser who paid the draft under Section 3—415.

(c) If a draft is accepted by a bank, the drawer is discharged, regardless of when or by whom acceptance was obtained.

(d) If a draft is accepted and the acceptor is not a bank, the obligation of the drawer to pay the draft if the draft is dishonored by the acceptor is the same as the obligation of an indorser under Section 3—415(a) and (c).

(e) If a draft states that it is drawn "without recourse" or otherwise disclaims liability of the drawer to pay the draft, the drawer is not liable under subsection (b) to pay the draft if the draft is not a check. A disclaimer of the liability stated in subsection (b) is not effective if the draft is a check.

(f) If (i) a check is not presented for payment or given to a depositary bank for collection within 30 days after its date, (ii) the drawee suspends payments after expiration of the 30-day period without paying the check, and (iii) because of the suspension of payments, the drawer is deprived of funds maintained with the drawee to cover payment of the check, the drawer to the extent deprived of funds may discharge its obligation to pay the check by assigning to the person entitled to enforce the check the rights of the drawer against the drawee with respect to the funds.

§3—415. OBLIGATION OF INDORSER

(a) Subject to subsections (b), (c), and (d) and to Section 3—419(d), if an instrument is dishonored, an indorser is obliged to pay the amount due on the instrument (i) according to the terms of the instrument at the time it was indorsed, or (ii) if the indorser indorsed an incomplete instrument, according to its terms when completed, to the extent stated in Sections 3—115 and 3—407. The obligation of the indorser is owed to a person entitled to enforce the instrument or to a subsequent indorser who paid the instrument under this section.

(b) If an indorsement states that it is made "without recourse" or otherwise disclaims liability of the indorser, the indorser is not liable under subsection (a) to pay the instrument.

(c) If notice of dishonor of an instrument is required by Section 3—503 and notice of dishonor complying with that section is not given to an indorser, the liability of the indorser under subsection (a) is discharged.

(d) If a draft is accepted by a bank after an indorsement is made, the liability of the indorser under subsection (a) is discharged.

(e) If an indorser of a check is liable under subsection (a) and the check is not presented for payment, or given to a depositary bank for collection, within 30 days after the day the indorsement was made, the liability of the indorser under subsection (a) is discharged.

As amended in 1993.

§3—416. TRANSFER WARRANTIES

(a) A person who transfers an instrument for consideration warrants to the transferee and, if the transfer is by indorsement, to any subsequent transferee that:

(1) the warrantor is a person entitled to enforce the instrument;

(2) all signatures on the instrument are authentic and authorized;

(3) the instrument has not been altered;

(4) the instrument is not subject to a defense or claim in recoupment of any party which can be asserted against the warrantor; and

(5) the warrantor has no knowledge of any insolvency proceeding commenced with respect to the maker or acceptor or, in the case of an unaccepted draft, the drawer.

(b) A person to whom the warranties under subsection (a) are made and who took the instrument in good faith may recover from the warrantor as damages for breach of warranty an amount equal to the loss suffered as a result of the breach, but not more than the amount of the instrument plus expenses and loss of interest incurred as a result of the breach.

(c) The warranties stated in subsection (a) cannot be disclaimed with respect to checks. Unless notice of a claim for breach of warranty is given to the warrantor within 30 days after the claimant has reason to know of the breach and the identity of the warrantor, the liability of the warrantor under subsection (b) is discharged to the extent of any loss caused by the delay in giving notice of the claim.

(d) A [cause of action] for breach of warranty under this section accrues when the claimant has reason to know of the breach.

§3—417. PRESENTMENT WARRANTIES

(a) If an unaccepted draft is presented to the drawee for payment or acceptance and the drawee pays or accepts the draft, (i) the person obtaining payment or acceptance, at the time of presentment, and (ii) a previous transferor of the draft, at the time of transfer, warrant to the drawee making payment or accepting the draft in good faith that:

(1) the warrantor is, or was, at the time the warrantor transferred the draft, a person entitled to enforce the draft or authorized to obtain payment or acceptance of the draft on behalf of a person entitled to enforce the draft;

(2) the draft has not been altered; and

(3) the warrantor has no knowledge that the signature of the drawer of the draft is unauthorized.

(b) A drawee making payment may recover from any warrantor damages for breach of warranty equal to the amount paid by the drawee less the amount the drawee received or is entitled to receive from the drawer because of the payment. In addition, the drawee is entitled to compensation for expenses and loss of interest resulting from the breach. The right of the drawee to recover damages under this subsection is not affected by any failure of the drawee to exercise ordinary care in making payment. If the drawee accepts the draft, breach of warranty is a defense to the obligation of the acceptor. If the acceptor makes payment with respect to the draft, the acceptor is entitled to recover from any warrantor for breach of warranty the amounts stated in this subsection.

(c) If a drawee asserts a claim for breach of warranty under subsection (a) based on an unauthorized indorsement of the draft or an alteration of the draft, the warrantor may defend by proving that the indorsement is effective under Section 3—404 or 3—405 or the drawer is precluded under Section 3—406 or 4—406 from asserting against the drawee the unauthorized indorsement or alteration.

(d) If (i) a dishonored draft is presented for payment to the drawer or an indorser or (ii) any other instrument is presented for payment to a party obliged to pay the instrument, and (iii) payment is received, the following rules apply:

(1) The person obtaining payment and a prior transferor of the instrument warrant to the person making payment in good faith that the warrantor is, or was, at the time the warrantor transferred the instrument, a person entitled to enforce the instrument or

authorized to obtain payment on behalf of a person entitled to enforce the instrument.

(2) The person making payment may recover from any warrantor for breach of warranty an amount equal to the amount paid plus expenses and loss of interest resulting from the breach.

(e) The warranties stated in subsections (a) and (d) cannot be disclaimed with respect to checks. Unless notice of a claim for breach of warranty is given to the warrantor within 30 days after the claimant has reason to know of the breach and the identity of the warrantor, the liability of the warrantor under subsection (b) or (d) is discharged to the extent of any loss caused by the delay in giving notice of the claim.

(f) A [cause of action] for breach of warranty under this section accrues when the claimant has reason to know of the breach.

§3—418. PAYMENT OR ACCEPTANCE BY MISTAKE

(a) Except as provided in subsection (c), if the drawee of a draft pays or accepts the draft and the drawee acted on the mistaken belief that (i) payment of the draft had not been stopped pursuant to Section 4—403 or (ii) the signature of the drawer of the draft was authorized, the drawee may recover the amount of the draft from the person to whom or for whose benefit payment was made or, in the case of acceptance, may revoke the acceptance. Rights of the drawee under this subsection are not affected by failure of the drawee to exercise ordinary care in paying or accepting the draft.

(b) Except as provided in subsection (c), if an instrument has been paid or accepted by mistake and the case is not covered by subsection (a), the person paying or accepting may, to the extent permitted by the law governing mistake and restitution, (i) recover the payment from the person to whom or for whose benefit payment was made or (ii) in the case of acceptance, may revoke the acceptance.

(c) The remedies provided by subsection (a) or (b) may not be asserted against a person who took the instrument in good faith and for value or who in good faith changed position in reliance on the payment or acceptance. This subsection does not limit remedies provided by Section 3—417 or 4—407.

(d) Notwithstanding Section 4—215, if an instrument is paid or accepted by mistake and the payor or acceptor recovers payment or revokes acceptance under subsection (a) or (b), the instrument is deemed not to have been paid or accepted and is treated as dishonored, and the person from whom payment is recovered has rights as a person entitled to enforce the dishonored instrument.

§3—419. INSTRUMENTS SIGNED FOR ACCOMMODATION

(a) If an instrument is issued for value given for the benefit of a party to the instrument ("accommodated party") and another party to the instrument ("accommodation party") signs the instrument for the purpose of incurring liability on the instrument without being a direct beneficiary of the value given for the instrument, the instrument is signed by the accommodation party "for accommodation."

(b) An accommodation party may sign the instrument as maker, drawer, acceptor, or indorser and, subject to subsection (d), is obliged to pay the instrument in the capacity in which the accommodation party signs. The obligation of an accommodation party may be enforced notwithstanding any statute of frauds and whether or not the accommodation party receives consideration for the accommodation.

* * * *

(e) An accommodation party who pays the instrument is entitled to reimbursement from the accommodated party and is entitled to enforce the instrument against the accommodated party. An accommodated party who pays the instrument has no right of recourse against, and is not entitled to contribution from, an accommodation party.

§3—420. CONVERSION OF INSTRUMENT

(a) The law applicable to conversion of personal property applies to instruments. An instrument is also converted if it is taken by transfer, other than a negotiation, from a person not entitled to enforce the instrument or a bank makes or obtains payment with respect to the instrument for a person not entitled to enforce the instrument or receive payment. An action for conversion of an instrument may not be brought by (i) the issuer or acceptor of the instrument or (ii) a payee or indorsee who did not receive delivery of the instrument either directly or through delivery to an agent or a co-payee.

(b) In an action under subsection (a), the measure of liability is presumed to be the amount payable on the instrument, but recovery may not exceed the amount of the plaintiff's interest in the instrument.

(c) A representative, other than a depositary bank, who has in good faith dealt with an instrument or its proceeds on behalf of one who was not the person entitled to enforce the instrument is not liable in conversion to that person beyond the amount of any proceeds that it has not paid out.

§3—501. PRESENTMENT

(a) "Presentment" means a demand made by or on behalf of a person entitled to enforce an instrument (i) to pay the instrument made to the drawee or a party obliged to pay the instrument or, in the case of a note or accepted draft payable at a bank, to the bank, or (ii) to accept a draft made to the drawee.

(b) The following rules are subject to Article 4, agreement of the parties, and clearing-house rules and the like:

(1) Presentment may be made at the place of payment of the instrument and must be made at the place of

payment if the instrument is payable at a bank in the United States; may be made by any commercially reasonable means, including an oral, written, or electronic communication; is effective when the demand for payment or acceptance is received by the person to whom presentment is made; and is effective if made to any one of two or more makers, acceptors, drawees, or other payors.

(2) Upon demand of the person to whom presentment is made, the person making presentment must (i) exhibit the instrument, (ii) give reasonable identification and, if presentment is made on behalf of another person, reasonable evidence of authority to do so, and (…) sign a receipt on the instrument for any payment made or surrender the instrument if full payment is made.

(3) Without dishonoring the instrument, the party to whom presentment is made may (i) return the instrument for lack of a necessary indorsement, or (ii) refuse payment or acceptance for failure of the presentment to comply with the terms of the instrument, an agreement of the parties, or other applicable law or rule.

(4) The party to whom presentment is made may treat presentment as occurring on the next business day after the day of presentment if the party to whom presentment is made has established a cut-off hour not earlier than 2 P.M. for the receipt and processing of instruments presented for payment or acceptance and presentment is made after the cut-off hour.

§3—502. DISHONOR

(a) Dishonor of a note is governed by the following rules:

(1) If the note is payable on demand, the note is dishonored if presentment is duly made to the maker and the note is not paid on the day of presentment.

(2) If the note is not payable on demand and is payable at or through a bank or the terms of the note require presentment, the note is dishonored if presentment is duly made and the note is not paid on the day it becomes payable or the day of presentment, whichever is later.

(3) If the note is not payable on demand and paragraph (2) does not apply, the note is dishonored if it is not paid on the day it becomes payable.

(b) Dishonor of an unaccepted draft other than a documentary draft is governed by the following rules:

(1) If a check is duly presented for payment to the payor bank otherwise than for immediate payment over the counter, the check is dishonored if the payor bank makes timely return of the check or sends timely notice of dishonor or nonpayment under Section 4—301 or 4—302, or becomes accountable for the amount of the check under Section 4—302.

(2) If a draft is payable on demand and paragraph (1) does not apply, the draft is dishonored if presentment for payment is duly made to the drawee and the draft is not paid on the day of presentment.

(3) If a draft is payable on a date stated in the draft, the draft is dishonored if (i) presentment for payment is duly made to the drawee and payment is not made on the day the draft becomes payable or the day of presentment, whichever is later, or (ii) presentment for acceptance is duly made before the day the draft becomes payable and the draft is not accepted on the day of presentment.

(4) If a draft is payable on elapse of a period of time after sight or acceptance, the draft is dishonored if presentment for acceptance is duly made and the draft is not accepted on the day of presentment.

(c) Dishonor of an unaccepted documentary draft occurs according to the rules stated in subsection (b)(2), (3), and (4), except that payment or acceptance may be delayed without dishonor until no later than the close of the third business day of the drawee following the day on which payment or acceptance is required by those paragraphs.

(d) Dishonor of an accepted draft is governed by the following rules:

(1) If the draft is payable on demand, the draft is dishonored if presentment for payment is duly made to the acceptor and the draft is not paid on the day of presentment.

(2) If the draft is not payable on demand, the draft is dishonored if presentment for payment is duly made to the acceptor and payment is not made on the day it becomes payable or the day of presentment, whichever is later.

(e) In any case in which presentment is otherwise required for dishonor under this section and presentment is excused under Section 3—504, dishonor occurs without presentment if the instrument is not duly accepted or paid.

(f) If a draft is dishonored because timely acceptance of the draft was not made and the person entitled to demand acceptance consents to a late acceptance, from the time of acceptance the draft is treated as never having been dishonored.

§3—503. NOTICE OF DISHONOR

(a) The obligation of an indorser stated in Section 3—415 (a) and the obligation of a drawer stated in Section 3—414 (d) may not be enforced unless (i) the indorser or drawer is given notice of dishonor of the instrument complying with this section or (ii) notice of dishonor is excused under Section 3—504(b).

(b) Notice of dishonor may be given by any person; may be given by any commercially reasonable means, including an oral, written, or electronic communication; and is sufficient if it reasonably identifies the instrument and indicates that the instrument has been dishonored or has not been paid or accepted. Return of an instrument given to a bank for collection is sufficient notice of dishonor.

(c) Subject to Section 3—504(c), with respect to an instrument taken for collection by a collecting bank, notice of dishonor must be given (i) by the bank before midnight of the next banking day following the banking day on which the bank receives notice of dishonor of the instrument, or (ii) by any other person within 30 days following the day on which the person receives notice of dishonor. With respect to any other instrument, notice of dishonor must be given within 30 days following the day on which dishonor occurs.

* * * *

§3—601. DISCHARGE AND EFFECT OF DISCHARGE

(a) The obligation of a party to pay the instrument is discharged as stated in this Article or by an act or agreement with the party which would discharge an obligation to pay money under a simple contract.

(b) Discharge of the obligation of a party is not effective against a person acquiring rights of a holder in due course of the instrument without notice of the discharge.

§3—602. PAYMENT

(a) Subject to subsection (b), an instrument is paid to the extent payment is made (i) by or on behalf of a party obliged to pay the instrument, and (ii) to a person entitled to enforce the instrument. To the extent of the payment, the obligation of the party obliged to pay the instrument is discharged even though payment is made with knowledge of a claim to the instrument under Section 3—306 by another person.

(b) The obligation of a party to pay the instrument is not discharged under subsection (a) if:

(1) a claim to the instrument under Section 3—306 is enforceable against the party receiving payment and (i) payment is made with knowledge by the payor that payment is prohibited by injunction or similar process of a court of competent jurisdiction, or (ii) in the case of an instrument other than a cashier's check, teller's check, or certified check, the party making payment accepted, from the person having a claim to the instrument, indemnity against loss resulting from refusal to pay the person entitled to enforce the instrument; or

(2) the person making payment knows that the instrument is a stolen instrument and pays a person it knows is in wrongful possession of the instrument.

§3—603. TENDER OF PAYMENT

(a) If tender of payment of an obligation to pay an instrument is made to a person entitled to enforce the instrument, the effect of tender is governed by principles of law applicable to tender of payment under a simple contract.

(b) If tender of payment of an obligation to pay an instrument is made to a person entitled to enforce the instrument and the tender is refused, there is discharge, to the extent of the amount of the tender, of the obligation of an indorser or accommodation party having a right of recourse with respect to the obligation to which the tender relates.

(c) If tender of payment of an amount due on an instrument is made to a person entitled to enforce the instrument, the obligation of the obligor to pay interest after the due date on the amount tendered is discharged. If presentment is required with respect to an instrument and the obligor is able and ready to pay on the due date at every place of payment stated in the instrument, the obligor is deemed to have made tender of payment on the due date to the person entitled to enforce the instrument.

§3—604. DISCHARGE BY CANCELLATION OR RENUNCIATION

(a) A person entitled to enforce an instrument, with or without consideration, may discharge the obligation of a party to pay the instrument (i) by an intentional voluntary act, such as surrender of the instrument to the party, destruction, mutilation, or cancellation of the instrument, cancellation or striking out of the party's signature, or the addition of words to the instrument indicating discharge, or (ii) by agreeing not to sue or otherwise renouncing rights against the party by a signed writing.

(b) Cancellation or striking out of an indorsement pursuant to subsection (a) does not affect the status and rights of a party derived from the indorsement.

§3—605. DISCHARGE OF INDORSERS AND ACCOMMODATION PARTIES

(a) In this section, the term "indorser" includes a drawer having the obligation described in Section 3—414(d).

(b) Discharge, under Section 3—604, of the obligation of a party to pay an instrument does not discharge the obligation of an indorser or accommodation party having a right of recourse against the discharged party.

(c) If a person entitled to enforce an instrument agrees, with or without consideration, to an extension of the due date of the obligation of a party to pay the instrument, the extension discharges an indorser or accommodation party having a right of recourse against the party whose obligation is extended to the extent the indorser or accommodation party proves that the extension caused loss to the indorser or accommodation party with respect to the right of recourse.

(d) If a person entitled to enforce an instrument agrees, with or without consideration, to a material modification of the obligation of a party other than an extension of the due date, the modification discharges the obligation of an indorser or accommodation party having a right of recourse against the person whose obligation is modified to the extent the modification causes loss to the indorser or accommodation party with respect to the right of recourse. The loss suffered by the indorser or accommodation party as a result of the modification is equal to the amount of the right of recourse unless the person enforcing the instrument proves that no loss was caused by the modification or that the loss caused by the modification was an amount less than the amount of the right of recourse.

(e) If the obligation of a party to pay an instrument is secured by an interest in collateral and a person entitled to enforce the instrument impairs the value of the interest in collateral, the obligation of an indorser or accommodation party having a right of recourse against the obligor is discharged to the extent of the impairment. The value of an interest in collateral is impaired to the extent (i) the value of the interest is reduced to an amount less than the amount of the right of recourse of the party asserting discharge, or (ii) the reduction in value of the interest causes an increase in the amount by which the amount of the right of recourse exceeds the value of the interest. The burden of proving impairment is on the party asserting discharge.

(f) If the obligation of a party is secured by an interest in collateral not provided by an accommodation party and a person entitled to enforce the instrument impairs the value of the interest in collateral, the obligation of any party who is jointly and severally liable with respect to the secured obligation is discharged to the extent the impairment causes the party asserting discharge to pay more than that party would have been obliged to pay, taking into account rights of contribution, if impairment had not occurred. If the party asserting discharge is an accommodation party not entitled to discharge under subsection (e), the party is deemed to have a right to contribution based on joint and several liability rather than a right to reimbursement. The burden of proving impairment is on the party asserting discharge.

* * * *

(h) An accommodation party is not discharged under subsection (c), (d), or (e) unless the person entitled to enforce the instrument knows of the accommodation or has notice under Section 3—419(c) that the instrument was signed for accommodation.

(i) A party is not discharged under this section if (i) the party asserting discharge consents to the event or conduct that is the basis of the discharge, or (ii) the instrument or a separate agreement of the party provides for waiver of discharge under this section either specifically or by general language indicating that parties waive defenses based on suretyship or impairment of collateral.

* * * *

Revised Article 4 Bank Deposits and Collections

Part 1 General Provisions and Definitions

§4—103. VARIATION BY AGREEMENT; MEASURE OF DAMAGES; ACTION CONSTITUTING ORDINARY CARE

(a) The effect of the provisions of this Article may be varied by agreement, but the parties to the agreement cannot disclaim a bank's responsibility for its lack of good faith or failure to exercise ordinary care or limit the measure of damages for the lack or failure. However, the parties may determine by agreement the standards by which the bank's responsibility is to be measured if those standards are not manifestly unreasonable.

(b) Federal Reserve regulations and operating circulars, clearing-house rules, and the like have the effect of agreements under subsection (a), whether or not specifically assented to by all parties interested in items handled.

* * * *

§4—104. DEFINITIONS AND INDEX OF DEFINITIONS

(1) "Account" means any deposit or credit account with a bank, including a demand, time, savings, passbook, share draft, or like account, other than an account evidenced by a certificate of deposit;

* * * *

(3) "Banking day" means the part of a day on which a bank is open to the public for carrying on substantially all of its banking functions;

(4) "Clearing house" means an association of banks or other payors regularly clearing items;

* * * *

(7) "Draft" means a draft as defined in Section 3 —104 or an item, other than an instrument, that is an order;

(8) "Drawee" means a person ordered in a draft to make payment;

* * * *

(10) "Midnight deadline" with respect to a bank is midnight on its next banking day following the banking day on which it receives the relevant item or notice or from which the time for taking action commences to run, whichever is later;

* * * *

§4—105. "BANK"; "DEPOSITARY BANK"; "PAYOR BANK"; "INTERMEDIARY BANK"; "COLLECTING BANK"; "PRESENTING BANK"

In this Article:

(1) "Bank" means a person engaged in the business of banking, including a savings bank, savings and loan association, credit union, or trust company;

(2) "Depositary bank" means the first bank to take an item even though it is also the payor bank, unless the item is presented for immediate payment over the counter;

(3) "Payor bank" means a bank that is the drawee of a draft;

(4) "Intermediary bank" means a bank to which an item is transferred in course of collection except the depositary or payor bank;

(5) "Collecting bank" means a bank handling an item for collection except the payor bank;

(6) "Presenting bank" means a bank presenting an item except a payor bank.

§4—106. PAYABLE THROUGH OR PAYABLE AT BANK: COLLECTING BANK

(a) If an item states that it is "payable through" a bank identified in the item, (i) the item designates the bank as a collecting bank and does not by itself authorize the bank to pay the item, and (ii) the item may be presented for payment only by or through the bank.

Alternative A

(b) If an item states that it is "payable at" a bank identified in the item, the item is equivalent to a draft drawn on the bank.

Alternative B

(b) If an item states that it is "payable at" a bank identified in the item, (i) the item designates the bank as a collecting bank and does not by itself authorize the bank to pay the item, and (ii) the item may be presented for payment only by or through the bank.

(c) If a draft names a nonbank drawee and it is unclear whether a bank named in the draft is a co-drawee or a collecting bank, the bank is a collecting bank.

§4—107. SEPARATE OFFICE OF BANK

A branch or separate office of a bank is a separate bank for the purpose of computing the time within which and determining the place at or to which action may be taken or notices or orders shall be given under this Article and under Article 3.

§4—108. TIME OF RECEIPT OF ITEMS

(a) For the purpose of allowing time to process items, prove balances, and make the necessary entries on its books to determine its position for the day, a bank may fix an afternoon hour of 2 P.M. or later as a cutoff hour for the handling of money and items and the making of entries on its books.

(b) An item or deposit of money received on any day after a cutoff hour so fixed or after the close of the banking day may be treated as being received at the opening of the next banking day.

§4—109. DELAYS

(a) Unless otherwise instructed, a collecting bank in a good faith effort to secure payment of a specific item drawn on a payor other than a bank, and with or without the approval of any person involved, may waive, modify, or extend time limits imposed or permitted by this [act] for a period not exceeding two additional banking days without discharge of drawers or indorsers or liability to its transferor or a prior party.

(b) Delay by a collecting bank or payor bank beyond time limits prescribed or permitted by this [act] or by instructions is excused if (i) the delay is caused by interruption of communication or computer facilities, suspension of payments by another bank, war, emergency conditions, failure of equipment, or other circumstances beyond the control of the bank, and (ii) the bank exercises such diligence as the circumstances require.

§4—110. ELECTRONIC PRESENTMENT

(a) "Agreement for electronic presentment" means an agreement, clearing-house rule, or Federal Reserve regulation or operating circular, providing that presentment of an item may be made by transmission of an image of an item or information describing the item ("presentment notice") rather than delivery of the item itself. The agreement may provide for procedures governing retention, presentment, payment, dishonor, and other matters concerning items subject to the agreement.

* * * *

§4—111. STATUTE OF LIMITATIONS

An action to enforce an obligation, duty, or right arising under this Article must be commenced within three years after the [cause of action] accrues.

§4—201. STATUS OF COLLECTING BANK AS AGENT AND PROVISIONAL STATUS OF CREDITS; APPLICABILITY OF ARTICLE; ITEM INDORSED "PAY ANY BANK"

(a) Unless a contrary intent clearly appears and before the time that a settlement given by a collecting bank for an item is or becomes final, the bank, with respect to an item, is an agent or sub-agent of the owner of the item and any settlement given for the item is provisional. This provision applies regardless of the form of indorsement or lack of indorsement and even though credit given for the item is subject to immediate withdrawal as of right or is in fact withdrawn; but the continuance of ownership of an item by its owner and any rights of the owner to proceeds of the item are subject to rights of a collecting bank, such as those resulting from outstanding advances on the item and rights of recoupment or setoff. If an item is handled by banks for purposes of presentment, payment, collection, or return, the relevant provisions of this Article apply even though action of the parties clearly establishes that a particular bank has purchased the item and is the owner of it.

(b) After an item has been indorsed with the words "pay any bank" or the like, only a bank may acquire the rights of a holder until the item has been:

(1) returned to the customer initiating collection; or

(2) specially indorsed by a bank to a person who is not a bank.

§4—202. RESPONSIBILITY FOR COLLECTION OR RETURN; WHEN ACTION TIMELY

(a) A collecting bank must exercise ordinary care in:

(1) presenting an item or sending it for presentment;

(2) sending notice of dishonor or nonpayment or returning an item other than a documentary draft to the bank's transferor after learning that the item has not been paid or accepted, as the case may be;

(3) settling for an item when the bank receives final settlement; and

(4) notifying its transferor of any loss or delay in transit within a reasonable time after discovery thereof.

(b) A collecting bank exercises ordinary care under subsection (a) by taking proper action before its midnight deadline following receipt of an item, notice, or settlement. Taking proper action within a reasonably longer time may constitute the exercise of ordinary care, but the bank has the burden of establishing timeliness.

(c) Subject to subsection (a)(1), a bank is not liable for the insolvency, neglect, misconduct, mistake, or default of another bank or person or for loss or destruction of an item in the possession of others or in transit.

* * * *

§4—205. DEPOSITARY BANK HOLDER OF UNINDORSED ITEM

If a customer delivers an item to a depositary bank for collection:

(1) the depositary bank becomes a holder of the item at the time it receives the item for collection if the customer at the time of delivery was a holder of the item, whether or not the customer indorses the item, and, if the bank satisfies the other requirements of Section 3—302, it is a holder in due course; and

(2) the depositary bank warrants to collecting banks, the payor bank or other payor, and the drawer that the amount of the item was paid to the customer or deposited to the customer's account.

* * * *

§4—207. TRANSFER WARRANTIES

(a) A customer or collecting bank that transfers an item and receives a settlement or other consideration warrants to the transferee and to any subsequent collecting bank that:

(1) the warrantor is a person entitled to enforce the item;

(2) all signatures on the item are authentic and authorized;

(3) the item has not been altered;

(4) the item is not subject to a defense or claim in recoupment (Section 3—305(a)) of any party that can be asserted against the warrantor; and

(5) the warrantor has no knowledge of any insolvency proceeding commenced with respect to the maker or acceptor or, in the case of an unaccepted draft, the drawer.

(b) If an item is dishonored, a customer or collecting bank transferring the item and receiving settlement or other consideration is obliged to pay the amount due on the item (i) according to the terms of the item at the time it was transferred, or (ii) if the transfer was of an incomplete item, according to its terms when completed as stated in Sections 3—115 and 3—407. The obligation of a transferor is owed to the transferee and to any subsequent collecting bank that takes the item in good faith. A transferor cannot disclaim its obligation under this subsection by an indorsement stating that it is made "without recourse" or otherwise disclaiming liability.

(c) A person to whom the warranties under subsection (a) are made and who took the item in good faith may recover from the warrantor as damages for breach of warranty an amount equal to the loss suffered as a result of the breach, but not more than the amount of the item plus expenses and loss of interest incurred as a result of the breach.

(d) The warranties stated in subsection (a) cannot be disclaimed with respect to checks. Unless notice of a claim for breach of warranty is given to the warrantor within 30 days after the claimant has reason to know of the breach and the identity of the warrantor, the warrantor is discharged to the extent of any loss caused by the delay in giving notice of the claim.

(e) A cause of action for breach of warranty under this section accrues when the claimant has reason to know of the breach.

§4—208. PRESENTMENT WARRANTIES

(a) If an unaccepted draft is presented to the drawee for payment or acceptance and the drawee pays or accepts the draft, (i) the person obtaining payment or acceptance, at the time of presentment, and (ii) a previous transferor of the draft, at the time of transfer, warrant to the drawee that pays or accepts the draft in good faith that:

(1) the warrantor is, or was, at the time the warrantor transferred the draft, a person entitled to enforce the draft or authorized to obtain payment or acceptance of the draft on behalf of a person entitled to enforce the draft;

(2) the draft has not been altered; and

(3) the warrantor has no knowledge that the signature of the purported drawer of the draft is unauthorized.

(b) A drawee making payment may recover from a warrantor damages for breach of warranty equal to the amount paid by the drawee less the amount the drawee received or is entitled to receive from the drawer because of the payment. In addition, the drawee is entitled to compensation for expenses and loss of interest resulting from the breach. The right of the drawee to recover damages under this subsection is not affected by any failure of the drawee to exercise ordinary care in making payment. If the drawee accepts the draft (i) breach of warranty is a defense to the obligation of the acceptor, and (ii) if the acceptor makes payment with respect to the draft, the acceptor is entitled to recover from a warrantor for breach of warranty the amounts stated in this subsection.

(c) If a drawee asserts a claim for breach of warranty under subsection (a) based on an unauthorized indorsement of the draft or an alteration of the draft, the warrantor may defend by proving that the indorsement is effective under Section 3—404 or 3—405 or the drawer is precluded under Section 3—406 or 4—406 from asserting against the drawee the unauthorized indorsement or alteration.

(d) If (i) a dishonored draft is presented for payment to the drawer or an indorser or (ii) any other item is presented for payment to a party obliged to pay the item, and the item is paid, the person obtaining payment and a prior transferor of the item warrant to the person making payment in good faith that the warrantor is, or was, at the time the warrantor transferred the item, a person entitled to enforce the item or authorized to obtain payment on behalf of a person entitled to enforce the item. The person making payment may recover from any warrantor for breach of warranty an amount equal to the amount paid plus expenses and loss of interest resulting from the breach.

(e) The warranties stated in subsections (a) and (d) cannot be disclaimed with respect to checks. Unless notice of a claim for breach of warranty is given to the warrantor within 30 days after the claimant has reason to know of the breach and the identity of the warrantor, the warrantor is discharged to the extent of any loss caused by the delay in giving notice of the claim.

(f) A cause of action for breach of warranty under this section accrues when the claimant has reason to know of the breach.

* * * *

§4—211. WHEN BANK GIVES VALUE FOR PURPOSES OF HOLDER IN DUE COURSE

For purposes of determining its status as a holder in due course, a bank has given value to the extent it has a security interest in an item, if the bank otherwise complies with the requirements of Section 3—302 on what constitutes a holder in due course.

As amended in 1990.

§4—212. PRESENTMENT BY NOTICE OF ITEM NOT PAYABLE BY, THROUGH, OR AT BANK; LIABILITY OF DRAWER OR INDORSER

(a) Unless otherwise instructed, a collecting bank may present an item not payable by, through, or at a bank by sending to the party to accept or pay a written notice that the bank holds the item for acceptance or payment. The notice must be sent in time to be received on or before the day when presentment is due and the bank must meet any requirement of the party to accept or pay under Section 3—501 by the close of the bank's next banking day after it knows of the requirement.

(b) If presentment is made by notice and payment, acceptance, or request for compliance with a requirement under Section 3—501 is not received by the close of business on the day after maturity or, in the case of demand items, by the close of business on the third banking day after notice was sent, the presenting bank may treat the item as dishonored and charge any drawer or indorser by sending it notice of the facts.

* * * *

§4—214. RIGHT OF CHARGE-BACK OR REFUND; LIABILITY OF COLLECTING BANK: RETURN OF ITEM

(a) If a collecting bank has made provisional settlement with its customer for an item and fails by reason of dishonor, suspension of payments by a bank, or otherwise to receive settlement for the item which is or becomes final, the bank may revoke the settlement given by it, charge back the amount of any credit given for the item to its customer's account, or obtain refund from its customer, whether or not it is able to return the item, if by its midnight deadline or within a longer reasonable time after it learns the facts it returns the item or sends notification of the facts. If the return or notice is delayed beyond the bank's midnight deadline or a longer reasonable time after it learns the facts, the bank may revoke the settlement, charge back the credit, or obtain refund from its customer, but it is liable for any loss resulting from the delay. These rights to revoke, charge back, and obtain refund terminate if and when a settlement for the item received by the bank is or becomes final.

(b) A collecting bank returns an item when it is sent or delivered to the bank's customer or transferor or pursuant to its instructions.

(c) A depositary bank that is also the payor may charge back the amount of an item to its customer's account or obtain refund in accordance with the section governing return of an item received by a payor bank for credit on its books (Section 4—301).

(d) The right to charge back is not affected by:

(1) previous use of a credit given for the item; or

(2) failure by any bank to exercise ordinary care with respect to the item, but a bank so failing remains liable.

(e) A failure to charge back or claim refund does not affect other rights of the bank against the customer or any other party.

(f) If credit is given in dollars as the equivalent of the value of an item payable in foreign money, the dollar amount of any charge-back or refund must be calculated on the basis of the bank-offered spot rate for the foreign money prevailing on the day when the person entitled to the charge-back or refund learns that it will not receive payment in ordinary course.

§4—215. FINAL PAYMENT OF ITEM BY PAYOR BANK; WHEN PROVISIONAL DEBITS AND CREDITS BECOME FINAL; WHEN CERTAIN CREDITS BECOME AVAILABLE FOR WITHDRAWAL

(a) An item is finally paid by a payor bank when the bank has first done any of the following:

(1) paid the item in cash;

(2) settled for the item without having a right to revoke the settlement under statute, clearing- house rule, or agreement; or

(3) made a provisional settlement for the item and failed to revoke the settlement in the time and manner permitted by statute, clearing-house rule, or agreement.

(b) If provisional settlement for an item does not become final, the item is not finally paid.

* * * *

§4—216. INSOLVENCY AND PREFERENCE

(a) If an item is in or comes into the possession of a payor or collecting bank that suspends payment and the item has not been finally paid, the item must be returned by the receiver, trustee, or agent in charge of the closed bank to the presenting bank or the closed bank's customer.

(b) If a payor bank finally pays an item and suspends payments without making a settlement for the item with its customer or the presenting bank which settlement is or becomes final, the owner of the item has a preferred claim against the payor bank.

(c) If a payor bank gives or a collecting bank gives or receives a provisional settlement for an item and thereafter suspends payments, the suspension does not prevent or interfere with the settlement's becoming final if the finality occurs automatically upon the lapse of certain time or the happening of certain events.

(d) If a collecting bank receives from subsequent parties settlement for an item, which settlement is or becomes final and the bank suspends payments without making a settlement for the item with its customer which settlement is or becomes final, the owner of the item has a preferred claim against the collecting bank.

§4—301. DEFERRED POSTING; RECOVERY OF PAYMENT BY RETURN OF ITEMS; TIME OF DISHONOR; RETURN OF ITEMS BY PAYOR BANK

(a) If a payor bank settles for a demand item other than a documentary draft presented otherwise than for immediate payment over the counter before midnight of the banking day of receipt, the payor bank may revoke the settlement and recover the settlement if, before it has made final payment and before its midnight deadline, it

(1) returns the item; or

(2) sends written notice of dishonor or nonpayment if the item is unavailable for return.

(b) If a demand item is received by a payor bank for credit on its books, it may return the item or send notice of dishonor and may revoke any credit given or recover the amount thereof withdrawn by its customer, if it acts within the time limit and in the manner specified in subsection (a).

(c) Unless previous notice of dishonor has been sent, an item is dishonored at the time when for purposes of dishonor it is returned or notice sent in accordance with this section.

(d) An item is returned:

(1) as to an item presented through a clearing house, when it is delivered to the presenting or last collecting bank or to the clearing house or is sent or delivered in accordance with clearing-house rules; or

(2) in all other cases, when it is sent or delivered to the bank's customer or transferor or pursuant to instructions.

§4—302. PAYOR BANK'S RESPONSIBILITY FOR LATE RETURN OF ITEM

(a) If an item is presented to and received by a payor bank, the bank is accountable for the amount of:

(1) a demand item, other than a documentary draft, whether properly payable or not, if the bank, in any case in which it is not also the depositary bank, retains the item beyond midnight of the banking day of

receipt without settling for it or, whether or not it is also the depositary bank, does not pay or return the item or send notice of dishonor until after its midnight deadline; or

(2) any other properly payable item unless, within the time allowed for acceptance or payment of that item, the bank either accepts or pays the item or returns it and accompanying documents.

(b) The liability of a payor bank to pay an item pursuant to subsection (a) is subject to defenses based on breach of a presentment warranty (Section 4—208) or proof that the person seeking enforcement of the liability presented or transferred the item for the purpose of defrauding the payor bank.

§4—303. WHEN ITEMS SUBJECT TO NOTICE, STOP-PAYMENT ORDER, LEGAL PROCESS, OR SETOFF; ORDER IN WHICH ITEMS MAY BE CHARGED OR CERTIFIED

(a) Any knowledge, notice, or stop-payment order received by, legal process served upon, or setoff exercised by a payor bank comes too late to terminate, suspend, or modify the bank's right or duty to pay an item or to charge its customer's account for the item if the knowledge, notice, stop-payment order, or legal process is received or served and a reasonable time for the bank to act thereon expires or the setoff is exercised after the earliest of the following:

(1) the bank accepts or certifies the item;

(2) the bank pays the item in cash;

(3) the bank settles for the item without having a right to revoke the settlement under statute, clearing-house rule, or agreement;

(4) the bank becomes accountable for the amount of the item under Section 4—302 dealing with the payor bank's responsibility for late return of items; or

(5) with respect to checks, a cutoff hour no earlier than one hour after the opening of the next banking day after the banking day on which the bank received the check and no later than the close of that next banking day or, if no cutoff hour is fixed, the close of the next banking day after the banking day on which the bank received the check.

(b) Subject to subsection (a), items may be accepted, paid, certified, or charged to the indicated account of its customer in any order.

§4—401. WHEN BANK MAY CHARGE CUSTOMER'S ACCOUNT

(a) A bank may charge against the account of a customer an item that is properly payable from the account even though the charge creates an overdraft. An item is properly payable if it is authorized by the customer and is in accordance with any agreement between the customer and bank.

(b) A customer is not liable for the amount of an overdraft if the customer neither signed the item nor benefited from the proceeds of the item.

(c) A bank may charge against the account of a customer a check that is otherwise properly payable from the account, even though payment was made before the date of the check, unless the customer has given notice to the bank of the postdating describing the check with reasonable certainty. The notice is effective for the period stated in Section 4—403(b) for stop-payment orders, and must be received at such time and in such manner as to afford the bank a reasonable opportunity to act on it before the bank takes any action with respect to the check described in Section 4—303. If a bank charges against the account of a customer a check before the date stated in the notice of postdating, the bank is liable for damages for the loss resulting from its act. The loss may include damages for dishonor of subsequent items under Section 4—402.

(d) A bank that in good faith makes payment to a holder may charge the indicated account of its customer according to:

(1) the original terms of the altered item; or

(2) the terms of the completed item, even though the bank knows the item has been completed unless the bank has notice that the completion was improper.

§4—402. BANK'S LIABILITY TO CUSTOMER FOR WRONGFUL DISHONOR; TIME OF DETERMINING INSUFFICIENCY OF ACCOUNT

(a) Except as otherwise provided in this Article, a payor bank wrongfully dishonors an item if it dishonors an item that is properly payable, but a bank may dishonor an item that would create an overdraft unless it has agreed to pay the overdraft.

(b) A payor bank is liable to its customer for damages proximately caused by the wrongful dishonor of an item. Liability is limited to actual damages proved and may include damages for an arrest or prosecution of the customer or other consequential damages. Whether any consequential damages are proximately caused by the wrongful dishonor is a question of fact to be determined in each case.

(c) A payor bank's determination of the customer's account balance on which a decision to dishonor for insufficiency of available funds is based may be made at any time between the time the item is received by the payor bank and the time that the payor bank returns the item or gives notice in lieu of return, and no more than one determination need be made. If, at the election of the payor bank, a subsequent balance determination is made for the purpose of reevaluating the bank's decision to dishonor the item, the account balance at that time is determinative of whether a dishonor for insufficiency of available funds is wrongful.

§4—403. CUSTOMER'S RIGHT TO STOP PAYMENT; BURDEN OF PROOF OF LOSS

(a) A customer or any person authorized to draw on the account if there is more than one person may stop payment of any item drawn on the customer's account or close the account by an order to the bank describing the item or account with reasonable certainty received at a time and in a manner that affords the bank a reasonable opportunity to act on it before any action by the bank with respect to the item described in Section 4—303. If the signature of more than one person is required to draw on an account, any of these persons may stop payment or close the account.

(b) A stop-payment order is effective for six months, but it lapses after 14 calendar days if the original order was oral and was not confirmed in writing within that period. A stop-payment order may be renewed for additional six-month periods by a writing given to the bank within a period during which the stop-payment order is effective.

(c) The burden of establishing the fact and amount of loss resulting from the payment of an item contrary to a stop-payment order or order to close an account is on the customer. The loss from payment of an item contrary to a stop-payment order may include damages for dishonor of subsequent items under Section 4—402.

§4—404. BANK NOT OBLIGED TO PAY CHECK MORE THAN SIX MONTHS OLD

A bank is under no obligation to a customer having a checking account to pay a check, other than a certified check, which is presented more than six months after its date, but it may charge its customer's account for a payment made thereafter in good faith.

§4—405. DEATH OR INCOMPETENCE OF CUSTOMER

(a) A payor or collecting bank's authority to accept, pay, or collect an item or to account for proceeds of its collection, if otherwise effective, is not rendered ineffective by incompetence of a customer of either bank existing at the time the item is issued or its collection is undertaken if the bank does not know of an adjudication of incompetence. Neither death nor incompetence of a customer revokes the authority to accept, pay, collect, or account until the bank knows of the fact of death or of an adjudication of incompetence and has reasonable opportunity to act on it.

(b) Even with knowledge, a bank may for 10 days after the date of death pay or certify checks drawn on or before the date unless ordered to stop payment by a person claiming an interest in the account.

§4—406. CUSTOMER'S DUTY TO DISCOVER AND REPORT UNAUTHORIZED SIGNATURE OR ALTERATION

(a) A bank that sends or makes available to a customer a statement of account showing payment of items for the account shall either return or make available to the customer the items paid or provide information in the statement of account sufficient to allow the customer reasonably to identify the items paid. The statement of account provides sufficient information if the item is described by item number, amount, and date of payment.

(b) If the items are not returned to the customer, the person retaining the items shall either retain the items or, if the items are destroyed, maintain the capacity to furnish legible copies of the items until the expiration of seven years after receipt of the items. A customer may request an item from the bank that paid the item, and that bank must provide in a reasonable time either the item or, if the item has been destroyed or is not otherwise obtainable, a legible copy of the item.

(c) If a bank sends or makes available a statement of account or items pursuant to subsection (a), the customer must exercise reasonable promptness in examining the statement or the items to determine whether any payment was not authorized because of an alteration of an item or because a purported signature by or on behalf of the customer was not authorized. If, based on the statement or items provided, the customer should reasonably have discovered the unauthorized payment, the customer must promptly notify the bank of the relevant facts.

(d) If the bank proves that the customer failed, with respect to an item, to comply with the duties imposed on the customer by subsection (c), the customer is precluded from asserting against the bank:

(1) the customer's unauthorized signature or any alteration on the item, if the bank also proves that it suffered a loss by reason of the failure; and

(2) the customer's unauthorized signature or alteration by the same wrongdoer on any other item paid in good faith by the bank if the payment was made before the bank received notice from the customer of the unauthorized signature or alteration and after the customer had been afforded a reasonable period of time, not exceeding 30 days, in which to examine the item or statement of account and notify the bank.

(e) If subsection (d) applies and the customer proves that the bank failed to exercise ordinary care in paying the item and that the failure substantially contributed to loss, the loss is allocated between the customer precluded and the bank asserting the preclusion according to the extent to which the failure of the customer to comply with subsection (c) and the failure of the bank to exercise ordinary care contributed to the loss. If the customer proves that the bank did not pay the item in good faith, the preclusion under subsection (d) does not apply.

(f) Without regard to care or lack of care of either the customer or the bank, a customer who does not within one year after the statement or items are made available to the customer (subsection (a)) discover and report the customer's unauthorized signature on or any alteration on the item is precluded from asserting against the bank the unauthorized signature or alteration. If there is a preclusion under this subsection, the payor bank may not recover for breach or warranty under Section 4—208 with respect to the unauthorized signature or alteration to which the preclusion applies.

§4—407. PAYOR BANK'S RIGHT TO SUBROGATION ON IMPROPER PAYMENT

If a payor has paid an item over the order of the drawer or maker to stop payment, or after an account has been closed, or otherwise under circumstances giving a basis for objection by the drawer or maker, to prevent unjust enrichment and only to the extent necessary to prevent loss to the bank by reason of its payment of the item, the payor bank is subrogated to the rights

(1) of any holder in due course on the item against the drawer or maker;

(2) of the payee or any other holder of the item against the drawer or maker either on the item or under the transaction out of which the item arose; and

(3) of the drawer or maker against the payee or any other holder of the item with respect to the transaction out of which the item arose.

* * * *

Article 4A Funds Transfers

Part 1 Subject Matter and Definitions

§4A—104. FUNDS TRANSFER—DEFINITIONS

(a) "Funds transfer" means the series of transactions, beginning with the originator's payment order, made for the purpose of making payment to the beneficiary of the order. The term includes any payment order issued by the originator's bank or an intermediary bank intended to carry out the originator's payment order. A funds transfer is completed by acceptance by the beneficiary's bank of a payment order for the benefit of the beneficiary of the originator's payment order.

(b) "Intermediary bank" means a receiving bank other than the originator's bank or the beneficiary's bank.

(c) "Originator" means the sender of the first payment order in a funds transfer.

(d) "Originator's bank" means (i) the receiving bank to which the payment order of the originator is issued if the originator is not a bank, or (ii) the originator if the originator is a bank.

§4A—105. OTHER DEFINITIONS

(1) "Authorized account" means a deposit account of a customer in a bank designated by the customer as a source of payment of payment orders issued by the customer to the bank. If a customer does not so designate an account, any account of the customer is an authorized account if payment of a payment order from that account is not inconsistent with a restriction on the use of that account.

(2) "Bank" means a person engaged in the business of banking and includes a savings bank, savings and loan association, credit union, and trust company. A branch or separate office of a bank is a separate bank for purposes of this Article.

(3) "Customer" means a person, including a bank, having an account with a bank or from whom a bank has agreed to receive payment orders.

(4) "Funds-transfer business day" of a receiving bank means the part of a day during which the receiving bank is open for the receipt, processing, and transmittal of payment orders and cancellations and amendments of payment orders.

(5) "Funds-transfer system" means a wire transfer network, automated clearing house, or other communication system of a clearing house or other association of banks through which a payment order by a bank may be transmitted to the bank to which the order is addressed.

(6) "Good faith" means honesty in fact and the observance of reasonable commercial standards of fair dealing.

(7) "Prove" with respect to a fact means to meet the burden of establishing the fact (Section 1—201(8)).

* * * *

§4A—106. TIME PAYMENT ORDER IS RECEIVED

(a) The time of receipt of a payment order or communication cancelling or amending a payment order is determined by the rules applicable to receipt of a notice stated in Section 1—201(27). A receiving bank may fix a cut-off time or times on a funds-transfer business day for the receipt and processing of payment orders and communications cancelling or amending payment orders. Different cut-off times may apply to payment orders, cancellations, or amendments, or to different categories of payment orders, cancellations, or amendments. A cut-off time may apply to senders generally or different cut-off times may apply to different senders or categories of payment orders. If a payment order or communication cancelling or amending a payment order is received after the close of a funds-transfer business day or after the appropriate cut-off time on a funds-transfer business day, the receiving bank may treat the payment order or communication as received at the opening of the next funds-transfer business day.

(b) If this Article refers to an execution date or payment date or states a day on which a receiving bank is required to take action, and the date or day does not fall on a funds-transfer business day, the next day that is a funds- transfer business day is treated as the date or day stated, unless the contrary is stated in this Article.

* * * *

§4A—108. EXCLUSION OF CONSUMER TRANSACTIONS GOVERNED BY FEDERAL LAW

This Article does not apply to a funds transfer any part of which is governed by the Electronic Fund Transfer Act of 1978 (Title XX, Public Law 95—630, 92 Stat. 3728, 15 U.S.C. §1693 et seq.) as amended from time to time.

* * * *

Revised Article 9 Secured Transactions

§9—102. DEFINITIONS AND INDEX OF DEFINITIONS

(1) "Accession" means goods that are physically united with other goods in such a manner that the identity of the original goods is not lost.

(2) "Account", except as used in "account for", means a right to payment of a monetary obligation, whether or not earned by performance, (i) for property that has been or is to be sold, leased, licensed, assigned, or otherwise disposed of, (ii) for services rendered or to be rendered, (iii) for a policy of insurance issued or to be issued, (iv) for a secondary obligation incurred or to be incurred, (v) for energy provided or to be provided, (vi) for the use or hire of a vessel under a charter or other contract, (vii) arising out of the use of a credit or charge card or information contained on or for use with the card, or (viii) as winnings in a lottery or other game of chance operated or sponsored by a State, governmental unit of a State, or person licensed or authorized to operate the game by a State or governmental unit of a State. The term includes health-care insurance receivables. The term does not include (i) rights to payment evidenced by chattel paper or an instrument, (ii) commercial tort claims, (iii) deposit accounts, (iv) investment property, (v) letter-of-credit rights or letters of credit, or (vi) rights to payment for money or funds advanced or sold, other than rights arising out of the use of a credit or charge card or information contained on or for use with the card.

* * * *

(5) "Agricultural lien" means an interest, other than a security interest, in farm products:

(A) which secures payment or performance of an obligation for:

(i) goods or services furnished in connection with a debtor's farming operation; or

(ii) rent on real property leased by a debtor in connection with its farming operation;

(B) which is created by statute in favor of a person that:

(i) in the ordinary course of its business furnished goods or services to a debtor in connection with a debtor's farming operation; or

(ii) leased real property to a debtor in connection with the debtor's farming operation; and

(C) whose effectiveness does not depend on the person's possession of the personal property.

(6) "As-extracted collateral" means:

(A) oil, gas, or other minerals that are subject to a security interest that:

(i) is created by a debtor having an interest in the minerals before extraction; and

(ii) attaches to the minerals as extracted; or

(B) accounts arising out of the sale at the wellhead or minehead of oil, gas, or other minerals in which the debtor had an interest before extraction.

(7) "Authenticate" means:

(A) to sign; or

(B) to execute or otherwise adopt a symbol, or encrypt or similarly process a record in whole or in part, with the present intent of the authenticating person to identify the person and adopt or accept a record.

* * * *

(11) "Chattel paper" means a record or records that evidence both a monetary obligation and a security interest in specific goods, a security interest in specific goods and software used in the goods, a security interest in specific goods and license of software used in the goods, a lease of specific goods, or a lease of specific goods and license of software used in the goods. In this paragraph, "monetary obligation" means a monetary obligation secured by the goods or owed under a lease of the goods and includes a monetary obligation with respect to software used in the goods. The term does not include (i) charters or other contracts involving the use or hire of a vessel or (ii) records that evidence a right to payment arising out of the use of a

credit or charge card or information contained on or for use with the card. If a transaction is evidenced by records that include an instrument or series of instruments, the group of records taken together constitutes chattel paper.

(12) "Collateral" means the property subject to a security interest or agricultural lien. The term includes:

(A) proceeds to which a security interest attaches;

(B) accounts, chattel paper, payment intangibles, and promissory notes that have been sold; and

(C) goods that are the subject of a consignment.

(13) "Commercial tort claim" means a claim arising in tort with respect to which:

(A) the claimant is an organization; or

(B) the claimant is an individual and the claim:

(i) arose in the course of the claimant's business or profession; and

(ii) does not include damages arising out of personal injury to or the death of an individual.

* * * *

(19) "Consignee" means a merchant to which goods are delivered in a consignment.

(20) "Consignment" means a transaction, regardless of its form, in which a person delivers goods to a merchant for the purpose of sale and:

(A) the merchant:

(i) deals in goods of that kind under a name other than the name of the person making delivery;

(ii) is not an auctioneer; and

(iii) is not generally known by its creditors to be substantially engaged in selling the goods of others;

(B) with respect to each delivery, the aggregate value of the goods is $1,000 or more at the time of delivery;

(C) the goods are not consumer goods immediately before delivery; and

(D) the transaction does not create a security interest that secures an obligation.

(21) "Consignor" means a person that delivers goods to a consignee in a consignment.

(22) "Consumer debtor" means a debtor in a consumer transaction.

(23) "Consumer goods" means goods that are used or bought for use primarily for personal, family, or household purposes.

(24) "Consumer-goods transaction" means a consumer transaction in which:

(A) an individual incurs an obligation primarily for personal, family, or household purposes; and

(B) a security interest in consumer goods secures the obligation.

(25) "Consumer obligor" means an obligor who is an individual and who incurred the obligation as part of a transaction entered into primarily for personal, family, or household purposes.

(26) "Consumer transaction" means a transaction in which (i) an individual incurs an obligation primarily for personal, family, or household purposes, (ii) a security interest secures the obligation, and (iii) the collateral is held or acquired primarily for personal, family, or household purposes. The term includes consumer-goods transactions.

(27) "Continuation statement" means an amendment of a financing statement which:

(A) identifies, by its file number, the initial financing statement to which it relates; and

(B) indicates that it is a continuation statement for, or that it is filed to continue the effectiveness of, the identified financing statement.

(28) "Debtor" means:

(A) a person having an interest, other than a security interest or other lien, in the collateral, whether or not the person is an obligor;

(B) a seller of accounts, chattel paper, payment intangibles, or promissory notes; or

(C) a consignee.

(29) "Deposit account" means a demand, time, savings, passbook, or similar account maintained with a bank. The term does not include investment property or accounts evidenced by an instrument.

(30) "Document" means a document of title or a receipt of the type described in Section 7—201(2).

(31) "Electronic chattel paper" means chattel paper evidenced by a record or records consisting of information stored in an electronic medium.

(32) "Encumbrance" means a right, other than an ownership interest, in real property. The term includes mortgages and other liens on real property.

(33) "Equipment" means goods other than inventory, farm products, or consumer goods.

(34) "Farm products" means goods, other than standing timber, with respect to which the debtor is engaged in a farming operation and which are:

(A) crops grown, growing, or to be grown, including:

(i) crops produced on trees, vines, and bushes; and

(ii) aquatic goods produced in aquacultural operations;

(B) livestock, born or unborn, including aquatic goods produced in aquacultural operations;

(C) supplies used or produced in a farming operation; or

(D) products of crops or livestock in their unmanufactured states.

(35) "Farming operation" means raising, cultivating, propagating, fattening, grazing, or any other farming, livestock, or aquacultural operation.

* * * *

(39) "Financing statement" means a record or records composed of an initial financing statement and any filed record relating to the initial financing statement.

(40) "Fixture filing" means the filing of a financing statement covering goods that are or are to become fixtures and satisfying Section 9—502(a) and (b). The term includes the filing of a financing statement covering goods of a transmitting utility which are or are to become fixtures.

(41) "Fixtures" means goods that have become so related to particular real property that an interest in them arises under real property law.

(42) "General intangible" means any personal property, including things in action, other than accounts, chattel paper, commercial tort claims, deposit accounts, documents, goods, instruments, investment property, letter-of-credit rights, letters of credit, money, and oil, gas, or other minerals before extraction. The term includes payment intangibles and software.

* * * *

(44) "Goods" means all things that are movable when a security interest attaches. The term includes (i) fixtures, (ii) standing timber that is to be cut and removed under a conveyance or contract for sale, (iii) the unborn young of animals, (iv) crops grown, growing, or to be grown, even if the crops are produced on trees, vines, or bushes, and (v) manufactured homes.

The term also includes a computer program embedded in goods and any supporting information provided in connection with a transaction relating to the program if (i) the program is associated with the goods in such a manner that it customarily is considered part of the goods, or (ii) by becoming the owner of the goods, a person acquires a right to use the program in connection with the goods. The term does not include a computer program embedded in goods that consist solely of the medium in which the program is embedded. The term also does not include accounts, chattel paper, commercial tort claims, deposit accounts, documents, general intangibles, instruments, investment property, letter-of-credit rights, letters of credit, money, or oil, gas, or other minerals before extraction.

* * * *

(46) "Health-care-insurance receivable" means an interest in or claim under a policy of insurance which is a right to payment of a monetary obligation for health-care goods or services provided.

(47) "Instrument" means a negotiable instrument or any other writing that evidences a right to the payment of a monetary obligation, is not itself a security agreement or lease, and is of a type that in ordinary course of business is transferred by delivery with any necessary indorsement or assignment. The term does not include (i) investment property, (ii) letters of credit, or (iii) writings that evidence a right to payment arising out of the use of a credit or charge card or information contained on or for use with the card.

(48) "Inventory" means goods, other than farm products, which:

(A) are leased by a person as lessor;

(B) are held by a person for sale or lease or to be furnished under a contract of service;

(C) are furnished by a person under a contract of service; or

(D) consist of raw materials, work in process, or materials used or consumed in a business.

(49) "Investment property" means a security, whether certificated or uncertificated, security entitlement, securities account, commodity contract, or commodity account.

* * * *

(51) "Letter-of-credit right" means a right to payment or performance under a letter of credit, whether or not the beneficiary has demanded or is at the time entitled to demand payment or performance. The term does not include the right of a beneficiary to demand payment or performance under a letter of credit.

(52) "Lien creditor" means:

(A) a creditor that has acquired a lien on the property involved by attachment, levy, or the like;

(B) an assignee for benefit of creditors from the time of assignment;

(C) a trustee in bankruptcy from the date of the filing of the petition; or

(D) a receiver in equity from the time of appointment.

* * * *

(55) "Mortgage" means a consensual interest in real property, including fixtures, which secures payment or performance of an obligation.

(56) "New debtor" means a person that becomes bound as debtor under Section 9—203(d) by a security agreement previously entered into by another person.

(57) "New value" means (i) money, (ii) money's worth in property, services, or new credit, or (iii) release by a transferee of an interest in property previously transferreed to the transferee. The term does not include an obligation substituted for another obligation.

* * * *

(61) "Payment intangible" means a general intangible under which the account debtor's principal obligation is a monetary obligation.

* * * *

(64) "Proceeds", except as used in Section 9—609 (b), means the following property:

(A) whatever is acquired upon the sale, lease, license, exchange, or other disposition of collateral;

(B) whatever is collected on, or distributed on account of, collateral;

(C) rights arising out of collateral;

(D) to the extent of the value of collateral, claims arising out of the loss, nonconformity, or interference with the use of, defects or infringement of rights in, or damage to, the collateral; or

(E) to the extent of the value of collateral and to the extent payable to the debtor or the secured party, insurance payable by reason of the loss or nonconformity of, defects or infringement of rights in, or damage to, the collateral.

* * * *

(69) "Record", except as used in "for record", "of record", "record or legal title", and "record owner", means information that is inscribed on a tangible medium or which is stored in an electronic or other medium and is retrievable in perceivable form.

* * * *

(72) "Secured party" means:

(A) a person in whose favor a security interest is created or provided for under a security agreement, whether or not any obligation to be secured is outstanding;

(B) a person that holds an agricultural lien;

(C) a consignor;

(D) a person to which accounts, chattel paper, payment intangibles, or promissory notes have been sold;

(E) a trustee, indenture trustee, agent, collateral agent, or other representative in whose favor a security interest or agricultural lien is created or provided for; or

(F) a person that holds a security interest arising under Section 2—401, 2—505, 2—711(3), 2A—508(5), 4—210, or 5—118.

(73) "Security agreement" means an agreement that creates or provides for a security interest.

* * * *

(78) "Tangible chattel paper" means chattel paper evidenced by a record or records consisting of information that is inscribed on a tangible medium.

(79) "Termination statement" means an amendment of a financing statement which:

(A) identifies, by its file number, the initial financing statement to which it relates; and

(B) indicates either that it is a termination statement or that the identified financing statement is no longer effective.

* * * *

§9—103. PURCHASE-MONEY SECURITY INTEREST; APPLICATION OF PAYMENTS; BURDEN OF ESTABLISHING

(a) In this section:

(1) "purchase-money collateral" means goods or software that secures a purchase-money obligation incurred with respect to that collateral; and

(2) "purchase-money obligation" means an obligation of an obligor incurred as all or part of the price of the collateral or for value given to enable the debtor to acquire rights in or the use of the collateral if the value is in fact so used.

(b) A security interest in goods is a purchase-money security interest:

(1) to the extent that the goods are purchase-money collateral with respect to that security interest;

(2) if the security interest is in inventory that is or was purchase-money collateral, also to the extent that the security interest secures a purchase-money obligation incurred with respect to other inventory in which the secured party holds or held a purchase-money security interest; and

(3) also to the extent that the security interest secures a purchase-money obligation incurred with respect to software in which the secured party holds or held a purchase-money security interest.

(c) A security interest in software is a purchase-money security interest to the extent that the security interest also secures a purchase-money obligation incurred with respect to goods in which the secured party holds or held a purchase-money security interest if:

(1) the debtor acquired its interest in the software in an integrated transaction in which it acquired an interest in the goods; and

(2) the debtor acquired its interest in the software for the principal purpose of using the software in the goods.

(d) The security interest of a consignor in goods that are the subject of a consignment is a purchase-money security interest in inventory.

(e) In a transaction other than a consumer-goods transaction, if the extent to which a security interest is a purchase-money security interest depends on the application of a payment to a particular obligation, the payment must be applied:

(1) in accordance with any reasonable method of application to which the parties agree;

(2) in the absence of the parties' agreement to a reasonable method, in accordance with any intention of the obligor manifested at or before the time of payment; or

(3) in the absence of an agreement to a reasonable method and a timely manifestation of the obligor's intention, in the following order:

(A) to obligations that are not secured; and

(B) if more than one obligation is secured, to obligations secured by purchase-money security interests in the order in which those obligations were incurred.

(f) In a transaction other than a consumer-goods transaction, a purchase-money security interest does not lose its status as such, even if:

(1) the purchase-money collateral also secures an obligation that is not a purchase-money obligation;

(2) collateral that is not purchase-money collateral also secures the purchase-money obligation; or

(3) the purchase-money obligation has been renewed, refinanced, consolidated, or restructured.

(g) In a transaction other than a consumer-goods transaction, a secured party claiming a purchase-money security interest has the burden of establishing the extent to which the security interest is a purchase-money security interest.

(h) The limitation of the rules in subsections (e), (f), and (g) to transactions other than consumer-goods transactions is intended to leave to the court the determination of the proper rules in consumer-goods transactions. The court may not infer from that limitation the nature of the proper rule in consumer-goods transactions and may continue to apply established approaches.

§9—104. CONTROL OF DEPOSIT ACCOUNT

(a) A secured party has control of a deposit account if:

(1) the secured party is the bank with which the deposit account is maintained;

(2) the debtor, secured party, and bank have agreed in an authenticated record that the bank will comply with instructions originated by the secured party directing disposition of the funds in the deposit account without further consent by the debtor; or

(3) the secured party becomes the bank's customer with respect to the deposit account.

(b) A secured party that has satisfied subsection (a) has control, even if the debtor retains the right to direct the disposition of funds from the deposit account.

§9—105. CONTROL OF ELECTRONIC CHATTEL PAPER

A secured party has control of electronic chattel paper if the record or records comprising the chattel paper are created, stored, and assigned in such a manner that:

(1) a single authoritative copy of the record or records exists which is unique, identifiable and, except as otherwise provided in paragraphs (4), (5), and (6), unalterable;

(2) the authoritative copy identifies the secured party as the assignee of the record or records;

(3) the authoritative copy is communicated to and maintained by the secured party or its designated custodian;

(4) copies or revisions that add or change an identified assignee of the authoritative copy can be made only with the participation of the secured party;

(5) each copy of the authoritative copy and any copy of a copy is readily identifiable as a copy that is not the authoritative copy; and

(6) any revision of the authoritative copy is readily identifiable as an authorized or unauthorized revision.

§9—106. CONTROL OF INVESTMENT PROPERTY

(a) A person has control of a certificated security, uncertificated security, or security entitlement as provided in Section 8—106.

(b) A secured party has control of a commodity contract if:

(1) the secured party is the commodity intermediary with which the commodity contract is carried; or

(2) the commodity customer, secured party, and commodity intermediary have agreed that the commodity intermediary will apply any value distributed on account of the commodity contract as directed by the secured party without further consent by the commodity customer.

(c) A secured party having control of all security entitlements or commodity contracts carried in a securities account or commodity account has control over the securities account or commodity account.

§9—107. CONTROL OF LETTER-OF-CREDIT RIGHT

A secured party has control of a letter-of-credit right to the extent of any right to payment or performance by the issuer or any nominated person if the issuer or nominated person has consented to an assignment of proceeds of the letter of credit under Section 5—114(c) or otherwise applicable law or practice.

§9—108. SUFFICIENCY OF DESCRIPTION

(a) Except as otherwise provided in subsections (c), (d), and (e), a description of personal or real property is sufficient, whether or not it is specific, if it reasonably identifies what is described.

(b) Except as otherwise provided in subsection (d), a description of collateral reasonably identifies the collateral if it identifies the collateral by:

(1) specific listing;

(2) category;

(3) except as otherwise provided in subsection (e), a type of collateral defined in [the Uniform Commercial Code];

(4) quantity;

(5) computational or allocational formula or procedure; or

(6) except as otherwise provided in subsection

(c) any other method, if the identity of the collateral is objectively determinable. (c) A description of collateral as "all the debtor's assets" or "all the debtor's personal property" or using words of similar import does not reasonably identify the collateral.

(d) Except as otherwise provided in subsection (e), a description of a security entitlement, securities account, or commodity account is sufficient if it describes:

(1) the collateral by those terms or as investment property; or

(2) the underlying financial asset or commodity contract.

(e) A description only by type of collateral defined in [the Uniform Commercial Code] is an insufficient description of:

(1) a commercial tort claim; or

(2) in a consumer transaction, consumer goods, a security entitlement, a securities account, or a commodity account.

§9-109 SCOPE

* * * *

This article does not apply to:

(1) a landlord's lien, other than an agricultural lien;

(2) a lien, other than an agricultural lien, given by statute or other rule of law for services or materials, but Section 9—333 applies with respect to priority of the lien;

(3) an assignment of a claim for wages, salary, or other compensation of an employee;

(4) a sale of accounts, chattel paper, payment intangibles, or promissory notes as part of a sale of the business out of which they arose;

(5) an assignment of accounts, chattel paper, payment intangibles, or promissory notes which is for the purpose of collection only;

(6) an assignment of a right to payment under a contract to an assignee that is also obligated to perform under the contract;

(7) an assignment of a single account, payment intangible, or promissory note to an assignee in full or partial satisfaction of a preexisting indebtedness;

(8) a transfer of an interest in or an assignment of a claim under a policy of insurance, other than an assignment by or to a health-care provider of a health-care-insurance receivable and any subsequent assignment of the right to payment, but Sections 9—315 and 9—322 apply with respect to proceeds and priorities in proceeds;

(9) an assignment of a right represented by a judgment, other than a judgment taken on a right to payment that was collateral;

(10) a right of recoupment or set-off, but:

(A) Section 9—340 applies with respect to the effectiveness of rights of recoupment or set-off against deposit accounts; and

(B) Section 9—404 applies with respect to defenses or claims of an account debtor;

(11) the creation or transfer of an interest in or lien on real property, including a lease or rents thereunder, except to the extent that provision is made for:

(A) liens on real property in Sections 9—203 and 9—308;

(B) fixtures in Section 9—334;

(C) fixture filings in Sections 9—501, 9—502, 9—512, 9—516, and 9—519; and

(D) security agreements covering personal and real property in Section 9—604;

(12) an assignment of a claim arising in tort, other than a commercial tort claim, but Sections 9—315 and 9—322 apply with respect to proceeds and priorities in proceeds; or

(13) an assignment of a deposit account in a consumer transaction, but Sections 9—315 and 9—322 apply with respect to proceeds and priorities in proceeds.

* * * *

§9—201. GENERAL EFFECTIVENESS OF SECURITY AGREEMENT

(a) Except as otherwise provided in [the Uniform Commercial Code], a security agreement is effective according to its terms between the parties, against purchasers of the collateral, and against creditors.

(b) A transaction subject to this article is subject to any applicable rule of law which establishes a different rule for consumers and [insert reference to (i) any other statute or regulation that regulates the rates, charges, agreements, and practices for loans, credit sales, or other extensions of credit and (ii) any consumer-protection statute or regulation].

(c) In case of conflict between this article and a rule of law, statute, or regulation described in subsection (b), the rule of law, statute, or regulation controls. Failure to comply with a statute or regulation described in subsection (b) has only the effect the statute or regulation specifies.

(d) This article does not:

(1) validate any rate, charge, agreement, or practice that violates a rule of law, statute, or regulation described in subsection (b); or

(2) extend the application of the rule of law, statute, or regulation to a transaction not otherwise subject to it.

§9—202. TITLE TO COLLATERAL IMMATERIAL

Except as otherwise provided with respect to consignments or sales of accounts, chattel paper, payment intangibles, or promissory notes, the provisions of this article with regard to rights and obligations apply whether title to collateral is in the secured party or the debtor.

§9—203. ATTACHMENT AND ENFORCEABILITY OF SECURITY INTEREST; PROCEEDS; SUPPORTING OBLIGATIONS; FORMAL REQUISITES

(a) A security interest attaches to collateral when it becomes enforceable against the debtor with respect to the collateral, unless an agreement expressly postpones the time of attachment.

(b) Except as otherwise provided in subsections (c) through (i), a security interest is enforceable against the debtor and third parties with respect to the collateral only if:

(1) value has been given;

(2) the debtor has rights in the collateral or the power to transfer rights in the collateral to a secured party; and

(3) one of the following conditions is met:

(A) the debtor has authenticated a security agreement that provides a description of the collateral and, if the security interest covers timber to be cut, a description of the land concerned;

(B) the collateral is not a certificated security and is in the possession of the secured party under Section 9—313 pursuant to the debtor's security agreement;

(C) the collateral is a certificated security in registered form and the security certificate has been delivered to the secured party under Section 8—301 pursuant to the debtor's security agreement; or

(D) the collateral is deposit accounts, electronic chattel paper, investment property, or letter-of-credit rights, and the secured party has control under Section 9—104, 9—105, 9 —106, or 9—107 pursuant to the debtor's security agreement.

(c) Subsection (b) is subject to Section 4—210 on the security interest of a collecting bank, Section 5—118 on the security interest of a letter-of-credit issuer or nominated person, Section 9—110 on a security interest arising under Article 2 or 2A, and Section 9—206 on security interests in investment property.

(d) A person becomes bound as debtor by a security agreement entered into by another person if, by operation of law other than this article or by contract:

(1) the security agreement becomes effective to create a security interest in the person's property; or

(2) the person becomes generally obligated for the obligations of the other person, including the obligation secured under the security agreement, and acquires or succeeds to all or substantially all of the assets of the other person.

(e) If a new debtor becomes bound as debtor by a security agreement entered into by another person:

(1) the agreement satisfies subsection (b)(3) with respect to existing or after-acquired property of the new debtor to the extent the property is described in the agreement; and

(2) another agreement is not necessary to make a security interest in the property enforceable.

(f) The attachment of a security interest in collateral gives the secured party the rights to proceeds provided by Section 9—315 and is also attachment of a security interest in a supporting obligation for the collateral.

(g) The attachment of a security interest in a right to payment or performance secured by a security interest or other lien on personal or real property is also attachment of a security interest in the security interest, mortgage, or other lien.

(h) The attachment of a security interest in a securities account is also attachment of a security interest in the security entitlements carried in the securities account.

(i) The attachment of a security interest in a commodity account is also attachment of a security interest in the commodity contracts carried in the commodity account.

§9—204. AFTER-ACQUIRED PROPERTY; FUTURE ADVANCES

(a) Except as otherwise provided in subsection (b), a security agreement may create or provide for a security interest in after-acquired collateral.

(b) A security interest does not attach under a term constituting an after-acquired property clause to:

(1) consumer goods, other than an accession when given as additional security, unless the debtor acquires rights in them within 10 days after the secured party gives value; or

(2) a commercial tort claim.

(c) A security agreement may provide that collateral secures, or that accounts, chattel paper, payment intangibles, or promissory notes are sold in connection with, future advances or other value, whether or not the advances or value are given pursuant to commitment.

§9—205. USE OR DISPOSITION OF COLLATERAL PERMISSIBLE

(a) A security interest is not invalid or fraudulent against creditors solely because:

(1) the debtor has the right or ability to:

(A) use, commingle, or dispose of all or part of the collateral, including returned or repossessed goods;

(B) collect, compromise, enforce, or otherwise deal with collateral;

(C) accept the return of collateral or make repossessions; or

(D) use, commingle, or dispose of proceeds; or

(2) the secured party fails to require the debtor to account for proceeds or replace collateral.

(b) This section does not relax the requirements of possession if attachment, perfection, or enforcement of a security interest depends upon possession of the collateral by the secured party.

§9—206. SECURITY INTEREST ARISING IN PURCHASE OR DELIVERY OF FINANCIAL ASSET

(a) A security interest in favor of a securities intermediary attaches to a person's security entitlement if:

(1) the person buys a financial asset through the securities intermediary in a transaction in which the person is obligated to pay the purchase price to the securities intermediary at the time of the purchase; and

(2) the securities intermediary credits the financial asset to the buyer's securities account before the buyer pays the securities intermediary.

(b) The security interest described in subsection (a) secures the person's obligation to pay for the financial asset.

* * * *

§9—207. RIGHTS AND DUTIES OF SECURED PARTY HAVING POSSESSION OR CONTROL OF COLLATERAL

(a) Except as otherwise provided in subsection (d), a secured party shall use reasonable care in the custody and preservation of collateral in the secured party's possession. In the case of chattel paper or an instrument, reasonable care includes taking necessary steps to preserve rights against prior parties unless otherwise agreed.

(b) Except as otherwise provided in subsection (d), if a secured party has possession of collateral:

(1) reasonable expenses, including the cost of insurance and payment of taxes or other charges, incurred in the custody, preservation, use, or operation of the collateral are chargeable to the debtor and are secured by the collateral;

(2) the risk of accidental loss or damage is on the debtor to the extent of a deficiency in any effective insurance coverage;

(3) the secured party shall keep the collateral identifiable, but fungible collateral may be commingled; and

(4) the secured party may use or operate the collateral:

(A) for the purpose of preserving the collateral or its value;

(B) as permitted by an order of a court having competent jurisdiction; or

(C) except in the case of consumer goods, in the manner and to the extent agreed by the debtor.

(c) Except as otherwise provided in subsection (d), a secured party having possession of collateral or control of collateral under Section 9—104, 9—105, 9—106, or 9—107:

(1) may hold as additional security any proceeds, except money or funds, received from the collateral;

(2) shall apply money or funds received from the collateral to reduce the secured obligation, unless remitted to the debtor; and

(3) may create a security interest in the collateral.

(d) If the secured party is a buyer of accounts, chattel paper, payment intangibles, or promissory notes or a consignor:

(1) subsection (a) does not apply unless the secured party is entitled under an agreement:

(A) to charge back uncollected collateral; or

(B) otherwise to full or limited recourse against the debtor or a secondary obligor based on the nonpayment or other default of an account debtor or other obligor on the collateral; and

(2) subsections (b) and (c) do not apply.

§9—208. ADDITIONAL DUTIES OF SECURED PARTY HAVING CONTROL OF COLLATERAL

(a) This section applies to cases in which there is no outstanding secured obligation and the secured party is not committed to make advances, incur obligations, or otherwise give value.

(b) Within 10 days after receiving an authenticated demand by the debtor:

(1) a secured party having control of a deposit account under Section 9—104(a)(2) shall send to the bank with which the deposit account is maintained an authenticated statement that releases the bank from any further obligation to comply with instructions originated by the secured party;

(2) a secured party having control of a deposit account under Section 9—104(a)(3) shall:

(A) pay the debtor the balance on deposit in the deposit account; or

(B) transfer the balance on deposit into a deposit account in the debtor's name;

(3) a secured party, other than a buyer, having control of electronic chattel paper under Section 9—105 shall:

(A) communicate the authoritative copy of the electronic chattel paper to the debtor or its designated custodian;

(B) if the debtor designates a custodian that is the designated custodian with which the authoritative copy of the electronic chattel paper is maintained for the secured party, communicate to the custodian an authenticated record releasing the designated custodian from any further obligation to comply with instructions originated by the secured party and instructing the custodian to comply with instructions originated by the debtor; and

(C) take appropriate action to enable the debtor or its designated custodian to make copies of or revisions to the authoritative copy which add or change an identified assignee of the authoritative copy without the consent of the secured party;

(4) a secured party having control of investment property under Section 8—106(d)(2) or 9—106 (b) shall send to the securities intermediary or commodity intermediary with which the security entitlement or commodity contract is maintained an authenticated record that releases the securities intermediary or commodity intermediary from any further obligation to comply with entitlement orders or directions originated by the secured party; and

(5) a secured party having control of a letter-of-credit right under Section 9—107 shall send to each person having an unfulfilled obligation to pay or deliver proceeds of the letter of credit to the secured party an authenticated release from any further obligation to pay or deliver proceeds of the letter of credit to the secured party.

§9—209. DUTIES OF SECURED PARTY IF ACCOUNT DEBTOR HAS BEEN NOTIFIED OF ASSIGNMENT

(a) Except as otherwise provided in subsection (c), this section applies if:

(1) there is no outstanding secured obligation; and

(2) the secured party is not committed to make advances, incur obligations, or otherwise give value.

(b) Within 10 days after receiving an authenticated demand by the debtor, a secured party shall send to an account debtor that has received notification of an assignment to the secured party as assignee under Section 9—406(a) an authenticated record that releases the account debtor from any further obligation to the secured party.

* * * *

§9—301. LAW GOVERNING PERFECTION AND PRIORITY OF SECURITY INTERESTS

Except as otherwise provided in Sections 9—303 through 9—306, the following rules determine the law governing perfection, the effect of perfection or nonperfection, and the priority of a security interest in collateral:

(1) Except as otherwise provided in this section, while a debtor is located in a jurisdiction, the local law of that jurisdiction governs perfection, the effect of perfection or nonperfection, and the priority of a security interest in collateral.

(2) While collateral is located in a jurisdiction, the local law of that jurisdiction governs perfection, the effect of perfection or nonperfection, and the priority of a possessory security interest in that collateral.

(3) Except as otherwise provided in paragraph (4), while negotiable documents, goods, instruments, money, or tangible chattel paper is located in a jurisdiction, the local law of that jurisdiction governs:

(A) perfection of a security interest in the goods by filing a fixture filing;

(B) perfection of a security interest in timber to be cut; and

(C) the effect of perfection or nonperfection and the priority of a nonpossessory security interest in the collateral.

(4) The local law of the jurisdiction in which the wellhead or minehead is located governs perfection, the effect of perfection or nonperfection, and the priority of a security interest in as-extracted collateral.

* * * *

§9—309. SECURITY INTEREST PERFECTED UPON ATTACHMENT

The following security interests are perfected when they attach:

(1) a purchase-money security interest in consumer goods, except as otherwise provided in Section 9—311(b) with respect to consumer goods that are subject to a statute or treaty described in Section 9—311(a);

(2) an assignment of accounts or payment intangibles which does not by itself or in conjunction with other assignments to the same assignee transfer a significant part of the assignor's outstanding accounts or payment intangibles;

(3) a sale of a payment intangible;

(4) a sale of a promissory note;

(5) a security interest created by the assignment of a health-care-insurance receivable to the provider of the health-care goods or services;

(6) a security interest arising under Section 2—401, 2—505, 2—711(3), or 2A—508(5), until the debtor obtains possession of the collateral;

(7) a security interest of a collecting bank arising under Section 4—210;

(8) a security interest of an issuer or nominated person arising under Section 5—118;

(9) a security interest arising in the delivery of a financial asset under Section 9—206(c);

(10) a security interest in investment property created by a broker or securities intermediary;

(11) a security interest in a commodity contract or a commodity account created by a commodity intermediary;

(12) an assignment for the benefit of all creditors of the transferor and subsequent transfers by the assignee thereunder; and

(13) a security interest created by an assignment of a beneficial interest in a decedent's estate; and

(14) a sale by an individual of an account that is a right to payment of winnings in a lottery or other game of chance.

§9—310. WHEN FILING REQUIRED TO PERFECT SECURITY INTEREST OR AGRICULTURAL LIEN; SECURITY INTERESTS AND AGRICULTURAL LIENS TO WHICH FILING PROVISIONS DO NOT APPLY

(a) Except as otherwise provided in subsection (b) and Section 9—312(b), a financing statement must be filed to perfect all security interests and agricultural liens.

(b) The filing of a financing statement is not necessary to perfect a security interest:

(1) that is perfected under Section 9—308(d), (e), (f), or (g);

(2) that is perfected under Section 9—309 when it attaches;

(3) in property subject to a statute, regulation, or treaty described in Section 9—311(a);

(4) in goods in possession of a bailee which is perfected under Section 9—312(d)(1) or (2);

(5) in certificated securities, documents, goods, or instruments which is perfected without filing or possession under Section 9—312(e), (f), or (g);

(6) in collateral in the secured party's possession under Section 9—313;

(7) in a certificated security which is perfected by delivery of the security certificate to the secured party under Section 9—313;

(8) in deposit accounts, electronic chattel paper, investment property, or letter-of-credit rights which is perfected by control under Section 9—314;

(9) in proceeds which is perfected under Section 9—315; or

(10) that is perfected under Section 9—316.

(c) If a secured party assigns a perfected security interest or agricultural lien, a filing under this article is not required to continue the perfected status of the security interest against creditors of and transferees from the original debtor.

§9—311. PERFECTION OF SECURITY INTERESTS IN PROPERTY SUBJECT TO CERTAIN STATUTES, REGULATIONS, AND TREATIES

(a) Except as otherwise provided in subsection (d), the filing of a financing statement is not necessary or effective to perfect a security interest in property subject to:

(1) a statute, regulation, or treaty of the United States whose requirements for a security interest's obtaining priority over the rights of a lien creditor with respect to the property preempt Section 9—310(a);

(2) [list any certificate-of-title statute covering automobiles, trailers, mobile homes, boats, farm tractors, or the like, which provides for a security interest to be indicated on the certificate as a condition or result of perfection, and any non Uniform Commercial Code central filing statute]; or

(3) a certificate-of-title statute of another jurisdiction which provides for a security interest to be indicated on the certificate as a condition or result of the security interest's obtaining priority over the rights of a lien creditor with respect to the property.

* * * *

§9—312. PERFECTION OF SECURITY INTERESTS IN CHATTEL PAPER, DEPOSIT ACCOUNTS, DOCUMENTS, GOODS COVERED BY DOCUMENTS, INSTRUMENTS, INVESTMENT PROPERTY, LETTER-OF-CREDIT RIGHTS, AND MONEY; PERFECTION BY PERMISSIVE FILING; TEMPORARY PERFECTION WITHOUT FILING OR TRANSFER OF POSSESSION

(a) A security interest in chattel paper, negotiable documents, instruments, or investment property may be perfected by filing.

(b) Except as otherwise provided in Section 9—315 (c) and (d) for proceeds:

(1) a security interest in a deposit account may be perfected only by control under Section 9—314;

(2) and except as otherwise provided in Section 9—308(d), a security interest in a letter-of-credit right may be perfected only by control under Section 9—314; and

(3) a security interest in money may be perfected only by the secured party's taking possession under Section 9—313.

(c) While goods are in the possession of a bailee that has issued a negotiable document covering the goods:

(1) a security interest in the goods may be perfected by perfecting a security interest in the document; and

(2) a security interest perfected in the document has priority over any security interest that becomes perfected in the goods by another method during that time.

(d) While goods are in the possession of a bailee that has issued a nonnegotiable document covering the goods, a security interest in the goods may be perfected by:

(1) issuance of a document in the name of the secured party;

(2) the bailee's receipt of notification of the secured party's interest; or

(3) filing as to the goods.

(e) A security interest in certificated securities, negotiable documents, or instruments is perfected without filing or the taking of possession for a period of 20 days from the time it attaches to the extent that it arises for new value given under an authenticated security agreement.

(f) A perfected security interest in a negotiable document or goods in possession of a bailee, other than one that has issued a negotiable document for the goods, remains perfected for 20 days without filing if the secured party makes available to the debtor the goods or documents representing the goods for the purpose of:

(1) ultimate sale or exchange; or

(2) loading, unloading, storing, shipping, transshipping, manufacturing, processing, or otherwise dealing with them in a manner preliminary to their sale or exchange.

(g) A perfected security interest in a certificated security or instrument remains perfected for 20 days without filing if the secured party delivers the security certificate or instrument to the debtor for the purpose of:

(1) ultimate sale or exchange; or

(2) presentation, collection, enforcement, renewal, or registration of transfer.

(h) After the 20-day period specified in subsection (e), (f), or (g) expires, perfection depends upon compliance with this article.

§9—313. WHEN POSSESSION BY OR DELIVERY TO SECURED PARTY PERFECTS SECURITY INTEREST WITHOUT FILING

(a) Except as otherwise provided in subsection (b), a secured party may perfect a security interest in negotiable documents, goods, instruments, money, or tangible chattel paper by taking possession of the collateral. A secured party may perfect a security interest in certificated securities by taking delivery of the certificated securities under Section 8—301.

(b) With respect to goods covered by a certificate of title issued by this State, a secured party may perfect a security interest in the goods by taking possession of the goods only in the circumstances described in Section 9—316(d).

(c) With respect to collateral other than certificated securities and goods covered by a document, a secured party takes possession of collateral in the possession of a person other than the debtor, the secured party, or a lessee of the collateral from the debtor in the ordinary course of the debtor's business, when:

(1) the person in possession authenticates a record acknowledging that it holds possession of the collateral for the secured party's benefit; or

(2) the person takes possession of the collateral after having authenticated a record acknowledging that it will hold possession of collateral for the secured party's benefit.

(d) If perfection of a security interest depends upon possession of the collateral by a secured party, perfection occurs no earlier than the time the secured party takes possession and continues only while the secured party retains possession.

(e) A security interest in a certificated security in registered form is perfected by delivery when delivery of the certificated security occurs under Section 8—301 and remains perfected by delivery until the debtor obtains possession of the security certificate.

(f) A person in possession of collateral is not required to acknowledge that it holds possession for a secured party's benefit.

(g) If a person acknowledges that it holds possession for the secured party's benefit:

(1) the acknowledgment is effective under subsection (c) or Section 8—301(a), even if the acknowledgment violates the rights of a debtor; and

(2) unless the person otherwise agrees or law other than this article otherwise provides, the person does not owe any duty to the secured party and is not required to confirm the acknowledgment to another person.

(h) A secured party having possession of collateral does not relinquish possession by delivering the collateral to a person other than the debtor or a lessee of the collateral from the debtor in the ordinary course of the debtor's business if the person was instructed before the delivery or is instructed contemporaneously with the delivery:

(1) to hold possession of the collateral for the secured party's benefit; or

(2) to redeliver the collateral to the secured party.

(i) A secured party does not relinquish possession, even if a delivery under subsection (h) violates the rights of a debtor. A person to which collateral is delivered under subsection (h) does not owe any duty to the secured party and is not required to confirm the delivery to another person unless the person otherwise agrees or law other than this article otherwise provides.

§9—314. PERFECTION BY CONTROL

(a) A security interest in investment property, deposit accounts, letter-of-credit rights, or electronic chattel paper may be perfected by control of the collateral under Section 9—104, 9—105, 9—106, or 9—107.

(b) A security interest in deposit accounts, electronic chattel paper, or letter-of-credit rights is perfected by control under Section 9—104, 9—105, or 9—107 when the secured party obtains control and remains perfected by control only while the secured party retains control.

(c) A security interest in investment property is perfected by control under Section 9—106 from the time the secured party obtains control and remains perfected by control until:

(1) the secured party does not have control; and

(2) one of the following occurs:

(A) if the collateral is a certificated security, the debtor has or acquires possession of the security certificate;

(B) if the collateral is an uncertificated security, the issuer has registered or registers the debtor as the registered owner; or

(C) if the collateral is a security entitlement, the debtor is or becomes the entitlement holder.

§9—315. SECURED PARTY'S RIGHTS ON DISPOSITION OF COLLATERAL AND IN PROCEEDS

(a) Except as otherwise provided in this article and in Section 2—403(2):

(1) a security interest or agricultural lien continues in collateral notwithstanding sale, lease, license, exchange, or other disposition thereof unless the secured party authorized the disposition free of the security interest or agricultural lien; and

(2) a security interest attaches to any identifiable proceeds of collateral.

(b) Proceeds that are commingled with other property are identifiable proceeds:

(1) if the proceeds are goods, to the extent provided by Section 9—336; and

(2) if the proceeds are not goods, to the extent that the secured party identifies the proceeds by a method of tracing, including application of equitable principles, that is permitted under law other than this article with respect to commingled property of the type involved.

(c) A security interest in proceeds is a perfected security interest if the security interest in the original collateral was perfected.

(d) A perfected security interest in proceeds becomes unperfected on the 21st day after the security interest attaches to the proceeds unless:

(1) the following conditions are satisfied:

(A) a filed financing statement covers the original collateral;

(B) the proceeds are collateral in which a security interest may be perfected by filing in the office in which the financing statement has been filed; and

(C) the proceeds are not acquired with cash proceeds;

(2) the proceeds are identifiable cash proceeds; or

(3) the security interest in the proceeds is perfected other than under subsection (c) when the security interest attaches to the proceeds or within 20 days thereafter.

(e) If a filed financing statement covers the original collateral, a security interest in proceeds which remains perfected under subsection (d)(1) becomes unperfected at the later of:

(1) when the effectiveness of the filed financing statement lapses under Section 9—515 or is terminated under Section 9—513; or

(2) the 21st day after the security interest attaches to the proceeds.

§9—316. CONTINUED PERFECTION OF SECURITY INTEREST FOLLOWING CHANGE IN GOVERNING LAW

(a) A security interest perfected pursuant to the law of the jurisdiction designated in Section 9—301(1) or 9—305(c) remains perfected until the earliest of:

(1) the time perfection would have ceased under the law of that jurisdiction;

(2) the expiration of four months after a change of the debtor's location to another jurisdiction; or

(3) the expiration of one year after a transfer of collateral to a person that thereby becomes a debtor and is located in another jurisdiction.

(b) If a security interest described in subsection (a) becomes perfected under the law of the other jurisdiction before the earliest time or event described in that subsection, it remains perfected thereafter. If the security interest does not become perfected under the law of the other jurisdiction before the earliest time or event, it becomes unperfected and is deemed never to have been perfected as against a purchaser of the collateral for value.

(c) A possessory security interest in collateral, other than goods covered by a certificate of title and as-extracted collateral consisting of goods, remains continuously perfected if:

(1) the collateral is located in one jurisdiction and subject to a security interest perfected under the law of that jurisdiction;

(2) thereafter the collateral is brought into another jurisdiction; and

(3) upon entry into the other jurisdiction, the security interest is perfected under the law of the other jurisdiction.

(d) Except as otherwise provided in subsection (e), a security interest in goods covered by a certificate of title which is perfected by any method under the law of another jurisdiction when the goods become covered by a certificate of title from this State remains perfected until the security interest would have become unperfected under the law of the other jurisdiction had the goods not become so covered.

(e) A security interest described in subsection (d) becomes unperfected as against a purchaser of the goods for value and is deemed never to have been perfected as against a purchaser of the goods for value if the applicable requirements for perfection under Section 9—311(b) or 9—313 are not satisfied before the earlier of:

(1) the time the security interest would have become unperfected under the law of the other jurisdiction had the goods not become covered by a certificate of title from this State; or

(2) the expiration of four months after the goods had become so covered.

(f) A security interest in deposit accounts, letter-of-credit rights, or investment property which is perfected under the law of the bank's jurisdiction, the issuer's jurisdiction, a nominated person's jurisdiction, the securities intermediary's jurisdiction, or the commodity intermediary's jurisdiction, as applicable, remains perfected until the earlier of:

(1) the time the security interest would have become unperfected under the law of that jurisdiction; or

(2) the expiration of four months after a change of the applicable jurisdiction to another jurisdiction.

(g) If a security interest described in subsection (f) becomes perfected under the law of the other jurisdiction before the earlier of the time or the end of the period described in that subsection, it remains perfected thereafter. If the security interest does not become perfected under the law of the other jurisdiction before the earlier of that time or the end of that period, it becomes unperfected and is deemed never to have been perfected as against a purchaser of the collateral for value.

§9—317. INTERESTS THAT TAKE PRIORITY OVER OR TAKE FREE OF SECURITY INTEREST OR AGRICULTURAL LIEN

(a) A security interest or agricultural lien is subordinate to the rights of:

(1) a person entitled to priority under Section 9—322; and

(2) except as otherwise provided in subsection (e), a person that becomes a lien creditor before the earlier of the time:

(A) the security interest or agricultural lien is perfected; or

(B) one of the conditions specified in Section 9—203(b)(3) is met and a financing statement covering the collateral is filed.

(b) Except as otherwise provided in subsection (e), a buyer, other than a secured party, of tangible chattel paper, documents, goods, instruments, or a security certificate takes free of a security interest or agricultural lien if the buyer gives value and receives delivery of the collateral without knowledge of the security interest or agricultural lien and before it is perfected.

(c) Except as otherwise provided in subsection (e), a lessee of goods takes free of a security interest or agricultural lien if the lessee gives value and receives delivery of the collateral without knowledge of the security interest or agricultural lien and before it is perfected.

(d) A licensee of a general intangible or a buyer, other than a secured party, of accounts, electronic chattel paper, general intangibles, or investment property other than a certificated security takes free of a security interest if the licensee or buyer gives value without knowledge of the security interest and before it is perfected.

(e) Except as otherwise provided in Sections 9—320 and 9—321, if a person files a financing statement with respect to a purchase-money security interest before or within 20 days after the debtor receives delivery of the collateral, the security interest takes priority over the rights of a buyer, lessee, or lien creditor which arise between the time the security interest attaches and the time of filing.

§9—318. NO INTEREST RETAINED IN RIGHT TO PAYMENT THAT IS SOLD; RIGHTS AND TITLE OF SELLER OF ACCOUNT OR CHATTEL PAPER WITH RESPECT TO CREDITORS AND PURCHASERS

(a) A debtor that has sold an account, chattel paper, payment intangible, or promissory note does not retain a legal or equitable interest in the collateral sold.

(b) For purposes of determining the rights of creditors of, and purchasers for value of an account or chattel paper from, a debtor that has sold an account or chattel paper, while the buyer's security interest is unperfected, the debtor is deemed to have rights and title to the account or chattel paper identical to those the debtor sold.

§9—319. RIGHTS AND TITLE OF CONSIGNEE WITH RESPECT TO CREDITORS AND PURCHASERS

(a) Except as otherwise provided in subsection (b), for purposes of determining the rights of creditors of, and purchasers for value of goods from, a consignee, while the goods are in the possession of the consignee, the consignee is deemed to have rights and title to the goods identical to those the consignor had or had power to transfer.

(b) For purposes of determining the rights of a creditor of a consignee, law other than this article determines the rights and title of a consignee while goods are in the consignee's possession if, under this part, a perfected security interest held by the consignor would have priority over the rights of the creditor.

§9—320. BUYER OF GOODS

(a) Except as otherwise provided in subsection (e), a buyer in ordinary course of business, other than a person buying farm products from a person engaged in farming operations, takes free of a security interest created by the buyer's seller, even if the security interest is perfected and the buyer knows of its existence.

(b) Except as otherwise provided in subsection (e), a buyer of goods from a person who used or bought the goods for use primarily for personal, family, or household purposes takes free of a security interest, even if perfected, if the buyer buys:

(1) without knowledge of the security interest;

(2) for value;

(3) primarily for the buyer's personal, family, or household purposes; and

(4) before the filing of a financing statement covering the goods.

(c) To the extent that it affects the priority of a security interest over a buyer of goods under subsection (b), the period of effectiveness of a filing made in the jurisdiction in which the seller is located is governed by Section 9—316(a) and (b).

(d) A buyer in ordinary course of business buying oil, gas, or other minerals at the wellhead or minehead or after extraction takes free of an interest arising out of an encumbrance.

(e) Subsections (a) and (b) do not affect a security interest in goods in the possession of the secured party under Section 9—313.

* * * *

§9—322. PRIORITIES AMONG CONFLICTING SECURITY INTERESTS IN AND AGRICULTURAL LIENS ON SAME COLLATERAL

(a) Except as otherwise provided in this section, priority among conflicting security interests and agricultural liens in the same collateral is determined according to the following rules:

(1) Conflicting perfected security interests and agricultural liens rank according to priority in time of filing or perfection. Priority dates from the earlier of the time a filing covering the collateral is first made or the security interest or agricultural lien is first perfected, if there is no period thereafter when there is neither filing nor perfection.

(2) A perfected security interest or agricultural lien has priority over a conflicting unperfected security interest or agricultural lien.

(3) The first security interest or agricultural lien to attach or become effective has priority if conflicting security interests and agricultural liens are unperfected.

(b) For the purposes of subsection (a)(1):

(1) the time of filing or perfection as to a security interest in collateral is also the time of filing or perfection as to a security interest in proceeds; and

(2) the time of filing or perfection as to a security interest in collateral supported by a supporting obligation is also the time of filing or perfection as to a security interest in the supporting obligation.

(c) Except as otherwise provided in subsection (f), a security interest in collateral which qualifies for priority over a conflicting security interest under Section 9—327, 9—328, 9—329, 9—330, or 9—331 also has priority over a conflicting security interest in:

(1) any supporting obligation for the collateral; and

(2) proceeds of the collateral if:

(A) the security interest in proceeds is perfected;

(B) the proceeds are cash proceeds or of the same type as the collateral; and

(C) in the case of proceeds that are proceeds of proceeds, all intervening proceeds are cash proceeds, proceeds of the same type as the collateral, or an account relating to the collateral.

(d) Subject to subsection (e) and except as otherwise provided in subsection (f), if a security interest in chattel paper, deposit accounts, negotiable documents, instruments, investment property, or letter-of-credit rights is perfected by a method other than filing, conflicting perfected security interests in proceeds of the collateral rank according to priority in time of filing.

(e) Subsection (d) applies only if the proceeds of the collateral are not cash proceeds, chattel paper, negotiable documents, instruments, investment property, or letter-of-credit rights.

(f) Subsections (a) through (e) are subject to:

(1) subsection (g) and the other provisions of this part;

(2) Section 4—210 with respect to a security interest of a collecting bank;

(3) Section 5—118 with respect to a security interest of an issuer or nominated person; and

(4) Section 9—110 with respect to a security interest arising under Article 2 or 2A.

(g) A perfected agricultural lien on collateral has priority over a conflicting security interest in or agricultural lien on the same collateral if the statute creating the agricultural lien so provides.

§9—323. FUTURE ADVANCES

(a) Except as otherwise provided in subsection (c), for purposes of determining the priority of a perfected security interest under Section 9—322(a)(1), perfection of the security interest dates from the time an advance is made to the extent that the security interest secures an advance that:

(1) is made while the security interest is perfected only:

(A) under Section 9—309 when it attaches; or

(B) temporarily under Section 9—312(e), (f), or (g); and

(2) is not made pursuant to a commitment entered into before or while the security interest is perfected by a method other than under Section 9—309 or 9—312(e), (f), or (g).

(b) Except as otherwise provided in subsection (c), a security interest is subordinate to the rights of a person that becomes a lien creditor to the extent that the security interest secures an advance made more than 45 days after the person becomes a lien creditor unless the advance is made:

(1) without knowledge of the lien; or

(2) pursuant to a commitment entered into without knowledge of the lien.

(c) Subsections (a) and (b) do not apply to a security interest held by a secured party that is a buyer of accounts, chattel paper, payment intangibles, or promissory notes or a consignor.

(d) Except as otherwise provided in subsection (e), a buyer of goods other than a buyer in ordinary course of business takes free of a security interest to the extent that it secures advances made after the earlier of:

(1) the time the secured party acquires knowledge of the buyer's purchase; or

(2) 45 days after the purchase.

(e) Subsection (d) does not apply if the advance is made pursuant to a commitment entered into without knowledge of the buyer's purchase and before the expiration of the 45-day period.

(f) Except as otherwise provided in subsection (g), a lessee of goods, other than a lessee in ordinary course of business, takes the leasehold interest free of a security interest to the extent that it secures advances made after the earlier of:

(1) the time the secured party acquires knowledge of the lease; or

(2) 45 days after the lease contract becomes enforceable.

(g) Subsection (f) does not apply if the advance is made pursuant to a commitment entered into without knowledge of the lease and before the expiration of the 45 day period.

§9—324. PRIORITY OF PURCHASE-MONEY SECURITY INTERESTS

(a) Except as otherwise provided in subsection (g), a perfected purchase-money security interest in goods other than inventory or livestock has priority over a conflicting security interest in the same goods, and, except as otherwise provided in Section 9—327, a perfected security interest in its identifiable proceeds also has priority, if the purchase-money security interest is perfected when the debtor receives possession of the collateral or within 20 days thereafter.

(b) Subject to subsection (c) and except as otherwise provided in subsection (g), a perfected purchase-money security interest in inventory has priority over a conflicting security interest in the same inventory, has priority over a conflicting security interest in chattel paper or an instrument constituting proceeds of the inventory and in proceeds of the chattel paper, if so provided in Section 9—330, and, except as otherwise provided in Section 9—327, also has priority in identifiable cash proceeds of the inventory to the extent the identifiable cash proceeds are received on or before the delivery of the inventory to a buyer, if:

(1) the purchase-money security interest is perfected when the debtor receives possession of the inventory;

(2) the purchase-money secured party sends an authenticated notification to the holder of the conflicting security interest;

(3) the holder of the conflicting security interest receives the notification within five years before the debtor receives possession of the inventory; and

(4) the notification states that the person sending the notification has or expects to acquire a purchase-money security interest in inventory of the debtor and describes the inventory.

(c) Subsections (b)(2) through (4) apply only if the holder of the conflicting security interest had filed a financing statement covering the same types of inventory:

(1) if the purchase-money security interest is perfected by filing, before the date of the filing; or

(2) if the purchase-money security interest is temporarily perfected without filing or possession under Section 9—312(f), before the beginning of the 20-day period thereunder.

(d) Subject to subsection (e) and except as otherwise provided in subsection (g), a perfected purchase-money security interest in livestock that are farm products has priority over a conflicting security interest in the same livestock, and, except as otherwise provided in Section 9—327, a perfected security interest in their identifiable proceeds and identifiable products in their unmanufactured states also has priority, if:

(1) the purchase-money security interest is perfected when the debtor receives possession of the livestock;

(2) the purchase-money secured party sends an authenticated notification to the holder of the conflicting security interest;

(3) the holder of the conflicting security interest receives the notification within six months before the debtor receives possession of the livestock; and

(4) the notification states that the person sending the notification has or expects to acquire a purchase-money security interest in livestock of the debtor and describes the livestock.

(e) Subsections (d)(2) through (4) apply only if the holder of the conflicting security interest had filed a financing statement covering the same types of livestock:

(1) if the purchase-money security interest is perfected by filing, before the date of the filing; or

(2) if the purchase-money security interest is temporarily perfected without filing or possession under Section 9—312(f), before the beginning of the 20-day period thereunder.

(f) Except as otherwise provided in subsection (g), a perfected purchase-money security interest in software has priority over a conflicting security interest in the same collateral, and, except as otherwise provided in Section 9—327, a perfected security interest in its identifiable proceeds also has priority, to the extent that the purchase-money security interest in the goods in which the software was acquired for use has priority in the goods and proceeds of the goods under this section.

(g) If more than one security interest qualifies for priority in the same collateral under subsection (a), (b), (d), or (f):

(1) a security interest securing an obligation incurred as all or part of the price of the collateral has priority over a security interest securing an obligation incurred for value given to enable the debtor to acquire rights in or the use of collateral; and

(2) in all other cases, Section 9—322(a) applies to the qualifying security interests.

§9—325. PRIORITY OF SECURITY INTERESTS IN TRANSFERRED COLLATERAL

(a) Except as otherwise provided in subsection (b), a security interest created by a debtor is subordinate to a security interest in the same collateral created by another person if:

(1) the debtor acquired the collateral subject to the security interest created by the other person;

(2) the security interest created by the other person was perfected when the debtor acquired the collateral; and

(3) there is no period thereafter when the security interest is unperfected.

(b) Subsection (a) subordinates a security interest only if the security interest:

(1) otherwise would have priority solely under Section 9—322(a) or 9—324; or

(2) arose solely under Section 2—711(3) or 2A—508(5).

§9—326. PRIORITY OF SECURITY INTERESTS CREATED BY NEW DEBTOR

(a) Subject to subsection (b), a security interest created by a new debtor which is perfected by a filed financing statement that is effective solely under Section 9—508 in collateral in which a new debtor has or acquires rights is subordinate to a security interest in the same collateral which is perfected other than by a filed financing statement that is effective solely under Section 9—508.

(b) The other provisions of this part determine the priority among conflicting security interests in the same collateral perfected by filed financing statements that are effective solely under Section 9—508. However, if the security agreements to which a new debtor became bound as debtor were not entered into by the same original debtor, the conflicting security interests rank according to priority in time of the new debtor's having become bound.

* * * *

§9—330. PRIORITY OF PURCHASER OF CHATTEL PAPER OR INSTRUMENT

(a) A purchaser of chattel paper has priority over a security interest in the chattel paper which is claimed merely as proceeds of inventory subject to a security interest if:

(1) in good faith and in the ordinary course of the purchaser's business, the purchaser gives new value and takes possession of the chattel paper or obtains control of the chattel paper under Section 9—105; and

(2) the chattel paper does not indicate that it has been assigned to an identified assignee other than the purchaser.

(b) A purchaser of chattel paper has priority over a security interest in the chattel paper which is claimed other than merely as proceeds of inventory subject to a security interest if the purchaser gives new value and takes possession of the chattel paper or obtains control of the chattel paper under Section 9—105 in good faith, in the ordinary course of the purchaser's business, and without knowledge that the purchase violates the rights of the secured party.

(c) Except as otherwise provided in Section 9—327, a purchaser having priority in chattel paper under subsection (a) or (b) also has priority in proceeds of the chattel paper to the extent that:

(1) Section 9—322 provides for priority in the proceeds; or

(2) the proceeds consist of the specific goods covered by the chattel paper or cash proceeds of the specific goods, even if the purchaser's security interest in the proceeds is unperfected.

(d) Except as otherwise provided in Section 9—331 (a), a purchaser of an instrument has priority over a security interest in the instrument perfected by a method other than possession if the purchaser gives value and takes possession of the instrument in good faith and without knowledge that the purchase violates the rights of the secured party.

(e) For purposes of subsections (a) and (b), the holder of a purchase-money security interest in inventory gives new value for chattel paper constituting proceeds of the inventory.

(f) For purposes of subsections (b) and (d), if chattel paper or an instrument indicates that it has been assigned to an identified secured party other than the purchaser, a purchaser of the chattel paper or instrument has knowledge that the purchase violates the rights of the secured party.

* * * *

§9—333. PRIORITY OF CERTAIN LIENS ARISING BY OPERATION OF LAW

(a) In this section, "possessory lien" means an interest, other than a security interest or an agricultural lien:

(1) which secures payment or performance of an obligation for services or materials furnished with respect to goods by a person in the ordinary course of the person's business;

(2) which is created by statute or rule of law in favor of the person; and

(3) whose effectiveness depends on the person's possession of the goods.

(b) A possessory lien on goods has priority over a security interest in the goods unless the lien is created by a statute that expressly provides otherwise.

§9—334. PRIORITY OF SECURITY INTERESTS IN FIXTURES AND CROPS

(a) A security interest under this article may be created in goods that are fixtures or may continue in goods that become fixtures. A security interest does not exist under this article in ordinary building materials incorporated into an improvement on land.

(b) This article does not prevent creation of an encumbrance upon fixtures under real property law.

(c) In cases not governed by subsections (d) through (h), a security interest in fixtures is subordinate to a conflicting interest of an encumbrancer or owner of the related real property other than the debtor.

(d) Except as otherwise provided in subsection (h), a perfected security interest in fixtures has priority over a conflicting interest of an encumbrancer or owner of the real property if the debtor has an interest of record in or is in possession of the real property and:

(1) the security interest is a purchase-money security interest;

(2) the interest of the encumbrancer or owner arises before the goods become fixtures; and

(3) the security interest is perfected by a fixture filing before the goods become fixtures or within 20 days thereafter.

(e) A perfected security interest in fixtures has priority over a conflicting interest of an encumbrancer or owner of the real property if:

(1) the debtor has an interest of record in the real property or is in possession of the real property and the security interest:

(A) is perfected by a fixture filing before the interest of the encumbrancer or owner is of record; and

(B) has priority over any conflicting interest of a predecessor in title of the encumbrancer or owner;

(2) before the goods become fixtures, the security interest is perfected by any method permitted by this article and the fixtures are readily removable:

(A) factory or office machines;

(B) equipment that is not primarily used or leased for use in the operation of the real property; or

(C) replacements of domestic appliances that are consumer goods;

(3) the conflicting interest is a lien on the real property obtained by legal or equitable proceedings after the security interest was perfected by any method permitted by this article; or

(4) the security interest is:

(A) created in a manufactured home in a manufactured-home transaction; and

(B) perfected pursuant to a statute described in Section 9—311(a)(2).

(f) A security interest in fixtures, whether or not perfected, has priority over a conflicting interest of an encumbrancer or owner of the real property if:

(1) the encumbrancer or owner has, in an authenticated record, consented to the security interest or disclaimed an interest in the goods as fixtures; or

(2) the debtor has a right to remove the goods as against the encumbrancer or owner.

(g) The priority of the security interest under paragraph (f)(2) continues for a reasonable time if the debtor's right to remove the goods as against the encumbrancer or owner terminates.

(h) A mortgage is a construction mortgage to the extent that it secures an obligation incurred for the construction of an improvement on land, including the acquisition cost of the land, if a recorded record of the mortgage so indicates. Except as otherwise provided in subsections (e) and (f), a security interest in fixtures is subordinate to a construction mortgage if a record of the mortgage is recorded before the goods become fixtures and the goods become fixtures before the completion of the construction. A mortgage has this priority to the same extent as a construction mortgage to the extent that it is given to refinance a construction mortgage.

(i) A perfected security interest in crops growing on real property has priority over a conflicting interest of an encumbrancer or owner of the real property if the debtor has an interest of record in or is in possession of the real property.

* * * *

§9—336. COMMINGLED GOODS

(a) In this section, "commingled goods" means goods that are physically united with other goods in such a manner that their identity is lost in a product or mass.

(b) A security interest does not exist in commingled goods as such. However, a security interest may attach to a product or mass that results when goods become commingled goods.

(c) If collateral becomes commingled goods, a security interest attaches to the product or mass.

(d) If a security interest in collateral is perfected before the collateral becomes commingled goods, the security interest that attaches to the product or mass under subsection (c) is perfected.

(e) Except as otherwise provided in subsection (f), the other provisions of this part determine the priority of a security interest that attaches to the product or mass under subsection (c).

(f) If more than one security interest attaches to the product or mass under subsection (c), the following rules determine priority:

(1) A security interest that is perfected under subsection (d) has priority over a security interest that is unperfected at the time the collateral becomes commingled goods.

(2) If more than one security interest is perfected under subsection (d), the security interests rank equally in proportion to the value of the collateral at the time it became commingled goods.

* * * *

§9—501. FILING OFFICE

(a) Except as otherwise provided in subsection (b), if the local law of this State governs perfection of a security interest or agricultural lien, the office in which to file a financing statement to perfect the security interest or agricultural lien is:

(1) the office designated for the filing or recording of a record of a mortgage on the related real property, if:

(A) the collateral is as-extracted collateral or timber to be cut; or

(B) the financing statement is filed as a fixture filing and the collateral is goods that are or are to become fixtures; or

(2) the office of [ ] [or any office duly authorized by [ ]], in all other cases, including a case in which the collateral is goods that are or are to become fixtures and the financing statement is not filed as a fixture filing.

(b) The office in which to file a financing statement to perfect a security interest in collateral, including fixtures, of a transmitting utility is the office of [ ]. The financing statement also constitutes a fixture filing as to the collateral indicated in the financing statement which is or is to become fixtures.

Legislative Note: The State should designate the filing office where the brackets appear. The filing office may be that of a governmental official (e.g., the Secretary of State) or a private party that maintains the State's filing system.

§9—502. CONTENTS OF FINANCING STATEMENT; RECORD OF MORTGAGE AS FINANCING STATEMENT; TIME OF FILING FINANCING STATEMENT

(a) Subject to subsection (b), a financing statement is sufficient only if it:

(1) provides the name of the debtor;

(2) provides the name of the secured party or a representative of the secured party; and

(3) indicates the collateral covered by the financing statement.

(b) Except as otherwise provided in Section 9—501 (b), to be sufficient, a financing statement that covers as-extracted collateral or timber to be cut, or which is filed as a fixture filing and covers goods that are or are to become fixtures, must satisfy subsection (a) and also:

(1) indicate that it covers this type of collateral;

(2) indicate that it is to be filed [for record] in the real property records;

(3) provide a description of the real property to which the collateral is related [sufficient to give constructive notice of a mortgage under the law of this State if the description were contained in a record of the mortgage of the real property]; and

(4) if the debtor does not have an interest of record in the real property, provide the name of a record owner.

(c) A record of a mortgage is effective, from the date of recording, as a financing statement filed as a fixture filing or as a financing statement covering as-extracted collateral or timber to be cut only if:

(1) the record indicates the goods or accounts that it covers;

(2) the goods are or are to become fixtures related to the real property described in the record or the collateral is related to the real property described in the record and is as-extracted collateral or timber to be cut;

(3) the record satisfies the requirements for a financing statement in this section other than an indication that it is to be filed in the real property records; and

(4) the record is [duly] recorded.

(d) A financing statement may be filed before a security agreement is made or a security interest otherwise attaches.

Legislative Note: Language in brackets is optional. Where the State has any special recording system for real property other than the usual grantor-grantee index (as, for instance, a tract system or a title registration or Torrens system) local adaptations of subsection (b) and Section 9—519(d) and (e) may be necessary. See, e.g., Mass. Gen. Laws Chapter 106, Section 9—410.

§9—503. NAME OF DEBTOR AND SECURED PARTY

(a) A financing statement sufficiently provides the name of the debtor:

(1) if the debtor is a registered organization, only if the financing statement provides the name of the debtor indicated on the public record of the debtor's jurisdiction of organization which shows the debtor to have been organized;

(2) if the debtor is a decedent's estate, only if the financing statement provides the name of the decedent and indicates that the debtor is an estate;

(3) if the debtor is a trust or a trustee acting with respect to property held in trust, only if the financing statement:

(A) provides the name specified for the trust in its organic documents or, if no name is specified, provides the name of the settlor and additional information sufficient to distinguish the debtor from other trusts having one or more of the same settlors; and

(B) indicates, in the debtor's name or otherwise, that the debtor is a trust or is a trustee acting with respect to property held in trust; and

(4) in other cases:

(A) if the debtor has a name, only if it provides the individual or organizational name of the debtor; and

(B) if the debtor does not have a name, only if it provides the names of the partners, members, associates, or other persons comprising the debtor.

(b) A financing statement that provides the name of the debtor in accordance with subsection (a) is not rendered ineffective by the absence of:

(1) a trade name or other name of the debtor; or

(2) unless required under subsection (a)(4)(B), names of partners, members, associates, or other persons comprising the debtor.

(c) A financing statement that provides only the debtor's trade name does not sufficiently provide the name of the debtor.

(d) Failure to indicate the representative capacity of a secured party or representative of a secured party does not affect the sufficiency of a financing statement.

(e) A financing statement may provide the name of more than one debtor and the name of more than one secured party.

§9—504. INDICATION OF COLLATERAL

A financing statement sufficiently indicates the collateral that it covers if the financing statement provides:

(1) a description of the collateral pursuant to Section 9—108; or

(2) an indication that the financing statement covers all assets or all personal property.

As amended in 1999.

* * * *

§9—506. EFFECT OF ERRORS OR OMISSIONS

(a) A financing statement substantially satisfying the requirements of this part is effective, even if it has minor errors or omissions, unless the errors or omissions make the financing statement seriously misleading.

(b) Except as otherwise provided in subsection (c), a financing statement that fails sufficiently to provide the name of the debtor in accordance with Section 9—503(a) is seriously misleading.

(c) If a search of the records of the filing office under the debtor's correct name, using the filing office's standard search logic, if any, would disclose a financing statement that fails sufficiently to provide the name of the debtor in accordance with Section 9—503(a), the name provided does not make the financing statement seriously misleading.

(d) For purposes of Section 9—508(b), the "debtor's correct name" in subsection (c) means the correct name of the new debtor.

* * * *

§9—509. PERSONS ENTITLED TO FILE A RECORD

(a) A person may file an initial financing statement, amendment that adds collateral covered by a financing statement, or amendment that adds a debtor to a financing statement only if:

(1) the debtor authorizes the filing in an authenticated record or pursuant to subsection (b) or (c); or

(2) the person holds an agricultural lien that has become effective at the time of filing and the financing statement covers only collateral in which the person holds an agricultural lien.

(b) By authenticating or becoming bound as debtor by a security agreement, a debtor or new debtor authorizes the filing of an initial financing statement, and an amendment, covering:

(1) the collateral described in the security agreement; and

(2) property that becomes collateral under Section 9—315(a)(2), whether or not the security agreement expressly covers proceeds.

(c) By acquiring collateral in which a security interest or agricultural lien continues under Section 9—315(a)(1), a debtor authorizes the filing of an initial financing statement, and an amendment, covering the collateral and property that becomes collateral under Section 9—315(a)(2).

(d) A person may file an amendment other than an amendment that adds collateral covered by a financing statement or an amendment that adds a debtor to a financing statement only if:

(1) the secured party of record authorizes the filing; or

(2) the amendment is a termination statement for a financing statement as to which the secured party of record has failed to file or send a termination statement as required by Section 9—513(a) or (c), the debtor authorizes the filing, and the termination statement indicates that the debtor authorized it to be filed.

(e) If there is more than one secured party of record for a financing statement, each secured party of record may authorize the filing of an amendment under subsection (d).

§9—510. EFFECTIVENESS OF FILED RECORD

(a) A filed record is effective only to the extent that it was filed by a person that may file it under Section 9—509.

(b) A record authorized by one secured party of record does not affect the financing statement with respect to another secured party of record.

(c) A continuation statement that is not filed within the six-month period prescribed by Section 9—515(d) is ineffective.

* * * *

§9—513. TERMINATION STATEMENT

(a) A secured party shall cause the secured party of record for a financing statement to file a termination statement for the financing statement if the financing statement covers consumer goods and:

(1) there is no obligation secured by the collateral covered by the financing statement and no commitment to make an advance, incur an obligation, or otherwise give value; or

(2) the debtor did not authorize the filing of the initial financing statement.

(b) To comply with subsection (a), a secured party shall cause the secured party of record to file the termination statement:

(1) within one month after there is no obligation secured by the collateral covered by the financing statement and no commitment to make an advance, incur an obligation, or otherwise give value; or

(2) if earlier, within 20 days after the secured party receives an authenticated demand from a debtor.

(c) In cases not governed by subsection (a), within 20 days after a secured party receives an authenticated demand from a debtor, the secured party shall cause the secured party of record for a financing statement to send to the debtor a termination statement for the financing statement or file the termination statement in the filing office if:

(1) except in the case of a financing statement covering accounts or chattel paper that has been sold or goods that are the subject of a consignment, there is no obligation secured by the collateral covered by the financing statement and no commitment to make an advance, incur an obligation, or otherwise give value;

(2) the financing statement covers accounts or chattel paper that has been sold but as to which the account debtor or other person obligated has discharged its obligation;

(3) the financing statement covers goods that were the subject of a consignment to the debtor but are not in the debtor's possession; or

(4) the debtor did not authorize the filing of the initial financing statement.

(d) Except as otherwise provided in Section 9—510, upon the filing of a termination statement with the filing office, the financing statement to which the termination statement relates ceases to be effective. Except as otherwise provided in Section 9—510, for purposes of Sections 9—519(g), 9—522(a), and 9—523(c), the filing with the filing office of a termination statement relating to a financing statement that indicates that the debtor is a transmitting utility also causes the effectiveness of the financing statement to lapse.

* * * *

§9—515. DURATION AND EFFECTIVENESS OF FINANCING STATEMENT; EFFECT OF LAPSED FINANCING STATEMENT

(a) Except as otherwise provided in subsections (b), (e), (f), and (g), a filed financing statement is effective for a period of five years after the date of filing.

(b) Except as otherwise provided in subsections (e), (f), and (g), an initial financing statement filed in connection with a public-finance transaction or manufactured-home transaction is effective for a period of 30 years after the date of filing if it indicates that it is filed in connection with a public-finance transaction or manufactured-home transaction.

(c) The effectiveness of a filed financing statement lapses on the expiration of the period of its effectiveness unless before the lapse a continuation statement is filed pursuant to subsection (d). Upon lapse, a financing statement ceases to be effective and any security interest or agricultural lien that was perfected by the financing statement becomes unperfected, unless the security interest is perfected otherwise. If the security interest or agricultural lien becomes unperfected upon lapse, it is deemed never to have been perfected as against a purchaser of the collateral for value.

(d) A continuation statement may be filed only within six months before the expiration of the five-year period specified in subsection (a) or the 30-year period specified in subsection (b), whichever is applicable.

(e) Except as otherwise provided in Section 9—510, upon timely filing of a continuation statement, the effectiveness of the initial financing statement continues for a period of five years commencing on the day on which the financing statement would have become ineffective in the absence of the filing. Upon the expiration of the five-year period, the financing statement lapses in the same manner as provided in subsection (c), unless, before the lapse, another continuation statement is filed pursuant to subsection (d). Succeeding continuation statements may be filed in the same manner to continue the effectiveness of the initial financing statement.

(f) If a debtor is a transmitting utility and a filed financing statement so indicates, the financing statement is effective until a termination statement is filed.

(g) A record of a mortgage that is effective as a financing statement filed as a fixture filing under Section 9—502(c) remains effective as a financing statement filed as a fixture filing until the mortgage is released or satisfied of record or its effectiveness otherwise terminates as to the real property.

* * * *

§9—601. RIGHTS AFTER DEFAULT; JUDICIAL ENFORCEMENT; CONSIGNOR OR BUYER OF ACCOUNTS, CHATTEL PAPER, PAYMENT INTANGIBLES, OR PROMISSORY NOTES

(a) After default, a secured party has the rights provided in this part and, except as otherwise provided in Section 9—602, those provided by agreement of the parties. A secured party:

(1) may reduce a claim to judgment, foreclose, or otherwise enforce the claim, security interest, or agricultural lien by any available judicial procedure; and

(2) if the collateral is documents, may proceed either as to the documents or as to the goods they cover.

(b) A secured party in possession of collateral or control of collateral under Section 9—104, 9—105, 9—106, or 9—107 has the rights and duties provided in Section 9—207.

(c) The rights under subsections (a) and (b) are cumulative and may be exercised simultaneously.

(d) Except as otherwise provided in subsection (g) and Section 9—605, after default, a debtor and an obligor have the rights provided in this part and by agreement of the parties.

(e) If a secured party has reduced its claim to judgment, the lien of any levy that may be made upon the collateral by virtue of an execution based upon the judgment relates back to the earliest of:

(1) the date of perfection of the security interest or agricultural lien in the collateral;

(2) the date of filing a financing statement covering the collateral; or

(3) any date specified in a statute under which the agricultural lien was created.

(f) A sale pursuant to an execution is a foreclosure of the security interest or agricultural lien by judicial procedure within the meaning of this section. A secured party may purchase at the sale and thereafter hold the collateral free of any other requirements of this article.

(g) Except as otherwise provided in Section 9—607 (c), this part imposes no duties upon a secured party that is a consignor or is a buyer of accounts, chattel paper, payment intangibles, or promissory notes.

* * * *

§9—604. PROCEDURE IF SECURITY AGREEMENT COVERS REAL PROPERTY OR FIXTURES

(a) If a security agreement covers both personal and real property, a secured party may proceed:

(1) under this part as to the personal property without prejudicing any rights with respect to the real property; or

(2) as to both the personal property and the real property in accordance with the rights with respect to the real property, in which case the other provisions of this part do not apply.

(b) Subject to subsection (c), if a security agreement covers goods that are or become fixtures, a secured party may proceed:

(1) under this part; or

(2) in accordance with the rights with respect to real property, in which case the other provisions of this part do not apply.

(c) Subject to the other provisions of this part, if a secured party holding a security interest in fixtures has priority over all owners and encumbrancers of the real property, the secured party, after default, may remove the collateral from the real property.

(d) A secured party that removes collateral shall promptly reimburse any encumbrancer or owner of the real property, other than the debtor, for the cost of repair of any physical injury caused by the removal. The secured party need not reimburse the encumbrancer or owner for any diminution in value of the real property caused by the absence of the goods removed or by any necessity of replacing them. A person entitled to reimbursement may refuse permission to remove until the secured party gives adequate assurance for the performance of the obligation to reimburse.

* * * *

§9—607. COLLECTION AND ENFORCEMENT BY SECURED PARTY

(a) If so agreed, and in any event after default, a secured party:

(1) may notify an account debtor or other person obligated on collateral to make payment or otherwise render performance to or for the benefit of the secured party;

(2) may take any proceeds to which the secured party is entitled under Section 9—315;

(3) may enforce the obligations of an account debtor or other person obligated on collateral and exercise the rights of the debtor with respect to the obligation of the account debtor or other person obligated on collateral to make payment or otherwise render performance to the debtor, and with respect to any property that secures the obligations of the account debtor or other person obligated on the collateral;

(4) if it holds a security interest in a deposit account perfected by control under Section 9—104(a)(1), may apply the balance of the deposit account to the obligation secured by the deposit account; and

(5) if it holds a security interest in a deposit account perfected by control under Section 9—104(a)(2) or (3), may instruct the bank to pay the balance of the deposit account to or for the benefit of the secured party.

(b) If necessary to enable a secured party to exercise under subsection (a)(3) the right of a debtor to enforce a mortgage nonjudicially, the secured party may record in the office in which a record of the mortgage is recorded:

(1) a copy of the security agreement that creates or provides for a security interest in the obligation secured by the mortgage; and

(2) the secured party's sworn affidavit in recordable form stating that:

(A) a default has occurred; and

(B) the secured party is entitled to enforce the mortgage nonjudicially.

(c) A secured party shall proceed in a commercially reasonable manner if the secured party:

(1) undertakes to collect from or enforce an obligation of an account debtor or other person obligated on collateral; and

(2) is entitled to charge back uncollected collateral or otherwise to full or limited recourse against the debtor or a secondary obligor.

(d) A secured party may deduct from the collections made pursuant to subsection (c) reasonable expenses of collection and enforcement, including reasonable attorney's fees and legal expenses incurred by the secured party.

(e) This section does not determine whether an account debtor, bank, or other person obligated on collateral owes a duty to a secured party.

§9—608. APPLICATION OF PROCEEDS OF COLLECTION OR ENFORCEMENT; LIABILITY FOR DEFICIENCY AND RIGHT TO SURPLUS

(a) If a security interest or agricultural lien secures payment or performance of an obligation, the following rules apply:

(1) A secured party shall apply or pay over for application the cash proceeds of collection or enforcement under Section 9—607 in the following order to:

(A) the reasonable expenses of collection and enforcement and, to the extent provided for by agreement and not prohibited by law, reasonable attorney's fees and legal expenses incurred by the secured party;

(B) the satisfaction of obligations secured by the security interest or agricultural lien under which the collection or enforcement is made; and

(C) the satisfaction of obligations secured by any subordinate security interest in or other lien on the collateral subject to the security interest or agricultural lien under which the collection or enforcement is made if the secured party receives an authenticated demand for proceeds before distribution of the proceeds is completed.

(2) If requested by a secured party, a holder of a subordinate security interest or other lien shall furnish reasonable proof of the interest or lien within a reasonable time. Unless the holder complies, the secured party need not comply with the holder's demand under paragraph (1)(C).

(3) A secured party need not apply or pay over for application noncash proceeds of collection and

enforcement under Section 9—607 unless the failure to do so would be commercially unreasonable. A secured party that applies or pays over for application noncash proceeds shall do so in a commercially reasonable manner.

(4) A secured party shall account to and pay a debtor for any surplus, and the obligor is liable for any deficiency.

(b) If the underlying transaction is a sale of accounts, chattel paper, payment intangibles, or promissory notes, the debtor is not entitled to any surplus, and the obligor is not liable for any deficiency.

§9—609. SECURED PARTY'S RIGHT TO TAKE POSSESSION AFTER DEFAULT

(a) After default, a secured party:

(1) may take possession of the collateral; and

(2) without removal, may render equipment unusable and dispose of collateral on a debtor's premises under Section 9—610.

(b) A secured party may proceed under subsection (a):

(1) pursuant to judicial process; or

(2) without judicial process, if it proceeds without breach of the peace.

(c) If so agreed, and in any event after default, a secured party may require the debtor to assemble the collateral and make it available to the secured party at a place to be designated by the secured party which is reasonably convenient to both parties.

§9—610. DISPOSITION OF COLLATERAL AFTER DEFAULT

(a) After default, a secured party may sell, lease, license, or otherwise dispose of any or all of the collateral in its present condition or following any commercially reasonable preparation or processing.

(b) Every aspect of a disposition of collateral, including the method, manner, time, place, and other terms, must be commercially reasonable. If commercially reasonable, a secured party may dispose of collateral by public or private proceedings, by one or more contracts, as a unit or in parcels, and at any time and place and on any terms.

(c) A secured party may purchase collateral:

(1) at a public disposition; or

(2) at a private disposition only if the collateral is of a kind that is customarily sold on a recognized market or the subject of widely distributed standard price quotations.

(d) A contract for sale, lease, license, or other disposition includes the warranties relating to title, possession, quiet enjoyment, and the like which by operation of law accompany a voluntary disposition of property of the kind subject to the contract.

(e) A secured party may disclaim or modify warranties under subsection (d):

(1) in a manner that would be effective to disclaim or modify the warranties in a voluntary disposition of property of the kind subject to the contract of disposition; or

(2) by communicating to the purchaser a record evidencing the contract for disposition and including an express disclaimer or modification of the warranties.

(f) A record is sufficient to disclaim warranties under subsection (e) if it indicates "There is no warranty relating to title, possession, quiet enjoyment, or the like in this disposition" or uses words of similar import.

§9—611. NOTIFICATION BEFORE DISPOSITION OF COLLATERAL

(a) In this section, "notification date" means the earlier of the date on which:

(1) a secured party sends to the debtor and any secondary obligor an authenticated notification of disposition; or

(2) the debtor and any secondary obligor waive the right to notification.

(b) Except as otherwise provided in subsection (d), a secured party that disposes of collateral under Section 9—610 shall send to the persons specified in subsection (c) a reasonable authenticated notification of disposition.

(c) To comply with subsection (b), the secured party shall send an authenticated notification of disposition to:

(1) the debtor;

(2) any secondary obligor; and

(3) if the collateral is other than consumer goods:

(A) any other person from which the secured party has received, before the notification date, an authenticated notification of a claim of an interest in the collateral;

(B) any other secured party or lienholder that, 10 days before the notification date, held a security interest in or other lien on the collateral perfected by the filing of a financing statement that:

(i) identified the collateral;

(ii) was indexed under the debtor's name as of that date; and

(iii) was filed in the office in which to file a financing statement against the debtor covering the collateral as of that date; and

(C) any other secured party that, 10 days before the notification date, held a security interest in the collateral perfected by compliance with a statute, regulation, or treaty described in Section 9—311(a).

(d) Subsection (b) does not apply if the collateral is perishable or threatens to decline speedily in value or is of a type customarily sold on a recognized market.

(e) A secured party complies with the requirement for notification prescribed by subsection (c)(3)(B) if:

(1) not later than 20 days or earlier than 30 days before the notification date, the secured party requests, in a commercially reasonable manner, information concerning financing statements indexed under the debtor's name in the office indicated in subsection (c)(3)(B); and

(2) before the notification date, the secured party:

(A) did not receive a response to the request for information; or

(B) received a response to the request for information and sent an authenticated notification of disposition to each secured party or other lienholder named in that response whose financing statement covered the collateral.

§9—612. TIMELINESS OF NOTIFICATION BEFORE DISPOSITION OF COLLATERAL

(a) Except as otherwise provided in subsection (b), whether a notification is sent within a reasonable time is a question of fact.

(b) In a transaction other than a consumer transaction, a notification of disposition sent after default and 10 days or more before the earliest time of disposition set forth in the notification is sent within a reasonable time before the disposition.

* * * *

§9—615. APPLICATION OF PROCEEDS OF DISPOSITION; LIABILITY FOR DEFICIENCY AND RIGHT TO SURPLUS

(a) A secured party shall apply or pay over for application the cash proceeds of disposition under Section 9—610 in the following order to:

(1) the reasonable expenses of retaking, holding, preparing for disposition, processing, and disposing, and, to the extent provided for by agreement and not prohibited by law, reasonable attorney's fees and legal expenses incurred by the secured party;

(2) the satisfaction of obligations secured by the security interest or agricultural lien under which the disposition is made;

(3) the satisfaction of obligations secured by any subordinate security interest in or other subordinate lien on the collateral if:

(A) the secured party receives from the holder of the subordinate security interest or other lien an authenticated demand for proceeds before distribution of the proceeds is completed; and

(B) in a case in which a consignor has an interest in the collateral, the subordinate security interest or other lien is senior to the interest of the consignor; and

(4) a secured party that is a consignor of the collateral if the secured party receives from the consignor an authenticated demand for proceeds before distribution of the proceeds is completed.

(b) If requested by a secured party, a holder of a subordinate security interest or other lien shall furnish reasonable proof of the interest or lien within a reasonable time. Unless the holder does so, the secured party need not comply with the holder's demand under subsection (a)(3).

(c) A secured party need not apply or pay over for application noncash proceeds of disposition under Section 9—610 unless the failure to do so would be commercially unreasonable. A secured party that applies or pays over for application noncash proceeds shall do so in a commercially reasonable manner.

(d) If the security interest under which a disposition is made secures payment or performance of an obligation, after making the payments and applications required by subsection (a) and permitted by subsection (c):

(1) unless subsection (a)(4) requires the secured party to apply or pay over cash proceeds to a consignor, the secured party shall account to and pay a debtor for any surplus; and

(2) the obligor is liable for any deficiency.

(e) If the underlying transaction is a sale of accounts, chattel paper, payment intangibles, or promissory notes:

(1) the debtor is not entitled to any surplus; and

(2) the obligor is not liable for any deficiency.

(f) The surplus or deficiency following a disposition is calculated based on the amount of proceeds that would have been realized in a disposition complying with this part to a transferee other than the secured party, a person related to the secured party, or a secondary obligor if:

(1) the transferee in the disposition is the secured party, a person related to the secured party, or a secondary obligor; and

(2) the amount of proceeds of the disposition is significantly below the range of proceeds that a complying disposition to a person other than the secured party, a person related to the secured party, or a secondary obligor would have brought.

(g) A secured party that receives cash proceeds of a disposition in good faith and without knowledge that the receipt violates the rights of the holder of a security interest or other lien that is not subordinate to the security interest or agricultural lien under which the disposition is made:

(1) takes the cash proceeds free of the security interest or other lien;

(2) is not obligated to apply the proceeds of the disposition to the satisfaction of obligations secured by the security interest or other lien; and

(3) is not obligated to account to or pay the holder of the security interest or other lien for any surplus.

* * * *

§9—617. RIGHTS OF TRANSFEREE OF COLLATERAL

(a) A secured party's disposition of collateral after default:

1) transfers to a transferee for value all of the debtor's rights in the collateral;

2) discharges the security interest under which the disposition is made; and

3) discharges any subordinate security interest or other subordinate lien [other than liens created under [cite acts or statutes providing for liens, if any, that are not to be discharged]].

(b) A transferee that acts in good faith takes free of the rights and interests described in subsection (a), even if the secured party fails to comply with this article or the requirements of any judicial proceeding.

(c) If a transferee does not take free of the rights and interests described in subsection (a), the transferee takes the collateral subject to:

(1) the debtor's rights in the collateral;

(2) the security interest or agricultural lien under which the disposition is made; and

(3) any other security interest or other lien.

* * * *

§9—620. ACCEPTANCE OF COLLATERAL IN FULL OR PARTIAL SATISFACTION OF OBLIGATION; COMPULSORY DISPOSITION OF COLLATERAL

(a) Except as otherwise provided in subsection (g), a secured party may accept collateral in full or partial satisfaction of the obligation it secures only if:

(1) the debtor consents to the acceptance under subsection (c);

(2) the secured party does not receive, within the time set forth in subsection (d), a notification of objection to the proposal authenticated by:

(A) a person to which the secured party was required to send a proposal under Section 9—621; or

(B) any other person, other than the debtor, holding an interest in the collateral subordinate to the security interest that is the subject of the proposal;

(3) if the collateral is consumer goods, the collateral is not in the possession of the debtor when the debtor consents to the acceptance; and

(4) subsection (e) does not require the secured party to dispose of the collateral or the debtor waives the requirement pursuant to Section 9—624.

(b) A purported or apparent acceptance of collateral under this section is ineffective unless:

(1) the secured party consents to the acceptance in an authenticated record or sends a proposal to the debtor; and

(2) the conditions of subsection (a) are met.

(c) For purposes of this section:

(1) a debtor consents to an acceptance of collateral in partial satisfaction of the obligation it secures only if the debtor agrees to the terms of the acceptance in a record authenticated after default; and

(2) a debtor consents to an acceptance of collateral in full satisfaction of the obligation it secures only if the debtor agrees to the terms of the acceptance in a record authenticated after default or the secured party:

(A) sends to the debtor after default a proposal that is unconditional or subject only to a condition that collateral not in the possession of the secured party be preserved or maintained;

(B) in the proposal, proposes to accept collateral in full satisfaction of the obligation it secures; and

(C) does not receive a notification of objection authenticated by the debtor within 20 days after the proposal is sent.

(d) To be effective under subsection (a)(2), a notification of objection must be received by the secured party:

(1) in the case of a person to which the proposal was sent pursuant to Section 9—621, within 20 days after notification was sent to that person; and

(2) in other cases:

(A) within 20 days after the last notification was sent pursuant to Section 9—621; or

(B) if a notification was not sent, before the debtor consents to the acceptance under subsection (c).

(e) A secured party that has taken possession of collateral shall dispose of the collateral pursuant to Section 9—610 within the time specified in subsection (f) if:

(1) 60 percent of the cash price has been paid in the case of a purchase-money security interest in consumer goods; or

(2) 60 percent of the principal amount of the obligation secured has been paid in the case of a non-purchase-money security interest in consumer goods.

(f) To comply with subsection (e), the secured party shall dispose of the collateral:

(1) within 90 days after taking possession; or

(2) within any longer period to which the debtor and all secondary obligors have agreed in an agreement to that effect entered into and authenticated after default.

(g) In a consumer transaction, a secured party may not accept collateral in partial satisfaction of the obligation it secures.

* * * *

§9—623. RIGHT TO REDEEM COLLATERAL

(a) A debtor, any secondary obligor, or any other secured party or lienholder may redeem collateral.

(b) To redeem collateral, a person shall tender:

(1) fulfillment of all obligations secured by the collateral; and

(2) the reasonable expenses and attorney's fees described in Section 9—615(a)(1).

(c) A redemption may occur at any time before a secured party:

(1) has collected collateral under Section 9—607;

(2) has disposed of collateral or entered into a contract for its disposition under Section 9—610; or

(3) has accepted collateral in full or partial satisfaction of the obligation it secures under Section 9—622.

* * * *

§9—625. REMEDIES FOR SECURED PARTY'S FAILURE TO COMPLY WITH ARTICLE

(a) If it is established that a secured party is not proceeding in accordance with this article, a court may order or restrain collection, enforcement, or disposition of collateral on appropriate terms and conditions.

(b) Subject to subsections (c), (d), and (f), a person is liable for damages in the amount of any loss caused by a failure to comply with this article. Loss caused by a failure to comply may include loss resulting from the debtor's inability to obtain, or increased costs of, alternative financing.

(c) Except as otherwise provided in Section 9—628:

(1) a person that, at the time of the failure, was a debtor, was an obligor, or held a security interest in or other lien on the collateral may recover damages under subsection (b) for its loss; and

(2) if the collateral is consumer goods, a person that was a debtor or a secondary obligor at the time a secured party failed to comply with this part may recover for that failure in any event an amount not less than the credit service charge plus 10 percent of the principal amount of the obligation or the time-price differential plus 10 percent of the cash price.

(d) A debtor whose deficiency is eliminated under Section 9—626 may recover damages for the loss of any surplus. However, a debtor or secondary obligor whose deficiency is eliminated or reduced under Section 9—626 may not otherwise recover under subsection (b) for noncompliance with the provisions of this part relating to collection, enforcement, disposition, or acceptance.

(e) In addition to any damages recoverable under subsection (b), the debtor, consumer obligor, or person named as a debtor in a filed record, as applicable, may recover $500 in each case from a person that:

(1) fails to comply with Section 9—208;

(2) fails to comply with Section 9—209;

(3) files a record that the person is not entitled to file under Section 9—509(a);

(4) fails to cause the secured party of record to file or send a termination statement as required by Section 9—513(a) or (c);

(5) fails to comply with Section 9—616(b)(1) and whose failure is part of a pattern, or consistent with a practice, of noncompliance; or

(6) fails to comply with Section 9—616(b)(2).

(f) A debtor or consumer obligor may recover damages under subsection (b) and, in addition, $500 in each case from a person that, without reasonable cause, fails to comply with a request under Section 9—210. A recipient of a request under Section 9—210 which never claimed an interest in the collateral or obligations that are the subject of a request under that section has a reasonable excuse for failure to comply with the request within the meaning of this subsection.

(g) If a secured party fails to comply with a request regarding a list of collateral or a statement of account under Section 9—210, the secured party may claim a security interest only as shown in the list or statement included in the request as against a person that is reasonably misled by the failure.

* * * *

§9—627. DETERMINATION OF WHETHER CONDUCT WAS COMMERCIALLY REASONABLE

(a) The fact that a greater amount could have been obtained by a collection, enforcement, disposition, or acceptance at a different time or in a different method from that selected by the secured party is not of itself sufficient to preclude the secured party from establishing that the collection, enforcement, disposition, or acceptance was made in a commercially reasonable manner.

(b) A disposition of collateral is made in a commercially reasonable manner if the disposition is made:

(1) in the usual manner on any recognized market;

(2) at the price current in any recognized market at the time of the disposition; or

(3) otherwise in conformity with reasonable commercial practices among dealers in the type of property that was the subject of the disposition.

(c) A collection, enforcement, disposition, or acceptance is commercially reasonable if it has been approved:

(1) in a judicial proceeding;

(2) by a bona fide creditors' committee;

(3) by a representative of creditors; or

(4) by an assignee for the benefit of creditors.

(d) Approval under subsection (c) need not be obtained, and lack of approval does not mean that the collection, enforcement, disposition, or acceptance is not commercially reasonable.

case index

Opinion cases are in boldface type at the case summary; cited cases are in Roman type.

A

B

Q

R

S

T

U

V

W

Y

Z

glossary

A

abate—put a stop to a nuisance; reduce or cancel a legacy because the estate of the decedent is insufficient to make payment in full.

absolute guaranty—agreement that creates an obligation for a guarantor similar to that promised by a surety in suretyship relationships. The ability to demand payment immediately from a guarantor in an absolute guaranty situation distinguishes it from suretyship.

absolute privilege—complete defense against the tort of defamation, as in the speeches of members of Congress on the floor and witnesses in a trial.

abstract of title—history of the transfers of title to a given piece of land, briefly stating the parties to and the effect of all deeds, wills, and judicial proceedings relating to the land.

acceptance—unqualified assent to the act or proposal of another; as the acceptance of a draft (bill of exchange), of an offer to make a contract, of goods delivered by the seller, or of a gift or deed.

acceptor—drawee who has accepted the liability of paying the amount of money specified in a draft.

accommodation party—person who signs an instrument to lend credit to another party to the paper.

accord and satisfaction—agreement to substitute for an existing debt some alternative form of discharging that debt, coupled with the actual discharge of the debt by the substituted performance.

acknowledgment—admission or confirmation, generally of an instrument and usually made before a person authorized to administer oaths, such as a notary public; used to establish that the instrument was executed by the person making the instrument, that it was a voluntary act, or that the instrument is recorded.

acquired distinctiveness—through advertising, use and association, over time, an ordinary descriptive word or phase has taken on a new source identifying meaning and functions as a mark in the eyes of the public.

act-of-state doctrine—doctrine whereby every sovereign state is bound to respect the independence of every other sovereign state, and the courts of one country will not sit in judgment of another government's acts done within its own territory.

adeemed—canceled; as in a specifically bequeathed property being sold or given away by the testator prior to death, thus canceling the bequest.

adjustable rate mortgage (ARM)—mortgage with variable financing charges over the life of the loan.

administrative agency—government body charged with administering and implementing legislation.

administrative law—law governing administrative agencies.

Administrative Procedure Act—federal law that establishes the operating rules for administrative agencies.

administrative regulations—rules made by state and federal administrative agencies.

administrator, administratrix—person (man, woman) appointed to wind up and settle the estate of a person who has died without a will.

admissibility—the quality of the evidence in a case that allows it to be presented to the jury.

adverse possession—hostile possession of real estate, which when actual, visible, notorious, exclusive, and continued for the required time, will vest the title to the land in the person in such adverse possession.

advising bank—bank that tells beneficiary that letter of credit has been issued.

affidavit—statement of facts set forth in written form and supported by the oath or affirmation of the person making the statement setting forth that such facts are true on the basis of actual knowledge or on information and belief. The affidavit is executed before a notary public or other person authorized to administer oaths.

affirm—action taken by an appellate court that approves the decision of the court below.

affirmative action plan (AAP)—plan to have a diverse and representative workforce.

after-acquired goods—goods acquired after a security interest has attached.

agency—the relationship that exists between a person identified as a principal and another by virtue of which the latter may make contracts with third persons on behalf of the principal. (Parties—principal, agent, third person) *agent*—person or firm who is authorized by the principal or by operation of law to make contracts with third persons on behalf of the principal.

airbill—document of title issued to a shipper whose goods are being sent via air.

alteration—unauthorized change or completion of a negotiable instrument designed to modify the obligation of a party to the instrument.

alternative payees—those persons to whom a negotiable instrument is made payable, any one of whom may indorse and take delivery of it.

ambiguous—having more than one reasonable interpretation.

answer—what a defendant must file to admit or deny facts asserted by the plaintiff.

anticipatory breach—promisor's repudiation of the contract prior to the time that performance is required.

anticipatory repudiation—repudiation made in advance of the time for performance of the contract obligations.

antilapse statutes—statutes providing that the children or heirs of a deceased beneficiary may take the legacy in the place of the deceased beneficiary.

apparent authority—appearance of authority created by the principal's words or conduct.

appeal—taking a case to a reviewing court to determine whether the judgment of the lower court or administrative agency was correct. (Parties—appellant, appellee)

appellate jurisdiction—the power of a court to hear and decide a given class of cases on appeal from another court or administrative agency.

appropriation—taking of an image, likeness, or name for commercial advantage.

arbitration—the settlement of disputed questions, whether of law or fact, by one or more arbitrators by whose decision the parties agree to be bound.

Article 2—section of the Uniform Commercial Code that governs contracts for the sale of goods.

articles of copartnership—See *Partnership Agreement.*

articles of incorporation—See *Certificate of Incorporation.*

articles of partnership—See *Partnership Agreement.*

assignee—third party to whom contract benefits are transferred.

assignment—transfer of a right. Generally used in connection with personal property rights, as rights under a contract, commercial paper, an insurance policy, a mortgage, or a lease. (Parties—assignor, assignee)

assignor—party who assigns contract rights to a third party.

association tribunal—a court created by a trade association or group for the resolution of disputes among its members.

assumption—mortgage transfers in which the transferee and mortgagor are liable and the property is subject to foreclosure by the mortgagee if payments are not made.

attestation clause—clause that indicates a witness has observed either the execution of the will or the testator's acknowledgment of the writing as the testator's will.

attorney in fact—agent authorized to act for another under a power of attorney.

attorney-client privilege—right of individual to have discussions with his/her attorney kept private and confidential.

attractive nuisance doctrine—a rule imposing liability upon a landowner for injuries sustained by small children playing on the land when the landowner permits a condition to exist or maintains equipment that a reasonable person should realize would attract small children who could not realize the danger. The rule does not apply if an unreasonable burden would be imposed upon the landowner in taking steps to protect the children.

authorities—corporations formed by government that perform public service.

automatic perfection—perfection given by statute without specific filing or possession requirements on the part of the creditor.

automatic stay—order to prevent creditors from taking action such as filing suits or seeking foreclosure against the debtor.

B

bad check laws—laws making it a criminal offense to issue a bad check with intent to defraud.

bailee—person who accepts possession of a property.

bailee's lien—specific, possessory lien of the bailee upon the goods for work done to them. Commonly extended by statute to any bailee's claim for compensation, eliminating the necessity of retention of possession.

bailment—relationship that exists when personal property is delivered into the possession of another under an agreement, express or implied, that the identical property will be returned or will be delivered in accordance with the agreement. (Parties—bailor, bailee)

bailment for mutual benefit—bailment in which the bailor and bailee derive a benefit from the bailment.

bailor—person who turns over the possession of a property.

balance sheet test—comparison of assets to liabilities made to determine solvency.

bankruptcy—procedure by which one unable to pay debts may surrender all assets in excess of any exemption claim to the court for administration and distribution to creditors, and the debtor is given a discharge that releases him from the unpaid balance due on most debts.

bankruptcy courts—court of special jurisdiction to determine bankruptcy issues.

battle of the forms—merchants' exchanges of invoices and purchase orders with differing boilerplate terms.

bearer—person in physical possession of commercial paper payable to bearer, a document of title directing delivery to bearer, or an investment security in bearer form.

bearer paper—instrument with no payee, payable to cash or payable to bearer.

bedrock view—a strict constructionist interpretation of a constitution.

beneficiary—person to whom the proceeds of a life insurance policy are payable, a person for whose benefit property is held in trust, or a person given property by a will; the ultimate recipient of the benefit of a funds transfer.

beneficiary's bank—the final bank, which carries out the payment order, in the chain of a transfer of funds.

bequest—gift of personal property by will.

best available treatment—in environmental law, a requirement that state-of-the-art methods be used for treating water.

best conventional treatment—in environmental law, a requirement that water be treated with the most commonly used method.

bicameral—a two-house form of the legislative branch of government.

bilateral contract—agreement under which one promise is given in exchange for another.

bill of lading—document issued by a carrier acknowledging the receipt of goods and the terms of the contract of transportation.

bill of sale—writing signed by the seller reciting that the personal property therein described has been sold to the buyer.

blackmail—extortion demands made by a nonpublic official.

blank indorsement—an indorsement that does not name the person to whom the paper, document of title, or investment security is negotiated.

blocking laws—laws that prohibit the disclosure, copying, inspection, or removal of documents located in the enacting country in compliance with orders from foreign authorities.

blue sky laws—state statutes designed to protect the public from the sale of worthless stocks and bonds.

bona fide—in good faith; without any fraud or deceit.

bond—obligation or promise in writing and sealed, generally of corporations, personal representatives, and trustees; fidelity bonds.

bond indenture—agreement setting forth the contractual terms of a particular bond issue.

book value—value found by dividing the value of the corporate assets by the number of shares outstanding.

breach—failure to act or perform in the manner called for in a contract.

breach of the peace—violation of the law in the repossession of the collateral.

brownfields—land that is a designated Superfund cleanup site but which lies fallow because no one is willing to risk liability by buying the property, even when the hazardous waste has been removed or property no one is willing to spend the money to remove the hazardous waste.

bubble concept—method for determining total emissions in one area; all sources are considered in an area.

business ethics—balancing the goal of profits with values of individuals and society.

business judgment rule (BJR)—rule that allows board immunity from liability for corporate acts where there is a reasonable indication that the acts were made in good faith with due care.

bylaws—rules and regulations enacted by a corporation to govern the affairs of the corporation and its shareholders, directors, and officers.

C

cancellation provision—crossing out of a part of an instrument or a destruction of all legal effect of the instrument, whether by act of party, upon breach by the other party, or pursuant to agreement or decree of court.

capital stock—declared money value of the outstanding stock of the corporation.

cargo insurance—insurance that protects a cargo owner against financial loss if goods being shipped are lost or damaged at sea.

carrier—individual or organization undertaking the transportation of goods.

case law—law that includes principles that are expressed for the first time in court decisions.

cashier's check—draft (check) drawn by a bank on itself.

cash surrender value—sum paid the insured upon the surrender of a policy to the insurer.

cash tender offer—general offer to all shareholders of a target corporation to purchase their shares for cash at a specified price.

cause of action—right to damages or other judicial relief when a legally protected right of the plaintiff is violated by an unlawful act of the defendant.

cease-and-desist order—order issued by a court or administrative agency to stop a practice that it decides is improper.

certificate of deposit (CD)—promise to pay instrument issued by a bank.

certificate of incorporation—written approval from the state or national government for a corporation to be formed.

certificate of stock—document evidencing a shareholder's ownership of stock issued by a corporation.

certified check—check for which the bank has set aside in a special account sufficient funds to pay it; payment is made when check is presented regardless of amount in drawer's account at that time; discharges all parties except certifying bank when holder requests certification.

cestui que trust—beneficiary or person for whose benefit the property is held in trust.

CF—cost and freight.

Chapter 11 bankruptcy—reorganization form of bankruptcy under federal law.

Chapter 7 bankruptcy—liquidation form of bankruptcy under federal law.

Chapter 13 bankruptcy—proceeding of consumer debt readjustment plan bankruptcy.

charging order—order by a court, after a business partner's personal assets are exhausted, requiring that the partner's share of the profits be paid to a creditor until the debt is discharged.

charter—grant of authority from a government to exist as a corporation. Generally replaced today by a certificate of incorporation approving the articles of incorporation.

check—order by a depositor on a bank to pay a sum of money to a payee; a draft drawn on a bank and payable on demand.

choice-of-law clause—clause in an agreement that specifies which law will govern should a dispute arise.

chose in action—intangible personal property in the nature of claims against another, such as a claim for accounts receivable or wages.

CIF—cost, insurance, and freight.

civil disobedience—the term used when natural law proponents violate positive law.

civil law—the law that defines the rights of one person against another.

claim—right to payment.

Clayton Act—a federal law that prohibits price discrimination.

Clean Air Act—federal legislation that establishes standards for air pollution levels and prevents further deterioration of air quality.

Clean Water Act—federal legislation that regulates water pollution through a control system.

close corporation—corporation whose shares are held by a single shareholder or a small group of shareholders.

close-connection doctrine—circumstantial evidence, such as an ongoing or a close relationship, that can serve as notice of a problem with an instrument.

COD—cash on delivery.

coinsurance clause—clause requiring the insured to maintain insurance on property up to a stated amount and providing that to the extent that this is not done, the insured is to be deemed a coinsurer with the insurer, so that the latter is liable only for its proportionate share of the amount of insurance required to be carried.

collateral—property pledged by a borrower as security for a debt.

comity—principle of international and national law that the laws of all nations and states deserve the respect legitimately demanded by equal participants.

commerce clause—that section of the U.S. Constitution allocating the power for business regulation between the federal government and the states.

commercial impracticability—situation that occurs when costs of performance rise suddenly and performance of a contract will result in a substantial loss.

commercial lease—any nonconsumer lease.

commercial paper—written, transferable, signed promise or order to pay a specified sum of money; a negotiable instrument.

commercial unit—standard of the trade for shipment or packaging of a good.

commission merchant—bailee to whom goods are consigned for sale.

commission or factorage—consignee's compensation.

common carrier—carrier that holds out its facilities to serve the general public for compensation without discrimination.

common law—the body of unwritten principles originally based upon the usages and customs of the community that were recognized and enforced by the courts.

common stock—stock that has no right or priority over any other stock of the corporation as to dividends or distribution of assets upon dissolution.

community property—cotenancy held by husband and wife in property acquired during their marriage under the law of some of the states, principally in the southwestern United States.

comparative negligence—defense to negligence that allows plaintiff to recover reduced damages based on his level of fault.

compensatory damages—sum of money that will compensate an injured plaintiff for actual loss.

complaint—the initial pleading filed by the plaintiff in many actions, which in many states may be served as original process to acquire jurisdiction over the defendant.

composition of creditors—agreement among creditors that each shall accept a partial payment as full payment in consideration of the other creditors doing the same.

Comprehensive Environmental Response, Compensation, and Liability Act (CERCLA)—federal law that authorizes the president to issue funds for the cleanup of areas that were once disposal sites for hazardous wastes.

computer crimes—wrongs committed using a computer or with knowledge of computers.

concealment—failure to volunteer information not requested.

condition—stipulation or prerequisite in a contract, will, or other instrument.

condition precedent—event that must take place before the duty to perform under a contract arises.

condition subsequent—event whose occurrence or lack thereof terminates a contract.

condominium—combination of co-ownership and individual ownership.

confidential relationship—relationship in which, because of the legal status of the parties or their respective physical or mental conditions or knowledge, one party places full confidence and trust in the other.

conflict of interest—conduct that compromises an employee's allegiance to that company.

conglomerate—relationship of a parent corporation to subsidiary corporations engaged in diversified fields of activity unrelated to the field of activity of the parent corporation.

consent decrees—informal settlements of enforcement actions brought by agencies.

consequential damages—damages the buyer experiences as a result of the seller's breach with respect to a third party; also called *special damages.*

consideration—promise or performance that the promisor demands as the price of the promise.

consignee—(1) person to whom goods are shipped, (2) dealer who sells goods for others.

consignment—bailment made for the purpose of sale by the bailee. (Parties —consignor, consignee)

consignor—(1) person who delivers goods to the carrier for shipment, (2) party with title who turns goods over to another for sale.

consolidation (of corporations)—combining of two or more corporations in which the corporate existence of each one ceases and a new corporation is created.

conspiracy—agreement between two or more persons to commit an unlawful act.

constitution—a body of principles that establishes the structure of a government and the relationship of the government to the people who are governed.

constructive bailment—bailment imposed by law as opposed to one created by contract, whereby the bailee must preserve the property and redeliver it to the owner.

constructive delivery—See *symbolic delivery.*

constructive eviction—act or omission of the landlord that substantially deprives the tenant of the use and enjoyment of the premises.

consumer—any buyer afforded special protections by statute or regulation.

consumer credit—credit for personal, family, and household use.

consumer goods—goods used or bought primarily for personal, family, or household use.

consumer lease—lease of goods by a natural person for personal, family, or household use.

Consumer Product Safety Improvement Act—federal law that sets standards for the types of paints used in toys; a response to the lead paint found in toys made in China; requires tracking for international production; increases penalties.

contract—a binding agreement based on the genuine assent of the parties, made for a lawful object, between competent parties, in the form required by law, and generally supported by consideration.

contract carrier—carrier that transports on the basis of individual contracts that it makes with each shipper.

contract interference—tort in which a third party interferes with others' freedom to contract.

contract of adhesion—contract offered by a dominant party to a party with inferior bargaining power on a take-it-or-leave-it basis.

contract under seal—contract executed by affixing a seal or making an impression on the paper or on some adhering substance such as wax attached to the document.

contracting agent—agent with authority to make contracts; person with whom the buyer deals.

Contracts for the International Sale of Goods (CISG)—uniform international contract code contracts for international sale of goods.

contractual capacity—ability to understand that a contract is being made and to understand its general meaning.

contribution—right of a co-obligor who has paid more than a proportionate share to demand that the other obligor pay the amount of the excess payment made.

contributory negligence—negligence of the plaintiff that contributes to injury and at common law bars recovery from the defendant although the defendant may have been more negligent than the plaintiff.

conversion—act of taking personal property by a person not entitled to it and keeping it from its true owner or prior possessor without consent.

cooperative—group of two or more persons or enterprises that acts through a common agent with respect to a common objective, such as buying or selling.

copyright—exclusive right given by federal statute to the creator of a literary or an artistic work to use, reproduce, and display the work.

corporation—artificial being created by government grant, which for many purposes is treated as a natural person.

corporation by estoppel—corporation that comes about when parties estop themselves from denying that the corporation exists.

corporation de jure—corporation with a legal right to exist by virtue of law.

correspondent bank—will honor the letter of credit from the domestic bank of the buyer.

cost plus—method of determining the purchase price or contract price equal to the seller's or contractor's costs plus a stated percentage as the profit.

co-sureties—sureties for the same debtor and obligor.

cotenancy—when two or more persons hold concurrent rights and interests in the same property.

Council on Environmental Quality (CEQ)—federal agency that establishes national policies on environmental quality and then recommends legislation to implement these policies.

counterclaim—a claim that the defendant in an action may make against the plaintiff.

counteroffer—proposal by an offeree to the offeror that changes the terms of, and thus rejects, the original offer.

course of dealing—pattern of performance between two parties to a contract.

court—a tribunal established by government to hear evidence, decide cases brought before it, and provide remedies when a wrong has been committed.

covenant against encumbrances—guarantee that conveyed land is not subject to any right or interest of a third person.

covenant of further assurances—promise that the grantor of an interest in land will execute any additional documents required to perfect the title of the grantee.

covenant of quiet enjoyment—covenant by the grantor of an interest in land that the grantee's possession of the land shall not be disturbed.

covenant of right to convey—guarantee that the grantor of an interest in land, if not the owner, has the right or authority to make the conveyance to a new owner.

covenant of seisin—guarantee that the grantor of an interest in land owns the estate conveyed to a new owner.

covenants (or warranties) of title—grantor's covenants of a deed that guarantee such matters as the right to make the conveyance, to ownership of the property, to freedom of the property from encumbrances, or that the grantee will not be disturbed in the quiet enjoyment of the land.

credit transfer—transaction in which a person making payment, such as a buyer, requests payment be made to the beneficiary's bank.

creditor—person (seller or lender) who is owed money; also may be a secured party.

crime—violation of the law that is punished as an offense against the state or government.

criminal law—the law that defines wrongs against society.

cross-examination—the examination made of a witness by the attorney for the adverse party.

cumulative voting—system of voting for directors in which each shareholder has as many votes as the number of voting shares owned multiplied by the number of directors to be elected, and such votes can be distributed for the various candidates as desired.

customary authority—authority of an agent to do any act that, according to the custom of the community, usually accompanies the transaction for which the agent is authorized to act.

cyberlaw—laws and precedent applicable to Internet transactions and communications.

cyberspace—World Wide Web and Internet communication.

cybersquatters—term for those who register and set up domain names on the Internet for resale to the famous users of the names in question.

D

de facto—existing in fact as distinguished from as of right, as in the case of an officer or a corporation purporting to act as such without being elected to the office or having been properly incorporated.

debenture—unsecured bond of a corporation, with no specific corporate assets pledged as security for payment.

debit transfer—transaction in which a beneficiary entitled to money requests payment from a bank according to a prior agreement.

debtor—buyer on credit (i.e., a borrower).

decedent—upon death, person whose estate is being administered.

deed—instrument by which the grantor (owner of land) conveys or transfers the title to a grantee.

defamation—untrue statement by one party about another to a third party.

defendant—party charged with a violation of civil or criminal law in a proceeding.

defined benefit plan—an employer commitment to make specified future payments to participants upon retirement.

defined contribution plan—a plan that provides for an individual account for each plan participant and for benefits based solely on the amount contributed to the participant's account; also known as an *individual account plan.*

definite time—time of payment computable from the face of the instrument.

delegated powers—powers expressly granted the national government by the Constitution.

delegation—transfer to another of the right and power to do an act.

delegation of duties—transfer of duties by a contracting party to another person who is to perform them.

delivery—constructive or actual possession.

demand draft—draft that is payable upon presentment.

demurrer—a pleading to dismiss the adverse party's pleading for not stating a cause of action or a defense.

deposition—the testimony of a witness taken out of court but under oath.

depositor—person, or bailor, who gives property for storage.

derivative (secondary) action—secondary action for damages or breach of contract brought by one or more corporate shareholders against directors, officers, or third persons.

development statement—statement that sets forth significant details of a real estate or property development as required by the federal Interstate Land Sales Act.

devise—gift of real estate made by will.

devisee—beneficiary of a devise.

direct damages—losses that are caused by breach of a contract.

direct examination—examination of a witness by his or her attorney.

directed verdict—a direction by the trial judge to the jury to return a verdict in favor of a specified party to the action.

disability—any incapacity resulting from bodily injury or disease to engage in any occupation for remuneration or profit.

discharge in bankruptcy—order of the bankruptcy court relieving the debtor from obligation to pay the unpaid balance of most claims.

disclosed principal—principal whose identity is made known by the agent as well as the fact that the agent is acting on the principal's behalf.

discovery—procedures for ascertaining facts prior to the time of trial in order to eliminate the element of surprise in litigation.

dishonor—status when the primary party refuses to pay the instrument according to its terms.

disinherited—excluded from sharing in the estate of a decedent.

Dispute Settlement Body (DSB)—means, provided by the World Trade Organization, for member countries to resolve trade disputes rather than engage in unilateral trade sanctions or a trade war.

distinctiveness—capable of serving the source-identifying function of a mark.

distribution per stirpes—distribution of an estate made in as many equal parts as there are family lines represented in the nearest generation; also known as *stirpital distribution.*

distributor—entity that takes title to goods and bears the financial and commercial risks for the subsequent sale of the goods.

divestiture order—a court order to dispose of interests that could lead to a monopoly.

divisible contract—agreement consisting of two or more parts, each calling for corresponding performances of each part by the parties.

document of title—document treated as evidence that a person is entitled to receive, hold, and dispose of the document and the goods it covers.

domestic corporation—corporation that has been incorporated by the state in question as opposed to incorporation by another state.

dominant tenement—land that is benefited by an easement.

donee—recipient of a gift.

donor—person making a gift.

double indemnity—provision for payment of double the amount specified by the insurance contract if death is caused by an accident and occurs under specified circumstances.

draft or bill of exchange—an unconditional order in writing by one person upon another, signed by the person giving it, and ordering the person to whom it is directed to pay upon demand or at a definite time a sum certain in money to order or to bearer.

drawee—person to whom the draft is addressed and who is ordered to pay the amount of money specified in the draft.

drawer—person who writes out and creates a draft or bill of exchange, including a check.

due diligence—process of checking the environmental history and nature of land prior to purchase.

due process—the constitutional right to be heard, question witnesses, and present evidence.

due process clause—in the Fifth and Fourteenth Amendments, a guarantee of protection from unreasonable procedures and unreasonable laws.

dumping—selling goods in another country at less than their fair value.

duress—conduct that deprives the victim of free will and that generally gives the victim the right to set aside any transaction entered into under such circumstances.

duty—an obligation of law imposed on a person to perform or refrain from performing a certain act.

E

easement—permanent right that one has in the land of another, as the right to cross another's land or an easement of way.

easement by implication—easement not specifically created by deed that arises from the circumstances of the parties and the land location and access.

economic duress—threat of financial loss.

Economic Espionage Act (EEA)—federal law that makes it a felony to copy, download, transmit, or in anyway transfer proprietary files, documents, and information from a computer to an unauthorized person.

economic strikers—union strikers trying to enforce bargaining demands when an impasse has been reached in the negotiation process for a collective bargaining agreement.

effects doctrine—doctrine that U.S. courts will assume jurisdiction and will apply antitrust laws to conduct outside of the United States when the activity of business firms has direct and substantial effect on U.S. commerce; the rule has been modified to require that the effect on U.S. commerce also be foreseeable.

effluent guidelines—EPA standards for maximum ranges of discharge into water.

electronic funds transfer (EFT)—any transfer of funds (other than a transaction originated by a check, draft, or similar paper instrument) that is initiated through an electronic terminal, telephone, computer, or magnetic tape so as to authorize a financial institution to debit or credit an account.

Electronic Funds Transfer Act (EFTA)—federal law that provides consumers with rights and protections in electronic funds transfers.

eleemosynary corporation—corporation organized for a charitable or benevolent purpose.

embezzlement—statutory offense consisting of the unlawful conversion of property entrusted to the wrongdoer.

eminent domain—power of government and certain kinds of corporations to take private property against the objection of the owner, provided the taking is for a public purpose and just compensation is made for it.

emissions offset policy—controls whether new factories can be built in a nonattainment area.

employment-at-will doctrine—doctrine in which the employer has historically been allowed to terminate the employment contract at any time for any reason or for no reason.

en banc—the term used when the full panel of judges on the appellate court hears a case.

encoding warranty—warranty made by any party who encodes electronic information on an instrument; a warranty of accuracy.

Endangered Species Act (ESA)—federal law that identifies and protects species that are endangered from development or other acts that threaten their existence.

endowment insurance—insurance that pays the face amount of the policy if the insured dies within the policy period.

entitlement theory—also known as *rights theory*; Nozick's theory that (1) everyone has a set of rights, and (2) it is up to the governments to protect those rights.

environmental impact statement (EIS)—formal report prepared under NEPA to document findings on the impact of a federal project on the environment.

equitable title—beneficial interest in a trust.

equity—the body of principles that originally developed because of the inadequacy of the rules then applied by the common law courts of England.

escalation clause—provision for the automatic increase of the rent at periodic intervals.

escheat—transfer to the state of the title to a decedent's property when the owner of the property dies intestate and is not survived by anyone capable of taking the property as heir.

E-sign—signature over the Internet.

estate in fee—largest estate possible, in which the owner has absolute and entire interest in the land.

estoppel—principle by which a person is barred from pursuing a certain course of action or of disputing the truth of certain matters.

ethical egoism—Ayn Rand theory of ethics that we should all act in our own best interests.

ethics—a branch of philosophy dealing with values that relate to the nature of human conduct and values associated with that conduct.

ex post facto *law*—a law making criminal an act that was lawful when done or that increases the penalty when done. Such laws are generally prohibited by constitutional provisions.

exculpatory clause—provision in a contract stating that one of the parties is not liable for damages in case of breach; also called *limitation-of-liability clause.*

executed contract—agreement that has been completely performed.

execution—the carrying out of a judgment of a court, generally directing that property owned by the defendant be sold and the proceeds first be used to pay the execution or judgment creditor.

executive branch—the branch of government (e.g., the president) formed to execute the laws.

executor, executrix—person (man, woman) named in a will to administer the estate of the decedent.

executory contract—contract in which something remains to be done by one or both parties.

exhaustion of administrative remedies—requirement that an agency make its final decision before the issue can be taken to court.

existing goods—goods that physically exist and are owned by the seller at the time of a transaction.

exoneration—agreement or provision in an agreement that one party will not be held liable for loss; the right of the surety to demand that those primarily liable pay the claim for which the surety is secondarily liable.

expert witness—one who has acquired special knowledge in a particular field as through practical experience or study, or both, whose opinion is admissible as an aid to the trier of fact.

export sale—direct sale to customers in a foreign country.

express authority—authority of an agent to perform a certain act.

express authorization—authorization of an agent to perform a certain act.

express contract—agreement of the parties manifested by their words, whether spoken or written.

express warranty—statement by the defendant relating to the goods, which statement is part of the basis of the bargain.

extortion—illegal demand by a public officer acting with apparent authority.

F

facilitation payments—(or grease payments) legal payments to speed up or ensure performance of normal government duties.

factor—bailee to whom goods are consigned for sale.

false imprisonment—intentional detention of a person without that person's consent; called the shopkeeper's tort when shoplifters are unlawfully detained.

FAS—free alongside the named vessel.

federal district court—the general trial court of the federal system.

Federal Register—government publication issued five days a week that lists all administrative regulations, all presidential proclamations and executive orders, and other documents and classes of documents that the president or Congress direct to be published.

Federal Register Act—federal law requiring agencies to make public disclosure of proposed rules, passed rules, and activities.

Federal Sentencing Guidelines—federal standards used by judges in determining mandatory sentence terms for those convicted of federal crimes.

federal system—the system of government in which a central government is given power to administer to national concerns while individual states retain the power to administer to local concerns.

fee simple defeasibles—fee simple interest that can be lost if restrictions on its use are violated.

fee simple estate—highest level of land ownership; full interest of unlimited duration.

felony—criminal offense that is punishable by confinement in prison for more than one year or by death, or that is expressly stated by statute to be a felony.

field warehousing—stored goods under the exclusive control of a warehouse but kept on the owner's premises rather than in a warehouse.

Fifth Amendment—constitutional protection against self-incrimination; also guarantees due process.

finance lease—three-party lease agreement in which there is a lessor, a lessee, and a financier.

financing statement—brief statement (record) that gives sufficient information to alert third persons that a particular creditor may have a security interest in the collateral described.

fire insurance policy—a contract that indemnifies the insured for property destruction or damage caused by fire.

firm offer—offer stated to be held open for a specified time, which must be so held in some states even in the absence of an option contract, or under the UCC, with respect to merchants.

first-in-time provision—creditor whose interest attached first has priority in the collateral when two creditors have a secured interest.

first-to-perfect basis—rule of priorities that holds that first in time in perfecting a security interest, mortgage, judgment, lien, or other property attachment right should have priority.

fixture—personal property that has become so attached to or adapted to real estate that it has lost its character as personal property and is part of the real estate.

floating lien—claim in a changing or shifting stock of goods of the buyer.

FOB place of destination—shipping contract that requires seller to deliver goods to buyer.

FOB place of shipment—contract that requires the seller to arrange for shipment only.

forbearance—refraining from doing an act.

forcible entry and detainer—action by the landlord to have the tenant removed for nonpayment of rent.

foreclosure—procedure for enforcing a mortgage resulting in the public sale of the mortgaged property and, less commonly, in merely barring the right of the mortgagor to redeem the property from the mortgage.

foreign corporation—corporation incorporated under the laws of another state.

Foreign Corrupt Practices Act (FCPA)—federal law that makes it a felony to influence decision makers in other countries for the purpose of obtaining business, such as contracts for sales and services; also imposes financial reporting requirements on certain U.S. corporations.

forged or unauthorized indorsement—instrument indorsed by an agent for a principal without authorization or authority.

forgery—fraudulently making or altering an instrument that apparently creates or alters a legal liability of another.

formal contracts—written contracts or agreements whose formality signifies the parties' intention to abide by the terms.

Fourth Amendment—privacy protection in the U.S. Constitution; prohibits unauthorized searches and seizures.

franchise—(1) privilege or authorization, generally exclusive, to engage in a particular activity within a particular geographic area, such as a government franchise to operate a taxi company within a specified city, or a private franchise as the grant by a manufacturer of a right to sell products within a particular territory or for a particular number of years; (2) right to vote.

franchise agreement—sets forth rights of franchisee to use trademarks, etc., of franchisor.

franchisee—person to whom franchise is granted.

Franchise Rule—rule requiring detailed disclosures and prohibiting certain practices.

franchising—granting of permission to use a trademark, trade name, or copyright under specified conditions; a form of licensing.

franchisor—party granting the franchise.

fraud—making of a false statement of a past or existing fact, with knowledge of its falsity or with reckless indifference as to its truth, with the intent to cause another to rely thereon, and such person does rely thereon and is harmed thereby.

fraud in the inducement—fraud that occurs when a person is persuaded or induced to execute an instrument because of fraudulent statements.

fraud-on-the-market—a theory that in an open and developed securities market, the price of a stock is determined by the information on the company available to the public, and misleading statements will defraud purchasers of stock even if they do not directly rely on these statements.

Freedom of Information Act—federal law permitting citizens to request documents and records from administrative agencies.

freight forwarder—one who contracts to have goods transported and, in turn, contracts with carriers for such transportation.

freight insurance—insures that ship owner will receive payment for transportation charges.

full warranty—obligation of a seller to fix or replace a defective product within a reasonable time without cost to the buyer.

funds transfer—communication of instructions or requests to pay a specific sum of money to the credit of a specified account or person without an actual physical passing of money.

fungible goods—homogeneous goods of which any unit is the equivalent of any other unit.

future goods—goods that exist physically but are not owned by the seller and goods that have not yet been produced.

G

garnishment—the name given in some states to attachment proceedings.

general agent—agent authorized by the principal to transact all affairs in connection with a particular type of business or trade or to transact all business at a certain place.

general corporation code—state's code listing certain requirements for creation of a corporation.

general jurisdiction—the power to hear and decide most controversies involving legal rights and duties.

general legacies—certain sums of money bequeathed to named persons by the testator; to be paid out of the decedent's assets generally without specifying any particular fund or source from which the payment is to be made.

general partnership—partnership in which the partners conduct as co-owners a business for profit, and each partner has a right to take part in the management of the business and has unlimited liability.

general partners—partners who publicly and actively engage in the transaction of firm business.

general partners—partnership in which the partners conduct as co-owners a business for profit, and each partner has a right to take part in the management of the business and has unlimited liability; general partners publicly and actively engage in the transaction of firm business.

gift—title to an owner's personal property voluntarily transferred by a party not receiving anything in exchange.

gift causa mortis—gift, made by the donor in the belief that death was immediate and impending, that is revoked or is revocable under certain circumstances.

good faith—absence of knowledge of any defects or problems; "pure heart and an empty head."

goods—anything movable at the time it is identified as the subject of a transaction.

grantee—new owner of a land conveyance.

grantor—owner who transfers or conveys an interest in land to a new owner.

gratuitous bailment—bailment in which the bailee does not receive any compensation or advantage.

gray market goods—foreign-made goods with U.S. trademarks brought into the United States by a third party without the consent of the trademark owners to compete with these owners.

grease payments—(or facilitation payments) legal payments to speed up or ensure performance of normal government duties.

guarantor—one who undertakes the obligation of guaranty.

guaranty—agreement or promise to answer for a debt; an undertaking to pay the debt of another if the creditor first sues the debtor.

guaranty of collection—form of guaranty in which creditor cannot proceed against guarantor until after proceeding against debtor.

guaranty of payment—absolute promise to pay when a debtor defaults.

guest—transient who contracts for a room or site at a hotel.

H

hearsay evidence—statements made out of court that are offered in court as proof of the information contained in the statements and that, subject to many exceptions, are not admissible in evidence.

holder—someone in possession of an instrument that runs to that person (i.e., is made payable to that person, is indorsed to that person, or is bearer paper).

holder in due course—a holder who has given value, taken in good faith without notice of dishonor, defenses, or that instrument is overdue, and who is afforded special rights or status.

holder through a holder in due course—holder of an instrument who attains holder-in-due-course status because a holder in due course has held it previous to him or her.

holographic will—unwitnessed will written by hand.

homeowners insurance policy—combination of standard fire insurance and comprehensive personal liability insurance.

hotelkeeper—one regularly engaged in the business of offering living accommodations to all transient persons.

hull insurance—insurance that covers physical damage on a freight-moving vessel.

I

identification—point in the transaction when the buyer acquires an interest in the goods subject to the contract.

identified—term applied to particular goods selected by either the buyer or the seller as the goods called for by the sales contract.

identity theft—use of another's credit tools, social security number, or other IDs to obtain cash, goods, or credit without permission.

illusory promise—promise that in fact does not impose any obligation on the promisor.

impeach—using prior inconsistent evidence to challenge the credibility of a witness.

implied contract—contract expressed by conduct or implied or deduced from the facts.

implied warranty—warranty that was not made but is implied by law.

implied warranty of merchantability—group of promises made by the seller, the most important of which is that the goods are fit for the ordinary purposes for which they are sold.

impostor rule—an exception to the rules on liability for forgery that covers situations such as the embezzling payroll clerk.

in pari delicto—equally guilty; used in reference to a transaction as to which relief will not be granted to either party because both are equally guilty of wrongdoing.

incidental authority—authority of an agent that is reasonably necessary to execute express authority.

incidental damages—incurred by the nonbreaching party as part of the process of trying to cover (buy substitute goods) or sell (selling subject matter of contract to another); includes storage fees, commissions, and the like.

income—money earned by the principal, or property in trust, and distributed by the trustee.

incontestability clause—provision that after the lapse of a specified time the insurer cannot dispute the policy on the ground of misrepresentation or fraud of the insured or similar wrongful conduct.

incorporation by reference—contract consisting of both the original or skeleton document and the detailed statement that is incorporated in it.

incorporator—one or more natural persons or corporations who sign and file appropriate incorporation forms with a designated government official.

indemnity—right of a person secondarily liable to require that a person primarily liable pay for loss sustained when the secondary party discharges the obligation that the primary party should have discharged; the right of an agent to be paid the amount of any loss or damage sustained without fault because of obedience to the principal's instructions; an undertaking by one person for a consideration to pay another person a sum of money to indemnify that person when a specified loss is incurred.

indemnity contract—agreement by one person, for consideration, to pay another person a sum of money in the event that the other person sustains a specified loss.

indenture trustee—usually a commercial banking institution, to represent the interests of the bondholders and ensure that the terms and covenants of the bond issue are met by the corporation.

independent contractor—contractor who undertakes to perform a specified task according to the terms of a contract but over whom the other contracting party has no control except as provided for by the contract.

indorsee—party to whom special indorsement is made.

indorsement—signature of the payee on an instrument.

indorser—secondary party (or obligor) on a note.

informal contract—simple oral or written contract.

informal settlements—negotiated disposition of a matter before an administrative agency, generally without public sanctions.

injunction—order of a court of equity to refrain from doing (negative injunction) or to do (affirmative or mandatory injunction) a specified act.

inland marine—insurance that covers domestic shipments of goods over land and inland waterways.

insider—full-time corporate employee or a director or their relatives.

insider information—privileged information on company business only known to employees.

insolvency—excess of debts and liabilities over assets, or inability to pay debts as they mature.

instruction—summary of the law given to jurors by the judge before deliberation begins.

insurable interest—the right to hold a valid insurance policy on a person or property.

insurance—a plan of security against risks by charging the loss against a fund created by the payments made by policyholders.

insurance agent—agent of an insurance company.

insurance broker—independent contractor who is not employed by any one insurance company.

insured—person to whom the promise in an insurance contract is made.

insurer—promisor in an insurance contract.

integrity—the adherence to one's values and principles despite the costs and consequences.

intellectual property rights—trademark, copyright, and patent rights protected by law.

intended beneficiary—third person of a contract whom the contract is intended to benefit.

intentional infliction of emotional distress—tort that produces mental anguish caused by conduct that exceeds all bounds of decency.

intentional tort—civil wrong that results from intentional conduct.

intervivos gift—any transaction that takes place between living persons and creates rights prior to the death of any of them.

interest in the authority—form of agency in which an agent has been given or paid for the right to exercise authority.

interest in the subject matter—form of agency in which an agent is given an interest in the property with which that agent is dealing.

interlineation—writing between the lines or adding to the provisions of a document, the effect thereof depending upon the nature of the document.

intermediary bank—bank between the originator and the beneficiary bank in the transfer of funds.

interrogatories—written questions used as a discovery tool that must be answered under oath.

intestate—condition of dying without a will as to any property.

intestate succession—distribution, made as directed by statute, of a decedent's property not effectively disposed of by will.

invasion of privacy—tort of intentional intrusion into the private affairs of another.

invitee—person who enters another's land by invitation.

involuntary bankruptcy—proceeding in which a creditor or creditors file the petition for relief with the bankruptcy court.

issuer—party who issues a document such as a letter of credit or a document of title such as a warehouse receipt or bill of lading.

J

joint and several liability—disproportionate satisfaction of partnership debt rendering each partner liable for the entire debt with the right to contribution from other partners.

joint liability—apportions partners' responsibility for debt equally.

joint tenancy—estate held jointly by two or more with the right of survivorship as between them, unless modified by statute.

joint venture—relationship in which two or more persons or firms combine their labor or property for a single undertaking and share profits and losses equally unless otherwise agreed.

judge—primary officer of the court.

judgment lien—lien by a creditor who has won a verdict against the landowner in court.

judgment n.o.v. (or non obstante veredicto, *"notwithstanding the verdict"*)— a judgment entered after verdict upon the motion of the losing party on the ground that the verdict is so wrong that a judgment should be entered the opposite of the verdict.

judicial branch—the branch of government (courts) formed to interpret the laws.

judicial triage—court management tool used by judges to expedite certain cases in which time is of the essence, such as asbestos cases in which the plaintiffs are gravely ill.

jurisdiction—the authority of courts to hear and determine a given class of cases; the power to act over a particular defendant.

jurisdictional rule of reason—rule that balances the vital interests, including laws and policies, of the United States with those of a foreign country.

jury—a body of citizens sworn by a court to determine by verdict the issues of fact submitted to them.

K

Kant's categorical imperative—theory of ethical thought that asks individuals to be governed by the same set of rules in all circumstances; whether you are buyer or seller, the standards for full and fair disclosure are the same.

L

land—earth, including all things embedded in or attached thereto, whether naturally or by the act of humans.

landlord—one who leases real property to another.

law—the order or pattern of rules that society establishes to govern the conduct of individuals and the relationships among them.

lease—agreement between the owner of property and a tenant by which the former agrees to give possession of the property to the latter in consideration of the payment of rent. (Parties—landlord or lessor, tenant or lessee)

leasehold estate—interest of a tenant in rented land.

legacy—gift of money made by will.

legal title—title held by the trustee in a trust situation.

legatee—beneficiary who receives a gift of personal property by will.

legislative branch—the branch of government (e.g., Congress) formed to make the laws.

lessee—one who has a possessory interest in real or personal property under a lease; a tenant.

lessor—one who conveys real or personal property by a lease; a landlord.

letter of credit—commercial device used to guarantee payment to a seller, primarily in an international business transaction.

letters of administration—written authorization given to an administrator of an estate as evidence of appointment and authority.

letters testamentary—written authorization given to an executor of an estate as evidence of appointment and authority.

liability insurance—covers the ship owner's liability if the ship causes damage to another ship or its cargo.

libel—written or visual defamation without legal justification.

license—personal privilege to do some act or series of acts upon the land of another, as the placing of a sign there on, not amounting to an ease mentor a right of possession.

licensee—someone on another's premises with the permission of the occupier, whose duty is to warn the licensee of nonobvious dangers.

licensing—transfer of technology rights to a product so that it may be produced by a different business organization in a foreign country in exchange for royalties and other payments as agreed.

lien—claim or right, against property, existing by virtue of the entry of a judgment against its owner or by the entry of a judgment and a levy there under on the property, or because of the relationship of the claimant to the particular property, such as an unpaid seller.

life estate—an estate for the duration of a life.

limitation-of-liability clause—provision in a contract stating that one of the parties shall not be liable for damages in case of breach; also called an *exculpatory clause.*

limited covenant—any covenant that does not provide the complete protection of a full covenant.

limited defenses—defenses available to secondary parties if the presenting party is a holder in due course.

limited liability company (LLC)—a partnership for federal tax treatment and the limited liability feature of the corporate form of business organization.

limited liability partnership (LLP)—partnership in which at least one partner has a liability limited to the loss of the capital contribution made to the partnership.

limited partner—partner who neither takes part in the management of the partnership nor appears to the public to be a general partner.

limited partnership—partnership that can be formed by "one or more general partners and one or more limited partners."

limited (special) jurisdiction—the authority to hear only particular kinds of cases.

limited warranty—any warranty that does not provide the complete protection of a full warranty.

lineals—relationship that exists when one person is a direct descendant of the other; also called *lineal descendants.*

liquidated damages—damages established in advance of breach as an alternative to establishing compensatory damages at the time of the breach.

liquidated damages clause—specification of exact compensation in case of a breach of contract.

liquidation—process of converting property into money whether of particular items of property or of all the assets of a business or an estate.

living trust—trust created to take effect within the lifetime of the settlor; also called *inter vivos* trust.

living will—document by which individuals may indicate that if they become unable to express their wishes and are in an irreversible, incurable condition, they do not want life-sustaining medical treatments.

living-document view—the term when a constitution is interpreted according to changes in conditions.

lottery—any plan by which a consideration is given for a chance to win a prize; it consists of three elements: (1) there must be a payment of money or something of value for an opportunity to win, (2) a prize must be available, and (3) the prize must be offered by lot or chance.

M

mailbox rule—timing for acceptance tied to proper acceptance.

maker—party who writes or creates a promissory note.

malpractice—basis for liability when services are not properly rendered in accordance with commonly accepted standards; negligence by a professional in performing his or her skill.

marine insurance—policies that cover perils relating to the transportation of goods.

market power—the ability to control price and exclude competitors.

market value—price at which a share of stock can be voluntarily bought or sold in the open market.

mask work—specific form of expression embodied in a chip design, including the stencils used in manufacturing semiconductor chip products.

mass picketing—illegal tactic of employees massing together in great numbers to effectively shut down entrances of the employer's facility.

maturity date—date that a corporation is required to repay a loan to a bondholder.

means test—new standard under the Reform Act that requires the court to find that the debtor does not have the means to repay creditors; goes beyond the past requirement of petitions being granted on the simple assertion of the debtor saying, "I have debts."

mechanic's lien—protection afforded by statute to various kinds of laborers and persons supplying materials, by giving them a lien on the building and land that has been improved or added to by them.

mediation—the settlement of a dispute through the use of a messenger who carries to each side of the dispute the issues and offers in the case.

merchant—seller who deals in specific goods classified by the UCC.

merger (of corporations)—combining of corporations by which one absorbs the other and continues to exist, preserving its original charter and identity while the other corporation ceases to exist.

minitrial—a trial held on portions of the case or certain issues in the case.

Miranda warnings—warnings required to prevent self-incrimination in a criminal matter.

mirror image rule—common law contract rule on acceptance that requires language to be absolutely the same as the offer, unequivocal and unconditional.

misdemeanor—criminal offense with a sentence of less than one year that is neither treason nor a felony.

misrepresentation—false statement of fact made innocently without any intent to deceive.

mistrial—a court's declaration that terminates a trial and postpones it to a later date; commonly entered when evidence has been of a highly prejudicial character or when a juror has been guilty of misconduct.

money—medium of exchange.

money order—draft issued by a bank or a nonbank.

moral relativists—group of ethical theorists who believe that ethical choices are determined according to the circumstances and not according to any predetermined set of standards.

mortgage—interest in land given by the owner to a creditor as security for the payment of the creditor for a debt, the nature of the interest depending upon the law of the state where the land is located. (Parties—mortgagor, mortgagee)

most-favored-nation clause—clause in treaties between countries whereby any privilege subsequently granted to a third country in relation to a given treaty subject is extended to the other party to the treaty.

motion for summary judgment—request that the court decide a case on basis of law only because there are no material issues disputed by the parties.

motion to dismiss—a pleading that may be filed to attack the adverse party's pleading as not stating a cause of action or a defense.

N

National Environmental Policy Act (NEPA)—federal law that mandates study of a project's impact on the environment before it can be undertaken by any federal agency.

National Pollutant Discharge Elimination System (NPDES)—federal law that regulates discharge into bodies of water.

natural law—a system of principles to guide human conduct independent of, and sometimes contrary to, enacted law and discovered by man's rational intelligence.

necessaries—things indispensable or absolutely necessary for the sustenance of human life.

negligence—failure to exercise due care under the circumstances in consequence of which harm is proximately caused to one to whom the defendant owed a duty to exercise due care.

negotiability—quality of an instrument that affords special rights and standing.

negotiable bill of lading—document of title that by its terms calls for goods to be delivered "to the bearer" or "to the order of" a named person.

negotiable instruments—drafts, promissory notes, checks, and certificates of deposit that, in proper form, give special rights as "negotiable commercial paper."

negotiable warehouse receipt—receipt that states the covered goods will be delivered "to the bearer" or "to the order of."

negotiation—the transfer of commercial paper by indorsement and delivery by the person to whom it is then payable in the case of order paper and by physical transfer in the case of bearer paper.

Noise Control Act—federal law that controls noise emissions from low-flying aircraft.

nominal damages—nominal sum awarded the plaintiff in order to establish that legal rights have been violated although the plaintiff in fact has not sustained any actual loss or damages.

nonattainment areas—"dirty" areas that do not meet federal standards under the Clean Air Act.

nonconforming use—use of land that conflicts with a zoning ordinance at the time the ordinance goes into effect.

nonconsumer lease—lease that does not satisfy the definition of a consumer lease; also known as a *commercial lease.*

nonnegotiable bill of lading—See *straight bill of lading.*

nonnegotiable instrument—contract, note, or draft that does not meet negotiability requirements of Article 3.

nonnegotiable warehouse receipt—receipt that states the covered goods received will be delivered to a specific person.

notice of dishonor—notice that an instrument has been dishonored; such notice can be oral, written, or electronic but is subject to time limitations.

notice statute—statute under which the last good faith or bona fide purchaser holds the title.

notice-race statute—statute under which the first bona fide purchaser to record the deed holds the title.

novation—substitution for an old contract with a new one that either replaces an existing obligation with a new obligation or replaces an original party with a new party.

nuisance—conduct that harms or prejudices another in the use of land or that harms or prejudices the public.

O

obligee—promisee who can claim the benefit of the obligation.

obligor—promisor.

ocean marine—policies that cover transportation of goods in vessels in international and coastal trade.

offer—expression of an offeror's willingness to enter into a contractual agreement.

offeree—person to whom an offer is made.

offeror—person who makes an offer.

Oil Pollution Act—federal law that assigns cleanup liability for oil spills in U.S. waters.

open meeting law—law that requires advance notice of agency meeting and public access.

opening statements—statements by opposing attorneys that tell the jury what their cases will prove.

operation of law—attaching of certain consequences to certain facts because of legal principles that operate automatically as contrasted with consequences that arise because of the voluntary action of a party designed to create those consequences.

option contract—contract to hold an offer to make a contract open for a fixed period of time.

order of relief—the order from the bankruptcy judge that starts the protection for the debtor; when the order of relief is entered by the court, the debtor's creditors must stop all proceedings and work through the bankruptcy court to recover debts (if possible). Court finding that creditors have met the standards for bankruptcy petitions.

order paper—instrument payable to the order of a party.

original jurisdiction—the authority of courts to hear the original proceedings in a case.

originator—party who originates the funds transfer.

output contract—contract of a producer to sell its entire production or output to a buyer.

outstanding—name for shares of a company that have been issued to stockholders.

overdraft—negative balance in a drawer's account.

P

par value—specified monetary amount assigned by an issuing corporation for each share of its stock.

parol evidence rule—rule that prohibits the introduction into evidence of oral or written statements made prior to or contemporaneously with the execution of a complete written contract, deed, or instrument, in the absence of clear proof of fraud, accident, or mistake causing the omission of the statement in question.

partially disclosed principal—principal whose existence is made known but whose identity is not.

partner—one of two or more persons who jointly own and carry on a business for profit.

partnership—pooling of capital resources and the business or professional talents of two or more individuals (partners) with the goal of making a profit.

partnership agreement—document prepared to evidence the contract of the parties. (Parties—partners or general partners)

party—person involved in a legal transaction; may be a natural person, an artificial person (e.g., a corporation), or an unincorporated enterprise (e.g., a government agency).

past consideration—something that has been performed in the past and which, therefore, cannot be consideration for a promise made in the present.

payable to order—term stating that a negotiable instrument is payable to the order of any person described in it or to a person or order.

payee—party to whom payment is to be made.

payment order—direction given by an originator to his or her bank or by any bank to a subsequent bank to make a specified funds transfer.

Pension Benefit Guaranty Corporation (PBGC)—a federal insurance plan established by ERISA that protects employees covered under defined benefit plans should the employer go out of business.

per capita—method of distributing estate assets on an equal-per-person basis.

per stirpes—method for distribution of an estate that divides property equally down family lines.

perfected security interest—security interest with priority because of filing, possession, automatic or temporary priority status.

periodic tenancy—tenancy that continues indefinitely for a specified rental period until terminated; often called a month-to-month tenancy.

personal property—property that is movable or intangible, or rights in such things.

personal representative—administrator or executor who represents decedents under the UPC.

physical duress—threat of physical harm to person or property.

plaintiff—the party who initiates a lawsuit.

pleadings—the papers filed by the parties in an action in order to set forth the facts and frame the issues to be tried, although, under some systems, the pleadings merely give notice or a general indication of the nature of the issues.

pledge—bailment given as security for the payment of a debt or the performance of an obligation owed to the pledgee. (Parties—pledgor, pledgee)

police power—the power to govern; the power to adopt laws for the protection of the public health, welfare, safety, and morals.

policy—paper evidencing the contract of insurance.

positive law—law enacted and codified by governmental authority.

possession—exclusive dominion and control of property.

possibility of reverter—nature of the interest held by the grantor after conveying land outright but subject to a condition or provision that may cause the grantee's interest to become forfeited and the interest to revert to the grantor or heirs.

postdate—to insert or place on an instrument a later date than the actual date on which it was executed.

power of attorney—written authorization to an agent by the principal.

precedent—a decision of a court that stands as the law for a particular problem in the future.

predatory lending—a practice on the part of the subprime lending market whereby lenders take advantage of less sophisticated consumers or those who are desperate for funds by using the lenders' superior bargaining positions to obtain credit terms that go well beyond compensating them for their risk.

predicate act—qualifying underlying offense for RICO liability.

preemption—the federal government's superior regulatory position over state laws on the same subject area.

preemptive right—shareholder's right upon the increase of a corporation's capital stock to be allowed to subscribe to such a percentage of the new shares as the shareholder's old shares bore to the former total capital stock.

preferences—transfers of property by a debtor to one or more specific creditors to enable these creditors to obtain payment for debts owed.

preferential transfers—certain transfers of money or security interests in the time frame just prior to bankruptcy that can be set aside if voidable.

preferred stock—stock that has a priority or preference as to payment of dividends or upon liquidation, or both.

prescription—acquisition of a right to use the land of another, as an easement, by making hostile, visible, and notorious use of the land, continuing for the period specified by the local law.

presentment—formal request for payment on an instrument.

price discrimination—the charging practice by a seller of different prices to different buyers for commodities of similar grade and quality, resulting in reduced competition or a tendency to create a monopoly.

prima facie—evidence that, if believed, is sufficient by itself to lead to a particular conclusion.

primary party—party to whom the holder or holder in due course must turn first to obtain payment.

primary picketing—legal presentations in front of a business notifying the public of a labor dispute.

primum non nocere—"above all do no harm."

principal—person or firm who employs an agent; person who, with respect to a surety, is primarily liable to the third person or creditor; property held in trust.

principal debtor—original borrower or debtor.

prior art—a showing that an invention as a whole would have been obvious to a person of ordinary skill in the art when the invention was patented.

private carrier—carrier owned by the shipper, such as a company's own fleet of trucks.

private corporation—corporation organized for charitable and benevolent purposes or for purposes of finance, industry, and commerce.

private law—the rules and regulations parties agree to as part of their contractual relationships.

private nuisance—nuisance that affects only one or a few individuals.

privileges and immunities clause—a clause that entitles a person going into another state to make contracts, own property, and engage in business to the same extent as citizens of that state.

privity—succession or chain of relationship to the same thing or right, such as privity of contract, privity of estate, privity of possession.

privity of contract—relationship between a promisor and the promisee.

privity rule—succession or chain of relationship to the same thing or right, such as privity of contract, privity of estate, privity of possession.

pro rata—proportionately, or divided according to a rate or standard.

probate—procedure for formally establishing or proving that a given writing is the last will and testament of the person who purportedly signed it.

procedural law—the law that specifies the steps that must be followed in enforcing rights and liabilities.

process—paperwork served personally on a defendant in a civil case.

product disparagement—false statements made about a product or business.

profit—right to take a part of the soil or produce of another's land, such as timber or water.

promisee—person to whom a promise is made.

promisor—person who makes a promise.

promissory estoppel—doctrine that a promise will be enforced although it is not supported by consideration when the promisor should have reasonably expected that the promise would induce action or forbearance of a definite and substantial character on the part of the promised and injustice can be avoided only by enforcement of the promise.

promissory note—unconditional promise in writing made by one person to another, signed by the maker engaging to pay on demand, or at a definite time, a sum certain in money to order or to bearer. (Parties—maker, payee)

promoters—persons who plan the formation of the corporation and sell or promote the idea to others.

proof of claim—written statement, signed by the creditor or an authorized representative, setting forth any claim made against the debtor and the basis for it.

property report—condensed version of a property development statement filed with the secretary of HUD and given to a prospective customer at least 48 hours before signing a contract to buy or lease property.

prosecutor—party who originates a criminal proceeding.

prospectus—information provided to each potential purchaser of securities setting forth the key information contained in the registration statement.

proxy—written authorization by a shareholder to another person to vote the stock owned by the shareholder; the person who is the holder of such a written authorization.

public corporation—corporation that has been established for governmental purposes and for the administration of public affairs.

public nuisance—nuisance that affects the community or public at large.

public policy—certain objectives relating to health, morals, and integrity of government that the law seeks to advance by declaring invalid any contract that conflicts with those objectives even though there is no statute expressly declaring such a contract illegal.

public warehouses—entities that serve the public generally without discrimination.

punitive damages—damages, in excess of those required to compensate the plaintiff for the wrong done, that are imposed in order to punish the defendant because of the particularly wanton or willful character of wrongdoing; also called *exemplary damages.*

purchase money security interest (PMSI)—the security interest in the goods a seller sells on credit that become the collateral for the creditor/seller.

Q

qualified indorsement—an indorsement that includes words such as "without recourse" that disclaims certain liability of the indorser to a maker or a drawee.

qualified privilege—media privilege to print inaccurate information without liability for defamation, so long as a retraction is printed and there was no malice.

quantum meruit—"as much as deserved"; an action brought for the value of the services rendered the defendant when there was no express contract as to the purchase price.

quasi contract—court-imposed obligation to prevent unjust enrichment in the absence of a contract.

quasi-judicial proceedings—forms of hearings in which the rules of evidence and procedure are more relaxed but each side still has a chance to be heard.

quasi-public corporation—private corporation furnishing services on which the public is particularly dependent, for example, a gas and electric company.

quitclaim deed—deed by which the grantor purports to give up only whatever right or title the grantor may have in the property without specifying or warranting transfer of any particular interest.

quorum—minimum number of persons, shares represented, or directors who must be present at a meeting in order to lawfully transact business.

R

race statute—statute under which the first party to record the deed holds the title.

race-notice statute—See *notice-race statute.*

Racketeer Influenced and Corrupt Organizations (RICO) Act—federal law, initially targeting organized crime, that has expanded in scope and provides penalties and civil recovery for multiple criminal offenses, or a pattern of racketeering.

real property—land and all rights in land.

recognizance—obligation entered into before a court to do some act, such as to appear at a later date for a hearing. Also called a *contract of record.*

recorder—public official in charge of deeds.

recross-examination—an examination by the other side's attorney that follows the redirect examination.

redemption—buying back of one's property, which has been sold because of a default, upon paying the amount that had been originally due together with interest and costs.

redirect examination—questioning after cross-examination, in which the attorney for the witness testifying may ask the same witness other questions to overcome effects of the cross-examination.

reference to a third person—settlement that allows a nonparty to resolve the dispute.

reformation—remedy by which a written instrument is corrected when it fails to express the actual intent of both parties because of fraud, accident, or mistake.

registered bonds—bonds held by owners whose names and addresses are registered on the books of the corporation.

registration requirements—provisions of the Securities Act of 1933 requiring advance disclosure to the public of a new securities issue through filing a statement with the SEC and sending a prospectus to each potential purchaser.

registration statement—document disclosing specific financial information regarding the security, the issuer, and the underwriter.

remainder interest—land interest that follows a life estate.

remand—term used when an appellate court sends a case back to trial court for additional hearings or a new trial.

remedy—action or procedure that is followed in order to enforce a right or to obtain damages for injury to a right.

rent-a-judge plan—dispute resolution through private courts with judges paid to be referees for the cases.

representative capacity—action taken by one on behalf of another, as the act of a personal representative on behalf of a decedent's estate, or action taken both on one's behalf and on behalf of others, as a shareholder bringing a representative action.

repudiation—result of a buyer or seller refusing to perform the contract as stated.

request for production of documents—discovery tool for uncovering paper or electronic evidence in a case.

requirements contract—contract in which the buyer buys its needs (requirements) from the seller.

rescission—action of one party to a contract to set the contract aside when the other party is guilty of a breach of the contract.

reservation of rights—assertion by a party to a contract that even though a tendered performance (e.g., a defective product) is accepted, the right to damages for nonconformity to the contract is reserved.

Resource Conservation and Recovery Act (RCRA)—federal law that regulates the disposal of potentially harmful substances and encourages resource conservation and recovery.

Resource Recovery Act—early federal solid waste disposal legislation that provided funding for states and local governments with recycling programs.

respondeat superior—doctrine that the principal or employer is vicariously liable for the unauthorized torts committed by an agent or employee while acting within the scope of the agency or the course of the employment, respectively.

restrictive covenants—covenants in a deed by which the grantee agrees to refrain from doing specified acts.

restrictive indorsement—an indorsement that restricts further transfer, such as in trust for or to the use of some other person, is conditional, or for collection or deposit.

reverse—the term used when the appellate court sets aside the verdict or judgment of a lower court.

reverse mortgage—mortgage in which the owners get their equity out of their home over a period of time and return the house to the lender upon their deaths.

reversible error—an error or defect in court proceedings of so serious a nature that on appeal the appellate court will set aside the proceedings of the lower court.

reversionary interest—interest that a lessor has in property that is subject to an outstanding lease.

revoke—testator's act of taking back his or her will and its provisions.

right—legal capacity to require another person to perform or refrain from an action.

right of escheat—right of the state to take the property of a decedent that has not been distributed.

right of first refusal—right of a party to meet the terms of a proposed contract before it is executed, such as a real estate purchase agreement.

right of privacy—the right to be free from unreasonable intrusion by others.

rights theory—Nozick's theory of ethics that (1) everyone has a set of rights, and (2) it is up to the governments to protect those rights.

right to cure—second chance for a seller to make a proper tender of conforming goods.

right-to-work laws—laws restricting unions and employees from negotiating clauses in their collective bargaining agreements that make union membership compulsory.

risk—peril or contingency against which the insured is protected by the contract of insurance.

risk of loss—in contract performance, the cost of damage or injury to the goods contracted for.

Robinson-Patman Act—a federal statute designed to eliminate price discrimination in interstate commerce.

run with the land—concept that certain covenants in a deed to land are deemed to run or pass with the land so that whoever owns the land is bound by or entitled to the benefit of the covenants.

S

Safe Drinking Water Act—a federal law that establishes national standards for contaminants in drinking water.

sale on approval—term indicating that no sale takes place until the buyer approves or accepts the goods.

sale or return—sale in which the title to the property passes to the buyer at the time of the transaction but the buyer is given the option of returning the property and restoring the title to the seller.

search engine—Internet service used to locate Web sites.

search warrant—judicial authorization for a search of property where there is the expectation of privacy.

seasonable—timely.

secondary meaning—a legal term signifying the words in question have taken on a new meaning with the public, capable of serving a source-identifying function of a mark.

secondary parties—called *secondary obligors* under Revised Article 3; parties to an instrument to whom holders turn when the primary party, for whatever reason, fails to pay the instrument.

secondary picketing—picketing an employer with which a union has no dispute to persuade the employer to stop doing business with a party to the dispute; generally illegal under the NLRA.

secrecy laws—confidentiality laws applied to home-country banks.

secured party—person owed the money, whether as a seller or a lender, in a secured transaction in personal property.

secured transaction—credit sale of goods or a secured loan that provides special protection for the creditor.

securities—stocks and bonds issued by a corporation. Under some investor protection laws, the term includes any interest in an enterprise that provides unearned income to its owner.

security agreement—agreement of the creditor and the debtor that the creditor will have a security interest.

security interest—property right that enables the creditor to take possession of the property if the debtor does not pay the amount owed.

self-help repossession—creditor's right to repossess the collateral without judicial proceedings.

self-proved wills—wills that eliminate some formalities of proof by being executed according to statutory requirements.

selling on consignment—entrusting a person with possession of property for the purpose of sale.

semiconductor chip product—product placed on a piece of semiconductor material in accordance with a predetermined pattern that is intended to perform electronic circuitry functions.

service mark—mark that identifies a service.

servient tenement—land that is subject to an easement.

settlor—one who settles property in trust or creates a trust estate.

severalty—ownership of property by one person.

shared powers—powers that are held by both state and national governments.

Sherman Antitrust Act—a federal statute prohibiting combinations and contracts in restraint of interstate trade, now generally inapplicable to labor union activity.

shop right—right of an employer to use in business without charge an invention discovered by an employee during working hours and with the employer's material and equipment.

shopkeeper's privilege—right of a store owner to detain a suspected shoplifter based on reasonable cause and for a reasonable time without resulting liability for false imprisonment.

short-swing profit—profit realized by a corporate insider from selling securities less than six months after purchase.

sinking fund—fixed amount of money set aside each year by the borrowing corporation toward the ultimate payment of bonds.

situational ethics—a flexible standard of ethics that permits an examination of circumstances and motivation before attaching the label of right or wrong to conduct.

Sixth Amendment—the U.S. constitutional amendment that guarantees a speedy trial.

slander—defamation of character by spoken words or gestures.

slander of title—malicious making of false statements as to a seller's title.

small claims courts—courts that resolve disputes between parties when those disputes do not exceed a minimal level; no lawyers are permitted; the parties represent themselves.

social contract—theory of ethics that focuses on social norms; what is ethical is the standard set by implied agreement; for example, we disapprove of people who cut in line ahead of us.

sole or individual proprietorship—form of business ownership in which one individual owns the business.

soliciting agent—salesperson.

sovereign compliance doctrine—doctrine that allows a defendant to raise as an affirmative defense to an antitrust action the fact that the defendant's actions were compelled by a foreign state.

sovereign immunity doctrine—doctrine that states that a foreign sovereign generally cannot be sued unless an exception to the Foreign Sovereign Immunities Act of 1976 applies.

special agent—agent authorized to transact a specific transaction or to do a specific act.

special drawing rights (SDRs)—rights that allow a country to borrow enough money from other International Money Fund (IMF) members to permit that country to maintain the stability of its currency's relationship to other world currencies.

special indorsement—an indorsement that specifies the person to whom the instrument is indorsed.

specific legacies—identified property bequeathed by a testator; also called *specific devises.*

specific lien—right of a creditor to hold particular property or assert a lien on particular property of the debtor because of the creditor's having done work on or having some other association with the property, as distinguished from having a lien generally against the assets of the debtor merely because the debtor is indebted to the lien holder.

specific performance—action brought to compel the adverse party to perform a contract on the theory that merely suing for damages for its breach will not be an adequate remedy.

spendthrift trust—a trust that, to varying degrees, provides that creditors of the beneficiary shall not be able to reach the principal or income held by the trustee and that the beneficiary shall not be able to assign any interest in the trust.

spot zoning—allowing individual variation in zoning.

stakeholder analysis—the term used when a decision maker views a problem from different perspectives and measures the impact of a decision on various groups.

stakeholders—those who have a stake, or interest, in the activities of a corporation; stakeholders include employees, members of the community in which the corporation operates, vendors, customers, and any others who are affected by the actions and decisions of the corporation.

stale check—a check whose date is longer than six months ago.

standby letter—letter of credit for a contractor ensuring he will complete the project as contracted.

stare decisis—"let the decision stand"; the principle that the decision of a court should serve as a guide or precedent and control the decision of a similar case in the future.

status quo ante—original positions of the parties.

statute of frauds—statute that, in order to prevent fraud through the use of perjured testimony, requires that certain kinds of transactions be evidenced in writing in order to be binding or enforceable.

statute of limitations—statute that restricts the period of time within which an action may be brought.

statutory law—laws enacted by a legislative body.

stay (or delay) of foreclosure—delay of foreclosure obtained by the mortgagor to prevent undue hardship.

stirpes—family lines; distribution *per stirpes* refers to the manner in which descendants take property by right of representation.

stock subscription—contract or agreement to buy a specific number and kind of shares when they are issued by the corporation.

stop payment order—order by a depositor to the bank to refuse to make payment of a check when presented for payment.

straight (or nonnegotiable) bill of lading—document of title that consigns transported goods to a named person.

strict liability—civil wrong for which there is absolute liability because of the inherent danger in the underlying activity, for example, the use of explosives.

strict tort liability—product liability theory that imposes liability upon the manufacturer, seller, or distributor of goods for harm caused by defective goods.

subject matter jurisdiction—judicial authority to hear a particular type of case.

sublease—a transfer of the premises by the lessee to a third person, the sublessee or subtenant, for a period of less than the term of the original lease.

sublessee—person with lease rights for a period of less than the term of the original lease (also *subtenant*).

subprime lending market—a credit market that makes loans to high-risk consumers (those who have bankruptcies, no credit history, or a poor credit history), often loaning money to pay off other debts the consumer has due.

subrogation—right of a party secondarily liable to stand in the place of the creditor after making payment to the creditor and to enforce the creditor's right against the party primarily liable in order to obtain indemnity from such primary party.

substantial impairment—material defect in a good.

substantial performance—equitable rule that if a good-faith attempt to perform does not precisely meet the terms of the agreement, the agreement will still be considered complete if the essential purpose of the contract is accomplished.

substantive law—the law that creates, defines, and regulates rights and liabilities.

substitute check—electronic image of a paper check that a bank can create and that has the same legal effect as the original instrument.

substitution—substitution of a new contract between the same parties.

sum certain—amount due under an instrument that can be computed from its face with only reference to interest rates.

summary jury trial—a mock or dry-run trial for parties to get a feel for how their cases will play to a jury.

summation—the attorney address to a jury that is given after all the evidence is presented in court and sums up a case and urges the jury to reach a particular verdict.

Superfund Amendment and Reauthorization Act—federal law that authorizes the EPA to collect cleanup costs from those responsible for the ownership, leasing, dumping, or security of hazardous waste sites.

Superfund sites—areas designated by the EPA for cleanup of hazardous waste.

surety—obligor of a suretyship; primarily liable for the debt or obligation of the principal debtor.

suretyship—undertaking to pay the debt or be liable for the default of another.

symbolic delivery—delivery of goods by delivery of the means of control, such as a key or a relevant document of title, such as a negotiable bill of lading; also called *constructive delivery.*

T

takeover laws—laws that guard against unfairness in corporate takeover situations.

tariff—(1) domestically—government-approved schedule of charges that may be made by a regulated business, such as a common carrier or warehouser; (2) internationally—tax imposed by a country on goods crossing its borders, without regard to whether the purpose is to raise revenue or to discourage the traffic in the taxed goods.

tax lien—lien on property by a government agency for nonpayment of taxes.

teller's check—draft drawn by a bank on another bank in which it has an account.

temporary insider—someone retained by a corporation for professional services on an as-needed basis, such as an attorney, accountant, or investment banker.

temporary perfection—perfection given for a limited period of time to creditors.

tenancy at sufferance—lease arrangement in which the tenant occupies the property at the discretion of the landlord.

tenancy at will—holding of land for an indefinite period that may be terminated at any time by the landlord or by the landlord and tenant acting together.

tenancy by entirety or tenancy by entireties—transfer of property to both husband and wife.

tenancy for years—tenancy for a fixed period of time, even though the time is less than a year.

tenancy in common—relationship that exists when two or more persons own undivided interests in property.

tenancy in partnership—ownership relationship that exists between partners under the Uniform Partnership Act.

tenant—one who holds or possesses real property by any kind of right or title; one who pays rent for the temporary use and occupation of another's real property under a lease.

tender—goods have arrived, are available for pickup, and buyer is notified.

term insurance—policy written for a specified number of years that terminates at the end of that period.

termination statement—document (record), which may be requested by a debtor who has paid in full, stating that a security interest is no longer claimed under the specified financing statement.

testamentary capacity—sufficient mental capacity to understand that a writing being executed is a will and what that entails.

testamentary intent—designed to take effect at death, as by disposing of property or appointing a personal representative.

testamentary trust—trust that becomes effective only when the settlor's will takes effect after death.

testate—condition of leaving a will upon death.

testate distribution—distribution of an estate in accordance with the will of the decedent.

testator, testatrix—man, woman who makes a will.

third-party beneficiary—third person whom the parties to a contract intend to benefit by the making of the contract and to confer upon such person the right to sue for breach of contract.

time draft—bill of exchange payable at a stated time after sight or at a definite time.

tippee—individual who receives information about a corporation from an insider or temporary insider.

tort—civil wrong that interferes with one's property or person.

Toxic Substances Control Act (TOSCA)—first federal law to control the manufacture, use, and disposal of toxic substances.

trade dress—product's total image including its overall packaging look.

trade libel—written defamation about a product or service.

trade name—name under which a business is carried on and, if fictitious, must be registered.

trade secret—any formula, device, or compilation of information that is used in one's business and is of such a nature that it provides an advantage over competitors who do not have the information.

trademark—mark that identifies a product.

transferee—buyer or vendee.

traveler's check—check that is payable on demand provided it is countersigned by the person whose specimen signature appears on the check.

treasury stock—corporate stock that the corporation has reacquired.

treble damages—three times the damages actually sustained.

trespass—an unauthorized action with respect to person or property.

trial de novo—a trial required to preserve the constitutional right to a jury trial by allowing an appeal to proceed as though there never had been any prior hearing or decision.

tripartite—three-part division (of government).

trust—transfer of property by one person to another with the understanding or declaration that such property be held for the benefit of another; the holding of property by the owner in trust for another, upon a declaration of trust, without a transfer to another person. (Parties—settlor, trustee, beneficiary)

trust agreement—instrument creating a trust; also called *deed of trust.*

trust corpus—fund or property that is transferred to the trustee or held by the settlor as the body or subject matter of the trust; also called *trust fund, trust estate*, and *trust res.*

trustee—party who has legal title to estate and manages it.

trustee in bankruptcy—impartial person elected to administer the debtor's estate.

trustor—donor or settlor who is the owner of property and creates a trust in the property.

tying—the anticompetitive practice of requiring buyers to purchase one product in order to get another.

U

ultra vires—act or contract that the corporation does not have authority to do or make.

unconscionable—unreasonable, not guided or restrained by conscience and often referring to a contract grossly unfair to one party because of the superior bargaining powers of the other party.

underwriter—insurer.

undisclosed principal—principal on whose behalf an agent acts without disclosing to the third person the fact of agency or the identity of the principal.

undue influence—influence that is asserted upon another person by one who dominates that person.

Uniform Probate Code (UPC)—uniform statute on wills and administration of estates.

Uniform Simultaneous Death Act—law providing that when survivorship cannot be established, the property of each person shall be disposed of as though he or she had survived the other.

unilateral contract—contract under which only one party makes a promise.

unincorporated association—combination of two or more persons for the furtherance of a common nonprofit purpose.

universal agent—agent authorized by the principal to do all acts that can lawfully be delegated to a representative.

universal defenses—defenses that are regarded as so basic that the social interest in preserving them outweighs the social interest of giving negotiable instruments the freely transferable qualities of money; accordingly, such defenses are given universal effect and may be raised against all holders.

USA Patriot Act—federal law that, among other things, imposes reporting requirements on banks.

usage of trade—language and customs of an industry.

usury—lending money at an interest rate that is higher than the maximum rate allowed by law.

utilitarians—those who support the ethical theory of resolving dilemmas by doing the most good for the most people.

uttering—crime of issuing or delivering a forged instrument to another person.

V

valid—legal.

valid contract—agreement that is binding and enforceable.

value—consideration or antecedent debt or security given in exchange for the transfer of a negotiable instrument or creation of a security interest.

variance—permission of a landowner to use the land in a specified manner that is inconsistent with the zoning ordinance.

vicarious liability—imposing liability for the fault of another.

void agreement—agreement that cannot be enforced.

voidable contract—agreement that is otherwise binding and enforceable but may be rejected at the option of one of the parties as the result of specific circumstances.

voidable title—title of goods that carries with it the contingency of an underlying problem.

voir dire *examination*—the preliminary examination of a juror or a witness to ascertain fitness to act as such.

voluntary bankruptcy—proceeding in which the debtor files the petition for relief.

voting by proxy—authorizing someone else to vote the shares owned by the shareholder.

voting trust—transfer by two or more persons of their shares of stock of a corporation to a trustee who is to vote the shares and act for such shareholders.

W

waiver—release or relinquishment of a known right or objection.

warehouse—entity engaged in the business of storing the goods of others for compensation.

warehouse receipt—receipt issued by the warehouse for stored goods. Regulated by the UCC, which clothes the receipt with some degree of negotiability.

warranty—promise either express or implied about the nature, quality, or performance of the goods.

warranty against encumbrances—warranty that there are no liens or other encumbrances to goods except those noted by seller.

warranty deed—deed by which the grantor conveys a specific estate or interest to the grantee and makes one or more of the covenants of title.

warranty of habitability—implied warranty that the leased property is fit for dwelling by tenants.

warranty of title—implied warranty that title to the goods is good and transfer is proper.

wasting assets corporation—corporation designed to exhaust or use up the assets of the corporation, such as by extracting oil, coal, iron, and other ores.

way of necessity—grantee's right to use land retained by the grantor for going to and from the conveyed land.

White-Collar Crime Penalty Enhancement Act of 2002—federal reforms passed as a result of the collapses of companies such as Enron; provides for longer sentences and higher fines for both executives and companies.

white-collar crimes—crimes committed generally in the course of doing business and usually involving some form of deceit used to get gains.

whole life insurance—ordinary life insurance providing lifetime insurance protection.

will—instrument executed with the formality required by law by which a person makes a disposition of his or her property to take effect upon death.

writ of certiorari—order by the U.S. Supreme Court granting a right of review by the court of a lower court decision.

wrongfully dishonored—error by a bank in refusing to pay a check.

Z

zoning—restrictions imposed by government on the use of designated land to ensure an orderly physical development of the regulated area.

subject index

A

B

C

E

F

G

M

N

O

P

S